TheStreet Ratings' Guide to Exchange-Traded Funds

A Quarterly Compilation of Investment Ratings and Analyses Covering ETFs and Other Closed-End Mutual Funds

Spring 2012

GREY HOUSE PUBLISHING

TheStreet, Inc.
14 Wall Street, 15th Floor
New York, NY 10005
800-289-9222

The Street Ratings

Published by Grey House Publishing, Inc. located at 4919 Route 22, Amenia, NY, 12501; telephone 518-789-8700. Grey House Publishing neither guarantees the accuracy of the data contained herein nor assumes any responsibility for errors, omissions or discrepancies. Grey House Publishing accepts no payment for listing; inclusion in the publication of any organization agency, institution, publication, service or individual does not imply endorsement of the publisher.

Grey House
Publishing
4919 Route 22
PO Box 56
Amenia, NY 12501-0056

Edition No. 36, Spring 2012

ISBN: 978-1-59237-890-6
ISSN: 2158-6101

Contents

* Includes other Closed-End Funds

Terms and Conditions

This Document is prepared strictly for the confidential use of our customer(s). It has been provided to you at your specific request. It is not directed to, or intended for distribution to or use by, any person or entity who is a citizen or resident of or located in any locality, state, country or other jurisdiction where such distribution, publication, availability or use would be contrary to law or regulation or which would subject TheStreet or its affiliates to any registration or licensing requirement within such jurisdiction.

No part of the analysts' compensation was, is, or will be, directly or indirectly, related to the specific recommendations or views expressed in this research report.

This Document is not intended for the direct or indirect solicitation of business. TheStreet, Inc. and its affiliates disclaims any and all liability to any person or entity for any loss or damage caused, in whole or in part, by any error (negligent or otherwise) or other circumstances involved in, resulting from or relating to the procurement, compilation, analysis, interpretation, editing, transcribing, publishing and/or dissemination or transmittal of any information contained herein.

TheStreet has not taken any steps to ensure that the securities or investment vehicle referred to in this report are suitable for any particular investor. The investment or services contained or referred to in this report may not be suitable for you and it is recommended that you consult an independent investment advisor if you are in doubt about such investments or investment services. Nothing in this report constitutes investment, legal, accounting or tax advice or a representation that any investment or strategy is suitable or appropriate to your individual circumstances or otherwise constitutes a personal recommendation to you.

The ratings and other opinions contained in this Document must be construed solely as statements of opinion from TheStreet, Inc., and not statements of fact. Each rating or opinion must be weighed solely as a factor in your choice of an institution and should not be construed as a recommendation to buy, sell or otherwise act with respect to the particular product or company involved.

Past performance should not be taken as an indication or guarantee of future performance, and no representation or warranty, expressed or implied, is made regarding future performance. Information, opinions and estimates contained in this report reflect a judgment at its original date of publication and are subject to change without notice. TheStreet offers a notification service for rating changes on companies you specify. For more information call 1-800-289-9222 or visit www.thestreet.com/ratings. The price, value and income from any of the securities or financial instruments mentioned in this report can fall as well as rise.

This Document and the information contained herein is copyrighted by TheStreet, Inc. Any copying, displaying, selling, distributing or otherwise delivering of this information or any part of this Document to any other person, without the express written consent of TheStreet, Inc. except by a reviewer or editor who may quote brief passages in connection with a review or a news story, is prohibited.

Welcome to TheStreet Ratings
Guide to Exchange-Traded Funds

With the growing popularity of mutual fund investing, consumers need a reliable source to help them track and evaluate the performance of their mutual fund holdings. Plus, they need a way of identifying and monitoring other funds as potential new investments. Unfortunately, the hundreds of performance and risk measures available – multiplied by the vast number of mutual fund investments on the market today – can make this a daunting task for even the most sophisticated investor.

TheStreet Investment Ratings simplify the evaluation process. We condense all of the available mutual fund data into a single composite opinion of each fund's risk-adjusted performance. This allows you to instantly identify those funds that have historically done well and those that have underperformed the market. While there is no guarantee of future performance, TheStreet Investment Ratings provide a solid framework for making informed investment decisions.

TheStreet Ratings' Mission Statement

TheStreet Ratings' mission is to empower consumers, professionals, and institutions with high quality advisory information for selecting or monitoring a financial services company or financial investment.

In doing so, TheStreet Ratings will adhere to the highest ethical standards by maintaining our independent, unbiased outlook and approach to advising our customers.

Why rely on TheStreet Ratings?

TheStreet Ratings provides financial strength ratings evaluating the financial stability of insurance companies and banks in addition to TheStreet Investment Ratings. Our goal is to provide fair, objective information to help professionals and consumers alike make educated purchasing decisions.

At TheStreet Ratings, objectivity and total independence are never compromised. We never take a penny from rated companies for issuing our ratings, and we publish them without regard for the companies' preferences. TheStreet's ratings are more frequently reviewed and updated than any other ratings, so you can be sure that the information you receive is accurate and current.

Our rating scale, from A to E, is easy to understand as follows:

	Rating	Description
Top 10% of funds	A	Excellent
Next 20% of funds	B	Good
Middle 40% of funds	C	Fair
Next 20% of funds	D	Weak
Bottom 10% of funds	E	Very Weak

In addition, a plus or minus sign designates that a fund is in the top third or bottom third of funds with the same letter grade.

Thank you for your trust and purchase of this Guide. If you have any comments, or wish to review other products from TheStreet Ratings, please call 1-800-289-9222 or visit www.thestreetratings.com. We look forward to hearing from you.

How to Use This Guide

The purpose of the *Guide to Exchange-Traded Funds* is to provide investors with a reliable source of investment ratings and analyses on a timely basis. We realize that past performance is an important factor to consider when making the decision to purchase shares in a mutual fund. The ratings and analyses in this Guide can make that evaluation easier when you are considering ETF and other closed-end:

- growth funds

- sector or international funds

- municipal bond funds

- corporate bond funds

- or other ETFs and closed-end funds

However, this Guide does not include open-end mutual funds since they represent a whole separate class of investments with unique risk profiles and performance expectations. For information on open-end equity funds, refer to *TheStreet Ratings' Guide to Stock Mutual Funds*. And if you are interested in open-end bond or money market funds, refer to *TheStreet Ratings' Guide to Bond and Money Market Mutual Funds*.

The rating for a particular fund indicates our opinion regarding that fund's past risk-adjusted performance. When evaluating a specific mutual fund, we recommend you follow these steps:

Step 1   **Confirm the fund name and ticker symbol.** To ensure you evaluate the correct mutual fund, verify the fund's exact name and ticker symbol as it was given to you in its prospectus or appears on your account statement. Many funds have similar names, so you want to make sure the fund you look up is really the one you are interested in evaluating.

Step 2   **Check the fund's Investment Rating.** Turn to Section I, the Index of Exchange-Traded Funds, and locate the fund you are evaluating. This section contains all ETFs and other closed-end mutual funds analyzed by TheStreet Ratings, including those that did not receive a Investment Rating. All funds are listed in alphabetical order by the name of the fund with the ticker symbol following the name for additional verification. Once you have located your specific fund, the first column after the ticker symbol shows its Investment Rating. Turn to *About TheStreet Investment Ratings* on page 7 for information about what this rating means.

Step 3   **Analyze the supporting data.** Following TheStreet Investment Rating are some of the various measures we have used in rating the fund. Refer to the Section I introduction (beginning on page 15) to see what each of these factors measures. In most cases, lower rated funds will have a low performance rating and/or a low risk rating (i.e., high volatility). Bear in mind, however, that TheStreet Investment Rating is the result of a complex computer-generated analysis which cannot be reproduced using only the data provided here.

When looking to identify a mutual fund that achieves your specific investing goals, we recommend the following:

Step 4   **View the top-performing funds.** If your priority is to achieve the highest return, regardless of the amount of risk, turn to Section V which lists the ETFs and other closed-end mutual funds with the best financial performance. Keep in mind that past performance alone is not always a true indicator of the future since these funds have already experienced a run up in price and could be due for a correction.

Step 5   **View the top-rated funds by fund type.** If you are looking to invest in a particular type of mutual fund (e.g., corporate high-yield bond or emerging market), turn to Section VI, Top-Rated ETFs and Other Closed-End Mutual Funds by Fund Type. There you will find the ETFs and other closed-end mutual funds with the highest performance rating in each category. Please be careful to also consider the risk component when selecting a fund from one of these lists.

Step 6   **Refer back to Section I.** Once you have identified a particular fund that interests you, refer back to Section I, the Index of ETFs and Other Closed-End Mutual Funds, for a more thorough analysis.

Always remember:

Step 7   **Read our warnings and cautions.** In order to use TheStreet Investment Ratings most effectively, we strongly recommend you consult the Important Warnings and Cautions listed on page 11. These are more than just "standard disclaimers." They are very important factors you should be aware of before using this Guide.

Step 8   **Stay up to date.** Periodically review the latest TheStreet Investment Ratings for the funds that you own to make sure they are still in line with your investment goals and level of risk tolerance. For information on how to acquire follow-up reports on a particular mutual fund, call 1-800-289-9222 or visit www.thestreetratings.com.

Data Source: Thomson Wealth Management
1455 Research Boulevard
Rockville, MD 20850

Date of data analyzed: March 31, 2012

About TheStreet Investment Ratings

TheStreet Investment Ratings represent a completely independent, unbiased opinion of a mutual fund's historical risk-adjusted performance. Each fund's rating is based on two primary components:

Primary Component #1

A fund's **Performance Rating** is based on its total return to shareholders over a period of up to three years, including share price appreciation and distributions to shareholders. This total return figure is stated net of the expenses and fees charged by the fund.

This adjusted return is then weighted to give more recent performance a slightly greater emphasis. Thus, two mutual funds may have provided identical returns to their shareholders over the last three years, but the one with the better performance in the last 12 months will receive a slightly higher performance rating.

Primary Component #2

The **Risk Rating** is based on the level of volatility in the fund's monthly returns, also over a period of up to three years. We use several statistical measures – standard deviation, semi-deviation and a drawdown factor – as our barometer of volatility. Funds with more volatility relative to other mutual funds are considered riskier, and thus receive a lower risk rating. By contrast, funds with very stable returns are considered less risky and receive a higher risk rating. In addition to considering the fund's volatility, the risk rating also considers the fund's discount/premium as compared to its historical average, as well as an assessment of the valuation and quality of the fund's holdings.

Note that none of the mutual funds listed in this publication have received a risk rating in the A (Excellent) range. This is because all closed-end mutual fund investments, by their very nature, involve at least some degree of risk.

Rarely will you ever find a mutual fund that has both a very high Performance Rating plus, at the same time, a very high Risk Rating. Therefore, the funds that receive the highest overall Investment Ratings are those that attain the ideal combination of both primary components. There is always a tradeoff between risk and reward.

Keep in mind that while TheStreet Investment Ratings use the same rating scale as TheStreet Financial Strength Ratings of financial institutions, the two ratings have totally independent meanings. TheStreet Financial Strength Ratings assess the *future* financial stability of an insurer or bank as a way of helping investors place their money with a financially sound company and minimize the risk of loss. These ratings are derived without regard to the performance of the individual investments offered by the insurance companies, banks, or thrifts.

On the other hand, TheStreet Investment Ratings employ a ranking system to evaluate both safety and performance. Based on these measures, funds are divided into percentiles, and an individual performance rating and a risk rating are assigned to each fund. Then these measures are combined to derive a fund's composite percentile ranking. Finally, TheStreet Investment Ratings are assigned to their corresponding percentile rankings as shown on page 3.

How Our Ratings Differ From Those of Other Services

Balanced approach: TheStreet Investment Ratings are designed to meet the needs of aggressive *as well as* conservative investors. We realize that your investment goals can be different from those of other investors based upon your age, income, and tolerance for risk. Therefore, our ratings balance a fund's performance against the amount of risk it poses to identify those funds that have achieved the optimum mix of both factors. Some of these top funds have achieved excellent returns with only average risk. Others have achieved average returns with only moderate risk. Whatever your personal preferences, we can help you identify a top notch fund that meets your investing style.

Other investment rating firms give a far greater weight to performance and insufficient consideration to risk. In effect, they bet too heavily on a rising market and do not give enough consideration to the risk of a decline. While performance is obviously a very important factor to consider, we believe that the riskiness of a fund is also very important. Therefore, we weigh these two components more equally when assigning TheStreet Investment Ratings.

But we don't stop there. We also assign a separate performance rating and risk rating to each fund so you can focus on the component that is most important to you.

Easy to use: Unlike those of other services, TheStreet Investment Ratings are extremely intuitive and easy to use. Our rating scale (A to E) is easily understood by members of the general public based on their familiarity with school grades. So, there are no stars to count and no numbering systems to interpret.

More funds: *TheStreet Ratings Guide to Exchange-Traded Funds* tracks more closed-end mutual funds than any other publication – with updates that come out more frequently than those of other rating agencies. We've included more than 1,500 funds in this edition, all of which are updated every three months.

Recency: Recognizing that every fund's performance is going to have its peaks and valleys, superior long-term performance is a major consideration in TheStreet Investment Ratings. Even so, we do not give a fund a top rating solely because it did well 10 or 15 years ago. Times change and the top performing funds in the current economic environment are often very different from those of a decade ago. Thus, our ratings are designed to keep you abreast of the best funds available *today* and in the *near future,* not the distant past.

Thoroughness: One of the unique characteristics of closed-end funds is that they often trade either above (premium) or below (discount) their net asset value (NAV). Our ratings not only consider performance and risk factors of each fund, but we also evaluate the current premium or discount of each fund as compared to its historical average. This evaluation is factored into the overall rating and can help investors identify funds that may be overvalued or undervalued.

What Our Ratings Mean

A   **Excellent**. The mutual fund has an excellent track record for maximizing performance while minimizing risk, thus delivering the best possible combination of total return on investment and reduced volatility. It has made the most of the recent economic environment to maximize risk-adjusted returns compared to other mutual funds. While past performance is just an indication – not a guarantee – we believe this fund is among the most likely to deliver superior performance relative to risk in the future.

B   **Good.** The mutual fund has a good track record for balancing performance with risk. Compared to other mutual funds, it has achieved above-average returns given the level of risk in its underlying investments. While the risk-adjusted performance of any mutual fund is subject to change, we believe that this fund has proven to be a good investment in the recent past.

C   **Fair.** In the trade-off between performance and risk, the mutual fund has a track record which is about average. It is neither significantly better nor significantly worse than most other mutual funds. With some funds in this category, the total return may be better than average, but this can be misleading since the higher return was achieved with higher than average risk. With other funds, the risk may be lower than average, but the returns are also lower. In short, based on recent history, there is no particular advantage to investing in this fund.

D   **Weak.** The mutual fund has underperformed the universe of other funds given the level of risk in its underlying investments, resulting in a weak risk-adjusted performance. Thus, its investment strategy and/or management has not been attuned to capitalize on the recent economic environment. While the risk-adjusted performance of any mutual fund is subject to change, we believe that this fund has proven to be a bad investment over the recent past.

E   **Very Weak.** The mutual fund has significantly underperformed most other funds given the level of risk in its underlying investments, resulting in a very weak risk-adjusted performance. Thus, its investment strategy and/or management has done just the opposite of what was needed to maximize returns in the recent economic environment. While the risk-adjusted performance of any mutual fund is subject to change, we believe this fund has proven to be a very bad investment in the recent past.

+   **The plus sign** is an indication that the fund is in the top third of its letter grade.

-   **The minus sign** is an indication that the fund is in the bottom third of its letter grade.

U   **Unrated.** The mutual fund is unrated because it is too new to make a reliable assessment of its risk-adjusted performance.

Important Warnings and Cautions

1. **A rating alone cannot tell the whole story.** Please read the explanatory information contained here, in the section introductions and in the appendix. It is provided in order to give you an understanding of our rating methodology as well as to paint a more complete picture of a mutual fund's strengths and weaknesses.

2. **Investment ratings shown in this Guide were current as of the publication date.** In the meantime, the rating may have been updated based on more recent data. TheStreet Ratings offers a notification service for ratings changes on companies that you specify. For more information call 1-800-289-9222 or visit www.thestreet.com/ratings.

3. **When deciding to buy or sell shares in a specific mutual fund, your decision must be based on a wide variety of factors in addition to TheStreet Investment Rating.** These include any charges you may incur from switching funds, to what degree it meets your long-term planning needs, and what other choices are available to you.

4. **TheStreet Investment Ratings represent our opinion of a mutual fund's past risk-adjusted performance.** As such, a high rating means we feel that the mutual fund has performed very well for its shareholders compared to other closed-end mutual funds. A high rating is not a guarantee that a fund will continue to perform well, nor is a low rating a prediction of continued weak performance. TheStreet Investment Ratings are not deemed to be a recommendation concerning the purchase or sale of any mutual fund.

5. **A mutual fund's individual performance is not the only factor in determining its rating.** Since TheStreet Investment Ratings are based on performance relative to other funds, it is possible for a fund's rating to be upgraded or downgraded based strictly on the improved or deteriorated performance of other funds.

6. **All funds that have the same TheStreet Investment Rating should be considered to be essentially equal from a risk/reward perspective.** This is true regardless of any differences in the underlying numbers which might appear to indicate greater strengths.

7. **Our rating standards are more consumer-oriented than those used by other rating agencies.** We make more conservative assumptions as we attempt to identify those funds that have historically provided superior returns with only little or moderate risk.

8. **We are an independent rating agency and do not depend on the cooperation of the managers operating the mutual funds we rate.** Our data are derived, for the most part, from price quotes obtained and documented on the open market. This is supplemented by information collected from the mutual fund prospectuses and regulatory filings. Although we seek to maintain an open line of communication with the mutual fund managers, we do not grant them the right to stop or influence publication of the ratings. This policy stems from the fact that this Guide is designed for the information of the consumer.

9. **This Guide does not cover open-end funds.** Because open-end funds represent a whole separate class of investments with unique risk profiles and performance expectations, they are available in separate publications. Please see our *Guide to Stock Mutual Funds* and our *Guide to Bond and Money Market Mutual Funds* for our analyses of open-end mutual funds.

Section I

Index of ETFs and Other Closed-End Funds

An analysis of all rated and unrated

Exchange-Traded Funds and

Other Closed-End Mutual Funds.

Funds are listed in alphabetical order.

Section I Contents

1.   Fund Type   The mutual fund's peer category based on an analysis of its investment portfolio.

COH	Corporate – High Yield	HL	Health
COI	Corporate – Inv. Grade	IN	Income
EM	Emerging Market	LP	Loan Participation
EN	Energy/Natural Resources	MTG	Mortgage
FS	Financial Services	MUH	Municipal – High Yield
FO	Foreign	MUN	Municipal – National
GEI	General – Inv. Grade	MUS	Municipal – Single State
GEN	General Bond	PM	Precious Metals
GL	Global	USA	U.S. Gov. – Agency
GR	Growth	UT	Utilities
GI	Growth and Income		

A blank fund type means that the mutual fund has not yet been categorized.

2.   Fund Name   The name of the mutual fund as stated in its prospectus, which can sometimes differ slightly from the name that the company uses for advertising. If you cannot find the particular mutual fund you are interested in, or if you have any doubts regarding the precise name, verify the information with your broker or on your account statement. Also, use the fund's ticker symbol for confirmation. (See column 3.)

3.   Ticker Symbol   The unique alphabetic symbol used for identifying and trading a specific mutual fund. No two funds can have the same ticker symbol.

4.   Overall Investment Rating   Our overall rating is measured on a scale from A to E based on each fund's risk-adjusted performance. Please see page 10 for specific descriptions of each letter grade. Also, refer to page 7 for information on how our ratings are derived. Most important, when using this rating, please be sure to consider the warnings beginning on page 11 regarding the ratings' limitations and the underlying assumptions.

5.	**Price**	Closing price of the fund on the date shown.

6.	**52-Week High**	Highest price at which the fund has traded in the last 52 weeks.

7.	**52-Week Low**	Lowest price at which the fund has traded in the last 52 weeks.

8.	**Performance Rating/Points**	A letter grade rating based solely on the mutual fund's financial performance over the trailing three years, without any consideration for the amount of risk the fund poses. Like the overall Investment Rating, the Performance Rating is measured on a scale from A to E for ease of interpretation. The points score indicates where the Performance Rating falls on a scale of 0 to 10.

9.	**3-Month Total Return**	The total return the fund has provided to investors over the preceding 13 weeks. This total return figure is computed based on the fund's dividend distributions and share price appreciation/depreciation during the period, net of the expenses and fees it imposes on its shareholders. The 3-Month Total Return shown here is not annualized.

10.	**6-Month Total Return**	The total return the fund has provided investors over the preceding 26 weeks, not annualized.

11.	**1-Year Total Return**	The total return the fund has provided investors over the preceding 52 weeks.

12.	**1-Year Total Return Percentile**	The fund's percentile rank based on its one-year performance compared to that of all other closed-end funds in existence for at least one year. A score of 99 is the best possible, indicating that the fund outperformed 99% of the closed-end mutual funds. Zero is the worst possible percentile score.

13.	**3-Year Total Return**	The total annual return the fund has provided investors over the preceding 156 weeks.

14.	**3-Year Total Return Percentile**	The fund's percentile rank based on its three-year performance compared to that of all other closed-end funds in existence for at least three years. A score of 99 is the best possible, indicating that the fund outperformed 99% of the closed-end mutual funds. Zero is the worst possible percentile score.

15.	**5-Year Total Return**	The total annual return the fund has provided investors over the preceding 260 weeks.

16.	**5-Year Total Return Percentile**	The fund's percentile rank based on its five-year performance compared to that of all other closed-end funds in existence for at least five years. A score of 99 is the best possible, indicating that the fund outperformed 99% of the closed-end mutual funds. Zero is the worst possible percentile score.

Right Pages

1. Dividend Yield

Most recent quarterly dividend to fund investors annualized, expressed as a percent of the fund's current share price. The dividend yield of a fund can have little correlation to the amount of dividends the fund has received from its underlying investments. Rather, dividend distributions are based on a fund's need to pass earnings from both dividends and gains on the sale of investments along to shareholders. Thus, these dividend distributions are included as a part of the fund's total return.

Keep in mind that dividend income may be taxed at a different rate than capital gains depending on your income tax bracket.

2. Expense Ratio

The expense ratio is taken directly from each fund's annual report with no further calculation. It indicates the percentage of the fund's assets that are deducted each fiscal year to cover its expenses, although for practical purposes, it is actually accrued daily. Typical fund expenses include management fees and other costs incurred by the fund. Brokerage costs incurred by the fund to buy or sell shares of the underlying securities are not included in the expense ratio.

If a mutual fund's net assets are small, its expense ratio can be quite high because the fund must cover its expenses from a smaller asset base. Conversely, as the net assets of the fund grow, the expense percentage should ideally diminish since the expenses are being spread across a larger asset base.

Funds with higher expense ratios are generally less attractive since the expense ratio represents a hurdle that must be met before the investment becomes profitable to its shareholders. Since a fund's expenses affect its total return though, they are already factored into its TheStreet Investment Rating.

3. Risk Rating/Points

A letter grade rating based solely on the mutual fund's risk as determined by its monthly performance volatility over the trailing three years. The risk rating does not take into consideration the overall financial performance the fund has achieved or the total return it has provided to its shareholders. Like the overall Investment Rating, the Risk Rating is measured on a scale from A to E for ease of interpretation. The points score indicates where the Risk Rating falls on a scale of 0 to 10.

| 4. | **Standard Deviation** | A statistical measure of the amount of volatility in a fund's monthly performance over the last trailing 36 months. In absolute terms, standard deviation provides a historical measure of a fund's deviation from its mean, or average, monthly total return over the period. |

A high standard deviation indicates a high degree of volatility in the past, which usually means you should expect to see a high degree of volatility in the future as well. This translates into higher risk since a large negative swing could easily become a sizable loss in the event you need to liquidate your shares.

| 5. | **Beta** | The level of correlation between the fund's monthly performance over the last trailing 36 months and the performance of its investment category as a whole. |

A beta of 1.00 means that the fund's returns have matched those of the index one for one during the stock market's ups and downs. A beta of 1.10 means that on average the fund has outperformed the index by 10% during rising markets and underperformed it by 10% during falling markets. Conversely, a beta of 0.85 means that the fund has typically performed 15% worse than the overall market during up markets and 15% better during down markets.

| 6. | **Average Duration** | Expressed in years, duration is a measure of a bond fund's sensitivity to interest rate fluctuations, or its level of interest rate risk. |

The longer a fund's duration, the more sensitive the fund is to shifts in interest rates. For example, a fund with a duration of eight years is twice as sensitive to a change in rates as a fund with a four year duration.

| 7. | **NAV** | The fund's net asset value (NAV) as of the date indicated. A fund's NAV is computed by dividing the value of the fund's asset holdings, less accrued fees and expenses, by the number of its shares outstanding. |

Because a closed-end fund's shares trade on an exchange and the price is based on investor demand, the fund may trade at a price higher or lower than its NAV.

| 8. | **Net Assets** | The total value (stated in millions of dollars) of all of the fund's asset holdings including stocks, bonds, cash, and other financial instruments, less accrued expenses and fees. |

Larger funds have the advantage of being able to spread their expenses over a greater asset base so that the effect per share is lessened. On the other hand, if a fund becomes too large, it can be more difficult for the fund manager to buy and sell investments for the benefit of shareholders.

www.thestreetratings.com

9.	Premium/ Discount	A comparison of the fund's price to its NAV as of the date indicated. The premium (+) or discount (-) indicates the percentage the shares are trading above or below the fund's NAV per share.

If the price is above the fund's NAV, the fund is said to be trading at a premium. If the price is lower than the fund's NAV, the fund is trading at a discount.

10.	1-Year Average Premium/ Discount	The average of the fund's premium/discount over the preceding year.

It can be useful to compare the fund's current premium/discount to its one-year average. If the fund is currently trading at a premium/discount that is lower/higher than its one-year average, then there has been less demand for the fund in more recent times than over the past year. Conversely, if the fund is currently trading at a premium/discount that is higher/lower than its one-year average, this indicates that there has been greater demand for the fund in more recent times than over the past year.

11.	Weighted Average Price-to-Earnings	The average of the price-to-earnings (P/E) ratios for the equity securities of the fund, where larger holdings are weighted more heavily than smaller holdings. A high P/E multiple indicates that investors have high expectations for future growth of the securities of that fund.

Compare this number to that of funds of the same type to get a feel for whether the equity securities of the fund might be overvalued or undervalued.

12.	Cash %	The percentage of the fund's assets held in cash or money market funds as of the last reporting period. Investments in this area will tend to hamper the fund's returns while adding to its stability during market swings.

13.	Stocks %	The percentage of the fund's assets held in common or preferred stocks as of the last reporting period. Since stocks are inherently riskier investments than the other categories, it is common for funds invested primarily or exclusively in stocks to receive a lower risk rating.

14.	Bonds %	The percentage of the fund's assets held in bonds as of the last reporting period. This category includes corporate bonds, municipal bonds, and government bonds such as T-bills and T-bonds.

15.	Other %	The percentage of the fund's assets invested as of the last reporting period in other types of financial instruments such as convertible securities, options, and warrants.

16. Portfolio Turnover Ratio

The average annual portion of the fund's holdings that have been moved from one specific investment to another over the past three years. This indicates the amount of buying and selling the fund manager engages in. A portfolio turnover ratio of 100% signifies that on average, the entire value of the fund's assets is turned over once during the course of a year.

A high portfolio turnover ratio has implications for shareholders since the fund is required to pass all realized earnings along to shareholders each year. Thus a high portfolio turnover ratio will result in higher annual distributions for shareholders, effectively increasing their annual taxable income. In contrast, a low turnover ratio means a higher level of unrealized gains that will not be taxable until you sell your shares in the fund.

17. Manager Quality Percentile

The manager quality percentile is based on a ranking of the fund's alpha, a statistical measure representing the difference between a fund's actual returns and its expected performance given its level of risk. Fund managers who have been able to exceed the fund's statistically expected performance receive a high percentile rank with 99 representing the highest possible score. At the other end of the spectrum, fund managers who have actually detracted from the fund's expected performance receive a low percentile rank with 0 representing the lowest possible score.

18. Manager Tenure

The number of years the current manager has been managing the fund. Since fund managers who deliver substandard returns are usually replaced, a long tenure is usually a good sign that shareholders are satisfied that the fund is achieving its stated objectives.

Fund Type	Fund Name	Ticker Symbol	Overall Investment Rating	PRICE Price As of 3/31/12	52 Week High	52 Week Low	PERFORMANCE Performance Rating/Pts	3 Mo	6 Mo	1Yr/Pct	Annualized 3Yr/Pct	5Yr/Pct
GI	*2x Levered CS Mrg Arb Lq Idx	CSMB	U	19.63	N/A	N/A	U /	-0.30	0.41	--	--	--
GL	*Accuvest Global Opportunities ET	ACCU	U	26.11	N/A	N/A	U /	--	--	--	--	--
GR	*Active Bear ETF	HDGE	D-	20.61	30.35	20.02	E / 0.4	-17.63	-28.54	-13.57 / 17	--	--
EN	*Alps Alerian MLP ETF	AMLP	C	16.67	17.19	13.10	C- / 3.0	1.75	12.77	8.10 / 64	--	--
IN	*Alps Equal Sector Weight ETF	EQL	C	39.18	39.51	30.21	C / 4.9	10.49	22.32	6.66 / 60	--	--
GL	*Alps Jefferies / TR/J CRB Gl Cm	CRBQ	D	45.83	54.72	36.50	D- / 1.4	8.02	17.50	-13.47 / 17	--	--
EN	*Alps Jefferies/TR/J CRB WE & PE	WCAT	E+	40.62	57.76	28.23	E+ / 0.9	1.20	22.78	-28.14 / 6	--	--
GR	*Barclays ETN + VEQTOR ETN	VQT	D+	133.97	137.85	102.46	C / 4.6	6.35	7.20	18.48 / 81	--	--
FO	*BLDRS Asia 50 ADR Index	ADRA	D+	25.64	28.87	21.21	D+ / 2.9	14.33	15.68	-5.56 / 29	11.89 / 19	-2.38 / 18
FO	*BLDRS Developed Mkts 100 ADR Ind	ADRD	D+	20.37	23.76	16.86	C- / 3.0	9.02	16.12	-6.44 / 28	13.07 / 22	-4.00 / 14
EM	*BLDRS Emerging Market 50 ADR Ind	ADRE	D+	42.22	49.89	17.56	C- / 3.3	10.90	18.25	-11.30 / 20	14.93 / 27	3.04 / 44
FO	*BLDRS Europe Select ADR Index	ADRU	D+	19.79	23.55	16.44	C- / 3.0	6.23	15.39	-8.42 / 24	13.97 / 24	-4.21 / 14
GR	*Brclys ETN+ Inv S&P500 VIX STF E	XXV	D	36.38	36.62	28.69	C / 4.6	10.24	22.24	5.60 / 57	--	--
IN	*Brclys ETN+ Lg B Lv S&P500 TR ET	BXUB	C+	97.75	98.10	49.28	A+ / 9.9	29.03	71.49	16.86 / 80	--	--
IN	*Brclys ETN+ Lg C Lv S&P500 TR ET	BXUC	C+	164.34	166.13	100.38	A+ / 9.6	21.16	49.36	12.97 / 73	--	--
IN	*Brclys ETN+ Sh B Lv I S&P500 TR	BXDB	E	65.01	103.23	65.01	E / 0.4	-18.61	-29.38	-14.47 / 15	--	--
IN	*Brclys ETN+ Sh C Lv I S&P500 TR	BXDC	E-	21.27	63.38	19.77	E- / 0.0	-48.09	-62.99	-39.27 / 3	--	--
IN	*Brclys ETN+InvS&P500 VIX STF ETN	IVOP	U	31.55	N/A	N/A	U /	38.74	124.88	--	--	--
IN	*C-Tracks ETN Citi Volatility Idx	CVOL	E-	11.00	98.04	10.50	E- / 0.0	-61.29	-85.25	-72.12 / 0	--	--
GI	*Cambria Global Tactical ETF Fund	GTAA	D	24.30	27.39	22.07	D- / 1.1	3.45	2.40	-6.86 / 27	--	--
GI	*Cohen & Steers Global Realty Maj	GRI	C+	36.55	38.46	27.99	B- / 7.4	12.62	21.21	2.66 / 48	27.87 / 76	--
GEI	*Columbia Core Bond Strategy	GMTB	C-	52.44	54.40	49.95	D / 1.8	-1.82	1.04	8.22 / 65	--	--
GR	*Columbia Growth Equity Strategy	RPX	C	30.16	37.64	23.10	C / 4.5	7.71	23.91	5.30 / 56	--	--
MUN	*Columbia Intermediate Muni Bd St	GMMB	U	60.60	81.43	48.00	U /	14.79	--	--	--	--
GR	*Columbia Large-Cap Growth Eq Str	RWG	C+	31.59	34.37	24.53	C+ / 6.3	20.30	22.92	5.71 / 58	--	--
GR	*Consumer Discretionary Sel Sec S	XLY	B+	45.09	45.56	33.07	B+ / 8.6	15.91	30.47	16.54 / 79	30.21 / 82	4.66 / 55
GR	*Consumer Staples Select Sector S	XLP	C+	34.08	34.15	28.07	C / 5.2	5.45	16.52	16.59 / 79	19.36 / 40	7.51 / 71
EN	*Credit Suisse Cushing 30 MLP ETN	MLPN	D-	24.65	37.58	20.32	D / 1.7	0.09	13.41	-1.53 / 37	--	--
GR	*Credit Suisse L/S Liq Idx ETN	CSLS	D-	22.70	23.55	19.95	D / 1.9	4.85	8.66	0.18 / 41	--	--
GR	*Credit Suisse Merger Arb Lq Id E	CSMA	D-	20.36	21.29	18.80	D- / 1.1	-3.04	0.55	-1.82 / 36	--	--
GL	*Credit Suisse Mkt Neutral Glbl E	CSMN	U	19.17	N/A	N/A	U /	-4.39	-2.94	--	--	--
GI	*db-X 2010 Target Date Fund	TDD	C-	23.50	24.03	22.18	D- / 1.5	1.34	-0.55	1.78 / 46	3.88 / 9	--
GI	*db-X 2020 Target Date Fund	TDH	C-	22.33	23.65	20.51	D+ / 2.3	1.45	3.86	-2.09 / 35	10.18 / 16	--
GI	*db-X 2030 Target Date Fund	TDN	C-	20.96	22.22	18.45	C- / 3.1	5.97	9.55	2.10 / 47	13.14 / 22	--
GI	*db-X 2040 Target Date Fund	TDV	C	21.99	22.18	17.01	C / 4.9	12.77	22.16	5.34 / 56	19.00 / 39	--
GI	*db-X In-Target Date Fund	TDX	C-	26.53	27.55	23.16	D / 1.8	2.39	8.47	3.55 / 50	4.79 / 10	--
FO	*DBX MSCI Brazil Currency-Hedged	DBBR	U	23.50	N/A	N/A	U /	--	10.28	--	--	--
FO	*DBX MSCI EAFE Currency-Hedged Eq	DBEF	U	24.53	N/A	N/A	U /	12.27	14.34	--	--	--
EM	*DBX MSCI Emg Mkt Currency-Hedged	DBEM	U	23.38	N/A	N/A	U /	--	13.40	--	--	--
FO	*DBX MSCI Japan Currency-Hedged E	DBJP	U	26.59	N/A	N/A	U /	21.64	17.48	--	--	--
GL	*Dent Tactical ETF Fund	DENT	D	18.28	22.06	18.11	E+ / 0.6	-2.48	-9.12	-15.84 / 14	--	--
GI	*Direxion All Cap Insider Sentime	KNOW	U	45.59	N/A	N/A	U /	--	--	--	--	--
GL	*Direxion Daily 20+ Yr Treas Bear	TYBS	D-	29.92	41.27	28.02	E+ / 0.7	5.58	0.11	-25.61 / 8	--	--
USA	*Direxion Daily 20+ Yr Treas Bear	TMV	E	81.19	233.50	64.73	E / 0.4	19.47	4.97	-62.32 / 0	--	--
USA	*Direxion Daily 20+ Yr Treas Bull	TMF	C+	56.36	80.31	30.22	B+ / 8.7	-21.13	-20.57	73.73 / 99	--	--
GL	*Direxion Daily 7-10 Yr Treas Br	TYNS	D	34.98	40.88	34.13	E+ / 0.8	--	0.03	-13.42 / 17	--	--
USA	*Direxion Daily 7-10 Yr Trs Bear	TYO	E+	28.33	46.89	26.51	E / 0.5	3.47	-2.55	-37.69 / 3	--	--
USA	*Direxion Daily 7-10 Yr Trs Bull	TYD	B	73.33	80.71	51.10	B / 8.1	-5.83	-0.84	46.45 / 99	--	--
GI	*Direxion Daily Agribusiness Bear	COWS	U	20.91	N/A	N/A	U /	-33.03	-58.29	--	--	--
GI	*Direxion Daily Agribusiness Bull	COWL	U	30.69	N/A	N/A	U /	37.17	63.22	--	--	--
GI	*Direxion Daily Basic Mat Bear 3x	MATS	U	24.10	N/A	N/A	U /	-29.51	-62.49	--	--	--
IN	*Direxion Daily Basic Mat Bull 3x	MATL	U	29.22	N/A	N/A	U /	31.94	79.82	--	--	--

99 Pct = Best
0 Pct = Worst

* Denotes ETF Fund, N/A denotes number is not available

Incl. in Returns		RISK				NET ASSETS		VALUATION				ASSET					FUND MANAGER	
		Risk	3 Year					Premium / Discount										
Dividend Yield %	Expense Ratio	Rating/ Pts	Standard Deviation	Beta	Avg Dura- tion	NAV as of 3/31/12	Total $(Mil)	As of 3/31/12	1 Year Average	Wtd Avg P/E	Cash %	Stocks %	Bonds %	Other %	Portfolio Turnover Ratio	Manager Quality Pct	Manager Tenure (Years)
0.00	0.55	U /	N/A	N/A	N/A	19.65	24	-0.10	N/A	N/A	0	0	0	100	N/A	N/A	1
0.00	1.78	U /	N/A	N/A	N/A	26.06	6	0.19	N/A	N/A	0	0	0	100	N/A	N/A	0
0.00	3.07	C+/ 6.8	N/A	N/A	N/A	20.61	132	0.00	0.08	N/A	12	88	0	0	N/A	28	N/A
5.83	0.85	B+/ 9.2	N/A	N/A	N/A	16.64	2,747	0.18	0.07	N/A	0	100	0	0	N/A	85	1
1.58	0.34	B / 8.4	N/A	N/A	N/A	39.16	84	0.05	0.02	N/A	0	100	0	0	2	42	3
1.06	0.65	B- / 7.0	N/A	N/A	N/A	45.72	95	0.24	-0.15	N/A	0	100	0	0	10	19	1
0.11	0.65	C / 5.4	N/A	N/A	N/A	40.95	11	-0.81	-0.46	N/A	0	98	0	2	7	7	1
0.00	0.95	C+/ 5.8	N/A	N/A	N/A	133.86	325	0.08	-0.01	N/A	0	0	0	100	N/A	92	2
2.39	0.30	B- / 7.6	20.5	0.89	N/A	25.77	34	-0.50	-0.23	N/A	0	100	0	0	7	46	N/A
0.10	0.30	B- / 7.4	22.2	1.04	N/A	20.37	57	0.00	-0.08	58.0	0	99	0	1	14	34	N/A
2.76	0.30	B- / 7.3	25.1	0.95	N/A	42.27	470	-0.12	-0.05	N/A	0	99	0	1	8	24	N/A
4.26	0.30	B- / 7.3	23.6	1.09	N/A	19.87	14	-0.40	-0.09	58.0	0	100	0	0	17	29	N/A
0.00	0.89	C / 5.0	N/A	N/A	N/A	36.43	16	-0.14	-0.04	N/A	0	0	0	100	N/A	32	N/A
0.00	N/A	C- / 3.8	N/A	N/A	N/A	97.75	9	0.00	-0.05	N/A	0	0	0	100	N/A	23	3
0.00	N/A	C / 4.3	N/A	N/A	N/A	164.34	18	0.00	N/A	N/A	0	0	0	100	N/A	35	3
0.00	N/A	C- / 3.7	N/A	N/A	N/A	65.03	5	-0.03	0.10	N/A	0	0	0	100	N/A	22	3
0.00	N/A	D / 1.9	N/A	N/A	N/A	20.98	7	1.38	0.21	N/A	0	0	0	100	N/A	7	3
0.00	0.89	U /	N/A	N/A	N/A	31.76	7	-0.66	N/A	N/A	0	0	0	100	N/A	N/A	1
0.00	1.15	D / 1.9	N/A	N/A	N/A	10.68	9	3.00	-0.33	N/A	0	0	0	100	N/A	N/A	N/A
0.81	1.02	B / 8.8	N/A	N/A	N/A	24.35	119	-0.21	-0.07	N/A	33	56	11	0	187	15	N/A
1.64	0.55	B- / 7.3	22.7	1.24	N/A	36.50	62	0.14	0.17	86.8	0	100	0	0	11	58	1
2.68	0.35	B+/ 9.7	N/A	N/A	N/A	52.23	5	0.40	0.53	N/A	9	0	90	1	116	66	1
0.00	0.89	B- / 7.7	N/A	N/A	N/A	30.83	1	-2.17	-0.40	N/A	4	95	0	1	110	32	1
2.49	0.35	U /	N/A	N/A	N/A	53.53	5	13.21	1.16	N/A	0	0	100	0	6	98	2
0.00	0.89	B- / 7.8	N/A	N/A	N/A	31.73	8	-0.44	-0.61	N/A	0	99	0	1	51	28	1
1.22	0.19	B / 8.2	19.9	1.12	N/A	45.07	3,277	0.04	-0.01	43.7	0	100	0	0	7	77	14
2.09	0.19	B+/ 9.2	10.2	0.52	N/A	34.08	5,524	0.00	0.01	25.2	0	100	0	0	4	82	14
1.35	0.85	C / 5.1	N/A	N/A	N/A	24.69	269	-0.16	0.10	N/A	0	0	0	100	N/A	59	2
0.00	0.45	C / 5.4	N/A	N/A	N/A	22.66	34	0.18	-0.04	N/A	0	0	0	100	N/A	27	2
0.00	0.55	C+/ 5.8	N/A	N/A	N/A	20.40	92	-0.20	0.14	N/A	0	0	0	100	N/A	31	N/A
0.00	1.05	U /	N/A	N/A	N/A	19.16	16	0.05	N/A	N/A	0	0	0	100	N/A	N/A	1
0.00	0.65	B+/ 9.5	6.0	0.10	3.3	23.84	14	-1.43	-1.78	51.7	26	15	57	2	58	62	3
0.00	0.65	B / 8.9	10.6	0.58	4.4	23.88	33	-6.49	-2.99	51.9	0	62	36	2	49	36	3
2.29	0.65	B / 8.5	13.1	0.74	15.6	22.40	31	-6.43	-3.07	52.2	0	84	14	2	39	37	3
1.73	0.65	B / 8.2	16.7	0.98	25.3	21.82	30	0.78	-1.79	51.9	0	95	4	1	35	36	3
0.68	0.65	B+/ 9.3	7.9	0.26	3.3	26.49	16	0.15	-1.55	51.7	27	27	44	2	60	40	3
1.63	0.60	U /	N/A	N/A	N/A	23.40	5	0.43	N/A	N/A	0	94	0	6	N/A	N/A	1
0.52	0.35	U /	N/A	N/A	N/A	24.51	34	0.08	N/A	N/A	0	95	0	5	N/A	N/A	1
0.32	0.65	U /	N/A	N/A	N/A	23.12	5	1.12	N/A	N/A	0	93	0	7	N/A	N/A	1
0.86	0.50	U /	N/A	N/A	N/A	25.97	5	2.39	N/A	N/A	0	96	0	4	N/A	N/A	1
0.00	1.49	B / 8.4	N/A	N/A	N/A	18.32	8	-0.22	-0.12	N/A	61	38	0	1	456	10	N/A
0.72	0.65	U /	N/A	N/A	N/A	45.74	7	-0.33	N/A	N/A	0	100	0	0	N/A	5	1
0.00	0.65	C+/ 6.7	N/A	N/A	N/A	29.80	3	0.40	N/A	N/A	100	0	0	0	N/A	5	1
0.00	0.92	D+/ 2.6	N/A	N/A	N/A	81.24	308	-0.06	0.06	N/A	100	0	0	0	N/A	8	N/A
0.00	0.95	C / 5.1	N/A	N/A	N/A	56.35	23	0.02	-0.04	N/A	24	0	75	1	128	11	N/A
0.00	0.65	B / 8.8	N/A	N/A	N/A	35.02	3	-0.11	-0.03	N/A	100	0	0	0	N/A	12	1
0.00	0.95	C / 4.5	N/A	N/A	N/A	28.37	53	-0.14	0.03	N/A	100	0	0	0	N/A	7	4
0.00	0.95	B- / 7.5	N/A	N/A	N/A	73.42	4	-0.12	-0.04	N/A	15	0	84	1	536	90	4
0.00	0.95	U /	N/A	N/A	N/A	20.82	2	0.43	N/A	N/A	100	0	0	0	N/A	N/A	N/A
0.00	0.95	U /	N/A	N/A	N/A	30.73	5	-0.13	N/A	N/A	0	99	0	1	N/A	N/A	N/A
0.00	0.95	U /	N/A	N/A	N/A	24.22	2	-0.50	N/A	N/A	100	0	0	0	N/A	N/A	N/A
0.00	0.95	U /	N/A	N/A	N/A	29.28	6	-0.20	N/A	N/A	0	99	0	1	N/A	N/A	N/A

* Denotes ETF Fund, N/A denotes number is not available

Fund Type	Fund Name	Ticker Symbol	Overall Investment Rating	PRICE Price As of 3/31/12	52 Week High	52 Week Low	Performance Rating/Pts		3 Mo	6 Mo	1Yr/Pct	Annualized 3Yr/Pct	5Yr/Pct
FO	*Direxion Daily BRIC Bear 3X	BRIS	E	20.75	43.86	17.40	E	0.3	-33.13	-46.18	-8.68 / 24	--	--
EM	*Direxion Daily BRIC Bull 3X	BRIL	D-	32.95	49.96	21.10	C-	3.5	38.11	43.44	-31.51 / 5	--	--
FO	*Direxion Daily China Bear 3x ETF	YANG	E-	12.34	32.00	10.88	E-	0.2	-35.09	-53.17	-11.60 / 19	--	--
FO	*Direxion Daily China Bull 3x ETF	YINN	E-	22.25	59.52	13.49	E+	0.8	35.92	33.31	-58.41 / 1	--	--
PM	*Direxion Daily Gold Miners Bear	DUST	E+	42.04	51.99	27.44	D-	1.2	-9.57	11.97	-1.33 / 37	--	--
PM	*Direxion Daily Gold Miners Bull	NUGT	E-	16.36	43.63	14.94	E-	0.1	-16.40	-41.13	-52.83 / 1	--	--
HL	*Direxion Daily Healthcare Bear 3	SICK	U	23.57	N/A	N/A	U		-23.60	-45.60	--	--	--
HL	*Direxion Daily Healthcare Bull 3	CURE	U	44.57	N/A	N/A	U		27.02	60.38	--	--	--
FO	*Direxion Daily India Bear 3X	INDZ	E	24.70	47.34	19.43	E	0.4	-43.45	-32.95	-3.52 / 33	--	--
EM	*Direxion Daily India Bull 3X	INDL	E-	23.95	46.38	15.60	E+	0.7	44.98	-0.75	-46.75 / 2	--	--
FO	*Direxion Daily Latin Amer Bear 3	LHB	E-	11.10	33.11	10.14	E-	0.1	-33.13	-60.71	-23.27 / 9	--	--
FO	*Direxion Daily Latin Amer Bull 3	LBJ	E+	97.81	212.00	53.31	C-	3.6	35.69	68.19	-46.41 / 2	--	--
GR	*Direxion Daily Mid Cap Bear 3X	MWN	E-	21.23	63.26	20.62	E-	0.1	-31.80	-58.60	-40.11 / 3	-64.94 / 0	--
GR	*Direxion Daily Mid Cap Bull 3X	MWJ	C-	41.17	62.82	21.25	A+	9.9	40.96	85.31	-14.80 / 15	67.22 / 99	--
GR	*Direxion Daily Nat Gas Rel Bear	GASX	E-	18.65	34.65	14.38	E+	0.9	-2.43	-33.98	12.79 / 73	--	--
GR	*Direxion Daily Nat Gas Rel Bull	GASL	E-	34.66	83.26	28.18	E	0.3	-12.32	0.69	-57.45 / 1	--	--
GR	*Direxion Daily Real Estate Bear	DRV	E-	27.76	104.25	27.59	E-	0.0	-28.57	-62.10	-61.04 / 0	--	--
GR	*Direxion Daily Real Estate Bull	DRN	C-	68.61	83.89	30.59	A+	9.9	33.05	99.99	16.70 / 79	--	--
GR	*Direxion Daily Retail Bear 3X	RETS	E	12.66	30.18	12.23	E-	0.0	-34.98	-47.25	-49.26 / 1	--	--
GR	*Direxion Daily Retail Bull 3X	RETL	A+	87.91	91.62	46.77	A+	9.9	48.72	71.07	59.72 / 99	--	--
GI	*Direxion Daily Russia Bear 3x	RUSS	U	21.60	N/A	N/A	U		-43.81	-70.52	--	--	--
FO	*Direxion Daily Russia Bull 3x	RUSL	U	45.03	N/A	N/A	U		45.07	45.96	--	--	--
IN	*Direxion Daily Semiconductor Bea	SOXS	E-	29.95	115.50	28.77	E-	0.0	-47.40	-65.88	-50.17 / 1	--	--
IN	*Direxion Daily Semiconductor Bul	SOXL	C-	44.07	62.10	19.60	A+	9.9	69.76	91.53	-20.52 / 11	--	--
GR	*Direxion Daily Small Cap Bear 3x	TZA	E-	17.68	68.31	16.60	E-	0.0	-33.23	-66.62	-48.95 / 1	-69.01 / 0	--
GR	*Direxion Daily Small Cap Bull 3x	TNA	C	62.40	96.25	26.67	A+	9.8	39.17	89.10	-30.06 / 5	48.01 / 98	--
GR	*Direxion Daily Technology Bear 3	TYP	E-	8.71	29.68	8.41	E-	0.1	-46.56	-62.60	-58.82 / 0	-62.59 / 1	--
GR	*Direxion Daily Technology Bull 3	TYH	C-	65.50	67.93	26.58	A+	9.9	79.70	113.42	39.24 / 96	70.71 / 99	--
GR	*Direxion Daily Total Market Bear	TOTS	U	32.93	N/A	N/A	U		-10.39	-23.72	--	--	--
GL	*Direxion Developed Markets Bear	DPK	E-	24.33	55.41	23.13	E-	0.1	-29.99	-49.44	-29.11 / 6	-56.22 / 1	--
GL	*Direxion Developed Markets Bull	DZK	D-	39.92	86.00	26.84	C	4.5	32.35	38.49	-39.66 / 3	20.62 / 46	--
GL	*Direxion Emerging Markets Bear 3	EDZ	E-	12.68	37.92	11.41	E-	0.1	-35.60	-61.33	-25.63 / 8	-64.84 / 0	--
GL	*Direxion Emerging Markets Bull 3	EDC	D-	104.23	227.75	56.10	C	5.1	39.69	56.69	-51.53 / 1	21.84 / 52	--
EN	*Direxion Energy Bear 3x Shares	ERY	E-	9.75	28.12	8.41	E-	0.1	-13.79	-57.57	-26.14 / 7	-59.72 / 1	--
EN	*Direxion Energy Bull 3x Shares	ERX	D	51.32	93.27	24.82	C+	6.6	9.54	63.28	-43.33 / 2	27.50 / 75	--
FS	*Direxion Financial Bear 3x Share	FAZ	E-	20.65	81.50	19.92	E-	0.0	-44.71	-68.70	-47.42 / 1	-70.20 / 0	--
FS	*Direxion Financial Bull 3x Share	FAS	D+	109.15	160.75	42.15	B+	8.3	68.27	105.56	-29.49 / 6	22.85 / 56	--
GR	*Direxion Large Cap Bear 3x Share	BGZ	E-	20.16	57.00	19.68	E-	0.1	-31.73	-56.44	-42.56 / 2	-57.44 / 1	--
GR	*Direxion Large Cap Bull 3x Share	BGU	C+	86.18	92.65	39.24	A+	9.9	41.65	85.85	1.51 / 45	55.23 / 99	--
GI	*Direxion S&P RC 1500 Vol Respons	VSPR	U	42.81	N/A	N/A	U		--	--	--	--	--
GI	*Direxion S&P RC 500 Vol Response	VSPY	U	43.04	N/A	N/A	U		--	--	--	--	--
GL	*EGShares Basic Materials GEMS ET	LGEM	U	15.70	N/A	N/A	U		--	4.68	--	--	--
FO	*EGShares Brazil Infrastructure E	BRXX	C-	24.09	27.43	18.84	C	4.3	17.34	28.43	-4.60 / 31	--	--
FO	*EGShares China Infrastructure ET	CHXX	E+	16.41	23.38	12.20	D-	1.0	8.23	23.67	-25.45 / 8	--	--
GL	*EGShares Consumer Goods GEMS ETF	GGEM	U	22.19	N/A	N/A	U		11.90	22.35	--	--	--
GL	*EGShares COnsumer Services GEMS	VGEM	U	20.90	N/A	N/A	U		--	29.50	--	--	--
EM	*EGShares Em Mkts Metals&Mining E	EMT	E	15.98	23.72	14.01	E+	0.8	10.82	8.72	-28.68 / 6	--	--
EM	*EGShares Emerging Markets Cons E	ECON	C+	24.85	25.06	18.95	C+	6.2	13.06	25.68	7.70 / 63	--	--
EM	*EGShares Energy GEMS ETF	OGEM	E+	24.44	31.99	19.56	D-	1.3	12.94	18.77	-18.20 / 12	--	--
FS	*EGShares Financials GEMS ETF	FGEM	E+	20.30	25.66	15.57	D	1.7	15.54	23.30	-17.56 / 12	--	--
EM	*EGShares GEMS Composite ETF	AGEM	E+	23.22	28.32	18.72	D-	1.5	12.56	20.15	-15.68 / 14	--	--
HL	*EGShares Health Care GEMS ETF	HGEM	U	19.16	N/A	N/A	U		18.56	15.97	--	--	--

* Denotes ETF Fund, N/A denotes number is not available

www.thestreetratings.com

I. Index of ETFs and Other Closed-End Funds

		RISK				NET ASSETS		VALUATION			ASSET					FUND MANAGER	
Incl. in Returns		Risk Rating/ Pts	3 Year		Avg Dura-tion	NAV as of 3/31/12	Total $(Mil)	Premium / Discount		Wtd Avg P/E	Cash %	Stocks %	Bonds %	Other %	Portfolio Turnover Ratio	Manager Quality Pct	Manager Tenure (Years)
Dividend Yield %	Expense Ratio		Standard Deviation	Beta				As of 3/31/12	1 Year Average								
0.00	0.95	D+ / 2.7	N/A	N/A	N/A	20.30	2	2.22	0.28	N/A	100	0	0	0	N/A	4	2
0.67	0.95	C- / 3.8	N/A	N/A	N/A	33.11	8	-0.48	-0.23	N/A	47	52	0	1	7	12	2
0.00	0.95	D / 1.9	N/A	N/A	N/A	12.31	10	0.24	0.09	N/A	100	0	0	0	N/A	3	3
0.00	0.95	D / 1.9	N/A	N/A	N/A	22.12	56	0.59	-0.04	N/A	0	100	0	0	131	1	3
0.00	0.95	C- / 3.7	N/A	N/A	N/A	39.49	12	6.46	-0.12	N/A	100	0	0	0	N/A	99	2
0.00	0.95	D+ / 2.4	N/A	N/A	N/A	16.39	142	-0.18	0.01	N/A	0	100	0	0	N/A	N/A	2
0.00	0.95	U /	N/A	N/A	N/A	23.65	3	-0.34	N/A	N/A	100	0	0	0	N/A	N/A	1
0.05	0.95	U /	N/A	N/A	N/A	44.45	4	0.27	N/A	N/A	75	24	0	1	N/A	N/A	1
0.00	0.95	D+ / 2.9	N/A	N/A	N/A	24.59	4	0.45	0.02	N/A	100	0	0	0	N/A	8	2
0.00	0.95	D / 2.2	N/A	N/A	N/A	24.02	21	-0.29	-0.11	N/A	67	32	0	1	N/A	2	2
0.00	1.07	D / 1.9	N/A	N/A	N/A	11.10	5	0.00	0.05	N/A	100	0	0	0	N/A	1	3
1.98	0.95	D / 1.9	N/A	N/A	N/A	97.76	47	0.05	-0.01	N/A	60	39	0	1	102	3	3
0.00	0.95	D / 1.9	60.3	-3.33	N/A	21.20	13	0.14	0.03	N/A	100	0	0	0	N/A	2	3
0.00	1.10	D / 1.9	64.0	3.59	N/A	41.31	59	-0.34	-0.06	N/A	73	26	0	1	63	9	3
0.00	0.95	D / 2.0	N/A	N/A	N/A	18.67	2	-0.11	0.04	N/A	100	0	0	0	N/A	99	2
0.22	0.95	D+ / 2.5	N/A	N/A	N/A	34.65	13	0.03	-0.15	N/A	42	57	0	1	40	N/A	2
0.00	0.95	D / 1.9	N/A	N/A	N/A	27.78	29	-0.07	-0.03	N/A	100	0	0	0	N/A	N/A	3
0.00	0.95	D / 1.9	N/A	N/A	N/A	68.63	116	-0.03	N/A	N/A	72	27	0	1	110	10	3
0.00	0.95	C- / 3.2	N/A	N/A	N/A	12.68	2	-0.16	-0.08	N/A	100	0	0	0	N/A	1	2
0.00	0.95	B / 8.5	N/A	N/A	N/A	87.95	7	-0.05	0.06	N/A	65	34	0	1	111	98	2
0.00	0.95	U /	N/A	N/A	N/A	21.61	8	-0.05	N/A	N/A	100	0	0	0	N/A	N/A	N/A
0.24	0.95	U /	N/A	N/A	N/A	45.16	23	-0.29	N/A	N/A	54	45	0	1	N/A	N/A	N/A
0.00	1.01	D / 1.9	N/A	N/A	N/A	30.01	29	-0.20	0.01	N/A	100	0	0	0	N/A	3	2
0.00	0.95	D / 1.9	N/A	N/A	N/A	44.09	117	-0.05	-0.04	N/A	59	40	0	1	69	1	2
0.00	0.95	D / 1.9	70.9	-3.74	N/A	17.70	929	-0.11	-0.01	N/A	100	0	0	0	N/A	2	4
0.00	0.95	D+ / 2.5	75.0	3.99	N/A	62.47	854	-0.11	-0.02	N/A	90	9	0	1	305	3	4
0.00	0.95	D / 1.9	59.9	-3.16	N/A	8.71	42	0.00	-0.03	N/A	100	0	0	0	N/A	2	4
0.00	0.95	D / 1.9	64.1	3.40	N/A	65.52	156	-0.03	-0.04	N/A	71	28	0	1	12	13	3
0.00	0.65	U /	N/A	N/A	N/A	32.58	3	1.07	N/A	N/A	100	0	0	0	N/A	N/A	1
0.00	0.95	D / 1.9	65.4	-2.85	N/A	24.30	14	0.12	-0.02	N/A	100	0	0	0	N/A	2	4
1.42	1.01	D+ / 2.4	73.3	3.22	N/A	39.96	24	-0.10	-0.01	N/A	54	46	0	0	116	6	4
0.00	0.95	D / 1.9	87.0	-3.25	N/A	12.68	150	0.00	-0.06	N/A	100	0	0	0	187	N/A	N/A
0.18	0.95	D / 1.9	90.0	3.53	N/A	104.10	402	0.12	0.06	N/A	82	17	0	1	187	5	7
0.00	1.02	D / 1.9	70.3	-2.86	N/A	9.72	99	0.31	-0.06	N/A	100	0	0	0	N/A	1	4
0.00	0.95	D / 2.2	76.0	3.10	N/A	51.48	363	-0.31	N/A	N/A	60	39	0	1	302	6	4
0.00	0.95	D / 1.9	89.5	-3.27	N/A	20.65	985	0.00	-0.06	N/A	100	0	0	0	N/A	N/A	4
0.00	0.95	D / 1.9	74.9	2.91	N/A	109.24	1,459	-0.08	0.02	N/A	84	15	0	1	63	4	4
0.00	0.95	D+ / 2.3	50.5	-2.94	N/A	20.13	186	0.15	-0.04	N/A	100	0	0	0	N/A	4	4
0.00	0.95	C / 4.5	54.2	3.17	N/A	86.37	257	-0.22	-0.03	N/A	87	12	0	1	116	10	4
0.00	0.45	U /	N/A	N/A	N/A	42.80	4	0.02	N/A	N/A	0	0	0	100	N/A	N/A	0
0.00	0.45	U /	N/A	N/A	N/A	42.96	4	0.19	N/A	N/A	0	0	0	100	N/A	N/A	0
2.55	0.85	U /	N/A	N/A	N/A	15.76	2	-0.38	N/A	N/A	0	99	0	1	N/A	N/A	3
4.07	0.85	B- / 7.1	N/A	N/A	N/A	24.21	90	-0.50	0.51	N/A	1	98	0	1	35	70	2
2.47	0.85	C / 5.3	N/A	N/A	N/A	16.40	14	0.06	-0.24	N/A	1	98	0	1	34	9	2
1.35	0.85	U /	N/A	N/A	N/A	22.01	1	0.82	N/A	N/A	0	99	0	1	N/A	N/A	3
0.15	0.85	U /	N/A	N/A	N/A	20.87	1	0.14	N/A	N/A	0	99	0	1	N/A	N/A	3
3.70	0.85	D / 2.2	N/A	N/A	N/A	15.97	16	0.06	-0.42	N/A	0	99	0	1	35	7	3
0.49	0.85	B- / 7.7	N/A	N/A	N/A	24.77	370	0.32	0.20	N/A	0	99	0	1	9	91	2
2.11	0.85	C- / 3.8	N/A	N/A	N/A	24.58	12	-0.57	-0.51	N/A	2	97	0	1	19	16	3
1.71	0.85	C- / 3.1	N/A	N/A	N/A	20.23	3	0.35	-0.51	N/A	0	99	0	1	39	8	3
1.68	0.75	C- / 3.5	N/A	N/A	N/A	23.31	16	-0.39	-0.49	N/A	1	99	0	0	39	20	3
0.26	0.85	U /	N/A	N/A	N/A	19.09	2	0.37	N/A	N/A	0	99	0	1	N/A	N/A	3

* Denotes ETF Fund, N/A denotes number is not available

Data as of March 31, 2012

Fund Type	Fund Name	Ticker Symbol	Overall Investment Rating	PRICE Price As of 3/31/12	52 Week High	52 Week Low	Performance Rating/Pts	3 Mo	6 Mo	1Yr/Pct	3Yr/Pct	5Yr/Pct
	99 Pct = Best *0 Pct = Worst*									% Total Return Through 3/31/12 Annualized		
GI	*EGShares India Consumer ETF	INCO	U	19.02	N/A	N/A	U /	18.58	6.63	--	--	--
GL	*EGShares India Infrastructure ET	INXX	E+	14.88	20.18	11.54	D- / 1.0	28.28	5.46	-24.21 / 9	--	--
FO	*EGShares India Small Cap ETF	SCIN	E+	14.49	21.20	11.10	E+ / 0.9	29.61	0.26	-26.34 / 7	--	--
GL	*EGShares Industrials GEMS ETF	IGEM	U	18.12	N/A	N/A	U /	19.05	--	--	--	--
GI	*EGShares Low Vol Em Mkts Div ETF	HILO	U	20.17	N/A	N/A	U /	10.54	19.44	--	--	--
GR	*EGShares Technology GEMS ETF	QGEM	U	18.93	N/A	N/A	U /	--	17.43	--	--	--
GL	*EGShares Telecom GEMS ETF	TGEM	U	20.47	N/A	N/A	U /	13.22	11.93	--	--	--
UT	*EGShares Utilities GEMS ETF	UGEM	U	18.62	N/A	N/A	U /	16.67	25.70	--	--	--
EN	*ELEMENTS MLCX Biofuels Tot Ret	FUE	D-	11.38	16.78	9.78	D+ / 2.9	5.37	9.53	-5.01 / 30	13.27 / 22	--
EN	*ELEMENTS MLCX Grains Idx Tot Ret	GRU	E+	6.40	7.88	5.64	D- / 1.2	2.40	6.84	-15.79 / 14	2.06 / 8	--
EN	*ELEMENTS RIC Energy Total Return	RJN	D-	7.08	8.02	5.66	D+ / 2.8	5.36	20.61	-6.35 / 28	12.14 / 19	--
EN	*ELEMENTS RIC Index Agri Total Re	RJA	E+	9.13	11.54	8.34	D / 1.6	2.01	1.33	-19.20 / 11	7.59 / 13	--
EN	*ELEMENTS RIC Index Total Return	RJI	D-	8.95	10.51	7.90	D+ / 2.7	5.12	10.86	-11.95 / 19	12.88 / 21	--
EN	*ELEMENTS RIC Metals Total Return	RJZ	D-	10.95	14.46	9.71	C- / 3.4	7.93	6.83	-13.85 / 17	17.15 / 33	--
EN	*Energy Select Sector SPDR	XLE	C-	71.75	80.90	54.26	C- / 4.0	4.20	23.61	-8.85 / 23	17.97 / 36	4.68 / 55
PM	*ETFS Physical Asian Gold Shares	AGOL	C-	164.75	190.43	144.57	C- / 3.3	5.67	1.90	15.46 / 78	--	--
PM	*ETFS Physical Palladium Shares	PALL	D-	64.47	83.90	52.96	E+ / 0.9	-0.15	7.45	-16.01 / 14	--	--
PM	*ETFS Physical Platinum Shares	PPLT	D	161.72	189.16	133.50	D / 1.7	17.34	7.58	-7.79 / 25	--	--
PM	*ETFS Physical PM Basket Shares	GLTR	D	95.27	116.78	83.50	D / 1.9	10.46	5.22	-0.54 / 39	--	--
GL	*ETFS Physical Silver Shares	SIVR	E+	32.05	49.28	26.19	D- / 1.2	16.46	8.57	-14.69 / 15	--	--
PM	*ETFS Physical Swiss Gold Shares	SGOL	C-	165.23	189.30	142.30	C- / 3.7	6.65	2.57	16.45 / 79	--	--
PM	*ETFS Physical WM Basket Shares	WITE	D-	53.55	73.94	44.71	D- / 1.3	14.69	8.18	-12.96 / 18	--	--
PM	*FactorShares Gold Bull S&P 500 B	FSG	E+	23.38	55.00	22.87	E / 0.5	-12.50	-37.51	-2.30 / 35	--	--
GI	*FactorShares Oil Bull S&P 500 Be	FOL	E+	17.34	30.74	17.29	E / 0.4	-19.26	-6.32	-37.87 / 3	--	--
GI	*FactorShares S&P 500 Bull Tbd Be	FSE	E	14.63	25.93	9.42	D- / 1.0	22.79	34.31	-41.48 / 3	--	--
GR	*FactorShares Tbd Bull S&P 500 Be	FSA	E+	21.64	47.45	20.96	E / 0.3	-29.07	-47.22	-10.43 / 21	--	--
GR	*Fidelity Nasdaq Comp Tracker Sto	ONEQ	C+	121.86	123.52	90.00	B- / 7.4	18.49	28.76	12.29 / 73	25.15 / 65	5.39 / 58
FS	*Financial Select Sector SPDR	XLF	C	15.80	16.75	10.95	C / 5.4	21.89	35.00	-2.80 / 34	19.34 / 40	-13.11 / 5
HL	*First Trust AMEX Biotechnology	FBT	B	42.27	45.50	29.94	B+ / 8.5	29.42	27.86	2.08 / 47	30.77 / 83	11.60 / 94
FO	*First Trust AsiaPac Ex-Jpn Alpha	FPA	U	25.52	N/A	N/A	U /	11.88	20.44	--	--	--
FO	*First Trust BICK Index	BICK	D-	26.28	35.30	20.57	D- / 1.2	15.87	19.40	-23.05 / 9	--	--
FO	*First Trust Brazil AlphaDEX	FBZ	U	27.23	N/A	N/A	U /	17.86	31.10	--	--	--
FO	*First Trust Canada AlphaDEX	FCAN	U	30.35	N/A	N/A	U /	--	--	--	--	--
FO	*First Trust China AlphaDEX	FCA	U	21.67	N/A	N/A	U /	10.39	27.53	--	--	--
IN	*First Trust Consumer Dis AlphaDE	FXD	A-	22.85	23.32	16.88	B+ / 8.9	15.17	27.68	8.09 / 64	34.09 / 89	--
IN	*First Trust Consumer Stap AlphaD	FXG	B-	25.05	25.63	21.12	C+ / 6.2	5.92	12.87	7.95 / 64	24.09 / 61	--
FO	*First Trust Dev Mkt Ex-US AlphaD	FDT	U	42.10	N/A	N/A	U /	7.79	14.22	--	--	--
GL	*First Trust DJ Glb Sel Div Idx F	FGD	C+	23.59	26.20	19.99	C+ / 6.5	7.83	13.80	-1.12 / 38	25.84 / 68	--
GR	*First Trust Dow Jones Internet I	FDN	C+	37.10	38.25	27.62	B+ / 8.4	14.86	26.54	1.49 / 45	32.11 / 86	9.45 / 83
GR	*First Trust Dow Jones Sel Micro	FDM	C	22.56	24.35	15.88	C / 5.5	12.35	32.31	-4.81 / 30	21.49 / 50	-0.85 / 23
EM	*First Trust EM Small Cap AlphaDE	FEMS	U	30.77	N/A	N/A	U /	--	--	--	--	--
EM	*First Trust Emerg Mkt AlphaDEX	FEM	U	26.02	N/A	N/A	U /	16.47	23.69	--	--	--
EN	*First Trust Energy AlphaDEX	FXN	C-	20.20	25.34	15.02	C / 5.1	4.61	22.33	-18.74 / 11	23.76 / 59	--
IN	*First Trust Enhanced 130/30 Lg C	JFT	D	35.59	43.39	28.00	C- / 3.7	8.77	9.51	-4.33 / 32	16.93 / 32	--
FO	*First Trust Europe AlphaDEX	FEP	U	24.85	N/A	N/A	U /	14.10	15.02	--	--	--
FS	*First Trust Financial AlphaDEX	FXO	B	15.47	15.85	11.00	B- / 7.5	17.29	32.62	1.56 / 45	26.98 / 73	--
GI	*First Trust FTSE EPRA/NAREIT Glb	FFR	C+	35.70	38.01	28.00	C+ / 6.8	11.98	21.36	1.05 / 44	25.79 / 68	--
HL	*First Trust Health Care AlphaDEX	FXH	B+	30.81	31.21	23.70	B / 8.1	13.61	20.30	7.17 / 62	30.23 / 83	--
IN	*First Trust Industrials AlphaDEX	FXR	C+	19.35	20.54	13.81	C+ / 6.9	-12.70	31.67	-3.39 / 33	25.84 / 68	--
IN	*First Trust ISE Chindia Index Fu	FNI	C-	21.90	27.86	17.28	C / 5.3	20.68	19.25	-17.16 / 13	22.68 / 55	--
GL	*First Trust ISE Cloud Computing	SKYY	U	21.36	N/A	N/A	U /	24.19	34.00	--	--	--
GL	*First Trust ISE Glb Eng & Constr	FLM	D	41.13	50.66	31.78	C- / 3.0	14.25	22.37	-15.09 / 15	13.40 / 23	--

* Denotes ETF Fund, N/A denotes number is not available

www.thestreetratings.com

Incl. in Returns Dividend Yield %	Expense Ratio	Risk Rating/ Pts	3 Year Standard Deviation	Beta	Avg Dura-tion	NAV as of 3/31/12	Total $(Mil)	Premium/Discount As of 3/31/12	1 Year Average	Wtd Avg P/E	Cash %	Stocks %	Bonds %	Other %	Portfolio Turnover Ratio	Manager Quality Pct	Manager Tenure (Years)
0.11	0.89	U /	N/A	N/A	N/A	19.08	2	-0.31	N/A	N/A	0	0	0	100	N/A	N/A	N/A
0.56	0.85	C / 4.9	N/A	N/A	N/A	14.99	63	-0.73	-0.47	N/A	0	100	0	0	9	8	N/A
1.13	0.90	C- / 4.2	N/A	N/A	N/A	14.39	27	0.69	0.15	N/A	0	100	0	0	1	8	N/A
0.27	0.85	U /	N/A	N/A	N/A	18.57	3	-2.42	N/A	N/A	0	99	0	1	N/A	N/A	3
0.96	0.85	U /	N/A	N/A	N/A	20.09	51	0.40	N/A	N/A	0	0	0	100	N/A	N/A	3
0.00	0.85	U /	N/A	N/A	N/A	18.84	2	0.48	N/A	N/A	0	99	0	1	N/A	N/A	3
1.37	0.85	U /	N/A	N/A	N/A	20.09	2	1.89	N/A	N/A	0	99	0	1	N/A	N/A	3
1.43	0.85	U /	N/A	N/A	N/A	18.59	3	0.16	N/A	N/A	0	99	0	1	N/A	N/A	3
0.00	0.75	C / 4.6	30.2	0.72	N/A	11.14	2	2.15	-0.38	N/A	0	0	0	100	N/A	73	4
0.00	0.75	C- / 4.1	35.5	0.81	N/A	6.04	16	5.96	0.05	N/A	0	0	0	100	N/A	15	4
0.00	0.75	C / 4.4	25.5	0.88	N/A	7.05	53	0.43	0.05	N/A	0	0	0	100	N/A	30	5
0.00	0.75	C / 4.5	23.8	0.62	N/A	8.88	303	2.82	-0.05	N/A	0	0	0	100	N/A	31	5
0.00	0.75	C / 4.6	20.9	0.76	N/A	8.83	511	1.36	-0.02	N/A	0	0	0	100	N/A	42	5
0.00	0.75	C / 4.6	23.5	0.78	N/A	10.88	58	0.64	-0.17	N/A	0	0	0	100	N/A	70	5
1.59	0.19	B- / 7.5	24.2	1.06	N/A	71.76	7,884	-0.01	0.01	18.3	0	100	0	0	3	48	14
0.00	0.39	B / 8.0	N/A	N/A	N/A	164.97	79	-0.13	-0.10	N/A	0	0	0	100	N/A	54	1
0.00	0.60	C+ / 6.6	N/A	N/A	N/A	64.23	531	0.37	N/A	N/A	0	0	0	100	N/A	6	2
0.00	0.60	B- / 7.0	N/A	N/A	N/A	161.82	886	-0.06	0.13	N/A	0	0	0	100	N/A	7	2
0.00	0.60	C+ / 6.7	N/A	N/A	N/A	95.19	214	0.08	0.14	N/A	0	0	0	100	N/A	9	N/A
0.00	0.30	C / 5.1	N/A	N/A	N/A	32.17	687	-0.37	0.12	N/A	0	0	0	100	N/A	22	3
0.00	0.39	B / 8.2	N/A	N/A	N/A	164.60	1,972	0.38	0.17	N/A	0	0	0	100	N/A	56	3
0.00	0.60	C / 5.2	N/A	N/A	N/A	53.61	48	-0.11	0.06	N/A	0	0	0	100	N/A	3	2
0.00	0.75	C / 4.5	N/A	N/A	N/A	23.38	11	0.00	0.21	N/A	99	0	0	1	N/A	5	1
0.00	0.75	C / 4.9	N/A	N/A	N/A	17.02	2	1.88	0.09	N/A	100	0	0	0	N/A	1	1
0.00	0.75	D+ / 2.7	N/A	N/A	N/A	14.62	1	0.07	-0.14	N/A	94	0	0	6	N/A	N/A	1
0.00	0.75	C- / 4.2	N/A	N/A	N/A	21.21	2	2.03	0.05	N/A	0	0	0	100	N/A	89	1
0.69	0.35	B- / 7.5	19.1	1.12	N/A	121.80	187	0.05	-0.05	99.7	0	100	0	0	12	50	8
1.26	0.19	B- / 7.5	25.7	1.07	N/A	15.80	7,395	0.00	-0.01	19.5	0	99	0	1	7	36	14
0.00	0.60	C+ / 6.9	29.1	1.16	N/A	42.24	234	0.07	0.03	79.7	0	99	0	1	35	55	6
1.85	0.80	U /	N/A	N/A	N/A	25.65	3	-0.51	N/A	N/A	0	100	0	0	N/A	N/A	1
0.00	0.64	C+ / 6.0	N/A	N/A	N/A	26.16	53	0.46	0.02	N/A	0	98	0	2	96	11	2
1.58	0.80	U /	N/A	N/A	N/A	27.17	9	0.22	N/A	N/A	1	95	0	4	N/A	N/A	1
1.58	0.80	U /	N/A	N/A	N/A	30.37	3	-0.07	N/A	N/A	0	0	0	100	N/A	N/A	0
0.45	0.80	U /	N/A	N/A	N/A	21.64	4	0.14	N/A	N/A	0	99	0	1	N/A	N/A	1
0.81	0.70	B / 8.0	25.3	1.38	N/A	22.83	568	0.09	0.01	35.9	0	99	0	1	90	64	5
0.99	0.70	B / 8.7	13.5	0.67	N/A	25.03	325	0.08	0.05	44.2	0	99	0	1	108	83	5
0.63	0.80	U /	N/A	N/A	N/A	42.12	45	-0.05	N/A	N/A	0	100	0	0	N/A	N/A	1
1.70	0.60	B / 8.2	23.9	1.03	N/A	23.47	170	0.51	0.21	18.4	0	100	0	0	22	86	5
0.06	0.60	C+ / 6.4	22.3	1.24	N/A	37.07	524	0.08	0.01	152.9	0	100	0	0	16	69	6
0.94	0.60	B- / 7.2	25.4	1.39	N/A	22.45	56	0.49	-0.01	40.3	0	100	0	0	86	18	7
0.00	0.80	U /	N/A	N/A	N/A	30.72	3	0.16	N/A	N/A	0	0	0	100	N/A	N/A	0
0.87	0.80	U /	N/A	N/A	N/A	25.92	66	0.39	N/A	N/A	0	100	0	0	N/A	N/A	1
0.66	0.70	C+ / 6.8	33.5	1.38	N/A	20.20	96	0.00	-0.02	19.1	0	99	0	1	101	50	5
0.00	0.95	C / 4.6	27.7	0.57	N/A	37.47	4	-5.02	-2.48	N/A	0	0	0	100	N/A	71	4
0.09	0.80	U /	N/A	N/A	N/A	24.65	4	0.81	N/A	N/A	0	100	0	0	N/A	N/A	1
1.54	0.70	B- / 7.9	22.3	0.92	N/A	15.46	126	0.06	N/A	23.2	0	99	0	1	62	80	5
1.13	0.60	B- / 7.4	23.6	1.30	N/A	35.80	80	-0.28	0.04	83.6	0	99	0	1	11	44	5
0.10	0.70	B / 8.4	14.7	0.78	N/A	30.78	568	0.10	0.05	49.7	0	99	0	1	116	86	5
0.64	0.70	B- / 7.5	23.7	1.35	N/A	19.34	124	0.05	0.01	35.0	0	99	0	1	102	30	5
1.83	0.60	C+ / 6.3	31.8	1.53	N/A	21.91	98	-0.05	-0.12	91.3	0	100	0	0	34	16	5
0.00	0.60	U /	N/A	N/A	N/A	21.36	78	0.00	N/A	N/A	0	0	0	100	N/A	N/A	1
0.26	0.70	C+ / 6.8	25.7	1.13	N/A	41.00	38	0.32	-0.16	N/A	0	99	0	1	22	27	4

* Denotes ETF Fund, N/A denotes number is not available

Fund Type	Fund Name	Ticker Symbol	Overall Investment Rating	PRICE Price As of 3/31/12	52 Week High	52 Week Low	PERFORMANCE Perform-ance Rating/Pts		% Total Return Through 3/31/12 3 Mo	6 Mo	1Yr/Pct	Annualized 3Yr/Pct	5Yr/Pct
EN	*First Trust ISE Glb Wind Energy	FAN	E+	7.83	12.28	7.54	E+	0.7	-1.14	-2.85	-34.22 / 4	-10.88 / 6	--
PM	*First Trust ISE Global Copper Id	CU	E+	31.17	46.83	23.63	E+	0.8	6.42	18.70	-29.35 / 6	--	--
PM	*First Trust ISE Global Platinum	PLTM	E+	19.33	34.54	17.32	E	0.5	8.35	1.57	-42.14 / 2	--	--
IN	*First Trust ISE Water Index Fund	FIW	C	23.98	24.40	17.42	C	5.2	15.46	28.70	2.05 / 46	19.32 / 40	--
IN	*First Trust ISE-Revere Natural G	FCG	D	17.67	23.75	14.25	D+	2.9	-2.86	11.85	-24.43 / 8	16.70 / 32	--
FO	*First Trust Japan AlphaDEX	FJP	U	39.82	N/A	N/A	U		6.30	-0.67	--	--	--
GR	*First Trust Large Cap Gro AlphaD	FTC	C	30.13	31.42	23.92	C	5.2	9.64	20.33	-0.97 / 38	21.06 / 47	--
IN	*First Trust Large Cap Val AlphaD	FTA	B	29.78	30.47	22.33	B-	7.4	12.59	26.82	5.06 / 55	27.05 / 73	--
FO	*First Trust Latin America AlphaD	FLN	U	28.47	N/A	N/A	U		17.26	30.48	--	--	--
GI	*First Trust Lrg Cap Core AlphaDE	FEX	C+	30.27	30.70	23.18	C+	6.5	11.41	24.27	2.59 / 48	24.30 / 62	--
IN	*First Trust Materials AlphaDEX	FXZ	B	25.20	26.09	16.88	B+	8.4	18.70	37.93	-1.19 / 38	30.83 / 84	--
GR	*First Trust Mega Cap AlphaDEX	FMK	U	19.81	N/A	N/A	U		10.32	22.22	--	--	--
GR	*First Trust Mid Cap Core AlphaDE	FNX	B	36.69	37.41	26.63	B	7.8	12.48	29.30	1.86 / 46	29.11 / 80	--
GR	*First Trust Mid Cap Growth Alpha	FNY	U	20.90	N/A	N/A	U		11.07	23.55	--	--	--
GR	*First Trust Mid Cap Val AlphaDEX	FNK	U	21.29	N/A	N/A	U		13.79	31.76	--	--	--
IN	*First Trust Morningstar Div Lead	FDL	B	17.73	17.98	14.57	C+	6.3	1.74	11.87	10.00 / 68	24.80 / 64	-1.60 / 21
GR	*First Trust Multi Cap Grth Alpha	FAD	C+	32.99	34.09	24.72	C+	6.2	10.18	23.70	0.23 / 42	23.78 / 60	--
IN	*First Trust Multi Cap Val AlphaD	FAB	B	32.00	32.75	23.51	B	7.7	12.35	28.44	3.65 / 51	28.29 / 77	--
GR	*First Trust NASD Cln Edge Smt Gd	GRID	D-	27.79	35.55	22.16	D-	1.0	11.47	13.57	-20.99 / 10	--	--
IN	*First Trust NASDAQ ABA Community	QABA	C+	25.94	26.56	18.36	C+	6.5	12.96	35.08	2.55 / 48	--	--
GL	*First Trust NASDAQ CEA Smartphon	FONE	C-	27.63	29.35	21.33	C-	3.7	16.53	21.56	-2.67 / 34	--	--
IN	*First Trust NASDAQ Cln Edg US Li	QCLN	D-	10.75	17.28	9.00	E+	0.9	12.10	7.39	-35.42 / 4	-2.19 / 7	-12.58 / 5
GL	*First Trust NASDAQ Global Auto	CARZ	U	27.95	N/A	N/A	U		22.37	24.50	--	--	--
GR	*First Trust NASDAQ-100 Equal Wei	QQEW	B-	26.97	27.28	20.50	B-	7.4	17.52	25.33	6.70 / 60	26.38 / 70	5.40 / 58
IN	*First Trust NASDAQ-100 Ex-Tech S	QQXT	C+	24.14	24.51	18.99	C+	6.9	16.17	19.86	6.71 / 60	25.37 / 65	4.73 / 56
GR	*First Trust NASDAQ-100-Technolog	QTEC	B	28.69	28.97	20.73	B	7.8	18.95	32.09	6.42 / 59	27.32 / 74	7.18 / 68
IN	*First Trust S&P REIT Index Fund	FRI	A-	17.14	17.15	12.55	A-	9.1	10.65	27.40	12.48 / 73	36.42 / 92	--
GR	*First Trust Small Cap Core Alpha	FYX	B	33.48	34.20	23.84	B	7.8	11.94	31.08	4.02 / 52	28.68 / 79	--
GR	*First Trust Small Cap Gro AlphaD	FYC	U	21.11	N/A	N/A	U		10.06	26.95	--	--	--
GR	*First Trust Small Cap Val AlphaD	FYT	U	21.82	N/A	N/A	U		12.88	29.56	--	--	--
FO	*First Trust South Korea AlphaDEX	FKO	U	25.10	N/A	N/A	U		9.89	15.40	--	--	--
FO	*First Trust STOXX European Sel D	FDD	D+	12.54	15.86	10.90	D+	2.9	6.13	8.67	-9.75 / 22	14.31 / 25	--
IN	*First Trust Strategic Value Inde	FDV	C+	25.44	25.95	18.98	C+	5.9	16.44	29.23	4.04 / 52	21.28 / 49	3.45 / 48
FO	*First Trust Switz AlphaDEX	FSZ	U	30.41	N/A	N/A	U		--	--	--	--	--
GR	*First Trust Technology AlphaDEX	FXL	C+	23.68	25.53	17.35	B-	7.4	18.16	29.75	-1.93 / 36	27.41 / 75	--
FO	*First Trust UK AlphaDEX	FKU	U	30.84	N/A	N/A	U		--	--	--	--	--
GR	*First Trust US IPO Index Fund	FPX	B+	28.86	29.06	20.21	B+	8.5	20.40	35.62	14.09 / 76	29.30 / 81	5.39 / 58
UT	*First Trust Utilities AlphaDEX	FXU	C	17.66	18.67	15.10	C-	3.5	-1.51	6.03	2.00 / 46	16.50 / 31	--
GR	*First Trust Value Line 100 Fund	FVL	C-	13.95	15.34	9.89	C	4.5	12.55	32.13	-5.87 / 29	18.19 / 36	-2.27 / 18
GI	*First Trust Value Line Dividend	FVD	C+	16.90	17.01	13.66	C	5.4	6.19	18.55	8.64 / 66	21.12 / 48	2.60 / 42
GI	*First Trust Value Line Equity AI	FVI	C	19.82	21.70	15.82	C-	4.2	8.72	19.69	-5.93 / 29	18.59 / 38	0.72 / 30
USA	*FlexShs iB 3Y Tgt Dur TIPS Idx	TDTT	U	25.38	N/A	N/A	U		1.28	1.39	--	--	--
USA	*FlexShs iB 5Y Tgt Dur TIPS Idx	TDTF	U	25.61	N/A	N/A	U		1.23	2.57	--	--	--
EN	*FlexShs Morningstar Gl Upstream	GUNR	U	35.54	N/A	N/A	U		7.70	16.56	--	--	--
IN	*FlexShs Morningstar US Mkt Fac T	TILT	U	58.74	N/A	N/A	U		12.74	27.29	--	--	--
GI	*Focus Mstar Basic Mat Id ETF	FBM	D	22.10	38.74	16.92	D	2.1	9.90	25.82	-12.80 / 18	--	--
GR	*Focus Mstar Comm Svc Id ETF	FCQ	C	25.89	38.62	20.29	C-	3.8	10.17	17.60	4.10 / 52	--	--
GI	*Focus Mstar Cons Cyc Id ETF	FCL	B+	29.07	29.51	21.60	B+	8.5	16.09	30.27	14.62 / 76	--	--
GI	*Focus Mstar Cons Def Id ETF	FCD	C+	28.77	28.80	24.14	C	5.2	5.23	15.49	15.54 / 78	--	--
EN	*Focus Mstar Energy Id ETF	FEG	D	23.37	26.12	17.78	D	2.2	4.42	23.46	-7.09 / 27	--	--
LP	*Focus Mstar Finl Svc Id ETF	FFL	C+	24.66	27.11	17.25	C+	6.5	21.24	34.10	-1.91 / 36	--	--
HL	*Focus Mstar Hlth Care Id ETF	FHC	B-	28.86	29.99	22.82	C+	6.1	9.32	18.42	14.64 / 77	--	--

* Denotes ETF Fund, N/A denotes number is not available

Incl. in Returns Dividend Yield %	Expense Ratio	RISK Risk Rating/ Pts	3 Year Standard Deviation	Beta	Avg Dura-tion	NET ASSETS NAV as of 3/31/12	Total $(Mil)	VALUATION Premium / Discount As of 3/31/12	1 Year Average	Wtd Avg P/E	ASSET Cash %	Stocks %	Bonds %	Other %	Portfolio Turnover Ratio	FUND MANAGER Manager Quality Pct	Manager Tenure (Years)
0.74	0.60	C / 5.1	30.4	1.01	N/A	7.89	29	-0.76	-0.54	N/A	0	99	0	1	35	5	4
0.00	0.70	C / 4.9	N/A	N/A	N/A	31.29	61	-0.38	-0.21	N/A	0	100	0	0	22	1	2
2.48	0.70	C / 4.7	N/A	N/A	N/A	19.37	12	-0.21	-0.12	N/A	0	99	0	1	29	N/A	2
0.53	0.60	B- / 7.8	20.4	1.15	N/A	23.93	66	0.21	-0.03	49.9	0	99	0	1	38	24	5
0.29	0.60	C+/ 6.9	33.2	1.53	N/A	17.71	359	-0.23	-0.02	17.0	0	100	0	0	93	12	5
0.87	0.80	U /	N/A	N/A	N/A	39.41	4	1.04	N/A	N/A	0	100	0	0	N/A	N/A	1
0.81	0.70	B / 8.0	17.3	1.01	N/A	30.11	130	0.07	0.02	53.1	0	99	0	1	146	38	5
1.50	0.70	B / 8.4	20.2	1.15	N/A	29.74	218	0.13	0.08	16.6	0	99	0	1	76	64	5
3.08	0.80	U /	N/A	N/A	N/A	28.50	4	-0.11	N/A	N/A	0	100	0	0	N/A	N/A	1
1.19	0.70	B / 8.2	18.2	1.09	N/A	30.26	323	0.03	0.08	32.5	0	99	0	1	81	53	5
0.30	0.70	B- / 7.3	27.7	1.55	N/A	25.17	159	0.12	-0.02	28.7	0	99	0	1	116	32	5
1.04	0.70	U /	N/A	N/A	N/A	19.80	6	0.05	N/A	N/A	0	99	0	1	N/A	N/A	1
0.60	0.70	B / 8.0	21.7	1.24	N/A	36.68	310	0.03	0.03	30.8	0	99	0	1	86	57	5
0.03	0.70	U /	N/A	N/A	N/A	20.82	14	0.38	N/A	N/A	0	99	0	1	N/A	N/A	1
0.50	0.70	U /	N/A	N/A	N/A	21.23	8	0.28	N/A	N/A	0	99	0	1	N/A	N/A	1
3.54	0.45	B+/ 9.3	13.4	0.65	N/A	17.72	471	0.06	0.10	19.6	0	99	0	1	30	86	15
0.44	0.70	B- / 7.9	18.9	1.06	N/A	32.90	27	0.27	-0.01	51.4	0	99	0	1	149	45	5
0.59	0.70	B / 8.2	21.7	1.23	N/A	32.05	51	-0.16	0.07	20.1	0	99	0	1	74	61	5
0.00	0.70	C+/ 6.7	N/A	N/A	N/A	28.05	14	-0.93	-0.28	N/A	0	100	0	0	28	3	3
0.00	0.60	B- / 7.1	N/A	N/A	N/A	25.87	7	0.27	-0.02	N/A	0	99	0	1	26	16	3
0.00	0.70	B- / 7.7	N/A	N/A	N/A	27.60	15	0.11	-0.08	N/A	0	99	0	1	29	62	1
0.00	0.60	C+/ 6.0	32.1	1.71	N/A	10.76	20	-0.09	-0.17	38.4	0	100	0	0	22	3	1
0.00	0.70	U /	N/A	N/A	N/A	27.79	4	0.58	N/A	N/A	0	99	0	1	N/A	N/A	1
0.20	0.60	B- / 7.8	20.5	1.19	N/A	26.94	92	0.11	0.01	65.9	0	100	0	0	24	47	6
0.34	0.60	B- / 7.8	19.1	1.08	N/A	24.12	36	0.08	0.02	81.0	0	99	0	1	19	58	6
0.00	0.60	B- / 7.8	22.9	1.29	N/A	28.71	176	-0.07	N/A	49.6	0	100	0	0	26	40	6
1.70	0.50	B- / 7.9	26.0	1.28	N/A	17.11	397	0.18	0.04	59.7	0	99	0	1	16	84	5
0.27	0.70	B- / 7.8	23.1	1.28	N/A	33.43	164	0.15	0.03	39.6	0	99	0	1	90	48	5
0.01	0.70	U /	N/A	N/A	N/A	21.19	5	-0.38	N/A	N/A	0	99	0	1	N/A	N/A	1
0.30	0.70	U /	N/A	N/A	N/A	21.71	4	0.51	N/A	N/A	0	99	0	1	N/A	N/A	1
3.43	0.80	U /	N/A	N/A	N/A	24.78	1	1.29	N/A	N/A	0	100	0	0	N/A	N/A	1
1.48	0.60	B- / 7.4	23.0	1.00	N/A	12.39	11	1.21	0.42	N/A	0	96	0	4	27	44	N/A
2.20	0.65	B / 8.1	19.8	1.17	N/A	25.52	34	-0.31	-0.01	19.7	0	99	0	1	197	30	6
1.78	0.80	U /	N/A	N/A	N/A	30.48	3	-0.23	N/A	N/A	0	0	0	100	N/A	N/A	0
0.60	0.70	B- / 7.4	23.7	1.32	N/A	23.65	238	0.13	0.02	46.4	0	99	0	1	109	36	5
5.45	0.80	U /	N/A	N/A	N/A	30.81	3	0.10	N/A	N/A	0	0	0	100	N/A	N/A	0
1.29	0.60	B / 8.1	19.1	1.11	N/A	28.72	17	0.49	0.01	N/A	0	99	0	1	43	66	6
1.75	0.70	B+/ 9.0	12.0	0.97	N/A	17.67	272	-0.06	0.11	23.1	0	99	0	1	66	56	5
0.94	0.70	B- / 7.3	22.2	1.18	N/A	13.89	59	0.43	-0.03	35.5	0	99	0	1	205	18	9
2.39	0.70	B / 8.9	12.8	0.76	N/A	16.87	418	0.18	0.10	23.5	0	99	0	1	55	72	9
1.34	0.70	B- / 7.9	17.2	1.00	N/A	19.77	7	0.25	0.02	37.3	0	99	0	1	205	29	6
0.05	0.20	U /	N/A	N/A	N/A	25.34	183	0.16	N/A	N/A	0	0	0	100	N/A	N/A	1
0.27	0.20	U /	N/A	N/A	N/A	25.57	185	0.16	N/A	N/A	0	0	0	100	N/A	N/A	1
0.50	0.48	U /	N/A	N/A	N/A	35.43	248	0.31	N/A	N/A	0	0	0	100	N/A	N/A	1
0.41	0.27	U /	N/A	N/A	N/A	58.57	48	0.29	N/A	N/A	0	0	0	100	N/A	N/A	1
1.63	0.19	C+/ 6.2	N/A	N/A	N/A	22.18	4	-0.36	0.10	N/A	0	100	0	0	19	4	1
3.49	0.19	B / 8.3	N/A	N/A	N/A	25.91	5	-0.08	0.04	N/A	0	100	0	0	N/A	38	1
1.20	0.19	B / 8.3	N/A	N/A	N/A	29.06	6	0.03	-0.12	N/A	0	100	0	0	4	74	1
2.27	0.19	B+/ 9.3	N/A	N/A	N/A	28.74	6	0.10	0.03	N/A	0	100	0	0	4	88	1
1.24	0.19	B- / 7.1	N/A	N/A	N/A	23.36	5	0.04	0.02	N/A	0	100	0	0	13	44	1
1.36	0.19	B- / 7.1	N/A	N/A	N/A	24.67	5	-0.04	0.12	N/A	0	100	0	0	5	99	1
1.34	0.19	B+/ 9.0	N/A	N/A	N/A	28.81	6	0.17	-0.02	N/A	0	100	0	0	6	85	1

Fund Type	Fund Name	Ticker Symbol	Overall Investment Rating	PRICE Price As of 3/31/12	52 Week High	52 Week Low	PERFORMANCE Performance Rating/Pts	3 Mo	6 Mo	1Yr/Pct	3Yr/Pct	5Yr/Pct
	99 Pct = Best 0 Pct = Worst							% Total Return Through 3/31/12 (Annualized)				
GR	*Focus Mstar Indus Id ETF	FIL	C-	25.34	26.23	19.21	C / 4.5	10.62	29.36	0.12 / 41	--	--
GR	*Focus Mstar Large Cap Id ETF	FLG	C+	27.11	29.00	20.76	C+ / 6.1	12.02	24.94	8.52 / 65	--	--
GR	*Focus Mstar Mid Cap Id ETF	FMM	C	26.02	26.50	19.91	C / 4.8	12.84	25.44	2.81 / 49	--	--
GI	*Focus Mstar Real Est Id ETF	FRL	C+	27.26	27.42	20.86	C+ / 5.9	10.90	23.17	9.65 / 68	--	--
GR	*Focus Mstar Small Cap Id ETF	FOS	C	25.45	27.99	18.78	C / 4.7	11.87	29.33	0.32 / 42	--	--
GR	*Focus Mstar Technology Id ETF	FTQ	A	29.11	29.40	21.00	A- / 9.1	21.34	31.12	15.94 / 78	--	--
GR	*Focus Mstar US Market Id ETF	FMU	C+	26.76	27.09	20.37	C+ / 5.7	11.97	25.49	6.63 / 60	--	--
UT	*Focus Mstar Utilities Id ETF	FUI	C-	27.62	28.44	22.12	D+ / 2.3	-2.75	5.13	10.68 / 69	--	--
GL	*Global X Aluminm ETF	ALUM	E+	10.30	16.36	8.64	E+ / 0.7	14.06	10.46	-34.19 / 4	--	--
GL	*Global X Auto ETF	VROM	U	14.43	N/A	N/A	U /	25.87	26.56	--	--	--
FO	*Global X Brazil Consumer ETF	BRAQ	C	18.78	20.43	13.14	B- / 7.1	24.54	37.21	-3.25 / 33	--	--
FO	*Global X Brazil Financials ETF	BRAF	D	14.99	17.97	11.78	C- / 3.0	15.04	28.06	-10.59 / 21	--	--
FO	*Global X Brazil Mid Cap ETF	BRAZ	C	17.26	19.58	12.52	C+ / 5.7	21.29	35.84	-5.97 / 29	--	--
FO	*Global X Canada Preferred ETF	CNPF	U	14.32	N/A	N/A	U /	0.12	8.19	--	--	--
FO	*Global X China Consumer ETF	CHIQ	D-	14.90	18.84	11.76	D- / 1.4	8.68	17.90	-13.62 / 17	--	--
EN	*Global X China Energy ETF	CHIE	D-	13.56	17.92	10.98	E+ / 0.9	4.23	17.14	-22.08 / 10	--	--
FS	*Global X China Financials ETF	CHIX	D-	11.00	14.50	7.80	D- / 1.3	5.91	31.56	-22.45 / 9	--	--
FO	*Global X China Industrials ETF	CHII	E+	11.60	17.25	7.99	D- / 1.2	12.84	31.36	-28.98 / 6	--	--
FO	*Global X China Materials ETF	CHIM	E+	8.77	14.76	7.13	E+ / 0.6	0.69	12.23	-36.86 / 4	--	--
PM	*Global X Copper Miners ETF	COPX	E+	13.64	20.97	10.35	D- / 1.0	6.23	25.96	-25.53 / 8	--	--
GL	*Global X Fertilizers/Potash ETF	SOIL	U	13.90	N/A	N/A	U /	13.61	17.10	--	--	--
FO	*Global X FTSE Andean 40 ETF	AND	C	14.92	15.67	11.09	C+ / 5.7	19.84	26.46	1.33 / 44	--	--
FO	*Global X FTSE Argentina 20 ETF	ARGT	E+	10.70	15.87	9.21	E+ / 0.7	1.89	10.77	-28.55 / 6	--	--
GL	*Global X FTSE ASEAN 40 ETF	ASEA	C-	16.22	17.68	13.00	C / 4.5	12.87	22.21	3.41 / 50	--	--
GL	*Global X FTSE Nordic Region ETF	GXF	D	18.54	23.08	14.35	C- / 3.0	18.59	25.09	-10.45 / 21	--	--
FO	*Global X FTSE Norway 30 ETF	NORW	D	14.64	17.89	10.83	D+ / 2.9	16.75	27.27	-11.80 / 19	--	--
GL	*Global X Gold Explorers ETF	GLDX	E	9.96	19.36	9.55	E / 0.3	-7.35	-11.07	-43.67 / 2	--	--
GR	*Global X Lithium ETF	LIT	D-	16.73	22.79	12.20	D- / 1.3	16.75	24.26	-24.24 / 8	--	--
GR	*Global X NASDAQ 400 Mid Cap ETF	QQQM	U	28.41	N/A	N/A	U /	--	--	--	--	--
IN	*Global X NASDAQ 500 ETF	QQQV	U	29.42	N/A	N/A	U /	--	--	--	--	--
FO	*Global X NASDAQ China Tech ETF	QQQC	D	15.76	20.00	12.47	D / 2.2	20.49	19.76	-13.92 / 16	--	--
GI	*Global X Permanent ETF	PERM	U	24.70	N/A	N/A	U /	--	--	--	--	--
PM	*Global X Pure Gold Miners ETF	GGGG	D-	11.98	16.95	11.69	E+ / 0.6	-2.29	-8.32	-22.37 / 10	--	--
EN	*Global X S-P/TSX Venture 30 Can	TSXV	E+	10.76	45.00	7.60	E+ / 0.9	10.25	26.09	-34.11 / 4	--	--
PM	*Global X Silver Miners ETF	SIL	D-	22.23	31.34	19.05	E+ / 0.8	5.28	6.94	-20.93 / 10	--	--
GL	*Global X Social Media Index ETF	SOCL	U	15.39	N/A	N/A	U /	17.48	--	--	--	--
GL	*Global X SuperDividend ETF	SDIV	U	22.40	N/A	N/A	U /	9.91	18.17	--	--	--
GL	*Global X Uranium ETF	URA	E	9.40	15.66	7.06	E+ / 0.8	15.34	18.84	-37.50 / 4	--	--
FO	*Global X/InterBolsa FTSE Col 20	GXG	C	21.20	21.95	10.13	A / 9.5	18.97	19.50	5.01 / 55	41.61 / 96	--
GI	*GreenHaven Continuous Commodity	GCC	D+	30.28	36.51	28.98	D / 2.0	1.20	-0.20	-14.20 / 16	10.50 / 17	--
GR	*GS Cnct S&P GSCI Enh Cmd TR Str	GSC	D+	51.70	58.57	43.14	D+ / 2.7	5.77	16.97	-8.21 / 25	12.28 / 20	--
IN	*Guggenheim 2x S&P 500 ETF	RSU	B+	49.99	50.70	29.29	A+ / 9.6	26.63	54.83	10.01 / 68	39.78 / 95	--
FO	*Guggenheim ABC High Dividend ETF	ABCS	U	23.20	N/A	N/A	U /	18.82	32.12	--	--	--
GL	*Guggenheim Airline ETF	FAA	D	29.20	39.18	23.82	C- / 3.1	11.24	10.92	-18.74 / 11	15.91 / 29	--
FO	*Guggenheim Australian Dollar Sha	FXA	C	103.87	110.99	93.92	C- / 3.8	2.11	8.99	3.27 / 49	16.89 / 32	7.91 / 74
COI	*Guggenheim BltShs 2012 Corp Bd E	BSCC	C-	20.48	20.69	20.15	D- / 1.2	-0.09	0.38	0.42 / 42	--	--
COI	*Guggenheim BltShs 2013 Corp Bd E	BSCD	C-	20.93	20.99	20.46	D- / 1.4	1.26	1.79	2.50 / 48	--	--
COI	*Guggenheim BltShs 2014 Corp Bd E	BSCE	C-	21.14	21.30	20.62	D / 1.6	1.45	2.59	3.20 / 49	--	--
COI	*Guggenheim BltShs 2015 Corp Bd E	BSCF	C-	21.50	22.40	20.64	D / 2.0	2.76	3.88	5.71 / 58	--	--
COI	*Guggenheim BltShs 2016 Corp Bd E	BSCG	C-	21.69	22.69	20.73	D / 2.1	2.43	4.61	6.49 / 60	--	--
COI	*Guggenheim BltShs 2017 Corp Bd E	BSCH	C	22.02	22.17	20.70	D+ / 2.6	3.80	6.11	8.41 / 65	--	--
IN	*Guggenheim BRIC ETF	EEB	D+	39.48	48.96	32.27	C- / 3.8	12.70	19.44	-14.77 / 15	17.30 / 33	6.44 / 64

* Denotes ETF Fund, N/A denotes number is not available

www.thestreetratings.com

I. Index of ETFs and Other Closed-End Funds

Incl. in Returns		RISK Risk Rating/ Pts	3 Year		Avg Dura-tion	NET ASSETS NAV as of 3/31/12	Total $(Mil)	VALUATION Premium / Discount As of 3/31/12	1 Year Average	Wtd Avg P/E	ASSET Cash %	Stocks %	Bonds %	Other %	Portfolio Turnover Ratio	Manager Quality Pct	Manager Tenure (Years)
Dividend Yield %	Expense Ratio		Standard Deviation	Beta													
1.54	0.19	B- / 7.5	N/A	N/A	N/A	25.30	5	0.16	0.05	N/A	0	100	0	0	6	15	1
1.75	0.05	B / 8.4	N/A	N/A	N/A	27.12	5	-0.04	0.03	N/A	0	100	0	0	4	50	1
1.23	0.12	B- / 7.8	N/A	N/A	N/A	26.00	5	0.08	-0.06	N/A	0	100	0	0	16	20	1
5.86	0.12	B / 8.0	N/A	N/A	N/A	27.25	5	0.04	-0.05	N/A	0	100	0	0	21	51	1
1.37	0.12	B- / 7.4	N/A	N/A	N/A	25.40	5	0.20	-0.03	N/A	0	100	0	0	21	14	1
0.72	0.19	B / 8.5	N/A	N/A	N/A	29.02	6	0.31	-0.03	N/A	0	100	0	0	5	79	1
1.44	0.05	B / 8.2	N/A	N/A	N/A	26.82	16	-0.22	0.03	N/A	0	100	0	0	9	34	1
2.66	0.19	B+ / 9.5	N/A	N/A	N/A	27.60	7	0.07	-0.03	N/A	0	100	0	0	4	26	1
1.02	0.69	C / 4.8	N/A	N/A	N/A	10.27	3	0.29	-0.37	N/A	0	99	0	1	15	4	1
0.57	0.65	U /	N/A	N/A	N/A	14.28	1	1.05	N/A	N/A	0	100	0	0	N/A	N/A	1
1.16	0.77	C+ / 6.1	N/A	N/A	N/A	18.84	42	-0.32	0.23	N/A	0	100	0	0	37	84	2
4.27	0.77	C+ / 6.2	N/A	N/A	N/A	15.05	6	-0.40	-0.27	N/A	0	95	0	5	37	40	2
1.98	0.69	C+ / 6.5	N/A	N/A	N/A	17.31	25	-0.29	-0.18	N/A	0	100	0	0	17	73	2
2.47	0.58	U /	N/A	N/A	N/A	14.57	13	-1.72	N/A	N/A	0	0	0	100	N/A	N/A	1
0.38	0.65	C+ / 5.9	N/A	N/A	N/A	15.06	135	-1.06	-0.10	N/A	0	99	0	1	12	20	3
1.93	0.65	C+ / 6.4	N/A	N/A	N/A	13.68	5	-0.88	-0.41	N/A	0	99	0	1	11	10	3
0.10	0.65	C / 5.2	N/A	N/A	N/A	11.14	13	-1.26	-0.40	N/A	0	99	0	1	42	5	3
0.19	0.65	C / 4.8	N/A	N/A	N/A	11.76	5	-1.36	-0.06	N/A	0	99	0	1	20	6	3
0.00	0.65	C / 4.9	N/A	N/A	N/A	8.94	3	-1.90	-0.13	N/A	0	99	0	1	37	3	2
4.15	0.65	C / 4.7	N/A	N/A	N/A	13.70	34	-0.44	-0.27	N/A	0	100	0	0	16	2	2
0.89	N/A	U /	N/A	N/A	N/A	13.91	30	-0.07	N/A	N/A	0	100	0	0	N/A	N/A	1
1.61	0.72	B- / 7.1	N/A	N/A	N/A	14.95	7	-0.20	-0.02	N/A	0	99	0	1	16	84	1
2.74	0.75	C+ / 5.6	N/A	N/A	N/A	10.71	4	-0.09	-0.02	N/A	0	99	0	1	41	6	1
2.28	0.65	B- / 7.2	N/A	N/A	N/A	16.14	27	0.50	0.30	N/A	0	99	0	1	3	86	1
2.84	0.50	C+ / 6.7	N/A	N/A	N/A	18.45	26	0.49	-0.21	N/A	0	99	0	1	4	29	3
2.45	0.50	C+ / 6.3	N/A	N/A	N/A	14.61	54	0.21	-0.09	N/A	0	99	0	1	24	28	2
2.55	0.65	C- / 4.0	N/A	N/A	N/A	9.90	26	0.61	0.31	N/A	0	100	0	0	N/A	1	2
0.11	0.75	C / 5.5	N/A	N/A	N/A	16.78	97	-0.30	-0.48	N/A	0	100	0	0	25	2	2
0.00	0.48	U /	N/A	N/A	N/A	28.56	1	-0.53	N/A	N/A	0	0	0	100	N/A	N/A	1
0.00	0.48	U /	N/A	N/A	N/A	29.59	1	-0.57	N/A	N/A	0	0	0	100	N/A	N/A	1
1.22	0.65	C+ / 6.6	N/A	N/A	N/A	15.97	5	-1.31	-0.66	N/A	1	98	0	1	17	21	3
0.00	0.48	U /	N/A	N/A	N/A	24.62	5	0.32	N/A	N/A	0	0	0	100	N/A	N/A	0
2.07	0.59	C+ / 6.0	N/A	N/A	N/A	12.05	6	-0.58	0.10	N/A	0	99	0	1	8	2	1
2.67	0.75	C- / 4.0	N/A	N/A	N/A	11.04	3	-2.54	-0.44	N/A	0	100	0	0	28	5	1
0.16	0.65	C+ / 6.0	N/A	N/A	N/A	22.34	321	-0.49	-0.14	N/A	0	99	0	1	27	2	2
0.00	0.65	U /	N/A	N/A	N/A	15.31	8	0.52	N/A	N/A	0	0	0	100	N/A	N/A	1
3.37	0.79	U /	N/A	N/A	N/A	22.26	56	0.63	N/A	N/A	0	100	0	0	N/A	N/A	1
0.00	0.69	D+ / 2.5	N/A	N/A	N/A	9.46	184	-0.63	0.05	N/A	0	99	0	1	24	3	2
0.98	0.81	C- / 3.6	25.2	0.86	N/A	21.23	147	-0.14	0.08	N/A	1	98	0	1	63	96	3
0.00	1.09	B / 8.0	17.8	0.64	N/A	30.35	677	-0.23	-0.01	N/A	100	0	0	0	N/A	29	4
0.00	1.25	B- / 7.4	22.0	0.93	N/A	51.70	71	0.00	N/A	N/A	0	0	0	100	N/A	20	5
1.85	0.71	C+ / 6.8	33.7	2.03	N/A	50.00	80	-0.02	-0.04	46.3	16	83	0	1	41	22	5
3.14	0.65	U /	N/A	N/A	N/A	22.98	8	0.96	N/A	N/A	0	100	0	0	N/A	N/A	1
1.04	0.70	C+ / 6.2	34.2	0.89	N/A	29.23	15	-0.10	-0.19	N/A	0	100	0	0	38	71	N/A
3.51	0.40	B / 8.6	15.1	0.63	N/A	103.92	837	-0.05	-0.02	N/A	100	0	0	0	N/A	79	6
0.94	0.24	B+ / 9.9	N/A	N/A	N/A	20.50	98	-0.10	0.43	N/A	0	0	100	0	N/A	52	N/A
1.43	0.24	B+ / 9.9	N/A	N/A	N/A	20.86	119	0.34	0.51	N/A	0	0	100	0	N/A	58	N/A
1.76	0.24	B+ / 9.9	N/A	N/A	N/A	21.12	114	0.09	0.59	N/A	0	0	100	0	N/A	42	N/A
2.12	0.24	B+ / 9.8	N/A	N/A	N/A	21.46	93	0.19	0.61	N/A	0	0	100	0	N/A	38	N/A
2.43	0.24	B+ / 9.7	N/A	N/A	N/A	21.64	91	0.23	0.60	N/A	0	0	100	0	N/A	37	N/A
2.83	0.24	B+ / 9.7	N/A	N/A	N/A	21.95	79	0.32	0.43	N/A	0	0	100	0	N/A	35	N/A
3.51	0.64	B- / 7.0	28.5	1.45	N/A	39.52	490	-0.10	-0.04	N/A	0	100	0	0	15	13	N/A

* Denotes ETF Fund, N/A denotes number is not available

Fund Type	Fund Name	Ticker Symbol	Overall Investment Rating	Price As of 3/31/12	52 Week High	52 Week Low	Performance Rating	Pts	3 Mo	6 Mo	1Yr/Pct	3Yr/Pct	5Yr/Pct
FO	*Guggenheim Brit Pnd Sterling	FXB	D+	158.58	166.12	151.18	D-	1.4	2.91	2.50	-0.97 / 38	2.28 / 8	-3.73 / 15
FO	*Guggenheim Canadian Dollar Shs	FXC	D+	99.69	105.59	93.29	D	1.9	2.15	5.15	-3.18 / 33	7.12 / 13	3.11 / 45
EN	*Guggenheim Canadian Energy Inc E	ENY	D+	17.20	23.69	12.46	C	4.3	2.76	23.76	-23.34 / 9	21.75 / 51	--
FO	*Guggenheim China All-Cap ETF	YAO	D-	23.63	29.99	18.24	D	1.6	10.68	22.82	-15.97 / 14	--	--
GI	*Guggenheim China Real Estate ETF	TAO	D	16.94	20.55	12.37	C-	3.3	15.71	29.73	-14.05 / 16	13.62 / 23	--
FO	*Guggenheim China Small Cap ETF	HAO	D-	21.57	31.03	16.65	D+	2.8	11.76	22.93	-24.28 / 8	13.57 / 23	--
FO	*Guggenheim China Technology ETF	CQQQ	D-	24.14	32.94	18.26	D	1.9	18.16	25.16	-18.32 / 11	--	--
GI	*Guggenheim Chinese Renminbi Shs	FXCH	U	79.91	N/A	N/A	U		0.20	--	--	--	--
IN	*Guggenheim Defensive Equity ETF	DEF	B-	28.03	28.15	23.03	C+	5.7	2.53	14.03	8.89 / 66	22.67 / 55	3.28 / 46
GEI	*Guggenheim Enhanced Core Bond ET	GIY	C-	51.55	59.39	51.10	D	2.1	-0.22	1.74	5.87 / 58	8.15 / 14	--
GR	*Guggenheim Enhanced Sh Bd ETF	GSY	C-	49.89	49.93	49.54	D-	1.2	0.49	--	--	0.28 / 7	--
FO	*Guggenheim Euro Shares	FXE	D	132.72	148.81	125.75	D-	1.1	2.95	-0.50	-6.11 / 28	-0.45 / 7	0.32 / 29
GL	*Guggenheim Frontier Markets ETF	FRN	C+	21.52	23.72	16.89	B-	7.1	18.63	23.61	0.17 / 41	26.38 / 70	--
IN	*Guggenheim Insider Sentiment ETF	NFO	B	34.95	37.33	25.47	B	8.0	13.51	29.10	2.38 / 47	29.40 / 81	5.54 / 59
FO	*Guggenheim Intl Multi-Asset Inc	HGI	C	17.67	20.51	14.22	C	4.8	10.09	19.16	-5.65 / 29	20.73 / 46	--
IN	*Guggenheim Inverse 2x S&P 500 ET	RSW	E	24.47	46.48	24.08	E	0.3	-21.57	-40.69	-27.07 / 7	-39.85 / 2	--
FO	*Guggenheim Japanese Yen Trust	FXY	D+	118.78	130.22	115.54	D	1.6	-7.15	-7.06	1.13 / 44	6.15 / 11	7.11 / 68
GR	*Guggenheim Mid-Cap Core ETF	CZA	B	32.81	33.02	24.71	B-	7.4	10.29	26.20	4.31 / 53	27.50 / 75	--
EM	*Guggenheim MSCI EAFE Eq Weight E	EWEF	D	38.40	45.49	32.22	D	1.8	12.86	11.97	-7.40 / 26	--	--
EM	*Guggenheim MSCI Em Mkt Eq Weight	EWEM	D	35.74	43.07	28.00	D+	2.6	15.75	25.78	-12.15 / 19	--	--
IN	*Guggenheim Multi-Asset Income ET	CVY	B+	21.85	22.33	17.48	B	7.9	8.14	19.93	8.02 / 64	29.90 / 82	1.98 / 38
IN	*Guggenheim Raymond James SB1 Eq	RYJ	B	23.70	24.03	16.18	B	8.1	15.44	32.91	3.14 / 49	29.22 / 80	7.53 / 71
GR	*Guggenheim Russell 1000 Eq Wght	EWRI	C	34.45	34.77	25.83	C	5.3	12.82	26.96	3.57 / 50	--	--
GR	*Guggenheim Russell 2000 Eq Wght	EWRS	C-	32.83	35.28	23.93	C-	3.9	12.16	27.36	-2.53 / 35	--	--
GR	*Guggenheim Russell MC Eq Wght ET	EWRM	C	34.50	35.07	25.67	C	4.9	12.54	26.73	2.28 / 47	--	--
IN	*Guggenheim Russell Top 50 ETF	XLG	C+	103.12	103.89	78.50	C	5.5	14.05	27.12	13.01 / 74	18.93 / 39	1.65 / 35
GR	*Guggenheim S&P 500 Eq WgCon Dsc	RCD	A	54.80	55.81	39.35	A-	9.2	16.37	31.96	14.68 / 77	35.94 / 92	3.94 / 50
GR	*Guggenheim S&P 500 Eq WgCon St E	RHS	B-	66.16	66.82	54.93	C+	5.9	5.47	16.33	13.12 / 74	22.23 / 53	7.54 / 71
EN	*Guggenheim S&P 500 Eq Wght Engy	RYE	C	64.03	76.49	47.60	C	5.2	4.35	23.26	-14.44 / 15	23.24 / 58	4.79 / 56
FS	*Guggenheim S&P 500 Eq Wght Finl	RYF	B	28.35	29.76	19.91	B	7.8	20.48	33.57	-0.28 / 40	28.06 / 77	-9.01 / 7
GR	*Guggenheim S&P 500 Eq Wght HC ET	RYH	B	75.41	75.50	58.75	B-	7.1	13.82	21.61	10.44 / 69	25.17 / 65	7.61 / 72
GR	*Guggenheim S&P 500 Eq Wght Ind E	RGI	B-	57.50	59.44	42.50	B-	7.0	11.43	28.15	0.18 / 41	26.07 / 69	4.17 / 51
GR	*Guggenheim S&P 500 Eq Wght Mat E	RTM	C+	62.75	68.50	45.70	B-	7.1	12.28	29.17	-4.45 / 32	26.83 / 72	4.28 / 52
GR	*Guggenheim S&P 500 Eq Wght Tech	RYT	C+	58.74	60.41	43.04	B-	7.0	18.03	30.11	3.63 / 51	24.74 / 63	3.53 / 48
UT	*Guggenheim S&P 500 Eq Wght Util	RYU	C	54.57	56.29	46.62	C-	4.0	--	6.79	8.45 / 65	17.32 / 33	1.31 / 32
IN	*Guggenheim S&P 500 Equal Wght	RSP	B-	51.87	52.48	39.03	B-	7.2	12.86	26.67	4.15 / 52	26.32 / 70	2.60 / 42
GR	*Guggenheim S&P 500 Pure Growth	RPG	B	49.24	49.50	37.38	B	8.0	14.26	25.16	6.12 / 59	29.36 / 81	6.37 / 63
IN	*Guggenheim S&P 500 Pure Value	RPV	A	32.29	33.38	23.50	A-	9.2	16.88	28.43	5.49 / 57	37.75 / 94	0.69 / 30
IN	*Guggenheim S&P Gl Div Opps Idx E	LVL	C	13.91	16.64	11.94	C	5.2	5.79	11.84	-7.20 / 26	23.21 / 58	--
EN	*Guggenheim S&P Global Water Idx	CGW	C	21.11	22.44	17.52	C	4.9	12.63	17.73	0.98 / 43	20.10 / 44	--
GR	*Guggenheim S&P Mid Cap 400 Eq Wg	EWMD	U	31.80	N/A	N/A	U		12.91	--	--	--	--
GR	*Guggenheim S&P Mid Cap 400 Pure	RFV	B+	36.06	37.25	25.75	B+	8.7	14.69	31.78	0.16 / 41	33.14 / 88	1.61 / 35
GR	*Guggenheim S&P Mid Cap 400 Pure	RFG	B+	89.64	92.67	67.99	B+	8.5	14.38	22.65	3.57 / 50	32.78 / 87	10.56 / 90
GR	*Guggenheim S&P Sm Cap 600 Eq Wgh	EWSM	U	32.52	N/A	N/A	U		13.76	32.02	--	--	--
GR	*Guggenheim S&P Sm Cap 600 Pure G	RZG	B	55.42	56.59	40.25	B	8.2	10.90	29.16	7.22 / 62	30.26 / 83	5.93 / 61
GR	*Guggenheim S&P Sm Cap 600 Pure V	RZV	B+	40.99	42.36	28.42	A	9.4	14.27	33.86	1.08 / 44	39.57 / 95	0.32 / 29
GL	*Guggenheim Shipping ETF	SEA	D-	19.04	27.25	13.37	D	2.2	28.65	29.71	-26.12 / 7	--	--
EN	*Guggenheim Solar ETF	TAN	E	24.88	88.70	24.20	E	0.4	0.73	-16.39	-69.14 / 0	-28.67 / 3	--
IN	*Guggenheim Spin-Off ETF	CSD	A-	26.57	26.70	19.50	B+	8.6	12.97	28.19	9.06 / 67	31.80 / 85	0.41 / 29
FO	*Guggenheim Swedish Krona	FXS	D+	150.11	168.44	141.44	D	1.8	4.16	3.99	-3.93 / 32	6.78 / 12	1.53 / 34
FO	*Guggenheim Swiss Franc	FXF	D+	109.28	139.91	103.10	D	2.0	3.98	0.21	2.01 / 46	7.36 / 13	6.08 / 62
GL	*Guggenheim Timber ETF	CUT	C	18.84	23.56	15.02	C+	5.9	13.91	21.11	-17.57 / 12	25.23 / 65	--

* Denotes ETF Fund, N/A denotes number is not available

Incl. in Returns Dividend Yield %	Expense Ratio	RISK Risk Rating/ Pts	3 Year Standard Deviation	3 Year Beta	Avg Dura-tion	NET ASSETS NAV as of 3/31/12	NET ASSETS Total $(Mil)	VALUATION Premium/Discount As of 3/31/12	VALUATION Premium/Discount 1 Year Average	Wtd Avg P/E	Cash %	Stocks %	Bonds %	Other %	Portfolio Turnover Ratio	Manager Quality Pct	Manager Tenure (Years)
0.01	0.40	B / 8.8	10.2	0.34	N/A	158.39	113	0.12	0.03	N/A	100	0	0	0	N/A	32	6
0.10	0.40	B+ / 9.0	11.7	0.47	N/A	99.50	586	0.19	-0.02	N/A	100	0	0	0	N/A	46	6
2.74	0.70	C+ / 6.5	33.1	1.32	N/A	17.15	117	0.29	-0.17	15.1	0	100	0	0	34	37	2
2.45	0.70	C+ / 6.5	N/A	N/A	N/A	23.88	61	-1.05	-0.08	N/A	0	99	0	1	16	17	N/A
1.14	0.70	C+ / 6.0	38.3	1.53	N/A	17.16	21	-1.28	-0.27	N/A	0	100	0	0	17	10	N/A
2.87	0.75	C / 4.4	36.2	1.32	N/A	21.65	179	-0.37	-0.22	182.6	0	100	0	0	11	22	N/A
2.34	0.70	C+ / 5.8	N/A	N/A	N/A	24.24	26	-0.41	-0.21	N/A	0	100	0	0	28	15	N/A
0.00	0.40	U /	N/A	N/A	N/A	79.07	4	1.06	N/A	N/A	0	0	0	100	N/A	N/A	1
1.34	0.65	B+ / 9.2	10.1	0.55	N/A	28.04	61	-0.04	0.04	26.5	0	100	0	0	32	85	N/A
1.17	0.32	B+ / 9.4	8.4	0.46	N/A	51.98	5	-0.83	0.21	N/A	0	0	100	0	458	82	4
0.09	0.27	B+ / 9.9	0.4	N/A	2.7	49.91	150	-0.04	-0.08	N/A	55	0	43	2	N/A	48	1
0.09	0.40	B / 8.2	12.5	0.46	N/A	132.55	333	0.13	N/A	N/A	100	0	0	0	N/A	18	7
3.83	0.70	B- / 7.4	22.4	0.77	N/A	21.37	135	0.70	-0.42	N/A	0	100	0	0	9	88	N/A
1.55	0.65	B- / 7.7	24.7	1.39	N/A	34.90	100	0.14	-0.04	40.3	0	100	0	0	53	42	N/A
4.19	0.70	B- / 7.8	22.6	1.04	N/A	17.54	101	0.74	0.25	8.7	0	100	0	0	44	72	N/A
0.41	0.71	C- / 3.5	32.4	-1.94	N/A	24.45	38	0.08	0.02	N/A	100	0	0	0	N/A	11	5
0.00	0.40	B+ / 9.0	9.9	N/A	N/A	119.53	328	-0.63	-0.02	N/A	100	0	0	0	N/A	75	4
0.21	0.65	B / 8.2	17.2	1.00	N/A	32.73	34	0.24	0.13	32.7	0	100	0	0	45	71	N/A
2.06	0.56	B- / 7.1	N/A	N/A	N/A	38.70	12	-0.78	-0.02	N/A	1	98	0	1	24	40	N/A
0.90	0.63	C+ / 5.9	N/A	N/A	N/A	35.17	14	1.62	1.15	N/A	3	96	0	1	63	47	N/A
4.85	0.65	B / 8.7	17.8	0.96	N/A	21.82	667	0.14	0.07	24.0	0	95	0	5	83	84	N/A
0.12	0.75	B- / 7.8	22.7	1.31	N/A	23.67	95	0.13	0.03	30.7	0	100	0	0	47	50	N/A
2.16	0.41	B- / 7.8	N/A	N/A	N/A	34.33	39	0.35	N/A	N/A	0	99	0	1	25	20	N/A
1.18	0.41	B- / 7.3	N/A	N/A	N/A	32.77	20	0.18	0.12	N/A	0	99	0	1	38	11	N/A
1.63	0.41	B- / 7.8	N/A	N/A	N/A	34.46	57	0.12	0.05	N/A	0	99	0	1	30	18	N/A
3.96	0.20	B / 8.3	14.9	0.91	N/A	103.11	464	0.01	0.05	55.3	0	99	0	1	6	46	N/A
1.94	0.50	B / 8.0	25.6	1.37	N/A	54.70	63	0.18	-0.04	43.1	0	99	0	1	26	74	N/A
3.31	0.50	B+ / 9.0	11.3	0.60	N/A	66.07	36	0.14	-0.02	24.4	0	99	0	1	15	83	N/A
1.62	0.50	B- / 7.1	29.7	1.25	N/A	64.03	35	0.00	-0.03	19.4	0	99	0	1	23	54	N/A
5.91	0.50	B- / 7.7	26.4	1.09	N/A	28.39	16	-0.14	-0.08	19.5	0	99	0	1	18	75	N/A
1.11	0.50	B / 8.4	14.5	0.79	N/A	75.36	90	0.07	0.01	44.3	0	99	0	1	19	76	N/A
3.30	0.50	B- / 7.9	22.3	1.26	N/A	57.42	34	0.14	-0.02	29.1	0	99	0	1	15	38	N/A
2.02	0.50	B- / 7.5	27.0	1.51	N/A	62.79	38	-0.06	-0.08	25.0	0	99	0	1	21	23	N/A
1.35	0.50	B- / 7.5	22.2	1.27	N/A	58.68	150	0.10	-0.04	65.3	0	99	0	1	29	31	N/A
7.06	0.50	B+ / 9.3	10.7	0.93	N/A	54.59	44	-0.04	-0.01	20.8	0	99	0	1	15	66	N/A
2.79	0.40	B / 8.1	20.2	1.20	N/A	51.89	3,182	-0.04	N/A	34.6	0	99	0	1	21	52	N/A
1.37	0.35	B- / 7.6	19.7	1.15	N/A	49.18	315	0.12	0.03	82.9	0	99	0	1	21	66	N/A
2.68	0.35	B / 8.1	26.7	1.42	N/A	32.31	94	-0.06	0.04	13.4	0	99	0	1	23	76	N/A
3.05	0.65	B- / 7.6	25.4	1.32	N/A	13.81	63	0.72	0.53	N/A	0	100	0	0	51	31	2
1.95	0.70	B / 8.2	18.6	0.63	N/A	21.11	193	0.00	-0.27	35.6	0	100	0	0	8	83	N/A
2.13	0.40	U /	N/A	N/A	N/A	31.95	3	-0.47	N/A	N/A	0	0	0	100	N/A	N/A	N/A
2.80	0.35	B- / 7.8	27.8	1.50	N/A	36.09	42	-0.08	0.01	18.9	0	99	0	1	49	51	N/A
0.42	0.35	B / 8.0	21.7	1.19	N/A	89.70	614	-0.07	N/A	53.3	0	99	0	1	45	78	N/A
2.02	0.40	U /	N/A	N/A	N/A	32.65	6	-0.40	N/A	N/A	0	0	0	100	N/A	N/A	N/A
0.47	0.35	B- / 7.7	24.1	1.25	N/A	55.19	83	0.42	0.02	66.4	0	99	0	1	33	68	N/A
1.76	0.35	B- / 7.3	38.4	1.85	N/A	41.04	80	-0.12	-0.06	19.7	0	99	0	1	76	28	N/A
2.16	0.65	C / 5.3	N/A	N/A	N/A	18.98	32	0.32	0.09	N/A	0	100	0	0	N/A	6	N/A
8.48	0.70	C- / 3.7	55.5	1.64	N/A	24.94	87	-0.24	-0.14	2.8	0	100	0	0	38	1	N/A
0.42	0.65	B / 8.5	18.6	1.04	N/A	26.55	36	0.08	0.10	23.3	0	100	0	0	2	82	N/A
1.06	0.40	B / 8.5	14.2	0.57	N/A	150.06	76	0.03	-0.01	N/A	100	0	0	0	N/A	35	6
0.00	0.40	B / 8.3	13.7	0.42	N/A	109.16	444	0.11	-0.02	N/A	100	0	0	0	N/A	49	6
2.05	0.70	B- / 7.3	30.5	1.24	N/A	18.81	123	0.16	-0.14	14.7	0	100	0	0	29	74	N/A

* Denotes ETF Fund, N/A denotes number is not available

Fund Type	Fund Name	Ticker Symbol	Overall Investment Rating	PRICE Price As of 3/31/12	52 Week High	52 Week Low	Performance Rating/Pts	PERFORMANCE % Total Return Through 3/31/12 3 Mo	6 Mo	1Yr/Pct	Annualized 3Yr/Pct	5Yr/Pct
	99 Pct = Best 0 Pct = Worst											
IN	*Guggenheim Wilshire Micro-Cap ET	WMCR	C	18.20	20.41	13.53	C / 5.4	19.34	30.51	-6.20 / 28	20.63 / 46	-6.48 / 10
GI	*Guggenheim Wilshire US REIT ETF	WREI	C+	34.69	34.96	25.86	C+ / 6.5	9.07	24.80	11.90 / 72	--	--
GR	*Guggenheim Wilshire5000 Tot Mkt	WFVK	C+	31.24	31.50	24.11	C / 5.5	12.29	24.61	6.52 / 60	--	--
GL	*Guggenheim Yuan Bond ETF	RMB	U	25.20	N/A	N/A	U /	1.08	1.35	--	--	--
COH	*Guggenhm BltShs 2012 HY Corp Bd	BSJC	C-	25.49	26.74	24.43	D / 1.7	1.19	4.89	3.47 / 50	--	--
COH	*Guggenhm BltShs 2013 HY Corp Bd	BSJD	C-	25.77	26.14	23.85	D / 2.2	2.93	7.42	5.29 / 56	--	--
COH	*Guggenhm BltShs 2014 HY Corp Bd	BSJE	C	25.92	26.13	23.76	D+ / 2.5	3.30	8.38	6.78 / 61	--	--
COH	*Guggenhm BltShs 2015 HY Corp Bd	BSJF	C	25.89	26.00	23.40	D+ / 2.7	3.65	9.66	6.76 / 61	--	--
HL	*Health Care Select Sector SPDR	XLV	C+	37.61	37.66	29.64	C / 5.1	8.96	19.77	15.38 / 78	18.62 / 38	3.66 / 49
GL	*IndexIQ Emerging Mkts MC ETF	EMER	U	17.59	N/A	N/A	U /	19.01	25.41	--	--	--
GR	*Industrial Select Sector SPDR	XLI	B-	37.42	38.98	27.67	B- / 7.1	11.39	29.48	0.70 / 43	26.40 / 71	3.23 / 46
FO	*iPath Asian & Gulf Currncy Reval	PGD	D-	50.21	52.23	49.17	D- / 1.2	--	-0.69	-1.45 / 37	0.41 / 7	--
GR	*iPath CBOE S&P 500 BuyWrite Idx	BWV	C	52.57	52.85	39.40	C- / 3.6	4.30	22.00	8.13 / 64	13.63 / 23	--
EN	*iPath Cptl Glbl Carbon Tot Ret E	GRN	E-	10.00	33.00	9.51	E / 0.4	-3.29	-42.13	-65.51 / 0	-24.73 / 4	--
EN	*iPath DJ UBS Agri Tot Ret Sub	JJA	D-	55.10	67.61	48.87	D / 2.2	3.15	5.92	-15.98 / 14	11.38 / 18	--
EN	*iPath DJ UBS Almin Tot Ret Sub	JJU	E+	26.19	36.94	24.56	D- / 1.4	3.52	-3.89	-24.65 / 8	7.08 / 12	--
EN	*iPath DJ UBS Cocoa Tot Ret Sub	NIB	E	30.09	47.47	27.23	E+ / 0.7	4.66	-16.81	-30.02 / 5	-11.51 / 6	--
EN	*iPath DJ UBS Coffee Tot Ret Sub	JO	E	44.76	81.13	42.81	D- / 1.1	-20.82	-22.21	-35.29 / 4	6.69 / 12	--
EN	*iPath DJ UBS Copper Total Ret Su	JJC	D	49.07	60.04	38.99	C / 4.7	11.42	22.03	-12.89 / 18	20.93 / 47	--
EN	*iPath DJ UBS Cotton Tot Ret Sub	BAL	D-	56.63	111.58	52.13	C / 4.4	0.30	-7.93	-44.11 / 2	28.23 / 77	--
EN	*iPath DJ UBS Energy Tot Ret Sub	JJE	E+	17.99	26.53	17.86	E+ / 0.8	-6.06	-4.16	-28.04 / 7	-8.08 / 6	--
EN	*iPath DJ UBS Grains Tot Ret	JJG	E+	47.41	56.50	40.32	D / 1.6	5.29	10.75	-13.26 / 17	5.39 / 11	--
EN	*iPath DJ UBS Ind Me Tot Ret Sub	JJM	D-	36.75	48.98	32.85	D+ / 2.5	5.91	8.37	-20.76 / 11	13.61 / 23	--
EN	*iPath DJ UBS Lead Tot Ret Sub	LD	E+	48.77	72.86	44.17	D / 1.9	-0.57	-0.18	-28.85 / 6	11.70 / 19	--
EN	*iPath DJ UBS Live Stk TR Sub	COW	E+	28.11	33.06	27.39	E+ / 0.9	-5.54	-9.85	-14.92 / 15	-4.01 / 6	--
EN	*iPath DJ UBS Nkl Tot Ret Sub	JJN	E+	25.37	41.42	24.12	D+ / 2.3	-4.91	0.99	-32.80 / 5	16.01 / 30	--
EN	*iPath DJ UBS Ntrl Gas Tot Ret Su	GAZ	E-	3.80	9.05	2.90	E / 0.3	0.80	-32.62	-57.16 / 1	-41.52 / 2	--
EN	*iPath DJ UBS Platinum Tot Ret Su	PGM	D-	37.64	45.87	30.91	D+ / 2.3	17.53	7.14	-12.93 / 18	9.88 / 16	--
EN	*iPath DJ UBS Precious Mtls Tot R	JJP	C-	91.44	109.66	77.09	C+ / 6.4	8.44	3.33	6.46 / 59	25.58 / 67	--
EN	*iPath DJ UBS Softs Tot Ret Sub	JJS	D-	66.73	91.00	64.83	C- / 3.9	-3.71	-8.33	-24.05 / 9	23.60 / 59	--
EN	*iPath DJ UBS Sugar Tot Ret Sub	SGG	D	89.67	107.06	65.34	B- / 7.0	9.62	1.07	5.77 / 58	28.09 / 77	--
EN	*iPath DJ UBS Tin Tot Ret Sub	JJT	D	52.43	79.90	42.32	C+ / 6.2	19.95	12.83	-29.65 / 6	28.17 / 77	--
GR	*iPath DJ-UBS Commodity Index Tot	DJP	D	42.32	53.22	40.47	D- / 1.5	0.19	1.39	-17.81 / 12	7.18 / 13	-3.79 / 15
USA	*iPath ETN US Treasury 5Yr Bear E	DFVS	U	43.77	N/A	N/A	U /	3.33	-1.55	--	--	--
FO	*iPath EUR/USD Exch Rate ETN	ERO	D	51.87	58.11	49.38	D- / 1.1	3.04	-0.44	-6.22 / 28	-0.40 / 7	--
GR	*iPath GBP/USD Exchange Rate ETN	GBB	D+	42.89	45.12	41.15	D- / 1.5	3.52	2.44	-0.65 / 39	3.96 / 9	--
FO	*iPath GEMS Asia 8 ETN	AYT	D-	48.08	50.74	46.39	D- / 1.5	2.61	2.53	-2.50 / 35	4.19 / 9	--
GI	*iPath GEMS Index ETN	JEM	D-	43.91	48.77	40.89	D / 2.0	5.73	6.73	-2.42 / 35	7.29 / 13	--
FO	*iPath JPY/USD Exchange Rate ETN	JYN	D+	71.20	78.65	66.98	D / 1.6	-6.86	-7.07	1.78 / 46	6.11 / 11	--
GI	*iPath LngEnh S&P500 VIX MT Fut I	VZZB	U	28.35	N/A	N/A	U /	-38.28	-53.35	--	--	--
IN	*iPath Long Ext Rus 2000 TR Idx E	RTLA	C	71.24	78.12	24.03	A+ / 9.9	33.28	120.42	-3.26 / 33	--	--
IN	*iPath Long Ext S&P 500 TR Idx ET	SFLA	C+	81.24	82.00	37.08	A+ / 9.9	32.26	81.79	18.03 / 81	--	--
EM	*iPath MSCI India Index ETN	INP	D	56.47	74.50	45.91	C- / 3.6	21.13	4.90	-22.90 / 9	18.44 / 37	2.32 / 40
GL	*iPath Optimized Currency Carry E	ICI	D+	46.08	47.93	43.38	D- / 1.3	-0.04	3.30	-1.12 / 38	1.19 / 8	--
IN	*iPath Pure Beta Agriculture ETN	DIRT	U	43.74	N/A	N/A	U /	2.94	3.65	--	--	--
IN	*iPath Pure Beta Broad Commodity	BCM	U	45.34	N/A	N/A	U /	5.54	10.13	--	--	--
IN	*iPath Pure Beta Cocoa ETN	CHOC	U	34.16	N/A	N/A	U /	1.97	-16.60	--	--	--
IN	*iPath Pure Beta Coffee ETN	CAFE	U	28.78	N/A	N/A	U /	-20.06	-23.21	--	--	--
GI	*iPath Pure Beta Copper ETN	CUPM	U	42.93	N/A	N/A	U /	9.40	16.03	--	--	--
IN	*iPath Pure Beta Cotton ETN	CTNN	U	36.34	N/A	N/A	U /	1.57	-6.82	--	--	--
IN	*iPath Pure Beta Crude Oil ETN	OLEM	U	45.10	N/A	N/A	U /	2.57	25.10	--	--	--
IN	*iPath Pure Beta Grains ETN	WEET	U	43.93	N/A	N/A	U /	3.12	5.20	--	--	--

* Denotes ETF Fund, N/A denotes number is not available

www.thestreetratings.com

Incl. in Returns		RISK				NET ASSETS		VALUATION			ASSET					FUND MANAGER	
			3 Year					Premium / Discount									
Dividend Yield %	Expense Ratio	Risk Rating/ Pts	Standard Deviation	Beta	Avg Dura-tion	NAV as of 3/31/12	Total $(Mil)	As of 3/31/12	1 Year Average	Wtd Avg P/E	Cash %	Stocks %	Bonds %	Other %	Portfolio Turnover Ratio	Manager Quality Pct	Manager Tenure (Years)
3.57	0.50	B- / 7.4	24.7	1.37	N/A	18.29	16	-0.49	-0.24	33.8	0	100	0	0	37	18	N/A
2.14	0.32	B / 8.0	N/A	N/A	N/A	34.79	8	-0.29	-0.01	N/A	0	100	0	0	12	54	N/A
1.50	0.12	B / 8.3	N/A	N/A	N/A	31.29	6	-0.16	0.08	N/A	0	100	0	0	4	33	N/A
0.99	0.65	U /	N/A	N/A	N/A	25.16	5	0.16	N/A	N/A	0	0	0	100	N/A	N/A	1
3.67	0.42	B+ / 9.7	N/A	N/A	N/A	25.43	71	0.24	0.63	N/A	0	0	100	0	N/A	57	N/A
4.38	0.42	B+ / 9.6	N/A	N/A	N/A	25.67	116	0.39	0.44	N/A	0	0	100	0	N/A	60	N/A
4.81	0.42	B+ / 9.6	N/A	N/A	N/A	25.85	78	0.27	0.41	N/A	0	0	100	0	N/A	67	N/A
3.80	0.42	B+ / 9.4	N/A	N/A	N/A	25.77	96	0.47	0.54	N/A	0	0	100	0	N/A	63	N/A
1.98	0.19	B / 8.7	12.7	0.58	N/A	37.62	4,118	-0.03	N/A	40.7	0	100	0	0	7	71	14
1.99	0.75	U /	N/A	N/A	N/A	17.17	2	2.45	N/A	N/A	0	100	0	0	N/A	N/A	1
1.89	0.19	B- / 7.8	22.3	1.30	N/A	37.41	2,790	0.03	N/A	25.2	0	100	0	0	4	37	14
0.00	0.89	C+ / 5.8	4.5	0.10	N/A	50.88	4	-1.32	-0.21	N/A	0	0	0	100	N/A	38	4
0.00	0.75	B / 8.7	12.5	0.65	N/A	52.73	10	-0.30	-0.03	N/A	0	0	0	100	N/A	43	5
0.00	0.75	D / 1.9	44.9	0.28	N/A	11.30	4	-11.50	-5.12	N/A	0	0	0	100	N/A	4	4
0.00	0.75	C / 4.6	27.1	0.67	N/A	55.08	68	0.04	-0.03	N/A	0	0	0	100	N/A	44	5
0.00	0.75	C- / 4.2	26.1	0.64	N/A	26.24	7	-0.19	-0.11	N/A	0	0	0	100	N/A	26	4
0.00	0.75	C- / 3.2	32.5	0.67	N/A	30.03	28	0.20	0.02	N/A	0	0	0	100	N/A	7	4
0.00	0.75	C- / 3.3	33.7	0.50	N/A	44.75	8	0.02	-0.01	N/A	0	0	0	100	N/A	37	4
0.00	0.75	C- / 4.0	31.1	0.98	N/A	49.08	130	-0.02	0.05	N/A	0	0	0	100	N/A	68	5
0.00	0.75	C- / 3.1	36.4	0.66	N/A	56.90	23	-0.47	-0.01	N/A	0	0	0	100	N/A	90	4
0.00	0.75	C- / 4.0	24.2	0.74	N/A	17.93	11	0.33	-0.16	N/A	0	0	0	100	N/A	7	5
0.00	0.75	C / 4.4	32.5	0.76	N/A	47.35	57	0.13	0.02	N/A	0	0	0	100	N/A	19	5
0.00	0.75	C- / 4.1	28.8	0.91	N/A	36.80	50	-0.14	-0.08	N/A	0	0	0	100	N/A	36	5
0.00	0.75	C- / 4.2	36.3	1.03	N/A	48.64	14	0.27	-0.04	N/A	0	0	0	100	N/A	20	4
0.00	0.75	C / 5.1	14.3	0.09	N/A	28.08	110	0.11	-0.07	N/A	0	0	0	100	N/A	23	5
0.00	0.75	C- / 3.5	40.3	1.13	N/A	25.44	15	-0.28	-0.09	N/A	0	0	0	100	N/A	30	5
0.00	0.75	D / 1.9	46.0	0.52	N/A	2.11	208	80.09	14.86	N/A	0	0	0	100	N/A	N/A	5
0.00	0.75	C / 4.3	28.1	0.70	N/A	37.68	103	-0.11	0.28	N/A	0	0	0	100	N/A	32	4
0.00	0.75	C / 4.8	26.6	0.44	N/A	91.82	8	-0.41	0.06	N/A	0	0	0	100	N/A	90	4
0.00	0.75	C / 4.3	25.6	0.48	N/A	66.88	5	-0.22	-0.14	N/A	0	0	0	100	N/A	89	4
0.00	0.75	D+ / 2.8	48.0	0.35	N/A	89.69	27	-0.02	-0.07	N/A	0	0	0	100	N/A	93	4
0.00	0.75	C- / 3.4	35.1	0.98	N/A	52.42	2	0.02	-0.49	N/A	0	0	0	100	N/A	83	4
0.00	0.75	B- / 7.7	19.4	0.80	N/A	42.31	1,897	0.02	0.10	N/A	0	99	0	1	N/A	17	6
0.00	0.75	U /	N/A	N/A	N/A	43.71	1	0.14	N/A	N/A	0	0	0	100	N/A	N/A	1
0.00	0.40	B / 8.1	13.3	0.47	N/A	51.79	8	0.15	-0.14	N/A	0	0	0	100	N/A	18	5
0.00	0.40	B / 8.7	11.3	0.25	N/A	42.85	2	0.09	-0.14	N/A	0	0	0	100	N/A	36	5
0.77	0.89	C+ / 5.6	11.5	0.32	N/A	48.08	22	0.00	-0.05	N/A	0	0	0	100	N/A	38	4
4.08	0.89	C / 5.3	12.5	0.60	N/A	43.80	2	0.25	0.01	N/A	0	0	0	100	N/A	21	4
0.00	0.40	B+ / 9.0	10.2	N/A	N/A	71.31	11	-0.15	-0.08	N/A	0	0	0	100	N/A	76	5
0.00	0.89	U /	N/A	N/A	N/A	27.50	5	3.09	N/A	N/A	0	0	0	100	N/A	N/A	1
0.00	N/A	D+ / 2.4	N/A	N/A	N/A	71.96	8	-1.00	-0.01	N/A	0	0	0	100	N/A	3	N/A
0.00	N/A	C- / 3.6	N/A	N/A	N/A	81.25	8	-0.01	-0.03	N/A	0	0	0	100	N/A	22	N/A
0.00	0.89	C+ / 5.9	37.9	1.30	N/A	56.48	1,059	-0.02	0.04	N/A	0	0	0	100	N/A	16	6
0.00	0.65	B+ / 9.6	4.6	0.08	N/A	46.19	27	-0.24	-0.12	N/A	0	0	0	100	N/A	44	4
0.00	0.75	U /	N/A	N/A	N/A	43.90	2	-0.36	N/A	N/A	0	0	0	100	N/A	N/A	1
0.00	0.75	U /	N/A	N/A	N/A	45.31	17	0.07	N/A	N/A	0	0	0	100	N/A	N/A	1
0.00	0.75	U /	N/A	N/A	N/A	34.50	2	-0.99	N/A	N/A	0	0	0	100	N/A	N/A	1
0.00	0.75	U /	N/A	N/A	N/A	28.98	2	-0.69	N/A	N/A	0	0	0	100	N/A	N/A	1
0.00	0.75	U /	N/A	N/A	N/A	42.99	2	-0.14	N/A	N/A	0	0	0	100	N/A	N/A	1
0.00	0.75	U /	N/A	N/A	N/A	36.98	2	-1.73	N/A	N/A	0	0	0	100	N/A	N/A	1
0.00	0.75	U /	N/A	N/A	N/A	44.95	2	0.33	N/A	N/A	0	0	0	100	N/A	N/A	1
0.00	0.75	U /	N/A	N/A	N/A	44.35	2	-0.95	N/A	N/A	0	0	0	100	N/A	N/A	1

* Denotes ETF Fund, N/A denotes number is not available

Fund Type	Fund Name	Ticker Symbol	Overall Investment Rating	Price As of 3/31/12	52 Week High	52 Week Low	Performance Rating/Pts		3 Mo	6 Mo	1Yr/Pct	3Yr/Pct	5Yr/Pct
											% Total Return Through 3/31/12 / Annualized		
IN	*iPath Pure Beta Indus Metals ETN	HEVY	U	41.25	N/A	N/A	U	/	9.94	8.55	--	--	--
IN	*iPath Pure Beta Lead ETN	LEDD	U	37.08	N/A	N/A	U	/	--	-3.91	--	--	--
IN	*iPath Pure Beta Livestock ETN	LSTK	U	46.26	N/A	N/A	U	/	-3.00	-3.62	--	--	--
PM	*iPath Pure Beta Precious Metals	BLNG	U	50.33	N/A	N/A	U	/	5.71	2.59	--	--	--
IN	*iPath Pure Beta Softs ETN	GRWN	U	41.92	N/A	N/A	U	/	-1.36	-8.55	--	--	--
GL	*iPath S&P 500 Dynamic VIX ETN	XVZ	U	57.86	N/A	N/A	U	/	2.32	-8.26	--	--	--
IN	*iPath S&P 500 VIX Mid-Trm Futr E	VXZ	E-	46.23	77.65	45.48	E	/ 0.5	-23.79	-36.84	-15.42 / 15	-25.39 / 4	--
IN	*iPath S&P 500 VIX Sm-Trm Futr ET	VXX	E-	16.78	59.18	15.57	E-	/ 0.0	-52.77	-68.56	-42.31 / 2	-66.07 / 0	--
EN	*iPath S&P GSCI Crude Oil TotRet	OIL	D	25.88	30.27	18.87	D+	/ 2.3	3.03	30.44	-9.48 / 22	8.66 / 14	-7.39 / 9
GR	*iPath S&P GSCI Total Return ETN	GSP	D+	35.62	40.60	29.71	D+	/ 2.6	5.54	16.98	-7.50 / 26	11.16 / 18	-3.32 / 16
EN	*iPath Seasonal Natural Gas ETN	DCNG	U	27.31	N/A	N/A	U		--	-33.21	--	--	--
IN	*iPath Shrt Ext Rus 1000 TR Idx E	ROSA	E-	16.01	61.36	14.52	E-	/ 0.0	-44.39	-69.61	-46.60 / 2	--	--
IN	*iPath Shrt Ext Rus 2000 TR Idx E	RTSA	E-	22.95	72.00	19.62	E-	/ 0.1	-45.77	-64.24	-7.91 / 25	--	--
IN	*iPath Shrt Ext S&P 500 TR Idx ET	SFSA	E-	16.47	66.00	14.49	E-	/ 0.0	-54.80	-69.50	-46.07 / 2	--	--
USA	*iPath US Treas 10Yr Bear ETN	DTYS	E	33.78	54.42	30.60	E	/ 0.5	4.71	-1.60	-36.44 / 4	--	--
USA	*iPath US Treas 10Yr Bull ETN	DTYL	C	65.40	67.97	45.06	B	/ 7.9	-2.02	1.36	41.47 / 97	--	--
USA	*iPath US Treas 2Yr Bear ETN	DTUS	E+	41.65	49.90	40.60	E+	/ 0.8	0.34	-0.48	-16.11 / 14	--	--
USA	*iPath US Treas 2Yr Bull ETN	DTUL	D	57.03	58.36	49.64	D+	/ 2.6	-0.92	-0.40	15.84 / 78	--	--
USA	*iPath US Treas Flattener ETN	FLAT	D	57.08	59.40	44.96	C-	/ 3.9	-2.14	0.05	23.90 / 84	--	--
USA	*iPath US Treas Lng Bd Bear ETN	DLBS	E	35.77	54.81	31.10	E+	/ 0.7	11.89	6.59	-32.56 / 5	--	--
USA	*iPath US Treas Lng Bd Bull ETN	DLBL	C-	63.59	67.94	44.66	C+	/ 6.1	-4.83	-2.57	37.52 / 95	--	--
USA	*iPath US Treas Steepen ETN	STPP	E+	40.77	54.41	39.23	E+	/ 0.6	1.39	-2.88	-23.59 / 9	--	--
FO	*IQ Australia Small Cap ETF	KROO	D-	23.36	31.78	19.70	D+	/ 2.3	15.93	25.42	-13.90 / 16	--	--
FO	*IQ Canada Small Cap ETF	CNDA	D-	26.50	36.59	21.41	E+	/ 0.9	4.62	14.01	-24.27 / 8	--	--
GL	*IQ Global Agribusiness SmCp ETF	CROP	D+	25.43	27.72	20.82	D+	/ 2.5	12.72	17.38	-5.03 / 30	--	--
GL	*IQ Global Oil Small Cap ETF	IOIL	U	18.13	N/A	N/A	U	/	17.27	34.69	--	--	--
EN	*IQ Global Resources ETF	GRES	D	29.10	33.87	26.21	D-	/ 1.1	3.86	9.64	-10.20 / 21	--	--
GL	*IQ Hedge Macro Tracker ETF	MCRO	D+	27.29	28.46	25.52	D-	/ 1.5	3.88	5.38	-0.83 / 39	--	--
GL	*IQ Hedge Multi-Strategy Tracker	QAI	C-	27.73	28.24	26.59	D	/ 1.7	2.40	4.34	2.58 / 48	4.80 / 10	--
GL	*IQ Merger Arbitrage ETF	MNA	C-	25.67	26.71	21.52	D	/ 1.8	4.43	6.82	0.66 / 43	--	--
IN	*IQ Real Return ETF	CPI	C-	26.18	28.53	24.25	D-	/ 1.4	0.68	1.99	2.99 / 49	--	--
FO	*IQ South Korea Small Cap ETF	SKOR	D-	25.96	35.68	22.90	E+	/ 0.9	-0.06	9.14	-18.39 / 11	--	--
GI	*IQ US Real Estate SmCp ETF	ROOF	U	20.07	N/A	N/A	U	/	14.37	29.08	--	--	--
GL	*iShares 10+ Year Credit Bond	CLY	C	57.77	60.12	51.55	D+	/ 2.7	-1.33	2.74	14.90 / 77	--	--
GL	*iShares 10+ Year Govt/Credit Bd	GLJ	C-	58.89	62.69	50.97	D+	/ 2.7	-2.37	-0.66	17.91 / 80	--	--
GEI	*iShares 2012 S&P AMT-Free Muni S	MUAA	C-	50.84	51.40	49.65	D-	/ 1.3	0.32	0.93	0.44 / 42	--	--
GEI	*iShares 2013 S&P AMT-Free Muni S	MUAB	C-	51.23	54.02	50.01	D-	/ 1.4	1.05	1.49	1.68 / 45	--	--
GEI	*iShares 2014 S&P AMT-Free Muni S	MUAC	C-	51.90	56.78	50.50	D-	/ 1.5	0.61	2.07	3.51 / 50	--	--
GEI	*iShares 2015 S&P AMT-Free Muni S	MUAD	C-	53.46	58.00	51.20	D	/ 1.7	0.91	2.49	5.25 / 56	--	--
GEI	*iShares 2016 S&P AMT-Free Muni S	MUAE	C-	53.58	54.17	50.50	D	/ 2.1	0.88	3.87	7.72 / 63	--	--
GEI	*iShares 2017 S&P AMT-Free Muni S	MUAF	C-	54.67	81.63	51.09	D	/ 2.1	-0.21	2.86	8.92 / 66	--	--
COI	*iShares Aaa-A Rated Corporate Bo	QLTA	U	49.78	N/A	N/A	U	/	--	--	--	--	--
FO	*iShares Asia/Pacific Dividend 30	DVYA	U	50.98	N/A	N/A	U	/	--	--	--	--	--
USA	*iShares Barclays 0-5 Year TIPS B	STIP	C-	103.32	104.33	100.38	D-	/ 1.5	1.28	2.04	3.34 / 50	--	--
COI	*iShares Barclays 1-3 Year Credit	CSJ	C-	105.09	105.25	103.35	D	/ 1.6	1.14	1.94	2.62 / 48	4.90 / 10	4.20 / 51
USA	*iShares Barclays 1-3Yr Treasury	SHY	C-	84.32	84.85	83.66	D-	/ 1.3	-0.13	--	1.35 / 45	1.48 / 8	3.26 / 46
USA	*iShares Barclays 10-20 Yr Treasu	TLH	C-	127.76	135.13	109.84	D	/ 2.1	-3.49	-2.13	17.58 / 80	7.17 / 13	8.94 / 79
USA	*iShares Barclays 20+Yr Treasury	TLT	D+	112.20	125.03	89.65	D	/ 2.1	-7.02	-5.66	26.12 / 86	7.02 / 12	9.42 / 83
USA	*iShares Barclays 3-7 Yr Treasury	IEI	C-	121.10	122.84	113.60	D	/ 1.6	-0.58	0.33	7.68 / 63	4.46 / 10	6.58 / 65
USA	*iShares Barclays 7-10Yr Treasury	IEF	C-	103.28	106.66	91.94	D	/ 1.9	-1.83	-0.60	13.71 / 75	6.13 / 11	8.28 / 76
USA	*iShares Barclays Agency Bond	AGZ	C-	112.64	113.67	108.46	D-	/ 1.5	-0.04	0.68	4.64 / 54	3.43 / 9	--
GEI	*iShares Barclays Aggregate Bd	AGG	C-	109.85	111.07	104.53	D	/ 1.9	0.14	1.29	7.71 / 63	6.66 / 12	6.04 / 62

* Denotes ETF Fund, N/A denotes number is not available

www.thestreetratings.com

99 Pct = Best
0 Pct = Worst

Incl. in Returns		RISK	3 Year		Avg Dura-tion	NET ASSETS		VALUATION Premium / Discount		Wtd Avg P/E	ASSET				Portfolio Turnover Ratio	FUND MANAGER	
Dividend Yield %	Expense Ratio	Risk Rating/ Pts	Standard Deviation	Beta		NAV as of 3/31/12	Total $(Mil)	As of 3/31/12	1 Year Average		Cash %	Stocks %	Bonds %	Other %		Manager Quality Pct	Manager Tenure (Years)
0.00	0.75	U /	N/A	N/A	N/A	41.14	3	0.27	N/A	N/A	0	0	0	100	N/A	N/A	1
0.00	0.75	U /	N/A	N/A	N/A	36.94	3	0.38	N/A	N/A	0	0	0	100	N/A	N/A	1
0.00	0.75	U /	N/A	N/A	N/A	46.19	1	0.15	N/A	N/A	0	0	0	100	N/A	N/A	1
0.00	0.75	U /	N/A	N/A	N/A	50.48	5	-0.30	N/A	N/A	0	0	0	100	N/A	N/A	1
0.00	0.75	U /	N/A	N/A	N/A	41.67	3	0.60	N/A	N/A	0	0	0	100	N/A	N/A	1
0.00	0.95	U /	N/A	N/A	N/A	57.46	187	0.70	N/A	N/A	0	0	0	100	N/A	66	3
0.00	0.89	D+ / 2.4	35.7	-1.58	N/A	45.63	29	1.31	0.09	N/A	0	0	0	100	N/A	2	3
0.00	0.89	D / 1.9	69.2	-3.15	N/A	16.68	665	0.60	0.14	N/A	0	0	0	100	N/A	17	6
0.00	0.75	C+ / 6.4	31.3	1.04	N/A	25.87	564	0.04	0.16	N/A	0	0	0	100	N/A	19	6
0.00	0.75	B- / 7.4	22.9	0.94	N/A	35.46	79	0.45	0.15	N/A	0	0	0	100	N/A	N/A	1
0.00	0.75	U /	N/A	N/A	N/A	27.53	2	-0.80	N/A	N/A	0	0	0	100	N/A	2	N/A
0.00	N/A	D / 1.9	N/A	N/A	N/A	15.47	2	3.49	1.11	N/A	0	0	0	100	N/A	97	N/A
0.00	N/A	D / 2.0	N/A	N/A	N/A	22.85	6	0.44	-0.02	N/A	0	0	0	100	N/A	4	N/A
0.00	N/A	D / 1.9	N/A	N/A	N/A	16.00	9	2.94	0.02	N/A	0	0	0	100	N/A	8	2
0.00	0.75	C- / 3.4	N/A	N/A	N/A	33.76	70	0.06	0.04	N/A	0	0	0	100	N/A	94	2
0.00	0.75	C / 5.2	N/A	N/A	N/A	65.44	5	-0.06	-0.12	N/A	0	0	0	100	N/A	11	2
0.00	0.75	C / 4.9	N/A	N/A	N/A	41.73	18	-0.19	N/A	N/A	0	0	0	100	N/A	85	2
0.00	0.75	C+ / 5.8	N/A	N/A	N/A	56.99	4	0.07	-0.01	N/A	0	0	0	100	N/A	78	2
0.00	0.75	C / 5.2	N/A	N/A	N/A	57.19	35	-0.19	-0.03	N/A	0	0	0	100	N/A	30	2
0.00	0.75	C- / 3.4	N/A	N/A	N/A	35.63	21	0.39	0.07	N/A	0	0	0	100	N/A	84	2
0.00	0.75	C / 5.1	N/A	N/A	N/A	63.80	1	-0.33	-0.09	N/A	0	0	0	100	N/A	14	2
0.00	0.75	C / 4.4	N/A	N/A	N/A	41.27	13	-1.21	0.08	N/A	0	0	0	100	N/A	22	N/A
7.56	0.69	C+ / 5.7	N/A	N/A	N/A	23.35	17	0.04	-0.25	N/A	0	100	0	0	49	8	N/A
1.16	0.69	C+ / 6.2	N/A	N/A	N/A	26.54	35	-0.15	-0.19	N/A	0	100	0	0	52	43	N/A
0.82	0.75	B- / 7.8	N/A	N/A	N/A	25.42	38	0.04	-0.15	N/A	0	100	0	0	N/A	N/A	N/A
0.82	0.75	U /	N/A	N/A	N/A	17.98	2	0.83	N/A	N/A	0	100	0	0	N/A	20	1
0.70	0.76	B / 8.2	N/A	N/A	N/A	29.07	71	0.10	0.09	36.3	0	100	0	0	117	60	3
0.99	0.77	B+ / 9.2	N/A	N/A	N/A	27.28	39	0.04	0.05	N/A	1	98	0	1	54	55	4
1.34	0.77	B+ / 9.5	5.4	0.22	N/A	27.71	197	0.07	0.09	N/A	0	81	0	19	145	58	1
0.00	0.76	B+ / 9.2	N/A	N/A	N/A	25.70	26	-0.12	-0.11	N/A	0	100	0	0	365	63	1
0.00	0.49	B+ / 9.9	N/A	N/A	N/A	26.16	24	0.08	0.01	N/A	0	100	0	0	52	15	N/A
0.40	0.80	C+ / 6.0	N/A	N/A	N/A	26.23	10	-1.03	-0.25	N/A	0	100	0	0	73	N/A	1
1.09	0.69	U /	N/A	N/A	N/A	20.04	31	0.15	N/A	N/A	0	100	0	0	N/A	89	2
5.01	0.20	B+ / 9.4	N/A	N/A	N/A	57.88	196	-0.19	1.45	N/A	1	0	96	3	18	92	2
4.20	0.20	B+ / 9.2	N/A	N/A	N/A	59.14	24	-0.42	0.12	N/A	1	0	98	1	9	57	2
0.67	0.30	B+ / 9.8	N/A	N/A	N/A	50.72	28	0.24	-0.27	N/A	0	0	100	0	2	54	2
1.00	0.30	B+ / 9.9	N/A	N/A	N/A	50.96	36	0.53	0.15	N/A	0	0	100	0	N/A	72	2
1.09	0.30	B+ / 9.7	N/A	N/A	N/A	51.62	36	0.54	0.17	N/A	0	0	100	0	N/A	63	2
1.48	0.30	B+ / 9.8	N/A	N/A	N/A	53.12	37	0.64	0.22	N/A	1	0	98	1	2	74	2
1.75	0.30	B+ / 9.7	N/A	N/A	N/A	53.19	32	0.73	0.20	N/A	0	0	100	0	4	43	2
1.91	0.30	B+ / 9.4	N/A	N/A	N/A	54.64	42	0.05	0.39	N/A	0	0	100	0	2	N/A	0
0.00	0.15	U /	N/A	N/A	N/A	49.58	10	0.40	N/A	N/A	0	0	0	100	N/A	N/A	0
13.42	0.49	U /	N/A	N/A	N/A	51.19	5	-0.41	N/A	N/A	0	0	0	100	N/A	75	2
0.23	0.20	B+ / 9.9	N/A	N/A	N/A	103.16	279	0.16	0.13	N/A	0	0	100	0	34	47	2
1.79	0.20	B+ / 9.8	2.2	0.38	4.0	104.83	9,132	0.25	0.15	N/A	0	0	98	2	2	53	2
0.50	0.15	B+ / 9.9	1.0	0.05	2.6	84.31	10,652	0.01	0.02	N/A	0	0	100	0	30	52	2
2.46	0.15	B+ / 9.1	9.5	0.76	15.6	127.91	513	-0.12	0.03	N/A	0	0	100	0	9	29	2
2.85	0.15	B / 8.4	15.2	1.24	15.6	112.52	3,038	-0.28	0.03	N/A	0	0	100	0	17	61	2
1.09	0.15	B+ / 9.7	3.9	0.23	4.2	121.06	2,256	0.03	0.04	N/A	0	0	100	0	22	57	2
1.97	0.15	B+ / 9.3	6.9	0.51	6.9	103.29	4,637	-0.01	0.04	N/A	0	0	100	0	52	62	2
1.48	0.20	B+ / 9.9	2.0	0.12	4.6	112.32	361	0.28	0.07	N/A	0	0	100	0	31	41	2
3.02	0.20	B+ / 9.8	2.9	1.05	9.8	109.64	14,774	0.19	0.15	N/A	0	0	99	1	406		

* Denotes ETF Fund, N/A denotes number is not available

Fund Type	Fund Name	Ticker Symbol	Overall Investment Rating	PRICE Price As of 3/31/12	52 Week High	52 Week Low	Perform-ance Rating/Pts		PERFORMANCE % Total Return Through 3/31/12 3 Mo	6 Mo	1Yr/Pct	Annualized 3Yr/Pct	5Yr/Pct
COI	*iShares Barclays CMBS Bond	CMBS	U	50.67	N/A	N/A	U	/	--	--	--	--	--
COI	*iShares Barclays Credit Bond Fd	CFT	C	109.72	111.49	103.67	D+	/ 2.8	1.32	3.80	9.19 / 67	11.86 / 19	6.72 / 66
GEI	*iShares Barclays GNMA Bond	GNMA	U	50.00	N/A	N/A	U	/	--	--	--	--	--
USA	*iShares Barclays Govt/Credit Bd	GBF	C-	112.96	114.78	106.26	D	/ 1.9	-0.31	1.57	8.66 / 66	6.84 / 12	6.22 / 63
COI	*iShares Barclays Intrm Credit Bd	CIU	C	108.85	109.51	104.87	D+	/ 2.4	2.14	3.76	6.87 / 61	9.50 / 15	6.21 / 62
GEI	*iShares Barclays Intrm Govt/Crdt	GVI	C-	111.12	112.30	107.04	D	/ 1.7	0.24	1.18	5.93 / 58	5.52 / 11	5.60 / 59
MTG	*iShares Barclays MBS Bond	MBB	C-	107.95	109.20	104.55	D	/ 1.7	0.44	1.36	5.86 / 58	5.02 / 10	5.83 / 61
USA	*iShares Barclays Short Treasury	SHV	C-	110.19	110.29	109.94	D-	/ 1.2	-0.04	-0.04	-0.01 / 41	0.11 / 7	1.38 / 33
USA	*iShares Barclays TIPS Bond	TIP	C	117.65	119.44	108.46	D+	/ 2.4	0.82	3.61	11.75 / 72	8.78 / 15	7.49 / 71
IN	*iShares Cohen & Steers Realty Ma	ICF	A-	76.64	77.03	56.83	A-	/ 9.2	10.00	26.92	12.50 / 73	37.33 / 93	-1.95 / 19
GL	*iShares Diversified Alternatives	ALT	D+	48.72	52.95	47.34	D-	/ 1.0	-0.06	-0.14	-4.81 / 31	--	--
FO	*iShares DJ Intl Select Dividend	IDV	C+	32.60	38.41	27.01	C+	/ 5.8	10.67	16.97	-5.05 / 30	24.00 / 61	--
IN	*iShares DJ Select Dividend	DVY	B-	55.96	56.62	44.80	C+	/ 6.2	5.01	18.01	10.51 / 69	23.25 / 58	-1.12 / 22
IN	*iShares DJ Transportation	IYT	C	93.69	101.60	70.82	C+	/ 5.6	4.91	25.15	-2.16 / 35	22.57 / 54	2.65 / 43
IN	*iShares DJ US Aerospace & Def Id	ITA	B-	67.13	68.11	50.91	C+	/ 6.9	9.99	23.91	4.99 / 55	25.50 / 66	4.30 / 52
IN	*iShares DJ US Basic Material	IYM	C	70.36	84.81	52.69	C+	/ 5.7	9.75	26.15	-12.22 / 18	23.91 / 60	3.24 / 46
FS	*iShares DJ US Broker-Dealers Idx	IAI	D	25.36	30.72	18.54	D	/ 2.1	21.68	28.45	-15.66 / 14	6.50 / 12	-12.96 / 5
IN	*iShares DJ US Consumer Goods	IYK	B-	74.12	74.33	60.22	C+	/ 6.3	8.68	19.13	13.45 / 75	22.71 / 55	6.16 / 62
IN	*iShares DJ US Consumer Services	IYC	B	80.99	81.98	60.88	B-	/ 7.5	13.70	27.38	15.26 / 78	25.76 / 67	4.18 / 51
EN	*iShares DJ US Energy	IYE	C-	41.52	46.12	31.44	C-	/ 3.8	4.61	23.40	-7.65 / 25	16.58 / 31	4.45 / 53
FS	*iShares DJ US Financial Sector	IYF	C	58.52	60.42	40.93	C	/ 5.3	19.66	33.81	-0.18 / 40	19.21 / 40	-10.79 / 6
FS	*iShares DJ US Financial Services	IYG	C-	57.22	60.43	37.90	C	/ 4.6	26.70	40.13	-2.00 / 35	15.77 / 29	-13.45 / 5
HL	*iShares DJ US Health Care Provid	IHF	B	66.88	67.58	47.76	B	/ 8.0	13.88	30.15	7.25 / 62	28.62 / 79	2.98 / 44
HL	*iShares DJ US Healthcare	IYH	C+	78.20	78.32	61.02	C	/ 5.2	9.73	20.78	14.40 / 76	18.87 / 39	4.26 / 52
IN	*iShares DJ US Home Cons Idx	ITB	C	14.72	15.48	8.21	C+	/ 6.0	24.05	64.96	11.47 / 71	16.26 / 30	-14.68 / 3
IN	*iShares DJ US Index	IYY	C+	70.73	71.40	53.52	C+	/ 6.0	12.81	26.23	6.93 / 61	21.72 / 51	1.94 / 37
IN	*iShares DJ US Industrial	IYJ	C+	71.38	73.40	51.88	B-	/ 7.1	12.58	30.98	1.23 / 44	25.89 / 68	2.84 / 43
IN	*iShares DJ US Insurance Idx	IAK	C+	32.05	33.61	23.50	C+	/ 6.1	12.53	27.85	-0.32 / 40	22.98 / 57	-8.27 / 8
HL	*iShares DJ US Medical Devices Id	IHI	C	67.84	69.67	53.14	C+	/ 6.1	15.51	20.42	4.81 / 54	22.68 / 55	4.90 / 57
EN	*iShares DJ US Oil & Gas Exp & Pr	IEO	C-	65.79	75.45	46.51	C	/ 4.6	7.28	28.97	-11.42 / 20	20.36 / 44	4.77 / 56
EN	*iShares DJ US Oil Equip & Svcs	IEZ	C-	53.50	69.39	39.37	C	/ 5.2	3.15	23.64	-20.97 / 10	24.33 / 62	2.05 / 38
HL	*iShares DJ US Pharmaceuticals	IHE	B+	83.06	83.55	61.12	B	/ 8.1	9.04	25.97	25.66 / 85	27.75 / 75	10.02 / 87
IN	*iShares DJ US Real Estate	IYR	B+	62.30	63.00	46.70	B+	/ 8.8	10.60	25.53	8.70 / 66	33.76 / 89	-1.93 / 19
FS	*iShares DJ US Regional Banks	IAT	C-	24.80	25.32	16.95	C	/ 4.4	17.52	38.35	2.59 / 48	15.32 / 28	-10.89 / 6
GR	*iShares DJ US Technology	IYW	B-	77.81	78.78	55.93	B	/ 7.9	21.93	31.97	18.02 / 81	25.79 / 68	7.66 / 72
IN	*iShares DJ US Telecommunications	IYZ	C-	22.20	25.89	18.97	D+	/ 2.8	6.22	10.50	-4.59 / 31	12.43 / 20	-3.84 / 14
UT	*iShares DJ US Utilities	IDU	C	86.16	89.18	72.21	C-	/ 3.7	-1.56	7.16	11.57 / 71	15.72 / 29	0.69 / 30
GL	*iShares Emerging Mkts Lcl Cur Bo	LEMB	U	51.95	N/A	N/A	U	/	4.42	--	--	--	--
COI	*iShares Financials Sector Bond	MONY	U	50.50	N/A	N/A	U	/	--	--	--	--	--
COI	*iShares Floating Rate Note	FLOT	U	50.09	N/A	N/A	U	/	2.41	2.14	--	--	--
FO	*iShares FTSE China 25	FXI	D	36.67	46.40	28.61	D	/ 1.8	5.15	19.20	-17.90 / 12	7.49 / 13	2.18 / 39
FO	*iShares FTSE China Index	FCHI	D	43.75	54.74	34.50	D	/ 2.2	5.70	18.91	-16.72 / 13	9.55 / 16	--
FO	*iShares FTSE Dev Sm Cap ex-North	IFSM	C	35.54	42.41	28.92	C	/ 4.6	16.46	16.70	-8.49 / 24	19.84 / 42	--
GI	*iShares FTSE EPRA/NAREIT Asia In	IFAS	C-	28.25	31.90	22.45	C-	/ 4.2	17.93	20.78	-5.04 / 30	17.27 / 33	--
GI	*iShares FTSE EPRA/NAREIT Dev RE	IFGL	D+	28.74	33.03	23.36	C	/ 4.4	14.69	15.88	-5.28 / 30	18.93 / 39	--
GI	*iShares FTSE EPRA/NAREIT Europe	IFEU	D+	28.10	35.68	23.46	C-	/ 3.7	14.47	10.55	-10.42 / 21	16.99 / 32	--
GI	*iShares FTSE EPRA/NAREIT NA Idx	IFNA	A-	45.93	48.57	33.44	A	/ 9.5	9.86	23.77	10.24 / 69	41.41 / 96	--
IN	*iShares FTSE NAREIT Indl/Off Idx	FNIO	B	28.26	30.42	20.90	B+	/ 8.4	13.52	25.11	2.17 / 47	32.40 / 86	--
IN	*iShares FTSE NAREIT Mtge+Capped	REM	C-	13.52	15.48	11.28	C-	/ 3.1	10.07	15.95	0.44 / 42	12.26 / 20	--
IN	*iShares FTSE NAREIT Real Estate	FTY	A-	38.18	38.45	28.99	B+	/ 8.9	8.94	22.66	11.17 / 70	35.41 / 91	--
IN	*iShares FTSE NAREIT Residential	REZ	A-	46.41	46.70	36.14	A-	/ 9.0	5.84	21.66	14.30 / 76	35.75 / 92	--
IN	*iShares FTSE NAREIT Retail Idx	RTL	A+	32.64	32.87	23.39	A+	/ 9.6	13.74	30.40	18.72 / 81	41.95 / 96	--

* Denotes ETF Fund, N/A denotes number is not available

Incl. in Returns Dividend Yield %	Expense Ratio	RISK Risk Rating/ Pts	3 Year Standard Deviation	Beta	Avg Dura-tion	NET ASSETS NAV as of 3/31/12	Total $(Mil)	VALUATION Premium / Discount As of 3/31/12	1 Year Average	Wtd Avg P/E	Cash %	Stocks %	Bonds %	Other %	Portfolio Turnover Ratio	Manager Quality Pct	Manager Tenure (Years)
0.00	0.25	U /	N/A	N/A	N/A	50.25	8	0.84	N/A	N/A	0	0	0	100	N/A	N/A	0
3.82	0.20	B+/ 9.4	4.6	0.99	12.1	109.09	1,170	0.58	0.50	N/A	0	0	98	2	4	41	2
0.00	0.25	U /	N/A	N/A	N/A	49.89	5	0.22	N/A	N/A	0	0	0	100	N/A	N/A	0
2.74	0.20	B+/ 9.7	3.3	0.20	8.0	112.61	137	0.31	0.13	N/A	0	0	98	2	18	73	2
3.51	0.20	B+/ 9.7	3.7	0.75	4.6	108.32	4,462	0.49	0.35	N/A	1	0	97	2	3	48	2
2.30	0.20	B+/ 9.8	2.5	0.89	4.8	110.93	725	0.17	0.21	N/A	2	0	96	2	14	41	2
3.37	0.25	B+/ 9.7	2.2	1.02	15.2	107.84	4,595	0.10	0.08	N/A	0	0	97	3	258	43	2
0.00	0.15	B+/ 9.9	0.1	N/A	N/A	110.18	2,435	0.01	0.02	N/A	6	0	92	2	70	46	2
1.84	0.20	B+/ 9.7	4.9	0.14	8.1	117.38	22,889	0.23	0.12	N/A	0	0	99	1	13	80	2
3.11	0.35	B-/ 7.8	26.3	1.29	N/A	76.62	2,644	0.03	N/A	59.5	0	99	0	1	9	86	4
0.00	1.01	B+/ 9.5	N/A	N/A	N/A	48.78	73	-0.12	-0.14	N/A	0	0	0	100	N/A	28	N/A
3.10	0.50	B-/ 7.7	24.7	1.13	N/A	32.41	898	0.59	0.32	17.4	0	99	0	1	38	77	4
3.62	0.40	B+/ 9.0	13.6	0.78	N/A	55.96	10,119	0.00	0.02	20.6	0	99	0	1	18	79	4
0.74	0.47	B-/ 7.7	23.0	1.27	N/A	93.65	447	0.04	-0.01	30.2	0	99	0	1	8	29	4
1.03	0.47	B / 8.1	20.4	1.12	N/A	67.09	110	0.06	-0.02	41.7	0	99	0	1	10	50	4
1.19	0.47	B-/ 7.0	29.4	1.63	N/A	70.41	656	-0.07	N/A	25.0	1	98	0	1	7	16	4
1.49	0.47	B-/ 7.0	25.3	0.98	N/A	25.33	66	0.12	0.01	19.1	0	99	0	1	32	13	4
1.64	0.47	B / 8.9	12.7	0.73	N/A	74.10	394	0.03	0.01	31.4	0	99	0	1	7	79	4
1.01	0.47	B / 8.4	17.3	0.99	N/A	81.01	284	-0.02	N/A	43.1	0	99	0	1	4	71	4
1.42	0.47	B-/ 7.6	23.1	1.02	N/A	41.54	1,029	-0.05	N/A	18.5	0	99	0	1	6	44	4
1.20	0.47	B-/ 7.6	23.9	1.01	N/A	58.54	444	-0.03	-0.01	25.2	0	99	0	1	8	44	4
0.96	0.47	B-/ 7.2	26.5	1.10	N/A	57.22	208	0.00	0.01	18.5	0	99	0	1	5	22	4
0.81	0.47	B / 8.1	18.4	0.93	N/A	66.83	236	0.07	-0.01	26.7	4	95	0	1	13	78	4
1.72	0.47	B / 8.6	12.9	0.61	N/A	78.21	618	-0.01	-0.01	43.3	0	99	0	1	8	69	4
0.47	0.47	C+/ 6.5	35.6	1.61	N/A	14.71	535	0.07	-0.01	7.5	1	98	0	1	22	10	4
1.61	0.20	B / 8.1	16.8	1.03	N/A	70.74	596	-0.01	0.04	45.7	0	99	0	1	5	45	4
1.37	0.47	B-/ 7.8	22.5	1.32	N/A	71.38	419	0.00	N/A	27.6	0	99	0	1	6	32	4
1.13	0.47	B / 8.0	22.1	1.25	N/A	32.00	67	0.16	0.05	13.5	0	99	0	1	15	28	4
0.21	0.47	B-/ 7.2	17.8	0.92	N/A	67.85	327	-0.01	-0.02	104.3	0	99	0	1	33	54	4
0.60	0.47	B-/ 7.1	30.9	1.25	N/A	65.80	403	-0.02	N/A	17.5	0	99	0	1	21	45	4
0.44	0.47	C+/ 6.4	36.9	1.51	N/A	53.55	541	-0.09	N/A	28.9	0	99	0	1	30	38	4
1.44	0.47	B / 8.1	13.5	0.54	N/A	83.09	375	-0.04	0.01	98.2	2	97	0	1	25	89	4
3.42	0.47	B-/ 7.9	24.3	1.23	N/A	62.30	3,704	0.00	0.01	53.6	1	98	0	1	17	82	4
1.08	0.47	B-/ 7.4	24.8	0.91	N/A	24.78	114	0.08	0.02	10.2	0	99	0	1	11	32	4
0.52	0.47	B-/ 7.4	19.7	1.11	N/A	77.78	1,576	0.04	N/A	113.6	0	99	0	1	8	58	4
1.93	0.47	B / 8.2	17.6	0.84	N/A	22.21	573	-0.05	0.01	16.9	0	99	0	1	29	27	4
3.64	0.47	B+/ 9.2	10.0	0.94	N/A	86.19	675	-0.03	0.01	19.6	0	99	0	1	8	51	4
2.94	0.60	U /	N/A	N/A	N/A	50.85	31	2.16	N/A	N/A	0	0	0	100	N/A	N/A	1
0.00	0.30	U /	N/A	N/A	N/A	50.34	10	0.32	N/A	N/A	0	0	0	100	N/A	N/A	0
0.83	0.20	U /	N/A	N/A	N/A	49.79	65	0.60	N/A	N/A	0	0	0	100	N/A	N/A	1
0.43	0.72	C+/ 6.7	26.6	0.94	N/A	36.90	7,047	-0.62	0.01	N/A	0	99	0	1	23	22	4
0.97	0.72	C+/ 6.8	25.8	0.91	N/A	44.41	39	-1.49	-0.13	N/A	0	99	0	1	8	27	4
2.72	0.50	B-/ 7.7	24.0	1.10	N/A	35.39	36	0.42	-0.26	0.4	0	99	0	1	25	65	4
2.39	0.48	B-/ 7.3	26.3	1.26	N/A	28.24	24	0.04	-0.28	N/A	0	99	0	1	8	18	4
2.26	0.48	C+/ 5.7	23.3	1.19	N/A	28.69	399	0.17	0.23	309.6	0	99	0	1	7	24	4
2.27	0.48	C+/ 6.7	29.4	1.43	N/A	27.97	12	0.46	0.09	N/A	0	99	0	1	11	15	4
3.16	0.48	B-/ 7.7	26.4	1.21	N/A	46.11	16	-0.39	0.09	83.8	0	99	0	1	12	88	4
3.02	0.48	B-/ 7.5	29.2	1.35	N/A	28.34	10	-0.28	-0.02	42.1	0	99	0	1	22	62	4
15.34	0.48	B / 8.2	13.3	0.66	N/A	13.52	280	0.00	0.06	12.6	0	97	0	3	63	41	4
3.49	0.48	B / 8.1	23.0	1.16	N/A	38.22	54	-0.10	N/A	54.0	0	99	0	1	18	84	4
3.37	0.48	B / 8.0	20.7	0.98	N/A	46.41	169	0.00	0.04	67.9	0	99	0	1	16	90	4
3.40	0.48	B / 8.0	31.1	1.34	N/A	32.61	14	0.09	-0.02	54.1	0	99	0	1	28	89	4

* Denotes ETF Fund, N/A denotes number is not available

				PRICE			PERFORMANCE					
	99 Pct = Best 0 Pct = Worst		Overall Investment Rating	Price As of 3/31/12	52 Week		Perform-ance Rating/Pts	% Total Return Through 3/31/12			Annualized	
Fund Type	Fund Name	Ticker Symbol			High	Low		3 Mo	6 Mo	1Yr/Pct	3Yr/Pct	5Yr/Pct
GL	*iShares Global Inflation-Linked	GTIP	U	50.78	N/A	N/A	U /	2.54	4.44	--	--	--
PM	*iShares Gold Trust	IAU	D-	16.27	18.63	13.97	C+ / 5.9	6.83	2.78	16.63 / 79	22.86 / 56	19.43 / 99
GL	*iShares High Dividend Equity	HDV	C+	57.15	57.52	46.00	C / 5.2	3.92	16.26	15.68 / 78	--	--
COH	*iShares iBoxx $ High Yld Corp Bo	HYG	C-	90.72	92.85	77.90	C / 4.3	2.62	13.59	6.39 / 59	18.10 / 36	--
COI	*iShares iBoxx $ Inves Grade Corp	LQD	C	115.63	117.87	107.90	C- / 3.1	2.34	5.15	11.14 / 70	12.81 / 21	6.95 / 67
COI	*iShares Industrials Sector Bond	ENGN	U	49.72	N/A	N/A	U /	--	--	--	--	--
GL	*iShares Internat Inflation-Link	ITIP	U	49.82	N/A	N/A	U /	9.14	9.29	--	--	--
EM	*iShares JPMorgan USD Emg Mkts Bo	EMB	C	112.71	115.00	102.50	C- / 3.6	3.51	9.50	10.74 / 70	15.00 / 27	--
GR	*iShares Morningstar Large Core	JKD	C+	80.15	80.47	61.06	C+ / 5.8	12.57	26.24	10.37 / 69	20.45 / 45	3.20 / 45
GR	*iShares Morningstar Large Growth	JKE	C+	77.14	77.97	57.31	C+ / 6.8	17.15	28.77	13.75 / 75	22.64 / 55	3.89 / 50
IN	*iShares Morningstar Large Value	JKF	C	63.23	65.97	49.87	C- / 4.1	8.08	21.71	2.27 / 47	16.63 / 32	-2.69 / 17
GR	*iShares Morningstar Mid Core	JKG	B	96.43	97.90	70.07	B / 7.7	13.57	29.46	5.67 / 57	27.78 / 75	3.54 / 48
GR	*iShares Morningstar Mid Growth	JKH	B-	107.56	111.10	80.29	C+ / 6.9	15.29	23.63	2.09 / 47	25.68 / 67	3.84 / 50
GR	*iShares Morningstar Mid Value	JKI	C+	80.16	83.33	60.22	C+ / 6.8	11.71	26.30	0.61 / 42	25.39 / 66	0.28 / 28
GR	*iShares Morningstar Small Core	JKJ	C+	94.75	100.34	68.14	B- / 7.0	13.35	30.61	-2.25 / 35	25.94 / 68	2.21 / 40
GR	*iShares Morningstar Small Growth	JKK	C+	93.73	96.16	68.60	B- / 7.1	12.72	28.20	2.18 / 47	25.97 / 69	4.01 / 51
GR	*iShares Morningstar Small Value	JKL	B	87.64	89.84	63.48	B / 7.8	11.66	30.61	1.96 / 46	29.02 / 80	3.23 / 46
FO	*iShares MSCI AC Asia xJapan SC I	AXJS	U	57.11	N/A	N/A	U /	--	--	--	--	--
GL	*iShares MSCI ACW Minimum Vol Ind	ACWV	U	54.53	N/A	N/A	U /	6.40	--	--	--	--
EN	*iShares MSCI ACWI ex US Enrgy Id	AXEN	D-	58.65	70.87	46.35	D- / 1.4	7.14	19.19	-13.69 / 17	--	--
FS	*iShares MSCI ACWI ex US Fn Sctr	AXFN	D-	20.87	26.26	17.19	E+ / 0.9	--	10.96	-16.88 / 13	--	--
HL	*iShares MSCI ACWI ex US HlthCre	AXHE	C	60.33	63.92	51.08	C- / 3.7	7.60	11.68	9.45 / 67	--	--
FO	*iShares MSCI ACWI ex US Index	ACWX	C-	40.83	47.95	33.23	C- / 3.4	10.92	18.09	-8.54 / 24	15.23 / 27	--
FO	*iShares MSCI ACWI ex US Indsl In	AXID	D	55.10	67.02	45.99	D / 1.9	13.66	17.63	-10.56 / 21	--	--
EM	*iShares MSCI ACWI ex US IT Index	AXIT	C-	57.32	61.45	44.90	C / 4.3	19.07	23.60	-2.24 / 35	--	--
PM	*iShares MSCI ACWI ex US Mtls Ind	AXMT	D-	55.22	73.45	46.21	E+ / 0.9	9.32	8.71	-19.87 / 11	--	--
EM	*iShares MSCI ACWI ex US TS Index	AXTE	D	52.89	62.77	50.91	D- / 1.1	1.89	3.93	-6.14 / 28	--	--
UT	*iShares MSCI ACWI ex US Utl Sct	AXUT	D	45.09	56.86	40.79	D- / 1.1	9.28	2.93	-10.34 / 21	--	--
GL	*iShares MSCI ACWI Index Fund	ACWI	C	47.20	50.99	37.09	C / 4.4	11.93	21.95	-0.92 / 38	17.95 / 35	--
FO	*iShares MSCI ACWI xUS Cnsmr Dis	AXDI	C-	64.72	69.00	51.02	C / 4.7	20.10	17.30	3.81 / 51	--	--
FO	*iShares MSCI ACWI xUS Cnsmr Stp	AXSL	C+	67.32	68.33	55.52	C / 5.0	8.28	16.59	12.32 / 73	--	--
FO	*iShares MSCI All Cntry Asia ex J	AAXJ	C-	56.44	65.31	44.27	C- / 4.0	13.11	21.96	-10.33 / 21	17.65 / 34	--
FO	*iShares MSCI All Peru Capped Idx	EPU	B-	46.70	46.70	33.29	B / 7.9	21.71	33.75	5.18 / 56	--	--
FO	*iShares MSCI Australia	EWA	C-	23.51	28.36	18.91	C / 5.0	9.65	20.78	-8.44 / 24	21.78 / 52	1.75 / 36
FO	*iShares MSCI Australia Sm Cap In	EWAS	U	26.35	N/A	N/A	U /	--	--	--	--	--
FO	*iShares MSCI Austria Inv Mkt	EWO	D-	16.42	24.50	12.97	D / 2.0	15.47	11.03	-28.27 / 6	10.26 / 16	-13.56 / 4
FO	*iShares MSCI Belgium Inv Mkt	EWK	D+	12.34	15.65	10.23	C- / 3.7	16.52	15.64	-9.33 / 22	16.21 / 30	-11.36 / 6
FO	*iShares MSCI Brazil	EWZ	D+	64.66	80.23	49.25	C- / 4.0	12.67	25.24	-16.53 / 13	18.33 / 37	8.19 / 75
FO	*iShares MSCI Brazil Small Cap In	EWZS	D+	27.39	31.79	19.89	C / 4.8	22.22	32.07	-7.40 / 26	--	--
FO	*iShares MSCI BRIC	BKF	D	40.88	52.25	31.78	C- / 3.3	12.71	21.61	-19.00 / 11	15.58 / 28	--
FO	*iShares MSCI Canada	EWC	C-	28.34	34.57	23.48	C- / 3.9	6.54	12.68	-14.78 / 15	18.89 / 39	2.89 / 44
FO	*iShares MSCI Canada Small Cap In	EWCS	U	24.97	N/A	N/A	U /	--	--	--	--	--
FO	*iShares MSCI Chile Inv Market	ECH	C+	68.30	78.42	48.25	C+ / 6.9	18.35	28.57	-5.88 / 29	26.15 / 70	--
FO	*iShares MSCI China Index	MCHI	D-	43.52	54.26	33.44	D- / 1.4	8.18	20.81	-15.48 / 15	--	--
FO	*iShares MSCI China Small Cap Ind	ECNS	E+	36.55	56.51	30.57	E+ / 0.8	10.11	14.97	-30.54 / 5	--	--
FO	*iShares MSCI EAFE	EFA	D+	54.89	64.35	45.45	C- / 3.2	10.82	16.22	-6.63 / 28	13.91 / 24	-3.98 / 14
FO	*iShares MSCI EAFE Growth	EFG	C-	58.64	66.66	47.43	C- / 3.6	12.75	18.77	-4.51 / 31	15.32 / 28	-2.43 / 18
FO	*iShares MSCI EAFE Minimum Vol Id	EFAV	U	52.48	N/A	N/A	U /	4.49	--	--	--	--
FO	*iShares MSCI EAFE Small Cap Idx	SCZ	C	40.13	46.13	33.13	C / 5.2	15.45	16.80	-4.77 / 31	21.46 / 50	--
FO	*iShares MSCI EAFE Value	EFV	D+	47.00	56.56	39.41	D+ / 2.9	10.07	15.19	-8.42 / 24	12.88 / 21	-5.57 / 11
EM	*iShares MSCI EM Cons Discrt Sect	EMDI	U	51.00	N/A	N/A	U /	--	--	--	--	--
EM	*iShares MSCI EM Eastern Europe	ESR	D-	27.79	37.68	20.90	D / 1.6	18.15	25.96	-21.76 / 10	--	--

* Denotes ETF Fund, N/A denotes number is not available

Incl. in Returns		RISK				NET ASSETS		VALUATION			ASSET					FUND MANAGER	
Dividend Yield %	Expense Ratio	Risk Rating/ Pts	3 Year Standard Deviation	Beta	Avg Dura-tion	NAV as of 3/31/12	Total $(Mil)	Premium / Discount As of 3/31/12	1 Year Average	Wtd Avg P/E	Cash %	Stocks %	Bonds %	Other %	Portfolio Turnover Ratio	Manager Quality Pct	Manager Tenure (Years)
0.96	0.40	U /	N/A	N/A	N/A	51.37	16	-1.15	N/A	N/A	0	0	0	100	N/A	N/A	1
0.00	0.25	D / 1.9	21.0	0.95	N/A	16.20	10,328	0.43	0.24	N/A	0	0	0	100	N/A	51	7
4.60	0.40	B+ / 9.4	N/A	N/A	N/A	57.14	1,253	0.02	0.06	N/A	0	99	0	1	N/A	90	1
7.10	0.50	B- / 7.1	12.2	1.09	4.8	90.28	14,259	0.49	0.59	N/A	1	0	97	2	16	24	2
4.18	0.15	B+ / 9.4	6.0	1.26	13.2	115.26	19,563	0.32	0.49	N/A	0	0	97	3	7	29	2
0.00	0.30	U /	N/A	N/A	N/A	49.37	10	0.71	N/A	N/A	0	0	0	100	N/A	N/A	0
2.30	0.40	U /	N/A	N/A	N/A	48.31	49	3.13	N/A	N/A	0	0	0	100	N/A	N/A	1
4.83	0.60	B / 8.9	8.2	0.54	10.9	112.04	4,085	0.60	0.57	N/A	2	0	96	2	12	87	2
1.68	0.20	B / 8.5	15.5	0.95	N/A	80.20	272	-0.06	0.02	26.0	0	99	0	1	38	50	4
0.62	0.25	B- / 7.5	17.7	1.05	N/A	77.14	413	0.00	-0.01	104.6	0	99	0	1	24	44	4
2.73	0.25	B / 8.4	15.4	0.92	N/A	63.27	252	-0.06	0.02	15.8	0	99	0	1	30	32	4
1.14	0.25	B / 8.1	19.9	1.18	N/A	96.49	156	-0.06	0.02	32.7	0	99	0	1	47	59	4
0.16	0.30	B / 8.0	18.8	1.07	N/A	107.62	174	-0.06	0.02	51.2	0	99	0	1	47	62	4
1.86	0.30	B / 8.0	20.6	1.20	N/A	80.05	102	0.14	-0.02	22.8	0	99	0	1	46	47	4
0.92	0.25	B- / 7.5	23.8	1.35	N/A	94.50	149	0.26	-0.07	37.0	0	99	0	1	69	31	4
0.65	0.30	B- / 7.2	21.4	1.21	N/A	93.43	91	0.32	-0.05	89.6	0	99	0	1	64	42	4
2.11	0.30	B- / 7.9	23.7	1.34	N/A	87.56	164	0.09	0.02	21.5	0	99	0	1	55	49	4
0.00	0.75	U /	N/A	N/A	N/A	57.39	12	-0.49	N/A	N/A	0	0	0	100	N/A	N/A	0
1.16	0.35	U /	N/A	N/A	N/A	53.99	32	1.00	N/A	N/A	0	0	0	100	N/A	N/A	1
2.58	0.48	C+ / 6.9	N/A	N/A	N/A	58.45	6	0.34	-0.15	N/A	0	99	0	1	7	22	2
2.82	0.48	C+ / 6.7	N/A	N/A	N/A	21.43	2	-2.61	-0.32	N/A	0	99	0	1	6	9	2
0.58	0.48	B / 8.5	N/A	N/A	N/A	59.80	9	0.89	0.18	N/A	0	99	0	1	8	67	2
2.44	0.34	B- / 7.6	22.8	1.06	N/A	40.71	940	0.29	0.06	32.0	0	99	0	1	7	44	4
2.74	0.48	B- / 7.0	N/A	N/A	N/A	55.55	3	-0.81	-0.42	N/A	0	99	0	1	9	25	2
2.60	0.48	B- / 7.5	N/A	N/A	N/A	57.46	3	-0.24	-1.22	N/A	0	99	0	1	4	65	2
1.93	0.48	C+ / 6.5	N/A	N/A	N/A	55.58	3	-0.65	-0.26	N/A	0	99	0	1	5	4	2
4.72	0.48	B / 8.3	N/A	N/A	N/A	53.64	3	-1.40	-0.11	N/A	0	99	0	1	5	33	2
3.35	0.48	B- / 7.5	N/A	N/A	N/A	44.31	4	1.76	0.16	N/A	0	99	0	1	6	16	2
1.91	0.34	B- / 7.8	20.1	0.93	N/A	47.11	2,420	0.19	0.06	43.2	0	99	0	1	5	68	4
1.23	0.48	B- / 7.1	N/A	N/A	N/A	64.47	6	0.39	-0.98	N/A	0	99	0	1	7	86	2
1.57	0.48	B / 8.7	N/A	N/A	N/A	66.83	3	0.73	0.25	N/A	0	99	0	1	4	91	2
1.39	0.66	B- / 7.1	26.8	1.10	N/A	56.52	2,469	-0.14	0.07	N/A	0	99	0	1	41	56	4
2.62	0.51	B- / 7.0	N/A	N/A	N/A	45.99	496	1.54	-0.21	49.5	0	99	0	1	9	83	3
5.55	0.52	C+ / 6.9	28.2	1.19	N/A	23.41	2,916	0.43	-0.06	N/A	0	99	0	1	9	65	4
0.00	0.59	U /	N/A	N/A	N/A	26.24	3	0.42	N/A	N/A	0	0	0	100	N/A	N/A	0
2.57	0.52	C+ / 5.8	34.3	1.47	N/A	16.42	78	0.00	-0.22	N/A	0	99	0	1	12	13	4
5.24	0.52	C+ / 6.8	25.1	1.08	N/A	12.31	26	0.24	-0.04	N/A	0	97	0	3	12	44	4
1.30	0.59	C+ / 6.4	34.1	1.36	N/A	64.92	10,569	-0.40	0.32	N/A	0	99	0	1	12	39	4
1.26	0.59	C+ / 6.1	N/A	N/A	N/A	27.63	58	-0.87	0.70	N/A	0	99	0	1	77	69	2
1.33	0.67	C+ / 6.6	31.3	1.25	N/A	41.16	967	-0.68	-0.26	N/A	0	99	0	1	13	33	4
2.49	0.52	B- / 7.6	25.1	0.98	N/A	28.27	4,816	0.25	-0.06	35.8	0	99	0	1	8	68	4
0.00	0.59	U /	N/A	N/A	N/A	24.99	5	-0.08	N/A	N/A	0	0	0	100	N/A	N/A	0
0.18	0.59	C+ / 6.7	26.9	0.79	N/A	68.68	707	-0.55	-0.24	N/A	0	99	0	1	38	87	4
0.44	0.61	C+ / 6.1	N/A	N/A	N/A	43.71	338	-0.43	0.17	N/A	0	99	0	1	N/A	17	1
1.60	0.59	C / 5.2	N/A	N/A	N/A	37.00	18	-1.22	-0.06	N/A	0	99	0	1	47	5	2
2.07	0.34	B- / 7.6	21.7	1.02	N/A	54.76	39,416	0.24	0.01	40.2	0	99	0	1	6	39	4
1.66	0.40	B- / 7.6	21.0	0.97	N/A	58.39	1,236	0.43	-0.04	40.2	0	99	0	1	27	48	4
1.06	0.20	U /	N/A	N/A	N/A	52.25	21	0.44	N/A	N/A	0	0	0	100	N/A	N/A	1
2.89	0.40	B- / 7.9	22.8	1.05	N/A	39.94	1,427	0.48	-0.02	11.3	0	99	0	1	12	73	4
3.02	0.40	B- / 7.3	23.4	1.09	N/A	46.73	1,342	0.58	-0.07	N/A	0	99	0	1	29	31	4
0.00	0.68	U /	N/A	N/A	N/A	51.17	10	-0.33	N/A	N/A	0	0	0	100	N/A	N/A	0
3.11	0.68	C+ / 5.7	N/A	N/A	N/A	27.66	31	0.47	-0.09	N/A	0	99	0	1	24	15	3

* Denotes ETF Fund, N/A denotes number is not available

Fund Type	Fund Name	Ticker Symbol	Overall Investment Rating	PRICE Price As of 3/31/12	52 Week High	52 Week Low	PERFORMANCE Performance Rating/Pts	% Total Return Through 3/31/12 3 Mo	6 Mo	1Yr/Pct	Annualized 3Yr/Pct	5Yr/Pct
FO	*iShares MSCI Em Mkts Lat Amer In	EEML	U	54.69	N/A	N/A	U /	--	--	--	--	--
EM	*iShares MSCI Emerg Markets Divid	DVYE	U	54.65	N/A	N/A	U /	--	--	--	--	--
EM	*iShares MSCI Emerging Markets	EEM	C-	42.95	50.43	33.42	C- / 4.1	13.19	23.49	-11.48 / 19	18.15 / 36	3.17 / 45
EM	*iShares MSCI Emg Mkts Asia Index	EEMA	U	53.79	N/A	N/A	U /	--	--	--	--	--
EM	*iShares MSCI Emg Mkts EMEA Index	EEME	U	56.42	N/A	N/A	U /	--	--	--	--	--
EM	*iShares MSCI Emg Mkts Finls Sctr	EMFN	D	24.24	30.26	18.87	D+ / 2.3	16.15	23.52	-12.91 / 18	--	--
EM	*iShares MSCI Emg Mkts Matl Sctr	EMMT	D-	21.46	28.98	17.69	D- / 1.0	11.25	15.75	-22.42 / 10	--	--
EM	*iShares MSCI Emg Mkts Min Vol In	EEMV	U	56.60	N/A	N/A	U /	12.97	--	--	--	--
EM	*iShares MSCI Emg Mkts Sm Cap Ind	EEMS	U	46.62	N/A	N/A	U /	13.16	15.48	--	--	--
FO	*iShares MSCI EMU	EZU	D	31.55	42.22	25.57	D / 2.2	13.08	16.77	-16.69 / 13	9.11 / 15	-7.56 / 9
FS	*iShares MSCI Europ Finls Sctr Id	EUFN	D-	17.78	25.11	13.71	D- / 1.1	17.34	16.90	-22.49 / 9	--	--
FS	*iShares MSCI Far East Finls Sctr	FEFN	D	24.61	25.85	20.53	D- / 1.2	--	--	1.00 / 44	--	--
FO	*iShares MSCI France	EWQ	D	22.07	29.16	17.88	D / 2.2	12.72	16.91	-16.75 / 13	9.03 / 15	-6.55 / 10
FO	*iShares MSCI Germany	EWG	D+	23.28	29.05	16.96	C- / 3.8	21.12	27.42	-9.45 / 22	14.86 / 26	-2.48 / 18
FO	*iShares MSCI Germany Small Cap I	EWGS	U	28.23	N/A	N/A	U /	--	--	--	--	--
PM	*iShares MSCI Gl Sel M&MP	PICK	U	23.60	N/A	N/A	U /	--	--	--	--	--
GL	*iShares MSCI Global Agri Pro	VEGI	U	25.97	N/A	N/A	U /	--	--	--	--	--
EN	*iShares MSCI Global Engy Pro	FILL	U	25.05	N/A	N/A	U /	--	--	--	--	--
PM	*iShares MSCI Global Gold Miners	RING	U	22.01	N/A	N/A	U /	--	--	--	--	--
PM	*iShares MSCI Global Silver Miner	SLVP	U	22.08	N/A	N/A	U /	--	--	--	--	--
FO	*iShares MSCI Hong Kong	EWH	C-	17.45	19.67	13.30	C / 4.5	12.77	23.11	-6.32 / 28	19.19 / 39	3.90 / 50
FO	*iShares MSCI Hong Kong Sm Cap In	EWHS	U	28.20	N/A	N/A	U /	--	--	--	--	--
FO	*iShares MSCI India Index	INDA	U	24.85	N/A	N/A	U /	--	--	--	--	--
FO	*iShares MSCI India Small Cap Ind	SMIN	U	24.92	N/A	N/A	U /	--	--	--	--	--
FO	*iShares MSCI Indonesia Inv Mkt I	EIDO	D+	30.94	35.16	23.33	C- / 3.4	5.56	20.47	2.84 / 49	--	--
FO	*iShares MSCI Irlnd Capd Inv Mkt	EIRL	B-	23.11	23.80	16.92	B / 7.9	21.70	28.96	8.11 / 64	--	--
FO	*iShares MSCI Israel Capped Inv M	EIS	D	43.07	60.52	38.00	D / 2.0	8.87	8.92	-25.69 / 7	10.66 / 17	--
FO	*iShares MSCI Italy	EWI	D-	13.08	20.15	10.88	D- / 1.1	9.09	11.62	-27.46 / 7	1.21 / 8	-14.40 / 4
FO	*iShares MSCI Japan	EWJ	D+	10.18	10.91	8.83	D+ / 2.3	11.69	8.83	0.83 / 43	8.57 / 14	-5.71 / 11
FO	*iShares MSCI Japan Small Cap	SCJ	C-	46.89	49.49	41.82	C- / 3.2	8.23	4.28	6.32 / 59	13.68 / 23	--
IN	*iShares MSCI KLD 400 Social Idx	DSI	C+	51.90	52.18	40.35	C / 5.4	11.06	23.54	8.16 / 65	20.02 / 43	1.65 / 35
GL	*iShares MSCI Kokusai Index	TOK	C	41.88	44.79	32.82	C / 4.6	10.76	21.03	-1.65 / 37	19.19 / 40	--
FO	*iShares MSCI Malaysia	EWM	B	14.60	15.48	11.95	B / 7.6	8.96	23.82	2.03 / 46	28.83 / 79	8.84 / 79
FO	*iShares MSCI Mexico Inv Market	EWW	B-	62.52	64.65	46.65	B / 7.7	16.29	28.47	-0.57 / 39	28.71 / 79	3.74 / 49
FO	*iShares MSCI Netherlands Inv Mar	EWN	D	18.99	24.04	15.36	C- / 3.1	10.21	16.78	-15.84 / 14	14.88 / 26	-5.25 / 12
FO	*iShares MSCI New Zealand Inv Mk	ENZL	C+	31.66	34.45	26.41	C+ / 5.6	14.88	14.94	12.00 / 72	--	--
FO	*iShares MSCI Pacific ex-Japan	EPP	C	43.52	51.06	34.60	C / 5.3	11.79	21.32	-7.17 / 27	21.95 / 52	2.44 / 41
FO	*iShares MSCI Philipps Invst Mkt	EPHE	B+	28.74	29.07	20.10	A / 9.4	21.93	35.74	18.49 / 81	--	--
FO	*iShares MSCI Poland Invstbl Mkt	EPOL	E+	25.95	39.75	20.86	D- / 1.1	19.89	16.72	-25.40 / 8	--	--
FO	*iShares MSCI Russia Capped Index	ERUS	D-	24.88	31.98	17.49	D+ / 2.4	18.99	31.92	-19.68 / 11	--	--
FO	*iShares MSCI Singapore	EWS	C+	12.89	14.61	10.28	B- / 7.3	19.02	20.16	-2.44 / 35	27.81 / 76	3.75 / 49
FO	*iShares MSCI Singapore Sm Cp Ind	EWSS	U	29.89	N/A	N/A	U /	--	--	--	--	--
FO	*iShares MSCI South Africa	EZA	C	68.91	77.58	54.64	C+ / 6.1	12.84	24.03	-4.31 / 32	23.70 / 59	5.11 / 57
FO	*iShares MSCI South Korea	EWY	C	59.54	69.99	44.67	C+ / 6.2	13.93	28.76	-8.31 / 24	24.26 / 62	3.69 / 49
FO	*iShares MSCI Spain	EWP	D-	29.30	45.99	28.53	D- / 1.1	-3.20	-2.92	-25.37 / 8	2.65 / 8	-7.88 / 8
FO	*iShares MSCI Sweden	EWD	C	29.01	36.14	21.41	C+ / 6.2	15.39	26.19	-9.25 / 23	24.58 / 63	-0.29 / 26
FO	*iShares MSCI Switzerland	EWL	C-	25.03	28.57	20.67	C / 4.4	10.65	15.65	1.00 / 43	18.32 / 37	0.82 / 30
FO	*iShares MSCI Taiwan	EWT	C-	13.42	16.06	11.19	C- / 4.0	14.56	18.16	-7.59 / 26	17.52 / 34	2.41 / 41
FO	*iShares MSCI Thailand Inv Market	THD	A-	72.79	73.93	49.43	A+ / 9.8	21.09	38.52	9.88 / 68	50.49 / 99	--
FO	*iShares MSCI Turkey Inv Market	TUR	C	53.05	70.74	39.82	B- / 7.0	28.95	11.89	-17.69 / 12	28.50 / 78	--
FO	*iShares MSCI UK Small Cap Index	EWUS	U	28.58	N/A	N/A	U /	--	--	--	--	--
FO	*iShares MSCI United Kingdom	EWU	C-	17.30	19.22	14.04	C / 4.3	7.05	18.83	-1.59 / 37	18.44 / 37	-3.31 / 16

		RISK				NET ASSETS		VALUATION			ASSET				FUND MANAGER		
Incl. in Returns		Risk Rating/ Pts	3 Year		Avg Dura-tion	NAV as of 3/31/12	Total $(Mil)	Premium / Discount		Wtd Avg P/E	Cash %	Stocks %	Bonds %	Other %	Portfolio Turnover Ratio	Manager Quality Pct	Manager Tenure (Years)
Dividend Yield %	Expense Ratio		Standard Deviation	Beta				As of 3/31/12	1 Year Average								
0.00	0.49	U /	N/A	N/A	N/A	55.25	6	-1.01	N/A	N/A	0	0	0	100	N/A	N/A	0
3.13	0.49	U /	N/A	N/A	N/A	54.31	6	0.63	N/A	N/A	0	0	0	100	N/A	N/A	0
1.62	0.67	B- / 7.1	27.5	1.06	N/A	43.02	41,057	-0.16	0.04	41.8	0	99	0	1	17	25	4
0.00	0.49	U /	N/A	N/A	N/A	54.18	11	-0.72	N/A	N/A	0	0	0	100	N/A	N/A	0
0.00	0.49	U /	N/A	N/A	N/A	55.61	6	1.46	N/A	N/A	0	0	0	100	N/A	N/A	0
9.53	0.67	C+ / 6.6	N/A	N/A	N/A	23.86	4	1.59	0.34	N/A	0	99	0	1	6	36	2
3.95	0.67	C+ / 6.1	N/A	N/A	N/A	21.56	9	-0.46	-0.46	N/A	0	99	0	1	6	12	2
3.02	0.25	U /	N/A	N/A	N/A	56.20	102	0.71	N/A	N/A	0	0	0	100	N/A	N/A	1
1.67	0.69	U /	N/A	N/A	N/A	47.00	39	-0.81	N/A	N/A	0	0	0	100	N/A	N/A	1
1.95	0.52	C+ / 6.7	29.2	1.33	N/A	31.47	725	0.25	-0.05	40.2	0	99	0	1	8	14	4
0.67	0.48	C+ / 5.6	N/A	N/A	N/A	17.84	20	-0.34	0.11	N/A	0	99	0	1	10	6	2
2.10	0.48	B- / 7.5	N/A	N/A	N/A	24.56	2	0.20	-0.04	N/A	0	99	0	1	9	49	2
1.60	0.52	C+ / 6.3	29.6	1.33	N/A	22.02	271	0.23	-0.08	N/A	0	99	0	1	6	14	4
2.90	0.51	C+ / 6.6	30.4	1.33	N/A	23.22	3,143	0.26	-0.02	40.2	0	99	0	1	13	24	4
0.00	0.59	U /	N/A	N/A	N/A	28.00	3	0.82	N/A	N/A	0	0	0	100	N/A	N/A	0
0.00	0.39	U /	N/A	N/A	N/A	23.40	3	0.85	N/A	N/A	0	0	0	100	N/A	N/A	0
0.00	0.39	U /	N/A	N/A	N/A	25.69	5	1.09	N/A	N/A	0	0	0	100	N/A	N/A	0
0.00	0.39	U /	N/A	N/A	N/A	24.96	5	0.36	N/A	N/A	0	0	0	100	N/A	N/A	0
0.00	0.39	U /	N/A	N/A	N/A	22.11	27	-0.45	N/A	N/A	0	0	0	100	N/A	N/A	0
0.00	0.39	U /	N/A	N/A	N/A	22.47	5	-1.74	N/A	N/A	0	0	0	100	N/A	N/A	0
1.99	0.52	B- / 7.2	25.9	0.98	N/A	17.50	1,984	-0.29	0.04	N/A	0	99	0	1	15	72	4
0.00	0.59	U /	N/A	N/A	N/A	27.83	6	1.33	N/A	N/A	0	0	0	100	N/A	N/A	0
0.00	0.65	U /	N/A	N/A	N/A	24.81	10	0.16	N/A	N/A	0	0	0	100	N/A	N/A	0
0.00	0.74	U /	N/A	N/A	N/A	24.93	5	-0.04	N/A	N/A	0	0	0	100	N/A	N/A	0
1.16	0.59	C+ / 6.9	N/A	N/A	N/A	31.08	331	-0.45	-0.42	N/A	0	99	0	1	16	86	2
0.99	0.52	B- / 7.3	N/A	N/A	N/A	22.65	8	2.03	0.34	N/A	0	99	0	1	24	92	2
2.78	0.59	C+ / 6.6	25.0	0.95	N/A	42.76	96	0.72	-0.20	N/A	0	99	0	1	17	26	4
2.49	0.51	C+ / 5.6	34.1	1.50	N/A	13.06	147	0.15	-0.06	N/A	0	99	0	1	16	7	4
2.08	0.51	B- / 7.9	15.9	0.57	N/A	10.14	5,082	0.39	-0.09	N/A	0	99	0	1	4	51	4
3.11	0.51	B / 8.6	14.6	0.41	N/A	46.99	55	-0.21	-0.12	N/A	0	99	0	1	10	80	4
1.34	0.50	B / 8.4	16.1	0.98	N/A	51.92	169	-0.04	0.01	37.4	0	99	0	1	10	42	4
2.04	0.25	B- / 7.9	18.9	0.86	N/A	41.60	616	0.67	0.60	45.4	0	99	0	1	4	75	4
6.08	0.52	B- / 7.9	19.8	0.76	N/A	14.66	956	-0.41	-0.03	N/A	0	99	0	1	49	91	4
1.11	0.52	B- / 7.5	23.7	0.95	N/A	62.49	1,332	0.05	-0.04	N/A	0	99	0	1	5	90	4
1.42	0.52	C+ / 6.8	26.7	1.20	N/A	18.97	68	0.11	-0.04	N/A	0	99	0	1	6	28	4
8.94	0.51	B- / 7.9	N/A	N/A	N/A	31.54	105	0.38	0.05	N/A	0	99	0	1	13	92	2
4.47	0.50	B- / 7.1	26.6	1.14	N/A	43.49	3,520	0.07	-0.07	N/A	0	99	0	1	10	70	4
0.68	0.59	B- / 7.3	N/A	N/A	N/A	28.58	100	0.56	-0.17	N/A	0	99	0	1	29	97	2
7.72	0.59	C / 5.0	N/A	N/A	N/A	25.86	139	0.35	-0.07	N/A	0	98	0	2	23	9	2
1.39	0.58	C / 5.2	N/A	N/A	N/A	24.70	121	0.73	0.05	N/A	0	98	0	2	22	15	2
4.30	0.52	B- / 7.3	28.2	1.10	N/A	12.90	1,557	-0.08	-0.11	N/A	0	99	0	1	10	84	4
0.00	0.59	U /	N/A	N/A	N/A	29.58	3	1.05	N/A	N/A	0	0	0	100	N/A	N/A	0
3.10	0.59	B- / 7.1	28.0	1.04	N/A	68.29	596	0.91	0.03	N/A	0	99	0	1	4	80	4
1.25	0.59	C+ / 6.5	32.6	1.26	N/A	59.71	3,485	-0.28	-0.35	N/A	0	99	0	1	18	74	4
14.48	0.52	C+ / 5.6	33.1	1.35	N/A	29.29	113	0.03	-0.08	N/A	0	99	0	1	14	10	4
3.58	0.51	C+ / 6.5	30.4	1.31	N/A	28.92	361	0.31	-0.19	N/A	0	99	0	1	9	77	4
0.14	0.52	B- / 7.6	20.0	0.86	N/A	25.00	553	0.12	-0.02	N/A	0	99	0	1	7	70	4
3.52	0.59	B- / 7.1	29.4	1.17	N/A	13.44	2,580	-0.15	-0.04	N/A	0	98	0	2	23	49	4
2.15	0.59	B- / 7.1	29.9	0.98	N/A	72.70	647	0.12	0.13	N/A	0	99	0	1	22	97	4
0.55	0.59	C+ / 5.7	36.6	1.24	N/A	52.78	437	0.51	-0.20	N/A	0	99	0	1	12	82	4
0.00	0.59	U /	N/A	N/A	N/A	28.37	3	0.74	N/A	N/A	0	0	0	100	N/A	N/A	0
2.67	0.52	B- / 7.7	22.7	1.04	N/A	17.29	1,526	0.06	0.31	N/A	0	99	0	1	4	63	4

* Denotes ETF Fund, N/A denotes number is not available

				PRICE			PERFORMANCE					
99 Pct = Best / 0 Pct = Worst			Overall Investment Rating	Price As of 3/31/12	52 Week High	52 Week Low	Performance Rating/Pts	% Total Return Through 3/31/12			Annualized	
Fund Type	Fund Name	Ticker Symbol						3 Mo	6 Mo	1Yr/Pct	3Yr/Pct	5Yr/Pct
IN	*iShares MSCI USA	EUSA	C+	30.28	30.75	23.87	C+ / 5.8	11.80	24.77	7.61 / 63	--	--
GR	*iShares MSCI USA ESG Select Soc	KLD	C+	61.59	61.95	47.51	C+ / 5.8	12.26	24.22	8.62 / 65	21.15 / 48	2.37 / 40
IN	*iShares MSCI USA Minimum Vol Idx	USMV	U	28.23	N/A	N/A	U /	6.10	--	--	--	--
GL	*iShares MSCI World Index	URTH	U	54.98	N/A	N/A	U /	--	--	--	--	--
HL	*iShares Nasdaq Biotechnology	IBB	C+	123.30	124.66	83.96	B- / 7.5	18.19	32.13	22.26 / 83	24.02 / 61	9.58 / 84
IN	*iShares NYSE 100	NY	C	65.64	66.28	50.93	C / 4.4	9.80	22.46	5.57 / 57	17.34 / 34	-0.28 / 26
IN	*iShares NYSE Composite	NYC	C	75.03	79.76	58.74	C / 4.4	10.19	20.18	-0.72 / 39	18.25 / 36	-0.28 / 26
IN	*iShares PHLX SOX Semicon Sector	SOXX	C+	59.47	61.01	43.63	C+ / 6.2	20.60	29.90	2.60 / 48	21.68 / 51	0.16 / 28
GR	*iShares Russell 1000	IWB	C+	77.96	78.68	59.20	C+ / 5.9	12.85	25.91	7.13 / 62	21.45 / 50	1.74 / 36
GR	*iShares Russell 1000 Growth	IWF	C+	66.08	66.61	49.96	C+ / 6.6	14.68	26.56	10.31 / 69	22.65 / 55	4.51 / 54
IN	*iShares Russell 1000 Value	IWD	C+	70.07	71.08	53.44	C / 5.3	10.95	25.33	3.89 / 51	20.10 / 44	-1.20 / 21
GR	*iShares Russell 2000	IWM	C+	82.81	86.81	60.09	C+ / 6.4	12.62	29.80	-0.60 / 39	23.59 / 59	1.92 / 37
GR	*iShares Russell 2000 Growth	IWO	C+	95.38	99.40	68.55	B- / 7.0	13.44	30.40	0.45 / 42	25.61 / 67	3.79 / 49
GR	*iShares Russell 2000 Value	IWN	C	72.97	77.00	53.40	C+ / 5.6	11.62	29.31	-1.65 / 36	21.64 / 51	-0.30 / 25
IN	*iShares Russell 3000	IWV	C+	83.28	84.11	63.05	C+ / 5.9	12.71	26.01	6.41 / 59	21.59 / 51	1.73 / 36
GR	*iShares Russell 3000 Growth	IWZ	C+	53.88	54.35	40.60	C+ / 6.6	14.50	26.86	9.39 / 67	23.01 / 57	4.42 / 53
IN	*iShares Russell 3000 Value	IWW	C+	91.79	93.09	69.75	C / 5.3	10.97	25.52	3.46 / 50	20.16 / 44	-1.15 / 22
GR	*iShares Russell Micro Cap	IWC	C+	51.40	54.20	36.82	C+ / 6.2	15.40	31.58	-2.44 / 35	22.93 / 56	-1.94 / 19
GR	*iShares Russell Mid Cap	IWR	B-	110.72	112.92	82.76	B- / 7.0	12.86	26.52	2.49 / 48	25.86 / 68	2.56 / 42
GR	*iShares Russell Mid Cap Growth	IWP	B-	62.87	63.88	46.63	B- / 7.1	14.42	27.27	3.52 / 50	25.95 / 68	3.82 / 50
GR	*iShares Russell Mid Cap Value	IWS	B-	48.13	49.58	36.23	C+ / 6.9	11.38	26.19	1.28 / 44	25.65 / 67	0.85 / 30
GR	*iShares Russell Top 200 Growth	IWY	B+	35.16	35.44	26.82	B / 7.6	14.47	25.69	13.37 / 75	--	--
IN	*iShares Russell Top 200 Idx	IWL	C+	32.69	32.88	25.09	C+ / 6.2	12.56	24.23	8.93 / 66	--	--
IN	*iShares Russell Top 200 Value Id	IWX	C	30.22	30.63	23.23	C / 5.0	10.56	25.11	5.14 / 55	--	--
GR	*iShares S&P 100	OEF	C+	64.04	64.63	48.90	C / 5.5	12.80	25.84	9.88 / 68	19.78 / 42	1.64 / 35
IN	*iShares S&P 1500	ISI	C+	64.02	64.51	48.73	C+ / 5.9	12.42	26.09	7.15 / 62	21.49 / 50	1.81 / 37
GR	*iShares S&P 500	IVV	C+	141.21	142.41	107.80	C+ / 5.8	12.61	25.52	7.90 / 64	21.08 / 47	1.63 / 35
GR	*iShares S&P 500 Growth	IVW	C+	75.37	75.81	58.38	C+ / 6.0	12.17	24.14	11.21 / 71	21.44 / 50	4.22 / 52
IN	*iShares S&P 500 Value	IVE	C+	64.93	65.86	48.73	C+ / 5.6	12.86	27.39	4.44 / 53	20.58 / 45	-1.19 / 21
GI	*iShares S&P Aggressive Allocatio	AOA	C	36.45	37.28	28.76	C / 4.8	10.61	20.94	3.15 / 49	19.16 / 39	--
FO	*iShares S&P Asia 50 Index	AIA	C	44.50	49.92	34.75	C / 4.9	13.67	25.65	-5.47 / 30	20.04 / 43	--
MUS	*iShares S&P CA AMT-Free Muni Bon	CMF	C	112.65	120.00	100.00	C- / 3.2	2.25	4.76	15.86 / 85	6.67 / 16	--
GI	*iShares S&P Conservative Allocat	AOK	C	30.18	30.37	28.18	D / 2.2	3.01	6.37	5.23 / 56	8.55 / 14	--
FO	*iShares S&P Dev ex-US Property	WPS	D+	31.56	36.18	26.42	C / 4.7	15.22	16.02	-4.51 / 31	20.11 / 44	--
GL	*iShares S&P Emerging Mkts Infr	EMIF	C-	33.21	37.39	24.50	C- / 3.9	15.15	30.08	-6.21 / 28	--	--
FO	*iShares S&P Europe 350	IEV	D+	37.35	45.58	30.16	C- / 3.2	10.70	18.31	-8.90 / 23	13.96 / 24	-4.64 / 13
GL	*iShares S&P Gl Cons Staples Sect	KXI	C+	70.77	70.97	57.00	C / 5.5	6.33	15.53	13.46 / 75	20.83 / 47	6.61 / 65
GL	*iShares S&P Glb Infrastructure	IGF	C	35.41	39.07	30.41	C- / 3.8	6.65	13.84	-0.47 / 39	16.28 / 30	--
GL	*iShares S&P Glb Timber & Forestr	WOOD	C	41.39	51.56	32.39	C / 4.9	11.30	20.81	-17.43 / 12	22.42 / 54	--
GR	*iShares S&P Global 100	IOO	C-	63.59	69.28	51.00	C- / 3.8	9.75	19.97	-0.42 / 40	15.55 / 28	-0.78 / 24
EN	*iShares S&P Global Clean Energy	ICLN	E+	9.10	19.00	8.12	E+ / 0.6	6.56	0.81	-49.65 / 1	-19.67 / 5	--
GL	*iShares S&P Global Cons Disc	RXI	B-	59.04	59.56	44.12	C+ / 6.9	18.20	26.49	9.24 / 67	23.91 / 60	1.32 / 32
EN	*iShares S&P Global Energy	IXC	D+	39.78	45.61	30.78	C- / 3.2	4.16	21.27	-9.24 / 23	14.29 / 25	3.24 / 46
FS	*iShares S&P Global Financials	IXG	D+	42.66	49.92	32.17	C- / 3.5	19.23	25.05	-9.72 / 22	14.38 / 25	-11.40 / 6
HL	*iShares S&P Global Healthcare	IXJ	C	60.15	60.18	49.32	C / 4.6	7.18	16.68	12.95 / 73	17.82 / 35	2.53 / 42
GL	*iShares S&P Global Industrials	EXI	C	54.23	60.31	41.38	C / 5.3	12.44	25.05	-4.66 / 31	21.48 / 50	0.12 / 27
GL	*iShares S&P Global Materials	MXI	D+	63.17	78.50	50.36	C- / 3.8	10.44	18.96	-14.21 / 16	17.72 / 35	1.23 / 32
EN	*iShares S&P Global Nuclear	NUCL	D	35.17	42.47	30.35	D / 1.7	8.75	10.62	-12.57 / 18	5.86 / 11	--
GL	*iShares S&P Global Technology	IXN	C+	70.79	71.58	52.16	C+ / 6.7	20.58	30.27	14.33 / 76	21.86 / 52	4.63 / 55
GL	*iShares S&P Global Telecom	IXP	C-	56.51	64.11	52.25	D+ / 2.6	1.28	6.53	-4.14 / 32	12.33 / 20	0.61 / 29
UT	*iShares S&P Global Utilities	JXI	D+	42.67	48.40	38.67	D / 2.0	1.84	5.15	-2.84 / 34	7.97 / 14	-3.86 / 14
GI	*iShares S&P Growth Allocation	AOR	C	33.34	33.55	27.84	C- / 3.5	7.35	14.49	4.38 / 53	14.31 / 25	--

* Denotes ETF Fund, N/A denotes number is not available

www.thestreetratings.com

| Incl. in Returns | | RISK | | | Avg Dura-tion | NET ASSETS | | VALUATION | | Wtd Avg P/E | ASSET | | | | Portfolio Turnover Ratio | FUND MANAGER | |
| Dividend Yield % | Expense Ratio | Risk Rating/ Pts | 3 Year | | | NAV as of 3/31/12 | Total $(Mil) | Premium / Discount | | | Cash % | Stocks % | Bonds % | Other % | | Manager Quality Pct | Manager Tenure (Years) |
			Standard Deviation	Beta				As of 3/31/12	1 Year Average								
1.71	0.15	B / 8.3	N/A	N/A	N/A	30.30	128	-0.07	0.03	46.1	0	99	0	1	8	50	2
1.23	0.50	B / 8.4	16.2	0.99	N/A	61.51	177	0.13	0.01	39.2	0	99	0	1	35	46	4
2.03	0.15	U /	N/A	N/A	N/A	28.22	14	0.04	N/A	N/A	0	0	0	100	N/A	N/A	1
0.00	0.24	U /	N/A	N/A	N/A	54.95	22	0.05	N/A	N/A	0	0	0	100	N/A	N/A	0
0.04	0.48	C+ / 6.9	18.2	0.80	N/A	123.34	1,746	-0.03	-0.02	144.3	0	99	0	1	13	69	4
2.15	0.20	B / 8.5	15.0	0.91	N/A	65.65	55	-0.02	-0.02	24.1	0	99	0	1	7	34	4
2.05	0.25	B / 8.1	18.2	1.10	N/A	74.98	74	0.07	N/A	29.1	0	99	0	1	5	25	4
0.70	0.48	B- / 7.4	26.8	1.39	N/A	59.49	242	-0.03	N/A	31.0	0	99	0	1	52	19	4
1.65	0.15	B / 8.2	16.7	1.03	N/A	78.02	6,808	-0.08	-0.01	45.5	0	99	0	1	7	45	4
1.17	0.20	B / 8.0	16.6	1.01	N/A	66.11	16,039	-0.05	N/A	68.1	0	99	0	1	24	55	4
2.07	0.20	B / 8.3	17.2	1.05	N/A	70.16	11,972	-0.13	-0.01	20.3	0	99	0	1	24	34	4
1.21	0.20	B- / 7.5	22.6	1.29	N/A	82.84	16,018	-0.04	0.01	47.3	0	99	0	1	20	27	4
0.73	0.25	B- / 7.3	22.6	1.28	N/A	95.38	3,999	0.00	-0.01	71.5	0	99	0	1	36	34	4
1.65	0.25	B- / 7.6	22.7	1.30	N/A	73.02	4,211	-0.07	0.04	27.8	0	99	0	1	32	23	4
1.59	0.20	B / 8.2	17.0	1.05	N/A	83.37	3,366	-0.11	N/A	45.6	0	99	0	1	6	43	4
1.14	0.25	B- / 7.9	16.8	1.02	N/A	53.89	335	-0.02	-0.01	68.2	0	99	0	1	24	54	4
2.04	0.25	B / 8.2	17.5	1.07	N/A	91.88	305	-0.10	-0.03	20.7	0	99	0	1	25	33	4
0.98	0.60	B- / 7.4	24.4	1.35	N/A	51.35	463	0.10	-0.04	38.5	0	99	0	1	35	22	4
1.30	0.20	B / 8.0	19.6	1.17	N/A	110.75	6,668	-0.03	0.04	35.2	0	99	0	1	12	53	4
0.74	0.25	B- / 7.9	19.7	1.16	N/A	62.91	3,423	-0.06	-0.01	46.6	0	99	0	1	29	54	4
1.74	0.25	B / 8.1	19.9	1.18	N/A	48.14	3,166	-0.02	-0.01	23.8	0	99	0	1	25	51	4
1.37	0.20	B / 8.5	N/A	N/A	N/A	35.18	328	-0.06	0.07	N/A	0	99	0	1	19	76	3
1.75	0.15	B / 8.5	N/A	N/A	N/A	32.67	124	0.06	0.03	N/A	0	99	0	1	7	59	3
3.02	0.20	B / 8.1	N/A	N/A	N/A	30.22	62	0.00	N/A	N/A	0	99	0	1	24	28	3
1.81	0.20	B / 8.3	15.5	0.95	N/A	64.12	3,387	-0.12	N/A	49.5	0	99	0	1	7	43	4
1.56	0.20	B / 8.2	16.7	1.03	N/A	63.98	386	0.06	0.02	45.2	0	99	0	1	4	45	4
1.79	0.09	B / 8.2	16.2	1.00	N/A	141.28	28,477	-0.05	N/A	46.1	0	99	0	1	5	46	4
1.42	0.18	B / 8.1	15.5	0.95	N/A	75.41	6,896	-0.05	N/A	66.7	0	99	0	1	22	55	4
2.08	0.18	B / 8.2	17.6	1.07	N/A	64.97	4,385	-0.06	0.06	19.0	0	99	0	1	23	36	4
1.13	0.11	B / 8.2	16.5	1.01	N/A	36.41	93	0.11	0.08	N/A	0	99	0	1	13	33	4
3.21	0.50	B- / 7.2	25.2	1.03	N/A	44.67	206	-0.38	-0.27	N/A	0	99	0	1	7	69	4
3.49	0.25	B+ / 9.1	6.8	1.18	10.6	112.09	210	0.50	-0.13	N/A	0	0	100	0	21	32	5
1.03	0.11	B+ / 9.8	4.2	0.23	N/A	30.14	98	0.13	0.03	N/A	0	21	78	1	7	67	4
2.03	0.48	C+ / 5.7	23.5	1.06	N/A	31.45	131	0.35	-0.11	292.5	0	99	0	1	8	71	4
2.17	0.70	B- / 7.1	N/A	N/A	N/A	33.15	120	0.18	-0.06	N/A	0	98	0	2	10	61	3
1.69	0.60	B- / 7.2	25.0	1.16	N/A	37.27	1,100	0.21	-0.08	40.2	0	99	0	1	5	28	4
1.93	0.48	B+ / 9.0	12.7	0.51	N/A	70.88	451	-0.16	0.09	25.8	0	99	0	1	4	88	4
4.70	0.48	B / 8.3	17.9	0.79	N/A	35.44	439	-0.08	-0.04	21.4	0	99	0	1	17	66	4
1.52	0.48	B- / 7.3	26.4	1.02	N/A	41.22	158	0.41	0.01	18.6	0	99	0	1	23	77	4
2.11	0.40	B / 8.0	19.3	1.13	N/A	63.57	1,058	0.03	-0.03	23.3	0	99	0	1	6	18	4
5.02	0.48	C / 4.6	37.5	1.19	N/A	9.10	35	0.00	-0.27	18.4	0	99	0	1	39	2	4
1.32	0.48	B / 8.1	20.8	0.87	N/A	58.82	137	0.37	-0.03	43.2	0	99	0	1	4	87	4
2.20	0.48	B- / 7.6	23.8	1.02	N/A	39.68	1,240	0.25	-0.02	17.0	0	99	0	1	5	31	4
2.19	0.48	B- / 7.3	27.6	1.10	N/A	42.45	162	0.49	-0.15	19.3	0	99	0	1	7	21	4
1.40	0.48	B / 8.6	12.9	0.59	N/A	60.12	534	0.05	-0.02	40.5	0	99	0	1	6	67	4
1.78	0.48	B- / 7.6	22.4	0.98	N/A	54.12	200	0.20	-0.05	24.6	0	99	0	1	6	79	4
1.77	0.48	C+ / 6.8	28.9	1.22	N/A	62.78	563	0.62	-0.04	55.3	0	99	0	1	4	41	4
2.35	0.48	B- / 7.3	21.1	0.69	N/A	35.29	12	-0.34	-0.56	31.1	0	99	0	1	40	22	4
0.94	0.48	B- / 7.2	19.9	0.83	N/A	70.72	625	0.10	-0.06	114.9	0	99	0	1	3	83	4
4.63	0.48	B / 8.6	14.1	0.58	N/A	56.35	426	0.28	0.13	20.7	0	99	0	1	6	68	4
3.85	0.48	B / 8.5	13.9	1.07	N/A	42.55	256	0.28	0.16	18.7	0	99	0	1	9	17	4
1.03	0.11	B / 8.9	10.6	0.65	N/A	33.30	139	0.12	0.06	N/A	0	57	42	1	10	52	4

* Denotes ETF Fund, N/A denotes number is not available

	99 Pct = Best / 0 Pct = Worst			PRICE			PERFORMANCE						
					52 Week			% Total Return Through 3/31/12					
												Annualized	
Fund Type	Fund Name	Ticker Symbol	Overall Investment Rating	Price As of 3/31/12	High	Low	Performance Rating/Pts		3 Mo	6 Mo	1Yr/Pct	3Yr/Pct	5Yr/Pct
IN	*iShares S&P GSCI Commodity-Index	GSG	D	34.78	39.37	29.02	D+ /	2.4	5.46	15.20	-7.92 / 25	10.10 / 16	-3.48 / 15
EM	*iShares S&P India Nifty 50	INDY	D-	23.71	30.65	19.48	D- /	1.0	20.05	6.23	-20.97 / 10	--	--
COI	*iShares S&P Intl Preferred Stock	IPFF	U	26.01	N/A	N/A	U /		4.42	--	--	--	--
FO	*iShares S&P Latin American 40	ILF	C	47.63	55.38	36.73	C /	4.9	11.89	24.41	-10.09 / 22	20.97 / 47	7.64 / 72
GR	*iShares S&P Mid Cap 400	IJH	C+	99.22	101.75	72.99	C+ /	6.9	13.55	28.07	1.08 / 44	25.33 / 65	4.34 / 53
GR	*iShares S&P Mid Cap 400 Growth	IJK	B-	112.44	115.49	83.83	B- /	7.3	14.06	25.63	2.11 / 47	26.94 / 72	6.31 / 63
GR	*iShares S&P Mid Cap 400 Value	IJJ	C+	85.41	88.25	62.00	C+ /	6.5	12.82	30.58	-0.02 / 40	23.69 / 59	2.25 / 40
GI	*iShares S&P Moderate Allocation	AOM	C	31.22	31.40	28.35	D+ /	2.9	4.64	8.89	4.21 / 52	12.34 / 20	--
EN	*iShares S&P NA Natural Resource	IGE	D+	39.42	47.81	30.82	C- /	3.6	3.96	18.57	-14.96 / 15	17.35 / 34	3.08 / 44
GR	*iShares S&P NA Tech-Multimedia N	IGN	C-	31.23	36.31	24.15	C- /	4.1	14.19	24.37	-9.81 / 22	17.87 / 35	-0.80 / 23
GR	*iShares S&P NA Technology Sector	IGM	C+	70.83	71.72	52.56	B- /	7.2	19.38	28.38	13.32 / 74	23.99 / 60	6.63 / 65
IN	*iShares S&P NA Technology-Softwa	IGV	C	65.87	66.20	48.20	C+ /	6.7	21.80	26.41	5.51 / 57	23.29 / 58	7.47 / 71
MUN	*iShares S&P Natl AMT-Free Muni B	MUB	C	109.40	113.99	99.20	C- /	3.0	1.59	4.24	13.16 / 82	6.68 / 17	--
MUS	*iShares S&P NY AMT-Free Muni Bon	NYF	C-	109.30	111.00	101.63	D+ /	2.5	1.53	3.22	10.35 / 78	5.29 / 14	--
MUN	*iShares S&P Sh Tm Ntl AMT-Fr Mun	SUB	C-	106.60	108.31	100.65	D- /	1.3	0.06	0.60	2.48 / 51	1.08 / 8	--
GR	*iShares S&P Small Cap 600	IJR	B-	76.31	77.84	55.01	B- /	7.2	12.06	31.20	4.63 / 54	25.69 / 67	3.27 / 46
GR	*iShares S&P Small Cap 600 Growth	IJT	B-	82.59	84.11	60.26	B- /	7.4	11.23	28.80	5.04 / 55	27.17 / 73	4.70 / 55
GR	*iShares S&P Small Cap 600 Value	IJS	C+	78.57	80.17	55.54	C+ /	6.8	12.93	33.71	4.25 / 53	24.29 / 62	1.77 / 36
GI	*iShares S&P Target Date 2010 Ind	TZD	C	32.39	32.56	29.01	D+ /	2.9	5.12	9.08	4.95 / 55	12.14 / 19	--
GI	*iShares S&P Target Date 2015 Ind	TZE	C	33.59	42.41	29.26	C- /	3.5	6.46	12.41	4.17 / 52	14.55 / 25	--
GI	*iShares S&P Target Date 2020 Ind	TZG	C	34.62	35.54	29.42	C- /	3.8	7.59	14.14	4.57 / 54	15.58 / 28	--
GI	*iShares S&P Target Date 2025 Ind	TZI	C	35.15	36.01	29.32	C /	4.3	9.33	16.45	3.85 / 51	17.82 / 35	--
GI	*iShares S&P Target Date 2030 Ind	TZL	C	35.31	36.16	29.77	C- /	4.1	9.25	14.43	3.33 / 50	17.31 / 33	--
GI	*iShares S&P Target Date 2035 Ind	TZO	C	35.50	36.36	28.84	C /	4.8	10.19	18.73	3.39 / 50	19.41 / 40	--
GI	*iShares S&P Target Date 2040 Ind	TZV	C	35.76	37.14	28.60	C /	4.6	10.52	20.50	2.80 / 49	18.71 / 38	--
GL	*iShares S&P Target Date 2045 Ind	TZW	U	27.42	N/A	N/A	U /		--	16.95	--	--	--
GL	*iShares S&P Target Date 2050 Ind	TZY	U	27.83	N/A	N/A	U /		12.24	21.00	--	--	--
GI	*iShares S&P Target Date Ret Inco	TGR	C	31.03	31.36	28.96	D+ /	2.6	3.62	6.60	5.11 / 55	10.34 / 17	--
IN	*iShares S&P USPreferred Stock	PFF	B	39.04	40.15	32.88	C+ /	6.9	10.53	12.92	4.43 / 53	26.87 / 72	2.56 / 42
GL	*iShares S&P/Citigroup 1-3 Year I	ISHG	D+	99.22	112.00	95.98	D- /	1.4	2.71	0.06	-3.20 / 33	2.91 / 8	--
GL	*iShares S&P/Citigroup Intl Treas	IGOV	D+	99.83	110.94	95.69	D- /	1.4	0.30	-2.33	-0.59 / 39	4.14 / 9	--
FO	*iShares S&P/Topix 150	ITF	D+	43.46	47.07	37.68	D+ /	2.3	12.35	9.29	-0.54 / 39	8.30 / 14	-6.08 / 10
PM	*iShares Silver Trust	SLV	C+	31.38	48.35	25.65	B+ /	8.3	16.48	8.54	-14.87 / 15	35.55 / 91	18.10 / 99
COI	*iShares Utilities Sector Bond	AMPS	U	49.75	N/A	N/A	U /		--	--	--	--	--
EN	*JPMorgan Alerian MLP Idx ETN	AMJ	D	39.14	41.68	31.52	C- /	3.6	1.61	17.81	8.03 / 64	--	--
GR	*JPMorgan Dbl Short 10 Year Trs E	DSXJ	E+	42.05	54.73	40.90	E+ /	0.7	1.11	-1.71	-22.46 / 9	--	--
GR	*JPMorgan Dbl Short US Long Trs E	DSTJ	E	39.37	59.97	36.82	E+ /	0.6	5.68	0.45	-31.92 / 5	--	--
GR	*Madrona Domestic ETF	FWDD	U	27.12	N/A	N/A	U /		15.06	25.04	--	--	--
GL	*Madrona Global Bond ETF	FWDB	U	25.71	N/A	N/A	U /		2.85	4.48	--	--	--
FO	*Madrona International ETF	FWDI	U	23.37	N/A	N/A	U /		14.61	19.43	--	--	--
GL	*Market Vector RVE Hard Asst Prd	HAP	D+	36.50	43.44	29.12	C- /	3.3	8.21	19.66	-13.17 / 17	15.54 / 28	--
FO	*Market Vectors Africa Index ETF	AFK	C-	29.50	34.75	25.24	C- /	3.4	14.56	18.10	-8.91 / 23	14.94 / 27	--
GL	*Market Vectors Agribusiness ETF	MOO	C	52.83	57.53	39.86	C /	5.2	12.05	22.99	-6.41 / 28	21.40 / 49	--
IN	*Market Vectors Bank and Brokerag	RKH	U	43.48	N/A	N/A	U /		--	--	--	--	--
IN	*Market Vectors Biotech ETF	BBH	U	44.50	N/A	N/A	U /		--	--	--	--	--
FO	*Market Vectors Brazil Small-Cap	BRF	D	43.93	60.41	35.53	D+ /	2.9	20.55	27.89	-13.97 / 16	--	--
MUN	*Market Vectors CEF Muni Inc ETF	XMPT	U	27.32	N/A	N/A	U /		2.40	9.10	--	--	--
FO	*Market Vectors China ETF	PEK	D-	34.00	47.26	30.10	E+ /	0.7	7.46	1.01	-24.44 / 8	--	--
FO	*Market Vectors Chinese RMB USD E	CNY	C-	41.00	42.04	40.08	D- /	1.2	0.12	1.03	1.73 / 45	0.01 / 7	--
EN	*Market Vectors Coal ETF	KOL	D+	31.88	51.87	27.42	C /	4.9	-1.15	6.58	-36.85 / 4	27.85 / 76	--
GL	*Market Vectors Colombia ETF	COLX	D+	19.29	21.37	15.86	D+ /	2.7	18.05	16.57	-5.97 / 29	--	--
FO	*Market Vectors Double Long Euro	URR	D-	27.77	36.98	25.10	D- /	1.0	5.82	-4.26	-13.88 / 16	-2.41 / 6	--

* Denotes ETF Fund, N/A denotes number is not available

		RISK				NET ASSETS		VALUATION			ASSET					FUND MANAGER	
Incl. in Returns		Risk Rating/ Pts	3 Year		Avg Dura-tion	NAV as of 3/31/12	Total $(Mil)	Premium / Discount		Wtd Avg P/E	Cash %	Stocks %	Bonds %	Other %	Portfolio Turnover Ratio	Manager Quality Pct	Manager Tenure (Years)
Dividend Yield %	Expense Ratio		Standard Deviation	Beta				As of 3/31/12	1 Year Average								
0.00	0.75	B- / 7.5	22.4	0.91	N/A	35.00	1,437	-0.63	-0.12	N/A	0	100	0	0	N/A	17	6
0.22	0.91	C+/ 6.1	N/A	N/A	N/A	23.65	365	0.25	0.19	N/A	0	99	0	1	13	11	3
2.78	0.55	U /	N/A	N/A	N/A	25.90	95	0.42	N/A	N/A	0	0	0	100	N/A	N/A	1
2.77	0.50	B- / 7.2	28.4	1.16	N/A	47.68	2,166	-0.10	-0.03	42.7	0	99	0	1	6	70	4
1.04	0.20	B- / 7.9	20.0	1.17	N/A	99.26	10,706	-0.04	N/A	35.4	0	99	0	1	14	48	4
0.62	0.25	B- / 7.9	19.7	1.14	N/A	112.48	3,014	-0.04	N/A	46.0	0	99	0	1	41	59	4
1.45	0.25	B- / 7.8	20.8	1.21	N/A	85.46	2,193	-0.06	-0.01	24.6	0	99	0	1	22	35	4
0.87	0.11	B+ / 9.4	6.9	0.42	N/A	31.21	145	0.03	0.05	N/A	0	32	67	1	9	60	4
0.84	0.48	B- / 7.2	26.1	1.09	N/A	39.44	1,970	-0.05	0.01	29.4	0	99	0	1	11	38	4
0.63	0.48	B- / 7.0	28.6	1.51	N/A	31.22	265	0.03	N/A	37.8	0	99	0	1	28	13	4
0.53	0.48	B- / 7.6	19.8	1.14	N/A	70.82	410	0.01	0.01	93.8	0	99	0	1	12	46	4
0.15	0.48	C+/ 6.6	19.6	1.05	N/A	65.82	523	0.08	N/A	148.2	0	99	0	1	18	52	4
3.13	0.25	B+ / 9.4	5.8	1.24	10.1	108.57	2,834	0.76	0.54	N/A	0	0	98	2	9	30	2
3.29	0.25	B+ / 9.4	6.1	0.78	11.0	108.93	99	0.34	0.44	N/A	0	0	98	2	14	33	2
1.02	0.25	B+ / 9.8	1.6	0.18	N/A	106.40	496	0.19	0.14	N/A	2	0	96	2	23	48	2
1.18	0.20	B- / 7.7	21.8	1.23	N/A	76.32	7,543	-0.01	0.01	45.8	0	99	0	1	21	45	4
1.16	0.25	B- / 7.7	20.8	1.16	N/A	82.58	1,669	0.01	-0.03	60.5	0	99	0	1	46	61	4
1.06	0.25	B- / 7.8	23.1	1.30	N/A	78.54	2,202	0.04	N/A	31.7	0	99	0	1	31	31	4
0.94	0.11	B+ / 9.4	8.2	0.42	N/A	32.47	5	-0.25	-0.08	N/A	0	43	55	2	28	64	4
1.01	0.11	B+ / 9.0	10.0	0.57	N/A	33.65	10	-0.18	0.08	N/A	0	54	44	2	24	56	4
1.02	0.11	B / 8.9	11.1	0.66	N/A	34.45	19	0.49	0.11	N/A	0	64	34	2	20	55	4
1.10	0.11	B / 8.7	12.8	0.76	N/A	34.98	31	0.49	0.02	N/A	0	72	26	2	17	54	4
1.12	0.11	B / 8.7	13.5	0.77	N/A	35.31	14	0.00	-0.02	N/A	0	78	20	2	23	55	4
1.15	0.11	B / 8.3	15.4	0.89	N/A	35.39	9	0.31	0.07	N/A	0	83	15	2	30	39	4
1.16	0.11	B / 8.2	16.8	0.99	N/A	35.71	18	0.14	-0.03	N/A	0	86	12	2	15	35	4
1.38	0.32	U /	N/A	N/A	N/A	27.50	4	-0.29	N/A	N/A	0	0	0	100	N/A	N/A	1
1.41	0.32	U /	N/A	N/A	N/A	27.94	4	-0.39	N/A	N/A	0	0	0	100	N/A	N/A	1
1.09	0.11	B+ / 9.7	5.1	0.30	N/A	31.13	8	-0.32	0.07	N/A	0	30	67	3	20	69	4
4.57	0.48	B / 8.9	17.4	0.64	N/A	38.93	8,262	0.28	0.04	N/A	2	0	0	98	33	88	4
2.11	0.35	B / 8.7	10.1	1.00	N/A	97.39	167	1.88	0.53	N/A	2	0	95	3	49	26	2
1.95	0.35	B / 8.7	9.9	1.02	N/A	99.58	301	0.25	0.40	N/A	1	0	96	3	21	31	2
2.64	0.50	B- / 7.8	16.3	0.60	N/A	43.90	78	-1.00	-0.61	N/A	0	99	0	1	6	46	4
0.00	0.50	C / 5.1	46.5	1.68	N/A	31.49	11,687	-0.35	0.18	N/A	0	0	0	100	N/A	27	6
0.00	0.30	U /	N/A	N/A	N/A	49.27	10	0.97	N/A	N/A	0	0	0	100	N/A	N/A	0
4.83	0.85	C / 5.2	N/A	N/A	N/A	39.17	4,061	-0.08	-0.02	N/A	0	0	0	100	N/A	88	3
0.00	0.85	C / 4.4	N/A	N/A	N/A	42.15	8	-0.24	0.01	N/A	0	0	0	100	N/A	4	N/A
0.00	0.85	C- / 3.7	N/A	N/A	N/A	39.33	8	0.10	-0.10	N/A	0	0	0	100	N/A	2	N/A
0.32	1.25	U /	N/A	N/A	N/A	26.95	16	0.63	N/A	N/A	0	100	0	0	N/A	N/A	1
1.95	0.95	U /	N/A	N/A	N/A	25.58	16	0.51	N/A	N/A	6	0	89	5	N/A	N/A	1
0.46	1.25	U /	N/A	N/A	N/A	23.21	13	0.69	N/A	N/A	1	98	0	1	N/A	N/A	1
1.81	0.61	B- / 7.3	25.6	1.07	N/A	36.56	187	-0.16	0.08	37.1	0	99	0	1	15	40	4
3.29	0.81	B- / 7.7	25.1	1.00	N/A	29.25	74	0.85	-0.61	9.9	0	99	0	1	24	39	4
0.58	0.53	B- / 7.4	26.8	1.04	N/A	52.79	6,115	0.08	0.09	45.2	0	99	0	1	22	72	5
0.00	0.35	U /	N/A	N/A	N/A	43.50	28	-0.05	N/A	N/A	0	0	0	100	N/A	N/A	1
0.00	0.35	U /	N/A	N/A	N/A	44.40	107	0.23	N/A	N/A	0	0	0	100	N/A	N/A	1
2.54	0.62	C+/ 5.7	N/A	N/A	N/A	44.04	786	-0.25	0.09	N/A	0	75	0	25	64	27	3
4.46	1.43	U /	N/A	N/A	N/A	27.27	8	0.18	N/A	N/A	0	0	0	100	N/A	N/A	1
0.00	0.72	C+/ 6.4	N/A	N/A	N/A	31.60	17	7.59	7.80	N/A	100	0	0	0	N/A	7	2
0.00	0.55	B+ / 9.8	2.5	0.04	N/A	41.07	27	-0.17	-0.17	N/A	0	0	0	100	N/A	40	4
1.52	0.59	C+/ 6.0	44.3	1.60	N/A	32.04	322	-0.50	-0.33	33.1	0	100	0	0	47	50	4
0.73	0.75	B- / 7.2	N/A	N/A	N/A	19.06	2	1.21	0.32	N/A	0	97	0	3	22	46	1
0.00	0.65	C+/ 6.3	26.0	0.94	N/A	28.15	5	-1.35	-0.42	N/A	0	0	0	100	N/A	9	4

* Denotes ETF Fund, N/A denotes number is not available

Fund Type	Fund Name	Ticker Symbol	Overall Investment Rating	Price As of 3/31/12	52 Week High	52 Week Low	Performance Rating/Pts	3 Mo	6 Mo	1Yr/Pct	Annualized 3Yr/Pct	Annualized 5Yr/Pct
FO	*Market Vectors Double Shrt Euro	DRR	D-	42.61	47.99	35.64	D- / 1.0	-6.68	-1.21	7.60 / 63	-4.10 / 6	--
EM	*Market Vectors Egypt Index ETF	EGPT	D-	12.67	16.45	9.24	D+ / 2.3	33.93	18.19	-19.88 / 11	--	--
GL	*Market Vectors EM Lcl Curr Bnd E	EMLC	D+	26.28	27.94	23.51	D+ / 2.4	8.01	9.51	2.55 / 48	--	--
IN	*Market Vectors Environment Svc E	EVX	C	52.76	55.70	41.77	C / 5.3	13.24	17.94	-1.43 / 37	21.31 / 49	3.96 / 50
GL	*Market Vectors Gaming ETF	BJK	C+	35.83	37.20	25.63	B+ / 8.6	19.16	31.82	12.05 / 72	30.92 / 84	--
FO	*Market Vectors Germany SmallCap	GERJ	U	20.95	N/A	N/A	U /	20.47	17.54	--	--	--
EN	*Market Vectors Global Alt Enrgy	GEX	E+	11.84	22.70	10.59	E+ / 0.6	8.52	-0.18	-45.70 / 2	-15.30 / 5	--
PM	*Market Vectors Gold Miners ETF	GDX	D-	49.54	66.98	48.05	D / 2.1	-3.67	-9.98	-16.87 / 13	12.86 / 21	4.35 / 53
FO	*Market Vectors Gulf States ETF	MES	D+	20.92	23.50	18.73	D+ / 2.8	6.95	9.70	-1.06 / 38	12.23 / 19	--
MUH	*Market Vectors Hi-Yld Mun Idx ET	HYD	B-	31.34	31.41	27.28	C+ / 5.9	6.07	6.89	16.71 / 86	12.81 / 42	--
FO	*Market Vectors India Small-Cap E	SCIF	E	12.13	18.56	8.73	D- / 1.1	38.95	4.12	-28.85 / 6	--	--
FO	*Market Vectors Indian Rupee USD	INR	D	38.50	42.76	35.00	D- / 1.4	7.84	0.76	-7.49 / 26	3.23 / 9	--
FO	*Market Vectors Indonesia Idx ETF	IDX	C+	29.86	34.99	23.16	A+ / 9.7	4.88	19.90	-0.18 / 40	48.88 / 99	--
MUN	*Market Vectors Interm Muni Idx E	ITM	C	22.98	24.50	20.83	C- / 3.1	1.00	3.93	13.19 / 82	7.22 / 18	--
COI	*Market Vectors Invest Grade FR E	FLTR	U	23.81	N/A	N/A	U /	3.71	1.27	--	--	--
PM	*Market Vectors Junior Gold Mnrs	GDXJ	E+	24.55	42.97	22.59	E / 0.5	-0.61	-7.13	-32.97 / 5	--	--
FO	*Market Vectors Lat Am SC Index E	LATM	D-	25.50	33.47	20.42	D / 1.6	16.23	20.43	-17.63 / 12	--	--
GEI	*Market Vectors LatAm Aggrgte Bd	BONO	U	25.26	N/A	N/A	U /	7.40	11.04	--	--	--
MUN	*Market Vectors Long Muni Index E	MLN	C+	19.50	20.09	16.72	C / 4.7	3.18	6.25	20.09 / 89	10.18 / 29	--
MTG	*Market Vectors Mtge REIT Income	MORT	U	25.23	N/A	N/A	U /	10.52	16.75	--	--	--
IN	*Market Vectors Oil Services ETF	OIH	U	40.62	N/A	N/A	U /	--	--	--	--	--
IN	*Market Vectors Pharmaceutical ET	PPH	U	38.46	N/A	N/A	U /	--	--	--	--	--
EM	*Market Vectors Poland ETF	PLND	E+	20.60	31.45	16.64	D- / 1.0	19.91	15.49	-26.31 / 7	--	--
MUN	*Market Vectors Pre-Refnded Muni	PRB	C-	25.20	25.48	24.52	D- / 1.5	0.25	1.36	3.71 / 58	2.15 / 9	--
EM	*Market Vectors Renminbi Bond ETF	CHLC	U	25.68	N/A	N/A	U /	-0.12	--	--	--	--
IN	*Market Vectors Retail ETF	RTH	U	41.89	N/A	N/A	U /	--	--	--	--	--
FO	*Market Vectors Russia ETF	RSX	C-	30.88	43.16	23.23	C+ / 5.6	15.85	24.74	-25.79 / 7	25.00 / 64	--
FO	*Market Vectors Russia SmallCap E	RSXJ	U	17.98	N/A	N/A	U /	12.68	14.30	--	--	--
IN	*Market Vectors Semiconductor ETF	SMH	U	35.80	N/A	N/A	U /	--	--	--	--	--
MUN	*Market Vectors Short Muni Index	SMB	C-	17.74	25.54	16.97	D / 1.8	0.46	1.14	5.78 / 66	3.46 / 10	--
EN	*Market Vectors Solar Energy ETF	KWT	E	3.75	13.56	3.61	E / 0.4	1.62	-13.14	-70.11 / 0	-30.82 / 3	--
IN	*Market Vectors Steel Index ETF	SLX	D+	53.03	76.70	39.52	C- / 4.1	11.52	25.59	-27.25 / 7	20.15 / 44	0.20 / 28
GL	*Market Vectors Uranium+Nuc Engy	NLR	D-	16.45	23.57	14.55	D- / 1.3	10.85	9.11	-19.73 / 11	2.38 / 8	--
FO	*Market Vectors Vietnam ETF	VNM	D-	19.14	24.75	14.15	D / 1.8	31.55	12.20	-18.51 / 11	--	--
GR	*Materials Select Sector SPDR	XLB	C-	36.97	41.28	27.77	C / 4.5	10.78	27.27	-5.92 / 29	18.93 / 39	1.84 / 37
GI	*Meidell Tactical Advantage ETF	MATH	U	27.01	N/A	N/A	U /	9.42	10.06	--	--	--
EN	*Mk Vectors Unconv O&G ETF	FRAK	U	24.23	N/A	N/A	U /	--	--	--	--	--
GR	*Morgan Stanley Technology ETF	MTK	C+	71.45	71.89	53.02	C+ / 6.6	21.92	28.96	6.29 / 59	22.64 / 55	5.19 / 58
GR	*Mrkt Vectors Rare Earth/Str Met	REMX	E+	17.16	28.91	13.83	E+ / 0.9	15.01	18.85	-31.39 / 5	--	--
GR	*Nuveen Diversified Commodity	CFD	D	23.08	29.40	18.59	D / 2.0	15.85	17.00	-11.05 / 20	--	--
FO	*Pax MSCI EAFE ESG Index ETF	EAPS	D	23.46	31.48	19.17	D / 2.2	11.24	14.20	-4.59 / 31	--	--
GR	*Pax MSCI North America ESG Idx E	NASI	C	29.95	32.04	23.65	C- / 4.2	10.85	19.94	4.83 / 54	--	--
COH	*Peritus High Yield ETF	HYLD	C-	49.75	52.79	45.12	D+ / 2.4	6.63	10.77	2.47 / 48	--	--
COI	*PIMCO 0-5 Year Hi Yield Corp Bd	HYS	U	99.84	N/A	N/A	U /	3.10	9.47	--	--	--
USA	*PIMCO 1-3 Year US Treasury Index	TUZ	C-	50.93	51.34	50.62	D- / 1.3	-0.25	0.01	1.43 / 45	--	--
USA	*PIMCO 1-5 Year US TIPS Index	STPZ	C-	54.06	54.31	52.87	D / 1.6	1.35	2.32	3.66 / 51	--	--
USA	*PIMCO 15 Plus Year US TIPS Index	LTPZ	C	64.65	67.50	54.10	C- / 4.0	-0.80	3.66	21.86 / 83	--	--
USA	*PIMCO 25+ Year Zero Coupon US Tr	ZROZ	C	97.14	117.55	65.49	C+ / 6.0	-12.22	-10.27	46.83 / 99	--	--
USA	*PIMCO 3-7 Year US Treasury Index	FIVZ	C-	80.83	82.07	76.17	D / 1.8	-0.09	0.51	8.03 / 64	--	--
USA	*PIMCO 7-15 Year US Treasury Inde	TENZ	C-	84.44	87.52	75.28	D+ / 2.5	-1.09	0.06	14.70 / 77	--	--
GL	*PIMCO Australia Bond Index	AUD	U	99.33	N/A	N/A	U /	1.76	--	--	--	--
USA	*PIMCO Broad US TIPS Index	TIPZ	C	58.65	59.62	53.81	D+ / 2.5	0.62	3.35	11.88 / 72	--	--

* Denotes ETF Fund, N/A denotes number is not available

www.thestreetratings.com

Incl. in Returns Dividend Yield %	Expense Ratio	RISK Risk Rating/Pts	3 Year Standard Deviation	Beta	Avg Dura-tion	NAV as of 3/31/12	Total $(Mil)	Premium / Discount As of 3/31/12	1 Year Average	Wtd Avg P/E	Cash %	Stocks %	Bonds %	Other %	Portfolio Turnover Ratio	Manager Quality Pct	Manager Tenure (Years)
0.00	0.65	C+ / 6.4	25.6	-0.92	N/A	42.74	28	-0.30	-0.01	N/A	0	0	0	100	N/A	85	4
2.30	0.94	C / 4.4	N/A	N/A	N/A	12.89	54	-1.71	-0.60	N/A	0	100	0	0	54	14	2
4.68	0.49	B / 8.5	N/A	N/A	N/A	26.16	599	0.46	0.45	N/A	0	0	0	100	3	26	2
1.18	0.55	B / 8.1	17.6	0.95	N/A	52.90	25	-0.26	-0.07	54.8	0	99	0	1	1	59	6
1.76	0.65	C / 5.5	30.1	1.19	N/A	36.00	85	-0.47	-0.31	206.2	0	99	0	1	19	87	4
0.74	0.55	U /	N/A	N/A	N/A	20.94	3	0.05	N/A	N/A	0	95	0	5	17	N/A	1
2.94	0.62	C / 5.0	32.5	1.07	N/A	11.86	63	-0.17	-0.44	42.9	0	99	0	1	26	3	5
0.30	0.52	C+ / 5.9	37.0	1.41	N/A	49.55	8,990	-0.02	N/A	146.5	0	100	0	0	9	9	6
3.82	0.98	B- / 7.6	22.8	0.70	N/A	21.32	14	-1.88	-1.77	N/A	0	100	0	0	29	54	4
5.00	0.35	B+ / 9.1	8.6	1.48	N/A	31.13	452	0.67	0.32	N/A	1	0	98	1	42	53	4
1.32	0.85	C- / 3.4	N/A	N/A	N/A	12.02	53	0.92	-0.05	N/A	0	100	0	0	76	7	2
0.00	0.55	B / 8.5	10.9	0.38	N/A	38.36	7	0.36	-0.37	N/A	0	0	0	100	N/A	31	4
1.52	0.61	C / 4.7	34.5	1.22	N/A	29.98	543	-0.40	-0.27	N/A	0	100	0	0	18	96	3
2.70	0.24	B+ / 9.4	6.1	1.32	6.5	22.89	431	0.39	0.12	N/A	1	0	98	1	19	31	5
0.77	0.19	U /	N/A	N/A	N/A	24.28	7	-1.94	N/A	N/A	0	0	0	100	N/A	N/A	1
4.94	0.54	C / 5.1	N/A	N/A	N/A	24.37	2,414	0.74	0.27	N/A	0	99	0	1	60	1	3
1.93	0.63	C+ / 6.2	N/A	N/A	N/A	25.60	17	-0.39	-0.23	N/A	0	90	0	10	58	15	2
4.07	0.49	U /	N/A	N/A	N/A	25.35	8	-0.36	N/A	N/A	0	0	0	100	N/A	N/A	1
3.82	0.24	B+ / 9.1	8.0	1.71	9.3	19.46	80	0.21	-0.31	N/A	1	0	98	1	27	28	4
8.42	0.40	U /	N/A	N/A	N/A	25.18	26	0.20	N/A	N/A	0	0	0	100	N/A	N/A	1
0.00	0.35	U /	N/A	N/A	N/A	40.67	1,091	-0.12	N/A	N/A	0	0	0	100	N/A	N/A	1
0.00	0.35	U /	N/A	N/A	N/A	38.49	276	-0.08	N/A	N/A	0	0	0	100	N/A	N/A	1
3.66	0.61	C / 5.1	N/A	N/A	N/A	20.51	34	0.44	-0.10	N/A	0	100	0	0	27	10	3
1.45	0.24	B+ / 9.7	3.0	0.54	N/A	25.24	33	-0.16	-0.45	N/A	1	0	98	1	28	34	4
1.53	0.39	U /	N/A	N/A	N/A	25.63	5	0.20	N/A	N/A	0	0	0	100	N/A	N/A	1
0.00	0.35	U /	N/A	N/A	N/A	41.91	83	-0.05	N/A	N/A	0	0	0	100	N/A	N/A	1
1.89	0.62	C+ / 5.6	41.1	1.58	N/A	30.69	2,169	0.62	-0.06	N/A	0	99	0	1	29	56	5
0.42	0.67	U /	N/A	N/A	N/A	17.70	5	1.58	N/A	N/A	0	94	0	6	41	N/A	1
0.00	0.35	U /	N/A	N/A	N/A	35.82	310	-0.06	N/A	N/A	0	0	0	100	N/A	N/A	1
1.68	0.20	B+ / 9.7	2.8	0.52	4.0	17.70	126	0.23	0.11	N/A	0	0	100	0	35	46	4
6.21	0.65	C- / 3.7	55.2	1.63	N/A	3.71	15	1.08	0.22	2.9	0	99	0	1	35	N/A	4
2.15	0.55	C+ / 6.4	39.5	2.06	N/A	53.02	178	0.02	N/A	9.8	0	100	0	0	3	8	6
11.74	0.62	C+ / 6.1	28.2	1.10	N/A	16.52	102	-0.42	-0.31	32.7	0	99	0	1	51	11	5
0.85	0.76	C / 5.2	N/A	N/A	N/A	19.09	276	0.26	0.72	N/A	3	96	0	1	43	11	3
1.53	0.19	B- / 7.3	26.2	1.48	N/A	36.97	1,778	0.00	N/A	36.4	0	100	0	0	3	13	14
0.09	1.35	U /	N/A	N/A	N/A	26.85	4	0.60	N/A	N/A	14	85	0	1	N/A	N/A	1
0.00	0.54	U /	N/A	N/A	N/A	24.16	5	0.29	N/A	N/A	0	0	0	100	N/A	N/A	0
0.40	0.53	B- / 7.2	22.2	1.27	N/A	71.35	193	0.14	-0.02	96.4	0	100	0	0	10	28	12
5.55	0.57	C / 4.5	N/A	N/A	N/A	17.27	229	-0.64	-0.29	N/A	0	97	0	3	35	1	2
7.54	N/A	C+ / 6.7	N/A	N/A	N/A	23.55	213	-2.00	-4.60	N/A	0	0	0	100	N/A	7	2
1.18	0.55	B- / 7.5	N/A	N/A	N/A	23.30	7	0.69	0.08	N/A	4	95	0	1	11	46	1
0.78	0.50	B / 8.4	N/A	N/A	N/A	29.76	7	0.64	0.40	N/A	0	99	0	1	10	27	2
6.35	1.34	B+ / 9.0	N/A	N/A	N/A	49.54	76	0.42	0.24	N/A	9	0	90	1	81	38	N/A
4.81	0.55	U /	N/A	N/A	N/A	99.77	204	0.07	N/A	N/A	0	0	0	100	N/A	N/A	1
0.47	0.09	B+ / 9.9	N/A	N/A	N/A	50.95	138	-0.04	-0.01	N/A	5	0	95	0	18	53	3
0.57	0.20	B+ / 9.9	N/A	N/A	N/A	54.05	954	0.02	0.02	N/A	25	0	75	0	17	76	3
1.11	0.20	B+ / 9.1	N/A	N/A	N/A	64.59	314	0.09	0.08	N/A	1	0	99	0	38	91	3
3.05	0.15	B- / 7.1	N/A	N/A	N/A	97.09	70	0.05	-0.19	N/A	0	0	100	0	50	21	3
1.63	0.15	B+ / 9.6	N/A	N/A	N/A	80.68	22	0.19	-0.04	N/A	1	0	99	0	48	72	3
1.56	0.15	B+ / 9.3	N/A	N/A	N/A	83.89	16	0.66	-0.02	N/A	2	0	98	0	76	74	3
6.40	0.45	U /	N/A	N/A	N/A	99.16	29	0.17	N/A	N/A	0	0	0	100	N/A	N/A	1
1.36	0.20	B+ / 9.7	N/A	N/A	N/A	58.63	103	0.03	0.03	N/A	10	0	90	0	20	87	3

* Denotes ETF Fund, N/A denotes number is not available

				PRICE			PERFORMANCE						
	99 Pct = Best				52 Week		Perform-		% Total Return Through 3/31/12				
	0 Pct = Worst		Overall	Price			ance					Annualized	
Fund		Ticker	Investment	As of			Rating/Pts						
Type	Fund Name	Symbol	Rating	3/31/12	High	Low			3 Mo	6 Mo	1Yr/Pct	3Yr/Pct	5Yr/Pct
USA	*PIMCO Broad US Treasury Index	TRSY	U	104.55	N/A	N/A	U /		-2.02	-0.41	--	--	--
USA	*PIMCO Build America Bond Strateg	BABZ	C+	54.45	56.99	46.67	C / 4.8		2.82	2.59	24.43 / 85	--	--
GL	*PIMCO Canada Bond Index	CAD	U	103.04	N/A	N/A	U /		0.59	--	--	--	--
COI	*PIMCO Enhanced Short Maturity St	MINT	C-	101.03	101.29	99.90	D- / 1.3		1.16	1.24	1.06 / 44	--	--
GL	*PIMCO Germany Bond Index	BUND	U	99.92	N/A	N/A	U /		4.33	--	--	--	--
MUN	*PIMCO Intermediate Muncipal Bd S	MUNI	C	53.21	53.99	50.13	D+ / 2.8		0.72	2.83	8.46 / 74	--	--
COI	*PIMCO Investment Grade Corp Bond	CORP	C	103.88	105.66	98.07	D+ / 2.5		3.91	4.30	9.23 / 67	--	--
MUN	*PIMCO Short Term Muncipal Bond S	SMMU	C-	50.57	51.46	49.89	D- / 1.4		0.55	0.64	2.14 / 50	--	--
USA	*PowerShares 1-30 Laddered Treasu	PLW	C-	31.11	33.01	27.09	D / 1.9		-3.64	-2.49	16.22 / 79	6.22 / 12	--
GI	*PowerShares Act US Real Estate	PSR	A-	54.33	57.96	41.18	A- / 9.0		8.37	23.49	11.69 / 72	35.50 / 91	--
GI	*PowerShares Active Low Dur Fd	PLK	C-	25.45	26.06	24.29	D- / 1.3		0.26	-0.12	1.83 / 46	1.74 / 8	--
GR	*PowerShares Active Mega-Cap Fd	PMA	C+	29.51	29.51	22.50	C+ / 6.0		12.29	23.49	12.01 / 72	21.23 / 48	--
IN	*PowerShares Aerospace & Defense	PPA	C	20.15	20.80	15.57	C / 4.7		10.77	23.31	-0.44 / 40	19.21 / 40	1.45 / 34
USA	*PowerShares Build America Bond	BAB	C+	29.06	29.59	25.06	C / 4.3		2.55	3.44	21.74 / 83	--	--
IN	*PowerShares Buyback Achievers	PKW	B	29.35	30.29	22.38	B- / 7.3		10.78	25.05	13.26 / 74	25.49 / 66	3.91 / 50
IN	*PowerShares CEF Inc Composite Po	PCEF	C	24.97	26.43	21.57	C- / 3.5		8.33	14.60	6.17 / 59	--	--
GL	*PowerShares Chinese YDS Bd	DSUM	U	24.45	N/A	N/A	U /		4.32	3.52	--	--	--
IN	*PowerShares Cleantech Portfolio	PZD	D	23.88	30.20	18.87	D+ / 2.4		11.12	15.71	-18.22 / 12	11.20 / 18	-1.85 / 20
GI	*PowerShares Convertible Secs Por	CVRT	U	23.25	N/A	N/A	U /		5.49	5.25	--	--	--
GL	*PowerShares DB 3x German Bd Fut	BUNT	B-	30.36	30.79	19.01	A+ / 9.6		2.08	5.75	54.98 / 99	--	--
GL	*PowerShares DB 3x Inv Jpnese Gvt	JGBD	U	19.84	N/A	N/A	U /		-0.49	--	--	--	--
GL	*PowerShares DB 3x Itn Trs B Fut	ITLT	C+	22.00	24.87	12.00	A+ / 9.6		55.81	24.29	10.72 / 70	--	--
GL	*PowerShares DB 3x Jpne GvBd Fut	JGBT	D-	21.37	21.82	19.67	D / 1.6		-0.70	-0.23	6.96 / 61	--	--
USA	*PowerShares DB 3x Lg 25+ Yr Tr E	LBND	C+	37.10	48.64	19.60	A / 9.5		-18.94	-16.14	78.97 / 99	--	--
GI	*PowerShares DB 3x Lng USD I Fut	UUPT	U	20.13	N/A	N/A	U /		-7.61	-5.80	--	--	--
USA	*PowerShares DB 3x Sh 25+ Yr Tr E	SBND	E-	10.80	28.10	8.45	E / 0.5		20.40	12.03	-58.60 / 1	--	--
GI	*PowerShares DB 3x Sht USD I Fut	UDNT	U	18.29	N/A	N/A	U /		6.77	1.11	--	--	--
GR	*PowerShares DB Agri Double Long	DAG	E+	11.11	16.49	9.25	D- / 1.3		2.97	-3.98	-26.01 / 7	5.99 / 11	--
GR	*PowerShares DB Agri Double Sht	AGA	E-	16.98	22.50	13.66	E / 0.5		-4.56	-9.97	4.04 / 52	-28.06 / 3	--
IN	*PowerShares DB Agriculture Fund	DBA	D	28.10	34.83	27.56	D- / 1.2		-2.70	-5.28	-18.15 / 12	3.97 / 9	2.65 / 43
GR	*PowerShares DB Agriculture Long	AGF	E+	18.77	22.93	16.66	D- / 1.4		0.32	1.35	-14.41 / 15	4.94 / 10	--
GR	*PowerShares DB Agriculture Sht E	ADZ	E	24.00	26.86	19.90	E+ / 0.8		-1.55	-3.80	5.78 / 58	-12.27 / 6	--
IN	*PowerShares DB Base Metals Fund	DBB	D	20.09	25.76	17.82	D+ / 2.6		7.72	8.30	-17.70 / 12	13.34 / 22	-3.78 / 15
PM	*PowerShares DB Base Metals Sht E	BOS	E	20.12	33.03	17.44	E+ / 0.7		-9.11	-11.35	13.04 / 74	-18.86 / 5	--
PM	*PowerShares DB Base Mtls Dbl Lg	BDD	D-	12.12	21.68	9.87	C- / 3.7		15.72	12.33	-37.16 / 4	20.82 / 47	--
PM	*PowerShares DB Base Mtls Dbl Sh	BOM	E-	12.24	16.80	9.37	E / 0.4		-18.13	-22.48	17.58 / 80	-37.33 / 3	--
GR	*PowerShares DB Commodity Double	DEE	E-	30.42	40.06	25.16	E / 0.5		-0.75	-20.14	5.41 / 57	-26.72 / 4	--
GR	*PowerShares DB Commodity Double	DYY	D-	10.01	13.79	7.46	C- / 3.7		9.04	28.66	-19.98 / 11	17.19 / 33	--
GR	*PowerShares DB Commodity Idx Tra	DBC	D+	28.80	32.02	25.19	D+ / 2.5		7.30	11.84	-6.25 / 28	11.03 / 18	3.42 / 47
GR	*PowerShares DB Commodity Lg ETN	DPU	D-	18.45	21.79	15.09	D+ / 2.4		6.03	12.16	-8.37 / 24	10.59 / 17	--
GR	*PowerShares DB Commodity Short E	DDP	E	31.50	38.05	27.73	E+ / 0.8		0.38	-11.04	7.28 / 62	-12.36 / 5	--
GR	*PowerShares DB Crude Oil Dbl Sh	DTO	E-	37.92	80.67	32.64	E / 0.4		-8.45	-48.81	-8.85 / 23	-36.70 / 3	--
GR	*PowerShares DB Crude Oil Long ET	OLO	D-	14.84	16.94	10.88	C- / 3.1		5.86	30.08	-7.53 / 26	12.69 / 21	--
GR	*PowerShares DB Crude Oil Short E	SZO	E	39.11	55.48	36.42	E+ / 0.6		-4.00	-26.07	-0.43 / 40	-16.56 / 5	--
EN	*PowerShares DB Energy Fund	DBE	D+	30.05	33.70	24.85	C- / 3.1		8.80	16.88	-5.53 / 29	13.25 / 22	2.54 / 42
IN	*PowerShares DB G10 Currency Harv	DBV	D+	25.01	25.68	21.80	D / 1.9		5.26	8.98	1.54 / 45	6.12 / 11	-0.85 / 23
GL	*PowerShares DB German Bond Fut E	BUNL	D	23.12	23.79	19.67	C- / 3.1		0.70	2.17	16.53 / 79	--	--
PM	*PowerShares DB Gold Double Lg ET	DGP	C+	53.17	73.71	42.82	A / 9.5		11.68	1.24	24.67 / 85	41.85 / 96	--
PM	*PowerShares DB Gold Double Sht E	DZZ	E-	4.61	7.74	3.83	E / 0.3		-15.43	-12.78	-40.73 / 3	-42.23 / 2	--
PM	*PowerShares DB Gold Fund	DGL	C+	57.78	66.80	50.33	C / 5.3		6.12	1.67	15.15 / 77	21.24 / 49	17.51 / 99
PM	*PowerShares DB Gold Short ETN	DGZ	E	11.95	14.95	10.82	E+ / 0.6		-7.29	-5.16	-20.23 / 11	-22.25 / 4	--
GL	*PowerShares DB Inv Jpnese Gvt Bd	JGBS	U	19.92	N/A	N/A	U /		-0.45	--	--	--	--

* Denotes ETF Fund, N/A denotes number is not available

Incl. in Returns		RISK Risk Rating/ Pts	3 Year		Avg Dura-tion	NET ASSETS		VALUATION Premium / Discount		Wtd Avg P/E	ASSET				Portfolio Turnover Ratio	FUND MANAGER	
Dividend Yield %	Expense Ratio		Standard Deviation	Beta		NAV as of 3/31/12	Total $(Mil)	As of 3/31/12	1 Year Average		Cash %	Stocks %	Bonds %	Other %		Manager Quality Pct	Manager Tenure (Years)
0.92	0.15	U /	N/A	N/A	N/A	104.70	19	-0.14	N/A	N/A	0	0	0	100	219	N/A	2
3.97	0.45	B+ / 9.4	N/A	N/A	N/A	54.46	42	-0.02	-0.08	N/A	0	0	0	100	N/A	88	1
1.28	0.45	U /	N/A	N/A	N/A	102.79	14	0.24	N/A	N/A	0	0	0	100	N/A	N/A	1
1.19	0.35	B+ / 9.9	N/A	N/A	N/A	101.02	1,430	0.01	0.01	N/A	6	0	94	0	280	52	3
0.12	0.45	U /	N/A	N/A	N/A	99.83	13	0.09	N/A	N/A	0	0	0	100	N/A	N/A	1
2.10	0.35	B+ / 9.7	N/A	N/A	N/A	53.14	127	0.13	0.02	N/A	2	0	98	0	44	35	1
3.00	0.20	B+ / 9.7	N/A	N/A	N/A	103.60	213	0.27	0.09	N/A	0	0	0	100	69	35	2
0.87	0.35	B+ / 9.9	N/A	N/A	N/A	50.49	38	0.16	N/A	N/A	0	0	100	0	35	57	1
2.55	0.25	B+ / 9.1	9.0	0.74	13.3	31.16	158	-0.16	N/A	N/A	4	0	95	1	4	47	5
1.67	0.80	B / 8.1	24.4	1.19	N/A	54.46	24	-0.24	0.03	59.9	0	100	0	0	37	85	4
0.64	0.29	B+ / 9.9	1.5	-0.02	2.7	25.42	8	0.12	-0.05	N/A	15	0	84	1	119	58	3
1.22	0.75	B / 8.5	15.1	0.90	N/A	29.43	10	0.27	0.21	41.4	0	100	0	0	89	56	4
0.16	0.66	B / 8.0	19.3	1.11	N/A	20.13	58	0.10	-0.03	29.7	0	99	0	1	12	24	5
5.16	0.28	B+ / 9.3	N/A	N/A	N/A	29.05	871	0.03	0.05	N/A	3	0	96	1	15	87	3
0.53	0.70	B / 8.6	15.6	0.93	N/A	29.30	117	0.17	0.05	34.2	0	100	0	0	26	75	5
8.61	0.50	B / 8.6	N/A	N/A	N/A	24.93	271	0.16	0.08	N/A	0	100	0	0	32	55	2
3.03	0.45	U /	N/A	N/A	N/A	24.09	7	1.49	N/A	N/A	0	0	0	100	N/A	N/A	1
0.34	0.67	B- / 7.0	26.1	1.46	N/A	23.92	107	-0.17	-0.34	41.1	0	100	0	0	24	9	5
2.55	0.35	U /	N/A	N/A	N/A	24.01	10	-3.17	N/A	N/A	0	0	0	100	N/A	N/A	1
0.00	0.95	C+ / 5.6	N/A	N/A	N/A	30.39	38	-0.10	-0.05	N/A	0	0	0	100	N/A	99	1
0.00	N/A	U /	N/A	N/A	N/A	19.93	22	-0.45	N/A	N/A	0	0	0	100	N/A	N/A	1
0.00	0.95	C- / 4.0	N/A	N/A	N/A	21.24	34	3.58	-7.03	N/A	0	0	0	100	N/A	69	1
0.00	0.95	C+ / 5.9	N/A	N/A	N/A	21.51	4	-0.65	0.03	N/A	0	0	0	100	N/A	76	1
0.00	0.95	C / 4.8	N/A	N/A	N/A	37.25	27	-0.40	-0.08	N/A	0	0	0	100	N/A	23	2
0.00	0.95	U /	N/A	N/A	N/A	20.25	9	-0.59	N/A	N/A	0	0	0	100	N/A	N/A	1
0.00	0.95	D / 1.9	N/A	N/A	N/A	10.71	20	0.84	0.17	N/A	0	0	0	100	N/A	14	2
0.00	0.95	U /	N/A	N/A	N/A	18.31	4	-0.11	N/A	N/A	0	0	0	100	N/A	N/A	1
0.00	0.75	C- / 3.2	52.1	1.30	N/A	10.84	87	2.49	2.23	N/A	0	0	0	100	N/A	8	4
0.00	0.75	D / 1.9	54.0	-1.33	N/A	17.17	4	-1.11	0.21	N/A	0	0	0	100	N/A	19	4
0.00	0.93	B- / 7.9	17.9	0.56	N/A	28.11	2,088	-0.04	-0.06	N/A	0	0	0	100	N/A	19	N/A
0.00	0.75	C / 4.3	26.6	0.77	N/A	19.06	5	-1.52	0.48	N/A	0	0	0	100	N/A	15	4
0.00	0.75	C- / 3.2	25.3	-0.71	N/A	24.08	3	-0.33	0.05	N/A	0	0	0	100	N/A	52	4
0.00	0.76	C+ / 6.9	27.5	1.28	N/A	20.10	382	-0.05	-0.07	N/A	0	0	0	100	N/A	12	N/A
0.00	0.75	D+ / 2.6	27.7	-0.31	N/A	20.26	3	-0.69	0.06	N/A	0	0	0	100	N/A	10	4
0.00	0.75	C- / 3.0	58.3	0.81	N/A	12.16	23	-0.33	0.07	N/A	0	0	0	100	N/A	77	4
0.00	0.75	D / 1.9	57.6	-0.64	N/A	12.28	2	-0.33	-0.10	N/A	0	0	0	100	N/A	3	4
0.00	0.75	D / 1.9	45.3	-1.63	N/A	28.57	6	6.48	0.26	N/A	0	0	0	100	N/A	50	4
0.00	0.75	C- / 3.7	50.7	1.83	N/A	9.94	43	0.70	0.33	N/A	0	0	0	100	N/A	8	4
0.00	0.88	B- / 7.8	20.6	0.85	N/A	28.71	6,519	0.31	0.07	N/A	0	0	0	100	N/A	21	N/A
0.00	0.75	C / 4.7	21.3	0.84	N/A	18.04	7	2.27	-0.32	N/A	0	0	0	100	N/A	19	4
0.00	0.75	C- / 3.3	24.4	-0.93	N/A	30.03	10	4.90	0.28	N/A	0	0	0	100	N/A	76	4
0.00	0.75	D / 1.9	71.9	-2.28	N/A	37.98	97	-0.16	-0.19	N/A	0	0	0	100	N/A	30	4
0.00	0.75	C- / 4.0	27.4	1.09	N/A	14.67	15	1.16	-0.03	N/A	0	0	0	100	N/A	16	4
0.00	0.75	C- / 3.0	30.8	-1.06	N/A	39.21	14	-0.26	-0.07	N/A	0	0	0	100	N/A	60	4
0.00	0.78	B- / 7.4	24.1	0.84	N/A	30.02	178	0.10	0.09	N/A	0	0	0	100	N/A	43	N/A
0.00	0.80	B+ / 9.0	10.8	0.53	N/A	25.06	353	-0.20	-0.01	N/A	65	0	0	35	N/A	24	N/A
0.00	0.50	C+ / 5.9	N/A	N/A	N/A	23.07	31	0.22	-0.01	N/A	0	0	0	100	N/A	90	1
0.00	0.75	C- / 4.2	43.3	1.89	N/A	53.28	570	-0.21	0.18	N/A	0	0	0	100	N/A	24	4
0.00	0.75	D / 1.9	45.4	-1.97	N/A	4.61	81	0.00	-0.26	N/A	0	0	0	100	N/A	11	4
0.00	0.76	B / 8.2	21.0	0.95	N/A	57.89	428	-0.19	0.10	N/A	0	0	0	100	N/A	42	N/A
0.00	0.75	D+ / 2.6	21.3	-0.96	N/A	11.94	41	0.08	-0.12	N/A	0	0	0	100	N/A	22	4
0.00	N/A	U /	N/A	N/A	N/A	19.82	23	0.50	N/A	N/A	0	0	0	100	N/A	N/A	1

* Denotes ETF Fund, N/A denotes number is not available

Fund Type	Fund Name	Ticker Symbol	Overall Investment Rating	Price As of 3/31/12	52 Week High	52 Week Low	Performance Rating/Pts	3 Mo	6 Mo	1Yr/Pct	3Yr/Pct	5Yr/Pct
GL	*PowerShares DB Itn Trs B Fut ETN	ITLY	D	21.23	21.86	16.38	C- / 4.0	18.27	9.77	6.31 / 59	--	--
GL	*PowerShares DB Japanese GvBd Fut	JGBL	D-	20.35	20.69	19.88	D- / 1.3	-0.10	--	1.75 / 46	--	--
EN	*PowerShares DB Oil Fund	DBO	D	29.91	34.57	22.07	C- / 3.0	4.69	29.82	-8.59 / 24	12.48 / 21	3.28 / 47
PM	*PowerShares DB Precious Metals F	DBP	C+	58.33	69.52	52.36	C+ / 5.9	8.26	3.28	7.54 / 62	23.90 / 60	17.58 / 99
PM	*PowerShares DB Silver Fund	DBS	C	56.24	86.98	45.74	B / 8.2	17.19	8.89	-15.25 / 15	34.82 / 90	16.79 / 99
USA	*PowerShares DB US Deflation ETN	DEFL	U	48.15	N/A	N/A	U /	--	--	--	--	--
GR	*PowerShares DB US Dollar Bearish	UDN	D+	27.43	29.33	26.37	D- / 1.3	2.16	0.99	-2.63 / 34	2.40 / 8	1.88 / 37
GR	*PowerShares DB US Dollar Bullish	UUP	D	21.91	22.85	20.84	D- / 1.0	-2.49	-1.77	0.64 / 43	-4.61 / 6	-2.12 / 19
USA	*PowerShares DB US Inflation ETN	INFL	U	51.16	N/A	N/A	U /	--	--	--	--	--
IN	*PowerShares Div Achievers	PFM	C+	15.82	15.85	12.81	C / 5.0	6.17	18.74	9.23 / 67	19.45 / 40	0.87 / 31
FO	*PowerShares DWA Dev Mkt Tech Lea	PIZ	C-	19.52	23.91	15.56	C- / 4.1	11.92	19.94	-10.98 / 20	18.59 / 38	--
EM	*PowerShares DWA Emg Mkts Tech Le	PIE	C+	17.94	19.84	12.86	C+ / 6.7	12.55	26.35	-3.78 / 33	25.56 / 66	--
IN	*PowerShares DWA Technical Leader	PDP	B-	27.30	27.53	20.54	B- / 7.2	14.56	24.43	5.99 / 58	26.09 / 69	1.86 / 37
FS	*PowerShares Dynamic Banking Port	PJB	D	13.50	13.81	8.98	D+ / 2.4	14.91	42.36	5.32 / 56	4.99 / 10	-8.65 / 7
IN	*PowerShares Dynamic Basic Materi	PYZ	B-	38.03	40.96	25.50	B / 8.1	19.00	37.18	-1.88 / 36	29.75 / 81	5.87 / 61
HL	*PowerShares Dynamic Biotech&Geno	PBE	C-	22.68	23.79	17.30	C+ / 5.6	13.06	23.87	3.42 / 50	21.38 / 49	4.37 / 53
IN	*PowerShares Dynamic Bldg & Cons	PKB	C-	14.12	14.67	9.23	C / 4.6	17.86	41.83	-2.81 / 34	16.38 / 31	-2.44 / 18
IN	*PowerShares Dynamic Consumer Dis	PEZ	B-	29.59	29.99	21.07	B- / 7.1	15.95	30.79	13.24 / 74	24.06 / 61	1.39 / 33
IN	*PowerShares Dynamic Consumer Sta	PSL	C+	32.68	32.80	27.11	C / 5.3	5.17	14.25	10.17 / 69	20.93 / 47	5.05 / 57
EN	*PowerShares Dynamic Energy	PXI	B-	40.76	45.79	28.62	B / 7.9	6.84	29.97	-7.17 / 27	31.23 / 84	6.57 / 64
EN	*PowerShares Dynamic Enrg Exp & P	PXE	C+	25.06	28.36	17.24	C+ / 6.6	11.95	32.85	-8.60 / 24	25.41 / 66	4.63 / 55
FS	*PowerShares Dynamic Financial	PFI	C-	20.30	20.54	14.57	C- / 3.7	13.28	30.74	1.01 / 44	13.59 / 23	-3.37 / 16
IN	*PowerShares Dynamic Food & Bever	PBJ	C	19.83	20.60	16.95	C / 4.5	3.44	11.24	4.56 / 54	19.46 / 41	4.58 / 54
HL	*PowerShares Dynamic Hlthcare	PTH	C+	32.43	32.94	24.22	C+ / 6.5	13.04	25.07	8.56 / 65	23.12 / 57	2.76 / 43
IN	*PowerShares Dynamic Industrials	PRN	C	30.15	32.90	21.95	C / 5.5	10.56	29.75	-6.58 / 28	21.99 / 52	2.16 / 39
IN	*PowerShares Dynamic Insurance	PIC	C-	16.43	17.28	12.40	C- / 3.8	9.69	25.00	-1.39 / 37	15.09 / 27	-0.30 / 26
GR	*PowerShares Dynamic Large Cap Gr	PWB	C+	18.61	18.81	13.67	C+ / 6.2	15.50	29.87	9.28 / 67	21.41 / 50	2.40 / 41
IN	*PowerShares Dynamic Large Cap Va	PWV	C+	20.81	20.85	16.36	C / 5.2	8.40	22.87	8.15 / 64	19.69 / 42	3.22 / 45
IN	*PowerShares Dynamic Leisure&Ente	PEJ	A-	21.89	22.05	15.21	A- / 9.0	17.12	35.90	15.69 / 78	33.02 / 88	4.90 / 56
IN	*PowerShares Dynamic MagniQuant	PIQ	C	26.55	27.54	19.20	C / 5.1	12.03	29.66	2.06 / 46	19.39 / 40	-0.11 / 27
GR	*PowerShares Dynamic Market	PWC	C-	46.66	48.71	34.03	C- / 4.2	13.86	27.36	-0.37 / 40	16.34 / 31	-0.96 / 23
IN	*PowerShares Dynamic Media	PBS	B-	15.16	15.73	11.00	B / 7.6	14.49	29.36	0.03 / 41	28.02 / 76	-0.55 / 24
GR	*PowerShares Dynamic Networking	PXQ	B+	28.58	29.55	19.67	B+ / 8.9	17.66	37.40	3.17 / 49	33.57 / 88	9.48 / 83
EN	*PowerShares Dynamic Oil & Gas Sv	PXJ	D+	20.85	26.82	14.50	C / 4.7	3.42	28.96	-21.16 / 10	22.40 / 54	-0.29 / 26
GR	*PowerShares Dynamic OTC Portfoli	PWO	C-	51.60	54.60	39.62	C / 4.3	13.56	22.17	-1.28 / 38	17.63 / 34	-0.81 / 23
HL	*PowerShares Dynamic Pharmaceutic	PJP	B	31.43	31.56	22.67	A- / 9.0	11.60	28.29	29.39 / 88	32.53 / 87	12.03 / 96
IN	*PowerShares Dynamic Retail	PMR	B	25.61	26.19	17.74	B / 7.8	16.65	35.20	26.22 / 86	24.32 / 62	5.50 / 59
IN	*PowerShares Dynamic Semiconducto	PSI	C-	16.21	18.53	11.46	C / 4.5	16.70	34.74	-6.45 / 28	17.72 / 35	-2.09 / 19
GR	*PowerShares Dynamic Software	PSJ	C	26.96	27.84	19.97	C+ / 5.8	14.96	23.89	-1.75 / 36	22.52 / 54	5.73 / 60
GR	*PowerShares Dynamic Technology	PTF	C	27.54	27.96	19.89	C / 4.9	18.30	31.64	-0.29 / 40	18.35 / 37	0.25 / 28
UT	*PowerShares Dynamic Utilities	PUI	C-	16.74	17.72	14.22	D+ / 2.9	3.42	10.14	4.21 / 52	12.43 / 21	-0.36 / 25
EM	*PowerShares Emg Mkts Infrastruct	PXR	C-	42.88	56.59	31.83	C / 4.8	15.56	25.53	-20.23 / 11	21.85 / 52	--
EM	*PowerShares Emrg Mkt Sovereign D	PCY	C	28.02	28.56	25.62	C- / 4.0	3.77	10.01	11.49 / 71	16.71 / 32	--
FS	*PowerShares Financial Preferred	PGF	B+	17.90	18.45	14.70	B / 8.0	12.89	15.06	5.66 / 57	30.74 / 83	1.59 / 34
FO	*PowerShares FTSE RAFI Asia Pac E	PAF	C+	51.92	61.86	41.09	C+ / 6.4	12.02	22.04	-8.79 / 23	25.64 / 67	--
FO	*PowerShares FTSE RAFI DM exUS Sm	PDN	C-	22.53	26.27	19.63	C / 4.8	9.64	9.94	-8.45 / 24	22.14 / 53	--
FO	*PowerShares FTSE RAFI Dvlp Mkt e	PXF	D+	35.83	44.09	29.87	C- / 3.4	11.67	15.31	-12.10 / 19	15.85 / 29	--
EM	*PowerShares FTSE RAFI Emg Mkts	PXH	C-	22.92	27.44	18.01	C- / 4.1	13.41	21.89	-12.24 / 18	18.13 / 36	--
IN	*PowerShares FTSE RAFI US 1000	PRF	B-	60.50	61.22	46.23	B- / 7.2	11.18	24.90	3.86 / 51	26.52 / 71	2.31 / 40
IN	*PowerShares FTSE RAFI US 1500 Sm	PRFZ	B	68.07	70.84	49.00	B+ / 8.4	13.56	30.48	-0.92 / 38	32.11 / 86	4.73 / 56
COH	*PowerShares Fundamental High Yie	PHB	C-	18.62	18.90	17.00	C- / 3.7	2.19	8.95	6.33 / 59	15.90 / 29	--
GR	*PowerShares Fundamental Pure Lg	PXLC	C	26.59	26.78	21.35	C / 4.7	9.24	20.51	6.91 / 61	18.50 / 38	2.06 / 38

99 Pct = Best
0 Pct = Worst

* Denotes ETF Fund, N/A denotes number is not available

www.thestreetratings.com

Incl. in Returns		RISK Risk Rating/ Pts	3 Year		Avg Dura-tion	NET ASSETS		VALUATION Premium / Discount		Wtd Avg P/E	ASSET				Portfolio Turnover Ratio	FUND MANAGER	
Dividend Yield %	Expense Ratio		Standard Deviation	Beta		NAV as of 3/31/12	Total $(Mil)	As of 3/31/12	1 Year Average		Cash %	Stocks %	Bonds %	Other %		Manager Quality Pct	Manager Tenure (Years)
0.00	0.50	C / 5.3	N/A	N/A	N/A	22.15	39	-4.15	9.20	N/A	0	0	0	100	N/A	68	1
0.00	0.50	C+ / 5.9	N/A	N/A	N/A	20.46	5	-0.54	0.09	N/A	0	0	0	100	N/A	55	1
0.00	0.77	C+ / 6.6	28.2	1.00	N/A	29.87	759	0.13	0.07	N/A	0	0	0	100	N/A	26	N/A
0.00	0.78	B- / 7.6	25.6	1.11	N/A	58.41	447	-0.14	0.08	N/A	0	0	0	100	N/A	36	N/A
0.00	0.77	C / 5.0	47.1	1.71	N/A	56.50	84	-0.46	0.05	N/A	0	0	0	100	N/A	25	N/A
0.00	0.75	U /	N/A	N/A	N/A	48.08	20	0.15	N/A	N/A	0	0	0	100	N/A	N/A	1
0.00	0.80	B / 8.7	9.9	0.43	N/A	27.43	93	0.00	0.01	N/A	100	0	0	0	N/A	20	N/A
0.00	0.81	B / 8.4	10.0	-0.42	N/A	21.91	1,255	0.00	-0.03	N/A	1	0	0	99	N/A	67	N/A
0.00	0.75	U /	N/A	N/A	N/A	51.06	20	0.20	N/A	N/A	0	0	0	100	N/A	N/A	1
1.61	0.60	B / 8.9	12.3	0.74	N/A	15.81	286	0.06	0.01	26.6	0	99	0	1	11	68	5
0.65	0.80	B- / 7.1	26.3	1.16	N/A	19.43	64	0.46	-0.02	29.2	1	98	0	1	93	43	5
1.14	0.90	C+ / 6.9	27.8	1.02	N/A	17.91	195	0.17	-0.12	74.8	0	100	0	0	147	58	5
0.16	0.70	B- / 7.9	18.4	1.05	N/A	27.27	522	0.11	0.01	60.4	0	99	0	1	42	64	5
1.40	0.65	B- / 7.4	20.6	0.67	N/A	13.48	13	0.15	-0.06	10.6	0	100	0	0	114	17	5
0.91	0.65	B- / 7.0	27.8	1.58	N/A	38.00	64	0.08	-0.02	41.5	0	99	0	1	28	23	5
0.00	0.63	C+ / 5.9	20.6	1.03	N/A	22.70	141	-0.09	-0.12	189.0	0	100	0	0	81	32	5
0.06	0.63	B- / 7.2	27.3	1.44	N/A	14.09	29	0.21	-0.07	28.3	0	99	0	1	75	12	5
1.02	0.65	B / 8.0	21.2	1.12	N/A	29.63	21	-0.14	-0.01	42.8	0	100	0	0	68	44	5
0.61	0.65	B / 8.9	12.6	0.68	N/A	32.65	38	0.09	-0.02	31.1	0	99	0	1	54	78	5
0.25	0.65	B- / 7.3	27.5	1.14	N/A	40.78	163	-0.05	N/A	23.7	0	100	0	0	35	84	5
0.79	0.63	B- / 7.3	27.7	1.15	N/A	25.09	75	-0.12	-0.07	11.2	0	100	0	0	57	75	5
0.22	0.65	B / 8.1	18.1	0.68	N/A	20.28	19	0.10	0.02	14.3	0	100	0	0	59	48	5
1.68	0.63	B / 8.9	11.7	0.58	N/A	19.83	159	0.00	N/A	26.4	0	99	0	1	73	80	5
0.00	0.65	B- / 7.6	15.7	0.80	N/A	32.34	42	0.28	0.01	89.6	0	99	0	1	63	71	5
0.58	0.65	B- / 7.5	23.8	1.34	N/A	30.16	33	-0.03	N/A	27.7	0	100	0	0	48	21	5
0.29	0.63	B / 8.2	17.8	0.99	N/A	16.36	7	0.43	-0.02	12.1	0	99	0	1	66	23	5
0.20	0.63	B- / 7.7	17.4	1.03	N/A	18.62	183	-0.05	-0.05	72.7	0	100	0	0	45	37	5
1.72	0.61	B / 8.6	15.0	0.91	N/A	20.83	420	-0.10	-0.01	19.7	0	99	0	1	40	52	5
0.99	0.63	B- / 7.9	23.4	1.27	N/A	21.84	47	0.23	-0.04	50.5	0	100	0	0	58	73	5
0.57	0.65	B- / 7.6	21.6	1.22	N/A	26.56	18	-0.04	-0.13	44.9	0	100	0	0	93	20	5
0.40	0.60	B- / 7.8	17.8	1.04	N/A	46.60	134	0.13	-0.03	35.6	0	100	0	0	107	22	5
0.32	0.63	B- / 7.6	24.8	1.38	N/A	15.14	136	0.13	N/A	31.6	0	100	0	0	53	34	5
0.00	0.63	B- / 7.3	27.0	1.41	N/A	28.59	92	-0.03	-0.02	50.9	0	100	0	0	61	58	5
0.01	0.63	C+ / 6.1	38.8	1.56	N/A	20.88	169	-0.14	-0.04	42.1	0	100	0	0	39	26	5
0.07	0.60	B- / 7.6	19.3	1.06	N/A	51.47	27	0.25	-0.01	68.1	0	100	0	0	75	23	5
0.23	0.63	C+ / 6.9	13.7	0.62	N/A	31.40	251	0.10	0.07	179.9	0	99	0	1	9	90	5
0.10	0.63	B / 8.2	20.7	1.02	N/A	25.62	60	-0.04	-0.02	38.0	0	99	0	1	102	62	5
0.21	0.63	C+ / 6.8	30.4	1.59	N/A	16.15	22	0.37	-0.04	32.7	0	100	0	0	64	11	5
0.00	0.63	B- / 7.4	18.7	1.00	N/A	26.90	51	0.22	-0.02	94.0	0	100	0	0	46	53	5
0.00	0.65	B- / 7.4	22.7	1.28	N/A	27.45	31	0.33	0.07	62.2	0	100	0	0	67	17	5
1.56	0.63	B / 8.8	11.5	0.95	N/A	16.74	46	0.00	-0.04	23.8	0	99	0	1	68	31	5
0.26	0.75	C+ / 6.4	34.7	1.33	N/A	42.98	131	-0.23	-0.17	36.7	0	99	0	1	34	19	4
5.32	0.50	B / 8.8	8.8	0.53	12.1	28.02	1,491	0.00	-0.03	N/A	1	0	98	1	4	88	5
6.44	0.66	B / 8.7	20.6	0.49	N/A	17.85	1,589	0.28	-0.02	N/A	0	0	0	100	26	93	5
1.55	0.80	B- / 7.0	27.3	1.16	N/A	52.03	62	-0.21	-0.17	N/A	0	99	0	1	22	77	N/A
0.15	0.75	B- / 7.2	22.5	1.02	N/A	23.14	63	-2.64	-0.77	94.3	0	99	0	1	75	77	5
0.81	0.75	B- / 7.4	26.5	1.22	N/A	35.61	278	0.62	0.13	25.6	0	99	0	1	17	34	5
0.39	0.85	B- / 7.0	27.2	1.04	N/A	22.90	416	0.09	0.26	N/A	0	99	0	1	20	26	5
1.22	0.39	B / 8.2	20.8	1.21	N/A	60.52	1,346	-0.03	0.02	26.8	0	99	0	1	9	52	5
0.38	0.39	B- / 7.5	27.1	1.50	N/A	68.05	452	0.03	0.02	39.6	0	99	0	1	19	44	5
5.37	0.50	B / 8.0	9.8	0.87	5.1	18.67	878	-0.27	0.14	N/A	1	0	98	1	27	30	5
1.77	0.65	B / 8.6	14.7	0.88	N/A	26.60	25	-0.04	-0.05	22.9	0	99	0	1	41	45	5

* Denotes ETF Fund, N/A denotes number is not available

Fund Type	Fund Name	Ticker Symbol	Overall Investment Rating	Price As of 3/31/12	52 Week High	52 Week Low	Performance Rating/Pts	3 Mo	6 Mo	1Yr/Pct	3Yr/Pct	5Yr/Pct
	99 Pct = Best *0 Pct = Worst*											
GR	*PowerShares Fundamental Pure Lg	PXLG	U	22.41	N/A	N/A	U /	14.10	25.06	--	--	--
GR	*PowerShares Fundamental Pure Lg	PXLV	U	20.96	N/A	N/A	U /	11.16	24.59	--	--	--
GR	*PowerShares Fundamental Pure Md	PXMG	C	22.95	24.27	17.33	C / 5.0	12.86	25.49	-1.37 / 37	19.72 / 42	2.09 / 39
GR	*PowerShares Fundamental Pure Md	PXMV	C+	17.18	17.43	12.64	C / 5.5	11.72	28.61	3.78 / 51	20.62 / 46	-1.17 / 22
GR	*PowerShares Fundamental Pure Md	PXMC	C+	26.93	27.40	20.55	C+ / 5.6	11.56	24.25	2.49 / 48	21.44 / 50	0.48 / 29
GR	*PowerShares Fundamental Pure Sm	PXSC	C	24.56	25.39	18.03	C+ / 5.6	11.78	27.40	0.46 / 42	21.38 / 49	-0.79 / 24
GR	*PowerShares Fundamental Pure Sm	PXSG	C	17.92	19.22	13.30	C / 5.4	12.63	25.48	-3.66 / 33	21.43 / 50	-0.46 / 25
GR	*PowerShares Fundamental Pure Sm	PXSV	C+	16.69	17.13	11.78	C+ / 5.8	13.46	33.49	1.88 / 46	21.16 / 48	-0.31 / 25
COI	*PowerShares Fundmntl Inv Gr Corp	PFIG	U	25.12	N/A	N/A	U /	1.09	3.25	--	--	--
EN	*PowerShares Gb Nuclear Energy Po	PKN	D	17.03	20.71	14.19	D / 2.1	9.38	13.03	-13.41 / 17	9.08 / 15	--
PM	*PowerShares Glb Gold & Precious	PSAU	D	39.70	52.00	37.95	D+ / 2.9	-0.13	-3.09	-18.01 / 12	17.19 / 33	--
GL	*PowerShares Gldn Drgn Hltr USX C	PGJ	D	21.62	29.33	17.87	D+ / 2.3	10.34	12.99	-21.63 / 10	11.77 / 19	1.56 / 34
GL	*PowerShares Global Agriculture P	PAGG	C-	30.20	34.29	23.74	C- / 4.0	12.44	18.84	-9.24 / 23	17.65 / 34	--
EN	*PowerShares Global Clean Energy	PBD	E+	8.99	15.86	7.91	E+ / 0.8	9.42	3.44	-41.93 / 3	-8.56 / 6	--
EN	*PowerShares Global Coal Portfoli	PKOL	D+	24.82	38.44	21.22	C- / 3.9	1.23	6.77	-33.62 / 4	22.90 / 56	--
IN	*PowerShares Global Listed Priv E	PSP	C-	9.48	12.36	7.09	C+ / 5.6	18.65	23.28	-13.63 / 17	23.26 / 58	-14.01 / 4
GL	*PowerShares Global Steel Portfol	PSTL	D	16.43	24.35	13.51	D / 1.9	10.82	10.92	-30.38 / 5	9.78 / 16	--
EN	*PowerShares Global Water Portfol	PIO	C-	18.10	21.50	14.76	C- / 3.7	16.10	16.40	-10.67 / 21	16.40 / 31	--
EN	*PowerShares Global Wind Energy P	PWND	E+	6.99	11.76	6.59	E+ / 0.6	2.04	-0.94	-39.59 / 3	-14.98 / 5	--
IN	*PowerShares High Yld Eq Div Ach	PEY	B-	9.42	9.56	7.50	C+ / 6.0	2.83	17.04	9.57 / 68	23.10 / 57	-5.50 / 11
GL	*PowerShares Ibbotson Altv Comp	PTO	C-	11.59	12.50	9.32	C- / 3.5	8.63	10.02	-1.64 / 37	15.48 / 28	--
FO	*PowerShares India Portfolio	PIN	D	18.83	24.59	15.96	D+ / 2.6	15.63	3.44	-22.12 / 10	13.57 / 23	--
MUN	*PowerShares Insured CA Mun Bond	PWZ	C	24.67	26.49	21.82	C- / 4.0	2.97	4.95	16.86 / 86	9.00 / 24	--
MUN	*PowerShares Insured National Mun	PZA	C	24.78	25.31	22.18	C- / 4.0	2.47	4.43	16.43 / 85	9.18 / 24	--
MUN	*PowerShares Insured NY Mun Bond	PZT	C	24.15	24.60	21.83	C- / 3.8	2.11	4.37	15.22 / 84	8.62 / 22	--
GL	*PowerShares International Corp B	PICB	C-	27.87	29.21	25.53	D+ / 2.3	6.26	7.80	4.21 / 53	--	--
FO	*PowerShares Intl Dividend Ach	PID	C	15.36	16.99	13.15	C / 4.7	5.91	13.21	-3.02 / 33	21.21 / 48	-1.31 / 21
IN	*PowerShares KBW Bank	KBWB	U	25.33	N/A	N/A	U /	26.86	--	--	--	--
IN	*PowerShares KBW Capital Markets	KBWC	U	35.02	N/A	N/A	U /	22.36	--	--	--	--
GI	*PowerShares KBW High Div Yield F	KBWD	C+	23.93	24.77	19.01	C+ / 6.1	12.66	22.34	9.92 / 68	--	--
IN	*PowerShares KBW Insurance	KBWI	U	42.74	N/A	N/A	U /	12.78	--	--	--	--
FO	*PowerShares KBW International Fn	KBWX	U	22.57	28.06	17.86	U /	--	--	--	--	--
IN	*PowerShares KBW Premium Yld Eq R	KBWY	C	25.71	28.75	19.67	C / 5.0	13.25	23.20	4.87 / 55	--	--
IN	*PowerShares KBW Regional Banking	KBWR	U	28.52	N/A	N/A	U /	15.06	--	--	--	--
GR	*PowerShares Lux Nanotech	PXN	D-	6.55	9.70	5.41	E+ / 0.9	8.20	11.52	-30.80 / 5	-4.73 / 6	-17.72 / 3
FO	*PowerShares MENA Frontier Countr	PMNA	D	11.33	13.17	9.96	D / 1.6	8.96	8.39	-4.53 / 31	4.73 / 10	--
IN	*PowerShares Mrnngstr StockInv Co	PYH	C	22.13	22.34	17.26	C- / 3.9	9.06	22.01	5.07 / 55	15.02 / 27	-3.78 / 15
IN	*PowerShares NASDAQ Internet Port	PNQI	B	41.63	42.57	29.82	A / 9.3	20.54	30.87	5.39 / 57	37.23 / 93	--
GEI	*PowerShares Preferred Port	PGX	C+	14.37	14.54	12.38	C / 5.0	6.73	9.36	6.81 / 61	20.78 / 46	--
GR	*PowerShares QQQ	QQQ	B	67.55	68.51	49.94	B+ / 8.4	21.19	28.88	18.00 / 80	28.55 / 78	9.21 / 81
GI	*PowerShares RiverFront Tact Bal	PAO	C-	12.42	13.67	10.29	C- / 3.3	8.89	16.24	-4.76 / 31	14.44 / 25	--
GI	*PowerShares RiverFront Tact Gr &	PCA	C-	13.00	13.97	10.53	C- / 3.0	5.02	11.93	-0.11 / 40	12.96 / 22	--
IN	*PowerShares S&P 500 BuyWrite Por	PBP	C	20.54	21.64	17.55	C- / 4.2	5.19	27.42	13.98 / 76	15.05 / 27	--
IN	*Powershares S&P 500 High Beta Po	SPHB	U	21.90	N/A	N/A	U /	16.91	33.54	--	--	--
GR	*Powershares S&P 500 Low Vol Port	SPLV	U	26.80	N/A	N/A	U /	4.16	14.96	--	--	--
EM	*PowerShares S&P EM Low Vol	EELV	U	27.13	N/A	N/A	U /	--	--	--	--	--
FO	*PowerShares S&P Intl Dev Low Vol	IDLV	U	26.77	N/A	N/A	U /	--	--	--	--	--
GR	*PowerShares S&P SC Cnsmr Discr	PSCD	B+	32.06	33.02	21.96	B+ / 8.9	18.37	35.61	13.09 / 74	--	--
GR	*PowerShares S&P SC Cnsmr Staples	PSCC	C	34.09	34.40	27.24	C / 4.5	8.48	17.35	9.25 / 67	--	--
GR	*PowerShares S&P SC Energy	PSCE	D	37.25	42.70	24.23	C- / 3.3	8.60	38.41	-11.36 / 20	--	--
GR	*PowerShares S&P SC Financials	PSCF	C+	29.95	30.16	21.69	B- / 7.0	10.90	31.33	8.58 / 65	--	--
GR	*PowerShares S&P SC Health Care	PSCH	B-	35.15	35.73	25.72	B- / 7.0	11.58	27.61	10.70 / 70	--	--

* Denotes ETF Fund, N/A denotes number is not available

Incl. in Returns		RISK Risk Rating/ Pts	3 Year		Avg Dura-tion	NET ASSETS		VALUATION Premium / Discount		Wtd Avg P/E	ASSET				Portfolio Turnover Ratio	Manager Quality Pct	Manager Tenure (Years)
Dividend Yield %	Expense Ratio		Standard Deviation	Beta		NAV as of 3/31/12	Total $(Mil)	As of 3/31/12	1 Year Average		Cash %	Stocks %	Bonds %	Other %			
0.39	0.29	U /	N/A	N/A	N/A	22.37	3	0.18	N/A	N/A	0	100	0	0	N/A	N/A	1
1.05	0.29	U /	N/A	N/A	N/A	20.94	8	0.10	N/A	N/A	0	100	0	0	N/A	N/A	1
0.18	0.63	B- / 7.7	20.0	1.11	N/A	22.96	91	-0.04	-0.07	44.7	0	99	0	1	49	25	5
1.15	0.63	B / 8.1	18.9	1.09	N/A	17.17	31	0.06	-0.02	18.6	0	99	0	1	65	32	5
0.26	0.65	B / 8.1	17.7	1.02	N/A	26.87	21	0.22	-0.02	43.6	0	100	0	0	47	41	5
1.02	0.65	B- / 7.7	21.7	1.20	N/A	24.50	16	0.24	N/A	39.9	0	99	0	1	68	26	5
0.00	0.63	B- / 7.2	21.2	1.12	N/A	17.91	33	0.06	-0.11	77.8	0	100	0	0	57	30	5
0.81	0.63	B- / 7.7	22.8	1.29	N/A	16.66	54	0.18	-0.11	21.7	0	100	0	0	90	23	5
1.93	0.22	U /	N/A	N/A	N/A	24.96	14	0.64	N/A	N/A	0	0	0	100	N/A	N/A	1
0.20	0.75	B- / 7.2	24.2	0.86	N/A	17.14	17	-0.64	-0.53	29.6	0	99	0	1	25	24	4
0.29	0.75	C+ / 6.0	33.7	1.28	N/A	39.29	49	1.04	-0.06	139.9	0	99	0	1	9	12	4
0.33	0.70	C+ / 6.5	28.5	1.11	N/A	21.68	266	-0.28	-0.23	74.0	0	100	0	0	15	26	5
0.23	0.75	B- / 7.2	27.8	1.07	N/A	30.21	116	-0.03	-0.02	57.6	0	100	0	0	16	52	4
0.69	0.75	C / 5.5	34.0	1.19	N/A	9.00	89	-0.11	-0.50	36.9	0	99	0	1	66	5	5
1.90	0.75	C+ / 6.5	40.1	1.42	N/A	24.85	19	-0.12	-0.45	18.5	0	99	0	1	36	41	4
1.09	0.70	C+ / 6.3	28.9	1.62	N/A	9.42	272	0.64	0.01	N/A	0	100	0	0	112	15	5
1.52	0.75	C+ / 6.6	35.0	1.45	N/A	16.62	4	-1.14	-0.42	6.8	0	99	0	1	41	14	4
1.17	0.75	B- / 7.4	22.5	0.76	N/A	18.12	253	-0.11	-0.30	48.5	0	99	0	1	26	71	5
0.33	0.75	C / 4.5	32.8	1.07	N/A	7.04	15	-0.71	-0.54	N/A	0	99	0	1	74	4	4
3.94	0.60	B+ / 9.0	16.2	0.82	N/A	9.42	332	0.00	0.01	19.2	0	99	0	1	44	79	5
3.18	0.25	B / 8.5	15.8	0.65	N/A	11.52	9	0.61	0.06	N/A	0	100	0	0	5	74	4
0.09	0.79	C+ / 6.3	33.8	1.16	N/A	18.81	425	0.11	-0.19	N/A	0	100	0	0	82	28	4
4.24	0.28	B+ / 9.3	6.6	1.41	15.2	24.62	45	0.20	0.02	N/A	2	0	97	1	33	34	5
4.44	0.28	B+ / 9.3	6.5	1.39	13.9	24.77	668	0.04	0.03	N/A	2	0	97	1	33	36	5
4.25	0.28	B+ / 9.3	6.2	1.33	16.0	24.11	46	0.17	N/A	N/A	3	0	96	1	37	37	5
3.50	0.50	B / 8.7	N/A	N/A	N/A	27.90	92	-0.11	0.29	N/A	0	0	100	0	12	39	2
1.85	0.58	B / 8.2	19.8	0.90	N/A	15.34	682	0.13	0.11	34.9	0	100	0	0	42	81	5
1.99	0.35	U /	N/A	N/A	N/A	25.34	80	-0.04	N/A	N/A	0	0	0	100	N/A	N/A	1
3.04	0.35	U /	N/A	N/A	N/A	34.99	3	0.09	N/A	N/A	0	0	0	100	N/A	N/A	1
11.04	0.37	B / 8.4	N/A	N/A	N/A	23.88	60	0.21	0.11	N/A	0	100	0	0	N/A	67	2
2.12	0.35	U /	N/A	N/A	N/A	42.90	4	-0.37	N/A	N/A	0	0	0	100	N/A	N/A	1
1.02	0.40	U /	N/A	N/A	N/A	22.48	3	0.40	-0.10	N/A	0	100	0	0	8	31	2
5.82	0.36	B- / 7.6	N/A	N/A	N/A	25.62	8	0.35	0.09	N/A	0	100	0	0	36	24	2
3.65	0.35	U /	N/A	N/A	N/A	28.47	12	0.18	N/A	N/A	0	0	0	100	N/A	N/A	1
0.38	0.70	C+ / 6.1	28.3	1.53	N/A	6.55	23	0.00	-0.05	31.9	0	100	0	0	58	3	5
1.50	0.70	B- / 7.3	21.2	0.73	N/A	11.43	20	-0.87	-1.01	N/A	0	99	0	1	60	21	4
1.56	0.53	B / 8.3	16.0	0.89	N/A	22.16	17	-0.14	-0.01	31.2	0	99	0	1	91	26	5
0.00	0.60	C+ / 6.6	24.1	1.25	N/A	41.51	57	0.29	0.07	128.9	0	99	0	1	20	81	4
6.65	0.50	B+ / 9.4	11.6	0.38	N/A	14.32	1,536	0.35	0.09	N/A	0	0	0	100	30	93	4
0.33	0.20	B- / 7.5	18.6	1.07	N/A	67.55	33,268	0.00	0.01	112.5	0	100	0	0	29	72	N/A
0.64	0.25	B / 8.1	15.5	0.91	N/A	12.43	22	-0.08	-0.06	N/A	0	100	0	0	195	25	4
1.99	0.25	B / 8.8	10.9	0.64	N/A	12.97	18	0.23	N/A	N/A	0	100	0	0	181	43	4
2.89	0.75	B / 8.4	12.2	0.63	N/A	20.51	117	0.15	-0.22	46.3	0	100	0	0	61	56	5
0.71	0.25	U /	N/A	N/A	N/A	21.91	69	-0.05	N/A	N/A	0	0	0	100	N/A	N/A	1
3.09	0.25	U /	N/A	N/A	N/A	26.80	1,320	0.00	N/A	N/A	0	0	0	100	N/A	N/A	1
0.00	0.29	U /	N/A	N/A	N/A	26.86	5	1.01	N/A	N/A	0	0	0	100	N/A	N/A	0
2.92	0.25	U /	N/A	N/A	N/A	26.53	3	0.90	N/A	N/A	0	0	0	100	N/A	N/A	0
0.23	0.29	B- / 7.4	N/A	N/A	N/A	31.97	60	0.28	0.03	N/A	0	100	0	0	3	56	2
0.30	0.29	B / 8.7	N/A	N/A	N/A	33.96	19	0.38	N/A	N/A	0	99	0	1	30	71	2
0.06	0.29	C+ / 5.9	N/A	N/A	N/A	37.23	61	0.05	-0.04	N/A	0	99	0	1	46	4	2
0.60	0.29	B- / 7.8	N/A	N/A	N/A	29.89	73	0.20	-0.02	N/A	0	100	0	0	13	36	2
0.09	0.29	B / 8.0	N/A	N/A	N/A	35.10	119	0.14	-0.04	N/A	0	100	0	0	15	58	2

* Denotes ETF Fund, N/A denotes number is not available

				PRICE			PERFORMANCE						
	99 Pct = Best 0 Pct = Worst			Price As of 3/31/12	52 Week		Perform- ance Rating/Pts	% Total Return Through 3/31/12					
												Annualized	
Fund Type	Fund Name	Ticker Symbol	Overall Investment Rating		High	Low		3 Mo	6 Mo	1Yr/Pct	3Yr/Pct	5Yr/Pct	
GR	*PowerShares S&P SC Industrials	PSCI	C	30.65	31.27	21.78	C / 5.1	12.08	32.22	-0.46 / 40	--	--	
GR	*PowerShares S&P SC Information T	PSCT	C	31.64	32.78	21.79	C / 5.5	12.87	34.89	-1.22 / 38	--	--	
GR	*PowerShares S&P SC Materials	PSCM	D+	29.11	31.05	21.50	C- / 3.4	12.82	25.68	-4.81 / 31	--	--	
GR	*PowerShares S&P SC Utilities	PSCU	C-	30.21	31.65	26.09	D+ / 2.5	-1.19	9.93	8.10 / 64	--	--	
LP	*PowerShares Senior Loan	BKLN	C-	24.58	25.36	22.50	D / 2.2	4.13	9.73	2.91 / 49	--	--	
MUH	*PowerShares VRDO Tax-Free Weekly	PVI	C-	24.99	25.35	24.94	D- / 1.2	-0.05	0.14	0.48 / 43	0.56 / 8	--	
IN	*PowerShares Water Resources	PHO	C-	19.20	20.61	14.01	C- / 3.8	14.07	28.02	-5.21 / 30	14.82 / 26	1.01 / 31	
EN	*PowerShares Wilder Clean Energy	PBW	E+	5.56	10.74	4.80	E+ / 0.7	10.13	2.97	-46.67 / 2	-12.13 / 6	-21.63 / 3	
EN	*PowerShares WilderHill Progr Ene	PUW	C-	26.26	31.01	18.22	C / 4.7	16.52	31.28	-13.53 / 17	20.01 / 43	-0.38 / 25	
GR	*PowerShares Zacks Micro Cap	PZI	C-	11.58	12.64	8.14	C- / 4.1	13.75	32.57	-5.93 / 29	16.44 / 31	-7.86 / 8	
GL	*Precidian Maxis Nikkei 225 Index	NKY	U	14.77	N/A	N/A	U /	13.09	10.64	--	--	--	
GEI	*ProShares 30 Year TIPS TSY Sprea	RINF	U	41.06	N/A	N/A	U /	--	--	--	--	--	
IN	*ProShares Alpha Cr Suisse 130/30	CSM	C	63.62	64.18	48.14	C / 4.9	12.32	24.20	4.13 / 52	--	--	
GL	*ProShares German Sovereign Sub S	GGOV	U	41.36	N/A	N/A	U /	--	--	--	--	--	
GL	*ProShares Hedge Replication ETF	HDG	U	39.67	N/A	N/A	U /	2.07	5.51	--	--	--	
IN	*ProShares RAFI Long/Short	RALS	D+	37.65	42.65	37.24	E+ / 0.9	-1.61	-0.96	-9.21 / 23	--	--	
USA	*ProShares Short 20+ Year Treas	TBF	D-	33.23	45.33	30.62	E+ / 0.7	6.61	3.36	-24.70 / 8	--	--	
GEI	*ProShares Short 7-10 Year Treasu	TBX	U	34.40	N/A	N/A	U /	0.41	-0.62	--	--	--	
GR	*ProShares Short Basic Materials	SBM	D-	35.41	51.02	33.88	E+ / 0.7	-9.69	-25.14	0.98 / 43	--	--	
GR	*ProShares Short Dow 30	DOG	E+	35.49	46.81	35.31	E+ / 0.6	-8.53	-20.16	-13.44 / 17	-20.92 / 5	-7.93 / 8	
FS	*ProShares Short Financials	SEF	E+	30.96	47.05	30.57	E / 0.5	-17.17	-29.23	-11.24 / 20	-25.62 / 4	--	
FO	*ProShares Short FTSE China 25	YXI	D-	42.30	58.27	38.36	E+ / 0.8	-6.64	-21.78	5.70 / 58	--	--	
GEI	*ProShares Short High Yield	SJB	D	35.84	43.68	35.54	E+ / 0.7	-3.45	-13.89	-10.17 / 21	--	--	
COI	*ProShares Short Inv Grade Corp	IGS	D	35.20	40.15	34.33	E+ / 0.7	-3.40	-5.78	-12.11 / 19	--	--	
FS	*ProShares Short KBW Regional Ban	KRS	E+	44.28	75.34	43.58	E / 0.3	-14.42	-37.85	-21.17 / 10	--	--	
GR	*ProShares Short Midcap 400	MYY	E+	26.98	38.27	26.65	E / 0.5	-12.54	-24.91	-9.92 / 22	-25.68 / 4	-11.22 / 6	
FO	*ProShares Short MSCI EAFE	EFZ	E+	46.02	58.62	44.67	E+ / 0.6	-10.64	-17.69	-3.14 / 33	-19.30 / 5	--	
EM	*ProShares Short MSCI Emg Mkts	EUM	E+	29.16	39.99	28.04	E / 0.5	-12.67	-23.50	0.03 / 41	-23.60 / 4	--	
IN	*ProShares Short Oil and Gas	DDG	E+	33.05	45.94	31.03	E+ / 0.6	-5.15	-21.28	-2.78 / 34	-20.86 / 5	--	
GR	*ProShares Short QQQ	PSQ	E+	25.65	36.59	25.30	E / 0.5	-18.02	-24.71	-21.20 / 10	-26.38 / 4	-14.27 / 4	
GI	*ProShares Short Real Estate	REK	D-	30.72	43.43	30.00	E / 0.5	-10.41	-23.73	-16.54 / 13	--	--	
GR	*ProShares Short Russell 2000	RWM	E+	26.07	38.20	25.50	E / 0.5	-12.16	-27.24	-11.21 / 20	-26.63 / 4	-11.73 / 5	
GR	*ProShares Short S-P 500	SH	E+	35.76	48.50	35.47	E+ / 0.6	-11.51	-22.43	-12.78 / 18	-21.31 / 5	-6.81 / 10	
GR	*ProShares Short Small Cap 600	SBB	E+	22.39	33.20	22.08	E / 0.5	-11.75	-27.77	-15.32 / 15	-27.50 / 4	-11.61 / 5	
GI	*ProShares Short VIX Sh-Tm Fut ET	SVXY	U	98.21	N/A	N/A	U /	87.85	--	--	--	--	
IN	*ProShares Ult Telecommunications	LTL	C-	48.80	67.00	36.31	C / 4.4	12.18	13.15	-14.02 / 16	20.68 / 46	--	
USA	*ProShares Ultra 20+ Year Treasur	UBT	C+	116.15	143.54	72.98	C+ / 6.5	-14.19	-12.88	51.62 / 99	--	--	
USA	*ProShares Ultra 7-10 Year Treasu	UST	C	102.77	109.84	78.82	C / 4.3	-3.41	-1.82	28.48 / 87	--	--	
IN	*ProShares Ultra Basic Materials	UYM	C+	38.29	60.07	22.04	A- / 9.0	19.21	50.81	-31.80 / 5	38.17 / 94	-10.67 / 6	
IN	*ProShares Ultra Consumer Goods	UGE	A+	92.52	92.73	60.43	A+ / 9.8	18.36	40.75	24.50 / 85	46.70 / 98	7.50 / 71	
IN	*ProShares Ultra Consumer Service	UCC	A-	68.31	69.83	39.10	A+ / 9.8	29.06	56.72	26.85 / 86	51.59 / 99	-0.15 / 27	
IN	*ProShares Ultra DJ-UBS Commodity	UCD	D-	25.90	42.52	24.00	D- / 1.5	1.01	0.90	-34.05 / 4	8.73 / 14	--	
EN	*ProShares Ultra DJ-UBS Crude Oil	UCO	E+	42.91	64.80	24.58	D / 1.8	4.81	58.40	-26.67 / 7	4.28 / 9	--	
EN	*ProShares Ultra DJ-UBS Natural G	BOIL	U	7.48	N/A	N/A	U /	-63.10	--	--	--	--	
GR	*ProShares Ultra Dow 30	DDM	B+	70.54	71.53	43.65	A+ / 9.6	17.94	46.76	13.63 / 75	40.78 / 96	-1.19 / 22	
FO	*ProShares Ultra Euro	ULE	D-	25.21	32.68	22.72	D- / 1.0	5.61	-2.10	-13.43 / 17	-2.33 / 7	--	
FS	*ProShares Ultra Financials	UYG	C+	62.82	72.93	31.66	B+ / 8.5	41.92	70.65	-10.93 / 20	27.16 / 73	-36.77 / 0	
FO	*ProShares Ultra FTSE China 25	XPP	E+	49.56	84.17	31.60	E+ / 0.9	9.16	33.12	-38.77 / 3	--	--	
PM	*ProShares Ultra Gold	UGL	B	88.40	122.13	70.75	A / 9.5	11.88	1.21	25.46 / 85	41.40 / 96	--	
HL	*ProShares Ultra Health Care	RXL	A-	73.10	73.27	44.73	A / 9.5	20.28	42.68	25.06 / 85	36.58 / 92	2.09 / 39	
COH	*ProShares Ultra High Yield	UJB	U	43.22	N/A	N/A	U /	6.74	25.57	--	--	--	
IN	*ProShares Ultra Industrials	UXI	B	51.98	57.95	27.88	A+ / 9.8	25.71	65.98	-5.72 / 29	48.22 / 98	-4.95 / 13	

* Denotes ETF Fund, N/A denotes number is not available

| Incl. in Returns | | RISK | 3 Year | | | NET ASSETS | | VALUATION | | | ASSET | | | | | FUND MANAGER | |
Dividend Yield %	Expense Ratio	Risk Rating/ Pts	Standard Deviation	Beta	Avg Dura-tion	NAV as of 3/31/12	Total $(Mil)	Premium/Discount As of 3/31/12	1 Year Average	Wtd Avg P/E	Cash %	Stocks %	Bonds %	Other %	Portfolio Turnover Ratio	Manager Quality Pct	Manager Tenure (Years)
0.54	0.29	B- / 7.2	N/A	N/A	N/A	30.52	34	0.43	N/A	N/A	0	100	0	0	9	12	2
0.05	0.29	B- / 7.0	N/A	N/A	N/A	31.50	123	0.44	N/A	N/A	0	99	0	1	9	11	2
0.58	0.31	B- / 7.2	N/A	N/A	N/A	29.15	4	-0.14	-0.07	N/A	0	100	0	0	17	11	2
2.31	0.29	B+ / 9.0	N/A	N/A	N/A	30.16	47	0.17	0.01	N/A	0	99	0	1	8	72	2
4.93	0.65	B+ / 9.5	N/A	N/A	N/A	24.40	260	0.74	0.44	N/A	0	0	0	100	49	90	1
0.15	0.25	B+ / 9.9	0.2	0.01	0.2	25.00	426	-0.04	-0.01	N/A	6	0	93	1	34	49	5
0.44	0.66	B- / 7.2	23.0	1.31	N/A	19.23	895	-0.16	-0.09	66.6	0	99	0	1	13	14	5
1.27	0.70	C / 5.2	34.2	1.14	N/A	5.57	211	-0.18	-0.16	43.9	0	99	0	1	32	4	5
1.42	0.70	C+ / 6.9	28.4	1.04	N/A	26.25	51	0.04	-0.10	30.7	0	100	0	0	22	65	5
0.39	0.70	B- / 7.1	26.5	1.49	N/A	11.57	36	0.09	-0.10	38.6	0	99	0	1	61	11	5
0.00	0.50	U /	N/A	N/A	N/A	14.67	193	0.68	N/A	N/A	0	0	0	100	N/A	N/A	1
0.00	0.75	U /	N/A	N/A	N/A	38.60	4	6.37	N/A	N/A	0	0	0	100	N/A	N/A	0
0.93	0.95	B / 8.2	N/A	N/A	N/A	63.63	89	-0.02	-0.02	N/A	0	97	0	3	86	24	2
0.00	0.45	U /	N/A	N/A	N/A	41.43	4	-0.17	N/A	N/A	0	0	0	100	N/A	N/A	0
0.00	0.95	U /	N/A	N/A	N/A	39.69	16	-0.05	N/A	N/A	0	0	0	100	N/A	N/A	0
1.13	0.95	B+ / 9.1	N/A	N/A	N/A	37.64	15	0.03	-0.07	N/A	0	0	0	100	N/A	13	2
0.00	0.95	C+ / 6.5	N/A	N/A	N/A	33.13	918	0.30	-0.01	N/A	9	0	0	91	N/A	27	3
0.00	0.95	U /	N/A	N/A	N/A	34.55	18	-0.43	N/A	N/A	0	0	0	100	N/A	N/A	1
0.00	0.95	C+ / 5.8	N/A	N/A	N/A	35.42	7	-0.03	0.02	N/A	2	0	0	98	N/A	91	1
0.00	0.95	C+ / 5.6	14.2	-0.86	N/A	35.50	269	-0.03	-0.04	N/A	8	0	0	92	N/A	18	3
0.00	0.95	C / 4.6	25.1	-1.04	N/A	30.94	77	0.06	-0.02	N/A	20	0	0	80	N/A	13	1
0.00	0.95	C+ / 6.8	N/A	N/A	N/A	42.27	8	0.07	0.04	N/A	23	0	0	77	N/A	28	2
0.00	0.95	B / 8.4	N/A	N/A	N/A	35.83	23	0.03	-0.02	N/A	0	0	0	100	N/A	12	1
0.00	0.95	B / 8.9	N/A	N/A	N/A	35.07	4	0.37	0.13	N/A	0	0	0	100	N/A	50	1
0.00	0.95	C+ / 5.6	N/A	N/A	N/A	44.19	7	0.20	-0.08	N/A	0	0	0	100	N/A	6	1
0.00	0.95	C / 4.8	19.8	-1.16	N/A	27.00	30	-0.07	N/A	N/A	0	0	0	100	N/A	17	2
0.00	0.95	C / 5.4	21.1	-0.99	N/A	46.00	131	0.04	N/A	N/A	11	0	0	89	N/A	17	3
0.00	0.95	C / 4.4	27.2	-1.04	N/A	29.14	234	0.07	N/A	N/A	14	0	0	86	N/A	19	3
0.00	0.95	C / 5.2	21.2	-1.12	N/A	33.09	7	-0.12	N/A	N/A	13	0	0	87	N/A	31	1
0.00	0.95	C / 4.8	18.1	-1.04	N/A	25.65	187	0.00	-0.01	N/A	10	0	0	90	N/A	13	3
0.00	0.95	C+ / 6.3	N/A	N/A	N/A	30.74	32	-0.07	0.01	N/A	0	0	0	100	N/A	16	1
0.00	0.95	C / 4.5	22.3	-1.27	N/A	26.05	352	0.08	0.04	N/A	7	0	0	93	N/A	19	3
0.00	0.90	C / 5.5	16.1	-0.99	N/A	35.73	1,841	0.08	-0.01	N/A	3	0	0	97	N/A	22	2
0.00	0.95	C / 4.5	21.6	-1.21	N/A	22.52	20	-0.58	-0.04	N/A	2	0	0	98	N/A	16	2
0.00	0.95	U /	N/A	N/A	N/A	98.98	9	-0.78	N/A	N/A	0	0	0	100	N/A	N/A	1
0.63	0.95	C+ / 6.7	36.5	1.62	N/A	48.75	4	0.10	-0.01	16.9	22	45	0	33	26	14	1
0.24	0.95	B- / 7.1	N/A	N/A	N/A	116.97	6	-0.70	-0.02	N/A	1	63	0	36	79	20	2
0.01	0.95	B+ / 9.0	N/A	N/A	N/A	102.75	15	0.02	0.07	N/A	14	0	9	77	314	82	2
0.13	0.95	C / 4.7	61.7	3.29	N/A	38.30	207	-0.03	-0.02	25.0	10	41	0	49	6	4	1
0.66	0.95	B / 8.0	26.8	1.51	N/A	92.33	14	0.21	-0.10	31.4	18	57	0	25	6	84	1
0.00	0.95	B- / 7.2	35.0	1.95	N/A	68.23	10	0.12	0.07	42.0	34	25	0	41	4	72	1
0.00	0.95	C / 5.5	38.4	1.56	N/A	26.10	9	-0.77	-0.16	N/A	0	100	0	0	N/A	7	4
0.00	0.99	C- / 3.5	60.8	1.90	N/A	42.81	261	0.23	0.17	N/A	0	100	0	0	N/A	5	4
0.00	0.95	U /	N/A	N/A	N/A	7.54	36	-0.80	N/A	N/A	0	0	0	100	N/A	N/A	1
0.53	0.95	B- / 7.0	29.8	1.77	N/A	70.54	259	0.00	0.03	N/A	41	48	0	11	30	49	5
0.00	0.95	C+ / 6.4	25.5	0.92	N/A	25.25	8	-0.16	-0.08	N/A	0	0	100	0	N/A	10	4
0.71	0.95	C / 5.5	48.6	1.97	N/A	62.92	960	-0.16	-0.01	25.2	10	64	0	26	8	13	1
0.00	0.95	C- / 3.9	N/A	N/A	N/A	49.53	30	0.06	0.03	N/A	80	0	0	20	N/A	4	3
0.00	0.95	C+ / 6.2	43.5	1.90	N/A	87.79	386	0.69	0.44	N/A	0	0	0	100	N/A	22	4
0.83	0.95	B- / 7.6	26.4	1.21	N/A	73.13	44	-0.04	-0.02	43.3	15	78	0	7	6	70	1
0.00	0.95	U /	N/A	N/A	N/A	43.45	4	-0.53	N/A	N/A	34	0	0	66	N/A	N/A	1
0.35	0.95	C+ / 5.8	47.1	2.68	N/A	52.05	27	-0.13	-0.03	27.6	8	63	0	29	40	13	1

* Denotes ETF Fund, N/A denotes number is not available

99 Pct = Best
0 Pct = Worst

Fund Type	Fund Name	Ticker Symbol	Overall Investment Rating	PRICE Price As of 3/31/12	52 Week High	52 Week Low	PERFORMANCE Performance Rating/Pts	3 Mo	6 Mo	1Yr/Pct	3Yr/Pct	5Yr/Pct
COI	*ProShares Ultra Invest Grade Cor	IGU	U	48.50	N/A	N/A	U /	--	10.40	--	--	--
FS	*ProShares Ultra KBW Regional Ban	KRU	C+	49.10	53.12	22.78	A+ / 9.9	28.80	99.55	-2.91 / 34	--	--
GR	*ProShares Ultra MidCap 400	MVV	B	70.84	79.61	39.24	A+ / 9.7	27.96	57.77	-7.02 / 27	46.43 / 98	-3.02 / 17
FO	*ProShares Ultra MSCI Brazil	UBR	E+	23.39	38.61	14.20	D / 2.0	25.35	48.79	-38.11 / 3	--	--
IN	*ProShares Ultra MSCI EAFE	EFO	D-	70.84	101.87	49.93	D / 2.1	21.76	27.94	-21.23 / 10	--	--
EM	*ProShares Ultra MSCI Emerging Mk	EET	D-	80.36	120.14	50.50	D+ / 2.5	25.72	43.09	-30.69 / 5	--	--
FO	*ProShares Ultra MSCI Europe	UPV	E+	29.16	45.70	19.53	D / 2.1	22.16	32.55	-24.32 / 8	--	--
FO	*ProShares Ultra MSCI Japan	EZJ	D	64.71	76.66	48.44	C- / 3.2	23.54	14.90	-5.38 / 30	--	--
FO	*ProShares Ultra MSCI Mex Invest	UMX	C	37.57	44.86	22.92	B / 8.1	29.06	57.59	-14.09 / 16	--	--
FO	*ProShares Ultra MSCI Pacific ex-	UXJ	D-	30.50	43.50	19.51	D+ / 2.8	22.10	38.83	-23.52 / 9	--	--
HL	*ProShares Ultra Nasdaq Biotech	BIB	B	96.07	97.76	36.10	A+ / 9.9	38.19	69.71	39.64 / 96	--	--
EN	*ProShares Ultra Oil and Gas	DIG	C-	47.59	63.63	28.05	C+ / 5.9	8.48	45.36	-23.54 / 9	24.52 / 63	-7.18 / 9
GR	*ProShares Ultra QQQ	QLD	B+	118.95	122.39	66.37	A+ / 9.9	46.02	63.06	32.11 / 90	57.20 / 99	8.17 / 75
IN	*ProShares Ultra Real Estate	URE	B+	61.79	65.20	34.60	A+ / 9.8	21.75	52.60	8.79 / 66	58.64 / 99	-26.00 / 2
GR	*ProShares Ultra Rus Mid Cap Grow	UKW	B	54.89	60.21	31.45	A+ / 9.8	30.07	56.69	-0.99 / 38	48.77 / 99	-2.53 / 18
GR	*ProShares Ultra Rus Mid Cap Valu	UVU	B+	39.62	43.66	22.93	A+ / 9.8	23.44	51.39	-4.98 / 30	47.51 / 98	-9.46 / 7
IN	*ProShares Ultra Russell 3000	UWC	B	91.97	93.14	54.27	A+ / 9.7	25.99	54.88	8.42 / 65	--	--
GR	*ProShares Ultra Russell1000 Grow	UKF	B+	64.55	65.71	37.57	A+ / 9.7	29.23	55.06	13.00 / 74	43.74 / 97	0.99 / 31
IN	*ProShares Ultra Russell1000 Valu	UVG	B	33.09	34.63	19.65	A / 9.3	22.18	47.90	0.82 / 43	36.56 / 92	-12.30 / 5
GR	*ProShares Ultra Russell2000	UWM	B-	43.76	52.16	23.74	A / 9.5	25.56	60.75	-11.81 / 19	40.34 / 95	-9.31 / 7
GR	*ProShares Ultra Russell2000 Grow	UKK	B-	50.97	61.27	27.40	A+ / 9.7	26.85	62.22	-10.01 / 22	44.82 / 97	-5.18 / 12
IN	*ProShares Ultra Russell2000 Valu	UVT	C+	30.91	36.71	16.91	A- / 9.0	23.99	55.65	-13.18 / 17	35.03 / 91	-13.48 / 4
GR	*ProShares Ultra S-P 500	SSO	B+	58.36	59.27	34.17	A+ / 9.6	26.10	54.09	9.26 / 67	39.26 / 95	-6.26 / 10
IN	*ProShares Ultra Semiconductors	USD	C+	45.45	48.10	26.18	A+ / 9.6	34.34	57.86	11.46 / 71	38.44 / 94	-6.55 / 10
EN	*ProShares Ultra Silver	AGQ	D+	54.46	191.04	38.25	B+ / 8.7	30.75	5.05	-51.76 / 1	42.17 / 97	--
GR	*ProShares Ultra SmallCap 600	SAA	B	52.31	56.54	28.09	A+ / 9.7	24.62	64.30	-1.60 / 37	45.25 / 98	-6.00 / 11
GR	*ProShares Ultra Technology	ROM	B+	86.97	89.11	46.29	A+ / 9.8	48.13	69.22	30.39 / 89	50.01 / 99	5.83 / 61
UT	*ProShares Ultra Utilities	UPW	B+	53.34	56.75	37.99	B / 7.8	-3.72	12.84	19.40 / 82	29.73 / 81	-5.87 / 11
GI	*ProShares Ultra VIX Sh-Tm Fut ET	UVXY	U	14.56	N/A	N/A	U /	-80.04	--	--	--	--
FO	*ProShares Ultra Yen	YCL	D	31.36	37.87	30.09	D / 2.0	-14.08	-14.32	0.90 / 43	10.82 / 17	--
GEI	*ProShares UltraPro 10 Year TIPS	UINF	U	41.09	N/A	N/A	U /	--	--	--	--	--
GR	*ProShares UltraPro Dow30	UDOW	B	166.24	169.80	82.64	A+ / 9.8	27.87	74.45	13.86 / 76	--	--
GR	*ProShares UltraPro MidCap400	UMDD	C-	81.52	109.20	35.05	A+ / 9.8	44.03	89.27	-20.39 / 11	--	--
GR	*ProShares UltraPro QQQ	TQQQ	C	119.62	124.75	51.29	A+ / 9.9	75.99	102.75	40.51 / 97	--	--
GR	*ProShares UltraPro Russell2000	URTY	C-	69.21	105.66	29.42	A / 9.5	39.88	90.30	-29.02 / 6	--	--
IN	*ProShares UltraPro S&P 500	UPRO	C-	84.88	88.00	38.97	A+ / 9.9	41.11	84.48	5.37 / 57	--	--
GR	*ProShares UltraPro Short Dow30	SDOW	E-	19.25	48.00	18.98	E- / 0.1	-23.64	-51.20	-41.95 / 3	--	--
GR	*ProShares UltraPro Short MidCap4	SMDD	E-	11.65	37.30	11.25	E- / 0.0	-33.69	-61.37	-41.25 / 3	--	--
GR	*ProShares UltraPro Short QQQ	SQQQ	E-	10.79	34.85	10.36	E- / 0.0	-45.20	-59.56	-57.44 / 1	--	--
GR	*ProShares UltraPro Short S&P 500	SPXU	E-	9.06	25.20	8.86	E- / 0.1	-31.00	-55.61	-42.40 / 2	--	--
GR	*ProShares UltraPro Shrt Russell2	SRTY	E-	8.80	33.51	8.27	E- / 0.0	-32.93	-66.41	-48.45 / 1	--	--
IN	*ProShares UltraShort 20+ Yr US T	TBT	E	20.45	39.18	17.48	E / 0.5	13.17	5.20	-44.89 / 2	-23.36 / 4	--
GEI	*ProShares UltraShort 3-7 Yr Trea	TBZ	U	33.93	N/A	N/A	U /	1.07	-2.53	--	--	--
IN	*ProShares UltraShort 7-10 Yr US	PST	D-	31.41	43.06	29.90	E+ / 0.6	2.95	-0.54	-25.55 / 8	-16.35 / 5	--
IN	*ProShares UltraShort Basic Mater	SMN	E-	14.99	32.15	13.96	E- / 0.2	-19.54	-46.96	-9.26 / 23	-52.21 / 1	-38.90 / 0
IN	*ProShares UltraShort Consumer Go	SZK	E	17.73	29.17	17.37	E / 0.3	-14.92	-31.54	-29.36 / 6	-39.30 / 3	-19.48 / 3
IN	*ProShares UltraShort Consumer Se	SCC	E	12.12	24.65	11.89	E- / 0.2	-23.96	-42.50	-37.14 / 4	-45.44 / 2	-23.66 / 2
IN	*ProShares UltraShort DJ-UBS Com	CMD	E	54.71	61.65	39.32	E+ / 0.6	-2.63	-7.74	27.26 / 87	-25.16 / 4	--
EN	*ProShares UltraShort DJ-UBS Cr O	SCO	E-	35.16	71.36	30.74	E / 0.4	-9.12	-46.11	-12.49 / 18	-36.37 / 3	--
IN	*ProShares UltraShort DJ-UBS Nat	KOLD	U	148.04	N/A	N/A	U /	105.95	--	--	--	--
GR	*ProShares UltraShort Dow 30	DXD	E	12.81	22.89	12.68	E / 0.3	-16.33	-37.18	-27.71 / 7	-38.98 / 3	-20.33 / 3
FO	*ProShares UltraShort Euro	EUO	D-	18.97	21.31	15.99	D- / 1.0	-6.78	-1.61	7.11 / 62	-4.24 / 6	--

* Denotes ETF Fund, N/A denotes number is not available

	RISK					NET ASSETS		VALUATION			ASSET					FUND MANAGER	
Incl. in Returns		Risk Rating/ Pts	3 Year		Avg Dura-tion	NAV as of 3/31/12	Total $(Mil)	Premium / Discount		Wtd Avg P/E	Cash %	Stocks %	Bonds %	Other %	Portfolio Turnover Ratio	Manager Quality Pct	Manager Tenure (Years)
Dividend Yield %	Expense Ratio		Standard Deviation	Beta				As of 3/31/12	1 Year Average								
0.00	0.95	U /	N/A	N/A	N/A	48.27	2	0.48	N/A	N/A	15	0	0	85	N/A	N/A	1
0.84	0.95	C- / 3.7	N/A	N/A	N/A	48.98	5	0.25	0.06	N/A	0	63	22	15	29	25	1
0.00	0.95	C+ / 6.1	42.0	2.39	N/A	70.91	314	-0.10	-0.02	35.4	20	49	0	31	12	19	2
0.00	0.95	C- / 3.0	N/A	N/A	N/A	23.34	14	0.21	-0.01	N/A	23	0	0	77	N/A	5	2
0.00	0.95	C / 5.0	N/A	N/A	N/A	71.05	11	-0.30	0.08	N/A	51	0	0	49	145	2	3
0.00	0.95	C- / 4.1	N/A	N/A	N/A	80.29	28	0.09	0.02	N/A	39	14	0	47	163	11	3
0.00	0.95	C- / 3.9	N/A	N/A	N/A	29.19	3	-0.10	-0.01	N/A	47	0	0	53	N/A	11	3
0.00	0.95	C+ / 5.7	N/A	N/A	N/A	65.00	23	-0.45	-0.12	N/A	12	0	0	88	N/A	41	3
0.00	0.95	C / 4.6	N/A	N/A	N/A	38.10	2	-1.39	-0.43	N/A	36	0	0	64	N/A	51	2
0.00	0.95	C- / 4.0	N/A	N/A	N/A	30.65	3	-0.49	0.13	N/A	50	0	0	50	N/A	14	2
0.00	0.95	C+ / 6.2	N/A	N/A	N/A	95.88	24	0.20	-0.13	N/A	21	59	0	20	8	95	1
0.10	0.95	C / 5.4	48.1	2.04	N/A	47.71	268	-0.25	-0.01	18.5	30	61	0	9	7	15	1
0.00	0.95	C+ / 6.9	38.6	2.17	N/A	118.98	687	-0.03	-0.01	112.4	25	50	0	25	23	68	3
1.46	0.95	C+ / 6.4	48.6	2.42	N/A	61.85	396	-0.10	N/A	53.6	17	56	0	27	11	72	1
0.00	0.95	C+ / 6.3	41.2	2.36	N/A	54.83	12	0.11	-0.08	46.6	32	43	0	25	73	21	3
0.23	0.95	C+ / 6.4	41.7	2.38	N/A	39.56	6	0.15	-0.10	23.8	39	43	0	18	92	20	3
0.00	0.95	C+ / 6.2	N/A	N/A	N/A	91.96	5	0.01	-0.14	N/A	21	40	0	39	42	13	5
0.20	0.95	C+ / 6.9	34.5	2.05	N/A	64.55	15	0.00	-0.05	67.4	26	58	0	16	59	28	3
0.53	0.95	C+ / 6.8	36.5	2.15	N/A	33.12	7	-0.09	0.04	20.3	18	59	0	23	30	14	3
0.03	0.95	C / 5.5	47.4	2.62	N/A	43.82	197	-0.14	-0.02	47.3	29	56	0	15	43	10	3
0.00	0.95	C+ / 5.6	48.0	2.61	N/A	50.61	15	0.71	-0.04	27.6	23	55	0	22	36	12	3
0.32	0.95	C / 5.5	47.1	2.60	N/A	30.78	9	0.42	0.06	71.5	31	42	0	27	37	8	3
0.94	0.92	C+ / 6.8	33.9	2.04	N/A	58.39	1,743	-0.05	-0.01	46.0	22	63	0	15	4	20	2
0.21	0.95	C / 5.2	51.7	2.55	N/A	45.44	48	0.02	-0.04	N/A	27	28	0	45	5	10	1
0.00	0.95	D / 1.9	104.8	2.34	N/A	54.90	837	-0.80	0.24	N/A	0	0	0	100	N/A	18	4
0.04	0.95	C+ / 5.9	46.1	2.52	N/A	52.28	27	0.06	-0.07	45.8	27	51	0	22	12	15	2
0.00	0.95	C+ / 6.5	41.4	2.27	N/A	86.95	117	0.02	-0.03	114.2	17	56	0	27	6	30	1
1.59	0.95	B / 8.4	20.4	1.89	N/A	53.44	20	-0.19	-0.01	19.6	20	71	0	9	5	34	1
0.00	0.95	U /	N/A	N/A	N/A	14.30	120	1.82	N/A	N/A	0	0	0	100	N/A	N/A	1
0.00	0.95	B- / 7.9	19.5	0.01	N/A	31.37	5	-0.03	-0.02	N/A	0	0	0	100	N/A	84	4
0.00	0.75	U /	N/A	N/A	N/A	40.73	4	0.88	N/A	N/A	0	0	0	100	N/A	N/A	0
0.69	0.95	C+ / 5.8	N/A	N/A	N/A	166.32	75	-0.05	N/A	26.2	11	63	0	26	N/A	18	3
0.00	0.95	D / 1.9	N/A	N/A	N/A	81.57	33	-0.06	-0.05	N/A	34	62	0	4	35	1	2
0.00	0.95	D / 2.2	N/A	N/A	N/A	119.67	233	-0.04	-0.03	N/A	23	61	0	16	31	85	2
0.00	0.95	D / 1.9	N/A	N/A	N/A	69.24	118	-0.04	-0.05	N/A	20	64	0	16	116	N/A	2
0.04	0.95	D / 1.9	N/A	N/A	N/A	85.06	272	-0.21	-0.02	N/A	30	58	0	12	70	8	2
0.00	0.95	D+ / 2.7	N/A	N/A	N/A	19.26	83	-0.05	-0.05	N/A	0	0	0	100	N/A	3	2
0.00	0.95	D / 1.9	N/A	N/A	N/A	11.68	9	-0.26	0.02	N/A	4	0	0	96	N/A	5	2
0.00	0.95	D / 1.9	N/A	N/A	N/A	10.79	136	0.00	-0.03	N/A	0	0	0	100	N/A	N/A	3
0.00	0.95	D+ / 2.4	N/A	N/A	N/A	9.05	606	0.11	-0.06	N/A	0	0	0	100	N/A	3	2
0.00	0.95	D / 1.9	N/A	N/A	N/A	8.81	61	-0.11	-0.03	N/A	0	0	0	100	N/A	3	2
0.00	0.93	C- / 3.8	31.5	1.36	N/A	20.34	3,864	0.54	-0.04	N/A	8	0	0	92	N/A	1	4
0.00	0.95	U /	N/A	N/A	N/A	33.99	5	-0.18	N/A	N/A	0	0	0	100	N/A	N/A	1
0.00	0.95	C+ / 6.1	13.7	0.51	N/A	31.38	365	0.10	-0.06	N/A	15	0	0	85	N/A	5	4
0.00	0.95	D / 2.1	60.2	-3.15	N/A	14.99	47	0.00	-0.01	N/A	2	0	0	98	N/A	11	1
0.00	0.95	C- / 3.8	26.1	-1.44	N/A	17.59	3	0.80	-0.05	N/A	0	0	0	100	N/A	6	1
0.00	0.95	C- / 3.4	33.8	-1.89	N/A	12.17	8	-0.41	-0.05	N/A	0	0	0	100	N/A	5	1
0.00	0.95	C- / 3.6	37.6	-1.53	N/A	55.01	9	-0.55	-0.01	N/A	0	0	0	100	N/A	43	4
0.00	1.01	D / 2.2	59.0	-1.85	N/A	35.24	170	-0.23	-0.21	N/A	0	0	0	100	N/A	9	4
0.00	0.95	U /	N/A	N/A	N/A	146.83	22	0.82	N/A	N/A	0	0	0	100	N/A	N/A	1
0.00	0.95	C- / 3.7	28.6	-1.69	N/A	12.82	287	-0.08	-0.03	N/A	22	0	0	78	N/A	9	3
0.00	0.95	C+ / 6.6	25.0	-0.90	N/A	18.97	820	0.00	0.05	N/A	0	0	0	100	N/A	83	4

* Denotes ETF Fund, N/A denotes number is not available

				PRICE	52 Week		PERFORMANCE	% Total Return Through 3/31/12			Annualized	
Fund Type	Fund Name	Ticker Symbol	Overall Investment Rating 99 Pct = Best 0 Pct = Worst	Price As of 3/31/12	High	Low	Performance Rating/Pts	3 Mo	6 Mo	1Yr/Pct	3Yr/Pct	5Yr/Pct
FS	*ProShares UltraShort Financials	SKF	E-	40.40	97.20	39.49	E- / 0.2	-31.89	-52.13	-28.58 / 6	-50.03 / 1	-32.57 / 0
FO	*ProShares UltraShort FTSE China	FXP	E-	26.09	52.30	21.57	E / 0.4	-14.09	-42.49	0.93 / 43	-38.26 / 3	--
EN	*ProShares UltraShort Gold	GLL	E	16.81	26.94	14.29	E / 0.3	-15.14	-12.31	-37.95 / 3	-41.82 / 2	--
HL	*ProShares UltraShort Health Care	RXD	E	16.89	30.67	16.89	E / 0.3	-17.81	-34.02	-33.58 / 4	-36.00 / 3	-17.46 / 3
IN	*ProShares UltraShort Industrials	SIJ	E	32.21	68.53	31.34	E- / 0.2	-22.50	-47.53	-23.80 / 9	-48.48 / 1	-25.37 / 2
GR	*ProShares UltraShort MidCap 400	MZZ	E	29.22	60.33	28.43	E- / 0.2	-23.17	-45.19	-24.10 / 9	-47.51 / 2	-28.04 / 1
FO	*ProShares UltraShort MSCI Brazil	BZQ	E-	14.27	29.18	12.09	E / 0.4	-24.70	-45.70	3.39 / 50	--	--
FO	*ProShares UltraShort MSCI EAFE	EFU	E	20.58	34.50	19.89	E / 0.3	-20.66	-34.23	-13.96 / 16	-38.91 / 3	--
EM	*ProShares UltraShort MSCI Emg Mk	EEV	E-	25.89	51.04	24.00	E- / 0.2	-24.56	-44.20	-9.06 / 23	-46.30 / 2	--
FO	*ProShares UltraShort MSCI Europe	EPV	E	35.92	68.98	34.08	E- / 0.2	-22.92	-41.40	-24.06 / 9	--	--
FO	*ProShares UltraShort MSCI Japan	EWV	E	29.83	42.31	29.69	E / 0.4	-21.33	-21.50	-17.53 / 12	-27.11 / 4	--
FO	*ProShares UltraShort MSCI Mex In	SMK	E	35.93	74.34	35.93	E- / 0.2	-27.33	-46.98	-25.22 / 8	--	--
FO	*ProShares UltraShort MSCI PXJ	JPX	E-	40.45	76.81	39.27	E / 0.3	-22.38	-39.46	-17.04 / 13	--	--
HL	*ProShares UltraShort Nasdaq Biot	BIS	E	22.90	56.38	22.61	E- / 0.1	-29.75	-47.62	-47.24 / 2	--	--
EN	*ProShares UltraShort Oil & Gas	DUG	E	22.97	45.48	20.77	E / 0.3	-10.38	-41.86	-12.66 / 18	-41.08 / 2	-36.92 / 0
GR	*ProShares UltraShort QQQ	QID	E	30.28	63.84	29.48	E- / 0.2	-32.90	-44.33	-40.56 / 3	-47.71 / 2	-32.20 / 1
IN	*ProShares UltraShort Real Estate	SRS	E-	29.54	61.95	29.37	E- / 0.1	-19.64	-43.44	-35.81 / 4	-62.75 / 0	-50.77 / 0
GR	*ProShares UltraShort Russell 300	TWQ	E	10.24	19.66	10.16	E- / 0.2	-22.72	-41.25	-26.33 / 7	--	--
GR	*ProShares UltraShort Russell MC	SJL	E	38.20	74.78	38.20	E- / 0.2	-19.80	-42.69	-23.06 / 9	-48.57 / 1	-23.76 / 2
GR	*ProShares UltraShort Russell1000	SFK	E	13.91	26.78	13.83	E / 0.3	-24.68	-42.04	-30.52 / 5	-41.83 / 2	-22.57 / 2
IN	*ProShares UltraShort Russell2000	SJH	E	34.07	76.00	33.40	E- / 0.2	-20.75	-48.67	-26.84 / 7	-49.26 / 1	-29.10 / 1
GR	*ProShares UltraShort Russell2000	SKK	E-	26.67	61.52	25.54	E- / 0.1	-24.64	-50.06	-31.49 / 5	-51.15 / 1	-31.53 / 1
GR	*ProShares UltraShort Russell2000	TWM	E	29.62	66.58	28.37	E- / 0.2	-23.28	-49.25	-28.49 / 6	-50.07 / 1	-30.75 / 1
GR	*ProShares UltraShort S-P 500	SDS	E	15.09	28.73	14.85	E / 0.3	-21.77	-40.80	-27.28 / 7	-40.07 / 2	-19.53 / 3
IN	*ProShares UltraShort Semiconduct	SSG	E-	32.65	71.10	32.01	E- / 0.2	-28.38	-46.31	-36.96 / 4	-47.80 / 2	-31.53 / 1
EN	*ProShares UltraShort Silver	ZSL	E-	10.55	24.49	8.12	E- / 0.0	-33.52	-38.34	-54.53 / 1	-72.05 / 0	--
GR	*ProShares UltraShort SmallCap 60	SDD	E	29.98	69.48	29.00	E- / 0.2	-22.14	-50.03	-33.86 / 4	-50.72 / 1	-29.61 / 1
GR	*ProShares UltraShort Technology	REW	E	33.69	73.57	32.97	E- / 0.2	-34.02	-46.87	-40.84 / 3	-45.87 / 2	-30.03 / 1
IN	*ProShares UltraShort Telecomncti	TLL	E	37.60	56.19	35.15	E / 0.4	-12.03	-21.44	-7.39 / 26	-31.40 / 3	--
GR	*ProShares UltraShort TIPS	TPS	D	29.00	37.14	28.21	E+ / 0.6	--	-6.45	-21.39 / 10	--	--
UT	*ProShares UltraShort Utilities	SDP	E	32.10	51.75	30.98	E / 0.4	3.08	-16.01	-28.04 / 6	-32.03 / 3	-14.61 / 4
FO	*ProShares UltraShort Yen	YCS	D-	47.05	51.48	39.72	E+ / 0.8	14.90	13.81	-5.69 / 29	-15.43 / 5	--
GEI	*ProShares VIX Mid-Term Futures E	VIXM	E+	56.82	95.00	56.07	E / 0.4	-23.35	-36.49	-15.27 / 15	--	--
GEI	*ProShares VIX Short-Term Futures	VIXY	E-	35.77	126.72	33.15	E- / 0.0	-52.77	-68.77	-43.37 / 2	--	--
GR	*QuantShares US Market Neutral Qu	QLT	U	24.06	N/A	N/A	U /	-0.62	-4.72	--	--	--
GR	*QuantShares US Market Neutral Si	SIZ	U	25.16	N/A	N/A	U /	--	3.99	--	--	--
IN	*QuantShares US Market Neutral Va	CHEP	U	24.82	N/A	N/A	U /	--	0.97	--	--	--
IN	*QuantShares US Mk Neutral Hi Bet	BTAH	U	26.77	N/A	N/A	U /	--	12.97	--	--	--
GR	*QuantShares US Mkt Neut Anti-Bet	BTAL	U	21.38	N/A	N/A	U /	-9.83	-16.29	--	--	--
GR	*QuantShares US Mkt Neut Anti-Mom	NOMO	U	24.26	N/A	N/A	U /	5.43	-3.74	--	--	--
GR	*QuantShares US Mkt Neutral Momen	MOM	U	23.64	N/A	N/A	U /	--	-0.24	--	--	--
GL	*RBS Global Big Pharma ETN	DRGS	U	27.99	N/A	N/A	U /	5.42	--	--	--	--
EN	*RBS Gold Trendpilot ETN	TBAR	D-	28.97	34.38	25.98	D+ / 2.3	2.84	-1.02	12.24 / 73	--	--
IN	*RBS NASDAQ 100 Trendpilot ETN	TNDQ	U	30.21	N/A	N/A	U /	--	--	--	--	--
GL	*RBS Oil Trendpilot ETN	TWTI	U	27.44	N/A	N/A	U /	5.12	9.76	--	--	--
GR	*RBS US Large Cap Trendpilot ETN	TRND	C-	27.03	28.04	22.76	D+ / 2.5	12.34	12.16	-1.13 / 38	--	--
GR	*RBS US Mid Cap Trendpilot ETN	TRNM	E+	24.10	27.60	21.07	D- / 1.1	7.97	7.78	-10.74 / 20	--	--
IN	*RevenueShares ADR Fund	RTR	D+	35.16	41.98	28.93	C- / 3.3	10.90	16.66	-9.62 / 22	14.70 / 26	--
FS	*RevenueShares Financials Sector	RWW	C	30.48	32.67	20.00	C+ / 6.1	27.48	36.21	-4.66 / 31	21.19 / 48	--
GR	*RevenueShares Large Cap Fund	RWL	C+	26.13	26.39	19.72	C+ / 6.0	12.27	24.98	5.18 / 56	21.98 / 52	--
GR	*RevenueShares Mid Cap Fund	RWK	B-	32.12	33.08	23.01	B- / 7.5	14.07	32.48	1.47 / 45	27.15 / 73	--
IN	*RevenueShares Navellier OA A100	RWV	C	39.90	43.52	31.50	C- / 4.2	11.04	19.32	0.16 / 41	17.54 / 34	--

| Incl. in Returns | | RISK | | | | NET ASSETS | | VALUATION | | | ASSET | | | | | FUND MANAGER | |
Dividend Yield %	Expense Ratio	Risk Rating/ Pts	Standard Deviation	Beta	Avg Dura-tion	NAV as of 3/31/12	Total $(Mil)	As of 3/31/12	1 Year Average	Wtd Avg P/E	Cash %	Stocks %	Bonds %	Other %	Portfolio Turnover Ratio	Manager Quality Pct	Manager Tenure (Years)
0.00	0.95	D+ / 2.7	54.5	-2.14	N/A	40.39	226	0.02	-0.03	N/A	55	0	0	45	N/A	4	1
0.00	0.95	D+ / 2.6	56.3	-1.85	N/A	26.14	207	-0.19	-0.05	N/A	9	0	0	91	N/A	6	3
0.00	0.95	C- / 3.1	42.8	-0.38	N/A	16.94	147	-0.77	-0.45	N/A	0	0	0	100	N/A	2	4
0.00	0.95	C- / 3.9	25.4	-1.15	N/A	16.94	4	-0.30	-0.08	N/A	12	0	0	88	N/A	8	1
0.00	0.95	D+ / 2.9	45.9	-2.58	N/A	32.22	5	-0.03	0.05	N/A	0	0	0	100	N/A	9	1
0.00	0.95	C- / 3.1	40.3	-2.28	N/A	29.21	27	0.03	-0.03	N/A	0	0	0	100	N/A	7	5
0.00	0.95	D / 2.0	N/A	N/A	N/A	14.23	13	0.28	-0.01	N/A	8	0	0	92	N/A	9	3
0.00	0.95	C- / 3.0	42.7	-1.93	N/A	20.58	19	0.00	-0.03	N/A	25	0	0	75	N/A	6	3
0.00	0.95	D+ / 2.3	55.9	-2.05	N/A	25.88	79	0.04	-0.03	N/A	0	0	0	100	N/A	6	3
0.00	0.95	C- / 3.2	N/A	N/A	N/A	35.88	120	0.11	0.09	N/A	0	0	0	100	N/A	2	3
0.00	0.95	C- / 4.0	30.6	-1.10	N/A	29.80	9	0.10	N/A	N/A	6	0	0	94	N/A	9	3
0.00	0.95	D+ / 2.8	N/A	N/A	N/A	35.74	2	0.53	0.13	N/A	0	0	0	100	N/A	2	3
0.00	0.95	D+ / 2.5	N/A	N/A	N/A	40.15	2	0.75	-0.18	N/A	18	0	0	82	N/A	3	3
0.00	0.95	C- / 3.3	N/A	N/A	N/A	22.88	5	0.09	0.12	N/A	0	0	0	100	N/A	1	1
0.00	0.95	D+ / 2.9	45.8	-1.94	N/A	22.91	87	0.26	-0.15	N/A	7	0	0	93	N/A	6	1
0.00	0.95	C- / 3.2	36.8	-2.05	N/A	30.30	599	-0.07	-0.03	N/A	22	0	0	78	N/A	5	5
0.00	0.95	D+ / 2.8	62.4	-2.70	N/A	29.47	132	0.24	-0.01	N/A	4	0	0	96	N/A	1	1
0.00	0.95	C- / 3.5	N/A	N/A	N/A	10.22	2	0.20	-0.07	N/A	24	0	0	76	N/A	10	3
0.00	0.95	C- / 3.0	43.1	-2.35	N/A	37.85	1	0.92	-0.12	N/A	0	0	0	100	N/A	7	3
0.00	0.95	C- / 3.5	32.2	-1.91	N/A	14.02	2	-0.78	-0.07	N/A	0	0	0	100	N/A	9	3
0.00	0.95	D+ / 2.8	47.7	-2.59	N/A	34.36	5	-0.84	-0.18	N/A	4	0	0	96	N/A	8	3
0.00	0.95	D+ / 2.7	46.1	-2.48	N/A	26.82	9	-0.56	0.06	N/A	0	0	0	100	N/A	6	3
0.00	0.95	D+ / 2.8	45.6	-2.51	N/A	29.62	260	0.00	-0.01	N/A	14	0	0	86	N/A	6	3
0.00	0.89	C- / 3.5	32.5	-1.95	N/A	15.07	2,014	0.13	-0.01	N/A	0	0	0	100	N/A	11	2
0.00	0.95	D+ / 2.5	50.1	-2.45	N/A	32.74	16	-0.27	-0.02	N/A	7	0	0	93	N/A	8	1
0.00	0.95	D / 1.9	88.3	-1.87	N/A	10.49	191	0.57	-0.42	N/A	0	0	0	100	N/A	N/A	4
0.00	0.95	D+ / 2.9	44.6	-2.40	N/A	30.15	12	-0.56	-0.03	N/A	18	0	0	82	N/A	5	2
0.00	0.95	C- / 3.1	39.4	-2.15	N/A	33.79	11	-0.30	-0.05	N/A	6	0	0	94	N/A	7	1
0.00	0.95	D+ / 2.9	35.8	-1.56	N/A	37.53	2	0.19	0.02	N/A	0	0	0	100	N/A	14	1
0.00	0.95	B- / 7.9	N/A	N/A	N/A	29.05	4	-0.17	-0.18	N/A	0	0	0	100	N/A	5	1
0.00	0.95	C- / 3.8	20.9	-1.92	N/A	32.04	3	0.19	N/A	N/A	3	0	0	97	N/A	14	1
0.00	0.95	C+ / 6.0	19.6	-0.01	N/A	47.05	280	0.00	N/A	N/A	0	0	0	100	N/A	10	4
0.00	0.85	C / 5.6	N/A	N/A	N/A	55.95	102	1.55	0.02	N/A	0	0	0	100	N/A	1	1
0.00	0.85	D / 1.9	N/A	N/A	N/A	35.50	125	0.76	0.15	N/A	0	0	0	100	N/A	N/A	1
0.00	0.80	U /	N/A	N/A	N/A	23.91	12	0.63	N/A	N/A	0	0	0	100	N/A	N/A	1
0.00	0.81	U /	N/A	N/A	N/A	25.08	8	0.32	N/A	N/A	0	0	0	100	N/A	N/A	1
0.00	0.81	U /	N/A	N/A	N/A	25.02	5	-0.80	N/A	N/A	0	0	0	100	N/A	N/A	1
0.00	0.81	U /	N/A	N/A	N/A	27.29	5	-1.91	N/A	N/A	0	0	0	100	N/A	N/A	1
0.23	0.81	U /	N/A	N/A	N/A	21.28	4	0.47	N/A	N/A	0	0	0	100	N/A	N/A	1
0.00	0.81	U /	N/A	N/A	N/A	24.27	5	-0.04	N/A	N/A	0	0	0	100	N/A	N/A	1
0.00	0.81	U /	N/A	N/A	N/A	23.62	5	0.08	N/A	N/A	0	0	0	100	N/A	N/A	1
0.00	0.60	U /	N/A	N/A	N/A	27.96	4	0.11	N/A	N/A	0	0	0	100	N/A	N/A	1
0.00	1.00	C / 5.1	N/A	N/A	N/A	28.97	28	0.00	0.13	N/A	0	0	0	100	N/A	89	1
0.00	N/A	U /	N/A	N/A	N/A	30.16	6	0.17	N/A	N/A	0	0	0	100	N/A	N/A	1
0.00	1.10	U /	N/A	N/A	N/A	27.38	5	0.22	N/A	N/A	0	0	0	100	N/A	N/A	1
0.00	0.50	B / 8.5	N/A	N/A	N/A	27.02	66	0.04	0.03	N/A	0	0	0	100	N/A	24	2
0.00	0.50	C / 4.8	N/A	N/A	N/A	24.05	32	0.21	0.12	N/A	0	0	0	100	N/A	10	1
8.12	0.49	B- / 7.4	24.1	1.37	N/A	35.16	41	0.00	-0.02	N/A	1	98	0	1	37	12	N/A
1.41	0.49	C+ / 6.8	28.8	1.19	N/A	30.47	8	0.03	0.07	N/A	0	99	0	1	16	29	4
1.74	0.49	B / 8.3	17.9	1.08	N/A	26.14	160	-0.04	0.02	27.0	0	99	0	1	13	41	4
4.04	0.54	B- / 7.8	23.3	1.34	N/A	32.08	139	0.12	-0.05	28.0	0	99	0	1	38	38	4
2.98	0.60	B- / 7.9	19.7	1.02	N/A	39.76	8	0.35	0.07	N/A	0	100	0	0	190	25	N/A

* Denotes ETF Fund, N/A denotes number is not available

Fund Type	Fund Name	Ticker Symbol	Overall Investment Rating	PRICE Price As of 3/31/12	52 Week High	52 Week Low	Performance Rating/Pts	3 Mo	6 Mo	1Yr/Pct	Annualized 3Yr/Pct	Annualized 5Yr/Pct
GR	*RevenueShares Small Cap Fund	RWJ	B+	36.34	38.00	25.43	B+ / 8.5	13.31	33.97	4.12 / 52	31.36 / 85	--
IN	*Rockledge SectorSAM ETF	SSAM	U	25.89	N/A	N/A	U /	--	--	--	--	--
IN	*Russell 1000 High Beta ETF	HBTA	U	49.79	N/A	N/A	U /	16.57	--	--	--	--
IN	*Russell 1000 High Momentum ETF	HMTM	U	52.22	N/A	N/A	U /	12.47	26.78	--	--	--
IN	*Russell 1000 Low Beta ETF	LBTA	U	52.41	N/A	N/A	U /	7.51	--	--	--	--
IN	*Russell 1000 Low Volatility ETF	LVOL	U	51.14	N/A	N/A	U /	3.97	15.80	--	--	--
IN	*Russell 2000 High Beta ETF	SHBT	U	46.47	N/A	N/A	U /	--	33.62	--	--	--
IN	*Russell 2000 High Momentum ETF	SHMO	U	51.74	N/A	N/A	U /	12.54	29.12	--	--	--
IN	*Russell 2000 High Volatility ETF	SHVY	U	43.73	N/A	N/A	U /	13.94	23.53	--	--	--
IN	*Russell 2000 Low Beta ETF	SLBT	U	51.70	N/A	N/A	U /	--	--	--	--	--
IN	*Russell 2000 Low Volatility ETF	SLVY	U	50.93	N/A	N/A	U /	8.33	--	--	--	--
GR	*Russell Aggressive Growth ETF	AGRG	U	52.60	N/A	N/A	U /	--	24.85	--	--	--
GR	*Russell Consistent Growth ETF	CONG	U	54.00	N/A	N/A	U /	15.44	27.31	--	--	--
IN	*Russell Contrarian ETF	CNTR	U	48.09	N/A	N/A	U /	14.09	--	--	--	--
GL	*Russell Developed ex-US Hi Mom E	XHMO	U	51.51	N/A	N/A	U /	7.69	--	--	--	--
GL	*Russell Developed ex-US Low Vol	XLVO	U	51.77	N/A	N/A	U /	6.38	--	--	--	--
GL	*Russell Equity ETF	ONEF	D+	28.43	30.65	23.15	D+ / 2.7	12.17	17.35	-3.49 / 33	--	--
IN	*Russell Equity Income ETF	EQIN	U	51.45	N/A	N/A	U /	10.12	21.84	--	--	--
GR	*Russell Low P/E ETF	LWPE	U	49.42	N/A	N/A	U /	11.07	22.77	--	--	--
GR	*Russell Sm Cp Aggressive Growth	SGGG	U	64.73	N/A	N/A	U /	14.87	--	--	--	--
GR	*Russell Small Cp Consistent Gro	SCOG	U	65.39	N/A	N/A	U /	12.45	--	--	--	--
FO	*Schwab Emerging Markets Equity E	SCHE	D	25.78	30.24	20.66	D / 2.1	12.72	21.59	-11.19 / 20	--	--
FO	*Schwab International Equity ETF	SCHF	D	26.02	30.72	21.88	D / 2.0	11.05	16.54	-7.60 / 26	--	--
FO	*Schwab Intl Small-Cap Equity ETF	SCHC	D	26.41	32.10	22.36	D / 1.8	12.96	15.97	-10.10 / 22	--	--
USA	*Schwab Intmdt-Term US Treasury E	SCHR	C-	52.83	55.61	48.74	D / 1.8	-1.09	-0.15	9.03 / 66	--	--
USA	*Schwab Short-Term US Treas ETF	SCHO	C-	50.42	50.62	49.91	D- / 1.2	-0.21	-0.07	1.31 / 44	--	--
GEN	*Schwab US Aggregate Bond ETF	SCHZ	U	51.49	N/A	N/A	U /	-0.26	0.67	--	--	--
IN	*Schwab US Broad Market ETF	SCHB	C+	33.92	34.22	25.67	C+ / 6.1	12.74	26.38	7.01 / 61	--	--
GI	*Schwab US Dividend Equity ETF	SCHD	U	27.89	N/A	N/A	U /	7.07	--	--	--	--
IN	*Schwab US Large-Cap ETF	SCHX	C+	33.51	33.77	25.46	C+ / 6.2	12.76	26.01	7.55 / 63	--	--
GR	*Schwab US Large-Cap Growth ETF	SCHG	B-	34.21	34.53	25.52	B- / 7.1	15.71	28.24	8.24 / 65	--	--
IN	*Schwab US Large-Cap Value ETF	SCHV	C+	31.18	31.37	24.39	C / 5.3	10.17	23.93	6.85 / 61	--	--
GR	*Schwab US Mid-Cap ETF	SCHM	C	27.25	27.89	19.88	C / 5.4	13.29	29.15	2.16 / 47	--	--
GI	*Schwab US REIT ETF	SCHH	B-	29.57	29.63	21.66	B- / 7.3	10.56	27.47	13.27 / 74	--	--
GR	*Schwab US Small-Cap ETF	SCHA	C	37.08	38.51	26.76	C / 5.1	13.25	29.98	0.52 / 42	--	--
GEI	*Schwab US TIPS ETF	SCHP	C	55.95	56.87	51.21	D+ / 2.3	0.59	2.96	10.46 / 69	--	--
FS	*SP Bank ETF	KBE	C-	23.85	26.55	16.17	C / 4.6	20.63	37.41	-6.63 / 28	17.45 / 34	-13.61 / 4
FS	*SP Capital Markets ETF	KCE	D	34.01	40.45	24.05	D+ / 2.6	22.06	34.72	-12.85 / 18	8.48 / 14	-11.52 / 6
IN	*SP Insurance ETF	KIE	C+	41.80	45.73	29.77	B- / 7.0	12.58	32.11	-4.95 / 30	26.42 / 71	-4.38 / 13
FS	*SP Regional Banking ETF	KRE	C-	28.47	29.36	18.31	C- / 4.2	17.03	48.79	7.82 / 63	12.73 / 21	-7.09 / 9
USA	*SPDR Barclays Cap 1-3 Month T-B	BIL	C-	45.82	45.87	45.76	D- / 1.2	-0.02	-0.06	-0.06 / 40	-0.01 / 7	--
GEI	*SPDR Barclays Cap Aggregate Bd E	LAG	C-	57.75	62.19	55.15	D / 1.8	0.13	1.19	7.76 / 63	6.20 / 11	--
GI	*SPDR Barclays Cap Conv Sec ETF	CWB	C-	39.86	42.94	32.93	D+ / 2.8	10.73	15.45	-0.34 / 40	--	--
GI	*SPDR Barclays Cap EM Loc Bond ET	EBND	D+	31.50	32.84	28.32	D+ / 2.3	6.67	6.86	4.10 / 52	--	--
COH	*SPDR Barclays Cap Hi Yld Bd ETF	JNK	C-	39.37	40.93	34.09	C / 4.9	3.57	13.57	6.23 / 59	20.40 / 45	--
GEI	*SPDR Barclays Cap Int Corp Bd ET	ITR	C	33.89	34.12	32.58	D+ / 2.4	2.61	4.29	7.40 / 62	9.64 / 16	--
USA	*SPDR Barclays Cap Int Tr Treas E	ITE	C-	60.60	62.06	58.11	D- / 1.5	-0.46	0.02	6.05 / 58	3.47 / 9	--
COI	*SPDR Barclays Cap Intl Corp Bd E	IBND	D+	33.96	35.87	31.01	D / 2.1	7.74	4.78	2.83 / 49	--	--
GL	*SPDR Barclays Cap Intl Treas Bd	BWX	D+	59.94	63.86	57.37	D / 1.9	2.21	2.11	4.06 / 52	6.71 / 12	--
COI	*SPDR Barclays Cap Inv Grade FR E	FLRN	U	30.80	N/A	N/A	U /	--	--	--	--	--
COI	*SPDR Barclays Cap Iss Sco Crp B	CBND	U	31.64	N/A	N/A	U /	1.97	2.30	--	--	--
GEI	*SPDR Barclays Cap Lng-T Corp Bd	LWC	C	38.65	44.38	34.62	C- / 3.3	-1.33	3.22	15.64 / 78	14.73 / 26	--

99 Pct = Best
0 Pct = Worst

* Denotes ETF Fund, N/A denotes number is not available

| Incl. in Returns | | RISK | | | | NET ASSETS | | VALUATION | | | ASSET | | | | | FUND MANAGER | |
Dividend Yield %	Expense Ratio	Risk Rating/ Pts	Standard Deviation	Beta	Avg Dura-tion	NAV as of 3/31/12	Total $(Mil)	As of 3/31/12	1 Year Average	Wtd Avg P/E	Cash %	Stocks %	Bonds %	Other %	Portfolio Turnover Ratio	Manager Quality Pct	Manager Tenure (Years)
0.52	0.54	B- / 7.7	26.7	1.48	N/A	36.23	133	0.30	-0.04	31.1	0	99	0	1	34	40	4
0.00	1.50	U /	N/A	N/A	N/A	25.82	3	0.27	N/A	N/A	0	0	0	100	N/A	N/A	0
0.64	0.20	U /	N/A	N/A	N/A	49.69	5	0.20	N/A	N/A	0	100	0	0	N/A	N/A	1
0.49	0.20	U /	N/A	N/A	N/A	52.28	5	-0.11	N/A	N/A	0	100	0	0	N/A	N/A	1
0.12	0.20	U /	N/A	N/A	N/A	52.41	5	0.00	N/A	N/A	0	100	0	0	N/A	N/A	1
0.44	0.20	U /	N/A	N/A	N/A	51.52	56	-0.74	N/A	N/A	0	100	0	0	N/A	N/A	1
0.13	0.30	U /	N/A	N/A	N/A	46.46	9	0.02	N/A	N/A	0	100	0	0	N/A	N/A	1
0.38	0.30	U /	N/A	N/A	N/A	51.26	5	0.94	N/A	N/A	0	100	0	0	N/A	N/A	1
0.00	0.30	U /	N/A	N/A	N/A	43.88	4	-0.34	N/A	N/A	0	100	0	0	N/A	N/A	1
0.45	0.30	U /	N/A	N/A	N/A	51.48	5	0.43	N/A	N/A	0	100	0	0	N/A	N/A	1
0.44	0.30	U /	N/A	N/A	N/A	50.88	10	0.10	N/A	N/A	0	100	0	0	N/A	N/A	1
0.14	0.37	U /	N/A	N/A	N/A	52.79	5	-0.36	N/A	N/A	0	100	0	0	N/A	N/A	1
0.21	0.37	U /	N/A	N/A	N/A	53.95	31	0.09	N/A	N/A	0	100	0	0	N/A	N/A	1
0.41	0.37	U /	N/A	N/A	N/A	48.20	5	-0.23	N/A	N/A	0	100	0	0	N/A	N/A	1
1.78	0.25	U /	N/A	N/A	N/A	51.18	5	0.64	N/A	N/A	0	0	0	100	N/A	N/A	1
2.06	0.25	U /	N/A	N/A	N/A	51.47	5	0.58	N/A	N/A	0	0	0	100	N/A	N/A	1
0.14	0.53	B- / 7.9	N/A	N/A	N/A	28.54	6	-0.39	-0.02	N/A	0	100	0	0	N/A	59	2
0.66	0.37	U /	N/A	N/A	N/A	51.50	60	-0.10	N/A	N/A	0	100	0	0	N/A	N/A	1
0.65	0.37	U /	N/A	N/A	N/A	49.60	5	-0.36	N/A	N/A	0	100	0	0	N/A	N/A	1
0.09	0.45	U /	N/A	N/A	N/A	65.21	6	-0.74	N/A	N/A	0	0	0	100	N/A	N/A	1
0.22	0.45	U /	N/A	N/A	N/A	65.37	6	0.03	N/A	N/A	0	0	0	100	N/A	N/A	1
2.20	0.25	B- / 7.0	N/A	N/A	N/A	25.62	563	0.62	0.32	N/A	0	97	0	3	9	27	2
2.88	0.13	B- / 7.6	N/A	N/A	N/A	25.85	757	0.66	0.44	30.3	0	97	0	3	6	36	3
3.12	0.35	C+ / 6.8	N/A	N/A	N/A	26.18	170	0.88	0.30	94.0	0	93	0	7	18	25	2
0.88	0.12	B+ / 9.7	N/A	N/A	N/A	52.84	160	-0.02	0.04	N/A	0	0	100	0	14	68	2
0.26	0.12	B+ / 9.9	N/A	N/A	N/A	50.42	182	0.00	0.04	N/A	1	0	98	1	40	51	2
0.87	0.10	U /	N/A	N/A	N/A	51.47	218	0.04	N/A	N/A	0	0	0	100	N/A	N/A	1
1.77	0.06	B / 8.1	N/A	N/A	N/A	33.91	993	0.03	0.02	N/A	0	99	0	1	3	36	3
2.37	0.17	U /	N/A	N/A	N/A	27.88	301	0.04	N/A	N/A	0	0	0	100	N/A	N/A	1
1.77	0.08	B / 8.2	N/A	N/A	N/A	33.51	824	0.00	0.02	N/A	0	99	0	1	5	41	3
0.88	0.13	B / 8.0	N/A	N/A	N/A	34.19	395	0.06	0.02	N/A	0	100	0	0	10	38	3
2.63	0.13	B / 8.3	N/A	N/A	N/A	31.18	306	0.00	0.02	N/A	0	99	0	1	7	44	3
1.29	0.13	B- / 7.5	N/A	N/A	N/A	27.25	198	0.00	0.05	N/A	0	99	0	1	9	17	1
2.54	0.13	B- / 7.8	N/A	N/A	N/A	29.59	279	-0.07	0.02	N/A	0	100	0	0	N/A	62	N/A
1.19	0.13	B- / 7.4	N/A	N/A	N/A	37.06	627	0.05	0.03	N/A	0	99	0	1	11	14	3
0.78	0.14	B+ / 9.8	N/A	N/A	N/A	55.89	350	0.11	0.12	N/A	0	0	99	1	13	65	2
1.19	0.36	B- / 7.0	29.7	1.16	N/A	23.93	1,873	-0.33	N/A	9.8	0	100	0	0	16	23	7
1.25	0.38	C+ / 6.9	25.8	0.99	N/A	33.97	37	0.12	-0.02	21.4	0	100	0	0	14	15	7
0.88	0.37	B- / 7.5	27.0	1.46	N/A	41.77	136	0.07	-0.01	22.5	0	100	0	0	9	24	7
1.36	0.36	B- / 7.3	26.6	0.88	N/A	28.44	1,180	0.11	N/A	10.5	0	100	0	0	13	26	N/A
0.00	0.15	B+ / 9.9	0.1	N/A	N/A	45.82	1,063	0.00	N/A	N/A	0	0	99	1	628	45	N/A
2.34	0.15	B+ / 9.7	3.1	1.10	N/A	57.72	306	0.05	0.12	N/A	0	0	99	1	310	36	N/A
4.04	0.41	B / 8.5	N/A	N/A	N/A	39.78	871	0.20	-0.05	N/A	0	0	0	100	33	19	N/A
3.46	0.50	B / 8.6	N/A	N/A	N/A	31.07	168	1.38	1.15	N/A	2	0	97	1	N/A	40	N/A
7.19	0.41	C+ / 6.9	12.7	1.21	4.7	39.42	12,028	-0.13	0.27	N/A	0	0	99	1	40	21	N/A
3.32	0.16	B+ / 9.7	4.0	0.96	N/A	33.66	256	0.68	0.50	N/A	0	0	100	0	37	62	N/A
1.64	0.16	B+ / 9.8	3.0	0.19	4.4	60.63	206	-0.05	-0.03	N/A	0	0	99	1	33	57	N/A
3.14	0.55	B / 8.7	N/A	N/A	N/A	33.66	64	0.89	0.28	N/A	0	0	99	1	21	16	N/A
1.53	0.52	B / 8.8	9.7	1.05	N/A	59.76	1,781	0.30	0.11	N/A	1	0	98	1	63	44	N/A
1.17	0.15	U /	N/A	N/A	N/A	30.37	6	1.42	N/A	N/A	0	0	100	0	N/A	N/A	1
3.58	0.16	U /	N/A	N/A	N/A	31.52	22	0.38	N/A	N/A	0	0	99	1	N/A	N/A	N/A
4.95	0.17	B+ / 9.0	9.4	2.43	N/A	38.50	73	0.39	0.77	N/A	0	0	99	1	58	33	N/A

* Denotes ETF Fund, N/A denotes number is not available

Fund Type	Fund Name	Ticker Symbol	Overall Investment Rating	Price As of 3/31/12	52 Week High	52 Week Low	Performance Rating/Pts	3 Mo	6 Mo	1Yr/Pct	3Yr/Pct	5Yr/Pct
USA	*SPDR Barclays Cap Lng-T Treas ET	TLO	D+	65.50	71.72	51.12	D / 2.2	-5.90	-4.64	23.20 / 84	7.74 / 13	--
MTG	*SPDR Barclays Cap Mortg Backed E	MBG	C-	27.52	28.30	26.72	D / 1.7	0.75	1.36	6.50 / 60	4.76 / 10	--
COI	*SPDR Barclays Cap S/T Corp Bd ET	SCPB	D-	30.53	30.60	30.02	D- / 1.5	1.68	1.77	2.74 / 48	--	--
GL	*SPDR Barclays Cap S/T Itl Treas	BWZ	D+	36.59	40.21	35.40	D / 1.6	2.81	1.00	-1.59 / 37	5.01 / 10	--
USA	*SPDR Barclays Cap ShTm Trs ETF	SST	U	30.01	N/A	N/A	U /	--	--	--	--	--
USA	*SPDR Barclays Capl TIPS ETF	IPE	C	58.35	59.37	53.58	D+ / 2.5	0.57	3.37	13.02 / 74	9.35 / 15	--
GL	*SPDR DB Intl Gvt Inflation Pt Bo	WIP	C-	60.45	63.62	55.03	D+ / 2.7	6.52	7.94	5.15 / 56	10.85 / 18	--
IN	*SPDR DJ REIT ETF	RWR	A-	70.83	71.00	52.32	A- / 9.2	10.67	27.34	13.17 / 74	37.02 / 93	-1.01 / 22
GR	*SPDR DJ Total Market ETF	TMW	C+	105.15	105.88	79.51	C+ / 6.0	12.85	26.07	6.94 / 61	21.59 / 51	2.02 / 38
GI	*SPDR DJ Wilshire Glb Real Est ET	RWO	B	39.14	40.71	30.34	B / 7.8	12.84	22.23	5.32 / 56	29.25 / 80	--
FO	*SPDR DJ Wilshire Intl Real Estat	RWX	C-	36.82	41.73	30.58	C+ / 5.6	16.43	17.22	-2.68 / 34	22.30 / 53	-7.33 / 9
GR	*SPDR DJ Wilshire Large Cap ETF	ELR	C+	66.11	66.51	50.32	C+ / 5.8	12.73	21.83	7.86 / 64	21.26 / 49	1.95 / 38
GR	*SPDR DJ Wilshire Mid Cap ETF	EMM	B-	65.49	66.90	48.02	B- / 7.5	13.30	29.28	2.26 / 47	27.33 / 74	4.18 / 51
GR	*SPDR Dow Jones Industrial Averag	DIA	C+	131.80	132.61	103.84	C+ / 5.8	8.79	22.53	9.48 / 67	21.53 / 51	3.89 / 50
FO	*SPDR Euro STOXX 50 ETF	FEZ	D-	32.45	44.42	26.10	D / 1.8	10.30	15.96	-17.99 / 12	7.17 / 13	-7.10 / 9
GL	*SPDR FTSE/Macquarie Glob Infr 10	GII	C-	40.54	45.15	35.67	D+ / 2.4	2.61	7.44	-0.91 / 38	10.34 / 17	-2.54 / 18
GL	*SPDR Global Dow ETF	DGT	D+	55.83	63.84	45.27	D+ / 2.8	11.63	17.20	-7.14 / 27	11.83 / 19	-3.47 / 16
PM	*SPDR Gold Shares	GLD	C+	162.12	185.85	139.45	C+ / 5.9	6.66	2.57	16.47 / 79	22.78 / 56	19.38 / 99
GL	*SPDR MSCI ACWI ex-US ETF	CWI	C-	31.43	37.15	25.65	C- / 3.5	10.44	17.58	-8.86 / 23	15.73 / 29	-1.93 / 20
MUN	*SPDR Nuveen Barclays Bld Amr Bd	BABS	A+	58.72	62.00	47.85	A- / 9.1	3.98	4.61	27.82 / 98	--	--
MUN	*SPDR Nuveen Barclays CA Muni Bd	CXA	C	23.92	24.36	21.01	C- / 3.9	2.67	6.31	17.58 / 87	7.96 / 20	--
MUN	*SPDR Nuveen Barclays Muni Bd ETF	TFI	C	23.84	24.33	21.79	D+ / 2.9	0.94	3.76	12.78 / 82	6.68 / 17	--
MUN	*SPDR Nuveen Barclays NY Muni Bd	INY	C	23.49	34.55	20.92	C- / 3.5	1.22	5.14	14.87 / 83	7.97 / 20	--
MUN	*SPDR Nuveen Barclays Sh Tm Muni	SHM	C-	24.37	24.55	23.78	D / 1.6	0.35	0.95	3.91 / 58	2.54 / 9	--
COH	*SPDR Nuveen S&P Hi Yld Muni Bd E	HYMB	U	54.77	N/A	N/A	U /	4.85	7.78	--	--	--
GEI	*SPDR Nuveen S&P VRDO Muni Bond E	VRD	C-	30.01	30.11	29.87	D- / 1.3	0.05	0.59	0.89 / 43	--	--
FO	*SPDR Russell/Nomura PRIME Japan	JPP	D+	38.65	41.51	33.99	D+ / 2.4	9.03	8.99	0.83 / 43	9.20 / 15	-5.25 / 12
FO	*SPDR Russell/Nomura Small Cap Ja	JSC	C	44.49	46.11	39.10	C- / 3.4	8.27	4.46	6.99 / 61	14.25 / 25	-1.79 / 21
GR	*SPDR S&P 400 Mid Cap Growth ETF	MDYG	B	83.90	85.55	62.80	B / 7.7	14.03	25.97	2.64 / 48	28.57 / 79	6.16 / 62
GR	*SPDR S&P 400 Mid Cap Value ETF	MDYV	C+	58.45	59.84	42.93	C+ / 6.7	13.02	29.41	0.63 / 42	24.79 / 63	1.35 / 33
GR	*SPDR S&P 500 ETF	SPY	C+	140.81	141.83	107.43	C+ / 5.8	12.69	25.76	7.97 / 64	21.08 / 48	1.54 / 34
GR	*SPDR S&P 500 Growth ETF	SPYG	C+	65.25	65.60	50.75	C+ / 6.6	12.00	23.60	11.11 / 70	23.17 / 57	4.61 / 54
IN	*SPDR S&P 500 Value ETF	SPYV	C+	70.54	71.25	53.41	C / 5.3	12.88	27.30	4.46 / 54	19.45 / 40	-0.84 / 23
GR	*SPDR S&P 600 Small Cap ETF	SLY	B	73.84	74.84	53.30	B / 8.0	12.07	31.90	5.05 / 55	29.06 / 80	4.30 / 52
GR	*SPDR S&P 600 Small Cap Growth ET	SLYG	B	124.36	126.07	90.77	B+ / 8.3	11.06	28.49	5.41 / 57	30.90 / 84	5.61 / 59
GR	*SPDR S&P 600 Small Cap Value ETF	SLYV	B-	75.60	76.73	53.21	B / 7.6	13.17	34.07	3.91 / 51	27.18 / 73	3.00 / 44
IN	*SPDR S&P Aerospace & Defense ETF	XAR	U	61.03	N/A	N/A	U /	9.30	--	--	--	--
HL	*SPDR S&P Biotech ETF	XBI	C+	80.46	82.69	54.71	C+ / 6.6	21.17	35.20	19.70 / 82	19.87 / 43	10.39 / 89
FO	*SPDR S&P BRIC 40 ETF	BIK	D+	24.66	30.48	19.11	C- / 3.7	12.50	22.08	-15.66 / 14	17.00 / 32	--
FO	*SPDR S&P China ETF	GXC	D	68.37	84.15	51.87	C- / 3.0	9.74	23.10	-14.13 / 16	13.48 / 23	5.62 / 60
IN	*SPDR S&P Dividend ETF	SDY	C+	56.64	57.29	45.72	C / 5.2	5.89	18.60	7.61 / 63	20.40 / 45	2.13 / 39
EM	*SPDR S&P Emerg Middle East&Afric	GAF	C	71.12	79.81	57.97	C / 5.1	13.34	20.86	-4.03 / 32	20.85 / 47	5.10 / 57
EM	*SPDR S&P Emerging Asia Pacific E	GMF	C-	74.15	89.05	61.80	C- / 4.2	12.37	18.96	-10.83 / 20	18.77 / 38	5.80 / 61
EM	*SPDR S&P Emerging Europe ETF	GUR	D+	42.93	58.35	33.47	C / 4.4	19.28	22.33	-21.36 / 10	20.41 / 45	-4.51 / 13
EM	*SPDR S&P Emerging Latin America	GML	C	78.87	91.61	59.85	C+ / 5.7	14.33	26.53	-10.29 / 21	23.05 / 57	7.39 / 70
EM	*SPDR S&P Emerging Markets ETF	GMM	C-	66.12	78.26	53.08	C / 4.7	13.59	20.68	-10.14 / 21	20.39 / 45	4.90 / 57
GI	*SPDR S&P Emg Markets Dividend ET	EDIV	D	50.85	56.10	42.00	D+ / 2.8	8.39	18.57	-1.37 / 37	--	--
GL	*SPDR S&P Emg Markets Sm Cap ETF	EWX	D+	45.93	56.85	35.97	C+ / 5.7	21.73	24.38	-11.45 / 20	22.76 / 56	--
EN	*SPDR S&P Glbl Natural Resources	GNR	D-	52.67	64.69	42.60	D- / 1.2	7.45	16.68	-15.72 / 14	--	--
HL	*SPDR S&P Health Care Equipment E	XHE	C	55.84	57.36	44.66	C / 4.7	13.18	19.58	6.10 / 59	--	--
HL	*SPDR S&P Health Care Services ET	XHS	U	61.96	N/A	N/A	U /	9.79	--	--	--	--
IN	*SPDR S&P Homebuilders ETF	XHB	B-	21.35	21.99	12.21	B / 8.2	25.08	61.37	17.44 / 80	24.02 / 61	-6.86 / 10

* Denotes ETF Fund, N/A denotes number is not available

Incl. in Returns — Dividend Yield %	Expense Ratio	Risk Rating/ Pts	3 Year — Standard Deviation	Beta	Avg Dura-tion	NAV as of 3/31/12	Total $(Mil)	Premium/Discount — As of 3/31/12	1 Year Average	Wtd Avg P/E	Cash %	Stocks %	Bonds %	Other %	Portfolio Turnover Ratio	Manager Quality Pct	Manager Tenure (Years)
2.76	0.15	B / 8.7	12.5	1.03	15.6	65.65	46	-0.23	-0.06	N/A	0	0	99	1	26	43	N/A
1.54	0.21	B+ / 9.6	3.8	1.36	N/A	27.52	33	0.00	0.03	N/A	0	0	99	1	1,107	31	N/A
1.65	0.13	B+ / 9.9	N/A	N/A	N/A	30.43	651	0.33	0.25	N/A	0	0	99	1	46	51	N/A
8.74	0.36	B / 8.8	9.4	0.82	N/A	36.48	244	0.30	0.20	N/A	1	0	98	1	85	45	N/A
0.21	0.12	U /	N/A	N/A	N/A	29.97	6	0.13	N/A	N/A	0	0	0	100	N/A	N/A	1
1.51	0.20	B+ / 9.7	5.2	0.16	8.3	58.31	601	0.07	0.03	N/A	0	0	99	1	21	81	N/A
6.77	0.52	B / 8.8	11.4	1.03	N/A	60.29	1,284	0.27	0.02	N/A	0	0	99	1	23	69	N/A
2.46	0.26	B- / 7.8	25.9	1.28	N/A	70.86	1,795	-0.04	N/A	61.4	0	100	0	0	10	85	N/A
1.54	0.22	B / 8.2	16.6	1.02	N/A	105.12	173	0.03	N/A	44.2	0	100	0	0	2	45	12
2.31	0.50	B- / 7.9	22.3	1.23	N/A	39.01	421	0.33	0.26	N/A	0	100	0	0	9	67	4
2.56	0.61	C+ / 6.1	23.1	1.03	N/A	36.67	2,663	0.41	0.25	161.2	0	99	0	1	10	77	N/A
1.61	0.22	B / 8.4	15.1	0.92	N/A	66.04	43	0.11	0.08	46.0	0	100	0	0	5	57	6
1.01	0.27	B- / 7.8	21.1	1.23	N/A	65.39	75	0.15	0.01	38.0	0	100	0	0	23	52	7
2.32	0.17	B / 8.6	14.4	0.88	N/A	131.84	12,603	-0.03	0.01	26.2	0	100	0	0	5	64	N/A
1.20	0.30	C+ / 6.2	30.0	1.35	N/A	32.34	454	0.34	N/A	N/A	0	100	0	0	7	12	10
4.25	0.60	B / 8.6	14.3	0.60	N/A	40.56	37	-0.05	-0.18	20.9	0	99	0	1	6	54	N/A
1.31	0.52	B- / 7.7	18.3	0.82	N/A	55.93	101	-0.18	-0.11	35.8	1	98	0	1	108	39	7
0.00	0.40	B / 8.2	21.0	0.95	N/A	161.48	73,592	0.40	0.15	N/A	0	0	0	100	N/A	51	8
1.92	0.35	B- / 7.6	22.7	1.06	N/A	31.45	472	-0.06	-0.01	28.2	0	99	0	1	4	48	N/A
4.54	0.35	B+ / 9.0	N/A	N/A	N/A	58.49	64	0.39	-1.05	N/A	0	0	99	1	58	26	N/A
3.51	0.20	B+ / 9.0	8.3	1.72	8.9	23.92	79	0.00	-0.63	N/A	1	0	98	1	29	23	N/A
3.12	0.22	B+ / 9.4	5.7	1.22	8.5	23.86	1,076	-0.08	-0.29	N/A	0	0	99	1	16	29	N/A
3.30	0.20	B+ / 9.3	7.1	1.28	9.7	23.53	28	-0.17	-0.68	N/A	0	0	99	1	37	35	N/A
1.44	0.20	B+ / 9.8	2.1	0.34	3.2	24.34	1,519	0.12	-0.01	N/A	0	0	100	0	25	45	N/A
5.39	0.45	U /	N/A	N/A	N/A	54.62	71	0.27	N/A	N/A	0	0	88	12	N/A	N/A	1
0.26	0.21	B+ / 9.9	N/A	N/A	N/A	30.02	15	-0.03	-0.13	N/A	0	0	99	1	77	54	N/A
2.06	0.51	B / 8.1	15.1	0.54	N/A	38.92	16	-0.69	-0.62	N/A	0	100	0	0	3	55	N/A
1.82	0.56	B / 8.7	14.8	0.37	N/A	44.52	96	-0.07	-0.29	N/A	0	100	0	0	10	82	N/A
0.62	0.28	B- / 7.9	21.2	1.23	N/A	83.62	67	0.33	-0.02	46.0	0	100	0	0	88	58	N/A
1.49	0.28	B- / 7.9	20.2	1.16	N/A	58.23	29	0.38	0.02	24.6	0	99	0	1	82	47	7
1.74	0.09	B / 8.2	16.2	1.00	N/A	140.79	105,621	0.01	N/A	46.3	0	100	0	0	4	45	N/A
1.40	0.22	B / 8.1	16.5	0.99	N/A	65.26	228	-0.02	-0.01	67.3	0	99	0	1	46	58	12
1.96	0.22	B / 8.3	16.4	0.99	N/A	70.57	180	-0.04	-0.06	19.0	0	100	0	0	41	35	7
1.15	0.24	B- / 7.7	22.8	1.30	N/A	73.49	103	0.48	0.06	45.8	0	99	0	1	82	53	7
1.10	0.27	B- / 7.6	22.9	1.28	N/A	124.23	162	0.10	-0.03	60.5	0	100	0	0	102	62	12
1.08	0.27	B- / 7.8	23.4	1.33	N/A	75.40	143	0.27	0.01	31.7	0	100	0	0	88	39	12
1.34	0.35	U /	N/A	N/A	N/A	61.47	15	-0.72	N/A	N/A	0	0	0	100	N/A	N/A	N/A
0.00	0.37	B- / 7.0	23.3	0.94	N/A	80.43	535	0.04	0.05	101.6	0	100	0	0	74	30	N/A
1.93	0.51	C+ / 6.8	28.0	1.12	N/A	24.72	403	-0.24	-0.14	N/A	0	100	0	0	10	52	N/A
0.88	0.60	C+ / 6.5	27.5	1.00	N/A	68.80	894	-0.63	0.08	87.9	0	100	0	0	9	38	N/A
2.84	0.36	B / 8.8	14.8	0.84	N/A	56.67	9,296	-0.05	0.01	21.4	0	100	0	0	52	65	7
5.15	0.60	B- / 7.4	23.9	0.81	N/A	70.95	99	0.24	-0.12	N/A	0	100	0	0	4	63	N/A
3.26	0.60	C+ / 6.9	28.3	1.07	N/A	74.42	469	-0.36	-0.14	73.1	0	100	0	0	20	24	N/A
3.75	0.61	C+ / 6.0	34.8	1.26	N/A	42.77	103	0.37	-0.24	N/A	0	100	0	0	10	21	N/A
3.11	0.60	B- / 7.0	31.8	1.18	N/A	79.04	150	-0.22	-0.12	49.5	0	100	0	0	12	33	N/A
2.55	0.60	B- / 7.2	26.3	1.02	N/A	66.17	179	-0.08	0.05	50.6	0	99	0	1	4	37	N/A
0.32	0.62	B- / 7.2	N/A	N/A	N/A	50.69	330	0.32	0.74	N/A	0	100	0	0	42	15	N/A
2.44	0.66	C / 5.1	30.1	1.23	N/A	45.52	933	0.90	-0.11	182.6	0	99	0	1	70	67	N/A
1.72	0.40	C+ / 6.9	N/A	N/A	N/A	52.38	254	0.55	0.18	N/A	2	97	0	1	32	16	N/A
0.15	0.35	B / 8.3	N/A	N/A	N/A	56.13	22	-0.52	0.11	N/A	0	100	0	0	N/A	43	N/A
0.99	0.35	U /	N/A	N/A	N/A	62.30	13	-0.55	N/A	N/A	0	100	0	0	N/A	N/A	N/A
0.72	0.37	B- / 7.1	33.7	1.61	N/A	21.36	1,393	-0.05	-0.01	21.2	0	100	0	0	38	16	N/A

* Denotes ETF Fund, N/A denotes number is not available

				PRICE			PERFORMANCE					
99 Pct = Best *0 Pct = Worst*			Overall Investment Rating	Price As of 3/31/12	52 Week High	52 Week Low	Perform-ance Rating/Pts	% Total Return Through 3/31/12			Annualized	
Fund Type	Fund Name	Ticker Symbol						3 Mo	6 Mo	1Yr/Pct	3Yr/Pct	5Yr/Pct
EM	*SPDR S&P International Div ETF	DWX	C-	49.97	64.33	42.50	C- / 4.2	8.21	14.17	-11.14 / 20	19.89 / 43	--
GL	*SPDR S&P International Mid Cap E	MDD	C-	28.29	33.94	23.79	C- / 4.2	13.70	15.43	-6.94 / 27	18.48 / 37	--
FO	*SPDR S&P International Small Cap	GWX	C	28.77	33.24	23.85	C / 5.1	14.30	17.70	-6.21 / 28	21.50 / 51	--
IN	*SPDR S&P Metals & Mining ETF	XME	D+	49.72	77.44	40.17	C- / 3.6	1.72	11.63	-32.58 / 5	21.16 / 48	-2.71 / 17
GR	*SPDR S&P MidCap 400 ETF	MDY	C+	180.71	184.97	132.94	C+ / 6.8	13.30	27.54	0.70 / 43	25.15 / 64	4.15 / 51
EN	*SPDR S&P Oil & Gas Equip & Serv	XES	C	36.41	44.61	25.58	C+ / 5.9	5.18	28.69	-16.88 / 13	25.32 / 65	3.13 / 45
IN	*SPDR S&P Oil & Gas Expl & Prod	XOP	C	56.91	65.76	37.67	C+ / 6.2	8.23	33.44	-11.45 / 20	24.75 / 63	7.07 / 67
HL	*SPDR S&P Pharmaceuticals ETF	XPH	B	57.10	57.46	42.32	B+ / 8.6	11.44	25.54	22.37 / 83	30.59 / 83	11.29 / 93
IN	*SPDR S&P Retail ETF	XRT	A	61.25	63.04	43.50	A / 9.4	16.75	33.31	21.16 / 83	36.88 / 93	8.27 / 76
EM	*SPDR S&P Russia	RBL	D-	30.93	41.29	22.84	D / 1.6	17.52	26.50	-22.13 / 10	--	--
EM	*SPDR S&P SC Emerging Asia Pac ET	GMFS	U	45.04	N/A	N/A	U /	--	--	--	--	--
IN	*SPDR S&P Semiconductor ETF	XSD	C	52.50	61.99	40.09	C / 5.3	18.56	24.48	-8.45 / 24	21.48 / 50	2.03 / 38
GR	*SPDR S&P Software & Services ETF	XSW	U	64.37	N/A	N/A	U /	14.46	--	--	--	--
GR	*SPDR S&P Telecom ETF	XTL	D	46.72	54.48	37.18	D / 2.2	11.91	21.39	-10.12 / 22	--	--
UT	*SPDR S&P Transportation ETF	XTN	D	49.25	55.29	36.13	D+ / 2.7	9.37	26.43	-7.67 / 25	--	--
GL	*SPDR S&P WORLD EX-US ETF	GWL	C-	24.47	28.61	20.09	C- / 3.5	12.30	17.32	-6.98 / 27	15.28 / 27	--
GL	*SPDR SP Intl Con Disc Sect ETF	IPD	C	29.30	31.80	22.92	C / 5.3	20.36	21.78	4.23 / 53	19.57 / 41	--
GL	*SPDR SP Intl Con Stap Sect ETF	IPS	C+	33.57	33.83	28.23	C+ / 5.8	7.79	13.59	10.47 / 69	22.34 / 53	--
EN	*SPDR SP Intl Energy Sector ETF	IPW	D+	26.12	31.58	20.53	D+ / 2.7	4.16	18.50	-12.45 / 18	12.88 / 21	--
FS	*SPDR SP Intl Finl Sector ETF	IPF	D+	17.46	22.04	14.30	D+ / 2.7	16.38	13.29	-14.34 / 16	11.96 / 19	--
HL	*SPDR SP Intl Health Care ETF	IRY	C	32.26	37.24	27.91	C- / 3.8	5.08	11.77	5.74 / 58	15.82 / 29	--
GL	*SPDR SP Intl Industrial ETF	IPN	C-	25.67	31.09	20.62	C- / 3.9	11.85	14.15	-11.01 / 20	17.92 / 35	--
GL	*SPDR SP Intl Materials Sec ETF	IRV	D+	25.46	33.23	20.77	C- / 3.7	10.86	14.85	-17.29 / 12	18.01 / 36	--
GL	*SPDR SP Intl Tech Sector ETF	IPK	D+	26.43	29.17	20.59	C- / 3.9	17.21	22.89	-4.05 / 32	15.84 / 29	--
GL	*SPDR SP Intl Telecom Sect ETF	IST	D+	22.83	27.77	21.45	D+ / 2.6	1.12	3.33	-8.37 / 24	12.81 / 21	--
UT	*SPDR SP Intl Utils Sector ETF	IPU	D	17.33	22.19	16.05	D- / 1.3	5.29	1.85	-13.95 / 16	3.20 / 8	--
FS	*SPDR SP Mortgage Finance ETF	KME	D-	37.74	41.52	27.61	E+ / 0.9	--	--	-7.60 / 26	--	--
FO	*SPDR STOXX Europe 50 ETF	FEU	D	32.03	38.85	26.37	D+ / 2.8	8.51	16.73	-7.18 / 26	12.25 / 20	-4.97 / 13
IN	*SPDR Wells Fargo Preferred Stk E	PSK	C-	44.92	48.96	38.62	D+ / 2.7	7.65	9.34	4.98 / 55	--	--
GR	*Technology Select Sector SPDR	XLK	C+	30.16	30.54	22.47	B- / 7.2	18.89	28.76	17.74 / 80	23.56 / 59	6.24 / 63
GR	*Teucrium Corn	CORN	D-	39.26	50.69	37.51	E+ / 0.8	-6.48	-1.55	-11.50 / 19	--	--
GR	*Teucrium Natural Gas	NAGS	E+	11.04	24.12	10.94	E- / 0.1	-20.46	-39.80	-53.90 / 1	--	--
GL	*Teucrium Soybean	SOYB	U	24.10	N/A	N/A	U /	9.25	8.90	--	--	--
GL	*Teucrium Sugar	CANE	U	23.79	N/A	N/A	U /	3.75	-2.36	--	--	--
GL	*Teucrium Wheat	WEAT	U	21.09	N/A	N/A	U /	-5.85	-7.09	--	--	--
GI	*Teucrium WTI Crude Oil	CRUD	D-	46.46	56.36	36.91	D- / 1.4	4.22	22.01	-13.53 / 17	--	--
IN	*TrimTabs Float Shrink ETF	TTFS	U	33.80	N/A	N/A	U /	12.60	--	--	--	--
IN	*UBS E Tracs Alerian MLP Infrast	MLPI	D	33.48	35.21	25.69	C- / 3.1	1.15	16.17	6.69 / 60	--	--
GR	*UBS E Tracs CMCI Agriculture TR	UAG	D-	28.74	34.25	24.74	C- / 3.0	3.87	3.16	-8.35 / 24	15.01 / 27	--
GR	*UBS E Tracs CMCI Energy TR	UBN	D-	16.50	23.43	13.89	D / 2.2	6.80	14.03	-8.44 / 24	9.20 / 15	--
GR	*UBS E Tracs CMCI Food Tr	FUD	D-	27.50	32.00	25.01	D+ / 2.3	2.88	2.15	-7.72 / 25	11.35 / 18	--
GR	*UBS E Tracs CMCI Gold TR	UBG	D+	44.17	52.14	38.42	C / 5.2	5.72	-1.19	14.97 / 77	21.28 / 49	--
GR	*UBS E Tracs CMCI Industrial Meta	UBM	D-	20.59	26.30	17.08	D+ / 2.8	5.76	2.96	-17.17 / 13	15.14 / 27	--
GR	*UBS E Tracs CMCI Livestock Tr	UBC	E+	19.81	23.50	19.81	D- / 1.0	-6.07	-9.50	-14.46 / 15	0.51 / 7	--
GR	*UBS E Tracs CMCI Silver TR	USV	C-	45.35	70.79	37.48	B / 8.1	16.23	6.76	-15.61 / 14	34.55 / 90	--
GR	*UBS E Tracs CMCI Total Return	UCI	D-	22.68	26.52	19.89	D+ / 2.6	5.21	9.25	-10.18 / 21	12.40 / 20	--
IN	*UBS E Tracs DJ-UBS Comm Idx Tot	DJCI	E+	26.68	33.66	25.60	E+ / 0.8	0.86	1.41	-17.19 / 12	--	--
GR	*UBS E Tracs Long Platinum ETN	PTM	D-	20.07	24.42	15.55	C- / 3.2	24.50	13.78	-3.60 / 33	12.31 / 20	--
IN	*UBS E-TRACS 1-Month S&P500VIX Fu	VXAA	U	41.00	N/A	N/A	U /	-52.28	-68.54	--	--	--
IN	*UBS E-TRACS 2-Month S&P500VIX Fu	VXBB	U	52.84	N/A	N/A	U /	-40.56	-57.11	--	--	--
EN	*UBS E-TRACS 2x Levd Lng Alerian	MLPL	C-	41.66	45.93	25.46	C+ / 6.7	2.36	33.10	11.42 / 71	--	--
GR	*UBS E-TRACS 2x Levd Long WF BDC	BDCL	U	21.00	N/A	N/A	U /	20.03	34.96	--	--	--

Dividend Yield %	Expense Ratio	Risk Rating/ Pts	Standard Deviation	Beta	Avg Dura-tion	NAV as of 3/31/12	Total $(Mil)	As of 3/31/12	1 Year Average	Wtd Avg P/E	Cash %	Stocks %	Bonds %	Other %	Portfolio Turnover Ratio	Manager Quality Pct	Manager Tenure (Years)
2.63	0.46	B- / 7.3	26.6	0.95	N/A	49.71	850	0.52	0.24	28.1	0	100	0	0	142	47	N/A
3.70	0.46	B- / 7.7	20.8	0.97	N/A	28.22	40	0.25	0.01	27.4	0	100	0	0	32	66	N/A
3.33	0.61	B- / 7.8	22.6	1.03	N/A	28.62	741	0.52	-0.02	18.8	0	100	0	0	22	75	N/A
0.91	0.36	C+ / 6.3	37.4	1.90	N/A	49.70	736	0.04	0.01	19.2	0	100	0	0	68	10	N/A
0.88	0.25	B- / 7.9	20.6	1.20	N/A	180.83	10,449	-0.07	-0.02	35.4	0	100	0	0	15	43	N/A
0.48	0.37	C+ / 6.4	35.8	1.46	N/A	36.39	344	0.05	N/A	37.2	0	100	0	0	96	49	N/A
0.80	0.36	C+ / 6.9	31.7	1.49	N/A	56.93	925	-0.04	-0.02	19.0	0	100	0	0	87	23	N/A
0.71	0.36	B- / 7.3	14.8	0.62	N/A	57.08	337	0.04	0.02	141.6	0	100	0	0	50	89	N/A
0.65	0.36	B / 8.1	22.8	1.18	N/A	61.25	793	0.00	0.01	43.6	0	100	0	0	69	84	N/A
2.80	0.59	C+ / 5.7	N/A	N/A	N/A	30.71	60	0.72	-0.11	N/A	0	100	0	0	15	14	N/A
0.00	0.65	U /	N/A	N/A	N/A	45.37	7	-0.73	N/A	N/A	0	0	0	100	N/A	N/A	0
0.35	0.37	C+ / 6.9	29.1	1.52	N/A	52.44	55	0.11	N/A	50.6	0	100	0	0	88	16	N/A
0.17	0.35	U /	N/A	N/A	N/A	64.20	22	0.26	N/A	N/A	0	0	0	100	N/A	N/A	N/A
0.51	0.35	C+ / 6.9	N/A	N/A	N/A	46.68	5	0.09	0.09	N/A	0	100	0	0	N/A	6	N/A
0.27	0.35	C+ / 6.9	N/A	N/A	N/A	50.06	12	-1.62	-0.01	N/A	0	100	0	0	N/A	9	N/A
2.39	0.35	B- / 7.5	22.3	1.04	N/A	24.30	165	0.70	0.25	44.3	0	100	0	0	2	44	N/A
0.39	0.50	B / 8.0	23.2	1.01	N/A	29.18	9	0.41	-0.33	17.8	0	100	0	0	9	77	N/A
2.15	0.51	B / 8.8	15.1	0.63	N/A	33.45	20	0.36	0.03	16.8	0	100	0	0	5	87	N/A
2.75	0.51	B- / 7.4	26.6	1.07	N/A	26.22	12	-0.38	-0.18	13.4	0	100	0	0	4	23	N/A
1.26	0.51	B- / 7.3	26.4	0.97	N/A	17.53	8	-0.40	-0.28	17.1	0	100	0	0	4	22	N/A
3.88	0.50	B / 8.5	14.7	0.69	N/A	32.40	19	-0.43	0.16	40.2	1	98	0	1	5	53	N/A
1.23	0.50	B- / 7.7	21.9	1.01	N/A	25.67	14	0.00	-0.29	24.5	1	98	0	1	20	64	N/A
1.61	0.51	C+ / 6.5	29.9	1.28	N/A	25.38	14	0.32	-0.45	84.5	0	100	0	0	1	37	N/A
0.08	0.51	B- / 7.0	23.2	1.00	N/A	26.48	15	-0.19	-0.36	88.2	0	99	0	1	1	54	N/A
0.19	0.51	B / 8.1	17.7	0.71	N/A	22.71	19	0.53	0.12	29.2	0	100	0	0	8	57	N/A
1.08	0.51	B- / 7.6	17.8	1.02	N/A	17.26	15	0.41	0.27	23.4	0	100	0	0	2	12	N/A
1.97	0.36	C+ / 5.9	N/A	N/A	N/A	37.77	4	-0.08	-0.10	N/A	0	100	0	0	35	18	N/A
3.69	0.31	B- / 7.1	24.6	1.13	N/A	31.84	30	0.60	-0.10	N/A	0	100	0	0	9	23	10
4.21	0.46	B+ / 9.1	N/A	N/A	N/A	44.78	190	0.31	0.10	N/A	3	0	0	97	26	57	N/A
1.28	0.19	B- / 7.6	17.7	1.01	N/A	30.16	9,815	0.00	N/A	104.2	0	100	0	0	5	60	14
0.00	3.50	B- / 7.0	N/A	N/A	N/A	39.17	70	0.23	-0.08	N/A	0	0	0	100	N/A	9	2
0.00	1.50	C / 4.5	N/A	N/A	N/A	11.02	2	0.18	-0.20	N/A	0	0	0	100	N/A	N/A	1
0.00	1.53	U /	N/A	N/A	N/A	24.06	2	0.17	N/A	N/A	0	0	0	100	N/A	N/A	1
0.00	1.53	U /	N/A	N/A	N/A	23.77	2	0.08	N/A	N/A	0	0	0	100	N/A	N/A	1
0.00	1.53	U /	N/A	N/A	N/A	21.42	2	-1.54	N/A	N/A	0	0	0	100	N/A	N/A	1
0.00	1.54	C+ / 6.3	N/A	N/A	N/A	46.43	4	0.06	0.11	N/A	0	0	0	100	N/A	6	1
0.10	0.99	U /	N/A	N/A	N/A	33.73	7	0.21	N/A	N/A	0	0	0	100	N/A	N/A	1
1.21	0.85	C / 5.4	N/A	N/A	N/A	33.54	245	-0.18	-0.03	N/A	0	0	0	100	N/A	66	2
0.00	0.65	C / 4.7	26.0	0.81	N/A	28.60	3	0.49	0.05	N/A	0	0	0	100	N/A	39	4
0.00	0.65	C / 4.6	20.7	0.54	N/A	16.21	4	1.79	0.06	N/A	0	0	0	100	N/A	30	4
0.00	0.65	C / 4.9	23.6	0.76	N/A	27.43	6	0.26	0.04	N/A	0	0	0	100	N/A	31	4
0.00	0.30	C / 5.1	19.7	0.04	N/A	44.15	5	0.05	0.17	N/A	0	0	0	100	N/A	92	4
0.00	0.65	C / 4.5	25.7	1.11	N/A	20.82	4	-1.10	-0.30	N/A	0	0	0	100	N/A	15	4
0.00	0.65	C / 5.1	13.1	-0.05	N/A	19.87	8	-0.30	-0.12	N/A	0	0	0	100	N/A	56	4
0.00	0.40	C- / 3.4	46.6	1.10	N/A	45.84	4	-1.07	-0.08	N/A	0	0	0	100	N/A	79	4
0.00	0.65	C / 4.9	19.2	0.91	N/A	22.66	12	0.09	0.07	N/A	0	0	0	100	N/A	23	4
0.00	0.50	C / 4.7	N/A	N/A	N/A	26.66	23	0.08	-0.09	N/A	0	0	0	100	N/A	5	3
0.00	0.65	C- / 4.1	28.4	0.99	N/A	18.97	66	5.80	1.84	N/A	0	0	0	100	N/A	17	4
0.00	0.85	U /	N/A	N/A	N/A	40.80	6	0.49	N/A	N/A	0	0	0	100	N/A	N/A	1
0.00	0.85	U /	N/A	N/A	N/A	52.27	7	1.09	N/A	N/A	0	0	0	100	N/A	N/A	1
2.30	0.85	C / 4.8	N/A	N/A	N/A	41.63	104	0.07	-0.09	N/A	0	0	0	100	N/A	94	2
0.00	0.85	U /	N/A	N/A	N/A	20.91	37	0.43	N/A	N/A	0	0	0	100	N/A	N/A	1

* Denotes ETF Fund, N/A denotes number is not available

Fund Type	Fund Name	Ticker Symbol	Overall Investment Rating	PRICE Price As of 3/31/12	52 Week High	52 Week Low	PERFORMANCE Performance Rating/Pts	3 Mo	6 Mo	1Yr/Pct	3Yr/Pct (Annualized)	5Yr/Pct (Annualized)
IN	*UBS E-TRACS 3-Month S&P500VIX Fu	VXCC	U	63.95	N/A	N/A	U /	-32.13	-46.53	--	--	--
IN	*UBS E-TRACS 4-Month S&P500VIX Fu	VXDD	U	68.71	N/A	N/A	U /	--	-41.09	--	--	--
IN	*UBS E-TRACS 5-Month S&P500VIX Fu	VXEE	U	75.07	N/A	N/A	U /	--	-32.92	--	--	--
IN	*UBS E-TRACS 6-Month S&P500VIX Fu	VXFF	U	79.35	N/A	N/A	U /	-16.98	-29.69	--	--	--
EN	*UBS E-TRACS Alerian Nat Gas MLP	MLPG	D-	30.28	31.66	25.47	D / 1.7	1.93	11.62	-1.70 / 36	--	--
IN	*UBS E-TRACS DS 1-Mo S&P500VIX Fu	AAVX	U	160.98	N/A	N/A	U /	85.76	120.01	--	--	--
IN	*UBS E-TRACS DS 2-Mo S&P500VIX Fu	BBVX	U	148.72	N/A	N/A	U /	54.90	83.47	--	--	--
IN	*UBS E-TRACS DS 3-Mo S&P500VIX Fu	CCVX	U	133.14	N/A	N/A	U /	40.19	61.89	--	--	--
IN	*UBS E-TRACS DS 4-Mo S&P500VIX Fu	DDVX	U	131.11	N/A	N/A	U /	36.33	50.70	--	--	--
IN	*UBS E-TRACS DS 5-Mo S&P500VIX Fu	EEVX	U	119.02	N/A	N/A	U /	22.37	34.93	--	--	--
IN	*UBS E-TRACS DS 6-Mo S&P500VIX Fu	FFVX	U	115.70	N/A	N/A	U /	--	30.10	--	--	--
IN	*UBS E-TRACS ISE Solid St Dr Id E	SSDD	U	33.40	N/A	N/A	U /	26.56	48.44	--	--	--
GL	*UBS E-TRACS Mo 2x Lvgd ISE SSD I	SSDL	U	42.47	N/A	N/A	U /	--	100.80	--	--	--
GL	*UBS E-TRACS Monthly 2X LISE CCTR	LSKY	U	43.04	N/A	N/A	U /	--	--	--	--	--
GR	*UBS E-TRACS Nat Gas Ft Contango	GASZ	U	31.61	N/A	N/A	U /	16.13	22.09	--	--	--
GR	*UBS E-TRACS Oil Fut Contago ETN	OILZ	U	25.49	N/A	N/A	U /	2.37	5.86	--	--	--
PM	*UBS E-TRACS S&P 500 Gold Hedged	SPGH	C+	51.27	80.00	36.96	A+ / 9.6	20.35	30.06	26.72 / 86	--	--
GR	*UBS E-TRACS Wells Fargo BDC Inde	BDCS	U	22.49	N/A	N/A	U /	10.62	15.22	--	--	--
EN	*UBS E-TRACS Wells Fargo MLP Inde	MLPW	D-	27.92	29.03	22.22	D+ / 2.4	--	14.91	3.25 / 49	--	--
IN	*UBS ETRACS FsherGartman Rsk Off	OFF	U	21.36	N/A	N/A	U /	--	--	--	--	--
IN	*UBS ETRACS FsherGartman Rsk On E	ONN	U	28.35	N/A	N/A	U /	--	--	--	--	--
EN	*United States 12 Month Oil Fund	USL	D	45.81	51.61	33.65	C- / 3.1	5.36	30.40	-6.64 / 27	12.49 / 21	--
EN	*United States Brent Oil Fund	BNO	B-	86.30	89.07	66.80	B- / 7.3	15.62	27.59	9.43 / 67	--	--
IN	*United States Commodity Index	USCI	D	61.27	73.01	56.34	D- / 1.0	4.97	5.37	-13.28 / 17	--	--
IN	*United States Copper Index	CPER	U	27.13	N/A	N/A	U /	10.74	--	--	--	--
EN	*United States Gasoline Fund LP	UGA	B	57.16	58.63	44.65	B+ / 8.5	18.29	24.42	11.64 / 72	31.17 / 84	--
EN	*United States Heating Oil Fund	UHN	C	35.99	38.67	30.73	C / 4.3	9.49	14.23	-0.80 / 39	18.79 / 39	--
EN	*United States Natural Gas Fund	UNG	E	15.92	50.56	15.92	E- / 0.1	-38.39	-55.80	-64.87 / 0	-49.36 / 1	--
EN	*United States Oil Fund	USO	D	39.23	45.60	29.10	D / 2.2	2.94	28.66	-9.13 / 23	8.25 / 14	-5.48 / 11
EN	*United States Short Oil Fund	DNO	D-	34.51	48.47	32.32	E+ / 0.7	-4.43	-25.65	-2.73 / 34	--	--
EN	*US 12 Month Natural Gas Fund	UNL	E	16.28	36.05	16.20	E- / 0.1	-22.92	-41.61	-52.15 / 1	--	--
UT	*Utilities Select Sector SPDR	XLU	C	35.05	36.27	29.45	C- / 3.6	-1.70	6.34	13.57 / 75	15.39 / 28	1.11 / 32
IN	*Vanguard 500 Index ETF	VOO	B	64.37	64.90	49.12	C+ / 6.2	12.54	25.66	7.90 / 64	--	--
IN	*Vanguard Consumer Discret ETF	VCR	A-	72.20	73.18	52.47	B+ / 8.7	16.81	31.28	15.12 / 77	31.53 / 85	4.37 / 53
IN	*Vanguard Consumer Staples ETF	VDC	C+	86.28	86.45	71.74	C / 5.4	5.90	15.82	16.11 / 79	20.04 / 43	7.64 / 72
GR	*Vanguard Div Appreciation ETF	VIG	C+	58.55	58.93	46.54	C / 4.9	7.63	21.37	7.05 / 61	19.11 / 39	3.68 / 49
EN	*Vanguard Energy ETF	VDE	C-	105.18	118.43	79.78	C- / 4.1	4.33	23.80	-8.82 / 23	18.60 / 38	4.58 / 54
GR	*Vanguard Extended Market Index E	VXF	C+	59.34	60.99	43.01	B- / 7.1	14.49	30.18	1.10 / 44	26.04 / 69	3.30 / 47
USA	*Vanguard Extnd Durtn Trea Idx ET	EDV	D	107.65	133.73	75.90	D+ / 2.4	-11.06	-9.47	43.33 / 98	7.41 / 13	--
FS	*Vanguard Financials ETF	VFH	C	32.97	34.64	23.00	C / 5.3	19.52	33.54	-1.63 / 37	19.16 / 39	-10.39 / 7
FO	*Vanguard FTSE All-Wld ex-US S/C	VSS	D	88.97	107.84	74.25	D / 2.0	14.70	17.10	-10.44 / 21	--	--
FO	*Vanguard FTSE All-World ex-US ET	VEU	C-	44.22	52.29	36.72	C- / 3.6	11.53	18.23	-8.22 / 25	16.08 / 30	-1.85 / 20
GL	*Vanguard Global ex-US RE I Fd ET	VNQI	D+	47.01	53.14	39.14	D+ / 2.9	15.50	18.46	-4.93 / 30	--	--
GR	*Vanguard Growth ETF	VUG	C+	70.97	71.52	53.09	C+ / 6.7	15.23	27.68	11.30 / 71	23.07 / 57	4.80 / 56
HL	*Vanguard HealthCare Index ETF	VHT	C+	67.57	67.67	52.70	C / 5.5	10.39	21.25	13.80 / 75	19.95 / 43	4.50 / 54
IN	*Vanguard High Dividend Yield ETF	VYM	B-	48.47	48.79	38.28	C+ / 6.1	7.81	21.72	12.07 / 72	22.19 / 53	1.65 / 35
IN	*Vanguard Industrials Index ETF	VIS	C+	69.54	72.60	50.93	B- / 7.0	12.00	31.32	-0.15 / 40	25.71 / 67	2.40 / 41
GR	*Vanguard Info Tech Ind ETF	VGT	B-	74.18	75.13	53.81	B / 7.9	20.87	31.73	16.75 / 80	26.03 / 69	7.34 / 70
GEI	*Vanguard Intermediate Term Bond	BIV	C-	86.96	88.93	81.32	D+ / 2.4	0.54	2.14	11.07 / 70	9.66 / 16	--
COI	*Vanguard Intm-Term Corp Bd Idx E	VCIT	C	83.75	85.05	78.63	D+ / 2.5	2.23	5.11	9.69 / 68	--	--
USA	*Vanguard Intm-Term Govt Bd Idx E	VGIT	C-	64.66	68.95	60.43	D / 1.8	-1.25	-0.07	8.72 / 66	--	--
GR	*Vanguard Large Cap ETF	VV	C+	64.43	65.00	48.92	C+ / 6.0	12.93	26.02	7.59 / 63	21.48 / 50	2.05 / 38

* Denotes ETF Fund, N/A denotes number is not available

www.thestreetratings.com

| Incl. in Returns | | RISK | | | | NET ASSETS | | VALUATION | | | ASSET | | | | | FUND MANAGER | |
Dividend Yield %	Expense Ratio	Risk Rating/ Pts	Standard Deviation	Beta	Avg Dura-tion	NAV as of 3/31/12	Total $(Mil)	As of 3/31/12	1 Year Average	Wtd Avg P/E	Cash %	Stocks %	Bonds %	Other %	Portfolio Turnover Ratio	Manager Quality Pct	Manager Tenure (Years)
0.00	0.85	U /	N/A	N/A	N/A	62.99	8	1.52	N/A	N/A	0	0	0	100	N/A	N/A	1
0.00	0.85	U /	N/A	N/A	N/A	67.99	8	1.06	N/A	N/A	0	0	0	100	N/A	N/A	1
0.00	0.85	U /	N/A	N/A	N/A	73.39	9	2.29	N/A	N/A	0	0	0	100	N/A	N/A	1
0.00	0.85	U /	N/A	N/A	N/A	77.68	9	2.15	N/A	N/A	0	0	0	100	N/A	N/A	1
1.39	0.85	C / 5.1	N/A	N/A	N/A	30.42	16	-0.46	-0.11	N/A	0	0	0	100	N/A	67	2
0.00	1.35	U /	N/A	N/A	N/A	162.40	12	-0.87	N/A	N/A	0	0	0	100	N/A	N/A	1
0.00	1.35	U /	N/A	N/A	N/A	150.37	11	-1.10	N/A	N/A	0	0	0	100	N/A	N/A	1
0.00	1.35	U /	N/A	N/A	N/A	134.19	11	-0.78	N/A	N/A	0	0	0	100	N/A	N/A	1
0.00	1.35	U /	N/A	N/A	N/A	131.82	11	-0.54	N/A	N/A	0	0	0	100	N/A	N/A	1
0.00	1.35	U /	N/A	N/A	N/A	121.16	10	-1.77	N/A	N/A	0	0	0	100	N/A	N/A	1
0.00	1.35	U /	N/A	N/A	N/A	116.09	10	-0.34	N/A	N/A	0	0	0	100	N/A	N/A	1
0.00	0.65	U /	N/A	N/A	N/A	33.34	13	0.18	N/A	N/A	0	0	0	100	N/A	N/A	1
0.00	0.65	U /	N/A	N/A	N/A	42.78	17	-0.72	N/A	N/A	0	0	0	100	N/A	N/A	1
0.00	0.60	U /	N/A	N/A	N/A	43.31	16	-0.62	N/A	N/A	0	0	0	100	N/A	N/A	1
0.00	0.85	U /	N/A	N/A	N/A	31.54	12	0.22	N/A	N/A	0	0	0	100	N/A	N/A	1
0.00	0.85	U /	N/A	N/A	N/A	25.40	10	0.35	N/A	N/A	0	0	0	100	N/A	N/A	1
0.00	0.85	C / 4.9	N/A	N/A	N/A	51.46	19	-0.37	0.30	N/A	0	0	0	100	N/A	87	2
0.00	0.85	U /	N/A	N/A	N/A	22.39	10	0.45	N/A	N/A	0	0	0	100	N/A	N/A	1
1.24	0.85	C / 5.3	N/A	N/A	N/A	28.09	20	-0.61	-0.04	N/A	0	0	0	100	N/A	82	N/A
0.00	1.15	U /	N/A	N/A	N/A	21.39	13	-0.14	N/A	N/A	0	0	0	100	N/A	N/A	1
0.00	0.85	U /	N/A	N/A	N/A	28.33	23	0.07	N/A	N/A	0	0	0	100	N/A	N/A	1
0.00	0.84	C+/ 6.8	25.6	0.90	N/A	45.81	175	0.00	0.04	N/A	87	0	0	13	N/A	31	5
0.00	0.99	B-/ 7.9	N/A	N/A	N/A	86.31	77	-0.01	0.02	N/A	0	0	0	100	N/A	91	N/A
0.00	1.16	B-/ 7.9	N/A	N/A	N/A	61.31	400	-0.07	0.03	N/A	0	0	0	100	N/A	8	N/A
0.00	0.95	U /	N/A	N/A	N/A	27.08	3	0.18	N/A	N/A	0	0	0	100	N/A	N/A	1
0.00	0.91	B-/ 7.5	28.0	0.83	N/A	56.89	157	0.47	0.20	N/A	91	0	0	9	N/A	90	4
0.00	0.90	B-/ 7.8	24.5	0.78	N/A	35.74	11	0.70	0.13	N/A	93	0	0	7	N/A	72	4
0.00	0.86	C-/ 3.0	36.9	0.30	N/A	16.01	910	-0.56	-0.02	N/A	100	0	0	0	N/A	N/A	N/A
0.00	0.66	C+/ 6.5	29.5	0.98	N/A	39.21	1,626	0.05	0.09	N/A	92	0	0	8	N/A	18	6
0.00	0.93	C+/ 6.3	N/A	N/A	N/A	34.56	7	-0.14	-0.12	N/A	0	0	0	100	N/A	13	3
0.00	0.93	C-/ 3.9	N/A	N/A	N/A	16.37	30	-0.55	-0.02	N/A	0	0	0	100	N/A	N/A	N/A
3.67	0.19	B+/ 9.1	10.1	0.96	N/A	35.05	6,347	0.00	N/A	18.5	0	99	0	1	3	48	14
1.77	0.05	B+/ 9.4	N/A	N/A	N/A	64.40	2,757	-0.05	0.01	46.1	0	0	0	100	4	46	21
1.18	1.90	B / 8.2	21.2	1.20	N/A	72.21	423	-0.01	N/A	43.3	0	100	0	0	7	74	2
2.20	0.19	B+/ 9.1	10.4	0.54	N/A	86.29	946	-0.01	0.02	28.8	0	99	0	1	7	83	2
1.86	0.18	B / 8.6	13.6	0.82	N/A	58.55	10,227	0.00	0.02	26.9	0	99	0	1	15	57	6
1.54	0.19	B-/ 7.5	24.5	1.07	N/A	105.20	1,957	-0.02	0.01	19.4	0	99	0	1	11	53	2
0.05	0.10	B-/ 7.7	21.8	1.27	N/A	59.34	1,367	0.00	-0.02	44.3	0	100	0	0	14	40	15
2.99	0.13	B-/ 7.0	25.4	2.00	N/A	107.12	168	0.49	0.43	N/A	0	0	100	0	22	17	5
0.51	0.19	B-/ 7.6	23.9	1.00	N/A	32.99	668	-0.06	0.02	22.0	0	99	0	1	10	42	2
2.78	0.28	C+/ 6.7	N/A	N/A	N/A	88.49	993	0.54	0.07	95.8	0	99	0	1	37	25	3
3.10	0.18	B-/ 7.6	23.2	1.08	N/A	44.14	6,683	0.18	0.10	34.6	0	99	0	1	6	47	4
2.84	0.35	B-/ 7.2	N/A	N/A	N/A	46.97	238	0.09	0.37	N/A	0	99	0	1	7	61	2
1.09	0.10	B-/ 7.9	17.0	1.03	N/A	70.98	6,870	-0.01	0.02	70.8	0	99	0	1	23	53	18
1.55	0.19	B / 8.6	13.1	0.65	N/A	67.53	786	0.06	0.01	45.8	0	100	0	0	9	70	8
2.71	0.13	B / 8.8	14.4	0.86	N/A	48.46	2,993	0.02	0.07	21.1	0	99	0	1	16	68	6
1.75	0.19	B-/ 7.7	23.2	1.35	N/A	69.53	502	0.01	N/A	26.5	0	99	0	1	5	29	2
0.65	0.19	B-/ 7.4	19.8	1.14	N/A	74.12	2,268	0.08	0.03	108.4	0	99	0	1	6	56	2
3.20	0.11	B+/ 9.6	4.5	1.65	8.5	86.75	2,984	0.24	0.30	N/A	0	0	100	0	61	33	4
3.44	0.14	B+/ 9.7	N/A	N/A	N/A	83.31	1,756	0.53	0.60	N/A	0	0	0	100	80	38	3
1.54	0.14	B+/ 9.6	N/A	N/A	N/A	64.70	95	-0.06	0.10	N/A	0	0	99	1	41	70	3
1.73	0.10	B / 8.2	16.6	1.02	N/A	64.45	3,300	-0.03	N/A	45.7	0	99	0	1	7	45	8

* Denotes ETF Fund, N/A denotes number is not available

Fund Type	Fund Name	Ticker Symbol	Overall Investment Rating	PRICE Price As of 3/31/12	52 Week High	52 Week Low	PERFORMANCE Performance Rating/Pts	3 Mo	6 Mo	1Yr/Pct	Annualized 3Yr/Pct	Annualized 5Yr/Pct
GEI	*Vanguard Long Term Bd Idx ETF	BLV	C	88.91	94.25	77.00	C- / 3.0	-2.72	-0.24	19.17 / 81	13.06 / 22	--
COI	*Vanguard Long-Term Corp Bd Idx E	VCLT	C-	84.98	89.36	76.03	D+ / 2.8	-1.28	2.97	15.29 / 78	--	--
USA	*Vanguard Long-Term Govt Bd Idx E	VGLT	C-	70.04	77.16	58.25	D+ / 2.5	-6.29	-5.22	21.44 / 83	--	--
IN	*Vanguard Materials ETF	VAW	C	82.21	90.18	60.58	C+ / 5.8	12.42	30.30	-4.36 / 32	22.38 / 54	2.97 / 44
IN	*Vanguard Mega Cap 300 ETF	MGC	C+	48.25	48.62	36.84	C+ / 5.7	12.69	25.78	8.78 / 66	20.59 / 45	--
GR	*Vanguard Mega Cap 300 Growth ETF	MGK	C+	55.28	55.64	41.48	C+ / 6.6	15.22	27.90	13.45 / 75	22.46 / 54	--
IN	*Vanguard Mega Cap 300 Value ETF	MGV	C	41.92	42.64	32.50	C / 4.8	10.50	23.94	4.22 / 53	18.78 / 38	--
GR	*Vanguard Mid Cap ETF	VO	B-	81.58	83.20	60.95	B- / 7.0	13.41	27.01	2.07 / 46	25.86 / 68	2.64 / 43
GR	*Vanguard Mid Cap Growth ETF	VOT	B-	68.92	70.39	50.67	B- / 7.2	15.77	27.49	1.88 / 46	26.14 / 70	3.56 / 48
GR	*Vanguard Mid Cap Value Index ETF	VOE	B-	57.46	59.02	43.53	C+ / 6.9	11.22	26.56	2.28 / 47	25.60 / 67	1.34 / 33
MTG	*Vanguard Mort-Backed Secs Idx ET	VMBS	C-	51.87	54.73	50.13	D / 1.6	0.27	1.34	5.52 / 57	--	--
FO	*Vanguard MSCI EAFE ETF	VEA	D	34.03	39.94	28.64	C- / 3.3	11.14	16.93	-6.52 / 28	14.23 / 25	--
EM	*Vanguard MSCI Emerging Markets E	VWO	C-	43.47	50.92	34.21	C / 4.8	13.77	24.24	-10.53 / 21	20.69 / 46	3.87 / 50
FO	*Vanguard MSCI Europe ETF	VGK	D	46.09	56.69	38.40	C- / 3.4	11.25	18.70	-8.26 / 24	14.96 / 27	-4.31 / 13
FO	*Vanguard MSCI Pacific Fund ETF	VPL	C-	53.14	58.24	46.58	C- / 3.2	11.66	13.39	-1.97 / 36	13.65 / 23	-2.57 / 18
IN	*Vanguard REIT ETF	VNQ	A-	63.65	63.97	47.10	A- / 9.1	10.61	27.51	12.74 / 73	36.60 / 92	0.15 / 28
GR	*Vanguard Russell 1000 Gro Idx ET	VONG	B	67.84	68.23	52.44	B- / 7.2	14.80	26.60	10.35 / 69	--	--
GR	*Vanguard Russell 1000 Index ETF	VONE	C+	64.36	64.87	49.38	C+ / 6.1	12.87	25.98	7.14 / 62	--	--
GR	*Vanguard Russell 1000 Val Index	VONV	C	61.35	61.93	47.03	C / 4.9	10.90	25.60	4.00 / 52	--	--
GR	*Vanguard Russell 2000 Gro Idx ET	VTWG	C	68.91	71.32	49.47	C / 5.0	13.10	29.92	0.16 / 41	--	--
GR	*Vanguard Russell 2000 Idx ETF	VTWO	C	65.82	68.58	48.42	C / 4.7	12.46	29.74	-0.52 / 39	--	--
GR	*Vanguard Russell 2000 Val Index	VTWV	C-	62.90	65.49	46.93	C / 4.3	10.99	29.58	-1.33 / 37	--	--
GR	*Vanguard Russell 3000 Index ETF	VTHR	C+	64.60	64.95	48.76	C+ / 6.2	12.89	26.79	7.10 / 62	--	--
GR	*Vanguard S&P 500 G Indx ETF	VOOG	B-	67.38	67.76	52.34	C+ / 6.5	11.99	23.23	11.23 / 71	--	--
GR	*Vanguard S&P 500 Val Indx ETF	VOOV	C+	62.20	62.87	47.14	C / 5.5	12.54	27.30	4.27 / 53	--	--
GR	*Vanguard S&P Mid-Cap 400 Gro ETF	IVOG	C	68.87	70.46	51.51	C / 5.1	14.12	25.86	2.60 / 48	--	--
GR	*Vanguard S&P Mid-Cap 400 Index E	IVOO	C	66.53	67.65	49.20	C / 4.8	13.42	26.98	1.45 / 45	--	--
GR	*Vanguard S&P Mid-Cap 400 Value E	IVOV	C	63.46	65.44	47.42	C / 4.7	11.51	29.67	0.17 / 41	--	--
GR	*Vanguard S&P SC 600 G Indx ETF	VIOG	C	70.50	71.78	51.80	C / 5.4	10.46	28.08	4.87 / 54	--	--
GR	*Vanguard S&P SC 600 Indx ETF	VIOO	C+	68.96	69.80	49.66	C+ / 6.1	11.59	31.51	4.33 / 53	--	--
GR	*Vanguard S&P SC 600 Val Indx ETF	VIOV	C+	67.29	68.21	47.66	C+ / 6.7	12.93	34.23	4.12 / 52	--	--
GEI	*Vanguard Short-Term Bd Idx ETF	BSV	C-	80.94	81.94	79.93	D- / 1.5	0.40	0.73	3.31 / 50	3.62 / 9	--
COI	*Vanguard Short-Term Crp Bd Idx E	VCSH	C-	79.04	79.36	77.15	D / 1.7	1.93	2.93	4.51 / 54	--	--
USA	*Vanguard Short-Term Gvt Bd Idx E	VGSH	C-	60.86	61.24	60.45	D- / 1.2	-0.12	--	1.26 / 44	--	--
GR	*Vanguard Small Cap ETF	VB	B-	78.72	81.85	57.25	B- / 7.3	13.02	30.03	0.58 / 42	26.92 / 72	3.36 / 47
GR	*Vanguard Small Cap Growth ETF	VBK	B-	86.95	89.84	62.27	B / 7.8	13.94	30.84	0.92 / 43	28.71 / 79	5.11 / 57
GR	*Vanguard Small Cap Value ETF	VBR	C+	70.38	73.50	51.93	C+ / 6.8	12.35	29.45	0.10 / 41	25.05 / 64	1.45 / 34
IN	*Vanguard Telecom Serv ETF	VOX	C-	65.01	73.14	57.01	C- / 3.2	4.57	10.65	-2.14 / 35	14.40 / 25	-0.68 / 24
GEI	*Vanguard Total Bond Market ETF	BND	C-	83.28	84.58	79.54	D / 1.9	0.17	1.40	7.71 / 63	6.72 / 12	--
GL	*Vanguard Total Intl Stock Index	VXUS	D	45.65	53.92	38.10	D / 2.0	11.61	16.90	-8.25 / 25	--	--
GI	*Vanguard Total Stock Market ETF	VTI	C+	72.26	72.99	54.58	C+ / 6.1	12.86	26.43	6.69 / 60	22.09 / 53	2.17 / 39
EM	*Vanguard Total World Stock ETF	VT	C	48.27	52.35	38.67	C / 4.4	11.79	21.58	-1.68 / 36	18.24 / 36	--
UT	*Vanguard Utilities Index ETF	VPU	C	74.84	77.57	62.94	C- / 3.6	-1.75	6.67	11.61 / 72	15.59 / 28	1.08 / 31
IN	*Vanguard Value ETF	VTV	C+	57.68	58.75	44.47	C / 5.1	10.54	24.28	3.86 / 51	19.82 / 42	-0.76 / 24
GL	*VelocityShares 2x Inv Copper ETN	SCPR	U	47.86	N/A	N/A	U /	--	--	--	--	--
GL	*VelocityShares 2x Inverse Pallad	IPAL	U	37.51	N/A	N/A	U /	-6.83	--	--	--	--
GL	*VelocityShares 2x Inverse Platin	IPLT	U	41.16	N/A	N/A	U /	-30.81	--	--	--	--
GL	*VelocityShares 2x Long Palladium	LPAL	U	51.13	N/A	N/A	U /	-2.31	--	--	--	--
GL	*VelocityShares 2x Long Platinum	LPLT	U	53.10	N/A	N/A	U /	32.92	--	--	--	--
GL	*VelocityShares 3x Inv Nat Gas ET	DGAZ	U	95.09	N/A	N/A	U /	--	--	--	--	--
GL	*VelocityShares 3x Inverse Crude	DWTI	U	38.26	N/A	N/A	U /	--	--	--	--	--
GL	*VelocityShares 3x Inverse Gold E	DGLD	U	46.04	N/A	N/A	U /	-17.98	--	--	--	--

99 Pct = Best
0 Pct = Worst

* Denotes ETF Fund, N/A denotes number is not available

Incl. in Returns		RISK	3 Year		Avg Dura-tion	NET ASSETS		VALUATION		Wtd Avg P/E	ASSET				Portfolio Turnover Ratio	FUND MANAGER	
Dividend Yield %	Expense Ratio	Risk Rating/ Pts	Standard Deviation	Beta		NAV as of 3/31/12	Total $(Mil)	As of 3/31/12	1 Year Average		Cash %	Stocks %	Bonds %	Other %		Manager Quality Pct	Manager Tenure (Years)
4.14	0.11	B+ / 9.0	8.7	2.58	21.6	88.70	633	0.24	0.33	N/A	1	0	98	1	45	21	4
4.86	0.14	B+ / 9.2	N/A	N/A	N/A	84.60	761	0.45	0.94	N/A	0	0	0	100	110	32	3
3.12	0.14	B / 8.7	N/A	N/A	N/A	70.32	66	-0.40	0.06	N/A	0	0	0	100	40	38	3
1.92	0.19	B- / 7.3	26.6	1.50	N/A	82.17	642	0.05	N/A	36.3	0	99	0	1	14	16	2
1.77	0.12	B / 8.2	16.0	0.99	N/A	48.26	375	-0.02	0.01	47.5	0	99	0	1	8	44	5
1.03	0.12	B- / 7.9	16.6	1.01	N/A	55.24	598	0.07	N/A	75.2	0	99	0	1	26	51	2
2.46	0.12	B / 8.4	16.4	0.99	N/A	41.90	384	0.05	0.01	17.5	0	100	0	0	24	35	2
0.02	0.10	B / 8.0	19.7	1.17	N/A	81.63	3,686	-0.06	N/A	36.0	0	99	0	1	22	52	14
0.02	0.10	B- / 7.8	20.3	1.18	N/A	68.95	1,216	-0.04	-0.01	46.2	0	99	0	1	41	51	6
0.02	0.10	B / 8.1	19.8	1.17	N/A	57.48	946	-0.03	0.01	25.9	0	99	0	1	41	53	6
1.60	0.15	B+ / 9.8	N/A	N/A	N/A	51.88	161	-0.02	0.22	N/A	0	0	0	100	344	37	3
0.06	0.12	C+ / 5.7	22.1	1.04	N/A	33.93	7,971	0.29	0.22	323.5	0	99	0	1	5	39	4
2.08	0.20	B- / 7.1	27.6	1.07	N/A	43.40	55,080	0.16	0.09	46.8	0	99	0	1	10	33	4
4.14	0.14	C / 5.4	25.3	1.18	N/A	45.98	2,670	0.24	0.12	320.2	0	100	0	0	6	30	4
2.98	0.14	B / 8.0	17.4	0.77	N/A	53.11	1,578	0.06	0.02	N/A	0	99	0	1	4	61	15
3.15	0.12	B- / 7.8	25.3	1.26	N/A	63.67	10,692	-0.03	N/A	60.3	0	99	0	1	12	85	16
1.12	0.15	B / 8.5	N/A	N/A	N/A	67.77	74	0.10	-0.04	N/A	0	99	0	1	N/A	59	N/A
1.59	0.12	B / 8.3	N/A	N/A	N/A	64.37	44	-0.02	N/A	N/A	0	99	0	1	20	37	2
1.60	0.15	B / 8.1	N/A	N/A	N/A	61.26	45	0.15	0.08	N/A	0	100	0	0	39	25	N/A
0.27	0.20	B- / 7.4	N/A	N/A	N/A	68.94	20	-0.04	-0.01	N/A	0	100	0	0	N/A	13	2
0.82	0.15	B- / 7.5	N/A	N/A	N/A	65.82	64	0.00	0.01	N/A	0	100	0	0	34	13	2
1.14	0.20	B- / 7.5	N/A	N/A	N/A	62.90	12	0.00	0.03	N/A	0	100	0	0	101	12	2
1.41	0.15	B / 8.2	N/A	N/A	N/A	64.43	25	0.26	0.03	N/A	0	100	0	0	32	34	2
1.40	0.15	B / 8.8	N/A	N/A	N/A	67.39	72	-0.01	0.03	N/A	0	100	0	0	26	67	2
1.90	0.15	B / 8.1	N/A	N/A	N/A	62.15	36	0.08	0.06	N/A	0	99	0	1	23	25	2
0.48	0.20	B- / 7.9	N/A	N/A	N/A	68.64	34	0.34	0.04	N/A	0	100	0	0	40	18	2
0.71	0.15	B- / 7.9	N/A	N/A	N/A	66.34	36	0.29	0.05	N/A	0	100	0	0	26	17	2
1.25	0.20	B- / 7.6	N/A	N/A	N/A	63.93	13	-0.74	-0.12	N/A	0	100	0	0	48	13	2
0.48	0.20	B- / 7.9	N/A	N/A	N/A	70.71	17	-0.30	N/A	N/A	0	100	0	0	106	23	2
0.69	0.15	B- / 7.8	N/A	N/A	N/A	68.64	17	0.47	0.03	N/A	0	99	0	1	42	21	2
0.97	0.20	B- / 7.7	N/A	N/A	N/A	66.93	16	0.54	-0.01	N/A	0	99	0	1	70	20	2
1.58	0.11	B+ / 9.8	1.6	0.52	4.1	80.93	7,665	0.01	0.09	N/A	1	0	98	1	67	46	7
2.32	0.14	B+ / 9.9	N/A	N/A	N/A	78.73	2,680	0.39	0.35	N/A	0	0	0	100	63	47	3
0.41	0.14	B+ / 9.9	N/A	N/A	N/A	60.83	167	0.05	0.06	N/A	0	0	0	100	69	53	3
0.05	0.10	B- / 7.6	23.1	1.33	N/A	78.71	4,229	0.01	-0.01	45.7	0	100	0	0	17	37	21
0.14	0.10	B- / 7.3	23.2	1.32	N/A	86.99	2,144	-0.05	-0.01	69.8	0	100	0	0	40	44	8
0.08	0.10	B- / 7.8	22.8	1.31	N/A	70.32	1,965	0.09	0.01	28.1	0	100	0	0	30	32	14
3.09	0.19	B / 8.5	16.0	0.76	N/A	65.05	424	-0.06	0.02	18.3	0	100	0	0	21	47	8
2.82	0.10	B+ / 9.7	2.7	0.99	12.3	83.08	15,026	0.24	0.21	N/A	0	0	100	0	73	44	20
2.83	0.18	B- / 7.3	N/A	N/A	N/A	45.50	674	0.33	0.53	42.3	0	99	0	1	3	33	4
1.70	0.05	B / 8.1	17.1	1.05	N/A	72.30	20,780	-0.06	0.01	45.6	0	100	0	0	5	45	18
2.11	0.22	B- / 7.8	20.2	0.74	N/A	48.20	1,141	0.15	0.22	44.7	0	100	0	0	10	60	4
3.78	0.19	B+ / 9.2	10.0	0.94	N/A	74.83	1,034	0.01	0.03	19.7	0	99	0	1	6	50	2
2.37	0.10	B / 8.3	16.6	1.01	N/A	57.69	5,635	-0.02	0.02	18.9	0	100	0	0	23	40	18
0.00	1.35	U /	N/A	N/A	N/A	49.12	1	-2.57	N/A	N/A	0	0	0	100	N/A	N/A	0
0.00	1.35	U /	N/A	N/A	N/A	37.66	2	-0.40	N/A	N/A	0	0	0	100	N/A	N/A	1
0.00	1.35	U /	N/A	N/A	N/A	41.05	2	0.27	N/A	N/A	0	0	0	100	N/A	N/A	1
0.00	1.35	U /	N/A	N/A	N/A	51.31	4	-0.35	N/A	N/A	0	0	0	100	N/A	N/A	1
0.00	1.35	U /	N/A	N/A	N/A	53.35	4	-0.47	N/A	N/A	0	0	0	100	N/A	N/A	1
0.00	1.65	U /	N/A	N/A	N/A	94.52	5	0.60	N/A	N/A	0	0	0	100	N/A	N/A	0
0.00	1.35	U /	N/A	N/A	N/A	38.10	1	0.42	N/A	N/A	0	0	0	100	N/A	N/A	0
0.00	1.35	U /	N/A	N/A	N/A	45.88	2	0.35	N/A	N/A	0	0	0	100	N/A	N/A	1

* Denotes ETF Fund, N/A denotes number is not available

Fund Type	Fund Name	Ticker Symbol	Overall Investment Rating	Price As of 3/31/12	52 Week High	52 Week Low	Performance Rating/Pts	3 Mo	6 Mo	1Yr/Pct	3Yr/Pct	5Yr/Pct
GL	*VelocityShares 3x Inverse Silver	DSLV	U	31.58	N/A	N/A	U /	-48.33	--	--	--	--
GL	*VelocityShares 3x Long Crude ETN	UWTI	U	53.77	N/A	N/A	U /	--	--	--	--	--
GL	*VelocityShares 3x Long Gold ETN	UGLD	U	45.12	N/A	N/A	U /	16.77	--	--	--	--
GL	*VelocityShares 3x Long Nat Gas E	UGAZ	U	20.92	N/A	N/A	U /	--	--	--	--	--
GL	*VelocityShares 3x Long Silver ET	USLV	U	39.33	N/A	N/A	U /	43.23	--	--	--	--
IN	*VelocityShares Daily 2x VIX S-T	TVIX	E-	7.24	109.14	5.85	E- / 0.0	-77.34	-91.88	-79.66 / 0	--	--
IN	*VelocityShares Dly 2x VIX Med-T	TVIZ	E-	34.55	101.88	33.47	E- / 0.0	-42.56	-64.57	-38.41 / 3	--	--
GEI	*VelocityShares Dly Invs VIX M-T	ZIV	C+	15.84	18.18	10.29	A- / 9.0	27.12	44.78	2.84 / 49	--	--
GI	*VelocityShares Dly Invs VIX ST E	XIV	C-	12.27	19.35	4.89	A+ / 9.9	88.48	124.03	-13.08 / 18	--	--
GL	*VelocityShares TM 3x Inv Brnt Cr	DOIL	U	40.97	N/A	N/A	U /	--	--	--	--	--
GL	*VelocityShares TM 3x Lng Brnt Cr	UOIL	U	58.82	N/A	N/A	U /	--	--	--	--	--
GI	*VelocityShares VIX Medium-Term E	VIIZ	U	66.24	100.70	64.24	U /	-20.50	-33.40	--	--	--
GI	*VelocityShares VIX Short-Term ET	VIIX	E-	36.42	127.94	33.79	E- / 0.0	-52.50	-68.49	-42.19 / 2	--	--
GL	*WCM/BNY Mellon Focused Gro ADR E	AADR	C-	30.95	32.25	24.62	C- / 3.4	10.10	20.90	0.41 / 42	--	--
GL	*WisdomTree Asia Local Debt	ALD	D	51.40	55.39	47.50	D / 1.7	2.81	4.87	2.36 / 47	--	--
FO	*WisdomTree Asia Pacific ex-Japan	AXJL	C	64.10	71.52	51.25	C / 5.4	10.80	20.80	-2.85 / 34	21.92 / 52	3.41 / 47
FO	*WisdomTree Australia and NZ Debt	AUNZ	D+	21.89	27.17	20.13	D / 2.0	2.59	-4.62	-4.54 / 31	9.34 / 15	--
FO	*WisdomTree Australia Divide	AUSE	C+	56.08	66.03	44.20	C+ / 6.6	12.42	22.49	-4.26 / 32	25.43 / 66	2.80 / 43
FO	*WisdomTree Commodity Country Equ	CCXE	C+	31.43	36.18	24.30	C+ / 6.3	13.12	23.88	-2.64 / 34	24.20 / 61	2.16 / 39
FO	*WisdomTree DEFA	DWM	D+	44.90	53.18	37.90	C- / 3.3	10.25	15.28	-5.42 / 30	14.63 / 26	-3.61 / 15
FO	*WisdomTree DEFA Equity Income	DTH	D+	38.95	47.61	33.63	C- / 3.0	7.18	13.22	-6.93 / 27	13.80 / 24	-5.00 / 13
IN	*WisdomTree Dividend Ex-Financial	DTN	B+	54.82	55.50	43.51	B / 7.9	6.30	19.99	13.66 / 75	28.92 / 80	2.15 / 39
FO	*WisdomTree Dr Brazilian Real Fun	BZF	D+	20.29	29.94	19.22	C- / 3.8	4.21	7.71	-5.42 / 30	18.13 / 36	--
FO	*WisdomTree Dr Chinese Yuan Fund	CYB	C-	25.35	25.85	24.91	D- / 1.4	0.64	4.72	4.26 / 53	1.59 / 8	--
GL	*WisdomTree Dr Commodity Curr Fun	CCX	D	21.38	29.44	20.04	D / 1.7	5.27	7.66	-0.87 / 38	--	--
FO	*WisdomTree Dr Emerg Curr Fd	CEW	D+	20.94	23.65	19.61	D+ / 2.3	6.29	12.42	1.01 / 44	--	--
FO	*WisdomTree Dr Indian Rupee Fund	ICN	D	21.44	27.99	19.90	D- / 1.4	6.56	0.46	-7.81 / 25	3.94 / 9	--
FO	*WisdomTree Dr Japanese Yen Fd	JYF	D+	30.94	35.15	30.50	D- / 1.5	-8.90	-8.24	0.52 / 42	5.75 / 11	--
FO	*WisdomTree Dr South African Rand	SZR	C-	24.88	30.06	22.63	C- / 3.4	7.15	16.41	-1.43 / 37	14.85 / 26	--
IN	*WisdomTree Earnings 500 Fund	EPS	C+	49.43	49.88	37.66	C+ / 6.1	12.71	27.16	10.89 / 70	21.40 / 49	1.95 / 38
EM	*WisdomTree Emg Mkts Eqty Inc Fd	DEM	C+	57.61	64.86	45.97	C+ / 6.4	12.77	23.30	-2.38 / 35	24.46 / 62	--
EM	*WisdomTree Emg Mkts Local Debt F	ELD	C-	51.89	54.65	47.12	D+ / 2.6	7.51	9.88	3.91 / 52	--	--
EM	*WisdomTree Emg Mkts SmCap Div Fd	DGS	C+	48.12	56.77	37.37	C+ / 6.7	16.57	25.99	-7.57 / 26	26.01 / 69	--
GI	*WisdomTree Equity Income Fund	DHS	B+	44.80	45.24	35.80	B- / 7.5	5.34	19.37	15.51 / 78	27.25 / 74	-0.94 / 23
FO	*WisdomTree Euro Debt	EU	D	20.89	24.45	19.05	D- / 1.1	5.83	-3.01	-7.97 / 25	-0.42 / 7	--
FO	*WisdomTree Europe Small Cap Div	DFE	C-	38.52	48.15	31.03	C / 5.0	18.33	19.31	-8.69 / 23	20.95 / 47	-6.06 / 11
GL	*WisdomTree Global Equity Income	DEW	C	41.68	48.14	35.30	C- / 4.1	6.66	15.96	-2.78 / 34	18.33 / 37	-3.47 / 16
GL	*WisdomTree Global ex-US Growth	DNL	C-	50.81	59.41	39.75	C- / 3.4	10.02	20.46	-6.66 / 27	14.65 / 26	-0.25 / 26
FO	*WisdomTree Global ex-US Real Est	DRW	C-	26.41	30.53	21.00	C+ / 6.1	13.79	19.07	-5.24 / 30	24.31 / 62	--
UT	*WisdomTree Global ex-US Utilitie	DBU	D	18.92	22.78	16.89	D / 1.9	6.88	9.45	-6.65 / 27	7.19 / 13	-5.03 / 12
EN	*WisdomTree Global Natural Resour	GNAT	D	25.20	31.42	19.51	D+ / 2.9	7.91	22.02	-13.84 / 17	13.13 / 22	1.30 / 32
GI	*WisdomTree Global Real Return Fu	RRF	U	47.50	N/A	N/A	U /	0.76	4.66	--	--	--
FO	*WisdomTree India Earnings Fund	EPI	D	19.28	25.58	15.44	C- / 3.5	23.66	6.28	-22.31 / 10	17.68 / 34	--
FO	*WisdomTree Intl Div Ex-Financial	DOO	D+	41.81	50.79	36.67	C- / 3.4	6.35	11.75	-7.65 / 25	15.95 / 30	-4.17 / 14
FO	*WisdomTree Intl Hedged Equity	HEDJ	D+	44.80	49.10	37.55	D / 2.1	9.16	12.98	-3.34 / 33	--	--
FO	*WisdomTree Intl LargeCap Dividen	DOL	D+	43.10	51.28	36.18	C- / 3.0	8.31	15.77	-5.63 / 29	13.02 / 22	-3.67 / 15
FO	*WisdomTree Intl MidCap Dividend	DIM	C-	48.09	57.23	40.58	C- / 3.7	12.16	14.50	-7.08 / 27	16.33 / 31	-3.37 / 16
FO	*WisdomTree Intl Small Cap Divide	DLS	C	49.55	56.05	41.50	C / 5.0	13.89	15.84	-2.12 / 35	20.71 / 46	-2.95 / 17
FO	*WisdomTree Japan Hedged Equity	DXJ	D	36.90	37.21	30.43	D / 2.0	17.74	15.42	2.20 / 47	4.74 / 10	-6.67 / 10
FO	*WisdomTree Japan SmallCap Div Fd	DFJ	C	45.58	45.80	39.34	C- / 3.6	9.44	6.39	10.52 / 69	14.76 / 26	-0.76 / 24
GI	*WisdomTree LargeCap Dividend Fun	DLN	B-	52.96	53.41	41.71	C+ / 6.4	8.68	23.12	13.13 / 74	22.74 / 55	1.08 / 31
GR	*WisdomTree LargeCap Growth Fund	ROI	C	41.00	41.56	30.49	C / 4.4	13.22	27.82	7.07 / 61	16.26 / 30	--

99 Pct = Best
0 Pct = Worst

* Denotes ETF Fund, N/A denotes number is not available

Incl. in Returns		RISK	3 Year		Avg Dura-tion	NET ASSETS		VALUATION Premium / Discount			ASSET				Portfolio Turnover Ratio	FUND MANAGER	
Dividend Yield %	Expense Ratio	Risk Rating/ Pts	Standard Deviation	Beta		NAV as of 3/31/12	Total $(Mil)	As of 3/31/12	1 Year Average	Wtd Avg P/E	Cash %	Stocks %	Bonds %	Other %		Manager Quality Pct	Manager Tenure (Years)
0.00	1.65	U /	N/A	N/A	N/A	31.10	8	1.54	N/A	N/A	0	0	0	100	N/A	N/A	1
0.00	1.35	U /	N/A	N/A	N/A	54.30	2	-0.98	N/A	N/A	0	0	0	100	N/A	N/A	0
0.00	1.35	U /	N/A	N/A	N/A	45.26	20	-0.31	N/A	N/A	0	0	0	100	N/A	N/A	1
0.00	1.65	U /	N/A	N/A	N/A	21.19	5	-1.27	N/A	N/A	0	0	0	100	N/A	N/A	0
0.00	1.65	U /	N/A	N/A	N/A	40.02	46	-1.72	N/A	N/A	0	0	0	100	N/A	N/A	1
0.00	1.65	D / 1.9	N/A	N/A	N/A	6.28	600	15.29	2.14	N/A	0	0	0	100	N/A	N/A	2
0.00	1.65	D / 2.0	N/A	N/A	N/A	33.61	7	2.80	0.04	N/A	0	0	0	100	N/A	16	2
0.00	1.35	C / 5.4	N/A	N/A	N/A	16.04	9	-1.25	0.01	N/A	0	0	0	100	N/A	99	2
0.00	1.35	D / 1.9	N/A	N/A	N/A	12.39	420	-0.97	-0.18	N/A	0	0	0	100	N/A	1	2
0.00	1.35	U /	N/A	N/A	N/A	40.75	1	0.54	N/A	N/A	0	0	0	100	N/A	N/A	0
0.00	1.35	U /	N/A	N/A	N/A	58.86	2	-0.07	N/A	N/A	0	0	0	100	N/A	N/A	0
0.00	0.89	U /	N/A	N/A	N/A	64.90	8	2.06	0.14	N/A	0	0	0	100	N/A	12	2
0.00	0.89	D / 1.9	N/A	N/A	N/A	36.08	16	0.94	0.17	N/A	0	0	0	100	N/A	9	2
0.24	1.25	B- / 7.8	N/A	N/A	N/A	31.02	8	-0.23	0.04	N/A	3	96	0	1	34	82	N/A
0.70	0.55	B / 8.0	N/A	N/A	N/A	51.45	419	-0.10	0.11	N/A	0	0	0	100	N/A	33	1
1.38	0.48	B- / 7.4	22.9	0.99	N/A	64.05	92	0.08	0.09	N/A	0	100	0	0	27	77	4
1.28	0.45	B- / 7.9	15.8	0.44	N/A	21.82	34	0.32	0.30	N/A	100	0	0	0	N/A	63	4
6.83	0.58	C+ / 6.9	27.4	1.17	N/A	55.87	61	0.38	0.04	N/A	0	100	0	0	46	78	4
3.08	0.58	B- / 7.4	28.6	1.27	N/A	31.44	32	-0.03	-0.30	16.7	0	100	0	0	35	70	4
1.88	0.48	B- / 7.4	21.7	1.01	N/A	44.53	363	0.83	0.08	N/A	0	100	0	0	30	41	N/A
2.37	0.58	B- / 7.3	23.5	1.07	N/A	38.64	171	0.80	0.43	N/A	0	100	0	0	34	33	4
3.33	0.38	B+ / 9.0	14.6	0.83	N/A	54.81	1,222	0.02	0.08	19.0	0	100	0	0	5	87	4
0.00	0.45	C+ / 6.3	19.3	0.68	N/A	20.33	94	-0.20	N/A	N/A	0	0	75	25	N/A	81	4
2.18	0.45	B+ / 9.8	3.4	0.07	N/A	25.40	413	-0.20	-0.07	N/A	0	0	72	28	8	48	4
0.00	0.55	C+ / 6.6	N/A	N/A	N/A	21.41	35	-0.14	-0.02	N/A	0	0	0	100	N/A	67	2
5.05	0.55	B / 8.4	N/A	N/A	N/A	20.94	347	0.00	-0.08	N/A	100	0	0	0	N/A	73	3
0.00	0.45	B- / 7.4	11.0	0.40	N/A	21.37	16	0.33	-0.02	N/A	0	0	70	30	N/A	32	4
0.00	0.35	B / 8.9	10.4	0.01	N/A	31.63	13	-2.18	-0.23	N/A	50	0	27	23	N/A	74	4
7.04	0.45	B- / 7.6	18.5	0.61	N/A	24.87	5	0.04	-0.19	N/A	98	0	0	2	N/A	76	4
1.58	0.28	B / 8.4	15.2	0.93	N/A	49.42	67	0.02	0.04	39.3	0	100	0	0	12	59	4
1.40	0.63	B- / 7.3	23.8	0.89	N/A	57.33	3,330	0.49	0.75	N/A	0	100	0	0	33	72	4
2.76	0.55	B / 8.6	N/A	N/A	N/A	51.72	1,222	0.33	0.20	N/A	14	0	85	1	30	32	2
0.57	0.63	C+ / 6.8	27.5	1.05	N/A	47.80	949	0.67	0.40	N/A	0	99	0	1	35	62	4
3.67	0.38	B+ / 9.1	14.7	0.79	N/A	44.81	414	-0.02	0.14	19.2	0	100	0	0	8	85	4
0.38	0.35	B / 8.1	13.1	0.47	N/A	21.87	5	-4.48	-1.16	N/A	49	0	50	1	N/A	17	4
1.18	0.58	C+ / 6.8	27.3	1.23	N/A	38.22	29	0.78	0.11	N/A	0	99	0	1	60	60	4
2.34	0.58	B- / 7.9	20.6	0.94	N/A	41.50	86	0.43	0.21	19.3	0	100	0	0	35	69	4
1.61	0.57	B- / 7.5	22.1	0.93	N/A	50.70	63	0.22	0.16	16.5	0	100	0	0	68	43	4
2.36	0.58	C / 5.4	25.7	1.14	N/A	26.40	122	0.04	0.14	272.7	0	99	0	1	18	78	4
1.83	0.58	B- / 7.7	19.8	1.25	N/A	18.90	32	0.11	-0.26	24.2	0	100	0	0	19	12	4
2.53	0.58	B- / 7.0	28.0	1.09	N/A	25.16	33	0.16	-0.15	22.9	0	100	0	0	32	20	4
1.35	0.60	U /	N/A	N/A	N/A	48.18	5	-1.41	N/A	N/A	0	0	0	100	N/A	N/A	1
0.15	0.88	C+ / 5.8	37.1	1.28	N/A	19.24	1,004	0.21	-0.07	N/A	0	100	0	0	38	36	4
2.67	0.58	B- / 7.5	22.2	1.01	N/A	41.64	343	0.41	0.30	N/A	0	100	0	0	52	54	4
1.52	0.58	B / 8.2	N/A	N/A	N/A	43.93	20	1.98	0.32	N/A	0	100	0	0	38	46	3
2.07	0.48	B- / 7.4	21.9	1.01	N/A	42.89	159	0.49	0.11	N/A	0	100	0	0	22	33	4
1.59	0.58	B- / 7.4	22.1	1.04	N/A	48.10	106	-0.02	-0.23	N/A	0	100	0	0	40	50	4
2.03	0.58	B- / 7.8	20.4	0.93	N/A	49.33	418	0.45	-0.25	N/A	0	100	0	0	55	77	4
2.93	0.48	B- / 7.6	15.5	0.48	N/A	36.66	520	0.65	-0.09	N/A	0	100	0	0	28	33	4
3.19	0.58	B / 8.8	14.6	0.34	N/A	45.45	187	0.29	-0.15	N/A	0	99	0	1	39	83	4
2.44	0.28	B / 8.8	13.8	0.83	N/A	52.98	1,187	-0.04	0.10	23.3	0	99	0	1	5	73	4
1.26	0.38	B / 8.2	16.1	0.95	N/A	40.92	20	0.20	0.08	N/A	0	99	0	1	10	29	4

* Denotes ETF Fund, N/A denotes number is not available

Fund Type	Fund Name	Ticker Symbol	Overall Investment Rating	PRICE Price As of 3/31/12	52 Week High	52 Week Low	Performance Rating/Pts	3 Mo	6 Mo	1Yr/Pct	Annualized 3Yr/Pct	Annualized 5Yr/Pct
IN	*WisdomTree LargeCap Value Fund	EZY	C+	44.34	44.77	33.85	C / 5.4	8.47	23.97	4.46 / 54	21.00 / 47	-0.39 / 25
GR	*WisdomTree Mgd Futures Strategy	WDTI	D	43.26	53.47	41.99	E+ / 0.7	-4.36	-6.03	-14.21 / 16	--	--
GR	*WisdomTree MidCap Dividend Fund	DON	B	56.29	57.17	43.22	B / 7.6	8.93	24.14	6.86 / 61	28.06 / 77	2.55 / 42
GR	*WisdomTree MidCap Earnings Fund	EZM	B+	61.14	62.35	44.09	B / 8.2	13.54	31.48	4.85 / 54	30.39 / 83	5.70 / 60
FO	*WisdomTree Middle East Dividend	GULF	D+	15.50	17.35	14.23	D+ / 2.7	7.04	9.43	-0.47 / 39	11.50 / 18	--
GR	*WisdomTree SmallCap Dividend Fd	DES	B	49.09	50.16	37.15	B- / 7.4	10.27	27.68	5.19 / 56	27.34 / 74	0.98 / 31
GR	*WisdomTree SmallCap Earnings Fun	EES	B+	56.79	58.00	40.83	B+ / 8.5	13.31	32.26	4.90 / 55	31.35 / 85	4.40 / 53
IN	*WisdomTree Total Dividend	DTD	B-	53.11	53.59	41.80	C+ / 6.6	8.98	23.74	12.25 / 73	23.50 / 58	1.33 / 33
IN	*WisdomTree Total Earnings Fund	EXT	C+	50.65	51.23	38.59	C+ / 6.5	12.92	27.97	10.08 / 68	22.64 / 55	2.46 / 41
GL	Aberdeen Asia-Pacific Income Fund	FAX	C	7.29	7.84	6.10	C / 5.2	0.86	8.88	11.19 / 70	21.25 / 49	10.25 / 88
FO	Aberdeen Australia Equity Fund	IAF	C	10.75	12.88	8.46	C+ / 6.7	22.10	19.00	-2.99 / 34	25.38 / 65	4.23 / 52
FO	Aberdeen Chile Fund	CH	B	19.23	22.39	12.34	A+ / 9.6	30.99	43.81	7.72 / 63	40.27 / 95	15.64 / 99
EM	Aberdeen Emerging Mkt Tele & Infr	ETF	C	19.37	19.67	16.12	C- / 4.2	10.50	15.51	4.72 / 54	17.08 / 33	1.50 / 34
GL	Aberdeen Global Income Fund	FCO	B	13.98	14.86	11.16	B- / 7.3	2.14	16.46	16.80 / 80	26.86 / 72	12.20 / 96
EM	Aberdeen Indonesia Fund	IF	A	12.74	14.47	10.83	A+ / 9.7	8.15	17.08	4.40 / 53	48.02 / 98	10.30 / 88
FO	Aberdeen Israel Fund	ISL	C-	13.99	18.22	12.46	C- / 4.2	9.73	8.06	-14.39 / 16	20.74 / 46	2.93 / 44
FO	Aberdeen Latin America Equity Fund	LAQ	B-	35.51	39.98	27.62	B+ / 8.4	18.06	29.08	-4.52 / 31	32.45 / 87	10.69 / 91
IN	Adams Express Company	ADX	C	10.98	11.52	8.63	C / 4.7	14.43	25.92	2.69 / 48	18.28 / 36	1.25 / 32
GI	Advent Claymore Cnv Sec & Inc	AVK	C+	16.31	20.10	13.16	C+ / 6.2	12.63	18.63	-11.72 / 19	25.75 / 67	-1.87 / 20
GL	Advent Claymore Enhanced Gr & Inc	LCM	C-	10.01	12.34	8.50	C- / 4.1	13.82	15.34	-8.07 / 25	18.48 / 37	-3.26 / 16
GI	Advent/Claymore Gbl Con Sec & Inc	AGC	D+	6.88	9.99	5.76	C- / 4.1	11.76	15.33	-22.63 / 9	20.55 / 45	--
GI	AGIC Convertible & Income Fund	NCV	B+	9.50	11.12	7.40	A / 9.3	15.80	22.46	-2.56 / 34	40.32 / 95	2.27 / 40
GI	AGIC Convertible & Income Fund II	NCZ	A-	8.76	10.18	6.85	A / 9.4	14.77	20.17	-1.74 / 36	41.62 / 96	1.76 / 36
IN	AGIC Equity & Convertible Income F	NIE	C+	17.77	19.88	14.05	C+ / 5.8	15.72	21.14	-3.14 / 33	22.86 / 56	1.64 / 35
GL	AGIC Global Equity & Conv Inc Fund	NGZ	C	14.23	17.33	11.98	C / 5.1	12.96	9.81	-7.22 / 26	22.46 / 54	--
FO	AGIC Intl & Premium Strategy Fund	NAI	D	10.97	14.57	9.41	C- / 3.5	15.01	16.98	-9.35 / 22	15.31 / 28	-5.08 / 12
MUS	Alliance CA Municipal Income Fund	AKP	B+	14.71	15.68	12.46	B / 7.9	2.99	11.94	21.32 / 91	17.09 / 70	6.05 / 82
MUS	Alliance NY Municipal Income Fund	AYN	B+	14.81	15.93	13.11	B- / 7.2	-1.61	9.03	14.72 / 83	17.02 / 70	5.95 / 81
GL	AllianceBernstein Global High Inc	AWF	B+	15.02	15.45	12.43	B+ / 8.5	7.44	23.16	11.43 / 71	31.85 / 85	13.94 / 98
GL	AllianceBernstein Income Fund	ACG	C	8.19	8.38	7.56	C- / 3.0	2.48	6.52	13.81 / 75	11.61 / 19	7.25 / 69
MUN	AllianceBernstein Nat Muni Inc Fun	AFB	B+	14.81	15.62	12.46	B- / 7.4	1.81	7.80	19.59 / 89	16.88 / 69	5.81 / 79
GL	Alpine Global Dynamic Div Fd	AGD	D-	6.06	7.89	4.90	D+ / 2.8	20.93	20.82	-11.69 / 19	11.15 / 18	-11.22 / 6
GI	Alpine Global Premier Properties F	AWP	B+	6.50	7.64	4.80	A- / 9.0	25.55	28.05	0.57 / 42	35.36 / 91	--
GL	Alpine Total Dynamic Dividend Fund	AOD	D-	4.74	6.39	4.15	D / 1.7	12.05	12.84	-12.53 / 18	5.41 / 11	-12.14 / 5
MTG	American Income Fund	MRF	C-	7.99	8.20	6.92	C / 5.1	5.26	12.89	8.99 / 66	20.53 / 45	7.88 / 73
MUN	American Municipal Income Portfoli	XAA	A	14.87	15.54	12.56	B+ / 8.7	3.25	9.58	24.02 / 94	19.91 / 83	5.59 / 77
MTG	American Select Portfolio	SLA	C	10.41	10.95	9.20	C / 4.8	5.48	10.95	10.82 / 70	19.66 / 41	5.32 / 58
MTG	American Strat Inc Portfolio	ASP	B-	11.67	11.76	9.55	C+ / 6.8	10.81	16.13	13.03 / 74	24.65 / 63	9.26 / 82
MTG	American Strat Inc Portfolio II	BSP	C-	8.30	9.32	7.70	C- / 3.1	4.24	5.58	1.22 / 44	14.25 / 25	2.97 / 44
MTG	American Strat Inc Portfolio III	CSP	D	7.00	7.95	6.42	D+ / 2.4	8.55	5.33	1.25 / 44	9.41 / 15	-0.08 / 27
LP	Apollo Senior Floating Rate Fd Inc	AFT	D+	17.91	20.09	14.93	D+ / 2.9	13.90	18.58	-4.16 / 32	--	--
PM	ASA Gold & Precious Metals Ltd	ASA	E+	25.77	33.81	24.88	D+ / 2.7	-1.59	-3.35	-17.10 / 13	15.95 / 29	5.46 / 59
FO	Asia Pacific Fund	APB	D+	10.58	12.63	8.51	C- / 3.5	12.55	13.09	-11.91 / 19	16.39 / 31	3.10 / 45
FO	Asia Tigers Fund	GRR	D	13.56	20.00	11.64	C- / 3.1	12.89	13.73	-12.08 / 19	14.58 / 25	0.20 / 28
LP	Avenue Income Credit Strategies	ACP	D	16.58	19.98	14.20	D / 1.8	9.25	12.14	-5.12 / 30	--	--
GI	Bancroft Fund Ltd.	BCV	C	16.69	18.18	14.10	C / 4.3	11.23	14.87	-1.96 / 36	18.46 / 37	2.75 / 43
MUN	BlackRock Build America Bond	BBN	A+	21.45	22.39	17.17	A+ / 9.7	1.68	10.18	31.67 / 99	--	--
MUS	BlackRock CA Muni 2018 Income Trus	BJZ	C+	16.45	17.13	15.23	C / 4.3	2.07	3.87	12.47 / 81	11.23 / 33	6.67 / 88
MUS	BlackRock CA Municipal Income Trus	BFZ	B+	15.02	15.90	12.37	B / 8.2	3.64	10.01	27.87 / 98	16.85 / 68	3.30 / 57
GEI	BlackRock Core Bond Trust	BHK	C	13.77	14.25	11.99	C / 4.8	2.83	9.35	20.01 / 82	18.81 / 39	8.50 / 77
COH	BlackRock Corporate High Yield Fun	COY	B	7.35	7.84	5.99	B+ / 8.5	3.37	16.67	11.48 / 71	32.92 / 87	8.63 / 78
COH	BlackRock Corporate High Yield III	CYE	B	7.59	7.93	6.05	A- / 9.1	8.69	22.91	15.39 / 78	36.91 / 93	9.56 / 84

99 Pct = Best
0 Pct = Worst

* Denotes ETF Fund, N/A denotes number is not available

Dividend Yield %	Expense Ratio	Risk Rating/ Pts	Standard Deviation	Beta	Avg Dura-tion	NAV as of 3/31/12	Total $(Mil)	As of 3/31/12	1 Year Average	Wtd Avg P/E	Cash %	Stocks %	Bonds %	Other %	Portfolio Turnover Ratio	Manager Quality Pct	Manager Tenure (Years)
1.76	0.38	B / 8.3	19.0	1.08	N/A	44.31	31	0.07	-0.04	24.9	0	100	0	0	6	40	4
1.80	0.95	B / 8.3	N/A	N/A	N/A	43.20	248	0.14	0.11	N/A	0	0	0	100	N/A	10	1
3.04	0.38	B / 8.4	19.1	1.09	N/A	56.25	344	0.07	0.10	25.4	0	99	0	1	10	73	4
0.75	0.38	B- / 7.9	22.1	1.25	N/A	61.00	154	0.23	0.07	38.9	0	99	0	1	18	65	4
2.07	0.88	B / 8.1	18.2	0.59	N/A	15.60	14	-0.64	-0.88	N/A	0	99	0	1	50	63	N/A
3.35	0.38	B / 8.1	22.1	1.20	N/A	49.03	296	0.12	0.10	22.5	0	99	0	1	11	63	4
1.50	0.38	B- / 7.8	24.8	1.35	N/A	56.59	143	0.35	0.02	34.4	0	99	0	1	19	61	4
2.57	0.28	B / 8.8	14.4	0.87	N/A	53.04	234	0.13	0.06	23.5	0	99	0	1	6	73	4
1.37	0.28	B / 8.3	15.9	0.96	N/A	50.62	37	0.06	0.02	39.3	0	100	0	0	9	61	4
5.76	1.49	B / 8.0	15.3	1.10	7.9	7.46	1,952	-2.28	-2.82	N/A	0	0	99	1	72	89	N/A
10.42	1.34	C+ / 6.6	36.2	1.38	N/A	9.88	230	8.81	4.71	N/A	1	90	0	9	30	62	N/A
8.94	2.07	C+ / 5.9	33.3	1.00	N/A	16.81	168	14.40	5.98	N/A	0	100	0	0	41	93	3
0.34	1.50	B / 8.4	20.5	0.74	N/A	21.88	165	-11.47	-10.49	N/A	2	97	0	1	50	49	N/A
6.01	2.13	B / 8.4	19.9	1.06	12.7	13.46	122	3.86	1.87	N/A	0	0	99	1	76	93	N/A
2.40	1.52	B- / 7.6	32.2	1.07	N/A	14.03	119	-9.19	-8.76	N/A	0	100	0	0	10	92	N/A
2.18	1.67	B- / 7.3	25.0	0.98	N/A	15.88	84	-11.90	-11.87	46.5	3	94	0	3	12	76	N/A
0.22	1.35	C+ / 6.8	30.0	1.20	N/A	38.56	312	-7.91	-9.05	N/A	1	98	0	1	8	88	3
1.09	0.58	B- / 7.9	18.3	1.10	N/A	12.92	1,125	-15.02	-14.61	46.6	4	95	0	1	16	22	26
7.48	1.58	B- / 7.4	21.4	1.09	N/A	17.61	413	-7.38	-8.06	N/A	8	1	23	68	93	59	9
8.39	2.11	B- / 7.4	18.7	0.74	N/A	10.95	145	-8.58	-7.70	N/A	1	17	18	64	121	79	5
8.20	1.99	C+ / 6.5	24.3	1.13	N/A	7.40	239	-7.03	-6.06	N/A	1	0	14	85	125	30	5
12.32	1.27	B- / 7.3	27.0	1.31	N/A	8.61	727	10.34	9.64	N/A	3	0	46	51	52	84	N/A
11.64	1.29	B- / 7.6	25.0	1.20	N/A	7.83	549	11.88	12.10	N/A	3	0	46	51	54	89	N/A
6.30	1.10	B- / 7.7	18.9	0.98	6.0	19.89	452	-10.66	-10.65	50.2	3	69	0	28	168	61	N/A
8.44	1.29	B- / 7.4	23.2	0.91	5.9	15.78	109	-9.82	-7.16	47.6	2	79	0	19	120	83	N/A
14.59	1.27	C+ / 6.0	26.0	1.03	N/A	11.26	146	-2.58	-3.65	N/A	0	98	0	2	47	42	N/A
6.22	1.30	B / 8.9	11.0	1.93	11.8	14.52	120	1.31	-1.95	N/A	1	0	98	1	14	56	N/A
5.75	1.44	B+ / 9.2	10.6	1.53	12.5	14.66	70	1.02	-1.12	N/A	2	0	97	1	15	73	N/A
7.99	1.01	B / 8.4	18.8	0.82	20.1	14.81	1,319	1.42	-1.13	N/A	0	0	98	2	52	96	20
5.86	0.71	B+ / 9.3	6.7	0.26	6.5	9.03	2,126	-9.30	-10.78	N/A	1	0	98	1	121	85	25
6.28	1.13	B / 8.9	11.1	1.79	12.4	14.76	409	0.34	-1.49	N/A	0	0	100	0	10	62	N/A
11.88	1.39	C / 5.1	39.5	1.43	N/A	5.61	143	8.02	4.37	27.6	0	100	0	0	299	14	6
9.23	1.29	B- / 7.1	32.5	1.65	N/A	7.41	759	-12.28	-13.75	35.6	0	100	0	0	67	48	5
13.92	1.35	C / 5.4	33.9	1.24	N/A	5.12	1,134	-7.42	-5.55	27.4	0	100	0	0	367	13	5
7.51	1.17	B- / 7.0	13.7	-0.75	13.5	8.49	80	-5.89	-8.29	N/A	0	0	100	0	265	96	N/A
6.26	1.37	B / 8.8	12.2	1.84	12.3	15.18	82	-2.04	-3.08	N/A	0	0	100	0	9	74	N/A
7.78	2.73	B / 8.0	13.3	-0.79	19.5	11.64	123	-10.57	-12.39	N/A	2	0	86	12	10	95	N/A
7.71	2.43	B / 8.2	14.4	-0.07	18.5	12.67	53	-7.89	-11.95	107.3	1	0	82	17	13	96	N/A
7.23	2.68	B- / 7.9	12.4	-1.24	19.7	9.82	160	-15.48	-15.52	107.3	1	0	89	10	11	94	N/A
6.43	2.72	B- / 7.5	12.6	-0.42	17.0	8.17	180	-14.32	-14.67	N/A	1	0	85	14	13	88	N/A
6.45	2.03	B- / 7.3	N/A	N/A	N/A	18.37	273	-2.50	-4.65	N/A	0	0	0	100	N/A	98	1
2.64	0.60	D+ / 2.8	30.5	1.06	N/A	27.35	626	-5.78	-9.24	67.6	0	99	0	1	6	18	N/A
0.00	2.01	B- / 7.2	27.8	1.11	N/A	11.67	135	-9.34	-9.11	N/A	0	99	0	1	136	42	8
0.00	2.36	C+ / 5.8	27.8	1.00	N/A	14.74	57	-8.01	-7.11	64.9	1	94	0	5	42	39	N/A
8.69	2.50	B- / 7.2	N/A	N/A	N/A	17.44	127	-4.93	-1.45	N/A	0	0	81	19	56	98	1
3.06	1.10	B / 8.4	14.6	0.77	N/A	19.40	98	-13.97	-13.29	N/A	2	0	0	98	43	59	16
7.37	1.06	B / 8.5	N/A	N/A	N/A	22.48	1,164	-4.58	-6.07	N/A	0	0	100	0	13	81	N/A
5.25	0.91	B+ / 9.4	8.0	0.34	6.9	15.49	100	6.20	6.13	N/A	0	0	100	0	28	84	6
6.21	1.39	B / 8.4	13.7	2.57	13.7	15.53	442	-3.28	-3.18	N/A	1	0	98	1	36	35	6
5.84	1.02	B / 8.5	9.5	2.20	15.0	14.24	372	-3.30	-6.54	N/A	2	0	95	3	824	61	N/A
8.33	1.18	B- / 7.1	16.3	1.11	5.0	7.23	258	1.66	1.12	196.9	0	6	90	4	83	78	6
8.06	1.37	B- / 7.0	15.5	1.25	5.0	7.35	282	3.27	-0.90	197.1	1	6	87	6	89	77	3

* Denotes ETF Fund, N/A denotes number is not available

				PRICE			PERFORMANCE						
99 Pct = Best 0 Pct = Worst					52 Week		Perform-ance	% Total Return Through 3/31/12				Annualized	
Fund Type	Fund Name	Ticker Symbol	Overall Investment Rating	Price As of 3/31/12	High	Low	Rating/Pts	3 Mo	6 Mo	1Yr/Pct	3Yr/Pct	5Yr/Pct	
COH	BlackRock Corporate High Yield V	HYV	B	12.55	13.07	10.10	A- / 9.0	8.86	21.64	14.89 / 77	35.42 / 91	9.30 / 82	
COH	BlackRock Corporate High Yield VI	HYT	B	12.42	12.84	9.94	B+ / 8.9	10.65	22.93	14.95 / 77	34.19 / 89	9.19 / 81	
IN	BlackRock Credit Alloc Inc Tr I	PSW	A+	9.88	10.32	8.56	A- / 9.2	7.62	17.07	16.62 / 79	37.91 / 94	-6.39 / 10	
IN	BlackRock Credit Alloc Inc Tr II	PSY	A+	10.51	10.78	9.08	B+ / 8.9	8.15	16.70	14.29 / 76	35.57 / 92	-3.89 / 14	
GL	BlackRock Credit Alloc Inc Tr III	BPP	A	11.23	11.45	9.71	B+ / 8.6	7.75	17.73	13.91 / 76	33.00 / 87	-7.48 / 9	
IN	BlackRock Credit Alloc Inc Tr IV	BTZ	A	13.07	13.34	11.18	B+ / 8.9	8.86	18.21	15.43 / 78	34.49 / 90	-1.19 / 22	
COH	BlackRock Debt Strategies Fund Inc	DSU	A	4.14	4.43	3.45	B+ / 8.9	8.10	12.90	11.60 / 72	36.55 / 92	-0.29 / 26	
LP	BlackRock Defined Opp Credit Trust	BHL	C	13.40	15.75	11.58	C / 4.5	8.69	12.71	-5.46 / 30	20.41 / 45	--	
LP	BlackRock Diversified Inc Strat	DVF	C+	10.28	12.02	8.84	C+ / 6.9	9.46	15.98	0.75 / 43	26.99 / 73	-2.67 / 17	
EN	BlackRock EcoSolutions Investment	BQR	C-	9.95	12.66	7.31	C / 4.4	30.40	30.64	-6.88 / 27	16.34 / 31	--	
EN	BlackRock Energy & Resources	BGR	C+	26.20	32.23	20.09	C+ / 6.3	8.81	20.33	-11.56 / 19	26.20 / 70	5.95 / 62	
GI	BlackRock Enhanced Capital and Inc	CII	C	13.49	15.70	10.84	C+ / 5.6	12.60	20.71	0.03 / 41	21.97 / 52	4.65 / 55	
IN	BlackRock Enhanced Equity Div	BDJ	C-	7.50	8.95	6.30	C- / 3.5	8.49	12.53	-7.85 / 25	16.16 / 30	-2.31 / 18	
USA	BlackRock Enhanced Government	EGF	D+	15.30	15.80	14.75	D / 1.7	1.25	3.12	4.86 / 54	4.58 / 10	1.77 / 36	
MUS	BlackRock FL Muni 2020 Term Tr	BFO	A-	15.43	15.67	13.30	B- / 7.5	2.65	6.47	19.30 / 89	17.45 / 72	6.76 / 89	
LP	BlackRock Floating Rate Inc Strat	FRA	C+	14.82	16.45	12.32	C+ / 6.5	12.10	20.37	1.70 / 45	24.52 / 63	3.60 / 48	
LP	BlackRock Floating Rate Inc Strt I	FRB	B-	13.95	14.79	11.38	B- / 7.3	14.37	24.15	5.60 / 57	26.71 / 72	3.09 / 44	
LP	BlackRock Floating Rt Income	BGT	C+	14.27	16.25	11.70	C+ / 6.1	7.10	17.99	3.88 / 51	23.73 / 59	3.56 / 48	
GL	BlackRock Global Opportunities Eq	BOE	C-	15.35	19.49	12.75	C / 5.0	20.50	22.01	-1.87 / 36	19.50 / 41	1.40 / 33	
HL	BlackRock Health Sciences Trust	BME	C+	27.47	29.95	22.77	C+ / 6.5	10.84	22.03	11.24 / 71	23.02 / 57	8.26 / 76	
COH	BlackRock High Income Shares	HIS	A	2.28	2.42	1.80	B+ / 8.6	5.92	22.81	15.98 / 79	32.42 / 86	8.02 / 74	
COH	BlackRock High Yield Trust	BHY	B+	7.24	7.32	5.90	B / 7.7	8.72	20.13	16.70 / 79	27.54 / 75	6.82 / 66	
GEI	BlackRock Income Opportunity Trust	BNA	C	10.48	10.81	9.30	C- / 4.0	3.57	10.16	18.14 / 81	14.93 / 26	6.77 / 66	
MTG	BlackRock Income Trust	BKT	C	7.42	7.58	6.68	C- / 3.1	2.33	6.22	16.88 / 80	11.90 / 19	8.91 / 79	
FO	BlackRock Intl Grth and Inc Tr	BGY	D	7.85	10.73	6.81	C- / 3.0	12.71	10.64	-11.13 / 20	14.19 / 24	--	
MUN	BlackRock Investment Qual Muni Tr	BKN	A	15.50	16.74	12.80	A- / 9.0	4.90	9.62	26.20 / 97	21.08 / 87	3.04 / 55	
MUS	BlackRock Invt Qual Muni Inc Tr	RFA	A+	13.43	15.04	10.83	A / 9.5	6.44	7.59	31.22 / 99	24.27 / 93	6.63 / 88	
GEN	BlackRock Limited Duration Income	BLW	C+	17.74	18.41	14.30	C / 5.5	12.46	16.42	11.50 / 71	20.51 / 45	5.94 / 61	
MUN	BlackRock Long Term Muni Adv	BTA	A+	12.39	12.89	9.86	A / 9.4	7.90	15.19	29.18 / 99	22.45 / 90	4.47 / 67	
MUS	BlackRock MD Muni Bond Trust	BZM	B	16.50	17.60	14.25	B- / 7.2	0.81	11.55	17.84 / 87	16.07 / 63	3.00 / 55	
MUN	BlackRock Muni 2020 Term Trust	BKK	B-	15.88	16.35	14.40	C+ / 5.7	1.87	5.23	14.92 / 84	13.99 / 51	5.72 / 79	
MUS	BlackRock Muni Bond Invt Trust	BIE	B+	15.36	16.60	13.00	B / 8.2	2.80	8.79	22.44 / 92	18.36 / 77	4.64 / 68	
MUN	BlackRock Muni Interm Duration	MUI	A	15.85	16.70	13.22	B+ / 8.3	4.85	11.23	21.97 / 92	18.04 / 75	7.32 / 92	
MUS	BlackRock Muni NY Interm Duration	MNE	A+	15.00	15.47	12.58	B+ / 8.9	5.60	11.15	23.32 / 94	20.89 / 86	6.89 / 90	
MUN	BlackRock MuniAssets Fund	MUA	B	13.01	13.34	10.96	B- / 7.0	5.33	12.08	21.40 / 91	13.74 / 48	3.30 / 57	
MUN	BlackRock Municipal 2018 Income Tr	BPK	C+	16.68	17.12	15.17	C / 4.6	2.02	5.79	13.56 / 82	11.50 / 34	6.14 / 83	
MUN	BlackRock Municipal Bond Trust	BBK	A+	16.28	17.46	13.49	A- / 9.0	5.30	10.30	20.97 / 90	21.83 / 88	4.21 / 64	
MUS	BlackRock Municipal Income Inv Qly	BAF	B+	15.23	16.18	12.64	B / 8.1	1.36	8.70	24.55 / 95	17.94 / 75	6.78 / 89	
MUS	BlackRock Municipal Income Invt Tr	BBF	B	14.59	15.25	12.03	B- / 7.2	3.57	8.51	25.59 / 96	14.37 / 53	4.48 / 67	
MUN	BlackRock Municipal Income Quality	BYM	B-	14.98	15.96	12.16	C+ / 6.9	2.48	8.14	22.60 / 93	14.53 / 53	5.69 / 78	
MUN	BlackRock Municipal Income Trust	BFK	A	14.49	15.37	12.02	B+ / 8.9	5.62	9.72	25.95 / 97	20.20 / 84	2.95 / 54	
MUN	BlackRock Municipal Income Trust I	BLE	A+	15.50	16.08	12.76	A- / 9.1	3.60	9.46	23.53 / 94	22.88 / 91	5.17 / 74	
MUN	BlackRock MuniEnhanced Fund	MEN	B	11.40	12.20	9.61	B- / 7.3	-0.64	5.71	22.81 / 93	16.59 / 66	7.04 / 91	
MUS	BlackRock MuniHoldings CA Qly	MUC	A	14.99	15.67	12.33	B+ / 8.9	2.27	9.11	27.55 / 98	20.50 / 85	7.14 / 92	
MUN	BlackRock MuniHoldings Fund	MHD	A+	17.76	18.45	14.16	A / 9.5	8.83	14.00	30.61 / 99	22.87 / 91	8.78 / 98	
MUN	BlackRock MuniHoldings Fund II	MUH	A+	15.72	16.72	13.08	B+ / 8.9	3.05	8.68	22.69 / 93	21.93 / 89	8.12 / 97	
MUS	BlackRock MuniHoldings Inv Quality	MFL	B+	14.59	15.40	12.21	B / 8.2	1.39	7.77	18.92 / 88	19.09 / 81	7.43 / 93	
MUS	BlackRock MuniHoldings New York Ql	MHN	A	15.15	16.14	12.74	B+ / 8.8	1.51	9.24	25.02 / 96	21.02 / 86	7.73 / 95	
MUS	BlackRock MuniHoldings NJ Qly	MUJ	B+	15.49	16.19	13.12	B / 7.7	-0.21	11.71	21.47 / 91	16.83 / 68	6.16 / 83	
MUN	BlackRock MuniHoldings Quality	MUS	B+	14.10	15.04	11.69	B / 8.0	1.40	8.13	24.22 / 95	17.68 / 73	7.51 / 94	
MUN	BlackRock MuniHoldings Quality II	MUE	B	13.97	14.94	11.45	B / 7.7	-0.81	8.96	21.78 / 92	17.68 / 74	7.79 / 95	
MUN	BlackRock MuniVest Fund	MVF	B+	10.42	11.01	8.74	B / 7.9	1.55	6.78	20.28 / 90	18.62 / 79	7.51 / 94	

* Denotes ETF Fund, N/A denotes number is not available

www.thestreetratings.com

		RISK				NET ASSETS		VALUATION			ASSET					FUND MANAGER	
Incl. in Returns		Risk Rating/ Pts	3 Year		Avg Dura-tion	NAV as of 3/31/12	Total $(Mil)	Premium / Discount		Wtd Avg P/E	Cash %	Stocks %	Bonds %	Other %	Portfolio Turnover Ratio	Manager Quality Pct	Manager Tenure (Years)
Dividend Yield %	Expense Ratio		Standard Deviation	Beta				As of 3/31/12	1 Year Average								
8.22	1.34	B- / 7.0	15.4	1.23	4.9	12.32	386	1.87	-1.40	197.0	1	5	87	7	87	78	N/A
8.07	1.41	B- / 7.1	15.5	1.22	5.0	12.04	406	3.16	-1.38	196.6	1	5	86	8	87	76	6
7.23	1.14	B / 8.7	22.0	0.62	20.6	10.75	109	-8.09	-11.32	N/A	1	0	82	17	53	95	1
6.96	1.12	B / 8.8	23.0	0.58	12.0	11.56	459	-9.08	-11.40	N/A	1	0	80	19	50	95	1
6.79	1.05	B / 8.8	23.4	0.71	N/A	12.41	223	-9.51	-12.06	N/A	1	0	82	17	48	94	1
7.21	1.09	B / 8.7	21.8	0.67	10.1	14.34	722	-8.86	-11.78	N/A	0	0	80	20	54	93	1
7.83	1.27	B / 8.6	20.2	1.55	5.0	4.12	461	0.49	-1.33	N/A	0	2	95	3	81	52	3
5.91	2.02	B / 8.2	14.1	-24.50	4.6	13.94	119	-3.87	-3.12	N/A	0	1	98	1	91	96	N/A
6.83	1.74	B- / 7.7	25.8	-11.40	4.5	10.70	126	-3.93	-4.23	N/A	0	3	95	2	93	98	3
9.45	1.40	C+ / 6.6	24.4	0.58	N/A	9.43	117	5.51	-1.95	47.9	0	100	0	0	86	79	5
6.18	1.15	B- / 7.3	28.0	1.06	N/A	27.34	843	-4.17	-5.64	31.1	0	100	0	0	111	76	N/A
10.67	0.93	B- / 7.8	19.3	0.86	N/A	14.56	612	-7.35	-5.80	20.2	0	100	0	0	190	71	N/A
9.07	1.14	B- / 7.9	19.0	0.77	N/A	8.42	576	-10.93	-6.89	20.4	0	100	0	0	231	49	2
5.49	1.22	B / 8.9	6.4	0.09	N/A	16.14	190	-5.20	-5.48	N/A	6	0	90	4	163	69	N/A
4.35	1.13	B+ / 9.4	7.3	1.30	8.2	15.69	83	-1.66	-3.52	N/A	0	0	99	1	6	77	6
6.23	1.60	B- / 7.7	20.5	-226.36	4.3	14.81	259	0.07	-2.45	N/A	0	0	98	2	91	99	3
6.28	1.56	B- / 7.6	20.5	-143.61	4.4	13.64	149	2.27	-2.97	N/A	0	0	98	2	100	99	3
6.52	1.60	B- / 7.8	17.3	-88.79	4.7	14.18	330	0.63	-0.32	N/A	0	1	98	1	89	98	5
14.82	1.09	C+ / 6.9	21.6	0.86	N/A	15.89	1,114	-3.40	-4.03	45.2	0	100	0	0	253	75	3
5.60	1.13	B- / 7.9	18.2	0.91	N/A	27.78	203	-1.12	-2.56	49.3	0	100	0	0	226	58	7
7.47	1.49	B / 8.7	14.6	1.14	5.0	2.22	119	2.70	-3.63	N/A	2	1	91	6	90	75	N/A
7.21	2.04	B / 8.9	13.2	0.94	5.0	7.15	44	1.26	-2.75	N/A	5	2	89	4	81	73	N/A
6.07	0.95	B / 8.6	7.9	1.71	16.9	11.09	371	-5.50	-8.41	N/A	3	0	94	3	774	57	N/A
6.55	1.05	B+ / 9.6	5.0	0.64	13.8	7.90	509	-6.08	-9.17	N/A	1	0	99	0	899	83	24
11.21	1.10	C+ / 6.5	26.1	0.95	N/A	8.59	959	-8.61	-5.34	19.5	0	100	0	0	217	51	5
6.50	1.08	B / 8.5	13.7	2.23	13.6	15.13	218	2.45	3.85	N/A	2	0	97	1	38	65	6
6.25	1.84	B / 8.5	16.1	2.79	14.5	13.14	13	2.21	1.09	N/A	2	0	97	1	27	45	6
7.10	1.00	B / 8.7	12.1	0.14	N/A	17.11	610	3.68	-1.21	N/A	2	1	95	2	106	93	5
6.39	1.43	B / 8.4	13.3	2.45	15.0	12.02	141	3.08	-1.67	N/A	0	0	99	1	12	64	N/A
5.75	1.45	B / 8.5	13.9	0.87	14.5	15.19	30	8.62	8.06	N/A	11	0	88	1	11	81	6
4.71	1.03	B+ / 9.4	7.9	1.16	8.3	16.18	296	-1.85	-0.28	N/A	0	0	100	0	9	76	6
6.33	1.66	B / 8.6	12.2	2.04	14.4	15.95	49	-3.70	-2.04	N/A	0	0	100	0	25	60	N/A
5.41	1.43	B / 8.9	10.8	1.96	9.7	15.98	550	-0.81	-3.67	N/A	2	0	97	1	21	65	6
5.00	1.23	B+ / 9.1	10.7	1.97	9.9	15.31	61	-2.02	-6.52	N/A	2	0	97	1	23	75	9
5.76	0.78	B / 8.4	9.6	1.82	13.7	13.29	434	-2.11	-4.77	N/A	2	0	97	1	24	47	N/A
5.61	0.85	B+ / 9.4	6.4	0.70	8.4	15.82	249	5.44	5.44	N/A	1	0	98	1	13	79	6
6.52	1.19	B / 8.6	13.4	1.91	12.5	15.95	151	2.07	2.46	N/A	1	0	98	1	27	80	6
5.87	1.23	B / 8.3	12.1	2.19	13.2	15.69	127	-2.93	-2.56	N/A	1	0	98	1	33	51	N/A
6.20	1.60	B / 8.3	12.8	2.43	14.2	14.99	90	-2.67	-1.62	N/A	2	0	97	1	24	28	6
6.25	1.24	B / 8.4	13.6	2.11	13.4	15.35	371	-2.41	-0.90	N/A	1	0	98	1	19	42	N/A
6.63	1.24	B / 8.4	14.1	2.61	13.8	14.34	541	1.05	1.85	N/A	1	0	98	1	18	47	6
6.58	1.10	B / 8.6	11.7	1.84	14.5	15.25	326	1.64	0.95	N/A	2	0	97	1	16	81	6
6.11	1.24	B / 8.8	11.8	2.06	13.1	11.95	303	-4.60	-2.77	N/A	1	0	98	1	9	46	23
6.32	1.25	B / 8.7	12.6	2.02	13.7	15.73	583	-4.70	-4.61	N/A	2	0	97	1	24	71	14
6.18	1.28	B / 8.9	10.9	1.57	13.9	17.11	205	3.80	0.24	N/A	1	0	98	1	15	85	N/A
6.34	1.23	B / 8.7	11.1	1.91	13.8	16.01	154	-1.81	-1.18	N/A	1	0	98	1	15	77	N/A
6.29	1.30	B / 8.6	11.6	1.83	13.9	15.08	528	-3.25	-1.85	N/A	5	0	94	1	32	74	N/A
6.30	1.36	B / 8.6	10.8	1.88	14.4	15.19	443	-0.26	-0.71	N/A	2	0	97	1	18	77	N/A
5.73	1.17	B / 8.8	10.9	1.79	10.9	15.84	313	-2.21	-4.05	N/A	1	0	98	1	12	64	N/A
6.30	1.25	B / 8.5	12.8	2.39	13.8	14.38	162	-1.95	-1.77	N/A	4	0	95	1	28	42	N/A
6.31	1.23	B / 8.4	14.1	2.23	14.1	14.41	293	-3.05	-0.97	N/A	5	0	94	1	24	45	N/A
6.79	1.28	B / 8.9	11.7	2.01	14.7	10.20	602	2.16	2.46	N/A	0	0	100	0	10	65	24

* Denotes ETF Fund, N/A denotes number is not available

	99 Pct = Best 0 Pct = Worst			PRICE			PERFORMANCE					
				Price As of 3/31/12	52 Week		Perform-ance Rating/Pts	% Total Return Through 3/31/12			Annualized	
Fund Type	Fund Name	Ticker Symbol	Overall Investment Rating		High	Low		3 Mo	6 Mo	1Yr/Pct	3Yr/Pct	5Yr/Pct
MUN	BlackRock MuniVest Fund II	MVT	A+	16.22	17.08	13.21	A / 9.4	3.88	11.97	25.46 / 96	23.85 / 92	7.99 / 97
MUS	BlackRock MuniYield AZ Fund	MZA	A+	14.59	14.78	12.09	A- / 9.2	4.84	16.69	27.36 / 98	20.95 / 86	6.14 / 83
MUS	BlackRock MuniYield CA Fund	MYC	A+	15.35	16.29	12.62	A- / 9.0	3.30	11.33	27.76 / 98	20.47 / 85	7.93 / 96
MUS	BlackRock MuniYield California Qly	MCA	A	14.86	15.65	12.28	B+ / 8.9	5.15	10.42	26.74 / 97	20.09 / 84	6.85 / 90
MUN	BlackRock MuniYield Fund	MYD	A+	15.31	15.98	12.73	A- / 9.1	5.24	8.35	25.00 / 96	22.18 / 89	6.38 / 85
MUS	BlackRock MuniYield Inv Quality	MFT	B+	14.21	15.09	11.76	B / 7.7	0.05	5.78	24.14 / 95	17.50 / 72	6.92 / 90
MUS	BlackRock MuniYield Invt Fund	MYF	A+	15.38	15.83	12.30	A / 9.3	6.31	12.50	30.41 / 99	21.31 / 87	8.56 / 98
MUS	BlackRock MuniYield Michigan Qly	MIY	B+	14.75	16.10	12.84	B / 7.9	-3.42	6.05	20.56 / 90	19.70 / 83	6.81 / 89
MUS	BlackRock MuniYield Michigan Qly I	MYM	A-	13.81	15.80	11.85	B / 8.1	-5.51	7.94	23.00 / 93	19.96 / 83	6.91 / 90
MUS	BlackRock MuniYield New Jersey Qly	MJI	A-	15.40	17.27	12.59	B+ / 8.3	0.33	13.29	25.47 / 96	17.76 / 74	6.89 / 90
MUS	BlackRock MuniYield New York Qly	MYN	B+	13.97	15.01	11.87	B / 8.2	0.70	9.50	21.44 / 91	18.98 / 80	6.71 / 88
MUS	BlackRock MuniYield NJ Fund	MYJ	A-	15.77	16.44	12.83	B+ / 8.3	2.48	13.70	26.62 / 97	16.95 / 69	6.73 / 88
MUS	BlackRock MuniYield PA Qly	MPA	B+	15.50	17.42	13.14	B- / 7.4	-0.43	9.82	18.59 / 88	17.25 / 71	6.53 / 87
MUN	BlackRock MuniYield Quality Fund	MQY	B	15.48	16.88	12.66	B- / 7.4	-0.71	7.41	24.25 / 95	16.42 / 65	7.92 / 96
MUN	BlackRock MuniYield Quality Fund I	MQT	A-	13.56	14.60	11.05	B+ / 8.4	0.44	8.88	25.98 / 97	19.03 / 80	7.76 / 95
MUN	BlackRock MuniYield Quality III	MYI	B+	14.21	15.07	11.58	B / 7.7	1.98	10.83	25.20 / 96	15.81 / 62	6.15 / 83
MUS	BlackRock New York Muni Inc Qly	BSE	A-	15.20	17.05	12.33	B+ / 8.3	3.43	9.64	28.16 / 98	17.25 / 71	6.28 / 84
MUS	BlackRock NJ Inv Qual Muni Tr	RNJ	A-	14.32	14.46	10.94	A+ / 9.6	7.92	21.91	37.08 / 99	22.00 / 89	2.09 / 45
MUS	BlackRock NJ Muni Bond Trust	BLJ	B	16.07	17.25	12.87	B / 8.0	6.39	18.06	31.42 / 99	13.28 / 45	3.10 / 56
MUS	BlackRock NJ Municipal Income Trus	BNJ	B+	15.70	17.25	13.07	B / 8.0	1.57	12.62	25.79 / 97	16.35 / 64	2.42 / 49
MUS	BlackRock NY Inv Qual Muni Tr	RNY	B+	14.81	15.47	12.72	B+ / 8.3	5.05	8.57	24.32 / 95	18.15 / 76	3.41 / 58
MUS	BlackRock NY Muni 2018 Income Trus	BLH	C	16.50	17.12	15.60	C- / 3.6	0.28	0.10	12.07 / 81	10.10 / 28	6.88 / 90
MUS	BlackRock NY Muni Bond Trust	BQH	B+	15.75	17.05	13.72	B / 7.6	1.81	9.64	20.52 / 90	16.98 / 69	4.24 / 64
MUS	BlackRock NY Municipal Income Tr I	BFY	A-	15.63	16.99	13.54	B+ / 8.3	0.86	9.34	21.52 / 91	19.25 / 81	6.78 / 89
MUS	BlackRock NY Municipal Income Trus	BNY	B+	15.67	16.39	13.79	B / 7.8	3.97	10.98	20.11 / 89	16.97 / 69	4.70 / 69
MUS	BlackRock PA Strategic Muni Tr	BPS	A	15.00	15.57	12.66	A- / 9.2	3.68	12.15	24.02 / 94	22.68 / 90	2.59 / 51
IN	BlackRock Real Asset Equity Trust	BCF	C+	12.05	16.03	9.25	C+ / 6.8	15.48	21.61	-16.56 / 13	28.27 / 77	4.77 / 56
IN	BlackRock Res & Commdty Strat Trus	BCX	D-	15.13	20.11	11.80	D- / 1.5	16.50	18.06	-16.90 / 13	--	--
GL	BlackRock S&P Qual Rkg Glob Eq Mgd	BQY	C+	12.97	14.36	10.91	C+ / 6.3	9.89	20.88	5.00 / 55	23.63 / 59	1.20 / 32
COH	BlackRock Senior High Income Fund	ARK	B+	4.11	4.31	3.40	B / 7.8	8.06	17.92	8.46 / 65	29.44 / 81	0.93 / 31
COH	BlackRock Strategic Bond Trust	BHD	B	14.07	14.41	11.66	C+ / 6.4	9.66	15.24	17.82 / 80	22.57 / 54	9.64 / 84
MUN	BlackRock Strategic Municipal Tr	BSD	A+	14.19	14.67	11.63	A / 9.3	5.36	11.43	27.11 / 97	22.67 / 90	1.20 / 37
GL	BlackRock Utility & Infrastructure	XBUIX	U	18.45	N/A	N/A	U /	-4.29	--	--	--	--
MUS	BlackRock VA Muni Bond Trust	BHV	C-	18.68	21.39	16.17	C- / 3.9	-5.89	4.52	14.79 / 83	10.87 / 32	4.79 / 70
LP	Blackstone / GSO Lng-Sht Credit In	BGX	D+	18.27	20.50	16.23	D / 1.8	9.00	9.80	-3.28 / 33	--	--
LP	Blackstone/GSO Sr Floating Rate Tr	BSL	C	19.95	21.69	17.11	C- / 4.1	9.90	17.29	6.71 / 60	--	--
GI	Boulder Growth&Income Fund	BIF	C-	6.27	6.67	5.18	C- / 3.2	9.23	14.84	-4.35 / 32	13.93 / 24	-8.21 / 8
IN	Boulder Total Return Fund	BTF	C+	17.05	17.28	12.69	C+ / 6.8	12.91	26.30	1.73 / 45	25.14 / 64	-1.98 / 19
GL	Brookfield Gl Lstd Infr Inc Fd	INF	U	19.34	N/A	N/A	U /	11.84	30.10	--	--	--
GI	Calamos Convertible Opport&Income	CHI	B-	12.78	13.62	10.54	C+ / 6.6	15.22	18.13	5.32 / 56	24.60 / 63	1.43 / 34
GI	Calamos Convertible&High Income	CHY	C+	12.76	13.80	10.32	C+ / 6.6	11.88	19.94	1.93 / 46	25.11 / 64	4.11 / 51
GL	Calamos Global Dynamic Income Fd	CHW	B-	8.80	9.11	6.51	B- / 7.5	22.31	29.53	8.89 / 66	25.55 / 66	--
GI	Calamos Global Total Return Fund	CGO	B	15.19	16.46	12.00	B- / 7.5	12.88	14.86	7.56 / 63	28.06 / 76	6.79 / 66
GI	Calamos Strategic Total Return Fun	CSQ	B	10.00	10.06	7.38	B / 8.2	21.49	30.66	10.16 / 69	28.65 / 79	0.67 / 29
FO	Canadian General Investments Ltd	T.CGI	D	16.92	20.25	13.97	C / 4.7	6.11	14.65	-10.66 / 21	22.07 / 53	-5.35 / 12
GL	Canadian World Fund Limited	T.CWF	D	3.75	4.30	3.28	C- / 3.4	5.34	6.53	-9.86 / 22	17.19 / 33	-10.58 / 6
GI	CBRE Clarion Global Real Estate In	IGR	A-	8.04	8.60	6.15	A+ / 9.6	19.58	25.48	5.27 / 56	41.95 / 96	-8.42 / 8
FO	Central Europe & Russia Fund	CEE	C+	35.02	47.93	27.84	B+ / 8.8	22.66	32.59	-12.64 / 18	35.37 / 91	-0.96 / 23
PM	Central Fund of Canada	CEF	C	21.95	26.40	18.44	C / 5.5	11.93	6.14	-1.22 / 38	23.58 / 59	18.25 / 99
PM	Central Gold-Trust	GTU	C-	63.75	77.56	53.39	C- / 3.6	7.74	-0.13	17.71 / 80	14.12 / 24	19.72 / 99
GR	Central Securities	CET	C+	22.12	24.82	18.52	C+ / 5.6	8.11	16.65	-1.75 / 36	23.09 / 57	3.40 / 47
FO	China Fund	CHN	D+	23.30	32.78	19.75	C- / 4.2	13.60	16.36	-15.73 / 14	19.66 / 41	9.92 / 86

		RISK				NET ASSETS		VALUATION			ASSET					FUND MANAGER	
Incl. in Returns		Risk Rating/ Pts	3 Year		Avg Dura-tion	NAV as of 3/31/12	Total $(Mil)	Premium / Discount		Wtd Avg P/E	Cash %	Stocks %	Bonds %	Other %	Portfolio Turnover Ratio	Manager Quality Pct	Manager Tenure (Years)
Dividend Yield %	Expense Ratio		Standard Deviation	Beta				As of 3/31/12	1 Year Average								
6.73	1.23	B / 8.7	12.9	1.62	14.4	15.65	278	3.64	3.10	N/A	0	0	100	0	16	86	13
5.72	1.52	B / 8.8	15.7	1.23	12.6	14.53	61	0.41	-3.80	N/A	3	0	96	1	16	87	19
6.18	1.49	B / 8.7	14.0	2.35	14.2	16.06	306	-4.42	-3.53	N/A	2	0	97	1	33	58	20
6.14	1.49	B / 8.6	12.2	2.13	13.9	15.87	492	-6.36	-6.57	N/A	2	0	97	1	26	64	20
6.54	1.15	B / 8.6	12.1	2.17	13.9	14.96	599	2.34	1.25	N/A	1	0	98	1	16	69	N/A
6.00	1.23	B / 8.8	11.6	1.95	13.5	14.83	113	-4.18	-2.64	N/A	5	0	94	1	29	63	N/A
6.16	1.45	B / 8.7	12.8	2.33	14.1	15.30	186	0.52	-1.35	N/A	1	0	98	1	27	64	N/A
6.22	1.36	B / 8.8	11.5	1.96	12.4	15.59	266	-5.39	-4.54	N/A	0	0	99	1	16	70	20
6.21	1.31	B / 8.8	13.4	2.13	13.1	14.55	163	-5.09	-3.41	N/A	0	0	99	1	18	66	20
5.61	1.12	B / 8.7	11.9	2.09	12.2	15.67	128	-1.72	-3.87	N/A	1	0	98	1	12	56	N/A
6.10	1.33	B / 8.6	10.8	1.98	14.2	14.52	530	-3.79	-3.90	N/A	2	0	97	1	18	66	20
5.63	1.26	B / 8.7	11.1	1.90	12.6	16.17	211	-2.47	-5.57	N/A	4	0	95	1	18	62	N/A
5.92	1.36	B / 8.8	11.2	1.58	12.9	16.02	172	-3.25	-2.83	N/A	2	0	97	1	11	73	20
6.20	1.21	B / 8.5	13.1	2.31	13.3	16.02	418	-3.37	-2.23	N/A	1	0	98	1	12	41	20
6.15	1.20	B / 8.5	12.2	2.41	13.9	13.92	266	-2.59	-2.44	N/A	1	0	98	1	10	47	N/A
6.08	1.32	B / 8.6	11.1	1.91	13.0	14.64	891	-2.94	-3.61	N/A	1	0	98	1	12	54	20
5.64	1.26	B / 8.6	14.7	2.38	14.8	15.01	92	1.27	-1.65	N/A	0	0	99	1	24	40	6
5.49	1.53	B- / 7.4	25.5	1.51	12.2	13.56	13	5.60	-1.08	N/A	2	0	97	1	26	87	6
5.82	1.43	B- / 7.9	14.8	2.09	12.9	15.86	34	1.32	-2.18	N/A	5	0	94	1	19	39	6
6.05	1.24	B / 8.4	14.1	2.14	13.0	15.46	107	1.55	1.60	N/A	3	0	96	1	20	49	6
5.91	1.39	B / 8.5	13.0	1.30	13.7	15.01	18	-1.33	-0.73	N/A	1	0	98	1	19	80	19
5.96	0.98	B+ / 9.4	5.6	0.53	10.0	15.63	57	5.57	6.46	N/A	2	0	97	1	16	75	6
6.25	1.37	B / 8.6	14.1	2.30	14.5	15.74	41	0.06	0.09	N/A	1	0	98	1	14	34	N/A
6.41	1.18	B / 8.9	10.9	1.46	14.5	15.49	73	0.90	1.75	N/A	1	0	98	1	20	82	6
6.32	1.27	B / 8.8	10.4	1.85	15.1	14.87	178	5.38	5.28	N/A	1	0	98	1	17	64	6
6.08	1.55	B / 8.4	13.3	2.42	14.4	14.90	27	0.67	-1.48	N/A	10	0	89	1	17	68	6
9.02	1.09	C+ / 6.9	27.3	1.42	N/A	12.11	712	-0.50	-3.33	29.1	0	100	0	0	79	28	6
9.25	1.13	C+ / 5.8	N/A	N/A	N/A	16.10	784	-6.02	-5.38	N/A	22	78	0	0	27	4	1
9.64	1.19	B / 8.2	17.2	0.72	N/A	13.79	82	-5.95	-6.72	24.6	0	100	0	0	97	88	2
7.30	1.13	B / 8.7	14.6	1.11	5.0	4.14	239	-0.72	-3.87	N/A	0	1	96	3	83	72	3
7.20	1.51	B+ / 9.1	10.9	0.64	6.4	14.12	95	-0.35	-4.38	N/A	2	1	93	4	72	80	5
6.26	1.39	B / 8.8	11.4	1.94	14.8	14.17	89	0.14	-1.44	N/A	3	0	96	1	20	79	6
11.79	N/A	U /	N/A	N/A	N/A	19.87	N/A	-7.15	N/A	N/A	0	0	0	100	N/A	N/A	1
5.33	1.52	B / 8.1	14.9	1.46	14.2	16.03	24	16.53	20.03	Wtd Avg P/E	1	0	98	1	12	52	6
7.09	1.78	B / 8.2	N/A	N/A	N/A	18.68	237	-2.19	0.72	N/A	0	0	99	1	N/A	99	1
6.62	2.79	B / 8.2	N/A	N/A	N/A	19.36	285	3.05	0.99	N/A	6	0	0	94	94	98	N/A
0.00	2.40	B / 8.2	16.3	0.81	N/A	7.70	188	-18.57	-18.46	N/A	7	88	1	4	6	34	40
0.00	2.12	B- / 7.9	20.8	1.01	N/A	21.27	234	-19.84	-18.10	N/A	5	93	1	1	3	68	19
6.21	0.47	U /	N/A	N/A	N/A	21.28	150	-9.12	N/A	N/A	0	0	0	100	N/A	N/A	1
8.92	1.55	B / 8.3	16.6	0.77	7.4	12.55	827	1.83	-0.58	N/A	4	1	58	37	44	79	10
7.99	1.61	B / 8.1	17.9	0.80	7.6	13.01	918	-1.92	-3.32	N/A	5	1	64	30	42	80	9
8.45	1.93	B- / 7.5	23.7	1.02	6.0	9.64	535	-8.71	-13.13	49.2	4	59	19	18	43	82	5
7.90	1.90	B / 8.0	18.5	0.92	6.2	14.86	120	2.22	0.73	29.9	3	44	21	32	89	79	7
8.40	1.93	B- / 7.7	20.7	1.17	7.3	10.82	1,568	-7.58	-12.75	23.5	1	54	21	24	30	60	8
1.42	3.57	C / 4.6	18.8	0.56	N/A	22.49	288	-24.77	-22.40	N/A	1	98	0	1	27	88	24
0.00	3.04	C / 4.9	16.7	0.43	N/A	5.58	20	-32.80	-31.83	110.8	4	95	0	1	19	81	N/A
6.72	1.03	B- / 7.6	32.3	1.50	N/A	8.88	950	-9.46	-11.07	42.3	0	74	0	26	2	81	6
2.12	1.11	C+ / 5.9	36.5	1.53	N/A	37.75	506	-7.23	-9.49	N/A	0	100	0	0	33	82	N/A
0.05	0.30	B- / 7.4	29.3	1.17	N/A	21.12	5,621	3.93	1.81	N/A	1	0	0	99	N/A	29	6
0.00	0.36	B- / 7.9	23.2	0.87	N/A	61.74	877	3.26	3.31	N/A	1	0	0	99	N/A	25	9
2.89	0.78	B / 8.1	16.8	0.93	N/A	26.57	594	-16.75	-16.37	32.6	0	99	0	1	7	61	39
0.75	1.01	C+ / 6.1	26.3	0.99	N/A	25.18	660	-7.47	-10.12	N/A	7	92	0	1	20	71	0

* Denotes ETF Fund, N/A denotes number is not available

Fund Type	Fund Name	Ticker Symbol	Overall Investment Rating	PRICE Price As of 3/31/12	52 Week High	52 Week Low	PERFORMANCE Perform-ance Rating/Pts	3 Mo	6 Mo	1Yr/Pct	Annualized 3Yr/Pct	5Yr/Pct
EN	ClearBridge Energy MLP Fund Inc	CEM	C+	23.60	24.00	17.62	C+ / 5.9	6.82	24.90	10.83 / 70	--	--
EN	ClearBridge Energy MLP Oppty Fd In	EMO	U	20.31	N/A	N/A	U /	8.18	26.56	--	--	--
GI	Clough Global Allocation Fund	GLV	C-	13.94	16.77	11.48	C- / 3.8	11.81	17.73	-6.97 / 27	16.39 / 31	1.10 / 31
GL	Clough Global Equity Fund	GLQ	C-	13.09	15.74	10.80	C- / 4.0	11.24	17.56	-8.02 / 25	17.93 / 35	0.55 / 29
GL	Clough Global Opportunities Fund	GLO	C-	11.78	14.06	9.80	C- / 3.8	14.18	17.31	-7.23 / 26	16.13 / 30	0.88 / 31
GL	Cohen & Steers Closed-End Opp Fd	FOF	C+	12.76	13.80	10.79	C+ / 5.8	8.77	14.38	2.31 / 47	23.47 / 58	0.13 / 27
GL	Cohen & Steers Global Inc Builder	INB	B	10.70	11.59	7.96	B+ / 8.4	18.06	30.31	5.82 / 58	30.84 / 84	--
IN	Cohen&Steers Dividend Majors	DVM	B	13.90	14.73	10.55	B+ / 8.3	16.87	27.31	11.77 / 72	29.75 / 81	-0.23 / 26
UT	Cohen&Steers Infrastructure Fund	UTF	B+	17.60	18.48	14.05	B+ / 8.6	13.67	17.98	7.30 / 62	32.89 / 87	1.51 / 34
GI	Cohen&Steers Quality Income Realty	RQI	A-	9.82	10.59	6.92	A+ / 9.9	18.06	33.15	6.55 / 60	68.30 / 99	-5.19 / 12
IN	Cohen&Steers REIT& Preferred Incom	RNP	A	16.31	17.20	11.28	A+ / 9.9	17.36	31.87	14.47 / 76	66.66 / 99	0.38 / 29
IN	Cohen&Steers Sel Preferred & Incom	PSF	C+	24.80	25.19	21.02	C / 4.8	16.85	11.16	10.09 / 68	--	--
GI	Cohen&Steers Total Return Realty	RFI	A	13.84	14.75	9.99	A+ / 9.6	18.13	26.13	6.31 / 59	42.82 / 97	4.40 / 53
GR	Columbia Seligman Prem Tech Gro	STK	B	18.90	19.99	13.85	B / 8.0	23.82	28.67	7.53 / 62		
IN	Cornerstone Progressive Return Fun	CFP	D	6.67	7.91	5.30	C- / 3.3	15.22	12.78	9.13 / 67	12.24 / 20	
IN	Cornerstone Strategic Value Fund	CLM	D+	7.61	11.00	6.33	C / 4.3	20.82	-4.96	-12.03 / 19	21.15 / 48	-9.47 / 7
IN	Cornerstone Total Return Fund	CRF	D	6.80	10.00	5.68	C- / 3.3	19.22	-9.24	-13.91 / 16	17.41 / 34	-14.07 / 4
COH	Credit Suisse Asset Mgmt Income	CIK	B	3.73	4.06	3.24	B- / 7.4	4.42	12.97	10.87 / 70	28.40 / 78	8.02 / 74
COH	Credit Suisse High Yield Bond Fund	DHY	A+	3.12	3.45	2.57	A- / 9.2	11.31	11.80	11.50 / 71	39.04 / 95	5.63 / 60
COI	Cutwater Select Income	BDF	C+	19.74	20.10	17.58	C / 5.2	5.00	11.33	15.40 / 78	20.08 / 44	8.13 / 75
GL	Delaware Enhanced Glb Div & Inc Fd	DEX	B+	12.83	13.84	9.60	A / 9.4	22.18	25.67	6.58 / 60	38.48 / 95	--
MUS	Delaware Inv CO Muni Inc	VCF	B	14.60	14.95	12.10	C+ / 6.4	8.40	10.85	21.93 / 92	11.54 / 35	3.47 / 58
GI	Delaware Inv Div & Inc	DDF	B+	8.15	8.38	5.99	B+ / 8.7	17.74	28.36	9.46 / 67	32.19 / 86	1.35 / 33
MUS	Delaware Inv MN Muni Inc Fund II	VMM	B	14.23	14.50	12.19	C+ / 6.0	6.47	10.89	18.11 / 87	11.96 / 37	4.05 / 63
MUN	Delaware Inv Nat Muni Inc	VFL	C+	13.24	13.45	11.95	C / 4.5	3.61	3.52	12.76 / 82	11.54 / 35	2.93 / 54
GI	Dividend and Income Fund Inc	DNI	C-	3.62	4.48	3.14	C / 4.7	9.15	9.20	-6.61 / 28	21.61 / 51	-8.27 / 8
UT	DNP Select Income Fund Inc	DNP	C+	10.10	11.47	8.52	C / 5.5	-5.77	4.85	15.11 / 77	22.96 / 56	6.67 / 65
GEI	DoubleLine Opportunistic Credit Fd	DBL	U	25.61	N/A	N/A	U /	--	--	--	--	--
IN	Dow 30 Enhanced Premium & Income F	DPO	C+	11.25	12.33	8.60	C+ / 6.0	12.88	23.06	5.39 / 57	22.35 / 54	--
IN	Dow 30 Premium & Dividend Income	DPD	C-	14.18	15.32	11.60	C- / 3.4	10.08	18.36	2.77 / 49	13.81 / 24	1.97 / 38
COH	Dreyfus High Yield Strategies Fund	DHF	B	4.65	5.14	3.96	A- / 9.0	6.89	14.45	9.70 / 68	37.00 / 93	13.28 / 98
MUN	Dreyfus Municipal Income	DMF	B+	9.92	10.64	8.20	B / 7.9	2.00	7.29	21.25 / 91	18.07 / 76	7.08 / 91
MUN	Dreyfus Strategic Muni Bond Fund	DSM	B+	8.69	9.17	7.32	B / 8.0	1.64	5.01	20.25 / 89	18.99 / 80	4.77 / 69
MUN	Dreyfus Strategic Municipals	LEO	A-	9.12	9.35	7.54	B+ / 8.5	4.29	11.00	22.16 / 92	18.85 / 80	5.98 / 81
MUN	DTF Tax Free Income	DTF	B+	16.60	17.12	14.17	B / 7.7	4.66	10.48	21.39 / 91	16.42 / 65	7.72 / 95
UT	Duff & Phelps Global Utility Incom	DPG	U	19.05	N/A	N/A	U /	7.18	11.79	--	--	--
GEI	Duff & Phelps Utilities & Crp Bd T	DUC	C-	11.81	12.78	10.60	D+ / 2.7	-0.16	6.25	16.33 / 79	9.62 / 16	8.29 / 76
GL	DWS Global High Income Fund	LBF	C	8.08	8.36	6.72	C / 4.5	8.42	16.09	9.73 / 68	17.75 / 35	5.58 / 59
GL	DWS High Income Opportunities Fund	DHG	A+	16.03	16.24	12.13	A+ / 9.7	18.15	28.64	20.22 / 82	42.68 / 97	-6.08 / 11
COH	DWS High Income Trust	KHI	C+	10.09	11.51	8.35	B / 8.0	0.89	15.27	8.44 / 65	31.14 / 84	6.35 / 63
GL	DWS Multi-Market Income Trust	KMM	B-	10.33	11.18	8.55	B / 8.1	4.62	13.04	7.13 / 62	31.79 / 85	9.71 / 85
MUN	DWS Municipal Income Trust	KTF	A+	13.82	14.34	11.10	A- / 9.2	1.71	12.00	27.13 / 97	22.45 / 90	11.23 / 99
GL	DWS Strategic Income Fund	KST	B+	14.55	14.55	11.28	B+ / 8.6	11.25	17.88	19.83 / 82	31.91 / 86	9.05 / 80
MUN	DWS Strategic Municipal Inc Tr	KSM	A+	13.95	14.53	11.22	A- / 9.2	2.15	13.58	25.77 / 96	22.18 / 89	9.70 / 99
GR	Eagle Capital Growth Fund	GRF	B-	6.76	8.03	5.30	C+ / 6.7	-5.82	19.91	9.57 / 68	26.02 / 69	--
MUS	Eaton Vance CA Muni Bond	EVM	C	11.96	13.55	10.35	C / 4.9	-5.31	0.71	23.18 / 94	12.71 / 41	1.69 / 42
MUS	Eaton Vance CA Muni Bond II	EIA	C+	12.50	13.45	10.19	C+ / 6.3	-0.59	5.41	28.53 / 98	12.80 / 42	3.00 / 55
MUS	Eaton Vance CA Muni Inc Tr	CEV	A-	13.46	14.32	10.84	B+ / 8.7	4.78	10.55	31.44 / 99	17.65 / 73	4.13 / 63
IN	Eaton Vance Enhanced Eqty Inc	EOI	D+	11.06	12.41	9.10	C- / 3.2	11.34	19.07	-0.71 / 39	12.93 / 21	-1.80 / 20
IN	Eaton Vance Enhanced Eqty Inc II	EOS	D+	10.88	12.50	9.07	C- / 3.4	9.23	16.21	-3.89 / 32	14.75 / 26	-1.03 / 22
LP	Eaton Vance Floating Rate Income T	EFT	B+	16.24	17.16	13.37	B+ / 8.3	15.37	19.50	4.52 / 54	31.64 / 85	4.65 / 55
GEN	Eaton Vance Limited Duration Incom	EVV	C+	16.05	16.79	13.92	C+ / 6.4	7.48	14.04	8.28 / 65	24.47 / 62	6.58 / 64

Incl. in Returns		RISK	3 Year		Avg Dura-tion	NET ASSETS		VALUATION Premium / Discount			ASSET				Portfolio Turnover Ratio	FUND MANAGER	
Dividend Yield %	Expense Ratio	Risk Rating/ Pts	Standard Deviation	Beta		NAV as of 3/31/12	Total $(Mil)	As of 3/31/12	1 Year Average	Wtd Avg P/E	Cash %	Stocks %	Bonds %	Other %		Manager Quality Pct	Manager Tenure (Years)
6.19	1.71	B / 8.2	N/A	N/A	N/A	22.55	1,363	4.66	2.55	N/A	0	99	0	1	14	90	N/A
6.50	6.31	U /	N/A	N/A	N/A	20.25	608	0.30	N/A	N/A	0	0	0	100	N/A	N/A	1
8.61	2.87	B- / 7.6	18.9	1.06	7.1	16.30	192	-14.48	-13.45	53.7	10	66	22	2	172	22	8
8.86	3.23	B- / 7.6	20.7	0.90	8.0	15.53	314	-15.71	-13.89	51.7	8	74	15	3	173	66	7
9.17	3.40	B- / 7.6	19.8	0.84	7.0	13.84	813	-14.88	-13.48	53.8	8	66	23	3	171	65	6
8.15	0.95	B / 8.4	16.5	0.60	N/A	13.85	389	-7.87	-8.03	46.9	1	65	18	16	79	89	N/A
10.47	2.01	B- / 7.4	23.3	0.99	N/A	11.60	246	-7.76	-10.06	N/A	0	95	0	5	56	89	N/A
6.62	0.95	B- / 7.8	22.2	1.19	N/A	14.96	173	-7.09	-7.85	52.1	0	99	0	1	61	70	7
8.18	2.09	B / 8.1	22.1	1.55	23.4	19.05	1,535	-7.61	-9.10	26.9	0	77	0	23	40	78	8
7.33	1.87	B- / 7.1	44.4	1.95	34.7	10.62	1,042	-7.53	-7.91	65.3	0	81	0	19	53	94	N/A
7.36	1.72	B- / 7.6	35.3	1.58	22.1	17.15	738	-4.90	-6.73	64.4	0	46	0	54	52	96	9
8.32	1.78	B / 8.7	N/A	N/A	N/A	24.54	271	1.06	0.12	N/A	1	0	6	93	48	80	N/A
6.36	0.91	B- / 7.6	25.2	1.24	N/A	13.31	117	3.98	1.93	N/A	0	82	0	18	72	89	N/A
9.79	1.10	B- / 7.7	N/A	N/A	N/A	19.39	261	-2.53	-3.44	N/A	0	100	0	0	71	32	N/A
16.44	1.61	C+ / 6.3	26.6	0.86	N/A	5.24	55	27.29	25.20	26.6	1	98	0	1	117	35	5
18.94	1.74	C+ / 5.6	33.6	1.01	N/A	6.44	64	18.17	35.00	51.0	0	99	0	1	25	42	11
17.22	2.37	C / 5.4	34.4	0.94	N/A	5.79	26	17.44	37.69	42.3	0	99	0	1	34	41	N/A
8.53	0.73	B / 8.6	15.7	1.13	4.4	3.72	180	0.27	0.69	N/A	0	0	96	4	57	61	N/A
10.19	2.00	B / 8.6	18.3	1.16	N/A	2.94	212	6.12	5.54	N/A	0	0	99	1	66	86	N/A
5.83	0.79	B+ / 9.6	6.8	0.64	18.1	20.38	214	-3.14	-7.09	N/A	0	0	99	1	20	87	7
9.59	1.98	B- / 7.2	24.8	0.87	25.1	12.12	179	5.86	-1.01	57.7	6	46	44	4	72	94	5
4.73	0.56	B+ / 9.1	9.4	0.85	13.9	15.01	65	-2.73	-6.75	N/A	0	0	100	0	10	79	8
8.47	1.51	B- / 7.7	19.6	0.95	25.2	8.50	72	-4.12	-6.61	27.2	1	53	32	14	45	86	11
4.85	0.56	B+ / 9.4	6.7	1.15	12.2	14.94	158	-4.75	-8.32	N/A	0	0	100	0	9	68	9
4.08	0.65	B+ / 9.0	9.7	1.60	12.8	14.02	31	-5.56	-5.49	N/A	0	0	100	0	50	39	9
16.91	2.00	B- / 7.2	19.3	0.94	5.1	4.09	71	-11.49	-10.61	22.0	6	40	51	3	24	54	1
7.72	1.95	B / 8.7	13.9	0.38	N/A	8.12	2,014	24.38	30.28	N/A	0	71	25	4	13	91	N/A
3.91	N/A	U /	N/A	N/A	N/A	24.02	N/A	6.62	N/A	N/A	0	0	0	100	N/A	N/A	N/A
7.75	1.01	B- / 7.5	24.0	0.98	N/A	11.81	306	-4.74	-2.33	26.0	5	94	0	1	3	64	1
7.50	1.02	B- / 7.8	17.4	0.82	N/A	15.02	171	-5.59	-3.90	26.2	0	100	0	0	6	27	1
9.46	2.00	C+ / 6.4	15.9	1.23	4.7	3.90	306	19.23	18.16	N/A	0	0	99	1	66	80	N/A
6.35	1.29	B / 8.8	11.1	1.62	12.0	9.88	195	0.40	0.28	N/A	0	0	100	0	23	76	3
6.49	0.85	B / 8.7	12.1	1.72	12.2	8.58	395	1.28	1.57	N/A	0	0	100	0	21	72	11
6.45	1.26	B / 8.5	11.8	1.71	12.3	8.81	515	3.52	1.31	N/A	0	0	100	0	18	74	3
5.48	1.23	B / 8.9	9.5	1.78	12.8	16.72	138	-0.72	-3.97	N/A	2	0	97	1	6	64	N/A
8.27	N/A	U /	N/A	N/A	N/A	19.24	725	-0.99	N/A	N/A	0	0	0	100	N/A	N/A	1
7.11	1.86	B / 8.7	9.6	1.55	7.5	11.74	321	0.60	-1.40	N/A	0	0	96	4	36	36	16
6.24	2.22	B- / 7.7	15.3	0.76	6.0	9.01	63	-10.32	-9.83	N/A	4	0	96	0	89	89	N/A
8.92	2.31	B / 8.8	17.1	0.65	4.8	15.62	234	2.62	-5.91	N/A	3	14	81	2	134	97	N/A
9.66	1.61	C+ / 6.7	16.6	1.16	4.7	9.68	148	4.24	6.61	N/A	2	0	98	0	60	66	14
8.94	1.49	B- / 7.1	13.6	0.52	5.1	10.00	228	3.30	5.29	N/A	0	0	100	0	55	96	N/A
6.08	1.23	B / 8.7	11.0	1.95	9.8	13.33	491	3.68	0.69	N/A	0	0	100	0	33	78	N/A
8.49	1.96	B- / 7.5	10.9	0.31	5.2	13.85	61	5.05	-1.03	N/A	1	0	99	0	56	97	N/A
6.62	1.29	B / 8.8	11.4	2.05	12.2	13.22	138	5.52	3.87	N/A	0	0	100	0	26	77	14
1.50	1.52	B / 8.4	24.8	0.74	N/A	7.70	23	-12.21	-12.87	23.6	5	94	0	1	62	82	N/A
6.18	1.99	B / 8.0	18.0	2.69	13.6	12.39	255	-3.47	2.83	N/A	0	0	100	0	21	18	10
6.16	1.62	B / 8.1	17.4	2.72	12.6	12.65	46	-1.19	2.14	N/A	0	0	100	0	34	19	10
6.58	2.00	B / 8.5	16.4	2.62	12.1	13.41	90	0.37	0.25	N/A	0	0	100	0	22	36	13
9.37	1.15	B- / 7.2	18.5	0.95	N/A	12.87	446	-14.06	-12.26	50.1	0	100	0	0	78	20	8
9.65	1.14	B- / 7.0	20.6	0.95	N/A	12.63	570	-13.86	-10.68	60.4	0	100	0	0	67	24	7
6.28	1.87	B / 8.2	18.7	-111.30	4.9	15.66	596	3.70	-1.29	N/A	0	0	0	100	50	99	8
7.79	1.76	B- / 7.5	13.3	0.78	4.9	16.55	2,001	-3.02	-5.15	N/A	1	0	66	33	46	92	9

* Denotes ETF Fund, N/A denotes number is not available

Fund Type	Fund Name	Ticker Symbol	Overall Investment Rating	PRICE Price As of 3/31/12	52 Week High	52 Week Low	PERFORMANCE Performance Rating/Pts	3 Mo	6 Mo	1Yr/Pct	Annualized 3Yr/Pct	5Yr/Pct
MUS	Eaton Vance MA Muni Bond	MAB	B+	15.51	17.38	12.46	B+ / 8.4	9.50	11.45	29.17 / 99	15.71 / 61	5.71 / 79
MUS	Eaton Vance MA Muni Inc Tr	MMV	C+	14.85	16.23	12.47	C+ / 6.0	4.09	3.98	21.62 / 92	12.84 / 42	5.99 / 81
MUS	Eaton Vance MI Muni Bond	MIW	B	15.05	15.93	12.30	B- / 7.5	3.49	14.04	10.37 / 78	17.61 / 73	6.98 / 91
MUS	Eaton Vance MI Muni Inc Tr	EMI	B+	13.49	13.90	11.31	B- / 7.5	6.10	12.66	26.81 / 97	13.85 / 49	5.48 / 77
MUN	Eaton Vance Muni Bond Fund	EIM	B-	13.00	13.44	10.97	C+ / 6.6	4.08	8.77	21.66 / 92	13.40 / 46	3.18 / 56
MUN	Eaton Vance Muni Bond II	EIV	A-	14.49	14.95	11.92	B+ / 8.3	6.28	13.12	24.02 / 94	17.08 / 70	5.54 / 77
MUN	Eaton Vance Municipal Inc Tr	EVN	A+	13.63	14.30	10.96	A / 9.5	9.02	16.60	25.83 / 97	23.32 / 92	4.61 / 68
MUN	Eaton Vance National Municipal Opp	EOT	A+	21.80	22.16	18.10	A / 9.4	5.67	13.50	23.36 / 94	--	--
MUS	Eaton Vance NJ Muni Bond	EMJ	B	14.65	15.76	12.53	B- / 7.5	4.88	13.00	24.16 / 95	14.53 / 54	5.16 / 74
MUS	Eaton Vance NJ Muni Inc Tr	EVJ	B+	13.89	14.58	11.88	B / 8.0	1.00	10.68	20.79 / 90	18.14 / 76	4.98 / 72
MUS	Eaton Vance NY Muni Bond	ENX	C+	13.47	15.50	11.69	C / 5.0	-2.30	3.07	20.63 / 90	12.53 / 40	3.72 / 60
MUS	Eaton Vance NY Muni Bond II	NYH	B-	13.64	15.20	11.72	C+ / 6.4	1.17	9.23	20.62 / 90	13.72 / 48	3.99 / 62
MUS	Eaton Vance NY Muni Inc Tr	EVY	A	14.64	15.39	11.87	B+ / 8.7	6.34	12.54	27.25 / 97	18.10 / 76	5.22 / 75
MUS	Eaton Vance OH Muni Bond	EIO	A	14.07	14.29	10.67	A- / 9.0	8.96	13.44	32.03 / 99	17.90 / 75	4.12 / 63
MUS	Eaton Vance OH Muni Inc Tr	EVO	A	15.05	15.49	11.62	A / 9.3	10.24	18.56	22.13 / 92	21.18 / 87	6.45 / 86
MUS	Eaton Vance PA Muni Bond	EIP	C+	13.80	14.69	11.88	C+ / 5.9	4.44	9.39	20.86 / 90	11.88 / 36	5.15 / 74
MUS	Eaton Vance PA Muni Inc Tr	EVP	A	14.15	14.46	12.08	B+ / 8.8	6.81	14.18	22.25 / 92	19.53 / 82	5.58 / 77
IN	Eaton Vance Risk Mgd Div Eq Inc	ETJ	D-	10.59	12.87	9.95	D- / 1.1	7.16	5.29	-5.34 / 30	-0.78 / 7	--
LP	Eaton Vance Senior Floating Rate	EFR	B-	15.24	17.69	13.31	B- / 7.5	7.18	11.04	-0.64 / 39	30.16 / 82	3.30 / 47
LP	Eaton Vance Senior Income Trust	EVF	B+	7.21	7.79	6.06	B+ / 8.3	11.57	18.24	3.67 / 51	32.27 / 86	3.44 / 47
GL	Eaton Vance Sh Dur Diversified Inc	EVG	C	17.08	17.67	15.44	C- / 4.1	6.55	9.64	7.84 / 63	17.33 / 33	5.57 / 59
GL	Eaton Vance Tax Adv Glob Div Inc	ETG	B	14.47	15.76	11.50	B / 8.2	20.10	24.47	5.68 / 57	30.14 / 82	-2.87 / 17
GL	Eaton Vance Tax Adv Global Div Opp	ETO	C+	19.58	23.08	15.14	B- / 7.0	16.56	24.58	-4.34 / 32	26.70 / 72	-1.44 / 21
IN	Eaton Vance Tax Advantage Div Inc	EVT	B	16.73	18.21	12.64	B / 8.2	16.08	27.65	1.78 / 46	30.85 / 84	-1.88 / 20
IN	Eaton Vance Tax Mgd Buy Write Opp	ETV	C	12.94	13.31	10.25	C / 5.1	13.24	24.99	11.96 / 72	18.29 / 37	3.36 / 47
IN	Eaton Vance Tax Mgd Div Eqty Inc	ETY	D+	9.53	11.34	7.87	C- / 3.1	13.58	21.98	-0.27 / 40	11.91 / 19	-1.53 / 21
IN	Eaton Vance Tax-Managed Buy-Write	ETB	C-	13.70	13.95	10.57	C / 5.0	9.28	24.02	9.10 / 67	18.65 / 38	2.31 / 40
GL	Eaton Vance Tax-Mgd Gbl Div Eq Inc	EXG	D+	8.91	11.12	7.45	C- / 3.7	14.42	22.06	-2.20 / 35	14.70 / 26	-1.85 / 20
MUN	Eaton Vance Tx Adv Bd&Option Str	EXD	C+	16.90	17.93	15.42	C+ / 5.7	4.68	7.28	12.56 / 82	--	--
GL	Eaton Vance Tx Mgd Glb Buy Wrt Opp	ETW	D+	11.04	12.54	9.20	C- / 4.1	10.23	19.52	0.30 / 42	17.00 / 32	0.42 / 29
GI	Ellsworth Fund Ltd	ECF	C	7.35	7.80	6.03	C / 4.8	12.31	16.39	0.15 / 41	20.12 / 44	3.11 / 45
IN	Equus Total Return	EQS	D-	2.27	2.99	1.79	D- / 1.0	1.34	20.74	-14.02 / 16	-4.18 / 6	-21.31 / 3
IN	F&C/Claymore Preferred Sec Inc Fun	FFC	A+	18.05	18.94	14.73	A+ / 9.8	5.81	18.87	16.54 / 79	52.62 / 99	7.06 / 67
IN	F&C/Claymore Total Return Fund	FLC	A+	19.01	19.90	15.50	A+ / 9.8	3.99	14.70	14.88 / 77	53.78 / 99	7.76 / 73
USA	Federated Enhanced Treasury Income	FTT	D	14.76	15.87	14.00	D / 1.6	4.43	1.49	2.46 / 47	--	--
MUN	Federated Prem Intermediate Muni	FPT	A	14.90	15.99	12.03	B+ / 8.7	9.58	15.49	25.50 / 96	17.26 / 71	7.53 / 94
MUN	Federated Premier Muni Income	FMN	A-	15.97	16.17	12.65	B+ / 8.8	7.26	15.25	28.65 / 98	17.38 / 72	7.33 / 93
EN	Fiduciary/Claymore MLP Opp	FMO	B-	22.66	24.34	16.21	B- / 7.1	7.35	22.38	7.35 / 62	26.60 / 71	5.76 / 60
FS	Financial Trends Fund	DHFT	A-	10.81	11.06	6.88	A- / 9.1	30.71	43.99	8.57 / 65	33.46 / 88	-5.12 / 12
FS	First Opportunity Fund	FOFI	C-	7.05	7.55	5.72	C- / 3.2	13.34	16.72	-2.76 / 34	13.31 / 22	-9.49 / 7
LP	First Tr Senior Floating Rte Inc I	FCT	B	14.97	15.62	12.05	B / 7.6	14.65	15.12	6.49 / 60	28.46 / 78	2.22 / 40
FS	First Tr Specialty Finance &Fin Op	FGB	B+	7.12	8.36	5.11	A- / 9.1	15.50	25.60	-4.72 / 31	38.97 / 95	--
GL	First Trust Active Dividend Inc Fd	FAV	D	8.70	11.53	7.39	D+ / 2.5	6.03	8.85	-15.63 / 14	12.84 / 21	--
EN	First Trust Energy Income&Growth	FEN	B	30.05	31.84	22.45	B- / 7.5	8.16	22.73	9.97 / 68	27.39 / 74	8.71 / 78
EN	First Trust Energy Infrastructure	XFIFX	U	21.29	N/A	N/A	U /	6.21	8.68	--	--	--
IN	First Trust Enhanced Equity Income	FFA	C+	12.08	12.95	9.49	C+ / 6.4	13.62	23.14	4.24 / 53	23.45 / 58	1.77 / 36
GL	First Trust High Income Long/Short	FSD	C	18.13	19.36	14.03	C / 5.4	20.44	18.80	5.21 / 56	--	--
MTG	First Trust Mortgage Income Fund	FMY	C-	19.62	21.40	16.61	C / 4.4	4.79	11.41	7.86 / 64	18.61 / 38	12.79 / 97
GEN	First Trust Strategic High Inc II	FHY	C	17.31	18.08	12.66	C+ / 6.5	16.06	31.53	31.95 / 90	15.05 / 27	-9.99 / 7
GL	First Trust/Aberdeen Emerg Opp Fd	FEO	B+	20.78	21.72	16.35	B+ / 8.8	18.57	27.23	8.25 / 65	33.32 / 88	11.56 / 94
GL	First Trust/Aberdeen Glob Opp Inc	FAM	B+	17.46	17.94	14.51	B / 8.1	13.38	13.58	13.75 / 75	29.77 / 81	9.31 / 82
IN	Flaherty&Crumrine Preferred Inc Op	PFO	A+	10.99	12.55	8.93	A+ / 9.6	0.18	10.00	14.90 / 77	45.22 / 98	6.69 / 65

99 Pct = Best
0 Pct = Worst

* Denotes ETF Fund, N/A denotes number is not available

www.thestreetratings.com

		RISK				NET ASSETS		VALUATION			ASSET					FUND MANAGER	
Incl. in Returns		Risk Rating/ Pts	3 Year		Avg Dura-tion	NAV as of 3/31/12	Total $(Mil)	Premium / Discount		Wtd Avg P/E	Cash %	Stocks %	Bonds %	Other %	Portfolio Turnover Ratio	Manager Quality Pct	Manager Tenure (Years)
Dividend Yield %	Expense Ratio		Standard Deviation	Beta				As of 3/31/12	1 Year Average								
5.42	1.65	B / 8.2	20.4	3.06	13.6	14.95	25	3.75	0.13	N/A	0	0	100	0	27	19	2
5.36	1.98	B / 8.6	12.2	1.74	13.3	14.89	38	-0.27	0.24	N/A	0	0	100	0	15	42	2
5.91	1.58	B / 8.6	15.3	1.58	13.6	14.59	21	3.15	0.40	N/A	0	0	100	0	5	78	10
5.70	2.04	B / 8.7	12.8	2.13	12.8	14.21	28	-5.07	-7.20	N/A	0	0	100	0	18	49	13
6.12	1.81	B / 8.4	14.0	2.29	11.8	13.24	856	-1.81	-0.58	N/A	0	0	100	0	18	27	2
6.61	1.63	B / 8.8	12.6	2.16	14.3	12.69	121	14.18	11.99	N/A	0	0	100	0	12	43	8
7.26	2.27	B / 8.4	15.6	2.62	14.3	11.92	244	14.35	13.02	N/A	0	0	100	0	15	56	13
5.14	0.94	B / 8.3	N/A	N/A	N/A	21.64	295	0.74	-3.22	N/A	0	0	100	0	10	83	3
5.32	1.57	B / 8.3	15.4	2.02	10.3	14.04	34	4.34	3.51	N/A	0	0	100	0	4	35	2
5.68	1.96	B / 8.5	15.5	2.60	12.4	13.97	61	-0.57	-0.41	N/A	0	0	100	0	11	34	2
5.48	1.91	B / 8.4	13.7	1.90	11.7	13.68	209	-1.54	1.96	N/A	0	0	100	0	29	37	7
6.18	1.75	B / 8.5	15.0	1.84	12.0	13.32	33	2.40	3.51	N/A	0	0	100	0	17	49	7
6.21	2.00	B / 8.5	18.3	3.04	14.2	14.17	73	3.32	0.42	N/A	0	0	100	0	13	27	13
5.48	1.44	B / 8.3	16.6	1.81	12.1	13.07	31	7.65	4.75	N/A	0	0	100	0	10	61	7
5.53	1.94	B / 8.2	16.7	2.45	12.9	14.50	38	3.79	-1.04	N/A	0	0	100	0	11	53	7
6.33	1.49	B / 8.2	19.1	3.07	13.3	13.81	39	-0.07	0.48	N/A	0	0	100	0	12	15	5
6.13	1.98	B / 8.7	13.4	2.13	13.3	13.96	36	1.36	-2.21	N/A	0	0	100	0	8	64	5
12.07	1.09	B- / 7.0	10.2	0.23	N/A	12.53	922	-15.48	-13.96	50.0	0	100	0	0	103	21	5
6.85	1.73	B- / 7.6	22.6	-4.55	5.1	15.33	503	-0.59	0.57	N/A	0	0	0	100	49	97	9
6.16	2.18	B / 8.5	17.5	-1.42	5.2	7.21	266	0.00	-3.48	N/A	3	1	7	89	53	98	14
6.32	1.89	B+ / 9.0	9.5	0.17	13.8	17.80	336	-4.04	-6.79	N/A	0	0	73	27	35	91	7
8.50	1.55	B- / 7.8	24.4	1.04	18.7	15.44	1,097	-6.28	-6.82	33.2	1	80	0	19	95	88	8
7.15	1.57	B- / 7.5	24.4	1.08	15.8	22.25	304	-12.00	-11.50	20.6	1	77	0	22	95	83	8
7.71	1.49	B- / 7.9	23.1	1.29	20.8	18.48	1,222	-9.47	-9.85	20.3	1	68	0	31	86	59	9
10.27	1.09	B- / 7.2	18.0	0.79	N/A	14.45	871	-10.45	-11.47	77.6	0	100	0	0	20	57	7
12.15	1.07	C+ / 6.8	18.6	0.96	N/A	11.24	1,652	-15.21	-12.59	50.3	0	100	0	0	63	17	6
9.46	1.15	B- / 7.1	21.5	0.81	N/A	15.38	362	-10.92	-10.98	46.2	0	100	0	0	20	49	7
12.76	1.05	C+ / 6.7	22.4	0.90	N/A	10.45	3,122	-14.74	-12.37	48.3	0	100	0	0	53	47	5
10.06	1.44	B / 8.0	N/A	N/A	N/A	17.87	189	-5.43	-8.21	N/A	21	0	78	1	11	35	2
10.58	1.08	C+ / 6.8	21.4	0.75	N/A	12.91	1,310	-14.48	-12.50	77.9	0	100	0	0	17	73	7
3.40	1.10	B / 8.4	14.2	0.77	N/A	8.45	100	-13.02	-13.23	N/A	2	6	0	92	47	62	26
0.00	8.26	C / 5.5	35.2	0.63	N/A	3.61	38	-37.12	-42.20	N/A	12	9	62	17	N/A	7	20
9.04	1.64	B+ / 9.0	20.7	0.64	30.8	17.36	1,063	3.97	5.11	13.8	1	0	4	95	24	98	9
8.81	1.98	B+ / 9.1	18.9	0.49	25.9	18.47	168	2.92	3.67	13.8	1	0	6	93	23	98	9
6.10	1.00	B- / 7.5	N/A	N/A	N/A	16.39	158	-9.95	-10.89	N/A	1	0	98	1	67	75	N/A
5.23	1.06	B / 8.9	12.7	2.03	7.3	14.45	97	3.11	-2.75	N/A	0	0	100	0	21	58	10
6.24	1.05	B / 8.4	18.0	3.00	12.3	14.78	86	8.05	2.65	N/A	0	0	100	0	38	25	10
6.41	2.06	B / 8.2	17.4	0.46	N/A	20.99	495	7.96	4.26	46.4	0	100	0	0	19	92	8
0.32	1.42	B- / 7.9	27.7	1.08	2.6	11.95	46	-9.54	-14.58	8.6	10	89	0	1	51	82	N/A
0.00	1.24	B / 8.3	18.4	0.58	N/A	9.30	264	-24.19	-24.81	14.8	1	97	0	2	97	71	2
6.01	1.98	B / 8.4	15.9	-35.13	N/A	14.68	374	1.98	-2.29	N/A	0	0	0	100	95	98	N/A
8.99	1.85	B- / 7.5	27.0	0.88	N/A	7.48	100	-4.81	-5.38	27.9	0	100	0	0	11	95	N/A
8.28	1.60	C+ / 6.5	26.5	0.82	N/A	9.59	76	-9.28	-3.54	22.6	0	100	0	0	1,297	40	N/A
6.39	2.41	B / 8.5	16.6	0.47	N/A	28.74	385	4.56	3.54	N/A	0	100	0	0	16	91	N/A
4.08	N/A	U /	N/A	N/A	N/A	22.52	N/A	-5.46	N/A	N/A	0	0	0	100	N/A	N/A	1
7.45	1.22	B- / 7.9	19.1	1.03	N/A	13.67	250	-11.63	-10.41	34.8	0	100	0	0	52	55	N/A
8.84	2.09	B- / 7.7	N/A	N/A	N/A	18.46	642	-1.79	-5.86	N/A	0	1	95	4	18	84	N/A
9.79	2.23	C+ / 6.9	10.0	-0.87	14.9	17.95	75	9.30	5.24	N/A	0	0	100	0	47	95	N/A
9.76	2.35	C+ / 6.7	22.0	-0.56	7.9	16.62	131	4.15	-6.96	N/A	0	0	99	1	49	93	N/A
5.05	1.68	B- / 7.9	21.5	0.77	8.5	22.32	108	-6.90	-9.69	N/A	0	43	56	1	51	92	N/A
8.93	2.13	B / 8.6	15.3	1.09	N/A	17.61	309	-0.85	-4.17	N/A	0	0	100	0	101	94	N/A
8.24	2.12	B / 8.9	18.9	0.53	26.2	10.22	114	7.53	10.43	14.1	1	0	3	96	24	97	N/A

* Denotes ETF Fund, N/A denotes number is not available

Fund Type	Fund Name	Ticker Symbol	Overall Investment Rating	Price As of 3/31/12	52 Week High	52 Week Low	Performance Rating/Pts	3 Mo	6 Mo	1Yr/Pct	3Yr/Pct	5Yr/Pct
IN	Flaherty&Crumrine Preferred Income	PFD	A+	14.22	16.10	11.05	A+ / 9.7	2.56	11.07	24.11 / 84	47.29 / 98	5.24 / 58
GEI	Fort Dearborn Inc. Secs.	FDI	B-	16.17	16.80	14.42	C+ / 6.1	3.51	14.47	31.33 / 90	19.82 / 42	11.62 / 94
IN	Foxby Corp	FXBY	B+	1.58	1.70	1.12	A / 9.5	27.42	30.58	37.39 / 95	32.45 / 87	-7.74 / 8
GEN	Franklin Templeton Ltd Duration In	FTF	B-	14.01	15.00	11.91	C+ / 6.4	8.58	11.99	13.68 / 75	23.59 / 59	8.01 / 74
GI	Franklin Universal Trust	FT	B	6.88	7.04	5.40	B / 8.0	4.55	14.04	13.40 / 75	30.61 / 83	7.23 / 69
GI	Gabelli Convertible&Income Sec Fun	GCV	C-	5.87	6.70	4.72	C- / 4.1	17.35	20.31	-1.10 / 38	16.66 / 32	0.70 / 30
IN	Gabelli Dividend & Income Trust	GDV	B+	16.38	17.19	12.32	B / 8.1	7.82	23.48	4.04 / 52	30.77 / 83	1.85 / 37
IN	Gabelli Equity Trust	GAB	B+	5.75	6.28	4.26	A- / 9.1	18.10	28.06	3.30 / 50	36.16 / 92	1.65 / 35
GL	Gabelli Global Multimedia Trust	GGT	B+	7.24	8.27	5.72	A- / 9.1	19.45	25.38	4.88 / 55	36.91 / 93	-4.57 / 13
UT	Gabelli Global Utility&Income Trus	GLU	B-	21.30	22.04	16.29	C+ / 5.7	3.23	13.87	11.27 / 71	22.39 / 54	5.83 / 61
HL	Gabelli Healthcare & WellnessRx Tr	GRX	B-	8.32	8.33	6.14	C+ / 6.6	16.69	24.55	8.76 / 66	23.06 / 57	--
EN	Gabelli Nat Res Gold & Income Trus	GNT	D	15.81	20.47	12.30	D / 2.2	20.89	14.87	-10.42 / 21	--	--
UT	Gabelli Utility Trust	GUT	C+	8.09	8.40	5.66	B / 7.9	5.79	22.89	32.62 / 91	24.99 / 64	5.69 / 60
PM	GAMCO Global Gold Nat ResandIncome	GGN	D+	16.16	19.35	12.70	C- / 3.4	17.68	19.33	-4.78 / 31	13.96 / 24	-0.49 / 25
GL	GDL Fund	GDL	D+	12.27	13.99	11.36	D+ / 2.6	6.70	8.50	0.29 / 42	10.50 / 17	0.74 / 30
GR	General American Investors	GAM	C+	29.00	29.23	20.57	C+ / 6.8	16.42	31.37	5.76 / 58	23.92 / 60	0.07 / 27
EM	Global High Income Fund	GHI	B	13.45	14.17	10.81	B+ / 8.6	13.57	18.92	18.89 / 81	31.34 / 84	8.35 / 76
GL	Global Income & Currency Fund	GCF	D+	13.73	16.20	12.42	D / 2.0	9.02	9.23	1.59 / 45	6.40 / 12	1.55 / 34
GL	Global Income Fund	GIFD	C+	4.05	4.48	3.46	C+ / 5.8	8.86	5.98	0.02 / 41	24.36 / 62	6.83 / 66
FO	Greater China Fund	GCH	D	11.50	13.17	9.00	D+ / 2.4	14.20	18.16	-9.62 / 22	9.14 / 15	0.73 / 30
GEI	Guggenheim Build America Bd Mgd Du	GBAB	B+	21.81	22.35	18.05	B- / 7.3	3.68	12.84	26.72 / 86	--	--
IN	Guggenheim Enhanced Equity Income	GPM	C+	9.40	9.87	7.16	C+ / 6.0	18.14	31.26	10.37 / 69	20.11 / 44	-2.04 / 19
IN	Guggenheim Enhanced Equity Strateg	GGE	B+	17.20	18.03	13.32	B+ / 8.8	9.26	25.52	10.13 / 69	34.49 / 90	-26.20 / 2
IN	Guggenheim Equal Weight Enh Eq Inc	GEQ	U	19.00	N/A	N/A	U /	9.51	--	--	--	--
GI	Guggenheim Strategic Opportunities	GOF	A+	20.55	22.47	16.50	A / 9.4	2.23	7.43	7.56 / 63	42.12 / 97	--
HL	H&Q Healthcare Investors	HQH	B	16.47	16.50	11.50	B / 8.1	18.92	30.23	24.53 / 85	26.15 / 70	6.75 / 66
HL	H&Q Life Sciences Investors	HQL	B+	13.83	13.87	9.75	A- / 9.1	22.84	42.56	29.16 / 88	31.15 / 84	8.26 / 76
GEN	Helios Advantage Income Fund Inc	HAV	B+	9.30	9.45	6.69	A / 9.5	21.46	28.56	31.59 / 90	36.61 / 92	-23.30 / 2
GEN	Helios High Income Fund Inc	HIH	B+	8.90	8.90	6.66	A- / 9.1	17.86	26.78	27.89 / 87	33.70 / 88	-23.95 / 2
COH	Helios High Yield Fund	HHY	A	10.45	10.83	7.90	B+ / 8.4	9.18	19.00	23.79 / 84	29.94 / 82	10.67 / 90
GEN	Helios Multi Sector High Income	HMH	B+	6.07	6.12	4.68	A- / 9.1	12.68	23.56	28.74 / 88	33.63 / 88	-28.14 / 1
GEN	Helios Strategic Income Fund Inc	HSA	C+	5.94	6.16	4.81	C+ / 6.8	10.13	15.87	21.29 / 83	23.69 / 59	-28.99 / 1
MTG	Helios Strategic Mortgage Income	HSM	C-	6.32	6.65	4.94	C- / 4.2	10.55	4.35	6.40 / 59	18.15 / 36	-3.21 / 16
MTG	Helios Total Return Fund Inc	HTR	C	6.02	6.35	5.30	C / 5.3	6.33	2.49	8.98 / 66	22.04 / 52	2.48 / 41
FO	Herzfeld Caribbean Basin Fund	CUBA	C	7.34	7.65	5.40	C / 4.4	14.37	22.29	-0.52 / 39	17.83 / 35	-4.09 / 14
FO	India Fund	IFN	D-	22.30	33.99	18.61	D / 1.7	17.12	-1.28	-29.73 / 6	8.59 / 14	-0.43 / 25
GL	ING Asia Pacific High Div Eq Inc F	IAE	C	16.13	19.72	11.69	C+ / 5.8	13.67	23.83	-4.43 / 32	23.00 / 57	0.04 / 27
EM	ING Emerging Markets High Div Eqty	IHD	U	16.02	N/A	N/A	U /	22.57	27.08	--	--	--
GL	ING Global Advantage and Premium O	IGA	D+	12.06	13.79	9.81	C- / 3.3	12.60	17.05	-3.11 / 33	13.88 / 24	0.38 / 29
GL	ING Gobal Equity Dividend Premium	IGD	D+	9.59	11.42	8.50	C- / 3.2	13.22	10.32	-1.54 / 37	13.79 / 23	-2.19 / 19
GR	ING Infrastructure Indus & Mtrls	IDE	D	18.48	21.99	13.78	C- / 3.1	20.08	22.27	-8.56 / 24	--	--
GL	ING International High Div Eq Inc	IID	C-	10.38	12.25	7.97	C / 4.6	19.24	21.62	-1.72 / 36	18.35 / 37	--
LP	ING Prime Rate Trust	PPR	C+	5.70	6.33	4.85	C+ / 5.7	12.96	14.94	0.09 / 41	22.98 / 57	1.60 / 35
EN	ING Risk Managed Nat Resources Fun	IRR	D	12.27	16.20	11.21	D- / 1.5	7.63	4.26	-16.01 / 14	5.43 / 11	1.37 / 33
MUS	Invesco California Muni Income Tr	IIC	A-	15.18	16.37	12.35	B+ / 8.3	1.10	10.59	28.72 / 98	17.72 / 74	6.83 / 90
MUS	Invesco California Municipal Sec	ICS	B-	14.54	15.35	12.20	C+ / 6.0	2.19	11.96	24.50 / 95	11.26 / 33	4.81 / 70
MUS	Invesco California Quality Muni Se	IQC	A	13.94	14.61	11.17	B+ / 8.8	3.11	11.78	30.62 / 99	18.68 / 79	4.78 / 70
COH	Invesco High Yield Investments Fun	MSY	B	6.36	6.83	5.25	B / 8.1	5.52	19.09	16.09 / 79	29.78 / 82	11.73 / 95
MUN	Invesco Municipal Income Opp II Tr	OIB	B-	7.53	7.75	6.39	C+ / 6.3	2.90	10.23	21.78 / 92	12.78 / 41	2.36 / 49
MUN	Invesco Municipal Income Opp III T	OIC	B	8.32	8.53	7.00	B- / 7.3	4.95	11.97	23.07 / 93	14.15 / 52	2.32 / 48
MUN	Invesco Municipal Income Opp Tr	OIA	B	6.86	7.11	5.84	C+ / 6.9	4.57	11.82	21.20 / 91	13.68 / 47	-0.50 / 25
MUN	Invesco Municipal Premium Income T	PIA	A	8.89	9.37	7.18	B+ / 8.7	0.94	14.92	28.51 / 98	18.39 / 77	5.09 / 73

* Denotes ETF Fund, N/A denotes number is not available

www.thestreetratings.com

	Incl. in Returns		RISK				NET ASSETS		VALUATION			ASSET					FUND MANAGER	
	Dividend Yield %	Expense Ratio	Risk Rating/ Pts	3 Year Standard Deviation	Beta	Avg Dura-tion	NAV as of 3/31/12	Total $(Mil)	Premium / Discount As of 3/31/12	1 Year Average	Wtd Avg P/E	Cash %	Stocks %	Bonds %	Other %	Portfolio Turnover Ratio	Manager Quality Pct	Manager Tenure (Years)
	7.85	2.08	B / 8.8	21.1	0.38	24.6	12.43	124	14.40	14.11	14.1	1	0	3	96	24	98	N/A
	8.66	0.70	B+ / 9.0	9.7	1.04	N/A	16.77	152	-3.58	-6.89	N/A	2	0	97	1	154	88	N/A
	0.00	2.28	B- / 7.3	22.1	0.65	N/A	2.09	4	-24.40	-29.17	113.8	3	92	2	3	4	90	7
	7.11	1.14	B / 8.6	15.3	-0.36	N/A	13.81	375	1.45	-2.18	N/A	1	0	98	1	263	96	N/A
	6.63	2.51	B- / 7.5	13.2	0.57	5.2	7.29	173	-5.62	-7.11	17.4	0	28	71	1	42	91	21
	8.18	2.05	B- / 7.7	17.4	0.63	4.5	5.78	80	1.56	-1.28	25.0	19	54	0	27	44	39	23
	5.86	1.40	B / 8.1	20.9	1.20	0.4	18.45	1,429	-11.22	-11.85	23.5	4	94	0	2	15	68	9
	9.74	1.50	B- / 7.8	24.1	1.25	N/A	5.69	1,059	1.05	-1.16	31.1	0	99	0	1	6	80	26
	11.05	3.19	B- / 7.1	25.6	1.04	N/A	8.04	124	-9.95	-12.52	50.1	6	93	0	1	9	92	18
	5.63	1.36	B+ / 9.1	11.8	0.70	N/A	20.58	63	3.50	-0.77	21.4	3	95	0	2	6	88	8
	0.00	2.11	B / 8.5	17.7	0.80	N/A	9.74	71	-14.58	-15.87	35.1	6	94	0	0	45	76	N/A
	10.63	1.17	C+ / 6.1	N/A	N/A	N/A	15.32	305	3.20	-2.03	N/A	0	0	0	100	N/A	24	1
	7.42	1.91	C+ / 6.4	30.5	1.02	N/A	5.54	168	46.03	32.38	25.3	0	98	0	2	1	81	13
	10.40	1.33	C+ / 6.8	29.5	0.88	0.2	14.70	1,020	9.93	2.63	81.9	2	90	4	4	52	21	7
	10.43	4.39	B / 8.2	10.2	0.35	0.2	14.07	318	-12.79	-12.99	61.9	56	42	0	2	365	72	5
	2.31	1.54	B- / 7.8	21.8	1.28	N/A	33.86	951	-14.35	-14.52	N/A	0	100	0	0	18	27	17
	7.93	1.44	B- / 7.3	21.3	1.24	9.2	13.07	281	2.91	-1.93	N/A	8	0	90	2	71	94	N/A
	6.55	1.21	B / 8.8	7.0	0.18	N/A	14.93	77	-8.04	-9.27	N/A	15	0	82	3	N/A	78	1
	6.42	2.00	B / 8.3	13.6	0.42	4.3	4.95	37	-18.18	-17.89	58.5	0	56	41	3	55	93	N/A
	0.00	1.85	C+ / 6.8	28.7	1.08	N/A	12.45	434	-7.63	-10.23	74.8	5	94	0	1	68	21	N/A
	7.10	1.05	B+ / 9.3	N/A	N/A	N/A	22.68	359	-3.84	-5.94	N/A	0	0	97	3	3	94	N/A
	10.21	1.80	B- / 7.6	18.5	0.90	N/A	9.69	183	-2.99	-4.71	N/A	0	100	0	0	497	50	N/A
	7.27	2.23	B- / 7.4	25.8	1.29	N/A	19.77	90	-13.00	-11.28	N/A	0	100	0	0	267	79	N/A
	5.53	N/A	U /	N/A	N/A	N/A	20.10	N/A	-5.47	N/A	N/A	0	0	0	100	N/A	N/A	1
	8.99	2.69	B / 8.7	16.3	0.41	27.1	19.46	187	5.60	6.72	N/A	7	10	73	10	64	97	5
	7.53	1.47	B / 8.0	16.9	0.73	N/A	17.87	379	-7.83	-9.45	51.7	7	82	0	11	94	81	8
	7.52	1.77	B- / 7.5	18.3	0.78	N/A	14.71	171	-5.98	-9.23	82.1	5	84	0	11	94	86	20
	8.06	2.61	B- / 7.2	13.5	-0.78	5.8	8.91	55	4.38	-6.42	2.4	0	1	99	0	62	99	N/A
	8.09	2.74	B- / 7.1	13.5	-0.52	6.0	8.48	39	4.95	-3.14	2.4	0	1	99	0	60	98	N/A
	9.33	1.95	B+ / 9.0	12.2	0.87	6.3	9.93	68	5.24	0.38	N/A	1	1	98	0	46	82	N/A
	8.40	2.71	B- / 7.4	13.1	-0.19	6.0	6.13	43	-0.98	-7.31	2.4	0	1	99	0	64	98	N/A
	7.07	2.75	B- / 7.8	15.4	0.29	7.2	6.62	36	-10.27	-11.99	18.0	0	4	96	0	55	95	N/A
	9.97	1.90	B- / 7.5	15.9	0.87	17.5	6.36	61	-0.63	-3.82	N/A	0	0	100	0	26	89	N/A
	9.47	1.71	B / 8.1	12.3	1.69	16.2	5.96	176	1.01	-0.44	N/A	0	0	100	0	43	88	N/A
	0.00	2.66	B / 8.2	24.8	0.88	N/A	7.84	30	-6.38	-9.67	14.7	1	98	0	1	22	58	18
	0.09	1.32	C / 5.1	37.8	1.08	N/A	24.85	1,581	-10.26	-8.00	N/A	2	96	0	2	51	19	N/A
	9.82	1.42	C+ / 6.6	31.2	1.14	N/A	16.16	226	-0.19	1.33	N/A	0	99	0	1	112	63	5
	8.17	N/A	U /	N/A	N/A	N/A	16.00	278	0.13	N/A	N/A	0	100	0	0	N/A	N/A	1
	11.11	0.99	B- / 7.4	16.2	0.54	N/A	12.80	252	-5.78	-4.34	45.0	0	99	0	1	164	69	7
	11.64	1.07	B- / 7.2	21.3	0.84	N/A	10.01	1,109	-4.20	-3.54	19.4	4	95	0	1	58	51	7
	9.74	1.19	C+ / 6.7	N/A	N/A	N/A	19.78	326	-6.57	-6.45	N/A	0	98	0	2	N/A	8	2
	9.94	1.25	C+ / 6.7	26.6	1.03	N/A	9.76	93	6.35	4.46	19.7	1	98	0	1	99	41	5
	6.32	1.93	B / 8.1	17.2	-75.26	N/A	5.83	894	-2.23	-3.32	N/A	0	0	0	100	60	98	12
	10.76	1.20	B- / 7.2	16.9	0.53	N/A	12.85	348	-4.51	-2.62	22.9	0	100	0	0	30	29	6
	5.34	0.85	B / 8.7	12.4	2.45	10.9	15.77	158	-3.74	-5.36	N/A	0	0	100	0	13	37	N/A
	4.54	0.72	B+ / 9.0	10.7	1.99	10.2	15.27	50	-4.78	-7.19	N/A	0	0	100	0	12	29	N/A
	6.03	0.93	B / 8.6	12.1	2.25	10.6	14.50	123	-3.86	-5.93	N/A	0	0	100	0	13	55	N/A
	8.49	1.52	B- / 7.3	15.2	1.19	9.0	6.20	71	2.58	2.16	N/A	5	0	94	1	109	56	N/A
	6.18	0.71	B / 8.5	10.5	1.70	12.9	7.85	115	-4.08	-5.15	N/A	0	0	100	0	18	42	N/A
	6.13	0.82	B / 8.5	10.9	1.86	12.7	8.48	65	-1.89	-4.74	N/A	0	0	100	0	16	48	N/A
	6.12	0.72	B / 8.8	8.5	1.36	13.3	7.12	126	-3.65	-4.94	N/A	0	0	100	0	12	70	N/A
	6.07	1.66	B / 8.6	12.5	2.40	10.8	8.91	131	-0.22	-3.66	N/A	0	0	100	0	5	41	N/A

* Denotes ETF Fund, N/A denotes number is not available

Fund Type	Fund Name	Ticker Symbol	Overall Investment Rating	PRICE Price As of 3/31/12	52 Week High	52 Week Low	PERFORMANCE Performance Rating/Pts	% Total Return Through 3/31/12 3 Mo	6 Mo	1Yr/Pct	Annualized 3Yr/Pct	5Yr/Pct
MUS	Invesco New York Quality Muni Sec	IQN	A+	15.79	16.40	12.96	B+ / 8.8	2.29	13.69	24.91 / 96	19.73 / 83	7.83 / 96
MUN	Invesco Quality Municipal Income T	IQI	A	13.90	14.47	11.56	B+ / 8.6	5.09	11.97	24.84 / 95	18.62 / 79	5.99 / 81
MUN	Invesco Quality Municipal Inv Tr	IQT	B+	13.99	14.82	11.96	B / 7.9	0.04	9.56	23.34 / 94	17.76 / 74	6.34 / 85
MUN	Invesco Quality Municipal Sec	IQM	B+	14.83	15.52	12.72	B / 7.9	2.39	7.14	22.10 / 92	17.88 / 75	6.42 / 86
MUN	Invesco Value Municipal Bond Trust	IMC	C	14.98	17.92	13.13	C- / 4.2	-12.03	1.50	15.88 / 85	13.85 / 49	7.30 / 92
MUN	Invesco Value Municipal Income Tr	IIM	B-	15.56	17.89	13.26	C+ / 6.3	-1.69	3.50	18.83 / 88	15.68 / 61	7.56 / 94
MUN	Invesco Value Municipal Securities	IMS	C-	14.33	15.91	12.87	D+ / 2.7	0.60	3.99	12.91 / 82	5.53 / 14	4.34 / 65
MUN	Invesco Value Municipal Trust	IMT	C+	14.69	16.27	12.62	C / 5.4	-4.13	1.74	17.41 / 86	14.71 / 54	6.28 / 84
MUN	Invesco Van Kampen Adv Muni Inc II	VKI	A	12.95	13.47	10.81	B+ / 8.7	5.74	10.43	22.53 / 92	19.54 / 82	5.97 / 81
GEI	Invesco Van Kampen Bond	VBF	C-	20.21	21.94	17.80	C- / 3.3	-2.15	6.98	19.31 / 82	13.35 / 22	9.01 / 80
MUS	Invesco Van Kampen CA Val Muni Inc	VCV	B+	13.15	14.30	10.95	B+ / 8.5	3.95	10.63	27.25 / 97	17.79 / 74	2.94 / 54
LP	Invesco Van Kampen Dynamic Cred Op	VTA	B	11.68	13.10	9.94	B- / 7.4	12.61	14.05	-2.44 / 35	29.36 / 81	--
COH	Invesco Van Kampen High Inc Tr II	VLT	A-	16.94	17.27	14.50	B+ / 8.8	11.65	12.59	10.77 / 70	34.53 / 90	6.68 / 65
MUS	Invesco Van Kampen MA Val Muni Inc	VMV	C-	12.70	13.80	11.17	C- / 3.8	1.52	1.78	11.97 / 81	9.98 / 28	2.42 / 49
MUN	Invesco Van Kampen Muni Opp	VMO	A-	14.58	15.88	12.52	B / 8.2	2.50	10.03	19.60 / 89	19.02 / 80	5.89 / 80
MUN	Invesco Van Kampen Muni Trust	VKQ	B+	14.23	15.01	12.28	B / 7.6	3.45	8.82	17.70 / 87	17.31 / 71	4.74 / 69
MUS	Invesco Van Kampen OH Qual Muni	VOQ	A+	16.56	16.85	13.48	B+ / 8.8	6.49	14.77	28.08 / 98	18.35 / 77	7.46 / 93
MUS	Invesco Van Kampen PA Val Muni Inc	VPV	A-	14.57	15.19	12.35	B+ / 8.4	4.04	10.51	20.70 / 90	18.98 / 80	6.31 / 85
MUN	Invesco Van Kampen Sel Sector Muni	VKL	A	12.84	13.34	10.49	B+ / 8.9	2.48	12.23	22.18 / 92	21.23 / 87	5.92 / 80
LP	Invesco Van Kampen Senior Inc Tr	VVR	A-	4.91	5.22	4.01	B+ / 8.7	16.60	20.25	3.60 / 50	34.18 / 89	-3.43 / 16
MUN	Invesco Van Kampen Tr Fr Inv Gr Mu	VGM	A	15.15	15.67	12.83	B+ / 8.6	2.95	9.20	21.09 / 91	20.45 / 85	6.51 / 86
MUS	Invesco Van Kampen Tr Fr Inv NJ Mu	VTJ	A+	17.78	18.44	14.30	A / 9.3	4.79	16.31	31.84 / 99	20.50 / 85	7.90 / 96
MUS	Invesco Van Kampen Tr Fr Inv NY Mu	VTN	A+	15.85	16.47	13.32	A- / 9.1	5.63	11.33	24.99 / 96	21.98 / 89	6.86 / 90
MUN	Invesco Van Kampen Tr Fr Val Muni	VIM	B-	13.94	14.69	11.64	C+ / 6.7	3.37	10.49	24.27 / 95	13.13 / 44	4.97 / 72
FS	J Hancock Bank & Thrift Oppty Fd	BTO	C+	17.25	17.71	11.41	C+ / 6.3	27.47	42.04	4.79 / 54	19.82 / 42	-5.31 / 12
GI	J Hancock Hedged Eqty & Inc Fd	HEQ	U	16.48	N/A	N/A	U /	14.47	19.35	--	--	--
GEI	J Hancock Income Securities Tr	JHS	B	15.25	15.85	12.86	C+ / 6.7	6.30	4.83	16.81 / 80	25.41 / 66	9.94 / 86
GEI	J Hancock Investors Trust	JHI	B	23.01	23.65	18.75	B / 8.1	6.02	12.38	13.36 / 75	31.05 / 84	14.72 / 98
IN	J Hancock Preferred Inc	HPI	A+	21.78	23.30	17.68	A- / 9.2	2.72	7.42	24.21 / 84	37.86 / 94	7.09 / 68
IN	J Hancock Preferred Income II	HPF	A+	21.85	22.60	17.70	A / 9.3	6.07	16.62	25.80 / 86	37.80 / 94	7.17 / 68
IN	J Hancock Preferred Income III	HPS	A+	17.80	18.99	14.18	A- / 9.0	5.57	14.64	14.11 / 76	36.79 / 93	4.42 / 53
GL	J Hancock Tax Adv Glb Shlr Yield	HTY	C+	13.07	15.73	10.71	C+ / 6.3	8.65	12.32	12.18 / 73	23.45 / 58	--
IN	J Hancock Tax Advantage Div Income	HTD	A+	17.72	18.26	13.22	A+ / 9.6	3.90	17.34	18.82 / 81	43.04 / 97	7.57 / 71
FO	Japan Equity Fund	JEQ	D+	5.67	6.40	4.89	D+ / 2.7	13.40	8.52	-6.83 / 27	11.51 / 19	-7.71 / 9
FO	Japan Smaller Cap Fund Inc.	JOF	D	7.83	8.96	6.99	D / 2.1	9.05	5.62	-11.98 / 19	9.33 / 15	-8.52 / 8
FO	JF China Region Fund	JFC	D	12.73	16.19	10.10	D+ / 2.5	15.52	18.09	-17.59 / 12	10.84 / 17	3.36 / 47
IN	John Hancock Premium Dividend	PDT	A+	13.47	14.32	10.70	A- / 9.2	1.34	16.89	23.91 / 84	37.61 / 94	10.78 / 91
EN	Kayne Anderson Energy Tot Ret	KYE	B	27.48	31.61	21.59	B+ / 8.4	7.70	15.54	-7.35 / 26	35.25 / 91	9.98 / 86
IN	Kayne Anderson Midstream/Energy	KMF	B+	27.42	27.48	19.43	B / 7.7	11.15	29.98	13.18 / 74	--	--
EN	Kayne Anderson MLP Inv Co	KYN	C+	31.15	33.10	22.87	C+ / 6.4	2.59	12.95	-0.84 / 39	26.35 / 70	5.21 / 58
FO	Korea Equity Fund	KEF	C	9.74	15.38	8.73	C+ / 6.9	7.27	15.42	-6.68 / 27	28.41 / 78	3.68 / 49
FO	Korea Fund	KF	C	40.55	52.69	35.02	C / 5.5	13.43	24.40	-5.67 / 29	22.12 / 53	2.01 / 38
FO	Latin American Discovery Fund	LDF	C	16.34	19.58	12.55	C+ / 5.9	15.89	24.32	-11.00 / 20	23.99 / 60	4.31 / 52
GL	Lazard Global Total Return&Income	LGI	C+	14.96	16.24	11.97	C+ / 5.7	13.58	20.90	4.29 / 53	21.54 / 51	-0.04 / 27
GL	Lazard World Div&Inc Fd	LOR	C+	12.20	13.99	10.03	C+ / 6.9	14.23	11.64	-1.99 / 35	27.27 / 74	-0.64 / 24
IN	Liberty All-Star Equity Fund	USA	C+	4.93	5.43	3.77	C+ / 6.9	18.76	24.50	-0.03 / 40	25.34 / 65	-1.87 / 20
IN	Liberty All-Star Growth Fund	ASG	C+	4.35	4.70	3.31	B / 7.7	16.04	25.03	0.05 / 41	28.53 / 78	3.60 / 48
GI	LMP Capital and Income Fund Inc	SCD	B+	13.39	14.14	10.61	B / 8.1	10.60	22.09	8.53 / 65	30.01 / 82	2.07 / 39
LP	LMP Corporate Loan Fund Inc	TLI	B-	11.90	12.80	10.13	C+ / 6.7	8.83	14.96	1.69 / 45	26.11 / 69	3.27 / 46
GI	LMP Real Estate Income Fund Inc	RIT	A	10.32	11.09	7.81	A+ / 9.8	13.55	23.29	6.42 / 59	50.88 / 99	-4.72 / 13
MUS	MA Health & Education Tax-Exempt T	MHE	A-	14.35	15.01	12.70	B / 8.2	-0.24	6.04	18.94 / 88	19.48 / 82	8.30 / 97
GL	Macquarie Global Infr Total Return	MGU	B	18.45	19.12	14.33	B / 7.6	10.01	23.43	4.42 / 53	28.35 / 78	-2.96 / 17

* Denotes ETF Fund, N/A denotes number is not available

Incl. in Returns		RISK				NET ASSETS		VALUATION			ASSET					FUND MANAGER	
Dividend Yield %	Expense Ratio	Risk Rating/ Pts	3 Year Standard Deviation	Beta	Avg Dura-tion	NAV as of 3/31/12	Total $(Mil)	Premium / Discount As of 3/31/12	1 Year Average	Wtd Avg P/E	Cash %	Stocks %	Bonds %	Other %	Portfolio Turnover Ratio	Manager Quality Pct	Manager Tenure (Years)
4.94	1.10	B / 8.9	11.1	1.98	11.0	16.21	63	-2.59	-6.37	N/A	0	0	100	0	21	67	N/A
6.37	0.92	B / 8.8	11.0	2.00	10.4	13.65	315	1.83	-2.06	N/A	0	0	100	0	11	59	N/A
6.33	0.89	B / 8.7	12.0	2.19	9.5	14.38	194	-2.71	-3.23	N/A	0	0	100	0	411	48	N/A
6.07	0.85	B / 8.8	11.8	2.22	9.5	15.31	200	-3.14	-3.32	N/A	0	0	100	0	11	46	N/A
5.81	1.22	B / 8.6	14.4	1.61	9.7	15.38	58	-2.60	3.66	N/A	0	0	100	0	7	57	N/A
5.78	0.88	B / 8.6	13.5	2.32	9.4	16.04	320	-2.99	-0.36	N/A	0	0	100	0	7	33	N/A
4.19	0.54	B / 8.8	10.9	1.73	10.8	14.94	96	-4.08	-3.48	N/A	0	0	100	0	9	18	N/A
6.13	0.90	B / 8.7	12.7	2.24	9.3	15.17	256	-3.16	-0.78	N/A	0	0	100	0	8	33	N/A
6.76	1.28	B / 8.8	12.3	1.96	10.9	12.56	547	3.11	0.62	N/A	0	0	98	2	9	69	10
4.75	0.52	B / 8.6	10.6	1.69	12.6	20.44	228	-1.13	-3.55	N/A	1	0	98	1	79	48	2
6.94	1.36	B / 8.4	14.5	2.55	10.5	13.01	281	1.08	2.39	N/A	0	0	97	3	12	35	10
7.71	2.22	B / 8.0	19.0	-130.76	N/A	12.46	984	-6.26	-6.87	N/A	0	0	0	100	88	99	2
8.22	2.57	B / 8.2	17.5	1.24	8.4	16.35	61	3.61	3.60	N/A	0	0	99	1	135	62	N/A
5.91	1.83	B / 8.2	16.0	1.61	9.8	13.14	34	-3.35	0.45	N/A	0	0	97	3	33	34	N/A
7.08	1.30	B / 8.7	12.1	1.77	10.6	13.98	468	4.29	3.57	N/A	0	0	97	3	10	67	10
6.75	1.12	B / 8.5	14.1	1.94	10.8	14.03	539	1.43	1.06	N/A	0	0	97	3	10	57	21
6.16	1.39	B / 8.9	11.9	1.57	8.1	15.76	90	5.08	0.54	N/A	0	0	97	3	14	75	N/A
6.18	1.23	B / 8.7	11.9	1.76	11.3	14.79	340	-1.49	-3.93	N/A	0	0	98	2	16	69	10
6.82	1.37	B / 8.6	12.4	1.93	10.8	12.39	186	3.63	0.94	N/A	0	0	96	4	12	74	10
6.48	2.14	B / 8.2	21.1	20.85	N/A	4.91	905	0.00	-3.85	N/A	1	0	3	96	50	97	N/A
6.97	1.23	B / 8.8	12.1	1.82	10.2	14.65	780	3.41	1.43	N/A	0	0	99	1	11	75	15
6.41	1.34	B / 8.8	11.6	1.91	9.9	16.81	99	5.77	1.35	N/A	0	0	99	1	17	78	10
6.36	1.35	B / 8.9	11.1	1.86	10.4	15.32	228	3.46	0.65	N/A	0	0	100	0	14	78	5
6.33	1.32	B / 8.4	13.8	2.35	11.7	13.96	132	-0.14	-2.17	N/A	0	0	97	3	5	20	10
4.94	1.37	B- / 7.5	25.2	0.96	15.6	18.88	298	-8.63	-9.84	12.0	1	96	0	3	23	49	6
7.07	1.18	U /	N/A	N/A	N/A	18.39	251	-10.39	N/A	N/A	7	92	0	1	N/A	N/A	1
6.92	1.56	B / 8.8	11.0	0.69	23.0	14.91	170	2.28	1.34	61.4	1	2	94	3	71	92	6
8.68	1.62	B- / 7.6	13.3	0.46	8.8	19.43	164	18.43	11.99	141.0	5	1	89	5	45	96	6
7.71	1.74	B / 8.9	19.0	0.38	N/A	21.39	536	1.82	2.00	N/A	3	1	1	95	16	96	10
7.69	1.72	B / 8.8	19.2	0.54	N/A	21.31	438	2.53	0.07	N/A	3	2	3	92	18	95	10
7.56	1.72	B / 8.8	19.6	0.60	N/A	18.41	558	-3.31	-2.71	N/A	4	0	3	93	19	94	9
9.79	1.28	B / 8.3	19.6	0.46	N/A	11.98	115	9.10	6.21	19.2	2	96	0	2	95	91	N/A
6.67	1.56	B / 8.9	19.4	0.77	N/A	19.21	690	-7.76	-7.42	21.0	0	61	0	39	16	95	N/A
0.92	1.38	B- / 7.6	18.5	0.65	N/A	6.38	87	-11.13	-9.75	N/A	0	99	0	1	59	52	3
0.45	1.44	B- / 7.6	19.6	0.48	N/A	9.15	208	-14.43	-11.23	N/A	0	100	0	0	57	59	N/A
0.80	1.99	C+ / 6.7	28.6	1.16	N/A	14.35	112	-11.29	-11.79	N/A	0	99	0	1	76	20	7
6.73	1.87	B+ / 9.1	15.3	0.41	N/A	13.83	660	-2.60	-3.36	N/A	2	33	0	65	13	96	7
6.99	4.30	B- / 7.4	21.1	0.60	5.4	27.53	884	-0.18	2.45	41.3	0	87	13	0	58	94	7
4.57	2.90	B / 8.5	N/A	N/A	N/A	29.07	562	-5.68	-6.52	N/A	0	84	16	0	74	76	N/A
6.55	4.90	B / 8.2	17.4	0.30	5.5	28.59	2,030	8.95	6.80	43.0	0	100	0	0	22	92	8
4.72	1.90	C+ / 5.8	28.0	1.03	N/A	10.67	121	-8.72	-8.84	N/A	2	97	0	1	75	87	7
0.00	1.10	C+ / 6.6	29.8	1.12	N/A	44.14	549	-8.13	-9.33	N/A	3	96	0	1	83	75	N/A
0.91	1.38	C+ / 6.8	30.9	1.26	N/A	17.67	168	-7.53	-8.07	74.9	0	100	0	0	32	72	10
6.47	1.59	B- / 7.8	20.5	0.91	3.0	17.05	162	-12.26	-11.62	25.2	0	67	32	1	32	81	1
6.53	2.11	B- / 7.8	21.9	0.96	N/A	13.65	96	-10.62	-8.24	22.5	1	71	27	1	67	86	N/A
6.49	1.08	B- / 7.5	23.2	1.32	10.6	5.65	1,039	-12.74	-11.98	52.3	1	99	0	0	52	27	N/A
6.44	1.79	B- / 7.0	20.0	1.06	N/A	4.79	137	-9.19	-8.29	107.4	2	97	0	1	80	69	26
8.36	1.53	B / 8.3	16.0	0.87	24.8	14.03	266	-4.56	-7.20	22.8	12	75	12	1	79	85	3
6.45	1.92	B / 8.6	15.2	-17.67	4.5	12.60	116	-5.56	-4.65	N/A	0	0	0	100	98	97	N/A
6.98	1.82	B- / 7.8	33.8	1.45	N/A	11.55	122	-10.65	-10.77	51.2	0	61	0	39	23	91	N/A
5.85	1.39	B / 8.9	11.1	1.18	14.5	13.91	31	3.16	5.17	N/A	1	0	98	1	10	85	N/A
5.20	2.11	B / 8.0	23.7	1.00	N/A	20.91	328	-11.76	-12.72	27.5	0	100	0	0	53	87	3

* Denotes ETF Fund, N/A denotes number is not available

Fund Type	Fund Name	Ticker Symbol	Overall Investment Rating	Price As of 3/31/12	52 Week High	52 Week Low	Performance Rating/Pts	3 Mo	6 Mo	1Yr/Pct	3Yr/Pct	5Yr/Pct
											Annualized	
GL	Macquarie/FTG Infr/ Util Div&Inc	MFD	A-	16.00	16.54	12.85	B+ / 8.9	15.14	23.91	10.25 / 69	34.83 / 90	-0.21 / 27
IN	Madison Strategic Sector Premium	MSP	C+	11.81	12.88	9.62	C / 5.4	13.44	19.58	1.34 / 45	21.19 / 48	-0.91 / 23
IN	Madison/Clym Cvd Call & Eq Strtg	MCN	C	8.27	8.89	6.61	C / 5.4	13.17	21.74	1.78 / 46	20.91 / 47	-1.86 / 20
FO	Malaysia Fund	MAY	B+	10.26	11.93	8.55	A- / 9.2	13.62	31.60	5.15 / 55	37.36 / 94	11.40 / 93
MUN	Managed Duration Investment Grd Mu	MZF	A+	15.32	15.82	12.11	A / 9.3	4.52	11.52	24.62 / 95	23.19 / 92	9.96 / 99
GL	Managed High Yield Plus Fund	HYF	A-	2.19	2.66	1.77	A / 9.3	5.23	20.13	5.72 / 58	40.56 / 96	-4.17 / 14
FO	Mexico Equity & Income Fund	MXE	B+	11.40	11.95	9.03	B+ / 8.6	14.57	18.87	-2.65 / 34	34.45 / 89	0.31 / 28
FO	Mexico Fund	MXF	B+	25.25	28.99	19.27	B+ / 8.8	15.56	24.82	-1.83 / 36	34.95 / 91	4.29 / 52
MUS	MFS CA Muni	CCA	B-	11.25	11.88	9.77	C+ / 6.8	3.55	6.86	16.41 / 85	15.56 / 60	1.81 / 43
GEI	MFS Charter Income Trust	MCR	C	9.57	9.78	8.25	C / 4.5	6.38	16.23	12.27 / 73	17.61 / 34	9.83 / 85
GL	MFS Government Markets Income Trus	MGF	D+	6.78	7.55	6.34	D / 2.1	-0.79	5.63	13.85 / 76	6.49 / 12	7.80 / 73
MUH	MFS High Inc Muni Tr	CXE	A+	5.35	5.64	4.54	A / 9.4	1.87	13.22	22.22 / 92	23.90 / 93	3.37 / 57
MUH	MFS High Yield Muni Trust	CMU	A+	4.90	5.07	4.14	A / 9.4	5.98	15.48	25.00 / 96	22.76 / 91	3.64 / 59
COH	MFS Interm High Inc	CIF	A+	3.18	3.22	2.49	A / 9.3	10.55	22.51	14.94 / 77	38.28 / 94	10.20 / 87
GL	MFS Intermediate Income Trust	MIN	C-	6.38	6.69	5.90	D+ / 2.9	3.43	10.98	14.82 / 77	9.49 / 15	9.20 / 81
GL	MFS InterMkt Inc Tr I	CMK	C	8.37	8.59	7.76	C- / 3.2	2.71	6.82	8.07 / 64	13.57 / 23	7.59 / 71
MUN	MFS Invst Gr Muni Tr	CXH	A	10.16	10.89	8.64	B+ / 8.8	5.79	12.59	23.55 / 94	19.61 / 82	5.14 / 73
GEN	MFS Multimarket Income Trust	MMT	C+	6.98	7.16	5.96	C / 5.0	5.75	15.19	11.45 / 71	19.70 / 42	10.97 / 92
MUN	MFS Municipal Income Trust	MFM	A+	7.29	7.58	6.15	A- / 9.0	4.39	12.06	23.99 / 94	20.93 / 86	4.31 / 65
GI	MFS Special Value Trust	MFV	B+	7.09	8.25	6.01	B / 8.2	12.98	14.62	-3.82 / 32	33.33 / 88	2.50 / 41
MUS	Minnesota Municipal Inc Portfolio	MXA	C+	15.77	17.31	13.86	C+ / 5.6	-5.17	2.17	14.58 / 83	14.71 / 55	8.40 / 97
MUS	Minnesota Municipal Income Fund II	MXN	B	15.99	17.24	13.65	C+ / 6.4	-3.29	8.24	17.41 / 86	15.53 / 60	8.32 / 97
EN	MLP & Strategic Equity Fund Inc.	MTP	C+	17.80	18.86	14.25	C+ / 6.7	5.63	19.34	0.27 / 42	26.61 / 71	--
GEI	Montgomery Street Inc. Sec.	MTS	C-	15.80	16.05	15.05	D+ / 2.5	2.40	3.47	5.50 / 57	10.24 / 16	3.46 / 48
FO	Morgan Stanley Asia Pacific Fund	APF	C-	14.86	17.90	12.87	C- / 4.2	13.44	14.78	-5.99 / 29	18.36 / 37	1.69 / 36
FO	Morgan Stanley China A Share Fund	CAF	D-	19.59	29.95	18.64	D- / 1.1	11.80	2.10	-24.32 / 8	0.65 / 7	7.70 / 72
FO	Morgan Stanley Eastern Europe	RNE	C+	16.58	20.05	12.58	C+ / 6.3	23.18	22.54	-16.22 / 13	25.29 / 65	-6.74 / 10
EM	Morgan Stanley Emerging Markets	MSF	C	14.63	16.49	12.07	C / 4.5	13.24	16.57	-9.69 / 22	20.10 / 44	2.85 / 43
EM	Morgan Stanley Emerging Mkts Debt	MSD	C+	10.85	11.24	9.50	C+ / 5.8	5.57	15.18	12.07 / 72	22.01 / 52	8.92 / 79
EM	Morgan Stanley Emg Mkts Dom Debt	EDD	B-	16.24	17.82	13.57	B / 7.6	16.87	16.60	7.68 / 63	27.87 / 76	--
GL	Morgan Stanley Frntier Emrg Mkt Fd	FFD	D+	11.39	14.46	9.74	D+ / 2.6	9.10	5.37	-16.86 / 13	13.57 / 23	--
GEN	Morgan Stanley Income Sec	ICB	C	17.79	18.12	16.08	C- / 4.0	3.80	5.96	14.95 / 77	16.64 / 32	7.85 / 73
FO	Morgan Stanley India Inv Fund	IIF	D-	16.56	24.49	13.59	D / 2.2	18.20	-1.37	-27.77 / 7	12.39 / 20	-0.77 / 24
IN	Nasdaq Premium Income & Growth Fun	QQQX	B-	15.74	15.85	11.94	B / 8.1	23.69	27.06	15.93 / 78	27.68 / 75	7.10 / 68
MUS	Neuberger Berman CA Inter Muni Fun	NBW	A-	16.04	16.28	13.50	B / 7.8	6.47	10.56	20.48 / 90	16.45 / 65	7.42 / 93
COH	Neuberger Berman High Yield Strat	NHS	B-	13.55	15.24	11.30	B+ / 8.8	1.42	10.95	1.44 / 45	37.73 / 94	9.12 / 80
MUN	Neuberger Berman Intermediate Muni	NBH	B+	16.10	16.20	13.43	B- / 7.4	2.65	11.78	21.39 / 91	15.70 / 61	8.84 / 98
MUS	Neuberger Berman NY Int Muni	NBO	C+	14.68	16.22	13.00	C / 4.9	-3.85	7.67	15.67 / 84	12.83 / 42	6.22 / 84
GI	Neuberger Berman Real Est Secs Inc	NRO	A+	4.28	4.46	3.19	A+ / 9.8	15.79	25.40	9.51 / 67	53.14 / 99	-10.96 / 6
COH	New America High Income Fund	HYB	B	10.29	11.13	8.39	A- / 9.1	2.07	21.41	11.08 / 70	37.27 / 93	12.43 / 97
FO	New Germany Fund	GF	B	15.08	18.90	12.06	B+ / 8.7	23.20	27.29	-7.52 / 26	34.59 / 90	0.85 / 30
GI	NFJ Dividend Interest & Premium St	NFJ	B	17.87	19.34	13.56	B / 7.6	14.36	27.48	7.93 / 64	27.26 / 74	0.21 / 28
MUN	Nuveen AMT/Fr Muni Income	NEA	C+	14.47	15.27	12.97	C / 5.1	0.43	4.56	16.64 / 85	12.71 / 41	4.80 / 70
MUS	Nuveen AZ Div Adv Muni	NFZ	B+	14.21	14.54	12.05	B / 7.6	4.90	10.18	18.08 / 87	16.72 / 67	4.21 / 64
MUS	Nuveen AZ Div Adv Muni Fund 2	NKR	B+	14.54	15.22	12.26	B / 7.6	4.01	10.37	22.56 / 93	15.89 / 62	4.82 / 70
MUS	Nuveen AZ Div Adv Muni Fund 3	NXE	A	13.90	14.75	12.05	B+ / 8.3	5.43	9.75	19.78 / 89	18.71 / 79	4.94 / 71
MUS	Nuveen AZ Prem Inc Muni	NAZ	B+	14.78	14.99	12.07	B / 8.2	5.89	10.25	27.58 / 98	16.24 / 64	6.11 / 82
MUN	Nuveen Build America Bond Fund	NBB	B-	20.18	21.25	17.99	C+ / 6.5	-0.08	4.62	19.16 / 88	--	--
GEI	Nuveen Build America Bond Oppty Fd	NBD	C	20.97	22.25	18.38	C- / 3.3	-1.39	2.65	19.00 / 81	--	--
MUS	Nuveen CA Div Adv Muni	NAC	A-	14.38	15.28	11.92	B+ / 8.5	2.57	9.74	26.53 / 97	18.58 / 79	5.36 / 76
MUS	Nuveen CA Div Adv Muni 2	NVX	A	14.93	15.72	12.58	B+ / 8.3	2.80	9.67	24.18 / 95	18.57 / 78	5.77 / 79
MUS	Nuveen CA Div Adv Muni 3	NZH	A-	13.77	14.46	11.58	B+ / 8.5	3.59	10.71	25.22 / 96	18.44 / 78	4.57 / 67

		RISK				NET ASSETS		VALUATION			ASSET					FUND MANAGER	
Incl. in Returns		Risk Rating/ Pts	3 Year		Avg Dura-tion	NAV as of 3/31/12	Total $(Mil)	Premium / Discount		Wtd Avg P/E	Cash %	Stocks %	Bonds %	Other %	Portfolio Turnover Ratio	Manager Quality Pct	Manager Tenure (Years)
Dividend Yield %	Expense Ratio		Standard Deviation	Beta				As of 3/31/12	1 Year Average								
8.75	2.24	B / 8.2	21.2	0.88	N/A	16.10	129	-0.62	-5.14	33.1	0	76	0	24	91	92	8
8.81	0.98	B / 8.2	17.3	0.93	2.2	13.54	73	-12.78	-12.12	26.5	0	100	0	0	61	60	7
8.71	1.36	B- / 7.8	19.0	1.07	N/A	9.31	167	-11.17	-11.35	34.6	0	100	0	0	68	37	N/A
1.90	1.11	B- / 7.6	20.7	0.75	N/A	10.60	110	-3.21	-8.40	N/A	0	100	0	0	2	95	4
6.46	1.46	B / 8.6	12.0	2.39	12.2	15.00	95	2.13	-0.38	N/A	0	0	100	0	8	68	9
8.55	1.59	B- / 7.6	24.8	0.85	N/A	2.14	140	2.34	5.68	N/A	1	0	98	1	64	98	3
0.00	1.51	B / 8.0	22.4	0.85	N/A	13.04	89	-12.58	-10.55	N/A	1	97	1	1	253	94	22
1.53	1.42	B- / 7.7	24.5	1.00	N/A	27.72	339	-8.91	-8.72	28.2	5	94	0	1	25	92	N/A
6.61	1.49	B / 8.2	16.6	2.86	10.9	11.56	30	-2.68	0.32	N/A	3	0	97	0	40	19	5
6.83	1.00	B / 8.8	9.9	0.58	18.4	10.07	526	-4.97	-7.10	N/A	0	0	99	1	47	89	8
7.49	0.80	B / 8.4	9.1	0.05	N/A	6.95	228	-2.45	-3.32	N/A	10	0	90	0	14	72	N/A
7.18	1.56	B / 8.7	14.1	2.49	N/A	5.11	149	4.70	4.09	N/A	0	0	100	0	22	67	5
7.10	1.43	B / 8.8	12.0	1.96	12.8	4.59	120	6.75	5.37	N/A	1	0	99	0	21	80	5
8.30	1.81	B / 8.7	18.1	1.21	N/A	3.01	59	5.65	-0.82	N/A	0	1	98	1	60	80	5
8.43	0.71	B / 8.6	9.6	0.26	N/A	6.29	746	1.43	-1.02	N/A	0	0	100	0	16	81	10
5.45	1.07	B+ / 9.5	7.1	0.43	N/A	9.27	97	-9.71	-10.02	N/A	0	0	100	0	38	85	5
6.44	1.30	B / 8.7	11.7	2.06	11.2	10.07	109	0.89	-0.51	N/A	0	0	100	0	29	65	5
7.22	1.12	B / 8.4	10.1	0.43	20.5	7.38	564	-5.42	-7.01	N/A	0	0	100	0	49	91	N/A
6.91	1.42	B / 8.6	10.1	1.55	13.1	7.00	271	4.14	2.78	N/A	1	0	99	0	22	81	19
9.66	1.39	B / 8.0	19.0	0.54	N/A	6.90	46	2.75	3.45	N/A	2	25	73	0	53	93	N/A
5.33	1.46	B / 8.9	11.5	1.56	10.0	15.57	60	1.28	5.34	N/A	0	0	100	0	10	59	N/A
5.07	2.25	B+ / 9.2	9.7	0.76	12.5	15.35	21	4.17	4.18	N/A	0	0	99	1	15	83	N/A
5.33	1.20	B / 8.1	17.9	0.52	N/A	18.49	263	-3.73	-5.89	N/A	0	100	0	0	37	90	N/A
3.80	0.71	B+ / 9.5	5.8	0.62	N/A	17.58	177	-10.13	-9.69	N/A	15	0	85	0	49	78	N/A
0.00	1.15	B- / 7.4	22.6	0.98	N/A	16.56	563	-10.27	-10.40	N/A	5	94	0	1	73	65	N/A
0.00	1.78	C / 5.5	34.3	1.02	N/A	21.71	610	-9.77	-7.38	64.9	0	99	0	1	94	12	6
0.00	2.01	B- / 7.3	32.9	1.41	N/A	18.45	85	-10.14	-11.86	4.2	4	94	0	2	44	59	16
0.00	1.54	B- / 7.6	27.0	1.03	N/A	16.25	303	-9.97	-9.55	44.3	3	96	0	1	61	30	21
5.16	1.19	B / 8.3	14.1	0.93	9.8	12.08	269	-10.18	-9.73	N/A	0	0	99	1	105	91	10
7.39	2.07	B- / 7.8	25.1	1.57	N/A	17.64	1,256	-7.94	-8.74	N/A	0	0	100	0	100	92	5
1.90	2.03	B- / 7.5	19.5	0.69	N/A	13.16	85	-13.45	-11.27	N/A	3	89	0	8	60	65	4
4.72	0.65	B+ / 9.2	8.2	0.81	N/A	18.65	162	-4.61	-5.61	N/A	1	0	98	1	52	86	4
0.00	1.33	C / 5.4	37.2	1.19	N/A	18.65	613	-11.21	-8.03	N/A	3	96	0	1	66	25	18
7.67	1.04	B- / 7.0	22.7	1.14	N/A	16.29	260	-3.38	-4.39	109.3	0	100	0	0	51	60	1
5.09	1.29	B+ / 9.2	10.2	1.62	7.4	15.48	83	3.62	-2.71	N/A	2	0	97	1	16	64	10
7.97	1.68	C+ / 6.5	22.4	1.77	5.7	13.41	253	1.04	3.81	N/A	0	0	100	0	100	23	7
5.22	1.05	B+ / 9.3	8.0	1.34	8.2	15.35	278	4.89	-0.30	N/A	2	0	97	1	23	75	10
5.31	1.29	B / 8.8	11.9	1.61	7.5	14.78	73	-0.68	-1.31	N/A	4	0	95	1	16	49	10
5.61	2.21	B- / 7.9	34.2	1.38	N/A	4.94	257	-13.36	-11.89	N/A	0	58	0	42	19	94	N/A
7.58	1.46	C+ / 6.6	18.0	1.43	7.5	10.18	222	1.08	1.22	16.5	0	0	96	4	59	70	24
1.87	1.09	C+ / 6.7	31.8	1.40	N/A	16.85	241	-10.50	-9.61	40.2	0	100	0	0	45	84	N/A
10.07	0.97	B- / 7.8	17.4	0.96	6.1	18.15	1,808	-1.54	-4.73	16.8	4	71	0	25	65	76	N/A
5.81	2.01	B / 8.7	10.2	1.96	12.2	15.14	327	-4.43	-4.51	N/A	1	0	93	6	2	32	6
5.45	2.23	B / 8.5	14.7	2.11	11.0	15.02	21	-5.39	-6.93	N/A	3	0	96	1	5	57	1
5.53	2.06	B+ / 9.0	11.0	1.96	10.8	15.22	34	-4.47	-7.07	N/A	2	0	97	1	7	54	1
5.44	1.43	B+ / 9.1	11.3	1.97	11.2	14.85	41	-6.40	-8.33	N/A	6	0	93	1	6	65	1
5.20	1.19	B / 8.5	12.9	1.75	11.5	14.76	59	0.14	-4.18	N/A	3	0	96	1	5	62	1
6.45	1.11	B / 8.8	N/A	N/A	N/A	21.39	499	-5.66	-4.72	N/A	8	0	91	1	100	21	N/A
6.09	0.84	B+ / 9.2	N/A	N/A	N/A	22.56	163	-7.05	-5.00	N/A	18	0	81	1	N/A	88	N/A
6.43	1.18	B / 8.5	13.6	2.68	11.9	14.79	298	-2.77	-2.98	N/A	9	0	90	1	20	34	10
6.43	1.28	B / 8.8	11.8	2.20	11.8	15.42	199	-3.18	-3.05	N/A	9	0	90	1	13	59	10
6.54	1.94	B / 8.6	14.0	2.33	11.9	13.83	293	-0.43	-1.81	N/A	8	0	91	1	16	47	10

* Denotes ETF Fund, N/A denotes number is not available

Fund Type	Fund Name	Ticker Symbol	Overall Investment Rating	PRICE Price As of 3/31/12	52 Week High	52 Week Low	Performance Rating/Pts	3 Mo	6 Mo	1Yr/Pct	3Yr/Pct	5Yr/Pct
MUS	Nuveen CA Inv Quality Muni	NQC	A+	15.24	15.93	12.08	A / 9.3	5.52	10.60	32.50 / 99	21.60 / 88	7.20 / 92
MUS	Nuveen CA Muni Market Opportunity	NCO	A+	15.50	16.11	12.13	A / 9.5	7.52	15.99	33.72 / 99	21.71 / 88	6.12 / 83
MUS	Nuveen CA Muni Value	NCA	C+	9.80	10.19	8.29	C / 5.0	4.27	10.94	21.33 / 91	9.46 / 25	4.68 / 69
MUS	Nuveen CA Performance Plus Muni	NCP	A+	15.18	16.03	12.01	A / 9.3	3.72	12.61	32.75 / 99	21.30 / 87	6.98 / 91
MUS	Nuveen CA Prem Inc Muni	NCU	A+	15.04	15.47	12.00	A / 9.5	7.29	16.02	32.72 / 99	22.55 / 90	7.37 / 93
MUS	Nuveen CA Quality Inc Muni	NUC	A	15.82	17.09	12.73	B+ / 8.8	0.89	9.67	31.09 / 99	19.46 / 82	7.36 / 93
MUS	Nuveen CA Select Quality Muni	NVC	A	15.56	16.47	12.74	A- / 9.1	4.83	10.03	28.52 / 98	20.63 / 85	7.71 / 95
MUS	Nuveen CA Select Tax-Free Inc Port	NXC	B	14.80	15.11	12.57	B- / 7.0	6.34	14.41	23.17 / 93	12.65 / 40	5.61 / 78
MUN	Nuveen California Municipal Value	NCB	A+	15.80	16.49	13.47	A- / 9.2	6.22	10.31	22.86 / 93	--	--
IN	Nuveen Core Equity Alpha Fund	JCE	B-	13.85	14.35	10.78	B- / 7.4	13.22	24.13	6.47 / 60	27.05 / 73	2.37 / 41
GI	Nuveen Credit Strategies Income	JQC	A+	8.98	9.44	7.33	A+ / 9.6	14.01	19.67	9.57 / 68	43.36 / 97	1.32 / 32
MUS	Nuveen CT Div Adv Muni	NFC	C	14.61	15.42	13.05	C- / 4.0	0.04	5.06	14.28 / 83	10.29 / 29	4.01 / 62
MUS	Nuveen CT Div Adv Muni Fund 2	NGK	C	14.55	15.34	13.48	C- / 3.9	-1.54	4.70	11.11 / 80	10.73 / 31	3.53 / 58
MUS	Nuveen CT Div Adv Muni Fund 3	NGO	C+	13.88	14.24	12.41	C / 5.1	2.63	6.91	15.23 / 84	12.07 / 38	4.44 / 66
MUS	Nuveen CT Prem Inc Muni	NTC	C+	14.25	14.68	12.72	C / 5.4	2.59	6.09	16.18 / 85	12.74 / 41	4.89 / 71
MUN	Nuveen Div Adv Muni	NAD	B+	14.58	15.19	12.32	B / 7.8	1.66	8.11	23.04 / 93	17.44 / 72	6.22 / 84
MUN	Nuveen Div Adv Muni 3	NZF	B+	14.77	15.42	12.91	B- / 7.4	2.04	6.81	18.83 / 88	17.30 / 71	5.37 / 76
MUN	Nuveen Div Adv Muni Income	NVG	B-	14.96	15.71	13.12	C+ / 6.0	0.86	7.40	19.15 / 88	13.50 / 46	5.48 / 77
GI	Nuveen Diversified Dividend&Income	JDD	A	11.73	12.27	8.94	A / 9.4	16.73	25.70	12.87 / 73	39.04 / 95	-0.20 / 27
MUN	Nuveen Dividend Advantage Muni 2	NXZ	B+	15.19	15.48	12.75	B / 7.8	4.54	12.53	25.35 / 96	15.47 / 60	4.65 / 68
GI	Nuveen Energy MLP Total Return Fun	JMF	D+	18.40	20.11	13.90	C- / 3.5	7.89	25.56	-1.29 / 38	--	--
GEI	Nuveen EnhancedMunicipal Value	NEV	B	15.05	16.00	12.02	B- / 7.3	7.47	10.91	25.94 / 86	--	--
IN	Nuveen Equity Premium & Growth Fun	JPG	C+	13.33	13.74	10.88	C / 5.2	12.78	21.23	6.47 / 60	19.62 / 41	1.29 / 32
IN	Nuveen Equity Premium Advantage	JLA	C-	12.12	12.93	10.40	C- / 3.9	8.24	15.77	3.60 / 51	15.92 / 29	1.71 / 36
IN	Nuveen Equity Premium Income Fund	JPZ	C	11.97	12.90	10.18	C- / 4.2	9.48	17.38	3.77 / 51	17.22 / 33	1.32 / 32
IN	Nuveen Equity Premium Opportunity	JSN	C-	12.18	12.85	10.25	C- / 3.9	9.11	17.43	5.25 / 56	15.67 / 29	2.19 / 40
LP	Nuveen Floating Rate Income Fund	JFR	B+	11.92	12.82	9.90	B+ / 8.7	11.73	23.59	5.36 / 57	34.20 / 89	4.31 / 53
LP	Nuveen Floating Rate Income Opp	JRO	A	12.05	12.91	10.01	A / 9.3	11.19	21.38	6.58 / 60	39.73 / 95	5.64 / 60
MUS	Nuveen GA Div Adv Muni	NZX	C+	15.28	16.25	13.28	C / 5.4	0.21	4.02	11.72 / 81	13.92 / 50	4.77 / 69
MUS	Nuveen GA Div Adv Muni Fund 2	NKG	C+	14.24	15.51	12.54	C+ / 5.7	-1.52	6.99	17.55 / 86	13.94 / 50	5.11 / 73
MUS	Nuveen GA Prem Inc Muni	NPG	B-	14.57	15.40	12.61	C+ / 6.3	1.83	5.00	18.88 / 88	14.57 / 54	5.75 / 79
GL	Nuveen Glob Govt Enhanced Inc	JGG	D+	14.33	15.37	13.36	D / 1.9	3.36	2.65	6.80 / 61	6.21 / 11	2.54 / 42
GL	Nuveen Global Value Opportunities	JGV	C-	16.31	20.22	15.84	C- / 3.9	-0.71	2.99	-11.54 / 19	20.66 / 46	6.05 / 62
MUS	Nuveen Insured CA Div Adv Muni Fun	NKL	B	15.32	17.32	12.91	B- / 7.3	-3.30	5.10	24.10 / 94	17.33 / 71	5.63 / 78
MUS	Nuveen Insured CA Prem Inc Muni	NPC	B-	15.10	16.43	12.79	C+ / 6.5	-5.27	8.06	21.03 / 91	15.53 / 60	5.88 / 80
MUS	Nuveen Insured CA Prem Inc Muni 2	NCL	B	14.58	16.80	12.14	B- / 7.2	-5.03	6.06	24.23 / 95	17.01 / 70	6.31 / 85
MUS	Nuveen Insured CA T/F Adv Muni Fd	NKX	B	14.32	15.19	11.43	B- / 7.2	-0.51	10.33	31.23 / 99	13.77 / 48	5.00 / 72
MUS	Nuveen Insured MA T/F Adv Muni Fd	NGX	C	14.80	15.00	12.51	C- / 4.1	8.18	8.39	17.92 / 87	7.24 / 18	5.60 / 78
MUN	Nuveen Investment Quality Muni Fun	NQM	B+	15.63	16.28	13.05	B / 7.7	1.72	9.17	24.42 / 95	16.60 / 66	6.51 / 86
MUS	Nuveen MA Div Adv Muni	NMB	C-	14.28	14.86	12.50	C- / 3.6	4.00	6.85	17.79 / 87	6.86 / 17	3.66 / 60
MUS	Nuveen MA Prem Inc Muni	NMT	B-	14.97	15.69	12.75	C+ / 6.4	3.77	10.25	21.44 / 91	12.71 / 41	6.11 / 82
MUS	Nuveen MD Div Adv Muni	NFM	C+	14.09	14.92	12.70	C / 4.6	-0.10	6.05	14.77 / 83	11.73 / 36	3.10 / 56
MUS	Nuveen MD Div Adv Muni 2	NZR	B-	14.65	15.52	12.90	C+ / 6.4	4.77	10.29	18.39 / 87	13.21 / 44	3.85 / 61
MUS	Nuveen MD Div Adv Muni Fund 3	NWI	C+	14.09	14.97	12.78	C / 5.0	1.07	5.37	13.12 / 82	12.91 / 43	4.27 / 64
MUS	Nuveen MD Prem Inc Muni Fund	NMY	B	15.30	15.97	12.96	C+ / 6.7	3.73	10.09	15.98 / 85	14.79 / 56	5.57 / 77
MUS	Nuveen MI Div Adv Muni	NZW	B+	13.87	14.58	12.12	B / 7.6	3.74	7.79	19.26 / 89	17.06 / 70	3.72 / 60
MUS	Nuveen MI Prem Inc Muni	NMP	A+	14.83	15.09	12.31	B+ / 8.8	6.65	11.02	23.13 / 93	19.48 / 82	6.69 / 88
MUS	Nuveen MI Quality Inc Muni	NUM	A+	15.11	15.70	12.62	B+ / 8.7	4.84	11.75	23.44 / 94	19.19 / 81	6.81 / 89
GL	Nuveen Mlt-Cur Sht-Tm Govt Inc	JGT	D+	13.22	15.14	11.50	D+ / 2.8	11.71	6.67	3.67 / 51	11.24 / 18	--
MUS	Nuveen MO Prem Inc Muni	NOM	B+	16.66	17.14	13.41	B / 7.7	2.70	13.52	17.18 / 86	16.85 / 68	5.96 / 81
MTG	Nuveen Mortgage Opportunity Term	JLS	C	23.38	25.22	19.89	C / 4.4	17.49	18.80	2.70 / 48	--	--
MTG	Nuveen Mortgage Opportunity Term 2	JMT	C+	23.46	25.00	19.81	C / 5.1	17.61	20.91	4.18 / 52	--	--

* Denotes ETF Fund, N/A denotes number is not available

www.thestreetratings.com

	RISK					NET ASSETS		VALUATION			ASSET					FUND MANAGER	
Incl. in Returns		Risk Rating/ Pts	3 Year		Avg Dura-tion	NAV as of 3/31/12	Total $(Mil)	Premium / Discount		Wtd Avg P/E	Cash %	Stocks %	Bonds %	Other %	Portfolio Turnover Ratio	Manager Quality Pct	Manager Tenure (Years)
Dividend Yield %	Expense Ratio		Standard Deviation	Beta				As of 3/31/12	1 Year Average								
6.54	1.36	B / 8.7	12.3	2.37	12.3	15.23	177	0.07	-2.15	N/A	8	0	91	1	16	61	10
6.19	1.77	B / 8.8	12.2	2.07	11.8	15.41	104	0.58	-2.57	N/A	10	0	89	1	18	74	10
4.78	0.65	B / 8.9	9.6	1.61	11.2	10.05	229	-2.49	-5.43	N/A	2	0	97	1	14	29	10
6.44	1.31	B / 8.7	11.7	2.19	11.8	15.20	169	-0.13	-2.50	N/A	9	0	90	1	15	68	10
5.78	1.69	B / 8.7	12.0	2.17	12.0	15.19	74	-0.99	-5.28	N/A	10	0	89	1	5	71	10
6.64	1.55	B / 8.4	13.5	2.23	12.0	15.86	300	-0.25	-0.30	N/A	8	0	91	1	16	60	10
6.63	1.50	B / 8.5	13.6	2.24	11.7	15.61	303	-0.32	-0.55	N/A	10	0	89	1	17	65	10
4.62	0.38	B+ / 9.0	10.3	1.56	8.8	15.07	84	-1.79	-5.51	N/A	3	0	96	1	8	49	20
5.05	0.72	B / 8.6	N/A	N/A	N/A	16.59	49	-4.76	-6.83	N/A	5	0	94	1	5	86	N/A
7.80	1.05	B- / 7.9	17.9	0.94	N/A	15.05	222	-7.97	-7.11	56.1	0	95	0	5	67	77	N/A
8.91	1.65	B / 8.6	19.9	0.87	21.5	9.78	1,250	-8.18	-11.21	42.3	5	36	0	59	37	94	9
4.85	3.08	B / 8.8	10.5	1.09	11.5	15.43	37	-5.31	-3.89	N/A	6	0	93	1	13	60	N/A
5.03	2.83	B / 8.4	13.6	1.41	11.1	15.29	33	-4.84	-2.33	N/A	4	0	95	1	11	54	N/A
4.97	2.87	B+ / 9.1	9.7	1.35	11.6	14.96	63	-7.22	-7.94	N/A	4	0	95	1	8	63	N/A
4.97	2.41	B+ / 9.0	10.7	1.84	11.1	15.06	76	-5.38	-6.60	N/A	3	0	93	4	9	39	N/A
6.26	2.02	B / 8.6	12.2	2.32	10.6	15.29	565	-4.64	-4.17	N/A	3	0	91	6	15	39	10
6.66	1.46	B / 8.8	9.9	1.54	11.5	15.19	587	-2.76	-2.93	N/A	1	0	91	8	30	74	6
6.02	1.84	B+ / 9.1	8.4	1.60	10.9	15.62	448	-4.23	-4.52	N/A	1	0	93	6	7	53	6
8.53	1.73	B / 8.1	20.7	0.97	10.3	12.36	227	-5.10	-7.60	43.0	3	0	0	97	67	90	9
6.32	1.75	B / 8.8	10.7	1.64	13.1	15.33	427	-0.91	-2.96	N/A	3	0	93	4	40	64	11
6.87	1.78	B- / 7.3	N/A	N/A	N/A	18.09	410	1.71	0.45	N/A	0	99	0	1	46	14	1
6.38	1.17	B / 8.2	N/A	N/A	N/A	14.90	269	1.01	-1.36	N/A	0	0	84	16	33	93	N/A
8.40	0.96	B / 8.3	14.0	0.68	N/A	14.58	226	-8.57	-10.73	43.8	0	99	0	1	4	75	N/A
9.37	0.94	B- / 7.7	13.4	0.60	N/A	13.63	341	-11.08	-10.36	80.5	1	99	0	0	14	70	N/A
9.06	0.84	B / 8.1	15.1	0.69	N/A	13.33	496	-10.20	-10.09	43.7	3	96	0	1	4	63	N/A
9.16	0.81	B- / 7.9	14.2	0.61	N/A	13.32	859	-8.56	-9.38	60.8	0	99	0	1	4	67	N/A
6.90	1.54	B / 8.1	18.4	-113.91	4.6	11.91	580	0.08	-2.70	N/A	5	2	6	87	99	99	N/A
7.22	1.56	B / 8.0	23.0	-40.13	4.6	11.88	365	1.43	-0.67	N/A	3	1	8	88	101	99	5
4.79	2.83	B / 8.6	15.2	1.16	11.1	15.31	28	-0.20	-0.76	N/A	1	0	96	3	9	73	5
4.72	2.75	B / 8.8	11.4	1.27	12.1	14.51	63	-1.86	-0.04	N/A	1	0	96	3	4	71	5
4.65	2.91	B / 8.9	10.9	1.49	12.0	14.89	53	-2.15	-2.36	N/A	24	0	75	1	5	66	5
8.65	1.06	B / 8.1	11.1	0.27	N/A	15.43	145	-7.13	-7.38	N/A	10	0	88	2	36	71	N/A
8.46	1.16	B- / 7.8	20.1	0.67	7.7	17.12	325	-4.73	-3.44	32.7	24	53	11	12	92	86	6
6.50	0.97	B / 8.6	13.9	2.35	10.8	15.81	209	-3.10	-0.78	N/A	1	0	93	6	7	41	10
6.24	1.77	B / 8.8	12.0	2.10	12.8	15.65	88	-3.51	-2.49	N/A	1	0	92	7	6	42	N/A
6.21	1.29	B / 8.6	14.4	2.46	11.0	15.21	165	-4.14	-1.95	N/A	1	0	90	9	26	33	N/A
5.95	1.97	B / 8.5	13.1	2.38	12.2	14.77	75	-3.05	-4.93	N/A	4	0	90	6	8	26	10
4.42	3.01	B / 8.4	12.1	0.71	13.3	14.81	39	-0.07	-5.61	N/A	4	0	93	3	4	60	N/A
6.45	1.50	B / 8.8	9.9	1.93	10.8	15.81	536	-1.14	-1.69	N/A	2	0	89	9	12	57	N/A
4.79	3.03	B / 8.4	14.4	2.17	12.9	14.98	27	-4.67	-5.18	N/A	2	0	89	9	16	19	N/A
4.97	2.51	B / 8.7	11.7	1.64	12.8	15.15	68	-1.19	-4.45	N/A	3	0	94	3	6	43	N/A
5.28	2.58	B / 8.8	9.4	1.36	12.0	14.98	58	-5.94	-5.06	N/A	2	0	93	5	13	53	N/A
5.41	2.55	B / 8.5	12.3	1.72	12.8	15.19	58	-3.55	-3.32	N/A	3	0	93	4	8	40	N/A
5.37	2.29	B / 8.8	10.9	1.92	12.5	15.09	76	-6.63	-5.30	N/A	3	0	93	4	7	34	N/A
5.06	2.10	B / 8.8	11.6	1.60	12.2	15.43	153	-0.84	-2.78	N/A	2	0	94	4	6	66	1
5.80	1.69	B+ / 9.1	9.8	1.54	11.5	15.00	28	-7.53	-8.28	N/A	1	0	96	3	6	73	N/A
5.91	1.20	B+ / 9.3	9.0	1.42	11.8	15.28	106	-2.95	-7.02	N/A	0	0	96	4	4	82	5
5.88	1.18	B+ / 9.1	9.3	1.50	11.3	15.75	164	-4.06	-7.30	N/A	1	0	96	3	6	81	5
9.47	1.06	B- / 7.3	17.3	1.27	N/A	14.94	606	-11.51	-11.04	N/A	8	0	91	1	41	63	N/A
4.68	2.30	B / 8.5	16.2	1.16	11.6	14.35	31	16.10	11.32	N/A	1	0	97	2	11	81	N/A
8.85	1.44	B / 8.3	N/A	N/A	N/A	23.72	347	-1.43	-3.52	N/A	7	0	93	0	23	87	N/A
8.82	1.58	B / 8.3	N/A	N/A	N/A	23.79	105	-1.39	-4.38	N/A	17	0	82	1	35	95	N/A

* Denotes ETF Fund, N/A denotes number is not available

Fund Type	Fund Name	Ticker Symbol	Overall Investment Rating	PRICE Price As of 3/31/12	52 Week High	52 Week Low	PERFORMANCE Performance Rating/Pts		3 Mo	6 Mo	1Yr/Pct	3Yr/Pct	5Yr/Pct
MUN	Nuveen Muni Advantage	NMA	B-	14.57	15.42	12.80	C+	6.8	0.86	4.91	19.07 / 88	16.08 / 63	5.13 / 73
MUH	Nuveen Muni High Income Opport	NMZ	B+	12.89	13.18	10.80	B	8.2	8.33	15.76	17.97 / 87	16.98 / 69	2.03 / 45
MUH	Nuveen Muni High Income Opport 2	NMD	B	12.10	12.34	9.98	B	7.8	7.51	14.66	18.72 / 88	15.69 / 61	--
MUN	Nuveen Muni Income	NMI	C	11.29	12.05	9.62	C	4.4	-0.83	5.12	19.52 / 89	10.44 / 30	5.94 / 81
MUN	Nuveen Muni Market Opportunity	NMO	B	14.09	14.78	12.14	B-	7.3	3.42	7.86	21.19 / 91	15.78 / 62	5.29 / 75
MUN	Nuveen Muni Opportunity	NIO	C+	14.61	15.30	12.61	C	5.5	-0.65	4.58	15.83 / 85	14.13 / 51	5.68 / 78
MUN	Nuveen Muni Value	NUV	C+	10.07	10.25	8.94	C	4.3	3.96	6.69	17.60 / 87	9.28 / 25	4.76 / 69
MUN	Nuveen Municipal Value Fund 2	NUW	C	16.67	18.38	14.64	C-	3.6	-2.57	1.85	16.19 / 85	9.58 / 26	--
MUS	Nuveen NC Div Adv Muni	NRB	B	17.00	17.21	13.80	B-	7.0	9.75	16.85	19.72 / 89	12.19 / 38	6.37 / 85
MUS	Nuveen NC Div Adv Muni 2	NNO	C	15.56	16.25	13.35	C	4.5	2.40	5.64	15.52 / 84	10.64 / 31	5.32 / 75
MUS	Nuveen NC Div Adv Muni Fund 3	NII	C+	15.43	16.06	13.59	C	4.9	2.81	8.68	17.73 / 87	10.74 / 31	5.85 / 80
MUS	Nuveen NC Prem Inc Muni	NNC	C+	15.43	16.00	13.36	C+	5.7	2.34	8.54	17.42 / 86	12.77 / 41	6.28 / 84
MUN	Nuveen New Jersey Municipal Value	NJV	A+	16.03	16.84	13.48	A-	9.2	5.41	9.96	23.74 / 94	--	--
MUN	Nuveen New York Municipal Value 2	NYV	B	15.30	15.33	13.26	B-	7.1	6.27	10.79	13.13 / 82	--	--
MUS	Nuveen NJ Div Adv Muni	NXJ	A	14.68	15.20	12.29	B+	8.5	6.28	13.04	24.90 / 96	17.58 / 73	4.45 / 66
MUS	Nuveen NJ Div Adv Muni Fund 2	NUJ	B+	14.70	15.85	12.24	B	7.9	2.53	11.84	24.34 / 95	16.32 / 64	4.39 / 66
MUS	Nuveen NJ Investment Quality Muni	NQJ	B+	14.57	15.25	12.41	B	7.7	3.48	9.96	22.81 / 93	16.35 / 64	6.46 / 86
MUS	Nuveen NJ Prem Inc Muni	NNJ	B+	15.60	15.94	12.94	B	7.9	2.11	13.32	22.43 / 92	16.56 / 66	6.59 / 87
MUS	Nuveen NY AMT/Fr Muni Income	NRK	C+	14.40	15.10	12.86	C	5.5	3.12	6.49	15.24 / 84	13.02 / 43	4.71 / 69
MUS	Nuveen NY Div Adv Muni	NAN	B	14.43	15.07	12.65	C+	6.7	2.67	8.28	18.60 / 88	14.74 / 55	4.83 / 70
MUS	Nuveen NY Div Adv Muni 2	NXK	B+	14.50	15.29	12.55	B-	7.3	3.03	9.60	19.52 / 89	15.88 / 62	4.84 / 70
MUS	Nuveen NY Div Adv Muni Income	NKO	B-	14.76	16.01	13.06	C+	6.2	0.13	7.16	15.17 / 84	14.94 / 57	4.63 / 68
MUS	Nuveen NY Investment Quality Muni	NQN	B-	14.94	16.13	13.00	C+	6.3	-1.77	7.19	19.12 / 88	14.84 / 56	6.57 / 87
MUS	Nuveen NY Muni Value	NNY	C	9.89	10.40	8.97	C-	3.5	0.74	6.68	13.95 / 83	8.00 / 20	5.09 / 73
MUS	Nuveen NY Performance Plus Muni	NNP	B	15.51	16.35	13.80	C+	6.7	1.81	6.86	15.31 / 84	15.71 / 61	5.21 / 74
MUS	Nuveen NY Prem Inc Muni	NNF	B	15.21	16.48	13.50	C+	6.6	-2.42	5.78	15.24 / 84	16.02 / 63	6.23 / 84
MUS	Nuveen NY Quality Inc Muni	NUN	C+	14.81	16.38	13.22	C+	5.6	-3.67	3.11	15.99 / 85	15.27 / 58	6.36 / 85
MUS	Nuveen NY Select Quality Muni	NVN	B-	15.11	16.45	13.25	C+	6.3	-2.13	5.45	17.28 / 86	15.73 / 61	6.06 / 82
MUS	Nuveen NY Select Tax-Free Inc Port	NXN	C	14.10	14.84	12.96	C-	3.2	0.27	5.83	12.52 / 81	7.42 / 18	4.66 / 68
MUS	Nuveen OH Div Adv Muni	NXI	B+	15.21	16.47	12.96	B-	7.3	1.41	12.00	22.74 / 93	15.37 / 59	5.66 / 78
MUS	Nuveen OH Div Adv Muni 2	NBJ	B+	14.88	15.15	12.74	B	7.6	6.42	11.21	20.73 / 90	15.54 / 60	6.52 / 87
MUS	Nuveen OH Div Adv Muni Fund 3	NVJ	B-	15.23	17.18	13.00	C+	6.6	2.12	9.35	18.34 / 87	14.44 / 53	6.34 / 85
MUS	Nuveen OH Quality Inc Muni	NUO	A-	17.38	17.55	14.25	B+	8.3	5.55	11.52	24.92 / 96	17.41 / 72	7.73 / 95
MUS	Nuveen PA Div Adv Muni	NXM	B	14.16	15.10	12.46	B-	7.2	2.32	8.44	18.33 / 87	16.33 / 64	3.98 / 62
MUS	Nuveen PA Div Adv Muni Fund 2	NVY	B-	14.40	15.00	12.74	C+	6.3	4.17	10.84	18.62 / 88	12.92 / 43	5.17 / 74
MUS	Nuveen PA Investment Quality Muni	NQP	A	15.56	15.86	12.84	B+	8.4	4.14	10.17	26.21 / 97	18.06 / 75	8.39 / 97
MUS	Nuveen PA Prem Inc Muni 2	NPY	A	14.30	14.69	12.00	B+	8.5	3.85	11.44	23.82 / 94	18.55 / 78	6.68 / 88
MUN	Nuveen Pennsylvania Municipal Valu	NPN	C	14.95	16.68	13.66	C-	3.6	-0.99	2.15	13.21 / 82	--	--
MUN	Nuveen Performance Plus Muni	NPP	B+	15.52	16.00	13.04	B	7.7	3.12	9.82	22.86 / 93	16.45 / 65	6.97 / 91
GI	Nuveen Preferref Income Opps	JPC	A+	8.88	9.16	7.11	A+	9.7	13.23	23.80	14.32 / 76	44.52 / 97	1.03 / 31
MUN	Nuveen Prem Inc Muni	NPI	B	14.49	14.97	12.33	C+	6.9	1.70	8.47	20.49 / 90	15.21 / 58	6.49 / 86
MUN	Nuveen Prem Inc Muni 4	NPT	B+	13.40	14.02	11.34	B	7.8	1.24	9.33	22.62 / 93	17.31 / 71	6.81 / 89
MUN	Nuveen Prem Inc Muni Oppty	NPX	B-	13.50	14.29	11.41	C+	6.6	-0.73	6.47	21.04 / 91	14.88 / 56	6.14 / 83
MUN	Nuveen Premier Muni Inc	NPF	B	14.59	15.43	12.48	B-	7.1	0.05	7.51	21.60 / 92	15.92 / 63	6.83 / 89
MUN	Nuveen Premier Muni Oppty	NIF	C	14.99	16.73	13.04	C	4.6	-6.29	3.78	10.49 / 79	13.02 / 43	6.06 / 82
MUN	Nuveen Premium Income Muni 2	NPM	B	15.00	15.45	12.73	B-	7.1	2.11	7.31	23.09 / 93	15.14 / 58	7.15 / 92
MUN	Nuveen Quality Inc Muni	NQU	B	14.94	15.48	12.71	B-	7.2	3.92	10.52	21.38 / 91	14.91 / 56	6.23 / 84
MUN	Nuveen Quality Municipal	NQI	C+	14.26	15.05	12.40	C	4.8	-3.49	3.00	19.47 / 89	12.66 / 41	5.36 / 75
IN	Nuveen Quality Preferred Income	JTP	A+	8.16	8.47	6.75	A-	9.2	9.78	12.55	14.26 / 76	38.22 / 94	-1.14 / 22
IN	Nuveen Quality Preferred Income 2	JPS	A+	8.62	8.96	6.95	A-	9.2	12.21	18.35	13.65 / 75	37.87 / 94	-0.32 / 25
IN	Nuveen Quality Preferred Income 3	JHP	A+	8.32	8.93	6.76	A	9.3	8.11	16.86	12.15 / 73	38.85 / 95	-1.37 / 21
GI	Nuveen Real Estate Inc Fund	JRS	A	11.29	12.19	7.91	A+	9.8	10.47	31.41	13.82 / 76	51.67 / 99	-3.40 / 16

* Denotes ETF Fund, N/A denotes number is not available

Incl. in Returns		RISK				NET ASSETS		VALUATION			ASSET					FUND MANAGER	
Dividend Yield %	Expense Ratio	Risk Rating/ Pts	3 Year Standard Deviation	Beta	Avg Dura-tion	NAV as of 3/31/12	Total $(Mil)	Premium / Discount As of 3/31/12	1 Year Average	Wtd Avg P/E	Cash %	Stocks %	Bonds %	Other %	Portfolio Turnover Ratio	Manager Quality Pct	Manager Tenure (Years)
6.51	2.01	B / 8.5	12.6	2.00	11.7	15.00	627	-2.87	-1.42	N/A	3	0	91	6	14	45	10
6.80	1.40	B / 8.3	15.5	2.44	12.8	12.50	323	3.12	3.61	N/A	2	0	88	10	32	35	9
6.50	1.61	B / 8.3	13.6	2.33	12.3	12.13	199	-0.25	-0.76	N/A	6	0	80	14	17	39	N/A
5.05	0.77	B / 8.8	8.4	1.31	11.7	11.23	88	0.53	1.25	N/A	3	0	92	5	16	50	N/A
6.26	2.10	B / 8.6	10.4	1.90	11.1	14.44	623	-2.42	-1.96	N/A	2	0	94	4	14	50	10
6.00	1.63	B / 8.9	10.3	1.85	11.4	15.33	1,405	-4.70	-4.06	N/A	1	0	92	7	10	46	6
4.65	0.65	B+ / 9.1	6.7	1.23	12.3	9.98	1,915	0.90	-0.69	N/A	2	0	94	4	10	48	25
4.82	0.71	B / 8.5	10.3	1.37	N/A	17.00	213	-1.94	0.98	N/A	2	0	92	6	1	39	3
4.45	2.95	B / 8.6	14.1	0.87	10.2	15.64	33	8.70	1.56	N/A	2	0	89	9	10	80	5
4.70	2.79	B / 8.7	10.9	0.99	10.5	15.47	55	0.58	-0.60	N/A	1	0	94	5	14	69	N/A
4.74	2.75	B / 8.8	11.1	1.52	11.1	15.17	56	1.71	0.07	N/A	1	0	92	7	17	51	5
4.43	2.49	B / 8.9	10.5	1.33	10.8	15.07	91	2.39	-0.01	N/A	1	0	96	3	6	67	5
4.34	0.85	B / 8.7	N/A	N/A	N/A	16.43	23	-2.43	-4.65	N/A	1	0	96	3	2	29	N/A
4.39	0.77	B / 8.7	N/A	N/A	N/A	15.79	36	-3.10	-6.25	N/A	1	0	92	7	8	86	N/A
5.68	1.27	B / 8.6	11.1	2.05	11.1	15.17	89	-3.23	-6.37	N/A	1	0	97	2	6	55	1
5.84	1.81	B / 8.4	15.4	2.26	12.0	15.08	62	-2.52	-4.09	N/A	0	0	98	2	7	40	N/A
5.81	1.55	B / 8.7	10.3	1.71	11.5	15.13	280	-3.70	-5.28	N/A	3	0	95	2	9	67	N/A
5.58	1.59	B / 8.8	9.3	1.33	11.4	15.69	171	-0.57	-3.72	N/A	1	0	97	2	7	78	N/A
4.87	2.89	B+ / 9.0	9.6	1.35	11.9	15.19	53	-5.20	-6.70	N/A	1	0	96	3	6	61	N/A
5.45	2.42	B+ / 9.0	9.5	1.71	12.0	15.45	139	-6.60	-7.66	N/A	4	0	88	8	10	60	N/A
5.50	2.41	B+ / 9.0	9.7	1.67	11.9	15.38	97	-5.72	-7.42	N/A	3	0	90	7	14	60	N/A
5.53	1.66	B+ / 9.0	10.1	1.80	12.2	15.59	122	-5.32	-5.93	N/A	1	0	93	6	12	50	N/A
5.54	1.73	B / 8.8	12.0	1.85	10.9	15.57	269	-4.05	-4.54	N/A	2	0	90	8	4	55	N/A
4.19	0.65	B+ / 9.1	7.6	0.97	12.3	10.13	151	-2.37	-3.18	N/A	1	0	97	2	10	51	N/A
5.69	1.77	B+ / 9.0	10.3	1.74	11.7	16.23	239	-4.44	-5.05	N/A	2	0	89	9	6	63	N/A
5.48	1.28	B+ / 9.0	10.0	1.60	11.3	15.93	129	-4.52	-4.02	N/A	5	0	87	8	3	66	N/A
5.91	1.62	B+ / 9.0	10.9	1.73	12.2	15.55	363	-4.76	-3.53	N/A	1	0	92	7	3	62	N/A
5.76	1.73	B / 8.8	10.6	1.78	12.2	15.85	366	-4.67	-4.10	N/A	2	0	92	6	5	61	N/A
4.64	0.41	B+ / 9.2	7.2	1.32	11.4	14.59	54	-3.36	-3.82	N/A	1	0	96	3	3	30	N/A
5.80	1.33	B / 8.8	10.5	1.72	11.5	15.65	61	-2.81	-4.55	N/A	2	0	96	2	14	57	5
5.65	1.10	B / 8.8	10.6	1.80	11.9	15.36	44	-3.13	-6.75	N/A	1	0	96	3	9	58	5
5.95	1.10	B / 8.6	11.6	1.91	11.5	15.54	31	-1.99	-3.08	N/A	3	0	96	1	12	38	5
5.52	1.14	B / 8.8	11.9	1.65	11.4	16.98	151	2.36	-3.04	N/A	2	0	97	1	14	73	N/A
5.89	1.87	B / 8.7	10.6	1.81	11.6	15.24	47	-7.09	-7.25	N/A	2	0	97	1	8	64	N/A
6.21	1.74	B / 8.7	12.2	1.62	11.6	15.03	52	-4.19	-6.20	N/A	5	0	94	1	7	58	N/A
6.02	1.60	B+ / 9.0	9.4	1.45	11.9	15.56	227	0.00	-3.85	N/A	7	0	92	1	8	79	N/A
5.87	1.56	B / 8.9	10.0	1.75	11.5	14.95	211	-4.35	-6.98	N/A	5	0	94	1	8	73	N/A
4.25	0.87	B / 8.7	N/A	N/A	N/A	16.17	18	-7.54	-4.65	N/A	5	0	94	1	3	11	N/A
6.19	1.62	B / 8.8	9.6	1.74	10.7	15.88	893	-2.27	-3.07	N/A	4	0	95	1	10	65	10
8.56	1.70	B / 8.1	20.7	0.92	20.2	9.37	841	-5.23	-9.88	42.4	6	36	57	1	34	94	9
6.34	1.66	B / 8.9	9.9	1.64	10.8	14.82	900	-2.23	-3.20	N/A	9	0	90	1	9	61	6
6.36	1.99	B / 8.7	11.4	2.05	12.0	13.83	566	-3.11	-3.22	N/A	7	0	92	1	11	55	N/A
5.51	1.80	B / 8.8	10.2	1.88	11.2	14.26	506	-5.33	-5.11	N/A	2	0	91	7	20	49	N/A
6.46	1.55	B / 8.8	10.6	2.13	9.2	15.11	287	-3.44	-3.87	N/A	9	0	90	1	10	43	N/A
6.04	1.65	B / 8.5	14.5	2.17	10.3	15.40	287	-2.66	1.54	N/A	9	0	90	1	8	29	6
6.36	1.48	B / 8.9	9.1	1.82	10.3	15.40	1,040	-2.60	-4.02	N/A	7	0	92	1	8	56	15
6.35	1.92	B / 8.8	9.2	1.65	11.7	15.36	781	-2.73	-2.82	N/A	5	0	94	1	16	60	10
6.31	1.66	B / 8.7	10.4	1.77	11.9	14.79	545	-3.58	-1.28	N/A	2	0	91	7	18	38	N/A
7.35	1.61	B / 8.9	19.5	0.52	23.9	8.31	533	-1.81	-3.36	19.8	8	0	0	92	9	96	N/A
7.66	1.58	B / 8.7	21.2	0.65	29.3	8.80	1,055	-2.05	-4.46	19.4	11	0	0	89	7	95	N/A
7.50	1.54	B / 8.6	21.5	0.68	27.2	8.50	201	-2.12	-3.31	16.7	13	0	0	87	8	95	N/A
8.15	1.65	B- / 7.5	33.5	1.34	N/A	10.44	276	8.14	6.70	65.0	0	66	0	34	49	95	N/A

* Denotes ETF Fund, N/A denotes number is not available

				PRICE			PERFORMANCE						
	99 Pct = Best *0 Pct = Worst*		**Overall Investment Rating**	Price As of 3/31/12	52 Week		**Perform-ance Rating/Pts**	% Total Return Through 3/31/12					
					High	Low					Annualized		
Fund Type	Fund Name	Ticker Symbol						3 Mo	6 Mo	1Yr/Pct	3Yr/Pct	5Yr/Pct	
MUN	Nuveen Select Maturities Muni	NIM	D+	10.23	11.26	9.68	D / 1.9	-3.40	-0.58	8.49 / 74	4.41 / 12	4.99 / 72
MUN	Nuveen Select Quality Muni	NQS	B+	15.37	16.11	12.96	B / 8.2	1.04	9.10	24.05 / 94	18.57 / 78	6.10 / 82
MUN	Nuveen Select T-F Inc Portf	NXP	C	14.57	15.12	12.80	C- / 3.2	0.67	6.18	15.02 / 84	7.01 / 17	4.77 / 69
MUN	Nuveen Select T-F Inc Portf 2	NXQ	C	13.63	14.00	11.96	C- / 3.2	1.66	7.46	14.48 / 83	6.38 / 16	4.24 / 64
MUN	Nuveen Select Tax-Free Inc 3	NXR	C-	14.34	14.80	12.66	C- / 3.0	1.35	6.84	15.29 / 84	5.59 / 14	5.29 / 75
GI	Nuveen Short Duration Credit Oppty	JSD	U	19.42	N/A	N/A	U /	13.08	17.60	--	--	--
LP	Nuveen Sr Inc	NSL	A-	7.13	7.93	6.06	B+ / 8.9	9.70	10.39	0.98 / 43	37.56 / 94	4.30 / 52
IN	Nuveen Tax-Advant Tot Ret Strat Fd	JTA	B	11.11	12.09	8.57	B / 7.6	18.50	18.50	3.90 / 51	28.16 / 77	-7.39 / 9
GI	Nuveen Tax-Advantaged Dividend Grt	JTD	A-	13.75	13.77	10.44	B+ / 8.8	14.02	27.88	11.81 / 72	33.15 / 88	--
LP	Nuveen Tax-Advantaged Floating Rat	JFP	D	2.43	2.68	1.83	D+ / 2.8	20.08	23.00	11.15 / 70	7.93 / 13	-22.32 / 3
MUS	Nuveen TX Quality Inc Muni	NTX	C+	16.24	17.18	14.86	C / 5.1	0.75	3.59	10.97 / 80	13.38 / 45	8.00 / 97
MUS	Nuveen VA Div Adv Muni 2	NNB	C+	15.81	16.54	13.44	C+ / 5.6	5.98	9.00	22.14 / 92	10.55 / 30	4.27 / 64
MUS	Nuveen VA Div Adv Muni Fund	NGB	C	15.07	16.19	12.79	C / 4.6	4.51	4.31	19.97 / 89	9.77 / 27	2.11 / 46
MUS	Nuveen VA Premium Income Municipal	NPV	B-	16.19	16.80	14.10	C+ / 6.4	6.34	9.15	20.75 / 90	12.46 / 39	5.68 / 78
COH	Pacholder High Yield Fund	PHF	A-	9.01	10.29	7.98	A+ / 9.7	3.58	6.67	16.38 / 79	46.57 / 98	10.12 / 87
MTG	PCM Fund	PCM	A+	11.01	11.58	9.46	A / 9.5	4.56	15.34	11.27 / 71	43.06 / 97	10.21 / 88
EN	Petroleum and Resources Corp.	PEO	C-	25.99	31.47	20.84	C- / 3.9	6.57	23.18	-8.77 / 23	17.00 / 32	2.45 / 41
MUS	PIMCO CA Municipal Income Fund	PCQ	B+	14.17	15.19	11.72	B / 8.0	7.21	11.34	27.28 / 98	15.28 / 58	2.68 / 51
MUS	PIMCO CA Municipal Income Fund II	PCK	B	9.87	10.40	8.71	B- / 7.5	7.04	9.66	20.22 / 89	15.59 / 60	-2.26 / 19
MUS	PIMCO CA Municipal Income Fund III	PZC	A-	10.40	11.05	8.70	B+ / 8.6	8.47	13.29	24.83 / 95	17.55 / 73	-2.63 / 18
COH	PIMCO Corporate and Income Oppty	PTY	A+	18.61	20.89	14.70	A+ / 9.7	9.18	22.96	7.23 / 62	46.86 / 98	14.88 / 99
COH	PIMCO Corporate and ncome Strategy	PCN	A	16.04	17.95	13.20	A / 9.4	2.56	23.15	10.34 / 69	40.11 / 95	11.61 / 94
GL	PIMCO Global StocksPLUS&Inc	PGP	B+	20.18	25.83	15.37	A+ / 9.7	10.55	19.74	-9.11 / 23	48.33 / 99	12.60 / 97
COH	PIMCO High Income Fund	PHK	A	12.84	14.88	10.52	A+ / 9.6	10.04	19.83	3.36 / 50	46.10 / 98	11.98 / 95
GL	Pimco Income Opportunity Fund	PKO	B+	26.35	29.54	23.57	B+ / 8.4	6.99	15.82	9.15 / 67	32.67 / 87	--
LP	PIMCO Income Strategy Fund	PFL	A	11.36	13.24	9.31	A / 9.4	11.52	20.16	4.22 / 53	41.97 / 96	0.19 / 28
LP	PIMCO Income Strategy Fund II	PFN	A	10.16	11.02	8.23	A / 9.5	13.29	20.78	4.97 / 55	42.03 / 97	-1.31 / 21
MUN	PIMCO Municipal Income Fund	PMF	B+	14.52	15.46	12.19	B / 8.0	3.88	10.85	16.76 / 86	18.43 / 78	3.60 / 59
MUN	PIMCO Municipal Income Fund II	PML	A+	12.18	13.06	9.79	A / 9.4	10.14	14.07	28.95 / 98	21.03 / 86	2.07 / 45
MUN	PIMCO Municipal Income Fund III	PMX	A	11.80	12.46	9.93	B+ / 8.6	8.74	14.06	19.32 / 89	18.55 / 78	1.43 / 40
MUS	PIMCO NY Muni Income Fund	PNF	B-	11.18	12.61	9.63	C+ / 6.8	0.50	10.13	20.66 / 90	14.85 / 56	1.63 / 42
MUS	PIMCO NY Municipal Income Fund II	PNI	B+	11.92	12.56	10.26	B / 7.6	5.26	11.18	22.92 / 93	15.40 / 59	1.17 / 36
MUS	PIMCO NY Municipal Income Fund III	PYN	B-	9.61	10.52	8.29	C+ / 6.6	3.14	10.46	19.77 / 89	13.54 / 47	-3.80 / 15
MTG	PIMCO Strategic Glob Gov Fund	RCS	B-	11.06	12.08	10.01	C+ / 6.8	1.32	13.37	14.44 / 76	25.87 / 68	11.65 / 94
GL	Pioneer Diversified High Income Tr	HNW	B+	20.59	22.83	17.27	B / 8.0	9.47	16.73	6.26 / 59	30.78 / 83	--
LP	Pioneer Floating Rate Trust	PHD	B	12.96	14.54	11.22	B- / 7.2	5.22	14.34	4.99 / 55	28.01 / 76	1.95 / 37
GL	Pioneer High Income Trust	PHT	A+	16.66	18.02	14.13	A / 9.3	-2.24	7.56	11.45 / 71	41.49 / 96	12.28 / 96
MUH	Pioneer Municipal High Income Adv	MAV	A+	14.72	15.37	12.45	A+ / 9.7	4.28	12.11	27.83 / 98	28.15 / 97	7.20 / 92
MUH	Pioneer Municipal High Income Trus	MHI	A+	14.73	15.44	13.01	A / 9.3	1.04	6.22	23.33 / 94	24.10 / 93	7.37 / 93
GEN	Putnam High Income Securities	PCF	C+	8.45	9.49	6.87	C+ / 6.8	11.80	17.38	5.66 / 57	25.49 / 66	6.61 / 65
MUN	Putnam Managed Muni Inc Tr	PMM	A-	7.70	7.91	6.58	B+ / 8.6	4.66	6.89	19.20 / 88	20.54 / 85	6.63 / 87
GEN	Putnam Master Intermediate Inc Tr	PIM	D	5.15	6.32	4.74	C- / 3.3	3.11	5.51	-5.78 / 29	16.13 / 30	4.04 / 51
MUN	Putnam Muni Opp Tr	PMO	A-	12.55	12.76	10.65	B+ / 8.3	3.91	10.71	22.96 / 93	18.14 / 76	7.12 / 91
GEN	Putnam Premier Income Trust	PPT	D+	5.51	6.75	5.00	C / 4.9	7.91	6.71	-7.59 / 26	22.64 / 55	6.38 / 64
GEN	Pyxis Credit Strategies Fund	HCF	C-	6.34	7.79	5.81	C- / 4.0	4.39	6.07	-9.79 / 22	19.80 / 42	-12.02 / 5
UT	Reaves Utility Income Trust	UTG	A+	26.00	28.22	19.92	A / 9.4	0.97	11.40	21.91 / 83	41.19 / 96	9.24 / 82
GI	RENN Global Entrepreneurs Fund Inc	RCG	E+	1.95	2.82	1.38	E+ / 0.8	7.14	20.37	-5.80 / 29	-12.49 / 5	-25.24 / 2
GI	RMR Real Estate Income	RAP	D+	16.10	19.76	12.44	C- / 3.3	16.33	22.88	-4.45 / 31	13.10 / 22	-12.95 / 5
GR	Royce Focus Trust	FUND	C-	6.96	8.59	5.68	C- / 3.9	12.06	18.91	-12.15 / 18	17.72 / 35	-2.82 / 17
GR	Royce Micro-Cap Trust	RMT	C+	9.41	10.47	7.02	C+ / 6.0	8.78	26.86	-2.62 / 34	23.25 / 58	-4.06 / 14
GR	Royce Value Trust	RVT	C+	13.89	15.87	10.15	C+ / 6.8	14.77	30.61	-3.44 / 33	25.40 / 66	-2.83 / 17
EN	Salient MLP & Energy Infrastructur	SMF	U	25.55	N/A	N/A	U /	9.66	22.82	--	--	--

| Incl. in Returns | | RISK | | | | NET ASSETS | | VALUATION | | | ASSET | | | | | FUND MANAGER | |
Dividend Yield %	Expense Ratio	Risk Rating/ Pts	3 Year Standard Deviation	Beta	Avg Dura-tion	NAV as of 3/31/12	Total $(Mil)	Premium / Discount As of 3/31/12	1 Year Average	Wtd Avg P/E	Cash %	Stocks %	Bonds %	Other %	Portfolio Turnover Ratio	Manager Quality Pct	Manager Tenure (Years)
3.70	0.59	B / 8.8	9.6	1.01	9.4	10.45	125	-2.11	1.02	N/A	1	0	98	1	8	30	N/A
6.71	1.53	B / 8.6	11.1	1.94	11.6	15.15	491	1.45	1.60	N/A	7	0	92	1	13	66	10
4.90	0.32	B / 8.9	7.7	1.15	11.0	14.55	224	0.14	0.22	N/A	1	0	98	1	6	37	13
4.62	0.39	B / 8.9	7.1	1.32	11.5	13.89	228	-1.87	-2.35	N/A	2	0	97	1	6	26	13
4.60	0.37	B / 8.8	7.8	0.78	10.7	14.43	176	-0.62	-0.99	N/A	1	0	98	1	4	52	13
6.65	1.16	U /	N/A	N/A	N/A	19.48	240	-0.31	N/A	N/A	0	0	0	100	N/A	N/A	1
7.24	1.78	B / 8.2	22.9	N/A	4.5	7.08	228	0.71	0.82	N/A	2	1	7	90	100	93	13
7.92	1.73	B / 8.2	20.6	0.96	N/A	12.23	152	-9.16	-9.18	17.3	7	68	0	25	56	80	8
7.56	1.87	B / 8.3	18.2	0.92	N/A	14.93	196	-7.90	-9.78	N/A	4	72	1	23	50	89	N/A
4.94	0.59	C+ / 6.3	30.1	N/A	10.3	2.76	38	-11.96	-8.88	N/A	14	0	0	86	28	4	N/A
5.06	1.92	B+ / 9.1	9.6	1.29	11.7	15.36	135	5.73	6.32	N/A	2	0	97	1	10	66	N/A
5.01	2.74	B / 8.8	10.5	1.67	11.6	15.26	81	3.60	0.71	N/A	6	0	93	1	8	28	N/A
4.82	2.96	B / 8.6	11.8	1.40	11.2	14.98	43	0.60	0.93	N/A	6	0	93	1	12	48	N/A
4.97	2.11	B / 8.5	12.5	1.40	11.1	15.36	130	5.40	2.96	N/A	5	0	94	1	12	56	N/A
9.32	2.17	B- / 7.4	19.0	1.32	28.1	8.28	102	8.82	10.91	N/A	0	0	100	0	50	86	N/A
9.45	2.44	B / 8.8	15.6	-1.13	N/A	10.22	109	7.73	9.43	N/A	1	0	97	2	26	99	11
0.62	0.64	B- / 7.5	24.7	1.06	N/A	29.90	762	-13.08	-13.17	19.5	3	97	0	0	17	38	2
6.52	1.48	B / 8.1	17.9	2.72	13.9	13.50	208	4.96	5.12	N/A	0	0	100	0	19	26	1
7.60	1.55	B / 8.5	17.3	2.74	13.7	8.37	231	17.92	21.74	N/A	1	0	98	1	15	27	1
6.92	1.48	B / 8.6	16.0	2.35	14.2	9.79	199	6.23	6.03	N/A	0	0	100	0	11	50	1
8.03	1.09	B / 8.0	22.2	1.50	N/A	15.47	967	20.30	21.26	N/A	0	0	94	6	53	83	N/A
8.62	1.30	B / 8.0	21.2	1.53	N/A	14.15	515	13.36	15.40	N/A	11	0	84	5	32	63	N/A
10.91	2.81	B- / 7.1	29.4	1.01	N/A	12.58	151	60.41	68.05	N/A	1	0	98	1	80	96	7
11.39	1.11	B- / 7.8	25.2	1.97	N/A	7.87	1,138	63.15	58.16	N/A	3	0	95	2	89	42	N/A
9.37	2.44	B / 8.5	15.8	0.56	N/A	24.97	360	5.53	6.74	N/A	0	0	94	6	194	97	5
8.58	1.51	B- / 7.9	26.4	-60.41	19.4	10.78	283	5.38	5.93	N/A	28	0	72	0	44	99	N/A
7.68	1.24	B / 8.1	24.9	9.86	N/A	9.80	584	3.67	2.91	N/A	35	0	65	0	42	99	3
6.72	1.44	B / 8.3	17.2	2.40	14.8	12.73	270	14.06	16.90	N/A	4	0	96	0	15	59	1
6.40	1.37	B / 8.5	15.9	2.85	14.6	11.57	611	5.27	3.45	N/A	8	0	92	0	21	37	1
7.12	1.44	B / 8.8	13.0	1.90	13.7	10.38	313	13.68	13.29	N/A	8	0	92	0	14	71	1
6.12	1.51	B / 8.6	15.8	2.50	13.3	11.23	76	-0.45	0.77	N/A	7	0	93	0	29	27	1
6.67	1.55	B / 8.6	15.2	2.22	14.1	11.08	109	7.58	7.43	N/A	9	0	91	0	7	55	1
6.56	1.73	B / 8.7	14.2	2.44	14.3	9.20	49	4.46	4.58	N/A	0	0	100	0	9	25	1
9.40	1.43	B / 8.5	17.3	2.33	14.8	9.31	395	18.80	21.55	N/A	2	0	97	1	168	89	7
10.10	2.20	B / 8.3	17.4	0.46	N/A	19.56	173	5.27	2.88	N/A	3	0	96	1	30	97	N/A
7.52	1.67	B / 8.3	17.6	-72.29	N/A	12.94	307	0.15	1.24	P/E	0	5	8	87	42	99	N/A
9.90	1.11	B+ / 9.0	16.7	0.68	N/A	13.46	401	23.77	26.00	N/A	0	0	93	7	10	98	N/A
8.39	1.35	B / 8.4	13.4	2.25	15.4	12.87	267	14.37	11.39	N/A	2	0	97	1	10	83	N/A
8.38	1.12	B / 8.5	12.2	2.08	14.0	13.93	291	5.74	5.01	N/A	2	0	97	1	10	80	N/A
6.23	0.91	C+ / 6.9	16.0	-0.01	14.2	8.30	139	1.81	-1.11	60.9	2	2	40	56	63	96	N/A
6.06	1.03	B / 8.5	10.5	1.77	12.7	7.73	424	-0.39	0.22	N/A	1	0	98	1	17	76	23
6.76	0.94	C+ / 6.1	13.9	1.72	7.3	5.46	351	-5.68	-3.76	N/A	0	0	100	0	171	68	18
6.34	1.31	B / 8.8	9.9	1.93	11.4	12.80	483	-1.95	-3.62	N/A	1	0	98	1	16	63	13
6.53	0.85	C+ / 5.8	15.4	0.76	14.6	5.80	874	-5.00	-2.16	N/A	0	0	100	0	294	90	20
6.62	3.15	B- / 7.7	18.0	0.14	4.8	7.18	443	-11.70	-7.83	4.5	0	10	28	62	52	93	N/A
5.77	1.93	B / 8.9	19.7	1.00	15.3	24.49	545	6.17	6.08	22.8	1	97	0	2	34	95	8
0.00	5.25	C / 5.4	31.6	0.46	N/A	2.46	10	-20.73	-21.53	N/A	1	87	0	12	7	7	18
3.91	1.72	C+ / 6.8	25.8	1.18	N/A	19.59	77	-17.82	-17.25	N/A	3	97	0	0	52	16	N/A
5.75	1.39	B- / 7.3	24.2	1.26	N/A	8.06	172	-13.65	-12.73	36.7	13	86	0	1	36	16	16
5.53	1.12	B- / 7.5	24.3	1.32	N/A	10.83	311	-13.11	-13.60	43.3	11	88	0	1	27	25	19
5.47	0.23	B- / 7.2	26.5	1.47	5.0	15.94	1,106	-12.86	-13.53	37.3	6	93	0	1	30	21	26
5.92	2.49	U /	N/A	N/A	N/A	25.24	144	1.23	N/A	N/A	0	0	0	100	N/A	N/A	1

* Denotes ETF Fund, N/A denotes number is not available

Fund Type	Fund Name	Ticker Symbol	Overall Investment Rating	Price As of 3/31/12	52 Week High	52 Week Low	Performance Rating/Pts		3 Mo	6 Mo	1Yr/Pct	3Yr/Pct	5Yr/Pct
FO	Singapore Fund	SGF	C+	12.96	15.22	10.50	B-	7.1	18.79	17.96	-8.05 / 25	28.06 / 76	-0.26 / 26
IN	Source Capital	SOR	C+	52.95	59.15	39.00	B-	7.0	12.83	29.73	-4.16 / 32	26.51 / 71	1.41 / 33
MUN	Special Opportunities Fund	SPE	B	16.06	16.38	13.89	C+	6.5	10.76	15.86	8.24 / 73	14.51 / 53	7.22 / 92
EM	Stone Harbor Emg Markets Income	EDF	C+	24.58	25.10	20.64	C+	6.5	20.43	15.15	11.75 / 72	--	--
GL	Strategic Global Income Fund	SGL	B-	10.68	11.58	9.71	B-	7.3	6.69	9.88	6.79 / 61	28.67 / 79	11.12 / 92
FO	Swiss Helvetia Fund	SWZ	D+	11.21	15.24	9.69	C-	4.0	12.66	12.93	-3.96 / 32	17.61 / 34	-2.09 / 19
FO	Taiwan Fund	TWN	C-	16.83	20.43	13.79	C	4.6	16.15	16.33	-7.84 / 25	19.93 / 43	3.04 / 44
GI	TCW Strategic Income Fund	TSI	B+	5.15	5.50	4.70	B+	8.4	7.97	18.11	11.77 / 72	31.90 / 86	13.29 / 98
FO	Templeton Dragon Fund	TDF	C	28.35	32.75	22.08	C	5.4	11.39	19.52	-1.79 / 36	22.03 / 52	10.12 / 87
EM	Templeton Emerging Markets Fd	EMF	C	19.56	24.56	15.32	C+	5.9	9.52	18.53	-16.21 / 14	25.77 / 67	8.08 / 75
EM	Templeton Emerging Markets Income	TEI	C+	15.68	18.12	13.82	B-	7.2	2.31	11.79	2.39 / 47	29.01 / 80	12.14 / 96
GL	Templeton Global Income Fd	GIM	C	9.65	12.88	8.82	C	4.3	4.10	12.88	3.21 / 49	18.49 / 38	12.15 / 96
FO	Templeton Russia&East European Fun	TRF	D	16.44	24.51	13.30	C-	3.7	20.79	12.30	-32.07 / 5	19.41 / 40	-10.19 / 7
FO	Thai Capital Fund	TF	B-	11.58	13.31	7.20	A+	9.7	34.77	37.98	19.28 / 81	41.48 / 96	11.78 / 95
FO	Thai Fund	TTF	A+	15.94	15.95	10.95	A+	9.8	30.02	38.88	22.18 / 83	47.49 / 98	13.33 / 98
GI	The Cushing MLP Total Return Fund	SRV	A-	9.96	10.87	8.01	A	9.4	13.25	18.14	1.30 / 44	42.52 / 97	--
GI	The Denali Fund Inc.	DNY	C+	14.74	16.60	12.80	C+	6.0	11.87	15.17	-1.36 / 37	24.15 / 61	-5.06 / 12
FO	The European Equity Fund	EEA	D+	6.78	8.85	5.67	C-	3.4	14.14	15.11	-16.34 / 13	16.31 / 30	-7.72 / 8
FO	The New Ireland Fund	IRL	C	8.12	8.77	6.49	C+	5.7	17.00	16.33	5.21 / 56	21.68 / 51	-13.96 / 4
EN	Tortoise Energy Capital	TYY	B-	28.34	29.61	21.24	B-	7.4	7.17	24.87	7.07 / 61	27.60 / 75	6.25 / 63
EN	Tortoise Energy Infrastr Corp	TYG	A	41.22	43.34	31.13	B+	8.7	4.53	25.03	9.85 / 68	33.82 / 89	8.32 / 76
GR	Tortoise MLP Fund Inc	NTG	C-	25.62	27.49	21.01	D+	2.6	0.97	17.31	2.91 / 49	--	--
EN	Tortoise North American Energy	TYN	A	25.65	27.75	19.76	B+	8.6	6.42	18.05	8.63 / 66	33.97 / 89	8.49 / 77
EN	Tortoise Pipeline & Enrgy Fund Inc	TTP	U	24.90	N/A	N/A	U		5.51	--	--	--	--
EN	Tortoise Power and Energy Inf Fund	TPZ	C-	25.39	26.62	20.13	C-	3.1	3.09	16.79	5.23 / 56	--	--
GL	Transamerica Income Shares	TAI	C+	21.79	22.54	19.55	C	4.6	2.58	4.79	10.20 / 69	19.93 / 43	8.54 / 77
IN	Tri-Continental Corporation	TY	B-	15.92	16.15	11.95	B-	7.1	12.62	26.66	10.82 / 70	24.71 / 63	-1.15 / 22
FO	Turkish Investment Fund	TKF	C+	13.65	17.91	10.81	B+	8.6	23.42	10.50	-15.78 / 14	36.26 / 92	-1.75 / 21
GI	Virtus Total Return	DCA	A+	3.80	3.99	3.05	A+	9.7	11.01	17.74	6.76 / 60	49.46 / 99	-16.16 / 3
GL	Wells Fargo Avtg Global Div Oppty	EOD	D+	8.52	10.47	7.34	C-	3.5	15.92	14.23	-1.67 / 36	14.54 / 25	-3.51 / 15
COH	Wells Fargo Avtg Income Oppty	EAD	B-	10.24	10.92	8.20	B	7.7	3.15	15.23	10.96 / 70	29.64 / 81	5.82 / 61
GL	Wells Fargo Avtg Multi-Sector Inc	ERC	C+	15.14	15.80	13.70	C+	5.6	4.43	10.86	8.33 / 65	22.67 / 55	8.48 / 77
UT	Wells Fargo Avtg Utilities&High In	ERH	C-	11.96	12.26	9.51	C	4.4	9.33	21.29	8.89 / 66	16.97 / 32	-5.82 / 11
EM	Western Asset Emerging Market Debt	ESD	B	20.13	20.68	17.00	B-	7.5	8.35	15.26	15.18 / 77	27.60 / 75	11.74 / 95
EM	Western Asset Emerging Mkts Inc	EMD	B	14.28	15.10	11.97	B	7.8	8.28	16.38	16.91 / 80	28.27 / 77	10.97 / 92
GL	Western Asset Global Corp Def Oppt	GDO	C+	19.28	19.49	15.62	C	5.5	9.28	16.22	13.81 / 75	--	--
GL	Western Asset Global High Income	EHI	B+	13.25	13.62	10.33	B+	8.9	7.50	19.35	12.20 / 73	35.46 / 91	8.77 / 79
GL	Western Asset Global Partners Inc	GDF	B	12.90	14.25	10.14	B+	8.7	0.64	20.89	9.78 / 68	34.72 / 90	10.48 / 89
GL	Western Asset High Inc Fd II	HIX	B+	9.99	10.45	8.35	A-	9.0	6.33	11.39	12.24 / 73	37.15 / 93	10.35 / 88
COH	Western Asset High Income Fund	HIF	C	9.64	11.06	8.36	C	5.3	10.17	5.00	4.77 / 54	22.29 / 53	9.09 / 80
COH	Western Asset High Income Opp Inc.	HIO	C+	6.16	6.63	5.34	C+	6.4	1.92	11.17	4.25 / 53	25.73 / 67	8.23 / 75
COH	Western Asset High Yld Def Opp	HYI	B+	19.69	19.86	15.33	B+	8.4	21.79	25.02	14.33 / 76	--	--
GEI	Western Asset Income Fund	PAI	C+	14.55	14.95	12.35	C+	5.7	6.71	12.80	17.32 / 80	21.24 / 49	6.78 / 66
GL	Western Asset Inflation Mgmt	IMF	C	17.75	18.05	16.77	D+	2.6	2.06	5.87	11.14 / 70	10.01 / 16	6.88 / 67
MUN	Western Asset Intermediate Muni	SBI	C+	10.03	10.36	8.76	C+	5.6	3.58	8.62	13.69 / 82	13.16 / 44	7.01 / 91
COH	Western Asset Managed High Income	MHY	B-	6.14	6.68	5.21	C+	6.3	3.85	13.10	5.83 / 58	24.88 / 64	7.79 / 73
MUN	Western Asset Managed Municipals	MMU	A-	13.67	14.44	11.31	B	8.0	3.40	7.45	23.76 / 94	17.41 / 72	9.89 / 99
MTG	Western Asset Mtge Defined Oppty	DMO	C	21.71	22.60	18.40	C	4.5	13.13	17.99	6.43 / 59	--	--
MUN	Western Asset Municipal Defined Op	MTT	C	22.41	23.64	19.35	C	4.3	2.74	9.10	17.11 / 86	9.14 / 24	--
MUH	Western Asset Municipal High Inc	MHF	C+	8.04	8.42	6.89	C	5.0	4.05	10.72	18.54 / 87	10.13 / 28	5.82 / 80
MUN	Western Asset Municipal Partners	MNP	A	15.79	16.37	12.89	B+	8.5	4.16	8.94	26.13 / 97	18.33 / 77	8.65 / 98
GEI	Western Asset Premier Bond Fund	WEA	B+	15.90	16.84	13.53	B+	8.4	1.84	10.52	13.29 / 74	33.09 / 88	11.64 / 94

* Denotes ETF Fund, N/A denotes number is not available

| Incl. in Returns | | RISK | | | | NET ASSETS | | VALUATION | | | ASSET | | | | | FUND MANAGER | |
Dividend Yield %	Expense Ratio	Risk Rating/ Pts	3 Year Standard Deviation	Beta	Avg Dura-tion	NAV as of 3/31/12	Total $(Mil)	Premium/Discount As of 3/31/12	1 Year Average	Wtd Avg P/E	Cash %	Stocks %	Bonds %	Other %	Portfolio Turnover Ratio	Manager Quality Pct	Manager Tenure (Years)
1.03	1.83	C+ / 6.7	29.1	1.10	N/A	14.21	138	-8.80	-7.25	N/A	4	95	0	1	76	84	1
5.29	0.98	B- / 7.5	23.2	1.26	6.6	60.54	578	-12.54	-11.09	23.9	4	89	4	3	13	40	16
1.64	1.50	B+ / 9.0	11.4	0.39	4.9	17.26	110	-6.95	-8.85	398.5	10	0	89	1	73	87	N/A
8.79	1.76	B / 8.0	N/A	N/A	N/A	23.65	N/A	3.93	1.21	N/A	0	0	0	100	157	93	N/A
0.86	1.17	B / 8.0	15.3	1.01	11.8	11.26	208	-5.15	-5.94	N/A	3	0	96	1	121	94	N/A
3.00	1.34	C+ / 6.7	19.8	0.82	N/A	12.69	467	-11.66	-10.67	N/A	0	96	0	4	61	66	16
0.00	1.43	B- / 7.0	29.4	1.08	N/A	17.97	375	-6.34	-9.48	N/A	14	86	0	0	54	63	N/A
6.72	1.26	B / 8.0	12.4	0.32	14.3	5.28	235	-2.46	-6.33	20.3	0	0	89	11	40	95	N/A
0.36	1.47	B- / 7.4	22.2	0.81	N/A	30.68	1,258	-7.59	-9.43	64.9	0	99	0	1	7	83	18
1.41	1.46	C+ / 6.6	34.4	1.29	N/A	21.22	397	-7.82	-5.83	N/A	0	80	0	20	3	24	21
6.38	1.20	B- / 7.2	20.5	1.24	6.5	15.81	790	-0.82	1.92	N/A	4	0	95	1	25	93	N/A
5.60	0.74	B / 8.0	18.0	1.23	N/A	9.17	1,339	5.23	6.34	N/A	5	0	94	1	21	85	24
0.00	1.79	C / 5.3	50.4	1.77	N/A	17.79	140	-7.59	-6.70	N/A	16	82	0	2	11	17	17
0.78	2.14	C / 5.4	25.2	0.70	N/A	12.16	51	-4.77	-12.40	N/A	1	98	0	1	245	96	N/A
1.66	1.59	B- / 7.9	27.8	0.86	N/A	17.82	235	-10.55	-14.28	N/A	2	97	0	1	11	97	4
9.04	3.39	B- / 7.6	27.3	0.97	4.7	7.73	256	28.85	20.82	43.7	0	90	9	1	241	91	N/A
0.14	2.64	B / 8.0	20.7	1.05	N/A	18.18	75	-18.92	-17.19	N/A	26	65	0	9	7	55	N/A
0.24	1.60	C+ / 6.6	27.9	1.25	N/A	7.52	72	-9.84	-9.39	N/A	0	100	0	0	73	26	N/A
0.25	2.22	C+ / 6.9	30.4	1.18	N/A	9.41	54	-13.71	-11.73	N/A	0	100	0	0	23	70	1
5.79	3.93	B- / 7.9	20.5	0.63	N/A	27.03	500	4.85	2.51	N/A	0	100	0	0	19	90	7
5.41	3.47	B / 8.5	17.1	0.60	N/A	35.49	925	16.15	13.75	N/A	0	100	0	0	18	93	8
6.44	2.33	B / 8.5	N/A	N/A	N/A	25.51	1,141	0.43	0.89	N/A	0	100	0	0	20	35	N/A
6.00	2.00	B / 8.8	16.4	0.34	N/A	25.94	156	-1.12	-4.22	30.8	0	100	0	0	27	97	7
0.00	1.77	U /	N/A	N/A	N/A	25.91	250	-3.90	N/A	N/A	0	0	0	100	N/A	N/A	1
5.91	1.65	B / 8.6	N/A	N/A	N/A	25.98	176	-2.27	-3.14	N/A	2	97	0	1	9	81	N/A
6.61	0.80	B+ / 9.1	9.4	0.08	N/A	22.23	142	-1.98	-2.41	N/A	2	0	90	8	67	91	N/A
2.64	0.60	B / 8.2	19.3	1.11	5.1	18.67	1,061	-14.73	-14.22	47.4	0	99	0	1	86	47	2
2.23	1.05	C+ / 6.2	38.7	1.35	N/A	15.48	108	-11.82	-10.46	N/A	5	94	0	1	29	88	15
6.16	1.38	B / 8.2	31.2	1.36	17.5	4.16	111	-8.65	-12.99	24.7	6	70	7	17	138	91	N/A
13.15	1.05	B- / 7.4	22.0	0.83	N/A	8.72	438	-2.29	-3.52	13.0	4	60	0	36	129	53	N/A
9.96	1.09	B- / 7.2	17.2	1.33	6.1	9.68	710	5.79	4.24	N/A	5	0	94	1	42	47	N/A
7.93	1.14	B / 8.7	13.2	0.65	9.3	16.42	679	-7.80	-8.09	N/A	1	0	98	1	35	92	N/A
7.53	1.24	C+ / 6.6	26.1	0.77	5.0	11.79	108	1.44	-3.82	34.0	9	52	28	11	64	74	8
6.86	1.02	B / 8.4	14.1	0.81	10.2	21.39	632	-5.89	-8.10	N/A	0	0	99	1	28	95	N/A
6.72	1.23	B / 8.4	16.7	1.04	N/A	15.14	430	-5.68	-7.35	N/A	0	0	99	1	35	94	N/A
7.94	1.40	B / 8.5	N/A	N/A	N/A	19.73	291	-2.28	-5.16	N/A	3	0	96	1	16	87	N/A
8.72	1.53	B- / 7.3	16.8	0.78	7.1	13.20	418	0.38	-1.98	N/A	3	0	96	1	75	97	N/A
8.84	1.66	B- / 7.0	21.9	1.04	9.1	11.86	179	8.77	8.79	N/A	4	0	95	1	56	96	N/A
9.91	1.61	B- / 7.5	17.3	0.72	12.4	8.86	807	12.75	12.05	N/A	3	0	96	1	84	97	N/A
7.78	1.11	B- / 7.4	14.4	0.86	14.0	9.29	46	3.77	4.85	N/A	3	0	97	0	58	69	6
8.28	0.89	B- / 7.4	14.3	1.02	13.7	6.14	433	0.33	1.13	N/A	3	0	96	1	68	56	6
8.96	0.91	B / 8.0	N/A	N/A	N/A	18.21	401	8.13	0.63	N/A	0	0	99	1	N/A	78	N/A
4.95	0.74	B / 8.7	12.3	0.71	19.9	14.20	130	2.46	-3.13	N/A	0	0	99	1	56	90	N/A
3.66	0.87	B+ / 9.6	5.4	0.14	8.5	19.47	127	-8.83	-8.73	N/A	2	0	97	1	48	82	6
4.79	0.91	B+ / 9.2	7.1	0.95	8.0	10.22	139	-1.86	-3.13	N/A	4	0	95	1	16	74	N/A
8.31	0.92	B / 8.6	14.7	1.00	N/A	5.94	291	3.37	2.94	N/A	4	0	96	0	96	55	N/A
5.71	0.95	B+ / 9.0	9.9	1.60	N/A	13.68	522	-0.07	-0.35	N/A	3	0	97	0	23	70	20
8.98	2.24	B / 8.7	N/A	N/A	N/A	21.61	197	0.46	-0.79	N/A	1	0	98	1	13	77	N/A
4.50	0.71	B / 8.9	7.5	1.01	N/A	22.34	257	0.31	-0.68	N/A	0	0	99	1	8	55	N/A
5.22	0.68	B / 8.9	8.8	1.48	13.4	7.97	164	0.88	-1.11	N/A	0	0	100	0	10	41	N/A
5.32	1.25	B / 8.9	10.3	1.79	11.7	16.11	148	-1.99	-3.77	N/A	0	0	99	1	34	70	N/A
8.30	1.38	B- / 7.9	14.6	0.28	12.0	13.63	164	16.65	14.60	N/A	4	0	95	1	33	97	N/A

* Denotes ETF Fund, N/A denotes number is not available

Fund Type	Fund Name	Ticker Symbol	Overall Investment Rating	PRICE Price As of 3/31/12	52 Week High	52 Week Low	PERFORMANCE Perform-ance Rating/Pts		% Total Return Through 3/31/12 3 Mo	6 Mo	1Yr/Pct	Annualized 3Yr/Pct	5Yr/Pct
GL	Western Asset Var Rt Strat Fd	GFY	C	16.62	17.41	14.28	C /	5.0	13.29	10.41	1.63 / 45	20.74 / 46	4.46 / 54
EM	Western Asset Worldwide Inc Fd	SBW	B	14.49	14.69	12.23	B- /	7.5	6.89	15.21	18.79 / 81	27.34 / 74	10.01 / 86
USA	Western Asset/Claymore Inf-Link O&	WIW	C	12.79	12.98	12.26	D+ /	2.6	1.96	3.60	7.47 / 62	10.47 / 17	6.91 / 67
USA	Western Asset/Claymore Inf-Link S&	WIA	C-	12.74	13.38	12.33	D /	2.0	1.29	2.82	4.62 / 54	7.36 / 13	6.89 / 67
COI	Western Asst Invst Grade Define Op	IGI	C-	21.40	23.24	19.60	D+ /	2.9	-0.99	3.42	15.24 / 77	--	--
IN	Zweig Fund	ZF	C	3.21	3.63	2.66	C /	4.8	13.74	20.46	-0.86 / 39	19.69 / 42	-0.70 / 24
GI	Zweig Total Return Fund	ZTR	C-	3.20	3.49	2.87	D+ /	2.8	8.71	11.93	2.95 / 49	11.30 / 18	-0.95 / 23

99 Pct = Best
0 Pct = Worst

Incl. in Returns		RISK				NET ASSETS		VALUATION			ASSET						FUND MANAGER	
		Risk Rating/ Pts	3 Year		Avg Dura-tion	NAV as of 3/31/12	Total $(Mil)	Premium / Discount		Wtd Avg P/E	Cash %	Stocks %	Bonds %	Other %	Portfolio Turnover Ratio	Manager Quality Pct	Manager Tenure (Years)
Dividend Yield %	Expense Ratio		Standard Deviation	Beta				As of 3/31/12	1 Year Average								
4.84	0.99	B / 8.3	10.0	0.18	4.6	17.66	112	-5.89	-8.41	N/A	1	0	98	1	31	92	N/A
6.54	1.37	B / 8.2	14.3	0.94	10.3	15.50	193	-6.52	-8.94	N/A	0	0	99	1	26	93	N/A
3.41	0.75	B+ / 9.6	6.8	0.05	8.6	14.33	812	-10.75	-10.29	N/A	0	0	91	9	48	84	N/A
3.27	0.76	B+ / 9.6	7.0	0.08	8.5	14.20	383	-10.28	-8.53	N/A	0	0	92	8	43	79	8
5.86	0.80	B / 8.9	N/A	N/A	N/A	21.51	220	-0.51	0.21	N/A	0	0	99	1	49	85	N/A
10.22	1.23	B- / 7.8	17.8	0.98	N/A	3.68	349	-12.77	-10.69	57.1	14	81	3	2	42	40	9
11.63	1.10	B / 8.3	11.0	0.51	5.7	3.67	457	-12.81	-12.27	42.3	24	44	30	2	25	53	9

* Denotes ETF Fund, N/A denotes number is not available

Section II

Analysis of ETFs and Other Closed-End Funds

A summary analysis of all

Exchange-Traded Funds and

Other Closed-End Mutual Funds

receiving a TheStreet Investment Rating.

Funds are listed in alphabetical order.

Section II Contents

1. Fund Name   The name of the mutual fund as stated in its prospectus, which can sometimes differ slightly from the name that the company uses for advertising. If you cannot find the paritcular mutual fund you are interested in, or if you have any doubts regarding the precise name, verify the information with your broker or on your account statement. Also, use the fund's ticker symbol for confirmation.

2. Ticker Symbol   The unique alphabetic symbol used for identifying and trading a specific mutual fund. No two funds can have the same ticker symbol.

3. Investment Rating   Our overall rating is measured on a scale from A to E based on each fund's risk-adjusted performance. Please see page 10 for specific descriptions of each letter grade. Also refer to page 7 for information on how our ratings are derived. Most important, when using this rating, please be sure to consider the warnings beginning on page 11 regarding the ratings' limitations and the underlying assumptions.

4. Fund Family   The umbrella group of mutual funds to which the fund belongs.

5. Fund Type   The mutual fund's peer category based on an analysis of its investment portfolio.

COH	Corporate – High Yield	HL	Health
COI	Corporate – Inv. Grade	IN	Income
EM	Emerging Market	LP	Loan Participation
EN	Energy/Natural Resources	MTG	Mortgage
FS	Financial Services	MUH	Municipal – High Yield
FO	Foreign	MUN	Municipal – National
GEI	General – Inv. Grade	MUS	Municipal – Single State
GEN	General Bond	PM	Precious Metals
GL	Global	USA	U.S. Gov. – Agency
GR	Growth	UT	Utilities
GI	Growth and Income		

A blank fund type means that the mutual fund has not yet been categorized.

6. Inception Date   The date on which the fund began.

7. Major Rating Factors   A synopsis of the key ratios and sub-factors that have most influenced the rating of a particular mutual fund, including an examination of the fund's performance, risk, and managerial performance. There may be additional factors which have influenced the rating but do not appear due to space limitations.

How to Read the Annualized Total Return Graph

The annualized total return graph provides a clearer picture of a fund's yearly financial performance. In addition to the solid line denoting the fund's calendar year returns for the last six years, the graph also shows the yearly return for a benchmark index for easy comparison using a dotted line. The S&P 500 Composite Index is used for ETFs and other closed-end mutual funds that are primarily invested in stocks. One of two indexes is shown for funds with the majority of their assets held in bonds. Municipal bond funds display the Lehman Brothers Municipals Index, and other bond funds will show the Lehman Brothers Aggregate Bond Index.

The top of the shaded area of the graph denotes the average returns for all funds within the same fund type. If the solid line falls into the shaded area, that means that the fund has performed below the average for its type.

How to Read the Historical Data Table

Data Date:
The quarter-end or year-end as of date used for evaluating the mutual fund.

Price:
The fund's share price as of the date indicated. A fund's price is determined by investor demand. The fund may trade at a price higher or lower than its net asset value (NAV).

Risk Rating/Pts:
A letter grade rating based solely on the mutual fund's risk as determined by its monthly performance volatility over the trailing three years. Pts are rating points where 0=worst and 10=best.

Data Date	Investment Rating	Net Assets ($Mil)	Price	Performance Rating/Pts	Total Return Y-T-D	Risk Rating/Pts
3-12	B+	126.6	8.91	A- / 9.2	52.38%	C+ / 6.0
2011	C+	178.56	7.43	C+ / 5.7	2.57%	C+ / 6.1
2010	B+	86.42	19.76	B / 7.8	8.78%	C+ / 6.8
2009	B	87.35	14.30	C / 5.4	4.71%	B / 8.3
2008	D+	284.1	6.90	C- / 3.2	5.19%	C / 4.6

Investment Rating:
Our overall opinion of the fund's risk-adjusted performance at the specified time period.

Net Assets $(Mil):
The total value of all of the fund's asset holdings (in millions) including stocks, bonds, cash, and other financial instruments, less accrued expenses and fees.

Performance Rating/Pts:
A letter grade rating based solely on the mutual fund's return to shareholders over the trailing three years, without any consideration for the amount of risk the fund poses. Pts are rating points where 0=worst and 10=best

Total Return Y-T-D:
The fund's total return to shareholders since the beginning of the calendar year specified.

*Active Bear ETF (HDGE)

D-   **Weak**

Fund Family: AdvisorShares Investments LLC
Fund Type: Growth
Inception Date: January 26, 2011

Major Rating Factors:
Very poor performance is the major factor driving the D- (Weak) TheStreet.com Investment Rating for *Active Bear ETF. The fund currently has a performance rating of E (Very Weak) based on an annualized return of 0.00% over the last three years and a total return of -17.63% year to date 2012. Factored into the performance evaluation is an expense ratio of 3.07% (high).

The fund's risk rating is currently C+ (Fair). It carries a beta of 0.00, meaning the fund's expected move will be 0.0% for every 10% move in the market. Volatility, as measured by both the semi-deviation and a drawdown factor, is considered low. As of March 31, 2012, *Active Bear ETF traded at a price exactly equal to its net asset value, which is better than its one-year historical average premium of .08%.

Brad H. Lamensdorf currently receives a manager quality ranking of 28 (0=worst, 99=best). This fund offers only a moderate level of risk but investors looking for strong performance are still waiting.

Data Date	Investment Rating	Net Assets ($Mil)	Price	Performance Rating/Pts	Total Return Y-T-D	Risk Rating/Pts
3-12	D-	131.99	20.61	E / 0.4	-17.63%	C+ / 6.8

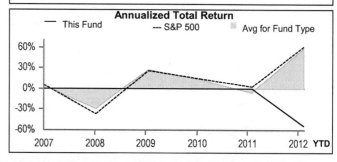
Annualized Total Return — This Fund --- S&P 500 Avg for Fund Type

*Alps Alerian MLP ETF (AMLP)

C   **Fair**

Fund Family: ALPS Advisors Inc
Fund Type: Energy/Natural Resources
Inception Date: August 25, 2010

Major Rating Factors: Middle of the road best describes *Alps Alerian MLP ETF whose TheStreet.com Investment Rating is currently a C (Fair). The fund currently has a performance rating of C- (Fair) based on an annualized return of 0.00% over the last three years and a total return of 1.75% year to date 2012. Factored into the performance evaluation is an expense ratio of 0.85% (very low).

The fund's risk rating is currently B+ (Good). It carries a beta of 0.00, meaning the fund's expected move will be 0.0% for every 10% move in the market. Volatility, as measured by both the semi-deviation and a drawdown factor, is considered very low. As of March 31, 2012, *Alps Alerian MLP ETF traded at a premium of .18% above its net asset value, which is worse than its one-year historical average premium of .07%.

Daniel Franciscus has been running the fund for 1 year and currently receives a manager quality ranking of 85 (0=worst, 99=best). If you desire an average level of risk, then this fund may be an option.

Data Date	Investment Rating	Net Assets ($Mil)	Price	Performance Rating/Pts	Total Return Y-T-D	Risk Rating/Pts
3-12	C	2,746.52	16.67	C- / 3.0	1.75%	B+ / 9.2
2011	B-	1,989.90	16.62	C+ / 6.0	0.60%	B+ / 9.2

Annualized Total Return — This Fund --- S&P 500 Avg for Fund Type

*Alps Equal Sector Weight ETF (EQL)

C   **Fair**

Fund Family: ALPS Advisors Inc
Fund Type: Income
Inception Date: July 7, 2009

Major Rating Factors: Middle of the road best describes *Alps Equal Sector Weight ETF whose TheStreet.com Investment Rating is currently a C (Fair). The fund currently has a performance rating of C (Fair) based on an annualized return of 0.00% over the last three years and a total return of 10.49% year to date 2012. Factored into the performance evaluation is an expense ratio of 0.34% (very low).

The fund's risk rating is currently B (Good). It carries a beta of 0.00, meaning the fund's expected move will be 0.0% for every 10% move in the market. Volatility, as measured by both the semi-deviation and a drawdown factor, is considered low. As of March 31, 2012, *Alps Equal Sector Weight ETF traded at a premium of .05% above its net asset value, which is worse than its one-year historical average premium of .02%.

Daniel Franciscus has been running the fund for 3 years and currently receives a manager quality ranking of 42 (0=worst, 99=best). If you desire an average level of risk, then this fund may be an option.

Data Date	Investment Rating	Net Assets ($Mil)	Price	Performance Rating/Pts	Total Return Y-T-D	Risk Rating/Pts
3-12	C	84.34	39.18	C / 4.9	10.49%	B / 8.4
2011	C-	62.30	35.60	D+ / 2.9	1.46%	B / 8.4
2010	A+	53.00	35.36	A- / 9.1	14.85%	B- / 7.9

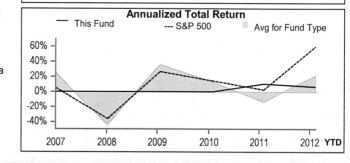
Annualized Total Return — This Fund --- S&P 500 Avg for Fund Type

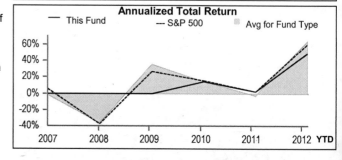

*Alps Jefferies / TR/J CRB Gl Cm (CRBQ)   D   Weak

Fund Family: ALPS Advisors Inc
Fund Type: Global
Inception Date: September 21, 2009

Data Date	Investment Rating	Net Assets ($Mil)	Price	Perfor-mance Rating/Pts	Total Return Y-T-D	Risk Rating/Pts
3-12	D	95.34	45.83	D- / 1.4	8.02%	B- / 7.0
2011	D	83.50	42.54	D- / 1.3	3.35%	B- / 7.1
2010	A+	111.00	49.58	A / 9.5	16.98%	B- / 7.3

Major Rating Factors:

Disappointing performance is the major factor driving the D (Weak) TheStreet.com Investment Rating for *Alps Jefferies / TR/J CRB Gl Cm. The fund currently has a performance rating of D- (Weak) based on an annualized return of 0.00% over the last three years and a total return of 8.02% year to date 2012. Factored into the performance evaluation is an expense ratio of 0.65% (very low).

The fund's risk rating is currently B- (Good). It carries a beta of 0.00, meaning the fund's expected move will be 0.0% for every 10% move in the market. Volatility, as measured by both the semi-deviation and a drawdown factor, is considered low. As of March 31, 2012, *Alps Jefferies / TR/J CRB Gl Cm traded at a premium of .24% above its net asset value, which is worse than its one-year historical average discount of .15%.

Daniel Franciscus has been running the fund for 1 year and currently receives a manager quality ranking of 19 (0=worst, 99=best). This fund offers only a moderate level of risk but investors looking for strong performance are still waiting.

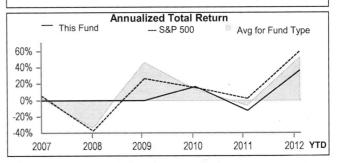

Annualized Total Return

---

*Alps Jefferies/TR/J CRB WE & PE (WCAT)   E+   Very Weak

Fund Family: ALPS Advisors Inc
Fund Type: Energy/Natural Resources
Inception Date: January 19, 2010

Data Date	Investment Rating	Net Assets ($Mil)	Price	Perfor-mance Rating/Pts	Total Return Y-T-D	Risk Rating/Pts
3-12	E+	10.98	40.62	E+ / 0.9	1.20%	C / 5.4
2011	D-	12.10	40.16	D- / 1.4	4.58%	C / 5.4

Major Rating Factors:

Very poor performance is the major factor driving the E+ (Very Weak) TheStreet.com Investment Rating for *Alps Jefferies/TR/J CRB WE & PE. The fund currently has a performance rating of E+ (Very Weak) based on an annualized return of 0.00% over the last three years and a total return of 1.20% year to date 2012. Factored into the performance evaluation is an expense ratio of 0.65% (very low).

The fund's risk rating is currently C (Fair). It carries a beta of 0.00, meaning the fund's expected move will be 0.0% for every 10% move in the market. Volatility, as measured by both the semi-deviation and a drawdown factor, is considered average. As of March 31, 2012, *Alps Jefferies/TR/J CRB WE & PE traded at a discount of .81% below its net asset value, which is better than its one-year historical average discount of .46%.

Daniel Franciscus has been running the fund for 1 year and currently receives a manager quality ranking of 7 (0=worst, 99=best). This fund offers an average level of risk but investors looking for strong performance will be frustrated.

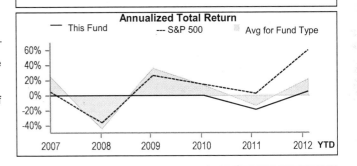

Annualized Total Return

---

*Barclays ETN + VEQTOR ETN (VQT)   D+   Weak

Fund Family: Barclays Bank PLC
Fund Type: Growth
Inception Date: August 31, 2010

Data Date	Investment Rating	Net Assets ($Mil)	Price	Perfor-mance Rating/Pts	Total Return Y-T-D	Risk Rating/Pts
3-12	D+	324.88	133.97	C / 4.6	6.35%	C+ / 5.8
2011	C	192.50	125.97	C+ / 6.8	0.73%	C+ / 5.8

Major Rating Factors: *Barclays ETN + VEQTOR ETN receives a TheStreet.com Investment Rating of D+ (Weak). The fund currently has a performance rating of C (Fair) based on an annualized return of 0.00% over the last three years and a total return of 6.35% year to date 2012. Factored into the performance evaluation is an expense ratio of 0.95% (low).

The fund's risk rating is currently C+ (Fair). It carries a beta of 0.00, meaning the fund's expected move will be 0.0% for every 10% move in the market. Volatility, as measured by both the semi-deviation and a drawdown factor, is considered low. As of March 31, 2012, *Barclays ETN + VEQTOR ETN traded at a premium of .08% above its net asset value, which is worse than its one-year historical average discount of .01%.

This fund has been team managed for 2 years and currently receives a manager quality ranking of 92 (0=worst, 99=best). If you desire an average level of risk, then this fund may be an option.

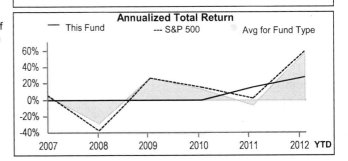

Annualized Total Return

*BLDRS Asia 50 ADR Index (ADRA)

D+ **Weak**

Fund Family: Bank of New York Mellon
Fund Type: Foreign
Inception Date: November 13, 2002

Major Rating Factors:
Disappointing performance is the major factor driving the D+ (Weak) TheStreet.com Investment Rating for *BLDRS Asia 50 ADR Index. The fund currently has a performance rating of D+ (Weak) based on an annualized return of 11.89% over the last three years and a total return of 14.33% year to date 2012. Factored into the performance evaluation is an expense ratio of 0.30% (very low).

The fund's risk rating is currently B- (Good). It carries a beta of 0.89, meaning the fund's expected move will be 8.9% for every 10% move in the market. Volatility, as measured by both the semi-deviation and a drawdown factor, is considered low. As of March 31, 2012, *BLDRS Asia 50 ADR Index traded at a discount of .50% below its net asset value, which is better than its one-year historical average discount of .23%.

Greg Metzmacher currently receives a manager quality ranking of 46 (0=worst, 99=best). This fund offers only a moderate level of risk but investors looking for strong performance are still waiting.

Data Date	Investment Rating	Net Assets ($Mil)	Price	Performance Rating/Pts	Total Return Y-T-D	Risk Rating/Pts
3-12	D+	33.87	25.64	D+ / 2.9	14.33%	B- / 7.6
2011	D+	29.40	22.43	D+ / 2.7	2.85%	B- / 7.6
2010	C-	50.10	28.66	C- / 3.9	14.13%	C / 5.1
2009	D+	65.75	25.72	D+ / 2.7	31.01%	C / 5.2

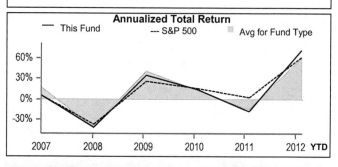

Annualized Total Return

*BLDRS Developed Mkts 100 ADR Ind (ADRD)

D+ **Weak**

Fund Family: Bank of New York Mellon
Fund Type: Foreign
Inception Date: November 13, 2002

Major Rating Factors: *BLDRS Developed Mkts 100 ADR Ind receives a TheStreet.com Investment Rating of D+ (Weak). The fund currently has a performance rating of C- (Fair) based on an annualized return of 13.07% over the last three years and a total return of 9.02% year to date 2012. Factored into the performance evaluation is an expense ratio of 0.30% (very low).

The fund's risk rating is currently B- (Good). It carries a beta of 1.04, meaning that its performance tracks fairly well with that of the overall stock market. Volatility, as measured by both the semi-deviation and a drawdown factor, is considered low. As of March 31, 2012, *BLDRS Developed Mkts 100 ADR Ind traded at a price exactly equal to its net asset value, which is worse than its one-year historical average discount of .08%.

Greg Metzmacher currently receives a manager quality ranking of 34 (0=worst, 99=best). If you desire an average level of risk, then this fund may be an option.

Data Date	Investment Rating	Net Assets ($Mil)	Price	Performance Rating/Pts	Total Return Y-T-D	Risk Rating/Pts
3-12	D+	57.32	20.37	C- / 3.0	9.02%	B- / 7.4
2011	D+	55.10	18.69	D+ / 2.4	0.02%	B- / 7.4
2010	D-	76.20	21.45	D- / 1.4	3.96%	C / 4.8
2009	D+	76.03	21.44	D / 2.2	26.46%	C+ / 5.6

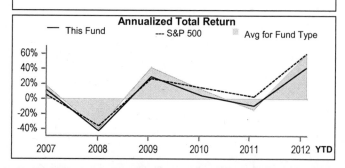

Annualized Total Return

*BLDRS Emerging Market 50 ADR Ind (ADRE)

D+ **Weak**

Fund Family: Bank of New York Mellon
Fund Type: Emerging Market
Inception Date: November 13, 2002

Major Rating Factors: *BLDRS Emerging Market 50 ADR Ind receives a TheStreet.com Investment Rating of D+ (Weak). The fund currently has a performance rating of C- (Fair) based on an annualized return of 14.93% over the last three years and a total return of 10.90% year to date 2012. Factored into the performance evaluation is an expense ratio of 0.30% (very low).

The fund's risk rating is currently B- (Good). It carries a beta of 0.95, meaning that its performance tracks fairly well with that of the overall stock market. Volatility, as measured by both the semi-deviation and a drawdown factor, is considered low. As of March 31, 2012, *BLDRS Emerging Market 50 ADR Ind traded at a discount of .12% below its net asset value, which is better than its one-year historical average discount of .05%.

Greg Metzmacher currently receives a manager quality ranking of 24 (0=worst, 99=best). If you desire an average level of risk, then this fund may be an option.

Data Date	Investment Rating	Net Assets ($Mil)	Price	Performance Rating/Pts	Total Return Y-T-D	Risk Rating/Pts
3-12	D+	470.42	42.22	C- / 3.3	10.90%	B- / 7.3
2011	C-	405.80	38.07	C- / 4.0	2.50%	B- / 7.3
2010	D+	674.10	48.15	C- / 3.8	11.58%	C / 4.5
2009	C+	627.30	44.13	B- / 7.3	57.25%	C / 4.8

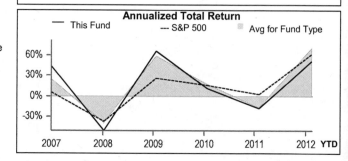

Annualized Total Return

*BLDRS Europe Select ADR Index (ADRU)   D+   Weak

Fund Family: Bank of New York Mellon
Fund Type: Foreign
Inception Date: November 13, 2002

Major Rating Factors: *BLDRS Europe Select ADR Index receives a TheStreet.com Investment Rating of D+ (Weak). The fund currently has a performance rating of C- (Fair) based on an annualized return of 13.97% over the last three years and a total return of 6.23% year to date 2012. Factored into the performance evaluation is an expense ratio of 0.30% (very low).

The fund's risk rating is currently B- (Good). It carries a beta of 1.09, meaning that its performance tracks fairly well with that of the overall stock market. Volatility, as measured by both the semi-deviation and a drawdown factor, is considered low. As of March 31, 2012, *BLDRS Europe Select ADR Index traded at a discount of .40% below its net asset value, which is better than its one-year historical average discount of .09%.

Greg Metzmacher currently receives a manager quality ranking of 29 (0=worst, 99=best). If you desire an average level of risk, then this fund may be an option.

Data Date	Investment Rating	Net Assets ($Mil)	Price	Performance Rating/Pts	Total Return Y-T-D	Risk Rating/Pts
3-12	D+	14.06	19.79	C- / 3.0	6.23%	B- / 7.3
2011	D+	14.80	18.63	D+ / 2.6	-0.64%	B- / 7.0
2010	D-	22.90	20.82	D- / 1.0	1.77%	C / 5.0
2009	D+	19.73	21.31	D+ / 2.5	28.00%	C / 5.4

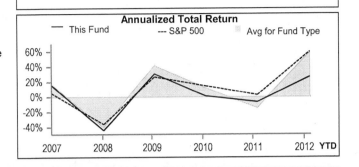

*Brclys ETN+ Inv S&P500 VIX STF E (XXV)   D   Weak

Fund Family: Barclays Bank PLC
Fund Type: Growth
Inception Date: July 20, 2010

Major Rating Factors: *Brclys ETN+ Inv S&P500 VIX STF E receives a TheStreet.com Investment Rating of D (Weak). The fund currently has a performance rating of C (Fair) based on an annualized return of 0.00% over the last three years and a total return of 10.24% year to date 2012. Factored into the performance evaluation is an expense ratio of 0.89% (low).

The fund's risk rating is currently C (Fair). It carries a beta of 0.00, meaning the fund's expected move will be 0.0% for every 10% move in the market. Volatility, as measured by both the semi-deviation and a drawdown factor, is considered average. As of March 31, 2012, *Brclys ETN+ Inv S&P500 VIX STF E traded at a discount of .14% below its net asset value, which is better than its one-year historical average discount of .04%.

This is team managed and currently receives a manager quality ranking of 32 (0=worst, 99=best). If you desire an average level of risk, then this fund may be an option.

Data Date	Investment Rating	Net Assets ($Mil)	Price	Performance Rating/Pts	Total Return Y-T-D	Risk Rating/Pts
3-12	D	15.62	36.38	C / 4.6	10.24%	C / 5.0
2011	D-	14.70	33.00	D+ / 2.3	1.79%	C / 5.0

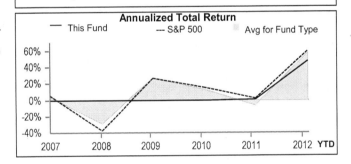

*Brclys ETN+ Lg B Lv S&P500 TR ET (BXUB)   C+   Fair

Fund Family: Barclays Bank PLC
Fund Type: Income
Inception Date: November 17, 2009

Major Rating Factors:
Exceptional performance is the major factor driving the C+ (Fair) TheStreet.com Investment Rating for *Brclys ETN+ Lg B Lv S&P500 TR ET. The fund currently has a performance rating of A+ (Excellent) based on an annualized return of 0.00% over the last three years and a total return of 29.03% year to date 2012.

The fund's risk rating is currently C- (Fair). It carries a beta of 0.00, meaning the fund's expected move will be 0.0% for every 10% move in the market. Volatility, as measured by both the semi-deviation and a drawdown factor, is considered average. As of March 31, 2012, *Brclys ETN+ Lg B Lv S&P500 TR ET traded at a price exactly equal to its net asset value, which is worse than its one-year historical average discount of .05%.

This fund has been team managed for 3 years and currently receives a manager quality ranking of 23 (0=worst, 99=best). If you desire an average level of risk and strong performance, then this fund is a good option.

Data Date	Investment Rating	Net Assets ($Mil)	Price	Performance Rating/Pts	Total Return Y-T-D	Risk Rating/Pts
3-12	C+	9.29	97.75	A+ / 9.9	29.03%	C- / 3.8
2011	D	7.70	75.76	C / 4.6	4.33%	C- / 3.8
2010	B	7.10	72.90	A+ / 9.8	40.08%	C- / 3.3

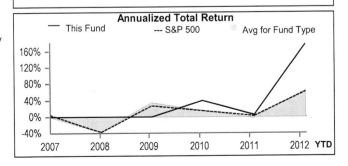

*Brclys ETN+ Lg C Lv S&P500 TR ET (BXUC)

C+   **Fair**

Fund Family: Barclays Bank PLC
Fund Type: Income
Inception Date: November 17, 2009

Major Rating Factors:

Exceptional performance is the major factor driving the C+ (Fair) TheStreet.com Investment Rating for *Brclys ETN+ Lg C Lv S&P500 TR ET. The fund currently has a performance rating of A+ (Excellent) based on an annualized return of 0.00% over the last three years and a total return of 21.16% year to date 2012.

   The fund's risk rating is currently C (Fair). It carries a beta of 0.00, meaning the fund's expected move will be 0.0% for every 10% move in the market. Volatility, as measured by both the semi-deviation and a drawdown factor, is considered average. As of March 31, 2012, *Brclys ETN+ Lg C Lv S&P500 TR ET traded at a price exactly equal to its net asset value.

   This fund has been team managed for 3 years and currently receives a manager quality ranking of 35 (0=worst, 99=best). If you desire an average level of risk and strong performance, then this fund is a good option.

Data Date	Investment Rating	Net Assets ($Mil)	Price	Perfor- mance Rating/Pts	Total Return Y-T-D	Risk Rating/Pts
3-12	C+	17.53	164.34	A+ / 9.6	21.16%	C / 4.3
2011	D	14.30	135.64	C- / 3.9	2.71%	C / 4.3
2010	B+	12.70	130.79	A+ / 9.7	27.35%	C- / 3.8

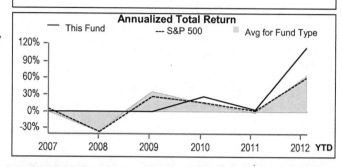

*Brclys ETN+ Sh B Lv I S&P500 TR (BXDB)

E   **Very Weak**

Fund Family: Barclays Bank PLC
Fund Type: Income
Inception Date: November 17, 2009

Major Rating Factors: Very poor performance is the major factor driving the E (Very Weak) TheStreet.com Investment Rating for *Brclys ETN+ Sh B Lv I S&P500 TR. The fund currently has a performance rating of E (Very Weak) based on an annualized return of 0.00% over the last three years and a total return of -18.61% year to date 2012.

   The fund's risk rating is currently C- (Fair). It carries a beta of 0.00, meaning the fund's expected move will be 0.0% for every 10% move in the market. Volatility, as measured by both the semi-deviation and a drawdown factor, is considered average. As of March 31, 2012, *Brclys ETN+ Sh B Lv I S&P500 TR traded at a discount of .03% below its net asset value, which is better than its one-year historical average premium of .10%.

   This fund has been team managed for 3 years and currently receives a manager quality ranking of 22 (0=worst, 99=best). This fund offers an average level of risk but investors looking for strong performance will be frustrated.

Data Date	Investment Rating	Net Assets ($Mil)	Price	Perfor- mance Rating/Pts	Total Return Y-T-D	Risk Rating/Pts
3-12	E	4.88	65.01	E / 0.4	-18.61%	C- / 3.7
2011	E+	5.60	79.87	D / 1.6	-0.26%	C- / 4.1
2010	E+	4.60	83.49	E / 0.4	-15.32%	C- / 4.0

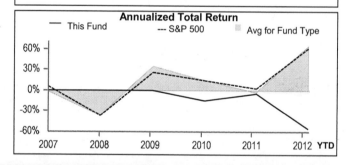

*Brclys ETN+ Sh C Lv I S&P500 TR (BXDC)

E-   **Very Weak**

Fund Family: Barclays Bank PLC
Fund Type: Income
Inception Date: November 17, 2009

Major Rating Factors: *Brclys ETN+ Sh C Lv I S&P500 TR has adopted a very risky asset allocation strategy and currently receives an overall TheStreet.com Investment Rating of E- (Very Weak). The fund has a high level of volatility, as measured by both semi-deviation and drawdown factors. It carries a beta of 0.00, meaning the fund's expected move will be 0.0% for every 10% move in the market. As of March 31, 2012, *Brclys ETN+ Sh C Lv I S&P500 TR traded at a premium of 1.38% above its net asset value, which is worse than its one-year historical average premium of .21%. Unfortunately, the high level of risk (D, Weak) failed to pay off as investors endured very poor performance.

   The fund's performance rating is currently E- (Very Weak). It has registered an annualized return of 0.00% over the last three years but is down -48.09% year to date 2012.

   This fund has been team managed for 3 years and currently receives a manager quality ranking of 7 (0=worst, 99=best). If you can tolerate very high levels of risk in the hope of improved future returns, holding this fund may be an option.

Data Date	Investment Rating	Net Assets ($Mil)	Price	Perfor- mance Rating/Pts	Total Return Y-T-D	Risk Rating/Pts
3-12	E-	7.16	21.27	E- / 0	-48.09%	D / 1.9
2011	E	5.70	40.97	D- / 1.2	-7.20%	D+ / 2.3
2010	E	8.00	44.81	E- / 0.1	-30.85%	C- / 3.1

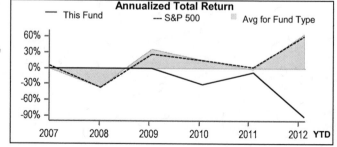

*C-Tracks ETN Citi Volatility Idx (CVOL)   E-   Very Weak

Fund Family: Citi Fund Management Inc
Fund Type: Income
Inception Date: November 15, 2010

Data Date	Investment Rating	Net Assets ($Mil)	Price	Performance Rating/Pts	Total Return Y-T-D	Risk Rating/Pts
3-12	E-	8.94	11.00	E- / 0	-61.29%	D / 1.9
2011	E-	0.00	28.41	E- / 0	-13.60%	D / 2.1

Major Rating Factors: *C-Tracks ETN Citi Volatility Idx has adopted a very risky asset allocation strategy and currently receives an overall TheStreet.com Investment Rating of E- (Very Weak). The fund has a high level of volatility, as measured by both semi-deviation and drawdown factors. It carries a beta of 0.00, meaning the fund's expected move will be 0.0% for every 10% move in the market. As of March 31, 2012, *C-Tracks ETN Citi Volatility Idx traded at a premium of 3.00% above its net asset value, which is worse than its one-year historical average discount of .33%. Unfortunately, the high level of risk (D, Weak) failed to pay off as investors endured very poor performance.

The fund's performance rating is currently E- (Very Weak). It has registered an annualized return of 0.00% over the last three years but is down -61.29% year to date 2012. Factored into the performance evaluation is an expense ratio of 1.15% (low).

This is team managed and currently receives a manager quality ranking of 0 (0=worst, 99=best). If you can tolerate very high levels of risk in the hope of improved future returns, holding this fund may be an option.

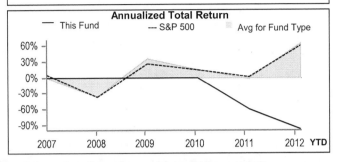

*Cambria Global Tactical ETF Fund (GTAA)   D   Weak

Fund Family: AdvisorShares Investments LLC
Fund Type: Growth and Income
Inception Date: October 25, 2010

Data Date	Investment Rating	Net Assets ($Mil)	Price	Performance Rating/Pts	Total Return Y-T-D	Risk Rating/Pts
3-12	D	118.97	24.30	D- / 1.1	3.45%	B / 8.8
2011	D+	140.70	23.49	D- / 1.2	-0.64%	B / 8.8

Major Rating Factors:
Disappointing performance is the major factor driving the D (Weak) TheStreet.com Investment Rating for *Cambria Global Tactical ETF Fund. The fund currently has a performance rating of D- (Weak) based on an annualized return of 0.00% over the last three years and a total return of 3.45% year to date 2012. Factored into the performance evaluation is an expense ratio of 1.02% (low).

The fund's risk rating is currently B (Good). It carries a beta of 0.00, meaning the fund's expected move will be 0.0% for every 10% move in the market. Volatility, as measured by both the semi-deviation and a drawdown factor, is considered low. As of March 31, 2012, *Cambria Global Tactical ETF Fund traded at a discount of .21% below its net asset value, which is better than its one-year historical average discount of .07%.

Mebane T. Faber currently receives a manager quality ranking of 15 (0=worst, 99=best). This fund offers only a moderate level of risk but investors looking for strong performance are still waiting.

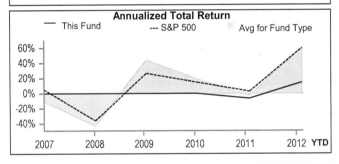

*Cohen & Steers Global Realty Maj (GRI)   C+   Fair

Fund Family: ALPS Advisors Inc
Fund Type: Growth and Income
Inception Date: May 7, 2008

Data Date	Investment Rating	Net Assets ($Mil)	Price	Performance Rating/Pts	Total Return Y-T-D	Risk Rating/Pts
3-12	C+	61.67	36.55	B- / 7.4	12.62%	B- / 7.3
2011	C-	50.50	32.59	C / 4.6	-0.25%	C+ / 6.3
2010	B+	40.90	35.86	A- / 9.2	20.75%	C / 4.5
2009	B-	5.01	31.43	B+ / 8.7	30.67%	C- / 4.0

Major Rating Factors: Strong performance is the major factor driving the C+ (Fair) TheStreet.com Investment Rating for *Cohen & Steers Global Realty Maj. The fund currently has a performance rating of B- (Good) based on an annualized return of 27.87% over the last three years and a total return of 12.62% year to date 2012. Factored into the performance evaluation is an expense ratio of 0.55% (very low).

The fund's risk rating is currently B- (Good). It carries a beta of 1.24, meaning it is expected to move 12.4% for every 10% move in the market. Volatility, as measured by both the semi-deviation and a drawdown factor, is considered low. As of March 31, 2012, *Cohen & Steers Global Realty Maj traded at a premium of .14% above its net asset value, which is better than its one-year historical average premium of .17%.

Daniel Franciscus has been running the fund for 1 year and currently receives a manager quality ranking of 58 (0=worst, 99=best). If you desire only a moderate level of risk and strong performance, then this fund is an excellent option.

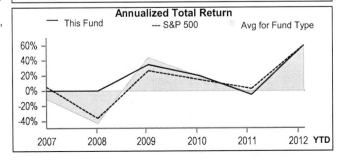

*Columbia Core Bond Strategy (GMTB)

C-   Fair

Fund Family: Columbia Management Inv Advisers LL
Fund Type: General - Investment Grade
Inception Date: January 29, 2010

Data Date	Investment Rating	Net Assets ($Mil)	Price	Performance Rating/Pts	Total Return Y-T-D	Risk Rating/Pts
3-12	C-	5.25	52.44	D / 1.8	-1.82%	B+ / 9.7

Major Rating Factors:

Disappointing performance is the major factor driving the C- (Fair) TheStreet.com Investment Rating for *Columbia Core Bond Strategy. The fund currently has a performance rating of D (Weak) based on an annualized return of 0.00% over the last three years and a total return of -1.82% year to date 2012. Factored into the performance evaluation is an expense ratio of 0.35% (very low).

The fund's risk rating is currently B+ (Good). It carries a beta of 0.00, meaning the fund's expected move will be 0.0% for every 10% move in the market. Volatility, as measured by both the semi-deviation and a drawdown factor, is considered very low. As of March 31, 2012, *Columbia Core Bond Strategy traded at a premium of .40% above its net asset value, which is better than its one-year historical average premium of .53%.

Orhan Imer has been running the fund for 1 year and currently receives a manager quality ranking of 66 (0=worst, 99=best). This fund offers only a moderate level of risk but investors looking for strong performance are still waiting.

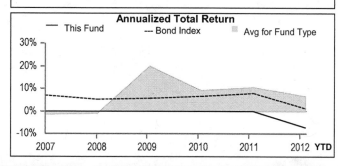

Annualized Total Return
— This Fund   --- Bond Index   ▨ Avg for Fund Type

*Columbia Growth Equity Strategy (RPX)

C   Fair

Fund Family: Columbia Management Inv Advisers LL
Fund Type: Growth
Inception Date: October 2, 2009

Data Date	Investment Rating	Net Assets ($Mil)	Price	Performance Rating/Pts	Total Return Y-T-D	Risk Rating/Pts
3-12	C	1.49	30.16	C / 4.5	7.71%	B- / 7.7
2011	D+	1.30	28.00	D / 1.7	-5.11%	B- / 7.7
2010	A+	4.70	31.22	B+ / 8.8	12.99%	B / 8.1

Major Rating Factors: Middle of the road best describes *Columbia Growth Equity Strategy whose TheStreet.com Investment Rating is currently a C (Fair). The fund currently has a performance rating of C (Fair) based on an annualized return of 0.00% over the last three years and a total return of 7.71% year to date 2012. Factored into the performance evaluation is an expense ratio of 0.89% (low).

The fund's risk rating is currently B- (Good). It carries a beta of 0.00, meaning the fund's expected move will be 0.0% for every 10% move in the market. Volatility, as measured by both the semi-deviation and a drawdown factor, is considered low. As of March 31, 2012, *Columbia Growth Equity Strategy traded at a discount of 2.17% below its net asset value, which is better than its one-year historical average discount of .40%.

Colin Moore has been running the fund for 1 year and currently receives a manager quality ranking of 32 (0=worst, 99=best). If you desire an average level of risk, then this fund may be an option.

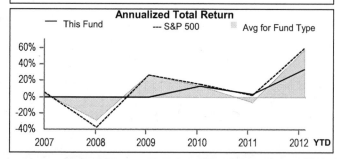

Annualized Total Return
— This Fund   --- S&P 500   ▨ Avg for Fund Type

*Columbia Large-Cap Growth Eq Str (RWG)

C+   Fair

Fund Family: Columbia Management Inv Advisers LL
Fund Type: Growth
Inception Date: October 2, 2009

Data Date	Investment Rating	Net Assets ($Mil)	Price	Performance Rating/Pts	Total Return Y-T-D	Risk Rating/Pts
3-12	C+	7.62	31.59	C+ / 6.3	20.30%	B- / 7.8
2011	D	8.00	26.26	D- / 1.2	0.04%	B- / 7.8
2010	A+	9.30	30.90	A- / 9.0	14.11%	B / 8.2

Major Rating Factors: Middle of the road best describes *Columbia Large-Cap Growth Eq Str whose TheStreet.com Investment Rating is currently a C+ (Fair). The fund currently has a performance rating of C+ (Fair) based on an annualized return of 0.00% over the last three years and a total return of 20.30% year to date 2012. Factored into the performance evaluation is an expense ratio of 0.89% (low).

The fund's risk rating is currently B- (Good). It carries a beta of 0.00, meaning the fund's expected move will be 0.0% for every 10% move in the market. Volatility, as measured by both the semi-deviation and a drawdown factor, is considered low. As of March 31, 2012, *Columbia Large-Cap Growth Eq Str traded at a discount of .44% below its net asset value, which is worse than its one-year historical average discount of .61%.

Colin Moore has been running the fund for 1 year and currently receives a manager quality ranking of 28 (0=worst, 99=best). If you desire an average level of risk, then this fund may be an option.

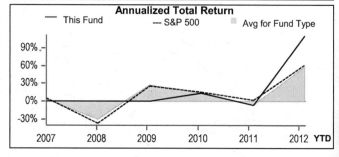

Annualized Total Return
— This Fund   --- S&P 500   ▨ Avg for Fund Type

*Consumer Discretionary Sel Sec S (XLY)   B+   Good

Fund Family: SSgA Funds Management Inc
Fund Type: Growth
Inception Date: December 16, 1998

Data Date	Investment Rating	Net Assets ($Mil)	Price	Performance Rating/Pts	Total Return Y-T-D	Risk Rating/Pts
3-12	B+	3,276.87	45.09	B+ / 8.6	15.91%	B / 8.2
2011	B	2,487.80	39.02	B / 7.7	2.64%	B- / 7.8
2010	B+	2,478.90	37.41	B / 8.0	27.50%	C+ / 5.9
2009	D+	1,268.30	29.77	D+ / 2.7	33.81%	C+ / 5.8

Major Rating Factors: Strong performance is the major factor driving the B+ (Good) TheStreet.com Investment Rating for *Consumer Discretionary Sel Sec S. The fund currently has a performance rating of B+ (Good) based on an annualized return of 30.21% over the last three years and a total return of 15.91% year to date 2012. Factored into the performance evaluation is an expense ratio of 0.19% (very low).

The fund's risk rating is currently B (Good). It carries a beta of 1.12, meaning it is expected to move 11.2% for every 10% move in the market. Volatility, as measured by both the semi-deviation and a drawdown factor, is considered low. As of March 31, 2012, *Consumer Discretionary Sel Sec S traded at a premium of .04% above its net asset value, which is worse than its one-year historical average discount of .01%.

John A. Tucker has been running the fund for 14 years and currently receives a manager quality ranking of 77 (0=worst, 99=best). If you desire only a moderate level of risk and strong performance, then this fund is an excellent option.

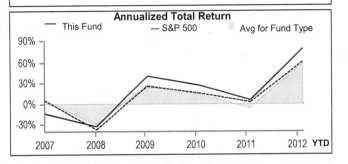

*Consumer Staples Select Sector S (XLP)   C+   Fair

Fund Family: SSgA Funds Management Inc
Fund Type: Growth
Inception Date: December 16, 1998

Data Date	Investment Rating	Net Assets ($Mil)	Price	Performance Rating/Pts	Total Return Y-T-D	Risk Rating/Pts
3-12	C+	5,524.42	34.08	C / 5.2	5.45%	B+ / 9.2
2011	B-	5,836.70	32.49	C+ / 5.9	-1.02%	B / 8.6
2010	B-	3,104.00	29.31	C+ / 5.9	13.81%	B- / 7.3
2009	C	1,885.36	26.47	C- / 3.9	12.61%	B- / 7.4

Major Rating Factors: Middle of the road best describes *Consumer Staples Select Sector S whose TheStreet.com Investment Rating is currently a C+ (Fair). The fund currently has a performance rating of C (Fair) based on an annualized return of 19.36% over the last three years and a total return of 5.45% year to date 2012. Factored into the performance evaluation is an expense ratio of 0.19% (very low).

The fund's risk rating is currently B+ (Good). It carries a beta of 0.52, meaning the fund's expected move will be 5.2% for every 10% move in the market. Volatility, as measured by both the semi-deviation and a drawdown factor, is considered very low. As of March 31, 2012, *Consumer Staples Select Sector S traded at a price exactly equal to its net asset value, which is better than its one-year historical average premium of .01%.

John A. Tucker has been running the fund for 14 years and currently receives a manager quality ranking of 82 (0=worst, 99=best). If you desire an average level of risk, then this fund may be an option.

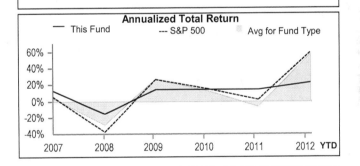

*Credit Suisse Cushing 30 MLP ETN (MLPN)   D-   Weak

Fund Family: Credit Suisse Asset Management LLC
Fund Type: Energy/Natural Resources
Inception Date: April 13, 2010

Data Date	Investment Rating	Net Assets ($Mil)	Price	Performance Rating/Pts	Total Return Y-T-D	Risk Rating/Pts
3-12	D-	268.69	24.65	D / 1.7	0.09%	C / 5.1
2011	C-	0.00	24.95	C / 5.4	2.12%	C / 5.1

Major Rating Factors:
Disappointing performance is the major factor driving the D- (Weak) TheStreet.com Investment Rating for *Credit Suisse Cushing 30 MLP ETN. The fund currently has a performance rating of D (Weak) based on an annualized return of 0.00% over the last three years and a total return of 0.09% year to date 2012. Factored into the performance evaluation is an expense ratio of 0.85% (very low).

The fund's risk rating is currently C (Fair). It carries a beta of 0.00, meaning the fund's expected move will be 0.0% for every 10% move in the market. Volatility, as measured by both the semi-deviation and a drawdown factor, is considered average. As of March 31, 2012, *Credit Suisse Cushing 30 MLP ETN traded at a discount of .16% below its net asset value, which is better than its one-year historical average premium of .10%.

This fund has been team managed for 2 years and currently receives a manager quality ranking of 59 (0=worst, 99=best). This fund offers an average level of risk but investors looking for strong performance will be frustrated.

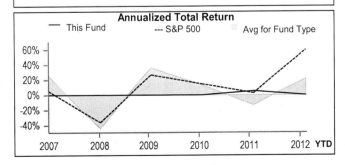

*Credit Suisse L/S Liq Idx ETN (CSLS)   D-   Weak

Fund Family: Credit Suisse Asset Management LLC
Fund Type: Growth
Inception Date: February 19, 2010

Major Rating Factors:
Disappointing performance is the major factor driving the D- (Weak) TheStreet.com Investment Rating for *Credit Suisse L/S Liq Idx ETN. The fund currently has a performance rating of D (Weak) based on an annualized return of 0.00% over the last three years and a total return of 4.85% year to date 2012. Factored into the performance evaluation is an expense ratio of 0.45% (very low).

The fund's risk rating is currently C (Fair). It carries a beta of 0.00, meaning the fund's expected move will be 0.0% for every 10% move in the market. Volatility, as measured by both the semi-deviation and a drawdown factor, is considered average. As of March 31, 2012, *Credit Suisse L/S Liq Idx ETN traded at a premium of .18% above its net asset value, which is worse than its one-year historical average discount of .04%.

This fund has been team managed for 2 years and currently receives a manager quality ranking of 27 (0=worst, 99=best). This fund offers an average level of risk but investors looking for strong performance will be frustrated.

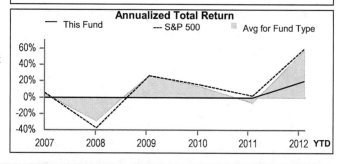

Data Date	Investment Rating	Net Assets ($Mil)	Price	Performance Rating/Pts	Total Return Y-T-D	Risk Rating/Pts
3-12	D-	33.87	22.70	D / 1.9	4.85%	C / 5.4
2011	D-	32.30	21.65	D / 1.7	0.14%	C / 5.4

Annualized Total Return

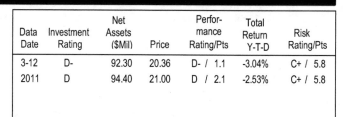

---

*Credit Suisse Merger Arb Lq Id E (CSMA)   D-   Weak

Fund Family: Credit Suisse Asset Management LLC
Fund Type: Growth
Inception Date: October 1, 2010

Major Rating Factors:
Disappointing performance is the major factor driving the D- (Weak) TheStreet.com Investment Rating for *Credit Suisse Merger Arb Lq Id E. The fund currently has a performance rating of D- (Weak) based on an annualized return of 0.00% over the last three years and a total return of -3.04% year to date 2012. Factored into the performance evaluation is an expense ratio of 0.55% (very low).

The fund's risk rating is currently C+ (Fair). It carries a beta of 0.00, meaning the fund's expected move will be 0.0% for every 10% move in the market. Volatility, as measured by both the semi-deviation and a drawdown factor, is considered low. As of March 31, 2012, *Credit Suisse Merger Arb Lq Id E traded at a discount of .20% below its net asset value, which is better than its one-year historical average premium of .14%.

This is team managed and currently receives a manager quality ranking of 31 (0=worst, 99=best). This fund offers only a moderate level of risk but investors looking for strong performance are still waiting.

Data Date	Investment Rating	Net Assets ($Mil)	Price	Performance Rating/Pts	Total Return Y-T-D	Risk Rating/Pts
3-12	D-	92.30	20.36	D- / 1.1	-3.04%	C+ / 5.8
2011	D	94.40	21.00	D / 2.1	-2.53%	C+ / 5.8

Annualized Total Return

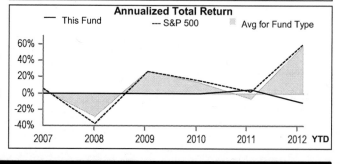

---

*db-X 2010 Target Date Fund (TDD)   C-   Fair

Fund Family: DBX Strategic Advisors LLC
Fund Type: Growth and Income
Inception Date: October 1, 2007

Major Rating Factors:
Disappointing performance is the major factor driving the C- (Fair) TheStreet.com Investment Rating for *db-X 2010 Target Date Fund. The fund currently has a performance rating of D- (Weak) based on an annualized return of 3.88% over the last three years and a total return of 1.34% year to date 2012. Factored into the performance evaluation is an expense ratio of 0.65% (very low).

The fund's risk rating is currently B+ (Good). It carries a beta of 0.10, meaning the fund's expected move will be 1.0% for every 10% move in the market. Volatility, as measured by both the semi-deviation and a drawdown factor, is considered very low. As of March 31, 2012, *db-X 2010 Target Date Fund traded at a discount of 1.43% below its net asset value, which is worse than its one-year historical average discount of 1.78%.

Glenn S. Davis has been running the fund for 3 years and currently receives a manager quality ranking of 62 (0=worst, 99=best). This fund offers only a moderate level of risk but investors looking for strong performance are still waiting.

Data Date	Investment Rating	Net Assets ($Mil)	Price	Performance Rating/Pts	Total Return Y-T-D	Risk Rating/Pts
3-12	C-	14.29	23.50	D- / 1.5	1.34%	B+ / 9.5
2011	C	14.10	23.19	D+ / 2.7	1.25%	B+ / 9.5
2010	C-	14.10	22.74	D+ / 2.3	2.54%	B- / 7.7
2009	C+	17.69	22.82	C- / 4.1	5.70%	B- / 7.8

Annualized Total Return

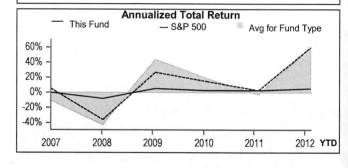

*db-X 2020 Target Date Fund (TDH)

C-   **Fair**

Fund Family: DBX Strategic Advisors LLC
Fund Type: Growth and Income
Inception Date: October 1, 2007

Major Rating Factors:
Disappointing performance is the major factor driving the C- (Fair) TheStreet.com Investment Rating for *db-X 2020 Target Date Fund. The fund currently has a performance rating of D+ (Weak) based on an annualized return of 10.18% over the last three years and a total return of 1.45% year to date 2012. Factored into the performance evaluation is an expense ratio of 0.65% (very low).

The fund's risk rating is currently B (Good). It carries a beta of 0.58, meaning the fund's expected move will be 5.8% for every 10% move in the market. Volatility, as measured by both the semi-deviation and a drawdown factor, is considered low. As of March 31, 2012, *db-X 2020 Target Date Fund traded at a discount of 6.49% below its net asset value, which is better than its one-year historical average discount of 2.99%.

Glenn S. Davis has been running the fund for 3 years and currently receives a manager quality ranking of 36 (0=worst, 99=best). This fund offers only a moderate level of risk but investors looking for strong performance are still waiting.

Data Date	Investment Rating	Net Assets ($Mil)	Price	Perfor-mance Rating/Pts	Total Return Y-T-D	Risk Rating/Pts
3-12	C-	33.05	22.33	D+ / 2.3	1.45%	B / 8.9
2011	C	36.00	22.01	C- / 3.4	1.27%	B / 8.7
2010	C-	40.80	22.18	C- / 3.1	8.50%	C+ / 6.8
2009	C+	37.14	20.93	C+ / 5.9	9.83%	C+ / 6.9

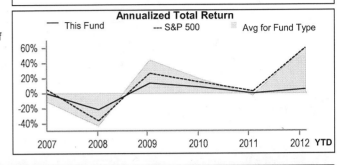

Annualized Total Return

*db-X 2030 Target Date Fund (TDN)

C-   **Fair**

Fund Family: DBX Strategic Advisors LLC
Fund Type: Growth and Income
Inception Date: October 1, 2007

Major Rating Factors: Middle of the road best describes *db-X 2030 Target Date Fund whose TheStreet.com Investment Rating is currently a C- (Fair). The fund currently has a performance rating of C- (Fair) based on an annualized return of 13.14% over the last three years and a total return of 5.97% year to date 2012. Factored into the performance evaluation is an expense ratio of 0.65% (very low).

The fund's risk rating is currently B (Good). It carries a beta of 0.74, meaning the fund's expected move will be 7.4% for every 10% move in the market. Volatility, as measured by both the semi-deviation and a drawdown factor, is considered low. As of March 31, 2012, *db-X 2030 Target Date Fund traded at a discount of 6.43% below its net asset value, which is better than its one-year historical average discount of 3.07%.

Glenn S. Davis has been running the fund for 3 years and currently receives a manager quality ranking of 37 (0=worst, 99=best). If you desire an average level of risk, then this fund may be an option.

Data Date	Investment Rating	Net Assets ($Mil)	Price	Perfor-mance Rating/Pts	Total Return Y-T-D	Risk Rating/Pts
3-12	C-	31.07	20.96	C- / 3.1	5.97%	B / 8.5
2011	C-	29.00	19.78	C- / 3.0	-1.42%	B- / 7.9
2010	D+	33.00	19.71	D / 1.8	6.74%	C+ / 6.1
2009	B	28.94	18.85	B- / 7.4	16.18%	C+ / 6.0

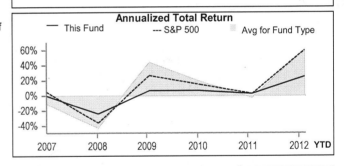

Annualized Total Return

*db-X 2040 Target Date Fund (TDV)

C   **Fair**

Fund Family: DBX Strategic Advisors LLC
Fund Type: Growth and Income
Inception Date: October 1, 2007

Major Rating Factors: Middle of the road best describes *db-X 2040 Target Date Fund whose TheStreet.com Investment Rating is currently a C (Fair). The fund currently has a performance rating of C (Fair) based on an annualized return of 19.00% over the last three years and a total return of 12.77% year to date 2012. Factored into the performance evaluation is an expense ratio of 0.65% (very low).

The fund's risk rating is currently B (Good). It carries a beta of 0.98, meaning that its performance tracks fairly well with that of the overall stock market. Volatility, as measured by both the semi-deviation and a drawdown factor, is considered low. As of March 31, 2012, *db-X 2040 Target Date Fund traded at a premium of .78% above its net asset value, which is worse than its one-year historical average discount of 1.79%.

Glenn S. Davis has been running the fund for 3 years and currently receives a manager quality ranking of 36 (0=worst, 99=best). If you desire an average level of risk, then this fund may be an option.

Data Date	Investment Rating	Net Assets ($Mil)	Price	Perfor-mance Rating/Pts	Total Return Y-T-D	Risk Rating/Pts
3-12	C	30.01	21.99	C / 4.9	12.77%	B / 8.2
2011	C-	27.60	19.50	C- / 3.7	-1.03%	B- / 7.8
2010	D+	32.30	19.61	D / 2.2	10.09%	C+ / 5.8
2009	B+	27.65	18.14	B / 7.8	21.30%	C+ / 5.8

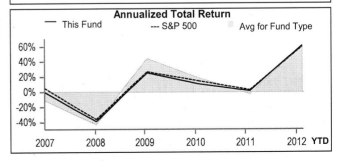

Annualized Total Return

*db-X In-Target Date Fund (TDX)

C-   **Fair**

Fund Family: DBX Strategic Advisors LLC
Fund Type: Growth and Income
Inception Date: October 1, 2007

Data Date	Investment Rating	Net Assets ($Mil)	Price	Performance Rating/Pts	Total Return Y-T-D	Risk Rating/Pts
3-12	C-	15.83	26.53	D / 1.8	2.39%	B+ / 9.3
2011	C-	15.40	25.91	D+ / 2.3	-3.13%	B+ / 9.3
2010	C	15.60	24.76	D+ / 2.6	1.45%	B / 8.6
2009	B	24.40	24.79	C / 4.4	8.95%	B / 8.9

Major Rating Factors:

Disappointing performance is the major factor driving the C- (Fair) TheStreet.com Investment Rating for *db-X In-Target Date Fund. The fund currently has a performance rating of D (Weak) based on an annualized return of 4.79% over the last three years and a total return of 2.39% year to date 2012. Factored into the performance evaluation is an expense ratio of 0.65% (very low).

The fund's risk rating is currently B+ (Good). It carries a beta of 0.26, meaning the fund's expected move will be 2.6% for every 10% move in the market. Volatility, as measured by both the semi-deviation and a drawdown factor, is considered very low. As of March 31, 2012, *db-X In-Target Date Fund traded at a premium of .15% above its net asset value, which is worse than its one-year historical average discount of 1.55%.

Vishal Bhatia has been running the fund for 3 years and currently receives a manager quality ranking of 40 (0=worst, 99=best). This fund offers only a moderate level of risk but investors looking for strong performance are still waiting.

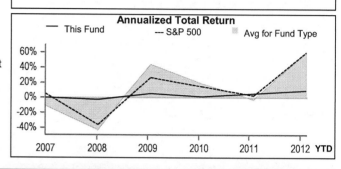

Annualized Total Return

*Dent Tactical ETF Fund (DENT)

D   **Weak**

Fund Family: AdvisorShares Investments LLC
Fund Type: Global
Inception Date: September 16, 2009

Data Date	Investment Rating	Net Assets ($Mil)	Price	Performance Rating/Pts	Total Return Y-T-D	Risk Rating/Pts
3-12	D	8.22	18.28	E+ / 0.6	-2.48%	B / 8.4
2011	D+	13.20	18.75	D- / 1.2	0.03%	B / 8.5
2010	B	22.40	20.52	C+ / 6.5	3.79%	B / 8.0

Major Rating Factors:

Very poor performance is the major factor driving the D (Weak) TheStreet.com Investment Rating for *Dent Tactical ETF Fund. The fund currently has a performance rating of E+ (Very Weak) based on an annualized return of 0.00% over the last three years and a total return of -2.48% year to date 2012. Factored into the performance evaluation is an expense ratio of 1.49% (average).

The fund's risk rating is currently B (Good). It carries a beta of 0.00, meaning the fund's expected move will be 0.0% for every 10% move in the market. Volatility, as measured by both the semi-deviation and a drawdown factor, is considered low. As of March 31, 2012, *Dent Tactical ETF Fund traded at a discount of .22% below its net asset value, which is better than its one-year historical average discount of .12%.

Harry S. Dent, Jr. currently receives a manager quality ranking of 10 (0=worst, 99=best). This fund offers only a moderate level of risk but investors looking for strong performance are still waiting.

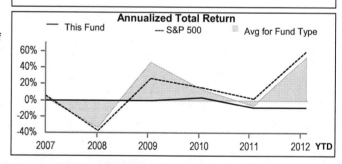

Annualized Total Return

*Direxion Daily 20+ Yr Treas Bear (TMV)

E   **Very Weak**

Fund Family: Rafferty Asset Management LLC
Fund Type: US Government/Agency
Inception Date: April 16, 2009

Data Date	Investment Rating	Net Assets ($Mil)	Price	Performance Rating/Pts	Total Return Y-T-D	Risk Rating/Pts
3-12	E	308.07	81.19	E / 0.4	19.47%	D+ / 2.6
2011	E-	258.60	67.96	E- / 0	6.18%	D+ / 2.6
2010	E+	303.90	43.21	E+ / 0.7	-36.69%	C- / 3.5

Major Rating Factors: *Direxion Daily 20+ Yr Treas Bear has adopted a risky asset allocation strategy and currently receives an overall TheStreet.com Investment Rating of E (Very Weak). The fund has an above average level of volatility, as measured by both semi-deviation and drawdown factors. It carries a beta of 0.00, meaning the fund's expected move will be 0.0% for every 10% move in the market. As of March 31, 2012, *Direxion Daily 20+ Yr Treas Bear traded at a discount of .06% below its net asset value, which is better than its one-year historical average premium of .06%. Unfortunately, the high level of risk (D+, Weak) failed to pay off as investors endured very poor performance.

The fund's performance rating is currently E (Very Weak). It has registered an annualized return of 0.00% over the last three years and is up 19.47% year to date 2012. Factored into the performance evaluation is an expense ratio of 0.92% (low).

Paul Brigandi currently receives a manager quality ranking of 8 (0=worst, 99=best). If you can tolerate high levels of risk in the hope of improved future returns, holding this fund may be an option.

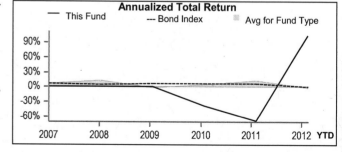

Annualized Total Return

---

* Denotes ETF Fund

*Direxion Daily 20+ Yr Treas Bear (TYBS)   D-   Weak

Fund Family: Rafferty Asset Management LLC
Fund Type: Global
Inception Date: March 23, 2011

Data Date	Investment Rating	Net Assets ($Mil)	Price	Performance Rating/Pts	Total Return Y-T-D	Risk Rating/Pts
3-12	D-	2.91	29.92	E+ / 0.7	5.58%	C+ / 6.7

Major Rating Factors:
Very poor performance is the major factor driving the D- (Weak) TheStreet.com Investment Rating for *Direxion Daily 20+ Yr Treas Bear. The fund currently has a performance rating of E+ (Very Weak) based on an annualized return of 0.00% over the last three years and a total return of 5.58% year to date 2012. Factored into the performance evaluation is an expense ratio of 0.65% (very low).

The fund's risk rating is currently C+ (Fair). It carries a beta of 0.00, meaning the fund's expected move will be 0.0% for every 10% move in the market. Volatility, as measured by both the semi-deviation and a drawdown factor, is considered low. As of March 31, 2012, *Direxion Daily 20+ Yr Treas Bear traded at a premium of .40% above its net asset value.

Paul Brigandi has been running the fund for 1 year and currently receives a manager quality ranking of 5 (0=worst, 99=best). This fund offers only a moderate level of risk but investors looking for strong performance are still waiting.

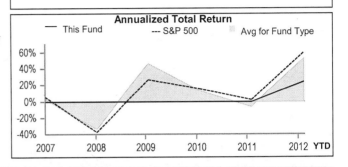

*Direxion Daily 20+ Yr Treas Bull (TMF)   C+   Fair

Fund Family: Rafferty Asset Management LLC
Fund Type: US Government/Agency
Inception Date: April 16, 2009

Data Date	Investment Rating	Net Assets ($Mil)	Price	Performance Rating/Pts	Total Return Y-T-D	Risk Rating/Pts
3-12	C+	22.66	56.36	B+ / 8.7	-21.13%	C / 5.1
2011	B-	42.90	71.52	A+ / 9.9	-6.21%	C / 5.2
2010	D-	19.30	34.45	D- / 1.1	19.49%	C / 5.0

Major Rating Factors: Strong performance is the major factor driving the C+ (Fair) TheStreet.com Investment Rating for *Direxion Daily 20+ Yr Treas Bull. The fund currently has a performance rating of B+ (Good) based on an annualized return of 0.00% over the last three years and a total return of -21.13% year to date 2012. Factored into the performance evaluation is an expense ratio of 0.95% (low).

The fund's risk rating is currently C (Fair). It carries a beta of 0.00, meaning the fund's expected move will be 0.0% for every 10% move in the market. Volatility, as measured by both the semi-deviation and a drawdown factor, is considered average. As of March 31, 2012, *Direxion Daily 20+ Yr Treas Bull traded at a premium of .02% above its net asset value, which is worse than its one-year historical average discount of .04%.

Paul Brigandi currently receives a manager quality ranking of 11 (0=worst, 99=best). If you desire an average level of risk and strong performance, then this fund is a good option.

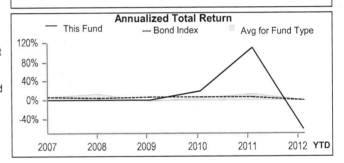

*Direxion Daily 7-10 Yr Treas Br (TYNS)   D   Weak

Fund Family: Rafferty Asset Management LLC
Fund Type: Global
Inception Date: March 23, 2011

Data Date	Investment Rating	Net Assets ($Mil)	Price	Performance Rating/Pts	Total Return Y-T-D	Risk Rating/Pts
3-12	D	3.44	34.98	E+ / 0.8	2.16%	B / 8.8

Major Rating Factors:
Very poor performance is the major factor driving the D (Weak) TheStreet.com Investment Rating for *Direxion Daily 7-10 Yr Treas Br. The fund currently has a performance rating of E+ (Very Weak) based on an annualized return of 0.00% over the last three years and a total return of 2.16% year to date 2012. Factored into the performance evaluation is an expense ratio of 0.65% (very low).

The fund's risk rating is currently B (Good). It carries a beta of 0.00, meaning the fund's expected move will be 0.0% for every 10% move in the market. Volatility, as measured by both the semi-deviation and a drawdown factor, is considered low. As of March 31, 2012, *Direxion Daily 7-10 Yr Treas Br traded at a discount of .11% below its net asset value, which is better than its one-year historical average discount of .03%.

Paul Brigandi has been running the fund for 1 year and currently receives a manager quality ranking of 12 (0=worst, 99=best). This fund offers only a moderate level of risk but investors looking for strong performance are still waiting.

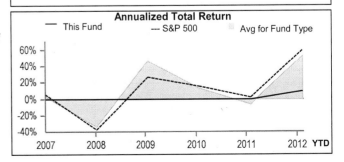

*Direxion Daily 7-10 Yr Trs Bear (TYO)

E+   **Very Weak**

Fund Family: Rafferty Asset Management LLC
Fund Type: US Government/Agency
Inception Date: April 16, 2009

Major Rating Factors:

Very poor performance is the major factor driving the E+ (Very Weak) TheStreet.com Investment Rating for *Direxion Daily 7-10 Yr Trs Bear. The fund currently has a performance rating of E (Very Weak) based on an annualized return of 0.00% over the last three years and a total return of 3.47% year to date 2012. Factored into the performance evaluation is an expense ratio of 0.95% (low).

The fund's risk rating is currently C (Fair). It carries a beta of 0.00, meaning the fund's expected move will be 0.0% for every 10% move in the market. Volatility, as measured by both the semi-deviation and a drawdown factor, is considered average. As of March 31, 2012, *Direxion Daily 7-10 Yr Trs Bear traded at a discount of .14% below its net asset value, which is better than its one-year historical average premium of .03%.

Milu E. Komer has been running the fund for 4 years and currently receives a manager quality ranking of 7 (0=worst, 99=best). This fund offers an average level of risk but investors looking for strong performance will be frustrated.

Data Date	Investment Rating	Net Assets ($Mil)	Price	Performance Rating/Pts	Total Return Y-T-D	Risk Rating/Pts
3-12	E+	53.08	28.33	E / 0.5	3.47%	C / 4.5
2011	E+	57.30	27.38	E- / 0.2	1.35%	C / 4.5
2010	D-	68.40	45.84	E+ / 0.6	-28.62%	C+ / 5.6

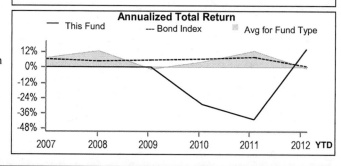

*Direxion Daily 7-10 Yr Trs Bull (TYD)

B   **Good**

Fund Family: Rafferty Asset Management LLC
Fund Type: US Government/Agency
Inception Date: April 16, 2009

Major Rating Factors: Strong performance is the major factor driving the B (Good) TheStreet.com Investment Rating for *Direxion Daily 7-10 Yr Trs Bull. The fund currently has a performance rating of B (Good) based on an annualized return of 0.00% over the last three years and a total return of -5.83% year to date 2012. Factored into the performance evaluation is an expense ratio of 0.95% (low).

The fund's risk rating is currently B- (Good). It carries a beta of 0.00, meaning the fund's expected move will be 0.0% for every 10% move in the market. Volatility, as measured by both the semi-deviation and a drawdown factor, is considered low. As of March 31, 2012, *Direxion Daily 7-10 Yr Trs Bull traded at a discount of .12% below its net asset value, which is better than its one-year historical average discount of .04%.

Milu E. Komer has been running the fund for 4 years and currently receives a manager quality ranking of 90 (0=worst, 99=best). If you desire only a moderate level of risk and strong performance, then this fund is an excellent option.

Data Date	Investment Rating	Net Assets ($Mil)	Price	Performance Rating/Pts	Total Return Y-T-D	Risk Rating/Pts
3-12	B	3.86	73.33	B / 8.1	-5.83%	B- / 7.5
2011	A-	3.90	77.87	A+ / 9.9	-1.71%	B- / 7.6
2010	A	10.90	54.11	B+ / 8.5	28.71%	C+ / 6.9

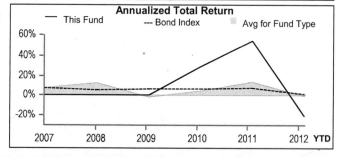

*Direxion Daily BRIC Bear 3X (BRIS)

E   **Very Weak**

Fund Family: Rafferty Asset Management LLC
Fund Type: Foreign
Inception Date: March 11, 2010

Major Rating Factors: *Direxion Daily BRIC Bear 3X has adopted a risky asset allocation strategy and currently receives an overall TheStreet.com Investment Rating of E (Very Weak). The fund has an above average level of volatility, as measured by both semi-deviation and drawdown factors. It carries a beta of 0.00, meaning the fund's expected move will be 0.0% for every 10% move in the market. As of March 31, 2012, *Direxion Daily BRIC Bear 3X traded at a premium of 2.22% above its net asset value, which is worse than its one-year historical average premium of .28%. Unfortunately, the high level of risk (D+, Weak) failed to pay off as investors endured very poor performance.

The fund's performance rating is currently E (Very Weak). It has registered an annualized return of 0.00% over the last three years but is down -33.13% year to date 2012. Factored into the performance evaluation is an expense ratio of 0.95% (low).

Paul Brigandi has been running the fund for 2 years and currently receives a manager quality ranking of 4 (0=worst, 99=best). If you can tolerate high levels of risk in the hope of improved future returns, holding this fund may be an option.

Data Date	Investment Rating	Net Assets ($Mil)	Price	Performance Rating/Pts	Total Return Y-T-D	Risk Rating/Pts
3-12	E	1.80	20.75	E / 0.3	-33.13%	D+ / 2.7
2011	D-	3.10	31.03	D / 1.9	-12.19%	C / 4.4

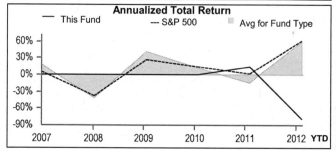

*Direxion Daily BRIC Bull 3X (BRIL)   D-   Weak

Fund Family: Rafferty Asset Management LLC
Fund Type: Emerging Market
Inception Date: March 11, 2010

Data Date	Investment Rating	Net Assets ($Mil)	Price	Performance Rating/Pts	Total Return Y-T-D	Risk Rating/Pts
3-12	D-	7.69	32.95	C- / 3.5	38.11%	C- / 3.8
2011	E	3.60	23.86	E- / 0.2	7.69%	C- / 3.9

Major Rating Factors: *Direxion Daily BRIC Bull 3X receives a TheStreet.com Investment Rating of D- (Weak). The fund currently has a performance rating of C- (Fair) based on an annualized return of 0.00% over the last three years and a total return of 38.11% year to date 2012. Factored into the performance evaluation is an expense ratio of 0.95% (low).

The fund's risk rating is currently C- (Fair). It carries a beta of 0.00, meaning the fund's expected move will be 0.0% for every 10% move in the market. Volatility, as measured by both the semi-deviation and a drawdown factor, is considered average. As of March 31, 2012, *Direxion Daily BRIC Bull 3X traded at a discount of .48% below its net asset value, which is better than its one-year historical average discount of .23%.

Paul Brigandi has been running the fund for 2 years and currently receives a manager quality ranking of 12 (0=worst, 99=best). If you desire an average level of risk, then this fund may be an option.

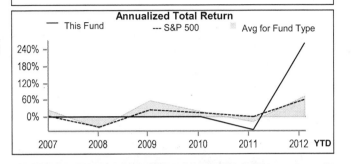

Annualized Total Return — This Fund --- S&P 500 ▨ Avg for Fund Type

*Direxion Daily China Bear 3x ETF (YANG)   E-   Very Weak

Fund Family: Rafferty Asset Management LLC
Fund Type: Foreign
Inception Date: December 3, 2009

Data Date	Investment Rating	Net Assets ($Mil)	Price	Performance Rating/Pts	Total Return Y-T-D	Risk Rating/Pts
3-12	E-	10.32	12.34	E- / 0.2	-35.09%	D / 1.9
2011	E+	12.40	19.01	D+ / 2.4	-8.89%	D / 2.1
2010	E-	11.90	18.41	E- / 0.1	-56.32%	D / 1.9

Major Rating Factors: *Direxion Daily China Bear 3x ETF has adopted a very risky asset allocation strategy and currently receives an overall TheStreet.com Investment Rating of E- (Very Weak). The fund has a high level of volatility, as measured by both semi-deviation and drawdown factors. It carries a beta of 0.00, meaning the fund's expected move will be 0.0% for every 10% move in the market. As of March 31, 2012, *Direxion Daily China Bear 3x ETF traded at a premium of .24% above its net asset value, which is worse than its one-year historical average premium of .09%. Unfortunately, the high level of risk (D, Weak) failed to pay off as investors endured very poor performance.

The fund's performance rating is currently E- (Very Weak). It has registered an annualized return of 0.00% over the last three years but is down -35.09% year to date 2012. Factored into the performance evaluation is an expense ratio of 0.95% (low).

Paul Brigandi has been running the fund for 3 years and currently receives a manager quality ranking of 3 (0=worst, 99=best). If you can tolerate very high levels of risk in the hope of improved future returns, holding this fund may be an option.

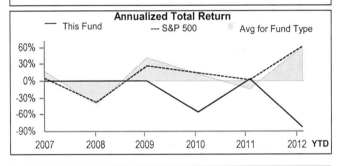

Annualized Total Return — This Fund --- S&P 500 ▨ Avg for Fund Type

*Direxion Daily China Bull 3x ETF (YINN)   E-   Very Weak

Fund Family: Rafferty Asset Management LLC
Fund Type: Foreign
Inception Date: December 3, 2009

Data Date	Investment Rating	Net Assets ($Mil)	Price	Performance Rating/Pts	Total Return Y-T-D	Risk Rating/Pts
3-12	E-	56.23	22.25	E+ / 0.8	35.92%	D / 1.9
2011	E-	35.90	16.37	E- / 0	6.29%	D / 1.9
2010	A-	65.50	43.51	A+ / 9.6	25.05%	C / 4.9

Major Rating Factors: *Direxion Daily China Bull 3x ETF has adopted a very risky asset allocation strategy and currently receives an overall TheStreet.com Investment Rating of E- (Very Weak). The fund has a high level of volatility, as measured by both semi-deviation and drawdown factors. It carries a beta of 0.00, meaning the fund's expected move will be 0.0% for every 10% move in the market. As of March 31, 2012, *Direxion Daily China Bull 3x ETF traded at a premium of .59% above its net asset value, which is worse than its one-year historical average discount of .04%. Unfortunately, the high level of risk (D, Weak) failed to pay off as investors endured very poor performance.

The fund's performance rating is currently E+ (Very Weak). It has registered an annualized return of 0.00% over the last three years and is up 35.92% year to date 2012. Factored into the performance evaluation is an expense ratio of 0.95% (low).

Paul Brigandi has been running the fund for 3 years and currently receives a manager quality ranking of 1 (0=worst, 99=best). If you can tolerate very high levels of risk in the hope of improved future returns, holding this fund may be an option.

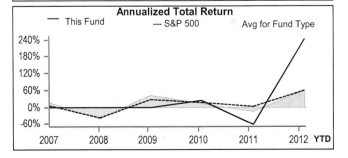

Annualized Total Return — This Fund --- S&P 500 ▨ Avg for Fund Type

*Direxion Daily Gold Miners Bear (DUST)   E+   Very Weak

Fund Family: Rafferty Asset Management LLC
Fund Type: Precious Metals
Inception Date: December 8, 2010

Data Date	Investment Rating	Net Assets ($Mil)	Price	Performance Rating/Pts	Total Return Y-T-D	Risk Rating/Pts
3-12	E+	12.45	42.04	D- / 1.2	-7.30%	C- / 3.7
2011	E+	6.40	42.60	D- / 1.2	-13.66%	C / 4.3

Major Rating Factors:
Disappointing performance is the major factor driving the E+ (Very Weak)
TheStreet.com Investment Rating for *Direxion Daily Gold Miners Bear. The fund
currently has a performance rating of D- (Weak) based on an annualized return of
0.00% over the last three years and a total return of -7.30% year to date 2012.
Factored into the performance evaluation is an expense ratio of 0.95% (low).

The fund's risk rating is currently C- (Fair). It carries a beta of 0.00, meaning the
fund's expected move will be 0.0% for every 10% move in the market. Volatility, as
measured by both the semi-deviation and a drawdown factor, is considered average.
As of March 31, 2012, *Direxion Daily Gold Miners Bear traded at a premium of
6.46% above its net asset value, which is worse than its one-year historical average
discount of .12%.

Paul Brigandi has been running the fund for 2 years and currently receives a
manager quality ranking of 99 (0=worst, 99=best). This fund offers an average level
of risk but investors looking for strong performance will be frustrated.

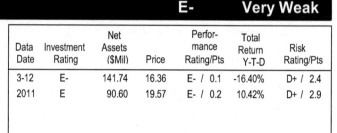

*Direxion Daily Gold Miners Bull (NUGT)   E-   Very Weak

Fund Family: Rafferty Asset Management LLC
Fund Type: Precious Metals
Inception Date: December 8, 2010

Data Date	Investment Rating	Net Assets ($Mil)	Price	Performance Rating/Pts	Total Return Y-T-D	Risk Rating/Pts
3-12	E-	141.74	16.36	E- / 0.1	-16.40%	D+ / 2.4
2011	E	90.60	19.57	E- / 0.2	10.42%	D+ / 2.9

Major Rating Factors: *Direxion Daily Gold Miners Bull has adopted a risky asset
allocation strategy and currently receives an overall TheStreet.com Investment Rating
of E- (Very Weak). The fund has an above average level of volatility, as measured by
both semi-deviation and drawdown factors. It carries a beta of 0.00, meaning the
fund's expected move will be 0.0% for every 10% move in the market. As of March
31, 2012, *Direxion Daily Gold Miners Bull traded at a discount of .18% below its net
asset value, which is better than its one-year historical average premium of .01%.
Unfortunately, the high level of risk (D+, Weak) failed to pay off as investors endured
very poor performance.

The fund's performance rating is currently E- (Very Weak). It has registered an
annualized return of 0.00% over the last three years but is down -16.40% year to date
2012. Factored into the performance evaluation is an expense ratio of 0.95% (low).

Paul Brigandi has been running the fund for 2 years and currently receives a
manager quality ranking of 0 (0=worst, 99=best). If you can tolerate high levels of risk
in the hope of improved future returns, holding this fund may be an option.

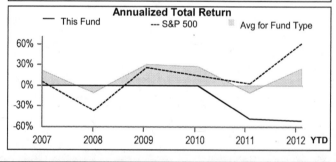

*Direxion Daily India Bear 3X (INDZ)   E   Very Weak

Fund Family: Rafferty Asset Management LLC
Fund Type: Foreign
Inception Date: March 11, 2010

Data Date	Investment Rating	Net Assets ($Mil)	Price	Performance Rating/Pts	Total Return Y-T-D	Risk Rating/Pts
3-12	E	4.36	24.70	E / 0.4	-43.45%	D+ / 2.9
2011	B-	4.40	43.68	A+ / 9.9	-11.74%	C / 4.5

Major Rating Factors: *Direxion Daily India Bear 3X has adopted a risky asset
allocation strategy and currently receives an overall TheStreet.com Investment Rating
of E (Very Weak). The fund has an above average level of volatility, as measured by
both semi-deviation and drawdown factors. It carries a beta of 0.00, meaning the
fund's expected move will be 0.0% for every 10% move in the market. As of March
31, 2012, *Direxion Daily India Bear 3X traded at a premium of .45% above its net
asset value, which is worse than its one-year historical average premium of .02%.
Unfortunately, the high level of risk (D+, Weak) failed to pay off as investors endured
very poor performance.

The fund's performance rating is currently E (Very Weak). It has registered an
annualized return of 0.00% over the last three years but is down -43.45% year to date
2012. Factored into the performance evaluation is an expense ratio of 0.95% (low).

Paul Brigandi has been running the fund for 2 years and currently receives a
manager quality ranking of 8 (0=worst, 99=best). If you can tolerate high levels of risk
in the hope of improved future returns, holding this fund may be an option.

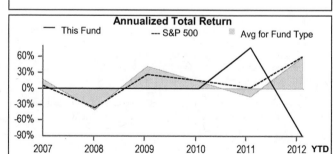

*Direxion Daily India Bull 3X (INDL)

E-   Very Weak

Fund Family: Rafferty Asset Management LLC
Fund Type: Emerging Market
Inception Date: March 11, 2010

Data Date	Investment Rating	Net Assets ($Mil)	Price	Performance Rating/Pts	Total Return Y-T-D	Risk Rating/Pts
3-12	E-	20.66	23.95	E+ / 0.7	44.98%	D / 2.2
2011	E-	10.70	16.52	E- / 0	10.17%	D+ / 2.4

Major Rating Factors: *Direxion Daily India Bull 3X has adopted a very risky asset allocation strategy and currently receives an overall TheStreet.com Investment Rating of E- (Very Weak). The fund has a high level of volatility, as measured by both semi-deviation and drawdown factors. It carries a beta of 0.00, meaning the fund's expected move will be 0.0% for every 10% move in the market. As of March 31, 2012, *Direxion Daily India Bull 3X traded at a discount of .29% below its net asset value, which is better than its one-year historical average discount of .11%. Unfortunately, the high level of risk (D, Weak) failed to pay off as investors endured very poor performance.

The fund's performance rating is currently E+ (Very Weak). It has registered an annualized return of 0.00% over the last three years and is up 44.98% year to date 2012. Factored into the performance evaluation is an expense ratio of 0.95% (low).

Paul Brigandi has been running the fund for 2 years and currently receives a manager quality ranking of 2 (0=worst, 99=best). If you can tolerate very high levels of risk in the hope of improved future returns, holding this fund may be an option.

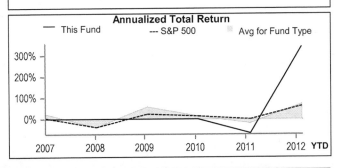

Annualized Total Return

*Direxion Daily Latin Amer Bear 3 (LHB)

E-   Very Weak

Fund Family: Rafferty Asset Management LLC
Fund Type: Foreign
Inception Date: December 3, 2009

Data Date	Investment Rating	Net Assets ($Mil)	Price	Performance Rating/Pts	Total Return Y-T-D	Risk Rating/Pts
3-12	E-	5.37	11.10	E- / 0.1	-33.13%	D / 1.9
2011	E-	6.60	16.60	E+ / 0.9	-4.52%	D / 1.9
2010	E-	3.30	16.62	E- / 0	-56.34%	D- / 1.4

Major Rating Factors: *Direxion Daily Latin Amer Bear 3 has adopted a very risky asset allocation strategy and currently receives an overall TheStreet.com Investment Rating of E- (Very Weak). The fund has a high level of volatility, as measured by both semi-deviation and drawdown factors. It carries a beta of 0.00, meaning the fund's expected move will be 0.0% for every 10% move in the market. As of March 31, 2012, *Direxion Daily Latin Amer Bear 3 traded at a price exactly equal to its net asset value, which is better than its one-year historical average premium of .05%. Unfortunately, the high level of risk (D, Weak) failed to pay off as investors endured very poor performance.

The fund's performance rating is currently E- (Very Weak). It has registered an annualized return of 0.00% over the last three years but is down -33.13% year to date 2012. Factored into the performance evaluation is an expense ratio of 1.07% (low).

Paul Brigandi has been running the fund for 3 years and currently receives a manager quality ranking of 1 (0=worst, 99=best). If you can tolerate very high levels of risk in the hope of improved future returns, holding this fund may be an option.

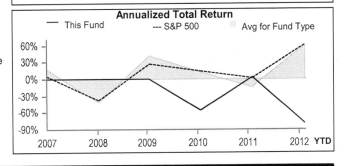

Annualized Total Return

*Direxion Daily Latin Amer Bull 3 (LBJ)

E+   Very Weak

Fund Family: Rafferty Asset Management LLC
Fund Type: Foreign
Inception Date: December 3, 2009

Data Date	Investment Rating	Net Assets ($Mil)	Price	Performance Rating/Pts	Total Return Y-T-D	Risk Rating/Pts
3-12	E+	46.83	97.81	C- / 3.6	35.69%	D / 1.9
2011	E-	43.00	72.83	E- / 0.1	3.60%	D / 1.9
2010	B	44.80	40.60	A+ / 9.8	25.82%	C- / 3.4

Major Rating Factors: *Direxion Daily Latin Amer Bull 3 has adopted a very risky asset allocation strategy and currently receives an overall TheStreet.com Investment Rating of E+ (Very Weak). The fund has a high level of volatility, as measured by both semi-deviation and drawdown factors. It carries a beta of 0.00, meaning the fund's expected move will be 0.0% for every 10% move in the market. As of March 31, 2012, *Direxion Daily Latin Amer Bull 3 traded at a premium of .05% above its net asset value, which is worse than its one-year historical average discount of .01%. Unfortunately, the high level of risk (D, Weak) has only provided investors with average performance.

The fund's performance rating is currently C- (Fair). It has registered an annualized return of 0.00% over the last three years and is up 35.69% year to date 2012. Factored into the performance evaluation is an expense ratio of 0.95% (low).

Paul Brigandi has been running the fund for 3 years and currently receives a manager quality ranking of 3 (0=worst, 99=best). If you are comfortable owning a very high risk investment, then this fund may be an option.

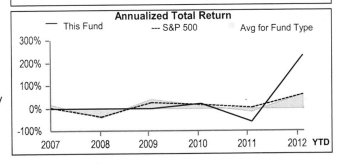

Annualized Total Return

*Direxion Daily Mid Cap Bear 3X (MWN)

E-   **Very Weak**

Fund Family: Rafferty Asset Management LLC
Fund Type: Growth
Inception Date: January 8, 2009

Major Rating Factors: *Direxion Daily Mid Cap Bear 3X has adopted a very risky asset allocation strategy and currently receives an overall TheStreet.com Investment Rating of E- (Very Weak). The fund has a high level of volatility, as measured by both semi-deviation and drawdown factors. It carries a beta of -3.33, meaning the fund's expected move will be -33.3% for every 10% move in the market. As of March 31, 2012, *Direxion Daily Mid Cap Bear 3X traded at a premium of .14% above its net asset value, which is worse than its one-year historical average premium of .03%. Unfortunately, the high level of risk (D, Weak) failed to pay off as investors endured very poor performance.

The fund's performance rating is currently E- (Very Weak). It has registered an annualized return of -64.94% over the last three years and is down -31.80% year to date 2012. Factored into the performance evaluation is an expense ratio of 0.95% (low).

Paul Brigandi has been running the fund for 3 years and currently receives a manager quality ranking of 2 (0=worst, 99=best). If you can tolerate very high levels of risk in the hope of improved future returns, holding this fund may be an option.

Data Date	Investment Rating	Net Assets ($Mil)	Price	Performance Rating/Pts	Total Return Y-T-D	Risk Rating/Pts
3-12	E-	13.17	21.23	E- / 0.1	-31.80%	D / 1.9
2011	E-	16.40	31.13	E / 0.3	-3.89%	D / 1.9
2010	E-	12.40	9.36	E- / 0	-62.04%	D- / 1.0

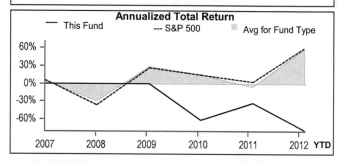
Annualized Total Return

*Direxion Daily Mid Cap Bull 3X (MWJ)

C-   **Fair**

Fund Family: Rafferty Asset Management LLC
Fund Type: Growth
Inception Date: January 8, 2009

Major Rating Factors: *Direxion Daily Mid Cap Bull 3X has adopted a very risky asset allocation strategy and currently receives an overall TheStreet.com Investment Rating of C- (Fair). The fund has shown a high level of volatility, as measured by both semi-deviation and drawdown factors. It carries a beta of 3.59, meaning it is expected to move 35.9% for every 10% move in the market. As of March 31, 2012, *Direxion Daily Mid Cap Bull 3X traded at a discount of .34% below its net asset value, which is better than its one-year historical average discount of .06%. The high level of risk (D, Weak) did however, reward investors with excellent performance.

The fund's performance rating is currently A+ (Excellent). It has registered an annualized return of 67.22% over the last three years and is up 40.96% year to date 2012. Factored into the performance evaluation is an expense ratio of 1.10% (low).

Paul Brigandi has been running the fund for 3 years and currently receives a manager quality ranking of 9 (0=worst, 99=best). If you are comfortable owning a very high risk investment, this fund may be an option.

Data Date	Investment Rating	Net Assets ($Mil)	Price	Performance Rating/Pts	Total Return Y-T-D	Risk Rating/Pts
3-12	C-	58.67	41.17	A+ / 9.9	40.96%	D / 1.9
2011	E-	56.70	31.44	E+ / 0.8	4.55%	D / 1.9
2010	C	52.20	47.61	A+ / 9.9	75.27%	D- / 1.1

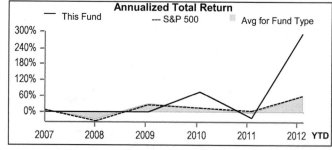
Annualized Total Return

*Direxion Daily Nat Gas Rel Bear (GASX)

E-   **Very Weak**

Fund Family: Rafferty Asset Management LLC
Fund Type: Growth
Inception Date: July 14, 2010

Major Rating Factors: *Direxion Daily Nat Gas Rel Bear has adopted a very risky asset allocation strategy and currently receives an overall TheStreet.com Investment Rating of E- (Very Weak). The fund has a high level of volatility, as measured by both semi-deviation and drawdown factors. It carries a beta of 0.00, meaning the fund's expected move will be 0.0% for every 10% move in the market. As of March 31, 2012, *Direxion Daily Nat Gas Rel Bear traded at a discount of .11% below its net asset value, which is better than its one-year historical average premium of .04%. Unfortunately, the high level of risk (D, Weak) failed to pay off as investors endured very poor performance.

The fund's performance rating is currently E+ (Very Weak). It has registered an annualized return of 0.00% over the last three years but is down -2.43% year to date 2012. Factored into the performance evaluation is an expense ratio of 0.95% (low).

Paul Brigandi has been running the fund for 2 years and currently receives a manager quality ranking of 99 (0=worst, 99=best). If you can tolerate very high levels of risk in the hope of improved future returns, holding this fund may be an option.

Data Date	Investment Rating	Net Assets ($Mil)	Price	Performance Rating/Pts	Total Return Y-T-D	Risk Rating/Pts
3-12	E-	2.35	18.65	E+ / 0.9	-2.43%	D / 2.0
2011	E-	2.90	19.11	E / 0.4	-8.18%	D+ / 2.3

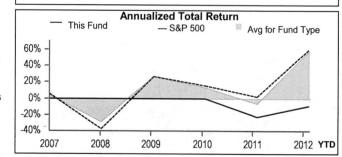
Annualized Total Return

*Direxion Daily Nat Gas Rel Bull (GASL)   E-   Very Weak

Fund Family: Rafferty Asset Management LLC
Fund Type: Growth
Inception Date: July 14, 2010

Data Date	Investment Rating	Net Assets ($Mil)	Price	Performance Rating/Pts	Total Return Y-T-D	Risk Rating/Pts
3-12	E-	13.11	34.66	E / 0.3	-12.32%	D+ / 2.5
2011	E	9.90	39.53	E+ / 0.6	7.46%	D+ / 2.7

Major Rating Factors: *Direxion Daily Nat Gas Rel Bull has adopted a risky asset allocation strategy and currently receives an overall TheStreet.com Investment Rating of E- (Very Weak). The fund has an above average level of volatility, as measured by both semi-deviation and drawdown factors. It carries a beta of 0.00, meaning the fund's expected move will be 0.0% for every 10% move in the market. As of March 31, 2012, *Direxion Daily Nat Gas Rel Bull traded at a premium of .03% above its net asset value, which is worse than its one-year historical average discount of .15%. Unfortunately, the high level of risk (D+, Weak) failed to pay off as investors endured very poor performance.

The fund's performance rating is currently E (Very Weak). It has registered an annualized return of 0.00% over the last three years but is down -12.32% year to date 2012. Factored into the performance evaluation is an expense ratio of 0.95% (low).

Paul Brigandi has been running the fund for 2 years and currently receives a manager quality ranking of 0 (0=worst, 99=best). If you can tolerate high levels of risk in the hope of improved future returns, holding this fund may be an option.

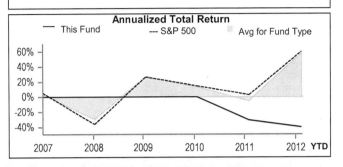

*Direxion Daily Real Estate Bear (DRV)   E-   Very Weak

Fund Family: Rafferty Asset Management LLC
Fund Type: Growth
Inception Date: July 16, 2009

Data Date	Investment Rating	Net Assets ($Mil)	Price	Performance Rating/Pts	Total Return Y-T-D	Risk Rating/Pts
3-12	E-	28.89	27.76	E- / 0	-28.57%	D / 1.9
2011	E-	26.70	38.86	E- / 0	0.72%	D / 1.9
2010	E-	55.50	18.01	E- / 0	-71.73%	D- / 1.3

Major Rating Factors: *Direxion Daily Real Estate Bear has adopted a very risky asset allocation strategy and currently receives an overall TheStreet.com Investment Rating of E- (Very Weak). The fund has a high level of volatility, as measured by both semi-deviation and drawdown factors. It carries a beta of 0.00, meaning the fund's expected move will be 0.0% for every 10% move in the market. As of March 31, 2012, *Direxion Daily Real Estate Bear traded at a discount of .07% below its net asset value, which is better than its one-year historical average discount of .03%. Unfortunately, the high level of risk (D, Weak) failed to pay off as investors endured very poor performance.

The fund's performance rating is currently E- (Very Weak). It has registered an annualized return of 0.00% over the last three years but is down -28.57% year to date 2012. Factored into the performance evaluation is an expense ratio of 0.95% (low).

Paul Brigandi has been running the fund for 3 years and currently receives a manager quality ranking of 0 (0=worst, 99=best). If you can tolerate very high levels of risk in the hope of improved future returns, holding this fund may be an option.

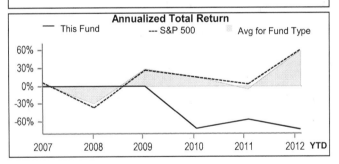

*Direxion Daily Real Estate Bull (DRN)   C-   Fair

Fund Family: Rafferty Asset Management LLC
Fund Type: Growth
Inception Date: July 16, 2009

Data Date	Investment Rating	Net Assets ($Mil)	Price	Performance Rating/Pts	Total Return Y-T-D	Risk Rating/Pts
3-12	C-	115.85	68.61	A+ / 9.9	33.05%	D / 1.9
2011	D-	118.50	51.57	C / 5.2	-1.36%	D / 1.9
2010	C	170.20	56.82	A+ / 9.9	63.42%	D- / 1.0

Major Rating Factors: *Direxion Daily Real Estate Bull has adopted a very risky asset allocation strategy and currently receives an overall TheStreet.com Investment Rating of C- (Fair). The fund has shown a high level of volatility, as measured by both semi-deviation and drawdown factors. It carries a beta of 0.00, meaning the fund's expected move will be 0.0% for every 10% move in the market. As of March 31, 2012, *Direxion Daily Real Estate Bull traded at a discount of .03% below its net asset value. The high level of risk (D, Weak) did however, reward investors with excellent performance.

The fund's performance rating is currently A+ (Excellent). It has registered an annualized return of 0.00% over the last three years and is up 33.05% year to date 2012. Factored into the performance evaluation is an expense ratio of 0.95% (low).

Paul Brigandi has been running the fund for 3 years and currently receives a manager quality ranking of 10 (0=worst, 99=best). If you are comfortable owning a very high risk investment, this fund may be an option.

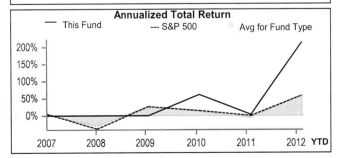

*Direxion Daily Retail Bear 3X (RETS)   E   Very Weak

Fund Family: Rafferty Asset Management LLC
Fund Type: Growth
Inception Date: July 14, 2010

Major Rating Factors: Very poor performance is the major factor driving the E (Very Weak) TheStreet.com Investment Rating for *Direxion Daily Retail Bear 3X. The fund currently has a performance rating of E- (Very Weak) based on an annualized return of 0.00% over the last three years and a total return of -34.98% year to date 2012. Factored into the performance evaluation is an expense ratio of 0.95% (low).

The fund's risk rating is currently C- (Fair). It carries a beta of 0.00, meaning the fund's expected move will be 0.0% for every 10% move in the market. Volatility, as measured by both the semi-deviation and a drawdown factor, is considered average. As of March 31, 2012, *Direxion Daily Retail Bear 3X traded at a discount of .16% below its net asset value, which is better than its one-year historical average discount of .08%.

Paul Brigandi has been running the fund for 2 years and currently receives a manager quality ranking of 1 (0=worst, 99=best). This fund offers an average level of risk but investors looking for strong performance will be frustrated.

Data Date	Investment Rating	Net Assets ($Mil)	Price	Performance Rating/Pts	Total Return Y-T-D	Risk Rating/Pts
3-12	E	1.53	12.66	E- / 0	-34.98%	C- / 3.2
2011	E+	2.00	19.47	E / 0.5	-2.11%	C / 4.5

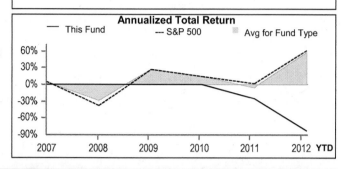

*Direxion Daily Retail Bull 3X (RETL)   A+   Excellent

Fund Family: Rafferty Asset Management LLC
Fund Type: Growth
Inception Date: July 14, 2010

Major Rating Factors:
Exceptional performance is the major factor driving the A+ (Excellent) TheStreet.com Investment Rating for *Direxion Daily Retail Bull 3X. The fund currently has a performance rating of A+ (Excellent) based on an annualized return of 0.00% over the last three years and a total return of 48.72% year to date 2012. Factored into the performance evaluation is an expense ratio of 0.95% (low).

The fund's risk rating is currently B (Good). It carries a beta of 0.00, meaning the fund's expected move will be 0.0% for every 10% move in the market. Volatility, as measured by both the semi-deviation and a drawdown factor, is considered low. As of March 31, 2012, *Direxion Daily Retail Bull 3X traded at a discount of .05% below its net asset value, which is better than its one-year historical average premium of .06%.

Paul Brigandi has been running the fund for 2 years and currently receives a manager quality ranking of 98 (0=worst, 99=best). If you desire only a moderate level of risk and strong performance, then this fund is an excellent option.

Data Date	Investment Rating	Net Assets ($Mil)	Price	Performance Rating/Pts	Total Return Y-T-D	Risk Rating/Pts
3-12	A+	7.37	87.91	A+ / 9.9	48.72%	B / 8.5
2011	C+	5.90	59.11	C+ / 5.9	2.47%	B / 8.4

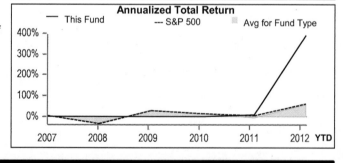

*Direxion Daily Semiconductor Bea (SOXS)   E-   Very Weak

Fund Family: Rafferty Asset Management LLC
Fund Type: Income
Inception Date: March 11, 2010

Major Rating Factors: *Direxion Daily Semiconductor Bea has adopted a very risky asset allocation strategy and currently receives an overall TheStreet.com Investment Rating of E- (Very Weak). The fund has a high level of volatility, as measured by both semi-deviation and drawdown factors. It carries a beta of 0.00, meaning the fund's expected move will be 0.0% for every 10% move in the market. As of March 31, 2012, *Direxion Daily Semiconductor Bea traded at a discount of .20% below its net asset value, which is better than its one-year historical average premium of .01%. Unfortunately, the high level of risk (D, Weak) failed to pay off as investors endured very poor performance.

The fund's performance rating is currently E- (Very Weak). It has registered an annualized return of 0.00% over the last three years but is down -47.40% year to date 2012. Factored into the performance evaluation is an expense ratio of 1.01% (low).

Paul Brigandi has been running the fund for 2 years and currently receives a manager quality ranking of 3 (0=worst, 99=best). If you can tolerate very high levels of risk in the hope of improved future returns, holding this fund may be an option.

Data Date	Investment Rating	Net Assets ($Mil)	Price	Performance Rating/Pts	Total Return Y-T-D	Risk Rating/Pts
3-12	E-	28.79	29.95	E- / 0	-47.40%	D / 1.9
2011	E-	17.00	56.94	E / 0.4	-8.87%	D / 1.9

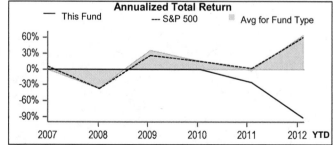

*Direxion Daily Semiconductor Bul (SOXL)

C-   **Fair**

Fund Family: Rafferty Asset Management LLC
Fund Type: Income
Inception Date: March 11, 2010

Data Date	Investment Rating	Net Assets ($Mil)	Price	Perfor-mance Rating/Pts	Total Return Y-T-D	Risk Rating/Pts
3-12	C-	116.84	44.07	A+ / 9.9	69.76%	D / 1.9
2011	E-	109.20	25.96	E- / 0.1	9.01%	D / 1.9

Major Rating Factors: *Direxion Daily Semiconductor Bul has adopted a very risky asset allocation strategy and currently receives an overall TheStreet.com Investment Rating of C- (Fair). The fund has shown a high level of volatility, as measured by both semi-deviation and drawdown factors. It carries a beta of 0.00, meaning the fund's expected move will be 0.0% for every 10% move in the market. As of March 31, 2012, *Direxion Daily Semiconductor Bul traded at a discount of .05% below its net asset value, which is better than its one-year historical average discount of .04%. The high level of risk (D, Weak) did however, reward investors with excellent performance.

The fund's performance rating is currently A+ (Excellent). It has registered an annualized return of 0.00% over the last three years and is up 69.76% year to date 2012. Factored into the performance evaluation is an expense ratio of 0.95% (low).

Paul Brigandi has been running the fund for 2 years and currently receives a manager quality ranking of 1 (0=worst, 99=best). If you are comfortable owning a very high risk investment, this fund may be an option.

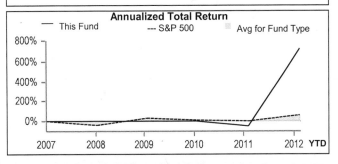

Annualized Total Return — This Fund --- S&P 500 · Avg for Fund Type

*Direxion Daily Small Cap Bear 3x (TZA)

E-   **Very Weak**

Fund Family: Rafferty Asset Management LLC
Fund Type: Growth
Inception Date: November 5, 2008

Data Date	Investment Rating	Net Assets ($Mil)	Price	Perfor-mance Rating/Pts	Total Return Y-T-D	Risk Rating/Pts
3-12	E-	929.31	17.68	E- / 0	-33.23%	D / 1.9
2011	E-	741.80	26.48	E- / 0	-3.88%	D / 1.9
2010	E-	635.20	15.61	E- / 0	-68.34%	D- / 1.0
2009	E-	199.35	9.86	E- / 0	-78.57%	D- / 1.1

Major Rating Factors: *Direxion Daily Small Cap Bear 3x has adopted a very risky asset allocation strategy and currently receives an overall TheStreet.com Investment Rating of E- (Very Weak). The fund has a high level of volatility, as measured by both semi-deviation and drawdown factors. It carries a beta of -3.74, meaning the fund's expected move will be -37.4% for every 10% move in the market. As of March 31, 2012, *Direxion Daily Small Cap Bear 3x traded at a discount of .11% below its net asset value, which is better than its one-year historical average discount of .01%. Unfortunately, the high level of risk (D, Weak) failed to pay off as investors endured very poor performance.

The fund's performance rating is currently E- (Very Weak). It has registered an annualized return of -69.01% over the last three years and is down -33.23% year to date 2012. Factored into the performance evaluation is an expense ratio of 0.95% (low).

Paul Brigandi has been running the fund for 4 years and currently receives a manager quality ranking of 2 (0=worst, 99=best). If you can tolerate very high levels of risk in the hope of improved future returns, holding this fund may be an option.

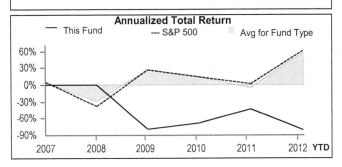

Annualized Total Return — This Fund --- S&P 500 · Avg for Fund Type

*Direxion Daily Small Cap Bull 3x (TNA)

C   **Fair**

Fund Family: Rafferty Asset Management LLC
Fund Type: Growth
Inception Date: November 5, 2008

Data Date	Investment Rating	Net Assets ($Mil)	Price	Perfor-mance Rating/Pts	Total Return Y-T-D	Risk Rating/Pts
3-12	C	853.52	62.40	A+ / 9.8	39.17%	D+ / 2.5
2011	D-	1,027.30	44.84	C / 4.3	3.84%	D / 2.2
2010	B+	565.00	72.43	A+ / 9.9	69.80%	C- / 3.7
2009	C+	219.09	42.74	A+ / 9.6	35.68%	C- / 3.0

Major Rating Factors: *Direxion Daily Small Cap Bull 3x has adopted a risky asset allocation strategy and currently receives an overall TheStreet.com Investment Rating of C (Fair). The fund has shown an above average level of volatility, as measured by both semi-deviation and drawdown factors. It carries a beta of 3.99, meaning it is expected to move 39.9% for every 10% move in the market. As of March 31, 2012, *Direxion Daily Small Cap Bull 3x traded at a discount of .11% below its net asset value, which is better than its one-year historical average discount of .02%. The high level of risk (D+, Weak) did however, reward investors with excellent performance.

The fund's performance rating is currently A+ (Excellent). It has registered an annualized return of 48.01% over the last three years and is up 39.17% year to date 2012. Factored into the performance evaluation is an expense ratio of 0.95% (low).

Paul Brigandi has been running the fund for 4 years and currently receives a manager quality ranking of 3 (0=worst, 99=best). If you are comfortable owning a high risk investment, this fund may be an option.

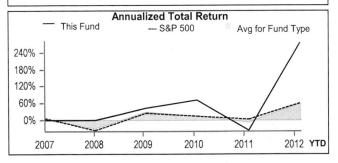

Annualized Total Return — This Fund --- S&P 500 · Avg for Fund Type

*Direxion Daily Technology Bear 3 (TYP)

E- **Very Weak**

Fund Family: Rafferty Asset Management LLC
Fund Type: Growth
Inception Date: December 17, 2008

Major Rating Factors: *Direxion Daily Technology Bear 3 has adopted a very risky asset allocation strategy and currently receives an overall TheStreet.com Investment Rating of E- (Very Weak). The fund has a high level of volatility, as measured by both semi-deviation and drawdown factors. It carries a beta of -3.16, meaning the fund's expected move will be -31.6% for every 10% move in the market. As of March 31, 2012, *Direxion Daily Technology Bear 3 traded at a price exactly equal to its net asset value, which is worse than its one-year historical average discount of .03%. Unfortunately, the high level of risk (D, Weak) failed to pay off as investors endured very poor performance.

The fund's performance rating is currently E- (Very Weak). It has registered an annualized return of -62.59% over the last three years and is down -46.56% year to date 2012. Factored into the performance evaluation is an expense ratio of 0.95% (low).

Paul Brigandi has been running the fund for 4 years and currently receives a manager quality ranking of 2 (0=worst, 99=best). If you can tolerate very high levels of risk in the hope of improved future returns, holding this fund may be an option.

Data Date	Investment Rating	Net Assets ($Mil)	Price	Performance Rating/Pts	Total Return Y-T-D	Risk Rating/Pts
3-12	E-	42.17	8.71	E- / 0.1	-46.56%	D / 1.9
2011	E-	32.00	16.30	E- / 0	-8.22%	D / 1.9
2010	E-	44.50	23.91	E- / 0	-45.29%	D- / 1.0
2009	E-	9.69	8.74	E- / 0	-84.58%	D- / 1.1

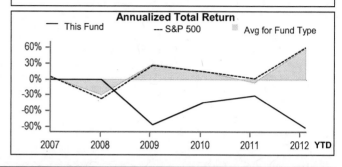

*Direxion Daily Technology Bull 3 (TYH)

C- **Fair**

Fund Family: Rafferty Asset Management LLC
Fund Type: Growth
Inception Date: December 17, 2008

Major Rating Factors: *Direxion Daily Technology Bull 3 has adopted a very risky asset allocation strategy and currently receives an overall TheStreet.com Investment Rating of C- (Fair). The fund has shown a high level of volatility, as measured by both semi-deviation and drawdown factors. It carries a beta of 3.40, meaning it is expected to move 34.0% for every 10% move in the market. As of March 31, 2012, *Direxion Daily Technology Bull 3 traded at a discount of .03% below its net asset value, which is worse than its one-year historical average discount of .04%. The high level of risk (D, Weak) did however, reward investors with excellent performance.

The fund's performance rating is currently A+ (Excellent). It has registered an annualized return of 70.71% over the last three years and is up 79.70% year to date 2012. Factored into the performance evaluation is an expense ratio of 0.95% (low).

Paul Brigandi has been running the fund for 3 years and currently receives a manager quality ranking of 13 (0=worst, 99=best). If you are comfortable owning a very high risk investment, this fund may be an option.

Data Date	Investment Rating	Net Assets ($Mil)	Price	Performance Rating/Pts	Total Return Y-T-D	Risk Rating/Pts
3-12	C-	155.62	65.50	A+ / 9.9	79.70%	D / 1.9
2011	C-	178.80	36.45	A+ / 9.9	8.50%	D / 1.9
2010	C	208.60	45.50	A+ / 9.8	21.21%	D- / 1.0
2009	A+	41.33	157.96	A+ / 9.9	203.65%	B- / 7.3

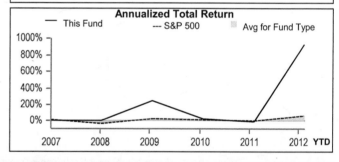

*Direxion Developed Markets Bear (DPK)

E- **Very Weak**

Fund Family: Rafferty Asset Management LLC
Fund Type: Global
Inception Date: December 17, 2008

Major Rating Factors: *Direxion Developed Markets Bear has adopted a very risky asset allocation strategy and currently receives an overall TheStreet.com Investment Rating of E- (Very Weak). The fund has a high level of volatility, as measured by both semi-deviation and drawdown factors. It carries a beta of -2.85, meaning the fund's expected move will be -28.5% for every 10% move in the market. As of March 31, 2012, *Direxion Developed Markets Bear traded at a premium of .12% above its net asset value, which is worse than its one-year historical average discount of .02%. Unfortunately, the high level of risk (D, Weak) failed to pay off as investors endured very poor performance.

The fund's performance rating is currently E- (Very Weak). It has registered an annualized return of -56.22% over the last three years and is down -29.99% year to date 2012. Factored into the performance evaluation is an expense ratio of 0.95% (low).

Paul Brigandi has been running the fund for 4 years and currently receives a manager quality ranking of 2 (0=worst, 99=best). If you can tolerate very high levels of risk in the hope of improved future returns, holding this fund may be an option.

Data Date	Investment Rating	Net Assets ($Mil)	Price	Performance Rating/Pts	Total Return Y-T-D	Risk Rating/Pts
3-12	E-	13.53	24.33	E- / 0.1	-29.99%	D / 1.9
2011	E-	17.00	34.75	E- / 0.2	1.27%	D / 1.9
2010	E-	15.20	8.22	E- / 0.1	-46.41%	D- / 1.0
2009	E-	4.91	15.34	E- / 0	-73.28%	D- / 1.1

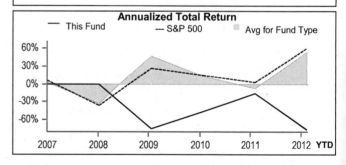

*Direxion Developed Markets Bull (DZK)   D-   Weak

Fund Family: Rafferty Asset Management LLC
Fund Type: Global
Inception Date: December 17, 2008

Data Date	Investment Rating	Net Assets ($Mil)	Price	Perfor-mance Rating/Pts	Total Return Y-T-D	Risk Rating/Pts
3-12	D-	24.13	39.92	C / 4.5	32.35%	D+ / 2.4
2011	E	19.70	30.35	D- / 1.1	-2.67%	D+ / 2.3
2010	C+	23.50	67.07	A+ / 9.8	11.84%	D+ / 2.5
2009	B	5.92	72.94	A+ / 9.6	41.40%	C- / 3.9

Major Rating Factors: *Direxion Developed Markets Bull has adopted a risky asset allocation strategy and currently receives an overall TheStreet.com Investment Rating of D- (Weak). The fund has an above average level of volatility, as measured by both semi-deviation and drawdown factors. It carries a beta of 3.22, meaning it is expected to move 32.2% for every 10% move in the market. As of March 31, 2012, *Direxion Developed Markets Bull traded at a discount of .10% below its net asset value, which is better than its one-year historical average discount of .01%. Unfortunately, the high level of risk (D+, Weak) has only provided investors with average performance.

The fund's performance rating is currently C (Fair). It has registered an annualized return of 20.62% over the last three years and is up 32.35% year to date 2012. Factored into the performance evaluation is an expense ratio of 1.01% (low).

Adam Gould has been running the fund for 4 years and currently receives a manager quality ranking of 6 (0=worst, 99=best). If you are comfortable owning a high risk investment, then this fund may be an option.

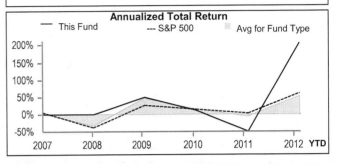

*Direxion Emerging Markets Bear 3 (EDZ)   E-   Very Weak

Fund Family: Rafferty Asset Management LLC
Fund Type: Global
Inception Date: December 17, 2008

Data Date	Investment Rating	Net Assets ($Mil)	Price	Perfor-mance Rating/Pts	Total Return Y-T-D	Risk Rating/Pts
3-12	E-	150.41	12.68	E- / 0.1	-35.60%	D / 1.9
2011	E-	125.90	19.69	E- / 0	-3.00%	D / 1.9
2010	E-	87.20	20.29	E- / 0	-59.34%	D- / 1.0
2009	E-	19.06	4.99	E- / 0	-91.17%	D- / 1.1

Major Rating Factors: *Direxion Emerging Markets Bear 3 has adopted a very risky asset allocation strategy and currently receives an overall TheStreet.com Investment Rating of E- (Very Weak). The fund has a high level of volatility, as measured by both semi-deviation and drawdown factors. It carries a beta of -3.25, meaning the fund's expected move will be -32.5% for every 10% move in the market. As of March 31, 2012, *Direxion Emerging Markets Bear 3 traded at a price exactly equal to its net asset value, which is worse than its one-year historical average discount of .06%. Unfortunately, the high level of risk (D, Weak) failed to pay off as investors endured very poor performance.

The fund's performance rating is currently E- (Very Weak). It has registered an annualized return of -64.84% over the last three years and is down -35.60% year to date 2012. Factored into the performance evaluation is an expense ratio of 0.95% (low).

David A. Plecha currently receives a manager quality ranking of 0 (0=worst, 99=best). If you can tolerate very high levels of risk in the hope of improved future returns, holding this fund may be an option.

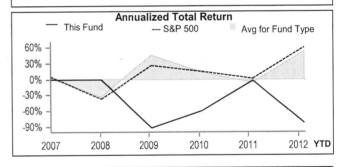

*Direxion Emerging Markets Bull 3 (EDC)   D-   Weak

Fund Family: Rafferty Asset Management LLC
Fund Type: Global
Inception Date: December 17, 2008

Data Date	Investment Rating	Net Assets ($Mil)	Price	Perfor-mance Rating/Pts	Total Return Y-T-D	Risk Rating/Pts
3-12	D-	402.36	104.23	C / 5.1	39.69%	D / 1.9
2011	E	369.70	74.61	D / 1.9	2.16%	D / 1.9
2010	C	426.80	41.31	A+ / 9.8	24.29%	D- / 1.0
2009	A+	63.36	134.35	A+ / 9.9	166.37%	C+ / 5.7

Major Rating Factors: *Direxion Emerging Markets Bull 3 has adopted a very risky asset allocation strategy and currently receives an overall TheStreet.com Investment Rating of D- (Weak). The fund has a high level of volatility, as measured by both semi-deviation and drawdown factors. It carries a beta of 3.53, meaning it is expected to move 35.3% for every 10% move in the market. As of March 31, 2012, *Direxion Emerging Markets Bull 3 traded at a premium of .12% above its net asset value, which is worse than its one-year historical average premium of .06%. Unfortunately, the high level of risk (D, Weak) has only provided investors with average performance.

The fund's performance rating is currently C (Fair). It has registered an annualized return of 21.84% over the last three years and is up 39.69% year to date 2012. Factored into the performance evaluation is an expense ratio of 0.95% (low).

Paul Brigandi has been running the fund for 7 years and currently receives a manager quality ranking of 5 (0=worst, 99=best). If you are comfortable owning a very high risk investment, then this fund may be an option.

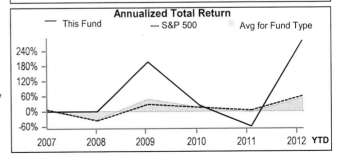

*Direxion Energy Bear 3x Shares (ERY)

E- Very Weak

Fund Family: Rafferty Asset Management LLC
Fund Type: Energy/Natural Resources
Inception Date: November 6, 2008

Major Rating Factors: *Direxion Energy Bear 3x Shares has adopted a very risky asset allocation strategy and currently receives an overall TheStreet.com Investment Rating of E- (Very Weak). The fund has a high level of volatility, as measured by both semi-deviation and drawdown factors. It carries a beta of -2.86, meaning the fund's expected move will be -28.6% for every 10% move in the market. As of March 31, 2012, *Direxion Energy Bear 3x Shares traded at a premium of .31% above its net asset value, which is worse than its one-year historical average discount of .06%. Unfortunately, the high level of risk (D, Weak) failed to pay off as investors endured very poor performance.

The fund's performance rating is currently E- (Very Weak). It has registered an annualized return of -59.72% over the last three years and is down -13.79% year to date 2012. Factored into the performance evaluation is an expense ratio of 1.02% (low).

Paul Brigandi has been running the fund for 4 years and currently receives a manager quality ranking of 1 (0=worst, 99=best). If you can tolerate very high levels of risk in the hope of improved future returns, holding this fund may be an option.

Data Date	Investment Rating	Net Assets ($Mil)	Price	Performance Rating/Pts	Total Return Y-T-D	Risk Rating/Pts
3-12	E-	98.72	9.75	E- / 0.1	-13.79%	D / 1.9
2011	E-	94.90	11.31	E- / 0	-5.66%	D / 1.9
2010	E-	50.60	22.55	E- / 0	-60.02%	D- / 1.1
2009	E-	37.07	11.28	E- / 0	-65.40%	D / 1.6

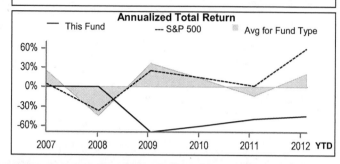

*Direxion Energy Bull 3x Shares (ERX)

D Weak

Fund Family: Rafferty Asset Management LLC
Fund Type: Energy/Natural Resources
Inception Date: November 6, 2008

Major Rating Factors: *Direxion Energy Bull 3x Shares has adopted a very risky asset allocation strategy and currently receives an overall TheStreet.com Investment Rating of D (Weak). The fund has a high level of volatility, as measured by both semi-deviation and drawdown factors. It carries a beta of 3.10, meaning it is expected to move 31.0% for every 10% move in the market. As of March 31, 2012, *Direxion Energy Bull 3x Shares traded at a discount of .31% below its net asset value. Unfortunately, the high level of risk (D, Weak) has only provided investors with average performance.

The fund's performance rating is currently C+ (Fair). It has registered an annualized return of 27.50% over the last three years and is up 9.54% year to date 2012. Factored into the performance evaluation is an expense ratio of 0.95% (low).

Paul Brigandi has been running the fund for 4 years and currently receives a manager quality ranking of 6 (0=worst, 99=best). If you are comfortable owning a very high risk investment, then this fund may be an option.

Data Date	Investment Rating	Net Assets ($Mil)	Price	Performance Rating/Pts	Total Return Y-T-D	Risk Rating/Pts
3-12	D	362.69	51.32	C+ / 6.6	9.54%	D / 2.2
2011	E+	384.20	46.85	C- / 3.9	4.97%	D / 2.1
2010	B	241.40	58.45	A+ / 9.9	48.98%	C- / 3.3
2009	B-	130.44	39.68	B+ / 8.8	-0.04%	C- / 3.9

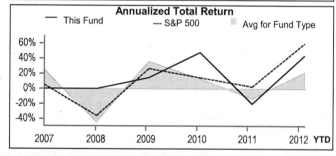

*Direxion Financial Bear 3x Share (FAZ)

E- Very Weak

Fund Family: Rafferty Asset Management LLC
Fund Type: Financial Services
Inception Date: November 6, 2008

Major Rating Factors: *Direxion Financial Bear 3x Share has adopted a very risky asset allocation strategy and currently receives an overall TheStreet.com Investment Rating of E- (Very Weak). The fund has a high level of volatility, as measured by both semi-deviation and drawdown factors. It carries a beta of -3.27, meaning the fund's expected move will be -32.7% for every 10% move in the market. As of March 31, 2012, *Direxion Financial Bear 3x Share traded at a price exactly equal to its net asset value, which is worse than its one-year historical average discount of .06%. Unfortunately, the high level of risk (D, Weak) failed to pay off as investors endured very poor performance.

The fund's performance rating is currently E- (Very Weak). It has registered an annualized return of -70.20% over the last three years and is down -44.71% year to date 2012. Factored into the performance evaluation is an expense ratio of 0.95% (low).

Paul Brigandi has been running the fund for 4 years and currently receives a manager quality ranking of 0 (0=worst, 99=best). If you can tolerate very high levels of risk in the hope of improved future returns, holding this fund may be an option.

Data Date	Investment Rating	Net Assets ($Mil)	Price	Performance Rating/Pts	Total Return Y-T-D	Risk Rating/Pts
3-12	E-	984.72	20.65	E- / 0	-44.71%	D / 1.9
2011	E-	823.80	37.35	E- / 0	-7.32%	D / 1.9
2010	E-	971.50	9.45	E- / 0	-51.36%	D- / 1.0
2009	E-	1,433.17	19.43	E- / 0	-94.34%	D- / 1.1

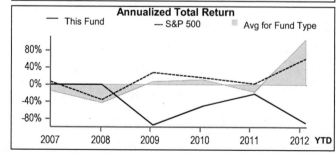

*Direxion Financial Bull 3x Share (FAS)   D+   Weak

Fund Family: Rafferty Asset Management LLC
Fund Type: Financial Services
Inception Date: November 6, 2008

Major Rating Factors: *Direxion Financial Bull 3x Share has adopted a very risky asset allocation strategy and currently receives an overall TheStreet.com Investment Rating of D+ (Weak). The fund has shown a high level of volatility, as measured by both semi-deviation and drawdown factors. It carries a beta of 2.91, meaning it is expected to move 29.1% for every 10% move in the market. As of March 31, 2012, *Direxion Financial Bull 3x Share traded at a discount of .08% below its net asset value, which is better than its one-year historical average premium of .02%. The high level of risk (D, Weak) did however, reward investors with excellent performance.

The fund's performance rating is currently B+ (Good). It has registered an annualized return of 22.85% over the last three years and is up 68.27% year to date 2012. Factored into the performance evaluation is an expense ratio of 0.95% (low).

Paul Brigandi has been running the fund for 4 years and currently receives a manager quality ranking of 4 (0=worst, 99=best). If you are comfortable owning a very high risk investment, this fund may be an option.

Data Date	Investment Rating	Net Assets ($Mil)	Price	Performance Rating/Pts	Total Return Y-T-D	Risk Rating/Pts
3-12	D+	1,458.75	109.15	B+ / 8.3	68.27%	D / 1.9
2011	E-	1,391.00	64.87	E+ / 0.6	7.13%	D / 1.9
2010	C	1,921.20	27.84	A+ / 9.6	12.75%	D- / 1.0
2009	D-	1,072.79	74.13	C / 4.6	-42.39%	D- / 1.2

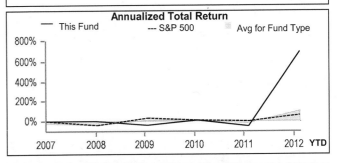

*Direxion Large Cap Bear 3x Share (BGZ)   E-   Very Weak

Fund Family: Rafferty Asset Management LLC
Fund Type: Growth
Inception Date: November 5, 2008

Major Rating Factors: *Direxion Large Cap Bear 3x Share has adopted a risky asset allocation strategy and currently receives an overall TheStreet.com Investment Rating of E- (Very Weak). The fund has an above average level of volatility, as measured by both semi-deviation and drawdown factors. It carries a beta of -2.94, meaning the fund's expected move will be -29.4% for every 10% move in the market. As of March 31, 2012, *Direxion Large Cap Bear 3x Share traded at a premium of .15% above its net asset value, which is worse than its one-year historical average discount of .04%. Unfortunately, the high level of risk (D+, Weak) failed to pay off as investors endured very poor performance.

The fund's performance rating is currently E- (Very Weak). It has registered an annualized return of -57.44% over the last three years and is down -31.73% year to date 2012. Factored into the performance evaluation is an expense ratio of 0.95% (low).

Paul Brigandi has been running the fund for 4 years and currently receives a manager quality ranking of 4 (0=worst, 99=best). If you can tolerate high levels of risk in the hope of improved future returns, holding this fund may be an option.

Data Date	Investment Rating	Net Assets ($Mil)	Price	Performance Rating/Pts	Total Return Y-T-D	Risk Rating/Pts
3-12	E-	185.50	20.16	E- / 0.1	-31.73%	D+ / 2.3
2011	E-	155.90	29.53	E- / 0.1	-5.25%	D / 2.1
2010	E-	194.00	8.77	E- / 0	-48.74%	D- / 1.0
2009	E-	364.97	17.11	E- / 0	-67.89%	D- / 1.2

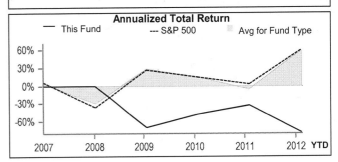

*Direxion Large Cap Bull 3x Share (BGU)   C+   Fair

Fund Family: Rafferty Asset Management LLC
Fund Type: Growth
Inception Date: November 5, 2008

Major Rating Factors:
Exceptional performance is the major factor driving the C+ (Fair) TheStreet.com Investment Rating for *Direxion Large Cap Bull 3x Share. The fund currently has a performance rating of A+ (Excellent) based on an annualized return of 55.23% over the last three years and a total return of 41.65% year to date 2012. Factored into the performance evaluation is an expense ratio of 0.95% (low).

The fund's risk rating is currently C (Fair). It carries a beta of 3.17, meaning it is expected to move 31.7% for every 10% move in the market. Volatility, as measured by both the semi-deviation and a drawdown factor, is considered average. As of March 31, 2012, *Direxion Large Cap Bull 3x Share traded at a discount of .22% below its net asset value, which is better than its one-year historical average discount of .03%.

Paul Brigandi has been running the fund for 4 years and currently receives a manager quality ranking of 10 (0=worst, 99=best). If you desire an average level of risk and strong performance, then this fund is a good option.

Data Date	Investment Rating	Net Assets ($Mil)	Price	Performance Rating/Pts	Total Return Y-T-D	Risk Rating/Pts
3-12	C+	257.43	86.18	A+ / 9.9	41.65%	C / 4.5
2011	C-	307.50	60.84	B / 7.7	5.13%	C- / 4.1
2010	A-	235.20	71.50	A+ / 9.9	39.78%	C / 4.6
2009	B+	284.63	52.51	A+ / 9.8	50.44%	C- / 4.2

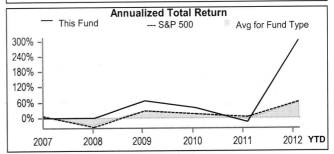

*EGShares Brazil Infrastructure E (BRXX)

C-   **Fair**

Fund Family: ALPS Advisors Inc
Fund Type: Foreign
Inception Date: February 24, 2010

Data Date	Investment Rating	Net Assets ($Mil)	Price	Performance Rating/Pts	Total Return Y-T-D	Risk Rating/Pts
3-12	C-	89.53	24.09	C / 4.3	17.34%	B- / 7.1
2011	D	65.70	20.53	D- / 1.2	1.07%	B- / 7.1

Major Rating Factors: Middle of the road best describes *EGShares Brazil Infrastructure E whose TheStreet.com Investment Rating is currently a C- (Fair). The fund currently has a performance rating of C (Fair) based on an annualized return of 0.00% over the last three years and a total return of 17.34% year to date 2012. Factored into the performance evaluation is an expense ratio of 0.85% (very low).

The fund's risk rating is currently B- (Good). It carries a beta of 0.00, meaning the fund's expected move will be 0.0% for every 10% move in the market. Volatility, as measured by both the semi-deviation and a drawdown factor, is considered low. As of March 31, 2012, *EGShares Brazil Infrastructure E traded at a discount of .50% below its net asset value, which is better than its one-year historical average premium of .51%.

Richard Kang has been running the fund for 2 years and currently receives a manager quality ranking of 70 (0=worst, 99=best). If you desire an average level of risk, then this fund may be an option.

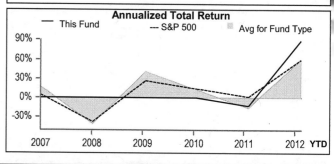

*EGShares China Infrastructure ET (CHXX)

E+   **Very Weak**

Fund Family: ALPS Advisors Inc
Fund Type: Foreign
Inception Date: February 17, 2010

Data Date	Investment Rating	Net Assets ($Mil)	Price	Performance Rating/Pts	Total Return Y-T-D	Risk Rating/Pts
3-12	E+	14.20	16.41	D- / 1.0	8.23%	C / 5.3
2011	E+	12.20	15.16	E / 0.5	-2.18%	C / 5.5

Major Rating Factors:
Disappointing performance is the major factor driving the E+ (Very Weak) TheStreet.com Investment Rating for *EGShares China Infrastructure ET. The fund currently has a performance rating of D- (Weak) based on an annualized return of 0.00% over the last three years and a total return of 8.23% year to date 2012. Factored into the performance evaluation is an expense ratio of 0.85% (very low).

The fund's risk rating is currently C (Fair). It carries a beta of 0.00, meaning the fund's expected move will be 0.0% for every 10% move in the market. Volatility, as measured by both the semi-deviation and a drawdown factor, is considered average. As of March 31, 2012, *EGShares China Infrastructure ET traded at a premium of .06% above its net asset value, which is worse than its one-year historical average discount of .24%.

Richard Kang has been running the fund for 2 years and currently receives a manager quality ranking of 9 (0=worst, 99=best). This fund offers an average level of risk but investors looking for strong performance will be frustrated.

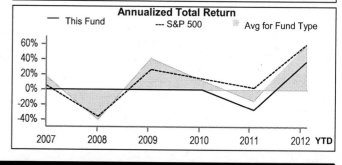

*EGShares Em Mkts Metals&Mining E (EMT)

E   **Very Weak**

Fund Family: ALPS Advisors Inc
Fund Type: Emerging Market
Inception Date: May 21, 2009

Data Date	Investment Rating	Net Assets ($Mil)	Price	Performance Rating/Pts	Total Return Y-T-D	Risk Rating/Pts
3-12	E	15.85	15.98	E+ / 0.8	10.82%	D / 2.2
2011	E-	13.10	14.42	E / 0.4	2.64%	D+ / 2.3
2010	C	24.80	23.40	A / 9.5	19.31%	D / 1.6

Major Rating Factors: *EGShares Em Mkts Metals&Mining E has adopted a very risky asset allocation strategy and currently receives an overall TheStreet.com Investment Rating of E (Very Weak). The fund has a high level of volatility, as measured by both semi-deviation and drawdown factors. It carries a beta of 0.00, meaning the fund's expected move will be 0.0% for every 10% move in the market. As of March 31, 2012, *EGShares Em Mkts Metals&Mining E traded at a premium of .06% above its net asset value, which is worse than its one-year historical average discount of .42%. Unfortunately, the high level of risk (D, Weak) failed to pay off as investors endured very poor performance.

The fund's performance rating is currently E+ (Very Weak). It has registered an annualized return of 0.00% over the last three years and is up 10.82% year to date 2012. Factored into the performance evaluation is an expense ratio of 0.85% (very low).

Richard Kang has been running the fund for 3 years and currently receives a manager quality ranking of 7 (0=worst, 99=best). If you can tolerate very high levels of risk in the hope of improved future returns, holding this fund may be an option.

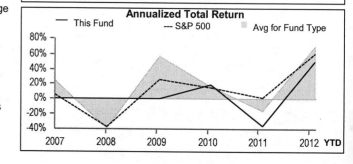

*EGShares Emerging Markets Cons E (ECON)   C+   Fair

Fund Family: ALPS Advisors Inc
Fund Type: Emerging Market
Inception Date: September 14, 2010

Data Date	Investment Rating	Net Assets ($Mil)	Price	Performance Rating/Pts	Total Return Y-T-D	Risk Rating/Pts
3-12	C+	370.31	24.85	C+ / 6.2	13.06%	B- / 7.7
2011	D	293.90	21.98	D- / 1.5	0.00%	B- / 7.7

Major Rating Factors: Middle of the road best describes *EGShares Emerging Markets Cons E whose TheStreet.com Investment Rating is currently a C+ (Fair). The fund currently has a performance rating of C+ (Fair) based on an annualized return of 0.00% over the last three years and a total return of 13.06% year to date 2012. Factored into the performance evaluation is an expense ratio of 0.85% (very low).

The fund's risk rating is currently B- (Good). It carries a beta of 0.00, meaning the fund's expected move will be 0.0% for every 10% move in the market. Volatility, as measured by both the semi-deviation and a drawdown factor, is considered low. As of March 31, 2012, *EGShares Emerging Markets Cons E traded at a premium of .32% above its net asset value, which is worse than its one-year historical average premium of .20%.

Richard Kang has been running the fund for 2 years and currently receives a manager quality ranking of 91 (0=worst, 99=best). If you desire an average level of risk, then this fund may be an option.

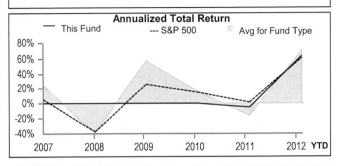

*EGShares Energy GEMS ETF (OGEM)   E+   Very Weak

Fund Family: ALPS Advisors Inc
Fund Type: Emerging Market
Inception Date: May 21, 2009

Data Date	Investment Rating	Net Assets ($Mil)	Price	Performance Rating/Pts	Total Return Y-T-D	Risk Rating/Pts
3-12	E+	11.98	24.44	D- / 1.3	12.94%	C- / 3.8
2011	E+	13.10	21.64	D- / 1.0	3.42%	C- / 3.8
2010	B	9.90	27.27	A- / 9.2	16.79%	C- / 3.7

Major Rating Factors:
Disappointing performance is the major factor driving the E+ (Very Weak) TheStreet.com Investment Rating for *EGShares Energy GEMS ETF. The fund currently has a performance rating of D- (Weak) based on an annualized return of 0.00% over the last three years and a total return of 12.94% year to date 2012. Factored into the performance evaluation is an expense ratio of 0.85% (very low).

The fund's risk rating is currently C- (Fair). It carries a beta of 0.00, meaning the fund's expected move will be 0.0% for every 10% move in the market. Volatility, as measured by both the semi-deviation and a drawdown factor, is considered average. As of March 31, 2012, *EGShares Energy GEMS ETF traded at a discount of .57% below its net asset value, which is better than its one-year historical average discount of .51%.

Richard Kang has been running the fund for 3 years and currently receives a manager quality ranking of 16 (0=worst, 99=best). This fund offers an average level of risk but investors looking for strong performance will be frustrated.

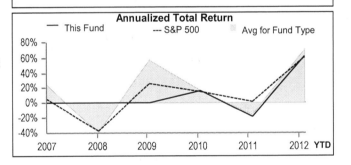

*EGShares Financials GEMS ETF (FGEM)   E+   Very Weak

Fund Family: ALPS Advisors Inc
Fund Type: Financial Services
Inception Date: September 16, 2009

Data Date	Investment Rating	Net Assets ($Mil)	Price	Performance Rating/Pts	Total Return Y-T-D	Risk Rating/Pts
3-12	E+	3.22	20.30	D / 1.7	15.54%	C- / 3.1
2011	E	2.70	17.57	E+ / 0.7	1.20%	C- / 3.1
2010	C+	12.20	24.86	B / 8.2	11.18%	C- / 3.6

Major Rating Factors:
Disappointing performance is the major factor driving the E+ (Very Weak) TheStreet.com Investment Rating for *EGShares Financials GEMS ETF. The fund currently has a performance rating of D (Weak) based on an annualized return of 0.00% over the last three years and a total return of 15.54% year to date 2012. Factored into the performance evaluation is an expense ratio of 0.85% (very low).

The fund's risk rating is currently C- (Fair). It carries a beta of 0.00, meaning the fund's expected move will be 0.0% for every 10% move in the market. Volatility, as measured by both the semi-deviation and a drawdown factor, is considered average. As of March 31, 2012, *EGShares Financials GEMS ETF traded at a premium of .35% above its net asset value, which is worse than its one-year historical average discount of .51%.

Richard Kang has been running the fund for 3 years and currently receives a manager quality ranking of 8 (0=worst, 99=best). This fund offers an average level of risk but investors looking for strong performance will be frustrated.

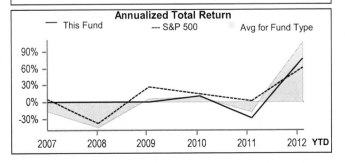

*EGShares GEMS Composite ETF (AGEM)

E+   **Very Weak**

Fund Family: ALPS Advisors Inc
Fund Type: Emerging Market
Inception Date: July 22, 2009

Data Date	Investment Rating	Net Assets ($Mil)	Price	Perfor-mance Rating/Pts	Total Return Y-T-D	Risk Rating/Pts
3-12	E+	15.84	23.22	D- / 1.5	12.56%	C- / 3.5
2011	E+	16.60	20.63	E+ / 0.9	2.03%	C- / 3.5
2010	C+	28.10	26.90	B+ / 8.7	10.75%	C- / 3.6

Major Rating Factors:
Disappointing performance is the major factor driving the E+ (Very Weak) TheStreet.com Investment Rating for *EGShares GEMS Composite ETF. The fund currently has a performance rating of D- (Weak) based on an annualized return of 0.00% over the last three years and a total return of 12.56% year to date 2012. Factored into the performance evaluation is an expense ratio of 0.75% (very low).

The fund's risk rating is currently C- (Fair). It carries a beta of 0.00, meaning the fund's expected move will be 0.0% for every 10% move in the market. Volatility, as measured by both the semi-deviation and a drawdown factor, is considered average. As of March 31, 2012, *EGShares GEMS Composite ETF traded at a discount of .39% below its net asset value, which is worse than its one-year historical average discount of .49%.

Richard Kang has been running the fund for 3 years and currently receives a manager quality ranking of 20 (0=worst, 99=best). This fund offers an average level of risk but investors looking for strong performance will be frustrated.

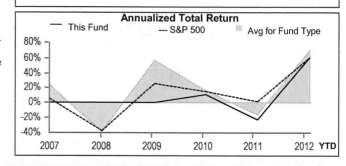

*EGShares India Infrastructure ET (INXX)

E+   **Very Weak**

Fund Family: ALPS Advisors Inc
Fund Type: Global
Inception Date: August 11, 2010

Data Date	Investment Rating	Net Assets ($Mil)	Price	Perfor-mance Rating/Pts	Total Return Y-T-D	Risk Rating/Pts
3-12	E+	62.59	14.88	D- / 1.0	28.28%	C / 4.9
2011	E+	48.60	11.60	E- / 0.1	3.10%	C / 4.8

Major Rating Factors:
Disappointing performance is the major factor driving the E+ (Very Weak) TheStreet.com Investment Rating for *EGShares India Infrastructure ET. The fund currently has a performance rating of D- (Weak) based on an annualized return of 0.00% over the last three years and a total return of 28.28% year to date 2012. Factored into the performance evaluation is an expense ratio of 0.85% (very low).

The fund's risk rating is currently C (Fair). It carries a beta of 0.00, meaning the fund's expected move will be 0.0% for every 10% move in the market. Volatility, as measured by both the semi-deviation and a drawdown factor, is considered average. As of March 31, 2012, *EGShares India Infrastructure ET traded at a discount of .73% below its net asset value, which is better than its one-year historical average discount of .47%.

Richard Kang currently receives a manager quality ranking of 8 (0=worst, 99=best). This fund offers an average level of risk but investors looking for strong performance will be frustrated.

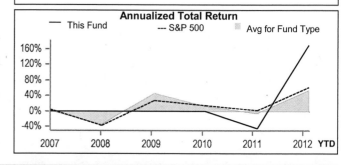

*EGShares India Small Cap ETF (SCIN)

E+   **Very Weak**

Fund Family: ALPS Advisors Inc
Fund Type: Foreign
Inception Date: July 7, 2010

Data Date	Investment Rating	Net Assets ($Mil)	Price	Perfor-mance Rating/Pts	Total Return Y-T-D	Risk Rating/Pts
3-12	E+	26.90	14.49	E+ / 0.9	29.61%	C- / 4.2
2011	E	17.00	11.18	E- / 0	4.11%	C- / 4.1

Major Rating Factors:
Very poor performance is the major factor driving the E+ (Very Weak) TheStreet.com Investment Rating for *EGShares India Small Cap ETF. The fund currently has a performance rating of E+ (Very Weak) based on an annualized return of 0.00% over the last three years and a total return of 29.61% year to date 2012. Factored into the performance evaluation is an expense ratio of 0.90% (low).

The fund's risk rating is currently C- (Fair). It carries a beta of 0.00, meaning the fund's expected move will be 0.0% for every 10% move in the market. Volatility, as measured by both the semi-deviation and a drawdown factor, is considered average. As of March 31, 2012, *EGShares India Small Cap ETF traded at a premium of .69% above its net asset value, which is worse than its one-year historical average premium of .15%.

Richard Kang currently receives a manager quality ranking of 8 (0=worst, 99=best). This fund offers an average level of risk but investors looking for strong performance will be frustrated.

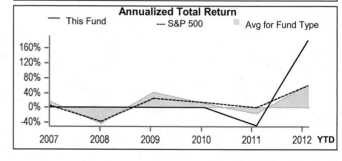

*ELEMENTS MLCX Biofuels Tot Ret (FUE)   D-   Weak

Fund Family: Swedish Export Credit Corporation
Fund Type: Energy/Natural Resources
Inception Date: February 5, 2008

Data Date	Investment Rating	Net Assets ($Mil)	Price	Performance Rating/Pts	Total Return Y-T-D	Risk Rating/Pts
3-12	D-	1.86	11.38	D+ / 2.9	5.37%	C / 4.6
2011	D	2.40	10.80	C- / 3.9	-2.78%	C / 4.6
2010	C+	2.50	11.35	A+ / 9.7	27.82%	D+ / 2.6
2009	C	1.59	8.50	B / 8.1	25.00%	D+ / 2.8

Major Rating Factors:
Disappointing performance is the major factor driving the D- (Weak) TheStreet.com Investment Rating for *ELEMENTS MLCX Biofuels Tot Ret. The fund currently has a performance rating of D+ (Weak) based on an annualized return of 13.27% over the last three years and a total return of 5.37% year to date 2012. Factored into the performance evaluation is an expense ratio of 0.75% (very low).

The fund's risk rating is currently C (Fair). It carries a beta of 0.72, meaning the fund's expected move will be 7.2% for every 10% move in the market. Volatility, as measured by both the semi-deviation and a drawdown factor, is considered average. As of March 31, 2012, *ELEMENTS MLCX Biofuels Tot Ret traded at a premium of 2.15% above its net asset value, which is worse than its one-year historical average discount of .38%.

This fund has been team managed for 4 years and currently receives a manager quality ranking of 73 (0=worst, 99=best). This fund offers an average level of risk but investors looking for strong performance will be frustrated.

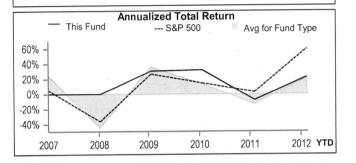

Annualized Total Return

---

*ELEMENTS MLCX Grains Idx Tot Ret (GRU)   E+   Very Weak

Fund Family: Swedish Export Credit Corporation
Fund Type: Energy/Natural Resources
Inception Date: February 5, 2008

Data Date	Investment Rating	Net Assets ($Mil)	Price	Performance Rating/Pts	Total Return Y-T-D	Risk Rating/Pts
3-12	E+	15.58	6.40	D- / 1.2	2.40%	C- / 4.1
2011	E+	17.90	6.25	D / 1.6	-1.84%	C- / 4.0
2010	C+	18.50	7.24	A+ / 9.7	27.24%	D / 2.2
2009	E	5.37	5.71	D / 1.8	-11.88%	D+ / 2.6

Major Rating Factors:
Disappointing performance is the major factor driving the E+ (Very Weak) TheStreet.com Investment Rating for *ELEMENTS MLCX Grains Idx Tot Ret. The fund currently has a performance rating of D- (Weak) based on an annualized return of 2.06% over the last three years and a total return of 2.40% year to date 2012. Factored into the performance evaluation is an expense ratio of 0.75% (very low).

The fund's risk rating is currently C- (Fair). It carries a beta of 0.81, meaning the fund's expected move will be 8.1% for every 10% move in the market. Volatility, as measured by both the semi-deviation and a drawdown factor, is considered average. As of March 31, 2012, *ELEMENTS MLCX Grains Idx Tot Ret traded at a premium of 5.96% above its net asset value, which is worse than its one-year historical average premium of .05%.

This fund has been team managed for 4 years and currently receives a manager quality ranking of 15 (0=worst, 99=best). This fund offers an average level of risk but investors looking for strong performance will be frustrated.

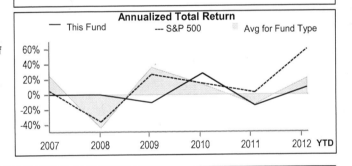

Annualized Total Return

---

*ELEMENTS RIC Energy Total Return (RJN)   D-   Weak

Fund Family: Swedish Export Credit Corporation
Fund Type: Energy/Natural Resources
Inception Date: October 17, 2007

Data Date	Investment Rating	Net Assets ($Mil)	Price	Performance Rating/Pts	Total Return Y-T-D	Risk Rating/Pts
3-12	D-	53.46	7.08	D+ / 2.8	5.36%	C / 4.4
2011	D	75.90	6.72	C / 4.5	3.72%	C / 4.4
2010	E-	56.60	6.38	E+ / 0.7	0.00%	D- / 1.3
2009	D+	38.41	6.35	C+ / 6.7	17.59%	D / 1.6

Major Rating Factors:
Disappointing performance is the major factor driving the D- (Weak) TheStreet.com Investment Rating for *ELEMENTS RIC Energy Total Return. The fund currently has a performance rating of D+ (Weak) based on an annualized return of 12.14% over the last three years and a total return of 5.36% year to date 2012. Factored into the performance evaluation is an expense ratio of 0.75% (very low).

The fund's risk rating is currently C (Fair). It carries a beta of 0.88, meaning the fund's expected move will be 8.8% for every 10% move in the market. Volatility, as measured by both the semi-deviation and a drawdown factor, is considered average. As of March 31, 2012, *ELEMENTS RIC Energy Total Return traded at a premium of .43% above its net asset value, which is worse than its one-year historical average premium of .05%.

This fund has been team managed for 5 years and currently receives a manager quality ranking of 30 (0=worst, 99=best). This fund offers an average level of risk but investors looking for strong performance will be frustrated.

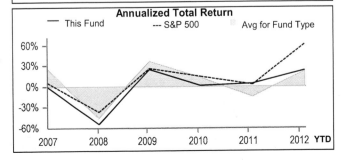

Annualized Total Return

*ELEMENTS RIC Index Agri Total Re (RJA)

E+   **Very Weak**

Fund Family: Swedish Export Credit Corporation
Fund Type: Energy/Natural Resources
Inception Date: October 17, 2007

Data Date	Investment Rating	Net Assets ($Mil)	Price	Performance Rating/Pts	Total Return Y-T-D	Risk Rating/Pts
3-12	E+	302.91	9.13	D / 1.6	2.01%	C / 4.5
2011	D-	420.40	8.95	D / 2.1	-0.56%	C / 4.5
2010	C-	408.50	10.67	C+ / 6.8	34.05%	D+ / 2.6
2009	D+	244.95	7.94	C+ / 5.6	4.75%	D+ / 2.8

Major Rating Factors:
Disappointing performance is the major factor driving the E+ (Very Weak) TheStreet.com Investment Rating for *ELEMENTS RIC Index Agri Total Re. The fund currently has a performance rating of D (Weak) based on an annualized return of 7.59% over the last three years and a total return of 2.01% year to date 2012. Factored into the performance evaluation is an expense ratio of 0.75% (very low).

The fund's risk rating is currently C (Fair). It carries a beta of 0.62, meaning the fund's expected move will be 6.2% for every 10% move in the market. Volatility, as measured by both the semi-deviation and a drawdown factor, is considered average. As of March 31, 2012, *ELEMENTS RIC Index Agri Total Re traded at a premium of 2.82% above its net asset value, which is worse than its one-year historical average discount of .05%.

This fund has been team managed for 5 years and currently receives a manager quality ranking of 31 (0=worst, 99=best). This fund offers an average level of risk but investors looking for strong performance will be frustrated.

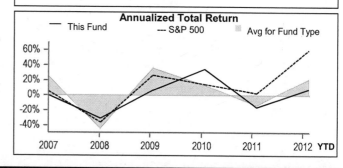

*ELEMENTS RIC Index Total Return (RJI)

D-   **Weak**

Fund Family: Swedish Export Credit Corporation
Fund Type: Energy/Natural Resources
Inception Date: October 17, 2007

Data Date	Investment Rating	Net Assets ($Mil)	Price	Performance Rating/Pts	Total Return Y-T-D	Risk Rating/Pts
3-12	D-	510.91	8.95	D+ / 2.7	5.12%	C / 4.6
2011	D	666.30	8.51	C- / 3.8	1.88%	C / 4.6
2010	E+	566.30	9.16	D+ / 2.5	16.24%	D / 2.1
2009	C-	303.18	7.84	B / 7.8	21.74%	D+ / 2.3

Major Rating Factors:
Disappointing performance is the major factor driving the D- (Weak) TheStreet.com Investment Rating for *ELEMENTS RIC Index Total Return. The fund currently has a performance rating of D+ (Weak) based on an annualized return of 12.88% over the last three years and a total return of 5.12% year to date 2012. Factored into the performance evaluation is an expense ratio of 0.75% (very low).

The fund's risk rating is currently C (Fair). It carries a beta of 0.76, meaning the fund's expected move will be 7.6% for every 10% move in the market. Volatility, as measured by both the semi-deviation and a drawdown factor, is considered average. As of March 31, 2012, *ELEMENTS RIC Index Total Return traded at a premium of 1.36% above its net asset value, which is worse than its one-year historical average discount of .02%.

This fund has been team managed for 5 years and currently receives a manager quality ranking of 42 (0=worst, 99=best). This fund offers an average level of risk but investors looking for strong performance will be frustrated.

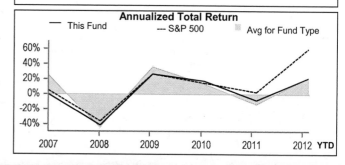

*ELEMENTS RIC Metals Total Return (RJZ)

D-   **Weak**

Fund Family: Swedish Export Credit Corporation
Fund Type: Energy/Natural Resources
Inception Date: October 17, 2007

Data Date	Investment Rating	Net Assets ($Mil)	Price	Performance Rating/Pts	Total Return Y-T-D	Risk Rating/Pts
3-12	D-	57.91	10.95	C- / 3.4	7.93%	C / 4.6
2011	D+	46.30	10.15	C / 4.8	1.03%	C / 4.6
2010	C	57.20	12.25	B / 8.1	23.36%	D+ / 2.5
2009	C+	46.75	9.90	A+ / 9.6	64.45%	D+ / 2.7

Major Rating Factors: *ELEMENTS RIC Metals Total Return receives a TheStreet.com Investment Rating of D- (Weak). The fund currently has a performance rating of C- (Fair) based on an annualized return of 17.15% over the last three years and a total return of 7.93% year to date 2012. Factored into the performance evaluation is an expense ratio of 0.75% (very low).

The fund's risk rating is currently C (Fair). It carries a beta of 0.78, meaning the fund's expected move will be 7.8% for every 10% move in the market. Volatility, as measured by both the semi-deviation and a drawdown factor, is considered average. As of March 31, 2012, *ELEMENTS RIC Metals Total Return traded at a premium of .64% above its net asset value, which is worse than its one-year historical average discount of .17%.

This fund has been team managed for 5 years and currently receives a manager quality ranking of 70 (0=worst, 99=best). If you desire an average level of risk, then this fund may be an option.

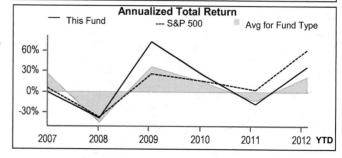

*Energy Select Sector SPDR (XLE)   C-   Fair

Fund Family: SSgA Funds Management Inc
Fund Type: Energy/Natural Resources
Inception Date: December 16, 1998

Data Date	Investment Rating	Net Assets ($Mil)	Price	Performance Rating/Pts	Total Return Y-T-D	Risk Rating/Pts
3-12	C-	7,884.28	71.75	C- / 4.0	4.20%	B- / 7.5
2011	C	6,717.60	69.13	C / 5.3	1.89%	B- / 7.1
2010	C	8,385.10	68.25	C / 5.1	21.81%	C+ / 5.6
2009	C-	5,219.00	57.01	C- / 4.1	16.02%	C+ / 5.9

Major Rating Factors: Middle of the road best describes *Energy Select Sector SPDR whose TheStreet.com Investment Rating is currently a C- (Fair). The fund currently has a performance rating of C- (Fair) based on an annualized return of 17.97% over the last three years and a total return of 4.20% year to date 2012. Factored into the performance evaluation is an expense ratio of 0.19% (very low).

The fund's risk rating is currently B- (Good). It carries a beta of 1.06, meaning that its performance tracks fairly well with that of the overall stock market. Volatility, as measured by both the semi-deviation and a drawdown factor, is considered low. As of March 31, 2012, *Energy Select Sector SPDR traded at a discount of .01% below its net asset value, which is better than its one-year historical average premium of .01%.

John A. Tucker has been running the fund for 14 years and currently receives a manager quality ranking of 48 (0=worst, 99=best). If you desire an average level of risk, then this fund may be an option.

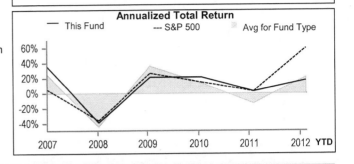

*ETFS Physical Asian Gold Shares (AGOL)   C-   Fair

Fund Family: ETF Securities USA LLC
Fund Type: Precious Metals
Inception Date: January 11, 2011

Data Date	Investment Rating	Net Assets ($Mil)	Price	Performance Rating/Pts	Total Return Y-T-D	Risk Rating/Pts
3-12	C-	79.30	164.75	C- / 3.3	5.67%	B / 8.0

Major Rating Factors: Middle of the road best describes *ETFS Physical Asian Gold Shares whose TheStreet.com Investment Rating is currently a C- (Fair). The fund currently has a performance rating of C- (Fair) based on an annualized return of 0.00% over the last three years and a total return of 5.67% year to date 2012. Factored into the performance evaluation is an expense ratio of 0.39% (very low).

The fund's risk rating is currently B (Good). It carries a beta of 0.00, meaning the fund's expected move will be 0.0% for every 10% move in the market. Volatility, as measured by both the semi-deviation and a drawdown factor, is considered low. As of March 31, 2012, *ETFS Physical Asian Gold Shares traded at a discount of .13% below its net asset value, which is better than its one-year historical average discount of .10%.

This fund has been team managed for 1 year and currently receives a manager quality ranking of 54 (0=worst, 99=best). If you desire an average level of risk, then this fund may be an option.

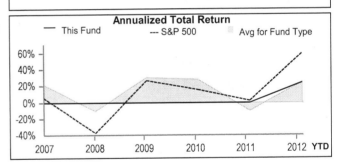

*ETFS Physical Palladium Shares (PALL)   D-   Weak

Fund Family: ETF Securities USA LLC
Fund Type: Precious Metals
Inception Date: January 7, 2010

Data Date	Investment Rating	Net Assets ($Mil)	Price	Performance Rating/Pts	Total Return Y-T-D	Risk Rating/Pts
3-12	D-	530.99	64.47	E+ / 0.9	-0.15%	C+ / 6.6
2011	D-	373.90	64.57	E+ / 0.8	-5.68%	C+ / 6.6

Major Rating Factors:
Very poor performance is the major factor driving the D- (Weak) TheStreet.com Investment Rating for *ETFS Physical Palladium Shares. The fund currently has a performance rating of E+ (Very Weak) based on an annualized return of 0.00% over the last three years and a total return of -0.15% year to date 2012. Factored into the performance evaluation is an expense ratio of 0.60% (very low).

The fund's risk rating is currently C+ (Fair). It carries a beta of 0.00, meaning the fund's expected move will be 0.0% for every 10% move in the market. Volatility, as measured by both the semi-deviation and a drawdown factor, is considered low. As of March 31, 2012, *ETFS Physical Palladium Shares traded at a premium of .37% above its net asset value.

This fund has been team managed for 2 years and currently receives a manager quality ranking of 6 (0=worst, 99=best). This fund offers only a moderate level of risk but investors looking for strong performance are still waiting.

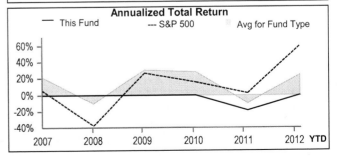

*ETFS Physical Platinum Shares (PPLT)

D   **Weak**

Fund Family: ETF Securities USA LLC
Fund Type: Precious Metals
Inception Date: January 7, 2010

Major Rating Factors:

Disappointing performance is the major factor driving the D (Weak) TheStreet.com Investment Rating for *ETFS Physical Platinum Shares. The fund currently has a performance rating of D (Weak) based on an annualized return of 0.00% over the last three years and a total return of 17.34% year to date 2012. Factored into the performance evaluation is an expense ratio of 0.60% (very low).

The fund's risk rating is currently B- (Good). It carries a beta of 0.00, meaning the fund's expected move will be 0.0% for every 10% move in the market. Volatility, as measured by both the semi-deviation and a drawdown factor, is considered low. As of March 31, 2012, *ETFS Physical Platinum Shares traded at a discount of .06% below its net asset value, which is better than its one-year historical average premium of .13%.

This fund has been team managed for 2 years and currently receives a manager quality ranking of 7 (0=worst, 99=best). This fund offers only a moderate level of risk but investors looking for strong performance are still waiting.

Data Date	Investment Rating	Net Assets ($Mil)	Price	Performance Rating/Pts	Total Return Y-T-D	Risk Rating/Pts
3-12	D	886.01	161.72	D / 1.7	17.34%	B- / 7.0
2011	D-	607.30	137.82	E+ / 0.7	0.54%	B- / 7.0

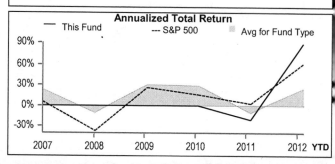

Annualized Total Return

*ETFS Physical PM Basket Shares (GLTR)

D   **Weak**

Fund Family: ETF Securities USA LLC
Fund Type: Precious Metals
Inception Date: October 21, 2010

Major Rating Factors:

Disappointing performance is the major factor driving the D (Weak) TheStreet.com Investment Rating for *ETFS Physical PM Basket Shares. The fund currently has a performance rating of D (Weak) based on an annualized return of 0.00% over the last three years and a total return of 10.46% year to date 2012. Factored into the performance evaluation is an expense ratio of 0.60% (very low).

The fund's risk rating is currently C+ (Fair). It carries a beta of 0.00, meaning the fund's expected move will be 0.0% for every 10% move in the market. Volatility, as measured by both the semi-deviation and a drawdown factor, is considered low. As of March 31, 2012, *ETFS Physical PM Basket Shares traded at a premium of .08% above its net asset value, which is better than its one-year historical average premium of .14%.

This is team managed and currently receives a manager quality ranking of 9 (0=worst, 99=best). This fund offers only a moderate level of risk but investors looking for strong performance are still waiting.

Data Date	Investment Rating	Net Assets ($Mil)	Price	Performance Rating/Pts	Total Return Y-T-D	Risk Rating/Pts
3-12	D	214.08	95.27	D / 1.9	10.46%	C+ / 6.7
2011	D	0.00	86.25	D / 1.9	3.81%	C+ / 6.6

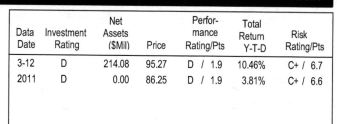

Annualized Total Return

*ETFS Physical Silver Shares (SIVR)

E+   **Very Weak**

Fund Family: ETF Securities USA LLC
Fund Type: Global
Inception Date: July 20, 2009

Major Rating Factors:

Disappointing performance is the major factor driving the E+ (Very Weak) TheStreet.com Investment Rating for *ETFS Physical Silver Shares. The fund currently has a performance rating of D- (Weak) based on an annualized return of 0.00% over the last three years and a total return of 16.46% year to date 2012. Factored into the performance evaluation is an expense ratio of 0.30% (very low).

The fund's risk rating is currently C (Fair). It carries a beta of 0.00, meaning the fund's expected move will be 0.0% for every 10% move in the market. Volatility, as measured by both the semi-deviation and a drawdown factor, is considered average. As of March 31, 2012, *ETFS Physical Silver Shares traded at a discount of .37% below its net asset value, which is better than its one-year historical average premium of .12%.

This fund has been team managed for 3 years and currently receives a manager quality ranking of 22 (0=worst, 99=best). This fund offers an average level of risk but investors looking for strong performance will be frustrated.

Data Date	Investment Rating	Net Assets ($Mil)	Price	Performance Rating/Pts	Total Return Y-T-D	Risk Rating/Pts
3-12	E+	687.08	32.05	D- / 1.2	16.46%	C / 5.1
2011	D-	534.30	27.52	D- / 1.1	3.52%	C / 5.2
2010	A+	391.80	30.73	A+ / 9.9	82.16%	B / 8.4

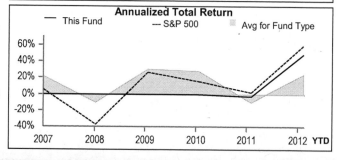
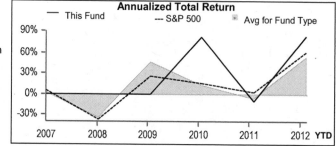

Annualized Total Return

*ETFS Physical Swiss Gold Shares (SGOL)

C-   **Fair**

Fund Family: ETF Securities USA LLC
Fund Type: Precious Metals
Inception Date: September 8, 2009

Major Rating Factors: Middle of the road best describes *ETFS Physical Swiss Gold Shares whose TheStreet.com Investment Rating is currently a C- (Fair). The fund currently has a performance rating of C- (Fair) based on an annualized return of 0.00% over the last three years and a total return of 6.65% year to date 2012. Factored into the performance evaluation is an expense ratio of 0.39% (very low).

The fund's risk rating is currently B (Good). It carries a beta of 0.00, meaning the fund's expected move will be 0.0% for every 10% move in the market. Volatility, as measured by both the semi-deviation and a drawdown factor, is considered low. As of March 31, 2012, *ETFS Physical Swiss Gold Shares traded at a premium of .38% above its net asset value, which is worse than its one-year historical average premium of .17%.

This fund has been team managed for 3 years and currently receives a manager quality ranking of 56 (0=worst, 99=best). If you desire an average level of risk, then this fund may be an option.

Data Date	Investment Rating	Net Assets ($Mil)	Price	Performance Rating/Pts	Total Return Y-T-D	Risk Rating/Pts
3-12	C-	1,972.13	165.23	C- / 3.7	6.65%	B / 8.2
2011	C+	1,677.40	154.93	C / 5.3	3.40%	B / 8.2
2010	A+	1,087.70	141.39	A / 9.3	29.23%	B / 8.4

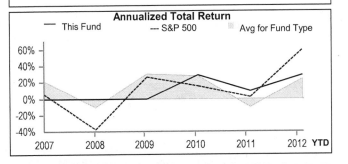

*ETFS Physical WM Basket Shares (WITE)

D-   **Weak**

Fund Family: ETF Securities USA LLC
Fund Type: Precious Metals
Inception Date: December 2, 2010

Major Rating Factors:
Disappointing performance is the major factor driving the D- (Weak) TheStreet.com Investment Rating for *ETFS Physical WM Basket Shares. The fund currently has a performance rating of D- (Weak) based on an annualized return of 0.00% over the last three years and a total return of 14.69% year to date 2012. Factored into the performance evaluation is an expense ratio of 0.60% (very low).

The fund's risk rating is currently C (Fair). It carries a beta of 0.00, meaning the fund's expected move will be 0.0% for every 10% move in the market. Volatility, as measured by both the semi-deviation and a drawdown factor, is considered average. As of March 31, 2012, *ETFS Physical WM Basket Shares traded at a discount of .11% below its net asset value, which is better than its one-year historical average premium of .06%.

This fund has been team managed for 2 years and currently receives a manager quality ranking of 3 (0=worst, 99=best). This fund offers an average level of risk but investors looking for strong performance will be frustrated.

Data Date	Investment Rating	Net Assets ($Mil)	Price	Performance Rating/Pts	Total Return Y-T-D	Risk Rating/Pts
3-12	D-	47.85	53.55	D- / 1.3	14.69%	C / 5.2
2011	E+	39.80	46.69	E+ / 0.9	1.62%	C / 5.1

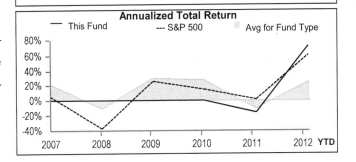

*FactorShares Gold Bull S&P 500 B (FSG)

E+   **Very Weak**

Fund Family: Factor Capital Management LLC
Fund Type: Precious Metals
Inception Date: February 22, 2011

Major Rating Factors:
Very poor performance is the major factor driving the E+ (Very Weak) TheStreet.com Investment Rating for *FactorShares Gold Bull S&P 500 B. The fund currently has a performance rating of E (Very Weak) based on an annualized return of 0.00% over the last three years and a total return of -12.50% year to date 2012. Factored into the performance evaluation is an expense ratio of 0.75% (very low).

The fund's risk rating is currently C (Fair). It carries a beta of 0.00, meaning the fund's expected move will be 0.0% for every 10% move in the market. Volatility, as measured by both the semi-deviation and a drawdown factor, is considered average. As of March 31, 2012, *FactorShares Gold Bull S&P 500 B traded at a price exactly equal to its net asset value, which is better than its one-year historical average premium of .21%.

This fund has been team managed for 1 year and currently receives a manager quality ranking of 5 (0=worst, 99=best). This fund offers an average level of risk but investors looking for strong performance will be frustrated.

Data Date	Investment Rating	Net Assets ($Mil)	Price	Performance Rating/Pts	Total Return Y-T-D	Risk Rating/Pts
3-12	E+	10.53	23.38	E / 0.5	-12.50%	C / 4.5

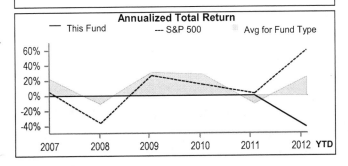

*FactorShares Oil Bull S&P 500 Be (FOL)

E+ **Very Weak**

Fund Family: Factor Capital Management LLC
Fund Type: Growth and Income
Inception Date: February 22, 2011

Data Date	Investment Rating	Net Assets ($Mil)	Price	Perfor-mance Rating/Pts	Total Return Y-T-D	Risk Rating/Pts
3-12	E+	2.01	17.34	E / 0.4	-19.26%	C / 4.9

Major Rating Factors:
Very poor performance is the major factor driving the E+ (Very Weak) TheStreet.com Investment Rating for *FactorShares Oil Bull S&P 500 Be. The fund currently has a performance rating of E (Very Weak) based on an annualized return of 0.00% over the last three years and a total return of -19.26% year to date 2012. Factored into the performance evaluation is an expense ratio of 0.75% (very low).

The fund's risk rating is currently C (Fair). It carries a beta of 0.00, meaning the fund's expected move will be 0.0% for every 10% move in the market. Volatility, as measured by both the semi-deviation and a drawdown factor, is considered average. As of March 31, 2012, *FactorShares Oil Bull S&P 500 Be traded at a premium of 1.88% above its net asset value, which is worse than its one-year historical average premium of .09%.

This fund has been team managed for 1 year and currently receives a manager quality ranking of 1 (0=worst, 99=best). This fund offers an average level of risk but investors looking for strong performance will be frustrated.

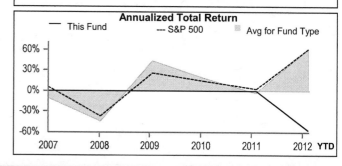
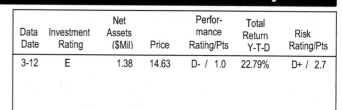

*FactorShares S&P 500 Bull Tbd Be (FSE)

E **Very Weak**

Fund Family: Factor Capital Management LLC
Fund Type: Growth and Income
Inception Date: February 22, 2011

Data Date	Investment Rating	Net Assets ($Mil)	Price	Perfor-mance Rating/Pts	Total Return Y-T-D	Risk Rating/Pts
3-12	E	1.38	14.63	D- / 1.0	22.79%	D+ / 2.7

Major Rating Factors: *FactorShares S&P 500 Bull Tbd Be has adopted a risky asset allocation strategy and currently receives an overall TheStreet.com Investment Rating of E (Very Weak). The fund has an above average level of volatility, as measured by both semi-deviation and drawdown factors. It carries a beta of 0.00, meaning the fund's expected move will be 0.0% for every 10% move in the market. As of March 31, 2012, *FactorShares S&P 500 Bull Tbd Be traded at a premium of .07% above its net asset value, which is worse than its one-year historical average discount of .14%. Unfortunately, the high level of risk (D+, Weak) failed to pay off as investors endured poor performance.

The fund's performance rating is currently D- (Weak). It has registered an annualized return of 0.00% over the last three years and is up 22.79% year to date 2012. Factored into the performance evaluation is an expense ratio of 0.75% (very low).

This fund has been team managed for 1 year and currently receives a manager quality ranking of 0 (0=worst, 99=best). If you can tolerate high levels of risk in the hope of improved future returns, holding this fund may be an option.

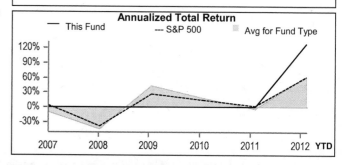
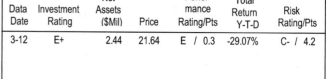

*FactorShares Tbd Bull S&P 500 Be (FSA)

E+ **Very Weak**

Fund Family: Factor Capital Management LLC
Fund Type: Growth
Inception Date: February 22, 2011

Data Date	Investment Rating	Net Assets ($Mil)	Price	Perfor-mance Rating/Pts	Total Return Y-T-D	Risk Rating/Pts
3-12	E+	2.44	21.64	E / 0.3	-29.07%	C- / 4.2

Major Rating Factors:
Very poor performance is the major factor driving the E+ (Very Weak) TheStreet.com Investment Rating for *FactorShares Tbd Bull S&P 500 Be. The fund currently has a performance rating of E (Very Weak) based on an annualized return of 0.00% over the last three years and a total return of -29.07% year to date 2012. Factored into the performance evaluation is an expense ratio of 0.75% (very low).

The fund's risk rating is currently C- (Fair). It carries a beta of 0.00, meaning the fund's expected move will be 0.0% for every 10% move in the market. Volatility, as measured by both the semi-deviation and a drawdown factor, is considered average. As of March 31, 2012, *FactorShares Tbd Bull S&P 500 Be traded at a premium of 2.03% above its net asset value, which is worse than its one-year historical average premium of .05%.

This fund has been team managed for 1 year and currently receives a manager quality ranking of 89 (0=worst, 99=best). This fund offers an average level of risk but investors looking for strong performance will be frustrated.

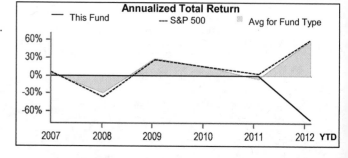

*Fidelity Nasdaq Comp Tracker Sto (ONEQ)   C+   Fair

Fund Family: Fidelity Management & Research Comp
Fund Type: Growth
Inception Date: September 25, 2003

Data Date	Investment Rating	Net Assets ($Mil)	Price	Perfor-mance Rating/Pts	Total Return Y-T-D	Risk Rating/Pts
3-12	C+	187.23	121.86	B- / 7.4	18.49%	B- / 7.5
2011	C+	154.00	103.02	C+ / 6.4	2.39%	B- / 7.2
2010	C+	156.80	104.77	C+ / 6.3	17.79%	C / 5.5
2009	C-	90.90	89.60	C- / 4.2	39.92%	C+ / 5.6

Major Rating Factors: Strong performance is the major factor driving the C+ (Fair) TheStreet.com Investment Rating for *Fidelity Nasdaq Comp Tracker Sto. The fund currently has a performance rating of B- (Good) based on an annualized return of 25.15% over the last three years and a total return of 18.49% year to date 2012. Factored into the performance evaluation is an expense ratio of 0.35% (very low).

The fund's risk rating is currently B- (Good). It carries a beta of 1.12, meaning it is expected to move 11.2% for every 10% move in the market. Volatility, as measured by both the semi-deviation and a drawdown factor, is considered low. As of March 31, 2012, *Fidelity Nasdaq Comp Tracker Sto traded at a premium of .05% above its net asset value, which is worse than its one-year historical average discount of .05%.

Patrick J. Waddell has been running the fund for 8 years and currently receives a manager quality ranking of 50 (0=worst, 99=best). If you desire only a moderate level of risk and strong performance, then this fund is an excellent option.

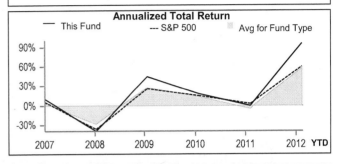

*Financial Select Sector SPDR (XLF)   C   Fair

Fund Family: SSgA Funds Management Inc
Fund Type: Financial Services
Inception Date: December 16, 1998

Data Date	Investment Rating	Net Assets ($Mil)	Price	Perfor-mance Rating/Pts	Total Return Y-T-D	Risk Rating/Pts
3-12	C	7,395.04	15.80	C / 5.4	21.89%	B- / 7.5
2011	D	5,373.30	13.00	D+ / 2.7	3.04%	C+ / 6.6
2010	D-	7,470.50	15.95	E+ / 0.8	11.91%	C- / 4.1
2009	E+	7,494.11	14.40	E+ / 0.6	16.19%	C- / 4.2

Major Rating Factors: Middle of the road best describes *Financial Select Sector SPDR whose TheStreet.com Investment Rating is currently a C (Fair). The fund currently has a performance rating of C (Fair) based on an annualized return of 19.34% over the last three years and a total return of 21.89% year to date 2012. Factored into the performance evaluation is an expense ratio of 0.19% (very low).

The fund's risk rating is currently B- (Good). It carries a beta of 1.07, meaning that its performance tracks fairly well with that of the overall stock market. Volatility, as measured by both the semi-deviation and a drawdown factor, is considered low. As of March 31, 2012, *Financial Select Sector SPDR traded at a price exactly equal to its net asset value, which is worse than its one-year historical average discount of .01%.

John A. Tucker has been running the fund for 14 years and currently receives a manager quality ranking of 36 (0=worst, 99=best). If you desire an average level of risk, then this fund may be an option.

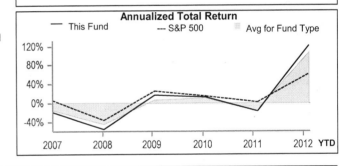

*First Trust AMEX Biotechnology (FBT)   B   Good

Fund Family: First Trust Advisors LP
Fund Type: Health
Inception Date: June 19, 2006

Data Date	Investment Rating	Net Assets ($Mil)	Price	Perfor-mance Rating/Pts	Total Return Y-T-D	Risk Rating/Pts
3-12	B	233.89	42.27	B+ / 8.5	29.42%	C+ / 6.9
2011	C	183.00	32.66	C+ / 5.8	6.52%	C+ / 6.2
2010	A	201.20	39.11	A- / 9.1	36.94%	C+ / 6.0
2009	C+	60.38	28.56	C+ / 6.9	42.94%	C+ / 6.2

Major Rating Factors: Strong performance is the major factor driving the B (Good) TheStreet.com Investment Rating for *First Trust AMEX Biotechnology. The fund currently has a performance rating of B+ (Good) based on an annualized return of 30.77% over the last three years and a total return of 29.42% year to date 2012. Factored into the performance evaluation is an expense ratio of 0.60% (very low).

The fund's risk rating is currently C+ (Fair). It carries a beta of 1.16, meaning it is expected to move 11.6% for every 10% move in the market. Volatility, as measured by both the semi-deviation and a drawdown factor, is considered low. As of March 31, 2012, *First Trust AMEX Biotechnology traded at a premium of .07% above its net asset value, which is worse than its one-year historical average premium of .03%.

Jonathan Erickson has been running the fund for 6 years and currently receives a manager quality ranking of 55 (0=worst, 99=best). If you desire only a moderate level of risk and strong performance, then this fund is an excellent option.

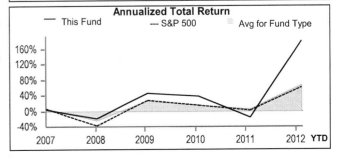

*First Trust BICK Index (BICK)

D-   **Weak**

Fund Family: First Trust Advisors LP
Fund Type: Foreign
Inception Date: April 12, 2010

Major Rating Factors:

Disappointing performance is the major factor driving the D- (Weak) TheStreet.com Investment Rating for *First Trust BICK Index. The fund currently has a performance rating of D- (Weak) based on an annualized return of 0.00% over the last three years and a total return of 15.87% year to date 2012. Factored into the performance evaluation is an expense ratio of 0.64% (very low).

The fund's risk rating is currently C+ (Fair). It carries a beta of 0.00, meaning the fund's expected move will be 0.0% for every 10% move in the market. Volatility, as measured by both the semi-deviation and a drawdown factor, is considered low. As of March 31, 2012, *First Trust BICK Index traded at a premium of .46% above its net asset value, which is worse than its one-year historical average premium of .02%.

Jonathan Erickson has been running the fund for 2 years and currently receives a manager quality ranking of 11 (0=worst, 99=best). This fund offers only a moderate level of risk but investors looking for strong performance are still waiting.

Data Date	Investment Rating	Net Assets ($Mil)	Price	Performance Rating/Pts	Total Return Y-T-D	Risk Rating/Pts
3-12	D-	52.74	26.28	D- / 1.2	15.87%	C+ / 6.0
2011	D-	43.30	22.68	E / 0.5	2.07%	C+ / 6.0

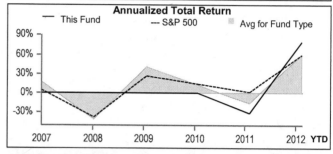

*First Trust Consumer Dis AlphaDE (FXD)

A-   **Excellent**

Fund Family: First Trust Advisors LP
Fund Type: Income
Inception Date: May 8, 2007

Major Rating Factors:

Strong performance is the major factor driving the A- (Excellent) TheStreet.com Investment Rating for *First Trust Consumer Dis AlphaDE. The fund currently has a performance rating of B+ (Good) based on an annualized return of 34.09% over the last three years and a total return of 15.17% year to date 2012. Factored into the performance evaluation is an expense ratio of 0.70% (very low).

The fund's risk rating is currently B (Good). It carries a beta of 1.38, meaning it is expected to move 13.8% for every 10% move in the market. Volatility, as measured by both the semi-deviation and a drawdown factor, is considered low. As of March 31, 2012, *First Trust Consumer Dis AlphaDE traded at a premium of .09% above its net asset value, which is worse than its one-year historical average premium of .01%.

Jonathan Erickson has been running the fund for 5 years and currently receives a manager quality ranking of 64 (0=worst, 99=best). If you desire only a moderate level of risk and strong performance, then this fund is an excellent option.

Data Date	Investment Rating	Net Assets ($Mil)	Price	Performance Rating/Pts	Total Return Y-T-D	Risk Rating/Pts
3-12	A-	567.91	22.85	B+ / 8.9	15.17%	B / 8.0
2011	B	461.80	19.84	B / 7.9	1.26%	B- / 7.8
2010	B	401.00	19.78	B / 8.2	32.01%	C / 5.1
2009	A	6.39	15.06	A / 9.3	51.60%	C / 5.3

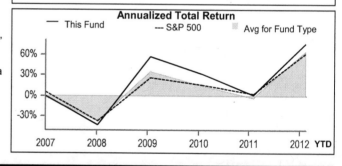

*First Trust Consumer Stap AlphaD (FXG)

B-   **Good**

Fund Family: First Trust Advisors LP
Fund Type: Income
Inception Date: May 8, 2007

Major Rating Factors: *First Trust Consumer Stap AlphaD receives a TheStreet.com Investment Rating of B- (Good). The fund currently has a performance rating of C+ (Fair) based on an annualized return of 24.09% over the last three years and a total return of 5.92% year to date 2012. Factored into the performance evaluation is an expense ratio of 0.70% (very low).

The fund's risk rating is currently B (Good). It carries a beta of 0.67, meaning the fund's expected move will be 6.7% for every 10% move in the market. Volatility, as measured by both the semi-deviation and a drawdown factor, is considered low. As of March 31, 2012, *First Trust Consumer Stap AlphaD traded at a premium of .08% above its net asset value, which is worse than its one-year historical average premium of .05%.

Jonathan Erickson has been running the fund for 5 years and currently receives a manager quality ranking of 83 (0=worst, 99=best). If you desire an average level of risk, then this fund may be an option.

Data Date	Investment Rating	Net Assets ($Mil)	Price	Performance Rating/Pts	Total Return Y-T-D	Risk Rating/Pts
3-12	B-	325.12	25.05	C+ / 6.2	5.92%	B / 8.7
2011	B-	206.70	23.65	C+ / 6.7	-0.63%	B / 8.4
2010	B+	33.70	21.10	B- / 7.0	19.75%	C+ / 6.9
2009	A+	9.02	17.82	B / 8.0	24.83%	C+ / 6.9

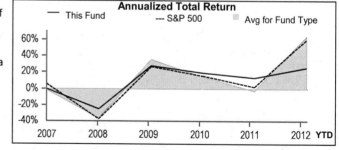

*First Trust DJ Glb Sel Div Idx F (FGD)

C+   **Fair**

Fund Family: First Trust Advisors LP
Fund Type: Global
Inception Date: November 21, 2007

Major Rating Factors: Middle of the road best describes *First Trust DJ Glb Sel Div Idx F whose TheStreet.com Investment Rating is currently a C+ (Fair). The fund currently has a performance rating of C+ (Fair) based on an annualized return of 25.84% over the last three years and a total return of 7.83% year to date 2012. Factored into the performance evaluation is an expense ratio of 0.60% (very low).

The fund's risk rating is currently B (Good). It carries a beta of 1.03, meaning that its performance tracks fairly well with that of the overall stock market. Volatility, as measured by both the semi-deviation and a drawdown factor, is considered low. As of March 31, 2012, *First Trust DJ Glb Sel Div Idx F traded at a premium of .51% above its net asset value, which is worse than its one-year historical average premium of .21%.

Jonathan Erickson has been running the fund for 5 years and currently receives a manager quality ranking of 86 (0=worst, 99=best). If you desire an average level of risk, then this fund may be an option.

Data Date	Investment Rating	Net Assets ($Mil)	Price	Performance Rating/Pts	Total Return Y-T-D	Risk Rating/Pts
3-12	C+	170.31	23.59	C+ / 6.5	7.83%	B / 8.2
2011	C+	124.60	21.97	C+ / 6.3	-1.09%	B- / 7.9
2010	D	59.80	23.67	D+ / 2.9	12.56%	C / 5.0
2009	A	28.79	22.04	A / 9.4	58.09%	C / 5.1

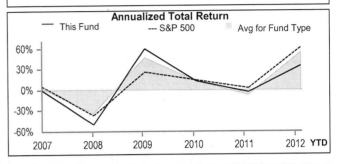

---

*First Trust Dow Jones Internet I (FDN)

C+   **Fair**

Fund Family: First Trust Advisors LP
Fund Type: Growth
Inception Date: June 19, 2006

Major Rating Factors: Strong performance is the major factor driving the C+ (Fair) TheStreet.com Investment Rating for *First Trust Dow Jones Internet I. The fund currently has a performance rating of B+ (Good) based on an annualized return of 32.11% over the last three years and a total return of 14.86% year to date 2012. Factored into the performance evaluation is an expense ratio of 0.60% (very low).

The fund's risk rating is currently C+ (Fair). It carries a beta of 1.24, meaning it is expected to move 12.4% for every 10% move in the market. Volatility, as measured by both the semi-deviation and a drawdown factor, is considered low. As of March 31, 2012, *First Trust Dow Jones Internet I traded at a premium of .08% above its net asset value, which is worse than its one-year historical average premium of .01%.

Jonathan Erickson has been running the fund for 6 years and currently receives a manager quality ranking of 69 (0=worst, 99=best). If you desire only a moderate level of risk and strong performance, then this fund is an excellent option.

Data Date	Investment Rating	Net Assets ($Mil)	Price	Performance Rating/Pts	Total Return Y-T-D	Risk Rating/Pts
3-12	C+	524.34	37.10	B+ / 8.4	14.86%	C+ / 6.4
2011	C+	519.70	32.30	B / 8.1	1.11%	C+ / 6.2
2010	B-	589.50	34.32	B+ / 8.7	36.72%	C- / 4.0
2009	C+	33.65	25.13	B- / 7.3	73.19%	C / 4.6

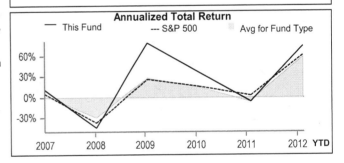

---

*First Trust Dow Jones Sel Micro (FDM)

C   **Fair**

Fund Family: First Trust Advisors LP
Fund Type: Growth
Inception Date: September 27, 2005

Major Rating Factors: Middle of the road best describes *First Trust Dow Jones Sel Micro whose TheStreet.com Investment Rating is currently a C (Fair). The fund currently has a performance rating of C (Fair) based on an annualized return of 21.49% over the last three years and a total return of 12.35% year to date 2012. Factored into the performance evaluation is an expense ratio of 0.60% (very low).

The fund's risk rating is currently B- (Good). It carries a beta of 1.39, meaning it is expected to move 13.9% for every 10% move in the market. Volatility, as measured by both the semi-deviation and a drawdown factor, is considered low. As of March 31, 2012, *First Trust Dow Jones Sel Micro traded at a premium of .49% above its net asset value, which is worse than its one-year historical average discount of .01%.

Jonathan Erickson has been running the fund for 7 years and currently receives a manager quality ranking of 18 (0=worst, 99=best). If you desire an average level of risk, then this fund may be an option.

Data Date	Investment Rating	Net Assets ($Mil)	Price	Performance Rating/Pts	Total Return Y-T-D	Risk Rating/Pts
3-12	C	56.29	22.56	C / 5.5	12.35%	B- / 7.2
2011	C-	52.30	20.08	C / 4.5	1.84%	B- / 7.0
2010	C+	153.00	22.15	C+ / 6.9	25.58%	C+ / 5.7
2009	D	14.44	17.71	D- / 1.5	20.02%	C / 5.4

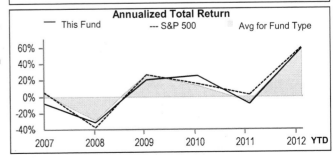

*First Trust Energy AlphaDEX (FXN)

C-   **Fair**

Fund Family: First Trust Advisors LP
Fund Type: Energy/Natural Resources
Inception Date: May 8, 2007

Major Rating Factors: Middle of the road best describes *First Trust Energy AlphaDEX whose TheStreet.com Investment Rating is currently a C- (Fair). The fund currently has a performance rating of C (Fair) based on an annualized return of 23.76% over the last three years and a total return of 4.61% year to date 2012. Factored into the performance evaluation is an expense ratio of 0.70% (very low).

The fund's risk rating is currently C+ (Fair). It carries a beta of 1.38, meaning it is expected to move 13.8% for every 10% move in the market. Volatility, as measured by both the semi-deviation and a drawdown factor, is considered low. As of March 31, 2012, *First Trust Energy AlphaDEX traded at a price exactly equal to its net asset value, which is worse than its one-year historical average discount of .02%.

Jonathan Erickson has been running the fund for 5 years and currently receives a manager quality ranking of 50 (0=worst, 99=best). If you desire an average level of risk, then this fund may be an option.

Data Date	Investment Rating	Net Assets ($Mil)	Price	Performance Rating/Pts	Total Return Y-T-D	Risk Rating/Pts
3-12	C-	95.77	20.20	C / 5.1	4.61%	C+ / 6.8
2011	C	90.80	19.31	C+ / 6.0	3.00%	C+ / 6.6
2010	C	86.60	21.17	C+ / 5.9	27.63%	C / 4.3
2009	B+	9.53	16.69	A- / 9.2	40.63%	C / 4.6

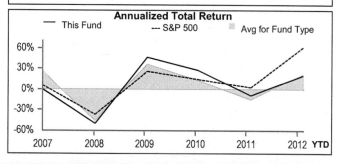

Annualized Total Return
— This Fund   --- S&P 500   ▨ Avg for Fund Type

*First Trust Enhanced 130/30 Lg C (JFT)

D   **Weak**

Fund Family: JP Morgan & Chase Co
Fund Type: Income
Inception Date: May 21, 2008

Major Rating Factors: *First Trust Enhanced 130/30 Lg C receives a TheStreet.com Investment Rating of D (Weak). The fund currently has a performance rating of C- (Fair) based on an annualized return of 16.93% over the last three years and a total return of 8.77% year to date 2012. Factored into the performance evaluation is an expense ratio of 0.95% (low).

The fund's risk rating is currently C (Fair). It carries a beta of 0.57, meaning the fund's expected move will be 5.7% for every 10% move in the market. Volatility, as measured by both the semi-deviation and a drawdown factor, is considered average. As of March 31, 2012, *First Trust Enhanced 130/30 Lg C traded at a discount of 5.02% below its net asset value, which is better than its one-year historical average discount of 2.48%.

This fund has been team managed for 4 years and currently receives a manager quality ranking of 71 (0=worst, 99=best). If you desire an average level of risk, then this fund may be an option.

Data Date	Investment Rating	Net Assets ($Mil)	Price	Performance Rating/Pts	Total Return Y-T-D	Risk Rating/Pts
3-12	D	3.71	35.59	C- / 3.7	8.77%	C / 4.6
2010	C+	4.90	34.33	A / 9.5	31.33%	D / 2.1
2009	D	0.00	26.14	C / 5.1	14.15%	D+ / 2.3

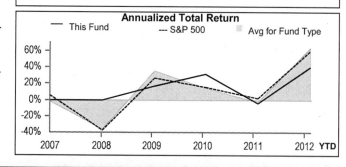

Annualized Total Return
— This Fund   --- S&P 500   ▨ Avg for Fund Type

*First Trust Financial AlphaDEX (FXO)

B   **Good**

Fund Family: First Trust Advisors LP
Fund Type: Financial Services
Inception Date: May 8, 2007

Major Rating Factors: Strong performance is the major factor driving the B (Good) TheStreet.com Investment Rating for *First Trust Financial AlphaDEX. The fund currently has a performance rating of B- (Good) based on an annualized return of 26.98% over the last three years and a total return of 17.29% year to date 2012. Factored into the performance evaluation is an expense ratio of 0.70% (very low).

The fund's risk rating is currently B- (Good). It carries a beta of 0.92, meaning that its performance tracks fairly well with that of the overall stock market. Volatility, as measured by both the semi-deviation and a drawdown factor, is considered low. As of March 31, 2012, *First Trust Financial AlphaDEX traded at a premium of .06% above its net asset value.

Jonathan Erickson has been running the fund for 5 years and currently receives a manager quality ranking of 80 (0=worst, 99=best). If you desire only a moderate level of risk and strong performance, then this fund is an excellent option.

Data Date	Investment Rating	Net Assets ($Mil)	Price	Performance Rating/Pts	Total Return Y-T-D	Risk Rating/Pts
3-12	B	125.69	15.47	B- / 7.5	17.29%	B- / 7.9
2011	C	77.80	13.19	C / 4.9	1.67%	B- / 7.3
2010	C-	330.00	14.61	C / 4.9	19.25%	C / 5.1
2009	B+	8.30	12.42	B+ / 8.7	30.64%	C / 5.0

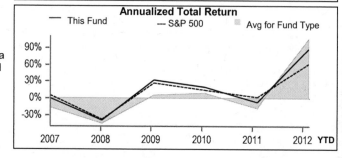

Annualized Total Return
— This Fund   --- S&P 500   ▨ Avg for Fund Type

*First Trust FTSE EPRA/NAREIT Glb (FFR)

C+ **Fair**

Fund Family: First Trust Advisors LP
Fund Type: Growth and Income
Inception Date: August 27, 2007

Data Date	Investment Rating	Net Assets ($Mil)	Price	Performance Rating/Pts	Total Return Y-T-D	Risk Rating/Pts
3-12	C+	79.79	35.70	C+ / 6.8	11.98%	B- / 7.4
2011	C-	71.70	32.00	C / 4.6	-0.37%	C+ / 6.1
2010	D	59.20	34.93	C- / 3.1	19.23%	C- / 4.2
2009	B-	15.24	30.52	B+ / 8.8	33.85%	C- / 4.1

Major Rating Factors: Middle of the road best describes *First Trust FTSE EPRA/NAREIT Glb whose TheStreet.com Investment Rating is currently a C+ (Fair). The fund currently has a performance rating of C+ (Fair) based on an annualized return of 25.79% over the last three years and a total return of 11.98% year to date 2012. Factored into the performance evaluation is an expense ratio of 0.60% (very low).

The fund's risk rating is currently B- (Good). It carries a beta of 1.30, meaning it is expected to move 13.0% for every 10% move in the market. Volatility, as measured by both the semi-deviation and a drawdown factor, is considered low. As of March 31, 2012, *First Trust FTSE EPRA/NAREIT Glb traded at a discount of .28% below its net asset value, which is better than its one-year historical average premium of .04%.

Daniel J. Lindquist has been running the fund for 5 years and currently receives a manager quality ranking of 44 (0=worst, 99=best). If you desire an average level of risk, then this fund may be an option.

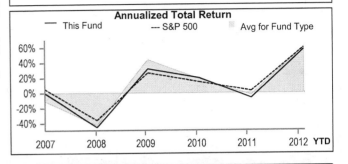

*First Trust Health Care AlphaDEX (FXH)

B+ **Good**

Fund Family: First Trust Advisors LP
Fund Type: Health
Inception Date: May 8, 2007

Data Date	Investment Rating	Net Assets ($Mil)	Price	Performance Rating/Pts	Total Return Y-T-D	Risk Rating/Pts
3-12	B+	568.14	30.81	B / 8.1	13.61%	B / 8.4
2011	B	401.20	27.12	B- / 7.5	1.70%	B- / 7.8
2010	A-	59.00	25.69	B / 7.6	19.02%	C+ / 6.8
2009	A+	15.02	21.61	A / 9.3	48.93%	C+ / 6.8

Major Rating Factors: Strong performance is the major factor driving the B+ (Good) TheStreet.com Investment Rating for *First Trust Health Care AlphaDEX. The fund currently has a performance rating of B (Good) based on an annualized return of 30.23% over the last three years and a total return of 13.61% year to date 2012. Factored into the performance evaluation is an expense ratio of 0.70% (very low).

The fund's risk rating is currently B (Good). It carries a beta of 0.78, meaning the fund's expected move will be 7.8% for every 10% move in the market. Volatility, as measured by both the semi-deviation and a drawdown factor, is considered low. As of March 31, 2012, *First Trust Health Care AlphaDEX traded at a premium of .10% above its net asset value, which is worse than its one-year historical average premium of .05%.

Jonathan Erickson has been running the fund for 5 years and currently receives a manager quality ranking of 86 (0=worst, 99=best). If you desire only a moderate level of risk and strong performance, then this fund is an excellent option.

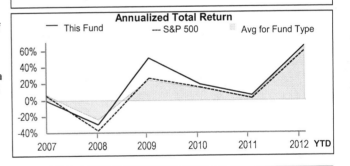

*First Trust Industrials AlphaDEX (FXR)

C+ **Fair**

Fund Family: First Trust Advisors LP
Fund Type: Income
Inception Date: May 8, 2007

Data Date	Investment Rating	Net Assets ($Mil)	Price	Performance Rating/Pts	Total Return Y-T-D	Risk Rating/Pts
3-12	C+	124.31	19.35	C+ / 6.9	12.70%	B- / 7.5
2011	C	54.20	17.17	C+ / 5.8	2.27%	B- / 7.2
2010	C	43.20	18.48	C+ / 6.2	26.08%	C / 4.3
2009	A-	5.41	14.75	A- / 9.1	39.18%	C / 5.1

Major Rating Factors: Middle of the road best describes *First Trust Industrials AlphaDEX whose TheStreet.com Investment Rating is currently a C+ (Fair). The fund currently has a performance rating of C+ (Fair) based on an annualized return of 25.84% year to date 2012. Factored into the performance evaluation is an expense ratio of 0.70% (very low).

The fund's risk rating is currently B- (Good). It carries a beta of 1.35, meaning it is expected to move 13.5% for every 10% move in the market. Volatility, as measured by both the semi-deviation and a drawdown factor, is considered low. As of March 31, 2012, *First Trust Industrials AlphaDEX traded at a premium of .05% above its net asset value, which is worse than its one-year historical average premium of .01%.

This fund has been team managed for 5 years and currently receives a manager quality ranking of 30 (0=worst, 99=best). If you desire an average level of risk, then this fund may be an option.

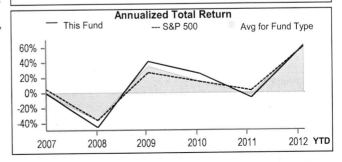

*First Trust ISE Chindia Index Fu (FNI)   C-   Fair

Fund Family: First Trust Advisors LP
Fund Type: Income
Inception Date: May 8, 2007

Major Rating Factors: Middle of the road best describes *First Trust ISE Chindia Index Fu whose TheStreet.com Investment Rating is currently a C- (Fair). The fund currently has a performance rating of C (Fair) based on an annualized return of 22.68% over the last three years and a total return of 20.68% year to date 2012. Factored into the performance evaluation is an expense ratio of 0.60% (very low).

The fund's risk rating is currently C+ (Fair). It carries a beta of 1.53, meaning it is expected to move 15.3% for every 10% move in the market. Volatility, as measured by both the semi-deviation and a drawdown factor, is considered low. As of March 31, 2012, *First Trust ISE Chindia Index Fu traded at a discount of .05% below its net asset value, which is worse than its one-year historical average discount of .12%.

Jonathan Erickson has been running the fund for 5 years and currently receives a manager quality ranking of 16 (0=worst, 99=best). If you desire an average level of risk, then this fund may be an option.

Data Date	Investment Rating	Net Assets ($Mil)	Price	Perfor-mance Rating/Pts	Total Return Y-T-D	Risk Rating/Pts
3-12	C-	97.76	21.90	C / 5.3	20.68%	C+ / 6.3
2011	D+	79.30	18.15	C / 4.3	3.31%	C+ / 5.9
2010	D	176.30	25.02	C- / 3.7	18.17%	C- / 4.1
2009	C+	67.11	21.34	A+ / 9.6	71.88%	D+ / 2.9

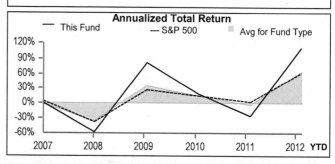

*First Trust ISE Glb Eng & Constr (FLM)   D   Weak

Fund Family: First Trust Advisors LP
Fund Type: Global
Inception Date: October 13, 2008

Major Rating Factors: *First Trust ISE Glb Eng & Constr receives a TheStreet.com Investment Rating of D (Weak). The fund currently has a performance rating of C- (Fair) based on an annualized return of 13.40% over the last three years and a total return of 14.25% year to date 2012. Factored into the performance evaluation is an expense ratio of 0.70% (very low).

The fund's risk rating is currently C+ (Fair). It carries a beta of 1.13, meaning it is expected to move 11.3% for every 10% move in the market. Volatility, as measured by both the semi-deviation and a drawdown factor, is considered low. As of March 31, 2012, *First Trust ISE Glb Eng & Constr traded at a premium of .32% above its net asset value, which is worse than its one-year historical average discount of .16%.

Jonathan Erickson has been running the fund for 4 years and currently receives a manager quality ranking of 27 (0=worst, 99=best). If you desire an average level of risk, then this fund may be an option.

Data Date	Investment Rating	Net Assets ($Mil)	Price	Perfor-mance Rating/Pts	Total Return Y-T-D	Risk Rating/Pts
3-12	D	37.78	41.13	C- / 3.0	14.25%	C+ / 6.8
2011	D	25.30	36.03	D+ / 2.3	0.70%	C+ / 6.7
2010	A	37.90	44.71	A / 9.4	17.63%	C+ / 6.6
2009	A	35.78	38.64	B / 7.6	22.86%	C+ / 6.8

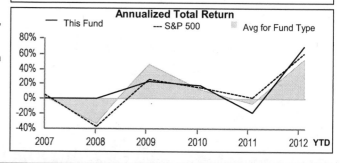

*First Trust ISE Glb Wind Energy (FAN)   E+   Very Weak

Fund Family: First Trust Advisors LP
Fund Type: Energy/Natural Resources
Inception Date: June 16, 2008

Major Rating Factors:
Very poor performance is the major factor driving the E+ (Very Weak) TheStreet.com Investment Rating for *First Trust ISE Glb Wind Energy. The fund currently has a performance rating of E+ (Very Weak) based on an annualized return of -10.88% over the last three years and a total return of -1.14% year to date 2012. Factored into the performance evaluation is an expense ratio of 0.60% (very low).

The fund's risk rating is currently C (Fair). It carries a beta of 1.01, meaning that its performance tracks fairly well with that of the overall stock market. Volatility, as measured by both the semi-deviation and a drawdown factor, is considered average. As of March 31, 2012, *First Trust ISE Glb Wind Energy traded at a discount of .76% below its net asset value, which is better than its one-year historical average discount of .54%.

Jonathan Erickson has been running the fund for 4 years and currently receives a manager quality ranking of 5 (0=worst, 99=best). This fund offers an average level of risk but investors looking for strong performance will be frustrated.

Data Date	Investment Rating	Net Assets ($Mil)	Price	Perfor-mance Rating/Pts	Total Return Y-T-D	Risk Rating/Pts
3-12	E+	28.91	7.83	E+ / 0.7	-1.14%	C / 5.1
2011	D-	29.20	7.92	D- / 1.0	-1.64%	C / 5.5
2010	E+	51.80	10.25	E / 0.5	-31.11%	C- / 3.8
2009	C-	100.85	15.02	C+ / 5.9	19.40%	C- / 3.6

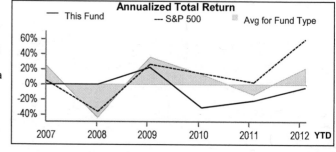

*First Trust ISE Global Copper Id (CU)   E+   Very Weak

Fund Family: First Trust Advisors LP
Fund Type: Precious Metals
Inception Date: March 11, 2010

Data Date	Investment Rating	Net Assets ($Mil)	Price	Performance Rating/Pts	Total Return Y-T-D	Risk Rating/Pts
3-12	E+	60.84	31.17	E+ / 0.8	6.42%	C / 4.9
2011	E+	51.30	29.29	E / 0.5	2.90%	C / 4.9

Major Rating Factors:
Very poor performance is the major factor driving the E+ (Very Weak) TheStreet.com Investment Rating for *First Trust ISE Global Copper Id. The fund currently has a performance rating of E+ (Very Weak) based on an annualized return of 0.00% over the last three years and a total return of 6.42% year to date 2012. Factored into the performance evaluation is an expense ratio of 0.70% (very low).

The fund's risk rating is currently C (Fair). It carries a beta of 0.00, meaning the fund's expected move will be 0.0% for every 10% move in the market. Volatility, as measured by both the semi-deviation and a drawdown factor, is considered average. As of March 31, 2012, *First Trust ISE Global Copper Id traded at a discount of .38% below its net asset value, which is better than its one-year historical average discount of .21%.

Jonathan Erickson has been running the fund for 2 years and currently receives a manager quality ranking of 1 (0=worst, 99=best). This fund offers an average level of risk but investors looking for strong performance will be frustrated.

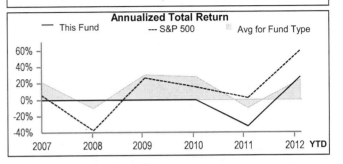

*First Trust ISE Global Platinum (PLTM)   E+   Very Weak

Fund Family: First Trust Advisors LP
Fund Type: Precious Metals
Inception Date: March 11, 2010

Data Date	Investment Rating	Net Assets ($Mil)	Price	Performance Rating/Pts	Total Return Y-T-D	Risk Rating/Pts
3-12	E+	11.65	19.33	E / 0.5	8.35%	C / 4.7
2011	E+	7.20	17.84	E- / 0.1	4.20%	C / 4.7

Major Rating Factors:
Very poor performance is the major factor driving the E+ (Very Weak) TheStreet.com Investment Rating for *First Trust ISE Global Platinum. The fund currently has a performance rating of E (Very Weak) based on an annualized return of 0.00% over the last three years and a total return of 8.35% year to date 2012. Factored into the performance evaluation is an expense ratio of 0.70% (very low).

The fund's risk rating is currently C (Fair). It carries a beta of 0.00, meaning the fund's expected move will be 0.0% for every 10% move in the market. Volatility, as measured by both the semi-deviation and a drawdown factor, is considered average. As of March 31, 2012, *First Trust ISE Global Platinum traded at a discount of .21% below its net asset value, which is better than its one-year historical average discount of .12%.

Jonathan Erickson has been running the fund for 2 years and currently receives a manager quality ranking of 0 (0=worst, 99=best). This fund offers an average level of risk but investors looking for strong performance will be frustrated.

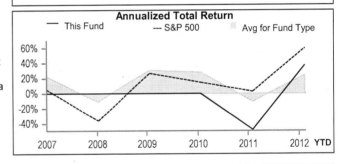

*First Trust ISE Water Index Fund (FIW)   C   Fair

Fund Family: First Trust Advisors LP
Fund Type: Income
Inception Date: May 8, 2007

Data Date	Investment Rating	Net Assets ($Mil)	Price	Performance Rating/Pts	Total Return Y-T-D	Risk Rating/Pts
3-12	C	66.41	23.98	C / 5.2	15.46%	B- / 7.8
2011	C-	58.00	20.77	C- / 4.2	1.76%	C+ / 6.7
2010	C+	53.10	22.17	C+ / 6.2	19.90%	C / 5.4
2009	B-	32.94	18.63	B / 7.6	17.77%	C / 5.3

Major Rating Factors: Middle of the road best describes *First Trust ISE Water Index Fund whose TheStreet.com Investment Rating is currently a C (Fair). The fund currently has a performance rating of C (Fair) based on an annualized return of 19.32% over the last three years and a total return of 15.46% year to date 2012. Factored into the performance evaluation is an expense ratio of 0.60% (very low).

The fund's risk rating is currently B- (Good). It carries a beta of 1.15, meaning it is expected to move 11.5% for every 10% move in the market. Volatility, as measured by both the semi-deviation and a drawdown factor, is considered low. As of March 31, 2012, *First Trust ISE Water Index Fund traded at a premium of .21% above its net asset value, which is worse than its one-year historical average discount of .03%.

Jonathan Erickson has been running the fund for 5 years and currently receives a manager quality ranking of 24 (0=worst, 99=best). If you desire an average level of risk, then this fund may be an option.

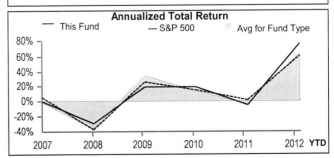

*First Trust ISE-Revere Natural G (FCG)

D **Weak**

Fund Family: First Trust Advisors LP
Fund Type: Income
Inception Date: May 8, 2007

Major Rating Factors:
Disappointing performance is the major factor driving the D (Weak) TheStreet.com Investment Rating for *First Trust ISE-Revere Natural G. The fund currently has a performance rating of D+ (Weak) based on an annualized return of 16.70% over the last three years and a total return of -2.86% year to date 2012. Factored into the performance evaluation is an expense ratio of 0.60% (very low).

The fund's risk rating is currently C+ (Fair). It carries a beta of 1.53, meaning it is expected to move 15.3% for every 10% move in the market. Volatility, as measured by both the semi-deviation and a drawdown factor, is considered low. As of March 31, 2012, *First Trust ISE-Revere Natural G traded at a discount of .23% below its net asset value, which is better than its one-year historical average discount of .02%.

Jonathan Erickson has been running the fund for 5 years and currently receives a manager quality ranking of 12 (0=worst, 99=best). This fund offers only a moderate level of risk but investors looking for strong performance are still waiting.

Data Date	Investment Rating	Net Assets ($Mil)	Price	Performance Rating/Pts	Total Return Y-T-D	Risk Rating/Pts
3-12	D	359.39	17.67	D+ / 2.9	-2.86%	C+ / 6.9
2011	C-	346.50	18.19	C / 4.5	2.53%	C+ / 6.7
2010	D	396.90	19.68	C- / 3.4	12.23%	C / 4.5
2009	B+	85.84	17.59	A- / 9.2	40.85%	C / 4.7

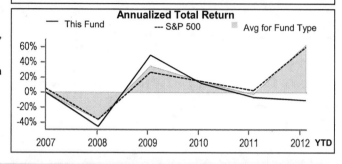
Annualized Total Return

*First Trust Large Cap Gro AlphaD (FTC)

C **Fair**

Fund Family: First Trust Advisors LP
Fund Type: Growth
Inception Date: May 8, 2007

Major Rating Factors: Middle of the road best describes *First Trust Large Cap Gro AlphaD whose TheStreet.com Investment Rating is currently a C (Fair). The fund currently has a performance rating of C (Fair) based on an annualized return of 21.06% over the last three years and a total return of 9.64% year to date 2012. Factored into the performance evaluation is an expense ratio of 0.70% (very low).

The fund's risk rating is currently B (Good). It carries a beta of 1.01, meaning that its performance tracks fairly well with that of the overall stock market. Volatility, as measured by both the semi-deviation and a drawdown factor, is considered low. As of March 31, 2012, *First Trust Large Cap Gro AlphaD traded at a premium of .07% above its net asset value, which is worse than its one-year historical average premium of .02%.

Jonathan Erickson has been running the fund for 5 years and currently receives a manager quality ranking of 38 (0=worst, 99=best). If you desire an average level of risk, then this fund may be an option.

Data Date	Investment Rating	Net Assets ($Mil)	Price	Performance Rating/Pts	Total Return Y-T-D	Risk Rating/Pts
3-12	C	130.14	30.13	C / 5.2	9.64%	B / 8.0
2011	C	125.10	27.48	C / 5.1	1.06%	B- / 7.6
2010	C	82.50	28.48	C / 5.1	23.63%	C+ / 5.7
2009	A-	13.96	23.17	B+ / 8.5	26.59%	C+ / 5.8

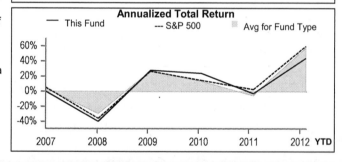
Annualized Total Return

*First Trust Large Cap Val AlphaD (FTA)

B **Good**

Fund Family: First Trust Advisors LP
Fund Type: Income
Inception Date: May 8, 2007

Major Rating Factors: Strong performance is the major factor driving the B (Good) TheStreet.com Investment Rating for *First Trust Large Cap Val AlphaD. The fund currently has a performance rating of B- (Good) based on an annualized return of 27.05% over the last three years and a total return of 12.59% year to date 2012. Factored into the performance evaluation is an expense ratio of 0.70% (very low).

The fund's risk rating is currently B (Good). It carries a beta of 1.15, meaning it is expected to move 11.5% for every 10% move in the market. Volatility, as measured by both the semi-deviation and a drawdown factor, is considered low. As of March 31, 2012, *First Trust Large Cap Val AlphaD traded at a premium of .13% above its net asset value, which is worse than its one-year historical average premium of .08%.

Jonathan Erickson has been running the fund for 5 years and currently receives a manager quality ranking of 64 (0=worst, 99=best). If you desire only a moderate level of risk and strong performance, then this fund is an excellent option.

Data Date	Investment Rating	Net Assets ($Mil)	Price	Performance Rating/Pts	Total Return Y-T-D	Risk Rating/Pts
3-12	B	218.44	29.78	B- / 7.4	12.59%	B / 8.4
2011	C+	184.90	26.45	C+ / 6.4	1.89%	B- / 7.8
2010	C+	92.50	26.45	C+ / 6.5	18.69%	C+ / 5.7
2009	A	18.14	22.60	B+ / 8.9	36.27%	C+ / 5.6

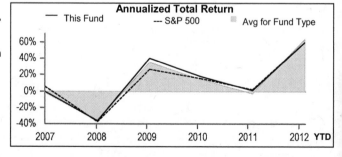
Annualized Total Return

*First Trust Lrg Cap Core AlphaDE (FEX)   C+   Fair

Fund Family: First Trust Advisors LP
Fund Type: Growth and Income
Inception Date: May 8, 2007

Data Date	Investment Rating	Net Assets ($Mil)	Price	Performance Rating/Pts	Total Return Y-T-D	Risk Rating/Pts
3-12	C+	323.07	30.27	C+ / 6.5	11.41%	B / 8.2
2011	C+	267.70	27.17	C+ / 6.1	1.58%	B- / 7.9
2010	C+	128.00	27.58	C+ / 5.9	20.67%	C+ / 5.8
2009	A	13.72	23.08	B+ / 8.7	32.18%	C+ / 5.9

Major Rating Factors: Middle of the road best describes *First Trust Lrg Cap Core AlphaDE whose TheStreet.com Investment Rating is currently a C+ (Fair). The fund currently has a performance rating of C+ (Fair) based on an annualized return of 24.30% over the last three years and a total return of 11.41% year to date 2012. Factored into the performance evaluation is an expense ratio of 0.70% (very low).

The fund's risk rating is currently B (Good). It carries a beta of 1.09, meaning that its performance tracks fairly well with that of the overall stock market. Volatility, as measured by both the semi-deviation and a drawdown factor, is considered low. As of March 31, 2012, *First Trust Lrg Cap Core AlphaDE traded at a premium of .03% above its net asset value, which is better than its one-year historical average premium of .08%.

Jonathan Erickson has been running the fund for 5 years and currently receives a manager quality ranking of 53 (0=worst, 99=best). If you desire an average level of risk, then this fund may be an option.

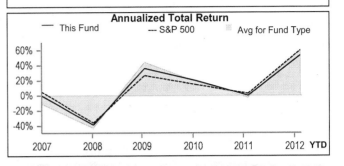

*First Trust Materials AlphaDEX (FXZ)   B   Good

Fund Family: First Trust Advisors LP
Fund Type: Income
Inception Date: May 8, 2007

Data Date	Investment Rating	Net Assets ($Mil)	Price	Performance Rating/Pts	Total Return Y-T-D	Risk Rating/Pts
3-12	B	158.52	25.20	B+ / 8.4	18.70%	B- / 7.3
2011	C+	121.10	21.23	B- / 7.0	4.00%	B- / 7.1
2010	C+	417.20	23.76	B / 7.6	28.28%	C / 4.7
2009	A	9.92	18.84	A / 9.4	53.07%	C / 5.0

Major Rating Factors: Strong performance is the major factor driving the B (Good) TheStreet.com Investment Rating for *First Trust Materials AlphaDEX. The fund currently has a performance rating of B+ (Good) based on an annualized return of 30.83% over the last three years and a total return of 18.70% year to date 2012. Factored into the performance evaluation is an expense ratio of 0.70% (very low).

The fund's risk rating is currently B- (Good). It carries a beta of 1.55, meaning it is expected to move 15.5% for every 10% move in the market. Volatility, as measured by both the semi-deviation and a drawdown factor, is considered low. As of March 31, 2012, *First Trust Materials AlphaDEX traded at a premium of .12% above its net asset value, which is worse than its one-year historical average discount of .02%.

Jonathan Erickson has been running the fund for 5 years and currently receives a manager quality ranking of 32 (0=worst, 99=best). If you desire only a moderate level of risk and strong performance, then this fund is an excellent option.

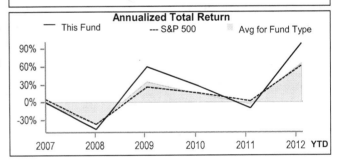

*First Trust Mid Cap Core AlphaDE (FNX)   B   Good

Fund Family: First Trust Advisors LP
Fund Type: Growth
Inception Date: May 8, 2007

Data Date	Investment Rating	Net Assets ($Mil)	Price	Performance Rating/Pts	Total Return Y-T-D	Risk Rating/Pts
3-12	B	310.32	36.69	B / 7.8	12.48%	B / 8.0
2011	B-	244.70	32.62	B- / 7.3	1.47%	B- / 7.8
2010	B+	151.20	32.51	B / 7.8	26.64%	C+ / 5.7
2009	A+	8.80	25.80	A- / 9.1	46.78%	C+ / 6.0

Major Rating Factors: Strong performance is the major factor driving the B (Good) TheStreet.com Investment Rating for *First Trust Mid Cap Core AlphaDE. The fund currently has a performance rating of B (Good) based on an annualized return of 29.11% over the last three years and a total return of 12.48% year to date 2012. Factored into the performance evaluation is an expense ratio of 0.70% (very low).

The fund's risk rating is currently B (Good). It carries a beta of 1.24, meaning it is expected to move 12.4% for every 10% move in the market. Volatility, as measured by both the semi-deviation and a drawdown factor, is considered low. As of March 31, 2012, *First Trust Mid Cap Core AlphaDE traded at a premium of .03% above its net asset value, which is in line with its one-year historical average premium of .03%.

Jonathan Erickson has been running the fund for 5 years and currently receives a manager quality ranking of 57 (0=worst, 99=best). If you desire only a moderate level of risk and strong performance, then this fund is an excellent option.

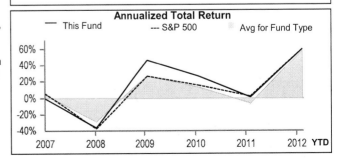

*First Trust Morningstar Div Lead (FDL)

B   **Good**

Fund Family: First Trust Advisors LP
Fund Type: Income
Inception Date: March 9, 2006

Major Rating Factors: *First Trust Morningstar Div Lead receives a TheStreet.com Investment Rating of B (Good). The fund currently has a performance rating of C+ (Fair) based on an annualized return of 24.80% over the last three years and a total return of 1.74% year to date 2012. Factored into the performance evaluation is an expense ratio of 0.45% (very low).

The fund's risk rating is currently B+ (Good). It carries a beta of 0.65, meaning the fund's expected move will be 6.5% for every 10% move in the market. Volatility, as measured by both the semi-deviation and a drawdown factor, is considered very low. As of March 31, 2012, *First Trust Morningstar Div Lead traded at a premium of .06% above its net asset value, which is better than its one-year historical average premium of .10%.

Jonathan Erickson has been running the fund for 15 years and currently receives a manager quality ranking of 86 (0=worst, 99=best). If you desire an average level of risk, then this fund may be an option.

Data Date	Investment Rating	Net Assets ($Mil)	Price	Performance Rating/Pts	Total Return Y-T-D	Risk Rating/Pts
3-12	B	471.17	17.73	C+ / 6.3	1.74%	B+ / 9.3
2011	C+	447.00	17.58	C+ / 6.2	-1.14%	B- / 7.4
2010	C-	143.30	15.94	C- / 3.5	16.19%	C / 5.4
2009	D-	40.48	14.27	D- / 1.1	12.02%	C / 5.3

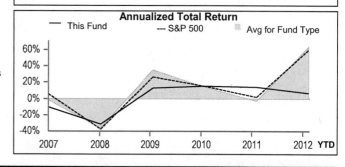

Annualized Total Return
— This Fund   --- S&P 500   ▒ Avg for Fund Type

*First Trust Multi Cap Grth Alpha (FAD)

C+   **Fair**

Fund Family: First Trust Advisors LP
Fund Type: Growth
Inception Date: May 8, 2007

Major Rating Factors: Middle of the road best describes *First Trust Multi Cap Grth Alpha whose TheStreet.com Investment Rating is currently a C+ (Fair). The fund currently has a performance rating of C+ (Fair) based on an annualized return of 23.78% over the last three years and a total return of 10.18% year to date 2012. Factored into the performance evaluation is an expense ratio of 0.70% (very low).

The fund's risk rating is currently B- (Good). It carries a beta of 1.06, meaning that its performance tracks fairly well with that of the overall stock market. Volatility, as measured by both the semi-deviation and a drawdown factor, is considered low. As of March 31, 2012, *First Trust Multi Cap Grth Alpha traded at a premium of .27% above its net asset value, which is worse than its one-year historical average discount of .01%.

Jonathan Erickson has been running the fund for 5 years and currently receives a manager quality ranking of 45 (0=worst, 99=best). If you desire an average level of risk, then this fund may be an option.

Data Date	Investment Rating	Net Assets ($Mil)	Price	Performance Rating/Pts	Total Return Y-T-D	Risk Rating/Pts
3-12	C+	27.21	32.99	C+ / 6.2	10.18%	B- / 7.9
2011	C+	25.40	29.94	C+ / 6.0	0.69%	B- / 7.5
2010	C+	18.10	30.27	C+ / 6.4	25.14%	C+ / 5.6
2009	A-	5.20	24.26	B+ / 8.6	30.89%	C+ / 5.7

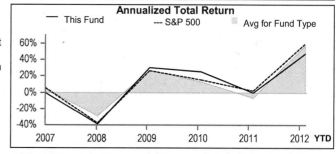

Annualized Total Return
— This Fund   --- S&P 500   ▒ Avg for Fund Type

*First Trust Multi Cap Val AlphaD (FAB)

B   **Good**

Fund Family: First Trust Advisors LP
Fund Type: Income
Inception Date: May 8, 2007

Major Rating Factors: Strong performance is the major factor driving the B (Good) TheStreet.com Investment Rating for *First Trust Multi Cap Val AlphaD. The fund currently has a performance rating of B (Good) based on an annualized return of 28.29% over the last three years and a total return of 12.35% year to date 2012. Factored into the performance evaluation is an expense ratio of 0.70% (very low).

The fund's risk rating is currently B (Good). It carries a beta of 1.23, meaning it is expected to move 12.3% for every 10% move in the market. Volatility, as measured by both the semi-deviation and a drawdown factor, is considered low. As of March 31, 2012, *First Trust Multi Cap Val AlphaD traded at a discount of .16% below its net asset value, which is better than its one-year historical average premium of .07%.

Jonathan Erickson has been running the fund for 5 years and currently receives a manager quality ranking of 61 (0=worst, 99=best). If you desire only a moderate level of risk and strong performance, then this fund is an excellent option.

Data Date	Investment Rating	Net Assets ($Mil)	Price	Performance Rating/Pts	Total Return Y-T-D	Risk Rating/Pts
3-12	B	50.64	32.00	B / 7.7	12.35%	B / 8.2
2011	B-	39.70	28.48	B- / 7.1	1.82%	B- / 7.8
2010	B	25.70	28.69	B- / 7.3	22.42%	C+ / 5.7
2009	A+	10.10	23.75	A- / 9.1	48.31%	C+ / 5.6

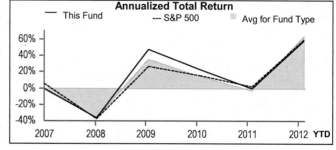

Annualized Total Return
— This Fund   --- S&P 500   ▒ Avg for Fund Type

*First Trust NASD Cln Edge Smt Gd (GRID)   D-   Weak

Fund Family: First Trust Advisors LP
Fund Type: Growth
Inception Date: November 16, 2009

Major Rating Factors:
Disappointing performance is the major factor driving the D- (Weak) TheStreet.com Investment Rating for *First Trust NASD Cln Edge Smt Gd. The fund currently has a performance rating of D- (Weak) based on an annualized return of 0.00% over the last three years and a total return of 11.47% year to date 2012. Factored into the performance evaluation is an expense ratio of 0.70% (very low).

The fund's risk rating is currently C+ (Fair). It carries a beta of 0.00, meaning the fund's expected move will be 0.0% for every 10% move in the market. Volatility, as measured by both the semi-deviation and a drawdown factor, is considered low. As of March 31, 2012, *First Trust NASD Cln Edge Smt Gd traded at a discount of .93% below its net asset value, which is better than its one-year historical average discount of .28%.

Jonathan Erickson has been running the fund for 3 years and currently receives a manager quality ranking of 3 (0=worst, 99=best). This fund offers only a moderate level of risk but investors looking for strong performance are still waiting.

Data Date	Investment Rating	Net Assets ($Mil)	Price	Performance Rating/Pts	Total Return Y-T-D	Risk Rating/Pts
3-12	D-	14.21	27.79	D- / 1.0	11.47%	C+ / 6.7
2011	D-	14.90	24.93	E+ / 0.7	0.32%	C+ / 6.7
2010	B-	28.60	31.77	C+ / 6.5	-1.06%	B- / 7.2

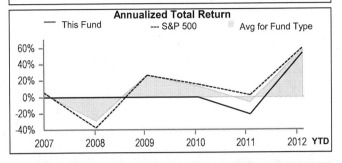

Annualized Total Return

---

*First Trust NASDAQ ABA Community (QABA)   C+   Fair

Fund Family: First Trust Advisors LP
Fund Type: Income
Inception Date: June 29, 2009

Major Rating Factors: Middle of the road best describes *First Trust NASDAQ ABA Community whose TheStreet.com Investment Rating is currently a C+ (Fair). The fund currently has a performance rating of C+ (Fair) based on an annualized return of 0.00% over the last three years and a total return of 12.96% year to date 2012. Factored into the performance evaluation is an expense ratio of 0.60% (very low).

The fund's risk rating is currently B- (Good). It carries a beta of 0.00, meaning the fund's expected move will be 0.0% for every 10% move in the market. Volatility, as measured by both the semi-deviation and a drawdown factor, is considered low. As of March 31, 2012, *First Trust NASDAQ ABA Community traded at a premium of .27% above its net asset value, which is worse than its one-year historical average discount of .02%.

Cynthia J. Clemson has been running the fund for 3 years and currently receives a manager quality ranking of 16 (0=worst, 99=best). If you desire an average level of risk, then this fund may be an option.

Data Date	Investment Rating	Net Assets ($Mil)	Price	Performance Rating/Pts	Total Return Y-T-D	Risk Rating/Pts
3-12	C+	7.33	25.94	C+ / 6.5	12.96%	B- / 7.1
2011	D+	12.60	22.96	D+ / 2.7	4.14%	B- / 7.1
2010	A	10.00	25.05	B+ / 8.7	11.73%	C+ / 6.9

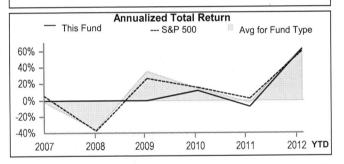

Annualized Total Return

---

*First Trust NASDAQ CEA Smartphon (FONE)   C-   Fair

Fund Family: First Trust Advisors LP
Fund Type: Global
Inception Date: February 17, 2011

Major Rating Factors: Middle of the road best describes *First Trust NASDAQ CEA Smartphon whose TheStreet.com Investment Rating is currently a C- (Fair). The fund currently has a performance rating of C- (Fair) based on an annualized return of 0.00% over the last three years and a total return of 16.53% year to date 2012. Factored into the performance evaluation is an expense ratio of 0.70% (very low).

The fund's risk rating is currently B- (Good). It carries a beta of 0.00, meaning the fund's expected move will be 0.0% for every 10% move in the market. Volatility, as measured by both the semi-deviation and a drawdown factor, is considered low. As of March 31, 2012, *First Trust NASDAQ CEA Smartphon traded at a premium of .11% above its net asset value, which is worse than its one-year historical average discount of .08%.

Jonathan Erickson has been running the fund for 1 year and currently receives a manager quality ranking of 62 (0=worst, 99=best). If you desire an average level of risk, then this fund may be an option.

Data Date	Investment Rating	Net Assets ($Mil)	Price	Performance Rating/Pts	Total Return Y-T-D	Risk Rating/Pts
3-12	C-	15.17	27.63	C- / 3.7	16.53%	B- / 7.7

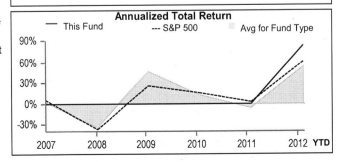

Annualized Total Return

---

*First Trust NASDAQ Cln Edg US Li (QCLN)

D- **Weak**

Fund Family: First Trust Advisors LP
Fund Type: Income
Inception Date: February 8, 2007

Major Rating Factors:
Very poor performance is the major factor driving the D- (Weak) TheStreet.com Investment Rating for *First Trust NASDAQ Cln Edg US Li. The fund currently has a performance rating of E+ (Very Weak) based on an annualized return of -2.19% over the last three years and a total return of 12.10% year to date 2012. Factored into the performance evaluation is an expense ratio of 0.60% (very low).

The fund's risk rating is currently C+ (Fair). It carries a beta of 1.71, meaning it is expected to move 17.1% for every 10% move in the market. Volatility, as measured by both the semi-deviation and a drawdown factor, is considered low. As of March 31, 2012, *First Trust NASDAQ Cln Edg US Li traded at a discount of .09% below its net asset value, which is worse than its one-year historical average discount of .17%.

Jonathan Erickson has been running the fund for 5 years and currently receives a manager quality ranking of 3 (0=worst, 99=best). This fund offers only a moderate level of risk but investors looking for strong performance are still waiting.

Data Date	Investment Rating	Net Assets ($Mil)	Price	Performance Rating/Pts	Total Return Y-T-D	Risk Rating/Pts
3-12	D-	20.27	10.75	E+ / 0.9	12.10%	C+ / 6.0
2011	D-	20.70	9.59	D- / 1.1	2.10%	C+ / 5.7
2010	E+	36.10	16.42	E+ / 0.7	2.18%	C- / 4.0
2009	C+	38.05	16.07	B+ / 8.5	34.59%	C- / 3.8

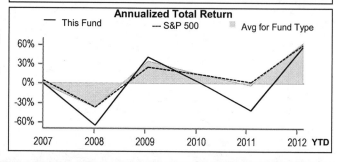

*First Trust NASDAQ-100 Equal Wei (QQEW)

B- **Good**

Fund Family: First Trust Advisors LP
Fund Type: Growth
Inception Date: April 19, 2006

Major Rating Factors: Strong performance is the major factor driving the B- (Good) TheStreet.com Investment Rating for *First Trust NASDAQ-100 Equal Wei. The fund currently has a performance rating of B- (Good) based on an annualized return of 26.38% over the last three years and a total return of 17.52% year to date 2012. Factored into the performance evaluation is an expense ratio of 0.60% (very low).

The fund's risk rating is currently B- (Good). It carries a beta of 1.19, meaning it is expected to move 11.9% for every 10% move in the market. Volatility, as measured by both the semi-deviation and a drawdown factor, is considered low. As of March 31, 2012, *First Trust NASDAQ-100 Equal Wei traded at a premium of .11% above its net asset value, which is worse than its one-year historical average premium of .01%.

Jonathan Erickson has been running the fund for 6 years and currently receives a manager quality ranking of 47 (0=worst, 99=best). If you desire only a moderate level of risk and strong performance, then this fund is an excellent option.

Data Date	Investment Rating	Net Assets ($Mil)	Price	Performance Rating/Pts	Total Return Y-T-D	Risk Rating/Pts
3-12	B-	91.84	26.97	B- / 7.4	17.52%	B- / 7.8
2011	B-	73.50	22.95	C+ / 6.9	2.66%	B- / 7.7
2010	C+	76.00	23.72	C+ / 6.9	20.10%	C / 5.5
2009	C	22.94	19.75	C / 4.6	53.21%	C+ / 5.6

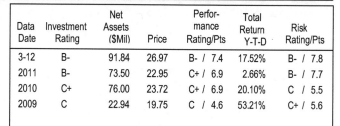

*First Trust NASDAQ-100 Ex-Tech S (QQXT)

C+ **Fair**

Fund Family: First Trust Advisors LP
Fund Type: Income
Inception Date: February 8, 2007

Major Rating Factors: Middle of the road best describes *First Trust NASDAQ-100 Ex-Tech S whose TheStreet.com Investment Rating is currently a C+ (Fair). The fund currently has a performance rating of C+ (Fair) based on an annualized return of 25.37% over the last three years and a total return of 16.17% year to date 2012. Factored into the performance evaluation is an expense ratio of 0.60% (very low).

The fund's risk rating is currently B- (Good). It carries a beta of 1.08, meaning that its performance tracks fairly well with that of the overall stock market. Volatility, as measured by both the semi-deviation and a drawdown factor, is considered low. As of March 31, 2012, *First Trust NASDAQ-100 Ex-Tech S traded at a premium of .08% above its net asset value, which is worse than its one-year historical average premium of .02%.

Jonathan Erickson has been running the fund for 6 years and currently receives a manager quality ranking of 58 (0=worst, 99=best). If you desire an average level of risk, then this fund may be an option.

Data Date	Investment Rating	Net Assets ($Mil)	Price	Performance Rating/Pts	Total Return Y-T-D	Risk Rating/Pts
3-12	C+	35.52	24.14	C+ / 6.9	16.17%	B- / 7.8
2011	C+	30.20	20.78	C+ / 6.3	2.60%	B- / 7.7
2010	C+	22.20	21.10	C+ / 5.7	19.48%	C+ / 5.7
2009	A	6.35	17.66	B+ / 8.9	40.33%	C+ / 5.8

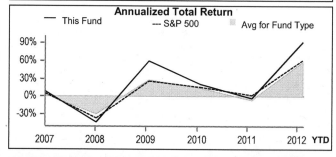

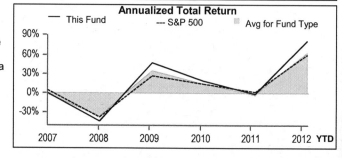

*First Trust NASDAQ-100-Technolog (QTEC)   B   Good

Fund Family: First Trust Advisors LP
Fund Type: Growth
Inception Date: April 19, 2006

Data Date	Investment Rating	Net Assets ($Mil)	Price	Performance Rating/Pts	Total Return Y-T-D	Risk Rating/Pts
3-12	B	175.64	28.69	B / 7.8	18.95%	B- / 7.8
2011	B-	149.70	24.12	B / 7.6	2.65%	B- / 7.6
2010	B+	453.40	25.71	B / 8.0	21.22%	C / 5.5
2009	B-	21.30	21.21	B- / 7.2	73.54%	C+ / 5.7

Major Rating Factors: Strong performance is the major factor driving the B (Good) TheStreet.com Investment Rating for *First Trust NASDAQ-100-Technolog. The fund currently has a performance rating of B (Good) based on an annualized return of 27.32% over the last three years and a total return of 18.95% year to date 2012. Factored into the performance evaluation is an expense ratio of 0.60% (very low).

The fund's risk rating is currently B- (Good). It carries a beta of 1.29, meaning it is expected to move 12.9% for every 10% move in the market. Volatility, as measured by both the semi-deviation and a drawdown factor, is considered low. As of March 31, 2012, *First Trust NASDAQ-100-Technolog traded at a discount of .07% below its net asset value.

Jonathan Erickson has been running the fund for 6 years and currently receives a manager quality ranking of 40 (0=worst, 99=best). If you desire only a moderate level of risk and strong performance, then this fund is an excellent option.

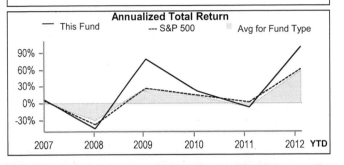

*First Trust S&P REIT Index Fund (FRI)   A-   Excellent

Fund Family: First Trust Advisors LP
Fund Type: Income
Inception Date: May 8, 2007

Data Date	Investment Rating	Net Assets ($Mil)	Price	Performance Rating/Pts	Total Return Y-T-D	Risk Rating/Pts
3-12	A-	396.56	17.14	A- / 9.1	10.65%	B- / 7.9
2011	C+	325.00	15.49	B / 7.7	-0.45%	C+ / 6.4
2010	C	71.10	14.65	B- / 7.0	27.73%	C- / 4.2
2009	B	4.44	11.72	A- / 9.2	30.49%	C- / 4.2

Major Rating Factors:
Exceptional performance is the major factor driving the A- (Excellent) TheStreet.com Investment Rating for *First Trust S&P REIT Index Fund. The fund currently has a performance rating of A- (Excellent) based on an annualized return of 36.42% over the last three years and a total return of 10.65% year to date 2012. Factored into the performance evaluation is an expense ratio of 0.50% (very low).

The fund's risk rating is currently B- (Good). It carries a beta of 1.28, meaning it is expected to move 12.8% for every 10% move in the market. Volatility, as measured by both the semi-deviation and a drawdown factor, is considered low. As of March 31, 2012, *First Trust S&P REIT Index Fund traded at a premium of .18% above its net asset value, which is worse than its one-year historical average premium of .04%.

Jonathan Erickson has been running the fund for 5 years and currently receives a manager quality ranking of 84 (0=worst, 99=best). If you desire only a moderate level of risk and strong performance, then this fund is an excellent option.

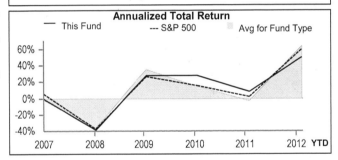

*First Trust Small Cap Core Alpha (FYX)   B   Good

Fund Family: First Trust Advisors LP
Fund Type: Growth
Inception Date: May 8, 2007

Data Date	Investment Rating	Net Assets ($Mil)	Price	Performance Rating/Pts	Total Return Y-T-D	Risk Rating/Pts
3-12	B	164.24	33.48	B / 7.8	11.94%	B- / 7.8
2011	B-	125.60	29.91	C+ / 6.9	1.47%	B- / 7.5
2010	B	82.50	30.08	B / 7.8	27.35%	C / 5.5
2009	B+	8.31	23.72	B+ / 8.5	34.43%	C / 5.5

Major Rating Factors: Strong performance is the major factor driving the B (Good) TheStreet.com Investment Rating for *First Trust Small Cap Core Alpha. The fund currently has a performance rating of B (Good) based on an annualized return of 28.68% over the last three years and a total return of 11.94% year to date 2012. Factored into the performance evaluation is an expense ratio of 0.70% (very low).

The fund's risk rating is currently B- (Good). It carries a beta of 1.28, meaning it is expected to move 12.8% for every 10% move in the market. Volatility, as measured by both the semi-deviation and a drawdown factor, is considered low. As of March 31, 2012, *First Trust Small Cap Core Alpha traded at a premium of .15% above its net asset value, which is worse than its one-year historical average premium of .03%.

Jonathan Erickson has been running the fund for 5 years and currently receives a manager quality ranking of 48 (0=worst, 99=best). If you desire only a moderate level of risk and strong performance, then this fund is an excellent option.

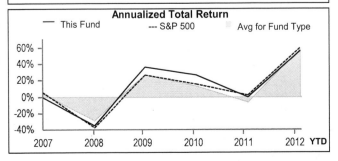

*First Trust STOXX European Sel D (FDD)

D+　　**Weak**

Fund Family: First Trust Advisors LP
Fund Type: Foreign
Inception Date: August 27, 2007

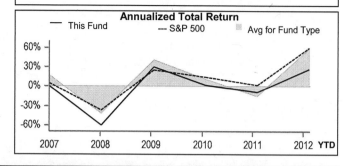

Data Date	Investment Rating	Net Assets ($Mil)	Price	Performance Rating/Pts	Total Return Y-T-D	Risk Rating/Pts
3-12	D+	10.54	12.54	D+ / 2.9	6.13%	B- / 7.4
2011	D+	9.90	11.86	D / 2.2	-3.74%	B- / 7.4
2010	E+	9.60	13.69	E+ / 0.6	1.93%	C- / 3.7
2009	C+	8.33	14.05	B+ / 8.5	31.16%	C- / 3.7

Major Rating Factors:
Disappointing performance is the major factor driving the D+ (Weak) TheStreet.com Investment Rating for *First Trust STOXX European Sel D. The fund currently has a performance rating of D+ (Weak) based on an annualized return of 14.31% over the last three years and a total return of 6.13% year to date 2012. Factored into the performance evaluation is an expense ratio of 0.60% (very low).

The fund's risk rating is currently B- (Good). It carries a beta of 1.00, meaning that its performance tracks fairly well with that of the overall stock market. Volatility, as measured by both the semi-deviation and a drawdown factor, is considered low. As of March 31, 2012, *First Trust STOXX European Sel D traded at a premium of 1.21% above its net asset value, which is worse than its one-year historical average premium of .42%.

Daniel J. Lindquist currently receives a manager quality ranking of 44 (0=worst, 99=best). This fund offers only a moderate level of risk but investors looking for strong performance are still waiting.

Annualized Total Return

---

*First Trust Strategic Value Inde (FDV)

C+　　**Fair**

Fund Family: First Trust Advisors LP
Fund Type: Income
Inception Date: July 6, 2006

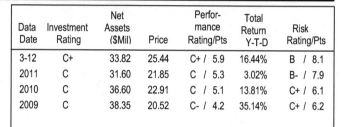

Data Date	Investment Rating	Net Assets ($Mil)	Price	Performance Rating/Pts	Total Return Y-T-D	Risk Rating/Pts
3-12	C+	33.82	25.44	C+ / 5.9	16.44%	B / 8.1
2011	C	31.60	21.85	C / 5.3	3.02%	B- / 7.9
2010	C	36.60	22.91	C / 5.1	13.81%	C+ / 6.1
2009	C	38.35	20.52	C- / 4.2	35.14%	C+ / 6.2

Major Rating Factors: Middle of the road best describes *First Trust Strategic Value Inde whose TheStreet.com Investment Rating is currently a C+ (Fair). The fund currently has a performance rating of C+ (Fair) based on an annualized return of 21.28% over the last three years and a total return of 16.44% year to date 2012. Factored into the performance evaluation is an expense ratio of 0.65% (very low).

The fund's risk rating is currently B (Good). It carries a beta of 1.17, meaning it is expected to move 11.7% for every 10% move in the market. Volatility, as measured by both the semi-deviation and a drawdown factor, is considered low. As of March 31, 2012, *First Trust Strategic Value Inde traded at a discount of .31% below its net asset value, which is better than its one-year historical average discount of .01%.

Jonathan Erickson has been running the fund for 6 years and currently receives a manager quality ranking of 30 (0=worst, 99=best). If you desire an average level of risk, then this fund may be an option.

Annualized Total Return

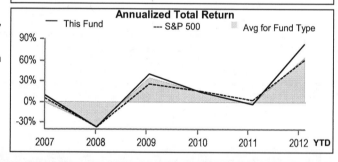

---

*First Trust Technology AlphaDEX (FXL)

C+　　**Fair**

Fund Family: First Trust Advisors LP
Fund Type: Growth
Inception Date: May 8, 2007

Data Date	Investment Rating	Net Assets ($Mil)	Price	Performance Rating/Pts	Total Return Y-T-D	Risk Rating/Pts
3-12	C+	237.86	23.68	B- / 7.4	18.16%	B- / 7.4
2011	C+	188.30	20.04	C+ / 6.5	2.69%	B- / 7.2
2010	C+	119.10	22.70	B- / 7.2	26.64%	C / 4.8
2009	A	12.37	17.93	A / 9.5	60.38%	C / 5.0

Major Rating Factors: Strong performance is the major factor driving the C+ (Fair) TheStreet.com Investment Rating for *First Trust Technology AlphaDEX. The fund currently has a performance rating of B- (Good) based on an annualized return of 27.41% over the last three years and a total return of 18.16% year to date 2012. Factored into the performance evaluation is an expense ratio of 0.70% (very low).

The fund's risk rating is currently B- (Good). It carries a beta of 1.32, meaning it is expected to move 13.2% for every 10% move in the market. Volatility, as measured by both the semi-deviation and a drawdown factor, is considered low. As of March 31, 2012, *First Trust Technology AlphaDEX traded at a premium of .13% above its net asset value, which is worse than its one-year historical average premium of .02%.

Jonathan Erickson has been running the fund for 5 years and currently receives a manager quality ranking of 36 (0=worst, 99=best). If you desire only a moderate level of risk and strong performance, then this fund is an excellent option.

Annualized Total Return

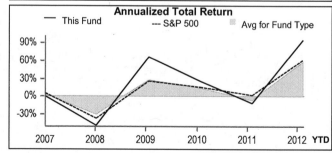

---

*First Trust US IPO Index Fund (FPX)   B+   Good

Fund Family: First Trust Advisors LP
Fund Type: Growth
Inception Date: April 12, 2006

Data Date	Investment Rating	Net Assets ($Mil)	Price	Performance Rating/Pts	Total Return Y-T-D	Risk Rating/Pts
3-12	B+	16.72	28.86	B+ / 8.5	20.40%	B / 8.1
2011	B-	15.60	23.97	C+ / 6.6	1.38%	B / 8.2
2010	C	15.30	23.51	C / 5.2	18.17%	C / 5.1
2009	D+	8.75	20.10	C- / 4.1	41.66%	C / 4.5

Major Rating Factors: Strong performance is the major factor driving the B+ (Good) TheStreet.com Investment Rating for *First Trust US IPO Index Fund. The fund currently has a performance rating of B+ (Good) based on an annualized return of 29.30% over the last three years and a total return of 20.40% year to date 2012. Factored into the performance evaluation is an expense ratio of 0.60% (very low).

The fund's risk rating is currently B (Good). It carries a beta of 1.11, meaning it is expected to move 11.1% for every 10% move in the market. Volatility, as measured by both the semi-deviation and a drawdown factor, is considered low. As of March 31, 2012, *First Trust US IPO Index Fund traded at a premium of .49% above its net asset value, which is worse than its one-year historical average premium of .01%.

Jonathan Erickson has been running the fund for 6 years and currently receives a manager quality ranking of 66 (0=worst, 99=best). If you desire only a moderate level of risk and strong performance, then this fund is an excellent option.

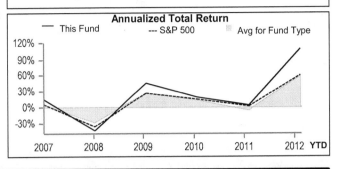

Annualized Total Return
— This Fund   --- S&P 500   Avg for Fund Type

*First Trust Utilities AlphaDEX (FXU)   C   Fair

Fund Family: First Trust Advisors LP
Fund Type: Utilities
Inception Date: May 8, 2007

Data Date	Investment Rating	Net Assets ($Mil)	Price	Performance Rating/Pts	Total Return Y-T-D	Risk Rating/Pts
3-12	C	271.98	17.66	C- / 3.5	-1.51%	B+ / 9.0
2011	C+	331.30	17.93	C / 4.9	-1.56%	B / 8.4
2010	C	39.70	16.53	C- / 3.6	10.47%	C+ / 6.8
2009	A	13.66	15.40	B / 7.9	18.95%	C+ / 6.6

Major Rating Factors: Middle of the road best describes *First Trust Utilities AlphaDEX whose TheStreet.com Investment Rating is currently a C (Fair). The fund currently has a performance rating of C- (Fair) based on an annualized return of 16.50% over the last three years and a total return of -1.51% year to date 2012. Factored into the performance evaluation is an expense ratio of 0.70% (very low).

The fund's risk rating is currently B+ (Good). It carries a beta of 0.97, meaning that its performance tracks fairly well with that of the overall stock market. Volatility, as measured by both the semi-deviation and a drawdown factor, is considered very low. As of March 31, 2012, *First Trust Utilities AlphaDEX traded at a discount of .06% below its net asset value, which is better than its one-year historical average premium of .11%.

Jonathan Erickson has been running the fund for 5 years and currently receives a manager quality ranking of 56 (0=worst, 99=best). If you desire an average level of risk, then this fund may be an option.

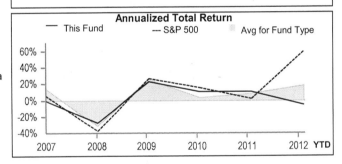

Annualized Total Return
— This Fund   --- S&P 500   Avg for Fund Type

*First Trust Value Line 100 Fund (FVL)   C-   Fair

Fund Family: First Trust Advisors LP
Fund Type: Growth
Inception Date: June 12, 2003

Data Date	Investment Rating	Net Assets ($Mil)	Price	Performance Rating/Pts	Total Return Y-T-D	Risk Rating/Pts
3-12	C-	59.39	13.95	C / 4.5	12.55%	B- / 7.3
2011	C-	55.50	12.39	C- / 4.1	3.00%	B- / 7.2
2010	D	88.40	13.52	D+ / 2.6	28.27%	C / 5.2
2009	D-	63.08	10.54	D- / 1.3	11.77%	C / 4.9

Major Rating Factors: Middle of the road best describes *First Trust Value Line 100 Fund whose TheStreet.com Investment Rating is currently a C- (Fair). The fund currently has a performance rating of C (Fair) based on an annualized return of 18.19% over the last three years and a total return of 12.55% year to date 2012. Factored into the performance evaluation is an expense ratio of 0.70% (very low).

The fund's risk rating is currently B- (Good). It carries a beta of 1.18, meaning it is expected to move 11.8% for every 10% move in the market. Volatility, as measured by both the semi-deviation and a drawdown factor, is considered low. As of March 31, 2012, *First Trust Value Line 100 Fund traded at a premium of .43% above its net asset value, which is worse than its one-year historical average discount of .03%.

Jonathan Erickson has been running the fund for 9 years and currently receives a manager quality ranking of 18 (0=worst, 99=best). If you desire an average level of risk, then this fund may be an option.

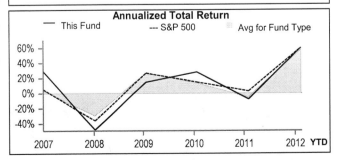

Annualized Total Return
— This Fund   --- S&P 500   Avg for Fund Type

*First Trust Value Line Dividend (FVD)

C+ **Fair**

Fund Family: First Trust Advisors LP
Fund Type: Growth and Income
Inception Date: August 19, 2003

Data Date	Investment Rating	Net Assets ($Mil)	Price	Performance Rating/Pts	Total Return Y-T-D	Risk Rating/Pts
3-12	C+	417.58	16.90	C / 5.4	6.19%	B / 8.9
2011	C+	366.40	16.01	C / 5.4	-0.25%	B / 8.1
2010	C+	218.50	15.09	C+ / 5.7	16.07%	C+ / 6.5
2009	C-	121.90	13.38	D+ / 2.3	16.74%	C+ / 6.4

Major Rating Factors: Middle of the road best describes *First Trust Value Line Dividend whose TheStreet.com Investment Rating is currently a C+ (Fair). The fund currently has a performance rating of C (Fair) based on an annualized return of 21.12% over the last three years and a total return of 6.19% year to date 2012. Factored into the performance evaluation is an expense ratio of 0.70% (very low).

The fund's risk rating is currently B (Good). It carries a beta of 0.76, meaning the fund's expected move will be 7.6% for every 10% move in the market. Volatility, as measured by both the semi-deviation and a drawdown factor, is considered low. As of March 31, 2012, *First Trust Value Line Dividend traded at a premium of .18% above its net asset value, which is worse than its one-year historical average premium of .10%.

Jonathan Erickson has been running the fund for 9 years and currently receives a manager quality ranking of 72 (0=worst, 99=best). If you desire an average level of risk, then this fund may be an option.

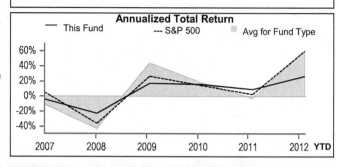

*First Trust Value Line Equity AI (FVI)

C **Fair**

Fund Family: First Trust Advisors LP
Fund Type: Growth and Income
Inception Date: December 5, 2006

Data Date	Investment Rating	Net Assets ($Mil)	Price	Performance Rating/Pts	Total Return Y-T-D	Risk Rating/Pts
3-12	C	6.78	19.82	C- / 4.2	8.72%	B- / 7.9
2011	C	6.40	18.23	C / 4.3	0.49%	B- / 7.7
2010	C+	7.10	20.35	C+ / 6.0	19.25%	C+ / 6.0
2009	C-	5.43	17.34	C- / 3.8	35.37%	C+ / 6.1

Major Rating Factors: Middle of the road best describes *First Trust Value Line Equity AI whose TheStreet.com Investment Rating is currently a C (Fair). The fund currently has a performance rating of C- (Fair) based on an annualized return of 18.59% over the last three years and a total return of 8.72% year to date 2012. Factored into the performance evaluation is an expense ratio of 0.70% (very low).

The fund's risk rating is currently B- (Good). It carries a beta of 1.00, meaning that its performance tracks fairly well with that of the overall stock market. Volatility, as measured by both the semi-deviation and a drawdown factor, is considered low. As of March 31, 2012, *First Trust Value Line Equity AI traded at a premium of .25% above its net asset value, which is worse than its one-year historical average premium of .02%.

Jonathan Erickson has been running the fund for 6 years and currently receives a manager quality ranking of 29 (0=worst, 99=best). If you desire an average level of risk, then this fund may be an option.

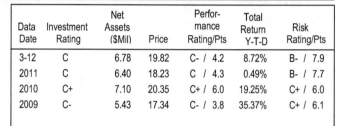

*Focus Mstar Basic Mat Id ETF (FBM)

D **Weak**

Fund Family: FocusShares LLC
Fund Type: Growth and Income
Inception Date: March 30, 2011

Data Date	Investment Rating	Net Assets ($Mil)	Price	Performance Rating/Pts	Total Return Y-T-D	Risk Rating/Pts
3-12	D	4.48	22.10	D / 2.1	9.90%	C+ / 6.2

Major Rating Factors:
Disappointing performance is the major factor driving the D (Weak) TheStreet.com Investment Rating for *Focus Mstar Basic Mat Id ETF. The fund currently has a performance rating of D (Weak) based on an annualized return of 0.00% over the last three years and a total return of 9.90% year to date 2012. Factored into the performance evaluation is an expense ratio of 0.19% (very low).

The fund's risk rating is currently C+ (Fair). It carries a beta of 0.00, meaning the fund's expected move will be 0.0% for every 10% move in the market. Volatility, as measured by both the semi-deviation and a drawdown factor, is considered low. As of March 31, 2012, *Focus Mstar Basic Mat Id ETF traded at a discount of .36% below its net asset value, which is better than its one-year historical average premium of .10%.

Kristopher A. Wallace has been running the fund for 1 year and currently receives a manager quality ranking of 4 (0=worst, 99=best). This fund offers only a moderate level of risk but investors looking for strong performance are still waiting.

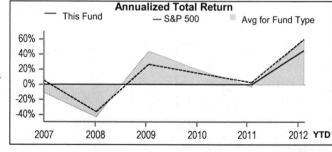

*Focus Mstar Comm Svc Id ETF (FCQ)

C   **Fair**

Fund Family: FocusShares LLC
Fund Type: Growth
Inception Date: March 30, 2011

Data Date	Investment Rating	Net Assets ($Mil)	Price	Performance Rating/Pts	Total Return Y-T-D	Risk Rating/Pts
3-12	C	5.09	25.89	C- / 3.8	10.17%	B / 8.3

Major Rating Factors: Middle of the road best describes *Focus Mstar Comm Svc Id ETF whose TheStreet.com Investment Rating is currently a C (Fair). The fund currently has a performance rating of C- (Fair) based on an annualized return of 0.00% over the last three years and a total return of 10.17% year to date 2012. Factored into the performance evaluation is an expense ratio of 0.19% (very low).

The fund's risk rating is currently B (Good). It carries a beta of 0.00, meaning the fund's expected move will be 0.0% for every 10% move in the market. Volatility, as measured by both the semi-deviation and a drawdown factor, is considered low. As of March 31, 2012, *Focus Mstar Comm Svc Id ETF traded at a discount of .08% below its net asset value, which is better than its one-year historical average premium of .04%.

Kristopher A. Wallace has been running the fund for 1 year and currently receives a manager quality ranking of 38 (0=worst, 99=best). If you desire an average level of risk, then this fund may be an option.

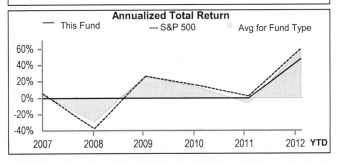

*Focus Mstar Cons Cyc Id ETF (FCL)

B+   **Good**

Fund Family: FocusShares LLC
Fund Type: Growth and Income
Inception Date: March 30, 2011

Data Date	Investment Rating	Net Assets ($Mil)	Price	Performance Rating/Pts	Total Return Y-T-D	Risk Rating/Pts
3-12	B+	5.59	29.07	B+ / 8.5	16.09%	B / 8.3

Major Rating Factors: Strong performance is the major factor driving the B+ (Good) TheStreet.com Investment Rating for *Focus Mstar Cons Cyc Id ETF. The fund currently has a performance rating of B+ (Good) based on an annualized return of 0.00% over the last three years and a total return of 16.09% year to date 2012. Factored into the performance evaluation is an expense ratio of 0.19% (very low).

The fund's risk rating is currently B (Good). It carries a beta of 0.00, meaning the fund's expected move will be 0.0% for every 10% move in the market. Volatility, as measured by both the semi-deviation and a drawdown factor, is considered low. As of March 31, 2012, *Focus Mstar Cons Cyc Id ETF traded at a premium of .03% above its net asset value, which is worse than its one-year historical average discount of .12%.

Kristopher A. Wallace has been running the fund for 1 year and currently receives a manager quality ranking of 74 (0=worst, 99=best). If you desire only a moderate level of risk and strong performance, then this fund is an excellent option.

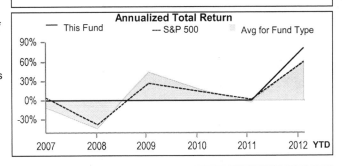

*Focus Mstar Cons Def Id ETF (FCD)

C+   **Fair**

Fund Family: FocusShares LLC
Fund Type: Growth and Income
Inception Date: March 30, 2011

Data Date	Investment Rating	Net Assets ($Mil)	Price	Performance Rating/Pts	Total Return Y-T-D	Risk Rating/Pts
3-12	C+	5.60	28.77	C / 5.2	5.23%	B+ / 9.3

Major Rating Factors: Middle of the road best describes *Focus Mstar Cons Def Id ETF whose TheStreet.com Investment Rating is currently a C+ (Fair). The fund currently has a performance rating of C (Fair) based on an annualized return of 0.00% over the last three years and a total return of 5.23% year to date 2012. Factored into the performance evaluation is an expense ratio of 0.19% (very low).

The fund's risk rating is currently B+ (Good). It carries a beta of 0.00, meaning the fund's expected move will be 0.0% for every 10% move in the market. Volatility, as measured by both the semi-deviation and a drawdown factor, is considered very low. As of March 31, 2012, *Focus Mstar Cons Def Id ETF traded at a premium of .10% above its net asset value, which is worse than its one-year historical average premium of .03%.

Kristopher A. Wallace has been running the fund for 1 year and currently receives a manager quality ranking of 88 (0=worst, 99=best). If you desire an average level of risk, then this fund may be an option.

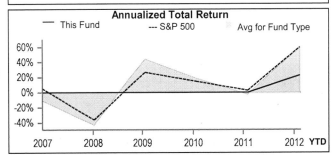

*Focus Mstar Energy Id ETF (FEG)

D   **Weak**

Fund Family: FocusShares LLC
Fund Type: Energy/Natural Resources
Inception Date: March 30, 2011

Data Date	Investment Rating	Net Assets ($Mil)	Price	Perfor-mance Rating/Pts	Total Return Y-T-D	Risk Rating/Pts
3-12	D	4.86	23.37	D / 2.2	4.42%	B- / 7.1

Major Rating Factors:
Disappointing performance is the major factor driving the D (Weak) TheStreet.com Investment Rating for *Focus Mstar Energy Id ETF. The fund currently has a performance rating of D (Weak) based on an annualized return of 0.00% over the last three years and a total return of 4.42% year to date 2012. Factored into the performance evaluation is an expense ratio of 0.19% (very low).

The fund's risk rating is currently B- (Good). It carries a beta of 0.00, meaning the fund's expected move will be 0.0% for every 10% move in the market. Volatility, as measured by both the semi-deviation and a drawdown factor, is considered low. As of March 31, 2012, *Focus Mstar Energy Id ETF traded at a premium of .04% above its net asset value, which is worse than its one-year historical average premium of .02%.

Kristopher A. Wallace has been running the fund for 1 year and currently receives a manager quality ranking of 44 (0=worst, 99=best). This fund offers only a moderate level of risk but investors looking for strong performance are still waiting.

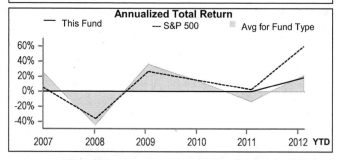

*Focus Mstar Finl Svc Id ETF (FFL)

C+   **Fair**

Fund Family: FocusShares LLC
Fund Type: Loan Participation
Inception Date: March 30, 2011

Data Date	Investment Rating	Net Assets ($Mil)	Price	Perfor-mance Rating/Pts	Total Return Y-T-D	Risk Rating/Pts
3-12	C+	4.62	24.66	C+ / 6.5	21.24%	B- / 7.1

Major Rating Factors: Middle of the road best describes *Focus Mstar Finl Svc Id ETF whose TheStreet.com Investment Rating is currently a C+ (Fair). The fund currently has a performance rating of C+ (Fair) based on an annualized return of 0.00% over the last three years and a total return of 21.24% year to date 2012. Factored into the performance evaluation is an expense ratio of 0.19% (very low).

The fund's risk rating is currently B- (Good). It carries a beta of 0.00, meaning the fund's expected move will be 0.0% for every 10% move in the market. Volatility, as measured by both the semi-deviation and a drawdown factor, is considered low. As of March 31, 2012, *Focus Mstar Finl Svc Id ETF traded at a discount of .04% below its net asset value, which is better than its one-year historical average premium of .12%.

Kristopher A. Wallace has been running the fund for 1 year and currently receives a manager quality ranking of 99 (0=worst, 99=best). If you desire an average level of risk, then this fund may be an option.

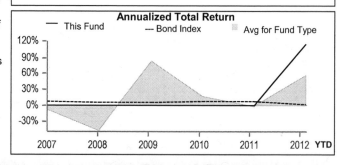
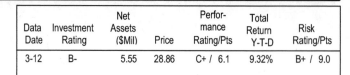

*Focus Mstar Hlth Care Id ETF (FHC)

B-   **Good**

Fund Family: FocusShares LLC
Fund Type: Health
Inception Date: March 30, 2011

Data Date	Investment Rating	Net Assets ($Mil)	Price	Perfor-mance Rating/Pts	Total Return Y-T-D	Risk Rating/Pts
3-12	B-	5.55	28.86	C+ / 6.1	9.32%	B+ / 9.0

Major Rating Factors: *Focus Mstar Hlth Care Id ETF receives a TheStreet.com Investment Rating of B- (Good). The fund currently has a performance rating of C+ (Fair) based on an annualized return of 0.00% over the last three years and a total return of 9.32% year to date 2012. Factored into the performance evaluation is an expense ratio of 0.19% (very low).

The fund's risk rating is currently B+ (Good). It carries a beta of 0.00, meaning the fund's expected move will be 0.0% for every 10% move in the market. Volatility, as measured by both the semi-deviation and a drawdown factor, is considered very low. As of March 31, 2012, *Focus Mstar Hlth Care Id ETF traded at a premium of .17% above its net asset value, which is worse than its one-year historical average discount of .02%.

Kristopher A. Wallace has been running the fund for 1 year and currently receives a manager quality ranking of 85 (0=worst, 99=best). If you desire an average level of risk, then this fund may be an option.

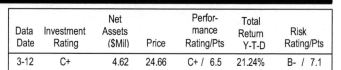
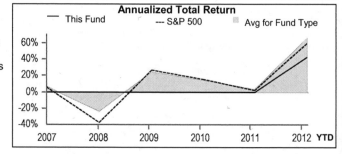

*Focus Mstar Indus Id ETF (FIL)

| | | | | C- | | Fair |

Fund Family: FocusShares LLC
Fund Type: Growth
Inception Date: March 30, 2011

Data Date	Investment Rating	Net Assets ($Mil)	Price	Performance Rating/Pts	Total Return Y-T-D	Risk Rating/Pts
3-12	C-	5.02	25.34	C / 4.5	10.62%	B- / 7.5

Major Rating Factors: Middle of the road best describes *Focus Mstar Indus Id ETF whose TheStreet.com Investment Rating is currently a C- (Fair). The fund currently has a performance rating of C (Fair) based on an annualized return of 0.00% over the last three years and a total return of 10.62% year to date 2012. Factored into the performance evaluation is an expense ratio of 0.19% (very low).

The fund's risk rating is currently B- (Good). It carries a beta of 0.00, meaning the fund's expected move will be 0.0% for every 10% move in the market. Volatility, as measured by both the semi-deviation and a drawdown factor, is considered low. As of March 31, 2012, *Focus Mstar Indus Id ETF traded at a premium of .16% above its net asset value, which is worse than its one-year historical average premium of .05%.

Kristopher A. Wallace has been running the fund for 1 year and currently receives a manager quality ranking of 15 (0=worst, 99=best). If you desire an average level of risk, then this fund may be an option.

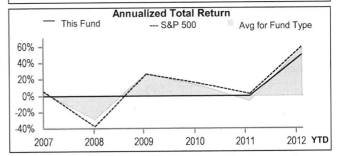

*Focus Mstar Large Cap Id ETF (FLG)

| | | | | C+ | | Fair |

Fund Family: FocusShares LLC
Fund Type: Growth
Inception Date: March 30, 2011

Data Date	Investment Rating	Net Assets ($Mil)	Price	Performance Rating/Pts	Total Return Y-T-D	Risk Rating/Pts
3-12	C+	5.26	27.11	C+ / 6.1	12.02%	B / 8.4

Major Rating Factors: Middle of the road best describes *Focus Mstar Large Cap Id ETF whose TheStreet.com Investment Rating is currently a C+ (Fair). The fund currently has a performance rating of C+ (Fair) based on an annualized return of 0.00% over the last three years and a total return of 12.02% year to date 2012. Factored into the performance evaluation is an expense ratio of 0.05% (very low).

The fund's risk rating is currently B (Good). It carries a beta of 0.00, meaning the fund's expected move will be 0.0% for every 10% move in the market. Volatility, as measured by both the semi-deviation and a drawdown factor, is considered low. As of March 31, 2012, *Focus Mstar Large Cap Id ETF traded at a discount of .04% below its net asset value, which is better than its one-year historical average premium of .03%.

Kristopher A. Wallace has been running the fund for 1 year and currently receives a manager quality ranking of 50 (0=worst, 99=best). If you desire an average level of risk, then this fund may be an option.

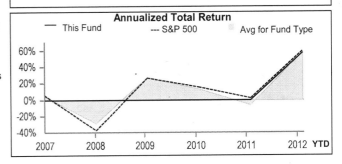

*Focus Mstar Mid Cap Id ETF (FMM)

| | | | | C | | Fair |

Fund Family: FocusShares LLC
Fund Type: Growth
Inception Date: March 30, 2011

Data Date	Investment Rating	Net Assets ($Mil)	Price	Performance Rating/Pts	Total Return Y-T-D	Risk Rating/Pts
3-12	C	5.11	26.02	C / 4.8	12.84%	B- / 7.8

Major Rating Factors: Middle of the road best describes *Focus Mstar Mid Cap Id ETF whose TheStreet.com Investment Rating is currently a C (Fair). The fund currently has a performance rating of C (Fair) based on an annualized return of 0.00% over the last three years and a total return of 12.84% year to date 2012. Factored into the performance evaluation is an expense ratio of 0.12% (very low).

The fund's risk rating is currently B- (Good). It carries a beta of 0.00, meaning the fund's expected move will be 0.0% for every 10% move in the market. Volatility, as measured by both the semi-deviation and a drawdown factor, is considered low. As of March 31, 2012, *Focus Mstar Mid Cap Id ETF traded at a premium of .08% above its net asset value, which is worse than its one-year historical average discount of .06%.

Kristopher A. Wallace has been running the fund for 1 year and currently receives a manager quality ranking of 20 (0=worst, 99=best). If you desire an average level of risk, then this fund may be an option.

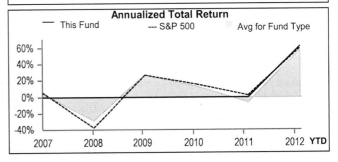

*Focus Mstar Real Est Id ETF (FRL)

C+ **Fair**

Fund Family: FocusShares LLC
Fund Type: Growth and Income
Inception Date: March 30, 2011

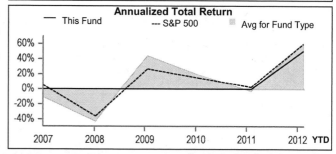

Data Date	Investment Rating	Net Assets ($Mil)	Price	Performance Rating/Pts	Total Return Y-T-D	Risk Rating/Pts
3-12	C+	5.23	27.26	C+ / 5.9	10.90%	B / 8.0

Major Rating Factors: Middle of the road best describes *Focus Mstar Real Est Id ETF whose TheStreet.com Investment Rating is currently a C+ (Fair). The fund currently has a performance rating of C+ (Fair) based on an annualized return of 0.00% over the last three years and a total return of 10.90% year to date 2012. Factored into the performance evaluation is an expense ratio of 0.12% (very low).

The fund's risk rating is currently B (Good). It carries a beta of 0.00, meaning the fund's expected move will be 0.0% for every 10% move in the market. Volatility, as measured by both the semi-deviation and a drawdown factor, is considered low. As of March 31, 2012, *Focus Mstar Real Est Id ETF traded at a premium of .04% above its net asset value, which is worse than its one-year historical average discount of .05%.

Kristopher A. Wallace has been running the fund for 1 year and currently receives a manager quality ranking of 51 (0=worst, 99=best). If you desire an average level of risk, then this fund may be an option.

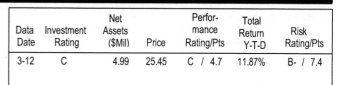

Annualized Total Return
— This Fund — S&P 500 — Avg for Fund Type

*Focus Mstar Small Cap Id ETF (FOS)

C **Fair**

Fund Family: FocusShares LLC
Fund Type: Growth
Inception Date: March 30, 2011

Data Date	Investment Rating	Net Assets ($Mil)	Price	Performance Rating/Pts	Total Return Y-T-D	Risk Rating/Pts
3-12	C	4.99	25.45	C / 4.7	11.87%	B- / 7.4

Major Rating Factors: Middle of the road best describes *Focus Mstar Small Cap Id ETF whose TheStreet.com Investment Rating is currently a C (Fair). The fund currently has a performance rating of C (Fair) based on an annualized return of 0.00% over the last three years and a total return of 11.87% year to date 2012. Factored into the performance evaluation is an expense ratio of 0.12% (very low).

The fund's risk rating is currently B- (Good). It carries a beta of 0.00, meaning the fund's expected move will be 0.0% for every 10% move in the market. Volatility, as measured by both the semi-deviation and a drawdown factor, is considered low. As of March 31, 2012, *Focus Mstar Small Cap Id ETF traded at a premium of .20% above its net asset value, which is worse than its one-year historical average discount of .03%.

Kristopher A. Wallace has been running the fund for 1 year and currently receives a manager quality ranking of 14 (0=worst, 99=best). If you desire an average level of risk, then this fund may be an option.

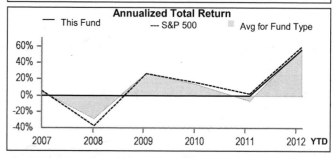

Annualized Total Return
— This Fund — S&P 500 — Avg for Fund Type

*Focus Mstar Technology Id ETF (FTQ)

A **Excellent**

Fund Family: FocusShares LLC
Fund Type: Growth
Inception Date: March 30, 2011

Data Date	Investment Rating	Net Assets ($Mil)	Price	Performance Rating/Pts	Total Return Y-T-D	Risk Rating/Pts
3-12	A	5.54	29.11	A- / 9.1	21.34%	B / 8.5

Major Rating Factors:
Exceptional performance is the major factor driving the A (Excellent) TheStreet.com Investment Rating for *Focus Mstar Technology Id ETF. The fund currently has a performance rating of A- (Excellent) based on an annualized return of 0.00% over the last three years and a total return of 21.34% year to date 2012. Factored into the performance evaluation is an expense ratio of 0.19% (very low).

The fund's risk rating is currently B (Good). It carries a beta of 0.00, meaning the fund's expected move will be 0.0% for every 10% move in the market. Volatility, as measured by both the semi-deviation and a drawdown factor, is considered low. As of March 31, 2012, *Focus Mstar Technology Id ETF traded at a premium of .31% above its net asset value, which is worse than its one-year historical average discount of .03%.

Kristopher A. Wallace has been running the fund for 1 year and currently receives a manager quality ranking of 79 (0=worst, 99=best). If you desire only a moderate level of risk and strong performance, then this fund is an excellent option.

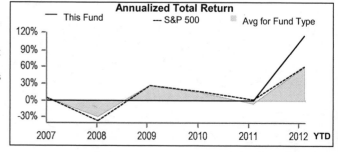

Annualized Total Return
— This Fund — S&P 500 — Avg for Fund Type

*Focus Mstar US Market Id ETF (FMU)

C+   Fair

Fund Family: FocusShares LLC
Fund Type: Growth
Inception Date: March 30, 2011

Data Date	Investment Rating	Net Assets ($Mil)	Price	Performance Rating/Pts	Total Return Y-T-D	Risk Rating/Pts
3-12	C+	15.77	26.76	C+ / 5.7	11.97%	B / 8.2

Major Rating Factors: Middle of the road best describes *Focus Mstar US Market Id ETF whose TheStreet.com Investment Rating is currently a C+ (Fair). The fund currently has a performance rating of C+ (Fair) based on an annualized return of 0.00% over the last three years and a total return of 11.97% year to date 2012. Factored into the performance evaluation is an expense ratio of 0.05% (very low).

The fund's risk rating is currently B (Good). It carries a beta of 0.00, meaning the fund's expected move will be 0.0% for every 10% move in the market. Volatility, as measured by both the semi-deviation and a drawdown factor, is considered low. As of March 31, 2012, *Focus Mstar US Market Id ETF traded at a discount of .22% below its net asset value, which is better than its one-year historical average premium of .03%.

Kristopher A. Wallace has been running the fund for 1 year and currently receives a manager quality ranking of 34 (0=worst, 99=best). If you desire an average level of risk, then this fund may be an option.

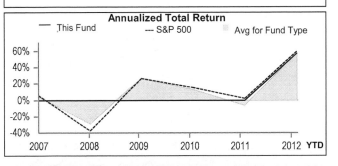

*Focus Mstar Utilities Id ETF (FUI)

C-   Fair

Fund Family: FocusShares LLC
Fund Type: Utilities
Inception Date: March 30, 2011

Data Date	Investment Rating	Net Assets ($Mil)	Price	Performance Rating/Pts	Total Return Y-T-D	Risk Rating/Pts
3-12	C-	6.87	27.62	D+ / 2.3	-2.75%	B+ / 9.5

Major Rating Factors:
Disappointing performance is the major factor driving the C- (Fair) TheStreet.com Investment Rating for *Focus Mstar Utilities Id ETF. The fund currently has a performance rating of D+ (Weak) based on an annualized return of 0.00% over the last three years and a total return of -2.75% year to date 2012. Factored into the performance evaluation is an expense ratio of 0.19% (very low).

The fund's risk rating is currently B+ (Good). It carries a beta of 0.00, meaning the fund's expected move will be 0.0% for every 10% move in the market. Volatility, as measured by both the semi-deviation and a drawdown factor, is considered very low. As of March 31, 2012, *Focus Mstar Utilities Id ETF traded at a premium of .07% above its net asset value, which is worse than its one-year historical average discount of .03%.

Kristopher A. Wallace has been running the fund for 1 year and currently receives a manager quality ranking of 26 (0=worst, 99=best). This fund offers only a moderate level of risk but investors looking for strong performance are still waiting.

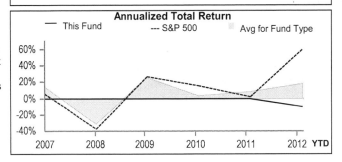

*Global X Aluminm ETF (ALUM)

E+   Very Weak

Fund Family: Global X Management Company LLC
Fund Type: Global
Inception Date: January 4, 2011

Data Date	Investment Rating	Net Assets ($Mil)	Price	Performance Rating/Pts	Total Return Y-T-D	Risk Rating/Pts
3-12	E+	3.29	10.30	E+ / 0.7	14.06%	C / 4.8

Major Rating Factors:
Very poor performance is the major factor driving the E+ (Very Weak) TheStreet.com Investment Rating for *Global X Aluminm ETF. The fund currently has a performance rating of E+ (Very Weak) based on an annualized return of 0.00% over the last three years and a total return of 14.06% year to date 2012. Factored into the performance evaluation is an expense ratio of 0.69% (very low).

The fund's risk rating is currently C (Fair). It carries a beta of 0.00, meaning the fund's expected move will be 0.0% for every 10% move in the market. Volatility, as measured by both the semi-deviation and a drawdown factor, is considered average. As of March 31, 2012, *Global X Aluminm ETF traded at a premium of .29% above its net asset value, which is worse than its one-year historical average discount of .37%.

Bruno Del Ama has been running the fund for 1 year and currently receives a manager quality ranking of 4 (0=worst, 99=best). This fund offers an average level of risk but investors looking for strong performance will be frustrated.

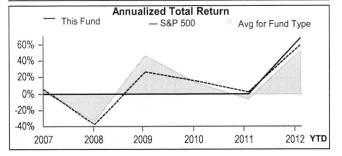

*Global X Brazil Consumer ETF (BRAQ)

C | **Fair**

Fund Family: Global X Management Company LLC
Fund Type: Foreign
Inception Date: July 7, 2010

Major Rating Factors: Strong performance is the major factor driving the C (Fair) TheStreet.com Investment Rating for *Global X Brazil Consumer ETF. The fund currently has a performance rating of B- (Good) based on an annualized return of 0.00% over the last three years and a total return of 24.54% year to date 2012. Factored into the performance evaluation is an expense ratio of 0.77% (very low).

The fund's risk rating is currently C+ (Fair). It carries a beta of 0.00, meaning the fund's expected move will be 0.0% for every 10% move in the market. Volatility, as measured by both the semi-deviation and a drawdown factor, is considered low. As of March 31, 2012, *Global X Brazil Consumer ETF traded at a discount of .32% below its net asset value, which is better than its one-year historical average premium of .23%.

Bruno Del Ama has been running the fund for 2 years and currently receives a manager quality ranking of 84 (0=worst, 99=best). If you desire only a moderate level of risk and strong performance, then this fund is an excellent option.

Data Date	Investment Rating	Net Assets ($Mil)	Price	Perfor-mance Rating/Pts	Total Return Y-T-D	Risk Rating/Pts
3-12	C	42.39	18.78	B- / 7.1	24.54%	C+ / 6.1
2011	D-	27.00	15.08	E+ / 0.8	1.95%	C+ / 6.1

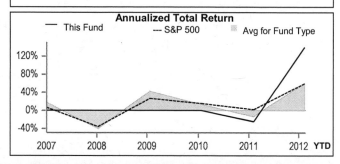

*Global X Brazil Financials ETF (BRAF)

D | **Weak**

Fund Family: Global X Management Company LLC
Fund Type: Foreign
Inception Date: July 28, 2010

Major Rating Factors: *Global X Brazil Financials ETF receives a TheStreet.com Investment Rating of D (Weak). The fund currently has a performance rating of C- (Fair) based on an annualized return of 0.00% over the last three years and a total return of 15.04% year to date 2012. Factored into the performance evaluation is an expense ratio of 0.77% (very low).

The fund's risk rating is currently C+ (Fair). It carries a beta of 0.00, meaning the fund's expected move will be 0.0% for every 10% move in the market. Volatility, as measured by both the semi-deviation and a drawdown factor, is considered low. As of March 31, 2012, *Global X Brazil Financials ETF traded at a discount of .40% below its net asset value, which is better than its one-year historical average discount of .27%.

Bruno Del Ama has been running the fund for 2 years and currently receives a manager quality ranking of 40 (0=worst, 99=best). If you desire an average level of risk, then this fund may be an option.

Data Date	Investment Rating	Net Assets ($Mil)	Price	Perfor-mance Rating/Pts	Total Return Y-T-D	Risk Rating/Pts
3-12	D	6.02	14.99	C- / 3.0	15.04%	C+ / 6.2
2011	D-	5.20	13.03	D- / 1.3	5.14%	C+ / 6.3

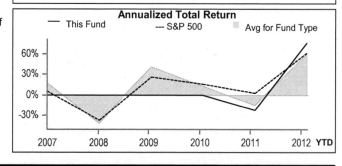

*Global X Brazil Mid Cap ETF (BRAZ)

C | **Fair**

Fund Family: Global X Management Company LLC
Fund Type: Foreign
Inception Date: June 21, 2010

Major Rating Factors: Middle of the road best describes *Global X Brazil Mid Cap ETF whose TheStreet.com Investment Rating is currently a C (Fair). The fund currently has a performance rating of C+ (Fair) based on an annualized return of 0.00% over the last three years and a total return of 21.29% year to date 2012. Factored into the performance evaluation is an expense ratio of 0.69% (very low).

The fund's risk rating is currently C+ (Fair). It carries a beta of 0.00, meaning the fund's expected move will be 0.0% for every 10% move in the market. Volatility, as measured by both the semi-deviation and a drawdown factor, is considered low. As of March 31, 2012, *Global X Brazil Mid Cap ETF traded at a discount of .29% below its net asset value, which is better than its one-year historical average discount of .18%.

Bruno Del Ama has been running the fund for 2 years and currently receives a manager quality ranking of 73 (0=worst, 99=best). If you desire an average level of risk, then this fund may be an option.

Data Date	Investment Rating	Net Assets ($Mil)	Price	Perfor-mance Rating/Pts	Total Return Y-T-D	Risk Rating/Pts
3-12	C	25.11	17.26	C+ / 5.7	21.29%	C+ / 6.5
2011	D-	20.70	14.23	D- / 1.0	2.24%	C+ / 6.4

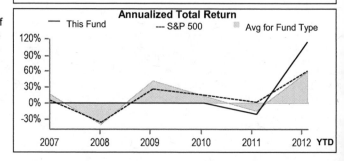

*Global X China Consumer ETF (CHIQ)

D-   Weak

Fund Family: Global X Management Company LLC
Fund Type: Foreign
Inception Date: November 30, 2009

Major Rating Factors:
Disappointing performance is the major factor driving the D- (Weak) TheStreet.com Investment Rating for *Global X China Consumer ETF. The fund currently has a performance rating of D- (Weak) based on an annualized return of 0.00% over the last three years and a total return of 8.68% year to date 2012. Factored into the performance evaluation is an expense ratio of 0.65% (very low).

The fund's risk rating is currently C+ (Fair). It carries a beta of 0.00, meaning the fund's expected move will be 0.0% for every 10% move in the market. Volatility, as measured by both the semi-deviation and a drawdown factor, is considered low. As of March 31, 2012, *Global X China Consumer ETF traded at a discount of 1.06% below its net asset value, which is better than its one-year historical average discount of .10%.

Bruno Del Ama has been running the fund for 3 years and currently receives a manager quality ranking of 20 (0=worst, 99=best). This fund offers only a moderate level of risk but investors looking for strong performance are still waiting.

Data Date	Investment Rating	Net Assets ($Mil)	Price	Performance Rating/Pts	Total Return Y-T-D	Risk Rating/Pts
3-12	D-	134.76	14.90	D- / 1.4	8.68%	C+ / 5.9
2011	D-	119.20	13.71	E+ / 0.6	-0.51%	C+ / 5.8
2010	B-	165.00	18.09	C+ / 6.0	9.64%	B- / 7.5

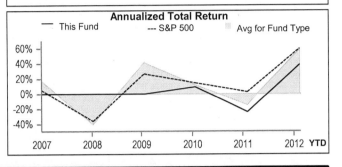

*Global X China Energy ETF (CHIE)

D-   Weak

Fund Family: Global X Management Company LLC
Fund Type: Energy/Natural Resources
Inception Date: December 15, 2009

Major Rating Factors:
Very poor performance is the major factor driving the D- (Weak) TheStreet.com Investment Rating for *Global X China Energy ETF. The fund currently has a performance rating of E+ (Very Weak) based on an annualized return of 0.00% over the last three years and a total return of 4.23% year to date 2012. Factored into the performance evaluation is an expense ratio of 0.65% (very low).

The fund's risk rating is currently C+ (Fair). It carries a beta of 0.00, meaning the fund's expected move will be 0.0% for every 10% move in the market. Volatility, as measured by both the semi-deviation and a drawdown factor, is considered low. As of March 31, 2012, *Global X China Energy ETF traded at a discount of .88% below its net asset value, which is better than its one-year historical average discount of .41%.

Bruno Del Ama has been running the fund for 3 years and currently receives a manager quality ranking of 10 (0=worst, 99=best). This fund offers only a moderate level of risk but investors looking for strong performance are still waiting.

Data Date	Investment Rating	Net Assets ($Mil)	Price	Performance Rating/Pts	Total Return Y-T-D	Risk Rating/Pts
3-12	D-	5.47	13.56	E+ / 0.9	4.23%	C+ / 6.4
2011	D-	3.90	13.01	D- / 1.1	1.80%	C+ / 6.4
2010	A	7.10	15.75	B / 8.1	5.07%	B- / 7.5

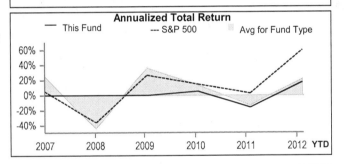

*Global X China Financials ETF (CHIX)

D-   Weak

Fund Family: Global X Management Company LLC
Fund Type: Financial Services
Inception Date: December 10, 2009

Major Rating Factors:
Disappointing performance is the major factor driving the D- (Weak) TheStreet.com Investment Rating for *Global X China Financials ETF. The fund currently has a performance rating of D- (Weak) based on an annualized return of 0.00% over the last three years and a total return of 5.91% year to date 2012. Factored into the performance evaluation is an expense ratio of 0.65% (very low).

The fund's risk rating is currently C (Fair). It carries a beta of 0.00, meaning the fund's expected move will be 0.0% for every 10% move in the market. Volatility, as measured by both the semi-deviation and a drawdown factor, is considered average. As of March 31, 2012, *Global X China Financials ETF traded at a discount of 1.26% below its net asset value, which is better than its one-year historical average discount of .40%.

Bruno Del Ama has been running the fund for 3 years and currently receives a manager quality ranking of 5 (0=worst, 99=best). This fund offers an average level of risk but investors looking for strong performance will be frustrated.

Data Date	Investment Rating	Net Assets ($Mil)	Price	Performance Rating/Pts	Total Return Y-T-D	Risk Rating/Pts
3-12	D-	13.37	11.00	D- / 1.3	5.91%	C / 5.2
2011	E+	14.00	10.39	E+ / 0.8	-2.30%	C / 5.2
2010	D+	67.40	13.35	D- / 1.2	-6.58%	B- / 7.4

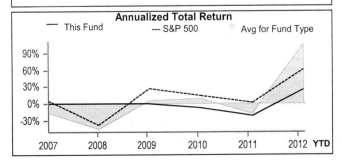

*Global X China Industrials ETF (CHII)

E+   **Very Weak**

Fund Family: Global X Management Company LLC
Fund Type: Foreign
Inception Date: November 30, 2009

Major Rating Factors:
Disappointing performance is the major factor driving the E+ (Very Weak) TheStreet.com Investment Rating for *Global X China Industrials ETF. The fund currently has a performance rating of D- (Weak) based on an annualized return of 0.00% over the last three years and a total return of 12.84% year to date 2012. Factored into the performance evaluation is an expense ratio of 0.65% (very low).

The fund's risk rating is currently C (Fair). It carries a beta of 0.00, meaning the fund's expected move will be 0.0% for every 10% move in the market. Volatility, as measured by both the semi-deviation and a drawdown factor, is considered average. As of March 31, 2012, *Global X China Industrials ETF traded at a discount of 1.36% below its net asset value, which is better than its one-year historical average discount of .06%.

Bruno Del Ama has been running the fund for 3 years and currently receives a manager quality ranking of 6 (0=worst, 99=best). This fund offers an average level of risk but investors looking for strong performance will be frustrated.

Data Date	Investment Rating	Net Assets ($Mil)	Price	Performance Rating/Pts	Total Return Y-T-D	Risk Rating/Pts
3-12	E+	4.70	11.60	D- / 1.2	12.84%	C / 4.8
2011	E+	4.10	10.28	E / 0.4	-2.52%	C / 4.8
2010	A	10.70	16.40	B / 8.0	6.01%	B- / 7.6

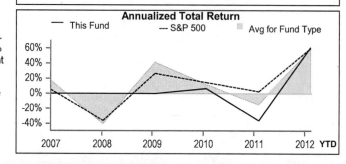

Annualized Total Return

*Global X China Materials ETF (CHIM)

E+   **Very Weak**

Fund Family: Global X Management Company LLC
Fund Type: Foreign
Inception Date: January 12, 2010

Major Rating Factors:
Very poor performance is the major factor driving the E+ (Very Weak) TheStreet.com Investment Rating for *Global X China Materials ETF. The fund currently has a performance rating of E+ (Very Weak) based on an annualized return of 0.00% over the last three years and a total return of 0.69% year to date 2012. Factored into the performance evaluation is an expense ratio of 0.65% (very low).

The fund's risk rating is currently C (Fair). It carries a beta of 0.00, meaning the fund's expected move will be 0.0% for every 10% move in the market. Volatility, as measured by both the semi-deviation and a drawdown factor, is considered average. As of March 31, 2012, *Global X China Materials ETF traded at a discount of 1.90% below its net asset value, which is better than its one-year historical average discount of .13%.

Bruno Del Ama has been running the fund for 2 years and currently receives a manager quality ranking of 3 (0=worst, 99=best). This fund offers an average level of risk but investors looking for strong performance will be frustrated.

Data Date	Investment Rating	Net Assets ($Mil)	Price	Performance Rating/Pts	Total Return Y-T-D	Risk Rating/Pts
3-12	E+	2.68	8.77	E+ / 0.6	0.69%	C / 4.9
2011	E+	2.20	8.71	E- / 0.2	-2.08%	C / 5.0

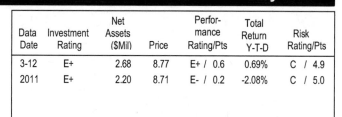
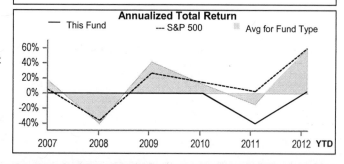

Annualized Total Return

*Global X Copper Miners ETF (COPX)

E+   **Very Weak**

Fund Family: Global X Management Company LLC
Fund Type: Precious Metals
Inception Date: April 19, 2010

Major Rating Factors:
Disappointing performance is the major factor driving the E+ (Very Weak) TheStreet.com Investment Rating for *Global X Copper Miners ETF. The fund currently has a performance rating of D- (Weak) based on an annualized return of 0.00% over the last three years and a total return of 6.23% year to date 2012. Factored into the performance evaluation is an expense ratio of 0.65% (very low).

The fund's risk rating is currently C (Fair). It carries a beta of 0.00, meaning the fund's expected move will be 0.0% for every 10% move in the market. Volatility, as measured by both the semi-deviation and a drawdown factor, is considered average. As of March 31, 2012, *Global X Copper Miners ETF traded at a discount of .44% below its net asset value, which is better than its one-year historical average discount of .27%.

Bruno Del Ama has been running the fund for 2 years and currently receives a manager quality ranking of 2 (0=worst, 99=best). This fund offers an average level of risk but investors looking for strong performance will be frustrated.

Data Date	Investment Rating	Net Assets ($Mil)	Price	Performance Rating/Pts	Total Return Y-T-D	Risk Rating/Pts
3-12	E+	34.26	13.64	D- / 1.0	6.23%	C / 4.7
2011	E+	38.00	12.84	E+ / 0.7	3.74%	C / 4.7

Annualized Total Return

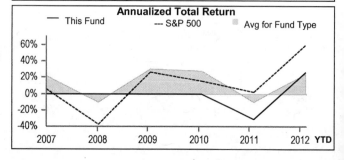

*Global X FTSE Andean 40 ETF (AND)

C   **Fair**

Fund Family: Global X Management Company LLC
Fund Type: Foreign
Inception Date: February 2, 2011

Data Date	Investment Rating	Net Assets ($Mil)	Price	Perfor- mance Rating/Pts	Total Return Y-T-D	Risk Rating/Pts
3-12	C	7.37	14.92	C+ / 5.7	19.84%	B- / 7.1

Major Rating Factors: Middle of the road best describes *Global X FTSE Andean 40 ETF whose TheStreet.com Investment Rating is currently a C (Fair). The fund currently has a performance rating of C+ (Fair) based on an annualized return of 0.00% over the last three years and a total return of 19.84% year to date 2012. Factored into the performance evaluation is an expense ratio of 0.72% (very low).

    The fund's risk rating is currently B- (Good). It carries a beta of 0.00, meaning the fund's expected move will be 0.0% for every 10% move in the market. Volatility, as measured by both the semi-deviation and a drawdown factor, is considered low. As of March 31, 2012, *Global X FTSE Andean 40 ETF traded at a discount of .20% below its net asset value, which is better than its one-year historical average discount of .02%.

    Bruno Del Ama has been running the fund for 1 year and currently receives a manager quality ranking of 84 (0=worst, 99=best). If you desire an average level of risk, then this fund may be an option.

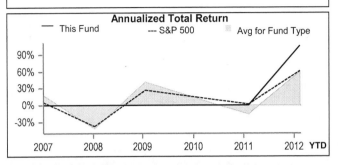

*Global X FTSE Argentina 20 ETF (ARGT)

E+   **Very Weak**

Fund Family: Global X Management Company LLC
Fund Type: Foreign
Inception Date: March 3, 2011

Data Date	Investment Rating	Net Assets ($Mil)	Price	Perfor- mance Rating/Pts	Total Return Y-T-D	Risk Rating/Pts
3-12	E+	3.93	10.70	E+ / 0.7	1.89%	C+ / 5.6

Major Rating Factors:
Very poor performance is the major factor driving the E+ (Very Weak) TheStreet.com Investment Rating for *Global X FTSE Argentina 20 ETF. The fund currently has a performance rating of E+ (Very Weak) based on an annualized return of 0.00% over the last three years and a total return of 1.89% year to date 2012. Factored into the performance evaluation is an expense ratio of 0.75% (very low).

    The fund's risk rating is currently C+ (Fair). It carries a beta of 0.00, meaning the fund's expected move will be 0.0% for every 10% move in the market. Volatility, as measured by both the semi-deviation and a drawdown factor, is considered low. As of March 31, 2012, *Global X FTSE Argentina 20 ETF traded at a discount of .09% below its net asset value, which is better than its one-year historical average discount of .02%.

    Bruno Del Ama has been running the fund for 1 year and currently receives a manager quality ranking of 6 (0=worst, 99=best). This fund offers only a moderate level of risk but investors looking for strong performance are still waiting.

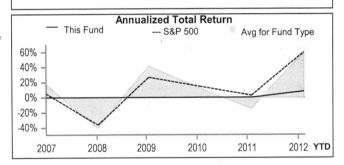

*Global X FTSE ASEAN 40 ETF (ASEA)

C-   **Fair**

Fund Family: Global X Management Company LLC
Fund Type: Global
Inception Date: February 17, 2011

Data Date	Investment Rating	Net Assets ($Mil)	Price	Perfor- mance Rating/Pts	Total Return Y-T-D	Risk Rating/Pts
3-12	C-	27.30	16.22	C / 4.5	12.87%	B- / 7.2

Major Rating Factors: Middle of the road best describes *Global X FTSE ASEAN 40 ETF whose TheStreet.com Investment Rating is currently a C- (Fair). The fund currently has a performance rating of C (Fair) based on an annualized return of 0.00% over the last three years and a total return of 12.87% year to date 2012. Factored into the performance evaluation is an expense ratio of 0.65% (very low).

    The fund's risk rating is currently B- (Good). It carries a beta of 0.00, meaning the fund's expected move will be 0.0% for every 10% move in the market. Volatility, as measured by both the semi-deviation and a drawdown factor, is considered low. As of March 31, 2012, *Global X FTSE ASEAN 40 ETF traded at a premium of .50% above its net asset value, which is worse than its one-year historical average premium of .30%.

    Bruno Del Ama has been running the fund for 1 year and currently receives a manager quality ranking of 86 (0=worst, 99=best). If you desire an average level of risk, then this fund may be an option.

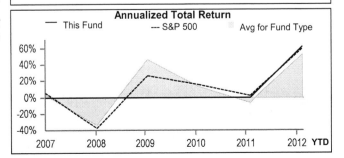

*Global X FTSE Nordic Region ETF (GXF)

D   **Weak**

Fund Family: Global X Management Company LLC
Fund Type: Global
Inception Date: August 19, 2009

Major Rating Factors: *Global X FTSE Nordic Region ETF receives a TheStreet.com Investment Rating of D (Weak). The fund currently has a performance rating of C- (Fair) based on an annualized return of 0.00% over the last three years and a total return of 18.59% year to date 2012. Factored into the performance evaluation is an expense ratio of 0.50% (very low).

The fund's risk rating is currently C+ (Fair). It carries a beta of 0.00, meaning the fund's expected move will be 0.0% for every 10% move in the market. Volatility, as measured by both the semi-deviation and a drawdown factor, is considered low. As of March 31, 2012, *Global X FTSE Nordic Region ETF traded at a premium of .49% above its net asset value, which is worse than its one-year historical average discount of .21%.

Bruno Del Ama has been running the fund for 3 years and currently receives a manager quality ranking of 29 (0=worst, 99=best). If you desire an average level of risk, then this fund may be an option.

Data Date	Investment Rating	Net Assets ($Mil)	Price	Performance Rating/Pts	Total Return Y-T-D	Risk Rating/Pts
3-12	D	26.02	18.54	C- / 3.0	18.59%	C+ / 6.7
2011	D-	22.20	15.64	E+ / 0.9	0.80%	C+ / 6.7
2010	A+	18.20	20.08	A / 9.4	25.42%	B- / 7.5

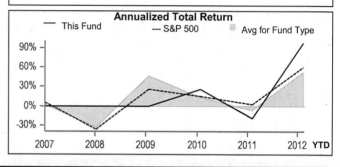

Annualized Total Return

---

*Global X FTSE Norway 30 ETF (NORW)

D   **Weak**

Fund Family: Global X Management Company LLC
Fund Type: Foreign
Inception Date: November 9, 2010

Major Rating Factors:
Disappointing performance is the major factor driving the D (Weak) TheStreet.com Investment Rating for *Global X FTSE Norway 30 ETF. The fund currently has a performance rating of D+ (Weak) based on an annualized return of 0.00% over the last three years and a total return of 16.75% year to date 2012. Factored into the performance evaluation is an expense ratio of 0.50% (very low).

The fund's risk rating is currently C+ (Fair). It carries a beta of 0.00, meaning the fund's expected move will be 0.0% for every 10% move in the market. Volatility, as measured by both the semi-deviation and a drawdown factor, is considered low. As of March 31, 2012, *Global X FTSE Norway 30 ETF traded at a premium of .21% above its net asset value, which is worse than its one-year historical average discount of .09%.

Bruno Del Ama has been running the fund for 2 years and currently receives a manager quality ranking of 28 (0=worst, 99=best). This fund offers only a moderate level of risk but investors looking for strong performance are still waiting.

Data Date	Investment Rating	Net Assets ($Mil)	Price	Performance Rating/Pts	Total Return Y-T-D	Risk Rating/Pts
3-12	D	54.07	14.64	D+ / 2.9	16.75%	C+ / 6.3
2011	D-	44.00	12.54	D- / 1.0	0.40%	C+ / 6.2

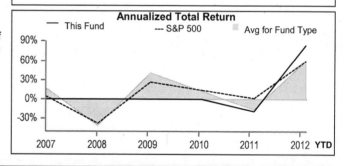

Annualized Total Return

---

*Global X Gold Explorers ETF (GLDX)

E   **Very Weak**

Fund Family: Global X Management Company LLC
Fund Type: Global
Inception Date: November 3, 2010

Major Rating Factors: Very poor performance is the major factor driving the E (Very Weak) TheStreet.com Investment Rating for *Global X Gold Explorers ETF. The fund currently has a performance rating of E (Very Weak) based on an annualized return of 0.00% over the last three years and a total return of -7.35% year to date 2012. Factored into the performance evaluation is an expense ratio of 0.65% (very low).

The fund's risk rating is currently C- (Fair). It carries a beta of 0.00, meaning the fund's expected move will be 0.0% for every 10% move in the market. Volatility, as measured by both the semi-deviation and a drawdown factor, is considered average. As of March 31, 2012, *Global X Gold Explorers ETF traded at a premium of .61% above its net asset value, which is worse than its one-year historical average premium of .31%.

Bruno Del Ama has been running the fund for 2 years and currently receives a manager quality ranking of 1 (0=worst, 99=best). This fund offers an average level of risk but investors looking for strong performance will be frustrated.

Data Date	Investment Rating	Net Assets ($Mil)	Price	Performance Rating/Pts	Total Return Y-T-D	Risk Rating/Pts
3-12	E	26.22	9.96	E / 0.3	-7.35%	C- / 4.0
2011	E+	24.00	10.75	E / 0.4	2.05%	C / 4.3

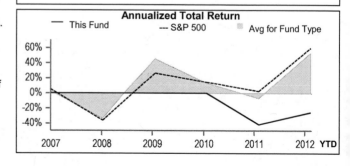

Annualized Total Return

---

*Global X Lithium ETF (LIT)   D-   Weak

Fund Family: Global X Management Company LLC
Fund Type: Growth
Inception Date: July 22, 2010

Data Date	Investment Rating	Net Assets ($Mil)	Price	Performance Rating/Pts	Total Return Y-T-D	Risk Rating/Pts
3-12	D-	97.30	16.73	D- / 1.3	16.75%	C / 5.5
2011	E+	86.70	14.33	E / 0.5	4.05%	C / 5.4

Major Rating Factors:
Disappointing performance is the major factor driving the D- (Weak) TheStreet.com Investment Rating for *Global X Lithium ETF. The fund currently has a performance rating of D- (Weak) based on an annualized return of 0.00% over the last three years and a total return of 16.75% year to date 2012. Factored into the performance evaluation is an expense ratio of 0.75% (very low).

The fund's risk rating is currently C (Fair). It carries a beta of 0.00, meaning the fund's expected move will be 0.0% for every 10% move in the market. Volatility, as measured by both the semi-deviation and a drawdown factor, is considered average. As of March 31, 2012, *Global X Lithium ETF traded at a discount of .30% below its net asset value, which is worse than its one-year historical average discount of .48%.

Bruno Del Ama has been running the fund for 2 years and currently receives a manager quality ranking of 2 (0=worst, 99=best). This fund offers an average level of risk but investors looking for strong performance will be frustrated.

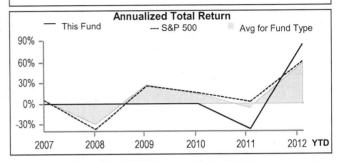

Annualized Total Return

*Global X NASDAQ China Tech ETF (QQQC)   D   Weak

Fund Family: Global X Management Company LLC
Fund Type: Foreign
Inception Date: December 8, 2009

Data Date	Investment Rating	Net Assets ($Mil)	Price	Performance Rating/Pts	Total Return Y-T-D	Risk Rating/Pts
3-12	D	4.75	15.76	D / 2.2	20.49%	C+ / 6.6
2010	A	4.90	16.50	B+ / 8.3	8.34%	B- / 7.7

Major Rating Factors:
Disappointing performance is the major factor driving the D (Weak) TheStreet.com Investment Rating for *Global X NASDAQ China Tech ETF. The fund currently has a performance rating of D (Weak) based on an annualized return of 0.00% over the last three years and a total return of 20.49% year to date 2012. Factored into the performance evaluation is an expense ratio of 0.65% (very low).

The fund's risk rating is currently C+ (Fair). It carries a beta of 0.00, meaning the fund's expected move will be 0.0% for every 10% move in the market. Volatility, as measured by both the semi-deviation and a drawdown factor, is considered low. As of March 31, 2012, *Global X NASDAQ China Tech ETF traded at a discount of 1.31% below its net asset value, which is better than its one-year historical average discount of .66%.

Bruno Del Ama has been running the fund for 3 years and currently receives a manager quality ranking of 21 (0=worst, 99=best). This fund offers only a moderate level of risk but investors looking for strong performance are still waiting.

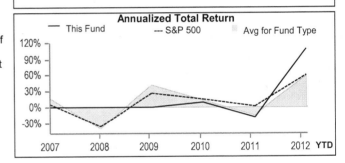

Annualized Total Return

*Global X Pure Gold Miners ETF (GGGG)   D-   Weak

Fund Family: Global X Management Company LLC
Fund Type: Precious Metals
Inception Date: March 14, 2011

Data Date	Investment Rating	Net Assets ($Mil)	Price	Performance Rating/Pts	Total Return Y-T-D	Risk Rating/Pts
3-12	D-	5.51	11.98	E+ / 0.6	-2.29%	C+ / 6.0

Major Rating Factors:
Very poor performance is the major factor driving the D- (Weak) TheStreet.com Investment Rating for *Global X Pure Gold Miners ETF. The fund currently has a performance rating of E+ (Very Weak) based on an annualized return of 0.00% over the last three years and a total return of -2.29% year to date 2012. Factored into the performance evaluation is an expense ratio of 0.59% (very low).

The fund's risk rating is currently C+ (Fair). It carries a beta of 0.00, meaning the fund's expected move will be 0.0% for every 10% move in the market. Volatility, as measured by both the semi-deviation and a drawdown factor, is considered low. As of March 31, 2012, *Global X Pure Gold Miners ETF traded at a discount of .58% below its net asset value, which is better than its one-year historical average premium of .10%.

Bruno Del Ama has been running the fund for 1 year and currently receives a manager quality ranking of 2 (0=worst, 99=best). This fund offers only a moderate level of risk but investors looking for strong performance are still waiting.

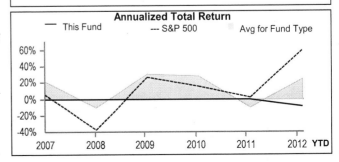

Annualized Total Return

*Global X S-P/TSX Venture 30 Can (TSXV)

| | E+ | Very Weak |

Fund Family: Global X Management Company LLC
Fund Type: Energy/Natural Resources
Inception Date: March 16, 2011

Data Date	Investment Rating	Net Assets ($Mil)	Price	Perfor- mance Rating/Pts	Total Return Y-T-D	Risk Rating/Pts
3-12	E+	2.95	10.76	E+ / 0.9	10.25%	C- / 4.0

Major Rating Factors:

Very poor performance is the major factor driving the E+ (Very Weak) TheStreet.com Investment Rating for *Global X S-P/TSX Venture 30 Can. The fund currently has a performance rating of E+ (Very Weak) based on an annualized return of 0.00% over the last three years and a total return of 10.25% year to date 2012. Factored into the performance evaluation is an expense ratio of 0.75% (very low).

The fund's risk rating is currently C- (Fair). It carries a beta of 0.00, meaning the fund's expected move will be 0.0% for every 10% move in the market. Volatility, as measured by both the semi-deviation and a drawdown factor, is considered average. As of March 31, 2012, *Global X S-P/TSX Venture 30 Can traded at a discount of 2.54% below its net asset value, which is better than its one-year historical average discount of .44%.

Bruno Del Ama has been running the fund for 1 year and currently receives a manager quality ranking of 5 (0=worst, 99=best). This fund offers an average level of risk but investors looking for strong performance will be frustrated.

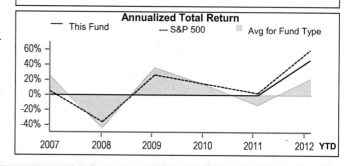

Annualized Total Return

*Global X Silver Miners ETF (SIL)

| | D- | Weak |

Fund Family: Global X Management Company LLC
Fund Type: Precious Metals
Inception Date: April 19, 2010

Data Date	Investment Rating	Net Assets ($Mil)	Price	Perfor- mance Rating/Pts	Total Return Y-T-D	Risk Rating/Pts
3-12	D-	320.51	22.23	E+ / 0.8	5.28%	C+ / 6.0
2011	D-	314.10	21.12	D- / 1.2	3.91%	C+ / 6.1

Major Rating Factors:

Very poor performance is the major factor driving the D- (Weak) TheStreet.com Investment Rating for *Global X Silver Miners ETF. The fund currently has a performance rating of E+ (Very Weak) based on an annualized return of 0.00% over the last three years and a total return of 5.28% year to date 2012. Factored into the performance evaluation is an expense ratio of 0.65% (very low).

The fund's risk rating is currently C+ (Fair). It carries a beta of 0.00, meaning the fund's expected move will be 0.0% for every 10% move in the market. Volatility, as measured by both the semi-deviation and a drawdown factor, is considered low. As of March 31, 2012, *Global X Silver Miners ETF traded at a discount of .49% below its net asset value, which is better than its one-year historical average discount of .14%.

Bruno Del Ama has been running the fund for 2 years and currently receives a manager quality ranking of 2 (0=worst, 99=best). This fund offers only a moderate level of risk but investors looking for strong performance are still waiting.

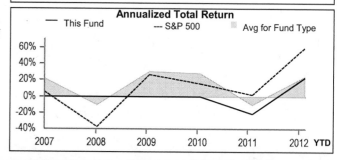

Annualized Total Return

*Global X Uranium ETF (URA)

| | E | Very Weak |

Fund Family: Global X Management Company LLC
Fund Type: Global
Inception Date: November 3, 2010

Data Date	Investment Rating	Net Assets ($Mil)	Price	Perfor- mance Rating/Pts	Total Return Y-T-D	Risk Rating/Pts
3-12	E	184.07	9.40	E+ / 0.8	15.34%	D+ / 2.5
2011	E-	164.00	8.15	E- / 0.1	3.44%	D+ / 2.3

Major Rating Factors: *Global X Uranium ETF has adopted a risky asset allocation strategy and currently receives an overall TheStreet.com Investment Rating of E (Very Weak). The fund has an above average level of volatility, as measured by both semi-deviation and drawdown factors. It carries a beta of 0.00, meaning the fund's expected move will be 0.0% for every 10% move in the market. As of March 31, 2012, *Global X Uranium ETF traded at a discount of .63% below its net asset value, which is better than its one-year historical average premium of .05%. Unfortunately, the high level of risk (D+, Weak) failed to pay off as investors endured very poor performance.

The fund's performance rating is currently E+ (Very Weak). It has registered an annualized return of 0.00% over the last three years and is up 15.34% year to date 2012. Factored into the performance evaluation is an expense ratio of 0.69% (very low).

Bruno Del Ama has been running the fund for 2 years and currently receives a manager quality ranking of 3 (0=worst, 99=best). If you can tolerate high levels of risk in the hope of improved future returns, holding this fund may be an option.

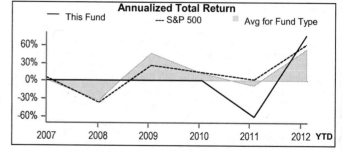

Annualized Total Return

*Global X/InterBolsa FTSE Col 20 (GXG)   C   Fair

Fund Family: Global X Management Company LLC
Fund Type: Foreign
Inception Date: February 5, 2009

Data Date	Investment Rating	Net Assets ($Mil)	Price	Performance Rating/Pts	Total Return Y-T-D	Risk Rating/Pts
3-12	C	147.47	21.20	A / 9.5	18.97%	C- / 3.6
2011	E+	121.60	17.82	D- / 1.2	3.48%	C- / 3.6
2010	A+	170.40	42.53	A+ / 9.6	50.18%	B- / 7.9

Major Rating Factors:
Exceptional performance is the major factor driving the C (Fair) TheStreet.com Investment Rating for *Global X/InterBolsa FTSE Col 20. The fund currently has a performance rating of A (Excellent) based on an annualized return of 41.61% over the last three years and a total return of 18.97% year to date 2012. Factored into the performance evaluation is an expense ratio of 0.81% (very low).

The fund's risk rating is currently C- (Fair). It carries a beta of 0.86, meaning the fund's expected move will be 8.6% for every 10% move in the market. Volatility, as measured by both the semi-deviation and a drawdown factor, is considered average. As of March 31, 2012, *Global X/InterBolsa FTSE Col 20 traded at a discount of .14% below its net asset value, which is better than its one-year historical average premium of .08%.

Bruno Del Ama has been running the fund for 3 years and currently receives a manager quality ranking of 96 (0=worst, 99=best). If you desire an average level of risk and strong performance, then this fund is a good option.

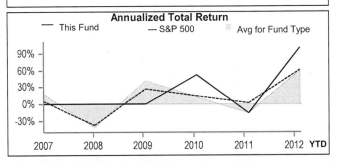

*GreenHaven Continuous Commodity (GCC)   D+   Weak

Fund Family: Greenhaven Commodity Services LLC
Fund Type: Growth and Income
Inception Date: January 24, 2008

Data Date	Investment Rating	Net Assets ($Mil)	Price	Performance Rating/Pts	Total Return Y-T-D	Risk Rating/Pts
3-12	D+	676.79	30.28	D / 2.0	1.20%	B / 8.0
2011	C-	581.20	29.92	C- / 3.4	0.77%	B / 8.1
2010	A	442.10	32.95	A / 9.5	25.19%	C+ / 5.7
2009	B+	143.21	26.32	B / 7.8	18.83%	C+ / 5.8

Major Rating Factors:
Disappointing performance is the major factor driving the D+ (Weak) TheStreet.com Investment Rating for *GreenHaven Continuous Commodity. The fund currently has a performance rating of D (Weak) based on an annualized return of 10.50% over the last three years and a total return of 1.20% year to date 2012. Factored into the performance evaluation is an expense ratio of 1.09% (low).

The fund's risk rating is currently B (Good). It carries a beta of 0.64, meaning the fund's expected move will be 6.4% for every 10% move in the market. Volatility, as measured by both the semi-deviation and a drawdown factor, is considered low. As of March 31, 2012, *GreenHaven Continuous Commodity traded at a discount of .23% below its net asset value, which is better than its one-year historical average discount of .01%.

Greenhaven Commodity Services has been running the fund for 4 years and currently receives a manager quality ranking of 29 (0=worst, 99=best). This fund offers only a moderate level of risk but investors looking for strong performance are still waiting.

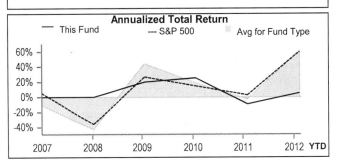

*GS Cnct S&P GSCI Enh Cmd TR Str (GSC)   D+   Weak

Fund Family: Goldman Sachs & Co/GSAM
Fund Type: Growth
Inception Date: July 31, 2007

Data Date	Investment Rating	Net Assets ($Mil)	Price	Performance Rating/Pts	Total Return Y-T-D	Risk Rating/Pts
3-12	D+	71.25	51.70	D+ / 2.7	5.77%	B- / 7.4
2011	C-	0.00	48.88	C- / 4.2	2.19%	B- / 7.4
2010	D-	0.00	48.82	D- / 1.4	10.33%	C / 4.4
2009	C+	0.00	44.25	B- / 7.5	20.70%	C / 4.8

Major Rating Factors:
Disappointing performance is the major factor driving the D+ (Weak) TheStreet.com Investment Rating for *GS Cnct S&P GSCI Enh Cmd TR Str. The fund currently has a performance rating of D+ (Weak) based on an annualized return of 12.28% over the last three years and a total return of 5.77% year to date 2012. Factored into the performance evaluation is an expense ratio of 1.25% (average).

The fund's risk rating is currently B- (Good). It carries a beta of 0.93, meaning that its performance tracks fairly well with that of the overall stock market. Volatility, as measured by both the semi-deviation and a drawdown factor, is considered low. As of March 31, 2012, *GS Cnct S&P GSCI Enh Cmd TR Str traded at a price exactly equal to its net asset value.

This fund has been team managed for 5 years and currently receives a manager quality ranking of 20 (0=worst, 99=best). This fund offers only a moderate level of risk but investors looking for strong performance are still waiting.

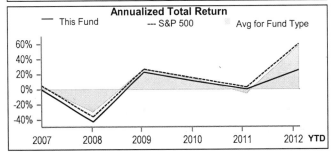

*Guggenheim 2x S&P 500 ETF (RSU)

| | | | | | B+ | Good |

Fund Family: Security Investors LLC
Fund Type: Income
Inception Date: November 5, 2007

Data Date	Investment Rating	Net Assets ($Mil)	Price	Performance Rating/Pts	Total Return Y-T-D	Risk Rating/Pts
3-12	B+	79.99	49.99	A+ / 9.6	26.63%	C+ / 6.8
2011	C+	73.50	39.66	B- / 7.4	3.28%	C+ / 6.3
2010	D-	90.40	41.10	D / 1.6	27.31%	C- / 3.5
2009	B-	146.78	32.62	A / 9.4	38.23%	C- / 3.5

Major Rating Factors:
Exceptional performance is the major factor driving the B+ (Good) TheStreet.com Investment Rating for *Guggenheim 2x S&P 500 ETF. The fund currently has a performance rating of A+ (Excellent) based on an annualized return of 39.78% over the last three years and a total return of 26.63% year to date 2012. Factored into the performance evaluation is an expense ratio of 0.71% (very low).

The fund's risk rating is currently C+ (Fair). It carries a beta of 2.03, meaning it is expected to move 20.3% for every 10% move in the market. Volatility, as measured by both the semi-deviation and a drawdown factor, is considered low. As of March 31, 2012, *Guggenheim 2x S&P 500 ETF traded at a discount of .02% below its net asset value, which is worse than its one-year historical average discount of .04%.

Michael Dellapa has been running the fund for 5 years and currently receives a manager quality ranking of 22 (0=worst, 99=best). If you desire only a moderate level of risk and strong performance, then this fund is an excellent option.

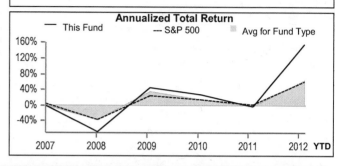

---

*Guggenheim Airline ETF (FAA)

| | | | | | D | Weak |

Fund Family: Guggenheim Funds Investment Advisor
Fund Type: Global
Inception Date: January 26, 2009

Data Date	Investment Rating	Net Assets ($Mil)	Price	Performance Rating/Pts	Total Return Y-T-D	Risk Rating/Pts
3-12	D	14.65	29.20	C- / 3.1	11.24%	C+ / 6.2
2011	D-	14.50	26.25	E / 0.5	0.76%	C+ / 5.9
2010	A	37.60	39.56	A / 9.4	29.54%	C+ / 6.5

Major Rating Factors: *Guggenheim Airline ETF receives a TheStreet.com Investment Rating of D (Weak). The fund currently has a performance rating of C- (Fair) based on an annualized return of 15.91% over the last three years and a total return of 11.24% year to date 2012. Factored into the performance evaluation is an expense ratio of 0.70% (very low).

The fund's risk rating is currently C+ (Fair). It carries a beta of 0.89, meaning the fund's expected move will be 8.9% for every 10% move in the market. Volatility, as measured by both the semi-deviation and a drawdown factor, is considered low. As of March 31, 2012, *Guggenheim Airline ETF traded at a discount of .10% below its net asset value, which is worse than its one-year historical average discount of .19%.

Michael P. Byrum currently receives a manager quality ranking of 71 (0=worst, 99=best). If you desire an average level of risk, then this fund may be an option.

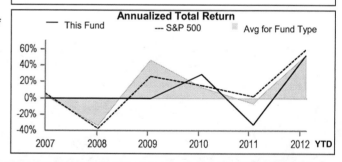

---

*Guggenheim Australian Dollar Sha (FXA)

| | | | | | C | Fair |

Fund Family: Security Investors LLC
Fund Type: Foreign
Inception Date: June 26, 2006

Data Date	Investment Rating	Net Assets ($Mil)	Price	Performance Rating/Pts	Total Return Y-T-D	Risk Rating/Pts
3-12	C	837.39	103.87	C- / 3.8	2.11%	B / 8.6
2011	B-	784.40	102.62	C+ / 5.8	0.03%	B / 8.7
2010	B+	735.50	102.66	B / 7.7	18.23%	C+ / 6.4
2009	C+	557.97	90.07	C+ / 5.9	29.41%	C+ / 6.8

Major Rating Factors: Middle of the road best describes *Guggenheim Australian Dollar Sha whose TheStreet.com Investment Rating is currently a C (Fair). The fund currently has a performance rating of C- (Fair) based on an annualized return of 16.89% over the last three years and a total return of 2.11% year to date 2012. Factored into the performance evaluation is an expense ratio of 0.40% (very low).

The fund's risk rating is currently B (Good). It carries a beta of 0.63, meaning the fund's expected move will be 6.3% for every 10% move in the market. Volatility, as measured by both the semi-deviation and a drawdown factor, is considered low. As of March 31, 2012, *Guggenheim Australian Dollar Sha traded at a discount of .05% below its net asset value, which is better than its one-year historical average discount of .02%.

This fund has been team managed for 6 years and currently receives a manager quality ranking of 79 (0=worst, 99=best). If you desire an average level of risk, then this fund may be an option.

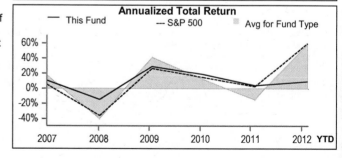

*Guggenheim BltShs 2012 Corp Bd E (BSCC)   C-   Fair

Fund Family: Guggenheim Funds Investment Advisor
Fund Type: Corporate - Investment Grade
Inception Date: June 4, 2010

Data Date	Investment Rating	Net Assets ($Mil)	Price	Performance Rating/Pts	Total Return Y-T-D	Risk Rating/Pts
3-12	C-	98.38	20.48	D- / 1.2	-0.09%	B+ / 9.9
2011	C	98.00	20.53	D / 2.1	0.15%	B+ / 9.9

Major Rating Factors:
Disappointing performance is the major factor driving the C- (Fair) TheStreet.com Investment Rating for *Guggenheim BltShs 2012 Corp Bd E. The fund currently has a performance rating of D- (Weak) based on an annualized return of 0.00% over the last three years and a total return of -0.09% year to date 2012. Factored into the performance evaluation is an expense ratio of 0.24% (very low).

The fund's risk rating is currently B+ (Good). It carries a beta of 0.00, meaning the fund's expected move will be 0.0% for every 10% move in the market. Volatility, as measured by both the semi-deviation and a drawdown factor, is considered very low. As of March 31, 2012, *Guggenheim BltShs 2012 Corp Bd E traded at a discount of .10% below its net asset value, which is better than its one-year historical average premium of .43%.

Michael P. Byrum currently receives a manager quality ranking of 52 (0=worst, 99=best). This fund offers only a moderate level of risk but investors looking for strong performance are still waiting.

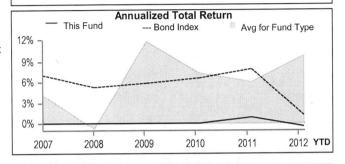

Annualized Total Return

---

*Guggenheim BltShs 2013 Corp Bd E (BSCD)   C-   Fair

Fund Family: Guggenheim Funds Investment Advisor
Fund Type: Corporate - Investment Grade
Inception Date: June 4, 2010

Data Date	Investment Rating	Net Assets ($Mil)	Price	Performance Rating/Pts	Total Return Y-T-D	Risk Rating/Pts
3-12	C-	118.88	20.93	D- / 1.4	1.26%	B+ / 9.9
2011	C	111.40	20.72	D / 2.2	0.24%	B+ / 9.9

Major Rating Factors:
Disappointing performance is the major factor driving the C- (Fair) TheStreet.com Investment Rating for *Guggenheim BltShs 2013 Corp Bd E. The fund currently has a performance rating of D- (Weak) based on an annualized return of 0.00% over the last three years and a total return of 1.26% year to date 2012. Factored into the performance evaluation is an expense ratio of 0.24% (very low).

The fund's risk rating is currently B+ (Good). It carries a beta of 0.00, meaning the fund's expected move will be 0.0% for every 10% move in the market. Volatility, as measured by both the semi-deviation and a drawdown factor, is considered very low. As of March 31, 2012, *Guggenheim BltShs 2013 Corp Bd E traded at a premium of .34% above its net asset value, which is better than its one-year historical average premium of .51%.

Michael P. Byrum currently receives a manager quality ranking of 58 (0=worst, 99=best). This fund offers only a moderate level of risk but investors looking for strong performance are still waiting.

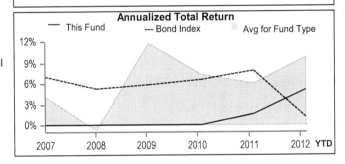

Annualized Total Return

---

*Guggenheim BltShs 2014 Corp Bd E (BSCE)   C-   Fair

Fund Family: Guggenheim Funds Investment Advisor
Fund Type: Corporate - Investment Grade
Inception Date: June 4, 2010

Data Date	Investment Rating	Net Assets ($Mil)	Price	Performance Rating/Pts	Total Return Y-T-D	Risk Rating/Pts
3-12	C-	114.00	21.14	D / 1.6	1.45%	B+ / 9.9
2011	C	96.30	20.90	D+ / 2.4	0.00%	B+ / 9.9

Major Rating Factors:
Disappointing performance is the major factor driving the C- (Fair) TheStreet.com Investment Rating for *Guggenheim BltShs 2014 Corp Bd E. The fund currently has a performance rating of D (Weak) based on an annualized return of 0.00% over the last three years and a total return of 1.45% year to date 2012. Factored into the performance evaluation is an expense ratio of 0.24% (very low).

The fund's risk rating is currently B+ (Good). It carries a beta of 0.00, meaning the fund's expected move will be 0.0% for every 10% move in the market. Volatility, as measured by both the semi-deviation and a drawdown factor, is considered very low. As of March 31, 2012, *Guggenheim BltShs 2014 Corp Bd E traded at a premium of .09% above its net asset value, which is better than its one-year historical average premium of .59%.

Michael P. Byrum currently receives a manager quality ranking of 42 (0=worst, 99=best). This fund offers only a moderate level of risk but investors looking for strong performance are still waiting.

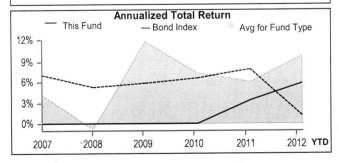

Annualized Total Return

*Guggenheim BltShs 2015 Corp Bd E (BSCF)

C-   **Fair**

Fund Family: Guggenheim Funds Investment Advisor
Fund Type: Corporate - Investment Grade
Inception Date: June 4, 2010

Major Rating Factors:
Disappointing performance is the major factor driving the C- (Fair) TheStreet.com Investment Rating for *Guggenheim BltShs 2015 Corp Bd E. The fund currently has a performance rating of D (Weak) based on an annualized return of 0.00% over the last three years and a total return of 2.76% year to date 2012. Factored into the performance evaluation is an expense ratio of 0.24% (very low).

The fund's risk rating is currently B+ (Good). It carries a beta of 0.00, meaning the fund's expected move will be 0.0% for every 10% move in the market. Volatility, as measured by both the semi-deviation and a drawdown factor, is considered very low. As of March 31, 2012, *Guggenheim BltShs 2015 Corp Bd E traded at a premium of .19% above its net asset value, which is better than its one-year historical average premium of .61%.

Michael P. Byrum currently receives a manager quality ranking of 38 (0=worst, 99=best). This fund offers only a moderate level of risk but investors looking for strong performance are still waiting.

Data Date	Investment Rating	Net Assets ($Mil)	Price	Performance Rating/Pts	Total Return Y-T-D	Risk Rating/Pts
3-12	C-	93.34	21.50	D / 2.0	2.76%	B+ / 9.8
2011	C	68.80	21.00	D+ / 2.5	-0.10%	B+ / 9.8

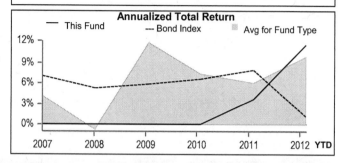

*Guggenheim BltShs 2016 Corp Bd E (BSCG)

C-   **Fair**

Fund Family: Guggenheim Funds Investment Advisor
Fund Type: Corporate - Investment Grade
Inception Date: June 4, 2010

Major Rating Factors:
Disappointing performance is the major factor driving the C- (Fair) TheStreet.com Investment Rating for *Guggenheim BltShs 2016 Corp Bd E. The fund currently has a performance rating of D (Weak) based on an annualized return of 0.00% over the last three years and a total return of 2.43% year to date 2012. Factored into the performance evaluation is an expense ratio of 0.24% (very low).

The fund's risk rating is currently B+ (Good). It carries a beta of 0.00, meaning the fund's expected move will be 0.0% for every 10% move in the market. Volatility, as measured by both the semi-deviation and a drawdown factor, is considered very low. As of March 31, 2012, *Guggenheim BltShs 2016 Corp Bd E traded at a premium of .23% above its net asset value, which is better than its one-year historical average premium of .60%.

Michael P. Byrum currently receives a manager quality ranking of 37 (0=worst, 99=best). This fund offers only a moderate level of risk but investors looking for strong performance are still waiting.

Data Date	Investment Rating	Net Assets ($Mil)	Price	Performance Rating/Pts	Total Return Y-T-D	Risk Rating/Pts
3-12	C-	91.02	21.69	D / 2.1	2.43%	B+ / 9.7
2011	C	66.30	21.26	D+ / 2.9	-0.02%	B+ / 9.8

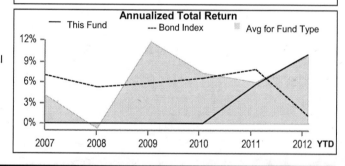

*Guggenheim BltShs 2017 Corp Bd E (BSCH)

C   **Fair**

Fund Family: Guggenheim Funds Investment Advisor
Fund Type: Corporate - Investment Grade
Inception Date: June 4, 2010

Major Rating Factors:
Disappointing performance is the major factor driving the C (Fair) TheStreet.com Investment Rating for *Guggenheim BltShs 2017 Corp Bd E. The fund currently has a performance rating of D+ (Weak) based on an annualized return of 0.00% over the last three years and a total return of 3.80% year to date 2012. Factored into the performance evaluation is an expense ratio of 0.24% (very low).

The fund's risk rating is currently B+ (Good). It carries a beta of 0.00, meaning the fund's expected move will be 0.0% for every 10% move in the market. Volatility, as measured by both the semi-deviation and a drawdown factor, is considered very low. As of March 31, 2012, *Guggenheim BltShs 2017 Corp Bd E traded at a premium of .32% above its net asset value, which is better than its one-year historical average premium of .43%.

Michael P. Byrum currently receives a manager quality ranking of 35 (0=worst, 99=best). This fund offers only a moderate level of risk but investors looking for strong performance are still waiting.

Data Date	Investment Rating	Net Assets ($Mil)	Price	Performance Rating/Pts	Total Return Y-T-D	Risk Rating/Pts
3-12	C	78.99	22.02	D+ / 2.6	3.80%	B+ / 9.7
2011	C	53.90	21.32	C- / 3.0	0.07%	B+ / 9.8

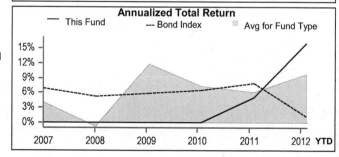

*Guggenheim BRIC ETF (EEB)

D+ **Weak**

Fund Family: Guggenheim Funds Investment Advisor
Fund Type: Income
Inception Date: September 21, 2006

Major Rating Factors: *Guggenheim BRIC ETF receives a TheStreet.com Investment Rating of D+ (Weak). The fund currently has a performance rating of C- (Fair) based on an annualized return of 17.30% over the last three years and a total return of 12.70% year to date 2012. Factored into the performance evaluation is an expense ratio of 0.64% (very low).

The fund's risk rating is currently B- (Good). It carries a beta of 1.45, meaning it is expected to move 14.5% for every 10% move in the market. Volatility, as measured by both the semi-deviation and a drawdown factor, is considered low. As of March 31, 2012, *Guggenheim BRIC ETF traded at a discount of .10% below its net asset value, which is better than its one-year historical average discount of .04%.

Michael P. Byrum currently receives a manager quality ranking of 13 (0=worst, 99=best). If you desire an average level of risk, then this fund may be an option.

Data Date	Investment Rating	Net Assets ($Mil)	Price	Performance Rating/Pts	Total Return Y-T-D	Risk Rating/Pts
3-12	D+	489.73	39.48	C- / 3.8	12.70%	B- / 7.0
2011	C-	418.90	35.03	C / 4.6	2.80%	B- / 7.0
2010	D	1,054.70	46.14	C- / 3.5	10.49%	C- / 4.2
2009	C+	753.72	42.46	B / 8.1	73.91%	C / 4.3

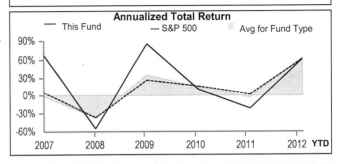

*Guggenheim Brit Pnd Sterling (FXB)

D+ **Weak**

Fund Family: Security Investors LLC
Fund Type: Foreign
Inception Date: June 26, 2006

Major Rating Factors:
Disappointing performance is the major factor driving the D+ (Weak) TheStreet.com Investment Rating for *Guggenheim Brit Pnd Sterling. The fund currently has a performance rating of D- (Weak) based on an annualized return of 2.28% over the last three years and a total return of 2.91% year to date 2012. Factored into the performance evaluation is an expense ratio of 0.40% (very low).

The fund's risk rating is currently B (Good). It carries a beta of 0.34, meaning the fund's expected move will be 3.4% for every 10% move in the market. Volatility, as measured by both the semi-deviation and a drawdown factor, is considered low. As of March 31, 2012, *Guggenheim Brit Pnd Sterling traded at a premium of .12% above its net asset value, which is worse than its one-year historical average premium of .03%.

This fund has been team managed for 6 years and currently receives a manager quality ranking of 32 (0=worst, 99=best). This fund offers only a moderate level of risk but investors looking for strong performance are still waiting.

Data Date	Investment Rating	Net Assets ($Mil)	Price	Performance Rating/Pts	Total Return Y-T-D	Risk Rating/Pts
3-12	D+	113.36	158.58	D- / 1.4	2.91%	B / 8.8
2011	C-	92.50	154.10	D / 1.9	-0.70%	B / 8.8
2010	D+	124.50	155.77	D- / 1.0	-3.33%	B- / 7.1
2009	C-	157.26	161.13	D / 1.6	11.30%	B- / 7.3

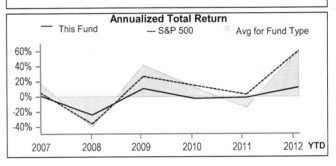

*Guggenheim Canadian Dollar Shs (FXC)

D+ **Weak**

Fund Family: Security Investors LLC
Fund Type: Foreign
Inception Date: June 26, 2006

Major Rating Factors:
Disappointing performance is the major factor driving the D+ (Weak) TheStreet.com Investment Rating for *Guggenheim Canadian Dollar Shs. The fund currently has a performance rating of D (Weak) based on an annualized return of 7.12% over the last three years and a total return of 2.15% year to date 2012. Factored into the performance evaluation is an expense ratio of 0.40% (very low).

The fund's risk rating is currently B+ (Good). It carries a beta of 0.47, meaning the fund's expected move will be 4.7% for every 10% move in the market. Volatility, as measured by both the semi-deviation and a drawdown factor, is considered very low. As of March 31, 2012, *Guggenheim Canadian Dollar Shs traded at a premium of .19% above its net asset value, which is worse than its one-year historical average discount of .02%.

This fund has been team managed for 6 years and currently receives a manager quality ranking of 46 (0=worst, 99=best). This fund offers only a moderate level of risk but investors looking for strong performance are still waiting.

Data Date	Investment Rating	Net Assets ($Mil)	Price	Performance Rating/Pts	Total Return Y-T-D	Risk Rating/Pts
3-12	D+	585.57	99.69	D / 1.9	2.15%	B+ / 9.0
2011	C-	576.20	97.62	D+ / 2.5	-0.83%	B+ / 9.0
2010	C	590.50	99.54	C- / 3.0	4.97%	B- / 7.4
2009	C+	489.42	94.85	C / 4.6	15.22%	B- / 7.5

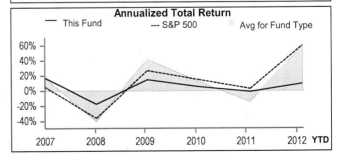

*Guggenheim Canadian Energy Inc E (ENY)

D+   **Weak**

Fund Family: Guggenheim Funds Investment Advisor
Fund Type: Energy/Natural Resources
Inception Date: July 3, 2007

Major Rating Factors: *Guggenheim Canadian Energy Inc E receives a TheStreet.com Investment Rating of D+ (Weak). The fund currently has a performance rating of C (Fair) based on an annualized return of 21.75% over the last three years and a total return of 2.76% year to date 2012. Factored into the performance evaluation is an expense ratio of 0.70% (very low).

The fund's risk rating is currently C+ (Fair). It carries a beta of 1.32, meaning it is expected to move 13.2% for every 10% move in the market. Volatility, as measured by both the semi-deviation and a drawdown factor, is considered low. As of March 31, 2012, *Guggenheim Canadian Energy Inc E traded at a premium of .29% above its net asset value, which is worse than its one-year historical average discount of .17%.

Saroj Kanuri has been running the fund for 2 years and currently receives a manager quality ranking of 37 (0=worst, 99=best). If you desire an average level of risk, then this fund may be an option.

Data Date	Investment Rating	Net Assets ($Mil)	Price	Performance Rating/Pts	Total Return Y-T-D	Risk Rating/Pts
3-12	D+	117.40	17.20	C / 4.3	2.76%	C+ / 6.5
2011	C-	114.70	16.85	C / 5.0	1.42%	C+ / 6.4
2010	D	97.90	20.15	C- / 4.0	22.45%	C- / 3.6
2009	B+	37.79	16.98	A / 9.4	50.27%	C / 4.3

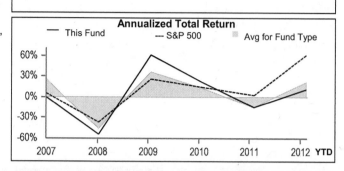

---

*Guggenheim China All-Cap ETF (YAO)

D-   **Weak**

Fund Family: Guggenheim Funds Investment Advisor
Fund Type: Foreign
Inception Date: October 19, 2009

Major Rating Factors:
Disappointing performance is the major factor driving the D- (Weak) TheStreet.com Investment Rating for *Guggenheim China All-Cap ETF. The fund currently has a performance rating of D (Weak) based on an annualized return of 0.00% over the last three years and a total return of 10.68% year to date 2012. Factored into the performance evaluation is an expense ratio of 0.70% (very low).

The fund's risk rating is currently C+ (Fair). It carries a beta of 0.00, meaning the fund's expected move will be 0.0% for every 10% move in the market. Volatility, as measured by both the semi-deviation and a drawdown factor, is considered low. As of March 31, 2012, *Guggenheim China All-Cap ETF traded at a discount of 1.05% below its net asset value, which is better than its one-year historical average discount of .08%.

Michael P. Byrum currently receives a manager quality ranking of 17 (0=worst, 99=best). This fund offers only a moderate level of risk but investors looking for strong performance are still waiting.

Data Date	Investment Rating	Net Assets ($Mil)	Price	Performance Rating/Pts	Total Return Y-T-D	Risk Rating/Pts
3-12	D-	61.32	23.63	D / 1.6	10.68%	C+ / 6.5
2011	D-	53.80	21.35	E+ / 0.8	0.76%	C+ / 6.5
2010	A	84.10	27.16	B / 8.1	8.81%	B- / 7.9

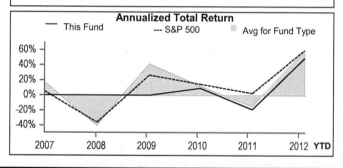

---

*Guggenheim China Real Estate ETF (TAO)

D   **Weak**

Fund Family: Guggenheim Funds Investment Advisor
Fund Type: Growth and Income
Inception Date: December 18, 2007

Major Rating Factors: *Guggenheim China Real Estate ETF receives a TheStreet.com Investment Rating of D (Weak). The fund currently has a performance rating of C- (Fair) based on an annualized return of 13.62% over the last three years and a total return of 15.71% year to date 2012. Factored into the performance evaluation is an expense ratio of 0.70% (very low).

The fund's risk rating is currently C+ (Fair). It carries a beta of 1.53, meaning it is expected to move 15.3% for every 10% move in the market. Volatility, as measured by both the semi-deviation and a drawdown factor, is considered low. As of March 31, 2012, *Guggenheim China Real Estate ETF traded at a discount of 1.28% below its net asset value, which is better than its one-year historical average discount of .27%.

Michael P. Byrum currently receives a manager quality ranking of 10 (0=worst, 99=best). If you desire an average level of risk, then this fund may be an option.

Data Date	Investment Rating	Net Assets ($Mil)	Price	Performance Rating/Pts	Total Return Y-T-D	Risk Rating/Pts
3-12	D	20.96	16.94	C- / 3.3	15.71%	C+ / 6.0
2011	D	17.90	14.64	C- / 3.2	0.07%	C+ / 6.1
2010	D-	65.40	19.94	D / 2.0	10.10%	C- / 4.0
2009	B	39.80	18.15	A / 9.3	68.65%	C- / 4.2

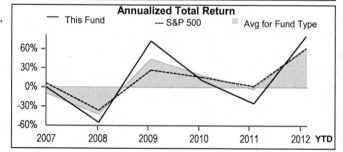

---

*Guggenheim China Small Cap ETF (HAO)   D-   Weak

Fund Family: Guggenheim Funds Investment Advisor
Fund Type: Foreign
Inception Date: January 30, 2008

Major Rating Factors:
Disappointing performance is the major factor driving the D- (Weak) TheStreet.com Investment Rating for *Guggenheim China Small Cap ETF. The fund currently has a performance rating of D+ (Weak) based on an annualized return of 13.57% over the last three years and a total return of 11.76% year to date 2012. Factored into the performance evaluation is an expense ratio of 0.75% (very low).

The fund's risk rating is currently C (Fair). It carries a beta of 1.32, meaning it is expected to move 13.2% for every 10% move in the market. Volatility, as measured by both the semi-deviation and a drawdown factor, is considered average. As of March 31, 2012, *Guggenheim China Small Cap ETF traded at a discount of .37% below its net asset value, which is better than its one-year historical average discount of .22%.

Michael P. Byrum currently receives a manager quality ranking of 22 (0=worst, 99=best). This fund offers an average level of risk but investors looking for strong performance will be frustrated.

Data Date	Investment Rating	Net Assets ($Mil)	Price	Performance Rating/Pts	Total Return Y-T-D	Risk Rating/Pts
3-12	D-	178.78	21.57	D+ / 2.8	11.76%	C / 4.4
2011	D-	142.00	19.30	C- / 3.2	-1.55%	C / 4.4
2010	B-	438.70	30.06	B+ / 8.9	15.32%	C- / 3.7
2009	B	62.94	26.33	A+ / 9.8	88.42%	C- / 3.5

Annualized Total Return

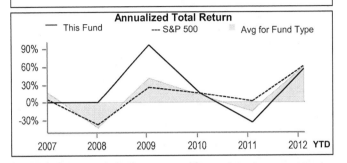

*Guggenheim China Technology ETF (CQQQ)   D-   Weak

Fund Family: Guggenheim Funds Investment Advisor
Fund Type: Foreign
Inception Date: December 8, 2009

Major Rating Factors:
Disappointing performance is the major factor driving the D- (Weak) TheStreet.com Investment Rating for *Guggenheim China Technology ETF. The fund currently has a performance rating of D (Weak) based on an annualized return of 0.00% over the last three years and a total return of 18.16% year to date 2012. Factored into the performance evaluation is an expense ratio of 0.70% (very low).

The fund's risk rating is currently C+ (Fair). It carries a beta of 0.00, meaning the fund's expected move will be 0.0% for every 10% move in the market. Volatility, as measured by both the semi-deviation and a drawdown factor, is considered low. As of March 31, 2012, *Guggenheim China Technology ETF traded at a discount of .41% below its net asset value, which is better than its one-year historical average discount of .21%.

Michael P. Byrum currently receives a manager quality ranking of 15 (0=worst, 99=best). This fund offers only a moderate level of risk but investors looking for strong performance are still waiting.

Data Date	Investment Rating	Net Assets ($Mil)	Price	Performance Rating/Pts	Total Return Y-T-D	Risk Rating/Pts
3-12	D-	25.98	24.14	D / 1.9	18.16%	C+ / 5.8
2011	D-	21.60	20.43	E+ / 0.6	-0.10%	C+ / 5.8
2010	A	37.10	27.58	B / 8.0	7.08%	B- / 7.4

Annualized Total Return

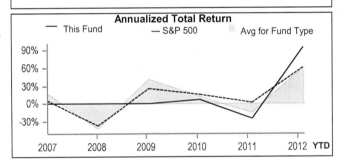

*Guggenheim Defensive Equity ETF (DEF)   B-   Good

Fund Family: Guggenheim Funds Investment Advisor
Fund Type: Income
Inception Date: December 15, 2006

Major Rating Factors: *Guggenheim Defensive Equity ETF receives a TheStreet.com Investment Rating of B- (Good). The fund currently has a performance rating of C+ (Fair) based on an annualized return of 22.67% over the last three years and a total return of 2.53% year to date 2012. Factored into the performance evaluation is an expense ratio of 0.65% (very low).

The fund's risk rating is currently B+ (Good). It carries a beta of 0.55, meaning the fund's expected move will be 5.5% for every 10% move in the market. Volatility, as measured by both the semi-deviation and a drawdown factor, is considered very low. As of March 31, 2012, *Guggenheim Defensive Equity ETF traded at a discount of .04% below its net asset value, which is better than its one-year historical average premium of .04%.

Michael P. Byrum currently receives a manager quality ranking of 85 (0=worst, 99=best). If you desire an average level of risk, then this fund may be an option.

Data Date	Investment Rating	Net Assets ($Mil)	Price	Performance Rating/Pts	Total Return Y-T-D	Risk Rating/Pts
3-12	B-	60.90	28.03	C+ / 5.7	2.53%	B+ / 9.2
2011	B-	47.60	27.34	C+ / 6.6	-0.84%	B / 8.5
2010	C+	19.60	24.53	C / 5.4	18.77%	C+ / 6.0
2009	C-	15.52	20.86	D+ / 2.5	19.95%	C+ / 6.3

Annualized Total Return

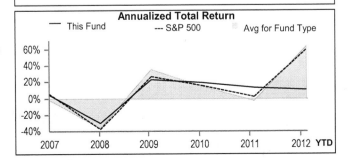

*Guggenheim Enhanced Core Bond ET (GIY)

C-   **Fair**

Fund Family: Guggenheim Funds Investment Advisor
Fund Type: General - Investment Grade
Inception Date: February 12, 2008

Data Date	Investment Rating	Net Assets ($Mil)	Price	Performance Rating/Pts	Total Return Y-T-D	Risk Rating/Pts
3-12	C-	5.21	51.55	D / 2.1	-0.22%	B+ / 9.4
2011	C	5.20	51.81	C- / 3.8	-0.86%	B / 8.9
2010	B-	10.40	51.71	C / 4.3	8.30%	B / 8.2
2009	B	5.04	49.00	C / 5.3	11.22%	B / 8.4

Major Rating Factors:

Disappointing performance is the major factor driving the C- (Fair) TheStreet.com Investment Rating for *Guggenheim Enhanced Core Bond ET. The fund currently has a performance rating of D (Weak) based on an annualized return of 8.15% over the last three years and a total return of -0.22% year to date 2012. Factored into the performance evaluation is an expense ratio of 0.32% (very low).

The fund's risk rating is currently B+ (Good). It carries a beta of 0.46, meaning the fund's expected move will be 4.6% for every 10% move in the market. Volatility, as measured by both the semi-deviation and a drawdown factor, is considered very low. As of March 31, 2012, *Guggenheim Enhanced Core Bond ET traded at a discount of .83% below its net asset value, which is better than its one-year historical average premium of .21%.

David C. Kwan has been running the fund for 4 years and currently receives a manager quality ranking of 82 (0=worst, 99=best). This fund offers only a moderate level of risk but investors looking for strong performance are still waiting.

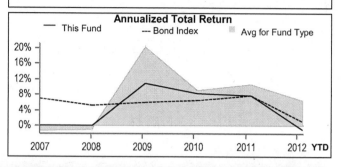

Annualized Total Return
— This Fund   --- Bond Index   Avg for Fund Type

*Guggenheim Enhanced Sh Bd ETF (GSY)

C-   **Fair**

Fund Family: Guggenheim Funds Investment Advisor
Fund Type: Growth
Inception Date: February 12, 2008

Data Date	Investment Rating	Net Assets ($Mil)	Price	Performance Rating/Pts	Total Return Y-T-D	Risk Rating/Pts
3-12	C-	149.55	49.89	D- / 1.2	0.49%	B+ / 9.9
2011	C-	14.90	49.66	D / 2.0	-0.02%	B+ / 9.9
2010	C	5.00	49.77	D / 2.2	-0.17%	B+ / 9.0
2009	C	9.97	49.86	D / 1.9	0.06%	B+ / 9.1

Major Rating Factors:

Disappointing performance is the major factor driving the C- (Fair) TheStreet.com Investment Rating for *Guggenheim Enhanced Sh Bd ETF. The fund currently has a performance rating of D- (Weak) based on an annualized return of 0.28% over the last three years and a total return of 0.49% year to date 2012. Factored into the performance evaluation is an expense ratio of 0.27% (very low).

The fund's risk rating is currently B+ (Good). It carries a beta of 0.00, meaning the fund's expected move will be 0.0% for every 10% move in the market. Volatility, as measured by both the semi-deviation and a drawdown factor, is considered very low. As of March 31, 2012, *Guggenheim Enhanced Sh Bd ETF traded at a discount of .04% below its net asset value, which is worse than its one-year historical average discount of .08%.

Anne Walsh has been running the fund for 1 year and currently receives a manager quality ranking of 48 (0=worst, 99=best). This fund offers only a moderate level of risk but investors looking for strong performance are still waiting.

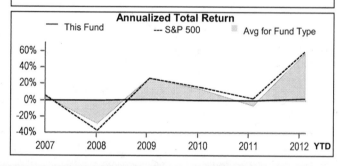

Annualized Total Return
— This Fund   --- S&P 500   Avg for Fund Type

*Guggenheim Euro Shares (FXE)

D   **Weak**

Fund Family: Security Investors LLC
Fund Type: Foreign
Inception Date: December 9, 2005

Data Date	Investment Rating	Net Assets ($Mil)	Price	Performance Rating/Pts	Total Return Y-T-D	Risk Rating/Pts
3-12	D	332.95	132.72	D- / 1.1	2.95%	B / 8.2
2011	D+	278.00	128.92	D / 1.6	-1.71%	B / 8.2
2010	D+	354.10	133.09	D- / 1.5	-6.87%	B- / 7.2
2009	C	616.52	142.91	C- / 3.5	3.32%	B- / 7.9

Major Rating Factors:

Disappointing performance is the major factor driving the D (Weak) TheStreet.com Investment Rating for *Guggenheim Euro Shares. The fund currently has a performance rating of D- (Weak) based on an annualized return of -0.45% over the last three years and a total return of 2.95% year to date 2012. Factored into the performance evaluation is an expense ratio of 0.40% (very low).

The fund's risk rating is currently B (Good). It carries a beta of 0.46, meaning the fund's expected move will be 4.6% for every 10% move in the market. Volatility, as measured by both the semi-deviation and a drawdown factor, is considered low. As of March 31, 2012, *Guggenheim Euro Shares traded at a premium of .13% above its net asset value.

This fund has been team managed for 7 years and currently receives a manager quality ranking of 18 (0=worst, 99=best). This fund offers only a moderate level of risk but investors looking for strong performance are still waiting.

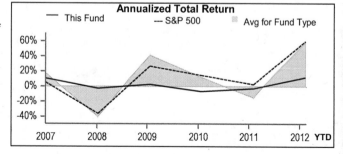

Annualized Total Return
— This Fund   --- S&P 500   Avg for Fund Type

*Guggenheim Frontier Markets ETF (FRN)   C+   Fair

Fund Family: Guggenheim Funds Investment Advisor
Fund Type: Global
Inception Date: June 12, 2008

Major Rating Factors: Strong performance is the major factor driving the C+ (Fair) TheStreet.com Investment Rating for *Guggenheim Frontier Markets ETF. The fund currently has a performance rating of B- (Good) based on an annualized return of 26.38% over the last three years and a total return of 18.63% year to date 2012. Factored into the performance evaluation is an expense ratio of 0.70% (very low).

The fund's risk rating is currently B- (Good). It carries a beta of 0.77, meaning the fund's expected move will be 7.7% for every 10% move in the market. Volatility, as measured by both the semi-deviation and a drawdown factor, is considered low. As of March 31, 2012, *Guggenheim Frontier Markets ETF traded at a premium of .70% above its net asset value, which is worse than its one-year historical average discount of .42%.

Michael P. Byrum currently receives a manager quality ranking of 88 (0=worst, 99=best). If you desire only a moderate level of risk and strong performance, then this fund is an excellent option.

Data Date	Investment Rating	Net Assets ($Mil)	Price	Performance Rating/Pts	Total Return Y-T-D	Risk Rating/Pts
3-12	C+	134.57	21.52	B- / 7.1	18.63%	B- / 7.4
2011	C-	121.20	18.14	C / 4.4	1.93%	B- / 7.3
2010	B+	242.00	24.44	A+ / 9.6	33.59%	C / 4.5
2009	B+	15.07	18.35	A- / 9.0	50.14%	C / 4.7

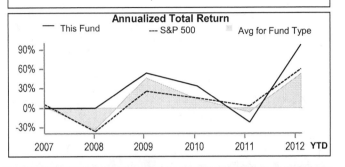

Annualized Total Return

*Guggenheim Insider Sentiment ETF (NFO)   B   Good

Fund Family: Guggenheim Funds Investment Advisor
Fund Type: Income
Inception Date: September 21, 2006

Major Rating Factors: Strong performance is the major factor driving the B (Good) TheStreet.com Investment Rating for *Guggenheim Insider Sentiment ETF. The fund currently has a performance rating of B (Good) based on an annualized return of 29.40% over the last three years and a total return of 13.51% year to date 2012. Factored into the performance evaluation is an expense ratio of 0.65% (very low).

The fund's risk rating is currently B- (Good). It carries a beta of 1.39, meaning it is expected to move 13.9% for every 10% move in the market. Volatility, as measured by both the semi-deviation and a drawdown factor, is considered low. As of March 31, 2012, *Guggenheim Insider Sentiment ETF traded at a premium of .14% above its net asset value, which is worse than its one-year historical average discount of .04%.

Michael P. Byrum currently receives a manager quality ranking of 42 (0=worst, 99=best). If you desire only a moderate level of risk and strong performance, then this fund is an excellent option.

Data Date	Investment Rating	Net Assets ($Mil)	Price	Performance Rating/Pts	Total Return Y-T-D	Risk Rating/Pts
3-12	B	99.60	34.95	B / 8.0	13.51%	B- / 7.7
2011	C+	97.00	30.79	C+ / 6.8	2.50%	B- / 7.5
2010	B	127.00	32.65	B / 7.9	25.48%	C / 5.4
2009	C	56.46	25.91	C+ / 5.8	45.07%	C / 5.5

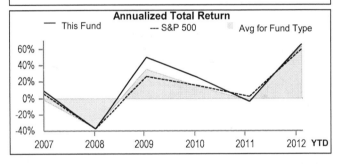

Annualized Total Return

*Guggenheim Intl Multi-Asset Inc (HGI)   C   Fair

Fund Family: Guggenheim Funds Investment Advisor
Fund Type: Foreign
Inception Date: July 11, 2007

Major Rating Factors: Middle of the road best describes *Guggenheim Intl Multi-Asset Inc whose TheStreet.com Investment Rating is currently a C (Fair). The fund currently has a performance rating of C (Fair) based on an annualized return of 20.73% over the last three years and a total return of 10.09% year to date 2012. Factored into the performance evaluation is an expense ratio of 0.70% (very low).

The fund's risk rating is currently B- (Good). It carries a beta of 1.04, meaning that its performance tracks fairly well with that of the overall stock market. Volatility, as measured by both the semi-deviation and a drawdown factor, is considered low. As of March 31, 2012, *Guggenheim Intl Multi-Asset Inc traded at a premium of .74% above its net asset value, which is worse than its one-year historical average premium of .25%.

Michael P. Byrum currently receives a manager quality ranking of 72 (0=worst, 99=best). If you desire an average level of risk, then this fund may be an option.

Data Date	Investment Rating	Net Assets ($Mil)	Price	Performance Rating/Pts	Total Return Y-T-D	Risk Rating/Pts
3-12	C	100.97	17.67	C / 4.8	10.09%	B- / 7.8
2011	C-	85.70	16.22	C- / 4.2	0.49%	B- / 7.3
2010	C-	80.30	19.24	C- / 3.8	12.13%	C / 5.4
2009	B	14.31	17.90	A- / 9.1	45.77%	C / 4.5

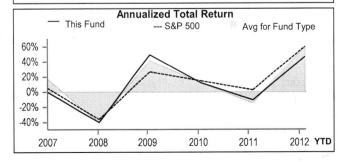

Annualized Total Return

*Guggenheim Inverse 2x S&P 500 ET (RSW)

E **Very Weak**

Fund Family: Security Investors LLC
Fund Type: Income
Inception Date: November 5, 2007

Major Rating Factors: Very poor performance is the major factor driving the E (Very Weak) TheStreet.com Investment Rating for *Guggenheim Inverse 2x S&P 500 ET. The fund currently has a performance rating of E (Very Weak) based on an annualized return of -39.85% over the last three years and a total return of -21.57% year to date 2012. Factored into the performance evaluation is an expense ratio of 0.71% (very low).

The fund's risk rating is currently C- (Fair). It carries a beta of -1.94, meaning the fund's expected move will be -19.4% for every 10% move in the market. Volatility, as measured by both the semi-deviation and a drawdown factor, is considered average. As of March 31, 2012, *Guggenheim Inverse 2x S&P 500 ET traded at a premium of .08% above its net asset value, which is worse than its one-year historical average premium of .02%.

Michael Dellapa has been running the fund for 5 years and currently receives a manager quality ranking of 11 (0=worst, 99=best). This fund offers an average level of risk but investors looking for strong performance will be frustrated.

Data Date	Investment Rating	Net Assets ($Mil)	Price	Performance Rating/Pts	Total Return Y-T-D	Risk Rating/Pts
3-12	E	37.89	24.47	E / 0.3	-21.57%	C- / 3.5
2011	E	51.60	31.20	E / 0.5	-3.08%	C- / 3.4
2010	E	67.50	38.53	E / 0.4	-31.79%	D+ / 2.9
2009	E	97.55	56.49	E- / 0.2	-47.15%	C- / 4.0

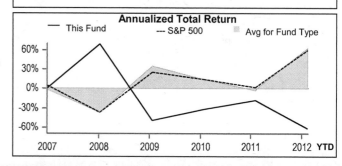

Annualized Total Return

---

*Guggenheim Japanese Yen Trust (FXY)

D+ **Weak**

Fund Family: Security Investors LLC
Fund Type: Foreign
Inception Date: February 13, 2007

Major Rating Factors:
Disappointing performance is the major factor driving the D+ (Weak) TheStreet.com Investment Rating for *Guggenheim Japanese Yen Trust. The fund currently has a performance rating of D (Weak) based on an annualized return of 6.15% over the last three years and a total return of -7.15% year to date 2012. Factored into the performance evaluation is an expense ratio of 0.40% (very low).

The fund's risk rating is currently B+ (Good). It carries a beta of 0.00, meaning the fund's expected move will be 0.0% for every 10% move in the market. Volatility, as measured by both the semi-deviation and a drawdown factor, is considered very low. As of March 31, 2012, *Guggenheim Japanese Yen Trust traded at a discount of .63% below its net asset value, which is better than its one-year historical average discount of .02%.

David C. Kwan has been running the fund for 4 years and currently receives a manager quality ranking of 75 (0=worst, 99=best). This fund offers only a moderate level of risk but investors looking for strong performance are still waiting.

Data Date	Investment Rating	Net Assets ($Mil)	Price	Performance Rating/Pts	Total Return Y-T-D	Risk Rating/Pts
3-12	D+	328.24	118.78	D / 1.6	-7.15%	B+ / 9.0
2011	C	729.50	127.93	C- / 3.1	-0.03%	B+ / 9.0
2010	A	207.20	121.75	B- / 7.4	14.20%	B / 8.2
2009	C	553.53	106.61	D / 1.7	-1.09%	B / 8.5

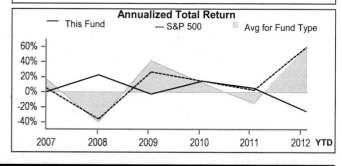

Annualized Total Return

---

*Guggenheim Mid-Cap Core ETF (CZA)

B **Good**

Fund Family: Guggenheim Funds Investment Advisor
Fund Type: Growth
Inception Date: April 2, 2007

Major Rating Factors: Strong performance is the major factor driving the B (Good) TheStreet.com Investment Rating for *Guggenheim Mid-Cap Core ETF. The fund currently has a performance rating of B- (Good) based on an annualized return of 27.50% over the last three years and a total return of 10.29% year to date 2012. Factored into the performance evaluation is an expense ratio of 0.65% (very low).

The fund's risk rating is currently B (Good). It carries a beta of 1.00, meaning that its performance tracks fairly well with that of the overall stock market. Volatility, as measured by both the semi-deviation and a drawdown factor, is considered low. As of March 31, 2012, *Guggenheim Mid-Cap Core ETF traded at a premium of .24% above its net asset value, which is worse than its one-year historical average premium of .13%.

Michael P. Byrum currently receives a manager quality ranking of 71 (0=worst, 99=best). If you desire only a moderate level of risk and strong performance, then this fund is an excellent option.

Data Date	Investment Rating	Net Assets ($Mil)	Price	Performance Rating/Pts	Total Return Y-T-D	Risk Rating/Pts
3-12	B	33.91	32.81	B- / 7.4	10.29%	B / 8.2
2011	B-	26.70	29.75	B- / 7.1	0.91%	B / 8.0
2010	B+	11.50	28.75	B- / 7.1	22.60%	C+ / 6.4
2009	A	4.13	23.61	B+ / 8.9	40.07%	C+ / 5.7

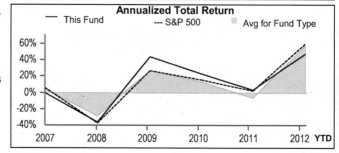

Annualized Total Return

*Guggenheim MSCI EAFE Eq Weight E　(EWEF)　　　D　　Weak

Fund Family: Security Investors LLC
Fund Type: Emerging Market
Inception Date: December 3, 2010

Data Date	Investment Rating	Net Assets ($Mil)	Price	Perfor-mance Rating/Pts	Total Return Y-T-D	Risk Rating/Pts
3-12	D	11.61	38.40	D / 1.8	12.86%	B- / 7.1
2011	D	10.30	34.20	E+ / 0.9	-0.26%	B- / 7.0

Major Rating Factors:
Disappointing performance is the major factor driving the D (Weak) TheStreet.com Investment Rating for *Guggenheim MSCI EAFE Eq Weight E. The fund currently has a performance rating of D (Weak) based on an annualized return of 0.00% over the last three years and a total return of 12.86% year to date 2012. Factored into the performance evaluation is an expense ratio of 0.56% (very low).

The fund's risk rating is currently B- (Good). It carries a beta of 0.00, meaning the fund's expected move will be 0.0% for every 10% move in the market. Volatility, as measured by both the semi-deviation and a drawdown factor, is considered low. As of March 31, 2012, *Guggenheim MSCI EAFE Eq Weight E traded at a discount of .78% below its net asset value, which is better than its one-year historical average discount of .02%.

Adrian G.W. Duffy currently receives a manager quality ranking of 40 (0=worst, 99=best). This fund offers only a moderate level of risk but investors looking for strong performance are still waiting.

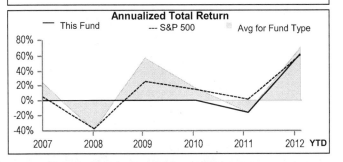

*Guggenheim MSCI Em Mkt Eq Weight　(EWEM)　　　D　　Weak

Fund Family: Security Investors LLC
Fund Type: Emerging Market
Inception Date: December 3, 2010

Data Date	Investment Rating	Net Assets ($Mil)	Price	Perfor-mance Rating/Pts	Total Return Y-T-D	Risk Rating/Pts
3-12	D	14.07	35.74	D+ / 2.6	15.75%	C+ / 5.9
2011	D-	12.30	30.97	E+ / 0.7	0.65%	C+ / 5.7

Major Rating Factors:
Disappointing performance is the major factor driving the D (Weak) TheStreet.com Investment Rating for *Guggenheim MSCI Em Mkt Eq Weight. The fund currently has a performance rating of D+ (Weak) based on an annualized return of 0.00% over the last three years and a total return of 15.75% year to date 2012. Factored into the performance evaluation is an expense ratio of 0.63% (very low).

The fund's risk rating is currently C+ (Fair). It carries a beta of 0.00, meaning the fund's expected move will be 0.0% for every 10% move in the market. Volatility, as measured by both the semi-deviation and a drawdown factor, is considered low. As of March 31, 2012, *Guggenheim MSCI Em Mkt Eq Weight traded at a premium of 1.62% above its net asset value, which is worse than its one-year historical average premium of 1.15%.

Adrian G.W. Duffy currently receives a manager quality ranking of 47 (0=worst, 99=best). This fund offers only a moderate level of risk but investors looking for strong performance are still waiting.

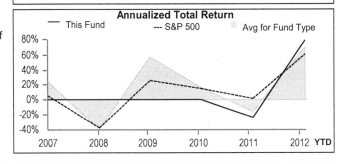

*Guggenheim Multi-Asset Income ET　(CVY)　　　B+　　Good

Fund Family: Guggenheim Funds Investment Advisor
Fund Type: Income
Inception Date: September 21, 2006

Data Date	Investment Rating	Net Assets ($Mil)	Price	Perfor-mance Rating/Pts	Total Return Y-T-D	Risk Rating/Pts
3-12	B+	667.28	21.85	B / 7.9	8.14%	B / 8.7
2011	B	474.80	20.45	B- / 7.5	1.22%	B / 8.0
2010	C	358.70	20.07	C+ / 5.7	16.98%	C / 4.9
2009	D+	121.12	17.92	C- / 3.2	45.19%	C / 5.3

Major Rating Factors: Strong performance is the major factor driving the B+ (Good) TheStreet.com Investment Rating for *Guggenheim Multi-Asset Income ET. The fund currently has a performance rating of B (Good) based on an annualized return of 29.90% over the last three years and a total return of 8.14% year to date 2012. Factored into the performance evaluation is an expense ratio of 0.65% (very low).

The fund's risk rating is currently B (Good). It carries a beta of 0.96, meaning that its performance tracks fairly well with that of the overall stock market. Volatility, as measured by both the semi-deviation and a drawdown factor, is considered low. As of March 31, 2012, *Guggenheim Multi-Asset Income ET traded at a premium of .14% above its net asset value, which is worse than its one-year historical average premium of .07%.

Michael P. Byrum currently receives a manager quality ranking of 84 (0=worst, 99=best). If you desire only a moderate level of risk and strong performance, then this fund is an excellent option.

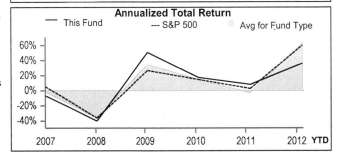

*Guggenheim Raymond James SB1 Eq (RYJ)   B   Good

Fund Family: Guggenheim Funds Investment Advisor
Fund Type: Income
Inception Date: May 19, 2006

Major Rating Factors: Strong performance is the major factor driving the B (Good) TheStreet.com Investment Rating for *Guggenheim Raymond James SB1 Eq. The fund currently has a performance rating of B (Good) based on an annualized return of 29.22% over the last three years and a total return of 15.44% year to date 2012. Factored into the performance evaluation is an expense ratio of 0.75% (very low).

The fund's risk rating is currently B- (Good). It carries a beta of 1.31, meaning it is expected to move 13.1% for every 10% move in the market. Volatility, as measured by both the semi-deviation and a drawdown factor, is considered low. As of March 31, 2012, *Guggenheim Raymond James SB1 Eq traded at a premium of .13% above its net asset value, which is worse than its one-year historical average premium of .03%.

Michael P. Byrum currently receives a manager quality ranking of 50 (0=worst, 99=best). If you desire only a moderate level of risk and strong performance, then this fund is an excellent option.

Data Date	Investment Rating	Net Assets ($Mil)	Price	Perfor-mance Rating/Pts	Total Return Y-T-D	Risk Rating/Pts
3-12	B	94.99	23.70	B / 8.1	15.44%	B- / 7.8
2011	B-	82.50	20.53	B- / 7.3	2.43%	B- / 7.6
2010	B-	63.40	21.03	B / 8.1	27.45%	C / 4.6
2009	C	39.56	16.51	C+ / 6.1	98.92%	C / 4.7

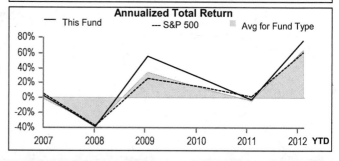

Annualized Total Return — This Fund --- S&P 500 ▨ Avg for Fund Type

*Guggenheim Russell 1000 Eq Wght (EWRI)   C   Fair

Fund Family: Security Investors LLC
Fund Type: Growth
Inception Date: December 3, 2010

Major Rating Factors: Middle of the road best describes *Guggenheim Russell 1000 Eq Wght whose TheStreet.com Investment Rating is currently a C (Fair). The fund currently has a performance rating of C (Fair) based on an annualized return of 0.00% over the last three years and a total return of 12.82% year to date 2012. Factored into the performance evaluation is an expense ratio of 0.41% (very low).

The fund's risk rating is currently B- (Good). It carries a beta of 0.00, meaning the fund's expected move will be 0.0% for every 10% move in the market. Volatility, as measured by both the semi-deviation and a drawdown factor, is considered low. As of March 31, 2012, *Guggenheim Russell 1000 Eq Wght traded at a premium of .35% above its net asset value.

Adrian G.W. Duffy currently receives a manager quality ranking of 20 (0=worst, 99=best). If you desire an average level of risk, then this fund may be an option.

Data Date	Investment Rating	Net Assets ($Mil)	Price	Perfor-mance Rating/Pts	Total Return Y-T-D	Risk Rating/Pts
3-12	C	39.48	34.45	C / 5.3	12.82%	B- / 7.8
2011	D+	35.30	30.70	D+ / 2.3	1.82%	B- / 7.8

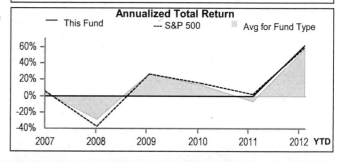

Annualized Total Return — This Fund --- S&P 500 ▨ Avg for Fund Type

*Guggenheim Russell 2000 Eq Wght (EWRS)   C-   Fair

Fund Family: Security Investors LLC
Fund Type: Growth
Inception Date: December 3, 2010

Major Rating Factors: Middle of the road best describes *Guggenheim Russell 2000 Eq Wght whose TheStreet.com Investment Rating is currently a C- (Fair). The fund currently has a performance rating of C- (Fair) based on an annualized return of 0.00% over the last three years and a total return of 12.16% year to date 2012. Factored into the performance evaluation is an expense ratio of 0.41% (very low).

The fund's risk rating is currently B- (Good). It carries a beta of 0.00, meaning the fund's expected move will be 0.0% for every 10% move in the market. Volatility, as measured by both the semi-deviation and a drawdown factor, is considered low. As of March 31, 2012, *Guggenheim Russell 2000 Eq Wght traded at a premium of .18% above its net asset value, which is worse than its one-year historical average premium of .12%.

Adrian G.W. Duffy currently receives a manager quality ranking of 11 (0=worst, 99=best). If you desire an average level of risk, then this fund may be an option.

Data Date	Investment Rating	Net Assets ($Mil)	Price	Perfor-mance Rating/Pts	Total Return Y-T-D	Risk Rating/Pts
3-12	C-	19.66	32.83	C- / 3.9	12.16%	B- / 7.3
2011	D	17.60	29.36	D / 1.6	1.37%	B- / 7.3

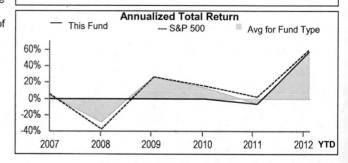

Annualized Total Return — This Fund --- S&P 500 ▨ Avg for Fund Type

*Guggenheim Russell MC Eq Wght ET (EWRM)   C   Fair

Fund Family: Security Investors LLC
Fund Type: Growth
Inception Date: December 3, 2010

Major Rating Factors: Middle of the road best describes *Guggenheim Russell MC Eq Wght ET whose TheStreet.com Investment Rating is currently a C (Fair). The fund currently has a performance rating of C (Fair) based on an annualized return of 0.00% over the last three years and a total return of 12.54% year to date 2012. Factored into the performance evaluation is an expense ratio of 0.41% (very low).

The fund's risk rating is currently B- (Good). It carries a beta of 0.00, meaning the fund's expected move will be 0.0% for every 10% move in the market. Volatility, as measured by both the semi-deviation and a drawdown factor, is considered low. As of March 31, 2012, *Guggenheim Russell MC Eq Wght ET traded at a premium of .12% above its net asset value, which is worse than its one-year historical average premium of .05%.

Adrian G.W. Duffy currently receives a manager quality ranking of 18 (0=worst, 99=best). If you desire an average level of risk, then this fund may be an option.

Data Date	Investment Rating	Net Assets ($Mil)	Price	Perfor- mance Rating/Pts	Total Return Y-T-D	Risk Rating/Pts
3-12	C	56.85	34.50	C / 4.9	12.54%	B- / 7.8
2011	D+	49.20	30.78	D / 2.2	1.69%	B- / 7.7

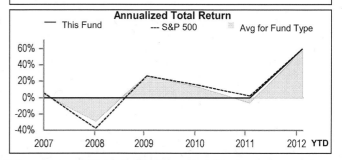

*Guggenheim Russell Top 50 ETF (XLG)   C+   Fair

Fund Family: Security Investors LLC
Fund Type: Income
Inception Date: May 4, 2005

Major Rating Factors: Middle of the road best describes *Guggenheim Russell Top 50 ETF whose TheStreet.com Investment Rating is currently a C+ (Fair). The fund currently has a performance rating of C (Fair) based on an annualized return of 18.93% over the last three years and a total return of 14.05% year to date 2012. Factored into the performance evaluation is an expense ratio of 0.20% (very low).

The fund's risk rating is currently B (Good). It carries a beta of 0.91, meaning that its performance tracks fairly well with that of the overall stock market. Volatility, as measured by both the semi-deviation and a drawdown factor, is considered low. As of March 31, 2012, *Guggenheim Russell Top 50 ETF traded at a premium of .01% above its net asset value, which is better than its one-year historical average premium of .05%.

Adrian G.W. Duffy currently receives a manager quality ranking of 46 (0=worst, 99=best). If you desire an average level of risk, then this fund may be an option.

Data Date	Investment Rating	Net Assets ($Mil)	Price	Perfor- mance Rating/Pts	Total Return Y-T-D	Risk Rating/Pts
3-12	C+	464.09	103.12	C / 5.5	14.05%	B / 8.3
2011	C	461.20	91.31	C / 4.8	1.91%	B- / 7.9
2010	D+	331.20	89.50	D+ / 2.4	9.32%	C+ / 6.2
2009	D+	307.38	83.59	D / 1.8	16.90%	C+ / 6.2

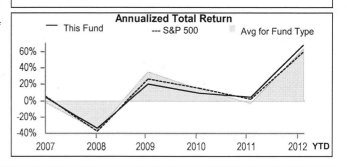

*Guggenheim S&P 500 Eq WgCon Dsc (RCD)   A   Excellent

Fund Family: Security Investors LLC
Fund Type: Growth
Inception Date: November 1, 2006

Major Rating Factors:
Exceptional performance is the major factor driving the A (Excellent) TheStreet.com Investment Rating for *Guggenheim S&P 500 Eq WgCon Dsc. The fund currently has a performance rating of A- (Excellent) based on an annualized return of 35.94% over the last three years and a total return of 16.37% year to date 2012. Factored into the performance evaluation is an expense ratio of 0.50% (very low).

The fund's risk rating is currently B (Good). It carries a beta of 1.37, meaning it is expected to move 13.7% for every 10% move in the market. Volatility, as measured by both the semi-deviation and a drawdown factor, is considered low. As of March 31, 2012, *Guggenheim S&P 500 Eq WgCon Dsc traded at a premium of .18% above its net asset value, which is worse than its one-year historical average discount of .04%.

Adrian G.W. Duffy currently receives a manager quality ranking of 74 (0=worst, 99=best). If you desire only a moderate level of risk and strong performance, then this fund is an excellent option.

Data Date	Investment Rating	Net Assets ($Mil)	Price	Perfor- mance Rating/Pts	Total Return Y-T-D	Risk Rating/Pts
3-12	A	62.90	54.80	A- / 9.2	16.37%	B / 8.0
2011	B	26.00	47.32	B / 8.2	2.07%	B- / 7.7
2010	B+	27.50	45.86	B+ / 8.3	26.07%	C / 5.3
2009	C-	5.36	36.76	C- / 3.9	56.80%	C / 5.2

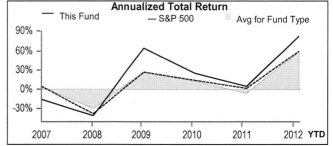

*Guggenheim S&P 500 Eq WgCon St E (RHS) | B- Good

Fund Family: Security Investors LLC
Fund Type: Growth
Inception Date: November 1, 2006

Major Rating Factors: *Guggenheim S&P 500 Eq WgCon St E receives a
TheStreet.com Investment Rating of B- (Good). The fund currently has a performance
rating of C+ (Fair) based on an annualized return of 22.23% over the last three years
and a total return of 5.47% year to date 2012. Factored into the performance
evaluation is an expense ratio of 0.50% (very low).

The fund's risk rating is currently B+ (Good). It carries a beta of 0.60, meaning
the fund's expected move will be 6.0% for every 10% move in the market. Volatility,
as measured by both the semi-deviation and a drawdown factor, is considered very
low. As of March 31, 2012, *Guggenheim S&P 500 Eq WgCon St E traded at a
premium of .14% above its net asset value, which is worse than its one-year historical
average discount of .02%.

Adrian G.W. Duffy currently receives a manager quality ranking of 83 (0=worst,
99=best). If you desire an average level of risk, then this fund may be an option.

Data Date	Investment Rating	Net Assets ($Mil)	Price	Performance Rating/Pts	Total Return Y-T-D	Risk Rating/Pts
3-12	B-	36.34	66.16	C+ / 5.9	5.47%	B+ / 9.0
2011	B	28.40	63.25	C+ / 6.6	-0.95%	B / 8.7
2010	A-	14.30	57.22	B- / 7.3	17.03%	B- / 7.1
2009	C+	8.06	49.92	C / 4.8	26.18%	B- / 7.2

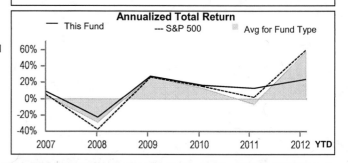

*Guggenheim S&P 500 Eq Wght Engy (RYE) | C Fair

Fund Family: Security Investors LLC
Fund Type: Energy/Natural Resources
Inception Date: November 1, 2006

Major Rating Factors: Middle of the road best describes *Guggenheim S&P 500 Eq
Wght Engy whose TheStreet.com Investment Rating is currently a C (Fair). The fund
currently has a performance rating of C (Fair) based on an annualized return of
23.24% over the last three years and a total return of 4.35% year to date 2012.
Factored into the performance evaluation is an expense ratio of 0.50% (very low).

The fund's risk rating is currently B- (Good). It carries a beta of 1.25, meaning it is
expected to move 12.5% for every 10% move in the market. Volatility, as measured
by both the semi-deviation and a drawdown factor, is considered low. As of March 31,
2012, *Guggenheim S&P 500 Eq Wght Engy traded at a price exactly equal to its net
asset value, which is worse than its one-year historical average discount of .03%.

Adrian G.W. Duffy currently receives a manager quality ranking of 54 (0=worst,
99=best). If you desire an average level of risk, then this fund may be an option.

Data Date	Investment Rating	Net Assets ($Mil)	Price	Performance Rating/Pts	Total Return Y-T-D	Risk Rating/Pts
3-12	C	35.22	64.03	C / 5.2	4.35%	B- / 7.1
2011	C+	33.80	61.61	C+ / 6.6	2.39%	C+ / 6.9
2010	C	22.00	62.84	C+ / 6.0	26.08%	C / 4.9
2009	C	5.55	50.24	C+ / 6.1	38.51%	C / 5.2

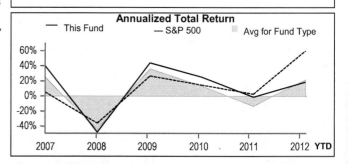

*Guggenheim S&P 500 Eq Wght Finl (RYF) | B Good

Fund Family: Security Investors LLC
Fund Type: Financial Services
Inception Date: November 1, 2006

Major Rating Factors: Strong performance is the major factor driving the B (Good)
TheStreet.com Investment Rating for *Guggenheim S&P 500 Eq Wght Finl. The fund
currently has a performance rating of B (Good) based on an annualized return of
28.06% over the last three years and a total return of 20.48% year to date 2012.
Factored into the performance evaluation is an expense ratio of 0.50% (very low).

The fund's risk rating is currently B- (Good). It carries a beta of 1.09, meaning
that its performance tracks fairly well with that of the overall stock market. Volatility,
as measured by both the semi-deviation and a drawdown factor, is considered low.
As of March 31, 2012, *Guggenheim S&P 500 Eq Wght Finl traded at a discount
of .14% below its net asset value, which is better than its one-year historical average
discount of .08%.

Adrian G.W. Duffy currently receives a manager quality ranking of 75 (0=worst,
99=best). If you desire only a moderate level of risk and strong performance, then this
fund is an excellent option.

Data Date	Investment Rating	Net Assets ($Mil)	Price	Performance Rating/Pts	Total Return Y-T-D	Risk Rating/Pts
3-12	B	15.61	28.35	B / 7.8	20.48%	B- / 7.7
2011	C-	15.60	23.99	C- / 4.1	2.88%	C+ / 6.9
2010	D-	18.10	27.84	D / 1.8	22.41%	C / 4.3
2009	E+	8.91	23.03	E+ / 0.7	32.97%	C / 4.3

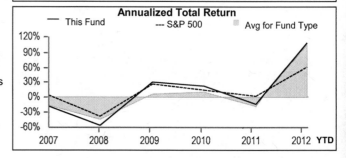

*Guggenheim S&P 500 Eq Wght HC ET (RYH)

B **Good**

Fund Family: Security Investors LLC
Fund Type: Growth
Inception Date: November 1, 2006

Major Rating Factors: Strong performance is the major factor driving the B (Good) TheStreet.com Investment Rating for *Guggenheim S&P 500 Eq Wght HC ET. The fund currently has a performance rating of B- (Good) based on an annualized return of 25.17% over the last three years and a total return of 13.82% year to date 2012. Factored into the performance evaluation is an expense ratio of 0.50% (very low).

The fund's risk rating is currently B (Good). It carries a beta of 0.79, meaning the fund's expected move will be 7.9% for every 10% move in the market. Volatility, as measured by both the semi-deviation and a drawdown factor, is considered low. As of March 31, 2012, *Guggenheim S&P 500 Eq Wght HC ET traded at a premium of .07% above its net asset value, which is worse than its one-year historical average premium of .01%.

Adrian G.W. Duffy currently receives a manager quality ranking of 76 (0=worst, 99=best). If you desire only a moderate level of risk and strong performance, then this fund is an excellent option.

Data Date	Investment Rating	Net Assets ($Mil)	Price	Performance Rating/Pts	Total Return Y-T-D	Risk Rating/Pts
3-12	B	89.85	75.41	B- / 7.1	13.82%	B / 8.4
2011	C+	46.60	66.44	C+ / 6.3	2.14%	B / 8.1
2010	C+	50.30	62.81	C+ / 6.1	10.67%	C+ / 6.7
2009	C+	37.51	56.96	C+ / 5.8	34.99%	C+ / 6.8

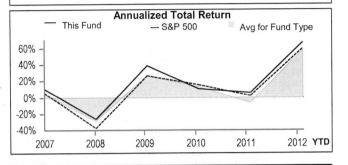

*Guggenheim S&P 500 Eq Wght Ind E (RGI)

B- **Good**

Fund Family: Security Investors LLC
Fund Type: Growth
Inception Date: November 1, 2006

Major Rating Factors: Strong performance is the major factor driving the B- (Good) TheStreet.com Investment Rating for *Guggenheim S&P 500 Eq Wght Ind E. The fund currently has a performance rating of B- (Good) based on an annualized return of 26.07% over the last three years and a total return of 11.43% year to date 2012. Factored into the performance evaluation is an expense ratio of 0.50% (very low).

The fund's risk rating is currently B- (Good). It carries a beta of 1.26, meaning it is expected to move 12.6% for every 10% move in the market. Volatility, as measured by both the semi-deviation and a drawdown factor, is considered low. As of March 31, 2012, *Guggenheim S&P 500 Eq Wght Ind E traded at a premium of .14% above its net asset value, which is worse than its one-year historical average discount of .02%.

Adrian G.W. Duffy currently receives a manager quality ranking of 38 (0=worst, 99=best). If you desire only a moderate level of risk and strong performance, then this fund is an excellent option.

Data Date	Investment Rating	Net Assets ($Mil)	Price	Performance Rating/Pts	Total Return Y-T-D	Risk Rating/Pts
3-12	B-	34.45	57.50	B- / 7.0	11.43%	B- / 7.9
2011	C+	13.00	52.03	C+ / 5.6	2.18%	B- / 7.6
2010	C+	48.70	54.21	C+ / 6.5	26.13%	C / 5.5
2009	C-	11.91	43.56	C- / 3.5	29.62%	C+ / 5.9

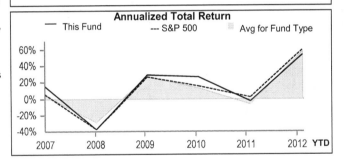

*Guggenheim S&P 500 Eq Wght Mat E (RTM)

C+ **Fair**

Fund Family: Security Investors LLC
Fund Type: Growth
Inception Date: November 1, 2006

Major Rating Factors: Strong performance is the major factor driving the C+ (Fair) TheStreet.com Investment Rating for *Guggenheim S&P 500 Eq Wght Mat E. The fund currently has a performance rating of B- (Good) based on an annualized return of 26.83% over the last three years and a total return of 12.28% year to date 2012. Factored into the performance evaluation is an expense ratio of 0.50% (very low).

The fund's risk rating is currently B- (Good). It carries a beta of 1.51, meaning it is expected to move 15.1% for every 10% move in the market. Volatility, as measured by both the semi-deviation and a drawdown factor, is considered low. As of March 31, 2012, *Guggenheim S&P 500 Eq Wght Mat E traded at a discount of .06% below its net asset value, which is worse than its one-year historical average discount of .08%.

Adrian G.W. Duffy currently receives a manager quality ranking of 23 (0=worst, 99=best). If you desire only a moderate level of risk and strong performance, then this fund is an excellent option.

Data Date	Investment Rating	Net Assets ($Mil)	Price	Performance Rating/Pts	Total Return Y-T-D	Risk Rating/Pts
3-12	C+	37.67	62.75	B- / 7.1	12.28%	B- / 7.5
2011	C+	33.70	56.17	B- / 7.1	3.43%	B- / 7.3
2010	B	40.90	63.00	B / 7.9	23.12%	C / 5.4
2009	B-	5.60	52.73	B- / 7.0	61.99%	C+ / 5.7

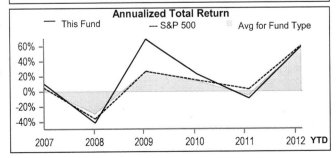

*Guggenheim S&P 500 Eq Wght Tech (RYT)

C+   **Fair**

Fund Family: Security Investors LLC
Fund Type: Growth
Inception Date: November 1, 2006

Data Date	Investment Rating	Net Assets ($Mil)	Price	Performance Rating/Pts	Total Return Y-T-D	Risk Rating/Pts
3-12	C+	149.62	58.74	B- / 7.0	18.03%	B- / 7.5
2011	C+	102.40	49.99	C+ / 6.5	1.66%	B- / 7.4
2010	B-	102.30	53.77	B- / 7.0	17.89%	C / 5.4
2009	C	8.25	45.75	C / 4.8	69.07%	C / 5.5

Major Rating Factors: Strong performance is the major factor driving the C+ (Fair) TheStreet.com Investment Rating for *Guggenheim S&P 500 Eq Wght Tech. The fund currently has a performance rating of B- (Good) based on an annualized return of 24.74% over the last three years and a total return of 18.03% year to date 2012. Factored into the performance evaluation is an expense ratio of 0.50% (very low).

The fund's risk rating is currently B- (Good). It carries a beta of 1.27, meaning it is expected to move 12.7% for every 10% move in the market. Volatility, as measured by both the semi-deviation and a drawdown factor, is considered low. As of March 31, 2012, *Guggenheim S&P 500 Eq Wght Tech traded at a premium of .10% above its net asset value, which is worse than its one-year historical average discount of .04%.

Adrian G.W. Duffy currently receives a manager quality ranking of 31 (0=worst, 99=best). If you desire only a moderate level of risk and strong performance, then this fund is an excellent option.

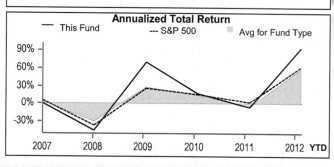

*Guggenheim S&P 500 Eq Wght Util (RYU)

C   **Fair**

Fund Family: Security Investors LLC
Fund Type: Utilities
Inception Date: November 1, 2006

Data Date	Investment Rating	Net Assets ($Mil)	Price	Performance Rating/Pts	Total Return Y-T-D	Risk Rating/Pts
3-12	C	43.68	54.57	C- / 4.0	0.00%	B+ / 9.3
2011	C+	33.30	55.53	C / 4.9	-2.36%	B / 8.8
2010	C-	20.40	51.10	C- / 3.3	12.70%	C+ / 6.7
2009	C-	5.70	47.10	C- / 3.0	20.77%	C+ / 6.7

Major Rating Factors: Middle of the road best describes *Guggenheim S&P 500 Eq Wght Util whose TheStreet.com Investment Rating is currently a C (Fair). The fund currently has a performance rating of C- (Fair) based on an annualized return of 17.32% over the last three years and a total return of 0.00% year to date 2012. Factored into the performance evaluation is an expense ratio of 0.50% (very low).

The fund's risk rating is currently B+ (Good). It carries a beta of 0.93, meaning that its performance tracks fairly well with that of the overall stock market. Volatility, as measured by both the semi-deviation and a drawdown factor, is considered very low. As of March 31, 2012, *Guggenheim S&P 500 Eq Wght Util traded at a discount of .04% below its net asset value, which is better than its one-year historical average discount of .01%.

Adrian G.W. Duffy currently receives a manager quality ranking of 66 (0=worst, 99=best). If you desire an average level of risk, then this fund may be an option.

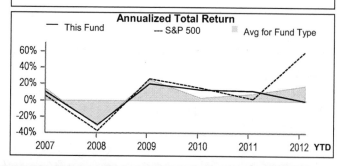

*Guggenheim S&P 500 Equal Wght (RSP)

B-   **Good**

Fund Family: Security Investors LLC
Fund Type: Income
Inception Date: April 24, 2003

Data Date	Investment Rating	Net Assets ($Mil)	Price	Performance Rating/Pts	Total Return Y-T-D	Risk Rating/Pts
3-12	B-	3,181.56	51.87	B- / 7.2	12.86%	B / 8.1
2011	C+	2,640.10	46.28	C+ / 6.5	1.73%	B- / 7.8
2010	C+	3,181.20	47.31	C+ / 6.6	21.39%	C+ / 5.7
2009	C-	890.08	39.53	C- / 3.4	39.81%	C+ / 5.7

Major Rating Factors: Strong performance is the major factor driving the B- (Good) TheStreet.com Investment Rating for *Guggenheim S&P 500 Equal Wght. The fund currently has a performance rating of B- (Good) based on an annualized return of 26.32% over the last three years and a total return of 12.86% year to date 2012. Factored into the performance evaluation is an expense ratio of 0.40% (very low).

The fund's risk rating is currently B (Good). It carries a beta of 1.20, meaning it is expected to move 12.0% for every 10% move in the market. Volatility, as measured by both the semi-deviation and a drawdown factor, is considered low. As of March 31, 2012, *Guggenheim S&P 500 Equal Wght traded at a discount of .04% below its net asset value.

Adrian G.W. Duffy currently receives a manager quality ranking of 52 (0=worst, 99=best). If you desire only a moderate level of risk and strong performance, then this fund is an excellent option.

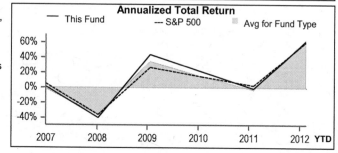

*Guggenheim S&P 500 Pure Growth (RPG)   B   Good

Fund Family: Security Investors LLC
Fund Type: Growth
Inception Date: March 1, 2006

Major Rating Factors: Strong performance is the major factor driving the B (Good) TheStreet.com Investment Rating for *Guggenheim S&P 500 Pure Growth. The fund currently has a performance rating of B (Good) based on an annualized return of 29.36% over the last three years and a total return of 14.26% year to date 2012. Factored into the performance evaluation is an expense ratio of 0.35% (very low).

The fund's risk rating is currently B- (Good). It carries a beta of 1.15, meaning it is expected to move 11.5% for every 10% move in the market. Volatility, as measured by both the semi-deviation and a drawdown factor, is considered low. As of March 31, 2012, *Guggenheim S&P 500 Pure Growth traded at a premium of .12% above its net asset value, which is worse than its one-year historical average premium of .03%.

Adrian G.W. Duffy currently receives a manager quality ranking of 66 (0=worst, 99=best). If you desire only a moderate level of risk and strong performance, then this fund is an excellent option.

Data Date	Investment Rating	Net Assets ($Mil)	Price	Performance Rating/Pts	Total Return Y-T-D	Risk Rating/Pts
3-12	B	314.77	49.24	B / 8.0	14.26%	B- / 7.6
2011	C+	257.40	43.24	B- / 7.2	2.00%	B- / 7.0
2010	B	197.00	43.25	B / 7.8	26.91%	C / 5.3
2009	C	31.22	34.23	C / 4.5	43.07%	C+ / 5.8

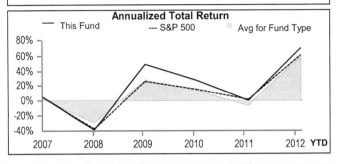

*Guggenheim S&P 500 Pure Value (RPV)   A   Excellent

Fund Family: Security Investors LLC
Fund Type: Income
Inception Date: March 1, 2006

Major Rating Factors:
Exceptional performance is the major factor driving the A (Excellent) TheStreet.com Investment Rating for *Guggenheim S&P 500 Pure Value. The fund currently has a performance rating of A- (Excellent) based on an annualized return of 37.75% over the last three years and a total return of 16.88% year to date 2012. Factored into the performance evaluation is an expense ratio of 0.35% (very low).

The fund's risk rating is currently B (Good). It carries a beta of 1.42, meaning it is expected to move 14.2% for every 10% move in the market. Volatility, as measured by both the semi-deviation and a drawdown factor, is considered low. As of March 31, 2012, *Guggenheim S&P 500 Pure Value traded at a discount of .06% below its net asset value, which is better than its one-year historical average premium of .04%.

Adrian G.W. Duffy currently receives a manager quality ranking of 76 (0=worst, 99=best). If you desire only a moderate level of risk and strong performance, then this fund is an excellent option.

Data Date	Investment Rating	Net Assets ($Mil)	Price	Performance Rating/Pts	Total Return Y-T-D	Risk Rating/Pts
3-12	A	93.79	32.29	A- / 9.2	16.88%	B / 8.1
2011	C+	77.80	27.81	C+ / 6.8	1.97%	B- / 7.1
2010	C	62.90	28.59	C+ / 6.1	22.52%	C / 4.7
2009	D+	13.85	23.65	C- / 3.1	47.44%	C / 4.9

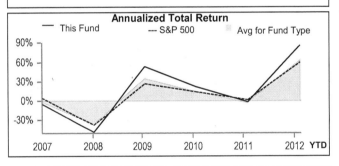

*Guggenheim S&P Gl Div Opps Idx E (LVL)   C   Fair

Fund Family: Guggenheim Funds Investment Advisor
Fund Type: Income
Inception Date: June 25, 2007

Major Rating Factors: Middle of the road best describes *Guggenheim S&P Gl Div Opps Idx E whose TheStreet.com Investment Rating is currently a C (Fair). The fund currently has a performance rating of C (Fair) based on an annualized return of 23.21% over the last three years and a total return of 5.79% year to date 2012. Factored into the performance evaluation is an expense ratio of 0.65% (very low).

The fund's risk rating is currently B- (Good). It carries a beta of 1.32, meaning it is expected to move 13.2% for every 10% move in the market. Volatility, as measured by both the semi-deviation and a drawdown factor, is considered low. As of March 31, 2012, *Guggenheim S&P Gl Div Opps Idx E traded at a premium of .72% above its net asset value, which is worse than its one-year historical average premium of .53%.

Saroj Kanuri has been running the fund for 2 years and currently receives a manager quality ranking of 31 (0=worst, 99=best). If you desire an average level of risk, then this fund may be an option.

Data Date	Investment Rating	Net Assets ($Mil)	Price	Performance Rating/Pts	Total Return Y-T-D	Risk Rating/Pts
3-12	C	62.60	13.91	C / 5.2	5.79%	B- / 7.6
2011	C	53.00	13.25	C / 5.1	0.15%	B- / 7.5
2010	D	27.20	14.80	D+ / 2.4	6.00%	C- / 4.1
2009	B+	5.54	14.90	A / 9.5	59.39%	C / 4.6

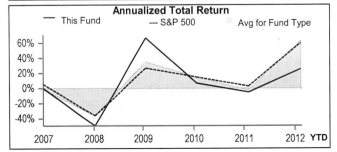

*Guggenheim S&P Global Water Idx (CGW)

C   **Fair**

Fund Family: Guggenheim Funds Investment Advisor
Fund Type: Energy/Natural Resources
Inception Date: May 14, 2007

Major Rating Factors: Middle of the road best describes *Guggenheim S&P Global Water Idx whose TheStreet.com Investment Rating is currently a C (Fair). The fund currently has a performance rating of C (Fair) based on an annualized return of 20.10% over the last three years and a total return of 12.63% year to date 2012. Factored into the performance evaluation is an expense ratio of 0.70% (very low).

The fund's risk rating is currently B (Good). It carries a beta of 0.63, meaning the fund's expected move will be 6.3% for every 10% move in the market. Volatility, as measured by both the semi-deviation and a drawdown factor, is considered low. As of March 31, 2012, *Guggenheim S&P Global Water Idx traded at a price exactly equal to its net asset value, which is worse than its one-year historical average discount of .27%.

Michael P. Byrum currently receives a manager quality ranking of 83 (0=worst, 99=best). If you desire an average level of risk, then this fund may be an option.

Data Date	Investment Rating	Net Assets ($Mil)	Price	Performance Rating/Pts	Total Return Y-T-D	Risk Rating/Pts
3-12	C	193.11	21.11	C / 4.9	12.63%	B / 8.2
2011	D+	179.80	18.74	C- / 3.8	0.21%	C+ / 6.1
2010	D+	220.00	20.77	C- / 3.6	14.46%	C / 4.9
2009	B-	178.94	18.42	B+ / 8.3	27.62%	C / 4.7

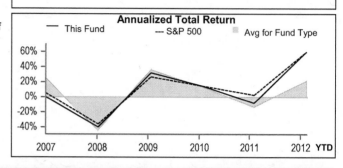

Annualized Total Return

*Guggenheim S&P Mid Cap 400 Pure (RFV)

B+   **Good**

Fund Family: Security Investors LLC
Fund Type: Growth
Inception Date: March 1, 2006

Major Rating Factors: Strong performance is the major factor driving the B+ (Good) TheStreet.com Investment Rating for *Guggenheim S&P Mid Cap 400 Pure. The fund currently has a performance rating of B+ (Good) based on an annualized return of 33.14% over the last three years and a total return of 14.69% year to date 2012. Factored into the performance evaluation is an expense ratio of 0.35% (very low).

The fund's risk rating is currently B- (Good). It carries a beta of 1.50, meaning it is expected to move 15.0% for every 10% move in the market. Volatility, as measured by both the semi-deviation and a drawdown factor, is considered low. As of March 31, 2012, *Guggenheim S&P Mid Cap 400 Pure traded at a discount of .08% below its net asset value, which is better than its one-year historical average premium of .01%.

Adrian G.W. Duffy currently receives a manager quality ranking of 51 (0=worst, 99=best). If you desire only a moderate level of risk and strong performance, then this fund is an excellent option.

Data Date	Investment Rating	Net Assets ($Mil)	Price	Performance Rating/Pts	Total Return Y-T-D	Risk Rating/Pts
3-12	B+	41.52	36.06	B+ / 8.7	14.69%	B- / 7.8
2011	B-	39.60	31.66	C+ / 6.9	2.37%	B- / 7.5
2010	B-	45.90	34.01	B- / 7.5	22.34%	C / 5.0
2009	C-	8.36	28.11	C / 4.4	54.62%	C / 5.1

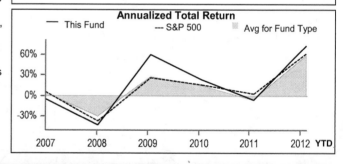

Annualized Total Return

*Guggenheim S&P Mid Cap 400 Pure (RFG)

B+   **Good**

Fund Family: Security Investors LLC
Fund Type: Growth
Inception Date: March 1, 2006

Major Rating Factors: Strong performance is the major factor driving the B+ (Good) TheStreet.com Investment Rating for *Guggenheim S&P Mid Cap 400 Pure. The fund currently has a performance rating of B+ (Good) based on an annualized return of 32.78% over the last three years and a total return of 14.38% year to date 2012. Factored into the performance evaluation is an expense ratio of 0.35% (very low).

The fund's risk rating is currently B (Good). It carries a beta of 1.19, meaning it is expected to move 11.9% for every 10% move in the market. Volatility, as measured by both the semi-deviation and a drawdown factor, is considered low. As of March 31, 2012, *Guggenheim S&P Mid Cap 400 Pure traded at a discount of .07% below its net asset value.

Adrian G.W. Duffy currently receives a manager quality ranking of 78 (0=worst, 99=best). If you desire only a moderate level of risk and strong performance, then this fund is an excellent option.

Data Date	Investment Rating	Net Assets ($Mil)	Price	Performance Rating/Pts	Total Return Y-T-D	Risk Rating/Pts
3-12	B+	614.43	89.64	B+ / 8.5	14.38%	B / 8.0
2011	B	514.80	78.48	B / 8.0	1.58%	B- / 7.6
2010	B+	477.40	78.35	B+ / 8.7	34.84%	C / 4.8
2009	C+	19.05	58.17	C+ / 6.8	53.85%	C+ / 6.2

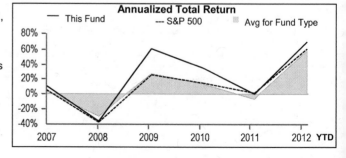

Annualized Total Return

*Guggenheim S&P Sm Cap 600 Pure G (RZG)

B **Good**

Fund Family: Security Investors LLC
Fund Type: Growth
Inception Date: March 1, 2006

Major Rating Factors: Strong performance is the major factor driving the B (Good) TheStreet.com Investment Rating for *Guggenheim S&P Sm Cap 600 Pure G. The fund currently has a performance rating of B (Good) based on an annualized return of 30.26% over the last three years and a total return of 10.90% year to date 2012. Factored into the performance evaluation is an expense ratio of 0.35% (very low).

The fund's risk rating is currently B- (Good). It carries a beta of 1.25, meaning it is expected to move 12.5% for every 10% move in the market. Volatility, as measured by both the semi-deviation and a drawdown factor, is considered low. As of March 31, 2012, *Guggenheim S&P Sm Cap 600 Pure G traded at a premium of .42% above its net asset value, which is worse than its one-year historical average premium of .02%.

Adrian G.W. Duffy currently receives a manager quality ranking of 68 (0=worst, 99=best). If you desire only a moderate level of risk and strong performance, then this fund is an excellent option.

Data Date	Investment Rating	Net Assets ($Mil)	Price	Performance Rating/Pts	Total Return Y-T-D	Risk Rating/Pts
3-12	B	82.79	55.42	B / 8.2	10.90%	B- / 7.7
2011	C+	55.10	50.21	B- / 7.0	-0.08%	C+ / 6.7
2010	B+	26.30	47.88	B / 8.0	28.38%	C / 5.3
2009	C-	5.77	37.42	C- / 3.6	34.23%	C+ / 5.7

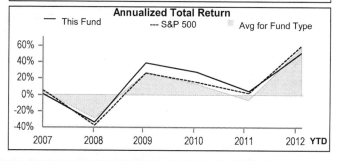

*Guggenheim S&P Sm Cap 600 Pure V (RZV)

B+ **Good**

Fund Family: Security Investors LLC
Fund Type: Growth
Inception Date: March 1, 2006

Major Rating Factors:
Exceptional performance is the major factor driving the B+ (Good) TheStreet.com Investment Rating for *Guggenheim S&P Sm Cap 600 Pure V. The fund currently has a performance rating of A (Excellent) based on an annualized return of 39.57% over the last three years and a total return of 14.27% year to date 2012. Factored into the performance evaluation is an expense ratio of 0.35% (very low).

The fund's risk rating is currently B- (Good). It carries a beta of 1.85, meaning it is expected to move 18.5% for every 10% move in the market. Volatility, as measured by both the semi-deviation and a drawdown factor, is considered low. As of March 31, 2012, *Guggenheim S&P Sm Cap 600 Pure V traded at a discount of .12% below its net asset value, which is better than its one-year historical average discount of .06%.

Adrian G.W. Duffy currently receives a manager quality ranking of 28 (0=worst, 99=best). If you desire only a moderate level of risk and strong performance, then this fund is an excellent option.

Data Date	Investment Rating	Net Assets ($Mil)	Price	Performance Rating/Pts	Total Return Y-T-D	Risk Rating/Pts
3-12	B+	80.03	40.99	A / 9.4	14.27%	B- / 7.3
2011	C+	63.20	36.08	B- / 7.0	1.43%	C+ / 6.3
2010	B	106.20	39.40	B+ / 8.4	28.57%	C / 4.4
2009	D	23.71	30.81	D+ / 2.9	59.83%	C / 4.5

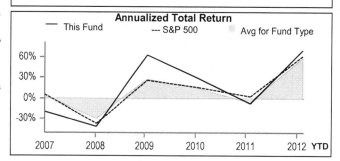

*Guggenheim Shipping ETF (SEA)

D- **Weak**

Fund Family: Guggenheim Funds Investment Advisor
Fund Type: Global
Inception Date: June 11, 2010

Major Rating Factors:
Disappointing performance is the major factor driving the D- (Weak) TheStreet.com Investment Rating for *Guggenheim Shipping ETF. The fund currently has a performance rating of D (Weak) based on an annualized return of 0.00% over the last three years and a total return of 28.65% year to date 2012. Factored into the performance evaluation is an expense ratio of 0.65% (very low).

The fund's risk rating is currently C (Fair). It carries a beta of 0.00, meaning the fund's expected move will be 0.0% for every 10% move in the market. Volatility, as measured by the semi-deviation and a drawdown factor, is considered average. As of March 31, 2012, *Guggenheim Shipping ETF traded at a premium of .32% above its net asset value, which is worse than its one-year historical average premium of .09%.

Michael P. Byrum currently receives a manager quality ranking of 6 (0=worst, 99=best). This fund offers an average level of risk but investors looking for strong performance will be frustrated.

Data Date	Investment Rating	Net Assets ($Mil)	Price	Performance Rating/Pts	Total Return Y-T-D	Risk Rating/Pts
3-12	D-	32.37	19.04	D / 2.2	28.65%	C / 5.3
2011	E+	34.10	14.88	E- / 0.2	0.94%	C / 5.1

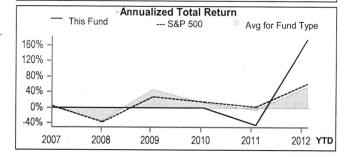

*Guggenheim Solar ETF (TAN)

E   **Very Weak**

Fund Family: Guggenheim Funds Investment Advisor
Fund Type: Energy/Natural Resources
Inception Date: April 15, 2008

Major Rating Factors: Very poor performance is the major factor driving the E (Very Weak) TheStreet.com Investment Rating for *Guggenheim Solar ETF. The fund currently has a performance rating of E (Very Weak) based on an annualized return of -28.67% over the last three years and a total return of 0.73% year to date 2012. Factored into the performance evaluation is an expense ratio of 0.70% (very low).

The fund's risk rating is currently C- (Fair). It carries a beta of 1.64, meaning it is expected to move 16.4% for every 10% move in the market. Volatility, as measured by both the semi-deviation and a drawdown factor, is considered average. As of March 31, 2012, *Guggenheim Solar ETF traded at a discount of .24% below its net asset value, which is better than its one-year historical average discount of .14%.

Michael P. Byrum currently receives a manager quality ranking of 1 (0=worst, 99=best). This fund offers an average level of risk but investors looking for strong performance will be frustrated.

Data Date	Investment Rating	Net Assets ($Mil)	Price	Performance Rating/Pts	Total Return Y-T-D	Risk Rating/Pts
3-12	E	86.55	24.88	E / 0.4	0.73%	C- / 3.7
2011	E	59.30	2.47	E / 0.4	3.64%	C- / 3.7
2010	E	142.70	7.30	E / 0.5	-28.64%	D+ / 2.8
2009	C-	166.57	10.25	C+ / 6.2	10.57%	D+ / 2.7

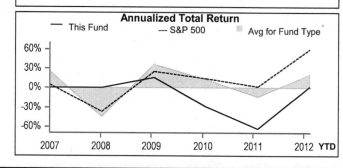

Annualized Total Return — This Fund — S&P 500 — Avg for Fund Type

*Guggenheim Spin-Off ETF (CSD)

A-   **Excellent**

Fund Family: Guggenheim Funds Investment Advisor
Fund Type: Income
Inception Date: December 15, 2006

Major Rating Factors:
Strong performance is the major factor driving the A- (Excellent) TheStreet.com Investment Rating for *Guggenheim Spin-Off ETF. The fund currently has a performance rating of B+ (Good) based on an annualized return of 31.80% over the last three years and a total return of 12.97% year to date 2012. Factored into the performance evaluation is an expense ratio of 0.65% (very low).

The fund's risk rating is currently B (Good). It carries a beta of 1.04, meaning that its performance tracks fairly well with that of the overall stock market. Volatility, as measured by both the semi-deviation and a drawdown factor, is considered low. As of March 31, 2012, *Guggenheim Spin-Off ETF traded at a premium of .08% above its net asset value, which is better than its one-year historical average premium of .10%.

Michael P. Byrum currently receives a manager quality ranking of 82 (0=worst, 99=best). If you desire only a moderate level of risk and strong performance, then this fund is an excellent option.

Data Date	Investment Rating	Net Assets ($Mil)	Price	Performance Rating/Pts	Total Return Y-T-D	Risk Rating/Pts
3-12	A-	36.25	26.57	B+ / 8.6	12.97%	B / 8.5
2011	B+	29.30	23.52	B / 8.0	1.19%	B / 8.4
2010	C-	15.90	22.78	C / 4.4	21.35%	C / 4.8
2009	C-	8.07	18.76	C / 4.3	65.69%	C / 5.0

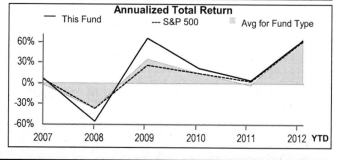

Annualized Total Return — This Fund — S&P 500 — Avg for Fund Type

*Guggenheim Swedish Krona (FXS)

D+   **Weak**

Fund Family: Security Investors LLC
Fund Type: Foreign
Inception Date: June 26, 2006

Major Rating Factors:
Disappointing performance is the major factor driving the D+ (Weak) TheStreet.com Investment Rating for *Guggenheim Swedish Krona. The fund currently has a performance rating of D (Weak) based on an annualized return of 6.78% over the last three years and a total return of 4.16% year to date 2012. Factored into the performance evaluation is an expense ratio of 0.40% (very low).

The fund's risk rating is currently B (Good). It carries a beta of 0.57, meaning the fund's expected move will be 5.7% for every 10% move in the market. Volatility, as measured by both the semi-deviation and a drawdown factor, is considered low. As of March 31, 2012, *Guggenheim Swedish Krona traded at a premium of .03% above its net asset value, which is worse than its one-year historical average discount of .01%.

This fund has been team managed for 6 years and currently receives a manager quality ranking of 35 (0=worst, 99=best). This fund offers only a moderate level of risk but investors looking for strong performance are still waiting.

Data Date	Investment Rating	Net Assets ($Mil)	Price	Performance Rating/Pts	Total Return Y-T-D	Risk Rating/Pts
3-12	D+	75.65	150.11	D / 1.8	4.16%	B / 8.5
2011	C-	87.10	144.57	D+ / 2.6	-0.89%	B / 8.5
2010	C-	51.80	148.96	D+ / 2.7	7.00%	C+ / 6.6
2009	C-	34.29	139.35	D+ / 2.9	8.89%	B- / 7.0

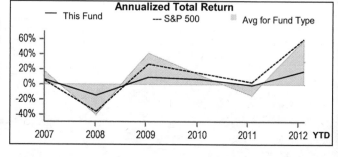

Annualized Total Return — This Fund — S&P 500 — Avg for Fund Type

*Guggenheim Swiss Franc (FXF)   D+   Weak

Fund Family: Security Investors LLC
Fund Type: Foreign
Inception Date: June 26, 2006

Data Date	Investment Rating	Net Assets ($Mil)	Price	Performance Rating/Pts	Total Return Y-T-D	Risk Rating/Pts
3-12	D+	443.72	109.28	D / 2.0	3.98%	B / 8.3
2011	C-	427.70	105.10	D+ / 2.4	-1.62%	B / 8.4
2010	B-	393.60	106.25	C+ / 6.3	10.54%	B- / 7.7
2009	C+	352.07	96.12	C- / 4.0	4.08%	B / 8.1

Major Rating Factors:
Disappointing performance is the major factor driving the D+ (Weak) Investment Rating for *Guggenheim Swiss Franc. The fund currently has a performance rating of D (Weak) based on an annualized return of 7.36% over the last three years and a total return of 3.98% year to date 2012. Factored into the performance evaluation is an expense ratio of 0.40% (very low).

The fund's risk rating is currently B (Good). It carries a beta of 0.42, meaning the fund's expected move will be 4.2% for every 10% move in the market. Volatility, as measured by both the semi-deviation and a drawdown factor, is considered low. As of March 31, 2012, *Guggenheim Swiss Franc traded at a premium of .11% above its net asset value, which is worse than its one-year historical average discount of .02%.

This fund has been team managed for 6 years and currently receives a manager quality ranking of 49 (0=worst, 99=best). This fund offers only a moderate level of risk but investors looking for strong performance are still waiting.

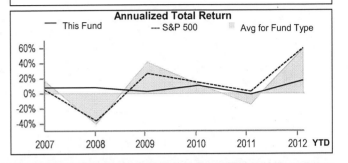

*Guggenheim Timber ETF (CUT)   C   Fair

Fund Family: Guggenheim Funds Investment Advisor
Fund Type: Global
Inception Date: November 9, 2007

Data Date	Investment Rating	Net Assets ($Mil)	Price	Performance Rating/Pts	Total Return Y-T-D	Risk Rating/Pts
3-12	C	122.72	18.84	C+ / 5.9	13.91%	B- / 7.3
2011	C-	103.60	16.54	C- / 3.8	1.09%	B- / 7.1
2010	C-	142.80	20.63	C- / 3.8	17.21%	C / 5.2
2009	A-	45.92	17.96	A- / 9.2	46.77%	C / 5.0

Major Rating Factors: Middle of the road best describes *Guggenheim Timber ETF whose TheStreet.com Investment Rating is currently a C (Fair). The fund currently has a performance rating of C+ (Fair) based on an annualized return of 25.23% over the last three years and a total return of 13.91% year to date 2012. Factored into the performance evaluation is an expense ratio of 0.70% (very low).

The fund's risk rating is currently B- (Good). It carries a beta of 1.24, meaning it is expected to move 12.4% for every 10% move in the market. Volatility, as measured by both the semi-deviation and a drawdown factor, is considered low. As of March 31, 2012, *Guggenheim Timber ETF traded at a premium of .16% above its net asset value, which is worse than its one-year historical average discount of .14%.

Michael P. Byrum currently receives a manager quality ranking of 74 (0=worst, 99=best). If you desire an average level of risk, then this fund may be an option.

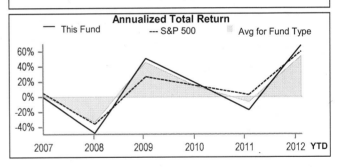

*Guggenheim Wilshire Micro-Cap ET (WMCR)   C   Fair

Fund Family: Guggenheim Funds Investment Advisor
Fund Type: Income
Inception Date: September 21, 2006

Data Date	Investment Rating	Net Assets ($Mil)	Price	Performance Rating/Pts	Total Return Y-T-D	Risk Rating/Pts
3-12	C	15.63	18.20	C / 5.4	19.34%	B- / 7.4
2011	D+	13.80	15.25	C- / 3.1	2.62%	B- / 7.1
2010	C-	39.90	19.14	C / 5.0	24.27%	C / 5.2
2009	E+	3.56	15.45	E+ / 0.9	18.46%	C- / 3.5

Major Rating Factors: Middle of the road best describes *Guggenheim Wilshire Micro-Cap ET whose TheStreet.com Investment Rating is currently a C (Fair). The fund currently has a performance rating of C (Fair) based on an annualized return of 20.63% over the last three years and a total return of 19.34% year to date 2012. Factored into the performance evaluation is an expense ratio of 0.50% (very low).

The fund's risk rating is currently B- (Good). It carries a beta of 1.37, meaning it is expected to move 13.7% for every 10% move in the market. Volatility, as measured by both the semi-deviation and a drawdown factor, is considered low. As of March 31, 2012, *Guggenheim Wilshire Micro-Cap ET traded at a discount of .49% below its net asset value, which is better than its one-year historical average discount of .24%.

Michael P. Byrum currently receives a manager quality ranking of 18 (0=worst, 99=best). If you desire an average level of risk, then this fund may be an option.

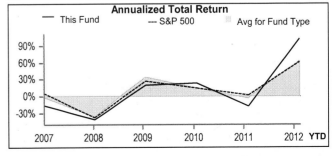

*Guggenheim Wilshire US REIT ETF (WREI)   C+   Fair

Fund Family: Guggenheim Funds Investment Advisor
Fund Type: Growth and Income
Inception Date: March 8, 2010

Data Date	Investment Rating	Net Assets ($Mil)	Price	Performance Rating/Pts	Total Return Y-T-D	Risk Rating/Pts
3-12	C+	8.39	34.69	C+ / 6.5	9.07%	B / 8.0
2011	C	8.00	31.97	C- / 4.0	-0.69%	B / 8.0

Major Rating Factors: Middle of the road best describes *Guggenheim Wilshire US REIT ETF whose TheStreet.com Investment Rating is currently a C+ (Fair). The fund currently has a performance rating of C+ (Fair) based on an annualized return of 0.00% over the last three years and a total return of 9.07% year to date 2012. Factored into the performance evaluation is an expense ratio of 0.32% (very low).

The fund's risk rating is currently B (Good). It carries a beta of 0.00, meaning the fund's expected move will be 0.0% for every 10% move in the market. Volatility, as measured by both the semi-deviation and a drawdown factor, is considered low. As of March 31, 2012, *Guggenheim Wilshire US REIT ETF traded at a discount of .29% below its net asset value, which is better than its one-year historical average discount of .01%.

Michael P. Byrum currently receives a manager quality ranking of 54 (0=worst, 99=best). If you desire an average level of risk, then this fund may be an option.

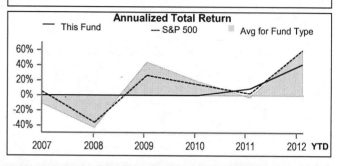

Annualized Total Return

— This Fund   --- S&P 500   ▓ Avg for Fund Type

*Guggenheim Wilshire5000 Tot Mkt (WFVK)   C+   Fair

Fund Family: Guggenheim Funds Investment Advisor
Fund Type: Growth
Inception Date: March 8, 2010

Data Date	Investment Rating	Net Assets ($Mil)	Price	Performance Rating/Pts	Total Return Y-T-D	Risk Rating/Pts
3-12	C+	6.07	31.24	C / 5.5	12.29%	B / 8.3
2011	C-	5.50	27.82	D+ / 2.6	1.69%	B / 8.3

Major Rating Factors: Middle of the road best describes *Guggenheim Wilshire5000 Tot Mkt whose TheStreet.com Investment Rating is currently a C+ (Fair). The fund currently has a performance rating of C (Fair) based on an annualized return of 0.00% over the last three years and a total return of 12.29% year to date 2012. Factored into the performance evaluation is an expense ratio of 0.12% (very low).

The fund's risk rating is currently B (Good). It carries a beta of 0.00, meaning the fund's expected move will be 0.0% for every 10% move in the market. Volatility, as measured by both the semi-deviation and a drawdown factor, is considered low. As of March 31, 2012, *Guggenheim Wilshire5000 Tot Mkt traded at a discount of .16% below its net asset value, which is better than its one-year historical average premium of .08%.

Michael P. Byrum currently receives a manager quality ranking of 33 (0=worst, 99=best). If you desire an average level of risk, then this fund may be an option.

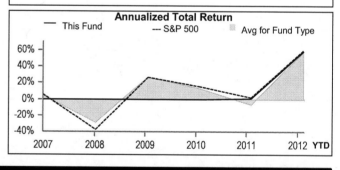

Annualized Total Return

— This Fund   --- S&P 500   ▓ Avg for Fund Type

*Guggenhm BltShs 2012 HY Corp Bd (BSJC)   C-   Fair

Fund Family: Guggenheim Funds Investment Advisor
Fund Type: Corporate - High Yield
Inception Date: January 24, 2011

Data Date	Investment Rating	Net Assets ($Mil)	Price	Performance Rating/Pts	Total Return Y-T-D	Risk Rating/Pts
3-12	C-	71.14	25.49	D / 1.7	1.19%	B+ / 9.7

Major Rating Factors:
Disappointing performance is the major factor driving the C- (Fair) TheStreet.com Investment Rating for *Guggenhm BltShs 2012 HY Corp Bd. The fund currently has a performance rating of D (Weak) based on an annualized return of 0.00% over the last three years and a total return of 1.19% year to date 2012. Factored into the performance evaluation is an expense ratio of 0.42% (very low).

The fund's risk rating is currently B+ (Good). It carries a beta of 0.00, meaning the fund's expected move will be 0.0% for every 10% move in the market. Volatility, as measured by both the semi-deviation and a drawdown factor, is considered very low. As of March 31, 2012, *Guggenhm BltShs 2012 HY Corp Bd traded at a premium of .24% above its net asset value, which is better than its one-year historical average premium of .63%.

Mark A. Mitchell currently receives a manager quality ranking of 57 (0=worst, 99=best). This fund offers only a moderate level of risk but investors looking for strong performance are still waiting.

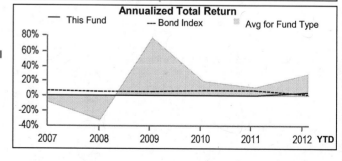

Annualized Total Return

— This Fund   --- Bond Index   ▓ Avg for Fund Type

*Guggenhm BltShs 2013 HY Corp Bd (BSJD)   C-   Fair

Fund Family: Guggenheim Funds Investment Advisor
Fund Type: Corporate - High Yield
Inception Date: January 24, 2011

Data Date	Investment Rating	Net Assets ($Mil)	Price	Perfor-mance Rating/Pts	Total Return Y-T-D	Risk Rating/Pts
3-12	C-	115.75	25.77	D / 2.2	2.93%	B+ / 9.6

Major Rating Factors:
Disappointing performance is the major factor driving the C- (Fair) TheStreet.com Investment Rating for *Guggenhm BltShs 2013 HY Corp Bd. The fund currently has a performance rating of D (Weak) based on an annualized return of 0.00% over the last three years and a total return of 2.93% year to date 2012. Factored into the performance evaluation is an expense ratio of 0.42% (very low).

The fund's risk rating is currently B+ (Good). It carries a beta of 0.00, meaning the fund's expected move will be 0.0% for every 10% move in the market. Volatility, as measured by both the semi-deviation and a drawdown factor, is considered very low. As of March 31, 2012, *Guggenhm BltShs 2013 HY Corp Bd traded at a premium of .39% above its net asset value, which is better than its one-year historical average premium of .44%.

Michael P. Byrum currently receives a manager quality ranking of 60 (0=worst, 99=best). This fund offers only a moderate level of risk but investors looking for strong performance are still waiting.

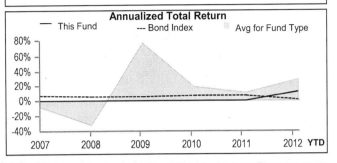

*Guggenhm BltShs 2014 HY Corp Bd (BSJE)   C   Fair

Fund Family: Guggenheim Funds Investment Advisor
Fund Type: Corporate - High Yield
Inception Date: January 24, 2011

Data Date	Investment Rating	Net Assets ($Mil)	Price	Perfor-mance Rating/Pts	Total Return Y-T-D	Risk Rating/Pts
3-12	C	77.67	25.92	D+ / 2.5	3.30%	B+ / 9.6

Major Rating Factors:
Disappointing performance is the major factor driving the C (Fair) TheStreet.com Investment Rating for *Guggenhm BltShs 2014 HY Corp Bd. The fund currently has a performance rating of D+ (Weak) based on an annualized return of 0.00% over the last three years and a total return of 3.30% year to date 2012. Factored into the performance evaluation is an expense ratio of 0.42% (very low).

The fund's risk rating is currently B+ (Good). It carries a beta of 0.00, meaning the fund's expected move will be 0.0% for every 10% move in the market. Volatility, as measured by both the semi-deviation and a drawdown factor, is considered very low. As of March 31, 2012, *Guggenhm BltShs 2014 HY Corp Bd traded at a premium of .27% above its net asset value, which is better than its one-year historical average premium of .41%.

Michael P. Byrum currently receives a manager quality ranking of 67 (0=worst, 99=best). This fund offers only a moderate level of risk but investors looking for strong performance are still waiting.

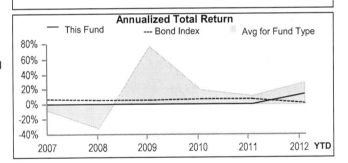

*Guggenhm BltShs 2015 HY Corp Bd (BSJF)   C   Fair

Fund Family: Guggenheim Funds Investment Advisor
Fund Type: Corporate - High Yield
Inception Date: January 24, 2011

Data Date	Investment Rating	Net Assets ($Mil)	Price	Perfor-mance Rating/Pts	Total Return Y-T-D	Risk Rating/Pts
3-12	C	95.74	25.89	D+ / 2.7	3.65%	B+ / 9.4

Major Rating Factors:
Disappointing performance is the major factor driving the C (Fair) TheStreet.com Investment Rating for *Guggenhm BltShs 2015 HY Corp Bd. The fund currently has a performance rating of D+ (Weak) based on an annualized return of 0.00% over the last three years and a total return of 3.65% year to date 2012. Factored into the performance evaluation is an expense ratio of 0.42% (very low).

The fund's risk rating is currently B+ (Good). It carries a beta of 0.00, meaning the fund's expected move will be 0.0% for every 10% move in the market. Volatility, as measured by both the semi-deviation and a drawdown factor, is considered very low. As of March 31, 2012, *Guggenhm BltShs 2015 HY Corp Bd traded at a premium of .47% above its net asset value, which is better than its one-year historical average premium of .54%.

Michael P. Byrum currently receives a manager quality ranking of 63 (0=worst, 99=best). This fund offers only a moderate level of risk but investors looking for strong performance are still waiting.

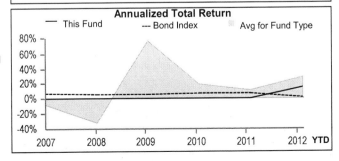

*Health Care Select Sector SPDR (XLV)

C+   **Fair**

Fund Family: SSgA Funds Management Inc
Fund Type: Health
Inception Date: December 16, 1998

Major Rating Factors: Middle of the road best describes *Health Care Select Sector SPDR whose TheStreet.com Investment Rating is currently a C+ (Fair). The fund currently has a performance rating of C (Fair) based on an annualized return of 18.62% over the last three years and a total return of 8.96% year to date 2012. Factored into the performance evaluation is an expense ratio of 0.19% (very low).

The fund's risk rating is currently B (Good). It carries a beta of 0.58, meaning the fund's expected move will be 5.8% for every 10% move in the market. Volatility, as measured by both the semi-deviation and a drawdown factor, is considered low. As of March 31, 2012, *Health Care Select Sector SPDR traded at a discount of .03% below its net asset value.

John A. Tucker has been running the fund for 14 years and currently receives a manager quality ranking of 71 (0=worst, 99=best). If you desire an average level of risk, then this fund may be an option.

Data Date	Investment Rating	Net Assets ($Mil)	Price	Performance Rating/Pts	Total Return Y-T-D	Risk Rating/Pts
3-12	C+	4,117.65	37.61	C / 5.1	8.96%	B / 8.7
2011	C	3,400.80	34.69	C / 4.9	1.27%	B / 8.2
2010	C-	2,705.80	31.50	D+ / 2.5	3.32%	C+ / 6.9
2009	C-	1,979.59	31.07	C- / 3.2	17.10%	C+ / 6.8

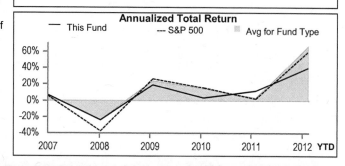

*Industrial Select Sector SPDR (XLI)

B-   **Good**

Fund Family: SSgA Funds Management Inc
Fund Type: Growth
Inception Date: December 16, 1998

Major Rating Factors: Strong performance is the major factor driving the B- (Good) TheStreet.com Investment Rating for *Industrial Select Sector SPDR. The fund currently has a performance rating of B- (Good) based on an annualized return of 26.40% over the last three years and a total return of 11.39% year to date 2012. Factored into the performance evaluation is an expense ratio of 0.19% (very low).

The fund's risk rating is currently B- (Good). It carries a beta of 1.30, meaning it is expected to move 13.0% for every 10% move in the market. Volatility, as measured by both the semi-deviation and a drawdown factor, is considered low. As of March 31, 2012, *Industrial Select Sector SPDR traded at a premium of .03% above its net asset value.

John A. Tucker has been running the fund for 14 years and currently receives a manager quality ranking of 37 (0=worst, 99=best). If you desire only a moderate level of risk and strong performance, then this fund is an excellent option.

Data Date	Investment Rating	Net Assets ($Mil)	Price	Performance Rating/Pts	Total Return Y-T-D	Risk Rating/Pts
3-12	B-	2,789.76	37.42	B- / 7.1	11.39%	B- / 7.8
2011	C	2,711.00	33.75	C+ / 5.8	2.49%	B- / 7.3
2010	C	3,744.30	34.87	C+ / 5.8	27.85%	C / 5.4
2009	D+	2,010.29	27.79	D / 2.2	17.67%	C+ / 5.7

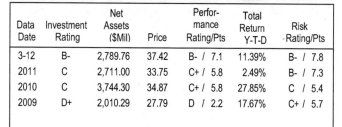

*iPath Asian & Gulf Curncy Reval (PGD)

D-   **Weak**

Fund Family: Barclays Bank PLC
Fund Type: Foreign
Inception Date: February 5, 2008

Major Rating Factors:
Disappointing performance is the major factor driving the D- (Weak) TheStreet.com Investment Rating for *iPath Asian & Gulf Curncy Reval. The fund currently has a performance rating of D- (Weak) based on an annualized return of 0.41% over the last three years and a total return of 0.02% year to date 2012. Factored into the performance evaluation is an expense ratio of 0.89% (low).

The fund's risk rating is currently C+ (Fair). It carries a beta of 0.10, meaning the fund's expected move will be 1.0% for every 10% move in the market. Volatility, as measured by both the semi-deviation and a drawdown factor, is considered low. As of March 31, 2012, *iPath Asian & Gulf Curncy Reval traded at a discount of 1.32% below its net asset value, which is better than its one-year historical average discount of .21%.

This fund has been team managed for 4 years and currently receives a manager quality ranking of 38 (0=worst, 99=best). This fund offers only a moderate level of risk but investors looking for strong performance are still waiting.

Data Date	Investment Rating	Net Assets ($Mil)	Price	Performance Rating/Pts	Total Return Y-T-D	Risk Rating/Pts
3-12	D-	4.06	50.21	D- / 1.2	0.02%	C+ / 5.8
2011	D-	4.00	50.20	D / 2.0	0.22%	C+ / 5.9
2010	D+	4.00	51.21	C- / 3.7	0.85%	C / 4.9
2009	C	0.00	50.78	C- / 3.1	1.63%	B / 8.1

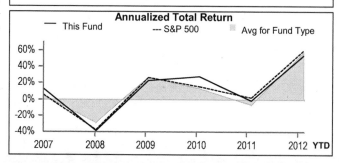

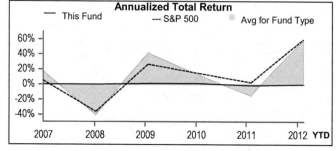

*iPath CBOE S&P 500 BuyWrite Idx (BWV)   C   Fair

Fund Family: Barclays Bank PLC
Fund Type: Growth
Inception Date: May 22, 2007

Data Date	Investment Rating	Net Assets ($Mil)	Price	Performance Rating/Pts	Total Return Y-T-D	Risk Rating/Pts
3-12	C	10.45	52.57	C- / 3.6	4.30%	B / 8.7
2011	C+	18.80	50.40	C / 4.7	0.63%	B / 8.7
2010	C-	16.70	47.83	D+ / 2.8	4.80%	C+ / 6.4
2009	A	10.45	45.64	B / 8.1	23.72%	C+ / 6.7

Major Rating Factors: Middle of the road best describes *iPath CBOE S&P 500 BuyWrite Idx whose TheStreet.com Investment Rating is currently a C (Fair). The fund currently has a performance rating of C- (Fair) based on an annualized return of 13.63% over the last three years and a total return of 4.30% year to date 2012. Factored into the performance evaluation is an expense ratio of 0.75% (very low).

The fund's risk rating is currently B (Good). It carries a beta of 0.65, meaning the fund's expected move will be 6.5% for every 10% move in the market. Volatility, as measured by both the semi-deviation and a drawdown factor, is considered low. As of March 31, 2012, *iPath CBOE S&P 500 BuyWrite Idx traded at a discount of .30% below its net asset value, which is better than its one-year historical average discount of .03%.

This fund has been team managed for 5 years and currently receives a manager quality ranking of 43 (0=worst, 99=best). If you desire an average level of risk, then this fund may be an option.

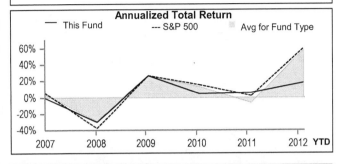

*iPath Cptl Glbl Carbon Tot Ret E (GRN)   E-   Very Weak

Fund Family: Barclays Bank PLC
Fund Type: Energy/Natural Resources
Inception Date: June 24, 2008

Data Date	Investment Rating	Net Assets ($Mil)	Price	Performance Rating/Pts	Total Return Y-T-D	Risk Rating/Pts
3-12	E-	4.10	10.00	E / 0.4	-3.29%	D / 1.9
2011	E-	1.20	10.34	E / 0.4	3.97%	D / 1.9
2010	E+	3.80	25.54	D+ / 2.4	11.67%	D- / 1.4
2009	D-	4.10	22.87	E / 0.5	-20.86%	C+ / 5.7

Major Rating Factors: *iPath Cptl Glbl Carbon Tot Ret E has adopted a very risky asset allocation strategy and currently receives an overall TheStreet.com Investment Rating of E- (Very Weak). The fund has a high level of volatility, as measured by both semi-deviation and drawdown factors. It carries a beta of 0.28, meaning the fund's expected move will be 2.8% for every 10% move in the market. As of March 31, 2012, *iPath Cptl Glbl Carbon Tot Ret E traded at a discount of 11.50% below its net asset value, which is better than its one-year historical average discount of 5.12%. Unfortunately, the high level of risk (D, Weak) failed to pay off as investors endured very poor performance.

The fund's performance rating is currently E (Very Weak). It has registered an annualized return of -24.73% over the last three years and is down -3.29% year to date 2012. Factored into the performance evaluation is an expense ratio of 0.75% (very low).

This fund has been team managed for 4 years and currently receives a manager quality ranking of 4 (0=worst, 99=best). If you can tolerate very high levels of risk in the hope of improved future returns, holding this fund may be an option.

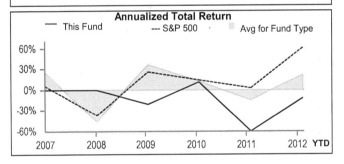

*iPath DJ UBS Agri Tot Ret Sub (JJA)   D-   Weak

Fund Family: Barclays Bank PLC
Fund Type: Energy/Natural Resources
Inception Date: October 23, 2007

Data Date	Investment Rating	Net Assets ($Mil)	Price	Performance Rating/Pts	Total Return Y-T-D	Risk Rating/Pts
3-12	D-	68.43	55.10	D / 2.2	3.15%	C / 4.6
2011	D-	135.50	53.42	D+ / 2.8	-1.10%	C / 4.6
2010	C	142.20	63.07	B / 8.2	38.40%	D+ / 2.6
2009	C-	68.43	45.57	B- / 7.0	12.08%	D+ / 2.9

Major Rating Factors:
Disappointing performance is the major factor driving the D- (Weak) TheStreet.com Investment Rating for *iPath DJ UBS Agri Tot Ret Sub. The fund currently has a performance rating of D (Weak) based on an annualized return of 11.38% over the last three years and a total return of 3.15% year to date 2012. Factored into the performance evaluation is an expense ratio of 0.75% (very low).

The fund's risk rating is currently C (Fair). It carries a beta of 0.67, meaning the fund's expected move will be 6.7% for every 10% move in the market. Volatility, as measured by both the semi-deviation and a drawdown factor, is considered average. As of March 31, 2012, *iPath DJ UBS Agri Tot Ret Sub traded at a premium of .04% above its net asset value, which is worse than its one-year historical average discount of .03%.

This fund has been team managed for 5 years and currently receives a manager quality ranking of 44 (0=worst, 99=best). This fund offers an average level of risk but investors looking for strong performance will be frustrated.

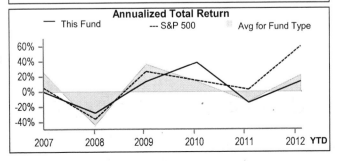

*iPath DJ UBS Almin Tot Ret Sub (JJU)

E+   **Very Weak**

Fund Family: Barclays Bank PLC
Fund Type: Energy/Natural Resources
Inception Date: June 24, 2008

Major Rating Factors:
Disappointing performance is the major factor driving the E+ (Very Weak) TheStreet.com Investment Rating for *iPath DJ UBS Almin Tot Ret Sub. The fund currently has a performance rating of D- (Weak) based on an annualized return of 7.08% over the last three years and a total return of 3.52% year to date 2012. Factored into the performance evaluation is an expense ratio of 0.75% (very low).

The fund's risk rating is currently C- (Fair). It carries a beta of 0.64, meaning the fund's expected move will be 6.4% for every 10% move in the market. Volatility, as measured by both the semi-deviation and a drawdown factor, is considered average. As of March 31, 2012, *iPath DJ UBS Almin Tot Ret Sub traded at a discount of .19% below its net asset value, which is better than its one-year historical average discount of .11%.

This fund has been team managed for 4 years and currently receives a manager quality ranking of 26 (0=worst, 99=best). This fund offers an average level of risk but investors looking for strong performance will be frustrated.

Data Date	Investment Rating	Net Assets ($Mil)	Price	Perfor-mance Rating/Pts	Total Return Y-T-D	Risk Rating/Pts
3-12	E+	6.79	26.19	D- / 1.4	3.52%	C- / 4.2
2011	E+	4.50	25.30	D / 1.6	1.54%	C- / 4.2
2010	C	11.60	33.10	B+ / 8.5	4.48%	D / 2.1
2009	C	6.79	31.68	A- / 9.0	32.55%	D+ / 2.4

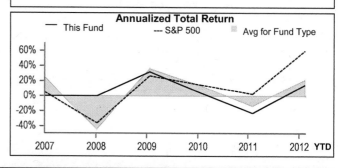

*iPath DJ UBS Cocoa Tot Ret Sub (NIB)

E   **Very Weak**

Fund Family: Barclays Bank PLC
Fund Type: Energy/Natural Resources
Inception Date: June 24, 2008

Major Rating Factors: Very poor performance is the major factor driving the E (Very Weak) TheStreet.com Investment Rating for *iPath DJ UBS Cocoa Tot Ret Sub. The fund currently has a performance rating of E+ (Very Weak) based on an annualized return of -11.51% over the last three years and a total return of 4.66% year to date 2012. Factored into the performance evaluation is an expense ratio of 0.75% (very low).

The fund's risk rating is currently C- (Fair). It carries a beta of 0.67, meaning the fund's expected move will be 6.7% for every 10% move in the market. Volatility, as measured by both the semi-deviation and a drawdown factor, is considered average. As of March 31, 2012, *iPath DJ UBS Cocoa Tot Ret Sub traded at a premium of .20% above its net asset value, which is worse than its one-year historical average premium of .02%.

This fund has been team managed for 4 years and currently receives a manager quality ranking of 7 (0=worst, 99=best). This fund offers an average level of risk but investors looking for strong performance will be frustrated.

Data Date	Investment Rating	Net Assets ($Mil)	Price	Perfor-mance Rating/Pts	Total Return Y-T-D	Risk Rating/Pts
3-12	E	27.73	30.09	E+ / 0.7	4.66%	C- / 3.2
2011	E	17.60	28.75	E+ / 0.9	-4.70%	C- / 3.1
2010	E+	15.20	43.18	D- / 1.1	-11.66%	C- / 3.6
2009	C+	27.73	48.88	B+ / 8.3	25.98%	C- / 3.8

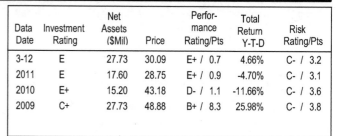

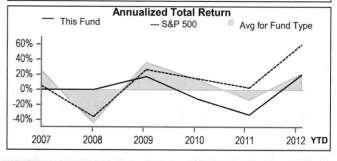

*iPath DJ UBS Coffee Tot Ret Sub (JO)

E   **Very Weak**

Fund Family: Barclays Bank PLC
Fund Type: Energy/Natural Resources
Inception Date: June 24, 2008

Major Rating Factors:
Disappointing performance is the major factor driving the E (Very Weak) TheStreet.com Investment Rating for *iPath DJ UBS Coffee Tot Ret Sub. The fund currently has a performance rating of D- (Weak) based on an annualized return of 6.69% over the last three years and a total return of -20.82% year to date 2012. Factored into the performance evaluation is an expense ratio of 0.75% (very low).

The fund's risk rating is currently C- (Fair). It carries a beta of 0.50, meaning the fund's expected move will be 5.0% for every 10% move in the market. Volatility, as measured by both the semi-deviation and a drawdown factor, is considered average. As of March 31, 2012, *iPath DJ UBS Coffee Tot Ret Sub traded at a premium of .02% above its net asset value, which is worse than its one-year historical average discount of .01%.

This fund has been team managed for 4 years and currently receives a manager quality ranking of 37 (0=worst, 99=best). This fund offers an average level of risk but investors looking for strong performance will be frustrated.

Data Date	Investment Rating	Net Assets ($Mil)	Price	Perfor-mance Rating/Pts	Total Return Y-T-D	Risk Rating/Pts
3-12	E	7.89	44.76	D- / 1.1	-20.82%	C- / 3.3
2011	D	25.70	56.52	C- / 3.7	-3.59%	C- / 4.2
2010	B	34.50	64.03	A+ / 9.8	65.37%	C- / 3.5
2009	C-	7.89	38.72	C / 5.4	10.44%	C- / 3.7

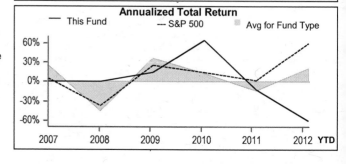

*iPath DJ UBS Copper Total Ret Su (JJC)   D   Weak

Fund Family: Barclays Bank PLC
Fund Type: Energy/Natural Resources
Inception Date: October 23, 2007

Data Date	Investment Rating	Net Assets ($Mil)	Price	Perfor-mance Rating/Pts	Total Return Y-T-D	Risk Rating/Pts
3-12	D	130.36	49.07	C / 4.7	11.42%	C- / 4.0
2011	D+	127.80	44.04	C+ / 6.4	-0.57%	C- / 4.0
2010	C	252.40	59.10	B+ / 8.6	29.04%	D / 1.8
2009	C+	130.36	45.80	A+ / 9.9	122.44%	D / 2.0

Major Rating Factors: *iPath DJ UBS Copper Total Ret Su receives a TheStreet.com Investment Rating of D (Weak). The fund currently has a performance rating of C (Fair) based on an annualized return of 20.93% over the last three years and a total return of 11.42% year to date 2012. Factored into the performance evaluation is an expense ratio of 0.75% (very low).

The fund's risk rating is currently C- (Fair). It carries a beta of 0.98, meaning that its performance tracks fairly well with that of the overall stock market. Volatility, as measured by both the semi-deviation and a drawdown factor, is considered average. As of March 31, 2012, *iPath DJ UBS Copper Total Ret Su traded at a discount of .02% below its net asset value, which is better than its one-year historical average premium of .05%.

This fund has been team managed for 5 years and currently receives a manager quality ranking of 68 (0=worst, 99=best). If you desire an average level of risk, then this fund may be an option.

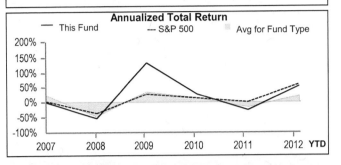

*iPath DJ UBS Cotton Tot Ret Sub (BAL)   D-   Weak

Fund Family: Barclays Bank PLC
Fund Type: Energy/Natural Resources
Inception Date: June 24, 2008

Data Date	Investment Rating	Net Assets ($Mil)	Price	Perfor-mance Rating/Pts	Total Return Y-T-D	Risk Rating/Pts
3-12	D-	22.72	56.63	C / 4.4	0.30%	C- / 3.1
2011	D+	45.50	56.46	C+ / 6.6	3.67%	C- / 3.1
2010	B-	56.40	73.05	A+ / 9.9	96.21%	D+ / 2.7
2009	C	22.72	37.23	B+ / 8.5	29.90%	D+ / 2.9

Major Rating Factors: *iPath DJ UBS Cotton Tot Ret Sub receives a TheStreet.com Investment Rating of D- (Weak). The fund currently has a performance rating of C (Fair) based on an annualized return of 28.23% over the last three years and a total return of 0.30% year to date 2012. Factored into the performance evaluation is an expense ratio of 0.75% (very low).

The fund's risk rating is currently C- (Fair). It carries a beta of 0.66, meaning the fund's expected move will be 6.6% for every 10% move in the market. Volatility, as measured by both the semi-deviation and a drawdown factor, is considered average. As of March 31, 2012, *iPath DJ UBS Cotton Tot Ret Sub traded at a discount of .47% below its net asset value, which is better than its one-year historical average discount of .01%.

This fund has been team managed for 4 years and currently receives a manager quality ranking of 90 (0=worst, 99=best). If you desire an average level of risk, then this fund may be an option.

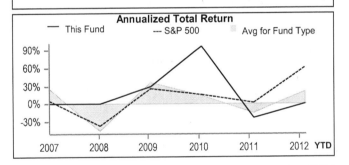

*iPath DJ UBS Energy Tot Ret Sub (JJE)   E+   Very Weak

Fund Family: Barclays Bank PLC
Fund Type: Energy/Natural Resources
Inception Date: October 23, 2007

Data Date	Investment Rating	Net Assets ($Mil)	Price	Perfor-mance Rating/Pts	Total Return Y-T-D	Risk Rating/Pts
3-12	E+	10.54	17.99	E+ / 0.8	-6.06%	C- / 4.0
2011	E+	19.00	19.15	D- / 1.2	3.13%	C- / 4.0
2010	E-	15.60	23.21	E / 0.5	-11.92%	D- / 1.2
2009	E	10.54	26.35	D / 1.6	-9.42%	D- / 1.5

Major Rating Factors:
Very poor performance is the major factor driving the E+ (Very Weak) TheStreet.com Investment Rating for *iPath DJ UBS Energy Tot Ret Sub. The fund currently has a performance rating of E+ (Very Weak) based on an annualized return of -8.08% over the last three years and a total return of -6.06% year to date 2012. Factored into the performance evaluation is an expense ratio of 0.75% (very low).

The fund's risk rating is currently C- (Fair). It carries a beta of 0.74, meaning the fund's expected move will be 7.4% for every 10% move in the market. Volatility, as measured by both the semi-deviation and a drawdown factor, is considered average. As of March 31, 2012, *iPath DJ UBS Energy Tot Ret Sub traded at a premium of .33% above its net asset value, which is worse than its one-year historical average discount of .16%.

This fund has been team managed for 5 years and currently receives a manager quality ranking of 7 (0=worst, 99=best). This fund offers an average level of risk but investors looking for strong performance will be frustrated.

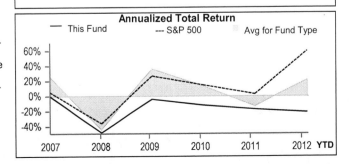

*iPath DJ UBS Grains Tot Ret (JJG)

E+   **Very Weak**

Fund Family: Barclays Bank PLC
Fund Type: Energy/Natural Resources
Inception Date: October 23, 2007

Major Rating Factors:

Disappointing performance is the major factor driving the E+ (Very Weak) TheStreet.com Investment Rating for *iPath DJ UBS Grains Tot Ret. The fund currently has a performance rating of D (Weak) based on an annualized return of 5.39% over the last three years and a total return of 5.29% year to date 2012. Factored into the performance evaluation is an expense ratio of 0.75% (very low).

The fund's risk rating is currently C (Fair). It carries a beta of 0.76, meaning the fund's expected move will be 7.6% for every 10% move in the market. Volatility, as measured by both the semi-deviation and a drawdown factor, is considered average. As of March 31, 2012, *iPath DJ UBS Grains Tot Ret traded at a premium of .13% above its net asset value, which is worse than its one-year historical average premium of .02%.

This fund has been team managed for 5 years and currently receives a manager quality ranking of 19 (0=worst, 99=best). This fund offers an average level of risk but investors looking for strong performance will be frustrated.

Data Date	Investment Rating	Net Assets ($Mil)	Price	Performance Rating/Pts	Total Return Y-T-D	Risk Rating/Pts
3-12	E+	57.16	47.41	D / 1.6	5.29%	C / 4.4
2011	D-	166.80	45.03	D / 1.8	-1.57%	C / 4.4
2010	D+	190.60	53.09	C+ / 5.9	29.87%	D+ / 2.4
2009	D	57.16	40.89	C / 4.4	-2.67%	D+ / 2.7

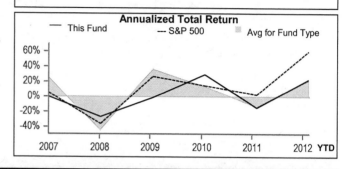

Annualized Total Return
— This Fund   --- S&P 500   ▨ Avg for Fund Type

*iPath DJ UBS Ind Me Tot Ret Sub (JJM)

D-   **Weak**

Fund Family: Barclays Bank PLC
Fund Type: Energy/Natural Resources
Inception Date: October 23, 2007

Major Rating Factors:

Disappointing performance is the major factor driving the D- (Weak) TheStreet.com Investment Rating for *iPath DJ UBS Ind Me Tot Ret Sub. The fund currently has a performance rating of D+ (Weak) based on an annualized return of 13.61% over the last three years and a total return of 5.91% year to date 2012. Factored into the performance evaluation is an expense ratio of 0.75% (very low).

The fund's risk rating is currently C- (Fair). It carries a beta of 0.91, meaning that its performance tracks fairly well with that of the overall stock market. Volatility, as measured by both the semi-deviation and a drawdown factor, is considered average. As of March 31, 2012, *iPath DJ UBS Ind Me Tot Ret Sub traded at a discount of .14% below its net asset value, which is better than its one-year historical average discount of .08%.

This fund has been team managed for 5 years and currently receives a manager quality ranking of 36 (0=worst, 99=best). This fund offers an average level of risk but investors looking for strong performance will be frustrated.

Data Date	Investment Rating	Net Assets ($Mil)	Price	Performance Rating/Pts	Total Return Y-T-D	Risk Rating/Pts
3-12	D-	49.69	36.75	D+ / 2.5	5.91%	C- / 4.1
2011	D-	31.50	34.70	C- / 3.4	0.58%	C- / 4.1
2010	D	71.70	46.87	C+ / 5.8	15.59%	D / 1.9
2009	C+	49.69	40.55	A+ / 9.7	72.92%	D / 2.1

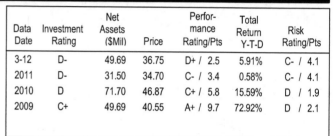

Annualized Total Return
— This Fund   --- S&P 500   ▨ Avg for Fund Type

*iPath DJ UBS Lead Tot Ret Sub (LD)

E+   **Very Weak**

Fund Family: Barclays Bank PLC
Fund Type: Energy/Natural Resources
Inception Date: June 24, 2008

Major Rating Factors:

Disappointing performance is the major factor driving the E+ (Very Weak) TheStreet.com Investment Rating for *iPath DJ UBS Lead Tot Ret Sub. The fund currently has a performance rating of D (Weak) based on an annualized return of 11.70% over the last three years and a total return of -0.57% year to date 2012. Factored into the performance evaluation is an expense ratio of 0.75% (very low).

The fund's risk rating is currently C- (Fair). It carries a beta of 1.03, meaning that its performance tracks fairly well with that of the overall stock market. Volatility, as measured by both the semi-deviation and a drawdown factor, is considered average. As of March 31, 2012, *iPath DJ UBS Lead Tot Ret Sub traded at a premium of .27% above its net asset value, which is worse than its one-year historical average discount of .04%.

This fund has been team managed for 4 years and currently receives a manager quality ranking of 20 (0=worst, 99=best). This fund offers an average level of risk but investors looking for strong performance will be frustrated.

Data Date	Investment Rating	Net Assets ($Mil)	Price	Performance Rating/Pts	Total Return Y-T-D	Risk Rating/Pts
3-12	E+	13.63	48.77	D / 1.9	-0.57%	C- / 4.2
2011	D-	4.20	49.05	C- / 3.5	1.43%	C- / 4.2
2010	C+	6.70	64.98	A / 9.3	3.22%	D / 2.2
2009	C+	13.63	62.95	A+ / 9.9	110.54%	D+ / 2.5

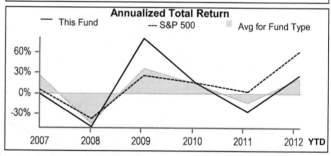
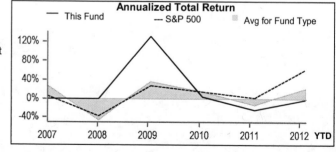

Annualized Total Return
— This Fund   --- S&P 500   ▨ Avg for Fund Type

*iPath DJ UBS Live Stk TR Sub (COW)   E+   Very Weak

Fund Family: Barclays Bank PLC
Fund Type: Energy/Natural Resources
Inception Date: October 23, 2007

Data Date	Investment Rating	Net Assets ($Mil)	Price	Performance Rating/Pts	Total Return Y-T-D	Risk Rating/Pts
3-12	E+	110.42	28.11	E+ / 0.9	-5.54%	C / 5.1
2011	D-	99.20	29.76	D- / 1.5	-0.38%	C / 4.8
2010	E+	65.00	30.75	E+ / 0.8	9.20%	D+ / 2.9
2009	E	110.42	28.16	E+ / 0.7	-19.08%	C- / 3.0

Major Rating Factors:
Very poor performance is the major factor driving the E+ (Very Weak) TheStreet.com Investment Rating for *iPath DJ UBS Live Stk TR Sub. The fund currently has a performance rating of E+ (Very Weak) based on an annualized return of -4.01% over the last three years and a total return of -5.54% year to date 2012. Factored into the performance evaluation is an expense ratio of 0.75% (very low).

The fund's risk rating is currently C (Fair). It carries a beta of 0.09, meaning the fund's expected move will be 0.9% for every 10% move in the market. Volatility, as measured by both the semi-deviation and a drawdown factor, is considered average. As of March 31, 2012, *iPath DJ UBS Live Stk TR Sub traded at a premium of .11% above its net asset value, which is worse than its one-year historical average discount of .07%.

This fund has been team managed for 5 years and currently receives a manager quality ranking of 23 (0=worst, 99=best). This fund offers an average level of risk but investors looking for strong performance will be frustrated.

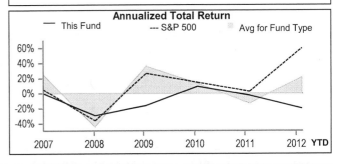

*iPath DJ UBS Nkl Tot Ret Sub (JJN)   E+   Very Weak

Fund Family: Barclays Bank PLC
Fund Type: Energy/Natural Resources
Inception Date: October 23, 2007

Data Date	Investment Rating	Net Assets ($Mil)	Price	Performance Rating/Pts	Total Return Y-T-D	Risk Rating/Pts
3-12	E+	14.87	25.37	D+ / 2.3	-4.91%	C- / 3.5
2011	D-	8.00	26.68	C- / 3.2	-0.45%	C- / 3.5
2010	E+	18.30	36.65	C- / 3.0	32.12%	D- / 1.5
2009	C	14.87	27.74	B+ / 8.5	40.10%	D / 1.7

Major Rating Factors:
Disappointing performance is the major factor driving the E+ (Very Weak) TheStreet.com Investment Rating for *iPath DJ UBS Nkl Tot Ret Sub. The fund currently has a performance rating of D+ (Weak) based on an annualized return of 16.01% over the last three years and a total return of -4.91% year to date 2012. Factored into the performance evaluation is an expense ratio of 0.75% (very low).

The fund's risk rating is currently C- (Fair). It carries a beta of 1.13, meaning it is expected to move 11.3% for every 10% move in the market. Volatility, as measured by both the semi-deviation and a drawdown factor, is considered average. As of March 31, 2012, *iPath DJ UBS Nkl Tot Ret Sub traded at a discount of .28% below its net asset value, which is better than its one-year historical average discount of .09%.

This fund has been team managed for 5 years and currently receives a manager quality ranking of 30 (0=worst, 99=best). This fund offers an average level of risk but investors looking for strong performance will be frustrated.

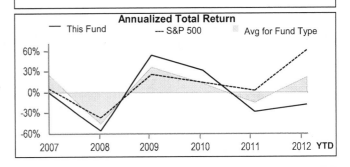

*iPath DJ UBS Ntrl Gas Tot Ret Su (GAZ)   E-   Very Weak

Fund Family: Barclays Bank PLC
Fund Type: Energy/Natural Resources
Inception Date: October 23, 2007

Data Date	Investment Rating	Net Assets ($Mil)	Price	Performance Rating/Pts	Total Return Y-T-D	Risk Rating/Pts
3-12	E-	208.19	3.80	E / 0.3	0.80%	D / 1.9
2011	E-	56.10	3.77	E- / 0.1	0.27%	D / 1.9
2010	E-	119.30	8.05	E- / 0.2	-43.63%	D- / 1.0
2009	E-	208.19	14.28	E / 0.3	-54.29%	D- / 1.1

Major Rating Factors: *iPath DJ UBS Ntrl Gas Tot Ret Su has adopted a very risky asset allocation strategy and currently receives an overall TheStreet.com Investment Rating of E- (Very Weak). The fund has a high level of volatility, as measured by both semi-deviation and drawdown factors. It carries a beta of 0.52, meaning the fund's expected move will be 5.2% for every 10% move in the market. As of March 31, 2012, *iPath DJ UBS Ntrl Gas Tot Ret Su traded at a premium of 80.09% above its net asset value, which is worse than its one-year historical average premium of 14.86%. Unfortunately, the high level of risk (D, Weak) failed to pay off as investors endured very poor performance.

The fund's performance rating is currently E (Very Weak). It has registered an annualized return of -41.52% over the last three years and is up 0.80% year to date 2012. Factored into the performance evaluation is an expense ratio of 0.75% (very low).

This fund has been team managed for 5 years and currently receives a manager quality ranking of 0 (0=worst, 99=best). If you can tolerate very high levels of risk in the hope of improved future returns, holding this fund may be an option.

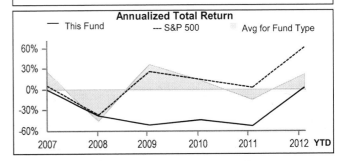

*iPath DJ UBS Platinum Tot Ret Su (PGM)   D-   Weak

Fund Family: Barclays Bank PLC
Fund Type: Energy/Natural Resources
Inception Date: June 24, 2008

Data Date	Investment Rating	Net Assets ($Mil)	Price	Performance Rating/Pts	Total Return Y-T-D	Risk Rating/Pts
3-12	D-	103.49	37.64	D+ / 2.3	17.53%	C / 4.3
2011	D-	30.80	32.03	D+ / 2.7	1.58%	C / 4.3
2010	C-	78.00	41.85	B+ / 8.4	8.59%	D / 1.6
2009	A+	103.49	38.54	A+ / 9.6	63.51%	C / 5.4

Major Rating Factors:
Disappointing performance is the major factor driving the D- (Weak) TheStreet.com Investment Rating for *iPath DJ UBS Platinum Tot Ret Su. The fund currently has a performance rating of D+ (Weak) based on an annualized return of 9.88% over the last three years and a total return of 17.53% year to date 2012. Factored into the performance evaluation is an expense ratio of 0.75% (very low).

The fund's risk rating is currently C (Fair). It carries a beta of 0.70, meaning the fund's expected move will be 7.0% for every 10% move in the market. Volatility, as measured by both the semi-deviation and a drawdown factor, is considered average. As of March 31, 2012, *iPath DJ UBS Platinum Tot Ret Su traded at a discount of .11% below its net asset value, which is better than its one-year historical average premium of .28%.

This fund has been team managed for 4 years and currently receives a manager quality ranking of 32 (0=worst, 99=best). This fund offers an average level of risk but investors looking for strong performance will be frustrated.

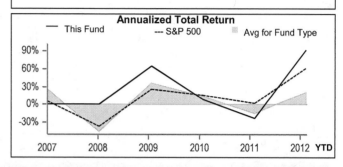

*iPath DJ UBS Precious Mtls Tot R (JJP)   C-   Fair

Fund Family: Barclays Bank PLC
Fund Type: Energy/Natural Resources
Inception Date: June 24, 2008

Data Date	Investment Rating	Net Assets ($Mil)	Price	Performance Rating/Pts	Total Return Y-T-D	Risk Rating/Pts
3-12	C-	8.23	91.44	C+ / 6.4	8.44%	C / 4.8
2011	C	73.20	84.32	B / 7.8	4.17%	C / 4.8
2010	B+	28.40	81.64	A+ / 9.7	41.91%	C- / 3.7
2009	C+	8.23	57.53	B+ / 8.3	29.43%	C- / 3.9

Major Rating Factors: Middle of the road best describes *iPath DJ UBS Precious Mtls Tot R whose TheStreet.com Investment Rating is currently a C- (Fair). The fund currently has a performance rating of C+ (Fair) based on an annualized return of 25.58% over the last three years and a total return of 8.44% year to date 2012. Factored into the performance evaluation is an expense ratio of 0.75% (very low).

The fund's risk rating is currently C (Fair). It carries a beta of 0.44, meaning the fund's expected move will be 4.4% for every 10% move in the market. Volatility, as measured by both the semi-deviation and a drawdown factor, is considered average. As of March 31, 2012, *iPath DJ UBS Precious Mtls Tot R traded at a discount of .41% below its net asset value, which is better than its one-year historical average premium of .06%.

This fund has been team managed for 4 years and currently receives a manager quality ranking of 90 (0=worst, 99=best). If you desire an average level of risk, then this fund may be an option.

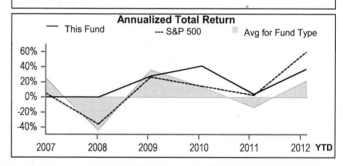

*iPath DJ UBS Softs Tot Ret Sub (JJS)   D-   Weak

Fund Family: Barclays Bank PLC
Fund Type: Energy/Natural Resources
Inception Date: June 24, 2008

Data Date	Investment Rating	Net Assets ($Mil)	Price	Performance Rating/Pts	Total Return Y-T-D	Risk Rating/Pts
3-12	D-	4.67	66.73	C- / 3.9	-3.71%	C / 4.3
2011	C-	17.40	69.30	C+ / 6.0	-1.30%	C / 4.5
2010	B+	43.50	81.05	A+ / 9.9	58.86%	C- / 3.6
2009	B-	4.67	51.02	A- / 9.0	43.60%	C- / 3.8

Major Rating Factors: *iPath DJ UBS Softs Tot Ret Sub receives a TheStreet.com Investment Rating of D- (Weak). The fund currently has a performance rating of C- (Fair) based on an annualized return of 23.60% over the last three years and a total return of -3.71% year to date 2012. Factored into the performance evaluation is an expense ratio of 0.75% (very low).

The fund's risk rating is currently C (Fair). It carries a beta of 0.48, meaning the fund's expected move will be 4.8% for every 10% move in the market. Volatility, as measured by both the semi-deviation and a drawdown factor, is considered average. As of March 31, 2012, *iPath DJ UBS Softs Tot Ret Sub traded at a discount of .22% below its net asset value, which is better than its one-year historical average discount of .14%.

This fund has been team managed for 4 years and currently receives a manager quality ranking of 89 (0=worst, 99=best). If you desire an average level of risk, then this fund may be an option.

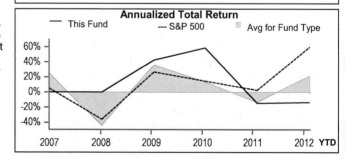

*iPath DJ UBS Sugar Tot Ret Sub (SGG)

D   **Weak**

Fund Family: Barclays Bank PLC
Fund Type: Energy/Natural Resources
Inception Date: June 24, 2008

Major Rating Factors: *iPath DJ UBS Sugar Tot Ret Sub has adopted a risky asset allocation strategy and currently receives an overall TheStreet.com Investment Rating of D (Weak). The fund has shown an above average level of volatility, as measured by both semi-deviation and drawdown factors. It carries a beta of 0.35, meaning the fund's expected move will be 3.5% for every 10% move in the market. As of March 31, 2012, *iPath DJ UBS Sugar Tot Ret Sub traded at a discount of .02% below its net asset value, which is worse than its one-year historical average discount of .07%. The high level of risk (D+, Weak) did however, reward investors with excellent performance.

The fund's performance rating is currently B- (Good). It has registered an annualized return of 28.09% over the last three years and is up 9.62% year to date 2012. Factored into the performance evaluation is an expense ratio of 0.75% (very low).

This fund has been team managed for 4 years and currently receives a manager quality ranking of 93 (0=worst, 99=best). If you are comfortable owning a high risk investment, this fund may be an option.

Data Date	Investment Rating	Net Assets ($Mil)	Price	Performance Rating/Pts	Total Return Y-T-D	Risk Rating/Pts
3-12	D	26.55	89.67	B- / 7.0	9.62%	D+ / 2.8
2011	D	32.90	81.80	C+ / 6.6	-0.56%	D+ / 2.7
2010	C+	81.10	93.55	A+ / 9.9	25.07%	D+ / 2.4
2009	B+	26.55	74.80	A+ / 9.8	82.62%	C- / 4.0

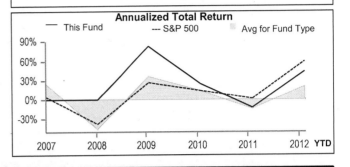

*iPath DJ UBS Tin Tot Ret Sub (JJT)

D   **Weak**

Fund Family: Barclays Bank PLC
Fund Type: Energy/Natural Resources
Inception Date: June 24, 2008

Major Rating Factors: *iPath DJ UBS Tin Tot Ret Sub receives a TheStreet.com Investment Rating of D (Weak). The fund currently has a performance rating of C+ (Fair) based on an annualized return of 28.17% over the last three years and a total return of 19.95% year to date 2012. Factored into the performance evaluation is an expense ratio of 0.75% (very low).

The fund's risk rating is currently C- (Fair). It carries a beta of 0.98, meaning that its performance tracks fairly well with that of the overall stock market. Volatility, as measured by both the semi-deviation and a drawdown factor, is considered average. As of March 31, 2012, *iPath DJ UBS Tin Tot Ret Sub traded at a premium of .02% above its net asset value, which is worse than its one-year historical average discount of .49%.

This fund has been team managed for 4 years and currently receives a manager quality ranking of 83 (0=worst, 99=best). If you desire an average level of risk, then this fund may be an option.

Data Date	Investment Rating	Net Assets ($Mil)	Price	Performance Rating/Pts	Total Return Y-T-D	Risk Rating/Pts
3-12	D	1.74	52.43	C+ / 6.2	19.95%	C- / 3.4
2011	D	7.50	43.71	C / 4.5	3.48%	C- / 3.3
2010	C+	33.40	63.37	A+ / 9.8	58.74%	D+ / 2.4
2009	C+	1.74	39.92	A- / 9.2	55.39%	D+ / 2.7

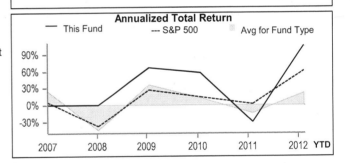

*iPath DJ-UBS Commodity Index Tot (DJP)

D   **Weak**

Fund Family: Barclays Bank PLC
Fund Type: Growth
Inception Date: June 6, 2006

Major Rating Factors:
Disappointing performance is the major factor driving the D (Weak) TheStreet.com Investment Rating for *iPath DJ-UBS Commodity Index Tot. The fund currently has a performance rating of D- (Weak) based on an annualized return of 7.18% over the last three years and a total return of 0.19% year to date 2012. Factored into the performance evaluation is an expense ratio of 0.75% (very low).

The fund's risk rating is currently B- (Good). It carries a beta of 0.80, meaning the fund's expected move will be 8.0% for every 10% move in the market. Volatility, as measured by both the semi-deviation and a drawdown factor, is considered low. As of March 31, 2012, *iPath DJ-UBS Commodity Index Tot traded at a premium of .02% above its net asset value, which is better than its one-year historical average premium of .10%.

This fund has been team managed for 6 years and currently receives a manager quality ranking of 17 (0=worst, 99=best). This fund offers only a moderate level of risk but investors looking for strong performance are still waiting.

Data Date	Investment Rating	Net Assets ($Mil)	Price	Performance Rating/Pts	Total Return Y-T-D	Risk Rating/Pts
3-12	D	1,897.33	42.32	D- / 1.5	0.19%	B- / 7.7
2011	D+	2,581.80	42.24	D+ / 2.4	0.76%	B- / 7.7
2010	D	2,854.70	49.12	C- / 3.0	16.23%	C / 4.9
2009	D+	1,897.33	42.26	D+ / 2.5	16.26%	C / 5.3

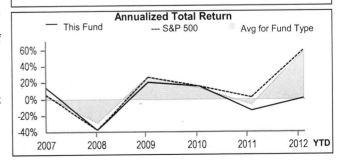

*iPath EUR/USD Exch Rate ETN (ERO)   D   Weak

Fund Family: Barclays Bank PLC
Fund Type: Foreign
Inception Date: May 8, 2007

Major Rating Factors:

Disappointing performance is the major factor driving the D (Weak) TheStreet.com Investment Rating for *iPath EUR/USD Exch Rate ETN. The fund currently has a performance rating of D- (Weak) based on an annualized return of -0.40% over the last three years and a total return of 3.04% year to date 2012. Factored into the performance evaluation is an expense ratio of 0.40% (very low).

The fund's risk rating is currently B (Good). It carries a beta of 0.47, meaning the fund's expected move will be 4.7% for every 10% move in the market. Volatility, as measured by both the semi-deviation and a drawdown factor, is considered low. As of March 31, 2012, *iPath EUR/USD Exch Rate ETN traded at a premium of .15% above its net asset value, which is worse than its one-year historical average discount of .14%.

This fund has been team managed for 5 years and currently receives a manager quality ranking of 18 (0=worst, 99=best). This fund offers only a moderate level of risk but investors looking for strong performance are still waiting.

Data Date	Investment Rating	Net Assets ($Mil)	Price	Performance Rating/Pts	Total Return Y-T-D	Risk Rating/Pts
3-12	D	8.45	51.87	D- / 1.1	3.04%	B / 8.1
2011	D+	4.80	50.34	D / 1.8	0.74%	B / 8.1
2010	D+	6.40	51.77	D- / 1.5	-7.50%	C+ / 6.8
2009	C-	8.45	55.97	D+ / 2.8	4.17%	B- / 7.2

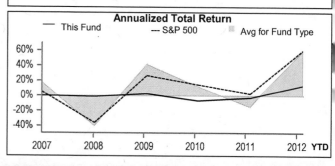

---

*iPath GBP/USD Exchange Rate ETN (GBB)   D+   Weak

Fund Family: Barclays Bank PLC
Fund Type: Growth
Inception Date: May 8, 2007

Major Rating Factors:

Disappointing performance is the major factor driving the D+ (Weak) TheStreet.com Investment Rating for *iPath GBP/USD Exchange Rate ETN. The fund currently has a performance rating of D- (Weak) based on an annualized return of 3.96% over the last three years and a total return of 3.52% year to date 2012. Factored into the performance evaluation is an expense ratio of 0.40% (very low).

The fund's risk rating is currently B (Good). It carries a beta of 0.25, meaning the fund's expected move will be 2.5% for every 10% move in the market. Volatility, as measured by both the semi-deviation and a drawdown factor, is considered low. As of March 31, 2012, *iPath GBP/USD Exchange Rate ETN traded at a premium of .09% above its net asset value, which is worse than its one-year historical average discount of .14%.

This fund has been team managed for 5 years and currently receives a manager quality ranking of 36 (0=worst, 99=best). This fund offers only a moderate level of risk but investors looking for strong performance are still waiting.

Data Date	Investment Rating	Net Assets ($Mil)	Price	Performance Rating/Pts	Total Return Y-T-D	Risk Rating/Pts
3-12	D+	1.78	42.89	D- / 1.5	3.52%	B / 8.7
2011	C-	2.50	41.43	D+ / 2.3	2.85%	B / 8.7
2010	D	6.80	41.40	E+ / 0.9	-3.77%	C+ / 6.5
2009	C	1.78	43.02	C- / 3.6	9.35%	C+ / 6.9

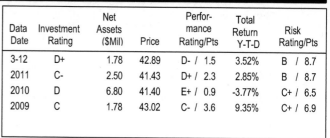
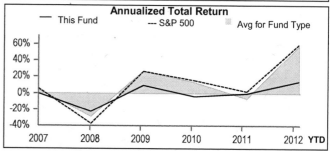

---

*iPath GEMS Asia 8 ETN (AYT)   D-   Weak

Fund Family: Barclays Bank PLC
Fund Type: Foreign
Inception Date: April 2, 2008

Major Rating Factors:

Disappointing performance is the major factor driving the D- (Weak) TheStreet.com Investment Rating for *iPath GEMS Asia 8 ETN. The fund currently has a performance rating of D- (Weak) based on an annualized return of 4.19% over the last three years and a total return of 2.61% year to date 2012. Factored into the performance evaluation is an expense ratio of 0.89% (low).

The fund's risk rating is currently C+ (Fair). It carries a beta of 0.32, meaning the fund's expected move will be 3.2% for every 10% move in the market. Volatility, as measured by both the semi-deviation and a drawdown factor, is considered low. As of March 31, 2012, *iPath GEMS Asia 8 ETN traded at a price exactly equal to its net asset value, which is worse than its one-year historical average discount of .05%.

This fund has been team managed for 4 years and currently receives a manager quality ranking of 38 (0=worst, 99=best). This fund offers only a moderate level of risk but investors looking for strong performance are still waiting.

Data Date	Investment Rating	Net Assets ($Mil)	Price	Performance Rating/Pts	Total Return Y-T-D	Risk Rating/Pts
3-12	D-	22.07	48.08	D- / 1.5	2.61%	C+ / 5.6
2011	D-	18.40	47.01	D / 2.2	0.68%	C+ / 5.6
2010	C+	10.00	48.99	C+ / 6.5	6.79%	C / 4.9

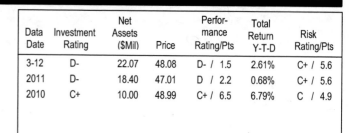
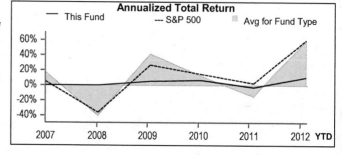

---

*iPath GEMS Index ETN (JEM)

D-　　**Weak**

Fund Family: Barclays Bank PLC
Fund Type: Growth and Income
Inception Date: February 1, 2008

Major Rating Factors:
Disappointing performance is the major factor driving the D- (Weak) TheStreet.com Investment Rating for *iPath GEMS Index ETN. The fund currently has a performance rating of D (Weak) based on an annualized return of 7.29% over the last three years and a total return of 5.73% year to date 2012. Factored into the performance evaluation is an expense ratio of 0.89% (low).

The fund's risk rating is currently C (Fair). It carries a beta of 0.60, meaning the fund's expected move will be 6.0% for every 10% move in the market. Volatility, as measured by both the semi-deviation and a drawdown factor, is considered average. As of March 31, 2012, *iPath GEMS Index ETN traded at a premium of .25% above its net asset value, which is worse than its one-year historical average premium of .01%.

Barclays Capital has been running the fund for 4 years and currently receives a manager quality ranking of 21 (0=worst, 99=best). This fund offers an average level of risk but investors looking for strong performance will be frustrated.

Data Date	Investment Rating	Net Assets ($Mil)	Price	Performance Rating/Pts	Total Return Y-T-D	Risk Rating/Pts
3-12	D-	1.51	43.91	D / 2.0	5.73%	C / 5.3
2011	D-	1.40	42.00	D / 2.1	-0.48%	C / 5.3
2010	C	4.10	46.50	B- / 7.4	6.69%	C- / 3.7
2009	D+	0.00	44.65	C- / 4.0	14.42%	C- / 3.9

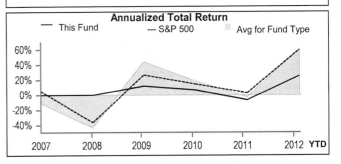

Annualized Total Return

*iPath JPY/USD Exchange Rate ETN (JYN)

D+　　**Weak**

Fund Family: Barclays Bank PLC
Fund Type: Foreign
Inception Date: May 8, 2007

Major Rating Factors:
Disappointing performance is the major factor driving the D+ (Weak) TheStreet.com Investment Rating for *iPath JPY/USD Exchange Rate ETN. The fund currently has a performance rating of D (Weak) based on an annualized return of 6.11% over the last three years and a total return of -6.86% year to date 2012. Factored into the performance evaluation is an expense ratio of 0.40% (very low).

The fund's risk rating is currently B+ (Good). It carries a beta of 0.00, meaning the fund's expected move will be 0.0% for every 10% move in the market. Volatility, as measured by both the semi-deviation and a drawdown factor, is considered very low. As of March 31, 2012, *iPath JPY/USD Exchange Rate ETN traded at a discount of .15% below its net asset value, which is better than its one-year historical average discount of .08%.

This fund has been team managed for 5 years and currently receives a manager quality ranking of 76 (0=worst, 99=best). This fund offers only a moderate level of risk but investors looking for strong performance are still waiting.

Data Date	Investment Rating	Net Assets ($Mil)	Price	Performance Rating/Pts	Total Return Y-T-D	Risk Rating/Pts
3-12	D+	11.27	71.20	D / 1.6	-6.86%	B+ / 9.0
2011	C	20.00	76.45	C- / 3.1	-0.12%	B+ / 9.0
2010	B	8.90	72.80	B- / 7.3	14.09%	C+ / 5.9
2009	D+	11.27	63.81	D / 1.7	-1.31%	C+ / 6.3

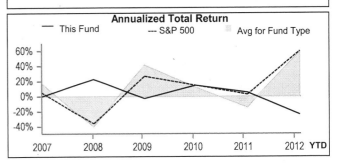

Annualized Total Return

*iPath Long Ext Rus 2000 TR Idx E (RTLA)

C　　**Fair**

Fund Family: Barclays Bank PLC
Fund Type: Income
Inception Date: November 29, 2010

Major Rating Factors: *iPath Long Ext Rus 2000 TR Idx E has adopted a risky asset allocation strategy and currently receives an overall TheStreet.com Investment Rating of C (Fair). The fund has shown an above average level of volatility, as measured by both semi-deviation and drawdown factors. It carries a beta of 0.00, meaning the fund's expected move will be 0.0% for every 10% move in the market. As of March 31, 2012, *iPath Long Ext Rus 2000 TR Idx E traded at a discount of 1.00% below its net asset value, which is better than its one-year historical average discount of .01%. The high level of risk (D+, Weak) did however, reward investors with excellent performance.

The fund's performance rating is currently A+ (Excellent). It has registered an annualized return of 0.00% over the last three years and is up 33.28% year to date 2012.

This is team managed and currently receives a manager quality ranking of 3 (0=worst, 99=best). If you are comfortable owning a high risk investment, this fund may be an option.

Data Date	Investment Rating	Net Assets ($Mil)	Price	Performance Rating/Pts	Total Return Y-T-D	Risk Rating/Pts
3-12	C	7.99	71.24	A+ / 9.9	33.28%	D+ / 2.4
2011	E+	4.50	53.45	D+ / 2.7	2.81%	D+ / 2.3

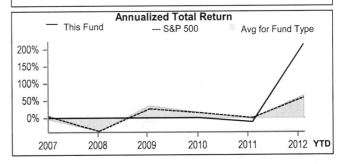

Annualized Total Return

*iPath Long Ext S&P 500 TR Idx ET (SFLA)

C+   **Fair**

Fund Family: Barclays Bank PLC
Fund Type: Income
Inception Date: November 29, 2010

Major Rating Factors:
Exceptional performance is the major factor driving the C+ (Fair) TheStreet.com Investment Rating for *iPath Long Ext S&P 500 TR Idx ET. The fund currently has a performance rating of A+ (Excellent) based on an annualized return of 0.00% over the last three years and a total return of 32.26% year to date 2012.

The fund's risk rating is currently C- (Fair). It carries a beta of 0.00, meaning the fund's expected move will be 0.0% for every 10% move in the market. Volatility, as measured by both the semi-deviation and a drawdown factor, is considered average. As of March 31, 2012, *iPath Long Ext S&P 500 TR Idx ET traded at a discount of .01% below its net asset value, which is worse than its one-year historical average discount of .03%.

This is team managed and currently receives a manager quality ranking of 22 (0=worst, 99=best). If you desire an average level of risk and strong performance, then this fund is a good option.

Data Date	Investment Rating	Net Assets ($Mil)	Price	Performance Rating/Pts	Total Return Y-T-D	Risk Rating/Pts
3-12	C+	7.92	81.24	A+ / 9.9	32.26%	C- / 3.6
2011	D	5.20	61.42	C / 5.0	4.60%	C- / 3.6

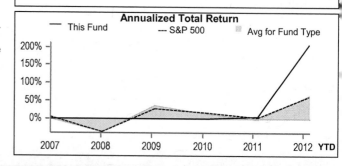

*iPath MSCI India Index ETN (INP)

D   **Weak**

Fund Family: Barclays Bank PLC
Fund Type: Emerging Market
Inception Date: December 19, 2006

Major Rating Factors: *iPath MSCI India Index ETN receives a TheStreet.com Investment Rating of D (Weak). The fund currently has a performance rating of C- (Fair) based on an annualized return of 18.44% over the last three years and a total return of 21.13% year to date 2012. Factored into the performance evaluation is an expense ratio of 0.89% (low).

The fund's risk rating is currently C+ (Fair). It carries a beta of 1.30, meaning it is expected to move 13.0% for every 10% move in the market. Volatility, as measured by both the semi-deviation and a drawdown factor, is considered low. As of March 31, 2012, *iPath MSCI India Index ETN traded at a discount of .02% below its net asset value, which is better than its one-year historical average premium of .04%.

This fund has been team managed for 6 years and currently receives a manager quality ranking of 16 (0=worst, 99=best). If you desire an average level of risk, then this fund may be an option.

Data Date	Investment Rating	Net Assets ($Mil)	Price	Performance Rating/Pts	Total Return Y-T-D	Risk Rating/Pts
3-12	D	1,058.84	56.47	C- / 3.6	21.13%	C+ / 5.9
2011	D	454.00	46.62	C- / 3.4	3.56%	C+ / 5.9
2010	D-	1,154.20	77.66	D / 2.1	21.23%	C- / 3.4
2009	C	1,058.84	64.06	B / 7.8	91.11%	C- / 3.6

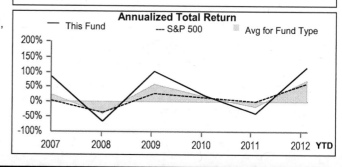

*iPath Optimized Currency Carry E (ICI)

D+   **Weak**

Fund Family: Barclays Bank PLC
Fund Type: Global
Inception Date: January 31, 2008

Major Rating Factors:
Disappointing performance is the major factor driving the D+ (Weak) TheStreet.com Investment Rating for *iPath Optimized Currency Carry E. The fund currently has a performance rating of D- (Weak) based on an annualized return of 1.19% over the last three years and a total return of -0.04% year to date 2012. Factored into the performance evaluation is an expense ratio of 0.65% (very low).

The fund's risk rating is currently B+ (Good). It carries a beta of 0.08, meaning the fund's expected move will be 0.8% for every 10% move in the market. Volatility, as measured by both the semi-deviation and a drawdown factor, is considered very low. As of March 31, 2012, *iPath Optimized Currency Carry E traded at a discount of .24% below its net asset value, which is better than its one-year historical average discount of .12%.

This fund has been team managed for 4 years and currently receives a manager quality ranking of 44 (0=worst, 99=best). This fund offers only a moderate level of risk but investors looking for strong performance are still waiting.

Data Date	Investment Rating	Net Assets ($Mil)	Price	Performance Rating/Pts	Total Return Y-T-D	Risk Rating/Pts
3-12	D+	27.19	46.08	D- / 1.3	-0.04%	B+ / 9.6
2011	C-	87.30	46.10	D+ / 2.3	0.48%	B+ / 9.6
2010	B	22.90	46.98	C / 4.7	3.07%	B / 8.2
2009	C+	27.19	45.58	C- / 3.5	4.76%	B / 8.4

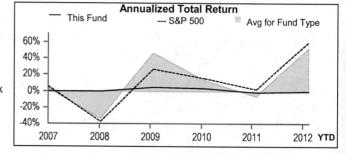

*IPath S&P 500 VIX Mid-Trm Futr E (VXZ)   E-   Very Weak

Fund Family: Barclays Bank PLC
Fund Type: Income
Inception Date: January 29, 2009

Data Date	Investment Rating	Net Assets ($Mil)	Price	Perfor-mance Rating/Pts	Total Return Y-T-D	Risk Rating/Pts
3-12	E-	28.95	46.23	E / 0.5	-23.79%	D+ / 2.4
2011	E	186.50	60.66	D- / 1.5	-4.86%	D+ / 2.4
2010	E	702.60	65.76	E / 0.3	-14.43%	D+ / 2.9

Major Rating Factors: *IPath S&P 500 VIX Mid-Trm Futr E has adopted a risky asset allocation strategy and currently receives an overall TheStreet.com Investment Rating of E- (Very Weak). The fund has an above average level of volatility, as measured by both semi-deviation and drawdown factors. It carries a beta of -1.58, meaning the fund's expected move will be -15.8% for every 10% move in the market. As of March 31, 2012, *IPath S&P 500 VIX Mid-Trm Futr E traded at a premium of 1.31% above its net asset value, which is worse than its one-year historical average premium of .09%. Unfortunately, the high level of risk (D+, Weak) failed to pay off as investors endured very poor performance.

The fund's performance rating is currently E (Very Weak). It has registered an annualized return of -25.39% over the last three years and is down -23.79% year to date 2012. Factored into the performance evaluation is an expense ratio of 0.89% (low).

This fund has been team managed for 3 years and currently receives a manager quality ranking of 66 (0=worst, 99=best). If you can tolerate high levels of risk in the hope of improved future returns, holding this fund may be an option.

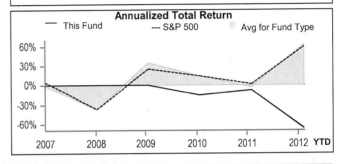

*IPath S&P 500 VIX Sm-Trm Futr ET (VXX)   E-   Very Weak

Fund Family: Barclays Bank PLC
Fund Type: Income
Inception Date: January 29, 2009

Data Date	Investment Rating	Net Assets ($Mil)	Price	Perfor-mance Rating/Pts	Total Return Y-T-D	Risk Rating/Pts
3-12	E-	664.55	16.78	E- / 0	-52.77%	D / 1.9
2011	E+	791.90	35.53	C- / 3.2	-9.23%	D / 1.9
2010	E-	1,994.20	37.61	E- / 0	-72.40%	D- / 1.0

Major Rating Factors: *IPath S&P 500 VIX Sm-Trm Futr ET has adopted a very risky asset allocation strategy and currently receives an overall TheStreet.com Investment Rating of E- (Very Weak). The fund has a high level of volatility, as measured by both semi-deviation and drawdown factors. It carries a beta of -3.15, meaning the fund's expected move will be -31.5% for every 10% move in the market. As of March 31, 2012, *IPath S&P 500 VIX Sm-Trm Futr ET traded at a premium of .60% above its net asset value, which is worse than its one-year historical average premium of .14%. Unfortunately, the high level of risk (D, Weak) failed to pay off as investors endured very poor performance.

The fund's performance rating is currently E- (Very Weak). It has registered an annualized return of -66.07% over the last three years and is down -52.77% year to date 2012. Factored into the performance evaluation is an expense ratio of 0.89% (low).

This fund has been team managed for 3 years and currently receives a manager quality ranking of 2 (0=worst, 99=best). If you can tolerate very high levels of risk in the hope of improved future returns, holding this fund may be an option.

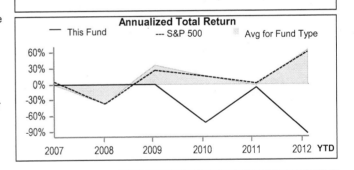

*iPath S&P GSCI Crude Oil TotRet (OIL)   D   Weak

Fund Family: Barclays Bank PLC
Fund Type: Energy/Natural Resources
Inception Date: August 15, 2006

Data Date	Investment Rating	Net Assets ($Mil)	Price	Perfor-mance Rating/Pts	Total Return Y-T-D	Risk Rating/Pts
3-12	D	564.45	25.88	D+ / 2.3	3.03%	C+ / 6.4
2011	D+	436.60	25.12	C- / 3.6	3.11%	C+ / 6.4
2010	E	643.90	25.61	E+ / 0.6	-1.04%	D+ / 2.4
2009	E	564.45	25.88	D- / 1.0	3.07%	C- / 3.1

Major Rating Factors:
Disappointing performance is the major factor driving the D (Weak) TheStreet.com Investment Rating for *iPath S&P GSCI Crude Oil TotRet. The fund currently has a performance rating of D+ (Weak) based on an annualized return of 8.66% over the last three years and a total return of 3.03% year to date 2012. Factored into the performance evaluation is an expense ratio of 0.75% (very low).

The fund's risk rating is currently C+ (Fair). It carries a beta of 1.04, meaning that its performance tracks fairly well with that of the overall stock market. Volatility, as measured by both the semi-deviation and a drawdown factor, is considered low. As of March 31, 2012, *iPath S&P GSCI Crude Oil TotRet traded at a premium of .04% above its net asset value, which is better than its one-year historical average premium of .16%.

This fund has been team managed for 6 years and currently receives a manager quality ranking of 17 (0=worst, 99=best). This fund offers only a moderate level of risk but investors looking for strong performance are still waiting.

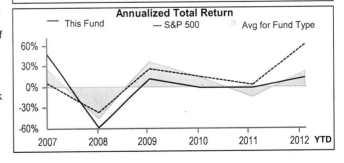

*iPath S&P GSCI Total Return ETN (GSP)

D+ **Weak**

Fund Family: Barclays Bank PLC
Fund Type: Growth
Inception Date: June 6, 2006

Major Rating Factors:

Disappointing performance is the major factor driving the D+ (Weak) TheStreet.com Investment Rating for *iPath S&P GSCI Total Return ETN. The fund currently has a performance rating of D+ (Weak) based on an annualized return of 11.16% over the last three years and a total return of 5.54% year to date 2012. Factored into the performance evaluation is an expense ratio of 0.75% (very low).

The fund's risk rating is currently B- (Good). It carries a beta of 0.94, meaning that its performance tracks fairly well with that of the overall stock market. Volatility, as measured by both the semi-deviation and a drawdown factor, is considered low. As of March 31, 2012, *iPath S&P GSCI Total Return ETN traded at a premium of .45% above its net asset value, which is worse than its one-year historical average premium of .15%.

This fund has been team managed for 6 years and currently receives a manager quality ranking of 19 (0=worst, 99=best). This fund offers only a moderate level of risk but investors looking for strong performance are still waiting.

Data Date	Investment Rating	Net Assets ($Mil)	Price	Performance Rating/Pts	Total Return Y-T-D	Risk Rating/Pts
3-12	D+	79.00	35.62	D+ / 2.6	5.54%	B- / 7.4
2011	C-	97.60	33.75	C- / 3.6	2.49%	B- / 7.4
2010	E+	102.50	34.23	E+ / 0.9	8.36%	C- / 3.5
2009	D-	79.00	31.59	D- / 1.5	9.54%	C- / 4.1

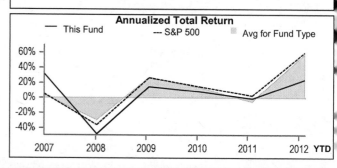

*iPath Shrt Ext Rus 1000 TR Idx E (ROSA)

E- **Very Weak**

Fund Family: Barclays Bank PLC
Fund Type: Income
Inception Date: November 29, 2010

Major Rating Factors: *iPath Shrt Ext Rus 1000 TR Idx E has adopted a very risky asset allocation strategy and currently receives an overall TheStreet.com Investment Rating of E- (Very Weak). The fund has a high level of volatility, as measured by both semi-deviation and drawdown factors. It carries a beta of 0.00, meaning the fund's expected move will be 0.0% for every 10% move in the market. As of March 31, 2012, *iPath Shrt Ext Rus 1000 TR Idx E traded at a premium of 3.49% above its net asset value, which is worse than its one-year historical average premium of 1.11%. Unfortunately, the high level of risk (D, Weak) failed to pay off as investors endured very poor performance.

The fund's performance rating is currently E- (Very Weak). It has registered an annualized return of 0.00% over the last three years but is down -44.39% year to date 2012.

This is team managed and currently receives a manager quality ranking of 2 (0=worst, 99=best). If you can tolerate very high levels of risk in the hope of improved future returns, holding this fund may be an option.

Data Date	Investment Rating	Net Assets ($Mil)	Price	Performance Rating/Pts	Total Return Y-T-D	Risk Rating/Pts
3-12	E-	2.07	16.01	E- / 0	-44.39%	D / 1.9
2011	E	3.40	28.79	D- / 1.2	15.04%	C- / 3.1

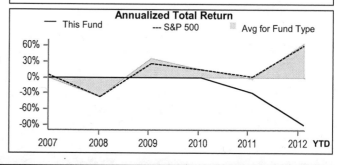

*iPath Shrt Ext Rus 2000 TR Idx E (RTSA)

E- **Very Weak**

Fund Family: Barclays Bank PLC
Fund Type: Income
Inception Date: November 29, 2010

Major Rating Factors: *iPath Shrt Ext Rus 2000 TR Idx E has adopted a very risky asset allocation strategy and currently receives an overall TheStreet.com Investment Rating of E- (Very Weak). The fund has a high level of volatility, as measured by both semi-deviation and drawdown factors. It carries a beta of 0.00, meaning the fund's expected move will be 0.0% for every 10% move in the market. As of March 31, 2012, *iPath Shrt Ext Rus 2000 TR Idx E traded at a premium of .44% above its net asset value, which is worse than its one-year historical average discount of .02%. Unfortunately, the high level of risk (D, Weak) failed to pay off as investors endured very poor performance.

The fund's performance rating is currently E- (Very Weak). It has registered an annualized return of 0.00% over the last three years but is down -45.77% year to date 2012.

This is team managed and currently receives a manager quality ranking of 97 (0=worst, 99=best). If you can tolerate very high levels of risk in the hope of improved future returns, holding this fund may be an option.

Data Date	Investment Rating	Net Assets ($Mil)	Price	Performance Rating/Pts	Total Return Y-T-D	Risk Rating/Pts
3-12	E-	6.45	22.95	E- / 0.1	-45.77%	D / 2.0
2011	C-	8.60	42.32	B+ / 8.6	-4.58%	C- / 3.0

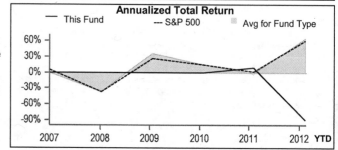

*iPath Shrt Ext S&P 500 TR Idx ET (SFSA)

E-   Very Weak

Fund Family: Barclays Bank PLC
Fund Type: Income
Inception Date: November 29, 2010

Major Rating Factors: *iPath Shrt Ext S&P 500 TR Idx ET has adopted a very risky asset allocation strategy and currently receives an overall TheStreet.com Investment Rating of E- (Very Weak). The fund has a high level of volatility, as measured by both semi-deviation and drawdown factors. It carries a beta of 0.00, meaning the fund's expected move will be 0.0% for every 10% move in the market. As of March 31, 2012, *iPath Shrt Ext S&P 500 TR Idx ET traded at a premium of 2.94% above its net asset value, which is worse than its one-year historical average premium of .02%. Unfortunately, the high level of risk (D, Weak) failed to pay off as investors endured very poor performance.

The fund's performance rating is currently E- (Very Weak). It has registered an annualized return of 0.00% over the last three years but is down -54.80% year to date 2012.

This is team managed and currently receives a manager quality ranking of 4 (0=worst, 99=best). If you can tolerate very high levels of risk in the hope of improved future returns, holding this fund may be an option.

Data Date	Investment Rating	Net Assets ($Mil)	Price	Performance Rating/Pts	Total Return Y-T-D	Risk Rating/Pts
3-12	E-	8.64	16.47	E- / 0	-54.80%	D / 1.9
2011	E+	13.50	36.44	D- / 1.1	-8.04%	C- / 4.0

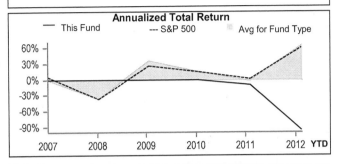

Annualized Total Return

— This Fund   --- S&P 500   Avg for Fund Type

*iPath US Treas 10Yr Bear ETN (DTYS)

E   Very Weak

Fund Family: Barclays Bank PLC
Fund Type: US Government/Agency
Inception Date: August 9, 2010

Major Rating Factors: Very poor performance is the major factor driving the E (Very Weak) TheStreet.com Investment Rating for *iPath US Treas 10Yr Bear ETN. The fund currently has a performance rating of E (Very Weak) based on an annualized return of 0.00% over the last three years and a total return of 4.71% year to date 2012. Factored into the performance evaluation is an expense ratio of 0.75% (very low).

The fund's risk rating is currently C- (Fair). It carries a beta of 0.00, meaning the fund's expected move will be 0.0% for every 10% move in the market. Volatility, as measured by both the semi-deviation and a drawdown factor, is considered average. As of March 31, 2012, *iPath US Treas 10Yr Bear ETN traded at a premium of .06% above its net asset value, which is worse than its one-year historical average premium of .04%.

This fund has been team managed for 2 years and currently receives a manager quality ranking of 8 (0=worst, 99=best). This fund offers an average level of risk but investors looking for strong performance will be frustrated.

Data Date	Investment Rating	Net Assets ($Mil)	Price	Performance Rating/Pts	Total Return Y-T-D	Risk Rating/Pts
3-12	E	70.30	33.78	E / 0.5	4.71%	C- / 3.4
2011	E	40.60	32.26	E / 0.3	1.92%	C- / 3.5

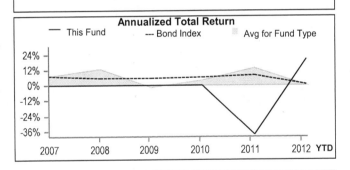

Annualized Total Return

— This Fund   --- Bond Index   Avg for Fund Type

*iPath US Treas 10Yr Bull ETN (DTYL)

C   Fair

Fund Family: Barclays Bank PLC
Fund Type: US Government/Agency
Inception Date: August 9, 2010

Major Rating Factors: Strong performance is the major factor driving the C (Fair) TheStreet.com Investment Rating for *iPath US Treas 10Yr Bull ETN. The fund currently has a performance rating of B (Good) based on an annualized return of 0.00% over the last three years and a total return of -2.02% year to date 2012. Factored into the performance evaluation is an expense ratio of 0.75% (very low).

The fund's risk rating is currently C (Fair). It carries a beta of 0.00, meaning the fund's expected move will be 0.0% for every 10% move in the market. Volatility, as measured by both a semi-deviation and a drawdown factor, is considered average. As of March 31, 2012, *iPath US Treas 10Yr Bull ETN traded at a discount of .06% below its net asset value, which is worse than its one-year historical average discount of .12%.

This fund has been team managed for 2 years and currently receives a manager quality ranking of 94 (0=worst, 99=best). If you desire an average level of risk and strong performance, then this fund is a good option.

Data Date	Investment Rating	Net Assets ($Mil)	Price	Performance Rating/Pts	Total Return Y-T-D	Risk Rating/Pts
3-12	C	4.81	65.40	B / 7.9	-2.02%	C / 5.2
2011	B-	4.80	66.75	A+ / 9.8	-1.14%	C / 5.2

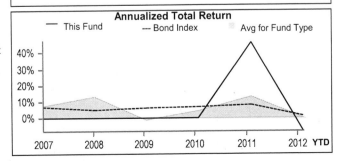

Annualized Total Return

— This Fund   --- Bond Index   Avg for Fund Type

203

* Denotes ETF Fund

*iPath US Treas 2Yr Bear ETN (DTUS)

E+   **Very Weak**

Fund Family: Barclays Bank PLC
Fund Type: US Government/Agency
Inception Date: August 9, 2010

Major Rating Factors:
Very poor performance is the major factor driving the E+ (Very Weak) TheStreet.com Investment Rating for *iPath US Treas 2Yr Bear ETN. The fund currently has a performance rating of E+ (Very Weak) based on an annualized return of 0.00% over the last three years and a total return of 0.34% year to date 2012. Factored into the performance evaluation is an expense ratio of 0.75% (very low).

The fund's risk rating is currently C (Fair). It carries a beta of 0.00, meaning the fund's expected move will be 0.0% for every 10% move in the market. Volatility, as measured by both the semi-deviation and a drawdown factor, is considered average. As of March 31, 2012, *iPath US Treas 2Yr Bear ETN traded at a discount of .19% below its net asset value.

This fund has been team managed for 2 years and currently receives a manager quality ranking of 11 (0=worst, 99=best). This fund offers an average level of risk but investors looking for strong performance will be frustrated.

Data Date	Investment Rating	Net Assets ($Mil)	Price	Performance Rating/Pts	Total Return Y-T-D	Risk Rating/Pts
3-12	E+	17.60	41.65	E+ / 0.8	0.34%	C / 4.9
2011	D-	13.00	41.51	D- / 1.1	-0.39%	C / 5.0

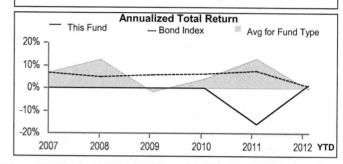

*iPath US Treas 2Yr Bull ETN (DTUL)

D   **Weak**

Fund Family: Barclays Bank PLC
Fund Type: US Government/Agency
Inception Date: August 9, 2010

Major Rating Factors:
Disappointing performance is the major factor driving the D (Weak) TheStreet.com Investment Rating for *iPath US Treas 2Yr Bull ETN. The fund currently has a performance rating of D+ (Weak) based on an annualized return of 0.00% over the last three years and a total return of -0.92% year to date 2012. Factored into the performance evaluation is an expense ratio of 0.75% (very low).

The fund's risk rating is currently C+ (Fair). It carries a beta of 0.00, meaning the fund's expected move will be 0.0% for every 10% move in the market. Volatility, as measured by both the semi-deviation and a drawdown factor, is considered low. As of March 31, 2012, *iPath US Treas 2Yr Bull ETN traded at a premium of .07% above its net asset value, which is worse than its one-year historical average discount of .01%.

This fund has been team managed for 2 years and currently receives a manager quality ranking of 85 (0=worst, 99=best). This fund offers only a moderate level of risk but investors looking for strong performance are still waiting.

Data Date	Investment Rating	Net Assets ($Mil)	Price	Performance Rating/Pts	Total Return Y-T-D	Risk Rating/Pts
3-12	D	4.09	57.03	D+ / 2.6	-0.92%	C+ / 5.8
2011	C-	8.60	57.56	C / 4.8	-0.17%	C+ / 5.8

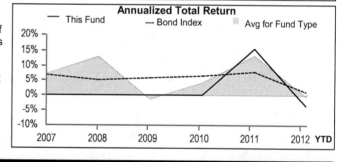

*iPath US Treas Flattener ETN (FLAT)

D   **Weak**

Fund Family: Barclays Bank PLC
Fund Type: US Government/Agency
Inception Date: August 9, 2010

Major Rating Factors: *iPath US Treas Flattener ETN receives a TheStreet.com Investment Rating of D (Weak). The fund currently has a performance rating of C- (Fair) based on an annualized return of 0.00% over the last three years and a total return of -2.14% year to date 2012. Factored into the performance evaluation is an expense ratio of 0.75% (very low).

The fund's risk rating is currently C (Fair). It carries a beta of 0.00, meaning the fund's expected move will be 0.0% for every 10% move in the market. Volatility, as measured by both the semi-deviation and a drawdown factor, is considered average. As of March 31, 2012, *iPath US Treas Flattener ETN traded at a discount of .19% below its net asset value, which is better than its one-year historical average discount of .03%.

This fund has been team managed for 2 years and currently receives a manager quality ranking of 78 (0=worst, 99=best). If you desire an average level of risk, then this fund may be an option.

Data Date	Investment Rating	Net Assets ($Mil)	Price	Performance Rating/Pts	Total Return Y-T-D	Risk Rating/Pts
3-12	D	35.48	57.08	C- / 3.9	-2.14%	C / 5.2
2011	C+	49.80	58.33	B+ / 8.4	-1.13%	C / 5.3

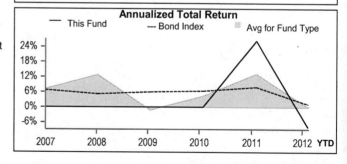

*iPath US Treas Lng Bd Bear ETN (DLBS)

E **Very Weak**

Fund Family: Barclays Bank PLC
Fund Type: US Government/Agency
Inception Date: August 9, 2010

Data Date	Investment Rating	Net Assets ($Mil)	Price	Performance Rating/Pts	Total Return Y-T-D	Risk Rating/Pts
3-12	E	21.05	35.77	E+ / 0.7	11.89%	C- / 3.4
2011	E	18.80	31.97	E / 0.3	5.20%	C- / 3.4

Major Rating Factors: Very poor performance is the major factor driving the E (Very Weak) TheStreet.com Investment Rating for *iPath US Treas Lng Bd Bear ETN. The fund currently has a performance rating of E+ (Very Weak) based on an annualized return of 0.00% over the last three years and a total return of 11.89% year to date 2012. Factored into the performance evaluation is an expense ratio of 0.75% (very low).

The fund's risk rating is currently C- (Fair). It carries a beta of 0.00, meaning the fund's expected move will be 0.0% for every 10% move in the market. Volatility, as measured by both the semi-deviation and a drawdown factor, is considered average. As of March 31, 2012, *iPath US Treas Lng Bd Bear ETN traded at a premium of .39% above its net asset value, which is worse than its one-year historical average premium of .07%.

This fund has been team managed for 2 years and currently receives a manager quality ranking of 30 (0=worst, 99=best). This fund offers an average level of risk but investors looking for strong performance will be frustrated.

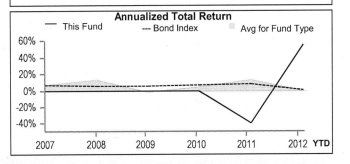

*iPath US Treas Lng Bd Bull ETN (DLBL)

C- **Fair**

Fund Family: Barclays Bank PLC
Fund Type: US Government/Agency
Inception Date: August 9, 2010

Data Date	Investment Rating	Net Assets ($Mil)	Price	Performance Rating/Pts	Total Return Y-T-D	Risk Rating/Pts
3-12	C-	1.40	63.59	C+ / 6.1	-4.83%	C / 5.1
2011	B-	10.70	66.82	A+ / 9.9	-1.65%	C / 5.1

Major Rating Factors: Middle of the road best describes *iPath US Treas Lng Bd Bull ETN whose TheStreet.com Investment Rating is currently a C- (Fair). The fund currently has a performance rating of C+ (Fair) based on an annualized return of 0.00% over the last three years and a total return of -4.83% year to date 2012. Factored into the performance evaluation is an expense ratio of 0.75% (very low).

The fund's risk rating is currently C (Fair). It carries a beta of 0.00, meaning the fund's expected move will be 0.0% for every 10% move in the market. Volatility, as measured by both the semi-deviation and a drawdown factor, is considered average. As of March 31, 2012, *iPath US Treas Lng Bd Bull ETN traded at a discount of .33% below its net asset value, which is better than its one-year historical average discount of .09%.

This fund has been team managed for 2 years and currently receives a manager quality ranking of 84 (0=worst, 99=best). If you desire an average level of risk, then this fund may be an option.

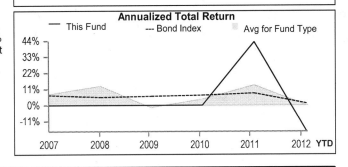

*iPath US Treas Steepen ETN (STPP)

E+ **Very Weak**

Fund Family: Barclays Bank PLC
Fund Type: US Government/Agency
Inception Date: August 9, 2010

Data Date	Investment Rating	Net Assets ($Mil)	Price	Performance Rating/Pts	Total Return Y-T-D	Risk Rating/Pts
3-12	E+	13.33	40.77	E+ / 0.6	1.39%	C / 4.4
2011	E+	2.50	40.21	E+ / 0.7	1.42%	C / 4.4

Major Rating Factors:
Very poor performance is the major factor driving the E+ (Very Weak) TheStreet.com Investment Rating for *iPath US Treas Steepen ETN. The fund currently has a performance rating of E+ (Very Weak) based on an annualized return of 0.00% over the last three years and a total return of 1.39% year to date 2012. Factored into the performance evaluation is an expense ratio of 0.75% (very low).

The fund's risk rating is currently C (Fair). It carries a beta of 0.00, meaning the fund's expected move will be 0.0% for every 10% move in the market. Volatility, as measured by both the semi-deviation and a drawdown factor, is considered average. As of March 31, 2012, *iPath US Treas Steepen ETN traded at a discount of 1.21% below its net asset value, which is better than its one-year historical average premium of .08%.

This fund has been team managed for 2 years and currently receives a manager quality ranking of 14 (0=worst, 99=best). This fund offers an average level of risk but investors looking for strong performance will be frustrated.

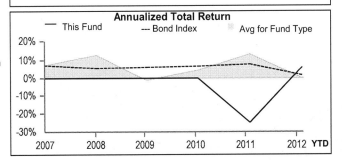

*IQ Australia Small Cap ETF (KROO)

D-   **Weak**

Fund Family: IndexIQ Advisors LLC
Fund Type: Foreign
Inception Date: March 22, 2010

Data Date	Investment Rating	Net Assets ($Mil)	Price	Performance Rating/Pts	Total Return Y-T-D	Risk Rating/Pts
3-12	D-	17.15	23.36	D+ / 2.3	15.93%	C+ / 5.7
2011	D-	15.10	20.15	E+ / 0.8	1.30%	C+ / 5.6

Major Rating Factors:
Disappointing performance is the major factor driving the D- (Weak) TheStreet.com Investment Rating for *IQ Australia Small Cap ETF. The fund currently has a performance rating of D+ (Weak) based on an annualized return of 0.00% over the last three years and a total return of 15.93% year to date 2012. Factored into the performance evaluation is an expense ratio of 0.69% (very low).

The fund's risk rating is currently C+ (Fair). It carries a beta of 0.00, meaning the fund's expected move will be 0.0% for every 10% move in the market. Volatility, as measured by both the semi-deviation and a drawdown factor, is considered low. As of March 31, 2012, *IQ Australia Small Cap ETF traded at a premium of .04% above its net asset value, which is worse than its one-year historical average discount of .25%.

Julie S. Abbett currently receives a manager quality ranking of 22 (0=worst, 99=best). This fund offers only a moderate level of risk but investors looking for strong performance are still waiting.

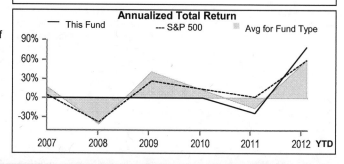

Annualized Total Return

*IQ Canada Small Cap ETF (CNDA)

D-   **Weak**

Fund Family: IndexIQ Advisors LLC
Fund Type: Foreign
Inception Date: March 22, 2010

Data Date	Investment Rating	Net Assets ($Mil)	Price	Performance Rating/Pts	Total Return Y-T-D	Risk Rating/Pts
3-12	D-	34.60	26.50	E+ / 0.9	4.62%	C+ / 6.2
2011	D-	31.80	25.33	E+ / 0.9	3.14%	C+ / 6.2

Major Rating Factors:
Very poor performance is the major factor driving the D- (Weak) TheStreet.com Investment Rating for *IQ Canada Small Cap ETF. The fund currently has a performance rating of E+ (Very Weak) based on an annualized return of 0.00% over the last three years and a total return of 4.62% year to date 2012. Factored into the performance evaluation is an expense ratio of 0.69% (very low).

The fund's risk rating is currently C+ (Fair). It carries a beta of 0.00, meaning the fund's expected move will be 0.0% for every 10% move in the market. Volatility, as measured by both the semi-deviation and a drawdown factor, is considered low. As of March 31, 2012, *IQ Canada Small Cap ETF traded at a discount of .15% below its net asset value, which is worse than its one-year historical average discount of .19%.

Julie S. Abbett currently receives a manager quality ranking of 8 (0=worst, 99=best). This fund offers only a moderate level of risk but investors looking for strong performance are still waiting.

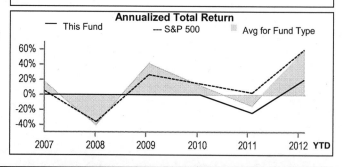

Annualized Total Return

*IQ Global Agribusiness SmCp ETF (CROP)

D+   **Weak**

Fund Family: IndexIQ Advisors LLC
Fund Type: Global
Inception Date: March 21, 2011

Data Date	Investment Rating	Net Assets ($Mil)	Price	Performance Rating/Pts	Total Return Y-T-D	Risk Rating/Pts
3-12	D+	38.08	25.43	D+ / 2.5	12.72%	B- / 7.8

Major Rating Factors:
Disappointing performance is the major factor driving the D+ (Weak) TheStreet.com Investment Rating for *IQ Global Agribusiness SmCp ETF. The fund currently has a performance rating of D+ (Weak) based on an annualized return of 0.00% over the last three years and a total return of 12.72% year to date 2012. Factored into the performance evaluation is an expense ratio of 0.75% (very low).

The fund's risk rating is currently B- (Good). It carries a beta of 0.00, meaning the fund's expected move will be 0.0% for every 10% move in the market. Volatility, as measured by both the semi-deviation and a drawdown factor, is considered low. As of March 31, 2012, *IQ Global Agribusiness SmCp ETF traded at a premium of .04% above its one-year historical average discount of .15%.

Julie S. Abbett currently receives a manager quality ranking of 43 (0=worst, 99=best). This fund offers only a moderate level of risk but investors looking for strong performance are still waiting.

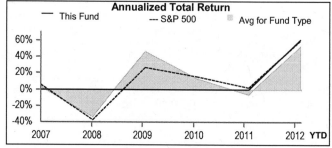

Annualized Total Return

*IQ Global Resources ETF (GRES)

D   **Weak**

Fund Family: IndexIQ Advisors LLC
Fund Type: Energy/Natural Resources
Inception Date: October 26, 2009

Major Rating Factors:
Disappointing performance is the major factor driving the D (Weak) TheStreet.com Investment Rating for *IQ Global Resources ETF. The fund currently has a performance rating of D- (Weak) based on an annualized return of 0.00% over the last three years and a total return of 3.86% year to date 2012. Factored into the performance evaluation is an expense ratio of 0.76% (very low).

The fund's risk rating is currently B (Good). It carries a beta of 0.00, meaning the fund's expected move will be 0.0% for every 10% move in the market. Volatility, as measured by both the semi-deviation and a drawdown factor, is considered low. As of March 31, 2012, *IQ Global Resources ETF traded at a premium of .10% above its net asset value, which is worse than its one-year historical average premium of .09%.

Julie S. Abbett has been running the fund for 1 year and currently receives a manager quality ranking of 20 (0=worst, 99=best). This fund offers only a moderate level of risk but investors looking for strong performance are still waiting.

Data Date	Investment Rating	Net Assets ($Mil)	Price	Performance Rating/Pts	Total Return Y-T-D	Risk Rating/Pts
3-12	D	70.57	29.10	D- / 1.1	3.86%	B / 8.2
2011	D	61.70	28.02	D- / 1.5	2.00%	B- / 7.2
2010	A+	42.50	31.83	A / 9.3	23.38%	B / 8.3

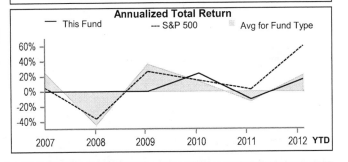

Annualized Total Return

---

*IQ Hedge Macro Tracker ETF (MCRO)

D+   **Weak**

Fund Family: IndexIQ Advisors LLC
Fund Type: Global
Inception Date: June 8, 2009

Major Rating Factors:
Disappointing performance is the major factor driving the D+ (Weak) TheStreet.com Investment Rating for *IQ Hedge Macro Tracker ETF. The fund currently has a performance rating of D- (Weak) based on an annualized return of 0.00% over the last three years and a total return of 3.88% year to date 2012. Factored into the performance evaluation is an expense ratio of 0.77% (very low).

The fund's risk rating is currently B+ (Good). It carries a beta of 0.00, meaning the fund's expected move will be 0.0% for every 10% move in the market. Volatility, as measured by both the semi-deviation and a drawdown factor, is considered very low. As of March 31, 2012, *IQ Hedge Macro Tracker ETF traded at a premium of .04% above its net asset value, which is better than its one-year historical average premium of .05%.

Denise Krisko has been running the fund for 3 years and currently receives a manager quality ranking of 60 (0=worst, 99=best). This fund offers only a moderate level of risk but investors looking for strong performance are still waiting.

Data Date	Investment Rating	Net Assets ($Mil)	Price	Performance Rating/Pts	Total Return Y-T-D	Risk Rating/Pts
3-12	D+	38.82	27.29	D- / 1.5	3.88%	B+ / 9.2
2011	C-	32.90	26.27	D / 1.6	0.80%	B+ / 9.3
2010	B	24.70	27.54	C / 5.5	4.88%	B / 8.8

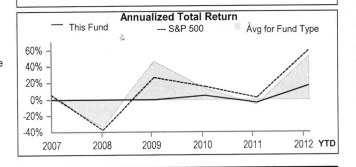

Annualized Total Return

---

*IQ Hedge Multi-Strategy Tracker (QAI)

C-   **Fair**

Fund Family: IndexIQ Advisors LLC
Fund Type: Global
Inception Date: March 24, 2009

Major Rating Factors:
Disappointing performance is the major factor driving the C- (Fair) TheStreet.com Investment Rating for *IQ Hedge Multi-Strategy Tracker. The fund currently has a performance rating of D (Weak) based on an annualized return of 4.80% over the last three years and a total return of 2.40% year to date 2012. Factored into the performance evaluation is an expense ratio of 0.77% (very low).

The fund's risk rating is currently B+ (Good). It carries a beta of 0.22, meaning the fund's expected move will be 2.2% for every 10% move in the market. Volatility, as measured by both the semi-deviation and a drawdown factor, is considered very low. As of March 31, 2012, *IQ Hedge Multi-Strategy Tracker traded at a premium of .07% above its net asset value, which is better than its one-year historical average premium of .09%.

Donald J. Mulvihill has been running the fund for 4 years and currently receives a manager quality ranking of 55 (0=worst, 99=best). This fund offers only a moderate level of risk but investors looking for strong performance are still waiting.

Data Date	Investment Rating	Net Assets ($Mil)	Price	Performance Rating/Pts	Total Return Y-T-D	Risk Rating/Pts
3-12	C-	196.84	27.73	D / 1.7	2.40%	B+ / 9.5
2011	C-	177.40	27.08	D / 2.0	0.37%	B+ / 9.6
2010	B	123.30	27.41	C- / 4.2	2.57%	B / 8.8

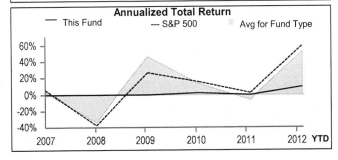

Annualized Total Return

*IQ Merger Arbitrage ETF (MNA)

C-   **Fair**

Fund Family: IndexIQ Advisors LLC
Fund Type: Global
Inception Date: November 16, 2009

Data Date	Investment Rating	Net Assets ($Mil)	Price	Performance Rating/Pts	Total Return Y-T-D	Risk Rating/Pts
3-12	C-	25.65	25.67	D / 1.8	4.43%	B+ / 9.2
2011	C-	24.80	24.58	D / 2.0	1.55%	B+ / 9.2
2010	C-	23.60	24.70	D- / 1.1	-3.05%	B / 8.6

Major Rating Factors:
Disappointing performance is the major factor driving the C- (Fair) TheStreet.com Investment Rating for *IQ Merger Arbitrage ETF. The fund currently has a performance rating of D (Weak) based on an annualized return of 0.00% over the last three years and a total return of 4.43% year to date 2012. Factored into the performance evaluation is an expense ratio of 0.76% (very low).

The fund's risk rating is currently B+ (Good). It carries a beta of 0.00, meaning the fund's expected move will be 0.0% for every 10% move in the market. Volatility, as measured by both the semi-deviation and a drawdown factor, is considered very low. As of March 31, 2012, *IQ Merger Arbitrage ETF traded at a discount of .12% below its net asset value, which is better than its one-year historical average discount of .11%.

Julie S. Abbett has been running the fund for 1 year and currently receives a manager quality ranking of 58 (0=worst, 99=best). This fund offers only a moderate level of risk but investors looking for strong performance are still waiting.

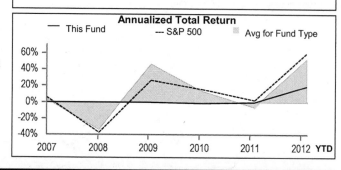
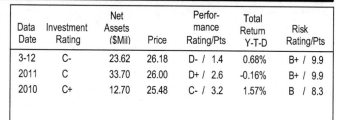

*IQ Real Return ETF (CPI)

C-   **Fair**

Fund Family: IndexIQ Advisors LLC
Fund Type: Income
Inception Date: October 26, 2009

Data Date	Investment Rating	Net Assets ($Mil)	Price	Performance Rating/Pts	Total Return Y-T-D	Risk Rating/Pts
3-12	C-	23.62	26.18	D- / 1.4	0.68%	B+ / 9.9
2011	C	33.70	26.00	D+ / 2.6	-0.16%	B+ / 9.9
2010	C+	12.70	25.48	C- / 3.2	1.57%	B / 8.3

Major Rating Factors:
Disappointing performance is the major factor driving the C- (Fair) TheStreet.com Investment Rating for *IQ Real Return ETF. The fund currently has a performance rating of D- (Weak) based on an annualized return of 0.00% over the last three years and a total return of 0.68% year to date 2012. Factored into the performance evaluation is an expense ratio of 0.49% (very low).

The fund's risk rating is currently B+ (Good). It carries a beta of 0.00, meaning the fund's expected move will be 0.0% for every 10% move in the market. Volatility, as measured by both the semi-deviation and a drawdown factor, is considered very low. As of March 31, 2012, *IQ Real Return ETF traded at a premium of .08% above its net asset value, which is worse than its one-year historical average premium of .01%.

Julie S. Abbett has been running the fund for 1 year and currently receives a manager quality ranking of 63 (0=worst, 99=best). This fund offers only a moderate level of risk but investors looking for strong performance are still waiting.

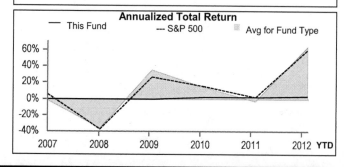

*IQ South Korea Small Cap ETF (SKOR)

D-   **Weak**

Fund Family: IndexIQ Advisors LLC
Fund Type: Foreign
Inception Date: April 13, 2010

Data Date	Investment Rating	Net Assets ($Mil)	Price	Performance Rating/Pts	Total Return Y-T-D	Risk Rating/Pts
3-12	D-	9.83	25.96	E+ / 0.9	-0.06%	C+ / 6.0
2011	D-	9.10	25.98	D- / 1.2	1.61%	C+ / 6.0

Major Rating Factors:
Very poor performance is the major factor driving the D- (Weak) TheStreet.com Investment Rating for *IQ South Korea Small Cap ETF. The fund currently has a performance rating of E+ (Very Weak) based on an annualized return of 0.00% over the last three years and a total return of -0.06% year to date 2012. Factored into the performance evaluation is an expense ratio of 0.80% (very low).

The fund's risk rating is currently C+ (Fair). It carries a beta of 0.00, meaning the fund's expected move will be 0.0% for every 10% move in the market. Volatility, as measured by both the semi-deviation and a drawdown factor, is considered low. As of March 31, 2012, *IQ South Korea Small Cap ETF traded at a discount of 1.03% below its net asset value, which is better than its one-year historical average discount of .25%.

Julie S. Abbett currently receives a manager quality ranking of 15 (0=worst, 99=best). This fund offers only a moderate level of risk but investors looking for strong performance are still waiting.

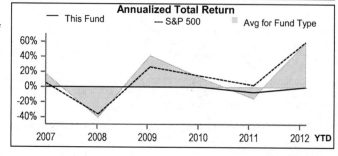

*iShares 10+ Year Credit Bond (CLY)   C   Fair

Fund Family: BlackRock Fund Advisors
Fund Type: Global
Inception Date: December 8, 2009

Major Rating Factors:
Disappointing performance is the major factor driving the C (Fair) TheStreet.com Investment Rating for *iShares 10+ Year Credit Bond. The fund currently has a performance rating of D+ (Weak) based on an annualized return of 0.00% over the last three years and a total return of -1.33% year to date 2012. Factored into the performance evaluation is an expense ratio of 0.20% (very low).

The fund's risk rating is currently B+ (Good). It carries a beta of 0.00, meaning the fund's expected move will be 0.0% for every 10% move in the market. Volatility, as measured by both the semi-deviation and a drawdown factor, is considered very low. As of March 31, 2012, *iShares 10+ Year Credit Bond traded at a discount of .19% below its net asset value, which is better than its one-year historical average premium of 1.45%.

Scott F. Radell has been running the fund for 2 years and currently receives a manager quality ranking of 89 (0=worst, 99=best). This fund offers only a moderate level of risk but investors looking for strong performance are still waiting.

Data Date	Investment Rating	Net Assets ($Mil)	Price	Performance Rating/Pts	Total Return Y-T-D	Risk Rating/Pts
3-12	C	196.42	57.77	D+ / 2.7	-1.33%	B+ / 9.4
2011	B	340.40	59.02	C+ / 6.6	-0.63%	B+ / 9.5
2010	B	15.80	52.98	C+ / 6.4	10.72%	B / 8.7

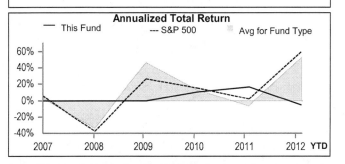

*iShares 10+ Year Govt/Credit Bd (GLJ)   C-   Fair

Fund Family: BlackRock Fund Advisors
Fund Type: Global
Inception Date: December 8, 2009

Major Rating Factors:
Disappointing performance is the major factor driving the C- (Fair) TheStreet.com Investment Rating for *iShares 10+ Year Govt/Credit Bd. The fund currently has a performance rating of D+ (Weak) based on an annualized return of 0.00% over the last three years and a total return of -2.37% year to date 2012. Factored into the performance evaluation is an expense ratio of 0.20% (very low).

The fund's risk rating is currently B+ (Good). It carries a beta of 0.00, meaning the fund's expected move will be 0.0% for every 10% move in the market. Volatility, as measured by both the semi-deviation and a drawdown factor, is considered very low. As of March 31, 2012, *iShares 10+ Year Govt/Credit Bd traded at a discount of .42% below its net asset value, which is better than its one-year historical average premium of .12%.

Scott F. Radell has been running the fund for 2 years and currently receives a manager quality ranking of 92 (0=worst, 99=best). This fund offers only a moderate level of risk but investors looking for strong performance are still waiting.

Data Date	Investment Rating	Net Assets ($Mil)	Price	Performance Rating/Pts	Total Return Y-T-D	Risk Rating/Pts
3-12	C-	24.44	58.89	D+ / 2.7	-2.37%	B+ / 9.2
2011	B+	24.30	60.74	B / 7.6	-1.47%	B+ / 9.3
2010	B	15.60	52.27	C / 4.3	9.17%	B / 8.5

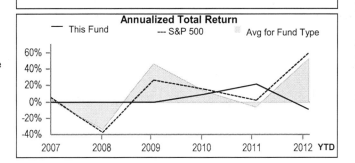

*iShares 2012 S&P AMT-Free Muni S (MUAA)   C-   Fair

Fund Family: BlackRock Fund Advisors
Fund Type: General - Investment Grade
Inception Date: January 7, 2010

Major Rating Factors:
Disappointing performance is the major factor driving the C- (Fair) TheStreet.com Investment Rating for *iShares 2012 S&P AMT-Free Muni S. The fund currently has a performance rating of D- (Weak) based on an annualized return of 0.00% over the last three years and a total return of 0.32% year to date 2012. Factored into the performance evaluation is an expense ratio of 0.30% (very low).

The fund's risk rating is currently B+ (Good). It carries a beta of 0.00, meaning the fund's expected move will be 0.0% for every 10% move in the market. Volatility, as measured by both the semi-deviation and a drawdown factor, is considered very low. As of March 31, 2012, *iShares 2012 S&P AMT-Free Muni S traded at a premium of .24% above its net asset value, which is worse than its one-year historical average discount of .27%.

Scott F. Radell has been running the fund for 2 years and currently receives a manager quality ranking of 57 (0=worst, 99=best). This fund offers only a moderate level of risk but investors looking for strong performance are still waiting.

Data Date	Investment Rating	Net Assets ($Mil)	Price	Performance Rating/Pts	Total Return Y-T-D	Risk Rating/Pts
3-12	C-	27.92	50.84	D- / 1.3	0.32%	B+ / 9.8
2011	C-	30.50	50.72	D / 2.1	0.06%	B+ / 9.9

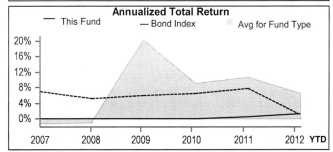

*iShares 2013 S&P AMT-Free Muni S (MUAB)   C-   Fair

Fund Family: BlackRock Fund Advisors
Fund Type: General - Investment Grade
Inception Date: January 7, 2010

Data Date	Investment Rating	Net Assets ($Mil)	Price	Performance Rating/Pts	Total Return Y-T-D	Risk Rating/Pts
3-12	C-	35.71	51.23	D- / 1.4	1.05%	B+ / 9.9
2011	C	33.10	50.77	D / 2.2	0.35%	B+ / 9.9

Major Rating Factors:
Disappointing performance is the major factor driving the C- (Fair) TheStreet.com
Investment Rating for *iShares 2013 S&P AMT-Free Muni S. The fund currently has a
performance rating of D- (Weak) based on an annualized return of 0.00% over the
last three years and a total return of 1.05% year to date 2012. Factored into the
performance evaluation is an expense ratio of 0.30% (very low).

The fund's risk rating is currently B+ (Good). It carries a beta of 0.00, meaning
the fund's expected move will be 0.0% for every 10% move in the market. Volatility,
as measured by both the semi-deviation and a drawdown factor, is considered very
low. As of March 31, 2012, *iShares 2013 S&P AMT-Free Muni S traded at a
premium of .53% above its net asset value, which is worse than its one-year historical
average premium of .15%.

Scott F. Radell has been running the fund for 2 years and currently receives a
manager quality ranking of 54 (0=worst, 99=best). This fund offers only a moderate
level of risk but investors looking for strong performance are still waiting.

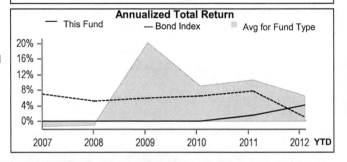

*iShares 2014 S&P AMT-Free Muni S (MUAC)   C-   Fair

Fund Family: BlackRock Fund Advisors
Fund Type: General - Investment Grade
Inception Date: January 7, 2010

Data Date	Investment Rating	Net Assets ($Mil)	Price	Performance Rating/Pts	Total Return Y-T-D	Risk Rating/Pts
3-12	C-	36.23	51.90	D- / 1.5	0.61%	B+ / 9.7
2011	C	33.40	51.67	D+ / 2.8	0.08%	B+ / 9.8

Major Rating Factors:
Disappointing performance is the major factor driving the C- (Fair) TheStreet.com
Investment Rating for *iShares 2014 S&P AMT-Free Muni S. The fund currently has a
performance rating of D- (Weak) based on an annualized return of 0.00% over the
last three years and a total return of 0.61% year to date 2012. Factored into the
performance evaluation is an expense ratio of 0.30% (very low).

The fund's risk rating is currently B+ (Good). It carries a beta of 0.00, meaning
the fund's expected move will be 0.0% for every 10% move in the market. Volatility,
as measured by both the semi-deviation and a drawdown factor, is considered very
low. As of March 31, 2012, *iShares 2014 S&P AMT-Free Muni S traded at a
premium of .54% above its net asset value, which is worse than its one-year historical
average premium of .17%.

Scott F. Radell has been running the fund for 2 years and currently receives a
manager quality ranking of 72 (0=worst, 99=best). This fund offers only a moderate
level of risk but investors looking for strong performance are still waiting.

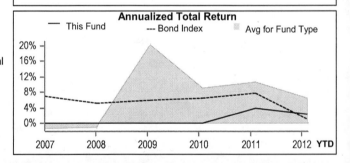

*iShares 2015 S&P AMT-Free Muni S (MUAD)   C-   Fair

Fund Family: BlackRock Fund Advisors
Fund Type: General - Investment Grade
Inception Date: January 7, 2010

Data Date	Investment Rating	Net Assets ($Mil)	Price	Performance Rating/Pts	Total Return Y-T-D	Risk Rating/Pts
3-12	C-	37.35	53.46	D / 1.7	0.91%	B+ / 9.8
2011	C	34.30	53.10	C- / 3.2	-0.04%	B+ / 9.8

Major Rating Factors:
Disappointing performance is the major factor driving the C- (Fair) TheStreet.com
Investment Rating for *iShares 2015 S&P AMT-Free Muni S. The fund currently has a
performance rating of D (Weak) based on an annualized return of 0.00% over the last
three years and a total return of 0.91% year to date 2012. Factored into the
performance evaluation is an expense ratio of 0.30% (very low).

The fund's risk rating is currently B+ (Good). It carries a beta of 0.00, meaning
the fund's expected move will be 0.0% for every 10% move in the market. Volatility,
as measured by both the semi-deviation and a drawdown factor, is considered very
low. As of March 31, 2012, *iShares 2015 S&P AMT-Free Muni S traded at a
premium of .64% above its net asset value, which is worse than its one-year historical
average premium of .22%.

Scott F. Radell has been running the fund for 2 years and currently receives a
manager quality ranking of 63 (0=worst, 99=best). This fund offers only a moderate
level of risk but investors looking for strong performance are still waiting.

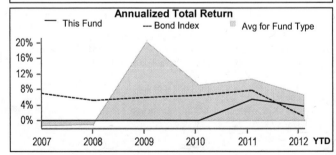

*iShares 2016 S&P AMT-Free Muni S (MUAE)   C-   Fair

Fund Family: BlackRock Fund Advisors
Fund Type: General - Investment Grade
Inception Date: January 7, 2010

Data Date	Investment Rating	Net Assets ($Mil)	Price	Perfor-mance Rating/Pts	Total Return Y-T-D	Risk Rating/Pts
3-12	C-	32.23	53.58	D / 2.1	0.88%	B+ / 9.7
2011	C+	26.50	53.26	C- / 3.9	0.04%	B+ / 9.8

Major Rating Factors:
Disappointing performance is the major factor driving the C- (Fair) TheStreet.com Investment Rating for *iShares 2016 S&P AMT-Free Muni S. The fund currently has a performance rating of D (Weak) based on an annualized return of 0.00% over the last three years and a total return of 0.88% year to date 2012. Factored into the performance evaluation is an expense ratio of 0.30% (very low).

The fund's risk rating is currently B+ (Good). It carries a beta of 0.00, meaning the fund's expected move will be 0.0% for every 10% move in the market. Volatility, as measured by both the semi-deviation and a drawdown factor, is considered very low. As of March 31, 2012, *iShares 2016 S&P AMT-Free Muni S traded at a premium of .73% above its net asset value, which is worse than its one-year historical average premium of .20%.

Scott F. Radell has been running the fund for 2 years and currently receives a manager quality ranking of 74 (0=worst, 99=best). This fund offers only a moderate level of risk but investors looking for strong performance are still waiting.

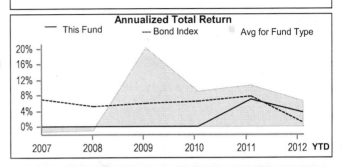

*iShares 2017 S&P AMT-Free Muni S (MUAF)   C-   Fair

Fund Family: BlackRock Fund Advisors
Fund Type: General - Investment Grade
Inception Date: January 7, 2010

Data Date	Investment Rating	Net Assets ($Mil)	Price	Perfor-mance Rating/Pts	Total Return Y-T-D	Risk Rating/Pts
3-12	C-	41.63	54.67	D / 2.1	-0.21%	B+ / 9.4
2011	C+	35.50	54.96	C / 4.4	0.15%	B+ / 9.5

Major Rating Factors:
Disappointing performance is the major factor driving the C- (Fair) TheStreet.com Investment Rating for *iShares 2017 S&P AMT-Free Muni S. The fund currently has a performance rating of D (Weak) based on an annualized return of 0.00% over the last three years and a total return of -0.21% year to date 2012. Factored into the performance evaluation is an expense ratio of 0.30% (very low).

The fund's risk rating is currently B+ (Good). It carries a beta of 0.00, meaning the fund's expected move will be 0.0% for every 10% move in the market. Volatility, as measured by both the semi-deviation and a drawdown factor, is considered very low. As of March 31, 2012, *iShares 2017 S&P AMT-Free Muni S traded at a premium of .05% above its net asset value, which is better than its one-year historical average premium of .39%.

Scott F. Radell has been running the fund for 2 years and currently receives a manager quality ranking of 43 (0=worst, 99=best). This fund offers only a moderate level of risk but investors looking for strong performance are still waiting.

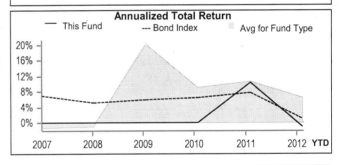

*iShares Barclays 0-5 Year TIPS B (STIP)   C-   Fair

Fund Family: BlackRock Fund Advisors
Fund Type: US Government/Agency
Inception Date: December 1, 2010

Data Date	Investment Rating	Net Assets ($Mil)	Price	Perfor-mance Rating/Pts	Total Return Y-T-D	Risk Rating/Pts
3-12	C-	278.96	103.32	D- / 1.5	1.28%	B+ / 9.9
2011	C	244.50	102.01	D+ / 2.6	0.42%	B+ / 9.9

Major Rating Factors:
Disappointing performance is the major factor driving the C- (Fair) TheStreet.com Investment Rating for *iShares Barclays 0-5 Year TIPS B. The fund currently has a performance rating of D- (Weak) based on an annualized return of 0.00% over the last three years and a total return of 1.28% year to date 2012. Factored into the performance evaluation is an expense ratio of 0.20% (very low).

The fund's risk rating is currently B+ (Good). It carries a beta of 0.00, meaning the fund's expected move will be 0.0% for every 10% move in the market. Volatility, as measured by both the semi-deviation and a drawdown factor, is considered very low. As of March 31, 2012, *iShares Barclays 0-5 Year TIPS B traded at a premium of .16% above its net asset value, which is worse than its one-year historical average premium of .13%.

Scott F. Radell has been running the fund for 2 years and currently receives a manager quality ranking of 75 (0=worst, 99=best). This fund offers only a moderate level of risk but investors looking for strong performance are still waiting.

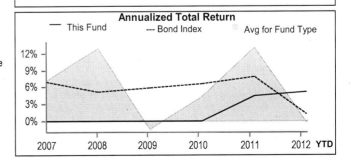

*iShares Barclays 1-3 Year Credit (CSJ)   C-   Fair

Fund Family: BlackRock Fund Advisors
Fund Type: Corporate - Investment Grade
Inception Date: January 5, 2007

Data Date	Investment Rating	Net Assets ($Mil)	Price	Performance Rating/Pts	Total Return Y-T-D	Risk Rating/Pts
3-12	C-	9,132.03	105.09	D / 1.6	1.14%	B+ / 9.8
2011	C	8,835.10	104.20	D+ / 2.5	0.04%	B+ / 9.9
2010	B	7,219.20	104.28	C / 4.3	2.88%	B / 8.8
2009	B-	3,228.95	103.96	C- / 4.1	7.26%	B / 8.9

Major Rating Factors:

Disappointing performance is the major factor driving the C- (Fair) TheStreet.com Investment Rating for *iShares Barclays 1-3 Year Credit. The fund currently has a performance rating of D (Weak) based on an annualized return of 4.90% over the last three years and a total return of 1.14% year to date 2012. Factored into the performance evaluation is an expense ratio of 0.20% (very low).

The fund's risk rating is currently B+ (Good). It carries a beta of 0.38, meaning the fund's expected move will be 3.8% for every 10% move in the market. Volatility, as measured by both the semi-deviation and a drawdown factor, is considered very low. As of March 31, 2012, *iShares Barclays 1-3 Year Credit traded at a premium of .25% above its net asset value, which is worse than its one-year historical average premium of .15%.

Scott F. Radell has been running the fund for 2 years and currently receives a manager quality ranking of 47 (0=worst, 99=best). This fund offers only a moderate level of risk but investors looking for strong performance are still waiting.

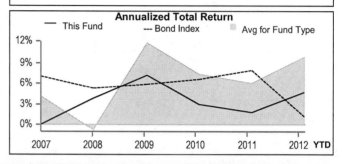

*iShares Barclays 1-3Yr Treasury (SHY)   C-   Fair

Fund Family: BlackRock Fund Advisors
Fund Type: US Government/Agency
Inception Date: July 22, 2002

Data Date	Investment Rating	Net Assets ($Mil)	Price	Performance Rating/Pts	Total Return Y-T-D	Risk Rating/Pts
3-12	C-	10,651.72	84.32	D- / 1.3	-0.13%	B+ / 9.9
2011	C	10,905.40	84.50	D / 2.2	-0.05%	B+ / 9.9
2010	B-	8,102.10	83.98	C- / 3.6	2.28%	B+ / 9.1
2009	C+	7,187.00	82.96	C- / 3.2	0.89%	B+ / 9.2

Major Rating Factors:

Disappointing performance is the major factor driving the C- (Fair) TheStreet.com Investment Rating for *iShares Barclays 1-3Yr Treasury. The fund currently has a performance rating of D- (Weak) based on an annualized return of 1.48% over the last three years and a total return of -0.13% year to date 2012. Factored into the performance evaluation is an expense ratio of 0.15% (very low).

The fund's risk rating is currently B+ (Good). It carries a beta of 0.05, meaning the fund's expected move will be 0.5% for every 10% move in the market. Volatility, as measured by both the semi-deviation and a drawdown factor, is considered very low. As of March 31, 2012, *iShares Barclays 1-3Yr Treasury traded at a premium of .01% above its net asset value, which is better than its one-year historical average premium of .02%.

Scott F. Radell has been running the fund for 2 years and currently receives a manager quality ranking of 53 (0=worst, 99=best). This fund offers only a moderate level of risk but investors looking for strong performance are still waiting.

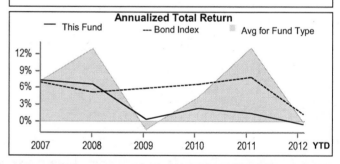

*iShares Barclays 10-20 Yr Treasu (TLH)   C-   Fair

Fund Family: BlackRock Fund Advisors
Fund Type: US Government/Agency
Inception Date: January 5, 2007

Data Date	Investment Rating	Net Assets ($Mil)	Price	Performance Rating/Pts	Total Return Y-T-D	Risk Rating/Pts
3-12	C-	513.12	127.76	D / 2.1	-3.49%	B+ / 9.1
2011	C+	505.20	132.93	C / 4.5	-0.98%	B / 8.9
2010	B	248.10	112.70	C / 4.6	9.71%	B / 8.4
2009	C-	243.39	106.47	E+ / 0.9	-6.98%	B / 8.6

Major Rating Factors:

Disappointing performance is the major factor driving the C- (Fair) TheStreet.com Investment Rating for *iShares Barclays 10-20 Yr Treasu. The fund currently has a performance rating of D (Weak) based on an annualized return of 7.17% over the last three years and a total return of -3.49% year to date 2012. Factored into the performance evaluation is an expense ratio of 0.15% (very low).

The fund's risk rating is currently B+ (Good). It carries a beta of 0.76, meaning the fund's expected move will be 7.6% for every 10% move in the market. Volatility, as measured by both the semi-deviation and a drawdown factor, is considered very low. As of March 31, 2012, *iShares Barclays 10-20 Yr Treasu traded at a discount of .12% below its net asset value, which is better than its one-year historical average premium of .03%.

Scott F. Radell has been running the fund for 2 years and currently receives a manager quality ranking of 52 (0=worst, 99=best). This fund offers only a moderate level of risk but investors looking for strong performance are still waiting.

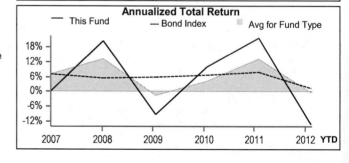

*iShares Barclays 20+Yr Treasury (TLT)

D+   **Weak**

Fund Family: BlackRock Fund Advisors
Fund Type: US Government/Agency
Inception Date: July 22, 2002

Data Date	Investment Rating	Net Assets ($Mil)	Price	Performance Rating/Pts	Total Return Y-T-D	Risk Rating/Pts
3-12	D+	3,038.27	112.20	D / 2.1	-7.02%	B / 8.4
2011	C+	3,382.10	121.25	C / 5.4	-2.08%	B- / 7.9
2010	C+	2,726.90	94.12	C- / 3.4	9.06%	B / 8.0
2009	C	2,202.01	89.89	D / 2.0	-19.74%	B / 8.2

Major Rating Factors:

Disappointing performance is the major factor driving the D+ (Weak) TheStreet.com Investment Rating for *iShares Barclays 20+Yr Treasury. The fund currently has a performance rating of D (Weak) based on an annualized return of 7.02% over the last three years and a total return of -7.02% year to date 2012. Factored into the performance evaluation is an expense ratio of 0.15% (very low).

The fund's risk rating is currently B (Good). It carries a beta of 1.24, meaning it is expected to move 12.4% for every 10% move in the market. Volatility, as measured by both the semi-deviation and a drawdown factor, is considered low. As of March 31, 2012, *iShares Barclays 20+Yr Treasury traded at a discount of .28% below its net asset value, which is better than its one-year historical average premium of .03%.

Scott F. Radell has been running the fund for 2 years and currently receives a manager quality ranking of 29 (0=worst, 99=best). This fund offers only a moderate level of risk but investors looking for strong performance are still waiting.

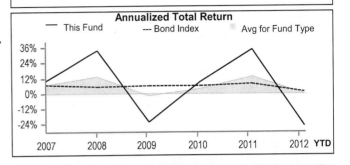

Annualized Total Return
— This Fund   --- Bond Index   Avg for Fund Type

*iShares Barclays 3-7 Yr Treasury (IEI)

C-   **Fair**

Fund Family: BlackRock Fund Advisors
Fund Type: US Government/Agency
Inception Date: January 5, 2007

Data Date	Investment Rating	Net Assets ($Mil)	Price	Performance Rating/Pts	Total Return Y-T-D	Risk Rating/Pts
3-12	C-	2,255.76	121.10	D / 1.6	-0.58%	B+ / 9.7
2011	C	2,816.00	122.04	C- / 3.0	-0.11%	B+ / 9.7
2010	B+	1,308.00	114.65	C / 4.6	6.32%	B+ / 9.0
2009	C	805.43	110.16	D / 1.7	-1.05%	B+ / 9.2

Major Rating Factors:

Disappointing performance is the major factor driving the C- (Fair) TheStreet.com Investment Rating for *iShares Barclays 3-7 Yr Treasury. The fund currently has a performance rating of D (Weak) based on an annualized return of 4.46% over the last three years and a total return of -0.58% year to date 2012. Factored into the performance evaluation is an expense ratio of 0.15% (very low).

The fund's risk rating is currently B+ (Good). It carries a beta of 0.23, meaning the fund's expected move will be 2.3% for every 10% move in the market. Volatility, as measured by both the semi-deviation and a drawdown factor, is considered very low. As of March 31, 2012, *iShares Barclays 3-7 Yr Treasury traded at a premium of .03% above its net asset value, which is better than its one-year historical average premium of .04%.

Scott F. Radell has been running the fund for 2 years and currently receives a manager quality ranking of 61 (0=worst, 99=best). This fund offers only a moderate level of risk but investors looking for strong performance are still waiting.

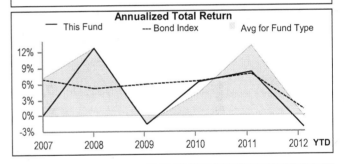

Annualized Total Return
— This Fund   --- Bond Index   Avg for Fund Type

*iShares Barclays 7-10Yr Treasury (IEF)

C-   **Fair**

Fund Family: BlackRock Fund Advisors
Fund Type: US Government/Agency
Inception Date: July 22, 2002

Data Date	Investment Rating	Net Assets ($Mil)	Price	Performance Rating/Pts	Total Return Y-T-D	Risk Rating/Pts
3-12	C-	4,637.40	103.28	D / 1.9	-1.83%	B+ / 9.3
2011	C	4,795.30	105.57	C- / 3.8	-0.54%	B+ / 9.2
2010	B+	3,039.30	93.82	C / 4.9	9.37%	B / 8.6
2009	C+	2,564.75	88.60	C- / 3.4	-5.21%	B / 8.9

Major Rating Factors:

Disappointing performance is the major factor driving the C- (Fair) TheStreet.com Investment Rating for *iShares Barclays 7-10Yr Treasury. The fund currently has a performance rating of D (Weak) based on an annualized return of 6.13% over the last three years and a total return of -1.83% year to date 2012. Factored into the performance evaluation is an expense ratio of 0.15% (very low).

The fund's risk rating is currently B+ (Good). It carries a beta of 0.51, meaning the fund's expected move will be 5.1% for every 10% move in the market. Volatility, as measured by both the semi-deviation and a drawdown factor, is considered very low. As of March 31, 2012, *iShares Barclays 7-10Yr Treasury traded at a discount of .01% below its net asset value, which is better than its one-year historical average premium of .04%.

Scott F. Radell has been running the fund for 2 years and currently receives a manager quality ranking of 57 (0=worst, 99=best). This fund offers only a moderate level of risk but investors looking for strong performance are still waiting.

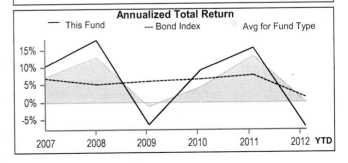

Annualized Total Return
— This Fund   --- Bond Index   Avg for Fund Type

*iShares Barclays Agency Bond (AGZ)

C- **Fair**

Fund Family: BlackRock Fund Advisors
Fund Type: US Government/Agency
Inception Date: November 5, 2008

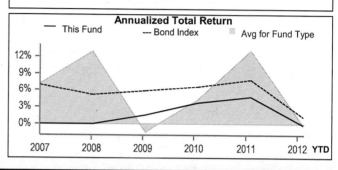

Data Date	Investment Rating	Net Assets ($Mil)	Price	Performance Rating/Pts	Total Return Y-T-D	Risk Rating/Pts
3-12	C-	360.97	112.64	D- / 1.5	-0.04%	B+ / 9.9
2011	C	360.50	112.95	D+ / 2.6	-0.26%	B+ / 9.9
2010	B-	361.40	109.52	C- / 3.4	3.75%	B+ / 9.1
2009	C	215.78	107.57	D+ / 2.4	2.08%	B+ / 9.2

Major Rating Factors:

Disappointing performance is the major factor driving the C- (Fair) TheStreet.com Investment Rating for *iShares Barclays Agency Bond. The fund currently has a performance rating of D- (Weak) based on an annualized return of 3.43% over the last three years and a total return of -0.04% year to date 2012. Factored into the performance evaluation is an expense ratio of 0.20% (very low).

The fund's risk rating is currently B+ (Good). It carries a beta of 0.12, meaning the fund's expected move will be 1.2% for every 10% move in the market. Volatility, as measured by both the semi-deviation and a drawdown factor, is considered very low. As of March 31, 2012, *iShares Barclays Agency Bond traded at a premium of .28% above its net asset value, which is worse than its one-year historical average premium of .07%.

Scott F. Radell has been running the fund for 2 years and currently receives a manager quality ranking of 62 (0=worst, 99=best). This fund offers only a moderate level of risk but investors looking for strong performance are still waiting.

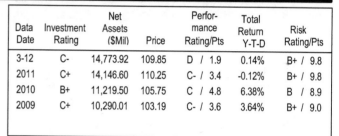

*iShares Barclays Aggregate Bd (AGG)

C- **Fair**

Fund Family: BlackRock Fund Advisors
Fund Type: General - Investment Grade
Inception Date: September 22, 2003

Data Date	Investment Rating	Net Assets ($Mil)	Price	Performance Rating/Pts	Total Return Y-T-D	Risk Rating/Pts
3-12	C-	14,773.92	109.85	D / 1.9	0.14%	B+ / 9.8
2011	C+	14,146.60	110.25	C- / 3.4	-0.12%	B+ / 9.8
2010	B+	11,219.50	105.75	C / 4.8	6.38%	B / 8.9
2009	C+	10,290.01	103.19	C- / 3.6	3.64%	B+ / 9.0

Major Rating Factors:

Disappointing performance is the major factor driving the C- (Fair) TheStreet.com Investment Rating for *iShares Barclays Aggregate Bd. The fund currently has a performance rating of D (Weak) based on an annualized return of 6.66% over the last three years and a total return of 0.14% year to date 2012. Factored into the performance evaluation is an expense ratio of 0.20% (very low).

The fund's risk rating is currently B+ (Good). It carries a beta of 1.05, meaning that its performance tracks fairly well with that of the overall stock market. Volatility, as measured by both the semi-deviation and a drawdown factor, is considered very low. As of March 31, 2012, *iShares Barclays Aggregate Bd traded at a premium of .19% above its net asset value, which is worse than its one-year historical average premium of .15%.

Scott F. Radell has been running the fund for 2 years and currently receives a manager quality ranking of 41 (0=worst, 99=best). This fund offers only a moderate level of risk but investors looking for strong performance are still waiting.

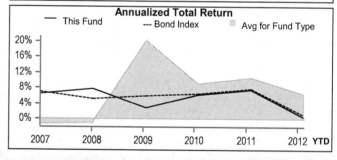

*iShares Barclays Credit Bond Fd (CFT)

C **Fair**

Fund Family: BlackRock Fund Advisors
Fund Type: Corporate - Investment Grade
Inception Date: January 5, 2007

Data Date	Investment Rating	Net Assets ($Mil)	Price	Performance Rating/Pts	Total Return Y-T-D	Risk Rating/Pts
3-12	C	1,169.56	109.72	D+ / 2.8	1.32%	B+ / 9.4
2011	C+	1,043.90	108.96	C- / 4.0	-0.57%	B+ / 9.3
2010	B	727.30	104.13	C / 5.3	8.43%	B / 8.1
2009	B	379.52	100.53	C / 4.8	11.31%	B / 8.4

Major Rating Factors:

Disappointing performance is the major factor driving the C (Fair) TheStreet.com Investment Rating for *iShares Barclays Credit Bond Fd. The fund currently has a performance rating of D+ (Weak) based on an annualized return of 11.86% over the last three years and a total return of 1.32% year to date 2012. Factored into the performance evaluation is an expense ratio of 0.20% (very low).

The fund's risk rating is currently B+ (Good). It carries a beta of 0.99, meaning that its performance tracks fairly well with that of the overall stock market. Volatility, as measured by both the semi-deviation and a drawdown factor, is considered very low. As of March 31, 2012, *iShares Barclays Credit Bond Fd traded at a premium of .58% above its net asset value, which is worse than its one-year historical average premium of .50%.

Scott F. Radell has been running the fund for 2 years and currently receives a manager quality ranking of 41 (0=worst, 99=best). This fund offers only a moderate level of risk but investors looking for strong performance are still waiting.

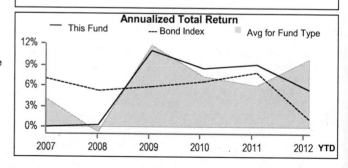

*iShares Barclays Govt/Credit Bd (GBF)   C-   Fair

Fund Family: BlackRock Fund Advisors
Fund Type: US Government/Agency
Inception Date: January 5, 2007

Major Rating Factors:
Disappointing performance is the major factor driving the C- (Fair) TheStreet.com Investment Rating for *iShares Barclays Govt/Credit Bd. The fund currently has a performance rating of D (Weak) based on an annualized return of 6.84% over the last three years and a total return of -0.31% year to date 2012. Factored into the performance evaluation is an expense ratio of 0.20% (very low).

The fund's risk rating is currently B+ (Good). It carries a beta of 0.20, meaning the fund's expected move will be 2.0% for every 10% move in the market. Volatility, as measured by both the semi-deviation and a drawdown factor, is considered very low. As of March 31, 2012, *iShares Barclays Govt/Credit Bd traded at a premium of .31% above its net asset value, which is worse than its one-year historical average premium of .13%.

Scott F. Radell has been running the fund for 2 years and currently receives a manager quality ranking of 73 (0=worst, 99=best). This fund offers only a moderate level of risk but investors looking for strong performance are still waiting.

Data Date	Investment Rating	Net Assets ($Mil)	Price	Performance Rating/Pts	Total Return Y-T-D	Risk Rating/Pts
3-12	C-	136.69	112.96	D / 1.9	-0.31%	B+ / 9.7
2011	C+	113.10	113.83	C- / 3.5	-0.12%	B+ / 9.7
2010	B	129.00	107.39	C / 4.5	5.72%	B / 8.8
2009	C+	126.09	104.86	C- / 3.0	3.49%	B+ / 9.0

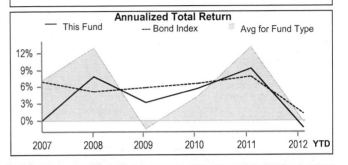

*iShares Barclays Intrm Credit Bd (CIU)   C   Fair

Fund Family: BlackRock Fund Advisors
Fund Type: Corporate - Investment Grade
Inception Date: January 5, 2007

Major Rating Factors:
Disappointing performance is the major factor driving the C (Fair) TheStreet.com Investment Rating for *iShares Barclays Intrm Credit Bd. The fund currently has a performance rating of D+ (Weak) based on an annualized return of 9.50% over the last three years and a total return of 2.14% year to date 2012. Factored into the performance evaluation is an expense ratio of 0.20% (very low).

The fund's risk rating is currently B+ (Good). It carries a beta of 0.75, meaning the fund's expected move will be 7.5% for every 10% move in the market. Volatility, as measured by both the semi-deviation and a drawdown factor, is considered very low. As of March 31, 2012, *iShares Barclays Intrm Credit Bd traded at a premium of .49% above its net asset value, which is worse than its one-year historical average premium of .35%.

Scott F. Radell has been running the fund for 2 years and currently receives a manager quality ranking of 48 (0=worst, 99=best). This fund offers only a moderate level of risk but investors looking for strong performance are still waiting.

Data Date	Investment Rating	Net Assets ($Mil)	Price	Performance Rating/Pts	Total Return Y-T-D	Risk Rating/Pts
3-12	C	4,462.38	108.85	D+ / 2.4	2.14%	B+ / 9.7
2011	C	4,475.90	107.18	C- / 3.5	-0.05%	B+ / 9.6
2010	B	2,950.70	105.18	C / 5.2	6.84%	B / 8.4
2009	B	1,625.94	102.71	C / 4.9	10.60%	B / 8.6

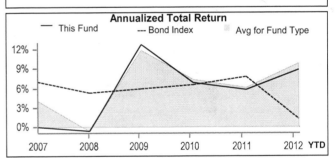

*iShares Barclays Intrm Govt/Crdt (GVI)   C-   Fair

Fund Family: BlackRock Fund Advisors
Fund Type: General - Investment Grade
Inception Date: January 5, 2007

Major Rating Factors:
Disappointing performance is the major factor driving the C- (Fair) TheStreet.com Investment Rating for *iShares Barclays Intrm Govt/Crdt. The fund currently has a performance rating of D (Weak) based on an annualized return of 5.52% over the last three years and a total return of 0.24% year to date 2012. Factored into the performance evaluation is an expense ratio of 0.20% (very low).

The fund's risk rating is currently B+ (Good). It carries a beta of 0.89, meaning the fund's expected move will be 8.9% for every 10% move in the market. Volatility, as measured by both the semi-deviation and a drawdown factor, is considered very low. As of March 31, 2012, *iShares Barclays Intrm Govt/Crdt traded at a premium of .17% above its net asset value, which is better than its one-year historical average premium of .21%.

Scott F. Radell has been running the fund for 2 years and currently receives a manager quality ranking of 41 (0=worst, 99=best). This fund offers only a moderate level of risk but investors looking for strong performance are still waiting.

Data Date	Investment Rating	Net Assets ($Mil)	Price	Performance Rating/Pts	Total Return Y-T-D	Risk Rating/Pts
3-12	C-	725.33	111.12	D / 1.7	0.24%	B+ / 9.8
2011	C	686.70	111.29	D+ / 2.9	-0.21%	B+ / 9.8
2010	B+	538.40	107.88	C / 4.5	5.47%	B / 8.9
2009	C+	357.64	105.26	D+ / 2.9	2.81%	B+ / 9.0

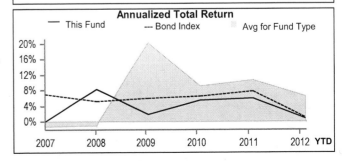

*iShares Barclays MBS Bond (MBB)

C-   **Fair**

Fund Family: BlackRock Fund Advisors
Fund Type: Mortgage
Inception Date: March 13, 2007

Major Rating Factors:

Disappointing performance is the major factor driving the C- (Fair) TheStreet.com Investment Rating for *iShares Barclays MBS Bond. The fund currently has a performance rating of D (Weak) based on an annualized return of 5.02% over the last three years and a total return of 0.44% year to date 2012. Factored into the performance evaluation is an expense ratio of 0.25% (very low).

The fund's risk rating is currently B+ (Good). It carries a beta of 1.02, meaning that its performance tracks fairly well with that of the overall stock market. Volatility, as measured by both the semi-deviation and a drawdown factor, is considered very low. As of March 31, 2012, *iShares Barclays MBS Bond traded at a premium of .10% above its net asset value, which is worse than its one-year historical average premium of .08%.

Scott F. Radell has been running the fund for 2 years and currently receives a manager quality ranking of 43 (0=worst, 99=best). This fund offers only a moderate level of risk but investors looking for strong performance are still waiting.

Data Date	Investment Rating	Net Assets ($Mil)	Price	Perfor- mance Rating/Pts	Total Return Y-T-D	Risk Rating/Pts
3-12	C-	4,595.10	107.95	D / 1.7	0.44%	B+ / 9.7
2011	C	4,057.40	108.07	C- / 3.1	0.03%	B+ / 9.7
2010	B+	2,224.20	105.58	C / 5.1	5.58%	B / 8.9
2009	C+	1,646.02	105.98	C- / 3.4	4.73%	B+ / 9.0

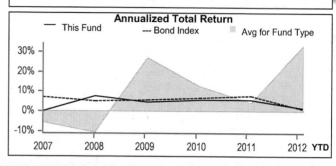

*iShares Barclays Short Treasury (SHV)

C-   **Fair**

Fund Family: BlackRock Fund Advisors
Fund Type: US Government/Agency
Inception Date: January 5, 2007

Major Rating Factors:

Disappointing performance is the major factor driving the C- (Fair) TheStreet.com Investment Rating for *iShares Barclays Short Treasury. The fund currently has a performance rating of D- (Weak) based on an annualized return of 0.11% over the last three years and a total return of -0.04% year to date 2012. Factored into the performance evaluation is an expense ratio of 0.15% (very low).

The fund's risk rating is currently B+ (Good). It carries a beta of 0.00, meaning the fund's expected move will be 0.0% for every 10% move in the market. Volatility, as measured by both the semi-deviation and a drawdown factor, is considered very low. As of March 31, 2012, *iShares Barclays Short Treasury traded at a premium of .01% above its net asset value, which is better than its one-year historical average premium of .02%.

Scott F. Radell has been running the fund for 2 years and currently receives a manager quality ranking of 46 (0=worst, 99=best). This fund offers only a moderate level of risk but investors looking for strong performance are still waiting.

Data Date	Investment Rating	Net Assets ($Mil)	Price	Perfor- mance Rating/Pts	Total Return Y-T-D	Risk Rating/Pts
3-12	C-	2,435.07	110.19	D- / 1.2	-0.04%	B+ / 9.9
2011	C-	2,589.70	110.23	D / 2.0	-0.01%	B+ / 9.9
2010	C+	4,000.20	110.24	D+ / 2.5	0.12%	B+ / 9.1
2009	C	1,785.08	110.19	D / 1.9	0.32%	B+ / 9.2

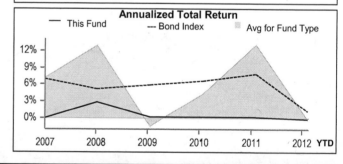

*iShares Barclays TIPS Bond (TIP)

C   **Fair**

Fund Family: BlackRock Fund Advisors
Fund Type: US Government/Agency
Inception Date: December 4, 2003

Major Rating Factors:

Disappointing performance is the major factor driving the C (Fair) TheStreet.com Investment Rating for *iShares Barclays TIPS Bond. The fund currently has a performance rating of D+ (Weak) based on an annualized return of 8.78% over the last three years and a total return of 0.82% year to date 2012. Factored into the performance evaluation is an expense ratio of 0.20% (very low).

The fund's risk rating is currently B+ (Good). It carries a beta of 0.14, meaning the fund's expected move will be 1.4% for every 10% move in the market. Volatility, as measured by both the semi-deviation and a drawdown factor, is considered very low. As of March 31, 2012, *iShares Barclays TIPS Bond traded at a premium of .23% above its net asset value, which is worse than its one-year historical average premium of .12%.

Scott F. Radell has been running the fund for 2 years and currently receives a manager quality ranking of 80 (0=worst, 99=best). This fund offers only a moderate level of risk but investors looking for strong performance are still waiting.

Data Date	Investment Rating	Net Assets ($Mil)	Price	Perfor- mance Rating/Pts	Total Return Y-T-D	Risk Rating/Pts
3-12	C	22,888.95	117.65	D+ / 2.4	0.82%	B+ / 9.7
2011	C+	22,164.20	116.69	C / 4.4	0.58%	B+ / 9.7
2010	B-	19,351.30	107.52	C / 4.5	6.14%	B / 8.3
2009	B-	15,405.47	103.90	C / 4.4	11.03%	B / 8.5

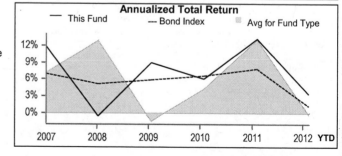

*iShares Cohen & Steers Realty Ma (ICF)   A-   Excellent

Fund Family: BlackRock Fund Advisors
Fund Type: Income
Inception Date: January 29, 2001

Major Rating Factors:
Exceptional performance is the major factor driving the A- (Excellent) TheStreet.com Investment Rating for *iShares Cohen & Steers Realty Ma. The fund currently has a performance rating of A- (Excellent) based on an annualized return of 37.33% over the last three years and a total return of 10.00% year to date 2012. Factored into the performance evaluation is an expense ratio of 0.35% (very low).

The fund's risk rating is currently B- (Good). It carries a beta of 1.29, meaning it is expected to move 12.9% for every 10% move in the market. Volatility, as measured by both the semi-deviation and a drawdown factor, is considered low. As of March 31, 2012, *iShares Cohen & Steers Realty Ma traded at a premium of .03% above its net asset value.

Diane Hsiung has been running the fund for 4 years and currently receives a manager quality ranking of 86 (0=worst, 99=best). If you desire only a moderate level of risk and strong performance, then this fund is an excellent option.

Data Date	Investment Rating	Net Assets ($Mil)	Price	Performance Rating/Pts	Total Return Y-T-D	Risk Rating/Pts
3-12	A-	2,643.50	76.64	A- / 9.2	10.00%	B- / 7.8
2011	C+	2,315.40	70.22	B / 7.8	-0.57%	C+ / 6.1
2010	C	2,212.70	65.72	B- / 7.1	29.14%	C- / 3.9
2009	E+	1,124.21	52.52	D- / 1.2	28.36%	C- / 3.9

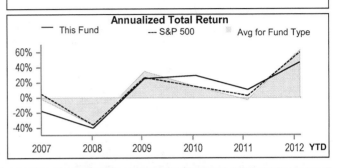

Annualized Total Return

*iShares Diversified Alternatives (ALT)   D+   Weak

Fund Family: BlackRock Fund Advisors
Fund Type: Global
Inception Date: October 6, 2009

Major Rating Factors:
Disappointing performance is the major factor driving the D+ (Weak) TheStreet.com Investment Rating for *iShares Diversified Alternatives. The fund currently has a performance rating of D- (Weak) based on an annualized return of 0.00% over the last three years and a total return of -0.06% year to date 2012. Factored into the performance evaluation is an expense ratio of 1.01% (low).

The fund's risk rating is currently B+ (Good). It carries a beta of 0.00, meaning the fund's expected move will be 0.0% for every 10% move in the market. Volatility, as measured by both the semi-deviation and a drawdown factor, is considered very low. As of March 31, 2012, *iShares Diversified Alternatives traded at a discount of .12% below its net asset value, which is worse than its one-year historical average discount of .14%.

Alan Mason currently receives a manager quality ranking of 28 (0=worst, 99=best). This fund offers only a moderate level of risk but investors looking for strong performance are still waiting.

Data Date	Investment Rating	Net Assets ($Mil)	Price	Performance Rating/Pts	Total Return Y-T-D	Risk Rating/Pts
3-12	D+	73.04	48.72	D- / 1.0	-0.06%	B+ / 9.5
2011	C-	87.90	48.75	D- / 1.5	0.39%	B+ / 9.5
2010	C+	110.90	50.55	C- / 3.3	1.61%	B+ / 9.0

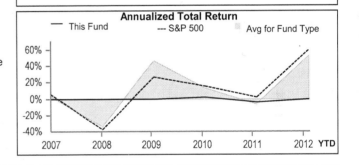

Annualized Total Return

*iShares DJ Intl Select Dividend (IDV)   C+   Fair

Fund Family: BlackRock Fund Advisors
Fund Type: Foreign
Inception Date: June 11, 2007

Major Rating Factors: Middle of the road best describes *iShares DJ Intl Select Dividend whose TheStreet.com Investment Rating is currently a C+ (Fair). The fund currently has a performance rating of C+ (Fair) based on an annualized return of 24.00% over the last three years and a total return of 10.67% year to date 2012. Factored into the performance evaluation is an expense ratio of 0.50% (very low).

The fund's risk rating is currently B- (Good). It carries a beta of 1.13, meaning it is expected to move 11.3% for every 10% move in the market. Volatility, as measured by both the semi-deviation and a drawdown factor, is considered low. As of March 31, 2012, *iShares DJ Intl Select Dividend traded at a premium of .59% above its net asset value, which is worse than its one-year historical average premium of .32%.

Diane Hsiung has been running the fund for 4 years and currently receives a manager quality ranking of 77 (0=worst, 99=best). If you desire an average level of risk, then this fund may be an option.

Data Date	Investment Rating	Net Assets ($Mil)	Price	Performance Rating/Pts	Total Return Y-T-D	Risk Rating/Pts
3-12	C+	897.51	32.60	C+ / 5.8	10.67%	B- / 7.7
2011	C+	698.80	29.69	C+ / 5.6	-0.77%	B- / 7.7
2010	D	347.20	33.64	D+ / 2.6	11.82%	C / 4.9
2009	A-	52.03	31.42	A / 9.4	57.77%	C / 4.9

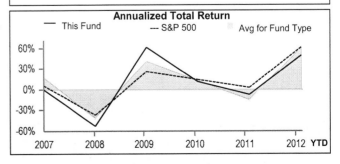

Annualized Total Return

*iShares DJ Select Dividend (DVY)

B-　　**Good**

Fund Family: BlackRock Fund Advisors
Fund Type: Income
Inception Date: November 3, 2003

Major Rating Factors: *iShares DJ Select Dividend receives a TheStreet.com Investment Rating of B- (Good). The fund currently has a performance rating of C+ (Fair) based on an annualized return of 23.25% over the last three years and a total return of 5.01% year to date 2012. Factored into the performance evaluation is an expense ratio of 0.40% (very low).

The fund's risk rating is currently B+ (Good). It carries a beta of 0.78, meaning the fund's expected move will be 7.8% for every 10% move in the market. Volatility, as measured by both the semi-deviation and a drawdown factor, is considered very low. As of March 31, 2012, *iShares DJ Select Dividend traded at a price exactly equal to its net asset value, which is better than its one-year historical average premium of .02%.

Diane Hsiung has been running the fund for 4 years and currently receives a manager quality ranking of 79 (0=worst, 99=best). If you desire an average level of risk, then this fund may be an option.

Data Date	Investment Rating	Net Assets ($Mil)	Price	Performance Rating/Pts	Total Return Y-T-D	Risk Rating/Pts
3-12	B-	10,119.48	55.96	C+ / 6.2	5.01%	B+ / 9.0
2011	C+	9,548.00	53.77	C+ / 5.8	-0.17%	B- / 7.6
2010	C-	6,011.90	49.86	C- / 3.3	17.79%	C+ / 5.7
2009	D-	2,961.00	43.91	D- / 1.1	9.19%	C / 5.4

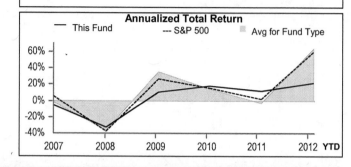

*iShares DJ Transportation (IYT)

C　　**Fair**

Fund Family: BlackRock Fund Advisors
Fund Type: Income
Inception Date: October 6, 2003

Major Rating Factors: Middle of the road best describes *iShares DJ Transportation whose TheStreet.com Investment Rating is currently a C (Fair). The fund currently has a performance rating of C+ (Fair) based on an annualized return of 22.57% over the last three years and a total return of 4.91% year to date 2012. Factored into the performance evaluation is an expense ratio of 0.47% (very low).

The fund's risk rating is currently B- (Good). It carries a beta of 1.27, meaning it is expected to move 12.7% for every 10% move in the market. Volatility, as measured by both the semi-deviation and a drawdown factor, is considered low. As of March 31, 2012, *iShares DJ Transportation traded at a premium of .04% above its net asset value, which is worse than its one-year historical average discount of .01%.

Diane Hsiung has been running the fund for 4 years and currently receives a manager quality ranking of 29 (0=worst, 99=best). If you desire an average level of risk, then this fund may be an option.

Data Date	Investment Rating	Net Assets ($Mil)	Price	Performance Rating/Pts	Total Return Y-T-D	Risk Rating/Pts
3-12	C	446.68	93.69	C+ / 5.6	4.91%	B- / 7.7
2011	C	411.70	89.47	C / 5.0	0.94%	B- / 7.2
2010	B+	673.20	92.32	B / 8.0	26.74%	C / 5.5
2009	C-	261.45	73.82	C- / 3.0	15.27%	C+ / 5.9

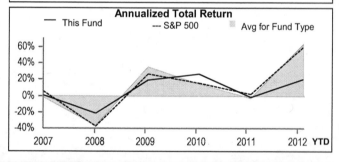

*iShares DJ US Aerospace & Def Id (ITA)

B-　　**Good**

Fund Family: BlackRock Fund Advisors
Fund Type: Income
Inception Date: May 1, 2006

Major Rating Factors: *iShares DJ US Aerospace & Def Id receives a TheStreet.com Investment Rating of B- (Good). The fund currently has a performance rating of C+ (Fair) based on an annualized return of 25.50% over the last three years and a total return of 9.99% year to date 2012. Factored into the performance evaluation is an expense ratio of 0.47% (very low).

The fund's risk rating is currently B (Good). It carries a beta of 1.12, meaning it is expected to move 11.2% for every 10% move in the market. Volatility, as measured by both the semi-deviation and a drawdown factor, is considered low. As of March 31, 2012, *iShares DJ US Aerospace & Def Id traded at a premium of .06% above its net asset value, which is worse than its one-year historical average discount of .02%.

Diane Hsiung has been running the fund for 4 years and currently receives a manager quality ranking of 50 (0=worst, 99=best). If you desire an average level of risk, then this fund may be an option.

Data Date	Investment Rating	Net Assets ($Mil)	Price	Performance Rating/Pts	Total Return Y-T-D	Risk Rating/Pts
3-12	B-	110.25	67.13	C+ / 6.9	9.99%	B / 8.1
2011	C	106.90	61.19	C / 5.2	1.08%	B- / 7.5
2010	D+	147.10	58.85	C- / 3.4	16.60%	C / 5.5
2009	C-	132.14	50.96	C- / 3.7	20.90%	C+ / 5.7

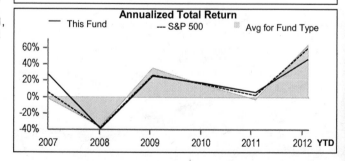

*iShares DJ US Basic Material (IYM)   C   Fair

Fund Family: BlackRock Fund Advisors
Fund Type: Income
Inception Date: June 12, 2000

Major Rating Factors: Middle of the road best describes *iShares DJ US Basic Material whose TheStreet.com Investment Rating is currently a C (Fair). The fund currently has a performance rating of C+ (Fair) based on an annualized return of 23.91% over the last three years and a total return of 9.75% year to date 2012. Factored into the performance evaluation is an expense ratio of 0.47% (very low).

    The fund's risk rating is currently B- (Good). It carries a beta of 1.63, meaning it is expected to move 16.3% for every 10% move in the market. Volatility, as measured by both the semi-deviation and a drawdown factor, is considered low. As of March 31, 2012, *iShares DJ US Basic Material traded at a discount of .07% below its net asset value.

    Diane Hsiung has been running the fund for 4 years and currently receives a manager quality ranking of 16 (0=worst, 99=best). If you desire an average level of risk, then this fund may be an option.

Data Date	Investment Rating	Net Assets ($Mil)	Price	Performance Rating/Pts	Total Return Y-T-D	Risk Rating/Pts
3-12	C	656.09	70.36	C+ / 5.7	9.75%	B- / 7.0
2011	C+	530.50	64.30	C+ / 6.4	3.45%	C+ / 6.9
2010	C+	1,114.50	77.46	B- / 7.5	31.02%	C / 4.7
2009	C+	402.11	59.91	B- / 7.1	57.73%	C / 5.1

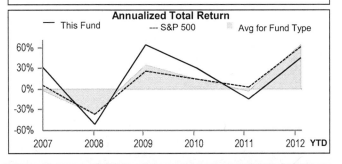

*iShares DJ US Broker-Dealers Idx (IAI)   D   Weak

Fund Family: BlackRock Fund Advisors
Fund Type: Financial Services
Inception Date: May 1, 2006

Major Rating Factors:
Disappointing performance is the major factor driving the D (Weak) TheStreet.com Investment Rating for *iShares DJ US Broker-Dealers Idx. The fund currently has a performance rating of D (Weak) based on an annualized return of 6.50% over the last three years and a total return of 21.68% year to date 2012. Factored into the performance evaluation is an expense ratio of 0.47% (very low).

    The fund's risk rating is currently B- (Good). It carries a beta of 0.98, meaning that its performance tracks fairly well with that of the overall stock market. Volatility, as measured by both the semi-deviation and a drawdown factor, is considered low. As of March 31, 2012, *iShares DJ US Broker-Dealers Idx traded at a premium of .12% above its net asset value, which is worse than its one-year historical average premium of .01%.

    Diane Hsiung has been running the fund for 4 years and currently receives a manager quality ranking of 13 (0=worst, 99=best). This fund offers only a moderate level of risk but investors looking for strong performance are still waiting.

Data Date	Investment Rating	Net Assets ($Mil)	Price	Performance Rating/Pts	Total Return Y-T-D	Risk Rating/Pts
3-12	D	65.52	25.36	D / 2.1	21.68%	B- / 7.0
2011	D	52.20	20.92	D / 1.9	2.20%	C+ / 6.9
2010	D-	100.10	29.02	E+ / 0.8	4.89%	C / 4.7
2009	D-	138.16	28.13	E+ / 0.7	39.55%	C / 4.9

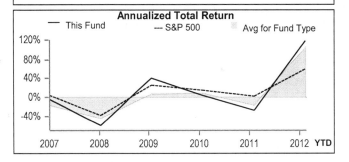

*iShares DJ US Consumer Goods (IYK)   B-   Good

Fund Family: BlackRock Fund Advisors
Fund Type: Income
Inception Date: June 12, 2000

Major Rating Factors: *iShares DJ US Consumer Goods receives a TheStreet.com Investment Rating of B- (Good). The fund currently has a performance rating of C+ (Fair) based on an annualized return of 22.71% over the last three years and a total return of 8.68% year to date 2012. Factored into the performance evaluation is an expense ratio of 0.47% (very low).

    The fund's risk rating is currently B (Good). It carries a beta of 0.73, meaning the fund's expected move will be 7.3% for every 10% move in the market. Volatility, as measured by both the semi-deviation and a drawdown factor, is considered low. As of March 31, 2012, *iShares DJ US Consumer Goods traded at a premium of .03% above its net asset value, which is worse than its one-year historical average premium of .01%.

    Diane Hsiung has been running the fund for 4 years and currently receives a manager quality ranking of 79 (0=worst, 99=best). If you desire an average level of risk, then this fund may be an option.

Data Date	Investment Rating	Net Assets ($Mil)	Price	Performance Rating/Pts	Total Return Y-T-D	Risk Rating/Pts
3-12	B-	393.76	74.12	C+ / 6.3	8.68%	B / 8.9
2011	B-	359.20	68.48	C+ / 6.1	0.26%	B / 8.5
2010	C+	306.70	64.55	C+ / 6.4	18.99%	C+ / 6.8
2009	C	308.32	55.53	C- / 3.4	20.43%	C+ / 6.8

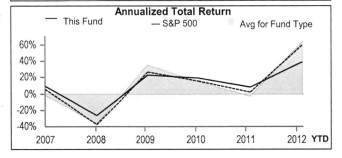

*iShares DJ US Consumer Services (IYC)   B   Good

Fund Family: BlackRock Fund Advisors
Fund Type: Income
Inception Date: June 12, 2000

Major Rating Factors: Strong performance is the major factor driving the B (Good) TheStreet.com Investment Rating for *iShares DJ US Consumer Services. The fund currently has a performance rating of B- (Good) based on an annualized return of 25.76% over the last three years and a total return of 13.70% year to date 2012. Factored into the performance evaluation is an expense ratio of 0.47% (very low).

The fund's risk rating is currently B (Good). It carries a beta of 0.99, meaning that its performance tracks fairly well with that of the overall stock market. Volatility, as measured by both the semi-deviation and a drawdown factor, is considered low. As of March 31, 2012, *iShares DJ US Consumer Services traded at a discount of .02% below its net asset value.

Diane Hsiung has been running the fund for 4 years and currently receives a manager quality ranking of 71 (0=worst, 99=best). If you desire only a moderate level of risk and strong performance, then this fund is an excellent option.

Data Date	Investment Rating	Net Assets ($Mil)	Price	Performance Rating/Pts	Total Return Y-T-D	Risk Rating/Pts
3-12	B	284.22	80.99	B- / 7.5	13.70%	B / 8.4
2011	B-	260.40	71.41	B- / 7.1	1.46%	B / 8.1
2010	B+	209.60	67.66	B- / 7.4	23.26%	C+ / 6.1
2009	C-	178.16	55.49	D+ / 2.6	28.24%	C+ / 6.2

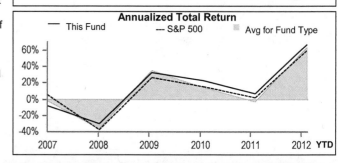

*iShares DJ US Energy (IYE)   C-   Fair

Fund Family: BlackRock Fund Advisors
Fund Type: Energy/Natural Resources
Inception Date: June 12, 2000

Major Rating Factors: Middle of the road best describes *iShares DJ US Energy whose TheStreet.com Investment Rating is currently a C- (Fair). The fund currently has a performance rating of C- (Fair) based on an annualized return of 16.58% over the last three years and a total return of 4.61% year to date 2012. Factored into the performance evaluation is an expense ratio of 0.47% (very low).

The fund's risk rating is currently B- (Good). It carries a beta of 1.02, meaning that its performance tracks fairly well with that of the overall stock market. Volatility, as measured by both the semi-deviation and a drawdown factor, is considered low. As of March 31, 2012, *iShares DJ US Energy traded at a discount of .05% below its net asset value.

Diane Hsiung has been running the fund for 4 years and currently receives a manager quality ranking of 44 (0=worst, 99=best). If you desire an average level of risk, then this fund may be an option.

Data Date	Investment Rating	Net Assets ($Mil)	Price	Performance Rating/Pts	Total Return Y-T-D	Risk Rating/Pts
3-12	C-	1,028.55	41.52	C- / 3.8	4.61%	B- / 7.6
2011	C	945.90	39.83	C / 5.0	1.78%	B- / 7.2
2010	D	806.00	38.96	C / 4.3	19.00%	D+ / 2.8
2009	D	597.62	33.24	C- / 3.9	13.74%	C- / 3.0

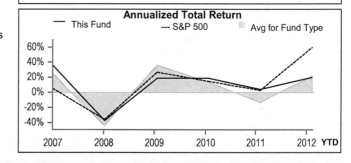

*iShares DJ US Financial Sector (IYF)   C   Fair

Fund Family: BlackRock Fund Advisors
Fund Type: Financial Services
Inception Date: May 22, 2000

Major Rating Factors: Middle of the road best describes *iShares DJ US Financial Sector whose TheStreet.com Investment Rating is currently a C (Fair). The fund currently has a performance rating of C (Fair) based on an annualized return of 19.21% over the last three years and a total return of 19.66% year to date 2012. Factored into the performance evaluation is an expense ratio of 0.47% (very low).

The fund's risk rating is currently B- (Good). It carries a beta of 1.01, meaning that its performance tracks fairly well with that of the overall stock market. Volatility, as measured by both the semi-deviation and a drawdown factor, is considered low. As of March 31, 2012, *iShares DJ US Financial Sector traded at a discount of .03% below its net asset value, which is better than its one-year historical average discount of .01%.

Diane Hsiung has been running the fund for 4 years and currently receives a manager quality ranking of 44 (0=worst, 99=best). If you desire an average level of risk, then this fund may be an option.

Data Date	Investment Rating	Net Assets ($Mil)	Price	Performance Rating/Pts	Total Return Y-T-D	Risk Rating/Pts
3-12	C	443.51	58.52	C / 5.3	19.66%	B- / 7.6
2011	D+	380.20	49.05	C- / 3.1	2.55%	C+ / 6.9
2010	D-	476.70	57.48	D- / 1.0	12.23%	C / 4.5
2009	E+	504.16	51.78	E+ / 0.6	16.17%	C / 4.5

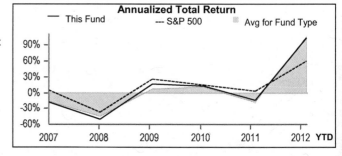

*iShares DJ US Financial Services (IYG)

C-   **Fair**

Fund Family: BlackRock Fund Advisors
Fund Type: Financial Services
Inception Date: June 12, 2000

Major Rating Factors: Middle of the road best describes *iShares DJ US Financial Services whose TheStreet.com Investment Rating is currently a C- (Fair). The fund currently has a performance rating of C (Fair) based on an annualized return of 15.77% over the last three years and a total return of 26.70% year to date 2012. Factored into the performance evaluation is an expense ratio of 0.47% (very low).

The fund's risk rating is currently B- (Good). It carries a beta of 1.10, meaning it is expected to move 11.0% for every 10% move in the market. Volatility, as measured by both the semi-deviation and a drawdown factor, is considered low. As of March 31, 2012, *iShares DJ US Financial Services traded at a price exactly equal to its net asset value, which is better than its one-year historical average premium of .01%.

Diane Hsiung has been running the fund for 4 years and currently receives a manager quality ranking of 22 (0=worst, 99=best). If you desire an average level of risk, then this fund may be an option.

Data Date	Investment Rating	Net Assets ($Mil)	Price	Performance Rating/Pts	Total Return Y-T-D	Risk Rating/Pts
3-12	C-	208.49	57.22	C / 4.6	26.70%	B- / 7.2
2011	D	172.10	45.27	D / 2.2	4.02%	C+ / 6.8
2010	D-	221.50	57.57	E+ / 0.8	7.71%	C / 4.3
2009	E+	317.11	53.71	E / 0.5	14.53%	C / 4.3

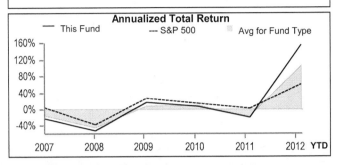

*iShares DJ US Health Care Provid (IHF)

B   **Good**

Fund Family: BlackRock Fund Advisors
Fund Type: Health
Inception Date: May 1, 2006

Major Rating Factors: Strong performance is the major factor driving the B (Good) TheStreet.com Investment Rating for *iShares DJ US Health Care Provid. The fund currently has a performance rating of B (Good) based on an annualized return of 28.62% over the last three years and a total return of 13.88% year to date 2012. Factored into the performance evaluation is an expense ratio of 0.47% (very low).

The fund's risk rating is currently B (Good). It carries a beta of 0.93, meaning that its performance tracks fairly well with that of the overall stock market. Volatility, as measured by both the semi-deviation and a drawdown factor, is considered low. As of March 31, 2012, *iShares DJ US Health Care Provid traded at a premium of .07% above its net asset value, which is worse than its one-year historical average discount of .01%.

Diane Hsiung has been running the fund for 4 years and currently receives a manager quality ranking of 78 (0=worst, 99=best). If you desire only a moderate level of risk and strong performance, then this fund is an excellent option.

Data Date	Investment Rating	Net Assets ($Mil)	Price	Performance Rating/Pts	Total Return Y-T-D	Risk Rating/Pts
3-12	B	236.23	66.88	B / 8.0	13.88%	B / 8.1
2011	B-	217.70	58.85	C+ / 6.9	3.64%	B- / 7.8
2010	D	110.40	53.87	D / 2.2	11.47%	C+ / 5.7
2009	C-	74.88	48.42	C- / 3.8	33.10%	C / 5.5

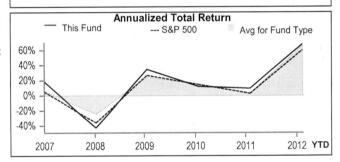

*iShares DJ US Healthcare (IYH)

C+   **Fair**

Fund Family: BlackRock Fund Advisors
Fund Type: Health
Inception Date: June 12, 2000

Major Rating Factors: Middle of the road best describes *iShares DJ US Healthcare whose TheStreet.com Investment Rating is currently a C+ (Fair). The fund currently has a performance rating of C (Fair) based on an annualized return of 18.87% over the last three years and a total return of 9.73% year to date 2012. Factored into the performance evaluation is an expense ratio of 0.47% (very low).

The fund's risk rating is currently B (Good). It carries a beta of 0.61, meaning the fund's expected move will be 6.1% for every 10% move in the market. Volatility, as measured by both the semi-deviation and a drawdown factor, is considered low. As of March 31, 2012, *iShares DJ US Healthcare traded at a discount of .01% below its net asset value, which is in line with its one-year historical average discount of .01%.

Diane Hsiung has been running the fund for 4 years and currently receives a manager quality ranking of 69 (0=worst, 99=best). If you desire an average level of risk, then this fund may be an option.

Data Date	Investment Rating	Net Assets ($Mil)	Price	Performance Rating/Pts	Total Return Y-T-D	Risk Rating/Pts
3-12	C+	617.85	78.20	C / 5.2	9.73%	B / 8.6
2011	C+	575.90	71.57	C / 5.0	1.17%	B / 8.2
2010	C-	552.10	65.37	D+ / 2.9	4.13%	B- / 7.0
2009	C	658.79	63.82	C- / 3.5	18.77%	C+ / 6.9

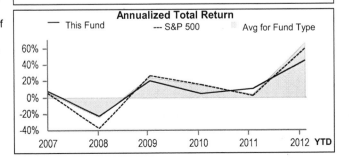

*iShares DJ US Home Cons Idx (ITB)   C   Fair

Fund Family: BlackRock Fund Advisors
Fund Type: Income
Inception Date: May 1, 2006

Major Rating Factors: Middle of the road best describes *iShares DJ US Home Cons Idx whose TheStreet.com Investment Rating is currently a C (Fair). The fund currently has a performance rating of C+ (Fair) based on an annualized return of 16.26% over the last three years and a total return of 24.05% year to date 2012. Factored into the performance evaluation is an expense ratio of 0.47% (very low).

The fund's risk rating is currently C+ (Fair). It carries a beta of 1.61, meaning it is expected to move 16.1% for every 10% move in the market. Volatility, as measured by both the semi-deviation and a drawdown factor, is considered low. As of March 31, 2012, *iShares DJ US Home Cons Idx traded at a premium of .07% above its net asset value, which is worse than its one-year historical average discount of .01%.

Diane Hsiung has been running the fund for 4 years and currently receives a manager quality ranking of 10 (0=worst, 99=best). If you desire an average level of risk, then this fund may be an option.

Data Date	Investment Rating	Net Assets ($Mil)	Price	Performance Rating/Pts	Total Return Y-T-D	Risk Rating/Pts
3-12	C	535.44	14.72	C+ / 6.0	24.05%	C+ / 6.5
2011	D+	374.60	11.88	C- / 3.6	4.88%	C+ / 6.4
2010	D	505.20	13.18	D+ / 2.4	10.43%	C / 4.5
2009	E	198.46	12.01	E / 0.5	20.18%	C- / 3.8

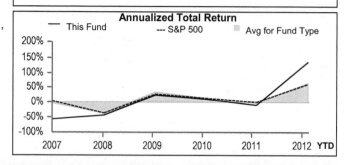

*iShares DJ US Index (IYY)   C+   Fair

Fund Family: BlackRock Fund Advisors
Fund Type: Income
Inception Date: June 12, 2000

Major Rating Factors: Middle of the road best describes *iShares DJ US Index whose TheStreet.com Investment Rating is currently a C+ (Fair). The fund currently has a performance rating of C+ (Fair) based on an annualized return of 21.72% over the last three years and a total return of 12.81% year to date 2012. Factored into the performance evaluation is an expense ratio of 0.20% (very low).

The fund's risk rating is currently B (Good). It carries a beta of 1.03, meaning that its performance tracks fairly well with that of the overall stock market. Volatility, as measured by both the semi-deviation and a drawdown factor, is considered low. As of March 31, 2012, *iShares DJ US Index traded at a discount of .01% below its net asset value, which is better than its one-year historical average premium of .04%.

Diane Hsiung has been running the fund for 4 years and currently receives a manager quality ranking of 45 (0=worst, 99=best). If you desire an average level of risk, then this fund may be an option.

Data Date	Investment Rating	Net Assets ($Mil)	Price	Performance Rating/Pts	Total Return Y-T-D	Risk Rating/Pts
3-12	C+	595.98	70.73	C+ / 6.0	12.81%	B / 8.1
2011	C+	582.20	62.95	C / 5.4	1.64%	B- / 7.9
2010	C	621.20	63.40	C / 4.4	16.50%	C+ / 5.9
2009	D+	487.85	55.39	D+ / 2.5	25.07%	C+ / 6.1

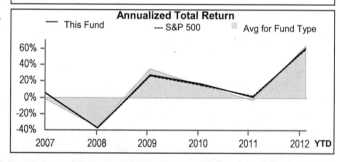

*iShares DJ US Industrial (IYJ)   C+   Fair

Fund Family: BlackRock Fund Advisors
Fund Type: Income
Inception Date: June 12, 2000

Major Rating Factors: Strong performance is the major factor driving the C+ (Fair) TheStreet.com Investment Rating for *iShares DJ US Industrial. The fund currently has a performance rating of B- (Good) based on an annualized return of 25.89% over the last three years and a total return of 12.58% year to date 2012. Factored into the performance evaluation is an expense ratio of 0.47% (very low).

The fund's risk rating is currently B- (Good). It carries a beta of 1.32, meaning it is expected to move 13.2% for every 10% move in the market. Volatility, as measured by both the semi-deviation and a drawdown factor, is considered low. As of March 31, 2012, *iShares DJ US Industrial traded at a price exactly equal to its net asset value.

Diane Hsiung has been running the fund for 4 years and currently receives a manager quality ranking of 32 (0=worst, 99=best). If you desire only a moderate level of risk and strong performance, then this fund is an excellent option.

Data Date	Investment Rating	Net Assets ($Mil)	Price	Performance Rating/Pts	Total Return Y-T-D	Risk Rating/Pts
3-12	C+	418.99	71.38	B- / 7.1	12.58%	B- / 7.8
2011	C	343.20	63.62	C+ / 5.6	2.14%	B- / 7.5
2010	C	369.30	65.40	C+ / 5.7	25.49%	C / 5.4
2009	D+	213.85	53.03	D+ / 2.5	21.44%	C+ / 5.7

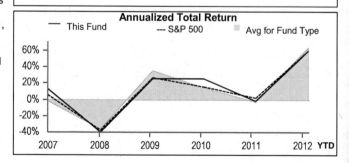

*iShares DJ US Insurance Idx (IAK)

C+ | Fair

Fund Family: BlackRock Fund Advisors
Fund Type: Income
Inception Date: May 1, 2006

Data Date	Investment Rating	Net Assets ($Mil)	Price	Performance Rating/Pts	Total Return Y-T-D	Risk Rating/Pts
3-12	C+	67.49	32.05	C+ / 6.1	12.53%	B / 8.0
2011	C-	59.80	28.57	C- / 3.7	1.48%	B- / 7.0
2010	D-	81.50	31.34	D- / 1.1	20.03%	C / 4.5
2009	E+	28.35	26.67	E+ / 0.7	12.63%	C / 4.6

Major Rating Factors: Middle of the road best describes *iShares DJ US Insurance Idx whose TheStreet.com Investment Rating is currently a C+ (Fair). The fund currently has a performance rating of C+ (Fair) based on an annualized return of 22.98% over the last three years and a total return of 12.53% year to date 2012. Factored into the performance evaluation is an expense ratio of 0.47% (very low).

The fund's risk rating is currently B (Good). It carries a beta of 1.25, meaning it is expected to move 12.5% for every 10% move in the market. Volatility, as measured by both the semi-deviation and a drawdown factor, is considered low. As of March 31, 2012, *iShares DJ US Insurance Idx traded at a premium of .16% above its net asset value, which is worse than its one-year historical average premium of .05%.

Diane Hsiung has been running the fund for 4 years and currently receives a manager quality ranking of 28 (0=worst, 99=best). If you desire an average level of risk, then this fund may be an option.

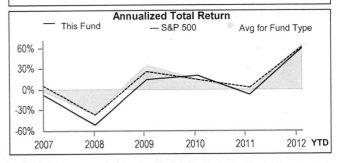

Annualized Total Return

*iShares DJ US Medical Devices Id (IHI)

C | Fair

Fund Family: BlackRock Fund Advisors
Fund Type: Health
Inception Date: May 1, 2006

Data Date	Investment Rating	Net Assets ($Mil)	Price	Performance Rating/Pts	Total Return Y-T-D	Risk Rating/Pts
3-12	C	327.16	67.84	C+ / 6.1	15.51%	B- / 7.2
2011	C	331.90	58.76	C / 5.3	1.14%	C+ / 6.9
2010	C-	338.80	58.91	C- / 3.7	11.35%	C+ / 5.6
2009	C	214.90	52.98	C / 5.1	35.04%	C+ / 5.7

Major Rating Factors: Middle of the road best describes *iShares DJ US Medical Devices Id whose TheStreet.com Investment Rating is currently a C (Fair). The fund currently has a performance rating of C+ (Fair) based on an annualized return of 22.68% over the last three years and a total return of 15.51% year to date 2012. Factored into the performance evaluation is an expense ratio of 0.47% (very low).

The fund's risk rating is currently B- (Good). It carries a beta of 0.92, meaning that its performance tracks fairly well with that of the overall stock market. Volatility, as measured by both the semi-deviation and a drawdown factor, is considered low. As of March 31, 2012, *iShares DJ US Medical Devices Id traded at a discount of .01% below its net asset value, which is worse than its one-year historical average discount of .02%.

Diane Hsiung has been running the fund for 4 years and currently receives a manager quality ranking of 54 (0=worst, 99=best). If you desire an average level of risk, then this fund may be an option.

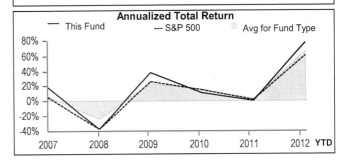

Annualized Total Return

*iShares DJ US Oil & Gas Exp & Pr (IEO)

C- | Fair

Fund Family: BlackRock Fund Advisors
Fund Type: Energy/Natural Resources
Inception Date: May 1, 2006

Data Date	Investment Rating	Net Assets ($Mil)	Price	Performance Rating/Pts	Total Return Y-T-D	Risk Rating/Pts
3-12	C-	402.77	65.79	C / 4.6	7.28%	B- / 7.1
2011	C	343.80	61.42	C+ / 6.0	3.79%	C+ / 6.9
2010	C	427.70	63.85	C / 5.5	18.64%	C / 4.9
2009	C	335.06	53.99	C / 5.5	33.25%	C / 4.9

Major Rating Factors: Middle of the road best describes *iShares DJ US Oil & Gas Exp & Pr whose TheStreet.com Investment Rating is currently a C- (Fair). The fund currently has a performance rating of C (Fair) based on an annualized return of 20.36% over the last three years and a total return of 7.28% year to date 2012. Factored into the performance evaluation is an expense ratio of 0.47% (very low).

The fund's risk rating is currently B- (Good). It carries a beta of 1.25, meaning it is expected to move 12.5% for every 10% move in the market. Volatility, as measured by both the semi-deviation and a drawdown factor, is considered low. As of March 31, 2012, *iShares DJ US Oil & Gas Exp & Pr traded at a discount of .02% below its net asset value.

Diane Hsiung has been running the fund for 4 years and currently receives a manager quality ranking of 45 (0=worst, 99=best). If you desire an average level of risk, then this fund may be an option.

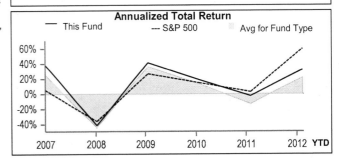

Annualized Total Return

*iShares DJ US Oil Equip & Svcs (IEZ)

C-   **Fair**

Fund Family: BlackRock Fund Advisors
Fund Type: Energy/Natural Resources
Inception Date: May 1, 2006

Major Rating Factors: Middle of the road best describes *iShares DJ US Oil Equip &
Svcs whose TheStreet.com Investment Rating is currently a C- (Fair). The fund
currently has a performance rating of C (Fair) based on an annualized return of
24.33% over the last three years and a total return of 3.15% year to date 2012.
Factored into the performance evaluation is an expense ratio of 0.47% (very low).

The fund's risk rating is currently C+ (Fair). It carries a beta of 1.51, meaning it is
expected to move 15.1% for every 10% move in the market. Volatility, as measured
by both the semi-deviation and a drawdown factor, is considered low. As of March 31,
2012, *iShares DJ US Oil Equip & Svcs traded at a discount of .09% below its net
asset value.

Diane Hsiung has been running the fund for 4 years and currently receives a
manager quality ranking of 38 (0=worst, 99=best). If you desire an average level of
risk, then this fund may be an option.

Data Date	Investment Rating	Net Assets ($Mil)	Price	Performance Rating/Pts	Total Return Y-T-D	Risk Rating/Pts
3-12	C-	540.91	53.50	C / 5.2	3.15%	C+ / 6.4
2011	C+	417.80	51.92	B- / 7.1	2.25%	C+ / 6.3
2010	C-	495.60	56.35	C+ / 5.9	31.77%	C- / 4.2
2009	C	194.24	43.02	C+ / 6.3	52.96%	C / 4.6

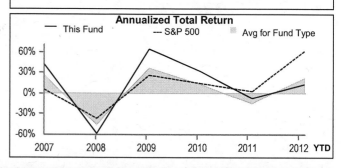

Annualized Total Return
— This Fund   --- S&P 500   ▨ Avg for Fund Type

*iShares DJ US Pharmaceuticals (IHE)

B+   **Good**

Fund Family: BlackRock Fund Advisors
Fund Type: Health
Inception Date: May 1, 2006

Major Rating Factors: Strong performance is the major factor driving the B+ (Good)
TheStreet.com Investment Rating for *iShares DJ US Pharmaceuticals. The fund
currently has a performance rating of B (Good) based on an annualized return of
27.75% over the last three years and a total return of 9.04% year to date 2012.
Factored into the performance evaluation is an expense ratio of 0.47% (very low).

The fund's risk rating is currently B (Good). It carries a beta of 0.54, meaning the
fund's expected move will be 5.4% for every 10% move in the market. Volatility, as
measured by both the semi-deviation and a drawdown factor, is considered low. As of
March 31, 2012, *iShares DJ US Pharmaceuticals traded at a discount of .04% below
its net asset value, which is better than its one-year historical average premium
of .01%.

Diane Hsiung has been running the fund for 4 years and currently receives a
manager quality ranking of 89 (0=worst, 99=best). If you desire only a moderate level
of risk and strong performance, then this fund is an excellent option.

Data Date	Investment Rating	Net Assets ($Mil)	Price	Performance Rating/Pts	Total Return Y-T-D	Risk Rating/Pts
3-12	B+	375.38	83.06	B / 8.1	9.04%	B / 8.1
2011	B-	344.10	76.45	B / 7.6	-0.16%	B- / 7.3
2010	B+	159.80	64.04	B- / 7.1	12.72%	C+ / 6.7
2009	C+	98.68	57.66	C / 5.5	28.19%	B- / 7.0

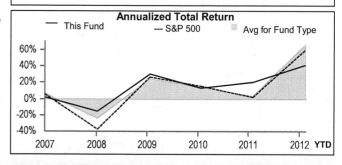

Annualized Total Return
— This Fund   --- S&P 500   ▨ Avg for Fund Type

*iShares DJ US Real Estate (IYR)

B+   **Good**

Fund Family: BlackRock Fund Advisors
Fund Type: Income
Inception Date: June 12, 2000

Major Rating Factors: Strong performance is the major factor driving the B+ (Good)
TheStreet.com Investment Rating for *iShares DJ US Real Estate. The fund currently
has a performance rating of B+ (Good) based on an annualized return of 33.76% over
the last three years and a total return of 10.60% year to date 2012. Factored into the
performance evaluation is an expense ratio of 0.47% (very low).

The fund's risk rating is currently B- (Good). It carries a beta of 1.23, meaning it is
expected to move 12.3% for every 10% move in the market. Volatility, as measured
by both the semi-deviation and a drawdown factor, is considered low. As of March 31,
2012, *iShares DJ US Real Estate traded at a price exactly equal to its net asset
value, which is better than its one-year historical average premium of .01%.

Diane Hsiung has been running the fund for 4 years and currently receives a
manager quality ranking of 82 (0=worst, 99=best). If you desire only a moderate level
of risk and strong performance, then this fund is an excellent option.

Data Date	Investment Rating	Net Assets ($Mil)	Price	Performance Rating/Pts	Total Return Y-T-D	Risk Rating/Pts
3-12	B+	3,704.01	62.30	B+ / 8.8	10.60%	B- / 7.9
2011	C+	3,294.80	56.81	B- / 7.4	0.04%	C+ / 6.6
2010	C+	3,080.10	55.96	B- / 7.1	26.59%	C / 4.3
2009	D-	1,721.08	45.92	D- / 1.5	34.13%	C- / 3.9

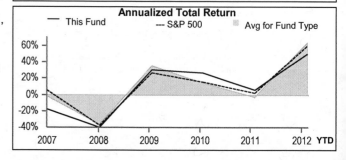

Annualized Total Return
— This Fund   --- S&P 500   ▨ Avg for Fund Type

*iShares DJ US Regional Banks (IAT)

C-   **Fair**

Fund Family: BlackRock Fund Advisors
Fund Type: Financial Services
Inception Date: May 1, 2006

Major Rating Factors: Middle of the road best describes *iShares DJ US Regional Banks whose TheStreet.com Investment Rating is currently a C- (Fair). The fund currently has a performance rating of C (Fair) based on an annualized return of 15.32% over the last three years and a total return of 17.52% year to date 2012. Factored into the performance evaluation is an expense ratio of 0.47% (very low).

The fund's risk rating is currently B- (Good). It carries a beta of 0.91, meaning that its performance tracks fairly well with that of the overall stock market. Volatility, as measured by both the semi-deviation and a drawdown factor, is considered low. As of March 31, 2012, *iShares DJ US Regional Banks traded at a premium of .08% above its net asset value, which is worse than its one-year historical average premium of .02%.

Diane Hsiung has been running the fund for 4 years and currently receives a manager quality ranking of 32 (0=worst, 99=best). If you desire an average level of risk, then this fund may be an option.

Data Date	Investment Rating	Net Assets ($Mil)	Price	Performance Rating/Pts	Total Return Y-T-D	Risk Rating/Pts
3-12	C-	113.68	24.80	C / 4.4	17.52%	B- / 7.4
2011	D+	95.10	21.16	D+ / 2.4	4.25%	C+ / 6.9
2010	D	135.90	24.74	D / 1.6	20.25%	C / 4.7
2009	E	121.02	20.82	E / 0.5	-11.00%	C- / 3.8

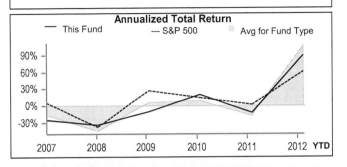

Annualized Total Return

*iShares DJ US Technology (IYW)

B-   **Good**

Fund Family: BlackRock Fund Advisors
Fund Type: Growth
Inception Date: May 15, 2000

Major Rating Factors: Strong performance is the major factor driving the B- (Good) TheStreet.com Investment Rating for *iShares DJ US Technology. The fund currently has a performance rating of B (Good) based on an annualized return of 25.79% over the last three years and a total return of 21.93% year to date 2012. Factored into the performance evaluation is an expense ratio of 0.47% (very low).

The fund's risk rating is currently B- (Good). It carries a beta of 1.11, meaning it is expected to move 11.1% for every 10% move in the market. Volatility, as measured by both the semi-deviation and a drawdown factor, is considered low. As of March 31, 2012, *iShares DJ US Technology traded at a premium of .04% above its net asset value.

Diane Hsiung has been running the fund for 4 years and currently receives a manager quality ranking of 58 (0=worst, 99=best). If you desire only a moderate level of risk and strong performance, then this fund is an excellent option.

Data Date	Investment Rating	Net Assets ($Mil)	Price	Performance Rating/Pts	Total Return Y-T-D	Risk Rating/Pts
3-12	B-	1,575.65	77.81	B / 7.9	21.93%	B- / 7.4
2011	C+	1,300.00	63.90	B- / 7.1	2.77%	B- / 7.3
2010	C+	1,451.40	64.38	C+ / 6.3	12.42%	C+ / 5.6
2009	C+	826.01	57.54	C+ / 6.6	57.55%	C+ / 5.6

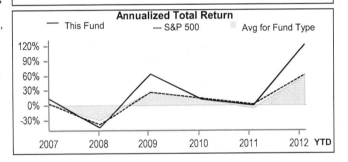

Annualized Total Return

*iShares DJ US Telecommunications (IYZ)

C-   **Fair**

Fund Family: BlackRock Fund Advisors
Fund Type: Income
Inception Date: May 22, 2000

Major Rating Factors:
Disappointing performance is the major factor driving the C- (Fair) TheStreet.com Investment Rating for *iShares DJ US Telecommunications. The fund currently has a performance rating of D+ (Weak) based on an annualized return of 12.43% over the last three years and a total return of 6.22% year to date 2012. Factored into the performance evaluation is an expense ratio of 0.47% (very low).

The fund's risk rating is currently B (Good). It carries a beta of 0.84, meaning the fund's expected move will be 8.4% for every 10% move in the market. Volatility, as measured by both the semi-deviation and a drawdown factor, is considered low. As of March 31, 2012, *iShares DJ US Telecommunications traded at a discount of .05% below its net asset value, which is better than its one-year historical average premium of .01%.

Diane Hsiung has been running the fund for 4 years and currently receives a manager quality ranking of 27 (0=worst, 99=best). This fund offers only a moderate level of risk but investors looking for strong performance are still waiting.

Data Date	Investment Rating	Net Assets ($Mil)	Price	Performance Rating/Pts	Total Return Y-T-D	Risk Rating/Pts
3-12	C-	572.57	22.20	D+ / 2.8	6.22%	B / 8.2
2011	C-	512.30	21.00	C- / 3.5	-0.57%	B / 8.1
2010	C-	761.10	23.37	C- / 3.8	20.72%	C+ / 6.1
2009	D-	531.48	20.02	D- / 1.4	22.35%	C / 5.4

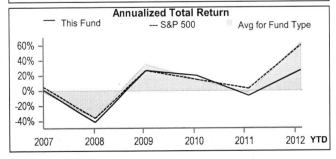

Annualized Total Return

*iShares DJ US Utilities (IDU)

C   Fair

Fund Family: BlackRock Fund Advisors
Fund Type: Utilities
Inception Date: June 12, 2000

Major Rating Factors: Middle of the road best describes *iShares DJ US Utilities whose TheStreet.com Investment Rating is currently a C (Fair). The fund currently has a performance rating of C- (Fair) based on an annualized return of 15.72% over the last three years and a total return of -1.56% year to date 2012. Factored into the performance evaluation is an expense ratio of 0.47% (very low).

The fund's risk rating is currently B+ (Good). It carries a beta of 0.94, meaning that its performance tracks fairly well with that of the overall stock market. Volatility, as measured by both the semi-deviation and a drawdown factor, is considered very low. As of March 31, 2012, *iShares DJ US Utilities traded at a discount of .03% below its net asset value, which is better than its one-year historical average premium of .01%.

Diane Hsiung has been running the fund for 4 years and currently receives a manager quality ranking of 51 (0=worst, 99=best). If you desire an average level of risk, then this fund may be an option.

Data Date	Investment Rating	Net Assets ($Mil)	Price	Performance Rating/Pts	Total Return Y-T-D	Risk Rating/Pts
3-12	C	674.56	86.16	C- / 3.7	-1.56%	B+ / 9.2
2011	C+	772.40	88.32	C / 4.9	-2.59%	B / 8.6
2010	D+	497.30	77.10	D / 1.6	7.21%	C+ / 6.6
2009	C-	405.86	74.79	D / 2.2	10.08%	C+ / 6.7

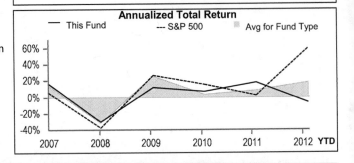

*iShares FTSE China 25 (FXI)

D   Weak

Fund Family: BlackRock Fund Advisors
Fund Type: Foreign
Inception Date: October 5, 2004

Major Rating Factors:
Disappointing performance is the major factor driving the D (Weak) TheStreet.com Investment Rating for *iShares FTSE China 25. The fund currently has a performance rating of D (Weak) based on an annualized return of 7.49% over the last three years and a total return of 5.15% year to date 2012. Factored into the performance evaluation is an expense ratio of 0.72% (very low).

The fund's risk rating is currently C+ (Fair). It carries a beta of 0.94, meaning that its performance tracks fairly well with that of the overall stock market. Volatility, as measured by both the semi-deviation and a drawdown factor, is considered low. As of March 31, 2012, *iShares FTSE China 25 traded at a discount of .62% below its net asset value, which is better than its one-year historical average premium of .01%.

Diane Hsiung has been running the fund for 4 years and currently receives a manager quality ranking of 22 (0=worst, 99=best). This fund offers only a moderate level of risk but investors looking for strong performance are still waiting.

Data Date	Investment Rating	Net Assets ($Mil)	Price	Performance Rating/Pts	Total Return Y-T-D	Risk Rating/Pts
3-12	D	7,047.15	36.67	D / 1.8	5.15%	C+ / 6.7
2011	D+	5,838.20	34.87	C- / 3.2	0.86%	C+ / 6.8
2010	E	8,139.90	43.09	D- / 1.3	3.51%	D- / 1.5
2009	D	11,300.67	42.26	C+ / 6.0	37.72%	D / 1.7

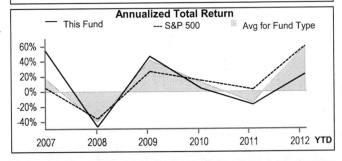

*iShares FTSE China Index (FCHI)

D   Weak

Fund Family: BlackRock Fund Advisors
Fund Type: Foreign
Inception Date: June 24, 2008

Major Rating Factors:
Disappointing performance is the major factor driving the D (Weak) TheStreet.com Investment Rating for *iShares FTSE China Index. The fund currently has a performance rating of D (Weak) based on an annualized return of 9.55% over the last three years and a total return of 5.70% year to date 2012. Factored into the performance evaluation is an expense ratio of 0.72% (very low).

The fund's risk rating is currently C+ (Fair). It carries a beta of 0.91, meaning that its performance tracks fairly well with that of the overall stock market. Volatility, as measured by both the semi-deviation and a drawdown factor, is considered low. As of March 31, 2012, *iShares FTSE China Index traded at a discount of 1.49% below its net asset value, which is better than its one-year historical average discount of .13%.

Diane Hsiung has been running the fund for 4 years and currently receives a manager quality ranking of 27 (0=worst, 99=best). This fund offers only a moderate level of risk but investors looking for strong performance are still waiting.

Data Date	Investment Rating	Net Assets ($Mil)	Price	Performance Rating/Pts	Total Return Y-T-D	Risk Rating/Pts
3-12	D	39.05	43.75	D / 2.2	5.70%	C+ / 6.8
2011	C-	37.30	41.39	C- / 3.4	0.90%	B- / 7.0
2010	B	56.60	51.20	B / 7.6	6.88%	C / 5.2
2009	B+	42.71	48.81	B+ / 8.6	39.80%	C / 5.2

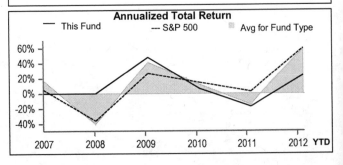

*iShares FTSE Dev Sm Cap ex-North (IFSM)   C   Fair

Fund Family: BlackRock Fund Advisors
Fund Type: Foreign
Inception Date: November 12, 2007

Data Date	Investment Rating	Net Assets ($Mil)	Price	Performance Rating/Pts	Total Return Y-T-D	Risk Rating/Pts
3-12	C	35.68	35.54	C / 4.6	16.46%	B- / 7.7
2011	C-	30.70	30.52	C- / 3.4	0.43%	B- / 7.7
2010	C-	38.70	38.69	C- / 4.1	20.80%	C / 5.4
2009	A-	23.33	32.89	B+ / 8.8	40.76%	C / 5.4

Major Rating Factors: Middle of the road best describes *iShares FTSE Dev Sm Cap ex-North whose TheStreet.com Investment Rating is currently a C (Fair). The fund currently has a performance rating of C (Fair) based on an annualized return of 19.84% over the last three years and a total return of 16.46% year to date 2012. Factored into the performance evaluation is an expense ratio of 0.50% (very low).

The fund's risk rating is currently B- (Good). It carries a beta of 1.10, meaning it is expected to move 11.0% for every 10% move in the market. Volatility, as measured by both the semi-deviation and a drawdown factor, is considered low. As of March 31, 2012, *iShares FTSE Dev Sm Cap ex-North traded at a premium of .42% above its net asset value, which is worse than its one-year historical average discount of .26%.

Diane Hsiung has been running the fund for 4 years and currently receives a manager quality ranking of 65 (0=worst, 99=best). If you desire an average level of risk, then this fund may be an option.

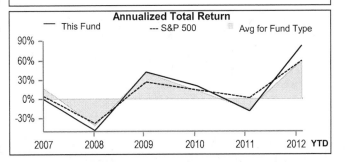

*iShares FTSE EPRA/NAREIT Asia In (IFAS)   C-   Fair

Fund Family: BlackRock Fund Advisors
Fund Type: Growth and Income
Inception Date: November 12, 2007

Data Date	Investment Rating	Net Assets ($Mil)	Price	Performance Rating/Pts	Total Return Y-T-D	Risk Rating/Pts
3-12	C-	23.89	28.25	C- / 4.2	17.93%	B- / 7.3
2011	D+	19.60	24.15	D+ / 2.8	2.19%	B- / 7.1
2010	D-	25.40	31.86	D / 2.0	16.32%	C- / 4.2
2009	C+	10.31	28.92	B+ / 8.4	37.63%	C- / 4.2

Major Rating Factors: Middle of the road best describes *iShares FTSE EPRA/NAREIT Asia In whose TheStreet.com Investment Rating is currently a C- (Fair). The fund currently has a performance rating of C- (Fair) based on an annualized return of 17.27% over the last three years and a total return of 17.93% year to date 2012. Factored into the performance evaluation is an expense ratio of 0.48% (very low).

The fund's risk rating is currently B- (Good). It carries a beta of 1.26, meaning it is expected to move 12.6% for every 10% move in the market. Volatility, as measured by both the semi-deviation and a drawdown factor, is considered low. As of March 31, 2012, *iShares FTSE EPRA/NAREIT Asia In traded at a premium of .04% above its net asset value, which is worse than its one-year historical average discount of .28%.

Diane Hsiung has been running the fund for 4 years and currently receives a manager quality ranking of 18 (0=worst, 99=best). If you desire an average level of risk, then this fund may be an option.

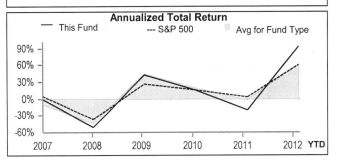

*iShares FTSE EPRA/NAREIT Dev RE (IFGL)   D+   Weak

Fund Family: BlackRock Fund Advisors
Fund Type: Growth and Income
Inception Date: November 12, 2007

Data Date	Investment Rating	Net Assets ($Mil)	Price	Performance Rating/Pts	Total Return Y-T-D	Risk Rating/Pts
3-12	D+	398.79	28.74	C / 4.4	14.69%	C+ / 5.7
2011	D	336.00	25.25	C- / 3.1	0.40%	C+ / 5.6
2010	E+	380.50	31.01	D / 1.6	14.55%	C- / 3.1
2009	C+	194.74	28.92	B+ / 8.6	36.54%	C- / 3.2

Major Rating Factors: *iShares FTSE EPRA/NAREIT Dev RE receives a TheStreet.com Investment Rating of D+ (Weak). The fund currently has a performance rating of C (Fair) based on an annualized return of 18.93% over the last three years and a total return of 14.69% year to date 2012. Factored into the performance evaluation is an expense ratio of 0.48% (very low).

The fund's risk rating is currently C+ (Fair). It carries a beta of 1.19, meaning it is expected to move 11.9% for every 10% move in the market. Volatility, as measured by both the semi-deviation and a drawdown factor, is considered low. As of March 31, 2012, *iShares FTSE EPRA/NAREIT Dev RE traded at a premium of .17% above its net asset value, which is better than its one-year historical average premium of .23%.

Diane Hsiung has been running the fund for 4 years and currently receives a manager quality ranking of 24 (0=worst, 99=best). If you desire an average level of risk, then this fund may be an option.

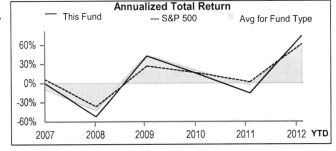

*iShares FTSE EPRA/NAREIT Europe (IFEU)   D+   Weak

Fund Family: BlackRock Fund Advisors
Fund Type: Growth and Income
Inception Date: November 12, 2007

Major Rating Factors: *iShares FTSE EPRA/NAREIT Europe receives a
TheStreet.com Investment Rating of D+ (Weak). The fund currently has a
performance rating of C- (Fair) based on an annualized return of 16.99% over the last
three years and a total return of 14.47% year to date 2012. Factored into the
performance evaluation is an expense ratio of 0.48% (very low).

The fund's risk rating is currently C+ (Fair). It carries a beta of 1.43, meaning it is
expected to move 14.3% for every 10% move in the market. Volatility, as measured
by both the semi-deviation and a drawdown factor, is considered low. As of March 31,
2012, *iShares FTSE EPRA/NAREIT Europe traded at a premium of .46% above its
net asset value, which is worse than its one-year historical average premium of .09%.

Diane Hsiung has been running the fund for 4 years and currently receives a
manager quality ranking of 15 (0=worst, 99=best). If you desire an average level of
risk, then this fund may be an option.

Data Date	Investment Rating	Net Assets ($Mil)	Price	Performance Rating/Pts	Total Return Y-T-D	Risk Rating/Pts
3-12	D+	12.16	28.10	C- / 3.7	14.47%	C+ / 6.7
2011	D	11.20	24.69	D / 1.8	-3.51%	C+ / 6.7
2010	E+	9.00	29.97	D- / 1.2	9.46%	C- / 3.6
2009	C+	3.16	29.30	B+ / 8.6	29.85%	C- / 3.9

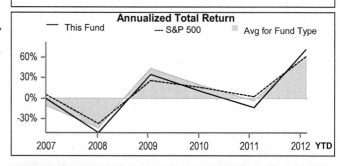

*iShares FTSE EPRA/NAREIT NA Idx (IFNA)   A-   Excellent

Fund Family: BlackRock Fund Advisors
Fund Type: Growth and Income
Inception Date: November 12, 2007

Major Rating Factors:
Exceptional performance is the major factor driving the A- (Excellent) TheStreet.com
Investment Rating for *iShares FTSE EPRA/NAREIT NA Idx. The fund currently has
a performance rating of A (Excellent) based on an annualized return of 41.41% over
the last three years and a total return of 9.86% year to date 2012. Factored into the
performance evaluation is an expense ratio of 0.48% (very low).

The fund's risk rating is currently B- (Good). It carries a beta of 1.21, meaning it is
expected to move 12.1% for every 10% move in the market. Volatility, as measured
by both the semi-deviation and a drawdown factor, is considered low. As of March 31,
2012, *iShares FTSE EPRA/NAREIT NA Idx traded at a discount of .39% below its
net asset value, which is better than its one-year historical average premium of .09%.

Diane Hsiung has been running the fund for 4 years and currently receives a
manager quality ranking of 88 (0=worst, 99=best). If you desire only a moderate level
of risk and strong performance, then this fund is an excellent option.

Data Date	Investment Rating	Net Assets ($Mil)	Price	Performance Rating/Pts	Total Return Y-T-D	Risk Rating/Pts
3-12	A-	15.58	45.93	A / 9.5	9.86%	B- / 7.7
2011	C+	12.60	42.14	B- / 7.5	0.12%	C+ / 6.0
2010	C	10.10	40.00	C+ / 6.9	24.46%	C- / 4.0
2009	B	2.28	33.20	A- / 9.2	33.80%	C- / 4.0

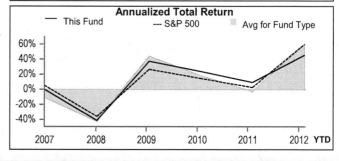

*iShares FTSE NAREIT Indl/Off Idx (FNIO)   B   Good

Fund Family: BlackRock Fund Advisors
Fund Type: Income
Inception Date: May 1, 2007

Major Rating Factors: Strong performance is the major factor driving the B (Good)
TheStreet.com Investment Rating for *iShares FTSE NAREIT Indl/Off Idx. The fund
currently has a performance rating of B+ (Good) based on an annualized return of
32.40% over the last three years and a total return of 13.52% year to date 2012.
Factored into the performance evaluation is an expense ratio of 0.48% (very low).

The fund's risk rating is currently B- (Good). It carries a beta of 1.35, meaning it is
expected to move 13.5% for every 10% move in the market. Volatility, as measured
by both the semi-deviation and a drawdown factor, is considered low. As of March 31,
2012, *iShares FTSE NAREIT Indl/Off Idx traded at a discount of .28% below its net
asset value, which is better than its one-year historical average discount of .02%.

Diane Hsiung has been running the fund for 4 years and currently receives a
manager quality ranking of 62 (0=worst, 99=best). If you desire only a moderate level
of risk and strong performance, then this fund is an excellent option.

Data Date	Investment Rating	Net Assets ($Mil)	Price	Performance Rating/Pts	Total Return Y-T-D	Risk Rating/Pts
3-12	B	9.58	28.26	B+ / 8.4	13.52%	B- / 7.5
2011	C-	10.00	25.08	C / 5.1	0.28%	C+ / 6.6
2010	D-	9.30	26.65	D / 2.1	16.27%	C- / 3.8
2009	B-	2.52	23.72	A- / 9.2	28.62%	C- / 3.8

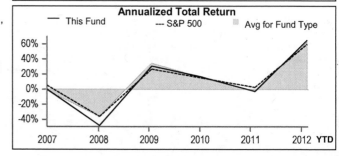

*iShares FTSE NAREIT Mtge+Capped (REM)   C-   Fair

Fund Family: BlackRock Fund Advisors
Fund Type: Income
Inception Date: May 1, 2007

Major Rating Factors: Middle of the road best describes *iShares FTSE NAREIT Mtge+Capped whose TheStreet.com Investment Rating is currently a C- (Fair). The fund currently has a performance rating of C- (Fair) based on an annualized return of 12.26% over the last three years and a total return of 10.07% year to date 2012. Factored into the performance evaluation is an expense ratio of 0.48% (very low).

The fund's risk rating is currently B (Good). It carries a beta of 0.66, meaning the fund's expected move will be 6.6% for every 10% move in the market. Volatility, as measured by both the semi-deviation and a drawdown factor, is considered low. As of March 31, 2012, *iShares FTSE NAREIT Mtge+Capped traded at a price exactly equal to its net asset value, which is better than its one-year historical average premium of .06%.

Diane Hsiung has been running the fund for 4 years and currently receives a manager quality ranking of 41 (0=worst, 99=best). If you desire an average level of risk, then this fund may be an option.

Data Date	Investment Rating	Net Assets ($Mil)	Price	Performance Rating/Pts	Total Return Y-T-D	Risk Rating/Pts
3-12	C-	279.67	13.52	C- / 3.1	10.07%	B / 8.2
2011	C-	215.00	12.66	D+ / 2.6	1.26%	B / 8.0
2010	D-	102.10	15.59	D- / 1.5	16.49%	C- / 4.2
2009	C	30.51	14.71	C+ / 6.9	13.12%	C / 4.4

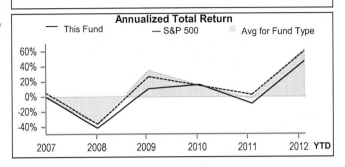

*iShares FTSE NAREIT Real Estate (FTY)   A-   Excellent

Fund Family: BlackRock Fund Advisors
Fund Type: Income
Inception Date: May 1, 2007

Major Rating Factors:
Strong performance is the major factor driving the A- (Excellent) TheStreet.com Investment Rating for *iShares FTSE NAREIT Real Estate. The fund currently has a performance rating of B+ (Good) based on an annualized return of 35.41% over the last three years and a total return of 8.94% year to date 2012. Factored into the performance evaluation is an expense ratio of 0.48% (very low).

The fund's risk rating is currently B (Good). It carries a beta of 1.16, meaning it is expected to move 11.6% for every 10% move in the market. Volatility, as measured by both the semi-deviation and a drawdown factor, is considered low. As of March 31, 2012, *iShares FTSE NAREIT Real Estate traded at a discount of .10% below its net asset value.

Diane Hsiung has been running the fund for 4 years and currently receives a manager quality ranking of 84 (0=worst, 99=best). If you desire only a moderate level of risk and strong performance, then this fund is an excellent option.

Data Date	Investment Rating	Net Assets ($Mil)	Price	Performance Rating/Pts	Total Return Y-T-D	Risk Rating/Pts
3-12	A-	53.56	38.18	B+ / 8.9	8.94%	B / 8.1
2011	C+	42.20	35.35	B- / 7.5	-0.83%	C+ / 6.7
2010	C+	50.40	33.72	B- / 7.2	26.21%	C / 4.3
2009	B	14.04	27.77	A- / 9.1	30.12%	C / 4.4

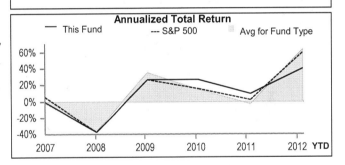

*iShares FTSE NAREIT Residential (REZ)   A-   Excellent

Fund Family: BlackRock Fund Advisors
Fund Type: Income
Inception Date: May 1, 2007

Major Rating Factors:
Exceptional performance is the major factor driving the A- (Excellent) TheStreet.com Investment Rating for *iShares FTSE NAREIT Residential. The fund currently has a performance rating of A- (Excellent) based on an annualized return of 35.75% over the last three years and a total return of 5.84% year to date 2012. Factored into the performance evaluation is an expense ratio of 0.48% (very low).

The fund's risk rating is currently B (Good). It carries a beta of 0.98, meaning that its performance tracks fairly well with that of the overall stock market. Volatility, as measured by both the semi-deviation and a drawdown factor, is considered low. As of March 31, 2012, *iShares FTSE NAREIT Residential traded at a price exactly equal to its net asset value, which is better than its one-year historical average premium of .04%.

Diane Hsiung has been running the fund for 4 years and currently receives a manager quality ranking of 90 (0=worst, 99=best). If you desire only a moderate level of risk and strong performance, then this fund is an excellent option.

Data Date	Investment Rating	Net Assets ($Mil)	Price	Performance Rating/Pts	Total Return Y-T-D	Risk Rating/Pts
3-12	A-	168.58	46.41	A- / 9.0	5.84%	B / 8.0
2011	C+	143.50	44.22	B / 8.2	-1.31%	C+ / 6.2
2010	B	70.90	39.39	B+ / 8.3	31.61%	C / 4.5
2009	B	14.23	30.94	A- / 9.0	25.84%	C / 4.4

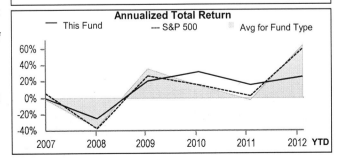

*iShares FTSE NAREIT Retail Idx (RTL)

A+   **Excellent**

Fund Family: BlackRock Fund Advisors
Fund Type: Income
Inception Date: May 1, 2007

Major Rating Factors:

Exceptional performance is the major factor driving the A+ (Excellent) TheStreet.com Investment Rating for *iShares FTSE NAREIT Retail Idx. The fund currently has a performance rating of A+ (Excellent) based on an annualized return of 41.95% over the last three years and a total return of 13.74% year to date 2012. Factored into the performance evaluation is an expense ratio of 0.48% (very low).

The fund's risk rating is currently B (Good). It carries a beta of 1.34, meaning it is expected to move 13.4% for every 10% move in the market. Volatility, as measured by both the semi-deviation and a drawdown factor, is considered low. As of March 31, 2012, *iShares FTSE NAREIT Retail Idx traded at a premium of .09% above its net asset value, which is worse than its one-year historical average discount of .02%.

Diane Hsiung has been running the fund for 4 years and currently receives a manager quality ranking of 89 (0=worst, 99=best). If you desire only a moderate level of risk and strong performance, then this fund is an excellent option.

Data Date	Investment Rating	Net Assets ($Mil)	Price	Performance Rating/Pts	Total Return Y-T-D	Risk Rating/Pts
3-12	A+	14.03	32.64	A+ / 9.6	13.74%	B / 8.0
2011	C+	8.60	28.94	B / 7.7	-0.21%	C+ / 6.2
2010	C-	14.00	28.13	C+ / 6.1	36.08%	C- / 3.7
2009	C+	1.63	21.36	B+ / 8.9	25.55%	D+ / 2.9

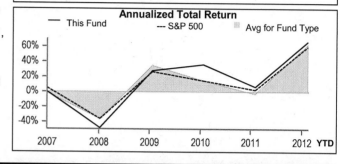

*iShares Gold Trust (IAU)

D-   **Weak**

Fund Family: BlackRock Fund Advisors
Fund Type: Precious Metals
Inception Date: January 21, 2005

Major Rating Factors: *iShares Gold Trust has adopted a very risky asset allocation strategy and currently receives an overall TheStreet.com Investment Rating of D- (Weak). The fund has a high level of volatility, as measured by both semi-deviation and drawdown factors. It carries a beta of 0.95, meaning that its performance tracks fairly well with that of the overall stock market. As of March 31, 2012, *iShares Gold Trust traded at a premium of .43% above its net asset value, which is worse than its one-year historical average premium of .24%. Unfortunately, the high level of risk (D, Weak) has only provided investors with average performance.

The fund's performance rating is currently C+ (Fair). It has registered an annualized return of 22.86% over the last three years and is up 6.83% year to date 2012. Factored into the performance evaluation is an expense ratio of 0.25% (very low).

Index Strategies Group has been running the fund for 7 years and currently receives a manager quality ranking of 51 (0=worst, 99=best). If you are comfortable owning a very high risk investment, then this fund may be an option.

Data Date	Investment Rating	Net Assets ($Mil)	Price	Performance Rating/Pts	Total Return Y-T-D	Risk Rating/Pts
3-12	D-	10,328.44	16.27	C+ / 5.9	6.83%	D / 1.9
2011	D+	8,416.90	15.23	B / 7.6	3.48%	D / 1.9
2010	C-	5,316.70	13.90	B+ / 8.9	29.46%	D- / 1.0
2009	A+	2,667.82	107.37	B- / 7.5	24.34%	B- / 7.2

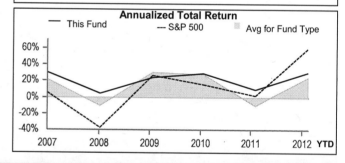

*iShares High Dividend Equity (HDV)

C+   **Fair**

Fund Family: BlackRock Fund Advisors
Fund Type: Global
Inception Date: March 28, 2011

Major Rating Factors: Middle of the road best describes *iShares High Dividend Equity whose TheStreet.com Investment Rating is currently a C+ (Fair). The fund currently has a performance rating of C (Fair) based on an annualized return of 0.00% over the last three years and a total return of 3.92% year to date 2012. Factored into the performance evaluation is an expense ratio of 0.40% (very low).

The fund's risk rating is currently B+ (Good). It carries a beta of 0.00, meaning the fund's expected move will be 0.0% for every 10% move in the market. Volatility, as measured by both the semi-deviation and a drawdown factor, is considered very low. As of March 31, 2012, *iShares High Dividend Equity traded at a premium of .02% above its net asset value, which is better than its one-year historical average premium of .06%.

Greg Savage has been running the fund for 1 year and currently receives a manager quality ranking of 90 (0=worst, 99=best). If you desire an average level of risk, then this fund may be an option.

Data Date	Investment Rating	Net Assets ($Mil)	Price	Performance Rating/Pts	Total Return Y-T-D	Risk Rating/Pts
3-12	C+	1,253.10	57.15	C / 5.2	3.92%	B+ / 9.4

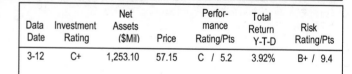
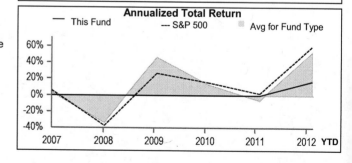

*iShares iBoxx $ High Yld Corp Bo (HYG)   C-   Fair

Fund Family: BlackRock Fund Advisors
Fund Type: Corporate - High Yield
Inception Date: April 4, 2007

Major Rating Factors: Middle of the road best describes *iShares iBoxx $ High Yld Corp Bo whose TheStreet.com Investment Rating is currently a C- (Fair). The fund currently has a performance rating of C (Fair) based on an annualized return of 18.10% over the last three years and a total return of 2.62% year to date 2012. Factored into the performance evaluation is an expense ratio of 0.50% (very low).

The fund's risk rating is currently B- (Good). It carries a beta of 1.09, meaning that its performance tracks fairly well with that of the overall stock market. Volatility, as measured by both the semi-deviation and a drawdown factor, is considered low. As of March 31, 2012, *iShares iBoxx $ High Yld Corp Bo traded at a premium of .49% above its net asset value, which is better than its one-year historical average premium of .59%.

Scott F. Radell has been running the fund for 2 years and currently receives a manager quality ranking of 24 (0=worst, 99=best). If you desire an average level of risk, then this fund may be an option.

Data Date	Investment Rating	Net Assets ($Mil)	Price	Performance Rating/Pts	Total Return Y-T-D	Risk Rating/Pts
3-12	C-	14,258.76	90.72	C / 4.3	2.62%	B- / 7.1
2011	C	10,636.60	89.43	C / 5.0	-0.59%	B- / 7.0
2010	C+	7,273.10	90.29	C+ / 6.7	11.98%	C / 5.2
2009	B	3,765.79	87.84	B / 8.2	29.16%	C / 5.2

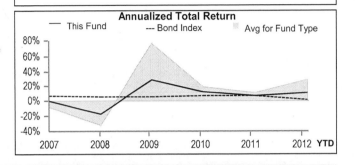

*iShares iBoxx $ Inves Grade Corp (LQD)   C   Fair

Fund Family: BlackRock Fund Advisors
Fund Type: Corporate - Investment Grade
Inception Date: July 22, 2002

Major Rating Factors: Middle of the road best describes *iShares iBoxx $ Inves Grade Corp whose TheStreet.com Investment Rating is currently a C (Fair). The fund currently has a performance rating of C- (Fair) based on an annualized return of 12.81% over the last three years and a total return of 2.34% year to date 2012. Factored into the performance evaluation is an expense ratio of 0.15% (very low).

The fund's risk rating is currently B+ (Good). It carries a beta of 1.26, meaning it is expected to move 12.6% for every 10% move in the market. Volatility, as measured by both the semi-deviation and a drawdown factor, is considered very low. As of March 31, 2012, *iShares iBoxx $ Inves Grade Corp traded at a premium of .32% above its net asset value, which is better than its one-year historical average premium of .49%.

Scott F. Radell has been running the fund for 2 years and currently receives a manager quality ranking of 29 (0=worst, 99=best). If you desire an average level of risk, then this fund may be an option.

Data Date	Investment Rating	Net Assets ($Mil)	Price	Performance Rating/Pts	Total Return Y-T-D	Risk Rating/Pts
3-12	C	19,563.38	115.63	C- / 3.1	2.34%	B+ / 9.4
2011	C+	16,990.80	113.76	C- / 4.0	-0.04%	B+ / 9.2
2010	B	13,098.30	108.44	C / 5.5	9.35%	B / 8.5
2009	B-	12,969.09	104.15	C- / 4.0	9.68%	B / 8.7

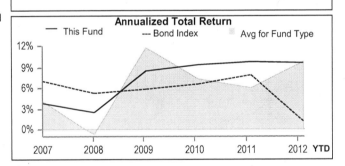

*iShares JPMorgan USD Emg Mkts Bo (EMB)   C   Fair

Fund Family: BlackRock Fund Advisors
Fund Type: Emerging Market
Inception Date: December 17, 2007

Major Rating Factors: Middle of the road best describes *iShares JPMorgan USD Emg Mkts Bo whose TheStreet.com Investment Rating is currently a C (Fair). The fund currently has a performance rating of C- (Fair) based on an annualized return of 15.00% over the last three years and a total return of 3.51% year to date 2012. Factored into the performance evaluation is an expense ratio of 0.60% (very low).

The fund's risk rating is currently B (Good). It carries a beta of 0.54, meaning the fund's expected move will be 5.4% for every 10% move in the market. Volatility, as measured by both the semi-deviation and a drawdown factor, is considered low. As of March 31, 2012, *iShares JPMorgan USD Emg Mkts Bo traded at a premium of .60% above its net asset value, which is worse than its one-year historical average premium of .57%.

Scott F. Radell has been running the fund for 2 years and currently receives a manager quality ranking of 87 (0=worst, 99=best). If you desire an average level of risk, then this fund may be an option.

Data Date	Investment Rating	Net Assets ($Mil)	Price	Performance Rating/Pts	Total Return Y-T-D	Risk Rating/Pts
3-12	C	4,084.63	112.71	C- / 3.6	3.51%	B / 8.9
2011	C+	3,554.20	109.75	C / 4.7	-1.23%	B / 8.6
2010	C+	2,187.50	107.08	C+ / 6.4	10.89%	C+ / 6.8
2009	B-	405.50	101.78	C+ / 5.9	13.50%	B- / 7.0

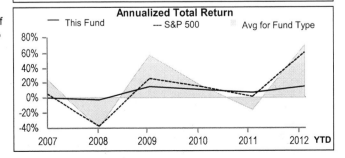

*iShares Morningstar Large Core (JKD)

C+　　**Fair**

Fund Family: BlackRock Fund Advisors
Fund Type: Growth
Inception Date: June 28, 2004

Data Date	Investment Rating	Net Assets ($Mil)	Price	Performance Rating/Pts	Total Return Y-T-D	Risk Rating/Pts
3-12	C+	271.56	80.15	C+ / 5.8	12.57%	B / 8.5
2011	C	285.80	71.50	C / 4.9	1.66%	B / 8.0
2010	C-	275.90	70.70	C- / 3.8	12.68%	C+ / 6.2
2009	C-	195.88	63.97	D+ / 2.5	18.04%	C+ / 6.3

Major Rating Factors: Middle of the road best describes *iShares Morningstar Large Core whose TheStreet.com Investment Rating is currently a C+ (Fair). The fund currently has a performance rating of C+ (Fair) based on an annualized return of 20.45% over the last three years and a total return of 12.57% year to date 2012. Factored into the performance evaluation is an expense ratio of 0.20% (very low).

The fund's risk rating is currently B (Good). It carries a beta of 0.95, meaning that its performance tracks fairly well with that of the overall stock market. Volatility, as measured by both the semi-deviation and a drawdown factor, is considered low. As of March 31, 2012, *iShares Morningstar Large Core traded at a discount of .06% below its net asset value, which is better than its one-year historical average premium of .02%.

Diane Hsiung has been running the fund for 4 years and currently receives a manager quality ranking of 50 (0=worst, 99=best). If you desire an average level of risk, then this fund may be an option.

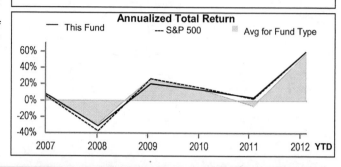

*iShares Morningstar Large Growth (JKE)

C+　　**Fair**

Fund Family: BlackRock Fund Advisors
Fund Type: Growth
Inception Date: June 28, 2004

Data Date	Investment Rating	Net Assets ($Mil)	Price	Performance Rating/Pts	Total Return Y-T-D	Risk Rating/Pts
3-12	C+	412.69	77.14	C+ / 6.8	17.15%	B- / 7.5
2011	C+	355.30	65.95	C+ / 6.2	1.88%	B- / 7.4
2010	C-	370.40	65.53	C / 4.3	12.57%	C+ / 5.7
2009	C-	331.59	58.69	C- / 3.9	39.27%	C+ / 5.8

Major Rating Factors: Middle of the road best describes *iShares Morningstar Large Growth whose TheStreet.com Investment Rating is currently a C+ (Fair). The fund currently has a performance rating of C+ (Fair) based on an annualized return of 22.64% over the last three years and a total return of 17.15% year to date 2012. Factored into the performance evaluation is an expense ratio of 0.25% (very low).

The fund's risk rating is currently B- (Good). It carries a beta of 1.05, meaning that its performance tracks fairly well with that of the overall stock market. Volatility, as measured by both the semi-deviation and a drawdown factor, is considered low. As of March 31, 2012, *iShares Morningstar Large Growth traded at a price exactly equal to its net asset value, which is worse than its one-year historical average discount of .01%.

Diane Hsiung has been running the fund for 4 years and currently receives a manager quality ranking of 44 (0=worst, 99=best). If you desire an average level of risk, then this fund may be an option.

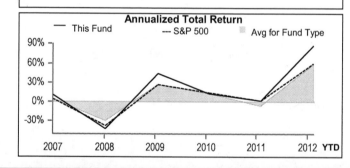

*iShares Morningstar Large Value (JKF)

C　　**Fair**

Fund Family: BlackRock Fund Advisors
Fund Type: Income
Inception Date: June 28, 2004

Data Date	Investment Rating	Net Assets ($Mil)	Price	Performance Rating/Pts	Total Return Y-T-D	Risk Rating/Pts
3-12	C	251.62	63.23	C- / 4.1	8.08%	B / 8.4
2011	C	244.40	58.90	C- / 4.1	1.21%	B / 8.0
2010	D+	208.20	59.53	D / 2.1	14.57%	C+ / 6.1
2009	D	159.31	53.41	D- / 1.1	8.17%	C+ / 5.7

Major Rating Factors: Middle of the road best describes *iShares Morningstar Large Value whose TheStreet.com Investment Rating is currently a C (Fair). The fund currently has a performance rating of C- (Fair) based on an annualized return of 16.63% over the last three years and a total return of 8.08% year to date 2012. Factored into the performance evaluation is an expense ratio of 0.25% (very low).

The fund's risk rating is currently B (Good). It carries a beta of 0.92, meaning that its performance tracks fairly well with that of the overall stock market. Volatility, as measured by both the semi-deviation and a drawdown factor, is considered low. As of March 31, 2012, *iShares Morningstar Large Value traded at a discount of .06% below its net asset value, which is better than its one-year historical average premium of .02%.

Diane Hsiung has been running the fund for 4 years and currently receives a manager quality ranking of 32 (0=worst, 99=best). If you desire an average level of risk, then this fund may be an option.

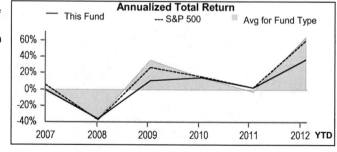

*iShares Morningstar Mid Core (JKG)   B   Good

Fund Family: BlackRock Fund Advisors
Fund Type: Growth
Inception Date: June 28, 2004

Major Rating Factors: Strong performance is the major factor driving the B (Good) TheStreet.com Investment Rating for *iShares Morningstar Mid Core. The fund currently has a performance rating of B (Good) based on an annualized return of 27.78% over the last three years and a total return of 13.57% year to date 2012. Factored into the performance evaluation is an expense ratio of 0.25% (very low).

The fund's risk rating is currently B (Good). It carries a beta of 1.18, meaning it is expected to move 11.8% for every 10% move in the market. Volatility, as measured by both the semi-deviation and a drawdown factor, is considered low. As of March 31, 2012, *iShares Morningstar Mid Core traded at a discount of .06% below its net asset value, which is better than its one-year historical average premium of .02%.

Diane Hsiung has been running the fund for 4 years and currently receives a manager quality ranking of 59 (0=worst, 99=best). If you desire only a moderate level of risk and strong performance, then this fund is an excellent option.

Data Date	Investment Rating	Net Assets ($Mil)	Price	Performance Rating/Pts	Total Return Y-T-D	Risk Rating/Pts
3-12	B	156.22	96.43	B / 7.7	13.57%	B / 8.1
2011	B-	140.60	85.15	B- / 7.0	1.59%	B- / 7.8
2010	B-	143.90	84.94	B- / 7.1	26.50%	C+ / 5.6
2009	C-	77.66	68.17	C- / 3.2	34.75%	C+ / 5.7

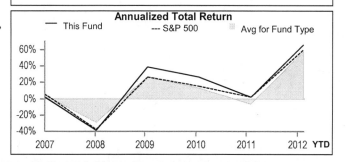

*iShares Morningstar Mid Growth (JKH)   B-   Good

Fund Family: BlackRock Fund Advisors
Fund Type: Growth
Inception Date: June 28, 2004

Major Rating Factors: *iShares Morningstar Mid Growth receives a TheStreet.com Investment Rating of B- (Good). The fund currently has a performance rating of C+ (Fair) based on an annualized return of 25.68% over the last three years and a total return of 15.29% year to date 2012. Factored into the performance evaluation is an expense ratio of 0.30% (very low).

The fund's risk rating is currently B (Good). It carries a beta of 1.07, meaning that its performance tracks fairly well with that of the overall stock market. Volatility, as measured by both the semi-deviation and a drawdown factor, is considered low. As of March 31, 2012, *iShares Morningstar Mid Growth traded at a discount of .06% below its net asset value, which is better than its one-year historical average premium of .02%.

Diane Hsiung has been running the fund for 4 years and currently receives a manager quality ranking of 62 (0=worst, 99=best). If you desire an average level of risk, then this fund may be an option.

Data Date	Investment Rating	Net Assets ($Mil)	Price	Performance Rating/Pts	Total Return Y-T-D	Risk Rating/Pts
3-12	B-	174.42	107.56	C+ / 6.9	15.29%	B / 8.0
2011	C+	158.70	93.33	C+ / 6.5	1.95%	B- / 7.5
2010	C	192.00	96.31	C+ / 6.1	27.84%	C / 4.9
2009	C-	195.61	75.60	C- / 3.5	36.46%	C / 5.5

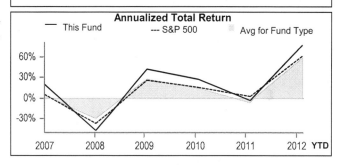

*iShares Morningstar Mid Value (JKI)   C+   Fair

Fund Family: BlackRock Fund Advisors
Fund Type: Growth
Inception Date: June 28, 2004

Major Rating Factors: Middle of the road best describes *iShares Morningstar Mid Value whose TheStreet.com Investment Rating is currently a C+ (Fair). The fund currently has a performance rating of C+ (Fair) based on an annualized return of 25.39% over the last three years and a total return of 11.71% year to date 2012. Factored into the performance evaluation is an expense ratio of 0.30% (very low).

The fund's risk rating is currently B (Good). It carries a beta of 1.20, meaning it is expected to move 12.0% for every 10% move in the market. Volatility, as measured by both the semi-deviation and a drawdown factor, is considered low. As of March 31, 2012, *iShares Morningstar Mid Value traded at a premium of .14% above its net asset value, which is worse than its one-year historical average discount of .02%.

Diane Hsiung has been running the fund for 4 years and currently receives a manager quality ranking of 47 (0=worst, 99=best). If you desire an average level of risk, then this fund may be an option.

Data Date	Investment Rating	Net Assets ($Mil)	Price	Performance Rating/Pts	Total Return Y-T-D	Risk Rating/Pts
3-12	C+	102.33	80.16	C+ / 6.8	11.71%	B / 8.0
2011	C+	93.50	72.09	C+ / 5.7	1.42%	B- / 7.7
2010	C+	109.70	75.75	C+ / 6.5	20.46%	C+ / 5.6
2009	D+	69.65	64.71	D+ / 2.6	31.64%	C+ / 5.6

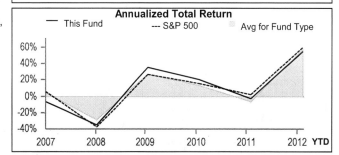

*iShares Morningstar Small Core (JKJ)   C+   Fair

Fund Family: BlackRock Fund Advisors
Fund Type: Growth
Inception Date: June 28, 2004

Data Date	Investment Rating	Net Assets ($Mil)	Price	Performance Rating/Pts	Total Return Y-T-D	Risk Rating/Pts
3-12	C+	148.75	94.75	B- / 7.0	13.35%	B- / 7.5
2011	C+	138.30	83.78	C+ / 6.4	1.73%	B- / 7.3
2010	B	173.60	89.11	B / 7.8	27.70%	C / 5.5
2009	D+	80.55	70.57	C- / 3.0	36.83%	C+ / 5.6

Major Rating Factors: Strong performance is the major factor driving the C+ (Fair) TheStreet.com Investment Rating for *iShares Morningstar Small Core. The fund currently has a performance rating of B- (Good) based on an annualized return of 25.94% over the last three years and a total return of 13.35% year to date 2012. Factored into the performance evaluation is an expense ratio of 0.25% (very low).

The fund's risk rating is currently B- (Good). It carries a beta of 1.35, meaning it is expected to move 13.5% for every 10% move in the market. Volatility, as measured by both the semi-deviation and a drawdown factor, is considered low. As of March 31, 2012, *iShares Morningstar Small Core traded at a premium of .26% above its net asset value, which is worse than its one-year historical average discount of .07%.

Diane Hsiung has been running the fund for 4 years and currently receives a manager quality ranking of 31 (0=worst, 99=best). If you desire only a moderate level of risk and strong performance, then this fund is an excellent option.

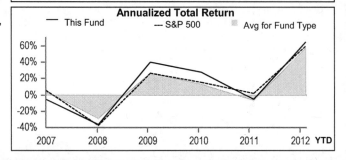

*iShares Morningstar Small Growth (JKK)   C+   Fair

Fund Family: BlackRock Fund Advisors
Fund Type: Growth
Inception Date: June 28, 2004

Data Date	Investment Rating	Net Assets ($Mil)	Price	Performance Rating/Pts	Total Return Y-T-D	Risk Rating/Pts
3-12	C+	91.43	93.73	B- / 7.1	12.72%	B- / 7.2
2011	C+	83.20	83.29	C+ / 6.4	0.62%	C+ / 6.8
2010	B-	109.80	84.51	B- / 7.2	31.19%	C / 5.3
2009	D+	66.16	64.58	D+ / 2.8	29.95%	C / 5.3

Major Rating Factors: Strong performance is the major factor driving the C+ (Fair) TheStreet.com Investment Rating for *iShares Morningstar Small Growth. The fund currently has a performance rating of B- (Good) based on an annualized return of 25.97% over the last three years and a total return of 12.72% year to date 2012. Factored into the performance evaluation is an expense ratio of 0.30% (very low).

The fund's risk rating is currently B- (Good). It carries a beta of 1.21, meaning it is expected to move 12.1% for every 10% move in the market. Volatility, as measured by both the semi-deviation and a drawdown factor, is considered low. As of March 31, 2012, *iShares Morningstar Small Growth traded at a premium of .32% above its net asset value, which is worse than its one-year historical average discount of .05%.

Diane Hsiung has been running the fund for 4 years and currently receives a manager quality ranking of 42 (0=worst, 99=best). If you desire only a moderate level of risk and strong performance, then this fund is an excellent option.

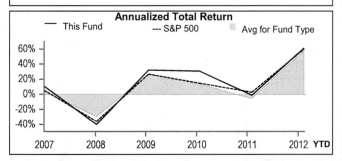

*iShares Morningstar Small Value (JKL)   B   Good

Fund Family: BlackRock Fund Advisors
Fund Type: Growth
Inception Date: June 28, 2004

Data Date	Investment Rating	Net Assets ($Mil)	Price	Performance Rating/Pts	Total Return Y-T-D	Risk Rating/Pts
3-12	B	163.51	87.64	B / 7.8	11.66%	B- / 7.9
2011	C+	153.80	78.90	C+ / 6.7	1.66%	B- / 7.5
2010	B+	185.90	82.67	B / 8.0	25.80%	C+ / 5.6
2009	C-	65.09	67.02	C- / 3.6	36.72%	C / 5.5

Major Rating Factors: Strong performance is the major factor driving the B (Good) TheStreet.com Investment Rating for *iShares Morningstar Small Value. The fund currently has a performance rating of B (Good) based on an annualized return of 29.02% over the last three years and a total return of 11.66% year to date 2012. Factored into the performance evaluation is an expense ratio of 0.30% (very low).

The fund's risk rating is currently B- (Good). It carries a beta of 1.34, meaning it is expected to move 13.4% for every 10% move in the market. Volatility, as measured by both the semi-deviation and a drawdown factor, is considered low. As of March 31, 2012, *iShares Morningstar Small Value traded at a premium of .09% above its net asset value, which is worse than its one-year historical average premium of .02%.

Diane Hsiung has been running the fund for 4 years and currently receives a manager quality ranking of 49 (0=worst, 99=best). If you desire only a moderate level of risk and strong performance, then this fund is an excellent option.

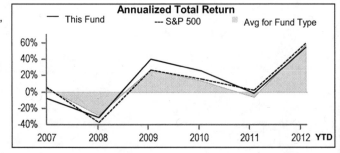

*iShares MSCI ACWI ex US Enrgy Id (AXEN)

D-   **Weak**

Fund Family: BlackRock Fund Advisors
Fund Type: Energy/Natural Resources
Inception Date: July 13, 2010

Data Date	Investment Rating	Net Assets ($Mil)	Price	Performance Rating/Pts	Total Return Y-T-D	Risk Rating/Pts
3-12	D-	6.21	58.65	D- / 1.4	7.14%	C+ / 6.9
2011	D	5.50	54.74	D / 1.7	3.05%	C+ / 6.9

Major Rating Factors:
Disappointing performance is the major factor driving the D- (Weak) TheStreet.com Investment Rating for *iShares MSCI ACWI ex US Enrgy Id. The fund currently has a performance rating of D- (Weak) based on an annualized return of 0.00% over the last three years and a total return of 7.14% year to date 2012. Factored into the performance evaluation is an expense ratio of 0.48% (very low).

The fund's risk rating is currently C+ (Fair). It carries a beta of 0.00, meaning the fund's expected move will be 0.0% for every 10% move in the market. Volatility, as measured by both the semi-deviation and a drawdown factor, is considered low. As of March 31, 2012, *iShares MSCI ACWI ex US Enrgy Id traded at a premium of .34% above its net asset value, which is worse than its one-year historical average discount of .15%.

Rene Casis has been running the fund for 2 years and currently receives a manager quality ranking of 22 (0=worst, 99=best). This fund offers only a moderate level of risk but investors looking for strong performance are still waiting.

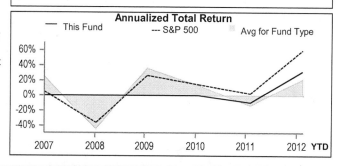

---

*iShares MSCI ACWI ex US Fn Sctr (AXFN)

D-   **Weak**

Fund Family: BlackRock Fund Advisors
Fund Type: Financial Services
Inception Date: January 20, 2010

Data Date	Investment Rating	Net Assets ($Mil)	Price	Performance Rating/Pts	Total Return Y-T-D	Risk Rating/Pts
3-12	D-	2.18	20.87	E+ / 0.9	14.42%	C+ / 6.7
2011	D-	1.90	18.24	E+ / 0.7	0.05%	C+ / 6.7

Major Rating Factors:
Very poor performance is the major factor driving the D- (Weak) TheStreet.com Investment Rating for *iShares MSCI ACWI ex US Fn Sctr. The fund currently has a performance rating of E+ (Very Weak) based on an annualized return of 0.00% over the last three years and a total return of 14.42% year to date 2012. Factored into the performance evaluation is an expense ratio of 0.48% (very low).

The fund's risk rating is currently C+ (Fair). It carries a beta of 0.00, meaning the fund's expected move will be 0.0% for every 10% move in the market. Volatility, as measured by both the semi-deviation and a drawdown factor, is considered low. As of March 31, 2012, *iShares MSCI ACWI ex US Fn Sctr traded at a discount of 2.61% below its net asset value, which is better than its one-year historical average discount of .32%.

Rene Casis has been running the fund for 2 years and currently receives a manager quality ranking of 9 (0=worst, 99=best). This fund offers only a moderate level of risk but investors looking for strong performance are still waiting.

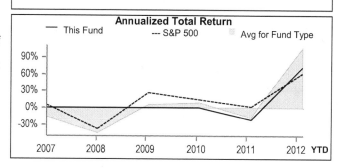

---

*iShares MSCI ACWI ex US HlthCre (AXHE)

C   **Fair**

Fund Family: BlackRock Fund Advisors
Fund Type: Health
Inception Date: July 13, 2010

Data Date	Investment Rating	Net Assets ($Mil)	Price	Performance Rating/Pts	Total Return Y-T-D	Risk Rating/Pts
3-12	C	8.86	60.33	C- / 3.7	7.60%	B / 8.5
2011	C-	8.50	56.07	D+ / 2.4	0.87%	B / 8.4

Major Rating Factors: Middle of the road best describes *iShares MSCI ACWI ex US HlthCre whose TheStreet.com Investment Rating is currently a C (Fair). The fund currently has a performance rating of C- (Fair) based on an annualized return of 0.00% over the last three years and a total return of 7.60% year to date 2012. Factored into the performance evaluation is an expense ratio of 0.48% (very low).

The fund's risk rating is currently B (Good). It carries a beta of 0.00, meaning the fund's expected move will be 0.0% for every 10% move in the market. Volatility, as measured by both the semi-deviation and a drawdown factor, is considered low. As of March 31, 2012, *iShares MSCI ACWI ex US HlthCre traded at a premium of .89% above its net asset value, which is worse than its one-year historical average premium of .18%.

Rene Casis has been running the fund for 2 years and currently receives a manager quality ranking of 67 (0=worst, 99=best). If you desire an average level of risk, then this fund may be an option.

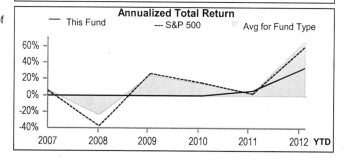

*iShares MSCI ACWI ex US Index (ACWX) · C- · Fair

Fund Family: BlackRock Fund Advisors
Fund Type: Foreign
Inception Date: March 26, 2008

Major Rating Factors: Middle of the road best describes *iShares MSCI ACWI ex US Index whose TheStreet.com Investment Rating is currently a C- (Fair). The fund currently has a performance rating of C- (Fair) based on an annualized return of 15.23% over the last three years and a total return of 10.92% year to date 2012. Factored into the performance evaluation is an expense ratio of 0.34% (very low).

The fund's risk rating is currently B- (Good). It carries a beta of 1.06, meaning that its performance tracks fairly well with that of the overall stock market. Volatility, as measured by both the semi-deviation and a drawdown factor, is considered low. As of March 31, 2012, *iShares MSCI ACWI ex US Index traded at a premium of .29% above its net asset value, which is worse than its one-year historical average premium of .06%.

Diane Hsiung has been running the fund for 4 years and currently receives a manager quality ranking of 44 (0=worst, 99=best). If you desire an average level of risk, then this fund may be an option.

Data Date	Investment Rating	Net Assets ($Mil)	Price	Performance Rating/Pts	Total Return Y-T-D	Risk Rating/Pts
3-12	C-	939.82	40.83	C- / 3.4	10.92%	B- / 7.6
2011	D+	835.90	36.81	C- / 3.0	-0.65%	B- / 7.3
2010	B+	771.80	44.04	B+ / 8.9	10.44%	C / 5.0
2009	B+	270.64	40.91	B+ / 8.6	34.14%	C / 5.3

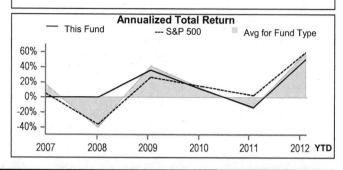

Annualized Total Return — This Fund · --- S&P 500 · Avg for Fund Type

*iShares MSCI ACWI ex US Indsl In (AXID) · D · Weak

Fund Family: BlackRock Fund Advisors
Fund Type: Foreign
Inception Date: July 13, 2010

Major Rating Factors:
Disappointing performance is the major factor driving the D (Weak) TheStreet.com Investment Rating for *iShares MSCI ACWI ex US Indsl In. The fund currently has a performance rating of D (Weak) based on an annualized return of 0.00% over the last three years and a total return of 13.66% year to date 2012. Factored into the performance evaluation is an expense ratio of 0.48% (very low).

The fund's risk rating is currently B- (Good). It carries a beta of 0.00, meaning the fund's expected move will be 0.0% for every 10% move in the market. Volatility, as measured by both the semi-deviation and a drawdown factor, is considered low. As of March 31, 2012, *iShares MSCI ACWI ex US Indsl In traded at a discount of .81% below its net asset value, which is better than its one-year historical average discount of .42%.

Rene Casis has been running the fund for 2 years and currently receives a manager quality ranking of 25 (0=worst, 99=best). This fund offers only a moderate level of risk but investors looking for strong performance are still waiting.

Data Date	Investment Rating	Net Assets ($Mil)	Price	Performance Rating/Pts	Total Return Y-T-D	Risk Rating/Pts
3-12	D	2.81	55.10	D / 1.9	13.66%	B- / 7.0

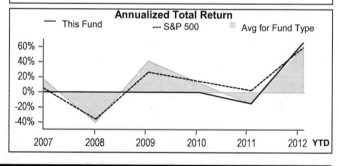

Annualized Total Return — This Fund · --- S&P 500 · Avg for Fund Type

*iShares MSCI ACWI ex US IT Index (AXIT) · C- · Fair

Fund Family: BlackRock Fund Advisors
Fund Type: Emerging Market
Inception Date: July 13, 2010

Major Rating Factors: Middle of the road best describes *iShares MSCI ACWI ex US IT Index whose TheStreet.com Investment Rating is currently a C- (Fair). The fund currently has a performance rating of C (Fair) based on an annualized return of 0.00% over the last three years and a total return of 19.07% year to date 2012. Factored into the performance evaluation is an expense ratio of 0.48% (very low).

The fund's risk rating is currently B- (Good). It carries a beta of 0.00, meaning the fund's expected move will be 0.0% for every 10% move in the market. Volatility, as measured by both the semi-deviation and a drawdown factor, is considered low. As of March 31, 2012, *iShares MSCI ACWI ex US IT Index traded at a discount of .24% below its net asset value, which is worse than its one-year historical average discount of 1.22%.

Rene Casis has been running the fund for 2 years and currently receives a manager quality ranking of 65 (0=worst, 99=best). If you desire an average level of risk, then this fund may be an option.

Data Date	Investment Rating	Net Assets ($Mil)	Price	Performance Rating/Pts	Total Return Y-T-D	Risk Rating/Pts
3-12	C-	2.80	57.32	C / 4.3	19.07%	B- / 7.5
2011	D	2.40	48.14	D- / 1.3	0.06%	B- / 7.4

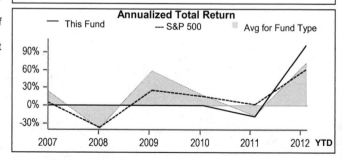

Annualized Total Return — This Fund · --- S&P 500 · Avg for Fund Type

*iShares MSCI ACWI ex US Mtls Ind (AXMT)   D-   Weak

Fund Family: BlackRock Fund Advisors
Fund Type: Precious Metals
Inception Date: July 13, 2010

Data Date	Investment Rating	Net Assets ($Mil)	Price	Performance Rating/Pts	Total Return Y-T-D	Risk Rating/Pts
3-12	D-	2.95	55.22	E+ / 0.9	9.32%	C+ / 6.5
2011	D-	2.50	50.51	E+ / 0.8	3.88%	C+ / 6.5

Major Rating Factors:
Very poor performance is the major factor driving the D- (Weak) TheStreet.com Investment Rating for *iShares MSCI ACWI ex US Mtls Ind. The fund currently has a performance rating of E+ (Very Weak) based on an annualized return of 0.00% over the last three years and a total return of 9.32% year to date 2012. Factored into the performance evaluation is an expense ratio of 0.48% (very low).

The fund's risk rating is currently C+ (Fair). It carries a beta of 0.00, meaning the fund's expected move will be 0.0% for every 10% move in the market. Volatility, as measured by both the semi-deviation and a drawdown factor, is considered low. As of March 31, 2012, *iShares MSCI ACWI ex US Mtls Ind traded at a discount of .65% below its net asset value, which is better than its one-year historical average discount of .26%.

Rene Casis has been running the fund for 2 years and currently receives a manager quality ranking of 4 (0=worst, 99=best). This fund offers only a moderate level of risk but investors looking for strong performance are still waiting.

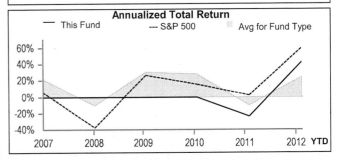

Annualized Total Return
— This Fund   --- S&P 500   Avg for Fund Type

*iShares MSCI ACWI ex US TS Index (AXTE)   D   Weak

Fund Family: BlackRock Fund Advisors
Fund Type: Emerging Market
Inception Date: July 13, 2010

Data Date	Investment Rating	Net Assets ($Mil)	Price	Performance Rating/Pts	Total Return Y-T-D	Risk Rating/Pts
3-12	D	2.69	52.89	D- / 1.1	1.89%	B / 8.3

Major Rating Factors:
Disappointing performance is the major factor driving the D (Weak) TheStreet.com Investment Rating for *iShares MSCI ACWI ex US TS Index. The fund currently has a performance rating of D- (Weak) based on an annualized return of 0.00% over the last three years and a total return of 1.89% year to date 2012. Factored into the performance evaluation is an expense ratio of 0.48% (very low).

The fund's risk rating is currently B (Good). It carries a beta of 0.00, meaning the fund's expected move will be 0.0% for every 10% move in the market. Volatility, as measured by both the semi-deviation and a drawdown factor, is considered low. As of March 31, 2012, *iShares MSCI ACWI ex US TS Index traded at a discount of 1.40% below its net asset value, which is better than its one-year historical average discount of .11%.

Rene Casis has been running the fund for 2 years and currently receives a manager quality ranking of 33 (0=worst, 99=best). This fund offers only a moderate level of risk but investors looking for strong performance are still waiting.

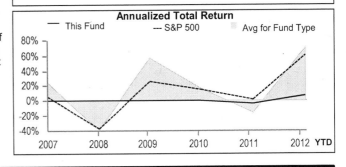

Annualized Total Return
— This Fund   --- S&P 500   Avg for Fund Type

*iShares MSCI ACWI ex US Utl Sct (AXUT)   D   Weak

Fund Family: BlackRock Fund Advisors
Fund Type: Utilities
Inception Date: July 13, 2010

Data Date	Investment Rating	Net Assets ($Mil)	Price	Performance Rating/Pts	Total Return Y-T-D	Risk Rating/Pts
3-12	D	4.45	45.09	D- / 1.1	9.28%	B- / 7.5
2011	D	2.10	41.26	E+ / 0.8	1.14%	B- / 7.4

Major Rating Factors:
Disappointing performance is the major factor driving the D (Weak) TheStreet.com Investment Rating for *iShares MSCI ACWI ex US Utl Sct. The fund currently has a performance rating of D- (Weak) based on an annualized return of 0.00% over the last three years and a total return of 9.28% year to date 2012. Factored into the performance evaluation is an expense ratio of 0.48% (very low).

The fund's risk rating is currently B- (Good). It carries a beta of 0.00, meaning the fund's expected move will be 0.0% for every 10% move in the market. Volatility, as measured by both the semi-deviation and a drawdown factor, is considered low. As of March 31, 2012, *iShares MSCI ACWI ex US Utl Sct traded at a premium of 1.76% above its net asset value, which is worse than its one-year historical average premium of .16%.

Rene Casis has been running the fund for 2 years and currently receives a manager quality ranking of 16 (0=worst, 99=best). This fund offers only a moderate level of risk but investors looking for strong performance are still waiting.

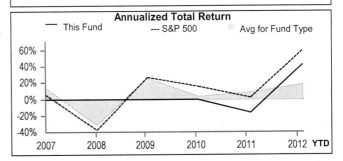

Annualized Total Return
— This Fund   --- S&P 500   Avg for Fund Type

*iShares MSCI ACWI Index Fund (ACWI)

C   **Fair**

Fund Family: BlackRock Fund Advisors
Fund Type: Global
Inception Date: March 26, 2008

Data Date	Investment Rating	Net Assets ($Mil)	Price	Performance Rating/Pts	Total Return Y-T-D	Risk Rating/Pts
3-12	C	2,419.60	47.20	C / 4.4	11.93%	B- / 7.8
2011	C-	2,189.90	42.17	C- / 4.0	0.71%	B- / 7.6
2010	A-	1,501.30	46.81	A- / 9.0	12.82%	C+ / 5.6
2009	A-	492.82	42.29	B+ / 8.4	29.48%	C+ / 5.7

Major Rating Factors: Middle of the road best describes *iShares MSCI ACWI Index Fund whose TheStreet.com Investment Rating is currently a C (Fair). The fund currently has a performance rating of C (Fair) based on an annualized return of 17.95% over the last three years and a total return of 11.93% year to date 2012. Factored into the performance evaluation is an expense ratio of 0.34% (very low).

The fund's risk rating is currently B- (Good). It carries a beta of 0.93, meaning that its performance tracks fairly well with that of the overall stock market. Volatility, as measured by both the semi-deviation and a drawdown factor, is considered low. As of March 31, 2012, *iShares MSCI ACWI Index Fund traded at a premium of .19% above its net asset value, which is worse than its one-year historical average premium of .06%.

Diane Hsiung has been running the fund for 4 years and currently receives a manager quality ranking of 68 (0=worst, 99=best). If you desire an average level of risk, then this fund may be an option.

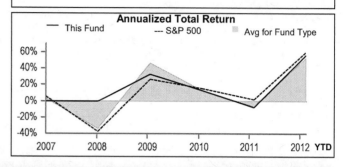

*iShares MSCI ACWI xUS Cnsmr Dis (AXDI)

C-   **Fair**

Fund Family: BlackRock Fund Advisors
Fund Type: Foreign
Inception Date: July 13, 2010

Data Date	Investment Rating	Net Assets ($Mil)	Price	Performance Rating/Pts	Total Return Y-T-D	Risk Rating/Pts
3-12	C-	6.36	64.72	C / 4.7	20.10%	B- / 7.1
2011	D	5.40	53.89	D- / 1.0	1.52%	B- / 7.1

Major Rating Factors: Middle of the road best describes *iShares MSCI ACWI xUS Cnsmr Dis whose TheStreet.com Investment Rating is currently a C- (Fair). The fund currently has a performance rating of C (Fair) based on an annualized return of 0.00% over the last three years and a total return of 20.10% year to date 2012. Factored into the performance evaluation is an expense ratio of 0.48% (very low).

The fund's risk rating is currently B- (Good). It carries a beta of 0.00, meaning the fund's expected move will be 0.0% for every 10% move in the market. Volatility, as measured by both the semi-deviation and a drawdown factor, is considered low. As of March 31, 2012, *iShares MSCI ACWI xUS Cnsmr Dis traded at a premium of .39% above its net asset value, which is worse than its one-year historical average discount of .98%.

Rene Casis has been running the fund for 2 years and currently receives a manager quality ranking of 86 (0=worst, 99=best). If you desire an average level of risk, then this fund may be an option.

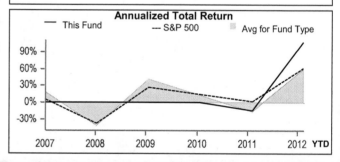

*iShares MSCI ACWI xUS Cnsmr Stp (AXSL)

C+   **Fair**

Fund Family: BlackRock Fund Advisors
Fund Type: Foreign
Inception Date: July 13, 2010

Data Date	Investment Rating	Net Assets ($Mil)	Price	Performance Rating/Pts	Total Return Y-T-D	Risk Rating/Pts
3-12	C+	3.25	67.32	C / 5.0	8.28%	B / 8.7
2011	C-	3.10	62.17	C- / 3.3	-0.77%	B / 8.7

Major Rating Factors: Middle of the road best describes *iShares MSCI ACWI xUS Cnsmr Stp whose TheStreet.com Investment Rating is currently a C+ (Fair). The fund currently has a performance rating of C (Fair) based on an annualized return of 0.00% over the last three years and a total return of 8.28% year to date 2012. Factored into the performance evaluation is an expense ratio of 0.48% (very low).

The fund's risk rating is currently B (Good). It carries a beta of 0.00, meaning the fund's expected move will be 0.0% for every 10% move in the market. Volatility, as measured by both the semi-deviation and a drawdown factor, is considered low. As of March 31, 2012, *iShares MSCI ACWI xUS Cnsmr Stp traded at a premium of .73% above its net asset value, which is worse than its one-year historical average premium of .25%.

Rene Casis has been running the fund for 2 years and currently receives a manager quality ranking of 91 (0=worst, 99=best). If you desire an average level of risk, then this fund may be an option.

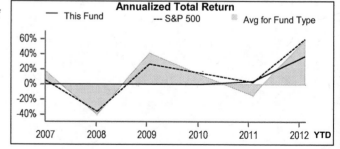

*iShares MSCI All Cntry Asia ex J (AAXJ)

C-   **Fair**

Fund Family: BlackRock Fund Advisors
Fund Type: Foreign
Inception Date: August 13, 2008

Major Rating Factors: Middle of the road best describes *iShares MSCI All Cntry Asia ex J whose TheStreet.com Investment Rating is currently a C- (Fair). The fund currently has a performance rating of C- (Fair) based on an annualized return of 17.65% over the last three years and a total return of 13.11% year to date 2012. Factored into the performance evaluation is an expense ratio of 0.66% (very low).

The fund's risk rating is currently B- (Good). It carries a beta of 1.10, meaning it is expected to move 11.0% for every 10% move in the market. Volatility, as measured by both the semi-deviation and a drawdown factor, is considered low. As of March 31, 2012, *iShares MSCI All Cntry Asia ex J traded at a discount of .14% below its net asset value, which is better than its one-year historical average premium of .07%.

Diane Hsiung has been running the fund for 4 years and currently receives a manager quality ranking of 56 (0=worst, 99=best). If you desire an average level of risk, then this fund may be an option.

Data Date	Investment Rating	Net Assets ($Mil)	Price	Performance Rating/Pts	Total Return Y-T-D	Risk Rating/Pts
3-12	C-	2,469.05	56.44	C- / 4.0	13.11%	B- / 7.1
2011	C-	2,006.60	49.90	C / 4.5	1.04%	B- / 7.1
2010	A-	2,657.90	63.70	A- / 9.0	16.22%	C+ / 6.0
2009	A+	1,045.35	55.71	A / 9.4	60.65%	C+ / 6.0

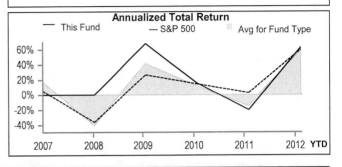

Annualized Total Return

---

*iShares MSCI All Peru Capped Idx (EPU)

B-   **Good**

Fund Family: BlackRock Fund Advisors
Fund Type: Foreign
Inception Date: June 19, 2009

Major Rating Factors: Strong performance is the major factor driving the B- (Good) TheStreet.com Investment Rating for *iShares MSCI All Peru Capped Idx. The fund currently has a performance rating of B (Good) based on an annualized return of 0.00% over the last three years and a total return of 21.71% year to date 2012. Factored into the performance evaluation is an expense ratio of 0.51% (very low).

The fund's risk rating is currently B- (Good). It carries a beta of 0.00, meaning the fund's expected move will be 0.0% for every 10% move in the market. Volatility, as measured by both the semi-deviation and a drawdown factor, is considered low. As of March 31, 2012, *iShares MSCI All Peru Capped Idx traded at a premium of 1.54% above its net asset value, which is worse than its one-year historical average discount of .21%.

Diane Hsiung has been running the fund for 3 years and currently receives a manager quality ranking of 83 (0=worst, 99=best). If you desire only a moderate level of risk and strong performance, then this fund is an excellent option.

Data Date	Investment Rating	Net Assets ($Mil)	Price	Performance Rating/Pts	Total Return Y-T-D	Risk Rating/Pts
3-12	B-	495.82	46.70	B / 7.9	21.71%	B- / 7.0
2011	D	429.60	38.37	D- / 1.4	2.35%	B- / 7.4
2010	A+	556.20	50.36	A+ / 9.8	57.46%	B / 8.3

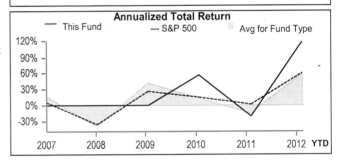

Annualized Total Return

---

*iShares MSCI Australia (EWA)

C-   **Fair**

Fund Family: BlackRock Fund Advisors
Fund Type: Foreign
Inception Date: March 12, 1996

Major Rating Factors: Middle of the road best describes *iShares MSCI Australia whose TheStreet.com Investment Rating is currently a C- (Fair). The fund currently has a performance rating of C (Fair) based on an annualized return of 21.78% over the last three years and a total return of 9.65% year to date 2012. Factored into the performance evaluation is an expense ratio of 0.52% (very low).

The fund's risk rating is currently C+ (Fair). It carries a beta of 1.19, meaning it is expected to move 11.9% for every 10% move in the market. Volatility, as measured by both the semi-deviation and a drawdown factor, is considered low. As of March 31, 2012, *iShares MSCI Australia traded at a premium of .43% above its net asset value, which is worse than its one-year historical average discount of .06%.

Diane Hsiung has been running the fund for 4 years and currently receives a manager quality ranking of 65 (0=worst, 99=best). If you desire an average level of risk, then this fund may be an option.

Data Date	Investment Rating	Net Assets ($Mil)	Price	Performance Rating/Pts	Total Return Y-T-D	Risk Rating/Pts
3-12	C-	2,916.29	23.51	C / 5.0	9.65%	C+ / 6.9
2011	C+	2,637.80	21.44	C+ / 6.3	1.49%	C+ / 6.9
2010	C-	2,958.40	25.44	C+ / 5.6	15.35%	C- / 4.1
2009	C+	1,593.68	22.84	B- / 7.4	66.12%	C / 4.3

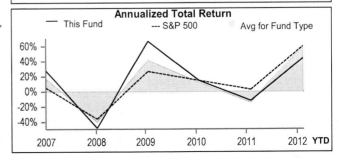

Annualized Total Return

---

*iShares MSCI Austria Inv Mkt (EWO)

D- **Weak**

Fund Family: BlackRock Fund Advisors
Fund Type: Foreign
Inception Date: March 12, 1996

Major Rating Factors:
Disappointing performance is the major factor driving the D- (Weak) TheStreet.com Investment Rating for *iShares MSCI Austria Inv Mkt. The fund currently has a performance rating of D (Weak) based on an annualized return of 10.26% over the last three years and a total return of 15.47% year to date 2012. Factored into the performance evaluation is an expense ratio of 0.52% (very low).

The fund's risk rating is currently C+ (Fair). It carries a beta of 1.47, meaning it is expected to move 14.7% for every 10% move in the market. Volatility, as measured by both the semi-deviation and a drawdown factor, is considered low. As of March 31, 2012, *iShares MSCI Austria Inv Mkt traded at a price exactly equal to its net asset value, which is worse than its one-year historical average discount of .22%.

Diane Hsiung has been running the fund for 4 years and currently receives a manager quality ranking of 13 (0=worst, 99=best). This fund offers only a moderate level of risk but investors looking for strong performance are still waiting.

Data Date	Investment Rating	Net Assets ($Mil)	Price	Performance Rating/Pts	Total Return Y-T-D	Risk Rating/Pts
3-12	D-	78.26	16.42	D / 2.0	15.47%	C+ / 5.8
2011	D-	53.90	14.22	D / 1.6	-3.31%	C+ / 5.7
2010	E+	119.50	22.33	D- / 1.3	15.81%	D+ / 2.8
2009	E+	159.67	19.56	D- / 1.2	52.05%	C- / 3.3

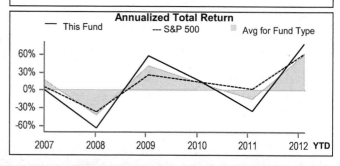

*iShares MSCI Belgium Inv Mkt (EWK)

D+ **Weak**

Fund Family: BlackRock Fund Advisors
Fund Type: Foreign
Inception Date: March 12, 1996

Major Rating Factors: *iShares MSCI Belgium Inv Mkt receives a TheStreet.com Investment Rating of D+ (Weak). The fund currently has a performance rating of C- (Fair) based on an annualized return of 16.21% over the last three years and a total return of 16.52% year to date 2012. Factored into the performance evaluation is an expense ratio of 0.52% (very low).

The fund's risk rating is currently C+ (Fair). It carries a beta of 1.08, meaning that its performance tracks fairly well with that of the overall stock market. Volatility, as measured by both the semi-deviation and a drawdown factor, is considered low. As of March 31, 2012, *iShares MSCI Belgium Inv Mkt traded at a premium of .24% above its net asset value, which is worse than its one-year historical average discount of .04%.

Diane Hsiung has been running the fund for 4 years and currently receives a manager quality ranking of 44 (0=worst, 99=best). If you desire an average level of risk, then this fund may be an option.

Data Date	Investment Rating	Net Assets ($Mil)	Price	Performance Rating/Pts	Total Return Y-T-D	Risk Rating/Pts
3-12	D+	26.22	12.34	C- / 3.7	16.52%	C+ / 6.8
2011	D+	23.40	10.59	D+ / 2.6	-1.79%	C+ / 6.8
2010	E+	50.40	13.13	E+ / 0.7	5.07%	C- / 3.3
2009	E+	53.04	12.76	D- / 1.0	44.41%	C- / 4.0

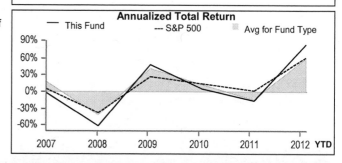

*iShares MSCI Brazil (EWZ)

D+ **Weak**

Fund Family: BlackRock Fund Advisors
Fund Type: Foreign
Inception Date: July 10, 2000

Major Rating Factors: *iShares MSCI Brazil receives a TheStreet.com Investment Rating of D+ (Weak). The fund currently has a performance rating of C- (Fair) based on an annualized return of 18.33% over the last three years and a total return of 12.67% year to date 2012. Factored into the performance evaluation is an expense ratio of 0.59% (very low).

The fund's risk rating is currently C+ (Fair). It carries a beta of 1.36, meaning it is expected to move 13.6% for every 10% move in the market. Volatility, as measured by both the semi-deviation and a drawdown factor, is considered low. As of March 31, 2012, *iShares MSCI Brazil traded at a discount of .40% below its net asset value, which is better than its one-year historical average premium of .32%.

Diane Hsiung has been running the fund for 4 years and currently receives a manager quality ranking of 39 (0=worst, 99=best). If you desire an average level of risk, then this fund may be an option.

Data Date	Investment Rating	Net Assets ($Mil)	Price	Performance Rating/Pts	Total Return Y-T-D	Risk Rating/Pts
3-12	D+	10,568.94	64.66	C- / 4.0	12.67%	C+ / 6.4
2011	C-	9,346.00	57.39	C / 4.9	1.97%	C+ / 6.5
2010	C-	11,699.30	77.40	C+ / 5.6	7.42%	C- / 3.6
2009	B-	8,777.37	74.61	B+ / 8.9	111.28%	C- / 4.2

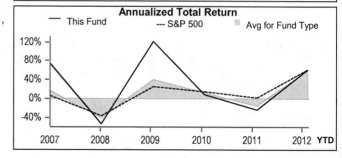

*iShares MSCI Brazil Small Cap In (EWZS)   D+   Weak

Fund Family: BlackRock Fund Advisors
Fund Type: Foreign
Inception Date: September 28, 2010

Data Date	Investment Rating	Net Assets ($Mil)	Price	Perfor-mance Rating/Pts	Total Return Y-T-D	Risk Rating/Pts
3-12	D+	57.99	27.39	C / 4.8	22.22%	C+ / 6.1
2011	D-	45.30	22.41	E+ / 0.7	1.07%	C+ / 6.1

Major Rating Factors: *iShares MSCI Brazil Small Cap In receives a TheStreet.com Investment Rating of D+ (Weak). The fund currently has a performance rating of C (Fair) based on an annualized return of 0.00% over the last three years and a total return of 22.22% year to date 2012. Factored into the performance evaluation is an expense ratio of 0.59% (very low).

The fund's risk rating is currently C+ (Fair). It carries a beta of 0.00, meaning the fund's expected move will be 0.0% for every 10% move in the market. Volatility, as measured by both the semi-deviation and a drawdown factor, is considered low. As of March 31, 2012, *iShares MSCI Brazil Small Cap In traded at a discount of .87% below its net asset value, which is better than its one-year historical average premium of .70%.

Diane Hsiung has been running the fund for 2 years and currently receives a manager quality ranking of 69 (0=worst, 99=best). If you desire an average level of risk, then this fund may be an option.

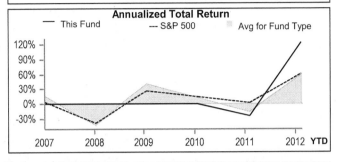

Annualized Total Return
— This Fund   --- S&P 500   Avg for Fund Type

*iShares MSCI BRIC (BKF)   D   Weak

Fund Family: BlackRock Fund Advisors
Fund Type: Foreign
Inception Date: November 12, 2007

Data Date	Investment Rating	Net Assets ($Mil)	Price	Perfor-mance Rating/Pts	Total Return Y-T-D	Risk Rating/Pts
3-12	D	966.53	40.88	C- / 3.3	12.71%	C+ / 6.6
2011	C-	683.90	36.27	C- / 4.0	1.96%	C+ / 6.7
2010	D-	1,188.10	49.13	D / 2.2	9.13%	C- / 4.0
2009	B+	497.84	45.85	A+ / 9.6	74.91%	C- / 4.0

Major Rating Factors: *iShares MSCI BRIC receives a TheStreet.com Investment Rating of D (Weak). The fund currently has a performance rating of C- (Fair) based on an annualized return of 15.58% over the last three years and a total return of 12.71% year to date 2012. Factored into the performance evaluation is an expense ratio of 0.67% (very low).

The fund's risk rating is currently C+ (Fair). It carries a beta of 1.25, meaning it is expected to move 12.5% for every 10% move in the market. Volatility, as measured by both the semi-deviation and a drawdown factor, is considered low. As of March 31, 2012, *iShares MSCI BRIC traded at a discount of .68% below its net asset value, which is better than its one-year historical average discount of .26%.

Diane Hsiung has been running the fund for 4 years and currently receives a manager quality ranking of 33 (0=worst, 99=best). If you desire an average level of risk, then this fund may be an option.

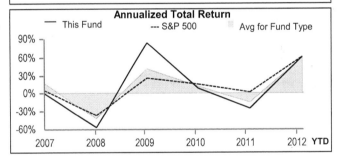

Annualized Total Return
— This Fund   --- S&P 500   Avg for Fund Type

*iShares MSCI Canada (EWC)   C-   Fair

Fund Family: BlackRock Fund Advisors
Fund Type: Foreign
Inception Date: March 12, 1996

Data Date	Investment Rating	Net Assets ($Mil)	Price	Perfor-mance Rating/Pts	Total Return Y-T-D	Risk Rating/Pts
3-12	C-	4,815.94	28.34	C- / 3.9	6.54%	B- / 7.6
2011	C	4,471.00	26.60	C / 4.6	1.13%	B- / 7.4
2010	C	4,647.50	31.00	C+ / 5.6	19.80%	C / 5.0
2009	C+	2,393.64	26.33	C+ / 6.3	49.22%	C / 5.4

Major Rating Factors: Middle of the road best describes *iShares MSCI Canada whose TheStreet.com Investment Rating is currently a C- (Fair). The fund currently has a performance rating of C- (Fair) based on an annualized return of 18.89% over the last three years and a total return of 6.54% year to date 2012. Factored into the performance evaluation is an expense ratio of 0.52% (very low).

The fund's risk rating is currently B- (Good). It carries a beta of 0.98, meaning that its performance tracks fairly well with that of the overall stock market. Volatility, as measured by both the semi-deviation and a drawdown factor, is considered low. As of March 31, 2012, *iShares MSCI Canada traded at a premium of .25% above its net asset value, which is worse than its one-year historical average discount of .06%.

Diane Hsiung has been running the fund for 4 years and currently receives a manager quality ranking of 68 (0=worst, 99=best). If you desire an average level of risk, then this fund may be an option.

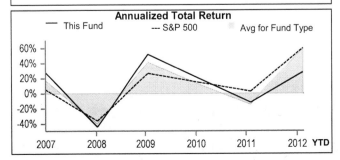

Annualized Total Return
— This Fund   --- S&P 500   Avg for Fund Type

*iShares MSCI Chile Inv Market (ECH)

C+ **Fair**

Fund Family: BlackRock Fund Advisors
Fund Type: Foreign
Inception Date: November 12, 2007

Major Rating Factors: Middle of the road best describes *iShares MSCI Chile Inv Market whose TheStreet.com Investment Rating is currently a C+ (Fair). The fund currently has a performance rating of C+ (Fair) based on an annualized return of 26.15% over the last three years and a total return of 18.35% year to date 2012. Factored into the performance evaluation is an expense ratio of 0.59% (very low).

The fund's risk rating is currently C+ (Fair). It carries a beta of 0.79, meaning the fund's expected move will be 7.9% for every 10% move in the market. Volatility, as measured by both the semi-deviation and a drawdown factor, is considered low. As of March 31, 2012, *iShares MSCI Chile Inv Market traded at a discount of .55% below its net asset value, which is better than its one-year historical average discount of .24%.

Diane Hsiung has been running the fund for 4 years and currently receives a manager quality ranking of 87 (0=worst, 99=best). If you desire an average level of risk, then this fund may be an option.

Data Date	Investment Rating	Net Assets ($Mil)	Price	Perfor-mance Rating/Pts	Total Return Y-T-D	Risk Rating/Pts
3-12	C+	707.03	68.30	C+ / 6.9	18.35%	C+ / 6.7
2011	C+	505.80	57.71	C+ / 6.5	2.55%	C+ / 6.7
2010	A-	1,006.80	79.60	A / 9.3	46.59%	C+ / 5.6
2009	A+	263.21	54.79	A+ / 9.7	82.77%	C+ / 5.8

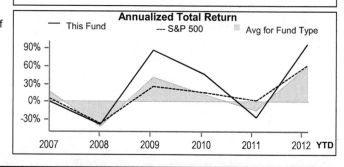

Annualized Total Return

*iShares MSCI China Index (MCHI)

D- **Weak**

Fund Family: BlackRock Fund Advisors
Fund Type: Foreign
Inception Date: March 29, 2011

Major Rating Factors:
Disappointing performance is the major factor driving the D- (Weak) TheStreet.com Investment Rating for *iShares MSCI China Index. The fund currently has a performance rating of D- (Weak) based on an annualized return of 0.00% over the last three years and a total return of 8.18% year to date 2012. Factored into the performance evaluation is an expense ratio of 0.61% (very low).

The fund's risk rating is currently C+ (Fair). It carries a beta of 0.00, meaning the fund's expected move will be 0.0% for every 10% move in the market. Volatility, as measured by both the semi-deviation and a drawdown factor, is considered low. As of March 31, 2012, *iShares MSCI China Index traded at a discount of .43% below its net asset value, which is better than its one-year historical average premium of .17%.

Christopher Bliss has been running the fund for 1 year and currently receives a manager quality ranking of 17 (0=worst, 99=best). This fund offers only a moderate level of risk but investors looking for strong performance are still waiting.

Data Date	Investment Rating	Net Assets ($Mil)	Price	Perfor-mance Rating/Pts	Total Return Y-T-D	Risk Rating/Pts
3-12	D-	338.16	43.52	D- / 1.4	8.18%	C+ / 6.1

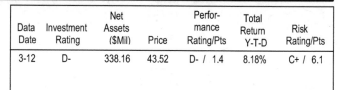

Annualized Total Return

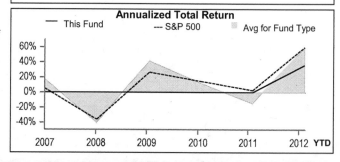

*iShares MSCI China Small Cap Ind (ECNS)

E+ **Very Weak**

Fund Family: BlackRock Fund Advisors
Fund Type: Foreign
Inception Date: September 28, 2010

Major Rating Factors:
Very poor performance is the major factor driving the E+ (Very Weak) TheStreet.com Investment Rating for *iShares MSCI China Small Cap Ind. The fund currently has a performance rating of E+ (Very Weak) based on an annualized return of 0.00% over the last three years and a total return of 10.11% year to date 2012. Factored into the performance evaluation is an expense ratio of 0.59% (very low).

The fund's risk rating is currently C (Fair). It carries a beta of 0.00, meaning the fund's expected move will be 0.0% for every 10% move in the market. Volatility, as measured by both the semi-deviation and a drawdown factor, is considered average. As of March 31, 2012, *iShares MSCI China Small Cap Ind traded at a discount of 1.22% below its net asset value, which is better than its one-year historical average discount of .06%.

Diane Hsiung has been running the fund for 2 years and currently receives a manager quality ranking of 5 (0=worst, 99=best). This fund offers an average level of risk but investors looking for strong performance will be frustrated.

Data Date	Investment Rating	Net Assets ($Mil)	Price	Perfor-mance Rating/Pts	Total Return Y-T-D	Risk Rating/Pts
3-12	E+	18.17	36.55	E+ / 0.8	10.11%	C / 5.2
2011	E+	15.10	33.19	E / 0.3	-1.02%	C / 5.2

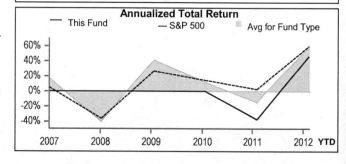

Annualized Total Return

*iShares MSCI EAFE (EFA)   D+   Weak

Fund Family: BlackRock Fund Advisors
Fund Type: Foreign
Inception Date: August 14, 2001

Data Date	Investment Rating	Net Assets ($Mil)	Price	Performance Rating/Pts	Total Return Y-T-D	Risk Rating/Pts
3-12	D+	39,415.90	54.89	C- / 3.2	10.82%	B- / 7.6
2011	D+	36,543.40	49.53	D+ / 2.6	-0.77%	B- / 7.4
2010	D	36,829.10	58.22	D / 1.7	8.25%	C / 5.2
2009	D	32,048.10	55.28	D / 2.0	25.26%	C / 5.0

Major Rating Factors: *iShares MSCI EAFE receives a TheStreet.com Investment Rating of D+ (Weak). The fund currently has a performance rating of C- (Fair) based on an annualized return of 13.91% over the last three years and a total return of 10.82% year to date 2012. Factored into the performance evaluation is an expense ratio of 0.34% (very low).

The fund's risk rating is currently B- (Good). It carries a beta of 1.02, meaning that its performance tracks fairly well with that of the overall stock market. Volatility, as measured by both the semi-deviation and a drawdown factor, is considered low. As of March 31, 2012, *iShares MSCI EAFE traded at a premium of .24% above its net asset value, which is worse than its one-year historical average premium of .01%.

Diane Hsiung has been running the fund for 4 years and currently receives a manager quality ranking of 39 (0=worst, 99=best). If you desire an average level of risk, then this fund may be an option.

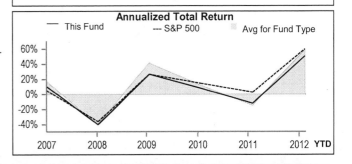

*iShares MSCI EAFE Growth (EFG)   C-   Fair

Fund Family: BlackRock Fund Advisors
Fund Type: Foreign
Inception Date: August 1, 2005

Data Date	Investment Rating	Net Assets ($Mil)	Price	Performance Rating/Pts	Total Return Y-T-D	Risk Rating/Pts
3-12	C-	1,236.06	58.64	C- / 3.6	12.75%	B- / 7.6
2011	D+	1,106.10	52.01	D+ / 2.8	0.00%	B- / 7.4
2010	D	1,338.40	61.08	D+ / 2.3	13.12%	C / 5.3
2009	D	1,198.70	55.12	D / 2.2	22.80%	C / 5.2

Major Rating Factors: Middle of the road best describes *iShares MSCI EAFE Growth whose TheStreet.com Investment Rating is currently a C- (Fair). The fund currently has a performance rating of C- (Fair) based on an annualized return of 15.32% over the last three years and a total return of 12.75% year to date 2012. Factored into the performance evaluation is an expense ratio of 0.40% (very low).

The fund's risk rating is currently B- (Good). It carries a beta of 0.97, meaning that its performance tracks fairly well with that of the overall stock market. Volatility, as measured by both the semi-deviation and a drawdown factor, is considered low. As of March 31, 2012, *iShares MSCI EAFE Growth traded at a premium of .43% above its net asset value, which is worse than its one-year historical average discount of .04%.

Diane Hsiung has been running the fund for 4 years and currently receives a manager quality ranking of 48 (0=worst, 99=best). If you desire an average level of risk, then this fund may be an option.

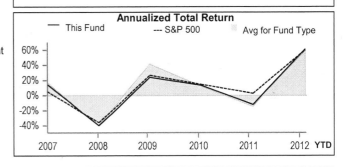

*iShares MSCI EAFE Small Cap Idx (SCZ)   C   Fair

Fund Family: BlackRock Fund Advisors
Fund Type: Foreign
Inception Date: December 10, 2007

Data Date	Investment Rating	Net Assets ($Mil)	Price	Performance Rating/Pts	Total Return Y-T-D	Risk Rating/Pts
3-12	C	1,426.90	40.13	C / 5.2	15.45%	B- / 7.9
2011	C-	1,231.60	34.76	C- / 3.9	-0.03%	B- / 7.9
2010	C-	1,373.40	42.21	C / 4.4	21.51%	C / 5.3
2009	A-	378.00	35.81	B+ / 8.7	41.30%	C / 5.5

Major Rating Factors: Middle of the road best describes *iShares MSCI EAFE Small Cap Idx whose TheStreet.com Investment Rating is currently a C (Fair). The fund currently has a performance rating of C (Fair) based on an annualized return of 21.46% over the last three years and a total return of 15.45% year to date 2012. Factored into the performance evaluation is an expense ratio of 0.40% (very low).

The fund's risk rating is currently B- (Good). It carries a beta of 1.05, meaning that its performance tracks fairly well with that of the overall stock market. Volatility, as measured by both the semi-deviation and a drawdown factor, is considered low. As of March 31, 2012, *iShares MSCI EAFE Small Cap Idx traded at a premium of .48% above its net asset value, which is worse than its one-year historical average discount of .02%.

Diane Hsiung has been running the fund for 4 years and currently receives a manager quality ranking of 73 (0=worst, 99=best). If you desire an average level of risk, then this fund may be an option.

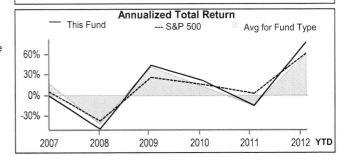

*iShares MSCI EAFE Value (EFV)   D+   Weak

Fund Family: BlackRock Fund Advisors
Fund Type: Foreign
Inception Date: August 1, 2005

Data Date	Investment Rating	Net Assets ($Mil)	Price	Performance Rating/Pts	Total Return Y-T-D	Risk Rating/Pts
3-12	D+	1,341.93	47.00	D+ / 2.9	10.07%	B- / 7.3
2011	D+	1,210.30	42.70	D+ / 2.3	-1.10%	B- / 7.2
2010	D-	1,355.20	50.77	D- / 1.4	4.59%	C / 4.7
2009	D-	1,142.40	50.34	D / 1.7	26.53%	C / 4.8

Major Rating Factors:
Disappointing performance is the major factor driving the D+ (Weak) TheStreet.com Investment Rating for *iShares MSCI EAFE Value. The fund currently has a performance rating of D+ (Weak) based on an annualized return of 12.88% over the last three years and a total return of 10.07% year to date 2012. Factored into the performance evaluation is an expense ratio of 0.40% (very low).

The fund's risk rating is currently B- (Good). It carries a beta of 1.09, meaning that its performance tracks fairly well with that of the overall stock market. Volatility, as measured by both the semi-deviation and a drawdown factor, is considered low. As of March 31, 2012, *iShares MSCI EAFE Value traded at a premium of .58% above its net asset value, which is worse than its one-year historical average discount of .07%.

Diane Hsiung has been running the fund for 4 years and currently receives a manager quality ranking of 31 (0=worst, 99=best). This fund offers only a moderate level of risk but investors looking for strong performance are still waiting.

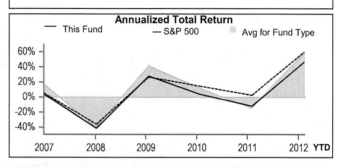

Annualized Total Return

---

*IShares MSCI EM Eastern Europe (ESR)   D-   Weak

Fund Family: BlackRock Fund Advisors
Fund Type: Emerging Market
Inception Date: September 30, 2009

Data Date	Investment Rating	Net Assets ($Mil)	Price	Performance Rating/Pts	Total Return Y-T-D	Risk Rating/Pts
3-12	D-	30.60	27.79	D / 1.6	18.15%	C+ / 5.7
2011	D-	22.30	23.52	E+ / 0.7	1.07%	C+ / 5.7
2010	A+	18.80	31.66	A / 9.4	17.16%	B- / 7.2

Major Rating Factors:
Disappointing performance is the major factor driving the D- (Weak) TheStreet.com Investment Rating for *IShares MSCI EM Eastern Europe. The fund currently has a performance rating of D (Weak) based on an annualized return of 0.00% over the last three years and a total return of 18.15% year to date 2012. Factored into the performance evaluation is an expense ratio of 0.68% (very low).

The fund's risk rating is currently C+ (Fair). It carries a beta of 0.00, meaning the fund's expected move will be 0.0% for every 10% move in the market. Volatility, as measured by both the semi-deviation and a drawdown factor, is considered low. As of March 31, 2012, *IShares MSCI EM Eastern Europe traded at a premium of .47% above its net asset value, which is worse than its one-year historical average discount of .09%.

Diane Hsiung has been running the fund for 3 years and currently receives a manager quality ranking of 15 (0=worst, 99=best). This fund offers only a moderate level of risk but investors looking for strong performance are still waiting.

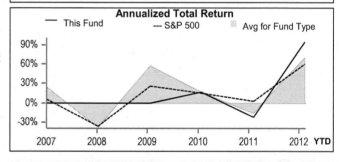

Annualized Total Return

---

*iShares MSCI Emerging Markets (EEM)   C-   Fair

Fund Family: BlackRock Fund Advisors
Fund Type: Emerging Market
Inception Date: April 7, 2003

Data Date	Investment Rating	Net Assets ($Mil)	Price	Performance Rating/Pts	Total Return Y-T-D	Risk Rating/Pts
3-12	C-	41,056.79	42.95	C- / 4.1	13.19%	B- / 7.1
2011	C-	32,493.30	37.94	C / 4.5	0.75%	B- / 7.5
2010	D+	47,459.00	47.64	C / 5.3	16.47%	D+ / 2.7
2009	C	30,268.12	41.50	B- / 7.2	61.14%	C- / 3.1

Major Rating Factors: Middle of the road best describes *iShares MSCI Emerging Markets whose TheStreet.com Investment Rating is currently a C- (Fair). The fund currently has a performance rating of C- (Fair) based on an annualized return of 18.15% over the last three years and a total return of 13.19% year to date 2012. Factored into the performance evaluation is an expense ratio of 0.67% (very low).

The fund's risk rating is currently B- (Good). It carries a beta of 1.06, meaning that its performance tracks fairly well with that of the overall stock market. Volatility, as measured by both the semi-deviation and a drawdown factor, is considered low. As of March 31, 2012, *iShares MSCI Emerging Markets traded at a discount of .16% below its net asset value, which is better than its one-year historical average premium of .04%.

Diane Hsiung has been running the fund for 4 years and currently receives a manager quality ranking of 25 (0=worst, 99=best). If you desire an average level of risk, then this fund may be an option.

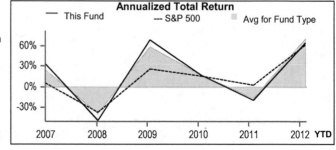

Annualized Total Return

---

*iShares MSCI Emg Mkts Finls Sctr (EMFN)   D   Weak

Fund Family: BlackRock Fund Advisors
Fund Type: Emerging Market
Inception Date: January 20, 2010

Major Rating Factors:
Disappointing performance is the major factor driving the D (Weak) TheStreet.com Investment Rating for *iShares MSCI Emg Mkts Finls Sctr. The fund currently has a performance rating of D+ (Weak) based on an annualized return of 0.00% over the last three years and a total return of 16.15% year to date 2012. Factored into the performance evaluation is an expense ratio of 0.67% (very low).

The fund's risk rating is currently C+ (Fair). It carries a beta of 0.00, meaning the fund's expected move will be 0.0% for every 10% move in the market. Volatility, as measured by both the semi-deviation and a drawdown factor, is considered low. As of March 31, 2012, *iShares MSCI Emg Mkts Finls Sctr traded at a premium of 1.59% above its net asset value, which is worse than its one-year historical average premium of .34%.

Rene Casis has been running the fund for 2 years and currently receives a manager quality ranking of 36 (0=worst, 99=best). This fund offers only a moderate level of risk but investors looking for strong performance are still waiting.

Data Date	Investment Rating	Net Assets ($Mil)	Price	Perfor-mance Rating/Pts	Total Return Y-T-D	Risk Rating/Pts
3-12	D	3.76	24.24	D+ / 2.3	16.15%	C+ / 6.6
2011	D-	3.10	20.87	D- / 1.0	5.03%	C+ / 6.6

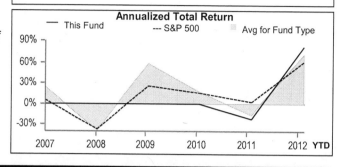

*iShares MSCI Emg Mkts Matl Sctr (EMMT)   D-   Weak

Fund Family: BlackRock Fund Advisors
Fund Type: Emerging Market
Inception Date: January 20, 2010

Major Rating Factors:
Disappointing performance is the major factor driving the D- (Weak) TheStreet.com Investment Rating for *iShares MSCI Emg Mkts Matl Sctr. The fund currently has a performance rating of D- (Weak) based on an annualized return of 0.00% over the last three years and a total return of 11.25% year to date 2012. Factored into the performance evaluation is an expense ratio of 0.67% (very low).

The fund's risk rating is currently C+ (Fair). It carries a beta of 0.00, meaning the fund's expected move will be 0.0% for every 10% move in the market. Volatility, as measured by both the semi-deviation and a drawdown factor, is considered low. As of March 31, 2012, *iShares MSCI Emg Mkts Matl Sctr traded at a discount of .46% below its net asset value, which is in line with its one-year historical average discount of .46%.

Rene Casis has been running the fund for 2 years and currently receives a manager quality ranking of 12 (0=worst, 99=best). This fund offers only a moderate level of risk but investors looking for strong performance are still waiting.

Data Date	Investment Rating	Net Assets ($Mil)	Price	Perfor-mance Rating/Pts	Total Return Y-T-D	Risk Rating/Pts
3-12	D-	9.24	21.46	D- / 1.0	11.25%	C+ / 6.1
2011	D-	7.80	19.29	E+ / 0.6	2.18%	C+ / 6.2

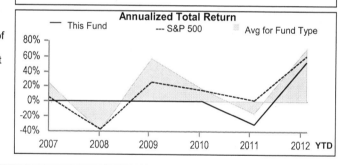

*iShares MSCI EMU (EZU)   D   Weak

Fund Family: BlackRock Fund Advisors
Fund Type: Foreign
Inception Date: July 25, 2000

Major Rating Factors:
Disappointing performance is the major factor driving the D (Weak) TheStreet.com Investment Rating for *iShares MSCI EMU. The fund currently has a performance rating of D (Weak) based on an annualized return of 9.11% over the last three years and a total return of 13.08% year to date 2012. Factored into the performance evaluation is an expense ratio of 0.52% (very low).

The fund's risk rating is currently C+ (Fair). It carries a beta of 1.33, meaning it is expected to move 13.3% for every 10% move in the market. Volatility, as measured by both the semi-deviation and a drawdown factor, is considered low. As of March 31, 2012, *iShares MSCI EMU traded at a premium of .25% above its net asset value, which is worse than its one-year historical average discount of .05%.

Diane Hsiung has been running the fund for 4 years and currently receives a manager quality ranking of 14 (0=worst, 99=best). This fund offers only a moderate level of risk but investors looking for strong performance are still waiting.

Data Date	Investment Rating	Net Assets ($Mil)	Price	Perfor-mance Rating/Pts	Total Return Y-T-D	Risk Rating/Pts
3-12	D	724.84	31.55	D / 2.2	13.08%	C+ / 6.7
2011	D	624.10	27.90	D- / 1.5	-2.15%	C+ / 6.4
2010	E	741.50	35.27	E+ / 0.8	-3.00%	D+ / 2.8
2009	E+	741.27	37.47	D / 1.9	24.42%	D+ / 2.9

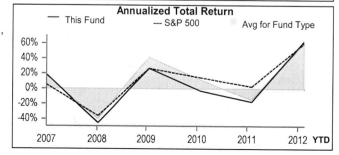

*iShares MSCI Europ Finls Sctr Id (EUFN)

D-   **Weak**

Fund Family: BlackRock Fund Advisors
Fund Type: Financial Services
Inception Date: January 20, 2010

Data Date	Investment Rating	Net Assets ($Mil)	Price	Performance Rating/Pts	Total Return Y-T-D	Risk Rating/Pts
3-12	D-	19.81	17.78	D- / 1.1	17.34%	C+ / 5.6
2011	E+	20.40	15.15	E / 0.4	-4.57%	C+ / 5.6

Major Rating Factors:

Disappointing performance is the major factor driving the D- (Weak) TheStreet.com Investment Rating for *iShares MSCI Europ Finls Sctr Id. The fund currently has a performance rating of D- (Weak) based on an annualized return of 0.00% over the last three years and a total return of 17.34% year to date 2012. Factored into the performance evaluation is an expense ratio of 0.48% (very low).

The fund's risk rating is currently C+ (Fair). It carries a beta of 0.00, meaning the fund's expected move will be 0.0% for every 10% move in the market. Volatility, as measured by both the semi-deviation and a drawdown factor, is considered low. As of March 31, 2012, *iShares MSCI Europ Finls Sctr Id traded at a discount of .34% below its net asset value, which is better than its one-year historical average premium of .11%.

Rene Casis has been running the fund for 2 years and currently receives a manager quality ranking of 6 (0=worst, 99=best). This fund offers only a moderate level of risk but investors looking for strong performance are still waiting.

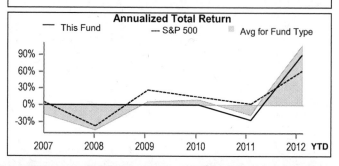

*iShares MSCI Far East Finls Sctr (FEFN)

D   **Weak**

Fund Family: BlackRock Fund Advisors
Fund Type: Financial Services
Inception Date: January 20, 2010

Data Date	Investment Rating	Net Assets ($Mil)	Price	Performance Rating/Pts	Total Return Y-T-D	Risk Rating/Pts
3-12	D	2.46	24.61	D- / 1.2	15.65%	B- / 7.5

Major Rating Factors:

Disappointing performance is the major factor driving the D (Weak) TheStreet.com Investment Rating for *iShares MSCI Far East Finls Sctr. The fund currently has a performance rating of D- (Weak) based on an annualized return of 0.00% over the last three years and a total return of 15.65% year to date 2012. Factored into the performance evaluation is an expense ratio of 0.48% (very low).

The fund's risk rating is currently B- (Good). It carries a beta of 0.00, meaning the fund's expected move will be 0.0% for every 10% move in the market. Volatility, as measured by both the semi-deviation and a drawdown factor, is considered low. As of March 31, 2012, *iShares MSCI Far East Finls Sctr traded at a premium of .20% above its net asset value, which is worse than its one-year historical average discount of .04%.

Rene Casis has been running the fund for 2 years and currently receives a manager quality ranking of 49 (0=worst, 99=best). This fund offers only a moderate level of risk but investors looking for strong performance are still waiting.

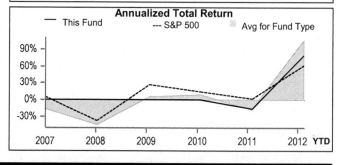

*iShares MSCI France (EWQ)

D   **Weak**

Fund Family: BlackRock Fund Advisors
Fund Type: Foreign
Inception Date: March 12, 1996

Data Date	Investment Rating	Net Assets ($Mil)	Price	Performance Rating/Pts	Total Return Y-T-D	Risk Rating/Pts
3-12	D	270.52	22.07	D / 2.2	12.72%	C+ / 6.3
2011	D	251.40	19.58	D- / 1.5	-2.71%	C+ / 6.3
2010	D-	286.50	24.45	D- / 1.0	-2.38%	C / 4.3
2009	D	184.51	25.85	D / 2.2	24.15%	C / 4.7

Major Rating Factors:

Disappointing performance is the major factor driving the D (Weak) TheStreet.com Investment Rating for *iShares MSCI France. The fund currently has a performance rating of D (Weak) based on an annualized return of 9.03% over the last three years and a total return of 12.72% year to date 2012. Factored into the performance evaluation is an expense ratio of 0.52% (very low).

The fund's risk rating is currently C+ (Fair). It carries a beta of 1.33, meaning it is expected to move 13.3% for every 10% move in the market. Volatility, as measured by both the semi-deviation and a drawdown factor, is considered low. As of March 31, 2012, *iShares MSCI France traded at a premium of .23% above its net asset value, which is worse than its one-year historical average discount of .08%.

Diane Hsiung has been running the fund for 4 years and currently receives a manager quality ranking of 14 (0=worst, 99=best). This fund offers only a moderate level of risk but investors looking for strong performance are still waiting.

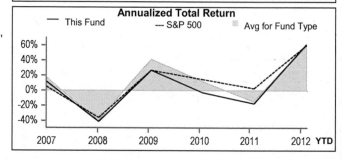

*iShares MSCI Germany (EWG)   D+   Weak

Fund Family: BlackRock Fund Advisors
Fund Type: Foreign
Inception Date: March 12, 1996

Data Date	Investment Rating	Net Assets ($Mil)	Price	Perfor-mance Rating/Pts	Total Return Y-T-D	Risk Rating/Pts
3-12	D+	3,143.08	23.28	C- / 3.8	21.12%	C+ / 6.6
2011	D	2,313.50	19.22	D / 2.0	0.36%	C+ / 6.3
2010	D-	1,892.70	23.94	D- / 1.3	8.31%	C / 4.7
2009	D	619.64	22.44	D+ / 2.8	19.62%	C- / 4.2

Major Rating Factors: *iShares MSCI Germany receives a TheStreet.com Investment Rating of D+ (Weak). The fund currently has a performance rating of C- (Fair) based on an annualized return of 14.86% over the last three years and a total return of 21.12% year to date 2012. Factored into the performance evaluation is an expense ratio of 0.51% (very low).

The fund's risk rating is currently C+ (Fair). It carries a beta of 1.33, meaning it is expected to move 13.3% for every 10% move in the market. Volatility, as measured by both the semi-deviation and a drawdown factor, is considered low. As of March 31, 2012, *iShares MSCI Germany traded at a premium of .26% above its net asset value, which is worse than its one-year historical average discount of .02%.

Diane Hsiung has been running the fund for 4 years and currently receives a manager quality ranking of 24 (0=worst, 99=best). If you desire an average level of risk, then this fund may be an option.

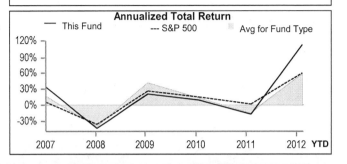

*iShares MSCI Hong Kong (EWH)   C-   Fair

Fund Family: BlackRock Fund Advisors
Fund Type: Foreign
Inception Date: March 12, 1996

Data Date	Investment Rating	Net Assets ($Mil)	Price	Perfor-mance Rating/Pts	Total Return Y-T-D	Risk Rating/Pts
3-12	C-	1,984.24	17.45	C / 4.5	12.77%	B- / 7.2
2011	C-	1,814.00	15.47	C / 4.5	0.52%	B- / 7.3
2010	C-	2,059.00	18.92	C / 4.7	24.16%	C / 5.0
2009	C	1,951.78	15.66	C+ / 5.6	48.91%	C / 5.0

Major Rating Factors: Middle of the road best describes *iShares MSCI Hong Kong whose TheStreet.com Investment Rating is currently a C- (Fair). The fund currently has a performance rating of C (Fair) based on an annualized return of 19.19% over the last three years and a total return of 12.77% year to date 2012. Factored into the performance evaluation is an expense ratio of 0.52% (very low).

The fund's risk rating is currently B- (Good). It carries a beta of 0.98, meaning that its performance tracks fairly well with that of the overall stock market. Volatility, as measured by both the semi-deviation and a drawdown factor, is considered low. As of March 31, 2012, *iShares MSCI Hong Kong traded at a discount of .29% below its net asset value, which is better than its one-year historical average premium of .04%.

Diane Hsiung has been running the fund for 4 years and currently receives a manager quality ranking of 72 (0=worst, 99=best). If you desire an average level of risk, then this fund may be an option.

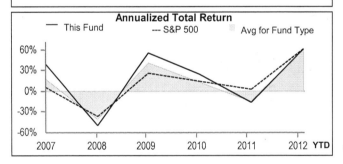

*iShares MSCI Indonesia Inv Mkt I (EIDO)   D+   Weak

Fund Family: BlackRock Fund Advisors
Fund Type: Foreign
Inception Date: May 5, 2010

Data Date	Investment Rating	Net Assets ($Mil)	Price	Perfor-mance Rating/Pts	Total Return Y-T-D	Risk Rating/Pts
3-12	D+	330.92	30.94	C- / 3.4	5.56%	C+ / 6.9
2011	D+	295.60	29.31	C- / 3.0	0.96%	C+ / 6.9

Major Rating Factors: *iShares MSCI Indonesia Inv Mkt I receives a TheStreet.com Investment Rating of D+ (Weak). The fund currently has a performance rating of C- (Fair) based on an annualized return of 0.00% over the last three years and a total return of 5.56% year to date 2012. Factored into the performance evaluation is an expense ratio of 0.59% (very low).

The fund's risk rating is currently C+ (Fair). It carries a beta of 0.00, meaning the fund's expected move will be 0.0% for every 10% move in the market. Volatility, as measured by both the semi-deviation and a drawdown factor, is considered low. As of March 31, 2012, *iShares MSCI Indonesia Inv Mkt I traded at a discount of .45% below its net asset value, which is better than its one-year historical average discount of .42%.

Diane Hsiung has been running the fund for 2 years and currently receives a manager quality ranking of 86 (0=worst, 99=best). If you desire an average level of risk, then this fund may be an option.

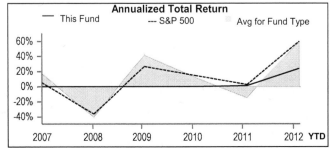

*iShares MSCI Irlnd Capd Inv Mkt (EIRL)

B-   **Good**

Fund Family: BlackRock Fund Advisors
Fund Type: Foreign
Inception Date: May 5, 2010

Major Rating Factors: Strong performance is the major factor driving the B- (Good) TheStreet.com Investment Rating for *iShares MSCI Irlnd Capd Inv Mkt. The fund currently has a performance rating of B (Good) based on an annualized return of 0.00% over the last three years and a total return of 21.70% year to date 2012. Factored into the performance evaluation is an expense ratio of 0.52% (very low).

The fund's risk rating is currently B- (Good). It carries a beta of 0.00, meaning the fund's expected move will be 0.0% for every 10% move in the market. Volatility, as measured by both the semi-deviation and a drawdown factor, is considered low. As of March 31, 2012, *iShares MSCI Irlnd Capd Inv Mkt traded at a premium of 2.03% above its net asset value, which is worse than its one-year historical average premium of .34%.

Diane Hsiung has been running the fund for 2 years and currently receives a manager quality ranking of 92 (0=worst, 99=best). If you desire only a moderate level of risk and strong performance, then this fund is an excellent option.

Data Date	Investment Rating	Net Assets ($Mil)	Price	Performance Rating/Pts	Total Return Y-T-D	Risk Rating/Pts
3-12	B-	7.85	23.11	B / 7.9	21.70%	B- / 7.3
2011	D	7.60	18.99	D- / 1.3	-1.95%	B- / 7.3

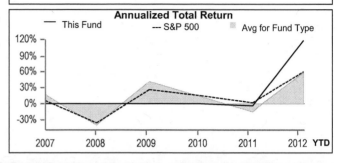

Annualized Total Return
— This Fund   --- S&P 500   ▨ Avg for Fund Type

*iShares MSCI Israel Capped Inv M (EIS)

D   **Weak**

Fund Family: BlackRock Fund Advisors
Fund Type: Foreign
Inception Date: March 26, 2008

Major Rating Factors:
Disappointing performance is the major factor driving the D (Weak) TheStreet.com Investment Rating for *iShares MSCI Israel Capped Inv M. The fund currently has a performance rating of D (Weak) based on an annualized return of 10.66% over the last three years and a total return of 8.87% year to date 2012. Factored into the performance evaluation is an expense ratio of 0.59% (very low).

The fund's risk rating is currently C+ (Fair). It carries a beta of 0.95, meaning that its performance tracks fairly well with that of the overall stock market. Volatility, as measured by both the semi-deviation and a drawdown factor, is considered low. As of March 31, 2012, *iShares MSCI Israel Capped Inv M traded at a premium of .72% above its net asset value, which is worse than its one-year historical average discount of .20%.

Diane Hsiung has been running the fund for 4 years and currently receives a manager quality ranking of 26 (0=worst, 99=best). This fund offers only a moderate level of risk but investors looking for strong performance are still waiting.

Data Date	Investment Rating	Net Assets ($Mil)	Price	Performance Rating/Pts	Total Return Y-T-D	Risk Rating/Pts
3-12	D	95.52	43.07	D / 2.0	8.87%	C+ / 6.6
2011	D+	75.20	39.56	D+ / 2.8	3.44%	C+ / 6.6
2010	A-	141.30	60.52	A / 9.3	15.39%	C+ / 5.6
2009	A+	107.79	54.40	A+ / 9.6	71.67%	C+ / 5.9

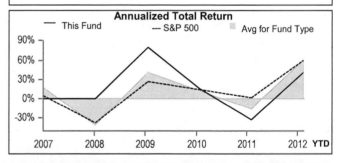

Annualized Total Return
— This Fund   --- S&P 500   ▨ Avg for Fund Type

*iShares MSCI Italy (EWI)

D-   **Weak**

Fund Family: BlackRock Fund Advisors
Fund Type: Foreign
Inception Date: March 12, 1996

Major Rating Factors:
Disappointing performance is the major factor driving the D- (Weak) TheStreet.com Investment Rating for *iShares MSCI Italy. The fund currently has a performance rating of D- (Weak) based on an annualized return of 1.21% over the last three years and a total return of 9.09% year to date 2012. Factored into the performance evaluation is an expense ratio of 0.51% (very low).

The fund's risk rating is currently C+ (Fair). It carries a beta of 1.50, meaning it is expected to move 15.0% for every 10% move in the market. Volatility, as measured by both the semi-deviation and a drawdown factor, is considered low. As of March 31, 2012, *iShares MSCI Italy traded at a premium of .15% above its net asset value, which is worse than its one-year historical average discount of .06%.

Diane Hsiung has been running the fund for 4 years and currently receives a manager quality ranking of 7 (0=worst, 99=best). This fund offers only a moderate level of risk but investors looking for strong performance are still waiting.

Data Date	Investment Rating	Net Assets ($Mil)	Price	Performance Rating/Pts	Total Return Y-T-D	Risk Rating/Pts
3-12	D-	146.99	13.08	D- / 1.1	9.09%	C+ / 5.6
2011	D-	100.80	11.99	D- / 1.1	-5.25%	C / 5.5
2010	E+	95.80	16.38	E+ / 0.6	-14.12%	C- / 3.8
2009	D-	125.72	19.51	D- / 1.1	20.86%	C / 4.3

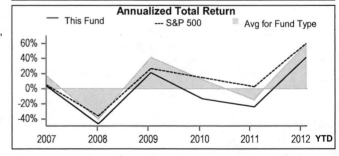

Annualized Total Return
— This Fund   --- S&P 500   ▨ Avg for Fund Type

*iShares MSCI Japan (EWJ)

D+ **Weak**

Fund Family: BlackRock Fund Advisors
Fund Type: Foreign
Inception Date: March 12, 1996

Major Rating Factors:
Disappointing performance is the major factor driving the D+ (Weak) TheStreet.com Investment Rating for *iShares MSCI Japan. The fund currently has a performance rating of D+ (Weak) based on an annualized return of 8.57% over the last three years and a total return of 11.69% year to date 2012. Factored into the performance evaluation is an expense ratio of 0.51% (very low).

The fund's risk rating is currently B- (Good). It carries a beta of 0.57, meaning the fund's expected move will be 5.7% for every 10% move in the market. Volatility, as measured by both the semi-deviation and a drawdown factor, is considered low. As of March 31, 2012, *iShares MSCI Japan traded at a premium of .39% above its net asset value, which is worse than its one-year historical average discount of .09%.

Diane Hsiung has been running the fund for 4 years and currently receives a manager quality ranking of 51 (0=worst, 99=best). This fund offers only a moderate level of risk but investors looking for strong performance are still waiting.

Data Date	Investment Rating	Net Assets ($Mil)	Price	Performance Rating/Pts	Total Return Y-T-D	Risk Rating/Pts
3-12	D+	5,081.89	10.18	D+ / 2.3	11.69%	B- / 7.9
2011	D+	5,345.00	9.11	D / 1.7	-0.49%	B- / 7.6
2010	D+	4,904.70	10.91	D+ / 2.4	13.61%	C+ / 5.6
2009	D-	6,164.17	9.74	E+ / 0.9	2.60%	C+ / 5.8

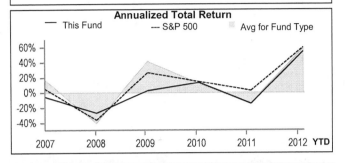

*iShares MSCI Japan Small Cap (SCJ)

C- **Fair**

Fund Family: BlackRock Fund Advisors
Fund Type: Foreign
Inception Date: December 20, 2007

Major Rating Factors: Middle of the road best describes *iShares MSCI Japan Small Cap whose TheStreet.com Investment Rating is currently a C- (Fair). The fund currently has a performance rating of C- (Fair) based on an annualized return of 13.68% over the last three years and a total return of 8.23% year to date 2012. Factored into the performance evaluation is an expense ratio of 0.51% (very low).

The fund's risk rating is currently B (Good). It carries a beta of 0.41, meaning the fund's expected move will be 4.1% for every 10% move in the market. Volatility, as measured by both the semi-deviation and a drawdown factor, is considered low. As of March 31, 2012, *iShares MSCI Japan Small Cap traded at a discount of .21% below its net asset value, which is better than its one-year historical average discount of .12%.

Diane Hsiung has been running the fund for 4 years and currently receives a manager quality ranking of 80 (0=worst, 99=best). If you desire an average level of risk, then this fund may be an option.

Data Date	Investment Rating	Net Assets ($Mil)	Price	Performance Rating/Pts	Total Return Y-T-D	Risk Rating/Pts
3-12	C-	54.91	46.89	C- / 3.2	8.23%	B / 8.6
2011	C-	52.20	43.33	C- / 3.0	0.08%	B- / 7.8
2010	C	42.00	46.66	C / 4.3	19.07%	C+ / 6.1
2009	D+	35.56	39.99	D / 2.1	3.32%	C+ / 6.3

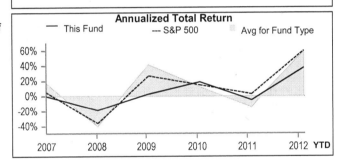

*iShares MSCI KLD 400 Social Idx (DSI)

C+ **Fair**

Fund Family: BlackRock Fund Advisors
Fund Type: Income
Inception Date: November 14, 2006

Major Rating Factors: Middle of the road best describes *iShares MSCI KLD 400 Social Idx whose TheStreet.com Investment Rating is currently a C+ (Fair). The fund currently has a performance rating of C (Fair) based on an annualized return of 20.02% over the last three years and a total return of 11.06% year to date 2012. Factored into the performance evaluation is an expense ratio of 0.50% (very low).

The fund's risk rating is currently B (Good). It carries a beta of 0.98, meaning that its performance tracks fairly well with that of the overall stock market. Volatility, as measured by both the semi-deviation and a drawdown factor, is considered low. As of March 31, 2012, *iShares MSCI KLD 400 Social Idx traded at a discount of .04% below its net asset value, which is better than its one-year historical average premium of .01%.

Diane Hsiung has been running the fund for 4 years and currently receives a manager quality ranking of 42 (0=worst, 99=best). If you desire an average level of risk, then this fund may be an option.

Data Date	Investment Rating	Net Assets ($Mil)	Price	Performance Rating/Pts	Total Return Y-T-D	Risk Rating/Pts
3-12	C+	169.23	51.90	C / 5.4	11.06%	B / 8.4
2011	C	161.20	46.89	C / 5.1	1.30%	B / 8.0
2010	C-	140.70	46.91	C- / 4.0	11.42%	C+ / 6.0
2009	C-	65.81	42.71	D+ / 2.8	27.31%	C+ / 6.1

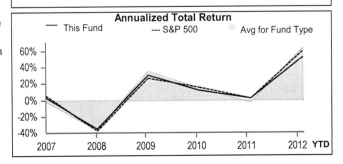

*iShares MSCI Kokusai Index (TOK)

C **Fair**

Fund Family: BlackRock Fund Advisors
Fund Type: Global
Inception Date: December 10, 2007

Major Rating Factors: Middle of the road best describes *iShares MSCI Kokusai Index whose TheStreet.com Investment Rating is currently a C (Fair). The fund currently has a performance rating of C (Fair) based on an annualized return of 19.19% over the last three years and a total return of 10.76% year to date 2012. Factored into the performance evaluation is an expense ratio of 0.25% (very low).

The fund's risk rating is currently B- (Good). It carries a beta of 0.86, meaning the fund's expected move will be 8.6% for every 10% move in the market. Volatility, as measured by both the semi-deviation and a drawdown factor, is considered low. As of March 31, 2012, *iShares MSCI Kokusai Index traded at a premium of .67% above its net asset value, which is worse than its one-year historical average premium of .60%.

Diane Hsiung has been running the fund for 4 years and currently receives a manager quality ranking of 75 (0=worst, 99=best). If you desire an average level of risk, then this fund may be an option.

Data Date	Investment Rating	Net Assets ($Mil)	Price	Performance Rating/Pts	Total Return Y-T-D	Risk Rating/Pts
3-12	C	615.97	41.88	C / 4.6	10.76%	B- / 7.9
2011	C	611.30	37.81	C / 4.3	0.50%	B- / 7.7
2010	D+	287.30	40.24	D+ / 2.9	11.45%	C+ / 5.7
2009	A	83.82	36.95	B+ / 8.6	31.91%	C+ / 5.8

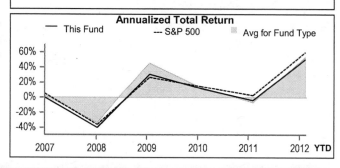

*iShares MSCI Malaysia (EWM)

B **Good**

Fund Family: BlackRock Fund Advisors
Fund Type: Foreign
Inception Date: March 12, 1996

Major Rating Factors: Strong performance is the major factor driving the B (Good) TheStreet.com Investment Rating for *iShares MSCI Malaysia. The fund currently has a performance rating of B (Good) based on an annualized return of 28.83% over the last three years and a total return of 8.96% year to date 2012. Factored into the performance evaluation is an expense ratio of 0.52% (very low).

The fund's risk rating is currently B- (Good). It carries a beta of 0.76, meaning the fund's expected move will be 7.6% for every 10% move in the market. Volatility, as measured by both the semi-deviation and a drawdown factor, is considered low. As of March 31, 2012, *iShares MSCI Malaysia traded at a discount of .41% below its net asset value, which is better than its one-year historical average discount of .03%.

Diane Hsiung has been running the fund for 4 years and currently receives a manager quality ranking of 91 (0=worst, 99=best). If you desire only a moderate level of risk and strong performance, then this fund is an excellent option.

Data Date	Investment Rating	Net Assets ($Mil)	Price	Performance Rating/Pts	Total Return Y-T-D	Risk Rating/Pts
3-12	B	955.55	14.60	B / 7.6	8.96%	B- / 7.9
2011	B	855.70	13.40	B- / 7.4	0.90%	B / 8.0
2010	B+	973.10	14.38	B+ / 8.4	38.97%	C+ / 5.7
2009	C+	513.00	10.62	C+ / 6.5	44.77%	C+ / 5.7

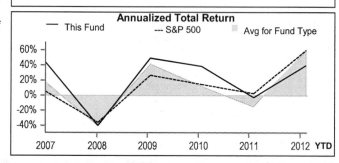

*iShares MSCI Mexico Inv Market (EWW)

B- **Good**

Fund Family: BlackRock Fund Advisors
Fund Type: Foreign
Inception Date: March 12, 1996

Major Rating Factors: Strong performance is the major factor driving the B- (Good) TheStreet.com Investment Rating for *iShares MSCI Mexico Inv Market. The fund currently has a performance rating of B (Good) based on an annualized return of 28.71% over the last three years and a total return of 16.29% year to date 2012. Factored into the performance evaluation is an expense ratio of 0.52% (very low).

The fund's risk rating is currently B- (Good). It carries a beta of 0.95, meaning that its performance tracks fairly well with that of the overall stock market. Volatility, as measured by both the semi-deviation and a drawdown factor, is considered low. As of March 31, 2012, *iShares MSCI Mexico Inv Market traded at a premium of .05% above its net asset value, which is worse than its one-year historical average discount of .04%.

Diane Hsiung has been running the fund for 4 years and currently receives a manager quality ranking of 90 (0=worst, 99=best). If you desire only a moderate level of risk and strong performance, then this fund is an excellent option.

Data Date	Investment Rating	Net Assets ($Mil)	Price	Performance Rating/Pts	Total Return Y-T-D	Risk Rating/Pts
3-12	B-	1,331.78	62.52	B / 7.7	16.29%	B- / 7.5
2011	C+	1,133.30	53.76	C+ / 6.1	1.00%	B- / 7.3
2010	B-	1,720.10	61.92	B / 7.8	27.91%	C / 4.6
2009	C	694.28	48.87	C+ / 6.3	47.42%	C / 4.6

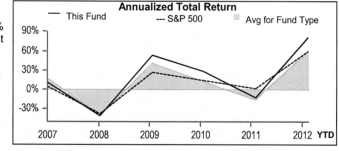

*iShares MSCI Netherlands Inv Mar (EWN)   D   Weak

Fund Family: BlackRock Fund Advisors
Fund Type: Foreign
Inception Date: March 12, 1996

Major Rating Factors: *iShares MSCI Netherlands Inv Mar receives a
TheStreet.com Investment Rating of D (Weak). The fund currently has a performance
rating of C- (Fair) based on an annualized return of 14.88% over the last three years
and a total return of 10.21% year to date 2012. Factored into the performance
evaluation is an expense ratio of 0.52% (very low).

The fund's risk rating is currently C+ (Fair). It carries a beta of 1.20, meaning it is
expected to move 12.0% for every 10% move in the market. Volatility, as measured
by both the semi-deviation and a drawdown factor, is considered low. As of March 31,
2012, *iShares MSCI Netherlands Inv Mar traded at a premium of .11% above its net
asset value, which is worse than its one-year historical average discount of .04%.

Diane Hsiung has been running the fund for 4 years and currently receives a
manager quality ranking of 28 (0=worst, 99=best). If you desire an average level of
risk, then this fund may be an option.

Data Date	Investment Rating	Net Assets ($Mil)	Price	Performance Rating/Pts	Total Return Y-T-D	Risk Rating/Pts
3-12	D	67.72	18.99	C- / 3.1	10.21%	C+ / 6.8
2011	D	73.50	17.23	D / 2.2	-3.02%	C+ / 6.7
2010	D-	172.20	21.09	D- / 1.3	4.95%	C- / 4.1
2009	D+	83.35	20.46	C- / 3.4	36.55%	C / 4.9

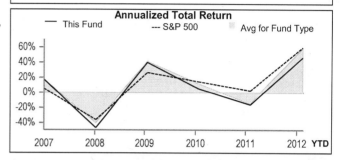

*iShares MSCI New Zealand Inv Mk (ENZL)   C+   Fair

Fund Family: BlackRock Fund Advisors
Fund Type: Foreign
Inception Date: September 1, 2010

Major Rating Factors: Middle of the road best describes *iShares MSCI New
Zealand Inv Mk whose TheStreet.com Investment Rating is currently a C+ (Fair). The
fund currently has a performance rating of C+ (Fair) based on an annualized return of
0.00% over the last three years and a total return of 14.88% year to date 2012.
Factored into the performance evaluation is an expense ratio of 0.51% (very low).

The fund's risk rating is currently B- (Good). It carries a beta of 0.00, meaning the
fund's expected move will be 0.0% for every 10% move in the market. Volatility, as
measured by both the semi-deviation and a drawdown factor, is considered low. As of
March 31, 2012, *iShares MSCI New Zealand Inv Mk traded at a premium of .38%
above its net asset value, which is worse than its one-year historical average
premium of .05%.

Diane Hsiung has been running the fund for 2 years and currently receives a
manager quality ranking of 92 (0=worst, 99=best). If you desire an average level of
risk, then this fund may be an option.

Data Date	Investment Rating	Net Assets ($Mil)	Price	Performance Rating/Pts	Total Return Y-T-D	Risk Rating/Pts
3-12	C+	104.78	31.66	C+ / 5.6	14.88%	B- / 7.9
2011	D	95.80	27.56	D- / 1.4	-0.51%	B- / 7.9

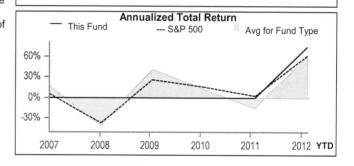

*iShares MSCI Pacific ex-Japan (EPP)   C   Fair

Fund Family: BlackRock Fund Advisors
Fund Type: Foreign
Inception Date: October 25, 2001

Major Rating Factors: Middle of the road best describes *iShares MSCI Pacific
ex-Japan whose TheStreet.com Investment Rating is currently a C (Fair). The fund
currently has a performance rating of C (Fair) based on an annualized return of
21.95% over the last three years and a total return of 11.79% year to date 2012.
Factored into the performance evaluation is an expense ratio of 0.50% (very low).

The fund's risk rating is currently B- (Good). It carries a beta of 1.14, meaning it is
expected to move 11.4% for every 10% move in the market. Volatility, as measured
by both the semi-deviation and a drawdown factor, is considered low. As of March 31,
2012, *iShares MSCI Pacific ex-Japan traded at a premium of .07% above its net
asset value, which is worse than its one-year historical average discount of .07%.

Diane Hsiung has been running the fund for 4 years and currently receives a
manager quality ranking of 70 (0=worst, 99=best). If you desire an average level of
risk, then this fund may be an option.

Data Date	Investment Rating	Net Assets ($Mil)	Price	Performance Rating/Pts	Total Return Y-T-D	Risk Rating/Pts
3-12	C	3,519.75	43.52	C / 5.3	11.79%	B- / 7.1
2011	C	3,099.70	38.93	C+ / 6.0	1.59%	B- / 7.1
2010	D	4,319.90	46.98	C+ / 5.7	17.77%	D- / 1.4
2009	C-	3,382.55	41.37	B- / 7.1	61.99%	D / 1.8

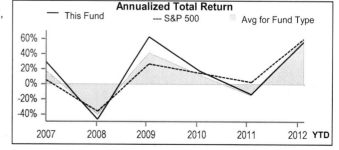

*iShares MSCI Philipps Invst Mkt (EPHE)

B+   **Good**

Fund Family: BlackRock Fund Advisors
Fund Type: Foreign
Inception Date: September 28, 2010

Data Date	Investment Rating	Net Assets ($Mil)	Price	Perfor-mance Rating/Pts	Total Return Y-T-D	Risk Rating/Pts
3-12	B+	99.75	28.74	A / 9.4	21.93%	B- / 7.3
2011	D+	69.80	23.57	D / 2.2	2.21%	B- / 7.3

Major Rating Factors:
Exceptional performance is the major factor driving the B+ (Good) TheStreet.com Investment Rating for *iShares MSCI Philipps Invst Mkt. The fund currently has a performance rating of A (Excellent) based on an annualized return of 0.00% over the last three years and a total return of 21.93% year to date 2012. Factored into the performance evaluation is an expense ratio of 0.59% (very low).

The fund's risk rating is currently B- (Good). It carries a beta of 0.00, meaning the fund's expected move will be 0.0% for every 10% move in the market. Volatility, as measured by both the semi-deviation and a drawdown factor, is considered low. As of March 31, 2012, *iShares MSCI Philipps Invst Mkt traded at a premium of .56% above its net asset value, which is worse than its one-year historical average discount of .17%.

Diane Hsiung has been running the fund for 2 years and currently receives a manager quality ranking of 97 (0=worst, 99=best). If you desire only a moderate level of risk and strong performance, then this fund is an excellent option.

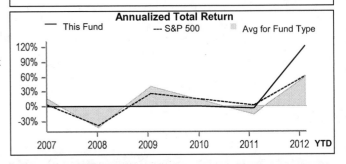

*iShares MSCI Poland Invstbl Mkt (EPOL)

E+   **Very Weak**

Fund Family: BlackRock Fund Advisors
Fund Type: Foreign
Inception Date: May 25, 2010

Data Date	Investment Rating	Net Assets ($Mil)	Price	Perfor-mance Rating/Pts	Total Return Y-T-D	Risk Rating/Pts
3-12	E+	138.92	25.95	D- / 1.1	19.89%	C / 5.0
2011	E+	109.80	21.64	E- / 0.2	-3.19%	C / 4.9

Major Rating Factors:
Disappointing performance is the major factor driving the E+ (Very Weak) TheStreet.com Investment Rating for *iShares MSCI Poland Invstbl Mkt. The fund currently has a performance rating of D- (Weak) based on an annualized return of 0.00% over the last three years and a total return of 19.89% year to date 2012. Factored into the performance evaluation is an expense ratio of 0.59% (very low).

The fund's risk rating is currently C (Fair). It carries a beta of 0.00, meaning the fund's expected move will be 0.0% for every 10% move in the market. Volatility, as measured by both the semi-deviation and a drawdown factor, is considered average. As of March 31, 2012, *iShares MSCI Poland Invstbl Mkt traded at a premium of .35% above its net asset value, which is worse than its one-year historical average discount of .07%.

Diane Hsiung has been running the fund for 2 years and currently receives a manager quality ranking of 9 (0=worst, 99=best). This fund offers an average level of risk but investors looking for strong performance will be frustrated.

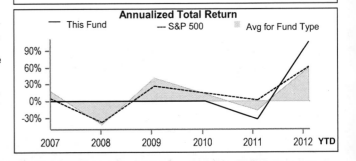

*iShares MSCI Russia Capped Index (ERUS)

D-   **Weak**

Fund Family: BlackRock Fund Advisors
Fund Type: Foreign
Inception Date: November 9, 2010

Data Date	Investment Rating	Net Assets ($Mil)	Price	Perfor-mance Rating/Pts	Total Return Y-T-D	Risk Rating/Pts
3-12	D-	120.54	24.88	D+ / 2.4	18.99%	C / 5.2

Major Rating Factors:
Disappointing performance is the major factor driving the D- (Weak) TheStreet.com Investment Rating for *iShares MSCI Russia Capped Index. The fund currently has a performance rating of D+ (Weak) based on an annualized return of 0.00% over the last three years and a total return of 18.99% year to date 2012. Factored into the performance evaluation is an expense ratio of 0.58% (very low).

The fund's risk rating is currently C (Fair). It carries a beta of 0.00, meaning the fund's expected move will be 0.0% for every 10% move in the market. Volatility, as measured by both the semi-deviation and a drawdown factor, is considered average. As of March 31, 2012, *iShares MSCI Russia Capped Index traded at a premium of .73% above its net asset value, which is worse than its one-year historical average premium of .05%.

Diane Hsiung has been running the fund for 2 years and currently receives a manager quality ranking of 15 (0=worst, 99=best). This fund offers an average level of risk but investors looking for strong performance will be frustrated.

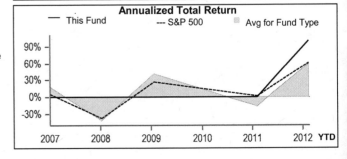

*iShares MSCI Singapore (EWS)

C+ **Fair**

Fund Family: BlackRock Fund Advisors
Fund Type: Foreign
Inception Date: March 12, 1996

Major Rating Factors: Strong performance is the major factor driving the C+ (Fair) TheStreet.com Investment Rating for *iShares MSCI Singapore. The fund currently has a performance rating of B- (Good) based on an annualized return of 27.81% over the last three years and a total return of 19.02% year to date 2012. Factored into the performance evaluation is an expense ratio of 0.52% (very low).

The fund's risk rating is currently B- (Good). It carries a beta of 1.10, meaning it is expected to move 11.0% for every 10% move in the market. Volatility, as measured by both the semi-deviation and a drawdown factor, is considered low. As of March 31, 2012, *iShares MSCI Singapore traded at a discount of .08% below its net asset value, which is worse than its one-year historical average discount of .11%.

Diane Hsiung has been running the fund for 4 years and currently receives a manager quality ranking of 84 (0=worst, 99=best). If you desire only a moderate level of risk and strong performance, then this fund is an excellent option.

Data Date	Investment Rating	Net Assets ($Mil)	Price	Performance Rating/Pts	Total Return Y-T-D	Risk Rating/Pts
3-12	C+	1,556.54	12.89	B- / 7.3	19.02%	B- / 7.3
2011	C	1,282.60	10.83	C+ / 5.6	2.40%	B- / 7.3
2010	C+	2,205.60	13.85	B / 7.7	24.51%	C / 4.5
2009	C+	1,294.04	11.49	B- / 7.2	63.20%	C / 4.6

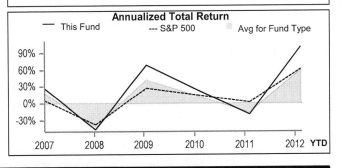

*iShares MSCI South Africa (EZA)

C **Fair**

Fund Family: BlackRock Fund Advisors
Fund Type: Foreign
Inception Date: February 3, 2003

Major Rating Factors: Middle of the road best describes *iShares MSCI South Africa whose TheStreet.com Investment Rating is currently a C (Fair). The fund currently has a performance rating of C+ (Fair) based on an annualized return of 23.70% over the last three years and a total return of 12.84% year to date 2012. Factored into the performance evaluation is an expense ratio of 0.59% (very low).

The fund's risk rating is currently B- (Good). It carries a beta of 1.04, meaning that its performance tracks fairly well with that of the overall stock market. Volatility, as measured by both the semi-deviation and a drawdown factor, is considered low. As of March 31, 2012, *iShares MSCI South Africa traded at a premium of .91% above its net asset value, which is worse than its one-year historical average premium of .03%.

Diane Hsiung has been running the fund for 4 years and currently receives a manager quality ranking of 80 (0=worst, 99=best). If you desire an average level of risk, then this fund may be an option.

Data Date	Investment Rating	Net Assets ($Mil)	Price	Performance Rating/Pts	Total Return Y-T-D	Risk Rating/Pts
3-12	C	595.75	68.91	C+ / 6.1	12.84%	B- / 7.1
2011	C+	504.20	61.07	C+ / 6.2	0.34%	B- / 7.1
2010	C	684.40	74.68	B+ / 8.5	36.91%	D+ / 2.3
2009	C-	488.73	55.97	C+ / 6.2	47.55%	D+ / 2.6

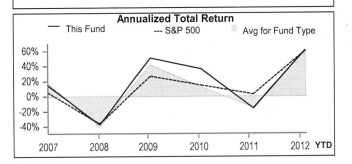

*iShares MSCI South Korea (EWY)

C **Fair**

Fund Family: BlackRock Fund Advisors
Fund Type: Foreign
Inception Date: May 9, 2000

Major Rating Factors: Middle of the road best describes *iShares MSCI South Korea whose TheStreet.com Investment Rating is currently a C (Fair). The fund currently has a performance rating of C+ (Fair) based on an annualized return of 24.26% over the last three years and a total return of 13.93% year to date 2012. Factored into the performance evaluation is an expense ratio of 0.59% (very low).

The fund's risk rating is currently C+ (Fair). It carries a beta of 1.26, meaning it is expected to move 12.6% for every 10% move in the market. Volatility, as measured by both the semi-deviation and a drawdown factor, is considered low. As of March 31, 2012, *iShares MSCI South Korea traded at a discount of .28% below its net asset value, which is worse than its one-year historical average discount of .35%.

Diane Hsiung has been running the fund for 4 years and currently receives a manager quality ranking of 74 (0=worst, 99=best). If you desire an average level of risk, then this fund may be an option.

Data Date	Investment Rating	Net Assets ($Mil)	Price	Performance Rating/Pts	Total Return Y-T-D	Risk Rating/Pts
3-12	C	3,485.03	59.54	C+ / 6.2	13.93%	C+ / 6.5
2011	C	3,038.60	52.26	C+ / 6.5	-0.13%	C+ / 6.3
2010	C	4,170.10	61.19	C+ / 6.7	29.58%	C- / 3.8
2009	C	2,398.55	47.64	C+ / 6.7	65.51%	C- / 3.8

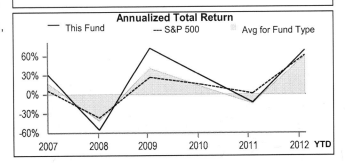

*iShares MSCI Spain (EWP)

D-   **Weak**

Fund Family: BlackRock Fund Advisors
Fund Type: Foreign
Inception Date: March 12, 1996

Major Rating Factors:
Disappointing performance is the major factor driving the D- (Weak) TheStreet.com Investment Rating for *iShares MSCI Spain. The fund currently has a performance rating of D- (Weak) based on an annualized return of 2.65% over the last three years and a total return of -3.20% year to date 2012. Factored into the performance evaluation is an expense ratio of 0.52% (very low).

The fund's risk rating is currently C+ (Fair). It carries a beta of 1.35, meaning it is expected to move 13.5% for every 10% move in the market. Volatility, as measured by both the semi-deviation and a drawdown factor, is considered low. As of March 31, 2012, *iShares MSCI Spain traded at a premium of .03% above its net asset value, which is worse than its one-year historical average discount of .08%.

Diane Hsiung has been running the fund for 4 years and currently receives a manager quality ranking of 10 (0=worst, 99=best). This fund offers only a moderate level of risk but investors looking for strong performance are still waiting.

Data Date	Investment Rating	Net Assets ($Mil)	Price	Performance Rating/Pts	Total Return Y-T-D	Risk Rating/Pts
3-12	D-	112.62	29.30	D- / 1.1	-3.20%	C+ / 5.6
2011	D-	99.70	30.27	D- / 1.5	-5.45%	C+ / 5.7
2010	E+	137.40	36.74	E+ / 0.7	-18.61%	C- / 4.2
2009	C-	278.73	48.04	C / 4.7	31.23%	C / 5.2

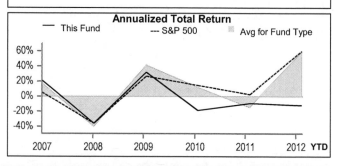

*iShares MSCI Sweden (EWD)

C   **Fair**

Fund Family: BlackRock Fund Advisors
Fund Type: Foreign
Inception Date: March 12, 1996

Major Rating Factors: Middle of the road best describes *iShares MSCI Sweden whose TheStreet.com Investment Rating is currently a C (Fair). The fund currently has a performance rating of C+ (Fair) based on an annualized return of 24.58% over the last three years and a total return of 15.39% year to date 2012. Factored into the performance evaluation is an expense ratio of 0.51% (very low).

The fund's risk rating is currently C+ (Fair). It carries a beta of 1.31, meaning it is expected to move 13.1% for every 10% move in the market. Volatility, as measured by both the semi-deviation and a drawdown factor, is considered low. As of March 31, 2012, *iShares MSCI Sweden traded at a premium of .31% above its net asset value, which is worse than its one-year historical average discount of .19%.

Diane Hsiung has been running the fund for 4 years and currently receives a manager quality ranking of 77 (0=worst, 99=best). If you desire an average level of risk, then this fund may be an option.

Data Date	Investment Rating	Net Assets ($Mil)	Price	Performance Rating/Pts	Total Return Y-T-D	Risk Rating/Pts
3-12	C	361.47	29.01	C+ / 6.2	15.39%	C+ / 6.5
2011	C	267.20	25.14	C+ / 5.8	0.08%	C+ / 6.5
2010	B-	421.90	31.23	B+ / 8.4	36.11%	C- / 4.1
2009	D+	190.33	23.50	C- / 3.2	48.14%	C / 4.7

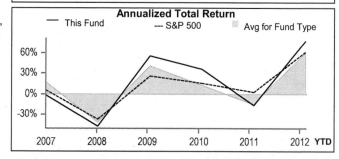

*iShares MSCI Switzerland (EWL)

C-   **Fair**

Fund Family: BlackRock Fund Advisors
Fund Type: Foreign
Inception Date: March 12, 1996

Major Rating Factors: Middle of the road best describes *iShares MSCI Switzerland whose TheStreet.com Investment Rating is currently a C- (Fair). The fund currently has a performance rating of C (Fair) based on an annualized return of 18.32% over the last three years and a total return of 10.65% year to date 2012. Factored into the performance evaluation is an expense ratio of 0.52% (very low).

The fund's risk rating is currently B- (Good). It carries a beta of 0.86, meaning the fund's expected move will be 8.6% for every 10% move in the market. Volatility, as measured by both the semi-deviation and a drawdown factor, is considered low. As of March 31, 2012, *iShares MSCI Switzerland traded at a premium of .12% above its net asset value, which is worse than its one-year historical average discount of .02%.

Diane Hsiung has been running the fund for 4 years and currently receives a manager quality ranking of 70 (0=worst, 99=best). If you desire an average level of risk, then this fund may be an option.

Data Date	Investment Rating	Net Assets ($Mil)	Price	Performance Rating/Pts	Total Return Y-T-D	Risk Rating/Pts
3-12	C-	553.48	25.03	C / 4.4	10.65%	B- / 7.6
2011	C-	475.80	22.62	C- / 3.4	-1.06%	B- / 7.5
2010	C	464.90	25.08	C / 5.2	14.48%	C / 5.5
2009	C-	271.86	22.26	C- / 3.1	22.38%	C+ / 5.8

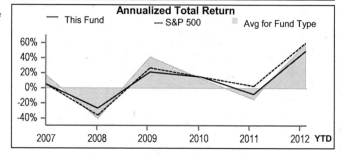

*iShares MSCI Taiwan (EWT)   C-   Fair

Fund Family: BlackRock Fund Advisors
Fund Type: Foreign
Inception Date: June 20, 2000

Data Date	Investment Rating	Net Assets ($Mil)	Price	Performance Rating/Pts	Total Return Y-T-D	Risk Rating/Pts
3-12	C-	2,580.02	13.42	C- / 4.0	14.56%	B- / 7.1
2011	C	2,193.10	11.71	C / 5.4	0.98%	B- / 7.1
2010	B-	3,435.30	15.62	B / 8.0	22.70%	C / 4.5
2009	C	3,035.33	12.97	C+ / 6.5	68.95%	C / 4.6

Major Rating Factors: Middle of the road best describes *iShares MSCI Taiwan whose TheStreet.com Investment Rating is currently a C- (Fair). The fund currently has a performance rating of C- (Fair) based on an annualized return of 17.52% over the last three years and a total return of 14.56% year to date 2012. Factored into the performance evaluation is an expense ratio of 0.59% (very low).

The fund's risk rating is currently B- (Good). It carries a beta of 1.17, meaning it is expected to move 11.7% for every 10% move in the market. Volatility, as measured by both the semi-deviation and a drawdown factor, is considered low. As of March 31, 2012, *iShares MSCI Taiwan traded at a discount of .15% below its net asset value, which is better than its one-year historical average discount of .04%.

Diane Hsiung has been running the fund for 4 years and currently receives a manager quality ranking of 49 (0=worst, 99=best). If you desire an average level of risk, then this fund may be an option.

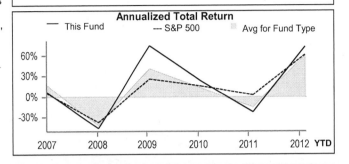

*iShares MSCI Thailand Inv Market (THD)   A-   Excellent

Fund Family: BlackRock Fund Advisors
Fund Type: Foreign
Inception Date: March 26, 2008

Data Date	Investment Rating	Net Assets ($Mil)	Price	Performance Rating/Pts	Total Return Y-T-D	Risk Rating/Pts
3-12	A-	647.42	72.79	A+ / 9.8	21.09%	B- / 7.1
2011	B+	459.40	60.11	A / 9.3	-0.07%	B- / 7.2
2010	B+	694.00	64.61	A+ / 9.8	56.76%	C- / 4.2
2009	B+	94.02	42.49	A / 9.5	74.19%	C- / 4.1

Major Rating Factors:
Exceptional performance is the major factor driving the A- (Excellent) TheStreet.com Investment Rating for *iShares MSCI Thailand Inv Market. The fund currently has a performance rating of A+ (Excellent) based on an annualized return of 50.49% over the last three years and a total return of 21.09% year to date 2012. Factored into the performance evaluation is an expense ratio of 0.59% (very low).

The fund's risk rating is currently B- (Good). It carries a beta of 0.98, meaning that its performance tracks fairly well with that of the overall stock market. Volatility, as measured by both the semi-deviation and a drawdown factor, is considered low. As of March 31, 2012, *iShares MSCI Thailand Inv Market traded at a premium of .12% above its net asset value, which is better than its one-year historical average premium of .13%.

Diane Hsiung has been running the fund for 4 years and currently receives a manager quality ranking of 97 (0=worst, 99=best). If you desire only a moderate level of risk and strong performance, then this fund is an excellent option.

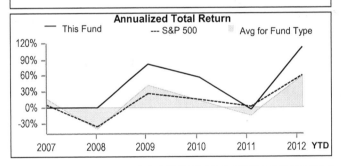

*iShares MSCI Turkey Inv Market (TUR)   C   Fair

Fund Family: BlackRock Fund Advisors
Fund Type: Foreign
Inception Date: March 26, 2008

Data Date	Investment Rating	Net Assets ($Mil)	Price	Performance Rating/Pts	Total Return Y-T-D	Risk Rating/Pts
3-12	C	437.04	53.05	B- / 7.0	28.95%	C+ / 5.7
2011	D	352.10	41.14	C- / 3.3	-2.14%	C+ / 5.8
2010	B	787.90	66.21	A- / 9.1	25.64%	C- / 3.8
2009	B+	242.44	53.90	A+ / 9.8	98.29%	C- / 3.9

Major Rating Factors: Strong performance is the major factor driving the C (Fair) TheStreet.com Investment Rating for *iShares MSCI Turkey Inv Market. The fund currently has a performance rating of B- (Good) based on an annualized return of 28.50% over the last three years and a total return of 28.95% year to date 2012. Factored into the performance evaluation is an expense ratio of 0.59% (very low).

The fund's risk rating is currently C+ (Fair). It carries a beta of 1.24, meaning it is expected to move 12.4% for every 10% move in the market. Volatility, as measured by both the semi-deviation and a drawdown factor, is considered low. As of March 31, 2012, *iShares MSCI Turkey Inv Market traded at a premium of .51% above its net asset value, which is worse than its one-year historical average discount of .20%.

Diane Hsiung has been running the fund for 4 years and currently receives a manager quality ranking of 82 (0=worst, 99=best). If you desire only a moderate level of risk and strong performance, then this fund is an excellent option.

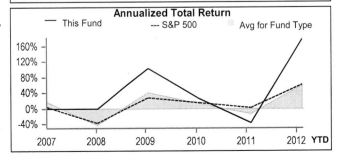

*iShares MSCI United Kingdom (EWU)   C-   Fair

Fund Family: BlackRock Fund Advisors
Fund Type: Foreign
Inception Date: March 12, 1996

Major Rating Factors: Middle of the road best describes *iShares MSCI United Kingdom whose TheStreet.com Investment Rating is currently a C- (Fair). The fund currently has a performance rating of C (Fair) based on an annualized return of 18.44% over the last three years and a total return of 7.05% year to date 2012. Factored into the performance evaluation is an expense ratio of 0.52% (very low).

The fund's risk rating is currently B- (Good). It carries a beta of 1.04, meaning that its performance tracks fairly well with that of the overall stock market. Volatility, as measured by both the semi-deviation and a drawdown factor, is considered low. As of March 31, 2012, *iShares MSCI United Kingdom traded at a premium of .06% above its net asset value, which is better than its one-year historical average premium of .31%.

Diane Hsiung has been running the fund for 4 years and currently receives a manager quality ranking of 63 (0=worst, 99=best). If you desire an average level of risk, then this fund may be an option.

Data Date	Investment Rating	Net Assets ($Mil)	Price	Performance Rating/Pts	Total Return Y-T-D	Risk Rating/Pts
3-12	C-	1,526.09	17.30	C / 4.3	7.05%	B- / 7.7
2011	C-	1,296.50	16.16	C- / 4.2	0.62%	B- / 7.6
2010	D	1,143.80	17.37	D / 1.8	10.28%	C / 4.8
2009	D	739.12	16.20	D / 2.1	35.56%	C / 4.9

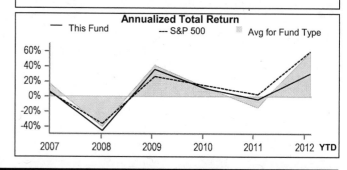

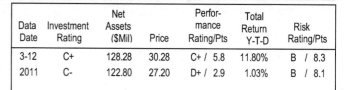

*iShares MSCI USA (EUSA)   C+   Fair

Fund Family: BlackRock Fund Advisors
Fund Type: Income
Inception Date: May 5, 2010

Major Rating Factors: Middle of the road best describes *iShares MSCI USA whose TheStreet.com Investment Rating is currently a C+ (Fair). The fund currently has a performance rating of C+ (Fair) based on an annualized return of 0.00% over the last three years and a total return of 11.80% year to date 2012. Factored into the performance evaluation is an expense ratio of 0.15% (very low).

The fund's risk rating is currently B (Good). It carries a beta of 0.00, meaning the fund's expected move will be 0.0% for every 10% move in the market. Volatility, as measured by both the semi-deviation and a drawdown factor, is considered low. As of March 31, 2012, *iShares MSCI USA traded at a discount of .07% below its net asset value, which is better than its one-year historical average premium of .03%.

Diane Hsiung has been running the fund for 2 years and currently receives a manager quality ranking of 50 (0=worst, 99=best). If you desire an average level of risk, then this fund may be an option.

Data Date	Investment Rating	Net Assets ($Mil)	Price	Performance Rating/Pts	Total Return Y-T-D	Risk Rating/Pts
3-12	C+	128.28	30.28	C+ / 5.8	11.80%	B / 8.3
2011	C-	122.80	27.20	D+ / 2.9	1.03%	B / 8.1

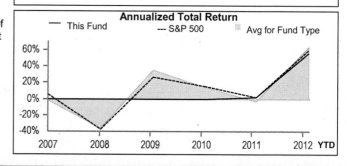

*iShares MSCI USA ESG Select Soc (KLD)   C+   Fair

Fund Family: BlackRock Fund Advisors
Fund Type: Growth
Inception Date: January 24, 2005

Major Rating Factors: Middle of the road best describes *iShares MSCI USA ESG Select Soc whose TheStreet.com Investment Rating is currently a C+ (Fair). The fund currently has a performance rating of C+ (Fair) based on an annualized return of 21.15% over the last three years and a total return of 12.26% year to date 2012. Factored into the performance evaluation is an expense ratio of 0.50% (very low).

The fund's risk rating is currently B (Good). It carries a beta of 0.99, meaning that its performance tracks fairly well with that of the overall stock market. Volatility, as measured by both the semi-deviation and a drawdown factor, is considered low. As of March 31, 2012, *iShares MSCI USA ESG Select Soc traded at a premium of .13% above its net asset value, which is worse than its one-year historical average premium of .01%.

Diane Hsiung has been running the fund for 4 years and currently receives a manager quality ranking of 46 (0=worst, 99=best). If you desire an average level of risk, then this fund may be an option.

Data Date	Investment Rating	Net Assets ($Mil)	Price	Performance Rating/Pts	Total Return Y-T-D	Risk Rating/Pts
3-12	C+	176.95	61.59	C+ / 5.8	12.26%	B / 8.4
2011	C+	164.80	55.03	C / 5.4	1.60%	B / 8.1
2010	C	145.50	54.91	C / 4.5	13.88%	C+ / 6.1
2009	C-	94.91	49.00	D+ / 2.8	26.93%	C+ / 6.1

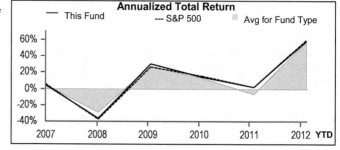

*iShares Nasdaq Biotechnology (IBB)

C+   **Fair**

Fund Family: BlackRock Fund Advisors
Fund Type: Health
Inception Date: February 5, 2001

Major Rating Factors: Strong performance is the major factor driving the C+ (Fair) TheStreet.com Investment Rating for *iShares Nasdaq Biotechnology. The fund currently has a performance rating of B- (Good) based on an annualized return of 24.02% over the last three years and a total return of 18.19% year to date 2012. Factored into the performance evaluation is an expense ratio of 0.48% (very low).

The fund's risk rating is currently C+ (Fair). It carries a beta of 0.80, meaning the fund's expected move will be 8.0% for every 10% move in the market. Volatility, as measured by both the semi-deviation and a drawdown factor, is considered low. As of March 31, 2012, *iShares Nasdaq Biotechnology traded at a discount of .03% below its net asset value, which is better than its one-year historical average discount of .02%.

Diane Hsiung has been running the fund for 4 years and currently receives a manager quality ranking of 69 (0=worst, 99=best). If you desire only a moderate level of risk and strong performance, then this fund is an excellent option.

Data Date	Investment Rating	Net Assets ($Mil)	Price	Performance Rating/Pts	Total Return Y-T-D	Risk Rating/Pts
3-12	C+	1,745.55	123.30	B- / 7.5	18.19%	C+ / 6.9
2011	C	1,393.90	104.35	C+ / 6.1	2.74%	C+ / 6.2
2010	C+	1,446.90	93.42	C+ / 6.8	14.84%	C+ / 5.9
2009	C-	1,627.16	81.83	C- / 3.3	13.54%	C+ / 5.9

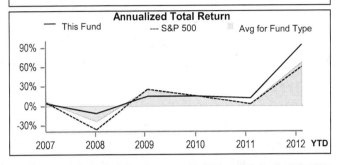

*iShares NYSE 100 (NY)

C   **Fair**

Fund Family: BlackRock Fund Advisors
Fund Type: Income
Inception Date: March 29, 2004

Major Rating Factors: Middle of the road best describes *iShares NYSE 100 whose TheStreet.com Investment Rating is currently a C (Fair). The fund currently has a performance rating of C (Fair) based on an annualized return of 17.34% over the last three years and a total return of 9.80% year to date 2012. Factored into the performance evaluation is an expense ratio of 0.20% (very low).

The fund's risk rating is currently B (Good). It carries a beta of 0.91, meaning that its performance tracks fairly well with that of the overall stock market. Volatility, as measured by both the semi-deviation and a drawdown factor, is considered low. As of March 31, 2012, *iShares NYSE 100 traded at a discount of .02% below its net asset value, which is in line with its one-year historical average discount of .02%.

Diane Hsiung has been running the fund for 4 years and currently receives a manager quality ranking of 34 (0=worst, 99=best). If you desire an average level of risk, then this fund may be an option.

Data Date	Investment Rating	Net Assets ($Mil)	Price	Performance Rating/Pts	Total Return Y-T-D	Risk Rating/Pts
3-12	C	54.50	65.64	C / 4.4	9.80%	B / 8.5
2011	C	54.00	60.10	C / 4.3	1.01%	B / 8.1
2010	D+	63.20	60.14	D+ / 2.5	12.35%	C+ / 6.2
2009	D	64.58	54.75	D- / 1.4	13.34%	C+ / 6.3

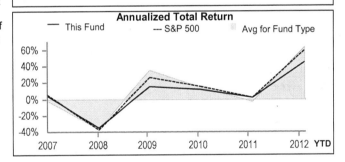

*iShares NYSE Composite (NYC)

C   **Fair**

Fund Family: BlackRock Fund Advisors
Fund Type: Income
Inception Date: March 30, 2004

Major Rating Factors: Middle of the road best describes *iShares NYSE Composite whose TheStreet.com Investment Rating is currently a C (Fair). The fund currently has a performance rating of C (Fair) based on an annualized return of 18.25% over the last three years and a total return of 10.19% year to date 2012. Factored into the performance evaluation is an expense ratio of 0.25% (very low).

The fund's risk rating is currently B (Good). It carries a beta of 1.10, meaning it is expected to move 11.0% for every 10% move in the market. Volatility, as measured by both the semi-deviation and a drawdown factor, is considered low. As of March 31, 2012, *iShares NYSE Composite traded at a premium of .07% above its net asset value.

Diane Hsiung has been running the fund for 4 years and currently receives a manager quality ranking of 25 (0=worst, 99=best). If you desire an average level of risk, then this fund may be an option.

Data Date	Investment Rating	Net Assets ($Mil)	Price	Performance Rating/Pts	Total Return Y-T-D	Risk Rating/Pts
3-12	C	74.38	75.03	C / 4.4	10.19%	B / 8.1
2011	C	71.70	68.45	C- / 4.2	0.91%	B- / 7.9
2010	D+	98.30	72.76	C- / 3.1	13.12%	C+ / 5.8
2009	D+	100.24	65.83	D+ / 2.4	25.08%	C+ / 5.9

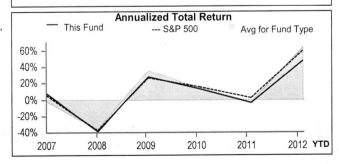

*iShares PHLX SOX Semicon Sector (SOXX)

C+   **Fair**

Fund Family: BlackRock Fund Advisors
Fund Type: Income
Inception Date: July 10, 2001

Major Rating Factors: Middle of the road best describes *iShares PHLX SOX Semicon Sector whose TheStreet.com Investment Rating is currently a C+ (Fair). The fund currently has a performance rating of C+ (Fair) based on an annualized return of 21.68% over the last three years and a total return of 20.60% year to date 2012. Factored into the performance evaluation is an expense ratio of 0.48% (very low).

The fund's risk rating is currently B- (Good). It carries a beta of 1.39, meaning it is expected to move 13.9% for every 10% move in the market. Volatility, as measured by both the semi-deviation and a drawdown factor, is considered low. As of March 31, 2012, *iShares PHLX SOX Semicon Sector traded at a discount of .03% below its net asset value.

Diane Hsiung has been running the fund for 4 years and currently receives a manager quality ranking of 19 (0=worst, 99=best). If you desire an average level of risk, then this fund may be an option.

Data Date	Investment Rating	Net Assets ($Mil)	Price	Performance Rating/Pts	Total Return Y-T-D	Risk Rating/Pts
3-12	C+	242.09	59.47	C+ / 6.2	20.60%	B- / 7.4
2011	C+	177.90	49.40	C+ / 6.3	2.89%	B- / 7.4
2010	C	230.90	55.70	C+ / 6.0	14.35%	C / 5.2
2009	C-	226.25	49.23	C / 4.3	67.14%	C / 4.9

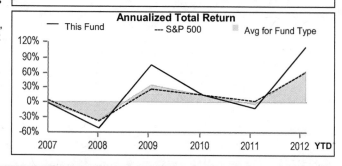

*iShares Russell 1000 (IWB)

C+   **Fair**

Fund Family: BlackRock Fund Advisors
Fund Type: Growth
Inception Date: May 15, 2000

Major Rating Factors: Middle of the road best describes *iShares Russell 1000 whose TheStreet.com Investment Rating is currently a C+ (Fair). The fund currently has a performance rating of C+ (Fair) based on an annualized return of 21.45% over the last three years and a total return of 12.85% year to date 2012. Factored into the performance evaluation is an expense ratio of 0.15% (very low).

The fund's risk rating is currently B (Good). It carries a beta of 1.03, meaning that its performance tracks fairly well with that of the overall stock market. Volatility, as measured by both the semi-deviation and a drawdown factor, is considered low. As of March 31, 2012, *iShares Russell 1000 traded at a discount of .08% below its net asset value, which is better than its one-year historical average discount of .01%.

Diane Hsiung has been running the fund for 4 years and currently receives a manager quality ranking of 45 (0=worst, 99=best). If you desire an average level of risk, then this fund may be an option.

Data Date	Investment Rating	Net Assets ($Mil)	Price	Performance Rating/Pts	Total Return Y-T-D	Risk Rating/Pts
3-12	C+	6,807.91	77.96	C+ / 5.9	12.85%	B / 8.2
2011	C+	6,300.80	69.37	C / 5.3	1.82%	B- / 7.9
2010	C-	6,452.00	69.86	C- / 4.2	16.02%	C+ / 5.9
2009	D+	4,885.21	61.31	D+ / 2.4	24.71%	C+ / 6.1

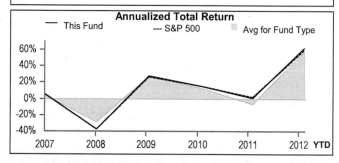

*iShares Russell 1000 Growth (IWF)

C+   **Fair**

Fund Family: BlackRock Fund Advisors
Fund Type: Growth
Inception Date: May 22, 2000

Major Rating Factors: Middle of the road best describes *iShares Russell 1000 Growth whose TheStreet.com Investment Rating is currently a C+ (Fair). The fund currently has a performance rating of C+ (Fair) based on an annualized return of 22.65% over the last three years and a total return of 14.68% year to date 2012. Factored into the performance evaluation is an expense ratio of 0.20% (very low).

The fund's risk rating is currently B (Good). It carries a beta of 1.01, meaning that its performance tracks fairly well with that of the overall stock market. Volatility, as measured by both the semi-deviation and a drawdown factor, is considered low. As of March 31, 2012, *iShares Russell 1000 Growth traded at a discount of .05% below its net asset value.

Diane Hsiung has been running the fund for 4 years and currently receives a manager quality ranking of 55 (0=worst, 99=best). If you desire an average level of risk, then this fund may be an option.

Data Date	Investment Rating	Net Assets ($Mil)	Price	Performance Rating/Pts	Total Return Y-T-D	Risk Rating/Pts
3-12	C+	16,038.91	66.08	C+ / 6.6	14.68%	B / 8.0
2011	C+	14,210.50	57.79	C+ / 6.2	1.77%	B- / 7.7
2010	C	12,576.60	57.26	C / 5.3	16.48%	C+ / 5.9
2009	C-	10,436.97	49.85	C- / 3.6	32.68%	C+ / 6.1

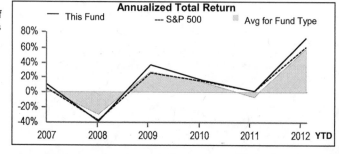

*iShares Russell 1000 Value (IWD)   C+   Fair

Fund Family: BlackRock Fund Advisors
Fund Type: Income
Inception Date: May 22, 2000

Data Date	Investment Rating	Net Assets ($Mil)	Price	Performance Rating/Pts	Total Return Y-T-D	Risk Rating/Pts
3-12	C+	11,972.00	70.07	C / 5.3	10.95%	B / 8.3
2011	C	11,359.00	63.48	C / 4.6	1.78%	B- / 7.8
2010	C-	10,698.20	64.87	C- / 3.1	15.44%	C+ / 5.9
2009	D	8,355.94	57.40	D- / 1.4	16.66%	C+ / 5.9

Major Rating Factors: Middle of the road best describes *iShares Russell 1000 Value whose TheStreet.com Investment Rating is currently a C+ (Fair). The fund currently has a performance rating of C (Fair) based on an annualized return of 20.10% over the last three years and a total return of 10.95% year to date 2012. Factored into the performance evaluation is an expense ratio of 0.20% (very low).

The fund's risk rating is currently B (Good). It carries a beta of 1.05, meaning that its performance tracks fairly well with that of the overall stock market. Volatility, as measured by both the semi-deviation and a drawdown factor, is considered low. As of March 31, 2012, *iShares Russell 1000 Value traded at a discount of .13% below its net asset value, which is better than its one-year historical average discount of .01%.

Diane Hsiung has been running the fund for 4 years and currently receives a manager quality ranking of 34 (0=worst, 99=best). If you desire an average level of risk, then this fund may be an option.

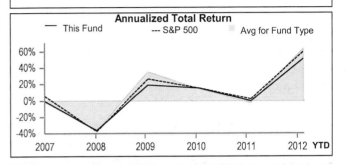

*iShares Russell 2000 (IWM)   C+   Fair

Fund Family: BlackRock Fund Advisors
Fund Type: Growth
Inception Date: May 22, 2000

Data Date	Investment Rating	Net Assets ($Mil)	Price	Performance Rating/Pts	Total Return Y-T-D	Risk Rating/Pts
3-12	C+	16,017.52	82.81	C+ / 6.4	12.62%	B- / 7.5
2011	C	14,101.20	73.75	C+ / 5.6	1.42%	B- / 7.2
2010	B	17,565.80	78.24	B- / 7.2	26.90%	C+ / 6.1
2009	D+	12,883.49	62.44	D+ / 2.3	26.02%	C+ / 5.6

Major Rating Factors: Middle of the road best describes *iShares Russell 2000 whose TheStreet.com Investment Rating is currently a C+ (Fair). The fund currently has a performance rating of C+ (Fair) based on an annualized return of 23.59% over the last three years and a total return of 12.62% year to date 2012. Factored into the performance evaluation is an expense ratio of 0.20% (very low).

The fund's risk rating is currently B- (Good). It carries a beta of 1.29, meaning it is expected to move 12.9% for every 10% move in the market. Volatility, as measured by both the semi-deviation and a drawdown factor, is considered low. As of March 31, 2012, *iShares Russell 2000 traded at a discount of .04% below its net asset value, which is better than its one-year historical average premium of .01%.

Diane Hsiung has been running the fund for 4 years and currently receives a manager quality ranking of 27 (0=worst, 99=best). If you desire an average level of risk, then this fund may be an option.

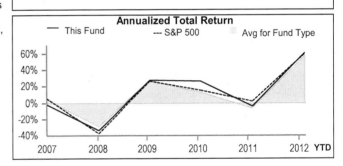

*iShares Russell 2000 Growth (IWO)   C+   Fair

Fund Family: BlackRock Fund Advisors
Fund Type: Growth
Inception Date: July 24, 2000

Data Date	Investment Rating	Net Assets ($Mil)	Price	Performance Rating/Pts	Total Return Y-T-D	Risk Rating/Pts
3-12	C+	3,998.91	95.38	B- / 7.0	13.44%	B- / 7.3
2011	C+	3,492.10	84.23	C+ / 6.3	1.14%	C+ / 6.9
2010	B-	4,134.90	87.42	B- / 7.4	29.35%	C / 5.4
2009	D+	3,313.21	68.07	C- / 3.0	31.86%	C / 5.0

Major Rating Factors: Strong performance is the major factor driving the C+ (Fair) TheStreet.com Investment Rating for *iShares Russell 2000 Growth. The fund currently has a performance rating of B- (Good) based on an annualized return of 25.61% over the last three years and a total return of 13.44% year to date 2012. Factored into the performance evaluation is an expense ratio of 0.25% (very low).

The fund's risk rating is currently B- (Good). It carries a beta of 1.28, meaning it is expected to move 12.8% for every 10% move in the market. Volatility, as measured by both the semi-deviation and a drawdown factor, is considered low. As of March 31, 2012, *iShares Russell 2000 Growth traded at a price exactly equal to its net asset value, which is worse than its one-year historical average discount of .01%.

Diane Hsiung has been running the fund for 4 years and currently receives a manager quality ranking of 34 (0=worst, 99=best). If you desire only a moderate level of risk and strong performance, then this fund is an excellent option.

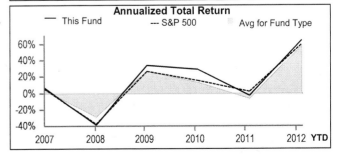

*iShares Russell 2000 Value (IWN)

C **Fair**

Fund Family: BlackRock Fund Advisors
Fund Type: Growth
Inception Date: July 24, 2000

Major Rating Factors: Middle of the road best describes *iShares Russell 2000 Value whose TheStreet.com Investment Rating is currently a C (Fair). The fund currently has a performance rating of C+ (Fair) based on an annualized return of 21.64% over the last three years and a total return of 11.62% year to date 2012. Factored into the performance evaluation is an expense ratio of 0.25% (very low).

The fund's risk rating is currently B- (Good). It carries a beta of 1.30, meaning it is expected to move 13.0% for every 10% move in the market. Volatility, as measured by both the semi-deviation and a drawdown factor, is considered low. As of March 31, 2012, *iShares Russell 2000 Value traded at a discount of .07% below its net asset value, which is better than its one-year historical average premium of .04%.

Diane Hsiung has been running the fund for 4 years and currently receives a manager quality ranking of 23 (0=worst, 99=best). If you desire an average level of risk, then this fund may be an option.

Data Date	Investment Rating	Net Assets ($Mil)	Price	Performance Rating/Pts	Total Return Y-T-D	Risk Rating/Pts
3-12	C	4,210.52	72.97	C+ / 5.6	11.62%	B- / 7.6
2011	C	3,887.90	65.64	C / 4.8	1.63%	B- / 7.4
2010	B-	4,728.40	71.09	B- / 7.1	24.68%	C+ / 5.7
2009	D	3,864.02	58.04	D / 1.6	20.27%	C+ / 5.6

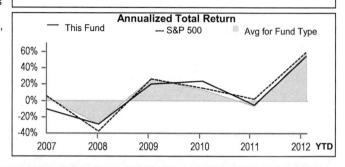

*iShares Russell 3000 (IWV)

C+ **Fair**

Fund Family: BlackRock Fund Advisors
Fund Type: Income
Inception Date: May 22, 2000

Major Rating Factors: Middle of the road best describes *iShares Russell 3000 whose TheStreet.com Investment Rating is currently a C+ (Fair). The fund currently has a performance rating of C+ (Fair) based on an annualized return of 21.59% over the last three years and a total return of 12.71% year to date 2012. Factored into the performance evaluation is an expense ratio of 0.20% (very low).

The fund's risk rating is currently B (Good). It carries a beta of 1.05, meaning that its performance tracks fairly well with that of the overall stock market. Volatility, as measured by both the semi-deviation and a drawdown factor, is considered low. As of March 31, 2012, *iShares Russell 3000 traded at a discount of .11% below its net asset value.

Diane Hsiung has been running the fund for 4 years and currently receives a manager quality ranking of 43 (0=worst, 99=best). If you desire an average level of risk, then this fund may be an option.

Data Date	Investment Rating	Net Assets ($Mil)	Price	Performance Rating/Pts	Total Return Y-T-D	Risk Rating/Pts
3-12	C+	3,366.28	83.28	C+ / 5.9	12.71%	B / 8.2
2011	C+	3,209.30	74.18	C / 5.3	1.70%	B- / 7.9
2010	C	3,250.80	74.95	C / 4.5	16.82%	C+ / 5.9
2009	D+	2,958.22	65.28	D+ / 2.3	24.83%	C+ / 6.0

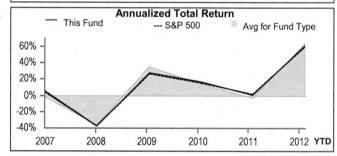

*iShares Russell 3000 Growth (IWZ)

C+ **Fair**

Fund Family: BlackRock Fund Advisors
Fund Type: Growth
Inception Date: July 24, 2000

Major Rating Factors: Middle of the road best describes *iShares Russell 3000 Growth whose TheStreet.com Investment Rating is currently a C+ (Fair). The fund currently has a performance rating of C+ (Fair) based on an annualized return of 23.01% over the last three years and a total return of 14.50% year to date 2012. Factored into the performance evaluation is an expense ratio of 0.25% (very low).

The fund's risk rating is currently B- (Good). It carries a beta of 1.02, meaning that its performance tracks fairly well with that of the overall stock market. Volatility, as measured by both the semi-deviation and a drawdown factor, is considered low. As of March 31, 2012, *iShares Russell 3000 Growth traded at a discount of .02% below its net asset value, which is better than its one-year historical average discount of .01%.

Diane Hsiung has been running the fund for 4 years and currently receives a manager quality ranking of 54 (0=worst, 99=best). If you desire an average level of risk, then this fund may be an option.

Data Date	Investment Rating	Net Assets ($Mil)	Price	Performance Rating/Pts	Total Return Y-T-D	Risk Rating/Pts
3-12	C+	335.23	53.88	C+ / 6.6	14.50%	B- / 7.9
2011	C+	346.90	47.19	C+ / 6.2	1.57%	B- / 7.7
2010	C+	333.00	46.93	C / 5.5	17.42%	C+ / 5.9
2009	C-	343.73	40.49	C- / 3.5	32.47%	C+ / 6.0

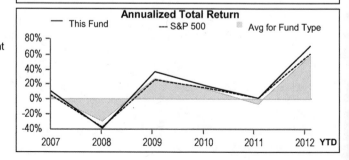

*iShares Russell 3000 Value (IWW)

C+ **Fair**

Fund Family: BlackRock Fund Advisors
Fund Type: Income
Inception Date: July 24, 2000

Major Rating Factors: Middle of the road best describes *iShares Russell 3000 Value whose TheStreet.com Investment Rating is currently a C+ (Fair). The fund currently has a performance rating of C (Fair) based on an annualized return of 20.16% over the last three years and a total return of 10.97% year to date 2012. Factored into the performance evaluation is an expense ratio of 0.25% (very low).

The fund's risk rating is currently B (Good). It carries a beta of 1.07, meaning that its performance tracks fairly well with that of the overall stock market. Volatility, as measured by both the semi-deviation and a drawdown factor, is considered low. As of March 31, 2012, *iShares Russell 3000 Value traded at a discount of .10% below its net asset value, which is better than its one-year historical average discount of .03%.

Diane Hsiung has been running the fund for 4 years and currently receives a manager quality ranking of 33 (0=worst, 99=best). If you desire an average level of risk, then this fund may be an option.

Data Date	Investment Rating	Net Assets ($Mil)	Price	Performance Rating/Pts	Total Return Y-T-D	Risk Rating/Pts
3-12	C+	304.99	91.79	C / 5.3	10.97%	B / 8.2
2011	C	307.60	83.14	C / 4.6	1.64%	B- / 7.8
2010	C-	324.00	85.25	C- / 3.4	15.76%	C+ / 5.9
2009	D	392.18	75.23	D- / 1.4	17.15%	C+ / 5.9

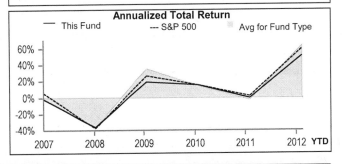

Annualized Total Return
— This Fund   --- S&P 500   Avg for Fund Type

*iShares Russell Micro Cap (IWC)

C+ **Fair**

Fund Family: BlackRock Fund Advisors
Fund Type: Growth
Inception Date: August 12, 2005

Major Rating Factors: Middle of the road best describes *iShares Russell Micro Cap whose TheStreet.com Investment Rating is currently a C+ (Fair). The fund currently has a performance rating of C+ (Fair) based on an annualized return of 22.93% over the last three years and a total return of 15.40% year to date 2012. Factored into the performance evaluation is an expense ratio of 0.60% (very low).

The fund's risk rating is currently B- (Good). It carries a beta of 1.35, meaning it is expected to move 13.5% for every 10% move in the market. Volatility, as measured by both the semi-deviation and a drawdown factor, is considered low. As of March 31, 2012, *iShares Russell Micro Cap traded at a premium of .10% above its net asset value, which is worse than its one-year historical average discount of .04%.

Diane Hsiung has been running the fund for 4 years and currently receives a manager quality ranking of 22 (0=worst, 99=best). If you desire an average level of risk, then this fund may be an option.

Data Date	Investment Rating	Net Assets ($Mil)	Price	Performance Rating/Pts	Total Return Y-T-D	Risk Rating/Pts
3-12	C+	462.74	51.40	C+ / 6.2	15.40%	B- / 7.4
2011	C-	388.90	44.65	C / 4.4	1.41%	B- / 7.1
2010	C+	529.90	50.11	C+ / 6.6	29.55%	C / 5.5
2009	D-	353.54	39.03	D- / 1.2	23.06%	C / 5.4

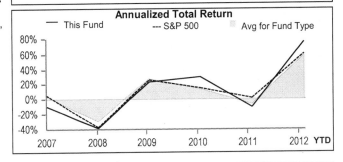

Annualized Total Return
— This Fund   --- S&P 500   Avg for Fund Type

*iShares Russell Mid Cap (IWR)

B- **Good**

Fund Family: BlackRock Fund Advisors
Fund Type: Growth
Inception Date: July 17, 2001

Major Rating Factors: Strong performance is the major factor driving the B- (Good) TheStreet.com Investment Rating for *iShares Russell Mid Cap. The fund currently has a performance rating of B- (Good) based on an annualized return of 25.86% over the last three years and a total return of 12.86% year to date 2012. Factored into the performance evaluation is an expense ratio of 0.20% (very low).

The fund's risk rating is currently B (Good). It carries a beta of 1.17, meaning it is expected to move 11.7% for every 10% move in the market. Volatility, as measured by both the semi-deviation and a drawdown factor, is considered low. As of March 31, 2012, *iShares Russell Mid Cap traded at a discount of .03% below its net asset value, which is better than its one-year historical average premium of .04%.

Diane Hsiung has been running the fund for 4 years and currently receives a manager quality ranking of 53 (0=worst, 99=best). If you desire only a moderate level of risk and strong performance, then this fund is an excellent option.

Data Date	Investment Rating	Net Assets ($Mil)	Price	Performance Rating/Pts	Total Return Y-T-D	Risk Rating/Pts
3-12	B-	6,668.35	110.72	B- / 7.0	12.86%	B / 8.0
2011	C+	6,009.40	98.42	C+ / 6.5	1.47%	B- / 7.8
2010	C+	6,018.40	101.75	C+ / 6.6	25.31%	C / 5.5
2009	C-	4,561.94	82.51	C- / 3.2	36.03%	C+ / 6.1

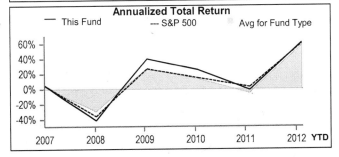

Annualized Total Return
— This Fund   --- S&P 500   Avg for Fund Type

*iShares Russell Mid Cap Growth (IWP)

B-   **Good**

Fund Family: BlackRock Fund Advisors
Fund Type: Growth
Inception Date: July 17, 2001

Data Date	Investment Rating	Net Assets ($Mil)	Price	Performance Rating/Pts	Total Return Y-T-D	Risk Rating/Pts
3-12	B-	3,423.00	62.87	B- / 7.1	14.42%	B- / 7.9
2011	C+	2,896.90	55.05	C+ / 6.7	1.80%	B- / 7.6
2010	C-	3,161.20	56.61	C+ / 6.7	26.03%	C- / 3.2
2009	D	2,542.46	45.34	C- / 3.7	40.24%	C- / 3.6

Major Rating Factors: Strong performance is the major factor driving the B- (Good) TheStreet.com Investment Rating for *iShares Russell Mid Cap Growth. The fund currently has a performance rating of B- (Good) based on an annualized return of 25.95% over the last three years and a total return of 14.42% year to date 2012. Factored into the performance evaluation is an expense ratio of 0.25% (very low).

The fund's risk rating is currently B- (Good). It carries a beta of 1.16, meaning it is expected to move 11.6% for every 10% move in the market. Volatility, as measured by both the semi-deviation and a drawdown factor, is considered low. As of March 31, 2012, *iShares Russell Mid Cap Growth traded at a discount of .06% below its net asset value, which is better than its one-year historical average discount of .01%.

Diane Hsiung has been running the fund for 4 years and currently receives a manager quality ranking of 54 (0=worst, 99=best). If you desire only a moderate level of risk and strong performance, then this fund is an excellent option.

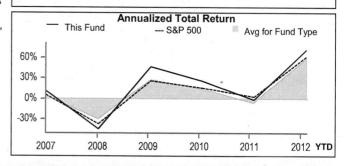

*iShares Russell Mid Cap Value (IWS)

B-   **Good**

Fund Family: BlackRock Fund Advisors
Fund Type: Growth
Inception Date: July 17, 2001

Data Date	Investment Rating	Net Assets ($Mil)	Price	Performance Rating/Pts	Total Return Y-T-D	Risk Rating/Pts
3-12	B-	3,165.76	48.13	C+ / 6.9	11.38%	B / 8.1
2011	C+	2,744.40	43.40	C+ / 6.1	1.29%	B- / 7.9
2010	C-	3,100.30	45.01	C+ / 6.5	24.43%	D+ / 2.8
2009	D-	2,890.41	36.95	D+ / 2.5	30.87%	C- / 3.0

Major Rating Factors: *iShares Russell Mid Cap Value receives a TheStreet.com Investment Rating of B- (Good). The fund currently has a performance rating of C+ (Fair) based on an annualized return of 25.65% over the last three years and a total return of 11.38% year to date 2012. Factored into the performance evaluation is an expense ratio of 0.25% (very low).

The fund's risk rating is currently B (Good). It carries a beta of 1.18, meaning it is expected to move 11.8% for every 10% move in the market. Volatility, as measured by both the semi-deviation and a drawdown factor, is considered low. As of March 31, 2012, *iShares Russell Mid Cap Value traded at a discount of .02% below its net asset value, which is better than its one-year historical average discount of .01%.

Diane Hsiung has been running the fund for 4 years and currently receives a manager quality ranking of 51 (0=worst, 99=best). If you desire an average level of risk, then this fund may be an option.

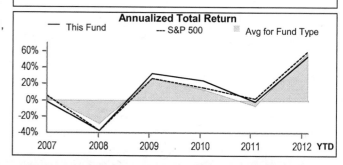

*iShares Russell Top 200 Growth (IWY)

B+   **Good**

Fund Family: BlackRock Fund Advisors
Fund Type: Growth
Inception Date: September 22, 2009

Data Date	Investment Rating	Net Assets ($Mil)	Price	Performance Rating/Pts	Total Return Y-T-D	Risk Rating/Pts
3-12	B+	328.49	35.16	B / 7.6	14.47%	B / 8.5
2011	C-	401.70	30.82	C- / 3.3	1.62%	B / 8.6
2010	A+	331.00	29.93	A- / 9.0	11.98%	B- / 7.8

Major Rating Factors: Strong performance is the major factor driving the B+ (Good) TheStreet.com Investment Rating for *iShares Russell Top 200 Growth. The fund currently has a performance rating of B (Good) based on an annualized return of 0.00% over the last three years and a total return of 14.47% year to date 2012. Factored into the performance evaluation is an expense ratio of 0.20% (very low).

The fund's risk rating is currently B (Good). It carries a beta of 0.00, meaning the fund's expected move will be 0.0% for every 10% move in the market. Volatility, as measured by both the semi-deviation and a drawdown factor, is considered low. As of March 31, 2012, *iShares Russell Top 200 Growth traded at a discount of .06% below its net asset value, which is better than its one-year historical average premium of .07%.

Diane Hsiung has been running the fund for 3 years and currently receives a manager quality ranking of 76 (0=worst, 99=best). If you desire only a moderate level of risk and strong performance, then this fund is an excellent option.

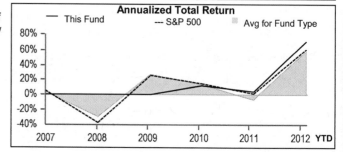

*iShares Russell Top 200 Idx (IWL)

C+   **Fair**

Fund Family: BlackRock Fund Advisors
Fund Type: Income
Inception Date: September 22, 2009

Major Rating Factors: Middle of the road best describes *iShares Russell Top 200 Idx whose TheStreet.com Investment Rating is currently a C+ (Fair). The fund currently has a performance rating of C+ (Fair) based on an annualized return of 0.00% over the last three years and a total return of 12.56% year to date 2012. Factored into the performance evaluation is an expense ratio of 0.15% (very low).

The fund's risk rating is currently B (Good). It carries a beta of 0.00, meaning the fund's expected move will be 0.0% for every 10% move in the market. Volatility, as measured by both the semi-deviation and a drawdown factor, is considered low. As of March 31, 2012, *iShares Russell Top 200 Idx traded at a premium of .06% above its net asset value, which is worse than its one-year historical average premium of .03%.

Diane Hsiung has been running the fund for 3 years and currently receives a manager quality ranking of 59 (0=worst, 99=best). If you desire an average level of risk, then this fund may be an option.

Data Date	Investment Rating	Net Assets ($Mil)	Price	Performance Rating/Pts	Total Return Y-T-D	Risk Rating/Pts
3-12	C+	123.67	32.69	C+ / 6.2	12.56%	B / 8.5
2011	C-	109.10	29.17	C- / 3.2	1.65%	B / 8.5
2010	A+	11.60	28.87	B+ / 8.9	11.26%	B- / 7.9

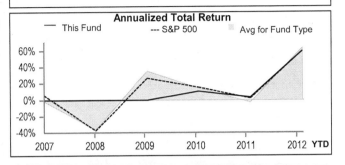

Annualized Total Return

*iShares Russell Top 200 Value Id (IWX)

C   **Fair**

Fund Family: BlackRock Fund Advisors
Fund Type: Income
Inception Date: September 22, 2009

Major Rating Factors: Middle of the road best describes *iShares Russell Top 200 Value Id whose TheStreet.com Investment Rating is currently a C (Fair). The fund currently has a performance rating of C (Fair) based on an annualized return of 0.00% over the last three years and a total return of 10.56% year to date 2012. Factored into the performance evaluation is an expense ratio of 0.20% (very low).

The fund's risk rating is currently B (Good). It carries a beta of 0.00, meaning the fund's expected move will be 0.0% for every 10% move in the market. Volatility, as measured by both the semi-deviation and a drawdown factor, is considered low. As of March 31, 2012, *iShares Russell Top 200 Value Id traded at a price exactly equal to its net asset value.

Diane Hsiung has been running the fund for 3 years and currently receives a manager quality ranking of 28 (0=worst, 99=best). If you desire an average level of risk, then this fund may be an option.

Data Date	Investment Rating	Net Assets ($Mil)	Price	Performance Rating/Pts	Total Return Y-T-D	Risk Rating/Pts
3-12	C	61.93	30.22	C / 5.0	10.56%	B / 8.1
2011	C-	137.30	27.54	D+ / 2.9	1.56%	B / 8.1
2010	A+	212.20	27.94	B+ / 8.8	10.59%	B- / 7.8

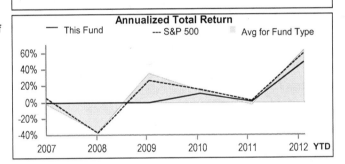

Annualized Total Return

*iShares S&P 100 (OEF)

C+   **Fair**

Fund Family: BlackRock Fund Advisors
Fund Type: Growth
Inception Date: October 23, 2000

Major Rating Factors: Middle of the road best describes *iShares S&P 100 whose TheStreet.com Investment Rating is currently a C+ (Fair). The fund currently has a performance rating of C (Fair) based on an annualized return of 19.78% over the last three years and a total return of 12.80% year to date 2012. Factored into the performance evaluation is an expense ratio of 0.20% (very low).

The fund's risk rating is currently B (Good). It carries a beta of 0.95, meaning that its performance tracks fairly well with that of the overall stock market. Volatility, as measured by both the semi-deviation and a drawdown factor, is considered low. As of March 31, 2012, *iShares S&P 100 traded at a discount of .12% below its net asset value.

Diane Hsiung has been running the fund for 4 years and currently receives a manager quality ranking of 43 (0=worst, 99=best). If you desire an average level of risk, then this fund may be an option.

Data Date	Investment Rating	Net Assets ($Mil)	Price	Performance Rating/Pts	Total Return Y-T-D	Risk Rating/Pts
3-12	C+	3,387.43	64.04	C / 5.5	12.80%	B / 8.3
2011	C	2,878.00	57.03	C / 4.9	1.93%	B- / 7.9
2010	C-	2,415.40	56.67	C- / 3.2	12.48%	C+ / 6.1
2009	D+	2,163.95	51.45	D / 1.9	18.80%	C+ / 6.1

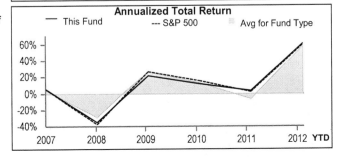

Annualized Total Return

*iShares S&P 1500 (ISI)

C+   **Fair**

Fund Family: BlackRock Fund Advisors
Fund Type: Income
Inception Date: January 20, 2004

Major Rating Factors: Middle of the road best describes *iShares S&P 1500 whose TheStreet.com Investment Rating is currently a C+ (Fair). The fund currently has a performance rating of C+ (Fair) based on an annualized return of 21.49% over the last three years and a total return of 12.42% year to date 2012. Factored into the performance evaluation is an expense ratio of 0.20% (very low).

The fund's risk rating is currently B (Good). It carries a beta of 1.03, meaning that its performance tracks fairly well with that of the overall stock market. Volatility, as measured by both the semi-deviation and a drawdown factor, is considered low. As of March 31, 2012, *iShares S&P 1500 traded at a premium of .06% above its net asset value, which is worse than its one-year historical average premium of .02%.

Diane Hsiung has been running the fund for 4 years and currently receives a manager quality ranking of 45 (0=worst, 99=best). If you desire an average level of risk, then this fund may be an option.

Data Date	Investment Rating	Net Assets ($Mil)	Price	Performance Rating/Pts	Total Return Y-T-D	Risk Rating/Pts
3-12	C+	386.13	64.02	C+ / 5.9	12.42%	B / 8.2
2011	C+	299.60	57.17	C / 5.3	1.45%	B- / 7.9
2010	D+	323.40	57.25	C- / 4.2	16.24%	C- / 3.7
2009	D-	290.33	50.14	D / 2.2	23.36%	C- / 4.2

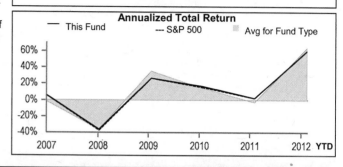

*iShares S&P 500 (IVV)

C+   **Fair**

Fund Family: BlackRock Fund Advisors
Fund Type: Growth
Inception Date: May 15, 2000

Major Rating Factors: Middle of the road best describes *iShares S&P 500 whose TheStreet.com Investment Rating is currently a C+ (Fair). The fund currently has a performance rating of C+ (Fair) based on an annualized return of 21.08% over the last three years and a total return of 12.61% year to date 2012. Factored into the performance evaluation is an expense ratio of 0.09% (very low).

The fund's risk rating is currently B (Good). It carries a beta of 1.00, meaning that its performance tracks fairly well with that of the overall stock market. Volatility, as measured by both the semi-deviation and a drawdown factor, is considered low. As of March 31, 2012, *iShares S&P 500 traded at a discount of .05% below its net asset value.

Diane Hsiung has been running the fund for 4 years and currently receives a manager quality ranking of 46 (0=worst, 99=best). If you desire an average level of risk, then this fund may be an option.

Data Date	Investment Rating	Net Assets ($Mil)	Price	Performance Rating/Pts	Total Return Y-T-D	Risk Rating/Pts
3-12	C+	28,477.25	141.21	C+ / 5.8	12.61%	B / 8.2
2011	C+	26,208.70	125.96	C / 5.3	1.83%	B- / 7.9
2010	C-	25,763.50	126.25	C- / 3.9	15.11%	C+ / 6.0
2009	D+	20,494.00	111.81	D / 2.2	22.60%	C+ / 6.1

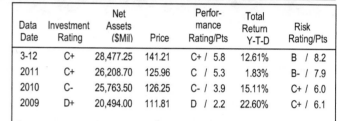
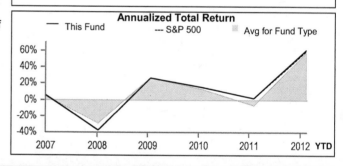

*iShares S&P 500 Growth (IVW)

C+   **Fair**

Fund Family: BlackRock Fund Advisors
Fund Type: Growth
Inception Date: May 22, 2000

Major Rating Factors: Middle of the road best describes *iShares S&P 500 Growth whose TheStreet.com Investment Rating is currently a C+ (Fair). The fund currently has a performance rating of C+ (Fair) based on an annualized return of 21.44% over the last three years and a total return of 12.17% year to date 2012. Factored into the performance evaluation is an expense ratio of 0.18% (very low).

The fund's risk rating is currently B (Good). It carries a beta of 0.95, meaning that its performance tracks fairly well with that of the overall stock market. Volatility, as measured by both the semi-deviation and a drawdown factor, is considered low. As of March 31, 2012, *iShares S&P 500 Growth traded at a discount of .05% below its net asset value.

Diane Hsiung has been running the fund for 4 years and currently receives a manager quality ranking of 55 (0=worst, 99=best). If you desire an average level of risk, then this fund may be an option.

Data Date	Investment Rating	Net Assets ($Mil)	Price	Performance Rating/Pts	Total Return Y-T-D	Risk Rating/Pts
3-12	C+	6,895.99	75.37	C+ / 6.0	12.17%	B / 8.1
2011	C+	6,403.90	67.43	C+ / 6.0	1.29%	B- / 7.8
2010	C	5,806.90	65.65	C / 5.0	14.91%	C+ / 6.1
2009	C-	5,513.11	57.99	C- / 3.3	27.19%	C+ / 6.3

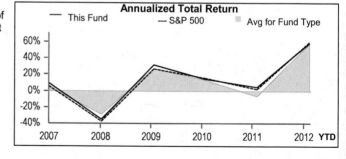

*iShares S&P 500 Value (IVE)   C+   Fair

Fund Family: BlackRock Fund Advisors
Fund Type: Income
Inception Date: May 22, 2000

Data Date	Investment Rating	Net Assets ($Mil)	Price	Performance Rating/Pts	Total Return Y-T-D	Risk Rating/Pts
3-12	C+	4,385.16	64.93	C+ / 5.6	12.86%	B / 8.2
2011	C	3,901.70	57.83	C / 4.7	2.21%	B- / 7.8
2010	D+	4,115.90	59.59	D+ / 2.7	14.97%	C+ / 5.7
2009	D	3,503.61	53.01	D- / 1.3	18.12%	C+ / 5.8

Major Rating Factors: Middle of the road best describes *iShares S&P 500 Value whose TheStreet.com Investment Rating is currently a C+ (Fair). The fund currently has a performance rating of C+ (Fair) based on an annualized return of 20.58% over the last three years and a total return of 12.86% year to date 2012. Factored into the performance evaluation is an expense ratio of 0.18% (very low).

The fund's risk rating is currently B (Good). It carries a beta of 1.07, meaning that its performance tracks fairly well with that of the overall stock market. Volatility, as measured by both the semi-deviation and a drawdown factor, is considered low. As of March 31, 2012, *iShares S&P 500 Value traded at a discount of .06% below its net asset value, which is better than its one-year historical average premium of .06%.

Diane Hsiung has been running the fund for 4 years and currently receives a manager quality ranking of 36 (0=worst, 99=best). If you desire an average level of risk, then this fund may be an option.

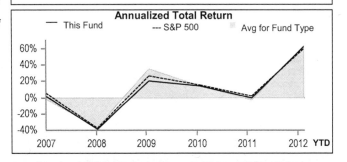

Annualized Total Return — This Fund --- S&P 500 — Avg for Fund Type

*iShares S&P Aggressive Allocatio (AOA)   C   Fair

Fund Family: BlackRock Fund Advisors
Fund Type: Growth and Income
Inception Date: November 4, 2008

Data Date	Investment Rating	Net Assets ($Mil)	Price	Performance Rating/Pts	Total Return Y-T-D	Risk Rating/Pts
3-12	C	93.41	36.45	C / 4.8	10.61%	B / 8.2
2011	C	82.50	33.05	C / 4.7	1.05%	B / 8.1
2010	A+	56.70	34.37	A- / 9.2	16.77%	B- / 7.5
2009	A+	18.88	29.97	B / 8.1	23.89%	B- / 7.8

Major Rating Factors: Middle of the road best describes *iShares S&P Aggressive Allocatio whose TheStreet.com Investment Rating is currently a C (Fair). The fund currently has a performance rating of C (Fair) based on an annualized return of 19.16% over the last three years and a total return of 10.61% year to date 2012. Factored into the performance evaluation is an expense ratio of 0.11% (very low).

The fund's risk rating is currently B (Good). It carries a beta of 1.01, meaning that its performance tracks fairly well with that of the overall stock market. Volatility, as measured by both the semi-deviation and a drawdown factor, is considered low. As of March 31, 2012, *iShares S&P Aggressive Allocatio traded at a premium of .11% above its net asset value, which is worse than its one-year historical average premium of .08%.

Diane Hsiung has been running the fund for 4 years and currently receives a manager quality ranking of 33 (0=worst, 99=best). If you desire an average level of risk, then this fund may be an option.

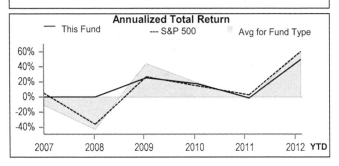

Annualized Total Return — This Fund --- S&P 500 — Avg for Fund Type

*iShares S&P Asia 50 Index (AIA)   C   Fair

Fund Family: BlackRock Fund Advisors
Fund Type: Foreign
Inception Date: November 13, 2007

Data Date	Investment Rating	Net Assets ($Mil)	Price	Performance Rating/Pts	Total Return Y-T-D	Risk Rating/Pts
3-12	C	206.22	44.50	C / 4.9	13.67%	B- / 7.2
2011	C	177.10	39.15	C / 5.2	1.10%	B- / 7.3
2010	C	209.60	46.95	C+ / 6.3	19.62%	C / 4.9
2009	A-	111.28	39.95	A- / 9.1	51.24%	C / 5.1

Major Rating Factors: Middle of the road best describes *iShares S&P Asia 50 Index whose TheStreet.com Investment Rating is currently a C (Fair). The fund currently has a performance rating of C (Fair) based on an annualized return of 20.04% over the last three years and a total return of 13.67% year to date 2012. Factored into the performance evaluation is an expense ratio of 0.50% (very low).

The fund's risk rating is currently B- (Good). It carries a beta of 1.03, meaning that its performance tracks fairly well with that of the overall stock market. Volatility, as measured by both the semi-deviation and a drawdown factor, is considered low. As of March 31, 2012, *iShares S&P Asia 50 Index traded at a discount of .38% below its net asset value, which is better than its one-year historical average discount of .27%.

Diane Hsiung has been running the fund for 4 years and currently receives a manager quality ranking of 69 (0=worst, 99=best). If you desire an average level of risk, then this fund may be an option.

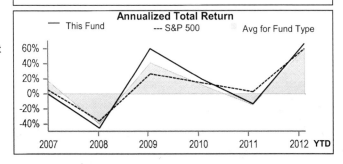

Annualized Total Return — This Fund --- S&P 500 — Avg for Fund Type

*iShares S&P CA AMT-Free Muni Bon (CMF)

C   **Fair**

Fund Family: BlackRock Fund Advisors
Fund Type: Municipal - Single State
Inception Date: October 4, 2007

Major Rating Factors: Middle of the road best describes *iShares S&P CA AMT-Free Muni Bon whose TheStreet.com Investment Rating is currently a C (Fair). The fund currently has a performance rating of C- (Fair) based on an annualized return of 6.67% over the last three years and a total return of 2.25% year to date 2012. Factored into the performance evaluation is an expense ratio of 0.25% (very low).

The fund's risk rating is currently B+ (Good). It carries a beta of 1.18, meaning it is expected to move 11.8% for every 10% move in the market. Volatility, as measured by both the semi-deviation and a drawdown factor, is considered very low. As of March 31, 2012, *iShares S&P CA AMT-Free Muni Bon traded at a premium of .50% above its net asset value, which is worse than its one-year historical average discount of .13%.

Joel Silva has been running the fund for 5 years and currently receives a manager quality ranking of 32 (0=worst, 99=best). If you desire an average level of risk, then this fund may be an option.

Data Date	Investment Rating	Net Assets ($Mil)	Price	Performance Rating/Pts	Total Return Y-T-D	Risk Rating/Pts
3-12	C	209.60	112.65	C- / 3.2	2.25%	B+ / 9.1
2011	B-	193.00	110.79	C / 5.5	0.59%	B+ / 9.2
2010	C	225.30	98.85	D / 2.2	-2.64%	B / 8.5
2009	B	167.56	105.55	C / 5.3	8.17%	B / 8.9

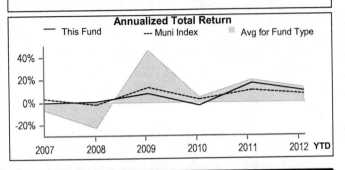

Annualized Total Return — This Fund, Muni Index, Avg for Fund Type

*iShares S&P Conservative Allocat (AOK)

C   **Fair**

Fund Family: BlackRock Fund Advisors
Fund Type: Growth and Income
Inception Date: November 4, 2008

Major Rating Factors:
Disappointing performance is the major factor driving the C (Fair) TheStreet.com Investment Rating for *iShares S&P Conservative Allocat. The fund currently has a performance rating of D (Weak) based on an annualized return of 8.55% over the last three years and a total return of 3.01% year to date 2012. Factored into the performance evaluation is an expense ratio of 0.11% (very low).

The fund's risk rating is currently B+ (Good). It carries a beta of 0.23, meaning the fund's expected move will be 2.3% for every 10% move in the market. Volatility, as measured by both the semi-deviation and a drawdown factor, is considered very low. As of March 31, 2012, *iShares S&P Conservative Allocat traded at a premium of .13% above its net asset value, which is worse than its one-year historical average premium of .03%.

Diane Hsiung has been running the fund for 4 years and currently receives a manager quality ranking of 67 (0=worst, 99=best). This fund offers only a moderate level of risk but investors looking for strong performance are still waiting.

Data Date	Investment Rating	Net Assets ($Mil)	Price	Performance Rating/Pts	Total Return Y-T-D	Risk Rating/Pts
3-12	C	97.92	30.18	D / 2.2	3.01%	B+ / 9.8
2011	C	95.30	29.35	C- / 3.4	0.20%	B+ / 9.6
2010	B	44.60	28.79	C+ / 6.6	7.08%	B / 8.7
2009	B+	10.51	27.30	C / 4.8	8.46%	B / 8.9

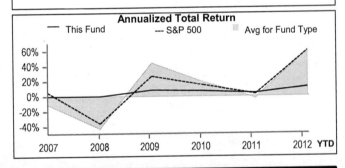

Annualized Total Return — This Fund, S&P 500, Avg for Fund Type

*iShares S&P Dev ex-US Property (WPS)

D+   **Weak**

Fund Family: BlackRock Fund Advisors
Fund Type: Foreign
Inception Date: July 30, 2007

Major Rating Factors: *iShares S&P Dev ex-US Property receives a TheStreet.com Investment Rating of D+ (Weak). The fund currently has a performance rating of C (Fair) based on an annualized return of 20.11% over the last three years and a total return of 15.22% year to date 2012. Factored into the performance evaluation is an expense ratio of 0.48% (very low).

The fund's risk rating is currently C+ (Fair). It carries a beta of 1.06, meaning that its performance tracks fairly well with that of the overall stock market. Volatility, as measured by both the semi-deviation and a drawdown factor, is considered low. As of March 31, 2012, *iShares S&P Dev ex-US Property traded at a premium of .35% above its net asset value, which is worse than its one-year historical average discount of .11%.

Diane Hsiung has been running the fund for 4 years and currently receives a manager quality ranking of 71 (0=worst, 99=best). If you desire an average level of risk, then this fund may be an option.

Data Date	Investment Rating	Net Assets ($Mil)	Price	Performance Rating/Pts	Total Return Y-T-D	Risk Rating/Pts
3-12	D+	131.11	31.56	C / 4.7	15.22%	C+ / 5.7
2011	D	116.30	27.53	C- / 3.2	0.41%	C / 5.5
2010	D-	143.30	34.25	D+ / 2.4	18.13%	C- / 3.1
2009	C	90.88	30.69	B+ / 8.4	33.92%	C- / 3.1

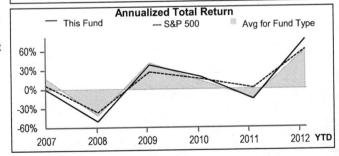

Annualized Total Return — This Fund, S&P 500, Avg for Fund Type

*iShares S&P Emerging Mkts Infr (EMIF)   C-   Fair

Fund Family: BlackRock Fund Advisors
Fund Type: Global
Inception Date: June 16, 2009

Data Date	Investment Rating	Net Assets ($Mil)	Price	Performance Rating/Pts	Total Return Y-T-D	Risk Rating/Pts
3-12	C-	120.33	33.21	C- / 3.9	15.15%	B- / 7.1
2011	D	102.60	28.84	D- / 1.3	2.01%	B- / 7.1
2010	A+	109.40	34.32	A- / 9.0	18.30%	B / 8.2

Major Rating Factors: Middle of the road best describes *iShares S&P Emerging Mkts Infr whose TheStreet.com Investment Rating is currently a C- (Fair). The fund currently has a performance rating of C- (Fair) based on an annualized return of 0.00% over the last three years and a total return of 15.15% year to date 2012. Factored into the performance evaluation is an expense ratio of 0.70% (very low).

The fund's risk rating is currently B- (Good). It carries a beta of 0.00, meaning the fund's expected move will be 0.0% for every 10% move in the market. Volatility, as measured by both the semi-deviation and a drawdown factor, is considered low. As of March 31, 2012, *iShares S&P Emerging Mkts Infr traded at a premium of .18% above its net asset value, which is worse than its one-year historical average discount of .06%.

Diane Hsiung has been running the fund for 3 years and currently receives a manager quality ranking of 61 (0=worst, 99=best). If you desire an average level of risk, then this fund may be an option.

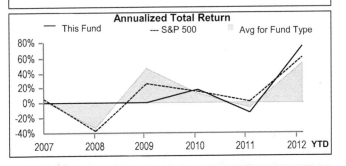

*iShares S&P Europe 350 (IEV)   D+   Weak

Fund Family: BlackRock Fund Advisors
Fund Type: Foreign
Inception Date: July 25, 2000

Data Date	Investment Rating	Net Assets ($Mil)	Price	Performance Rating/Pts	Total Return Y-T-D	Risk Rating/Pts
3-12	D+	1,099.88	37.35	C- / 3.2	10.70%	B- / 7.2
2011	D	915.60	33.74	D+ / 2.4	-1.04%	B- / 7.0
2010	E+	1,156.80	39.28	D- / 1.2	3.83%	C- / 3.0
2009	E+	1,509.85	38.96	D / 2.2	27.55%	C- / 3.1

Major Rating Factors: *iShares S&P Europe 350 receives a TheStreet.com Investment Rating of D+ (Weak). The fund currently has a performance rating of C- (Fair) based on an annualized return of 13.96% over the last three years and a total return of 10.70% year to date 2012. Factored into the performance evaluation is an expense ratio of 0.60% (very low).

The fund's risk rating is currently B- (Good). It carries a beta of 1.16, meaning it is expected to move 11.6% for every 10% move in the market. Volatility, as measured by both the semi-deviation and a drawdown factor, is considered low. As of March 31, 2012, *iShares S&P Europe 350 traded at a premium of .21% above its net asset value, which is worse than its one-year historical average discount of .08%.

Diane Hsiung has been running the fund for 4 years and currently receives a manager quality ranking of 28 (0=worst, 99=best). If you desire an average level of risk, then this fund may be an option.

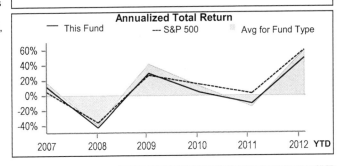

*iShares S&P Gl Cons Staples Sect (KXI)   C+   Fair

Fund Family: BlackRock Fund Advisors
Fund Type: Global
Inception Date: September 12, 2006

Data Date	Investment Rating	Net Assets ($Mil)	Price	Performance Rating/Pts	Total Return Y-T-D	Risk Rating/Pts
3-12	C+	450.71	70.77	C / 5.5	6.33%	B+ / 9.0
2011	C+	465.70	66.56	C+ / 5.7	-1.10%	B / 8.5
2010	C+	327.50	62.47	C / 5.4	13.19%	C+ / 6.9
2009	C	251.25	56.61	C / 4.5	20.16%	B- / 7.0

Major Rating Factors: Middle of the road best describes *iShares S&P Gl Cons Staples Sect whose TheStreet.com Investment Rating is currently a C+ (Fair). The fund currently has a performance rating of C (Fair) based on an annualized return of 20.83% over the last three years and a total return of 6.33% year to date 2012. Factored into the performance evaluation is an expense ratio of 0.48% (very low).

The fund's risk rating is currently B+ (Good). It carries a beta of 0.51, meaning the fund's expected move will be 5.1% for every 10% move in the market. Volatility, as measured by both the semi-deviation and a drawdown factor, is considered very low. As of March 31, 2012, *iShares S&P Gl Cons Staples Sect traded at a discount of .16% below its net asset value, which is better than its one-year historical average premium of .09%.

Diane Hsiung has been running the fund for 4 years and currently receives a manager quality ranking of 88 (0=worst, 99=best). If you desire an average level of risk, then this fund may be an option.

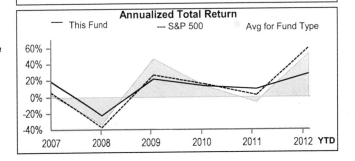

*iShares S&P Glb Infrastructure (IGF)

C   **Fair**

Fund Family: BlackRock Fund Advisors
Fund Type: Global
Inception Date: December 10, 2007

Major Rating Factors: Middle of the road best describes *iShares S&P Glb Infrastructure whose TheStreet.com Investment Rating is currently a C (Fair). The fund currently has a performance rating of C- (Fair) based on an annualized return of 16.28% over the last three years and a total return of 6.65% year to date 2012. Factored into the performance evaluation is an expense ratio of 0.48% (very low).

The fund's risk rating is currently B (Good). It carries a beta of 0.79, meaning the fund's expected move will be 7.9% for every 10% move in the market. Volatility, as measured by both the semi-deviation and a drawdown factor, is considered low. As of March 31, 2012, *iShares S&P Glb Infrastructure traded at a discount of .08% below its net asset value, which is better than its one-year historical average discount of .04%.

Diane Hsiung has been running the fund for 4 years and currently receives a manager quality ranking of 66 (0=worst, 99=best). If you desire an average level of risk, then this fund may be an option.

Data Date	Investment Rating	Net Assets ($Mil)	Price	Performance Rating/Pts	Total Return Y-T-D	Risk Rating/Pts
3-12	C	439.21	35.41	C- / 3.8	6.65%	B / 8.3
2011	C-	415.10	33.20	C- / 3.3	-1.33%	B- / 7.8
2010	D	468.90	35.06	D- / 1.3	7.05%	C+ / 5.7
2009	B	409.90	34.08	B / 7.6	16.96%	C+ / 5.8

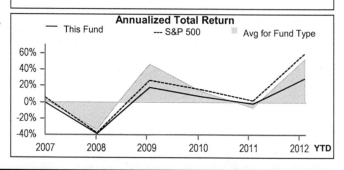

Annualized Total Return
— This Fund   --- S&P 500   Avg for Fund Type

*iShares S&P Glb Timber & Forestr (WOOD)

C   **Fair**

Fund Family: BlackRock Fund Advisors
Fund Type: Global
Inception Date: June 24, 2008

Major Rating Factors: Middle of the road best describes *iShares S&P Glb Timber & Forestr whose TheStreet.com Investment Rating is currently a C (Fair). The fund currently has a performance rating of C (Fair) based on an annualized return of 22.42% over the last three years and a total return of 11.30% year to date 2012. Factored into the performance evaluation is an expense ratio of 0.48% (very low).

The fund's risk rating is currently B- (Good). It carries a beta of 1.02, meaning that its performance tracks fairly well with that of the overall stock market. Volatility, as measured by both the semi-deviation and a drawdown factor, is considered low. As of March 31, 2012, *iShares S&P Glb Timber & Forestr traded at a premium of .41% above its net asset value, which is worse than its one-year historical average premium of .01%.

Diane Hsiung has been running the fund for 4 years and currently receives a manager quality ranking of 77 (0=worst, 99=best). If you desire an average level of risk, then this fund may be an option.

Data Date	Investment Rating	Net Assets ($Mil)	Price	Performance Rating/Pts	Total Return Y-T-D	Risk Rating/Pts
3-12	C	158.13	41.39	C / 4.9	11.30%	B- / 7.3
2011	C-	142.00	37.19	C- / 3.8	1.50%	B- / 7.0
2010	B+	166.70	44.95	A- / 9.1	16.19%	C / 5.0
2009	A-	35.72	39.68	A- / 9.2	38.44%	C / 4.9

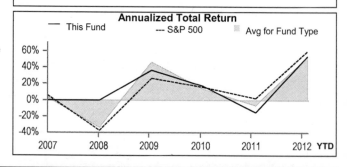

Annualized Total Return
— This Fund   --- S&P 500   Avg for Fund Type

*iShares S&P Global 100 (IOO)

C-   **Fair**

Fund Family: BlackRock Fund Advisors
Fund Type: Growth
Inception Date: December 5, 2000

Major Rating Factors: Middle of the road best describes *iShares S&P Global 100 whose TheStreet.com Investment Rating is currently a C- (Fair). The fund currently has a performance rating of C- (Fair) based on an annualized return of 15.55% over the last three years and a total return of 9.75% year to date 2012. Factored into the performance evaluation is an expense ratio of 0.40% (very low).

The fund's risk rating is currently B (Good). It carries a beta of 1.13, meaning it is expected to move 11.3% for every 10% move in the market. Volatility, as measured by both the semi-deviation and a drawdown factor, is considered low. As of March 31, 2012, *iShares S&P Global 100 traded at a premium of .03% above its net asset value, which is worse than its one-year historical average discount of .03%.

Diane Hsiung has been running the fund for 4 years and currently receives a manager quality ranking of 18 (0=worst, 99=best). If you desire an average level of risk, then this fund may be an option.

Data Date	Investment Rating	Net Assets ($Mil)	Price	Performance Rating/Pts	Total Return Y-T-D	Risk Rating/Pts
3-12	C-	1,057.65	63.59	C- / 3.8	9.75%	B / 8.0
2011	C-	975.50	57.94	C- / 3.5	0.57%	B- / 7.8
2010	D+	953.10	62.27	D / 1.9	5.96%	C+ / 6.0
2009	C-	707.27	60.25	D+ / 2.6	21.62%	C+ / 6.4

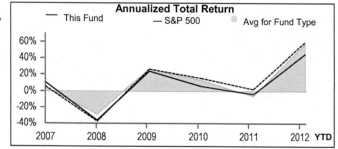

Annualized Total Return
— This Fund   --- S&P 500   Avg for Fund Type

*iShares S&P Global Clean Energy (ICLN)   E+   Very Weak

Fund Family: BlackRock Fund Advisors
Fund Type: Energy/Natural Resources
Inception Date: June 24, 2008

Data Date	Investment Rating	Net Assets ($Mil)	Price	Performance Rating/Pts	Total Return Y-T-D	Risk Rating/Pts
3-12	E+	35.37	9.10	E+ / 0.6	6.56%	C / 4.6
2011	E+	32.00	8.54	E+ / 0.6	0.00%	C / 4.3
2010	E+	50.60	15.84	E / 0.5	-27.64%	C- / 3.5
2009	E+	90.43	22.26	D / 2.0	-0.14%	C- / 3.3

Major Rating Factors:
Very poor performance is the major factor driving the E+ (Very Weak) TheStreet.com Investment Rating for *iShares S&P Global Clean Energy. The fund currently has a performance rating of E+ (Very Weak) based on an annualized return of -19.67% over the last three years and a total return of 6.56% year to date 2012. Factored into the performance evaluation is an expense ratio of 0.48% (very low).

The fund's risk rating is currently C (Fair). It carries a beta of 1.19, meaning it is expected to move 11.9% for every 10% move in the market. Volatility, as measured by both the semi-deviation and a drawdown factor, is considered average. As of March 31, 2012, *iShares S&P Global Clean Energy traded at a price exactly equal to its net asset value, which is worse than its one-year historical average discount of .27%.

Diane Hsiung has been running the fund for 4 years and currently receives a manager quality ranking of 2 (0=worst, 99=best). This fund offers an average level of risk but investors looking for strong performance will be frustrated.

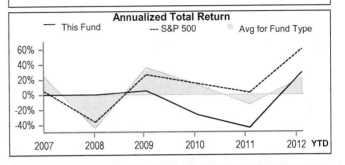

Annualized Total Return

*iShares S&P Global Cons Disc (RXI)   B-   Good

Fund Family: BlackRock Fund Advisors
Fund Type: Global
Inception Date: September 12, 2006

Data Date	Investment Rating	Net Assets ($Mil)	Price	Performance Rating/Pts	Total Return Y-T-D	Risk Rating/Pts
3-12	B-	136.85	59.04	C+ / 6.9	18.20%	B / 8.1
2011	C	112.60	49.95	C / 5.3	1.88%	B- / 7.8
2010	C+	130.60	53.41	C+ / 6.6	23.32%	C+ / 5.8
2009	D+	78.77	43.84	D+ / 2.4	33.34%	C+ / 5.7

Major Rating Factors: *iShares S&P Global Cons Disc receives a TheStreet.com Investment Rating of B- (Good). The fund currently has a performance rating of C+ (Fair) based on an annualized return of 23.91% over the last three years and a total return of 18.20% year to date 2012. Factored into the performance evaluation is an expense ratio of 0.48% (very low).

The fund's risk rating is currently B (Good). It carries a beta of 0.87, meaning the fund's expected move will be 8.7% for every 10% move in the market. Volatility, as measured by both the semi-deviation and a drawdown factor, is considered low. As of March 31, 2012, *iShares S&P Global Cons Disc traded at a premium of .37% above its net asset value, which is worse than its one-year historical average discount of .03%.

Diane Hsiung has been running the fund for 4 years and currently receives a manager quality ranking of 87 (0=worst, 99=best). If you desire an average level of risk, then this fund may be an option.

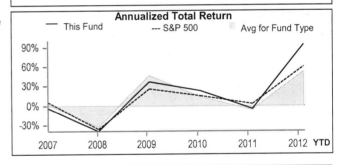

Annualized Total Return

*iShares S&P Global Energy (IXC)   D+   Weak

Fund Family: BlackRock Fund Advisors
Fund Type: Energy/Natural Resources
Inception Date: November 12, 2001

Data Date	Investment Rating	Net Assets ($Mil)	Price	Performance Rating/Pts	Total Return Y-T-D	Risk Rating/Pts
3-12	D+	1,239.60	39.78	C- / 3.2	4.16%	B- / 7.6
2011	C-	1,123.40	38.19	C / 4.3	1.44%	B- / 7.5
2010	D-	1,313.20	39.06	C- / 3.3	11.85%	D+ / 2.8
2009	D	930.27	35.68	C- / 4.2	18.86%	C- / 3.1

Major Rating Factors: *iShares S&P Global Energy receives a TheStreet.com Investment Rating of D+ (Weak). The fund currently has a performance rating of C- (Fair) based on an annualized return of 14.29% over the last three years and a total return of 4.16% year to date 2012. Factored into the performance evaluation is an expense ratio of 0.48% (very low).

The fund's risk rating is currently B- (Good). It carries a beta of 1.02, meaning that its performance tracks fairly well with that of the overall stock market. Volatility, as measured by both the semi-deviation and a drawdown factor, is considered low. As of March 31, 2012, *iShares S&P Global Energy traded at a premium of .25% above its net asset value, which is worse than its one-year historical average discount of .02%.

Diane Hsiung has been running the fund for 4 years and currently receives a manager quality ranking of 31 (0=worst, 99=best). If you desire an average level of risk, then this fund may be an option.

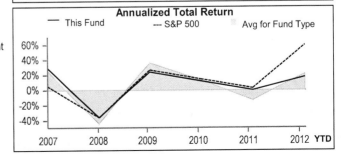

Annualized Total Return

*iShares S&P Global Financials (IXG)

D+   Weak

Fund Family: BlackRock Fund Advisors
Fund Type: Financial Services
Inception Date: November 12, 2001

Data Date	Investment Rating	Net Assets ($Mil)	Price	Performance Rating/Pts	Total Return Y-T-D	Risk Rating/Pts
3-12	D+	162.47	42.66	C- / 3.5	19.23%	B- / 7.3
2011	D	147.40	35.78	D / 2.0	0.70%	C+ / 6.8
2010	D-	287.80	46.13	E+ / 0.8	3.97%	C / 4.4
2009	E+	330.25	45.41	E+ / 0.8	30.85%	C / 4.5

Major Rating Factors: *iShares S&P Global Financials receives a TheStreet.com Investment Rating of D+ (Weak). The fund currently has a performance rating of C- (Fair) based on an annualized return of 14.38% over the last three years and a total return of 19.23% year to date 2012. Factored into the performance evaluation is an expense ratio of 0.48% (very low).

The fund's risk rating is currently B- (Good). It carries a beta of 1.10, meaning it is expected to move 11.0% for every 10% move in the market. Volatility, as measured by both the semi-deviation and a drawdown factor, is considered low. As of March 31, 2012, *iShares S&P Global Financials traded at a premium of .49% above its net asset value, which is worse than its one-year historical average discount of .15%.

Diane Hsiung has been running the fund for 4 years and currently receives a manager quality ranking of 21 (0=worst, 99=best). If you desire an average level of risk, then this fund may be an option.

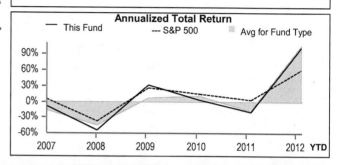

*iShares S&P Global Healthcare (IXJ)

C   Fair

Fund Family: BlackRock Fund Advisors
Fund Type: Health
Inception Date: November 13, 2001

Data Date	Investment Rating	Net Assets ($Mil)	Price	Performance Rating/Pts	Total Return Y-T-D	Risk Rating/Pts
3-12	C	533.53	60.15	C / 4.6	7.18%	B / 8.6
2011	C	530.40	56.12	C / 4.4	0.55%	B- / 7.9
2010	C-	477.00	51.76	D+ / 2.4	1.91%	C+ / 6.8
2009	C-	445.26	52.01	C- / 3.0	16.26%	C+ / 6.7

Major Rating Factors: Middle of the road best describes *iShares S&P Global Healthcare whose TheStreet.com Investment Rating is currently a C (Fair). The fund currently has a performance rating of C (Fair) based on an annualized return of 17.82% over the last three years and a total return of 7.18% year to date 2012. Factored into the performance evaluation is an expense ratio of 0.48% (very low).

The fund's risk rating is currently B (Good). It carries a beta of 0.59, meaning the fund's expected move will be 5.9% for every 10% move in the market. Volatility, as measured by both the semi-deviation and a drawdown factor, is considered low. As of March 31, 2012, *iShares S&P Global Healthcare traded at a premium of .05% above its net asset value, which is worse than its one-year historical average discount of .02%.

Diane Hsiung has been running the fund for 4 years and currently receives a manager quality ranking of 67 (0=worst, 99=best). If you desire an average level of risk, then this fund may be an option.

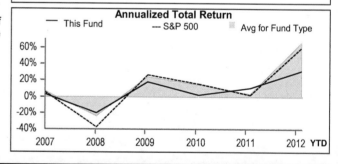

*iShares S&P Global Industrials (EXI)

C   Fair

Fund Family: BlackRock Fund Advisors
Fund Type: Global
Inception Date: September 12, 2006

Data Date	Investment Rating	Net Assets ($Mil)	Price	Performance Rating/Pts	Total Return Y-T-D	Risk Rating/Pts
3-12	C	199.96	54.23	C / 5.3	12.44%	B- / 7.6
2011	C-	167.10	48.23	C- / 4.1	1.24%	B- / 7.4
2010	C-	199.00	53.85	C / 4.6	23.33%	C / 5.3
2009	D+	124.62	44.41	D+ / 2.3	22.53%	C / 5.5

Major Rating Factors: Middle of the road best describes *iShares S&P Global Industrials whose TheStreet.com Investment Rating is currently a C (Fair). The fund currently has a performance rating of C (Fair) based on an annualized return of 21.48% over the last three years and a total return of 12.44% year to date 2012. Factored into the performance evaluation is an expense ratio of 0.48% (very low).

The fund's risk rating is currently B- (Good). It carries a beta of 0.98, meaning that its performance tracks fairly well with that of the overall stock market. Volatility, as measured by both the semi-deviation and a drawdown factor, is considered low. As of March 31, 2012, *iShares S&P Global Industrials traded at a premium of .20% above its net asset value, which is worse than its one-year historical average discount of .05%.

Diane Hsiung has been running the fund for 4 years and currently receives a manager quality ranking of 79 (0=worst, 99=best). If you desire an average level of risk, then this fund may be an option.

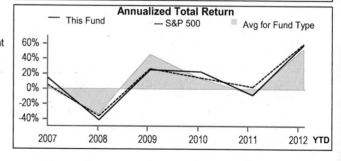

*iShares S&P Global Materials (MXI)   D+   Weak

Fund Family: BlackRock Fund Advisors
Fund Type: Global
Inception Date: September 12, 2006

Major Rating Factors: *iShares S&P Global Materials receives a TheStreet.com Investment Rating of D+ (Weak). The fund currently has a performance rating of C- (Fair) based on an annualized return of 17.72% over the last three years and a total return of 10.44% year to date 2012. Factored into the performance evaluation is an expense ratio of 0.48% (very low).

The fund's risk rating is currently C+ (Fair). It carries a beta of 1.22, meaning it is expected to move 12.2% for every 10% move in the market. Volatility, as measured by both the semi-deviation and a drawdown factor, is considered low. As of March 31, 2012, *iShares S&P Global Materials traded at a premium of .62% above its net asset value, which is worse than its one-year historical average discount of .04%.

Diane Hsiung has been running the fund for 4 years and currently receives a manager quality ranking of 41 (0=worst, 99=best). If you desire an average level of risk, then this fund may be an option.

Data Date	Investment Rating	Net Assets ($Mil)	Price	Perfor-mance Rating/Pts	Total Return Y-T-D	Risk Rating/Pts
3-12	D+	563.48	63.17	C- / 3.8	10.44%	C+ / 6.8
2011	C-	476.20	57.20	C- / 4.2	2.40%	C+ / 6.5
2010	C	777.40	73.25	C+ / 6.0	19.99%	C / 4.6
2009	C+	757.32	62.22	B- / 7.3	56.43%	C / 5.2

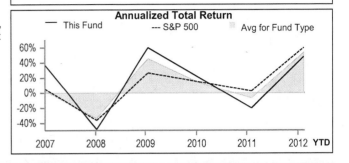

Annualized Total Return
— This Fund   --- S&P 500   Avg for Fund Type

*iShares S&P Global Nuclear (NUCL)   D   Weak

Fund Family: BlackRock Fund Advisors
Fund Type: Energy/Natural Resources
Inception Date: June 24, 2008

Major Rating Factors:
Disappointing performance is the major factor driving the D (Weak) TheStreet.com Investment Rating for *iShares S&P Global Nuclear. The fund currently has a performance rating of D (Weak) based on an annualized return of 5.86% over the last three years and a total return of 8.75% year to date 2012. Factored into the performance evaluation is an expense ratio of 0.48% (very low).

The fund's risk rating is currently B- (Good). It carries a beta of 0.69, meaning the fund's expected move will be 6.9% for every 10% move in the market. Volatility, as measured by both the semi-deviation and a drawdown factor, is considered low. As of March 31, 2012, *iShares S&P Global Nuclear traded at a discount of .34% below its net asset value, which is worse than its one-year historical average discount of .56%.

Diane Hsiung has been running the fund for 4 years and currently receives a manager quality ranking of 22 (0=worst, 99=best). This fund offers only a moderate level of risk but investors looking for strong performance are still waiting.

Data Date	Investment Rating	Net Assets ($Mil)	Price	Perfor-mance Rating/Pts	Total Return Y-T-D	Risk Rating/Pts
3-12	D	12.07	35.17	D / 1.7	8.75%	B- / 7.3
2011	D	11.10	32.34	D / 1.8	-0.46%	B- / 7.2
2010	A-	17.30	43.38	B+ / 8.9	7.11%	C+ / 5.9
2009	B+	16.19	41.90	B / 8.2	35.10%	C+ / 5.8

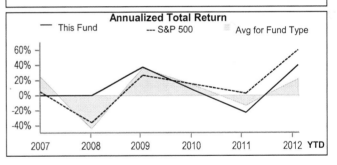

Annualized Total Return
— This Fund   --- S&P 500   Avg for Fund Type

*iShares S&P Global Technology (IXN)   C+   Fair

Fund Family: BlackRock Fund Advisors
Fund Type: Global
Inception Date: November 12, 2001

Major Rating Factors: Middle of the road best describes *iShares S&P Global Technology whose TheStreet.com Investment Rating is currently a C+ (Fair). The fund currently has a performance rating of C+ (Fair) based on an annualized return of 21.86% over the last three years and a total return of 20.58% year to date 2012. Factored into the performance evaluation is an expense ratio of 0.48% (very low).

The fund's risk rating is currently B- (Good). It carries a beta of 0.83, meaning the fund's expected move will be 8.3% for every 10% move in the market. Volatility, as measured by both the semi-deviation and a drawdown factor, is considered low. As of March 31, 2012, *iShares S&P Global Technology traded at a premium of .10% above its net asset value, which is worse than its one-year historical average discount of .06%.

Diane Hsiung has been running the fund for 4 years and currently receives a manager quality ranking of 83 (0=worst, 99=best). If you desire an average level of risk, then this fund may be an option.

Data Date	Investment Rating	Net Assets ($Mil)	Price	Perfor-mance Rating/Pts	Total Return Y-T-D	Risk Rating/Pts
3-12	C+	624.88	70.79	C+ / 6.7	20.58%	B- / 7.2
2011	C	475.80	58.71	C+ / 5.7	1.87%	B- / 7.1
2010	C-	601.00	61.42	C / 4.7	10.48%	C / 5.4
2009	C-	373.23	56.01	C / 4.5	48.00%	C / 5.5

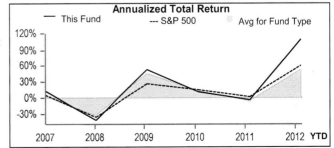

Annualized Total Return
— This Fund   --- S&P 500   Avg for Fund Type

*iShares S&P Global Telecom (IXP)　　　　　C-　　　　　Fair

Fund Family: BlackRock Fund Advisors
Fund Type: Global
Inception Date: November 12, 2001

Data Date	Investment Rating	Net Assets ($Mil)	Price	Performance Rating/Pts	Total Return Y-T-D	Risk Rating/Pts
3-12	C-	425.58	56.51	D+ / 2.6	1.28%	B / 8.6
2011	C-	440.60	55.79	C- / 3.5	-1.57%	B / 8.5
2010	D+	409.50	58.27	D+ / 2.3	11.74%	C+ / 6.4
2009	C-	243.98	54.68	D+ / 2.6	9.97%	C+ / 6.4

Major Rating Factors:
Disappointing performance is the major factor driving the C- (Fair) TheStreet.com Investment Rating for *iShares S&P Global Telecom. The fund currently has a performance rating of D+ (Weak) based on an annualized return of 12.33% over the last three years and a total return of 1.28% year to date 2012. Factored into the performance evaluation is an expense ratio of 0.48% (very low).

The fund's risk rating is currently B (Good). It carries a beta of 0.58, meaning the fund's expected move will be 5.8% for every 10% move in the market. Volatility, as measured by both the semi-deviation and a drawdown factor, is considered low. As of March 31, 2012, *iShares S&P Global Telecom traded at a premium of .28% above its net asset value, which is worse than its one-year historical average premium of .13%.

Diane Hsiung has been running the fund for 4 years and currently receives a manager quality ranking of 68 (0=worst, 99=best). This fund offers only a moderate level of risk but investors looking for strong performance are still waiting.

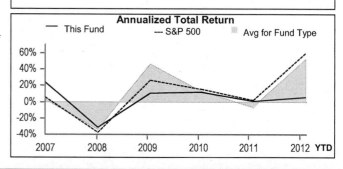

*iShares S&P Global Utilities (JXI)　　　　　D+　　　　　Weak

Fund Family: BlackRock Fund Advisors
Fund Type: Utilities
Inception Date: September 12, 2006

Data Date	Investment Rating	Net Assets ($Mil)	Price	Performance Rating/Pts	Total Return Y-T-D	Risk Rating/Pts
3-12	D+	256.09	42.67	D / 2.0	1.84%	B / 8.5
2011	D+	238.40	41.90	D / 1.9	-1.91%	B / 8.0
2010	D	252.70	45.08	E+ / 0.9	-1.70%	C+ / 6.3
2009	C-	157.41	47.99	D / 2.2	6.09%	C+ / 6.5

Major Rating Factors:
Disappointing performance is the major factor driving the D+ (Weak) TheStreet.com Investment Rating for *iShares S&P Global Utilities. The fund currently has a performance rating of D (Weak) based on an annualized return of 7.97% over the last three years and a total return of 1.84% year to date 2012. Factored into the performance evaluation is an expense ratio of 0.48% (very low).

The fund's risk rating is currently B (Good). It carries a beta of 1.07, meaning that its performance tracks fairly well with that of the overall stock market. Volatility, as measured by both the semi-deviation and a drawdown factor, is considered low. As of March 31, 2012, *iShares S&P Global Utilities traded at a premium of .28% above its net asset value, which is worse than its one-year historical average premium of .16%.

Diane Hsiung has been running the fund for 4 years and currently receives a manager quality ranking of 17 (0=worst, 99=best). This fund offers only a moderate level of risk but investors looking for strong performance are still waiting.

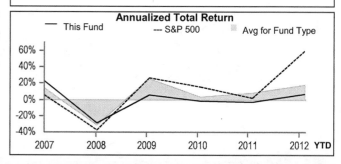

*iShares S&P Growth Allocation (AOR)　　　　　C　　　　　Fair

Fund Family: BlackRock Fund Advisors
Fund Type: Growth and Income
Inception Date: November 4, 2008

Data Date	Investment Rating	Net Assets ($Mil)	Price	Performance Rating/Pts	Total Return Y-T-D	Risk Rating/Pts
3-12	C	138.67	33.34	C- / 3.5	7.35%	B / 8.9
2011	C	118.20	31.14	C- / 4.0	0.64%	B / 8.8
2010	A+	81.90	31.54	B+ / 8.5	11.14%	B- / 7.8
2009	A+	26.80	28.94	B- / 7.3	17.44%	B- / 7.9

Major Rating Factors: Middle of the road best describes *iShares S&P Growth Allocation whose TheStreet.com Investment Rating is currently a C (Fair). The fund currently has a performance rating of C- (Fair) based on an annualized return of 14.31% over the last three years and a total return of 7.35% year to date 2012. Factored into the performance evaluation is an expense ratio of 0.11% (very low).

The fund's risk rating is currently B (Good). It carries a beta of 0.65, meaning the fund's expected move will be 6.5% for every 10% move in the market. Volatility, as measured by both the semi-deviation and a drawdown factor, is considered low. As of March 31, 2012, *iShares S&P Growth Allocation traded at a premium of .12% above its net asset value, which is worse than its one-year historical average premium of .06%.

Diane Hsiung has been running the fund for 4 years and currently receives a manager quality ranking of 52 (0=worst, 99=best). If you desire an average level of risk, then this fund may be an option.

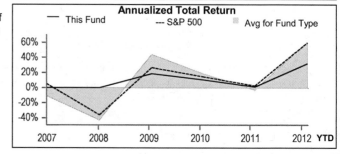

*iShares S&P GSCI Commodity-Index (GSG)   D   Weak

Fund Family: BlackRock Fund Advisors
Fund Type: Income
Inception Date: July 21, 2006

Major Rating Factors:
Disappointing performance is the major factor driving the D (Weak) TheStreet.com Investment Rating for *iShares S&P GSCI Commodity-Index. The fund currently has a performance rating of D+ (Weak) based on an annualized return of 10.10% over the last three years and a total return of 5.46% year to date 2012. Factored into the performance evaluation is an expense ratio of 0.75% (very low).

The fund's risk rating is currently B- (Good). It carries a beta of 0.91, meaning that its performance tracks fairly well with that of the overall stock market. Volatility, as measured by both the semi-deviation and a drawdown factor, is considered low. As of March 31, 2012, *iShares S&P GSCI Commodity-Index traded at a discount of .63% below its net asset value, which is better than its one-year historical average discount of .12%.

This fund has been team managed for 6 years and currently receives a manager quality ranking of 17 (0=worst, 99=best). This fund offers only a moderate level of risk but investors looking for strong performance are still waiting.

Data Date	Investment Rating	Net Assets ($Mil)	Price	Perfor-mance Rating/Pts	Total Return Y-T-D	Risk Rating/Pts
3-12	D	1,437.37	34.78	D+ / 2.4	5.46%	B- / 7.5
2011	C-	1,313.30	32.98	C- / 3.2	2.94%	B- / 7.6
2010	E+	1,799.90	34.10	E+ / 0.8	7.17%	C- / 3.7
2009	D-	1,092.84	31.82	D- / 1.4	7.46%	C / 4.3

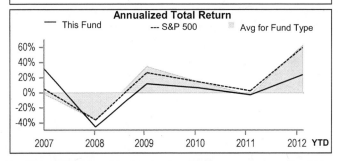

*iShares S&P India Nifty 50 (INDY)   D-   Weak

Fund Family: BlackRock Fund Advisors
Fund Type: Emerging Market
Inception Date: November 18, 2009

Major Rating Factors:
Disappointing performance is the major factor driving the D- (Weak) TheStreet.com Investment Rating for *iShares S&P India Nifty 50. The fund currently has a performance rating of D- (Weak) based on an annualized return of 0.00% over the last three years and a total return of 20.05% year to date 2012. Factored into the performance evaluation is an expense ratio of 0.91% (low).

The fund's risk rating is currently C+ (Fair). It carries a beta of 0.00, meaning the fund's expected move will be 0.0% for every 10% move in the market. Volatility, as measured by both the semi-deviation and a drawdown factor, is considered low. As of March 31, 2012, *iShares S&P India Nifty 50 traded at a premium of .25% above its net asset value, which is worse than its one-year historical average premium of .19%.

Diane Hsiung has been running the fund for 3 years and currently receives a manager quality ranking of 11 (0=worst, 99=best). This fund offers only a moderate level of risk but investors looking for strong performance are still waiting.

Data Date	Investment Rating	Net Assets ($Mil)	Price	Perfor-mance Rating/Pts	Total Return Y-T-D	Risk Rating/Pts
3-12	D-	364.62	23.71	D- / 1.0	20.05%	C+ / 6.1
2011	D-	214.40	19.75	E / 0.4	3.85%	C+ / 6.1
2010	A+	174.70	31.35	A- / 9.2	24.42%	B / 8.0

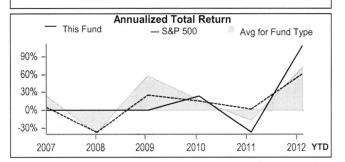

*iShares S&P Latin American 40 (ILF)   C   Fair

Fund Family: BlackRock Fund Advisors
Fund Type: Foreign
Inception Date: October 25, 2001

Major Rating Factors: Middle of the road best describes *iShares S&P Latin American 40 whose TheStreet.com Investment Rating is currently a C (Fair). The fund currently has a performance rating of C (Fair) based on an annualized return of 20.97% over the last three years and a total return of 11.89% year to date 2012. Factored into the performance evaluation is an expense ratio of 0.50% (very low).

The fund's risk rating is currently B- (Good). It carries a beta of 1.16, meaning it is expected to move 11.6% for every 10% move in the market. Volatility, as measured by both the semi-deviation and a drawdown factor, is considered low. As of March 31, 2012, *iShares S&P Latin American 40 traded at a discount of .10% below its net asset value, which is better than its one-year historical average discount of .03%.

Diane Hsiung has been running the fund for 4 years and currently receives a manager quality ranking of 70 (0=worst, 99=best). If you desire an average level of risk, then this fund may be an option.

Data Date	Investment Rating	Net Assets ($Mil)	Price	Perfor-mance Rating/Pts	Total Return Y-T-D	Risk Rating/Pts
3-12	C	2,165.58	47.63	C / 4.9	11.89%	B- / 7.2
2011	C	1,733.60	42.57	C / 5.5	1.25%	B- / 7.5
2010	C-	3,334.70	53.86	B- / 7.1	15.58%	D / 2.1
2009	C	2,557.89	47.79	B+ / 8.4	81.50%	D+ / 2.4

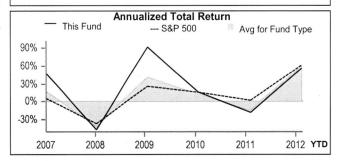

*iShares S&P Mid Cap 400 (IJH)   C+   Fair

Fund Family: BlackRock Fund Advisors
Fund Type: Growth
Inception Date: May 22, 2000

Major Rating Factors: Middle of the road best describes *iShares S&P Mid Cap 400 whose TheStreet.com Investment Rating is currently a C+ (Fair). The fund currently has a performance rating of C+ (Fair) based on an annualized return of 25.33% over the last three years and a total return of 13.55% year to date 2012. Factored into the performance evaluation is an expense ratio of 0.20% (very low).

The fund's risk rating is currently B- (Good). It carries a beta of 1.17, meaning it is expected to move 11.7% for every 10% move in the market. Volatility, as measured by both the semi-deviation and a drawdown factor, is considered low. As of March 31, 2012, *iShares S&P Mid Cap 400 traded at a discount of .04% below its net asset value.

Diane Hsiung has been running the fund for 4 years and currently receives a manager quality ranking of 48 (0=worst, 99=best). If you desire an average level of risk, then this fund may be an option.

Data Date	Investment Rating	Net Assets ($Mil)	Price	Performance Rating/Pts	Total Return Y-T-D	Risk Rating/Pts
3-12	C+	10,706.00	99.22	C+ / 6.9	13.55%	B- / 7.9
2011	C+	9,297.30	87.61	C+ / 6.4	1.48%	B- / 7.7
2010	B	9,360.60	90.69	B- / 7.4	26.73%	C+ / 5.7
2009	C-	6,099.88	72.41	C- / 3.8	34.21%	C+ / 6.0

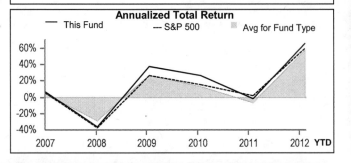

*iShares S&P Mid Cap 400 Growth (IJK)   B-   Good

Fund Family: BlackRock Fund Advisors
Fund Type: Growth
Inception Date: July 24, 2000

Major Rating Factors: Strong performance is the major factor driving the B- (Good) TheStreet.com Investment Rating for *iShares S&P Mid Cap 400 Growth. The fund currently has a performance rating of B- (Good) based on an annualized return of 26.94% over the last three years and a total return of 14.06% year to date 2012. Factored into the performance evaluation is an expense ratio of 0.25% (very low).

The fund's risk rating is currently B- (Good). It carries a beta of 1.14, meaning it is expected to move 11.4% for every 10% move in the market. Volatility, as measured by both the semi-deviation and a drawdown factor, is considered low. As of March 31, 2012, *iShares S&P Mid Cap 400 Growth traded at a discount of .04% below its net asset value.

Diane Hsiung has been running the fund for 4 years and currently receives a manager quality ranking of 59 (0=worst, 99=best). If you desire only a moderate level of risk and strong performance, then this fund is an excellent option.

Data Date	Investment Rating	Net Assets ($Mil)	Price	Performance Rating/Pts	Total Return Y-T-D	Risk Rating/Pts
3-12	B-	3,014.07	112.44	B- / 7.3	14.06%	B- / 7.9
2011	B-	2,632.90	98.73	C+ / 6.9	1.13%	B- / 7.7
2010	B	2,962.90	100.72	B / 7.7	30.44%	C / 5.5
2009	C	1,941.63	77.71	C / 4.3	37.15%	C+ / 6.1

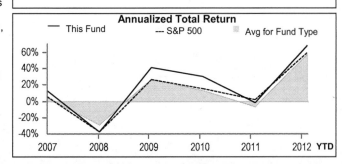

*iShares S&P Mid Cap 400 Value (IJJ)   C+   Fair

Fund Family: BlackRock Fund Advisors
Fund Type: Growth
Inception Date: July 24, 2000

Major Rating Factors: Middle of the road best describes *iShares S&P Mid Cap 400 Value whose TheStreet.com Investment Rating is currently a C+ (Fair). The fund currently has a performance rating of C+ (Fair) based on an annualized return of 23.69% over the last three years and a total return of 12.82% year to date 2012. Factored into the performance evaluation is an expense ratio of 0.25% (very low).

The fund's risk rating is currently B- (Good). It carries a beta of 1.21, meaning it is expected to move 12.1% for every 10% move in the market. Volatility, as measured by both the semi-deviation and a drawdown factor, is considered low. As of March 31, 2012, *iShares S&P Mid Cap 400 Value traded at a discount of .06% below its net asset value, which is better than its one-year historical average discount of .01%.

Diane Hsiung has been running the fund for 4 years and currently receives a manager quality ranking of 35 (0=worst, 99=best). If you desire an average level of risk, then this fund may be an option.

Data Date	Investment Rating	Net Assets ($Mil)	Price	Performance Rating/Pts	Total Return Y-T-D	Risk Rating/Pts
3-12	C+	2,192.77	85.41	C+ / 6.5	12.82%	B- / 7.8
2011	C+	1,988.30	75.98	C+ / 6.0	1.84%	B- / 7.6
2010	C+	2,082.10	79.46	C+ / 6.8	22.58%	C+ / 5.8
2009	C-	1,701.89	65.94	C- / 3.3	31.50%	C+ / 5.9

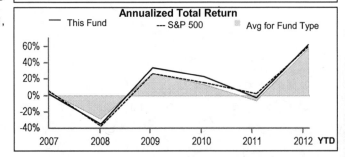

*iShares S&P Moderate Allocation (AOM)

C   **Fair**

Fund Family: BlackRock Fund Advisors
Fund Type: Growth and Income
Inception Date: November 4, 2008

Data Date	Investment Rating	Net Assets ($Mil)	Price	Performance Rating/Pts	Total Return Y-T-D	Risk Rating/Pts
3-12	C	144.66	31.22	D+ / 2.9	4.64%	B+ / 9.4
2011	C	125.40	29.90	C- / 3.6	0.30%	B+ / 9.2
2010	A	74.80	29.92	B- / 7.5	7.90%	B / 8.4
2009	B	18.59	28.23	C+ / 6.2	12.74%	B / 8.6

Major Rating Factors:
Disappointing performance is the major factor driving the C (Fair) TheStreet.com Investment Rating for *iShares S&P Moderate Allocation. The fund currently has a performance rating of D+ (Weak) based on an annualized return of 12.34% over the last three years and a total return of 4.64% year to date 2012. Factored into the performance evaluation is an expense ratio of 0.11% (very low).

The fund's risk rating is currently B+ (Good). It carries a beta of 0.42, meaning the fund's expected move will be 4.2% for every 10% move in the market. Volatility, as measured by both the semi-deviation and a drawdown factor, is considered very low. As of March 31, 2012, *iShares S&P Moderate Allocation traded at a premium of .03% above its net asset value, which is better than its one-year historical average premium of .05%.

Diane Hsiung has been running the fund for 4 years and currently receives a manager quality ranking of 60 (0=worst, 99=best). This fund offers only a moderate level of risk but investors looking for strong performance are still waiting.

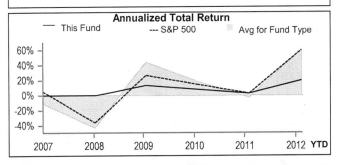

Annualized Total Return
— This Fund   --- S&P 500   Avg for Fund Type

*iShares S&P NA Natural Resource (IGE)

D+   **Weak**

Fund Family: BlackRock Fund Advisors
Fund Type: Energy/Natural Resources
Inception Date: October 22, 2001

Data Date	Investment Rating	Net Assets ($Mil)	Price	Performance Rating/Pts	Total Return Y-T-D	Risk Rating/Pts
3-12	D+	1,969.86	39.42	C- / 3.6	3.96%	B- / 7.2
2011	C	1,816.50	38.00	C / 5.1	2.47%	B- / 7.0
2010	D+	2,097.00	41.69	C+ / 5.8	23.35%	D+ / 2.6
2009	D+	1,427.86	34.31	C / 5.5	30.65%	D+ / 2.8

Major Rating Factors: *iShares S&P NA Natural Resource receives a TheStreet.com Investment Rating of D+ (Weak). The fund currently has a performance rating of C- (Fair) based on an annualized return of 17.35% over the last three years and a total return of 3.96% year to date 2012. Factored into the performance evaluation is an expense ratio of 0.48% (very low).

The fund's risk rating is currently B- (Good). It carries a beta of 1.09, meaning that its performance tracks fairly well with that of the overall stock market. Volatility, as measured by both the semi-deviation and a drawdown factor, is considered low. As of March 31, 2012, *iShares S&P NA Natural Resource traded at a discount of .05% below its net asset value, which is better than its one-year historical average premium of .01%.

Diane Hsiung has been running the fund for 4 years and currently receives a manager quality ranking of 38 (0=worst, 99=best). If you desire an average level of risk, then this fund may be an option.

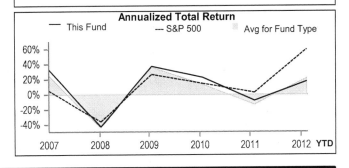

Annualized Total Return
— This Fund   --- S&P 500   Avg for Fund Type

*iShares S&P NA Tech-Multimedia N (IGN)

C-   **Fair**

Fund Family: BlackRock Fund Advisors
Fund Type: Growth
Inception Date: July 10, 2001

Data Date	Investment Rating	Net Assets ($Mil)	Price	Performance Rating/Pts	Total Return Y-T-D	Risk Rating/Pts
3-12	C-	264.52	31.23	C- / 4.1	14.19%	B- / 7.0
2011	C-	203.80	27.35	C / 4.3	1.68%	C+ / 6.8
2010	C+	217.60	33.51	C+ / 6.8	24.30%	C / 5.2
2009	D+	161.78	26.98	C- / 3.1	55.41%	C / 5.3

Major Rating Factors: Middle of the road best describes *iShares S&P NA Tech-Multimedia N whose TheStreet.com Investment Rating is currently a C- (Fair). The fund currently has a performance rating of C- (Fair) based on an annualized return of 17.87% over the last three years and a total return of 14.19% year to date 2012. Factored into the performance evaluation is an expense ratio of 0.48% (very low).

The fund's risk rating is currently B- (Good). It carries a beta of 1.51, meaning it is expected to move 15.1% for every 10% move in the market. Volatility, as measured by both the semi-deviation and a drawdown factor, is considered low. As of March 31, 2012, *iShares S&P NA Tech-Multimedia N traded at a premium of .03% above its net asset value.

Diane Hsiung has been running the fund for 4 years and currently receives a manager quality ranking of 13 (0=worst, 99=best). If you desire an average level of risk, then this fund may be an option.

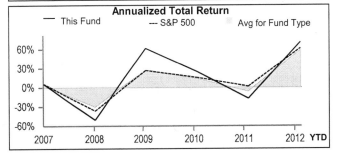

Annualized Total Return
— This Fund   --- S&P 500   Avg for Fund Type

*iShares S&P NA Technology Sector (IGM)

C+   **Fair**

Fund Family: BlackRock Fund Advisors
Fund Type: Growth
Inception Date: March 13, 2001

Major Rating Factors: Strong performance is the major factor driving the C+ (Fair) TheStreet.com Investment Rating for *iShares S&P NA Technology Sector. The fund currently has a performance rating of B- (Good) based on an annualized return of 23.99% over the last three years and a total return of 19.38% year to date 2012. Factored into the performance evaluation is an expense ratio of 0.48% (very low).

The fund's risk rating is currently B- (Good). It carries a beta of 1.14, meaning it is expected to move 11.4% for every 10% move in the market. Volatility, as measured by both the semi-deviation and a drawdown factor, is considered low. As of March 31, 2012, *iShares S&P NA Technology Sector traded at a premium of .01% above its net asset value, which is in line with its one-year historical average premium of .01%.

Diane Hsiung has been running the fund for 4 years and currently receives a manager quality ranking of 46 (0=worst, 99=best). If you desire only a moderate level of risk and strong performance, then this fund is an excellent option.

Data Date	Investment Rating	Net Assets ($Mil)	Price	Performance Rating/Pts	Total Return Y-T-D	Risk Rating/Pts
3-12	C+	410.37	70.83	B- / 7.2	19.38%	B- / 7.6
2011	C+	365.20	59.41	C+ / 6.7	2.41%	B- / 7.3
2010	C+	450.90	60.45	C+ / 6.0	11.98%	C / 5.5
2009	C+	332.97	54.22	C+ / 6.5	56.00%	C / 5.3

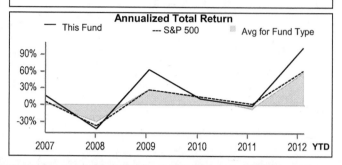

Annualized Total Return — This Fund --- S&P 500 — Avg for Fund Type

*iShares S&P NA Technology-Softwa (IGV)

C   **Fair**

Fund Family: BlackRock Fund Advisors
Fund Type: Income
Inception Date: July 10, 2001

Major Rating Factors: Middle of the road best describes *iShares S&P NA Technology-Softwa whose TheStreet.com Investment Rating is currently a C (Fair). The fund currently has a performance rating of C+ (Fair) based on an annualized return of 23.29% over the last three years and a total return of 21.80% year to date 2012. Factored into the performance evaluation is an expense ratio of 0.48% (very low).

The fund's risk rating is currently C+ (Fair). It carries a beta of 1.05, meaning that its performance tracks fairly well with that of the overall stock market. Volatility, as measured by both the semi-deviation and a drawdown factor, is considered low. As of March 31, 2012, *iShares S&P NA Technology-Softwa traded at a premium of .08% above its net asset value.

Diane Hsiung has been running the fund for 4 years and currently receives a manager quality ranking of 52 (0=worst, 99=best). If you desire an average level of risk, then this fund may be an option.

Data Date	Investment Rating	Net Assets ($Mil)	Price	Performance Rating/Pts	Total Return Y-T-D	Risk Rating/Pts
3-12	C	523.38	65.87	C+ / 6.7	21.80%	C+ / 6.6
2011	C-	492.40	54.12	C+ / 5.6	1.39%	C+ / 6.2
2010	C+	385.10	58.42	B- / 7.5	24.64%	C / 4.6
2009	C	301.15	46.87	C / 5.4	41.64%	C+ / 5.7

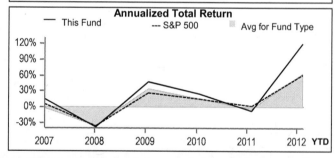

Annualized Total Return — This Fund --- S&P 500 — Avg for Fund Type

*iShares S&P Natl AMT-Free Muni B (MUB)

C   **Fair**

Fund Family: BlackRock Fund Advisors
Fund Type: Municipal - National
Inception Date: September 7, 2007

Major Rating Factors: Middle of the road best describes *iShares S&P Natl AMT-Free Muni B whose TheStreet.com Investment Rating is currently a C (Fair). The fund currently has a performance rating of C- (Fair) based on an annualized return of 6.68% and a total return of 1.59% year to date 2012. Factored into the performance evaluation is an expense ratio of 0.25% (very low).

The fund's risk rating is currently B+ (Good). It carries a beta of 1.24, meaning it is expected to move 12.4% for every 10% move in the market. Volatility, as measured by both the semi-deviation and a drawdown factor, is considered very low. As of March 31, 2012, *iShares S&P Natl AMT-Free Muni B traded at a premium of .76% above its net asset value, which is worse than its one-year historical average premium of .54%.

Scott F. Radell has been running the fund for 2 years and currently receives a manager quality ranking of 30 (0=worst, 99=best). If you desire an average level of risk, then this fund may be an option.

Data Date	Investment Rating	Net Assets ($Mil)	Price	Performance Rating/Pts	Total Return Y-T-D	Risk Rating/Pts
3-12	C	2,833.61	109.40	C- / 3.0	1.59%	B+ / 9.4
2011	B	2,512.30	108.25	C+ / 5.8	2.13%	B+ / 9.5
2010	C+	1,975.60	99.18	C- / 3.2	-0.22%	B / 8.7
2009	B+	1,409.80	102.75	C / 4.9	7.12%	B+ / 9.0

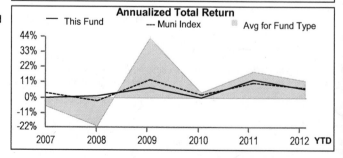

Annualized Total Return — This Fund --- Muni Index — Avg for Fund Type

*iShares S&P NY AMT-Free Muni Bon (NYF)

C-   **Fair**

Fund Family: BlackRock Fund Advisors
Fund Type: Municipal - Single State
Inception Date: October 4, 2007

Data Date	Investment Rating	Net Assets ($Mil)	Price	Performance Rating/Pts	Total Return Y-T-D	Risk Rating/Pts
3-12	C-	98.94	109.30	D+ / 2.5	1.53%	B+ / 9.4
2011	C+	97.10	108.23	C / 4.5	-0.13%	B+ / 9.4
2010	C+	70.90	99.98	C- / 3.4	-0.26%	B / 8.6
2009	B	56.54	103.87	C / 5.3	10.75%	B / 8.8

Major Rating Factors:
Disappointing performance is the major factor driving the C- (Fair) TheStreet.com Investment Rating for *iShares S&P NY AMT-Free Muni Bon. The fund currently has a performance rating of D+ (Weak) based on an annualized return of 5.29% over the last three years and a total return of 1.53% year to date 2012. Factored into the performance evaluation is an expense ratio of 0.25% (very low).

The fund's risk rating is currently B+ (Good). It carries a beta of 0.78, meaning the fund's expected move will be 7.8% for every 10% move in the market. Volatility, as measured by both the semi-deviation and a drawdown factor, is considered very low. As of March 31, 2012, *iShares S&P NY AMT-Free Muni Bon traded at a premium of .34% above its net asset value, which is better than its one-year historical average premium of .44%.

Scott F. Radell has been running the fund for 2 years and currently receives a manager quality ranking of 33 (0=worst, 99=best). This fund offers only a moderate level of risk but investors looking for strong performance are still waiting.

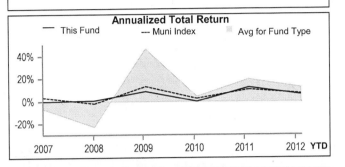

*iShares S&P Sh Tm Ntl AMT-Fr Mun (SUB)

C-   **Fair**

Fund Family: BlackRock Fund Advisors
Fund Type: Municipal - National
Inception Date: November 5, 2008

Data Date	Investment Rating	Net Assets ($Mil)	Price	Performance Rating/Pts	Total Return Y-T-D	Risk Rating/Pts
3-12	C-	496.47	106.60	D- / 1.3	0.06%	B+ / 9.8
2011	C	472.60	106.73	D+ / 2.9	0.23%	B+ / 9.9
2010	C	449.90	104.10	D / 2.0	0.36%	B / 8.9
2009	C+	156.17	105.05	C- / 3.0	4.31%	B+ / 9.1

Major Rating Factors:
Disappointing performance is the major factor driving the C- (Fair) TheStreet.com Investment Rating for *iShares S&P Sh Tm Ntl AMT-Fr Mun. The fund currently has a performance rating of D- (Weak) based on an annualized return of 1.08% over the last three years and a total return of 0.06% year to date 2012. Factored into the performance evaluation is an expense ratio of 0.25% (very low).

The fund's risk rating is currently B+ (Good). It carries a beta of 0.18, meaning the fund's expected move will be 1.8% for every 10% move in the market. Volatility, as measured by both the semi-deviation and a drawdown factor, is considered very low. As of March 31, 2012, *iShares S&P Sh Tm Ntl AMT-Fr Mun traded at a premium of .19% above its net asset value, which is worse than its one-year historical average premium of .14%.

Scott F. Radell has been running the fund for 2 years and currently receives a manager quality ranking of 48 (0=worst, 99=best). This fund offers only a moderate level of risk but investors looking for strong performance are still waiting.

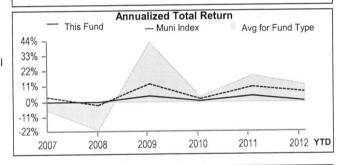

*iShares S&P Small Cap 600 (IJR)

B-   **Good**

Fund Family: BlackRock Fund Advisors
Fund Type: Growth
Inception Date: May 22, 2000

Data Date	Investment Rating	Net Assets ($Mil)	Price	Performance Rating/Pts	Total Return Y-T-D	Risk Rating/Pts
3-12	B-	7,543.35	76.31	B- / 7.2	12.06%	B- / 7.7
2011	C+	6,915.20	68.30	C+ / 6.4	1.29%	B- / 7.5
2010	B	6,785.10	68.47	B- / 7.3	26.61%	C+ / 5.7
2009	D+	4,901.74	54.72	D+ / 2.5	23.80%	C+ / 5.8

Major Rating Factors: Strong performance is the major factor driving the B- (Good) TheStreet.com Investment Rating for *iShares S&P Small Cap 600. The fund currently has a performance rating of B- (Good) based on an annualized return of 25.69% over the last three years and a total return of 12.06% year to date 2012. Factored into the performance evaluation is an expense ratio of 0.20% (very low).

The fund's risk rating is currently B- (Good). It carries a beta of 1.23, meaning it is expected to move 12.3% for every 10% move in the market. Volatility, as measured by both the semi-deviation and a drawdown factor, is considered low. As of March 31, 2012, *iShares S&P Small Cap 600 traded at a discount of .01% below its net asset value, which is better than its one-year historical average premium of .01%.

Diane Hsiung has been running the fund for 4 years and currently receives a manager quality ranking of 45 (0=worst, 99=best). If you desire only a moderate level of risk and strong performance, then this fund is an excellent option.

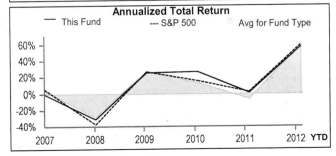

*iShares S&P Small Cap 600 Growth (IJT)

B-   **Good**

Fund Family: BlackRock Fund Advisors
Fund Type: Growth
Inception Date: July 24, 2000

Major Rating Factors: Strong performance is the major factor driving the B- (Good) TheStreet.com Investment Rating for *iShares S&P Small Cap 600 Growth. The fund currently has a performance rating of B- (Good) based on an annualized return of 27.17% over the last three years and a total return of 11.23% year to date 2012. Factored into the performance evaluation is an expense ratio of 0.25% (very low).

The fund's risk rating is currently B- (Good). It carries a beta of 1.16, meaning it is expected to move 11.6% for every 10% move in the market. Volatility, as measured by both the semi-deviation and a drawdown factor, is considered low. As of March 31, 2012, *iShares S&P Small Cap 600 Growth traded at a premium of .01% above its net asset value, which is worse than its one-year historical average discount of .03%.

Diane Hsiung has been running the fund for 4 years and currently receives a manager quality ranking of 61 (0=worst, 99=best). If you desire only a moderate level of risk and strong performance, then this fund is an excellent option.

Data Date	Investment Rating	Net Assets ($Mil)	Price	Performance Rating/Pts	Total Return Y-T-D	Risk Rating/Pts
3-12	B-	1,668.75	82.59	B- / 7.4	11.23%	B- / 7.7
2011	C+	1,561.20	74.47	C+ / 6.8	0.60%	B- / 7.2
2010	C	1,885.30	72.59	B- / 7.4	28.24%	C- / 3.4
2009	D	1,469.61	57.14	C- / 3.1	26.12%	C- / 3.8

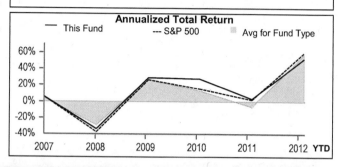
Annualized Total Return
— This Fund   --- S&P 500   Avg for Fund Type

*iShares S&P Small Cap 600 Value (IJS)

C+   **Fair**

Fund Family: BlackRock Fund Advisors
Fund Type: Growth
Inception Date: July 24, 2000

Major Rating Factors: Middle of the road best describes *iShares S&P Small Cap 600 Value whose TheStreet.com Investment Rating is currently a C+ (Fair). The fund currently has a performance rating of C+ (Fair) based on an annualized return of 24.29% over the last three years and a total return of 12.93% year to date 2012. Factored into the performance evaluation is an expense ratio of 0.25% (very low).

The fund's risk rating is currently B- (Good). It carries a beta of 1.30, meaning it is expected to move 13.0% for every 10% move in the market. Volatility, as measured by both the semi-deviation and a drawdown factor, is considered low. As of March 31, 2012, *iShares S&P Small Cap 600 Value traded at a premium of .04% above its net asset value.

Diane Hsiung has been running the fund for 4 years and currently receives a manager quality ranking of 31 (0=worst, 99=best). If you desire an average level of risk, then this fund may be an option.

Data Date	Investment Rating	Net Assets ($Mil)	Price	Performance Rating/Pts	Total Return Y-T-D	Risk Rating/Pts
3-12	C+	2,202.18	78.57	C+ / 6.8	12.93%	B- / 7.8
2011	C+	1,591.40	69.76	C+ / 6.1	2.05%	B- / 7.4
2010	B	1,792.50	71.89	B- / 7.2	24.70%	C+ / 5.7
2009	D	1,542.08	58.38	D / 2.0	21.43%	C+ / 5.6

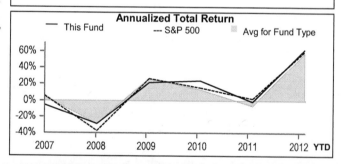
Annualized Total Return
— This Fund   --- S&P 500   Avg for Fund Type

*iShares S&P Target Date 2010 Ind (TZD)

C   **Fair**

Fund Family: BlackRock Fund Advisors
Fund Type: Growth and Income
Inception Date: November 4, 2008

Major Rating Factors:
Disappointing performance is the major factor driving the C (Fair) TheStreet.com Investment Rating for *iShares S&P Target Date 2010 Ind. The fund currently has a performance rating of D+ (Weak) based on an annualized return of 12.14% over the last three years and a total return of 5.12% year to date 2012. Factored into the performance evaluation is an expense ratio of 0.11% (very low).

The fund's risk rating is currently B+ (Good). It carries a beta of 0.42, meaning the fund's expected move will be 4.2% for every 10% move in the market. Volatility, as measured by both the semi-deviation and a drawdown factor, is considered very low. As of March 31, 2012, *iShares S&P Target Date 2010 Ind traded at a discount of .25% below its net asset value, which is better than its one-year historical average discount of .08%.

Diane Hsiung has been running the fund for 4 years and currently receives a manager quality ranking of 64 (0=worst, 99=best). This fund offers only a moderate level of risk but investors looking for strong performance are still waiting.

Data Date	Investment Rating	Net Assets ($Mil)	Price	Performance Rating/Pts	Total Return Y-T-D	Risk Rating/Pts
3-12	C	4.85	32.39	D+ / 2.9	5.12%	B+ / 9.4
2011	C+	6.20	30.86	C- / 3.9	0.84%	B+ / 9.4
2010	A+	6.20	30.93	B / 8.1	10.22%	B / 8.8
2009	A+	2.71	28.62	B- / 7.1	17.54%	B+ / 9.0

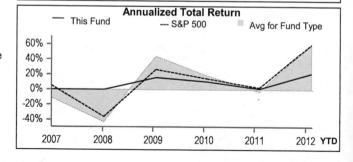
Annualized Total Return
— This Fund   --- S&P 500   Avg for Fund Type

*iShares S&P Target Date 2015 Ind (TZE)   C   Fair

Fund Family: BlackRock Fund Advisors
Fund Type: Growth and Income
Inception Date: November 4, 2008

Data Date	Investment Rating	Net Assets ($Mil)	Price	Performance Rating/Pts	Total Return Y-T-D	Risk Rating/Pts
3-12	C	10.05	33.59	C- / 3.5	6.46%	B+ / 9.0
2011	C	9.50	31.63	C- / 3.7	1.01%	B+ / 9.0
2010	A+	9.60	32.04	B+ / 8.5	11.35%	B / 8.5
2009	A+	2.72	29.24	B- / 7.3	19.00%	B / 8.8

Major Rating Factors: Middle of the road best describes *iShares S&P Target Date 2015 Ind whose TheStreet.com Investment Rating is currently a C (Fair). The fund currently has a performance rating of C- (Fair) based on an annualized return of 14.55% over the last three years and a total return of 6.46% year to date 2012. Factored into the performance evaluation is an expense ratio of 0.11% (very low).

The fund's risk rating is currently B+ (Good). It carries a beta of 0.57, meaning the fund's expected move will be 5.7% for every 10% move in the market. Volatility, as measured by both the semi-deviation and a drawdown factor, is considered very low. As of March 31, 2012, *iShares S&P Target Date 2015 Ind traded at a discount of .18% below its net asset value, which is better than its one-year historical average premium of .08%.

Diane Hsiung has been running the fund for 4 years and currently receives a manager quality ranking of 56 (0=worst, 99=best). If you desire an average level of risk, then this fund may be an option.

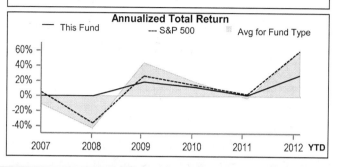

*iShares S&P Target Date 2020 Ind (TZG)   C   Fair

Fund Family: BlackRock Fund Advisors
Fund Type: Growth and Income
Inception Date: November 4, 2008

Data Date	Investment Rating	Net Assets ($Mil)	Price	Performance Rating/Pts	Total Return Y-T-D	Risk Rating/Pts
3-12	C	18.78	34.62	C- / 3.8	7.59%	B / 8.9
2011	C	17.60	32.26	C- / 4.1	-0.06%	B / 8.9
2010	A+	11.40	32.73	B+ / 8.7	12.58%	B / 8.4
2009	A+	2.72	29.67	B / 8.0	27.96%	B / 8.8

Major Rating Factors: Middle of the road best describes *iShares S&P Target Date 2020 Ind whose TheStreet.com Investment Rating is currently a C (Fair). The fund currently has a performance rating of C- (Fair) based on an annualized return of 15.58% over the last three years and a total return of 7.59% year to date 2012. Factored into the performance evaluation is an expense ratio of 0.11% (very low).

The fund's risk rating is currently B (Good). It carries a beta of 0.66, meaning the fund's expected move will be 6.6% for every 10% move in the market. Volatility, as measured by both the semi-deviation and a drawdown factor, is considered low. As of March 31, 2012, *iShares S&P Target Date 2020 Ind traded at a premium of .49% above its net asset value, which is worse than its one-year historical average premium of .11%.

Diane Hsiung has been running the fund for 4 years and currently receives a manager quality ranking of 55 (0=worst, 99=best). If you desire an average level of risk, then this fund may be an option.

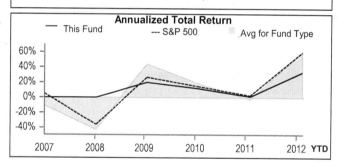

*iShares S&P Target Date 2025 Ind (TZI)   C   Fair

Fund Family: BlackRock Fund Advisors
Fund Type: Growth and Income
Inception Date: November 4, 2008

Data Date	Investment Rating	Net Assets ($Mil)	Price	Performance Rating/Pts	Total Return Y-T-D	Risk Rating/Pts
3-12	C	31.15	35.15	C / 4.3	9.33%	B / 8.7
2011	C	27.40	32.24	C- / 4.1	0.81%	B / 8.6
2010	A+	13.30	33.24	B+ / 8.8	13.02%	B / 8.1
2009	A+	4.08	29.90	B / 8.0	22.36%	B / 8.3

Major Rating Factors: Middle of the road best describes *iShares S&P Target Date 2025 Ind whose TheStreet.com Investment Rating is currently a C (Fair). The fund currently has a performance rating of C (Fair) based on an annualized return of 17.82% over the last three years and a total return of 9.33% year to date 2012. Factored into the performance evaluation is an expense ratio of 0.11% (very low).

The fund's risk rating is currently B (Good). It carries a beta of 0.76, meaning the fund's expected move will be 7.6% for every 10% move in the market. Volatility, as measured by both the semi-deviation and a drawdown factor, is considered low. As of March 31, 2012, *iShares S&P Target Date 2025 Ind traded at a premium of .49% above its net asset value, which is worse than its one-year historical average premium of .02%.

Diane Hsiung has been running the fund for 4 years and currently receives a manager quality ranking of 54 (0=worst, 99=best). If you desire an average level of risk, then this fund may be an option.

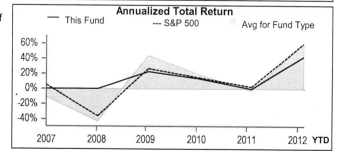

*iShares S&P Target Date 2030 Ind (TZL)   C   Fair

Fund Family: BlackRock Fund Advisors
Fund Type: Growth and Income
Inception Date: November 4, 2008

Data Date	Investment Rating	Net Assets ($Mil)	Price	Performance Rating/Pts	Total Return Y-T-D	Risk Rating/Pts
3-12	C	13.95	35.31	C- / 4.1	9.25%	B / 8.7
2011	C+	12.90	32.41	C / 4.6	0.56%	B / 8.6
2010	A+	10.00	33.57	B+ / 8.9	13.90%	B / 8.1
2009	A+	4.07	30.00	B+ / 8.3	28.66%	B / 8.4

Major Rating Factors: Middle of the road best describes *iShares S&P Target Date 2030 Ind whose TheStreet.com Investment Rating is currently a C (Fair). The fund currently has a performance rating of C- (Fair) based on an annualized return of 17.31% over the last three years and a total return of 9.25% year to date 2012. Factored into the performance evaluation is an expense ratio of 0.11% (very low).

The fund's risk rating is currently B (Good). It carries a beta of 0.77, meaning the fund's expected move will be 7.7% for every 10% move in the market. Volatility, as measured by both the semi-deviation and a drawdown factor, is considered low. As of March 31, 2012, *iShares S&P Target Date 2030 Ind traded at a price exactly equal to its net asset value, which is worse than its one-year historical average discount of .02%.

Diane Hsiung has been running the fund for 4 years and currently receives a manager quality ranking of 55 (0=worst, 99=best). If you desire an average level of risk, then this fund may be an option.

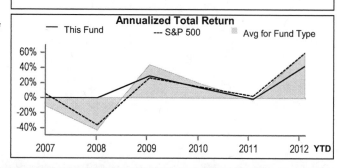

*iShares S&P Target Date 2035 Ind (TZO)   C   Fair

Fund Family: BlackRock Fund Advisors
Fund Type: Growth and Income
Inception Date: November 4, 2008

Data Date	Investment Rating	Net Assets ($Mil)	Price	Performance Rating/Pts	Total Return Y-T-D	Risk Rating/Pts
3-12	C	8.73	35.50	C / 4.8	10.19%	B / 8.3
2011	C	8.00	32.31	C- / 4.2	0.65%	B / 8.3
2010	A+	6.70	33.51	B+ / 8.9	14.19%	B- / 7.6
2009	A+	2.71	29.90	B / 8.1	25.09%	B- / 7.8

Major Rating Factors: Middle of the road best describes *iShares S&P Target Date 2035 Ind whose TheStreet.com Investment Rating is currently a C (Fair). The fund currently has a performance rating of C (Fair) based on an annualized return of 19.41% over the last three years and a total return of 10.19% year to date 2012. Factored into the performance evaluation is an expense ratio of 0.11% (very low).

The fund's risk rating is currently B (Good). It carries a beta of 0.89, meaning the fund's expected move will be 8.9% for every 10% move in the market. Volatility, as measured by both the semi-deviation and a drawdown factor, is considered low. As of March 31, 2012, *iShares S&P Target Date 2035 Ind traded at a premium of .31% above its net asset value, which is worse than its one-year historical average premium of .07%.

Diane Hsiung has been running the fund for 4 years and currently receives a manager quality ranking of 39 (0=worst, 99=best). If you desire an average level of risk, then this fund may be an option.

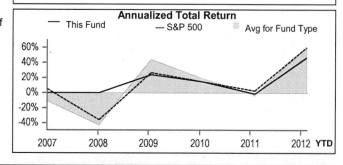

*iShares S&P Target Date 2040 Ind (TZV)   C   Fair

Fund Family: BlackRock Fund Advisors
Fund Type: Growth and Income
Inception Date: November 4, 2008

Data Date	Investment Rating	Net Assets ($Mil)	Price	Performance Rating/Pts	Total Return Y-T-D	Risk Rating/Pts
3-12	C	17.60	35.76	C / 4.6	10.52%	B / 8.2
2011	C	16.20	32.45	C- / 4.1	0.86%	B / 8.1
2010	A+	11.90	33.94	A- / 9.0	14.56%	B / 8.0
2009	A+	2.71	30.20	B / 8.1	23.48%	B / 8.4

Major Rating Factors: Middle of the road best describes *iShares S&P Target Date 2040 Ind whose TheStreet.com Investment Rating is currently a C (Fair). The fund currently has a performance rating of C (Fair) based on an annualized return of 18.71% over the last three years and a total return of 10.52% year to date 2012. Factored into the performance evaluation is an expense ratio of 0.11% (very low).

The fund's risk rating is currently B (Good). It carries a beta of 0.99, meaning that its performance tracks fairly well with that of the overall stock market. Volatility, as measured by both the semi-deviation and a drawdown factor, is considered low. As of March 31, 2012, *iShares S&P Target Date 2040 Ind traded at a premium of .14% above its net asset value, which is worse than its one-year historical average discount of .03%.

Daine Hsiung has been running the fund for 4 years and currently receives a manager quality ranking of 35 (0=worst, 99=best). If you desire an average level of risk, then this fund may be an option.

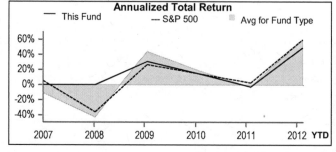

*iShares S&P Target Date Ret Inco (TGR)   C   Fair

Fund Family: BlackRock Fund Advisors
Fund Type: Growth and Income
Inception Date: November 4, 2008

Data Date	Investment Rating	Net Assets ($Mil)	Price	Performance Rating/Pts	Total Return Y-T-D	Risk Rating/Pts
3-12	C	7.76	31.03	D+ / 2.6	3.62%	B+ / 9.7
2011	C	9.00	30.00	C- / 3.6	0.54%	B+ / 9.4
2010	A	4.50	29.70	B- / 7.2	8.31%	B / 8.5
2009	B	2.66	28.00	C+ / 5.6	11.05%	B / 8.7

Major Rating Factors:
Disappointing performance is the major factor driving the C (Fair) TheStreet.com Investment Rating for *iShares S&P Target Date Ret Inco. The fund currently has a performance rating of D+ (Weak) based on an annualized return of 10.34% over the last three years and a total return of 3.62% year to date 2012. Factored into the performance evaluation is an expense ratio of 0.11% (very low).

The fund's risk rating is currently B+ (Good). It carries a beta of 0.30, meaning the fund's expected move will be 3.0% for every 10% move in the market. Volatility, as measured by both the semi-deviation and a drawdown factor, is considered very low. As of March 31, 2012, *iShares S&P Target Date Ret Inco traded at a discount of .32% below its net asset value, which is better than its one-year historical average premium of .07%.

Diane Hsiung has been running the fund for 4 years and currently receives a manager quality ranking of 69 (0=worst, 99=best). This fund offers only a moderate level of risk but investors looking for strong performance are still waiting.

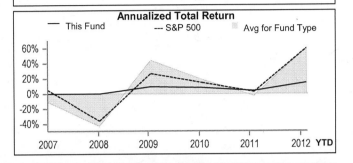

Annualized Total Return — This Fund --- S&P 500 Avg for Fund Type

*iShares S&P USPreferred Stock (PFF)   B   Good

Fund Family: BlackRock Fund Advisors
Fund Type: Income
Inception Date: March 26, 2007

Data Date	Investment Rating	Net Assets ($Mil)	Price	Performance Rating/Pts	Total Return Y-T-D	Risk Rating/Pts
3-12	B	8,261.83	39.04	C+ / 6.9	10.53%	B / 8.9
2011	C-	6,979.90	35.62	C / 4.7	3.34%	C+ / 6.6
2010	C	6,127.40	38.80	C+ / 6.2	13.87%	C / 4.4
2009	B-	2,763.48	36.70	B+ / 8.4	33.66%	C / 4.5

Major Rating Factors: *iShares S&P USPreferred Stock receives a TheStreet.com Investment Rating of B (Good). The fund currently has a performance rating of C+ (Fair) based on an annualized return of 26.87% over the last three years and a total return of 10.53% year to date 2012. Factored into the performance evaluation is an expense ratio of 0.48% (very low).

The fund's risk rating is currently B (Good). It carries a beta of 0.64, meaning the fund's expected move will be 6.4% for every 10% move in the market. Volatility, as measured by both the semi-deviation and a drawdown factor, is considered low. As of March 31, 2012, *iShares S&P USPreferred Stock traded at a premium of .28% above its net asset value, which is worse than its one-year historical average premium of .04%.

Diane Hsiung has been running the fund for 4 years and currently receives a manager quality ranking of 88 (0=worst, 99=best). If you desire an average level of risk, then this fund may be an option.

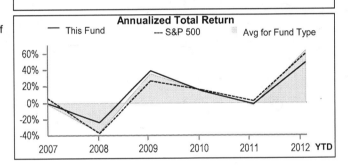

Annualized Total Return — This Fund --- S&P 500 Avg for Fund Type

*iShares S&P/Citigroup 1-3 Year I (ISHG)   D+   Weak

Fund Family: BlackRock Fund Advisors
Fund Type: Global
Inception Date: January 21, 2009

Data Date	Investment Rating	Net Assets ($Mil)	Price	Performance Rating/Pts	Total Return Y-T-D	Risk Rating/Pts
3-12	D+	167.30	99.22	D- / 1.4	2.71%	B / 8.7
2011	D+	154.80	96.99	D- / 1.5	-0.56%	B / 8.7
2010	C+	114.70	104.21	C- / 4.1	0.99%	B / 8.1

Major Rating Factors:
Disappointing performance is the major factor driving the D+ (Weak) TheStreet.com Investment Rating for *iShares S&P/Citigroup 1-3 Year I. The fund currently has a performance rating of D- (Weak) based on an annualized return of 2.91% over the last three years and a total return of 2.71% year to date 2012. Factored into the performance evaluation is an expense ratio of 0.35% (very low).

The fund's risk rating is currently B (Good). It carries a beta of 1.00, meaning that its performance tracks fairly well with that of the overall stock market. Volatility, as measured by both the semi-deviation and a drawdown factor, is considered low. As of March 31, 2012, *iShares S&P/Citigroup 1-3 Year I traded at a premium of 1.88% above its net asset value, which is worse than its one-year historical average premium of .53%.

Scott F. Radell has been running the fund for 2 years and currently receives a manager quality ranking of 26 (0=worst, 99=best). This fund offers only a moderate level of risk but investors looking for strong performance are still waiting.

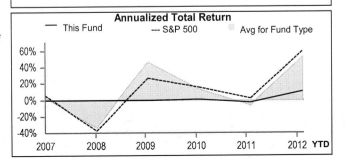

Annualized Total Return — This Fund --- S&P 500 Avg for Fund Type

*iShares S&P/Citigroup Intl Treas (IGOV)

D+   **Weak**

Fund Family: BlackRock Fund Advisors
Fund Type: Global
Inception Date: January 21, 2009

Major Rating Factors:

Disappointing performance is the major factor driving the D+ (Weak) TheStreet.com Investment Rating for *iShares S&P/Citigroup Intl Treas. The fund currently has a performance rating of D- (Weak) based on an annualized return of 4.14% over the last three years and a total return of 0.30% year to date 2012. Factored into the performance evaluation is an expense ratio of 0.35% (very low).

The fund's risk rating is currently B (Good). It carries a beta of 1.02, meaning that its performance tracks fairly well with that of the overall stock market. Volatility, as measured by both the semi-deviation and a drawdown factor, is considered low. As of March 31, 2012, *iShares S&P/Citigroup Intl Treas traded at a premium of .25% above its net asset value, which is better than its one-year historical average premium of .40%.

Scott F. Radell has been running the fund for 2 years and currently receives a manager quality ranking of 31 (0=worst, 99=best). This fund offers only a moderate level of risk but investors looking for strong performance are still waiting.

Data Date	Investment Rating	Net Assets ($Mil)	Price	Performance Rating/Pts	Total Return Y-T-D	Risk Rating/Pts
3-12	D+	300.78	99.83	D- / 1.4	0.30%	B / 8.7
2011	C-	273.90	99.90	D / 1.8	-2.15%	B / 8.8
2010	C+	163.30	102.27	C- / 3.3	1.40%	B / 8.1

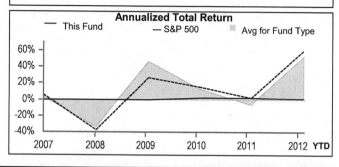

---

*iShares S&P/Topix 150 (ITF)

D+   **Weak**

Fund Family: BlackRock Fund Advisors
Fund Type: Foreign
Inception Date: October 23, 2001

Major Rating Factors:

Disappointing performance is the major factor driving the D+ (Weak) TheStreet.com Investment Rating for *iShares S&P/Topix 150. The fund currently has a performance rating of D+ (Weak) based on an annualized return of 8.30% over the last three years and a total return of 12.35% year to date 2012. Factored into the performance evaluation is an expense ratio of 0.50% (very low).

The fund's risk rating is currently B- (Good). It carries a beta of 0.60, meaning the fund's expected move will be 6.0% for every 10% move in the market. Volatility, as measured by both the semi-deviation and a drawdown factor, is considered low. As of March 31, 2012, *iShares S&P/Topix 150 traded at a discount of 1.00% below its net asset value, which is better than its one-year historical average discount of .61%.

Diane Hsiung has been running the fund for 4 years and currently receives a manager quality ranking of 46 (0=worst, 99=best). This fund offers only a moderate level of risk but investors looking for strong performance are still waiting.

Data Date	Investment Rating	Net Assets ($Mil)	Price	Performance Rating/Pts	Total Return Y-T-D	Risk Rating/Pts
3-12	D+	78.23	43.46	D+ / 2.3	12.35%	B- / 7.8
2011	D	70.50	38.68	D / 1.7	0.34%	B- / 7.6
2010	D-	100.20	47.53	D+ / 2.4	14.07%	D+ / 2.7
2009	E	116.70	42.34	E+ / 0.9	2.74%	C- / 3.1

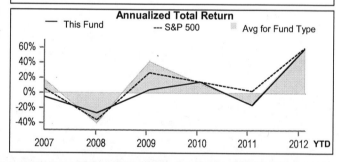

---

*iShares Silver Trust (SLV)

C+   **Fair**

Fund Family: BlackRock Fund Advisors
Fund Type: Precious Metals
Inception Date: April 28, 2006

Major Rating Factors: Strong performance is the major factor driving the C+ (Fair) TheStreet.com Investment Rating for *iShares Silver Trust. The fund currently has a performance rating of B+ (Good) based on an annualized return of 35.55% over the last three years and a total return of 16.48% year to date 2012. Factored into the performance evaluation is an expense ratio of 0.50% (very low).

The fund's risk rating is currently C (Fair). It carries a beta of 1.68, meaning it is expected to move 16.8% for every 10% move in the market. Volatility, as measured by both the semi-deviation and a drawdown factor, is considered average. As of March 31, 2012, *iShares Silver Trust traded at a discount of .35% below its net asset value, which is better than its one-year historical average premium of .18%.

This fund has been team managed for 6 years and currently receives a manager quality ranking of 27 (0=worst, 99=best). If you desire an average level of risk and strong performance, then this fund is a good option.

Data Date	Investment Rating	Net Assets ($Mil)	Price	Performance Rating/Pts	Total Return Y-T-D	Risk Rating/Pts
3-12	C+	11,686.53	31.38	B+ / 8.3	16.48%	C / 5.1
2011	C+	8,699.00	26.94	B+ / 8.5	3.60%	C / 5.2
2010	C	10,750.90	30.18	A+ / 9.7	82.47%	D- / 1.0
2009	D+	4,292.92	16.54	B- / 7.0	44.96%	D- / 1.5

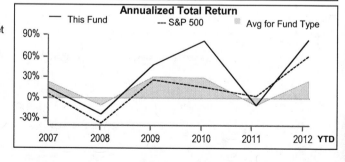

---

*JPMorgan Alerian MLP Idx ETN (AMJ)

D　**Weak**

Fund Family: JP Morgan Investment Management Inc
Fund Type: Energy/Natural Resources
Inception Date: April 2, 2009

Data Date	Investment Rating	Net Assets ($Mil)	Price	Performance Rating/Pts	Total Return Y-T-D	Risk Rating/Pts
3-12	D	4,061.07	39.14	C- / 3.6	1.61%	C / 5.2
2011	C	3,639.00	38.97	B- / 7.2	1.03%	C / 5.2
2010	A-	2,271.30	36.35	A / 9.5	34.55%	C / 4.7

Major Rating Factors: *JPMorgan Alerian MLP Idx ETN receives a TheStreet.com Investment Rating of D (Weak). The fund currently has a performance rating of C- (Fair) based on an annualized return of 0.00% over the last three years and a total return of 1.61% year to date 2012. Factored into the performance evaluation is an expense ratio of 0.85% (very low).

　　The fund's risk rating is currently C (Fair). It carries a beta of 0.00, meaning the fund's expected move will be 0.0% for every 10% move in the market. Volatility, as measured by both the semi-deviation and a drawdown factor, is considered average. As of March 31, 2012, *JPMorgan Alerian MLP Idx ETN traded at a discount of .08% below its net asset value, which is better than its one-year historical average discount of .02%.

　　This fund has been team managed for 3 years and currently receives a manager quality ranking of 88 (0=worst, 99=best). If you desire an average level of risk, then this fund may be an option.

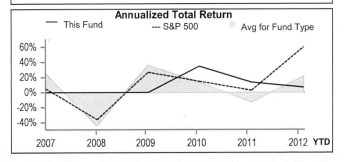

*JPMorgan Dbl Short 10 Year Trs E (DSXJ)

E+　**Very Weak**

Fund Family: JP Morgan Investment Management Inc
Fund Type: Growth
Inception Date: October 4, 2010

Data Date	Investment Rating	Net Assets ($Mil)	Price	Performance Rating/Pts	Total Return Y-T-D	Risk Rating/Pts
3-12	E+	8.31	42.05	E+ / 0.7	1.11%	C / 4.4
2011	E+	0.00	41.59	E+ / 0.7	0.75%	C / 4.5

Major Rating Factors:
Very poor performance is the major factor driving the E+ (Very Weak) TheStreet.com Investment Rating for *JPMorgan Dbl Short 10 Year Trs E. The fund currently has a performance rating of E+ (Very Weak) based on an annualized return of 0.00% over the last three years and a total return of 1.11% year to date 2012. Factored into the performance evaluation is an expense ratio of 0.85% (very low).

　　The fund's risk rating is currently C (Fair). It carries a beta of 0.00, meaning the fund's expected move will be 0.0% for every 10% move in the market. Volatility, as measured by both the semi-deviation and a drawdown factor, is considered average. As of March 31, 2012, *JPMorgan Dbl Short 10 Year Trs E traded at a discount of .24% below its net asset value, which is better than its one-year historical average premium of .01%.

　　This is team managed and currently receives a manager quality ranking of 4 (0=worst, 99=best). This fund offers an average level of risk but investors looking for strong performance will be frustrated.

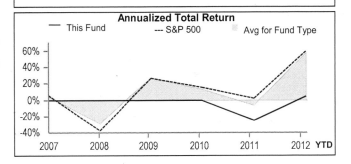

*JPMorgan Dbl Short US Long Trs E (DSTJ)

E　**Very Weak**

Fund Family: JP Morgan Investment Management Inc
Fund Type: Growth
Inception Date: October 4, 2010

Data Date	Investment Rating	Net Assets ($Mil)	Price	Performance Rating/Pts	Total Return Y-T-D	Risk Rating/Pts
3-12	E	7.63	39.37	E+ / 0.6	5.68%	C- / 3.7

Major Rating Factors: Very poor performance is the major factor driving the E (Very Weak) TheStreet.com Investment Rating for *JPMorgan Dbl Short US Long Trs E. The fund currently has a performance rating of E+ (Very Weak) based on an annualized return of 0.00% over the last three years and a total return of 5.68% year to date 2012. Factored into the performance evaluation is an expense ratio of 0.85% (very low).

　　The fund's risk rating is currently C- (Fair). It carries a beta of 0.00, meaning the fund's expected move will be 0.0% for every 10% move in the market. Volatility, as measured by both the semi-deviation and a drawdown factor, is considered average. As of March 31, 2012, *JPMorgan Dbl Short US Long Trs E traded at a premium of .10% above its net asset value, which is worse than its one-year historical average discount of .10%.

　　This is team managed and currently receives a manager quality ranking of 2 (0=worst, 99=best). This fund offers an average level of risk but investors looking for strong performance will be frustrated.

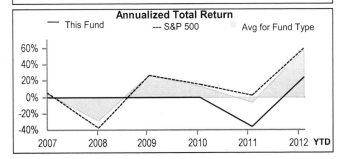

*Market Vector RVE Hard Asst Prd (HAP)

D+   **Weak**

Fund Family: Van Eck Associates Corporation
Fund Type: Global
Inception Date: August 29, 2008

Major Rating Factors: *Market Vector RVE Hard Asst Prd receives a TheStreet.com Investment Rating of D+ (Weak). The fund currently has a performance rating of C- (Fair) based on an annualized return of 15.54% over the last three years and a total return of 8.21% year to date 2012. Factored into the performance evaluation is an expense ratio of 0.61% (very low).

The fund's risk rating is currently B- (Good). It carries a beta of 1.07, meaning that its performance tracks fairly well with that of the overall stock market. Volatility, as measured by both the semi-deviation and a drawdown factor, is considered low. As of March 31, 2012, *Market Vector RVE Hard Asst Prd traded at a discount of .16% below its net asset value, which is better than its one-year historical average premium of .08%.

George Cao has been running the fund for 4 years and currently receives a manager quality ranking of 40 (0=worst, 99=best). If you desire an average level of risk, then this fund may be an option.

Data Date	Investment Rating	Net Assets ($Mil)	Price	Performance Rating/Pts	Total Return Y-T-D	Risk Rating/Pts
3-12	D+	186.67	36.50	C- / 3.3	8.21%	B- / 7.3
2011	C-	158.70	33.73	C- / 4.2	2.55%	B- / 7.1
2010	A+	209.70	38.95	A / 9.5	16.52%	C+ / 6.9
2009	A+	47.89	33.70	B+ / 8.9	38.05%	B- / 7.0

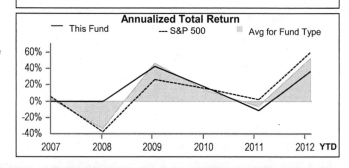

*Market Vectors Africa Index ETF (AFK)

C-   **Fair**

Fund Family: Van Eck Associates Corporation
Fund Type: Foreign
Inception Date: July 10, 2008

Major Rating Factors: Middle of the road best describes *Market Vectors Africa Index ETF whose TheStreet.com Investment Rating is currently a C- (Fair). The fund currently has a performance rating of C- (Fair) based on an annualized return of 14.94% over the last three years and a total return of 14.56% year to date 2012. Factored into the performance evaluation is an expense ratio of 0.81% (very low).

The fund's risk rating is currently B- (Good). It carries a beta of 1.00, meaning that its performance tracks fairly well with that of the overall stock market. Volatility, as measured by both the semi-deviation and a drawdown factor, is considered low. As of March 31, 2012, *Market Vectors Africa Index ETF traded at a premium of .85% above its net asset value, which is worse than its one-year historical average discount of .61%.

George Cao has been running the fund for 4 years and currently receives a manager quality ranking of 39 (0=worst, 99=best). If you desire an average level of risk, then this fund may be an option.

Data Date	Investment Rating	Net Assets ($Mil)	Price	Performance Rating/Pts	Total Return Y-T-D	Risk Rating/Pts
3-12	C-	74.09	29.50	C- / 3.4	14.56%	B- / 7.7
2011	C-	63.80	25.75	D+ / 2.9	0.89%	B- / 7.7
2010	B	107.50	35.18	A / 9.4	25.26%	C- / 3.4
2009	C	18.60	28.40	B- / 7.5	29.79%	C- / 3.4

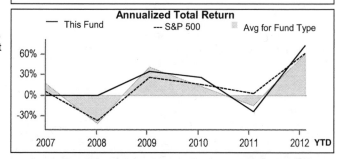

*Market Vectors Agribusiness ETF (MOO)

C   **Fair**

Fund Family: Van Eck Associates Corporation
Fund Type: Global
Inception Date: August 31, 2007

Major Rating Factors: Middle of the road best describes *Market Vectors Agribusiness ETF whose TheStreet.com Investment Rating is currently a C (Fair). The fund currently has a performance rating of C (Fair) based on an annualized return of 21.40% over the last three years and a total return of 12.05% year to date 2012. Factored into the performance evaluation is an expense ratio of 0.53% (very low).

The fund's risk rating is currently B- (Good). It carries a beta of 1.04, meaning that its performance tracks fairly well with that of the overall stock market. Volatility, as measured by both the semi-deviation and a drawdown factor, is considered low. As of March 31, 2012, *Market Vectors Agribusiness ETF traded at a premium of .08% above its net asset value, which is better than its one-year historical average premium of .09%.

Hao-Hung Liao has been running the fund for 5 years and currently receives a manager quality ranking of 72 (0=worst, 99=best). If you desire an average level of risk, then this fund may be an option.

Data Date	Investment Rating	Net Assets ($Mil)	Price	Performance Rating/Pts	Total Return Y-T-D	Risk Rating/Pts
3-12	C	6,114.91	52.83	C / 5.2	12.05%	B- / 7.4
2011	C	5,530.60	47.15	C+ / 5.6	3.46%	B- / 7.3
2010	C	2,624.20	53.54	C+ / 5.8	23.02%	C / 4.7
2009	B+	1,389.32	43.79	A / 9.3	50.12%	C / 4.6

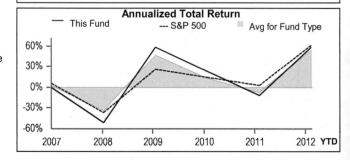

*Market Vectors Brazil Small-Cap (BRF)

D **Weak**

Fund Family: Van Eck Associates Corporation
Fund Type: Foreign
Inception Date: May 12, 2009

Major Rating Factors:
Disappointing performance is the major factor driving the D (Weak) TheStreet.com Investment Rating for *Market Vectors Brazil Small-Cap. The fund currently has a performance rating of D+ (Weak) based on an annualized return of 0.00% over the last three years and a total return of 20.55% year to date 2012. Factored into the performance evaluation is an expense ratio of 0.62% (very low).

The fund's risk rating is currently C+ (Fair). It carries a beta of 0.00, meaning the fund's expected move will be 0.0% for every 10% move in the market. Volatility, as measured by both the semi-deviation and a drawdown factor, is considered low. As of March 31, 2012, *Market Vectors Brazil Small-Cap traded at a discount of .25% below its net asset value, which is better than its one-year historical average premium of .09%.

George Cao has been running the fund for 3 years and currently receives a manager quality ranking of 27 (0=worst, 99=best). This fund offers only a moderate level of risk but investors looking for strong performance are still waiting.

Data Date	Investment Rating	Net Assets ($Mil)	Price	Performance Rating/Pts	Total Return Y-T-D	Risk Rating/Pts
3-12	D	785.56	43.93	D+ / 2.9	20.55%	C+ / 5.7
2011	D-	512.60	36.44	E+ / 0.6	1.21%	C+ / 5.7
2010	A+	1,078.10	57.68	A / 9.5	24.05%	C+ / 6.6

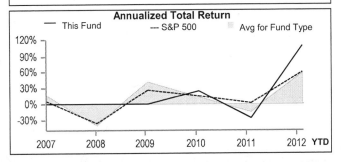

Annualized Total Return

*Market Vectors China ETF (PEK)

D- **Weak**

Fund Family: Van Eck Associates Corporation
Fund Type: Foreign
Inception Date: October 13, 2010

Major Rating Factors:
Very poor performance is the major factor driving the D- (Weak) TheStreet.com Investment Rating for *Market Vectors China ETF. The fund currently has a performance rating of E+ (Very Weak) based on an annualized return of 0.00% over the last three years and a total return of 7.46% year to date 2012. Factored into the performance evaluation is an expense ratio of 0.72% (very low).

The fund's risk rating is currently C+ (Fair). It carries a beta of 0.00, meaning the fund's expected move will be 0.0% for every 10% move in the market. Volatility, as measured by both the semi-deviation and a drawdown factor, is considered low. As of March 31, 2012, *Market Vectors China ETF traded at a premium of 7.59% above its net asset value, which is better than its one-year historical average premium of 7.80%.

George Cao has been running the fund for 2 years and currently receives a manager quality ranking of 7 (0=worst, 99=best). This fund offers only a moderate level of risk but investors looking for strong performance are still waiting.

Data Date	Investment Rating	Net Assets ($Mil)	Price	Performance Rating/Pts	Total Return Y-T-D	Risk Rating/Pts
3-12	D-	16.96	34.00	E+ / 0.7	7.46%	C+ / 6.4
2011	D-	15.10	31.64	E / 0.4	-1.49%	C+ / 6.4

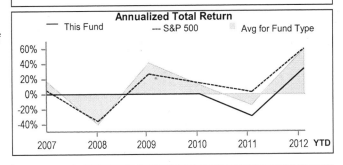

Annualized Total Return

*Market Vectors Chinese RMB USD E (CNY)

C- **Fair**

Fund Family: Morgan Stanley Investment Mgmt Inc
Fund Type: Foreign
Inception Date: March 14, 2008

Major Rating Factors:
Disappointing performance is the major factor driving the C- (Fair) TheStreet.com Investment Rating for *Market Vectors Chinese RMB USD E. The fund currently has a performance rating of D- (Weak) based on an annualized return of 0.01% over the last three years and a total return of 0.12% year to date 2012. Factored into the performance evaluation is an expense ratio of 0.55% (very low).

The fund's risk rating is currently B+ (Good). It carries a beta of 0.04, meaning the fund's expected move will be 0.4% for every 10% move in the market. Volatility, as measured by both the semi-deviation and a drawdown factor, is considered very low. As of March 31, 2012, *Market Vectors Chinese RMB USD E traded at a discount of .17% below its net asset value, which is in line with its one-year historical average discount of .17%.

This fund has been team managed for 4 years and currently receives a manager quality ranking of 40 (0=worst, 99=best). This fund offers only a moderate level of risk but investors looking for strong performance are still waiting.

Data Date	Investment Rating	Net Assets ($Mil)	Price	Performance Rating/Pts	Total Return Y-T-D	Risk Rating/Pts
3-12	C-	27.05	41.00	D- / 1.2	0.12%	B+ / 9.8
2011	C	27.05	40.95	D / 2.2	0.15%	B+ / 9.8
2010	C+	27.05	40.57	D+ / 2.9	0.87%	B / 8.8
2009	C	27.05	40.22	D / 2.1	1.69%	B+ / 9.0

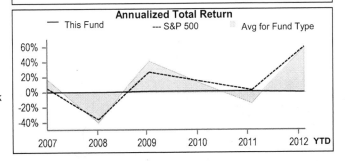

Annualized Total Return

* Denotes ETF Fund

*Market Vectors Coal ETF (KOL)

D+   **Weak**

Fund Family: Van Eck Associates Corporation
Fund Type: Energy/Natural Resources
Inception Date: January 10, 2008

Major Rating Factors: *Market Vectors Coal ETF receives a TheStreet.com Investment Rating of D+ (Weak). The fund currently has a performance rating of C (Fair) based on an annualized return of 27.85% over the last three years and a total return of -1.15% year to date 2012. Factored into the performance evaluation is an expense ratio of 0.59% (very low).

The fund's risk rating is currently C+ (Fair). It carries a beta of 1.60, meaning it is expected to move 16.0% for every 10% move in the market. Volatility, as measured by both the semi-deviation and a drawdown factor, is considered low. As of March 31, 2012, *Market Vectors Coal ETF traded at a discount of .50% below its net asset value, which is better than its one-year historical average discount of .33%.

George Cao has been running the fund for 4 years and currently receives a manager quality ranking of 50 (0=worst, 99=best). If you desire an average level of risk, then this fund may be an option.

Data Date	Investment Rating	Net Assets ($Mil)	Price	Performance Rating/Pts	Total Return Y-T-D	Risk Rating/Pts
3-12	D+	321.78	31.88	C / 4.9	-1.15%	C+ / 6.0
2011	C	314.40	32.25	B- / 7.1	3.01%	C+ / 5.9
2010	B	529.60	47.24	A+ / 9.8	31.33%	C- / 3.1
2009	B-	268.98	36.12	A+ / 9.9	123.90%	C- / 3.2

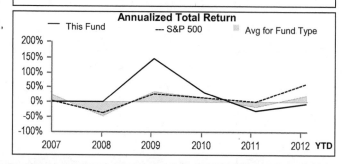

*Market Vectors Colombia ETF (COLX)

D+   **Weak**

Fund Family: Van Eck Associates Corporation
Fund Type: Global
Inception Date: March 14, 2011

Major Rating Factors:
Disappointing performance is the major factor driving the D+ (Weak) TheStreet.com Investment Rating for *Market Vectors Colombia ETF. The fund currently has a performance rating of D+ (Weak) based on an annualized return of 0.00% over the last three years and a total return of 18.05% year to date 2012. Factored into the performance evaluation is an expense ratio of 0.75% (very low).

The fund's risk rating is currently B- (Good). It carries a beta of 0.00, meaning the fund's expected move will be 0.0% for every 10% move in the market. Volatility, as measured by both the semi-deviation and a drawdown factor, is considered low. As of March 31, 2012, *Market Vectors Colombia ETF traded at a premium of 1.21% above its net asset value, which is worse than its one-year historical average premium of .32%.

George Cao has been running the fund for 1 year and currently receives a manager quality ranking of 46 (0=worst, 99=best). This fund offers only a moderate level of risk but investors looking for strong performance are still waiting.

Data Date	Investment Rating	Net Assets ($Mil)	Price	Performance Rating/Pts	Total Return Y-T-D	Risk Rating/Pts
3-12	D+	1.91	19.29	D+ / 2.7	18.05%	B- / 7.2

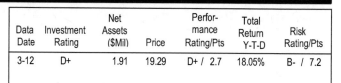

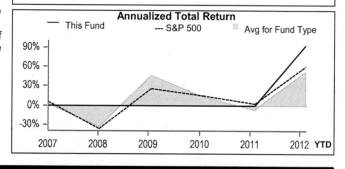

*Market Vectors Double Long Euro (URR)

D-   **Weak**

Fund Family: Morgan Stanley Investment Mgmt Inc
Fund Type: Foreign
Inception Date: May 7, 2008

Major Rating Factors:
Disappointing performance is the major factor driving the D- (Weak) TheStreet.com Investment Rating for *Market Vectors Double Long Euro. The fund currently has a performance rating of D- (Weak) based on an annualized return of -2.41% over the last three years and a total return of 5.82% year to date 2012. Factored into the performance evaluation is an expense ratio of 0.65% (very low).

The fund's risk rating is currently C+ (Fair). It carries a beta of 0.94, meaning that its performance tracks fairly well with that of the overall stock market. Volatility, as measured by both the semi-deviation and a drawdown factor, is considered low. As of March 31, 2012, *Market Vectors Double Long Euro traded at a discount of 1.35% below its net asset value, which is better than its one-year historical average discount of .42%.

This fund has been team managed for 4 years and currently receives a manager quality ranking of 9 (0=worst, 99=best). This fund offers only a moderate level of risk but investors looking for strong performance are still waiting.

Data Date	Investment Rating	Net Assets ($Mil)	Price	Performance Rating/Pts	Total Return Y-T-D	Risk Rating/Pts
3-12	D-	4.84	27.77	D- / 1.0	5.82%	C+ / 6.3
2011	D-	4.84	26.24	D- / 1.3	-1.87%	C+ / 6.4
2010	D	4.84	29.10	D- / 1.1	-14.24%	C / 5.3
2009	C-	4.84	33.93	C- / 3.2	5.97%	C+ / 5.9

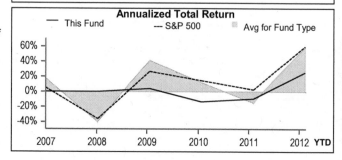

*Market Vectors Double Shrt Euro (DRR)

D- **Weak**

Fund Family: Morgan Stanley Investment Mgmt Inc
Fund Type: Foreign
Inception Date: May 7, 2008

Major Rating Factors:

Disappointing performance is the major factor driving the D- (Weak) TheStreet.com Investment Rating for *Market Vectors Double Shrt Euro. The fund currently has a performance rating of D- (Weak) based on an annualized return of -4.10% over the last three years and a total return of -6.68% year to date 2012. Factored into the performance evaluation is an expense ratio of 0.65% (very low).

The fund's risk rating is currently C+ (Fair). It carries a beta of -0.92, meaning the fund's expected move will be -9.2% for every 10% move in the market. Volatility, as measured by both the semi-deviation and a drawdown factor, is considered low. As of March 31, 2012, *Market Vectors Double Shrt Euro traded at a discount of .30% below its net asset value, which is better than its one-year historical average discount of .01%.

This fund has been team managed for 4 years and currently receives a manager quality ranking of 85 (0=worst, 99=best). This fund offers only a moderate level of risk but investors looking for strong performance are still waiting.

Data Date	Investment Rating	Net Assets ($Mil)	Price	Performance Rating/Pts	Total Return Y-T-D	Risk Rating/Pts
3-12	D-	28.43	42.61	D- / 1.0	-6.68%	C+ / 6.4
2011	D	28.43	45.66	D / 2.0	3.57%	C+ / 6.4
2010	C-	28.43	45.64	C- / 3.2	9.24%	C+ / 5.9
2009	D	28.43	41.78	E+ / 0.8	-11.91%	C+ / 6.3

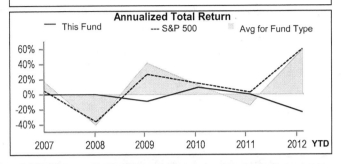

Annualized Total Return

*Market Vectors Egypt Index ETF (EGPT)

D- **Weak**

Fund Family: Van Eck Associates Corporation
Fund Type: Emerging Market
Inception Date: February 16, 2010

Major Rating Factors:

Disappointing performance is the major factor driving the D- (Weak) TheStreet.com Investment Rating for *Market Vectors Egypt Index ETF. The fund currently has a performance rating of D+ (Weak) based on an annualized return of 0.00% over the last three years and a total return of 33.93% year to date 2012. Factored into the performance evaluation is an expense ratio of 0.94% (low).

The fund's risk rating is currently C (Fair). It carries a beta of 0.00, meaning the fund's expected move will be 0.0% for every 10% move in the market. Volatility, as measured by both the semi-deviation and a drawdown factor, is considered average. As of March 31, 2012, *Market Vectors Egypt Index ETF traded at a discount of 1.71% below its net asset value, which is better than its one-year historical average discount of .60%.

George Cao has been running the fund for 2 years and currently receives a manager quality ranking of 14 (0=worst, 99=best). This fund offers an average level of risk but investors looking for strong performance will be frustrated.

Data Date	Investment Rating	Net Assets ($Mil)	Price	Performance Rating/Pts	Total Return Y-T-D	Risk Rating/Pts
3-12	D-	54.40	12.67	D+ / 2.3	33.93%	C / 4.4
2011	E+	36.20	9.46	E- / 0	0.42%	C / 4.4

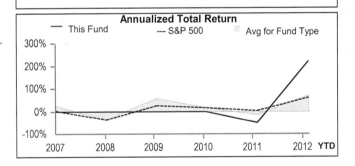

Annualized Total Return

*Market Vectors EM Lcl Curr Bnd E (EMLC)

D+ **Weak**

Fund Family: Van Eck Associates Corporation
Fund Type: Global
Inception Date: July 22, 2010

Major Rating Factors:

Disappointing performance is the major factor driving the D+ (Weak) TheStreet.com Investment Rating for *Market Vectors EM Lcl Curr Bnd E. The fund currently has a performance rating of D+ (Weak) based on an annualized return of 0.00% over the last three years and a total return of 8.01% year to date 2012. Factored into the performance evaluation is an expense ratio of 0.49% (very low).

The fund's risk rating is currently B (Good). It carries a beta of 0.00, meaning the fund's expected move will be 0.0% for every 10% move in the market. Volatility, as measured by both the semi-deviation and a drawdown factor, is considered low. As of March 31, 2012, *Market Vectors EM Lcl Curr Bnd E traded at a premium of .46% above its net asset value, which is worse than its one-year historical average premium of .45%.

Michael F. Mazier has been running the fund for 2 years and currently receives a manager quality ranking of 26 (0=worst, 99=best). This fund offers only a moderate level of risk but investors looking for strong performance are still waiting.

Data Date	Investment Rating	Net Assets ($Mil)	Price	Performance Rating/Pts	Total Return Y-T-D	Risk Rating/Pts
3-12	D+	599.32	26.28	D+ / 2.4	8.01%	B / 8.5
2011	D+	491.80	24.51	D- / 1.3	-0.16%	B / 8.5

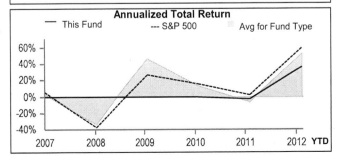

Annualized Total Return

*Market Vectors Environment Svc E (EVX)

| | **C** | **Fair** |

Fund Family: Van Eck Associates Corporation
Fund Type: Income
Inception Date: October 10, 2006

Major Rating Factors: Middle of the road best describes *Market Vectors Environment Svc E whose TheStreet.com Investment Rating is currently a C (Fair). The fund currently has a performance rating of C (Fair) based on an annualized return of 21.31% over the last three years and a total return of 13.24% year to date 2012. Factored into the performance evaluation is an expense ratio of 0.55% (very low).

The fund's risk rating is currently B (Good). It carries a beta of 0.95, meaning that its performance tracks fairly well with that of the overall stock market. Volatility, as measured by both the semi-deviation and a drawdown factor, is considered low. As of March 31, 2012, *Market Vectors Environment Svc E traded at a discount of .26% below its net asset value, which is better than its one-year historical average discount of .07%.

Hao-Hung Liao has been running the fund for 6 years and currently receives a manager quality ranking of 59 (0=worst, 99=best). If you desire an average level of risk, then this fund may be an option.

Data Date	Investment Rating	Net Assets ($Mil)	Price	Performance Rating/Pts	Total Return Y-T-D	Risk Rating/Pts
3-12	C	25.08	52.76	C / 5.3	13.24%	B / 8.1
2011	C-	23.30	46.59	C- / 3.4	0.04%	B- / 7.1
2010	C+	30.90	51.60	C+ / 6.2	22.10%	C / 5.3
2009	C-	19.56	42.67	C- / 3.7	19.57%	C / 5.5

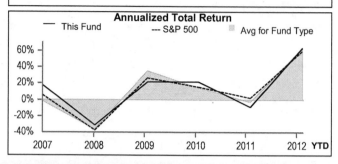

*Market Vectors Gaming ETF (BJK)

| | **C+** | **Fair** |

Fund Family: Van Eck Associates Corporation
Fund Type: Global
Inception Date: January 22, 2008

Major Rating Factors: Strong performance is the major factor driving the C+ (Fair) TheStreet.com Investment Rating for *Market Vectors Gaming ETF. The fund currently has a performance rating of B+ (Good) based on an annualized return of 30.92% over the last three years and a total return of 19.16% year to date 2012. Factored into the performance evaluation is an expense ratio of 0.65% (very low).

The fund's risk rating is currently C (Fair). It carries a beta of 1.19, meaning it is expected to move 11.9% for every 10% move in the market. Volatility, as measured by both the semi-deviation and a drawdown factor, is considered average. As of March 31, 2012, *Market Vectors Gaming ETF traded at a discount of .47% below its net asset value, which is better than its one-year historical average discount of .31%.

George Cao has been running the fund for 4 years and currently receives a manager quality ranking of 87 (0=worst, 99=best). If you desire an average level of risk and strong performance, then this fund is a good option.

Data Date	Investment Rating	Net Assets ($Mil)	Price	Performance Rating/Pts	Total Return Y-T-D	Risk Rating/Pts
3-12	C+	84.66	35.83	B+ / 8.6	19.16%	C / 5.5
2011	C-	96.70	30.07	C+ / 6.1	-0.19%	C / 5.5
2010	B+	129.10	31.49	A+ / 9.7	37.89%	C / 4.4
2009	C+	104.09	23.45	B / 8.0	30.79%	C / 4.7

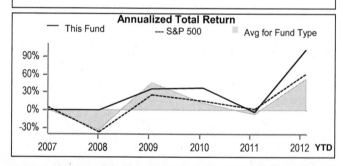

*Market Vectors Global Alt Enrgy (GEX)

| | **E+** | **Very Weak** |

Fund Family: Van Eck Associates Corporation
Fund Type: Energy/Natural Resources
Inception Date: May 3, 2007

Major Rating Factors:
Very poor performance is the major factor driving the E+ (Very Weak) TheStreet.com Investment Rating for *Market Vectors Global Alt Enrgy. The fund currently has a performance rating of E+ (Very Weak) based on an annualized return of -15.30% over the last three years and a total return of 8.52% year to date 2012. Factored into the performance evaluation is an expense ratio of 0.62% (very low).

The fund's risk rating is currently C (Fair). It carries a beta of 1.07, meaning that its performance tracks fairly well with that of the overall stock market. Volatility, as measured by both the semi-deviation and a drawdown factor, is considered average. As of March 31, 2012, *Market Vectors Global Alt Enrgy traded at a discount of .17% below its net asset value, which is worse than its one-year historical average discount of .44%.

Hao-Hung Liao has been running the fund for 5 years and currently receives a manager quality ranking of 3 (0=worst, 99=best). This fund offers an average level of risk but investors looking for strong performance will be frustrated.

Data Date	Investment Rating	Net Assets ($Mil)	Price	Performance Rating/Pts	Total Return Y-T-D	Risk Rating/Pts
3-12	E+	62.50	11.84	E+ / 0.6	8.52%	C / 5.0
2011	E+	58.60	10.91	E+ / 0.6	0.46%	C / 4.8
2010	E+	134.50	20.01	E / 0.4	-19.20%	C- / 3.5
2009	D	231.99	25.00	C- / 3.4	1.88%	C- / 3.6

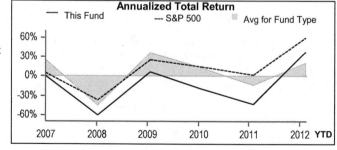

*Market Vectors Gold Miners ETF (GDX)

D-   **Weak**

Fund Family: Van Eck Associates Corporation
Fund Type: Precious Metals
Inception Date: May 16, 2006

Major Rating Factors:
Disappointing performance is the major factor driving the D- (Weak) TheStreet.com Investment Rating for *Market Vectors Gold Miners ETF. The fund currently has a performance rating of D (Weak) based on an annualized return of 12.86% over the last three years and a total return of -3.67% year to date 2012. Factored into the performance evaluation is an expense ratio of 0.52% (very low).

The fund's risk rating is currently C+ (Fair). It carries a beta of 1.41, meaning it is expected to move 14.1% for every 10% move in the market. Volatility, as measured by both the semi-deviation and a drawdown factor, is considered low. As of March 31, 2012, *Market Vectors Gold Miners ETF traded at a discount of .02% below its net asset value.

Hao-Hung Liao has been running the fund for 6 years and currently receives a manager quality ranking of 9 (0=worst, 99=best). This fund offers only a moderate level of risk but investors looking for strong performance are still waiting.

Data Date	Investment Rating	Net Assets ($Mil)	Price	Perfor-mance Rating/Pts	Total Return Y-T-D	Risk Rating/Pts
3-12	D-	8,989.80	49.54	D / 2.1	-3.67%	C+ / 5.9
2011	C	8,772.70	51.43	C+ / 6.0	3.73%	B- / 7.1
2010	C+	7,677.40	61.47	B+ / 8.4	33.90%	C- / 3.3
2009	C-	4,322.09	46.21	C+ / 6.4	39.02%	C- / 3.2

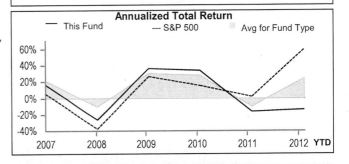

Annualized Total Return

*Market Vectors Gulf States ETF (MES)

D+   **Weak**

Fund Family: Van Eck Associates Corporation
Fund Type: Foreign
Inception Date: July 22, 2008

Major Rating Factors:
Disappointing performance is the major factor driving the D+ (Weak) TheStreet.com Investment Rating for *Market Vectors Gulf States ETF. The fund currently has a performance rating of D+ (Weak) based on an annualized return of 12.23% over the last three years and a total return of 6.95% year to date 2012. Factored into the performance evaluation is an expense ratio of 0.98% (low).

The fund's risk rating is currently B- (Good). It carries a beta of 0.70, meaning the fund's expected move will be 7.0% for every 10% move in the market. Volatility, as measured by both the semi-deviation and a drawdown factor, is considered low. As of March 31, 2012, *Market Vectors Gulf States ETF traded at a discount of 1.88% below its net asset value, which is better than its one-year historical average discount of 1.77%.

George Cao has been running the fund for 4 years and currently receives a manager quality ranking of 54 (0=worst, 99=best). This fund offers only a moderate level of risk but investors looking for strong performance are still waiting.

Data Date	Investment Rating	Net Assets ($Mil)	Price	Perfor-mance Rating/Pts	Total Return Y-T-D	Risk Rating/Pts
3-12	D+	13.72	20.92	D+ / 2.8	6.95%	B- / 7.6
2011	D+	14.10	19.56	D+ / 2.4	-0.26%	B- / 7.3
2010	B	22.10	23.81	A / 9.4	23.81%	C- / 3.8
2009	E+	8.06	19.42	D- / 1.0	1.62%	C- / 3.7

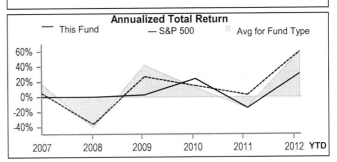

Annualized Total Return

*Market Vectors Hi-Yld Mun Idx ET (HYD)

B-   **Good**

Fund Family: Van Eck Associates Corporation
Fund Type: Municipal - High Yield
Inception Date: February 4, 2009

Major Rating Factors: *Market Vectors Hi-Yld Mun Idx ET receives a TheStreet.com Investment Rating of B- (Good). The fund currently has a performance rating of C+ (Fair) based on an annualized return of 12.81% over the last three years and a total return of 6.07% year to date 2012. Factored into the performance evaluation is an expense ratio of 0.35% (very low).

The fund's risk rating is currently B+ (Good). It carries a beta of 1.48, meaning it is expected to move 14.8% for every 10% move in the market. Volatility, as measured by both the semi-deviation and a drawdown factor, is considered very low. As of March 31, 2012, *Market Vectors Hi-Yld Mun Idx ET traded at a premium of .67% above its net asset value, which is worse than its one-year historical average premium of .32%.

Jeffrey A. Herrmann has been running the fund for 4 years and currently receives a manager quality ranking of 53 (0=worst, 99=best). If you desire an average level of risk, then this fund may be an option.

Data Date	Investment Rating	Net Assets ($Mil)	Price	Perfor-mance Rating/Pts	Total Return Y-T-D	Risk Rating/Pts
3-12	B-	452.09	31.34	C+ / 5.9	6.07%	B+ / 9.1
2011	B	340.80	29.80	C+ / 6.8	0.64%	B+ / 9.1
2010	C-	175.50	28.51	D- / 1.0	-0.40%	B / 8.4

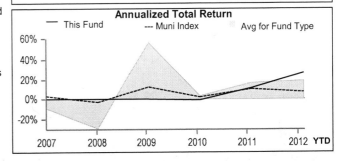

Annualized Total Return

*Market Vectors India Small-Cap E (SCIF)

E   **Very Weak**

Fund Family: Van Eck Associates Corporation
Fund Type: Foreign
Inception Date: August 24, 2010

Major Rating Factors:

Disappointing performance is the major factor driving the E (Very Weak) TheStreet.com Investment Rating for *Market Vectors India Small-Cap E. The fund currently has a performance rating of D- (Weak) based on an annualized return of 0.00% over the last three years and a total return of 38.95% year to date 2012. Factored into the performance evaluation is an expense ratio of 0.85% (very low).

The fund's risk rating is currently C- (Fair). It carries a beta of 0.00, meaning the fund's expected move will be 0.0% for every 10% move in the market. Volatility, as measured by both the semi-deviation and a drawdown factor, is considered average. As of March 31, 2012, *Market Vectors India Small-Cap E traded at a premium of .92% above its net asset value, which is worse than its one-year historical average discount of .05%.

George Cao has been running the fund for 2 years and currently receives a manager quality ranking of 7 (0=worst, 99=best). This fund offers an average level of risk but investors looking for strong performance will be frustrated.

Data Date	Investment Rating	Net Assets ($Mil)	Price	Performance Rating/Pts	Total Return Y-T-D	Risk Rating/Pts
3-12	E	52.80	12.13	D- / 1.1	38.95%	C- / 3.4
2011	E	30.90	8.73	E- / 0	5.38%	C- / 3.3

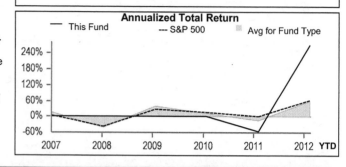

*Market Vectors Indian Rupee USD (INR)

D   **Weak**

Fund Family: Morgan Stanley Investment Mgmt Inc
Fund Type: Foreign
Inception Date: March 14, 2008

Major Rating Factors:

Disappointing performance is the major factor driving the D (Weak) TheStreet.com Investment Rating for *Market Vectors Indian Rupee USD. The fund currently has a performance rating of D- (Weak) based on an annualized return of 3.23% over the last three years and a total return of 7.84% year to date 2012. Factored into the performance evaluation is an expense ratio of 0.55% (very low).

The fund's risk rating is currently B (Good). It carries a beta of 0.38, meaning the fund's expected move will be 3.8% for every 10% move in the market. Volatility, as measured by both the semi-deviation and a drawdown factor, is considered low. As of March 31, 2012, *Market Vectors Indian Rupee USD traded at a premium of .36% above its net asset value, which is worse than its one-year historical average discount of .37%.

This fund has been team managed for 4 years and currently receives a manager quality ranking of 31 (0=worst, 99=best). This fund offers only a moderate level of risk but investors looking for strong performance are still waiting.

Data Date	Investment Rating	Net Assets ($Mil)	Price	Performance Rating/Pts	Total Return Y-T-D	Risk Rating/Pts
3-12	D	6.60	38.50	D- / 1.4	7.84%	B / 8.5
2011	D+	6.60	35.70	D / 1.6	-0.90%	B / 8.5
2010	A-	6.60	40.85	B- / 7.0	7.78%	B- / 7.8
2009	C+	6.60	37.90	C / 4.4	8.13%	B / 8.0

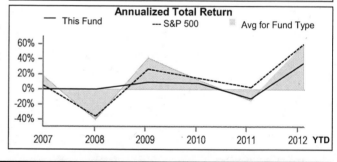

*Market Vectors Indonesia Idx ETF (IDX)

C+   **Fair**

Fund Family: Van Eck Associates Corporation
Fund Type: Foreign
Inception Date: January 15, 2009

Major Rating Factors:

Exceptional performance is the major factor driving the C+ (Fair) TheStreet.com Investment Rating for *Market Vectors Indonesia Idx ETF. The fund currently has a performance rating of A+ (Excellent) based on an annualized return of 48.88% over the last three years and a total return of 4.88% year to date 2012. Factored into the performance evaluation is an expense ratio of 0.61% (very low).

The fund's risk rating is currently C (Fair). It carries a beta of 1.22, meaning it is expected to move 12.2% for every 10% move in the market. Volatility, as measured by both the semi-deviation and a drawdown factor, is considered average. As of March 31, 2012, *Market Vectors Indonesia Idx ETF traded at a discount of .40% below its net asset value, which is better than its one-year historical average discount of .27%.

George Cao has been running the fund for 3 years and currently receives a manager quality ranking of 96 (0=worst, 99=best). If you desire an average level of risk and strong performance, then this fund is a good option.

Data Date	Investment Rating	Net Assets ($Mil)	Price	Performance Rating/Pts	Total Return Y-T-D	Risk Rating/Pts
3-12	C+	542.87	29.86	A+ / 9.7	4.88%	C / 4.7
2011	D-	471.30	28.47	D+ / 2.5	1.40%	C / 4.9
2010	A+	623.50	87.31	A / 9.5	41.77%	B- / 7.9

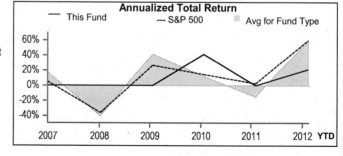

*Market Vectors Interm Muni Idx E (ITM)

C **Fair**

Fund Family: Van Eck Associates Corporation
Fund Type: Municipal - National
Inception Date: December 4, 2007

Major Rating Factors: Middle of the road best describes *Market Vectors Interm Muni Idx E whose TheStreet.com Investment Rating is currently a C (Fair). The fund currently has a performance rating of C- (Fair) based on an annualized return of 7.22% over the last three years and a total return of 1.00% year to date 2012. Factored into the performance evaluation is an expense ratio of 0.24% (very low).

The fund's risk rating is currently B+ (Good). It carries a beta of 1.32, meaning it is expected to move 13.2% for every 10% move in the market. Volatility, as measured by both the semi-deviation and a drawdown factor, is considered very low. As of March 31, 2012, *Market Vectors Interm Muni Idx E traded at a premium of .39% above its net asset value, which is worse than its one-year historical average premium of .12%.

James T. Colby, III has been running the fund for 5 years and currently receives a manager quality ranking of 31 (0=worst, 99=best). If you desire an average level of risk, then this fund may be an option.

Data Date	Investment Rating	Net Assets ($Mil)	Price	Perfor-mance Rating/Pts	Total Return Y-T-D	Risk Rating/Pts
3-12	C	430.75	22.98	C- / 3.1	1.00%	B+ / 9.4
2011	B-	351.40	22.86	C+ / 5.8	0.52%	B+ / 9.4
2010	D	209.70	20.89	C- / 4.1	1.47%	D+ / 2.7
2009	D+	51.92	21.29	C+ / 5.8	10.41%	D+ / 2.6

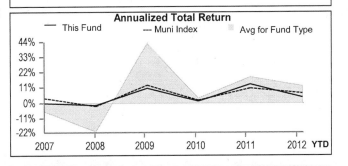

Annualized Total Return

*Market Vectors Junior Gold Mnrs (GDXJ)

E+ **Very Weak**

Fund Family: Van Eck Associates Corporation
Fund Type: Precious Metals
Inception Date: November 10, 2009

Major Rating Factors:
Very poor performance is the major factor driving the E+ (Very Weak) TheStreet.com Investment Rating for *Market Vectors Junior Gold Mnrs. The fund currently has a performance rating of E (Very Weak) based on an annualized return of 0.00% over the last three years and a total return of -0.61% year to date 2012. Factored into the performance evaluation is an expense ratio of 0.54% (very low).

The fund's risk rating is currently C (Fair). It carries a beta of 0.00, meaning the fund's expected move will be 0.0% for every 10% move in the market. Volatility, as measured by both the semi-deviation and a drawdown factor, is considered average. As of March 31, 2012, *Market Vectors Junior Gold Mnrs traded at a premium of .74% above its net asset value, which is worse than its one-year historical average premium of .27%.

George Cao has been running the fund for 3 years and currently receives a manager quality ranking of 1 (0=worst, 99=best). This fund offers an average level of risk but investors looking for strong performance will be frustrated.

Data Date	Investment Rating	Net Assets ($Mil)	Price	Perfor-mance Rating/Pts	Total Return Y-T-D	Risk Rating/Pts
3-12	E+	2,414.20	24.55	E / 0.5	-0.61%	C / 5.1
2011	E+	1,922.70	24.70	E+ / 0.6	3.72%	C / 5.2
2010	A+	2,123.90	39.89	A+ / 9.9	66.53%	B- / 7.6

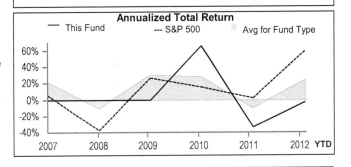

Annualized Total Return

*Market Vectors Lat Am SC Index E (LATM)

D- **Weak**

Fund Family: Van Eck Associates Corporation
Fund Type: Foreign
Inception Date: April 6, 2010

Major Rating Factors:
Disappointing performance is the major factor driving the D- (Weak) TheStreet.com Investment Rating for *Market Vectors Lat Am SC Index E. The fund currently has a performance rating of D (Weak) based on an annualized return of 0.00% over the last three years and a total return of 16.23% year to date 2012. Factored into the performance evaluation is an expense ratio of 0.63% (very low).

The fund's risk rating is currently C+ (Fair). It carries a beta of 0.00, meaning the fund's expected move will be 0.0% for every 10% move in the market. Volatility, as measured by both the semi-deviation and a drawdown factor, is considered low. As of March 31, 2012, *Market Vectors Lat Am SC Index E traded at a discount of .39% below its net asset value, which is better than its one-year historical average discount of .23%.

George Cao has been running the fund for 2 years and currently receives a manager quality ranking of 15 (0=worst, 99=best). This fund offers only a moderate level of risk but investors looking for strong performance are still waiting.

Data Date	Investment Rating	Net Assets ($Mil)	Price	Perfor-mance Rating/Pts	Total Return Y-T-D	Risk Rating/Pts
3-12	D-	17.30	25.50	D / 1.6	16.23%	C+ / 6.2
2011	D-	14.20	21.94	E+ / 0.6	3.01%	C+ / 6.2

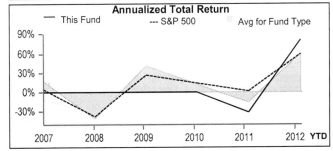

Annualized Total Return

*Market Vectors Long Muni Index E (MLN)

C+   **Fair**

Fund Family: Van Eck Associates Corporation
Fund Type: Municipal - National
Inception Date: January 2, 2008

Major Rating Factors: Middle of the road best describes *Market Vectors Long Muni Index E whose TheStreet.com Investment Rating is currently a C+ (Fair). The fund currently has a performance rating of C (Fair) based on an annualized return of 10.18% over the last three years and a total return of 3.18% year to date 2012. Factored into the performance evaluation is an expense ratio of 0.24% (very low).

The fund's risk rating is currently B+ (Good). It carries a beta of 1.71, meaning it is expected to move 17.1% for every 10% move in the market. Volatility, as measured by both the semi-deviation and a drawdown factor, is considered very low. As of March 31, 2012, *Market Vectors Long Muni Index E traded at a premium of .21% above its net asset value, which is worse than its one-year historical average discount of .31%.

James T. Colby, III has been running the fund for 4 years and currently receives a manager quality ranking of 28 (0=worst, 99=best). If you desire an average level of risk, then this fund may be an option.

Data Date	Investment Rating	Net Assets ($Mil)	Price	Performance Rating/Pts	Total Return Y-T-D	Risk Rating/Pts
3-12	C+	79.61	19.50	C / 4.7	3.18%	B+ / 9.1
2011	B	67.30	19.03	C+ / 6.9	0.60%	B+ / 9.1
2010	E	56.00	17.17	E+ / 0.9	-1.26%	D+ / 2.7
2009	C-	30.25	18.18	B- / 7.4	17.84%	D+ / 2.5

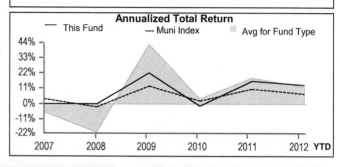
Annualized Total Return

---

*Market Vectors Poland ETF (PLND)

E+   **Very Weak**

Fund Family: Van Eck Associates Corporation
Fund Type: Emerging Market
Inception Date: November 24, 2009

Major Rating Factors:
Disappointing performance is the major factor driving the E+ (Very Weak) TheStreet.com Investment Rating for *Market Vectors Poland ETF. The fund currently has a performance rating of D- (Weak) based on an annualized return of 0.00% over the last three years and a total return of 19.91% year to date 2012. Factored into the performance evaluation is an expense ratio of 0.61% (very low).

The fund's risk rating is currently C (Fair). It carries a beta of 0.00, meaning the fund's expected move will be 0.0% for every 10% move in the market. Volatility, as measured by both the semi-deviation and a drawdown factor, is considered average. As of March 31, 2012, *Market Vectors Poland ETF traded at a premium of .44% above its net asset value, which is worse than its one-year historical average discount of .10%.

George Cao has been running the fund for 3 years and currently receives a manager quality ranking of 10 (0=worst, 99=best). This fund offers an average level of risk but investors looking for strong performance will be frustrated.

Data Date	Investment Rating	Net Assets ($Mil)	Price	Performance Rating/Pts	Total Return Y-T-D	Risk Rating/Pts
3-12	E+	34.49	20.60	D- / 1.0	19.91%	C / 5.1
2011	E+	31.00	17.18	E- / 0.2	-3.14%	C / 5.1
2010	A	52.80	27.02	A- / 9.1	12.50%	C+ / 6.5

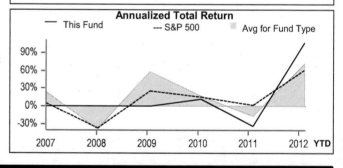
Annualized Total Return

---

*Market Vectors Pre-Refnded Muni (PRB)

C-   **Fair**

Fund Family: Van Eck Associates Corporation
Fund Type: Municipal - National
Inception Date: February 2, 2009

Major Rating Factors:
Disappointing performance is the major factor driving the C- (Fair) TheStreet.com Investment Rating for *Market Vectors Pre-Refnded Muni. The fund currently has a performance rating of D- (Weak) based on an annualized return of 2.15% over the last three years and a total return of 0.25% year to date 2012. Factored into the performance evaluation is an expense ratio of 0.24% (very low).

The fund's risk rating is currently B+ (Good). It carries a beta of 0.54, meaning the fund's expected move will be 5.4% for every 10% move in the market. Volatility, as measured by both the semi-deviation and a drawdown factor, is considered very low. As of March 31, 2012, *Market Vectors Pre-Refnded Muni traded at a discount of .16% below its net asset value, which is worse than its one-year historical average discount of .45%.

Jack W. Bauer has been running the fund for 4 years and currently receives a manager quality ranking of 34 (0=worst, 99=best). This fund offers only a moderate level of risk but investors looking for strong performance are still waiting.

Data Date	Investment Rating	Net Assets ($Mil)	Price	Performance Rating/Pts	Total Return Y-T-D	Risk Rating/Pts
3-12	C-	33.07	25.20	D- / 1.5	0.25%	B+ / 9.7
2011	C	35.40	25.20	C- / 3.1	0.09%	B+ / 9.8
2010	D	37.20	24.76	D / 2.0	0.49%	C / 4.9

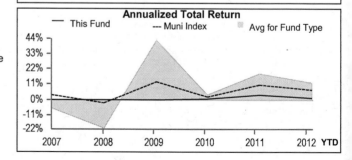
Annualized Total Return

*Market Vectors Russia ETF (RSX)

C-   Fair

Fund Family: Van Eck Associates Corporation
Fund Type: Foreign
Inception Date: April 24, 2007

Major Rating Factors: Middle of the road best describes *Market Vectors Russia ETF whose TheStreet.com Investment Rating is currently a C- (Fair). The fund currently has a performance rating of C+ (Fair) based on an annualized return of 25.00% over the last three years and a total return of 15.85% year to date 2012. Factored into the performance evaluation is an expense ratio of 0.62% (very low).

The fund's risk rating is currently C+ (Fair). It carries a beta of 1.58, meaning it is expected to move 15.8% for every 10% move in the market. Volatility, as measured by both the semi-deviation and a drawdown factor, is considered low. As of March 31, 2012, *Market Vectors Russia ETF traded at a premium of .62% above its net asset value, which is worse than its one-year historical average discount of .06%.

Hao-Hung Liao has been running the fund for 5 years and currently receives a manager quality ranking of 56 (0=worst, 99=best). If you desire an average level of risk, then this fund may be an option.

Data Date	Investment Rating	Net Assets ($Mil)	Price	Performance Rating/Pts	Total Return Y-T-D	Risk Rating/Pts
3-12	C-	2,169.23	30.88	C+ / 5.6	15.85%	C+ / 5.6
2011	C-	1,557.00	26.65	C+ / 6.2	1.61%	C+ / 5.8
2010	E+	2,609.60	37.91	D / 2.0	22.14%	D+ / 2.3
2009	C+	726.96	31.19	A+ / 9.9	120.06%	D+ / 2.6

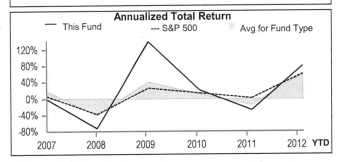

Annualized Total Return
— This Fund   --- S&P 500   Avg for Fund Type

*Market Vectors Short Muni Index (SMB)

C-   Fair

Fund Family: Van Eck Associates Corporation
Fund Type: Municipal - National
Inception Date: February 22, 2008

Major Rating Factors:
Disappointing performance is the major factor driving the C- (Fair) TheStreet.com Investment Rating for *Market Vectors Short Muni Index. The fund currently has a performance rating of D (Weak) based on an annualized return of 3.46% over the last three years and a total return of 0.46% year to date 2012. Factored into the performance evaluation is an expense ratio of 0.20% (very low).

The fund's risk rating is currently B+ (Good). It carries a beta of 0.52, meaning the fund's expected move will be 5.2% for every 10% move in the market. Volatility, as measured by both the semi-deviation and a drawdown factor, is considered very low. As of March 31, 2012, *Market Vectors Short Muni Index traded at a premium of .23% above its net asset value, which is worse than its one-year historical average premium of .11%.

James T. Colby, III has been running the fund for 4 years and currently receives a manager quality ranking of 46 (0=worst, 99=best). This fund offers only a moderate level of risk but investors looking for strong performance are still waiting.

Data Date	Investment Rating	Net Assets ($Mil)	Price	Performance Rating/Pts	Total Return Y-T-D	Risk Rating/Pts
3-12	C-	125.57	17.74	D / 1.8	0.46%	B+ / 9.7
2011	C+	113.80	17.71	C- / 3.6	0.17%	B+ / 9.7
2010	D-	102.40	17.12	D / 2.0	0.86%	C- / 3.8
2009	D+	24.54	17.32	C / 5.0	7.88%	C- / 3.5

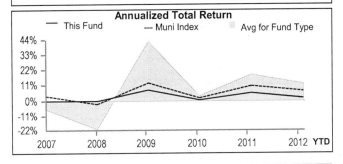

Annualized Total Return
— This Fund   --- Muni Index   Avg for Fund Type

*Market Vectors Solar Energy ETF (KWT)

E   Very Weak

Fund Family: Van Eck Associates Corporation
Fund Type: Energy/Natural Resources
Inception Date: April 21, 2008

Major Rating Factors: Very poor performance is the major factor driving the E (Very Weak) TheStreet.com Investment Rating for *Market Vectors Solar Energy ETF. The fund currently has a performance rating of E (Very Weak) based on an annualized return of -30.82% over the last three years and a total return of 1.62% year to date 2012. Factored into the performance evaluation is an expense ratio of 0.65% (very low).

The fund's risk rating is currently C- (Fair). It carries a beta of 1.63, meaning it is expected to move 16.3% for every 10% move in the market. Volatility, as measured by both the semi-deviation and a drawdown factor, is considered average. As of March 31, 2012, *Market Vectors Solar Energy ETF traded at a premium of 1.08% above its net asset value, which is worse than its one-year historical average premium of .22%.

George Cao has been running the fund for 4 years and currently receives a manager quality ranking of 0 (0=worst, 99=best). This fund offers an average level of risk but investors looking for strong performance will be frustrated.

Data Date	Investment Rating	Net Assets ($Mil)	Price	Performance Rating/Pts	Total Return Y-T-D	Risk Rating/Pts
3-12	E	14.70	3.75	E / 0.4	1.62%	C- / 3.7
2011	E	9.90	3.69	E / 0.3	2.98%	C- / 3.8
2010	E	24.90	10.99	E / 0.5	-28.71%	C- / 3.0
2009	D	29.87	15.51	C / 4.4	2.47%	C- / 3.0

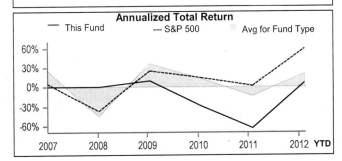

Annualized Total Return
— This Fund   --- S&P 500   Avg for Fund Type

*Market Vectors Steel Index ETF (SLX)

D+   **Weak**

Fund Family: Van Eck Associates Corporation
Fund Type: Income
Inception Date: October 10, 2006

Data Date	Investment Rating	Net Assets ($Mil)	Price	Performance Rating/Pts	Total Return Y-T-D	Risk Rating/Pts
3-12	D+	177.67	53.03	C- / 4.1	11.52%	C+ / 6.4
2011	C-	181.00	47.55	C- / 4.2	4.65%	C+ / 6.3
2010	C-	279.10	72.58	C / 5.4	19.65%	C- / 3.7
2009	B-	227.48	61.52	B+ / 8.6	97.08%	C- / 4.1

Major Rating Factors: *Market Vectors Steel Index ETF receives a TheStreet.com Investment Rating of D+ (Weak). The fund currently has a performance rating of C- (Fair) based on an annualized return of 20.15% over the last three years and a total return of 11.52% year to date 2012. Factored into the performance evaluation is an expense ratio of 0.55% (very low).

The fund's risk rating is currently C+ (Fair). It carries a beta of 2.06, meaning it is expected to move 20.6% for every 10% move in the market. Volatility, as measured by both the semi-deviation and a drawdown factor, is considered low. As of March 31, 2012, *Market Vectors Steel Index ETF traded at a premium of .02% above its net asset value.

Hao-Hung Liao has been running the fund for 6 years and currently receives a manager quality ranking of 8 (0=worst, 99=best). If you desire an average level of risk, then this fund may be an option.

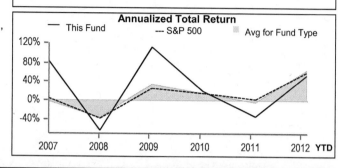

*Market Vectors Uranium+Nuc Engy (NLR)

D-   **Weak**

Fund Family: Van Eck Associates Corporation
Fund Type: Global
Inception Date: August 13, 2007

Data Date	Investment Rating	Net Assets ($Mil)	Price	Performance Rating/Pts	Total Return Y-T-D	Risk Rating/Pts
3-12	D-	101.86	16.45	D- / 1.3	10.85%	C+ / 6.1
2011	D-	86.70	14.84	D- / 1.3	-0.27%	C+ / 5.8
2010	D	260.40	25.35	D+ / 2.3	16.59%	C / 5.1
2009	C-	164.63	22.66	C / 5.1	12.63%	C / 4.8

Major Rating Factors:
Disappointing performance is the major factor driving the D- (Weak) TheStreet.com Investment Rating for *Market Vectors Uranium+Nuc Engy. The fund currently has a performance rating of D- (Weak) based on an annualized return of 2.38% over the last three years and a total return of 10.85% year to date 2012. Factored into the performance evaluation is an expense ratio of 0.62% (very low).

The fund's risk rating is currently C+ (Fair). It carries a beta of 1.10, meaning it is expected to move 11.0% for every 10% move in the market. Volatility, as measured by both the semi-deviation and a drawdown factor, is considered low. As of March 31, 2012, *Market Vectors Uranium+Nuc Engy traded at a discount of .42% below its net asset value, which is better than its one-year historical average discount of .31%.

Hao-Hung Liao has been running the fund for 5 years and currently receives a manager quality ranking of 11 (0=worst, 99=best). This fund offers only a moderate level of risk but investors looking for strong performance are still waiting.

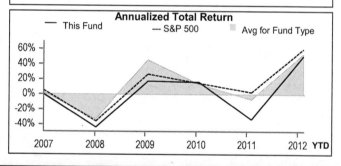

*Market Vectors Vietnam ETF (VNM)

D-   **Weak**

Fund Family: Van Eck Associates Corporation
Fund Type: Foreign
Inception Date: August 11, 2009

Data Date	Investment Rating	Net Assets ($Mil)	Price	Performance Rating/Pts	Total Return Y-T-D	Risk Rating/Pts
3-12	D-	275.73	19.14	D / 1.8	31.55%	C / 5.2
2011	E+	198.50	14.55	E- / 0.1	-1.03%	C / 5.1
2010	B-	243.30	26.18	C+ / 6.8	4.10%	B- / 7.3

Major Rating Factors:
Disappointing performance is the major factor driving the D- (Weak) TheStreet.com Investment Rating for *Market Vectors Vietnam ETF. The fund currently has a performance rating of D (Weak) based on an annualized return of 0.00% over the last three years and a total return of 31.55% year to date 2012. Factored into the performance evaluation is an expense ratio of 0.76% (very low).

The fund's risk rating is currently C (Fair). It carries a beta of 0.00, meaning the fund's expected move will be 0.0% for every 10% move in the market. Volatility, as measured by both the semi-deviation and a drawdown factor, is considered average. As of March 31, 2012, *Market Vectors Vietnam ETF traded at a premium of .26% above its net asset value, which is better than its one-year historical average premium of .72%.

George Cao has been running the fund for 3 years and currently receives a manager quality ranking of 11 (0=worst, 99=best). This fund offers an average level of risk but investors looking for strong performance will be frustrated.

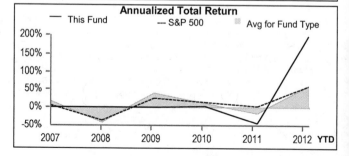

*Materials Select Sector SPDR (XLB)

C-   **Fair**

Fund Family: SSgA Funds Management Inc
Fund Type: Growth
Inception Date: December 16, 1998

Major Rating Factors: Middle of the road best describes *Materials Select Sector SPDR whose TheStreet.com Investment Rating is currently a C- (Fair). The fund currently has a performance rating of C (Fair) based on an annualized return of 18.93% over the last three years and a total return of 10.78% year to date 2012. Factored into the performance evaluation is an expense ratio of 0.19% (very low).

The fund's risk rating is currently B- (Good). It carries a beta of 1.48, meaning it is expected to move 14.8% for every 10% move in the market. Volatility, as measured by both the semi-deviation and a drawdown factor, is considered low. As of March 31, 2012, *Materials Select Sector SPDR traded at a price exactly equal to its net asset value.

John A. Tucker has been running the fund for 14 years and currently receives a manager quality ranking of 13 (0=worst, 99=best). If you desire an average level of risk, then this fund may be an option.

Data Date	Investment Rating	Net Assets ($Mil)	Price	Performance Rating/Pts	Total Return Y-T-D	Risk Rating/Pts
3-12	C-	1,777.50	36.97	C / 4.5	10.78%	B- / 7.3
2011	C	1,635.40	33.50	C / 5.3	3.79%	B- / 7.1
2010	C+	2,594.70	38.41	C+ / 6.4	20.56%	C / 5.3
2009	C	1,725.05	32.99	C+ / 5.8	42.89%	C / 5.5

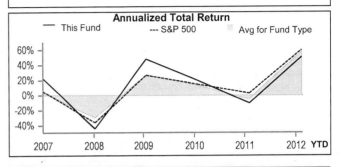

*Morgan Stanley Technology ETF (MTK)

C+   **Fair**

Fund Family: SSgA Funds Management Inc
Fund Type: Growth
Inception Date: September 25, 2000

Major Rating Factors: Middle of the road best describes *Morgan Stanley Technology ETF whose TheStreet.com Investment Rating is currently a C+ (Fair). The fund currently has a performance rating of C+ (Fair) based on an annualized return of 22.64% over the last three years and a total return of 21.92% year to date 2012. Factored into the performance evaluation is an expense ratio of 0.53% (very low).

The fund's risk rating is currently B- (Good). It carries a beta of 1.27, meaning it is expected to move 12.7% for every 10% move in the market. Volatility, as measured by both the semi-deviation and a drawdown factor, is considered low. As of March 31, 2012, *Morgan Stanley Technology ETF traded at a premium of .14% above its net asset value, which is worse than its one-year historical average discount of .02%.

John A. Tucker has been running the fund for 12 years and currently receives a manager quality ranking of 28 (0=worst, 99=best). If you desire an average level of risk, then this fund may be an option.

Data Date	Investment Rating	Net Assets ($Mil)	Price	Performance Rating/Pts	Total Return Y-T-D	Risk Rating/Pts
3-12	C+	192.66	71.45	C+ / 6.6	21.92%	B- / 7.2
2011	C	155.30	58.66	C+ / 5.7	1.99%	B- / 7.0
2010	C+	218.00	66.08	C+ / 6.9	15.31%	C / 4.7
2009	C+	197.82	57.61	C+ / 6.5	63.10%	C / 5.2

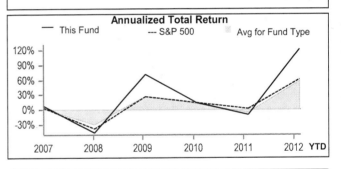

*Mrkt Vectors Rare Earth/Str Met (REMX)

E+   **Very Weak**

Fund Family: Van Eck Associates Corporation
Fund Type: Growth
Inception Date: October 27, 2010

Major Rating Factors:
Very poor performance is the major factor driving the E+ (Very Weak) TheStreet.com Investment Rating for *Mrkt Vectors Rare Earth/Str Met. The fund currently has a performance rating of E+ (Very Weak) based on an annualized return of 0.00% over the last three years and a total return of 15.01% year to date 2012. Factored into the performance evaluation is an expense ratio of 0.57% (very low).

The fund's risk rating is currently C (Fair). It carries a beta of 0.00, meaning the fund's expected move will be 0.0% for every 10% move in the market. Volatility, as measured by both the semi-deviation and a drawdown factor, is considered average. As of March 31, 2012, *Mrkt Vectors Rare Earth/Str Met traded at a discount of .64% below its net asset value, which is better than its one-year historical average discount of .29%.

George Cao has been running the fund for 2 years and currently receives a manager quality ranking of 1 (0=worst, 99=best). This fund offers an average level of risk but investors looking for strong performance will be frustrated.

Data Date	Investment Rating	Net Assets ($Mil)	Price	Performance Rating/Pts	Total Return Y-T-D	Risk Rating/Pts
3-12	E+	228.99	17.16	E+ / 0.9	15.01%	C / 4.5
2011	E+	198.50	14.92	E / 0.5	3.95%	C / 4.3

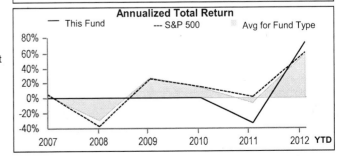

*Nuveen Diversified Commodity (CFD)

D   **Weak**

Fund Family: Nuveen Commodities Asset Management
Fund Type: Growth
Inception Date: September 28, 2010

Major Rating Factors:

Disappointing performance is the major factor driving the D (Weak) TheStreet.com Investment Rating for *Nuveen Diversified Commodity. The fund currently has a performance rating of D (Weak) based on an annualized return of 0.00% over the last three years and a total return of 15.85% year to date 2012.

The fund's risk rating is currently C+ (Fair). It carries a beta of 0.00, meaning the fund's expected move will be 0.0% for every 10% move in the market. Volatility, as measured by both the semi-deviation and a drawdown factor, is considered low. As of March 31, 2012, *Nuveen Diversified Commodity traded at a discount of 2.00% below its net asset value, which is worse than its one-year historical average discount of 4.60%.

This fund has been team managed for 2 years and currently receives a manager quality ranking of 7 (0=worst, 99=best). This fund offers only a moderate level of risk but investors looking for strong performance are still waiting.

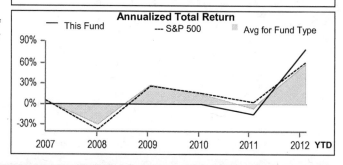

Data Date	Investment Rating	Net Assets ($Mil)	Price	Performance Rating/Pts	Total Return Y-T-D	Risk Rating/Pts
3-12	D	212.73	23.08	D / 2.0	15.85%	C+ / 6.7
2011	D-	214.30	20.30	D- / 1.0	2.61%	C+ / 6.6

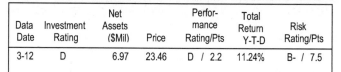

Annualized Total Return

---

*Pax MSCI EAFE ESG Index ETF (EAPS)

D   **Weak**

Fund Family: Pax World Management LLC
Fund Type: Foreign
Inception Date: January 28, 2011

Major Rating Factors:

Disappointing performance is the major factor driving the D (Weak) TheStreet.com Investment Rating for *Pax MSCI EAFE ESG Index ETF. The fund currently has a performance rating of D (Weak) based on an annualized return of 0.00% over the last three years and a total return of 11.24% year to date 2012. Factored into the performance evaluation is an expense ratio of 0.55% (very low).

The fund's risk rating is currently B- (Good). It carries a beta of 0.00, meaning the fund's expected move will be 0.0% for every 10% move in the market. Volatility, as measured by both the semi-deviation and a drawdown factor, is considered low. As of March 31, 2012, *Pax MSCI EAFE ESG Index ETF traded at a premium of .69% above its net asset value, which is worse than its one-year historical average premium of .08%.

Christopher H. Brown has been running the fund for 1 year and currently receives a manager quality ranking of 46 (0=worst, 99=best). This fund offers only a moderate level of risk but investors looking for strong performance are still waiting.

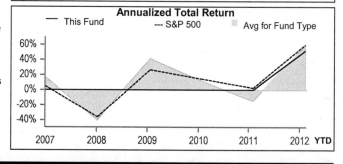

Data Date	Investment Rating	Net Assets ($Mil)	Price	Performance Rating/Pts	Total Return Y-T-D	Risk Rating/Pts
3-12	D	6.97	23.46	D / 2.2	11.24%	B- / 7.5

Annualized Total Return

---

*Pax MSCI North America ESG Idx E (NASI)

C   **Fair**

Fund Family: Pax World Management LLC
Fund Type: Growth
Inception Date: May 18, 2010

Major Rating Factors: Middle of the road best describes *Pax MSCI North America ESG Idx E whose TheStreet.com Investment Rating is currently a C (Fair). The fund currently has a performance rating of C- (Fair) based on an annualized return of 0.00% over the last three years and a total return of 10.85% year to date 2012. Factored into the performance evaluation is an expense ratio of 0.50% (very low).

The fund's risk rating is currently B (Good). It carries a beta of 0.00, meaning the fund's expected move will be 0.0% for every 10% move in the market. Volatility, as measured by both the semi-deviation and a drawdown factor, is considered low. As of March 31, 2012, *Pax MSCI North America ESG Idx E traded at a premium of .64% above its net asset value, which is worse than its one-year historical average premium of .40%.

Christopher H. Brown has been running the fund for 2 years and currently receives a manager quality ranking of 27 (0=worst, 99=best). If you desire an average level of risk, then this fund may be an option.

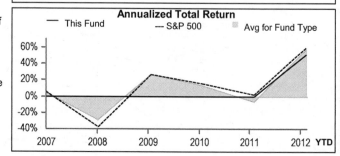

Data Date	Investment Rating	Net Assets ($Mil)	Price	Performance Rating/Pts	Total Return Y-T-D	Risk Rating/Pts
3-12	C	7.29	29.95	C- / 4.2	10.85%	B / 8.4
2011	C-	5.40	27.09	D+ / 2.3	1.77%	B / 8.4

Annualized Total Return

---

*Peritus High Yield ETF (HYLD)   C-   Fair

Fund Family: AdvisorShares Investments LLC
Fund Type: Corporate - High Yield
Inception Date: December 1, 2010

Data Date	Investment Rating	Net Assets ($Mil)	Price	Perfor-mance Rating/Pts	Total Return Y-T-D	Risk Rating/Pts
3-12	C-	75.93	49.75	D+ / 2.4	6.63%	B+ / 9.0
2011	C-	61.40	47.52	D / 1.9	0.23%	B+ / 9.0

Major Rating Factors:
Disappointing performance is the major factor driving the C- (Fair) TheStreet.com Investment Rating for *Peritus High Yield ETF. The fund currently has a performance rating of D+ (Weak) based on an annualized return of 0.00% over the last three years and a total return of 6.63% year to date 2012. Factored into the performance evaluation is an expense ratio of 1.34% (average).

The fund's risk rating is currently B+ (Good). It carries a beta of 0.00, meaning the fund's expected move will be 0.0% for every 10% move in the market. Volatility, as measured by both the semi-deviation and a drawdown factor, is considered very low. As of March 31, 2012, *Peritus High Yield ETF traded at a premium of .42% above its net asset value, which is worse than its one-year historical average premium of .24%.

Ronald J. Heller currently receives a manager quality ranking of 38 (0=worst, 99=best). This fund offers only a moderate level of risk but investors looking for strong performance are still waiting.

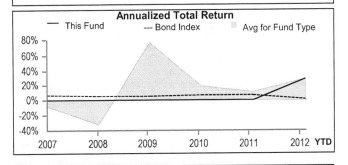

*PIMCO 1-3 Year US Treasury Index (TUZ)   C-   Fair

Fund Family: PIMCO
Fund Type: US Government/Agency
Inception Date: June 1, 2009

Data Date	Investment Rating	Net Assets ($Mil)	Price	Perfor-mance Rating/Pts	Total Return Y-T-D	Risk Rating/Pts
3-12	C-	137.80	50.93	D- / 1.3	-0.25%	B+ / 9.9
2011	C	143.10	51.12	D / 2.2	-0.11%	B+ / 9.9
2010	C+	106.80	50.92	C- / 3.1	2.37%	B+ / 9.0

Major Rating Factors:
Disappointing performance is the major factor driving the C- (Fair) TheStreet.com Investment Rating for *PIMCO 1-3 Year US Treasury Index. The fund currently has a performance rating of D- (Weak) based on an annualized return of 0.00% over the last three years and a total return of -0.25% year to date 2012. Factored into the performance evaluation is an expense ratio of 0.09% (very low).

The fund's risk rating is currently B+ (Good). It carries a beta of 0.00, meaning the fund's expected move will be 0.0% for every 10% move in the market. Volatility, as measured by both the semi-deviation and a drawdown factor, is considered very low. As of March 31, 2012, *PIMCO 1-3 Year US Treasury Index traded at a discount of .04% below its net asset value, which is better than its one-year historical average discount of .01%.

Vineer Bhansali has been running the fund for 3 years and currently receives a manager quality ranking of 53 (0=worst, 99=best). This fund offers only a moderate level of risk but investors looking for strong performance are still waiting.

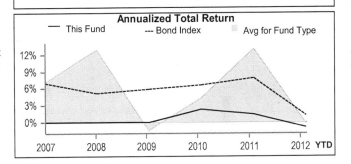

*PIMCO 1-5 Year US TIPS Index (STPZ)   C-   Fair

Fund Family: PIMCO
Fund Type: US Government/Agency
Inception Date: August 20, 2009

Data Date	Investment Rating	Net Assets ($Mil)	Price	Perfor-mance Rating/Pts	Total Return Y-T-D	Risk Rating/Pts
3-12	C-	953.60	54.06	D / 1.6	1.35%	B+ / 9.9
2011	C	933.90	53.34	D+ / 2.8	0.41%	B+ / 9.9
2010	B	672.80	52.58	C- / 4.0	3.40%	B+ / 9.0

Major Rating Factors:
Disappointing performance is the major factor driving the C- (Fair) TheStreet.com Investment Rating for *PIMCO 1-5 Year US TIPS Index. The fund currently has a performance rating of D (Weak) based on an annualized return of 0.00% over the last three years and a total return of 1.35% year to date 2012. Factored into the performance evaluation is an expense ratio of 0.20% (very low).

The fund's risk rating is currently B+ (Good). It carries a beta of 0.00, meaning the fund's expected move will be 0.0% for every 10% move in the market. Volatility, as measured by both the semi-deviation and a drawdown factor, is considered very low. As of March 31, 2012, *PIMCO 1-5 Year US TIPS Index traded at a premium of .02% above its net asset value, which is in line with its one-year historical average premium of .02%.

Vineer Bhansali has been running the fund for 3 years and currently receives a manager quality ranking of 76 (0=worst, 99=best). This fund offers only a moderate level of risk but investors looking for strong performance are still waiting.

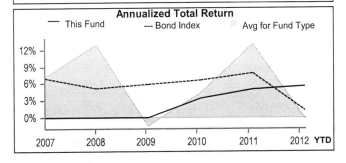

*PIMCO 15 Plus Year US TIPS Index (LTPZ)

C   **Fair**

Fund Family: PIMCO
Fund Type: US Government/Agency
Inception Date: September 3, 2009

Major Rating Factors: Middle of the road best describes *PIMCO 15 Plus Year US TIPS Index whose TheStreet.com Investment Rating is currently a C (Fair). The fund currently has a performance rating of C- (Fair) based on an annualized return of 0.00% over the last three years and a total return of -0.80% year to date 2012. Factored into the performance evaluation is an expense ratio of 0.20% (very low).

The fund's risk rating is currently B+ (Good). It carries a beta of 0.00, meaning the fund's expected move will be 0.0% for every 10% move in the market. Volatility, as measured by both the semi-deviation and a drawdown factor, is considered very low. As of March 31, 2012, *PIMCO 15 Plus Year US TIPS Index traded at a premium of .09% above its net asset value, which is worse than its one-year historical average premium of .08%.

Vineer Bhansali has been running the fund for 3 years and currently receives a manager quality ranking of 91 (0=worst, 99=best). If you desire an average level of risk, then this fund may be an option.

Data Date	Investment Rating	Net Assets ($Mil)	Price	Performance Rating/Pts	Total Return Y-T-D	Risk Rating/Pts
3-12	C	314.35	64.65	C- / 4.0	-0.80%	B+ / 9.1
2011	A	360.50	65.25	B+ / 8.7	0.92%	B+ / 9.1
2010	B	250.80	54.35	C / 5.2	8.49%	B / 8.4

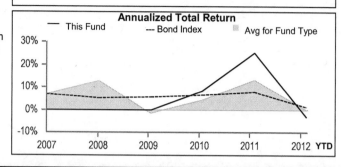

*PIMCO 25+ Year Zero Coupon US Tr (ZROZ)

C   **Fair**

Fund Family: PIMCO
Fund Type: US Government/Agency
Inception Date: October 30, 2009

Major Rating Factors: Middle of the road best describes *PIMCO 25+ Year Zero Coupon US Tr whose TheStreet.com Investment Rating is currently a C (Fair). The fund currently has a performance rating of C+ (Fair) based on an annualized return of 0.00% over the last three years and a total return of -12.22% year to date 2012. Factored into the performance evaluation is an expense ratio of 0.15% (very low).

The fund's risk rating is currently B- (Good). It carries a beta of 0.00, meaning the fund's expected move will be 0.0% for every 10% move in the market. Volatility, as measured by both the semi-deviation and a drawdown factor, is considered low. As of March 31, 2012, *PIMCO 25+ Year Zero Coupon US Tr traded at a premium of .05% above its net asset value, which is worse than its one-year historical average discount of .19%.

Vineer Bhansali has been running the fund for 3 years and currently receives a manager quality ranking of 21 (0=worst, 99=best). If you desire an average level of risk, then this fund may be an option.

Data Date	Investment Rating	Net Assets ($Mil)	Price	Performance Rating/Pts	Total Return Y-T-D	Risk Rating/Pts
3-12	C	69.58	97.14	C+ / 6.0	-12.22%	B- / 7.1
2011	B+	64.50	111.50	A+ / 9.9	-3.82%	B- / 7.2
2010	D	53.50	72.30	D- / 1.0	8.61%	C+ / 6.8

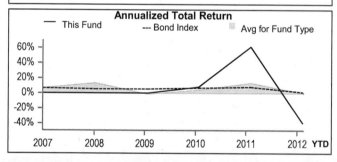

*PIMCO 3-7 Year US Treasury Index (FIVZ)

C-   **Fair**

Fund Family: PIMCO
Fund Type: US Government/Agency
Inception Date: October 30, 2009

Major Rating Factors:
Disappointing performance is the major factor driving the C- (Fair) TheStreet.com Investment Rating for *PIMCO 3-7 Year US Treasury Index. The fund currently has a performance rating of D (Weak) based on an annualized return of 0.00% over the last three years and a total return of -0.09% year to date 2012. Factored into the performance evaluation is an expense ratio of 0.15% (very low).

The fund's risk rating is currently B+ (Good). It carries a beta of 0.00, meaning the fund's expected move will be 0.0% for every 10% move in the market. Volatility, as measured by both the semi-deviation and a drawdown factor, is considered very low. As of March 31, 2012, *PIMCO 3-7 Year US Treasury Index traded at a premium of .19% above its net asset value, which is worse than its one-year historical average discount of .04%.

Vineer Bhansali has been running the fund for 3 years and currently receives a manager quality ranking of 72 (0=worst, 99=best). This fund offers only a moderate level of risk but investors looking for strong performance are still waiting.

Data Date	Investment Rating	Net Assets ($Mil)	Price	Performance Rating/Pts	Total Return Y-T-D	Risk Rating/Pts
3-12	C-	21.69	80.83	D / 1.8	-0.09%	B+ / 9.6
2011	C+	21.70	81.26	C- / 3.7	0.14%	B+ / 9.7
2010	B-	51.30	76.95	C- / 4.0	6.22%	B / 8.8

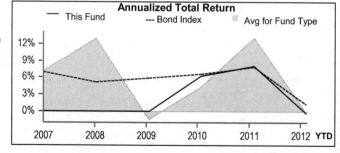

*PIMCO 7-15 Year US Treasury Inde (TENZ)   C-   Fair

Fund Family: PIMCO
Fund Type: US Government/Agency
Inception Date: September 10, 2009

Data Date	Investment Rating	Net Assets ($Mil)	Price	Performance Rating/Pts	Total Return Y-T-D	Risk Rating/Pts
3-12	C-	15.95	84.44	D+ / 2.5	-1.09%	B+ / 9.3
2011	B	16.00	85.79	C+ / 6.0	-0.49%	B+ / 9.3
2010	C+	14.30	76.37	C- / 3.7	8.28%	B / 8.4

Major Rating Factors:
Disappointing performance is the major factor driving the C- (Fair) TheStreet.com Investment Rating for *PIMCO 7-15 Year US Treasury Inde. The fund currently has a performance rating of D+ (Weak) based on an annualized return of 0.00% over the last three years and a total return of -1.09% year to date 2012. Factored into the performance evaluation is an expense ratio of 0.15% (very low).

The fund's risk rating is currently B+ (Good). It carries a beta of 0.00, meaning the fund's expected move will be 0.0% for every 10% move in the market. Volatility, as measured by both the semi-deviation and a drawdown factor, is considered very low. As of March 31, 2012, *PIMCO 7-15 Year US Treasury Inde traded at a premium of .66% above its net asset value, which is worse than its one-year historical average discount of .02%.

Vineer Bhansali has been running the fund for 3 years and currently receives a manager quality ranking of 74 (0=worst, 99=best). This fund offers only a moderate level of risk but investors looking for strong performance are still waiting.

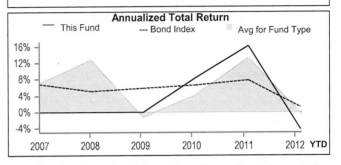

*PIMCO Broad US TIPS Index (TIPZ)   C   Fair

Fund Family: PIMCO
Fund Type: US Government/Agency
Inception Date: September 3, 2009

Data Date	Investment Rating	Net Assets ($Mil)	Price	Performance Rating/Pts	Total Return Y-T-D	Risk Rating/Pts
3-12	C	102.61	58.65	D+ / 2.5	0.62%	B+ / 9.7
2011	B	95.00	58.29	C+ / 5.7	0.63%	B+ / 9.7
2010	B	38.80	53.13	C / 4.5	5.94%	B / 8.8

Major Rating Factors:
Disappointing performance is the major factor driving the C (Fair) TheStreet.com Investment Rating for *PIMCO Broad US TIPS Index. The fund currently has a performance rating of D+ (Weak) based on an annualized return of 0.00% over the last three years and a total return of 0.62% year to date 2012. Factored into the performance evaluation is an expense ratio of 0.20% (very low).

The fund's risk rating is currently B+ (Good). It carries a beta of 0.00, meaning the fund's expected move will be 0.0% for every 10% move in the market. Volatility, as measured by both the semi-deviation and a drawdown factor, is considered very low. As of March 31, 2012, *PIMCO Broad US TIPS Index traded at a premium of .03% above its net asset value, which is in line with its one-year historical average premium of .03%.

Vineer Bhansali has been running the fund for 3 years and currently receives a manager quality ranking of 87 (0=worst, 99=best). This fund offers only a moderate level of risk but investors looking for strong performance are still waiting.

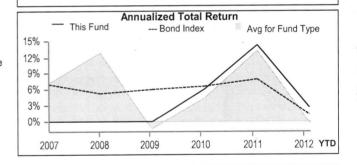

*PIMCO Build America Bond Strateg (BABZ)   C+   Fair

Fund Family: PIMCO
Fund Type: US Government/Agency
Inception Date: September 20, 2010

Data Date	Investment Rating	Net Assets ($Mil)	Price	Performance Rating/Pts	Total Return Y-T-D	Risk Rating/Pts
3-12	C+	42.15	54.45	C / 4.8	2.82%	B+ / 9.4
2011	B+	24.60	53.47	B- / 7.2	-0.97%	B+ / 9.5

Major Rating Factors: Middle of the road best describes *PIMCO Build America Bond Strateg whose TheStreet.com Investment Rating is currently a C+ (Fair). The fund currently has a performance rating of C (Fair) based on an annualized return of 0.00% over the last three years and a total return of 2.82% year to date 2012. Factored into the performance evaluation is an expense ratio of 0.45% (very low).

The fund's risk rating is currently B+ (Good). It carries a beta of 0.00, meaning the fund's expected move will be 0.0% for every 10% move in the market. Volatility, as measured by both the semi-deviation and a drawdown factor, is considered very low. As of March 31, 2012, *PIMCO Build America Bond Strateg traded at a discount of .02% below its net asset value, which is worse than its one-year historical average discount of .08%.

Joseph P. Deane has been running the fund for 1 year and currently receives a manager quality ranking of 88 (0=worst, 99=best). If you desire an average level of risk, then this fund may be an option.

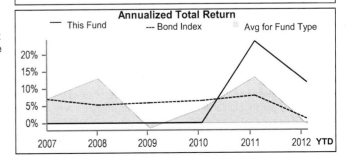

*PIMCO Enhanced Short Maturity St (MINT)

C-   **Fair**

Fund Family: PIMCO
Fund Type: Corporate - Investment Grade
Inception Date: November 16, 2009

Data Date	Investment Rating	Net Assets ($Mil)	Price	Performance Rating/Pts	Total Return Y-T-D	Risk Rating/Pts
3-12	C-	1,429.95	101.03	D- / 1.3	1.16%	B+ / 9.9
2011	C-	1,803.30	100.16	D / 2.0	-0.03%	B+ / 9.9
2010	C+	785.20	100.71	C- / 3.0	1.61%	B+ / 9.0

Major Rating Factors:
Disappointing performance is the major factor driving the C- (Fair) TheStreet.com Investment Rating for *PIMCO Enhanced Short Maturity St. The fund currently has a performance rating of D- (Weak) based on an annualized return of 0.00% over the last three years and a total return of 1.16% year to date 2012. Factored into the performance evaluation is an expense ratio of 0.35% (very low).

The fund's risk rating is currently B+ (Good). It carries a beta of 0.00, meaning the fund's expected move will be 0.0% for every 10% move in the market. Volatility, as measured by both the semi-deviation and a drawdown factor, is considered very low. As of March 31, 2012, *PIMCO Enhanced Short Maturity St traded at a premium of .01% above its net asset value, which is in line with its one-year historical average premium of .01%.

Jerome M. Schneider has been running the fund for 3 years and currently receives a manager quality ranking of 52 (0=worst, 99=best). This fund offers only a moderate level of risk but investors looking for strong performance are still waiting.

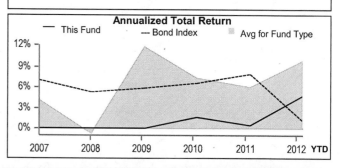

*PIMCO Intermediate Muncipal Bd S (MUNI)

C   **Fair**

Fund Family: PIMCO
Fund Type: Municipal - National
Inception Date: November 30, 2009

Data Date	Investment Rating	Net Assets ($Mil)	Price	Performance Rating/Pts	Total Return Y-T-D	Risk Rating/Pts
3-12	C	126.86	53.21	D+ / 2.8	0.72%	B+ / 9.7
2011	B	98.60	53.12	C+ / 5.6	0.17%	B+ / 9.8
2010	C+	63.40	50.37	C- / 3.4	3.50%	B / 8.9

Major Rating Factors:
Disappointing performance is the major factor driving the C (Fair) TheStreet.com Investment Rating for *PIMCO Intermediate Muncipal Bd S. The fund currently has a performance rating of D+ (Weak) based on an annualized return of 0.00% over the last three years and a total return of 0.72% year to date 2012. Factored into the performance evaluation is an expense ratio of 0.35% (very low).

The fund's risk rating is currently B+ (Good). It carries a beta of 0.00, meaning the fund's expected move will be 0.0% for every 10% move in the market. Volatility, as measured by both the semi-deviation and a drawdown factor, is considered very low. As of March 31, 2012, *PIMCO Intermediate Muncipal Bd S traded at a premium of .13% above its net asset value, which is worse than its one-year historical average premium of .02%.

Joseph P. Deane has been running the fund for 1 year and currently receives a manager quality ranking of 35 (0=worst, 99=best). This fund offers only a moderate level of risk but investors looking for strong performance are still waiting.

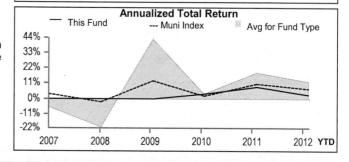

*PIMCO Investment Grade Corp Bond (CORP)

C   **Fair**

Fund Family: PIMCO
Fund Type: Corporate - Investment Grade
Inception Date: September 20, 2010

Data Date	Investment Rating	Net Assets ($Mil)	Price	Performance Rating/Pts	Total Return Y-T-D	Risk Rating/Pts
3-12	C	212.77	103.88	D+ / 2.5	3.91%	B+ / 9.7
2011	C+	186.40	100.71	C- / 3.4	1.00%	B+ / 9.8

Major Rating Factors:
Disappointing performance is the major factor driving the C (Fair) TheStreet.com Investment Rating for *PIMCO Investment Grade Corp Bond. The fund currently has a performance rating of D+ (Weak) based on an annualized return of 0.00% over the last three years and a total return of 3.91% year to date 2012. Factored into the performance evaluation is an expense ratio of 0.20% (very low).

The fund's risk rating is currently B+ (Good). It carries a beta of 0.00, meaning the fund's expected move will be 0.0% for every 10% move in the market. Volatility, as measured by both the semi-deviation and a drawdown factor, is considered very low. As of March 31, 2012, *PIMCO Investment Grade Corp Bond traded at a premium of .27% above its net asset value, which is worse than its one-year historical average premium of .09%.

Vineer Bhansali has been running the fund for 2 years and currently receives a manager quality ranking of 35 (0=worst, 99=best). This fund offers only a moderate level of risk but investors looking for strong performance are still waiting.

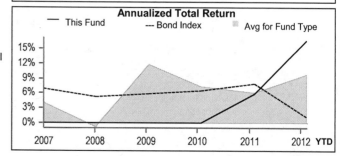

*PIMCO Short Term Muncipal Bond S (SMMU)

C- **Fair**

Fund Family: PIMCO
Fund Type: Municipal - National
Inception Date: February 1, 2010

Data Date	Investment Rating	Net Assets ($Mil)	Price	Performance Rating/Pts	Total Return Y-T-D	Risk Rating/Pts
3-12	C-	38.42	50.57	D- / 1.4	0.55%	B+ / 9.9
2011	C	38.30	50.44	D+ / 2.4	-0.10%	B+ / 9.9

Major Rating Factors:
Disappointing performance is the major factor driving the C- (Fair) TheStreet.com Investment Rating for *PIMCO Short Term Muncipal Bond S. The fund currently has a performance rating of D- (Weak) based on an annualized return of 0.00% over the last three years and a total return of 0.55% year to date 2012. Factored into the performance evaluation is an expense ratio of 0.35% (very low).

The fund's risk rating is currently B+ (Good). It carries a beta of 0.00, meaning the fund's expected move will be 0.0% for every 10% move in the market. Volatility, as measured by both the semi-deviation and a drawdown factor, is considered very low. As of March 31, 2012, *PIMCO Short Term Muncipal Bond S traded at a premium of .16% above its net asset value.

Joseph P. Deane has been running the fund for 1 year and currently receives a manager quality ranking of 57 (0=worst, 99=best). This fund offers only a moderate level of risk but investors looking for strong performance are still waiting.

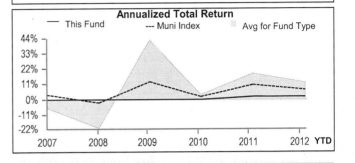

*PowerShares 1-30 Laddered Treasu (PLW)

C- **Fair**

Fund Family: Invesco Powershares Capital Mgmt LL
Fund Type: US Government/Agency
Inception Date: October 11, 2007

Data Date	Investment Rating	Net Assets ($Mil)	Price	Performance Rating/Pts	Total Return Y-T-D	Risk Rating/Pts
3-12	C-	158.44	31.11	D / 1.9	-3.64%	B+ / 9.1
2011	C	0.00	32.47	C- / 4.2	-0.80%	B / 8.8
2010	B-	280.30	27.95	C / 4.4	9.11%	B / 8.3
2009	C-	89.22	26.57	E+ / 0.8	-9.60%	B / 8.5

Major Rating Factors:
Disappointing performance is the major factor driving the C- (Fair) TheStreet.com Investment Rating for *PowerShares 1-30 Laddered Treasu. The fund currently has a performance rating of D (Weak) based on an annualized return of 6.22% over the last three years and a total return of -3.64% year to date 2012. Factored into the performance evaluation is an expense ratio of 0.25% (very low).

The fund's risk rating is currently B+ (Good). It carries a beta of 0.74, meaning the fund's expected move will be 7.4% for every 10% move in the market. Volatility, as measured by both the semi-deviation and a drawdown factor, is considered very low. As of March 31, 2012, *PowerShares 1-30 Laddered Treasu traded at a discount of .16% below its net asset value.

Peter Hubbard has been running the fund for 5 years and currently receives a manager quality ranking of 47 (0=worst, 99=best). This fund offers only a moderate level of risk but investors looking for strong performance are still waiting.

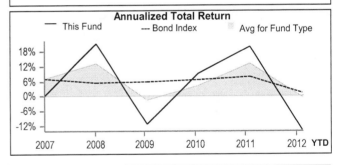

*PowerShares Act US Real Estate (PSR)

A- **Excellent**

Fund Family: Invesco Powershares Capital Mgmt LL
Fund Type: Growth and Income
Inception Date: November 19, 2008

Data Date	Investment Rating	Net Assets ($Mil)	Price	Performance Rating/Pts	Total Return Y-T-D	Risk Rating/Pts
3-12	A-	23.70	54.33	A- / 9.0	8.37%	B / 8.1
2011	C+	20.10	50.42	B / 7.6	-0.09%	C+ / 6.8
2010	A	16.00	45.81	A / 9.4	26.87%	C+ / 6.6
2009	A+	2.62	37.42	A- / 9.1	29.23%	C+ / 6.5

Major Rating Factors:
Exceptional performance is the major factor driving the A- (Excellent) TheStreet.com Investment Rating for *PowerShares Act US Real Estate. The fund currently has a performance rating of A- (Excellent) based on an annualized return of 35.50% over the last three years and a total return of 8.37% year to date 2012. Factored into the performance evaluation is an expense ratio of 0.80% (very low).

The fund's risk rating is currently B (Good). It carries a beta of 1.19, meaning it is expected to move 11.9% for every 10% move in the market. Volatility, as measured by both the semi-deviation and a drawdown factor, is considered low. As of March 31, 2012, *PowerShares Act US Real Estate traded at a discount of .24% below its net asset value, which is better than its one-year historical average premium of .03%.

Joseph V. Rodriguez, Jr. has been running the fund for 4 years and currently receives a manager quality ranking of 85 (0=worst, 99=best). If you desire only a moderate level of risk and strong performance, then this fund is an excellent option.

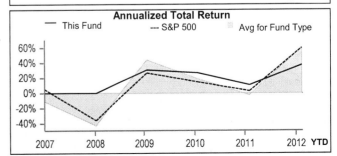

*PowerShares Active Low Dur Fd (PLK)

C-   **Fair**

Fund Family: Invesco Powershares Capital Mgmt LL
Fund Type: Growth and Income
Inception Date: April 8, 2008

Major Rating Factors:
Disappointing performance is the major factor driving the C- (Fair) TheStreet.com Investment Rating for *PowerShares Active Low Dur Fd. The fund currently has a performance rating of D- (Weak) based on an annualized return of 1.74% over the last three years and a total return of 0.26% year to date 2012. Factored into the performance evaluation is an expense ratio of 0.29% (very low).

The fund's risk rating is currently B+ (Good). It carries a beta of -0.02, meaning the fund's expected move will be -0.2% for every 10% move in the market. Volatility, as measured by both the semi-deviation and a drawdown factor, is considered very low. As of March 31, 2012, *PowerShares Active Low Dur Fd traded at a premium of .12% above its net asset value, which is worse than its one-year historical average discount of .05%.

Brian Schneider has been running the fund for 3 years and currently receives a manager quality ranking of 58 (0=worst, 99=best). This fund offers only a moderate level of risk but investors looking for strong performance are still waiting.

Data Date	Investment Rating	Net Assets ($Mil)	Price	Perfor-mance Rating/Pts	Total Return Y-T-D	Risk Rating/Pts
3-12	C-	7.64	25.45	D- / 1.3	0.26%	B+ / 9.9
2011	C	7.60	25.43	D / 2.1	-0.51%	B+ / 9.9
2010	C+	10.10	25.33	D+ / 2.6	1.68%	B+ / 9.1
2009	C	6.32	25.32	D / 2.1	1.52%	B+ / 9.2

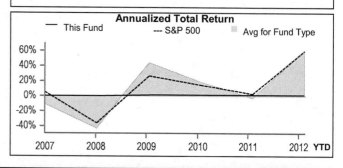

*PowerShares Active Mega-Cap Fd (PMA)

C+   **Fair**

Fund Family: Invesco Powershares Capital Mgmt LL
Fund Type: Growth
Inception Date: April 8, 2008

Major Rating Factors: Middle of the road best describes *PowerShares Active Mega-Cap Fd whose TheStreet.com Investment Rating is currently a C+ (Fair). The fund currently has a performance rating of C+ (Fair) based on an annualized return of 21.23% over the last three years and a total return of 12.29% year to date 2012. Factored into the performance evaluation is an expense ratio of 0.75% (very low).

The fund's risk rating is currently B (Good). It carries a beta of 0.90, meaning that its performance tracks fairly well with that of the overall stock market. Volatility, as measured by both the semi-deviation and a drawdown factor, is considered low. As of March 31, 2012, *PowerShares Active Mega-Cap Fd traded at a premium of .27% above its net asset value, which is worse than its one-year historical average premium of .21%.

Anthony J. Munchak has been running the fund for 4 years and currently receives a manager quality ranking of 56 (0=worst, 99=best). If you desire an average level of risk, then this fund may be an option.

Data Date	Investment Rating	Net Assets ($Mil)	Price	Perfor-mance Rating/Pts	Total Return Y-T-D	Risk Rating/Pts
3-12	C+	10.00	29.51	C+ / 6.0	12.29%	B / 8.5
2011	C+	5.30	26.36	C+ / 5.8	1.63%	B / 8.2
2010	A	3.70	24.90	A- / 9.0	11.55%	C+ / 6.4
2009	A	1.82	22.83	B / 8.0	22.63%	C+ / 6.4

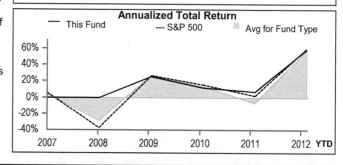

*PowerShares Aerospace & Defense (PPA)

C   **Fair**

Fund Family: Invesco Powershares Capital Mgmt LL
Fund Type: Income
Inception Date: October 26, 2005

Major Rating Factors: Middle of the road best describes *PowerShares Aerospace & Defense whose TheStreet.com Investment Rating is currently a C (Fair). The fund currently has a performance rating of C (Fair) based on an annualized return of 19.21% over the last three years and a total return of 10.77% year to date 2012. Factored into the performance evaluation is an expense ratio of 0.66% (very low).

The fund's risk rating is currently B (Good). It carries a beta of 1.11, meaning it is expected to move 11.1% for every 10% move in the market. Volatility, as measured by both the semi-deviation and a drawdown factor, is considered low. As of March 31, 2012, *PowerShares Aerospace & Defense traded at a premium of .10% above its net asset value, which is worse than its one-year historical average discount of .03%.

Peter Hubbard has been running the fund for 5 years and currently receives a manager quality ranking of 24 (0=worst, 99=best). If you desire an average level of risk, then this fund may be an option.

Data Date	Investment Rating	Net Assets ($Mil)	Price	Perfor-mance Rating/Pts	Total Return Y-T-D	Risk Rating/Pts
3-12	C	58.00	20.15	C / 4.7	10.77%	B / 8.0
2011	C-	53.70	18.20	C- / 3.7	1.21%	B- / 7.7
2010	D+	110.40	18.71	D+ / 2.3	10.93%	C+ / 5.8
2009	C-	116.43	17.07	C- / 3.0	18.16%	C+ / 5.9

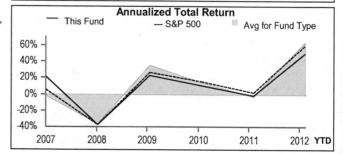

*PowerShares Build America Bond (BAB)

C+ **Fair**

Fund Family: Invesco Powershares Capital Mgmt LL
Fund Type: US Government/Agency
Inception Date: November 17, 2009

Major Rating Factors: Middle of the road best describes *PowerShares Build America Bond whose TheStreet.com Investment Rating is currently a C+ (Fair). The fund currently has a performance rating of C (Fair) based on an annualized return of 0.00% over the last three years and a total return of 2.55% year to date 2012. Factored into the performance evaluation is an expense ratio of 0.28% (very low).

The fund's risk rating is currently B+ (Good). It carries a beta of 0.00, meaning the fund's expected move will be 0.0% for every 10% move in the market. Volatility, as measured by both the semi-deviation and a drawdown factor, is considered very low. As of March 31, 2012, *PowerShares Build America Bond traded at a premium of .03% above its net asset value, which is better than its one-year historical average premium of .05%.

Peter Hubbard has been running the fund for 3 years and currently receives a manager quality ranking of 87 (0=worst, 99=best). If you desire an average level of risk, then this fund may be an option.

Data Date	Investment Rating	Net Assets ($Mil)	Price	Performance Rating/Pts	Total Return Y-T-D	Risk Rating/Pts
3-12	C+	870.51	29.06	C / 4.3	2.55%	B+ / 9.3
2011	B+	777.10	28.70	B- / 7.2	-0.42%	B+ / 9.4
2010	B-	606.70	25.08	C- / 4.0	8.81%	B / 8.6

Annualized Total Return

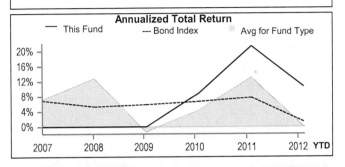

— This Fund   --- Bond Index   Avg for Fund Type

*PowerShares Buyback Achievers (PKW)

B **Good**

Fund Family: Invesco Powershares Capital Mgmt LL
Fund Type: Income
Inception Date: December 20, 2006

Major Rating Factors: Strong performance is the major factor driving the B (Good) TheStreet.com Investment Rating for *PowerShares Buyback Achievers. The fund currently has a performance rating of B- (Good) based on an annualized return of 25.49% over the last three years and a total return of 10.78% year to date 2012. Factored into the performance evaluation is an expense ratio of 0.70% (very low).

The fund's risk rating is currently B (Good). It carries a beta of 0.93, meaning that its performance tracks fairly well with that of the overall stock market. Volatility, as measured by both the semi-deviation and a drawdown factor, is considered low. As of March 31, 2012, *PowerShares Buyback Achievers traded at a premium of .17% above its net asset value, which is worse than its one-year historical average premium of .05%.

Peter Hubbard has been running the fund for 5 years and currently receives a manager quality ranking of 75 (0=worst, 99=best). If you desire only a moderate level of risk and strong performance, then this fund is an excellent option.

Data Date	Investment Rating	Net Assets ($Mil)	Price	Performance Rating/Pts	Total Return Y-T-D	Risk Rating/Pts
3-12	B	116.98	29.35	B- / 7.3	10.78%	B / 8.6
2011	B-	74.20	26.53	C+ / 6.9	1.06%	B / 8.1
2010	C+	35.20	24.32	C+ / 6.1	18.11%	C / 5.2
2009	C-	27.46	20.70	D+ / 2.7	29.72%	C+ / 6.2

Annualized Total Return

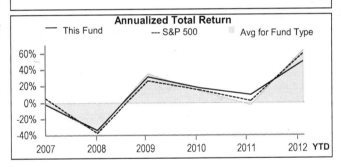

— This Fund   --- S&P 500   Avg for Fund Type

*PowerShares CEF Inc Composite Po (PCEF)

C **Fair**

Fund Family: Invesco Powershares Capital Mgmt LL
Fund Type: Income
Inception Date: February 18, 2010

Major Rating Factors: Middle of the road best describes *PowerShares CEF Inc Composite Po whose TheStreet.com Investment Rating is currently a C (Fair). The fund currently has a performance rating of C- (Fair) based on an annualized return of 0.00% over the last three years and a total return of 8.33% year to date 2012. Factored into the performance evaluation is an expense ratio of 0.50% (very low).

The fund's risk rating is currently B (Good). It carries a beta of 0.00, meaning the fund's expected move will be 0.0% for every 10% move in the market. Volatility, as measured by both the semi-deviation and a drawdown factor, is considered low. As of March 31, 2012, *PowerShares CEF Inc Composite Po traded at a premium of .16% above its net asset value, which is worse than its one-year historical average premium of .08%.

This fund has been team managed for 2 years and currently receives a manager quality ranking of 55 (0=worst, 99=best). If you desire an average level of risk, then this fund may be an option.

Data Date	Investment Rating	Net Assets ($Mil)	Price	Performance Rating/Pts	Total Return Y-T-D	Risk Rating/Pts
3-12	C	271.22	24.97	C- / 3.5	8.33%	B / 8.6
2011	C-	233.40	23.51	D+ / 2.6	1.61%	B / 8.6

Annualized Total Return

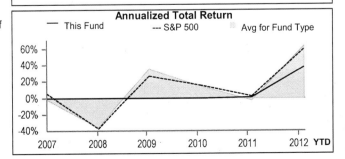

— This Fund   --- S&P 500   Avg for Fund Type

*PowerShares Cleantech Portfolio (PZD)   D   Weak

Fund Family: Invesco Powershares Capital Mgmt LL
Fund Type: Income
Inception Date: October 24, 2006

Major Rating Factors:
Disappointing performance is the major factor driving the D (Weak) TheStreet.com Investment Rating for *PowerShares Cleantech Portfolio. The fund currently has a performance rating of D+ (Weak) based on an annualized return of 11.20% over the last three years and a total return of 11.12% year to date 2012. Factored into the performance evaluation is an expense ratio of 0.67% (very low).

The fund's risk rating is currently B- (Good). It carries a beta of 1.46, meaning it is expected to move 14.6% for every 10% move in the market. Volatility, as measured by both the semi-deviation and a drawdown factor, is considered low. As of March 31, 2012, *PowerShares Cleantech Portfolio traded at a discount of .17% below its net asset value, which is worse than its one-year historical average discount of .34%.

Peter Hubbard has been running the fund for 5 years and currently receives a manager quality ranking of 9 (0=worst, 99=best). This fund offers only a moderate level of risk but investors looking for strong performance are still waiting.

Data Date	Investment Rating	Net Assets ($Mil)	Price	Perfor-mance Rating/Pts	Total Return Y-T-D	Risk Rating/Pts
3-12	D	106.62	23.88	D+ / 2.4	11.12%	B- / 7.0
2011	D	97.30	21.51	D / 2.2	0.69%	C+ / 6.5
2010	D-	147.10	26.40	D- / 1.5	7.61%	C / 4.4
2009	D+	111.67	24.54	C- / 3.9	30.82%	C / 4.6

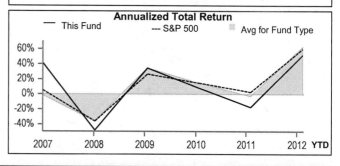

Annualized Total Return

*PowerShares DB 3x German Bd Fut (BUNT)   B-   Good

Fund Family: DB Commodity Services LLC
Fund Type: Global
Inception Date: March 22, 2011

Major Rating Factors:
Exceptional performance is the major factor driving the B- (Good) TheStreet.com Investment Rating for *PowerShares DB 3x German Bd Fut. The fund currently has a performance rating of A+ (Excellent) based on an annualized return of 0.00% over the last three years and a total return of 2.08% year to date 2012. Factored into the performance evaluation is an expense ratio of 0.95% (low).

The fund's risk rating is currently C+ (Fair). It carries a beta of 0.00, meaning the fund's expected move will be 0.0% for every 10% move in the market. Volatility, as measured by both the semi-deviation and a drawdown factor, is considered low. As of March 31, 2012, *PowerShares DB 3x German Bd Fut traded at a discount of .10% below its net asset value, which is better than its one-year historical average discount of .05%.

This fund has been team managed for 1 year and currently receives a manager quality ranking of 99 (0=worst, 99=best). If you desire only a moderate level of risk and strong performance, then this fund is an excellent option.

Data Date	Investment Rating	Net Assets ($Mil)	Price	Perfor-mance Rating/Pts	Total Return Y-T-D	Risk Rating/Pts
3-12	B-	37.86	30.36	A+ / 9.6	2.08%	C+ / 5.6

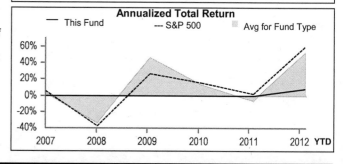

Annualized Total Return

*PowerShares DB 3x Itn Trs B Fut (ITLT)   C+   Fair

Fund Family: DB Commodity Services LLC
Fund Type: Global
Inception Date: March 22, 2011

Major Rating Factors:
Exceptional performance is the major factor driving the C+ (Fair) TheStreet.com Investment Rating for *PowerShares DB 3x Itn Trs B Fut. The fund currently has a performance rating of A+ (Excellent) based on an annualized return of 0.00% over the last three years and a total return of 55.81% year to date 2012. Factored into the performance evaluation is an expense ratio of 0.95% (low).

The fund's risk rating is currently C- (Fair). It carries a beta of 0.00, meaning the fund's expected move will be 0.0% for every 10% move in the market. Volatility, as measured by both the semi-deviation and a drawdown factor, is considered average. As of March 31, 2012, *PowerShares DB 3x Itn Trs B Fut traded at a premium of 3.58% above its net asset value, which is worse than its one-year historical average discount of 7.03%.

This fund has been team managed for 1 year and currently receives a manager quality ranking of 69 (0=worst, 99=best). If you desire an average level of risk and strong performance, then this fund is a good option.

Data Date	Investment Rating	Net Assets ($Mil)	Price	Perfor-mance Rating/Pts	Total Return Y-T-D	Risk Rating/Pts
3-12	C+	34.13	22.00	A+ / 9.6	55.81%	C- / 4.0

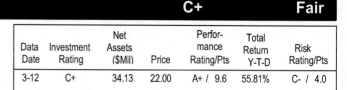

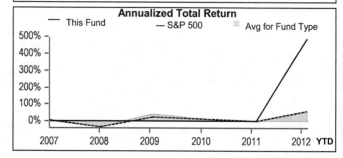

Annualized Total Return

*PowerShares DB 3x Jpne GvBd Fut (JGBT)

D-   Weak

Fund Family: DB Commodity Services LLC
Fund Type: Global
Inception Date: March 22, 2011

Data Date	Investment Rating	Net Assets ($Mil)	Price	Performance Rating/Pts	Total Return Y-T-D	Risk Rating/Pts
3-12	D-	4.34	21.37	D / 1.6	-0.70%	C+ / 5.9

Major Rating Factors:
Disappointing performance is the major factor driving the D- (Weak) TheStreet.com Investment Rating for *PowerShares DB 3x Jpne GvBd Fut. The fund currently has a performance rating of D (Weak) based on an annualized return of 0.00% over the last three years and a total return of -0.70% year to date 2012. Factored into the performance evaluation is an expense ratio of 0.95% (low).

The fund's risk rating is currently C+ (Fair). It carries a beta of 0.00, meaning the fund's expected move will be 0.0% for every 10% move in the market. Volatility, as measured by both the semi-deviation and a drawdown factor, is considered low. As of March 31, 2012, *PowerShares DB 3x Jpne GvBd Fut traded at a discount of .65% below its net asset value, which is better than its one-year historical average premium of .03%.

This fund has been team managed for 1 year and currently receives a manager quality ranking of 76 (0=worst, 99=best). This fund offers only a moderate level of risk but investors looking for strong performance are still waiting.

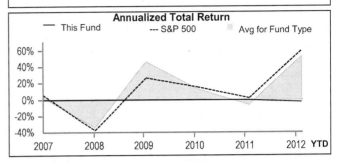
Annualized Total Return

---

*PowerShares DB 3x Lg 25+ Yr Tr E (LBND)

C+   Fair

Fund Family: DB Commodity Services LLC
Fund Type: US Government/Agency
Inception Date: June 28, 2010

Data Date	Investment Rating	Net Assets ($Mil)	Price	Performance Rating/Pts	Total Return Y-T-D	Risk Rating/Pts
3-12	C+	27.13	37.10	A / 9.5	-18.94%	C / 4.8
2011	B	0.00	45.77	A+ / 9.9	-7.78%	C / 5.4

Major Rating Factors:
Exceptional performance is the major factor driving the C+ (Fair) TheStreet.com Investment Rating for *PowerShares DB 3x Lg 25+ Yr Tr E. The fund currently has a performance rating of A (Excellent) based on an annualized return of 0.00% over the last three years and a total return of -18.94% year to date 2012. Factored into the performance evaluation is an expense ratio of 0.95% (low).

The fund's risk rating is currently C (Fair). It carries a beta of 0.00, meaning the fund's expected move will be 0.0% for every 10% move in the market. Volatility, as measured by both the semi-deviation and a drawdown factor, is considered average. As of March 31, 2012, *PowerShares DB 3x Lg 25+ Yr Tr E traded at a discount of .40% below its net asset value, which is better than its one-year historical average discount of .08%.

This fund has been team managed for 2 years and currently receives a manager quality ranking of 23 (0=worst, 99=best). If you desire an average level of risk and strong performance, then this fund is a good option.

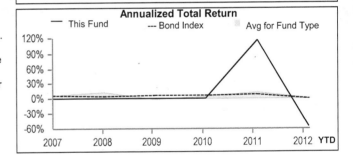
Annualized Total Return

---

*PowerShares DB 3x Sh 25+ Yr Tr E (SBND)

E-   Very Weak

Fund Family: DB Commodity Services LLC
Fund Type: US Government/Agency
Inception Date: June 28, 2010

Data Date	Investment Rating	Net Assets ($Mil)	Price	Performance Rating/Pts	Total Return Y-T-D	Risk Rating/Pts
3-12	E-	20.22	10.80	E / 0.5	20.40%	D / 1.9
2011	E-	0.00	8.97	E- / 0	7.80%	D / 1.9

Major Rating Factors: *PowerShares DB 3x Sh 25+ Yr Tr E has adopted a very risky asset allocation strategy and currently receives an overall TheStreet.com Investment Rating of E- (Very Weak). The fund has a high level of volatility, as measured by both semi-deviation and drawdown factors. It carries a beta of 0.00, meaning the fund's expected move will be 0.0% for every 10% move in the market. As of March 31, 2012, *PowerShares DB 3x Sh 25+ Yr Tr E traded at a premium of .84% above its net asset value, which is worse than its one-year historical average premium of .17%. Unfortunately, the high level of risk (D, Weak) failed to pay off as investors endured very poor performance.

The fund's performance rating is currently E (Very Weak). It has registered an annualized return of 0.00% over the last three years and is up 20.40% year to date 2012. Factored into the performance evaluation is an expense ratio of 0.95% (low).

This fund has been team managed for 2 years and currently receives a manager quality ranking of 14 (0=worst, 99=best). If you can tolerate very high levels of risk in the hope of improved future returns, holding this fund may be an option.

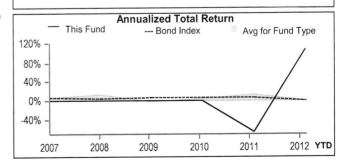
Annualized Total Return

* Denotes ETF Fund

*PowerShares DB Agri Double Long (DAG)

E+   **Very Weak**

Fund Family: Deutsche Bank AG (London)
Fund Type: Growth
Inception Date: April 15, 2008

Major Rating Factors:
Disappointing performance is the major factor driving the E+ (Very Weak) TheStreet.com Investment Rating for *PowerShares DB Agri Double Long. The fund currently has a performance rating of D- (Weak) based on an annualized return of 5.99% over the last three years and a total return of 2.97% year to date 2012. Factored into the performance evaluation is an expense ratio of 0.75% (very low).

The fund's risk rating is currently C- (Fair). It carries a beta of 1.30, meaning it is expected to move 13.0% for every 10% move in the market. Volatility, as measured by both the semi-deviation and a drawdown factor, is considered average. As of March 31, 2012, *PowerShares DB Agri Double Long traded at a premium of 2.49% above its net asset value, which is worse than its one-year historical average premium of 2.23%.

This fund has been team managed for 4 years and currently receives a manager quality ranking of 8 (0=worst, 99=best). This fund offers an average level of risk but investors looking for strong performance will be frustrated.

Data Date	Investment Rating	Net Assets ($Mil)	Price	Performance Rating/Pts	Total Return Y-T-D	Risk Rating/Pts
3-12	E+	87.09	11.11	D- / 1.3	2.97%	C- / 3.2
2011	E+	87.09	10.79	D- / 1.5	-0.83%	C- / 3.1
2010	C	87.09	14.07	A+ / 9.9	30.88%	D- / 1.2
2009	C-	87.09	10.75	B- / 7.4	5.29%	D / 1.8

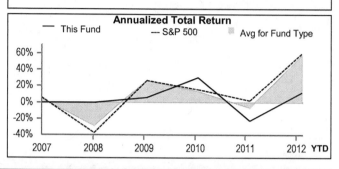

Annualized Total Return

---

*PowerShares DB Agri Double Sht (AGA)

E-   **Very Weak**

Fund Family: Deutsche Bank AG (London)
Fund Type: Growth
Inception Date: April 15, 2008

Major Rating Factors: *PowerShares DB Agri Double Sht has adopted a very risky asset allocation strategy and currently receives an overall TheStreet.com Investment Rating of E- (Very Weak). The fund has a high level of volatility, as measured by both semi-deviation and drawdown factors. It carries a beta of -1.33, meaning the fund's expected move will be -13.3% for every 10% move in the market. As of March 31, 2012, *PowerShares DB Agri Double Sht traded at a discount of 1.11% below its net asset value, which is better than its one-year historical average premium of .21%. Unfortunately, the high level of risk (D, Weak) failed to pay off as investors endured very poor performance.

The fund's performance rating is currently E (Very Weak). It has registered an annualized return of -28.06% over the last three years and is down -4.56% year to date 2012. Factored into the performance evaluation is an expense ratio of 0.75% (very low).

This fund has been team managed for 4 years and currently receives a manager quality ranking of 19 (0=worst, 99=best). If you can tolerate very high levels of risk in the hope of improved future returns, holding this fund may be an option.

Data Date	Investment Rating	Net Assets ($Mil)	Price	Performance Rating/Pts	Total Return Y-T-D	Risk Rating/Pts
3-12	E-	3.98	16.98	E / 0.5	-4.56%	D / 1.9
2011	E-	3.98	17.79	E+ / 0.9	3.42%	D / 1.9
2010	E-	3.98	18.00	E- / 0	-47.14%	D / 1.7
2009	E	3.98	34.05	E / 0.4	-19.90%	C- / 3.5

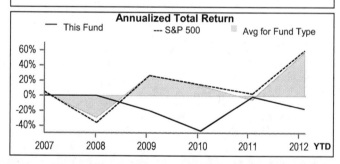

Annualized Total Return

---

*PowerShares DB Agriculture Fund (DBA)

D   **Weak**

Fund Family: DB Commodity Services LLC
Fund Type: Income
Inception Date: January 3, 2007

Major Rating Factors:
Disappointing performance is the major factor driving the D (Weak) TheStreet.com Investment Rating for *PowerShares DB Agriculture Fund. The fund currently has a performance rating of D- (Weak) based on an annualized return of 3.97% over the last three years and a total return of -2.70% year to date 2012. Factored into the performance evaluation is an expense ratio of 0.93% (low).

The fund's risk rating is currently B- (Good). It carries a beta of 0.56, meaning the fund's expected move will be 5.6% for every 10% move in the market. Volatility, as measured by both the semi-deviation and a drawdown factor, is considered low. As of March 31, 2012, *PowerShares DB Agriculture Fund traded at a discount of .04% below its net asset value, which is worse than its one-year historical average discount of .06%.

Kevin Parker currently receives a manager quality ranking of 19 (0=worst, 99=best). This fund offers only a moderate level of risk but investors looking for strong performance are still waiting.

Data Date	Investment Rating	Net Assets ($Mil)	Price	Performance Rating/Pts	Total Return Y-T-D	Risk Rating/Pts
3-12	D	2,088.45	28.10	D- / 1.2	-2.70%	B- / 7.9
2011	D+	2,034.30	28.88	D / 1.8	-1.84%	B / 8.1
2010	C	2,712.70	32.35	C / 5.3	22.35%	C+ / 5.6
2009	C-	2,327.02	26.44	C- / 4.1	1.15%	C+ / 6.0

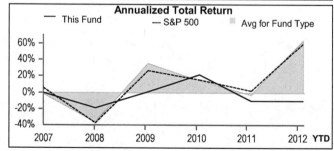

Annualized Total Return

*PowerShares DB Agriculture Long (AGF)   E+   Very Weak

Fund Family: Deutsche Bank AG (London)
Fund Type: Growth
Inception Date: April 15, 2008

Major Rating Factors:
Disappointing performance is the major factor driving the E+ (Very Weak) TheStreet.com Investment Rating for *PowerShares DB Agriculture Long. The fund currently has a performance rating of D- (Weak) based on an annualized return of 4.94% over the last three years and a total return of 0.32% year to date 2012. Factored into the performance evaluation is an expense ratio of 0.75% (very low).

The fund's risk rating is currently C (Fair). It carries a beta of 0.77, meaning the fund's expected move will be 7.7% for every 10% move in the market. Volatility, as measured by both the semi-deviation and a drawdown factor, is considered average. As of March 31, 2012, *PowerShares DB Agriculture Long traded at a discount of 1.52% below its net asset value, which is better than its one-year historical average premium of .48%.

This fund has been team managed for 4 years and currently receives a manager quality ranking of 15 (0=worst, 99=best). This fund offers an average level of risk but investors looking for strong performance will be frustrated.

Data Date	Investment Rating	Net Assets ($Mil)	Price	Performance Rating/Pts	Total Return Y-T-D	Risk Rating/Pts
3-12	E+	4.96	18.77	D- / 1.4	0.32%	C / 4.3
2011	E+	4.96	18.71	D / 1.9	-1.92%	C- / 4.1
2010	C+	4.96	20.96	A+ / 9.6	19.57%	D+ / 2.5
2009	D	4.96	17.53	C / 4.5	1.15%	C- / 3.2

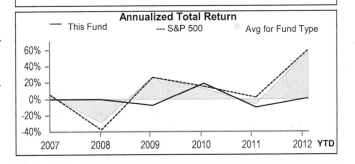

*PowerShares DB Agriculture Sht E (ADZ)   E   Very Weak

Fund Family: Deutsche Bank AG (London)
Fund Type: Growth
Inception Date: April 15, 2008

Major Rating Factors: Very poor performance is the major factor driving the E (Very Weak) TheStreet.com Investment Rating for *PowerShares DB Agriculture Sht E. The fund currently has a performance rating of E+ (Very Weak) based on an annualized return of -12.27% over the last three years and a total return of -1.55% year to date 2012. Factored into the performance evaluation is an expense ratio of 0.75% (very low).

The fund's risk rating is currently C- (Fair). It carries a beta of -0.71, meaning the fund's expected move will be -7.1% for every 10% move in the market. Volatility, as measured by both the semi-deviation and a drawdown factor, is considered average. As of March 31, 2012, *PowerShares DB Agriculture Sht E traded at a discount of .33% below its net asset value, which is better than its one-year historical average premium of .05%.

This fund has been team managed for 4 years and currently receives a manager quality ranking of 52 (0=worst, 99=best). This fund offers an average level of risk but investors looking for strong performance will be frustrated.

Data Date	Investment Rating	Net Assets ($Mil)	Price	Performance Rating/Pts	Total Return Y-T-D	Risk Rating/Pts
3-12	E	3.34	24.00	E+ / 0.8	-1.55%	C- / 3.2
2011	E+	3.34	24.38	D- / 1.4	1.61%	C- / 3.1
2010	E	3.34	23.93	E- / 0.2	-23.05%	C- / 3.1
2009	E+	3.34	31.10	E+ / 0.6	-8.02%	C / 4.4

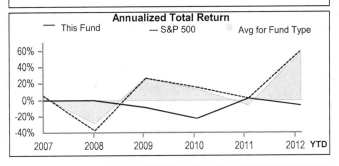

*PowerShares DB Base Metals Fund (DBB)   D   Weak

Fund Family: DB Commodity Services LLC
Fund Type: Income
Inception Date: January 3, 2007

Major Rating Factors:
Disappointing performance is the major factor driving the D (Weak) TheStreet.com Investment Rating for *PowerShares DB Base Metals Fund. The fund currently has a performance rating of D+ (Weak) based on an annualized return of 13.34% over the last three years and a total return of 7.72% year to date 2012. Factored into the performance evaluation is an expense ratio of 0.76% (very low).

The fund's risk rating is currently C+ (Fair). It carries a beta of 1.28, meaning it is expected to move 12.8% for every 10% move in the market. Volatility, as measured by both the semi-deviation and a drawdown factor, is considered low. As of March 31, 2012, *PowerShares DB Base Metals Fund traded at a discount of .05% below its net asset value, which is worse than its one-year historical average discount of .07%.

Kevin Parker currently receives a manager quality ranking of 12 (0=worst, 99=best). This fund offers only a moderate level of risk but investors looking for strong performance are still waiting.

Data Date	Investment Rating	Net Assets ($Mil)	Price	Performance Rating/Pts	Total Return Y-T-D	Risk Rating/Pts
3-12	D	382.32	20.09	D+ / 2.6	7.72%	C+ / 6.9
2011	C-	366.90	18.65	C- / 3.4	0.70%	B- / 7.0
2010	C	511.70	24.43	C+ / 6.1	8.58%	C / 4.4
2009	A	441.46	22.50	A+ / 9.8	81.01%	C / 4.9

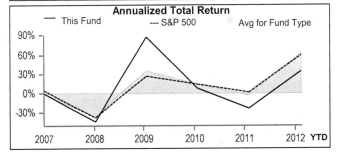

*PowerShares DB Base Metals Sht E (BOS)

E   **Very Weak**

Fund Family: Deutsche Bank AG (London)
Fund Type: Precious Metals
Inception Date: June 16, 2008

Data Date	Investment Rating	Net Assets ($Mil)	Price	Perfor-mance Rating/Pts	Total Return Y-T-D	Risk Rating/Pts
3-12	E	2.52	20.12	E+ / 0.7	-9.11%	D+ / 2.6
2011	E	2.52	22.14	D- / 1.2	0.29%	D / 2.0
2010	E-	2.52	18.49	E / 0.4	-13.44%	D / 2.0
2009	E-	2.52	21.36	E- / 0.2	-49.29%	D+ / 2.5

Major Rating Factors: *PowerShares DB Base Metals Sht E has adopted a risky asset allocation strategy and currently receives an overall TheStreet.com Investment Rating of E (Very Weak). The fund has an above average level of volatility, as measured by both semi-deviation and drawdown factors. It carries a beta of -0.31, meaning the fund's expected move will be -3.1% for every 10% move in the market. As of March 31, 2012, *PowerShares DB Base Metals Sht E traded at a discount of .69% below its net asset value, which is better than its one-year historical average premium of .06%. Unfortunately, the high level of risk (D+, Weak) failed to pay off as investors endured very poor performance.

The fund's performance rating is currently E+ (Very Weak). It has registered an annualized return of -18.86% over the last three years and is down -9.11% year to date 2012. Factored into the performance evaluation is an expense ratio of 0.75% (very low).

This fund has been team managed for 4 years and currently receives a manager quality ranking of 10 (0=worst, 99=best). If you can tolerate high levels of risk in the hope of improved future returns, holding this fund may be an option.

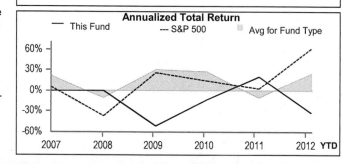

*PowerShares DB Base Mtls Dbl Lg (BDD)

D-   **Weak**

Fund Family: Deutsche Bank AG (London)
Fund Type: Precious Metals
Inception Date: June 16, 2008

Data Date	Investment Rating	Net Assets ($Mil)	Price	Perfor-mance Rating/Pts	Total Return Y-T-D	Risk Rating/Pts
3-12	D-	22.78	12.12	C- / 3.7	15.72%	C- / 3.0
2011	E+	22.78	10.47	C- / 3.1	1.05%	D+ / 2.9
2010	C	22.78	19.27	A+ / 9.7	9.12%	D- / 1.0
2009	C	22.78	17.66	A+ / 9.9	202.40%	D- / 1.2

Major Rating Factors: *PowerShares DB Base Mtls Dbl Lg receives a TheStreet.com Investment Rating of D- (Weak). The fund currently has a performance rating of C- (Fair) based on an annualized return of 20.82% over the last three years and a total return of 15.72% year to date 2012. Factored into the performance evaluation is an expense ratio of 0.75% (very low).

The fund's risk rating is currently C- (Fair). It carries a beta of 0.81, meaning the fund's expected move will be 8.1% for every 10% move in the market. Volatility, as measured by both the semi-deviation and a drawdown factor, is considered average. As of March 31, 2012, *PowerShares DB Base Mtls Dbl Lg traded at a discount of .33% below its net asset value, which is better than its one-year historical average premium of .07%.

This fund has been team managed for 4 years and currently receives a manager quality ranking of 77 (0=worst, 99=best). If you desire an average level of risk, then this fund may be an option.

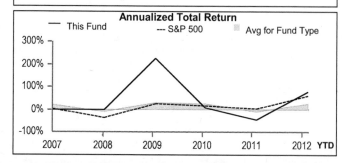

*PowerShares DB Base Mtls Dbl Sh (BOM)

E-   **Very Weak**

Fund Family: Deutsche Bank AG (London)
Fund Type: Precious Metals
Inception Date: June 16, 2008

Data Date	Investment Rating	Net Assets ($Mil)	Price	Perfor-mance Rating/Pts	Total Return Y-T-D	Risk Rating/Pts
3-12	E-	2.20	12.24	E / 0.4	-18.13%	D / 1.9
2011	E-	2.20	14.95	E+ / 0.8	-0.33%	D / 1.9
2010	E-	2.20	10.54	E- / 0.1	-33.71%	D- / 1.0
2009	E-	2.20	15.90	E- / 0	-75.52%	D- / 1.2

Major Rating Factors: *PowerShares DB Base Mtls Dbl Sh has adopted a very risky asset allocation strategy and currently receives an overall TheStreet.com Investment Rating of E- (Very Weak). The fund has a high level of volatility, as measured by both semi-deviation and drawdown factors. It carries a beta of -0.64, meaning the fund's expected move will be -6.4% for every 10% move in the market. As of March 31, 2012, *PowerShares DB Base Mtls Dbl Sh traded at a discount of .33% below its net asset value, which is better than its one-year historical average discount of .10%. Unfortunately, the high level of risk (D, Weak) failed to pay off as investors endured very poor performance.

The fund's performance rating is currently E (Very Weak). It has registered an annualized return of -37.33% over the last three years and is down -18.13% year to date 2012. Factored into the performance evaluation is an expense ratio of 0.75% (very low).

This fund has been team managed for 4 years and currently receives a manager quality ranking of 3 (0=worst, 99=best). If you can tolerate very high levels of risk in the hope of improved future returns, holding this fund may be an option.

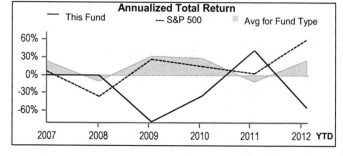

*PowerShares DB Commodity Double (DEE)

E-   **Very Weak**

Fund Family: Deutsche Bank AG (London)
Fund Type: Growth
Inception Date: April 28, 2008

Major Rating Factors: *PowerShares DB Commodity Double has adopted a very risky asset allocation strategy and currently receives an overall TheStreet.com Investment Rating of E- (Very Weak). The fund has a high level of volatility, as measured by both semi-deviation and drawdown factors. It carries a beta of -1.63, meaning the fund's expected move will be -16.3% for every 10% move in the market. As of March 31, 2012, *PowerShares DB Commodity Double traded at a premium of 6.48% above its net asset value, which is worse than its one-year historical average premium of .26%. Unfortunately, the high level of risk (D, Weak) failed to pay off as investors endured very poor performance.

The fund's performance rating is currently E (Very Weak). It has registered an annualized return of -26.72% over the last three years and is down -0.75% year to date 2012. Factored into the performance evaluation is an expense ratio of 0.75% (very low).

This fund has been team managed for 4 years and currently receives a manager quality ranking of 50 (0=worst, 99=best). If you can tolerate very high levels of risk in the hope of improved future returns, holding this fund may be an option.

Data Date	Investment Rating	Net Assets ($Mil)	Price	Performance Rating/Pts	Total Return Y-T-D	Risk Rating/Pts
3-12	E-	5.65	30.42	E / 0.5	-0.75%	D / 1.9
2011	E-	5.65	30.65	E+ / 0.6	-6.30%	D / 1.9
2010	E-	5.65	35.00	E- / 0.1	-30.83%	D / 1.9
2009	E	5.65	50.60	E / 0.3	-27.24%	C- / 3.0

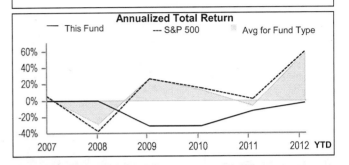

*PowerShares DB Commodity Double (DYY)

D-   **Weak**

Fund Family: Deutsche Bank AG (London)
Fund Type: Growth
Inception Date: April 28, 2008

Major Rating Factors: *PowerShares DB Commodity Double receives a TheStreet.com Investment Rating of D- (Weak). The fund currently has a performance rating of C- (Fair) based on an annualized return of 17.19% over the last three years and a total return of 9.04% year to date 2012. Factored into the performance evaluation is an expense ratio of 0.75% (very low).

The fund's risk rating is currently C- (Fair). It carries a beta of 1.83, meaning it is expected to move 18.3% for every 10% move in the market. Volatility, as measured by both the semi-deviation and a drawdown factor, is considered average. As of March 31, 2012, *PowerShares DB Commodity Double traded at a premium of .70% above its net asset value, which is worse than its one-year historical average premium of .33%.

This fund has been team managed for 4 years and currently receives a manager quality ranking of 8 (0=worst, 99=best). If you desire an average level of risk, then this fund may be an option.

Data Date	Investment Rating	Net Assets ($Mil)	Price	Performance Rating/Pts	Total Return Y-T-D	Risk Rating/Pts
3-12	D-	43.11	10.01	C- / 3.7	9.04%	C- / 3.7
2011	D	43.11	9.18	C / 4.6	4.03%	C- / 3.7
2010	C	43.11	10.00	A+ / 9.7	19.62%	D- / 1.0
2009	C-	43.11	8.36	B+ / 8.8	24.59%	D- / 1.1

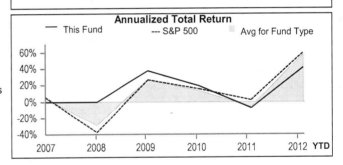

*PowerShares DB Commodity Idx Tra (DBC)

D+   **Weak**

Fund Family: DB Commodity Services LLC
Fund Type: Growth
Inception Date: February 3, 2006

Major Rating Factors:
Disappointing performance is the major factor driving the D+ (Weak) TheStreet.com Investment Rating for *PowerShares DB Commodity Idx Tra. The fund currently has a performance rating of D+ (Weak) based on an annualized return of 11.03% over the last three years and a total return of 7.30% year to date 2012. Factored into the performance evaluation is an expense ratio of 0.88% (low).

The fund's risk rating is currently B- (Good). It carries a beta of 0.85, meaning the fund's expected move will be 8.5% for every 10% move in the market. Volatility, as measured by both the semi-deviation and a drawdown factor, is considered low. As of March 31, 2012, *PowerShares DB Commodity Idx Tra traded at a premium of .31% above its net asset value, which is worse than its one-year historical average premium of .07%.

Kevin Parker currently receives a manager quality ranking of 21 (0=worst, 99=best). This fund offers only a moderate level of risk but investors looking for strong performance are still waiting.

Data Date	Investment Rating	Net Assets ($Mil)	Price	Performance Rating/Pts	Total Return Y-T-D	Risk Rating/Pts
3-12	D+	6,519.35	28.80	D+ / 2.5	7.30%	B- / 7.8
2011	C-	5,456.80	26.84	C- / 3.6	2.79%	B- / 7.8
2010	D	5,106.80	27.55	D+ / 2.7	11.90%	C / 4.7
2009	C-	3,731.03	24.62	C- / 4.0	12.27%	C / 5.2

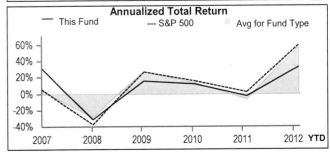

* Denotes ETF Fund

*PowerShares DB Commodity Lg ETN (DPU)

D-   **Weak**

Fund Family: Deutsche Bank AG (London)
Fund Type: Growth
Inception Date: April 28, 2008

Major Rating Factors:
Disappointing performance is the major factor driving the D- (Weak) TheStreet.com Investment Rating for *PowerShares DB Commodity Lg ETN. The fund currently has a performance rating of D+ (Weak) based on an annualized return of 10.59% over the last three years and a total return of 6.03% year to date 2012. Factored into the performance evaluation is an expense ratio of 0.75% (very low).

The fund's risk rating is currently C (Fair). It carries a beta of 0.84, meaning the fund's expected move will be 8.4% for every 10% move in the market. Volatility, as measured by both the semi-deviation and a drawdown factor, is considered average. As of March 31, 2012, *PowerShares DB Commodity Lg ETN traded at a premium of 2.27% above its net asset value, which is worse than its one-year historical average discount of .32%.

This fund has been team managed for 4 years and currently receives a manager quality ranking of 19 (0=worst, 99=best). This fund offers an average level of risk but investors looking for strong performance will be frustrated.

Data Date	Investment Rating	Net Assets ($Mil)	Price	Performance Rating/Pts	Total Return Y-T-D	Risk Rating/Pts
3-12	D-	6.87	18.45	D+ / 2.4	6.03%	C / 4.7
2011	D	6.87	17.40	C- / 3.6	2.76%	C / 4.7
2010	C	6.87	18.00	A- / 9.1	9.89%	D / 2.1
2009	C-	6.87	16.38	B- / 7.5	17.00%	D+ / 2.3

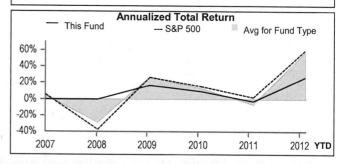

*PowerShares DB Commodity Short E (DDP)

E   **Very Weak**

Fund Family: Deutsche Bank AG (London)
Fund Type: Growth
Inception Date: April 28, 2008

Major Rating Factors: Very poor performance is the major factor driving the E (Very Weak) TheStreet.com Investment Rating for *PowerShares DB Commodity Short E. The fund currently has a performance rating of E+ (Very Weak) based on an annualized return of -12.36% over the last three years and a total return of 0.38% year to date 2012. Factored into the performance evaluation is an expense ratio of 0.75% (very low).

The fund's risk rating is currently C- (Fair). It carries a beta of -0.93, meaning the fund's expected move will be -9.3% for every 10% move in the market. Volatility, as measured by both the semi-deviation and a drawdown factor, is considered average. As of March 31, 2012, *PowerShares DB Commodity Short E traded at a premium of 4.90% above its net asset value, which is worse than its one-year historical average premium of .28%.

This fund has been team managed for 4 years and currently receives a manager quality ranking of 76 (0=worst, 99=best). This fund offers an average level of risk but investors looking for strong performance will be frustrated.

Data Date	Investment Rating	Net Assets ($Mil)	Price	Performance Rating/Pts	Total Return Y-T-D	Risk Rating/Pts
3-12	E	10.11	31.50	E+ / 0.8	0.38%	C- / 3.3
2011	E	10.11	31.38	D- / 1.2	-1.24%	C- / 3.1
2010	E+	10.11	32.50	E / 0.4	-14.16%	C- / 3.2
2009	E+	10.11	37.86	E / 0.5	-13.46%	C- / 4.0

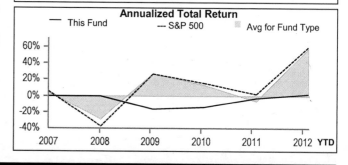

*PowerShares DB Crude Oil Dbl Sh (DTO)

E-   **Very Weak**

Fund Family: Deutsche Bank AG (London)
Fund Type: Growth
Inception Date: June 16, 2008

Major Rating Factors: *PowerShares DB Crude Oil Dbl Sh has adopted a very risky asset allocation strategy and currently receives an overall TheStreet.com Investment Rating of E- (Very Weak). The fund has a high level of volatility, as measured by both semi-deviation and drawdown factors. It carries a beta of -2.28, meaning the fund's expected move will be -22.8% for every 10% move in the market. As of March 31, 2012, *PowerShares DB Crude Oil Dbl Sh traded at a discount of .16% below its net asset value, which is worse than its one-year historical average discount of .19%. Unfortunately, the high level of risk (D, Weak) failed to pay off as investors endured very poor performance.

The fund's performance rating is currently E (Very Weak). It has registered an annualized return of -36.70% over the last three years and is down -8.45% year to date 2012. Factored into the performance evaluation is an expense ratio of 0.75% (very low).

This fund has been team managed for 4 years and currently receives a manager quality ranking of 30 (0=worst, 99=best). If you can tolerate very high levels of risk in the hope of improved future returns, holding this fund may be an option.

Data Date	Investment Rating	Net Assets ($Mil)	Price	Performance Rating/Pts	Total Return Y-T-D	Risk Rating/Pts
3-12	E-	97.05	37.92	E / 0.4	-8.45%	D / 1.9
2011	E-	97.05	41.42	E / 0.4	-5.55%	D / 1.9
2010	E-	97.05	53.35	E / 0.3	-20.25%	D- / 1.3
2009	E-	97.05	66.90	E / 0.3	-46.99%	D / 1.9

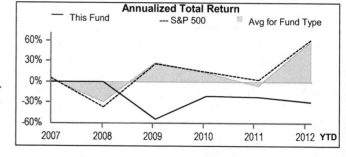

*PowerShares DB Crude Oil Long ET (OLO) D- Weak

Fund Family: Deutsche Bank AG (London)
Fund Type: Growth
Inception Date: June 16, 2008

Major Rating Factors: *PowerShares DB Crude Oil Long ET receives a TheStreet.com Investment Rating of D- (Weak). The fund currently has a performance rating of C- (Fair) based on an annualized return of 12.69% over the last three years and a total return of 5.86% year to date 2012. Factored into the performance evaluation is an expense ratio of 0.75% (very low).

The fund's risk rating is currently C- (Fair). It carries a beta of 1.09, meaning that its performance tracks fairly well with that of the overall stock market. Volatility, as measured by both the semi-deviation and a drawdown factor, is considered average. As of March 31, 2012, *PowerShares DB Crude Oil Long ET traded at a premium of 1.16% above its net asset value, which is worse than its one-year historical average discount of .03%.

This fund has been team managed for 4 years and currently receives a manager quality ranking of 16 (0=worst, 99=best). If you desire an average level of risk, then this fund may be an option.

Data Date	Investment Rating	Net Assets ($Mil)	Price	Performance Rating/Pts	Total Return Y-T-D	Risk Rating/Pts
3-12	D-	14.59	14.84	C- / 3.1	5.86%	C- / 4.0
2011	D+	14.59	14.02	C / 5.4	3.08%	C- / 4.0
2010	C	14.59	14.00	B+ / 8.5	3.09%	D / 2.0
2009	C	14.59	13.58	B+ / 8.4	32.62%	D / 2.2

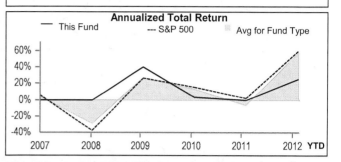

*PowerShares DB Crude Oil Short E (SZO) E Very Weak

Fund Family: Deutsche Bank AG (London)
Fund Type: Growth
Inception Date: June 16, 2008

Major Rating Factors: Very poor performance is the major factor driving the E (Very Weak) TheStreet.com Investment Rating for *PowerShares DB Crude Oil Short E. The fund currently has a performance rating of E+ (Very Weak) based on an annualized return of -16.56% over the last three years and a total return of -4.00% year to date 2012. Factored into the performance evaluation is an expense ratio of 0.75% (very low).

The fund's risk rating is currently C- (Fair). It carries a beta of -1.06, meaning the fund's expected move will be -10.6% for every 10% move in the market. Volatility, as measured by both the semi-deviation and a drawdown factor, is considered average. As of March 31, 2012, *PowerShares DB Crude Oil Short E traded at a discount of .26% below its net asset value, which is better than its one-year historical average discount of .07%.

This fund has been team managed for 4 years and currently receives a manager quality ranking of 60 (0=worst, 99=best). This fund offers an average level of risk but investors looking for strong performance will be frustrated.

Data Date	Investment Rating	Net Assets ($Mil)	Price	Performance Rating/Pts	Total Return Y-T-D	Risk Rating/Pts
3-12	E	14.43	39.11	E+ / 0.6	-4.00%	C- / 3.0
2011	E	14.43	40.74	D- / 1.0	-2.80%	D+ / 2.7
2010	E	14.43	44.31	E+ / 0.6	-7.69%	D+ / 2.9
2009	E	14.43	48.00	E / 0.5	-20.83%	C- / 3.3

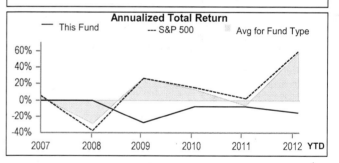

*PowerShares DB Energy Fund (DBE) D+ Weak

Fund Family: DB Commodity Services LLC
Fund Type: Energy/Natural Resources
Inception Date: January 3, 2007

Major Rating Factors: *PowerShares DB Energy Fund receives a TheStreet.com Investment Rating of D+ (Weak). The fund currently has a performance rating of C- (Fair) based on an annualized return of 13.25% over the last three years and a total return of 8.80% year to date 2012. Factored into the performance evaluation is an expense ratio of 0.78% (very low).

The fund's risk rating is currently B- (Good). It carries a beta of 0.84, meaning the fund's expected move will be 8.4% for every 10% move in the market. Volatility, as measured by both the semi-deviation and a drawdown factor, is considered low. As of March 31, 2012, *PowerShares DB Energy Fund traded at a premium of .10% above its net asset value, which is worse than its one-year historical average premium of .09%.

Kevin Parker currently receives a manager quality ranking of 43 (0=worst, 99=best). If you desire an average level of risk, then this fund may be an option.

Data Date	Investment Rating	Net Assets ($Mil)	Price	Performance Rating/Pts	Total Return Y-T-D	Risk Rating/Pts
3-12	D+	177.66	30.05	C- / 3.1	8.80%	B- / 7.4
2011	C	149.10	27.62	C / 4.6	5.32%	B- / 7.5
2010	E+	161.40	26.88	D- / 1.2	2.63%	C- / 3.8
2009	C+	364.70	26.19	B / 7.7	21.70%	C / 4.4

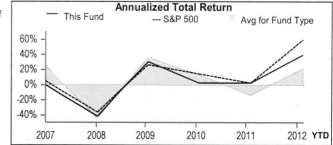

*PowerShares DB G10 Currency Harv (DBV)   D+   Weak

Fund Family: DB Commodity Services LLC
Fund Type: Income
Inception Date: September 18, 2006

Data Date	Investment Rating	Net Assets ($Mil)	Price	Performance Rating/Pts	Total Return Y-T-D	Risk Rating/Pts
3-12	D+	353.01	25.01	D / 1.9	5.26%	B+ / 9.0
2011	C	286.00	23.76	C- / 3.2	0.76%	B+ / 9.0
2010	D+	356.10	23.74	D / 1.6	0.85%	C+ / 6.7
2009	C-	411.67	23.54	D+ / 2.6	19.80%	C+ / 6.8

Major Rating Factors:
Disappointing performance is the major factor driving the D+ (Weak) TheStreet.com Investment Rating for *PowerShares DB G10 Currency Harv. The fund currently has a performance rating of D (Weak) based on an annualized return of 6.12% over the last three years and a total return of 5.26% year to date 2012. Factored into the performance evaluation is an expense ratio of 0.80% (very low).

The fund's risk rating is currently B+ (Good). It carries a beta of 0.53, meaning the fund's expected move will be 5.3% for every 10% move in the market. Volatility, as measured by both the semi-deviation and a drawdown factor, is considered very low. As of March 31, 2012, *PowerShares DB G10 Currency Harv traded at a discount of .20% below its net asset value, which is better than its one-year historical average discount of .01%.

Kevin Parker currently receives a manager quality ranking of 24 (0=worst, 99=best). This fund offers only a moderate level of risk but investors looking for strong performance are still waiting.

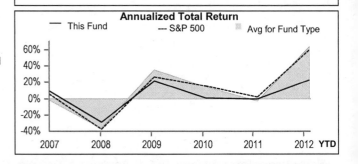

*PowerShares DB German Bond Fut E (BUNL)   D   Weak

Fund Family: DB Commodity Services LLC
Fund Type: Global
Inception Date: March 22, 2011

Data Date	Investment Rating	Net Assets ($Mil)	Price	Performance Rating/Pts	Total Return Y-T-D	Risk Rating/Pts
3-12	D	31.06	23.12	C- / 3.1	0.70%	C+ / 5.9

Major Rating Factors: *PowerShares DB German Bond Fut E receives a TheStreet.com Investment Rating of D (Weak). The fund currently has a performance rating of C- (Fair) based on an annualized return of 0.00% over the last three years and a total return of 0.70% year to date 2012. Factored into the performance evaluation is an expense ratio of 0.50% (very low).

The fund's risk rating is currently C+ (Fair). It carries a beta of 0.00, meaning the fund's expected move will be 0.0% for every 10% move in the market. Volatility, as measured by both the semi-deviation and a drawdown factor, is considered low. As of March 31, 2012, *PowerShares DB German Bond Fut E traded at a premium of .22% above its net asset value, which is worse than its one-year historical average discount of .01%.

This fund has been team managed for 1 year and currently receives a manager quality ranking of 90 (0=worst, 99=best). If you desire an average level of risk, then this fund may be an option.

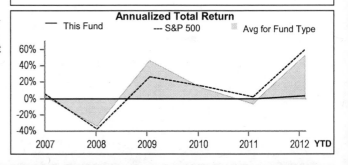

*PowerShares DB Gold Double Lg ET (DGP)   C+   Fair

Fund Family: Deutsche Bank AG (London)
Fund Type: Precious Metals
Inception Date: February 28, 2008

Data Date	Investment Rating	Net Assets ($Mil)	Price	Performance Rating/Pts	Total Return Y-T-D	Risk Rating/Pts
3-12	C+	569.70	53.17	A / 9.5	11.68%	C- / 4.2
2011	C+	0.00	47.61	A+ / 9.8	7.50%	C- / 4.2
2010	B-	0.10	42.93	A+ / 9.8	62.37%	D+ / 2.8
2009	C+	0.00	26.44	A- / 9.2	46.48%	C- / 3.0

Major Rating Factors:
Exceptional performance is the major factor driving the C+ (Fair) TheStreet.com Investment Rating for *PowerShares DB Gold Double Lg ET. The fund currently has a performance rating of A (Excellent) based on an annualized return of 41.85% over the last three years and a total return of 11.68% year to date 2012. Factored into the performance evaluation is an expense ratio of 0.75% (very low).

The fund's risk rating is currently C- (Fair). It carries a beta of 1.89, meaning it is expected to move 18.9% for every 10% move in the market. Volatility, as measured by both the semi-deviation and a drawdown factor, is considered average. As of March 31, 2012, *PowerShares DB Gold Double Lg ET traded at a discount of .21% below its net asset value, which is better than its one-year historical average premium of .18%.

This fund has been team managed for 4 years and currently receives a manager quality ranking of 24 (0=worst, 99=best). If you desire an average level of risk and strong performance, then this fund is a good option.

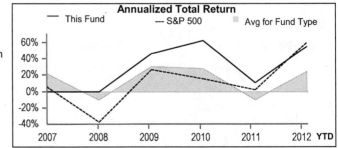

*PowerShares DB Gold Double Sht E (DZZ)　　　　E-　　Very Weak

Fund Family: Deutsche Bank AG (London)
Fund Type: Precious Metals
Inception Date: February 28, 2008

Major Rating Factors: *PowerShares DB Gold Double Sht E has adopted a very risky asset allocation strategy and currently receives an overall TheStreet.com Investment Rating of E- (Very Weak). The fund has a high level of volatility, as measured by both semi-deviation and drawdown factors. It carries a beta of -1.97, meaning the fund's expected move will be -19.7% for every 10% move in the market. As of March 31, 2012, *PowerShares DB Gold Double Sht E traded at a price exactly equal to its net asset value, which is worse than its one-year historical average discount of .26%. Unfortunately, the high level of risk (D, Weak) failed to pay off as investors endured very poor performance.

The fund's performance rating is currently E (Very Weak). It has registered an annualized return of -42.23% over the last three years and is down -15.43% year to date 2012. Factored into the performance evaluation is an expense ratio of 0.75% (very low).

This fund has been team managed for 4 years and currently receives a manager quality ranking of 11 (0=worst, 99=best). If you can tolerate very high levels of risk in the hope of improved future returns, holding this fund may be an option.

Data Date	Investment Rating	Net Assets ($Mil)	Price	Performance Rating/Pts	Total Return Y-T-D	Risk Rating/Pts
3-12	E-	80.91	4.61	E / 0.3	-15.43%	D / 1.9
2011	E-	0.00	5.45	E / 0.3	-7.62%	D / 1.9
2010	E-	0.10	7.98	E- / 0.2	-43.08%	D- / 1.0
2009	E-	0.00	14.02	E- / 0.2	-44.08%	D / 1.8

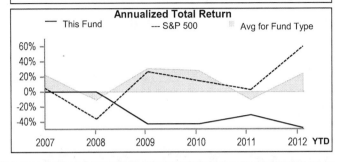

*PowerShares DB Gold Fund (DGL)　　　　　　C+　　　　Fair

Fund Family: DB Commodity Services LLC
Fund Type: Precious Metals
Inception Date: January 3, 2007

Major Rating Factors: Middle of the road best describes *PowerShares DB Gold Fund whose TheStreet.com Investment Rating is currently a C+ (Fair). The fund currently has a performance rating of C (Fair) based on an annualized return of 21.24% over the last three years and a total return of 6.12% year to date 2012. Factored into the performance evaluation is an expense ratio of 0.76% (very low).

The fund's risk rating is currently B (Good). It carries a beta of 0.95, meaning that its performance tracks fairly well with that of the overall stock market. Volatility, as measured by both the semi-deviation and a drawdown factor, is considered low. As of March 31, 2012, *PowerShares DB Gold Fund traded at a discount of .19% below its net asset value, which is better than its one-year historical average premium of .10%.

Kevin Parker currently receives a manager quality ranking of 42 (0=worst, 99=best). If you desire an average level of risk, then this fund may be an option.

Data Date	Investment Rating	Net Assets ($Mil)	Price	Performance Rating/Pts	Total Return Y-T-D	Risk Rating/Pts
3-12	C+	427.75	57.78	C / 5.3	6.12%	B / 8.2
2011	B	458.10	54.45	B- / 7.3	3.40%	B / 8.2
2010	A	331.30	50.16	B+ / 8.7	27.89%	C+ / 6.9
2009	A+	149.38	39.22	B / 7.9	22.99%	B- / 7.2

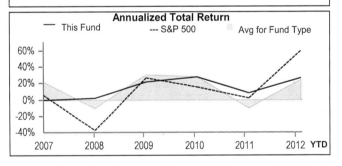

*PowerShares DB Gold Short ETN (DGZ)　　　　　E　　Very Weak

Fund Family: Deutsche Bank AG (London)
Fund Type: Precious Metals
Inception Date: February 29, 2008

Major Rating Factors: *PowerShares DB Gold Short ETN has adopted a risky asset allocation strategy and currently receives an overall TheStreet.com Investment Rating of E (Very Weak). The fund has an above average level of volatility, as measured by both semi-deviation and drawdown factors. It carries a beta of -0.96, meaning the fund's expected move will be -9.6% for every 10% move in the market. As of March 31, 2012, *PowerShares DB Gold Short ETN traded at a premium of .08% above its net asset value, which is worse than its one-year historical average discount of .12%. Unfortunately, the high level of risk (D+, Weak) failed to pay off as investors endured very poor performance.

The fund's performance rating is currently E+ (Very Weak). It has registered an annualized return of -22.25% over the last three years and is down -7.29% year to date 2012. Factored into the performance evaluation is an expense ratio of 0.75% (very low).

This fund has been team managed for 4 years and currently receives a manager quality ranking of 22 (0=worst, 99=best). If you can tolerate high levels of risk in the hope of improved future returns, holding this fund may be an option.

Data Date	Investment Rating	Net Assets ($Mil)	Price	Performance Rating/Pts	Total Return Y-T-D	Risk Rating/Pts
3-12	E	41.16	11.95	E+ / 0.6	-7.29%	D+ / 2.6
2011	E	0.00	12.89	E+ / 0.8	-3.72%	D+ / 2.5
2010	E	0.10	15.16	E / 0.4	-24.05%	D+ / 2.4
2009	E	0.00	19.96	E / 0.4	-23.52%	C- / 3.1

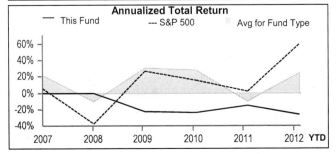

*PowerShares DB ltn Trs B Fut ETN (ITLY)　　　　D　　　Weak

Fund Family: DB Commodity Services LLC
Fund Type: Global
Inception Date: March 22, 2011

Data Date	Investment Rating	Net Assets ($Mil)	Price	Performance Rating/Pts	Total Return Y-T-D	Risk Rating/Pts
3-12	D	38.81	21.23	C- / 4.0	18.27%	C / 5.3

Major Rating Factors: *PowerShares DB ltn Trs B Fut ETN receives a TheStreet.com Investment Rating of D (Weak). The fund currently has a performance rating of C- (Fair) based on an annualized return of 0.00% over the last three years and a total return of 18.27% year to date 2012. Factored into the performance evaluation is an expense ratio of 0.50% (very low).

The fund's risk rating is currently C (Fair). It carries a beta of 0.00, meaning the fund's expected move will be 0.0% for every 10% move in the market. Volatility, as measured by both the semi-deviation and a drawdown factor, is considered average. As of March 31, 2012, *PowerShares DB ltn Trs B Fut ETN traded at a discount of 4.15% below its net asset value, which is better than its one-year historical average premium of 9.20%.

This fund has been team managed for 1 year and currently receives a manager quality ranking of 68 (0=worst, 99=best). If you desire an average level of risk, then this fund may be an option.

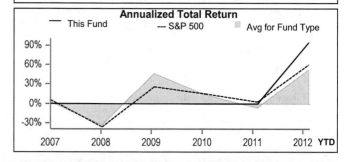

*PowerShares DB Japanese GvBd Fut (JGBL)　　　　D-　　　Weak

Fund Family: DB Commodity Services LLC
Fund Type: Global
Inception Date: March 22, 2011

Data Date	Investment Rating	Net Assets ($Mil)	Price	Performance Rating/Pts	Total Return Y-T-D	Risk Rating/Pts
3-12	D-	5.13	20.35	D- / 1.3	-0.10%	C+ / 5.9

Major Rating Factors:
Disappointing performance is the major factor driving the D- (Weak) TheStreet.com Investment Rating for *PowerShares DB Japanese GvBd Fut. The fund currently has a performance rating of D- (Weak) based on an annualized return of 0.00% over the last three years and a total return of -0.10% year to date 2012. Factored into the performance evaluation is an expense ratio of 0.50% (very low).

The fund's risk rating is currently C+ (Fair). It carries a beta of 0.00, meaning the fund's expected move will be 0.0% for every 10% move in the market. Volatility, as measured by both the semi-deviation and a drawdown factor, is considered low. As of March 31, 2012, *PowerShares DB Japanese GvBd Fut traded at a discount of .54% below its net asset value, which is better than its one-year historical average premium of .09%.

This fund has been team managed for 1 year and currently receives a manager quality ranking of 55 (0=worst, 99=best). This fund offers only a moderate level of risk but investors looking for strong performance are still waiting.

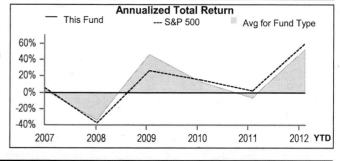

*PowerShares DB Oil Fund (DBO)　　　　D　　　Weak

Fund Family: DB Commodity Services LLC
Fund Type: Energy/Natural Resources
Inception Date: January 3, 2007

Data Date	Investment Rating	Net Assets ($Mil)	Price	Performance Rating/Pts	Total Return Y-T-D	Risk Rating/Pts
3-12	D	759.33	29.91	C- / 3.0	4.69%	C+ / 6.6
2011	C	508.40	28.57	C / 5.4	3.36%	C+ / 6.7
2010	D-	597.80	28.22	D- / 1.4	2.36%	C- / 3.7
2009	B-	302.15	27.57	B+ / 8.4	32.61%	C / 4.4

Major Rating Factors: *PowerShares DB Oil Fund receives a TheStreet.com Investment Rating of D (Weak). The fund currently has a performance rating of C- (Fair) based on an annualized return of 12.48% over the last three years and a total return of 4.69% year to date 2012. Factored into the performance evaluation is an expense ratio of 0.77% (very low).

The fund's risk rating is currently C+ (Fair). It carries a beta of 1.00, meaning that its performance tracks fairly well with that of the overall stock market. Volatility, as measured by both the semi-deviation and a drawdown factor, is considered low. As of March 31, 2012, *PowerShares DB Oil Fund traded at a premium of .13% above its net asset value, which is worse than its one-year historical average premium of .07%.

Kevin Parker currently receives a manager quality ranking of 26 (0=worst, 99=best). If you desire an average level of risk, then this fund may be an option.

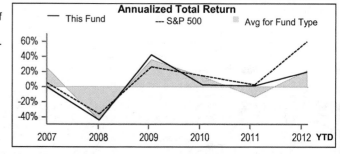

*PowerShares DB Precious Metals F (DBP)

C+   **Fair**

Fund Family: DB Commodity Services LLC
Fund Type: Precious Metals
Inception Date: January 3, 2007

Major Rating Factors: Middle of the road best describes *PowerShares DB Precious Metals F whose TheStreet.com Investment Rating is currently a C+ (Fair). The fund currently has a performance rating of C+ (Fair) based on an annualized return of 23.90% over the last three years and a total return of 8.26% year to date 2012. Factored into the performance evaluation is an expense ratio of 0.78% (very low).

The fund's risk rating is currently B- (Good). It carries a beta of 1.11, meaning it is expected to move 11.1% for every 10% move in the market. Volatility, as measured by both the semi-deviation and a drawdown factor, is considered low. As of March 31, 2012, *PowerShares DB Precious Metals F traded at a discount of .14% below its net asset value, which is better than its one-year historical average premium of .08%.

Kevin Parker currently receives a manager quality ranking of 36 (0=worst, 99=best). If you desire an average level of risk, then this fund may be an option.

Data Date	Investment Rating	Net Assets ($Mil)	Price	Perfor-mance Rating/Pts	Total Return Y-T-D	Risk Rating/Pts
3-12	C+	447.18	58.33	C+ / 5.9	8.26%	B- / 7.6
2011	B-	454.10	53.88	B- / 7.5	3.36%	B- / 7.7
2010	A	404.20	51.82	A- / 9.1	37.56%	C+ / 6.5
2009	A+	201.07	37.67	B / 8.2	27.05%	C+ / 6.8

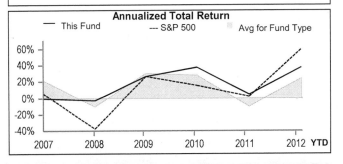

*PowerShares DB Silver Fund (DBS)

C   **Fair**

Fund Family: DB Commodity Services LLC
Fund Type: Precious Metals
Inception Date: January 3, 2007

Major Rating Factors: Strong performance is the major factor driving the C (Fair) TheStreet.com Investment Rating for *PowerShares DB Silver Fund. The fund currently has a performance rating of B (Good) based on an annualized return of 34.82% over the last three years and a total return of 17.19% year to date 2012. Factored into the performance evaluation is an expense ratio of 0.77% (very low).

The fund's risk rating is currently C (Fair). It carries a beta of 1.71, meaning it is expected to move 17.1% for every 10% move in the market. Volatility, as measured by both the semi-deviation and a drawdown factor, is considered average. As of March 31, 2012, *PowerShares DB Silver Fund traded at a discount of .46% below its net asset value, which is better than its one-year historical average premium of .05%.

Kevin Parker currently receives a manager quality ranking of 25 (0=worst, 99=best). If you desire an average level of risk and strong performance, then this fund is a good option.

Data Date	Investment Rating	Net Assets ($Mil)	Price	Perfor-mance Rating/Pts	Total Return Y-T-D	Risk Rating/Pts
3-12	C	84.45	56.24	B / 8.2	17.19%	C / 5.0
2011	C+	77.70	47.99	B+ / 8.4	3.83%	C / 5.1
2010	A-	207.60	54.51	A+ / 9.7	81.16%	C / 4.8
2009	B+	81.26	30.09	B+ / 8.9	45.93%	C / 5.1

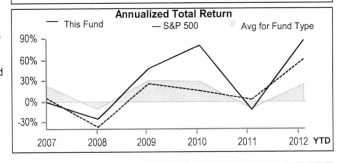

*PowerShares DB US Dollar Bearish (UDN)

D+   **Weak**

Fund Family: DB Commodity Services LLC
Fund Type: Growth
Inception Date: February 15, 2007

Major Rating Factors:
Disappointing performance is the major factor driving the D+ (Weak) TheStreet.com Investment Rating for *PowerShares DB US Dollar Bearish. The fund currently has a performance rating of D- (Weak) based on an annualized return of 2.40% over the last three years and a total return of 2.16% year to date 2012. Factored into the performance evaluation is an expense ratio of 0.80% (very low).

The fund's risk rating is currently B (Good). It carries a beta of 0.43, meaning the fund's expected move will be 4.3% for every 10% move in the market. Volatility, as measured by both the semi-deviation and a drawdown factor, is considered low. As of March 31, 2012, *PowerShares DB US Dollar Bearish traded at a price exactly equal to its net asset value, which is better than its one-year historical average premium of .01%.

Kevin Parker currently receives a manager quality ranking of 20 (0=worst, 99=best). This fund offers only a moderate level of risk but investors looking for strong performance are still waiting.

Data Date	Investment Rating	Net Assets ($Mil)	Price	Perfor-mance Rating/Pts	Total Return Y-T-D	Risk Rating/Pts
3-12	D+	93.23	27.43	D- / 1.3	2.16%	B / 8.7
2011	C-	102.20	26.85	D / 2.0	-1.27%	B / 8.7
2010	C-	151.50	27.10	D / 2.1	-1.60%	B- / 7.8
2009	C+	382.19	27.54	C- / 3.5	6.00%	B / 8.2

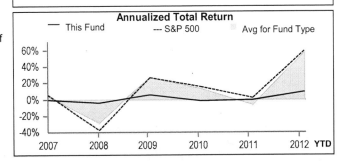

*PowerShares DB US Dollar Bullish (UUP)

D   **Weak**

Fund Family: DB Commodity Services LLC
Fund Type: Growth
Inception Date: February 15, 2007

Major Rating Factors:
Disappointing performance is the major factor driving the D (Weak) TheStreet.com Investment Rating for *PowerShares DB US Dollar Bullish. The fund currently has a performance rating of D- (Weak) based on an annualized return of -4.61% over the last three years and a total return of -2.49% year to date 2012. Factored into the performance evaluation is an expense ratio of 0.81% (very low).

The fund's risk rating is currently B (Good). It carries a beta of -0.42, meaning the fund's expected move will be -4.2% for every 10% move in the market. Volatility, as measured by both the semi-deviation and a drawdown factor, is considered low. As of March 31, 2012, *PowerShares DB US Dollar Bullish traded at a price exactly equal to its net asset value, which is worse than its one-year historical average discount of .03%.

Kevin Parker currently receives a manager quality ranking of 67 (0=worst, 99=best). This fund offers only a moderate level of risk but investors looking for strong performance are still waiting.

Data Date	Investment Rating	Net Assets ($Mil)	Price	Performance Rating/Pts	Total Return Y-T-D	Risk Rating/Pts
3-12	D	1,254.97	21.91	D- / 1.0	-2.49%	B / 8.4
2011	D+	0.00	22.47	D / 1.7	1.11%	B / 8.2
2010	C-	997.50	22.71	D / 1.8	-1.60%	B- / 7.8
2009	C-	770.21	23.08	D- / 1.0	-7.38%	B / 8.2

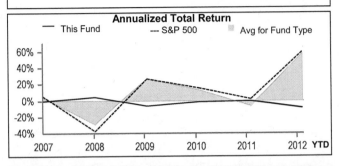

*PowerShares Div Achievers (PFM)

C+   **Fair**

Fund Family: Invesco Powershares Capital Mgmt LL
Fund Type: Income
Inception Date: September 15, 2005

Major Rating Factors: Middle of the road best describes *PowerShares Div Achievers whose TheStreet.com Investment Rating is currently a C+ (Fair). The fund currently has a performance rating of C (Fair) based on an annualized return of 19.45% over the last three years and a total return of 6.17% year to date 2012. Factored into the performance evaluation is an expense ratio of 0.60% (very low).

The fund's risk rating is currently B (Good). It carries a beta of 0.74, meaning the fund's expected move will be 7.4% for every 10% move in the market. Volatility, as measured by both the semi-deviation and a drawdown factor, is considered low. As of March 31, 2012, *PowerShares Div Achievers traded at a premium of .06% above its net asset value, which is worse than its one-year historical average premium of .01%.

Peter Hubbard has been running the fund for 5 years and currently receives a manager quality ranking of 68 (0=worst, 99=best). If you desire an average level of risk, then this fund may be an option.

Data Date	Investment Rating	Net Assets ($Mil)	Price	Performance Rating/Pts	Total Return Y-T-D	Risk Rating/Pts
3-12	C+	286.30	15.82	C / 5.0	6.17%	B / 8.9
2011	C	256.30	14.96	C / 5.0	0.00%	B / 8.0
2010	C-	193.50	14.02	C- / 3.5	15.87%	C+ / 6.1
2009	D+	85.45	12.47	D- / 1.3	8.45%	C+ / 6.5

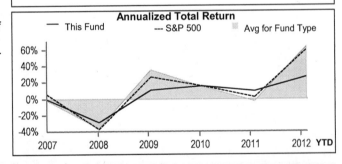

*PowerShares DWA Dev Mkt Tech Lea (PIZ)

C-   **Fair**

Fund Family: Invesco Powershares Capital Mgmt LL
Fund Type: Foreign
Inception Date: December 27, 2007

Major Rating Factors: Middle of the road best describes *PowerShares DWA Dev Mkt Tech Lea whose TheStreet.com Investment Rating is currently a C- (Fair). The fund currently has a performance rating of C- (Fair) based on an annualized return of 18.59% over the last three years and a total return of 11.92% year to date 2012. Factored into the performance evaluation is an expense ratio of 0.80% (very low).

The fund's risk rating is currently B- (Good). It carries a beta of 1.16, meaning it is expected to move 11.6% for every 10% move in the market. Volatility, as measured by both the semi-deviation and a drawdown factor, is considered low. As of March 31, 2012, *PowerShares DWA Dev Mkt Tech Lea traded at a premium of .46% above its net asset value, which is worse than its one-year historical average discount of .02%.

Peter Hubbard has been running the fund for 5 years and currently receives a manager quality ranking of 43 (0=worst, 99=best). If you desire an average level of risk, then this fund may be an option.

Data Date	Investment Rating	Net Assets ($Mil)	Price	Performance Rating/Pts	Total Return Y-T-D	Risk Rating/Pts
3-12	C-	64.22	19.52	C- / 4.1	11.92%	B- / 7.1
2011	D+	54.30	17.47	C- / 3.3	-0.11%	C+ / 6.9
2010	C-	120.70	22.15	C / 4.4	21.32%	C / 5.3
2009	B+	16.83	18.39	B+ / 8.9	36.06%	C / 5.2

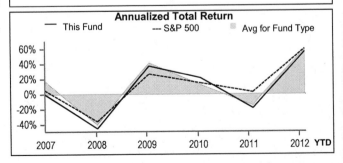

*PowerShares DWA Emg Mkts Tech Le (PIE)

C+   **Fair**

Fund Family: Invesco Powershares Capital Mgmt LL
Fund Type: Emerging Market
Inception Date: December 27, 2007

Major Rating Factors: Middle of the road best describes *PowerShares DWA Emg Mkts Tech Le whose TheStreet.com Investment Rating is currently a C+ (Fair). The fund currently has a performance rating of C+ (Fair) based on an annualized return of 25.56% over the last three years and a total return of 12.55% year to date 2012. Factored into the performance evaluation is an expense ratio of 0.90% (low).

The fund's risk rating is currently C+ (Fair). It carries a beta of 1.02, meaning that its performance tracks fairly well with that of the overall stock market. Volatility, as measured by both the semi-deviation and a drawdown factor, is considered low. As of March 31, 2012, *PowerShares DWA Emg Mkts Tech Le traded at a premium of .17% above its net asset value, which is worse than its one-year historical average discount of .12%.

Peter Hubbard has been running the fund for 5 years and currently receives a manager quality ranking of 58 (0=worst, 99=best). If you desire an average level of risk, then this fund may be an option.

Data Date	Investment Rating	Net Assets ($Mil)	Price	Performance Rating/Pts	Total Return Y-T-D	Risk Rating/Pts
3-12	C+	195.24	17.94	C+ / 6.7	12.55%	C+ / 6.9
2011	C	147.90	15.94	C+ / 6.0	0.56%	B- / 7.0
2010	D-	392.00	18.37	D / 1.7	25.56%	C- / 3.8
2009	B	14.94	14.73	A / 9.4	53.10%	C- / 4.2

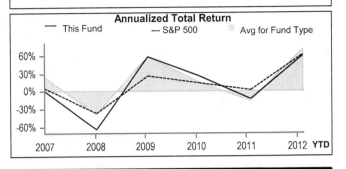

Annualized Total Return — This Fund --- S&P 500 — Avg for Fund Type

*PowerShares DWA Technical Leader (PDP)

B-   **Good**

Fund Family: Invesco Powershares Capital Mgmt LL
Fund Type: Income
Inception Date: March 1, 2007

Major Rating Factors: Strong performance is the major factor driving the B- (Good) TheStreet.com Investment Rating for *PowerShares DWA Technical Leader. The fund currently has a performance rating of B- (Good) based on an annualized return of 26.09% over the last three years and a total return of 14.56% year to date 2012. Factored into the performance evaluation is an expense ratio of 0.70% (very low).

The fund's risk rating is currently B- (Good). It carries a beta of 1.05, meaning that its performance tracks fairly well with that of the overall stock market. Volatility, as measured by both the semi-deviation and a drawdown factor, is considered low. As of March 31, 2012, *PowerShares DWA Technical Leader traded at a premium of .11% above its net asset value, which is worse than its one-year historical average premium of .01%.

Peter Hubbard has been running the fund for 5 years and currently receives a manager quality ranking of 64 (0=worst, 99=best). If you desire only a moderate level of risk and strong performance, then this fund is an excellent option.

Data Date	Investment Rating	Net Assets ($Mil)	Price	Performance Rating/Pts	Total Return Y-T-D	Risk Rating/Pts
3-12	B-	522.30	27.30	B- / 7.2	14.56%	B- / 7.9
2011	C+	441.40	23.83	C+ / 6.2	1.26%	B- / 7.3
2010	D+	323.90	23.51	C- / 4.2	26.79%	C / 4.6
2009	B+	138.55	18.62	B+ / 8.5	24.87%	C / 5.4

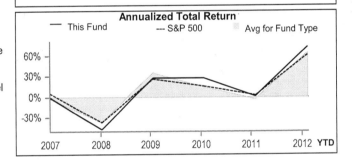

Annualized Total Return — This Fund --- S&P 500 — Avg for Fund Type

*PowerShares Dynamic Banking Port (PJB)

D   **Weak**

Fund Family: Invesco Powershares Capital Mgmt LL
Fund Type: Financial Services
Inception Date: October 12, 2006

Major Rating Factors:
Disappointing performance is the major factor driving the D (Weak) TheStreet.com Investment Rating for *PowerShares Dynamic Banking Port. The fund currently has a performance rating of D+ (Weak) based on an annualized return of 4.99% over the last three years and a total return of 14.91% year to date 2012. Factored into the performance evaluation is an expense ratio of 0.65% (very low).

The fund's risk rating is currently B- (Good). It carries a beta of 0.67, meaning the fund's expected move will be 6.7% for every 10% move in the market. Volatility, as measured by both the semi-deviation and a drawdown factor, is considered low. As of March 31, 2012, *PowerShares Dynamic Banking Port traded at a premium of .15% above its net asset value, which is worse than its one-year historical average discount of .06%.

Peter Hubbard has been running the fund for 5 years and currently receives a manager quality ranking of 17 (0=worst, 99=best). This fund offers only a moderate level of risk but investors looking for strong performance are still waiting.

Data Date	Investment Rating	Net Assets ($Mil)	Price	Performance Rating/Pts	Total Return Y-T-D	Risk Rating/Pts
3-12	D	12.79	13.50	D+ / 2.4	14.91%	B- / 7.4
2011	D	11.80	11.79	D / 1.8	3.39%	C+ / 6.8
2010	D	24.50	13.27	D / 1.6	12.42%	C+ / 5.9
2009	D-	74.77	12.00	E / 0.5	-21.61%	C+ / 5.8

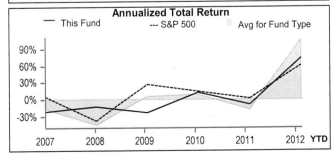

Annualized Total Return — This Fund --- S&P 500 — Avg for Fund Type

* Denotes ETF Fund

*PowerShares Dynamic Basic Materi (PYZ)   B-   Good

Fund Family: Invesco Powershares Capital Mgmt LL
Fund Type: Income
Inception Date: October 12, 2006

Major Rating Factors: Strong performance is the major factor driving the B- (Good) TheStreet.com Investment Rating for *PowerShares Dynamic Basic Materi. The fund currently has a performance rating of B (Good) based on an annualized return of 29.75% over the last three years and a total return of 19.00% year to date 2012. Factored into the performance evaluation is an expense ratio of 0.65% (very low).

The fund's risk rating is currently B- (Good). It carries a beta of 1.58, meaning it is expected to move 15.8% for every 10% move in the market. Volatility, as measured by both the semi-deviation and a drawdown factor, is considered low. As of March 31, 2012, *PowerShares Dynamic Basic Materi traded at a premium of .08% above its net asset value, which is worse than its one-year historical average discount of .02%.

Peter Hubbard has been running the fund for 5 years and currently receives a manager quality ranking of 23 (0=worst, 99=best). If you desire only a moderate level of risk and strong performance, then this fund is an excellent option.

Data Date	Investment Rating	Net Assets ($Mil)	Price	Performance Rating/Pts	Total Return Y-T-D	Risk Rating/Pts
3-12	B-	63.82	38.03	B / 8.1	19.00%	B- / 7.0
2011	C+	54.40	32.03	C+ / 6.7	4.28%	B- / 7.0
2010	B-	76.20	35.44	B / 7.7	30.88%	C / 4.9
2009	C	18.13	28.30	C+ / 6.3	42.86%	C / 5.2

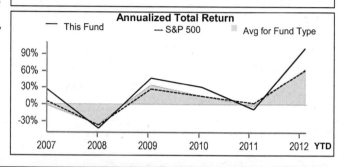

*PowerShares Dynamic Biotech&Geno (PBE)   C-   Fair

Fund Family: Invesco Powershares Capital Mgmt LL
Fund Type: Health
Inception Date: June 23, 2005

Major Rating Factors: Middle of the road best describes *PowerShares Dynamic Biotech&Geno whose TheStreet.com Investment Rating is currently a C- (Fair). The fund currently has a performance rating of C+ (Fair) based on an annualized return of 21.38% over the last three years and a total return of 13.06% year to date 2012. Factored into the performance evaluation is an expense ratio of 0.63% (very low).

The fund's risk rating is currently C+ (Fair). It carries a beta of 1.03, meaning that its performance tracks fairly well with that of the overall stock market. Volatility, as measured by both the semi-deviation and a drawdown factor, is considered low. As of March 31, 2012, *PowerShares Dynamic Biotech&Geno traded at a discount of .09% below its net asset value, which is worse than its one-year historical average discount of .12%.

Peter Hubbard has been running the fund for 5 years and currently receives a manager quality ranking of 32 (0=worst, 99=best). If you desire an average level of risk, then this fund may be an option.

Data Date	Investment Rating	Net Assets ($Mil)	Price	Performance Rating/Pts	Total Return Y-T-D	Risk Rating/Pts
3-12	C-	141.29	22.68	C+ / 5.6	13.06%	C+ / 5.9
2011	C-	135.40	20.06	C / 4.8	2.59%	C+ / 5.8
2010	B	205.30	21.89	B+ / 8.4	31.47%	C / 4.5
2009	D	139.30	16.65	D+ / 2.8	19.13%	C / 4.8

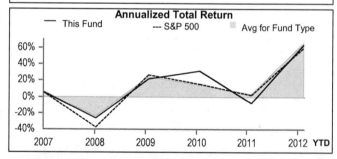

*PowerShares Dynamic Bldg & Cons (PKB)   C-   Fair

Fund Family: Invesco Powershares Capital Mgmt LL
Fund Type: Income
Inception Date: October 26, 2005

Major Rating Factors: Middle of the road best describes *PowerShares Dynamic Bldg & Cons whose TheStreet.com Investment Rating is currently a C- (Fair). The fund currently has a performance rating of C (Fair) based on an annualized return of 16.38% over the last three years and a total return of 17.86% year to date 2012. Factored into the performance evaluation is an expense ratio of 0.63% (very low).

The fund's risk rating is currently B- (Good). It carries a beta of 1.44, meaning it is expected to move 14.4% for every 10% move in the market. Volatility, as measured by both the semi-deviation and a drawdown factor, is considered low. As of March 31, 2012, *PowerShares Dynamic Bldg & Cons traded at a premium of .21% above its net asset value, which is worse than its one-year historical average discount of .07%.

Peter Hubbard has been running the fund for 5 years and currently receives a manager quality ranking of 12 (0=worst, 99=best). If you desire an average level of risk, then this fund may be an option.

Data Date	Investment Rating	Net Assets ($Mil)	Price	Performance Rating/Pts	Total Return Y-T-D	Risk Rating/Pts
3-12	C-	28.60	14.12	C / 4.6	17.86%	B- / 7.2
2011	D+	25.80	11.98	D+ / 2.9	1.84%	C+ / 6.9
2010	D+	42.50	13.00	C- / 3.5	22.05%	C / 5.1
2009	D-	49.14	11.94	D- / 1.0	-1.11%	C / 5.2

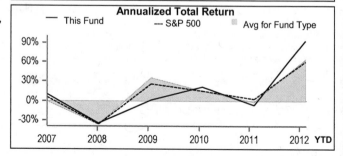

*PowerShares Dynamic Consumer Dis (PEZ)

B- **Good**

Fund Family: Invesco Powershares Capital Mgmt LL
Fund Type: Income
Inception Date: October 12, 2006

Major Rating Factors: Strong performance is the major factor driving the B- (Good) TheStreet.com Investment Rating for *PowerShares Dynamic Consumer Dis. The fund currently has a performance rating of B- (Good) based on an annualized return of 24.06% over the last three years and a total return of 15.95% year to date 2012. Factored into the performance evaluation is an expense ratio of 0.65% (very low).

The fund's risk rating is currently B (Good). It carries a beta of 1.12, meaning it is expected to move 11.2% for every 10% move in the market. Volatility, as measured by both the semi-deviation and a drawdown factor, is considered low. As of March 31, 2012, *PowerShares Dynamic Consumer Dis traded at a discount of .14% below its net asset value, which is better than its one-year historical average discount of .01%.

Peter Hubbard has been running the fund for 5 years and currently receives a manager quality ranking of 44 (0=worst, 99=best). If you desire only a moderate level of risk and strong performance, then this fund is an excellent option.

Data Date	Investment Rating	Net Assets ($Mil)	Price	Performance Rating/Pts	Total Return Y-T-D	Risk Rating/Pts
3-12	B-	21.22	29.59	B- / 7.1	15.95%	B / 8.0
2011	C+	17.70	25.52	C+ / 6.2	1.02%	B- / 7.8
2010	B+	22.80	25.42	B / 7.6	29.87%	C+ / 6.2
2009	D	13.66	19.81	D- / 1.3	22.42%	C+ / 5.8

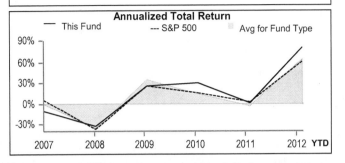

*PowerShares Dynamic Consumer Sta (PSL)

C+ **Fair**

Fund Family: Invesco Powershares Capital Mgmt LL
Fund Type: Income
Inception Date: October 12, 2006

Major Rating Factors: Middle of the road best describes *PowerShares Dynamic Consumer Sta whose TheStreet.com Investment Rating is currently a C+ (Fair). The fund currently has a performance rating of C (Fair) based on an annualized return of 20.93% over the last three years and a total return of 5.17% year to date 2012. Factored into the performance evaluation is an expense ratio of 0.65% (very low).

The fund's risk rating is currently B (Good). It carries a beta of 0.68, meaning the fund's expected move will be 6.8% for every 10% move in the market. Volatility, as measured by both the semi-deviation and a drawdown factor, is considered low. As of March 31, 2012, *PowerShares Dynamic Consumer Sta traded at a premium of .09% above its net asset value, which is worse than its one-year historical average discount of .02%.

Peter Hubbard has been running the fund for 5 years and currently receives a manager quality ranking of 78 (0=worst, 99=best). If you desire an average level of risk, then this fund may be an option.

Data Date	Investment Rating	Net Assets ($Mil)	Price	Performance Rating/Pts	Total Return Y-T-D	Risk Rating/Pts
3-12	C+	38.33	32.68	C / 5.3	5.17%	B / 8.9
2011	B-	38.80	31.12	C+ / 6.0	-1.09%	B / 8.4
2010	C+	40.40	28.98	C+ / 6.8	20.56%	C+ / 6.9
2009	C-	37.45	24.67	C- / 3.1	18.05%	B- / 7.0

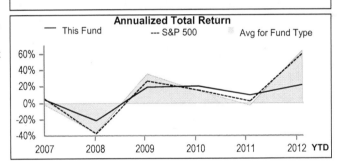

*PowerShares Dynamic Energy (PXI)

B- **Good**

Fund Family: Invesco Powershares Capital Mgmt LL
Fund Type: Energy/Natural Resources
Inception Date: October 12, 2006

Major Rating Factors: Strong performance is the major factor driving the B- (Good) TheStreet.com Investment Rating for *PowerShares Dynamic Energy. The fund currently has a performance rating of B (Good) based on an annualized return of 31.23% over the last three years and a total return of 6.84% year to date 2012. Factored into the performance evaluation is an expense ratio of 0.65% (very low).

The fund's risk rating is currently B- (Good). It carries a beta of 1.14, meaning it is expected to move 11.4% for every 10% move in the market. Volatility, as measured by both the semi-deviation and a drawdown factor, is considered low. As of March 31, 2012, *PowerShares Dynamic Energy traded at a discount of .05% below its net asset value.

Peter Hubbard has been running the fund for 5 years and currently receives a manager quality ranking of 84 (0=worst, 99=best). If you desire only a moderate level of risk and strong performance, then this fund is an excellent option.

Data Date	Investment Rating	Net Assets ($Mil)	Price	Performance Rating/Pts	Total Return Y-T-D	Risk Rating/Pts
3-12	B-	162.94	40.76	B / 7.9	6.84%	B- / 7.3
2011	B-	135.50	38.15	B / 7.9	3.07%	B- / 7.1
2010	B-	106.50	37.41	B / 7.6	40.04%	C / 4.9
2009	C	25.88	26.98	C / 5.2	33.80%	C / 5.1

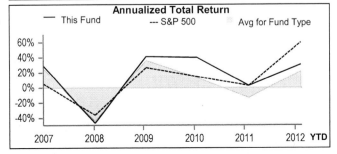

*PowerShares Dynamic Enrg Exp & P (PXE)

C+   **Fair**

Fund Family: Invesco Powershares Capital Mgmt LL
Fund Type: Energy/Natural Resources
Inception Date: October 26, 2005

Major Rating Factors: Middle of the road best describes *PowerShares Dynamic Enrg Exp & P whose TheStreet.com Investment Rating is currently a C+ (Fair). The fund currently has a performance rating of C+ (Fair) based on an annualized return of 25.41% over the last three years and a total return of 11.95% year to date 2012. Factored into the performance evaluation is an expense ratio of 0.63% (very low).

The fund's risk rating is currently B- (Good). It carries a beta of 1.15, meaning it is expected to move 11.5% for every 10% move in the market. Volatility, as measured by both the semi-deviation and a drawdown factor, is considered low. As of March 31, 2012, *PowerShares Dynamic Enrg Exp & P traded at a discount of .12% below its net asset value, which is better than its one-year historical average discount of .07%.

Peter Hubbard has been running the fund for 5 years and currently receives a manager quality ranking of 75 (0=worst, 99=best). If you desire an average level of risk, then this fund may be an option.

Data Date	Investment Rating	Net Assets ($Mil)	Price	Performance Rating/Pts	Total Return Y-T-D	Risk Rating/Pts
3-12	C+	75.08	25.06	C+ / 6.6	11.95%	B- / 7.3
2011	C+	67.30	22.43	C+ / 6.2	3.21%	B- / 7.0
2010	C+	76.10	23.07	C+ / 6.8	40.36%	C / 4.9
2009	D+	51.34	16.58	D+ / 2.7	13.13%	C / 5.2

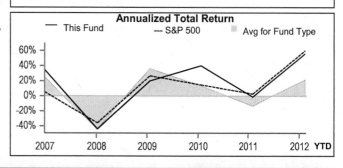

*PowerShares Dynamic Financial (PFI)

C-   **Fair**

Fund Family: Invesco Powershares Capital Mgmt LL
Fund Type: Financial Services
Inception Date: October 12, 2006

Major Rating Factors: Middle of the road best describes *PowerShares Dynamic Financial whose TheStreet.com Investment Rating is currently a C- (Fair). The fund currently has a performance rating of C- (Fair) based on an annualized return of 13.59% over the last three years and a total return of 13.28% year to date 2012. Factored into the performance evaluation is an expense ratio of 0.65% (very low).

The fund's risk rating is currently B (Good). It carries a beta of 0.68, meaning the fund's expected move will be 6.8% for every 10% move in the market. Volatility, as measured by both the semi-deviation and a drawdown factor, is considered low. As of March 31, 2012, *PowerShares Dynamic Financial traded at a premium of .10% above its net asset value, which is worse than its one-year historical average premium of .02%.

Peter Hubbard has been running the fund for 5 years and currently receives a manager quality ranking of 48 (0=worst, 99=best). If you desire an average level of risk, then this fund may be an option.

Data Date	Investment Rating	Net Assets ($Mil)	Price	Performance Rating/Pts	Total Return Y-T-D	Risk Rating/Pts
3-12	C-	18.57	20.30	C- / 3.7	13.28%	B / 8.1
2011	D+	17.00	17.93	D+ / 2.7	1.76%	B- / 7.5
2010	D+	19.00	19.01	D / 2.2	15.84%	C+ / 6.0
2009	D-	14.63	16.87	E+ / 0.8	-5.95%	C+ / 5.9

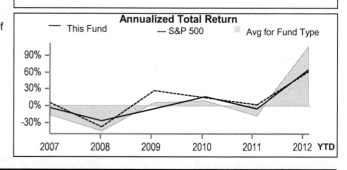

*PowerShares Dynamic Food & Bever (PBJ)

C   **Fair**

Fund Family: Invesco Powershares Capital Mgmt LL
Fund Type: Income
Inception Date: June 23, 2005

Major Rating Factors: Middle of the road best describes *PowerShares Dynamic Food & Bever whose TheStreet.com Investment Rating is currently a C (Fair). The fund currently has a performance rating of C (Fair) based on an annualized return of 19.46% over the last three years and a total return of 3.44% year to date 2012. Factored into the performance evaluation is an expense ratio of 0.63% (very low).

The fund's risk rating is currently B (Good). It carries a beta of 0.58, meaning the fund's expected move will be 5.8% for every 10% move in the market. Volatility, as measured by both the semi-deviation and a drawdown factor, is considered low. As of March 31, 2012, *PowerShares Dynamic Food & Bever traded at a price exactly equal to its net asset value.

Peter Hubbard has been running the fund for 5 years and currently receives a manager quality ranking of 80 (0=worst, 99=best). If you desire an average level of risk, then this fund may be an option.

Data Date	Investment Rating	Net Assets ($Mil)	Price	Performance Rating/Pts	Total Return Y-T-D	Risk Rating/Pts
3-12	C	159.49	19.83	C / 4.5	3.44%	B / 8.9
2011	C+	190.90	19.17	C / 5.5	-0.94%	B / 8.5
2010	A	126.70	18.23	B / 8.2	30.78%	B- / 7.0
2009	C-	86.59	14.20	D / 1.9	8.78%	B- / 7.0

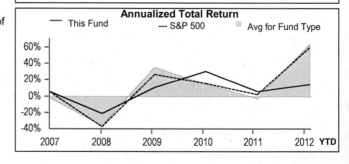

*PowerShares Dynamic Hlthcare (PTH)   C+   Fair

Fund Family: Invesco Powershares Capital Mgmt LL
Fund Type: Health
Inception Date: October 12, 2006

Major Rating Factors: Middle of the road best describes *PowerShares Dynamic Hlthcare whose TheStreet.com Investment Rating is currently a C+ (Fair). The fund currently has a performance rating of C+ (Fair) based on an annualized return of 23.12% over the last three years and a total return of 13.04% year to date 2012. Factored into the performance evaluation is an expense ratio of 0.65% (very low).

The fund's risk rating is currently B- (Good). It carries a beta of 0.80, meaning the fund's expected move will be 8.0% for every 10% move in the market. Volatility, as measured by both the semi-deviation and a drawdown factor, is considered low. As of March 31, 2012, *PowerShares Dynamic Hlthcare traded at a premium of .28% above its net asset value, which is worse than its one-year historical average premium of .01%.

Peter Hubbard has been running the fund for 5 years and currently receives a manager quality ranking of 71 (0=worst, 99=best). If you desire an average level of risk, then this fund may be an option.

Data Date	Investment Rating	Net Assets ($Mil)	Price	Performance Rating/Pts	Total Return Y-T-D	Risk Rating/Pts
3-12	C+	42.00	32.43	C+ / 6.5	13.04%	B- / 7.6
2011	C+	45.90	28.69	C+ / 5.6	1.92%	B- / 7.8
2010	D+	49.70	26.85	D+ / 2.7	13.58%	C+ / 5.9
2009	C-	71.58	23.64	D+ / 2.9	19.54%	C+ / 6.0

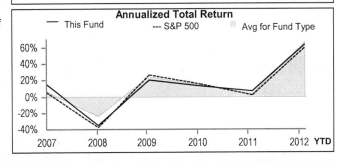

*PowerShares Dynamic Industrials (PRN)   C   Fair

Fund Family: Invesco Powershares Capital Mgmt LL
Fund Type: Income
Inception Date: October 12, 2006

Major Rating Factors: Middle of the road best describes *PowerShares Dynamic Industrials whose TheStreet.com Investment Rating is currently a C (Fair). The fund currently has a performance rating of C (Fair) based on an annualized return of 21.99% over the last three years and a total return of 10.56% year to date 2012. Factored into the performance evaluation is an expense ratio of 0.65% (very low).

The fund's risk rating is currently B- (Good). It carries a beta of 1.34, meaning it is expected to move 13.4% for every 10% move in the market. Volatility, as measured by both the semi-deviation and a drawdown factor, is considered low. As of March 31, 2012, *PowerShares Dynamic Industrials traded at a discount of .03% below its net asset value.

Peter Hubbard has been running the fund for 5 years and currently receives a manager quality ranking of 21 (0=worst, 99=best). If you desire an average level of risk, then this fund may be an option.

Data Date	Investment Rating	Net Assets ($Mil)	Price	Performance Rating/Pts	Total Return Y-T-D	Risk Rating/Pts
3-12	C	32.87	30.15	C / 5.5	10.56%	B- / 7.5
2011	C-	46.30	27.31	C / 4.4	2.00%	B- / 7.2
2010	B-	55.60	29.35	B- / 7.0	33.38%	C / 5.5
2009	D	60.32	22.25	D / 1.8	12.95%	C+ / 5.6

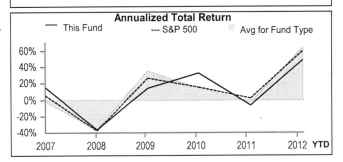

*PowerShares Dynamic Insurance (PIC)   C-   Fair

Fund Family: Invesco Powershares Capital Mgmt LL
Fund Type: Income
Inception Date: October 26, 2005

Major Rating Factors: Middle of the road best describes *PowerShares Dynamic Insurance whose TheStreet.com Investment Rating is currently a C- (Fair). The fund currently has a performance rating of C- (Fair) based on an annualized return of 15.09% over the last three years and a total return of 9.69% year to date 2012. Factored into the performance evaluation is an expense ratio of 0.63% (very low).

The fund's risk rating is currently B (Good). It carries a beta of 0.99, meaning that its performance tracks fairly well with that of the overall stock market. Volatility, as measured by both the semi-deviation and a drawdown factor, is considered low. As of March 31, 2012, *PowerShares Dynamic Insurance traded at a premium of .43% above its net asset value, which is worse than its one-year historical average discount of .02%.

Peter Hubbard has been running the fund for 5 years and currently receives a manager quality ranking of 23 (0=worst, 99=best). If you desire an average level of risk, then this fund may be an option.

Data Date	Investment Rating	Net Assets ($Mil)	Price	Performance Rating/Pts	Total Return Y-T-D	Risk Rating/Pts
3-12	C-	7.21	16.43	C- / 3.8	9.69%	B / 8.2
2011	C-	6.70	14.99	C- / 3.0	0.93%	B- / 7.6
2010	C+	18.80	16.36	C+ / 6.9	23.35%	C+ / 6.5
2009	D	26.81	13.68	D- / 1.1	-3.54%	C+ / 6.2

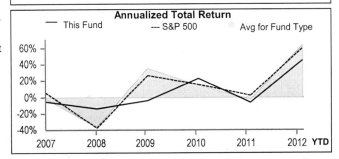

*PowerShares Dynamic Large Cap Gr (PWB)

C+ **Fair**

Fund Family: Invesco Powershares Capital Mgmt LL
Fund Type: Growth
Inception Date: March 3, 2005

Major Rating Factors: Middle of the road best describes *PowerShares Dynamic Large Cap Gr whose TheStreet.com Investment Rating is currently a C+ (Fair). The fund currently has a performance rating of C+ (Fair) based on an annualized return of 21.41% over the last three years and a total return of 15.50% year to date 2012. Factored into the performance evaluation is an expense ratio of 0.63% (very low).

The fund's risk rating is currently B- (Good). It carries a beta of 1.03, meaning that its performance tracks fairly well with that of the overall stock market. Volatility, as measured by both the semi-deviation and a drawdown factor, is considered low. As of March 31, 2012, *PowerShares Dynamic Large Cap Gr traded at a discount of .05% below its net asset value, which is in line with its one-year historical average discount of .05%.

Peter Hubbard has been running the fund for 5 years and currently receives a manager quality ranking of 37 (0=worst, 99=best). If you desire an average level of risk, then this fund may be an option.

Data Date	Investment Rating	Net Assets ($Mil)	Price	Performance Rating/Pts	Total Return Y-T-D	Risk Rating/Pts
3-12	C+	182.76	18.61	C+ / 6.2	15.50%	B- / 7.7
2011	C	163.70	16.12	C / 5.1	0.87%	B- / 7.5
2010	C-	215.50	16.25	C- / 3.6	14.11%	C+ / 5.9
2009	C-	281.17	14.39	C- / 3.0	30.17%	C+ / 5.9

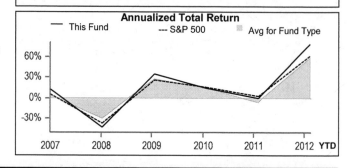

*PowerShares Dynamic Large Cap Va (PWV)

C+ **Fair**

Fund Family: Invesco Powershares Capital Mgmt LL
Fund Type: Income
Inception Date: March 3, 2005

Major Rating Factors: Middle of the road best describes *PowerShares Dynamic Large Cap Va whose TheStreet.com Investment Rating is currently a C+ (Fair). The fund currently has a performance rating of C (Fair) based on an annualized return of 19.69% over the last three years and a total return of 8.40% year to date 2012. Factored into the performance evaluation is an expense ratio of 0.61% (very low).

The fund's risk rating is currently B (Good). It carries a beta of 0.91, meaning that its performance tracks fairly well with that of the overall stock market. Volatility, as measured by both the semi-deviation and a drawdown factor, is considered low. As of March 31, 2012, *PowerShares Dynamic Large Cap Va traded at a discount of .10% below its net asset value, which is better than its one-year historical average discount of .01%.

Peter Hubbard has been running the fund for 5 years and currently receives a manager quality ranking of 52 (0=worst, 99=best). If you desire an average level of risk, then this fund may be an option.

Data Date	Investment Rating	Net Assets ($Mil)	Price	Performance Rating/Pts	Total Return Y-T-D	Risk Rating/Pts
3-12	C+	419.81	20.81	C / 5.2	8.40%	B / 8.6
2011	C+	393.90	19.28	C / 5.1	1.02%	B / 8.1
2010	C	374.50	18.53	C / 4.6	14.34%	C+ / 6.6
2009	C-	262.70	16.75	D+ / 2.6	15.25%	C+ / 6.6

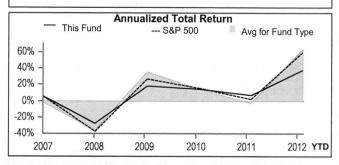

*PowerShares Dynamic Leisure&Ente (PEJ)

A- **Excellent**

Fund Family: Invesco Powershares Capital Mgmt LL
Fund Type: Income
Inception Date: June 23, 2005

Major Rating Factors:
Exceptional performance is the major factor driving the A- (Excellent) TheStreet.com Investment Rating for *PowerShares Dynamic Leisure&Ente. The fund currently has a performance rating of A- (Excellent) based on an annualized return of 33.02% over the last three years and a total return of 17.12% year to date 2012. Factored into the performance evaluation is an expense ratio of 0.63% (very low).

The fund's risk rating is currently B- (Good). It carries a beta of 1.27, meaning it is expected to move 12.7% for every 10% move in the market. Volatility, as measured by both the semi-deviation and a drawdown factor, is considered low. As of March 31, 2012, *PowerShares Dynamic Leisure&Ente traded at a premium of .23% above its net asset value, which is worse than its one-year historical average discount of .04%.

Peter Hubbard has been running the fund for 5 years and currently receives a manager quality ranking of 73 (0=worst, 99=best). If you desire only a moderate level of risk and strong performance, then this fund is an excellent option.

Data Date	Investment Rating	Net Assets ($Mil)	Price	Performance Rating/Pts	Total Return Y-T-D	Risk Rating/Pts
3-12	A-	47.49	21.89	A- / 9.0	17.12%	B- / 7.9
2011	B	35.50	18.69	B / 7.7	0.64%	B- / 7.6
2010	A-	66.30	18.47	B+ / 8.8	39.93%	C+ / 5.6
2009	D	12.78	13.39	D / 2.1	37.52%	C / 5.4

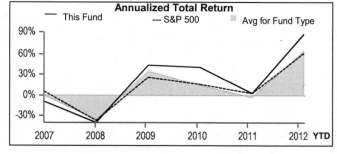

*PowerShares Dynamic MagniQuant (PIQ)   C   Fair

Fund Family: Invesco Powershares Capital Mgmt LL
Fund Type: Income
Inception Date: October 12, 2006

Major Rating Factors: Middle of the road best describes *PowerShares Dynamic MagniQuant whose TheStreet.com Investment Rating is currently a C (Fair). The fund currently has a performance rating of C (Fair) based on an annualized return of 19.39% over the last three years and a total return of 12.03% year to date 2012. Factored into the performance evaluation is an expense ratio of 0.65% (very low).

The fund's risk rating is currently B- (Good). It carries a beta of 1.22, meaning it is expected to move 12.2% for every 10% move in the market. Volatility, as measured by both the semi-deviation and a drawdown factor, is considered low. As of March 31, 2012, *PowerShares Dynamic MagniQuant traded at a discount of .04% below its net asset value, which is worse than its one-year historical average discount of .13%.

Peter Hubbard has been running the fund for 5 years and currently receives a manager quality ranking of 20 (0=worst, 99=best). If you desire an average level of risk, then this fund may be an option.

Data Date	Investment Rating	Net Assets ($Mil)	Price	Performance Rating/Pts	Total Return Y-T-D	Risk Rating/Pts
3-12	C	18.13	26.55	C / 5.1	12.03%	B- / 7.6
2011	C-	16.50	23.70	C / 4.4	0.42%	B- / 7.5
2010	C	25.60	24.54	C / 5.2	20.68%	C+ / 6.0
2009	D	28.65	20.59	D / 1.6	16.89%	C+ / 6.0

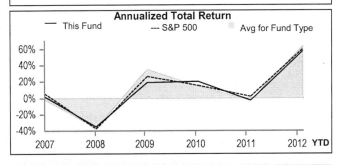

*PowerShares Dynamic Market (PWC)   C-   Fair

Fund Family: Invesco Powershares Capital Mgmt LL
Fund Type: Growth
Inception Date: May 1, 2003

Major Rating Factors: Middle of the road best describes *PowerShares Dynamic Market whose TheStreet.com Investment Rating is currently a C- (Fair). The fund currently has a performance rating of C- (Fair) based on an annualized return of 16.34% over the last three years and a total return of 13.86% year to date 2012. Factored into the performance evaluation is an expense ratio of 0.60% (very low).

The fund's risk rating is currently B- (Good). It carries a beta of 1.04, meaning that its performance tracks fairly well with that of the overall stock market. Volatility, as measured by both the semi-deviation and a drawdown factor, is considered low. As of March 31, 2012, *PowerShares Dynamic Market traded at a premium of .13% above its net asset value, which is worse than its one-year historical average discount of .03%.

Peter Hubbard has been running the fund for 5 years and currently receives a manager quality ranking of 22 (0=worst, 99=best). If you desire an average level of risk, then this fund may be an option.

Data Date	Investment Rating	Net Assets ($Mil)	Price	Performance Rating/Pts	Total Return Y-T-D	Risk Rating/Pts
3-12	C-	134.14	46.66	C- / 4.2	13.86%	B- / 7.8
2011	C-	131.10	41.02	C- / 3.7	1.27%	B- / 7.7
2010	C-	195.80	44.01	C- / 3.8	18.15%	C+ / 6.3
2009	D	260.78	38.05	D- / 1.4	15.86%	C+ / 6.2

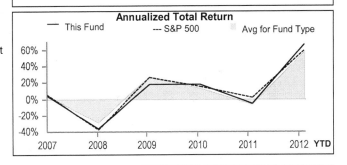

*PowerShares Dynamic Media (PBS)   B-   Good

Fund Family: Invesco Powershares Capital Mgmt LL
Fund Type: Income
Inception Date: June 23, 2005

Major Rating Factors: Strong performance is the major factor driving the B- (Good) TheStreet.com Investment Rating for *PowerShares Dynamic Media. The fund currently has a performance rating of B (Good) based on an annualized return of 28.02% over the last three years and a total return of 14.49% year to date 2012. Factored into the performance evaluation is an expense ratio of 0.63% (very low).

The fund's risk rating is currently B- (Good). It carries a beta of 1.38, meaning it is expected to move 13.8% for every 10% move in the market. Volatility, as measured by both the semi-deviation and a drawdown factor, is considered low. As of March 31, 2012, *PowerShares Dynamic Media traded at a premium of .13% above its net asset value.

Peter Hubbard has been running the fund for 5 years and currently receives a manager quality ranking of 34 (0=worst, 99=best). If you desire only a moderate level of risk and strong performance, then this fund is an excellent option.

Data Date	Investment Rating	Net Assets ($Mil)	Price	Performance Rating/Pts	Total Return Y-T-D	Risk Rating/Pts
3-12	B-	135.98	15.16	B / 7.6	14.49%	B- / 7.6
2011	B-	124.00	13.25	B- / 7.0	2.03%	B- / 7.5
2010	C+	84.10	13.92	C+ / 6.1	20.54%	C / 5.4
2009	D+	8.25	11.64	D+ / 2.7	55.05%	C / 5.1

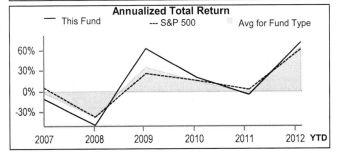

*PowerShares Dynamic Networking (PXQ)

B+ **Good**

Fund Family: Invesco Powershares Capital Mgmt LL
Fund Type: Growth
Inception Date: June 23, 2005

Major Rating Factors: Strong performance is the major factor driving the B+ (Good) TheStreet.com Investment Rating for *PowerShares Dynamic Networking. The fund currently has a performance rating of B+ (Good) based on an annualized return of 33.57% over the last three years and a total return of 17.66% year to date 2012. Factored into the performance evaluation is an expense ratio of 0.63% (very low).

The fund's risk rating is currently B- (Good). It carries a beta of 1.41, meaning it is expected to move 14.1% for every 10% move in the market. Volatility, as measured by both the semi-deviation and a drawdown factor, is considered low. As of March 31, 2012, *PowerShares Dynamic Networking traded at a discount of .03% below its net asset value, which is better than its one-year historical average discount of .02%.

Peter Hubbard has been running the fund for 5 years and currently receives a manager quality ranking of 58 (0=worst, 99=best). If you desire only a moderate level of risk and strong performance, then this fund is an excellent option.

Data Date	Investment Rating	Net Assets ($Mil)	Price	Performance Rating/Pts	Total Return Y-T-D	Risk Rating/Pts
3-12	B+	91.54	28.58	B+ / 8.9	17.66%	B- / 7.3
2011	B-	81.40	24.29	B / 7.6	0.95%	B- / 7.0
2010	A	116.10	26.46	A- / 9.2	47.05%	C+ / 5.8
2009	C	16.28	18.14	C+ / 6.1	63.13%	C / 5.5

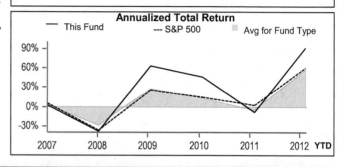

*PowerShares Dynamic Oil & Gas Sv (PXJ)

D+ **Weak**

Fund Family: Invesco Powershares Capital Mgmt LL
Fund Type: Energy/Natural Resources
Inception Date: October 26, 2005

Major Rating Factors: *PowerShares Dynamic Oil & Gas Sv receives a TheStreet.com Investment Rating of D+ (Weak). The fund currently has a performance rating of C (Fair) based on an annualized return of 22.40% over the last three years and a total return of 3.42% year to date 2012. Factored into the performance evaluation is an expense ratio of 0.63% (very low).

The fund's risk rating is currently C+ (Fair). It carries a beta of 1.56, meaning it is expected to move 15.6% for every 10% move in the market. Volatility, as measured by both the semi-deviation and a drawdown factor, is considered low. As of March 31, 2012, *PowerShares Dynamic Oil & Gas Sv traded at a discount of .14% below its net asset value, which is better than its one-year historical average discount of .04%.

Peter Hubbard has been running the fund for 5 years and currently receives a manager quality ranking of 26 (0=worst, 99=best). If you desire an average level of risk, then this fund may be an option.

Data Date	Investment Rating	Net Assets ($Mil)	Price	Performance Rating/Pts	Total Return Y-T-D	Risk Rating/Pts
3-12	D+	168.86	20.85	C / 4.7	3.42%	C+ / 6.1
2011	C	169.50	20.16	C+ / 6.6	2.93%	C+ / 6.0
2010	D+	199.50	21.83	C- / 4.0	29.63%	C- / 4.1
2009	D+	155.72	16.96	C- / 3.9	43.35%	C / 4.4

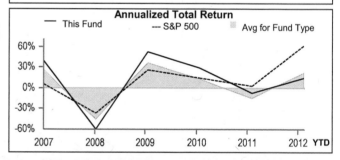

*PowerShares Dynamic OTC Portfoli (PWO)

C- **Fair**

Fund Family: Invesco Powershares Capital Mgmt LL
Fund Type: Growth
Inception Date: May 1, 2003

Major Rating Factors: Middle of the road best describes *PowerShares Dynamic OTC Portfoli whose TheStreet.com Investment Rating is currently a C- (Fair). The fund currently has a performance rating of C (Fair) based on an annualized return of 17.63% over the last three years and a total return of 13.56% year to date 2012. Factored into the performance evaluation is an expense ratio of 0.60% (very low).

The fund's risk rating is currently B- (Good). It carries a beta of 1.06, meaning that its performance tracks fairly well with that of the overall stock market. Volatility, as measured by both the semi-deviation and a drawdown factor, is considered low. As of March 31, 2012, *PowerShares Dynamic OTC Portfoli traded at a premium of .25% above its net asset value, which is worse than its one-year historical average discount of .01%.

Peter Hubbard has been running the fund for 5 years and currently receives a manager quality ranking of 23 (0=worst, 99=best). If you desire an average level of risk, then this fund may be an option.

Data Date	Investment Rating	Net Assets ($Mil)	Price	Performance Rating/Pts	Total Return Y-T-D	Risk Rating/Pts
3-12	C-	27.22	51.60	C / 4.3	13.56%	B- / 7.6
2011	C-	27.20	45.44	C- / 3.9	1.47%	B- / 7.4
2010	C+	37.20	49.80	C / 5.5	23.64%	C+ / 6.0
2009	D	39.39	40.45	D- / 1.4	17.93%	C+ / 5.6

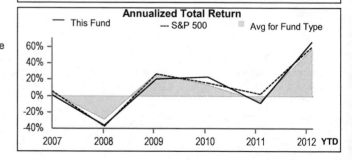

*PowerShares Dynamic Pharmaceutic (PJP)

B **Good**

Fund Family: Invesco Powershares Capital Mgmt LL
Fund Type: Health
Inception Date: June 23, 2005

Major Rating Factors:
Exceptional performance is the major factor driving the B (Good) TheStreet.com Investment Rating for *PowerShares Dynamic Pharmaceutic. The fund currently has a performance rating of A- (Excellent) based on an annualized return of 32.53% over the last three years and a total return of 11.60% year to date 2012. Factored into the performance evaluation is an expense ratio of 0.63% (very low).

The fund's risk rating is currently C+ (Fair). It carries a beta of 0.62, meaning the fund's expected move will be 6.2% for every 10% move in the market. Volatility, as measured by both the semi-deviation and a drawdown factor, is considered low. As of March 31, 2012, *PowerShares Dynamic Pharmaceutic traded at a premium of .10% above its net asset value, which is worse than its one-year historical average premium of .07%.

Peter Hubbard has been running the fund for 5 years and currently receives a manager quality ranking of 90 (0=worst, 99=best). If you desire only a moderate level of risk and strong performance, then this fund is an excellent option.

Data Date	Investment Rating	Net Assets ($Mil)	Price	Perfor-mance Rating/Pts	Total Return Y-T-D	Risk Rating/Pts
3-12	B	251.00	31.43	A- / 9.0	11.60%	C+ / 6.9
2011	B	182.80	28.18	B / 7.9	0.50%	B- / 7.5
2010	A-	94.60	23.64	B+ / 8.3	27.81%	C+ / 5.9
2009	C-	104.35	18.65	C- / 3.8	15.07%	C / 5.2

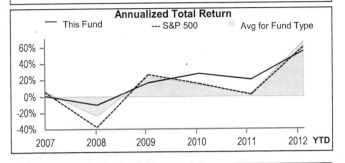

*PowerShares Dynamic Retail (PMR)

B **Good**

Fund Family: Invesco Powershares Capital Mgmt LL
Fund Type: Income
Inception Date: October 26, 2005

Major Rating Factors: Strong performance is the major factor driving the B (Good) TheStreet.com Investment Rating for *PowerShares Dynamic Retail. The fund currently has a performance rating of B (Good) based on an annualized return of 24.32% over the last three years and a total return of 16.65% year to date 2012. Factored into the performance evaluation is an expense ratio of 0.63% (very low).

The fund's risk rating is currently B (Good). It carries a beta of 1.02, meaning that its performance tracks fairly well with that of the overall stock market. Volatility, as measured by both the semi-deviation and a drawdown factor, is considered low. As of March 31, 2012, *PowerShares Dynamic Retail traded at a discount of .04% below its net asset value, which is better than its one-year historical average discount of .02%.

Peter Hubbard has been running the fund for 5 years and currently receives a manager quality ranking of 62 (0=worst, 99=best). If you desire only a moderate level of risk and strong performance, then this fund is an excellent option.

Data Date	Investment Rating	Net Assets ($Mil)	Price	Perfor-mance Rating/Pts	Total Return Y-T-D	Risk Rating/Pts
3-12	B	59.95	25.61	B / 7.8	16.65%	B / 8.2
2011	B	29.70	21.96	B / 8.0	1.46%	B / 8.0
2010	A-	13.60	19.45	B+ / 8.3	24.90%	C+ / 6.7
2009	D+	77.61	15.82	D / 1.9	27.20%	C+ / 6.2

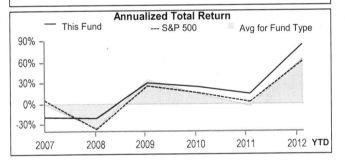

*PowerShares Dynamic Semiconducto (PSI)

C- **Fair**

Fund Family: Invesco Powershares Capital Mgmt LL
Fund Type: Income
Inception Date: June 23, 2005

Major Rating Factors: Middle of the road best describes *PowerShares Dynamic Semiconducto whose TheStreet.com Investment Rating is currently a C- (Fair). The fund currently has a performance rating of C (Fair) based on an annualized return of 17.72% over the last three years and a total return of 16.70% year to date 2012. Factored into the performance evaluation is an expense ratio of 0.63% (very low).

The fund's risk rating is currently C+ (Fair). It carries a beta of 1.59, meaning it is expected to move 15.9% for every 10% move in the market. Volatility, as measured by both the semi-deviation and a drawdown factor, is considered low. As of March 31, 2012, *PowerShares Dynamic Semiconducto traded at a premium of .37% above its net asset value, which is worse than its one-year historical average discount of .04%.

Peter Hubbard has been running the fund for 5 years and currently receives a manager quality ranking of 11 (0=worst, 99=best). If you desire an average level of risk, then this fund may be an option.

Data Date	Investment Rating	Net Assets ($Mil)	Price	Perfor-mance Rating/Pts	Total Return Y-T-D	Risk Rating/Pts
3-12	C-	21.70	16.21	C / 4.5	16.70%	C+ / 6.8
2011	C-	22.30	13.89	C / 4.4	1.73%	C+ / 6.7
2010	C+	37.40	16.28	C+ / 6.6	20.74%	C / 5.3
2009	D+	36.37	13.53	D+ / 2.6	41.71%	C / 5.2

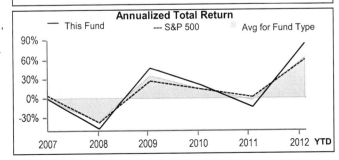

* Denotes ETF Fund

*PowerShares Dynamic Software (PSJ)   C   Fair

Fund Family: Invesco Powershares Capital Mgmt LL
Fund Type: Growth
Inception Date: June 23, 2005

Major Rating Factors: Middle of the road best describes *PowerShares Dynamic Software whose TheStreet.com Investment Rating is currently a C (Fair). The fund currently has a performance rating of C+ (Fair) based on an annualized return of 22.52% over the last three years and a total return of 14.96% year to date 2012. Factored into the performance evaluation is an expense ratio of 0.63% (very low).

The fund's risk rating is currently B- (Good). It carries a beta of 1.00, meaning that its performance tracks fairly well with that of the overall stock market. Volatility, as measured by both the semi-deviation and a drawdown factor, is considered low. As of March 31, 2012, *PowerShares Dynamic Software traded at a premium of .22% above its net asset value, which is worse than its one-year historical average discount of .02%.

Peter Hubbard has been running the fund for 5 years and currently receives a manager quality ranking of 53 (0=worst, 99=best). If you desire an average level of risk, then this fund may be an option.

Data Date	Investment Rating	Net Assets ($Mil)	Price	Performance Rating/Pts	Total Return Y-T-D	Risk Rating/Pts
3-12	C	50.78	26.96	C+ / 5.8	14.96%	B- / 7.4
2011	C+	50.20	23.45	C+ / 5.9	-0.99%	B- / 7.4
2010	A-	66.00	24.96	B / 7.9	20.06%	C+ / 6.4
2009	C+	36.90	20.79	C+ / 6.2	51.42%	C+ / 5.9

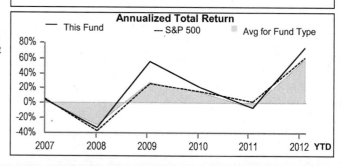

Annualized Total Return

*PowerShares Dynamic Technology (PTF)   C   Fair

Fund Family: Invesco Powershares Capital Mgmt LL
Fund Type: Growth
Inception Date: October 12, 2006

Major Rating Factors: Middle of the road best describes *PowerShares Dynamic Technology whose TheStreet.com Investment Rating is currently a C (Fair). The fund currently has a performance rating of C (Fair) based on an annualized return of 18.35% over the last three years and a total return of 18.30% year to date 2012. Factored into the performance evaluation is an expense ratio of 0.65% (very low).

The fund's risk rating is currently B- (Good). It carries a beta of 1.28, meaning it is expected to move 12.8% for every 10% move in the market. Volatility, as measured by both the semi-deviation and a drawdown factor, is considered low. As of March 31, 2012, *PowerShares Dynamic Technology traded at a premium of .33% above its net asset value, which is worse than its one-year historical average premium of .07%.

Peter Hubbard has been running the fund for 5 years and currently receives a manager quality ranking of 17 (0=worst, 99=best). If you desire an average level of risk, then this fund may be an option.

Data Date	Investment Rating	Net Assets ($Mil)	Price	Performance Rating/Pts	Total Return Y-T-D	Risk Rating/Pts
3-12	C	30.52	27.54	C / 4.9	18.30%	B- / 7.4
2011	C-	27.70	23.28	C- / 4.0	0.83%	B- / 7.1
2010	C	42.30	25.63	C / 4.9	11.21%	C+ / 5.7
2009	C-	25.93	23.07	C- / 3.5	38.89%	C+ / 5.6

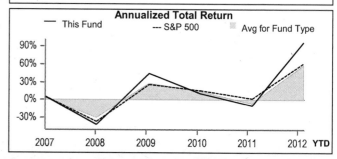

Annualized Total Return

*PowerShares Dynamic Utilities (PUI)   C-   Fair

Fund Family: Invesco Powershares Capital Mgmt LL
Fund Type: Utilities
Inception Date: October 26, 2005

Major Rating Factors:
Disappointing performance is the major factor driving the C- (Fair) TheStreet.com Investment Rating for *PowerShares Dynamic Utilities. The fund currently has a performance rating of D+ (Weak) based on an annualized return of 12.43% over the last three years and a total return of 3.42% year to date 2012. Factored into the performance evaluation is an expense ratio of 0.63% (very low).

The fund's risk rating is currently B (Good). It carries a beta of 0.95, meaning that its performance tracks fairly well with that of the overall stock market. Volatility, as measured by both the semi-deviation and a drawdown factor, is considered low. As of March 31, 2012, *PowerShares Dynamic Utilities traded at a price exactly equal to its net asset value, which is worse than its one-year historical average discount of .04%.

Peter Hubbard has been running the fund for 5 years and currently receives a manager quality ranking of 31 (0=worst, 99=best). This fund offers only a moderate level of risk but investors looking for strong performance are still waiting.

Data Date	Investment Rating	Net Assets ($Mil)	Price	Performance Rating/Pts	Total Return Y-T-D	Risk Rating/Pts
3-12	C-	46.40	16.74	D+ / 2.9	3.42%	B / 8.8
2011	C-	47.10	16.25	C- / 3.2	-1.48%	B / 8.3
2010	C-	41.30	15.59	D+ / 2.3	8.56%	C+ / 6.8
2009	D+	42.07	15.04	D / 1.6	1.82%	C+ / 6.9

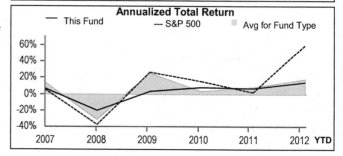

Annualized Total Return

*PowerShares Emg Mkts Infrastruct (PXR)

C-   **Fair**

Fund Family: Invesco Powershares Capital Mgmt LL
Fund Type: Emerging Market
Inception Date: October 15, 2008

Major Rating Factors: Middle of the road best describes *PowerShares Emg Mkts Infrastruct whose TheStreet.com Investment Rating is currently a C- (Fair). The fund currently has a performance rating of C (Fair) based on an annualized return of 21.85% over the last three years and a total return of 15.56% year to date 2012. Factored into the performance evaluation is an expense ratio of 0.75% (very low).

The fund's risk rating is currently C+ (Fair). It carries a beta of 1.33, meaning it is expected to move 13.3% for every 10% move in the market. Volatility, as measured by both the semi-deviation and a drawdown factor, is considered low. As of March 31, 2012, *PowerShares Emg Mkts Infrastruct traded at a discount of .23% below its net asset value, which is better than its one-year historical average discount of .17%.

Brian McGreal has been running the fund for 4 years and currently receives a manager quality ranking of 19 (0=worst, 99=best). If you desire an average level of risk, then this fund may be an option.

Data Date	Investment Rating	Net Assets ($Mil)	Price	Performance Rating/Pts	Total Return Y-T-D	Risk Rating/Pts
3-12	C-	131.46	42.88	C / 4.8	15.56%	C+ / 6.4
2011	C-	112.20	37.13	C- / 4.1	0.57%	C+ / 6.4
2010	A+	192.00	53.62	A+ / 9.6	27.00%	B- / 7.6
2009	A+	21.23	42.84	A+ / 9.7	77.81%	B / 8.0

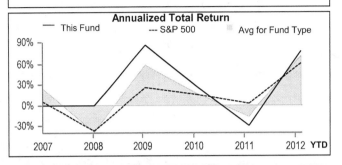

Annualized Total Return

*PowerShares Emrg Mkt Sovereign D (PCY)

C   **Fair**

Fund Family: Invesco Powershares Capital Mgmt LL
Fund Type: Emerging Market
Inception Date: October 11, 2007

Major Rating Factors: Middle of the road best describes *PowerShares Emrg Mkt Sovereign D whose TheStreet.com Investment Rating is currently a C (Fair). The fund currently has a performance rating of C- (Fair) based on an annualized return of 16.71% over the last three years and a total return of 3.77% year to date 2012. Factored into the performance evaluation is an expense ratio of 0.50% (very low).

The fund's risk rating is currently B (Good). It carries a beta of 0.53, meaning the fund's expected move will be 5.3% for every 10% move in the market. Volatility, as measured by both the semi-deviation and a drawdown factor, is considered low. As of March 31, 2012, *PowerShares Emrg Mkt Sovereign D traded at a price exactly equal to its net asset value, which is worse than its one-year historical average discount of .03%.

Peter Hubbard has been running the fund for 5 years and currently receives a manager quality ranking of 88 (0=worst, 99=best). If you desire an average level of risk, then this fund may be an option.

Data Date	Investment Rating	Net Assets ($Mil)	Price	Performance Rating/Pts	Total Return Y-T-D	Risk Rating/Pts
3-12	C	1,490.73	28.02	C- / 4.0	3.77%	B / 8.8
2011	C+	1,405.50	27.36	C / 5.2	-0.88%	B / 8.8
2010	C+	893.80	26.67	C+ / 6.4	11.40%	C+ / 6.2
2009	B+	133.19	25.53	B / 7.7	29.03%	C+ / 6.1

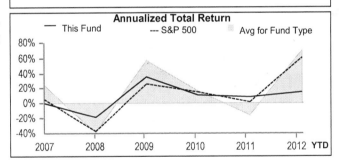

Annualized Total Return

*PowerShares Financial Preferred (PGF)

B+   **Good**

Fund Family: Invesco Powershares Capital Mgmt LL
Fund Type: Financial Services
Inception Date: December 1, 2006

Major Rating Factors: Strong performance is the major factor driving the B+ (Good) TheStreet.com Investment Rating for *PowerShares Financial Preferred. The fund currently has a performance rating of B (Good) based on an annualized return of 30.74% over the last three years and a total return of 12.89% year to date 2012. Factored into the performance evaluation is an expense ratio of 0.66% (very low).

The fund's risk rating is currently B (Good). It carries a beta of 0.49, meaning the fund's expected move will be 4.9% for every 10% move in the market. Volatility, as measured by both the semi-deviation and a drawdown factor, is considered low. As of March 31, 2012, *PowerShares Financial Preferred traded at a premium of .28% above its net asset value, which is worse than its one-year historical average discount of .02%.

Peter Hubbard has been running the fund for 5 years and currently receives a manager quality ranking of 93 (0=worst, 99=best). If you desire only a moderate level of risk and strong performance, then this fund is an excellent option.

Data Date	Investment Rating	Net Assets ($Mil)	Price	Performance Rating/Pts	Total Return Y-T-D	Risk Rating/Pts
3-12	B+	1,589.27	17.90	B / 8.0	12.89%	B / 8.7
2011	D+	1,423.20	16.12	C / 4.6	4.09%	C+ / 5.6
2010	C-	1,735.70	17.61	C+ / 5.6	16.71%	C- / 3.4
2009	D-	773.64	16.32	D+ / 2.3	30.76%	C- / 3.7

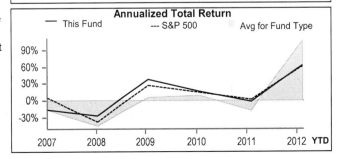

Annualized Total Return

*PowerShares FTSE RAFI Asia Pac E (PAF)

C+   **Fair**

Fund Family: Invesco Powershares Capital Mgmt LL
Fund Type: Foreign
Inception Date: June 25, 2007

Major Rating Factors: Middle of the road best describes *PowerShares FTSE RAFI Asia Pac E whose TheStreet.com Investment Rating is currently a C+ (Fair). The fund currently has a performance rating of C+ (Fair) based on an annualized return of 25.64% over the last three years and a total return of 12.02% year to date 2012. Factored into the performance evaluation is an expense ratio of 0.80% (very low).

The fund's risk rating is currently B- (Good). It carries a beta of 1.16, meaning it is expected to move 11.6% for every 10% move in the market. Volatility, as measured by both the semi-deviation and a drawdown factor, is considered low. As of March 31, 2012, *PowerShares FTSE RAFI Asia Pac E traded at a discount of .21% below its net asset value, which is better than its one-year historical average discount of .17%.

Peter Hubbard currently receives a manager quality ranking of 77 (0=worst, 99=best). If you desire an average level of risk, then this fund may be an option.

Data Date	Investment Rating	Net Assets ($Mil)	Price	Performance Rating/Pts	Total Return Y-T-D	Risk Rating/Pts
3-12	C+	61.86	51.92	C+ / 6.4	12.02%	B- / 7.0
2011	C+	53.70	46.53	C+ / 6.2	1.31%	B- / 7.0
2010	C+	49.50	55.67	B- / 7.2	23.18%	C / 4.6
2009	A-	15.59	46.81	A+ / 9.7	71.61%	C / 4.6

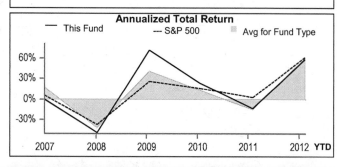

*PowerShares FTSE RAFI DM exUS Sm (PDN)

C-   **Fair**

Fund Family: Invesco Powershares Capital Mgmt LL
Fund Type: Foreign
Inception Date: September 27, 2007

Major Rating Factors: Middle of the road best describes *PowerShares FTSE RAFI DM exUS Sm whose TheStreet.com Investment Rating is currently a C- (Fair). The fund currently has a performance rating of C (Fair) based on an annualized return of 22.14% over the last three years and a total return of 9.64% year to date 2012. Factored into the performance evaluation is an expense ratio of 0.75% (very low).

The fund's risk rating is currently B- (Good). It carries a beta of 1.02, meaning that its performance tracks fairly well with that of the overall stock market. Volatility, as measured by both the semi-deviation and a drawdown factor, is considered low. As of March 31, 2012, *PowerShares FTSE RAFI DM exUS Sm traded at a discount of 2.64% below its net asset value, which is better than its one-year historical average discount of .77%.

Peter Hubbard has been running the fund for 5 years and currently receives a manager quality ranking of 77 (0=worst, 99=best). If you desire an average level of risk, then this fund may be an option.

Data Date	Investment Rating	Net Assets ($Mil)	Price	Performance Rating/Pts	Total Return Y-T-D	Risk Rating/Pts
3-12	C-	62.64	22.53	C / 4.8	9.64%	B- / 7.2
2011	C-	60.30	20.56	C / 4.6	0.19%	C+ / 6.6
2010	C+	70.20	24.49	C+ / 6.9	20.35%	C / 5.3
2009	B+	14.70	21.04	A- / 9.0	51.55%	C / 5.0

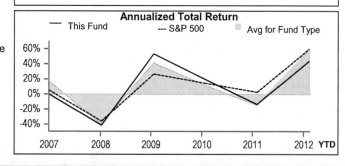

*PowerShares FTSE RAFI Dvlp Mkt e (PXF)

D+   **Weak**

Fund Family: Invesco Powershares Capital Mgmt LL
Fund Type: Foreign
Inception Date: June 25, 2007

Major Rating Factors: *PowerShares FTSE RAFI Dvlp Mkt e receives a TheStreet.com Investment Rating of D+ (Weak). The fund currently has a performance rating of C- (Fair) based on an annualized return of 15.85% over the last three years and a total return of 11.67% year to date 2012. Factored into the performance evaluation is an expense ratio of 0.75% (very low).

The fund's risk rating is currently B- (Good). It carries a beta of 1.22, meaning it is expected to move 12.2% for every 10% move in the market. Volatility, as measured by both the semi-deviation and a drawdown factor, is considered low. As of March 31, 2012, *PowerShares FTSE RAFI Dvlp Mkt e traded at a premium of .62% above its net asset value, which is worse than its one-year historical average premium of .13%.

Peter Hubbard has been running the fund for 5 years and currently receives a manager quality ranking of 34 (0=worst, 99=best). If you desire an average level of risk, then this fund may be an option.

Data Date	Investment Rating	Net Assets ($Mil)	Price	Performance Rating/Pts	Total Return Y-T-D	Risk Rating/Pts
3-12	D+	278.26	35.83	C- / 3.4	11.67%	B- / 7.4
2011	D+	229.70	32.15	D+ / 2.5	-0.56%	B- / 7.2
2010	D	214.60	39.41	D+ / 2.5	8.95%	C / 5.4
2009	A-	93.57	37.86	B+ / 8.7	37.76%	C / 5.5

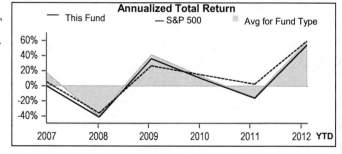

*PowerShares FTSE RAFI Emg Mkts (PXH)

C-   **Fair**

Fund Family: Invesco Powershares Capital Mgmt LL
Fund Type: Emerging Market
Inception Date: September 27, 2007

Data Date	Investment Rating	Net Assets ($Mil)	Price	Performance Rating/Pts	Total Return Y-T-D	Risk Rating/Pts
3-12	C-	416.21	22.92	C- / 4.1	13.41%	B- / 7.0
2011	C-	327.50	20.23	C / 4.4	1.29%	B- / 7.0
2010	C	533.90	25.78	C+ / 5.9	14.23%	C / 4.6
2009	B+	102.87	23.01	A / 9.5	60.22%	C / 4.6

Major Rating Factors: Middle of the road best describes *PowerShares FTSE RAFI Emg Mkts whose TheStreet.com Investment Rating is currently a C- (Fair). The fund currently has a performance rating of C- (Fair) based on an annualized return of 18.13% over the last three years and a total return of 13.41% year to date 2012. Factored into the performance evaluation is an expense ratio of 0.85% (very low).

The fund's risk rating is currently B- (Good). It carries a beta of 1.04, meaning that its performance tracks fairly well with that of the overall stock market. Volatility, as measured by both the semi-deviation and a drawdown factor, is considered low. As of March 31, 2012, *PowerShares FTSE RAFI Emg Mkts traded at a premium of .09% above its net asset value, which is better than its one-year historical average premium of .26%.

Peter Hubbard has been running the fund for 5 years and currently receives a manager quality ranking of 26 (0=worst, 99=best). If you desire an average level of risk, then this fund may be an option.

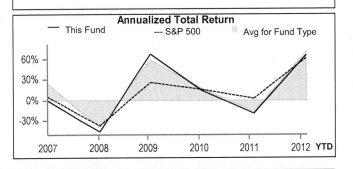

*PowerShares FTSE RAFI US 1000 (PRF)

B-   **Good**

Fund Family: Invesco Powershares Capital Mgmt LL
Fund Type: Income
Inception Date: December 19, 2005

Data Date	Investment Rating	Net Assets ($Mil)	Price	Performance Rating/Pts	Total Return Y-T-D	Risk Rating/Pts
3-12	B-	1,345.97	60.50	B- / 7.2	11.18%	B / 8.2
2011	B-	1,164.80	54.58	C+ / 6.5	1.48%	B- / 7.9
2010	C+	927.40	55.95	C+ / 6.1	20.41%	C+ / 5.8
2009	C-	396.44	47.47	C- / 3.2	37.47%	C+ / 6.3

Major Rating Factors: Strong performance is the major factor driving the B- (Good) TheStreet.com Investment Rating for *PowerShares FTSE RAFI US 1000. The fund currently has a performance rating of B- (Good) based on an annualized return of 26.52% over the last three years and a total return of 11.18% year to date 2012. Factored into the performance evaluation is an expense ratio of 0.39% (very low).

The fund's risk rating is currently B (Good). It carries a beta of 1.21, meaning it is expected to move 12.1% for every 10% move in the market. Volatility, as measured by both the semi-deviation and a drawdown factor, is considered low. As of March 31, 2012, *PowerShares FTSE RAFI US 1000 traded at a discount of .03% below its net asset value, which is better than its one-year historical average premium of .02%.

Peter Hubbard has been running the fund for 5 years and currently receives a manager quality ranking of 52 (0=worst, 99=best). If you desire only a moderate level of risk and strong performance, then this fund is an excellent option.

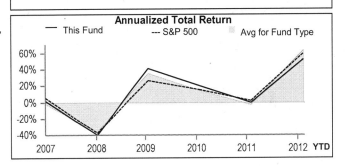

*PowerShares FTSE RAFI US 1500 Sm (PRFZ)

B   **Good**

Fund Family: Invesco Powershares Capital Mgmt LL
Fund Type: Income
Inception Date: September 20, 2006

Data Date	Investment Rating	Net Assets ($Mil)	Price	Performance Rating/Pts	Total Return Y-T-D	Risk Rating/Pts
3-12	B	452.06	68.07	B+ / 8.4	13.56%	B- / 7.5
2011	B-	344.40	60.00	B- / 7.4	1.35%	B- / 7.2
2010	B+	389.60	64.47	B+ / 8.3	28.81%	C / 5.4
2009	C	94.40	50.64	C / 4.7	55.35%	C+ / 5.6

Major Rating Factors: Strong performance is the major factor driving the B (Good) TheStreet.com Investment Rating for *PowerShares FTSE RAFI US 1500 Sm. The fund currently has a performance rating of B+ (Good) based on an annualized return of 32.11% over the last three years and a total return of 13.56% year to date 2012. Factored into the performance evaluation is an expense ratio of 0.39% (very low).

The fund's risk rating is currently B- (Good). It carries a beta of 1.50, meaning it is expected to move 15.0% for every 10% move in the market. Volatility, as measured by both the semi-deviation and a drawdown factor, is considered low. As of March 31, 2012, *PowerShares FTSE RAFI US 1500 Sm traded at a premium of .03% above its net asset value, which is worse than its one-year historical average premium of .02%.

Peter Hubbard has been running the fund for 5 years and currently receives a manager quality ranking of 44 (0=worst, 99=best). If you desire only a moderate level of risk and strong performance, then this fund is an excellent option.

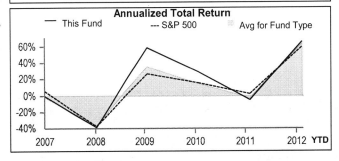

*PowerShares Fundamental High Yie (PHB)

C-   **Fair**

Fund Family: Invesco Powershares Capital Mgmt LL
Fund Type: Corporate - High Yield
Inception Date: November 13, 2007

Data Date	Investment Rating	Net Assets ($Mil)	Price	Performance Rating/Pts	Total Return Y-T-D	Risk Rating/Pts
3-12	C-	877.63	18.62	C- / 3.7	2.19%	B / 8.0
2011	C	637.10	18.47	C / 4.7	-1.14%	B- / 7.7
2010	D	407.30	18.19	D+ / 2.5	9.83%	C / 5.2
2009	C+	95.70	18.01	B / 7.7	21.99%	C / 4.8

Major Rating Factors: Middle of the road best describes *PowerShares Fundamental High Yie whose TheStreet.com Investment Rating is currently a C- (Fair). The fund currently has a performance rating of C- (Fair) based on an annualized return of 15.90% over the last three years and a total return of 2.19% year to date 2012. Factored into the performance evaluation is an expense ratio of 0.50% (very low).

The fund's risk rating is currently B (Good). It carries a beta of 0.87, meaning the fund's expected move will be 8.7% for every 10% move in the market. Volatility, as measured by both the semi-deviation and a drawdown factor, is considered low. As of March 31, 2012, *PowerShares Fundamental High Yie traded at a discount of .27% below its net asset value, which is better than its one-year historical average premium of .14%.

Peter Hubbard has been running the fund for 5 years and currently receives a manager quality ranking of 30 (0=worst, 99=best). If you desire an average level of risk, then this fund may be an option.

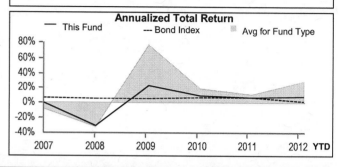

*PowerShares Fundamental Pure Lg (PXLC)

C   **Fair**

Fund Family: Invesco Powershares Capital Mgmt LL
Fund Type: Growth
Inception Date: December 1, 2006

Data Date	Investment Rating	Net Assets ($Mil)	Price	Performance Rating/Pts	Total Return Y-T-D	Risk Rating/Pts
3-12	C	24.78	26.59	C / 4.7	9.24%	B / 8.6
2011	C+	23.20	24.44	C / 4.8	1.29%	B / 8.3
2010	C-	32.80	24.27	C- / 3.8	14.84%	C+ / 6.3
2009	D+	33.36	21.67	D / 2.2	16.53%	C+ / 6.4

Major Rating Factors: Middle of the road best describes *PowerShares Fundamental Pure Lg whose TheStreet.com Investment Rating is currently a C (Fair). The fund currently has a performance rating of C (Fair) based on an annualized return of 18.50% over the last three years and a total return of 9.24% year to date 2012. Factored into the performance evaluation is an expense ratio of 0.65% (very low).

The fund's risk rating is currently B (Good). It carries a beta of 0.88, meaning the fund's expected move will be 8.8% for every 10% move in the market. Volatility, as measured by both the semi-deviation and a drawdown factor, is considered low. As of March 31, 2012, *PowerShares Fundamental Pure Lg traded at a discount of .04% below its net asset value, which is worse than its one-year historical average discount of .05%.

Peter Hubbard has been running the fund for 5 years and currently receives a manager quality ranking of 45 (0=worst, 99=best). If you desire an average level of risk, then this fund may be an option.

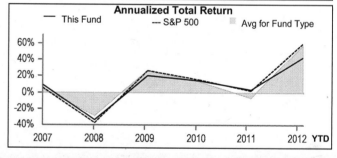

*PowerShares Fundamental Pure Md (PXMC)

C+   **Fair**

Fund Family: Invesco Powershares Capital Mgmt LL
Fund Type: Growth
Inception Date: December 1, 2006

Data Date	Investment Rating	Net Assets ($Mil)	Price	Performance Rating/Pts	Total Return Y-T-D	Risk Rating/Pts
3-12	C+	21.11	26.93	C+ / 5.6	11.56%	B / 8.1
2011	C+	20.50	24.16	C / 5.5	1.59%	B- / 7.8
2010	C	22.20	24.76	C / 4.7	21.78%	C+ / 5.8
2009	D+	17.93	20.62	D / 2.1	27.00%	C+ / 5.7

Major Rating Factors: Middle of the road best describes *PowerShares Fundamental Pure Md whose TheStreet.com Investment Rating is currently a C+ (Fair). The fund currently has a performance rating of C+ (Fair) based on an annualized return of 21.44% over the last three years and a total return of 11.56% year to date 2012. Factored into the performance evaluation is an expense ratio of 0.65% (very low).

The fund's risk rating is currently B (Good). It carries a beta of 1.02, meaning that its performance tracks fairly well with that of the overall stock market. Volatility, as measured by both the semi-deviation and a drawdown factor, is considered low. As of March 31, 2012, *PowerShares Fundamental Pure Md traded at a premium of .22% above its net asset value, which is worse than its one-year historical average discount of .02%.

Peter Hubbard has been running the fund for 5 years and currently receives a manager quality ranking of 41 (0=worst, 99=best). If you desire an average level of risk, then this fund may be an option.

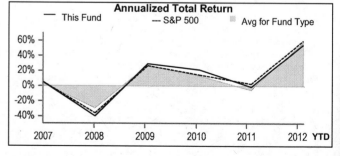

*PowerShares Fundamental Pure Md (PXMG)   C   Fair

Fund Family: Invesco Powershares Capital Mgmt LL
Fund Type: Growth
Inception Date: March 3, 2005

Major Rating Factors: Middle of the road best describes *PowerShares Fundamental Pure Md whose TheStreet.com Investment Rating is currently a C (Fair). The fund currently has a performance rating of C (Fair) based on an annualized return of 19.72% over the last three years and a total return of 12.86% year to date 2012. Factored into the performance evaluation is an expense ratio of 0.63% (very low).

The fund's risk rating is currently B- (Good). It carries a beta of 1.11, meaning it is expected to move 11.1% for every 10% move in the market. Volatility, as measured by both the semi-deviation and a drawdown factor, is considered low. As of March 31, 2012, *PowerShares Fundamental Pure Md traded at a discount of .04% below its net asset value, which is worse than its one-year historical average discount of .07%.

Peter Hubbard has been running the fund for 5 years and currently receives a manager quality ranking of 25 (0=worst, 99=best). If you desire an average level of risk, then this fund may be an option.

Data Date	Investment Rating	Net Assets ($Mil)	Price	Performance Rating/Pts	Total Return Y-T-D	Risk Rating/Pts
3-12	C	91.21	22.95	C / 5.0	12.86%	B- / 7.7
2011	C	86.40	20.35	C / 4.9	2.01%	B- / 7.5
2010	C-	131.10	21.66	C / 5.1	29.95%	C / 4.6
2009	D+	140.04	16.76	D+ / 2.4	19.98%	C+ / 5.6

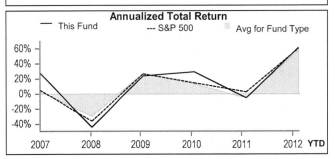

Annualized Total Return

*PowerShares Fundamental Pure Md (PXMV)   C+   Fair

Fund Family: Invesco Powershares Capital Mgmt LL
Fund Type: Growth
Inception Date: March 3, 2005

Major Rating Factors: Middle of the road best describes *PowerShares Fundamental Pure Md whose TheStreet.com Investment Rating is currently a C+ (Fair). The fund currently has a performance rating of C (Fair) based on an annualized return of 20.62% over the last three years and a total return of 11.72% year to date 2012. Factored into the performance evaluation is an expense ratio of 0.63% (very low).

The fund's risk rating is currently B (Good). It carries a beta of 1.09, meaning that its performance tracks fairly well with that of the overall stock market. Volatility, as measured by both the semi-deviation and a drawdown factor, is considered low. As of March 31, 2012, *PowerShares Fundamental Pure Md traded at a premium of .06% above its net asset value, which is worse than its one-year historical average discount of .02%.

Peter Hubbard has been running the fund for 5 years and currently receives a manager quality ranking of 32 (0=worst, 99=best). If you desire an average level of risk, then this fund may be an option.

Data Date	Investment Rating	Net Assets ($Mil)	Price	Performance Rating/Pts	Total Return Y-T-D	Risk Rating/Pts
3-12	C+	31.21	17.18	C / 5.5	11.72%	B / 8.1
2011	C	32.30	15.42	C / 4.7	0.91%	B- / 7.8
2010	C-	39.40	15.79	C- / 3.6	15.31%	C+ / 5.7
2009	D	39.06	13.90	D / 1.7	21.68%	C / 5.5

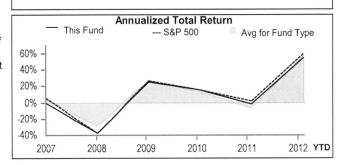

Annualized Total Return

*PowerShares Fundamental Pure Sm (PXSG)   C   Fair

Fund Family: Invesco Powershares Capital Mgmt LL
Fund Type: Growth
Inception Date: March 3, 2005

Major Rating Factors: Middle of the road best describes *PowerShares Fundamental Pure Sm whose TheStreet.com Investment Rating is currently a C (Fair). The fund currently has a performance rating of C (Fair) based on an annualized return of 21.43% over the last three years and a total return of 12.63% year to date 2012. Factored into the performance evaluation is an expense ratio of 0.63% (very low).

The fund's risk rating is currently B- (Good). It carries a beta of 1.12, meaning it is expected to move 11.2% for every 10% move in the market. Volatility, as measured by both the semi-deviation and a drawdown factor, is considered low. As of March 31, 2012, *PowerShares Fundamental Pure Sm traded at a premium of .06% above its net asset value, which is worse than its one-year historical average discount of .11%.

Peter Hubbard has been running the fund for 5 years and currently receives a manager quality ranking of 30 (0=worst, 99=best). If you desire an average level of risk, then this fund may be an option.

Data Date	Investment Rating	Net Assets ($Mil)	Price	Performance Rating/Pts	Total Return Y-T-D	Risk Rating/Pts
3-12	C	33.36	17.92	C / 5.4	12.63%	B- / 7.2
2011	C-	33.30	15.91	C / 5.0	1.45%	C+ / 6.8
2010	C+	38.70	16.13	C+ / 5.7	27.31%	C+ / 5.8
2009	D-	31.48	12.67	D- / 1.2	16.22%	C / 5.5

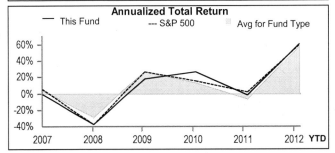

Annualized Total Return

*PowerShares Fundamental Pure Sm (PXSV)

C+   **Fair**

Fund Family: Invesco Powershares Capital Mgmt LL
Fund Type: Growth
Inception Date: March 3, 2005

Data Date	Investment Rating	Net Assets ($Mil)	Price	Performance Rating/Pts	Total Return Y-T-D	Risk Rating/Pts
3-12	C+	54.34	16.69	C+ / 5.8	13.46%	B- / 7.7
2011	C	52.30	14.74	C / 4.6	1.42%	B- / 7.4
2010	C+	65.60	15.08	C+ / 5.8	19.92%	C+ / 5.7
2009	D	62.25	12.84	D- / 1.3	16.77%	C+ / 5.7

Major Rating Factors: Middle of the road best describes *PowerShares Fundamental Pure Sm whose TheStreet.com Investment Rating is currently a C+ (Fair). The fund currently has a performance rating of C+ (Fair) based on an annualized return of 21.16% over the last three years and a total return of 13.46% year to date 2012. Factored into the performance evaluation is an expense ratio of 0.63% (very low).

The fund's risk rating is currently B- (Good). It carries a beta of 1.29, meaning it is expected to move 12.9% for every 10% move in the market. Volatility, as measured by both the semi-deviation and a drawdown factor, is considered low. As of March 31, 2012, *PowerShares Fundamental Pure Sm traded at a premium of .18% above its net asset value, which is worse than its one-year historical average discount of .11%.

Peter Hubbard has been running the fund for 5 years and currently receives a manager quality ranking of 23 (0=worst, 99=best). If you desire an average level of risk, then this fund may be an option.

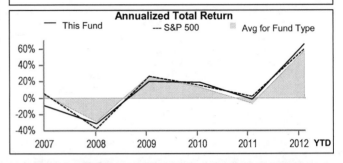

Annualized Total Return

*PowerShares Fundamental Pure Sm (PXSC)

C   **Fair**

Fund Family: Invesco Powershares Capital Mgmt LL
Fund Type: Growth
Inception Date: December 1, 2006

Data Date	Investment Rating	Net Assets ($Mil)	Price	Performance Rating/Pts	Total Return Y-T-D	Risk Rating/Pts
3-12	C	15.58	24.56	C+ / 5.6	11.78%	B- / 7.7
2011	C-	14.20	21.98	C / 4.5	0.79%	B- / 7.4
2010	C	17.80	22.45	C+ / 5.6	23.30%	C+ / 5.6
2009	D	13.53	18.35	D- / 1.2	15.57%	C+ / 5.6

Major Rating Factors: Middle of the road best describes *PowerShares Fundamental Pure Sm whose TheStreet.com Investment Rating is currently a C (Fair). The fund currently has a performance rating of C+ (Fair) based on an annualized return of 21.38% over the last three years and a total return of 11.78% year to date 2012. Factored into the performance evaluation is an expense ratio of 0.65% (very low).

The fund's risk rating is currently B- (Good). It carries a beta of 1.20, meaning it is expected to move 12.0% for every 10% move in the market. Volatility, as measured by both the semi-deviation and a drawdown factor, is considered low. As of March 31, 2012, *PowerShares Fundamental Pure Sm traded at a premium of .24% above its net asset value.

Peter Hubbard has been running the fund for 5 years and currently receives a manager quality ranking of 26 (0=worst, 99=best). If you desire an average level of risk, then this fund may be an option.

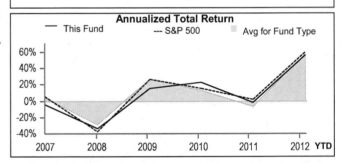

Annualized Total Return

*PowerShares Gb Nuclear Energy Po (PKN)

D   **Weak**

Fund Family: Invesco Powershares Capital Mgmt LL
Fund Type: Energy/Natural Resources
Inception Date: April 1, 2008

Data Date	Investment Rating	Net Assets ($Mil)	Price	Performance Rating/Pts	Total Return Y-T-D	Risk Rating/Pts
3-12	D	16.85	17.03	D / 2.1	9.38%	B- / 7.2
2011	D	14.90	15.58	D / 1.8	0.26%	B- / 7.0
2010	A-	36.80	21.15	A / 9.5	20.01%	C / 5.1
2009	C+	28.57	18.70	B- / 7.3	21.35%	C / 5.0

Major Rating Factors:
Disappointing performance is the major factor driving the D (Weak) TheStreet.com Investment Rating for *PowerShares Gb Nuclear Energy Po. The fund currently has a performance rating of D (Weak) based on an annualized return of 9.08% over the last three years and a total return of 9.38% year to date 2012. Factored into the performance evaluation is an expense ratio of 0.75% (very low).

The fund's risk rating is currently B- (Good). It carries a beta of 0.86, meaning the fund's expected move will be 8.6% for every 10% move in the market. Volatility, as measured by both the semi-deviation and a drawdown factor, is considered low. As of March 31, 2012, *PowerShares Gb Nuclear Energy Po traded at a discount of .64% below its net asset value, which is better than its one-year historical average discount of .53%.

Peter Hubbard has been running the fund for 4 years and currently receives a manager quality ranking of 24 (0=worst, 99=best). This fund offers only a moderate level of risk but investors looking for strong performance are still waiting.

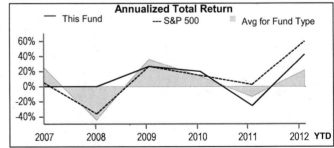

Annualized Total Return

*PowerShares Glb Gold & Precious (PSAU)

D **Weak**

Fund Family: Invesco Powershares Capital Mgmt LL
Fund Type: Precious Metals
Inception Date: September 16, 2008

Data Date	Investment Rating	Net Assets ($Mil)	Price	Performance Rating/Pts	Total Return Y-T-D	Risk Rating/Pts
3-12	D	49.12	39.70	D+ / 2.9	-0.13%	C+ / 6.0
2011	C-	47.80	39.81	C+ / 5.7	2.66%	C / 5.4
2010	A-	67.50	50.01	A+ / 9.6	37.48%	C / 5.3
2009	B+	7.73	38.21	A- / 9.0	45.33%	C / 4.6

Major Rating Factors:
Disappointing performance is the major factor driving the D (Weak) TheStreet.com Investment Rating for *PowerShares Glb Gold & Precious. The fund currently has a performance rating of D+ (Weak) based on an annualized return of 17.19% over the last three years and a total return of -0.13% year to date 2012. Factored into the performance evaluation is an expense ratio of 0.75% (very low).

The fund's risk rating is currently C+ (Fair). It carries a beta of 1.28, meaning it is expected to move 12.8% for every 10% move in the market. Volatility, as measured by both the semi-deviation and a drawdown factor, is considered low. As of March 31, 2012, *PowerShares Glb Gold & Precious traded at a premium of 1.04% above its net asset value, which is worse than its one-year historical average discount of .06%.

Brian McGreal has been running the fund for 4 years and currently receives a manager quality ranking of 12 (0=worst, 99=best). This fund offers only a moderate level of risk but investors looking for strong performance are still waiting.

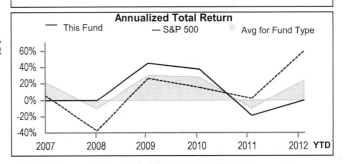

*PowerShares Gldn Drgn Hltr USX C (PGJ)

D **Weak**

Fund Family: Invesco Powershares Capital Mgmt LL
Fund Type: Global
Inception Date: December 9, 2004

Data Date	Investment Rating	Net Assets ($Mil)	Price	Performance Rating/Pts	Total Return Y-T-D	Risk Rating/Pts
3-12	D	265.79	21.62	D+ / 2.3	10.34%	C+ / 6.5
2011	D+	228.90	19.61	C- / 3.1	1.53%	C+ / 6.3
2010	D-	450.30	26.64	D / 1.7	11.77%	C / 4.4
2009	C-	279.49	24.10	C+ / 6.4	54.14%	C- / 3.3

Major Rating Factors:
Disappointing performance is the major factor driving the D (Weak) TheStreet.com Investment Rating for *PowerShares Gldn Drgn Hltr USX C. The fund currently has a performance rating of D+ (Weak) based on an annualized return of 11.77% over the last three years and a total return of 10.34% year to date 2012. Factored into the performance evaluation is an expense ratio of 0.70% (very low).

The fund's risk rating is currently C+ (Fair). It carries a beta of 1.11, meaning it is expected to move 11.1% for every 10% move in the market. Volatility, as measured by both the semi-deviation and a drawdown factor, is considered low. As of March 31, 2012, *PowerShares Gldn Drgn Hltr USX C traded at a discount of .28% below its net asset value, which is better than its one-year historical average discount of .23%.

Peter Hubbard has been running the fund for 5 years and currently receives a manager quality ranking of 26 (0=worst, 99=best). This fund offers only a moderate level of risk but investors looking for strong performance are still waiting.

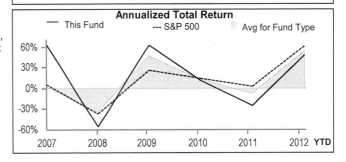

*PowerShares Global Agriculture P (PAGG)

C- **Fair**

Fund Family: Invesco Powershares Capital Mgmt LL
Fund Type: Global
Inception Date: September 16, 2008

Data Date	Investment Rating	Net Assets ($Mil)	Price	Performance Rating/Pts	Total Return Y-T-D	Risk Rating/Pts
3-12	C-	115.77	30.20	C- / 4.0	12.44%	B- / 7.2
2011	C-	106.40	26.88	C / 4.4	2.55%	C+ / 6.9
2010	A	68.50	32.03	A+ / 9.7	21.91%	C+ / 6.2
2009	A+	9.56	26.74	A / 9.3	51.75%	C+ / 6.6

Major Rating Factors: Middle of the road best describes *PowerShares Global Agriculture P whose TheStreet.com Investment Rating is currently a C- (Fair). The fund currently has a performance rating of C- (Fair) based on an annualized return of 17.65% over the last three years and a total return of 12.44% year to date 2012. Factored into the performance evaluation is an expense ratio of 0.75% (very low).

The fund's risk rating is currently B- (Good). It carries a beta of 1.07, meaning that its performance tracks fairly well with that of the overall stock market. Volatility, as measured by both the semi-deviation and a drawdown factor, is considered low. As of March 31, 2012, *PowerShares Global Agriculture P traded at a discount of .03% below its net asset value, which is better than its one-year historical average discount of .02%.

Brian McGreal has been running the fund for 4 years and currently receives a manager quality ranking of 52 (0=worst, 99=best). If you desire an average level of risk, then this fund may be an option.

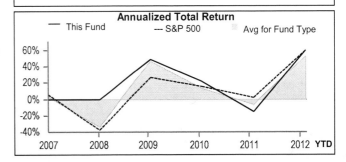

*PowerShares Global Clean Energy (PBD)   E+   Very Weak

Fund Family: Invesco Powershares Capital Mgmt LL
Fund Type: Energy/Natural Resources
Inception Date: June 13, 2007

Data Date	Investment Rating	Net Assets ($Mil)	Price	Perfor- mance Rating/Pts	Total Return Y-T-D	Risk Rating/Pts
3-12	E+	89.01	8.99	E+ / 0.8	9.42%	C / 5.5
2011	D-	97.00	8.23	E+ / 0.9	0.49%	C / 5.4
2010	E+	147.40	13.96	E / 0.5	-15.98%	C- / 4.0
2009	C+	140.69	16.66	B / 7.9	28.38%	C- / 3.9

Major Rating Factors:
Very poor performance is the major factor driving the E+ (Very Weak) TheStreet.com Investment Rating for *PowerShares Global Clean Energy. The fund currently has a performance rating of E+ (Very Weak) based on an annualized return of -8.56% over the last three years and a total return of 9.42% year to date 2012. Factored into the performance evaluation is an expense ratio of 0.75% (very low).

The fund's risk rating is currently C (Fair). It carries a beta of 1.19, meaning it is expected to move 11.9% for every 10% move in the market. Volatility, as measured by both the semi-deviation and a drawdown factor, is considered average. As of March 31, 2012, *PowerShares Global Clean Energy traded at a discount of .11% below its net asset value, which is worse than its one-year historical average discount of .50%.

Peter Hubbard has been running the fund for 5 years and currently receives a manager quality ranking of 5 (0=worst, 99=best). This fund offers an average level of risk but investors looking for strong performance will be frustrated.

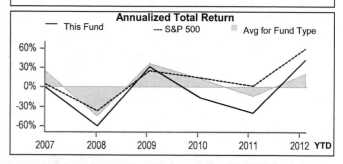

Annualized Total Return

*PowerShares Global Coal Portfoli (PKOL)   D+   Weak

Fund Family: Invesco Powershares Capital Mgmt LL
Fund Type: Energy/Natural Resources
Inception Date: September 16, 2008

Data Date	Investment Rating	Net Assets ($Mil)	Price	Perfor- mance Rating/Pts	Total Return Y-T-D	Risk Rating/Pts
3-12	D+	19.33	24.82	C- / 3.9	1.23%	C+ / 6.5
2011	C	14.90	24.52	C+ / 6.1	3.47%	C+ / 6.5
2010	A	27.80	37.40	A+ / 9.7	31.63%	C+ / 6.3
2009	A+	4.78	28.92	A+ / 9.9	119. 44%	C+ / 6.1

Major Rating Factors: *PowerShares Global Coal Portfoli receives a TheStreet.com Investment Rating of D+ (Weak). The fund currently has a performance rating of C- (Fair) based on an annualized return of 22.90% over the last three years and a total return of 1.23% year to date 2012. Factored into the performance evaluation is an expense ratio of 0.75% (very low).

The fund's risk rating is currently C+ (Fair). It carries a beta of 1.42, meaning it is expected to move 14.2% for every 10% move in the market. Volatility, as measured by both the semi-deviation and a drawdown factor, is considered low. As of March 31, 2012, *PowerShares Global Coal Portfoli traded at a discount of .12% below its net asset value, which is worse than its one-year historical average discount of .45%.

Brian McGreal has been running the fund for 4 years and currently receives a manager quality ranking of 41 (0=worst, 99=best). If you desire an average level of risk, then this fund may be an option.

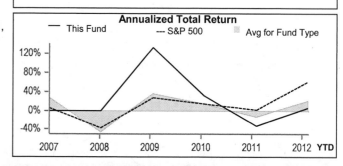

Annualized Total Return

*PowerShares Global Listed Priv E (PSP)   C-   Fair

Fund Family: Invesco Powershares Capital Mgmt LL
Fund Type: Income
Inception Date: October 24, 2006

Data Date	Investment Rating	Net Assets ($Mil)	Price	Perfor- mance Rating/Pts	Total Return Y-T-D	Risk Rating/Pts
3-12	C-	271.98	9.48	C+ / 5.6	18.65%	C+ / 6.3
2011	D	240.60	7.99	D / 2.0	1.00%	C+ / 6.4
2010	E+	309.90	10.75	D- / 1.3	30.23%	C- / 3.5
2009	E	60.48	9.01	E+ / 0.6	25.84%	C- / 3.6

Major Rating Factors: Middle of the road best describes *PowerShares Global Listed Priv E whose TheStreet.com Investment Rating is currently a C- (Fair). The fund currently has a performance rating of C+ (Fair) based on an annualized return of 23.26% over the last three years and a total return of 18.65% year to date 2012. Factored into the performance evaluation is an expense ratio of 0.70% (very low).

The fund's risk rating is currently C+ (Fair). It carries a beta of 1.62, meaning it is expected to move 16.2% for every 10% move in the market. Volatility, as measured by both the semi-deviation and a drawdown factor, is considered low. As of March 31, 2012, *PowerShares Global Listed Priv E traded at a premium of .64% above its net asset value, which is worse than its one-year historical average premium of .01%.

Peter Hubbard has been running the fund for 5 years and currently receives a manager quality ranking of 15 (0=worst, 99=best). If you desire an average level of risk, then this fund may be an option.

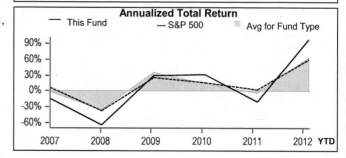

Annualized Total Return

*PowerShares Global Steel Portfol (PSTL)   D   Weak

Fund Family: Invesco Powershares Capital Mgmt LL
Fund Type: Global
Inception Date: September 16, 2008

Major Rating Factors:
Disappointing performance is the major factor driving the D (Weak) TheStreet.com Investment Rating for *PowerShares Global Steel Portfol. The fund currently has a performance rating of D (Weak) based on an annualized return of 9.78% over the last three years and a total return of 10.82% year to date 2012. Factored into the performance evaluation is an expense ratio of 0.75% (very low).

The fund's risk rating is currently C+ (Fair). It carries a beta of 1.45, meaning it is expected to move 14.5% for every 10% move in the market. Volatility, as measured by both the semi-deviation and a drawdown factor, is considered low. As of March 31, 2012, *PowerShares Global Steel Portfol traded at a discount of 1.14% below its net asset value, which is better than its one-year historical average discount of .42%.

Brian McGreal has been running the fund for 4 years and currently receives a manager quality ranking of 14 (0=worst, 99=best). This fund offers only a moderate level of risk but investors looking for strong performance are still waiting.

Data Date	Investment Rating	Net Assets ($Mil)	Price	Performance Rating/Pts	Total Return Y-T-D	Risk Rating/Pts
3-12	D	4.42	16.43	D / 1.9	10.82%	C+ / 6.6
2011	D	3.80	14.88	D / 1.8	2.96%	C+ / 6.5
2010	A	5.90	23.82	A- / 9.2	8.29%	C+ / 6.3
2009	A+	1.38	22.38	A+ / 9.6	66.07%	C+ / 6.3

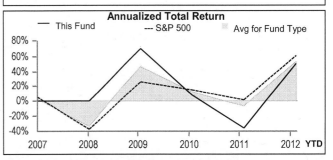

Annualized Total Return

*PowerShares Global Water Portfol (PIO)   C-   Fair

Fund Family: Invesco Powershares Capital Mgmt LL
Fund Type: Energy/Natural Resources
Inception Date: June 13, 2007

Major Rating Factors: Middle of the road best describes *PowerShares Global Water Portfol whose TheStreet.com Investment Rating is currently a C- (Fair). The fund currently has a performance rating of C- (Fair) based on an annualized return of 16.40% over the last three years and a total return of 16.10% year to date 2012. Factored into the performance evaluation is an expense ratio of 0.75% (very low).

The fund's risk rating is currently B- (Good). It carries a beta of 0.76, meaning the fund's expected move will be 7.6% for every 10% move in the market. Volatility, as measured by both the semi-deviation and a drawdown factor, is considered low. As of March 31, 2012, *PowerShares Global Water Portfol traded at a discount of .11% below its net asset value, which is worse than its one-year historical average discount of .30%.

Peter Hubbard has been running the fund for 5 years and currently receives a manager quality ranking of 71 (0=worst, 99=best). If you desire an average level of risk, then this fund may be an option.

Data Date	Investment Rating	Net Assets ($Mil)	Price	Performance Rating/Pts	Total Return Y-T-D	Risk Rating/Pts
3-12	C-	252.67	18.10	C- / 3.7	16.10%	B- / 7.4
2011	D	234.10	15.59	D+ / 2.4	0.77%	C / 5.5
2010	D	352.70	20.01	D+ / 2.5	11.80%	C / 4.3
2009	C+	179.20	18.16	B+ / 8.7	36.57%	C- / 3.8

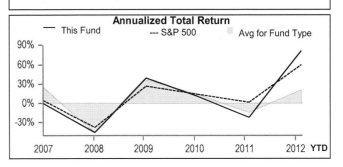

Annualized Total Return

*PowerShares Global Wind Energy P (PWND)   E+   Very Weak

Fund Family: Invesco Powershares Capital Mgmt LL
Fund Type: Energy/Natural Resources
Inception Date: June 27, 2008

Major Rating Factors:
Very poor performance is the major factor driving the E+ (Very Weak) TheStreet.com Investment Rating for *PowerShares Global Wind Energy P. The fund currently has a performance rating of E+ (Very Weak) based on an annualized return of -14.98% over the last three years and a total return of 2.04% year to date 2012. Factored into the performance evaluation is an expense ratio of 0.75% (very low).

The fund's risk rating is currently C (Fair). It carries a beta of 1.07, meaning that its performance tracks fairly well with that of the overall stock market. Volatility, as measured by both the semi-deviation and a drawdown factor, is considered average. As of March 31, 2012, *PowerShares Global Wind Energy P traded at a discount of .71% below its net asset value, which is better than its one-year historical average discount of .54%.

Peter Hubbard has been running the fund for 4 years and currently receives a manager quality ranking of 4 (0=worst, 99=best). This fund offers an average level of risk but investors looking for strong performance will be frustrated.

Data Date	Investment Rating	Net Assets ($Mil)	Price	Performance Rating/Pts	Total Return Y-T-D	Risk Rating/Pts
3-12	E+	15.17	6.99	E+ / 0.6	2.04%	C / 4.5
2011	D-	14.90	6.85	E+ / 0.8	-0.47%	C / 5.3
2010	E+	25.90	9.87	E / 0.4	-35.81%	C / 4.5
2009	C	27.53	15.43	C+ / 6.9	26.49%	C / 4.6

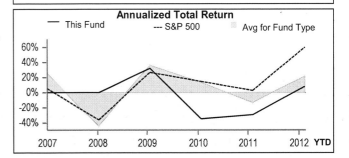

Annualized Total Return

*PowerShares High Yld Eq Div Ach (PEY)   B-   Good

Fund Family: Invesco Powershares Capital Mgmt LL
Fund Type: Income
Inception Date: December 9, 2004

Major Rating Factors: *PowerShares High Yld Eq Div Ach receives a TheStreet.com Investment Rating of B- (Good). The fund currently has a performance rating of C+ (Fair) based on an annualized return of 23.10% over the last three years and a total return of 2.83% year to date 2012. Factored into the performance evaluation is an expense ratio of 0.60% (very low).

The fund's risk rating is currently B+ (Good). It carries a beta of 0.82, meaning the fund's expected move will be 8.2% for every 10% move in the market. Volatility, as measured by both the semi-deviation and a drawdown factor, is considered very low. As of March 31, 2012, *PowerShares High Yld Eq Div Ach traded at a price exactly equal to its net asset value, which is better than its one-year historical average premium of .01%.

Peter Hubbard has been running the fund for 5 years and currently receives a manager quality ranking of 79 (0=worst, 99=best). If you desire an average level of risk, then this fund may be an option.

Data Date	Investment Rating	Net Assets ($Mil)	Price	Performance Rating/Pts	Total Return Y-T-D	Risk Rating/Pts
3-12	B-	331.57	9.42	C+ / 6.0	2.83%	B+ / 9.0
2011	C	357.50	9.25	C / 5.3	-0.11%	C+ / 6.9
2010	D	182.60	8.86	D / 1.9	21.32%	C / 4.7
2009	D-	86.85	7.65	E+ / 0.7	3.21%	C / 4.8

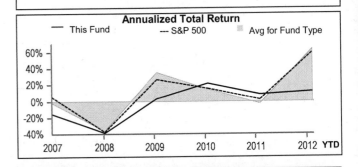
Annualized Total Return

---

*PowerShares Ibbotson Altv Comp (PTO)   C-   Fair

Fund Family: Invesco Powershares Capital Mgmt LL
Fund Type: Global
Inception Date: May 16, 2008

Major Rating Factors: Middle of the road best describes *PowerShares Ibbotson Altv Comp whose TheStreet.com Investment Rating is currently a C- (Fair). The fund currently has a performance rating of C- (Fair) based on an annualized return of 15.48% over the last three years and a total return of 8.63% year to date 2012. Factored into the performance evaluation is an expense ratio of 0.25% (very low).

The fund's risk rating is currently B (Good). It carries a beta of 0.65, meaning the fund's expected move will be 6.5% for every 10% move in the market. Volatility, as measured by both the semi-deviation and a drawdown factor, is considered low. As of March 31, 2012, *PowerShares Ibbotson Altv Comp traded at a premium of .61% above its net asset value, which is worse than its one-year historical average premium of .06%.

Peter Hubbard has been running the fund for 4 years and currently receives a manager quality ranking of 74 (0=worst, 99=best). If you desire an average level of risk, then this fund may be an option.

Data Date	Investment Rating	Net Assets ($Mil)	Price	Performance Rating/Pts	Total Return Y-T-D	Risk Rating/Pts
3-12	C-	8.86	11.59	C- / 3.5	8.63%	B / 8.5
2011	C-	8.20	10.75	C- / 3.8	2.79%	B / 8.1
2010	B+	9.40	11.70	B+ / 8.9	13.32%	C / 5.1
2009	B-	7.70	10.72	B / 7.8	21.67%	C / 5.1

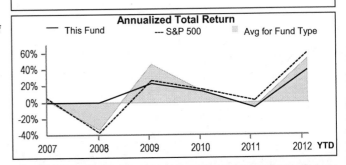
Annualized Total Return

---

*PowerShares India Portfolio (PIN)   D   Weak

Fund Family: Invesco Powershares Capital Mgmt LL
Fund Type: Foreign
Inception Date: March 4, 2008

Major Rating Factors:
Disappointing performance is the major factor driving the D (Weak) TheStreet.com Investment Rating for *PowerShares India Portfolio. The fund currently has a performance rating of D+ (Weak) based on an annualized return of 13.57% over the last three years and a total return of 15.63% year to date 2012. Factored into the performance evaluation is an expense ratio of 0.79% (very low).

The fund's risk rating is currently C+ (Fair). It carries a beta of 1.16, meaning it is expected to move 11.6% for every 10% move in the market. Volatility, as measured by both the semi-deviation and a drawdown factor, is considered low. As of March 31, 2012, *PowerShares India Portfolio traded at a premium of .11% above its net asset value, which is worse than its one-year historical average discount of .19%.

Peter Hubbard has been running the fund for 4 years and currently receives a manager quality ranking of 28 (0=worst, 99=best). This fund offers only a moderate level of risk but investors looking for strong performance are still waiting.

Data Date	Investment Rating	Net Assets ($Mil)	Price	Performance Rating/Pts	Total Return Y-T-D	Risk Rating/Pts
3-12	D	425.18	18.83	D+ / 2.6	15.63%	C+ / 6.3
2011	D	286.00	16.30	D+ / 2.9	3.68%	C+ / 6.4
2010	B-	566.00	25.42	B+ / 8.5	16.25%	C- / 4.2
2009	B+	97.45	22.07	A / 9.5	70.44%	C- / 4.1

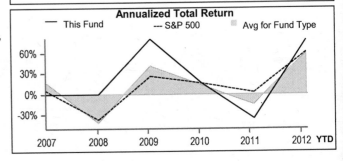
Annualized Total Return

*PowerShares Insured CA Mun Bond (PWZ)   C   Fair

Fund Family: Invesco Powershares Capital Mgmt LL
Fund Type: Municipal - National
Inception Date: October 11, 2007

Data Date	Investment Rating	Net Assets ($Mil)	Price	Performance Rating/Pts	Total Return Y-T-D	Risk Rating/Pts
3-12	C	44.69	24.67	C- / 4.0	2.97%	B+ / 9.3
2011	B-	39.90	24.21	C+ / 5.9	0.52%	B+ / 9.3
2010	C	38.30	22.57	D+ / 2.4	1.06%	B / 8.1
2009	B	27.02	23.45	C+ / 6.8	14.62%	B / 8.3

Major Rating Factors: Middle of the road best describes *PowerShares Insured CA Mun Bond whose TheStreet.com Investment Rating is currently a C (Fair). The fund currently has a performance rating of C- (Fair) based on an annualized return of 9.00% over the last three years and a total return of 2.97% year to date 2012. Factored into the performance evaluation is an expense ratio of 0.28% (very low).

The fund's risk rating is currently B+ (Good). It carries a beta of 1.41, meaning it is expected to move 14.1% for every 10% move in the market. Volatility, as measured by both the semi-deviation and a drawdown factor, is considered very low. As of March 31, 2012, *PowerShares Insured CA Mun Bond traded at a premium of .20% above its net asset value, which is worse than its one-year historical average premium of .02%.

Peter Hubbard has been running the fund for 5 years and currently receives a manager quality ranking of 34 (0=worst, 99=best). If you desire an average level of risk, then this fund may be an option.

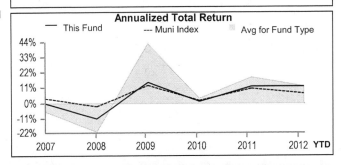

Annualized Total Return

*PowerShares Insured National Mun (PZA)   C   Fair

Fund Family: Invesco Powershares Capital Mgmt LL
Fund Type: Municipal - National
Inception Date: October 11, 2007

Data Date	Investment Rating	Net Assets ($Mil)	Price	Performance Rating/Pts	Total Return Y-T-D	Risk Rating/Pts
3-12	C	667.50	24.78	C- / 4.0	2.47%	B+ / 9.3
2011	B	588.30	24.45	C+ / 6.4	0.41%	B+ / 9.3
2010	C	507.10	22.54	D / 2.2	-0.09%	B / 8.2
2009	A+	303.83	23.72	B / 7.6	17.92%	B / 8.3

Major Rating Factors: Middle of the road best describes *PowerShares Insured National Mun whose TheStreet.com Investment Rating is currently a C (Fair). The fund currently has a performance rating of C- (Fair) based on an annualized return of 9.18% over the last three years and a total return of 2.47% year to date 2012. Factored into the performance evaluation is an expense ratio of 0.28% (very low).

The fund's risk rating is currently B+ (Good). It carries a beta of 1.39, meaning it is expected to move 13.9% for every 10% move in the market. Volatility, as measured by both the semi-deviation and a drawdown factor, is considered very low. As of March 31, 2012, *PowerShares Insured National Mun traded at a premium of .04% above its net asset value, which is worse than its one-year historical average premium of .03%.

Peter Hubbard has been running the fund for 5 years and currently receives a manager quality ranking of 36 (0=worst, 99=best). If you desire an average level of risk, then this fund may be an option.

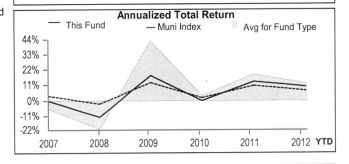

Annualized Total Return

*PowerShares Insured NY Mun Bond (PZT)   C   Fair

Fund Family: Invesco Powershares Capital Mgmt LL
Fund Type: Municipal - National
Inception Date: October 11, 2007

Data Date	Investment Rating	Net Assets ($Mil)	Price	Performance Rating/Pts	Total Return Y-T-D	Risk Rating/Pts
3-12	C	46.34	24.15	C- / 3.8	2.11%	B+ / 9.3
2011	B	40.60	23.90	C+ / 6.1	0.54%	B+ / 9.4
2010	C-	37.80	22.15	D / 2.1	0.22%	B / 8.1
2009	A+	28.72	23.22	B- / 7.4	16.89%	B / 8.3

Major Rating Factors: Middle of the road best describes *PowerShares Insured NY Mun Bond whose TheStreet.com Investment Rating is currently a C (Fair). The fund currently has a performance rating of C- (Fair) based on an annualized return of 8.62% over the last three years and a total return of 2.11% year to date 2012. Factored into the performance evaluation is an expense ratio of 0.28% (very low).

The fund's risk rating is currently B+ (Good). It carries a beta of 1.33, meaning it is expected to move 13.3% for every 10% move in the market. Volatility, as measured by both the semi-deviation and a drawdown factor, is considered very low. As of March 31, 2012, *PowerShares Insured NY Mun Bond traded at a premium of .17% above its net asset value.

Peter Hubbard has been running the fund for 5 years and currently receives a manager quality ranking of 37 (0=worst, 99=best). If you desire an average level of risk, then this fund may be an option.

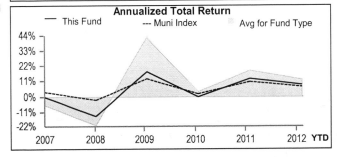

Annualized Total Return

*PowerShares International Corp B (PICB)

C-   **Fair**

Fund Family: Invesco Powershares Capital Mgmt LL
Fund Type: Global
Inception Date: June 2, 2010

Major Rating Factors:
Disappointing performance is the major factor driving the C- (Fair) TheStreet.com Investment Rating for *PowerShares International Corp B. The fund currently has a performance rating of D+ (Weak) based on an annualized return of 0.00% over the last three years and a total return of 6.26% year to date 2012. Factored into the performance evaluation is an expense ratio of 0.50% (very low).

The fund's risk rating is currently B (Good). It carries a beta of 0.00, meaning the fund's expected move will be 0.0% for every 10% move in the market. Volatility, as measured by both the semi-deviation and a drawdown factor, is considered low. As of March 31, 2012, *PowerShares International Corp B traded at a discount of .11% below its net asset value, which is better than its one-year historical average premium of .29%.

Peter Hubbard has been running the fund for 2 years and currently receives a manager quality ranking of 39 (0=worst, 99=best). This fund offers only a moderate level of risk but investors looking for strong performance are still waiting.

Data Date	Investment Rating	Net Assets ($Mil)	Price	Perfor-mance Rating/Pts	Total Return Y-T-D	Risk Rating/Pts
3-12	C-	92.49	27.87	D+ / 2.3	6.26%	B / 8.7
2011	C-	77.50	26.46	D / 1.9	-1.32%	B / 8.7

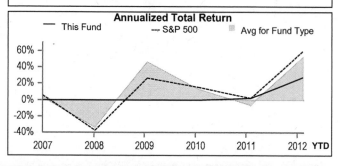

Annualized Total Return
— This Fund   --- S&P 500   Avg for Fund Type

*PowerShares Intl Dividend Ach (PID)

C   **Fair**

Fund Family: Invesco Powershares Capital Mgmt LL
Fund Type: Foreign
Inception Date: September 15, 2005

Major Rating Factors: Middle of the road best describes *PowerShares Intl Dividend Ach whose TheStreet.com Investment Rating is currently a C (Fair). The fund currently has a performance rating of C (Fair) based on an annualized return of 21.21% over the last three years and a total return of 5.91% year to date 2012. Factored into the performance evaluation is an expense ratio of 0.58% (very low).

The fund's risk rating is currently B (Good). It carries a beta of 0.90, meaning that its performance tracks fairly well with that of the overall stock market. Volatility, as measured by both the semi-deviation and a drawdown factor, is considered low. As of March 31, 2012, *PowerShares Intl Dividend Ach traded at a premium of .13% above its net asset value, which is worse than its one-year historical average premium of .11%.

Peter Hubbard has been running the fund for 5 years and currently receives a manager quality ranking of 81 (0=worst, 99=best). If you desire an average level of risk, then this fund may be an option.

Data Date	Investment Rating	Net Assets ($Mil)	Price	Perfor-mance Rating/Pts	Total Return Y-T-D	Risk Rating/Pts
3-12	C	681.68	15.36	C / 4.7	5.91%	B / 8.2
2011	C	585.20	14.57	C / 4.8	0.27%	B / 8.0
2010	D	468.80	15.40	D+ / 2.4	15.04%	C / 5.1
2009	D	256.58	13.97	D+ / 2.6	34.13%	C / 5.0

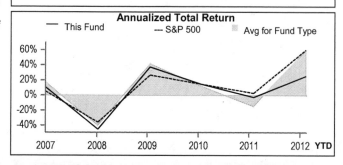

Annualized Total Return
— This Fund   --- S&P 500   Avg for Fund Type

*PowerShares KBW High Div Yield F (KBWD)

C+   **Fair**

Fund Family: Invesco Powershares Capital Mgmt LL
Fund Type: Growth and Income
Inception Date: December 1, 2010

Major Rating Factors: Middle of the road best describes *PowerShares KBW High Div Yield F whose TheStreet.com Investment Rating is currently a C+ (Fair). The fund currently has a performance rating of C+ (Fair) based on an annualized return of 0.00% over the last three years and a total return of 12.66% year to date 2012. Factored into the performance evaluation is an expense ratio of 0.37% (very low).

The fund's risk rating is currently B (Good). It carries a beta of 0.00, meaning the fund's expected move will be 0.0% for every 10% move in the market. Volatility, as measured by both the semi-deviation and a drawdown factor, is considered low. As of March 31, 2012, *PowerShares KBW High Div Yield F traded at a premium of .21% above its net asset value, which is worse than its one-year historical average premium of .11%.

Michael C. Jeanette has been running the fund for 2 years and currently receives a manager quality ranking of 67 (0=worst, 99=best). If you desire an average level of risk, then this fund may be an option.

Data Date	Investment Rating	Net Assets ($Mil)	Price	Perfor-mance Rating/Pts	Total Return Y-T-D	Risk Rating/Pts
3-12	C+	59.67	23.93	C+ / 6.1	12.66%	B / 8.4
2011	C-	33.60	21.76	C- / 3.1	2.21%	B / 8.3

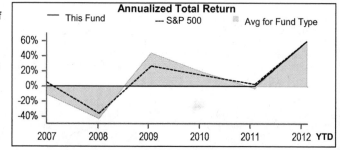

Annualized Total Return
— This Fund   --- S&P 500   Avg for Fund Type

*PowerShares KBW Premium Yld Eq R (KBWY)

C   **Fair**

Fund Family: Invesco Powershares Capital Mgmt LL
Fund Type: Income
Inception Date: December 1, 2010

Data Date	Investment Rating	Net Assets ($Mil)	Price	Performance Rating/Pts	Total Return Y-T-D	Risk Rating/Pts
3-12	C	7.52	25.71	C / 5.0	13.25%	B- / 7.6
2011	D+	6.90	23.04	D / 2.1	2.34%	B- / 7.6

Major Rating Factors: Middle of the road best describes *PowerShares KBW Premium Yld Eq R whose TheStreet.com Investment Rating is currently a C (Fair). The fund currently has a performance rating of C (Fair) based on an annualized return of 0.00% over the last three years and a total return of 13.25% year to date 2012. Factored into the performance evaluation is an expense ratio of 0.36% (very low).

The fund's risk rating is currently B- (Good). It carries a beta of 0.00, meaning the fund's expected move will be 0.0% for every 10% move in the market. Volatility, as measured by both the semi-deviation and a drawdown factor, is considered low. As of March 31, 2012, *PowerShares KBW Premium Yld Eq R traded at a premium of .35% above its net asset value, which is worse than its one-year historical average premium of .09%.

Michael C. Jeanette has been running the fund for 2 years and currently receives a manager quality ranking of 24 (0=worst, 99=best). If you desire an average level of risk, then this fund may be an option.

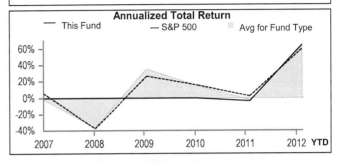

*PowerShares Lux Nanotech (PXN)

D-   **Weak**

Fund Family: Invesco Powershares Capital Mgmt LL
Fund Type: Growth
Inception Date: October 26, 2005

Data Date	Investment Rating	Net Assets ($Mil)	Price	Performance Rating/Pts	Total Return Y-T-D	Risk Rating/Pts
3-12	D-	22.72	6.55	E+ / 0.9	8.20%	C+ / 6.1
2011	D-	22.10	6.05	D- / 1.1	1.49%	C+ / 5.8
2010	D-	46.10	9.80	E+ / 0.8	-6.58%	C / 4.9
2009	D-	39.48	10.49	E+ / 0.9	32.41%	C / 5.1

Major Rating Factors:
Very poor performance is the major factor driving the D- (Weak) TheStreet.com Investment Rating for *PowerShares Lux Nanotech. The fund currently has a performance rating of E+ (Very Weak) based on an annualized return of -4.73% over the last three years and a total return of 8.20% year to date 2012. Factored into the performance evaluation is an expense ratio of 0.70% (very low).

The fund's risk rating is currently C+ (Fair). It carries a beta of 1.53, meaning it is expected to move 15.3% for every 10% move in the market. Volatility, as measured by both the semi-deviation and a drawdown factor, is considered low. As of March 31, 2012, *PowerShares Lux Nanotech traded at a price exactly equal to its net asset value, which is worse than its one-year historical average discount of .05%.

Peter Hubbard has been running the fund for 5 years and currently receives a manager quality ranking of 3 (0=worst, 99=best). This fund offers only a moderate level of risk but investors looking for strong performance are still waiting.

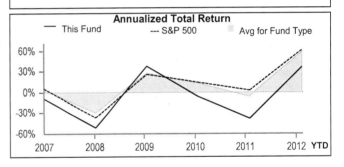

*PowerShares MENA Frontier Countr (PMNA)

D   **Weak**

Fund Family: Invesco Powershares Capital Mgmt LL
Fund Type: Foreign
Inception Date: July 7, 2008

Data Date	Investment Rating	Net Assets ($Mil)	Price	Performance Rating/Pts	Total Return Y-T-D	Risk Rating/Pts
3-12	D	19.87	11.33	D / 1.6	8.96%	B- / 7.3
2011	D	18.70	10.45	D- / 1.4	-2.30%	B- / 7.3
2010	B-	21.80	13.71	B+ / 8.5	9.76%	C / 4.3
2009	D-	10.34	12.90	D / 1.6	4.07%	C- / 4.1

Major Rating Factors:
Disappointing performance is the major factor driving the D (Weak) TheStreet.com Investment Rating for *PowerShares MENA Frontier Countr. The fund currently has a performance rating of D (Weak) based on an annualized return of 4.73% over the last three years and a total return of 8.96% year to date 2012. Factored into the performance evaluation is an expense ratio of 0.70% (very low).

The fund's risk rating is currently B- (Good). It carries a beta of 0.73, meaning the fund's expected move will be 7.3% for every 10% move in the market. Volatility, as measured by both the semi-deviation and a drawdown factor, is considered low. As of March 31, 2012, *PowerShares MENA Frontier Countr traded at a discount of .87% below its net asset value, which is worse than its one-year historical average discount of 1.01%.

Peter Hubbard has been running the fund for 4 years and currently receives a manager quality ranking of 21 (0=worst, 99=best). This fund offers only a moderate level of risk but investors looking for strong performance are still waiting.

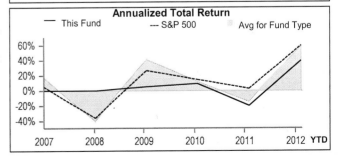

*PowerShares Mrnngstr StockInv Co (PYH)   C   Fair

Fund Family: Invesco Powershares Capital Mgmt LL
Fund Type: Income
Inception Date: December 1, 2006

Major Rating Factors: Middle of the road best describes *PowerShares Mrnngstr StockInv Co whose TheStreet.com Investment Rating is currently a C (Fair). The fund currently has a performance rating of C- (Fair) based on an annualized return of 15.02% over the last three years and a total return of 9.06% year to date 2012. Factored into the performance evaluation is an expense ratio of 0.53% (very low).

The fund's risk rating is currently B (Good). It carries a beta of 0.89, meaning the fund's expected move will be 8.9% for every 10% move in the market. Volatility, as measured by both the semi-deviation and a drawdown factor, is considered low. As of March 31, 2012, *PowerShares Mrnngstr StockInv Co traded at a discount of .14% below its net asset value, which is better than its one-year historical average discount of .01%.

Peter Hubbard has been running the fund for 5 years and currently receives a manager quality ranking of 26 (0=worst, 99=best). If you desire an average level of risk, then this fund may be an option.

Data Date	Investment Rating	Net Assets ($Mil)	Price	Perfor-mance Rating/Pts	Total Return Y-T-D	Risk Rating/Pts
3-12	C	17.12	22.13	C- / 3.9	9.06%	B / 8.3
2011	C-	16.30	20.37	C- / 3.8	0.54%	B / 8.1
2010	D	18.00	20.04	D- / 1.0	10.63%	C+ / 5.7
2009	D-	26.51	18.33	D- / 1.1	8.44%	C / 5.5

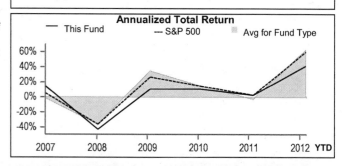

*PowerShares NASDAQ Internet Port (PNQI)   B   Good

Fund Family: Invesco Powershares Capital Mgmt LL
Fund Type: Income
Inception Date: June 10, 2008

Major Rating Factors:
Exceptional performance is the major factor driving the B (Good) TheStreet.com Investment Rating for *PowerShares NASDAQ Internet Port. The fund currently has a performance rating of A (Excellent) based on an annualized return of 37.23% over the last three years and a total return of 20.54% year to date 2012. Factored into the performance evaluation is an expense ratio of 0.60% (very low).

The fund's risk rating is currently C+ (Fair). It carries a beta of 1.25, meaning it is expected to move 12.5% for every 10% move in the market. Volatility, as measured by both the semi-deviation and a drawdown factor, is considered low. As of March 31, 2012, *PowerShares NASDAQ Internet Port traded at a premium of .29% above its net asset value, which is worse than its one-year historical average premium of .07%.

Peter Hubbard has been running the fund for 4 years and currently receives a manager quality ranking of 81 (0=worst, 99=best). If you desire only a moderate level of risk and strong performance, then this fund is an excellent option.

Data Date	Investment Rating	Net Assets ($Mil)	Price	Perfor-mance Rating/Pts	Total Return Y-T-D	Risk Rating/Pts
3-12	B	56.87	41.63	A / 9.3	20.54%	C+ / 6.6
2011	B	53.50	34.54	B+ / 8.8	1.69%	C+ / 6.5
2010	B+	31.10	34.69	A+ / 9.6	34.20%	C- / 3.9
2009	A-	1.79	25.85	A+ / 9.8	88.03%	C / 4.3

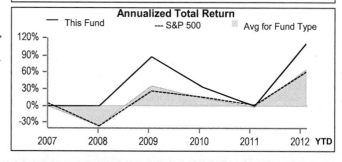

*PowerShares Preferred Port (PGX)   C+   Fair

Fund Family: Invesco Powershares Capital Mgmt LL
Fund Type: General - Investment Grade
Inception Date: January 28, 2008

Major Rating Factors: Middle of the road best describes *PowerShares Preferred Port whose TheStreet.com Investment Rating is currently a C+ (Fair). The fund currently has a performance rating of C (Fair) based on an annualized return of 20.78% over the last three years and a total return of 6.73% year to date 2012. Factored into the performance evaluation is an expense ratio of 0.50% (very low).

The fund's risk rating is currently B+ (Good). It carries a beta of 0.38, meaning the fund's expected move will be 3.8% for every 10% move in the market. Volatility, as measured by both the semi-deviation and a drawdown factor, is considered very low. As of March 31, 2012, *PowerShares Preferred Port traded at a premium of .35% above its net asset value, which is worse than its one-year historical average premium of .09%.

Peter Hubbard has been running the fund for 4 years and currently receives a manager quality ranking of 93 (0=worst, 99=best). If you desire an average level of risk, then this fund may be an option.

Data Date	Investment Rating	Net Assets ($Mil)	Price	Perfor-mance Rating/Pts	Total Return Y-T-D	Risk Rating/Pts
3-12	C+	1,536.06	14.37	C / 5.0	6.73%	B+ / 9.4
2011	C-	1,359.70	13.69	C- / 3.8	2.34%	C+ / 6.8
2010	C+	1,353.90	14.12	B- / 7.3	12.18%	C / 4.4
2009	C	387.66	13.55	C+ / 6.6	14.01%	C / 4.3

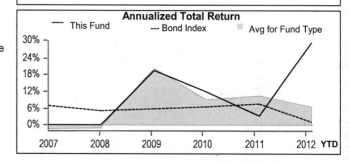

*PowerShares QQQ (QQQ)   B   Good

Fund Family: Bank of New York Mellon
Fund Type: Growth
Inception Date: March 10, 1999

Major Rating Factors: Strong performance is the major factor driving the B (Good) TheStreet.com Investment Rating for *PowerShares QQQ. The fund currently has a performance rating of B+ (Good) based on an annualized return of 28.55% over the last three years and a total return of 21.19% year to date 2012. Factored into the performance evaluation is an expense ratio of 0.20% (very low).

The fund's risk rating is currently B- (Good). It carries a beta of 1.07, meaning that its performance tracks fairly well with that of the overall stock market. Volatility, as measured by both the semi-deviation and a drawdown factor, is considered low. As of March 31, 2012, *PowerShares QQQ traded at a price exactly equal to its net asset value, which is better than its one-year historical average premium of .01%.

Bruce T. Duncan currently receives a manager quality ranking of 72 (0=worst, 99=best). If you desire only a moderate level of risk and strong performance, then this fund is an excellent option.

Data Date	Investment Rating	Net Assets ($Mil)	Price	Performance Rating/Pts	Total Return Y-T-D	Risk Rating/Pts
3-12	B	33,268.32	67.55	B+ / 8.4	21.19%	B- / 7.5
2011	B	25,574.40	55.83	B- / 7.5	3.55%	B / 8.6
2010	C+	22,061.00	54.46	C+ / 6.9	20.16%	C+ / 5.6
2009	C	13,357.13	45.75	C+ / 6.0	48.21%	C / 5.5

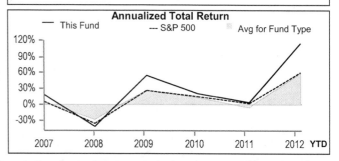

Annualized Total Return

*PowerShares RiverFront Tact Bal (PAO)   C-   Fair

Fund Family: Invesco Powershares Capital Mgmt LL
Fund Type: Growth and Income
Inception Date: May 16, 2008

Major Rating Factors: Middle of the road best describes *PowerShares RiverFront Tact Bal whose TheStreet.com Investment Rating is currently a C- (Fair). The fund currently has a performance rating of C- (Fair) based on an annualized return of 14.44% over the last three years and a total return of 8.89% year to date 2012. Factored into the performance evaluation is an expense ratio of 0.25% (very low).

The fund's risk rating is currently B (Good). It carries a beta of 0.91, meaning that its performance tracks fairly well with that of the overall stock market. Volatility, as measured by both the semi-deviation and a drawdown factor, is considered low. As of March 31, 2012, *PowerShares RiverFront Tact Bal traded at a discount of .08% below its net asset value, which is better than its one-year historical average discount of .06%.

Peter Hubbard has been running the fund for 4 years and currently receives a manager quality ranking of 25 (0=worst, 99=best). If you desire an average level of risk, then this fund may be an option.

Data Date	Investment Rating	Net Assets ($Mil)	Price	Performance Rating/Pts	Total Return Y-T-D	Risk Rating/Pts
3-12	C-	22.29	12.42	C- / 3.3	8.89%	B / 8.1
2011	C-	20.60	11.43	C- / 3.4	0.91%	B- / 7.9
2010	A-	18.20	12.63	B+ / 8.9	13.24%	C / 5.5
2009	B	8.32	11.44	B / 7.8	20.46%	C+ / 5.6

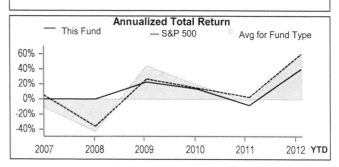

Annualized Total Return

*PowerShares RiverFront Tact Gr & (PCA)   C-   Fair

Fund Family: Invesco Powershares Capital Mgmt LL
Fund Type: Growth and Income
Inception Date: May 16, 2008

Major Rating Factors: Middle of the road best describes *PowerShares RiverFront Tact Gr & whose TheStreet.com Investment Rating is currently a C- (Fair). The fund currently has a performance rating of C- (Fair) based on an annualized return of 12.96% over the last three years and a total return of 5.02% year to date 2012. Factored into the performance evaluation is an expense ratio of 0.25% (very low).

The fund's risk rating is currently B (Good). It carries a beta of 0.64, meaning the fund's expected move will be 6.4% for every 10% move in the market. Volatility, as measured by both the semi-deviation and a drawdown factor, is considered low. As of March 31, 2012, *PowerShares RiverFront Tact Gr & traded at a premium of .23% above its net asset value.

Peter Hubbard has been running the fund for 4 years and currently receives a manager quality ranking of 43 (0=worst, 99=best). If you desire an average level of risk, then this fund may be an option.

Data Date	Investment Rating	Net Assets ($Mil)	Price	Performance Rating/Pts	Total Return Y-T-D	Risk Rating/Pts
3-12	C-	18.19	13.00	C- / 3.0	5.02%	B / 8.8
2011	C	29.10	12.44	C- / 3.7	-0.16%	B / 8.4
2010	A-	17.90	12.81	B+ / 8.6	11.98%	C+ / 6.3
2009	B	10.05	11.84	B- / 7.3	15.43%	C+ / 6.1

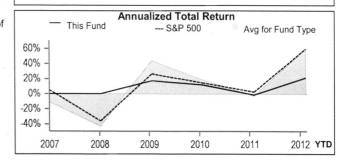

Annualized Total Return

*PowerShares S&P 500 BuyWrite Por (PBP)

C   Fair

Fund Family: Invesco Powershares Capital Mgmt LL
Fund Type: Income
Inception Date: December 20, 2007

Data Date	Investment Rating	Net Assets ($Mil)	Price	Performance Rating/Pts	Total Return Y-T-D	Risk Rating/Pts
3-12	C	116.78	20.54	C- / 4.2	5.19%	B / 8.4
2011	C+	89.50	19.62	C+ / 5.8	1.38%	B / 8.2
2010	C-	140.70	20.89	D+ / 2.8	5.51%	C+ / 6.4
2009	A	84.21	21.51	B / 7.9	21.32%	C+ / 6.5

Major Rating Factors: Middle of the road best describes *PowerShares S&P 500 BuyWrite Por whose TheStreet.com Investment Rating is currently a C (Fair). The fund currently has a performance rating of C- (Fair) based on an annualized return of 15.05% over the last three years and a total return of 5.19% year to date 2012. Factored into the performance evaluation is an expense ratio of 0.75% (very low).

The fund's risk rating is currently B (Good). It carries a beta of 0.63, meaning the fund's expected move will be 6.3% for every 10% move in the market. Volatility, as measured by both the semi-deviation and a drawdown factor, is considered low. As of March 31, 2012, *PowerShares S&P 500 BuyWrite Por traded at a premium of .15% above its net asset value, which is worse than its one-year historical average discount of .22%.

Peter Hubbard has been running the fund for 5 years and currently receives a manager quality ranking of 56 (0=worst, 99=best). If you desire an average level of risk, then this fund may be an option.

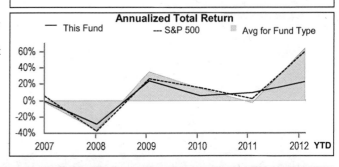

*PowerShares S&P SC Cnsmr Discr (PSCD)

B+   Good

Fund Family: Invesco Powershares Capital Mgmt LL
Fund Type: Growth
Inception Date: April 6, 2010

Data Date	Investment Rating	Net Assets ($Mil)	Price	Performance Rating/Pts	Total Return Y-T-D	Risk Rating/Pts
3-12	B+	59.96	32.06	B+ / 8.9	18.37%	B- / 7.4
2011	D	43.30	27.10	D / 1.8	0.92%	B- / 7.3

Major Rating Factors: Strong performance is the major factor driving the B+ (Good) TheStreet.com Investment Rating for *PowerShares S&P SC Cnsmr Discr. The fund currently has a performance rating of B+ (Good) based on an annualized return of 0.00% over the last three years and a total return of 18.37% year to date 2012. Factored into the performance evaluation is an expense ratio of 0.29% (very low).

The fund's risk rating is currently B- (Good). It carries a beta of 0.00, meaning the fund's expected move will be 0.0% for every 10% move in the market. Volatility, as measured by both the semi-deviation and a drawdown factor, is considered low. As of March 31, 2012, *PowerShares S&P SC Cnsmr Discr traded at a premium of .28% above its net asset value, which is worse than its one-year historical average premium of .03%.

Michael C. Jeanette has been running the fund for 2 years and currently receives a manager quality ranking of 56 (0=worst, 99=best). If you desire only a moderate level of risk and strong performance, then this fund is an excellent option.

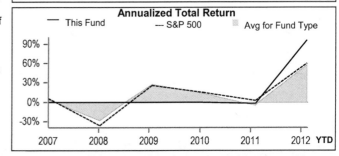

*PowerShares S&P SC Cnsmr Staples (PSCC)

C   Fair

Fund Family: Invesco Powershares Capital Mgmt LL
Fund Type: Growth
Inception Date: April 6, 2010

Data Date	Investment Rating	Net Assets ($Mil)	Price	Performance Rating/Pts	Total Return Y-T-D	Risk Rating/Pts
3-12	C	19.35	34.09	C / 4.5	8.48%	B / 8.7
2011	C	20.30	31.45	C- / 3.3	-1.24%	B / 8.7

Major Rating Factors: Middle of the road best describes *PowerShares S&P SC Cnsmr Staples whose TheStreet.com Investment Rating is currently a C (Fair). The fund currently has a performance rating of C (Fair) based on an annualized return of 0.00% over the last three years and a total return of 8.48% year to date 2012. Factored into the performance evaluation is an expense ratio of 0.29% (very low).

The fund's risk rating is currently B (Good). It carries a beta of 0.00, meaning the fund's expected move will be 0.0% for every 10% move in the market. Volatility, as measured by both the semi-deviation and a drawdown factor, is considered low. As of March 31, 2012, *PowerShares S&P SC Cnsmr Staples traded at a premium of .38% above its net asset value.

Michael C. Jeanette has been running the fund for 2 years and currently receives a manager quality ranking of 71 (0=worst, 99=best). If you desire an average level of risk, then this fund may be an option.

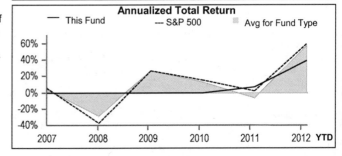

*PowerShares S&P SC Energy (PSCE) — D — Weak

Fund Family: Invesco Powershares Capital Mgmt LL
Fund Type: Growth
Inception Date: April 6, 2010

Major Rating Factors: *PowerShares S&P SC Energy receives a TheStreet.com Investment Rating of D (Weak). The fund currently has a performance rating of C- (Fair) based on an annualized return of 0.00% over the last three years and a total return of 8.60% year to date 2012. Factored into the performance evaluation is an expense ratio of 0.29% (very low).

The fund's risk rating is currently C+ (Fair). It carries a beta of 0.00, meaning the fund's expected move will be 0.0% for every 10% move in the market. Volatility, as measured by both the semi-deviation and a drawdown factor, is considered low. As of March 31, 2012, *PowerShares S&P SC Energy traded at a premium of .05% above its net asset value, which is worse than its one-year historical average discount of .04%.

Michael C. Jeanette has been running the fund for 2 years and currently receives a manager quality ranking of 4 (0=worst, 99=best). If you desire an average level of risk, then this fund may be an option.

Data Date	Investment Rating	Net Assets ($Mil)	Price	Performance Rating/Pts	Total Return Y-T-D	Risk Rating/Pts
3-12	D	61.09	37.25	C- / 3.3	8.60%	C+ / 5.9
2011	D+	54.80	34.30	C- / 4.0	2.33%	C+ / 5.8

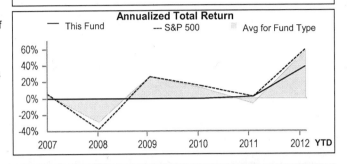
Annualized Total Return
— This Fund   --- S&P 500   Avg for Fund Type

*PowerShares S&P SC Financials (PSCF) — C+ — Fair

Fund Family: Invesco Powershares Capital Mgmt LL
Fund Type: Growth
Inception Date: April 6, 2010

Major Rating Factors: Strong performance is the major factor driving the C+ (Fair) TheStreet.com Investment Rating for *PowerShares S&P SC Financials. The fund currently has a performance rating of B- (Good) based on an annualized return of 0.00% over the last three years and a total return of 10.90% year to date 2012. Factored into the performance evaluation is an expense ratio of 0.29% (very low).

The fund's risk rating is currently B- (Good). It carries a beta of 0.00, meaning the fund's expected move will be 0.0% for every 10% move in the market. Volatility, as measured by both the semi-deviation and a drawdown factor, is considered low. As of March 31, 2012, *PowerShares S&P SC Financials traded at a premium of .20% above its net asset value, which is worse than its one-year historical average discount of .02%.

Michael C. Jeanette has been running the fund for 2 years and currently receives a manager quality ranking of 36 (0=worst, 99=best). If you desire only a moderate level of risk and strong performance, then this fund is an excellent option.

Data Date	Investment Rating	Net Assets ($Mil)	Price	Performance Rating/Pts	Total Return Y-T-D	Risk Rating/Pts
3-12	C+	73.26	29.95	B- / 7.0	10.90%	B- / 7.8
2011	C	62.00	27.04	C / 4.3	1.47%	B- / 7.8

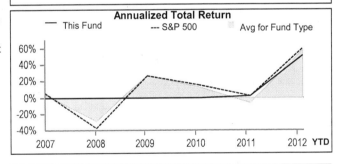
Annualized Total Return
— This Fund   --- S&P 500   Avg for Fund Type

*PowerShares S&P SC Health Care (PSCH) — B- — Good

Fund Family: Invesco Powershares Capital Mgmt LL
Fund Type: Growth
Inception Date: April 6, 2010

Major Rating Factors: Strong performance is the major factor driving the B- (Good) TheStreet.com Investment Rating for *PowerShares S&P SC Health Care. The fund currently has a performance rating of B- (Good) based on an annualized return of 0.00% over the last three years and a total return of 11.58% year to date 2012. Factored into the performance evaluation is an expense ratio of 0.29% (very low).

The fund's risk rating is currently B (Good). It carries a beta of 0.00, meaning the fund's expected move will be 0.0% for every 10% move in the market. Volatility, as measured by both the semi-deviation and a drawdown factor, is considered low. As of March 31, 2012, *PowerShares S&P SC Health Care traded at a premium of .14% above its net asset value, which is worse than its one-year historical average discount of .04%.

Michael C. Jeanette has been running the fund for 2 years and currently receives a manager quality ranking of 58 (0=worst, 99=best). If you desire only a moderate level of risk and strong performance, then this fund is an excellent option.

Data Date	Investment Rating	Net Assets ($Mil)	Price	Performance Rating/Pts	Total Return Y-T-D	Risk Rating/Pts
3-12	B-	118.68	35.15	B- / 7.0	11.58%	B / 8.0
2011	C	103.80	31.53	C- / 4.1	0.33%	B / 8.0

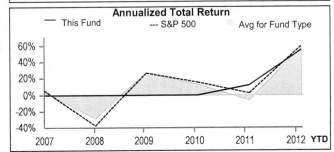
Annualized Total Return
— This Fund   --- S&P 500   Avg for Fund Type

*PowerShares S&P SC Industrials (PSCI)   C   Fair

Fund Family: Invesco Powershares Capital Mgmt LL
Fund Type: Growth
Inception Date: April 6, 2010

Major Rating Factors: Middle of the road best describes *PowerShares S&P SC Industrials whose TheStreet.com Investment Rating is currently a C (Fair). The fund currently has a performance rating of C (Fair) based on an annualized return of 0.00% over the last three years and a total return of 12.08% year to date 2012. Factored into the performance evaluation is an expense ratio of 0.29% (very low).

The fund's risk rating is currently B- (Good). It carries a beta of 0.00, meaning the fund's expected move will be 0.0% for every 10% move in the market. Volatility, as measured by both the semi-deviation and a drawdown factor, is considered low. As of March 31, 2012, *PowerShares S&P SC Industrials traded at a premium of .43% above its net asset value.

Michael C. Jeanette has been running the fund for 2 years and currently receives a manager quality ranking of 12 (0=worst, 99=best). If you desire an average level of risk, then this fund may be an option.

Data Date	Investment Rating	Net Assets ($Mil)	Price	Performance Rating/Pts	Total Return Y-T-D	Risk Rating/Pts
3-12	C	34.24	30.65	C / 5.1	12.08%	B- / 7.2
2011	D	25.90	27.38	D / 1.9	1.61%	B- / 7.2

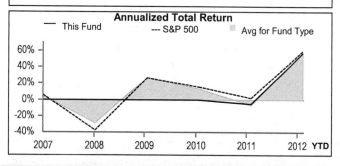

Annualized Total Return
— This Fund   --- S&P 500   ▨ Avg for Fund Type

*PowerShares S&P SC Information T (PSCT)   C   Fair

Fund Family: Invesco Powershares Capital Mgmt LL
Fund Type: Growth
Inception Date: April 6, 2010

Major Rating Factors: Middle of the road best describes *PowerShares S&P SC Information T whose TheStreet.com Investment Rating is currently a C (Fair). The fund currently has a performance rating of C (Fair) based on an annualized return of 0.00% over the last three years and a total return of 12.87% year to date 2012. Factored into the performance evaluation is an expense ratio of 0.29% (very low).

The fund's risk rating is currently B- (Good). It carries a beta of 0.00, meaning the fund's expected move will be 0.0% for every 10% move in the market. Volatility, as measured by both the semi-deviation and a drawdown factor, is considered low. As of March 31, 2012, *PowerShares S&P SC Information T traded at a premium of .44% above its net asset value.

Michael C. Jeanette has been running the fund for 2 years and currently receives a manager quality ranking of 11 (0=worst, 99=best). If you desire an average level of risk, then this fund may be an option.

Data Date	Investment Rating	Net Assets ($Mil)	Price	Performance Rating/Pts	Total Return Y-T-D	Risk Rating/Pts
3-12	C	123.20	31.64	C / 5.5	12.87%	B- / 7.0
2011	D	78.10	28.03	D / 1.7	0.88%	B- / 7.0

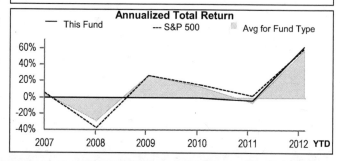

Annualized Total Return
— This Fund   --- S&P 500   ▨ Avg for Fund Type

*PowerShares S&P SC Materials (PSCM)   D+   Weak

Fund Family: Invesco Powershares Capital Mgmt LL
Fund Type: Growth
Inception Date: April 6, 2010

Major Rating Factors: *PowerShares S&P SC Materials receives a TheStreet.com Investment Rating of D+ (Weak). The fund currently has a performance rating of C- (Fair) based on an annualized return of 0.00% over the last three years and a total return of 12.82% year to date 2012. Factored into the performance evaluation is an expense ratio of 0.31% (very low).

The fund's risk rating is currently B- (Good). It carries a beta of 0.00, meaning the fund's expected move will be 0.0% for every 10% move in the market. Volatility, as measured by both the semi-deviation and a drawdown factor, is considered low. As of March 31, 2012, *PowerShares S&P SC Materials traded at a discount of .14% below its net asset value, which is better than its one-year historical average discount of .07%.

Michael C. Jeanette has been running the fund for 2 years and currently receives a manager quality ranking of 11 (0=worst, 99=best). If you desire an average level of risk, then this fund may be an option.

Data Date	Investment Rating	Net Assets ($Mil)	Price	Performance Rating/Pts	Total Return Y-T-D	Risk Rating/Pts
3-12	D+	4.29	29.11	C- / 3.4	12.82%	B- / 7.2
2011	D	3.90	25.84	D- / 1.4	1.47%	B- / 7.2

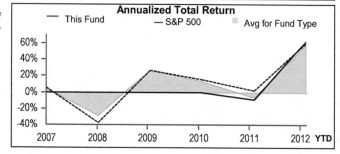

Annualized Total Return
— This Fund   --- S&P 500   ▨ Avg for Fund Type

*PowerShares S&P SC Utilities (PSCU)　　　　　C-　　　Fair

Fund Family: Invesco Powershares Capital Mgmt LL
Fund Type: Growth
Inception Date: April 6, 2010

Data Date	Investment Rating	Net Assets ($Mil)	Price	Performance Rating/Pts	Total Return Y-T-D	Risk Rating/Pts
3-12	C-	47.49	30.21	D+ / 2.5	-1.19%	B+ / 9.0
2011	C+	46.10	30.75	C / 4.8	-1.17%	B+ / 9.0

Major Rating Factors:
Disappointing performance is the major factor driving the C- (Fair) TheStreet.com Investment Rating for *PowerShares S&P SC Utilities. The fund currently has a performance rating of D+ (Weak) based on an annualized return of 0.00% over the last three years and a total return of -1.19% year to date 2012. Factored into the performance evaluation is an expense ratio of 0.29% (very low).

The fund's risk rating is currently B+ (Good). It carries a beta of 0.00, meaning the fund's expected move will be 0.0% for every 10% move in the market. Volatility, as measured by both the semi-deviation and a drawdown factor, is considered very low. As of March 31, 2012, *PowerShares S&P SC Utilities traded at a premium of .17% above its net asset value, which is worse than its one-year historical average premium of .01%.

Michael C. Jeanette has been running the fund for 2 years and currently receives a manager quality ranking of 72 (0=worst, 99=best). This fund offers only a moderate level of risk but investors looking for strong performance are still waiting.

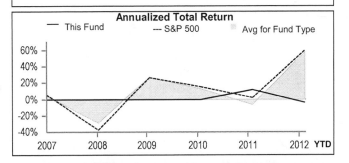

Annualized Total Return

*PowerShares Senior Loan (BKLN)　　　　　　C-　　　Fair

Fund Family: Invesco Powershares Capital Mgmt LL
Fund Type: Loan Participation
Inception Date: March 1, 2011

Data Date	Investment Rating	Net Assets ($Mil)	Price	Performance Rating/Pts	Total Return Y-T-D	Risk Rating/Pts
3-12	C-	260.46	24.58	D / 2.2	4.13%	B+ / 9.5

Major Rating Factors:
Disappointing performance is the major factor driving the C- (Fair) TheStreet.com Investment Rating for *PowerShares Senior Loan. The fund currently has a performance rating of D (Weak) based on an annualized return of 0.00% over the last three years and a total return of 4.13% year to date 2012. Factored into the performance evaluation is an expense ratio of 0.65% (very low).

The fund's risk rating is currently B+ (Good). It carries a beta of 0.00, meaning the fund's expected move will be 0.0% for every 10% move in the market. Volatility, as measured by both the semi-deviation and a drawdown factor, is considered very low. As of March 31, 2012, *PowerShares Senior Loan traded at a premium of .74% above its net asset value, which is worse than its one-year historical average premium of .44%.

Peter Hubbard has been running the fund for 1 year and currently receives a manager quality ranking of 90 (0=worst, 99=best). This fund offers only a moderate level of risk but investors looking for strong performance are still waiting.

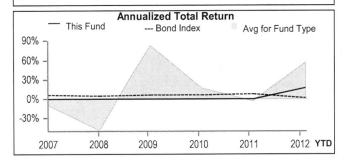

Annualized Total Return

*PowerShares VRDO Tax-Free Weekly (PVI)　　　　C-　　　Fair

Fund Family: Invesco Powershares Capital Mgmt LL
Fund Type: Municipal - High Yield
Inception Date: November 14, 2007

Data Date	Investment Rating	Net Assets ($Mil)	Price	Performance Rating/Pts	Total Return Y-T-D	Risk Rating/Pts
3-12	C-	426.25	24.99	D- / 1.2	-0.05%	B+ / 9.9
2011	C	436.20	25.02	D / 2.1	-0.12%	B+ / 9.9
2010	B-	566.30	24.99	C- / 3.3	0.32%	B+ / 9.1
2009	C	380.13	25.00	D+ / 2.3	0.96%	B+ / 9.2

Major Rating Factors:
Disappointing performance is the major factor driving the C- (Fair) TheStreet.com Investment Rating for *PowerShares VRDO Tax-Free Weekly. The fund currently has a performance rating of D- (Weak) based on an annualized return of 0.56% over the last three years and a total return of -0.05% year to date 2012. Factored into the performance evaluation is an expense ratio of 0.25% (very low).

The fund's risk rating is currently B+ (Good). It carries a beta of 0.01, meaning the fund's expected move will be 0.1% for every 10% move in the market. Volatility, as measured by both the semi-deviation and a drawdown factor, is considered very low. As of March 31, 2012, *PowerShares VRDO Tax-Free Weekly traded at a discount of .04% below its net asset value, which is better than its one-year historical average discount of .01%.

Peter Hubbard has been running the fund for 5 years and currently receives a manager quality ranking of 49 (0=worst, 99=best). This fund offers only a moderate level of risk but investors looking for strong performance are still waiting.

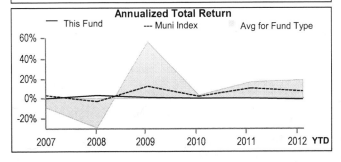

Annualized Total Return

*PowerShares Water Resources (PHO)

C-   **Fair**

Fund Family: Invesco Powershares Capital Mgmt LL
Fund Type: Income
Inception Date: December 6, 2005

Data Date	Investment Rating	Net Assets ($Mil)	Price	Perfor- mance Rating/Pts	Total Return Y-T-D	Risk Rating/Pts
3-12	C-	894.91	19.20	C- / 3.8	14.07%	B- / 7.2
2011	D+	808.80	16.85	C- / 3.1	2.14%	C+ / 6.4
2010	D+	1,162.50	18.99	C- / 3.9	13.73%	C / 5.0
2009	D	1,220.03	16.86	D+ / 2.7	13.90%	C / 4.9

Major Rating Factors: Middle of the road best describes *PowerShares Water Resources whose TheStreet.com Investment Rating is currently a C- (Fair). The fund currently has a performance rating of C- (Fair) based on an annualized return of 14.82% over the last three years and a total return of 14.07% year to date 2012. Factored into the performance evaluation is an expense ratio of 0.66% (very low).

The fund's risk rating is currently B- (Good). It carries a beta of 1.31, meaning it is expected to move 13.1% for every 10% move in the market. Volatility, as measured by both the semi-deviation and a drawdown factor, is considered low. As of March 31, 2012, *PowerShares Water Resources traded at a discount of .16% below its net asset value, which is better than its one-year historical average discount of .09%.

Peter Hubbard has been running the fund for 5 years and currently receives a manager quality ranking of 14 (0=worst, 99=best). If you desire an average level of risk, then this fund may be an option.

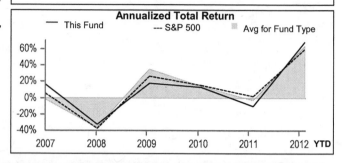

*PowerShares Wilder Clean Energy (PBW)

E+   **Very Weak**

Fund Family: Invesco Powershares Capital Mgmt LL
Fund Type: Energy/Natural Resources
Inception Date: March 3, 2005

Data Date	Investment Rating	Net Assets ($Mil)	Price	Perfor- mance Rating/Pts	Total Return Y-T-D	Risk Rating/Pts
3-12	E+	210.74	5.56	E+ / 0.7	10.13%	C / 5.2
2011	E+	194.50	5.07	E+ / 0.8	2.96%	C / 4.8
2010	E+	547.20	10.39	E / 0.5	-5.55%	C- / 3.7
2009	E+	658.40	11.00	E+ / 0.9	21.28%	C- / 3.7

Major Rating Factors:
Very poor performance is the major factor driving the E+ (Very Weak) TheStreet.com Investment Rating for *PowerShares Wilder Clean Energy. The fund currently has a performance rating of E+ (Very Weak) based on an annualized return of -12.13% over the last three years and a total return of 10.13% year to date 2012. Factored into the performance evaluation is an expense ratio of 0.70% (very low).

The fund's risk rating is currently C (Fair). It carries a beta of 1.14, meaning it is expected to move 11.4% for every 10% move in the market. Volatility, as measured by both the semi-deviation and a drawdown factor, is considered average. As of March 31, 2012, *PowerShares Wilder Clean Energy traded at a discount of .18% below its net asset value, which is better than its one-year historical average discount of .16%.

Peter Hubbard has been running the fund for 5 years and currently receives a manager quality ranking of 4 (0=worst, 99=best). This fund offers an average level of risk but investors looking for strong performance will be frustrated.

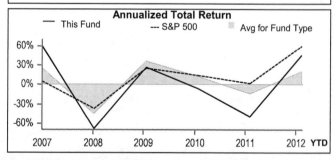

*PowerShares WilderHill Progr Ene (PUW)

C-   **Fair**

Fund Family: Invesco Powershares Capital Mgmt LL
Fund Type: Energy/Natural Resources
Inception Date: October 24, 2006

Data Date	Investment Rating	Net Assets ($Mil)	Price	Perfor- mance Rating/Pts	Total Return Y-T-D	Risk Rating/Pts
3-12	C-	50.52	26.26	C / 4.7	16.52%	C+ / 6.9
2011	C-	43.90	22.53	C / 4.3	3.32%	C+ / 6.8
2010	C	61.70	28.13	C+ / 5.8	20.44%	C / 5.1
2009	C-	39.97	23.54	C / 4.5	51.77%	C / 5.3

Major Rating Factors: Middle of the road best describes *PowerShares WilderHill Progr Ene whose TheStreet.com Investment Rating is currently a C- (Fair). The fund currently has a performance rating of C (Fair) based on an annualized return of 20.01% over the last three years and a total return of 16.52% year to date 2012. Factored into the performance evaluation is an expense ratio of 0.70% (very low).

The fund's risk rating is currently C+ (Fair). It carries a beta of 1.04, meaning that its performance tracks fairly well with that of the overall stock market. Volatility, as measured by both the semi-deviation and a drawdown factor, is considered low. As of March 31, 2012, *PowerShares WilderHill Progr Ene traded at a premium of .04% above its net asset value, which is worse than its one-year historical average discount of .10%.

Peter Hubbard has been running the fund for 5 years and currently receives a manager quality ranking of 65 (0=worst, 99=best). If you desire an average level of risk, then this fund may be an option.

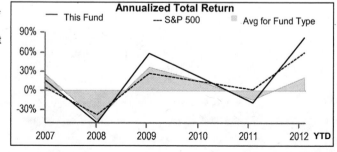

*PowerShares Zacks Micro Cap (PZI)

C-   **Fair**

Fund Family: Invesco Powershares Capital Mgmt LL
Fund Type: Growth
Inception Date: August 18, 2005

Major Rating Factors: Middle of the road best describes *PowerShares Zacks Micro Cap whose TheStreet.com Investment Rating is currently a C- (Fair). The fund currently has a performance rating of C- (Fair) based on an annualized return of 16.44% over the last three years and a total return of 13.75% year to date 2012. Factored into the performance evaluation is an expense ratio of 0.70% (very low).

The fund's risk rating is currently B- (Good). It carries a beta of 1.49, meaning it is expected to move 14.9% for every 10% move in the market. Volatility, as measured by both the semi-deviation and a drawdown factor, is considered low. As of March 31, 2012, *PowerShares Zacks Micro Cap traded at a premium of .09% above its net asset value, which is worse than its one-year historical average discount of .10%.

Peter Hubbard has been running the fund for 5 years and currently receives a manager quality ranking of 11 (0=worst, 99=best). If you desire an average level of risk, then this fund may be an option.

Data Date	Investment Rating	Net Assets ($Mil)	Price	Performance Rating/Pts	Total Return Y-T-D	Risk Rating/Pts
3-12	C-	35.58	11.58	C- / 4.1	13.75%	B- / 7.1
2011	D+	31.60	10.19	D+ / 2.9	0.98%	C+ / 6.8
2010	C-	110.70	12.01	C- / 4.0	23.70%	C / 5.3
2009	D-	46.96	9.80	E+ / 0.7	9.89%	C / 5.1

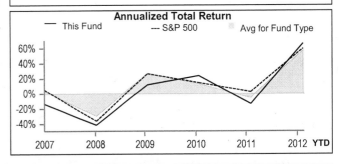

Annualized Total Return

*ProShares Alpha Cr Suisse 130/30 (CSM)

C   **Fair**

Fund Family: ProShare Advisors LLC
Fund Type: Income
Inception Date: July 13, 2009

Major Rating Factors: Middle of the road best describes *ProShares Alpha Cr Suisse 130/30 whose TheStreet.com Investment Rating is currently a C (Fair). The fund currently has a performance rating of C (Fair) based on an annualized return of 0.00% over the last three years and a total return of 12.32% year to date 2012. Factored into the performance evaluation is an expense ratio of 0.95% (low).

The fund's risk rating is currently B (Good). It carries a beta of 0.00, meaning the fund's expected move will be 0.0% for every 10% move in the market. Volatility, as measured by both the semi-deviation and a drawdown factor, is considered low. As of March 31, 2012, *ProShares Alpha Cr Suisse 130/30 traded at a discount of .02% below its net asset value, which is in line with its one-year historical average discount of .02%.

Ryan Dofflemeyer has been running the fund for 2 years and currently receives a manager quality ranking of 24 (0=worst, 99=best). If you desire an average level of risk, then this fund may be an option.

Data Date	Investment Rating	Net Assets ($Mil)	Price	Performance Rating/Pts	Total Return Y-T-D	Risk Rating/Pts
3-12	C	89.08	63.62	C / 4.9	12.32%	B / 8.2
2011	D+	91.00	56.77	D / 2.1	1.41%	B / 8.2
2010	A+	62.70	57.03	A- / 9.0	14.17%	B- / 7.9

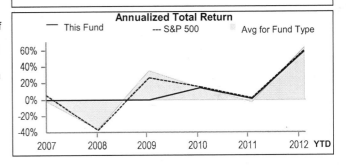

Annualized Total Return

*ProShares RAFI Long/Short (RALS)

D+   **Weak**

Fund Family: ProShare Advisors LLC
Fund Type: Income
Inception Date: December 2, 2010

Major Rating Factors:
Very poor performance is the major factor driving the D+ (Weak) TheStreet.com Investment Rating for *ProShares RAFI Long/Short. The fund currently has a performance rating of E+ (Very Weak) based on an annualized return of 0.00% over the last three years and a total return of -1.61% year to date 2012. Factored into the performance evaluation is an expense ratio of 0.95% (low).

The fund's risk rating is currently B+ (Good). It carries a beta of 0.00, meaning the fund's expected move will be 0.0% for every 10% move in the market. Volatility, as measured by both the semi-deviation and a drawdown factor, is considered very low. As of March 31, 2012, *ProShares RAFI Long/Short traded at a premium of .03% above its net asset value, which is worse than its one-year historical average discount of .07%.

Ryan Dofflemeyer has been running the fund for 2 years and currently receives a manager quality ranking of 13 (0=worst, 99=best). This fund offers only a moderate level of risk but investors looking for strong performance are still waiting.

Data Date	Investment Rating	Net Assets ($Mil)	Price	Performance Rating/Pts	Total Return Y-T-D	Risk Rating/Pts
3-12	D+	15.06	37.65	E+ / 0.9	-1.61%	B+ / 9.1
2011	C-	15.40	38.37	D- / 1.4	0.21%	B+ / 9.1

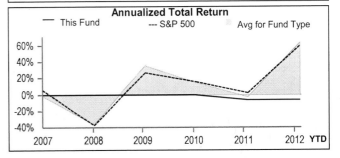

Annualized Total Return

*ProShares Short 20+ Year Treas (TBF)

D-   **Weak**

Fund Family: ProShare Advisors LLC
Fund Type: US Government/Agency
Inception Date: August 18, 2009

Data Date	Investment Rating	Net Assets ($Mil)	Price	Performance Rating/Pts	Total Return Y-T-D	Risk Rating/Pts
3-12	D-	917.58	33.23	E+ / 0.7	6.61%	C+ / 6.5
2011	D-	712.30	31.17	E / 0.5	2.09%	C+ / 6.5
2010	D+	812.00	44.25	D- / 1.4	-12.39%	B- / 7.3

Major Rating Factors:
Very poor performance is the major factor driving the D- (Weak) TheStreet.com Investment Rating for *ProShares Short 20+ Year Treas. The fund currently has a performance rating of E+ (Very Weak) based on an annualized return of 0.00% over the last three years and a total return of 6.61% year to date 2012. Factored into the performance evaluation is an expense ratio of 0.95% (low).

The fund's risk rating is currently C+ (Fair). It carries a beta of 0.00, meaning the fund's expected move will be 0.0% for every 10% move in the market. Volatility, as measured by both the semi-deviation and a drawdown factor, is considered low. As of March 31, 2012, *ProShares Short 20+ Year Treas traded at a premium of .30% above its net asset value, which is worse than its one-year historical average discount of .01%.

Howard S. Rubin has been running the fund for 3 years and currently receives a manager quality ranking of 27 (0=worst, 99=best). This fund offers only a moderate level of risk but investors looking for strong performance are still waiting.

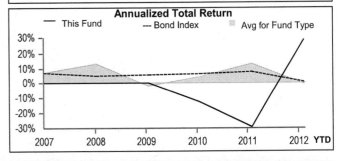

---

*ProShares Short Basic Materials (SBM)

D-   **Weak**

Fund Family: ProShare Advisors LLC
Fund Type: Growth
Inception Date: March 16, 2010

Data Date	Investment Rating	Net Assets ($Mil)	Price	Performance Rating/Pts	Total Return Y-T-D	Risk Rating/Pts
3-12	D-	7.06	35.41	E+ / 0.7	-9.69%	C+ / 5.8
2011	D-	7.80	39.21	D / 1.6	-3.55%	C+ / 5.9

Major Rating Factors:
Very poor performance is the major factor driving the D- (Weak) TheStreet.com Investment Rating for *ProShares Short Basic Materials. The fund currently has a performance rating of E+ (Very Weak) based on an annualized return of 0.00% over the last three years and a total return of -9.69% year to date 2012. Factored into the performance evaluation is an expense ratio of 0.95% (low).

The fund's risk rating is currently C+ (Fair). It carries a beta of 0.00, meaning the fund's expected move will be 0.0% for every 10% move in the market. Volatility, as measured by both the semi-deviation and a drawdown factor, is considered low. As of March 31, 2012, *ProShares Short Basic Materials traded at a discount of .03% below its net asset value, which is better than its one-year historical average premium of .02%.

Hratch Najarian has been running the fund for 1 year and currently receives a manager quality ranking of 91 (0=worst, 99=best). This fund offers only a moderate level of risk but investors looking for strong performance are still waiting.

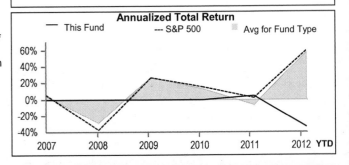

---

*ProShares Short Dow 30 (DOG)

E+   **Very Weak**

Fund Family: ProShare Advisors LLC
Fund Type: Growth
Inception Date: June 19, 2006

Data Date	Investment Rating	Net Assets ($Mil)	Price	Performance Rating/Pts	Total Return Y-T-D	Risk Rating/Pts
3-12	E+	268.93	35.49	E+ / 0.6	-8.53%	C+ / 5.6
2011	D-	293.90	38.80	D- / 1.0	-1.39%	C / 5.5
2010	D	246.20	44.33	E+ / 0.8	-15.29%	C+ / 5.7
2009	D	234.48	52.33	D- / 1.0	-21.40%	C+ / 6.7

Major Rating Factors:
Very poor performance is the major factor driving the E+ (Very Weak) TheStreet.com Investment Rating for *ProShares Short Dow 30. The fund currently has a performance rating of E+ (Very Weak) based on an annualized return of -20.92% over the last three years and a total return of -8.53% year to date 2012. Factored into the performance evaluation is an expense ratio of 0.95% (low).

The fund's risk rating is currently C+ (Fair). It carries a beta of -0.86, meaning the fund's expected move will be -8.6% for every 10% move in the market. Volatility, as measured by both the semi-deviation and a drawdown factor, is considered low. As of March 31, 2012, *ProShares Short Dow 30 traded at a discount of .03% below its net asset value, which is worse than its one-year historical average discount of .04%.

Hratch Najarian has been running the fund for 3 years and currently receives a manager quality ranking of 18 (0=worst, 99=best). This fund offers only a moderate level of risk but investors looking for strong performance are still waiting.

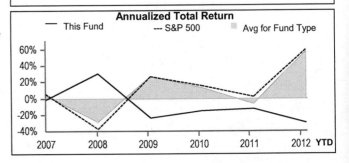

---

*ProShares Short Financials (SEF)   E+   Very Weak

Fund Family: ProShare Advisors LLC
Fund Type: Financial Services
Inception Date: June 10, 2008

Major Rating Factors:
Very poor performance is the major factor driving the E+ (Very Weak) TheStreet.com Investment Rating for *ProShares Short Financials. The fund currently has a performance rating of E (Very Weak) based on an annualized return of -25.62% over the last three years and a total return of -17.17% year to date 2012. Factored into the performance evaluation is an expense ratio of 0.95% (low).

The fund's risk rating is currently C (Fair). It carries a beta of -1.04, meaning the fund's expected move will be -10.4% for every 10% move in the market. Volatility, as measured by both the semi-deviation and a drawdown factor, is considered average. As of March 31, 2012, *ProShares Short Financials traded at a premium of .06% above its net asset value, which is worse than its one-year historical average discount of .02%.

Hratch Najarian has been running the fund for 1 year and currently receives a manager quality ranking of 13 (0=worst, 99=best). This fund offers an average level of risk but investors looking for strong performance will be frustrated.

Data Date	Investment Rating	Net Assets ($Mil)	Price	Performance Rating/Pts	Total Return Y-T-D	Risk Rating/Pts
3-12	E+	76.58	30.96	E / 0.5	-17.17%	C / 4.6
2011	E+	131.90	37.38	E+ / 0.8	-2.49%	C- / 3.9
2010	E+	96.30	36.66	E / 0.4	-17.43%	C- / 3.7
2009	E+	157.37	44.40	E / 0.3	-40.93%	C- / 4.1

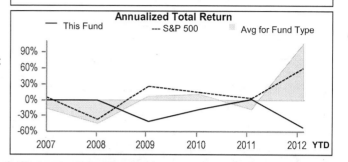

*ProShares Short FTSE China 25 (YXI)   D-   Weak

Fund Family: ProShare Advisors LLC
Fund Type: Foreign
Inception Date: March 16, 2010

Major Rating Factors:
Very poor performance is the major factor driving the D- (Weak) TheStreet.com Investment Rating for *ProShares Short FTSE China 25. The fund currently has a performance rating of E+ (Very Weak) based on an annualized return of 0.00% over the last three years and a total return of -6.64% year to date 2012. Factored into the performance evaluation is an expense ratio of 0.95% (low).

The fund's risk rating is currently C+ (Fair). It carries a beta of 0.00, meaning the fund's expected move will be 0.0% for every 10% move in the market. Volatility, as measured by both the semi-deviation and a drawdown factor, is considered low. As of March 31, 2012, *ProShares Short FTSE China 25 traded at a premium of .07% above its net asset value, which is worse than its one-year historical average premium of .04%.

Alexander V. Ilyasov has been running the fund for 2 years and currently receives a manager quality ranking of 28 (0=worst, 99=best). This fund offers only a moderate level of risk but investors looking for strong performance are still waiting.

Data Date	Investment Rating	Net Assets ($Mil)	Price	Performance Rating/Pts	Total Return Y-T-D	Risk Rating/Pts
3-12	D-	8.45	42.30	E+ / 0.8	-6.64%	C+ / 6.8
2011	D+	11.30	45.31	D / 2.1	-0.88%	B- / 7.4

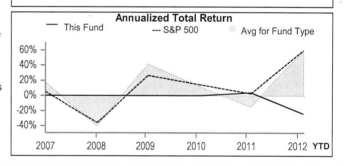

*ProShares Short High Yield (SJB)   D   Weak

Fund Family: ProShare Advisors LLC
Fund Type: General - Investment Grade
Inception Date: March 21, 2011

Major Rating Factors:
Very poor performance is the major factor driving the D (Weak) TheStreet.com Investment Rating for *ProShares Short High Yield. The fund currently has a performance rating of E+ (Very Weak) based on an annualized return of 0.00% over the last three years and a total return of -3.45% year to date 2012. Factored into the performance evaluation is an expense ratio of 0.95% (low).

The fund's risk rating is currently B (Good). It carries a beta of 0.00, meaning the fund's expected move will be 0.0% for every 10% move in the market. Volatility, as measured by both the semi-deviation and a drawdown factor, is considered low. As of March 31, 2012, *ProShares Short High Yield traded at a premium of .03% above its net asset value, which is worse than its one-year historical average discount of .02%.

Jeff Ploshnick has been running the fund for 1 year and currently receives a manager quality ranking of 12 (0=worst, 99=best). This fund offers only a moderate level of risk but investors looking for strong performance are still waiting.

Data Date	Investment Rating	Net Assets ($Mil)	Price	Performance Rating/Pts	Total Return Y-T-D	Risk Rating/Pts
3-12	D	23.29	35.84	E+ / 0.7	-3.45%	B / 8.4

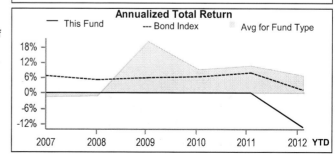

*ProShares Short Inv Grade Corp (IGS)   D   Weak

Fund Family: ProShare Advisors LLC
Fund Type: Corporate - Investment Grade
Inception Date: March 28, 2011

Data Date	Investment Rating	Net Assets ($Mil)	Price	Performance Rating/Pts	Total Return Y-T-D	Risk Rating/Pts
3-12	D	3.51	35.20	E+ / 0.7	-3.40%	B / 8.9

Major Rating Factors:
Very poor performance is the major factor driving the D (Weak) TheStreet.com Investment Rating for *ProShares Short Inv Grade Corp. The fund currently has a performance rating of E+ (Very Weak) based on an annualized return of 0.00% over the last three years and a total return of -3.40% year to date 2012. Factored into the performance evaluation is an expense ratio of 0.95% (low).

The fund's risk rating is currently B (Good). It carries a beta of 0.00, meaning the fund's expected move will be 0.0% for every 10% move in the market. Volatility, as measured by both the semi-deviation and a drawdown factor, is considered low. As of March 31, 2012, *ProShares Short Inv Grade Corp traded at a premium of .37% above its net asset value, which is worse than its one-year historical average premium of .13%.

Jeff Ploshnick has been running the fund for 1 year and currently receives a manager quality ranking of 50 (0=worst, 99=best). This fund offers only a moderate level of risk but investors looking for strong performance are still waiting.

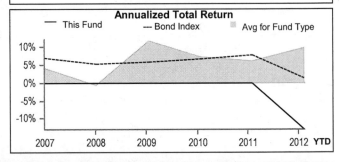

*ProShares Short KBW Regional Ban (KRS)   E+   Very Weak

Fund Family: ProShare Advisors LLC
Fund Type: Financial Services
Inception Date: April 20, 2010

Data Date	Investment Rating	Net Assets ($Mil)	Price	Performance Rating/Pts	Total Return Y-T-D	Risk Rating/Pts
3-12	E+	6.74	44.28	E / 0.3	-14.42%	C+ / 5.6
2011	D-	10.50	51.74	E+ / 0.6	-3.34%	C+ / 6.3

Major Rating Factors:
Very poor performance is the major factor driving the E+ (Very Weak) TheStreet.com Investment Rating for *ProShares Short KBW Regional Ban. The fund currently has a performance rating of E (Very Weak) based on an annualized return of 0.00% over the last three years and a total return of -14.42% year to date 2012. Factored into the performance evaluation is an expense ratio of 0.95% (low).

The fund's risk rating is currently C+ (Fair). It carries a beta of 0.00, meaning the fund's expected move will be 0.0% for every 10% move in the market. Volatility, as measured by both the semi-deviation and a drawdown factor, is considered low. As of March 31, 2012, *ProShares Short KBW Regional Ban traded at a premium of .20% above its net asset value, which is worse than its one-year historical average discount of .08%.

Hratch Najarian has been running the fund for 1 year and currently receives a manager quality ranking of 6 (0=worst, 99=best). This fund offers only a moderate level of risk but investors looking for strong performance are still waiting.

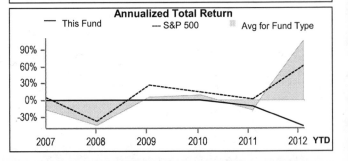

*ProShares Short Midcap 400 (MYY)   E+   Very Weak

Fund Family: ProShare Advisors LLC
Fund Type: Growth
Inception Date: June 19, 2006

Data Date	Investment Rating	Net Assets ($Mil)	Price	Performance Rating/Pts	Total Return Y-T-D	Risk Rating/Pts
3-12	E+	30.37	26.98	E / 0.5	-12.54%	C / 4.8
2011	E+	32.40	30.85	E+ / 0.8	-1.46%	C / 4.5
2010	D-	32.40	33.15	E / 0.5	-25.40%	C / 4.5
2009	D-	30.63	44.44	E+ / 0.7	-33.39%	C+ / 5.7

Major Rating Factors:
Very poor performance is the major factor driving the E+ (Very Weak) TheStreet.com Investment Rating for *ProShares Short Midcap 400. The fund currently has a performance rating of E (Very Weak) based on an annualized return of -25.68% over the last three years and a total return of -12.54% year to date 2012. Factored into the performance evaluation is an expense ratio of 0.95% (low).

The fund's risk rating is currently C (Fair). It carries a beta of -1.16, meaning the fund's expected move will be -11.6% for every 10% move in the market. Volatility, as measured by both the semi-deviation and a drawdown factor, is considered average. As of March 31, 2012, *ProShares Short Midcap 400 traded at a discount of .07% below its net asset value.

Hratch Najarian has been running the fund for 2 years and currently receives a manager quality ranking of 17 (0=worst, 99=best). This fund offers an average level of risk but investors looking for strong performance will be frustrated.

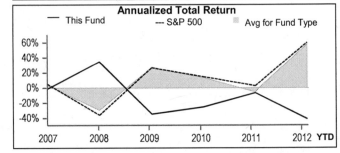

*ProShares Short MSCI EAFE (EFZ)   E+   Very Weak

Fund Family: ProShare Advisors LLC
Fund Type: Foreign
Inception Date: October 23, 2007

Major Rating Factors:
Very poor performance is the major factor driving the E+ (Very Weak) TheStreet.com Investment Rating for *ProShares Short MSCI EAFE. The fund currently has a performance rating of E+ (Very Weak) based on an annualized return of -19.30% over the last three years and a total return of -10.64% year to date 2012. Factored into the performance evaluation is an expense ratio of 0.95% (low).

The fund's risk rating is currently C (Fair). It carries a beta of -0.99, meaning the fund's expected move will be -9.9% for every 10% move in the market. Volatility, as measured by both the semi-deviation and a drawdown factor, is considered average. As of March 31, 2012, *ProShares Short MSCI EAFE traded at a premium of .04% above its net asset value.

Alexander V. Ilyasov has been running the fund for 3 years and currently receives a manager quality ranking of 17 (0=worst, 99=best). This fund offers an average level of risk but investors looking for strong performance will be frustrated.

Data Date	Investment Rating	Net Assets ($Mil)	Price	Performance Rating/Pts	Total Return Y-T-D	Risk Rating/Pts
3-12	E+	131.10	46.02	E+ / 0.6	-10.64%	C / 5.4
2011	D-	251.10	51.50	D- / 1.2	0.61%	C / 4.9
2010	D-	105.20	50.06	E+ / 0.8	-14.24%	C / 4.6
2009	D-	60.46	58.37	E / 0.3	-29.66%	C / 5.4

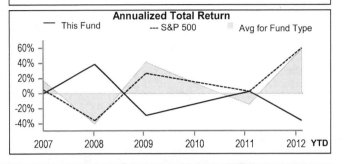

*ProShares Short MSCI Emg Mkts (EUM)   E+   Very Weak

Fund Family: ProShare Advisors LLC
Fund Type: Emerging Market
Inception Date: October 30, 2007

Major Rating Factors:
Very poor performance is the major factor driving the E+ (Very Weak) TheStreet.com Investment Rating for *ProShares Short MSCI Emg Mkts. The fund currently has a performance rating of E (Very Weak) based on an annualized return of -23.60% over the last three years and a total return of -12.67% year to date 2012. Factored into the performance evaluation is an expense ratio of 0.95% (low).

The fund's risk rating is currently C (Fair). It carries a beta of -1.04, meaning the fund's expected move will be -10.4% for every 10% move in the market. Volatility, as measured by both the semi-deviation and a drawdown factor, is considered average. As of March 31, 2012, *ProShares Short MSCI Emg Mkts traded at a premium of .07% above its net asset value.

Alexander V. Ilyasov has been running the fund for 3 years and currently receives a manager quality ranking of 19 (0=worst, 99=best). This fund offers an average level of risk but investors looking for strong performance will be frustrated.

Data Date	Investment Rating	Net Assets ($Mil)	Price	Performance Rating/Pts	Total Return Y-T-D	Risk Rating/Pts
3-12	E+	233.87	29.16	E / 0.5	-12.67%	C / 4.4
2011	E+	280.80	33.39	E+ / 0.9	-0.93%	C- / 4.0
2010	E+	200.20	30.66	E / 0.4	-20.92%	C- / 3.7
2009	E+	54.70	38.77	E- / 0.2	-48.04%	C / 4.4

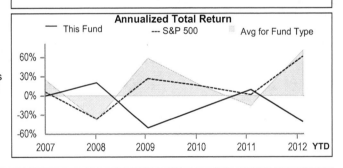

*ProShares Short Oil and Gas (DDG)   E+   Very Weak

Fund Family: ProShare Advisors LLC
Fund Type: Income
Inception Date: June 10, 2008

Major Rating Factors:
Very poor performance is the major factor driving the E+ (Very Weak) TheStreet.com Investment Rating for *ProShares Short Oil and Gas. The fund currently has a performance rating of E+ (Very Weak) based on an annualized return of -20.86% over the last three years and a total return of -5.15% year to date 2012. Factored into the performance evaluation is an expense ratio of 0.95% (low).

The fund's risk rating is currently C (Fair). It carries a beta of -1.12, meaning the fund's expected move will be -11.2% for every 10% move in the market. Volatility, as measured by both the semi-deviation and a drawdown factor, is considered average. As of March 31, 2012, *ProShares Short Oil and Gas traded at a discount of .12% below its net asset value.

Hratch Najarian has been running the fund for 1 year and currently receives a manager quality ranking of 31 (0=worst, 99=best). This fund offers an average level of risk but investors looking for strong performance will be frustrated.

Data Date	Investment Rating	Net Assets ($Mil)	Price	Performance Rating/Pts	Total Return Y-T-D	Risk Rating/Pts
3-12	E+	7.44	33.05	E+ / 0.6	-5.15%	C / 5.2
2011	D-	7.90	34.85	E+ / 0.9	-1.81%	C / 5.2
2010	E+	12.10	40.38	E / 0.3	-21.02%	C / 4.5
2009	D-	4.44	51.13	E / 0.4	-20.86%	C / 5.3

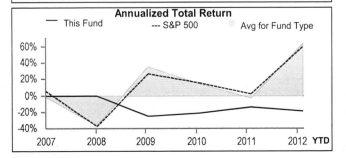

*ProShares Short QQQ (PSQ)

E+   **Very Weak**

Fund Family: ProShare Advisors LLC
Fund Type: Growth
Inception Date: June 19, 2006

Data Date	Investment Rating	Net Assets ($Mil)	Price	Perfor-mance Rating/Pts	Total Return Y-T-D	Risk Rating/Pts
3-12	E+	186.61	25.65	E / 0.5	-18.02%	C / 4.8
2011	E+	293.30	31.29	E+ / 0.8	-3.39%	C / 4.8
2010	D-	200.30	34.67	E+ / 0.6	-20.61%	C / 4.9
2009	D-	174.68	43.67	E+ / 0.6	-37.79%	C+ / 6.0

Major Rating Factors:
Very poor performance is the major factor driving the E+ (Very Weak) TheStreet.com Investment Rating for *ProShares Short QQQ. The fund currently has a performance rating of E (Very Weak) based on an annualized return of -26.38% over the last three years and a total return of -18.02% year to date 2012. Factored into the performance evaluation is an expense ratio of 0.95% (low).

The fund's risk rating is currently C (Fair). It carries a beta of -1.04, meaning the fund's expected move will be -10.4% for every 10% move in the market. Volatility, as measured by both the semi-deviation and a drawdown factor, is considered average. As of March 31, 2012, *ProShares Short QQQ traded at a price exactly equal to its net asset value, which is worse than its one-year historical average discount of .01%.

Hratch Najarian has been running the fund for 3 years and currently receives a manager quality ranking of 13 (0=worst, 99=best). This fund offers an average level of risk but investors looking for strong performance will be frustrated.

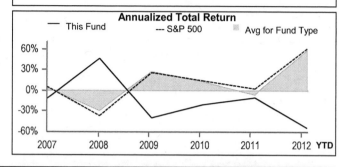

Annualized Total Return
— This Fund --- S&P 500 ▨ Avg for Fund Type

*ProShares Short Real Estate (REK)

D-   **Weak**

Fund Family: ProShare Advisors LLC
Fund Type: Growth and Income
Inception Date: March 16, 2010

Data Date	Investment Rating	Net Assets ($Mil)	Price	Perfor-mance Rating/Pts	Total Return Y-T-D	Risk Rating/Pts
3-12	D-	32.28	30.72	E / 0.5	-10.41%	C+ / 6.3
2011	D-	42.90	34.29	D- / 1.0	-0.09%	C+ / 6.8

Major Rating Factors:
Very poor performance is the major factor driving the D- (Weak) TheStreet.com Investment Rating for *ProShares Short Real Estate. The fund currently has a performance rating of E (Very Weak) based on an annualized return of 0.00% over the last three years and a total return of -10.41% year to date 2012. Factored into the performance evaluation is an expense ratio of 0.95% (low).

The fund's risk rating is currently C+ (Fair). It carries a beta of 0.00, meaning the fund's expected move will be 0.0% for every 10% move in the market. Volatility, as measured by both the semi-deviation and a drawdown factor, is considered low. As of March 31, 2012, *ProShares Short Real Estate traded at a discount of .07% below its net asset value, which is better than its one-year historical average premium of .01%.

Hratch Najarian has been running the fund for 1 year and currently receives a manager quality ranking of 16 (0=worst, 99=best). This fund offers only a moderate level of risk but investors looking for strong performance are still waiting.

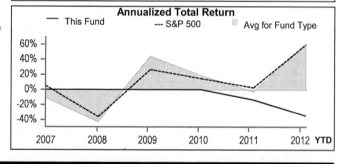

Annualized Total Return
— This Fund --- S&P 500 ▨ Avg for Fund Type

*ProShares Short Russell 2000 (RWM)

E+   **Very Weak**

Fund Family: ProShare Advisors LLC
Fund Type: Growth
Inception Date: January 23, 2007

Data Date	Investment Rating	Net Assets ($Mil)	Price	Perfor-mance Rating/Pts	Total Return Y-T-D	Risk Rating/Pts
3-12	E+	351.73	26.07	E / 0.5	-12.16%	C / 4.5
2011	E+	475.30	29.68	E+ / 0.8	-1.45%	C / 4.3
2010	E+	224.60	32.18	E / 0.5	-27.39%	C- / 3.7
2009	E+	78.49	44.32	E / 0.3	-31.44%	C / 4.9

Major Rating Factors:
Very poor performance is the major factor driving the E+ (Very Weak) TheStreet.com Investment Rating for *ProShares Short Russell 2000. The fund currently has a performance rating of E (Very Weak) based on an annualized return of -26.63% over the last three years and a total return of -12.16% year to date 2012. Factored into the performance evaluation is an expense ratio of 0.95% (low).

The fund's risk rating is currently C (Fair). It carries a beta of -1.27, meaning the fund's expected move will be -12.7% for every 10% move in the market. Volatility, as measured by both the semi-deviation and a drawdown factor, is considered average. As of March 31, 2012, *ProShares Short Russell 2000 traded at a premium of .08% above its net asset value, which is worse than its one-year historical average premium of .04%.

Hratch Najarian has been running the fund for 3 years and currently receives a manager quality ranking of 19 (0=worst, 99=best). This fund offers an average level of risk but investors looking for strong performance will be frustrated.

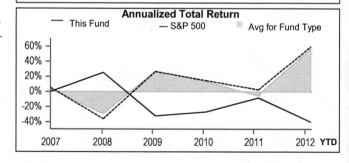

Annualized Total Return
— This Fund --- S&P 500 ▨ Avg for Fund Type

*ProShares Short S-P 500 (SH)

E+ **Very Weak**

Fund Family: ProShare Advisors LLC
Fund Type: Growth
Inception Date: June 19, 2006

Major Rating Factors:
Very poor performance is the major factor driving the E+ (Very Weak) TheStreet.com Investment Rating for *ProShares Short S-P 500. The fund currently has a performance rating of E+ (Very Weak) based on an annualized return of -21.31% over the last three years and a total return of -11.51% year to date 2012. Factored into the performance evaluation is an expense ratio of 0.90% (low).

The fund's risk rating is currently C (Fair). It carries a beta of -0.99, meaning the fund's expected move will be -9.9% for every 10% move in the market. Volatility, as measured by both the semi-deviation and a drawdown factor, is considered average. As of March 31, 2012, *ProShares Short S-P 500 traded at a premium of .08% above its net asset value, which is worse than its one-year historical average discount of .01%.

Hratch Najarian has been running the fund for 2 years and currently receives a manager quality ranking of 22 (0=worst, 99=best). This fund offers an average level of risk but investors looking for strong performance will be frustrated.

Data Date	Investment Rating	Net Assets ($Mil)	Price	Performance Rating/Pts	Total Return Y-T-D	Risk Rating/Pts
3-12	E+	1,841.21	35.76	E+ / 0.6	-11.51%	C / 5.5
2011	D-	2,366.70	40.41	D- / 1.0	-1.76%	C / 5.4
2010	D-	1,553.90	43.84	E+ / 0.7	-16.59%	C / 5.4
2009	D	1,282.50	52.56	D- / 1.1	-24.87%	C+ / 6.4

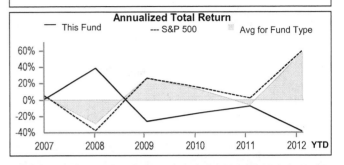

Annualized Total Return

*ProShares Short Small Cap 600 (SBB)

E+ **Very Weak**

Fund Family: ProShare Advisors LLC
Fund Type: Growth
Inception Date: January 23, 2007

Major Rating Factors:
Very poor performance is the major factor driving the E+ (Very Weak) TheStreet.com Investment Rating for *ProShares Short Small Cap 600. The fund currently has a performance rating of E (Very Weak) based on an annualized return of -27.50% over the last three years and a total return of -11.75% year to date 2012. Factored into the performance evaluation is an expense ratio of 0.95% (low).

The fund's risk rating is currently C (Fair). It carries a beta of -1.21, meaning the fund's expected move will be -12.1% for every 10% move in the market. Volatility, as measured by both the semi-deviation and a drawdown factor, is considered average. As of March 31, 2012, *ProShares Short Small Cap 600 traded at a discount of .58% below its net asset value, which is better than its one-year historical average discount of .04%.

Hratch Najarian has been running the fund for 2 years and currently receives a manager quality ranking of 16 (0=worst, 99=best). This fund offers an average level of risk but investors looking for strong performance will be frustrated.

Data Date	Investment Rating	Net Assets ($Mil)	Price	Performance Rating/Pts	Total Return Y-T-D	Risk Rating/Pts
3-12	E+	20.27	22.39	E / 0.5	-11.75%	C / 4.5
2011	E+	28.60	25.37	E+ / 0.7	-1.19%	C / 4.3
2010	E+	23.80	28.76	E / 0.5	-26.33%	C- / 3.3
2009	E+	23.16	39.04	E / 0.3	-29.68%	C / 4.4

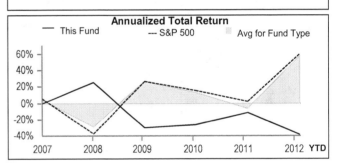

Annualized Total Return

*ProShares Ult Telecommunications (LTL)

C- **Fair**

Fund Family: ProShare Advisors LLC
Fund Type: Income
Inception Date: March 25, 2008

Major Rating Factors: Middle of the road best describes *ProShares Ult Telecommunications whose TheStreet.com Investment Rating is currently a C- (Fair). The fund currently has a performance rating of C (Fair) based on an annualized return of 20.68% over the last three years and a total return of 12.18% year to date 2012. Factored into the performance evaluation is an expense ratio of 0.95% (low).

The fund's risk rating is currently C+ (Fair). It carries a beta of 1.62, meaning it is expected to move 16.2% for every 10% move in the market. Volatility, as measured by both the semi-deviation and a drawdown factor, is considered low. As of March 31, 2012, *ProShares Ult Telecommunications traded at a premium of .10% above its net asset value, which is worse than its one-year historical average discount of .01%.

Hratch Najarian has been running the fund for 1 year and currently receives a manager quality ranking of 14 (0=worst, 99=best). If you desire an average level of risk, then this fund may be an option.

Data Date	Investment Rating	Net Assets ($Mil)	Price	Performance Rating/Pts	Total Return Y-T-D	Risk Rating/Pts
3-12	C-	3.66	48.80	C / 4.4	12.18%	C+ / 6.7
2011	C-	3.30	43.59	C- / 3.7	-1.06%	C+ / 6.7
2010	B+	8.20	54.58	A+ / 9.8	40.39%	C- / 3.6
2009	B-	11.65	39.55	A- / 9.2	38.86%	C- / 3.5

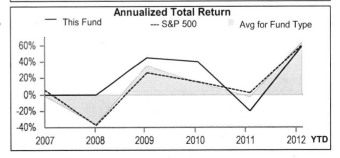

Annualized Total Return

*ProShares Ultra 20+ Year Treasur (UBT)   C+   Fair

Fund Family: ProShare Advisors LLC
Fund Type: US Government/Agency
Inception Date: January 19, 2010

Data Date	Investment Rating	Net Assets ($Mil)	Price	Performance Rating/Pts	Total Return Y-T-D	Risk Rating/Pts
3-12	C+	5.85	116.15	C+ / 6.5	-14.19%	B- / 7.1
2011	B+	33.90	135.46	A+ / 9.9	-4.22%	B- / 7.2

Major Rating Factors: Middle of the road best describes *ProShares Ultra 20+ Year Treasur whose TheStreet.com Investment Rating is currently a C+ (Fair). The fund currently has a performance rating of C+ (Fair) based on an annualized return of 0.00% over the last three years and a total return of -14.19% year to date 2012. Factored into the performance evaluation is an expense ratio of 0.95% (low).

The fund's risk rating is currently B- (Good). It carries a beta of 0.00, meaning the fund's expected move will be 0.0% for every 10% move in the market. Volatility, as measured by both the semi-deviation and a drawdown factor, is considered low. As of March 31, 2012, *ProShares Ultra 20+ Year Treasur traded at a discount of .70% below its net asset value, which is better than its one-year historical average discount of .02%.

Michelle Lui has been running the fund for 2 years and currently receives a manager quality ranking of 20 (0=worst, 99=best). If you desire an average level of risk, then this fund may be an option.

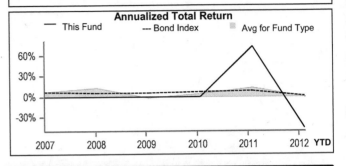

*ProShares Ultra 7-10 Year Treasu (UST)   C   Fair

Fund Family: ProShare Advisors LLC
Fund Type: US Government/Agency
Inception Date: January 19, 2010

Data Date	Investment Rating	Net Assets ($Mil)	Price	Performance Rating/Pts	Total Return Y-T-D	Risk Rating/Pts
3-12	C	15.41	102.77	C / 4.3	-3.41%	B+ / 9.0
2011	A+	181.10	106.40	A- / 9.1	-0.70%	B+ / 9.1

Major Rating Factors: Middle of the road best describes *ProShares Ultra 7-10 Year Treasu whose TheStreet.com Investment Rating is currently a C (Fair). The fund currently has a performance rating of C (Fair) based on an annualized return of 0.00% over the last three years and a total return of -3.41% year to date 2012. Factored into the performance evaluation is an expense ratio of 0.95% (low).

The fund's risk rating is currently B+ (Good). It carries a beta of 0.00, meaning the fund's expected move will be 0.0% for every 10% move in the market. Volatility, as measured by both the semi-deviation and a drawdown factor, is considered very low. As of March 31, 2012, *ProShares Ultra 7-10 Year Treasu traded at a premium of .02% above its net asset value, which is better than its one-year historical average premium of .07%.

Michelle Lui has been running the fund for 2 years and currently receives a manager quality ranking of 82 (0=worst, 99=best). If you desire an average level of risk, then this fund may be an option.

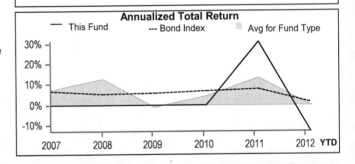

*ProShares Ultra Basic Materials (UYM)   C+   Fair

Fund Family: ProShare Advisors LLC
Fund Type: Income
Inception Date: January 30, 2007

Data Date	Investment Rating	Net Assets ($Mil)	Price	Performance Rating/Pts	Total Return Y-T-D	Risk Rating/Pts
3-12	C+	206.82	38.29	A- / 9.0	19.21%	C / 4.7
2011	C	224.00	32.12	B / 7.6	6.82%	C / 4.5
2010	D+	368.30	50.65	C+ / 5.8	57.39%	D+ / 2.3
2009	C+	466.53	32.23	A+ / 9.9	106.64%	D+ / 2.6

Major Rating Factors:
Exceptional performance is the major factor driving the C+ (Fair) TheStreet.com Investment Rating for *ProShares Ultra Basic Materials. The fund currently has a performance rating of A- (Excellent) based on an annualized return of 38.17% over the last three years and a total return of 19.21% year to date 2012. Factored into the performance evaluation is an expense ratio of 0.95% (low).

The fund's risk rating is currently C (Fair). It carries a beta of 3.29, meaning it is expected to move 32.9% for every 10% move in the market. Volatility, as measured by both the semi-deviation and a drawdown factor, is considered average. As of March 31, 2012, *ProShares Ultra Basic Materials traded at a discount of .03% below its net asset value, which is better than its one-year historical average discount of .02%.

Hratch Najarian has been running the fund for 1 year and currently receives a manager quality ranking of 4 (0=worst, 99=best). If you desire an average level of risk and strong performance, then this fund is a good option.

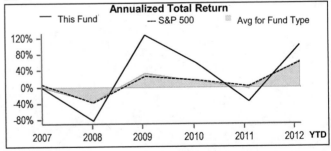

*ProShares Ultra Consumer Goods (UGE)

A+　　Excellent

Fund Family: ProShare Advisors LLC
Fund Type: Income
Inception Date: January 30, 2007

Major Rating Factors:
Exceptional performance is the major factor driving the A+ (Excellent) TheStreet.com Investment Rating for *ProShares Ultra Consumer Goods. The fund currently has a performance rating of A+ (Excellent) based on an annualized return of 46.70% over the last three years and a total return of 18.36% year to date 2012. Factored into the performance evaluation is an expense ratio of 0.95% (low).

The fund's risk rating is currently B (Good). It carries a beta of 1.51, meaning it is expected to move 15.1% for every 10% move in the market. Volatility, as measured by both the semi-deviation and a drawdown factor, is considered low. As of March 31, 2012, *ProShares Ultra Consumer Goods traded at a premium of .21% above its net asset value, which is worse than its one-year historical average discount of .10%.

Hratch Najarian has been running the fund for 1 year and currently receives a manager quality ranking of 84 (0=worst, 99=best). If you desire only a moderate level of risk and strong performance, then this fund is an excellent option.

Data Date	Investment Rating	Net Assets ($Mil)	Price	Perfor-mance Rating/Pts	Total Return Y-T-D	Risk Rating/Pts
3-12	A+	13.85	92.52	A+ / 9.8	18.36%	B / 8.0
2011	B+	11.80	78.34	B+ / 8.9	0.80%	B- / 7.4
2010	C+	20.80	69.61	B- / 7.4	36.67%	C / 4.8
2009	B+	15.92	51.46	A / 9.3	41.11%	C / 4.8

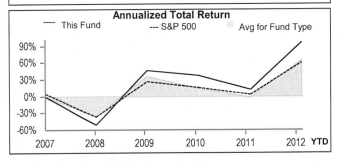
Annualized Total Return

---

*ProShares Ultra Consumer Service (UCC)

A-　　Excellent

Fund Family: ProShare Advisors LLC
Fund Type: Income
Inception Date: January 30, 2007

Major Rating Factors:
Exceptional performance is the major factor driving the A- (Excellent) TheStreet.com Investment Rating for *ProShares Ultra Consumer Service. The fund currently has a performance rating of A+ (Excellent) based on an annualized return of 51.59% over the last three years and a total return of 29.06% year to date 2012. Factored into the performance evaluation is an expense ratio of 0.95% (low).

The fund's risk rating is currently B- (Good). It carries a beta of 1.95, meaning it is expected to move 19.5% for every 10% move in the market. Volatility, as measured by both the semi-deviation and a drawdown factor, is considered low. As of March 31, 2012, *ProShares Ultra Consumer Service traded at a premium of .12% above its net asset value, which is worse than its one-year historical average premium of .07%.

Hratch Najarian has been running the fund for 1 year and currently receives a manager quality ranking of 72 (0=worst, 99=best). If you desire only a moderate level of risk and strong performance, then this fund is an excellent option.

Data Date	Investment Rating	Net Assets ($Mil)	Price	Perfor-mance Rating/Pts	Total Return Y-T-D	Risk Rating/Pts
3-12	A-	10.23	68.31	A+ / 9.8	29.06%	B- / 7.2
2011	B+	7.90	52.93	A / 9.5	2.57%	B- / 7.1
2010	C+	11.00	49.20	B / 8.1	46.07%	C- / 3.8
2009	B	11.44	33.73	A+ / 9.7	54.04%	C- / 3.9

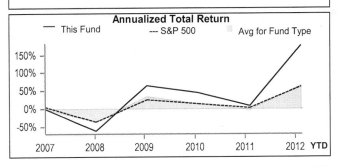
Annualized Total Return

---

*ProShares Ultra DJ-UBS Commodity (UCD)

D-　　Weak

Fund Family: ProShare Advisors LLC
Fund Type: Income
Inception Date: November 25, 2008

Major Rating Factors:
Disappointing performance is the major factor driving the D- (Weak) TheStreet.com Investment Rating for *ProShares Ultra DJ-UBS Commodity. The fund currently has a performance rating of D- (Weak) based on an annualized return of 8.73% over the last three years and a total return of 1.01% year to date 2012. Factored into the performance evaluation is an expense ratio of 0.95% (low).

The fund's risk rating is currently C (Fair). It carries a beta of 1.56, meaning it is expected to move 15.6% for every 10% move in the market. Volatility, as measured by both the semi-deviation and a drawdown factor, is considered average. As of March 31, 2012, *ProShares Ultra DJ-UBS Commodity traded at a discount of .77% below its net asset value, which is better than its one-year historical average discount of .16%.

This fund has been team managed for 4 years and currently receives a manager quality ranking of 7 (0=worst, 99=best). This fund offers an average level of risk but investors looking for strong performance will be frustrated.

Data Date	Investment Rating	Net Assets ($Mil)	Price	Perfor-mance Rating/Pts	Total Return Y-T-D	Risk Rating/Pts
3-12	D-	9.14	25.90	D- / 1.5	1.01%	C / 5.5
2011	D-	9.10	25.64	D / 2.0	3.74%	C+ / 5.6
2010	A+	18.20	36.27	A+ / 9.8	27.58%	C+ / 6.6
2009	A+	3.33	28.43	B+ / 8.6	21.08%	B- / 7.2

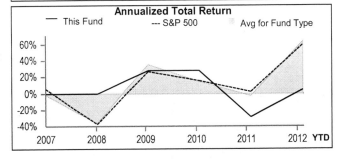
Annualized Total Return

*ProShares Ultra DJ-UBS Crude Oil (UCO)

E+   **Very Weak**

Fund Family: ProShare Advisors LLC
Fund Type: Energy/Natural Resources
Inception Date: November 25, 2008

Data Date	Investment Rating	Net Assets ($Mil)	Price	Performance Rating/Pts		Total Return Y-T-D	Risk Rating/Pts	
3-12	E+	261.12	42.91	D	/ 1.8	4.81%	C-	/ 3.5
2011	E+	251.40	40.94	D	/ 1.7	5.94%	C-	/ 3.4
2010	B-	228.10	12.50	A-	/ 9.2	-1.42%	C-	/ 3.2
2009	E+	99.77	12.68	D-	/ 1.2	-19.03%	C-	/ 4.1

Major Rating Factors:
Disappointing performance is the major factor driving the E+ (Very Weak) TheStreet.com Investment Rating for *ProShares Ultra DJ-UBS Crude Oil. The fund currently has a performance rating of D (Weak) based on an annualized return of 4.28% over the last three years and a total return of 4.81% year to date 2012. Factored into the performance evaluation is an expense ratio of 0.99% (low).

The fund's risk rating is currently C- (Fair). It carries a beta of 1.90, meaning it is expected to move 19.0% for every 10% move in the market. Volatility, as measured by both the semi-deviation and a drawdown factor, is considered average. As of March 31, 2012, *ProShares Ultra DJ-UBS Crude Oil traded at a premium of .23% above its net asset value, which is worse than its one-year historical average premium of .17%.

This fund has been team managed for 4 years and currently receives a manager quality ranking of 5 (0=worst, 99=best). This fund offers an average level of risk but investors looking for strong performance will be frustrated.

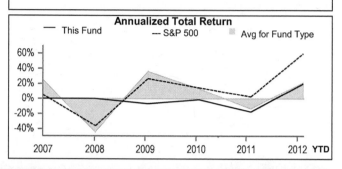

Annualized Total Return — This Fund --- S&P 500 Avg for Fund Type

*ProShares Ultra Dow 30 (DDM)

B+   **Good**

Fund Family: ProShare Advisors LLC
Fund Type: Growth
Inception Date: June 19, 2006

Data Date	Investment Rating	Net Assets ($Mil)	Price	Performance Rating/Pts		Total Return Y-T-D	Risk Rating/Pts	
3-12	B+	259.25	70.54	A+	/ 9.6	17.94%	B-	/ 7.0
2011	B-	269.80	59.89	B	/ 8.2	2.71%	C+	/ 6.2
2010	E+	314.20	54.52	D	/ 1.9	25.37%	C-	/ 3.0
2009	E+	602.47	43.81	D-	/ 1.3	32.45%	C-	/ 3.2

Major Rating Factors:
Exceptional performance is the major factor driving the B+ (Good) TheStreet.com Investment Rating for *ProShares Ultra Dow 30. The fund currently has a performance rating of A+ (Excellent) based on an annualized return of 40.78% over the last three years and a total return of 17.94% year to date 2012. Factored into the performance evaluation is an expense ratio of 0.95% (low).

The fund's risk rating is currently B- (Good). It carries a beta of 1.77, meaning it is expected to move 17.7% for every 10% move in the market. Volatility, as measured by both the semi-deviation and a drawdown factor, is considered low. As of March 31, 2012, *ProShares Ultra Dow 30 traded at a price exactly equal to its net asset value, which is better than its one-year historical average premium of .03%.

Howard Rubin has been running the fund for 5 years and currently receives a manager quality ranking of 49 (0=worst, 99=best). If you desire only a moderate level of risk and strong performance, then this fund is an excellent option.

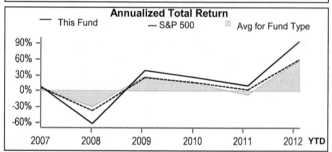

Annualized Total Return — This Fund --- S&P 500 Avg for Fund Type

*ProShares Ultra Euro (ULE)

D-   **Weak**

Fund Family: ProShare Advisors LLC
Fund Type: Foreign
Inception Date: November 25, 2008

Data Date	Investment Rating	Net Assets ($Mil)	Price	Performance Rating/Pts		Total Return Y-T-D	Risk Rating/Pts	
3-12	D-	7.57	25.21	D-	/ 1.0	5.61%	C+	/ 6.4
2011	D-	9.60	23.87	D-	/ 1.3	-3.27%	C+	/ 6.5
2010	D	7.70	25.86	D-	/ 1.0	-14.29%	C+	/ 5.9
2009	C-	4.39	30.17	D+	/ 2.8	3.39%	B-	/ 7.2

Major Rating Factors:
Disappointing performance is the major factor driving the D- (Weak) TheStreet.com Investment Rating for *ProShares Ultra Euro. The fund currently has a performance rating of D- (Weak) based on an annualized return of -2.33% over the last three years and a total return of 5.61% year to date 2012. Factored into the performance evaluation is an expense ratio of 0.95% (low).

The fund's risk rating is currently C+ (Fair). It carries a beta of 0.92, meaning that its performance tracks fairly well with that of the overall stock market. Volatility, as measured by both the semi-deviation and a drawdown factor, is considered low. As of March 31, 2012, *ProShares Ultra Euro traded at a discount of .16% below its net asset value, which is better than its one-year historical average discount of .08%.

This fund has been team managed for 4 years and currently receives a manager quality ranking of 10 (0=worst, 99=best). This fund offers only a moderate level of risk but investors looking for strong performance are still waiting.

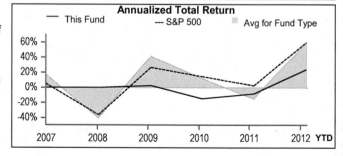

Annualized Total Return — This Fund --- S&P 500 Avg for Fund Type

*ProShares Ultra Financials (UYG)   C+   Fair

Fund Family: ProShare Advisors LLC
Fund Type: Financial Services
Inception Date: January 30, 2007

Data Date	Investment Rating	Net Assets ($Mil)	Price	Performance Rating/Pts	Total Return Y-T-D	Risk Rating/Pts
3-12	C+	960.21	62.82	B+ / 8.5	41.92%	C / 5.5
2011	E+	770.40	44.37	D- / 1.4	4.82%	C- / 4.2
2010	E	1,372.70	66.38	E / 0.3	18.04%	D+ / 2.4
2009	C-	2,517.92	5.63	B- / 7.4	-6.27%	D+ / 2.4

Major Rating Factors: Strong performance is the major factor driving the C+ (Fair) TheStreet.com Investment Rating for *ProShares Ultra Financials. The fund currently has a performance rating of B+ (Good) based on an annualized return of 27.16% over the last three years and a total return of 41.92% year to date 2012. Factored into the performance evaluation is an expense ratio of 0.95% (low).

The fund's risk rating is currently C (Fair). It carries a beta of 1.97, meaning it is expected to move 19.7% for every 10% move in the market. Volatility, as measured by both the semi-deviation and a drawdown factor, is considered average. As of March 31, 2012, *ProShares Ultra Financials traded at a discount of .16% below its net asset value, which is better than its one-year historical average discount of .01%.

Hratch Najarian has been running the fund for 1 year and currently receives a manager quality ranking of 13 (0=worst, 99=best). If you desire an average level of risk and strong performance, then this fund is a good option.

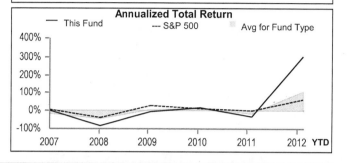

*ProShares Ultra FTSE China 25 (XPP)   E+   Very Weak

Fund Family: ProShare Advisors LLC
Fund Type: Foreign
Inception Date: June 2, 2009

Data Date	Investment Rating	Net Assets ($Mil)	Price	Performance Rating/Pts	Total Return Y-T-D	Risk Rating/Pts
3-12	E+	29.72	49.56	E+ / 0.9	9.16%	C- / 3.9
2011	E+	24.90	45.40	E / 0.5	1.23%	C- / 4.0
2010	B+	47.50	73.12	B- / 7.5	2.74%	C+ / 6.3

Major Rating Factors:
Very poor performance is the major factor driving the E+ (Very Weak) TheStreet.com Investment Rating for *ProShares Ultra FTSE China 25. The fund currently has a performance rating of E+ (Very Weak) based on an annualized return of 0.00% over the last three years and a total return of 9.16% year to date 2012. Factored into the performance evaluation is an expense ratio of 0.95% (low).

The fund's risk rating is currently C- (Fair). It carries a beta of 0.00, meaning the fund's expected move will be 0.0% for every 10% move in the market. Volatility, as measured by both the semi-deviation and a drawdown factor, is considered average. As of March 31, 2012, *ProShares Ultra FTSE China 25 traded at a premium of .06% above its net asset value, which is worse than its one-year historical average premium of .03%.

Alexander V. Ilyasov has been running the fund for 3 years and currently receives a manager quality ranking of 4 (0=worst, 99=best). This fund offers an average level of risk but investors looking for strong performance will be frustrated.

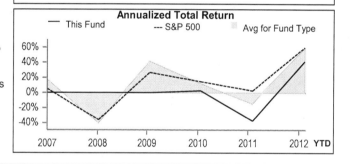

*ProShares Ultra Gold (UGL)   B   Good

Fund Family: ProShare Advisors LLC
Fund Type: Precious Metals
Inception Date: December 2, 2008

Data Date	Investment Rating	Net Assets ($Mil)	Price	Performance Rating/Pts	Total Return Y-T-D	Risk Rating/Pts
3-12	B	386.28	88.40	A / 9.5	11.88%	C+ / 6.2
2011	B	322.60	79.01	A+ / 9.8	6.73%	C+ / 6.3
2010	A+	252.80	70.72	A+ / 9.8	58.28%	B- / 7.1
2009	A+	27.74	44.68	A- / 9.2	42.29%	B- / 7.2

Major Rating Factors:
Exceptional performance is the major factor driving the B (Good) TheStreet.com Investment Rating for *ProShares Ultra Gold. The fund currently has a performance rating of A (Excellent) based on an annualized return of 41.40% over the last three years and a total return of 11.88% year to date 2012. Factored into the performance evaluation is an expense ratio of 0.95% (low).

The fund's risk rating is currently C+ (Fair). It carries a beta of 1.90, meaning it is expected to move 19.0% for every 10% move in the market. Volatility, as measured by both the semi-deviation and a drawdown factor, is considered low. As of March 31, 2012, *ProShares Ultra Gold traded at a premium of .69% above its net asset value, which is worse than its one-year historical average premium of .44%.

Howard S. Rubin has been running the fund for 4 years and currently receives a manager quality ranking of 22 (0=worst, 99=best). If you desire only a moderate level of risk and strong performance, then this fund is an excellent option.

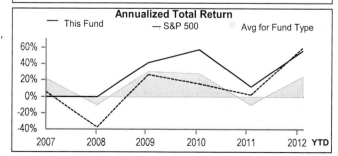

*ProShares Ultra Health Care (RXL)

A-　　**Excellent**

Fund Family: ProShare Advisors LLC
Fund Type: Health
Inception Date: January 30, 2007

Data Date	Investment Rating	Net Assets ($Mil)	Price	Performance Rating/Pts	Total Return Y-T-D	Risk Rating/Pts
3-12	A-	43.88	73.10	A / 9.5	20.28%	B- / 7.6
2011	B-	36.60	60.90	B- / 7.5	2.63%	B- / 7.1
2010	D	46.80	52.02	D- / 1.5	5.01%	C / 4.9
2009	B+	48.66	49.96	A / 9.3	35.65%	C / 4.8

Major Rating Factors:

Exceptional performance is the major factor driving the A- (Excellent) TheStreet.com Investment Rating for *ProShares Ultra Health Care. The fund currently has a performance rating of A (Excellent) based on an annualized return of 36.58% over the last three years and a total return of 20.28% year to date 2012. Factored into the performance evaluation is an expense ratio of 0.95% (low).

The fund's risk rating is currently B- (Good). It carries a beta of 1.21, meaning it is expected to move 12.1% for every 10% move in the market. Volatility, as measured by both the semi-deviation and a drawdown factor, is considered low. As of March 31, 2012, *ProShares Ultra Health Care traded at a discount of .04% below its net asset value, which is better than its one-year historical average discount of .02%.

Hratch Najarian has been running the fund for 1 year and currently receives a manager quality ranking of 70 (0=worst, 99=best). If you desire only a moderate level of risk and strong performance, then this fund is an excellent option.

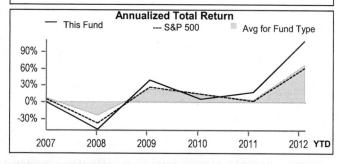

*ProShares Ultra Industrials (UXI)

B　　**Good**

Fund Family: ProShare Advisors LLC
Fund Type: Income
Inception Date: January 30, 2007

Data Date	Investment Rating	Net Assets ($Mil)	Price	Performance Rating/Pts	Total Return Y-T-D	Risk Rating/Pts
3-12	B	27.33	51.98	A+ / 9.8	25.71%	C+ / 5.8
2011	C	24.80	41.42	B- / 7.3	4.42%	C / 5.4
2010	D	34.70	46.31	C- / 3.9	49.21%	D+ / 2.9
2009	B-	30.23	31.13	A / 9.5	30.86%	C- / 3.3

Major Rating Factors:

Exceptional performance is the major factor driving the B (Good) TheStreet.com Investment Rating for *ProShares Ultra Industrials. The fund currently has a performance rating of A+ (Excellent) based on an annualized return of 48.22% over the last three years and a total return of 25.71% year to date 2012. Factored into the performance evaluation is an expense ratio of 0.95% (low).

The fund's risk rating is currently C+ (Fair). It carries a beta of 2.68, meaning it is expected to move 26.8% for every 10% move in the market. Volatility, as measured by both the semi-deviation and a drawdown factor, is considered low. As of March 31, 2012, *ProShares Ultra Industrials traded at a discount of .13% below its net asset value, which is better than its one-year historical average discount of .03%.

Hratch Najarian has been running the fund for 1 year and currently receives a manager quality ranking of 13 (0=worst, 99=best). If you desire only a moderate level of risk and strong performance, then this fund is an excellent option.

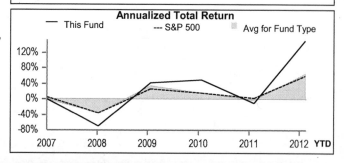

*ProShares Ultra KBW Regional Ban (KRU)

C+　　**Fair**

Fund Family: ProShare Advisors LLC
Fund Type: Financial Services
Inception Date: April 20, 2010

Data Date	Investment Rating	Net Assets ($Mil)	Price	Performance Rating/Pts	Total Return Y-T-D	Risk Rating/Pts
3-12	C+	4.90	49.10	A+ / 9.9	28.80%	C- / 3.7
2011	D-	3.80	38.20	C- / 3.9	7.41%	D+ / 2.8

Major Rating Factors:

Exceptional performance is the major factor driving the C+ (Fair) TheStreet.com Investment Rating for *ProShares Ultra KBW Regional Ban. The fund currently has a performance rating of A+ (Excellent) based on an annualized return of 0.00% over the last three years and a total return of 28.80% year to date 2012. Factored into the performance evaluation is an expense ratio of 0.95% (low).

The fund's risk rating is currently C- (Fair). It carries a beta of 0.00, meaning the fund's expected move will be 0.0% for every 10% move in the market. Volatility, as measured by both the semi-deviation and a drawdown factor, is considered average. As of March 31, 2012, *ProShares Ultra KBW Regional Ban traded at a premium of .25% above its net asset value, which is worse than its one-year historical average premium of .06%.

Hratch Najarian has been running the fund for 1 year and currently receives a manager quality ranking of 25 (0=worst, 99=best). If you desire an average level of risk and strong performance, then this fund is a good option.

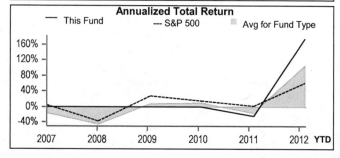

*ProShares Ultra MidCap 400 (MVV)

B   **Good**

Fund Family: ProShare Advisors LLC
Fund Type: Growth
Inception Date: June 19, 2006

Major Rating Factors:
Exceptional performance is the major factor driving the B (Good) TheStreet.com Investment Rating for *ProShares Ultra MidCap 400. The fund currently has a performance rating of A+ (Excellent) based on an annualized return of 46.43% over the last three years and a total return of 27.96% year to date 2012. Factored into the performance evaluation is an expense ratio of 0.95% (low).

The fund's risk rating is currently C+ (Fair). It carries a beta of 2.39, meaning it is expected to move 23.9% for every 10% move in the market. Volatility, as measured by both the semi-deviation and a drawdown factor, is considered low. As of March 31, 2012, *ProShares Ultra MidCap 400 traded at a discount of .10% below its net asset value, which is better than its one-year historical average discount of .02%.

Hratch Najarian has been running the fund for 2 years and currently receives a manager quality ranking of 19 (0=worst, 99=best). If you desire only a moderate level of risk and strong performance, then this fund is an excellent option.

Data Date	Investment Rating	Net Assets ($Mil)	Price	Performance Rating/Pts	Total Return Y-T-D	Risk Rating/Pts
3-12	B	313.79	70.84	A+ / 9.7	27.96%	C+ / 6.1
2011	C+	91.50	55.36	B / 8.2	3.03%	C+ / 5.9
2010	C	137.90	63.68	B- / 7.4	52.88%	C- / 3.1
2009	E+	158.90	41.69	D / 1.8	60.55%	C- / 3.5

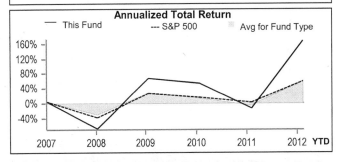

Annualized Total Return

---

*ProShares Ultra MSCI Brazil (UBR)

E+   **Very Weak**

Fund Family: ProShare Advisors LLC
Fund Type: Foreign
Inception Date: April 27, 2010

Major Rating Factors:
Disappointing performance is the major factor driving the E+ (Very Weak) TheStreet.com Investment Rating for *ProShares Ultra MSCI Brazil. The fund currently has a performance rating of D (Weak) based on an annualized return of 0.00% over the last three years and a total return of 25.35% year to date 2012. Factored into the performance evaluation is an expense ratio of 0.95% (low).

The fund's risk rating is currently C- (Fair). It carries a beta of 0.00, meaning the fund's expected move will be 0.0% for every 10% move in the market. Volatility, as measured by both the semi-deviation and a drawdown factor, is considered average. As of March 31, 2012, *ProShares Ultra MSCI Brazil traded at a premium of .21% above its net asset value, which is worse than its one-year historical average discount of .01%.

Alexander V. Ilyasov has been running the fund for 2 years and currently receives a manager quality ranking of 5 (0=worst, 99=best). This fund offers an average level of risk but investors looking for strong performance will be frustrated.

Data Date	Investment Rating	Net Assets ($Mil)	Price	Performance Rating/Pts	Total Return Y-T-D	Risk Rating/Pts
3-12	E+	14.01	23.39	D / 2.0	25.35%	C- / 3.0
2011	E	10.30	18.66	E- / 0.2	3.54%	C- / 3.0

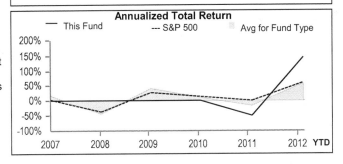

Annualized Total Return

---

*ProShares Ultra MSCI EAFE (EFO)

D-   **Weak**

Fund Family: ProShare Advisors LLC
Fund Type: Income
Inception Date: June 2, 2009

Major Rating Factors:
Disappointing performance is the major factor driving the D- (Weak) TheStreet.com Investment Rating for *ProShares Ultra MSCI EAFE. The fund currently has a performance rating of D (Weak) based on an annualized return of 0.00% over the last three years and a total return of 21.76% year to date 2012. Factored into the performance evaluation is an expense ratio of 0.95% (low).

The fund's risk rating is currently C (Fair). It carries a beta of 0.00, meaning the fund's expected move will be 0.0% for every 10% move in the market. Volatility, as measured by both the semi-deviation and a drawdown factor, is considered average. As of March 31, 2012, *ProShares Ultra MSCI EAFE traded at a discount of .30% below its net asset value, which is better than its one-year historical average premium of .08%.

Alexander V. Ilyasov has been running the fund for 3 years and currently receives a manager quality ranking of 2 (0=worst, 99=best). This fund offers an average level of risk but investors looking for strong performance will be frustrated.

Data Date	Investment Rating	Net Assets ($Mil)	Price	Performance Rating/Pts	Total Return Y-T-D	Risk Rating/Pts
3-12	D-	10.71	70.84	D / 2.1	21.76%	C / 5.0
2011	E+	5.90	58.18	E / 0.4	-0.62%	C / 5.0
2010	A	8.50	85.89	A / 9.5	9.53%	C+ / 5.9

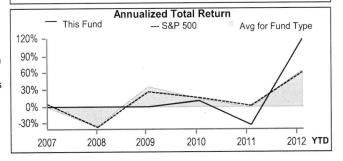

Annualized Total Return

*ProShares Ultra MSCI Emerging Mk (EET)   D-   Weak

Fund Family: ProShare Advisors LLC
Fund Type: Emerging Market
Inception Date: June 2, 2009

Major Rating Factors:

Disappointing performance is the major factor driving the D- (Weak) TheStreet.com Investment Rating for *ProShares Ultra MSCI Emerging Mk. The fund currently has a performance rating of D+ (Weak) based on an annualized return of 0.00% over the last three years and a total return of 25.72% year to date 2012. Factored into the performance evaluation is an expense ratio of 0.95% (low).

The fund's risk rating is currently C- (Fair). It carries a beta of 0.00, meaning the fund's expected move will be 0.0% for every 10% move in the market. Volatility, as measured by both the semi-deviation and a drawdown factor, is considered average. As of March 31, 2012, *ProShares Ultra MSCI Emerging Mk traded at a premium of .09% above its net asset value, which is worse than its one-year historical average premium of .02%.

Alexander V. Ilyasov has been running the fund for 3 years and currently receives a manager quality ranking of 11 (0=worst, 99=best). This fund offers an average level of risk but investors looking for strong performance will be frustrated.

Data Date	Investment Rating	Net Assets ($Mil)	Price	Performance Rating/Pts	Total Return Y-T-D	Risk Rating/Pts
3-12	D-	28.10	80.36	D+ / 2.5	25.72%	C- / 4.1
2011	E	22.20	63.92	E- / 0.2	0.91%	C- / 4.1
2010	A	43.80	109.55	A+ / 9.6	25.18%	C+ / 6.3

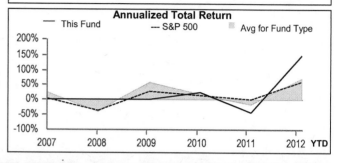

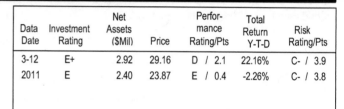

*ProShares Ultra MSCI Europe (UPV)   E+   Very Weak

Fund Family: ProShare Advisors LLC
Fund Type: Foreign
Inception Date: April 27, 2010

Major Rating Factors:

Disappointing performance is the major factor driving the E+ (Very Weak) TheStreet.com Investment Rating for *ProShares Ultra MSCI Europe. The fund currently has a performance rating of D (Weak) based on an annualized return of 0.00% over the last three years and a total return of 22.16% year to date 2012. Factored into the performance evaluation is an expense ratio of 0.95% (low).

The fund's risk rating is currently C- (Fair). It carries a beta of 0.00, meaning the fund's expected move will be 0.0% for every 10% move in the market. Volatility, as measured by both the semi-deviation and a drawdown factor, is considered average. As of March 31, 2012, *ProShares Ultra MSCI Europe traded at a discount of .10% below its net asset value, which is better than its one-year historical average discount of .01%.

Alexander V. Ilyasov has been running the fund for 3 years and currently receives a manager quality ranking of 11 (0=worst, 99=best). This fund offers an average level of risk but investors looking for strong performance will be frustrated.

Data Date	Investment Rating	Net Assets ($Mil)	Price	Performance Rating/Pts	Total Return Y-T-D	Risk Rating/Pts
3-12	E+	2.92	29.16	D / 2.1	22.16%	C- / 3.9
2011	E	2.40	23.87	E / 0.4	-2.26%	C- / 3.8

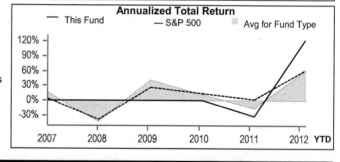

*ProShares Ultra MSCI Japan (EZJ)   D   Weak

Fund Family: ProShare Advisors LLC
Fund Type: Foreign
Inception Date: June 2, 2009

Major Rating Factors: *ProShares Ultra MSCI Japan receives a TheStreet.com Investment Rating of D (Weak). The fund currently has a performance rating of C- (Fair) based on an annualized return of 0.00% over the last three years and a total return of 23.54% year to date 2012. Factored into the performance evaluation is an expense ratio of 0.95% (low).

The fund's risk rating is currently C+ (Fair). It carries a beta of 0.00, meaning the fund's expected move will be 0.0% for every 10% move in the market. Volatility, as measured by both the semi-deviation and a drawdown factor, is considered low. As of March 31, 2012, *ProShares Ultra MSCI Japan traded at a discount of .45% below its net asset value, which is better than its one-year historical average discount of .12%.

Alexander V. Ilyasov has been running the fund for 3 years and currently receives a manager quality ranking of 41 (0=worst, 99=best). If you desire an average level of risk, then this fund may be an option.

Data Date	Investment Rating	Net Assets ($Mil)	Price	Performance Rating/Pts	Total Return Y-T-D	Risk Rating/Pts
3-12	D	22.75	64.71	C- / 3.2	23.54%	C+ / 5.7
2011	D-	23.60	52.38	E / 0.4	-1.16%	C+ / 5.7
2010	A+	11.70	78.49	A+ / 9.6	24.81%	C+ / 6.8

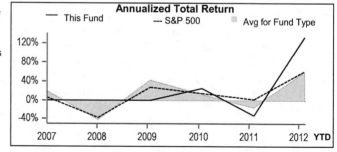

*ProShares Ultra MSCI Mex Invest (UMX)   C   Fair

Fund Family: ProShare Advisors LLC
Fund Type: Foreign
Inception Date: April 27, 2010

Data Date	Investment Rating	Net Assets ($Mil)	Price	Performance Rating/Pts	Total Return Y-T-D	Risk Rating/Pts
3-12	C	1.95	37.57	B / 8.1	29.06%	C / 4.6
2011	E+	1.50	29.11	E+ / 0.6	1.79%	C / 4.5

Major Rating Factors: Strong performance is the major factor driving the C (Fair) TheStreet.com Investment Rating for *ProShares Ultra MSCI Mex Invest. The fund currently has a performance rating of B (Good) based on an annualized return of 0.00% over the last three years and a total return of 29.06% year to date 2012. Factored into the performance evaluation is an expense ratio of 0.95% (low).

The fund's risk rating is currently C (Fair). It carries a beta of 0.00, meaning the fund's expected move will be 0.0% for every 10% move in the market. Volatility, as measured by both the semi-deviation and a drawdown factor, is considered average. As of March 31, 2012, *ProShares Ultra MSCI Mex Invest traded at a discount of 1.39% below its net asset value, which is better than its one-year historical average discount of .43%.

Alexander V. Ilyasov has been running the fund for 2 years and currently receives a manager quality ranking of 51 (0=worst, 99=best). If you desire an average level of risk and strong performance, then this fund is a good option.

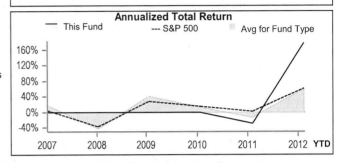

Annualized Total Return
— This Fund   --- S&P 500   Avg for Fund Type

*ProShares Ultra MSCI Pacific ex- (UXJ)   D-   Weak

Fund Family: ProShare Advisors LLC
Fund Type: Foreign
Inception Date: April 27, 2010

Data Date	Investment Rating	Net Assets ($Mil)	Price	Performance Rating/Pts	Total Return Y-T-D	Risk Rating/Pts
3-12	D-	3.07	30.50	D+ / 2.8	22.10%	C- / 4.0
2011	E+	2.50	24.98	E / 0.5	2.36%	C- / 4.0

Major Rating Factors:
Disappointing performance is the major factor driving the D- (Weak) TheStreet.com Investment Rating for *ProShares Ultra MSCI Pacific ex-. The fund currently has a performance rating of D+ (Weak) based on an annualized return of 0.00% over the last three years and a total return of 22.10% year to date 2012. Factored into the performance evaluation is an expense ratio of 0.95% (low).

The fund's risk rating is currently C- (Fair). It carries a beta of 0.00, meaning the fund's expected move will be 0.0% for every 10% move in the market. Volatility, as measured by both the semi-deviation and a drawdown factor, is considered average. As of March 31, 2012, *ProShares Ultra MSCI Pacific ex- traded at a discount of .49% below its net asset value, which is better than its one-year historical average premium of .13%.

Alexander V. Ilyasov has been running the fund for 2 years and currently receives a manager quality ranking of 14 (0=worst, 99=best). This fund offers an average level of risk but investors looking for strong performance will be frustrated.

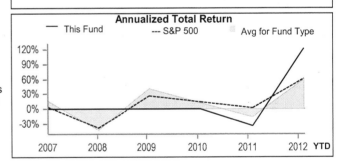

Annualized Total Return
— This Fund   --- S&P 500   Avg for Fund Type

*ProShares Ultra Nasdaq Biotech (BIB)   B   Good

Fund Family: ProShare Advisors LLC
Fund Type: Health
Inception Date: April 7, 2010

Data Date	Investment Rating	Net Assets ($Mil)	Price	Performance Rating/Pts	Total Return Y-T-D	Risk Rating/Pts
3-12	B	23.97	96.07	A+ / 9.9	38.19%	C+ / 6.2
2011	C+	13.90	69.52	B- / 7.1	5.16%	C+ / 6.2

Major Rating Factors:
Exceptional performance is the major factor driving the B (Good) TheStreet.com Investment Rating for *ProShares Ultra Nasdaq Biotech. The fund currently has a performance rating of A+ (Excellent) based on an annualized return of 0.00% over the last three years and a total return of 38.19% year to date 2012. Factored into the performance evaluation is an expense ratio of 0.95% (low).

The fund's risk rating is currently C+ (Fair). It carries a beta of 0.00, meaning the fund's expected move will be 0.0% for every 10% move in the market. Volatility, as measured by both the semi-deviation and a drawdown factor, is considered low. As of March 31, 2012, *ProShares Ultra Nasdaq Biotech traded at a premium of .20% above its net asset value, which is worse than its one-year historical average discount of .13%.

Hratch Najarian has been running the fund for 1 year and currently receives a manager quality ranking of 95 (0=worst, 99=best). If you desire only a moderate level of risk and strong performance, then this fund is an excellent option.

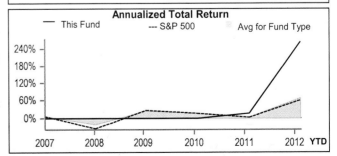

Annualized Total Return
— This Fund   --- S&P 500   Avg for Fund Type

*ProShares Ultra Oil and Gas (DIG)　　　　　　　C-　　　　Fair

Fund Family: ProShare Advisors LLC
Fund Type: Energy/Natural Resources
Inception Date: January 30, 2007

Major Rating Factors: Middle of the road best describes *ProShares Ultra Oil and Gas whose TheStreet.com Investment Rating is currently a C- (Fair). The fund currently has a performance rating of C+ (Fair) based on an annualized return of 24.52% over the last three years and a total return of 8.48% year to date 2012. Factored into the performance evaluation is an expense ratio of 0.95% (low).

The fund's risk rating is currently C (Fair). It carries a beta of 2.04, meaning it is expected to move 20.4% for every 10% move in the market. Volatility, as measured by both the semi-deviation and a drawdown factor, is considered average. As of March 31, 2012, *ProShares Ultra Oil and Gas traded at a discount of .25% below its net asset value, which is better than its one-year historical average discount of .01%.

Hratch Najarian has been running the fund for 1 year and currently receives a manager quality ranking of 15 (0=worst, 99=best). If you desire an average level of risk, then this fund may be an option.

Data Date	Investment Rating	Net Assets ($Mil)	Price	Perfor-mance Rating/Pts	Total Return Y-T-D	Risk Rating/Pts
3-12	C-	268.35	47.59	C+ / 5.9	8.48%	C / 5.4
2011	D+	254.00	43.91	C / 5.5	3.67%	C / 4.5
2010	E	366.70	45.81	D- / 1.1	33.69%	D / 1.7
2009	C+	818.55	34.53	B+ / 8.3	10.42%	C- / 3.4

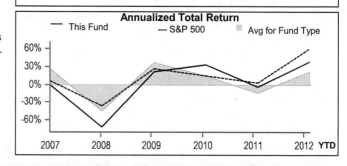

*ProShares Ultra QQQ (QLD)　　　　　　　　　B+　　　　Good

Fund Family: ProShare Advisors LLC
Fund Type: Growth
Inception Date: June 19, 2006

Major Rating Factors:
Exceptional performance is the major factor driving the B+ (Good) TheStreet.com Investment Rating for *ProShares Ultra QQQ. The fund currently has a performance rating of A+ (Excellent) based on an annualized return of 57.20% over the last three years and a total return of 46.02% year to date 2012. Factored into the performance evaluation is an expense ratio of 0.95% (low).

The fund's risk rating is currently C+ (Fair). It carries a beta of 2.17, meaning it is expected to move 21.7% for every 10% move in the market. Volatility, as measured by both the semi-deviation and a drawdown factor, is considered low. As of March 31, 2012, *ProShares Ultra QQQ traded at a discount of .03% below its net asset value, which is better than its one-year historical average discount of .01%.

Hratch Najarian has been running the fund for 3 years and currently receives a manager quality ranking of 68 (0=worst, 99=best). If you desire only a moderate level of risk and strong performance, then this fund is an excellent option.

Data Date	Investment Rating	Net Assets ($Mil)	Price	Perfor-mance Rating/Pts	Total Return Y-T-D	Risk Rating/Pts
3-12	B+	687.14	118.95	A+ / 9.9	46.02%	C+ / 6.9
2011	B+	678.20	81.46	A+ / 9.8	7.00%	C+ / 6.8
2010	C-	842.00	81.43	C+ / 6.8	36.90%	C- / 3.1
2009	D+	1,080.61	59.48	C / 5.2	103.28%	C- / 3.1

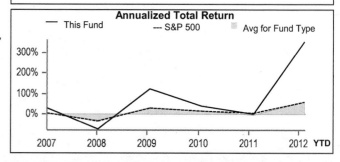

*ProShares Ultra Real Estate (URE)　　　　　　B+　　　　Good

Fund Family: ProShare Advisors LLC
Fund Type: Income
Inception Date: January 30, 2007

Major Rating Factors:
Exceptional performance is the major factor driving the B+ (Good) TheStreet.com Investment Rating for *ProShares Ultra Real Estate. The fund currently has a performance rating of A+ (Excellent) based on an annualized return of 58.64% over the last three years and a total return of 21.75% year to date 2012. Factored into the performance evaluation is an expense ratio of 0.95% (low).

The fund's risk rating is currently C+ (Fair). It carries a beta of 2.42, meaning it is expected to move 24.2% for every 10% move in the market. Volatility, as measured by both the semi-deviation and a drawdown factor, is considered low. As of March 31, 2012, *ProShares Ultra Real Estate traded at a discount of .10% below its net asset value.

Hratch Najarian has been running the fund for 1 year and currently receives a manager quality ranking of 72 (0=worst, 99=best). If you desire only a moderate level of risk and strong performance, then this fund is an excellent option.

Data Date	Investment Rating	Net Assets ($Mil)	Price	Perfor-mance Rating/Pts	Total Return Y-T-D	Risk Rating/Pts
3-12	B+	396.09	61.79	A+ / 9.8	21.75%	C+ / 6.4
2011	C	353.40	51.00	B / 7.9	-0.22%	C- / 4.2
2010	E	535.30	50.62	E+ / 0.7	48.36%	D / 2.1
2009	C+	451.44	6.89	A+ / 9.7	19.77%	D / 2.1

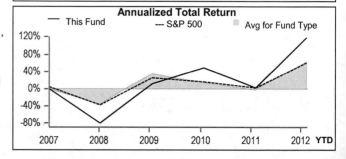

*ProShares Ultra Rus Mid Cap Grow (UKW)   B   Good

Fund Family: ProShare Advisors LLC
Fund Type: Growth
Inception Date: February 20, 2007

Major Rating Factors:
Exceptional performance is the major factor driving the B (Good) TheStreet.com
Investment Rating for *ProShares Ultra Rus Mid Cap Grow. The fund currently has a
performance rating of A+ (Excellent) based on an annualized return of 48.77% over
the last three years and a total return of 30.07% year to date 2012. Factored into the
performance evaluation is an expense ratio of 0.95% (low).

The fund's risk rating is currently C+ (Fair). It carries a beta of 2.36, meaning it is
expected to move 23.6% for every 10% move in the market. Volatility, as measured
by both the semi-deviation and a drawdown factor, is considered low. As of March 31,
2012, *ProShares Ultra Rus Mid Cap Grow traded at a premium of .11% above its net
asset value, which is worse than its one-year historical average discount of .08%.

Hratch Najarian has been running the fund for 3 years and currently receives a
manager quality ranking of 21 (0=worst, 99=best). If you desire only a moderate level
of risk and strong performance, then this fund is an excellent option.

Data Date	Investment Rating	Net Assets ($Mil)	Price	Performance Rating/Pts	Total Return Y-T-D	Risk Rating/Pts
3-12	B	12.34	54.89	A+ / 9.8	30.07%	C+ / 6.3
2011	B-	12.60	42.20	B+ / 8.8	3.08%	C+ / 6.1
2010	C-	14.30	48.03	C+ / 6.4	51.71%	D+ / 2.9
2009	B-	15.46	31.66	A+ / 9.8	78.84%	C- / 3.2

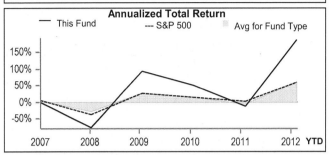

*ProShares Ultra Rus Mid Cap Valu (UVU)   B+   Good

Fund Family: ProShare Advisors LLC
Fund Type: Growth
Inception Date: February 20, 2007

Major Rating Factors:
Exceptional performance is the major factor driving the B+ (Good) TheStreet.com
Investment Rating for *ProShares Ultra Rus Mid Cap Valu. The fund currently has a
performance rating of A+ (Excellent) based on an annualized return of 47.51% over
the last three years and a total return of 23.44% year to date 2012. Factored into the
performance evaluation is an expense ratio of 0.95% (low).

The fund's risk rating is currently C+ (Fair). It carries a beta of 2.38, meaning it is
expected to move 23.8% for every 10% move in the market. Volatility, as measured
by both the semi-deviation and a drawdown factor, is considered low. As of March 31,
2012, *ProShares Ultra Rus Mid Cap Valu traded at a premium of .15% above its net
asset value, which is worse than its one-year historical average discount of .10%.

Hratch Najarian has been running the fund for 3 years and currently receives a
manager quality ranking of 20 (0=worst, 99=best). If you desire only a moderate level
of risk and strong performance, then this fund is an excellent option.

Data Date	Investment Rating	Net Assets ($Mil)	Price	Performance Rating/Pts	Total Return Y-T-D	Risk Rating/Pts
3-12	B+	5.93	39.62	A+ / 9.8	23.44%	C+ / 6.4
2011	C+	7.20	32.17	B / 7.9	3.29%	C+ / 6.0
2010	D+	8.10	36.22	C / 4.9	46.79%	C- / 3.1
2009	B-	13.78	24.76	A+ / 9.7	50.94%	C- / 3.3

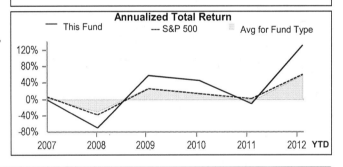

*ProShares Ultra Russell 3000 (UWC)   B   Good

Fund Family: ProShare Advisors LLC
Fund Type: Income
Inception Date: June 30, 2009

Major Rating Factors:
Exceptional performance is the major factor driving the B (Good) TheStreet.com
Investment Rating for *ProShares Ultra Russell 3000. The fund currently has a
performance rating of A+ (Excellent) based on an annualized return of 0.00% over the
last three years and a total return of 25.99% year to date 2012. Factored into the
performance evaluation is an expense ratio of 0.95% (low).

The fund's risk rating is currently C+ (Fair). It carries a beta of 0.00, meaning the
fund's expected move will be 0.0% for every 10% move in the market. Volatility, as
measured by both the semi-deviation and a drawdown factor, is considered low. As of
March 31, 2012, *ProShares Ultra Russell 3000 traded at a premium of .01% above
its net asset value, which is worse than its one-year historical average discount
of .14%.

Howard Rubin has been running the fund for 5 years and currently receives a
manager quality ranking of 13 (0=worst, 99=best). If you desire only a moderate level
of risk and strong performance, then this fund is an excellent option.

Data Date	Investment Rating	Net Assets ($Mil)	Price	Performance Rating/Pts	Total Return Y-T-D	Risk Rating/Pts
3-12	B	4.60	91.97	A+ / 9.7	25.99%	C+ / 6.2
2011	D	7.30	73.00	D / 1.8	3.48%	C+ / 6.2
2010	A	7.70	76.69	A+ / 9.7	27.20%	C+ / 6.3

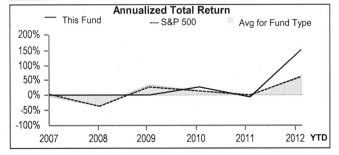

*ProShares Ultra Russell1000 Grow (UKF)

B+ **Good**

Fund Family: ProShare Advisors LLC
Fund Type: Growth
Inception Date: February 20, 2007

Data Date	Investment Rating	Net Assets ($Mil)	Price	Performance Rating/Pts	Total Return Y-T-D	Risk Rating/Pts
3-12	B+	14.60	64.55	A+ / 9.7	29.23%	C+ / 6.9
2011	B-	14.90	50.00	B+ / 8.5	2.86%	C+ / 6.7
2010	D	15.20	50.68	C- / 4.0	30.70%	C- / 3.6
2009	B	29.07	38.90	A+ / 9.8	63.98%	C- / 3.7

Major Rating Factors:
Exceptional performance is the major factor driving the B+ (Good) TheStreet.com Investment Rating for *ProShares Ultra Russell1000 Grow. The fund currently has a performance rating of A+ (Excellent) based on an annualized return of 43.74% over the last three years and a total return of 29.23% year to date 2012. Factored into the performance evaluation is an expense ratio of 0.95% (low).

The fund's risk rating is currently C+ (Fair). It carries a beta of 2.05, meaning it is expected to move 20.5% for every 10% move in the market. Volatility, as measured by both the semi-deviation and a drawdown factor, is considered low. As of March 31, 2012, *ProShares Ultra Russell1000 Grow traded at a price exactly equal to its net asset value, which is worse than its one-year historical average discount of .05%.

Hratch Najarian has been running the fund for 3 years and currently receives a manager quality ranking of 28 (0=worst, 99=best). If you desire only a moderate level of risk and strong performance, then this fund is an excellent option.

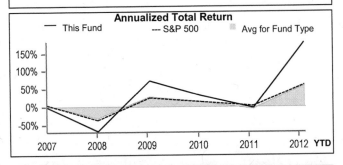

Annualized Total Return
— This Fund   --- S&P 500   ▨ Avg for Fund Type

*ProShares Ultra Russell1000 Valu (UVG)

B **Good**

Fund Family: ProShare Advisors LLC
Fund Type: Income
Inception Date: February 20, 2007

Data Date	Investment Rating	Net Assets ($Mil)	Price	Performance Rating/Pts	Total Return Y-T-D	Risk Rating/Pts
3-12	B	7.45	33.09	A / 9.3	22.18%	C+ / 6.8
2011	C	6.10	27.12	C+ / 6.1	3.25%	C+ / 5.9
2010	E+	13.10	29.14	E+ / 0.9	25.43%	C- / 3.4
2009	C+	20.48	23.42	A- / 9.1	23.90%	C- / 3.6

Major Rating Factors:
Exceptional performance is the major factor driving the B (Good) TheStreet.com Investment Rating for *ProShares Ultra Russell1000 Valu. The fund currently has a performance rating of A (Excellent) based on an annualized return of 36.56% over the last three years and a total return of 22.18% year to date 2012. Factored into the performance evaluation is an expense ratio of 0.95% (low).

The fund's risk rating is currently C+ (Fair). It carries a beta of 2.15, meaning it is expected to move 21.5% for every 10% move in the market. Volatility, as measured by both the semi-deviation and a drawdown factor, is considered low. As of March 31, 2012, *ProShares Ultra Russell1000 Valu traded at a discount of .09% below its net asset value, which is better than its one-year historical average premium of .04%.

Hratch Najarian has been running the fund for 3 years and currently receives a manager quality ranking of 14 (0=worst, 99=best). If you desire only a moderate level of risk and strong performance, then this fund is an excellent option.

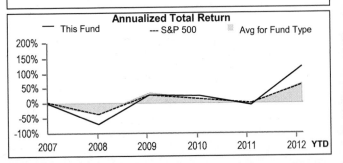

Annualized Total Return
— This Fund   --- S&P 500   ▨ Avg for Fund Type

*ProShares Ultra Russell2000 (UWM)

B- **Good**

Fund Family: ProShare Advisors LLC
Fund Type: Growth
Inception Date: January 23, 2007

Data Date	Investment Rating	Net Assets ($Mil)	Price	Performance Rating/Pts	Total Return Y-T-D	Risk Rating/Pts
3-12	B-	197.19	43.76	A / 9.5	25.56%	C / 5.5
2011	C-	204.40	34.86	C+ / 6.6	2.61%	C / 5.2
2010	C-	275.70	42.69	C+ / 6.5	50.63%	C- / 3.0
2009	C+	303.99	28.35	A / 9.3	37.44%	C- / 3.1

Major Rating Factors:
Exceptional performance is the major factor driving the B- (Good) TheStreet.com Investment Rating for *ProShares Ultra Russell2000. The fund currently has a performance rating of A (Excellent) based on an annualized return of 40.34% over the last three years and a total return of 25.56% year to date 2012. Factored into the performance evaluation is an expense ratio of 0.95% (low).

The fund's risk rating is currently C (Fair). It carries a beta of 2.62, meaning it is expected to move 26.2% for every 10% move in the market. Volatility, as measured by both the semi-deviation and a drawdown factor, is considered average. As of March 31, 2012, *ProShares Ultra Russell2000 traded at a discount of .14% below its net asset value, which is better than its one-year historical average discount of .02%.

Hratch Najarian has been running the fund for 3 years and currently receives a manager quality ranking of 10 (0=worst, 99=best). If you desire an average level of risk and strong performance, then this fund is a good option.

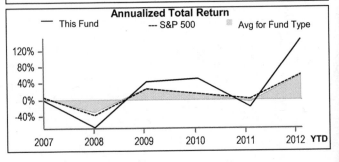

Annualized Total Return
— This Fund   --- S&P 500   ▨ Avg for Fund Type

*ProShares Ultra Russell2000 Grow (UKK)

B-   **Good**

Fund Family: ProShare Advisors LLC
Fund Type: Growth
Inception Date: February 20, 2007

Data Date	Investment Rating	Net Assets ($Mil)	Price	Perfor-mance Rating/Pts	Total Return Y-T-D	Risk Rating/Pts
3-12	B-	15.18	50.97	A+ / 9.7	26.85%	C+ / 5.6
2011	C	17.90	40.18	B / 7.7	1.05%	C / 5.4
2010	C-	28.80	47.94	B- / 7.2	55.80%	D+ / 2.8
2009	C+	23.18	30.77	A / 9.5	54.42%	D+ / 2.8

Major Rating Factors:
Exceptional performance is the major factor driving the B- (Good) TheStreet.com Investment Rating for *ProShares Ultra Russell2000 Grow. The fund currently has a performance rating of A+ (Excellent) based on an annualized return of 44.82% over the last three years and a total return of 26.85% year to date 2012. Factored into the performance evaluation is an expense ratio of 0.95% (low).

The fund's risk rating is currently C+ (Fair). It carries a beta of 2.61, meaning it is expected to move 26.1% for every 10% move in the market. Volatility, as measured by both the semi-deviation and a drawdown factor, is considered low. As of March 31, 2012, *ProShares Ultra Russell2000 Grow traded at a premium of .71% above its net asset value, which is worse than its one-year historical average discount of .04%.

Hratch Najarian has been running the fund for 3 years and currently receives a manager quality ranking of 12 (0=worst, 99=best). If you desire only a moderate level of risk and strong performance, then this fund is an excellent option.

Annualized Total Return

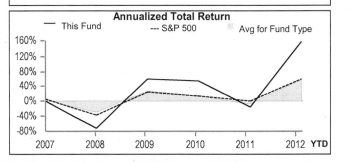

*ProShares Ultra Russell2000 Valu (UVT)

C+   **Fair**

Fund Family: ProShare Advisors LLC
Fund Type: Income
Inception Date: February 20, 2007

Data Date	Investment Rating	Net Assets ($Mil)	Price	Perfor-mance Rating/Pts	Total Return Y-T-D	Risk Rating/Pts
3-12	C+	9.23	30.91	A- / 9.0	23.99%	C / 5.5
2011	D+	9.40	24.97	C / 4.8	3.36%	C / 5.1
2010	D+	23.70	31.80	C+ / 5.7	44.93%	D+ / 2.9
2009	C+	18.45	22.02	A- / 9.1	22.37%	C- / 3.1

Major Rating Factors:
Exceptional performance is the major factor driving the C+ (Fair) TheStreet.com Investment Rating for *ProShares Ultra Russell2000 Valu. The fund currently has a performance rating of A- (Excellent) based on an annualized return of 35.03% over the last three years and a total return of 23.99% year to date 2012. Factored into the performance evaluation is an expense ratio of 0.95% (low).

The fund's risk rating is currently C (Fair). It carries a beta of 2.60, meaning it is expected to move 26.0% for every 10% move in the market. Volatility, as measured by both the semi-deviation and a drawdown factor, is considered average. As of March 31, 2012, *ProShares Ultra Russell2000 Valu traded at a premium of .42% above its net asset value, which is worse than its one-year historical average premium of .06%.

Hratch Najarian has been running the fund for 3 years and currently receives a manager quality ranking of 8 (0=worst, 99=best). If you desire an average level of risk and strong performance, then this fund is a good option.

Annualized Total Return

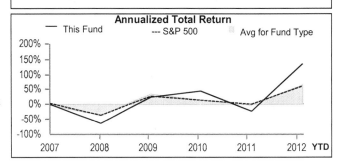

*ProShares Ultra S-P 500 (SSO)

B+   **Good**

Fund Family: ProShare Advisors LLC
Fund Type: Growth
Inception Date: June 19, 2006

Data Date	Investment Rating	Net Assets ($Mil)	Price	Perfor-mance Rating/Pts	Total Return Y-T-D	Risk Rating/Pts
3-12	B+	1,742.83	58.36	A+ / 9.6	26.10%	C+ / 6.8
2011	C+	1,654.20	46.39	B- / 7.4	3.56%	C+ / 6.5
2010	D-	1,589.60	48.05	D / 1.6	26.86%	C- / 3.5
2009	E+	2,398.03	38.24	E+ / 0.9	38.72%	C- / 3.7

Major Rating Factors:
Exceptional performance is the major factor driving the B+ (Good) TheStreet.com Investment Rating for *ProShares Ultra S-P 500. The fund currently has a performance rating of A+ (Excellent) based on an annualized return of 39.26% over the last three years and a total return of 26.10% year to date 2012. Factored into the performance evaluation is an expense ratio of 0.92% (low).

The fund's risk rating is currently C+ (Fair). It carries a beta of 2.04, meaning it is expected to move 20.4% for every 10% move in the market. Volatility, as measured by both the semi-deviation and a drawdown factor, is considered low. As of March 31, 2012, *ProShares Ultra S-P 500 traded at a discount of .05% below its net asset value, which is better than its one-year historical average discount of .01%.

Hratch Najarian has been running the fund for 2 years and currently receives a manager quality ranking of 20 (0=worst, 99=best). If you desire only a moderate level of risk and strong performance, then this fund is an excellent option.

Annualized Total Return

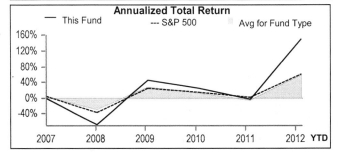

*ProShares Ultra Semiconductors (USD)

C+   **Fair**

Fund Family: ProShare Advisors LLC
Fund Type: Income
Inception Date: January 30, 2007

Major Rating Factors:
Exceptional performance is the major factor driving the C+ (Fair) TheStreet.com Investment Rating for *ProShares Ultra Semiconductors. The fund currently has a performance rating of A+ (Excellent) based on an annualized return of 38.44% over the last three years and a total return of 34.34% year to date 2012. Factored into the performance evaluation is an expense ratio of 0.95% (low).

The fund's risk rating is currently C (Fair). It carries a beta of 2.55, meaning it is expected to move 25.5% for every 10% move in the market. Volatility, as measured by both the semi-deviation and a drawdown factor, is considered average. As of March 31, 2012, *ProShares Ultra Semiconductors traded at a premium of .02% above its net asset value, which is worse than its one-year historical average discount of .04%.

Hratch Najarian has been running the fund for 1 year and currently receives a manager quality ranking of 10 (0=worst, 99=best). If you desire an average level of risk and strong performance, then this fund is a good option.

Data Date	Investment Rating	Net Assets ($Mil)	Price	Performance Rating/Pts	Total Return Y-T-D	Risk Rating/Pts
3-12	C+	47.71	45.45	A+ / 9.6	34.34%	C / 5.2
2011	C+	43.30	33.90	B+ / 8.8	6.52%	C / 5.3
2010	E+	74.60	39.82	D+ / 2.6	19.43%	D / 1.6
2009	C+	105.49	33.44	A+ / 9.9	124.24%	D / 1.9

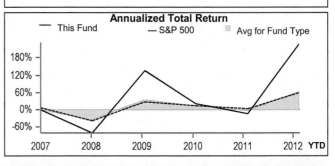

*ProShares Ultra Silver (AGQ)

D+   **Weak**

Fund Family: ProShare Advisors LLC
Fund Type: Energy/Natural Resources
Inception Date: December 2, 2008

Major Rating Factors: *ProShares Ultra Silver has adopted a very risky asset allocation strategy and currently receives an overall TheStreet.com Investment Rating of D+ (Weak). The fund has shown a high level of volatility, as measured by both semi-deviation and drawdown factors. It carries a beta of 2.34, meaning it is expected to move 23.4% for every 10% move in the market. As of March 31, 2012, *ProShares Ultra Silver traded at a discount of .80% below its net asset value, which is better than its one-year historical average premium of .24%. The high level of risk (D, Weak) did however, reward investors with excellent performance.

The fund's performance rating is currently B+ (Good). It has registered an annualized return of 42.17% over the last three years and is up 30.75% year to date 2012. Factored into the performance evaluation is an expense ratio of 0.95% (low).

This fund has been team managed for 4 years and currently receives a manager quality ranking of 18 (0=worst, 99=best). If you are comfortable owning a very high risk investment, this fund may be an option.

Data Date	Investment Rating	Net Assets ($Mil)	Price	Performance Rating/Pts	Total Return Y-T-D	Risk Rating/Pts
3-12	D+	837.14	54.46	B+ / 8.7	30.75%	D / 1.9
2011	D+	600.40	41.65	B / 8.2	7.20%	D / 1.9
2010	A	546.70	158.59	A+ / 9.9	182.44%	C+ / 5.8
2009	A+	10.01	56.15	A+ / 9.6	71.35%	C / 5.5

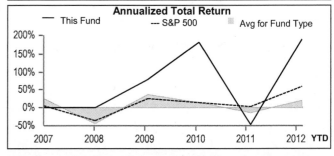

*ProShares Ultra SmallCap 600 (SAA)

B   **Good**

Fund Family: ProShare Advisors LLC
Fund Type: Growth
Inception Date: January 23, 2007

Major Rating Factors:
Exceptional performance is the major factor driving the B (Good) TheStreet.com Investment Rating for *ProShares Ultra SmallCap 600. The fund currently has a performance rating of A+ (Excellent) based on an annualized return of 45.25% over the last three years and a total return of 24.62% year to date 2012. Factored into the performance evaluation is an expense ratio of 0.95% (low).

The fund's risk rating is currently C+ (Fair). It carries a beta of 2.52, meaning it is expected to move 25.2% for every 10% move in the market. Volatility, as measured by both the semi-deviation and a drawdown factor, is considered low. As of March 31, 2012, *ProShares Ultra SmallCap 600 traded at a premium of .06% above its net asset value, which is worse than its one-year historical average discount of .07%.

Hratch Najarian has been running the fund for 2 years and currently receives a manager quality ranking of 15 (0=worst, 99=best). If you desire only a moderate level of risk and strong performance, then this fund is an excellent option.

Data Date	Investment Rating	Net Assets ($Mil)	Price	Performance Rating/Pts	Total Return Y-T-D	Risk Rating/Pts
3-12	B	27.45	52.31	A+ / 9.7	24.62%	C+ / 5.9
2011	C+	37.90	41.99	B / 7.8	2.50%	C+ / 5.6
2010	C-	48.50	46.37	B- / 7.1	49.95%	C- / 3.0
2009	C+	54.57	30.93	A / 9.3	34.54%	C- / 3.2

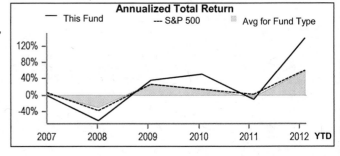

*ProShares Ultra Technology (ROM)   B+   Good

Fund Family: ProShare Advisors LLC
Fund Type: Growth
Inception Date: January 30, 2007

Major Rating Factors:
Exceptional performance is the major factor driving the B+ (Good) TheStreet.com
Investment Rating for *ProShares Ultra Technology. The fund currently has a
performance rating of A+ (Excellent) based on an annualized return of 50.01% over
the last three years and a total return of 48.13% year to date 2012. Factored into the
performance evaluation is an expense ratio of 0.95% (low).

The fund's risk rating is currently C+ (Fair). It carries a beta of 2.27, meaning it is
expected to move 22.7% for every 10% move in the market. Volatility, as measured
by both the semi-deviation and a drawdown factor, is considered low. As of March 31,
2012, *ProShares Ultra Technology traded at a premium of .02% above its net asset
value, which is worse than its one-year historical average discount of .03%.

Hratch Najarian has been running the fund for 1 year and currently receives a
manager quality ranking of 30 (0=worst, 99=best). If you desire only a moderate level
of risk and strong performance, then this fund is an excellent option.

Data Date	Investment Rating	Net Assets ($Mil)	Price	Performance Rating/Pts	Total Return Y-T-D	Risk Rating/Pts
3-12	B+	117.38	86.97	A+ / 9.8	48.13%	C+ / 6.5
2011	B	88.10	58.71	A / 9.4	5.65%	C+ / 6.5
2010	D+	151.80	63.37	C / 5.4	19.91%	C- / 3.2
2009	B-	128.44	52.85	A+ / 9.9	127.15%	C- / 3.2

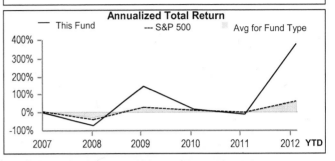
Annualized Total Return
This Fund --- S&P 500   Avg for Fund Type

*ProShares Ultra Utilities (UPW)   B+   Good

Fund Family: ProShare Advisors LLC
Fund Type: Utilities
Inception Date: January 30, 2007

Major Rating Factors: Strong performance is the major factor driving the B+ (Good)
TheStreet.com Investment Rating for *ProShares Ultra Utilities. The fund currently
has a performance rating of B (Good) based on an annualized return of 29.73% over
the last three years and a total return of -3.72% year to date 2012. Factored into the
performance evaluation is an expense ratio of 0.95% (low).

The fund's risk rating is currently B (Good). It carries a beta of 1.89, meaning it is
expected to move 18.9% for every 10% move in the market. Volatility, as measured
by both the semi-deviation and a drawdown factor, is considered low. As of March 31,
2012, *ProShares Ultra Utilities traded at a discount of .19% below its net asset
value, which is better than its one-year historical average discount of .01%.

Hratch Najarian has been running the fund for 1 year and currently receives a
manager quality ranking of 34 (0=worst, 99=best). If you desire only a moderate level
of risk and strong performance, then this fund is an excellent option.

Data Date	Investment Rating	Net Assets ($Mil)	Price	Performance Rating/Pts	Total Return Y-T-D	Risk Rating/Pts
3-12	B+	20.04	53.34	B / 7.8	-3.72%	B / 8.4
2011	B-	20.80	55.62	B- / 7.5	-5.17%	B- / 7.3
2010	D-	22.10	42.00	E+ / 0.7	11.49%	C / 4.4
2009	B-	25.18	38.77	B+ / 8.3	14.29%	C / 4.4

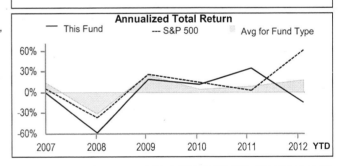
Annualized Total Return
This Fund --- S&P 500   Avg for Fund Type

*ProShares Ultra Yen (YCL)   D   Weak

Fund Family: ProShare Advisors LLC
Fund Type: Foreign
Inception Date: November 25, 2008

Major Rating Factors:
Disappointing performance is the major factor driving the D (Weak) TheStreet.com
Investment Rating for *ProShares Ultra Yen. The fund currently has a performance
rating of D (Weak) based on an annualized return of 10.82% over the last three years
and a total return of -14.08% year to date 2012. Factored into the performance
evaluation is an expense ratio of 0.95% (low).

The fund's risk rating is currently B- (Good). It carries a beta of 0.01, meaning the
fund's expected move will be 0.1% for every 10% move in the market. Volatility, as
measured by both the semi-deviation and a drawdown factor, is considered low. As of
March 31, 2012, *ProShares Ultra Yen traded at a discount of .03% below its net
asset value, which is better than its one-year historical average discount of .02%.

This fund has been team managed for 4 years and currently receives a manager
quality ranking of 84 (0=worst, 99=best). This fund offers only a moderate level of risk
but investors looking for strong performance are still waiting.

Data Date	Investment Rating	Net Assets ($Mil)	Price	Performance Rating/Pts	Total Return Y-T-D	Risk Rating/Pts
3-12	D	4.71	31.36	D / 2.0	-14.08%	B- / 7.9
2011	C-	5.50	36.50	C- / 4.0	-0.11%	B- / 7.8
2010	A+	5.00	33.29	A- / 9.1	25.24%	B- / 7.0
2009	D+	2.85	26.58	D- / 1.4	-3.90%	B- / 7.1

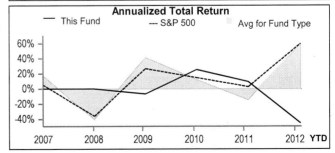
Annualized Total Return
This Fund --- S&P 500   Avg for Fund Type

*ProShares UltraPro Dow30 (UDOW)   B   Good

Fund Family: ProShare Advisors LLC
Fund Type: Growth
Inception Date: February 9, 2010

Major Rating Factors:
Exceptional performance is the major factor driving the B (Good) TheStreet.com Investment Rating for *ProShares UltraPro Dow30. The fund currently has a performance rating of A+ (Excellent) based on an annualized return of 0.00% over the last three years and a total return of 27.87% year to date 2012. Factored into the performance evaluation is an expense ratio of 0.95% (low).

The fund's risk rating is currently C+ (Fair). It carries a beta of 0.00, meaning the fund's expected move will be 0.0% for every 10% move in the market. Volatility, as measured by both the semi-deviation and a drawdown factor, is considered low. As of March 31, 2012, *ProShares UltraPro Dow30 traded at a discount of .05% below its net asset value.

Hratch Najarian has been running the fund for 3 years and currently receives a manager quality ranking of 18 (0=worst, 99=best). If you desire only a moderate level of risk and strong performance, then this fund is an excellent option.

Data Date	Investment Rating	Net Assets ($Mil)	Price	Performance Rating/Pts	Total Return Y-T-D	Risk Rating/Pts
3-12	B	74.85	166.24	A+ / 9.8	27.87%	C+ / 5.8
2011	C-	58.80	130.31	C+ / 5.7	4.01%	C+ / 5.7

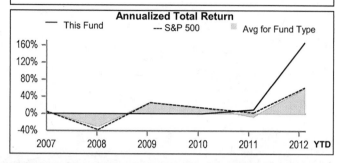

*ProShares UltraPro MidCap400 (UMDD)   C-   Fair

Fund Family: ProShare Advisors LLC
Fund Type: Growth
Inception Date: February 9, 2010

Major Rating Factors: *ProShares UltraPro MidCap400 has adopted a very risky asset allocation strategy and currently receives an overall TheStreet.com Investment Rating of C- (Fair). The fund has shown a high level of volatility, as measured by both semi-deviation and drawdown factors. It carries a beta of 0.00, meaning the fund's expected move will be 0.0% for every 10% move in the market. As of March 31, 2012, *ProShares UltraPro MidCap400 traded at a discount of .06% below its net asset value, which is better than its one-year historical average discount of .05%. The high level of risk (D, Weak) did however, reward investors with excellent performance.

The fund's performance rating is currently A+ (Excellent). It has registered an annualized return of 0.00% over the last three years and is up 44.03% year to date 2012. Factored into the performance evaluation is an expense ratio of 0.95% (low).

This fund has been team managed for 2 years and currently receives a manager quality ranking of 1 (0=worst, 99=best). If you are comfortable owning a very high risk investment, this fund may be an option.

Data Date	Investment Rating	Net Assets ($Mil)	Price	Performance Rating/Pts	Total Return Y-T-D	Risk Rating/Pts
3-12	C-	32.63	81.52	A+ / 9.8	44.03%	D / 1.9
2011	E-	34.00	56.60	E+ / 0.7	4.47%	D / 1.9

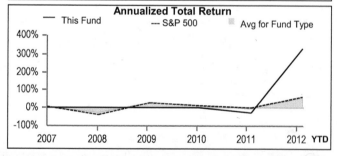

*ProShares UltraPro QQQ (TQQQ)   C   Fair

Fund Family: ProShare Advisors LLC
Fund Type: Growth
Inception Date: February 9, 2010

Major Rating Factors: *ProShares UltraPro QQQ has adopted a very risky asset allocation strategy and currently receives an overall TheStreet.com Investment Rating of C (Fair). The fund has shown a high level of volatility, as measured by both semi-deviation and drawdown factors. It carries a beta of 0.00, meaning the fund's expected move will be 0.0% for every 10% move in the market. As of March 31, 2012, *ProShares UltraPro QQQ traded at a discount of .04% below its net asset value, which is better than its one-year historical average discount of .03%. The high level of risk (D, Weak) did however, reward investors with excellent performance.

The fund's performance rating is currently A+ (Excellent). It has registered an annualized return of 0.00% over the last three years and is up 75.99% year to date 2012. Factored into the performance evaluation is an expense ratio of 0.95% (low).

Hratch Najarian has been running the fund for 2 years and currently receives a manager quality ranking of 85 (0=worst, 99=best). If you are comfortable owning a very high risk investment, this fund may be an option.

Data Date	Investment Rating	Net Assets ($Mil)	Price	Performance Rating/Pts	Total Return Y-T-D	Risk Rating/Pts
3-12	C	233.35	119.62	A+ / 9.9	75.99%	D / 2.2
2011	E	183.70	67.97	D- / 1.5	10.74%	D / 2.1

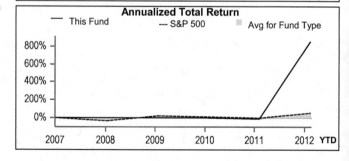

*ProShares UltraPro Russell2000 (URTY) | C- | Fair

Fund Family: ProShare Advisors LLC
Fund Type: Growth
Inception Date: February 9, 2010

Major Rating Factors: *ProShares UltraPro Russell2000 has adopted a very risky asset allocation strategy and currently receives an overall TheStreet.com Investment Rating of C- (Fair). The fund has shown a high level of volatility, as measured by both semi-deviation and drawdown factors. It carries a beta of 0.00, meaning the fund's expected move will be 0.0% for every 10% move in the market. As of March 31, 2012, *ProShares UltraPro Russell2000 traded at a discount of .04% below its net asset value, which is worse than its one-year historical average discount of .05%. The high level of risk (D, Weak) did however, reward investors with excellent performance.

The fund's performance rating is currently A (Excellent). It has registered an annualized return of 0.00% over the last three years and is up 39.88% year to date 2012. Factored into the performance evaluation is an expense ratio of 0.95% (low).

This fund has been team managed for 2 years and currently receives a manager quality ranking of 0 (0=worst, 99=best). If you are comfortable owning a very high risk investment, this fund may be an option.

Data Date	Investment Rating	Net Assets ($Mil)	Price	Performance Rating/Pts	Total Return Y-T-D	Risk Rating/Pts
3-12	C-	117.71	69.21	A / 9.5	39.88%	D / 1.9
2011	E-	99.40	49.48	E+ / 0.6	3.88%	D / 1.9

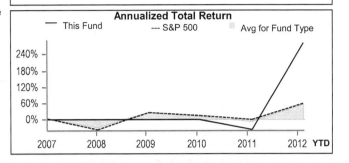

*ProShares UltraPro S&P 500 (UPRO) | C- | Fair

Fund Family: ProShare Advisors LLC
Fund Type: Income
Inception Date: June 23, 2009

Major Rating Factors: *ProShares UltraPro S&P 500 has adopted a very risky asset allocation strategy and currently receives an overall TheStreet.com Investment Rating of C- (Fair). The fund has shown a high level of volatility, as measured by both semi-deviation and drawdown factors. It carries a beta of 0.00, meaning the fund's expected move will be 0.0% for every 10% move in the market. As of March 31, 2012, *ProShares UltraPro S&P 500 traded at a discount of .21% below its net asset value, which is better than its one-year historical average discount of .02%. The high level of risk (D, Weak) did however, reward investors with excellent performance.

The fund's performance rating is currently A+ (Excellent). It has registered an annualized return of 0.00% over the last three years and is up 41.11% year to date 2012. Factored into the performance evaluation is an expense ratio of 0.95% (low).

Hratch Najarian has been running the fund for 2 years and currently receives a manager quality ranking of 8 (0=worst, 99=best). If you are comfortable owning a very high risk investment, this fund may be an option.

Data Date	Investment Rating	Net Assets ($Mil)	Price	Performance Rating/Pts	Total Return Y-T-D	Risk Rating/Pts
3-12	C-	272.18	84.88	A+ / 9.9	41.11%	D / 1.9
2011	E	343.60	60.15	D- / 1.4	5.29%	D / 1.9
2010	A-	204.50	204.91	A+ / 9.9	36.37%	C / 5.1

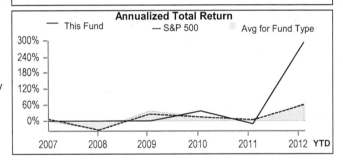

*ProShares UltraPro Short Dow30 (SDOW) | E- | Very Weak

Fund Family: ProShare Advisors LLC
Fund Type: Growth
Inception Date: February 9, 2010

Major Rating Factors: *ProShares UltraPro Short Dow30 has adopted a risky asset allocation strategy and currently receives an overall TheStreet.com Investment Rating of E- (Very Weak). The fund has an above average level of volatility, as measured by both semi-deviation and drawdown factors. It carries a beta of 0.00, meaning the fund's expected move will be 0.0% for every 10% move in the market. As of March 31, 2012, *ProShares UltraPro Short Dow30 traded at a discount of .05% below its net asset value, which is in line with its one-year historical average discount of .05%. Unfortunately, the high level of risk (D+, Weak) failed to pay off as investors endured very poor performance.

The fund's performance rating is currently E- (Very Weak). It has registered an annualized return of 0.00% over the last three years but is down -23.64% year to date 2012. Factored into the performance evaluation is an expense ratio of 0.95% (low).

Hratch Najarian has been running the fund for 2 years and currently receives a manager quality ranking of 3 (0=worst, 99=best). If you can tolerate high levels of risk in the hope of improved future returns, holding this fund may be an option.

Data Date	Investment Rating	Net Assets ($Mil)	Price	Performance Rating/Pts	Total Return Y-T-D	Risk Rating/Pts
3-12	E-	82.81	19.25	E- / 0.1	-23.64%	D+ / 2.7
2011	E	68.00	25.21	E- / 0.1	-4.28%	D+ / 2.9

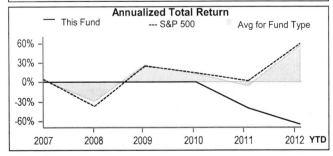

*ProShares UltraPro Short MidCap4 (SMDD)   E-   Very Weak

Fund Family: ProShare Advisors LLC
Fund Type: Growth
Inception Date: February 9, 2010

Data Date	Investment Rating	Net Assets ($Mil)	Price	Performance Rating/Pts	Total Return Y-T-D	Risk Rating/Pts
3-12	E-	8.76	11.65	E- / 0	-33.69%	D / 1.9
2011	E-	11.40	17.57	E- / 0.2	-4.38%	D / 1.9

Major Rating Factors: *ProShares UltraPro Short MidCap4 has adopted a very risky asset allocation strategy and currently receives an overall TheStreet.com Investment Rating of E- (Very Weak). The fund has a high level of volatility, as measured by both semi-deviation and drawdown factors. It carries a beta of 0.00, meaning the fund's expected move will be 0.0% for every 10% move in the market. As of March 31, 2012, *ProShares UltraPro Short MidCap4 traded at a discount of .26% below its net asset value, which is better than its one-year historical average premium of .02%. Unfortunately, the high level of risk (D, Weak) failed to pay off as investors endured very poor performance.

The fund's performance rating is currently E- (Very Weak). It has registered an annualized return of 0.00% over the last three years but is down -33.69% year to date 2012. Factored into the performance evaluation is an expense ratio of 0.95% (low).

Hratch Najarian has been running the fund for 2 years and currently receives a manager quality ranking of 5 (0=worst, 99=best). If you can tolerate very high levels of risk in the hope of improved future returns, holding this fund may be an option.

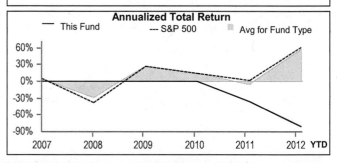

*ProShares UltraPro Short QQQ (SQQQ)   E-   Very Weak

Fund Family: ProShare Advisors LLC
Fund Type: Growth
Inception Date: February 9, 2010

Data Date	Investment Rating	Net Assets ($Mil)	Price	Performance Rating/Pts	Total Return Y-T-D	Risk Rating/Pts
3-12	E-	136.47	10.79	E- / 0	-45.20%	D / 1.9
2011	E-	94.50	19.69	E- / 0.1	-9.95%	D+ / 2.3

Major Rating Factors: *ProShares UltraPro Short QQQ has adopted a very risky asset allocation strategy and currently receives an overall TheStreet.com Investment Rating of E- (Very Weak). The fund has a high level of volatility, as measured by both semi-deviation and drawdown factors. It carries a beta of 0.00, meaning the fund's expected move will be 0.0% for every 10% move in the market. As of March 31, 2012, *ProShares UltraPro Short QQQ traded at a price exactly equal to its net asset value, which is worse than its one-year historical average discount of .03%. Unfortunately, the high level of risk (D, Weak) failed to pay off as investors endured very poor performance.

The fund's performance rating is currently E- (Very Weak). It has registered an annualized return of 0.00% over the last three years but is down -45.20% year to date 2012. Factored into the performance evaluation is an expense ratio of 0.95% (low).

Hratch Najarian has been running the fund for 3 years and currently receives a manager quality ranking of 0 (0=worst, 99=best). If you can tolerate very high levels of risk in the hope of improved future returns, holding this fund may be an option.

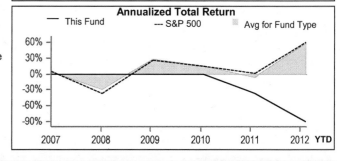

*ProShares UltraPro Short S&P 500 (SPXU)   E-   Very Weak

Fund Family: ProShare Advisors LLC
Fund Type: Growth
Inception Date: June 23, 2009

Data Date	Investment Rating	Net Assets ($Mil)	Price	Performance Rating/Pts	Total Return Y-T-D	Risk Rating/Pts
3-12	E-	605.52	9.06	E- / 0.1	-31.00%	D+ / 2.4
2011	E-	596.80	13.13	E- / 0.2	-5.18%	D+ / 2.6
2010	E-	290.10	19.41	E- / 0	-46.51%	D+ / 2.3

Major Rating Factors: *ProShares UltraPro Short S&P 500 has adopted a risky asset allocation strategy and currently receives an overall TheStreet.com Investment Rating of E- (Very Weak). The fund has an above average level of volatility, as measured by both semi-deviation and drawdown factors. It carries a beta of 0.00, meaning the fund's expected move will be 0.0% for every 10% move in the market. As of March 31, 2012, *ProShares UltraPro Short S&P 500 traded at a premium of .11% above its net asset value, which is worse than its one-year historical average discount of .06%. Unfortunately, the high level of risk (D+, Weak) failed to pay off as investors endured very poor performance.

The fund's performance rating is currently E- (Very Weak). It has registered an annualized return of 0.00% over the last three years but is down -31.00% year to date 2012. Factored into the performance evaluation is an expense ratio of 0.95% (low).

Hratch Najarian has been running the fund for 2 years and currently receives a manager quality ranking of 3 (0=worst, 99=best). If you can tolerate high levels of risk in the hope of improved future returns, holding this fund may be an option.

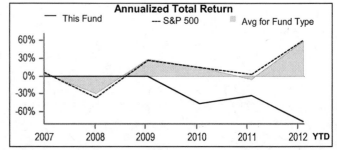

*ProShares UltraPro Shrt Russell2 (SRTY)   E-   Very Weak

Fund Family: ProShare Advisors LLC
Fund Type: Growth
Inception Date: February 9, 2010

Data Date	Investment Rating	Net Assets ($Mil)	Price	Perfor-mance Rating/Pts	Total Return Y-T-D	Risk Rating/Pts
3-12	E-	61.20	8.80	E- / 0	-32.93%	D / 1.9
2011	E-	66.90	13.12	E- / 0	-3.73%	D / 1.9

Major Rating Factors: *ProShares UltraPro Shrt Russell2 has adopted a very risky asset allocation strategy and currently receives an overall TheStreet.com Investment Rating of E- (Very Weak). The fund has a high level of volatility, as measured by both semi-deviation and drawdown factors. It carries a beta of 0.00, meaning the fund's expected move will be 0.0% for every 10% move in the market. As of March 31, 2012, *ProShares UltraPro Shrt Russell2 traded at a discount of .11% below its net asset value, which is better than its one-year historical average discount of .03%. Unfortunately, the high level of risk (D, Weak) failed to pay off as investors endured very poor performance.

The fund's performance rating is currently E- (Very Weak). It has registered an annualized return of 0.00% over the last three years but is down -32.93% year to date 2012. Factored into the performance evaluation is an expense ratio of 0.95% (low).

This fund has been team managed for 2 years and currently receives a manager quality ranking of 3 (0=worst, 99=best). If you can tolerate very high levels of risk in the hope of improved future returns, holding this fund may be an option.

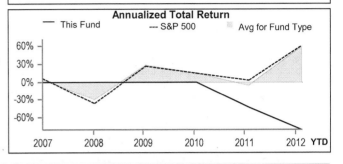

*ProShares UltraShort 20+ Yr US T (TBT)   E   Very Weak

Fund Family: ProShare Advisors LLC
Fund Type: Income
Inception Date: April 29, 2008

Data Date	Investment Rating	Net Assets ($Mil)	Price	Perfor-mance Rating/Pts	Total Return Y-T-D	Risk Rating/Pts
3-12	E	3,863.83	20.45	E / 0.5	13.17%	C- / 3.8
2011	E+	3,106.50	18.07	E+ / 0.6	4.15%	C- / 3.9
2010	E+	5,392.20	37.04	E+ / 0.8	-25.74%	C- / 4.2
2009	C+	4,058.21	49.88	B / 7.7	27.90%	C / 5.0

Major Rating Factors: Very poor performance is the major factor driving the E (Very Weak) TheStreet.com Investment Rating for *ProShares UltraShort 20+ Yr US T. The fund currently has a performance rating of E (Very Weak) based on an annualized return of -23.36% over the last three years and a total return of 13.17% year to date 2012. Factored into the performance evaluation is an expense ratio of 0.93% (low).

The fund's risk rating is currently C- (Fair). It carries a beta of 1.36, meaning it is expected to move 13.6% for every 10% move in the market. Volatility, as measured by both the semi-deviation and a drawdown factor, is considered average. As of March 31, 2012, *ProShares UltraShort 20+ Yr US T traded at a premium of .54% above its net asset value, which is worse than its one-year historical average discount of .04%.

Michelle Lui has been running the fund for 4 years and currently receives a manager quality ranking of 1 (0=worst, 99=best). This fund offers an average level of risk but investors looking for strong performance will be frustrated.

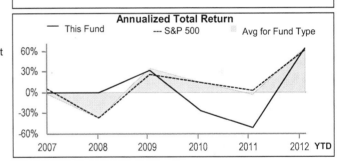

*ProShares UltraShort 7-10 Yr US (PST)   D-   Weak

Fund Family: ProShare Advisors LLC
Fund Type: Income
Inception Date: April 29, 2008

Data Date	Investment Rating	Net Assets ($Mil)	Price	Perfor-mance Rating/Pts	Total Return Y-T-D	Risk Rating/Pts
3-12	D-	364.75	31.41	E+ / 0.6	2.95%	C+ / 6.1
2011	D-	380.80	30.51	E+ / 0.9	1.11%	C+ / 6.2
2010	D	451.30	42.34	E+ / 0.6	-21.51%	C+ / 5.8
2009	C-	445.82	53.94	D / 1.9	0.04%	C+ / 6.8

Major Rating Factors:
Very poor performance is the major factor driving the D- (Weak) TheStreet.com Investment Rating for *ProShares UltraShort 7-10 Yr US. The fund currently has a performance rating of E+ (Very Weak) based on an annualized return of -16.35% over the last three years and a total return of 2.95% year to date 2012. Factored into the performance evaluation is an expense ratio of 0.95% (low).

The fund's risk rating is currently C+ (Fair). It carries a beta of 0.51, meaning the fund's expected move will be 5.1% for every 10% move in the market. Volatility, as measured by both the semi-deviation and a drawdown factor, is considered low. As of March 31, 2012, *ProShares UltraShort 7-10 Yr US traded at a premium of .10% above its net asset value, which is worse than its one-year historical average discount of .06%.

Michelle Lui has been running the fund for 4 years and currently receives a manager quality ranking of 5 (0=worst, 99=best). This fund offers only a moderate level of risk but investors looking for strong performance are still waiting.

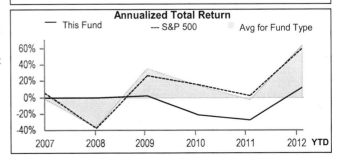

*ProShares UltraShort Basic Mater (SMN)

E-   **Very Weak**

Fund Family: ProShare Advisors LLC
Fund Type: Income
Inception Date: January 30, 2007

Major Rating Factors: *ProShares UltraShort Basic Mater has adopted a very risky asset allocation strategy and currently receives an overall TheStreet.com Investment Rating of E- (Very Weak). The fund has a high level of volatility, as measured by both semi-deviation and drawdown factors. It carries a beta of -3.15, meaning the fund's expected move will be -31.5% for every 10% move in the market. As of March 31, 2012, *ProShares UltraShort Basic Mater traded at a price exactly equal to its net asset value, which is worse than its one-year historical average discount of .01%. Unfortunately, the high level of risk (D, Weak) failed to pay off as investors endured very poor performance.

The fund's performance rating is currently E- (Very Weak). It has registered an annualized return of -52.21% over the last three years and is down -19.54% year to date 2012. Factored into the performance evaluation is an expense ratio of 0.95% (low).

Hratch Najarian has been running the fund for 1 year and currently receives a manager quality ranking of 11 (0=worst, 99=best). If you can tolerate very high levels of risk in the hope of improved future returns, holding this fund may be an option.

Data Date	Investment Rating	Net Assets ($Mil)	Price	Perfor-mance Rating/Pts	Total Return Y-T-D	Risk Rating/Pts
3-12	E-	47.45	14.99	E- / 0.2	-19.54%	D / 2.1
2011	E-	64.50	18.63	E- / 0.1	-7.03%	D / 1.9
2010	E-	73.90	19.24	E- / 0.1	-54.68%	D- / 1.0
2009	E-	62.69	8.49	E- / 0	-75.87%	D- / 1.4

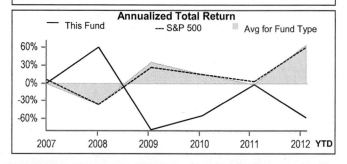

*ProShares UltraShort Consumer Go (SZK)

E   **Very Weak**

Fund Family: ProShare Advisors LLC
Fund Type: Income
Inception Date: January 30, 2007

Major Rating Factors: Very poor performance is the major factor driving the E (Very Weak) TheStreet.com Investment Rating for *ProShares UltraShort Consumer Go. The fund currently has a performance rating of E (Very Weak) based on an annualized return of -39.30% over the last three years and a total return of -14.92% year to date 2012. Factored into the performance evaluation is an expense ratio of 0.95% (low).

The fund's risk rating is currently C- (Fair). It carries a beta of -1.44, meaning the fund's expected move will be -14.4% for every 10% move in the market. Volatility, as measured by both the semi-deviation and a drawdown factor, is considered average. As of March 31, 2012, *ProShares UltraShort Consumer Go traded at a premium of .80% above its net asset value, which is worse than its one-year historical average discount of .05%.

Hratch Najarian has been running the fund for 1 year and currently receives a manager quality ranking of 6 (0=worst, 99=best). This fund offers an average level of risk but investors looking for strong performance will be frustrated.

Data Date	Investment Rating	Net Assets ($Mil)	Price	Perfor-mance Rating/Pts	Total Return Y-T-D	Risk Rating/Pts
3-12	E	2.61	17.73	E / 0.3	-14.92%	C- / 3.8
2011	E	4.70	20.84	E / 0.5	-1.34%	C- / 3.8
2010	E+	8.30	27.52	E / 0.4	-34.86%	C- / 3.3
2009	E+	19.67	42.25	E / 0.3	-40.09%	C / 4.8

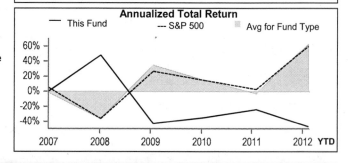

*ProShares UltraShort Consumer Se (SCC)

E   **Very Weak**

Fund Family: ProShare Advisors LLC
Fund Type: Income
Inception Date: January 30, 2007

Major Rating Factors: Very poor performance is the major factor driving the E (Very Weak) TheStreet.com Investment Rating for *ProShares UltraShort Consumer Se. The fund currently has a performance rating of E- (Very Weak) based on an annualized return of -45.44% over the last three years and a total return of -23.96% year to date 2012. Factored into the performance evaluation is an expense ratio of 0.95% (low).

The fund's risk rating is currently C- (Fair). It carries a beta of -1.89, meaning the fund's expected move will be -18.9% for every 10% move in the market. Volatility, as measured by both the semi-deviation and a drawdown factor, is considered average. As of March 31, 2012, *ProShares UltraShort Consumer Se traded at a discount of .41% below its net asset value, which is better than its one-year historical average discount of .05%.

Hratch Najarian has been running the fund for 1 year and currently receives a manager quality ranking of 5 (0=worst, 99=best). This fund offers an average level of risk but investors looking for strong performance will be frustrated.

Data Date	Investment Rating	Net Assets ($Mil)	Price	Perfor-mance Rating/Pts	Total Return Y-T-D	Risk Rating/Pts
3-12	E	8.22	12.12	E- / 0.2	-23.96%	C- / 3.4
2011	E	12.00	15.94	E / 0.3	-3.33%	C- / 3.2
2010	E-	22.90	21.81	E / 0.3	-42.09%	D / 2.0
2009	E	72.41	37.66	E- / 0.1	-52.35%	C- / 3.3

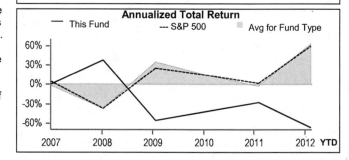

*ProShares UltraShort DJ-UBS Com (CMD)

E   **Very Weak**

Fund Family: ProShare Advisors LLC
Fund Type: Income
Inception Date: November 25, 2008

Major Rating Factors: Very poor performance is the major factor driving the E (Very Weak) TheStreet.com Investment Rating for *ProShares UltraShort DJ-UBS Com. The fund currently has a performance rating of E+ (Very Weak) based on an annualized return of -25.16% over the last three years and a total return of -2.63% year to date 2012. Factored into the performance evaluation is an expense ratio of 0.95% (low).

The fund's risk rating is currently C- (Fair). It carries a beta of -1.53, meaning the fund's expected move will be -15.3% for every 10% move in the market. Volatility, as measured by both the semi-deviation and a drawdown factor, is considered average. As of March 31, 2012, *ProShares UltraShort DJ-UBS Com traded at a discount of .55% below its net asset value, which is better than its one-year historical average discount of .01%.

This fund has been team managed for 4 years and currently receives a manager quality ranking of 43 (0=worst, 99=best). This fund offers an average level of risk but investors looking for strong performance will be frustrated.

Data Date	Investment Rating	Net Assets ($Mil)	Price	Performance Rating/Pts	Total Return Y-T-D	Risk Rating/Pts
3-12	E	8.80	54.71	E+ / 0.6	-2.63%	C- / 3.6
2011	E+	9.10	56.19	E+ / 0.9	-1.76%	C- / 3.8
2010	E	1.40	9.66	E- / 0.1	-34.06%	C- / 3.5
2009	E+	2.68	14.65	E- / 0.2	-42.64%	C / 5.0

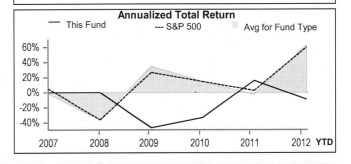

*ProShares UltraShort DJ-UBS Cr O (SCO)

E-   **Very Weak**

Fund Family: ProShare Advisors LLC
Fund Type: Energy/Natural Resources
Inception Date: November 25, 2008

Major Rating Factors: *ProShares UltraShort DJ-UBS Cr O has adopted a very risky asset allocation strategy and currently receives an overall TheStreet.com Investment Rating of E- (Very Weak). The fund has a high level of volatility, as measured by both semi-deviation and drawdown factors. It carries a beta of -1.85, meaning the fund's expected move will be -18.5% for every 10% move in the market. As of March 31, 2012, *ProShares UltraShort DJ-UBS Cr O traded at a discount of .23% below its net asset value, which is better than its one-year historical average discount of .21%. Unfortunately, the high level of risk (D, Weak) failed to pay off as investors endured very poor performance.

The fund's performance rating is currently E (Very Weak). It has registered an annualized return of -36.37% over the last three years and is down -9.12% year to date 2012. Factored into the performance evaluation is an expense ratio of 1.01% (low).

This fund has been team managed for 4 years and currently receives a manager quality ranking of 9 (0=worst, 99=best). If you can tolerate very high levels of risk in the hope of improved future returns, holding this fund may be an option.

Data Date	Investment Rating	Net Assets ($Mil)	Price	Performance Rating/Pts	Total Return Y-T-D	Risk Rating/Pts
3-12	E-	169.87	35.16	E / 0.4	-9.12%	D / 2.2
2011	E-	144.40	38.69	E / 0.3	-6.25%	D+ / 2.4
2010	E-	132.20	10.17	E- / 0.2	-25.49%	D / 1.9
2009	E-	14.50	13.65	E- / 0.2	-49.82%	D+ / 2.3

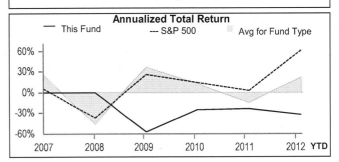

*ProShares UltraShort Dow 30 (DXD)

E   **Very Weak**

Fund Family: ProShare Advisors LLC
Fund Type: Growth
Inception Date: July 11, 2006

Major Rating Factors: Very poor performance is the major factor driving the E (Very Weak) TheStreet.com Investment Rating for *ProShares UltraShort Dow 30. The fund currently has a performance rating of E (Very Weak) based on an annualized return of -38.98% over the last three years and a total return of -16.33% year to date 2012. Factored into the performance evaluation is an expense ratio of 0.95% (low).

The fund's risk rating is currently C- (Fair). It carries a beta of -1.69, meaning the fund's expected move will be -16.9% for every 10% move in the market. Volatility, as measured by both the semi-deviation and a drawdown factor, is considered average. As of March 31, 2012, *ProShares UltraShort Dow 30 traded at a discount of .08% below its net asset value, which is better than its one-year historical average discount of .03%.

Hratch Najarian has been running the fund for 3 years and currently receives a manager quality ranking of 9 (0=worst, 99=best). This fund offers an average level of risk but investors looking for strong performance will be frustrated.

Data Date	Investment Rating	Net Assets ($Mil)	Price	Performance Rating/Pts	Total Return Y-T-D	Risk Rating/Pts
3-12	E	287.38	12.81	E / 0.3	-16.33%	C- / 3.7
2011	E	288.20	15.31	E / 0.5	-2.68%	C- / 3.6
2010	E	379.70	20.70	E / 0.4	-29.76%	C- / 3.1
2009	E+	639.20	29.47	E / 0.5	-41.74%	C / 4.3

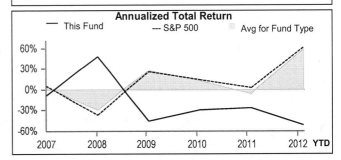

*ProShares UltraShort Euro (EUO)

D-   **Weak**

Fund Family: ProShare Advisors LLC
Fund Type: Foreign
Inception Date: November 25, 2008

Major Rating Factors:
Disappointing performance is the major factor driving the D- (Weak) TheStreet.com Investment Rating for *ProShares UltraShort Euro. The fund currently has a performance rating of D- (Weak) based on an annualized return of -4.24% over the last three years and a total return of -6.78% year to date 2012. Factored into the performance evaluation is an expense ratio of 0.95% (low).

The fund's risk rating is currently C+ (Fair). It carries a beta of -0.90, meaning the fund's expected move will be -9.0% for every 10% move in the market. Volatility, as measured by both the semi-deviation and a drawdown factor, is considered low. As of March 31, 2012, *ProShares UltraShort Euro traded at a price exactly equal to its net asset value, which is better than its one-year historical average premium of .05%.

This fund has been team managed for 4 years and currently receives a manager quality ranking of 83 (0=worst, 99=best). This fund offers only a moderate level of risk but investors looking for strong performance are still waiting.

Data Date	Investment Rating	Net Assets ($Mil)	Price	Performance Rating/Pts	Total Return Y-T-D	Risk Rating/Pts
3-12	D-	819.57	18.97	D- / 1.0	-6.78%	C+ / 6.6
2011	D	1,095.10	20.35	D / 2.0	3.24%	C+ / 6.6
2010	D+	444.40	20.31	D+ / 2.8	8.61%	C+ / 5.9
2009	D	7.33	18.70	E+ / 0.7	-12.90%	C+ / 6.1

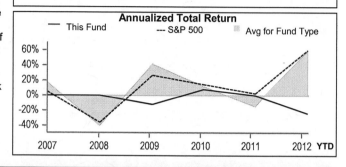

*ProShares UltraShort Financials (SKF)

E-   **Very Weak**

Fund Family: ProShare Advisors LLC
Fund Type: Financial Services
Inception Date: January 30, 2007

Major Rating Factors: *ProShares UltraShort Financials has adopted a risky asset allocation strategy and currently receives an overall TheStreet.com Investment Rating of E- (Very Weak). The fund has an above average level of volatility, as measured by both semi-deviation and drawdown factors. It carries a beta of -2.14, meaning the fund's expected move will be -21.4% for every 10% move in the market. As of March 31, 2012, *ProShares UltraShort Financials traded at a premium of .02% above its net asset value, which is worse than its one-year historical average discount of .03%. Unfortunately, the high level of risk (D+, Weak) failed to pay off as investors endured very poor performance.

The fund's performance rating is currently E- (Very Weak). It has registered an annualized return of -50.03% over the last three years and is down -31.89% year to date 2012. Factored into the performance evaluation is an expense ratio of 0.95% (low).

Hratch Najarian has been running the fund for 1 year and currently receives a manager quality ranking of 4 (0=worst, 99=best). If you can tolerate high levels of risk in the hope of improved future returns, holding this fund may be an option.

Data Date	Investment Rating	Net Assets ($Mil)	Price	Performance Rating/Pts	Total Return Y-T-D	Risk Rating/Pts
3-12	E-	226.36	40.40	E- / 0.2	-31.89%	D+ / 2.7
2011	E-	350.30	59.32	E- / 0.2	-5.09%	D / 1.9
2010	E-	389.10	15.67	E- / 0.2	-35.33%	D- / 1.0
2009	E-	1,204.27	24.23	E- / 0.1	-76.26%	D- / 1.5

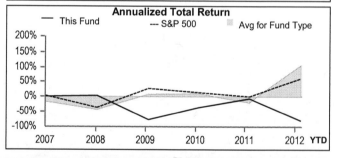

*ProShares UltraShort FTSE China (FXP)

E-   **Very Weak**

Fund Family: ProShare Advisors LLC
Fund Type: Foreign
Inception Date: November 6, 2007

Major Rating Factors: *ProShares UltraShort FTSE China has adopted a risky asset allocation strategy and currently receives an overall TheStreet.com Investment Rating of E- (Very Weak). The fund has an above average level of volatility, as measured by both semi-deviation and drawdown factors. It carries a beta of -1.85, meaning the fund's expected move will be -18.5% for every 10% move in the market. As of March 31, 2012, *ProShares UltraShort FTSE China traded at a discount of .19% below its net asset value, which is better than its one-year historical average discount of .05%. Unfortunately, the high level of risk (D+, Weak) failed to pay off as investors endured very poor performance.

The fund's performance rating is currently E (Very Weak). It has registered an annualized return of -38.26% over the last three years and is down -14.09% year to date 2012. Factored into the performance evaluation is an expense ratio of 0.95% (low).

Alexander V. Ilyasov has been running the fund for 3 years and currently receives a manager quality ranking of 6 (0=worst, 99=best). If you can tolerate high levels of risk in the hope of improved future returns, holding this fund may be an option.

Data Date	Investment Rating	Net Assets ($Mil)	Price	Performance Rating/Pts	Total Return Y-T-D	Risk Rating/Pts
3-12	E-	207.00	26.09	E / 0.4	-14.09%	D+ / 2.6
2011	E-	192.70	30.37	E / 0.4	-2.21%	D / 2.2
2010	E-	211.10	30.08	E- / 0.1	-28.29%	D- / 1.0
2009	E-	169.69	8.39	E- / 0.1	-72.69%	D- / 1.1

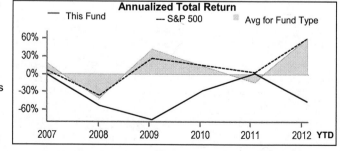

*ProShares UltraShort Gold (GLL)

E   Very Weak

Fund Family: ProShare Advisors LLC
Fund Type: Energy/Natural Resources
Inception Date: December 2, 2008

Data Date	Investment Rating	Net Assets ($Mil)	Price	Perfor-mance Rating/Pts	Total Return Y-T-D	Risk Rating/Pts
3-12	E	147.17	16.81	E / 0.3	-15.14%	C- / 3.1
2011	E	194.20	19.81	E / 0.3	-7.12%	C- / 3.4
2010	E+	81.10	27.80	E- / 0.1	-46.28%	C / 4.5
2009	E+	3.88	10.35	E- / 0.2	-46.29%	C / 4.4

Major Rating Factors: Very poor performance is the major factor driving the E (Very Weak) TheStreet.com Investment Rating for *ProShares UltraShort Gold. The fund currently has a performance rating of E (Very Weak) based on an annualized return of -41.82% over the last three years and a total return of -15.14% year to date 2012. Factored into the performance evaluation is an expense ratio of 0.95% (low).

The fund's risk rating is currently C- (Fair). It carries a beta of -0.38, meaning the fund's expected move will be -3.8% for every 10% move in the market. Volatility, as measured by both the semi-deviation and a drawdown factor, is considered average. As of March 31, 2012, *ProShares UltraShort Gold traded at a discount of .77% below its net asset value, which is better than its one-year historical average discount of .45%.

This fund has been team managed for 4 years and currently receives a manager quality ranking of 2 (0=worst, 99=best). This fund offers an average level of risk but investors looking for strong performance will be frustrated.

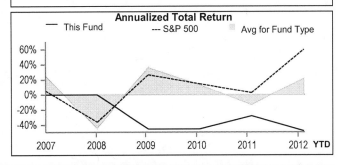

*ProShares UltraShort Health Care (RXD)

E   Very Weak

Fund Family: ProShare Advisors LLC
Fund Type: Health
Inception Date: January 30, 2007

Data Date	Investment Rating	Net Assets ($Mil)	Price	Perfor-mance Rating/Pts	Total Return Y-T-D	Risk Rating/Pts
3-12	E	3.81	16.89	E / 0.3	-17.81%	C- / 3.9
2011	E+	3.10	20.55	E / 0.5	-2.19%	C- / 4.0
2010	E	4.40	29.22	E+ / 0.6	-15.62%	D+ / 2.8
2009	E	12.34	34.63	E / 0.3	-37.01%	C- / 3.6

Major Rating Factors: Very poor performance is the major factor driving the E (Very Weak) TheStreet.com Investment Rating for *ProShares UltraShort Health Care. The fund currently has a performance rating of E (Very Weak) based on an annualized return of -36.00% over the last three years and a total return of -17.81% year to date 2012. Factored into the performance evaluation is an expense ratio of 0.95% (low).

The fund's risk rating is currently C- (Fair). It carries a beta of -1.15, meaning the fund's expected move will be -11.5% for every 10% move in the market. Volatility, as measured by both the semi-deviation and a drawdown factor, is considered average. As of March 31, 2012, *ProShares UltraShort Health Care traded at a discount of .30% below its net asset value, which is better than its one-year historical average discount of .08%.

Hratch Najarian has been running the fund for 1 year and currently receives a manager quality ranking of 8 (0=worst, 99=best). This fund offers an average level of risk but investors looking for strong performance will be frustrated.

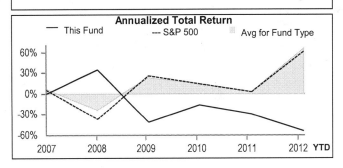

*ProShares UltraShort Industrials (SIJ)

E   Very Weak

Fund Family: ProShare Advisors LLC
Fund Type: Income
Inception Date: January 30, 2007

Data Date	Investment Rating	Net Assets ($Mil)	Price	Perfor-mance Rating/Pts	Total Return Y-T-D	Risk Rating/Pts
3-12	E	5.43	32.21	E- / 0.2	-22.50%	D+ / 2.9
2011	E-	7.00	41.56	E / 0.3	-4.33%	D+ / 2.6
2010	E-	8.90	13.07	E / 0.3	-46.26%	D- / 1.3
2009	E-	35.75	24.32	E- / 0.1	-52.04%	D+ / 2.3

Major Rating Factors: *ProShares UltraShort Industrials has adopted a risky asset allocation strategy and currently receives an overall TheStreet.com Investment Rating of E (Very Weak). The fund has an above average level of volatility, as measured by both semi-deviation and drawdown factors. It carries a beta of -2.58, meaning the fund's expected move will be -25.8% for every 10% move in the market. As of March 31, 2012, *ProShares UltraShort Industrials traded at a discount of .03% below its net asset value, which is better than its one-year historical average premium of .05%. Unfortunately, the high level of risk (D+, Weak) failed to pay off as investors endured very poor performance.

The fund's performance rating is currently E- (Very Weak). It has registered an annualized return of -48.48% over the last three years and is down -22.50% year to date 2012. Factored into the performance evaluation is an expense ratio of 0.95% (low).

Hratch Najarian has been running the fund for 1 year and currently receives a manager quality ranking of 9 (0=worst, 99=best). If you can tolerate high levels of risk in the hope of improved future returns, holding this fund may be an option.

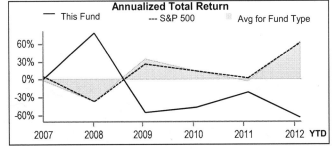

*ProShares UltraShort MidCap 400 (MZZ)   E   Very Weak

Fund Family: ProShare Advisors LLC
Fund Type: Growth
Inception Date: July 11, 2006

Data Date	Investment Rating	Net Assets ($Mil)	Price	Performance Rating/Pts	Total Return Y-T-D	Risk Rating/Pts
3-12	E	26.84	29.22	E- / 0.2	-23.17%	C- / 3.1
2011	E	40.80	38.03	E / 0.3	-2.34%	D+ / 2.9
2010	E-	19.60	11.89	E- / 0.2	-46.22%	D / 1.8
2009	E	61.46	22.11	E / 0.4	-59.99%	D+ / 2.8

Major Rating Factors: Very poor performance is the major factor driving the E (Very Weak) TheStreet.com Investment Rating for *ProShares UltraShort MidCap 400. The fund currently has a performance rating of E- (Very Weak) based on an annualized return of -47.51% over the last three years and a total return of -23.17% year to date 2012. Factored into the performance evaluation is an expense ratio of 0.95% (low).

The fund's risk rating is currently C- (Fair). It carries a beta of -2.28, meaning the fund's expected move will be -22.8% for every 10% move in the market. Volatility, as measured by both the semi-deviation and a drawdown factor, is considered average. As of March 31, 2012, *ProShares UltraShort MidCap 400 traded at a premium of .03% above its net asset value, which is worse than its one-year historical average discount of .03%.

Howard Rubin has been running the fund for 5 years and currently receives a manager quality ranking of 7 (0=worst, 99=best). This fund offers an average level of risk but investors looking for strong performance will be frustrated.

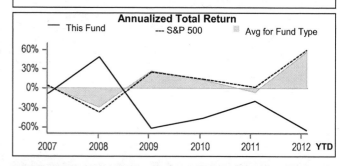

*ProShares UltraShort MSCI Brazil (BZQ)   E-   Very Weak

Fund Family: ProShare Advisors LLC
Fund Type: Foreign
Inception Date: June 16, 2009

Data Date	Investment Rating	Net Assets ($Mil)	Price	Performance Rating/Pts	Total Return Y-T-D	Risk Rating/Pts
3-12	E-	12.81	14.27	E / 0.4	-24.70%	D / 2.0
2011	D-	17.00	18.95	C- / 3.9	-4.64%	D+ / 2.4
2010	E-	18.80	15.06	E- / 0.2	-34.97%	D / 1.9

Major Rating Factors: *ProShares UltraShort MSCI Brazil has adopted a very risky asset allocation strategy and currently receives an overall TheStreet.com Investment Rating of E- (Very Weak). The fund has a high level of volatility, as measured by both semi-deviation and drawdown factors. It carries a beta of 0.00, meaning the fund's expected move will be 0.0% for every 10% move in the market. As of March 31, 2012, *ProShares UltraShort MSCI Brazil traded at a premium of .28% above its net asset value, which is worse than its one-year historical average discount of .01%. Unfortunately, the high level of risk (D, Weak) failed to pay off as investors endured very poor performance.

The fund's performance rating is currently E (Very Weak). It has registered an annualized return of 0.00% over the last three years but is down -24.70% year to date 2012. Factored into the performance evaluation is an expense ratio of 0.95% (low).

Alexander V. Ilyasov has been running the fund for 3 years and currently receives a manager quality ranking of 9 (0=worst, 99=best). If you can tolerate very high levels of risk in the hope of improved future returns, holding this fund may be an option.

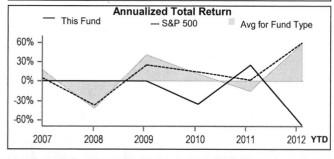

*ProShares UltraShort MSCI EAFE (EFU)   E   Very Weak

Fund Family: ProShare Advisors LLC
Fund Type: Foreign
Inception Date: October 23, 2007

Data Date	Investment Rating	Net Assets ($Mil)	Price	Performance Rating/Pts	Total Return Y-T-D	Risk Rating/Pts
3-12	E	18.52	20.58	E / 0.3	-20.66%	C- / 3.0
2011	E	27.20	25.94	E+ / 0.6	1.12%	D+ / 2.9
2010	E-	18.00	26.70	E / 0.3	-30.72%	D / 1.9
2009	E	56.21	38.54	E- / 0.2	-55.40%	D+ / 2.7

Major Rating Factors: Very poor performance is the major factor driving the E (Very Weak) TheStreet.com Investment Rating for *ProShares UltraShort MSCI EAFE. The fund currently has a performance rating of E (Very Weak) based on an annualized return of -38.91% over the last three years and a total return of -20.66% year to date 2012. Factored into the performance evaluation is an expense ratio of 0.95% (low).

The fund's risk rating is currently C- (Fair). It carries a beta of -1.93, meaning the fund's expected move will be -19.3% for every 10% move in the market. Volatility, as measured by both the semi-deviation and a drawdown factor, is considered average. As of March 31, 2012, *ProShares UltraShort MSCI EAFE traded at a price exactly equal to its net asset value, which is worse than its one-year historical average discount of .03%.

Alexander V. Ilyasov has been running the fund for 3 years and currently receives a manager quality ranking of 6 (0=worst, 99=best). This fund offers an average level of risk but investors looking for strong performance will be frustrated.

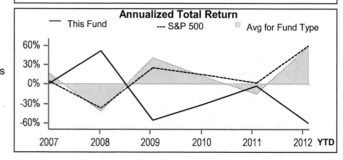

*ProShares UltraShort MSCI Emg Mk (EEV)   E-   Very Weak

Fund Family: ProShare Advisors LLC
Fund Type: Emerging Market
Inception Date: October 30, 2007

Major Rating Factors: *ProShares UltraShort MSCI Emg Mk has adopted a risky asset allocation strategy and currently receives an overall TheStreet.com Investment Rating of E- (Very Weak). The fund has an above average level of volatility, as measured by both semi-deviation and drawdown factors. It carries a beta of -2.05, meaning the fund's expected move will be -20.5% for every 10% move in the market. As of March 31, 2012, *ProShares UltraShort MSCI Emg Mk traded at a premium of .04% above its net asset value, which is worse than its one-year historical average discount of .03%. Unfortunately, the high level of risk (D+, Weak) failed to pay off as investors endured very poor performance.

The fund's performance rating is currently E- (Very Weak). It has registered an annualized return of -46.30% over the last three years and is down -24.56% year to date 2012. Factored into the performance evaluation is an expense ratio of 0.95% (low).

Alexander V. Ilyasov has been running the fund for 3 years and currently receives a manager quality ranking of 6 (0=worst, 99=best). If you can tolerate high levels of risk in the hope of improved future returns, holding this fund may be an option.

Data Date	Investment Rating	Net Assets ($Mil)	Price	Performance Rating/Pts	Total Return Y-T-D	Risk Rating/Pts
3-12	E-	78.78	25.89	E- / 0.2	-24.56%	D+ / 2.3
2011	E-	91.60	34.32	E / 0.3	-2.13%	D / 2.0
2010	E-	103.80	31.71	E- / 0.1	-41.82%	D- / 1.2
2009	E-	207.08	10.90	E- / 0	-76.97%	D- / 1.3

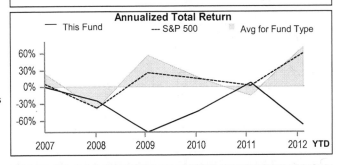

Annualized Total Return

*ProShares UltraShort MSCI Europe (EPV)   E   Very Weak

Fund Family: ProShare Advisors LLC
Fund Type: Foreign
Inception Date: June 16, 2009

Major Rating Factors: Very poor performance is the major factor driving the E (Very Weak) TheStreet.com Investment Rating for *ProShares UltraShort MSCI Europe. The fund currently has a performance rating of E- (Very Weak) based on an annualized return of 0.00% over the last three years and a total return of -22.92% year to date 2012. Factored into the performance evaluation is an expense ratio of 0.95% (low).

The fund's risk rating is currently C- (Fair). It carries a beta of 0.00, meaning the fund's expected move will be 0.0% for every 10% move in the market. Volatility, as measured by both the semi-deviation and a drawdown factor, is considered average. As of March 31, 2012, *ProShares UltraShort MSCI Europe traded at a premium of .11% above its net asset value, which is worse than its one-year historical average premium of .09%.

Howard Rubin has been running the fund for 3 years and currently receives a manager quality ranking of 2 (0=worst, 99=best). This fund offers an average level of risk but investors looking for strong performance will be frustrated.

Data Date	Investment Rating	Net Assets ($Mil)	Price	Performance Rating/Pts	Total Return Y-T-D	Risk Rating/Pts
3-12	E	120.18	35.92	E- / 0.2	-22.92%	C- / 3.2
2011	E	149.20	46.60	D- / 1.0	1.67%	C- / 3.3
2010	E	51.40	14.29	E- / 0.1	-34.66%	C- / 3.2

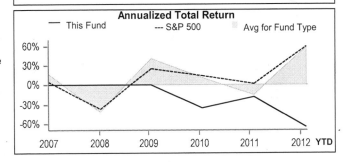

Annualized Total Return

*ProShares UltraShort MSCI Japan (EWV)   E   Very Weak

Fund Family: ProShare Advisors LLC
Fund Type: Foreign
Inception Date: November 6, 2007

Major Rating Factors: Very poor performance is the major factor driving the E (Very Weak) TheStreet.com Investment Rating for *ProShares UltraShort MSCI Japan. The fund currently has a performance rating of E (Very Weak) based on an annualized return of -27.11% over the last three years and a total return of -21.33% year to date 2012. Factored into the performance evaluation is an expense ratio of 0.95% (low).

The fund's risk rating is currently C- (Fair). It carries a beta of -1.10, meaning the fund's expected move will be -11.0% for every 10% move in the market. Volatility, as measured by both the semi-deviation and a drawdown factor, is considered average. As of March 31, 2012, *ProShares UltraShort MSCI Japan traded at a premium of .10% above its net asset value.

Alexander V. Ilyasov has been running the fund for 3 years and currently receives a manager quality ranking of 9 (0=worst, 99=best). This fund offers an average level of risk but investors looking for strong performance will be frustrated.

Data Date	Investment Rating	Net Assets ($Mil)	Price	Performance Rating/Pts	Total Return Y-T-D	Risk Rating/Pts
3-12	E	8.94	29.83	E / 0.4	-21.33%	C- / 4.0
2011	E+	17.10	37.92	D- / 1.1	0.47%	C- / 3.9
2010	E	12.80	34.00	E / 0.4	-30.85%	C- / 3.2
2009	E+	13.23	49.17	E / 0.4	-26.12%	C- / 4.1

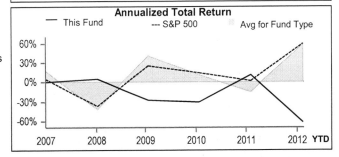

Annualized Total Return

*ProShares UltraShort MSCI Mex In (SMK)

E   Very Weak

Fund Family: ProShare Advisors LLC
Fund Type: Foreign
Inception Date: June 16, 2009

Major Rating Factors: *ProShares UltraShort MSCI Mex In has adopted a risky asset allocation strategy and currently receives an overall TheStreet.com Investment Rating of E (Very Weak). The fund has an above average level of volatility, as measured by both semi-deviation and drawdown factors. It carries a beta of 0.00, meaning the fund's expected move will be 0.0% for every 10% move in the market. As of March 31, 2012, *ProShares UltraShort MSCI Mex In traded at a premium of .53% above its net asset value, which is worse than its one-year historical average premium of .13%. Unfortunately, the high level of risk (D+, Weak) failed to pay off as investors endured very poor performance.

The fund's performance rating is currently E- (Very Weak). It has registered an annualized return of 0.00% over the last three years but is down -27.33% year to date 2012. Factored into the performance evaluation is an expense ratio of 0.95% (low).

Alexander V. Ilyasov has been running the fund for 3 years and currently receives a manager quality ranking of 2 (0=worst, 99=best). If you can tolerate high levels of risk in the hope of improved future returns, holding this fund may be an option.

Data Date	Investment Rating	Net Assets ($Mil)	Price	Perfor-mance Rating/Pts	Total Return Y-T-D	Risk Rating/Pts
3-12	E	1.79	35.93	E- / 0.2	-27.33%	D+ / 2.8
2011	E	2.50	49.44	D- / 1.2	-1.13%	C- / 3.1
2010	E	2.60	13.26	E- / 0.1	-49.66%	D+ / 2.5

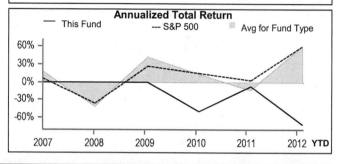

*ProShares UltraShort MSCI PXJ (JPX)

E-   Very Weak

Fund Family: ProShare Advisors LLC
Fund Type: Foreign
Inception Date: June 16, 2009

Major Rating Factors: *ProShares UltraShort MSCI PXJ has adopted a risky asset allocation strategy and currently receives an overall TheStreet.com Investment Rating of E- (Very Weak). The fund has an above average level of volatility, as measured by both semi-deviation and drawdown factors. It carries a beta of 0.00, meaning the fund's expected move will be 0.0% for every 10% move in the market. As of March 31, 2012, *ProShares UltraShort MSCI PXJ traded at a premium of .75% above its net asset value, which is worse than its one-year historical average discount of .18%. Unfortunately, the high level of risk (D+, Weak) failed to pay off as investors endured very poor performance.

The fund's performance rating is currently E (Very Weak). It has registered an annualized return of 0.00% over the last three years but is down -22.38% year to date 2012. Factored into the performance evaluation is an expense ratio of 0.95% (low).

Alexander V. Ilyasov has been running the fund for 3 years and currently receives a manager quality ranking of 3 (0=worst, 99=best). If you can tolerate high levels of risk in the hope of improved future returns, holding this fund may be an option.

Data Date	Investment Rating	Net Assets ($Mil)	Price	Perfor-mance Rating/Pts	Total Return Y-T-D	Risk Rating/Pts
3-12	E-	2.05	40.45	E / 0.3	-22.38%	D+ / 2.5
2011	E	2.60	52.11	D- / 1.1	-2.80%	D+ / 2.7
2010	E	2.70	10.88	E- / 0.1	-43.22%	D+ / 2.4

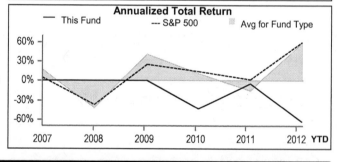

*ProShares UltraShort Nasdaq Biot (BIS)

E   Very Weak

Fund Family: ProShare Advisors LLC
Fund Type: Health
Inception Date: April 7, 2010

Major Rating Factors: Very poor performance is the major factor driving the E (Very Weak) TheStreet.com Investment Rating for *ProShares UltraShort Nasdaq Biot. The fund currently has a performance rating of E- (Very Weak) based on an annualized return of 0.00% over the last three years and a total return of -29.75% year to date 2012. Factored into the performance evaluation is an expense ratio of 0.95% (low).

The fund's risk rating is currently C- (Fair). It carries a beta of 0.00, meaning the fund's expected move will be 0.0% for every 10% move in the market. Volatility, as measured by both the semi-deviation and a drawdown factor, is considered average. As of March 31, 2012, *ProShares UltraShort Nasdaq Biot traded at a premium of .09% above its net asset value, which is better than its one-year historical average premium of .12%.

Hratch Najarian has been running the fund for 1 year and currently receives a manager quality ranking of 1 (0=worst, 99=best). This fund offers an average level of risk but investors looking for strong performance will be frustrated.

Data Date	Investment Rating	Net Assets ($Mil)	Price	Perfor-mance Rating/Pts	Total Return Y-T-D	Risk Rating/Pts
3-12	E	4.58	22.90	E- / 0.1	-29.75%	C- / 3.3
2011	E	1.60	32.60	E / 0.3	-4.39%	C- / 4.0

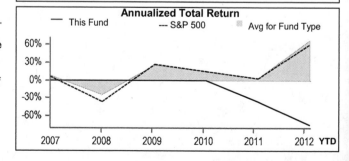

*ProShares UltraShort Oil & Gas (DUG)　　　　　E　　Very Weak

Fund Family: ProShare Advisors LLC
Fund Type: Energy/Natural Resources
Inception Date: January 30, 2007

Data Date	Investment Rating	Net Assets ($Mil)	Price	Perfor-mance Rating/Pts	Total Return Y-T-D	Risk Rating/Pts
3-12	E	86.94	22.97	E / 0.3	-10.38%	D+ / 2.9
2011	E	89.50	25.63	E / 0.3	-3.75%	C- / 3.0
2010	E	86.20	37.42	E- / 0.2	-41.26%	D+ / 2.6
2009	E	219.57	12.74	E- / 0.2	-43.88%	D+ / 2.7

Major Rating Factors: *ProShares UltraShort Oil & Gas has adopted a risky asset allocation strategy and currently receives an overall TheStreet.com Investment Rating of E (Very Weak). The fund has an above average level of volatility, as measured by both semi-deviation and drawdown factors. It carries a beta of -1.94, meaning the fund's expected move will be -19.4% for every 10% move in the market. As of March 31, 2012, *ProShares UltraShort Oil & Gas traded at a premium of .26% above its net asset value, which is worse than its one-year historical average discount of .15%. Unfortunately, the high level of risk (D+, Weak) failed to pay off as investors endured very poor performance.

The fund's performance rating is currently E (Very Weak). It has registered an annualized return of -41.08% over the last three years and is down -10.38% year to date 2012. Factored into the performance evaluation is an expense ratio of 0.95% (low).

Hratch Najarian has been running the fund for 1 year and currently receives a manager quality ranking of 6 (0=worst, 99=best). If you can tolerate high levels of risk in the hope of improved future returns, holding this fund may be an option.

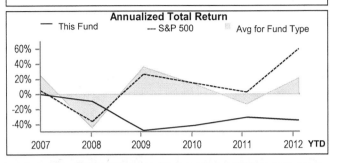

*ProShares UltraShort QQQ (QID)　　　　　E　　Very Weak

Fund Family: ProShare Advisors LLC
Fund Type: Growth
Inception Date: July 11, 2006

Data Date	Investment Rating	Net Assets ($Mil)	Price	Perfor-mance Rating/Pts	Total Return Y-T-D	Risk Rating/Pts
3-12	E	599.47	30.28	E- / 0.2	-32.90%	C- / 3.2
2011	E	601.70	45.13	E- / 0.2	-6.82%	C- / 3.1
2010	E	629.70	11.63	E / 0.3	-38.92%	D / 2.2
2009	E	956.42	19.04	E / 0.4	-63.73%	C- / 3.3

Major Rating Factors: Very poor performance is the major factor driving the E (Very Weak) TheStreet.com Investment Rating for *ProShares UltraShort QQQ. The fund currently has a performance rating of E- (Very Weak) based on an annualized return of -47.71% over the last three years and a total return of -32.90% year to date 2012. Factored into the performance evaluation is an expense ratio of 0.95% (low).

The fund's risk rating is currently C- (Fair). It carries a beta of -2.05, meaning the fund's expected move will be -20.5% for every 10% move in the market. Volatility, as measured by both the semi-deviation and a drawdown factor, is considered average. As of March 31, 2012, *ProShares UltraShort QQQ traded at a discount of .07% below its net asset value, which is better than its one-year historical average discount of .03%.

Howard Rubin has been running the fund for 5 years and currently receives a manager quality ranking of 5 (0=worst, 99=best). This fund offers an average level of risk but investors looking for strong performance will be frustrated.

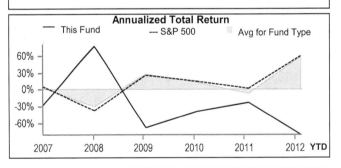

*ProShares UltraShort Real Estate (SRS)　　　　　E-　　Very Weak

Fund Family: ProShare Advisors LLC
Fund Type: Income
Inception Date: January 30, 2007

Data Date	Investment Rating	Net Assets ($Mil)	Price	Perfor-mance Rating/Pts	Total Return Y-T-D	Risk Rating/Pts
3-12	E-	132.38	29.54	E- / 0.1	-19.64%	D+ / 2.8
2011	E-	134.80	36.76	E- / 0	-0.16%	D / 1.9
2010	E-	242.40	18.14	E- / 0	-51.63%	D- / 1.0
2009	E-	1,239.19	7.50	E- / 0	-85.91%	D- / 1.1

Major Rating Factors: *ProShares UltraShort Real Estate has adopted a risky asset allocation strategy and currently receives an overall TheStreet.com Investment Rating of E- (Very Weak). The fund has an above average level of volatility, as measured by both semi-deviation and drawdown factors. It carries a beta of -2.70, meaning the fund's expected move will be -27.0% for every 10% move in the market. As of March 31, 2012, *ProShares UltraShort Real Estate traded at a premium of .24% above its net asset value, which is worse than its one-year historical average discount of .01%. Unfortunately, the high level of risk (D+, Weak) failed to pay off as investors endured very poor performance.

The fund's performance rating is currently E- (Very Weak). It has registered an annualized return of -62.75% over the last three years and is down -19.64% year to date 2012. Factored into the performance evaluation is an expense ratio of 0.95% (low).

Hratch Najarian has been running the fund for 1 year and currently receives a manager quality ranking of 1 (0=worst, 99=best). If you can tolerate high levels of risk in the hope of improved future returns, holding this fund may be an option.

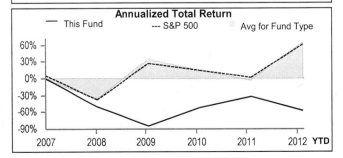

*ProShares UltraShort Russell 300 (TWQ)

E   Very Weak

Fund Family: ProShare Advisors LLC
Fund Type: Growth
Inception Date: June 30, 2009

Major Rating Factors: Very poor performance is the major factor driving the E (Very Weak) TheStreet.com Investment Rating for *ProShares UltraShort Russell 300. The fund currently has a performance rating of E- (Very Weak) based on an annualized return of 0.00% over the last three years and a total return of -22.72% year to date 2012. Factored into the performance evaluation is an expense ratio of 0.95% (low).

The fund's risk rating is currently C- (Fair). It carries a beta of 0.00, meaning the fund's expected move will be 0.0% for every 10% move in the market. Volatility, as measured by both the semi-deviation and a drawdown factor, is considered average. As of March 31, 2012, *ProShares UltraShort Russell 300 traded at a premium of .20% above its net asset value, which is worse than its one-year historical average discount of .07%.

Hratch Najarian has been running the fund for 3 years and currently receives a manager quality ranking of 10 (0=worst, 99=best). This fund offers an average level of risk but investors looking for strong performance will be frustrated.

Data Date	Investment Rating	Net Assets ($Mil)	Price	Performance Rating/Pts	Total Return Y-T-D	Risk Rating/Pts
3-12	E	1.53	10.24	E- / 0.2	-22.72%	C- / 3.5
2011	E+	2.00	13.25	E+ / 0.7	-4.53%	C- / 3.9
2010	E+	1.60	16.28	E- / 0.1	-33.82%	C- / 4.2

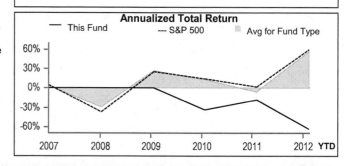

*ProShares UltraShort Russell MC (SJL)

E   Very Weak

Fund Family: ProShare Advisors LLC
Fund Type: Growth
Inception Date: February 20, 2007

Major Rating Factors: Very poor performance is the major factor driving the E (Very Weak) TheStreet.com Investment Rating for *ProShares UltraShort Russell MC. The fund currently has a performance rating of E- (Very Weak) based on an annualized return of -48.57% over the last three years and a total return of -19.80% year to date 2012. Factored into the performance evaluation is an expense ratio of 0.95% (low).

The fund's risk rating is currently C- (Fair). It carries a beta of -2.35, meaning the fund's expected move will be -23.5% for every 10% move in the market. Volatility, as measured by both the semi-deviation and a drawdown factor, is considered average. As of March 31, 2012, *ProShares UltraShort Russell MC traded at a premium of .92% above its net asset value, which is worse than its one-year historical average discount of .12%.

Hratch Najarian has been running the fund for 3 years and currently receives a manager quality ranking of 7 (0=worst, 99=best). This fund offers an average level of risk but investors looking for strong performance will be frustrated.

Data Date	Investment Rating	Net Assets ($Mil)	Price	Performance Rating/Pts	Total Return Y-T-D	Risk Rating/Pts
3-12	E	1.44	38.20	E- / 0.2	-19.80%	C- / 3.0
2011	E	1.80	47.63	E / 0.4	1.30%	D+ / 2.6
2010	E-	2.20	14.60	E- / 0.2	-45.07%	D- / 1.4
2009	E-	4.09	26.58	E- / 0.1	-59.92%	D / 2.0

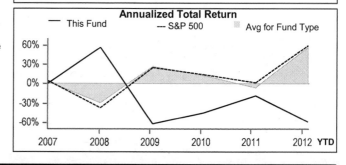

*ProShares UltraShort Russell1000 (SFK)

E   Very Weak

Fund Family: ProShare Advisors LLC
Fund Type: Growth
Inception Date: February 20, 2007

Major Rating Factors: Very poor performance is the major factor driving the E (Very Weak) TheStreet.com Investment Rating for *ProShares UltraShort Russell1000. The fund currently has a performance rating of E (Very Weak) based on an annualized return of -41.83% over the last three years and a total return of -24.68% year to date 2012. Factored into the performance evaluation is an expense ratio of 0.95% (low).

The fund's risk rating is currently C- (Fair). It carries a beta of -1.91, meaning the fund's expected move will be -19.1% for every 10% move in the market. Volatility, as measured by both the semi-deviation and a drawdown factor, is considered average. As of March 31, 2012, *ProShares UltraShort Russell1000 traded at a discount of .78% below its net asset value, which is better than its one-year historical average discount of .07%.

Hratch Najarian has been running the fund for 3 years and currently receives a manager quality ranking of 9 (0=worst, 99=best). This fund offers an average level of risk but investors looking for strong performance will be frustrated.

Data Date	Investment Rating	Net Assets ($Mil)	Price	Performance Rating/Pts	Total Return Y-T-D	Risk Rating/Pts
3-12	E	2.09	13.91	E / 0.3	-24.68%	C- / 3.5
2011	E	5.60	18.47	E / 0.4	-3.18%	C- / 3.4
2010	E	5.20	23.21	E / 0.4	-33.91%	D+ / 2.4
2009	E	17.25	35.12	E- / 0.2	-53.28%	C- / 3.5

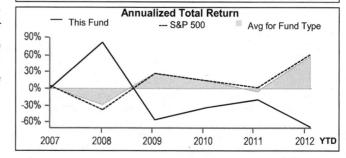

*ProShares UltraShort Russell2000 (SJH) E Very Weak

Fund Family: ProShare Advisors LLC
Fund Type: Income
Inception Date: February 20, 2007

Data Date	Investment Rating	Net Assets ($Mil)	Price	Performance Rating/Pts	Total Return Y-T-D	Risk Rating/Pts
3-12	E	4.51	34.07	E- / 0.2	-20.75%	D+ / 2.8
2011	E-	5.70	42.99	E- / 0.2	-1.86%	D+ / 2.4
2010	E-	7.20	13.56	E- / 0.2	-49.00%	D- / 1.3
2009	E-	14.77	26.59	E- / 0.1	-57.75%	D+ / 2.4

Major Rating Factors: *ProShares UltraShort Russell2000 has adopted a risky asset allocation strategy and currently receives an overall TheStreet.com Investment Rating of E (Very Weak). The fund has an above average level of volatility, as measured by both semi-deviation and drawdown factors. It carries a beta of -2.59, meaning the fund's expected move will be -25.9% for every 10% move in the market. As of March 31, 2012, *ProShares UltraShort Russell2000 traded at a discount of .84% below its net asset value, which is better than its one-year historical average discount of .18%. Unfortunately, the high level of risk (D+, Weak) failed to pay off as investors endured very poor performance.

The fund's performance rating is currently E- (Very Weak). It has registered an annualized return of -49.26% over the last three years and is down -20.75% year to date 2012. Factored into the performance evaluation is an expense ratio of 0.95% (low).

Hratch Najarian has been running the fund for 3 years and currently receives a manager quality ranking of 8 (0=worst, 99=best). If you can tolerate high levels of risk in the hope of improved future returns, holding this fund may be an option.

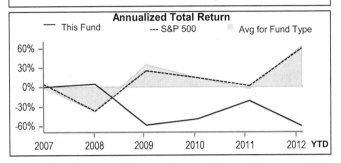

Annualized Total Return — This Fund --- S&P 500 Avg for Fund Type

*ProShares UltraShort Russell2000 (SKK) E- Very Weak

Fund Family: ProShare Advisors LLC
Fund Type: Growth
Inception Date: February 20, 2007

Data Date	Investment Rating	Net Assets ($Mil)	Price	Performance Rating/Pts	Total Return Y-T-D	Risk Rating/Pts
3-12	E-	9.25	26.67	E- / 0.1	-24.64%	D+ / 2.7
2011	E-	17.50	35.39	E- / 0.1	-2.75%	D+ / 2.3
2010	E-	8.00	9.64	E- / 0.2	-51.56%	D- / 1.2
2009	E-	11.43	19.90	E- / 0.1	-60.06%	D / 1.9

Major Rating Factors: *ProShares UltraShort Russell2000 has adopted a risky asset allocation strategy and currently receives an overall TheStreet.com Investment Rating of E- (Very Weak). The fund has an above average level of volatility, as measured by both semi-deviation and drawdown factors. It carries a beta of -2.48, meaning the fund's expected move will be -24.8% for every 10% move in the market. As of March 31, 2012, *ProShares UltraShort Russell2000 traded at a discount of .56% below its net asset value, which is better than its one-year historical average premium of .06%. Unfortunately, the high level of risk (D+, Weak) failed to pay off as investors endured very poor performance.

The fund's performance rating is currently E- (Very Weak). It has registered an annualized return of -51.15% over the last three years and is down -24.64% year to date 2012. Factored into the performance evaluation is an expense ratio of 0.95% (low).

Hratch Najarian has been running the fund for 3 years and currently receives a manager quality ranking of 6 (0=worst, 99=best). If you can tolerate high levels of risk in the hope of improved future returns, holding this fund may be an option.

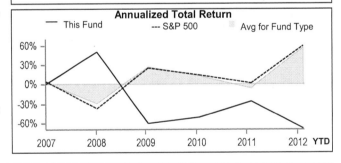

Annualized Total Return — This Fund --- S&P 500 Avg for Fund Type

*ProShares UltraShort Russell2000 (TWM) E Very Weak

Fund Family: ProShare Advisors LLC
Fund Type: Growth
Inception Date: January 23, 2007

Data Date	Investment Rating	Net Assets ($Mil)	Price	Performance Rating/Pts	Total Return Y-T-D	Risk Rating/Pts
3-12	E	260.37	29.62	E- / 0.2	-23.28%	D+ / 2.8
2011	E-	297.60	38.61	E- / 0.2	-2.95%	D+ / 2.6
2010	E-	299.00	12.56	E- / 0.2	-50.14%	D / 1.6
2009	E	578.47	25.19	E- / 0.1	-59.03%	D+ / 2.7

Major Rating Factors: *ProShares UltraShort Russell2000 has adopted a risky asset allocation strategy and currently receives an overall TheStreet.com Investment Rating of E (Very Weak). The fund has an above average level of volatility, as measured by both semi-deviation and drawdown factors. It carries a beta of -2.51, meaning the fund's expected move will be -25.1% for every 10% move in the market. As of March 31, 2012, *ProShares UltraShort Russell2000 traded at a price exactly equal to its net asset value, which is worse than its one-year historical average discount of .01%. Unfortunately, the high level of risk (D+, Weak) failed to pay off as investors endured very poor performance.

The fund's performance rating is currently E- (Very Weak). It has registered an annualized return of -50.07% over the last three years and is down -23.28% year to date 2012. Factored into the performance evaluation is an expense ratio of 0.95% (low).

Hratch Najarian has been running the fund for 3 years and currently receives a manager quality ranking of 6 (0=worst, 99=best). If you can tolerate high levels of risk in the hope of improved future returns, holding this fund may be an option.

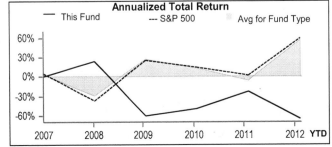

Annualized Total Return — This Fund --- S&P 500 Avg for Fund Type

* Denotes ETF Fund

*ProShares UltraShort S-P 500 (SDS)

E   **Very Weak**

Fund Family: ProShare Advisors LLC
Fund Type: Growth
Inception Date: July 11, 2006

Major Rating Factors: Very poor performance is the major factor driving the E (Very Weak) TheStreet.com Investment Rating for *ProShares UltraShort S-P 500. The fund currently has a performance rating of E (Very Weak) based on an annualized return of -40.07% over the last three years and a total return of -21.77% year to date 2012. Factored into the performance evaluation is an expense ratio of 0.89% (low).

The fund's risk rating is currently C- (Fair). It carries a beta of -1.95, meaning the fund's expected move will be -19.5% for every 10% move in the market. Volatility, as measured by both the semi-deviation and a drawdown factor, is considered average. As of March 31, 2012, *ProShares UltraShort S-P 500 traded at a premium of .13% above its net asset value, which is worse than its one-year historical average discount of .01%.

Hratch Najarian has been running the fund for 2 years and currently receives a manager quality ranking of 11 (0=worst, 99=best). This fund offers an average level of risk but investors looking for strong performance will be frustrated.

Data Date	Investment Rating	Net Assets ($Mil)	Price	Perfor-mance Rating/Pts	Total Return Y-T-D	Risk Rating/Pts
3-12	E	2,013.54	15.09	E / 0.3	-21.77%	C- / 3.5
2011	E	2,013.10	19.29	E / 0.5	-3.57%	C- / 3.4
2010	E	2,052.80	23.76	E / 0.4	-32.21%	D+ / 2.9
2009	E+	3,872.85	35.05	E / 0.5	-47.35%	C- / 4.2

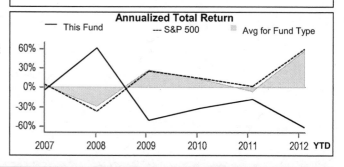

*ProShares UltraShort Semiconduct (SSG)

E-   **Very Weak**

Fund Family: ProShare Advisors LLC
Fund Type: Income
Inception Date: January 30, 2007

Major Rating Factors: *ProShares UltraShort Semiconduct has adopted a risky asset allocation strategy and currently receives an overall TheStreet.com Investment Rating of E- (Very Weak). The fund has an above average level of volatility, as measured by both semi-deviation and drawdown factors. It carries a beta of -2.45, meaning the fund's expected move will be -24.5% for every 10% move in the market. As of March 31, 2012, *ProShares UltraShort Semiconduct traded at a discount of .27% below its net asset value, which is better than its one-year historical average discount of .02%. Unfortunately, the high level of risk (D+, Weak) failed to pay off as investors endured very poor performance.

The fund's performance rating is currently E- (Very Weak). It has registered an annualized return of -47.80% over the last three years and is down -28.38% year to date 2012. Factored into the performance evaluation is an expense ratio of 0.95% (low).

Hratch Najarian has been running the fund for 1 year and currently receives a manager quality ranking of 8 (0=worst, 99=best). If you can tolerate high levels of risk in the hope of improved future returns, holding this fund may be an option.

Data Date	Investment Rating	Net Assets ($Mil)	Price	Perfor-mance Rating/Pts	Total Return Y-T-D	Risk Rating/Pts
3-12	E-	15.71	32.65	E- / 0.2	-28.38%	D+ / 2.5
2011	E-	15.00	45.59	E- / 0.1	-6.01%	D+ / 2.3
2010	E-	20.10	11.17	E- / 0.2	-38.59%	D- / 1.1
2009	E-	34.53	18.19	E- / 0	-74.59%	D / 1.7

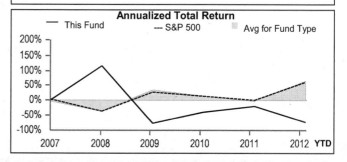

*ProShares UltraShort Silver (ZSL)

E-   **Very Weak**

Fund Family: ProShare Advisors LLC
Fund Type: Energy/Natural Resources
Inception Date: December 2, 2008

Major Rating Factors: *ProShares UltraShort Silver has adopted a very risky asset allocation strategy and currently receives an overall TheStreet.com Investment Rating of E- (Very Weak). The fund has a high level of volatility, as measured by both semi-deviation and drawdown factors. It carries a beta of -1.87, meaning the fund's expected move will be -18.7% for every 10% move in the market. As of March 31, 2012, *ProShares UltraShort Silver traded at a premium of .57% above its net asset value, which is worse than its one-year historical average discount of .42%. Unfortunately, the high level of risk (D, Weak) failed to pay off as investors endured very poor performance.

The fund's performance rating is currently E- (Very Weak). It has registered an annualized return of -72.05% over the last three years and is down -33.52% year to date 2012. Factored into the performance evaluation is an expense ratio of 0.95% (low).

This fund has been team managed for 4 years and currently receives a manager quality ranking of 0 (0=worst, 99=best). If you can tolerate very high levels of risk in the hope of improved future returns, holding this fund may be an option.

Data Date	Investment Rating	Net Assets ($Mil)	Price	Perfor-mance Rating/Pts	Total Return Y-T-D	Risk Rating/Pts
3-12	E-	191.33	10.55	E- / 0	-33.52%	D / 1.9
2011	E-	245.30	15.87	E- / 0	-7.56%	D / 1.9
2010	E-	99.10	9.82	E- / 0	-79.50%	D- / 1.4
2009	E-	1.96	4.79	E- / 0	-71.91%	D / 1.8

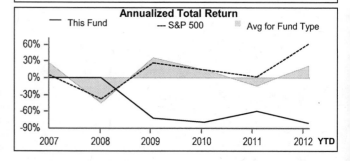

*ProShares UltraShort SmallCap 60 (SDD)   E   Very Weak

Fund Family: ProShare Advisors LLC
Fund Type: Growth
Inception Date: January 23, 2007

Data Date	Investment Rating	Net Assets ($Mil)	Price	Performance Rating/Pts	Total Return Y-T-D	Risk Rating/Pts
3-12	E	11.87	29.98	E- / 0.2	-22.14%	D+ / 2.9
2011	E-	18.10	38.51	E- / 0.1	-2.30%	D+ / 2.6
2010	E-	15.30	13.59	E- / 0.2	-48.39%	D- / 1.5
2009	E-	24.73	26.33	E- / 0.1	-56.67%	D+ / 2.7

Major Rating Factors: *ProShares UltraShort SmallCap 60 has adopted a risky asset allocation strategy and currently receives an overall TheStreet.com Investment Rating of E (Very Weak). The fund has an above average level of volatility, as measured by both semi-deviation and drawdown factors. It carries a beta of -2.40, meaning the fund's expected move will be -24.0% for every 10% move in the market. As of March 31, 2012, *ProShares UltraShort SmallCap 60 traded at a discount of .56% below its net asset value, which is better than its one-year historical average discount of .03%. Unfortunately, the high level of risk (D+, Weak) failed to pay off as investors endured very poor performance.

The fund's performance rating is currently E- (Very Weak). It has registered an annualized return of -50.72% over the last three years and is down -22.14% year to date 2012. Factored into the performance evaluation is an expense ratio of 0.95% (low).

Hratch Najarian has been running the fund for 2 years and currently receives a manager quality ranking of 5 (0=worst, 99=best). If you can tolerate high levels of risk in the hope of improved future returns, holding this fund may be an option.

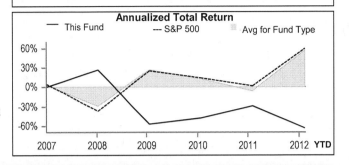

*ProShares UltraShort Technology (REW)   E   Very Weak

Fund Family: ProShare Advisors LLC
Fund Type: Growth
Inception Date: January 30, 2007

Data Date	Investment Rating	Net Assets ($Mil)	Price	Performance Rating/Pts	Total Return Y-T-D	Risk Rating/Pts
3-12	E	11.40	33.69	E- / 0.2	-34.02%	C- / 3.1
2011	E	13.40	51.06	E / 0.3	-5.56%	C- / 3.0
2010	E-	18.60	15.51	E / 0.3	-30.82%	D / 2.0
2009	E-	36.39	22.42	E- / 0	-68.81%	D+ / 2.7

Major Rating Factors: Very poor performance is the major factor driving the E (Very Weak) TheStreet.com Investment Rating for *ProShares UltraShort Technology. The fund currently has a performance rating of E- (Very Weak) based on an annualized return of -45.87% over the last three years and a total return of -34.02% year to date 2012. Factored into the performance evaluation is an expense ratio of 0.95% (low).

The fund's risk rating is currently C- (Fair). It carries a beta of -2.15, meaning the fund's expected move will be -21.5% for every 10% move in the market. Volatility, as measured by both the semi-deviation and a drawdown factor, is considered average. As of March 31, 2012, *ProShares UltraShort Technology traded at a discount of .30% below its net asset value, which is better than its one-year historical average discount of .05%.

Hratch Najarian has been running the fund for 1 year and currently receives a manager quality ranking of 7 (0=worst, 99=best). This fund offers an average level of risk but investors looking for strong performance will be frustrated.

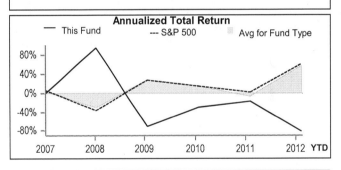

*ProShares UltraShort Telecomncti (TLL)   E   Very Weak

Fund Family: ProShare Advisors LLC
Fund Type: Income
Inception Date: March 25, 2008

Data Date	Investment Rating	Net Assets ($Mil)	Price	Performance Rating/Pts	Total Return Y-T-D	Risk Rating/Pts
3-12	E	2.26	37.60	E / 0.4	-12.03%	D+ / 2.9
2011	E	2.60	42.74	E+ / 0.7	0.98%	D+ / 2.8
2010	E-	2.00	8.84	E- / 0.1	-37.96%	D- / 1.3
2009	E-	2.33	14.25	E- / 0.2	-50.15%	D- / 1.1

Major Rating Factors: *ProShares UltraShort Telecomncti has adopted a risky asset allocation strategy and currently receives an overall TheStreet.com Investment Rating of E (Very Weak). The fund has an above average level of volatility, as measured by both semi-deviation and drawdown factors. It carries a beta of -1.56, meaning the fund's expected move will be -15.6% for every 10% move in the market. As of March 31, 2012, *ProShares UltraShort Telecomncti traded at a premium of .19% above its net asset value, which is worse than its one-year historical average premium of .02%. Unfortunately, the high level of risk (D+, Weak) failed to pay off as investors endured very poor performance.

The fund's performance rating is currently E (Very Weak). It has registered an annualized return of -31.40% over the last three years and is down -12.03% year to date 2012. Factored into the performance evaluation is an expense ratio of 0.95% (low).

Hratch Najarian has been running the fund for 1 year and currently receives a manager quality ranking of 14 (0=worst, 99=best). If you can tolerate high levels of risk in the hope of improved future returns, holding this fund may be an option.

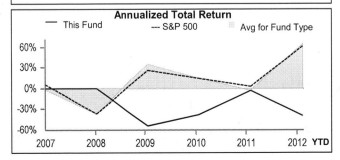

*ProShares UltraShort TIPS (TPS)

D   **Weak**

Fund Family: ProShare Advisors LLC
Fund Type: Growth
Inception Date: February 9, 2011

Major Rating Factors:
Very poor performance is the major factor driving the D (Weak) TheStreet.com Investment Rating for *ProShares UltraShort TIPS. The fund currently has a performance rating of E+ (Very Weak) based on an annualized return of 0.00% over the last three years and a total return of -2.09% year to date 2012. Factored into the performance evaluation is an expense ratio of 0.95% (low).

   The fund's risk rating is currently B- (Good). It carries a beta of 0.00, meaning the fund's expected move will be 0.0% for every 10% move in the market. Volatility, as measured by both the semi-deviation and a drawdown factor, is considered low. As of March 31, 2012, *ProShares UltraShort TIPS traded at a discount of .17% below its net asset value, which is worse than its one-year historical average discount of .18%.

   Michelle Lui has been running the fund for 1 year and currently receives a manager quality ranking of 5 (0=worst, 99=best). This fund offers only a moderate level of risk but investors looking for strong performance are still waiting.

Data Date	Investment Rating	Net Assets ($Mil)	Price	Performance Rating/Pts	Total Return Y-T-D	Risk Rating/Pts
3-12	D	4.36	29.00	E+ / 0.6	-2.09%	B- / 7.9

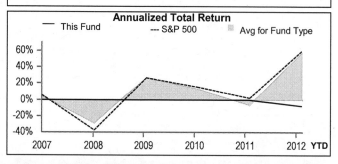

Annualized Total Return

--- This Fund   --- S&P 500   Avg for Fund Type

---

*ProShares UltraShort Utilities (SDP)

E   **Very Weak**

Fund Family: ProShare Advisors LLC
Fund Type: Utilities
Inception Date: January 30, 2007

Major Rating Factors: Very poor performance is the major factor driving the E (Very Weak) TheStreet.com Investment Rating for *ProShares UltraShort Utilities. The fund currently has a performance rating of E (Very Weak) based on an annualized return of -32.03% over the last three years and a total return of 3.08% year to date 2012. Factored into the performance evaluation is an expense ratio of 0.95% (low).

   The fund's risk rating is currently C- (Fair). It carries a beta of -1.92, meaning the fund's expected move will be -19.2% for every 10% move in the market. Volatility, as measured by both the semi-deviation and a drawdown factor, is considered average. As of March 31, 2012, *ProShares UltraShort Utilities traded at a premium of .19% above its net asset value.

   Hratch Najarian has been running the fund for 1 year and currently receives a manager quality ranking of 14 (0=worst, 99=best). This fund offers an average level of risk but investors looking for strong performance will be frustrated.

Data Date	Investment Rating	Net Assets ($Mil)	Price	Performance Rating/Pts	Total Return Y-T-D	Risk Rating/Pts
3-12	E	3.20	32.10	E / 0.4	3.08%	C- / 3.8
2011	E+	3.10	31.14	E+ / 0.6	5.94%	C- / 3.8
2010	E	6.20	16.44	E+ / 0.7	-19.80%	D+ / 2.4
2009	E	12.32	20.50	E / 0.3	-29.85%	C- / 3.1

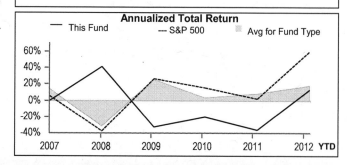

Annualized Total Return

--- This Fund   --- S&P 500   Avg for Fund Type

---

*ProShares UltraShort Yen (YCS)

D-   **Weak**

Fund Family: ProShare Advisors LLC
Fund Type: Foreign
Inception Date: November 25, 2008

Major Rating Factors:
Very poor performance is the major factor driving the D- (Weak) TheStreet.com Investment Rating for *ProShares UltraShort Yen. The fund currently has a performance rating of E+ (Very Weak) based on an annualized return of -15.43% over the last three years and a total return of 14.90% year to date 2012. Factored into the performance evaluation is an expense ratio of 0.95% (low).

   The fund's risk rating is currently C+ (Fair). It carries a beta of -0.01, meaning the fund's expected move will be -0.1% for every 10% move in the market. Volatility, as measured by both the semi-deviation and a drawdown factor, is considered low. As of March 31, 2012, *ProShares UltraShort Yen traded at a price exactly equal to its net asset value.

   This fund has been team managed for 4 years and currently receives a manager quality ranking of 10 (0=worst, 99=best). This fund offers only a moderate level of risk but investors looking for strong performance are still waiting.

Data Date	Investment Rating	Net Assets ($Mil)	Price	Performance Rating/Pts	Total Return Y-T-D	Risk Rating/Pts
3-12	D-	279.89	47.05	E+ / 0.8	14.90%	C+ / 6.0
2011	D-	221.20	40.95	D- / 1.1	0.02%	C+ / 6.0
2010	D	207.70	15.67	E / 0.3	-26.43%	C+ / 6.0
2009	D+	2.17	21.30	D- / 1.2	-3.97%	B- / 7.0

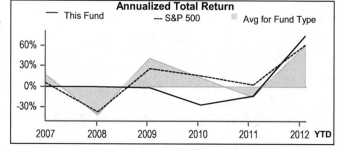

Annualized Total Return

--- This Fund   --- S&P 500   Avg for Fund Type

---

*ProShares VIX Mid-Term Futures E (VIXM)

E+ **Very Weak**

Fund Family: ProShare Advisors LLC
Fund Type: General - Investment Grade
Inception Date: January 3, 2011

Data Date	Investment Rating	Net Assets ($Mil)	Price	Performance Rating/Pts	Total Return Y-T-D	Risk Rating/Pts
3-12	E+	102.11	56.82	E / 0.4	-23.35%	C / 5.6

Major Rating Factors:
Very poor performance is the major factor driving the E+ (Very Weak) TheStreet.com Investment Rating for *ProShares VIX Mid-Term Futures E. The fund currently has a performance rating of E (Very Weak) based on an annualized return of 0.00% over the last three years and a total return of -23.35% year to date 2012. Factored into the performance evaluation is an expense ratio of 0.85% (very low).

The fund's risk rating is currently C (Fair). It carries a beta of 0.00, meaning the fund's expected move will be 0.0% for every 10% move in the market. Volatility, as measured by both the semi-deviation and a drawdown factor, is considered average. As of March 31, 2012, *ProShares VIX Mid-Term Futures E traded at a premium of 1.55% above its net asset value, which is worse than its one-year historical average premium of .02%.

Michelle Liu has been running the fund for 1 year and currently receives a manager quality ranking of 1 (0=worst, 99=best). This fund offers an average level of risk but investors looking for strong performance will be frustrated.

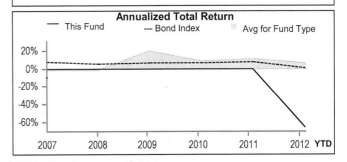

Annualized Total Return
— This Fund   --- Bond Index   Avg for Fund Type

*ProShares VIX Short-Term Futures (VIXY)

E- **Very Weak**

Fund Family: ProShare Advisors LLC
Fund Type: General - Investment Grade
Inception Date: January 3, 2011

Data Date	Investment Rating	Net Assets ($Mil)	Price	Performance Rating/Pts	Total Return Y-T-D	Risk Rating/Pts
3-12	E-	125.12	35.77	E- / 0	-52.77%	D / 1.9

Major Rating Factors: *ProShares VIX Short-Term Futures has adopted a very risky asset allocation strategy and currently receives an overall TheStreet.com Investment Rating of E- (Very Weak). The fund has a high level of volatility, as measured by both semi-deviation and drawdown factors. It carries a beta of 0.00, meaning the fund's expected move will be 0.0% for every 10% move in the market. As of March 31, 2012, *ProShares VIX Short-Term Futures traded at a premium of .76% above its net asset value, which is worse than its one-year historical average premium of .15%. Unfortunately, the high level of risk (D, Weak) failed to pay off as investors endured very poor performance.

The fund's performance rating is currently E- (Very Weak). It has registered an annualized return of 0.00% over the last three years but is down -52.77% year to date 2012. Factored into the performance evaluation is an expense ratio of 0.85% (very low).

Michelle Liu has been running the fund for 1 year and currently receives a manager quality ranking of 0 (0=worst, 99=best). If you can tolerate very high levels of risk in the hope of improved future returns, holding this fund may be an option.

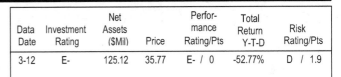

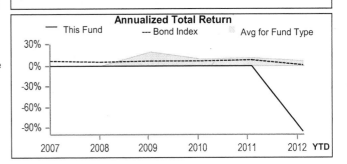

Annualized Total Return
— This Fund   --- Bond Index   Avg for Fund Type

*RBS Gold Trendpilot ETN (TBAR)

D- **Weak**

Fund Family: Royal Bank of Scotland NV
Fund Type: Energy/Natural Resources
Inception Date: February 17, 2011

Data Date	Investment Rating	Net Assets ($Mil)	Price	Performance Rating/Pts	Total Return Y-T-D	Risk Rating/Pts
3-12	D-	27.53	28.97	D+ / 2.3	2.84%	C / 5.1

Major Rating Factors:
Disappointing performance is the major factor driving the D- (Weak) TheStreet.com Investment Rating for *RBS Gold Trendpilot ETN. The fund currently has a performance rating of D+ (Weak) based on an annualized return of 0.00% over the last three years and a total return of 2.84% year to date 2012. Factored into the performance evaluation is an expense ratio of 1.00% (low).

The fund's risk rating is currently C (Fair). It carries a beta of 0.00, meaning the fund's expected move will be 0.0% for every 10% move in the market. Volatility, as measured by both the semi-deviation and a drawdown factor, is considered average. As of March 31, 2012, *RBS Gold Trendpilot ETN traded at a price exactly equal to its net asset value, which is better than its one-year historical average premium of .13%.

This fund has been team managed for 1 year and currently receives a manager quality ranking of 89 (0=worst, 99=best). This fund offers an average level of risk but investors looking for strong performance will be frustrated.

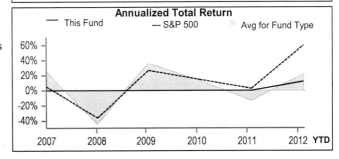

Annualized Total Return
— This Fund   --- S&P 500   Avg for Fund Type

*RBS US Large Cap Trendpilot ETN (TRND)

C-   **Fair**

Fund Family: Royal Bank of Scotland NV
Fund Type: Growth
Inception Date: December 6, 2010

Data Date	Investment Rating	Net Assets ($Mil)	Price	Performance Rating/Pts	Total Return Y-T-D	Risk Rating/Pts
3-12	C-	65.82	27.03	D+ / 2.5	12.34%	B / 8.5
2011	D+	0.00	24.06	D- / 1.3	1.89%	B / 8.5

Major Rating Factors:
Disappointing performance is the major factor driving the C- (Fair) TheStreet.com Investment Rating for *RBS US Large Cap Trendpilot ETN. The fund currently has a performance rating of D+ (Weak) based on an annualized return of 0.00% over the last three years and a total return of 12.34% year to date 2012. Factored into the performance evaluation is an expense ratio of 0.50% (very low).

The fund's risk rating is currently B (Good). It carries a beta of 0.00, meaning the fund's expected move will be 0.0% for every 10% move in the market. Volatility, as measured by both the semi-deviation and a drawdown factor, is considered low. As of March 31, 2012, *RBS US Large Cap Trendpilot ETN traded at a premium of .04% above its net asset value, which is worse than its one-year historical average premium of .03%.

This fund has been team managed for 2 years and currently receives a manager quality ranking of 24 (0=worst, 99=best). This fund offers only a moderate level of risk but investors looking for strong performance are still waiting.

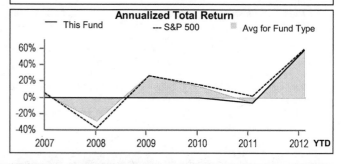

Annualized Total Return
— This Fund   --- S&P 500   Avg for Fund Type

*RBS US Mid Cap Trendpilot ETN (TRNM)

E+   **Very Weak**

Fund Family: Royal Bank of Scotland NV
Fund Type: Growth
Inception Date: January 27, 2011

Data Date	Investment Rating	Net Assets ($Mil)	Price	Performance Rating/Pts	Total Return Y-T-D	Risk Rating/Pts
3-12	E+	32.36	24.10	D- / 1.1	7.97%	C / 4.8

Major Rating Factors:
Disappointing performance is the major factor driving the E+ (Very Weak) TheStreet.com Investment Rating for *RBS US Mid Cap Trendpilot ETN. The fund currently has a performance rating of D- (Weak) based on an annualized return of 0.00% over the last three years and a total return of 7.97% year to date 2012. Factored into the performance evaluation is an expense ratio of 0.50% (very low).

The fund's risk rating is currently C (Fair). It carries a beta of 0.00, meaning the fund's expected move will be 0.0% for every 10% move in the market. Volatility, as measured by both the semi-deviation and a drawdown factor, is considered average. As of March 31, 2012, *RBS US Mid Cap Trendpilot ETN traded at a premium of .21% above its net asset value, which is worse than its one-year historical average premium of .12%.

This fund has been team managed for 1 year and currently receives a manager quality ranking of 10 (0=worst, 99=best). This fund offers an average level of risk but investors looking for strong performance will be frustrated.

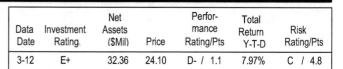

Annualized Total Return
— This Fund   --- S&P 500   Avg for Fund Type

*RevenueShares ADR Fund (RTR)

D+   **Weak**

Fund Family: VTL Associates LLC
Fund Type: Income
Inception Date: November 18, 2008

Data Date	Investment Rating	Net Assets ($Mil)	Price	Performance Rating/Pts	Total Return Y-T-D	Risk Rating/Pts
3-12	D+	41.08	35.16	C- / 3.3	10.90%	B- / 7.4
2011	C-	38.10	31.71	C- / 3.2	1.83%	B- / 7.4
2010	A	59.10	38.13	B+ / 8.6	6.85%	B- / 7.1
2009	A+	7.52	36.38	B+ / 8.7	38.63%	B- / 7.4

Major Rating Factors: *RevenueShares ADR Fund receives a TheStreet.com Investment Rating of D+ (Weak). The fund currently has a performance rating of C- (Fair) based on an annualized return of 14.70% over the last three years and a total return of 10.90% year to date 2012. Factored into the performance evaluation is an expense ratio of 0.49% (very low).

The fund's risk rating is currently B- (Good). It carries a beta of 1.37, meaning it is expected to move 13.7% for every 10% move in the market. Volatility, as measured by both the semi-deviation and a drawdown factor, is considered low. As of March 31, 2012, *RevenueShares ADR Fund traded at a price exactly equal to its net asset value, which is worse than its one-year historical average discount of .02%.

Michael Gompers currently receives a manager quality ranking of 12 (0=worst, 99=best). If you desire an average level of risk, then this fund may be an option.

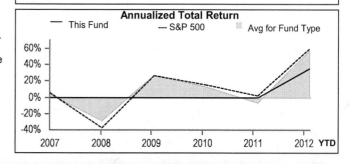

Annualized Total Return
— This Fund   --- S&P 500   Avg for Fund Type

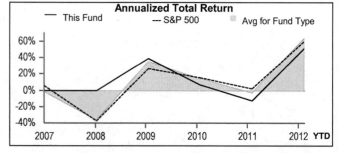

*RevenueShares Financials Sector (RWW)   C   Fair

Fund Family: VTL Associates LLC
Fund Type: Financial Services
Inception Date: November 10, 2008

Major Rating Factors: Middle of the road best describes *RevenueShares Financials Sector whose TheStreet.com Investment Rating is currently a C (Fair). The fund currently has a performance rating of C+ (Fair) based on an annualized return of 21.19% over the last three years and a total return of 27.48% year to date 2012. Factored into the performance evaluation is an expense ratio of 0.49% (very low).

The fund's risk rating is currently C+ (Fair). It carries a beta of 1.19, meaning it is expected to move 11.9% for every 10% move in the market. Volatility, as measured by both the semi-deviation and a drawdown factor, is considered low. As of March 31, 2012, *RevenueShares Financials Sector traded at a premium of .03% above its net asset value, which is better than its one-year historical average premium of .07%.

Vincent T. Lowry has been running the fund for 4 years and currently receives a manager quality ranking of 29 (0=worst, 99=best). If you desire an average level of risk, then this fund may be an option.

Data Date	Investment Rating	Net Assets ($Mil)	Price	Performance Rating/Pts	Total Return Y-T-D	Risk Rating/Pts
3-12	C	8.47	30.48	C+ / 6.1	27.48%	C+ / 6.8
2011	D	7.20	23.91	D / 2.1	2.80%	C+ / 6.1
2010	A-	20.70	31.84	A- / 9.0	15.52%	C / 5.3
2009	B	5.59	27.63	B / 8.2	27.10%	C / 5.2

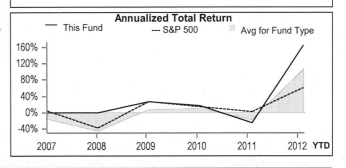

Annualized Total Return

*RevenueShares Large Cap Fund (RWL)   C+   Fair

Fund Family: VTL Associates LLC
Fund Type: Growth
Inception Date: February 22, 2008

Major Rating Factors: Middle of the road best describes *RevenueShares Large Cap Fund whose TheStreet.com Investment Rating is currently a C+ (Fair). The fund currently has a performance rating of C+ (Fair) based on an annualized return of 21.98% over the last three years and a total return of 12.27% year to date 2012. Factored into the performance evaluation is an expense ratio of 0.49% (very low).

The fund's risk rating is currently B (Good). It carries a beta of 1.08, meaning that its performance tracks fairly well with that of the overall stock market. Volatility, as measured by both the semi-deviation and a drawdown factor, is considered low. As of March 31, 2012, *RevenueShares Large Cap Fund traded at a discount of .04% below its net asset value, which is better than its one-year historical average premium of .02%.

Vincent T. Lowry has been running the fund for 4 years and currently receives a manager quality ranking of 41 (0=worst, 99=best). If you desire an average level of risk, then this fund may be an option.

Data Date	Investment Rating	Net Assets ($Mil)	Price	Performance Rating/Pts	Total Return Y-T-D	Risk Rating/Pts
3-12	C+	160.21	26.13	C+ / 6.0	12.27%	B / 8.3
2011	C	162.90	23.27	C / 5.1	1.80%	B / 8.0
2010	B-	188.90	23.64	A- / 9.2	16.38%	C- / 3.6
2009	C+	53.23	20.53	B+ / 8.4	26.40%	C- / 3.4

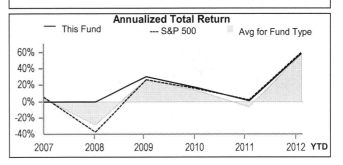

Annualized Total Return

*RevenueShares Mid Cap Fund (RWK)   B-   Good

Fund Family: VTL Associates LLC
Fund Type: Growth
Inception Date: February 22, 2008

Major Rating Factors: Strong performance is the major factor driving the B- (Good) TheStreet.com Investment Rating for *RevenueShares Mid Cap Fund. The fund currently has a performance rating of B- (Good) based on an annualized return of 27.15% over the last three years and a total return of 14.07% year to date 2012. Factored into the performance evaluation is an expense ratio of 0.54% (very low).

The fund's risk rating is currently B- (Good). It carries a beta of 1.34, meaning it is expected to move 13.4% for every 10% move in the market. Volatility, as measured by both the semi-deviation and a drawdown factor, is considered low. As of March 31, 2012, *RevenueShares Mid Cap Fund traded at a premium of .12% above its net asset value, which is worse than its one-year historical average discount of .05%.

Vincent T. Lowry has been running the fund for 4 years and currently receives a manager quality ranking of 38 (0=worst, 99=best). If you desire only a moderate level of risk and strong performance, then this fund is an excellent option.

Data Date	Investment Rating	Net Assets ($Mil)	Price	Performance Rating/Pts	Total Return Y-T-D	Risk Rating/Pts
3-12	B-	139.21	32.12	B- / 7.5	14.07%	B- / 7.8
2011	B-	126.70	28.16	C+ / 6.9	1.80%	B- / 7.6
2010	B-	138.60	29.51	A / 9.4	23.00%	C- / 3.3
2009	C+	30.17	24.10	A- / 9.1	47.01%	C- / 3.2

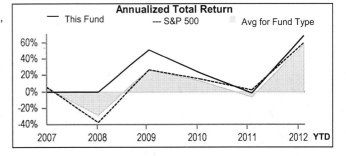

Annualized Total Return

*RevenueShares Navellier OA A100 (RWV)

C   **Fair**

Fund Family: VTL Associates LLC
Fund Type: Income
Inception Date: January 21, 2009

Major Rating Factors: Middle of the road best describes *RevenueShares Navellier OA A100 whose TheStreet.com Investment Rating is currently a C (Fair). The fund currently has a performance rating of C- (Fair) based on an annualized return of 17.54% over the last three years and a total return of 11.04% year to date 2012. Factored into the performance evaluation is an expense ratio of 0.60% (very low).

The fund's risk rating is currently B- (Good). It carries a beta of 1.02, meaning that its performance tracks fairly well with that of the overall stock market. Volatility, as measured by both the semi-deviation and a drawdown factor, is considered low. As of March 31, 2012, *RevenueShares Navellier OA A100 traded at a premium of .35% above its net asset value, which is worse than its one-year historical average premium of .07%.

Michael Gompers currently receives a manager quality ranking of 25 (0=worst, 99=best). If you desire an average level of risk, then this fund may be an option.

Data Date	Investment Rating	Net Assets ($Mil)	Price	Performance Rating/Pts	Total Return Y-T-D	Risk Rating/Pts
3-12	C	7.74	39.90	C- / 4.2	11.04%	B- / 7.9
2011	D	9.00	35.93	D- / 1.4	1.00%	B- / 7.9
2010	A+	9.60	38.66	A / 9.5	21.99%	B- / 7.8

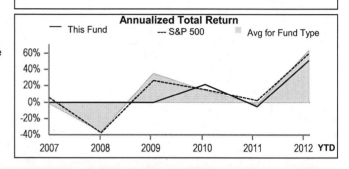

---

*RevenueShares Small Cap Fund (RWJ)

B+   **Good**

Fund Family: VTL Associates LLC
Fund Type: Growth
Inception Date: February 22, 2008

Major Rating Factors: Strong performance is the major factor driving the B+ (Good) TheStreet.com Investment Rating for *RevenueShares Small Cap Fund. The fund currently has a performance rating of B+ (Good) based on an annualized return of 31.36% over the last three years and a total return of 13.31% year to date 2012. Factored into the performance evaluation is an expense ratio of 0.54% (very low).

The fund's risk rating is currently B- (Good). It carries a beta of 1.48, meaning it is expected to move 14.8% for every 10% move in the market. Volatility, as measured by both the semi-deviation and a drawdown factor, is considered low. As of March 31, 2012, *RevenueShares Small Cap Fund traded at a premium of .30% above its net asset value, which is worse than its one-year historical average discount of .04%.

Vincent T. Lowry has been running the fund for 4 years and currently receives a manager quality ranking of 40 (0=worst, 99=best). If you desire only a moderate level of risk and strong performance, then this fund is an excellent option.

Data Date	Investment Rating	Net Assets ($Mil)	Price	Performance Rating/Pts	Total Return Y-T-D	Risk Rating/Pts
3-12	B+	132.83	36.34	B+ / 8.5	13.31%	B- / 7.7
2011	B-	104.30	32.07	B- / 7.3	1.40%	B- / 7.4
2010	B	128.20	32.49	A / 9.5	25.66%	C- / 3.3
2009	C+	32.10	25.90	A- / 9.0	44.07%	C- / 3.2

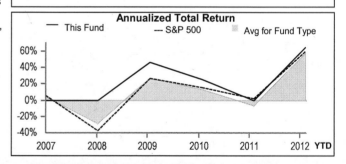

---

*Russell Equity ETF (ONEF)

D+   **Weak**

Fund Family: Russell Investment Management Compa
Fund Type: Global
Inception Date: May 11, 2010

Major Rating Factors:
Disappointing performance is the major factor driving the D+ (Weak) TheStreet.com Investment Rating for *Russell Equity ETF. The fund currently has a performance rating of D+ (Weak) based on an annualized return of 0.00% over the last three years and a total return of 12.17% year to date 2012. Factored into the performance evaluation is an expense ratio of 0.53% (very low).

The fund's risk rating is currently B- (Good). It carries a beta of 0.00, meaning the fund's expected move will be 0.0% for every 10% move in the market. Volatility, as measured by the semi-deviation and a drawdown factor, is considered low. As of March 31, 2012, *Russell Equity ETF traded at a discount of .39% below its net asset value, which is better than its one-year historical average discount of .02%.

Paul Hrabal has been running the fund for 2 years and currently receives a manager quality ranking of 59 (0=worst, 99=best). This fund offers only a moderate level of risk but investors looking for strong performance are still waiting.

Data Date	Investment Rating	Net Assets ($Mil)	Price	Performance Rating/Pts	Total Return Y-T-D	Risk Rating/Pts
3-12	D+	5.63	28.43	D+ / 2.7	12.17%	B- / 7.9
2011	D	6.40	25.38	D- / 1.3	1.30%	B- / 7.9

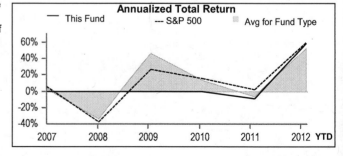

---

*Schwab Emerging Markets Equity E (SCHE)   D   Weak

Fund Family: Charles Schwab Investment Managemen
Fund Type: Foreign
Inception Date: January 13, 2010

Data Date	Investment Rating	Net Assets ($Mil)	Price	Perfor-mance Rating/Pts	Total Return Y-T-D	Risk Rating/Pts
3-12	D	562.88	25.78	D / 2.1	12.72%	B- / 7.0
2011	D	0.00	22.87	D- / 1.0	1.05%	B- / 7.0

Major Rating Factors:
Disappointing performance is the major factor driving the D (Weak) TheStreet.com Investment Rating for *Schwab Emerging Markets Equity E. The fund currently has a performance rating of D (Weak) based on an annualized return of 0.00% over the last three years and a total return of 12.72% year to date 2012. Factored into the performance evaluation is an expense ratio of 0.25% (very low).

The fund's risk rating is currently B- (Good). It carries a beta of 0.00, meaning the fund's expected move will be 0.0% for every 10% move in the market. Volatility, as measured by both the semi-deviation and a drawdown factor, is considered low. As of March 31, 2012, *Schwab Emerging Markets Equity E traded at a premium of .62% above its net asset value, which is worse than its one-year historical average premium of .32%.

Agnes Hong has been running the fund for 2 years and currently receives a manager quality ranking of 27 (0=worst, 99=best). This fund offers only a moderate level of risk but investors looking for strong performance are still waiting.

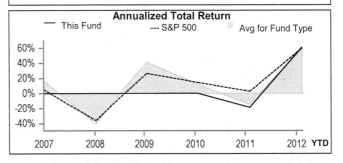

Annualized Total Return

*Schwab International Equity ETF (SCHF)   D   Weak

Fund Family: Charles Schwab Investment Managemen
Fund Type: Foreign
Inception Date: October 30, 2009

Data Date	Investment Rating	Net Assets ($Mil)	Price	Perfor-mance Rating/Pts	Total Return Y-T-D	Risk Rating/Pts
3-12	D	757.42	26.02	D / 2.0	11.05%	B- / 7.6
2011	D	632.50	23.43	D- / 1.1	-0.17%	B- / 7.4
2010	A+	359.70	27.69	B+ / 8.7	9.26%	B- / 7.7

Major Rating Factors:
Disappointing performance is the major factor driving the D (Weak) TheStreet.com Investment Rating for *Schwab International Equity ETF. The fund currently has a performance rating of D (Weak) based on an annualized return of 0.00% over the last three years and a total return of 11.05% year to date 2012. Factored into the performance evaluation is an expense ratio of 0.13% (very low).

The fund's risk rating is currently B- (Good). It carries a beta of 0.00, meaning the fund's expected move will be 0.0% for every 10% move in the market. Volatility, as measured by both the semi-deviation and a drawdown factor, is considered low. As of March 31, 2012, *Schwab International Equity ETF traded at a premium of .66% above its net asset value, which is worse than its one-year historical average premium of .44%.

Agnes Hong has been running the fund for 3 years and currently receives a manager quality ranking of 36 (0=worst, 99=best). This fund offers only a moderate level of risk but investors looking for strong performance are still waiting.

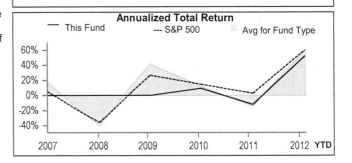

Annualized Total Return

*Schwab Intl Small-Cap Equity ETF (SCHC)   D   Weak

Fund Family: Charles Schwab Investment Managemen
Fund Type: Foreign
Inception Date: January 13, 2010

Data Date	Investment Rating	Net Assets ($Mil)	Price	Perfor-mance Rating/Pts	Total Return Y-T-D	Risk Rating/Pts
3-12	D	170.04	26.41	D / 1.8	12.96%	C+ / 6.8
2011	D-	137.80	23.38	E+ / 0.9	0.38%	C+ / 6.1

Major Rating Factors:
Disappointing performance is the major factor driving the D (Weak) TheStreet.com Investment Rating for *Schwab Intl Small-Cap Equity ETF. The fund currently has a performance rating of D (Weak) based on an annualized return of 0.00% over the last three years and a total return of 12.96% year to date 2012. Factored into the performance evaluation is an expense ratio of 0.35% (very low).

The fund's risk rating is currently C+ (Fair). It carries a beta of 0.00, meaning the fund's expected move will be 0.0% for every 10% move in the market. Volatility, as measured by both the semi-deviation and a drawdown factor, is considered low. As of March 31, 2012, *Schwab Intl Small-Cap Equity ETF traded at a premium of .88% above its net asset value, which is worse than its one-year historical average premium of .30%.

Agnes Hong has been running the fund for 2 years and currently receives a manager quality ranking of 25 (0=worst, 99=best). This fund offers only a moderate level of risk but investors looking for strong performance are still waiting.

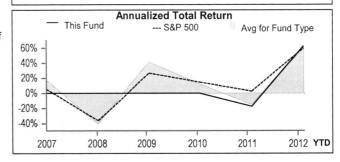

Annualized Total Return

*Schwab Intmdt-Term US Treasury E (SCHR)

C-   **Fair**

Fund Family: Charles Schwab Investment Managemen
Fund Type: US Government/Agency
Inception Date: August 4, 2010

Major Rating Factors:
Disappointing performance is the major factor driving the C- (Fair) TheStreet.com Investment Rating for *Schwab Intmdt-Term US Treasury E. The fund currently has a performance rating of D (Weak) based on an annualized return of 0.00% over the last three years and a total return of -1.09% year to date 2012. Factored into the performance evaluation is an expense ratio of 0.12% (very low).

The fund's risk rating is currently B+ (Good). It carries a beta of 0.00, meaning the fund's expected move will be 0.0% for every 10% move in the market. Volatility, as measured by both the semi-deviation and a drawdown factor, is considered very low. As of March 31, 2012, *Schwab Intmdt-Term US Treasury E traded at a discount of .02% below its net asset value, which is better than its one-year historical average premium of .04%.

Matthew Hastings has been running the fund for 2 years and currently receives a manager quality ranking of 68 (0=worst, 99=best). This fund offers only a moderate level of risk but investors looking for strong performance are still waiting.

Data Date	Investment Rating	Net Assets ($Mil)	Price	Performance Rating/Pts	Total Return Y-T-D	Risk Rating/Pts
3-12	C-	160.08	52.83	D / 1.8	-1.09%	B+ / 9.7
2011	C+	117.50	53.52	C- / 4.1	-0.32%	B+ / 9.7

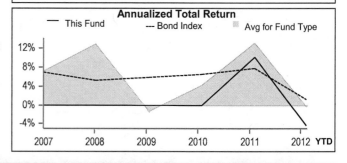

*Schwab Short-Term US Treas ETF (SCHO)

C-   **Fair**

Fund Family: Charles Schwab Investment Managemen
Fund Type: US Government/Agency
Inception Date: August 4, 2010

Major Rating Factors:
Disappointing performance is the major factor driving the C- (Fair) TheStreet.com Investment Rating for *Schwab Short-Term US Treas ETF. The fund currently has a performance rating of D- (Weak) based on an annualized return of 0.00% over the last three years and a total return of -0.21% year to date 2012. Factored into the performance evaluation is an expense ratio of 0.12% (very low).

The fund's risk rating is currently B+ (Good). It carries a beta of 0.00, meaning the fund's expected move will be 0.0% for every 10% move in the market. Volatility, as measured by both the semi-deviation and a drawdown factor, is considered very low. As of March 31, 2012, *Schwab Short-Term US Treas ETF traded at a price exactly equal to its net asset value, which is better than its one-year historical average premium of .04%.

Matthew Hastings has been running the fund for 2 years and currently receives a manager quality ranking of 51 (0=worst, 99=best). This fund offers only a moderate level of risk but investors looking for strong performance are still waiting.

Data Date	Investment Rating	Net Assets ($Mil)	Price	Performance Rating/Pts	Total Return Y-T-D	Risk Rating/Pts
3-12	C-	181.69	50.42	D- / 1.2	-0.21%	B+ / 9.9
2011	C	197.00	50.54	D / 2.2	-0.06%	B+ / 9.9

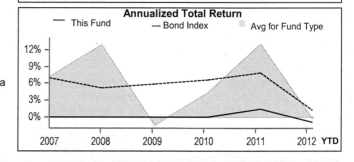

*Schwab US Broad Market ETF (SCHB)

C+   **Fair**

Fund Family: Charles Schwab Investment Managemen
Fund Type: Income
Inception Date: October 30, 2009

Major Rating Factors: Middle of the road best describes *Schwab US Broad Market ETF whose TheStreet.com Investment Rating is currently a C+ (Fair). The fund currently has a performance rating of C+ (Fair) based on an annualized return of 0.00% over the last three years and a total return of 12.74% year to date 2012. Factored into the performance evaluation is an expense ratio of 0.06% (very low).

The fund's risk rating is currently B (Good). It carries a beta of 0.00, meaning the fund's expected move will be 0.0% for every 10% move in the market. Volatility, as measured by both the semi-deviation and a drawdown factor, is considered low. As of March 31, 2012, *Schwab US Broad Market ETF traded at a premium of .03% above its net asset value, which is worse than its one-year historical average premium of .02%.

Agnes Hong has been running the fund for 3 years and currently receives a manager quality ranking of 36 (0=worst, 99=best). If you desire an average level of risk, then this fund may be an option.

Data Date	Investment Rating	Net Assets ($Mil)	Price	Performance Rating/Pts	Total Return Y-T-D	Risk Rating/Pts
3-12	C+	993.16	33.92	C+ / 6.1	12.74%	B / 8.1
2011	C-	815.30	30.22	D+ / 2.8	1.75%	B / 8.1
2010	A+	405.40	30.38	A- / 9.2	17.11%	B- / 7.8

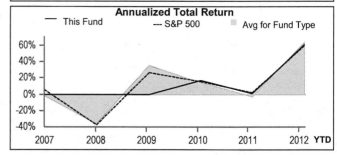

*Schwab US Large-Cap ETF (SCHX)   C+   Fair

Fund Family: Charles Schwab Investment Managemen
Fund Type: Income
Inception Date: October 30, 2009

Major Rating Factors: Middle of the road best describes *Schwab US Large-Cap ETF whose TheStreet.com Investment Rating is currently a C+ (Fair). The fund currently has a performance rating of C+ (Fair) based on an annualized return of 0.00% over the last three years and a total return of 12.76% year to date 2012. Factored into the performance evaluation is an expense ratio of 0.08% (very low).

The fund's risk rating is currently B (Good). It carries a beta of 0.00, meaning the fund's expected move will be 0.0% for every 10% move in the market. Volatility, as measured by both the semi-deviation and a drawdown factor, is considered low. As of March 31, 2012, *Schwab US Large-Cap ETF traded at a price exactly equal to its net asset value, which is better than its one-year historical average premium of .02%.

Agnes Hong has been running the fund for 3 years and currently receives a manager quality ranking of 41 (0=worst, 99=best). If you desire an average level of risk, then this fund may be an option.

Data Date	Investment Rating	Net Assets ($Mil)	Price	Performance Rating/Pts	Total Return Y-T-D	Risk Rating/Pts
3-12	C+	823.89	33.51	C+ / 6.2	12.76%	B / 8.2
2011	C-	704.30	29.85	D+ / 2.8	1.71%	B / 8.2
2010	A+	368.00	29.96	A- / 9.2	15.93%	B- / 7.8

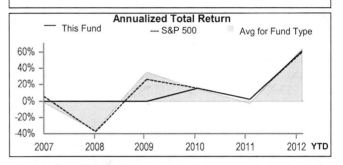

Annualized Total Return

---

*Schwab US Large-Cap Growth ETF (SCHG)   B-   Good

Fund Family: Charles Schwab Investment Managemen
Fund Type: Growth
Inception Date: December 9, 2009

Major Rating Factors: Strong performance is the major factor driving the B- (Good) TheStreet.com Investment Rating for *Schwab US Large-Cap Growth ETF. The fund currently has a performance rating of B- (Good) based on an annualized return of 0.00% over the last three years and a total return of 15.71% year to date 2012. Factored into the performance evaluation is an expense ratio of 0.13% (very low).

The fund's risk rating is currently B (Good). It carries a beta of 0.00, meaning the fund's expected move will be 0.0% for every 10% move in the market. Volatility, as measured by both the semi-deviation and a drawdown factor, is considered low. As of March 31, 2012, *Schwab US Large-Cap Growth ETF traded at a premium of .06% above its net asset value, which is worse than its one-year historical average premium of .02%.

Agnes Hong has been running the fund for 3 years and currently receives a manager quality ranking of 38 (0=worst, 99=best). If you desire only a moderate level of risk and strong performance, then this fund is an excellent option.

Data Date	Investment Rating	Net Assets ($Mil)	Price	Performance Rating/Pts	Total Return Y-T-D	Risk Rating/Pts
3-12	B-	394.93	34.21	B- / 7.1	15.71%	B / 8.0
2011	D+	324.40	29.63	D+ / 2.3	2.40%	B / 8.0
2010	A+	162.30	30.16	A- / 9.2	16.85%	B- / 7.6

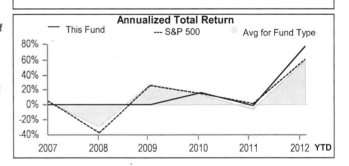

Annualized Total Return

---

*Schwab US Large-Cap Value ETF (SCHV)   C+   Fair

Fund Family: Charles Schwab Investment Managemen
Fund Type: Income
Inception Date: December 9, 2009

Major Rating Factors: Middle of the road best describes *Schwab US Large-Cap Value ETF whose TheStreet.com Investment Rating is currently a C+ (Fair). The fund currently has a performance rating of C (Fair) based on an annualized return of 0.00% over the last three years and a total return of 10.17% year to date 2012. Factored into the performance evaluation is an expense ratio of 0.13% (very low).

The fund's risk rating is currently B (Good). It carries a beta of 0.00, meaning the fund's expected move will be 0.0% for every 10% move in the market. Volatility, as measured by both the semi-deviation and a drawdown factor, is considered low. As of March 31, 2012, *Schwab US Large-Cap Value ETF traded at a price exactly equal to its net asset value, which is better than its one-year historical average premium of .02%.

Agnes Hong has been running the fund for 3 years and currently receives a manager quality ranking of 44 (0=worst, 99=best). If you desire an average level of risk, then this fund may be an option.

Data Date	Investment Rating	Net Assets ($Mil)	Price	Performance Rating/Pts	Total Return Y-T-D	Risk Rating/Pts
3-12	C+	306.32	31.18	C / 5.3	10.17%	B / 8.3
2011	C-	256.50	28.49	C- / 3.4	1.16%	B / 8.3
2010	A+	114.10	28.25	A- / 9.0	14.86%	B- / 7.8

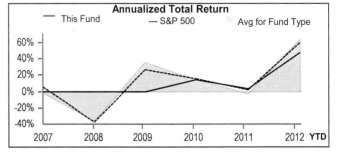

Annualized Total Return

*Schwab US Mid-Cap ETF (SCHM)   C   Fair

Fund Family: Charles Schwab Investment Managemen
Fund Type: Growth
Inception Date: January 12, 2011

Major Rating Factors: Middle of the road best describes *Schwab US Mid-Cap ETF whose TheStreet.com Investment Rating is currently a C (Fair). The fund currently has a performance rating of C (Fair) based on an annualized return of 0.00% over the last three years and a total return of 13.29% year to date 2012. Factored into the performance evaluation is an expense ratio of 0.13% (very low).

The fund's risk rating is currently B- (Good). It carries a beta of 0.00, meaning the fund's expected move will be 0.0% for every 10% move in the market. Volatility, as measured by both the semi-deviation and a drawdown factor, is considered low. As of March 31, 2012, *Schwab US Mid-Cap ETF traded at a price exactly equal to its net asset value, which is better than its one-year historical average premium of .05%.

Agnes Hong has been running the fund for 1 year and currently receives a manager quality ranking of 17 (0=worst, 99=best). If you desire an average level of risk, then this fund may be an option.

Data Date	Investment Rating	Net Assets ($Mil)	Price	Performance Rating/Pts	Total Return Y-T-D	Risk Rating/Pts
3-12	C	197.73	27.25	C / 5.4	13.29%	B- / 7.5

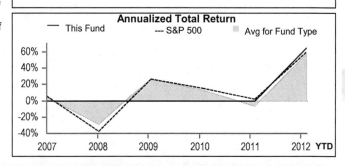

*Schwab US REIT ETF (SCHH)   B-   Good

Fund Family: Charles Schwab Investment Managemen
Fund Type: Growth and Income
Inception Date: January 12, 2011

Major Rating Factors: Strong performance is the major factor driving the B- (Good) TheStreet.com Investment Rating for *Schwab US REIT ETF. The fund currently has a performance rating of B- (Good) based on an annualized return of 0.00% over the last three years and a total return of 10.56% year to date 2012. Factored into the performance evaluation is an expense ratio of 0.13% (very low).

The fund's risk rating is currently B- (Good). It carries a beta of 0.00, meaning the fund's expected move will be 0.0% for every 10% move in the market. Volatility, as measured by both the semi-deviation and a drawdown factor, is considered low. As of March 31, 2012, *Schwab US REIT ETF traded at a discount of .07% below its net asset value, which is better than its one-year historical average premium of .02%.

Agnes Hong currently receives a manager quality ranking of 62 (0=worst, 99=best). If you desire only a moderate level of risk and strong performance, then this fund is an excellent option.

Data Date	Investment Rating	Net Assets ($Mil)	Price	Performance Rating/Pts	Total Return Y-T-D	Risk Rating/Pts
3-12	B-	278.78	29.57	B- / 7.3	10.56%	B- / 7.8

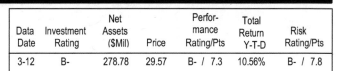
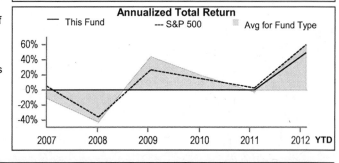

*Schwab US Small-Cap ETF (SCHA)   C   Fair

Fund Family: Charles Schwab Investment Managemen
Fund Type: Growth
Inception Date: October 30, 2009

Major Rating Factors: Middle of the road best describes *Schwab US Small-Cap ETF whose TheStreet.com Investment Rating is currently a C (Fair). The fund currently has a performance rating of C (Fair) based on an annualized return of 0.00% over the last three years and a total return of 13.25% year to date 2012. Factored into the performance evaluation is an expense ratio of 0.13% (very low).

The fund's risk rating is currently B- (Good). It carries a beta of 0.00, meaning the fund's expected move will be 0.0% for every 10% move in the market. Volatility, as measured by both the semi-deviation and a drawdown factor, is considered low. As of March 31, 2012, *Schwab US Small-Cap ETF traded at a premium of .05% above its net asset value, which is worse than its one-year historical average premium of .03%.

Agnes Hong has been running the fund for 3 years and currently receives a manager quality ranking of 14 (0=worst, 99=best). If you desire an average level of risk, then this fund may be an option.

Data Date	Investment Rating	Net Assets ($Mil)	Price	Performance Rating/Pts	Total Return Y-T-D	Risk Rating/Pts
3-12	C	626.78	37.08	C / 5.1	13.25%	B- / 7.4
2011	D	506.10	32.84	D / 1.9	1.64%	B- / 7.4
2010	A+	277.00	34.30	A+ / 9.6	28.64%	B- / 7.5

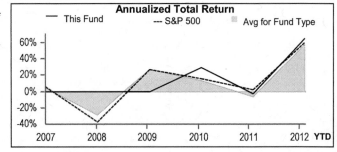

*Schwab US TIPS ETF (SCHP)

C   **Fair**

Fund Family: Charles Schwab Investment Managemen
Fund Type: General - Investment Grade
Inception Date: August 4, 2010

Major Rating Factors:
Disappointing performance is the major factor driving the C (Fair) TheStreet.com Investment Rating for *Schwab US TIPS ETF. The fund currently has a performance rating of D+ (Weak) based on an annualized return of 0.00% over the last three years and a total return of 0.59% year to date 2012. Factored into the performance evaluation is an expense ratio of 0.14% (very low).

The fund's risk rating is currently B+ (Good). It carries a beta of 0.00, meaning the fund's expected move will be 0.0% for every 10% move in the market. Volatility, as measured by both the semi-deviation and a drawdown factor, is considered very low. As of March 31, 2012, *Schwab US TIPS ETF traded at a premium of .11% above its net asset value, which is better than its one-year historical average premium of .12%.

Matthew Hastings has been running the fund for 2 years and currently receives a manager quality ranking of 65 (0=worst, 99=best). This fund offers only a moderate level of risk but investors looking for strong performance are still waiting.

Data Date	Investment Rating	Net Assets ($Mil)	Price	Performance Rating/Pts	Total Return Y-T-D	Risk Rating/Pts
3-12	C	350.49	55.95	D+ / 2.3	0.59%	B+ / 9.8
2011	B-	288.40	55.62	C / 4.9	0.50%	B+ / 9.8

Annualized Total Return

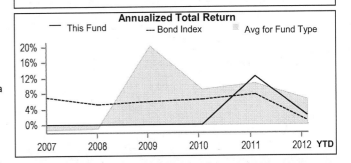

*SP Bank ETF (KBE)

C-   **Fair**

Fund Family: SSgA Funds Management Inc
Fund Type: Financial Services
Inception Date: November 8, 2005

Major Rating Factors: Middle of the road best describes *SP Bank ETF whose TheStreet.com Investment Rating is currently a C- (Fair). The fund currently has a performance rating of C (Fair) based on an annualized return of 17.45% over the last three years and a total return of 20.63% year to date 2012. Factored into the performance evaluation is an expense ratio of 0.36% (very low).

The fund's risk rating is currently B- (Good). It carries a beta of 1.16, meaning it is expected to move 11.6% for every 10% move in the market. Volatility, as measured by both the semi-deviation and a drawdown factor, is considered low. As of March 31, 2012, *SP Bank ETF traded at a discount of .33% below its net asset value.

John A. Tucker has been running the fund for 7 years and currently receives a manager quality ranking of 23 (0=worst, 99=best). If you desire an average level of risk, then this fund may be an option.

Data Date	Investment Rating	Net Assets ($Mil)	Price	Performance Rating/Pts	Total Return Y-T-D	Risk Rating/Pts
3-12	C-	1,873.40	23.85	C / 4.6	20.63%	B- / 7.0
2011	D	1,140.60	19.83	D / 2.1	4.84%	C+ / 6.4
2010	D-	1,988.30	25.91	D- / 1.0	23.06%	C- / 4.0
2009	E+	821.69	21.17	E / 0.5	-3.26%	C- / 4.1

Annualized Total Return

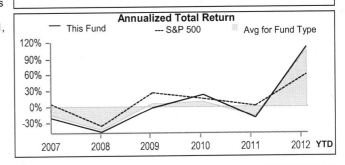

*SP Capital Markets ETF (KCE)

D   **Weak**

Fund Family: SSgA Funds Management Inc
Fund Type: Financial Services
Inception Date: November 8, 2005

Major Rating Factors:
Disappointing performance is the major factor driving the D (Weak) TheStreet.com Investment Rating for *SP Capital Markets ETF. The fund currently has a performance rating of D+ (Weak) based on an annualized return of 8.48% over the last three years and a total return of 22.06% year to date 2012. Factored into the performance evaluation is an expense ratio of 0.38% (very low).

The fund's risk rating is currently C+ (Fair). It carries a beta of 0.99, meaning that its performance tracks fairly well with that of the overall stock market. Volatility, as measured by both the semi-deviation and a drawdown factor, is considered low. As of March 31, 2012, *SP Capital Markets ETF traded at a premium of .12% above its net asset value, which is worse than its one-year historical average discount of .02%.

John A. Tucker has been running the fund for 7 years and currently receives a manager quality ranking of 15 (0=worst, 99=best). This fund offers only a moderate level of risk but investors looking for strong performance are still waiting.

Data Date	Investment Rating	Net Assets ($Mil)	Price	Performance Rating/Pts	Total Return Y-T-D	Risk Rating/Pts
3-12	D	37.36	34.01	D+ / 2.6	22.06%	C+ / 6.9
2011	D	22.40	27.95	D / 2.2	3.61%	C+ / 6.9
2010	D-	76.80	38.39	E+ / 0.9	6.23%	C / 4.8
2009	D-	80.19	36.78	E+ / 0.8	37.48%	C / 4.9

Annualized Total Return

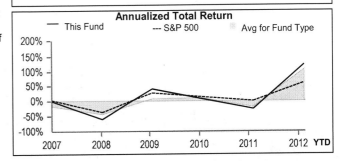

*SP Insurance ETF (KIE)

| | C+ | Fair |

Fund Family: SSgA Funds Management Inc
Fund Type: Income
Inception Date: November 8, 2005

Major Rating Factors: Strong performance is the major factor driving the C+ (Fair) TheStreet.com Investment Rating for *SP Insurance ETF. The fund currently has a performance rating of B- (Good) based on an annualized return of 26.42% over the last three years and a total return of 12.58% year to date 2012. Factored into the performance evaluation is an expense ratio of 0.37% (very low).

The fund's risk rating is currently B- (Good). It carries a beta of 1.46, meaning it is expected to move 14.6% for every 10% move in the market. Volatility, as measured by both the semi-deviation and a drawdown factor, is considered low. As of March 31, 2012, *SP Insurance ETF traded at a premium of .07% above its net asset value, which is worse than its one-year historical average discount of .01%.

John A. Tucker has been running the fund for 7 years and currently receives a manager quality ranking of 24 (0=worst, 99=best). If you desire only a moderate level of risk and strong performance, then this fund is an excellent option.

Data Date	Investment Rating	Net Assets ($Mil)	Price	Performance Rating/Pts	Total Return Y-T-D	Risk Rating/Pts
3-12	C+	135.76	41.80	B- / 7.0	12.58%	B- / 7.5
2011	C-	120.90	37.21	C / 4.3	0.59%	C+ / 6.7
2010	D+	236.80	43.03	C- / 3.7	26.06%	C / 4.5
2009	D-	139.21	34.71	D- / 1.1	26.28%	C / 4.5

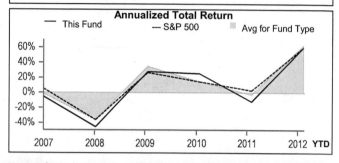

*SP Regional Banking ETF (KRE)

| | C- | Fair |

Fund Family: SSgA Funds Management Inc
Fund Type: Financial Services
Inception Date: June 19, 2006

Major Rating Factors: Middle of the road best describes *SP Regional Banking ETF whose TheStreet.com Investment Rating is currently a C- (Fair). The fund currently has a performance rating of C- (Fair) based on an annualized return of 12.73% over the last three years and a total return of 17.03% year to date 2012. Factored into the performance evaluation is an expense ratio of 0.36% (very low).

The fund's risk rating is currently B- (Good). It carries a beta of 0.88, meaning the fund's expected move will be 8.8% for every 10% move in the market. Volatility, as measured by both the semi-deviation and a drawdown factor, is considered low. As of March 31, 2012, *SP Regional Banking ETF traded at a premium of .11% above its net asset value.

John A. Tucker currently receives a manager quality ranking of 26 (0=worst, 99=best). If you desire an average level of risk, then this fund may be an option.

Data Date	Investment Rating	Net Assets ($Mil)	Price	Performance Rating/Pts	Total Return Y-T-D	Risk Rating/Pts
3-12	C-	1,180.48	28.47	C- / 4.2	17.03%	B- / 7.3
2011	D+	721.40	24.41	D+ / 2.9	4.59%	C+ / 6.8
2010	D	793.50	26.45	D+ / 2.3	20.66%	C / 5.3
2009	D-	434.94	22.25	E / 0.5	-21.83%	C / 5.2

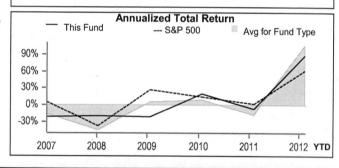

*SPDR Barclays Cap 1-3 Month T-B (BIL)

| | C- | Fair |

Fund Family: SSgA Funds Management Inc
Fund Type: US Government/Agency
Inception Date: May 25, 2007

Major Rating Factors:
Disappointing performance is the major factor driving the C- (Fair) TheStreet.com Investment Rating for *SPDR Barclays Cap 1-3 Month T-B. The fund currently has a performance rating of D- (Weak) based on an annualized return of -0.01% over the last three years and a total return of -0.02% year to date 2012. Factored into the performance evaluation is an expense ratio of 0.15% (very low).

The fund's risk rating is currently B+ (Good). It carries a beta of 0.00, meaning the fund's expected move will be 0.0% for every 10% move in the market. Volatility, as measured by both the semi-deviation and a drawdown factor, is considered very low. As of March 31, 2012, *SPDR Barclays Cap 1-3 Month T-B traded at a price exactly equal to its net asset value.

Steven R. Meier currently receives a manager quality ranking of 45 (0=worst, 99=best). This fund offers only a moderate level of risk but investors looking for strong performance are still waiting.

Data Date	Investment Rating	Net Assets ($Mil)	Price	Performance Rating/Pts	Total Return Y-T-D	Risk Rating/Pts
3-12	C-	1,063.09	45.82	D- / 1.2	-0.02%	B+ / 9.9
2011	C-	1,654.50	45.83	D / 1.9	-0.02%	B+ / 9.9
2010	C	1,013.40	45.85	D+ / 2.3	-0.04%	B+ / 9.0
2009	C	985.94	45.87	D / 1.9	0.25%	B+ / 9.1

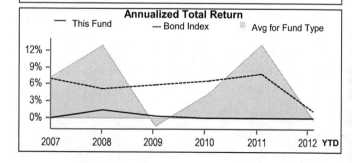

*SPDR Barclays Cap Aggregate Bd E (LAG)   C-   Fair

Fund Family: SSgA Funds Management Inc
Fund Type: General - Investment Grade
Inception Date: May 23, 2007

Data Date	Investment Rating	Net Assets ($Mil)	Price	Performance Rating/Pts	Total Return Y-T-D	Risk Rating/Pts
3-12	C-	305.91	57.75	D / 1.8	0.13%	B+ / 9.7
2011	C	306.20	57.90	C- / 3.2	-0.32%	B+ / 9.6
2010	B	222.40	55.56	C / 4.5	4.48%	B / 8.8
2009	C+	196.09	54.69	C- / 3.3	3.97%	B+ / 9.1

Major Rating Factors:
Disappointing performance is the major factor driving the C- (Fair) TheStreet.com Investment Rating for *SPDR Barclays Cap Aggregate Bd E. The fund currently has a performance rating of D (Weak) based on an annualized return of 6.20% over the last three years and a total return of 0.13% year to date 2012. Factored into the performance evaluation is an expense ratio of 0.15% (very low).

The fund's risk rating is currently B+ (Good). It carries a beta of 1.10, meaning it is expected to move 11.0% for every 10% move in the market. Volatility, as measured by both the semi-deviation and a drawdown factor, is considered very low. As of March 31, 2012, *SPDR Barclays Cap Aggregate Bd E traded at a premium of .05% above its net asset value, which is better than its one-year historical average premium of .12%.

John P. Kirby currently receives a manager quality ranking of 36 (0=worst, 99=best). This fund offers only a moderate level of risk but investors looking for strong performance are still waiting.

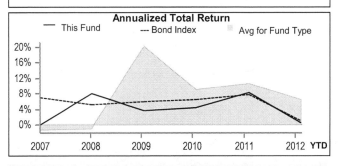

*SPDR Barclays Cap Conv Sec ETF (CWB)   C-   Fair

Fund Family: SSgA Funds Management Inc
Fund Type: Growth and Income
Inception Date: April 14, 2009

Data Date	Investment Rating	Net Assets ($Mil)	Price	Performance Rating/Pts	Total Return Y-T-D	Risk Rating/Pts
3-12	C-	871.18	39.86	D+ / 2.8	10.73%	B / 8.5
2011	D+	680.90	36.17	D- / 1.5	2.35%	B / 8.5
2010	A+	532.30	41.05	B+ / 8.6	13.01%	B / 8.4

Major Rating Factors:
Disappointing performance is the major factor driving the C- (Fair) TheStreet.com Investment Rating for *SPDR Barclays Cap Conv Sec ETF. The fund currently has a performance rating of D+ (Weak) based on an annualized return of 0.00% over the last three years and a total return of 10.73% year to date 2012. Factored into the performance evaluation is an expense ratio of 0.41% (very low).

The fund's risk rating is currently B (Good). It carries a beta of 0.00, meaning the fund's expected move will be 0.0% for every 10% move in the market. Volatility, as measured by both the semi-deviation and a drawdown factor, is considered low. As of March 31, 2012, *SPDR Barclays Cap Conv Sec ETF traded at a premium of .20% above its net asset value, which is worse than its one-year historical average discount of .05%.

Max DeSantis currently receives a manager quality ranking of 19 (0=worst, 99=best). This fund offers only a moderate level of risk but investors looking for strong performance are still waiting.

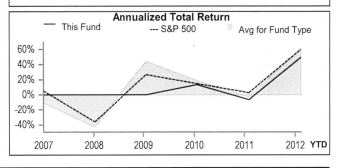

*SPDR Barclays Cap EM Loc Bond ET (EBND)   D+   Weak

Fund Family: SSgA Funds Management Inc
Fund Type: Growth and Income
Inception Date: February 23, 2011

Data Date	Investment Rating	Net Assets ($Mil)	Price	Performance Rating/Pts	Total Return Y-T-D	Risk Rating/Pts
3-12	D+	167.79	31.50	D+ / 2.3	6.67%	B / 8.6

Major Rating Factors:
Disappointing performance is the major factor driving the D+ (Weak) TheStreet.com Investment Rating for *SPDR Barclays Cap EM Loc Bond ET. The fund currently has a performance rating of D+ (Weak) based on an annualized return of 0.00% over the last three years and a total return of 6.67% year to date 2012. Factored into the performance evaluation is an expense ratio of 0.50% (very low).

The fund's risk rating is currently B (Good). It carries a beta of 0.00, meaning the fund's expected move will be 0.0% for every 10% move in the market. Volatility, as measured by both the semi-deviation and a drawdown factor, is considered low. As of March 31, 2012, *SPDR Barclays Cap EM Loc Bond ET traded at a premium of 1.38% above its net asset value, which is worse than its one-year historical average premium of 1.15%.

Abhishek Kumar currently receives a manager quality ranking of 40 (0=worst, 99=best). This fund offers only a moderate level of risk but investors looking for strong performance are still waiting.

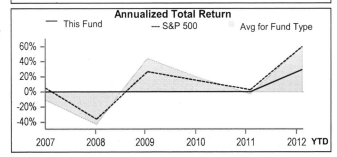

*SPDR Barclays Cap Hi Yld Bd ETF (JNK)

C- **Fair**

Fund Family: SSgA Funds Management Inc
Fund Type: Corporate - High Yield
Inception Date: November 28, 2007

Major Rating Factors: Middle of the road best describes *SPDR Barclays Cap Hi Yld Bd ETF whose TheStreet.com Investment Rating is currently a C- (Fair). The fund currently has a performance rating of C (Fair) based on an annualized return of 20.40% over the last three years and a total return of 3.57% year to date 2012. Factored into the performance evaluation is an expense ratio of 0.41% (very low).

The fund's risk rating is currently C+ (Fair). It carries a beta of 1.21, meaning it is expected to move 12.1% for every 10% move in the market. Volatility, as measured by both the semi-deviation and a drawdown factor, is considered low. As of March 31, 2012, *SPDR Barclays Cap Hi Yld Bd ETF traded at a discount of .13% below its net asset value, which is better than its one-year historical average premium of .27%.

John P. Kirby currently receives a manager quality ranking of 21 (0=worst, 99=best). If you desire an average level of risk, then this fund may be an option.

Data Date	Investment Rating	Net Assets ($Mil)	Price	Perfor- mance Rating/Pts	Total Return Y-T-D	Risk Rating/Pts
3-12	C-	12,027.91	39.37	C / 4.9	3.57%	C+ / 6.9
2011	B-	8,852.60	38.45	C+ / 6.1	0.05%	B / 8.6
2010	C+	6,315.30	39.71	C+ / 6.1	11.68%	C+ / 6.0
2009	B	1,900.71	38.81	B+ / 8.7	39.76%	C / 4.7

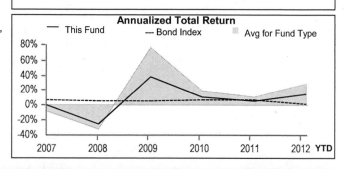

Annualized Total Return

*SPDR Barclays Cap Int Corp Bd ET (ITR)

C **Fair**

Fund Family: SSgA Funds Management Inc
Fund Type: General - Investment Grade
Inception Date: February 10, 2009

Major Rating Factors:
Disappointing performance is the major factor driving the C (Fair) TheStreet.com Investment Rating for *SPDR Barclays Cap Int Corp Bd ET. The fund currently has a performance rating of D+ (Weak) based on an annualized return of 9.64% over the last three years and a total return of 2.61% year to date 2012. Factored into the performance evaluation is an expense ratio of 0.16% (very low).

The fund's risk rating is currently B+ (Good). It carries a beta of 0.96, meaning that its performance tracks fairly well with that of the overall stock market. Volatility, as measured by both the semi-deviation and a drawdown factor, is considered very low. As of March 31, 2012, *SPDR Barclays Cap Int Corp Bd ET traded at a premium of .68% above its net asset value, which is worse than its one-year historical average premium of .50%.

Allen Kwong currently receives a manager quality ranking of 62 (0=worst, 99=best). This fund offers only a moderate level of risk but investors looking for strong performance are still waiting.

Data Date	Investment Rating	Net Assets ($Mil)	Price	Perfor- mance Rating/Pts	Total Return Y-T-D	Risk Rating/Pts
3-12	C	255.82	33.89	D+ / 2.4	2.61%	B+ / 9.7
2011	C	217.60	33.21	C- / 3.1	0.03%	B+ / 9.8
2010	B	143.10	32.56	C- / 4.2	6.35%	B / 8.9

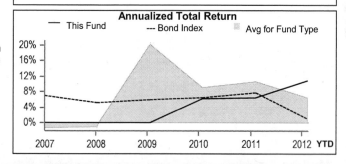

Annualized Total Return

*SPDR Barclays Cap Int Tr Treas E (ITE)

C- **Fair**

Fund Family: SSgA Funds Management Inc
Fund Type: US Government/Agency
Inception Date: May 23, 2007

Major Rating Factors:
Disappointing performance is the major factor driving the C- (Fair) TheStreet.com Investment Rating for *SPDR Barclays Cap Int Tr Treas E. The fund currently has a performance rating of D- (Weak) based on an annualized return of 3.47% over the last three years and a total return of -0.46% year to date 2012. Factored into the performance evaluation is an expense ratio of 0.16% (very low).

The fund's risk rating is currently B+ (Good). It carries a beta of 0.19, meaning the fund's expected move will be 1.9% for every 10% move in the market. Volatility, as measured by both the semi-deviation and a drawdown factor, is considered very low. As of March 31, 2012, *SPDR Barclays Cap Int Tr Treas E traded at a discount of .05% below its net asset value, which is better than its one-year historical average discount of .03%.

John P. Kirby currently receives a manager quality ranking of 57 (0=worst, 99=best). This fund offers only a moderate level of risk but investors looking for strong performance are still waiting.

Data Date	Investment Rating	Net Assets ($Mil)	Price	Perfor- mance Rating/Pts	Total Return Y-T-D	Risk Rating/Pts
3-12	C-	206.16	60.60	D- / 1.5	-0.46%	B+ / 9.8
2011	C	226.10	61.05	D+ / 2.8	-0.16%	B+ / 9.8
2010	B	205.30	58.57	C- / 3.9	4.53%	B+ / 9.1
2009	C	143.07	57.07	D / 1.7	-1.02%	B+ / 9.2

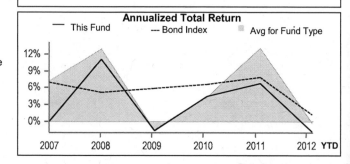

Annualized Total Return

*SPDR Barclays Cap Intl Corp Bd E (IBND)

D+   **Weak**

Fund Family: SSgA Funds Management Inc
Fund Type: Corporate - Investment Grade
Inception Date: May 19, 2010

Data Date	Investment Rating	Net Assets ($Mil)	Price	Performance Rating/Pts	Total Return Y-T-D	Risk Rating/Pts
3-12	D+	63.96	33.96	D / 2.1	7.74%	B / 8.7
2011	D+	53.60	31.52	D- / 1.4	-1.52%	B / 8.7

Major Rating Factors:
Disappointing performance is the major factor driving the D+ (Weak) TheStreet.com Investment Rating for *SPDR Barclays Cap Intl Corp Bd E. The fund currently has a performance rating of D (Weak) based on an annualized return of 0.00% over the last three years and a total return of 7.74% year to date 2012. Factored into the performance evaluation is an expense ratio of 0.55% (very low).

The fund's risk rating is currently B (Good). It carries a beta of 0.00, meaning the fund's expected move will be 0.0% for every 10% move in the market. Volatility, as measured by both the semi-deviation and a drawdown factor, is considered low. As of March 31, 2012, *SPDR Barclays Cap Intl Corp Bd E traded at a premium of .89% above its net asset value, which is worse than its one-year historical average premium of .28%.

John P. Philpot currently receives a manager quality ranking of 16 (0=worst, 99=best). This fund offers only a moderate level of risk but investors looking for strong performance are still waiting.

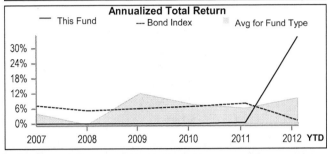

Annualized Total Return
— This Fund   --- Bond Index   Avg for Fund Type

*SPDR Barclays Cap Intl Treas Bd (BWX)

D+   **Weak**

Fund Family: SSgA Funds Management Inc
Fund Type: Global
Inception Date: October 2, 2007

Data Date	Investment Rating	Net Assets ($Mil)	Price	Performance Rating/Pts	Total Return Y-T-D	Risk Rating/Pts
3-12	D+	1,780.77	59.94	D / 1.9	2.21%	B / 8.8
2011	C-	1,616.60	58.83	D+ / 2.6	-1.58%	B / 8.8
2010	C+	1,342.40	58.46	C- / 4.1	3.17%	B- / 7.8
2009	C+	1,089.23	56.83	C- / 3.7	6.31%	B / 8.4

Major Rating Factors:
Disappointing performance is the major factor driving the D+ (Weak) TheStreet.com Investment Rating for *SPDR Barclays Cap Intl Treas Bd. The fund currently has a performance rating of D (Weak) based on an annualized return of 6.71% over the last three years and a total return of 2.21% year to date 2012. Factored into the performance evaluation is an expense ratio of 0.52% (very low).

The fund's risk rating is currently B (Good). It carries a beta of 1.05, meaning that its performance tracks fairly well with that of the overall stock market. Volatility, as measured by both the semi-deviation and a drawdown factor, is considered low. As of March 31, 2012, *SPDR Barclays Cap Intl Treas Bd traded at a premium of .30% above its net asset value, which is worse than its one-year historical average premium of .11%.

Karen Tsang currently receives a manager quality ranking of 44 (0=worst, 99=best). This fund offers only a moderate level of risk but investors looking for strong performance are still waiting.

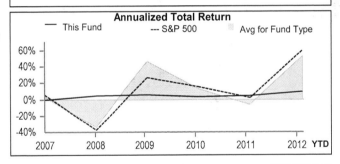

Annualized Total Return
— This Fund   --- S&P 500   Avg for Fund Type

*SPDR Barclays Cap Lng-T Corp Bd (LWC)

C   **Fair**

Fund Family: SSgA Funds Management Inc
Fund Type: General - Investment Grade
Inception Date: March 10, 2009

Data Date	Investment Rating	Net Assets ($Mil)	Price	Performance Rating/Pts	Total Return Y-T-D	Risk Rating/Pts
3-12	C	73.15	38.65	C- / 3.3	-1.33%	B+ / 9.0
2011	B	65.90	39.49	C+ / 6.8	-1.27%	B+ / 9.1
2010	C+	28.40	35.65	D+ / 2.9	6.18%	B / 8.5

Major Rating Factors: Middle of the road best describes *SPDR Barclays Cap Lng-T Corp Bd whose TheStreet.com Investment Rating is currently a C (Fair). The fund currently has a performance rating of C- (Fair) based on an annualized return of 14.73% over the last three years and a total return of -1.33% year to date 2012. Factored into the performance evaluation is an expense ratio of 0.17% (very low).

The fund's risk rating is currently B+ (Good). It carries a beta of 2.43, meaning it is expected to move 24.3% for every 10% move in the market. Volatility, as measured by both the semi-deviation and a drawdown factor, is considered very low. As of March 31, 2012, *SPDR Barclays Cap Lng-T Corp Bd traded at a premium of .39% above its net asset value, which is better than its one-year historical average premium of .77%.

John P. Kirby currently receives a manager quality ranking of 33 (0=worst, 99=best). If you desire an average level of risk, then this fund may be an option.

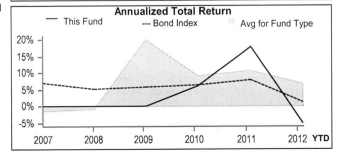

Annualized Total Return
— This Fund   --- Bond Index   Avg for Fund Type

*SPDR Barclays Cap Lng-T Treas ET (TLO)   D+   Weak

Fund Family: SSgA Funds Management Inc
Fund Type: US Government/Agency
Inception Date: May 23, 2007

Data Date	Investment Rating	Net Assets ($Mil)	Price	Performance Rating/Pts	Total Return Y-T-D	Risk Rating/Pts
3-12	D+	45.95	65.50	D / 2.2	-5.90%	B / 8.7
2011	C+	56.00	69.93	C / 5.5	-1.82%	B / 8.5
2010	C+	27.90	55.55	C- / 3.6	8.41%	B / 8.1
2009	C-	16.50	53.07	E+ / 0.7	-11.08%	B / 8.4

Major Rating Factors:
Disappointing performance is the major factor driving the D+ (Weak) TheStreet.com Investment Rating for *SPDR Barclays Cap Lng-T Treas ET. The fund currently has a performance rating of D (Weak) based on an annualized return of 7.74% over the last three years and a total return of -5.90% year to date 2012. Factored into the performance evaluation is an expense ratio of 0.15% (very low).

The fund's risk rating is currently B (Good). It carries a beta of 1.03, meaning that its performance tracks fairly well with that of the overall stock market. Volatility, as measured by both the semi-deviation and a drawdown factor, is considered low. As of March 31, 2012, *SPDR Barclays Cap Lng-T Treas ET traded at a discount of .23% below its net asset value, which is better than its one-year historical average discount of .06%.

John P. Kirby currently receives a manager quality ranking of 43 (0=worst, 99=best). This fund offers only a moderate level of risk but investors looking for strong performance are still waiting.

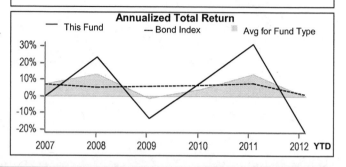

*SPDR Barclays Cap Mortg Backed E (MBG)   C-   Fair

Fund Family: SSgA Funds Management Inc
Fund Type: Mortgage
Inception Date: January 15, 2009

Data Date	Investment Rating	Net Assets ($Mil)	Price	Performance Rating/Pts	Total Return Y-T-D	Risk Rating/Pts
3-12	C-	33.02	27.52	D / 1.7	0.75%	B+ / 9.6
2011	C	41.10	27.38	C- / 3.5	0.21%	B+ / 9.6
2010	C	32.20	26.44	D / 1.9	2.55%	B / 8.8

Major Rating Factors:
Disappointing performance is the major factor driving the C- (Fair) TheStreet.com Investment Rating for *SPDR Barclays Cap Mortg Backed E. The fund currently has a performance rating of D (Weak) based on an annualized return of 4.76% over the last three years and a total return of 0.75% year to date 2012. Factored into the performance evaluation is an expense ratio of 0.21% (very low).

The fund's risk rating is currently B+ (Good). It carries a beta of 1.36, meaning it is expected to move 13.6% for every 10% move in the market. Volatility, as measured by both the semi-deviation and a drawdown factor, is considered very low. As of March 31, 2012, *SPDR Barclays Cap Mortg Backed E traded at a price exactly equal to its net asset value, which is better than its one-year historical average premium of .03%.

Karen Tsang currently receives a manager quality ranking of 31 (0=worst, 99=best). This fund offers only a moderate level of risk but investors looking for strong performance are still waiting.

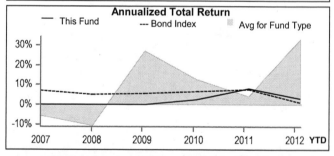

*SPDR Barclays Cap S/T Corp Bd ET (SCPB)   C-   Fair

Fund Family: SSgA Funds Management Inc
Fund Type: Corporate - Investment Grade
Inception Date: December 16, 2009

Data Date	Investment Rating	Net Assets ($Mil)	Price	Performance Rating/Pts	Total Return Y-T-D	Risk Rating/Pts
3-12	C-	651.21	30.53	D- / 1.5	1.68%	B+ / 9.9
2011	C	390.60	30.11	D+ / 2.3	0.60%	B+ / 9.9
2010	B-	196.40	30.25	C- / 3.4	2.52%	B+ / 9.0

Major Rating Factors:
Disappointing performance is the major factor driving the C- (Fair) TheStreet.com Investment Rating for *SPDR Barclays Cap S/T Corp Bd ET. The fund currently has a performance rating of D- (Weak) based on an annualized return of 0.00% over the last three years and a total return of 1.68% year to date 2012. Factored into the performance evaluation is an expense ratio of 0.13% (very low).

The fund's risk rating is currently B+ (Good). It carries a beta of 0.00, meaning the fund's expected move will be 0.0% for every 10% move in the market. Volatility, as measured by both the semi-deviation and a drawdown factor, is considered very low. As of March 31, 2012, *SPDR Barclays Cap S/T Corp Bd ET traded at a premium of .33% above its net asset value, which is worse than its one-year historical average premium of .25%.

Allen Kwong currently receives a manager quality ranking of 51 (0=worst, 99=best). This fund offers only a moderate level of risk but investors looking for strong performance are still waiting.

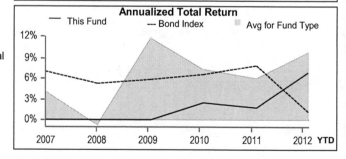

*SPDR Barclays Cap S/T Itl Treas (BWZ)

D+   Weak

Fund Family: SSgA Funds Management Inc
Fund Type: Global
Inception Date: January 15, 2009

Major Rating Factors:
Disappointing performance is the major factor driving the D+ (Weak) TheStreet.com Investment Rating for *SPDR Barclays Cap S/T Itl Treas. The fund currently has a performance rating of D (Weak) based on an annualized return of 5.01% over the last three years and a total return of 2.81% year to date 2012. Factored into the performance evaluation is an expense ratio of 0.36% (very low).

The fund's risk rating is currently B (Good). It carries a beta of 0.82, meaning the fund's expected move will be 8.2% for every 10% move in the market. Volatility, as measured by both the semi-deviation and a drawdown factor, is considered low. As of March 31, 2012, *SPDR Barclays Cap S/T Itl Treas traded at a premium of .30% above its net asset value, which is worse than its one-year historical average premium of .20%.

Michael J. Brunell currently receives a manager quality ranking of 45 (0=worst, 99=best). This fund offers only a moderate level of risk but investors looking for strong performance are still waiting.

Data Date	Investment Rating	Net Assets ($Mil)	Price	Performance Rating/Pts	Total Return Y-T-D	Risk Rating/Pts
3-12	D+	244.44	36.59	D / 1.6	2.81%	B / 8.8
2011	C-	218.90	35.59	D / 1.6	-0.24%	B / 8.9
2010	B	166.60	37.00	C / 4.7	1.59%	B / 8.2

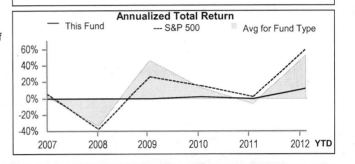

Annualized Total Return
— This Fund   --- S&P 500   Avg for Fund Type

*SPDR Barclays Capl TIPS ETF (IPE)

C   Fair

Fund Family: SSgA Funds Management Inc
Fund Type: US Government/Agency
Inception Date: May 25, 2007

Major Rating Factors:
Disappointing performance is the major factor driving the C (Fair) TheStreet.com Investment Rating for *SPDR Barclays Capl TIPS ETF. The fund currently has a performance rating of D+ (Weak) based on an annualized return of 9.35% over the last three years and a total return of 0.57% year to date 2012. Factored into the performance evaluation is an expense ratio of 0.20% (very low).

The fund's risk rating is currently B+ (Good). It carries a beta of 0.16, meaning the fund's expected move will be 1.6% for every 10% move in the market. Volatility, as measured by both the semi-deviation and a drawdown factor, is considered very low. As of March 31, 2012, *SPDR Barclays Capl TIPS ETF traded at a premium of .07% above its net asset value, which is worse than its one-year historical average premium of .03%.

Karen Tsang currently receives a manager quality ranking of 81 (0=worst, 99=best). This fund offers only a moderate level of risk but investors looking for strong performance are still waiting.

Data Date	Investment Rating	Net Assets ($Mil)	Price	Performance Rating/Pts	Total Return Y-T-D	Risk Rating/Pts
3-12	C	600.57	58.35	D+ / 2.5	0.57%	B+ / 9.7
2011	B-	613.60	58.02	C / 4.7	0.52%	B+ / 9.7
2010	B-	360.60	53.12	C / 4.3	6.03%	B / 8.3
2009	B	288.50	51.18	C / 5.0	11.53%	B / 8.5

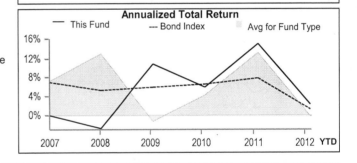

Annualized Total Return
— This Fund   --- Bond Index   Avg for Fund Type

*SPDR DB Intl Gvt Inflation Pt Bo (WIP)

C-   Fair

Fund Family: SSgA Funds Management Inc
Fund Type: Global
Inception Date: March 13, 2008

Major Rating Factors:
Disappointing performance is the major factor driving the C- (Fair) TheStreet.com Investment Rating for *SPDR DB Intl Gvt Inflation Pt Bo. The fund currently has a performance rating of D+ (Weak) based on an annualized return of 10.85% over the last three years and a total return of 6.52% year to date 2012. Factored into the performance evaluation is an expense ratio of 0.52% (very low).

The fund's risk rating is currently B (Good). It carries a beta of 1.03, meaning that its performance tracks fairly well with that of the overall stock market. Volatility, as measured by both the semi-deviation and a drawdown factor, is considered low. As of March 31, 2012, *SPDR DB Intl Gvt Inflation Pt Bo traded at a premium of .27% above its net asset value, which is worse than its one-year historical average premium of .02%.

David M. Kobuszewski currently receives a manager quality ranking of 69 (0=worst, 99=best). This fund offers only a moderate level of risk but investors looking for strong performance are still waiting.

Data Date	Investment Rating	Net Assets ($Mil)	Price	Performance Rating/Pts	Total Return Y-T-D	Risk Rating/Pts
3-12	C-	1,284.10	60.45	D+ / 2.7	6.52%	B / 8.8
2011	C	1,171.50	56.75	C- / 3.4	-0.42%	B / 8.8
2010	C+	893.40	58.11	C+ / 6.2	4.78%	C+ / 6.8
2009	B-	394.48	55.86	C+ / 6.0	17.38%	B- / 7.5

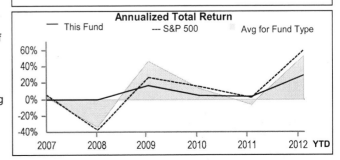

Annualized Total Return
— This Fund   --- S&P 500   Avg for Fund Type

*SPDR DJ REIT ETF (RWR)

A-　**Excellent**

Fund Family: SSgA Funds Management Inc
Fund Type: Income
Inception Date: April 23, 2001

Major Rating Factors:

Exceptional performance is the major factor driving the A- (Excellent) TheStreet.com Investment Rating for *SPDR DJ REIT ETF. The fund currently has a performance rating of A- (Excellent) based on an annualized return of 37.02% over the last three years and a total return of 10.67% year to date 2012. Factored into the performance evaluation is an expense ratio of 0.26% (very low).

The fund's risk rating is currently B- (Good). It carries a beta of 1.28, meaning it is expected to move 12.8% for every 10% move in the market. Volatility, as measured by both the semi-deviation and a drawdown factor, is considered low. As of March 31, 2012, *SPDR DJ REIT ETF traded at a discount of .04% below its net asset value.

Amos J. Rogers, III currently receives a manager quality ranking of 85 (0=worst, 99=best). If you desire only a moderate level of risk and strong performance, then this fund is an excellent option.

Data Date	Investment Rating	Net Assets ($Mil)	Price	Performance Rating/Pts	Total Return Y-T-D	Risk Rating/Pts
3-12	A-	1,795.13	70.83	A- / 9.2	10.67%	B- / 7.8
2011	C+	1,513.00	64.40	B / 7.9	-0.28%	C+ / 6.3
2010	C+	1,367.30	61.02	B- / 7.4	28.03%	C- / 4.1
2009	D-	908.89	49.21	D / 1.6	32.11%	C- / 4.0

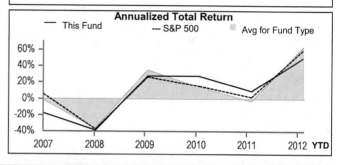

Annualized Total Return

*SPDR DJ Total Market ETF (TMW)

C+　**Fair**

Fund Family: SSgA Funds Management Inc
Fund Type: Growth
Inception Date: October 4, 2000

Major Rating Factors: Middle of the road best describes *SPDR DJ Total Market ETF whose TheStreet.com Investment Rating is currently a C+ (Fair). The fund currently has a performance rating of C+ (Fair) based on an annualized return of 21.59% over the last three years and a total return of 12.85% year to date 2012. Factored into the performance evaluation is an expense ratio of 0.22% (very low).

The fund's risk rating is currently B (Good). It carries a beta of 1.02, meaning that its performance tracks fairly well with that of the overall stock market. Volatility, as measured by both the semi-deviation and a drawdown factor, is considered low. As of March 31, 2012, *SPDR DJ Total Market ETF traded at a premium of .03% above its net asset value.

John A. Tucker has been running the fund for 12 years and currently receives a manager quality ranking of 45 (0=worst, 99=best). If you desire an average level of risk, then this fund may be an option.

Data Date	Investment Rating	Net Assets ($Mil)	Price	Performance Rating/Pts	Total Return Y-T-D	Risk Rating/Pts
3-12	C+	173.46	105.15	C+ / 6.0	12.85%	B / 8.2
2011	C+	163.90	93.54	C / 5.4	1.76%	B- / 7.9
2010	C	202.90	94.54	C / 4.7	17.34%	C+ / 5.9
2009	D+	158.24	81.95	D+ / 2.4	24.23%	C+ / 6.0

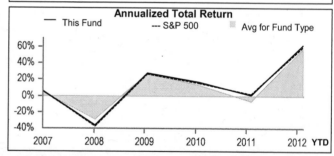

Annualized Total Return

*SPDR DJ Wilshire Glb Real Est ET (RWO)

B　**Good**

Fund Family: SSgA Funds Management Inc
Fund Type: Growth and Income
Inception Date: May 7, 2008

Major Rating Factors: Strong performance is the major factor driving the B (Good) TheStreet.com Investment Rating for *SPDR DJ Wilshire Glb Real Est ET. The fund currently has a performance rating of B (Good) based on an annualized return of 29.25% over the last three years and a total return of 12.84% year to date 2012. Factored into the performance evaluation is an expense ratio of 0.50% (very low).

The fund's risk rating is currently B- (Good). It carries a beta of 1.23, meaning it is expected to move 12.3% for every 10% move in the market. Volatility, as measured by both the semi-deviation and a drawdown factor, is considered low. As of March 31, 2012, *SPDR DJ Wilshire Glb Real Est ET traded at a premium of .33% above its net asset value, which is worse than its one-year historical average premium of .26%.

Amos J. Rogers III has been running the fund for 4 years and currently receives a manager quality ranking of 67 (0=worst, 99=best). If you desire only a moderate level of risk and strong performance, then this fund is an excellent option.

Data Date	Investment Rating	Net Assets ($Mil)	Price	Performance Rating/Pts	Total Return Y-T-D	Risk Rating/Pts
3-12	B	421.30	39.14	B / 7.8	12.84%	B- / 7.9
2011	C	323.70	34.89	C+ / 5.9	0.00%	B- / 7.0
2010	B	162.20	37.07	A / 9.3	24.01%	C- / 4.0
2009	B	81.08	32.13	B+ / 8.8	31.12%	C / 4.3

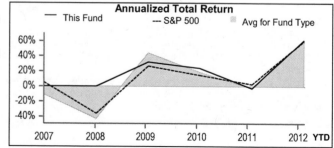

Annualized Total Return

*SPDR DJ Wilshire Intl Real Estat (RWX)   C-   Fair

Fund Family: SSgA Funds Management Inc
Fund Type: Foreign
Inception Date: December 15, 2006

Major Rating Factors: Middle of the road best describes *SPDR DJ Wilshire Intl Real Estat whose TheStreet.com Investment Rating is currently a C- (Fair). The fund currently has a performance rating of C+ (Fair) based on an annualized return of 22.30% over the last three years and a total return of 16.43% year to date 2012. Factored into the performance evaluation is an expense ratio of 0.61% (very low).

The fund's risk rating is currently C+ (Fair). It carries a beta of 1.03, meaning that its performance tracks fairly well with that of the overall stock market. Volatility, as measured by both the semi-deviation and a drawdown factor, is considered low. As of March 31, 2012, *SPDR DJ Wilshire Intl Real Estat traded at a premium of .41% above its net asset value, which is worse than its one-year historical average premium of .25%.

Amos J. Rogers, III currently receives a manager quality ranking of 77 (0=worst, 99=best). If you desire an average level of risk, then this fund may be an option.

Data Date	Investment Rating	Net Assets ($Mil)	Price	Performance Rating/Pts	Total Return Y-T-D	Risk Rating/Pts
3-12	C-	2,663.17	36.82	C+ / 5.6	16.43%	C+ / 6.1
2011	D	2,007.70	31.83	C- / 3.4	0.47%	C+ / 5.6
2010	D	1,430.50	38.93	D+ / 2.8	21.77%	C- / 3.9
2009	E+	939.27	34.89	D- / 1.1	31.75%	C- / 3.4

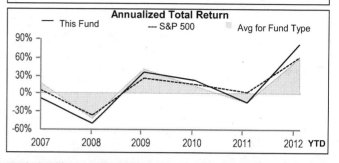

*SPDR DJ Wilshire Large Cap ETF (ELR)   C+   Fair

Fund Family: SSgA Funds Management Inc
Fund Type: Growth
Inception Date: November 8, 2005

Major Rating Factors: Middle of the road best describes *SPDR DJ Wilshire Large Cap ETF whose TheStreet.com Investment Rating is currently a C+ (Fair). The fund currently has a performance rating of C+ (Fair) based on an annualized return of 21.26% over the last three years and a total return of 12.73% year to date 2012. Factored into the performance evaluation is an expense ratio of 0.22% (very low).

The fund's risk rating is currently B (Good). It carries a beta of 0.92, meaning that its performance tracks fairly well with that of the overall stock market. Volatility, as measured by both the semi-deviation and a drawdown factor, is considered low. As of March 31, 2012, *SPDR DJ Wilshire Large Cap ETF traded at a premium of .11% above its net asset value, which is worse than its one-year historical average premium of .08%.

John A. Tucker has been running the fund for 6 years and currently receives a manager quality ranking of 57 (0=worst, 99=best). If you desire an average level of risk, then this fund may be an option.

Data Date	Investment Rating	Net Assets ($Mil)	Price	Performance Rating/Pts	Total Return Y-T-D	Risk Rating/Pts
3-12	C+	42.93	66.11	C+ / 5.8	12.73%	B / 8.4
2011	C+	35.30	58.88	C / 5.2	1.70%	B / 8.0
2010	C-	41.30	59.00	C- / 4.0	15.91%	C+ / 6.0
2009	D+	38.42	51.83	D+ / 2.4	24.27%	C+ / 6.1

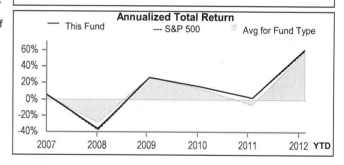

*SPDR DJ Wilshire Mid Cap ETF (EMM)   B-   Good

Fund Family: SSgA Funds Management Inc
Fund Type: Growth
Inception Date: November 8, 2005

Major Rating Factors: Strong performance is the major factor driving the B- (Good) TheStreet.com Investment Rating for *SPDR DJ Wilshire Mid Cap ETF. The fund currently has a performance rating of B- (Good) based on an annualized return of 27.33% over the last three years and a total return of 13.30% year to date 2012. Factored into the performance evaluation is an expense ratio of 0.27% (very low).

The fund's risk rating is currently B- (Good). It carries a beta of 1.23, meaning it is expected to move 12.3% for every 10% move in the market. Volatility, as measured by both the semi-deviation and a drawdown factor, is considered low. As of March 31, 2012, *SPDR DJ Wilshire Mid Cap ETF traded at a premium of .15% above its net asset value, which is worse than its one-year historical average premium of .01%.

John A. Tucker has been running the fund for 7 years and currently receives a manager quality ranking of 52 (0=worst, 99=best). If you desire only a moderate level of risk and strong performance, then this fund is an excellent option.

Data Date	Investment Rating	Net Assets ($Mil)	Price	Performance Rating/Pts	Total Return Y-T-D	Risk Rating/Pts
3-12	B-	75.20	65.49	B- / 7.5	13.30%	B- / 7.8
2011	B-	66.60	57.95	C+ / 6.8	1.69%	B- / 7.6
2010	B	59.10	59.43	B- / 7.3	24.63%	C+ / 5.8
2009	C-	31.26	48.30	C / 4.4	43.69%	C+ / 5.8

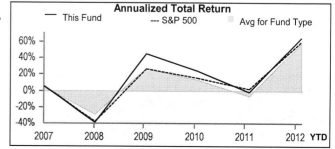

*SPDR Dow Jones Industrial Averag (DIA)

C+   **Fair**

Fund Family: State Street Bank and Trust Company
Fund Type: Growth
Inception Date: January 14, 1998

Major Rating Factors: Middle of the road best describes *SPDR Dow Jones Industrial Averag whose TheStreet.com Investment Rating is currently a C+ (Fair). The fund currently has a performance rating of C+ (Fair) based on an annualized return of 21.53% over the last three years and a total return of 8.79% year to date 2012. Factored into the performance evaluation is an expense ratio of 0.17% (very low).

    The fund's risk rating is currently B (Good). It carries a beta of 0.88, meaning the fund's expected move will be 8.8% for every 10% move in the market. Volatility, as measured by both the semi-deviation and a drawdown factor, is considered low. As of March 31, 2012, *SPDR Dow Jones Industrial Averag traded at a discount of .03% below its net asset value, which is better than its one-year historical average premium of .01%.

    David K. Chin currently receives a manager quality ranking of 64 (0=worst, 99=best). If you desire an average level of risk, then this fund may be an option.

Data Date	Investment Rating	Net Assets ($Mil)	Price	Perfor-mance Rating/Pts	Total Return Y-T-D	Risk Rating/Pts
3-12	C+	12,602.59	131.80	C+ / 5.8	8.79%	B / 8.6
2011	C+	10,842.40	121.85	C+ / 6.0	1.38%	B / 8.1
2010	C	8,721.10	115.63	C- / 4.1	14.26%	C+ / 6.3
2009	C-	7,500.73	104.07	D+ / 2.8	19.06%	C+ / 6.4

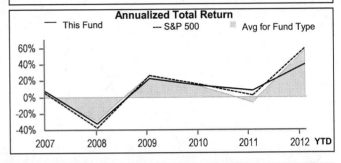

*SPDR Euro STOXX 50 ETF (FEZ)

D-   **Weak**

Fund Family: SSgA Funds Management Inc
Fund Type: Foreign
Inception Date: October 15, 2002

Major Rating Factors:
Disappointing performance is the major factor driving the D- (Weak) TheStreet.com Investment Rating for *SPDR Euro STOXX 50 ETF. The fund currently has a performance rating of D (Weak) based on an annualized return of 7.17% over the last three years and a total return of 10.30% year to date 2012. Factored into the performance evaluation is an expense ratio of 0.30% (very low).

    The fund's risk rating is currently C+ (Fair). It carries a beta of 1.35, meaning it is expected to move 13.5% for every 10% move in the market. Volatility, as measured by both the semi-deviation and a drawdown factor, is considered low. As of March 31, 2012, *SPDR Euro STOXX 50 ETF traded at a premium of .34% above its net asset value.

    John A. Tucker has been running the fund for 10 years and currently receives a manager quality ranking of 12 (0=worst, 99=best). This fund offers only a moderate level of risk but investors looking for strong performance are still waiting.

Data Date	Investment Rating	Net Assets ($Mil)	Price	Perfor-mance Rating/Pts	Total Return Y-T-D	Risk Rating/Pts
3-12	D-	454.33	32.45	D / 1.8	10.30%	C+ / 6.2
2011	D-	138.40	29.51	D- / 1.5	-3.12%	C+ / 6.2
2010	E+	163.70	36.84	E+ / 0.8	-7.75%	C- / 4.2
2009	D-	181.92	41.48	D / 1.6	18.75%	C / 4.6

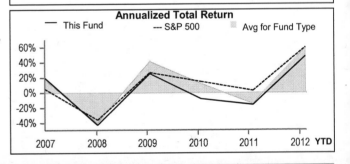

*SPDR FTSE/Macquarie Glob Infr 10 (GII)

C-   **Fair**

Fund Family: SSgA Funds Management Inc
Fund Type: Global
Inception Date: January 25, 2007

Major Rating Factors:
Disappointing performance is the major factor driving the C- (Fair) TheStreet.com Investment Rating for *SPDR FTSE/Macquarie Glob Infr 10. The fund currently has a performance rating of D+ (Weak) based on an annualized return of 10.34% over the last three years and a total return of 2.61% year to date 2012. Factored into the performance evaluation is an expense ratio of 0.60% (very low).

    The fund's risk rating is currently B (Good). It carries a beta of 0.60, meaning the fund's expected move will be 6.0% for every 10% move in the market. Volatility, as measured by both the semi-deviation and a drawdown factor, is considered low. As of March 31, 2012, *SPDR FTSE/Macquarie Glob Infr 10 traded at a discount of .05% below its net asset value, which is worse than its one-year historical average discount of .18%.

    John A. Tucker currently receives a manager quality ranking of 54 (0=worst, 99=best). This fund offers only a moderate level of risk but investors looking for strong performance are still waiting.

Data Date	Investment Rating	Net Assets ($Mil)	Price	Perfor-mance Rating/Pts	Total Return Y-T-D	Risk Rating/Pts
3-12	C-	36.50	40.54	D+ / 2.4	2.61%	B / 8.6
2011	C-	35.70	39.51	D+ / 2.6	-0.40%	B / 8.1
2010	D	49.70	41.32	D- / 1.0	1.22%	C+ / 6.3
2009	C+	67.10	42.52	C+ / 6.1	7.09%	C+ / 6.5

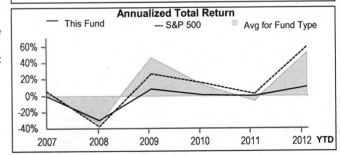

*SPDR Global Dow ETF (DGT)

D+ **Weak**

Fund Family: SSgA Funds Management Inc
Fund Type: Global
Inception Date: September 25, 2000

Major Rating Factors:
Disappointing performance is the major factor driving the D+ (Weak) TheStreet.com Investment Rating for *SPDR Global Dow ETF. The fund currently has a performance rating of D+ (Weak) based on an annualized return of 11.83% over the last three years and a total return of 11.63% year to date 2012. Factored into the performance evaluation is an expense ratio of 0.52% (very low).

The fund's risk rating is currently B- (Good). It carries a beta of 0.82, meaning the fund's expected move will be 8.2% for every 10% move in the market. Volatility, as measured by both the semi-deviation and a drawdown factor, is considered low. As of March 31, 2012, *SPDR Global Dow ETF traded at a discount of .18% below its net asset value, which is better than its one-year historical average discount of .11%.

John A. Tucker has been running the fund for 7 years and currently receives a manager quality ranking of 39 (0=worst, 99=best). This fund offers only a moderate level of risk but investors looking for strong performance are still waiting.

Data Date	Investment Rating	Net Assets ($Mil)	Price	Perfor-mance Rating/Pts	Total Return Y-T-D	Risk Rating/Pts
3-12	D+	100.70	55.83	D+ / 2.8	11.63%	B- / 7.7
2011	D+	98.20	50.18	D+ / 2.3	0.60%	B- / 7.6
2010	D	122.50	58.46	D / 1.6	4.99%	C+ / 5.9
2009	D+	70.92	57.02	D / 1.8	19.90%	C+ / 6.0

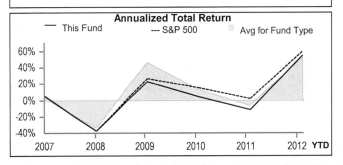

Annualized Total Return

*SPDR Gold Shares (GLD)

C+ **Fair**

Fund Family: SSgA Funds Management Inc
Fund Type: Precious Metals
Inception Date: November 18, 2004

Major Rating Factors: Middle of the road best describes *SPDR Gold Shares whose TheStreet.com Investment Rating is currently a C+ (Fair). The fund currently has a performance rating of C+ (Fair) based on an annualized return of 22.78% over the last three years and a total return of 6.66% year to date 2012. Factored into the performance evaluation is an expense ratio of 0.40% (very low).

The fund's risk rating is currently B (Good). It carries a beta of 0.95, meaning that its performance tracks fairly well with that of the overall stock market. Volatility, as measured by both the semi-deviation and a drawdown factor, is considered low. As of March 31, 2012, *SPDR Gold Shares traded at a premium of .40% above its net asset value, which is worse than its one-year historical average premium of .15%.

This fund has been team managed for 8 years and currently receives a manager quality ranking of 51 (0=worst, 99=best). If you desire an average level of risk, then this fund may be an option.

Data Date	Investment Rating	Net Assets ($Mil)	Price	Perfor-mance Rating/Pts	Total Return Y-T-D	Risk Rating/Pts
3-12	C+	73,592.21	162.12	C+ / 5.9	6.66%	B / 8.2
2011	B	63,484.30	151.99	B- / 7.5	3.43%	B / 8.3
2010	A	57,210.20	138.72	B+ / 8.8	29.27%	C+ / 6.9
2009	A+	36,885.82	107.31	B / 7.6	24.45%	B- / 7.2

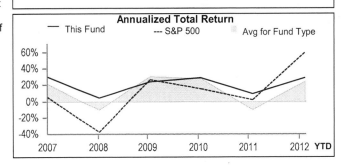

Annualized Total Return

*SPDR MSCI ACWI ex-US ETF (CWI)

C- **Fair**

Fund Family: SSgA Funds Management Inc
Fund Type: Global
Inception Date: January 10, 2007

Major Rating Factors: Middle of the road best describes *SPDR MSCI ACWI ex-US ETF whose TheStreet.com Investment Rating is currently a C- (Fair). The fund currently has a performance rating of C- (Fair) based on an annualized return of 15.73% over the last three years and a total return of 10.44% year to date 2012. Factored into the performance evaluation is an expense ratio of 0.35% (very low).

The fund's risk rating is currently B- (Good). It carries a beta of 1.06, meaning that its performance tracks fairly well with that of the overall stock market. Volatility, as measured by both the semi-deviation and a drawdown factor, is considered low. As of March 31, 2012, *SPDR MSCI ACWI ex-US ETF traded at a discount of .06% below its net asset value, which is better than its one-year historical average discount of .01%.

John A. Tucker currently receives a manager quality ranking of 48 (0=worst, 99=best). If you desire an average level of risk, then this fund may be an option.

Data Date	Investment Rating	Net Assets ($Mil)	Price	Perfor-mance Rating/Pts	Total Return Y-T-D	Risk Rating/Pts
3-12	C-	471.69	31.43	C- / 3.5	10.44%	B- / 7.6
2011	C-	527.50	28.46	C- / 3.3	-0.25%	B- / 7.5
2010	D+	410.90	33.91	C- / 3.0	11.59%	C / 5.5
2009	A-	309.90	31.20	B+ / 8.6	35.34%	C+ / 5.6

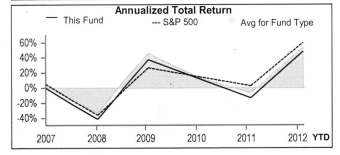

Annualized Total Return

*SPDR Nuveen Barclays Bld Amr Bd (BABS)

A+ **Excellent**

Fund Family: SSgA Funds Management Inc
Fund Type: Municipal - National
Inception Date: May 12, 2010

Major Rating Factors:
Exceptional performance is the major factor driving the A+ (Excellent) TheStreet.com Investment Rating for *SPDR Nuveen Barclays Bld Amr Bd. The fund currently has a performance rating of A- (Excellent) based on an annualized return of 0.00% over the last three years and a total return of 3.98% year to date 2012. Factored into the performance evaluation is an expense ratio of 0.35% (very low).

The fund's risk rating is currently B+ (Good). It carries a beta of 0.00, meaning the fund's expected move will be 0.0% for every 10% move in the market. Volatility, as measured by both the semi-deviation and a drawdown factor, is considered very low. As of March 31, 2012, *SPDR Nuveen Barclays Bld Amr Bd traded at a premium of .39% above its net asset value, which is worse than its one-year historical average discount of 1.05%.

Daniel J. Close currently receives a manager quality ranking of 26 (0=worst, 99=best). If you desire only a moderate level of risk and strong performance, then this fund is an excellent option.

Data Date	Investment Rating	Net Assets ($Mil)	Price	Performance Rating/Pts	Total Return Y-T-D	Risk Rating/Pts
3-12	A+	64.34	58.72	A- / 9.1	3.98%	B+ / 9.0
2011	A	39.90	56.90	A- / 9.1	-2.69%	B+ / 9.0

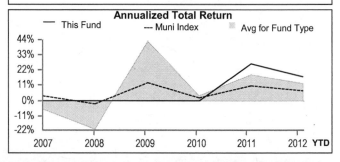

*SPDR Nuveen Barclays CA Muni Bd (CXA)

C **Fair**

Fund Family: SSgA Funds Management Inc
Fund Type: Municipal - National
Inception Date: October 10, 2007

Major Rating Factors: Middle of the road best describes *SPDR Nuveen Barclays CA Muni Bd whose TheStreet.com Investment Rating is currently a C (Fair). The fund currently has a performance rating of C- (Fair) based on an annualized return of 7.96% over the last three years and a total return of 2.67% year to date 2012. Factored into the performance evaluation is an expense ratio of 0.20% (very low).

The fund's risk rating is currently B+ (Good). It carries a beta of 1.72, meaning it is expected to move 17.2% for every 10% move in the market. Volatility, as measured by both the semi-deviation and a drawdown factor, is considered very low. As of March 31, 2012, *SPDR Nuveen Barclays CA Muni Bd traded at a price exactly equal to its net asset value, which is worse than its one-year historical average discount of .63%.

Daniel Farley currently receives a manager quality ranking of 23 (0=worst, 99=best). If you desire an average level of risk, then this fund may be an option.

Data Date	Investment Rating	Net Assets ($Mil)	Price	Performance Rating/Pts	Total Return Y-T-D	Risk Rating/Pts
3-12	C	78.94	23.92	C- / 3.9	2.67%	B+ / 9.0
2011	B	75.10	23.44	C+ / 6.4	0.99%	B+ / 9.0
2010	C	65.60	20.76	D / 2.0	-2.80%	B / 8.5
2009	B	40.38	22.18	C / 4.4	4.28%	B / 8.8

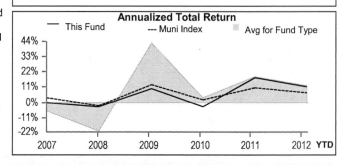

*SPDR Nuveen Barclays Muni Bd ETF (TFI)

C **Fair**

Fund Family: SSgA Funds Management Inc
Fund Type: Municipal - National
Inception Date: September 11, 2007

Major Rating Factors:
Disappointing performance is the major factor driving the C (Fair) TheStreet.com Investment Rating for *SPDR Nuveen Barclays Muni Bd ETF. The fund currently has a performance rating of D+ (Weak) based on an annualized return of 6.68% over the last three years and a total return of 0.94% year to date 2012. Factored into the performance evaluation is an expense ratio of 0.22% (very low).

The fund's risk rating is currently B+ (Good). It carries a beta of 1.22, meaning it is expected to move 12.2% for every 10% move in the market. Volatility, as measured by both the semi-deviation and a drawdown factor, is considered very low. As of March 31, 2012, *SPDR Nuveen Barclays Muni Bd ETF traded at a discount of .08% below its net asset value, which is worse than its one-year historical average discount of .29%.

Steve M. Hlavin currently receives a manager quality ranking of 29 (0=worst, 99=best). This fund offers only a moderate level of risk but investors looking for strong performance are still waiting.

Data Date	Investment Rating	Net Assets ($Mil)	Price	Performance Rating/Pts	Total Return Y-T-D	Risk Rating/Pts
3-12	C	1,076.29	23.84	D+ / 2.9	0.94%	B+ / 9.4
2011	B-	982.20	23.74	C / 5.2	0.21%	B+ / 9.4
2010	C+	862.00	21.63	D+ / 2.8	-1.42%	B / 8.6
2009	B	583.86	22.68	C+ / 5.8	10.82%	B / 8.9

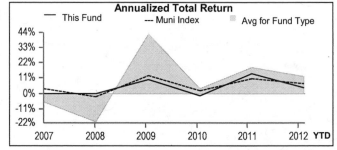

*SPDR Nuveen Barclays NY Muni Bd (INY)

C   Fair

Fund Family: SSgA Funds Management Inc
Fund Type: Municipal - National
Inception Date: October 11, 2007

Data Date	Investment Rating	Net Assets ($Mil)	Price	Performance Rating/Pts	Total Return Y-T-D	Risk Rating/Pts
3-12	C	28.23	23.49	C- / 3.5	1.22%	B+ / 9.3
2011	B-	25.70	23.34	C+ / 5.8	0.34%	B+ / 9.3
2010	C	26.00	21.42	D+ / 2.8	-0.91%	B / 8.3
2009	B	15.05	22.36	C+ / 6.6	14.34%	B / 8.5

Major Rating Factors: Middle of the road best describes *SPDR Nuveen Barclays NY Muni Bd whose TheStreet.com Investment Rating is currently a C (Fair). The fund currently has a performance rating of C- (Fair) based on an annualized return of 7.97% over the last three years and a total return of 1.22% year to date 2012. Factored into the performance evaluation is an expense ratio of 0.20% (very low).

The fund's risk rating is currently B+ (Good). It carries a beta of 1.28, meaning it is expected to move 12.8% for every 10% move in the market. Volatility, as measured by both the semi-deviation and a drawdown factor, is considered very low. As of March 31, 2012, *SPDR Nuveen Barclays NY Muni Bd traded at a discount of .17% below its net asset value, which is worse than its one-year historical average discount of .68%.

Daniel Farley currently receives a manager quality ranking of 35 (0=worst, 99=best). If you desire an average level of risk, then this fund may be an option.

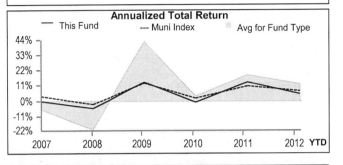

Annualized Total Return

*SPDR Nuveen Barclays Sh Tm Muni (SHM)

C-   Fair

Fund Family: SSgA Funds Management Inc
Fund Type: Municipal - National
Inception Date: October 10, 2007

Data Date	Investment Rating	Net Assets ($Mil)	Price	Performance Rating/Pts	Total Return Y-T-D	Risk Rating/Pts
3-12	C-	1,518.82	24.37	D / 1.6	0.35%	B+ / 9.8
2011	C	1,455.50	24.34	C- / 3.0	-0.12%	B+ / 9.9
2010	B+	1,300.60	23.81	C / 4.3	0.59%	B+ / 9.1
2009	B	501.79	24.02	C- / 4.1	4.28%	B+ / 9.2

Major Rating Factors:
Disappointing performance is the major factor driving the C- (Fair) TheStreet.com Investment Rating for *SPDR Nuveen Barclays Sh Tm Muni. The fund currently has a performance rating of D (Weak) based on an annualized return of 2.54% over the last three years and a total return of 0.35% year to date 2012. Factored into the performance evaluation is an expense ratio of 0.20% (very low).

The fund's risk rating is currently B+ (Good). It carries a beta of 0.34, meaning the fund's expected move will be 3.4% for every 10% move in the market. Volatility, as measured by both the semi-deviation and a drawdown factor, is considered very low. As of March 31, 2012, *SPDR Nuveen Barclays Sh Tm Muni traded at a premium of .12% above its net asset value, which is worse than its one-year historical average discount of .01%.

Daniel Farley currently receives a manager quality ranking of 45 (0=worst, 99=best). This fund offers only a moderate level of risk but investors looking for strong performance are still waiting.

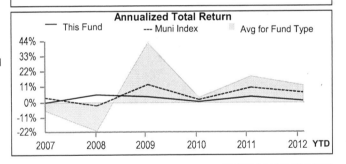

Annualized Total Return

*SPDR Nuveen S&P VRDO Muni Bond E (VRD)

C-   Fair

Fund Family: SSgA Funds Management Inc
Fund Type: General - Investment Grade
Inception Date: September 23, 2009

Data Date	Investment Rating	Net Assets ($Mil)	Price	Performance Rating/Pts	Total Return Y-T-D	Risk Rating/Pts
3-12	C-	15.01	30.01	D- / 1.3	0.05%	B+ / 9.9
2011	C	12.00	30.01	D / 2.1	-0.20%	B+ / 9.9
2010	C+	9.00	30.01	D+ / 2.4	0.42%	B+ / 9.0

Major Rating Factors:
Disappointing performance is the major factor driving the C- (Fair) TheStreet.com Investment Rating for *SPDR Nuveen S&P VRDO Muni Bond E. The fund currently has a performance rating of D- (Weak) based on an annualized return of 0.00% over the last three years and a total return of 0.05% year to date 2012. Factored into the performance evaluation is an expense ratio of 0.21% (very low).

The fund's risk rating is currently B+ (Good). It carries a beta of 0.00, meaning the fund's expected move will be 0.0% for every 10% move in the market. Volatility, as measured by both the semi-deviation and a drawdown factor, is considered very low. As of March 31, 2012, *SPDR Nuveen S&P VRDO Muni Bond E traded at a discount of .03% below its net asset value, which is worse than its one-year historical average discount of .13%.

Steve M. Hlavin currently receives a manager quality ranking of 54 (0=worst, 99=best). This fund offers only a moderate level of risk but investors looking for strong performance are still waiting.

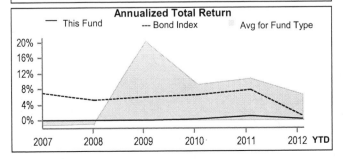

Annualized Total Return

*SPDR Russell/Nomura PRIME Japan (JPP)

D+   **Weak**

Fund Family: SSgA Funds Management Inc
Fund Type: Foreign
Inception Date: November 9, 2006

Major Rating Factors:
Disappointing performance is the major factor driving the D+ (Weak) TheStreet.com Investment Rating for *SPDR Russell/Nomura PRIME Japan. The fund currently has a performance rating of D+ (Weak) based on an annualized return of 9.20% over the last three years and a total return of 9.03% year to date 2012. Factored into the performance evaluation is an expense ratio of 0.51% (very low).

The fund's risk rating is currently B (Good). It carries a beta of 0.54, meaning the fund's expected move will be 5.4% for every 10% move in the market. Volatility, as measured by both the semi-deviation and a drawdown factor, is considered low. As of March 31, 2012, *SPDR Russell/Nomura PRIME Japan traded at a discount of .69% below its net asset value, which is better than its one-year historical average discount of .62%.

John A. Tucker currently receives a manager quality ranking of 55 (0=worst, 99=best). This fund offers only a moderate level of risk but investors looking for strong performance are still waiting.

Data Date	Investment Rating	Net Assets ($Mil)	Price	Perfor-mance Rating/Pts	Total Return Y-T-D	Risk Rating/Pts
3-12	D+	15.57	38.65	D+ / 2.4	9.03%	B / 8.1
2011	D+	14.10	35.45	D / 1.9	-0.14%	B- / 7.6
2010	D+	8.30	41.07	D+ / 2.5	12.14%	C+ / 5.7
2009	D-	15.36	37.45	E+ / 0.9	4.59%	C+ / 5.7

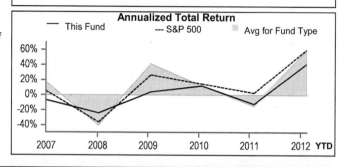

*SPDR Russell/Nomura Small Cap Ja (JSC)

C   **Fair**

Fund Family: SSgA Funds Management Inc
Fund Type: Foreign
Inception Date: November 9, 2006

Major Rating Factors: Middle of the road best describes *SPDR Russell/Nomura Small Cap Ja whose TheStreet.com Investment Rating is currently a C (Fair). The fund currently has a performance rating of C- (Fair) based on an annualized return of 14.25% over the last three years and a total return of 8.27% year to date 2012. Factored into the performance evaluation is an expense ratio of 0.56% (very low).

The fund's risk rating is currently B (Good). It carries a beta of 0.37, meaning the fund's expected move will be 3.7% for every 10% move in the market. Volatility, as measured by both the semi-deviation and a drawdown factor, is considered low. As of March 31, 2012, *SPDR Russell/Nomura Small Cap Ja traded at a discount of .07% below its net asset value, which is worse than its one-year historical average discount of .29%.

John A. Tucker currently receives a manager quality ranking of 82 (0=worst, 99=best). If you desire an average level of risk, then this fund may be an option.

Data Date	Investment Rating	Net Assets ($Mil)	Price	Perfor-mance Rating/Pts	Total Return Y-T-D	Risk Rating/Pts
3-12	C	95.71	44.49	C- / 3.4	8.27%	B / 8.7
2011	C-	88.90	41.09	C- / 3.2	0.38%	B- / 7.6
2010	C+	69.30	43.12	C+ / 6.4	17.94%	C+ / 6.1
2009	D	85.08	37.20	E+ / 0.9	3.01%	C+ / 6.0

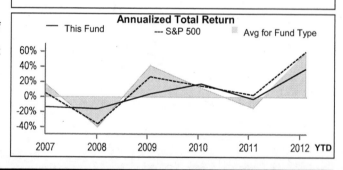

*SPDR S&P 400 Mid Cap Growth ETF (MDYG)

B   **Good**

Fund Family: SSgA Funds Management Inc
Fund Type: Growth
Inception Date: November 8, 2005

Major Rating Factors: Strong performance is the major factor driving the B (Good) TheStreet.com Investment Rating for *SPDR S&P 400 Mid Cap Growth ETF. The fund currently has a performance rating of B (Good) based on an annualized return of 28.57% over the last three years and a total return of 14.03% year to date 2012. Factored into the performance evaluation is an expense ratio of 0.28% (very low).

The fund's risk rating is currently B- (Good). It carries a beta of 1.23, meaning it is expected to move 12.3% for every 10% move in the market. Volatility, as measured by both the semi-deviation and a drawdown factor, is considered low. As of March 31, 2012, *SPDR S&P 400 Mid Cap Growth ETF traded at a premium of .33% above its net asset value, which is worse than its one-year historical average discount of .02%.

John A. Tucker currently receives a manager quality ranking of 58 (0=worst, 99=best). If you desire only a moderate level of risk and strong performance, then this fund is an excellent option.

Data Date	Investment Rating	Net Assets ($Mil)	Price	Perfor-mance Rating/Pts	Total Return Y-T-D	Risk Rating/Pts
3-12	B	66.90	83.90	B / 7.7	14.03%	B- / 7.9
2011	B-	58.80	73.69	B- / 7.2	0.88%	B- / 7.7
2010	B+	71.00	75.32	B / 7.9	27.62%	C / 5.5
2009	C+	42.94	59.22	C+ / 6.0	50.31%	C+ / 5.7

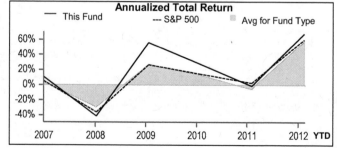

*SPDR S&P 400 Mid Cap Value ETF (MDYV)   C+   Fair

Fund Family: SSgA Funds Management Inc
Fund Type: Growth
Inception Date: November 8, 2005

Data Date	Investment Rating	Net Assets ($Mil)	Price	Performance Rating/Pts	Total Return Y-T-D	Risk Rating/Pts
3-12	C+	29.11	58.45	C+ / 6.7	13.02%	B- / 7.9
2011	C+	25.90	51.91	C+ / 5.7	1.73%	B- / 7.7
2010	C+	27.10	54.48	C+ / 6.2	21.37%	C+ / 5.7
2009	C-	8.82	46.00	C- / 3.0	31.68%	C+ / 5.7

Major Rating Factors: Middle of the road best describes *SPDR S&P 400 Mid Cap Value ETF whose TheStreet.com Investment Rating is currently a C+ (Fair). The fund currently has a performance rating of C+ (Fair) based on an annualized return of 24.79% over the last three years and a total return of 13.02% year to date 2012. Factored into the performance evaluation is an expense ratio of 0.28% (very low).

The fund's risk rating is currently B- (Good). It carries a beta of 1.16, meaning it is expected to move 11.6% for every 10% move in the market. Volatility, as measured by both the semi-deviation and a drawdown factor, is considered low. As of March 31, 2012, *SPDR S&P 400 Mid Cap Value ETF traded at a premium of .38% above its net asset value, which is worse than its one-year historical average premium of .02%.

John A. Tucker has been running the fund for 7 years and currently receives a manager quality ranking of 47 (0=worst, 99=best). If you desire an average level of risk, then this fund may be an option.

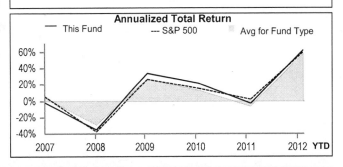

*SPDR S&P 500 ETF (SPY)   C+   Fair

Fund Family: State Street Bank and Trust Company
Fund Type: Growth
Inception Date: January 22, 1993

Data Date	Investment Rating	Net Assets ($Mil)	Price	Performance Rating/Pts	Total Return Y-T-D	Risk Rating/Pts
3-12	C+	105,621.24	140.81	C+ / 5.8	12.69%	B / 8.2
2011	C	95,397.40	125.50	C / 5.2	1.76%	B- / 7.9
2010	C-	89,875.00	125.75	C- / 3.8	15.08%	C+ / 6.0
2009	D+	63,691.96	111.44	D / 2.2	22.53%	C+ / 6.1

Major Rating Factors: Middle of the road best describes *SPDR S&P 500 ETF whose TheStreet.com Investment Rating is currently a C+ (Fair). The fund currently has a performance rating of C+ (Fair) based on an annualized return of 21.08% over the last three years and a total return of 12.69% year to date 2012. Factored into the performance evaluation is an expense ratio of 0.09% (very low).

The fund's risk rating is currently B (Good). It carries a beta of 1.00, meaning that its performance tracks fairly well with that of the overall stock market. Volatility, as measured by both the semi-deviation and a drawdown factor, is considered low. As of March 31, 2012, *SPDR S&P 500 ETF traded at a premium of .01% above its net asset value.

David K. Chin currently receives a manager quality ranking of 45 (0=worst, 99=best). If you desire an average level of risk, then this fund may be an option.

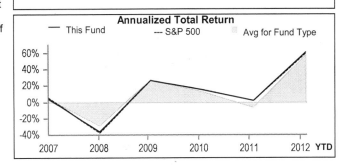

*SPDR S&P 500 Growth ETF (SPYG)   C+   Fair

Fund Family: SSgA Funds Management Inc
Fund Type: Growth
Inception Date: September 25, 2000

Data Date	Investment Rating	Net Assets ($Mil)	Price	Performance Rating/Pts	Total Return Y-T-D	Risk Rating/Pts
3-12	C+	228.42	65.25	C+ / 6.6	12.00%	B / 8.1
2011	C+	207.30	58.47	C+ / 6.3	1.12%	B- / 7.8
2010	C+	190.40	56.94	C / 5.5	16.50%	C+ / 5.8
2009	C-	154.82	49.26	C- / 3.8	32.07%	C+ / 6.1

Major Rating Factors: Middle of the road best describes *SPDR S&P 500 Growth ETF whose TheStreet.com Investment Rating is currently a C+ (Fair). The fund currently has a performance rating of C+ (Fair) based on an annualized return of 23.17% over the last three years and a total return of 12.00% year to date 2012. Factored into the performance evaluation is an expense ratio of 0.22% (very low).

The fund's risk rating is currently B (Good). It carries a beta of 0.99, meaning that its performance tracks fairly well with that of the overall stock market. Volatility, as measured by both the semi-deviation and a drawdown factor, is considered low. As of March 31, 2012, *SPDR S&P 500 Growth ETF traded at a discount of .02% below its net asset value, which is better than its one-year historical average discount of .01%.

John A. Tucker has been running the fund for 12 years and currently receives a manager quality ranking of 58 (0=worst, 99=best). If you desire an average level of risk, then this fund may be an option.

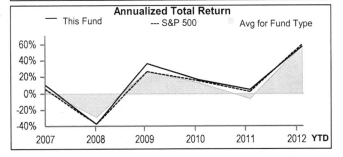

*SPDR S&P 500 Value ETF (SPYV)

C+   **Fair**

Fund Family: SSgA Funds Management Inc
Fund Type: Income
Inception Date: September 25, 2000

Major Rating Factors: Middle of the road best describes *SPDR S&P 500 Value ETF whose TheStreet.com Investment Rating is currently a C+ (Fair). The fund currently has a performance rating of C (Fair) based on an annualized return of 19.45% over the last three years and a total return of 12.88% year to date 2012. Factored into the performance evaluation is an expense ratio of 0.22% (very low).

The fund's risk rating is currently B (Good). It carries a beta of 0.99, meaning that its performance tracks fairly well with that of the overall stock market. Volatility, as measured by both the semi-deviation and a drawdown factor, is considered low. As of March 31, 2012, *SPDR S&P 500 Value ETF traded at a discount of .04% below its net asset value, which is worse than its one-year historical average discount of .06%.

John A. Tucker has been running the fund for 7 years and currently receives a manager quality ranking of 35 (0=worst, 99=best). If you desire an average level of risk, then this fund may be an option.

Data Date	Investment Rating	Net Assets ($Mil)	Price	Perfor-mance Rating/Pts	Total Return Y-T-D	Risk Rating/Pts
3-12	C+	180.00	70.54	C / 5.3	12.88%	B / 8.3
2011	C	160.30	62.80	C / 4.4	2.17%	B / 8.0
2010	D+	168.20	64.69	D+ / 2.8	15.51%	C+ / 6.0
2009	D	99.22	57.50	D- / 1.3	14.66%	C+ / 6.0

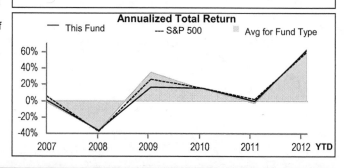

*SPDR S&P 600 Small Cap ETF (SLY)

B   **Good**

Fund Family: SSgA Funds Management Inc
Fund Type: Growth
Inception Date: November 8, 2005

Major Rating Factors: Strong performance is the major factor driving the B (Good) TheStreet.com Investment Rating for *SPDR S&P 600 Small Cap ETF. The fund currently has a performance rating of B (Good) based on an annualized return of 29.06% over the last three years and a total return of 12.07% year to date 2012. Factored into the performance evaluation is an expense ratio of 0.24% (very low).

The fund's risk rating is currently B- (Good). It carries a beta of 1.30, meaning it is expected to move 13.0% for every 10% move in the market. Volatility, as measured by both the semi-deviation and a drawdown factor, is considered low. As of March 31, 2012, *SPDR S&P 600 Small Cap ETF traded at a premium of .48% above its net asset value, which is worse than its one-year historical average premium of .06%.

John A. Tucker has been running the fund for 7 years and currently receives a manager quality ranking of 53 (0=worst, 99=best). If you desire only a moderate level of risk and strong performance, then this fund is an excellent option.

Data Date	Investment Rating	Net Assets ($Mil)	Price	Perfor-mance Rating/Pts	Total Return Y-T-D	Risk Rating/Pts
3-12	B	102.89	73.84	B / 8.0	12.07%	B- / 7.7
2011	B-	72.40	66.07	B- / 7.3	1.45%	B- / 7.5
2010	B	62.60	66.87	B / 7.8	28.92%	C / 5.4
2009	C-	22.65	52.54	C- / 3.6	38.80%	C+ / 5.6

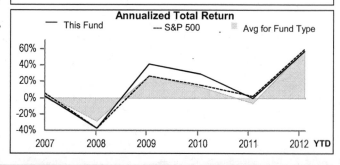

*SPDR S&P 600 Small Cap Growth ET (SLYG)

B   **Good**

Fund Family: SSgA Funds Management Inc
Fund Type: Growth
Inception Date: September 25, 2000

Major Rating Factors: Strong performance is the major factor driving the B (Good) TheStreet.com Investment Rating for *SPDR S&P 600 Small Cap Growth ET. The fund currently has a performance rating of B+ (Good) based on an annualized return of 30.90% over the last three years and a total return of 11.06% year to date 2012. Factored into the performance evaluation is an expense ratio of 0.27% (very low).

The fund's risk rating is currently B- (Good). It carries a beta of 1.28, meaning it is expected to move 12.8% for every 10% move in the market. Volatility, as measured by both the semi-deviation and a drawdown factor, is considered low. As of March 31, 2012, *SPDR S&P 600 Small Cap Growth ET traded at a premium of .10% above its net asset value, which is worse than its one-year historical average discount of .03%.

John A. Tucker has been running the fund for 12 years and currently receives a manager quality ranking of 62 (0=worst, 99=best). If you desire only a moderate level of risk and strong performance, then this fund is an excellent option.

Data Date	Investment Rating	Net Assets ($Mil)	Price	Perfor-mance Rating/Pts	Total Return Y-T-D	Risk Rating/Pts
3-12	B	161.51	124.36	B+ / 8.3	11.06%	B- / 7.6
2011	B-	145.80	112.28	B / 7.7	0.84%	B- / 7.2
2010	B	174.60	110.57	B / 8.0	32.09%	C / 5.2
2009	C-	94.08	83.96	C- / 4.2	43.53%	C / 5.3

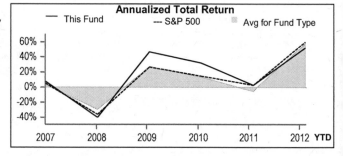

*SPDR S&P 600 Small Cap Value ETF (SLYV)

B-   **Good**

Fund Family: SSgA Funds Management Inc
Fund Type: Growth
Inception Date: September 25, 2000

Major Rating Factors: Strong performance is the major factor driving the B- (Good) TheStreet.com Investment Rating for *SPDR S&P 600 Small Cap Value ETF. The fund currently has a performance rating of B (Good) based on an annualized return of 27.18% over the last three years and a total return of 13.17% year to date 2012. Factored into the performance evaluation is an expense ratio of 0.27% (very low).

The fund's risk rating is currently B- (Good). It carries a beta of 1.33, meaning it is expected to move 13.3% for every 10% move in the market. Volatility, as measured by both the semi-deviation and a drawdown factor, is considered low. As of March 31, 2012, *SPDR S&P 600 Small Cap Value ETF traded at a premium of .27% above its net asset value, which is worse than its one-year historical average premium of .01%.

John A. Tucker has been running the fund for 12 years and currently receives a manager quality ranking of 39 (0=worst, 99=best). If you desire only a moderate level of risk and strong performance, then this fund is an excellent option.

Data Date	Investment Rating	Net Assets ($Mil)	Price	Perfor- mance Rating/Pts	Total Return Y-T-D	Risk Rating/Pts
3-12	B-	143.36	75.60	B / 7.6	13.17%	B- / 7.8
2011	B-	114.00	66.98	C+ / 6.9	2.56%	B- / 7.5
2010	B	134.50	69.75	B / 7.6	25.97%	C+ / 5.6
2009	C-	69.89	56.60	C- / 3.2	34.22%	C+ / 5.7

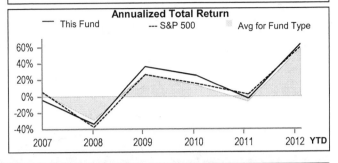

Annualized Total Return

*SPDR S&P Biotech ETF (XBI)

C+   **Fair**

Fund Family: SSgA Funds Management Inc
Fund Type: Health
Inception Date: January 31, 2006

Major Rating Factors: Middle of the road best describes *SPDR S&P Biotech ETF whose TheStreet.com Investment Rating is currently a C+ (Fair). The fund currently has a performance rating of C+ (Fair) based on an annualized return of 19.87% over the last three years and a total return of 21.17% year to date 2012. Factored into the performance evaluation is an expense ratio of 0.37% (very low).

The fund's risk rating is currently B- (Good). It carries a beta of 0.94, meaning that its performance tracks fairly well with that of the overall stock market. Volatility, as measured by both the semi-deviation and a drawdown factor, is considered low. As of March 31, 2012, *SPDR S&P Biotech ETF traded at a premium of .04% above its net asset value, which is better than its one-year historical average premium of .05%.

John A. Tucker currently receives a manager quality ranking of 30 (0=worst, 99=best). If you desire an average level of risk, then this fund may be an option.

Data Date	Investment Rating	Net Assets ($Mil)	Price	Perfor- mance Rating/Pts	Total Return Y-T-D	Risk Rating/Pts
3-12	C+	534.82	80.46	C+ / 6.6	21.17%	B- / 7.0
2011	D+	418.20	66.40	C- / 4.1	4.79%	C+ / 6.0
2010	C+	491.90	63.08	C+ / 5.9	17.60%	C+ / 6.0
2009	C-	428.51	53.64	C- / 3.7	-0.82%	C+ / 6.1

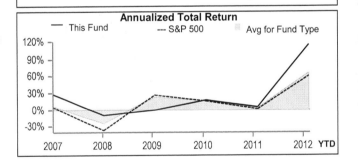

Annualized Total Return

*SPDR S&P BRIC 40 ETF (BIK)

D+   **Weak**

Fund Family: SSgA Funds Management Inc
Fund Type: Foreign
Inception Date: June 19, 2007

Major Rating Factors: *SPDR S&P BRIC 40 ETF receives a TheStreet.com Investment Rating of D+ (Weak). The fund currently has a performance rating of C- (Fair) based on an annualized return of 17.00% over the last three years and a total return of 12.50% year to date 2012. Factored into the performance evaluation is an expense ratio of 0.51% (very low).

The fund's risk rating is currently C+ (Fair). It carries a beta of 1.12, meaning it is expected to move 11.2% for every 10% move in the market. Volatility, as measured by both the semi-deviation and a drawdown factor, is considered low. As of March 31, 2012, *SPDR S&P BRIC 40 ETF traded at a discount of .24% below its net asset value, which is better than its one-year historical average discount of .14%.

John A. Tucker currently receives a manager quality ranking of 52 (0=worst, 99=best). If you desire an average level of risk, then this fund may be an option.

Data Date	Investment Rating	Net Assets ($Mil)	Price	Perfor- mance Rating/Pts	Total Return Y-T-D	Risk Rating/Pts
3-12	D+	403.00	24.66	C- / 3.7	12.50%	C+ / 6.8
2011	C-	342.00	21.92	C / 4.9	2.33%	C+ / 6.9
2010	D	503.00	27.43	C- / 3.1	11.36%	C- / 4.2
2009	B+	340.81	25.07	A / 9.5	67.09%	C- / 4.2

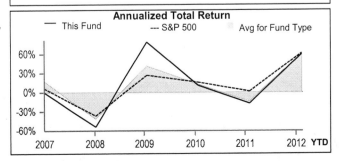

Annualized Total Return

*SPDR S&P China ETF (GXC)   D   Weak

Fund Family: SSgA Funds Management Inc
Fund Type: Foreign
Inception Date: March 20, 2007

Major Rating Factors: *SPDR S&P China ETF receives a TheStreet.com Investment Rating of D (Weak). The fund currently has a performance rating of C- (Fair) based on an annualized return of 13.48% over the last three years and a total return of 9.74% year to date 2012. Factored into the performance evaluation is an expense ratio of 0.60% (very low).

The fund's risk rating is currently C+ (Fair). It carries a beta of 1.00, meaning that its performance tracks fairly well with that of the overall stock market. Volatility, as measured by both the semi-deviation and a drawdown factor, is considered low. As of March 31, 2012, *SPDR S&P China ETF traded at a discount of .63% below its net asset value, which is better than its one-year historical average premium of .08%.

John A. Tucker currently receives a manager quality ranking of 38 (0=worst, 99=best). If you desire an average level of risk, then this fund may be an option.

Data Date	Investment Rating	Net Assets ($Mil)	Price	Performance Rating/Pts	Total Return Y-T-D	Risk Rating/Pts
3-12	D	894.42	68.37	C- / 3.0	9.74%	C+ / 6.5
2011	D+	584.70	62.30	C- / 4.0	0.88%	C+ / 6.1
2010	D	703.70	76.24	D / 2.1	7.57%	C / 4.6
2009	B	445.54	71.85	A- / 9.0	50.76%	C / 4.3

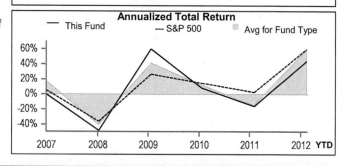

*SPDR S&P Dividend ETF (SDY)   C+   Fair

Fund Family: SSgA Funds Management Inc
Fund Type: Income
Inception Date: November 8, 2005

Major Rating Factors: Middle of the road best describes *SPDR S&P Dividend ETF whose TheStreet.com Investment Rating is currently a C+ (Fair). The fund currently has a performance rating of C (Fair) based on an annualized return of 20.40% over the last three years and a total return of 5.89% year to date 2012. Factored into the performance evaluation is an expense ratio of 0.36% (very low).

The fund's risk rating is currently B (Good). It carries a beta of 0.84, meaning the fund's expected move will be 8.4% for every 10% move in the market. Volatility, as measured by both the semi-deviation and a drawdown factor, is considered low. As of March 31, 2012, *SPDR S&P Dividend ETF traded at a discount of .05% below its net asset value, which is better than its one-year historical average premium of .01%.

John A. Tucker has been running the fund for 7 years and currently receives a manager quality ranking of 65 (0=worst, 99=best). If you desire an average level of risk, then this fund may be an option.

Data Date	Investment Rating	Net Assets ($Mil)	Price	Performance Rating/Pts	Total Return Y-T-D	Risk Rating/Pts
3-12	C+	9,296.30	56.64	C / 5.2	5.89%	B / 8.8
2011	C+	8,252.90	53.87	C / 5.5	0.09%	B- / 7.8
2010	C+	5,031.90	51.98	C+ / 6.0	16.43%	C+ / 6.1
2009	D+	658.66	46.25	D / 2.1	16.49%	C+ / 6.1

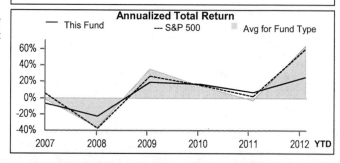

*SPDR S&P Emerg Middle East&Afric (GAF)   C   Fair

Fund Family: SSgA Funds Management Inc
Fund Type: Emerging Market
Inception Date: March 20, 2007

Major Rating Factors: Middle of the road best describes *SPDR S&P Emerg Middle East&Afric whose TheStreet.com Investment Rating is currently a C (Fair). The fund currently has a performance rating of C (Fair) based on an annualized return of 20.85% over the last three years and a total return of 13.34% year to date 2012. Factored into the performance evaluation is an expense ratio of 0.60% (very low).

The fund's risk rating is currently B- (Good). It carries a beta of 0.81, meaning the fund's expected move will be 8.1% for every 10% move in the market. Volatility, as measured by both the semi-deviation and a drawdown factor, is considered low. As of March 31, 2012, *SPDR S&P Emerg Middle East&Afric traded at a premium of .24% above its net asset value, which is worse than its one-year historical average discount of .12%.

John A. Tucker currently receives a manager quality ranking of 63 (0=worst, 99=best). If you desire an average level of risk, then this fund may be an option.

Data Date	Investment Rating	Net Assets ($Mil)	Price	Performance Rating/Pts	Total Return Y-T-D	Risk Rating/Pts
3-12	C	99.33	71.12	C / 5.1	13.34%	B- / 7.4
2011	C	94.70	62.75	C / 5.0	0.48%	B- / 7.4
2010	B+	181.70	79.59	B / 8.1	30.45%	C+ / 5.8
2009	A	129.23	62.39	A- / 9.0	46.98%	C+ / 5.8

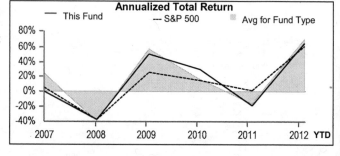

*SPDR S&P Emerging Asia Pacific E (GMF)   C-   Fair

Fund Family: SSgA Funds Management Inc
Fund Type: Emerging Market
Inception Date: March 20, 2007

Data Date	Investment Rating	Net Assets ($Mil)	Price	Performance Rating/Pts	Total Return Y-T-D	Risk Rating/Pts
3-12	C-	468.85	74.15	C- / 4.2	12.37%	C+ / 6.9
2011	C-	450.30	65.99	C / 5.2	1.73%	C+ / 6.5
2010	C	770.30	84.75	C+ / 5.9	19.44%	C / 4.8
2009	A-	436.77	74.18	A / 9.4	63.77%	C / 4.7

Major Rating Factors: Middle of the road best describes *SPDR S&P Emerging Asia Pacific E whose TheStreet.com Investment Rating is currently a C- (Fair). The fund currently has a performance rating of C- (Fair) based on an annualized return of 18.77% over the last three years and a total return of 12.37% year to date 2012. Factored into the performance evaluation is an expense ratio of 0.60% (very low).

The fund's risk rating is currently C+ (Fair). It carries a beta of 1.07, meaning that its performance tracks fairly well with that of the overall stock market. Volatility, as measured by both the semi-deviation and a drawdown factor, is considered low. As of March 31, 2012, *SPDR S&P Emerging Asia Pacific E traded at a discount of .36% below its net asset value, which is better than its one-year historical average discount of .14%.

John A. Tucker currently receives a manager quality ranking of 24 (0=worst, 99=best). If you desire an average level of risk, then this fund may be an option.

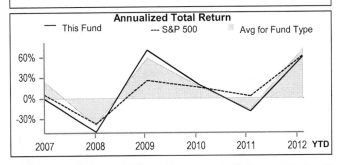

*SPDR S&P Emerging Europe ETF (GUR)   D+   Weak

Fund Family: SSgA Funds Management Inc
Fund Type: Emerging Market
Inception Date: March 20, 2007

Data Date	Investment Rating	Net Assets ($Mil)	Price	Performance Rating/Pts	Total Return Y-T-D	Risk Rating/Pts
3-12	D+	102.64	42.93	C / 4.4	19.28%	C+ / 6.0
2011	D+	86.00	35.99	C- / 3.6	0.58%	C+ / 6.1
2010	E+	217.30	49.55	D- / 1.4	15.70%	C- / 3.2
2009	B	137.98	43.34	A+ / 9.6	67.53%	C- / 3.6

Major Rating Factors: *SPDR S&P Emerging Europe ETF receives a TheStreet.com Investment Rating of D+ (Weak). The fund currently has a performance rating of C (Fair) based on an annualized return of 20.41% over the last three years and a total return of 19.28% year to date 2012. Factored into the performance evaluation is an expense ratio of 0.61% (very low).

The fund's risk rating is currently C+ (Fair). It carries a beta of 1.26, meaning it is expected to move 12.6% for every 10% move in the market. Volatility, as measured by both the semi-deviation and a drawdown factor, is considered low. As of March 31, 2012, *SPDR S&P Emerging Europe ETF traded at a premium of .37% above its net asset value, which is worse than its one-year historical average premium of .24%.

John A. Tucker currently receives a manager quality ranking of 21 (0=worst, 99=best). If you desire an average level of risk, then this fund may be an option.

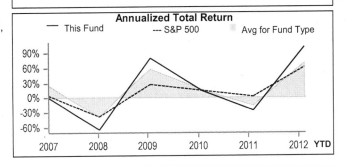

*SPDR S&P Emerging Latin America (GML)   C   Fair

Fund Family: SSgA Funds Management Inc
Fund Type: Emerging Market
Inception Date: March 20, 2007

Data Date	Investment Rating	Net Assets ($Mil)	Price	Performance Rating/Pts	Total Return Y-T-D	Risk Rating/Pts
3-12	C	150.17	78.87	C+ / 5.7	14.33%	B- / 7.0
2011	C	117.20	68.99	C+ / 5.7	2.01%	C+ / 6.9
2010	C+	276.80	89.74	B- / 7.2	15.38%	C / 4.5
2009	A+	132.84	80.06	A+ / 9.8	93.33%	C / 5.0

Major Rating Factors: Middle of the road best describes *SPDR S&P Emerging Latin America whose TheStreet.com Investment Rating is currently a C (Fair). The fund currently has a performance rating of C+ (Fair) based on an annualized return of 23.05% over the last three years and a total return of 14.33% year to date 2012. Factored into the performance evaluation is an expense ratio of 0.60% (very low).

The fund's risk rating is currently B- (Good). It carries a beta of 1.18, meaning it is expected to move 11.8% for every 10% move in the market. Volatility, as measured by both the semi-deviation and a drawdown factor, is considered low. As of March 31, 2012, *SPDR S&P Emerging Latin America traded at a discount of .22% below its net asset value, which is better than its one-year historical average discount of .12%.

John A. Tucker currently receives a manager quality ranking of 33 (0=worst, 99=best). If you desire an average level of risk, then this fund may be an option.

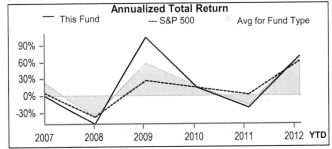

*SPDR S&P Emerging Markets ETF (GMM)

C-   **Fair**

Fund Family: SSgA Funds Management Inc
Fund Type: Emerging Market
Inception Date: March 20, 2007

Data Date	Investment Rating	Net Assets ($Mil)	Price	Performance Rating/Pts	Total Return Y-T-D	Risk Rating/Pts
3-12	C-	178.65	66.12	C / 4.7	13.59%	B- / 7.2
2011	C	139.10	58.21	C / 5.1	1.58%	B- / 7.1
2010	C	237.10	74.37	C+ / 5.9	18.75%	C / 5.0
2009	A	94.40	64.21	A / 9.5	65.38%	C / 5.1

Major Rating Factors: Middle of the road best describes *SPDR S&P Emerging Markets ETF whose TheStreet.com Investment Rating is currently a C- (Fair). The fund currently has a performance rating of C (Fair) based on an annualized return of 20.39% over the last three years and a total return of 13.59% year to date 2012. Factored into the performance evaluation is an expense ratio of 0.60% (very low).

The fund's risk rating is currently B- (Good). It carries a beta of 1.02, meaning that its performance tracks fairly well with that of the overall stock market. Volatility, as measured by both the semi-deviation and a drawdown factor, is considered low. As of March 31, 2012, *SPDR S&P Emerging Markets ETF traded at a discount of .08% below its net asset value, which is better than its one-year historical average premium of .05%.

John A. Tucker currently receives a manager quality ranking of 37 (0=worst, 99=best). If you desire an average level of risk, then this fund may be an option.

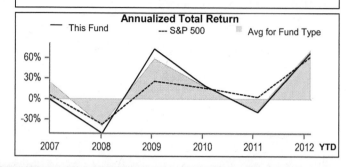

*SPDR S&P Emg Markets Dividend ET (EDIV)

D   **Weak**

Fund Family: SSgA Funds Management Inc
Fund Type: Growth and Income
Inception Date: February 23, 2011

Data Date	Investment Rating	Net Assets ($Mil)	Price	Performance Rating/Pts	Total Return Y-T-D	Risk Rating/Pts
3-12	D	329.51	50.85	D+ / 2.8	8.39%	B- / 7.2

Major Rating Factors:
Disappointing performance is the major factor driving the D (Weak) TheStreet.com Investment Rating for *SPDR S&P Emg Markets Dividend ET. The fund currently has a performance rating of D+ (Weak) based on an annualized return of 0.00% over the last three years and a total return of 8.39% year to date 2012. Factored into the performance evaluation is an expense ratio of 0.62% (very low).

The fund's risk rating is currently B- (Good). It carries a beta of 0.00, meaning the fund's expected move will be 0.0% for every 10% move in the market. Volatility, as measured by both the semi-deviation and a drawdown factor, is considered low. As of March 31, 2012, *SPDR S&P Emg Markets Dividend ET traded at a premium of .32% above its net asset value, which is better than its one-year historical average premium of .74%.

John A. Tucker currently receives a manager quality ranking of 15 (0=worst, 99=best). This fund offers only a moderate level of risk but investors looking for strong performance are still waiting.

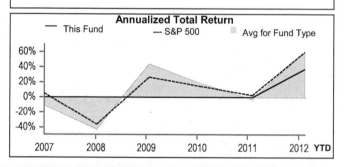

*SPDR S&P Emg Markets Sm Cap ETF (EWX)

D+   **Weak**

Fund Family: SSgA Funds Management Inc
Fund Type: Global
Inception Date: May 12, 2008

Data Date	Investment Rating	Net Assets ($Mil)	Price	Performance Rating/Pts	Total Return Y-T-D	Risk Rating/Pts
3-12	D+	933.20	45.93	C+ / 5.7	21.73%	C / 5.1
2011	D+	736.60	37.73	C / 4.7	1.33%	C / 5.0
2010	B+	1,245.10	57.01	A / 9.3	23.48%	C / 4.8
2009	A	65.67	47.60	A+ / 9.8	92.32%	C / 5.0

Major Rating Factors: *SPDR S&P Emg Markets Sm Cap ETF receives a TheStreet.com Investment Rating of D+ (Weak). The fund currently has a performance rating of C+ (Fair) based on an annualized return of 22.76% over the last three years and a total return of 21.73% year to date 2012. Factored into the performance evaluation is an expense ratio of 0.66% (very low).

The fund's risk rating is currently C (Fair). It carries a beta of 1.23, meaning it is expected to move 12.3% for every 10% move in the market. Volatility, as measured by both the semi-deviation and a drawdown factor, is considered average. As of March 31, 2012, *SPDR S&P Emg Markets Sm Cap ETF traded at a premium of .90% above its net asset value, which is worse than its one-year historical average discount of .11%.

John A. Tucker currently receives a manager quality ranking of 67 (0=worst, 99=best). If you desire an average level of risk, then this fund may be an option.

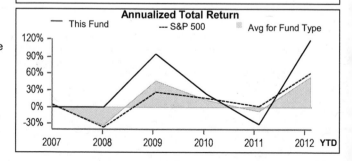

*SPDR S&P Glbl Natural Resources (GNR)   D-   Weak

Fund Family: SSgA Funds Management Inc
Fund Type: Energy/Natural Resources
Inception Date: September 13, 2010

Data Date	Investment Rating	Net Assets ($Mil)	Price	Perfor-mance Rating/Pts	Total Return Y-T-D	Risk Rating/Pts
3-12	D-	254.02	52.67	D- / 1.2	7.45%	C+ / 6.9
2011	D	171.40	49.02	D- / 1.1	2.75%	C+ / 6.8

Major Rating Factors:
Disappointing performance is the major factor driving the D- (Weak) TheStreet.com Investment Rating for *SPDR S&P Glbl Natural Resources. The fund currently has a performance rating of D- (Weak) based on an annualized return of 0.00% over the last three years and a total return of 7.45% year to date 2012. Factored into the performance evaluation is an expense ratio of 0.40% (very low).

The fund's risk rating is currently C+ (Fair). It carries a beta of 0.00, meaning the fund's expected move will be 0.0% for every 10% move in the market. Volatility, as measured by both the semi-deviation and a drawdown factor, is considered low. As of March 31, 2012, *SPDR S&P Glbl Natural Resources traded at a premium of .55% above its net asset value, which is worse than its one-year historical average premium of .18%.

John A. Tucker currently receives a manager quality ranking of 16 (0=worst, 99=best). This fund offers only a moderate level of risk but investors looking for strong performance are still waiting.

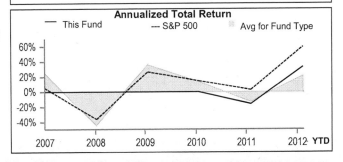

*SPDR S&P Health Care Equipment E (XHE)   C   Fair

Fund Family: SSgA Funds Management Inc
Fund Type: Health
Inception Date: January 26, 2011

Data Date	Investment Rating	Net Assets ($Mil)	Price	Perfor-mance Rating/Pts	Total Return Y-T-D	Risk Rating/Pts
3-12	C	22.48	55.84	C / 4.7	13.18%	B / 8.3

Major Rating Factors: Middle of the road best describes *SPDR S&P Health Care Equipment E whose TheStreet.com Investment Rating is currently a C (Fair). The fund currently has a performance rating of C (Fair) based on an annualized return of 0.00% over the last three years and a total return of 13.18% year to date 2012. Factored into the performance evaluation is an expense ratio of 0.35% (very low).

The fund's risk rating is currently B (Good). It carries a beta of 0.00, meaning the fund's expected move will be 0.0% for every 10% move in the market. Volatility, as measured by both the semi-deviation and a drawdown factor, is considered low. As of March 31, 2012, *SPDR S&P Health Care Equipment E traded at a discount of .52% below its net asset value, which is better than its one-year historical average premium of .11%.

John A. Tucker currently receives a manager quality ranking of 43 (0=worst, 99=best). If you desire an average level of risk, then this fund may be an option.

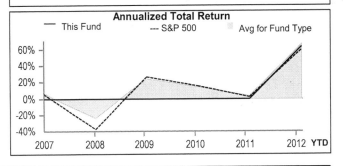

*SPDR S&P Homebuilders ETF (XHB)   B-   Good

Fund Family: SSgA Funds Management Inc
Fund Type: Income
Inception Date: January 31, 2006

Data Date	Investment Rating	Net Assets ($Mil)	Price	Perfor-mance Rating/Pts	Total Return Y-T-D	Risk Rating/Pts
3-12	B-	1,393.47	21.35	B / 8.2	25.08%	B- / 7.1
2011	C	876.90	17.10	C+ / 5.8	4.85%	B- / 7.0
2010	C	874.70	17.39	C+ / 6.1	17.40%	C / 4.9
2009	E+	556.11	15.11	E+ / 0.6	24.61%	C / 4.3

Major Rating Factors: Strong performance is the major factor driving the B- (Good) TheStreet.com Investment Rating for *SPDR S&P Homebuilders ETF. The fund currently has a performance rating of B (Good) based on an annualized return of 24.02% over the last three years and a total return of 25.08% year to date 2012. Factored into the performance evaluation is an expense ratio of 0.37% (very low).

The fund's risk rating is currently B- (Good). It carries a beta of 1.61, meaning it is expected to move 16.1% for every 10% move in the market. Volatility, as measured by both the semi-deviation and a drawdown factor, is considered low. As of March 31, 2012, *SPDR S&P Homebuilders ETF traded at a discount of .05% below its net asset value, which is better than its one-year historical average discount of .01%.

John A. Tucker currently receives a manager quality ranking of 16 (0=worst, 99=best). If you desire only a moderate level of risk and strong performance, then this fund is an excellent option.

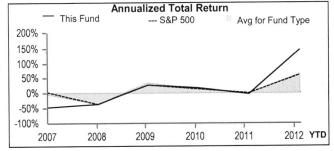

*SPDR S&P International Div ETF (DWX)

C-   Fair

Fund Family: SSgA Funds Management Inc
Fund Type: Emerging Market
Inception Date: February 12, 2008

Major Rating Factors: Middle of the road best describes *SPDR S&P International Div ETF whose TheStreet.com Investment Rating is currently a C- (Fair). The fund currently has a performance rating of C- (Fair) based on an annualized return of 19.89% over the last three years and a total return of 8.21% year to date 2012. Factored into the performance evaluation is an expense ratio of 0.46% (very low).

The fund's risk rating is currently B- (Good). It carries a beta of 0.95, meaning that its performance tracks fairly well with that of the overall stock market. Volatility, as measured by both the semi-deviation and a drawdown factor, is considered low. As of March 31, 2012, *SPDR S&P International Div ETF traded at a premium of .52% above its net asset value, which is worse than its one-year historical average premium of .24%.

John A. Tucker currently receives a manager quality ranking of 47 (0=worst, 99=best). If you desire an average level of risk, then this fund may be an option.

Data Date	Investment Rating	Net Assets ($Mil)	Price	Performance Rating/Pts	Total Return Y-T-D	Risk Rating/Pts
3-12	C-	850.14	49.97	C- / 4.2	8.21%	B- / 7.3
2011	C-	603.60	46.49	C- / 4.2	-0.17%	B- / 7.1
2010	B	351.30	56.00	B+ / 8.6	7.87%	C / 4.7
2009	A-	126.04	54.40	A / 9.3	56.71%	C / 4.9

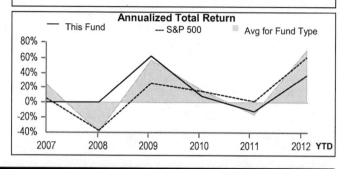

*SPDR S&P International Mid Cap E (MDD)

C-   Fair

Fund Family: SSgA Funds Management Inc
Fund Type: Global
Inception Date: May 7, 2008

Major Rating Factors: Middle of the road best describes *SPDR S&P International Mid Cap E whose TheStreet.com Investment Rating is currently a C- (Fair). The fund currently has a performance rating of C- (Fair) based on an annualized return of 18.48% over the last three years and a total return of 13.70% year to date 2012. Factored into the performance evaluation is an expense ratio of 0.46% (very low).

The fund's risk rating is currently B- (Good). It carries a beta of 0.97, meaning that its performance tracks fairly well with that of the overall stock market. Volatility, as measured by both the semi-deviation and a drawdown factor, is considered low. As of March 31, 2012, *SPDR S&P International Mid Cap E traded at a premium of .25% above its net asset value, which is worse than its one-year historical average premium of .01%.

John A. Tucker currently receives a manager quality ranking of 66 (0=worst, 99=best). If you desire an average level of risk, then this fund may be an option.

Data Date	Investment Rating	Net Assets ($Mil)	Price	Performance Rating/Pts	Total Return Y-T-D	Risk Rating/Pts
3-12	C-	39.51	28.29	C- / 4.2	13.70%	B- / 7.7
2011	C-	35.10	24.88	C- / 3.5	0.92%	B- / 7.4
2010	B+	40.10	31.00	A / 9.4	23.05%	C / 4.3
2009	B	21.72	26.24	B / 8.1	30.50%	C / 5.1

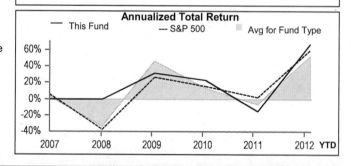

*SPDR S&P International Small Cap (GWX)

C   Fair

Fund Family: SSgA Funds Management Inc
Fund Type: Foreign
Inception Date: April 20, 2007

Major Rating Factors: Middle of the road best describes *SPDR S&P International Small Cap whose TheStreet.com Investment Rating is currently a C (Fair). The fund currently has a performance rating of C (Fair) based on an annualized return of 21.50% over the last three years and a total return of 14.30% year to date 2012. Factored into the performance evaluation is an expense ratio of 0.61% (very low).

The fund's risk rating is currently B- (Good). It carries a beta of 1.03, meaning that its performance tracks fairly well with that of the overall stock market. Volatility, as measured by both the semi-deviation and a drawdown factor, is considered low. As of March 31, 2012, *SPDR S&P International Small Cap traded at a premium of .52% above its net asset value, which is worse than its one-year historical average discount of .02%.

John A. Tucker currently receives a manager quality ranking of 75 (0=worst, 99=best). If you desire an average level of risk, then this fund may be an option.

Data Date	Investment Rating	Net Assets ($Mil)	Price	Performance Rating/Pts	Total Return Y-T-D	Risk Rating/Pts
3-12	C	741.26	28.77	C / 5.1	14.30%	B- / 7.8
2011	C-	656.90	25.17	C- / 3.9	0.20%	B- / 7.7
2010	C	806.70	30.84	C / 5.4	24.94%	C / 5.4
2009	B+	509.03	25.33	B+ / 8.5	35.65%	C / 5.3

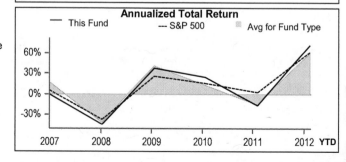

*SPDR S&P Metals & Mining ETF (XME)　　　　　　　D+　　　Weak

Fund Family: SSgA Funds Management Inc
Fund Type: Income
Inception Date: June 19, 2006

Major Rating Factors: *SPDR S&P Metals & Mining ETF receives a TheStreet.com Investment Rating of D+ (Weak). The fund currently has a performance rating of C- (Fair) based on an annualized return of 21.16% over the last three years and a total return of 1.72% year to date 2012. Factored into the performance evaluation is an expense ratio of 0.36% (very low).

The fund's risk rating is currently C+ (Fair). It carries a beta of 1.90, meaning it is expected to move 19.0% for every 10% move in the market. Volatility, as measured by both the semi-deviation and a drawdown factor, is considered low. As of March 31, 2012, *SPDR S&P Metals & Mining ETF traded at a premium of .04% above its net asset value, which is worse than its one-year historical average premium of .01%.

John A. Tucker currently receives a manager quality ranking of 10 (0=worst, 99=best). If you desire an average level of risk, then this fund may be an option.

Data Date	Investment Rating	Net Assets ($Mil)	Price	Perfor-mance Rating/Pts	Total Return Y-T-D	Risk Rating/Pts
3-12	D+	735.50	49.72	C- / 3.6	1.72%	C+ / 6.3
2011	C-	707.50	48.99	C / 5.1	4.74%	C+ / 6.2
2010	C+	1,220.90	68.78	B / 7.8	34.14%	C- / 3.7
2009	C+	602.42	51.61	B / 7.7	73.19%	C- / 4.1

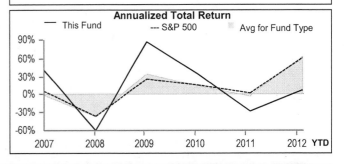

*SPDR S&P MidCap 400 ETF (MDY)　　　　　　　C+　　　Fair

Fund Family: Bank of New York Mellon
Fund Type: Growth
Inception Date: April 28, 1995

Major Rating Factors: Middle of the road best describes *SPDR S&P MidCap 400 ETF whose TheStreet.com Investment Rating is currently a C+ (Fair). The fund currently has a performance rating of C+ (Fair) based on an annualized return of 25.15% over the last three years and a total return of 13.30% year to date 2012. Factored into the performance evaluation is an expense ratio of 0.25% (very low).

The fund's risk rating is currently B- (Good). It carries a beta of 1.20, meaning it is expected to move 12.0% for every 10% move in the market. Volatility, as measured by both the semi-deviation and a drawdown factor, is considered low. As of March 31, 2012, *SPDR S&P MidCap 400 ETF traded at a discount of .07% below its net asset value, which is better than its one-year historical average discount of .02%.

Alistair Lowe currently receives a manager quality ranking of 43 (0=worst, 99=best). If you desire an average level of risk, then this fund may be an option.

Data Date	Investment Rating	Net Assets ($Mil)	Price	Perfor-mance Rating/Pts	Total Return Y-T-D	Risk Rating/Pts
3-12	C+	10,449.25	180.71	C+ / 6.8	13.30%	B- / 7.9
2011	C+	0.00	159.49	C+ / 6.4	1.53%	B- / 7.7
2010	B-	10,875.80	164.68	B- / 7.2	25.93%	C / 5.5
2009	C-	7,581.13	131.74	C- / 3.8	33.85%	C+ / 6.0

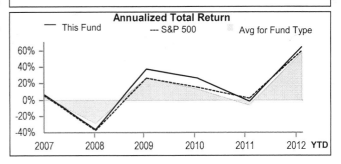

*SPDR S&P Oil & Gas Equip & Serv (XES)　　　　　C　　　Fair

Fund Family: SSgA Funds Management Inc
Fund Type: Energy/Natural Resources
Inception Date: June 19, 2006

Major Rating Factors: Middle of the road best describes *SPDR S&P Oil & Gas Equip & Serv whose TheStreet.com Investment Rating is currently a C (Fair). The fund currently has a performance rating of C+ (Fair) based on an annualized return of 25.32% over the last three years and a total return of 5.18% year to date 2012. Factored into the performance evaluation is an expense ratio of 0.37% (very low).

The fund's risk rating is currently C+ (Fair). It carries a beta of 1.46, meaning it is expected to move 14.6% for every 10% move in the market. Volatility, as measured by both the semi-deviation and a drawdown factor, is considered low. As of March 31, 2012, *SPDR S&P Oil & Gas Equip & Serv traded at a premium of .05% above its net asset value.

John A. Tucker currently receives a manager quality ranking of 49 (0=worst, 99=best). If you desire an average level of risk, then this fund may be an option.

Data Date	Investment Rating	Net Assets ($Mil)	Price	Perfor-mance Rating/Pts	Total Return Y-T-D	Risk Rating/Pts
3-12	C	343.91	36.41	C+ / 5.9	5.18%	C+ / 6.4
2011	C+	341.50	34.66	B- / 7.5	2.71%	C+ / 6.3
2010	C-	451.20	36.71	C+ / 6.0	30.10%	C- / 4.2
2009	C	199.10	28.48	C+ / 6.5	57.09%	C / 4.6

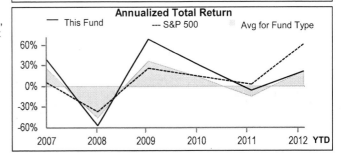

*SPDR S&P Oil & Gas Expl & Prod (XOP)

C **Fair**

Fund Family: SSgA Funds Management Inc
Fund Type: Income
Inception Date: June 19, 2006

Data Date	Investment Rating	Net Assets ($Mil)	Price	Performance Rating/Pts	Total Return Y-T-D	Risk Rating/Pts
3-12	C	925.17	56.91	C+ / 6.2	8.23%	C+ / 6.9
2011	C+	776.50	52.69	B- / 7.1	3.61%	C+ / 6.7
2010	C+	722.10	52.75	B- / 7.0	28.57%	C / 4.8
2009	C	280.28	41.21	C / 5.1	31.82%	C / 5.1

Major Rating Factors: Middle of the road best describes *SPDR S&P Oil & Gas Expl & Prod whose TheStreet.com Investment Rating is currently a C (Fair). The fund currently has a performance rating of C+ (Fair) based on an annualized return of 24.75% over the last three years and a total return of 8.23% year to date 2012. Factored into the performance evaluation is an expense ratio of 0.36% (very low).

The fund's risk rating is currently C+ (Fair). It carries a beta of 1.49, meaning it is expected to move 14.9% for every 10% move in the market. Volatility, as measured by both the semi-deviation and a drawdown factor, is considered low. As of March 31, 2012, *SPDR S&P Oil & Gas Expl & Prod traded at a discount of .04% below its net asset value, which is better than its one-year historical average discount of .02%.

John A. Tucker currently receives a manager quality ranking of 23 (0=worst, 99=best). If you desire an average level of risk, then this fund may be an option.

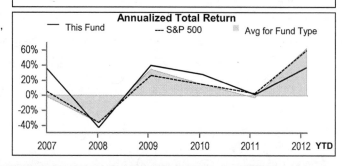

Annualized Total Return

*SPDR S&P Pharmaceuticals ETF (XPH)

B **Good**

Fund Family: SSgA Funds Management Inc
Fund Type: Health
Inception Date: June 19, 2006

Data Date	Investment Rating	Net Assets ($Mil)	Price	Performance Rating/Pts	Total Return Y-T-D	Risk Rating/Pts
3-12	B	336.78	57.10	B+ / 8.6	11.44%	B- / 7.3
2011	C+	289.90	51.33	B- / 7.3	0.66%	C+ / 6.3
2010	B+	209.50	46.09	B+ / 8.5	22.48%	C / 5.4
2009	C+	40.50	38.08	C / 4.8	25.17%	B- / 7.2

Major Rating Factors: Strong performance is the major factor driving the B (Good) TheStreet.com Investment Rating for *SPDR S&P Pharmaceuticals ETF. The fund currently has a performance rating of B+ (Good) based on an annualized return of 30.59% over the last three years and a total return of 11.44% year to date 2012. Factored into the performance evaluation is an expense ratio of 0.36% (very low).

The fund's risk rating is currently B- (Good). It carries a beta of 0.62, meaning the fund's expected move will be 6.2% for every 10% move in the market. Volatility, as measured by both the semi-deviation and a drawdown factor, is considered low. As of March 31, 2012, *SPDR S&P Pharmaceuticals ETF traded at a premium of .04% above its net asset value, which is worse than its one-year historical average premium of .02%.

John A. Tucker currently receives a manager quality ranking of 89 (0=worst, 99=best). If you desire only a moderate level of risk and strong performance, then this fund is an excellent option.

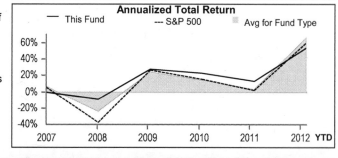

Annualized Total Return

*SPDR S&P Retail ETF (XRT)

A **Excellent**

Fund Family: SSgA Funds Management Inc
Fund Type: Income
Inception Date: June 19, 2006

Data Date	Investment Rating	Net Assets ($Mil)	Price	Performance Rating/Pts	Total Return Y-T-D	Risk Rating/Pts
3-12	A	793.25	61.25	A / 9.4	16.75%	B / 8.1
2011	A-	614.50	52.55	A / 9.3	-0.91%	B / 8.1
2010	A-	976.70	48.36	A- / 9.2	37.38%	C / 5.3
2009	C-	1,018.01	35.60	C / 4.7	70.31%	C / 5.4

Major Rating Factors:
Exceptional performance is the major factor driving the A (Excellent) TheStreet.com Investment Rating for *SPDR S&P Retail ETF. The fund currently has a performance rating of A (Excellent) based on an annualized return of 36.88% over the last three years and a total return of 16.75% year to date 2012. Factored into the performance evaluation is an expense ratio of 0.36% (very low).

The fund's risk rating is currently B (Good). It carries a beta of 1.18, meaning it is expected to move 11.8% for every 10% move in the market. Volatility, as measured by both the semi-deviation and a drawdown factor, is considered low. As of March 31, 2012, *SPDR S&P Retail ETF traded at a price exactly equal to its net asset value, which is better than its one-year historical average premium of .01%.

John A. Tucker currently receives a manager quality ranking of 84 (0=worst, 99=best). If you desire only a moderate level of risk and strong performance, then this fund is an excellent option.

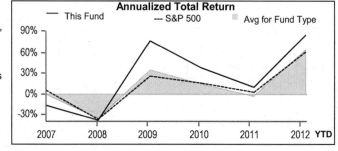

Annualized Total Return

*SPDR S&P Russia (RBL)   D-   Weak

Fund Family: SSgA Funds Management Inc
Fund Type: Emerging Market
Inception Date: March 10, 2010

Data Date	Investment Rating	Net Assets ($Mil)	Price	Perfor-mance Rating/Pts	Total Return Y-T-D	Risk Rating/Pts
3-12	D-	59.87	30.93	D / 1.6	17.52%	C+ / 5.7
2011	D-	35.20	26.32	E+ / 0.7	1.52%	C+ / 5.6

Major Rating Factors:
Disappointing performance is the major factor driving the D- (Weak) TheStreet.com Investment Rating for *SPDR S&P Russia. The fund currently has a performance rating of D (Weak) based on an annualized return of 0.00% over the last three years and a total return of 17.52% year to date 2012. Factored into the performance evaluation is an expense ratio of 0.59% (very low).

The fund's risk rating is currently C+ (Fair). It carries a beta of 0.00, meaning the fund's expected move will be 0.0% for every 10% move in the market. Volatility, as measured by both the semi-deviation and a drawdown factor, is considered low. As of March 31, 2012, *SPDR S&P Russia traded at a premium of .72% above its net asset value, which is worse than its one-year historical average discount of .11%.

John A. Tucker currently receives a manager quality ranking of 14 (0=worst, 99=best). This fund offers only a moderate level of risk but investors looking for strong performance are still waiting.

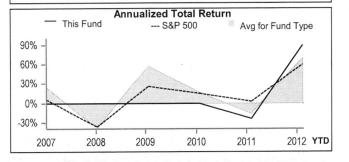
Annualized Total Return

*SPDR S&P Semiconductor ETF (XSD)   C   Fair

Fund Family: SSgA Funds Management Inc
Fund Type: Income
Inception Date: January 31, 2006

Data Date	Investment Rating	Net Assets ($Mil)	Price	Perfor-mance Rating/Pts	Total Return Y-T-D	Risk Rating/Pts
3-12	C	55.07	52.50	C / 5.3	18.56%	C+ / 6.9
2011	C	33.20	44.32	C+ / 6.2	2.30%	C+ / 6.7
2010	B	109.20	54.60	B / 8.1	15.71%	C / 5.0
2009	C	103.28	47.60	C+ / 6.2	91.09%	C / 4.9

Major Rating Factors: Middle of the road best describes *SPDR S&P Semiconductor ETF whose TheStreet.com Investment Rating is currently a C (Fair). The fund currently has a performance rating of C (Fair) based on an annualized return of 21.48% over the last three years and a total return of 18.56% year to date 2012. Factored into the performance evaluation is an expense ratio of 0.37% (very low).

The fund's risk rating is currently C+ (Fair). It carries a beta of 1.52, meaning it is expected to move 15.2% for every 10% move in the market. Volatility, as measured by both the semi-deviation and a drawdown factor, is considered low. As of March 31, 2012, *SPDR S&P Semiconductor ETF traded at a premium of .11% above its net asset value.

John A. Tucker currently receives a manager quality ranking of 16 (0=worst, 99=best). If you desire an average level of risk, then this fund may be an option.

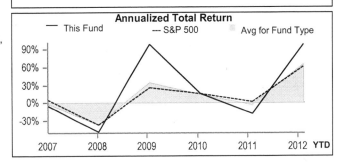
Annualized Total Return

*SPDR S&P Telecom ETF (XTL)   D   Weak

Fund Family: SSgA Funds Management Inc
Fund Type: Growth
Inception Date: January 26, 2011

Data Date	Investment Rating	Net Assets ($Mil)	Price	Perfor-mance Rating/Pts	Total Return Y-T-D	Risk Rating/Pts
3-12	D	4.64	46.72	D / 2.2	11.91%	C+ / 6.9

Major Rating Factors:
Disappointing performance is the major factor driving the D (Weak) TheStreet.com Investment Rating for *SPDR S&P Telecom ETF. The fund currently has a performance rating of D (Weak) based on an annualized return of 0.00% over the last three years and a total return of 11.91% year to date 2012. Factored into the performance evaluation is an expense ratio of 0.35% (very low).

The fund's risk rating is currently C+ (Fair). It carries a beta of 0.00, meaning the fund's expected move will be 0.0% for every 10% move in the market. Volatility, as measured by both the semi-deviation and a drawdown factor, is considered low. As of March 31, 2012, *SPDR S&P Telecom ETF traded at a premium of .09% above its net asset value, which is in line with its one-year historical average premium of .09%.

John A. Tucker currently receives a manager quality ranking of 6 (0=worst, 99=best). This fund offers only a moderate level of risk but investors looking for strong performance are still waiting.

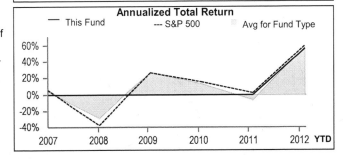
Annualized Total Return

*SPDR S&P Transportation ETF (XTN)

D **Weak**

Fund Family: SSgA Funds Management Inc
Fund Type: Utilities
Inception Date: January 26, 2011

Major Rating Factors:
Disappointing performance is the major factor driving the D (Weak) TheStreet.com Investment Rating for *SPDR S&P Transportation ETF. The fund currently has a performance rating of D+ (Weak) based on an annualized return of 0.00% over the last three years and a total return of 9.37% year to date 2012. Factored into the performance evaluation is an expense ratio of 0.35% (very low).

The fund's risk rating is currently C+ (Fair). It carries a beta of 0.00, meaning the fund's expected move will be 0.0% for every 10% move in the market. Volatility, as measured by both the semi-deviation and a drawdown factor, is considered low. As of March 31, 2012, *SPDR S&P Transportation ETF traded at a discount of 1.62% below its net asset value, which is better than its one-year historical average discount of .01%.

John A. Tucker currently receives a manager quality ranking of 9 (0=worst, 99=best). This fund offers only a moderate level of risk but investors looking for strong performance are still waiting.

Data Date	Investment Rating	Net Assets ($Mil)	Price	Performance Rating/Pts	Total Return Y-T-D	Risk Rating/Pts
3-12	D	12.44	49.25	D+ / 2.7	9.37%	C+ / 6.9

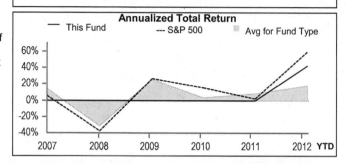

*SPDR S&P WORLD EX-US ETF (GWL)

C- **Fair**

Fund Family: SSgA Funds Management Inc
Fund Type: Global
Inception Date: April 20, 2007

Major Rating Factors: Middle of the road best describes *SPDR S&P WORLD EX-US ETF whose TheStreet.com Investment Rating is currently a C- (Fair). The fund currently has a performance rating of C- (Fair) based on an annualized return of 15.28% over the last three years and a total return of 12.30% year to date 2012. Factored into the performance evaluation is an expense ratio of 0.35% (very low).

The fund's risk rating is currently B- (Good). It carries a beta of 1.04, meaning that its performance tracks fairly well with that of the overall stock market. Volatility, as measured by both the semi-deviation and a drawdown factor, is considered low. As of March 31, 2012, *SPDR S&P WORLD EX-US ETF traded at a premium of .70% above its net asset value, which is worse than its one-year historical average premium of .25%.

John A. Tucker currently receives a manager quality ranking of 44 (0=worst, 99=best). If you desire an average level of risk, then this fund may be an option.

Data Date	Investment Rating	Net Assets ($Mil)	Price	Performance Rating/Pts	Total Return Y-T-D	Risk Rating/Pts
3-12	C-	165.23	24.47	C- / 3.5	12.30%	B- / 7.5
2011	D+	140.20	21.79	D+ / 2.7	-0.09%	B- / 7.2
2010	D	118.30	25.95	D+ / 2.3	11.26%	C / 5.4
2009	B+	84.89	23.93	B+ / 8.3	27.01%	C / 5.5

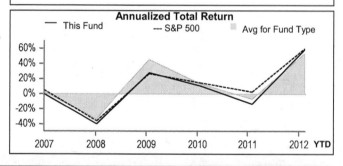

*SPDR SP Intl Con Disc Sect ETF (IPD)

C **Fair**

Fund Family: SSgA Funds Management Inc
Fund Type: Global
Inception Date: July 16, 2008

Major Rating Factors: Middle of the road best describes *SPDR SP Intl Con Disc Sect ETF whose TheStreet.com Investment Rating is currently a C (Fair). The fund currently has a performance rating of C (Fair) based on an annualized return of 19.57% over the last three years and a total return of 20.36% year to date 2012. Factored into the performance evaluation is an expense ratio of 0.50% (very low).

The fund's risk rating is currently B (Good). It carries a beta of 1.01, meaning that its performance tracks fairly well with that of the overall stock market. Volatility, as measured by both the semi-deviation and a drawdown factor, is considered low. As of March 31, 2012, *SPDR SP Intl Con Disc Sect ETF traded at a premium of .41% above its net asset value, which is worse than its one-year historical average discount of .33%.

John A. Tucker currently receives a manager quality ranking of 77 (0=worst, 99=best). If you desire an average level of risk, then this fund may be an option.

Data Date	Investment Rating	Net Assets ($Mil)	Price	Performance Rating/Pts	Total Return Y-T-D	Risk Rating/Pts
3-12	C	8.75	29.30	C / 5.3	20.36%	B / 8.0
2011	C	4.90	24.37	C / 5.0	0.86%	B- / 7.9
2010	A	22.00	29.34	A / 9.3	19.59%	C+ / 6.2
2009	A+	4.82	24.87	A / 9.3	61.86%	C+ / 6.2

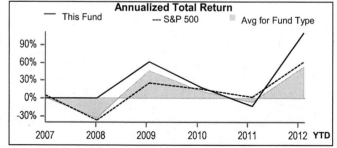

*SPDR SP Intl Con Stap Sect ETF (IPS)

C+ **Fair**

Fund Family: SSgA Funds Management Inc
Fund Type: Global
Inception Date: July 16, 2008

Major Rating Factors: Middle of the road best describes *SPDR SP Intl Con Stap Sect ETF whose TheStreet.com Investment Rating is currently a C+ (Fair). The fund currently has a performance rating of C+ (Fair) based on an annualized return of 22.34% over the last three years and a total return of 7.79% year to date 2012. Factored into the performance evaluation is an expense ratio of 0.51% (very low).

The fund's risk rating is currently B (Good). It carries a beta of 0.63, meaning the fund's expected move will be 6.3% for every 10% move in the market. Volatility, as measured by both the semi-deviation and a drawdown factor, is considered low. As of March 31, 2012, *SPDR SP Intl Con Stap Sect ETF traded at a premium of .36% above its net asset value, which is worse than its one-year historical average premium of .03%.

John A. Tucker currently receives a manager quality ranking of 87 (0=worst, 99=best). If you desire an average level of risk, then this fund may be an option.

Data Date	Investment Rating	Net Assets ($Mil)	Price	Performance Rating/Pts	Total Return Y-T-D	Risk Rating/Pts
3-12	C+	20.07	33.57	C+ / 5.8	7.79%	B / 8.8
2011	C+	17.20	31.31	C / 4.9	-1.09%	B / 8.3
2010	A	12.40	30.95	B+ / 8.6	11.72%	C+ / 6.8
2009	A+	5.26	28.32	B+ / 8.3	26.07%	B- / 7.0

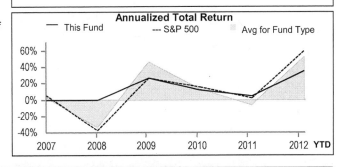

Annualized Total Return

*SPDR SP Intl Energy Sector ETF (IPW)

D+ **Weak**

Fund Family: SSgA Funds Management Inc
Fund Type: Energy/Natural Resources
Inception Date: July 16, 2008

Major Rating Factors:
Disappointing performance is the major factor driving the D+ (Weak) TheStreet.com Investment Rating for *SPDR SP Intl Energy Sector ETF. The fund currently has a performance rating of D+ (Weak) based on an annualized return of 12.88% over the last three years and a total return of 4.16% year to date 2012. Factored into the performance evaluation is an expense ratio of 0.51% (very low).

The fund's risk rating is currently B- (Good). It carries a beta of 1.07, meaning that its performance tracks fairly well with that of the overall stock market. Volatility, as measured by both the semi-deviation and a drawdown factor, is considered low. As of March 31, 2012, *SPDR SP Intl Energy Sector ETF traded at a discount of .38% below its net asset value, which is better than its one-year historical average discount of .18%.

John A. Tucker currently receives a manager quality ranking of 23 (0=worst, 99=best). This fund offers only a moderate level of risk but investors looking for strong performance are still waiting.

Data Date	Investment Rating	Net Assets ($Mil)	Price	Performance Rating/Pts	Total Return Y-T-D	Risk Rating/Pts
3-12	D+	11.80	26.12	D+ / 2.7	4.16%	B- / 7.4
2011	C-	10.20	25.25	C- / 3.7	1.60%	B- / 7.4
2010	A-	15.00	27.44	B+ / 8.9	4.68%	C+ / 6.1
2009	A+	6.37	26.86	B+ / 8.6	34.41%	C+ / 6.2

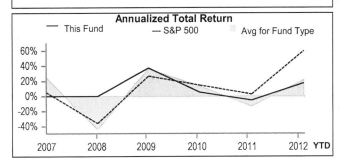

Annualized Total Return

*SPDR SP Intl Finl Sector ETF (IPF)

D+ **Weak**

Fund Family: SSgA Funds Management Inc
Fund Type: Financial Services
Inception Date: July 16, 2008

Major Rating Factors:
Disappointing performance is the major factor driving the D+ (Weak) TheStreet.com Investment Rating for *SPDR SP Intl Finl Sector ETF. The fund currently has a performance rating of D+ (Weak) based on an annualized return of 11.96% over the last three years and a total return of 16.38% year to date 2012. Factored into the performance evaluation is an expense ratio of 0.51% (very low).

The fund's risk rating is currently B- (Good). It carries a beta of 0.97, meaning that its performance tracks fairly well with that of the overall stock market. Volatility, as measured by both the semi-deviation and a drawdown factor, is considered low. As of March 31, 2012, *SPDR SP Intl Finl Sector ETF traded at a discount of .40% below its net asset value, which is better than its one-year historical average discount of .28%.

John A. Tucker currently receives a manager quality ranking of 22 (0=worst, 99=best). This fund offers only a moderate level of risk but investors looking for strong performance are still waiting.

Data Date	Investment Rating	Net Assets ($Mil)	Price	Performance Rating/Pts	Total Return Y-T-D	Risk Rating/Pts
3-12	D+	7.89	17.46	D+ / 2.7	16.38%	B- / 7.3
2011	D	4.60	15.05	D / 1.7	-0.98%	B- / 7.1
2010	C+	6.00	19.81	B- / 7.0	0.56%	C / 5.1
2009	B	5.35	20.45	B+ / 8.5	36.11%	C / 5.0

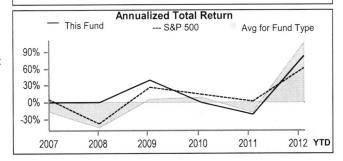

Annualized Total Return

*SPDR SP Intl Health Care ETF (IRY)

C   **Fair**

Fund Family: SSgA Funds Management Inc
Fund Type: Health
Inception Date: July 16, 2008

Major Rating Factors: Middle of the road best describes *SPDR SP Intl Health Care ETF whose TheStreet.com Investment Rating is currently a C (Fair). The fund currently has a performance rating of C- (Fair) based on an annualized return of 15.82% over the last three years and a total return of 5.08% year to date 2012. Factored into the performance evaluation is an expense ratio of 0.50% (very low).

The fund's risk rating is currently B (Good). It carries a beta of 0.69, meaning the fund's expected move will be 6.9% for every 10% move in the market. Volatility, as measured by both the semi-deviation and a drawdown factor, is considered low. As of March 31, 2012, *SPDR SP Intl Health Care ETF traded at a discount of .43% below its net asset value, which is better than its one-year historical average premium of .16%.

John A. Tucker currently receives a manager quality ranking of 53 (0=worst, 99=best). If you desire an average level of risk, then this fund may be an option.

Data Date	Investment Rating	Net Assets ($Mil)	Price	Performance Rating/Pts	Total Return Y-T-D	Risk Rating/Pts
3-12	C	19.43	32.26	C- / 3.8	5.08%	B / 8.5
2011	C-	15.50	31.00	C- / 3.7	-0.65%	B / 8.1
2010	C+	12.10	30.12	C+ / 6.9	3.51%	C+ / 6.5
2009	B+	5.70	29.75	B / 7.7	16.78%	C+ / 6.2

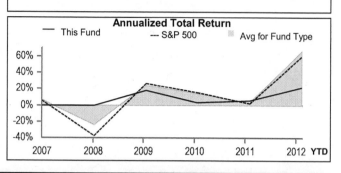

*SPDR SP Intl Industrial ETF (IPN)

C-   **Fair**

Fund Family: SSgA Funds Management Inc
Fund Type: Global
Inception Date: July 16, 2008

Major Rating Factors: Middle of the road best describes *SPDR SP Intl Industrial ETF whose TheStreet.com Investment Rating is currently a C- (Fair). The fund currently has a performance rating of C- (Fair) based on an annualized return of 17.92% over the last three years and a total return of 11.85% year to date 2012. Factored into the performance evaluation is an expense ratio of 0.50% (very low).

The fund's risk rating is currently B- (Good). It carries a beta of 1.01, meaning that its performance tracks fairly well with that of the overall stock market. Volatility, as measured by both the semi-deviation and a drawdown factor, is considered low. As of March 31, 2012, *SPDR SP Intl Industrial ETF traded at a price exactly equal to its net asset value, which is worse than its one-year historical average discount of .29%.

John A. Tucker currently receives a manager quality ranking of 64 (0=worst, 99=best). If you desire an average level of risk, then this fund may be an option.

Data Date	Investment Rating	Net Assets ($Mil)	Price	Performance Rating/Pts	Total Return Y-T-D	Risk Rating/Pts
3-12	C-	14.21	25.67	C- / 3.9	11.85%	B- / 7.7
2011	C-	12.80	23.02	C- / 3.0	-0.17%	B- / 7.6
2010	A-	28.30	28.28	A / 9.3	20.35%	C+ / 5.7
2009	A	4.65	23.88	B+ / 8.8	40.88%	C+ / 5.6

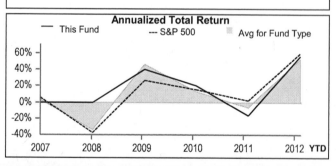

*SPDR SP Intl Materials Sec ETF (IRV)

D+   **Weak**

Fund Family: SSgA Funds Management Inc
Fund Type: Global
Inception Date: July 16, 2008

Major Rating Factors: *SPDR SP Intl Materials Sec ETF receives a TheStreet.com Investment Rating of D+ (Weak). The fund currently has a performance rating of C- (Fair) based on an annualized return of 18.01% over the last three years and a total return of 10.86% year to date 2012. Factored into the performance evaluation is an expense ratio of 0.51% (very low).

The fund's risk rating is currently C+ (Fair). It carries a beta of 1.28, meaning it is expected to move 12.8% for every 10% move in the market. Volatility, as measured by both the semi-deviation and a drawdown factor, is considered low. As of March 31, 2012, *SPDR SP Intl Materials Sec ETF traded at a premium of .32% above its net asset value, which is worse than its one-year historical average discount of .45%.

John A. Tucker currently receives a manager quality ranking of 37 (0=worst, 99=best). If you desire an average level of risk, then this fund may be an option.

Data Date	Investment Rating	Net Assets ($Mil)	Price	Performance Rating/Pts	Total Return Y-T-D	Risk Rating/Pts
3-12	D+	13.96	25.46	C- / 3.7	10.86%	C+ / 6.5
2011	D	12.80	23.06	C- / 3.5	1.97%	C+ / 5.8
2010	B	35.40	30.94	A+ / 9.6	21.94%	C- / 3.6
2009	B	9.22	25.69	A / 9.4	55.87%	C- / 4.1

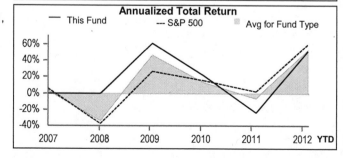

*SPDR SP Intl Tech Sector ETF (IPK)

D+ **Weak**

Fund Family: SSgA Funds Management Inc
Fund Type: Global
Inception Date: July 16, 2008

Major Rating Factors: *SPDR SP Intl Tech Sector ETF receives a TheStreet.com Investment Rating of D+ (Weak). The fund currently has a performance rating of C- (Fair) based on an annualized return of 15.84% over the last three years and a total return of 17.21% year to date 2012. Factored into the performance evaluation is an expense ratio of 0.51% (very low).

The fund's risk rating is currently B- (Good). It carries a beta of 1.00, meaning that its performance tracks fairly well with that of the overall stock market. Volatility, as measured by both the semi-deviation and a drawdown factor, is considered low. As of March 31, 2012, *SPDR SP Intl Tech Sector ETF traded at a discount of .19% below its net asset value, which is worse than its one-year historical average discount of .36%.

John A. Tucker currently receives a manager quality ranking of 54 (0=worst, 99=best). If you desire an average level of risk, then this fund may be an option.

Data Date	Investment Rating	Net Assets ($Mil)	Price	Perfor-mance Rating/Pts	Total Return Y-T-D	Risk Rating/Pts
3-12	D+	14.56	26.43	C- / 3.9	17.21%	B- / 7.0
2011	D+	12.50	22.55	C- / 3.1	0.22%	C+ / 6.6
2010	A-	26.40	27.79	A- / 9.1	15.11%	C / 5.3
2009	B+	11.06	24.48	B+ / 8.6	40.34%	C / 5.4

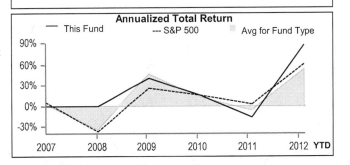

*SPDR SP Intl Telecom Sect ETF (IST)

D+ **Weak**

Fund Family: SSgA Funds Management Inc
Fund Type: Global
Inception Date: July 16, 2008

Major Rating Factors:
Disappointing performance is the major factor driving the D+ (Weak) TheStreet.com Investment Rating for *SPDR SP Intl Telecom Sect ETF. The fund currently has a performance rating of D+ (Weak) based on an annualized return of 12.81% over the last three years and a total return of 1.12% year to date 2012. Factored into the performance evaluation is an expense ratio of 0.51% (very low).

The fund's risk rating is currently B (Good). It carries a beta of 0.71, meaning the fund's expected move will be 7.1% for every 10% move in the market. Volatility, as measured by both the semi-deviation and a drawdown factor, is considered low. As of March 31, 2012, *SPDR SP Intl Telecom Sect ETF traded at a premium of .53% above its net asset value, which is worse than its one-year historical average premium of .12%.

John A. Tucker currently receives a manager quality ranking of 57 (0=worst, 99=best). This fund offers only a moderate level of risk but investors looking for strong performance are still waiting.

Data Date	Investment Rating	Net Assets ($Mil)	Price	Perfor-mance Rating/Pts	Total Return Y-T-D	Risk Rating/Pts
3-12	D+	19.30	22.83	D+ / 2.6	1.12%	B / 8.1
2011	C-	14.80	22.59	D+ / 2.9	-1.24%	B- / 7.9
2010	B	15.90	24.45	B+ / 8.3	9.02%	C / 4.7
2009	C	9.43	23.57	C+ / 6.5	11.21%	C / 4.8

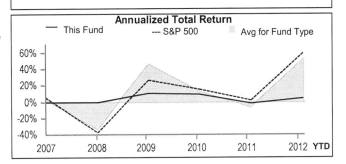

*SPDR SP Intl Utils Sector ETF (IPU)

D **Weak**

Fund Family: SSgA Funds Management Inc
Fund Type: Utilities
Inception Date: July 16, 2008

Major Rating Factors:
Disappointing performance is the major factor driving the D (Weak) TheStreet.com Investment Rating for *SPDR SP Intl Utils Sector ETF. The fund currently has a performance rating of D- (Weak) based on an annualized return of 3.20% over the last three years and a total return of 5.29% year to date 2012. Factored into the performance evaluation is an expense ratio of 0.51% (very low).

The fund's risk rating is currently B- (Good). It carries a beta of 1.02, meaning that its performance tracks fairly well with that of the overall stock market. Volatility, as measured by both the semi-deviation and a drawdown factor, is considered low. As of March 31, 2012, *SPDR SP Intl Utils Sector ETF traded at a premium of .41% above its net asset value, which is worse than its one-year historical average premium of .27%.

John A. Tucker currently receives a manager quality ranking of 12 (0=worst, 99=best). This fund offers only a moderate level of risk but investors looking for strong performance are still waiting.

Data Date	Investment Rating	Net Assets ($Mil)	Price	Perfor-mance Rating/Pts	Total Return Y-T-D	Risk Rating/Pts
3-12	D	14.67	17.33	D- / 1.3	5.29%	B- / 7.6
2011	D	11.60	16.50	D- / 1.3	-0.59%	B- / 7.4
2010	C-	8.40	20.86	C- / 3.8	-5.61%	C+ / 6.2
2009	C	4.56	22.98	C / 5.1	3.92%	C+ / 6.3

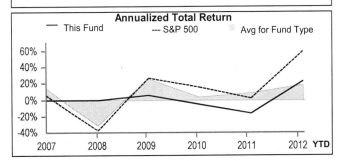

* Denotes ETF Fund

*SPDR SP Mortgage Finance ETF (KME)

D-   **Weak**

Fund Family: SSgA Funds Management Inc
Fund Type: Financial Services
Inception Date: April 29, 2009

Major Rating Factors:

Very poor performance is the major factor driving the D- (Weak) TheStreet.com Investment Rating for *SPDR SP Mortgage Finance ETF. The fund currently has a performance rating of E+ (Very Weak) based on an annualized return of 0.00% over the last three years and a total return of 13.96% year to date 2012. Factored into the performance evaluation is an expense ratio of 0.36% (very low).

The fund's risk rating is currently C+ (Fair). It carries a beta of 0.00, meaning the fund's expected move will be 0.0% for every 10% move in the market. Volatility, as measured by both the semi-deviation and a drawdown factor, is considered low. As of March 31, 2012, *SPDR SP Mortgage Finance ETF traded at a discount of .08% below its net asset value, which is worse than its one-year historical average discount of .10%.

John A. Tucker currently receives a manager quality ranking of 18 (0=worst, 99=best). This fund offers only a moderate level of risk but investors looking for strong performance are still waiting.

Data Date	Investment Rating	Net Assets ($Mil)	Price	Performance Rating/Pts	Total Return Y-T-D	Risk Rating/Pts
3-12	D-	3.75	37.74	E+ / 0.9	13.96%	C+ / 5.9
2011	D-	3.30	33.28	D- / 1.1	0.78%	C+ / 5.9
2010	B+	2.10	42.34	B- / 7.5	6.16%	C+ / 6.4

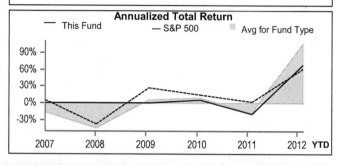

*SPDR STOXX Europe 50 ETF (FEU)

D   **Weak**

Fund Family: SSgA Funds Management Inc
Fund Type: Foreign
Inception Date: October 15, 2002

Major Rating Factors:

Disappointing performance is the major factor driving the D (Weak) TheStreet.com Investment Rating for *SPDR STOXX Europe 50 ETF. The fund currently has a performance rating of D+ (Weak) based on an annualized return of 12.25% over the last three years and a total return of 8.51% year to date 2012. Factored into the performance evaluation is an expense ratio of 0.31% (very low).

The fund's risk rating is currently B- (Good). It carries a beta of 1.13, meaning it is expected to move 11.3% for every 10% move in the market. Volatility, as measured by both the semi-deviation and a drawdown factor, is considered low. As of March 31, 2012, *SPDR STOXX Europe 50 ETF traded at a premium of .60% above its net asset value, which is worse than its one-year historical average discount of .10%.

John A. Tucker has been running the fund for 10 years and currently receives a manager quality ranking of 23 (0=worst, 99=best). This fund offers only a moderate level of risk but investors looking for strong performance are still waiting.

Data Date	Investment Rating	Net Assets ($Mil)	Price	Performance Rating/Pts	Total Return Y-T-D	Risk Rating/Pts
3-12	D	30.26	32.03	D+ / 2.8	8.51%	B- / 7.1
2011	D+	28.40	29.79	D+ / 2.3	-0.72%	B- / 7.0
2010	D-	39.00	33.80	E+ / 0.9	-3.15%	C / 4.7
2009	D	56.51	35.85	D+ / 2.3	27.29%	C / 5.3

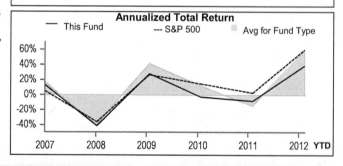

*SPDR Wells Fargo Preferred Stk E (PSK)

C-   **Fair**

Fund Family: SSgA Funds Management Inc
Fund Type: Income
Inception Date: September 16, 2009

Major Rating Factors:

Disappointing performance is the major factor driving the C- (Fair) TheStreet.com Investment Rating for *SPDR Wells Fargo Preferred Stk E. The fund currently has a performance rating of D+ (Weak) based on an annualized return of 0.00% over the last three years and a total return of 7.65% year to date 2012. Factored into the performance evaluation is an expense ratio of 0.46% (very low).

The fund's risk rating is currently B+ (Good). It carries a beta of 0.00, meaning the fund's expected move will be 0.0% for every 10% move in the market. Volatility, as measured by both the semi-deviation and a drawdown factor, is considered very low. As of March 31, 2012, *SPDR Wells Fargo Preferred Stk E traded at a premium of .31% above its net asset value, which is worse than its one-year historical average premium of .10%.

John A. Tucker currently receives a manager quality ranking of 57 (0=worst, 99=best). This fund offers only a moderate level of risk but investors looking for strong performance are still waiting.

Data Date	Investment Rating	Net Assets ($Mil)	Price	Performance Rating/Pts	Total Return Y-T-D	Risk Rating/Pts
3-12	C-	190.32	44.92	D+ / 2.7	7.65%	B+ / 9.1
2011	C-	126.40	42.17	D+ / 2.6	2.59%	B+ / 9.2
2010	A+	102.80	44.59	B / 7.9	13.95%	B / 8.9

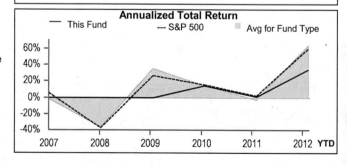

*Technology Select Sector SPDR (XLK)

C+   **Fair**

Fund Family: SSgA Funds Management Inc
Fund Type: Growth
Inception Date: December 16, 1998

Data Date	Investment Rating	Net Assets ($Mil)	Price	Performance Rating/Pts	Total Return Y-T-D	Risk Rating/Pts
3-12	C+	9,815.25	30.16	B- / 7.2	18.89%	B- / 7.6
2011	C+	8,195.60	25.45	C+ / 6.6	2.04%	B- / 7.5
2010	C	5,849.30	25.19	C / 5.1	11.41%	C+ / 5.7
2009	C	3,854.17	22.93	C+ / 5.7	45.76%	C+ / 5.8

Major Rating Factors: Strong performance is the major factor driving the C+ (Fair) TheStreet.com Investment Rating for *Technology Select Sector SPDR. The fund currently has a performance rating of B- (Good) based on an annualized return of 23.56% over the last three years and a total return of 18.89% year to date 2012. Factored into the performance evaluation is an expense ratio of 0.19% (very low).

The fund's risk rating is currently B- (Good). It carries a beta of 1.01, meaning that its performance tracks fairly well with that of the overall stock market. Volatility, as measured by both the semi-deviation and a drawdown factor, is considered low. As of March 31, 2012, *Technology Select Sector SPDR traded at a price exactly equal to its net asset value.

John A. Tucker has been running the fund for 14 years and currently receives a manager quality ranking of 60 (0=worst, 99=best). If you desire only a moderate level of risk and strong performance, then this fund is an excellent option.

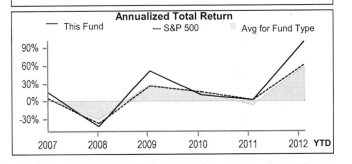

*Teucrium Corn (CORN)

D-   **Weak**

Fund Family: Teucrium Trading LLC
Fund Type: Growth
Inception Date: June 9, 2010

Data Date	Investment Rating	Net Assets ($Mil)	Price	Performance Rating/Pts	Total Return Y-T-D	Risk Rating/Pts
3-12	D-	70.03	39.26	E+ / 0.8	-6.48%	B- / 7.0
2011	D+	71.30	41.98	C- / 3.2	-1.50%	B- / 7.0

Major Rating Factors:
Very poor performance is the major factor driving the D- (Weak) TheStreet.com Investment Rating for *Teucrium Corn. The fund currently has a performance rating of E+ (Very Weak) based on an annualized return of 0.00% over the last three years and a total return of -6.48% year to date 2012. Factored into the performance evaluation is an expense ratio of 3.50% (high).

The fund's risk rating is currently B- (Good). It carries a beta of 0.00, meaning the fund's expected move will be 0.0% for every 10% move in the market. Volatility, as measured by both the semi-deviation and a drawdown factor, is considered low. As of March 31, 2012, *Teucrium Corn traded at a premium of .23% above its net asset value, which is worse than its one-year historical average discount of .08%.

Gilbertie/Teevan has been running the fund for 2 years and currently receives a manager quality ranking of 9 (0=worst, 99=best). This fund offers only a moderate level of risk but investors looking for strong performance are still waiting.

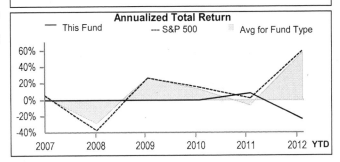

*Teucrium Natural Gas (NAGS)

E+   **Very Weak**

Fund Family: Teucrium Trading LLC
Fund Type: Growth
Inception Date: February 1, 2011

Data Date	Investment Rating	Net Assets ($Mil)	Price	Performance Rating/Pts	Total Return Y-T-D	Risk Rating/Pts
3-12	E+	1.81	11.04	E- / 0.1	-20.46%	C / 4.5

Major Rating Factors:
Very poor performance is the major factor driving the E+ (Very Weak) TheStreet.com Investment Rating for *Teucrium Natural Gas. The fund currently has a performance rating of E- (Very Weak) based on an annualized return of 0.00% over the last three years and a total return of -20.46% year to date 2012. Factored into the performance evaluation is an expense ratio of 1.50% (average).

The fund's risk rating is currently C (Fair). It carries a beta of 0.00, meaning the fund's expected move will be 0.0% for every 10% move in the market. Volatility, as measured by both the semi-deviation and a drawdown factor, is considered average. As of March 31, 2012, *Teucrium Natural Gas traded at a premium of .18% above its net asset value, which is worse than its one-year historical average discount of .20%.

This fund has been team managed for 1 year and currently receives a manager quality ranking of 0 (0=worst, 99=best). This fund offers an average level of risk but investors looking for strong performance will be frustrated.

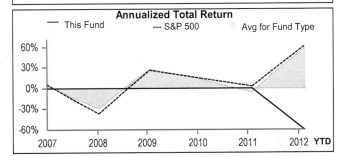

*Teucrium WTI Crude Oil (CRUD)

D-   **Weak**

Fund Family: Teucrium Trading LLC
Fund Type: Growth and Income
Inception Date: February 22, 2011

Data Date	Investment Rating	Net Assets ($Mil)	Price	Performance Rating/Pts	Total Return Y-T-D	Risk Rating/Pts
3-12	D-	3.59	46.46	D- / 1.4	4.22%	C+ / 6.3

Major Rating Factors:
Disappointing performance is the major factor driving the D- (Weak) TheStreet.com Investment Rating for *Teucrium WTI Crude Oil. The fund currently has a performance rating of D- (Weak) based on an annualized return of 0.00% over the last three years and a total return of 4.22% year to date 2012. Factored into the performance evaluation is an expense ratio of 1.54% (average).

The fund's risk rating is currently C+ (Fair). It carries a beta of 0.00, meaning the fund's expected move will be 0.0% for every 10% move in the market. Volatility, as measured by both the semi-deviation and a drawdown factor, is considered low. As of March 31, 2012, *Teucrium WTI Crude Oil traded at a premium of .06% above its net asset value, which is better than its one-year historical average premium of .11%.

This fund has been team managed for 1 year and currently receives a manager quality ranking of 6 (0=worst, 99=best). This fund offers only a moderate level of risk but investors looking for strong performance are still waiting.

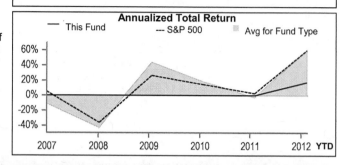

*UBS E Tracs Alerian MLP Infrast (MLPI)

D   **Weak**

Fund Family: UBS Global Asset Management
Fund Type: Income
Inception Date: April 1, 2010

Data Date	Investment Rating	Net Assets ($Mil)	Price	Performance Rating/Pts	Total Return Y-T-D	Risk Rating/Pts
3-12	D	245.22	33.48	C- / 3.1	1.15%	C / 5.4
2011	C	213.10	33.10	B- / 7.2	1.69%	C / 5.4

Major Rating Factors: *UBS E Tracs Alerian MLP Infrast receives a TheStreet.com Investment Rating of D (Weak). The fund currently has a performance rating of C- (Fair) based on an annualized return of 0.00% over the last three years and a total return of 1.15% year to date 2012. Factored into the performance evaluation is an expense ratio of 0.85% (very low).

The fund's risk rating is currently C (Fair). It carries a beta of 0.00, meaning the fund's expected move will be 0.0% for every 10% move in the market. Volatility, as measured by both the semi-deviation and a drawdown factor, is considered average. As of March 31, 2012, *UBS E Tracs Alerian MLP Infrast traded at a discount of .18% below its net asset value, which is better than its one-year historical average discount of .03%.

This fund has been team managed for 2 years and currently receives a manager quality ranking of 66 (0=worst, 99=best). If you desire an average level of risk, then this fund may be an option.

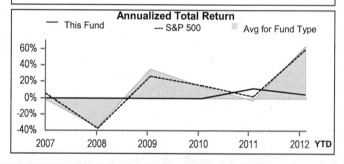

*UBS E Tracs CMCI Agriculture TR (UAG)

D-   **Weak**

Fund Family: UBS Global Asset Management
Fund Type: Growth
Inception Date: April 1, 2008

Data Date	Investment Rating	Net Assets ($Mil)	Price	Performance Rating/Pts	Total Return Y-T-D	Risk Rating/Pts
3-12	D-	3.43	28.74	C- / 3.0	3.87%	C / 4.7
2011	D	13.50	27.67	C- / 3.7	-1.16%	C / 4.7
2010	B	3.43	30.40	A+ / 9.8	35.17%	C- / 3.4
2009	C	3.43	22.49	B / 7.8	20.98%	C- / 3.6

Major Rating Factors: *UBS E Tracs CMCI Agriculture TR receives a TheStreet.com Investment Rating of D- (Weak). The fund currently has a performance rating of C- (Fair) based on an annualized return of 15.01% over the last three years and a total return of 3.87% year to date 2012. Factored into the performance evaluation is an expense ratio of 0.65% (very low).

The fund's risk rating is currently C (Fair). It carries a beta of 0.81, meaning the fund's expected move will be 8.1% for every 10% move in the market. Volatility, as measured by both the semi-deviation and a drawdown factor, is considered average. As of March 31, 2012, *UBS E Tracs CMCI Agriculture TR traded at a premium of .49% above its net asset value, which is worse than its one-year historical average premium of .05%.

This fund has been team managed for 4 years and currently receives a manager quality ranking of 39 (0=worst, 99=best). If you desire an average level of risk, then this fund may be an option.

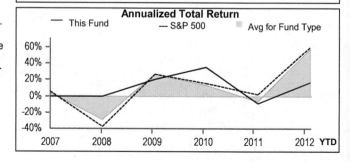

*UBS E Tracs CMCI Energy TR (UBN)   D-   Weak

Fund Family: UBS Global Asset Management
Fund Type: Growth
Inception Date: April 1, 2008

Data Date	Investment Rating	Net Assets ($Mil)	Price	Performance Rating/Pts	Total Return Y-T-D	Risk Rating/Pts
3-12	D-	4.37	16.50	D / 2.2	6.80%	C / 4.6
2011	D	3.10	15.45	C- / 3.2	3.75%	C / 4.6
2010	D+	4.37	15.21	C+ / 6.2	-0.59%	D / 1.9
2009	C-	4.37	15.30	B / 7.6	26.45%	D / 2.2

Major Rating Factors:
Disappointing performance is the major factor driving the D- (Weak) TheStreet.com Investment Rating for *UBS E Tracs CMCI Energy TR. The fund currently has a performance rating of D (Weak) based on an annualized return of 9.20% over the last three years and a total return of 6.80% year to date 2012. Factored into the performance evaluation is an expense ratio of 0.65% (very low).

The fund's risk rating is currently C (Fair). It carries a beta of 0.54, meaning the fund's expected move will be 5.4% for every 10% move in the market. Volatility, as measured by both the semi-deviation and a drawdown factor, is considered average. As of March 31, 2012, *UBS E Tracs CMCI Energy TR traded at a premium of 1.79% above its net asset value, which is worse than its one-year historical average premium of .06%.

This fund has been team managed for 4 years and currently receives a manager quality ranking of 30 (0=worst, 99=best). This fund offers an average level of risk but investors looking for strong performance will be frustrated.

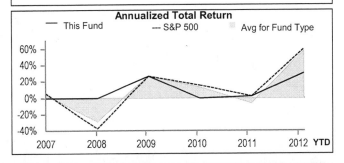

*UBS E Tracs CMCI Food Tr (FUD)   D-   Weak

Fund Family: UBS Global Asset Management
Fund Type: Growth
Inception Date: April 1, 2008

Data Date	Investment Rating	Net Assets ($Mil)	Price	Performance Rating/Pts	Total Return Y-T-D	Risk Rating/Pts
3-12	D-	6.32	27.50	D+ / 2.3	2.88%	C / 4.9
2011	D	41.60	26.73	C- / 3.5	-0.34%	C / 4.9
2010	B	6.32	29.23	A+ / 9.7	32.26%	C- / 3.1
2009	C	6.32	22.10	B- / 7.3	16.19%	C- / 3.3

Major Rating Factors:
Disappointing performance is the major factor driving the D- (Weak) TheStreet.com Investment Rating for *UBS E Tracs CMCI Food Tr. The fund currently has a performance rating of D+ (Weak) based on an annualized return of 11.35% over the last three years and a total return of 2.88% year to date 2012. Factored into the performance evaluation is an expense ratio of 0.65% (very low).

The fund's risk rating is currently C (Fair). It carries a beta of 0.76, meaning the fund's expected move will be 7.6% for every 10% move in the market. Volatility, as measured by both the semi-deviation and a drawdown factor, is considered average. As of March 31, 2012, *UBS E Tracs CMCI Food Tr traded at a premium of .26% above its net asset value, which is worse than its one-year historical average premium of .04%.

This fund has been team managed for 4 years and currently receives a manager quality ranking of 31 (0=worst, 99=best). This fund offers an average level of risk but investors looking for strong performance will be frustrated.

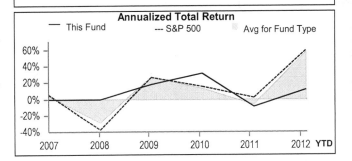

*UBS E Tracs CMCI Gold TR (UBG)   D+   Weak

Fund Family: UBS Global Asset Management
Fund Type: Growth
Inception Date: April 1, 2008

Data Date	Investment Rating	Net Assets ($Mil)	Price	Performance Rating/Pts	Total Return Y-T-D	Risk Rating/Pts
3-12	D+	4.56	44.17	C / 5.2	5.72%	C / 5.1
2011	C	8.00	41.78	B- / 7.5	4.00%	C / 5.1
2010	B	4.56	38.25	A / 9.3	28.05%	C- / 3.9
2009	C+	4.56	29.87	B / 8.1	27.54%	C- / 4.1

Major Rating Factors: *UBS E Tracs CMCI Gold TR receives a TheStreet.com Investment Rating of D+ (Weak). The fund currently has a performance rating of C (Fair) based on an annualized return of 21.28% over the last three years and a total return of 5.72% year to date 2012. Factored into the performance evaluation is an expense ratio of 0.30% (very low).

The fund's risk rating is currently C (Fair). It carries a beta of 0.04, meaning the fund's expected move will be 0.4% for every 10% move in the market. Volatility, as measured by both the semi-deviation and a drawdown factor, is considered average. As of March 31, 2012, *UBS E Tracs CMCI Gold TR traded at a premium of .05% above its net asset value, which is better than its one-year historical average premium of .17%.

This fund has been team managed for 4 years and currently receives a manager quality ranking of 92 (0=worst, 99=best). If you desire an average level of risk, then this fund may be an option.

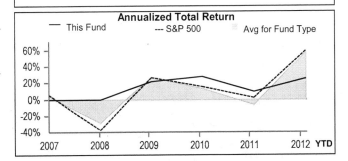

*UBS E Tracs CMCI Industrial Meta (UBM)

D-   **Weak**

Fund Family: UBS Global Asset Management
Fund Type: Growth
Inception Date: April 1, 2008

Major Rating Factors:

Disappointing performance is the major factor driving the D- (Weak) TheStreet.com Investment Rating for *UBS E Tracs CMCI Industrial Meta. The fund currently has a performance rating of D+ (Weak) based on an annualized return of 15.14% over the last three years and a total return of 5.76% year to date 2012. Factored into the performance evaluation is an expense ratio of 0.65% (very low).

The fund's risk rating is currently C (Fair). It carries a beta of 1.11, meaning it is expected to move 11.1% for every 10% move in the market. Volatility, as measured by both the semi-deviation and a drawdown factor, is considered average. As of March 31, 2012, *UBS E Tracs CMCI Industrial Meta traded at a discount of 1.10% below its net asset value, which is better than its one-year historical average discount of .30%.

This fund has been team managed for 4 years and currently receives a manager quality ranking of 15 (0=worst, 99=best). This fund offers an average level of risk but investors looking for strong performance will be frustrated.

Data Date	Investment Rating	Net Assets ($Mil)	Price	Perfor-mance Rating/Pts	Total Return Y-T-D	Risk Rating/Pts
3-12	D-	3.90	20.59	D+ / 2.8	5.76%	C / 4.5
2011	D	5.20	19.47	C- / 3.7	0.00%	C / 4.5
2010	C+	3.90	25.16	A+ / 9.6	18.46%	D+ / 2.4
2009	C+	3.90	21.24	A+ / 9.8	86.32%	D+ / 2.6

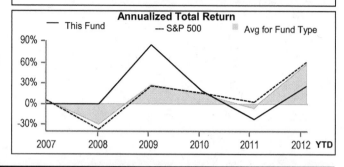

*UBS E Tracs CMCI Livestock Tr (UBC)

E+   **Very Weak**

Fund Family: UBS Global Asset Management
Fund Type: Growth
Inception Date: April 1, 2008

Major Rating Factors:

Disappointing performance is the major factor driving the E+ (Very Weak) TheStreet.com Investment Rating for *UBS E Tracs CMCI Livestock Tr. The fund currently has a performance rating of D- (Weak) based on an annualized return of 0.51% over the last three years and a total return of -6.07% year to date 2012. Factored into the performance evaluation is an expense ratio of 0.65% (very low).

The fund's risk rating is currently C (Fair). It carries a beta of -0.05, meaning the fund's expected move will be -0.5% for every 10% move in the market. Volatility, as measured by both the semi-deviation and a drawdown factor, is considered average. As of March 31, 2012, *UBS E Tracs CMCI Livestock Tr traded at a discount of .30% below its net asset value, which is better than its one-year historical average discount of .12%.

This fund has been team managed for 4 years and currently receives a manager quality ranking of 56 (0=worst, 99=best). This fund offers an average level of risk but investors looking for strong performance will be frustrated.

Data Date	Investment Rating	Net Assets ($Mil)	Price	Perfor-mance Rating/Pts	Total Return Y-T-D	Risk Rating/Pts
3-12	E+	7.84	19.81	D- / 1.0	-6.07%	C / 5.1
2011	D-	5.00	21.09	D / 1.8	-0.76%	C / 4.6
2010	C+	7.84	21.14	B+ / 8.6	16.60%	C- / 3.1
2009	E	7.84	18.13	E+ / 0.8	-16.37%	C- / 3.3

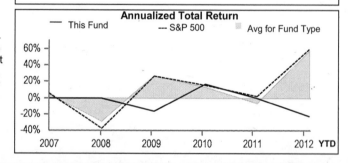

*UBS E Tracs CMCI Silver TR (USV)

C-   **Fair**

Fund Family: UBS Global Asset Management
Fund Type: Growth
Inception Date: April 1, 2008

Major Rating Factors: Strong performance is the major factor driving the C- (Fair) TheStreet.com Investment Rating for *UBS E Tracs CMCI Silver TR. The fund currently has a performance rating of B (Good) based on an annualized return of 34.55% over the last three years and a total return of 16.23% year to date 2012. Factored into the performance evaluation is an expense ratio of 0.40% (very low).

The fund's risk rating is currently C- (Fair). It carries a beta of 1.10, meaning it is expected to move 11.0% for every 10% move in the market. Volatility, as measured by both the semi-deviation and a drawdown factor, is considered average. As of March 31, 2012, *UBS E Tracs CMCI Silver TR traded at a discount of 1.07% below its net asset value, which is better than its one-year historical average discount of .08%.

This fund has been team managed for 4 years and currently receives a manager quality ranking of 79 (0=worst, 99=best). If you desire an average level of risk and strong performance, then this fund is a good option.

Data Date	Investment Rating	Net Assets ($Mil)	Price	Perfor-mance Rating/Pts	Total Return Y-T-D	Risk Rating/Pts
3-12	C-	3.74	45.35	B / 8.1	16.23%	C- / 3.4
2011	C	6.10	39.02	B+ / 8.7	5.89%	C- / 3.3
2010	B-	3.74	44.05	A+ / 9.9	80.74%	D+ / 2.7
2009	C	3.74	24.37	B+ / 8.7	43.69%	D+ / 2.9

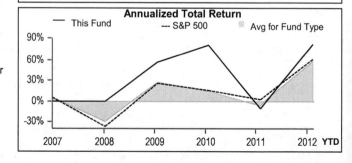

*UBS E Tracs CMCI Total Return (UCI)

D-   **Weak**

Fund Family: UBS Global Asset Management
Fund Type: Growth
Inception Date: April 1, 2008

Major Rating Factors:
Disappointing performance is the major factor driving the D- (Weak) TheStreet.com Investment Rating for *UBS E Tracs CMCI Total Return. The fund currently has a performance rating of D+ (Weak) based on an annualized return of 12.40% over the last three years and a total return of 5.21% year to date 2012. Factored into the performance evaluation is an expense ratio of 0.65% (very low).

The fund's risk rating is currently C (Fair). It carries a beta of 0.91, meaning that its performance tracks fairly well with that of the overall stock market. Volatility, as measured by both the semi-deviation and a drawdown factor, is considered average. As of March 31, 2012, *UBS E Tracs CMCI Total Return traded at a premium of .09% above its net asset value, which is worse than its one-year historical average premium of .07%.

This fund has been team managed for 4 years and currently receives a manager quality ranking of 23 (0=worst, 99=best). This fund offers an average level of risk but investors looking for strong performance will be frustrated.

Data Date	Investment Rating	Net Assets ($Mil)	Price	Performance Rating/Pts	Total Return Y-T-D	Risk Rating/Pts
3-12	D-	11.63	22.68	D+ / 2.6	5.21%	C / 4.9
2011	D	137.50	21.56	C- / 3.9	1.03%	C / 4.9
2010	C+	11.63	23.61	A / 9.4	18.61%	D+ / 2.5
2009	C	11.63	19.91	B+ / 8.7	40.61%	D+ / 2.7

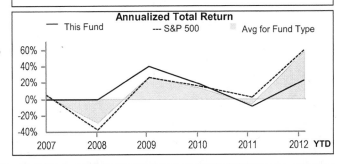

---

*UBS E Tracs DJ-UBS Comm Idx Tot (DJCI)

E+   **Very Weak**

Fund Family: UBS Global Asset Management
Fund Type: Income
Inception Date: October 29, 2009

Major Rating Factors:
Very poor performance is the major factor driving the E+ (Very Weak) TheStreet.com Investment Rating for *UBS E Tracs DJ-UBS Comm Idx Tot. The fund currently has a performance rating of E+ (Very Weak) based on an annualized return of 0.00% over the last three years and a total return of 0.86% year to date 2012. Factored into the performance evaluation is an expense ratio of 0.50% (very low).

The fund's risk rating is currently C (Fair). It carries a beta of 0.00, meaning the fund's expected move will be 0.0% for every 10% move in the market. Volatility, as measured by both the semi-deviation and a drawdown factor, is considered average. As of March 31, 2012, *UBS E Tracs DJ-UBS Comm Idx Tot traded at a premium of .08% above its net asset value, which is worse than its one-year historical average discount of .09%.

This fund has been team managed for 3 years and currently receives a manager quality ranking of 5 (0=worst, 99=best). This fund offers an average level of risk but investors looking for strong performance will be frustrated.

Data Date	Investment Rating	Net Assets ($Mil)	Price	Performance Rating/Pts	Total Return Y-T-D	Risk Rating/Pts
3-12	E+	23.15	26.68	E+ / 0.8	0.86%	C / 4.7
2011	E+	22.00	26.45	D- / 1.2	1.01%	C / 4.7
2010	B+	13.80	30.60	A / 9.3	14.86%	C / 4.7

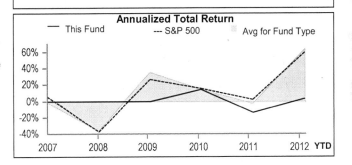

---

*UBS E Tracs Long Platinum ETN (PTM)

D-   **Weak**

Fund Family: UBS Global Asset Management
Fund Type: Growth
Inception Date: May 8, 2008

Major Rating Factors: *UBS E Tracs Long Platinum ETN receives a TheStreet.com Investment Rating of D- (Weak). The fund currently has a performance rating of C- (Fair) based on an annualized return of 12.31% over the last three years and a total return of 24.50% year to date 2012. Factored into the performance evaluation is an expense ratio of 0.65% (very low).

The fund's risk rating is currently C- (Fair). It carries a beta of 0.99, meaning that its performance tracks fairly well with that of the overall stock market. Volatility, as measured by both the semi-deviation and a drawdown factor, is considered average. As of March 31, 2012, *UBS E Tracs Long Platinum ETN traded at a premium of 5.80% above its net asset value, which is worse than its one-year historical average premium of 1.84%.

This fund has been team managed for 4 years and currently receives a manager quality ranking of 17 (0=worst, 99=best). If you desire an average level of risk, then this fund may be an option.

Data Date	Investment Rating	Net Assets ($Mil)	Price	Performance Rating/Pts	Total Return Y-T-D	Risk Rating/Pts
3-12	D-	66.49	20.07	C- / 3.2	24.50%	C- / 4.1
2011	D-	32.20	16.12	D+ / 2.5	1.74%	C- / 4.1
2010	C	66.49	20.92	B+ / 8.7	13.70%	D+ / 2.5
2009	C+	66.49	18.40	A / 9.4	55.80%	D+ / 2.7

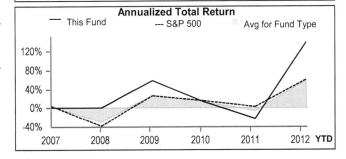

*UBS E-TRACS 2x Levd Lng Alerian (MLPL)

C-   **Fair**

Fund Family: UBS Global Asset Management
Fund Type: Energy/Natural Resources
Inception Date: July 7, 2010

Major Rating Factors: Middle of the road best describes *UBS E-TRACS 2x Levd Lng Alerian whose TheStreet.com Investment Rating is currently a C- (Fair). The fund currently has a performance rating of C+ (Fair) based on an annualized return of 0.00% over the last three years and a total return of 2.36% year to date 2012. Factored into the performance evaluation is an expense ratio of 0.85% (very low).

The fund's risk rating is currently C (Fair). It carries a beta of 0.00, meaning the fund's expected move will be 0.0% for every 10% move in the market. Volatility, as measured by both the semi-deviation and a drawdown factor, is considered average. As of March 31, 2012, *UBS E-TRACS 2x Levd Lng Alerian traded at a premium of .07% above its net asset value, which is worse than its one-year historical average discount of .09%.

This fund has been team managed for 2 years and currently receives a manager quality ranking of 94 (0=worst, 99=best). If you desire an average level of risk, then this fund may be an option.

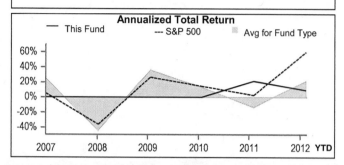

Data Date	Investment Rating	Net Assets ($Mil)	Price	Performance Rating/Pts	Total Return Y-T-D	Risk Rating/Pts
3-12	C-	103.79	41.66	C+ / 6.7	2.36%	C / 4.8
2011	B-	93.90	40.70	A+ / 9.8	2.97%	C / 4.8

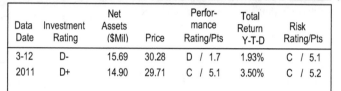

Annualized Total Return

—— This Fund   --- S&P 500   ▨ Avg for Fund Type

*UBS E-TRACS Alerian Nat Gas MLP (MLPG)

D-   **Weak**

Fund Family: UBS Global Asset Management
Fund Type: Energy/Natural Resources
Inception Date: July 14, 2010

Major Rating Factors:
Disappointing performance is the major factor driving the D- (Weak) TheStreet.com Investment Rating for *UBS E-TRACS Alerian Nat Gas MLP. The fund currently has a performance rating of D (Weak) based on an annualized return of 0.00% over the last three years and a total return of 1.93% year to date 2012. Factored into the performance evaluation is an expense ratio of 0.85% (very low).

The fund's risk rating is currently C (Fair). It carries a beta of 0.00, meaning the fund's expected move will be 0.0% for every 10% move in the market. Volatility, as measured by both the semi-deviation and a drawdown factor, is considered average. As of March 31, 2012, *UBS E-TRACS Alerian Nat Gas MLP traded at a discount of .46% below its net asset value, which is better than its one-year historical average discount of .11%.

This fund has been team managed for 2 years and currently receives a manager quality ranking of 67 (0=worst, 99=best). This fund offers an average level of risk but investors looking for strong performance will be frustrated.

Data Date	Investment Rating	Net Assets ($Mil)	Price	Performance Rating/Pts	Total Return Y-T-D	Risk Rating/Pts
3-12	D-	15.69	30.28	D / 1.7	1.93%	C / 5.1
2011	D+	14.90	29.71	C / 5.1	3.50%	C / 5.2

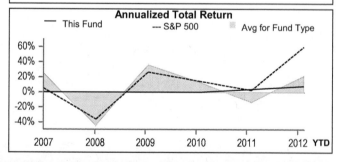

Annualized Total Return

—— This Fund   --- S&P 500   ▨ Avg for Fund Type

*UBS E-TRACS S&P 500 Gold Hedged (SPGH)

C+   **Fair**

Fund Family: UBS Global Asset Management
Fund Type: Precious Metals
Inception Date: January 28, 2010

Major Rating Factors:
Exceptional performance is the major factor driving the C+ (Fair) TheStreet.com Investment Rating for *UBS E-TRACS S&P 500 Gold Hedged. The fund currently has a performance rating of A+ (Excellent) based on an annualized return of 0.00% over the last three years and a total return of 20.35% year to date 2012. Factored into the performance evaluation is an expense ratio of 0.85% (very low).

The fund's risk rating is currently C (Fair). It carries a beta of 0.00, meaning the fund's expected move will be 0.0% for every 10% move in the market. Volatility, as measured by both the semi-deviation and a drawdown factor, is considered average. As of March 31, 2012, *UBS E-TRACS S&P 500 Gold Hedged traded at a discount of .37% below its net asset value, which is better than its one-year historical average premium of .30%.

This fund has been team managed for 2 years and currently receives a manager quality ranking of 87 (0=worst, 99=best). If you desire an average level of risk and strong performance, then this fund is a good option.

Data Date	Investment Rating	Net Assets ($Mil)	Price	Performance Rating/Pts	Total Return Y-T-D	Risk Rating/Pts
3-12	C+	18.58	51.27	A+ / 9.6	20.35%	C / 4.9
2011	C-	15.80	42.60	C+ / 6.4	3.71%	C / 4.9

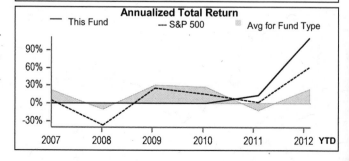

Annualized Total Return

—— This Fund   --- S&P 500   ▨ Avg for Fund Type

*UBS E-TRACS Wells Fargo MLP Inde (MLPW)　　　　　D-　　Weak

Fund Family: UBS Global Asset Management
Fund Type: Energy/Natural Resources
Inception Date: November 1, 2010

Major Rating Factors:
Disappointing performance is the major factor driving the D- (Weak) TheStreet.com Investment Rating for *UBS E-TRACS Wells Fargo MLP Inde. The fund currently has a performance rating of D+ (Weak) based on an annualized return of 0.00% over the last three years and a total return of 2.62% year to date 2012. Factored into the performance evaluation is an expense ratio of 0.85% (very low).

The fund's risk rating is currently C (Fair). It carries a beta of 0.00, meaning the fund's expected move will be 0.0% for every 10% move in the market. Volatility, as measured by both the semi-deviation and a drawdown factor, is considered average. As of March 31, 2012, *UBS E-TRACS Wells Fargo MLP Inde traded at a discount of .61% below its net asset value, which is better than its one-year historical average discount of .04%.

This is team managed and currently receives a manager quality ranking of 82 (0=worst, 99=best). This fund offers an average level of risk but investors looking for strong performance will be frustrated.

Data Date	Investment Rating	Net Assets ($Mil)	Price	Performance Rating/Pts	Total Return Y-T-D	Risk Rating/Pts
3-12	D-	20.35	27.92	D+ / 2.4	2.62%	C / 5.3
2011	C-	19.00	27.21	C+ / 5.9	2.81%	C / 5.3

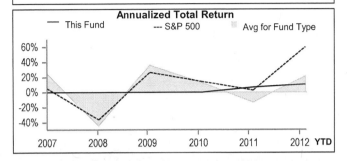

*United States 12 Month Oil Fund (USL)　　　　　　D　　Weak

Fund Family: United States Commodity Funds LLC
Fund Type: Energy/Natural Resources
Inception Date: December 6, 2007

Major Rating Factors: *United States 12 Month Oil Fund receives a TheStreet.com Investment Rating of D (Weak). The fund currently has a performance rating of C- (Fair) based on an annualized return of 12.49% over the last three years and a total return of 5.36% year to date 2012. Factored into the performance evaluation is an expense ratio of 0.84% (very low).

The fund's risk rating is currently C+ (Fair). It carries a beta of 0.90, meaning that its performance tracks fairly well with that of the overall stock market. Volatility, as measured by both the semi-deviation and a drawdown factor, is considered low. As of March 31, 2012, *United States 12 Month Oil Fund traded at a price exactly equal to its net asset value, which is better than its one-year historical average premium of .04%.

This fund has been team managed for 5 years and currently receives a manager quality ranking of 31 (0=worst, 99=best). If you desire an average level of risk, then this fund may be an option.

Data Date	Investment Rating	Net Assets ($Mil)	Price	Performance Rating/Pts	Total Return Y-T-D	Risk Rating/Pts
3-12	D	174.79	45.81	C- / 3.1	5.36%	C+ / 6.8
2011	C	169.50	43.48	C / 5.5	3.24%	C+ / 6.8
2010	D-	180.20	43.10	D- / 1.4	6.52%	C- / 3.6
2009	C+	181.22	40.46	B / 8.0	26.44%	C- / 3.8

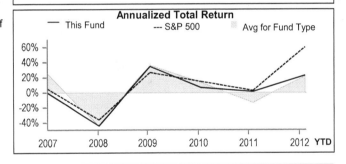

*United States Brent Oil Fund (BNO)　　　　　　　　B-　　Good

Fund Family: United States Commodity Funds LLC
Fund Type: Energy/Natural Resources
Inception Date: June 1, 2010

Major Rating Factors: Strong performance is the major factor driving the B- (Good) TheStreet.com Investment Rating for *United States Brent Oil Fund. The fund currently has a performance rating of B- (Good) based on an annualized return of 0.00% over the last three years and a total return of 15.62% year to date 2012. Factored into the performance evaluation is an expense ratio of 0.99% (low).

The fund's risk rating is currently B- (Good). It carries a beta of 0.00, meaning the fund's expected move will be 0.0% for every 10% move in the market. Volatility, as measured by both the semi-deviation and a drawdown factor, is considered low. As of March 31, 2012, *United States Brent Oil Fund traded at a discount of .01% below its net asset value, which is better than its one-year historical average premium of .02%.

Nicholas D. Gerber currently receives a manager quality ranking of 91 (0=worst, 99=best). If you desire only a moderate level of risk and strong performance, then this fund is an excellent option.

Data Date	Investment Rating	Net Assets ($Mil)	Price	Performance Rating/Pts	Total Return Y-T-D	Risk Rating/Pts
3-12	B-	77.02	86.30	B- / 7.3	15.62%	B- / 7.9
2011	B	37.30	74.64	B / 7.7	5.64%	B- / 7.9

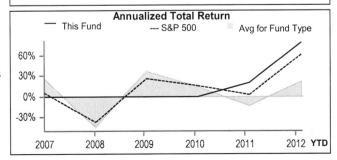

*United States Commodity Index (USCI)

D   **Weak**

Fund Family: United States Commodity Funds LLC
Fund Type: Income
Inception Date: August 9, 2010

Data Date	Investment Rating	Net Assets ($Mil)	Price	Performance Rating/Pts	Total Return Y-T-D	Risk Rating/Pts
3-12	D	400.18	61.27	D- / 1.0	4.97%	B- / 7.9
2011	D	350.80	58.37	D- / 1.4	2.88%	B- / 7.9

Major Rating Factors:
Disappointing performance is the major factor driving the D (Weak) TheStreet.com Investment Rating for *United States Commodity Index. The fund currently has a performance rating of D- (Weak) based on an annualized return of 0.00% over the last three years and a total return of 4.97% year to date 2012. Factored into the performance evaluation is an expense ratio of 1.16% (low).

The fund's risk rating is currently B- (Good). It carries a beta of 0.00, meaning the fund's expected move will be 0.0% for every 10% move in the market. Volatility, as measured by both the semi-deviation and a drawdown factor, is considered low. As of March 31, 2012, *United States Commodity Index traded at a discount of .07% below its net asset value, which is better than its one-year historical average premium of .03%.

Nicholas D. Gerber currently receives a manager quality ranking of 8 (0=worst, 99=best). This fund offers only a moderate level of risk but investors looking for strong performance are still waiting.

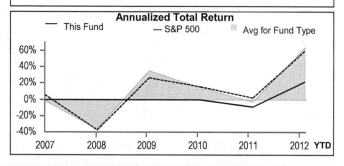

*United States Gasoline Fund LP (UGA)

B   **Good**

Fund Family: United States Commodity Funds LLC
Fund Type: Energy/Natural Resources
Inception Date: February 26, 2008

Data Date	Investment Rating	Net Assets ($Mil)	Price	Performance Rating/Pts	Total Return Y-T-D	Risk Rating/Pts
3-12	B	156.80	57.16	B+ / 8.5	18.29%	B- / 7.5
2011	B+	77.40	48.32	A- / 9.0	4.12%	B- / 7.6
2010	C+	67.30	42.11	A / 9.3	15.12%	C- / 3.0
2009	C+	91.54	36.58	A / 9.5	73.20%	C- / 3.1

Major Rating Factors: Strong performance is the major factor driving the B (Good) TheStreet.com Investment Rating for *United States Gasoline Fund LP. The fund currently has a performance rating of B+ (Good) based on an annualized return of 31.17% over the last three years and a total return of 18.29% year to date 2012. Factored into the performance evaluation is an expense ratio of 0.91% (low).

The fund's risk rating is currently B- (Good). It carries a beta of 0.83, meaning the fund's expected move will be 8.3% for every 10% move in the market. Volatility, as measured by both the semi-deviation and a drawdown factor, is considered low. As of March 31, 2012, *United States Gasoline Fund LP traded at a premium of .47% above its net asset value, which is worse than its one-year historical average premium of .20%.

This fund has been team managed for 4 years and currently receives a manager quality ranking of 90 (0=worst, 99=best). If you desire only a moderate level of risk and strong performance, then this fund is an excellent option.

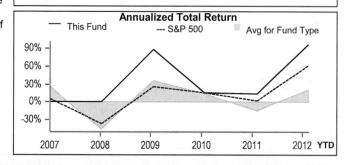

*United States Heating Oil Fund (UHN)

C   **Fair**

Fund Family: United States Commodity Funds LLC
Fund Type: Energy/Natural Resources
Inception Date: April 9, 2008

Data Date	Investment Rating	Net Assets ($Mil)	Price	Performance Rating/Pts	Total Return Y-T-D	Risk Rating/Pts
3-12	C	10.88	35.99	C / 4.3	9.49%	B- / 7.8
2011	C+	9.80	32.87	C+ / 5.7	4.96%	B- / 7.8
2010	C+	11.90	29.86	B+ / 8.8	8.15%	C- / 3.3
2009	C	7.71	27.61	B / 7.9	23.09%	C- / 3.4

Major Rating Factors: Middle of the road best describes *United States Heating Oil Fund whose TheStreet.com Investment Rating is currently a C (Fair). The fund currently has a performance rating of C (Fair) based on an annualized return of 18.79% over the last three years and a total return of 9.49% year to date 2012. Factored into the performance evaluation is an expense ratio of 0.90% (low).

The fund's risk rating is currently B- (Good). It carries a beta of 0.78, meaning the fund's expected move will be 7.8% for every 10% move in the market. Volatility, as measured by both the semi-deviation and a drawdown factor, is considered low. As of March 31, 2012, *United States Heating Oil Fund traded at a premium of .70% above its net asset value, which is worse than its one-year historical average premium of .13%.

Nicholas Gerber has been running the fund for 4 years and currently receives a manager quality ranking of 72 (0=worst, 99=best). If you desire an average level of risk, then this fund may be an option.

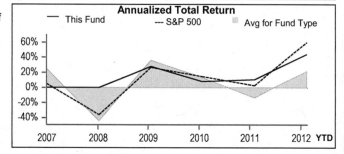

*United States Natural Gas Fund (UNG)   E   Very Weak

Fund Family: United States Commodity Funds LLC
Fund Type: Energy/Natural Resources
Inception Date: April 18, 2007

Data Date	Investment Rating	Net Assets ($Mil)	Price	Perfor-mance Rating/Pts	Total Return Y-T-D	Risk Rating/Pts
3-12	E	910.01	15.92	E- / 0.1	-38.39%	C- / 3.0
2011	E	1,072.10	6.46	E- / 0.1	2.79%	C- / 3.4
2010	E-	2,724.40	5.99	E- / 0.2	-40.58%	D / 2.1
2009	E-	3,722.20	10.08	E- / 0.2	-59.37%	D+ / 2.4

Major Rating Factors: Very poor performance is the major factor driving the E (Very Weak) TheStreet.com Investment Rating for *United States Natural Gas Fund. The fund currently has a performance rating of E- (Very Weak) based on an annualized return of -49.36% over the last three years and a total return of -38.39% year to date 2012. Factored into the performance evaluation is an expense ratio of 0.86% (very low).

The fund's risk rating is currently C- (Fair). It carries a beta of 0.30, meaning the fund's expected move will be 3.0% for every 10% move in the market. Volatility, as measured by both the semi-deviation and a drawdown factor, is considered average. As of March 31, 2012, *United States Natural Gas Fund traded at a discount of .56% below its net asset value, which is better than its one-year historical average discount of .02%.

Nicholas D. Gerber currently receives a manager quality ranking of 0 (0=worst, 99=best). This fund offers an average level of risk but investors looking for strong performance will be frustrated.

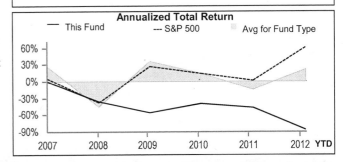

*United States Oil Fund (USO)   D   Weak

Fund Family: United States Commodity Funds LLC
Fund Type: Energy/Natural Resources
Inception Date: April 10, 2006

Data Date	Investment Rating	Net Assets ($Mil)	Price	Perfor-mance Rating/Pts	Total Return Y-T-D	Risk Rating/Pts
3-12	D	1,626.07	39.23	D / 2.2	2.94%	C+ / 6.5
2011	D+	1,134.60	38.11	C- / 3.7	2.91%	C+ / 6.6
2010	E	1,819.80	39.00	E+ / 0.6	-0.71%	D+ / 2.7
2009	E+	2,303.34	39.28	D- / 1.3	10.24%	C- / 3.4

Major Rating Factors:
Disappointing performance is the major factor driving the D (Weak) TheStreet.com Investment Rating for *United States Oil Fund. The fund currently has a performance rating of D (Weak) based on an annualized return of 8.25% over the last three years and a total return of 2.94% year to date 2012. Factored into the performance evaluation is an expense ratio of 0.66% (very low).

The fund's risk rating is currently C+ (Fair). It carries a beta of 0.98, meaning that its performance tracks fairly well with that of the overall stock market. Volatility, as measured by both the semi-deviation and a drawdown factor, is considered low. As of March 31, 2012, *United States Oil Fund traded at a premium of .05% above its net asset value, which is better than its one-year historical average premium of .09%.

Nicholas D.Gerber / John T. Hy has been running the fund for 6 years and currently receives a manager quality ranking of 18 (0=worst, 99=best). This fund offers only a moderate level of risk but investors looking for strong performance are still waiting.

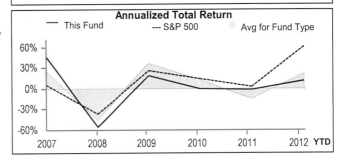

*United States Short Oil Fund (DNO)   D-   Weak

Fund Family: United States Commodity Funds LLC
Fund Type: Energy/Natural Resources
Inception Date: September 23, 2009

Data Date	Investment Rating	Net Assets ($Mil)	Price	Perfor-mance Rating/Pts	Total Return Y-T-D	Risk Rating/Pts
3-12	D-	6.65	34.51	E+ / 0.7	-4.43%	C+ / 6.3
2011	D-	10.80	36.11	E+ / 0.7	-3.05%	C+ / 6.4
2010	D	8.10	40.42	E / 0.5	-7.93%	C+ / 6.9

Major Rating Factors:
Very poor performance is the major factor driving the D- (Weak) TheStreet.com Investment Rating for *United States Short Oil Fund. The fund currently has a performance rating of E+ (Very Weak) based on an annualized return of 0.00% over the last three years and a total return of -4.43% year to date 2012. Factored into the performance evaluation is an expense ratio of 0.93% (low).

The fund's risk rating is currently C+ (Fair). It carries a beta of 0.00, meaning the fund's expected move will be 0.0% for every 10% move in the market. Volatility, as measured by both the semi-deviation and a drawdown factor, is considered low. As of March 31, 2012, *United States Short Oil Fund traded at a discount of .14% below its net asset value, which is better than its one-year historical average discount of .12%.

Nicholas Gerber has been running the fund for 3 years and currently receives a manager quality ranking of 13 (0=worst, 99=best). This fund offers only a moderate level of risk but investors looking for strong performance are still waiting.

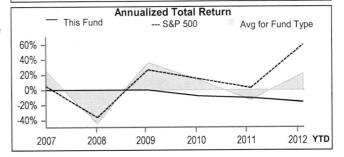

*US 12 Month Natural Gas Fund (UNL)

E **Very Weak**

Fund Family: United States Commodity Funds LLC
Fund Type: Energy/Natural Resources
Inception Date: November 19, 2009

Major Rating Factors: Very poor performance is the major factor driving the E (Very Weak) TheStreet.com Investment Rating for *US 12 Month Natural Gas Fund. The fund currently has a performance rating of E- (Very Weak) based on an annualized return of 0.00% over the last three years and a total return of -22.92% year to date 2012. Factored into the performance evaluation is an expense ratio of 0.93% (low).

The fund's risk rating is currently C- (Fair). It carries a beta of 0.00, meaning the fund's expected move will be 0.0% for every 10% move in the market. Volatility, as measured by both the semi-deviation and a drawdown factor, is considered average. As of March 31, 2012, *US 12 Month Natural Gas Fund traded at a discount of .55% below its net asset value, which is better than its one-year historical average discount of .02%.

Nicholas D. Gerber currently receives a manager quality ranking of 0 (0=worst, 99=best). This fund offers an average level of risk but investors looking for strong performance will be frustrated.

Data Date	Investment Rating	Net Assets ($Mil)	Price	Perfor-mance Rating/Pts	Total Return Y-T-D	Risk Rating/Pts
3-12	E	29.71	16.28	E- / 0.1	-22.92%	C- / 3.9
2011	E+	21.20	21.12	E- / 0.1	2.69%	C / 4.7
2010	D-	35.00	34.97	E / 0.3	-35.48%	C+ / 6.0

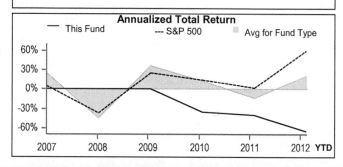

*Utilities Select Sector SPDR (XLU)

C **Fair**

Fund Family: SSgA Funds Management Inc
Fund Type: Utilities
Inception Date: December 16, 1998

Major Rating Factors: Middle of the road best describes *Utilities Select Sector SPDR whose TheStreet.com Investment Rating is currently a C (Fair). The fund currently has a performance rating of C- (Fair) based on an annualized return of 15.39% over the last three years and a total return of -1.70% year to date 2012. Factored into the performance evaluation is an expense ratio of 0.19% (very low).

The fund's risk rating is currently B+ (Good). It carries a beta of 0.96, meaning that its performance tracks fairly well with that of the overall stock market. Volatility, as measured by both the semi-deviation and a drawdown factor, is considered very low. As of March 31, 2012, *Utilities Select Sector SPDR traded at a price exactly equal to its net asset value.

John A. Tucker has been running the fund for 14 years and currently receives a manager quality ranking of 48 (0=worst, 99=best). If you desire an average level of risk, then this fund may be an option.

Data Date	Investment Rating	Net Assets ($Mil)	Price	Perfor-mance Rating/Pts	Total Return Y-T-D	Risk Rating/Pts
3-12	C	6,347.05	35.05	C- / 3.6	-1.70%	B+ / 9.1
2011	C+	7,662.30	35.98	C / 5.0	-2.67%	B / 8.6
2010	D+	3,756.60	31.34	D- / 1.5	5.35%	C+ / 6.7
2009	C-	2,462.73	31.02	D+ / 2.5	9.12%	C+ / 6.8

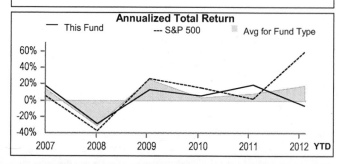

*Vanguard 500 Index ETF (VOO)

B **Good**

Fund Family: Vanguard Group Inc
Fund Type: Income
Inception Date: September 7, 2010

Major Rating Factors: *Vanguard 500 Index ETF receives a TheStreet.com Investment Rating of B (Good). The fund currently has a performance rating of C+ (Fair) based on an annualized return of 0.00% over the last three years and a total return of 12.54% year to date 2012. Factored into the performance evaluation is an expense ratio of 0.05% (very low).

The fund's risk rating is currently B+ (Good). It carries a beta of 0.00, meaning the fund's expected move will be 0.0% for every 10% move in the market. Volatility, as measured by both the semi-deviation and a drawdown factor, is considered very low. As of March 31, 2012, *Vanguard 500 Index ETF traded at a discount of .05% below its net asset value, which is better than its one-year historical average premium of .01%.

Michael H. Buek has been running the fund for 21 years and currently receives a manager quality ranking of 46 (0=worst, 99=best). If you desire an average level of risk, then this fund may be an option.

Data Date	Investment Rating	Net Assets ($Mil)	Price	Perfor-mance Rating/Pts	Total Return Y-T-D	Risk Rating/Pts
3-12	B	2,757.09	64.37	C+ / 6.2	12.54%	B+ / 9.4
2011	C	2,365.60	57.45	C- / 3.0	1.98%	B+ / 9.4

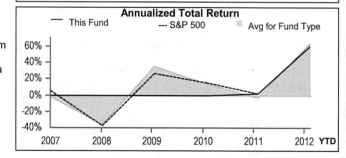

*Vanguard Consumer Discret ETF (VCR)   A-   Excellent

Fund Family: Vanguard Group Inc
Fund Type: Income
Inception Date: January 26, 2004

Major Rating Factors:
Strong performance is the major factor driving the A- (Excellent) TheStreet.com Investment Rating for *Vanguard Consumer Discret ETF. The fund currently has a performance rating of B+ (Good) based on an annualized return of 31.53% over the last three years and a total return of 16.81% year to date 2012. Factored into the performance evaluation is an expense ratio of 1.90% (above average).

The fund's risk rating is currently B (Good). It carries a beta of 1.20, meaning it is expected to move 12.0% for every 10% move in the market. Volatility, as measured by both the semi-deviation and a drawdown factor, is considered low. As of March 31, 2012, *Vanguard Consumer Discret ETF traded at a discount of .01% below its net asset value.

Michael A. Johnson has been running the fund for 2 years and currently receives a manager quality ranking of 74 (0=worst, 99=best). If you desire only a moderate level of risk and strong performance, then this fund is an excellent option.

Data Date	Investment Rating	Net Assets ($Mil)	Price	Performance Rating/Pts	Total Return Y-T-D	Risk Rating/Pts
3-12	A-	422.83	72.20	B+ / 8.7	16.81%	B / 8.2
2011	B	346.20	61.81	B / 7.9	2.44%	B- / 7.9
2010	B+	362.70	60.47	B / 8.2	30.57%	C+ / 5.6
2009	D+	140.76	46.77	D+ / 2.9	40.69%	C+ / 5.6

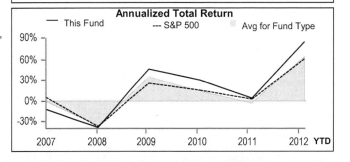

Annualized Total Return — This Fund --- S&P 500 · Avg for Fund Type

*Vanguard Consumer Staples ETF (VDC)   C+   Fair

Fund Family: Vanguard Group Inc
Fund Type: Income
Inception Date: January 26, 2004

Major Rating Factors: Middle of the road best describes *Vanguard Consumer Staples ETF whose TheStreet.com Investment Rating is currently a C+ (Fair). The fund currently has a performance rating of C (Fair) based on an annualized return of 20.04% over the last three years and a total return of 5.90% year to date 2012. Factored into the performance evaluation is an expense ratio of 0.19% (very low).

The fund's risk rating is currently B+ (Good). It carries a beta of 0.54, meaning the fund's expected move will be 5.4% for every 10% move in the market. Volatility, as measured by both the semi-deviation and a drawdown factor, is considered very low. As of March 31, 2012, *Vanguard Consumer Staples ETF traded at a discount of .01% below its net asset value, which is better than its one-year historical average premium of .02%.

Michael A. Johnson has been running the fund for 2 years and currently receives a manager quality ranking of 83 (0=worst, 99=best). If you desire an average level of risk, then this fund may be an option.

Data Date	Investment Rating	Net Assets ($Mil)	Price	Performance Rating/Pts	Total Return Y-T-D	Risk Rating/Pts
3-12	C+	946.01	86.28	C / 5.4	5.90%	B+ / 9.1
2011	B-	879.50	81.47	C+ / 6.0	-0.99%	B / 8.6
2010	B-	608.70	73.39	C+ / 6.2	14.62%	B- / 7.3
2009	C	552.45	65.69	C- / 4.0	15.05%	B- / 7.3

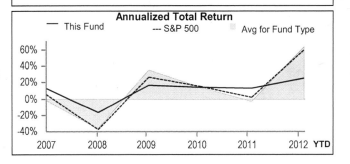

Annualized Total Return — This Fund --- S&P 500 · Avg for Fund Type

*Vanguard Div Appreciation ETF (VIG)   C+   Fair

Fund Family: Vanguard Group Inc
Fund Type: Growth
Inception Date: April 21, 2006

Major Rating Factors: Middle of the road best describes *Vanguard Div Appreciation ETF whose TheStreet.com Investment Rating is currently a C+ (Fair). The fund currently has a performance rating of C (Fair) based on an annualized return of 19.11% over the last three years and a total return of 7.63% year to date 2012. Factored into the performance evaluation is an expense ratio of 0.18% (very low).

The fund's risk rating is currently B (Good). It carries a beta of 0.82, meaning the fund's expected move will be 8.2% for every 10% move in the market. Volatility, as measured by both the semi-deviation and a drawdown factor, is considered low. As of March 31, 2012, *Vanguard Div Appreciation ETF traded at a price exactly equal to its net asset value, which is better than its one-year historical average premium of .02%.

Ryan E. Ludt has been running the fund for 6 years and currently receives a manager quality ranking of 57 (0=worst, 99=best). If you desire an average level of risk, then this fund may be an option.

Data Date	Investment Rating	Net Assets ($Mil)	Price	Performance Rating/Pts	Total Return Y-T-D	Risk Rating/Pts
3-12	C+	10,226.64	58.55	C / 4.9	7.63%	B / 8.6
2011	C+	8,964.40	54.65	C / 5.3	0.75%	B / 8.2
2010	C+	4,606.30	52.63	C / 5.0	14.76%	C+ / 6.6
2009	C-	1,203.27	46.86	D+ / 2.7	16.54%	B- / 7.1

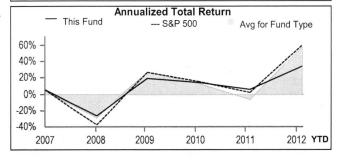

Annualized Total Return — This Fund --- S&P 500 · Avg for Fund Type

*Vanguard Energy ETF (VDE)

C-   **Fair**

Fund Family: Vanguard Group Inc
Fund Type: Energy/Natural Resources
Inception Date: September 23, 2004

Major Rating Factors: Middle of the road best describes *Vanguard Energy ETF whose TheStreet.com Investment Rating is currently a C- (Fair). The fund currently has a performance rating of C- (Fair) based on an annualized return of 18.60% over the last three years and a total return of 4.33% year to date 2012. Factored into the performance evaluation is an expense ratio of 0.19% (very low).

The fund's risk rating is currently B- (Good). It carries a beta of 1.07, meaning that its performance tracks fairly well with that of the overall stock market. Volatility, as measured by both the semi-deviation and a drawdown factor, is considered low. As of March 31, 2012, *Vanguard Energy ETF traded at a discount of .02% below its net asset value, which is better than its one-year historical average premium of .01%.

Jeffrey D. Miller has been running the fund for 2 years and currently receives a manager quality ranking of 53 (0=worst, 99=best). If you desire an average level of risk, then this fund may be an option.

Data Date	Investment Rating	Net Assets ($Mil)	Price	Performance Rating/Pts	Total Return Y-T-D	Risk Rating/Pts
3-12	C-	1,956.97	105.18	C- / 4.1	4.33%	B- / 7.5
2011	C	1,728.20	100.81	C+ / 5.6	1.95%	B- / 7.1
2010	C-	1,548.60	99.67	C / 5.0	21.05%	C / 4.8
2009	C-	869.27	83.37	C / 4.3	18.95%	C+ / 5.9

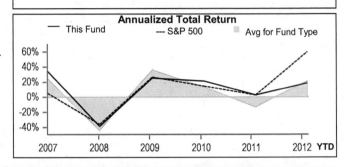

Annualized Total Return

*Vanguard Extended Market Index E (VXF)

C+   **Fair**

Fund Family: Vanguard Group Inc
Fund Type: Growth
Inception Date: December 27, 2001

Major Rating Factors: Strong performance is the major factor driving the C+ (Fair) TheStreet.com Investment Rating for *Vanguard Extended Market Index E. The fund currently has a performance rating of B- (Good) based on an annualized return of 26.04% over the last three years and a total return of 14.49% year to date 2012. Factored into the performance evaluation is an expense ratio of 0.10% (very low).

The fund's risk rating is currently B- (Good). It carries a beta of 1.27, meaning it is expected to move 12.7% for every 10% move in the market. Volatility, as measured by both the semi-deviation and a drawdown factor, is considered low. As of March 31, 2012, *Vanguard Extended Market Index E traded at a price exactly equal to its net asset value, which is worse than its one-year historical average discount of .02%.

Donald M. Butler has been running the fund for 15 years and currently receives a manager quality ranking of 40 (0=worst, 99=best). If you desire only a moderate level of risk and strong performance, then this fund is an excellent option.

Data Date	Investment Rating	Net Assets ($Mil)	Price	Performance Rating/Pts	Total Return Y-T-D	Risk Rating/Pts
3-12	C+	1,366.74	59.34	B- / 7.1	14.49%	B- / 7.7
2011	C+	1,148.20	51.84	C+ / 6.1	1.64%	B- / 7.4
2010	C	1,112.90	54.41	B- / 7.3	27.62%	C- / 3.2
2009	D	633.03	43.06	C- / 3.2	34.79%	C- / 3.6

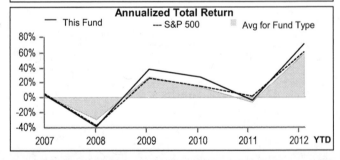

Annualized Total Return

*Vanguard Extnd Durtn Trea Idx ET (EDV)

D   **Weak**

Fund Family: Vanguard Group Inc
Fund Type: US Government/Agency
Inception Date: December 6, 2007

Major Rating Factors:
Disappointing performance is the major factor driving the D (Weak) TheStreet.com Investment Rating for *Vanguard Extnd Durtn Trea Idx ET. The fund currently has a performance rating of D+ (Weak) based on an annualized return of 7.41% over the last three years and a total return of -11.06% year to date 2012. Factored into the performance evaluation is an expense ratio of 0.13% (very low).

The fund's risk rating is currently B- (Good). It carries a beta of 2.00, meaning it is expected to move 20.0% for every 10% move in the market. Volatility, as measured by both the semi-deviation and a drawdown factor, is considered low. As of March 31, 2012, *Vanguard Extnd Durtn Trea Idx ET traded at a premium of .49% above its net asset value, which is worse than its one-year historical average premium of .43%.

Gregory Davis has been running the fund for 5 years and currently receives a manager quality ranking of 17 (0=worst, 99=best). This fund offers only a moderate level of risk but investors looking for strong performance are still waiting.

Data Date	Investment Rating	Net Assets ($Mil)	Price	Performance Rating/Pts	Total Return Y-T-D	Risk Rating/Pts
3-12	D	167.54	107.65	D+ / 2.4	-11.06%	B- / 7.0
2011	C+	187.90	121.94	B- / 7.2	-3.21%	C+ / 6.3
2010	D+	132.00	82.80	D / 2.0	9.79%	C+ / 5.9
2009	D-	45.86	78.87	E / 0.4	-31.22%	C+ / 6.1

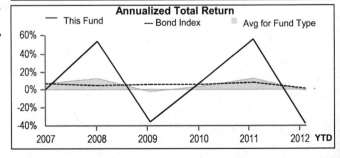

Annualized Total Return

*Vanguard Financials ETF (VFH)   C   Fair

Fund Family: Vanguard Group Inc
Fund Type: Financial Services
Inception Date: January 26, 2004

Data Date	Investment Rating	Net Assets ($Mil)	Price	Performance Rating/Pts	Total Return Y-T-D	Risk Rating/Pts
3-12	C	667.80	32.97	C / 5.3	19.52%	B- / 7.6
2011	D+	534.20	27.62	C- / 3.0	2.72%	C+ / 6.8
2010	D-	576.20	32.88	D- / 1.1	14.83%	C / 4.5
2009	E+	579.62	29.04	E+ / 0.6	13.97%	C / 4.5

Major Rating Factors: Middle of the road best describes *Vanguard Financials ETF whose TheStreet.com Investment Rating is currently a C (Fair). The fund currently has a performance rating of C (Fair) based on an annualized return of 19.16% over the last three years and a total return of 19.52% year to date 2012. Factored into the performance evaluation is an expense ratio of 0.19% (very low).

The fund's risk rating is currently B- (Good). It carries a beta of 1.00, meaning that its performance tracks fairly well with that of the overall stock market. Volatility, as measured by both the semi-deviation and a drawdown factor, is considered low. As of March 31, 2012, *Vanguard Financials ETF traded at a discount of .06% below its net asset value, which is better than its one-year historical average premium of .02%.

Jeffrey D. Miller has been running the fund for 2 years and currently receives a manager quality ranking of 42 (0=worst, 99=best). If you desire an average level of risk, then this fund may be an option.

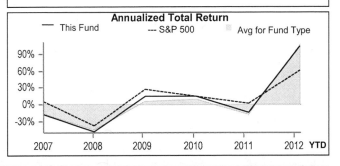

*Vanguard FTSE All-Wld ex-US S/C (VSS)   D   Weak

Fund Family: Vanguard Group Inc
Fund Type: Foreign
Inception Date: April 2, 2009

Data Date	Investment Rating	Net Assets ($Mil)	Price	Performance Rating/Pts	Total Return Y-T-D	Risk Rating/Pts
3-12	D	993.37	88.97	D / 2.0	14.70%	C+ / 6.7
2011	D-	814.40	77.57	E+ / 0.8	1.33%	C+ / 6.3
2010	A+	673.30	99.62	A / 9.5	25.62%	B- / 7.8

Major Rating Factors:
Disappointing performance is the major factor driving the D (Weak) TheStreet.com Investment Rating for *Vanguard FTSE All-Wld ex-US S/C. The fund currently has a performance rating of D (Weak) based on an annualized return of 0.00% over the last three years and a total return of 14.70% year to date 2012. Factored into the performance evaluation is an expense ratio of 0.28% (very low).

The fund's risk rating is currently C+ (Fair). It carries a beta of 0.00, meaning the fund's expected move will be 0.0% for every 10% move in the market. Volatility, as measured by both the semi-deviation and a drawdown factor, is considered low. As of March 31, 2012, *Vanguard FTSE All-Wld ex-US S/C traded at a premium of .54% above its net asset value, which is worse than its one-year historical average premium of .07%.

Ryan E. Ludt has been running the fund for 3 years and currently receives a manager quality ranking of 25 (0=worst, 99=best). This fund offers only a moderate level of risk but investors looking for strong performance are still waiting.

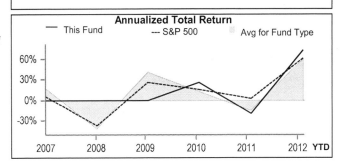

*Vanguard FTSE All-World ex-US ET (VEU)   C-   Fair

Fund Family: Vanguard Group Inc
Fund Type: Foreign
Inception Date: March 2, 2007

Data Date	Investment Rating	Net Assets ($Mil)	Price	Performance Rating/Pts	Total Return Y-T-D	Risk Rating/Pts
3-12	C-	6,682.54	44.22	C- / 3.6	11.53%	B- / 7.6
2011	C-	5,864.70	39.65	C- / 3.3	-0.10%	B- / 7.3
2010	D+	6,174.60	47.73	D+ / 2.7	11.80%	C / 5.3
2009	A-	2,600.53	43.61	B+ / 8.6	35.10%	C+ / 5.6

Major Rating Factors: Middle of the road best describes *Vanguard FTSE All-World ex-US ET whose TheStreet.com Investment Rating is currently a C- (Fair). The fund currently has a performance rating of C- (Fair) based on an annualized return of 16.08% over the last three years and a total return of 11.53% year to date 2012. Factored into the performance evaluation is an expense ratio of 0.18% (very low).

The fund's risk rating is currently B- (Good). It carries a beta of 1.08, meaning that its performance tracks fairly well with that of the overall stock market. Volatility, as measured by both the semi-deviation and a drawdown factor, is considered low. As of March 31, 2012, *Vanguard FTSE All-World ex-US ET traded at a premium of .18% above its net asset value, which is worse than its one-year historical average premium of .10%.

Ryan E. Ludt has been running the fund for 4 years and currently receives a manager quality ranking of 47 (0=worst, 99=best). If you desire an average level of risk, then this fund may be an option.

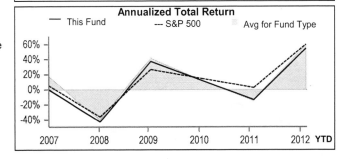

*Vanguard Global ex-US RE I Fd ET (VNQI)

D+　　　**Weak**

Fund Family: Vanguard Group Inc
Fund Type: Global
Inception Date: November 1, 2010

Major Rating Factors:
Disappointing performance is the major factor driving the D+ (Weak) TheStreet.com Investment Rating for *Vanguard Global ex-US RE I Fd ET. The fund currently has a performance rating of D+ (Weak) based on an annualized return of 0.00% over the last three years and a total return of 15.50% year to date 2012. Factored into the performance evaluation is an expense ratio of 0.35% (very low).

The fund's risk rating is currently B- (Good). It carries a beta of 0.00, meaning the fund's expected move will be 0.0% for every 10% move in the market. Volatility, as measured by both the semi-deviation and a drawdown factor, is considered low. As of March 31, 2012, *Vanguard Global ex-US RE I Fd ET traded at a premium of .09% above its net asset value, which is better than its one-year historical average premium of .37%.

Gerard C. O'Reilly has been running the fund for 2 years and currently receives a manager quality ranking of 61 (0=worst, 99=best). This fund offers only a moderate level of risk but investors looking for strong performance are still waiting.

Data Date	Investment Rating	Net Assets ($Mil)	Price	Performance Rating/Pts	Total Return Y-T-D	Risk Rating/Pts
3-12	D+	237.74	47.01	D+ / 2.9	15.50%	B- / 7.2
2011	D	166.70	40.70	D- / 1.0	1.55%	B- / 7.2

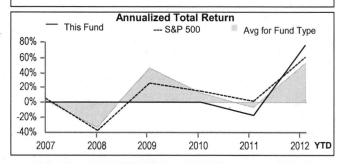

*Vanguard Growth ETF (VUG)

C+　　　**Fair**

Fund Family: Vanguard Group Inc
Fund Type: Growth
Inception Date: January 26, 2004

Major Rating Factors: Middle of the road best describes *Vanguard Growth ETF whose TheStreet.com Investment Rating is currently a C+ (Fair). The fund currently has a performance rating of C+ (Fair) based on an annualized return of 23.07% over the last three years and a total return of 15.23% year to date 2012. Factored into the performance evaluation is an expense ratio of 0.10% (very low).

The fund's risk rating is currently B- (Good). It carries a beta of 1.03, meaning that its performance tracks fairly well with that of the overall stock market. Volatility, as measured by both the semi-deviation and a drawdown factor, is considered low. As of March 31, 2012, *Vanguard Growth ETF traded at a discount of .01% below its net asset value, which is better than its one-year historical average premium of .02%.

Gerard C. O'Reilly has been running the fund for 18 years and currently receives a manager quality ranking of 53 (0=worst, 99=best). If you desire an average level of risk, then this fund may be an option.

Data Date	Investment Rating	Net Assets ($Mil)	Price	Performance Rating/Pts	Total Return Y-T-D	Risk Rating/Pts
3-12	C+	6,870.39	70.97	C+ / 6.7	15.23%	B- / 7.9
2011	C+	6,045.60	61.76	C+ / 6.2	1.98%	B- / 7.7
2010	C+	5,099.50	61.42	C / 5.5	17.23%	C+ / 5.9
2009	C-	3,294.13	53.06	C- / 3.7	32.17%	C+ / 6.1

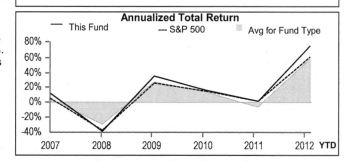

*Vanguard HealthCare Index ETF (VHT)

C+　　　**Fair**

Fund Family: Vanguard Group Inc
Fund Type: Health
Inception Date: January 26, 2004

Major Rating Factors: Middle of the road best describes *Vanguard HealthCare Index ETF whose TheStreet.com Investment Rating is currently a C+ (Fair). The fund currently has a performance rating of C (Fair) based on an annualized return of 19.95% over the last three years and a total return of 10.39% year to date 2012. Factored into the performance evaluation is an expense ratio of 0.19% (very low).

The fund's risk rating is currently B (Good). It carries a beta of 0.65, meaning the fund's expected move will be 6.5% for every 10% move in the market. Volatility, as measured by both the semi-deviation and a drawdown factor, is considered low. As of March 31, 2012, *Vanguard HealthCare Index ETF traded at a premium of .06% above its net asset value, which is worse than its one-year historical average premium of .01%.

Ryan E. Ludt has been running the fund for 8 years and currently receives a manager quality ranking of 70 (0=worst, 99=best). If you desire an average level of risk, then this fund may be an option.

Data Date	Investment Rating	Net Assets ($Mil)	Price	Performance Rating/Pts	Total Return Y-T-D	Risk Rating/Pts
3-12	C+	785.56	67.57	C / 5.5	10.39%	B / 8.6
2011	C+	728.90	61.21	C / 5.2	1.27%	B / 8.2
2010	C	614.30	56.25	C- / 3.4	5.60%	C+ / 6.9
2009	C	554.25	54.19	C- / 3.6	19.98%	C+ / 6.9

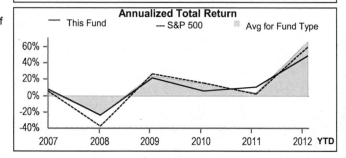

*Vanguard High Dividend Yield ETF (VYM)   B-   Good

Fund Family: Vanguard Group Inc
Fund Type: Income
Inception Date: November 10, 2006

Major Rating Factors: *Vanguard High Dividend Yield ETF receives a TheStreet.com Investment Rating of B- (Good). The fund currently has a performance rating of C+ (Fair) based on an annualized return of 22.19% over the last three years and a total return of 7.81% year to date 2012. Factored into the performance evaluation is an expense ratio of 0.13% (very low).

The fund's risk rating is currently B (Good). It carries a beta of 0.86, meaning the fund's expected move will be 8.6% for every 10% move in the market. Volatility, as measured by both the semi-deviation and a drawdown factor, is considered low. As of March 31, 2012, *Vanguard High Dividend Yield ETF traded at a premium of .02% above its net asset value, which is better than its one-year historical average premium of .07%.

Michael Perre has been running the fund for 6 years and currently receives a manager quality ranking of 68 (0=worst, 99=best). If you desire an average level of risk, then this fund may be an option.

Data Date	Investment Rating	Net Assets ($Mil)	Price	Performance Rating/Pts	Total Return Y-T-D	Risk Rating/Pts
3-12	B-	2,992.67	48.47	C+ / 6.1	7.81%	B / 8.8
2011	C+	2,407.50	45.26	C+ / 5.9	0.71%	B- / 7.8
2010	C-	931.40	42.22	C- / 3.5	14.25%	C+ / 6.0
2009	D	278.92	38.00	D / 1.6	14.68%	C+ / 6.1

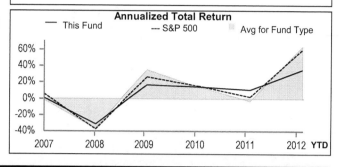

*Vanguard Industrials Index ETF (VIS)   C+   Fair

Fund Family: Vanguard Group Inc
Fund Type: Income
Inception Date: September 23, 2004

Major Rating Factors: Strong performance is the major factor driving the C+ (Fair) TheStreet.com Investment Rating for *Vanguard Industrials Index ETF. The fund currently has a performance rating of B- (Good) based on an annualized return of 25.71% over the last three years and a total return of 12.00% year to date 2012. Factored into the performance evaluation is an expense ratio of 0.19% (very low).

The fund's risk rating is currently B- (Good). It carries a beta of 1.35, meaning it is expected to move 13.5% for every 10% move in the market. Volatility, as measured by both the semi-deviation and a drawdown factor, is considered low. As of March 31, 2012, *Vanguard Industrials Index ETF traded at a premium of .01% above its net asset value.

Jeffrey D. Miller has been running the fund for 2 years and currently receives a manager quality ranking of 29 (0=worst, 99=best). If you desire only a moderate level of risk and strong performance, then this fund is an excellent option.

Data Date	Investment Rating	Net Assets ($Mil)	Price	Performance Rating/Pts	Total Return Y-T-D	Risk Rating/Pts
3-12	C+	501.93	69.54	B- / 7.0	12.00%	B- / 7.7
2011	C	435.10	62.09	C / 5.3	2.37%	B- / 7.3
2010	C	440.40	64.82	C / 5.5	27.32%	C / 5.3
2009	D	185.86	51.58	D / 2.1	17.86%	C+ / 5.6

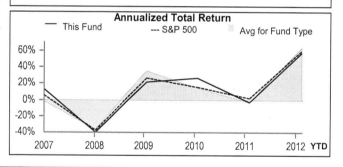

*Vanguard Info Tech Ind ETF (VGT)   B-   Good

Fund Family: Vanguard Group Inc
Fund Type: Growth
Inception Date: January 26, 2004

Major Rating Factors: Strong performance is the major factor driving the B- (Good) TheStreet.com Investment Rating for *Vanguard Info Tech Ind ETF. The fund currently has a performance rating of B (Good) based on an annualized return of 26.03% over the last three years and a total return of 20.87% year to date 2012. Factored into the performance evaluation is an expense ratio of 0.19% (very low).

The fund's risk rating is currently B- (Good). It carries a beta of 1.14, meaning it is expected to move 11.4% for every 10% move in the market. Volatility, as measured by both the semi-deviation and a drawdown factor, is considered low. As of March 31, 2012, *Vanguard Info Tech Ind ETF traded at a premium of .08% above its net asset value, which is worse than its one-year historical average premium of .03%.

Jeffrey D. Miller has been running the fund for 2 years and currently receives a manager quality ranking of 56 (0=worst, 99=best). If you desire only a moderate level of risk and strong performance, then this fund is an excellent option.

Data Date	Investment Rating	Net Assets ($Mil)	Price	Performance Rating/Pts	Total Return Y-T-D	Risk Rating/Pts
3-12	B-	2,268.07	74.18	B / 7.9	20.87%	B- / 7.4
2011	C+	1,891.00	61.37	B- / 7.0	2.31%	B- / 7.3
2010	C+	1,501.60	61.52	C+ / 6.3	12.78%	C+ / 5.6
2009	C+	639.19	54.87	C+ / 6.5	55.70%	C+ / 5.6

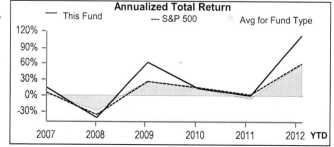

*Vanguard Intermediate Term Bond (BIV)   C-   Fair

Fund Family: Vanguard Group Inc
Fund Type: General - Investment Grade
Inception Date: April 3, 2007

Major Rating Factors:
Disappointing performance is the major factor driving the C- (Fair) TheStreet.com Investment Rating for *Vanguard Intermediate Term Bond. The fund currently has a performance rating of D+ (Weak) based on an annualized return of 9.66% over the last three years and a total return of 0.54% year to date 2012. Factored into the performance evaluation is an expense ratio of 0.11% (very low).

The fund's risk rating is currently B+ (Good). It carries a beta of 1.65, meaning it is expected to move 16.5% for every 10% move in the market. Volatility, as measured by both the semi-deviation and a drawdown factor, is considered very low. As of March 31, 2012, *Vanguard Intermediate Term Bond traded at a premium of .24% above its net asset value, which is better than its one-year historical average premium of .30%.

Joshua C. Barrickman has been running the fund for 4 years and currently receives a manager quality ranking of 33 (0=worst, 99=best). This fund offers only a moderate level of risk but investors looking for strong performance are still waiting.

Data Date	Investment Rating	Net Assets ($Mil)	Price	Performance Rating/Pts	Total Return Y-T-D	Risk Rating/Pts
3-12	C-	2,983.78	86.96	D+ / 2.4	0.54%	B+ / 9.6
2011	C+	2,780.90	86.97	C- / 3.9	-0.01%	B+ / 9.6
2010	B	1,931.90	82.49	C / 5.4	9.13%	B / 8.6
2009	C+	852.24	79.07	C- / 3.6	5.14%	B / 8.8

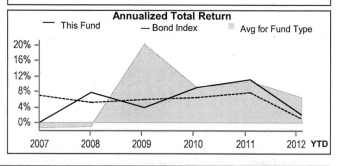

Annualized Total Return

*Vanguard Intm-Term Corp Bd Idx E (VCIT)   C   Fair

Fund Family: Vanguard Group Inc
Fund Type: Corporate - Investment Grade
Inception Date: November 19, 2009

Major Rating Factors:
Disappointing performance is the major factor driving the C (Fair) TheStreet.com Investment Rating for *Vanguard Intm-Term Corp Bd Idx E. The fund currently has a performance rating of D+ (Weak) based on an annualized return of 0.00% over the last three years and a total return of 2.23% year to date 2012. Factored into the performance evaluation is an expense ratio of 0.14% (very low).

The fund's risk rating is currently B+ (Good). It carries a beta of 0.00, meaning the fund's expected move will be 0.0% for every 10% move in the market. Volatility, as measured by both the semi-deviation and a drawdown factor, is considered very low. As of March 31, 2012, *Vanguard Intm-Term Corp Bd Idx E traded at a premium of .53% above its net asset value, which is better than its one-year historical average premium of .60%.

Joshua C. Barrickman has been running the fund for 3 years and currently receives a manager quality ranking of 38 (0=worst, 99=best). This fund offers only a moderate level of risk but investors looking for strong performance are still waiting.

Data Date	Investment Rating	Net Assets ($Mil)	Price	Performance Rating/Pts	Total Return Y-T-D	Risk Rating/Pts
3-12	C	1,755.78	83.75	D+ / 2.5	2.23%	B+ / 9.7
2011	C+	953.70	82.37	C- / 4.0	-0.11%	B+ / 9.7
2010	B	386.10	78.68	C+ / 6.2	9.96%	B / 8.9

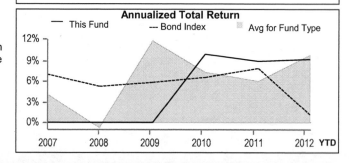

Annualized Total Return

*Vanguard Intm-Term Govt Bd Idx E (VGIT)   C-   Fair

Fund Family: Vanguard Group Inc
Fund Type: US Government/Agency
Inception Date: November 19, 2009

Major Rating Factors:
Disappointing performance is the major factor driving the C- (Fair) TheStreet.com Investment Rating for *Vanguard Intm-Term Govt Bd Idx E. The fund currently has a performance rating of D (Weak) based on an annualized return of 0.00% over the last three years and a total return of -1.25% year to date 2012. Factored into the performance evaluation is an expense ratio of 0.14% (very low).

The fund's risk rating is currently B+ (Good). It carries a beta of 0.00, meaning the fund's expected move will be 0.0% for every 10% move in the market. Volatility, as measured by both the semi-deviation and a drawdown factor, is considered very low. As of March 31, 2012, *Vanguard Intm-Term Govt Bd Idx E traded at a discount of .06% below its net asset value, which is better than its one-year historical average premium of .10%.

Gregory Davis has been running the fund for 3 years and currently receives a manager quality ranking of 70 (0=worst, 99=best). This fund offers only a moderate level of risk but investors looking for strong performance are still waiting.

Data Date	Investment Rating	Net Assets ($Mil)	Price	Performance Rating/Pts	Total Return Y-T-D	Risk Rating/Pts
3-12	C-	94.76	64.66	D / 1.8	-1.25%	B+ / 9.6
2011	C+	81.80	65.66	C- / 4.0	-0.32%	B+ / 9.6
2010	B	34.70	61.23	C / 4.5	7.51%	B / 8.8

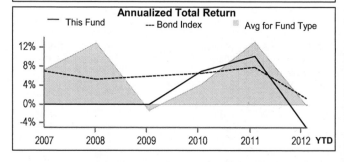

Annualized Total Return

*Vanguard Large Cap ETF (VV)

C+ **Fair**

Fund Family: Vanguard Group Inc
Fund Type: Growth
Inception Date: January 27, 2004

Major Rating Factors: Middle of the road best describes *Vanguard Large Cap ETF whose TheStreet.com Investment Rating is currently a C+ (Fair). The fund currently has a performance rating of C+ (Fair) based on an annualized return of 21.48% over the last three years and a total return of 12.93% year to date 2012. Factored into the performance evaluation is an expense ratio of 0.10% (very low).

The fund's risk rating is currently B (Good). It carries a beta of 1.02, meaning that its performance tracks fairly well with that of the overall stock market. Volatility, as measured by both the semi-deviation and a drawdown factor, is considered low. As of March 31, 2012, *Vanguard Large Cap ETF traded at a discount of .03% below its net asset value.

Ryan E. Ludt has been running the fund for 8 years and currently receives a manager quality ranking of 45 (0=worst, 99=best). If you desire an average level of risk, then this fund may be an option.

Data Date	Investment Rating	Net Assets ($Mil)	Price	Performance Rating/Pts	Total Return Y-T-D	Risk Rating/Pts
3-12	C+	3,300.01	64.43	C+ / 6.0	12.93%	B / 8.2
2011	C+	3,020.90	57.30	C / 5.3	1.78%	B- / 7.9
2010	C-	2,857.80	57.61	C- / 4.2	15.93%	C+ / 6.0
2009	D+	2,173.77	50.67	D+ / 2.5	24.07%	C+ / 6.1

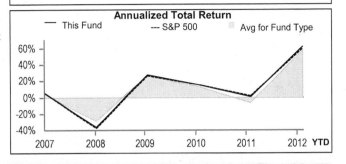

Annualized Total Return

---

*Vanguard Long Term Bd Idx ETF (BLV)

C **Fair**

Fund Family: Vanguard Group Inc
Fund Type: General - Investment Grade
Inception Date: April 3, 2007

Major Rating Factors: Middle of the road best describes *Vanguard Long Term Bd Idx ETF whose TheStreet.com Investment Rating is currently a C (Fair). The fund currently has a performance rating of C- (Fair) based on an annualized return of 13.06% over the last three years and a total return of -2.72% year to date 2012. Factored into the performance evaluation is an expense ratio of 0.11% (very low).

The fund's risk rating is currently B+ (Good). It carries a beta of 2.58, meaning it is expected to move 25.8% for every 10% move in the market. Volatility, as measured by both the semi-deviation and a drawdown factor, is considered very low. As of March 31, 2012, *Vanguard Long Term Bd Idx ETF traded at a premium of .24% above its net asset value, which is better than its one-year historical average premium of .33%.

Gregory Davis has been running the fund for 4 years and currently receives a manager quality ranking of 21 (0=worst, 99=best). If you desire an average level of risk, then this fund may be an option.

Data Date	Investment Rating	Net Assets ($Mil)	Price	Performance Rating/Pts	Total Return Y-T-D	Risk Rating/Pts
3-12	C	632.75	88.91	C- / 3.0	-2.72%	B+ / 9.0
2011	B-	511.80	92.01	C / 5.5	-0.85%	B+ / 9.1
2010	B	324.20	79.09	C / 5.1	10.01%	B / 8.2
2009	C	140.92	76.16	D+ / 2.7	2.26%	B / 8.4

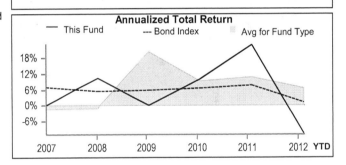

Annualized Total Return

---

*Vanguard Long-Term Corp Bd Idx E (VCLT)

C- **Fair**

Fund Family: Vanguard Group Inc
Fund Type: Corporate - Investment Grade
Inception Date: November 19, 2009

Major Rating Factors:
Disappointing performance is the major factor driving the C- (Fair) TheStreet.com Investment Rating for *Vanguard Long-Term Corp Bd Idx E. The fund currently has a performance rating of D+ (Weak) based on an annualized return of 0.00% over the last three years and a total return of -1.28% year to date 2012. Factored into the performance evaluation is an expense ratio of 0.14% (very low).

The fund's risk rating is currently B+ (Good). It carries a beta of 0.00, meaning the fund's expected move will be 0.0% for every 10% move in the market. Volatility, as measured by both the semi-deviation and a drawdown factor, is considered very low. As of March 31, 2012, *Vanguard Long-Term Corp Bd Idx E traded at a premium of .45% above its net asset value, which is better than its one-year historical average premium of .94%.

Joshua C. Barrickman has been running the fund for 3 years and currently receives a manager quality ranking of 32 (0=worst, 99=best). This fund offers only a moderate level of risk but investors looking for strong performance are still waiting.

Data Date	Investment Rating	Net Assets ($Mil)	Price	Performance Rating/Pts	Total Return Y-T-D	Risk Rating/Pts
3-12	C-	760.84	84.98	D+ / 2.8	-1.28%	B+ / 9.2
2011	B+	401.30	86.70	B- / 7.0	-0.36%	B+ / 9.3
2010	B	54.90	77.52	C+ / 6.2	10.62%	B / 8.6

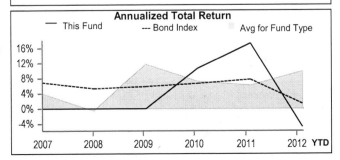

Annualized Total Return

*Vanguard Long-Term Govt Bd Idx E (VGLT)

C-   **Fair**

Fund Family: Vanguard Group Inc
Fund Type: US Government/Agency
Inception Date: November 19, 2009

Major Rating Factors:
Disappointing performance is the major factor driving the C- (Fair) TheStreet.com Investment Rating for *Vanguard Long-Term Govt Bd Idx E. The fund currently has a performance rating of D+ (Weak) based on an annualized return of 0.00% over the last three years and a total return of -6.29% year to date 2012. Factored into the performance evaluation is an expense ratio of 0.14% (very low).

The fund's risk rating is currently B (Good). It carries a beta of 0.00, meaning the fund's expected move will be 0.0% for every 10% move in the market. Volatility, as measured by both the semi-deviation and a drawdown factor, is considered low. As of March 31, 2012, *Vanguard Long-Term Govt Bd Idx E traded at a discount of .40% below its net asset value, which is better than its one-year historical average premium of .06%.

Gregory Davis has been running the fund for 3 years and currently receives a manager quality ranking of 38 (0=worst, 99=best). This fund offers only a moderate level of risk but investors looking for strong performance are still waiting.

Data Date	Investment Rating	Net Assets ($Mil)	Price	Performance Rating/Pts	Total Return Y-T-D	Risk Rating/Pts
3-12	C-	65.89	70.04	D+ / 2.5	-6.29%	B / 8.7
2011	A	63.90	75.11	A- / 9.0	-1.36%	B / 8.8
2010	C	72.30	60.27	D+ / 2.9	8.98%	B / 8.1

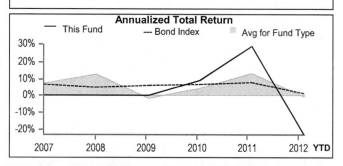

Annualized Total Return

---

*Vanguard Materials ETF (VAW)

C   **Fair**

Fund Family: Vanguard Group Inc
Fund Type: Income
Inception Date: January 26, 2004

Major Rating Factors: Middle of the road best describes *Vanguard Materials ETF whose TheStreet.com Investment Rating is currently a C (Fair). The fund currently has a performance rating of C+ (Fair) based on an annualized return of 22.38% over the last three years and a total return of 12.42% year to date 2012. Factored into the performance evaluation is an expense ratio of 0.19% (very low).

The fund's risk rating is currently B- (Good). It carries a beta of 1.50, meaning it is expected to move 15.0% for every 10% move in the market. Volatility, as measured by both the semi-deviation and a drawdown factor, is considered low. As of March 31, 2012, *Vanguard Materials ETF traded at a premium of .05% above its net asset value.

Michael D. Eyre has been running the fund for 2 years and currently receives a manager quality ranking of 16 (0=worst, 99=best). If you desire an average level of risk, then this fund may be an option.

Data Date	Investment Rating	Net Assets ($Mil)	Price	Performance Rating/Pts	Total Return Y-T-D	Risk Rating/Pts
3-12	C	641.93	82.21	C+ / 5.8	12.42%	B- / 7.3
2011	C+	530.10	73.13	C+ / 6.2	3.65%	B- / 7.0
2010	C+	614.30	82.60	C+ / 6.7	24.46%	C / 5.0
2009	C	375.30	67.82	C+ / 6.1	46.33%	C / 5.2

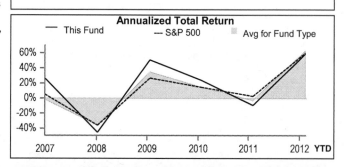

Annualized Total Return

---

*Vanguard Mega Cap 300 ETF (MGC)

C+   **Fair**

Fund Family: Vanguard Group Inc
Fund Type: Income
Inception Date: December 17, 2007

Major Rating Factors: Middle of the road best describes *Vanguard Mega Cap 300 ETF whose TheStreet.com Investment Rating is currently a C+ (Fair). The fund currently has a performance rating of C+ (Fair) based on an annualized return of 20.59% over the last three years and a total return of 12.69% year to date 2012. Factored into the performance evaluation is an expense ratio of 0.12% (very low).

The fund's risk rating is currently B (Good). It carries a beta of 0.99, meaning that its performance tracks fairly well with that of the overall stock market. Volatility, as measured by both the semi-deviation and a drawdown factor, is considered low. As of March 31, 2012, *Vanguard Mega Cap 300 ETF traded at a discount of .02% below its net asset value, which is better than its one-year historical average premium of .01%.

Ryan E. Ludt has been running the fund for 5 years and currently receives a manager quality ranking of 44 (0=worst, 99=best). If you desire an average level of risk, then this fund may be an option.

Data Date	Investment Rating	Net Assets ($Mil)	Price	Performance Rating/Pts	Total Return Y-T-D	Risk Rating/Pts
3-12	C+	375.05	48.25	C+ / 5.7	12.69%	B / 8.2
2011	C	331.00	43.01	C / 5.1	1.68%	B- / 7.9
2010	C-	246.60	42.92	C- / 3.7	13.77%	C+ / 6.1
2009	A-	198.72	38.50	B / 8.2	21.99%	C+ / 6.2

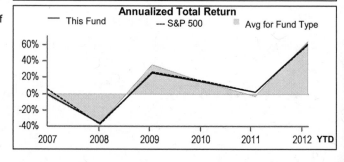

Annualized Total Return

---

*Vanguard Mega Cap 300 Growth ETF (MGK)　　　　　　C+　　　Fair

Fund Family: Vanguard Group Inc
Fund Type: Growth
Inception Date: December 17, 2007

Major Rating Factors: Middle of the road best describes *Vanguard Mega Cap 300 Growth ETF whose TheStreet.com Investment Rating is currently a C+ (Fair). The fund currently has a performance rating of C+ (Fair) based on an annualized return of 22.46% over the last three years and a total return of 15.22% year to date 2012. Factored into the performance evaluation is an expense ratio of 0.12% (very low).

The fund's risk rating is currently B- (Good). It carries a beta of 1.01, meaning that its performance tracks fairly well with that of the overall stock market. Volatility, as measured by both the semi-deviation and a drawdown factor, is considered low. As of March 31, 2012, *Vanguard Mega Cap 300 Growth ETF traded at a premium of .07% above its net asset value.

Michael D. Eyre has been running the fund for 2 years and currently receives a manager quality ranking of 51 (0=worst, 99=best). If you desire an average level of risk, then this fund may be an option.

Data Date	Investment Rating	Net Assets ($Mil)	Price	Performance Rating/Pts	Total Return Y-T-D	Risk Rating/Pts
3-12	C+	598.21	55.28	C+ / 6.6	15.22%	B- / 7.9
2011	C+	533.90	48.10	C+ / 6.1	1.85%	B- / 7.7
2010	C	346.90	47.31	C / 5.1	14.53%	C+ / 6.1
2009	A	36.25	41.87	B+ / 8.6	31.09%	C+ / 6.1

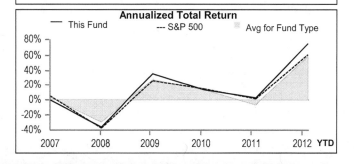

*Vanguard Mega Cap 300 Value ETF (MGV)　　　　　　C　　　Fair

Fund Family: Vanguard Group Inc
Fund Type: Income
Inception Date: December 17, 2007

Major Rating Factors: Middle of the road best describes *Vanguard Mega Cap 300 Value ETF whose TheStreet.com Investment Rating is currently a C (Fair). The fund currently has a performance rating of C (Fair) based on an annualized return of 18.78% over the last three years and a total return of 10.50% year to date 2012. Factored into the performance evaluation is an expense ratio of 0.12% (very low).

The fund's risk rating is currently B (Good). It carries a beta of 0.99, meaning that its performance tracks fairly well with that of the overall stock market. Volatility, as measured by both the semi-deviation and a drawdown factor, is considered low. As of March 31, 2012, *Vanguard Mega Cap 300 Value ETF traded at a premium of .05% above its net asset value, which is worse than its one-year historical average premium of .01%.

Michael D. Eyre has been running the fund for 2 years and currently receives a manager quality ranking of 35 (0=worst, 99=best). If you desire an average level of risk, then this fund may be an option.

Data Date	Investment Rating	Net Assets ($Mil)	Price	Performance Rating/Pts	Total Return Y-T-D	Risk Rating/Pts
3-12	C	384.46	41.92	C / 4.8	10.50%	B / 8.4
2011	C	347.40	38.17	C / 4.3	1.55%	B- / 7.8
2010	D+	259.50	38.72	D+ / 2.4	13.16%	C+ / 6.0
2009	B	163.14	35.10	B- / 7.5	13.22%	C+ / 6.1

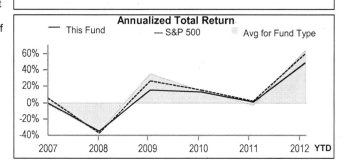

*Vanguard Mid Cap ETF (VO)　　　　　　　　　　　B-　　　Good

Fund Family: Vanguard Group Inc
Fund Type: Growth
Inception Date: January 26, 2004

Major Rating Factors: Strong performance is the major factor driving the B- (Good) TheStreet.com Investment Rating for *Vanguard Mid Cap ETF. The fund currently has a performance rating of B- (Good) based on an annualized return of 25.86% over the last three years and a total return of 13.41% year to date 2012. Factored into the performance evaluation is an expense ratio of 0.10% (very low).

The fund's risk rating is currently B (Good). It carries a beta of 1.17, meaning it is expected to move 11.7% for every 10% move in the market. Volatility, as measured by both the semi-deviation and a drawdown factor, is considered low. As of March 31, 2012, *Vanguard Mid Cap ETF traded at a discount of .06% below its net asset value.

Donald M. Butler has been running the fund for 14 years and currently receives a manager quality ranking of 52 (0=worst, 99=best). If you desire only a moderate level of risk and strong performance, then this fund is an excellent option.

Data Date	Investment Rating	Net Assets ($Mil)	Price	Performance Rating/Pts	Total Return Y-T-D	Risk Rating/Pts
3-12	B-	3,686.05	81.58	B- / 7.0	13.41%	B / 8.0
2011	C+	3,241.00	71.94	C+ / 6.5	1.83%	B- / 7.7
2010	C+	3,356.30	74.46	C+ / 6.7	25.68%	C / 5.4
2009	C-	1,482.72	59.95	C- / 3.3	36.24%	C+ / 5.7

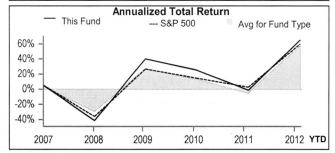

*Vanguard Mid Cap Growth ETF (VOT)

B-   **Good**

Fund Family: Vanguard Group Inc
Fund Type: Growth
Inception Date: August 17, 2006

Major Rating Factors: Strong performance is the major factor driving the B- (Good) TheStreet.com Investment Rating for *Vanguard Mid Cap Growth ETF. The fund currently has a performance rating of B- (Good) based on an annualized return of 26.14% over the last three years and a total return of 15.77% year to date 2012. Factored into the performance evaluation is an expense ratio of 0.10% (very low).

The fund's risk rating is currently B- (Good). It carries a beta of 1.18, meaning it is expected to move 11.8% for every 10% move in the market. Volatility, as measured by both the semi-deviation and a drawdown factor, is considered low. As of March 31, 2012, *Vanguard Mid Cap Growth ETF traded at a discount of .04% below its net asset value, which is better than its one-year historical average discount of .01%.

Gerard C. O'Reilly has been running the fund for 6 years and currently receives a manager quality ranking of 51 (0=worst, 99=best). If you desire only a moderate level of risk and strong performance, then this fund is an excellent option.

Data Date	Investment Rating	Net Assets ($Mil)	Price	Performance Rating/Pts	Total Return Y-T-D	Risk Rating/Pts
3-12	B-	1,216.14	68.92	B- / 7.2	15.77%	B- / 7.8
2011	C+	1,095.50	59.54	C+ / 6.6	2.27%	B- / 7.5
2010	C+	913.50	62.30	C+ / 6.5	29.14%	C / 5.1
2009	C-	523.74	48.49	C- / 3.5	37.89%	C / 5.5

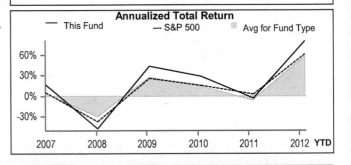

Annualized Total Return

*Vanguard Mid Cap Value Index ETF (VOE)

B-   **Good**

Fund Family: Vanguard Group Inc
Fund Type: Growth
Inception Date: August 17, 2006

Major Rating Factors: *Vanguard Mid Cap Value Index ETF receives a TheStreet.com Investment Rating of B- (Good). The fund currently has a performance rating of C+ (Fair) based on an annualized return of 25.60% over the last three years and a total return of 11.22% year to date 2012. Factored into the performance evaluation is an expense ratio of 0.10% (very low).

The fund's risk rating is currently B (Good). It carries a beta of 1.17, meaning it is expected to move 11.7% for every 10% move in the market. Volatility, as measured by both the semi-deviation and a drawdown factor, is considered low. As of March 31, 2012, *Vanguard Mid Cap Value Index ETF traded at a discount of .03% below its net asset value, which is better than its one-year historical average premium of .01%.

Donald M. Butler has been running the fund for 6 years and currently receives a manager quality ranking of 53 (0=worst, 99=best). If you desire an average level of risk, then this fund may be an option.

Data Date	Investment Rating	Net Assets ($Mil)	Price	Performance Rating/Pts	Total Return Y-T-D	Risk Rating/Pts
3-12	B-	945.72	57.46	C+ / 6.9	11.22%	B / 8.1
2011	C+	784.60	51.67	C+ / 6.3	1.41%	B- / 7.9
2010	C+	688.10	53.01	C+ / 6.7	21.76%	C+ / 5.7
2009	C-	492.35	44.37	C- / 3.0	34.58%	C+ / 5.7

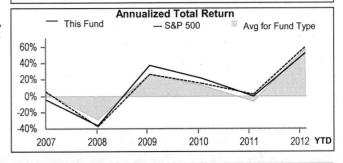

Annualized Total Return

*Vanguard Mort-Backed Secs Idx ET (VMBS)

C-   **Fair**

Fund Family: Vanguard Group Inc
Fund Type: Mortgage
Inception Date: November 19, 2009

Major Rating Factors:
Disappointing performance is the major factor driving the C- (Fair) TheStreet.com Investment Rating for *Vanguard Mort-Backed Secs Idx ET. The fund currently has a performance rating of D (Weak) based on an annualized return of 0.00% over the last three years and a total return of 0.27% year to date 2012. Factored into the performance evaluation is an expense ratio of 0.15% (very low).

The fund's risk rating is currently B+ (Good). It carries a beta of 0.00, meaning the fund's expected move will be 0.0% for every 10% move in the market. Volatility, as measured by both the semi-deviation and a drawdown factor, is considered very low. As of March 31, 2012, *Vanguard Mort-Backed Secs Idx ET traded at a discount of .02% below its net asset value, which is better than its one-year historical average premium of .22%.

Gregory Davis has been running the fund for 3 years and currently receives a manager quality ranking of 37 (0=worst, 99=best). This fund offers only a moderate level of risk but investors looking for strong performance are still waiting.

Data Date	Investment Rating	Net Assets ($Mil)	Price	Performance Rating/Pts	Total Return Y-T-D	Risk Rating/Pts
3-12	C-	160.89	51.87	D / 1.6	0.27%	B+ / 9.8
2011	C+	129.50	51.88	C- / 3.3	0.13%	B+ / 9.9
2010	B	36.00	50.28	C / 4.4	5.44%	B / 8.9

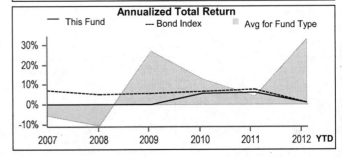

Annualized Total Return

*Vanguard MSCI EAFE ETF (VEA)   D   Weak

Fund Family: Vanguard Group Inc
Fund Type: Foreign
Inception Date: July 20, 2007

Major Rating Factors: *Vanguard MSCI EAFE ETF receives a TheStreet.com Investment Rating of D (Weak). The fund currently has a performance rating of C- (Fair) based on an annualized return of 14.23% over the last three years and a total return of 11.14% year to date 2012. Factored into the performance evaluation is an expense ratio of 0.12% (very low).

    The fund's risk rating is currently C+ (Fair). It carries a beta of 1.04, meaning that its performance tracks fairly well with that of the overall stock market. Volatility, as measured by both the semi-deviation and a drawdown factor, is considered low. As of March 31, 2012, *Vanguard MSCI EAFE ETF traded at a premium of .29% above its net asset value, which is worse than its one-year historical average premium of .22%.

    Donald M. Butler has been running the fund for 4 years and currently receives a manager quality ranking of 39 (0=worst, 99=best). If you desire an average level of risk, then this fund may be an option.

Data Date	Investment Rating	Net Assets ($Mil)	Price	Performance Rating/Pts	Total Return Y-T-D	Risk Rating/Pts
3-12	D	7,971.33	34.03	C- / 3.3	11.14%	C+ / 5.7
2011	D+	6,435.30	30.63	D+ / 2.6	-0.55%	B- / 7.4
2010	D-	4,829.40	36.15	D / 1.8	8.33%	C- / 3.6
2009	B	3,068.69	34.20	B / 8.2	26.41%	C / 4.9

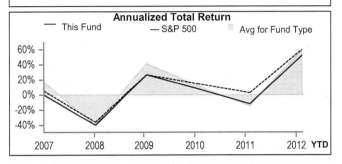

*Vanguard MSCI Emerging Markets E (VWO)   C-   Fair

Fund Family: Vanguard Group Inc
Fund Type: Emerging Market
Inception Date: March 4, 2005

Major Rating Factors: Middle of the road best describes *Vanguard MSCI Emerging Markets E whose TheStreet.com Investment Rating is currently a C- (Fair). The fund currently has a performance rating of C (Fair) based on an annualized return of 20.69% over the last three years and a total return of 13.77% year to date 2012. Factored into the performance evaluation is an expense ratio of 0.20% (very low).

    The fund's risk rating is currently B- (Good). It carries a beta of 1.07, meaning that its performance tracks fairly well with that of the overall stock market. Volatility, as measured by both the semi-deviation and a drawdown factor, is considered low. As of March 31, 2012, *Vanguard MSCI Emerging Markets E traded at a premium of .16% above its net asset value, which is worse than its one-year historical average premium of .09%.

    Michael Perre has been running the fund for 4 years and currently receives a manager quality ranking of 33 (0=worst, 99=best). If you desire an average level of risk, then this fund may be an option.

Data Date	Investment Rating	Net Assets ($Mil)	Price	Performance Rating/Pts	Total Return Y-T-D	Risk Rating/Pts
3-12	C-	55,080.25	43.47	C / 4.8	13.77%	B- / 7.1
2011	C	42,454.50	38.21	C / 5.2	0.94%	B- / 7.0
2010	D+	44,730.40	48.15	C / 5.3	19.46%	C- / 3.0
2009	C	6,767.32	41.00	B- / 7.4	66.71%	C- / 3.4

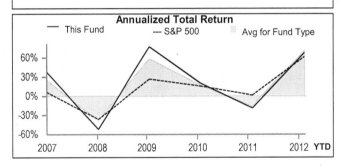

*Vanguard MSCI Europe ETF (VGK)   D   Weak

Fund Family: Vanguard Group Inc
Fund Type: Foreign
Inception Date: March 4, 2005

Major Rating Factors: *Vanguard MSCI Europe ETF receives a TheStreet.com Investment Rating of D (Weak). The fund currently has a performance rating of C- (Fair) based on an annualized return of 14.96% over the last three years and a total return of 11.25% year to date 2012. Factored into the performance evaluation is an expense ratio of 0.14% (very low).

    The fund's risk rating is currently C (Fair). It carries a beta of 1.18, meaning it is expected to move 11.8% for every 10% move in the market. Volatility, as measured by both the semi-deviation and a drawdown factor, is considered average. As of March 31, 2012, *Vanguard MSCI Europe ETF traded at a premium of .24% above its net asset value, which is worse than its one-year historical average premium of .12%.

    Gerard C. O'Reilly has been running the fund for 4 years and currently receives a manager quality ranking of 30 (0=worst, 99=best). If you desire an average level of risk, then this fund may be an option.

Data Date	Investment Rating	Net Assets ($Mil)	Price	Performance Rating/Pts	Total Return Y-T-D	Risk Rating/Pts
3-12	D	2,669.81	46.09	C- / 3.4	11.25%	C / 5.4
2011	D+	2,220.40	41.43	D+ / 2.7	-1.16%	B- / 7.1
2010	E+	2,784.40	49.09	D- / 1.4	6.05%	C- / 3.4
2009	D	1,544.20	48.48	D / 2.2	29.11%	C / 4.8

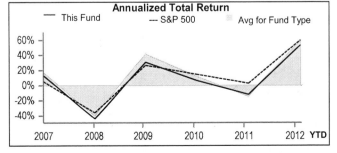

*Vanguard MSCI Pacific Fund ETF (VPL)

C-   **Fair**

Fund Family: Vanguard Group Inc
Fund Type: Foreign
Inception Date: March 4, 2005

Major Rating Factors: Middle of the road best describes *Vanguard MSCI Pacific Fund ETF whose TheStreet.com Investment Rating is currently a C- (Fair). The fund currently has a performance rating of C- (Fair) based on an annualized return of 13.65% over the last three years and a total return of 11.66% year to date 2012. Factored into the performance evaluation is an expense ratio of 0.14% (very low).

The fund's risk rating is currently B (Good). It carries a beta of 0.77, meaning the fund's expected move will be 7.7% for every 10% move in the market. Volatility, as measured by both the semi-deviation and a drawdown factor, is considered low. As of March 31, 2012, *Vanguard MSCI Pacific Fund ETF traded at a premium of .06% above its net asset value, which is worse than its one-year historical average premium of .02%.

Michael H. Buek has been running the fund for 15 years and currently receives a manager quality ranking of 61 (0=worst, 99=best). If you desire an average level of risk, then this fund may be an option.

Data Date	Investment Rating	Net Assets ($Mil)	Price	Performance Rating/Pts	Total Return Y-T-D	Risk Rating/Pts
3-12	C-	1,577.60	53.14	C- / 3.2	11.66%	B / 8.0
2011	C-	1,415.50	47.59	D+ / 2.7	0.25%	B- / 7.8
2010	C-	1,548.70	57.04	C- / 3.7	15.50%	C / 5.3
2009	D	1,130.26	51.32	D / 1.7	19.44%	C / 5.4

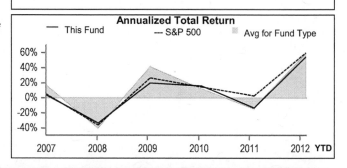

*Vanguard REIT ETF (VNQ)

A-   **Excellent**

Fund Family: Vanguard Group Inc
Fund Type: Income
Inception Date: September 23, 2004

Major Rating Factors:
Exceptional performance is the major factor driving the A- (Excellent) TheStreet.com Investment Rating for *Vanguard REIT ETF. The fund currently has a performance rating of A- (Excellent) based on an annualized return of 36.60% over the last three years and a total return of 10.61% year to date 2012. Factored into the performance evaluation is an expense ratio of 0.12% (very low).

The fund's risk rating is currently B- (Good). It carries a beta of 1.26, meaning it is expected to move 12.6% for every 10% move in the market. Volatility, as measured by both the semi-deviation and a drawdown factor, is considered low. As of March 31, 2012, *Vanguard REIT ETF traded at a discount of .03% below its net asset value.

Gerard C. O'Reilly has been running the fund for 16 years and currently receives a manager quality ranking of 85 (0=worst, 99=best). If you desire only a moderate level of risk and strong performance, then this fund is an excellent option.

Data Date	Investment Rating	Net Assets ($Mil)	Price	Performance Rating/Pts	Total Return Y-T-D	Risk Rating/Pts
3-12	A-	10,692.46	63.65	A- / 9.1	10.61%	B- / 7.8
2011	C+	9,307.90	58.00	B / 7.8	-0.28%	C+ / 6.4
2010	C+	7,532.70	55.37	B / 7.7	28.43%	C- / 4.2
2009	D-	2,491.89	44.74	D / 1.9	34.15%	C- / 4.1

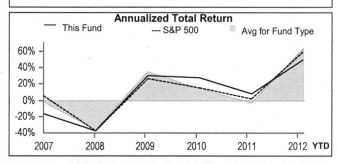

*Vanguard Russell 1000 Gro Idx ET (VONG)

B   **Good**

Fund Family: Vanguard Group Inc
Fund Type: Growth
Inception Date: September 20, 2010

Major Rating Factors: Strong performance is the major factor driving the B (Good) TheStreet.com Investment Rating for *Vanguard Russell 1000 Gro Idx ET. The fund currently has a performance rating of B- (Good) based on an annualized return of 0.00% over the last three years and a total return of 14.80% year to date 2012. Factored into the performance evaluation is an expense ratio of 0.15% (very low).

The fund's risk rating is currently B (Good). It carries a beta of 0.00, meaning the fund's expected move will be 0.0% for every 10% move in the market. Volatility, as measured by both the semi-deviation and a drawdown factor, is considered low. As of March 31, 2012, *Vanguard Russell 1000 Gro Idx ET traded at a premium of .10% above its net asset value, which is worse than its one-year historical average discount of .04%.

George U. Sauter currently receives a manager quality ranking of 59 (0=worst, 99=best). If you desire only a moderate level of risk and strong performance, then this fund is an excellent option.

Data Date	Investment Rating	Net Assets ($Mil)	Price	Performance Rating/Pts	Total Return Y-T-D	Risk Rating/Pts
3-12	B	74.14	67.84	B- / 7.2	14.80%	B / 8.5
2011	C-	53.40	59.26	D+ / 2.7	1.82%	B / 8.5

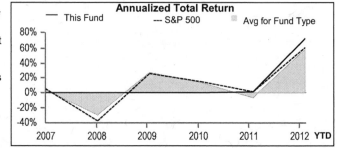

*Vanguard Russell 1000 Index ETF (VONE)

C+   **Fair**

Fund Family: Vanguard Group Inc
Fund Type: Growth
Inception Date: September 20, 2010

Major Rating Factors: Middle of the road best describes *Vanguard Russell 1000 Index ETF whose TheStreet.com Investment Rating is currently a C+ (Fair). The fund currently has a performance rating of C+ (Fair) based on an annualized return of 0.00% over the last three years and a total return of 12.87% year to date 2012. Factored into the performance evaluation is an expense ratio of 0.12% (very low).

   The fund's risk rating is currently B (Good). It carries a beta of 0.00, meaning the fund's expected move will be 0.0% for every 10% move in the market. Volatility, as measured by both the semi-deviation and a drawdown factor, is considered low. As of March 31, 2012, *Vanguard Russell 1000 Index ETF traded at a discount of .02% below its net asset value.

   Jeffrey D. Miller has been running the fund for 2 years and currently receives a manager quality ranking of 37 (0=worst, 99=best). If you desire an average level of risk, then this fund may be an option.

Data Date	Investment Rating	Net Assets ($Mil)	Price	Performance Rating/Pts	Total Return Y-T-D	Risk Rating/Pts
3-12	C+	43.87	64.36	C+ / 6.1	12.87%	B / 8.3
2011	C-	34.40	57.25	D+ / 2.8	1.99%	B / 8.3

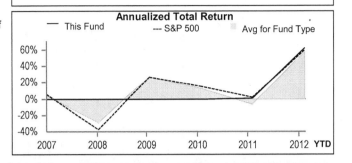

Annualized Total Return

*Vanguard Russell 1000 Val Index (VONV)

C   **Fair**

Fund Family: Vanguard Group Inc
Fund Type: Growth
Inception Date: September 20, 2010

Major Rating Factors: Middle of the road best describes *Vanguard Russell 1000 Val Index whose TheStreet.com Investment Rating is currently a C (Fair). The fund currently has a performance rating of C (Fair) based on an annualized return of 0.00% over the last three years and a total return of 10.90% year to date 2012. Factored into the performance evaluation is an expense ratio of 0.15% (very low).

   The fund's risk rating is currently B (Good). It carries a beta of 0.00, meaning the fund's expected move will be 0.0% for every 10% move in the market. Volatility, as measured by both the semi-deviation and a drawdown factor, is considered low. As of March 31, 2012, *Vanguard Russell 1000 Val Index traded at a premium of .15% above its net asset value, which is worse than its one-year historical average premium of .08%.

   George U. Sauter currently receives a manager quality ranking of 25 (0=worst, 99=best). If you desire an average level of risk, then this fund may be an option.

Data Date	Investment Rating	Net Assets ($Mil)	Price	Performance Rating/Pts	Total Return Y-T-D	Risk Rating/Pts
3-12	C	44.81	61.35	C / 4.9	10.90%	B / 8.1
2011	C-	36.00	55.54	D+ / 2.8	1.66%	B / 8.1

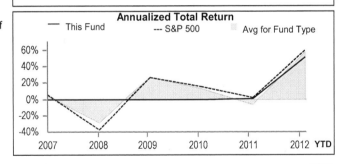

Annualized Total Return

*Vanguard Russell 2000 Gro Idx ET (VTWG)

C   **Fair**

Fund Family: Vanguard Group Inc
Fund Type: Growth
Inception Date: September 20, 2010

Major Rating Factors: Middle of the road best describes *Vanguard Russell 2000 Gro Idx ET whose TheStreet.com Investment Rating is currently a C (Fair). The fund currently has a performance rating of C (Fair) based on an annualized return of 0.00% over the last three years and a total return of 13.10% year to date 2012. Factored into the performance evaluation is an expense ratio of 0.20% (very low).

   The fund's risk rating is currently B- (Good). It carries a beta of 0.00, meaning the fund's expected move will be 0.0% for every 10% move in the market. Volatility, as measured by both the semi-deviation and a drawdown factor, is considered low. As of March 31, 2012, *Vanguard Russell 2000 Gro Idx ET traded at a discount of .04% below its net asset value, which is better than its one-year historical average discount of .01%.

   Andrew H. Maack has been running the fund for 2 years and currently receives a manager quality ranking of 13 (0=worst, 99=best). If you desire an average level of risk, then this fund may be an option.

Data Date	Investment Rating	Net Assets ($Mil)	Price	Performance Rating/Pts	Total Return Y-T-D	Risk Rating/Pts
3-12	C	20.26	68.91	C / 5.0	13.10%	B- / 7.4
2011	D	12.20	60.93	D / 1.8	1.10%	B- / 7.4

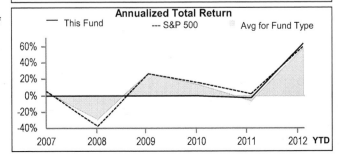

Annualized Total Return

*Vanguard Russell 2000 Idx ETF (VTWO)   C   Fair

Fund Family: Vanguard Group Inc
Fund Type: Growth
Inception Date: September 20, 2010

Major Rating Factors: Middle of the road best describes *Vanguard Russell 2000 Idx ETF whose TheStreet.com Investment Rating is currently a C (Fair). The fund currently has a performance rating of C (Fair) based on an annualized return of 0.00% over the last three years and a total return of 12.46% year to date 2012. Factored into the performance evaluation is an expense ratio of 0.15% (very low).

The fund's risk rating is currently B- (Good). It carries a beta of 0.00, meaning the fund's expected move will be 0.0% for every 10% move in the market. Volatility, as measured by both the semi-deviation and a drawdown factor, is considered low. As of March 31, 2012, *Vanguard Russell 2000 Idx ETF traded at a price exactly equal to its net asset value, which is better than its one-year historical average premium of .01%.

Andrew H. Maack has been running the fund for 2 years and currently receives a manager quality ranking of 13 (0=worst, 99=best). If you desire an average level of risk, then this fund may be an option.

Data Date	Investment Rating	Net Assets ($Mil)	Price	Performance Rating/Pts	Total Return Y-T-D	Risk Rating/Pts
3-12	C	64.17	65.82	C / 4.7	12.46%	B- / 7.5
2011	D	52.70	58.53	D / 1.7	1.54%	B- / 7.5

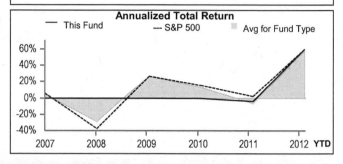

Annualized Total Return

*Vanguard Russell 2000 Val Index (VTWV)   C-   Fair

Fund Family: Vanguard Group Inc
Fund Type: Growth
Inception Date: September 20, 2010

Major Rating Factors: Middle of the road best describes *Vanguard Russell 2000 Val Index whose TheStreet.com Investment Rating is currently a C- (Fair). The fund currently has a performance rating of C (Fair) based on an annualized return of 0.00% over the last three years and a total return of 10.99% year to date 2012. Factored into the performance evaluation is an expense ratio of 0.20% (very low).

The fund's risk rating is currently B- (Good). It carries a beta of 0.00, meaning the fund's expected move will be 0.0% for every 10% move in the market. Volatility, as measured by both the semi-deviation and a drawdown factor, is considered low. As of March 31, 2012, *Vanguard Russell 2000 Val Index traded at a price exactly equal to its net asset value, which is better than its one-year historical average premium of .03%.

Andrew H. Maack has been running the fund for 2 years and currently receives a manager quality ranking of 12 (0=worst, 99=best). If you desire an average level of risk, then this fund may be an option.

Data Date	Investment Rating	Net Assets ($Mil)	Price	Performance Rating/Pts	Total Return Y-T-D	Risk Rating/Pts
3-12	C-	12.16	62.90	C / 4.3	10.99%	B- / 7.5
2011	D+	11.20	56.67	D / 1.9	0.97%	B- / 7.5

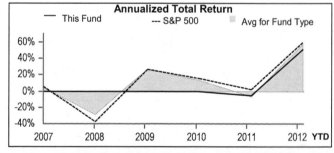

Annualized Total Return

*Vanguard Russell 3000 Index ETF (VTHR)   C+   Fair

Fund Family: Vanguard Group Inc
Fund Type: Growth
Inception Date: September 20, 2010

Major Rating Factors: Middle of the road best describes *Vanguard Russell 3000 Index ETF whose TheStreet.com Investment Rating is currently a C+ (Fair). The fund currently has a performance rating of C+ (Fair) based on an annualized return of 0.00% over the last three years and a total return of 12.89% year to date 2012. Factored into the performance evaluation is an expense ratio of 0.15% (very low).

The fund's risk rating is currently B (Good). It carries a beta of 0.00, meaning the fund's expected move will be 0.0% for every 10% move in the market. Volatility, as measured by both the semi-deviation and a drawdown factor, is considered low. As of March 31, 2012, *Vanguard Russell 3000 Index ETF traded at a premium of .26% above its net asset value, which is worse than its one-year historical average premium of .03%.

Jeffrey D. Miller has been running the fund for 2 years and currently receives a manager quality ranking of 34 (0=worst, 99=best). If you desire an average level of risk, then this fund may be an option.

Data Date	Investment Rating	Net Assets ($Mil)	Price	Performance Rating/Pts	Total Return Y-T-D	Risk Rating/Pts
3-12	C+	25.09	64.60	C+ / 6.2	12.89%	B / 8.2
2011	C-	22.90	57.42	D+ / 2.5	1.66%	B / 8.2

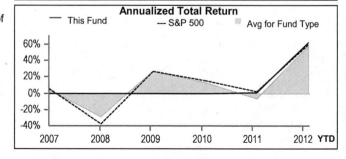

Annualized Total Return

*Vanguard S&P 500 G Indx ETF (VOOG)

<table>
<tr><td></td><td colspan="5" align="right">**B-**</td><td colspan="2" align="right">**Good**</td></tr>
</table>

Fund Family: Vanguard Group Inc
Fund Type: Growth
Inception Date: September 7, 2010

Data Date	Investment Rating	Net Assets ($Mil)	Price	Performance Rating/Pts	Total Return Y-T-D	Risk Rating/Pts
3-12	B-	72.08	67.38	C+ / 6.5	11.99%	B / 8.8
2011	C-	51.20	60.37	C- / 3.2	1.40%	B / 8.8

Major Rating Factors: *Vanguard S&P 500 G Indx ETF receives a TheStreet.com Investment Rating of B- (Good). The fund currently has a performance rating of C+ (Fair) based on an annualized return of 0.00% over the last three years and a total return of 11.99% year to date 2012. Factored into the performance evaluation is an expense ratio of 0.15% (very low).

The fund's risk rating is currently B (Good). It carries a beta of 0.00, meaning the fund's expected move will be 0.0% for every 10% move in the market. Volatility, as measured by both the semi-deviation and a drawdown factor, is considered low. As of March 31, 2012, *Vanguard S&P 500 G Indx ETF traded at a discount of .01% below its net asset value, which is better than its one-year historical average premium of .03%.

Ryan E. Ludt has been running the fund for 2 years and currently receives a manager quality ranking of 67 (0=worst, 99=best). If you desire an average level of risk, then this fund may be an option.

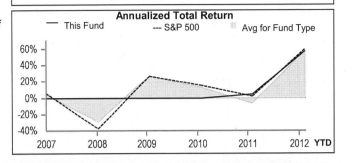

*Vanguard S&P 500 Val Indx ETF (VOOV)

<table>
<tr><td></td><td colspan="5" align="right">**C+**</td><td colspan="2" align="right">**Fair**</td></tr>
</table>

Fund Family: Vanguard Group Inc
Fund Type: Growth
Inception Date: September 7, 2010

Data Date	Investment Rating	Net Assets ($Mil)	Price	Performance Rating/Pts	Total Return Y-T-D	Risk Rating/Pts
3-12	C+	36.25	62.20	C / 5.5	12.54%	B / 8.1
2011	C-	33.20	55.53	D+ / 2.7	2.03%	B / 8.0

Major Rating Factors: Middle of the road best describes *Vanguard S&P 500 Val Indx ETF whose TheStreet.com Investment Rating is currently a C+ (Fair). The fund currently has a performance rating of C (Fair) based on an annualized return of 0.00% over the last three years and a total return of 12.54% year to date 2012. Factored into the performance evaluation is an expense ratio of 0.15% (very low).

The fund's risk rating is currently B (Good). It carries a beta of 0.00, meaning the fund's expected move will be 0.0% for every 10% move in the market. Volatility, as measured by both the semi-deviation and a drawdown factor, is considered low. As of March 31, 2012, *Vanguard S&P 500 Val Indx ETF traded at a premium of .08% above its net asset value, which is worse than its one-year historical average premium of .06%.

Ryan E. Ludt has been running the fund for 2 years and currently receives a manager quality ranking of 25 (0=worst, 99=best). If you desire an average level of risk, then this fund may be an option.

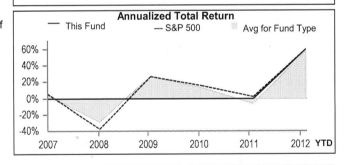

*Vanguard S&P Mid-Cap 400 Gro ETF (IVOG)

<table>
<tr><td></td><td colspan="5" align="right">**C**</td><td colspan="2" align="right">**Fair**</td></tr>
</table>

Fund Family: Vanguard Group Inc
Fund Type: Growth
Inception Date: September 7, 2010

Data Date	Investment Rating	Net Assets ($Mil)	Price	Performance Rating/Pts	Total Return Y-T-D	Risk Rating/Pts
3-12	C	33.76	68.87	C / 5.1	14.12%	B- / 7.9
2011	D+	30.10	60.35	D / 1.7	0.89%	B- / 7.9

Major Rating Factors: Middle of the road best describes *Vanguard S&P Mid-Cap 400 Gro ETF whose TheStreet.com Investment Rating is currently a C (Fair). The fund currently has a performance rating of C (Fair) based on an annualized return of 0.00% over the last three years and a total return of 14.12% year to date 2012. Factored into the performance evaluation is an expense ratio of 0.20% (very low).

The fund's risk rating is currently B- (Good). It carries a beta of 0.00, meaning the fund's expected move will be 0.0% for every 10% move in the market. Volatility, as measured by both the semi-deviation and a drawdown factor, is considered low. As of March 31, 2012, *Vanguard S&P Mid-Cap 400 Gro ETF traded at a premium of .34% above its net asset value, which is worse than its one-year historical average premium of .04%.

Donald M. Butler has been running the fund for 2 years and currently receives a manager quality ranking of 18 (0=worst, 99=best). If you desire an average level of risk, then this fund may be an option.

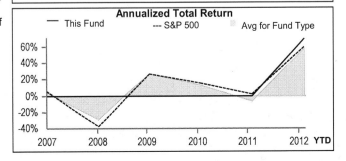

*Vanguard S&P Mid-Cap 400 Index E (IVOO)   C   Fair

Fund Family: Vanguard Group Inc
Fund Type: Growth
Inception Date: September 7, 2010

Major Rating Factors: Middle of the road best describes *Vanguard S&P Mid-Cap 400 Index E whose TheStreet.com Investment Rating is currently a C (Fair). The fund currently has a performance rating of C (Fair) based on an annualized return of 0.00% over the last three years and a total return of 13.42% year to date 2012. Factored into the performance evaluation is an expense ratio of 0.15% (very low).

The fund's risk rating is currently B- (Good). It carries a beta of 0.00, meaning the fund's expected move will be 0.0% for every 10% move in the market. Volatility, as measured by both the semi-deviation and a drawdown factor, is considered low. As of March 31, 2012, *Vanguard S&P Mid-Cap 400 Index E traded at a premium of .29% above its net asset value, which is worse than its one-year historical average premium of .05%.

Donald M. Butler has been running the fund for 2 years and currently receives a manager quality ranking of 17 (0=worst, 99=best). If you desire an average level of risk, then this fund may be an option.

Data Date	Investment Rating	Net Assets ($Mil)	Price	Perfor-mance Rating/Pts	Total Return Y-T-D	Risk Rating/Pts
3-12	C	35.82	66.53	C / 4.8	13.42%	B- / 7.9
2011	D+	26.30	58.66	D / 1.8	1.14%	B- / 7.8

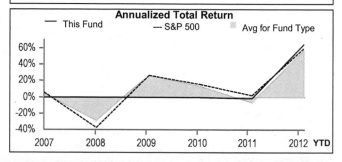

*Vanguard S&P Mid-Cap 400 Value E (IVOV)   C   Fair

Fund Family: Vanguard Group Inc
Fund Type: Growth
Inception Date: September 7, 2010

Major Rating Factors: Middle of the road best describes *Vanguard S&P Mid-Cap 400 Value E whose TheStreet.com Investment Rating is currently a C (Fair). The fund currently has a performance rating of C (Fair) based on an annualized return of 0.00% over the last three years and a total return of 11.51% year to date 2012. Factored into the performance evaluation is an expense ratio of 0.20% (very low).

The fund's risk rating is currently B- (Good). It carries a beta of 0.00, meaning the fund's expected move will be 0.0% for every 10% move in the market. Volatility, as measured by both the semi-deviation and a drawdown factor, is considered low. As of March 31, 2012, *Vanguard S&P Mid-Cap 400 Value E traded at a discount of .74% below its net asset value, which is better than its one-year historical average discount of .12%.

Donald M. Butler has been running the fund for 2 years and currently receives a manager quality ranking of 13 (0=worst, 99=best). If you desire an average level of risk, then this fund may be an option.

Data Date	Investment Rating	Net Assets ($Mil)	Price	Perfor-mance Rating/Pts	Total Return Y-T-D	Risk Rating/Pts
3-12	C	12.50	63.46	C / 4.7	11.51%	B- / 7.6
2011	D	11.30	56.91	D / 1.7	-0.93%	B- / 7.6

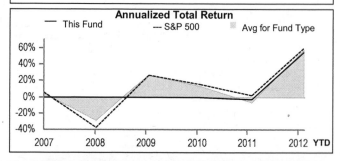

*Vanguard S&P SC 600 G Indx ETF (VIOG)   C   Fair

Fund Family: Vanguard Group Inc
Fund Type: Growth
Inception Date: September 7, 2010

Major Rating Factors: Middle of the road best describes *Vanguard S&P SC 600 G Indx ETF whose TheStreet.com Investment Rating is currently a C (Fair). The fund currently has a performance rating of C (Fair) based on an annualized return of 0.00% over the last three years and a total return of 10.46% year to date 2012. Factored into the performance evaluation is an expense ratio of 0.20% (very low).

The fund's risk rating is currently B- (Good). It carries a beta of 0.00, meaning the fund's expected move will be 0.0% for every 10% move in the market. Volatility, as measured by both the semi-deviation and a drawdown factor, is considered low. As of March 31, 2012, *Vanguard S&P SC 600 G Indx ETF traded at a discount of .30% below its net asset value.

Michael Perre has been running the fund for 2 years and currently receives a manager quality ranking of 23 (0=worst, 99=best). If you desire an average level of risk, then this fund may be an option.

Data Date	Investment Rating	Net Assets ($Mil)	Price	Perfor-mance Rating/Pts	Total Return Y-T-D	Risk Rating/Pts
3-12	C	17.14	70.50	C / 5.4	10.46%	B- / 7.9
2011	C-	19.10	63.82	D+ / 2.7	-0.28%	B- / 7.9

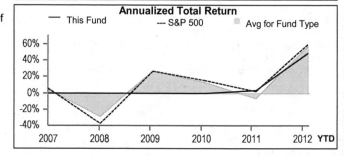

*Vanguard S&P SC 600 Indx ETF (VIOO)

C+ **Fair**

Fund Family: Vanguard Group Inc
Fund Type: Growth
Inception Date: September 7, 2010

Major Rating Factors: Middle of the road best describes *Vanguard S&P SC 600 Indx ETF whose TheStreet.com Investment Rating is currently a C+ (Fair). The fund currently has a performance rating of C+ (Fair) based on an annualized return of 0.00% over the last three years and a total return of 11.59% year to date 2012. Factored into the performance evaluation is an expense ratio of 0.15% (very low).

The fund's risk rating is currently B- (Good). It carries a beta of 0.00, meaning the fund's expected move will be 0.0% for every 10% move in the market. Volatility, as measured by both the semi-deviation and a drawdown factor, is considered low. As of March 31, 2012, *Vanguard S&P SC 600 Indx ETF traded at a premium of .47% above its net asset value, which is worse than its one-year historical average premium of .03%.

Michael H. Buek has been running the fund for 2 years and currently receives a manager quality ranking of 21 (0=worst, 99=best). If you desire an average level of risk, then this fund may be an option.

Data Date	Investment Rating	Net Assets ($Mil)	Price	Perfor-mance Rating/Pts	Total Return Y-T-D	Risk Rating/Pts
3-12	C+	16.68	68.96	C+ / 6.1	11.59%	B- / 7.8
2011	D+	12.30	61.80	D+ / 2.5	-0.23%	B- / 7.8

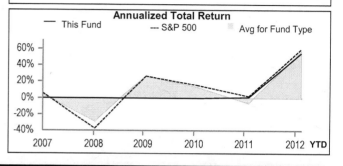

*Vanguard S&P SC 600 Val Indx ETF (VIOV)

C+ **Fair**

Fund Family: Vanguard Group Inc
Fund Type: Growth
Inception Date: September 7, 2010

Major Rating Factors: Middle of the road best describes *Vanguard S&P SC 600 Val Indx ETF whose TheStreet.com Investment Rating is currently a C+ (Fair). The fund currently has a performance rating of C+ (Fair) based on an annualized return of 0.00% over the last three years and a total return of 12.93% year to date 2012. Factored into the performance evaluation is an expense ratio of 0.20% (very low).

The fund's risk rating is currently B- (Good). It carries a beta of 0.00, meaning the fund's expected move will be 0.0% for every 10% move in the market. Volatility, as measured by both the semi-deviation and a drawdown factor, is considered low. As of March 31, 2012, *Vanguard S&P SC 600 Val Indx ETF traded at a premium of .54% above its net asset value, which is worse than its one-year historical average discount of .01%.

Michael H. Buek has been running the fund for 2 years and currently receives a manager quality ranking of 20 (0=worst, 99=best). If you desire an average level of risk, then this fund may be an option.

Data Date	Investment Rating	Net Assets ($Mil)	Price	Perfor-mance Rating/Pts	Total Return Y-T-D	Risk Rating/Pts
3-12	C+	16.28	67.29	C+ / 6.7	12.93%	B- / 7.7
2011	D+	14.80	59.59	D+ / 2.5	0.17%	B- / 7.7

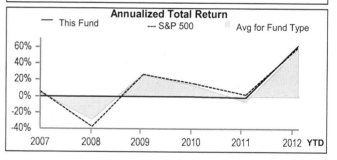

*Vanguard Short-Term Bd Idx ETF (BSV)

C- **Fair**

Fund Family: Vanguard Group Inc
Fund Type: General - Investment Grade
Inception Date: April 3, 2007

Major Rating Factors:
Disappointing performance is the major factor driving the C- (Fair) TheStreet.com Investment Rating for *Vanguard Short-Term Bd Idx ETF. The fund currently has a performance rating of D- (Weak) based on an annualized return of 3.62% over the last three years and a total return of 0.40% year to date 2012. Factored into the performance evaluation is an expense ratio of 0.11% (very low).

The fund's risk rating is currently B+ (Good). It carries a beta of 0.52, meaning the fund's expected move will be 5.2% for every 10% move in the market. Volatility, as measured by both the semi-deviation and a drawdown factor, is considered very low. As of March 31, 2012, *Vanguard Short-Term Bd Idx ETF traded at a premium of .01% above its net asset value, which is better than its one-year historical average premium of .09%.

Gregory Davis has been running the fund for 7 years and currently receives a manager quality ranking of 46 (0=worst, 99=best). This fund offers only a moderate level of risk but investors looking for strong performance are still waiting.

Data Date	Investment Rating	Net Assets ($Mil)	Price	Perfor-mance Rating/Pts	Total Return Y-T-D	Risk Rating/Pts
3-12	C-	7,664.95	80.94	D- / 1.5	0.40%	B+ / 9.8
2011	C	7,481.70	80.84	D+ / 2.5	0.11%	B+ / 9.8
2010	B	5,640.40	80.46	C / 4.3	3.89%	B / 8.9
2009	C+	1,904.50	79.54	D+ / 2.8	2.93%	B+ / 9.1

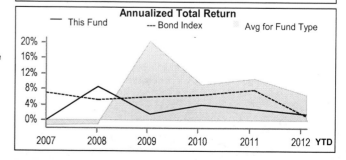

*Vanguard Short-Term Crp Bd Idx E (VCSH) C- Fair

Fund Family: Vanguard Group Inc
Fund Type: Corporate - Investment Grade
Inception Date: November 19, 2009

Major Rating Factors:
Disappointing performance is the major factor driving the C- (Fair) TheStreet.com Investment Rating for *Vanguard Short-Term Crp Bd Idx E. The fund currently has a performance rating of D (Weak) based on an annualized return of 0.00% over the last three years and a total return of 1.93% year to date 2012. Factored into the performance evaluation is an expense ratio of 0.14% (very low).

The fund's risk rating is currently B+ (Good). It carries a beta of 0.00, meaning the fund's expected move will be 0.0% for every 10% move in the market. Volatility, as measured by both the semi-deviation and a drawdown factor, is considered very low. As of March 31, 2012, *Vanguard Short-Term Crp Bd Idx E traded at a premium of .39% above its net asset value, which is worse than its one-year historical average premium of .35%.

Joshua C. Barrickman has been running the fund for 3 years and currently receives a manager quality ranking of 47 (0=worst, 99=best). This fund offers only a moderate level of risk but investors looking for strong performance are still waiting.

Data Date	Investment Rating	Net Assets ($Mil)	Price	Perfor-mance Rating/Pts	Total Return Y-T-D	Risk Rating/Pts
3-12	C-	2,680.11	79.04	D / 1.7	1.93%	B+ / 9.9
2011	C	2,230.20	77.83	D+ / 2.4	0.10%	B+ / 9.9
2010	B+	940.80	77.41	C / 4.5	5.27%	B+ / 9.0

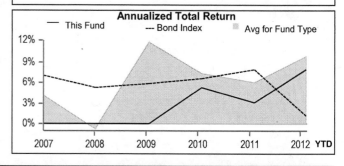

*Vanguard Short-Term Gvt Bd Idx E (VGSH) C- Fair

Fund Family: Vanguard Group Inc
Fund Type: US Government/Agency
Inception Date: November 19, 2009

Major Rating Factors:
Disappointing performance is the major factor driving the C- (Fair) TheStreet.com Investment Rating for *Vanguard Short-Term Gvt Bd Idx E. The fund currently has a performance rating of D- (Weak) based on an annualized return of 0.00% over the last three years and a total return of -0.12% year to date 2012. Factored into the performance evaluation is an expense ratio of 0.14% (very low).

The fund's risk rating is currently B+ (Good). It carries a beta of 0.00, meaning the fund's expected move will be 0.0% for every 10% move in the market. Volatility, as measured by both the semi-deviation and a drawdown factor, is considered very low. As of March 31, 2012, *Vanguard Short-Term Gvt Bd Idx E traded at a premium of .05% above its net asset value, which is better than its one-year historical average premium of .06%.

Gregory Davis has been running the fund for 3 years and currently receives a manager quality ranking of 53 (0=worst, 99=best). This fund offers only a moderate level of risk but investors looking for strong performance are still waiting.

Data Date	Investment Rating	Net Assets ($Mil)	Price	Perfor-mance Rating/Pts	Total Return Y-T-D	Risk Rating/Pts
3-12	C-	167.44	60.86	D- / 1.2	-0.12%	B+ / 9.9
2011	C	170.60	60.98	D / 2.2	-0.11%	B+ / 9.9
2010	C+	82.00	60.56	C- / 3.1	2.29%	B+ / 9.0

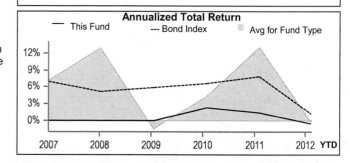

*Vanguard Small Cap ETF (VB) B- Good

Fund Family: Vanguard Group Inc
Fund Type: Growth
Inception Date: January 26, 2004

Major Rating Factors: Strong performance is the major factor driving the B- (Good) TheStreet.com Investment Rating for *Vanguard Small Cap ETF. The fund currently has a performance rating of B- (Good) based on an annualized return of 26.92% over the last three years and a total return of 13.02% year to date 2012. Factored into the performance evaluation is an expense ratio of 0.10% (very low).

The fund's risk rating is currently B- (Good). It carries a beta of 1.33, meaning it is expected to move 13.3% for every 10% move in the market. Volatility, as measured by both the semi-deviation and a drawdown factor, is considered low. As of March 31, 2012, *Vanguard Small Cap ETF traded at a premium of .01% above its net asset value, which is worse than its one-year historical average discount of .01%.

Michael H. Buek has been running the fund for 21 years and currently receives a manager quality ranking of 37 (0=worst, 99=best). If you desire only a moderate level of risk and strong performance, then this fund is an excellent option.

Data Date	Investment Rating	Net Assets ($Mil)	Price	Perfor-mance Rating/Pts	Total Return Y-T-D	Risk Rating/Pts
3-12	B-	4,229.37	78.72	B- / 7.3	13.02%	B- / 7.6
2011	C+	3,683.00	69.67	C+ / 6.5	1.42%	B- / 7.3
2010	B	4,843.10	72.63	B- / 7.5	28.12%	C / 5.5
2009	C-	1,621.53	57.35	C- / 3.3	34.18%	C+ / 5.6

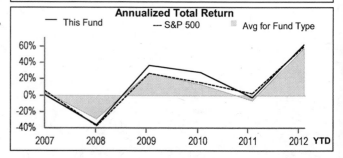

*Vanguard Small Cap Growth ETF (VBK)   B-   Good

Fund Family: Vanguard Group Inc
Fund Type: Growth
Inception Date: January 26, 2004

Data Date	Investment Rating	Net Assets ($Mil)	Price	Performance Rating/Pts	Total Return Y-T-D	Risk Rating/Pts
3-12	B-	2,143.98	86.95	B / 7.8	13.94%	B- / 7.3
2011	C+	1,857.30	76.36	B- / 7.0	1.13%	C+ / 6.9
2010	B	1,841.90	78.04	B / 7.8	30.95%	C / 5.3
2009	C-	993.12	59.87	C- / 4.0	39.29%	C / 5.4

Major Rating Factors: Strong performance is the major factor driving the B- (Good) TheStreet.com Investment Rating for *Vanguard Small Cap Growth ETF. The fund currently has a performance rating of B (Good) based on an annualized return of 28.71% over the last three years and a total return of 13.94% year to date 2012. Factored into the performance evaluation is an expense ratio of 0.10% (very low).

The fund's risk rating is currently B- (Good). It carries a beta of 1.32, meaning it is expected to move 13.2% for every 10% move in the market. Volatility, as measured by both the semi-deviation and a drawdown factor, is considered low. As of March 31, 2012, *Vanguard Small Cap Growth ETF traded at a discount of .05% below its net asset value, which is better than its one-year historical average discount of .01%.

Gerard C. O'Reilly has been running the fund for 8 years and currently receives a manager quality ranking of 44 (0=worst, 99=best). If you desire only a moderate level of risk and strong performance, then this fund is an excellent option.

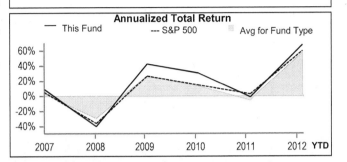

*Vanguard Small Cap Value ETF (VBR)   C+   Fair

Fund Family: Vanguard Group Inc
Fund Type: Growth
Inception Date: January 26, 2004

Data Date	Investment Rating	Net Assets ($Mil)	Price	Performance Rating/Pts	Total Return Y-T-D	Risk Rating/Pts
3-12	C+	1,965.34	70.38	C+ / 6.8	12.35%	B- / 7.8
2011	C	1,755.20	62.67	C / 5.4	1.88%	B- / 7.5
2010	B	1,851.20	66.86	B- / 7.4	25.12%	C / 5.5
2009	D+	1,023.31	54.48	D+ / 2.5	29.32%	C+ / 5.6

Major Rating Factors: Middle of the road best describes *Vanguard Small Cap Value ETF whose TheStreet.com Investment Rating is currently a C+ (Fair). The fund currently has a performance rating of C+ (Fair) based on an annualized return of 25.05% over the last three years and a total return of 12.35% year to date 2012. Factored into the performance evaluation is an expense ratio of 0.10% (very low).

The fund's risk rating is currently B- (Good). It carries a beta of 1.31, meaning it is expected to move 13.1% for every 10% move in the market. Volatility, as measured by both the semi-deviation and a drawdown factor, is considered low. As of March 31, 2012, *Vanguard Small Cap Value ETF traded at a premium of .09% above its net asset value, which is worse than its one-year historical average premium of .01%.

Michael H. Buek has been running the fund for 14 years and currently receives a manager quality ranking of 32 (0=worst, 99=best). If you desire an average level of risk, then this fund may be an option.

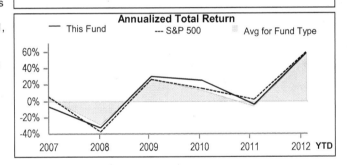

*Vanguard Telecom Serv ETF (VOX)   C-   Fair

Fund Family: Vanguard Group Inc
Fund Type: Income
Inception Date: September 23, 2004

Data Date	Investment Rating	Net Assets ($Mil)	Price	Performance Rating/Pts	Total Return Y-T-D	Risk Rating/Pts
3-12	C-	424.13	65.01	C- / 3.2	4.57%	B / 8.5
2011	C	373.10	62.17	C / 4.3	-1.34%	B / 8.4
2010	C	315.30	65.63	C / 4.7	19.52%	C+ / 6.4
2009	D+	146.79	56.51	D+ / 2.3	27.26%	C+ / 6.2

Major Rating Factors: Middle of the road best describes *Vanguard Telecom Serv ETF whose TheStreet.com Investment Rating is currently a C- (Fair). The fund currently has a performance rating of C- (Fair) based on an annualized return of 14.40% over the last three years and a total return of 4.57% year to date 2012. Factored into the performance evaluation is an expense ratio of 0.19% (very low).

The fund's risk rating is currently B (Good). It carries a beta of 0.76, meaning the fund's expected move will be 7.6% for every 10% move in the market. Volatility, as measured by both the semi-deviation and a drawdown factor, is considered low. As of March 31, 2012, *Vanguard Telecom Serv ETF traded at a discount of .06% below its net asset value, which is better than its one-year historical average premium of .02%.

Ryan E. Ludt has been running the fund for 8 years and currently receives a manager quality ranking of 47 (0=worst, 99=best). If you desire an average level of risk, then this fund may be an option.

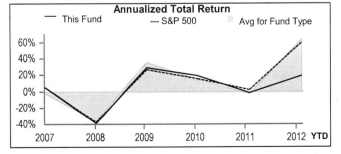

*Vanguard Total Bond Market ETF (BND)

C-   **Fair**

Fund Family: Vanguard Group Inc
Fund Type: General - Investment Grade
Inception Date: April 3, 2007

Major Rating Factors:

Disappointing performance is the major factor driving the C- (Fair) TheStreet.com Investment Rating for *Vanguard Total Bond Market ETF. The fund currently has a performance rating of D (Weak) based on an annualized return of 6.72% over the last three years and a total return of 0.17% year to date 2012. Factored into the performance evaluation is an expense ratio of 0.10% (very low).

The fund's risk rating is currently B+ (Good). It carries a beta of 0.99, meaning that its performance tracks fairly well with that of the overall stock market. Volatility, as measured by both the semi-deviation and a drawdown factor, is considered very low. As of March 31, 2012, *Vanguard Total Bond Market ETF traded at a premium of .24% above its net asset value, which is worse than its one-year historical average premium of .21%.

Kenneth E. Volpert has been running the fund for 20 years and currently receives a manager quality ranking of 44 (0=worst, 99=best). This fund offers only a moderate level of risk but investors looking for strong performance are still waiting.

Data Date	Investment Rating	Net Assets ($Mil)	Price	Performance Rating/Pts	Total Return Y-T-D	Risk Rating/Pts
3-12	C-	15,026.43	83.28	D / 1.9	0.17%	B+ / 9.7
2011	C	14,595.70	83.54	C- / 3.3	-0.24%	B+ / 9.7
2010	B+	9,047.80	80.27	C / 4.8	6.20%	B / 8.9
2009	C+	4,435.15	78.59	C- / 3.3	4.15%	B+ / 9.0

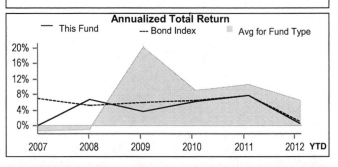

Annualized Total Return
— This Fund   --- Bond Index   Avg for Fund Type

*Vanguard Total Intl Stock Index (VXUS)

D   **Weak**

Fund Family: Vanguard Group Inc
Fund Type: Global
Inception Date: January 26, 2011

Major Rating Factors:

Disappointing performance is the major factor driving the D (Weak) TheStreet.com Investment Rating for *Vanguard Total Intl Stock Index. The fund currently has a performance rating of D (Weak) based on an annualized return of 0.00% over the last three years and a total return of 11.61% year to date 2012. Factored into the performance evaluation is an expense ratio of 0.18% (very low).

The fund's risk rating is currently B- (Good). It carries a beta of 0.00, meaning the fund's expected move will be 0.0% for every 10% move in the market. Volatility, as measured by both the semi-deviation and a drawdown factor, is considered low. As of March 31, 2012, *Vanguard Total Intl Stock Index traded at a premium of .33% above its net asset value, which is better than its one-year historical average premium of .53%.

Michael Perre has been running the fund for 4 years and currently receives a manager quality ranking of 33 (0=worst, 99=best). This fund offers only a moderate level of risk but investors looking for strong performance are still waiting.

Data Date	Investment Rating	Net Assets ($Mil)	Price	Performance Rating/Pts	Total Return Y-T-D	Risk Rating/Pts
3-12	D	674.44	45.65	D / 2.0	11.61%	B- / 7.3

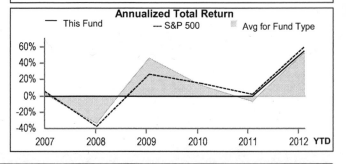

Annualized Total Return
— This Fund   --- S&P 500   Avg for Fund Type

*Vanguard Total Stock Market ETF (VTI)

C+   **Fair**

Fund Family: Vanguard Group Inc
Fund Type: Growth and Income
Inception Date: May 24, 2001

Major Rating Factors: Middle of the road best describes *Vanguard Total Stock Market ETF whose TheStreet.com Investment Rating is currently a C+ (Fair). The fund currently has a performance rating of C+ (Fair) based on an annualized return of 22.09% over the last three years and a total return of 12.86% year to date 2012. Factored into the performance evaluation is an expense ratio of 0.05% (very low).

The fund's risk rating is currently B (Good). It carries a beta of 1.05, meaning that its performance tracks fairly well with that of the overall stock market. Volatility, as measured by both the semi-deviation and a drawdown factor, is considered low. As of March 31, 2012, *Vanguard Total Stock Market ETF traded at a discount of .06% below its net asset value, which is better than its one-year historical average premium of .01%.

Gerard C. O'Reilly has been running the fund for 18 years and currently receives a manager quality ranking of 45 (0=worst, 99=best). If you desire an average level of risk, then this fund may be an option.

Data Date	Investment Rating	Net Assets ($Mil)	Price	Performance Rating/Pts	Total Return Y-T-D	Risk Rating/Pts
3-12	C+	20,780.30	72.26	C+ / 6.1	12.86%	B / 8.1
2011	C+	19,521.40	64.30	C / 5.5	1.68%	B- / 7.9
2010	D+	17,930.40	64.93	C / 4.8	17.45%	C- / 3.5
2009	D-	92,494.32	56.37	D+ / 2.5	25.19%	C- / 3.8

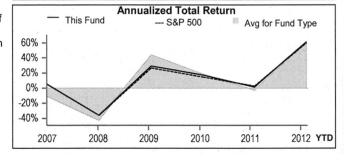

Annualized Total Return
— This Fund   --- S&P 500   Avg for Fund Type

*Vanguard Total World Stock ETF (VT)

C **Fair**

Fund Family: Vanguard Group Inc
Fund Type: Emerging Market
Inception Date: June 24, 2008

Major Rating Factors: Middle of the road best describes *Vanguard Total World Stock ETF whose TheStreet.com Investment Rating is currently a C (Fair). The fund currently has a performance rating of C (Fair) based on an annualized return of 18.24% over the last three years and a total return of 11.79% year to date 2012. Factored into the performance evaluation is an expense ratio of 0.22% (very low).

The fund's risk rating is currently B- (Good). It carries a beta of 0.74, meaning the fund's expected move will be 7.4% for every 10% move in the market. Volatility, as measured by both the semi-deviation and a drawdown factor, is considered low. As of March 31, 2012, *Vanguard Total World Stock ETF traded at a premium of .15% above its net asset value, which is better than its one-year historical average premium of .22%.

Ryan E. Ludt has been running the fund for 4 years and currently receives a manager quality ranking of 60 (0=worst, 99=best). If you desire an average level of risk, then this fund may be an option.

Data Date	Investment Rating	Net Assets ($Mil)	Price	Performance Rating/Pts	Total Return Y-T-D	Risk Rating/Pts
3-12	C	1,140.55	48.27	C / 4.4	11.79%	B- / 7.8
2011	C-	1,050.20	43.18	C- / 4.1	1.34%	B- / 7.7
2010	A-	742.10	47.80	A- / 9.0	13.09%	C+ / 5.9
2009	A-	114.19	43.09	B+ / 8.4	29.37%	C+ / 5.9

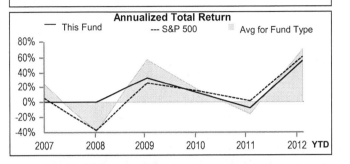

Annualized Total Return

*Vanguard Utilities Index ETF (VPU)

C **Fair**

Fund Family: Vanguard Group Inc
Fund Type: Utilities
Inception Date: January 26, 2004

Major Rating Factors: Middle of the road best describes *Vanguard Utilities Index ETF whose TheStreet.com Investment Rating is currently a C (Fair). The fund currently has a performance rating of C- (Fair) based on an annualized return of 15.59% over the last three years and a total return of -1.75% year to date 2012. Factored into the performance evaluation is an expense ratio of 0.19% (very low).

The fund's risk rating is currently B+ (Good). It carries a beta of 0.94, meaning that its performance tracks fairly well with that of the overall stock market. Volatility, as measured by both the semi-deviation and a drawdown factor, is considered very low. As of March 31, 2012, *Vanguard Utilities Index ETF traded at a premium of .01% above its net asset value, which is better than its one-year historical average premium of .03%.

Michael D. Eyre has been running the fund for 2 years and currently receives a manager quality ranking of 50 (0=worst, 99=best). If you desire an average level of risk, then this fund may be an option.

Data Date	Investment Rating	Net Assets ($Mil)	Price	Performance Rating/Pts	Total Return Y-T-D	Risk Rating/Pts
3-12	C	1,033.58	74.84	C- / 3.6	-1.75%	B+ / 9.2
2011	C+	1,048.80	76.89	C / 4.9	-2.74%	B / 8.5
2010	D+	647.00	67.08	D / 1.7	7.05%	C+ / 6.7
2009	C-	363.65	65.18	D+ / 2.5	9.30%	C+ / 6.8

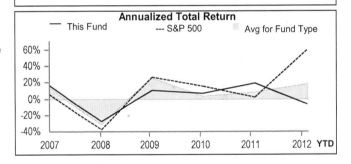

Annualized Total Return

*Vanguard Value ETF (VTV)

C+ **Fair**

Fund Family: Vanguard Group Inc
Fund Type: Income
Inception Date: January 26, 2004

Major Rating Factors: Middle of the road best describes *Vanguard Value ETF whose TheStreet.com Investment Rating is currently a C+ (Fair). The fund currently has a performance rating of C (Fair) based on an annualized return of 19.82% over the last three years and a total return of 10.54% year to date 2012. Factored into the performance evaluation is an expense ratio of 0.10% (very low).

The fund's risk rating is currently B (Good). It carries a beta of 1.01, meaning that its performance tracks fairly well with that of the overall stock market. Volatility, as measured by both the semi-deviation and a drawdown factor, is considered low. As of March 31, 2012, *Vanguard Value ETF traded at a discount of .02% below its net asset value, which is better than its one-year historical average premium of .02%.

Gerard C. O'Reilly has been running the fund for 18 years and currently receives a manager quality ranking of 40 (0=worst, 99=best). If you desire an average level of risk, then this fund may be an option.

Data Date	Investment Rating	Net Assets ($Mil)	Price	Performance Rating/Pts	Total Return Y-T-D	Risk Rating/Pts
3-12	C+	5,635.00	57.68	C / 5.1	10.54%	B / 8.3
2011	C	5,049.00	52.49	C / 4.6	1.58%	B- / 7.9
2010	C-	4,330.00	53.33	C- / 3.1	14.57%	C+ / 6.0
2009	D	2,357.82	47.75	D- / 1.5	16.53%	C+ / 6.0

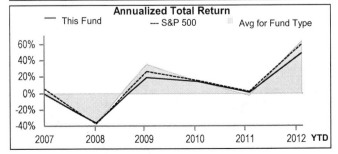

Annualized Total Return

*VelocityShares Daily 2x VIX S-T (TVIX)

E-   **Very Weak**

Fund Family: Credit Suisse AG
Fund Type: Income
Inception Date: November 29, 2010

Data Date	Investment Rating	Net Assets ($Mil)	Price	Performance Rating/Pts	Total Return Y-T-D	Risk Rating/Pts
3-12	E-	599.61	7.24	E- / 0	-77.34%	D / 1.9

Major Rating Factors: *VelocityShares Daily 2x VIX S-T has adopted a very risky asset allocation strategy and currently receives an overall TheStreet.com Investment Rating of E- (Very Weak). The fund has a high level of volatility, as measured by both semi-deviation and drawdown factors. It carries a beta of 0.00, meaning the fund's expected move will be 0.0% for every 10% move in the market. As of March 31, 2012, *VelocityShares Daily 2x VIX S-T traded at a premium of 15.29% above its net asset value, which is worse than its one-year historical average premium of 2.14%. Unfortunately, the high level of risk (D, Weak) failed to pay off as investors endured very poor performance.

The fund's performance rating is currently E- (Very Weak). It has registered an annualized return of 0.00% over the last three years but is down -77.34% year to date 2012. Factored into the performance evaluation is an expense ratio of 1.65% (above average).

This fund has been team managed for 2 years and currently receives a manager quality ranking of 0 (0=worst, 99=best). If you can tolerate very high levels of risk in the hope of improved future returns, holding this fund may be an option.

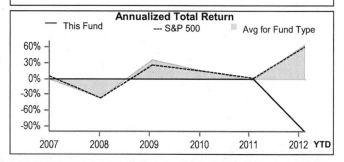

*VelocityShares Dly 2x VIX Med-T (TVIZ)

E-   **Very Weak**

Fund Family: Credit Suisse AG
Fund Type: Income
Inception Date: November 29, 2010

Data Date	Investment Rating	Net Assets ($Mil)	Price	Performance Rating/Pts	Total Return Y-T-D	Risk Rating/Pts
3-12	E-	7.49	34.55	E- / 0	-42.56%	D / 2.0

Major Rating Factors: *VelocityShares Dly 2x VIX Med-T has adopted a very risky asset allocation strategy and currently receives an overall TheStreet.com Investment Rating of E- (Very Weak). The fund has a high level of volatility, as measured by both semi-deviation and drawdown factors. It carries a beta of 0.00, meaning the fund's expected move will be 0.0% for every 10% move in the market. As of March 31, 2012, *VelocityShares Dly 2x VIX Med-T traded at a premium of 2.80% above its net asset value, which is worse than its one-year historical average premium of .04%. Unfortunately, the high level of risk (D, Weak) failed to pay off as investors endured very poor performance.

The fund's performance rating is currently E- (Very Weak). It has registered an annualized return of 0.00% over the last three years but is down -42.56% year to date 2012. Factored into the performance evaluation is an expense ratio of 1.65% (above average).

This fund has been team managed for 2 years and currently receives a manager quality ranking of 16 (0=worst, 99=best). If you can tolerate very high levels of risk in the hope of improved future returns, holding this fund may be an option.

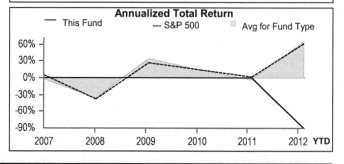

*VelocityShares Dly Invs VIX M-T (ZIV)

C+   **Fair**

Fund Family: Credit Suisse AG
Fund Type: General - Investment Grade
Inception Date: November 29, 2010

Data Date	Investment Rating	Net Assets ($Mil)	Price	Performance Rating/Pts	Total Return Y-T-D	Risk Rating/Pts
3-12	C+	8.98	15.84	A- / 9.0	27.12%	C / 5.4
2011	D-	7.10	12.46	D- / 1.3	5.77%	C / 5.4

Major Rating Factors:
Exceptional performance is the major factor driving the C+ (Fair) TheStreet.com Investment Rating for *VelocityShares Dly Invs VIX M-T. The fund currently has a performance rating of A- (Excellent) based on an annualized return of 0.00% over the last three years and a total return of 27.12% year to date 2012. Factored into the performance evaluation is an expense ratio of 1.35% (average).

The fund's risk rating is currently C (Fair). It carries a beta of 0.00, meaning the fund's expected move will be 0.0% for every 10% move in the market. Volatility, as measured by both the semi-deviation and a drawdown factor, is considered average. As of March 31, 2012, *VelocityShares Dly Invs VIX M-T traded at a discount of 1.25% below its net asset value, which is better than its one-year historical average premium of .01%.

This fund has been team managed for 2 years and currently receives a manager quality ranking of 99 (0=worst, 99=best). If you desire an average level of risk and strong performance, then this fund is a good option.

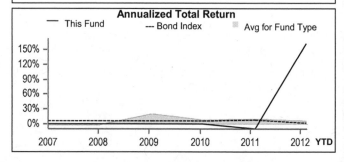

*VelocityShares Dly Invs VIX ST E (XIV)   C-   Fair

Fund Family: Credit Suisse AG
Fund Type: Growth and Income
Inception Date: November 29, 2010

Data Date	Investment Rating	Net Assets ($Mil)	Price	Performance Rating/Pts	Total Return Y-T-D	Risk Rating/Pts
3-12	C-	420.20	12.27	A+ / 9.9	88.48%	D / 1.9
2011	E-	387.60	6.51	E- / 0.2	11.37%	D / 1.9

Major Rating Factors: *VelocityShares Dly Invs VIX ST E has adopted a very risky asset allocation strategy and currently receives an overall TheStreet.com Investment Rating of C- (Fair). The fund has shown a high level of volatility, as measured by both semi-deviation and drawdown factors. It carries a beta of 0.00, meaning the fund's expected move will be 0.0% for every 10% move in the market. As of March 31, 2012, *VelocityShares Dly Invs VIX ST E traded at a discount of .97% below its net asset value, which is better than its one-year historical average discount of .18%. The high level of risk (D, Weak) did however, reward investors with excellent performance.

The fund's performance rating is currently A+ (Excellent). It has registered an annualized return of 0.00% over the last three years and is up 88.48% year to date 2012. Factored into the performance evaluation is an expense ratio of 1.35% (average).

This fund has been team managed for 2 years and currently receives a manager quality ranking of 1 (0=worst, 99=best). If you are comfortable owning a very high risk investment, this fund may be an option.

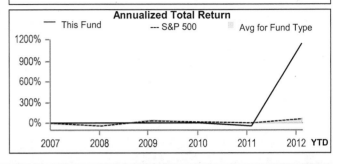

*VelocityShares VIX Short-Term ET (VIIX)   E-   Very Weak

Fund Family: Credit Suisse AG
Fund Type: Growth and Income
Inception Date: November 29, 2010

Data Date	Investment Rating	Net Assets ($Mil)	Price	Performance Rating/Pts	Total Return Y-T-D	Risk Rating/Pts
3-12	E-	16.08	36.42	E- / 0	-52.50%	D / 1.9
2011	D-	32.20	76.68	D+ / 2.5	-10.37%	C- / 3.9

Major Rating Factors: *VelocityShares VIX Short-Term ET has adopted a very risky asset allocation strategy and currently receives an overall TheStreet.com Investment Rating of E- (Very Weak). The fund has a high level of volatility, as measured by both semi-deviation and drawdown factors. It carries a beta of 0.00, meaning the fund's expected move will be 0.0% for every 10% move in the market. As of March 31, 2012, *VelocityShares VIX Short-Term ET traded at a premium of .94% above its net asset value, which is worse than its one-year historical average premium of .17%. Unfortunately, the high level of risk (D, Weak) failed to pay off as investors endured very poor performance.

The fund's performance rating is currently E- (Very Weak). It has registered an annualized return of 0.00% over the last three years but is down -52.50% year to date 2012. Factored into the performance evaluation is an expense ratio of 0.89% (low).

This fund has been team managed for 2 years and currently receives a manager quality ranking of 9 (0=worst, 99=best). If you can tolerate very high levels of risk in the hope of improved future returns, holding this fund may be an option.

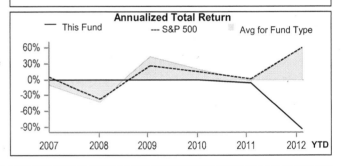

*WCM/BNY Mellon Focused Gro ADR E (AADR)   C-   Fair

Fund Family: AdvisorShares Investments LLC
Fund Type: Global
Inception Date: July 20, 2010

Data Date	Investment Rating	Net Assets ($Mil)	Price	Performance Rating/Pts	Total Return Y-T-D	Risk Rating/Pts
3-12	C-	7.63	30.95	C- / 3.4	10.10%	B- / 7.8
2011	D	6.30	28.11	D- / 1.4	-0.56%	B- / 7.8

Major Rating Factors: Middle of the road best describes *WCM/BNY Mellon Focused Gro ADR E whose TheStreet.com Investment Rating is currently a C- (Fair). The fund currently has a performance rating of C- (Fair) based on an annualized return of 0.00% over the last three years and a total return of 10.10% year to date 2012. Factored into the performance evaluation is an expense ratio of 1.25% (average).

The fund's risk rating is currently B- (Good). It carries a beta of 0.00, meaning the fund's expected move will be 0.0% for every 10% move in the market. Volatility, as measured by both the semi-deviation and a drawdown factor, is considered low. As of March 31, 2012, *WCM/BNY Mellon Focused Gro ADR E traded at a discount of .23% below its net asset value, which is better than its one-year historical average premium of .04%.

Kurt R. Winrich currently receives a manager quality ranking of 82 (0=worst, 99=best). If you desire an average level of risk, then this fund may be an option.

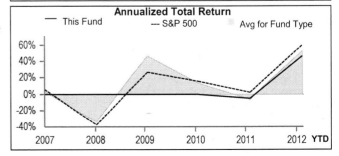

*WisdomTree Asia Local Debt (ALD)

D   **Weak**

Fund Family: WisdomTree Asset Management Inc
Fund Type: Global
Inception Date: March 17, 2011

Data Date	Investment Rating	Net Assets ($Mil)	Price	Perfor-mance Rating/Pts	Total Return Y-T-D	Risk Rating/Pts
3-12	D	419.16	51.40	D / 1.7	2.81%	B / 8.0

Major Rating Factors:
Disappointing performance is the major factor driving the D (Weak) TheStreet.com Investment Rating for *WisdomTree Asia Local Debt. The fund currently has a performance rating of D (Weak) based on an annualized return of 0.00% over the last three years and a total return of 2.81% year to date 2012. Factored into the performance evaluation is an expense ratio of 0.55% (very low).

The fund's risk rating is currently B (Good). It carries a beta of 0.00, meaning the fund's expected move will be 0.0% for every 10% move in the market. Volatility, as measured by both the semi-deviation and a drawdown factor, is considered low. As of March 31, 2012, *WisdomTree Asia Local Debt traded at a discount of .10% below its net asset value, which is better than its one-year historical average premium of .11%.

David C. Kwan has been running the fund for 1 year and currently receives a manager quality ranking of 33 (0=worst, 99=best). This fund offers only a moderate level of risk but investors looking for strong performance are still waiting.

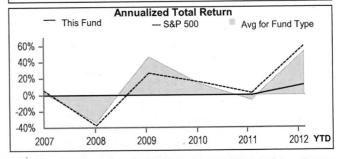

*WisdomTree Asia Pacific ex-Japan (AXJL)

C   **Fair**

Fund Family: WisdomTree Asset Management Inc
Fund Type: Foreign
Inception Date: June 16, 2006

Data Date	Investment Rating	Net Assets ($Mil)	Price	Perfor-mance Rating/Pts	Total Return Y-T-D	Risk Rating/Pts
3-12	C	92.20	64.10	C / 5.4	10.80%	B- / 7.4
2011	C+	72.50	58.05	C+ / 5.7	0.63%	B- / 7.5
2010	C-	89.80	66.42	C / 4.6	15.09%	C / 4.5
2009	C	151.37	60.00	C+ / 6.7	51.53%	C / 4.6

Major Rating Factors: Middle of the road best describes *WisdomTree Asia Pacific ex-Japan whose TheStreet.com Investment Rating is currently a C (Fair). The fund currently has a performance rating of C (Fair) based on an annualized return of 21.92% over the last three years and a total return of 10.80% year to date 2012. Factored into the performance evaluation is an expense ratio of 0.48% (very low).

The fund's risk rating is currently B- (Good). It carries a beta of 0.99, meaning that its performance tracks fairly well with that of the overall stock market. Volatility, as measured by both the semi-deviation and a drawdown factor, is considered low. As of March 31, 2012, *WisdomTree Asia Pacific ex-Japan traded at a premium of .08% above its net asset value, which is better than its one-year historical average premium of .09%.

Karen Q. Wong has been running the fund for 4 years and currently receives a manager quality ranking of 77 (0=worst, 99=best). If you desire an average level of risk, then this fund may be an option.

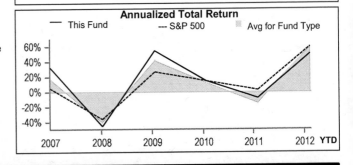

*WisdomTree Australia and NZ Debt (AUNZ)

D+   **Weak**

Fund Family: WisdomTree Asset Management Inc
Fund Type: Foreign
Inception Date: June 25, 2008

Data Date	Investment Rating	Net Assets ($Mil)	Price	Perfor-mance Rating/Pts	Total Return Y-T-D	Risk Rating/Pts
3-12	D+	33.89	21.89	D / 2.0	2.59%	B- / 7.9
2011	C-	25.90	21.50	D+ / 2.9	0.88%	B / 8.0
2010	A-	28.40	23.66	B+ / 8.3	9.97%	C+ / 6.5
2009	A-	9.47	22.65	B / 7.8	27.81%	C+ / 6.5

Major Rating Factors:
Disappointing performance is the major factor driving the D+ (Weak) TheStreet.com Investment Rating for *WisdomTree Australia and NZ Debt. The fund currently has a performance rating of D (Weak) based on an annualized return of 9.34% over the last three years and a total return of 2.59% year to date 2012. Factored into the performance evaluation is an expense ratio of 0.45% (very low).

The fund's risk rating is currently B- (Good). It carries a beta of 0.44, meaning the fund's expected move will be 4.4% for every 10% move in the market. Volatility, as measured by both the semi-deviation and a drawdown factor, is considered low. As of March 31, 2012, *WisdomTree Australia and NZ Debt traded at a premium of .32% above its net asset value, which is worse than its one-year historical average premium of .30%.

David C. Kwan has been running the fund for 4 years and currently receives a manager quality ranking of 63 (0=worst, 99=best). This fund offers only a moderate level of risk but investors looking for strong performance are still waiting.

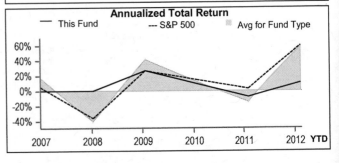

*WisdomTree Australia Divide (AUSE)

C+   Fair

Fund Family: WisdomTree Asset Management Inc
Fund Type: Foreign
Inception Date: June 16, 2006

Data Date	Investment Rating	Net Assets ($Mil)	Price	Performance Rating/Pts	Total Return Y-T-D	Risk Rating/Pts
3-12	C+	60.78	56.08	C+ / 6.6	12.42%	C+ / 6.9
2011	C+	50.70	50.74	C+ / 6.6	0.61%	B- / 7.0
2010	C-	78.50	60.41	C+ / 6.2	12.82%	C- / 4.0
2009	C+	103.32	56.34	B / 7.7	75.23%	C- / 4.2

Major Rating Factors: Middle of the road best describes *WisdomTree Australia Divide whose TheStreet.com Investment Rating is currently a C+ (Fair). The fund currently has a performance rating of C+ (Fair) based on an annualized return of 25.43% over the last three years and a total return of 12.42% year to date 2012. Factored into the performance evaluation is an expense ratio of 0.58% (very low).

The fund's risk rating is currently C+ (Fair). It carries a beta of 1.17, meaning it is expected to move 11.7% for every 10% move in the market. Volatility, as measured by both the semi-deviation and a drawdown factor, is considered low. As of March 31, 2012, *WisdomTree Australia Divide traded at a premium of .38% above its net asset value, which is worse than its one-year historical average premium of .04%.

Karen Q. Wong has been running the fund for 4 years and currently receives a manager quality ranking of 78 (0=worst, 99=best). If you desire an average level of risk, then this fund may be an option.

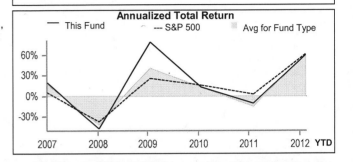

*WisdomTree Commodity Country Equ (CCXE)

C+   Fair

Fund Family: WisdomTree Asset Management Inc
Fund Type: Foreign
Inception Date: October 13, 2006

Data Date	Investment Rating	Net Assets ($Mil)	Price	Performance Rating/Pts	Total Return Y-T-D	Risk Rating/Pts
3-12	C+	32.39	31.43	C+ / 6.3	13.12%	B- / 7.4
2011	C	30.80	28.00	C / 5.2	0.36%	B- / 7.3
2010	C-	41.90	32.15	C / 5.1	16.76%	C- / 3.9
2009	C	41.79	28.12	B- / 7.0	51.62%	C / 4.4

Major Rating Factors: Middle of the road best describes *WisdomTree Commodity Country Equ whose TheStreet.com Investment Rating is currently a C+ (Fair). The fund currently has a performance rating of C+ (Fair) based on an annualized return of 24.20% over the last three years and a total return of 13.12% year to date 2012. Factored into the performance evaluation is an expense ratio of 0.58% (very low).

The fund's risk rating is currently B- (Good). It carries a beta of 1.27, meaning it is expected to move 12.7% for every 10% move in the market. Volatility, as measured by both the semi-deviation and a drawdown factor, is considered low. As of March 31, 2012, *WisdomTree Commodity Country Equ traded at a discount of .03% below its net asset value, which is worse than its one-year historical average discount of .30%.

Karen Q. Wong has been running the fund for 4 years and currently receives a manager quality ranking of 70 (0=worst, 99=best). If you desire an average level of risk, then this fund may be an option.

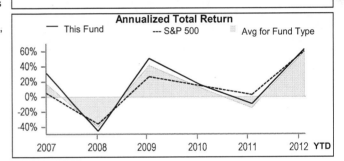

*WisdomTree DEFA (DWM)

D+   Weak

Fund Family: WisdomTree Asset Management Inc
Fund Type: Foreign
Inception Date: June 16, 2006

Data Date	Investment Rating	Net Assets ($Mil)	Price	Performance Rating/Pts	Total Return Y-T-D	Risk Rating/Pts
3-12	D+	362.86	44.90	C- / 3.3	10.25%	B- / 7.4
2011	D+	326.30	40.92	D+ / 2.7	-0.83%	B- / 7.4
2010	D-	426.80	47.37	D- / 1.4	5.19%	C / 4.8
2009	D	422.40	46.69	D+ / 2.3	24.55%	C / 5.0

Major Rating Factors: *WisdomTree DEFA receives a TheStreet.com Investment Rating of D+ (Weak). The fund currently has a performance rating of C- (Fair) based on an annualized return of 14.63% over the last three years and a total return of 10.25% year to date 2012. Factored into the performance evaluation is an expense ratio of 0.48% (very low).

The fund's risk rating is currently B- (Good). It carries a beta of 1.01, meaning that its performance tracks fairly well with that of the overall stock market. Volatility, as measured by both the semi-deviation and a drawdown factor, is considered low. As of March 31, 2012, *WisdomTree DEFA traded at a premium of .83% above its net asset value, which is worse than its one-year historical average premium of .08%.

Denise Krisko currently receives a manager quality ranking of 41 (0=worst, 99=best). If you desire an average level of risk, then this fund may be an option.

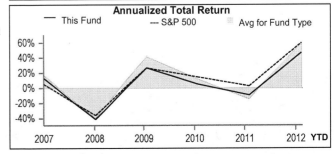

*WisdomTree DEFA Equity Income (DTH)

D+ **Weak**

Fund Family: WisdomTree Asset Management Inc
Fund Type: Foreign
Inception Date: June 16, 2006

Major Rating Factors: *WisdomTree DEFA Equity Income receives a TheStreet.com Investment Rating of D+ (Weak). The fund currently has a performance rating of C- (Fair) based on an annualized return of 13.80% over the last three years and a total return of 7.18% year to date 2012. Factored into the performance evaluation is an expense ratio of 0.58% (very low).

The fund's risk rating is currently B- (Good). It carries a beta of 1.07, meaning that its performance tracks fairly well with that of the overall stock market. Volatility, as measured by both the semi-deviation and a drawdown factor, is considered low. As of March 31, 2012, *WisdomTree DEFA Equity Income traded at a premium of .80% above its net asset value, which is worse than its one-year historical average premium of .43%.

Karen Q. Wong has been running the fund for 4 years and currently receives a manager quality ranking of 33 (0=worst, 99=best). If you desire an average level of risk, then this fund may be an option.

Data Date	Investment Rating	Net Assets ($Mil)	Price	Perfor-mance Rating/Pts	Total Return Y-T-D	Risk Rating/Pts
3-12	D+	170.55	38.95	C- / 3.0	7.18%	B- / 7.3
2011	D+	145.60	36.56	D+ / 2.8	-1.23%	B- / 7.3
2010	D-	120.50	41.10	D- / 1.0	-0.99%	C / 4.5
2009	D	155.16	43.50	D+ / 2.4	30.43%	C / 4.7

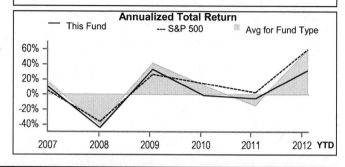

Annualized Total Return
— This Fund   --- S&P 500   ▨ Avg for Fund Type

*WisdomTree Dividend Ex-Financial (DTN)

B+ **Good**

Fund Family: WisdomTree Asset Management Inc
Fund Type: Income
Inception Date: June 16, 2006

Major Rating Factors: Strong performance is the major factor driving the B+ (Good) TheStreet.com Investment Rating for *WisdomTree Dividend Ex-Financial. The fund currently has a performance rating of B (Good) based on an annualized return of 28.92% over the last three years and a total return of 6.30% year to date 2012. Factored into the performance evaluation is an expense ratio of 0.38% (very low).

The fund's risk rating is currently B+ (Good). It carries a beta of 0.83, meaning the fund's expected move will be 8.3% for every 10% move in the market. Volatility, as measured by both the semi-deviation and a drawdown factor, is considered very low. As of March 31, 2012, *WisdomTree Dividend Ex-Financial traded at a premium of .02% above its net asset value, which is better than its one-year historical average premium of .08%.

Karen Q. Wong has been running the fund for 4 years and currently receives a manager quality ranking of 87 (0=worst, 99=best). If you desire only a moderate level of risk and strong performance, then this fund is an excellent option.

Data Date	Investment Rating	Net Assets ($Mil)	Price	Perfor-mance Rating/Pts	Total Return Y-T-D	Risk Rating/Pts
3-12	B+	1,222.46	54.82	B / 7.9	6.30%	B+ / 9.0
2011	B-	1,010.40	52.00	B- / 7.2	0.00%	B- / 7.7
2010	C	343.00	48.02	C / 5.4	21.44%	C+ / 5.6
2009	D	145.81	41.02	D / 2.0	22.73%	C+ / 5.7

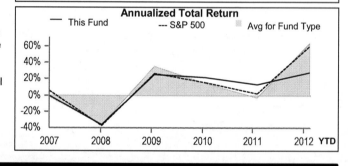

Annualized Total Return
— This Fund   --- S&P 500   ▨ Avg for Fund Type

*WisdomTree Dr Brazilian Real Fun (BZF)

D+ **Weak**

Fund Family: WisdomTree Asset Management Inc
Fund Type: Foreign
Inception Date: May 13, 2008

Major Rating Factors: *WisdomTree Dr Brazilian Real Fun receives a TheStreet.com Investment Rating of D+ (Weak). The fund currently has a performance rating of C- (Fair) based on an annualized return of 18.13% over the last three years and a total return of 4.21% year to date 2012. Factored into the performance evaluation is an expense ratio of 0.45% (very low).

The fund's risk rating is currently C+ (Fair). It carries a beta of 0.68, meaning the fund's expected move will be 6.8% for every 10% move in the market. Volatility, as measured by both the semi-deviation and a drawdown factor, is considered low. As of March 31, 2012, *WisdomTree Dr Brazilian Real Fun traded at a discount of .20% below its net asset value.

David C. Kwan has been running the fund for 4 years and currently receives a manager quality ranking of 81 (0=worst, 99=best). If you desire an average level of risk, then this fund may be an option.

Data Date	Investment Rating	Net Assets ($Mil)	Price	Perfor-mance Rating/Pts	Total Return Y-T-D	Risk Rating/Pts
3-12	D+	94.39	20.29	C- / 3.8	4.21%	C+ / 6.3
2011	C-	81.90	19.47	C / 5.4	0.57%	C+ / 6.4
2010	A	132.80	26.55	A / 9.4	24.53%	C+ / 6.4
2009	A+	112.57	26.53	B+ / 8.6	44.17%	C+ / 6.5

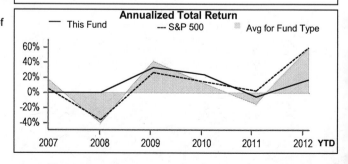

Annualized Total Return
— This Fund   --- S&P 500   ▨ Avg for Fund Type

*WisdomTree Dr Chinese Yuan Fund (CYB)

C-   **Fair**

Fund Family: WisdomTree Asset Management Inc
Fund Type: Foreign
Inception Date: May 13, 2008

Major Rating Factors:

Disappointing performance is the major factor driving the C- (Fair) TheStreet.com Investment Rating for *WisdomTree Dr Chinese Yuan Fund. The fund currently has a performance rating of D- (Weak) based on an annualized return of 1.59% over the last three years and a total return of 0.64% year to date 2012. Factored into the performance evaluation is an expense ratio of 0.45% (very low).

The fund's risk rating is currently B+ (Good). It carries a beta of 0.07, meaning the fund's expected move will be 0.7% for every 10% move in the market. Volatility, as measured by both the semi-deviation and a drawdown factor, is considered very low. As of March 31, 2012, *WisdomTree Dr Chinese Yuan Fund traded at a discount of .20% below its net asset value, which is better than its one-year historical average discount of .07%.

David C. Kwan has been running the fund for 4 years and currently receives a manager quality ranking of 48 (0=worst, 99=best). This fund offers only a moderate level of risk but investors looking for strong performance are still waiting.

Data Date	Investment Rating	Net Assets ($Mil)	Price	Performance Rating/Pts	Total Return Y-T-D	Risk Rating/Pts
3-12	C-	412.80	25.35	D- / 1.4	0.64%	B+ / 9.8
2011	C	448.50	25.19	C- / 3.0	0.60%	B+ / 9.8
2010	B-	639.60	25.37	C- / 3.6	1.79%	B / 8.9
2009	C	136.66	25.21	D / 2.0	1.16%	B+ / 9.1

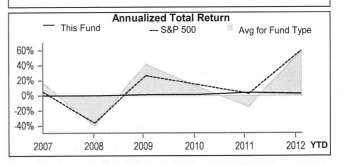

Annualized Total Return

---

*WisdomTree Dr Commodity Curr Fun (CCX)

D   **Weak**

Fund Family: WisdomTree Asset Management Inc
Fund Type: Global
Inception Date: September 21, 2010

Major Rating Factors:

Disappointing performance is the major factor driving the D (Weak) TheStreet.com Investment Rating for *WisdomTree Dr Commodity Curr Fun. The fund currently has a performance rating of D (Weak) based on an annualized return of 0.00% over the last three years and a total return of 5.27% year to date 2012. Factored into the performance evaluation is an expense ratio of 0.55% (very low).

The fund's risk rating is currently C+ (Fair). It carries a beta of 0.00, meaning the fund's expected move will be 0.0% for every 10% move in the market. Volatility, as measured by both the semi-deviation and a drawdown factor, is considered low. As of March 31, 2012, *WisdomTree Dr Commodity Curr Fun traded at a discount of .14% below its net asset value, which is better than its one-year historical average discount of .02%.

David C. Kwan has been running the fund for 2 years and currently receives a manager quality ranking of 67 (0=worst, 99=best). This fund offers only a moderate level of risk but investors looking for strong performance are still waiting.

Data Date	Investment Rating	Net Assets ($Mil)	Price	Performance Rating/Pts	Total Return Y-T-D	Risk Rating/Pts
3-12	D	35.15	21.38	D / 1.7	5.27%	C+ / 6.6
2011	D-	38.60	20.31	D- / 1.0	-0.24%	C+ / 6.5

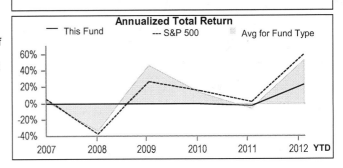

Annualized Total Return

---

*WisdomTree Dr Emerg Curr Fd (CEW)

D+   **Weak**

Fund Family: WisdomTree Asset Management Inc
Fund Type: Foreign
Inception Date: May 6, 2009

Major Rating Factors:

Disappointing performance is the major factor driving the D+ (Weak) TheStreet.com Investment Rating for *WisdomTree Dr Emerg Curr Fd. The fund currently has a performance rating of D+ (Weak) based on an annualized return of 0.00% over the last three years and a total return of 6.29% year to date 2012. Factored into the performance evaluation is an expense ratio of 0.55% (very low).

The fund's risk rating is currently B (Good). It carries a beta of 0.00, meaning the fund's expected move will be 0.0% for every 10% move in the market. Volatility, as measured by both the semi-deviation and a drawdown factor, is considered low. As of March 31, 2012, *WisdomTree Dr Emerg Curr Fd traded at a price exactly equal to its net asset value, which is worse than its one-year historical average discount of .08%.

David C. Kwan has been running the fund for 3 years and currently receives a manager quality ranking of 73 (0=worst, 99=best). This fund offers only a moderate level of risk but investors looking for strong performance are still waiting.

Data Date	Investment Rating	Net Assets ($Mil)	Price	Performance Rating/Pts	Total Return Y-T-D	Risk Rating/Pts
3-12	D+	347.18	20.94	D+ / 2.3	6.29%	B / 8.4
2011	D+	344.00	19.70	D / 1.8	0.41%	B / 8.4
2010	B	296.90	22.56	C+ / 6.9	6.40%	B / 8.8

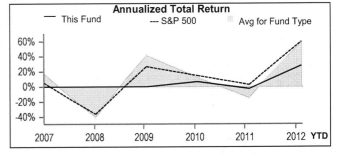

Annualized Total Return

*WisdomTree Dr Indian Rupee Fund (ICN) D Weak

Fund Family: WisdomTree Asset Management Inc
Fund Type: Foreign
Inception Date: May 13, 2008

Data Date	Investment Rating	Net Assets ($Mil)	Price	Perfor-mance Rating/Pts	Total Return Y-T-D	Risk Rating/Pts
3-12	D	15.53	21.44	D- / 1.4	6.56%	B- / 7.4
2011	D	16.10	20.12	D / 1.8	1.04%	B- / 7.4
2010	A-	21.20	26.58	B- / 7.0	7.89%	B / 8.0
2009	C+	11.89	25.17	C / 4.4	7.98%	B / 8.2

Major Rating Factors:
Disappointing performance is the major factor driving the D (Weak) TheStreet.com Investment Rating for *WisdomTree Dr Indian Rupee Fund. The fund currently has a performance rating of D- (Weak) based on an annualized return of 3.94% over the last three years and a total return of 6.56% year to date 2012. Factored into the performance evaluation is an expense ratio of 0.45% (very low).

The fund's risk rating is currently B- (Good). It carries a beta of 0.40, meaning the fund's expected move will be 4.0% for every 10% move in the market. Volatility, as measured by both the semi-deviation and a drawdown factor, is considered low. As of March 31, 2012, *WisdomTree Dr Indian Rupee Fund traded at a premium of .33% above its net asset value, which is worse than its one-year historical average discount of .02%.

David C. Kwan has been running the fund for 4 years and currently receives a manager quality ranking of 32 (0=worst, 99=best). This fund offers only a moderate level of risk but investors looking for strong performance are still waiting.

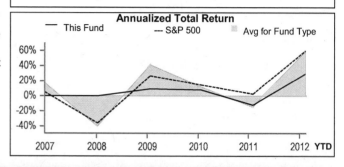

*WisdomTree Dr Japanese Yen Fd (JYF) D+ Weak

Fund Family: WisdomTree Asset Management Inc
Fund Type: Foreign
Inception Date: May 13, 2008

Data Date	Investment Rating	Net Assets ($Mil)	Price	Perfor-mance Rating/Pts	Total Return Y-T-D	Risk Rating/Pts
3-12	D+	12.87	30.94	D- / 1.5	-8.90%	B / 8.9
2011	C	13.50	33.96	C- / 3.3	-0.45%	B / 8.9
2010	A	12.90	31.83	B / 7.9	13.40%	B / 8.2
2009	C-	11.31	28.07	D / 1.8	-0.74%	B / 8.4

Major Rating Factors:
Disappointing performance is the major factor driving the D+ (Weak) TheStreet.com Investment Rating for *WisdomTree Dr Japanese Yen Fd. The fund currently has a performance rating of D- (Weak) based on an annualized return of 5.75% over the last three years and a total return of -8.90% year to date 2012. Factored into the performance evaluation is an expense ratio of 0.35% (very low).

The fund's risk rating is currently B (Good). It carries a beta of 0.01, meaning the fund's expected move will be 0.1% for every 10% move in the market. Volatility, as measured by both the semi-deviation and a drawdown factor, is considered low. As of March 31, 2012, *WisdomTree Dr Japanese Yen Fd traded at a discount of 2.18% below its net asset value, which is better than its one-year historical average discount of .23%.

David C. Kwan has been running the fund for 4 years and currently receives a manager quality ranking of 74 (0=worst, 99=best). This fund offers only a moderate level of risk but investors looking for strong performance are still waiting.

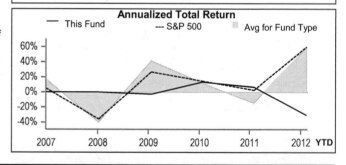

*WisdomTree Dr South African Rand (SZR) C- Fair

Fund Family: WisdomTree Asset Management Inc
Fund Type: Foreign
Inception Date: June 25, 2008

Data Date	Investment Rating	Net Assets ($Mil)	Price	Perfor-mance Rating/Pts	Total Return Y-T-D	Risk Rating/Pts
3-12	C-	5.10	24.88	C- / 3.4	7.15%	B- / 7.6
2011	C+	7.00	23.22	C+ / 6.2	-1.12%	B- / 7.6
2010	A+	11.70	29.44	A- / 9.1	19.45%	B- / 7.0
2009	A+	5.35	27.93	B / 8.1	34.57%	B- / 7.1

Major Rating Factors: Middle of the road best describes *WisdomTree Dr South African Rand whose TheStreet.com Investment Rating is currently a C- (Fair). The fund currently has a performance rating of C- (Fair) based on an annualized return of 14.85% over the last three years and a total return of 7.15% year to date 2012. Factored into the performance evaluation is an expense ratio of 0.45% (very low).

The fund's risk rating is currently B- (Good). It carries a beta of 0.61, meaning the fund's expected move will be 6.1% for every 10% move in the market. Volatility, as measured by both the semi-deviation and a drawdown factor, is considered low. As of March 31, 2012, *WisdomTree Dr South African Rand traded at a premium of .04% above its net asset value, which is worse than its one-year historical average discount of .19%.

David C. Kwan has been running the fund for 4 years and currently receives a manager quality ranking of 76 (0=worst, 99=best). If you desire an average level of risk, then this fund may be an option.

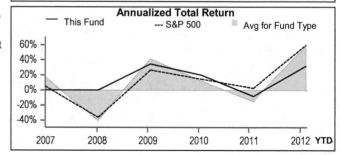

*WisdomTree Earnings 500 Fund (EPS)   C+   Fair

Fund Family: WisdomTree Asset Management Inc
Fund Type: Income
Inception Date: February 23, 2007

Major Rating Factors: Middle of the road best describes *WisdomTree Earnings 500 Fund whose TheStreet.com Investment Rating is currently a C+ (Fair). The fund currently has a performance rating of C+ (Fair) based on an annualized return of 21.40% over the last three years and a total return of 12.71% year to date 2012. Factored into the performance evaluation is an expense ratio of 0.28% (very low).

The fund's risk rating is currently B (Good). It carries a beta of 0.93, meaning that its performance tracks fairly well with that of the overall stock market. Volatility, as measured by both the semi-deviation and a drawdown factor, is considered low. As of March 31, 2012, *WisdomTree Earnings 500 Fund traded at a premium of .02% above its net asset value, which is better than its one-year historical average premium of .04%.

Karen Q. Wong has been running the fund for 4 years and currently receives a manager quality ranking of 59 (0=worst, 99=best). If you desire an average level of risk, then this fund may be an option.

Data Date	Investment Rating	Net Assets ($Mil)	Price	Performance Rating/Pts	Total Return Y-T-D	Risk Rating/Pts
3-12	C+	67.38	49.43	C+ / 6.1	12.71%	B / 8.4
2011	C+	61.50	44.03	C / 5.5	1.89%	B / 8.1
2010	C-	69.30	43.34	C- / 3.5	13.28%	C+ / 6.1
2009	A	55.24	38.97	B / 8.2	23.42%	C+ / 6.2

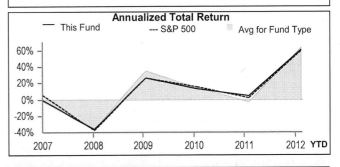

Annualized Total Return

*WisdomTree Emg Mkts Eqty Inc Fd (DEM)   C+   Fair

Fund Family: WisdomTree Asset Management Inc
Fund Type: Emerging Market
Inception Date: July 13, 2007

Major Rating Factors: Middle of the road best describes *WisdomTree Emg Mkts Eqty Inc Fd whose TheStreet.com Investment Rating is currently a C+ (Fair). The fund currently has a performance rating of C+ (Fair) based on an annualized return of 24.46% over the last three years and a total return of 12.77% year to date 2012. Factored into the performance evaluation is an expense ratio of 0.63% (very low).

The fund's risk rating is currently B- (Good). It carries a beta of 0.89, meaning the fund's expected move will be 8.9% for every 10% move in the market. Volatility, as measured by both the semi-deviation and a drawdown factor, is considered low. As of March 31, 2012, *WisdomTree Emg Mkts Eqty Inc Fd traded at a premium of .49% above its net asset value, which is better than its one-year historical average premium of .75%.

Karen Q. Wong has been running the fund for 4 years and currently receives a manager quality ranking of 72 (0=worst, 99=best). If you desire an average level of risk, then this fund may be an option.

Data Date	Investment Rating	Net Assets ($Mil)	Price	Performance Rating/Pts	Total Return Y-T-D	Risk Rating/Pts
3-12	C+	3,330.36	57.61	C+ / 6.4	12.77%	B- / 7.3
2011	C+	2,144.70	51.27	C+ / 6.4	0.35%	B- / 7.3
2010	B+	1,166.90	59.69	B+ / 8.3	25.43%	C / 5.2
2009	A	356.50	49.71	A- / 9.2	53.72%	C / 5.4

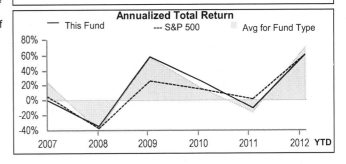

Annualized Total Return

*WisdomTree Emg Mkts Local Debt F (ELD)   C-   Fair

Fund Family: WisdomTree Asset Management Inc
Fund Type: Emerging Market
Inception Date: August 9, 2010

Major Rating Factors:
Disappointing performance is the major factor driving the C- (Fair) TheStreet.com Investment Rating for *WisdomTree Emg Mkts Local Debt F. The fund currently has a performance rating of D+ (Weak) based on an annualized return of 0.00% over the last three years and a total return of 7.51% year to date 2012. Factored into the performance evaluation is an expense ratio of 0.55% (very low).

The fund's risk rating is currently B (Good). It carries a beta of 0.00, meaning the fund's expected move will be 0.0% for every 10% move in the market. Volatility, as measured by both the semi-deviation and a drawdown factor, is considered low. As of March 31, 2012, *WisdomTree Emg Mkts Local Debt F traded at a premium of .33% above its net asset value, which is worse than its one-year historical average premium of .20%.

David C. Kwan has been running the fund for 2 years and currently receives a manager quality ranking of 32 (0=worst, 99=best). This fund offers only a moderate level of risk but investors looking for strong performance are still waiting.

Data Date	Investment Rating	Net Assets ($Mil)	Price	Performance Rating/Pts	Total Return Y-T-D	Risk Rating/Pts
3-12	C-	1,221.74	51.89	D+ / 2.6	7.51%	B / 8.6
2011	D+	1,078.10	48.64	D- / 1.5	0.12%	B / 8.6

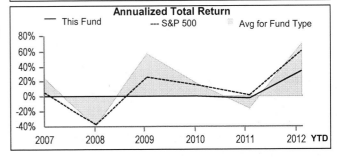

Annualized Total Return

*WisdomTree Emg Mkts SmCap Div Fd (DGS)

C+ **Fair**

Fund Family: WisdomTree Asset Management Inc
Fund Type: Emerging Market
Inception Date: October 30, 2007

Data Date	Investment Rating	Net Assets ($Mil)	Price	Performance Rating/Pts	Total Return Y-T-D	Risk Rating/Pts
3-12	C+	949.42	48.12	C+ / 6.7	16.57%	C+ / 6.8
2011	C+	739.40	41.34	C+ / 6.5	1.21%	C+ / 6.9
2010	B	929.70	54.50	B+ / 8.4	30.88%	C / 4.9
2009	A	203.24	43.05	A+ / 9.7	78.53%	C / 4.9

Major Rating Factors: Middle of the road best describes *WisdomTree Emg Mkts SmCap Div Fd whose TheStreet.com Investment Rating is currently a C+ (Fair). The fund currently has a performance rating of C+ (Fair) based on an annualized return of 26.01% over the last three years and a total return of 16.57% year to date 2012. Factored into the performance evaluation is an expense ratio of 0.63% (very low).

The fund's risk rating is currently C+ (Fair). It carries a beta of 1.05, meaning that its performance tracks fairly well with that of the overall stock market. Volatility, as measured by both the semi-deviation and a drawdown factor, is considered low. As of March 31, 2012, *WisdomTree Emg Mkts SmCap Div Fd traded at a premium of .67% above its net asset value, which is worse than its one-year historical average premium of .40%.

Karen Q. Wong has been running the fund for 4 years and currently receives a manager quality ranking of 62 (0=worst, 99=best). If you desire an average level of risk, then this fund may be an option.

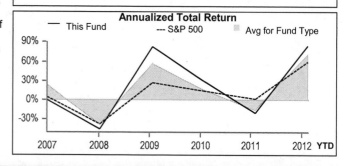

*WisdomTree Equity Income Fund (DHS)

B+ **Good**

Fund Family: WisdomTree Asset Management Inc
Fund Type: Growth and Income
Inception Date: June 16, 2006

Data Date	Investment Rating	Net Assets ($Mil)	Price	Performance Rating/Pts	Total Return Y-T-D	Risk Rating/Pts
3-12	B+	414.18	44.80	B- / 7.5	5.34%	B+ / 9.1
2011	C+	366.20	42.92	C+ / 6.8	-0.28%	B- / 7.4
2010	D	169.40	38.91	D+ / 2.6	17.63%	C / 5.1
2009	D-	141.20	34.57	D- / 1.1	14.64%	C / 5.2

Major Rating Factors: Strong performance is the major factor driving the B+ (Good) TheStreet.com Investment Rating for *WisdomTree Equity Income Fund. The fund currently has a performance rating of B- (Good) based on an annualized return of 27.25% over the last three years and a total return of 5.34% year to date 2012. Factored into the performance evaluation is an expense ratio of 0.38% (very low).

The fund's risk rating is currently B+ (Good). It carries a beta of 0.79, meaning the fund's expected move will be 7.9% for every 10% move in the market. Volatility, as measured by both the semi-deviation and a drawdown factor, is considered very low. As of March 31, 2012, *WisdomTree Equity Income Fund traded at a discount of .02% below its net asset value, which is better than its one-year historical average premium of .14%.

Karen Q. Wong has been running the fund for 4 years and currently receives a manager quality ranking of 85 (0=worst, 99=best). If you desire only a moderate level of risk and strong performance, then this fund is an excellent option.

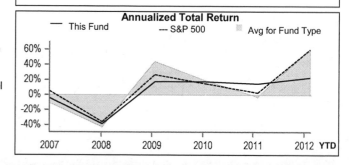

*WisdomTree Euro Debt (EU)

D **Weak**

Fund Family: WisdomTree Asset Management Inc
Fund Type: Foreign
Inception Date: May 13, 2008

Data Date	Investment Rating	Net Assets ($Mil)	Price	Performance Rating/Pts	Total Return Y-T-D	Risk Rating/Pts
3-12	D	4.92	20.89	D- / 1.1	5.83%	B / 8.1
2011	D+	4.70	19.80	D / 1.6	1.87%	B / 8.2
2010	D+	9.20	21.55	D- / 1.5	-6.59%	B- / 7.2
2009	C	9.86	23.07	D+ / 2.6	3.73%	B- / 7.6

Major Rating Factors:
Disappointing performance is the major factor driving the D (Weak) TheStreet.com Investment Rating for *WisdomTree Euro Debt. The fund currently has a performance rating of D- (Weak) based on an annualized return of -0.42% over the last three years and a total return of 5.83% year to date 2012. Factored into the performance evaluation is an expense ratio of 0.35% (very low).

The fund's risk rating is currently B (Good). It carries a beta of 0.47, meaning the fund's expected move will be 4.7% for every 10% move in the market. Volatility, as measured by both the semi-deviation and a drawdown factor, is considered low. As of March 31, 2012, *WisdomTree Euro Debt traded at a discount of 4.48% below its net asset value, which is better than its one-year historical average discount of 1.16%.

David C. Kwan has been running the fund for 4 years and currently receives a manager quality ranking of 17 (0=worst, 99=best). This fund offers only a moderate level of risk but investors looking for strong performance are still waiting.

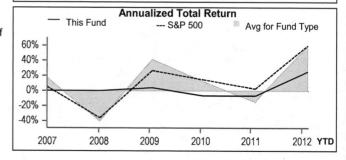

*WisdomTree Europe Small Cap Div (DFE)

C-   **Fair**

Fund Family: WisdomTree Asset Management Inc
Fund Type: Foreign
Inception Date: June 16, 2006

Major Rating Factors: Middle of the road best describes *WisdomTree Europe Small Cap Div whose TheStreet.com Investment Rating is currently a C- (Fair). The fund currently has a performance rating of C (Fair) based on an annualized return of 20.95% over the last three years and a total return of 18.33% year to date 2012. Factored into the performance evaluation is an expense ratio of 0.58% (very low).

The fund's risk rating is currently C+ (Fair). It carries a beta of 1.23, meaning it is expected to move 12.3% for every 10% move in the market. Volatility, as measured by both the semi-deviation and a drawdown factor, is considered low. As of March 31, 2012, *WisdomTree Europe Small Cap Div traded at a premium of .78% above its net asset value, which is worse than its one-year historical average premium of .11%.

Karen Q. Wong has been running the fund for 4 years and currently receives a manager quality ranking of 60 (0=worst, 99=best). If you desire an average level of risk, then this fund may be an option.

Data Date	Investment Rating	Net Assets ($Mil)	Price	Performance Rating/Pts	Total Return Y-T-D	Risk Rating/Pts
3-12	C-	28.63	38.52	C / 5.0	18.33%	C+ / 6.8
2011	D+	21.20	32.65	C- / 3.4	-0.56%	C+ / 6.8
2010	D	29.80	42.55	C- / 3.4	19.92%	C- / 4.1
2009	D-	25.71	36.50	D / 1.7	47.87%	C- / 4.1

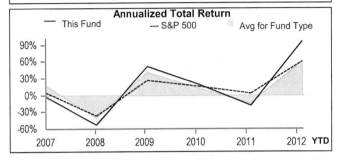

Annualized Total Return

*WisdomTree Global Equity Income (DEW)

C   **Fair**

Fund Family: WisdomTree Asset Management Inc
Fund Type: Global
Inception Date: June 16, 2006

Major Rating Factors: Middle of the road best describes *WisdomTree Global Equity Income whose TheStreet.com Investment Rating is currently a C (Fair). The fund currently has a performance rating of C- (Fair) based on an annualized return of 18.33% over the last three years and a total return of 6.66% year to date 2012. Factored into the performance evaluation is an expense ratio of 0.58% (very low).

The fund's risk rating is currently B- (Good). It carries a beta of 0.94, meaning that its performance tracks fairly well with that of the overall stock market. Volatility, as measured by both the semi-deviation and a drawdown factor, is considered low. As of March 31, 2012, *WisdomTree Global Equity Income traded at a premium of .43% above its net asset value, which is worse than its one-year historical average premium of .21%.

Karen Q. Wong has been running the fund for 4 years and currently receives a manager quality ranking of 69 (0=worst, 99=best). If you desire an average level of risk, then this fund may be an option.

Data Date	Investment Rating	Net Assets ($Mil)	Price	Performance Rating/Pts	Total Return Y-T-D	Risk Rating/Pts
3-12	C	85.89	41.68	C- / 4.1	6.66%	B- / 7.9
2011	C-	70.20	39.31	C- / 3.9	-1.14%	B- / 7.7
2010	D	69.30	42.15	D- / 1.3	5.82%	C / 5.3
2009	D-	38.13	41.36	D / 1.9	29.97%	C / 4.7

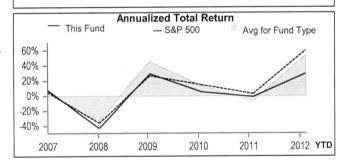

Annualized Total Return

*WisdomTree Global ex-US Growth (DNL)

C-   **Fair**

Fund Family: WisdomTree Asset Management Inc
Fund Type: Global
Inception Date: June 16, 2006

Major Rating Factors: Middle of the road best describes *WisdomTree Global ex-US Growth whose TheStreet.com Investment Rating is currently a C- (Fair). The fund currently has a performance rating of C- (Fair) based on an annualized return of 14.65% over the last three years and a total return of 10.02% year to date 2012. Factored into the performance evaluation is an expense ratio of 0.57% (very low).

The fund's risk rating is currently B- (Good). It carries a beta of 0.93, meaning that its performance tracks fairly well with that of the overall stock market. Volatility, as measured by both the semi-deviation and a drawdown factor, is considered low. As of March 31, 2012, *WisdomTree Global ex-US Growth traded at a premium of .22% above its net asset value, which is worse than its one-year historical average premium of .16%.

Karen Q. Wong has been running the fund for 4 years and currently receives a manager quality ranking of 43 (0=worst, 99=best). If you desire an average level of risk, then this fund may be an option.

Data Date	Investment Rating	Net Assets ($Mil)	Price	Performance Rating/Pts	Total Return Y-T-D	Risk Rating/Pts
3-12	C-	63.43	50.81	C- / 3.4	10.02%	B- / 7.5
2011	D+	55.50	46.37	D+ / 2.8	1.06%	B- / 7.4
2010	C+	37.80	54.19	C+ / 6.5	14.05%	C+ / 6.6
2009	C-	18.04	48.89	D+ / 2.5	11.74%	B- / 7.0

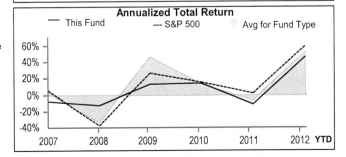

Annualized Total Return

*WisdomTree Global ex-US Real Est (DRW)   C-   Fair

Fund Family: WisdomTree Asset Management Inc
Fund Type: Foreign
Inception Date: June 5, 2007

Major Rating Factors: Middle of the road best describes *WisdomTree Global ex-US Real Est whose TheStreet.com Investment Rating is currently a C- (Fair). The fund currently has a performance rating of C+ (Fair) based on an annualized return of 24.31% over the last three years and a total return of 13.79% year to date 2012. Factored into the performance evaluation is an expense ratio of 0.58% (very low).

The fund's risk rating is currently C (Fair). It carries a beta of 1.14, meaning it is expected to move 11.4% for every 10% move in the market. Volatility, as measured by both the semi-deviation and a drawdown factor, is considered average. As of March 31, 2012, *WisdomTree Global ex-US Real Est traded at a premium of .04% above its net asset value, which is better than its one-year historical average premium of .14%.

Karen Q. Wong has been running the fund for 4 years and currently receives a manager quality ranking of 78 (0=worst, 99=best). If you desire an average level of risk, then this fund may be an option.

Data Date	Investment Rating	Net Assets ($Mil)	Price	Performance Rating/Pts	Total Return Y-T-D	Risk Rating/Pts
3-12	C-	122.15	26.41	C+ / 6.1	13.79%	C / 5.4
2011	D	102.80	23.21	C- / 3.9	0.39%	C / 5.3
2010	D	118.60	28.63	D+ / 2.8	24.49%	C- / 3.9
2009	C+	82.82	26.77	B+ / 8.7	38.41%	C- / 3.9

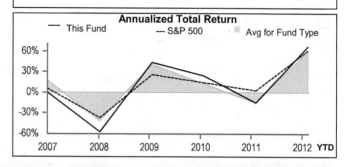

*WisdomTree Global ex-US Utilitie (DBU)   D   Weak

Fund Family: WisdomTree Asset Management Inc
Fund Type: Utilities
Inception Date: October 13, 2006

Major Rating Factors:
Disappointing performance is the major factor driving the D (Weak) TheStreet.com Investment Rating for *WisdomTree Global ex-US Utilitie. The fund currently has a performance rating of D (Weak) based on an annualized return of 7.19% over the last three years and a total return of 6.88% year to date 2012. Factored into the performance evaluation is an expense ratio of 0.58% (very low).

The fund's risk rating is currently B- (Good). It carries a beta of 1.25, meaning it is expected to move 12.5% for every 10% move in the market. Volatility, as measured by both the semi-deviation and a drawdown factor, is considered low. As of March 31, 2012, *WisdomTree Global ex-US Utilitie traded at a premium of .11% above its net asset value, which is worse than its one-year historical average discount of .26%.

Karen Q. Wong has been running the fund for 4 years and currently receives a manager quality ranking of 12 (0=worst, 99=best). This fund offers only a moderate level of risk but investors looking for strong performance are still waiting.

Data Date	Investment Rating	Net Assets ($Mil)	Price	Performance Rating/Pts	Total Return Y-T-D	Risk Rating/Pts
3-12	D	32.47	18.92	D / 1.9	6.88%	B- / 7.7
2011	D	30.30	17.78	D / 1.7	-0.50%	B- / 7.4
2010	D-	36.30	20.14	E+ / 0.8	-4.91%	C / 5.1
2009	D	38.57	22.50	D / 1.7	0.96%	C+ / 5.6

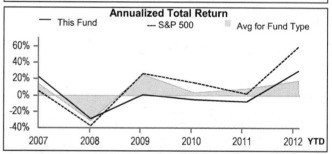

*WisdomTree Global Natural Resour (GNAT)   D   Weak

Fund Family: WisdomTree Asset Management Inc
Fund Type: Energy/Natural Resources
Inception Date: October 13, 2006

Major Rating Factors:
Disappointing performance is the major factor driving the D (Weak) TheStreet.com Investment Rating for *WisdomTree Global Natural Resour. The fund currently has a performance rating of D+ (Weak) based on an annualized return of 13.13% over the last three years and a total return of 7.91% year to date 2012. Factored into the performance evaluation is an expense ratio of 0.58% (very low).

The fund's risk rating is currently B- (Good). It carries a beta of 1.09, meaning that its performance tracks fairly well with that of the overall stock market. Volatility, as measured by both the semi-deviation and a drawdown factor, is considered low. As of March 31, 2012, *WisdomTree Global Natural Resour traded at a premium of .16% above its net asset value, which is worse than its one-year historical average discount of .15%.

Karen Q. Wong has been running the fund for 4 years and currently receives a manager quality ranking of 20 (0=worst, 99=best). This fund offers only a moderate level of risk but investors looking for strong performance are still waiting.

Data Date	Investment Rating	Net Assets ($Mil)	Price	Performance Rating/Pts	Total Return Y-T-D	Risk Rating/Pts
3-12	D	33.47	25.20	D+ / 2.9	7.91%	B- / 7.0
2011	C-	30.60	23.50	C- / 3.6	1.96%	C+ / 6.9
2010	D	52.20	26.65	C- / 3.0	7.25%	C / 4.7
2009	C-	38.97	25.60	C / 4.9	29.86%	C / 5.2

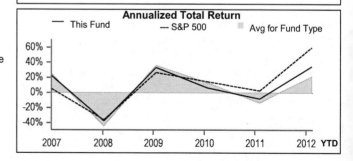

*WisdomTree India Earnings Fund (EPI)   D   Weak

Fund Family: WisdomTree Asset Management Inc
Fund Type: Foreign
Inception Date: February 22, 2008

Major Rating Factors: *WisdomTree India Earnings Fund receives a TheStreet.com Investment Rating of D (Weak). The fund currently has a performance rating of C- (Fair) based on an annualized return of 17.68% over the last three years and a total return of 23.66% year to date 2012. Factored into the performance evaluation is an expense ratio of 0.88% (low).

The fund's risk rating is currently C+ (Fair). It carries a beta of 1.28, meaning it is expected to move 12.8% for every 10% move in the market. Volatility, as measured by both the semi-deviation and a drawdown factor, is considered low. As of March 31, 2012, *WisdomTree India Earnings Fund traded at a premium of .21% above its net asset value, which is worse than its one-year historical average discount of .07%.

Karen Q. Wong has been running the fund for 4 years and currently receives a manager quality ranking of 36 (0=worst, 99=best). If you desire an average level of risk, then this fund may be an option.

Data Date	Investment Rating	Net Assets ($Mil)	Price	Performance Rating/Pts	Total Return Y-T-D	Risk Rating/Pts
3-12	D	1,004.46	19.28	C- / 3.5	23.66%	C+ / 5.8
2011	D	714.70	15.60	C- / 3.0	4.10%	C+ / 5.8
2010	B-	1,662.90	26.39	B+ / 8.7	20.34%	C- / 3.9
2009	B	553.94	22.07	A+ / 9.7	84.82%	C- / 3.9

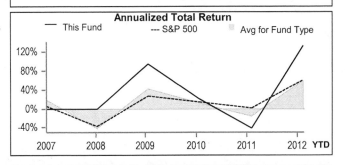

Annualized Total Return

*WisdomTree Intl Div Ex-Financial (DOO)   D+   Weak

Fund Family: WisdomTree Asset Management Inc
Fund Type: Foreign
Inception Date: June 16, 2006

Major Rating Factors: *WisdomTree Intl Div Ex-Financial receives a TheStreet.com Investment Rating of D+ (Weak). The fund currently has a performance rating of C- (Fair) based on an annualized return of 15.95% over the last three years and a total return of 6.35% year to date 2012. Factored into the performance evaluation is an expense ratio of 0.58% (very low).

The fund's risk rating is currently B- (Good). It carries a beta of 1.01, meaning that its performance tracks fairly well with that of the overall stock market. Volatility, as measured by both the semi-deviation and a drawdown factor, is considered low. As of March 31, 2012, *WisdomTree Intl Div Ex-Financial traded at a premium of .41% above its net asset value, which is worse than its one-year historical average premium of .30%.

Karen Q. Wong has been running the fund for 4 years and currently receives a manager quality ranking of 54 (0=worst, 99=best). If you desire an average level of risk, then this fund may be an option.

Data Date	Investment Rating	Net Assets ($Mil)	Price	Performance Rating/Pts	Total Return Y-T-D	Risk Rating/Pts
3-12	D+	342.81	41.81	C- / 3.4	6.35%	B- / 7.5
2011	C-	264.50	39.58	C- / 3.5	-1.47%	B- / 7.5
2010	D-	171.80	44.16	D- / 1.3	5.70%	C- / 4.2
2009	D	149.40	43.59	D+ / 2.4	31.21%	C / 4.5

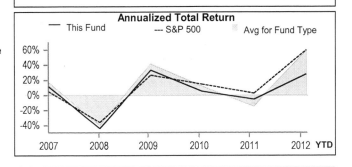

Annualized Total Return

*WisdomTree Intl Hedged Equity (HEDJ)   D+   Weak

Fund Family: WisdomTree Asset Management Inc
Fund Type: Foreign
Inception Date: December 31, 2009

Major Rating Factors:
Disappointing performance is the major factor driving the D+ (Weak) TheStreet.com Investment Rating for *WisdomTree Intl Hedged Equity. The fund currently has a performance rating of D (Weak) based on an annualized return of 0.00% over the last three years and a total return of 9.16% year to date 2012. Factored into the performance evaluation is an expense ratio of 0.58% (very low).

The fund's risk rating is currently B (Good). It carries a beta of 0.00, meaning the fund's expected move will be 0.0% for every 10% move in the market. Volatility, as measured by both the semi-deviation and a drawdown factor, is considered low. As of March 31, 2012, *WisdomTree Intl Hedged Equity traded at a premium of 1.98% above its net asset value, which is worse than its one-year historical average premium of .32%.

Karen Q. Wong has been running the fund for 3 years and currently receives a manager quality ranking of 46 (0=worst, 99=best). This fund offers only a moderate level of risk but investors looking for strong performance are still waiting.

Data Date	Investment Rating	Net Assets ($Mil)	Price	Performance Rating/Pts	Total Return Y-T-D	Risk Rating/Pts
3-12	D+	19.80	44.80	D / 2.1	9.16%	B / 8.2
2011	D+	18.40	41.20	D- / 1.3	0.46%	B / 8.2
2010	A-	21.00	46.85	B- / 7.1	3.53%	B- / 7.8

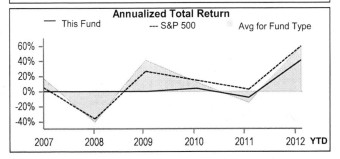

Annualized Total Return

*WisdomTree Intl LargeCap Dividen (DOL)

D+   **Weak**

Fund Family: WisdomTree Asset Management Inc
Fund Type: Foreign
Inception Date: June 16, 2006

Major Rating Factors: *WisdomTree Intl LargeCap Dividen receives a TheStreet.com Investment Rating of D+ (Weak). The fund currently has a performance rating of C- (Fair) based on an annualized return of 13.02% over the last three years and a total return of 8.31% year to date 2012. Factored into the performance evaluation is an expense ratio of 0.48% (very low).

The fund's risk rating is currently B- (Good). It carries a beta of 1.01, meaning that its performance tracks fairly well with that of the overall stock market. Volatility, as measured by both the semi-deviation and a drawdown factor, is considered low. As of March 31, 2012, *WisdomTree Intl LargeCap Dividen traded at a premium of .49% above its net asset value, which is worse than its one-year historical average premium of .11%.

Karen Q. Wong has been running the fund for 4 years and currently receives a manager quality ranking of 33 (0=worst, 99=best). If you desire an average level of risk, then this fund may be an option.

Data Date	Investment Rating	Net Assets ($Mil)	Price	Performance Rating/Pts	Total Return Y-T-D	Risk Rating/Pts
3-12	D+	158.97	43.10	C- / 3.0	8.31%	B- / 7.4
2011	D+	127.70	40.00	D+ / 2.6	-0.65%	B- / 7.3
2010	D-	149.30	45.49	D- / 1.2	1.87%	C / 4.8
2009	D	117.33	46.41	D+ / 2.3	22.43%	C / 5.0

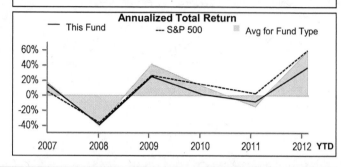

*WisdomTree Intl MidCap Dividend (DIM)

C-   **Fair**

Fund Family: WisdomTree Asset Management Inc
Fund Type: Foreign
Inception Date: June 16, 2006

Major Rating Factors: Middle of the road best describes *WisdomTree Intl MidCap Dividend whose TheStreet.com Investment Rating is currently a C- (Fair). The fund currently has a performance rating of C- (Fair) based on an annualized return of 16.33% over the last three years and a total return of 12.16% year to date 2012. Factored into the performance evaluation is an expense ratio of 0.58% (very low).

The fund's risk rating is currently B- (Good). It carries a beta of 1.04, meaning that its performance tracks fairly well with that of the overall stock market. Volatility, as measured by both the semi-deviation and a drawdown factor, is considered low. As of March 31, 2012, *WisdomTree Intl MidCap Dividend traded at a discount of .02% below its net asset value, which is worse than its one-year historical average discount of .23%.

Karen Q. Wong has been running the fund for 4 years and currently receives a manager quality ranking of 50 (0=worst, 99=best). If you desire an average level of risk, then this fund may be an option.

Data Date	Investment Rating	Net Assets ($Mil)	Price	Performance Rating/Pts	Total Return Y-T-D	Risk Rating/Pts
3-12	C-	106.38	48.09	C- / 3.7	12.16%	B- / 7.4
2011	C-	112.60	43.05	C- / 3.0	-0.33%	B- / 7.4
2010	D	153.40	51.85	D+ / 2.7	11.31%	C / 4.7
2009	D	128.53	48.12	D+ / 2.7	32.42%	C / 4.9

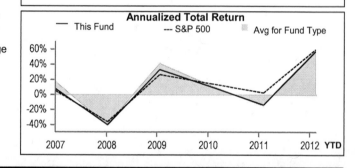

*WisdomTree Intl Small Cap Divide (DLS)

C   **Fair**

Fund Family: WisdomTree Asset Management Inc
Fund Type: Foreign
Inception Date: June 16, 2006

Major Rating Factors: Middle of the road best describes *WisdomTree Intl Small Cap Divide whose TheStreet.com Investment Rating is currently a C (Fair). The fund currently has a performance rating of C (Fair) based on an annualized return of 20.71% over the last three years and a total return of 13.89% year to date 2012. Factored into the performance evaluation is an expense ratio of 0.58% (very low).

The fund's risk rating is currently B- (Good). It carries a beta of 0.93, meaning that its performance tracks fairly well with that of the overall stock market. Volatility, as measured by both the semi-deviation and a drawdown factor, is considered low. As of March 31, 2012, *WisdomTree Intl Small Cap Divide traded at a premium of .45% above its net asset value, which is worse than its one-year historical average discount of .25%.

Karen Q. Wong has been running the fund for 4 years and currently receives a manager quality ranking of 77 (0=worst, 99=best). If you desire an average level of risk, then this fund may be an option.

Data Date	Investment Rating	Net Assets ($Mil)	Price	Performance Rating/Pts	Total Return Y-T-D	Risk Rating/Pts
3-12	C	418.03	49.55	C / 5.0	13.89%	B- / 7.8
2011	C-	363.80	43.73	C- / 3.9	0.16%	B- / 7.7
2010	D+	471.20	51.77	C- / 3.9	19.41%	C / 4.6
2009	D-	389.97	44.78	D / 2.1	34.92%	C / 4.7

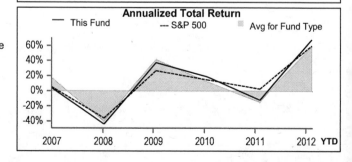

*WisdomTree Japan Hedged Equity (DXJ)

D   **Weak**

Fund Family: WisdomTree Asset Management Inc
Fund Type: Foreign
Inception Date: June 16, 2006

Major Rating Factors:
Disappointing performance is the major factor driving the D (Weak) TheStreet.com Investment Rating for *WisdomTree Japan Hedged Equity. The fund currently has a performance rating of D (Weak) based on an annualized return of 4.74% over the last three years and a total return of 17.74% year to date 2012. Factored into the performance evaluation is an expense ratio of 0.48% (very low).

The fund's risk rating is currently B- (Good). It carries a beta of 0.48, meaning the fund's expected move will be 4.8% for every 10% move in the market. Volatility, as measured by both the semi-deviation and a drawdown factor, is considered low. As of March 31, 2012, *WisdomTree Japan Hedged Equity traded at a premium of .65% above its net asset value, which is worse than its one-year historical average discount of .09%.

Karen Q. Wong has been running the fund for 4 years and currently receives a manager quality ranking of 33 (0=worst, 99=best). This fund offers only a moderate level of risk but investors looking for strong performance are still waiting.

Data Date	Investment Rating	Net Assets ($Mil)	Price	Performance Rating/Pts	Total Return Y-T-D	Risk Rating/Pts
3-12	D	520.42	36.90	D / 2.0	17.74%	B- / 7.6
2011	D	399.20	31.34	D- / 1.4	0.26%	B- / 7.4
2010	D	121.80	38.17	D- / 1.2	-1.78%	C+ / 5.8
2009	D	87.80	39.33	E+ / 0.9	0.22%	C+ / 6.0

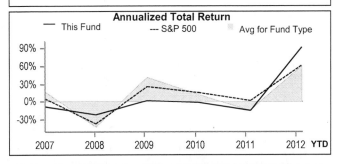

Annualized Total Return

*WisdomTree Japan SmallCap Div Fd (DFJ)

C   **Fair**

Fund Family: WisdomTree Asset Management Inc
Fund Type: Foreign
Inception Date: June 16, 2006

Major Rating Factors: Middle of the road best describes *WisdomTree Japan SmallCap Div Fd whose TheStreet.com Investment Rating is currently a C (Fair). The fund currently has a performance rating of C- (Fair) based on an annualized return of 14.76% over the last three years and a total return of 9.44% year to date 2012. Factored into the performance evaluation is an expense ratio of 0.58% (very low).

The fund's risk rating is currently B (Good). It carries a beta of 0.34, meaning the fund's expected move will be 3.4% for every 10% move in the market. Volatility, as measured by both the semi-deviation and a drawdown factor, is considered low. As of March 31, 2012, *WisdomTree Japan SmallCap Div Fd traded at a premium of .29% above its net asset value, which is worse than its one-year historical average discount of .15%.

Karen Q. Wong has been running the fund for 4 years and currently receives a manager quality ranking of 83 (0=worst, 99=best). If you desire an average level of risk, then this fund may be an option.

Data Date	Investment Rating	Net Assets ($Mil)	Price	Performance Rating/Pts	Total Return Y-T-D	Risk Rating/Pts
3-12	C	187.29	45.58	C- / 3.6	9.44%	B / 8.8
2011	C-	184.10	41.65	C- / 3.1	-0.31%	B- / 7.8
2010	C+	121.60	44.20	C+ / 6.3	17.37%	C+ / 6.3
2009	D	119.06	38.34	D- / 1.0	-0.93%	C+ / 6.3

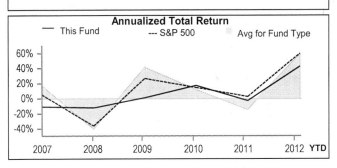

Annualized Total Return

*WisdomTree LargeCap Dividend Fun (DLN)

B-   **Good**

Fund Family: WisdomTree Asset Management Inc
Fund Type: Growth and Income
Inception Date: June 16, 2006

Major Rating Factors: *WisdomTree LargeCap Dividend Fun receives a TheStreet.com Investment Rating of B- (Good). The fund currently has a performance rating of C+ (Fair) based on an annualized return of 22.74% over the last three years and a total return of 8.68% year to date 2012. Factored into the performance evaluation is an expense ratio of 0.28% (very low).

The fund's risk rating is currently B (Good). It carries a beta of 0.83, meaning the fund's expected move will be 8.3% for every 10% move in the market. Volatility, as measured by both the semi-deviation and a drawdown factor, is considered low. As of March 31, 2012, *WisdomTree LargeCap Dividend Fun traded at a discount of .04% below its net asset value, which is better than its one-year historical average premium of .10%.

Karen Q. Wong has been running the fund for 4 years and currently receives a manager quality ranking of 73 (0=worst, 99=best). If you desire an average level of risk, then this fund may be an option.

Data Date	Investment Rating	Net Assets ($Mil)	Price	Performance Rating/Pts	Total Return Y-T-D	Risk Rating/Pts
3-12	B-	1,187.03	52.96	C+ / 6.4	8.68%	B / 8.8
2011	C+	930.90	49.03	C+ / 6.1	0.94%	B- / 7.9
2010	C-	554.90	46.10	C- / 3.0	14.98%	C+ / 5.9
2009	D	410.36	41.28	D- / 1.5	14.64%	C+ / 6.0

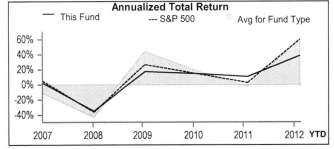

Annualized Total Return

*WisdomTree LargeCap Growth Fund (ROI)　　　　C　　　Fair

Fund Family: WisdomTree Asset Management Inc
Fund Type: Growth
Inception Date: December 4, 2008

Major Rating Factors: Middle of the road best describes *WisdomTree LargeCap Growth Fund whose TheStreet.com Investment Rating is currently a C (Fair). The fund currently has a performance rating of C (Fair) based on an annualized return of 16.26% over the last three years and a total return of 13.22% year to date 2012. Factored into the performance evaluation is an expense ratio of 0.38% (very low).

The fund's risk rating is currently B (Good). It carries a beta of 0.95, meaning that its performance tracks fairly well with that of the overall stock market. Volatility, as measured by both the semi-deviation and a drawdown factor, is considered low. As of March 31, 2012, *WisdomTree LargeCap Growth Fund traded at a premium of .20% above its net asset value, which is worse than its one-year historical average premium of .08%.

Karen Q. Wong has been running the fund for 4 years and currently receives a manager quality ranking of 29 (0=worst, 99=best). If you desire an average level of risk, then this fund may be an option.

Data Date	Investment Rating	Net Assets ($Mil)	Price	Performance Rating/Pts	Total Return Y-T-D	Risk Rating/Pts
3-12	C	20.16	41.00	C / 4.4	13.22%	B / 8.2
2011	C	18.10	36.33	C / 4.4	1.58%	B / 8.1
2010	A+	22.00	36.67	B+ / 8.7	9.11%	B- / 7.9
2009	A+	17.76	33.91	B / 8.1	21.99%	B / 8.4

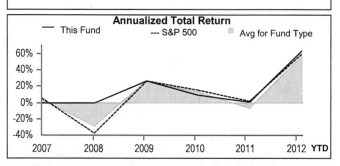

*WisdomTree LargeCap Value Fund (EZY)　　　　C+　　　Fair

Fund Family: WisdomTree Asset Management Inc
Fund Type: Income
Inception Date: February 23, 2007

Major Rating Factors: Middle of the road best describes *WisdomTree LargeCap Value Fund whose TheStreet.com Investment Rating is currently a C+ (Fair). The fund currently has a performance rating of C (Fair) based on an annualized return of 21.00% over the last three years and a total return of 8.47% year to date 2012. Factored into the performance evaluation is an expense ratio of 0.38% (very low).

The fund's risk rating is currently B (Good). It carries a beta of 1.08, meaning that its performance tracks fairly well with that of the overall stock market. Volatility, as measured by both the semi-deviation and a drawdown factor, is considered low. As of March 31, 2012, *WisdomTree LargeCap Value Fund traded at a premium of .07% above its net asset value, which is worse than its one-year historical average discount of .04%.

Karen Q. Wong has been running the fund for 4 years and currently receives a manager quality ranking of 40 (0=worst, 99=best). If you desire an average level of risk, then this fund may be an option.

Data Date	Investment Rating	Net Assets ($Mil)	Price	Performance Rating/Pts	Total Return Y-T-D	Risk Rating/Pts
3-12	C+	30.75	44.34	C / 5.4	8.47%	B / 8.3
2011	C+	30.70	41.06	C+ / 5.7	1.02%	B- / 7.9
2010	C-	23.80	39.68	C- / 3.4	14.24%	C+ / 5.7
2009	B+	28.00	35.26	B / 8.2	23.37%	C+ / 5.8

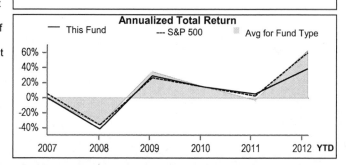

*WisdomTree Mgd Futures Strategy (WDTI)　　　　D　　　Weak

Fund Family: WisdomTree Asset Management Inc
Fund Type: Growth
Inception Date: January 5, 2011

Major Rating Factors:
Very poor performance is the major factor driving the D (Weak) TheStreet.com Investment Rating for *WisdomTree Mgd Futures Strategy. The fund currently has a performance rating of E+ (Very Weak) based on an annualized return of 0.00% over the last three years and a total return of -4.36% year to date 2012. Factored into the performance evaluation is an expense ratio of 0.95% (low).

The fund's risk rating is currently B (Good). It carries a beta of 0.00, meaning the fund's expected move will be 0.0% for every 10% move in the market. Volatility, as measured by both the semi-deviation and a drawdown factor, is considered low. As of March 31, 2012, *WisdomTree Mgd Futures Strategy traded at a premium of .14% above its net asset value, which is worse than its one-year historical average premium of .11%.

James H. Stavena has been running the fund for 1 year and currently receives a manager quality ranking of 10 (0=worst, 99=best). This fund offers only a moderate level of risk but investors looking for strong performance are still waiting.

Data Date	Investment Rating	Net Assets ($Mil)	Price	Performance Rating/Pts	Total Return Y-T-D	Risk Rating/Pts
3-12	D	248.06	43.26	E+ / 0.7	-4.36%	B / 8.3

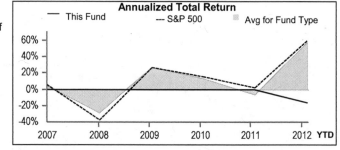

*WisdomTree MidCap Dividend Fund (DON)

B   **Good**

Fund Family: WisdomTree Asset Management Inc
Fund Type: Growth
Inception Date: June 16, 2006

Major Rating Factors: Strong performance is the major factor driving the B (Good) TheStreet.com Investment Rating for *WisdomTree MidCap Dividend Fund. The fund currently has a performance rating of B (Good) based on an annualized return of 28.06% over the last three years and a total return of 8.93% year to date 2012. Factored into the performance evaluation is an expense ratio of 0.38% (very low).

    The fund's risk rating is currently B (Good). It carries a beta of 1.09, meaning that its performance tracks fairly well with that of the overall stock market. Volatility, as measured by both the semi-deviation and a drawdown factor, is considered low. As of March 31, 2012, *WisdomTree MidCap Dividend Fund traded at a premium of .07% above its net asset value, which is better than its one-year historical average premium of .10%.

    Karen Q. Wong has been running the fund for 4 years and currently receives a manager quality ranking of 73 (0=worst, 99=best). If you desire only a moderate level of risk and strong performance, then this fund is an excellent option.

Data Date	Investment Rating	Net Assets ($Mil)	Price	Performance Rating/Pts	Total Return Y-T-D	Risk Rating/Pts
3-12	B	343.66	56.29	B / 7.6	8.93%	B / 8.4
2011	B-	288.30	52.07	C+ / 6.9	0.71%	B- / 7.6
2010	C+	233.00	50.70	C+ / 6.8	21.65%	C+ / 5.6
2009	D+	102.89	42.97	C- / 3.0	30.02%	C+ / 5.6

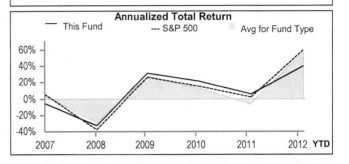

*WisdomTree MidCap Earnings Fund (EZM)

B+   **Good**

Fund Family: WisdomTree Asset Management Inc
Fund Type: Growth
Inception Date: February 23, 2007

Major Rating Factors: Strong performance is the major factor driving the B+ (Good) TheStreet.com Investment Rating for *WisdomTree MidCap Earnings Fund. The fund currently has a performance rating of B (Good) based on an annualized return of 30.39% over the last three years and a total return of 13.54% year to date 2012. Factored into the performance evaluation is an expense ratio of 0.38% (very low).

    The fund's risk rating is currently B- (Good). It carries a beta of 1.25, meaning it is expected to move 12.5% for every 10% move in the market. Volatility, as measured by both the semi-deviation and a drawdown factor, is considered low. As of March 31, 2012, *WisdomTree MidCap Earnings Fund traded at a premium of .23% above its net asset value, which is worse than its one-year historical average premium of .07%.

    Karen Q. Wong has been running the fund for 4 years and currently receives a manager quality ranking of 65 (0=worst, 99=best). If you desire only a moderate level of risk and strong performance, then this fund is an excellent option.

Data Date	Investment Rating	Net Assets ($Mil)	Price	Performance Rating/Pts	Total Return Y-T-D	Risk Rating/Pts
3-12	B+	154.27	61.14	B / 8.2	13.54%	B- / 7.9
2011	B-	121.20	53.95	B- / 7.4	1.93%	B- / 7.5
2010	B+	93.90	53.99	B / 8.0	25.60%	C+ / 5.8
2009	A+	22.35	43.65	A- / 9.2	46.05%	C+ / 5.8

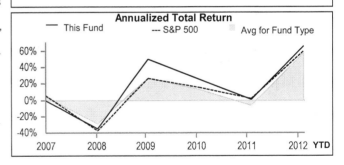

*WisdomTree Middle East Dividend (GULF)

D+   **Weak**

Fund Family: WisdomTree Asset Management Inc
Fund Type: Foreign
Inception Date: July 16, 2008

Major Rating Factors:
Disappointing performance is the major factor driving the D+ (Weak) TheStreet.com Investment Rating for *WisdomTree Middle East Dividend. The fund currently has a performance rating of D+ (Weak) based on an annualized return of 11.50% over the last three years and a total return of 7.04% year to date 2012. Factored into the performance evaluation is an expense ratio of 0.88% (low).

    The fund's risk rating is currently B (Good). It carries a beta of 0.59, meaning the fund's expected move will be 5.9% for every 10% move in the market. Volatility, as measured by both the semi-deviation and a drawdown factor, is considered low. As of March 31, 2012, *WisdomTree Middle East Dividend traded at a discount of .64% below its net asset value, which is worse than its one-year historical average discount of .88%.

    Michael C. Ho currently receives a manager quality ranking of 63 (0=worst, 99=best). This fund offers only a moderate level of risk but investors looking for strong performance are still waiting.

Data Date	Investment Rating	Net Assets ($Mil)	Price	Performance Rating/Pts	Total Return Y-T-D	Risk Rating/Pts
3-12	D+	13.96	15.50	D+ / 2.7	7.04%	B / 8.1
2011	C-	14.70	14.63	D+ / 2.8	-0.48%	B / 8.0
2010	A-	20.30	17.04	A- / 9.2	22.43%	C / 5.0
2009	D-	10.94	14.40	D- / 1.4	0.64%	C / 4.9

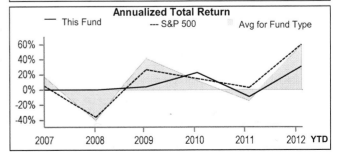

*WisdomTree SmallCap Dividend Fd (DES)   B   Good

Fund Family: WisdomTree Asset Management Inc
Fund Type: Growth
Inception Date: June 16, 2006

Major Rating Factors: Strong performance is the major factor driving the B (Good) TheStreet.com Investment Rating for *WisdomTree SmallCap Dividend Fd. The fund currently has a performance rating of B- (Good) based on an annualized return of 27.34% over the last three years and a total return of 10.27% year to date 2012. Factored into the performance evaluation is an expense ratio of 0.38% (very low).

The fund's risk rating is currently B (Good). It carries a beta of 1.20, meaning it is expected to move 12.0% for every 10% move in the market. Volatility, as measured by both the semi-deviation and a drawdown factor, is considered low. As of March 31, 2012, *WisdomTree SmallCap Dividend Fd traded at a premium of .12% above its net asset value, which is worse than its one-year historical average premium of .10%.

Karen Q. Wong has been running the fund for 4 years and currently receives a manager quality ranking of 63 (0=worst, 99=best). If you desire only a moderate level of risk and strong performance, then this fund is an excellent option.

Data Date	Investment Rating	Net Assets ($Mil)	Price	Performance Rating/Pts	Total Return Y-T-D	Risk Rating/Pts
3-12	B	296.27	49.09	B- / 7.4	10.27%	B / 8.1
2011	C	242.00	44.89	C / 5.2	1.69%	B- / 7.1
2010	B+	224.20	47.41	B / 8.2	27.05%	C / 5.4
2009	D	133.61	38.80	D / 1.7	20.06%	C / 5.4

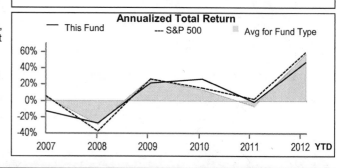
Annualized Total Return

*WisdomTree SmallCap Earnings Fun (EES)   B+   Good

Fund Family: WisdomTree Asset Management Inc
Fund Type: Growth
Inception Date: February 23, 2007

Major Rating Factors: Strong performance is the major factor driving the B+ (Good) TheStreet.com Investment Rating for *WisdomTree SmallCap Earnings Fun. The fund currently has a performance rating of B+ (Good) based on an annualized return of 31.35% over the last three years and a total return of 13.31% year to date 2012. Factored into the performance evaluation is an expense ratio of 0.38% (very low).

The fund's risk rating is currently B- (Good). It carries a beta of 1.35, meaning it is expected to move 13.5% for every 10% move in the market. Volatility, as measured by both the semi-deviation and a drawdown factor, is considered low. As of March 31, 2012, *WisdomTree SmallCap Earnings Fun traded at a premium of .35% above its net asset value, which is worse than its one-year historical average premium of .02%.

Karen Q. Wong has been running the fund for 4 years and currently receives a manager quality ranking of 61 (0=worst, 99=best). If you desire only a moderate level of risk and strong performance, then this fund is an excellent option.

Data Date	Investment Rating	Net Assets ($Mil)	Price	Performance Rating/Pts	Total Return Y-T-D	Risk Rating/Pts
3-12	B+	143.22	56.79	B+ / 8.5	13.31%	B- / 7.8
2011	B-	120.30	50.31	B- / 7.2	1.88%	B- / 7.4
2010	B+	116.40	51.95	B+ / 8.4	26.97%	C+ / 5.7
2009	A	62.23	41.41	A- / 9.0	44.03%	C / 5.5

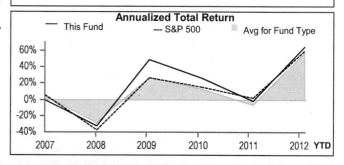
Annualized Total Return

*WisdomTree Total Dividend (DTD)   B-   Good

Fund Family: WisdomTree Asset Management Inc
Fund Type: Income
Inception Date: June 16, 2006

Major Rating Factors: *WisdomTree Total Dividend receives a TheStreet.com Investment Rating of B- (Good). The fund currently has a performance rating of C+ (Fair) based on an annualized return of 23.50% over the last three years and a total return of 8.98% year to date 2012. Factored into the performance evaluation is an expense ratio of 0.28% (very low).

The fund's risk rating is currently B (Good). It carries a beta of 0.87, meaning the fund's expected move will be 8.7% for every 10% move in the market. Volatility, as measured by both the semi-deviation and a drawdown factor, is considered low. As of March 31, 2012, *WisdomTree Total Dividend traded at a premium of .13% above its net asset value, which is worse than its one-year historical average premium of .06%.

Karen Q. Wong has been running the fund for 4 years and currently receives a manager quality ranking of 73 (0=worst, 99=best). If you desire an average level of risk, then this fund may be an option.

Data Date	Investment Rating	Net Assets ($Mil)	Price	Performance Rating/Pts	Total Return Y-T-D	Risk Rating/Pts
3-12	B-	233.81	53.11	C+ / 6.6	8.98%	B / 8.8
2011	C+	206.00	49.05	C+ / 6.1	0.92%	B- / 7.9
2010	C-	155.80	46.59	C- / 3.7	16.32%	C+ / 5.9
2009	D	124.25	41.32	D / 1.6	16.64%	C+ / 5.9

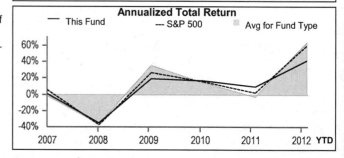
Annualized Total Return

*WisdomTree Total Earnings Fund (EXT)

C+ **Fair**

Fund Family: WisdomTree Asset Management Inc
Fund Type: Income
Inception Date: February 23, 2007

Major Rating Factors: Middle of the road best describes *WisdomTree Total Earnings Fund whose TheStreet.com Investment Rating is currently a C+ (Fair). The fund currently has a performance rating of C+ (Fair) based on an annualized return of 22.64% over the last three years and a total return of 12.92% year to date 2012. Factored into the performance evaluation is an expense ratio of 0.28% (very low).

The fund's risk rating is currently B (Good). It carries a beta of 0.96, meaning that its performance tracks fairly well with that of the overall stock market. Volatility, as measured by both the semi-deviation and a drawdown factor, is considered low. As of March 31, 2012, *WisdomTree Total Earnings Fund traded at a premium of .06% above its net asset value, which is worse than its one-year historical average premium of .02%.

Karen Q. Wong has been running the fund for 4 years and currently receives a manager quality ranking of 61 (0=worst, 99=best). If you desire an average level of risk, then this fund may be an option.

Data Date	Investment Rating	Net Assets ($Mil)	Price	Performance Rating/Pts	Total Return Y-T-D	Risk Rating/Pts
3-12	C+	37.03	50.65	C+ / 6.5	12.92%	B / 8.3
2011	C+	33.70	45.01	C+ / 6.0	1.98%	B / 8.0
2010	C-	51.20	44.62	C- / 4.1	13.78%	C+ / 5.9
2009	A	24.34	39.97	B+ / 8.5	29.03%	C+ / 6.0

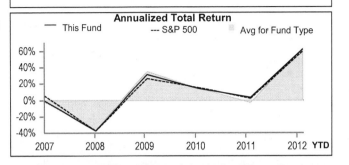

Aberdeen Asia-Pacific Income Fund (FAX)

C **Fair**

Fund Family: Aberdeen Asset Management Asia Ltd
Fund Type: Global
Inception Date: April 17, 1986

Major Rating Factors: Middle of the road best describes Aberdeen Asia-Pacific Income Fund whose TheStreet.com Investment Rating is currently a C (Fair). The fund currently has a performance rating of C (Fair) based on an annualized return of 21.25% over the last three years and a total return of 0.86% year to date 2012. Factored into the performance evaluation is an expense ratio of 1.49% (average).

The fund's risk rating is currently B (Good). It carries a beta of 1.10, meaning it is expected to move 11.0% for every 10% move in the market. Volatility, as measured by both the semi-deviation and a drawdown factor, is considered low. As of March 31, 2012, Aberdeen Asia-Pacific Income Fund traded at a discount of 2.28% below its net asset value, which is worse than its one-year historical average discount of 2.82%.

Anthony Michael currently receives a manager quality ranking of 89 (0=worst, 99=best). If you desire an average level of risk, then this fund may be an option.

Data Date	Investment Rating	Net Assets ($Mil)	Price	Performance Rating/Pts	Total Return Y-T-D	Risk Rating/Pts
3-12	C	1,951.74	7.29	C / 5.2	0.86%	B / 8.0
2011	B+	1,917.40	7.33	B / 8.0	1.50%	B / 8.6
2010	B+	1,777.77	6.75	B / 8.1	15.66%	C+ / 6.0
2009	C+	1,421.03	6.22	C+ / 6.4	49.04%	C+ / 6.3

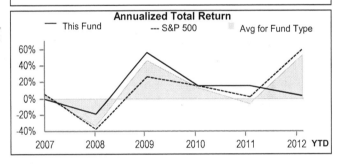

Aberdeen Australia Equity Fund (IAF)

C **Fair**

Fund Family: Aberdeen Asset Management Asia Ltd
Fund Type: Foreign
Inception Date: December 12, 1985

Major Rating Factors: Middle of the road best describes Aberdeen Australia Equity Fund whose TheStreet.com Investment Rating is currently a C (Fair). The fund currently has a performance rating of C+ (Fair) based on an annualized return of 25.38% over the last three years and a total return of 22.10% year to date 2012. Factored into the performance evaluation is an expense ratio of 1.34% (average).

The fund's risk rating is currently C+ (Fair). It carries a beta of 1.38, meaning it is expected to move 13.8% for every 10% move in the market. Volatility, as measured by both the semi-deviation and a drawdown factor, is considered low. As of March 31, 2012, Aberdeen Australia Equity Fund traded at a premium of 8.81% above its net asset value, which is worse than its one-year historical average premium of 4.71%.

Mark Daniels currently receives a manager quality ranking of 62 (0=worst, 99=best). If you desire an average level of risk, then this fund may be an option.

Data Date	Investment Rating	Net Assets ($Mil)	Price	Performance Rating/Pts	Total Return Y-T-D	Risk Rating/Pts
3-12	C	229.62	10.75	C+ / 6.7	22.10%	C+ / 6.6
2011	C-	207.70	9.05	C / 5.0	3.76%	C+ / 6.6
2010	C-	219.93	11.98	C / 4.8	8.15%	C / 4.4
2009	C+	155.02	12.17	B / 7.8	73.27%	C- / 4.0

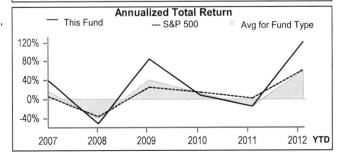

Aberdeen Chile Fund (CH)

B　　**Good**

Fund Family: Aberdeen Asset Management Inc
Fund Type: Foreign
Inception Date: September 27, 1989

Data Date	Investment Rating	Net Assets ($Mil)	Price	Performance Rating/Pts	Total Return Y-T-D	Risk Rating/Pts
3-12	B	168.15	19.23	A+ / 9.6	30.99%	C+ / 5.9
2011	C+	134.50	15.04	B / 8.2	1.60%	C+ / 5.9
2010	B+	190.85	22.67	A- / 9.1	48.63%	C / 4.7
2009	B	170.07	17.90	B / 8.2	93.26%	C / 5.1

Major Rating Factors:
Exceptional performance is the major factor driving the B (Good) TheStreet.com Investment Rating for Aberdeen Chile Fund. The fund currently has a performance rating of A+ (Excellent) based on an annualized return of 40.27% over the last three years and a total return of 30.99% year to date 2012. Factored into the performance evaluation is an expense ratio of 2.07% (high).

The fund's risk rating is currently C+ (Fair). It carries a beta of 1.00, meaning that its performance tracks fairly well with that of the overall stock market. Volatility, as measured by both the semi-deviation and a drawdown factor, is considered low. As of March 31, 2012, Aberdeen Chile Fund traded at a premium of 14.40% above its net asset value, which is worse than its one-year historical average premium of 5.98%.

Devan Kaloo has been running the fund for 3 years and currently receives a manager quality ranking of 93 (0=worst, 99=best). If you desire only a moderate level of risk and strong performance, then this fund is an excellent option.

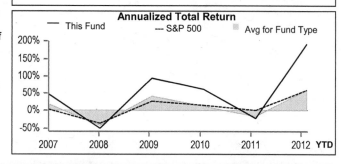

Aberdeen Emerging Mkt Tele & Infr (ETF)

C　　**Fair**

Fund Family: Aberdeen Asset Mgmt Inv Services Lt
Fund Type: Emerging Market
Inception Date: June 17, 1992

Data Date	Investment Rating	Net Assets ($Mil)	Price	Performance Rating/Pts	Total Return Y-T-D	Risk Rating/Pts
3-12	C	165.08	19.37	C- / 4.2	10.50%	B / 8.4
2011	C	161.40	17.53	C- / 4.2	1.60%	B / 8.0
2010	D-	157.63	19.36	D / 2.2	20.26%	C- / 3.3
2009	D-	125.36	16.58	D+ / 2.4	19.32%	C- / 4.1

Major Rating Factors: Middle of the road best describes Aberdeen Emerging Mkt Tele & Infr whose TheStreet.com Investment Rating is currently a C (Fair). The fund currently has a performance rating of C- (Fair) based on an annualized return of 17.08% over the last three years and a total return of 10.50% year to date 2012. Factored into the performance evaluation is an expense ratio of 1.50% (average).

The fund's risk rating is currently B (Good). It carries a beta of 0.74, meaning the fund's expected move will be 7.4% for every 10% move in the market. Volatility, as measured by both the semi-deviation and a drawdown factor, is considered low. As of March 31, 2012, Aberdeen Emerging Mkt Tele & Infr traded at a discount of 11.47% below its net asset value, which is better than its one-year historical average discount of 10.49%.

Allison R. Mortensen currently receives a manager quality ranking of 49 (0=worst, 99=best). If you desire an average level of risk, then this fund may be an option.

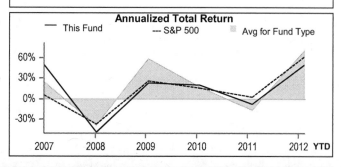

Aberdeen Global Income Fund (FCO)

B　　**Good**

Fund Family: Aberdeen Asset Management Asia Ltd
Fund Type: Global
Inception Date: February 20, 1992

Data Date	Investment Rating	Net Assets ($Mil)	Price	Performance Rating/Pts	Total Return Y-T-D	Risk Rating/Pts
3-12	B	121.65	13.98	B- / 7.3	2.14%	B / 8.4
2011	B+	119.80	13.90	B+ / 8.6	0.07%	B / 8.3
2010	B	108.85	12.31	B- / 7.5	5.93%	C+ / 5.6
2009	B-	87.89	12.46	B- / 7.2	54.30%	C+ / 5.6

Major Rating Factors: Strong performance is the major factor driving the B (Good) TheStreet.com Investment Rating for Aberdeen Global Income Fund. The fund currently has a performance rating of B- (Good) based on an annualized return of 26.86% over the last three years and a total return of 2.14% year to date 2012. Factored into the performance evaluation is an expense ratio of 2.13% (high).

The fund's risk rating is currently B (Good). It carries a beta of 1.06, meaning that its performance tracks fairly well with that of the overall stock market. Volatility, as measured by both the semi-deviation and a drawdown factor, is considered low. As of March 31, 2012, Aberdeen Global Income Fund traded at a premium of 3.86% above its net asset value, which is worse than its one-year historical average premium of 1.87%.

John A. Murphy currently receives a manager quality ranking of 93 (0=worst, 99=best). If you desire only a moderate level of risk and strong performance, then this fund is an excellent option.

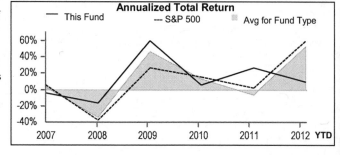

Aberdeen Indonesia Fund (IF)   A   Excellent

Fund Family: Aberdeen Asset Management Asia Ltd
Fund Type: Emerging Market
Inception Date: March 9, 1990

Major Rating Factors:
Exceptional performance is the major factor driving the A (Excellent) TheStreet.com Investment Rating for Aberdeen Indonesia Fund. The fund currently has a performance rating of A+ (Excellent) based on an annualized return of 48.02% over the last three years and a total return of 8.15% year to date 2012. Factored into the performance evaluation is an expense ratio of 1.52% (average).

The fund's risk rating is currently B- (Good). It carries a beta of 1.07, meaning that its performance tracks fairly well with that of the overall stock market. Volatility, as measured by both the semi-deviation and a drawdown factor, is considered low. As of March 31, 2012, Aberdeen Indonesia Fund traded at a discount of 9.19% below its net asset value, which is better than its one-year historical average discount of 8.76%.

Andrew Gillan currently receives a manager quality ranking of 92 (0=worst, 99=best). If you desire only a moderate level of risk and strong performance, then this fund is an excellent option.

Data Date	Investment Rating	Net Assets ($Mil)	Price	Performance Rating/Pts	Total Return Y-T-D	Risk Rating/Pts
3-12	A	119.04	12.74	A+ / 9.7	8.15%	B- / 7.6
2011	B+	106.50	11.78	A+ / 9.7	1.44%	B- / 7.5
2010	C+	84.14	13.31	B+ / 8.8	51.47%	D+ / 2.6
2009	C-	68.29	9.50	C+ / 6.2	102.19%	C- / 3.7

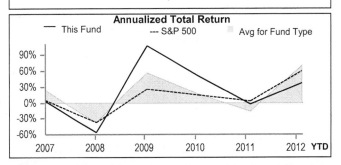

Aberdeen Israel Fund (ISL)   C-   Fair

Fund Family: Aberdeen Asset Management Inc
Fund Type: Foreign
Inception Date: October 22, 1992

Major Rating Factors: Middle of the road best describes Aberdeen Israel Fund whose TheStreet.com Investment Rating is currently a C- (Fair). The fund currently has a performance rating of C- (Fair) based on an annualized return of 20.74% over the last three years and a total return of 9.73% year to date 2012. Factored into the performance evaluation is an expense ratio of 1.67% (above average).

The fund's risk rating is currently B- (Good). It carries a beta of 0.98, meaning that its performance tracks fairly well with that of the overall stock market. Volatility, as measured by both the semi-deviation and a drawdown factor, is considered low. As of March 31, 2012, Aberdeen Israel Fund traded at a discount of 11.90% below its net asset value, which is better than its one-year historical average discount of 11.87%.

Andrew P.S. Brown currently receives a manager quality ranking of 76 (0=worst, 99=best). If you desire an average level of risk, then this fund may be an option.

Data Date	Investment Rating	Net Assets ($Mil)	Price	Performance Rating/Pts	Total Return Y-T-D	Risk Rating/Pts
3-12	C-	83.83	13.99	C- / 4.2	9.73%	B- / 7.3
2011	C-	62.40	12.75	C / 4.7	-0.24%	B- / 7.1
2010	C-	70.25	17.40	C- / 4.2	16.96%	C / 5.4
2009	B-	53.59	15.14	B / 7.6	81.32%	C / 5.3

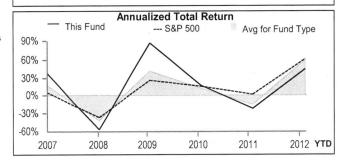

Aberdeen Latin America Equity Fund (LAQ)   B-   Good

Fund Family: Aberdeen Asset Management Inc
Fund Type: Foreign
Inception Date: October 30, 1991

Major Rating Factors: Strong performance is the major factor driving the B- (Good) TheStreet.com Investment Rating for Aberdeen Latin America Equity Fund. The fund currently has a performance rating of B+ (Good) based on an annualized return of 32.45% over the last three years and a total return of 18.06% year to date 2012. Factored into the performance evaluation is an expense ratio of 1.35% (average).

The fund's risk rating is currently C+ (Fair). It carries a beta of 1.20, meaning it is expected to move 12.0% for every 10% move in the market. Volatility, as measured by both the semi-deviation and a drawdown factor, is considered low. As of March 31, 2012, Aberdeen Latin America Equity Fund traded at a discount of 7.91% below its net asset value, which is worse than its one-year historical average discount of 9.05%.

Devan Kaloo has been running the fund for 3 years and currently receives a manager quality ranking of 88 (0=worst, 99=best). If you desire only a moderate level of risk and strong performance, then this fund is an excellent option.

Data Date	Investment Rating	Net Assets ($Mil)	Price	Performance Rating/Pts	Total Return Y-T-D	Risk Rating/Pts
3-12	B-	312.47	35.51	B+ / 8.4	18.06%	C+ / 6.8
2011	B-	247.50	30.10	B / 7.6	2.66%	C+ / 6.8
2010	C	265.10	38.72	B / 8.1	26.93%	D+ / 2.7
2009	C+	190.98	39.42	B+ / 8.5	107.90%	C- / 4.0

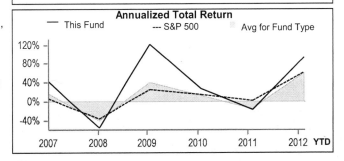

Adams Express Company (ADX)

C   **Fair**

Fund Family: Adams Express Company
Fund Type: Income
Inception Date: N/A

Data Date	Investment Rating	Net Assets ($Mil)	Price	Performance Rating/Pts	Total Return Y-T-D	Risk Rating/Pts
3-12	C	1,124.67	10.98	C / 4.7	14.43%	B- / 7.9
2011	C	1,050.70	9.64	C / 4.4	3.22%	B- / 7.7
2010	C	939.67	10.74	C- / 3.9	11.85%	C+ / 6.7
2009	C-	870.83	10.10	C- / 3.0	27.19%	C+ / 6.6

Major Rating Factors: Middle of the road best describes Adams Express Company whose TheStreet.com Investment Rating is currently a C (Fair). The fund currently has a performance rating of C (Fair) based on an annualized return of 18.28% over the last three years and a total return of 14.43% year to date 2012. Factored into the performance evaluation is an expense ratio of 0.58% (very low).

The fund's risk rating is currently B- (Good). It carries a beta of 1.10, meaning it is expected to move 11.0% for every 10% move in the market. Volatility, as measured by both the semi-deviation and a drawdown factor, is considered low. As of March 31, 2012, Adams Express Company traded at a discount of 15.02% below its net asset value, which is better than its one-year historical average discount of 14.61%.

Douglas G. Ober has been running the fund for 26 years and currently receives a manager quality ranking of 22 (0=worst, 99=best). If you desire an average level of risk, then this fund may be an option.

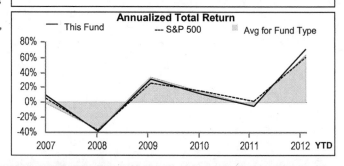

Advent Claymore Cnv Sec & Inc (AVK)

C+   **Fair**

Fund Family: Advent Capital Management LLC
Fund Type: Growth and Income
Inception Date: April 30, 2003

Data Date	Investment Rating	Net Assets ($Mil)	Price	Performance Rating/Pts	Total Return Y-T-D	Risk Rating/Pts
3-12	C+	413.04	16.31	C+ / 6.2	12.63%	B- / 7.4
2011	C	390.20	14.73	C+ / 6.2	6.59%	C+ / 6.6
2010	C	456.14	18.09	C+ / 6.9	27.15%	C- / 3.6
2009	D	304.08	15.59	D+ / 2.4	45.63%	C / 4.7

Major Rating Factors: Middle of the road best describes Advent Claymore Cnv Sec & Inc whose TheStreet.com Investment Rating is currently a C+ (Fair). The fund currently has a performance rating of C+ (Fair) based on an annualized return of 25.75% over the last three years and a total return of 12.63% year to date 2012. Factored into the performance evaluation is an expense ratio of 1.58% (above average).

The fund's risk rating is currently B- (Good). It carries a beta of 1.09, meaning that its performance tracks fairly well with that of the overall stock market. Volatility, as measured by both the semi-deviation and a drawdown factor, is considered low. As of March 31, 2012, Advent Claymore Cnv Sec & Inc traded at a discount of 7.38% below its net asset value, which is worse than its one-year historical average discount of 8.06%.

F. Barry Nelson has been running the fund for 9 years and currently receives a manager quality ranking of 59 (0=worst, 99=best). If you desire an average level of risk, then this fund may be an option.

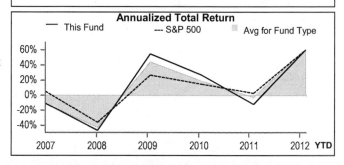

Advent Claymore Enhanced Gr & Inc (LCM)

C-   **Fair**

Fund Family: Guggenheim Funds Investment Advisor
Fund Type: Global
Inception Date: January 26, 2005

Data Date	Investment Rating	Net Assets ($Mil)	Price	Performance Rating/Pts	Total Return Y-T-D	Risk Rating/Pts
3-12	C-	144.53	10.01	C- / 4.1	13.82%	B- / 7.4
2011	C-	138.80	8.98	C- / 3.8	2.67%	B- / 7.3
2010	C-	171.50	11.80	C / 5.0	15.91%	C / 4.3
2009	D+	142.01	11.20	C- / 3.1	48.58%	C / 4.7

Major Rating Factors: Middle of the road best describes Advent Claymore Enhanced Gr & Inc whose TheStreet.com Investment Rating is currently a C- (Fair). The fund currently has a performance rating of C- (Fair) based on an annualized return of 18.48% over the last three years and a total return of 13.82% year to date 2012. Factored into the performance evaluation is an expense ratio of 2.11% (high).

The fund's risk rating is currently B- (Good). It carries a beta of 0.74, meaning the fund's expected move will be 7.4% for every 10% move in the market. Volatility, as measured by both the semi-deviation and a drawdown factor, is considered low. As of March 31, 2012, Advent Claymore Enhanced Gr & Inc traded at a discount of 8.58% below its net asset value, which is better than its one-year historical average discount of 7.70%.

Paul L. Latronica has been running the fund for 5 years and currently receives a manager quality ranking of 79 (0=worst, 99=best). If you desire an average level of risk, then this fund may be an option.

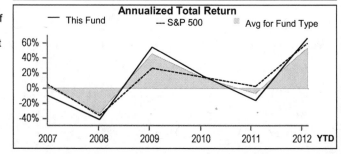

Advent/Claymore Gbl Con Sec & Inc (AGC)   D+   Weak

Fund Family: Guggenheim Funds Investment Advisor
Fund Type: Growth and Income
Inception Date: May 25, 2007

Major Rating Factors: Advent/Claymore Gbl Con Sec & Inc receives a
TheStreet.com Investment Rating of D+ (Weak). The fund currently has a
performance rating of C- (Fair) based on an annualized return of 20.55% over the last
three years and a total return of 11.76% year to date 2012. Factored into the
performance evaluation is an expense ratio of 1.99% (high).

The fund's risk rating is currently C+ (Fair). It carries a beta of 1.13, meaning it is
expected to move 11.3% for every 10% move in the market. Volatility, as measured
by both the semi-deviation and a drawdown factor, is considered low. As of March 31,
2012, Advent/Claymore Gbl Con Sec & Inc traded at a discount of 7.03% below its
net asset value, which is better than its one-year historical average discount of
6.06%.

Hart Woodson has been running the fund for 5 years and currently receives a
manager quality ranking of 30 (0=worst, 99=best). If you desire an average level of
risk, then this fund may be an option.

Data Date	Investment Rating	Net Assets ($Mil)	Price	Performance Rating/Pts	Total Return Y-T-D	Risk Rating/Pts
3-12	D+	238.69	6.88	C- / 4.1	11.76%	C+ / 6.5
2011	D+	224.90	6.30	C- / 3.6	2.70%	C+ / 6.1
2010	E+	300.46	9.17	D / 1.9	22.95%	C- / 3.0
2009	C+	211.61	8.17	A- / 9.1	47.85%	C- / 3.3

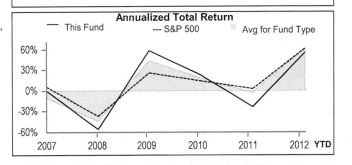

Annualized Total Return

AGIC Convertible & Income Fund (NCV)   B+   Good

Fund Family: Allianz Global Investors Fund Mgmt
Fund Type: Growth and Income
Inception Date: March 26, 2003

Major Rating Factors:
Exceptional performance is the major factor driving the B+ (Good) TheStreet.com
Investment Rating for AGIC Convertible & Income Fund. The fund currently has a
performance rating of A (Excellent) based on an annualized return of 40.32% over the
last three years and a total return of 15.80% year to date 2012. Factored into the
performance evaluation is an expense ratio of 1.27% (average).

The fund's risk rating is currently B- (Good). It carries a beta of 1.31, meaning it is
expected to move 13.1% for every 10% move in the market. Volatility, as measured
by both the semi-deviation and a drawdown factor, is considered low. As of March 31,
2012, AGIC Convertible & Income Fund traded at a premium of 10.34% above its net
asset value, which is worse than its one-year historical average premium of 9.64%.

Douglas G. Forsyth currently receives a manager quality ranking of 84 (0=worst,
99=best). If you desire only a moderate level of risk and strong performance, then this
fund is an excellent option.

Data Date	Investment Rating	Net Assets ($Mil)	Price	Performance Rating/Pts	Total Return Y-T-D	Risk Rating/Pts
3-12	B+	727.23	9.50	A / 9.3	15.80%	B- / 7.3
2011	B	595.10	8.45	B+ / 8.8	4.02%	C+ / 6.5
2010	C-	644.41	10.24	B / 7.9	24.09%	D / 1.7
2009	D+	573.98	9.27	C+ / 5.9	119.23%	D+ / 2.6

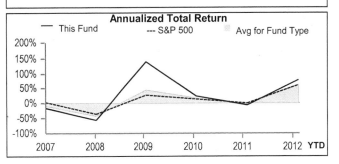

Annualized Total Return

AGIC Convertible & Income Fund II (NCZ)   A-   Excellent

Fund Family: Allianz Global Investors Fund Mgmt
Fund Type: Growth and Income
Inception Date: July 28, 2003

Major Rating Factors:
Exceptional performance is the major factor driving the A- (Excellent) TheStreet.com
Investment Rating for AGIC Convertible & Income Fund II. The fund currently has a
performance rating of A (Excellent) based on an annualized return of 41.62% over the
last three years and a total return of 14.77% year to date 2012. Factored into the
performance evaluation is an expense ratio of 1.29% (average).

The fund's risk rating is currently B- (Good). It carries a beta of 1.20, meaning it is
expected to move 12.0% for every 10% move in the market. Volatility, as measured
by both the semi-deviation and a drawdown factor, is considered low. As of March 31,
2012, AGIC Convertible & Income Fund II traded at a premium of 11.88% above its
net asset value, which is better than its one-year historical average premium of
12.10%.

Douglas G. Forsyth currently receives a manager quality ranking of 89 (0=worst,
99=best). If you desire only a moderate level of risk and strong performance, then this
fund is an excellent option.

Data Date	Investment Rating	Net Assets ($Mil)	Price	Performance Rating/Pts	Total Return Y-T-D	Risk Rating/Pts
3-12	A-	549.13	8.76	A / 9.4	14.77%	B- / 7.6
2011	B	449.50	7.87	A- / 9.0	3.81%	B- / 7.0
2010	C-	487.13	9.37	B- / 7.2	24.41%	D / 1.8
2009	D+	438.12	8.48	C / 5.4	114.55%	D+ / 2.4

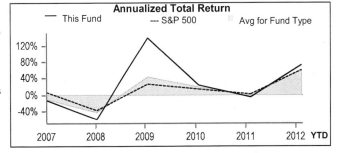

Annualized Total Return

AGIC Equity & Convertible Income F (NIE)

C+   **Fair**

Fund Family: Allianz Global Investors Fund Mgmt
Fund Type: Income
Inception Date: February 27, 2007

Major Rating Factors: Middle of the road best describes AGIC Equity & Convertible Income F whose TheStreet.com Investment Rating is currently a C+ (Fair). The fund currently has a performance rating of C+ (Fair) based on an annualized return of 22.86% over the last three years and a total return of 15.72% year to date 2012. Factored into the performance evaluation is an expense ratio of 1.10% (low).

The fund's risk rating is currently B- (Good). It carries a beta of 0.98, meaning that its performance tracks fairly well with that of the overall stock market. Volatility, as measured by both the semi-deviation and a drawdown factor, is considered low. As of March 31, 2012, AGIC Equity & Convertible Income F traded at a discount of 10.66% below its net asset value, which is better than its one-year historical average discount of 10.65%.

Douglas G. Forsyth currently receives a manager quality ranking of 61 (0=worst, 99=best). If you desire an average level of risk, then this fund may be an option.

Data Date	Investment Rating	Net Assets ($Mil)	Price	Performance Rating/Pts	Total Return Y-T-D	Risk Rating/Pts
3-12	C+	452.41	17.77	C+ / 5.8	15.72%	B- / 7.7
2011	C-	403.70	15.60	C- / 4.1	3.78%	B- / 7.4
2010	C	392.09	18.21	C+ / 5.6	15.68%	C / 5.1
2009	A-	361.94	16.56	B+ / 8.8	39.21%	C / 5.5

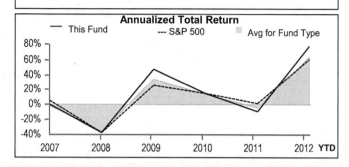

AGIC Global Equity & Conv Inc Fund (NGZ)

C   **Fair**

Fund Family: Allianz Global Investors Fund Mgmt
Fund Type: Global
Inception Date: September 26, 2007

Major Rating Factors: Middle of the road best describes AGIC Global Equity & Conv Inc Fund whose TheStreet.com Investment Rating is currently a C (Fair). The fund currently has a performance rating of C (Fair) based on an annualized return of 22.46% over the last three years and a total return of 12.96% year to date 2012. Factored into the performance evaluation is an expense ratio of 1.29% (average).

The fund's risk rating is currently B- (Good). It carries a beta of 0.91, meaning that its performance tracks fairly well with that of the overall stock market. Volatility, as measured by both the semi-deviation and a drawdown factor, is considered low. As of March 31, 2012, AGIC Global Equity & Conv Inc Fund traded at a discount of 9.82% below its net asset value, which is better than its one-year historical average discount of 7.16%.

Douglas G. Forsyth currently receives a manager quality ranking of 83 (0=worst, 99=best). If you desire an average level of risk, then this fund may be an option.

Data Date	Investment Rating	Net Assets ($Mil)	Price	Performance Rating/Pts	Total Return Y-T-D	Risk Rating/Pts
3-12	C	108.74	14.23	C / 5.1	12.96%	B- / 7.4
2011	C-	101.50	12.86	C / 4.6	2.57%	B- / 7.2
2010	C-	101.85	15.82	C- / 4.2	9.78%	C / 5.4
2009	B+	103.05	15.31	A / 9.5	58.23%	C / 4.5

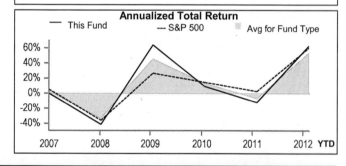

AGIC Intl & Premium Strategy Fund (NAI)

D   **Weak**

Fund Family: Allianz Global Investors Fund Mgmt
Fund Type: Foreign
Inception Date: April 27, 2005

Major Rating Factors: AGIC Intl & Premium Strategy Fund receives a TheStreet.com Investment Rating of D (Weak). The fund currently has a performance rating of C- (Fair) based on an annualized return of 15.31% over the last three years and a total return of 15.01% year to date 2012. Factored into the performance evaluation is an expense ratio of 1.27% (average).

The fund's risk rating is currently C+ (Fair). It carries a beta of 1.03, meaning that its performance tracks fairly well with that of the overall stock market. Volatility, as measured by both the semi-deviation and a drawdown factor, is considered low. As of March 31, 2012, AGIC Intl & Premium Strategy Fund traded at a discount of 2.58% below its net asset value, which is worse than its one-year historical average discount of 3.65%.

Michael E. Yee currently receives a manager quality ranking of 42 (0=worst, 99=best). If you desire an average level of risk, then this fund may be an option.

Data Date	Investment Rating	Net Assets ($Mil)	Price	Performance Rating/Pts	Total Return Y-T-D	Risk Rating/Pts
3-12	D	145.63	10.97	C- / 3.5	15.01%	C+ / 6.0
2011	D	106.50	9.89	D+ / 2.6	1.72%	C+ / 6.0
2010	D-	140.36	14.12	D / 1.9	0.23%	C- / 3.4
2009	C-	145.11	15.48	C- / 4.1	54.35%	C / 4.6

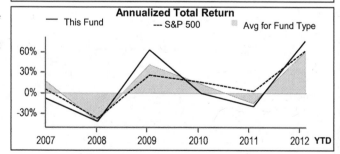

Alliance CA Municipal Income Fund (AKP)

B+   **Good**

Fund Family: AllianceBernstein LP
Fund Type: Municipal - Single State
Inception Date: January 28, 2002

Data Date	Investment Rating	Net Assets ($Mil)	Price	Perfor-mance Rating/Pts	Total Return Y-T-D	Risk Rating/Pts
3-12	B+	119.97	14.71	B / 7.9	2.99%	B / 8.9
2011	A	115.27	14.51	B+ / 8.9	-0.34%	B+ / 9.0
2010	C+	121.80	13.18	C / 4.8	10.12%	C+ / 6.5
2009	C+	112.32	12.80	C / 4.6	38.82%	B- / 7.6

Major Rating Factors: Strong performance is the major factor driving the B+ (Good) TheStreet.com Investment Rating for Alliance CA Municipal Income Fund. The fund currently has a performance rating of B (Good) based on an annualized return of 17.09% over the last three years and a total return of 2.99% year to date 2012. Factored into the performance evaluation is an expense ratio of 1.30% (average).

The fund's risk rating is currently B (Good). It carries a beta of 1.93, meaning it is expected to move 19.3% for every 10% move in the market. Volatility, as measured by both the semi-deviation and a drawdown factor, is considered low. As of March 31, 2012, Alliance CA Municipal Income Fund traded at a premium of 1.31% above its net asset value, which is worse than its one-year historical average discount of 1.95%.

Michael G. Brooks currently receives a manager quality ranking of 56 (0=worst, 99=best). If you desire only a moderate level of risk and strong performance, then this fund is an excellent option.

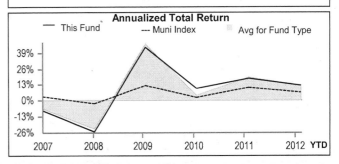

Alliance NY Municipal Income Fund (AYN)

B+   **Good**

Fund Family: AllianceBernstein LP
Fund Type: Municipal - Single State
Inception Date: January 28, 2002

Data Date	Investment Rating	Net Assets ($Mil)	Price	Perfor-mance Rating/Pts	Total Return Y-T-D	Risk Rating/Pts
3-12	B+	69.61	14.81	B- / 7.2	-1.61%	B+ / 9.2
2011	A	68.05	15.27	B+ / 8.8	-0.65%	B+ / 9.3
2010	B+	70.65	14.27	B / 7.8	15.62%	C+ / 6.2
2009	B-	66.38	13.11	C+ / 6.0	41.46%	B- / 7.7

Major Rating Factors: Strong performance is the major factor driving the B+ (Good) TheStreet.com Investment Rating for Alliance NY Municipal Income Fund. The fund currently has a performance rating of B- (Good) based on an annualized return of 17.02% over the last three years and a total return of -1.61% year to date 2012. Factored into the performance evaluation is an expense ratio of 1.44% (average).

The fund's risk rating is currently B+ (Good). It carries a beta of 1.53, meaning it is expected to move 15.3% for every 10% move in the market. Volatility, as measured by both the semi-deviation and a drawdown factor, is considered very low. As of March 31, 2012, Alliance NY Municipal Income Fund traded at a premium of 1.02% above its net asset value, which is worse than its one-year historical average discount of 1.12%.

Michael G. Brooks currently receives a manager quality ranking of 73 (0=worst, 99=best). If you desire only a moderate level of risk and strong performance, then this fund is an excellent option.

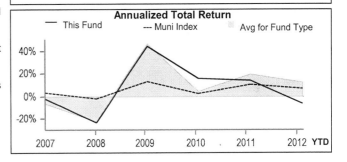

AllianceBernstein Global High Inc (AWF)

B+   **Good**

Fund Family: AllianceBernstein LP
Fund Type: Global
Inception Date: July 23, 1993

Data Date	Investment Rating	Net Assets ($Mil)	Price	Perfor-mance Rating/Pts	Total Return Y-T-D	Risk Rating/Pts
3-12	B+	1,318.65	15.02	B+ / 8.5	7.44%	B / 8.4
2011	B+	1,186.30	14.17	B+ / 8.9	1.48%	B / 8.1
2010	B	1,232.80	14.30	B+ / 8.3	16.34%	C / 5.0
2009	B-	1,144.75	13.29	B / 8.1	86.73%	C / 4.9

Major Rating Factors: Strong performance is the major factor driving the B+ (Good) TheStreet.com Investment Rating for AllianceBernstein Global High Inc. The fund currently has a performance rating of B+ (Good) based on an annualized return of 31.85% over the last three years and a total return of 7.44% year to date 2012. Factored into the performance evaluation is an expense ratio of 1.01% (low).

The fund's risk rating is currently B (Good). It carries a beta of 0.82, meaning the fund's expected move will be 8.2% for every 10% move in the market. Volatility, as measured by both the semi-deviation and a drawdown factor, is considered low. As of March 31, 2012, AllianceBernstein Global High Inc traded at a premium of 1.42% above its net asset value, which is worse than its one-year historical average discount of 1.13%.

Paul J. DeNoon has been running the fund for 20 years and currently receives a manager quality ranking of 96 (0=worst, 99=best). If you desire only a moderate level of risk and strong performance, then this fund is an excellent option.

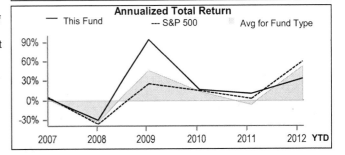

AllianceBernstein Income Fund (ACG)

C   **Fair**

Fund Family: AllianceBernstein LP
Fund Type: Global
Inception Date: August 21, 1987

Major Rating Factors: Middle of the road best describes AllianceBernstein Income Fund whose TheStreet.com Investment Rating is currently a C (Fair). The fund currently has a performance rating of C- (Fair) based on an annualized return of 11.61% over the last three years and a total return of 2.48% year to date 2012. Factored into the performance evaluation is an expense ratio of 0.71% (very low).

The fund's risk rating is currently B+ (Good). It carries a beta of 0.26, meaning the fund's expected move will be 2.6% for every 10% move in the market. Volatility, as measured by both the semi-deviation and a drawdown factor, is considered very low. As of March 31, 2012, AllianceBernstein Income Fund traded at a discount of 9.30% below its net asset value, which is worse than its one-year historical average discount of 10.78%.

Douglas J. Peebles has been running the fund for 25 years and currently receives a manager quality ranking of 85 (0=worst, 99=best). If you desire an average level of risk, then this fund may be an option.

Data Date	Investment Rating	Net Assets ($Mil)	Price	Performance Rating/Pts	Total Return Y-T-D	Risk Rating/Pts
3-12	C	2,126.00	8.19	C- / 3.0	2.48%	B+ / 9.3
2011	C+	2,168.20	8.07	C / 4.5	0.74%	B+ / 9.2
2010	B	2,099.85	7.93	C / 4.7	2.11%	B / 8.3
2009	C+	1,909.28	8.25	C / 5.2	24.26%	B- / 7.4

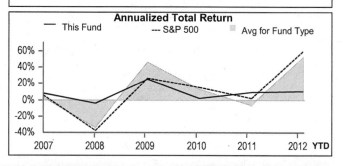

AllianceBernstein Nat Muni Inc Fun (AFB)

B+   **Good**

Fund Family: AllianceBernstein LP
Fund Type: Municipal - National
Inception Date: January 28, 2002

Major Rating Factors: Strong performance is the major factor driving the B+ (Good) TheStreet.com Investment Rating for AllianceBernstein Nat Muni Inc Fun. The fund currently has a performance rating of B- (Good) based on an annualized return of 16.88% over the last three years and a total return of 1.81% year to date 2012. Factored into the performance evaluation is an expense ratio of 1.13% (low).

The fund's risk rating is currently B (Good). It carries a beta of 1.79, meaning it is expected to move 17.9% for every 10% move in the market. Volatility, as measured by both the semi-deviation and a drawdown factor, is considered low. As of March 31, 2012, AllianceBernstein Nat Muni Inc Fun traded at a premium of .34% above its net asset value, which is worse than its one-year historical average discount of 1.49%.

Michael G. Brooks currently receives a manager quality ranking of 62 (0=worst, 99=best). If you desire only a moderate level of risk and strong performance, then this fund is an excellent option.

Data Date	Investment Rating	Net Assets ($Mil)	Price	Performance Rating/Pts	Total Return Y-T-D	Risk Rating/Pts
3-12	B+	409.20	14.81	B- / 7.4	1.81%	B / 8.9
2011	A+	386.44	14.78	A / 9.5	0.81%	B / 8.9
2010	C	403.45	12.94	C / 4.5	3.32%	C+ / 6.1
2009	C+	356.77	13.39	C+ / 6.5	46.57%	C+ / 6.9

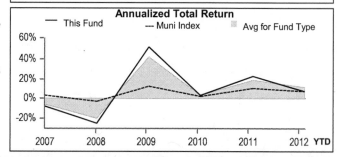

Alpine Global Dynamic Div Fd (AGD)

D-   **Weak**

Fund Family: Alpine Woods Capital Investors LLC
Fund Type: Global
Inception Date: July 26, 2006

Major Rating Factors:
Disappointing performance is the major factor driving the D- (Weak) TheStreet.com Investment Rating for Alpine Global Dynamic Div Fd. The fund currently has a performance rating of D+ (Weak) based on an annualized return of 11.15% over the last three years and a total return of 20.93% year to date 2012. Factored into the performance evaluation is an expense ratio of 1.39% (average).

The fund's risk rating is currently C (Fair). It carries a beta of 1.43, meaning it is expected to move 14.3% for every 10% move in the market. Volatility, as measured by both the semi-deviation and a drawdown factor, is considered average. As of March 31, 2012, Alpine Global Dynamic Div Fd traded at a premium of 8.02% above its net asset value, which is worse than its one-year historical average premium of 4.37%.

Jill K. Evans has been running the fund for 6 years and currently receives a manager quality ranking of 14 (0=worst, 99=best). This fund offers an average level of risk but investors looking for strong performance will be frustrated.

Data Date	Investment Rating	Net Assets ($Mil)	Price	Performance Rating/Pts	Total Return Y-T-D	Risk Rating/Pts
3-12	D-	142.83	6.06	D+ / 2.8	20.93%	C / 5.1
2011	D-	192.55	5.17	D / 1.6	2.90%	C / 4.8
2010	D-	177.05	7.29	E+ / 0.6	-17.71%	C / 4.6
2009	D	147.78	10.13	C- / 3.7	58.82%	C- / 3.3

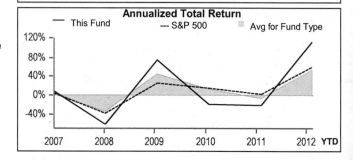

Alpine Global Premier Properties F (AWP) B+ Good

Fund Family: Alpine Woods Capital Investors LLC
Fund Type: Growth and Income
Inception Date: April 25, 2007

Major Rating Factors:
Exceptional performance is the major factor driving the B+ (Good) TheStreet.com Investment Rating for Alpine Global Premier Properties F. The fund currently has a performance rating of A- (Excellent) based on an annualized return of 35.36% over the last three years and a total return of 25.55% year to date 2012. Factored into the performance evaluation is an expense ratio of 1.29% (average).

The fund's risk rating is currently B- (Good). It carries a beta of 1.65, meaning it is expected to move 16.5% for every 10% move in the market. Volatility, as measured by both the semi-deviation and a drawdown factor, is considered low. As of March 31, 2012, Alpine Global Premier Properties F traded at a discount of 12.28% below its net asset value, which is worse than its one-year historical average discount of 13.75%.

Samuel A. Lieber has been running the fund for 5 years and currently receives a manager quality ranking of 48 (0=worst, 99=best). If you desire only a moderate level of risk and strong performance, then this fund is an excellent option.

Data Date	Investment Rating	Net Assets ($Mil)	Price	Performance Rating/Pts	Total Return Y-T-D	Risk Rating/Pts
3-12	B+	758.72	6.50	A- / 9.0	25.55%	B- / 7.1
2011	C	956.40	5.30	C / 5.5	3.02%	C+ / 6.7
2010	D-	794.94	7.09	D / 1.9	21.04%	C / 4.3
2009	B+	528.19	6.23	A+ / 9.7	73.64%	C- / 4.1

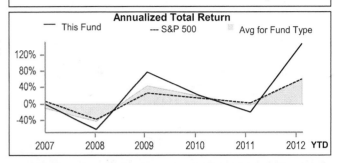

Alpine Total Dynamic Dividend Fund (AOD) D- Weak

Fund Family: Alpine Woods Capital Investors LLC
Fund Type: Global
Inception Date: January 26, 2007

Major Rating Factors:
Disappointing performance is the major factor driving the D- (Weak) TheStreet.com Investment Rating for Alpine Total Dynamic Dividend Fund. The fund currently has a performance rating of D (Weak) based on an annualized return of 5.41% over the last three years and a total return of 12.05% year to date 2012. Factored into the performance evaluation is an expense ratio of 1.35% (average).

The fund's risk rating is currently C (Fair). It carries a beta of 1.24, meaning it is expected to move 12.4% for every 10% move in the market. Volatility, as measured by both the semi-deviation and a drawdown factor, is considered average. As of March 31, 2012, Alpine Total Dynamic Dividend Fund traded at a discount of 7.42% below its net asset value, which is better than its one-year historical average discount of 5.55%.

Jill K. Evans has been running the fund for 5 years and currently receives a manager quality ranking of 13 (0=worst, 99=best). This fund offers an average level of risk but investors looking for strong performance will be frustrated.

Data Date	Investment Rating	Net Assets ($Mil)	Price	Performance Rating/Pts	Total Return Y-T-D	Risk Rating/Pts
3-12	D-	1,134.04	4.74	D / 1.7	12.05%	C / 5.4
2011	D-	1,504.33	4.38	D / 1.6	1.83%	C / 5.0
2010	D-	1,424.57	5.92	E+ / 0.7	-22.17%	C / 4.6
2009	B-	1,321.60	8.92	A / 9.4	61.13%	C- / 3.5

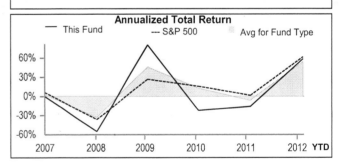

American Income Fund (MRF) C- Fair

Fund Family: US Bancorp Asset Management Inc
Fund Type: Mortgage
Inception Date: December 23, 1988

Major Rating Factors: Middle of the road best describes American Income Fund whose TheStreet.com Investment Rating is currently a C- (Fair). The fund currently has a performance rating of C (Fair) based on an annualized return of 20.53% over the last three years and a total return of 5.26% year to date 2012. Factored into the performance evaluation is an expense ratio of 1.17% (low).

The fund's risk rating is currently B- (Good). It carries a beta of -0.75, meaning the fund's expected move will be -7.5% for every 10% move in the market. Volatility, as measured by both the semi-deviation and a drawdown factor, is considered low. As of March 31, 2012, American Income Fund traded at a discount of 5.89% below its net asset value, which is worse than its one-year historical average discount of 8.29%.

Chris J. Neuharth currently receives a manager quality ranking of 96 (0=worst, 99=best). If you desire an average level of risk, then this fund may be an option.

Data Date	Investment Rating	Net Assets ($Mil)	Price	Performance Rating/Pts	Total Return Y-T-D	Risk Rating/Pts
3-12	C-	80.00	7.99	C / 5.1	5.26%	B- / 7.0
2011	C	77.80	7.69	C+ / 5.9	-1.30%	B- / 7.0
2010	B+	79.00	8.38	B / 7.8	22.25%	C+ / 5.7
2009	C	70.89	7.44	C+ / 5.6	41.22%	C+ / 5.7

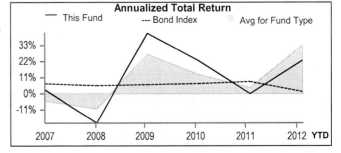

American Municipal Income Portfoli (XAA)

A   Excellent

Fund Family: US Bancorp Asset Management Inc
Fund Type: Municipal - National
Inception Date: June 18, 1993

Major Rating Factors:
Strong performance is the major factor driving the A (Excellent) TheStreet.com Investment Rating for American Municipal Income Portfoli. The fund currently has a performance rating of B+ (Good) based on an annualized return of 19.91% over the last three years and a total return of 3.25% year to date 2012. Factored into the performance evaluation is an expense ratio of 1.37% (average).

The fund's risk rating is currently B (Good). It carries a beta of 1.84, meaning it is expected to move 18.4% for every 10% move in the market. Volatility, as measured by both the semi-deviation and a drawdown factor, is considered low. As of March 31, 2012, American Municipal Income Portfoli traded at a discount of 2.04% below its net asset value, which is worse than its one-year historical average discount of 3.08%.

Christopher L. Drahn currently receives a manager quality ranking of 74 (0=worst, 99=best). If you desire only a moderate level of risk and strong performance, then this fund is an excellent option.

Data Date	Investment Rating	Net Assets ($Mil)	Price	Performance Rating/Pts	Total Return Y-T-D	Risk Rating/Pts
3-12	A	82.00	14.87	B+ / 8.7	3.25%	B / 8.8
2011	A+	84.30	14.55	A+ / 9.6	0.70%	B / 8.9
2010	C+	85.00	12.94	C / 5.4	-1.06%	C+ / 6.1
2009	A-	75.12	13.95	B / 7.8	71.92%	C+ / 6.3

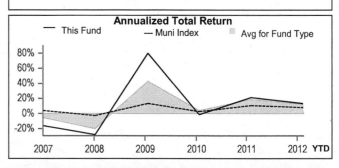

Annualized Total Return

American Select Portfolio (SLA)

C   Fair

Fund Family: US Bancorp Asset Management Inc
Fund Type: Mortgage
Inception Date: September 14, 1993

Major Rating Factors: Middle of the road best describes American Select Portfolio whose TheStreet.com Investment Rating is currently a C (Fair). The fund currently has a performance rating of C (Fair) based on an annualized return of 19.66% over the last three years and a total return of 5.48% year to date 2012. Factored into the performance evaluation is an expense ratio of 2.73% (high).

The fund's risk rating is currently B (Good). It carries a beta of -0.79, meaning the fund's expected move will be -7.9% for every 10% move in the market. Volatility, as measured by both the semi-deviation and a drawdown factor, is considered low. As of March 31, 2012, American Select Portfolio traded at a discount of 10.57% below its net asset value, which is worse than its one-year historical average discount of 12.39%.

Jason J. O'Brien currently receives a manager quality ranking of 95 (0=worst, 99=best). If you desire an average level of risk, then this fund may be an option.

Data Date	Investment Rating	Net Assets ($Mil)	Price	Performance Rating/Pts	Total Return Y-T-D	Risk Rating/Pts
3-12	C	123.00	10.41	C / 4.8	5.48%	B / 8.0
2011	C	121.80	10.00	C / 4.8	-0.30%	B- / 7.9
2010	C+	129.00	10.46	C / 4.9	3.75%	B- / 7.2
2009	C	131.42	11.37	C / 5.1	28.48%	C+ / 6.5

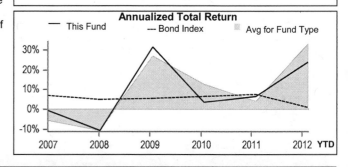

Annualized Total Return

American Strat Inc Portfolio (ASP)

B-   Good

Fund Family: US Bancorp Asset Management Inc
Fund Type: Mortgage
Inception Date: December 19, 1991

Major Rating Factors: American Strat Inc Portfolio receives a TheStreet.com Investment Rating of B- (Good). The fund currently has a performance rating of C+ (Fair) based on an annualized return of 24.65% over the last three years and a total return of 10.81% year to date 2012. Factored into the performance evaluation is an expense ratio of 2.43% (high).

The fund's risk rating is currently B (Good). It carries a beta of -0.07, meaning the fund's expected move will be -0.7% for every 10% move in the market. Volatility, as measured by both the semi-deviation and a drawdown factor, is considered low. As of March 31, 2012, American Strat Inc Portfolio traded at a discount of 7.89% below its net asset value, which is worse than its one-year historical average discount of 11.95%.

Jason J. O'Brien currently receives a manager quality ranking of 96 (0=worst, 99=best). If you desire an average level of risk, then this fund may be an option.

Data Date	Investment Rating	Net Assets ($Mil)	Price	Performance Rating/Pts	Total Return Y-T-D	Risk Rating/Pts
3-12	B-	53.00	11.67	C+ / 6.8	10.81%	B / 8.2
2011	C+	52.70	10.67	C+ / 5.6	0.37%	B- / 7.9
2010	B+	56.00	12.06	B / 7.6	16.86%	C+ / 5.8
2009	B-	52.66	11.31	C+ / 6.1	37.38%	B- / 7.1

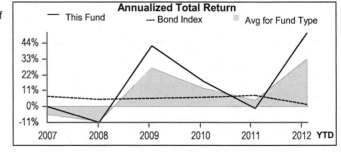

Annualized Total Return

American Strat Inc Portfolio II (BSP)

C-   **Fair**

Fund Family: US Bancorp Asset Management Inc
Fund Type: Mortgage
Inception Date: July 23, 1992

Major Rating Factors: Middle of the road best describes American Strat Inc Portfolio II whose TheStreet.com Investment Rating is currently a C- (Fair). The fund currently has a performance rating of C- (Fair) based on an annualized return of 14.25% over the last three years and a total return of 4.24% year to date 2012. Factored into the performance evaluation is an expense ratio of 2.68% (high).

    The fund's risk rating is currently B- (Good). It carries a beta of -1.24, meaning the fund's expected move will be -12.4% for every 10% move in the market. Volatility, as measured by both the semi-deviation and a drawdown factor, is considered low. As of March 31, 2012, American Strat Inc Portfolio II traded at a discount of 15.48% below its net asset value, which is worse than its one-year historical average discount of 15.52%.

    Jason J. O'Brien currently receives a manager quality ranking of 94 (0=worst, 99=best). If you desire an average level of risk, then this fund may be an option.

Data Date	Investment Rating	Net Assets ($Mil)	Price	Performance Rating/Pts	Total Return Y-T-D	Risk Rating/Pts
3-12	C-	160.00	8.30	C- / 3.1	4.24%	B- / 7.9
2011	C-	155.30	8.06	C- / 3.5	-0.74%	B- / 7.9
2010	C+	173.00	9.32	C / 4.6	4.13%	B- / 7.4
2009	C+	181.53	10.16	C / 5.0	29.23%	B- / 7.0

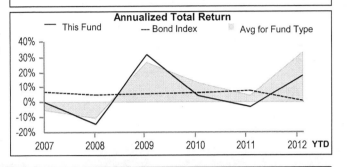

Annualized Total Return

American Strat Inc Portfolio III (CSP)

D   **Weak**

Fund Family: US Bancorp Asset Management Inc
Fund Type: Mortgage
Inception Date: March 18, 1993

Major Rating Factors:
Disappointing performance is the major factor driving the D (Weak) TheStreet.com Investment Rating for American Strat Inc Portfolio III. The fund currently has a performance rating of D+ (Weak) based on an annualized return of 9.41% over the last three years and a total return of 8.55% year to date 2012. Factored into the performance evaluation is an expense ratio of 2.72% (high).

    The fund's risk rating is currently B- (Good). It carries a beta of -0.42, meaning the fund's expected move will be -4.2% for every 10% move in the market. Volatility, as measured by both the semi-deviation and a drawdown factor, is considered low. As of March 31, 2012, American Strat Inc Portfolio III traded at a discount of 14.32% below its net asset value, which is worse than its one-year historical average discount of 14.67%.

    Jason J. O'Brien currently receives a manager quality ranking of 88 (0=worst, 99=best). This fund offers only a moderate level of risk but investors looking for strong performance are still waiting.

Data Date	Investment Rating	Net Assets ($Mil)	Price	Performance Rating/Pts	Total Return Y-T-D	Risk Rating/Pts
3-12	D	180.00	7.00	D+ / 2.4	8.55%	B- / 7.5
2011	D	172.80	6.52	D / 1.9	0.61%	B- / 7.3
2010	C-	196.00	7.65	D / 1.8	0.02%	B- / 7.2
2009	C-	227.89	8.79	D / 1.9	9.46%	C+ / 6.9

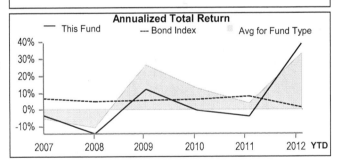

Annualized Total Return

Apollo Senior Floating Rate Fd Inc (AFT)

D+   **Weak**

Fund Family: Apollo Investment Management LP
Fund Type: Loan Participation
Inception Date: February 24, 2011

Major Rating Factors:
Disappointing performance is the major factor driving the D+ (Weak) TheStreet.com Investment Rating for Apollo Senior Floating Rate Fd Inc. The fund currently has a performance rating of D+ (Weak) based on an annualized return of 0.00% over the last three years and a total return of 13.90% year to date 2012. Factored into the performance evaluation is an expense ratio of 2.03% (high).

    The fund's risk rating is currently B- (Good). It carries a beta of 0.00, meaning the fund's expected move will be 0.0% for every 10% move in the market. Volatility, as measured by both the semi-deviation and a drawdown factor, is considered low. As of March 31, 2012, Apollo Senior Floating Rate Fd Inc traded at a discount of 2.50% below its net asset value, which is worse than its one-year historical average discount of 4.65%.

    This fund has been team managed for 1 year and currently receives a manager quality ranking of 98 (0=worst, 99=best). This fund offers only a moderate level of risk but investors looking for strong performance are still waiting.

Data Date	Investment Rating	Net Assets ($Mil)	Price	Performance Rating/Pts	Total Return Y-T-D	Risk Rating/Pts
3-12	D+	273.46	17.91	D+ / 2.9	13.90%	B- / 7.3

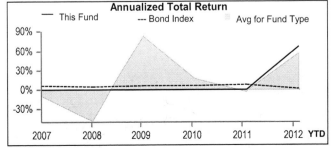

Annualized Total Return

ASA Gold & Precious Metals Ltd (ASA) E+ Very Weak

Fund Family: ASA Limited
Fund Type: Precious Metals
Inception Date: N/A

Major Rating Factors: ASA Gold & Precious Metals Ltd has adopted a risky asset allocation strategy and currently receives an overall TheStreet.com Investment Rating of E+ (Very Weak). The fund has an above average level of volatility, as measured by both semi-deviation and drawdown factors. It carries a beta of 1.06, meaning that its performance tracks fairly well with that of the overall stock market. As of March 31, 2012, ASA Gold & Precious Metals Ltd traded at a discount of 5.78% below its net asset value, which is worse than its one-year historical average discount of 9.24%. Unfortunately, the high level of risk (D+, Weak) failed to pay off as investors endured poor performance.

The fund's performance rating is currently D+ (Weak). It has registered an annualized return of 15.95% over the last three years but is down -1.59% year to date 2012. Factored into the performance evaluation is an expense ratio of 0.60% (very low).

David J. Christensen currently receives a manager quality ranking of 18 (0=worst, 99=best). If you can tolerate high levels of risk in the hope of improved future returns, holding this fund may be an option.

Data Date	Investment Rating	Net Assets ($Mil)	Price	Perfor-mance Rating/Pts	Total Return Y-T-D	Risk Rating/Pts
3-12	E+	626.08	25.77	D+ / 2.7	-1.59%	D+ / 2.8
2011	D	549.40	26.19	C+ / 6.3	2.90%	D+ / 2.5
2010	C	580.36	34.71	B+ / 8.9	35.98%	D / 1.6
2009	C	552.52	77.45	B / 7.6	57.73%	C- / 4.0

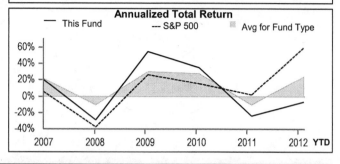

Asia Pacific Fund (APB) D+ Weak

Fund Family: Baring Asset Management (Asia) Limi
Fund Type: Foreign
Inception Date: April 24, 1987

Major Rating Factors: Asia Pacific Fund receives a TheStreet.com Investment Rating of D+ (Weak). The fund currently has a performance rating of C- (Fair) based on an annualized return of 16.39% over the last three years and a total return of 12.55% year to date 2012. Factored into the performance evaluation is an expense ratio of 2.01% (high).

The fund's risk rating is currently B- (Good). It carries a beta of 1.11, meaning it is expected to move 11.1% for every 10% move in the market. Volatility, as measured by both the semi-deviation and a drawdown factor, is considered low. As of March 31, 2012, Asia Pacific Fund traded at a discount of 9.34% below its net asset value, which is better than its one-year historical average discount of 9.11%.

Khiem T. Do has been running the fund for 8 years and currently receives a manager quality ranking of 42 (0=worst, 99=best). If you desire an average level of risk, then this fund may be an option.

Data Date	Investment Rating	Net Assets ($Mil)	Price	Perfor-mance Rating/Pts	Total Return Y-T-D	Risk Rating/Pts
3-12	D+	135.08	10.58	C- / 3.5	12.55%	B- / 7.2
2011	C-	107.30	9.40	C- / 3.6	1.06%	B- / 7.2
2010	D	113.44	11.95	C / 4.6	14.90%	C- / 3.3
2009	C-	105.97	10.40	C+ / 6.7	54.07%	D+ / 2.4

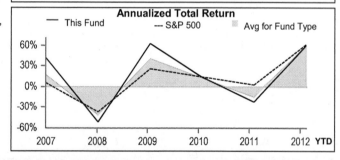

Asia Tigers Fund (GRR) D Weak

Fund Family: Aberdeen Asset Management Asia Ltd
Fund Type: Foreign
Inception Date: November 29, 1993

Major Rating Factors: Asia Tigers Fund receives a TheStreet.com Investment Rating of D (Weak). The fund currently has a performance rating of C- (Fair) based on an annualized return of 14.58% over the last three years and a total return of 12.89% year to date 2012. Factored into the performance evaluation is an expense ratio of 2.36% (high).

The fund's risk rating is currently C+ (Fair). It carries a beta of 1.00, meaning that its performance tracks fairly well with that of the overall stock market. Volatility, as measured by both the semi-deviation and a drawdown factor, is considered low. As of March 31, 2012, Asia Tigers Fund traded at a discount of 8.01% below its net asset value, which is better than its one-year historical average discount of 7.11%.

Gregory S. Geiling currently receives a manager quality ranking of 39 (0=worst, 99=best). If you desire an average level of risk, then this fund may be an option.

Data Date	Investment Rating	Net Assets ($Mil)	Price	Perfor-mance Rating/Pts	Total Return Y-T-D	Risk Rating/Pts
3-12	D	57.14	13.56	C- / 3.1	12.89%	C+ / 5.8
2011	D	79.92	12.01	C- / 3.3	2.25%	C / 5.5
2010	D-	77.15	19.68	D- / 1.3	2.50%	C- / 3.7
2009	C	54.83	19.20	B- / 7.2	70.92%	C / 4.3

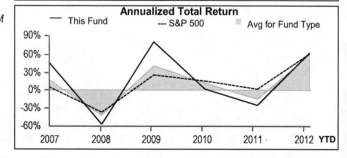

Avenue Income Credit Strategies (ACP)　　　　　D　　　Weak

Fund Family: Avenue Capital Management II LP
Fund Type: Loan Participation
Inception Date: January 27, 2011

Major Rating Factors:
Disappointing performance is the major factor driving the D (Weak) TheStreet.com Investment Rating for Avenue Income Credit Strategies. The fund currently has a performance rating of D (Weak) based on an annualized return of 0.00% over the last three years and a total return of 9.25% year to date 2012. Factored into the performance evaluation is an expense ratio of 2.50% (high).

　　The fund's risk rating is currently B- (Good). It carries a beta of 0.00, meaning the fund's expected move will be 0.0% for every 10% move in the market. Volatility, as measured by both the semi-deviation and a drawdown factor, is considered low. As of March 31, 2012, Avenue Income Credit Strategies traded at a discount of 4.93% below its net asset value, which is better than its one-year historical average discount of 1.45%.

　　Mr. Symington has been running the fund for 1 year and currently receives a manager quality ranking of 98 (0=worst, 99=best). This fund offers only a moderate level of risk but investors looking for strong performance are still waiting.

Data Date	Investment Rating	Net Assets ($Mil)	Price	Performance Rating/Pts	Total Return Y-T-D	Risk Rating/Pts
3-12	D	126.59	16.58	D / 1.8	9.25%	B- / 7.2

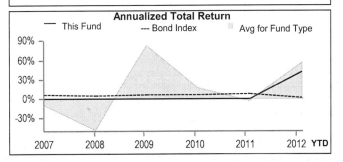

Bancroft Fund Ltd. (BCV)　　　　　　　　　　C　　　Fair

Fund Family: Dinsmore Capital Management Co
Fund Type: Growth and Income
Inception Date: April 20, 1971

Major Rating Factors: Middle of the road best describes Bancroft Fund Ltd. whose TheStreet.com Investment Rating is currently a C (Fair). The fund currently has a performance rating of C (Fair) based on an annualized return of 18.46% over the last three years and a total return of 11.23% year to date 2012. Factored into the performance evaluation is an expense ratio of 1.10% (low).

　　The fund's risk rating is currently B (Good). It carries a beta of 0.77, meaning the fund's expected move will be 7.7% for every 10% move in the market. Volatility, as measured by both the semi-deviation and a drawdown factor, is considered low. As of March 31, 2012, Bancroft Fund Ltd. traded at a discount of 13.97% below its net asset value, which is better than its one-year historical average discount of 13.29%.

　　Thomas H. Dinsmore has been running the fund for 16 years and currently receives a manager quality ranking of 59 (0=worst, 99=best). If you desire an average level of risk, then this fund may be an option.

Data Date	Investment Rating	Net Assets ($Mil)	Price	Performance Rating/Pts	Total Return Y-T-D	Risk Rating/Pts
3-12	C	98.21	16.69	C / 4.3	11.23%	B / 8.4
2011	C	95.00	15.12	C- / 4.2	2.31%	B / 8.3
2010	C	97.60	16.92	C / 4.9	17.38%	C+ / 5.7
2009	C	72.89	15.03	C- / 4.2	41.99%	C+ / 6.0

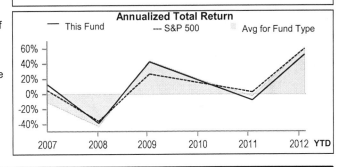

BlackRock Build America Bond (BBN)　　　　A+　　　Excellent

Fund Family: BlackRock Inc
Fund Type: Municipal - National
Inception Date: August 27, 2010

Major Rating Factors:
Exceptional performance is the major factor driving the A+ (Excellent) TheStreet.com Investment Rating for BlackRock Build America Bond. The fund currently has a performance rating of A+ (Excellent) based on an annualized return of 0.00% over the last three years and a total return of 1.68% year to date 2012. Factored into the performance evaluation is an expense ratio of 1.06% (low).

　　The fund's risk rating is currently B (Good). It carries a beta of 0.00, meaning the fund's expected move will be 0.0% for every 10% move in the market. Volatility, as measured by both the semi-deviation and a drawdown factor, is considered low. As of March 31, 2012, BlackRock Build America Bond traded at a discount of 4.58% below its net asset value, which is worse than its one-year historical average discount of 6.07%.

　　Jonathan A. Clark currently receives a manager quality ranking of 81 (0=worst, 99=best). If you desire only a moderate level of risk and strong performance, then this fund is an excellent option.

Data Date	Investment Rating	Net Assets ($Mil)	Price	Performance Rating/Pts	Total Return Y-T-D	Risk Rating/Pts
3-12	A+	1,164.02	21.45	A+ / 9.7	1.68%	B / 8.5
2011	A+	1,260.90	21.35	A+ / 9.9	0.23%	B / 8.5

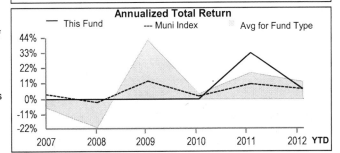

BlackRock CA Muni 2018 Income Trus (BJZ)

C+   Fair

Fund Family: BlackRock Inc
Fund Type: Municipal - Single State
Inception Date: October 25, 2001

Major Rating Factors: Middle of the road best describes BlackRock CA Muni 2018 Income Trus whose TheStreet.com Investment Rating is currently a C+ (Fair). The fund currently has a performance rating of C (Fair) based on an annualized return of 11.23% over the last three years and a total return of 2.07% year to date 2012. Factored into the performance evaluation is an expense ratio of 0.91% (low).

The fund's risk rating is currently B+ (Good). It carries a beta of 0.34, meaning the fund's expected move will be 3.4% for every 10% move in the market. Volatility, as measured by both the semi-deviation and a drawdown factor, is considered very low. As of March 31, 2012, BlackRock CA Muni 2018 Income Trus traded at a premium of 6.20% above its net asset value, which is worse than its one-year historical average premium of 6.13%.

Theodore R. Jaeckel, Jr. has been running the fund for 6 years and currently receives a manager quality ranking of 84 (0=worst, 99=best). If you desire an average level of risk, then this fund may be an option.

Data Date	Investment Rating	Net Assets ($Mil)	Price	Perfor-mance Rating/Pts	Total Return Y-T-D	Risk Rating/Pts
3-12	C+	100.35	16.45	C / 4.3	2.07%	B+ / 9.4
2011	B	100.30	16.34	C+ / 6.7	-0.18%	B+ / 9.4
2010	C+	94.69	15.38	C+ / 6.9	8.02%	C+ / 6.8
2009	B-	85.16	15.09	C+ / 6.4	39.10%	B- / 7.4

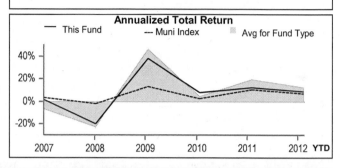
Annualized Total Return

BlackRock CA Municipal Income Trus (BFZ)

B+   Good

Fund Family: BlackRock Inc
Fund Type: Municipal - Single State
Inception Date: July 26, 2001

Major Rating Factors: Strong performance is the major factor driving the B+ (Good) TheStreet.com Investment Rating for BlackRock CA Municipal Income Trus. The fund currently has a performance rating of B (Good) based on an annualized return of 16.85% over the last three years and a total return of 3.64% year to date 2012. Factored into the performance evaluation is an expense ratio of 1.39% (average).

The fund's risk rating is currently B (Good). It carries a beta of 2.57, meaning it is expected to move 25.7% for every 10% move in the market. Volatility, as measured by both the semi-deviation and a drawdown factor, is considered low. As of March 31, 2012, BlackRock CA Municipal Income Trus traded at a discount of 3.28% below its net asset value, which is better than its one-year historical average discount of 3.18%.

Theodore R. Jaeckel, Jr. has been running the fund for 6 years and currently receives a manager quality ranking of 35 (0=worst, 99=best). If you desire only a moderate level of risk and strong performance, then this fund is an excellent option.

Data Date	Investment Rating	Net Assets ($Mil)	Price	Perfor-mance Rating/Pts	Total Return Y-T-D	Risk Rating/Pts
3-12	B+	441.75	15.02	B / 8.2	3.64%	B / 8.4
2011	A	472.90	14.71	A / 9.3	1.32%	B / 8.4
2010	D+	454.30	12.80	D / 1.7	3.76%	C+ / 6.7
2009	C	192.55	13.18	C / 4.3	47.74%	C+ / 6.7

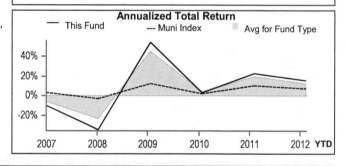
Annualized Total Return

BlackRock Core Bond Trust (BHK)

C   Fair

Fund Family: BlackRock Inc
Fund Type: General - Investment Grade
Inception Date: November 27, 2001

Major Rating Factors: Middle of the road best describes BlackRock Core Bond Trust whose TheStreet.com Investment Rating is currently a C (Fair). The fund currently has a performance rating of C (Fair) based on an annualized return of 18.81% over the last three years and a total return of 2.83% year to date 2012. Factored into the performance evaluation is an expense ratio of 1.02% (low).

The fund's risk rating is currently B (Good). It carries a beta of 2.20, meaning it is expected to move 22.0% for every 10% move in the market. Volatility, as measured by both the semi-deviation and a drawdown factor, is considered low. As of March 31, 2012, BlackRock Core Bond Trust traded at a discount of 3.30% below its net asset value, which is worse than its one-year historical average discount of 6.54%.

James E. Keenan currently receives a manager quality ranking of 61 (0=worst, 99=best). If you desire an average level of risk, then this fund may be an option.

Data Date	Investment Rating	Net Assets ($Mil)	Price	Perfor-mance Rating/Pts	Total Return Y-T-D	Risk Rating/Pts
3-12	C	372.30	13.77	C / 4.8	2.83%	B / 8.5
2011	B-	382.30	13.52	C+ / 6.3	-0.22%	B / 8.8
2010	C+	383.54	12.52	C+ / 6.1	12.69%	C+ / 6.6
2009	C	339.52	11.89	C / 4.4	14.41%	C+ / 6.8

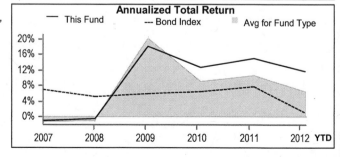
Annualized Total Return

BlackRock Corporate High Yield Fun (COY)

B   **Good**

Fund Family: BlackRock Inc
Fund Type: Corporate - High Yield
Inception Date: June 18, 1993

Major Rating Factors: Strong performance is the major factor driving the B (Good) TheStreet.com Investment Rating for BlackRock Corporate High Yield Fun. The fund currently has a performance rating of B+ (Good) based on an annualized return of 32.92% over the last three years and a total return of 3.37% year to date 2012. Factored into the performance evaluation is an expense ratio of 1.18% (low).

    The fund's risk rating is currently B- (Good). It carries a beta of 1.11, meaning it is expected to move 11.1% for every 10% move in the market. Volatility, as measured by both the semi-deviation and a drawdown factor, is considered low. As of March 31, 2012, BlackRock Corporate High Yield Fun traded at a premium of 1.66% above its net asset value, which is worse than its one-year historical average premium of 1.12%.

    James E. Keenan has been running the fund for 6 years and currently receives a manager quality ranking of 78 (0=worst, 99=best). If you desire only a moderate level of risk and strong performance, then this fund is an excellent option.

Data Date	Investment Rating	Net Assets ($Mil)	Price	Performance Rating/Pts	Total Return Y-T-D	Risk Rating/Pts
3-12	B	257.91	7.35	B+ / 8.5	3.37%	B- / 7.1
2011	B	237.10	7.21	B+ / 8.8	0.42%	B- / 7.0
2010	C	237.85	6.79	B- / 7.1	7.13%	C- / 3.3
2009	C+	202.65	6.89	B / 7.9	93.36%	C- / 3.8

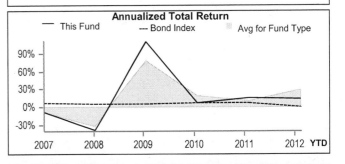

Annualized Total Return

BlackRock Corporate High Yield III (CYE)

B   **Good**

Fund Family: BlackRock Inc
Fund Type: Corporate - High Yield
Inception Date: January 27, 1998

Major Rating Factors:
Exceptional performance is the major factor driving the B (Good) TheStreet.com Investment Rating for BlackRock Corporate High Yield III. The fund currently has a performance rating of A- (Excellent) based on an annualized return of 36.91% over the last three years and a total return of 8.69% year to date 2012. Factored into the performance evaluation is an expense ratio of 1.37% (average).

    The fund's risk rating is currently B- (Good). It carries a beta of 1.25, meaning it is expected to move 12.5% for every 10% move in the market. Volatility, as measured by both the semi-deviation and a drawdown factor, is considered low. As of March 31, 2012, BlackRock Corporate High Yield III traded at a premium of 3.27% above its net asset value, which is worse than its one-year historical average discount of .90%.

    James E. Keenan has been running the fund for 3 years and currently receives a manager quality ranking of 77 (0=worst, 99=best). If you desire only a moderate level of risk and strong performance, then this fund is an excellent option.

Data Date	Investment Rating	Net Assets ($Mil)	Price	Performance Rating/Pts	Total Return Y-T-D	Risk Rating/Pts
3-12	B	282.26	7.59	A- / 9.1	8.69%	B- / 7.0
2011	B	257.80	7.08	B+ / 8.9	-0.56%	C+ / 6.8
2010	C	257.76	6.77	B / 7.7	16.70%	C- / 3.6
2009	C	215.35	6.35	B / 7.6	86.99%	C- / 3.4

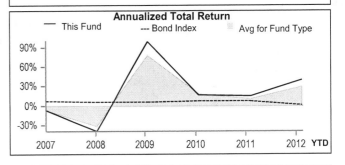

Annualized Total Return

BlackRock Corporate High Yield V (HYV)

B   **Good**

Fund Family: BlackRock Inc
Fund Type: Corporate - High Yield
Inception Date: November 27, 2001

Major Rating Factors:
Exceptional performance is the major factor driving the B (Good) TheStreet.com Investment Rating for BlackRock Corporate High Yield V. The fund currently has a performance rating of A- (Excellent) based on an annualized return of 35.42% over the last three years and a total return of 8.86% year to date 2012. Factored into the performance evaluation is an expense ratio of 1.34% (average).

    The fund's risk rating is currently B- (Good). It carries a beta of 1.23, meaning it is expected to move 12.3% for every 10% move in the market. Volatility, as measured by both the semi-deviation and a drawdown factor, is considered low. As of March 31, 2012, BlackRock Corporate High Yield V traded at a premium of 1.87% above its net asset value, which is worse than its one-year historical average discount of 1.40%.

    Robert C. Doll, Jr. currently receives a manager quality ranking of 78 (0=worst, 99=best). If you desire only a moderate level of risk and strong performance, then this fund is an excellent option.

Data Date	Investment Rating	Net Assets ($Mil)	Price	Performance Rating/Pts	Total Return Y-T-D	Risk Rating/Pts
3-12	B	385.69	12.55	A- / 9.0	8.86%	B- / 7.0
2011	B	380.60	11.69	A- / 9.0	1.37%	C+ / 6.9
2010	C+	382.60	11.54	B / 8.2	20.80%	C- / 3.7
2009	C	320.05	10.48	B / 7.6	84.43%	C- / 3.6

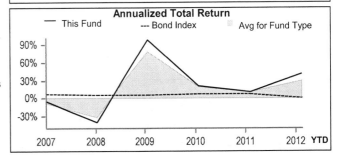

Annualized Total Return

BlackRock Corporate High Yield VI (HYT)   B   Good

Fund Family: BlackRock Inc
Fund Type: Corporate - High Yield
Inception Date: May 28, 2003

Major Rating Factors: Strong performance is the major factor driving the B (Good) TheStreet.com Investment Rating for BlackRock Corporate High Yield VI. The fund currently has a performance rating of B+ (Good) based on an annualized return of 34.19% over the last three years and a total return of 10.65% year to date 2012. Factored into the performance evaluation is an expense ratio of 1.41% (average).

The fund's risk rating is currently B- (Good). It carries a beta of 1.22, meaning it is expected to move 12.2% for every 10% move in the market. Volatility, as measured by both the semi-deviation and a drawdown factor, is considered low. As of March 31, 2012, BlackRock Corporate High Yield VI traded at a premium of 3.16% above its net asset value, which is worse than its one-year historical average discount of 1.38%.

James E. Keenan has been running the fund for 6 years and currently receives a manager quality ranking of 76 (0=worst, 99=best). If you desire only a moderate level of risk and strong performance, then this fund is an excellent option.

Data Date	Investment Rating	Net Assets ($Mil)	Price	Performance Rating/Pts	Total Return Y-T-D	Risk Rating/Pts
3-12	B	405.70	12.42	B+ / 8.9	10.65%	B- / 7.1
2011	B	399.40	11.38	B+ / 8.7	1.67%	B- / 7.1
2010	C+	401.76	11.63	B+ / 8.3	19.98%	C- / 3.7
2009	C	341.42	10.60	B / 7.7	84.31%	C- / 3.8

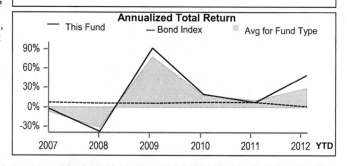

BlackRock Credit Alloc Inc Tr I (PSW)   A+   Excellent

Fund Family: BlackRock Inc
Fund Type: Income
Inception Date: July 29, 2003

Major Rating Factors:
Exceptional performance is the major factor driving the A+ (Excellent) TheStreet.com Investment Rating for BlackRock Credit Alloc Inc Tr I. The fund currently has a performance rating of A- (Excellent) based on an annualized return of 37.91% over the last three years and a total return of 7.62% year to date 2012. Factored into the performance evaluation is an expense ratio of 1.14% (low).

The fund's risk rating is currently B (Good). It carries a beta of 0.62, meaning the fund's expected move will be 6.2% for every 10% move in the market. Volatility, as measured by both the semi-deviation and a drawdown factor, is considered low. As of March 31, 2012, BlackRock Credit Alloc Inc Tr I traded at a discount of 8.09% below its net asset value, which is worse than its one-year historical average discount of 11.32%.

Jeffrey Cucunato has been running the fund for 1 year and currently receives a manager quality ranking of 95 (0=worst, 99=best). If you desire only a moderate level of risk and strong performance, then this fund is an excellent option.

Data Date	Investment Rating	Net Assets ($Mil)	Price	Performance Rating/Pts	Total Return Y-T-D	Risk Rating/Pts
3-12	A+	108.53	9.88	A- / 9.2	7.62%	B / 8.7
2011	B-	105.70	9.29	B- / 7.4	-0.65%	B- / 7.1
2010	D-	107.25	9.15	D- / 1.1	16.85%	C- / 3.9
2009	E+	57.85	8.38	E+ / 0.8	45.81%	C- / 3.6

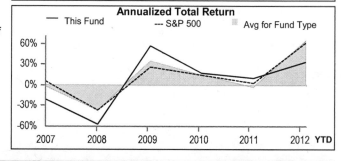

BlackRock Credit Alloc Inc Tr II (PSY)   A+   Excellent

Fund Family: BlackRock Inc
Fund Type: Income
Inception Date: March 25, 2003

Major Rating Factors:
Strong performance is the major factor driving the A+ (Excellent) TheStreet.com Investment Rating for BlackRock Credit Alloc Inc Tr II. The fund currently has a performance rating of B+ (Good) based on an annualized return of 35.57% over the last three years and a total return of 8.15% year to date 2012. Factored into the performance evaluation is an expense ratio of 1.12% (low).

The fund's risk rating is currently B (Good). It carries a beta of 0.58, meaning the fund's expected move will be 5.8% for every 10% move in the market. Volatility, as measured by both the semi-deviation and a drawdown factor, is considered low. As of March 31, 2012, BlackRock Credit Alloc Inc Tr II traded at a discount of 9.08% below its net asset value, which is worse than its one-year historical average discount of 11.40%.

Jeffrey Cucunato has been running the fund for 1 year and currently receives a manager quality ranking of 95 (0=worst, 99=best). If you desire only a moderate level of risk and strong performance, then this fund is an excellent option.

Data Date	Investment Rating	Net Assets ($Mil)	Price	Performance Rating/Pts	Total Return Y-T-D	Risk Rating/Pts
3-12	A+	459.28	10.51	B+ / 8.9	8.15%	B / 8.8
2011	B-	451.80	9.83	B- / 7.3	0.61%	B- / 7.4
2010	D-	463.33	9.83	D- / 1.4	12.62%	C- / 4.2
2009	E+	238.93	9.38	D / 1.6	60.13%	C- / 3.5

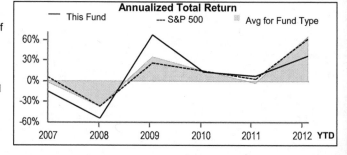

BlackRock Credit Alloc Inc Tr III (BPP)   A   Excellent

Fund Family: BlackRock Inc
Fund Type: Global
Inception Date: February 25, 2003

Major Rating Factors:
Strong performance is the major factor driving the A (Excellent) TheStreet.com Investment Rating for BlackRock Credit Alloc Inc Tr III. The fund currently has a performance rating of B+ (Good) based on an annualized return of 33.00% over the last three years and a total return of 7.75% year to date 2012. Factored into the performance evaluation is an expense ratio of 1.05% (low).

The fund's risk rating is currently B (Good). It carries a beta of 0.71, meaning the fund's expected move will be 7.1% for every 10% move in the market. Volatility, as measured by both the semi-deviation and a drawdown factor, is considered low. As of March 31, 2012, BlackRock Credit Alloc Inc Tr III traded at a discount of 9.51% below its net asset value, which is worse than its one-year historical average discount of 12.06%.

Jeffrey Cucunato has been running the fund for 1 year and currently receives a manager quality ranking of 94 (0=worst, 99=best). If you desire only a moderate level of risk and strong performance, then this fund is an excellent option.

Data Date	Investment Rating	Net Assets ($Mil)	Price	Performance Rating/Pts	Total Return Y-T-D	Risk Rating/Pts
3-12	A	222.94	11.23	B+ / 8.6	7.75%	B / 8.8
2011	C	218.40	10.54	C+ / 6.0	0.57%	C+ / 6.3
2010	D-	220.60	10.52	D- / 1.2	9.76%	C- / 3.9
2009	E+	122.75	10.27	E+ / 0.9	43.86%	C / 4.4

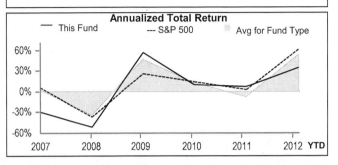

BlackRock Credit Alloc Inc Tr IV (BTZ)   A   Excellent

Fund Family: BlackRock Inc
Fund Type: Income
Inception Date: December 27, 2006

Major Rating Factors:
Strong performance is the major factor driving the A (Excellent) TheStreet.com Investment Rating for BlackRock Credit Alloc Inc Tr IV. The fund currently has a performance rating of B+ (Good) based on an annualized return of 34.49% over the last three years and a total return of 8.86% year to date 2012. Factored into the performance evaluation is an expense ratio of 1.09% (low).

The fund's risk rating is currently B (Good). It carries a beta of 0.67, meaning the fund's expected move will be 6.7% for every 10% move in the market. Volatility, as measured by both the semi-deviation and a drawdown factor, is considered low. As of March 31, 2012, BlackRock Credit Alloc Inc Tr IV traded at a discount of 8.86% below its net asset value, which is worse than its one-year historical average discount of 11.78%.

Jeffrey Cucunato has been running the fund for 1 year and currently receives a manager quality ranking of 93 (0=worst, 99=best). If you desire only a moderate level of risk and strong performance, then this fund is an excellent option.

Data Date	Investment Rating	Net Assets ($Mil)	Price	Performance Rating/Pts	Total Return Y-T-D	Risk Rating/Pts
3-12	A	722.34	13.07	B+ / 8.9	8.86%	B / 8.7
2011	C+	708.60	12.15	B- / 7.5	0.58%	C+ / 6.8
2010	D	723.87	12.10	D+ / 2.8	14.66%	C / 4.4
2009	D-	449.72	11.38	D- / 1.5	52.37%	C- / 3.9

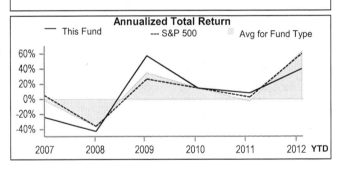

BlackRock Debt Strategies Fund Inc (DSU)   A   Excellent

Fund Family: BlackRock Inc
Fund Type: Corporate - High Yield
Inception Date: March 24, 1998

Major Rating Factors:
Strong performance is the major factor driving the A (Excellent) TheStreet.com Investment Rating for BlackRock Debt Strategies Fund Inc. The fund currently has a performance rating of B+ (Good) based on an annualized return of 36.55% over the last three years and a total return of 8.10% year to date 2012. Factored into the performance evaluation is an expense ratio of 1.27% (average).

The fund's risk rating is currently B (Good). It carries a beta of 1.55, meaning it is expected to move 15.5% for every 10% move in the market. Volatility, as measured by both the semi-deviation and a drawdown factor, is considered low. As of March 31, 2012, BlackRock Debt Strategies Fund Inc traded at a premium of .49% above its net asset value, which is worse than its one-year historical average discount of 1.33%.

Leland T. Hart has been running the fund for 3 years and currently receives a manager quality ranking of 52 (0=worst, 99=best). If you desire only a moderate level of risk and strong performance, then this fund is an excellent option.

Data Date	Investment Rating	Net Assets ($Mil)	Price	Performance Rating/Pts	Total Return Y-T-D	Risk Rating/Pts
3-12	A	461.25	4.14	B+ / 8.9	8.10%	B / 8.6
2011	C	428.20	3.88	B- / 7.2	2.58%	C / 5.0
2010	D	431.56	3.81	D+ / 2.6	14.79%	C- / 3.7
2009	E+	355.59	3.60	D / 2.0	49.66%	C- / 3.0

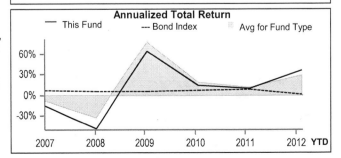

BlackRock Defined Opp Credit Trust (BHL)   C   Fair

Fund Family: BlackRock Inc
Fund Type: Loan Participation
Inception Date: January 31, 2008

Major Rating Factors: Middle of the road best describes BlackRock Defined Opp Credit Trust whose TheStreet.com Investment Rating is currently a C (Fair). The fund currently has a performance rating of C (Fair) based on an annualized return of 20.41% over the last three years and a total return of 8.69% year to date 2012. Factored into the performance evaluation is an expense ratio of 2.02% (high).

The fund's risk rating is currently B (Good). It carries a beta of -24.50, meaning the fund's expected move will be -245.0% for every 10% move in the market. Volatility, as measured by both the semi-deviation and a drawdown factor, is considered low. As of March 31, 2012, BlackRock Defined Opp Credit Trust traded at a discount of 3.87% below its net asset value, which is better than its one-year historical average discount of 3.12%.

James E. Keenan currently receives a manager quality ranking of 96 (0=worst, 99=best). If you desire an average level of risk, then this fund may be an option.

Data Date	Investment Rating	Net Assets ($Mil)	Price	Performance Rating/Pts	Total Return Y-T-D	Risk Rating/Pts
3-12	C	118.90	13.40	C / 4.5	8.69%	B / 8.2
2011	C	121.10	12.45	C / 4.8	2.65%	B / 8.2
2010	A	122.06	13.51	B+ / 8.7	19.14%	C+ / 6.8
2009	A+	112.86	11.94	B+ / 8.5	34.51%	C+ / 6.7

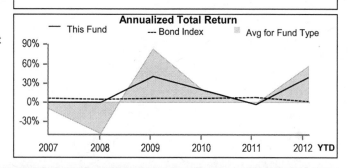

BlackRock Diversified Inc Strat (DVF)   C+   Fair

Fund Family: BlackRock Inc
Fund Type: Loan Participation
Inception Date: January 31, 2005

Major Rating Factors: Middle of the road best describes BlackRock Diversified Inc Strat whose TheStreet.com Investment Rating is currently a C+ (Fair). The fund currently has a performance rating of C+ (Fair) based on an annualized return of 26.99% over the last three years and a total return of 9.46% year to date 2012. Factored into the performance evaluation is an expense ratio of 1.74% (above average).

The fund's risk rating is currently B- (Good). It carries a beta of -11.40, meaning the fund's expected move will be -114.0% for every 10% move in the market. Volatility, as measured by both the semi-deviation and a drawdown factor, is considered low. As of March 31, 2012, BlackRock Diversified Inc Strat traded at a discount of 3.93% below its net asset value, which is worse than its one-year historical average discount of 4.23%.

C. Adrian Marshall has been running the fund for 3 years and currently receives a manager quality ranking of 98 (0=worst, 99=best). If you desire an average level of risk, then this fund may be an option.

Data Date	Investment Rating	Net Assets ($Mil)	Price	Performance Rating/Pts	Total Return Y-T-D	Risk Rating/Pts
3-12	C+	126.31	10.28	C+ / 6.9	9.46%	B- / 7.7
2011	C+	127.70	9.50	C+ / 6.7	0.32%	B- / 7.1
2010	C-	129.39	11.26	C+ / 6.7	26.22%	D+ / 2.8
2009	D	107.56	9.56	C- / 3.2	79.32%	C- / 4.0

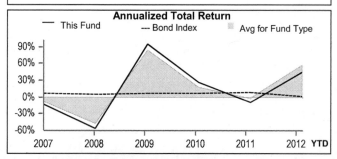

BlackRock EcoSolutions Investment (BQR)   C-   Fair

Fund Family: BlackRock Inc
Fund Type: Energy/Natural Resources
Inception Date: September 28, 2007

Major Rating Factors: Middle of the road best describes BlackRock EcoSolutions Investment whose TheStreet.com Investment Rating is currently a C- (Fair). The fund currently has a performance rating of C (Fair) based on an annualized return of 16.34% over the last three years and a total return of 30.40% year to date 2012. Factored into the performance evaluation is an expense ratio of 1.40% (average).

The fund's risk rating is currently C+ (Fair). It carries a beta of 0.58, meaning the fund's expected move will be 5.8% for every 10% move in the market. Volatility, as measured by both the semi-deviation and a drawdown factor, is considered low. As of March 31, 2012, BlackRock EcoSolutions Investment traded at a premium of 5.51% above its net asset value, which is worse than its one-year historical average discount of 1.95%.

Robert M. Shearer has been running the fund for 5 years and currently receives a manager quality ranking of 79 (0=worst, 99=best). If you desire an average level of risk, then this fund may be an option.

Data Date	Investment Rating	Net Assets ($Mil)	Price	Performance Rating/Pts	Total Return Y-T-D	Risk Rating/Pts
3-12	C-	117.50	9.95	C / 4.4	30.40%	C+ / 6.6
2011	D	110.10	7.82	D+ / 2.5	6.14%	C+ / 6.1
2010	D-	128.66	10.95	D / 1.9	12.25%	C- / 3.6
2009	C+	115.51	10.95	B+ / 8.3	42.30%	C- / 4.1

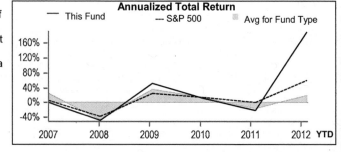

BlackRock Energy & Resources (BGR)   C+   Fair

Fund Family: BlackRock Inc
Fund Type: Energy/Natural Resources
Inception Date: December 23, 2004

Major Rating Factors: Middle of the road best describes BlackRock Energy & Resources whose TheStreet.com Investment Rating is currently a C+ (Fair). The fund currently has a performance rating of C+ (Fair) based on an annualized return of 26.20% over the last three years and a total return of 8.81% year to date 2012. Factored into the performance evaluation is an expense ratio of 1.15% (low).

    The fund's risk rating is currently B- (Good). It carries a beta of 1.06, meaning that its performance tracks fairly well with that of the overall stock market. Volatility, as measured by both the semi-deviation and a drawdown factor, is considered low. As of March 31, 2012, BlackRock Energy & Resources traded at a discount of 4.17% below its net asset value, which is worse than its one-year historical average discount of 5.64%.

    Daniel J. Rice, III currently receives a manager quality ranking of 76 (0=worst, 99=best). If you desire an average level of risk, then this fund may be an option.

Data Date	Investment Rating	Net Assets ($Mil)	Price	Performance Rating/Pts	Total Return Y-T-D	Risk Rating/Pts
3-12	C+	843.33	26.20	C+ / 6.3	8.81%	B- / 7.3
2011	C+	794.70	24.45	B- / 7.0	4.83%	B- / 7.1
2010	C	795.72	28.74	B- / 7.2	19.58%	C- / 3.9
2009	C+	554.46	25.63	B / 7.8	67.69%	C- / 4.1

Annualized Total Return

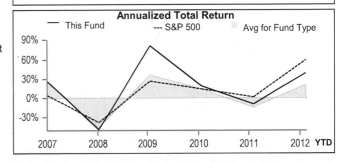

BlackRock Enhanced Capital and Inc (CII)   C   Fair

Fund Family: BlackRock Inc
Fund Type: Growth and Income
Inception Date: April 30, 2004

Major Rating Factors: Middle of the road best describes BlackRock Enhanced Capital and Inc whose TheStreet.com Investment Rating is currently a C (Fair). The fund currently has a performance rating of C+ (Fair) based on an annualized return of 21.97% over the last three years and a total return of 12.60% year to date 2012. Factored into the performance evaluation is an expense ratio of 0.93% (low).

    The fund's risk rating is currently B- (Good). It carries a beta of 0.86, meaning the fund's expected move will be 8.6% for every 10% move in the market. Volatility, as measured by both the semi-deviation and a drawdown factor, is considered low. As of March 31, 2012, BlackRock Enhanced Capital and Inc traded at a discount of 7.35% below its net asset value, which is better than its one-year historical average discount of 5.80%.

    Jonathan A. Clark currently receives a manager quality ranking of 71 (0=worst, 99=best). If you desire an average level of risk, then this fund may be an option.

Data Date	Investment Rating	Net Assets ($Mil)	Price	Performance Rating/Pts	Total Return Y-T-D	Risk Rating/Pts
3-12	C	612.15	13.49	C+ / 5.6	12.60%	B- / 7.8
2011	C	614.10	12.30	C / 5.1	3.01%	B- / 7.6
2010	C	659.60	14.85	C+ / 5.7	8.97%	C / 4.9
2009	C	552.92	15.57	C+ / 6.8	54.92%	C / 4.7

Annualized Total Return

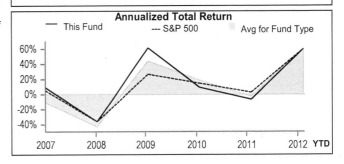

BlackRock Enhanced Equity Div (BDJ)   C-   Fair

Fund Family: BlackRock Inc
Fund Type: Income
Inception Date: August 25, 2005

Major Rating Factors: Middle of the road best describes BlackRock Enhanced Equity Div whose TheStreet.com Investment Rating is currently a C- (Fair). The fund currently has a performance rating of C- (Fair) based on an annualized return of 16.16% over the last three years and a total return of 8.49% year to date 2012. Factored into the performance evaluation is an expense ratio of 1.14% (low).

    The fund's risk rating is currently B- (Good). It carries a beta of 0.77, meaning the fund's expected move will be 7.7% for every 10% move in the market. Volatility, as measured by both the semi-deviation and a drawdown factor, is considered low. As of March 31, 2012, BlackRock Enhanced Equity Div traded at a discount of 10.93% below its net asset value, which is better than its one-year historical average discount of 6.89%.

    Kathleen M. Anderson has been running the fund for 2 years and currently receives a manager quality ranking of 49 (0=worst, 99=best). If you desire an average level of risk, then this fund may be an option.

Data Date	Investment Rating	Net Assets ($Mil)	Price	Performance Rating/Pts	Total Return Y-T-D	Risk Rating/Pts
3-12	C-	575.71	7.50	C- / 3.5	8.49%	B- / 7.9
2011	D+	578.80	7.07	D+ / 2.7	1.70%	B- / 7.2
2010	C	603.70	8.70	C+ / 5.8	11.31%	C / 4.9
2009	D-	526.67	8.80	D / 1.7	15.23%	C / 4.9

Annualized Total Return

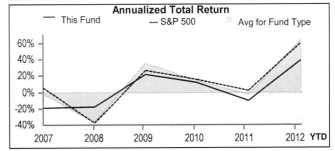

BlackRock Enhanced Government (EGF) D+ Weak

Fund Family: BlackRock Inc
Fund Type: US Government/Agency
Inception Date: October 27, 2005

Data Date	Investment Rating	Net Assets ($Mil)	Price	Performance Rating/Pts	Total Return Y-T-D	Risk Rating/Pts
3-12	D+	189.92	15.30	D / 1.7	1.25%	B / 8.9
2011	C-	187.90	15.25	D+ / 2.9	0.59%	B / 8.8
2010	C+	196.51	15.51	C- / 3.8	-4.02%	B / 8.2
2009	C	192.56	17.07	C- / 3.8	9.93%	B- / 7.5

Major Rating Factors:
Disappointing performance is the major factor driving the D+ (Weak) TheStreet.com Investment Rating for BlackRock Enhanced Government. The fund currently has a performance rating of D (Weak) based on an annualized return of 4.58% over the last three years and a total return of 1.25% year to date 2012. Factored into the performance evaluation is an expense ratio of 1.22% (average).

The fund's risk rating is currently B (Good). It carries a beta of 0.09, meaning the fund's expected move will be 0.9% for every 10% move in the market. Volatility, as measured by both the semi-deviation and a drawdown factor, is considered low. As of March 31, 2012, BlackRock Enhanced Government traded at a discount of 5.20% below its net asset value, which is worse than its one-year historical average discount of 5.48%.

Stuart Spodek currently receives a manager quality ranking of 69 (0=worst, 99=best). This fund offers only a moderate level of risk but investors looking for strong performance are still waiting.

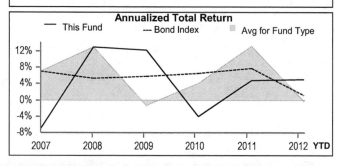

BlackRock FL Muni 2020 Term Tr (BFO) A- Excellent

Fund Family: BlackRock Inc
Fund Type: Municipal - Single State
Inception Date: September 26, 2003

Data Date	Investment Rating	Net Assets ($Mil)	Price	Performance Rating/Pts	Total Return Y-T-D	Risk Rating/Pts
3-12	A-	83.11	15.43	B- / 7.5	2.65%	B+ / 9.4
2011	B+	86.30	15.20	B / 7.9	-1.05%	B+ / 9.4
2010	C+	82.93	13.62	C+ / 6.0	7.01%	C+ / 6.6
2009	C+	74.26	13.35	C+ / 6.6	36.10%	C+ / 6.9

Major Rating Factors:
Strong performance is the major factor driving the A- (Excellent) TheStreet.com Investment Rating for BlackRock FL Muni 2020 Term Tr. The fund currently has a performance rating of B- (Good) based on an annualized return of 17.45% over the last three years and a total return of 2.65% year to date 2012. Factored into the performance evaluation is an expense ratio of 1.13% (low).

The fund's risk rating is currently B+ (Good). It carries a beta of 1.30, meaning it is expected to move 13.0% for every 10% move in the market. Volatility, as measured by both the semi-deviation and a drawdown factor, is considered very low. As of March 31, 2012, BlackRock FL Muni 2020 Term Tr traded at a discount of 1.66% below its net asset value, which is worse than its one-year historical average discount of 3.52%.

Theodore R. Jaeckel, Jr. has been running the fund for 6 years and currently receives a manager quality ranking of 77 (0=worst, 99=best). If you desire only a moderate level of risk and strong performance, then this fund is an excellent option.

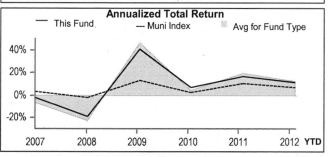

BlackRock Floating Rate Inc Strat (FRA) C+ Fair

Fund Family: BlackRock Inc
Fund Type: Loan Participation
Inception Date: October 28, 2003

Data Date	Investment Rating	Net Assets ($Mil)	Price	Performance Rating/Pts	Total Return Y-T-D	Risk Rating/Pts
3-12	C+	259.21	14.82	C+ / 6.5	12.10%	B- / 7.7
2011	C+	263.10	13.36	C+ / 6.7	3.29%	B- / 7.6
2010	C-	264.38	14.88	C+ / 5.9	10.94%	C- / 4.2
2009	C	237.16	14.23	B- / 7.0	66.45%	C / 4.5

Major Rating Factors: Middle of the road best describes BlackRock Floating Rate Inc Strat whose TheStreet.com Investment Rating is currently a C+ (Fair). The fund currently has a performance rating of C+ (Fair) based on an annualized return of 24.52% over the last three years and a total return of 12.10% year to date 2012. Factored into the performance evaluation is an expense ratio of 1.60% (above average).

The fund's risk rating is currently B- (Good). It carries a beta of -226.36, meaning the fund's expected move will be -2263.6% for every 10% move in the market. Volatility, as measured by both the semi-deviation and a drawdown factor, is considered low. As of March 31, 2012, BlackRock Floating Rate Inc Strat traded at a premium of .07% above its net asset value, which is worse than its one-year historical average discount of 2.45%.

C. Adrian Marshall has been running the fund for 3 years and currently receives a manager quality ranking of 99 (0=worst, 99=best). If you desire an average level of risk, then this fund may be an option.

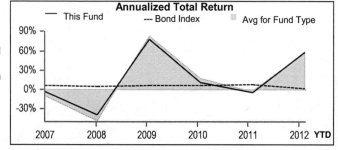

BlackRock Floating Rate Inc Strt I (FRB)   B-   Good

Fund Family: BlackRock Inc
Fund Type: Loan Participation
Inception Date: July 30, 2004

Major Rating Factors: Strong performance is the major factor driving the B- (Good) TheStreet.com Investment Rating for BlackRock Floating Rate Inc Strt I. The fund currently has a performance rating of B- (Good) based on an annualized return of 26.71% over the last three years and a total return of 14.37% year to date 2012. Factored into the performance evaluation is an expense ratio of 1.56% (average).

The fund's risk rating is currently B- (Good). It carries a beta of -143.61, meaning the fund's expected move will be -1436.1% for every 10% move in the market. Volatility, as measured by both the semi-deviation and a drawdown factor, is considered low. As of March 31, 2012, BlackRock Floating Rate Inc Strt I traded at a premium of 2.27% above its net asset value, which is worse than its one-year historical average discount of 2.97%.

C. Adrian Marshall has been running the fund for 3 years and currently receives a manager quality ranking of 99 (0=worst, 99=best). If you desire only a moderate level of risk and strong performance, then this fund is an excellent option.

Data Date	Investment Rating	Net Assets ($Mil)	Price	Performance Rating/Pts	Total Return Y-T-D	Risk Rating/Pts
3-12	B-	148.55	13.95	B- / 7.3	14.37%	B- / 7.6
2011	B-	138.90	12.33	B- / 7.0	3.49%	B- / 7.6
2010	D+	139.84	13.71	C / 4.3	6.08%	C- / 4.1
2009	C	126.20	13.73	B- / 7.2	74.16%	C- / 4.1

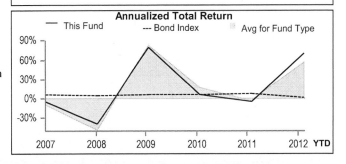

BlackRock Floating Rt Income (BGT)   C+   Fair

Fund Family: BlackRock Inc
Fund Type: Loan Participation
Inception Date: August 30, 2004

Major Rating Factors: Middle of the road best describes BlackRock Floating Rt Income whose TheStreet.com Investment Rating is currently a C+ (Fair). The fund currently has a performance rating of C+ (Fair) based on an annualized return of 23.73% over the last three years and a total return of 7.10% year to date 2012. Factored into the performance evaluation is an expense ratio of 1.60% (above average).

The fund's risk rating is currently B- (Good). It carries a beta of -88.79, meaning the fund's expected move will be -887.9% for every 10% move in the market. Volatility, as measured by both the semi-deviation and a drawdown factor, is considered low. As of March 31, 2012, BlackRock Floating Rt Income traded at a premium of .63% above its net asset value, which is worse than its one-year historical average discount of .32%.

James E. Keenan has been running the fund for 5 years and currently receives a manager quality ranking of 98 (0=worst, 99=best). If you desire an average level of risk, then this fund may be an option.

Data Date	Investment Rating	Net Assets ($Mil)	Price	Performance Rating/Pts	Total Return Y-T-D	Risk Rating/Pts
3-12	C+	329.83	14.27	C+ / 6.1	7.10%	B- / 7.8
2011	B-	320.00	13.47	B- / 7.1	0.52%	B- / 7.7
2010	B	337.34	16.55	B+ / 8.6	27.16%	C- / 4.2
2009	C	245.13	13.95	B- / 7.1	80.57%	C / 4.5

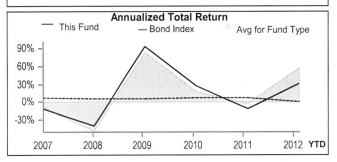

BlackRock Global Opportunities Eq (BOE)   C-   Fair

Fund Family: BlackRock Inc
Fund Type: Global
Inception Date: May 26, 2005

Major Rating Factors: Middle of the road best describes BlackRock Global Opportunities Eq whose TheStreet.com Investment Rating is currently a C- (Fair). The fund currently has a performance rating of C (Fair) based on an annualized return of 19.50% over the last three years and a total return of 20.50% year to date 2012. Factored into the performance evaluation is an expense ratio of 1.09% (low).

The fund's risk rating is currently C+ (Fair). It carries a beta of 0.86, meaning the fund's expected move will be 8.6% for every 10% move in the market. Volatility, as measured by both the semi-deviation and a drawdown factor, is considered low. As of March 31, 2012, BlackRock Global Opportunities Eq traded at a discount of 3.40% below its net asset value, which is worse than its one-year historical average discount of 4.03%.

Michael D. Carey has been running the fund for 3 years and currently receives a manager quality ranking of 75 (0=worst, 99=best). If you desire an average level of risk, then this fund may be an option.

Data Date	Investment Rating	Net Assets ($Mil)	Price	Performance Rating/Pts	Total Return Y-T-D	Risk Rating/Pts
3-12	C-	1,113.92	15.35	C / 5.0	20.50%	C+ / 6.9
2011	D+	1,056.00	13.21	D+ / 2.8	3.63%	C+ / 6.7
2010	D+	1,316.01	18.35	C- / 3.5	10.46%	C / 5.1
2009	D+	209.23	18.89	C- / 3.3	30.43%	C / 5.3

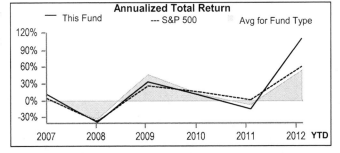

BlackRock Health Sciences Trust (BME)   C+   Fair

Fund Family: BlackRock Inc
Fund Type: Health
Inception Date: March 29, 2005

Data Date	Investment Rating	Net Assets ($Mil)	Price	Performance Rating/Pts	Total Return Y-T-D	Risk Rating/Pts
3-12	C+	202.68	27.47	C+ / 6.5	10.84%	B- / 7.9
2011	C+	196.00	25.13	C+ / 5.9	2.79%	B- / 7.6
2010	C+	213.38	26.22	C+ / 6.6	8.94%	C+ / 5.7
2009	C+	166.97	26.23	C+ / 6.7	38.58%	C+ / 6.5

Major Rating Factors: Middle of the road best describes BlackRock Health Sciences Trust whose TheStreet.com Investment Rating is currently a C+ (Fair). The fund currently has a performance rating of C+ (Fair) based on an annualized return of 23.02% over the last three years and a total return of 10.84% year to date 2012. Factored into the performance evaluation is an expense ratio of 1.13% (low).

The fund's risk rating is currently B- (Good). It carries a beta of 0.91, meaning that its performance tracks fairly well with that of the overall stock market. Volatility, as measured by both the semi-deviation and a drawdown factor, is considered low. As of March 31, 2012, BlackRock Health Sciences Trust traded at a discount of 1.12% below its net asset value, which is worse than its one-year historical average discount of 2.56%.

Erin Z. Xie has been running the fund for 7 years and currently receives a manager quality ranking of 58 (0=worst, 99=best). If you desire an average level of risk, then this fund may be an option.

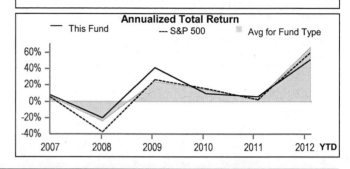

BlackRock High Income Shares (HIS)   A   Excellent

Fund Family: BlackRock Inc
Fund Type: Corporate - High Yield
Inception Date: August 10, 1988

Data Date	Investment Rating	Net Assets ($Mil)	Price	Performance Rating/Pts	Total Return Y-T-D	Risk Rating/Pts
3-12	A	118.81	2.28	B+ / 8.6	5.92%	B / 8.7
2011	A-	116.20	2.18	A- / 9.1	0.00%	B / 8.4
2010	C+	119.64	2.06	B / 7.8	20.50%	C- / 3.6
2009	C+	100.92	1.89	B- / 7.1	75.75%	C / 5.1

Major Rating Factors:
Strong performance is the major factor driving the A (Excellent) TheStreet.com Investment Rating for BlackRock High Income Shares. The fund currently has a performance rating of B+ (Good) based on an annualized return of 32.42% over the last three years and a total return of 5.92% year to date 2012. Factored into the performance evaluation is an expense ratio of 1.49% (average).

The fund's risk rating is currently B (Good). It carries a beta of 1.14, meaning it is expected to move 11.4% for every 10% move in the market. Volatility, as measured by both the semi-deviation and a drawdown factor, is considered low. As of March 31, 2012, BlackRock High Income Shares traded at a premium of 2.70% above its net asset value, which is worse than its one-year historical average discount of 3.63%.

Robert S. Kapito currently receives a manager quality ranking of 75 (0=worst, 99=best). If you desire only a moderate level of risk and strong performance, then this fund is an excellent option.

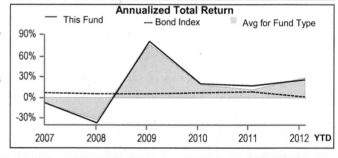

BlackRock High Yield Trust (BHY)   B+   Good

Fund Family: BlackRock Inc
Fund Type: Corporate - High Yield
Inception Date: December 17, 1998

Data Date	Investment Rating	Net Assets ($Mil)	Price	Performance Rating/Pts	Total Return Y-T-D	Risk Rating/Pts
3-12	B+	43.64	7.24	B / 7.7	8.72%	B / 8.9
2011	B	43.50	6.74	C+ / 6.6	1.78%	B / 8.8
2010	B-	42.98	6.60	B- / 7.3	17.23%	C / 5.3
2009	C	37.14	6.06	C / 5.3	42.96%	C+ / 5.8

Major Rating Factors: Strong performance is the major factor driving the B+ (Good) TheStreet.com Investment Rating for BlackRock High Yield Trust. The fund currently has a performance rating of B (Good) based on an annualized return of 27.54% over the last three years and a total return of 8.72% year to date 2012. Factored into the performance evaluation is an expense ratio of 2.04% (high).

The fund's risk rating is currently B (Good). It carries a beta of 0.94, meaning that its performance tracks fairly well with that of the overall stock market. Volatility, as measured by both the semi-deviation and a drawdown factor, is considered low. As of March 31, 2012, BlackRock High Yield Trust traded at a premium of 1.26% above its net asset value, which is worse than its one-year historical average discount of 2.75%.

Robert S. Kapito currently receives a manager quality ranking of 73 (0=worst, 99=best). If you desire only a moderate level of risk and strong performance, then this fund is an excellent option.

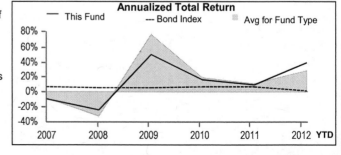

BlackRock Income Opportunity Trust (BNA)   C   Fair

Fund Family: BlackRock Inc
Fund Type: General - Investment Grade
Inception Date: December 20, 1991

Data Date	Investment Rating	Net Assets ($Mil)	Price	Performance Rating/Pts	Total Return Y-T-D	Risk Rating/Pts
3-12	C	371.18	10.48	C- / 4.0	3.57%	B / 8.6
2011	B-	381.20	10.22	C+ / 5.8	-0.29%	B+ / 9.0
2010	C+	381.38	9.69	C+ / 5.6	11.60%	C+ / 6.5
2009	C	345.10	9.27	C- / 3.9	14.47%	B- / 7.1

Major Rating Factors: Middle of the road best describes BlackRock Income Opportunity Trust whose TheStreet.com Investment Rating is currently a C (Fair). The fund currently has a performance rating of C- (Fair) based on an annualized return of 14.93% over the last three years and a total return of 3.57% year to date 2012. Factored into the performance evaluation is an expense ratio of 0.95% (low).

The fund's risk rating is currently B (Good). It carries a beta of 1.71, meaning it is expected to move 17.1% for every 10% move in the market. Volatility, as measured by both the semi-deviation and a drawdown factor, is considered low. As of March 31, 2012, BlackRock Income Opportunity Trust traded at a discount of 5.50% below its net asset value, which is worse than its one-year historical average discount of 8.41%.

Robert S. Kapito currently receives a manager quality ranking of 57 (0=worst, 99=best). If you desire an average level of risk, then this fund may be an option.

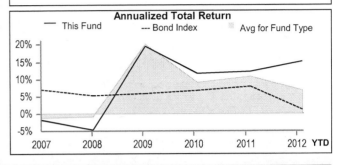

BlackRock Income Trust (BKT)   C   Fair

Fund Family: BlackRock Inc
Fund Type: Mortgage
Inception Date: July 22, 1988

Data Date	Investment Rating	Net Assets ($Mil)	Price	Performance Rating/Pts	Total Return Y-T-D	Risk Rating/Pts
3-12	C	508.77	7.42	C- / 3.1	2.33%	B+ / 9.6
2011	C+	509.30	7.33	C / 4.8	0.27%	B+ / 9.6
2010	A	496.26	6.84	B- / 7.2	11.86%	B / 8.1
2009	B-	455.53	6.36	C / 4.3	11.72%	B / 8.7

Major Rating Factors: Middle of the road best describes BlackRock Income Trust whose TheStreet.com Investment Rating is currently a C (Fair). The fund currently has a performance rating of C- (Fair) based on an annualized return of 11.90% over the last three years and a total return of 2.33% year to date 2012. Factored into the performance evaluation is an expense ratio of 1.05% (low).

The fund's risk rating is currently B+ (Good). It carries a beta of 0.64, meaning the fund's expected move will be 6.4% for every 10% move in the market. Volatility, as measured by both the semi-deviation and a drawdown factor, is considered very low. As of March 31, 2012, BlackRock Income Trust traded at a discount of 6.08% below its net asset value, which is worse than its one-year historical average discount of 9.17%.

Robert S. Kapito has been running the fund for 24 years and currently receives a manager quality ranking of 83 (0=worst, 99=best). If you desire an average level of risk, then this fund may be an option.

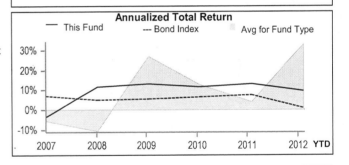

BlackRock Intl Grth and Inc Tr (BGY)   D   Weak

Fund Family: BlackRock Inc
Fund Type: Foreign
Inception Date: May 30, 2007

Data Date	Investment Rating	Net Assets ($Mil)	Price	Performance Rating/Pts	Total Return Y-T-D	Risk Rating/Pts
3-12	D	959.15	7.85	C- / 3.0	12.71%	C+ / 6.5
2011	D	890.80	7.16	D+ / 2.5	1.40%	C+ / 6.5
2010	D	1,158.58	10.17	D+ / 2.4	1.66%	C / 4.6
2009	B+	1,025.51	11.56	A- / 9.1	55.63%	C / 4.7

Major Rating Factors: BlackRock Intl Grth and Inc Tr receives a TheStreet.com Investment Rating of D (Weak). The fund currently has a performance rating of C- (Fair) based on an annualized return of 14.19% over the last three years and a total return of 12.71% year to date 2012. Factored into the performance evaluation is an expense ratio of 1.10% (low).

The fund's risk rating is currently C+ (Fair). It carries a beta of 0.95, meaning that its performance tracks fairly well with that of the overall stock market. Volatility, as measured by both the semi-deviation and a drawdown factor, is considered low. As of March 31, 2012, BlackRock Intl Grth and Inc Tr traded at a discount of 8.61% below its net asset value, which is better than its one-year historical average discount of 5.34%.

Michael D. Carey has been running the fund for 5 years and currently receives a manager quality ranking of 51 (0=worst, 99=best). If you desire an average level of risk, then this fund may be an option.

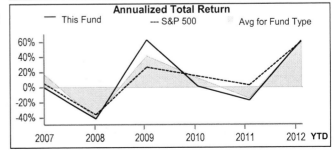

BlackRock Investment Qual Muni Tr (BKN)   A   Excellent

Fund Family: BlackRock Inc
Fund Type: Municipal - National
Inception Date: February 19, 1993

Data Date	Investment Rating	Net Assets ($Mil)	Price	Performance Rating/Pts	Total Return Y-T-D	Risk Rating/Pts
3-12	A	217.54	15.50	A- / 9.0	4.90%	B / 8.5
2011	A+	247.10	15.02	A+ / 9.8	3.73%	B / 8.6
2010	C-	232.47	13.14	D+ / 2.5	5.52%	C+ / 6.9
2009	C	196.81	13.40	C / 4.3	60.82%	C+ / 6.6

Major Rating Factors:
Exceptional performance is the major factor driving the A (Excellent) TheStreet.com Investment Rating for BlackRock Investment Qual Muni Tr. The fund currently has a performance rating of A- (Excellent) based on an annualized return of 21.08% over the last three years and a total return of 4.90% year to date 2012. Factored into the performance evaluation is an expense ratio of 1.08% (low).

The fund's risk rating is currently B (Good). It carries a beta of 2.23, meaning it is expected to move 22.3% for every 10% move in the market. Volatility, as measured by both the semi-deviation and a drawdown factor, is considered low. As of March 31, 2012, BlackRock Investment Qual Muni Tr traded at a premium of 2.45% above its net asset value, which is better than its one-year historical average premium of 3.85%.

Theodore R. Jaeckel, Jr. has been running the fund for 6 years and currently receives a manager quality ranking of 65 (0=worst, 99=best). If you desire only a moderate level of risk and strong performance, then this fund is an excellent option.

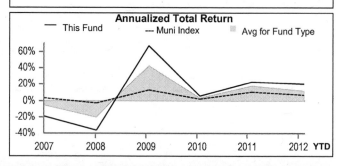

Annualized Total Return

BlackRock Invt Qual Muni Inc Tr (RFA)   A+   Excellent

Fund Family: BlackRock Inc
Fund Type: Municipal - Single State
Inception Date: May 28, 1993

Data Date	Investment Rating	Net Assets ($Mil)	Price	Performance Rating/Pts	Total Return Y-T-D	Risk Rating/Pts
3-12	A+	13.28	13.43	A / 9.5	6.44%	B / 8.5
2011	A+	14.20	12.82	A+ / 9.6	2.03%	B / 8.6
2010	C	13.86	11.22	C / 4.4	2.05%	C+ / 6.1
2009	C+	12.57	11.78	C / 5.5	57.13%	C+ / 6.3

Major Rating Factors:
Exceptional performance is the major factor driving the A+ (Excellent) TheStreet.com Investment Rating for BlackRock Invt Qual Muni Inc Tr. The fund currently has a performance rating of A (Excellent) based on an annualized return of 24.27% over the last three years and a total return of 6.44% year to date 2012. Factored into the performance evaluation is an expense ratio of 1.84% (above average).

The fund's risk rating is currently B (Good). It carries a beta of 2.79, meaning it is expected to move 27.9% for every 10% move in the market. Volatility, as measured by both the semi-deviation and a drawdown factor, is considered low. As of March 31, 2012, BlackRock Invt Qual Muni Inc Tr traded at a premium of 2.21% above its net asset value, which is worse than its one-year historical average premium of 1.09%.

Theodore R. Jaeckel, Jr. has been running the fund for 6 years and currently receives a manager quality ranking of 45 (0=worst, 99=best). If you desire only a moderate level of risk and strong performance, then this fund is an excellent option.

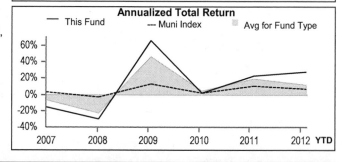

Annualized Total Return

BlackRock Limited Duration Income (BLW)   C+   Fair

Fund Family: BlackRock Inc
Fund Type: General Bond
Inception Date: July 30, 2003

Data Date	Investment Rating	Net Assets ($Mil)	Price	Performance Rating/Pts	Total Return Y-T-D	Risk Rating/Pts
3-12	C+	609.82	17.74	C / 5.5	12.46%	B / 8.7
2011	B	603.70	15.97	B- / 7.1	2.94%	B / 8.7
2010	C+	619.38	16.30	C+ / 6.7	17.46%	C+ / 5.8
2009	C	551.51	14.66	C- / 4.0	40.87%	C+ / 6.5

Major Rating Factors: Middle of the road best describes BlackRock Limited Duration Income whose TheStreet.com Investment Rating is currently a C+ (Fair). The fund currently has a performance rating of C (Fair) based on an annualized return of 20.51% over the last three years and a total return of 12.46% year to date 2012. Factored into the performance evaluation is an expense ratio of 1.00% (low).

The fund's risk rating is currently B (Good). It carries a beta of 0.14, meaning the fund's expected move will be 1.4% for every 10% move in the market. Volatility, as measured by both the semi-deviation and a drawdown factor, is considered low. As of March 31, 2012, BlackRock Limited Duration Income traded at a premium of 3.68% above its net asset value, which is worse than its one-year historical average discount of 1.21%.

James E. Keenan has been running the fund for 5 years and currently receives a manager quality ranking of 93 (0=worst, 99=best). If you desire an average level of risk, then this fund may be an option.

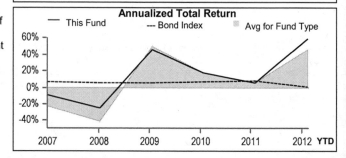

Annualized Total Return

BlackRock Long Term Muni Adv (BTA)

A+ **Excellent**

Fund Family: BlackRock Inc
Fund Type: Municipal - National
Inception Date: February 27, 2006

Major Rating Factors:
Exceptional performance is the major factor driving the A+ (Excellent) TheStreet.com Investment Rating for BlackRock Long Term Muni Adv. The fund currently has a performance rating of A (Excellent) based on an annualized return of 22.45% over the last three years and a total return of 7.90% year to date 2012. Factored into the performance evaluation is an expense ratio of 1.43% (average).

The fund's risk rating is currently B (Good). It carries a beta of 2.45, meaning it is expected to move 24.5% for every 10% move in the market. Volatility, as measured by both the semi-deviation and a drawdown factor, is considered low. As of March 31, 2012, BlackRock Long Term Muni Adv traded at a premium of 3.08% above its net asset value, which is worse than its one-year historical average discount of 1.67%.

Theodore R. Jaeckel, Jr. currently receives a manager quality ranking of 64 (0=worst, 99=best). If you desire only a moderate level of risk and strong performance, then this fund is an excellent option.

Data Date	Investment Rating	Net Assets ($Mil)	Price	Performance Rating/Pts	Total Return Y-T-D	Risk Rating/Pts
3-12	A+	140.51	12.39	A / 9.4	7.90%	B / 8.4
2011	A+	154.80	11.67	A+ / 9.7	0.69%	B / 8.4
2010	D	150.36	10.08	D / 1.8	5.39%	C+ / 5.9
2009	C-	127.08	10.22	C- / 3.4	53.14%	C+ / 5.9

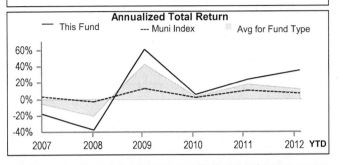

BlackRock MD Muni Bond Trust (BZM)

B **Good**

Fund Family: BlackRock Inc
Fund Type: Municipal - Single State
Inception Date: April 26, 2002

Major Rating Factors: Strong performance is the major factor driving the B (Good) TheStreet.com Investment Rating for BlackRock MD Muni Bond Trust. The fund currently has a performance rating of B- (Good) based on an annualized return of 16.07% over the last three years and a total return of 0.81% year to date 2012. Factored into the performance evaluation is an expense ratio of 1.45% (average).

The fund's risk rating is currently B (Good). It carries a beta of 0.87, meaning the fund's expected move will be 8.7% for every 10% move in the market. Volatility, as measured by both the semi-deviation and a drawdown factor, is considered low. As of March 31, 2012, BlackRock MD Muni Bond Trust traded at a premium of 8.62% above its net asset value, which is worse than its one-year historical average premium of 8.06%.

Theodore R. Jaeckel, Jr. has been running the fund for 6 years and currently receives a manager quality ranking of 81 (0=worst, 99=best). If you desire only a moderate level of risk and strong performance, then this fund is an excellent option.

Data Date	Investment Rating	Net Assets ($Mil)	Price	Performance Rating/Pts	Total Return Y-T-D	Risk Rating/Pts
3-12	B	30.20	16.50	B- / 7.2	0.81%	B / 8.5
2011	B+	30.80	16.61	B+ / 8.4	1.26%	B / 8.5
2010	C	31.35	14.67	C- / 3.0	8.04%	B- / 7.7
2009	C	28.31	14.44	C- / 3.1	35.37%	B- / 7.5

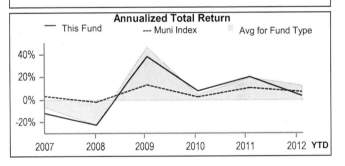

BlackRock Muni 2020 Term Trust (BKK)

B- **Good**

Fund Family: BlackRock Inc
Fund Type: Municipal - National
Inception Date: September 26, 2003

Major Rating Factors: BlackRock Muni 2020 Term Trust receives a TheStreet.com Investment Rating of B- (Good). The fund currently has a performance rating of C+ (Fair) based on an annualized return of 13.99% over the last three years and a total return of 1.87% year to date 2012. Factored into the performance evaluation is an expense ratio of 1.03% (low).

The fund's risk rating is currently B+ (Good). It carries a beta of 1.16, meaning it is expected to move 11.6% for every 10% move in the market. Volatility, as measured by both the semi-deviation and a drawdown factor, is considered very low. As of March 31, 2012, BlackRock Muni 2020 Term Trust traded at a discount of 1.85% below its net asset value, which is better than its one-year historical average discount of .28%.

Theodore R. Jaeckel, Jr. has been running the fund for 6 years and currently receives a manager quality ranking of 76 (0=worst, 99=best). If you desire an average level of risk, then this fund may be an option.

Data Date	Investment Rating	Net Assets ($Mil)	Price	Performance Rating/Pts	Total Return Y-T-D	Risk Rating/Pts
3-12	B-	296.08	15.88	C+ / 5.7	1.87%	B+ / 9.4
2011	B+	320.80	15.77	B / 8.0	1.14%	B+ / 9.3
2010	B-	293.55	14.67	C+ / 6.6	5.70%	B- / 7.1
2009	C+	243.57	14.60	C+ / 6.6	42.74%	C+ / 6.6

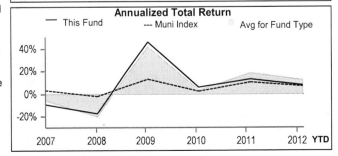

BlackRock Muni Bond Invt Trust (BIE)

B+   **Good**

Fund Family: BlackRock Inc
Fund Type: Municipal - Single State
Inception Date: April 26, 2002

Data Date	Investment Rating	Net Assets ($Mil)	Price	Performance Rating/Pts	Total Return Y-T-D	Risk Rating/Pts
3-12	B+	48.94	15.36	B / 8.2	2.80%	B / 8.6
2011	A	51.10	15.17	A- / 9.1	1.85%	B / 8.6
2010	C-	51.71	13.28	D / 2.0	6.26%	B- / 7.2
2009	C	47.20	13.33	C- / 4.1	42.09%	B- / 7.3

Major Rating Factors: Strong performance is the major factor driving the B+ (Good) TheStreet.com Investment Rating for BlackRock Muni Bond Invt Trust. The fund currently has a performance rating of B (Good) based on an annualized return of 18.36% over the last three years and a total return of 2.80% year to date 2012. Factored into the performance evaluation is an expense ratio of 1.66% (above average).

The fund's risk rating is currently B (Good). It carries a beta of 2.04, meaning it is expected to move 20.4% for every 10% move in the market. Volatility, as measured by both the semi-deviation and a drawdown factor, is considered low. As of March 31, 2012, BlackRock Muni Bond Invt Trust traded at a discount of 3.70% below its net asset value, which is better than its one-year historical average discount of 2.04%.

Robert S. Kapito currently receives a manager quality ranking of 60 (0=worst, 99=best). If you desire only a moderate level of risk and strong performance, then this fund is an excellent option.

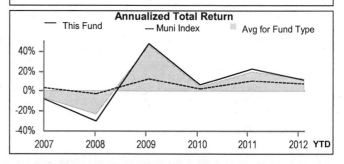

BlackRock Muni Interm Duration (MUI)

A   **Excellent**

Fund Family: BlackRock Inc
Fund Type: Municipal - National
Inception Date: July 29, 2003

Data Date	Investment Rating	Net Assets ($Mil)	Price	Performance Rating/Pts	Total Return Y-T-D	Risk Rating/Pts
3-12	A	549.52	15.85	B+ / 8.3	4.85%	B / 8.9
2011	A	596.00	15.32	A- / 9.1	2.61%	B+ / 9.0
2010	C+	561.14	13.79	C+ / 5.7	10.91%	C+ / 6.4
2009	C+	496.25	13.16	C / 4.9	30.77%	B- / 7.6

Major Rating Factors:
Strong performance is the major factor driving the A (Excellent) TheStreet.com Investment Rating for BlackRock Muni Interm Duration. The fund currently has a performance rating of B+ (Good) based on an annualized return of 18.04% over the last three years and a total return of 4.85% year to date 2012. Factored into the performance evaluation is an expense ratio of 1.43% (average).

The fund's risk rating is currently B (Good). It carries a beta of 1.96, meaning it is expected to move 19.6% for every 10% move in the market. Volatility, as measured by both the semi-deviation and a drawdown factor, is considered low. As of March 31, 2012, BlackRock Muni Interm Duration traded at a discount of .81% below its net asset value, which is worse than its one-year historical average discount of 3.67%.

Theodore R. Jaeckel, Jr. has been running the fund for 6 years and currently receives a manager quality ranking of 65 (0=worst, 99=best). If you desire only a moderate level of risk and strong performance, then this fund is an excellent option.

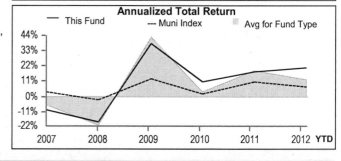

BlackRock Muni NY Interm Duration (MNE)

A+   **Excellent**

Fund Family: BlackRock Inc
Fund Type: Municipal - Single State
Inception Date: July 29, 2003

Data Date	Investment Rating	Net Assets ($Mil)	Price	Performance Rating/Pts	Total Return Y-T-D	Risk Rating/Pts
3-12	A+	61.02	15.00	B+ / 8.9	5.60%	B+ / 9.1
2011	A+	63.40	14.38	A / 9.3	1.39%	B+ / 9.1
2010	C+	61.01	12.85	C+ / 5.8	11.07%	C+ / 6.1
2009	B-	54.64	12.25	C+ / 5.9	43.61%	B- / 7.6

Major Rating Factors:
Strong performance is the major factor driving the A+ (Excellent) TheStreet.com Investment Rating for BlackRock Muni NY Interm Duration. The fund currently has a performance rating of B+ (Good) based on an annualized return of 20.89% over the last three years and a total return of 5.60% year to date 2012. Factored into the performance evaluation is an expense ratio of 1.23% (average).

The fund's risk rating is currently B+ (Good). It carries a beta of 1.97, meaning it is expected to move 19.7% for every 10% move in the market. Volatility, as measured by both the semi-deviation and a drawdown factor, is considered very low. As of March 31, 2012, BlackRock Muni NY Interm Duration traded at a discount of 2.02% below its net asset value, which is worse than its one-year historical average discount of 6.52%.

Timothy T. Browse has been running the fund for 9 years and currently receives a manager quality ranking of 75 (0=worst, 99=best). If you desire only a moderate level of risk and strong performance, then this fund is an excellent option.

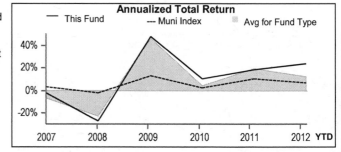

BlackRock MuniAssets Fund (MUA)

B **Good**

Fund Family: BlackRock Inc
Fund Type: Municipal - National
Inception Date: June 18, 1993

Major Rating Factors: Strong performance is the major factor driving the B (Good) TheStreet.com Investment Rating for BlackRock MuniAssets Fund. The fund currently has a performance rating of B- (Good) based on an annualized return of 13.74% over the last three years and a total return of 5.33% year to date 2012. Factored into the performance evaluation is an expense ratio of 0.78% (very low).

The fund's risk rating is currently B (Good). It carries a beta of 1.82, meaning it is expected to move 18.2% for every 10% move in the market. Volatility, as measured by both the semi-deviation and a drawdown factor, is considered low. As of March 31, 2012, BlackRock MuniAssets Fund traded at a discount of 2.11% below its net asset value, which is worse than its one-year historical average discount of 4.77%.

Robert C. Doll, Jr. currently receives a manager quality ranking of 47 (0=worst, 99=best). If you desire only a moderate level of risk and strong performance, then this fund is an excellent option.

Data Date	Investment Rating	Net Assets ($Mil)	Price	Performance Rating/Pts	Total Return Y-T-D	Risk Rating/Pts
3-12	B	433.89	13.01	B- / 7.0	5.33%	B / 8.4
2011	B+	456.80	12.53	B+ / 8.3	1.36%	B / 8.5
2010	C-	266.83	11.64	D+ / 2.9	1.63%	B- / 7.3
2009	C	221.90	12.18	C / 4.5	43.12%	C+ / 6.8

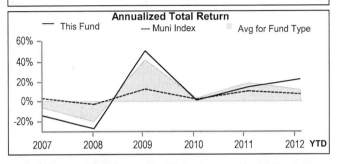

BlackRock Municipal 2018 Income Tr (BPK)

C+ **Fair**

Fund Family: BlackRock Inc
Fund Type: Municipal - National
Inception Date: October 25, 2001

Major Rating Factors: Middle of the road best describes BlackRock Municipal 2018 Income Tr whose TheStreet.com Investment Rating is currently a C+ (Fair). The fund currently has a performance rating of C (Fair) based on an annualized return of 11.50% over the last three years and a total return of 2.02% year to date 2012. Factored into the performance evaluation is an expense ratio of 0.85% (very low).

The fund's risk rating is currently B+ (Good). It carries a beta of 0.70, meaning the fund's expected move will be 7.0% for every 10% move in the market. Volatility, as measured by both the semi-deviation and a drawdown factor, is considered very low. As of March 31, 2012, BlackRock Municipal 2018 Income Tr traded at a premium of 5.44% above its net asset value, which is in line with its one-year historical average premium of 5.44%.

Theodore R. Jaeckel, Jr. has been running the fund for 6 years and currently receives a manager quality ranking of 79 (0=worst, 99=best). If you desire an average level of risk, then this fund may be an option.

Data Date	Investment Rating	Net Assets ($Mil)	Price	Performance Rating/Pts	Total Return Y-T-D	Risk Rating/Pts
3-12	C+	249.07	16.68	C / 4.6	2.02%	B+ / 9.4
2011	B	249.10	16.59	C+ / 6.7	0.24%	B+ / 9.4
2010	A-	235.85	15.72	B- / 7.1	10.28%	B- / 7.4
2009	C+	208.01	15.16	C / 4.7	20.30%	B- / 7.5

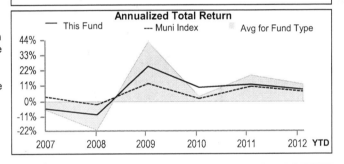

BlackRock Municipal Bond Trust (BBK)

A+ **Excellent**

Fund Family: BlackRock Inc
Fund Type: Municipal - National
Inception Date: April 26, 2002

Major Rating Factors:
Exceptional performance is the major factor driving the A+ (Excellent) TheStreet.com Investment Rating for BlackRock Municipal Bond Trust. The fund currently has a performance rating of A- (Excellent) based on an annualized return of 21.83% over the last three years and a total return of 5.30% year to date 2012. Factored into the performance evaluation is an expense ratio of 1.19% (average).

The fund's risk rating is currently B (Good). It carries a beta of 1.91, meaning it is expected to move 19.1% for every 10% move in the market. Volatility, as measured by both the semi-deviation and a drawdown factor, is considered low. As of March 31, 2012, BlackRock Municipal Bond Trust traded at a premium of 2.07% above its net asset value, which is better than its one-year historical average premium of 2.46%.

Theodore R. Jaeckel, Jr. has been running the fund for 6 years and currently receives a manager quality ranking of 80 (0=worst, 99=best). If you desire only a moderate level of risk and strong performance, then this fund is an excellent option.

Data Date	Investment Rating	Net Assets ($Mil)	Price	Performance Rating/Pts	Total Return Y-T-D	Risk Rating/Pts
3-12	A+	151.47	16.28	A- / 9.0	5.30%	B / 8.6
2011	A+	159.40	15.72	A / 9.5	1.59%	B / 8.6
2010	C-	159.22	13.73	D+ / 2.9	6.18%	B- / 7.1
2009	C	137.03	13.88	C- / 4.2	50.74%	C+ / 6.5

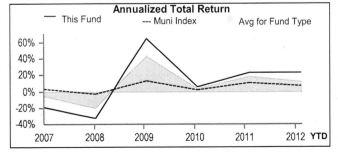

BlackRock Municipal Income Inv Qly (BAF)

B+   **Good**

Fund Family: BlackRock Inc
Fund Type: Municipal - Single State
Inception Date: October 28, 2002

Major Rating Factors: Strong performance is the major factor driving the B+ (Good) TheStreet.com Investment Rating for BlackRock Municipal Income Inv Qly. The fund currently has a performance rating of B (Good) based on an annualized return of 17.94% over the last three years and a total return of 1.36% year to date 2012. Factored into the performance evaluation is an expense ratio of 1.23% (average).

The fund's risk rating is currently B (Good). It carries a beta of 2.19, meaning it is expected to move 21.9% for every 10% move in the market. Volatility, as measured by both the semi-deviation and a drawdown factor, is considered low. As of March 31, 2012, BlackRock Municipal Income Inv Qly traded at a discount of 2.93% below its net asset value, which is better than its one-year historical average discount of 2.56%.

Robert S. Kapito currently receives a manager quality ranking of 51 (0=worst, 99=best). If you desire only a moderate level of risk and strong performance, then this fund is an excellent option.

Data Date	Investment Rating	Net Assets ($Mil)	Price	Performance Rating/Pts	Total Return Y-T-D	Risk Rating/Pts
3-12	B+	126.78	15.23	B / 8.1	1.36%	B / 8.3
2011	A-	132.60	15.24	A- / 9.2	1.25%	B / 8.4
2010	C	131.77	13.07	C / 4.5	3.44%	C+ / 6.4
2009	C+	122.83	13.43	C+ / 6.8	39.37%	C+ / 6.9

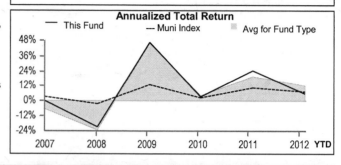

BlackRock Municipal Income Invt Tr (BBF)

B   **Good**

Fund Family: BlackRock Inc
Fund Type: Municipal - Single State
Inception Date: July 26, 2001

Major Rating Factors: Strong performance is the major factor driving the B (Good) TheStreet.com Investment Rating for BlackRock Municipal Income Invt Tr. The fund currently has a performance rating of B- (Good) based on an annualized return of 14.37% over the last three years and a total return of 3.57% year to date 2012. Factored into the performance evaluation is an expense ratio of 1.60% (above average).

The fund's risk rating is currently B (Good). It carries a beta of 2.43, meaning it is expected to move 24.3% for every 10% move in the market. Volatility, as measured by both the semi-deviation and a drawdown factor, is considered low. As of March 31, 2012, BlackRock Municipal Income Invt Tr traded at a discount of 2.67% below its net asset value, which is better than its one-year historical average discount of 1.62%.

Robert D. Sneeden has been running the fund for 6 years and currently receives a manager quality ranking of 28 (0=worst, 99=best). If you desire only a moderate level of risk and strong performance, then this fund is an excellent option.

Data Date	Investment Rating	Net Assets ($Mil)	Price	Performance Rating/Pts	Total Return Y-T-D	Risk Rating/Pts
3-12	B	89.73	14.59	B- / 7.2	3.57%	B / 8.3
2011	B+	96.10	14.30	B+ / 8.6	0.49%	B / 8.2
2010	C-	93.07	12.34	D / 1.8	3.01%	B- / 7.5
2009	C	85.05	12.80	C- / 3.2	37.79%	B- / 7.3

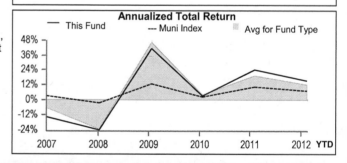

BlackRock Municipal Income Quality (BYM)

B-   **Good**

Fund Family: BlackRock Inc
Fund Type: Municipal - National
Inception Date: October 28, 2002

Major Rating Factors: BlackRock Municipal Income Quality receives a TheStreet.com Investment Rating of B- (Good). The fund currently has a performance rating of C+ (Fair) based on an annualized return of 14.53% over the last three years and a total return of 2.48% year to date 2012. Factored into the performance evaluation is an expense ratio of 1.24% (average).

The fund's risk rating is currently B (Good). It carries a beta of 2.11, meaning it is expected to move 21.1% for every 10% move in the market. Volatility, as measured by both the semi-deviation and a drawdown factor, is considered low. As of March 31, 2012, BlackRock Municipal Income Quality traded at a discount of 2.41% below its net asset value, which is better than its one-year historical average discount of .90%.

Robert S. Kapito currently receives a manager quality ranking of 42 (0=worst, 99=best). If you desire an average level of risk, then this fund may be an option.

Data Date	Investment Rating	Net Assets ($Mil)	Price	Performance Rating/Pts	Total Return Y-T-D	Risk Rating/Pts
3-12	B-	371.01	14.98	C+ / 6.9	2.48%	B / 8.4
2011	B+	388.20	14.84	B+ / 8.5	-0.54%	B / 8.5
2010	D+	384.56	12.95	D / 1.6	1.32%	C+ / 6.9
2009	C+	355.33	13.61	C / 5.4	32.69%	C+ / 6.9

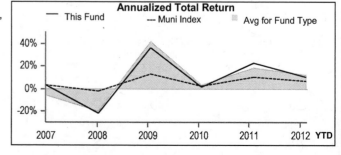

BlackRock Municipal Income Trust (BFK)   A   Excellent

Fund Family: BlackRock Inc
Fund Type: Municipal - National
Inception Date: July 27, 2001

Major Rating Factors:
Strong performance is the major factor driving the A (Excellent) TheStreet.com Investment Rating for BlackRock Municipal Income Trust. The fund currently has a performance rating of B+ (Good) based on an annualized return of 20.20% over the last three years and a total return of 5.62% year to date 2012. Factored into the performance evaluation is an expense ratio of 1.24% (average).

The fund's risk rating is currently B (Good). It carries a beta of 2.61, meaning it is expected to move 26.1% for every 10% move in the market. Volatility, as measured by both the semi-deviation and a drawdown factor, is considered low. As of March 31, 2012, BlackRock Municipal Income Trust traded at a premium of 1.05% above its net asset value, which is better than its one-year historical average premium of 1.85%.

Theodore R. Jaeckel, Jr. has been running the fund for 6 years and currently receives a manager quality ranking of 47 (0=worst, 99=best). If you desire only a moderate level of risk and strong performance, then this fund is an excellent option.

Data Date	Investment Rating	Net Assets ($Mil)	Price	Performance Rating/Pts	Total Return Y-T-D	Risk Rating/Pts
3-12	A	541.10	14.49	B+ / 8.9	5.62%	B / 8.4
2011	A+	609.10	13.95	A+ / 9.7	3.44%	B / 8.5
2010	C	587.25	12.69	C- / 3.5	6.50%	C+ / 6.8
2009	C	474.81	12.80	C / 4.4	61.74%	C+ / 6.2

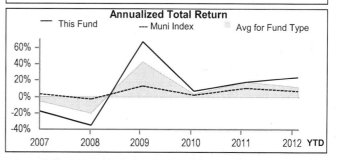

BlackRock Municipal Income Trust I (BLE)   A+   Excellent

Fund Family: BlackRock Inc
Fund Type: Municipal - National
Inception Date: July 25, 2002

Major Rating Factors:
Exceptional performance is the major factor driving the A+ (Excellent) TheStreet.com Investment Rating for BlackRock Municipal Income Trust I. The fund currently has a performance rating of A- (Excellent) based on an annualized return of 22.88% over the last three years and a total return of 3.60% year to date 2012. Factored into the performance evaluation is an expense ratio of 1.10% (low).

The fund's risk rating is currently B (Good). It carries a beta of 1.84, meaning it is expected to move 18.4% for every 10% move in the market. Volatility, as measured by both the semi-deviation and a drawdown factor, is considered low. As of March 31, 2012, BlackRock Municipal Income Trust I traded at a premium of 1.64% above its net asset value, which is worse than its one-year historical average premium of .95%.

Theodore R. Jaeckel, Jr. has been running the fund for 6 years and currently receives a manager quality ranking of 81 (0=worst, 99=best). If you desire only a moderate level of risk and strong performance, then this fund is an excellent option.

Data Date	Investment Rating	Net Assets ($Mil)	Price	Performance Rating/Pts	Total Return Y-T-D	Risk Rating/Pts
3-12	A+	325.71	15.50	A- / 9.1	3.60%	B / 8.6
2011	A+	340.50	15.21	A+ / 9.8	0.72%	B / 8.7
2010	C	340.27	13.10	C- / 3.2	2.63%	B- / 7.1
2009	C	296.07	13.69	C / 5.2	53.95%	C+ / 6.3

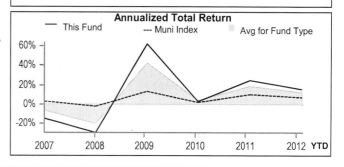

BlackRock MuniEnhanced Fund (MEN)   B   Good

Fund Family: BlackRock Inc
Fund Type: Municipal - National
Inception Date: February 23, 1989

Major Rating Factors: Strong performance is the major factor driving the B (Good) TheStreet.com Investment Rating for BlackRock MuniEnhanced Fund. The fund currently has a performance rating of B- (Good) based on an annualized return of 16.59% over the last three years and a total return of -0.64% year to date 2012. Factored into the performance evaluation is an expense ratio of 1.24% (average).

The fund's risk rating is currently B (Good). It carries a beta of 2.06, meaning it is expected to move 20.6% for every 10% move in the market. Volatility, as measured by both the semi-deviation and a drawdown factor, is considered low. As of March 31, 2012, BlackRock MuniEnhanced Fund traded at a discount of 4.60% below its net asset value, which is better than its one-year historical average discount of 2.77%.

Michael A. Kalinoski has been running the fund for 23 years and currently receives a manager quality ranking of 46 (0=worst, 99=best). If you desire only a moderate level of risk and strong performance, then this fund is an excellent option.

Data Date	Investment Rating	Net Assets ($Mil)	Price	Performance Rating/Pts	Total Return Y-T-D	Risk Rating/Pts
3-12	B	303.26	11.40	B- / 7.3	-0.64%	B / 8.8
2011	A	339.70	11.64	A- / 9.1	-1.20%	B / 8.8
2010	C+	320.08	10.45	C / 5.4	7.20%	C+ / 6.3
2009	B+	287.08	10.38	B- / 7.1	42.52%	C+ / 6.8

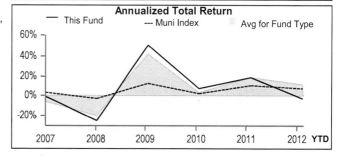

BlackRock MuniHoldings CA Qly (MUC)   A   Excellent

Fund Family: BlackRock Inc
Fund Type: Municipal - Single State
Inception Date: February 27, 1998

Data Date	Investment Rating	Net Assets ($Mil)	Price	Performance Rating/Pts	Total Return Y-T-D	Risk Rating/Pts
3-12	A	583.40	14.99	B+ / 8.9	2.27%	B / 8.7
2011	A	618.00	14.88	A / 9.3	0.81%	B / 8.7
2010	C+	254.00	13.05	C+ / 5.7	10.47%	C+ / 6.4
2009	B-	540.14	12.57	C+ / 5.6	39.83%	B- / 7.5

Major Rating Factors:
Strong performance is the major factor driving the A (Excellent) TheStreet.com Investment Rating for BlackRock MuniHoldings CA Qly. The fund currently has a performance rating of B+ (Good) based on an annualized return of 20.50% over the last three years and a total return of 2.27% year to date 2012. Factored into the performance evaluation is an expense ratio of 1.25% (average).

The fund's risk rating is currently B (Good). It carries a beta of 2.02, meaning it is expected to move 20.2% for every 10% move in the market. Volatility, as measured by both the semi-deviation and a drawdown factor, is considered low. As of March 31, 2012, BlackRock MuniHoldings CA Qly traded at a discount of 4.70% below its net asset value, which is better than its one-year historical average discount of 4.61%.

Walter O'Connor has been running the fund for 14 years and currently receives a manager quality ranking of 71 (0=worst, 99=best). If you desire only a moderate level of risk and strong performance, then this fund is an excellent option.

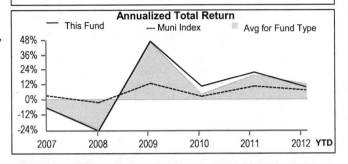

BlackRock MuniHoldings Fund (MHD)   A+   Excellent

Fund Family: BlackRock Inc
Fund Type: Municipal - National
Inception Date: April 29, 1997

Data Date	Investment Rating	Net Assets ($Mil)	Price	Performance Rating/Pts	Total Return Y-T-D	Risk Rating/Pts
3-12	A+	205.37	17.76	A / 9.5	8.83%	B / 8.9
2011	A+	229.90	16.58	A / 9.5	1.03%	B / 8.9
2010	C+	219.13	15.03	C+ / 6.7	11.71%	C+ / 5.9
2009	C+	184.69	14.49	C+ / 6.9	50.85%	C+ / 6.9

Major Rating Factors:
Exceptional performance is the major factor driving the A+ (Excellent) TheStreet.com Investment Rating for BlackRock MuniHoldings Fund. The fund currently has a performance rating of A (Excellent) based on an annualized return of 22.87% over the last three years and a total return of 8.83% year to date 2012. Factored into the performance evaluation is an expense ratio of 1.28% (average).

The fund's risk rating is currently B (Good). It carries a beta of 1.57, meaning it is expected to move 15.7% for every 10% move in the market. Volatility, as measured by both the semi-deviation and a drawdown factor, is considered low. As of March 31, 2012, BlackRock MuniHoldings Fund traded at a premium of 3.80% above its net asset value, which is worse than its one-year historical average premium of .24%.

Robert M. Shearer currently receives a manager quality ranking of 85 (0=worst, 99=best). If you desire only a moderate level of risk and strong performance, then this fund is an excellent option.

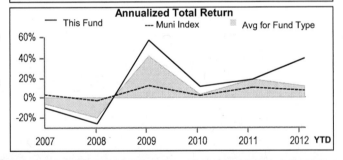

BlackRock MuniHoldings Fund II (MUH)   A+   Excellent

Fund Family: BlackRock Inc
Fund Type: Municipal - National
Inception Date: February 24, 1998

Data Date	Investment Rating	Net Assets ($Mil)	Price	Performance Rating/Pts	Total Return Y-T-D	Risk Rating/Pts
3-12	A+	154.26	15.72	B+ / 8.9	3.05%	B / 8.7
2011	A+	172.60	15.49	A+ / 9.6	1.25%	B / 8.7
2010	C+	163.72	13.66	C+ / 5.6	8.03%	C+ / 6.0
2009	B+	139.38	13.58	B- / 7.1	48.72%	C+ / 6.9

Major Rating Factors:
Strong performance is the major factor driving the A+ (Excellent) TheStreet.com Investment Rating for BlackRock MuniHoldings Fund II. The fund currently has a performance rating of B+ (Good) based on an annualized return of 21.93% over the last three years and a total return of 3.05% year to date 2012. Factored into the performance evaluation is an expense ratio of 1.23% (average).

The fund's risk rating is currently B (Good). It carries a beta of 1.91, meaning it is expected to move 19.1% for every 10% move in the market. Volatility, as measured by both the semi-deviation and a drawdown factor, is considered low. As of March 31, 2012, BlackRock MuniHoldings Fund II traded at a discount of 1.81% below its net asset value, which is better than its one-year historical average discount of 1.18%.

Robert M. Shearer currently receives a manager quality ranking of 77 (0=worst, 99=best). If you desire only a moderate level of risk and strong performance, then this fund is an excellent option.

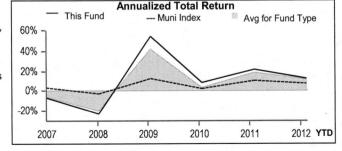

BlackRock MuniHoldings Inv Quality (MFL)   **B+**   **Good**

Fund Family: BlackRock Inc
Fund Type: Municipal - Single State
Inception Date: September 23, 1997

Data Date	Investment Rating	Net Assets ($Mil)	Price	Performance Rating/Pts	Total Return Y-T-D	Risk Rating/Pts
3-12	B+	528.17	14.59	B / 8.2	1.39%	B / 8.6
2011	A	550.70	14.61	A- / 9.2	-0.14%	B / 8.7
2010	C+	553.37	12.78	C+ / 5.8	4.98%	C+ / 6.3
2009	A-	511.01	12.97	B- / 7.0	46.26%	B- / 7.0

Major Rating Factors: Strong performance is the major factor driving the B+ (Good) TheStreet.com Investment Rating for BlackRock MuniHoldings Inv Quality. The fund currently has a performance rating of B (Good) based on an annualized return of 19.09% over the last three years and a total return of 1.39% year to date 2012. Factored into the performance evaluation is an expense ratio of 1.30% (average).

The fund's risk rating is currently B (Good). It carries a beta of 1.83, meaning it is expected to move 18.3% for every 10% move in the market. Volatility, as measured by both the semi-deviation and a drawdown factor, is considered low. As of March 31, 2012, BlackRock MuniHoldings Inv Quality traded at a discount of 3.25% below its net asset value, which is better than its one-year historical average discount of 1.85%.

Robert C. Doll, Jr. currently receives a manager quality ranking of 74 (0=worst, 99=best). If you desire only a moderate level of risk and strong performance, then this fund is an excellent option.

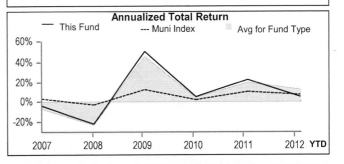

BlackRock MuniHoldings New York QI (MHN)   **A**   **Excellent**

Fund Family: BlackRock Inc
Fund Type: Municipal - Single State
Inception Date: September 16, 1997

Data Date	Investment Rating	Net Assets ($Mil)	Price	Performance Rating/Pts	Total Return Y-T-D	Risk Rating/Pts
3-12	A	443.33	15.15	B+ / 8.8	1.51%	B / 8.6
2011	A+	459.90	15.16	A / 9.5	0.20%	B / 8.7
2010	C+	464.85	13.46	C+ / 5.7	8.10%	C+ / 6.1
2009	A-	422.98	13.28	B- / 7.3	55.22%	C+ / 6.9

Major Rating Factors:
Strong performance is the major factor driving the A (Excellent) TheStreet.com Investment Rating for BlackRock MuniHoldings New York QI. The fund currently has a performance rating of B+ (Good) based on an annualized return of 21.02% over the last three years and a total return of 1.51% year to date 2012. Factored into the performance evaluation is an expense ratio of 1.36% (average).

The fund's risk rating is currently B (Good). It carries a beta of 1.88, meaning it is expected to move 18.8% for every 10% move in the market. Volatility, as measured by both the semi-deviation and a drawdown factor, is considered low. As of March 31, 2012, BlackRock MuniHoldings New York QI traded at a discount of .26% below its net asset value, which is worse than its one-year historical average discount of .71%.

Robert C. Doll, Jr. currently receives a manager quality ranking of 77 (0=worst, 99=best). If you desire only a moderate level of risk and strong performance, then this fund is an excellent option.

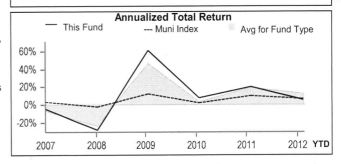

BlackRock MuniHoldings NJ Qly (MUJ)   **B+**   **Good**

Fund Family: BlackRock Inc
Fund Type: Municipal - Single State
Inception Date: March 6, 1998

Data Date	Investment Rating	Net Assets ($Mil)	Price	Performance Rating/Pts	Total Return Y-T-D	Risk Rating/Pts
3-12	B+	313.08	15.49	B / 7.7	-0.21%	B / 8.8
2011	A	330.80	15.74	A / 9.3	-0.19%	B / 8.8
2010	C+	322.68	13.49	C / 5.3	5.19%	C+ / 6.5
2009	B	305.86	13.61	C / 5.4	37.36%	B- / 7.7

Major Rating Factors: Strong performance is the major factor driving the B+ (Good) TheStreet.com Investment Rating for BlackRock MuniHoldings NJ Qly. The fund currently has a performance rating of B (Good) based on an annualized return of 16.83% over the last three years and a total return of -0.21% year to date 2012. Factored into the performance evaluation is an expense ratio of 1.17% (low).

The fund's risk rating is currently B (Good). It carries a beta of 1.79, meaning it is expected to move 17.9% for every 10% move in the market. Volatility, as measured by both the semi-deviation and a drawdown factor, is considered low. As of March 31, 2012, BlackRock MuniHoldings NJ Qly traded at a discount of 2.21% below its net asset value, which is worse than its one-year historical average discount of 4.05%.

Robert C. Doll, Jr. currently receives a manager quality ranking of 64 (0=worst, 99=best). If you desire only a moderate level of risk and strong performance, then this fund is an excellent option.

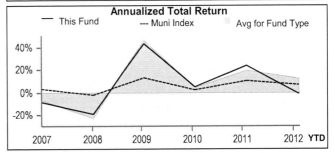

BlackRock MuniHoldings Quality (MUS)   **B+**   **Good**

Fund Family: BlackRock Inc
Fund Type: Municipal - National
Inception Date: April 28, 1998

Data Date	Investment Rating	Net Assets ($Mil)	Price	Performance Rating/Pts	Total Return Y-T-D	Risk Rating/Pts
3-12	B+	161.72	14.10	B / 8.0	1.40%	B / 8.5
2011	A	181.00	14.12	A / 9.4	0.42%	B / 8.5
2010	C	171.98	12.10	C / 4.5	1.24%	C+ / 6.5
2009	B+	158.06	12.77	B- / 7.2	42.01%	C+ / 6.8

Major Rating Factors: Strong performance is the major factor driving the B+ (Good) TheStreet.com Investment Rating for BlackRock MuniHoldings Quality. The fund currently has a performance rating of B (Good) based on an annualized return of 17.68% over the last three years and a total return of 1.40% year to date 2012. Factored into the performance evaluation is an expense ratio of 1.25% (average).

The fund's risk rating is currently B (Good). It carries a beta of 2.39, meaning it is expected to move 23.9% for every 10% move in the market. Volatility, as measured by both the semi-deviation and a drawdown factor, is considered low. As of March 31, 2012, BlackRock MuniHoldings Quality traded at a discount of 1.95% below its net asset value, which is better than its one-year historical average discount of 1.77%.

Robert M. Shearer currently receives a manager quality ranking of 42 (0=worst, 99=best). If you desire only a moderate level of risk and strong performance, then this fund is an excellent option.

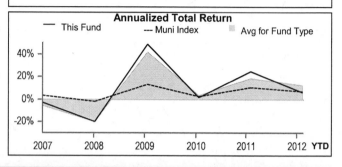

BlackRock MuniHoldings Quality II (MUE)   **B**   **Good**

Fund Family: BlackRock Inc
Fund Type: Municipal - National
Inception Date: February 23, 1999

Data Date	Investment Rating	Net Assets ($Mil)	Price	Performance Rating/Pts	Total Return Y-T-D	Risk Rating/Pts
3-12	B	293.36	13.97	B / 7.7	-0.81%	B / 8.4
2011	A	313.70	14.30	A+ / 9.6	1.61%	B / 8.5
2010	C	303.67	11.96	C- / 4.0	-1.83%	C+ / 6.4
2009	B+	274.34	13.01	B- / 7.5	44.33%	C+ / 6.5

Major Rating Factors: Strong performance is the major factor driving the B (Good) TheStreet.com Investment Rating for BlackRock MuniHoldings Quality II. The fund currently has a performance rating of B (Good) based on an annualized return of 17.68% over the last three years and a total return of -0.81% year to date 2012. Factored into the performance evaluation is an expense ratio of 1.23% (average).

The fund's risk rating is currently B (Good). It carries a beta of 2.23, meaning it is expected to move 22.3% for every 10% move in the market. Volatility, as measured by both the semi-deviation and a drawdown factor, is considered low. As of March 31, 2012, BlackRock MuniHoldings Quality II traded at a discount of 3.05% below its net asset value, which is better than its one-year historical average discount of .97%.

Robert M. Shearer currently receives a manager quality ranking of 45 (0=worst, 99=best). If you desire only a moderate level of risk and strong performance, then this fund is an excellent option.

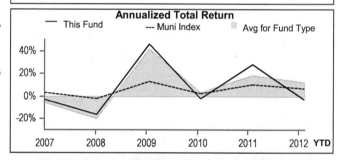

BlackRock MuniVest Fund (MVF)   **B+**   **Good**

Fund Family: BlackRock Inc
Fund Type: Municipal - National
Inception Date: September 22, 1988

Data Date	Investment Rating	Net Assets ($Mil)	Price	Performance Rating/Pts	Total Return Y-T-D	Risk Rating/Pts
3-12	B+	602.23	10.42	B / 7.9	1.55%	B / 8.9
2011	A+	626.10	10.44	A- / 9.2	0.38%	B / 8.9
2010	C+	625.20	9.46	C+ / 6.7	9.27%	C+ / 6.3
2009	B-	555.89	9.22	C+ / 6.6	39.12%	B- / 7.2

Major Rating Factors: Strong performance is the major factor driving the B+ (Good) TheStreet.com Investment Rating for BlackRock MuniVest Fund. The fund currently has a performance rating of B (Good) based on an annualized return of 18.62% over the last three years and a total return of 1.55% year to date 2012. Factored into the performance evaluation is an expense ratio of 1.28% (average).

The fund's risk rating is currently B (Good). It carries a beta of 2.01, meaning it is expected to move 20.1% for every 10% move in the market. Volatility, as measured by both the semi-deviation and a drawdown factor, is considered low. As of March 31, 2012, BlackRock MuniVest Fund traded at a premium of 2.16% above its net asset value, which is better than its one-year historical average premium of 2.46%.

Fred K. Stuebe has been running the fund for 24 years and currently receives a manager quality ranking of 65 (0=worst, 99=best). If you desire only a moderate level of risk and strong performance, then this fund is an excellent option.

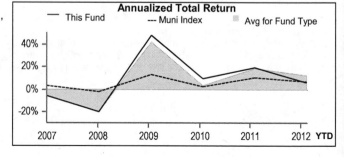

BlackRock MuniVest Fund II (MVT)

A+   **Excellent**

Fund Family: BlackRock Inc
Fund Type: Municipal - National
Inception Date: March 19, 1993

Data Date	Investment Rating	Net Assets ($Mil)	Price	Performance Rating/Pts	Total Return Y-T-D	Risk Rating/Pts
3-12	A+	278.28	16.22	A / 9.4	3.88%	B / 8.7
2011	A+	312.40	15.88	A+ / 9.8	3.02%	B / 8.6
2010	C+	295.47	14.00	C+ / 5.6	7.54%	C+ / 6.2
2009	B+	243.58	13.99	B- / 7.4	57.70%	C+ / 6.7

Major Rating Factors:
Exceptional performance is the major factor driving the A+ (Excellent) TheStreet.com Investment Rating for BlackRock MuniVest Fund II. The fund currently has a performance rating of A (Excellent) based on an annualized return of 23.85% over the last three years and a total return of 3.88% year to date 2012. Factored into the performance evaluation is an expense ratio of 1.23% (average).

The fund's risk rating is currently B (Good). It carries a beta of 1.62, meaning it is expected to move 16.2% for every 10% move in the market. Volatility, as measured by both the semi-deviation and a drawdown factor, is considered low. As of March 31, 2012, BlackRock MuniVest Fund II traded at a premium of 3.64% above its net asset value, which is worse than its one-year historical average premium of 3.10%.

Fred K. Stuebe has been running the fund for 13 years and currently receives a manager quality ranking of 86 (0=worst, 99=best). If you desire only a moderate level of risk and strong performance, then this fund is an excellent option.

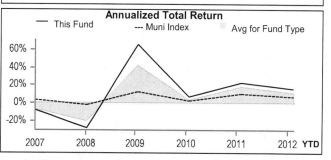

BlackRock MuniYield AZ Fund (MZA)

A+   **Excellent**

Fund Family: BlackRock Inc
Fund Type: Municipal - Single State
Inception Date: October 22, 1993

Data Date	Investment Rating	Net Assets ($Mil)	Price	Performance Rating/Pts	Total Return Y-T-D	Risk Rating/Pts
3-12	A+	61.09	14.59	A- / 9.2	4.84%	B / 8.8
2011	A+	64.90	14.12	A / 9.4	1.27%	B / 8.8
2010	C	62.62	12.62	C- / 3.9	8.80%	B- / 7.4
2009	C+	56.45	12.34	C / 5.0	48.15%	B- / 7.2

Major Rating Factors:
Exceptional performance is the major factor driving the A+ (Excellent) TheStreet.com Investment Rating for BlackRock MuniYield AZ Fund. The fund currently has a performance rating of A- (Excellent) based on an annualized return of 20.95% over the last three years and a total return of 4.84% year to date 2012. Factored into the performance evaluation is an expense ratio of 1.52% (average).

The fund's risk rating is currently B (Good). It carries a beta of 1.23, meaning it is expected to move 12.3% for every 10% move in the market. Volatility, as measured by both the semi-deviation and a drawdown factor, is considered low. As of March 31, 2012, BlackRock MuniYield AZ Fund traded at a premium of .41% above its net asset value, which is worse than its one-year historical average discount of 3.80%.

Michael A. Kalinoski has been running the fund for 19 years and currently receives a manager quality ranking of 87 (0=worst, 99=best). If you desire only a moderate level of risk and strong performance, then this fund is an excellent option.

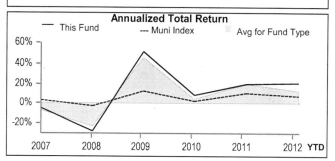

BlackRock MuniYield CA Fund (MYC)

A+   **Excellent**

Fund Family: BlackRock Inc
Fund Type: Municipal - Single State
Inception Date: February 21, 1992

Data Date	Investment Rating	Net Assets ($Mil)	Price	Performance Rating/Pts	Total Return Y-T-D	Risk Rating/Pts
3-12	A+	306.28	15.35	A- / 9.0	3.30%	B / 8.7
2011	A+	327.80	15.08	A / 9.3	1.33%	B / 8.8
2010	C+	314.33	13.28	C / 5.4	9.82%	C+ / 6.2
2009	B-	286.81	12.88	C+ / 6.3	42.95%	B- / 7.5

Major Rating Factors:
Exceptional performance is the major factor driving the A+ (Excellent) TheStreet.com Investment Rating for BlackRock MuniYield CA Fund. The fund currently has a performance rating of A- (Excellent) based on an annualized return of 20.47% over the last three years and a total return of 3.30% year to date 2012. Factored into the performance evaluation is an expense ratio of 1.49% (average).

The fund's risk rating is currently B (Good). It carries a beta of 2.35, meaning it is expected to move 23.5% for every 10% move in the market. Volatility, as measured by both the semi-deviation and a drawdown factor, is considered low. As of March 31, 2012, BlackRock MuniYield CA Fund traded at a discount of 4.42% below its net asset value, which is better than its one-year historical average discount of 3.53%.

Walter O'Connor has been running the fund for 20 years and currently receives a manager quality ranking of 58 (0=worst, 99=best). If you desire only a moderate level of risk and strong performance, then this fund is an excellent option.

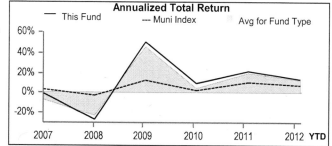

BlackRock MuniYield California Qly (MCA)

A   **Excellent**

Fund Family: BlackRock Inc
Fund Type: Municipal - Single State
Inception Date: October 23, 1992

Major Rating Factors:
Strong performance is the major factor driving the A (Excellent) TheStreet.com Investment Rating for BlackRock MuniYield California Qly. The fund currently has a performance rating of B+ (Good) based on an annualized return of 20.09% over the last three years and a total return of 5.15% year to date 2012. Factored into the performance evaluation is an expense ratio of 1.49% (average).

The fund's risk rating is currently B (Good). It carries a beta of 2.13, meaning it is expected to move 21.3% for every 10% move in the market. Volatility, as measured by both the semi-deviation and a drawdown factor, is considered low. As of March 31, 2012, BlackRock MuniYield California Qly traded at a discount of 6.36% below its net asset value, which is worse than its one-year historical average discount of 6.57%.

Walter O'Connor has been running the fund for 20 years and currently receives a manager quality ranking of 64 (0=worst, 99=best). If you desire only a moderate level of risk and strong performance, then this fund is an excellent option.

Data Date	Investment Rating	Net Assets ($Mil)	Price	Perfor-mance Rating/Pts	Total Return Y-T-D	Risk Rating/Pts
3-12	A	491.80	14.86	B+ / 8.9	5.15%	B / 8.6
2011	A-	523.90	14.34	B+ / 8.9	2.02%	B / 8.7
2010	C	503.87	12.79	C / 4.6	8.05%	C+ / 6.1
2009	B	461.51	12.57	C / 5.5	36.21%	B- / 7.7

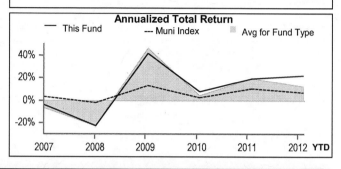

BlackRock MuniYield Fund (MYD)

A+   **Excellent**

Fund Family: BlackRock Inc
Fund Type: Municipal - National
Inception Date: November 21, 1991

Major Rating Factors:
Exceptional performance is the major factor driving the A+ (Excellent) TheStreet.com Investment Rating for BlackRock MuniYield Fund. The fund currently has a performance rating of A- (Excellent) based on an annualized return of 22.18% over the last three years and a total return of 5.24% year to date 2012. Factored into the performance evaluation is an expense ratio of 1.15% (low).

The fund's risk rating is currently B (Good). It carries a beta of 2.17, meaning it is expected to move 21.7% for every 10% move in the market. Volatility, as measured by both the semi-deviation and a drawdown factor, is considered low. As of March 31, 2012, BlackRock MuniYield Fund traded at a premium of 2.34% above its net asset value, which is worse than its one-year historical average premium of 1.25%.

Robert C. Doll, Jr. currently receives a manager quality ranking of 69 (0=worst, 99=best). If you desire only a moderate level of risk and strong performance, then this fund is an excellent option.

Data Date	Investment Rating	Net Assets ($Mil)	Price	Perfor-mance Rating/Pts	Total Return Y-T-D	Risk Rating/Pts
3-12	A+	598.98	15.31	A- / 9.1	5.24%	B / 8.6
2011	A-	660.60	14.79	B+ / 8.7	0.20%	B / 8.6
2010	C+	630.61	13.41	C / 4.7	11.94%	C+ / 6.8
2009	C+	523.59	12.82	C / 4.4	32.31%	B- / 7.3

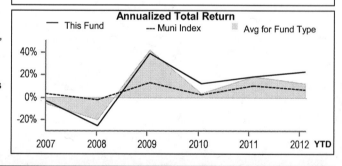

BlackRock MuniYield Inv Quality (MFT)

B+   **Good**

Fund Family: BlackRock Inc
Fund Type: Municipal - Single State
Inception Date: October 23, 1992

Major Rating Factors: Strong performance is the major factor driving the B+ (Good) TheStreet.com Investment Rating for BlackRock MuniYield Inv Quality. The fund currently has a performance rating of B (Good) based on an annualized return of 17.50% over the last three years and a total return of 0.05% year to date 2012. Factored into the performance evaluation is an expense ratio of 1.23% (average).

The fund's risk rating is currently B (Good). It carries a beta of 1.95, meaning it is expected to move 19.5% for every 10% move in the market. Volatility, as measured by both the semi-deviation and a drawdown factor, is considered low. As of March 31, 2012, BlackRock MuniYield Inv Quality traded at a discount of 4.18% below its net asset value, which is better than its one-year historical average discount of 2.64%.

Robert C. Doll, Jr. currently receives a manager quality ranking of 63 (0=worst, 99=best). If you desire only a moderate level of risk and strong performance, then this fund is an excellent option.

Data Date	Investment Rating	Net Assets ($Mil)	Price	Perfor-mance Rating/Pts	Total Return Y-T-D	Risk Rating/Pts
3-12	B+	113.42	14.21	B / 7.7	0.05%	B / 8.8
2011	A+	121.40	14.41	A / 9.4	0.35%	B / 8.8
2010	C-	117.34	12.31	C- / 4.1	2.49%	C / 5.4
2009	C+	108.43	12.78	C+ / 6.9	44.89%	C+ / 6.7

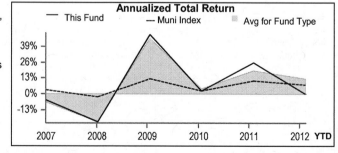

BlackRock MuniYield Invt Fund (MYF)

A+   **Excellent**

Fund Family: BlackRock Inc
Fund Type: Municipal - Single State
Inception Date: February 21, 1992

Major Rating Factors:

Exceptional performance is the major factor driving the A+ (Excellent) TheStreet.com Investment Rating for BlackRock MuniYield Invt Fund. The fund currently has a performance rating of A (Excellent) based on an annualized return of 21.31% over the last three years and a total return of 6.31% year to date 2012. Factored into the performance evaluation is an expense ratio of 1.45% (average).

The fund's risk rating is currently B (Good). It carries a beta of 2.33, meaning it is expected to move 23.3% for every 10% move in the market. Volatility, as measured by both the semi-deviation and a drawdown factor, is considered low. As of March 31, 2012, BlackRock MuniYield Invt Fund traded at a premium of .52% above its net asset value, which is worse than its one-year historical average discount of 1.35%.

Robert C. Doll, Jr. currently receives a manager quality ranking of 64 (0=worst, 99=best). If you desire only a moderate level of risk and strong performance, then this fund is an excellent option.

Data Date	Investment Rating	Net Assets ($Mil)	Price	Performance Rating/Pts	Total Return Y-T-D	Risk Rating/Pts
3-12	A+	186.13	15.38	A / 9.3	6.31%	B / 8.7
2011	A+	198.90	14.69	A+ / 9.7	2.45%	B / 8.8
2010	C+	193.27	12.98	C / 5.3	9.07%	C+ / 6.2
2009	B-	175.61	12.68	C+ / 6.8	45.37%	B- / 7.0

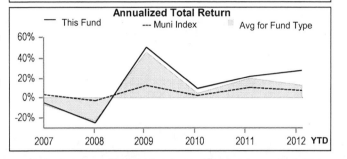

BlackRock MuniYield Michigan Qly (MIY)

B+   **Good**

Fund Family: BlackRock Inc
Fund Type: Municipal - Single State
Inception Date: October 23, 1992

Major Rating Factors: Strong performance is the major factor driving the B+ (Good) TheStreet.com Investment Rating for BlackRock MuniYield Michigan Qly. The fund currently has a performance rating of B (Good) based on an annualized return of 19.70% over the last three years and a total return of -3.42% year to date 2012. Factored into the performance evaluation is an expense ratio of 1.36% (average).

The fund's risk rating is currently B (Good). It carries a beta of 1.96, meaning it is expected to move 19.6% for every 10% move in the market. Volatility, as measured by both the semi-deviation and a drawdown factor, is considered low. As of March 31, 2012, BlackRock MuniYield Michigan Qly traded at a discount of 5.39% below its net asset value, which is better than its one-year historical average discount of 4.54%.

Fred K. Stuebe has been running the fund for 20 years and currently receives a manager quality ranking of 70 (0=worst, 99=best). If you desire only a moderate level of risk and strong performance, then this fund is an excellent option.

Data Date	Investment Rating	Net Assets ($Mil)	Price	Performance Rating/Pts	Total Return Y-T-D	Risk Rating/Pts
3-12	B+	266.33	14.75	B / 7.9	-3.42%	B / 8.8
2011	A+	279.40	15.50	A / 9.3	-2.00%	B / 8.9
2010	C+	271.61	13.35	C / 5.3	9.67%	C+ / 6.2
2009	B-	253.63	12.98	C+ / 6.4	40.50%	B- / 7.6

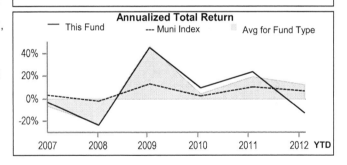

BlackRock MuniYield Michigan Qly I (MYM)

A-   **Excellent**

Fund Family: BlackRock Inc
Fund Type: Municipal - Single State
Inception Date: February 21, 1992

Major Rating Factors:

Strong performance is the major factor driving the A- (Excellent) TheStreet.com Investment Rating for BlackRock MuniYield Michigan Qly I. The fund currently has a performance rating of B (Good) based on an annualized return of 19.96% over the last three years and a total return of -5.51% year to date 2012. Factored into the performance evaluation is an expense ratio of 1.31% (average).

The fund's risk rating is currently B (Good). It carries a beta of 2.13, meaning it is expected to move 21.3% for every 10% move in the market. Volatility, as measured by both the semi-deviation and a drawdown factor, is considered low. As of March 31, 2012, BlackRock MuniYield Michigan Qly I traded at a discount of 5.09% below its net asset value, which is better than its one-year historical average discount of 3.41%.

Fred K. Stuebe has been running the fund for 20 years and currently receives a manager quality ranking of 66 (0=worst, 99=best). If you desire only a moderate level of risk and strong performance, then this fund is an excellent option.

Data Date	Investment Rating	Net Assets ($Mil)	Price	Performance Rating/Pts	Total Return Y-T-D	Risk Rating/Pts
3-12	A-	163.28	13.81	B / 8.1	-5.51%	B / 8.8
2011	A+	172.10	14.83	A+ / 9.7	-2.29%	B / 8.9
2010	C	166.77	12.11	C / 4.5	8.82%	C+ / 6.2
2009	B-	155.36	11.88	C+ / 5.7	40.26%	B- / 7.7

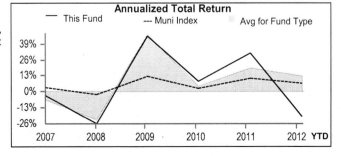

BlackRock MuniYield New Jersey Qly (MJI)   A-   Excellent

Fund Family: BlackRock Inc
Fund Type: Municipal - Single State
Inception Date: October 23, 1992

Data Date	Investment Rating	Net Assets ($Mil)	Price	Performance Rating/Pts	Total Return Y-T-D	Risk Rating/Pts
3-12	A-	128.48	15.40	B+ / 8.3	0.33%	B / 8.7
2011	A+	135.20	15.56	A+ / 9.6	1.03%	B / 8.7
2010	C-	132.28	13.34	C- / 3.6	5.58%	C+ / 6.6
2009	B-	123.81	13.40	C+ / 6.0	41.85%	B- / 7.6

Major Rating Factors:
Strong performance is the major factor driving the A- (Excellent) TheStreet.com Investment Rating for BlackRock MuniYield New Jersey Qly. The fund currently has a performance rating of B+ (Good) based on an annualized return of 17.76% over the last three years and a total return of 0.33% year to date 2012. Factored into the performance evaluation is an expense ratio of 1.12% (low).

The fund's risk rating is currently B (Good). It carries a beta of 2.09, meaning it is expected to move 20.9% for every 10% move in the market. Volatility, as measured by both the semi-deviation and a drawdown factor, is considered low. As of March 31, 2012, BlackRock MuniYield New Jersey Qly traded at a discount of 1.72% below its net asset value, which is worse than its one-year historical average discount of 3.87%.

Robert C. Doll, Jr. currently receives a manager quality ranking of 56 (0=worst, 99=best). If you desire only a moderate level of risk and strong performance, then this fund is an excellent option.

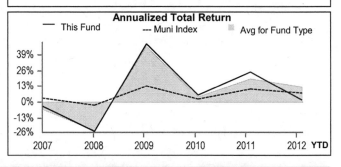

BlackRock MuniYield New York Qly (MYN)   B+   Good

Fund Family: BlackRock Inc
Fund Type: Municipal - Single State
Inception Date: February 21, 1992

Data Date	Investment Rating	Net Assets ($Mil)	Price	Performance Rating/Pts	Total Return Y-T-D	Risk Rating/Pts
3-12	B+	530.06	13.97	B / 8.2	0.70%	B / 8.6
2011	A	559.70	14.08	A / 9.4	0.00%	B / 8.6
2010	C	547.81	12.45	C / 5.5	12.09%	C / 5.4
2009	B-	499.09	11.80	C / 5.3	38.08%	B- / 7.7

Major Rating Factors: Strong performance is the major factor driving the B+ (Good) TheStreet.com Investment Rating for BlackRock MuniYield New York Qly. The fund currently has a performance rating of B (Good) based on an annualized return of 18.98% over the last three years and a total return of 0.70% year to date 2012. Factored into the performance evaluation is an expense ratio of 1.33% (average).

The fund's risk rating is currently B (Good). It carries a beta of 1.98, meaning it is expected to move 19.8% for every 10% move in the market. Volatility, as measured by both the semi-deviation and a drawdown factor, is considered low. As of March 31, 2012, BlackRock MuniYield New York Qly traded at a discount of 3.79% below its net asset value, which is worse than its one-year historical average discount of 3.90%.

Timothy T. Browse has been running the fund for 20 years and currently receives a manager quality ranking of 66 (0=worst, 99=best). If you desire only a moderate level of risk and strong performance, then this fund is an excellent option.

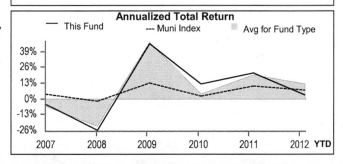

BlackRock MuniYield NJ Fund (MYJ)   A-   Excellent

Fund Family: BlackRock Inc
Fund Type: Municipal - Single State
Inception Date: April 23, 1992

Data Date	Investment Rating	Net Assets ($Mil)	Price	Performance Rating/Pts	Total Return Y-T-D	Risk Rating/Pts
3-12	A-	211.12	15.77	B+ / 8.3	2.48%	B / 8.7
2011	A-	224.80	15.60	B+ / 8.6	-1.60%	B / 8.8
2010	C	216.43	13.78	C- / 4.1	5.74%	C+ / 6.7
2009	B-	200.74	13.81	C+ / 5.7	38.87%	B- / 7.5

Major Rating Factors:
Strong performance is the major factor driving the A- (Excellent) TheStreet.com Investment Rating for BlackRock MuniYield NJ Fund. The fund currently has a performance rating of B+ (Good) based on an annualized return of 16.95% over the last three years and a total return of 2.48% year to date 2012. Factored into the performance evaluation is an expense ratio of 1.26% (average).

The fund's risk rating is currently B (Good). It carries a beta of 1.90, meaning it is expected to move 19.0% for every 10% move in the market. Volatility, as measured by both the semi-deviation and a drawdown factor, is considered low. As of March 31, 2012, BlackRock MuniYield NJ Fund traded at a discount of 2.47% below its net asset value, which is worse than its one-year historical average discount of 5.57%.

Robert C. Doll, Jr. currently receives a manager quality ranking of 62 (0=worst, 99=best). If you desire only a moderate level of risk and strong performance, then this fund is an excellent option.

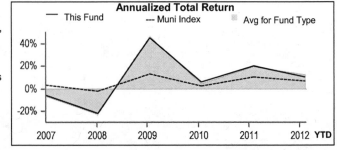

BlackRock MuniYield PA Qly (MPA)

B+ **Good**

Fund Family: BlackRock Inc
Fund Type: Municipal - Single State
Inception Date: October 23, 1992

Data Date	Investment Rating	Net Assets ($Mil)	Price	Performance Rating/Pts	Total Return Y-T-D	Risk Rating/Pts
3-12	B+	171.94	15.50	B- / 7.4	-0.43%	B / 8.8
2011	A+	180.10	15.79	A- / 9.2	0.06%	B / 8.9
2010	C	176.53	13.45	C- / 4.0	7.26%	C+ / 6.3
2009	B-	163.92	13.32	C+ / 6.0	43.71%	B- / 7.4

Major Rating Factors: Strong performance is the major factor driving the B+ (Good) TheStreet.com Investment Rating for BlackRock MuniYield PA Qly. The fund currently has a performance rating of B- (Good) based on an annualized return of 17.25% over the last three years and a total return of -0.43% year to date 2012. Factored into the performance evaluation is an expense ratio of 1.36% (average).

The fund's risk rating is currently B (Good). It carries a beta of 1.58, meaning it is expected to move 15.8% for every 10% move in the market. Volatility, as measured by both the semi-deviation and a drawdown factor, is considered low. As of March 31, 2012, BlackRock MuniYield PA Qly traded at a discount of 3.25% below its net asset value, which is better than its one-year historical average discount of 2.83%.

William R. Bock has been running the fund for 20 years and currently receives a manager quality ranking of 73 (0=worst, 99=best). If you desire only a moderate level of risk and strong performance, then this fund is an excellent option.

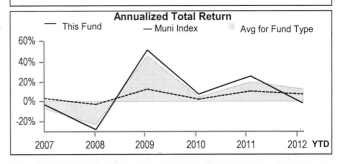

BlackRock MuniYield Quality Fund (MQY)

B **Good**

Fund Family: BlackRock Inc
Fund Type: Municipal - National
Inception Date: June 19, 1992

Data Date	Investment Rating	Net Assets ($Mil)	Price	Performance Rating/Pts	Total Return Y-T-D	Risk Rating/Pts
3-12	B	418.35	15.48	B- / 7.4	-0.71%	B / 8.5
2011	A-	470.20	15.82	A- / 9.1	-1.07%	B / 8.5
2010	C+	445.16	13.72	C+ / 6.0	5.54%	C+ / 5.9
2009	B-	403.80	13.84	C+ / 6.7	37.31%	B- / 7.1

Major Rating Factors: Strong performance is the major factor driving the B (Good) TheStreet.com Investment Rating for BlackRock MuniYield Quality Fund. The fund currently has a performance rating of B- (Good) based on an annualized return of 16.42% over the last three years and a total return of -0.71% year to date 2012. Factored into the performance evaluation is an expense ratio of 1.21% (average).

The fund's risk rating is currently B (Good). It carries a beta of 2.31, meaning it is expected to move 23.1% for every 10% move in the market. Volatility, as measured by both the semi-deviation and a drawdown factor, is considered low. As of March 31, 2012, BlackRock MuniYield Quality Fund traded at a discount of 3.37% below its net asset value, which is better than its one-year historical average discount of 2.23%.

Michael A. Kalinoski has been running the fund for 20 years and currently receives a manager quality ranking of 41 (0=worst, 99=best). If you desire only a moderate level of risk and strong performance, then this fund is an excellent option.

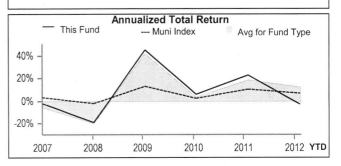

BlackRock MuniYield Quality Fund I (MQT)

A- **Excellent**

Fund Family: BlackRock Inc
Fund Type: Municipal - National
Inception Date: August 21, 1992

Data Date	Investment Rating	Net Assets ($Mil)	Price	Performance Rating/Pts	Total Return Y-T-D	Risk Rating/Pts
3-12	A-	265.92	13.56	B+ / 8.4	0.44%	B / 8.5
2011	A+	300.70	13.70	A+ / 9.7	-0.44%	B / 8.6
2010	C	284.40	11.35	C- / 4.2	2.87%	C+ / 6.3
2009	C+	258.26	11.76	C+ / 6.5	40.16%	C+ / 6.8

Major Rating Factors:
Strong performance is the major factor driving the A- (Excellent) TheStreet.com Investment Rating for BlackRock MuniYield Quality Fund I. The fund currently has a performance rating of B+ (Good) based on an annualized return of 19.03% over the last three years and a total return of 0.44% year to date 2012. Factored into the performance evaluation is an expense ratio of 1.20% (average).

The fund's risk rating is currently B (Good). It carries a beta of 2.41, meaning it is expected to move 24.1% for every 10% move in the market. Volatility, as measured by both the semi-deviation and a drawdown factor, is considered low. As of March 31, 2012, BlackRock MuniYield Quality Fund I traded at a discount of 2.59% below its net asset value, which is better than its one-year historical average discount of 2.44%.

Romualdo Roldan currently receives a manager quality ranking of 47 (0=worst, 99=best). If you desire only a moderate level of risk and strong performance, then this fund is an excellent option.

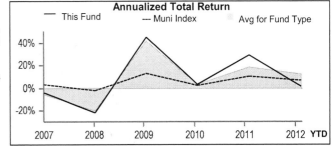

BlackRock MuniYield Quality III (MYI)

B+ **Good**

Fund Family: BlackRock Inc
Fund Type: Municipal - National
Inception Date: March 20, 1992

Data Date	Investment Rating	Net Assets ($Mil)	Price	Performance Rating/Pts	Total Return Y-T-D	Risk Rating/Pts
3-12	B+	890.99	14.21	B / 7.7	1.98%	B / 8.6
2011	A	955.20	14.14	A / 9.5	1.27%	B / 8.6
2010	D+	920.23	12.47	C- / 3.4	8.16%	C / 5.5
2009	C+	825.62	12.26	C / 5.1	37.13%	B- / 7.0

Major Rating Factors: Strong performance is the major factor driving the B+ (Good) TheStreet.com Investment Rating for BlackRock MuniYield Quality III. The fund currently has a performance rating of B (Good) based on an annualized return of 15.81% over the last three years and a total return of 1.98% year to date 2012. Factored into the performance evaluation is an expense ratio of 1.32% (average).

The fund's risk rating is currently B (Good). It carries a beta of 1.91, meaning it is expected to move 19.1% for every 10% move in the market. Volatility, as measured by both the semi-deviation and a drawdown factor, is considered low. As of March 31, 2012, BlackRock MuniYield Quality III traded at a discount of 2.94% below its net asset value, which is worse than its one-year historical average discount of 3.61%.

William R. Bock has been running the fund for 20 years and currently receives a manager quality ranking of 54 (0=worst, 99=best). If you desire only a moderate level of risk and strong performance, then this fund is an excellent option.

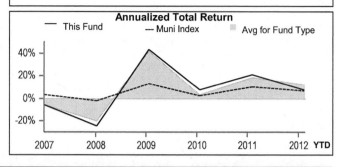

BlackRock New York Muni Inc Qly (BSE)

A- **Excellent**

Fund Family: BlackRock Inc
Fund Type: Municipal - Single State
Inception Date: October 28, 2002

Data Date	Investment Rating	Net Assets ($Mil)	Price	Performance Rating/Pts	Total Return Y-T-D	Risk Rating/Pts
3-12	A-	92.41	15.20	B+ / 8.3	3.43%	B / 8.6
2011	B+	95.80	14.91	B+ / 8.4	0.03%	B / 8.7
2010	C-	96.62	13.05	D / 2.1	3.27%	B- / 7.1
2009	B-	88.14	13.41	C+ / 6.2	47.95%	B- / 7.2

Major Rating Factors:
Strong performance is the major factor driving the A- (Excellent) TheStreet.com Investment Rating for BlackRock New York Muni Inc Qly. The fund currently has a performance rating of B+ (Good) based on an annualized return of 17.25% over the last three years and a total return of 3.43% year to date 2012. Factored into the performance evaluation is an expense ratio of 1.26% (average).

The fund's risk rating is currently B (Good). It carries a beta of 2.38, meaning it is expected to move 23.8% for every 10% move in the market. Volatility, as measured by both the semi-deviation and a drawdown factor, is considered low. As of March 31, 2012, BlackRock New York Muni Inc Qly traded at a premium of 1.27% above its net asset value, which is worse than its one-year historical average discount of 1.65%.

Timothy T. Browse has been running the fund for 6 years and currently receives a manager quality ranking of 40 (0=worst, 99=best). If you desire only a moderate level of risk and strong performance, then this fund is an excellent option.

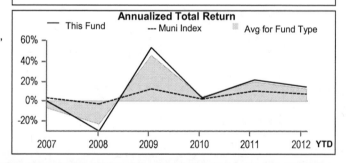

BlackRock NJ Inv Qual Muni Tr (RNJ)

A- **Excellent**

Fund Family: BlackRock Inc
Fund Type: Municipal - Single State
Inception Date: May 28, 1993

Data Date	Investment Rating	Net Assets ($Mil)	Price	Performance Rating/Pts	Total Return Y-T-D	Risk Rating/Pts
3-12	A-	12.53	14.32	A+ / 9.6	7.92%	B- / 7.4
2011	B+	13.40	13.46	A+ / 9.6	0.59%	B- / 7.5
2010	D	12.76	11.63	D- / 1.1	3.69%	C+ / 6.0
2009	C-	11.47	11.93	D+ / 2.8	53.15%	C+ / 6.4

Major Rating Factors:
Exceptional performance is the major factor driving the A- (Excellent) TheStreet.com Investment Rating for BlackRock NJ Inv Qual Muni Tr. The fund currently has a performance rating of A+ (Excellent) based on an annualized return of 22.00% over the last three years and a total return of 7.92% year to date 2012. Factored into the performance evaluation is an expense ratio of 1.53% (average).

The fund's risk rating is currently B- (Good). It carries a beta of 1.51, meaning it is expected to move 15.1% for every 10% move in the market. Volatility, as measured by both the semi-deviation and a drawdown factor, is considered low. As of March 31, 2012, BlackRock NJ Inv Qual Muni Tr traded at a premium of 5.60% above its net asset value, which is worse than its one-year historical average discount of 1.08%.

Theodore R. Jaeckel, Jr. has been running the fund for 6 years and currently receives a manager quality ranking of 87 (0=worst, 99=best). If you desire only a moderate level of risk and strong performance, then this fund is an excellent option.

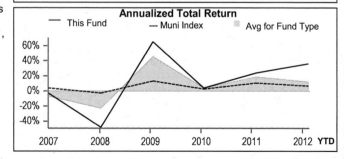

BlackRock NJ Muni Bond Trust (BLJ)

B **Good**

Fund Family: BlackRock Inc
Fund Type: Municipal - Single State
Inception Date: April 26, 2002

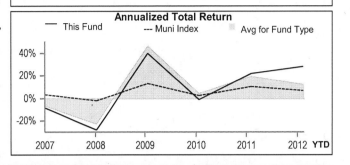

Data Date	Investment Rating	Net Assets ($Mil)	Price	Performance Rating/Pts	Total Return Y-T-D	Risk Rating/Pts
3-12	B	33.75	16.07	B / 8.0	6.39%	B- / 7.9
2011	A-	35.50	15.33	A / 9.3	1.37%	B / 8.0
2010	D+	35.28	13.38	D- / 1.3	-1.22%	C+ / 6.9
2009	C	31.24	14.47	C- / 3.6	33.40%	C+ / 6.8

Major Rating Factors: Strong performance is the major factor driving the B (Good) TheStreet.com Investment Rating for BlackRock NJ Muni Bond Trust. The fund currently has a performance rating of B (Good) based on an annualized return of 13.28% over the last three years and a total return of 6.39% year to date 2012. Factored into the performance evaluation is an expense ratio of 1.43% (average).

The fund's risk rating is currently B- (Good). It carries a beta of 2.09, meaning it is expected to move 20.9% for every 10% move in the market. Volatility, as measured by both the semi-deviation and a drawdown factor, is considered low. As of March 31, 2012, BlackRock NJ Muni Bond Trust traded at a premium of 1.32% above its net asset value, which is worse than its one-year historical average discount of 2.18%.

Theodore R. Jaeckel, Jr. has been running the fund for 6 years and currently receives a manager quality ranking of 39 (0=worst, 99=best). If you desire only a moderate level of risk and strong performance, then this fund is an excellent option.

BlackRock NJ Municipal Income Trus (BNJ)

B+ **Good**

Fund Family: BlackRock Inc
Fund Type: Municipal - Single State
Inception Date: July 26, 2001

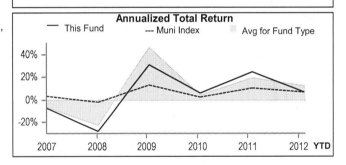

Data Date	Investment Rating	Net Assets ($Mil)	Price	Performance Rating/Pts	Total Return Y-T-D	Risk Rating/Pts
3-12	B+	107.23	15.70	B / 8.0	1.57%	B / 8.4
2011	B+	114.10	15.69	B+ / 8.8	1.02%	B / 8.4
2010	D+	109.26	13.43	D / 1.6	5.96%	C+ / 6.9
2009	C-	96.70	13.53	D / 1.8	25.91%	B- / 7.0

Major Rating Factors: Strong performance is the major factor driving the B+ (Good) TheStreet.com Investment Rating for BlackRock NJ Municipal Income Trus. The fund currently has a performance rating of B (Good) based on an annualized return of 16.35% over the last three years and a total return of 1.57% year to date 2012. Factored into the performance evaluation is an expense ratio of 1.24% (average).

The fund's risk rating is currently B (Good). It carries a beta of 2.14, meaning it is expected to move 21.4% for every 10% move in the market. Volatility, as measured by both the semi-deviation and a drawdown factor, is considered low. As of March 31, 2012, BlackRock NJ Municipal Income Trus traded at a premium of 1.55% above its net asset value, which is better than its one-year historical average premium of 1.60%.

Theodore R. Jaeckel, Jr. has been running the fund for 6 years and currently receives a manager quality ranking of 49 (0=worst, 99=best). If you desire only a moderate level of risk and strong performance, then this fund is an excellent option.

BlackRock NY Inv Qual Muni Tr (RNY)

B+ **Good**

Fund Family: BlackRock Inc
Fund Type: Municipal - Single State
Inception Date: May 28, 1993

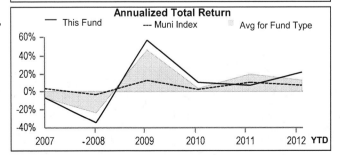

Data Date	Investment Rating	Net Assets ($Mil)	Price	Performance Rating/Pts	Total Return Y-T-D	Risk Rating/Pts
3-12	B+	18.08	14.81	B+ / 8.3	5.05%	B / 8.5
2011	B+	18.90	14.31	B+ / 8.5	1.92%	B / 8.6
2010	C+	18.58	14.27	C+ / 6.4	10.61%	C+ / 6.4
2009	C+	16.80	13.72	C / 5.0	53.14%	B- / 7.0

Major Rating Factors: Strong performance is the major factor driving the B+ (Good) TheStreet.com Investment Rating for BlackRock NY Inv Qual Muni Tr. The fund currently has a performance rating of B+ (Good) based on an annualized return of 18.15% over the last three years and a total return of 5.05% year to date 2012. Factored into the performance evaluation is an expense ratio of 1.39% (average).

The fund's risk rating is currently B (Good). It carries a beta of 1.30, meaning it is expected to move 13.0% for every 10% move in the market. Volatility, as measured by both the semi-deviation and a drawdown factor, is considered low. As of March 31, 2012, BlackRock NY Inv Qual Muni Tr traded at a discount of 1.33% below its net asset value, which is better than its one-year historical average discount of .73%.

Robert S. Kapito has been running the fund for 19 years and currently receives a manager quality ranking of 80 (0=worst, 99=best). If you desire only a moderate level of risk and strong performance, then this fund is an excellent option.

BlackRock NY Muni 2018 Income Trus (BLH) **C** **Fair**

Fund Family: BlackRock Inc
Fund Type: Municipal - Single State
Inception Date: October 25, 2001

Data Date	Investment Rating	Net Assets ($Mil)	Price	Performance Rating/Pts	Total Return Y-T-D	Risk Rating/Pts
3-12	C	56.81	16.50	C- / 3.6	0.28%	B+ / 9.4
2011	B	56.80	16.71	C+ / 6.2	1.56%	B+ / 9.5
2010	B-	56.98	16.10	C+ / 6.3	1.84%	B- / 7.3
2009	A	53.50	16.90	B- / 7.0	26.06%	B- / 7.5

Major Rating Factors: Middle of the road best describes BlackRock NY Muni 2018 Income Trus whose TheStreet.com Investment Rating is currently a C (Fair). The fund currently has a performance rating of C- (Fair) based on an annualized return of 10.10% over the last three years and a total return of 0.28% year to date 2012. Factored into the performance evaluation is an expense ratio of 0.98% (low).

The fund's risk rating is currently B+ (Good). It carries a beta of 0.53, meaning the fund's expected move will be 5.3% for every 10% move in the market. Volatility, as measured by both the semi-deviation and a drawdown factor, is considered very low. As of March 31, 2012, BlackRock NY Muni 2018 Income Trus traded at a premium of 5.57% above its net asset value, which is better than its one-year historical average premium of 6.46%.

F. Howard Downs has been running the fund for 6 years and currently receives a manager quality ranking of 75 (0=worst, 99=best). If you desire an average level of risk, then this fund may be an option.

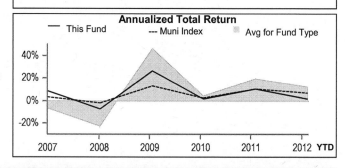

BlackRock NY Muni Bond Trust (BQH) **B+** **Good**

Fund Family: BlackRock Inc
Fund Type: Municipal - Single State
Inception Date: April 26, 2002

Data Date	Investment Rating	Net Assets ($Mil)	Price	Performance Rating/Pts	Total Return Y-T-D	Risk Rating/Pts
3-12	B+	41.40	15.75	B / 7.6	1.81%	B / 8.6
2011	B+	42.40	15.71	B+ / 8.4	-1.74%	B / 8.7
2010	C-	43.41	14.01	D / 1.9	-2.55%	B- / 7.1
2009	B-	40.20	15.33	C+ / 6.8	56.78%	B- / 7.1

Major Rating Factors: Strong performance is the major factor driving the B+ (Good) TheStreet.com Investment Rating for BlackRock NY Muni Bond Trust. The fund currently has a performance rating of B (Good) based on an annualized return of 16.98% over the last three years and a total return of 1.81% year to date 2012. Factored into the performance evaluation is an expense ratio of 1.37% (average).

The fund's risk rating is currently B (Good). It carries a beta of 2.30, meaning it is expected to move 23.0% for every 10% move in the market. Volatility, as measured by both the semi-deviation and a drawdown factor, is considered low. As of March 31, 2012, BlackRock NY Muni Bond Trust traded at a premium of .06% above its net asset value, which is better than its one-year historical average premium of .09%.

Robert S. Kapito currently receives a manager quality ranking of 34 (0=worst, 99=best). If you desire only a moderate level of risk and strong performance, then this fund is an excellent option.

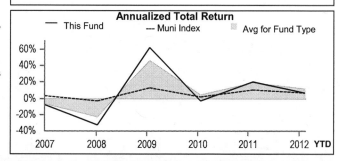

BlackRock NY Municipal Income Tr I (BFY) **A-** **Excellent**

Fund Family: BlackRock Inc
Fund Type: Municipal - Single State
Inception Date: July 25, 2002

Data Date	Investment Rating	Net Assets ($Mil)	Price	Performance Rating/Pts	Total Return Y-T-D	Risk Rating/Pts
3-12	A-	72.82	15.63	B+ / 8.3	0.86%	B / 8.9
2011	A+	74.70	15.75	A+ / 9.6	1.17%	B+ / 9.1
2010	C	75.87	14.09	C / 4.9	5.74%	C+ / 5.8
2009	B+	69.32	14.24	B- / 7.3	57.11%	C+ / 6.5

Major Rating Factors:
Strong performance is the major factor driving the A- (Excellent) TheStreet.com Investment Rating for BlackRock NY Municipal Income Tr I. The fund currently has a performance rating of B+ (Good) based on an annualized return of 19.25% over the last three years and a total return of 0.86% year to date 2012. Factored into the performance evaluation is an expense ratio of 1.18% (low).

The fund's risk rating is currently B (Good). It carries a beta of 1.46, meaning it is expected to move 14.6% for every 10% move in the market. Volatility, as measured by both the semi-deviation and a drawdown factor, is considered low. As of March 31, 2012, BlackRock NY Municipal Income Tr I traded at a premium of .90% above its net asset value, which is better than its one-year historical average premium of 1.75%.

Timothy T. Browse has been running the fund for 6 years and currently receives a manager quality ranking of 82 (0=worst, 99=best). If you desire only a moderate level of risk and strong performance, then this fund is an excellent option.

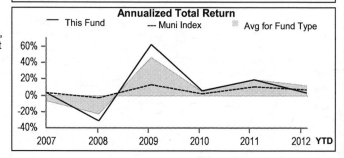

BlackRock NY Municipal Income Trus (BNY)   B+   Good

Fund Family: BlackRock Inc
Fund Type: Municipal - Single State
Inception Date: July 26, 2001

Data Date	Investment Rating	Net Assets ($Mil)	Price	Performance Rating/Pts	Total Return Y-T-D	Risk Rating/Pts
3-12	B+	177.99	15.67	B / 7.8	3.97%	B / 8.8
2011	B+	185.20	15.32	B+ / 8.3	0.00%	B / 8.9
2010	C-	182.37	13.63	D / 2.1	0.74%	B- / 7.1
2009	C	161.73	14.50	C / 4.7	47.20%	C+ / 6.8

Major Rating Factors: Strong performance is the major factor driving the B+ (Good) TheStreet.com Investment Rating for BlackRock NY Municipal Income Trus. The fund currently has a performance rating of B (Good) based on an annualized return of 16.97% over the last three years and a total return of 3.97% year to date 2012. Factored into the performance evaluation is an expense ratio of 1.27% (average).

The fund's risk rating is currently B (Good). It carries a beta of 1.85, meaning it is expected to move 18.5% for every 10% move in the market. Volatility, as measured by both the semi-deviation and a drawdown factor, is considered low. As of March 31, 2012, BlackRock NY Municipal Income Trus traded at a premium of 5.38% above its net asset value, which is worse than its one-year historical average premium of 5.28%.

Timothy T. Browse has been running the fund for 6 years and currently receives a manager quality ranking of 64 (0=worst, 99=best). If you desire only a moderate level of risk and strong performance, then this fund is an excellent option.

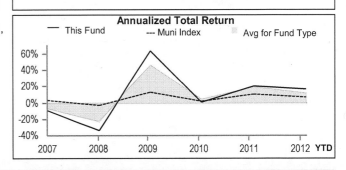

BlackRock PA Strategic Muni Tr (BPS)   A   Excellent

Fund Family: BlackRock Inc
Fund Type: Municipal - Single State
Inception Date: August 24, 1999

Data Date	Investment Rating	Net Assets ($Mil)	Price	Performance Rating/Pts	Total Return Y-T-D	Risk Rating/Pts
3-12	A	26.57	15.00	A- / 9.2	3.68%	B / 8.4
2011	A+	29.40	14.69	A+ / 9.7	0.00%	B / 8.4
2010	D+	28.04	12.44	D / 1.9	4.49%	C+ / 6.8
2009	C	24.02	12.68	C / 4.8	56.70%	C+ / 6.8

Major Rating Factors:
Exceptional performance is the major factor driving the A (Excellent) TheStreet.com Investment Rating for BlackRock PA Strategic Muni Tr. The fund currently has a performance rating of A- (Excellent) based on an annualized return of 22.68% over the last three years and a total return of 3.68% year to date 2012. Factored into the performance evaluation is an expense ratio of 1.55% (average).

The fund's risk rating is currently B (Good). It carries a beta of 2.42, meaning it is expected to move 24.2% for every 10% move in the market. Volatility, as measured by both the semi-deviation and a drawdown factor, is considered low. As of March 31, 2012, BlackRock PA Strategic Muni Tr traded at a premium of .67% above its net asset value, which is worse than its one-year historical average discount of 1.48%.

Theodore R. Jaeckel, Jr. has been running the fund for 6 years and currently receives a manager quality ranking of 68 (0=worst, 99=best). If you desire only a moderate level of risk and strong performance, then this fund is an excellent option.

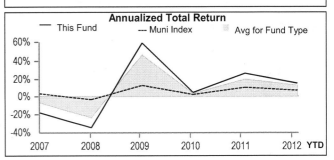

BlackRock Real Asset Equity Trust (BCF)   C+   Fair

Fund Family: BlackRock Inc
Fund Type: Income
Inception Date: September 29, 2006

Data Date	Investment Rating	Net Assets ($Mil)	Price	Performance Rating/Pts	Total Return Y-T-D	Risk Rating/Pts
3-12	C+	711.92	12.05	C+ / 6.8	15.48%	C+ / 6.9
2011	C+	664.50	10.67	C+ / 6.8	5.06%	C+ / 6.8
2010	C	664.93	14.62	B- / 7.5	25.56%	C- / 3.6
2009	C+	526.63	12.67	B / 8.1	90.33%	C- / 4.0

Major Rating Factors: Middle of the road best describes BlackRock Real Asset Equity Trust whose TheStreet.com Investment Rating is currently a C+ (Fair). The fund currently has a performance rating of C+ (Fair) based on an annualized return of 28.27% over the last three years and a total return of 15.48% year to date 2012. Factored into the performance evaluation is an expense ratio of 1.09% (low).

The fund's risk rating is currently C+ (Fair). It carries a beta of 1.42, meaning it is expected to move 14.2% for every 10% move in the market. Volatility, as measured by both the semi-deviation and a drawdown factor, is considered low. As of March 31, 2012, BlackRock Real Asset Equity Trust traded at a discount of .50% below its net asset value, which is worse than its one-year historical average discount of 3.33%.

Daniel J. Rice, III has been running the fund for 6 years and currently receives a manager quality ranking of 28 (0=worst, 99=best). If you desire an average level of risk, then this fund may be an option.

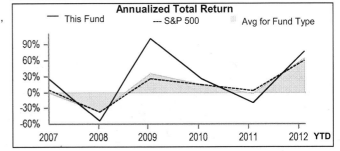

BlackRock Res & Commdty Strat Trus (BCX)

D-   **Weak**

Fund Family: BlackRock Inc
Fund Type: Income
Inception Date: March 30, 2011

Data Date	Investment Rating	Net Assets ($Mil)	Price	Performance Rating/Pts	Total Return Y-T-D	Risk Rating/Pts
3-12	D-	783.79	15.13	D- / 1.5	16.50%	C+ / 5.8

Major Rating Factors:
Disappointing performance is the major factor driving the D- (Weak) TheStreet.com Investment Rating for BlackRock Res & Commdty Strat Trus. The fund currently has a performance rating of D- (Weak) based on an annualized return of 0.00% over the last three years and a total return of 16.50% year to date 2012. Factored into the performance evaluation is an expense ratio of 1.13% (low).

The fund's risk rating is currently C+ (Fair). It carries a beta of 0.00, meaning the fund's expected move will be 0.0% for every 10% move in the market. Volatility, as measured by both the semi-deviation and a drawdown factor, is considered low. As of March 31, 2012, BlackRock Res & Commdty Strat Trus traded at a discount of 6.02% below its net asset value, which is better than its one-year historical average discount of 5.38%.

This fund has been team managed for 1 year and currently receives a manager quality ranking of 4 (0=worst, 99=best). This fund offers only a moderate level of risk but investors looking for strong performance are still waiting.

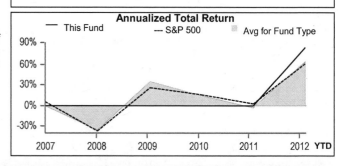

BlackRock S&P Qual Rkg Glob Eq Mgd (BQY)

C+   **Fair**

Fund Family: BlackRock Inc
Fund Type: Global
Inception Date: May 26, 2004

Data Date	Investment Rating	Net Assets ($Mil)	Price	Performance Rating/Pts	Total Return Y-T-D	Risk Rating/Pts
3-12	C+	82.10	12.97	C+ / 6.3	9.89%	B / 8.2
2011	C+	79.10	12.03	C+ / 5.7	1.58%	B- / 7.9
2010	C-	80.72	13.26	C / 4.3	13.87%	C / 4.9
2009	D+	67.40	12.52	D+ / 2.8	32.50%	C+ / 5.7

Major Rating Factors: Middle of the road best describes BlackRock S&P Qual Rkg Glob Eq Mgd whose TheStreet.com Investment Rating is currently a C+ (Fair). The fund currently has a performance rating of C+ (Fair) based on an annualized return of 23.63% over the last three years and a total return of 9.89% year to date 2012. Factored into the performance evaluation is an expense ratio of 1.19% (average).

The fund's risk rating is currently B (Good). It carries a beta of 0.72, meaning the fund's expected move will be 7.2% for every 10% move in the market. Volatility, as measured by both the semi-deviation and a drawdown factor, is considered low. As of March 31, 2012, BlackRock S&P Qual Rkg Glob Eq Mgd traded at a discount of 5.95% below its net asset value, which is worse than its one-year historical average discount of 6.72%.

Kathleen M. Anderson has been running the fund for 2 years and currently receives a manager quality ranking of 88 (0=worst, 99=best). If you desire an average level of risk, then this fund may be an option.

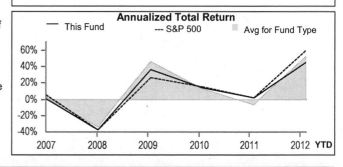

BlackRock Senior High Income Fund (ARK)

B+   **Good**

Fund Family: BlackRock Inc
Fund Type: Corporate - High Yield
Inception Date: April 30, 1993

Data Date	Investment Rating	Net Assets ($Mil)	Price	Performance Rating/Pts	Total Return Y-T-D	Risk Rating/Pts
3-12	B+	238.76	4.11	B / 7.8	8.06%	B / 8.7
2011	B-	226.90	3.85	C+ / 6.8	0.26%	B- / 7.6
2010	D+	225.89	3.89	C- / 3.3	19.17%	C / 4.8
2009	D-	196.31	3.50	D / 2.0	47.80%	C- / 3.9

Major Rating Factors: Strong performance is the major factor driving the B+ (Good) TheStreet.com Investment Rating for BlackRock Senior High Income Fund. The fund currently has a performance rating of B (Good) based on an annualized return of 29.44% over the last three years and a total return of 8.06% year to date 2012. Factored into the performance evaluation is an expense ratio of 1.13% (low).

The fund's risk rating is currently B (Good). It carries a beta of 1.11, meaning it is expected to move 11.1% for every 10% move in the market. Volatility, as measured by both the semi-deviation and a drawdown factor, is considered low. As of March 31, 2012, BlackRock Senior High Income Fund traded at a discount of .72% below its net asset value, which is worse than its one-year historical average discount of 3.87%.

Leland T. Hart has been running the fund for 3 years and currently receives a manager quality ranking of 72 (0=worst, 99=best). If you desire only a moderate level of risk and strong performance, then this fund is an excellent option.

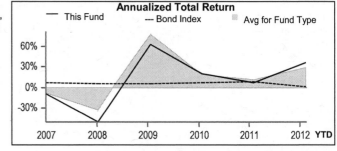

BlackRock Strategic Bond Trust (BHD)

B   **Good**

Fund Family: BlackRock Inc
Fund Type: Corporate - High Yield
Inception Date: February 26, 2002

Data Date	Investment Rating	Net Assets ($Mil)	Price	Performance Rating/Pts	Total Return Y-T-D	Risk Rating/Pts
3-12	B	95.13	14.07	C+ / 6.4	9.66%	B+ / 9.1
2011	B+	94.90	12.99	B- / 7.3	1.08%	B+ / 9.1
2010	C+	95.79	12.70	C+ / 6.9	12.20%	C+ / 5.8
2009	C+	85.58	12.08	C+ / 5.6	42.64%	C+ / 6.2

Major Rating Factors: BlackRock Strategic Bond Trust receives a TheStreet.com Investment Rating of B (Good). The fund currently has a performance rating of C+ (Fair) based on an annualized return of 22.57% over the last three years and a total return of 9.66% year to date 2012. Factored into the performance evaluation is an expense ratio of 1.51% (average).

The fund's risk rating is currently B+ (Good). It carries a beta of 0.64, meaning the fund's expected move will be 6.4% for every 10% move in the market. Volatility, as measured by both the semi-deviation and a drawdown factor, is considered very low. As of March 31, 2012, BlackRock Strategic Bond Trust traded at a discount of .35% below its net asset value, which is worse than its one-year historical average discount of 4.38%.

James E. Keenan has been running the fund for 5 years and currently receives a manager quality ranking of 80 (0=worst, 99=best). If you desire an average level of risk, then this fund may be an option.

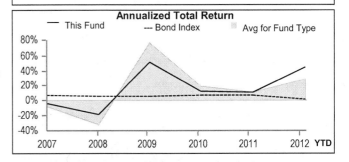

Annualized Total Return

BlackRock Strategic Municipal Tr (BSD)

A+   **Excellent**

Fund Family: BlackRock Inc
Fund Type: Municipal - National
Inception Date: August 24, 1999

Data Date	Investment Rating	Net Assets ($Mil)	Price	Performance Rating/Pts	Total Return Y-T-D	Risk Rating/Pts
3-12	A+	89.48	14.19	A / 9.3	5.36%	B / 8.8
2011	A+	99.10	13.68	A / 9.5	0.95%	B / 8.8
2010	C-	94.74	12.32	C- / 3.0	10.86%	B- / 7.0
2009	D+	79.82	11.89	D / 2.0	48.29%	C+ / 6.4

Major Rating Factors:
Exceptional performance is the major factor driving the A+ (Excellent) TheStreet.com Investment Rating for BlackRock Strategic Municipal Tr. The fund currently has a performance rating of A (Excellent) based on an annualized return of 22.67% over the last three years and a total return of 5.36% year to date 2012. Factored into the performance evaluation is an expense ratio of 1.39% (average).

The fund's risk rating is currently B (Good). It carries a beta of 1.94, meaning it is expected to move 19.4% for every 10% move in the market. Volatility, as measured by both the semi-deviation and a drawdown factor, is considered low. As of March 31, 2012, BlackRock Strategic Municipal Tr traded at a premium of .14% above its net asset value, which is worse than its one-year historical average discount of 1.44%.

Theodore R. Jaeckel, Jr. has been running the fund for 6 years and currently receives a manager quality ranking of 79 (0=worst, 99=best). If you desire only a moderate level of risk and strong performance, then this fund is an excellent option.

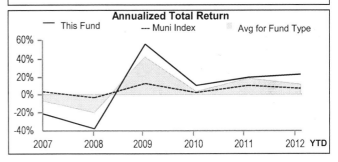

Annualized Total Return

BlackRock VA Muni Bond Trust (BHV)

C-   **Fair**

Fund Family: BlackRock Inc
Fund Type: Municipal - Single State
Inception Date: April 26, 2002

Data Date	Investment Rating	Net Assets ($Mil)	Price	Performance Rating/Pts	Total Return Y-T-D	Risk Rating/Pts
3-12	C-	24.16	18.68	C- / 3.9	-5.89%	B / 8.1
2011	B+	24.70	20.11	B+ / 8.3	2.78%	B / 8.2
2010	B-	25.14	17.66	C / 5.5	3.71%	B- / 7.3
2009	C+	23.48	18.07	C / 4.9	12.81%	B- / 7.7

Major Rating Factors: Middle of the road best describes BlackRock VA Muni Bond Trust whose TheStreet.com Investment Rating is currently a C- (Fair). The fund currently has a performance rating of C- (Fair) based on an annualized return of 10.87% over the last three years and a total return of -5.89% year to date 2012. Factored into the performance evaluation is an expense ratio of 1.52% (average).

The fund's risk rating is currently B (Good). It carries a beta of 1.46, meaning it is expected to move 14.6% for every 10% move in the market. Volatility, as measured by both the semi-deviation and a drawdown factor, is considered low. As of March 31, 2012, BlackRock VA Muni Bond Trust traded at a premium of 16.53% above its net asset value, which is better than its one-year historical average premium of 20.03%.

Theodore R. Jaeckel, Jr. has been running the fund for 6 years and currently receives a manager quality ranking of 52 (0=worst, 99=best). If you desire an average level of risk, then this fund may be an option.

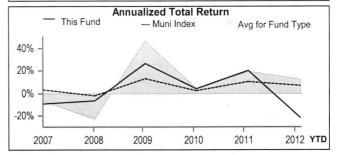

Annualized Total Return

Blackstone / GSO Lng-Sht Credit In (BGX) D+ Weak

Fund Family: GSO/Blackstone Debt Funds Managemen
Fund Type: Loan Participation
Inception Date: January 26, 2011

Data Date	Investment Rating	Net Assets ($Mil)	Price	Performance Rating/Pts	Total Return Y-T-D	Risk Rating/Pts
3-12	D+	237.20	18.27	D / 1.8	9.00%	B / 8.2

Major Rating Factors:
Disappointing performance is the major factor driving the D+ (Weak) TheStreet.com Investment Rating for Blackstone / GSO Lng-Sht Credit In. The fund currently has a performance rating of D (Weak) based on an annualized return of 0.00% over the last three years and a total return of 9.00% year to date 2012. Factored into the performance evaluation is an expense ratio of 1.78% (above average).

The fund's risk rating is currently B (Good). It carries a beta of 0.00, meaning the fund's expected move will be 0.0% for every 10% move in the market. Volatility, as measured by both the semi-deviation and a drawdown factor, is considered low. As of March 31, 2012, Blackstone / GSO Lng-Sht Credit In traded at a discount of 2.19% below its net asset value, which is better than its one-year historical average premium of .72%.

Brad Marshall has been running the fund for 1 year and currently receives a manager quality ranking of 99 (0=worst, 99=best). This fund offers only a moderate level of risk but investors looking for strong performance are still waiting.

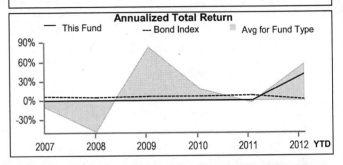

Annualized Total Return

Blackstone/GSO Sr Floating Rate Tr (BSL) C Fair

Fund Family: GSO/Blackstone Debt Funds Managemen
Fund Type: Loan Participation
Inception Date: May 26, 2010

Data Date	Investment Rating	Net Assets ($Mil)	Price	Performance Rating/Pts	Total Return Y-T-D	Risk Rating/Pts
3-12	C	285.30	19.95	C- / 4.1	9.90%	B / 8.2
2011	C-	285.10	18.36	D+ / 2.4	3.43%	B / 8.2

Major Rating Factors: Middle of the road best describes Blackstone/GSO Sr Floating Rate Tr whose TheStreet.com Investment Rating is currently a C (Fair). The fund currently has a performance rating of C- (Fair) based on an annualized return of 0.00% over the last three years and a total return of 9.90% year to date 2012. Factored into the performance evaluation is an expense ratio of 2.79% (high).

The fund's risk rating is currently B (Good). It carries a beta of 0.00, meaning the fund's expected move will be 0.0% for every 10% move in the market. Volatility, as measured by both the semi-deviation and a drawdown factor, is considered low. As of March 31, 2012, Blackstone/GSO Sr Floating Rate Tr traded at a premium of 3.05% above its net asset value, which is worse than its one-year historical average premium of .99%.

Debra Anderson currently receives a manager quality ranking of 98 (0=worst, 99=best). If you desire an average level of risk, then this fund may be an option.

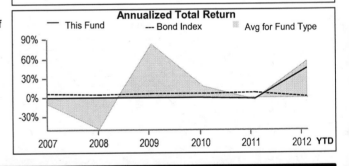

Annualized Total Return

Boulder Growth&Income Fund (BIF) C- Fair

Fund Family: Boulder Investment Advisors LLC
Fund Type: Growth and Income
Inception Date: December 7, 1972

Data Date	Investment Rating	Net Assets ($Mil)	Price	Performance Rating/Pts	Total Return Y-T-D	Risk Rating/Pts
3-12	C-	188.04	6.27	C- / 3.2	9.23%	B / 8.2
2011	C-	185.00	5.74	D+ / 2.7	1.05%	B / 8.0
2010	D	169.15	6.23	D- / 1.1	8.35%	C / 5.3
2009	D	148.23	5.75	D / 1.8	18.80%	C+ / 5.6

Major Rating Factors: Middle of the road best describes Boulder Growth&Income Fund whose TheStreet.com Investment Rating is currently a C- (Fair). The fund currently has a performance rating of C- (Fair) based on an annualized return of 13.93% over the last three years and a total return of 9.23% year to date 2012. Factored into the performance evaluation is an expense ratio of 2.40% (high).

The fund's risk rating is currently B (Good). It carries a beta of 0.81, meaning the fund's expected move will be 8.1% for every 10% move in the market. Volatility, as measured by both the semi-deviation and a drawdown factor, is considered low. As of March 31, 2012, Boulder Growth&Income Fund traded at a discount of 18.57% below its net asset value, which is better than its one-year historical average discount of 18.46%.

Stewart R. Horejsi has been running the fund for 40 years and currently receives a manager quality ranking of 34 (0=worst, 99=best). If you desire an average level of risk, then this fund may be an option.

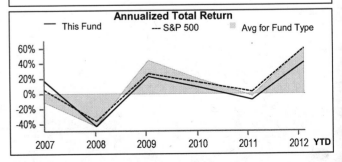

Annualized Total Return

Boulder Total Return Fund (BTF)   C+   Fair

Fund Family: Boulder Investment Advisors LLC
Fund Type: Income
Inception Date: February 19, 1993

Major Rating Factors: Middle of the road best describes Boulder Total Return Fund whose TheStreet.com Investment Rating is currently a C+ (Fair). The fund currently has a performance rating of C+ (Fair) based on an annualized return of 25.14% over the last three years and a total return of 12.91% year to date 2012. Factored into the performance evaluation is an expense ratio of 2.12% (high).

The fund's risk rating is currently B- (Good). It carries a beta of 1.01, meaning that its performance tracks fairly well with that of the overall stock market. Volatility, as measured by both the semi-deviation and a drawdown factor, is considered low. As of March 31, 2012, Boulder Total Return Fund traded at a discount of 19.84% below its net asset value, which is better than its one-year historical average discount of 18.10%.

Stewart R. Horejsi has been running the fund for 19 years and currently receives a manager quality ranking of 68 (0=worst, 99=best). If you desire an average level of risk, then this fund may be an option.

Data Date	Investment Rating	Net Assets ($Mil)	Price	Performance Rating/Pts	Total Return Y-T-D	Risk Rating/Pts
3-12	C+	234.10	17.05	C+ / 6.8	12.91%	B- / 7.9
2011	C-	235.10	15.10	C / 4.3	1.59%	B- / 7.6
2010	D	194.19	15.52	D / 1.9	22.01%	C / 4.9
2009	D-	155.03	12.72	D- / 1.3	24.11%	C / 5.2

Annualized Total Return

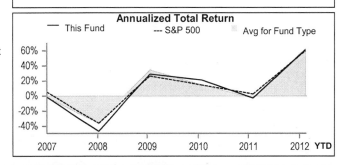

Calamos Convertible Opport&Income (CHI)   B-   Good

Fund Family: Calamos Advisors LLC
Fund Type: Growth and Income
Inception Date: June 25, 2002

Major Rating Factors: Calamos Convertible Opport&Income receives a TheStreet.com Investment Rating of B- (Good). The fund currently has a performance rating of C+ (Fair) based on an annualized return of 24.60% over the last three years and a total return of 15.22% year to date 2012. Factored into the performance evaluation is an expense ratio of 1.55% (average).

The fund's risk rating is currently B (Good). It carries a beta of 0.77, meaning the fund's expected move will be 7.7% for every 10% move in the market. Volatility, as measured by both the semi-deviation and a drawdown factor, is considered low. As of March 31, 2012, Calamos Convertible Opport&Income traded at a premium of 1.83% above its net asset value, which is worse than its one-year historical average discount of .58%.

John P. Calamos, Sr. has been running the fund for 10 years and currently receives a manager quality ranking of 79 (0=worst, 99=best). If you desire an average level of risk, then this fund may be an option.

Data Date	Investment Rating	Net Assets ($Mil)	Price	Performance Rating/Pts	Total Return Y-T-D	Risk Rating/Pts
3-12	B-	827.34	12.78	C+ / 6.6	15.22%	B / 8.3
2011	C+	860.64	11.26	C / 5.5	3.73%	B / 8.2
2010	B-	733.71	13.18	B- / 7.4	17.29%	C / 5.0
2009	C-	492.27	12.32	C- / 3.9	54.54%	C / 5.0

Annualized Total Return

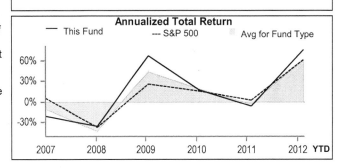

Calamos Convertible&High Income (CHY)   C+   Fair

Fund Family: Calamos Advisors LLC
Fund Type: Growth and Income
Inception Date: May 28, 2003

Major Rating Factors: Middle of the road best describes Calamos Convertible&High Income whose TheStreet.com Investment Rating is currently a C+ (Fair). The fund currently has a performance rating of C+ (Fair) based on an annualized return of 25.11% over the last three years and a total return of 11.88% year to date 2012. Factored into the performance evaluation is an expense ratio of 1.61% (above average).

The fund's risk rating is currently B (Good). It carries a beta of 0.80, meaning the fund's expected move will be 8.0% for every 10% move in the market. Volatility, as measured by both the semi-deviation and a drawdown factor, is considered low. As of March 31, 2012, Calamos Convertible&High Income traded at a discount of 1.92% below its net asset value, which is worse than its one-year historical average discount of 3.32%.

John P. Calamos, Sr. has been running the fund for 9 years and currently receives a manager quality ranking of 80 (0=worst, 99=best). If you desire an average level of risk, then this fund may be an option.

Data Date	Investment Rating	Net Assets ($Mil)	Price	Performance Rating/Pts	Total Return Y-T-D	Risk Rating/Pts
3-12	C+	917.54	12.76	C+ / 6.6	11.88%	B / 8.1
2011	B-	973.05	11.56	C+ / 6.6	4.76%	B / 8.0
2010	C+	896.19	12.66	B- / 7.3	19.18%	C / 5.0
2009	C-	658.52	11.54	C- / 4.0	45.58%	C / 5.1

Annualized Total Return

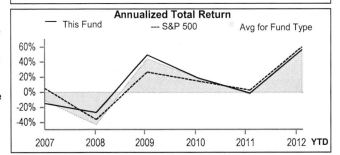

Calamos Global Dynamic Income Fd (CHW)   B-   Good

Fund Family: Calamos Advisors LLC
Fund Type: Global
Inception Date: June 26, 2007

Major Rating Factors: Strong performance is the major factor driving the B- (Good) TheStreet.com Investment Rating for Calamos Global Dynamic Income Fd. The fund currently has a performance rating of B- (Good) based on an annualized return of 25.55% over the last three years and a total return of 22.31% year to date 2012. Factored into the performance evaluation is an expense ratio of 1.93% (above average).

The fund's risk rating is currently B- (Good). It carries a beta of 1.02, meaning that its performance tracks fairly well with that of the overall stock market. Volatility, as measured by both the semi-deviation and a drawdown factor, is considered low. As of March 31, 2012, Calamos Global Dynamic Income Fd traded at a discount of 8.71% below its net asset value, which is worse than its one-year historical average discount of 13.13%.

John P. Calamos, Sr. has been running the fund for 5 years and currently receives a manager quality ranking of 82 (0=worst, 99=best). If you desire only a moderate level of risk and strong performance, then this fund is an excellent option.

Data Date	Investment Rating	Net Assets ($Mil)	Price	Performance Rating/Pts	Total Return Y-T-D	Risk Rating/Pts
3-12	B-	534.74	8.80	B- / 7.5	22.31%	B- / 7.5
2011	C	620.56	7.30	C / 4.9	2.88%	B- / 7.2
2010	D+	534.65	8.37	C- / 3.5	15.01%	C / 4.5
2009	B+	428.98	7.86	B+ / 8.9	45.02%	C / 4.8

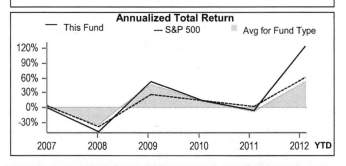

Calamos Global Total Return Fund (CGO)   B   Good

Fund Family: Calamos Advisors LLC
Fund Type: Growth and Income
Inception Date: October 27, 2005

Major Rating Factors: Strong performance is the major factor driving the B (Good) TheStreet.com Investment Rating for Calamos Global Total Return Fund. The fund currently has a performance rating of B- (Good) based on an annualized return of 28.06% over the last three years and a total return of 12.88% year to date 2012. Factored into the performance evaluation is an expense ratio of 1.90% (above average).

The fund's risk rating is currently B (Good). It carries a beta of 0.92, meaning that its performance tracks fairly well with that of the overall stock market. Volatility, as measured by both the semi-deviation and a drawdown factor, is considered low. As of March 31, 2012, Calamos Global Total Return Fund traded at a premium of 2.22% above its net asset value, which is worse than its one-year historical average premium of .73%.

John P. Calamos, Sr. has been running the fund for 7 years and currently receives a manager quality ranking of 79 (0=worst, 99=best). If you desire only a moderate level of risk and strong performance, then this fund is an excellent option.

Data Date	Investment Rating	Net Assets ($Mil)	Price	Performance Rating/Pts	Total Return Y-T-D	Risk Rating/Pts
3-12	B	119.60	15.19	B- / 7.5	12.88%	B / 8.0
2011	B-	131.71	13.64	C+ / 6.7	1.10%	B- / 7.8
2010	C-	117.48	14.60	C / 4.3	10.83%	C / 5.3
2009	C+	92.94	14.35	C+ / 6.6	56.52%	C / 5.1

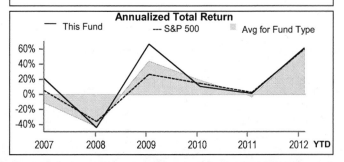

Calamos Strategic Total Return Fun (CSQ)   B   Good

Fund Family: Calamos Advisors LLC
Fund Type: Growth and Income
Inception Date: March 26, 2004

Major Rating Factors: Strong performance is the major factor driving the B (Good) TheStreet.com Investment Rating for Calamos Strategic Total Return Fun. The fund currently has a performance rating of B (Good) based on an annualized return of 28.65% over the last three years and a total return of 21.49% year to date 2012. Factored into the performance evaluation is an expense ratio of 1.93% (above average).

The fund's risk rating is currently B- (Good). It carries a beta of 1.17, meaning it is expected to move 11.7% for every 10% move in the market. Volatility, as measured by both the semi-deviation and a drawdown factor, is considered low. As of March 31, 2012, Calamos Strategic Total Return Fun traded at a discount of 7.58% below its net asset value, which is worse than its one-year historical average discount of 12.75%.

John P. Calamos, Sr. has been running the fund for 8 years and currently receives a manager quality ranking of 60 (0=worst, 99=best). If you desire only a moderate level of risk and strong performance, then this fund is an excellent option.

Data Date	Investment Rating	Net Assets ($Mil)	Price	Performance Rating/Pts	Total Return Y-T-D	Risk Rating/Pts
3-12	B	1,567.88	10.00	B / 8.2	21.49%	B- / 7.7
2011	C+	1,776.33	8.35	C+ / 5.8	3.59%	B- / 7.5
2010	D	1,596.21	9.26	C- / 3.1	13.63%	C / 4.6
2009	D	1,177.69	8.76	D+ / 2.5	47.54%	C / 5.0

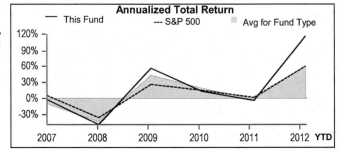

Canadian General Investments Ltd (T.CGI)   **D**   **Weak**

Fund Family: Morgan Meighen & Associates Limited
Fund Type: Foreign
Inception Date: N/A

Major Rating Factors: Canadian General Investments Ltd receives a TheStreet.com Investment Rating of D (Weak). The fund currently has a performance rating of C (Fair) based on an annualized return of 22.07% over the last three years and a total return of 6.11% year to date 2012. Factored into the performance evaluation is an expense ratio of 3.57% (high).

The fund's risk rating is currently C (Fair). It carries a beta of 0.56, meaning the fund's expected move will be 5.6% for every 10% move in the market. Volatility, as measured by both the semi-deviation and a drawdown factor, is considered average. As of March 31, 2012, Canadian General Investments Ltd traded at a discount of 24.77% below its net asset value, which is better than its one-year historical average discount of 22.40%.

Michael A. Smedley has been running the fund for 24 years and currently receives a manager quality ranking of 88 (0=worst, 99=best). If you desire an average level of risk, then this fund may be an option.

Data Date	Investment Rating	Net Assets ($Mil)	Price	Performance Rating/Pts	Total Return Y-T-D	Risk Rating/Pts
3-12	D	288.01	16.92	C / 4.7	6.11%	C / 4.6
2011	C	425.80	16.00	C+ / 6.8	0.63%	C / 5.2
2010	D-	288.01	19.18	C- / 3.2	27.89%	D+ / 2.9
2009	D-	288.01	15.83	D+ / 2.7	67.47%	D+ / 2.9

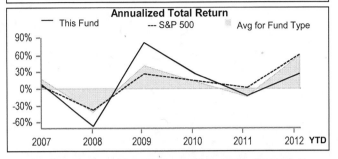

Annualized Total Return

Canadian World Fund Limited (T.CWF)   **D**   **Weak**

Fund Family: Morgan Meighen & Associates Limited
Fund Type: Global
Inception Date: February 25, 1994

Major Rating Factors: Canadian World Fund Limited receives a TheStreet.com Investment Rating of D (Weak). The fund currently has a performance rating of C- (Fair) based on an annualized return of 17.19% over the last three years and a total return of 5.34% year to date 2012. Factored into the performance evaluation is an expense ratio of 3.04% (high).

The fund's risk rating is currently C (Fair). It carries a beta of 0.43, meaning the fund's expected move will be 4.3% for every 10% move in the market. Volatility, as measured by both the semi-deviation and a drawdown factor, is considered average. As of March 31, 2012, Canadian World Fund Limited traded at a discount of 32.80% below its net asset value, which is better than its one-year historical average discount of 31.83%.

Alex Sulzer currently receives a manager quality ranking of 81 (0=worst, 99=best). If you desire an average level of risk, then this fund may be an option.

Data Date	Investment Rating	Net Assets ($Mil)	Price	Performance Rating/Pts	Total Return Y-T-D	Risk Rating/Pts
3-12	D	20.47	3.75	C- / 3.4	5.34%	C / 4.9
2011	D+	35.50	3.56	C / 5.2	0.84%	C / 4.9
2010	E	20.47	4.14	D- / 1.4	20.70%	D / 1.8
2009	E	20.47	3.43	D- / 1.0	43.51%	D+ / 2.5

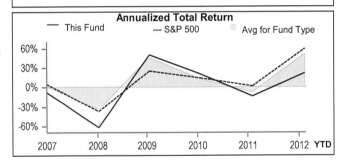

Annualized Total Return

CBRE Clarion Global Real Estate In (IGR)   **A-**   **Excellent**

Fund Family: CBRE Clarion Securities LLC
Fund Type: Growth and Income
Inception Date: February 25, 2004

Major Rating Factors:
Exceptional performance is the major factor driving the A- (Excellent) TheStreet.com Investment Rating for CBRE Clarion Global Real Estate In. The fund currently has a performance rating of A+ (Excellent) based on an annualized return of 41.95% over the last three years and a total return of 19.58% year to date 2012. Factored into the performance evaluation is an expense ratio of 1.03% (low).

The fund's risk rating is currently B- (Good). It carries a beta of 1.50, meaning it is expected to move 15.0% for every 10% move in the market. Volatility, as measured by both the semi-deviation and a drawdown factor, is considered low. As of March 31, 2012, CBRE Clarion Global Real Estate In traded at a discount of 9.46% below its net asset value, which is worse than its one-year historical average discount of 11.07%.

T. Ritson Ferguson has been running the fund for 6 years and currently receives a manager quality ranking of 81 (0=worst, 99=best). If you desire only a moderate level of risk and strong performance, then this fund is an excellent option.

Data Date	Investment Rating	Net Assets ($Mil)	Price	Performance Rating/Pts	Total Return Y-T-D	Risk Rating/Pts
3-12	A-	949.58	8.04	A+ / 9.6	19.58%	B- / 7.6
2011	C+	949.60	6.84	B / 7.6	3.36%	C+ / 6.7
2010	D-	839.24	7.75	D / 1.7	31.18%	C- / 3.6
2009	E+	570.07	6.37	E+ / 0.8	68.37%	C- / 3.6

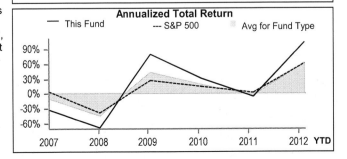

Annualized Total Return

Central Europe & Russia Fund (CEE)

C+　　**Fair**

Fund Family: Deutsche Asset Mgmt International G
Fund Type: Foreign
Inception Date: March 6, 1990

Major Rating Factors: Strong performance is the major factor driving the C+ (Fair) TheStreet.com Investment Rating for Central Europe & Russia Fund. The fund currently has a performance rating of B+ (Good) based on an annualized return of 35.37% over the last three years and a total return of 22.66% year to date 2012. Factored into the performance evaluation is an expense ratio of 1.11% (low).

The fund's risk rating is currently C+ (Fair). It carries a beta of 1.53, meaning it is expected to move 15.3% for every 10% move in the market. Volatility, as measured by both the semi-deviation and a drawdown factor, is considered low. As of March 31, 2012, Central Europe & Russia Fund traded at a discount of 7.23% below its net asset value, which is worse than its one-year historical average discount of 9.49%.

Rainer Vermehren currently receives a manager quality ranking of 82 (0=worst, 99=best). If you desire only a moderate level of risk and strong performance, then this fund is an excellent option.

Data Date	Investment Rating	Net Assets ($Mil)	Price	Performance Rating/Pts	Total Return Y-T-D	Risk Rating/Pts
3-12	C+	505.93	35.02	B+ / 8.8	22.66%	C+ / 5.9
2011	C	416.00	28.55	B- / 7.0	1.93%	C+ / 5.8
2010	D-	575.79	41.84	D / 2.1	27.56%	C- / 3.2
2009	D+	353.02	32.99	C / 4.9	91.61%	C- / 3.1

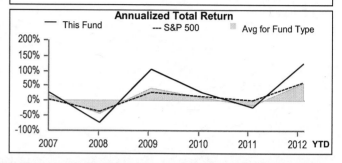

Central Fund of Canada (CEF)

C　　**Fair**

Fund Family: Central Group Alberta Ltd
Fund Type: Precious Metals
Inception Date: September 14, 1983

Major Rating Factors: Middle of the road best describes Central Fund of Canada whose TheStreet.com Investment Rating is currently a C (Fair). The fund currently has a performance rating of C (Fair) based on an annualized return of 23.58% over the last three years and a total return of 11.93% year to date 2012. Factored into the performance evaluation is an expense ratio of 0.30% (very low).

The fund's risk rating is currently B- (Good). It carries a beta of 1.17, meaning it is expected to move 11.7% for every 10% move in the market. Volatility, as measured by both the semi-deviation and a drawdown factor, is considered low. As of March 31, 2012, Central Fund of Canada traded at a premium of 3.93% above its net asset value, which is worse than its one-year historical average premium of 1.81%.

Philip M. Spicer has been running the fund for 6 years and currently receives a manager quality ranking of 29 (0=worst, 99=best). If you desire an average level of risk, then this fund may be an option.

Data Date	Investment Rating	Net Assets ($Mil)	Price	Performance Rating/Pts	Total Return Y-T-D	Risk Rating/Pts
3-12	C	5,620.88	21.95	C / 5.5	11.93%	B- / 7.4
2011	B-	4,902.00	19.61	B- / 7.2	1.84%	B- / 7.5
2010	A	2,382.34	20.73	A / 9.4	50.52%	C+ / 5.8
2009	B	1,204.00	13.78	B- / 7.1	26.29%	C+ / 6.3

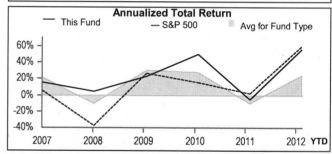

Central Gold-Trust (GTU)

C-　　**Fair**

Fund Family: Central Gold Trust
Fund Type: Precious Metals
Inception Date: September 22, 2006

Major Rating Factors: Middle of the road best describes Central Gold-Trust whose TheStreet.com Investment Rating is currently a C- (Fair). The fund currently has a performance rating of C- (Fair) based on an annualized return of 14.12% over the last three years and a total return of 7.74% year to date 2012. Factored into the performance evaluation is an expense ratio of 0.36% (very low).

The fund's risk rating is currently B- (Good). It carries a beta of 0.87, meaning the fund's expected move will be 8.7% for every 10% move in the market. Volatility, as measured by both the semi-deviation and a drawdown factor, is considered low. As of March 31, 2012, Central Gold-Trust traded at a premium of 3.26% above its net asset value, which is better than its one-year historical average premium of 3.31%.

This fund has been team managed for 9 years and currently receives a manager quality ranking of 25 (0=worst, 99=best). If you desire an average level of risk, then this fund may be an option.

Data Date	Investment Rating	Net Assets ($Mil)	Price	Performance Rating/Pts	Total Return Y-T-D	Risk Rating/Pts
3-12	C-	877.09	63.75	C- / 3.6	7.74%	B- / 7.9
2011	B	1,130.50	59.17	B- / 7.3	4.17%	B / 8.0
2010	A+	451.92	54.35	B+ / 8.8	22.44%	B- / 7.5
2009	A+	138.60	44.39	B- / 7.4	12.32%	B- / 7.8

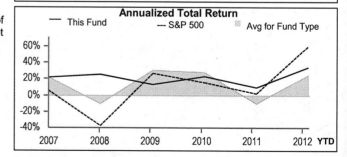

Central Securities (CET)

C+   Fair

Fund Family: Central Securities Corporation
Fund Type: Growth
Inception Date: N/A

Major Rating Factors: Middle of the road best describes Central Securities whose TheStreet.com Investment Rating is currently a C+ (Fair). The fund currently has a performance rating of C+ (Fair) based on an annualized return of 23.09% over the last three years and a total return of 8.11% year to date 2012. Factored into the performance evaluation is an expense ratio of 0.78% (very low).

The fund's risk rating is currently B (Good). It carries a beta of 0.93, meaning that its performance tracks fairly well with that of the overall stock market. Volatility, as measured by both the semi-deviation and a drawdown factor, is considered low. As of March 31, 2012, Central Securities traded at a discount of 16.75% below its net asset value, which is better than its one-year historical average discount of 16.37%.

Wilmot H. Kidd, III has been running the fund for 39 years and currently receives a manager quality ranking of 61 (0=worst, 99=best). If you desire an average level of risk, then this fund may be an option.

Data Date	Investment Rating	Net Assets ($Mil)	Price	Performance Rating/Pts	Total Return Y-T-D	Risk Rating/Pts
3-12	C+	593.52	22.12	C+ / 5.6	8.11%	B / 8.1
2011	C	574.20	20.46	C / 5.2	0.98%	B- / 7.8
2010	B+	499.95	21.97	B / 7.7	27.63%	C+ / 6.1
2009	C-	429.43	17.98	C- / 3.1	29.57%	C+ / 6.4

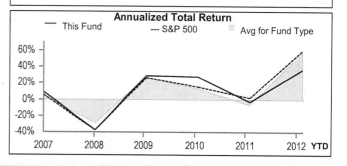

China Fund (CHN)

D+   Weak

Fund Family: Martin Currie Inc
Fund Type: Foreign
Inception Date: July 10, 1992

Major Rating Factors: China Fund receives a TheStreet.com Investment Rating of D+ (Weak). The fund currently has a performance rating of C- (Fair) based on an annualized return of 19.66% over the last three years and a total return of 13.60% year to date 2012. Factored into the performance evaluation is an expense ratio of 1.01% (low).

The fund's risk rating is currently C+ (Fair). It carries a beta of 0.99, meaning that its performance tracks fairly well with that of the overall stock market. Volatility, as measured by both the semi-deviation and a drawdown factor, is considered low. As of March 31, 2012, China Fund traded at a discount of 7.47% below its net asset value, which is worse than its one-year historical average discount of 10.12%.

Christina Chung currently receives a manager quality ranking of 71 (0=worst, 99=best). If you desire an average level of risk, then this fund may be an option.

Data Date	Investment Rating	Net Assets ($Mil)	Price	Performance Rating/Pts	Total Return Y-T-D	Risk Rating/Pts
3-12	D+	660.44	23.30	C- / 4.2	13.60%	C+ / 6.1
2011	D	529.60	20.51	D / 2.1	0.73%	C+ / 6.2
2010	C+	620.47	32.50	B / 8.2	23.60%	C- / 3.5
2009	C+	437.13	28.22	B+ / 8.3	65.10%	C- / 3.8

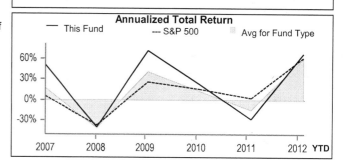

ClearBridge Energy MLP Fund Inc (CEM)

C+   Fair

Fund Family: Legg Mason Partners Fund Advisor LL
Fund Type: Energy/Natural Resources
Inception Date: June 25, 2010

Major Rating Factors: Middle of the road best describes ClearBridge Energy MLP Fund Inc whose TheStreet.com Investment Rating is currently a C+ (Fair). The fund currently has a performance rating of C+ (Fair) based on an annualized return of 0.00% over the last three years and a total return of 6.82% year to date 2012. Factored into the performance evaluation is an expense ratio of 1.71% (above average).

The fund's risk rating is currently B (Good). It carries a beta of 0.00, meaning the fund's expected move will be 0.0% for every 10% move in the market. Volatility, as measured by both the semi-deviation and a drawdown factor, is considered low. As of March 31, 2012, ClearBridge Energy MLP Fund Inc traded at a premium of 4.66% above its net asset value, which is worse than its one-year historical average premium of 2.55%.

Christopher Eades currently receives a manager quality ranking of 90 (0=worst, 99=best). If you desire an average level of risk, then this fund may be an option.

Data Date	Investment Rating	Net Assets ($Mil)	Price	Performance Rating/Pts	Total Return Y-T-D	Risk Rating/Pts
3-12	C+	1,363.00	23.60	C+ / 5.9	6.82%	B / 8.2
2011	C	1,441.10	22.44	C+ / 6.9	2.23%	C / 5.2

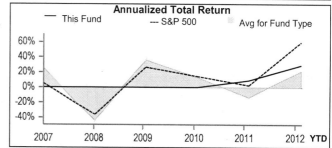

Clough Global Allocation Fund (GLV) C- Fair

Fund Family: Clough Capital Partners LP
Fund Type: Growth and Income
Inception Date: July 28, 2004

Major Rating Factors: Middle of the road best describes Clough Global Allocation Fund whose TheStreet.com Investment Rating is currently a C- (Fair). The fund currently has a performance rating of C- (Fair) based on an annualized return of 16.39% over the last three years and a total return of 11.81% year to date 2012. Factored into the performance evaluation is an expense ratio of 2.87% (high).

The fund's risk rating is currently B- (Good). It carries a beta of 1.06, meaning that its performance tracks fairly well with that of the overall stock market. Volatility, as measured by both the semi-deviation and a drawdown factor, is considered low. As of March 31, 2012, Clough Global Allocation Fund traded at a discount of 14.48% below its net asset value, which is better than its one-year historical average discount of 13.45%.

Charles I. Clough, Jr. has been running the fund for 8 years and currently receives a manager quality ranking of 22 (0=worst, 99=best). If you desire an average level of risk, then this fund may be an option.

Data Date	Investment Rating	Net Assets ($Mil)	Price	Performance Rating/Pts	Total Return Y-T-D	Risk Rating/Pts
3-12	C-	191.50	13.94	C- / 3.8	11.81%	B- / 7.6
2011	C-	156.20	12.75	C- / 4.2	1.25%	B- / 7.4
2010	D+	176.32	15.76	D+ / 2.9	10.41%	C / 5.5
2009	C-	177.64	15.17	C- / 4.0	49.89%	C+ / 5.6

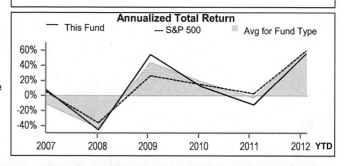

Annualized Total Return

Clough Global Equity Fund (GLQ) C- Fair

Fund Family: Clough Capital Partners LP
Fund Type: Global
Inception Date: April 26, 2005

Major Rating Factors: Middle of the road best describes Clough Global Equity Fund whose TheStreet.com Investment Rating is currently a C- (Fair). The fund currently has a performance rating of C- (Fair) based on an annualized return of 17.93% over the last three years and a total return of 11.24% year to date 2012. Factored into the performance evaluation is an expense ratio of 3.23% (high).

The fund's risk rating is currently B- (Good). It carries a beta of 0.90, meaning that its performance tracks fairly well with that of the overall stock market. Volatility, as measured by both the semi-deviation and a drawdown factor, is considered low. As of March 31, 2012, Clough Global Equity Fund traded at a discount of 15.71% below its net asset value, which is better than its one-year historical average discount of 13.89%.

Charles I. Clough, Jr. has been running the fund for 7 years and currently receives a manager quality ranking of 66 (0=worst, 99=best). If you desire an average level of risk, then this fund may be an option.

Data Date	Investment Rating	Net Assets ($Mil)	Price	Performance Rating/Pts	Total Return Y-T-D	Risk Rating/Pts
3-12	C-	314.36	13.09	C- / 4.0	11.24%	B- / 7.6
2011	C-	254.70	12.04	C / 4.4	1.25%	B- / 7.4
2010	C-	409.63	15.12	C- / 4.1	15.67%	C / 5.0
2009	C-	290.82	14.19	C- / 4.1	53.37%	C+ / 5.7

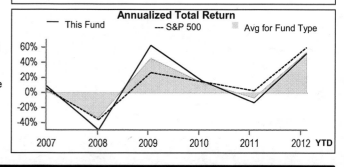

Annualized Total Return

Clough Global Opportunities Fund (GLO) C- Fair

Fund Family: Clough Capital Partners LP
Fund Type: Global
Inception Date: April 25, 2006

Major Rating Factors: Middle of the road best describes Clough Global Opportunities Fund whose TheStreet.com Investment Rating is currently a C- (Fair). The fund currently has a performance rating of C- (Fair) based on an annualized return of 16.13% over the last three years and a total return of 14.18% year to date 2012. Factored into the performance evaluation is an expense ratio of 3.40% (high).

The fund's risk rating is currently B- (Good). It carries a beta of 0.84, meaning the fund's expected move will be 8.4% for every 10% move in the market. Volatility, as measured by both the semi-deviation and a drawdown factor, is considered low. As of March 31, 2012, Clough Global Opportunities Fund traded at a discount of 14.88% below its net asset value, which is better than its one-year historical average discount of 13.48%.

Charles I. Clough, Jr. has been running the fund for 6 years and currently receives a manager quality ranking of 65 (0=worst, 99=best). If you desire an average level of risk, then this fund may be an option.

Data Date	Investment Rating	Net Assets ($Mil)	Price	Performance Rating/Pts	Total Return Y-T-D	Risk Rating/Pts
3-12	C-	813.18	11.78	C- / 3.8	14.18%	B- / 7.6
2011	C-	657.70	10.57	C- / 3.8	1.80%	B- / 7.3
2010	D+	759.60	13.45	C- / 3.7	13.63%	C / 5.2
2009	C-	769.65	12.88	C- / 4.2	48.12%	C+ / 5.7

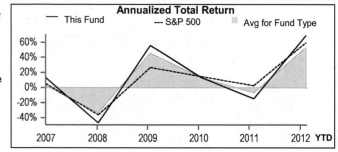

Annualized Total Return

Cohen & Steers Closed-End Opp Fd (FOF)

C+   Fair

Fund Family: Cohen & Steers Capital Management I
Fund Type: Global
Inception Date: November 24, 2006

Major Rating Factors: Middle of the road best describes Cohen & Steers Closed-End Opp Fd whose TheStreet.com Investment Rating is currently a C+ (Fair). The fund currently has a performance rating of C+ (Fair) based on an annualized return of 23.47% over the last three years and a total return of 8.77% year to date 2012. Factored into the performance evaluation is an expense ratio of 0.95% (low).

The fund's risk rating is currently B (Good). It carries a beta of 0.60, meaning the fund's expected move will be 6.0% for every 10% move in the market. Volatility, as measured by both the semi-deviation and a drawdown factor, is considered low. As of March 31, 2012, Cohen & Steers Closed-End Opp Fd traded at a discount of 7.87% below its net asset value, which is worse than its one-year historical average discount of 8.03%.

Douglas R. Bond currently receives a manager quality ranking of 89 (0=worst, 99=best). If you desire an average level of risk, then this fund may be an option.

Data Date	Investment Rating	Net Assets ($Mil)	Price	Perfor-mance Rating/Pts	Total Return Y-T-D	Risk Rating/Pts
3-12	C+	389.10	12.76	C+ / 5.8	8.77%	B / 8.4
2011	C+	389.10	11.97	C+ / 5.7	2.34%	B / 8.3
2010	C	344.90	13.03	C / 5.0	16.13%	C+ / 6.0
2009	D+	294.25	12.13	D+ / 2.6	38.37%	C / 5.4

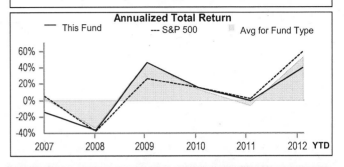

Cohen & Steers Global Inc Builder (INB)

B   Good

Fund Family: Cohen & Steers Capital Management I
Fund Type: Global
Inception Date: July 27, 2007

Major Rating Factors: Strong performance is the major factor driving the B (Good) TheStreet.com Investment Rating for Cohen & Steers Global Inc Builder. The fund currently has a performance rating of B+ (Good) based on an annualized return of 30.84% over the last three years and a total return of 18.06% year to date 2012. Factored into the performance evaluation is an expense ratio of 2.01% (high).

The fund's risk rating is currently B- (Good). It carries a beta of 0.99, meaning that its performance tracks fairly well with that of the overall stock market. Volatility, as measured by both the semi-deviation and a drawdown factor, is considered low. As of March 31, 2012, Cohen & Steers Global Inc Builder traded at a discount of 7.76% below its net asset value, which is worse than its one-year historical average discount of 10.06%.

Joseph M. Harvey currently receives a manager quality ranking of 89 (0=worst, 99=best). If you desire only a moderate level of risk and strong performance, then this fund is an excellent option.

Data Date	Investment Rating	Net Assets ($Mil)	Price	Perfor-mance Rating/Pts	Total Return Y-T-D	Risk Rating/Pts
3-12	B	245.70	10.70	B+ / 8.4	18.06%	B- / 7.4
2011	C	276.10	9.30	C / 5.4	2.47%	B- / 7.1
2010	D	224.60	11.21	C- / 3.1	10.13%	C / 4.4
2009	B+	227.62	11.29	A / 9.3	53.12%	C / 4.5

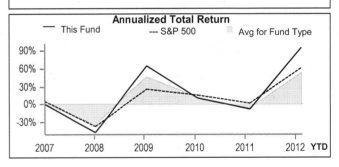

Cohen&Steers Dividend Majors (DVM)

B   Good

Fund Family: Cohen & Steers Capital Management I
Fund Type: Income
Inception Date: January 28, 2005

Major Rating Factors: Strong performance is the major factor driving the B (Good) TheStreet.com Investment Rating for Cohen&Steers Dividend Majors. The fund currently has a performance rating of B+ (Good) based on an annualized return of 29.75% over the last three years and a total return of 16.87% year to date 2012. Factored into the performance evaluation is an expense ratio of 0.95% (low).

The fund's risk rating is currently B- (Good). It carries a beta of 1.19, meaning it is expected to move 11.9% for every 10% move in the market. Volatility, as measured by both the semi-deviation and a drawdown factor, is considered low. As of March 31, 2012, Cohen&Steers Dividend Majors traded at a discount of 7.09% below its net asset value, which is worse than its one-year historical average discount of 7.85%.

Joseph M. Harvey has been running the fund for 7 years and currently receives a manager quality ranking of 70 (0=worst, 99=best). If you desire only a moderate level of risk and strong performance, then this fund is an excellent option.

Data Date	Investment Rating	Net Assets ($Mil)	Price	Perfor-mance Rating/Pts	Total Return Y-T-D	Risk Rating/Pts
3-12	B	172.80	13.90	B+ / 8.3	16.87%	B- / 7.8
2011	C	175.50	12.09	C+ / 5.7	3.89%	C+ / 6.7
2010	C	150.70	12.96	C+ / 6.5	31.87%	C- / 4.0
2009	D-	129.23	10.45	D- / 1.0	10.95%	C / 5.4

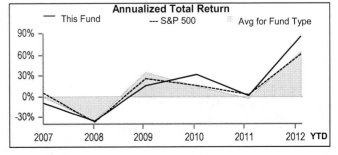

Cohen&Steers Infrastructure Fund (UTF)

B+   **Good**

Fund Family: Cohen & Steers Capital Management I
Fund Type: Utilities
Inception Date: March 26, 2004

Major Rating Factors: Strong performance is the major factor driving the B+ (Good) TheStreet.com Investment Rating for Cohen&Steers Infrastructure Fund. The fund currently has a performance rating of B+ (Good) based on an annualized return of 32.89% over the last three years and a total return of 13.67% year to date 2012. Factored into the performance evaluation is an expense ratio of 2.09% (high).

The fund's risk rating is currently B (Good). It carries a beta of 1.55, meaning it is expected to move 15.5% for every 10% move in the market. Volatility, as measured by both the semi-deviation and a drawdown factor, is considered low. As of March 31, 2012, Cohen&Steers Infrastructure Fund traded at a discount of 7.61% below its net asset value, which is worse than its one-year historical average discount of 9.10%.

Robert S. Becker has been running the fund for 8 years and currently receives a manager quality ranking of 78 (0=worst, 99=best). If you desire only a moderate level of risk and strong performance, then this fund is an excellent option.

Data Date	Investment Rating	Net Assets ($Mil)	Price	Performance Rating/Pts	Total Return Y-T-D	Risk Rating/Pts
3-12	B+	1,535.20	17.60	B+ / 8.6	13.67%	B / 8.1
2011	B-	1,593.10	15.80	B- / 7.0	3.10%	B- / 7.7
2010	D	1,314.10	16.42	D / 1.7	11.40%	C / 5.4
2009	C-	592.33	15.95	C / 4.6	54.65%	C / 4.6

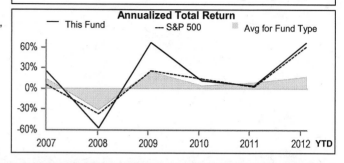

Annualized Total Return
— This Fund   --- S&P 500   Avg for Fund Type

Cohen&Steers Quality Income Realty (RQI)

A-   **Excellent**

Fund Family: Cohen & Steers Capital Management I
Fund Type: Growth and Income
Inception Date: February 25, 2002

Major Rating Factors:
Exceptional performance is the major factor driving the A- (Excellent) TheStreet.com Investment Rating for Cohen&Steers Quality Income Realty. The fund currently has a performance rating of A+ (Excellent) based on an annualized return of 68.30% over the last three years and a total return of 18.06% year to date 2012. Factored into the performance evaluation is an expense ratio of 1.87% (above average).

The fund's risk rating is currently B- (Good). It carries a beta of 1.95, meaning it is expected to move 19.5% for every 10% move in the market. Volatility, as measured by both the semi-deviation and a drawdown factor, is considered low. As of March 31, 2012, Cohen&Steers Quality Income Realty traded at a discount of 7.53% below its net asset value, which is worse than its one-year historical average discount of 7.91%.

Joseph M. Harvey currently receives a manager quality ranking of 94 (0=worst, 99=best). If you desire only a moderate level of risk and strong performance, then this fund is an excellent option.

Data Date	Investment Rating	Net Assets ($Mil)	Price	Performance Rating/Pts	Total Return Y-T-D	Risk Rating/Pts
3-12	A-	1,042.10	9.82	A+ / 9.9	18.06%	B- / 7.1
2011	B-	1,051.80	8.47	A+ / 9.7	1.06%	C / 5.0
2010	D+	852.60	8.65	C / 5.4	53.21%	C- / 3.0
2009	E	167.73	6.07	E+ / 0.8	67.00%	C- / 3.1

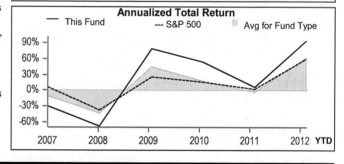

Annualized Total Return
— This Fund   --- S&P 500   Avg for Fund Type

Cohen&Steers REIT& Preferred Incom (RNP)

A   **Excellent**

Fund Family: Cohen & Steers Capital Management I
Fund Type: Income
Inception Date: June 25, 2003

Major Rating Factors:
Exceptional performance is the major factor driving the A (Excellent) TheStreet.com Investment Rating for Cohen&Steers REIT& Preferred Incom. The fund currently has a performance rating of A+ (Excellent) based on an annualized return of 66.66% over the last three years and a total return of 17.36% year to date 2012. Factored into the performance evaluation is an expense ratio of 1.72% (above average).

The fund's risk rating is currently B- (Good). It carries a beta of 1.58, meaning it is expected to move 15.8% for every 10% move in the market. Volatility, as measured by both the semi-deviation and a drawdown factor, is considered low. As of March 31, 2012, Cohen&Steers REIT& Preferred Incom traded at a discount of 4.90% below its net asset value, which is worse than its one-year historical average discount of 6.73%.

Joseph M. Harvey has been running the fund for 9 years and currently receives a manager quality ranking of 96 (0=worst, 99=best). If you desire only a moderate level of risk and strong performance, then this fund is an excellent option.

Data Date	Investment Rating	Net Assets ($Mil)	Price	Performance Rating/Pts	Total Return Y-T-D	Risk Rating/Pts
3-12	A	737.70	16.31	A+ / 9.9	17.36%	B- / 7.6
2011	B	750.90	14.15	A+ / 9.9	5.02%	C+ / 6.2
2010	C+	632.80	14.29	B+ / 8.6	49.38%	C- / 3.6
2009	D-	395.61	10.35	D- / 1.5	81.08%	C- / 3.9

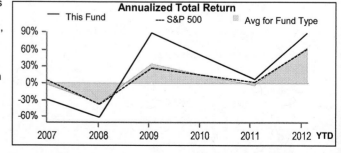

Annualized Total Return
— This Fund   --- S&P 500   Avg for Fund Type

Cohen&Steers Sel Preferred & Incom (PSF)

C+　　**Fair**

Fund Family: Cohen & Steers Capital Management I
Fund Type: Income
Inception Date: November 24, 2010

Data Date	Investment Rating	Net Assets ($Mil)	Price	Performance Rating/Pts	Total Return Y-T-D	Risk Rating/Pts
3-12	C+	271.40	24.80	C / 4.8	16.85%	B / 8.7
2011	D+	0.00	21.68	D / 1.6	4.38%	B / 8.7

Major Rating Factors: Middle of the road best describes Cohen&Steers Sel Preferred & Incom whose TheStreet.com Investment Rating is currently a C+ (Fair). The fund currently has a performance rating of C (Fair) based on an annualized return of 0.00% over the last three years and a total return of 16.85% year to date 2012. Factored into the performance evaluation is an expense ratio of 1.78% (above average).

The fund's risk rating is currently B (Good). It carries a beta of 0.00, meaning the fund's expected move will be 0.0% for every 10% move in the market. Volatility, as measured by both the semi-deviation and a drawdown factor, is considered low. As of March 31, 2012, Cohen&Steers Sel Preferred & Incom traded at a premium of 1.06% above its net asset value, which is worse than its one-year historical average premium of .12%.

Joseph M. Harvey currently receives a manager quality ranking of 80 (0=worst, 99=best). If you desire an average level of risk, then this fund may be an option.

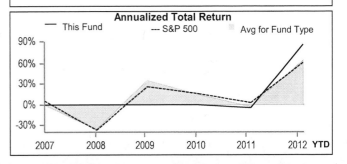

Cohen&Steers Total Return Realty (RFI)

A　　**Excellent**

Fund Family: Cohen & Steers Capital Management I
Fund Type: Growth and Income
Inception Date: September 17, 1993

Data Date	Investment Rating	Net Assets ($Mil)	Price	Performance Rating/Pts	Total Return Y-T-D	Risk Rating/Pts
3-12	A	117.00	13.84	A+ / 9.6	18.13%	B- / 7.6
2011	C+	117.90	11.91	B / 7.6	3.27%	C+ / 6.7
2010	B	107.40	14.88	A / 9.5	71.18%	C- / 3.4
2009	D-	73.26	9.68	D- / 1.5	36.20%	C / 4.8

Major Rating Factors:
Exceptional performance is the major factor driving the A (Excellent) TheStreet.com Investment Rating for Cohen&Steers Total Return Realty. The fund currently has a performance rating of A+ (Excellent) based on an annualized return of 42.82% over the last three years and a total return of 18.13% year to date 2012. Factored into the performance evaluation is an expense ratio of 0.91% (low).

The fund's risk rating is currently B- (Good). It carries a beta of 1.24, meaning it is expected to move 12.4% for every 10% move in the market. Volatility, as measured by both the semi-deviation and a drawdown factor, is considered low. As of March 31, 2012, Cohen&Steers Total Return Realty traded at a premium of 3.98% above its net asset value, which is worse than its one-year historical average premium of 1.93%.

Joseph M. Harvey currently receives a manager quality ranking of 89 (0=worst, 99=best). If you desire only a moderate level of risk and strong performance, then this fund is an excellent option.

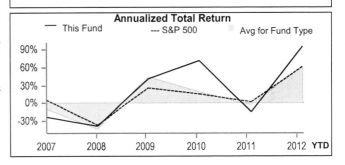

Columbia Seligman Prem Tech Gro (STK)

B　　**Good**

Fund Family: Columbia Management Inv Advisers LL
Fund Type: Growth
Inception Date: November 30, 2009

Data Date	Investment Rating	Net Assets ($Mil)	Price	Performance Rating/Pts	Total Return Y-T-D	Risk Rating/Pts
3-12	B	260.82	18.90	B / 8.0	23.82%	B- / 7.7
2011	D	260.80	15.66	D- / 1.4	3.51%	B- / 7.7
2010	A	0.00	19.17	B / 7.9	6.01%	B / 8.0

Major Rating Factors: Strong performance is the major factor driving the B (Good) TheStreet.com Investment Rating for Columbia Seligman Prem Tech Gro. The fund currently has a performance rating of B (Good) based on an annualized return of 0.00% over the last three years and a total return of 23.82% year to date 2012. Factored into the performance evaluation is an expense ratio of 1.10% (low).

The fund's risk rating is currently B- (Good). It carries a beta of 0.00, meaning the fund's expected move will be 0.0% for every 10% move in the market. Volatility, as measured by both the semi-deviation and a drawdown factor, is considered low. As of March 31, 2012, Columbia Seligman Prem Tech Gro traded at a discount of 2.53% below its net asset value, which is worse than its one-year historical average discount of 3.44%.

Ajay Diwan currently receives a manager quality ranking of 32 (0=worst, 99=best). If you desire only a moderate level of risk and strong performance, then this fund is an excellent option.

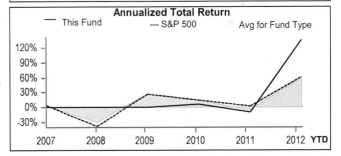

523

Cornerstone Progressive Return Fun (CFP)   D   Weak

Fund Family: Cornerstone Advisors Inc
Fund Type: Income
Inception Date: September 10, 2007

Major Rating Factors: Cornerstone Progressive Return Fun receives a TheStreet.com Investment Rating of D (Weak). The fund currently has a performance rating of C- (Fair) based on an annualized return of 12.24% over the last three years and a total return of 15.22% year to date 2012. Factored into the performance evaluation is an expense ratio of 1.61% (above average).

The fund's risk rating is currently C+ (Fair). It carries a beta of 0.86, meaning the fund's expected move will be 8.6% for every 10% move in the market. Volatility, as measured by both the semi-deviation and a drawdown factor, is considered low. As of March 31, 2012, Cornerstone Progressive Return Fun traded at a premium of 27.29% above its net asset value, which is worse than its one-year historical average premium of 25.20%.

Ralph W. Bradshaw has been running the fund for 5 years and currently receives a manager quality ranking of 35 (0=worst, 99=best). If you desire an average level of risk, then this fund may be an option.

Data Date	Investment Rating	Net Assets ($Mil)	Price	Performance Rating/Pts	Total Return Y-T-D	Risk Rating/Pts
3-12	D	55.28	6.67	C- / 3.3	15.22%	C+ / 6.3
2011	D	55.28	6.05	C- / 3.3	3.14%	C+ / 6.0
2010	D	48.87	7.50	D+ / 2.4	5.28%	C / 4.7
2009	C+	57.27	8.90	B+ / 8.7	55.21%	C- / 4.0

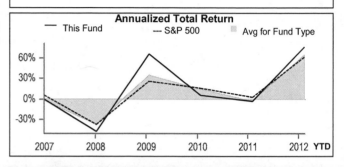

Cornerstone Strategic Value Fund (CLM)   D+   Weak

Fund Family: Cornerstone Advisors Inc
Fund Type: Income
Inception Date: June 30, 1987

Major Rating Factors: Cornerstone Strategic Value Fund receives a TheStreet.com Investment Rating of D+ (Weak). The fund currently has a performance rating of C (Fair) based on an annualized return of 21.15% over the last three years and a total return of 20.82% year to date 2012. Factored into the performance evaluation is an expense ratio of 1.74% (above average).

The fund's risk rating is currently C+ (Fair). It carries a beta of 1.01, meaning that its performance tracks fairly well with that of the overall stock market. Volatility, as measured by both the semi-deviation and a drawdown factor, is considered low. As of March 31, 2012, Cornerstone Strategic Value Fund traded at a premium of 18.17% above its net asset value, which is better than its one-year historical average premium of 35.00%.

Ralph W. Bradshaw has been running the fund for 11 years and currently receives a manager quality ranking of 42 (0=worst, 99=best). If you desire an average level of risk, then this fund may be an option.

Data Date	Investment Rating	Net Assets ($Mil)	Price	Performance Rating/Pts	Total Return Y-T-D	Risk Rating/Pts
3-12	D+	64.27	7.61	C / 4.3	20.82%	C+ / 5.6
2011	D-	64.27	6.60	D+ / 2.4	1.67%	C / 5.5
2010	D-	57.45	8.84	E+ / 0.8	-10.20%	C / 4.3
2009	D-	53.18	11.61	D / 2.0	78.06%	C- / 3.7

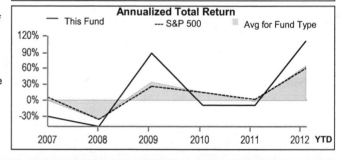

Cornerstone Total Return Fund (CRF)   D   Weak

Fund Family: Cornerstone Advisors Inc
Fund Type: Income
Inception Date: May 3, 1973

Major Rating Factors: Cornerstone Total Return Fund receives a TheStreet.com Investment Rating of D (Weak). The fund currently has a performance rating of C- (Fair) based on an annualized return of 17.41% over the last three years and a total return of 19.22% year to date 2012. Factored into the performance evaluation is an expense ratio of 2.37% (high).

The fund's risk rating is currently C (Fair). It carries a beta of 0.94, meaning that its performance tracks fairly well with that of the overall stock market. Volatility, as measured by both the semi-deviation and a drawdown factor, is considered average. As of March 31, 2012, Cornerstone Total Return Fund traded at a premium of 17.44% above its net asset value, which is better than its one-year historical average premium of 37.69%.

Ralph W. Bradshaw currently receives a manager quality ranking of 41 (0=worst, 99=best). If you desire an average level of risk, then this fund may be an option.

Data Date	Investment Rating	Net Assets ($Mil)	Price	Performance Rating/Pts	Total Return Y-T-D	Risk Rating/Pts
3-12	D	25.91	6.80	C- / 3.3	19.22%	C / 5.4
2011	D-	25.91	5.97	D / 1.7	1.68%	C / 5.0
2010	E+	17.08	7.88	E+ / 0.7	-9.94%	C- / 4.1
2009	E	19.08	10.25	E+ / 0.7	57.12%	C- / 3.4

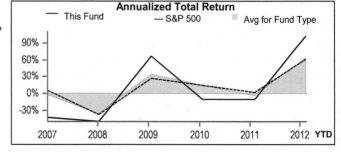

Credit Suisse Asset Mgmt Income (CIK)   B   Good

Fund Family: Credit Suisse Asset Management LLC
Fund Type: Corporate - High Yield
Inception Date: April 8, 1987

Data Date	Investment Rating	Net Assets ($Mil)	Price	Performance Rating/Pts	Total Return Y-T-D	Risk Rating/Pts
3-12	B	180.01	3.73	B- / 7.4	4.42%	B / 8.6
2011	B+	180.00	3.65	B / 7.8	0.82%	B / 8.4
2010	C+	176.38	3.56	B / 7.6	16.04%	C / 4.7
2009	C	152.99	3.36	C+ / 6.1	58.04%	C / 5.4

Major Rating Factors: Strong performance is the major factor driving the B (Good) TheStreet.com Investment Rating for Credit Suisse Asset Mgmt Income. The fund currently has a performance rating of B- (Good) based on an annualized return of 28.40% over the last three years and a total return of 4.42% year to date 2012. Factored into the performance evaluation is an expense ratio of 0.73% (very low).

The fund's risk rating is currently B (Good). It carries a beta of 1.13, meaning it is expected to move 11.3% for every 10% move in the market. Volatility, as measured by both the semi-deviation and a drawdown factor, is considered low. As of March 31, 2012, Credit Suisse Asset Mgmt Income traded at a premium of .27% above its net asset value, which is better than its one-year historical average premium of .69%.

Thomas J. Flannery currently receives a manager quality ranking of 61 (0=worst, 99=best). If you desire only a moderate level of risk and strong performance, then this fund is an excellent option.

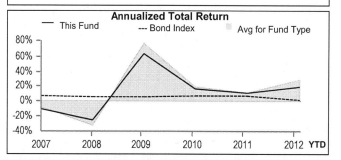

Credit Suisse High Yield Bond Fund (DHY)   A+   Excellent

Fund Family: Credit Suisse Asset Management LLC
Fund Type: Corporate - High Yield
Inception Date: July 28, 1998

Data Date	Investment Rating	Net Assets ($Mil)	Price	Performance Rating/Pts	Total Return Y-T-D	Risk Rating/Pts
3-12	A+	212.12	3.12	A- / 9.2	11.31%	B / 8.6
2011	B+	210.60	2.88	B+ / 8.8	1.04%	B / 8.0
2010	C-	165.31	2.89	C+ / 6.6	10.19%	C- / 3.1
2009	C	112.77	2.93	B / 7.7	102.64%	D+ / 2.6

Major Rating Factors:
Exceptional performance is the major factor driving the A+ (Excellent) TheStreet.com Investment Rating for Credit Suisse High Yield Bond Fund. The fund currently has a performance rating of A- (Excellent) based on an annualized return of 39.04% over the last three years and a total return of 11.31% year to date 2012. Factored into the performance evaluation is an expense ratio of 2.00% (high).

The fund's risk rating is currently B (Good). It carries a beta of 1.16, meaning it is expected to move 11.6% for every 10% move in the market. Volatility, as measured by both the semi-deviation and a drawdown factor, is considered low. As of March 31, 2012, Credit Suisse High Yield Bond Fund traded at a premium of 6.12% above its net asset value, which is worse than its one-year historical average premium of 5.54%.

Thomas J. Flannery currently receives a manager quality ranking of 86 (0=worst, 99=best). If you desire only a moderate level of risk and strong performance, then this fund is an excellent option.

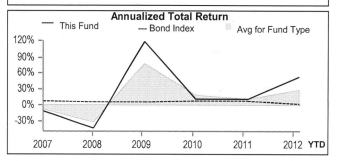

Cutwater Select Income (BDF)   C+   Fair

Fund Family: Cutwater Asset Management Corp
Fund Type: Corporate - Investment Grade
Inception Date: September 29, 1971

Data Date	Investment Rating	Net Assets ($Mil)	Price	Performance Rating/Pts	Total Return Y-T-D	Risk Rating/Pts
3-12	C+	214.27	19.74	C / 5.2	5.00%	B+ / 9.6
2010	B-	125.25	17.70	C+ / 6.6	15.48%	B- / 7.5
2009	C+	118.87	16.34	C- / 4.2	19.06%	B- / 7.6

Major Rating Factors: Middle of the road best describes Cutwater Select Income whose TheStreet.com Investment Rating is currently a C+ (Fair). The fund currently has a performance rating of C (Fair) based on an annualized return of 20.08% over the last three years and a total return of 5.00% year to date 2012. Factored into the performance evaluation is an expense ratio of 0.79% (very low).

The fund's risk rating is currently B+ (Good). It carries a beta of 0.64, meaning the fund's expected move will be 6.4% for every 10% move in the market. Volatility, as measured by both the semi-deviation and a drawdown factor, is considered very low. As of March 31, 2012, Cutwater Select Income traded at a discount of 3.14% below its net asset value, which is worse than its one-year historical average discount of 7.09%.

Gautam Khanna has been running the fund for 7 years and currently receives a manager quality ranking of 87 (0=worst, 99=best). If you desire an average level of risk, then this fund may be an option.

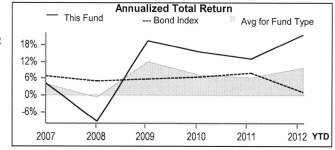

Delaware Enhanced Glb Div & Inc Fd (DEX)

B+   **Good**

Fund Family: Delaware Management Company
Fund Type: Global
Inception Date: June 29, 2007

Data Date	Investment Rating	Net Assets ($Mil)	Price	Perfor-mance Rating/Pts	Total Return Y-T-D	Risk Rating/Pts
3-12	B+	179.41	12.83	A / 9.4	22.18%	B- / 7.2
2011	B	180.90	10.77	B / 7.9	3.71%	B- / 7.5
2010	C-	149.94	12.40	C+ / 6.8	16.55%	C- / 3.2
2009	B	133.47	11.79	A+ / 9.7	78.76%	C- / 3.6

Major Rating Factors:
Exceptional performance is the major factor driving the B+ (Good) TheStreet.com Investment Rating for Delaware Enhanced Glb Div & Inc Fd. The fund currently has a performance rating of A (Excellent) based on an annualized return of 38.48% over the last three years and a total return of 22.18% year to date 2012. Factored into the performance evaluation is an expense ratio of 1.98% (high).

The fund's risk rating is currently B- (Good). It carries a beta of 0.87, meaning the fund's expected move will be 8.7% for every 10% move in the market. Volatility, as measured by both the semi-deviation and a drawdown factor, is considered low. As of March 31, 2012, Delaware Enhanced Glb Div & Inc Fd traded at a premium of 5.86% above its net asset value, which is worse than its one-year historical average discount of 1.01%.

Babak Zenouzi has been running the fund for 5 years and currently receives a manager quality ranking of 94 (0=worst, 99=best). If you desire only a moderate level of risk and strong performance, then this fund is an excellent option.

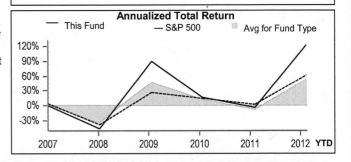

Annualized Total Return

Delaware Inv CO Muni Inc (VCF)

B   **Good**

Fund Family: Delaware Management Company
Fund Type: Municipal - Single State
Inception Date: July 22, 1993

Data Date	Investment Rating	Net Assets ($Mil)	Price	Perfor-mance Rating/Pts	Total Return Y-T-D	Risk Rating/Pts
3-12	B	64.69	14.60	C+ / 6.4	8.40%	B+ / 9.1
2011	C+	70.80	13.61	C+ / 5.6	1.44%	B / 8.7
2010	C-	67.65	12.86	D / 2.0	1.76%	B / 8.2
2009	C-	68.76	13.18	D- / 1.4	7.19%	B / 8.1

Major Rating Factors: Delaware Inv CO Muni Inc receives a TheStreet.com Investment Rating of B (Good). The fund currently has a performance rating of C+ (Fair) based on an annualized return of 11.54% over the last three years and a total return of 8.40% year to date 2012. Factored into the performance evaluation is an expense ratio of 0.56% (very low).

The fund's risk rating is currently B+ (Good). It carries a beta of 0.85, meaning the fund's expected move will be 8.5% for every 10% move in the market. Volatility, as measured by both the semi-deviation and a drawdown factor, is considered very low. As of March 31, 2012, Delaware Inv CO Muni Inc traded at a discount of 2.73% below its net asset value, which is worse than its one-year historical average discount of 6.75%.

Denise A. Franchetti has been running the fund for 8 years and currently receives a manager quality ranking of 79 (0=worst, 99=best). If you desire an average level of risk, then this fund may be an option.

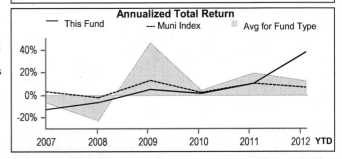

Annualized Total Return

Delaware Inv Div & Inc (DDF)

B+   **Good**

Fund Family: Delaware Management Company
Fund Type: Growth and Income
Inception Date: March 18, 1993

Data Date	Investment Rating	Net Assets ($Mil)	Price	Perfor-mance Rating/Pts	Total Return Y-T-D	Risk Rating/Pts
3-12	B+	72.39	8.15	B+ / 8.7	17.74%	B- / 7.7
2011	B	74.50	7.07	B / 7.8	4.34%	B- / 7.8
2010	D+	67.11	7.79	C / 5.3	16.18%	C- / 3.4
2009	D	58.09	7.36	C- / 3.9	54.31%	C- / 3.4

Major Rating Factors: Strong performance is the major factor driving the B+ (Good) TheStreet.com Investment Rating for Delaware Inv Div & Inc. The fund currently has a performance rating of B+ (Good) based on an annualized return of 32.19% over the last three years and a total return of 17.74% year to date 2012. Factored into the performance evaluation is an expense ratio of 1.51% (average).

The fund's risk rating is currently B- (Good). It carries a beta of 0.95, meaning that its performance tracks fairly well with that of the overall stock market. Volatility, as measured by both the semi-deviation and a drawdown factor, is considered low. As of March 31, 2012, Delaware Inv Div & Inc traded at a discount of 4.12% below its net asset value, which is worse than its one-year historical average discount of 6.61%.

Damon J. Andres has been running the fund for 11 years and currently receives a manager quality ranking of 86 (0=worst, 99=best). If you desire only a moderate level of risk and strong performance, then this fund is an excellent option.

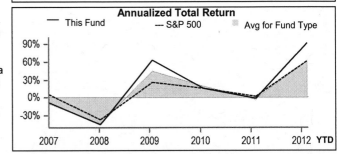

Annualized Total Return

Delaware Inv MN Muni Inc Fund II (VMM)

B   **Good**

Fund Family: Delaware Management Company
Fund Type: Municipal - Single State
Inception Date: February 19, 1993

Major Rating Factors: Delaware Inv MN Muni Inc Fund II receives a TheStreet.com Investment Rating of B (Good). The fund currently has a performance rating of C+ (Fair) based on an annualized return of 11.96% over the last three years and a total return of 6.47% year to date 2012. Factored into the performance evaluation is an expense ratio of 0.56% (very low).

The fund's risk rating is currently B+ (Good). It carries a beta of 1.15, meaning it is expected to move 11.5% for every 10% move in the market. Volatility, as measured by both the semi-deviation and a drawdown factor, is considered very low. As of March 31, 2012, Delaware Inv MN Muni Inc Fund II traded at a discount of 4.75% below its net asset value, which is worse than its one-year historical average discount of 8.32%.

Denise A. Franchetti has been running the fund for 9 years and currently receives a manager quality ranking of 68 (0=worst, 99=best). If you desire an average level of risk, then this fund may be an option.

Data Date	Investment Rating	Net Assets ($Mil)	Price	Performance Rating/Pts	Total Return Y-T-D	Risk Rating/Pts
3-12	B	157.66	14.23	C+ / 6.0	6.47%	B+ / 9.4
2011	B	170.00	13.51	C+ / 6.7	1.14%	B+ / 9.3
2010	C+	161.72	12.62	C- / 3.9	7.83%	B / 8.3
2009	C	163.21	12.23	D+ / 2.4	19.72%	B / 8.2

Annualized Total Return

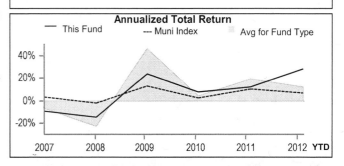

Delaware Inv Nat Muni Inc (VFL)

C+   **Fair**

Fund Family: Delaware Management Company
Fund Type: Municipal - National
Inception Date: February 19, 1993

Major Rating Factors: Middle of the road best describes Delaware Inv Nat Muni Inc whose TheStreet.com Investment Rating is currently a C+ (Fair). The fund currently has a performance rating of C (Fair) based on an annualized return of 11.54% over the last three years and a total return of 3.61% year to date 2012. Factored into the performance evaluation is an expense ratio of 0.65% (very low).

The fund's risk rating is currently B+ (Good). It carries a beta of 1.60, meaning it is expected to move 16.0% for every 10% move in the market. Volatility, as measured by both the semi-deviation and a drawdown factor, is considered very low. As of March 31, 2012, Delaware Inv Nat Muni Inc traded at a discount of 5.56% below its net asset value, which is better than its one-year historical average discount of 5.49%.

Denise A. Franchetti has been running the fund for 9 years and currently receives a manager quality ranking of 39 (0=worst, 99=best). If you desire an average level of risk, then this fund may be an option.

Data Date	Investment Rating	Net Assets ($Mil)	Price	Performance Rating/Pts	Total Return Y-T-D	Risk Rating/Pts
3-12	C+	30.56	13.24	C / 4.5	3.61%	B+ / 9.0
2011	B	61.90	12.91	B- / 7.2	0.31%	B / 8.9
2010	C-	31.65	12.09	C- / 3.7	2.62%	C+ / 6.1
2009	C	32.15	12.28	C- / 3.9	34.80%	C+ / 6.7

Annualized Total Return

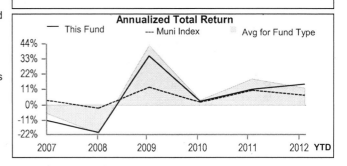

Dividend and Income Fund Inc (DNI)

C-   **Fair**

Fund Family: Bexil Advisers LLC
Fund Type: Growth and Income
Inception Date: June 23, 1998

Major Rating Factors: Middle of the road best describes Dividend and Income Fund Inc whose TheStreet.com Investment Rating is currently a C- (Fair). The fund currently has a performance rating of C (Fair) based on an annualized return of 21.61% over the last three years and a total return of 9.15% year to date 2012. Factored into the performance evaluation is an expense ratio of 2.00% (high).

The fund's risk rating is currently B- (Good). It carries a beta of 0.94, meaning that its performance tracks fairly well with that of the overall stock market. Volatility, as measured by both the semi-deviation and a drawdown factor, is considered low. As of March 31, 2012, Dividend and Income Fund Inc traded at a discount of 11.49% below its net asset value, which is better than its one-year historical average discount of 10.61%.

Heidi Keating has been running the fund for 1 year and currently receives a manager quality ranking of 54 (0=worst, 99=best). If you desire an average level of risk, then this fund may be an option.

Data Date	Investment Rating	Net Assets ($Mil)	Price	Performance Rating/Pts	Total Return Y-T-D	Risk Rating/Pts
3-12	C-	71.33	3.62	C / 4.7	9.15%	B- / 7.2
2011	C-	73.32	3.41	C- / 3.8	-2.05%	B- / 7.0
2010	D	70.85	4.27	D+ / 2.7	25.35%	C- / 4.1
2009	D-	63.00	3.77	E+ / 0.9	35.29%	C / 4.6

Annualized Total Return

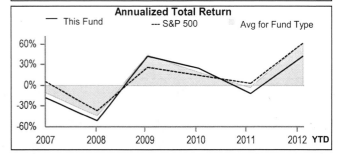

DNP Select Income Fund Inc (DNP)

C+   **Fair**

Fund Family: Duff & Phelps Investment Mgmt Co
Fund Type: Utilities
Inception Date: January 28, 1987

Major Rating Factors: Middle of the road best describes DNP Select Income Fund Inc whose TheStreet.com Investment Rating is currently a C+ (Fair). The fund currently has a performance rating of C (Fair) based on an annualized return of 22.96% over the last three years and a total return of -5.77% year to date 2012. Factored into the performance evaluation is an expense ratio of 1.95% (above average).

The fund's risk rating is currently B (Good). It carries a beta of 0.38, meaning the fund's expected move will be 3.8% for every 10% move in the market. Volatility, as measured by both the semi-deviation and a drawdown factor, is considered low. As of March 31, 2012, DNP Select Income Fund Inc traded at a premium of 24.38% above its net asset value, which is better than its one-year historical average premium of 30.28%.

Nathan I. Partain currently receives a manager quality ranking of 91 (0=worst, 99=best). If you desire an average level of risk, then this fund may be an option.

Data Date	Investment Rating	Net Assets ($Mil)	Price	Performance Rating/Pts	Total Return Y-T-D	Risk Rating/Pts
3-12	C+	2,013.93	10.10	C / 5.5	-5.77%	B / 8.7
2011	B+	2,014.00	10.92	B+ / 8.3	0.37%	B / 8.2
2010	C	1,703.40	9.14	C / 5.1	11.31%	C / 5.5
2009	C	1,467.93	8.95	C / 5.4	48.07%	C+ / 5.6

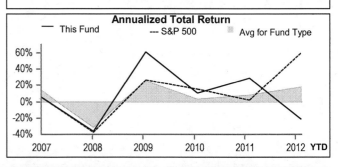

Annualized Total Return

Dow 30 Enhanced Premium & Income F (DPO)

C+   **Fair**

Fund Family: Nuveen Fund Advisors Inc
Fund Type: Income
Inception Date: May 30, 2007

Major Rating Factors: Middle of the road best describes Dow 30 Enhanced Premium & Income F whose TheStreet.com Investment Rating is currently a C+ (Fair). The fund currently has a performance rating of C+ (Fair) based on an annualized return of 22.35% over the last three years and a total return of 12.88% year to date 2012. Factored into the performance evaluation is an expense ratio of 1.01% (low).

The fund's risk rating is currently B- (Good). It carries a beta of 0.98, meaning that its performance tracks fairly well with that of the overall stock market. Volatility, as measured by both the semi-deviation and a drawdown factor, is considered low. As of March 31, 2012, Dow 30 Enhanced Premium & Income F traded at a discount of 4.74% below its net asset value, which is better than its one-year historical average discount of 2.33%.

James A. Colon has been running the fund for 1 year and currently receives a manager quality ranking of 64 (0=worst, 99=best). If you desire an average level of risk, then this fund may be an option.

Data Date	Investment Rating	Net Assets ($Mil)	Price	Performance Rating/Pts	Total Return Y-T-D	Risk Rating/Pts
3-12	C+	306.13	11.25	C+ / 6.0	12.88%	B- / 7.5
2011	C+	306.10	10.16	C+ / 6.3	1.57%	B- / 7.3
2010	C-	285.17	10.38	C- / 3.6	5.19%	C+ / 6.1
2009	B	244.94	10.94	B+ / 8.3	43.79%	C / 5.0

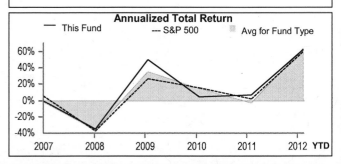

Annualized Total Return

Dow 30 Premium & Dividend Income (DPD)

C-   **Fair**

Fund Family: Nuveen Fund Advisors Inc
Fund Type: Income
Inception Date: May 6, 2005

Major Rating Factors: Middle of the road best describes Dow 30 Premium & Dividend Income whose TheStreet.com Investment Rating is currently a C- (Fair). The fund currently has a performance rating of C- (Fair) based on an annualized return of 13.81% over the last three years and a total return of 10.08% year to date 2012. Factored into the performance evaluation is an expense ratio of 1.02% (low).

The fund's risk rating is currently B- (Good). It carries a beta of 0.82, meaning the fund's expected move will be 8.2% for every 10% move in the market. Volatility, as measured by both the semi-deviation and a drawdown factor, is considered low. As of March 31, 2012, Dow 30 Premium & Dividend Income traded at a discount of 5.59% below its net asset value, which is better than its one-year historical average discount of 3.90%.

James A. Colon has been running the fund for 1 year and currently receives a manager quality ranking of 27 (0=worst, 99=best). If you desire an average level of risk, then this fund may be an option.

Data Date	Investment Rating	Net Assets ($Mil)	Price	Performance Rating/Pts	Total Return Y-T-D	Risk Rating/Pts
3-12	C-	171.00	14.18	C- / 3.4	10.08%	B- / 7.8
2011	C-	171.00	13.12	C- / 3.6	1.30%	B- / 7.5
2010	C	165.40	14.53	C+ / 5.6	7.76%	C / 5.3
2009	C-	144.47	14.74	D+ / 2.9	20.31%	C+ / 5.8

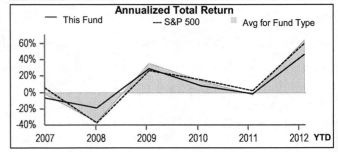

Annualized Total Return

Dreyfus High Yield Strategies Fund (DHF)   B   Good

Fund Family: Dreyfus Corporation
Fund Type: Corporate - High Yield
Inception Date: April 23, 1998

Major Rating Factors:
Exceptional performance is the major factor driving the B (Good) TheStreet.com Investment Rating for Dreyfus High Yield Strategies Fund. The fund currently has a performance rating of A- (Excellent) based on an annualized return of 37.00% over the last three years and a total return of 6.89% year to date 2012. Factored into the performance evaluation is an expense ratio of 2.00% (high).

The fund's risk rating is currently C+ (Fair). It carries a beta of 1.23, meaning it is expected to move 12.3% for every 10% move in the market. Volatility, as measured by both the semi-deviation and a drawdown factor, is considered low. As of March 31, 2012, Dreyfus High Yield Strategies Fund traded at a premium of 19.23% above its net asset value, which is worse than its one-year historical average premium of 18.16%.

Chris E. Barris currently receives a manager quality ranking of 80 (0=worst, 99=best). If you desire only a moderate level of risk and strong performance, then this fund is an excellent option.

Data Date	Investment Rating	Net Assets ($Mil)	Price	Performance Rating/Pts	Total Return Y-T-D	Risk Rating/Pts
3-12	B	306.18	4.65	A- / 9.0	6.89%	C+ / 6.4
2011	B	384.10	4.43	A- / 9.1	1.13%	C+ / 6.3
2010	C+	291.96	4.43	B+ / 8.9	33.00%	C- / 3.0
2009	C	273.02	3.76	B / 7.6	77.12%	C- / 3.8

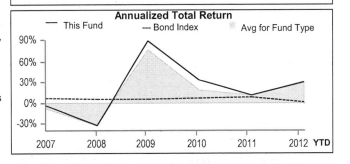

Dreyfus Municipal Income (DMF)   B+   Good

Fund Family: Dreyfus Corporation
Fund Type: Municipal - National
Inception Date: October 21, 1988

Major Rating Factors: Strong performance is the major factor driving the B+ (Good) TheStreet.com Investment Rating for Dreyfus Municipal Income. The fund currently has a performance rating of B (Good) based on an annualized return of 18.07% over the last three years and a total return of 2.00% year to date 2012. Factored into the performance evaluation is an expense ratio of 1.29% (average).

The fund's risk rating is currently B (Good). It carries a beta of 1.62, meaning it is expected to move 16.2% for every 10% move in the market. Volatility, as measured by both the semi-deviation and a drawdown factor, is considered low. As of March 31, 2012, Dreyfus Municipal Income traded at a premium of .40% above its net asset value, which is worse than its one-year historical average premium of .28%.

James S. Welch has been running the fund for 3 years and currently receives a manager quality ranking of 76 (0=worst, 99=best). If you desire only a moderate level of risk and strong performance, then this fund is an excellent option.

Data Date	Investment Rating	Net Assets ($Mil)	Price	Performance Rating/Pts	Total Return Y-T-D	Risk Rating/Pts
3-12	B+	194.79	9.92	B / 7.9	2.00%	B / 8.8
2011	A+	273.80	9.88	A+ / 9.6	2.63%	B / 8.8
2010	C+	199.20	8.93	C+ / 6.9	12.10%	C+ / 6.4
2009	B-	193.03	8.48	C / 5.5	28.94%	B- / 7.5

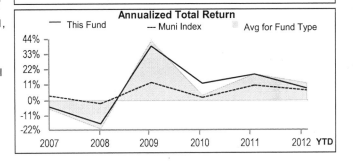

Dreyfus Strategic Muni Bond Fund (DSM)   B+   Good

Fund Family: Dreyfus Corporation
Fund Type: Municipal - National
Inception Date: November 22, 1989

Major Rating Factors: Strong performance is the major factor driving the B+ (Good) TheStreet.com Investment Rating for Dreyfus Strategic Muni Bond Fund. The fund currently has a performance rating of B (Good) based on an annualized return of 18.99% over the last three years and a total return of 1.64% year to date 2012. Factored into the performance evaluation is an expense ratio of 0.85% (very low).

The fund's risk rating is currently B (Good). It carries a beta of 1.72, meaning it is expected to move 17.2% for every 10% move in the market. Volatility, as measured by both the semi-deviation and a drawdown factor, is considered low. As of March 31, 2012, Dreyfus Strategic Muni Bond Fund traded at a premium of 1.28% above its net asset value, which is better than its one-year historical average premium of 1.57%.

James S. Welch has been running the fund for 11 years and currently receives a manager quality ranking of 72 (0=worst, 99=best). If you desire only a moderate level of risk and strong performance, then this fund is an excellent option.

Data Date	Investment Rating	Net Assets ($Mil)	Price	Performance Rating/Pts	Total Return Y-T-D	Risk Rating/Pts
3-12	B+	394.96	8.69	B / 8.0	1.64%	B / 8.7
2011	A+	545.10	8.69	A / 9.4	-0.01%	B / 8.7
2010	C-	384.46	7.58	C- / 3.2	5.39%	C+ / 6.2
2009	C+	363.86	7.69	C / 4.8	45.02%	C+ / 6.9

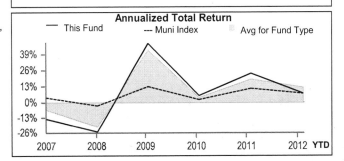

Dreyfus Strategic Municipals (LEO)

A-   **Excellent**

Fund Family: Dreyfus Corporation
Fund Type: Municipal - National
Inception Date: September 23, 1987

Data Date	Investment Rating	Net Assets ($Mil)	Price	Perfor-mance Rating/Pts	Total Return Y-T-D	Risk Rating/Pts
3-12	A-	515.40	9.12	B+ / 8.5	4.29%	B / 8.5
2011	A	738.90	8.89	A / 9.4	0.22%	B / 8.6
2010	C-	528.61	7.80	C- / 3.8	3.55%	C+ / 6.0
2009	C+	514.79	8.08	C+ / 6.8	46.73%	C+ / 6.8

Major Rating Factors:
Strong performance is the major factor driving the A- (Excellent) TheStreet.com Investment Rating for Dreyfus Strategic Municipals. The fund currently has a performance rating of B+ (Good) based on an annualized return of 18.85% over the last three years and a total return of 4.29% year to date 2012. Factored into the performance evaluation is an expense ratio of 1.26% (average).

The fund's risk rating is currently B (Good). It carries a beta of 1.71, meaning it is expected to move 17.1% for every 10% move in the market. Volatility, as measured by both the semi-deviation and a drawdown factor, is considered low. As of March 31, 2012, Dreyfus Strategic Municipals traded at a premium of 3.52% above its net asset value, which is worse than its one-year historical average premium of 1.31%.

James S. Welch has been running the fund for 3 years and currently receives a manager quality ranking of 74 (0=worst, 99=best). If you desire only a moderate level of risk and strong performance, then this fund is an excellent option.

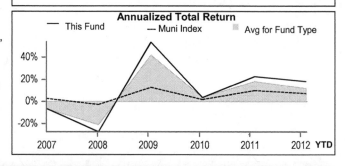

DTF Tax Free Income (DTF)

B+   **Good**

Fund Family: Duff & Phelps Investment Mgmt Co
Fund Type: Municipal - National
Inception Date: November 29, 1991

Data Date	Investment Rating	Net Assets ($Mil)	Price	Perfor-mance Rating/Pts	Total Return Y-T-D	Risk Rating/Pts
3-12	B+	138.11	16.60	B / 7.7	4.66%	B / 8.9
2011	B+	131.89	16.06	B / 8.2	1.00%	B / 8.9
2010	C+	136.53	14.82	C+ / 6.3	7.59%	C+ / 6.8
2009	B	128.43	14.56	C / 5.5	27.07%	B- / 7.6

Major Rating Factors: Strong performance is the major factor driving the B+ (Good) TheStreet.com Investment Rating for DTF Tax Free Income. The fund currently has a performance rating of B (Good) based on an annualized return of 16.42% over the last three years and a total return of 4.66% year to date 2012. Factored into the performance evaluation is an expense ratio of 1.23% (average).

The fund's risk rating is currently B (Good). It carries a beta of 1.78, meaning it is expected to move 17.8% for every 10% move in the market. Volatility, as measured by both the semi-deviation and a drawdown factor, is considered low. As of March 31, 2012, DTF Tax Free Income traded at a discount of .72% below its net asset value, which is worse than its one-year historical average discount of 3.97%.

Amy L. Robinson currently receives a manager quality ranking of 64 (0=worst, 99=best). If you desire only a moderate level of risk and strong performance, then this fund is an excellent option.

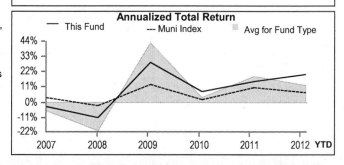

Duff & Phelps Utilities & Crp Bd T (DUC)

C-   **Fair**

Fund Family: Duff & Phelps Investment Mgmt Co
Fund Type: General - Investment Grade
Inception Date: January 22, 1993

Data Date	Investment Rating	Net Assets ($Mil)	Price	Perfor-mance Rating/Pts	Total Return Y-T-D	Risk Rating/Pts
3-12	C-	321.00	11.81	D+ / 2.7	-0.16%	B / 8.7
2011	C+	319.92	12.04	C / 5.5	1.16%	B / 8.8
2010	B-	318.39	11.39	C+ / 5.9	-0.60%	B- / 7.3
2009	B-	306.51	12.29	C / 5.3	27.90%	B- / 7.4

Major Rating Factors:
Disappointing performance is the major factor driving the C- (Fair) TheStreet.com Investment Rating for Duff & Phelps Utilities & Crp Bd T. The fund currently has a performance rating of D+ (Weak) based on an annualized return of 9.62% over the last three years and a total return of -0.16% year to date 2012. Factored into the performance evaluation is an expense ratio of 1.86% (above average).

The fund's risk rating is currently B (Good). It carries a beta of 1.55, meaning it is expected to move 15.5% for every 10% move in the market. Volatility, as measured by both the semi-deviation and a drawdown factor, is considered low. As of March 31, 2012, Duff & Phelps Utilities & Crp Bd T traded at a premium of .60% above its net asset value, which is worse than its one-year historical average discount of 1.40%.

Daniel J. Petrisko has been running the fund for 16 years and currently receives a manager quality ranking of 36 (0=worst, 99=best). This fund offers only a moderate level of risk but investors looking for strong performance are still waiting.

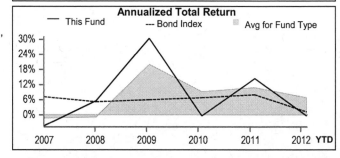

DWS Global High Income Fund (LBF)

C   **Fair**

Fund Family: DWS Investments
Fund Type: Global
Inception Date: July 24, 1992

Major Rating Factors: Middle of the road best describes DWS Global High Income Fund whose TheStreet.com Investment Rating is currently a C (Fair). The fund currently has a performance rating of C (Fair) based on an annualized return of 17.75% over the last three years and a total return of 8.42% year to date 2012. Factored into the performance evaluation is an expense ratio of 2.22% (high).

The fund's risk rating is currently B- (Good). It carries a beta of 0.76, meaning the fund's expected move will be 7.6% for every 10% move in the market. Volatility, as measured by both the semi-deviation and a drawdown factor, is considered low. As of March 31, 2012, DWS Global High Income Fund traded at a discount of 10.32% below its net asset value, which is better than its one-year historical average discount of 9.83%.

Gary A. Russell currently receives a manager quality ranking of 89 (0=worst, 99=best). If you desire an average level of risk, then this fund may be an option.

Data Date	Investment Rating	Net Assets ($Mil)	Price	Performance Rating/Pts	Total Return Y-T-D	Risk Rating/Pts
3-12	C	63.00	8.08	C / 4.5	8.42%	B- / 7.7
2011	C+	61.70	7.57	C+ / 6.6	2.11%	B- / 7.4
2010	C	84.00	7.80	C+ / 6.5	13.94%	C / 4.3
2009	C	68.95	7.29	C / 5.2	46.23%	C / 5.1

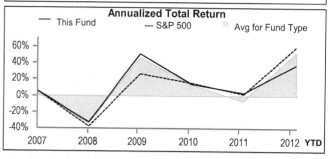

Annualized Total Return

DWS High Income Opportunities Fund (DHG)

A+   **Excellent**

Fund Family: DWS Investments
Fund Type: Global
Inception Date: November 22, 2006

Major Rating Factors:
Exceptional performance is the major factor driving the A+ (Excellent) TheStreet.com Investment Rating for DWS High Income Opportunities Fund. The fund currently has a performance rating of A+ (Excellent) based on an annualized return of 42.68% over the last three years and a total return of 18.15% year to date 2012. Factored into the performance evaluation is an expense ratio of 2.31% (high).

The fund's risk rating is currently B (Good). It carries a beta of 0.65, meaning the fund's expected move will be 6.5% for every 10% move in the market. Volatility, as measured by both the semi-deviation and a drawdown factor, is considered low. As of March 31, 2012, DWS High Income Opportunities Fund traded at a premium of 2.62% above its net asset value, which is worse than its one-year historical average discount of 5.91%.

Gary A. Russell currently receives a manager quality ranking of 97 (0=worst, 99=best). If you desire only a moderate level of risk and strong performance, then this fund is an excellent option.

Data Date	Investment Rating	Net Assets ($Mil)	Price	Performance Rating/Pts	Total Return Y-T-D	Risk Rating/Pts
3-12	A+	234.00	16.03	A+ / 9.7	18.15%	B / 8.8
2011	B+	252.50	13.86	B / 8.1	1.95%	B / 8.3
2010	E	365.00	14.08	D- / 1.2	25.15%	D / 2.0
2009	E	350.43	12.07	E+ / 0.8	57.98%	C- / 3.1

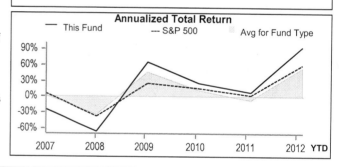

Annualized Total Return

DWS High Income Trust (KHI)

C+   **Fair**

Fund Family: DWS Investments
Fund Type: Corporate - High Yield
Inception Date: April 21, 1988

Major Rating Factors: Strong performance is the major factor driving the C+ (Fair) TheStreet.com Investment Rating for DWS High Income Trust. The fund currently has a performance rating of B (Good) based on an annualized return of 31.14% over the last three years and a total return of 0.89% year to date 2012. Factored into the performance evaluation is an expense ratio of 1.61% (above average).

The fund's risk rating is currently C+ (Fair). It carries a beta of 1.16, meaning it is expected to move 11.6% for every 10% move in the market. Volatility, as measured by both the semi-deviation and a drawdown factor, is considered low. As of March 31, 2012, DWS High Income Trust traded at a premium of 4.24% above its net asset value, which is better than its one-year historical average premium of 6.61%.

Gary A. Russell has been running the fund for 14 years and currently receives a manager quality ranking of 66 (0=worst, 99=best). If you desire only a moderate level of risk and strong performance, then this fund is an excellent option.

Data Date	Investment Rating	Net Assets ($Mil)	Price	Performance Rating/Pts	Total Return Y-T-D	Risk Rating/Pts
3-12	C+	148.00	10.09	B / 8.0	0.89%	C+ / 6.7
2011	B-	151.60	10.23	B+ / 8.6	-0.10%	C+ / 6.5
2010	C+	146.00	9.39	B- / 7.5	21.08%	C- / 4.1
2009	C	120.46	8.47	C+ / 5.9	60.93%	C / 4.5

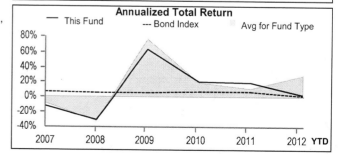

Annualized Total Return

DWS Multi-Market Income Trust (KMM)

B-   **Good**

Fund Family: DWS Investments
Fund Type: Global
Inception Date: January 23, 1989

Major Rating Factors: Strong performance is the major factor driving the B- (Good) TheStreet.com Investment Rating for DWS Multi-Market Income Trust. The fund currently has a performance rating of B (Good) based on an annualized return of 31.79% over the last three years and a total return of 4.62% year to date 2012. Factored into the performance evaluation is an expense ratio of 1.49% (average).

The fund's risk rating is currently B- (Good). It carries a beta of 0.52, meaning the fund's expected move will be 5.2% for every 10% move in the market. Volatility, as measured by both the semi-deviation and a drawdown factor, is considered low. As of March 31, 2012, DWS Multi-Market Income Trust traded at a premium of 3.30% above its net asset value, which is better than its one-year historical average premium of 5.29%.

Gary A. Russell currently receives a manager quality ranking of 96 (0=worst, 99=best). If you desire only a moderate level of risk and strong performance, then this fund is an excellent option.

Data Date	Investment Rating	Net Assets ($Mil)	Price	Perfor-mance Rating/Pts	Total Return Y-T-D	Risk Rating/Pts
3-12	B-	228.00	10.33	B / 8.1	4.62%	B- / 7.1
2011	B	234.40	10.10	B+ / 8.6	1.68%	B- / 7.0
2010	B	218.10	9.91	B+ / 8.6	26.07%	C / 4.3
2009	C+	190.98	8.61	C+ / 6.7	62.81%	C / 5.1

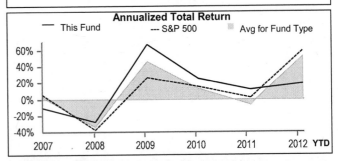

DWS Municipal Income Trust (KTF)

A+   **Excellent**

Fund Family: DWS Investments
Fund Type: Municipal - National
Inception Date: October 20, 1988

Major Rating Factors:
Exceptional performance is the major factor driving the A+ (Excellent) TheStreet.com Investment Rating for DWS Municipal Income Trust. The fund currently has a performance rating of A- (Excellent) based on an annualized return of 22.45% over the last three years and a total return of 1.71% year to date 2012. Factored into the performance evaluation is an expense ratio of 1.23% (average).

The fund's risk rating is currently B (Good). It carries a beta of 1.95, meaning it is expected to move 19.5% for every 10% move in the market. Volatility, as measured by both the semi-deviation and a drawdown factor, is considered low. As of March 31, 2012, DWS Municipal Income Trust traded at a premium of 3.68% above its net asset value, which is worse than its one-year historical average premium of .69%.

Philip G. Condon currently receives a manager quality ranking of 78 (0=worst, 99=best). If you desire only a moderate level of risk and strong performance, then this fund is an excellent option.

Data Date	Investment Rating	Net Assets ($Mil)	Price	Perfor-mance Rating/Pts	Total Return Y-T-D	Risk Rating/Pts
3-12	A+	491.00	13.82	A- / 9.2	1.71%	B / 8.7
2011	A+	505.20	13.80	A+ / 9.8	-1.45%	B / 8.8
2010	B+	465.33	11.42	B- / 7.0	3.85%	C+ / 6.5
2009	A+	440.43	11.78	B / 7.9	49.68%	C+ / 6.9

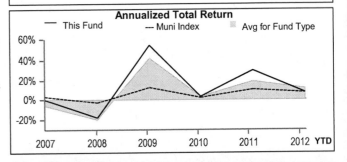

DWS Strategic Income Fund (KST)

B+   **Good**

Fund Family: DWS Investments
Fund Type: Global
Inception Date: April 29, 1994

Major Rating Factors: Strong performance is the major factor driving the B+ (Good) TheStreet.com Investment Rating for DWS Strategic Income Fund. The fund currently has a performance rating of B+ (Good) based on an annualized return of 31.91% over the last three years and a total return of 11.25% year to date 2012. Factored into the performance evaluation is an expense ratio of 1.96% (above average).

The fund's risk rating is currently B- (Good). It carries a beta of 0.31, meaning the fund's expected move will be 3.1% for every 10% move in the market. Volatility, as measured by both the semi-deviation and a drawdown factor, is considered low. As of March 31, 2012, DWS Strategic Income Fund traded at a premium of 5.05% above its net asset value, which is worse than its one-year historical average discount of 1.03%.

Gary A. Russell currently receives a manager quality ranking of 97 (0=worst, 99=best). If you desire only a moderate level of risk and strong performance, then this fund is an excellent option.

Data Date	Investment Rating	Net Assets ($Mil)	Price	Perfor-mance Rating/Pts	Total Return Y-T-D	Risk Rating/Pts
3-12	B+	61.00	14.55	B+ / 8.6	11.25%	B- / 7.5
2011	B	62.40	13.35	B+ / 8.4	0.15%	B- / 7.4
2010	B-	60.13	12.68	B / 8.0	19.44%	C / 4.8
2009	C-	51.68	11.57	C / 4.6	55.85%	C / 5.2

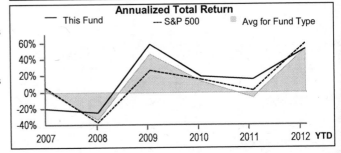

DWS Strategic Municipal Inc Tr (KSM)   A+   Excellent

Fund Family: DWS Investments
Fund Type: Municipal - National
Inception Date: March 22, 1989

Major Rating Factors:
Exceptional performance is the major factor driving the A+ (Excellent) TheStreet.com Investment Rating for DWS Strategic Municipal Inc Tr. The fund currently has a performance rating of A- (Excellent) based on an annualized return of 22.18% over the last three years and a total return of 2.15% year to date 2012. Factored into the performance evaluation is an expense ratio of 1.29% (average).

The fund's risk rating is currently B (Good). It carries a beta of 2.05, meaning it is expected to move 20.5% for every 10% move in the market. Volatility, as measured by both the semi-deviation and a drawdown factor, is considered low. As of March 31, 2012, DWS Strategic Municipal Inc Tr traded at a premium of 5.52% above its net asset value, which is worse than its one-year historical average premium of 3.87%.

Philip G. Condon has been running the fund for 14 years and currently receives a manager quality ranking of 77 (0=worst, 99=best). If you desire only a moderate level of risk and strong performance, then this fund is an excellent option.

Data Date	Investment Rating	Net Assets ($Mil)	Price	Performance Rating/Pts	Total Return Y-T-D	Risk Rating/Pts
3-12	A+	138.00	13.95	A- / 9.2	2.15%	B / 8.8
2011	A+	141.20	13.90	A+ / 9.9	2.81%	B / 8.9
2010	B+	138.00	12.28	B / 8.0	5.37%	C+ / 6.0
2009	A	121.32	12.60	B / 8.2	69.48%	C+ / 6.4

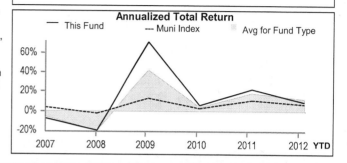

Eagle Capital Growth Fund (GRF)   B-   Good

Fund Family: Sims Capital Management LLC
Fund Type: Growth
Inception Date: July 2, 1990

Major Rating Factors: Eagle Capital Growth Fund receives a TheStreet.com Investment Rating of B- (Good). The fund currently has a performance rating of C+ (Fair) based on an annualized return of 26.02% over the last three years and a total return of -5.14% year to date 2012. Factored into the performance evaluation is an expense ratio of 1.52% (average).

The fund's risk rating is currently B (Good). It carries a beta of 0.74, meaning the fund's expected move will be 7.4% for every 10% move in the market. Volatility, as measured by both the semi-deviation and a drawdown factor, is considered low. As of March 31, 2012, Eagle Capital Growth Fund traded at a discount of 12.21% below its net asset value, which is worse than its one-year historical average discount of 12.87%.

David C. Sims currently receives a manager quality ranking of 82 (0=worst, 99=best). If you desire an average level of risk, then this fund may be an option.

Data Date	Investment Rating	Net Assets ($Mil)	Price	Performance Rating/Pts	Total Return Y-T-D	Risk Rating/Pts
3-12	B-	23.23	6.76	C+ / 6.7	-5.14%	B / 8.4
2011	B	22.20	7.00	B / 7.8	8.17%	B- / 7.7
2010	C-	21.00	6.62	C- / 3.3	9.34%	C+ / 6.3
2009	C-	16.80	6.39	C- / 3.3	28.82%	C / 5.5

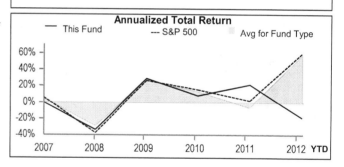

Eaton Vance CA Muni Bond (EVM)   C   Fair

Fund Family: Eaton Vance Management
Fund Type: Municipal - Single State
Inception Date: August 27, 2002

Major Rating Factors: Middle of the road best describes Eaton Vance CA Muni Bond whose TheStreet.com Investment Rating is currently a C (Fair). The fund currently has a performance rating of C (Fair) based on an annualized return of 12.71% over the last three years and a total return of -5.31% year to date 2012. Factored into the performance evaluation is an expense ratio of 1.99% (high).

The fund's risk rating is currently B (Good). It carries a beta of 2.69, meaning it is expected to move 26.9% for every 10% move in the market. Volatility, as measured by both the semi-deviation and a drawdown factor, is considered low. As of March 31, 2012, Eaton Vance CA Muni Bond traded at a discount of 3.47% below its net asset value, which is better than its one-year historical average premium of 2.83%.

Cynthia J. Clemson has been running the fund for 10 years and currently receives a manager quality ranking of 18 (0=worst, 99=best). If you desire an average level of risk, then this fund may be an option.

Data Date	Investment Rating	Net Assets ($Mil)	Price	Performance Rating/Pts	Total Return Y-T-D	Risk Rating/Pts
3-12	C	255.29	11.96	C / 4.9	-5.31%	B / 8.0
2011	B+	257.20	12.82	B+ / 8.8	-1.09%	B / 8.0
2010	D	273.91	11.25	D- / 1.5	5.61%	C+ / 6.2
2009	C-	280.74	11.43	C- / 3.4	43.32%	C+ / 6.5

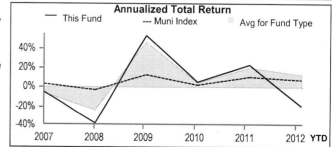

Eaton Vance CA Muni Bond II (EIA)   C+   Fair

Fund Family: Eaton Vance Management
Fund Type: Municipal - Single State
Inception Date: November 25, 2002

Major Rating Factors: Middle of the road best describes Eaton Vance CA Muni Bond II whose TheStreet.com Investment Rating is currently a C+ (Fair). The fund currently has a performance rating of C+ (Fair) based on an annualized return of 12.80% over the last three years and a total return of -0.59% year to date 2012. Factored into the performance evaluation is an expense ratio of 1.62% (above average).

The fund's risk rating is currently B (Good). It carries a beta of 2.72, meaning it is expected to move 27.2% for every 10% move in the market. Volatility, as measured by both the semi-deviation and a drawdown factor, is considered low. As of March 31, 2012, Eaton Vance CA Muni Bond II traded at a discount of 1.19% below its net asset value, which is better than its one-year historical average premium of 2.14%.

Cynthia J. Clemson has been running the fund for 10 years and currently receives a manager quality ranking of 19 (0=worst, 99=best). If you desire an average level of risk, then this fund may be an option.

Data Date	Investment Rating	Net Assets ($Mil)	Price	Performance Rating/Pts	Total Return Y-T-D	Risk Rating/Pts
3-12	C+	45.54	12.50	C+ / 6.3	-0.59%	B / 8.1
2011	B+	46.50	12.77	B+ / 8.9	-0.82%	B / 8.2
2010	D	48.53	11.00	D / 1.6	3.14%	C+ / 6.1
2009	C-	50.08	11.46	C- / 3.3	39.64%	C+ / 6.3

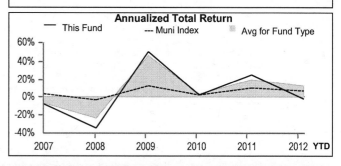

Annualized Total Return

Eaton Vance CA Muni Inc Tr (CEV)   A-   Excellent

Fund Family: Eaton Vance Management
Fund Type: Municipal - Single State
Inception Date: January 26, 1999

Major Rating Factors:
Strong performance is the major factor driving the A- (Excellent) TheStreet.com Investment Rating for Eaton Vance CA Muni Inc Tr. The fund currently has a performance rating of B+ (Good) based on an annualized return of 17.65% over the last three years and a total return of 4.78% year to date 2012. Factored into the performance evaluation is an expense ratio of 2.00% (high).

The fund's risk rating is currently B (Good). It carries a beta of 2.62, meaning it is expected to move 26.2% for every 10% move in the market. Volatility, as measured by both the semi-deviation and a drawdown factor, is considered low. As of March 31, 2012, Eaton Vance CA Muni Inc Tr traded at a premium of .37% above its net asset value, which is worse than its one-year historical average premium of .25%.

Cynthia J. Clemson has been running the fund for 13 years and currently receives a manager quality ranking of 36 (0=worst, 99=best). If you desire only a moderate level of risk and strong performance, then this fund is an excellent option.

Data Date	Investment Rating	Net Assets ($Mil)	Price	Performance Rating/Pts	Total Return Y-T-D	Risk Rating/Pts
3-12	A-	89.86	13.46	B+ / 8.7	4.78%	B / 8.5
2011	A	93.00	13.06	A / 9.3	-0.77%	B / 8.5
2010	D	93.25	11.67	D / 1.9	5.21%	C+ / 5.7
2009	C	84.48	11.90	C / 4.9	60.17%	C+ / 6.1

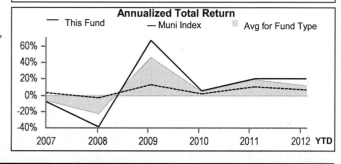

Annualized Total Return

Eaton Vance Enhanced Eqty Inc (EOI)   D+   Weak

Fund Family: Eaton Vance Management
Fund Type: Income
Inception Date: October 29, 2004

Major Rating Factors: Eaton Vance Enhanced Eqty Inc receives a TheStreet.com Investment Rating of D+ (Weak). The fund currently has a performance rating of C- (Fair) based on an annualized return of 12.93% over the last three years and a total return of 11.34% year to date 2012. Factored into the performance evaluation is an expense ratio of 1.15% (low).

The fund's risk rating is currently B- (Good). It carries a beta of 0.95, meaning that its performance tracks fairly well with that of the overall stock market. Volatility, as measured by both the semi-deviation and a drawdown factor, is considered low. As of March 31, 2012, Eaton Vance Enhanced Eqty Inc traded at a discount of 14.06% below its net asset value, which is better than its one-year historical average discount of 12.26%.

Walter A. Row, III has been running the fund for 8 years and currently receives a manager quality ranking of 20 (0=worst, 99=best). If you desire an average level of risk, then this fund may be an option.

Data Date	Investment Rating	Net Assets ($Mil)	Price	Performance Rating/Pts	Total Return Y-T-D	Risk Rating/Pts
3-12	D+	445.81	11.06	C- / 3.2	11.34%	B- / 7.2
2011	D	476.70	10.18	D+ / 2.4	1.57%	C+ / 6.8
2010	D	513.95	12.64	D / 2.1	-1.01%	C+ / 5.6
2009	C-	534.95	14.19	C- / 3.7	30.32%	C / 5.3

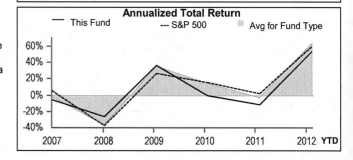

Annualized Total Return

Eaton Vance Enhanced Eqty Inc II (EOS)   D+   Weak

Fund Family: Eaton Vance Management
Fund Type: Income
Inception Date: January 26, 2005

Major Rating Factors: Eaton Vance Enhanced Eqty Inc II receives a TheStreet.com Investment Rating of D+ (Weak). The fund currently has a performance rating of C- (Fair) based on an annualized return of 14.75% over the last three years and a total return of 9.23% year to date 2012. Factored into the performance evaluation is an expense ratio of 1.14% (low).

The fund's risk rating is currently B- (Good). It carries a beta of 0.95, meaning that its performance tracks fairly well with that of the overall stock market. Volatility, as measured by both the semi-deviation and a drawdown factor, is considered low. As of March 31, 2012, Eaton Vance Enhanced Eqty Inc II traded at a discount of 13.86% below its net asset value, which is better than its one-year historical average discount of 10.68%.

Walter A. Row, III has been running the fund for 7 years and currently receives a manager quality ranking of 24 (0=worst, 99=best). If you desire an average level of risk, then this fund may be an option.

Data Date	Investment Rating	Net Assets ($Mil)	Price	Perfor- mance Rating/Pts	Total Return Y-T-D	Risk Rating/Pts
3-12	D+	569.63	10.88	C- / 3.4	9.23%	B- / 7.0
2011	C-	569.60	10.21	C / 4.3	1.76%	C+ / 6.4
2010	D+	563.82	12.21	D / 2.2	-4.47%	C+ / 5.9
2009	C	566.26	14.32	C+ / 5.6	45.56%	C / 4.7

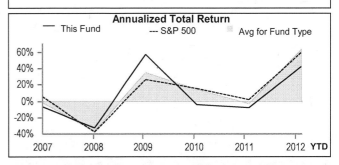

Annualized Total Return
— This Fund   --- S&P 500   Avg for Fund Type

Eaton Vance Floating Rate Income T (EFT)   B+   Good

Fund Family: Eaton Vance Management
Fund Type: Loan Participation
Inception Date: June 29, 2004

Major Rating Factors: Strong performance is the major factor driving the B+ (Good) TheStreet.com Investment Rating for Eaton Vance Floating Rate Income T. The fund currently has a performance rating of B+ (Good) based on an annualized return of 31.64% over the last three years and a total return of 15.37% year to date 2012. Factored into the performance evaluation is an expense ratio of 1.87% (above average).

The fund's risk rating is currently B (Good). It carries a beta of -111.30, meaning the fund's expected move will be -1113.0% for every 10% move in the market. Volatility, as measured by both the semi-deviation and a drawdown factor, is considered low. As of March 31, 2012, Eaton Vance Floating Rate Income T traded at a premium of 3.70% above its net asset value, which is worse than its one-year historical average discount of 1.29%.

Scott H. Page has been running the fund for 8 years and currently receives a manager quality ranking of 99 (0=worst, 99=best). If you desire only a moderate level of risk and strong performance, then this fund is an excellent option.

Data Date	Investment Rating	Net Assets ($Mil)	Price	Perfor- mance Rating/Pts	Total Return Y-T-D	Risk Rating/Pts
3-12	B+	595.89	16.24	B+ / 8.3	15.37%	B / 8.2
2011	B	564.10	14.23	B / 7.7	3.72%	B / 8.2
2010	C+	556.61	16.00	B / 7.6	20.23%	C / 4.3
2009	C	425.90	14.16	C+ / 5.8	83.29%	C / 4.9

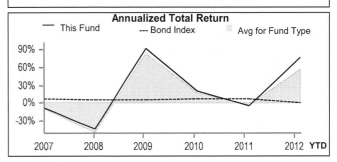

Annualized Total Return
— This Fund   --- Bond Index   Avg for Fund Type

Eaton Vance Limited Duration Incom (EVV)   C+   Fair

Fund Family: Eaton Vance Management
Fund Type: General Bond
Inception Date: May 30, 2003

Major Rating Factors: Middle of the road best describes Eaton Vance Limited Duration Incom whose TheStreet.com Investment Rating is currently a C+ (Fair). The fund currently has a performance rating of C+ (Fair) based on an annualized return of 24.47% over the last three years and a total return of 7.48% year to date 2012. Factored into the performance evaluation is an expense ratio of 1.76% (above average).

The fund's risk rating is currently B- (Good). It carries a beta of 0.78, meaning the fund's expected move will be 7.8% for every 10% move in the market. Volatility, as measured by both the semi-deviation and a drawdown factor, is considered low. As of March 31, 2012, Eaton Vance Limited Duration Incom traded at a discount of 3.02% below its net asset value, which is worse than its one-year historical average discount of 5.15%.

Payson F. Swaffield has been running the fund for 9 years and currently receives a manager quality ranking of 92 (0=worst, 99=best). If you desire an average level of risk, then this fund may be an option.

Data Date	Investment Rating	Net Assets ($Mil)	Price	Perfor- mance Rating/Pts	Total Return Y-T-D	Risk Rating/Pts
3-12	C+	2,001.37	16.05	C+ / 6.4	7.48%	B- / 7.5
2011	B-	1,899.70	15.23	B- / 7.1	1.58%	B- / 7.7
2010	C+	1,950.18	16.05	B / 7.6	16.59%	C / 4.4
2009	C	1,456.96	14.90	C+ / 6.4	60.33%	C / 5.1

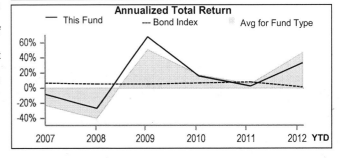

Annualized Total Return
— This Fund   --- Bond Index   Avg for Fund Type

Eaton Vance MA Muni Bond (MAB)

B+   **Good**

Fund Family: Eaton Vance Management
Fund Type: Municipal - Single State
Inception Date: November 25, 2002

Major Rating Factors: Strong performance is the major factor driving the B+ (Good) TheStreet.com Investment Rating for Eaton Vance MA Muni Bond. The fund currently has a performance rating of B+ (Good) based on an annualized return of 15.71% over the last three years and a total return of 9.50% year to date 2012. Factored into the performance evaluation is an expense ratio of 1.65% (above average).

The fund's risk rating is currently B (Good). It carries a beta of 3.06, meaning it is expected to move 30.6% for every 10% move in the market. Volatility, as measured by both the semi-deviation and a drawdown factor, is considered low. As of March 31, 2012, Eaton Vance MA Muni Bond traded at a premium of 3.75% above its net asset value, which is worse than its one-year historical average premium of .13%.

Craig R. Brandon has been running the fund for 2 years and currently receives a manager quality ranking of 19 (0=worst, 99=best). If you desire only a moderate level of risk and strong performance, then this fund is an excellent option.

Data Date	Investment Rating	Net Assets ($Mil)	Price	Performance Rating/Pts	Total Return Y-T-D	Risk Rating/Pts
3-12	B+	25.13	15.51	B+ / 8.4	9.50%	B / 8.2
2011	B-	25.60	14.36	C+ / 6.9	1.18%	B / 8.2
2010	C-	25.92	12.91	D / 1.8	-9.86%	B- / 7.3
2009	B+	25.77	15.20	B- / 7.5	53.12%	C+ / 6.3

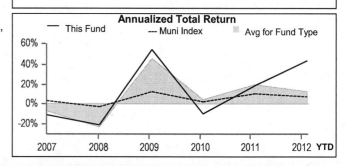

Eaton Vance MA Muni Inc Tr (MMV)

C+   **Fair**

Fund Family: Eaton Vance Management
Fund Type: Municipal - Single State
Inception Date: January 26, 1999

Major Rating Factors: Middle of the road best describes Eaton Vance MA Muni Inc Tr whose TheStreet.com Investment Rating is currently a C+ (Fair). The fund currently has a performance rating of C+ (Fair) based on an annualized return of 12.84% over the last three years and a total return of 4.09% year to date 2012. Factored into the performance evaluation is an expense ratio of 1.98% (high).

The fund's risk rating is currently B (Good). It carries a beta of 1.74, meaning it is expected to move 17.4% for every 10% move in the market. Volatility, as measured by both the semi-deviation and a drawdown factor, is considered low. As of March 31, 2012, Eaton Vance MA Muni Inc Tr traded at a discount of .27% below its net asset value, which is better than its one-year historical average premium of .24%.

Craig R. Brandon has been running the fund for 2 years and currently receives a manager quality ranking of 42 (0=worst, 99=best). If you desire an average level of risk, then this fund may be an option.

Data Date	Investment Rating	Net Assets ($Mil)	Price	Performance Rating/Pts	Total Return Y-T-D	Risk Rating/Pts
3-12	C+	38.37	14.85	C+ / 6.0	4.09%	B / 8.6
2011	A-	39.70	14.46	B+ / 8.7	3.53%	B / 8.7
2010	C+	39.13	13.50	C+ / 6.0	4.02%	C+ / 6.1
2009	B	34.26	13.84	B- / 7.0	54.15%	C+ / 6.2

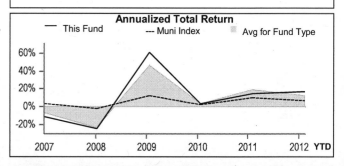

Eaton Vance MI Muni Bond (MIW)

B   **Good**

Fund Family: Eaton Vance Management
Fund Type: Municipal - Single State
Inception Date: November 25, 2002

Major Rating Factors: Strong performance is the major factor driving the B (Good) TheStreet.com Investment Rating for Eaton Vance MI Muni Bond. The fund currently has a performance rating of B- (Good) based on an annualized return of 17.61% over the last three years and a total return of 3.49% year to date 2012. Factored into the performance evaluation is an expense ratio of 1.58% (above average).

The fund's risk rating is currently B (Good). It carries a beta of 1.58, meaning it is expected to move 15.8% for every 10% move in the market. Volatility, as measured by both the semi-deviation and a drawdown factor, is considered low. As of March 31, 2012, Eaton Vance MI Muni Bond traded at a premium of 3.15% above its net asset value, which is worse than its one-year historical average premium of .40%.

William H. Ahern, Jr. has been running the fund for 10 years and currently receives a manager quality ranking of 78 (0=worst, 99=best). If you desire only a moderate level of risk and strong performance, then this fund is an excellent option.

Data Date	Investment Rating	Net Assets ($Mil)	Price	Performance Rating/Pts	Total Return Y-T-D	Risk Rating/Pts
3-12	B	21.23	15.05	B- / 7.5	3.49%	B / 8.6
2011	A+	21.60	14.76	A+ / 9.7	0.05%	B / 8.6
2010	D+	21.99	12.32	D+ / 2.3	-1.32%	C+ / 6.6
2009	B+	22.28	13.31	B- / 7.1	55.88%	C+ / 6.7

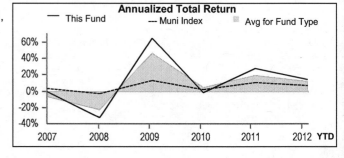

Eaton Vance MI Muni Inc Tr (EMI)

B+   **Good**

Fund Family: Eaton Vance Management
Fund Type: Municipal - Single State
Inception Date: January 26, 1999

Data Date	Investment Rating	Net Assets ($Mil)	Price	Performance Rating/Pts	Total Return Y-T-D	Risk Rating/Pts
3-12	B+	28.37	13.49	B- / 7.5	6.10%	B / 8.7
2011	A-	29.20	12.90	B+ / 8.8	-0.08%	B / 8.7
2010	D+	28.49	11.43	D / 2.2	3.24%	C+ / 5.9
2009	C+	26.11	11.86	C / 5.1	54.86%	C+ / 6.7

Major Rating Factors: Strong performance is the major factor driving the B+ (Good) TheStreet.com Investment Rating for Eaton Vance MI Muni Inc Tr. The fund currently has a performance rating of B- (Good) based on an annualized return of 13.85% over the last three years and a total return of 6.10% year to date 2012. Factored into the performance evaluation is an expense ratio of 2.04% (high).

The fund's risk rating is currently B (Good). It carries a beta of 2.13, meaning it is expected to move 21.3% for every 10% move in the market. Volatility, as measured by both the semi-deviation and a drawdown factor, is considered low. As of March 31, 2012, Eaton Vance MI Muni Inc Tr traded at a discount of 5.07% below its net asset value, which is worse than its one-year historical average discount of 7.20%.

William H. Ahern, Jr. has been running the fund for 13 years and currently receives a manager quality ranking of 49 (0=worst, 99=best). If you desire only a moderate level of risk and strong performance, then this fund is an excellent option.

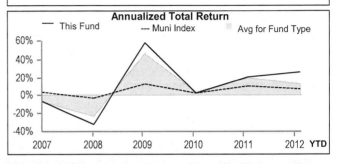

Eaton Vance Muni Bond Fund (EIM)

B-   **Good**

Fund Family: Eaton Vance Management
Fund Type: Municipal - National
Inception Date: August 27, 2002

Data Date	Investment Rating	Net Assets ($Mil)	Price	Performance Rating/Pts	Total Return Y-T-D	Risk Rating/Pts
3-12	B-	855.71	13.00	C+ / 6.6	4.08%	B / 8.4
2011	B+	866.50	12.68	B / 8.1	-0.32%	B / 8.4
2010	D+	889.54	11.48	D- / 1.3	-0.42%	C+ / 6.8
2009	C-	893.39	12.40	C- / 4.2	42.42%	C+ / 5.8

Major Rating Factors: Eaton Vance Muni Bond Fund receives a TheStreet.com Investment Rating of B- (Good). The fund currently has a performance rating of C+ (Fair) based on an annualized return of 13.40% over the last three years and a total return of 4.08% year to date 2012. Factored into the performance evaluation is an expense ratio of 1.81% (above average).

The fund's risk rating is currently B (Good). It carries a beta of 2.29, meaning it is expected to move 22.9% for every 10% move in the market. Volatility, as measured by both the semi-deviation and a drawdown factor, is considered low. As of March 31, 2012, Eaton Vance Muni Bond Fund traded at a discount of 1.81% below its net asset value, which is better than its one-year historical average discount of .58%.

William H. Ahern, Jr. has been running the fund for 2 years and currently receives a manager quality ranking of 27 (0=worst, 99=best). If you desire an average level of risk, then this fund may be an option.

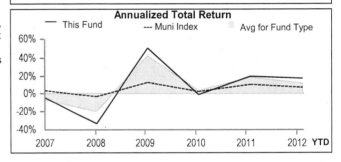

Eaton Vance Muni Bond II (EIV)

A-   **Excellent**

Fund Family: Eaton Vance Management
Fund Type: Municipal - National
Inception Date: November 25, 2002

Data Date	Investment Rating	Net Assets ($Mil)	Price	Performance Rating/Pts	Total Return Y-T-D	Risk Rating/Pts
3-12	A-	120.55	14.49	B+ / 8.3	6.28%	B / 8.8
2011	A+	121.50	13.87	A / 9.4	0.94%	B / 8.8
2010	D	126.81	12.00	D / 2.0	0.15%	C+ / 5.8
2009	C+	128.15	12.90	C+ / 6.0	46.32%	C+ / 5.9

Major Rating Factors:
Strong performance is the major factor driving the A- (Excellent) TheStreet.com Investment Rating for Eaton Vance Muni Bond II. The fund currently has a performance rating of B+ (Good) based on an annualized return of 17.08% over the last three years and a total return of 6.28% year to date 2012. Factored into the performance evaluation is an expense ratio of 1.63% (above average).

The fund's risk rating is currently B (Good). It carries a beta of 2.16, meaning it is expected to move 21.6% for every 10% move in the market. Volatility, as measured by both the semi-deviation and a drawdown factor, is considered low. As of March 31, 2012, Eaton Vance Muni Bond II traded at a premium of 14.18% above its net asset value, which is worse than its one-year historical average premium of 11.99%.

William H. Ahern, Jr. has been running the fund for 8 years and currently receives a manager quality ranking of 43 (0=worst, 99=best). If you desire only a moderate level of risk and strong performance, then this fund is an excellent option.

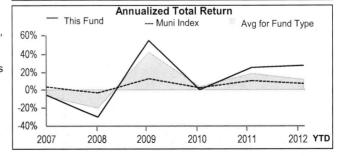

Eaton Vance Municipal Inc Tr (EVN)   A+   Excellent

Fund Family: Eaton Vance Management
Fund Type: Municipal - National
Inception Date: January 26, 1999

Data Date	Investment Rating	Net Assets ($Mil)	Price	Performance Rating/Pts	Total Return Y-T-D	Risk Rating/Pts
3-12	A+	243.94	13.63	A / 9.5	9.02%	B / 8.4
2011	A-	252.60	12.75	A- / 9.2	0.31%	B / 8.5
2010	D	260.25	11.13	D / 1.6	4.67%	C / 5.2
2009	C	214.07	11.53	C / 4.5	57.48%	C+ / 5.7

Major Rating Factors:
Exceptional performance is the major factor driving the A+ (Excellent) TheStreet.com Investment Rating for Eaton Vance Municipal Inc Tr. The fund currently has a performance rating of A (Excellent) based on an annualized return of 23.32% over the last three years and a total return of 9.02% year to date 2012. Factored into the performance evaluation is an expense ratio of 2.27% (high).

The fund's risk rating is currently B (Good). It carries a beta of 2.62, meaning it is expected to move 26.2% for every 10% move in the market. Volatility, as measured by both the semi-deviation and a drawdown factor, is considered low. As of March 31, 2012, Eaton Vance Municipal Inc Tr traded at a premium of 14.35% above its net asset value, which is worse than its one-year historical average premium of 13.02%.

Thomas M. Metzold has been running the fund for 13 years and currently receives a manager quality ranking of 56 (0=worst, 99=best). If you desire only a moderate level of risk and strong performance, then this fund is an excellent option.

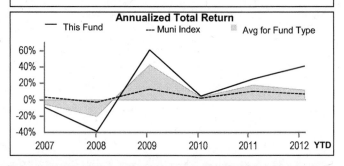

Eaton Vance National Municipal Opp (EOT)   A+   Excellent

Fund Family: Eaton Vance Management
Fund Type: Municipal - National
Inception Date: May 29, 2009

Data Date	Investment Rating	Net Assets ($Mil)	Price	Performance Rating/Pts	Total Return Y-T-D	Risk Rating/Pts
3-12	A+	295.50	21.80	A / 9.4	5.67%	B / 8.3
2011	A-	318.80	20.90	A- / 9.1	-0.43%	B / 8.4
2010	C-	324.33	19.09	D / 1.7	5.76%	B- / 7.9

Major Rating Factors:
Exceptional performance is the major factor driving the A+ (Excellent) TheStreet.com Investment Rating for Eaton Vance National Municipal Opp. The fund currently has a performance rating of A (Excellent) based on an annualized return of 0.00% over the last three years and a total return of 5.67% year to date 2012. Factored into the performance evaluation is an expense ratio of 0.94% (low).

The fund's risk rating is currently B (Good). It carries a beta of 0.00, meaning the fund's expected move will be 0.0% for every 10% move in the market. Volatility, as measured by both the semi-deviation and a drawdown factor, is considered low. As of March 31, 2012, Eaton Vance National Municipal Opp traded at a premium of .74% above its net asset value, which is worse than its one-year historical average discount of 3.22%.

Dan Wasiolek has been running the fund for 3 years and currently receives a manager quality ranking of 83 (0=worst, 99=best). If you desire only a moderate level of risk and strong performance, then this fund is an excellent option.

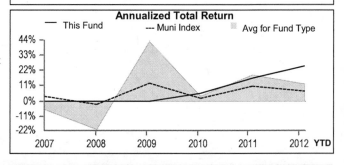

Eaton Vance NJ Muni Bond (EMJ)   B   Good

Fund Family: Eaton Vance Management
Fund Type: Municipal - Single State
Inception Date: November 25, 2002

Data Date	Investment Rating	Net Assets ($Mil)	Price	Performance Rating/Pts	Total Return Y-T-D	Risk Rating/Pts
3-12	B	34.19	14.65	B- / 7.5	4.88%	B / 8.3
2011	B	34.90	14.16	B / 7.7	-1.84%	B / 8.3
2010	D+	37.22	12.61	D- / 1.5	-6.04%	C+ / 6.7
2009	C+	37.63	14.33	C+ / 6.7	51.54%	C+ / 6.4

Major Rating Factors: Strong performance is the major factor driving the B (Good) TheStreet.com Investment Rating for Eaton Vance NJ Muni Bond. The fund currently has a performance rating of B- (Good) based on an annualized return of 14.53% over the last three years and a total return of 4.88% year to date 2012. Factored into the performance evaluation is an expense ratio of 1.57% (above average).

The fund's risk rating is currently B (Good). It carries a beta of 2.02, meaning it is expected to move 20.2% for every 10% move in the market. Volatility, as measured by both the semi-deviation and a drawdown factor, is considered low. As of March 31, 2012, Eaton Vance NJ Muni Bond traded at a premium of 4.34% above its net asset value, which is worse than its one-year historical average premium of 3.51%.

Adam Weigold has been running the fund for 2 years and currently receives a manager quality ranking of 35 (0=worst, 99=best). If you desire only a moderate level of risk and strong performance, then this fund is an excellent option.

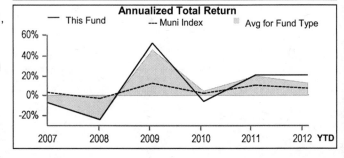

Eaton Vance NJ Muni Inc Tr (EVJ)   B+   Good

Fund Family: Eaton Vance Management
Fund Type: Municipal - Single State
Inception Date: January 26, 1999

Major Rating Factors: Strong performance is the major factor driving the B+ (Good) TheStreet.com Investment Rating for Eaton Vance NJ Muni Inc Tr. The fund currently has a performance rating of B (Good) based on an annualized return of 18.14% over the last three years and a total return of 1.00% year to date 2012. Factored into the performance evaluation is an expense ratio of 1.96% (above average).

The fund's risk rating is currently B (Good). It carries a beta of 2.60, meaning it is expected to move 26.0% for every 10% move in the market. Volatility, as measured by both the semi-deviation and a drawdown factor, is considered low. As of March 31, 2012, Eaton Vance NJ Muni Inc Tr traded at a discount of .57% below its net asset value, which is better than its one-year historical average discount of .41%.

Adam Weigold has been running the fund for 2 years and currently receives a manager quality ranking of 34 (0=worst, 99=best). If you desire only a moderate level of risk and strong performance, then this fund is an excellent option.

Data Date	Investment Rating	Net Assets ($Mil)	Price	Performance Rating/Pts	Total Return Y-T-D	Risk Rating/Pts
3-12	B+	60.73	13.89	B / 8.0	1.00%	B / 8.5
2011	B+	62.10	13.95	B+ / 8.8	-1.43%	B / 8.5
2010	C-	65.22	12.48	C- / 3.3	-2.98%	C+ / 5.8
2009	B+	57.62	13.78	B / 8.0	79.67%	C+ / 5.8

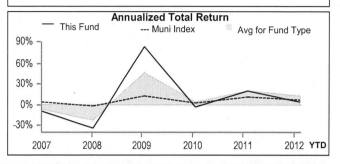

Eaton Vance NY Muni Bond (ENX)   C+   Fair

Fund Family: Eaton Vance Management
Fund Type: Municipal - Single State
Inception Date: August 27, 2002

Major Rating Factors: Middle of the road best describes Eaton Vance NY Muni Bond whose TheStreet.com Investment Rating is currently a C+ (Fair). The fund currently has a performance rating of C (Fair) based on an annualized return of 12.53% over the last three years and a total return of -2.30% year to date 2012. Factored into the performance evaluation is an expense ratio of 1.91% (above average).

The fund's risk rating is currently B (Good). It carries a beta of 1.90, meaning it is expected to move 19.0% for every 10% move in the market. Volatility, as measured by both the semi-deviation and a drawdown factor, is considered low. As of March 31, 2012, Eaton Vance NY Muni Bond traded at a discount of 1.54% below its net asset value, which is better than its one-year historical average premium of 1.96%.

Craig R. Brandon has been running the fund for 7 years and currently receives a manager quality ranking of 37 (0=worst, 99=best). If you desire an average level of risk, then this fund may be an option.

Data Date	Investment Rating	Net Assets ($Mil)	Price	Performance Rating/Pts	Total Return Y-T-D	Risk Rating/Pts
3-12	C+	209.00	13.47	C / 5.0	-2.30%	B / 8.4
2011	B+	212.70	13.97	B / 7.9	-2.86%	B / 8.6
2010	D+	215.45	12.18	D- / 1.5	-5.41%	B- / 7.0
2009	C+	215.30	13.71	C+ / 6.6	45.33%	C+ / 6.2

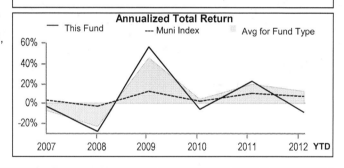

Eaton Vance NY Muni Bond II (NYH)   B-   Good

Fund Family: Eaton Vance Management
Fund Type: Municipal - Single State
Inception Date: November 25, 2002

Major Rating Factors: Eaton Vance NY Muni Bond II receives a TheStreet.com Investment Rating of B- (Good). The fund currently has a performance rating of C+ (Fair) based on an annualized return of 13.72% over the last three years and a total return of 1.17% year to date 2012. Factored into the performance evaluation is an expense ratio of 1.75% (above average).

The fund's risk rating is currently B (Good). It carries a beta of 1.84, meaning it is expected to move 18.4% for every 10% move in the market. Volatility, as measured by both the semi-deviation and a drawdown factor, is considered low. As of March 31, 2012, Eaton Vance NY Muni Bond II traded at a premium of 2.40% above its net asset value, which is better than its one-year historical average premium of 3.51%.

Craig R. Brandon has been running the fund for 7 years and currently receives a manager quality ranking of 49 (0=worst, 99=best). If you desire an average level of risk, then this fund may be an option.

Data Date	Investment Rating	Net Assets ($Mil)	Price	Performance Rating/Pts	Total Return Y-T-D	Risk Rating/Pts
3-12	B-	32.72	13.64	C+ / 6.4	1.17%	B / 8.5
2011	B+	33.50	13.69	B+ / 8.6	0.73%	B / 8.5
2010	D+	34.33	12.03	D / 1.9	-0.31%	C+ / 6.6
2009	C+	34.85	12.91	C+ / 5.7	46.59%	C+ / 6.2

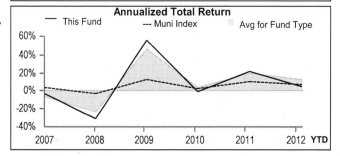

Eaton Vance NY Muni Inc Tr (EVY)   A   Excellent

Fund Family: Eaton Vance Management
Fund Type: Municipal - Single State
Inception Date: January 26, 1999

Data Date	Investment Rating	Net Assets ($Mil)	Price	Performance Rating/Pts	Total Return Y-T-D	Risk Rating/Pts
3-12	A	72.68	14.64	B+ / 8.7	6.34%	B / 8.5
2011	A+	74.80	13.99	A+ / 9.6	1.93%	B / 8.6
2010	D+	74.31	12.46	D+ / 2.7	-0.23%	C / 5.2
2009	B-	64.18	13.36	B / 7.6	83.39%	C / 5.2

Major Rating Factors:
Strong performance is the major factor driving the A (Excellent) TheStreet.com Investment Rating for Eaton Vance NY Muni Inc Tr. The fund currently has a performance rating of B+ (Good) based on an annualized return of 18.10% over the last three years and a total return of 6.34% year to date 2012. Factored into the performance evaluation is an expense ratio of 2.00% (high).

The fund's risk rating is currently B (Good). It carries a beta of 3.04, meaning it is expected to move 30.4% for every 10% move in the market. Volatility, as measured by both the semi-deviation and a drawdown factor, is considered low. As of March 31, 2012, Eaton Vance NY Muni Inc Tr traded at a premium of 3.32% above its net asset value, which is worse than its one-year historical average premium of .42%.

Craig R. Brandon has been running the fund for 13 years and currently receives a manager quality ranking of 27 (0=worst, 99=best). If you desire only a moderate level of risk and strong performance, then this fund is an excellent option.

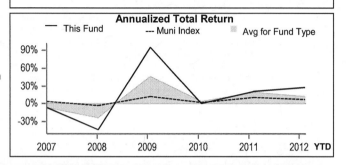

Eaton Vance OH Muni Bond (EIO)   A   Excellent

Fund Family: Eaton Vance Management
Fund Type: Municipal - Single State
Inception Date: November 25, 2002

Data Date	Investment Rating	Net Assets ($Mil)	Price	Performance Rating/Pts	Total Return Y-T-D	Risk Rating/Pts
3-12	A	30.92	14.07	A- / 9.0	8.96%	B / 8.3
2011	B+	31.70	13.10	B / 8.1	2.44%	B / 8.3
2010	D+	32.73	11.51	D / 1.7	-0.56%	C+ / 6.4
2009	C	32.71	12.30	C / 4.3	42.19%	C+ / 6.8

Major Rating Factors:
Exceptional performance is the major factor driving the A (Excellent) TheStreet.com Investment Rating for Eaton Vance OH Muni Bond. The fund currently has a performance rating of A- (Excellent) based on an annualized return of 17.90% over the last three years and a total return of 8.96% year to date 2012. Factored into the performance evaluation is an expense ratio of 1.44% (average).

The fund's risk rating is currently B (Good). It carries a beta of 1.81, meaning it is expected to move 18.1% for every 10% move in the market. Volatility, as measured by both the semi-deviation and a drawdown factor, is considered low. As of March 31, 2012, Eaton Vance OH Muni Bond traded at a premium of 7.65% above its net asset value, which is worse than its one-year historical average premium of 4.75%.

William H. Ahern, Jr. has been running the fund for 7 years and currently receives a manager quality ranking of 61 (0=worst, 99=best). If you desire only a moderate level of risk and strong performance, then this fund is an excellent option.

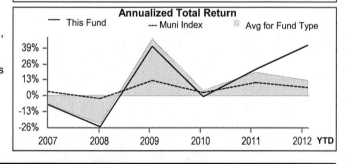

Eaton Vance OH Muni Inc Tr (EVO)   A   Excellent

Fund Family: Eaton Vance Management
Fund Type: Municipal - Single State
Inception Date: January 26, 1999

Data Date	Investment Rating	Net Assets ($Mil)	Price	Performance Rating/Pts	Total Return Y-T-D	Risk Rating/Pts
3-12	A	38.38	15.05	A / 9.3	10.24%	B / 8.2
2011	A-	39.70	13.85	A- / 9.2	1.52%	B / 8.3
2010	C-	39.19	12.50	C- / 4.0	-0.23%	C+ / 5.9
2009	B	35.50	13.38	B- / 7.0	55.89%	C+ / 6.4

Major Rating Factors:
Exceptional performance is the major factor driving the A (Excellent) TheStreet.com Investment Rating for Eaton Vance OH Muni Inc Tr. The fund currently has a performance rating of A (Excellent) based on an annualized return of 21.18% over the last three years and a total return of 10.24% year to date 2012. Factored into the performance evaluation is an expense ratio of 1.94% (above average).

The fund's risk rating is currently B (Good). It carries a beta of 2.45, meaning it is expected to move 24.5% for every 10% move in the market. Volatility, as measured by both the semi-deviation and a drawdown factor, is considered low. As of March 31, 2012, Eaton Vance OH Muni Inc Tr traded at a premium of 3.79% above its net asset value, which is worse than its one-year historical average discount of 1.04%.

William H. Ahern, Jr. has been running the fund for 7 years and currently receives a manager quality ranking of 53 (0=worst, 99=best). If you desire only a moderate level of risk and strong performance, then this fund is an excellent option.

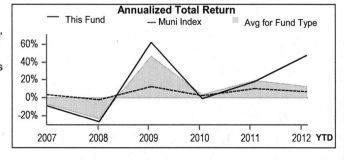

Eaton Vance PA Muni Bond (EIP)   C+   Fair

Fund Family: Eaton Vance Management
Fund Type: Municipal - Single State
Inception Date: November 25, 2002

Data Date	Investment Rating	Net Assets ($Mil)	Price	Performance Rating/Pts	Total Return Y-T-D	Risk Rating/Pts
3-12	C+	38.97	13.80	C+ / 5.9	4.44%	B / 8.2
2011	B+	39.50	13.42	B+ / 8.7	2.09%	B / 8.1
2010	D+	40.26	11.73	D- / 1.5	-10.91%	C+ / 6.8
2009	B	40.96	14.04	B / 7.9	71.36%	C+ / 5.6

Major Rating Factors: Middle of the road best describes Eaton Vance PA Muni Bond whose TheStreet.com Investment Rating is currently a C+ (Fair). The fund currently has a performance rating of C+ (Fair) based on an annualized return of 11.88% over the last three years and a total return of 4.44% year to date 2012. Factored into the performance evaluation is an expense ratio of 1.49% (average).

The fund's risk rating is currently B (Good). It carries a beta of 3.07, meaning it is expected to move 30.7% for every 10% move in the market. Volatility, as measured by both the semi-deviation and a drawdown factor, is considered low. As of March 31, 2012, Eaton Vance PA Muni Bond traded at a discount of .07% below its net asset value, which is better than its one-year historical average premium of .48%.

Adam Weigold has been running the fund for 5 years and currently receives a manager quality ranking of 15 (0=worst, 99=best). If you desire an average level of risk, then this fund may be an option.

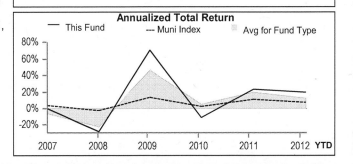

Annualized Total Return
— This Fund   --- Muni Index   ░ Avg for Fund Type

Eaton Vance PA Muni Inc Tr (EVP)   A   Excellent

Fund Family: Eaton Vance Management
Fund Type: Municipal - Single State
Inception Date: January 26, 1999

Data Date	Investment Rating	Net Assets ($Mil)	Price	Performance Rating/Pts	Total Return Y-T-D	Risk Rating/Pts
3-12	A	36.01	14.15	B+ / 8.8	6.81%	B / 8.7
2011	A	36.80	13.46	A- / 9.2	0.13%	B / 8.6
2010	D+	37.74	12.30	C- / 3.1	-0.20%	C / 5.5
2009	B+	34.18	13.14	B / 7.7	69.56%	C+ / 6.1

Major Rating Factors:
Strong performance is the major factor driving the A (Excellent) TheStreet.com Investment Rating for Eaton Vance PA Muni Inc Tr. The fund currently has a performance rating of B+ (Good) based on an annualized return of 19.53% over the last three years and a total return of 6.81% year to date 2012. Factored into the performance evaluation is an expense ratio of 1.98% (high).

The fund's risk rating is currently B (Good). It carries a beta of 2.13, meaning it is expected to move 21.3% for every 10% move in the market. Volatility, as measured by both the semi-deviation and a drawdown factor, is considered low. As of March 31, 2012, Eaton Vance PA Muni Inc Tr traded at a premium of 1.36% above its net asset value, which is worse than its one-year historical average discount of 2.21%.

Adam Weigold has been running the fund for 5 years and currently receives a manager quality ranking of 64 (0=worst, 99=best). If you desire only a moderate level of risk and strong performance, then this fund is an excellent option.

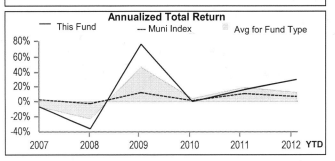

Annualized Total Return
— This Fund   --- Muni Index   ░ Avg for Fund Type

Eaton Vance Risk Mgd Div Eq Inc (ETJ)   D-   Weak

Fund Family: Eaton Vance Management
Fund Type: Income
Inception Date: July 31, 2007

Data Date	Investment Rating	Net Assets ($Mil)	Price	Performance Rating/Pts	Total Return Y-T-D	Risk Rating/Pts
3-12	D-	922.23	10.59	D- / 1.1	7.16%	B- / 7.0
2011	D	922.20	10.45	D- / 1.5	1.72%	C+ / 6.6
2010	C-	1,064.93	13.28	D / 2.1	-9.99%	B- / 7.9
2009	C	1,153.88	16.66	C- / 3.3	4.05%	B- / 7.3

Major Rating Factors:
Disappointing performance is the major factor driving the D- (Weak) TheStreet.com Investment Rating for Eaton Vance Risk Mgd Div Eq Inc. The fund currently has a performance rating of D- (Weak) based on an annualized return of -0.78% over the last three years and a total return of 7.16% year to date 2012. Factored into the performance evaluation is an expense ratio of 1.09% (low).

The fund's risk rating is currently B- (Good). It carries a beta of 0.23, meaning the fund's expected move will be 2.3% for every 10% move in the market. Volatility, as measured by both the semi-deviation and a drawdown factor, is considered low. As of March 31, 2012, Eaton Vance Risk Mgd Div Eq Inc traded at a discount of 15.48% below its net asset value, which is better than its one-year historical average discount of 13.96%.

Michael A. Allison has been running the fund for 5 years and currently receives a manager quality ranking of 21 (0=worst, 99=best). This fund offers only a moderate level of risk but investors looking for strong performance are still waiting.

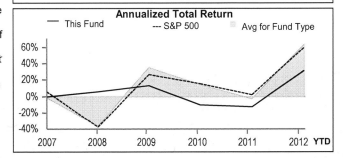

Annualized Total Return
— This Fund   --- S&P 500   ░ Avg for Fund Type

Eaton Vance Senior Floating Rate (EFR)

B-   **Good**

Fund Family: Eaton Vance Management
Fund Type: Loan Participation
Inception Date: November 28, 2003

Major Rating Factors: Strong performance is the major factor driving the B- (Good) TheStreet.com Investment Rating for Eaton Vance Senior Floating Rate. The fund currently has a performance rating of B- (Good) based on an annualized return of 30.16% over the last three years and a total return of 7.18% year to date 2012. Factored into the performance evaluation is an expense ratio of 1.73% (above average).

The fund's risk rating is currently B- (Good). It carries a beta of -4.55, meaning the fund's expected move will be -45.5% for every 10% move in the market. Volatility, as measured by both the semi-deviation and a drawdown factor, is considered low. As of March 31, 2012, Eaton Vance Senior Floating Rate traded at a discount of .59% below its net asset value, which is better than its one-year historical average premium of .57%.

Craig P. Russ has been running the fund for 9 years and currently receives a manager quality ranking of 97 (0=worst, 99=best). If you desire only a moderate level of risk and strong performance, then this fund is an excellent option.

Data Date	Investment Rating	Net Assets ($Mil)	Price	Performance Rating/Pts	Total Return Y-T-D	Risk Rating/Pts
3-12	B-	503.38	15.24	B- / 7.5	7.18%	B- / 7.6
2011	B	496.40	14.38	B / 7.8	2.50%	B- / 7.6
2010	C+	505.67	16.22	B / 7.9	19.54%	C- / 4.1
2009	C+	340.98	14.58	B / 7.7	91.29%	C / 4.4

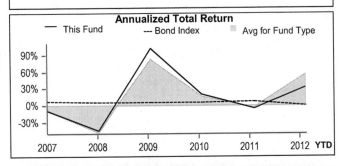

Eaton Vance Senior Income Trust (EVF)

B+   **Good**

Fund Family: Eaton Vance Management
Fund Type: Loan Participation
Inception Date: October 27, 1998

Major Rating Factors: Strong performance is the major factor driving the B+ (Good) TheStreet.com Investment Rating for Eaton Vance Senior Income Trust. The fund currently has a performance rating of B+ (Good) based on an annualized return of 32.27% over the last three years and a total return of 11.57% year to date 2012. Factored into the performance evaluation is an expense ratio of 2.18% (high).

The fund's risk rating is currently B (Good). It carries a beta of -1.42, meaning the fund's expected move will be -14.2% for every 10% move in the market. Volatility, as measured by both the semi-deviation and a drawdown factor, is considered low. As of March 31, 2012, Eaton Vance Senior Income Trust traded at a price exactly equal to its net asset value, which is worse than its one-year historical average discount of 3.48%.

Scott H. Page has been running the fund for 14 years and currently receives a manager quality ranking of 98 (0=worst, 99=best). If you desire only a moderate level of risk and strong performance, then this fund is an excellent option.

Data Date	Investment Rating	Net Assets ($Mil)	Price	Performance Rating/Pts	Total Return Y-T-D	Risk Rating/Pts
3-12	B+	265.93	7.21	B+ / 8.3	11.57%	B / 8.5
2011	B	254.50	6.53	B / 7.8	1.07%	B / 8.4
2010	C+	245.74	7.16	B- / 7.5	20.90%	C- / 4.1
2009	C	200.18	6.26	C+ / 5.6	84.34%	C / 4.9

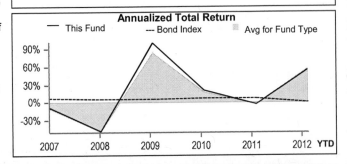

Eaton Vance Sh Dur Diversified Inc (EVG)

C   **Fair**

Fund Family: Eaton Vance Management
Fund Type: Global
Inception Date: February 23, 2005

Major Rating Factors: Middle of the road best describes Eaton Vance Sh Dur Diversified Inc whose TheStreet.com Investment Rating is currently a C (Fair). The fund currently has a performance rating of C- (Fair) based on an annualized return of 17.33% over the last three years and a total return of 6.55% year to date 2012. Factored into the performance evaluation is an expense ratio of 1.89% (above average).

The fund's risk rating is currently B+ (Good). It carries a beta of 0.17, meaning the fund's expected move will be 1.7% for every 10% move in the market. Volatility, as measured by both the semi-deviation and a drawdown factor, is considered very low. As of March 31, 2012, Eaton Vance Sh Dur Diversified Inc traded at a discount of 4.04% below its net asset value, which is worse than its one-year historical average discount of 6.79%.

Payson F. Swaffield has been running the fund for 7 years and currently receives a manager quality ranking of 91 (0=worst, 99=best). If you desire an average level of risk, then this fund may be an option.

Data Date	Investment Rating	Net Assets ($Mil)	Price	Performance Rating/Pts	Total Return Y-T-D	Risk Rating/Pts
3-12	C	336.17	17.08	C- / 4.1	6.55%	B+ / 9.0
2011	C	330.80	16.20	C+ / 5.6	1.79%	B- / 7.6
2010	C+	347.81	16.88	C+ / 6.6	11.53%	C+ / 6.1
2009	C+	293.17	16.12	C / 5.5	41.66%	C+ / 6.9

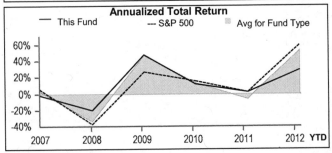

Eaton Vance Tax Adv Glob Div Inc (ETG)   B   Good

Fund Family: Eaton Vance Management
Fund Type: Global
Inception Date: January 30, 2004

Major Rating Factors: Strong performance is the major factor driving the B (Good) TheStreet.com Investment Rating for Eaton Vance Tax Adv Glob Div Inc. The fund currently has a performance rating of B (Good) based on an annualized return of 30.14% over the last three years and a total return of 20.10% year to date 2012. Factored into the performance evaluation is an expense ratio of 1.55% (average).

The fund's risk rating is currently B- (Good). It carries a beta of 1.04, meaning that its performance tracks fairly well with that of the overall stock market. Volatility, as measured by both the semi-deviation and a drawdown factor, is considered low. As of March 31, 2012, Eaton Vance Tax Adv Glob Div Inc traded at a discount of 6.28% below its net asset value, which is worse than its one-year historical average discount of 6.82%.

Judith A. Saryan has been running the fund for 8 years and currently receives a manager quality ranking of 88 (0=worst, 99=best). If you desire only a moderate level of risk and strong performance, then this fund is an excellent option.

Data Date	Investment Rating	Net Assets ($Mil)	Price	Perfor-mance Rating/Pts	Total Return Y-T-D	Risk Rating/Pts
3-12	B	1,097.14	14.47	B / 8.2	20.10%	B- / 7.8
2011	C-	1,064.30	12.22	C / 5.0	4.09%	C+ / 6.7
2010	E+	1,117.10	14.11	D- / 1.2	11.75%	C- / 3.7
2009	D-	837.49	13.73	D / 1.8	37.72%	C- / 4.2

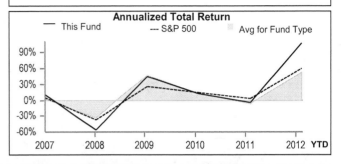

Eaton Vance Tax Adv Global Div Opp (ETO)   C+   Fair

Fund Family: Eaton Vance Management
Fund Type: Global
Inception Date: April 30, 2004

Major Rating Factors: Strong performance is the major factor driving the C+ (Fair) TheStreet.com Investment Rating for Eaton Vance Tax Adv Global Div Opp. The fund currently has a performance rating of B- (Good) based on an annualized return of 26.70% over the last three years and a total return of 16.56% year to date 2012. Factored into the performance evaluation is an expense ratio of 1.57% (above average).

The fund's risk rating is currently B- (Good). It carries a beta of 1.08, meaning that its performance tracks fairly well with that of the overall stock market. Volatility, as measured by both the semi-deviation and a drawdown factor, is considered low. As of March 31, 2012, Eaton Vance Tax Adv Global Div Opp traded at a discount of 12.00% below its net asset value, which is better than its one-year historical average discount of 11.50%.

Judith A. Saryan has been running the fund for 8 years and currently receives a manager quality ranking of 83 (0=worst, 99=best). If you desire only a moderate level of risk and strong performance, then this fund is an excellent option.

Data Date	Investment Rating	Net Assets ($Mil)	Price	Perfor-mance Rating/Pts	Total Return Y-T-D	Risk Rating/Pts
3-12	C+	303.82	19.58	B- / 7.0	16.56%	B- / 7.5
2011	C-	291.70	17.00	C / 4.4	2.97%	C+ / 6.8
2010	D-	319.53	20.52	D / 1.7	13.17%	C / 4.3
2009	D+	220.47	19.38	C- / 3.7	41.37%	C / 4.9

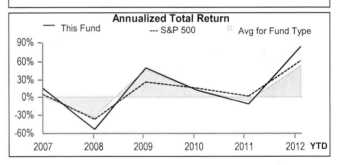

Eaton Vance Tax Advantage Div Inc (EVT)   B   Good

Fund Family: Eaton Vance Management
Fund Type: Income
Inception Date: September 30, 2003

Major Rating Factors: Strong performance is the major factor driving the B (Good) TheStreet.com Investment Rating for Eaton Vance Tax Advantage Div Inc. The fund currently has a performance rating of B (Good) based on an annualized return of 30.85% over the last three years and a total return of 16.08% year to date 2012. Factored into the performance evaluation is an expense ratio of 1.49% (average).

The fund's risk rating is currently B- (Good). It carries a beta of 1.29, meaning it is expected to move 12.9% for every 10% move in the market. Volatility, as measured by both the semi-deviation and a drawdown factor, is considered low. As of March 31, 2012, Eaton Vance Tax Advantage Div Inc traded at a discount of 9.47% below its net asset value, which is worse than its one-year historical average discount of 9.85%.

Judith A. Saryan has been running the fund for 9 years and currently receives a manager quality ranking of 59 (0=worst, 99=best). If you desire only a moderate level of risk and strong performance, then this fund is an excellent option.

Data Date	Investment Rating	Net Assets ($Mil)	Price	Perfor-mance Rating/Pts	Total Return Y-T-D	Risk Rating/Pts
3-12	B	1,222.19	16.73	B / 8.2	16.08%	B- / 7.9
2011	C	1,223.00	14.60	C+ / 5.9	3.77%	C+ / 6.7
2010	E+	1,161.72	16.55	D / 1.8	13.21%	D+ / 2.9
2009	D	1,116.18	15.78	D+ / 2.7	44.47%	C / 4.3

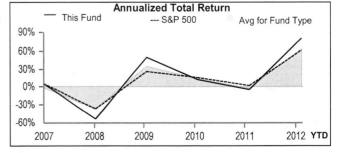

Eaton Vance Tax Mgd Buy Write Opp (ETV)

C   **Fair**

Fund Family: Eaton Vance Management
Fund Type: Income
Inception Date: June 27, 2005

Major Rating Factors: Middle of the road best describes Eaton Vance Tax Mgd Buy Write Opp whose TheStreet.com Investment Rating is currently a C (Fair). The fund currently has a performance rating of C (Fair) based on an annualized return of 18.29% over the last three years and a total return of 13.24% year to date 2012. Factored into the performance evaluation is an expense ratio of 1.09% (low).

The fund's risk rating is currently B- (Good). It carries a beta of 0.79, meaning the fund's expected move will be 7.9% for every 10% move in the market. Volatility, as measured by both the semi-deviation and a drawdown factor, is considered low. As of March 31, 2012, Eaton Vance Tax Mgd Buy Write Opp traded at a discount of 10.45% below its net asset value, which is worse than its one-year historical average discount of 11.47%.

David M. Stein has been running the fund for 7 years and currently receives a manager quality ranking of 57 (0=worst, 99=best). If you desire an average level of risk, then this fund may be an option.

Data Date	Investment Rating	Net Assets ($Mil)	Price	Performance Rating/Pts	Total Return Y-T-D	Risk Rating/Pts
3-12	C	871.18	12.94	C / 5.1	13.24%	B- / 7.2
2011	C	871.20	11.72	C+ / 5.6	2.56%	C+ / 6.9
2010	C	805.34	13.08	C / 4.4	-2.70%	C+ / 6.1
2009	C+	821.69	15.05	C+ / 6.8	57.78%	C / 5.4

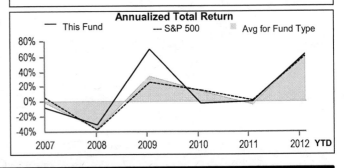

Eaton Vance Tax Mgd Div Eqty Inc (ETY)

D+   **Weak**

Fund Family: Eaton Vance Management
Fund Type: Income
Inception Date: November 30, 2006

Major Rating Factors: Eaton Vance Tax Mgd Div Eqty Inc receives a TheStreet.com Investment Rating of D+ (Weak). The fund currently has a performance rating of C- (Fair) based on an annualized return of 11.91% over the last three years and a total return of 13.58% year to date 2012. Factored into the performance evaluation is an expense ratio of 1.07% (low).

The fund's risk rating is currently C+ (Fair). It carries a beta of 0.96, meaning that its performance tracks fairly well with that of the overall stock market. Volatility, as measured by both the semi-deviation and a drawdown factor, is considered low. As of March 31, 2012, Eaton Vance Tax Mgd Div Eqty Inc traded at a discount of 15.21% below its net asset value, which is better than its one-year historical average discount of 12.59%.

Michael A. Allison has been running the fund for 6 years and currently receives a manager quality ranking of 17 (0=worst, 99=best). If you desire an average level of risk, then this fund may be an option.

Data Date	Investment Rating	Net Assets ($Mil)	Price	Performance Rating/Pts	Total Return Y-T-D	Risk Rating/Pts
3-12	D+	1,651.55	9.53	C- / 3.1	13.58%	C+ / 6.8
2011	D	1,612.60	8.87	D+ / 2.8	2.59%	C+ / 6.5
2010	D+	1,969.59	11.31	C- / 3.1	-1.22%	C+ / 5.8
2009	C-	1,742.10	13.13	C- / 3.9	37.09%	C+ / 5.6

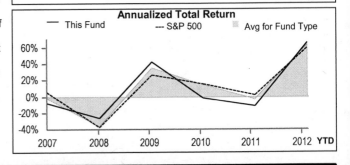

Eaton Vance Tax-Managed Buy-Write (ETB)

C-   **Fair**

Fund Family: Eaton Vance Management
Fund Type: Income
Inception Date: April 27, 2005

Major Rating Factors: Middle of the road best describes Eaton Vance Tax-Managed Buy-Write whose TheStreet.com Investment Rating is currently a C- (Fair). The fund currently has a performance rating of C (Fair) based on an annualized return of 18.65% over the last three years and a total return of 9.28% year to date 2012. Factored into the performance evaluation is an expense ratio of 1.15% (low).

The fund's risk rating is currently B- (Good). It carries a beta of 0.81, meaning the fund's expected move will be 8.1% for every 10% move in the market. Volatility, as measured by both the semi-deviation and a drawdown factor, is considered low. As of March 31, 2012, Eaton Vance Tax-Managed Buy-Write traded at a discount of 10.92% below its net asset value, which is worse than its one-year historical average discount of 10.98%.

David M. Stein has been running the fund for 7 years and currently receives a manager quality ranking of 49 (0=worst, 99=best). If you desire an average level of risk, then this fund may be an option.

Data Date	Investment Rating	Net Assets ($Mil)	Price	Performance Rating/Pts	Total Return Y-T-D	Risk Rating/Pts
3-12	C-	362.18	13.70	C / 5.0	9.28%	B- / 7.1
2011	C-	362.20	12.84	C / 5.0	2.80%	C+ / 6.8
2010	C-	335.31	14.41	C / 4.5	-3.39%	C / 5.4
2009	C+	343.03	16.85	C+ / 6.5	46.65%	C / 5.4

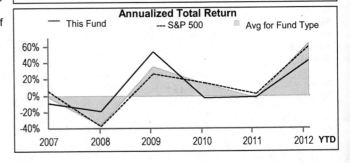

Eaton Vance Tax-Mgd Gbl Div Eq Inc (EXG)　　D+　　Weak

Fund Family: Eaton Vance Management
Fund Type: Global
Inception Date: February 27, 2007

Major Rating Factors: Eaton Vance Tax-Mgd Gbl Div Eq Inc receives a TheStreet.com Investment Rating of D+ (Weak). The fund currently has a performance rating of C- (Fair) based on an annualized return of 14.70% over the last three years and a total return of 14.42% year to date 2012. Factored into the performance evaluation is an expense ratio of 1.05% (low).

The fund's risk rating is currently C+ (Fair). It carries a beta of 0.90, meaning that its performance tracks fairly well with that of the overall stock market. Volatility, as measured by both the semi-deviation and a drawdown factor, is considered low. As of March 31, 2012, Eaton Vance Tax-Mgd Gbl Div Eq Inc traded at a discount of 14.74% below its net asset value, which is better than its one-year historical average discount of 12.37%.

Michael A. Allison has been running the fund for 5 years and currently receives a manager quality ranking of 47 (0=worst, 99=best). If you desire an average level of risk, then this fund may be an option.

Data Date	Investment Rating	Net Assets ($Mil)	Price	Performance Rating/Pts	Total Return Y-T-D	Risk Rating/Pts
3-12	D+	3,122.46	8.91	C- / 3.7	14.42%	C+ / 6.7
2011	D+	3,023.50	8.25	C- / 3.3	2.67%	C+ / 6.4
2010	D+	3,638.43	10.53	D+ / 2.5	-1.72%	C / 5.5
2009	A-	3,281.57	12.33	B+ / 8.9	42.90%	C / 5.3

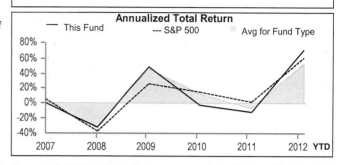

Eaton Vance Tx Adv Bd&Option Str (EXD)　　C+　　Fair

Fund Family: Eaton Vance Management
Fund Type: Municipal - National
Inception Date: June 29, 2010

Major Rating Factors: Middle of the road best describes Eaton Vance Tx Adv Bd&Option Str whose TheStreet.com Investment Rating is currently a C+ (Fair). The fund currently has a performance rating of C+ (Fair) based on an annualized return of 0.00% over the last three years and a total return of 4.68% year to date 2012. Factored into the performance evaluation is an expense ratio of 1.44% (average).

The fund's risk rating is currently B (Good). It carries a beta of 0.00, meaning the fund's expected move will be 0.0% for every 10% move in the market. Volatility, as measured by both the semi-deviation and a drawdown factor, is considered low. As of March 31, 2012, Eaton Vance Tx Adv Bd&Option Str traded at a discount of 5.43% below its net asset value, which is worse than its one-year historical average discount of 8.21%.

James H. Evans has been running the fund for 2 years and currently receives a manager quality ranking of 35 (0=worst, 99=best). If you desire an average level of risk, then this fund may be an option.

Data Date	Investment Rating	Net Assets ($Mil)	Price	Performance Rating/Pts	Total Return Y-T-D	Risk Rating/Pts
3-12	C+	188.85	16.90	C+ / 5.7	4.68%	B / 8.0
2011	C+	194.50	16.55	C / 5.3	2.42%	B / 8.0

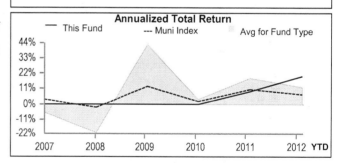

Eaton Vance Tx Mgd Glb Buy Wrt Opp (ETW)　　D+　　Weak

Fund Family: Eaton Vance Management
Fund Type: Global
Inception Date: September 27, 2005

Major Rating Factors: Eaton Vance Tx Mgd Glb Buy Wrt Opp receives a TheStreet.com Investment Rating of D+ (Weak). The fund currently has a performance rating of C- (Fair) based on an annualized return of 17.00% over the last three years and a total return of 10.23% year to date 2012. Factored into the performance evaluation is an expense ratio of 1.08% (low).

The fund's risk rating is currently C+ (Fair). It carries a beta of 0.75, meaning the fund's expected move will be 7.5% for every 10% move in the market. Volatility, as measured by both the semi-deviation and a drawdown factor, is considered low. As of March 31, 2012, Eaton Vance Tx Mgd Glb Buy Wrt Opp traded at a discount of 14.48% below its net asset value, which is better than its one-year historical average discount of 12.50%.

David M. Stein has been running the fund for 7 years and currently receives a manager quality ranking of 73 (0=worst, 99=best). If you desire an average level of risk, then this fund may be an option.

Data Date	Investment Rating	Net Assets ($Mil)	Price	Performance Rating/Pts	Total Return Y-T-D	Risk Rating/Pts
3-12	D+	1,309.94	11.04	C- / 4.1	10.23%	C+ / 6.8
2011	C-	1,310.00	10.28	C / 4.4	2.14%	C+ / 6.6
2010	D+	1,236.31	12.25	C- / 3.6	-0.83%	C / 5.3
2009	C	1,338.73	13.89	C+ / 5.7	51.30%	C / 5.2

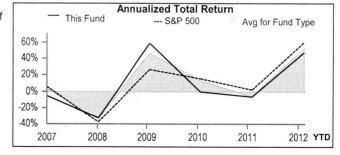

Ellsworth Fund Ltd (ECF)

C   **Fair**

Fund Family: Dinsmore Capital Management Co
Fund Type: Growth and Income
Inception Date: June 20, 1986

Data Date	Investment Rating	Net Assets ($Mil)	Price	Performance Rating/Pts	Total Return Y-T-D	Risk Rating/Pts
3-12	C	100.01	7.35	C / 4.8	12.31%	B / 8.4
2011	C	104.60	6.60	C / 4.5	3.62%	B / 8.3
2010	C	106.23	7.35	C / 5.1	16.86%	C+ / 6.1
2009	C	94.97	6.55	C / 4.3	38.58%	C+ / 6.1

Major Rating Factors: Middle of the road best describes Ellsworth Fund Ltd whose TheStreet.com Investment Rating is currently a C (Fair). The fund currently has a performance rating of C (Fair) based on an annualized return of 20.12% over the last three years and a total return of 12.31% year to date 2012. Factored into the performance evaluation is an expense ratio of 1.10% (low).

The fund's risk rating is currently B (Good). It carries a beta of 0.77, meaning the fund's expected move will be 7.7% for every 10% move in the market. Volatility, as measured by both the semi-deviation and a drawdown factor, is considered low. As of March 31, 2012, Ellsworth Fund Ltd traded at a discount of 13.02% below its net asset value, which is worse than its one-year historical average discount of 13.23%.

Thomas H. Dinsmore has been running the fund for 26 years and currently receives a manager quality ranking of 62 (0=worst, 99=best). If you desire an average level of risk, then this fund may be an option.

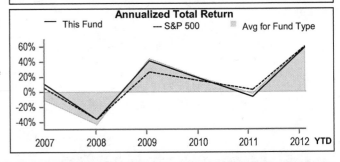

Annualized Total Return — This Fund --- S&P 500 · Avg for Fund Type

---

Equus Total Return (EQS)

D-   **Weak**

Fund Family: Equus Total Return Inc
Fund Type: Income
Inception Date: October 23, 1987

Data Date	Investment Rating	Net Assets ($Mil)	Price	Performance Rating/Pts	Total Return Y-T-D	Risk Rating/Pts
3-12	D-	38.05	2.27	D- / 1.0	1.34%	C / 5.5
2011	E+	38.05	2.24	E+ / 0.9	-2.23%	C- / 4.0
2010	E	50.90	2.50	E / 0.5	-21.87%	D / 2.0
2009	E+	73.00	3.20	E / 0.4	-31.94%	C / 4.3

Major Rating Factors:
Disappointing performance is the major factor driving the D- (Weak) TheStreet.com Investment Rating for Equus Total Return. The fund currently has a performance rating of D- (Weak) based on an annualized return of -4.18% over the last three years and a total return of 1.34% year to date 2012. Factored into the performance evaluation is an expense ratio of 8.26% (high).

The fund's risk rating is currently C (Fair). It carries a beta of 0.63, meaning the fund's expected move will be 6.3% for every 10% move in the market. Volatility, as measured by both the semi-deviation and a drawdown factor, is considered average. As of March 31, 2012, Equus Total Return traded at a discount of 37.12% below its net asset value, which is worse than its one-year historical average discount of 42.20%.

This fund has been team managed for 20 years and currently receives a manager quality ranking of 7 (0=worst, 99=best). This fund offers an average level of risk but investors looking for strong performance will be frustrated.

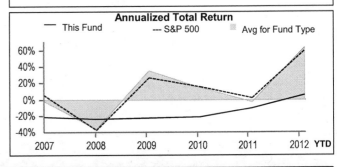

Annualized Total Return — This Fund --- S&P 500 · Avg for Fund Type

---

F&C/Claymore Preferred Sec Inc Fun (FFC)

A+   **Excellent**

Fund Family: Flaherty & Crumrine Inc
Fund Type: Income
Inception Date: January 28, 2003

Data Date	Investment Rating	Net Assets ($Mil)	Price	Performance Rating/Pts	Total Return Y-T-D	Risk Rating/Pts
3-12	A+	1,063.38	18.05	A+ / 9.8	5.81%	B+ / 9.0
2011	A-	699.40	17.46	A+ / 9.8	0.06%	B- / 7.6
2010	C	571.14	16.21	B+ / 8.3	27.69%	D+ / 2.5
2009	D+	419.99	13.97	C / 5.4	91.22%	D+ / 2.7

Major Rating Factors:
Exceptional performance is the major factor driving the A+ (Excellent) TheStreet.com Investment Rating for F&C/Claymore Preferred Sec Inc Fun. The fund currently has a performance rating of A+ (Excellent) based on an annualized return of 52.62% over the last three years and a total return of 5.81% year to date 2012. Factored into the performance evaluation is an expense ratio of 1.64% (above average).

The fund's risk rating is currently B+ (Good). It carries a beta of 0.64, meaning the fund's expected move will be 6.4% for every 10% move in the market. Volatility, as measured by both the semi-deviation and a drawdown factor, is considered very low. As of March 31, 2012, F&C/Claymore Preferred Sec Inc Fun traded at a premium of 3.97% above its net asset value, which is better than its one-year historical average premium of 5.11%.

Robert E. Chadwick has been running the fund for 9 years and currently receives a manager quality ranking of 98 (0=worst, 99=best). If you desire only a moderate level of risk and strong performance, then this fund is an excellent option.

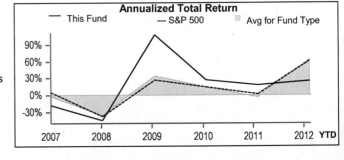

Annualized Total Return — This Fund --- S&P 500 · Avg for Fund Type

---

F&C/Claymore Total Return Fund (FLC)

A+   **Excellent**

Fund Family: Flaherty & Crumrine Inc
Fund Type: Income
Inception Date: August 29, 2003

Data Date	Investment Rating	Net Assets ($Mil)	Price	Performance Rating/Pts	Total Return Y-T-D	Risk Rating/Pts
3-12	A+	167.73	19.01	A+ / 9.8	3.99%	B+ / 9.1
2011	A-	170.50	18.70	A+ / 9.8	-0.16%	B- / 7.9
2010	C	140.59	17.26	B+ / 8.4	30.49%	D+ / 2.6
2009	C-	101.59	14.52	C+ / 5.8	92.26%	D+ / 2.9

Major Rating Factors:
Exceptional performance is the major factor driving the A+ (Excellent) TheStreet.com Investment Rating for F&C/Claymore Total Return Fund. The fund currently has a performance rating of A+ (Excellent) based on an annualized return of 53.78% over the last three years and a total return of 3.99% year to date 2012. Factored into the performance evaluation is an expense ratio of 1.98% (high).

The fund's risk rating is currently B+ (Good). It carries a beta of 0.49, meaning the fund's expected move will be 4.9% for every 10% move in the market. Volatility, as measured by both the semi-deviation and a drawdown factor, is considered very low. As of March 31, 2012, F&C/Claymore Total Return Fund traded at a premium of 2.92% above its net asset value, which is better than its one-year historical average premium of 3.67%.

Robert M. Ettinger has been running the fund for 9 years and currently receives a manager quality ranking of 98 (0=worst, 99=best). If you desire only a moderate level of risk and strong performance, then this fund is an excellent option.

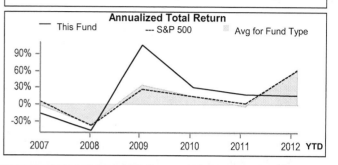

Federated Enhanced Treasury Income (FTT)

D   **Weak**

Fund Family: Federated Investors
Fund Type: US Government/Agency
Inception Date: January 28, 2010

Data Date	Investment Rating	Net Assets ($Mil)	Price	Performance Rating/Pts	Total Return Y-T-D	Risk Rating/Pts
3-12	D	158.25	14.76	D / 1.6	4.43%	B- / 7.5
2011	D	157.30	14.35	D- / 1.3	1.11%	B- / 7.5

Major Rating Factors:
Disappointing performance is the major factor driving the D (Weak) TheStreet.com Investment Rating for Federated Enhanced Treasury Income. The fund currently has a performance rating of D (Weak) based on an annualized return of 0.00% over the last three years and a total return of 4.43% year to date 2012. Factored into the performance evaluation is an expense ratio of 1.00% (low).

The fund's risk rating is currently B- (Good). It carries a beta of 0.00, meaning the fund's expected move will be 0.0% for every 10% move in the market. Volatility, as measured by both the semi-deviation and a drawdown factor, is considered low. As of March 31, 2012, Federated Enhanced Treasury Income traded at a discount of 9.95% below its net asset value, which is worse than its one-year historical average discount of 10.89%.

Donald T. Ellenberger currently receives a manager quality ranking of 75 (0=worst, 99=best). This fund offers only a moderate level of risk but investors looking for strong performance are still waiting.

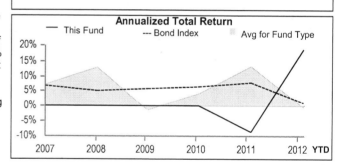

Federated Prem Intermediate Muni (FPT)

A   **Excellent**

Fund Family: Federated Investors
Fund Type: Municipal - National
Inception Date: December 19, 2002

Data Date	Investment Rating	Net Assets ($Mil)	Price	Performance Rating/Pts	Total Return Y-T-D	Risk Rating/Pts
3-12	A	97.17	14.90	B+ / 8.7	9.58%	B / 8.9
2011	A-	100.30	13.78	B+ / 8.6	1.89%	B / 8.9
2010	C+	93.60	12.59	C / 5.1	-2.48%	C+ / 6.4
2009	B+	88.99	13.75	B- / 7.5	49.23%	C+ / 6.5

Major Rating Factors:
Strong performance is the major factor driving the A (Excellent) TheStreet.com Investment Rating for Federated Prem Intermediate Muni. The fund currently has a performance rating of B+ (Good) based on an annualized return of 17.26% over the last three years and a total return of 9.58% year to date 2012. Factored into the performance evaluation is an expense ratio of 1.06% (low).

The fund's risk rating is currently B (Good). It carries a beta of 2.03, meaning it is expected to move 20.3% for every 10% move in the market. Volatility, as measured by both the semi-deviation and a drawdown factor, is considered low. As of March 31, 2012, Federated Prem Intermediate Muni traded at a premium of 3.11% above its net asset value, which is worse than its one-year historical average discount of 2.75%.

Lee R. Cunningham, II has been running the fund for 10 years and currently receives a manager quality ranking of 58 (0=worst, 99=best). If you desire only a moderate level of risk and strong performance, then this fund is an excellent option.

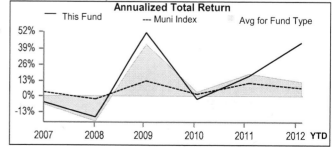

Federated Premier Muni Income (FMN)   A-   Excellent

Fund Family: Federated Investors
Fund Type: Municipal - National
Inception Date: December 19, 2002

Data Date	Investment Rating	Net Assets ($Mil)	Price	Performance Rating/Pts	Total Return Y-T-D	Risk Rating/Pts
3-12	A-	85.56	15.97	B+ / 8.8	7.26%	B / 8.4
2011	A	88.50	15.14	A / 9.5	-0.59%	B / 8.4
2010	C	81.44	13.36	C / 5.2	-3.27%	C+ / 5.8
2009	B+	76.04	14.88	B / 8.0	72.04%	C+ / 5.7

Major Rating Factors:
Strong performance is the major factor driving the A- (Excellent) TheStreet.com Investment Rating for Federated Premier Muni Income. The fund currently has a performance rating of B+ (Good) based on an annualized return of 17.38% over the last three years and a total return of 7.26% year to date 2012. Factored into the performance evaluation is an expense ratio of 1.05% (low).

The fund's risk rating is currently B (Good). It carries a beta of 3.00, meaning it is expected to move 30.0% for every 10% move in the market. Volatility, as measured by both the semi-deviation and a drawdown factor, is considered low. As of March 31, 2012, Federated Premier Muni Income traded at a premium of 8.05% above its net asset value, which is worse than its one-year historical average premium of 2.65%.

Lee R. Cunningham, II has been running the fund for 10 years and currently receives a manager quality ranking of 25 (0=worst, 99=best). If you desire only a moderate level of risk and strong performance, then this fund is an excellent option.

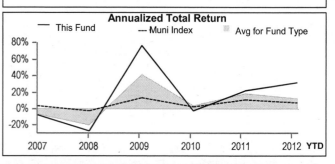

Fiduciary/Claymore MLP Opp (FMO)   B-   Good

Fund Family: Guggenheim Funds Investment Advisor
Fund Type: Energy/Natural Resources
Inception Date: December 22, 2004

Data Date	Investment Rating	Net Assets ($Mil)	Price	Performance Rating/Pts	Total Return Y-T-D	Risk Rating/Pts
3-12	B-	494.53	22.66	B- / 7.1	7.35%	B / 8.2
2011	B	523.10	21.47	B / 7.8	2.61%	B- / 7.8
2010	B-	282.09	21.59	B / 8.2	29.19%	C / 4.5
2009	C	242.16	17.94	C+ / 6.4	59.78%	C / 4.5

Major Rating Factors: Strong performance is the major factor driving the B- (Good) TheStreet.com Investment Rating for Fiduciary/Claymore MLP Opp. The fund currently has a performance rating of B- (Good) based on an annualized return of 26.60% over the last three years and a total return of 7.35% year to date 2012. Factored into the performance evaluation is an expense ratio of 2.06% (high).

The fund's risk rating is currently B (Good). It carries a beta of 0.46, meaning the fund's expected move will be 4.6% for every 10% move in the market. Volatility, as measured by both the semi-deviation and a drawdown factor, is considered low. As of March 31, 2012, Fiduciary/Claymore MLP Opp traded at a premium of 7.96% above its net asset value, which is worse than its one-year historical average premium of 4.26%.

James J. Cunnane, Jr. has been running the fund for 8 years and currently receives a manager quality ranking of 92 (0=worst, 99=best). If you desire only a moderate level of risk and strong performance, then this fund is an excellent option.

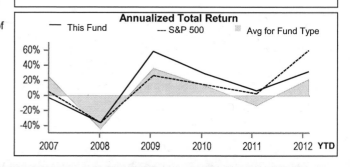

Financial Trends Fund (DHFT)   A-   Excellent

Fund Family: Diamond Hill Capital Management Inc
Fund Type: Financial Services
Inception Date: August 23, 1989

Data Date	Investment Rating	Net Assets ($Mil)	Price	Performance Rating/Pts	Total Return Y-T-D	Risk Rating/Pts
3-12	A-	46.00	10.81	A- / 9.1	30.71%	B- / 7.9
2011	C-	39.60	8.27	C- / 4.0	6.17%	C+ / 6.9
2010	D	39.21	9.81	D+ / 2.5	25.68%	C / 5.2
2009	D-	32.67	7.88	E+ / 0.6	20.49%	C / 5.1

Major Rating Factors:
Exceptional performance is the major factor driving the A- (Excellent) TheStreet.com Investment Rating for Financial Trends Fund. The fund currently has a performance rating of A- (Excellent) based on an annualized return of 33.46% over the last three years and a total return of 30.71% year to date 2012. Factored into the performance evaluation is an expense ratio of 1.42% (average).

The fund's risk rating is currently B- (Good). It carries a beta of 1.08, meaning that its performance tracks fairly well with that of the overall stock market. Volatility, as measured by both the semi-deviation and a drawdown factor, is considered low. As of March 31, 2012, Financial Trends Fund traded at a discount of 9.54% below its net asset value, which is worse than its one-year historical average discount of 14.58%.

Austin Hawley currently receives a manager quality ranking of 82 (0=worst, 99=best). If you desire only a moderate level of risk and strong performance, then this fund is an excellent option.

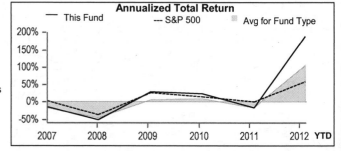

First Opportunity Fund (FOFI)

C-   **Fair**

Fund Family: Rocky Mountain Advisers LLC
Fund Type: Financial Services
Inception Date: May 1, 1986

Data Date	Investment Rating	Net Assets ($Mil)	Price	Performance Rating/Pts	Total Return Y-T-D	Risk Rating/Pts
3-12	C-	264.02	7.05	C- / 3.2	13.34%	B / 8.3
2011	C-	245.20	6.22	C- / 3.0	1.29%	B / 8.3
2010	D	234.57	7.43	D- / 1.5	23.42%	C / 5.1
2009	D-	219.74	6.02	E+ / 0.6	12.87%	C+ / 5.6

Major Rating Factors: Middle of the road best describes First Opportunity Fund whose TheStreet.com Investment Rating is currently a C- (Fair). The fund currently has a performance rating of C- (Fair) based on an annualized return of 13.31% over the last three years and a total return of 13.34% year to date 2012. Factored into the performance evaluation is an expense ratio of 1.24% (average).

The fund's risk rating is currently B (Good). It carries a beta of 0.58, meaning the fund's expected move will be 5.8% for every 10% move in the market. Volatility, as measured by both the semi-deviation and a drawdown factor, is considered low. As of March 31, 2012, First Opportunity Fund traded at a discount of 24.19% below its net asset value, which is worse than its one-year historical average discount of 24.81%.

Stewart R. Horejsi has been running the fund for 2 years and currently receives a manager quality ranking of 71 (0=worst, 99=best). If you desire an average level of risk, then this fund may be an option.

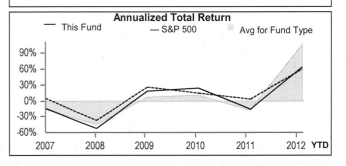

First Tr Senior Floating Rte Inc I (FCT)

B   **Good**

Fund Family: First Trust Advisors LP
Fund Type: Loan Participation
Inception Date: May 25, 2004

Data Date	Investment Rating	Net Assets ($Mil)	Price	Performance Rating/Pts	Total Return Y-T-D	Risk Rating/Pts
3-12	B	373.90	14.97	B / 7.6	14.65%	B / 8.4
2011	B	357.00	13.19	B / 7.9	5.76%	B / 8.3
2010	C	353.11	13.97	C+ / 6.7	22.37%	C- / 3.9
2009	C-	298.10	11.90	C- / 3.6	63.80%	C / 5.2

Major Rating Factors: Strong performance is the major factor driving the B (Good) TheStreet.com Investment Rating for First Tr Senior Floating Rte Inc I. The fund currently has a performance rating of B (Good) based on an annualized return of 28.46% over the last three years and a total return of 14.65% year to date 2012. Factored into the performance evaluation is an expense ratio of 1.98% (high).

The fund's risk rating is currently B (Good). It carries a beta of -35.13, meaning the fund's expected move will be -351.3% for every 10% move in the market. Volatility, as measured by both the semi-deviation and a drawdown factor, is considered low. As of March 31, 2012, First Tr Senior Floating Rte Inc I traded at a premium of 1.98% above its net asset value, which is worse than its one-year historical average discount of 2.29%.

Scott D. Fries currently receives a manager quality ranking of 98 (0=worst, 99=best). If you desire only a moderate level of risk and strong performance, then this fund is an excellent option.

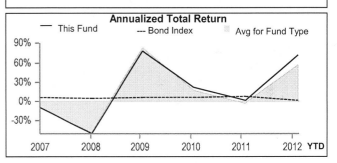

First Tr Specialty Finance &Fin Op (FGB)

B+   **Good**

Fund Family: First Trust Advisors LP
Fund Type: Financial Services
Inception Date: May 24, 2007

Data Date	Investment Rating	Net Assets ($Mil)	Price	Performance Rating/Pts	Total Return Y-T-D	Risk Rating/Pts
3-12	B+	99.70	7.12	A- / 9.1	15.50%	B- / 7.5
2010	C-	85.07	7.62	C+ / 5.7	39.34%	C- / 3.5
2009	B-	62.88	5.98	A+ / 9.6	58.86%	C- / 3.3

Major Rating Factors:
Exceptional performance is the major factor driving the B+ (Good) TheStreet.com Investment Rating for First Tr Specialty Finance &Fin Op. The fund currently has a performance rating of A- (Excellent) based on an annualized return of 38.97% over the last three years and a total return of 15.50% year to date 2012. Factored into the performance evaluation is an expense ratio of 1.85% (above average).

The fund's risk rating is currently B- (Good). It carries a beta of 0.88, meaning the fund's expected move will be 8.8% for every 10% move in the market. Volatility, as measured by both the semi-deviation and a drawdown factor, is considered low. As of March 31, 2012, First Tr Specialty Finance &Fin Op traded at a discount of 4.81% below its net asset value, which is worse than its one-year historical average discount of 5.38%.

David B. Miyazaki currently receives a manager quality ranking of 95 (0=worst, 99=best). If you desire only a moderate level of risk and strong performance, then this fund is an excellent option.

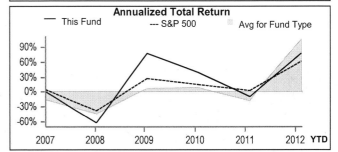

First Trust Active Dividend Inc Fd (FAV)

D   **Weak**

Fund Family: First Trust Advisors LP
Fund Type: Global
Inception Date: September 20, 2007

Major Rating Factors:
Disappointing performance is the major factor driving the D (Weak) TheStreet.com Investment Rating for First Trust Active Dividend Inc Fd. The fund currently has a performance rating of D+ (Weak) based on an annualized return of 12.84% over the last three years and a total return of 6.03% year to date 2012. Factored into the performance evaluation is an expense ratio of 1.60% (above average).

The fund's risk rating is currently C+ (Fair). It carries a beta of 0.82, meaning the fund's expected move will be 8.2% for every 10% move in the market. Volatility, as measured by both the semi-deviation and a drawdown factor, is considered low. As of March 31, 2012, First Trust Active Dividend Inc Fd traded at a discount of 9.28% below its net asset value, which is better than its one-year historical average discount of 3.54%.

Christian C. Bertelsen currently receives a manager quality ranking of 40 (0=worst, 99=best). This fund offers only a moderate level of risk but investors looking for strong performance are still waiting.

Data Date	Investment Rating	Net Assets ($Mil)	Price	Perfor-mance Rating/Pts	Total Return Y-T-D	Risk Rating/Pts
3-12	D	75.98	8.70	D+ / 2.5	6.03%	C+ / 6.5
2011	D	77.40	8.38	D / 2.0	1.19%	C+ / 6.0
2010	D	76.20	11.02	C- / 3.6	-0.73%	C- / 4.0
2009	B-	71.15	12.63	B+ / 8.9	42.88%	C- / 4.1

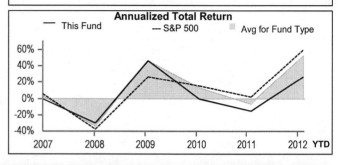

Annualized Total Return

First Trust Energy Income&Growth (FEN)

B   **Good**

Fund Family: First Trust Advisors LP
Fund Type: Energy/Natural Resources
Inception Date: June 24, 2004

Major Rating Factors: Strong performance is the major factor driving the B (Good) TheStreet.com Investment Rating for First Trust Energy Income&Growth. The fund currently has a performance rating of B- (Good) based on an annualized return of 27.39% over the last three years and a total return of 8.16% year to date 2012. Factored into the performance evaluation is an expense ratio of 2.41% (high).

The fund's risk rating is currently B (Good). It carries a beta of 0.47, meaning the fund's expected move will be 4.7% for every 10% move in the market. Volatility, as measured by both the semi-deviation and a drawdown factor, is considered low. As of March 31, 2012, First Trust Energy Income&Growth traded at a premium of 4.56% above its net asset value, which is worse than its one-year historical average premium of 3.54%.

James J. Murchie currently receives a manager quality ranking of 91 (0=worst, 99=best). If you desire only a moderate level of risk and strong performance, then this fund is an excellent option.

Data Date	Investment Rating	Net Assets ($Mil)	Price	Perfor-mance Rating/Pts	Total Return Y-T-D	Risk Rating/Pts
3-12	B	385.33	30.05	B- / 7.5	8.16%	B / 8.5
2011	B+	409.30	28.25	B+ / 8.8	3.01%	B / 8.3
2010	B+	136.52	26.88	B+ / 8.4	24.14%	C / 5.1
2009	C+	114.29	23.37	B- / 7.2	75.68%	C / 4.9

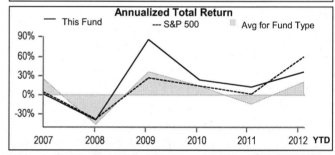

Annualized Total Return

First Trust Enhanced Equity Income (FFA)

C+   **Fair**

Fund Family: First Trust Advisors LP
Fund Type: Income
Inception Date: August 27, 2004

Major Rating Factors: Middle of the road best describes First Trust Enhanced Equity Income whose TheStreet.com Investment Rating is currently a C+ (Fair). The fund currently has a performance rating of C+ (Fair) based on an annualized return of 23.45% over the last three years and a total return of 13.62% year to date 2012. Factored into the performance evaluation is an expense ratio of 1.22% (average).

The fund's risk rating is currently B- (Good). It carries a beta of 1.03, meaning that its performance tracks fairly well with that of the overall stock market. Volatility, as measured by both the semi-deviation and a drawdown factor, is considered low. As of March 31, 2012, First Trust Enhanced Equity Income traded at a discount of 11.63% below its net asset value, which is better than its one-year historical average discount of 10.41%.

Douglas W. Kugler currently receives a manager quality ranking of 55 (0=worst, 99=best). If you desire an average level of risk, then this fund may be an option.

Data Date	Investment Rating	Net Assets ($Mil)	Price	Perfor-mance Rating/Pts	Total Return Y-T-D	Risk Rating/Pts
3-12	C+	249.77	12.08	C+ / 6.4	13.62%	B- / 7.9
2011	C	249.80	10.83	C / 5.2	2.03%	B- / 7.8
2010	C+	225.65	12.64	C+ / 6.4	16.50%	C / 5.0
2009	C-	213.19	11.70	C- / 4.1	39.18%	C+ / 5.6

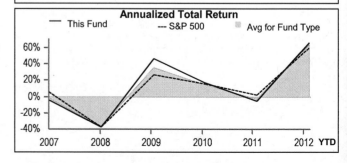

Annualized Total Return

First Trust High Income Long/Short (FSD)   C   Fair

Fund Family: First Trust Advisors LP
Fund Type: Global
Inception Date: September 27, 2010

Major Rating Factors: Middle of the road best describes First Trust High Income Long/Short whose TheStreet.com Investment Rating is currently a C (Fair). The fund currently has a performance rating of C (Fair) based on an annualized return of 0.00% over the last three years and a total return of 20.44% year to date 2012. Factored into the performance evaluation is an expense ratio of 2.09% (high).

The fund's risk rating is currently B- (Good). It carries a beta of 0.00, meaning the fund's expected move will be 0.0% for every 10% move in the market. Volatility, as measured by both the semi-deviation and a drawdown factor, is considered low. As of March 31, 2012, First Trust High Income Long/Short traded at a discount of 1.79% below its net asset value, which is worse than its one-year historical average discount of 5.86%.

Dan C. Roberts currently receives a manager quality ranking of 84 (0=worst, 99=best). If you desire an average level of risk, then this fund may be an option.

Data Date	Investment Rating	Net Assets ($Mil)	Price	Performance Rating/Pts	Total Return Y-T-D	Risk Rating/Pts
3-12	C	642.41	18.13	C / 5.4	20.44%	B- / 7.7
2011	D	613.70	15.27	D- / 1.4	2.82%	B- / 7.7

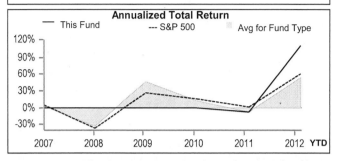

First Trust Mortgage Income Fund (FMY)   C-   Fair

Fund Family: First Trust Advisors LP
Fund Type: Mortgage
Inception Date: May 25, 2005

Major Rating Factors: Middle of the road best describes First Trust Mortgage Income Fund whose TheStreet.com Investment Rating is currently a C- (Fair). The fund currently has a performance rating of C (Fair) based on an annualized return of 18.61% over the last three years and a total return of 4.79% year to date 2012. Factored into the performance evaluation is an expense ratio of 2.23% (high).

The fund's risk rating is currently C+ (Fair). It carries a beta of -0.87, meaning the fund's expected move will be -8.7% for every 10% move in the market. Volatility, as measured by both the semi-deviation and a drawdown factor, is considered low. As of March 31, 2012, First Trust Mortgage Income Fund traded at a premium of 9.30% above its net asset value, which is worse than its one-year historical average premium of 5.24%.

Anthony Breaks currently receives a manager quality ranking of 95 (0=worst, 99=best). If you desire an average level of risk, then this fund may be an option.

Data Date	Investment Rating	Net Assets ($Mil)	Price	Performance Rating/Pts	Total Return Y-T-D	Risk Rating/Pts
3-12	C-	75.01	19.62	C / 4.4	4.79%	C+ / 6.9
2011	C	71.40	19.04	C+ / 5.9	0.16%	B- / 7.0
2010	B	82.10	19.40	B / 8.1	16.83%	C / 5.1
2009	B-	68.08	18.24	C+ / 5.8	20.93%	B- / 7.8

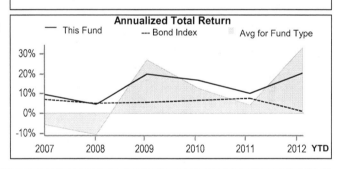

First Trust Strategic High Inc II (FHY)   C   Fair

Fund Family: First Trust Advisors LP
Fund Type: General Bond
Inception Date: March 28, 2006

Major Rating Factors: Middle of the road best describes First Trust Strategic High Inc II whose TheStreet.com Investment Rating is currently a C (Fair). The fund currently has a performance rating of C+ (Fair) based on an annualized return of 15.05% over the last three years and a total return of 16.06% year to date 2012. Factored into the performance evaluation is an expense ratio of 2.35% (high).

The fund's risk rating is currently C+ (Fair). It carries a beta of -0.56, meaning the fund's expected move will be -5.6% for every 10% move in the market. Volatility, as measured by both the semi-deviation and a drawdown factor, is considered low. As of March 31, 2012, First Trust Strategic High Inc II traded at a premium of 4.15% above its net asset value, which is worse than its one-year historical average discount of 6.96%.

Anthony Breaks currently receives a manager quality ranking of 93 (0=worst, 99=best). If you desire an average level of risk, then this fund may be an option.

Data Date	Investment Rating	Net Assets ($Mil)	Price	Performance Rating/Pts	Total Return Y-T-D	Risk Rating/Pts
3-12	C	131.11	17.31	C+ / 6.5	16.06%	C+ / 6.7
2011	C-	129.70	15.28	C / 4.7	-0.46%	C+ / 5.9
2010	E+	48.16	4.68	E+ / 0.7	11.78%	C- / 4.1
2009	E	53.64	4.61	E / 0.5	-9.29%	C- / 3.2

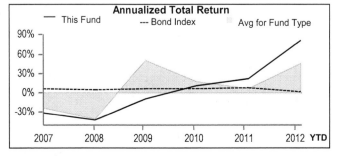

First Trust/Aberdeen Emerg Opp Fd (FEO)

B+   **Good**

Fund Family: First Trust Advisors LP
Fund Type: Global
Inception Date: August 28, 2006

Data Date	Investment Rating	Net Assets ($Mil)	Price	Performance Rating/Pts	Total Return Y-T-D	Risk Rating/Pts
3-12	B+	108.17	20.78	B+ / 8.8	18.57%	B- / 7.9
2011	B	108.20	17.82	B / 7.6	2.49%	B- / 7.8
2010	B-	106.39	21.31	B+ / 8.4	26.55%	C- / 4.0
2009	B-	94.44	18.04	B / 7.7	78.12%	C / 5.0

Major Rating Factors: Strong performance is the major factor driving the B+ (Good) TheStreet.com Investment Rating for First Trust/Aberdeen Emerg Opp Fd. The fund currently has a performance rating of B+ (Good) based on an annualized return of 33.32% over the last three years and a total return of 18.57% year to date 2012. Factored into the performance evaluation is an expense ratio of 1.68% (above average).

The fund's risk rating is currently B- (Good). It carries a beta of 0.77, meaning the fund's expected move will be 7.7% for every 10% move in the market. Volatility, as measured by both the semi-deviation and a drawdown factor, is considered low. As of March 31, 2012, First Trust/Aberdeen Emerg Opp Fd traded at a discount of 6.90% below its net asset value, which is worse than its one-year historical average discount of 9.69%.

Andrew P.S. Brown currently receives a manager quality ranking of 92 (0=worst, 99=best). If you desire only a moderate level of risk and strong performance, then this fund is an excellent option.

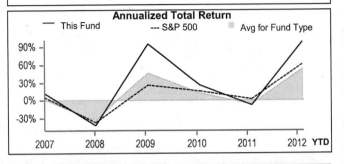

Annualized Total Return

First Trust/Aberdeen Glob Opp Inc (FAM)

B+   **Good**

Fund Family: First Trust Advisors LP
Fund Type: Global
Inception Date: November 23, 2004

Data Date	Investment Rating	Net Assets ($Mil)	Price	Performance Rating/Pts	Total Return Y-T-D	Risk Rating/Pts
3-12	B+	309.34	17.46	B / 8.1	13.38%	B / 8.6
2011	B+	294.50	15.76	B / 7.8	1.59%	B / 8.6
2010	B	290.78	17.36	B / 8.2	18.95%	C / 4.9
2009	C+	259.99	16.03	B- / 7.1	69.35%	C / 5.5

Major Rating Factors: Strong performance is the major factor driving the B+ (Good) TheStreet.com Investment Rating for First Trust/Aberdeen Glob Opp Inc. The fund currently has a performance rating of B (Good) based on an annualized return of 29.77% over the last three years and a total return of 13.38% year to date 2012. Factored into the performance evaluation is an expense ratio of 2.13% (high).

The fund's risk rating is currently B (Good). It carries a beta of 1.09, meaning that its performance tracks fairly well with that of the overall stock market. Volatility, as measured by both the semi-deviation and a drawdown factor, is considered low. As of March 31, 2012, First Trust/Aberdeen Glob Opp Inc traded at a discount of .85% below its net asset value, which is worse than its one-year historical average discount of 4.17%.

Esther S.E. Chan currently receives a manager quality ranking of 94 (0=worst, 99=best). If you desire only a moderate level of risk and strong performance, then this fund is an excellent option.

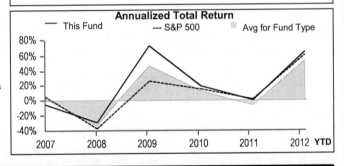

Annualized Total Return

Flaherty&Crumrine Preferred Inc Op (PFO)

A+   **Excellent**

Fund Family: Flaherty & Crumrine Inc
Fund Type: Income
Inception Date: February 13, 1992

Data Date	Investment Rating	Net Assets ($Mil)	Price	Performance Rating/Pts	Total Return Y-T-D	Risk Rating/Pts
3-12	A+	113.61	10.99	A+ / 9.6	0.18%	B / 8.9
2011	A+	114.70	11.20	A+ / 9.8	0.98%	B / 8.9
2010	C+	95.02	9.48	B- / 7.0	25.08%	C / 4.3
2009	C-	67.90	8.27	C / 5.0	83.81%	C- / 4.1

Major Rating Factors:
Exceptional performance is the major factor driving the A+ (Excellent) TheStreet.com Investment Rating for Flaherty&Crumrine Preferred Inc Op. The fund currently has a performance rating of A+ (Excellent) based on an annualized return of 45.22% over the last three years and a total return of 0.18% year to date 2012. Factored into the performance evaluation is an expense ratio of 2.12% (high).

The fund's risk rating is currently B (Good). It carries a beta of 0.53, meaning the fund's expected move will be 5.3% for every 10% move in the market. Volatility, as measured by both the semi-deviation and a drawdown factor, is considered low. As of March 31, 2012, Flaherty&Crumrine Preferred Inc Op traded at a premium of 7.53% above its net asset value, which is better than its one-year historical average premium of 10.43%.

Robert E. Chadwick currently receives a manager quality ranking of 97 (0=worst, 99=best). If you desire only a moderate level of risk and strong performance, then this fund is an excellent option.

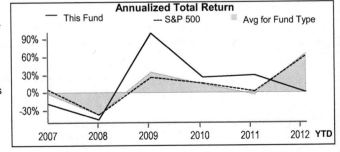

Annualized Total Return

Flaherty&Crumrine Preferred Income (PFD)   **A+**   **Excellent**

Fund Family: Flaherty & Crumrine Inc
Fund Type: Income
Inception Date: January 31, 1991

Major Rating Factors:
Exceptional performance is the major factor driving the A+ (Excellent) TheStreet.com
Investment Rating for Flaherty&Crumrine Preferred Income. The fund currently has a
performance rating of A+ (Excellent) based on an annualized return of 47.29% over
the last three years and a total return of 2.56% year to date 2012. Factored into the
performance evaluation is an expense ratio of 2.08% (high).

The fund's risk rating is currently B (Good). It carries a beta of 0.38, meaning the
fund's expected move will be 3.8% for every 10% move in the market. Volatility, as
measured by both the semi-deviation and a drawdown factor, is considered low. As of
March 31, 2012, Flaherty&Crumrine Preferred Income traded at a premium of 14.40%
above its net asset value, which is worse than its one-year historical average
premium of 14.11%.

Robert E. Chadwick currently receives a manager quality ranking of 98 (0=worst,
99=best). If you desire only a moderate level of risk and strong performance, then this
fund is an excellent option.

Data Date	Investment Rating	Net Assets ($Mil)	Price	Perfor-mance Rating/Pts	Total Return Y-T-D	Risk Rating/Pts
3-12	A+	124.10	14.22	A+ / 9.7	2.56%	B / 8.8
2011	B+	125.40	14.14	A / 9.5	1.56%	B- / 7.4
2010	C-	104.76	11.62	C+ / 6.8	21.26%	C- / 3.4
2009	D+	76.36	10.47	C / 4.5	78.67%	C- / 3.8

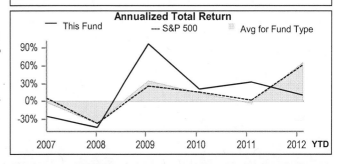

Fort Dearborn Inc. Secs. (FDI)   **B-**   **Good**

Fund Family: UBS Global Asset Management
Fund Type: General - Investment Grade
Inception Date: December 15, 1972

Major Rating Factors: Fort Dearborn Inc. Secs. receives a TheStreet.com
Investment Rating of B- (Good). The fund currently has a performance rating of C+
(Fair) based on an annualized return of 19.82% over the last three years and a total
return of 3.51% year to date 2012. Factored into the performance evaluation is an
expense ratio of 0.70% (very low).

The fund's risk rating is currently B+ (Good). It carries a beta of 1.04, meaning
that its performance tracks fairly well with that of the overall stock market. Volatility,
as measured by both the semi-deviation and a drawdown factor, is considered very
low. As of March 31, 2012, Fort Dearborn Inc. Secs. traded at a discount of 3.58%
below its net asset value, which is worse than its one-year historical average discount
of 6.89%.

Michael G. Dow currently receives a manager quality ranking of 88 (0=worst,
99=best). If you desire an average level of risk, then this fund may be an option.

Data Date	Investment Rating	Net Assets ($Mil)	Price	Perfor-mance Rating/Pts	Total Return Y-T-D	Risk Rating/Pts
3-12	B-	151.70	16.17	C+ / 6.1	3.51%	B+ / 9.0
2011	B+	151.70	15.96	B- / 7.4	-0.13%	B+ / 9.0
2010	B+	152.20	15.46	B / 7.6	17.35%	C+ / 6.4
2009	C+	144.77	14.48	C / 4.6	11.63%	B- / 7.9

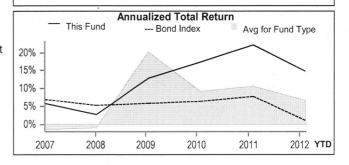

Foxby Corp (FXBY)   **B+**   **Good**

Fund Family: CEF Advisers Inc
Fund Type: Income
Inception Date: October 26, 1999

Major Rating Factors:
Exceptional performance is the major factor driving the B+ (Good) TheStreet.com
Investment Rating for Foxby Corp. The fund currently has a performance rating of A
(Excellent) based on an annualized return of 32.45% over the last three years and a
total return of 27.42% year to date 2012. Factored into the performance evaluation is
an expense ratio of 2.28% (high).

The fund's risk rating is currently B- (Good). It carries a beta of 0.65, meaning the
fund's expected move will be 6.5% for every 10% move in the market. Volatility, as
measured by both the semi-deviation and a drawdown factor, is considered low. As of
March 31, 2012, Foxby Corp traded at a discount of 24.40% below its net asset
value, which is worse than its one-year historical average discount of 29.17%.

Thomas B. Winmill has been running the fund for 7 years and currently receives
a manager quality ranking of 90 (0=worst, 99=best). If you desire only a moderate
level of risk and strong performance, then this fund is an excellent option.

Data Date	Investment Rating	Net Assets ($Mil)	Price	Perfor-mance Rating/Pts	Total Return Y-T-D	Risk Rating/Pts
3-12	B+	4.49	1.58	A / 9.5	27.42%	B- / 7.3
2011	C+	4.70	1.24	B- / 7.1	0.81%	B- / 7.0
2010	E	3.71	1.10	E / 0.5	7.84%	D+ / 2.3
2009	E	3.59	1.02	E+ / 0.8	82.14%	D+ / 2.6

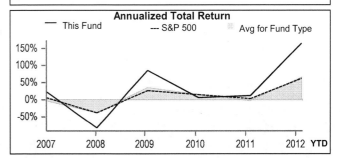

Franklin Templeton Ltd Duration In (FTF)

B-   Good

Fund Family: Franklin Advisers Inc
Fund Type: General Bond
Inception Date: August 27, 2003

Data Date	Investment Rating	Net Assets ($Mil)	Price	Performance Rating/Pts	Total Return Y-T-D	Risk Rating/Pts
3-12	B-	375.02	14.01	C+ / 6.4	8.58%	B / 8.6
2011	B	357.50	13.14	B- / 7.2	-1.07%	B / 8.6
2010	B-	360.80	13.10	B / 7.9	16.73%	C / 4.7
2009	C+	341.73	12.00	C+ / 6.2	52.91%	C+ / 6.0

Major Rating Factors: Franklin Templeton Ltd Duration In receives a TheStreet.com Investment Rating of B- (Good). The fund currently has a performance rating of C+ (Fair) based on an annualized return of 23.59% over the last three years and a total return of 8.58% year to date 2012. Factored into the performance evaluation is an expense ratio of 1.14% (low).

The fund's risk rating is currently B (Good). It carries a beta of -0.36, meaning the fund's expected move will be -3.6% for every 10% move in the market. Volatility, as measured by both the semi-deviation and a drawdown factor, is considered low. As of March 31, 2012, Franklin Templeton Ltd Duration In traded at a premium of 1.45% above its net asset value, which is worse than its one-year historical average discount of 2.18%.

Christopher J. Molumphy currently receives a manager quality ranking of 96 (0=worst, 99=best). If you desire an average level of risk, then this fund may be an option.

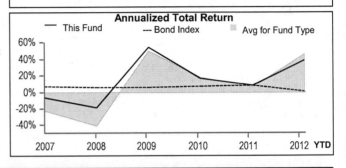

Franklin Universal Trust (FT)

B   Good

Fund Family: Franklin Advisers Inc
Fund Type: Growth and Income
Inception Date: September 23, 1988

Data Date	Investment Rating	Net Assets ($Mil)	Price	Performance Rating/Pts	Total Return Y-T-D	Risk Rating/Pts
3-12	B	172.76	6.88	B / 8.0	4.55%	B- / 7.5
2011	B	179.20	6.69	B / 8.0	-1.05%	B- / 7.3
2010	C	165.08	6.33	C+ / 6.7	17.60%	C- / 4.2
2009	C	147.07	5.80	C+ / 6.6	59.54%	C / 4.9

Major Rating Factors: Strong performance is the major factor driving the B (Good) TheStreet.com Investment Rating for Franklin Universal Trust. The fund currently has a performance rating of B (Good) based on an annualized return of 30.61% over the last three years and a total return of 4.55% year to date 2012. Factored into the performance evaluation is an expense ratio of 2.51% (high).

The fund's risk rating is currently B- (Good). It carries a beta of 0.57, meaning the fund's expected move will be 5.7% for every 10% move in the market. Volatility, as measured by both the semi-deviation and a drawdown factor, is considered low. As of March 31, 2012, Franklin Universal Trust traded at a discount of 5.62% below its net asset value, which is worse than its one-year historical average discount of 7.11%.

Christopher J. Molumphy has been running the fund for 21 years and currently receives a manager quality ranking of 91 (0=worst, 99=best). If you desire only a moderate level of risk and strong performance, then this fund is an excellent option.

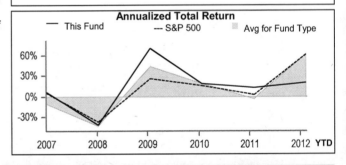

Gabelli Convertible&Income Sec Fun (GCV)

C-   Fair

Fund Family: Gabelli Funds LLC
Fund Type: Growth and Income
Inception Date: July 3, 1989

Data Date	Investment Rating	Net Assets ($Mil)	Price	Performance Rating/Pts	Total Return Y-T-D	Risk Rating/Pts
3-12	C-	80.41	5.87	C- / 4.1	17.35%	B- / 7.7
2011	D+	98.20	5.11	D / 2.0	2.54%	B- / 7.6
2010	C+	74.08	6.12	C / 5.2	15.79%	C+ / 6.3
2009	D+	67.67	5.83	D / 1.8	8.95%	C+ / 6.8

Major Rating Factors: Middle of the road best describes Gabelli Convertible&Income Sec Fun whose TheStreet.com Investment Rating is currently a C- (Fair). The fund currently has a performance rating of C- (Fair) based on an annualized return of 16.66% over the last three years and a total return of 17.35% year to date 2012. Factored into the performance evaluation is an expense ratio of 2.05% (high).

The fund's risk rating is currently B- (Good). It carries a beta of 0.63, meaning the fund's expected move will be 6.3% for every 10% move in the market. Volatility, as measured by both the semi-deviation and a drawdown factor, is considered low. As of March 31, 2012, Gabelli Convertible&Income Sec Fun traded at a premium of 1.56% above its net asset value, which is worse than its one-year historical average discount of 1.28%.

Mario J. Gabelli has been running the fund for 23 years and currently receives a manager quality ranking of 39 (0=worst, 99=best). If you desire an average level of risk, then this fund may be an option.

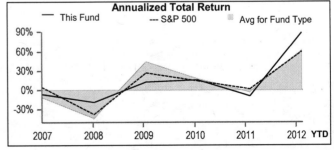

Gabelli Dividend & Income Trust (GDV)

B+   **Good**

Fund Family: Gabelli Funds LLC
Fund Type: Income
Inception Date: November 24, 2003

Major Rating Factors: Strong performance is the major factor driving the B+ (Good) TheStreet.com Investment Rating for Gabelli Dividend & Income Trust. The fund currently has a performance rating of B (Good) based on an annualized return of 30.77% over the last three years and a total return of 7.82% year to date 2012. Factored into the performance evaluation is an expense ratio of 1.40% (average).

The fund's risk rating is currently B (Good). It carries a beta of 1.20, meaning it is expected to move 12.0% for every 10% move in the market. Volatility, as measured by both the semi-deviation and a drawdown factor, is considered low. As of March 31, 2012, Gabelli Dividend & Income Trust traded at a discount of 11.22% below its net asset value, which is worse than its one-year historical average discount of 11.85%.

Barbara G. Marcin has been running the fund for 9 years and currently receives a manager quality ranking of 68 (0=worst, 99=best). If you desire only a moderate level of risk and strong performance, then this fund is an excellent option.

Data Date	Investment Rating	Net Assets ($Mil)	Price	Performance Rating/Pts	Total Return Y-T-D	Risk Rating/Pts
3-12	B+	1,429.40	16.38	B / 8.1	7.82%	B / 8.1
2011	C+	1,888.80	15.42	B- / 7.0	-0.32%	B- / 7.3
2010	C	1,168.13	15.36	C / 5.4	24.50%	C / 5.1
2009	D+	1,023.81	13.11	D+ / 2.6	32.13%	C+ / 5.7

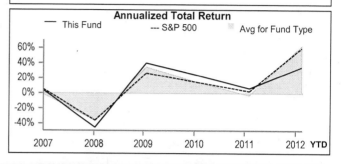

Gabelli Equity Trust (GAB)

B+   **Good**

Fund Family: Gabelli Funds LLC
Fund Type: Income
Inception Date: August 14, 1986

Major Rating Factors:
Exceptional performance is the major factor driving the B+ (Good) TheStreet.com Investment Rating for Gabelli Equity Trust. The fund currently has a performance rating of A- (Excellent) based on an annualized return of 36.16% over the last three years and a total return of 18.10% year to date 2012. Factored into the performance evaluation is an expense ratio of 1.50% (average).

The fund's risk rating is currently B- (Good). It carries a beta of 1.25, meaning it is expected to move 12.5% for every 10% move in the market. Volatility, as measured by both the semi-deviation and a drawdown factor, is considered low. As of March 31, 2012, Gabelli Equity Trust traded at a premium of 1.05% above its net asset value, which is worse than its one-year historical average discount of 1.16%.

Mario J. Gabelli has been running the fund for 26 years and currently receives a manager quality ranking of 80 (0=worst, 99=best). If you desire only a moderate level of risk and strong performance, then this fund is an excellent option.

Data Date	Investment Rating	Net Assets ($Mil)	Price	Performance Rating/Pts	Total Return Y-T-D	Risk Rating/Pts
3-12	B+	1,058.82	5.75	A- / 9.1	18.10%	B- / 7.8
2011	C+	1,265.50	4.99	B- / 7.2	2.61%	B- / 7.2
2010	C	822.41	5.67	C+ / 5.6	27.14%	C / 5.1
2009	D	711.52	5.04	D+ / 2.7	50.72%	C / 4.7

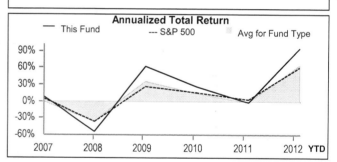

Gabelli Global Multimedia Trust (GGT)

B+   **Good**

Fund Family: Gabelli Funds LLC
Fund Type: Global
Inception Date: October 11, 1994

Major Rating Factors:
Exceptional performance is the major factor driving the B+ (Good) TheStreet.com Investment Rating for Gabelli Global Multimedia Trust. The fund currently has a performance rating of A- (Excellent) based on an annualized return of 36.91% over the last three years and a total return of 19.45% year to date 2012. Factored into the performance evaluation is an expense ratio of 3.19% (high).

The fund's risk rating is currently B- (Good). It carries a beta of 1.04, meaning that its performance tracks fairly well with that of the overall stock market. Volatility, as measured by both the semi-deviation and a drawdown factor, is considered low. As of March 31, 2012, Gabelli Global Multimedia Trust traded at a discount of 9.95% below its net asset value, which is worse than its one-year historical average discount of 12.52%.

Lawrence J. Haverty, Jr. has been running the fund for 18 years and currently receives a manager quality ranking of 92 (0=worst, 99=best). If you desire only a moderate level of risk and strong performance, then this fund is an excellent option.

Data Date	Investment Rating	Net Assets ($Mil)	Price	Performance Rating/Pts	Total Return Y-T-D	Risk Rating/Pts
3-12	B+	124.46	7.24	A- / 9.1	19.45%	B- / 7.1
2011	C	170.00	6.23	C+ / 6.6	5.14%	C+ / 6.6
2010	D-	106.39	8.21	C- / 3.0	34.34%	D+ / 2.7
2009	D-	80.51	6.61	D- / 1.3	39.45%	C- / 4.1

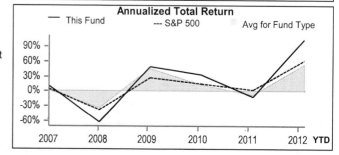

* Denotes ETF Fund

Gabelli Global Utility&Income Trus (GLU)   B-   Good

Fund Family: Gabelli Funds LLC
Fund Type: Utilities
Inception Date: May 26, 2004

Data Date	Investment Rating	Net Assets ($Mil)	Price	Performance Rating/Pts	Total Return Y-T-D	Risk Rating/Pts
3-12	B-	63.33	21.30	C+ / 5.7	3.23%	B+ / 9.1
2011	C+	63.30	21.04	C+ / 6.4	1.05%	B- / 7.9
2010	C	55.20	20.46	C / 5.3	12.68%	C / 5.2
2009	C	53.65	19.42	C / 5.1	28.04%	C / 5.2

Major Rating Factors: Gabelli Global Utility&Income Trus receives a TheStreet.com Investment Rating of B- (Good). The fund currently has a performance rating of C+ (Fair) based on an annualized return of 22.39% over the last three years and a total return of 3.23% year to date 2012. Factored into the performance evaluation is an expense ratio of 1.36% (average).

The fund's risk rating is currently B+ (Good). It carries a beta of 0.70, meaning the fund's expected move will be 7.0% for every 10% move in the market. Volatility, as measured by both the semi-deviation and a drawdown factor, is considered very low. As of March 31, 2012, Gabelli Global Utility&Income Trus traded at a premium of 3.50% above its net asset value, which is worse than its one-year historical average discount of .77%.

Mario J. Gabelli has been running the fund for 8 years and currently receives a manager quality ranking of 88 (0=worst, 99=best). If you desire an average level of risk, then this fund may be an option.

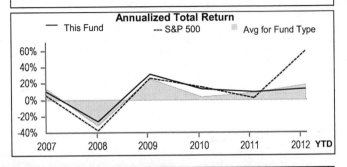

Gabelli Healthcare & WellnessRx Tr (GRX)   B-   Good

Fund Family: Gabelli Funds LLC
Fund Type: Health
Inception Date: June 28, 2007

Data Date	Investment Rating	Net Assets ($Mil)	Price	Performance Rating/Pts	Total Return Y-T-D	Risk Rating/Pts
3-12	B-	71.44	8.32	C+ / 6.6	16.69%	B / 8.5
2011	C+	125.60	7.13	C / 5.4	1.54%	B / 8.3
2010	C+	63.00	7.10	C / 4.7	6.72%	B- / 7.3
2009	A+	55.89	6.70	B+ / 8.8	30.10%	C+ / 6.1

Major Rating Factors: Gabelli Healthcare & WellnessRx Tr receives a TheStreet.com Investment Rating of B- (Good). The fund currently has a performance rating of C+ (Fair) based on an annualized return of 23.06% over the last three years and a total return of 16.69% year to date 2012. Factored into the performance evaluation is an expense ratio of 2.11% (high).

The fund's risk rating is currently B (Good). It carries a beta of 0.80, meaning the fund's expected move will be 8.0% for every 10% move in the market. Volatility, as measured by both the semi-deviation and a drawdown factor, is considered low. As of March 31, 2012, Gabelli Healthcare & WellnessRx Tr traded at a discount of 14.58% below its net asset value, which is worse than its one-year historical average discount of 15.87%.

Kevin V. Dreyer currently receives a manager quality ranking of 76 (0=worst, 99=best). If you desire an average level of risk, then this fund may be an option.

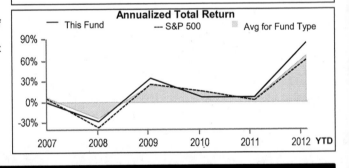

Gabelli Nat Res Gold & Income Trus (GNT)   D   Weak

Fund Family: Gabelli Funds LLC
Fund Type: Energy/Natural Resources
Inception Date: January 31, 2011

Data Date	Investment Rating	Net Assets ($Mil)	Price	Performance Rating/Pts	Total Return Y-T-D	Risk Rating/Pts
3-12	D	305.25	15.81	D / 2.2	20.89%	C+ / 6.1

Major Rating Factors:
Disappointing performance is the major factor driving the D (Weak) TheStreet.com Investment Rating for Gabelli Nat Res Gold & Income Trus. The fund currently has a performance rating of D (Weak) based on an annualized return of 0.00% over the last three years and a total return of 20.89% year to date 2012. Factored into the performance evaluation is an expense ratio of 1.17% (low).

The fund's risk rating is currently C+ (Fair). It carries a beta of 0.00, meaning the fund's expected move will be 0.0% for every 10% move in the market. Volatility, as measured by both the semi-deviation and a drawdown factor, is considered low. As of March 31, 2012, Gabelli Nat Res Gold & Income Trus traded at a premium of 3.20% above its net asset value, which is worse than its one-year historical average discount of 2.03%.

CAESAR M.P. BRYAN has been running the fund for 1 year and currently receives a manager quality ranking of 24 (0=worst, 99=best). This fund offers only a moderate level of risk but investors looking for strong performance are still waiting.

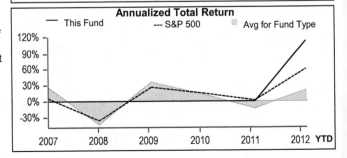

Gabelli Utility Trust (GUT)

C+   Fair

Fund Family: Gabelli Funds LLC
Fund Type: Utilities
Inception Date: July 9, 1999

Data Date	Investment Rating	Net Assets ($Mil)	Price	Performance Rating/Pts	Total Return Y-T-D	Risk Rating/Pts
3-12	C+	167.51	8.09	B / 7.9	5.79%	C+ / 6.4
2011	C+	232.50	7.80	B / 8.1	1.67%	C+ / 6.2
2010	D	142.39	6.39	D- / 1.1	-20.15%	C+ / 6.1
2009	B-	138.32	8.95	B- / 7.5	60.52%	C / 5.2

Major Rating Factors: Strong performance is the major factor driving the C+ (Fair) TheStreet.com Investment Rating for Gabelli Utility Trust. The fund currently has a performance rating of B (Good) based on an annualized return of 24.99% over the last three years and a total return of 5.79% year to date 2012. Factored into the performance evaluation is an expense ratio of 1.91% (above average).

The fund's risk rating is currently C+ (Fair). It carries a beta of 1.02, meaning that its performance tracks fairly well with that of the overall stock market. Volatility, as measured by both the semi-deviation and a drawdown factor, is considered low. As of March 31, 2012, Gabelli Utility Trust traded at a premium of 46.03% above its net asset value, which is worse than its one-year historical average premium of 32.38%.

Mario J. Gabelli has been running the fund for 13 years and currently receives a manager quality ranking of 81 (0=worst, 99=best). If you desire only a moderate level of risk and strong performance, then this fund is an excellent option.

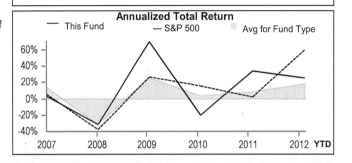

Annualized Total Return
— This Fund   --- S&P 500   Avg for Fund Type

GAMCO Global Gold Nat ResandIncome (GGN)

D+   Weak

Fund Family: Gabelli Funds LLC
Fund Type: Precious Metals
Inception Date: March 29, 2005

Data Date	Investment Rating	Net Assets ($Mil)	Price	Performance Rating/Pts	Total Return Y-T-D	Risk Rating/Pts
3-12	D+	1,020.35	16.16	C- / 3.4	17.68%	C+ / 6.8
2011	D+	1,206.10	14.11	C- / 3.7	6.31%	C+ / 5.9
2010	D	664.32	19.27	C / 4.9	32.00%	D / 2.2
2009	D	280.71	16.33	C- / 3.4	26.96%	C- / 3.5

Major Rating Factors: GAMCO Global Gold Nat ResandIncome receives a TheStreet.com Investment Rating of D+ (Weak). The fund currently has a performance rating of C- (Fair) based on an annualized return of 13.96% over the last three years and a total return of 17.68% year to date 2012. Factored into the performance evaluation is an expense ratio of 1.33% (average).

The fund's risk rating is currently C+ (Fair). It carries a beta of 0.88, meaning the fund's expected move will be 8.8% for every 10% move in the market. Volatility, as measured by both the semi-deviation and a drawdown factor, is considered low. As of March 31, 2012, GAMCO Global Gold Nat ResandIncome traded at a premium of 9.93% above its net asset value, which is worse than its one-year historical average premium of 2.63%.

Caesar M. P. Bryan has been running the fund for 7 years and currently receives a manager quality ranking of 21 (0=worst, 99=best). If you desire an average level of risk, then this fund may be an option.

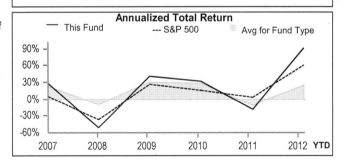

Annualized Total Return
— This Fund   --- S&P 500   Avg for Fund Type

GDL Fund (GDL)

D+   Weak

Fund Family: Gabelli Funds LLC
Fund Type: Global
Inception Date: January 26, 2007

Data Date	Investment Rating	Net Assets ($Mil)	Price	Performance Rating/Pts	Total Return Y-T-D	Risk Rating/Pts
3-12	D+	317.98	12.27	D+ / 2.6	6.70%	B / 8.2
2011	C-	438.10	11.80	D+ / 2.9	0.68%	B / 8.1
2010	C+	315.08	13.37	C / 4.6	4.19%	C+ / 6.8
2009	C+	339.63	14.41	C+ / 6.4	17.32%	C+ / 6.8

Major Rating Factors:
Disappointing performance is the major factor driving the D+ (Weak) TheStreet.com Investment Rating for GDL Fund. The fund currently has a performance rating of D+ (Weak) based on an annualized return of 10.50% over the last three years and a total return of 6.70% year to date 2012. Factored into the performance evaluation is an expense ratio of 4.39% (high).

The fund's risk rating is currently B (Good). It carries a beta of 0.35, meaning the fund's expected move will be 3.5% for every 10% move in the market. Volatility, as measured by both the semi-deviation and a drawdown factor, is considered low. As of March 31, 2012, GDL Fund traded at a discount of 12.79% below its net asset value, which is worse than its one-year historical average discount of 12.99%.

Mario J. Gabelli has been running the fund for 5 years and currently receives a manager quality ranking of 72 (0=worst, 99=best). This fund offers only a moderate level of risk but investors looking for strong performance are still waiting.

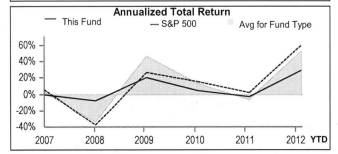

Annualized Total Return
— This Fund   --- S&P 500   Avg for Fund Type

General American Investors (GAM)

C+   **Fair**

Fund Family: General American Investors Company
Fund Type: Growth
Inception Date: N/A

Major Rating Factors: Middle of the road best describes General American Investors whose TheStreet.com Investment Rating is currently a C+ (Fair). The fund currently has a performance rating of C+ (Fair) based on an annualized return of 23.92% over the last three years and a total return of 16.42% year to date 2012. Factored into the performance evaluation is an expense ratio of 1.54% (average).

The fund's risk rating is currently B- (Good). It carries a beta of 1.28, meaning it is expected to move 12.8% for every 10% move in the market. Volatility, as measured by both the semi-deviation and a drawdown factor, is considered low. As of March 31, 2012, General American Investors traded at a discount of 14.35% below its net asset value, which is worse than its one-year historical average discount of 14.52%.

Spencer Davidson has been running the fund for 17 years and currently receives a manager quality ranking of 27 (0=worst, 99=best). If you desire an average level of risk, then this fund may be an option.

Data Date	Investment Rating	Net Assets ($Mil)	Price	Performance Rating/Pts	Total Return Y-T-D	Risk Rating/Pts
3-12	C+	950.94	29.00	C+ / 6.8	16.42%	B- / 7.8
2011	C	1,076.70	24.91	C / 4.9	2.17%	B- / 7.6
2010	D+	864.32	26.82	D+ / 2.6	16.16%	C+ / 5.7
2009	D	732.06	23.46	D / 1.8	28.31%	C / 5.4

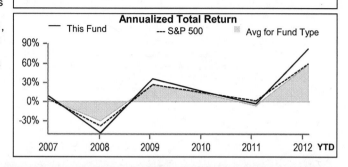

Global High Income Fund (GHI)

B   **Good**

Fund Family: UBS Global Asset Management
Fund Type: Emerging Market
Inception Date: September 30, 1993

Major Rating Factors: Strong performance is the major factor driving the B (Good) TheStreet.com Investment Rating for Global High Income Fund. The fund currently has a performance rating of B+ (Good) based on an annualized return of 31.34% over the last three years and a total return of 13.57% year to date 2012. Factored into the performance evaluation is an expense ratio of 1.44% (average).

The fund's risk rating is currently B- (Good). It carries a beta of 1.24, meaning it is expected to move 12.4% for every 10% move in the market. Volatility, as measured by both the semi-deviation and a drawdown factor, is considered low. As of March 31, 2012, Global High Income Fund traded at a premium of 2.91% above its net asset value, which is worse than its one-year historical average discount of 1.93%.

John C. Leonard currently receives a manager quality ranking of 94 (0=worst, 99=best). If you desire only a moderate level of risk and strong performance, then this fund is an excellent option.

Data Date	Investment Rating	Net Assets ($Mil)	Price	Performance Rating/Pts	Total Return Y-T-D	Risk Rating/Pts
3-12	B	280.80	13.45	B+ / 8.6	13.57%	B- / 7.3
2011	B-	270.80	12.08	B / 7.7	1.24%	B- / 7.4
2010	B	291.28	13.05	B- / 7.5	23.01%	C / 5.4
2009	C	292.26	12.15	C / 5.4	57.81%	C+ / 5.7

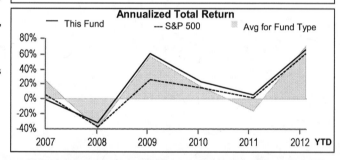

Global Income & Currency Fund (GCF)

D+   **Weak**

Fund Family: Nuveen Fund Advisors Inc
Fund Type: Global
Inception Date: April 25, 2006

Major Rating Factors:
Disappointing performance is the major factor driving the D+ (Weak) TheStreet.com Investment Rating for Global Income & Currency Fund. The fund currently has a performance rating of D (Weak) based on an annualized return of 6.40% over the last three years and a total return of 9.02% year to date 2012. Factored into the performance evaluation is an expense ratio of 1.21% (average).

The fund's risk rating is currently B (Good). It carries a beta of 0.18, meaning the fund's expected move will be 1.8% for every 10% move in the market. Volatility, as measured by both the semi-deviation and a drawdown factor, is considered low. As of March 31, 2012, Global Income & Currency Fund traded at a discount of 8.04% below its net asset value, which is worse than its one-year historical average discount of 9.27%.

Timothy A. Palmer has been running the fund for 1 year and currently receives a manager quality ranking of 78 (0=worst, 99=best). This fund offers only a moderate level of risk but investors looking for strong performance are still waiting.

Data Date	Investment Rating	Net Assets ($Mil)	Price	Performance Rating/Pts	Total Return Y-T-D	Risk Rating/Pts
3-12	D+	76.85	13.73	D / 2.0	9.02%	B / 8.8
2011	C-	76.80	12.80	D+ / 2.4	1.59%	B / 8.7
2010	C+	89.14	14.47	C- / 3.8	9.00%	B / 8.0
2009	C	103.99	14.04	D+ / 2.6	5.68%	B- / 7.9

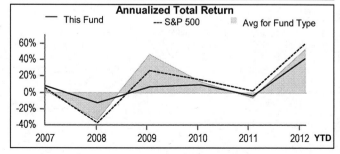

Global Income Fund (GIFD)   C+   Fair

Fund Family: CEF Advisers Inc
Fund Type: Global
Inception Date: August 30, 1983

Data Date	Investment Rating	Net Assets ($Mil)	Price	Perfor-mance Rating/Pts	Total Return Y-T-D	Risk Rating/Pts
3-12	C+	37.07	4.05	C+ / 5.8	8.86%	B / 8.3
2011	C	34.10	3.78	C / 4.8	-1.59%	B- / 7.8
2010	A-	31.19	4.17	B / 7.7	21.03%	B- / 7.0
2009	C+	28.99	3.65	C / 5.3	35.47%	C+ / 6.7

Major Rating Factors: Middle of the road best describes Global Income Fund whose TheStreet.com Investment Rating is currently a C+ (Fair). The fund currently has a performance rating of C+ (Fair) based on an annualized return of 24.36% over the last three years and a total return of 8.86% year to date 2012. Factored into the performance evaluation is an expense ratio of 2.00% (high).

The fund's risk rating is currently B (Good). It carries a beta of 0.42, meaning the fund's expected move will be 4.2% for every 10% move in the market. Volatility, as measured by both the semi-deviation and a drawdown factor, is considered low. As of March 31, 2012, Global Income Fund traded at a discount of 18.18% below its net asset value, which is better than its one-year historical average discount of 17.89%.

Heidi Keating currently receives a manager quality ranking of 93 (0=worst, 99=best). If you desire an average level of risk, then this fund may be an option.

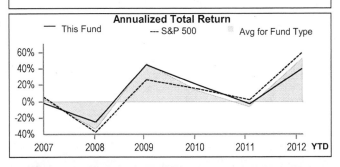

Greater China Fund (GCH)   D   Weak

Fund Family: Baring Asset Management (Asia) Limi
Fund Type: Foreign
Inception Date: July 15, 1992

Data Date	Investment Rating	Net Assets ($Mil)	Price	Perfor-mance Rating/Pts	Total Return Y-T-D	Risk Rating/Pts
3-12	D	434.15	11.50	D+ / 2.4	14.20%	C+ / 6.8
2011	D	273.60	10.07	D+ / 2.5	1.79%	C+ / 6.4
2010	E+	368.48	13.15	D- / 1.4	-5.41%	C- / 3.1
2009	C-	273.67	13.92	B- / 7.2	58.49%	D / 2.0

Major Rating Factors:
Disappointing performance is the major factor driving the D (Weak) TheStreet.com Investment Rating for Greater China Fund. The fund currently has a performance rating of D+ (Weak) based on an annualized return of 9.14% over the last three years and a total return of 14.20% year to date 2012. Factored into the performance evaluation is an expense ratio of 1.85% (above average).

The fund's risk rating is currently C+ (Fair). It carries a beta of 1.08, meaning that its performance tracks fairly well with that of the overall stock market. Volatility, as measured by both the semi-deviation and a drawdown factor, is considered low. As of March 31, 2012, Greater China Fund traded at a discount of 7.63% below its net asset value, which is worse than its one-year historical average discount of 10.23%.

Agnes Deng currently receives a manager quality ranking of 21 (0=worst, 99=best). This fund offers only a moderate level of risk but investors looking for strong performance are still waiting.

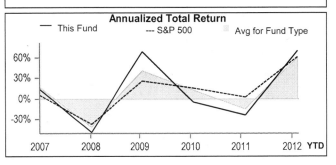

Guggenheim Build America Bd Mgd Du (GBAB)   B+   Good

Fund Family: Guggenheim Funds Investment Advisor
Fund Type: General - Investment Grade
Inception Date: October 28, 2010

Data Date	Investment Rating	Net Assets ($Mil)	Price	Perfor-mance Rating/Pts	Total Return Y-T-D	Risk Rating/Pts
3-12	B+	359.44	21.81	B- / 7.3	3.68%	B+ / 9.3
2011	A	359.44	21.41	B+ / 8.5	0.26%	B+ / 9.3

Major Rating Factors: Strong performance is the major factor driving the B+ (Good) TheStreet.com Investment Rating for Guggenheim Build America Bd Mgd Du. The fund currently has a performance rating of B- (Good) based on an annualized return of 0.00% over the last three years and a total return of 3.68% year to date 2012. Factored into the performance evaluation is an expense ratio of 1.05% (low).

The fund's risk rating is currently B+ (Good). It carries a beta of 0.00, meaning the fund's expected move will be 0.0% for every 10% move in the market. Volatility, as measured by both the semi-deviation and a drawdown factor, is considered very low. As of March 31, 2012, Guggenheim Build America Bd Mgd Du traded at a discount of 3.84% below its net asset value, which is worse than its one-year historical average discount of 5.94%.

Anne Walsh currently receives a manager quality ranking of 94 (0=worst, 99=best). If you desire only a moderate level of risk and strong performance, then this fund is an excellent option.

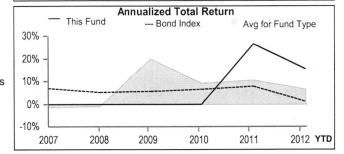

Guggenheim Enhanced Equity Income (GPM)   C+   Fair

Fund Family: Guggenheim Funds Investment Advisor
Fund Type: Income
Inception Date: August 25, 2005

Data Date	Investment Rating	Net Assets ($Mil)	Price	Performance Rating/Pts	Total Return Y-T-D	Risk Rating/Pts
3-12	C+	183.26	9.40	C+ / 6.0	18.14%	B- / 7.6
2011	C-	176.70	8.16	C- / 4.1	2.21%	B- / 7.5
2010	D	154.55	9.33	C- / 3.8	22.63%	C- / 3.4
2009	D-	177.78	8.50	D- / 1.1	17.22%	C / 5.5

Major Rating Factors: Middle of the road best describes Guggenheim Enhanced Equity Income whose TheStreet.com Investment Rating is currently a C+ (Fair). The fund currently has a performance rating of C+ (Fair) based on an annualized return of 20.11% over the last three years and a total return of 18.14% year to date 2012. Factored into the performance evaluation is an expense ratio of 1.80% (above average).

The fund's risk rating is currently B- (Good). It carries a beta of 0.90, meaning that its performance tracks fairly well with that of the overall stock market. Volatility, as measured by both the semi-deviation and a drawdown factor, is considered low. As of March 31, 2012, Guggenheim Enhanced Equity Income traded at a discount of 2.99% below its net asset value, which is worse than its one-year historical average discount of 4.71%.

Byron S. Minerd currently receives a manager quality ranking of 50 (0=worst, 99=best). If you desire an average level of risk, then this fund may be an option.

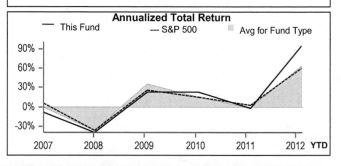

Guggenheim Enhanced Equity Strateg (GGE)   B+   Good

Fund Family: Guggenheim Funds Investment Advisor
Fund Type: Income
Inception Date: January 28, 2004

Data Date	Investment Rating	Net Assets ($Mil)	Price	Performance Rating/Pts	Total Return Y-T-D	Risk Rating/Pts
3-12	B+	90.33	17.20	B+ / 8.8	9.26%	B- / 7.4
2011	C+	93.70	16.03	B- / 7.3	2.15%	C+ / 6.1
2010	E	134.88	15.03	E / 0.3	-0.60%	C- / 3.0
2009	E-	104.28	15.65	E / 0.4	61.97%	D / 1.7

Major Rating Factors: Strong performance is the major factor driving the B+ (Good) TheStreet.com Investment Rating for Guggenheim Enhanced Equity Strateg. The fund currently has a performance rating of B+ (Good) based on an annualized return of 34.49% over the last three years and a total return of 9.26% year to date 2012. Factored into the performance evaluation is an expense ratio of 2.23% (high).

The fund's risk rating is currently B- (Good). It carries a beta of 1.29, meaning it is expected to move 12.9% for every 10% move in the market. Volatility, as measured by both the semi-deviation and a drawdown factor, is considered low. As of March 31, 2012, Guggenheim Enhanced Equity Strateg traded at a discount of 13.00% below its net asset value, which is better than its one-year historical average discount of 11.28%.

Byron S. Minerd currently receives a manager quality ranking of 79 (0=worst, 99=best). If you desire only a moderate level of risk and strong performance, then this fund is an excellent option.

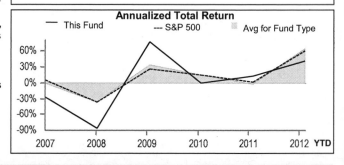

Guggenheim Strategic Opportunities (GOF)   A+   Excellent

Fund Family: Guggenheim Funds Investment Advisor
Fund Type: Growth and Income
Inception Date: July 27, 2007

Data Date	Investment Rating	Net Assets ($Mil)	Price	Performance Rating/Pts	Total Return Y-T-D	Risk Rating/Pts
3-12	A+	187.33	20.55	A / 9.4	2.23%	B / 8.7
2011	A	174.10	20.59	A / 9.5	0.64%	B / 8.5
2010	B-	161.78	19.93	B+ / 8.8	31.55%	C- / 4.0
2009	A-	113.08	16.80	A+ / 9.7	78.82%	C / 4.3

Major Rating Factors:
Exceptional performance is the major factor driving the A+ (Excellent) TheStreet.com Investment Rating for Guggenheim Strategic Opportunities. The fund currently has a performance rating of A (Excellent) based on an annualized return of 42.12% over the last three years and a total return of 2.23% year to date 2012. Factored into the performance evaluation is an expense ratio of 2.69% (high).

The fund's risk rating is currently B (Good). It carries a beta of 0.41, meaning the fund's expected move will be 4.1% for every 10% move in the market. Volatility, as measured by both the semi-deviation and a drawdown factor, is considered low. As of March 31, 2012, Guggenheim Strategic Opportunities traded at a premium of 5.60% above its net asset value, which is better than its one-year historical average premium of 6.72%.

Byron S. Minerd has been running the fund for 5 years and currently receives a manager quality ranking of 97 (0=worst, 99=best). If you desire only a moderate level of risk and strong performance, then this fund is an excellent option.

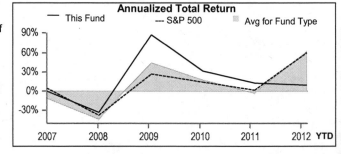

H&Q Healthcare Investors (HQH)   B   Good

Fund Family: Hambrecht & Quist Capital Mgmt LLC
Fund Type: Health
Inception Date: April 23, 1987

Major Rating Factors: Strong performance is the major factor driving the B (Good) TheStreet.com Investment Rating for H&Q Healthcare Investors. The fund currently has a performance rating of B (Good) based on an annualized return of 26.15% over the last three years and a total return of 18.92% year to date 2012. Factored into the performance evaluation is an expense ratio of 1.47% (average).

The fund's risk rating is currently B (Good). It carries a beta of 0.73, meaning the fund's expected move will be 7.3% for every 10% move in the market. Volatility, as measured by both the semi-deviation and a drawdown factor, is considered low. As of March 31, 2012, H&Q Healthcare Investors traded at a discount of 7.83% below its net asset value, which is worse than its one-year historical average discount of 9.45%.

Daniel R. Omstead has been running the fund for 8 years and currently receives a manager quality ranking of 81 (0=worst, 99=best). If you desire only a moderate level of risk and strong performance, then this fund is an excellent option.

Data Date	Investment Rating	Net Assets ($Mil)	Price	Performance Rating/Pts	Total Return Y-T-D	Risk Rating/Pts
3-12	B	379.00	16.47	B / 8.1	18.92%	B / 8.0
2011	C+	404.80	14.11	C+ / 5.9	1.28%	B- / 7.4
2010	C+	365.00	13.37	C+ / 5.6	20.68%	C+ / 5.7
2009	D	356.28	11.85	D / 1.7	4.89%	C+ / 5.6

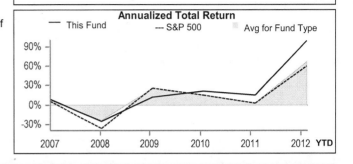

H&Q Life Sciences Investors (HQL)   B+   Good

Fund Family: Hambrecht & Quist Capital Mgmt LLC
Fund Type: Health
Inception Date: May 8, 1992

Major Rating Factors:
Exceptional performance is the major factor driving the B+ (Good) TheStreet.com Investment Rating for H&Q Life Sciences Investors. The fund currently has a performance rating of A- (Excellent) based on an annualized return of 31.15% over the last three years and a total return of 22.84% year to date 2012. Factored into the performance evaluation is an expense ratio of 1.77% (above average).

The fund's risk rating is currently B- (Good). It carries a beta of 0.78, meaning the fund's expected move will be 7.8% for every 10% move in the market. Volatility, as measured by both the semi-deviation and a drawdown factor, is considered low. As of March 31, 2012, H&Q Life Sciences Investors traded at a discount of 5.98% below its net asset value, which is worse than its one-year historical average discount of 9.23%.

Daniel R. Omstead has been running the fund for 20 years and currently receives a manager quality ranking of 86 (0=worst, 99=best). If you desire only a moderate level of risk and strong performance, then this fund is an excellent option.

Data Date	Investment Rating	Net Assets ($Mil)	Price	Performance Rating/Pts	Total Return Y-T-D	Risk Rating/Pts
3-12	B+	171.00	13.83	A- / 9.1	22.84%	B- / 7.5
2011	C+	178.80	11.47	B- / 7.3	2.70%	C+ / 6.1
2010	C	251.00	10.77	C+ / 5.9	21.84%	C / 4.5
2009	D-	248.58	9.44	D / 1.7	8.41%	C / 5.1

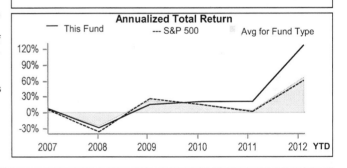

Helios Advantage Income Fund Inc (HAV)   B+   Good

Fund Family: Brookfield Investment Management In
Fund Type: General Bond
Inception Date: November 8, 2004

Major Rating Factors:
Exceptional performance is the major factor driving the B+ (Good) TheStreet.com Investment Rating for Helios Advantage Income Fund Inc. The fund currently has a performance rating of A (Excellent) based on an annualized return of 36.61% over the last three years and a total return of 21.46% year to date 2012. Factored into the performance evaluation is an expense ratio of 2.61% (high).

The fund's risk rating is currently B- (Good). It carries a beta of -0.78, meaning the fund's expected move will be -7.8% for every 10% move in the market. Volatility, as measured by both the semi-deviation and a drawdown factor, is considered low. As of March 31, 2012, Helios Advantage Income Fund Inc traded at a premium of 4.38% above its net asset value, which is worse than its one-year historical average discount of 6.42%.

Dana E. Erikson currently receives a manager quality ranking of 99 (0=worst, 99=best). If you desire only a moderate level of risk and strong performance, then this fund is an excellent option.

Data Date	Investment Rating	Net Assets ($Mil)	Price	Performance Rating/Pts	Total Return Y-T-D	Risk Rating/Pts
3-12	B+	55.24	9.30	A / 9.5	21.46%	B- / 7.2
2011	B	55.70	7.82	B+ / 8.6	2.81%	B- / 7.2
2010	E	49.02	7.65	E+ / 0.8	28.60%	D+ / 2.7
2009	E-	46.91	6.59	E / 0.4	58.89%	D+ / 2.3

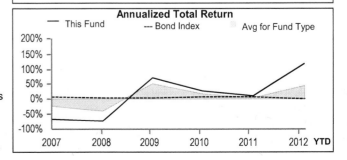

Helios High Income Fund Inc (HIH)

B+ **Good**

Fund Family: Brookfield Investment Management In
Fund Type: General Bond
Inception Date: June 26, 2003

Data Date	Investment Rating	Net Assets ($Mil)	Price	Performance Rating/Pts	Total Return Y-T-D	Risk Rating/Pts
3-12	B+	38.83	8.90	A- / 9.1	17.86%	B- / 7.1
2011	B	39.30	7.71	B+ / 8.5	1.50%	B- / 7.1
2010	E	37.04	7.24	E+ / 0.6	18.85%	D+ / 2.5
2009	E-	35.08	6.74	E / 0.4	55.76%	D / 1.8

Major Rating Factors:

Exceptional performance is the major factor driving the B+ (Good) TheStreet.com Investment Rating for Helios High Income Fund Inc. The fund currently has a performance rating of A- (Excellent) based on an annualized return of 33.70% over the last three years and a total return of 17.86% year to date 2012. Factored into the performance evaluation is an expense ratio of 2.74% (high).

The fund's risk rating is currently B- (Good). It carries a beta of -0.52, meaning the fund's expected move will be -5.2% for every 10% move in the market. Volatility, as measured by both the semi-deviation and a drawdown factor, is considered low. As of March 31, 2012, Helios High Income Fund Inc traded at a premium of 4.95% above its net asset value, which is worse than its one-year historical average discount of 3.14%.

Dana E. Erikson currently receives a manager quality ranking of 98 (0=worst, 99=best). If you desire only a moderate level of risk and strong performance, then this fund is an excellent option.

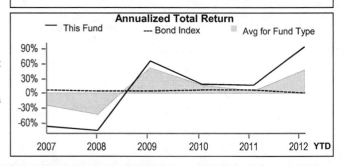

Helios High Yield Fund (HHY)

A **Excellent**

Fund Family: Brookfield Investment Management In
Fund Type: Corporate - High Yield
Inception Date: July 27, 1998

Data Date	Investment Rating	Net Assets ($Mil)	Price	Performance Rating/Pts	Total Return Y-T-D	Risk Rating/Pts
3-12	A	67.87	10.45	B+ / 8.4	9.18%	B+ / 9.0
2011	B+	65.00	9.79	B / 8.1	1.93%	B / 8.8
2010	B-	63.26	8.94	B / 7.9	25.40%	C / 4.8
2009	C-	57.53	7.83	C / 4.7	31.73%	C / 5.0

Major Rating Factors:

Strong performance is the major factor driving the A (Excellent) TheStreet.com Investment Rating for Helios High Yield Fund. The fund currently has a performance rating of B+ (Good) based on an annualized return of 29.94% over the last three years and a total return of 9.18% year to date 2012. Factored into the performance evaluation is an expense ratio of 1.95% (above average).

The fund's risk rating is currently B+ (Good). It carries a beta of 0.87, meaning the fund's expected move will be 8.7% for every 10% move in the market. Volatility, as measured by both the semi-deviation and a drawdown factor, is considered very low. As of March 31, 2012, Helios High Yield Fund traded at a premium of 5.24% above its net asset value, which is worse than its one-year historical average premium of .38%.

Dana E. Erikson currently receives a manager quality ranking of 82 (0=worst, 99=best). If you desire only a moderate level of risk and strong performance, then this fund is an excellent option.

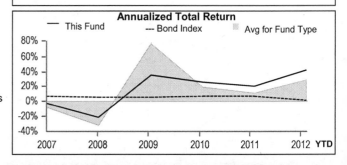

Helios Multi Sector High Income (HMH)

B+ **Good**

Fund Family: Brookfield Investment Management In
Fund Type: General Bond
Inception Date: January 19, 2006

Data Date	Investment Rating	Net Assets ($Mil)	Price	Performance Rating/Pts	Total Return Y-T-D	Risk Rating/Pts
3-12	B+	43.12	6.07	A- / 9.1	12.68%	B- / 7.4
2011	B	44.40	5.50	B+ / 8.4	-0.55%	B- / 7.3
2010	E	37.04	5.03	E / 0.5	20.56%	D / 2.0
2009	E-	38.80	4.60	E / 0.3	49.04%	D / 2.0

Major Rating Factors:

Exceptional performance is the major factor driving the B+ (Good) TheStreet.com Investment Rating for Helios Multi Sector High Income. The fund currently has a performance rating of A- (Excellent) based on an annualized return of 33.63% over the last three years and a total return of 12.68% year to date 2012. Factored into the performance evaluation is an expense ratio of 2.71% (high).

The fund's risk rating is currently B- (Good). It carries a beta of -0.19, meaning the fund's expected move will be -1.9% for every 10% move in the market. Volatility, as measured by both the semi-deviation and a drawdown factor, is considered low. As of March 31, 2012, Helios Multi Sector High Income traded at a discount of .98% below its net asset value, which is worse than its one-year historical average discount of 7.31%.

Dana E. Erikson currently receives a manager quality ranking of 98 (0=worst, 99=best). If you desire only a moderate level of risk and strong performance, then this fund is an excellent option.

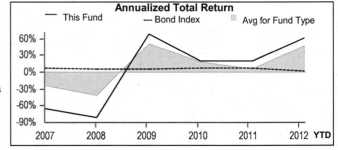

Helios Strategic Income Fund Inc (HSA)

C+   **Fair**

Fund Family: Brookfield Investment Management In
Fund Type: General Bond
Inception Date: March 18, 2004

Major Rating Factors: Middle of the road best describes Helios Strategic Income Fund Inc whose TheStreet.com Investment Rating is currently a C+ (Fair). The fund currently has a performance rating of C+ (Fair) based on an annualized return of 23.69% over the last three years and a total return of 10.13% year to date 2012. Factored into the performance evaluation is an expense ratio of 2.75% (high).

The fund's risk rating is currently B- (Good). It carries a beta of 0.29, meaning the fund's expected move will be 2.9% for every 10% move in the market. Volatility, as measured by both the semi-deviation and a drawdown factor, is considered low. As of March 31, 2012, Helios Strategic Income Fund Inc traded at a discount of 10.27% below its net asset value, which is worse than its one-year historical average discount of 11.99%.

Dana E. Erikson currently receives a manager quality ranking of 95 (0=worst, 99=best). If you desire an average level of risk, then this fund may be an option.

Data Date	Investment Rating	Net Assets ($Mil)	Price	Performance Rating/Pts	Total Return Y-T-D	Risk Rating/Pts
3-12	C+	35.98	5.94	C+ / 6.8	10.13%	B- / 7.8
2011	B-	37.60	5.49	C+ / 6.7	1.09%	B- / 7.8
2010	E	34.97	5.33	E / 0.5	11.47%	D+ / 2.4
2009	E-	33.54	5.23	E / 0.3	44.16%	D+ / 2.3

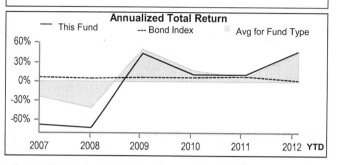

Helios Strategic Mortgage Income (HSM)

C-   **Fair**

Fund Family: Brookfield Investment Management In
Fund Type: Mortgage
Inception Date: July 23, 2002

Major Rating Factors: Middle of the road best describes Helios Strategic Mortgage Income whose TheStreet.com Investment Rating is currently a C- (Fair). The fund currently has a performance rating of C- (Fair) based on an annualized return of 18.15% over the last three years and a total return of 10.74% year to date 2012. Factored into the performance evaluation is an expense ratio of 1.90% (above average).

The fund's risk rating is currently B- (Good). It carries a beta of 0.87, meaning the fund's expected move will be 8.7% for every 10% move in the market. Volatility, as measured by both the semi-deviation and a drawdown factor, is considered low. As of March 31, 2012, Helios Strategic Mortgage Income traded at a discount of .63% below its net asset value, which is worse than its one-year historical average discount of 3.82%.

Michelle L. Russell-Dowe currently receives a manager quality ranking of 89 (0=worst, 99=best). If you desire an average level of risk, then this fund may be an option.

Data Date	Investment Rating	Net Assets ($Mil)	Price	Performance Rating/Pts	Total Return Y-T-D	Risk Rating/Pts
3-12	C-	61.24	6.32	C- / 4.2	10.74%	B- / 7.5
2011	C-	62.30	5.77	C- / 3.6	-0.87%	B- / 7.5
2010	D	61.58	6.19	D / 2.0	14.56%	C+ / 5.6
2009	D-	56.93	5.96	E+ / 0.7	15.24%	C / 4.8

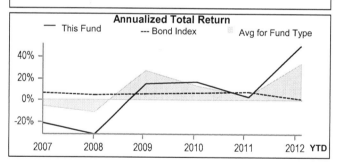

Helios Total Return Fund Inc (HTR)

C   **Fair**

Fund Family: Brookfield Investment Management In
Fund Type: Mortgage
Inception Date: July 28, 1989

Major Rating Factors: Middle of the road best describes Helios Total Return Fund Inc whose TheStreet.com Investment Rating is currently a C (Fair). The fund currently has a performance rating of C (Fair) based on an annualized return of 22.04% over the last three years and a total return of 7.63% year to date 2012. Factored into the performance evaluation is an expense ratio of 1.71% (above average).

The fund's risk rating is currently B (Good). It carries a beta of 1.69, meaning it is expected to move 16.9% for every 10% move in the market. Volatility, as measured by both the semi-deviation and a drawdown factor, is considered low. As of March 31, 2012, Helios Total Return Fund Inc traded at a premium of 1.01% above its net asset value, which is worse than its one-year historical average discount of .44%.

Michelle L. Russell-Dowe currently receives a manager quality ranking of 88 (0=worst, 99=best). If you desire an average level of risk, then this fund may be an option.

Data Date	Investment Rating	Net Assets ($Mil)	Price	Performance Rating/Pts	Total Return Y-T-D	Risk Rating/Pts
3-12	C	176.46	6.02	C / 5.3	7.63%	B / 8.1
2011	B-	178.20	5.72	C+ / 6.3	0.52%	B / 8.1
2010	C+	168.91	5.68	C+ / 6.2	21.84%	C+ / 6.8
2009	D	154.61	5.17	D- / 1.2	18.20%	C+ / 5.8

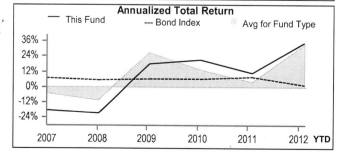

Herzfeld Caribbean Basin Fund (CUBA)

C   **Fair**

Fund Family: Thomas J Herzfeld Advisors Inc
Fund Type: Foreign
Inception Date: September 10, 1993

Major Rating Factors: Middle of the road best describes Herzfeld Caribbean Basin Fund whose TheStreet.com Investment Rating is currently a C (Fair). The fund currently has a performance rating of C (Fair) based on an annualized return of 17.83% over the last three years and a total return of 14.37% year to date 2012. Factored into the performance evaluation is an expense ratio of 2.66% (high).

The fund's risk rating is currently B (Good). It carries a beta of 0.88, meaning the fund's expected move will be 8.8% for every 10% move in the market. Volatility, as measured by both the semi-deviation and a drawdown factor, is considered low. As of March 31, 2012, Herzfeld Caribbean Basin Fund traded at a discount of 6.38% below its net asset value, which is worse than its one-year historical average discount of 9.67%.

Thomas J. Herzfeld has been running the fund for 18 years and currently receives a manager quality ranking of 58 (0=worst, 99=best). If you desire an average level of risk, then this fund may be an option.

Data Date	Investment Rating	Net Assets ($Mil)	Price	Performance Rating/Pts	Total Return Y-T-D	Risk Rating/Pts
3-12	C	30.17	7.34	C / 4.4	14.37%	B / 8.2
2011	C-	26.60	6.42	C- / 3.5	2.06%	B / 8.0
2010	D+	22.71	7.17	C- / 3.4	11.68%	C / 5.4
2009	D-	19.88	6.42	E+ / 0.8	45.91%	C / 4.8

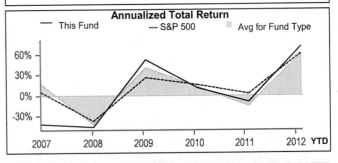

India Fund (IFN)

D-   **Weak**

Fund Family: Aberdeen Asset Management Asia Ltd
Fund Type: Foreign
Inception Date: February 14, 1994

Major Rating Factors:
Disappointing performance is the major factor driving the D- (Weak) TheStreet.com Investment Rating for India Fund. The fund currently has a performance rating of D (Weak) based on an annualized return of 8.59% over the last three years and a total return of 17.12% year to date 2012. Factored into the performance evaluation is an expense ratio of 1.32% (average).

The fund's risk rating is currently C (Fair). It carries a beta of 1.08, meaning that its performance tracks fairly well with that of the overall stock market. Volatility, as measured by both the semi-deviation and a drawdown factor, is considered average. As of March 31, 2012, India Fund traded at a discount of 10.26% below its net asset value, which is better than its one-year historical average discount of 8.00%.

Gregory S. Geiling currently receives a manager quality ranking of 19 (0=worst, 99=best). This fund offers an average level of risk but investors looking for strong performance will be frustrated.

Data Date	Investment Rating	Net Assets ($Mil)	Price	Performance Rating/Pts	Total Return Y-T-D	Risk Rating/Pts
3-12	D-	1,581.37	22.30	D / 1.7	17.12%	C / 5.1
2011	D-	1,581.37	19.04	D / 1.6	2.94%	C / 5.1
2010	E+	1,608.62	35.11	D / 1.8	14.63%	D+ / 2.7
2009	C-	1,003.13	30.70	C+ / 5.9	59.56%	C- / 3.6

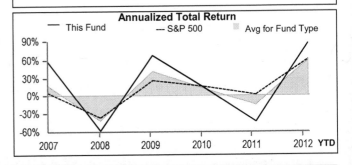

ING Asia Pacific High Div Eq Inc F (IAE)

C   **Fair**

Fund Family: ING Investments LLC
Fund Type: Global
Inception Date: March 30, 2007

Major Rating Factors: Middle of the road best describes ING Asia Pacific High Div Eq Inc F whose TheStreet.com Investment Rating is currently a C (Fair). The fund currently has a performance rating of C+ (Fair) based on an annualized return of 23.00% over the last three years and a total return of 13.67% year to date 2012. Factored into the performance evaluation is an expense ratio of 1.42% (average).

The fund's risk rating is currently C+ (Fair). It carries a beta of 1.14, meaning it is expected to move 11.4% for every 10% move in the market. Volatility, as measured by both the semi-deviation and a drawdown factor, is considered low. As of March 31, 2012, ING Asia Pacific High Div Eq Inc F traded at a discount of .19% below its net asset value, which is better than its one-year historical average premium of 1.33%.

Bas Peeters has been running the fund for 5 years and currently receives a manager quality ranking of 63 (0=worst, 99=best). If you desire an average level of risk, then this fund may be an option.

Data Date	Investment Rating	Net Assets ($Mil)	Price	Performance Rating/Pts	Total Return Y-T-D	Risk Rating/Pts
3-12	C	225.98	16.13	C+ / 5.8	13.67%	C+ / 6.6
2011	C	179.00	14.19	C+ / 5.9	1.13%	C+ / 6.7
2010	C-	208.61	19.65	C+ / 6.2	11.12%	C- / 3.5
2009	B+	197.51	19.01	A+ / 9.8	85.35%	C- / 3.9

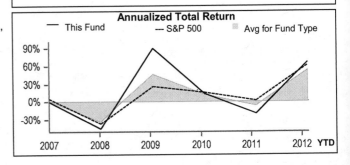

ING Global Advantage and Premium O (IGA)

D+   **Weak**

Fund Family: ING Investments LLC
Fund Type: Global
Inception Date: October 26, 2005

Major Rating Factors: ING Global Advantage and Premium O receives a TheStreet.com Investment Rating of D+ (Weak). The fund currently has a performance rating of C- (Fair) based on an annualized return of 13.88% over the last three years and a total return of 12.60% year to date 2012. Factored into the performance evaluation is an expense ratio of 0.99% (low).

The fund's risk rating is currently B- (Good). It carries a beta of 0.54, meaning the fund's expected move will be 5.4% for every 10% move in the market. Volatility, as measured by both the semi-deviation and a drawdown factor, is considered low. As of March 31, 2012, ING Global Advantage and Premium O traded at a discount of 5.78% below its net asset value, which is better than its one-year historical average discount of 4.34%.

Jody I. Hrazanek has been running the fund for 7 years and currently receives a manager quality ranking of 69 (0=worst, 99=best). If you desire an average level of risk, then this fund may be an option.

Data Date	Investment Rating	Net Assets ($Mil)	Price	Performance Rating/Pts	Total Return Y-T-D	Risk Rating/Pts
3-12	D+	251.55	12.06	C- / 3.3	12.60%	B- / 7.4
2011	C-	218.20	10.71	C- / 3.3	1.68%	B- / 7.2
2010	D+	242.43	13.55	C- / 3.5	7.04%	C / 5.1
2009	C-	238.91	13.69	C / 4.6	36.15%	C / 5.1

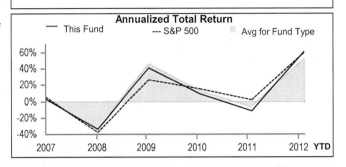

Annualized Total Return

ING Gobal Equity Dividend Premium (IGD)

D+   **Weak**

Fund Family: ING Investments LLC
Fund Type: Global
Inception Date: March 29, 2005

Major Rating Factors: ING Gobal Equity Dividend Premium receives a TheStreet.com Investment Rating of D+ (Weak). The fund currently has a performance rating of C- (Fair) based on an annualized return of 13.79% over the last three years and a total return of 13.22% year to date 2012. Factored into the performance evaluation is an expense ratio of 1.07% (low).

The fund's risk rating is currently B- (Good). It carries a beta of 0.84, meaning the fund's expected move will be 8.4% for every 10% move in the market. Volatility, as measured by both the semi-deviation and a drawdown factor, is considered low. As of March 31, 2012, ING Gobal Equity Dividend Premium traded at a discount of 4.20% below its net asset value, which is better than its one-year historical average discount of 3.54%.

Nicolas Simar has been running the fund for 7 years and currently receives a manager quality ranking of 51 (0=worst, 99=best). If you desire an average level of risk, then this fund may be an option.

Data Date	Investment Rating	Net Assets ($Mil)	Price	Performance Rating/Pts	Total Return Y-T-D	Risk Rating/Pts
3-12	D+	1,108.70	9.59	C- / 3.2	13.22%	B- / 7.2
2011	D+	947.30	8.64	D+ / 2.9	2.43%	C+ / 6.9
2010	D	1,117.91	10.85	D+ / 2.3	-0.57%	C / 5.5
2009	D+	1,130.16	12.17	D+ / 2.9	40.82%	C / 5.5

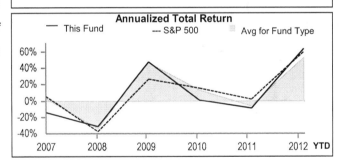

Annualized Total Return

ING Infrastructure Indus & Mtrls (IDE)

D   **Weak**

Fund Family: ING Investments LLC
Fund Type: Growth
Inception Date: January 26, 2010

Major Rating Factors: ING Infrastructure Indus & Mtrls receives a TheStreet.com Investment Rating of D (Weak). The fund currently has a performance rating of C- (Fair) based on an annualized return of 0.00% over the last three years and a total return of 20.08% year to date 2012. Factored into the performance evaluation is an expense ratio of 1.19% (average).

The fund's risk rating is currently C+ (Fair). It carries a beta of 0.00, meaning the fund's expected move will be 0.0% for every 10% move in the market. Volatility, as measured by both the semi-deviation and a drawdown factor, is considered low. As of March 31, 2012, ING Infrastructure Indus & Mtrls traded at a discount of 6.57% below its net asset value, which is better than its one-year historical average discount of 6.45%.

Martin J. Jansen has been running the fund for 2 years and currently receives a manager quality ranking of 8 (0=worst, 99=best). If you desire an average level of risk, then this fund may be an option.

Data Date	Investment Rating	Net Assets ($Mil)	Price	Performance Rating/Pts	Total Return Y-T-D	Risk Rating/Pts
3-12	D	326.18	18.48	C- / 3.1	20.08%	C+ / 6.7
2011	D-	354.20	15.39	D- / 1.1	4.29%	C+ / 6.7

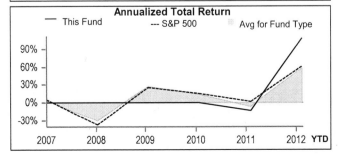

Annualized Total Return

ING International High Div Eq Inc (IID)   C-   Fair

Fund Family: ING Investments LLC
Fund Type: Global
Inception Date: September 26, 2007

Major Rating Factors: Middle of the road best describes ING International High Div Eq Inc whose TheStreet.com Investment Rating is currently a C- (Fair). The fund currently has a performance rating of C (Fair) based on an annualized return of 18.35% over the last three years and a total return of 19.24% year to date 2012. Factored into the performance evaluation is an expense ratio of 1.25% (average).

The fund's risk rating is currently C+ (Fair). It carries a beta of 1.03, meaning that its performance tracks fairly well with that of the overall stock market. Volatility, as measured by both the semi-deviation and a drawdown factor, is considered low. As of March 31, 2012, ING International High Div Eq Inc traded at a premium of 6.35% above its net asset value, which is worse than its one-year historical average premium of 4.46%.

Martin J. Jansen has been running the fund for 5 years and currently receives a manager quality ranking of 41 (0=worst, 99=best). If you desire an average level of risk, then this fund may be an option.

Data Date	Investment Rating	Net Assets ($Mil)	Price	Performance Rating/Pts	Total Return Y-T-D	Risk Rating/Pts
3-12	C-	92.55	10.38	C / 4.6	19.24%	C+ / 6.7
2011	D+	73.80	8.86	C- / 3.6	3.27%	C+ / 6.3
2010	D+	86.22	11.40	C / 4.4	6.43%	C / 4.4
2009	B-	86.65	11.87	B+ / 8.3	54.97%	C / 4.5

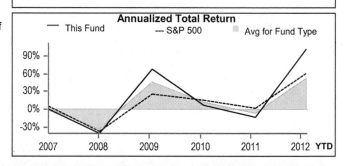

ING Prime Rate Trust (PPR)   C+   Fair

Fund Family: ING Investments LLC
Fund Type: Loan Participation
Inception Date: May 2, 1988

Major Rating Factors: Middle of the road best describes ING Prime Rate Trust whose TheStreet.com Investment Rating is currently a C+ (Fair). The fund currently has a performance rating of C+ (Fair) based on an annualized return of 22.98% over the last three years and a total return of 12.96% year to date 2012. Factored into the performance evaluation is an expense ratio of 1.93% (above average).

The fund's risk rating is currently B (Good). It carries a beta of -75.26, meaning the fund's expected move will be -752.6% for every 10% move in the market. Volatility, as measured by both the semi-deviation and a drawdown factor, is considered low. As of March 31, 2012, ING Prime Rate Trust traded at a discount of 2.23% below its net asset value, which is worse than its one-year historical average discount of 3.32%.

Daniel A. Norman has been running the fund for 12 years and currently receives a manager quality ranking of 98 (0=worst, 99=best). If you desire an average level of risk, then this fund may be an option.

Data Date	Investment Rating	Net Assets ($Mil)	Price	Performance Rating/Pts	Total Return Y-T-D	Risk Rating/Pts
3-12	C+	893.66	5.70	C+ / 5.7	12.96%	B / 8.1
2011	C+	822.30	5.10	C+ / 5.9	4.51%	B- / 7.9
2010	C-	830.79	5.69	C+ / 5.8	14.73%	C / 4.4
2009	C-	761.30	5.22	C / 4.3	55.82%	C / 5.4

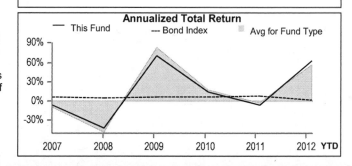

ING Risk Managed Nat Resources Fun (IRR)   D   Weak

Fund Family: ING Investments LLC
Fund Type: Energy/Natural Resources
Inception Date: October 24, 2006

Major Rating Factors:
Disappointing performance is the major factor driving the D (Weak) TheStreet.com Investment Rating for ING Risk Managed Nat Resources Fun. The fund currently has a performance rating of D- (Weak) based on an annualized return of 5.43% over the last three years and a total return of 7.63% year to date 2012. Factored into the performance evaluation is an expense ratio of 1.20% (average).

The fund's risk rating is currently B- (Good). It carries a beta of 0.53, meaning the fund's expected move will be 5.3% for every 10% move in the market. Volatility, as measured by both the semi-deviation and a drawdown factor, is considered low. As of March 31, 2012, ING Risk Managed Nat Resources Fun traded at a discount of 4.51% below its net asset value, which is better than its one-year historical average discount of 2.62%.

Jody I. Hrazanek has been running the fund for 6 years and currently receives a manager quality ranking of 29 (0=worst, 99=best). This fund offers only a moderate level of risk but investors looking for strong performance are still waiting.

Data Date	Investment Rating	Net Assets ($Mil)	Price	Performance Rating/Pts	Total Return Y-T-D	Risk Rating/Pts
3-12	D	347.95	12.27	D- / 1.5	7.63%	B- / 7.2
2011	D+	289.10	11.40	D+ / 2.3	1.67%	B- / 7.1
2010	C+	357.35	15.33	C / 5.0	-3.43%	B- / 7.2
2009	C+	360.74	17.08	C+ / 5.6	36.95%	C+ / 6.5

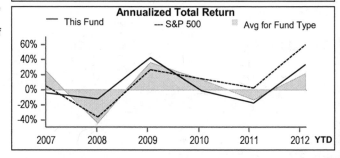

Invesco California Muni Income Tr (IIC)

A-   **Excellent**

Fund Family: Invesco Advisers Inc
Fund Type: Municipal - Single State
Inception Date: February 26, 1993

Major Rating Factors:
Strong performance is the major factor driving the A- (Excellent) TheStreet.com Investment Rating for Invesco California Muni Income Tr. The fund currently has a performance rating of B+ (Good) based on an annualized return of 17.72% over the last three years and a total return of 1.10% year to date 2012. Factored into the performance evaluation is an expense ratio of 0.85% (very low).

The fund's risk rating is currently B (Good). It carries a beta of 2.45, meaning it is expected to move 24.5% for every 10% move in the market. Volatility, as measured by both the semi-deviation and a drawdown factor, is considered low. As of March 31, 2012, Invesco California Muni Income Tr traded at a discount of 3.74% below its net asset value, which is worse than its one-year historical average discount of 5.36%.

Stephen D. Turman currently receives a manager quality ranking of 37 (0=worst, 99=best). If you desire only a moderate level of risk and strong performance, then this fund is an excellent option.

Data Date	Investment Rating	Net Assets ($Mil)	Price	Performance Rating/Pts	Total Return Y-T-D	Risk Rating/Pts
3-12	A-	157.81	15.18	B+ / 8.3	1.10%	B / 8.7
2011	A	160.00	15.21	A / 9.3	1.05%	B / 8.8
2010	C	152.63	12.96	C- / 3.2	9.11%	B- / 7.7
2009	B-	145.53	12.56	C / 5.2	35.74%	B- / 7.8

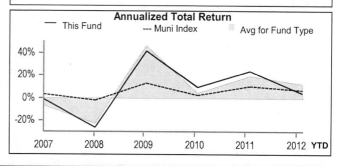

Invesco California Municipal Sec (ICS)

B-   **Good**

Fund Family: Invesco Advisers Inc
Fund Type: Municipal - Single State
Inception Date: February 18, 1994

Major Rating Factors: Invesco California Municipal Sec receives a TheStreet.com Investment Rating of B- (Good). The fund currently has a performance rating of C+ (Fair) based on an annualized return of 11.26% over the last three years and a total return of 2.19% year to date 2012. Factored into the performance evaluation is an expense ratio of 0.72% (very low).

The fund's risk rating is currently B+ (Good). It carries a beta of 1.99, meaning it is expected to move 19.9% for every 10% move in the market. Volatility, as measured by both the semi-deviation and a drawdown factor, is considered very low. As of March 31, 2012, Invesco California Municipal Sec traded at a discount of 4.78% below its net asset value, which is worse than its one-year historical average discount of 7.19%.

Robert J. Stryker currently receives a manager quality ranking of 29 (0=worst, 99=best). If you desire an average level of risk, then this fund may be an option.

Data Date	Investment Rating	Net Assets ($Mil)	Price	Performance Rating/Pts	Total Return Y-T-D	Risk Rating/Pts
3-12	B-	50.44	14.54	C+ / 6.0	2.19%	B+ / 9.0
2011	B+	50.70	14.39	B / 8.0	0.58%	B+ / 9.1
2010	C	50.20	12.72	D+ / 2.7	2.26%	B / 8.7
2009	B	48.54	12.99	C / 5.0	20.47%	B / 8.6

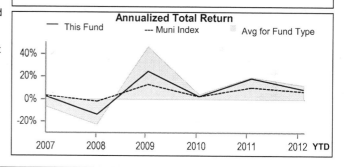

Invesco California Quality Muni Se (IQC)

A   **Excellent**

Fund Family: Invesco Advisers Inc
Fund Type: Municipal - Single State
Inception Date: September 29, 1993

Major Rating Factors:
Strong performance is the major factor driving the A (Excellent) TheStreet.com Investment Rating for Invesco California Quality Muni Se. The fund currently has a performance rating of B+ (Good) based on an annualized return of 18.68% over the last three years and a total return of 3.11% year to date 2012. Factored into the performance evaluation is an expense ratio of 0.93% (low).

The fund's risk rating is currently B (Good). It carries a beta of 2.25, meaning it is expected to move 22.5% for every 10% move in the market. Volatility, as measured by both the semi-deviation and a drawdown factor, is considered low. As of March 31, 2012, Invesco California Quality Muni Se traded at a discount of 3.86% below its net asset value, which is worse than its one-year historical average discount of 5.93%.

Robert J. Stryker currently receives a manager quality ranking of 55 (0=worst, 99=best). If you desire only a moderate level of risk and strong performance, then this fund is an excellent option.

Data Date	Investment Rating	Net Assets ($Mil)	Price	Performance Rating/Pts	Total Return Y-T-D	Risk Rating/Pts
3-12	A	122.59	13.94	B+ / 8.8	3.11%	B / 8.6
2011	A+	124.00	13.72	A / 9.5	1.31%	B / 8.7
2010	D+	116.84	11.79	D / 1.8	7.29%	B- / 7.1
2009	C	107.56	11.70	C- / 4.0	42.86%	B- / 7.4

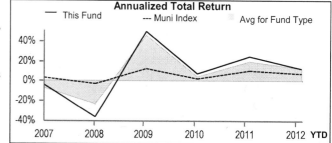

Invesco High Yield Investments Fun (MSY)   B   Good

Fund Family: Invesco Advisers Inc
Fund Type: Corporate - High Yield
Inception Date: November 30, 1993

Data Date	Investment Rating	Net Assets ($Mil)	Price	Performance Rating/Pts	Total Return Y-T-D	Risk Rating/Pts
3-12	B	71.09	6.36	B / 8.1	5.52%	B- / 7.3
2011	B	67.10	6.16	B / 7.9	0.32%	B- / 7.6
2010	B	66.61	5.96	B / 8.0	17.57%	C / 4.9
2009	C	60.64	5.56	B- / 7.2	54.15%	C / 4.3

Major Rating Factors: Strong performance is the major factor driving the B (Good) TheStreet.com Investment Rating for Invesco High Yield Investments Fun. The fund currently has a performance rating of B (Good) based on an annualized return of 29.78% over the last three years and a total return of 5.52% year to date 2012. Factored into the performance evaluation is an expense ratio of 1.52% (average).

The fund's risk rating is currently B- (Good). It carries a beta of 1.19, meaning it is expected to move 11.9% for every 10% move in the market. Volatility, as measured by both the semi-deviation and a drawdown factor, is considered low. As of March 31, 2012, Invesco High Yield Investments Fun traded at a premium of 2.58% above its net asset value, which is worse than its one-year historical average premium of 2.16%.

Darren S. Hughes currently receives a manager quality ranking of 56 (0=worst, 99=best). If you desire only a moderate level of risk and strong performance, then this fund is an excellent option.

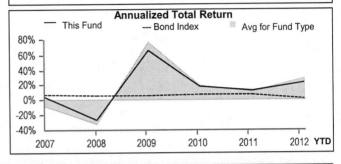

Invesco Municipal Income Opp II Tr (OIB)   B-   Good

Fund Family: Invesco Advisers Inc
Fund Type: Municipal - National
Inception Date: June 22, 1989

Data Date	Investment Rating	Net Assets ($Mil)	Price	Performance Rating/Pts	Total Return Y-T-D	Risk Rating/Pts
3-12	B-	114.58	7.53	C+ / 6.3	2.90%	B / 8.5
2011	B+	122.80	7.43	B / 8.2	0.00%	B / 8.6
2010	C-	119.98	6.82	D / 1.9	5.39%	B- / 7.4
2009	C	110.05	6.90	C- / 3.8	39.65%	B- / 7.3

Major Rating Factors: Invesco Municipal Income Opp II Tr receives a TheStreet.com Investment Rating of B- (Good). The fund currently has a performance rating of C+ (Fair) based on an annualized return of 12.78% over the last three years and a total return of 2.90% year to date 2012. Factored into the performance evaluation is an expense ratio of 0.71% (very low).

The fund's risk rating is currently B (Good). It carries a beta of 1.70, meaning it is expected to move 17.0% for every 10% move in the market. Volatility, as measured by both the semi-deviation and a drawdown factor, is considered low. As of March 31, 2012, Invesco Municipal Income Opp II Tr traded at a discount of 4.08% below its net asset value, which is worse than its one-year historical average discount of 5.15%.

Franklin Ruben currently receives a manager quality ranking of 42 (0=worst, 99=best). If you desire an average level of risk, then this fund may be an option.

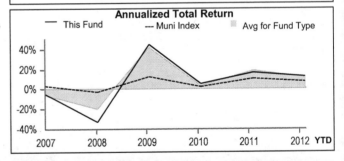

Invesco Municipal Income Opp III T (OIC)   B   Good

Fund Family: Invesco Advisers Inc
Fund Type: Municipal - National
Inception Date: April 20, 1990

Data Date	Investment Rating	Net Assets ($Mil)	Price	Performance Rating/Pts	Total Return Y-T-D	Risk Rating/Pts
3-12	B	64.55	8.32	B- / 7.3	4.95%	B / 8.5
2011	B+	69.80	8.05	B+ / 8.4	0.99%	B / 8.6
2010	C-	67.94	7.32	D / 1.7	4.31%	B- / 7.5
2009	C-	68.88	7.49	D+ / 2.9	33.50%	B- / 7.3

Major Rating Factors: Strong performance is the major factor driving the B (Good) TheStreet.com Investment Rating for Invesco Municipal Income Opp III T. The fund currently has a performance rating of B- (Good) based on an annualized return of 14.15% over the last three years and a total return of 4.95% year to date 2012. Factored into the performance evaluation is an expense ratio of 0.82% (very low).

The fund's risk rating is currently B (Good). It carries a beta of 1.86, meaning it is expected to move 18.6% for every 10% move in the market. Volatility, as measured by both the semi-deviation and a drawdown factor, is considered low. As of March 31, 2012, Invesco Municipal Income Opp III T traded at a discount of 1.89% below its net asset value, which is worse than its one-year historical average discount of 4.74%.

Franklin Ruben currently receives a manager quality ranking of 48 (0=worst, 99=best). If you desire only a moderate level of risk and strong performance, then this fund is an excellent option.

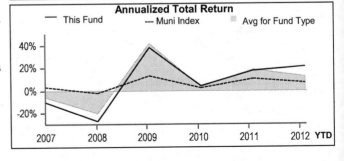

Invesco Municipal Income Opp Tr (OIA)

B   **Good**

Fund Family: Invesco Advisers Inc
Fund Type: Municipal - National
Inception Date: August 12, 1988

Major Rating Factors: Invesco Municipal Income Opp Tr receives a TheStreet.com Investment Rating of B (Good). The fund currently has a performance rating of C+ (Fair) based on an annualized return of 13.68% over the last three years and a total return of 4.57% year to date 2012. Factored into the performance evaluation is an expense ratio of 0.72% (very low).

   The fund's risk rating is currently B (Good). It carries a beta of 1.36, meaning it is expected to move 13.6% for every 10% move in the market. Volatility, as measured by both the semi-deviation and a drawdown factor, is considered low. As of March 31, 2012, Invesco Municipal Income Opp Tr traded at a discount of 3.65% below its net asset value, which is worse than its one-year historical average discount of 4.94%.

   Franklin Ruben currently receives a manager quality ranking of 70 (0=worst, 99=best). If you desire an average level of risk, then this fund may be an option.

Data Date	Investment Rating	Net Assets ($Mil)	Price	Perfor-mance Rating/Pts	Total Return Y-T-D	Risk Rating/Pts
3-12	B	125.78	6.86	C+ / 6.9	4.57%	B / 8.8
2011	B+	135.00	6.66	B+ / 8.3	1.05%	B / 8.8
2010	C-	133.20	6.18	D / 2.2	6.65%	B- / 7.3
2009	D+	115.78	6.18	D / 1.6	37.04%	C+ / 6.6

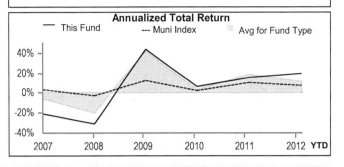

Invesco Municipal Premium Income T (PIA)

A   **Excellent**

Fund Family: Invesco Advisers Inc
Fund Type: Municipal - National
Inception Date: December 29, 1988

Major Rating Factors:
Strong performance is the major factor driving the A (Excellent) TheStreet.com Investment Rating for Invesco Municipal Premium Income T. The fund currently has a performance rating of B+ (Good) based on an annualized return of 18.39% over the last three years and a total return of 0.94% year to date 2012. Factored into the performance evaluation is an expense ratio of 1.66% (above average).

   The fund's risk rating is currently B (Good). It carries a beta of 2.40, meaning it is expected to move 24.0% for every 10% move in the market. Volatility, as measured by both the semi-deviation and a drawdown factor, is considered low. As of March 31, 2012, Invesco Municipal Premium Income T traded at a discount of .22% below its net asset value, which is worse than its one-year historical average discount of 3.66%.

   Richard A. Berry currently receives a manager quality ranking of 41 (0=worst, 99=best). If you desire only a moderate level of risk and strong performance, then this fund is an excellent option.

Data Date	Investment Rating	Net Assets ($Mil)	Price	Perfor-mance Rating/Pts	Total Return Y-T-D	Risk Rating/Pts
3-12	A	130.52	8.89	B+ / 8.7	0.94%	B / 8.6
2011	A+	145.10	8.94	A+ / 9.6	-0.45%	B / 8.7
2010	D+	141.00	7.58	D+ / 2.7	1.84%	C+ / 6.0
2009	C+	128.68	7.95	C+ / 5.7	40.65%	C+ / 6.3

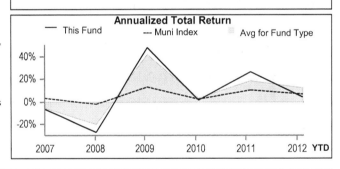

Invesco New York Quality Muni Sec (IQN)

A+   **Excellent**

Fund Family: Invesco Advisers Inc
Fund Type: Municipal - Single State
Inception Date: September 29, 1993

Major Rating Factors:
Strong performance is the major factor driving the A+ (Excellent) TheStreet.com Investment Rating for Invesco New York Quality Muni Sec. The fund currently has a performance rating of B+ (Good) based on an annualized return of 19.73% over the last three years and a total return of 2.29% year to date 2012. Factored into the performance evaluation is an expense ratio of 1.10% (low).

   The fund's risk rating is currently B (Good). It carries a beta of 1.98, meaning it is expected to move 19.8% for every 10% move in the market. Volatility, as measured by both the semi-deviation and a drawdown factor, is considered low. As of March 31, 2012, Invesco New York Quality Muni Sec traded at a discount of 2.59% below its net asset value, which is worse than its one-year historical average discount of 6.37%.

   Stephen D. Turman currently receives a manager quality ranking of 67 (0=worst, 99=best). If you desire only a moderate level of risk and strong performance, then this fund is an excellent option.

Data Date	Investment Rating	Net Assets ($Mil)	Price	Perfor-mance Rating/Pts	Total Return Y-T-D	Risk Rating/Pts
3-12	A+	62.98	15.79	B+ / 8.8	2.29%	B / 8.9
2011	A+	64.00	15.63	A / 9.5	0.45%	B / 8.9
2010	C+	58.62	13.32	C / 4.8	6.22%	C+ / 6.6
2009	B-	54.61	13.20	C+ / 6.5	41.52%	B- / 7.5

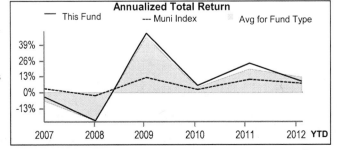

Invesco Quality Municipal Income T (IQI) — A Excellent

Fund Family: Invesco Advisers Inc
Fund Type: Municipal - National
Inception Date: September 29, 1992

Major Rating Factors:
Strong performance is the major factor driving the A (Excellent) TheStreet.com Investment Rating for Invesco Quality Municipal Income T. The fund currently has a performance rating of B+ (Good) based on an annualized return of 18.62% over the last three years and a total return of 5.09% year to date 2012. Factored into the performance evaluation is an expense ratio of 0.92% (low).

The fund's risk rating is currently B (Good). It carries a beta of 2.00, meaning it is expected to move 20.0% for every 10% move in the market. Volatility, as measured by both the semi-deviation and a drawdown factor, is considered low. As of March 31, 2012, Invesco Quality Municipal Income T traded at a premium of 1.83% above its net asset value, which is worse than its one-year historical average discount of 2.06%.

Richard A. Berry currently receives a manager quality ranking of 59 (0=worst, 99=best). If you desire only a moderate level of risk and strong performance, then this fund is an excellent option.

Data Date	Investment Rating	Net Assets ($Mil)	Price	Performance Rating/Pts	Total Return Y-T-D	Risk Rating/Pts
3-12	A	314.90	13.90	B+ / 8.6	5.09%	B / 8.8
2011	A+	314.70	13.44	A / 9.5	2.23%	B / 8.8
2010	C	296.50	12.30	C / 4.9	9.06%	C+ / 6.0
2009	C+	271.06	12.06	C / 5.1	32.90%	C+ / 6.6

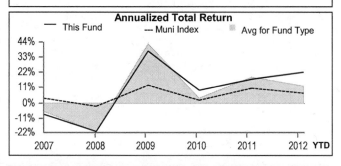

Invesco Quality Municipal Inv Tr (IQT) — B+ Good

Fund Family: Invesco Advisers Inc
Fund Type: Municipal - National
Inception Date: September 27, 1991

Major Rating Factors: Strong performance is the major factor driving the B+ (Good) TheStreet.com Investment Rating for Invesco Quality Municipal Inv Tr. The fund currently has a performance rating of B (Good) based on an annualized return of 17.76% over the last three years and a total return of 0.04% year to date 2012. Factored into the performance evaluation is an expense ratio of 0.89% (low).

The fund's risk rating is currently B (Good). It carries a beta of 2.19, meaning it is expected to move 21.9% for every 10% move in the market. Volatility, as measured by both the semi-deviation and a drawdown factor, is considered low. As of March 31, 2012, Invesco Quality Municipal Inv Tr traded at a discount of 2.71% below its net asset value, which is worse than its one-year historical average discount of 3.23%.

Richard A. Berry currently receives a manager quality ranking of 48 (0=worst, 99=best). If you desire only a moderate level of risk and strong performance, then this fund is an excellent option.

Data Date	Investment Rating	Net Assets ($Mil)	Price	Performance Rating/Pts	Total Return Y-T-D	Risk Rating/Pts
3-12	B+	194.12	13.99	B / 7.9	0.04%	B / 8.7
2011	A	194.70	14.20	A- / 9.0	-1.34%	B / 8.7
2010	C-	183.54	12.50	C- / 4.1	5.38%	C+ / 5.7
2009	C+	169.23	12.65	C+ / 6.6	39.92%	C+ / 6.9

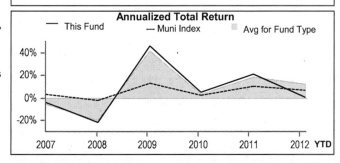

Invesco Quality Municipal Sec (IQM) — B+ Good

Fund Family: Invesco Advisers Inc
Fund Type: Municipal - National
Inception Date: September 22, 1993

Major Rating Factors: Strong performance is the major factor driving the B+ (Good) TheStreet.com Investment Rating for Invesco Quality Municipal Sec. The fund currently has a performance rating of B (Good) based on an annualized return of 17.88% over the last three years and a total return of 2.39% year to date 2012. Factored into the performance evaluation is an expense ratio of 0.85% (very low).

The fund's risk rating is currently B (Good). It carries a beta of 2.22, meaning it is expected to move 22.2% for every 10% move in the market. Volatility, as measured by both the semi-deviation and a drawdown factor, is considered low. As of March 31, 2012, Invesco Quality Municipal Sec traded at a discount of 3.14% below its net asset value, which is worse than its one-year historical average discount of 3.32%.

Richard A. Berry currently receives a manager quality ranking of 46 (0=worst, 99=best). If you desire only a moderate level of risk and strong performance, then this fund is an excellent option.

Data Date	Investment Rating	Net Assets ($Mil)	Price	Performance Rating/Pts	Total Return Y-T-D	Risk Rating/Pts
3-12	B+	199.53	14.83	B / 7.9	2.39%	B / 8.8
2011	A-	201.40	14.70	B+ / 8.7	0.27%	B / 8.9
2010	C	187.99	13.12	C / 4.3	5.54%	C+ / 6.4
2009	C+	174.06	13.21	C+ / 6.4	39.73%	C+ / 6.9

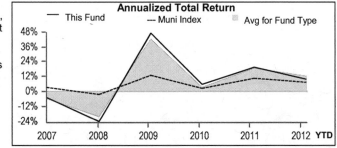

Invesco Value Municipal Bond Trust (IMC)

C   **Fair**

Fund Family: Invesco Advisers Inc
Fund Type: Municipal - National
Inception Date: February 28, 1991

Major Rating Factors: Middle of the road best describes Invesco Value Municipal Bond Trust whose TheStreet.com Investment Rating is currently a C (Fair). The fund currently has a performance rating of C- (Fair) based on an annualized return of 13.85% over the last three years and a total return of -12.03% year to date 2012. Factored into the performance evaluation is an expense ratio of 1.22% (average).

The fund's risk rating is currently B (Good). It carries a beta of 1.61, meaning it is expected to move 16.1% for every 10% move in the market. Volatility, as measured by both the semi-deviation and a drawdown factor, is considered low. As of March 31, 2012, Invesco Value Municipal Bond Trust traded at a discount of 2.60% below its net asset value, which is better than its one-year historical average premium of 3.66%.

Richard A. Berry currently receives a manager quality ranking of 57 (0=worst, 99=best). If you desire an average level of risk, then this fund may be an option.

Data Date	Investment Rating	Net Assets ($Mil)	Price	Performance Rating/Pts	Total Return Y-T-D	Risk Rating/Pts
3-12	C	58.27	14.98	C- / 4.2	-12.03%	B / 8.6
2011	A+	59.30	17.27	A+ / 9.9	0.58%	B / 8.8
2010	C+	55.23	13.00	C+ / 6.1	5.29%	C+ / 6.7
2009	B-	51.94	13.10	C+ / 6.1	37.81%	B- / 7.3

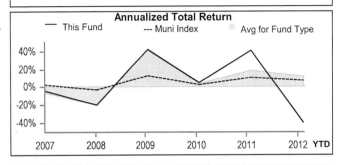

Annualized Total Return — This Fund — Muni Index — Avg for Fund Type

Invesco Value Municipal Income Tr (IIM)

B-   **Good**

Fund Family: Invesco Advisers Inc
Fund Type: Municipal - National
Inception Date: February 19, 1993

Major Rating Factors: Invesco Value Municipal Income Tr receives a TheStreet.com Investment Rating of B- (Good). The fund currently has a performance rating of C+ (Fair) based on an annualized return of 15.68% over the last three years and a total return of -1.69% year to date 2012. Factored into the performance evaluation is an expense ratio of 0.88% (low).

The fund's risk rating is currently B (Good). It carries a beta of 2.32, meaning it is expected to move 23.2% for every 10% move in the market. Volatility, as measured by both the semi-deviation and a drawdown factor, is considered low. As of March 31, 2012, Invesco Value Municipal Income Tr traded at a discount of 2.99% below its net asset value, which is better than its one-year historical average discount of .36%.

Richard A. Berry currently receives a manager quality ranking of 33 (0=worst, 99=best). If you desire an average level of risk, then this fund may be an option.

Data Date	Investment Rating	Net Assets ($Mil)	Price	Performance Rating/Pts	Total Return Y-T-D	Risk Rating/Pts
3-12	B-	320.04	15.56	C+ / 6.3	-1.69%	B / 8.6
2011	A+	325.00	16.05	A+ / 9.7	4.36%	B / 8.7
2010	C+	303.16	13.50	C / 4.7	2.39%	C+ / 6.6
2009	B-	287.53	14.00	C+ / 6.6	34.89%	B- / 7.2

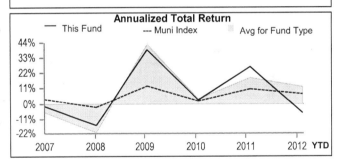

Annualized Total Return — This Fund — Muni Index — Avg for Fund Type

Invesco Value Municipal Securities (IMS)

C-   **Fair**

Fund Family: Invesco Advisers Inc
Fund Type: Municipal - National
Inception Date: February 18, 1994

Major Rating Factors:
Disappointing performance is the major factor driving the C- (Fair) TheStreet.com Investment Rating for Invesco Value Municipal Securities. The fund currently has a performance rating of D+ (Weak) based on an annualized return of 5.53% over the last three years and a total return of 0.60% year to date 2012. Factored into the performance evaluation is an expense ratio of 0.54% (very low).

The fund's risk rating is currently B (Good). It carries a beta of 1.73, meaning it is expected to move 17.3% for every 10% move in the market. Volatility, as measured by both the semi-deviation and a drawdown factor, is considered low. As of March 31, 2012, Invesco Value Municipal Securities traded at a discount of 4.08% below its net asset value, which is better than its one-year historical average discount of 3.48%.

Richard A. Berry currently receives a manager quality ranking of 18 (0=worst, 99=best). This fund offers only a moderate level of risk but investors looking for strong performance are still waiting.

Data Date	Investment Rating	Net Assets ($Mil)	Price	Performance Rating/Pts	Total Return Y-T-D	Risk Rating/Pts
3-12	C-	96.40	14.33	D+ / 2.7	0.60%	B / 8.8
2011	B-	97.40	14.39	C+ / 6.2	0.76%	B / 8.9
2010	C	93.22	12.86	D / 2.2	-4.54%	B / 8.5
2009	B-	90.06	14.04	C / 5.2	19.03%	B- / 7.6

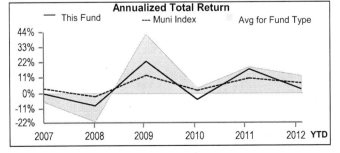

Annualized Total Return — This Fund — Muni Index — Avg for Fund Type

Invesco Value Municipal Trust (IMT)

C+　**Fair**

Fund Family: Invesco Advisers Inc
Fund Type: Municipal - National
Inception Date: February 28, 1992

Major Rating Factors: Middle of the road best describes Invesco Value Municipal Trust whose TheStreet.com Investment Rating is currently a C+ (Fair). The fund currently has a performance rating of C (Fair) based on an annualized return of 14.71% over the last three years and a total return of -4.13% year to date 2012. Factored into the performance evaluation is an expense ratio of 0.90% (low).

The fund's risk rating is currently B (Good). It carries a beta of 2.24, meaning it is expected to move 22.4% for every 10% move in the market. Volatility, as measured by both the semi-deviation and a drawdown factor, is considered low. As of March 31, 2012, Invesco Value Municipal Trust traded at a discount of 3.16% below its net asset value, which is better than its one-year historical average discount of .78%.

Richard A. Berry currently receives a manager quality ranking of 33 (0=worst, 99=best). If you desire an average level of risk, then this fund may be an option.

Data Date	Investment Rating	Net Assets ($Mil)	Price	Perfor- mance Rating/Pts	Total Return Y-T-D	Risk Rating/Pts
3-12	C+	256.43	14.69	C / 5.4	-4.13%	B / 8.7
2011	A-	260.40	15.55	A- / 9.0	-1.80%	B / 8.7
2010	C+	246.19	12.94	C / 5.0	3.18%	C+ / 6.7
2009	B-	235.26	13.35	C+ / 6.3	35.35%	B- / 7.5

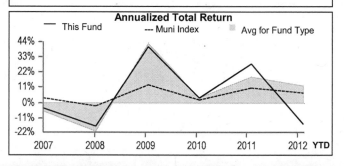

Invesco Van Kampen Adv Muni Inc II (VKI)

A　**Excellent**

Fund Family: Invesco Advisers Inc
Fund Type: Municipal - National
Inception Date: August 27, 1993

Major Rating Factors:
Strong performance is the major factor driving the A (Excellent) TheStreet.com Investment Rating for Invesco Van Kampen Adv Muni Inc II. The fund currently has a performance rating of B+ (Good) based on an annualized return of 19.54% over the last three years and a total return of 5.74% year to date 2012. Factored into the performance evaluation is an expense ratio of 1.28% (average).

The fund's risk rating is currently B (Good). It carries a beta of 1.96, meaning it is expected to move 19.6% for every 10% move in the market. Volatility, as measured by both the semi-deviation and a drawdown factor, is considered low. As of March 31, 2012, Invesco Van Kampen Adv Muni Inc II traded at a premium of 3.11% above its net asset value, which is worse than its one-year historical average premium of .62%.

Robert W. Wimmell has been running the fund for 10 years and currently receives a manager quality ranking of 69 (0=worst, 99=best). If you desire only a moderate level of risk and strong performance, then this fund is an excellent option.

Data Date	Investment Rating	Net Assets ($Mil)	Price	Perfor- mance Rating/Pts	Total Return Y-T-D	Risk Rating/Pts
3-12	A	547.10	12.95	B+ / 8.7	5.74%	B / 8.8
2011	A+	544.80	12.46	A / 9.4	0.56%	B / 8.8
2010	C-	512.04	11.35	C- / 3.4	6.65%	C+ / 5.7
2009	C+	447.53	11.45	C+ / 6.8	55.30%	C+ / 6.1

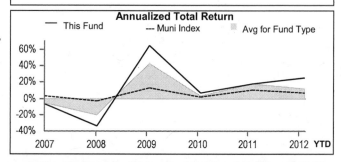

Invesco Van Kampen Bond (VBF)

C-　**Fair**

Fund Family: Invesco Advisers Inc
Fund Type: General - Investment Grade
Inception Date: October 15, 1970

Major Rating Factors: Middle of the road best describes Invesco Van Kampen Bond whose TheStreet.com Investment Rating is currently a C- (Fair). The fund currently has a performance rating of C- (Fair) based on an annualized return of 13.35% over the last three years and a total return of -2.15% year to date 2012. Factored into the performance evaluation is an expense ratio of 0.52% (very low).

The fund's risk rating is currently B (Good). It carries a beta of 1.69, meaning it is expected to move 16.9% for every 10% move in the market. Volatility, as measured by both the semi-deviation and a drawdown factor, is considered low. As of March 31, 2012, Invesco Van Kampen Bond traded at a discount of 1.13% below its net asset value, which is worse than its one-year historical average discount of 3.55%.

Chuck Burge has been running the fund for 2 years and currently receives a manager quality ranking of 48 (0=worst, 99=best). If you desire an average level of risk, then this fund may be an option.

Data Date	Investment Rating	Net Assets ($Mil)	Price	Perfor- mance Rating/Pts	Total Return Y-T-D	Risk Rating/Pts
3-12	C-	227.80	20.21	C- / 3.3	-2.15%	B / 8.6
2011	C+	227.50	20.90	C / 5.0	-5.41%	B / 8.7
2010	B-	223.60	18.64	C+ / 5.8	3.81%	B- / 7.0
2009	C+	202.99	18.90	C / 5.1	18.86%	B- / 7.2

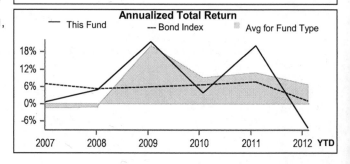

Invesco Van Kampen CA Val Muni Inc (VCV)　　　　　　　B+　　　　Good

Fund Family: Invesco Advisers Inc
Fund Type: Municipal - Single State
Inception Date: April 30, 1993

Major Rating Factors: Strong performance is the major factor driving the B+ (Good) TheStreet.com Investment Rating for Invesco Van Kampen CA Val Muni Inc. The fund currently has a performance rating of B+ (Good) based on an annualized return of 17.79% over the last three years and a total return of 3.95% year to date 2012. Factored into the performance evaluation is an expense ratio of 1.36% (average).

The fund's risk rating is currently B (Good). It carries a beta of 2.55, meaning it is expected to move 25.5% for every 10% move in the market. Volatility, as measured by both the semi-deviation and a drawdown factor, is considered low. As of March 31, 2012, Invesco Van Kampen CA Val Muni Inc traded at a premium of 1.08% above its net asset value, which is better than its one-year historical average premium of 2.39%.

Robert W. Wimmell has been running the fund for 10 years and currently receives a manager quality ranking of 35 (0=worst, 99=best). If you desire only a moderate level of risk and strong performance, then this fund is an excellent option.

Data Date	Investment Rating	Net Assets ($Mil)	Price	Performance Rating/Pts	Total Return Y-T-D	Risk Rating/Pts
3-12	B+	280.90	13.15	B+ / 8.5	3.95%	B / 8.4
2011	A	278.00	12.87	A / 9.5	1.79%	B / 8.5
2010	D	259.74	11.28	D- / 1.2	1.81%	C+ / 6.5
2009	C	225.69	11.94	C / 4.5	55.72%	C+ / 6.0

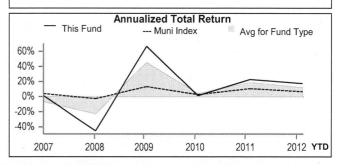
Annualized Total Return

Invesco Van Kampen Dynamic Cred Op (VTA)　　　　　　B　　　　Good

Fund Family: Invesco Advisers Inc
Fund Type: Loan Participation
Inception Date: June 26, 2007

Major Rating Factors: Strong performance is the major factor driving the B (Good) TheStreet.com Investment Rating for Invesco Van Kampen Dynamic Cred Op. The fund currently has a performance rating of B- (Good) based on an annualized return of 29.36% over the last three years and a total return of 12.61% year to date 2012. Factored into the performance evaluation is an expense ratio of 2.22% (high).

The fund's risk rating is currently B (Good). It carries a beta of -130.76, meaning the fund's expected move will be -1307.6% for every 10% move in the market. Volatility, as measured by both the semi-deviation and a drawdown factor, is considered low. As of March 31, 2012, Invesco Van Kampen Dynamic Cred Op traded at a discount of 6.26% below its net asset value, which is worse than its one-year historical average discount of 6.87%.

Scott Baskind has been running the fund for 2 years and currently receives a manager quality ranking of 99 (0=worst, 99=best). If you desire only a moderate level of risk and strong performance, then this fund is an excellent option.

Data Date	Investment Rating	Net Assets ($Mil)	Price	Performance Rating/Pts	Total Return Y-T-D	Risk Rating/Pts
3-12	B	983.82	11.68	B- / 7.4	12.61%	B / 8.0
2011	B-	877.50	10.57	C+ / 6.8	2.74%	B- / 7.9
2010	C-	927.10	12.21	C / 5.4	12.20%	C / 4.5
2009	B+	814.40	11.84	A+ / 9.6	76.63%	C / 4.3

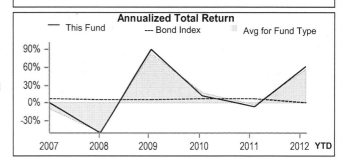
Annualized Total Return

Invesco Van Kampen High Inc Tr II (VLT)　　　　　　A-　　　　Excellent

Fund Family: Invesco Advisers Inc
Fund Type: Corporate - High Yield
Inception Date: April 28, 1989

Major Rating Factors:
Strong performance is the major factor driving the A- (Excellent) TheStreet.com Investment Rating for Invesco Van Kampen High Inc Tr II. The fund currently has a performance rating of B+ (Good) based on an annualized return of 34.53% over the last three years and a total return of 11.65% year to date 2012. Factored into the performance evaluation is an expense ratio of 2.57% (high).

The fund's risk rating is currently B (Good). It carries a beta of 1.24, meaning it is expected to move 12.4% for every 10% move in the market. Volatility, as measured by both the semi-deviation and a drawdown factor, is considered low. As of March 31, 2012, Invesco Van Kampen High Inc Tr II traded at a premium of 3.61% above its net asset value, which is worse than its one-year historical average premium of 3.60%.

Darren S. Hughes currently receives a manager quality ranking of 62 (0=worst, 99=best). If you desire only a moderate level of risk and strong performance, then this fund is an excellent option.

Data Date	Investment Rating	Net Assets ($Mil)	Price	Performance Rating/Pts	Total Return Y-T-D	Risk Rating/Pts
3-12	A-	60.90	16.94	B+ / 8.8	11.65%	B / 8.2
2011	B	57.40	15.50	B+ / 8.5	2.58%	B- / 7.7
2010	C-	58.00	16.02	C+ / 6.3	22.05%	C- / 3.2
2009	C-	48.63	14.48	C / 5.0	70.00%	C- / 3.8

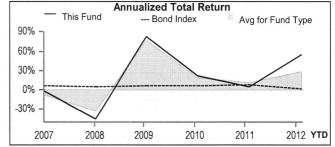
Annualized Total Return

Invesco Van Kampen MA Val Muni Inc (VMV)   C-   Fair

Fund Family: Invesco Advisers Inc
Fund Type: Municipal - Single State
Inception Date: April 23, 1993

Data Date	Investment Rating	Net Assets ($Mil)	Price	Performance Rating/Pts	Total Return Y-T-D	Risk Rating/Pts
3-12	C-	34.00	12.70	C- / 3.8	1.52%	B / 8.2
2011	B+	34.80	12.69	B+ / 8.4	2.13%	B / 8.3
2010	D+	32.18	11.50	D- / 1.5	0.88%	B- / 7.1
2009	C	29.88	12.19	C- / 3.5	27.78%	C+ / 6.7

Major Rating Factors: Middle of the road best describes Invesco Van Kampen MA Val Muni Inc whose TheStreet.com Investment Rating is currently a C- (Fair). The fund currently has a performance rating of C- (Fair) based on an annualized return of 9.98% over the last three years and a total return of 1.52% year to date 2012. Factored into the performance evaluation is an expense ratio of 1.83% (above average).

The fund's risk rating is currently B (Good). It carries a beta of 1.61, meaning it is expected to move 16.1% for every 10% move in the market. Volatility, as measured by both the semi-deviation and a drawdown factor, is considered low. As of March 31, 2012, Invesco Van Kampen MA Val Muni Inc traded at a discount of 3.35% below its net asset value, which is better than its one-year historical average premium of .45%.

Julius D. Williams currently receives a manager quality ranking of 34 (0=worst, 99=best). If you desire an average level of risk, then this fund may be an option.

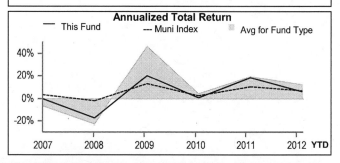

Invesco Van Kampen Muni Opp (VMO)   A-   Excellent

Fund Family: Invesco Advisers Inc
Fund Type: Municipal - National
Inception Date: April 24, 1992

Data Date	Investment Rating	Net Assets ($Mil)	Price	Performance Rating/Pts	Total Return Y-T-D	Risk Rating/Pts
3-12	A-	467.70	14.58	B / 8.2	2.50%	B / 8.7
2011	A+	462.60	14.48	A+ / 9.6	0.90%	B / 8.8
2010	C-	439.37	13.04	C- / 3.3	5.26%	C+ / 6.1
2009	C+	388.12	13.37	C+ / 6.3	44.98%	C+ / 6.3

Major Rating Factors:
Strong performance is the major factor driving the A- (Excellent) TheStreet.com Investment Rating for Invesco Van Kampen Muni Opp. The fund currently has a performance rating of B (Good) based on an annualized return of 19.02% over the last three years and a total return of 2.50% year to date 2012. Factored into the performance evaluation is an expense ratio of 1.30% (average).

The fund's risk rating is currently B (Good). It carries a beta of 1.77, meaning it is expected to move 17.7% for every 10% move in the market. Volatility, as measured by both the semi-deviation and a drawdown factor, is considered low. As of March 31, 2012, Invesco Van Kampen Muni Opp traded at a premium of 4.29% above its net asset value, which is worse than its one-year historical average premium of 3.57%.

Robert W. Wimmell has been running the fund for 10 years and currently receives a manager quality ranking of 67 (0=worst, 99=best). If you desire only a moderate level of risk and strong performance, then this fund is an excellent option.

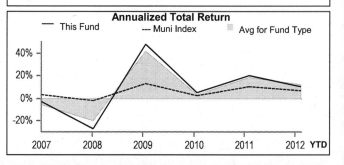

Invesco Van Kampen Muni Trust (VKQ)   B+   Good

Fund Family: Invesco Advisers Inc
Fund Type: Municipal - National
Inception Date: September 20, 1991

Data Date	Investment Rating	Net Assets ($Mil)	Price	Performance Rating/Pts	Total Return Y-T-D	Risk Rating/Pts
3-12	B+	539.10	14.23	B / 7.6	3.45%	B / 8.5
2011	A	535.40	13.99	A- / 9.2	0.50%	B / 8.5
2010	D+	505.46	12.49	D / 1.7	2.88%	C+ / 6.9
2009	C	440.00	13.04	C+ / 6.0	49.25%	C+ / 5.6

Major Rating Factors: Strong performance is the major factor driving the B+ (Good) TheStreet.com Investment Rating for Invesco Van Kampen Muni Trust. The fund currently has a performance rating of B (Good) based on an annualized return of 17.31% over the last three years and a total return of 3.45% year to date 2012. Factored into the performance evaluation is an expense ratio of 1.12% (low).

The fund's risk rating is currently B (Good). It carries a beta of 1.94, meaning it is expected to move 19.4% for every 10% move in the market. Volatility, as measured by both the semi-deviation and a drawdown factor, is considered low. As of March 31, 2012, Invesco Van Kampen Muni Trust traded at a premium of 1.43% above its net asset value, which is worse than its one-year historical average premium of 1.06%.

This fund has been team managed for 21 years and currently receives a manager quality ranking of 57 (0=worst, 99=best). If you desire only a moderate level of risk and strong performance, then this fund is an excellent option.

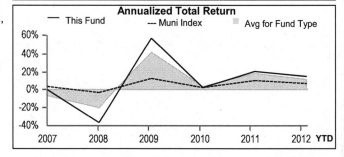

Invesco Van Kampen OH Qual Muni (VOQ)   A+   Excellent

Fund Family: Invesco Advisers Inc
Fund Type: Municipal - Single State
Inception Date: September 20, 1991

Data Date	Investment Rating	Net Assets ($Mil)	Price	Performance Rating/Pts	Total Return Y-T-D	Risk Rating/Pts
3-12	A+	90.00	16.56	B+ / 8.8	6.49%	B / 8.9
2011	B+	89.80	15.80	B / 8.1	0.00%	B / 8.9
2010	C+	85.68	14.48	C / 5.2	7.52%	C+ / 6.9
2009	C+	78.70	14.41	C / 5.0	18.36%	B- / 7.7

Major Rating Factors:
Strong performance is the major factor driving the A+ (Excellent) TheStreet.com Investment Rating for Invesco Van Kampen OH Qual Muni. The fund currently has a performance rating of B+ (Good) based on an annualized return of 18.35% over the last three years and a total return of 6.49% year to date 2012. Factored into the performance evaluation is an expense ratio of 1.39% (average).

The fund's risk rating is currently B (Good). It carries a beta of 1.57, meaning it is expected to move 15.7% for every 10% move in the market. Volatility, as measured by both the semi-deviation and a drawdown factor, is considered low. As of March 31, 2012, Invesco Van Kampen OH Qual Muni traded at a premium of 5.08% above its net asset value, which is worse than its one-year historical average premium of .54%.

Stephen D. Turman currently receives a manager quality ranking of 75 (0=worst, 99=best). If you desire only a moderate level of risk and strong performance, then this fund is an excellent option.

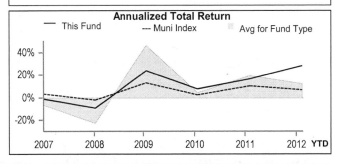

Invesco Van Kampen PA Val Muni Inc (VPV)   A-   Excellent

Fund Family: Invesco Advisers Inc
Fund Type: Municipal - Single State
Inception Date: April 23, 1993

Data Date	Investment Rating	Net Assets ($Mil)	Price	Performance Rating/Pts	Total Return Y-T-D	Risk Rating/Pts
3-12	A-	340.00	14.57	B+ / 8.4	4.04%	B / 8.7
2011	A+	343.00	14.22	A / 9.4	-0.39%	B / 8.7
2010	C-	321.18	12.65	C- / 3.6	6.03%	C+ / 6.2
2009	B+	294.63	12.74	B- / 7.1	52.07%	C+ / 6.6

Major Rating Factors:
Strong performance is the major factor driving the A- (Excellent) TheStreet.com Investment Rating for Invesco Van Kampen PA Val Muni Inc. The fund currently has a performance rating of B+ (Good) based on an annualized return of 18.98% over the last three years and a total return of 4.04% year to date 2012. Factored into the performance evaluation is an expense ratio of 1.23% (average).

The fund's risk rating is currently B (Good). It carries a beta of 1.76, meaning it is expected to move 17.6% for every 10% move in the market. Volatility, as measured by both the semi-deviation and a drawdown factor, is considered low. As of March 31, 2012, Invesco Van Kampen PA Val Muni Inc traded at a discount of 1.49% below its net asset value, which is worse than its one-year historical average discount of 3.93%.

Robert W. Wimmell has been running the fund for 10 years and currently receives a manager quality ranking of 69 (0=worst, 99=best). If you desire only a moderate level of risk and strong performance, then this fund is an excellent option.

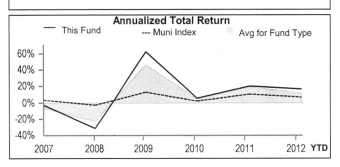

Invesco Van Kampen Sel Sector Muni (VKL)   A   Excellent

Fund Family: Invesco Advisers Inc
Fund Type: Municipal - National
Inception Date: November 26, 1993

Data Date	Investment Rating	Net Assets ($Mil)	Price	Performance Rating/Pts	Total Return Y-T-D	Risk Rating/Pts
3-12	A	185.90	12.84	B+ / 8.9	2.48%	B / 8.6
2011	A+	184.00	12.75	A+ / 9.7	-0.71%	B / 8.7
2010	C-	174.21	11.22	C- / 3.3	5.66%	C+ / 6.4
2009	B+	152.68	11.43	B- / 7.4	59.36%	C+ / 6.2

Major Rating Factors:
Strong performance is the major factor driving the A (Excellent) TheStreet.com Investment Rating for Invesco Van Kampen Sel Sector Muni. The fund currently has a performance rating of B+ (Good) based on an annualized return of 21.23% over the last three years and a total return of 2.48% year to date 2012. Factored into the performance evaluation is an expense ratio of 1.37% (average).

The fund's risk rating is currently B (Good). It carries a beta of 1.93, meaning it is expected to move 19.3% for every 10% move in the market. Volatility, as measured by both the semi-deviation and a drawdown factor, is considered low. As of March 31, 2012, Invesco Van Kampen Sel Sector Muni traded at a premium of 3.63% above its net asset value, which is worse than its one-year historical average premium of .94%.

Robert W. Wimmell has been running the fund for 10 years and currently receives a manager quality ranking of 74 (0=worst, 99=best). If you desire only a moderate level of risk and strong performance, then this fund is an excellent option.

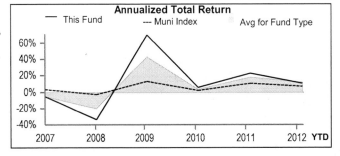

Invesco Van Kampen Senior Inc Tr (VVR)   A-   Excellent

Fund Family: Invesco Advisers Inc
Fund Type: Loan Participation
Inception Date: June 23, 1998

Data Date	Investment Rating	Net Assets ($Mil)	Price	Performance Rating/Pts	Total Return Y-T-D	Risk Rating/Pts
3-12	A-	904.60	4.91	B+ / 8.7	16.60%	B / 8.2
2011	B	849.20	4.28	B / 7.6	3.74%	B / 8.3
2010	D-	836.90	4.69	D / 2.2	18.70%	C- / 3.2
2009	D-	717.10	4.22	D / 2.1	66.80%	C / 4.3

Major Rating Factors:
Strong performance is the major factor driving the A- (Excellent) TheStreet.com Investment Rating for Invesco Van Kampen Senior Inc Tr. The fund currently has a performance rating of B+ (Good) based on an annualized return of 34.18% over the last three years and a total return of 16.60% year to date 2012. Factored into the performance evaluation is an expense ratio of 2.14% (high).

The fund's risk rating is currently B (Good). It carries a beta of 20.85, meaning it is expected to move 208.5% for every 10% move in the market. Volatility, as measured by both the semi-deviation and a drawdown factor, is considered low. As of March 31, 2012, Invesco Van Kampen Senior Inc Tr traded at a price exactly equal to its net asset value, which is worse than its one-year historical average discount of 3.85%.

Philip Yarrow currently receives a manager quality ranking of 97 (0=worst, 99=best). If you desire only a moderate level of risk and strong performance, then this fund is an excellent option.

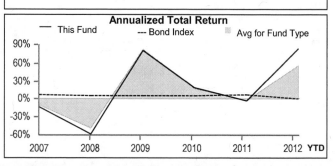

Invesco Van Kampen Tr Fr Inv Gr Mu (VGM)   A   Excellent

Fund Family: Invesco Advisers Inc
Fund Type: Municipal - National
Inception Date: January 24, 1992

Data Date	Investment Rating	Net Assets ($Mil)	Price	Performance Rating/Pts	Total Return Y-T-D	Risk Rating/Pts
3-12	A	780.20	15.15	B+ / 8.6	2.95%	B / 8.8
2011	A+	775.90	14.98	A / 9.4	-0.40%	B / 8.8
2010	C	733.60	13.35	C / 4.8	3.84%	C+ / 5.7
2009	B	646.45	13.86	B- / 7.4	55.46%	C+ / 6.0

Major Rating Factors:
Strong performance is the major factor driving the A (Excellent) TheStreet.com Investment Rating for Invesco Van Kampen Tr Fr Inv Gr Mu. The fund currently has a performance rating of B+ (Good) based on an annualized return of 20.45% over the last three years and a total return of 2.95% year to date 2012. Factored into the performance evaluation is an expense ratio of 1.23% (average).

The fund's risk rating is currently B (Good). It carries a beta of 1.82, meaning it is expected to move 18.2% for every 10% move in the market. Volatility, as measured by both the semi-deviation and a drawdown factor, is considered low. As of March 31, 2012, Invesco Van Kampen Tr Fr Inv Gr Mu traded at a premium of 3.41% above its net asset value, which is worse than its one-year historical average premium of 1.43%.

Thomas M. Byron has been running the fund for 15 years and currently receives a manager quality ranking of 75 (0=worst, 99=best). If you desire only a moderate level of risk and strong performance, then this fund is an excellent option.

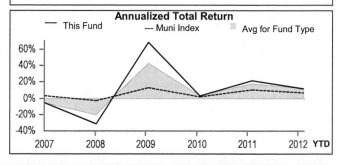

Invesco Van Kampen Tr Fr Inv NJ Mu (VTJ)   A+   Excellent

Fund Family: Invesco Advisers Inc
Fund Type: Municipal - Single State
Inception Date: March 27, 1992

Data Date	Investment Rating	Net Assets ($Mil)	Price	Performance Rating/Pts	Total Return Y-T-D	Risk Rating/Pts
3-12	A+	98.50	17.78	A / 9.3	4.79%	B / 8.8
2011	A	99.80	17.25	A- / 9.2	0.06%	B / 8.8
2010	C+	93.86	15.55	C+ / 5.8	7.57%	C+ / 6.3
2009	C+	86.44	15.47	C+ / 6.7	38.78%	C+ / 6.8

Major Rating Factors:
Exceptional performance is the major factor driving the A+ (Excellent) TheStreet.com Investment Rating for Invesco Van Kampen Tr Fr Inv NJ Mu. The fund currently has a performance rating of A (Excellent) based on an annualized return of 20.50% over the last three years and a total return of 4.79% year to date 2012. Factored into the performance evaluation is an expense ratio of 1.34% (average).

The fund's risk rating is currently B (Good). It carries a beta of 1.91, meaning it is expected to move 19.1% for every 10% move in the market. Volatility, as measured by both the semi-deviation and a drawdown factor, is considered low. As of March 31, 2012, Invesco Van Kampen Tr Fr Inv NJ Mu traded at a premium of 5.77% above its net asset value, which is worse than its one-year historical average premium of 1.35%.

Robert W. Wimmell has been running the fund for 10 years and currently receives a manager quality ranking of 78 (0=worst, 99=best). If you desire only a moderate level of risk and strong performance, then this fund is an excellent option.

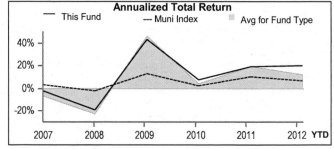

Invesco Van Kampen Tr Fr Inv NY Mu (VTN)   A+   Excellent

Fund Family: Invesco Advisers Inc
Fund Type: Municipal - Single State
Inception Date: March 20, 1992

Data Date	Investment Rating	Net Assets ($Mil)	Price	Performance Rating/Pts	Total Return Y-T-D	Risk Rating/Pts
3-12	A+	228.00	15.85	A- / 9.1	5.63%	B / 8.9
2011	A+	228.00	15.25	A / 9.5	1.31%	B / 8.8
2010	C	212.05	13.63	C / 4.8	2.52%	C+ / 5.7
2009	B	190.53	14.25	B / 7.7	62.54%	C+ / 5.8

Major Rating Factors:
Exceptional performance is the major factor driving the A+ (Excellent) TheStreet.com Investment Rating for Invesco Van Kampen Tr Fr Inv NY Mu. The fund currently has a performance rating of A- (Excellent) based on an annualized return of 21.98% over the last three years and a total return of 5.63% year to date 2012. Factored into the performance evaluation is an expense ratio of 1.35% (average).

The fund's risk rating is currently B (Good). It carries a beta of 1.86, meaning it is expected to move 18.6% for every 10% move in the market. Volatility, as measured by both the semi-deviation and a drawdown factor, is considered low. As of March 31, 2012, Invesco Van Kampen Tr Fr Inv NY Mu traded at a premium of 3.46% above its net asset value, which is worse than its one-year historical average premium of .65%.

Robert J. Stryker has been running the fund for 5 years and currently receives a manager quality ranking of 78 (0=worst, 99=best). If you desire only a moderate level of risk and strong performance, then this fund is an excellent option.

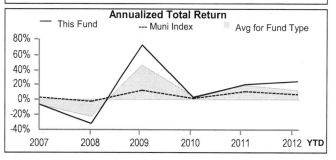

Invesco Van Kampen Tr Fr Val Muni (VIM)   B-   Good

Fund Family: Invesco Advisers Inc
Fund Type: Municipal - National
Inception Date: January 24, 1992

Data Date	Investment Rating	Net Assets ($Mil)	Price	Performance Rating/Pts	Total Return Y-T-D	Risk Rating/Pts
3-12	B-	131.60	13.94	C+ / 6.7	3.37%	B / 8.4
2011	B+	132.60	13.70	B / 8.2	0.53%	B / 8.4
2010	C-	125.44	12.08	D / 1.8	-3.14%	B- / 7.7
2009	C+	114.10	13.30	C+ / 6.1	34.16%	C+ / 6.7

Major Rating Factors: Invesco Van Kampen Tr Fr Val Muni receives a TheStreet.com Investment Rating of B- (Good). The fund currently has a performance rating of C+ (Fair) based on an annualized return of 13.13% over the last three years and a total return of 3.37% year to date 2012. Factored into the performance evaluation is an expense ratio of 1.32% (average).

The fund's risk rating is currently B (Good). It carries a beta of 2.35, meaning it is expected to move 23.5% for every 10% move in the market. Volatility, as measured by both the semi-deviation and a drawdown factor, is considered low. As of March 31, 2012, Invesco Van Kampen Tr Fr Val Muni traded at a discount of .14% below its net asset value, which is worse than its one-year historical average discount of 2.17%.

Robert W. Wimmell has been running the fund for 10 years and currently receives a manager quality ranking of 20 (0=worst, 99=best). If you desire an average level of risk, then this fund may be an option.

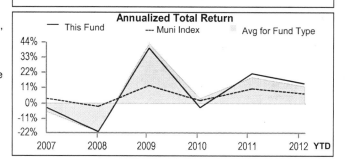

J Hancock Bank & Thrift Oppty Fd (BTO)   C+   Fair

Fund Family: John Hancock Advisers LLC
Fund Type: Financial Services
Inception Date: August 16, 1994

Data Date	Investment Rating	Net Assets ($Mil)	Price	Performance Rating/Pts	Total Return Y-T-D	Risk Rating/Pts
3-12	C+	298.00	17.25	C+ / 6.3	27.47%	B- / 7.5
2011	C-	300.00	13.70	C- / 3.8	7.45%	B- / 7.2
2010	C	418.00	17.22	C / 4.7	29.28%	C+ / 6.0
2009	D-	290.68	14.10	E+ / 0.6	4.44%	C+ / 6.0

Major Rating Factors: Middle of the road best describes J Hancock Bank & Thrift Oppty Fd whose TheStreet.com Investment Rating is currently a C+ (Fair). The fund currently has a performance rating of C+ (Fair) based on an annualized return of 19.82% over the last three years and a total return of 27.47% year to date 2012. Factored into the performance evaluation is an expense ratio of 1.37% (average).

The fund's risk rating is currently B- (Good). It carries a beta of 0.96, meaning that its performance tracks fairly well with that of the overall stock market. Volatility, as measured by both the semi-deviation and a drawdown factor, is considered low. As of March 31, 2012, J Hancock Bank & Thrift Oppty Fd traded at a discount of 8.63% below its net asset value, which is worse than its one-year historical average discount of 9.84%.

Susan Curry has been running the fund for 6 years and currently receives a manager quality ranking of 49 (0=worst, 99=best). If you desire an average level of risk, then this fund may be an option.

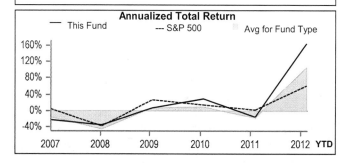

J Hancock Income Securities Tr (JHS)

B   Good

Fund Family: John Hancock Advisers LLC
Fund Type: General - Investment Grade
Inception Date: February 14, 1973

Data Date	Investment Rating	Net Assets ($Mil)	Price	Perfor-mance Rating/Pts	Total Return Y-T-D	Risk Rating/Pts
3-12	B	170.00	15.25	C+ / 6.7	6.30%	B / 8.8
2011	B+	253.60	14.60	B- / 7.4	1.23%	B+ / 9.0
2010	B+	164.00	15.10	B+ / 8.3	21.62%	C+ / 5.6
2009	C+	120.58	13.45	C+ / 6.4	49.48%	C+ / 5.8

Major Rating Factors: J Hancock Income Securities Tr receives a TheStreet.com Investment Rating of B (Good). The fund currently has a performance rating of C+ (Fair) based on an annualized return of 25.41% over the last three years and a total return of 6.30% year to date 2012. Factored into the performance evaluation is an expense ratio of 1.56% (average).

The fund's risk rating is currently B (Good). It carries a beta of 0.69, meaning the fund's expected move will be 6.9% for every 10% move in the market. Volatility, as measured by both the semi-deviation and a drawdown factor, is considered low. As of March 31, 2012, J Hancock Income Securities Tr traded at a premium of 2.28% above its net asset value, which is worse than its one-year historical average premium of 1.34%.

Howard C. Greene has been running the fund for 6 years and currently receives a manager quality ranking of 92 (0=worst, 99=best). If you desire an average level of risk, then this fund may be an option.

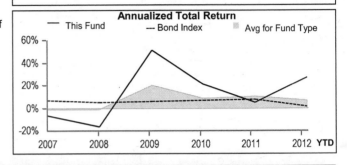

J Hancock Investors Trust (JHI)

B   Good

Fund Family: John Hancock Advisers LLC
Fund Type: General - Investment Grade
Inception Date: January 29, 1971

Data Date	Investment Rating	Net Assets ($Mil)	Price	Perfor-mance Rating/Pts	Total Return Y-T-D	Risk Rating/Pts
3-12	B	164.00	23.01	B / 8.1	6.02%	B- / 7.6
2011	B+	247.30	22.20	B+ / 8.9	0.32%	B- / 7.7
2010	B+	166.00	20.05	B / 8.1	21.55%	C+ / 5.9
2009	C+	119.03	18.27	C+ / 6.9	53.70%	C+ / 6.0

Major Rating Factors: Strong performance is the major factor driving the B (Good) TheStreet.com Investment Rating for J Hancock Investors Trust. The fund currently has a performance rating of B (Good) based on an annualized return of 31.05% over the last three years and a total return of 6.02% year to date 2012. Factored into the performance evaluation is an expense ratio of 1.62% (above average).

The fund's risk rating is currently B- (Good). It carries a beta of 0.46, meaning the fund's expected move will be 4.6% for every 10% move in the market. Volatility, as measured by both the semi-deviation and a drawdown factor, is considered low. As of March 31, 2012, J Hancock Investors Trust traded at a premium of 18.43% above its net asset value, which is worse than its one-year historical average premium of 11.99%.

John F. Iles has been running the fund for 6 years and currently receives a manager quality ranking of 96 (0=worst, 99=best). If you desire only a moderate level of risk and strong performance, then this fund is an excellent option.

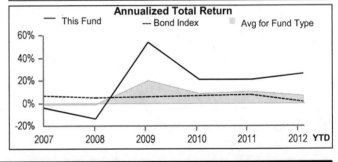

J Hancock Preferred Inc (HPI)

A+   Excellent

Fund Family: John Hancock Advisers LLC
Fund Type: Income
Inception Date: August 22, 2002

Data Date	Investment Rating	Net Assets ($Mil)	Price	Perfor-mance Rating/Pts	Total Return* Y-T-D	Risk Rating/Pts
3-12	A+	536.00	21.78	A- / 9.2	2.72%	B / 8.9
2011	B-	786.50	21.48	B- / 7.5	0.42%	B- / 7.3
2010	B-	510.00	18.68	B- / 7.0	18.39%	C+ / 5.8
2009	D+	422.64	17.10	D+ / 2.9	28.20%	C+ / 5.6

Major Rating Factors:
Exceptional performance is the major factor driving the A+ (Excellent) TheStreet.com Investment Rating for J Hancock Preferred Inc. The fund currently has a performance rating of A- (Excellent) based on an annualized return of 37.86% over the last three years and a total return of 2.72% year to date 2012. Factored into the performance evaluation is an expense ratio of 1.74% (above average).

The fund's risk rating is currently B (Good). It carries a beta of 0.38, meaning the fund's expected move will be 3.8% for every 10% move in the market. Volatility, as measured by both the semi-deviation and a drawdown factor, is considered low. As of March 31, 2012, J Hancock Preferred Inc traded at a premium of 1.82% above its net asset value, which is better than its one-year historical average premium of 2.00%.

Gregory K. Phelps has been running the fund for 10 years and currently receives a manager quality ranking of 96 (0=worst, 99=best). If you desire only a moderate level of risk and strong performance, then this fund is an excellent option.

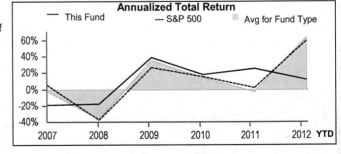

J Hancock Preferred Income II (HPF)

A+   Excellent

Fund Family: John Hancock Advisers LLC
Fund Type: Income
Inception Date: November 25, 2002

Data Date	Investment Rating	Net Assets ($Mil)	Price	Perfor-mance Rating/Pts		Total Return Y-T-D	Risk Rating/Pts	
3-12	A+	438.00	21.85	A	/ 9.3	6.07%	B	/ 8.8
2011	B	644.00	20.87	B	/ 7.8	0.34%	B-	/ 7.9
2010	B	414.00	18.59	B-	/ 7.1	19.23%	C+	/ 5.9
2009	C-	343.55	17.03	C-	/ 3.1	33.74%	C+	/ 5.7

Major Rating Factors:
Exceptional performance is the major factor driving the A+ (Excellent) TheStreet.com Investment Rating for J Hancock Preferred Income II. The fund currently has a performance rating of A (Excellent) based on an annualized return of 37.80% over the last three years and a total return of 6.07% year to date 2012. Factored into the performance evaluation is an expense ratio of 1.72% (above average).

The fund's risk rating is currently B (Good). It carries a beta of 0.54, meaning the fund's expected move will be 5.4% for every 10% move in the market. Volatility, as measured by both the semi-deviation and a drawdown factor, is considered low. As of March 31, 2012, J Hancock Preferred Income II traded at a premium of 2.53% above its net asset value, which is worse than its one-year historical average premium of .07%.

Gregory K. Phelps has been running the fund for 10 years and currently receives a manager quality ranking of 95 (0=worst, 99=best). If you desire only a moderate level of risk and strong performance, then this fund is an excellent option.

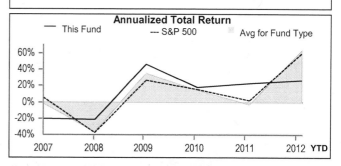

J Hancock Preferred Income III (HPS)

A+   Excellent

Fund Family: John Hancock Advisers LLC
Fund Type: Income
Inception Date: June 19, 2003

Data Date	Investment Rating	Net Assets ($Mil)	Price	Perfor-mance Rating/Pts		Total Return Y-T-D	Risk Rating/Pts	
3-12	A+	558.00	17.80	A-	/ 9.0	5.57%	B	/ 8.8
2011	B-	819.80	17.07	B-	/ 7.4	1.52%	B-	/ 7.6
2010	C-	530.00	15.99	C	/ 4.8	15.17%	C-	/ 4.2
2009	D+	441.56	15.09	C-	/ 3.8	43.13%	C	/ 4.7

Major Rating Factors:
Exceptional performance is the major factor driving the A+ (Excellent) TheStreet.com Investment Rating for J Hancock Preferred Income III. The fund currently has a performance rating of A- (Excellent) based on an annualized return of 36.79% over the last three years and a total return of 5.57% year to date 2012. Factored into the performance evaluation is an expense ratio of 1.72% (above average).

The fund's risk rating is currently B (Good). It carries a beta of 0.60, meaning the fund's expected move will be 6.0% for every 10% move in the market. Volatility, as measured by both the semi-deviation and a drawdown factor, is considered low. As of March 31, 2012, J Hancock Preferred Income III traded at a discount of 3.31% below its net asset value, which is better than its one-year historical average discount of 2.71%.

Gregory K. Phelps has been running the fund for 9 years and currently receives a manager quality ranking of 94 (0=worst, 99=best). If you desire only a moderate level of risk and strong performance, then this fund is an excellent option.

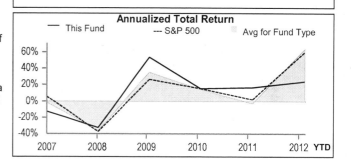

J Hancock Tax Adv Glb Shlr Yield (HTY)

C+   Fair

Fund Family: John Hancock Advisers LLC
Fund Type: Global
Inception Date: September 26, 2007

Data Date	Investment Rating	Net Assets ($Mil)	Price	Perfor-mance Rating/Pts		Total Return Y-T-D	Risk Rating/Pts	
3-12	C+	115.00	13.07	C+	/ 6.3	8.65%	B	/ 8.3
2011	B-	115.30	12.34	C+	/ 6.7	2.27%	B	/ 8.0
2010	C+	115.00	12.73	C+	/ 6.1	7.95%	C	/ 5.4
2009	A-	105.82	13.25	B+	/ 8.8	33.81%	C	/ 5.5

Major Rating Factors: Middle of the road best describes J Hancock Tax Adv Glb Shlr Yield whose TheStreet.com Investment Rating is currently a C+ (Fair). The fund currently has a performance rating of C+ (Fair) based on an annualized return of 23.45% over the last three years and a total return of 8.65% year to date 2012. Factored into the performance evaluation is an expense ratio of 1.28% (average).

The fund's risk rating is currently B (Good). It carries a beta of 0.46, meaning the fund's expected move will be 4.6% for every 10% move in the market. Volatility, as measured by both the semi-deviation and a drawdown factor, is considered low. As of March 31, 2012, J Hancock Tax Adv Glb Shlr Yield traded at a premium of 9.10% above its net asset value, which is worse than its one-year historical average premium of 6.21%.

Dennis M. Bein currently receives a manager quality ranking of 91 (0=worst, 99=best). If you desire an average level of risk, then this fund may be an option.

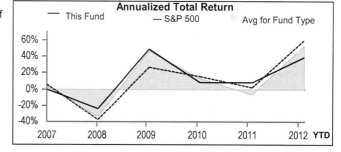

* Denotes ETF Fund

J Hancock Tax Advantage Div Income (HTD)   A+   Excellent

Fund Family: John Hancock Advisers LLC
Fund Type: Income
Inception Date: February 27, 2004

Data Date	Investment Rating	Net Assets ($Mil)	Price	Performance Rating/Pts	Total Return Y-T-D	Risk Rating/Pts
3-12	A+	690.00	17.72	A+ / 9.6	3.90%	B / 8.9
2011	B	1,052.90	17.34	B+ / 8.8	1.27%	B- / 7.2
2010	B-	594.00	14.91	B- / 7.3	24.73%	C / 5.1
2009	C-	447.79	12.92	C- / 3.6	35.72%	C / 5.1

Major Rating Factors:
Exceptional performance is the major factor driving the A+ (Excellent) TheStreet.com Investment Rating for J Hancock Tax Advantage Div Income. The fund currently has a performance rating of A+ (Excellent) based on an annualized return of 43.04% over the last three years and a total return of 3.90% year to date 2012. Factored into the performance evaluation is an expense ratio of 1.56% (average).

The fund's risk rating is currently B (Good). It carries a beta of 0.77, meaning the fund's expected move will be 7.7% for every 10% move in the market. Volatility, as measured by both the semi-deviation and a drawdown factor, is considered low. As of March 31, 2012, J Hancock Tax Advantage Div Income traded at a discount of 7.76% below its net asset value, which is better than its one-year historical average discount of 7.42%.

Dennis M. Bein currently receives a manager quality ranking of 95 (0=worst, 99=best). If you desire only a moderate level of risk and strong performance, then this fund is an excellent option.

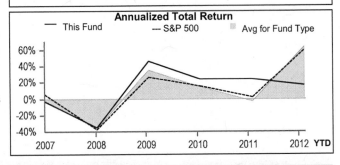

Japan Equity Fund (JEQ)   D+   Weak

Fund Family: Daiwa SB Investments
Fund Type: Foreign
Inception Date: July 24, 1992

Data Date	Investment Rating	Net Assets ($Mil)	Price	Performance Rating/Pts	Total Return Y-T-D	Risk Rating/Pts
3-12	D+	86.90	5.67	D+ / 2.7	13.40%	B- / 7.6
2011	D	82.40	5.00	D / 1.7	2.60%	B- / 7.4
2010	D+	94.00	6.12	D+ / 2.6	17.85%	C+ / 6.3
2009	D	74.32	5.24	E+ / 0.7	2.69%	C+ / 6.4

Major Rating Factors:
Disappointing performance is the major factor driving the D+ (Weak) TheStreet.com Investment Rating for Japan Equity Fund. The fund currently has a performance rating of D+ (Weak) based on an annualized return of 11.51% over the last three years and a total return of 13.40% year to date 2012. Factored into the performance evaluation is an expense ratio of 1.38% (average).

The fund's risk rating is currently B- (Good). It carries a beta of 0.65, meaning the fund's expected move will be 6.5% for every 10% move in the market. Volatility, as measured by both the semi-deviation and a drawdown factor, is considered low. As of March 31, 2012, Japan Equity Fund traded at a discount of 11.13% below its net asset value, which is better than its one-year historical average discount of 9.75%.

Takahiro Ueno has been running the fund for 3 years and currently receives a manager quality ranking of 52 (0=worst, 99=best). This fund offers only a moderate level of risk but investors looking for strong performance are still waiting.

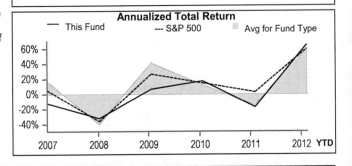

Japan Smaller Cap Fund Inc. (JOF)   D   Weak

Fund Family: Nomura Asset Management USA Inc
Fund Type: Foreign
Inception Date: March 14, 1990

Data Date	Investment Rating	Net Assets ($Mil)	Price	Performance Rating/Pts	Total Return Y-T-D	Risk Rating/Pts
3-12	D	208.21	7.83	D / 2.1	9.05%	B- / 7.6
2011	D	238.30	7.18	D / 1.7	1.95%	B- / 7.5
2010	C+	179.38	8.97	C+ / 6.2	23.86%	C+ / 6.1
2009	D-	190.28	7.32	E+ / 0.6	-2.22%	C+ / 5.8

Major Rating Factors:
Disappointing performance is the major factor driving the D (Weak) TheStreet.com Investment Rating for Japan Smaller Cap Fund Inc.. The fund currently has a performance rating of D (Weak) based on an annualized return of 9.33% over the last three years and a total return of 9.05% year to date 2012. Factored into the performance evaluation is an expense ratio of 1.44% (average).

The fund's risk rating is currently B- (Good). It carries a beta of 0.48, meaning the fund's expected move will be 4.8% for every 10% move in the market. Volatility, as measured by both the semi-deviation and a drawdown factor, is considered low. As of March 31, 2012, Japan Smaller Cap Fund Inc. traded at a discount of 14.43% below its net asset value, which is better than its one-year historical average discount of 11.23%.

Department Investment currently receives a manager quality ranking of 59 (0=worst, 99=best). This fund offers only a moderate level of risk but investors looking for strong performance are still waiting.

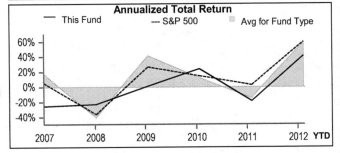

JF China Region Fund (JFC)

| | | **D** | | | **Weak** |

Fund Family: JF International Management Inc
Fund Type: Foreign
Inception Date: July 16, 1992

Data Date	Investment Rating	Net Assets ($Mil)	Price	Performance Rating/Pts	Total Return Y-T-D	Risk Rating/Pts
3-12	D	112.25	12.73	D+ / 2.5	15.52%	C+ / 6.7
2011	D+	112.25	11.02	C- / 3.0	4.36%	C+ / 6.7
2010	D	89.71	15.79	C / 4.9	14.73%	D+ / 2.3
2009	C-	81.70	13.78	C+ / 6.6	49.97%	D+ / 2.6

Major Rating Factors:
Disappointing performance is the major factor driving the D (Weak) TheStreet.com Investment Rating for JF China Region Fund. The fund currently has a performance rating of D+ (Weak) based on an annualized return of 10.84% over the last three years and a total return of 15.52% year to date 2012. Factored into the performance evaluation is an expense ratio of 1.99% (high).

The fund's risk rating is currently C+ (Fair). It carries a beta of 1.16, meaning it is expected to move 11.6% for every 10% move in the market. Volatility, as measured by both the semi-deviation and a drawdown factor, is considered low. As of March 31, 2012, JF China Region Fund traded at a discount of 11.29% below its net asset value, which is worse than its one-year historical average discount of 11.79%.

Howard H. Wang has been running the fund for 7 years and currently receives a manager quality ranking of 20 (0=worst, 99=best). This fund offers only a moderate level of risk but investors looking for strong performance are still waiting.

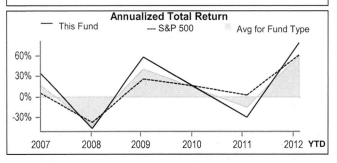

John Hancock Premium Dividend (PDT)

| | | **A+** | | | **Excellent** |

Fund Family: John Hancock Advisers LLC
Fund Type: Income
Inception Date: December 14, 1989

Data Date	Investment Rating	Net Assets ($Mil)	Price	Performance Rating/Pts	Total Return Y-T-D	Risk Rating/Pts
3-12	A+	660.00	13.47	A- / 9.2	1.34%	B+ / 9.1
2011	B+	991.20	13.44	A- / 9.1	-1.56%	B / 8.0
2010	B+	573.00	11.56	B+ / 8.5	25.73%	C / 5.3
2009	C+	385.52	9.96	C+ / 6.3	46.75%	C / 5.3

Major Rating Factors:
Exceptional performance is the major factor driving the A+ (Excellent) TheStreet.com Investment Rating for John Hancock Premium Dividend. The fund currently has a performance rating of A- (Excellent) based on an annualized return of 37.61% over the last three years and a total return of 1.34% year to date 2012. Factored into the performance evaluation is an expense ratio of 1.87% (above average).

The fund's risk rating is currently B+ (Good). It carries a beta of 0.41, meaning the fund's expected move will be 4.1% for every 10% move in the market. Volatility, as measured by both the semi-deviation and a drawdown factor, is considered very low. As of March 31, 2012, John Hancock Premium Dividend traded at a discount of 2.60% below its net asset value, which is worse than its one-year historical average discount of 3.36%.

Gregory K. Phelps has been running the fund for 7 years and currently receives a manager quality ranking of 96 (0=worst, 99=best). If you desire only a moderate level of risk and strong performance, then this fund is an excellent option.

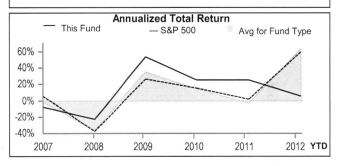

Kayne Anderson Energy Tot Ret (KYE)

| | | **B** | | | **Good** |

Fund Family: KA Fund Advisors LLC
Fund Type: Energy/Natural Resources
Inception Date: June 28, 2005

Data Date	Investment Rating	Net Assets ($Mil)	Price	Performance Rating/Pts	Total Return Y-T-D	Risk Rating/Pts
3-12	B	883.97	27.48	B+ / 8.4	7.74%	B- / 7.4
2011	B	915.06	25.31	B+ / 8.9	3.44%	B- / 7.3
2010	B-	677.68	29.11	B+ / 8.8	35.68%	C- / 3.6
2009	C+	547.78	23.10	B+ / 8.4	124.18%	C- / 3.9

Major Rating Factors: Strong performance is the major factor driving the B (Good) TheStreet.com Investment Rating for Kayne Anderson Energy Tot Ret. The fund currently has a performance rating of B+ (Good) based on an annualized return of 35.25% over the last three years and a total return of 7.74% year to date 2012. Factored into the performance evaluation is an expense ratio of 4.30% (high).

The fund's risk rating is currently B- (Good). It carries a beta of 0.60, meaning the fund's expected move will be 6.0% for every 10% move in the market. Volatility, as measured by both the semi-deviation and a drawdown factor, is considered low. As of March 31, 2012, Kayne Anderson Energy Tot Ret traded at a discount of .18% below its net asset value, which is better than its one-year historical average premium of 2.45%.

John C. Frey has been running the fund for 7 years and currently receives a manager quality ranking of 94 (0=worst, 99=best). If you desire only a moderate level of risk and strong performance, then this fund is an excellent option.

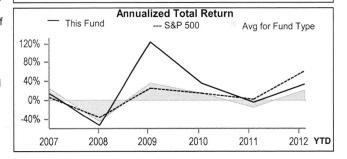

Kayne Anderson Midstream/Energy (KMF)

B+   **Good**

Fund Family: KA Fund Advisors LLC
Fund Type: Income
Inception Date: November 24, 2010

Data Date	Investment Rating	Net Assets ($Mil)	Price	Perfor-mance Rating/Pts	Total Return Y-T-D	Risk Rating/Pts
3-12	B+	562.04	27.42	B / 7.7	11.46%	B / 8.5
2011	C-	0.00	24.60	C- / 3.1	1.71%	B / 8.5

Major Rating Factors: Strong performance is the major factor driving the B+ (Good) TheStreet.com Investment Rating for Kayne Anderson Midstream/Energy. The fund currently has a performance rating of B (Good) based on an annualized return of 0.00% over the last three years and a total return of 11.46% year to date 2012. Factored into the performance evaluation is an expense ratio of 2.90% (high).

The fund's risk rating is currently B (Good). It carries a beta of 0.00, meaning the fund's expected move will be 0.0% for every 10% move in the market. Volatility, as measured by both the semi-deviation and a drawdown factor, is considered low. As of March 31, 2012, Kayne Anderson Midstream/Energy traded at a discount of 5.68% below its net asset value, which is worse than its one-year historical average discount of 6.52%.

Robert V. Sinnott currently receives a manager quality ranking of 76 (0=worst, 99=best). If you desire only a moderate level of risk and strong performance, then this fund is an excellent option.

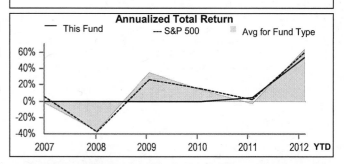

Kayne Anderson MLP Inv Co (KYN)

C+   **Fair**

Fund Family: KA Fund Advisors LLC
Fund Type: Energy/Natural Resources
Inception Date: September 27, 2004

Data Date	Investment Rating	Net Assets ($Mil)	Price	Perfor-mance Rating/Pts	Total Return Y-T-D	Risk Rating/Pts
3-12	C+	2,029.60	31.15	C+ / 6.4	2.83%	B / 8.2
2011	B+	1,825.89	30.37	B+ / 8.6	1.02%	B / 8.1
2010	B-	1,038.28	0.00	B+ / 8.8	35.72%	C- / 4.0
2009	C+	763.65	25.04	B- / 7.0	65.38%	C / 4.8

Major Rating Factors: Middle of the road best describes Kayne Anderson MLP Inv Co whose TheStreet.com Investment Rating is currently a C+ (Fair). The fund currently has a performance rating of C+ (Fair) based on an annualized return of 26.35% over the last three years and a total return of 2.83% year to date 2012. Factored into the performance evaluation is an expense ratio of 4.90% (high).

The fund's risk rating is currently B (Good). It carries a beta of 0.30, meaning the fund's expected move will be 3.0% for every 10% move in the market. Volatility, as measured by both the semi-deviation and a drawdown factor, is considered low. As of March 31, 2012, Kayne Anderson MLP Inv Co traded at a premium of 8.95% above its net asset value, which is worse than its one-year historical average premium of 6.80%.

John C. Frey has been running the fund for 8 years and currently receives a manager quality ranking of 92 (0=worst, 99=best). If you desire an average level of risk, then this fund may be an option.

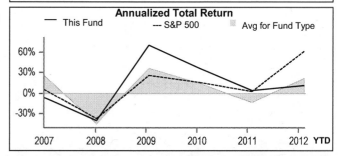

Korea Equity Fund (KEF)

C   **Fair**

Fund Family: Nomura Asset Management USA Inc
Fund Type: Foreign
Inception Date: November 24, 1993

Data Date	Investment Rating	Net Assets ($Mil)	Price	Perfor-mance Rating/Pts	Total Return Y-T-D	Risk Rating/Pts
3-12	C	121.20	9.74	C+ / 6.9	7.27%	C+ / 5.8
2011	C+	103.50	9.08	B / 8.0	0.77%	C+ / 5.8
2010	C-	109.46	12.23	C+ / 5.8	32.22%	C- / 4.0
2009	C-	84.14	9.25	C- / 4.1	55.59%	C / 4.5

Major Rating Factors: Middle of the road best describes Korea Equity Fund whose TheStreet.com Investment Rating is currently a C (Fair). The fund currently has a performance rating of C+ (Fair) based on an annualized return of 28.41% over the last three years and a total return of 7.27% year to date 2012. Factored into the performance evaluation is an expense ratio of 1.90% (above average).

The fund's risk rating is currently C+ (Fair). It carries a beta of 1.03, meaning that its performance tracks fairly well with that of the overall stock market. Volatility, as measured by both the semi-deviation and a drawdown factor, is considered low. As of March 31, 2012, Korea Equity Fund traded at a discount of 8.72% below its net asset value, which is worse than its one-year historical average discount of 8.84%.

Shigeto Kasahara has been running the fund for 7 years and currently receives a manager quality ranking of 87 (0=worst, 99=best). If you desire an average level of risk, then this fund may be an option.

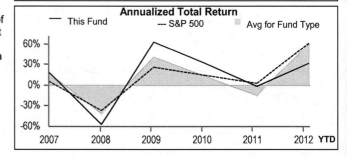

Korea Fund (KF)   C   Fair

Fund Family: RCM Capital Management LLC
Fund Type: Foreign
Inception Date: August 22, 1984

Data Date	Investment Rating	Net Assets ($Mil)	Price	Performance Rating/Pts	Total Return Y-T-D	Risk Rating/Pts
3-12	C	549.09	40.55	C / 5.5	13.43%	C+ / 6.6
2011	D	549.09	35.75	C- / 3.0	-0.06%	C / 5.2
2010	D	393.37	44.11	C- / 3.1	24.08%	C- / 3.7
2009	E	307.21	35.55	D- / 1.4	0.12%	D+ / 2.7

Major Rating Factors: Middle of the road best describes Korea Fund whose TheStreet.com Investment Rating is currently a C (Fair). The fund currently has a performance rating of C (Fair) based on an annualized return of 22.12% over the last three years and a total return of 13.43% year to date 2012. Factored into the performance evaluation is an expense ratio of 1.10% (low).

The fund's risk rating is currently C+ (Fair). It carries a beta of 1.12, meaning it is expected to move 11.2% for every 10% move in the market. Volatility, as measured by both the semi-deviation and a drawdown factor, is considered low. As of March 31, 2012, Korea Fund traded at a discount of 8.13% below its net asset value, which is worse than its one-year historical average discount of 9.33%.

Raymond Chan currently receives a manager quality ranking of 75 (0=worst, 99=best). If you desire an average level of risk, then this fund may be an option.

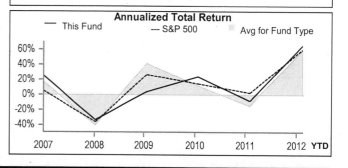

Latin American Discovery Fund (LDF)   C   Fair

Fund Family: Morgan Stanley Investment Mgmt Inc
Fund Type: Foreign
Inception Date: June 23, 1992

Data Date	Investment Rating	Net Assets ($Mil)	Price	Performance Rating/Pts	Total Return Y-T-D	Risk Rating/Pts
3-12	C	167.83	16.34	C+ / 5.9	15.89%	C+ / 6.8
2011	C	125.60	14.10	C / 5.5	3.19%	C+ / 6.9
2010	D+	130.76	19.17	C / 5.4	15.09%	C- / 3.5
2009	C	104.44	17.23	B / 8.1	86.30%	C- / 3.0

Major Rating Factors: Middle of the road best describes Latin American Discovery Fund whose TheStreet.com Investment Rating is currently a C (Fair). The fund currently has a performance rating of C+ (Fair) based on an annualized return of 23.99% over the last three years and a total return of 15.89% year to date 2012. Factored into the performance evaluation is an expense ratio of 1.38% (average).

The fund's risk rating is currently C+ (Fair). It carries a beta of 1.26, meaning it is expected to move 12.6% for every 10% move in the market. Volatility, as measured by both the semi-deviation and a drawdown factor, is considered low. As of March 31, 2012, Latin American Discovery Fund traded at a discount of 7.53% below its net asset value, which is worse than its one-year historical average discount of 8.07%.

Ana Cristina Piedrahita has been running the fund for 10 years and currently receives a manager quality ranking of 72 (0=worst, 99=best). If you desire an average level of risk, then this fund may be an option.

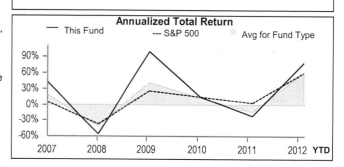

Lazard Global Total Return&Income (LGI)   C+   Fair

Fund Family: Lazard Asset Management LLC
Fund Type: Global
Inception Date: April 27, 2004

Data Date	Investment Rating	Net Assets ($Mil)	Price	Performance Rating/Pts	Total Return Y-T-D	Risk Rating/Pts
3-12	C+	161.65	14.96	C+ / 5.7	13.58%	B- / 7.8
2011	C-	148.80	13.39	C- / 3.8	0.90%	B- / 7.3
2010	D	139.30	15.06	D / 2.0	8.90%	C / 5.0
2009	D+	139.04	14.89	D+ / 2.7	29.89%	C+ / 5.8

Major Rating Factors: Middle of the road best describes Lazard Global Total Return&Income whose TheStreet.com Investment Rating is currently a C+ (Fair). The fund currently has a performance rating of C+ (Fair) based on an annualized return of 21.54% over the last three years and a total return of 13.58% year to date 2012. Factored into the performance evaluation is an expense ratio of 1.59% (above average).

The fund's risk rating is currently B- (Good). It carries a beta of 0.91, meaning that its performance tracks fairly well with that of the overall stock market. Volatility, as measured by both the semi-deviation and a drawdown factor, is considered low. As of March 31, 2012, Lazard Global Total Return&Income traded at a discount of 12.26% below its net asset value, which is better than its one-year historical average discount of 11.62%.

Ronald S. Temple has been running the fund for 1 year and currently receives a manager quality ranking of 81 (0=worst, 99=best). If you desire an average level of risk, then this fund may be an option.

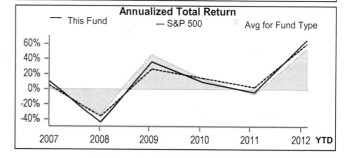

Lazard World Div&Inc Fd (LOR)

C+   Fair

Fund Family: Lazard Asset Management LLC
Fund Type: Global
Inception Date: June 27, 2005

Data Date	Investment Rating	Net Assets ($Mil)	Price	Performance Rating/Pts	Total Return Y-T-D	Risk Rating/Pts
3-12	C+	95.62	12.20	C+ / 6.9	14.23%	B- / 7.8
2011	C	84.30	10.86	C / 4.8	0.00%	B- / 7.6
2010	C-	78.78	12.85	C- / 4.1	23.81%	C / 4.9
2009	D+	72.22	11.17	D+ / 2.6	36.31%	C / 5.4

Major Rating Factors: Middle of the road best describes Lazard World Div&Inc Fd whose TheStreet.com Investment Rating is currently a C+ (Fair). The fund currently has a performance rating of C+ (Fair) based on an annualized return of 27.27% over the last three years and a total return of 14.23% year to date 2012. Factored into the performance evaluation is an expense ratio of 2.11% (high).

The fund's risk rating is currently B- (Good). It carries a beta of 0.96, meaning that its performance tracks fairly well with that of the overall stock market. Volatility, as measured by both the semi-deviation and a drawdown factor, is considered low. As of March 31, 2012, Lazard World Div&Inc Fd traded at a discount of 10.62% below its net asset value, which is better than its one-year historical average discount of 8.24%.

Andrew D. Lacey currently receives a manager quality ranking of 86 (0=worst, 99=best). If you desire an average level of risk, then this fund may be an option.

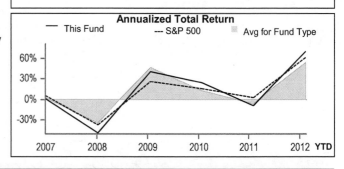

Liberty All-Star Equity Fund (USA)

C+   Fair

Fund Family: ALPS Advisors Inc
Fund Type: Income
Inception Date: October 24, 1986

Data Date	Investment Rating	Net Assets ($Mil)	Price	Performance Rating/Pts	Total Return Y-T-D	Risk Rating/Pts
3-12	C+	1,039.00	4.93	C+ / 6.9	18.76%	B- / 7.5
2011	C-	911.80	4.22	C / 4.9	4.27%	B- / 7.0
2010	C-	840.00	4.93	C / 4.6	21.80%	C / 5.4
2009	D	796.41	4.33	D- / 1.5	31.08%	C / 5.4

Major Rating Factors: Middle of the road best describes Liberty All-Star Equity Fund whose TheStreet.com Investment Rating is currently a C+ (Fair). The fund currently has a performance rating of C+ (Fair) based on an annualized return of 25.34% over the last three years and a total return of 18.76% year to date 2012. Factored into the performance evaluation is an expense ratio of 1.08% (low).

The fund's risk rating is currently B- (Good). It carries a beta of 1.32, meaning it is expected to move 13.2% for every 10% move in the market. Volatility, as measured by both the semi-deviation and a drawdown factor, is considered low. As of March 31, 2012, Liberty All-Star Equity Fund traded at a discount of 12.74% below its net asset value, which is better than its one-year historical average discount of 11.98%.

David A. Katz currently receives a manager quality ranking of 27 (0=worst, 99=best). If you desire an average level of risk, then this fund may be an option.

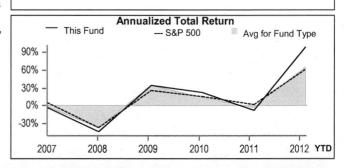

Liberty All-Star Growth Fund (ASG)

C+   Fair

Fund Family: ALPS Advisors Inc
Fund Type: Income
Inception Date: March 6, 1986

Data Date	Investment Rating	Net Assets ($Mil)	Price	Performance Rating/Pts	Total Return Y-T-D	Risk Rating/Pts
3-12	C+	137.00	4.35	B / 7.7	16.04%	B- / 7.0
2011	C	127.60	3.81	C+ / 6.3	2.36%	C+ / 6.5
2010	C	113.00	4.25	C+ / 5.6	34.99%	C / 5.0
2009	D+	102.47	3.36	D+ / 2.9	30.11%	C+ / 5.7

Major Rating Factors: Strong performance is the major factor driving the C+ (Fair) TheStreet.com Investment Rating for Liberty All-Star Growth Fund. The fund currently has a performance rating of B (Good) based on an annualized return of 28.53% over the last three years and a total return of 16.04% year to date 2012. Factored into the performance evaluation is an expense ratio of 1.79% (above average).

The fund's risk rating is currently B- (Good). It carries a beta of 1.06, meaning that its performance tracks fairly well with that of the overall stock market. Volatility, as measured by both the semi-deviation and a drawdown factor, is considered low. As of March 31, 2012, Liberty All-Star Growth Fund traded at a discount of 9.19% below its net asset value, which is better than its one-year historical average discount of 8.29%.

Matthew A. Weatherbie has been running the fund for 26 years and currently receives a manager quality ranking of 69 (0=worst, 99=best). If you desire only a moderate level of risk and strong performance, then this fund is an excellent option.

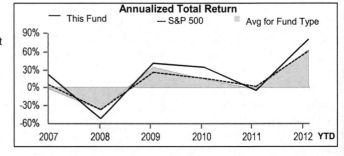

LMP Capital and Income Fund Inc (SCD)　　　　　B+　　　Good

Fund Family: Legg Mason Partners Fund Advisor LL
Fund Type: Growth and Income
Inception Date: February 24, 2004

Major Rating Factors: Strong performance is the major factor driving the B+ (Good) TheStreet.com Investment Rating for LMP Capital and Income Fund Inc. The fund currently has a performance rating of B (Good) based on an annualized return of 30.01% over the last three years and a total return of 10.60% year to date 2012. Factored into the performance evaluation is an expense ratio of 1.53% (average).

The fund's risk rating is currently B (Good). It carries a beta of 0.87, meaning the fund's expected move will be 8.7% for every 10% move in the market. Volatility, as measured by both the semi-deviation and a drawdown factor, is considered low. As of March 31, 2012, LMP Capital and Income Fund Inc traded at a discount of 4.56% below its net asset value, which is worse than its one-year historical average discount of 7.20%.

Harry D. Cohen has been running the fund for 3 years and currently receives a manager quality ranking of 85 (0=worst, 99=best). If you desire only a moderate level of risk and strong performance, then this fund is an excellent option.

Data Date	Investment Rating	Net Assets ($Mil)	Price	Performance Rating/Pts	Total Return Y-T-D	Risk Rating/Pts
3-12	B+	266.27	13.39	B / 8.1	10.60%	B / 8.3
2011	B-	268.30	12.36	C+ / 6.9	0.32%	B / 8.1
2010	C-	372.89	12.45	C- / 4.1	26.27%	C / 4.9
2009	D	325.30	10.35	D / 2.0	33.94%	C+ / 5.6

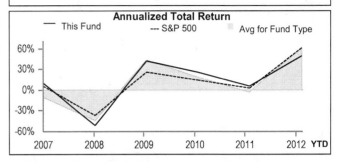

Annualized Total Return
— This Fund　--- S&P 500　Avg for Fund Type

LMP Corporate Loan Fund Inc (TLI)　　　　　　B-　　　Good

Fund Family: Legg Mason Partners Fund Advisor LL
Fund Type: Loan Participation
Inception Date: November 19, 1998

Major Rating Factors: LMP Corporate Loan Fund Inc receives a TheStreet.com Investment Rating of B- (Good). The fund currently has a performance rating of C+ (Fair) based on an annualized return of 26.11% over the last three years and a total return of 8.83% year to date 2012. Factored into the performance evaluation is an expense ratio of 1.92% (above average).

The fund's risk rating is currently B (Good). It carries a beta of -17.67, meaning the fund's expected move will be -176.7% for every 10% move in the market. Volatility, as measured by both the semi-deviation and a drawdown factor, is considered low. As of March 31, 2012, LMP Corporate Loan Fund Inc traded at a discount of 5.56% below its net asset value, which is better than its one-year historical average discount of 4.65%.

Jerry Pascucci currently receives a manager quality ranking of 97 (0=worst, 99=best). If you desire an average level of risk, then this fund may be an option.

Data Date	Investment Rating	Net Assets ($Mil)	Price	Performance Rating/Pts	Total Return Y-T-D	Risk Rating/Pts
3-12	B-	116.00	11.90	C+ / 6.7	8.83%	B / 8.6
2011	B+	120.00	11.11	B / 8.2	4.68%	B / 8.6
2010	C+	119.00	11.73	B- / 7.2	22.84%	C / 4.7
2009	C	111.29	10.04	C / 4.5	68.54%	C+ / 5.7

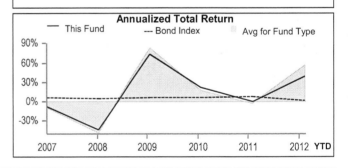

Annualized Total Return
— This Fund　--- Bond Index　Avg for Fund Type

LMP Real Estate Income Fund Inc (RIT)　　　　　A　　　Excellent

Fund Family: Legg Mason Partners Fund Advisor LL
Fund Type: Growth and Income
Inception Date: July 31, 2002

Major Rating Factors:
Exceptional performance is the major factor driving the A (Excellent) TheStreet.com Investment Rating for LMP Real Estate Income Fund Inc. The fund currently has a performance rating of A+ (Excellent) based on an annualized return of 50.88% over the last three years and a total return of 13.55% year to date 2012. Factored into the performance evaluation is an expense ratio of 1.82% (above average).

The fund's risk rating is currently B- (Good). It carries a beta of 1.45, meaning it is expected to move 14.5% for every 10% move in the market. Volatility, as measured by both the semi-deviation and a drawdown factor, is considered low. As of March 31, 2012, LMP Real Estate Income Fund Inc traded at a discount of 10.65% below its net asset value, which is worse than its one-year historical average discount of 10.77%.

Matthew A. Troxell currently receives a manager quality ranking of 91 (0=worst, 99=best). If you desire only a moderate level of risk and strong performance, then this fund is an excellent option.

Data Date	Investment Rating	Net Assets ($Mil)	Price	Performance Rating/Pts	Total Return Y-T-D	Risk Rating/Pts
3-12	A	122.00	10.32	A+ / 9.8	13.55%	B- / 7.8
2011	B	122.30	9.25	A- / 9.0	1.08%	C+ / 6.7
2010	C+	102.69	10.10	B / 8.1	35.86%	C- / 3.5
2009	E+	69.43	8.05	D / 2.1	89.96%	D+ / 2.5

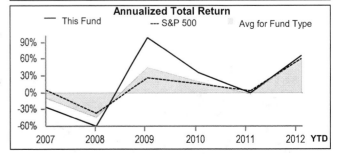

Annualized Total Return
— This Fund　--- S&P 500　Avg for Fund Type

MA Health & Education Tax-Exempt T (MHE)   A-   Excellent

Fund Family: BlackRock Inc
Fund Type: Municipal - Single State
Inception Date: July 23, 1993

Data Date	Investment Rating	Net Assets ($Mil)	Price	Perfor-mance Rating/Pts	Total Return Y-T-D	Risk Rating/Pts
3-12	A-	30.61	14.35	B / 8.2	-0.24%	B / 8.9
2011	A+	32.00	14.60	A+ / 9.7	1.71%	B+ / 9.0
2010	A-	31.74	13.29	B+ / 8.5	18.59%	C+ / 6.3
2009	B-	28.58	12.00	C+ / 6.3	43.06%	B- / 7.0

Major Rating Factors:
Strong performance is the major factor driving the A- (Excellent) TheStreet.com Investment Rating for MA Health & Education Tax-Exempt T. The fund currently has a performance rating of B (Good) based on an annualized return of 19.48% over the last three years and a total return of -0.24% year to date 2012. Factored into the performance evaluation is an expense ratio of 1.39% (average).

The fund's risk rating is currently B (Good). It carries a beta of 1.18, meaning it is expected to move 11.8% for every 10% move in the market. Volatility, as measured by both the semi-deviation and a drawdown factor, is considered low. As of March 31, 2012, MA Health & Education Tax-Exempt T traded at a premium of 3.16% above its net asset value, which is better than its one-year historical average premium of 5.17%.

Thomas M. Metzold currently receives a manager quality ranking of 85 (0=worst, 99=best). If you desire only a moderate level of risk and strong performance, then this fund is an excellent option.

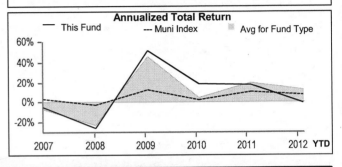
Annualized Total Return — This Fund / Muni Index / Avg for Fund Type

Macquarie Global Infr Total Return (MGU)   B   Good

Fund Family: Macquarie Capital Investment Mgmt L
Fund Type: Global
Inception Date: August 26, 2005

Data Date	Investment Rating	Net Assets ($Mil)	Price	Perfor-mance Rating/Pts	Total Return Y-T-D	Risk Rating/Pts
3-12	B	327.99	18.45	B / 7.6	10.01%	B / 8.0
2011	C	330.80	16.99	C+ / 5.6	0.82%	B- / 7.3
2010	D-	280.77	17.28	D- / 1.2	15.34%	C / 5.0
2009	D-	266.79	15.85	D / 1.6	31.62%	C / 5.1

Major Rating Factors: Strong performance is the major factor driving the B (Good) TheStreet.com Investment Rating for Macquarie Global Infr Total Return. The fund currently has a performance rating of B (Good) based on an annualized return of 28.35% over the last three years and a total return of 10.01% year to date 2012. Factored into the performance evaluation is an expense ratio of 2.11% (high).

The fund's risk rating is currently B (Good). It carries a beta of 1.00, meaning that its performance tracks fairly well with that of the overall stock market. Volatility, as measured by both the semi-deviation and a drawdown factor, is considered low. As of March 31, 2012, Macquarie Global Infr Total Return traded at a discount of 11.76% below its net asset value, which is worse than its one-year historical average discount of 12.72%.

Andrew Maple-Brown has been running the fund for 3 years and currently receives a manager quality ranking of 87 (0=worst, 99=best). If you desire only a moderate level of risk and strong performance, then this fund is an excellent option.

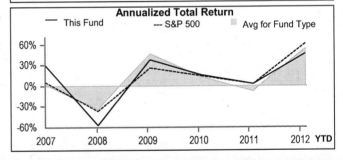
Annualized Total Return — This Fund / S&P 500 / Avg for Fund Type

Macquarie/FTG Infr/ Util Div&Inc (MFD)   A-   Excellent

Fund Family: First Trust Advisors LP
Fund Type: Global
Inception Date: March 25, 2004

Data Date	Investment Rating	Net Assets ($Mil)	Price	Perfor-mance Rating/Pts	Total Return Y-T-D	Risk Rating/Pts
3-12	A-	129.06	16.00	B+ / 8.9	15.14%	B / 8.2
2011	C+	130.30	14.21	C+ / 6.7	3.45%	B- / 7.2
2010	D-	117.04	14.48	D / 1.8	23.62%	C- / 3.6
2009	E+	111.30	12.37	D- / 1.3	26.14%	C- / 4.0

Major Rating Factors:
Strong performance is the major factor driving the A- (Excellent) TheStreet.com Investment Rating for Macquarie/FTG Infr/ Util Div&Inc. The fund currently has a performance rating of B+ (Good) based on an annualized return of 34.83% over the last three years and a total return of 15.14% year to date 2012. Factored into the performance evaluation is an expense ratio of 2.24% (high).

The fund's risk rating is currently B (Good). It carries a beta of 0.88, meaning the fund's expected move will be 8.8% for every 10% move in the market. Volatility, as measured by both the semi-deviation and a drawdown factor, is considered low. As of March 31, 2012, Macquarie/FTG Infr/ Util Div&Inc traded at a discount of .62% below its net asset value, which is worse than its one-year historical average discount of 5.14%.

Justin Lannen has been running the fund for 8 years and currently receives a manager quality ranking of 92 (0=worst, 99=best). If you desire only a moderate level of risk and strong performance, then this fund is an excellent option.

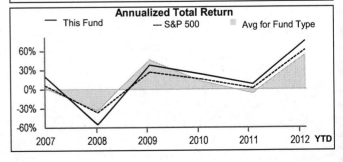
Annualized Total Return — This Fund / S&P 500 / Avg for Fund Type

Madison Strategic Sector Premium (MSP)   C+   Fair

Fund Family: Madison Asset Management LLC
Fund Type: Income
Inception Date: April 28, 2005

Data Date	Investment Rating	Net Assets ($Mil)	Price	Perfor-mance Rating/Pts	Total Return Y-T-D	Risk Rating/Pts
3-12	C+	73.21	11.81	C / 5.4	13.44%	B / 8.2
2011	C+	73.20	10.64	C / 5.2	4.04%	B- / 7.9
2010	C+	80.18	12.82	C+ / 6.3	14.04%	C / 5.4
2009	C-	69.89	12.23	C- / 3.2	49.47%	C+ / 5.8

Major Rating Factors: Middle of the road best describes Madison Strategic Sector Premium whose TheStreet.com Investment Rating is currently a C+ (Fair). The fund currently has a performance rating of C (Fair) based on an annualized return of 21.19% over the last three years and a total return of 13.44% year to date 2012. Factored into the performance evaluation is an expense ratio of 0.98% (low).

The fund's risk rating is currently B (Good). It carries a beta of 0.93, meaning that its performance tracks fairly well with that of the overall stock market. Volatility, as measured by both the semi-deviation and a drawdown factor, is considered low. As of March 31, 2012, Madison Strategic Sector Premium traded at a discount of 12.78% below its net asset value, which is better than its one-year historical average discount of 12.12%.

Frank E. Burgess has been running the fund for 7 years and currently receives a manager quality ranking of 60 (0=worst, 99=best). If you desire an average level of risk, then this fund may be an option.

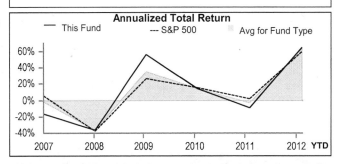

Madison/Clym Cvd Call & Eq Strtg (MCN)   C   Fair

Fund Family: Guggenheim Funds Investment Advisor
Fund Type: Income
Inception Date: July 28, 2004

Data Date	Investment Rating	Net Assets ($Mil)	Price	Perfor-mance Rating/Pts	Total Return Y-T-D	Risk Rating/Pts
3-12	C	166.76	8.27	C / 5.4	13.17%	B- / 7.8
2011	C	167.00	7.47	C / 4.7	1.34%	B- / 7.5
2010	C	185.39	9.05	C+ / 5.6	10.55%	C / 4.9
2009	C-	162.11	8.90	C- / 3.8	55.38%	C / 5.3

Major Rating Factors: Middle of the road best describes Madison/Clym Cvd Call & Eq Strtg whose TheStreet.com Investment Rating is currently a C (Fair). The fund currently has a performance rating of C (Fair) based on an annualized return of 20.91% over the last three years and a total return of 13.17% year to date 2012. Factored into the performance evaluation is an expense ratio of 1.36% (average).

The fund's risk rating is currently B- (Good). It carries a beta of 1.07, meaning that its performance tracks fairly well with that of the overall stock market. Volatility, as measured by both the semi-deviation and a drawdown factor, is considered low. As of March 31, 2012, Madison/Clym Cvd Call & Eq Strtg traded at a discount of 11.17% below its net asset value, which is worse than its one-year historical average discount of 11.35%.

Frank E. Burgess currently receives a manager quality ranking of 37 (0=worst, 99=best). If you desire an average level of risk, then this fund may be an option.

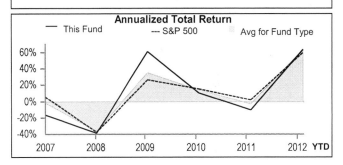

Malaysia Fund (MAY)   B+   Good

Fund Family: Morgan Stanley Investment Mgmt Inc
Fund Type: Foreign
Inception Date: May 8, 1987

Data Date	Investment Rating	Net Assets ($Mil)	Price	Perfor-mance Rating/Pts	Total Return Y-T-D	Risk Rating/Pts
3-12	B+	109.69	10.26	A- / 9.2	13.62%	B- / 7.6
2011	B	71.40	9.03	B / 8.0	1.11%	B- / 7.7
2010	B+	90.12	11.25	A- / 9.0	58.72%	C / 4.7
2009	C+	70.55	7.55	C+ / 6.4	40.82%	C+ / 6.2

Major Rating Factors:
Exceptional performance is the major factor driving the B+ (Good) TheStreet.com Investment Rating for Malaysia Fund. The fund currently has a performance rating of A- (Excellent) based on an annualized return of 37.36% over the last three years and a total return of 13.62% year to date 2012. Factored into the performance evaluation is an expense ratio of 1.11% (low).

The fund's risk rating is currently B- (Good). It carries a beta of 0.75, meaning the fund's expected move will be 7.5% for every 10% move in the market. Volatility, as measured by both the semi-deviation and a drawdown factor, is considered low. As of March 31, 2012, Malaysia Fund traded at a discount of 3.21% below its net asset value, which is worse than its one-year historical average discount of 8.40%.

James K.K. Cheng has been running the fund for 4 years and currently receives a manager quality ranking of 95 (0=worst, 99=best). If you desire only a moderate level of risk and strong performance, then this fund is an excellent option.

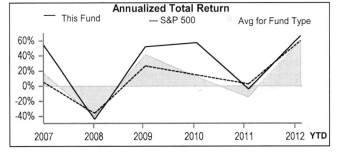

Managed Duration Investment Grd Mu (MZF)

A+   Excellent

Fund Family: Cutwater Asset Management Corp
Fund Type: Municipal - National
Inception Date: August 26, 2003

Data Date	Investment Rating	Net Assets ($Mil)	Price	Performance Rating/Pts	Total Return Y-T-D	Risk Rating/Pts
3-12	A+	94.91	15.32	A / 9.3	4.52%	B / 8.6
2011	A+	98.90	14.90	A+ / 9.8	0.00%	B / 8.6
2010	C+	97.19	13.11	C+ / 6.9	6.65%	C+ / 6.1
2009	A-	101.02	13.19	B / 8.0	61.84%	C+ / 6.2

Major Rating Factors:
Exceptional performance is the major factor driving the A+ (Excellent) TheStreet.com Investment Rating for Managed Duration Investment Grd Mu. The fund currently has a performance rating of A (Excellent) based on an annualized return of 23.19% over the last three years and a total return of 4.52% year to date 2012. Factored into the performance evaluation is an expense ratio of 1.46% (average).

The fund's risk rating is currently B (Good). It carries a beta of 2.39, meaning it is expected to move 23.9% for every 10% move in the market. Volatility, as measured by both the semi-deviation and a drawdown factor, is considered low. As of March 31, 2012, Managed Duration Investment Grd Mu traded at a premium of 2.13% above its net asset value, which is worse than its one-year historical average discount of .38%.

Clifford D. Corso has been running the fund for 9 years and currently receives a manager quality ranking of 68 (0=worst, 99=best). If you desire only a moderate level of risk and strong performance, then this fund is an excellent option.

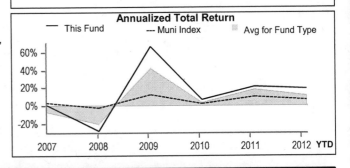

Managed High Yield Plus Fund (HYF)

A-   Excellent

Fund Family: UBS Global Asset Management
Fund Type: Global
Inception Date: June 24, 1998

Data Date	Investment Rating	Net Assets ($Mil)	Price	Performance Rating/Pts	Total Return Y-T-D	Risk Rating/Pts
3-12	A-	139.53	2.19	A / 9.3	5.23%	B- / 7.6
2011	C+	126.90	2.13	B+ / 8.3	0.94%	C+ / 6.0
2010	D-	127.31	2.20	D+ / 2.7	23.34%	D+ / 2.3
2009	E+	103.92	1.99	D / 1.7	67.25%	C- / 3.3

Major Rating Factors:
Exceptional performance is the major factor driving the A- (Excellent) TheStreet.com Investment Rating for Managed High Yield Plus Fund. The fund currently has a performance rating of A (Excellent) based on an annualized return of 40.56% over the last three years and a total return of 5.23% year to date 2012. Factored into the performance evaluation is an expense ratio of 1.59% (above average).

The fund's risk rating is currently B- (Good). It carries a beta of 0.85, meaning the fund's expected move will be 8.5% for every 10% move in the market. Volatility, as measured by both the semi-deviation and a drawdown factor, is considered low. As of March 31, 2012, Managed High Yield Plus Fund traded at a premium of 2.34% above its net asset value, which is better than its one-year historical average premium of 5.68%.

Matthew A. Iannucci has been running the fund for 3 years and currently receives a manager quality ranking of 98 (0=worst, 99=best). If you desire only a moderate level of risk and strong performance, then this fund is an excellent option.

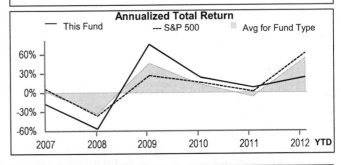

Mexico Equity & Income Fund (MXE)

B+   Good

Fund Family: Pichardo Asset Management SA de CV
Fund Type: Foreign
Inception Date: August 14, 1990

Data Date	Investment Rating	Net Assets ($Mil)	Price	Performance Rating/Pts	Total Return Y-T-D	Risk Rating/Pts
3-12	B+	89.18	11.40	B+ / 8.6	14.57%	B / 8.0
2011	D+	89.18	9.95	C / 4.7	0.20%	C+ / 5.7
2010	C-	74.61	11.33	B+ / 8.5	48.41%	D- / 1.5
2009	D-	61.43	7.65	C- / 3.4	15.91%	D+ / 2.5

Major Rating Factors: Strong performance is the major factor driving the B+ (Good) TheStreet.com Investment Rating for Mexico Equity & Income Fund. The fund currently has a performance rating of B+ (Good) based on an annualized return of 34.45% over the last three years and a total return of 14.57% year to date 2012. Factored into the performance evaluation is an expense ratio of 1.51% (average).

The fund's risk rating is currently B (Good). It carries a beta of 0.85, meaning the fund's expected move will be 8.5% for every 10% move in the market. Volatility, as measured by both the semi-deviation and a drawdown factor, is considered low. As of March 31, 2012, Mexico Equity & Income Fund traded at a discount of 12.58% below its net asset value, which is better than its one-year historical average discount of 10.55%.

Maria-Eugenia Pichardo has been running the fund for 22 years and currently receives a manager quality ranking of 94 (0=worst, 99=best). If you desire only a moderate level of risk and strong performance, then this fund is an excellent option.

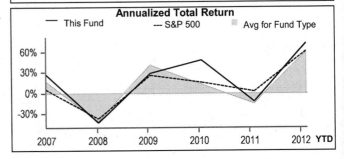

Mexico Fund (MXF)

B+   **Good**

Fund Family: Impulsora Del Fondo Mexico SA De CV
Fund Type: Foreign
Inception Date: June 3, 1981

Major Rating Factors: Strong performance is the major factor driving the B+ (Good) TheStreet.com Investment Rating for Mexico Fund. The fund currently has a performance rating of B+ (Good) based on an annualized return of 34.95% over the last three years and a total return of 15.56% year to date 2012. Factored into the performance evaluation is an expense ratio of 1.42% (average).

The fund's risk rating is currently B- (Good). It carries a beta of 1.00, meaning that its performance tracks fairly well with that of the overall stock market. Volatility, as measured by both the semi-deviation and a drawdown factor, is considered low. As of March 31, 2012, Mexico Fund traded at a discount of 8.91% below its net asset value, which is better than its one-year historical average discount of 8.72%.

José Luis Gómez Pimienta currently receives a manager quality ranking of 92 (0=worst, 99=best). If you desire only a moderate level of risk and strong performance, then this fund is an excellent option.

Data Date	Investment Rating	Net Assets ($Mil)	Price	Performance Rating/Pts	Total Return Y-T-D	Risk Rating/Pts
3-12	B+	339.05	25.25	B+ / 8.8	15.56%	B- / 7.7
2011	C+	318.50	21.85	C+ / 6.9	1.83%	B- / 7.3
2010	B-	383.24	28.27	B+ / 8.7	42.37%	C- / 3.8
2009	D+	282.00	21.91	C / 4.3	52.65%	C / 4.3

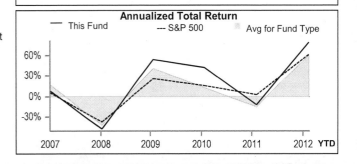

Annualized Total Return

MFS CA Muni (CCA)

B-   **Good**

Fund Family: MFS Investment Management
Fund Type: Municipal - Single State
Inception Date: October 26, 1999

Major Rating Factors: MFS CA Muni receives a TheStreet.com Investment Rating of B- (Good). The fund currently has a performance rating of C+ (Fair) based on an annualized return of 15.56% over the last three years and a total return of 3.55% year to date 2012. Factored into the performance evaluation is an expense ratio of 1.49% (average).

The fund's risk rating is currently B (Good). It carries a beta of 2.86, meaning it is expected to move 28.6% for every 10% move in the market. Volatility, as measured by both the semi-deviation and a drawdown factor, is considered low. As of March 31, 2012, MFS CA Muni traded at a discount of 2.68% below its net asset value, which is better than its one-year historical average premium of .32%.

Geoffrey L. Schechter has been running the fund for 5 years and currently receives a manager quality ranking of 19 (0=worst, 99=best). If you desire an average level of risk, then this fund may be an option.

Data Date	Investment Rating	Net Assets ($Mil)	Price	Performance Rating/Pts	Total Return Y-T-D	Risk Rating/Pts
3-12	B-	29.85	11.25	C+ / 6.8	3.55%	B / 8.2
2011	B+	31.00	11.04	B+ / 8.7	1.90%	B / 8.3
2010	D	30.90	10.16	D / 1.6	-1.39%	C+ / 5.6
2009	C-	29.32	11.09	C / 4.6	53.70%	C / 5.5

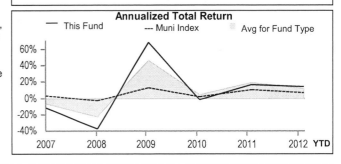

Annualized Total Return

MFS Charter Income Trust (MCR)

C   **Fair**

Fund Family: MFS Investment Management
Fund Type: General - Investment Grade
Inception Date: July 20, 1989

Major Rating Factors: Middle of the road best describes MFS Charter Income Trust whose TheStreet.com Investment Rating is currently a C (Fair). The fund currently has a performance rating of C (Fair) based on an annualized return of 17.61% over the last three years and a total return of 6.38% year to date 2012. Factored into the performance evaluation is an expense ratio of 1.00% (low).

The fund's risk rating is currently B (Good). It carries a beta of 0.58, meaning the fund's expected move will be 5.8% for every 10% move in the market. Volatility, as measured by both the semi-deviation and a drawdown factor, is considered low. As of March 31, 2012, MFS Charter Income Trust traded at a discount of 4.97% below its net asset value, which is worse than its one-year historical average discount of 7.10%.

Richard O. Hawkins has been running the fund for 8 years and currently receives a manager quality ranking of 89 (0=worst, 99=best). If you desire an average level of risk, then this fund may be an option.

Data Date	Investment Rating	Net Assets ($Mil)	Price	Performance Rating/Pts	Total Return Y-T-D	Risk Rating/Pts
3-12	C	526.32	9.57	C / 4.5	6.38%	B / 8.8
2011	B-	535.80	9.15	C+ / 5.8	1.53%	B / 8.9
2010	A-	525.25	9.42	B / 7.6	11.32%	C+ / 6.6
2009	C+	473.08	9.18	C+ / 5.8	30.03%	C+ / 6.2

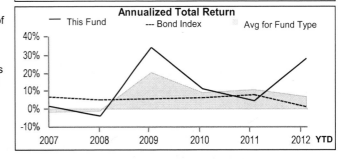

Annualized Total Return

MFS Government Markets Income Trus (MGF)

D+   **Weak**

Fund Family: MFS Investment Management
Fund Type: Global
Inception Date: May 20, 1987

Data Date	Investment Rating	Net Assets ($Mil)	Price	Performance Rating/Pts	Total Return Y-T-D	Risk Rating/Pts
3-12	D+	227.61	6.78	D / 2.1	-0.79%	B / 8.4
2011	C	228.00	6.96	C- / 3.8	0.43%	B / 8.4
2010	C+	232.78	6.80	C / 4.6	-1.88%	B- / 7.6
2009	C+	230.65	7.45	C / 4.9	0.84%	B- / 7.5

Major Rating Factors:
Disappointing performance is the major factor driving the D+ (Weak) TheStreet.com Investment Rating for MFS Government Markets Income Trus. The fund currently has a performance rating of D (Weak) based on an annualized return of 6.49% over the last three years and a total return of -0.79% year to date 2012. Factored into the performance evaluation is an expense ratio of 0.80% (very low).

The fund's risk rating is currently B (Good). It carries a beta of 0.05, meaning the fund's expected move will be 0.5% for every 10% move in the market. Volatility, as measured by both the semi-deviation and a drawdown factor, is considered low. As of March 31, 2012, MFS Government Markets Income Trus traded at a discount of 2.45% below its net asset value, which is worse than its one-year historical average discount of 3.32%.

Geoffrey L. Schechter currently receives a manager quality ranking of 72 (0=worst, 99=best). This fund offers only a moderate level of risk but investors looking for strong performance are still waiting.

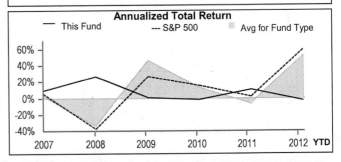

MFS High Inc Muni Tr (CXE)

A+   **Excellent**

Fund Family: MFS Investment Management
Fund Type: Municipal - High Yield
Inception Date: February 16, 1989

Data Date	Investment Rating	Net Assets ($Mil)	Price	Performance Rating/Pts	Total Return Y-T-D	Risk Rating/Pts
3-12	A+	149.23	5.35	A / 9.4	1.87%	B / 8.7
2011	A+	152.20	5.35	A+ / 9.9	-1.12%	B / 8.7
2010	D+	153.04	4.71	C- / 3.2	5.60%	C / 5.0
2009	C	134.11	4.83	C / 5.1	75.05%	C / 5.4

Major Rating Factors:
Exceptional performance is the major factor driving the A+ (Excellent) TheStreet.com Investment Rating for MFS High Inc Muni Tr. The fund currently has a performance rating of A (Excellent) based on an annualized return of 23.90% over the last three years and a total return of 1.87% year to date 2012. Factored into the performance evaluation is an expense ratio of 1.56% (average).

The fund's risk rating is currently B (Good). It carries a beta of 2.49, meaning it is expected to move 24.9% for every 10% move in the market. Volatility, as measured by both the semi-deviation and a drawdown factor, is considered low. As of March 31, 2012, MFS High Inc Muni Tr traded at a premium of 4.70% above its net asset value, which is worse than its one-year historical average premium of 4.09%.

Gary A. Lasman has been running the fund for 5 years and currently receives a manager quality ranking of 67 (0=worst, 99=best). If you desire only a moderate level of risk and strong performance, then this fund is an excellent option.

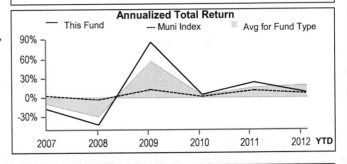

MFS High Yield Muni Trust (CMU)

A+   **Excellent**

Fund Family: MFS Investment Management
Fund Type: Municipal - High Yield
Inception Date: March 19, 1987

Data Date	Investment Rating	Net Assets ($Mil)	Price	Performance Rating/Pts	Total Return Y-T-D	Risk Rating/Pts
3-12	A+	119.85	4.90	A / 9.4	5.98%	B / 8.8
2011	A+	122.30	4.71	A+ / 9.8	1.06%	B / 8.8
2010	C-	122.46	4.32	C- / 3.7	5.92%	C+ / 5.7
2009	C	106.85	4.42	C / 5.2	65.78%	C+ / 5.7

Major Rating Factors:
Exceptional performance is the major factor driving the A+ (Excellent) TheStreet.com Investment Rating for MFS High Yield Muni Trust. The fund currently has a performance rating of A (Excellent) based on an annualized return of 22.76% over the last three years and a total return of 5.98% year to date 2012. Factored into the performance evaluation is an expense ratio of 1.43% (average).

The fund's risk rating is currently B (Good). It carries a beta of 1.96, meaning it is expected to move 19.6% for every 10% move in the market. Volatility, as measured by both the semi-deviation and a drawdown factor, is considered low. As of March 31, 2012, MFS High Yield Muni Trust traded at a premium of 6.75% above its net asset value, which is worse than its one-year historical average premium of 5.37%.

Gary A. Lasman has been running the fund for 5 years and currently receives a manager quality ranking of 80 (0=worst, 99=best). If you desire only a moderate level of risk and strong performance, then this fund is an excellent option.

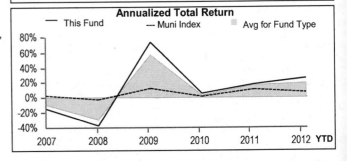

MFS Interm High Inc (CIF)

A+   **Excellent**

Fund Family: MFS Investment Management
Fund Type: Corporate - High Yield
Inception Date: July 21, 1988

Data Date	Investment Rating	Net Assets ($Mil)	Price	Performance Rating/Pts	Total Return Y-T-D	Risk Rating/Pts
3-12	A+	59.41	3.18	A / 9.3	10.55%	B / 8.7
2011	B+	60.50	2.94	B+ / 8.7	-0.34%	B- / 7.8
2010	C	58.49	2.95	B / 8.0	14.37%	C- / 3.0
2009	C	45.51	2.87	B / 7.9	82.47%	D+ / 2.8

Major Rating Factors:
Exceptional performance is the major factor driving the A+ (Excellent) TheStreet.com Investment Rating for MFS Interm High Inc. The fund currently has a performance rating of A (Excellent) based on an annualized return of 38.28% over the last three years and a total return of 10.55% year to date 2012. Factored into the performance evaluation is an expense ratio of 1.81% (above average).

The fund's risk rating is currently B (Good). It carries a beta of 1.21, meaning it is expected to move 12.1% for every 10% move in the market. Volatility, as measured by both the semi-deviation and a drawdown factor, is considered low. As of March 31, 2012, MFS Interm High Inc traded at a premium of 5.65% above its net asset value, which is worse than its one-year historical average discount of .82%.

David P. Cole has been running the fund for 5 years and currently receives a manager quality ranking of 80 (0=worst, 99=best). If you desire only a moderate level of risk and strong performance, then this fund is an excellent option.

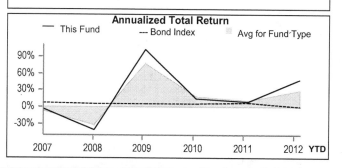

Annualized Total Return

MFS Intermediate Income Trust (MIN)

C-   **Fair**

Fund Family: MFS Investment Management
Fund Type: Global
Inception Date: March 10, 1988

Data Date	Investment Rating	Net Assets ($Mil)	Price	Performance Rating/Pts	Total Return Y-T-D	Risk Rating/Pts
3-12	C-	745.54	6.38	D+ / 2.9	3.43%	B / 8.6
2011	C	735.30	6.30	C- / 4.1	0.00%	B / 8.7
2010	B-	792.81	6.31	C+ / 6.4	2.59%	B- / 7.6
2009	B-	774.71	6.70	C / 5.0	15.12%	B- / 7.9

Major Rating Factors:
Disappointing performance is the major factor driving the C- (Fair) TheStreet.com Investment Rating for MFS Intermediate Income Trust. The fund currently has a performance rating of D+ (Weak) based on an annualized return of 9.49% over the last three years and a total return of 3.43% year to date 2012. Factored into the performance evaluation is an expense ratio of 0.71% (very low).

The fund's risk rating is currently B (Good). It carries a beta of 0.26, meaning the fund's expected move will be 2.6% for every 10% move in the market. Volatility, as measured by both the semi-deviation and a drawdown factor, is considered low. As of March 31, 2012, MFS Intermediate Income Trust traded at a premium of 1.43% above its net asset value, which is worse than its one-year historical average discount of 1.02%.

James J. Calmas has been running the fund for 10 years and currently receives a manager quality ranking of 81 (0=worst, 99=best). This fund offers only a moderate level of risk but investors looking for strong performance are still waiting.

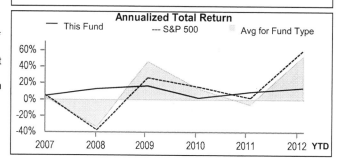

Annualized Total Return

MFS InterMkt Inc Tr I (CMK)

C   **Fair**

Fund Family: MFS Investment Management
Fund Type: Global
Inception Date: September 22, 1989

Data Date	Investment Rating	Net Assets ($Mil)	Price	Performance Rating/Pts	Total Return Y-T-D	Risk Rating/Pts
3-12	C	96.94	8.37	C- / 3.2	2.71%	B+ / 9.5
2011	C+	98.10	8.26	C / 4.6	-1.21%	B+ / 9.5
2010	B+	96.05	8.43	B- / 7.0	12.12%	C+ / 6.4
2009	C+	87.57	8.00	C / 4.7	18.49%	B- / 7.0

Major Rating Factors: Middle of the road best describes MFS InterMkt Inc Tr I whose TheStreet.com Investment Rating is currently a C (Fair). The fund currently has a performance rating of C- (Fair) based on an annualized return of 13.57% over the last three years and a total return of 2.71% year to date 2012. Factored into the performance evaluation is an expense ratio of 1.07% (low).

The fund's risk rating is currently B+ (Good). It carries a beta of 0.43, meaning the fund's expected move will be 4.3% for every 10% move in the market. Volatility, as measured by both the semi-deviation and a drawdown factor, is considered very low. As of March 31, 2012, MFS InterMkt Inc Tr I traded at a discount of 9.71% below its net asset value, which is worse than its one-year historical average discount of 10.02%.

James J. Calmas has been running the fund for 5 years and currently receives a manager quality ranking of 85 (0=worst, 99=best). If you desire an average level of risk, then this fund may be an option.

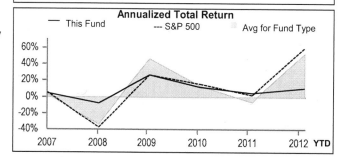

Annualized Total Return

MFS Invst Gr Muni Tr (CXH) A Excellent

Fund Family: MFS Investment Management
Fund Type: Municipal - National
Inception Date: May 19, 1989

Major Rating Factors:
Strong performance is the major factor driving the A (Excellent) TheStreet.com Investment Rating for MFS Invst Gr Muni Tr. The fund currently has a performance rating of B+ (Good) based on an annualized return of 19.61% over the last three years and a total return of 5.79% year to date 2012. Factored into the performance evaluation is an expense ratio of 1.30% (average).

The fund's risk rating is currently B (Good). It carries a beta of 2.06, meaning it is expected to move 20.6% for every 10% move in the market. Volatility, as measured by both the semi-deviation and a drawdown factor, is considered low. As of March 31, 2012, MFS Invst Gr Muni Tr traded at a premium of .89% above its net asset value, which is worse than its one-year historical average discount of .51%.

Geoffrey L. Schechter has been running the fund for 5 years and currently receives a manager quality ranking of 65 (0=worst, 99=best). If you desire only a moderate level of risk and strong performance, then this fund is an excellent option.

Data Date	Investment Rating	Net Assets ($Mil)	Price	Performance Rating/Pts	Total Return Y-T-D	Risk Rating/Pts
3-12	A	109.45	10.16	B+ / 8.8	5.79%	B / 8.7
2011	A	111.90	9.76	A- / 9.2	1.64%	B / 8.8
2010	C-	111.17	8.82	C- / 3.8	1.97%	C+ / 5.9
2009	C+	101.79	9.26	C+ / 6.9	56.01%	C+ / 6.3

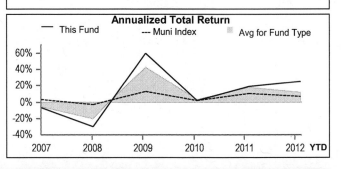

MFS Multimarket Income Trust (MMT) C+ Fair

Fund Family: MFS Investment Management
Fund Type: General Bond
Inception Date: March 5, 1987

Major Rating Factors: Middle of the road best describes MFS Multimarket Income Trust whose TheStreet.com Investment Rating is currently a C+ (Fair). The fund currently has a performance rating of C (Fair) based on an annualized return of 19.70% over the last three years and a total return of 5.75% year to date 2012. Factored into the performance evaluation is an expense ratio of 1.12% (low).

The fund's risk rating is currently B (Good). It carries a beta of 0.43, meaning the fund's expected move will be 4.3% for every 10% move in the market. Volatility, as measured by both the semi-deviation and a drawdown factor, is considered low. As of March 31, 2012, MFS Multimarket Income Trust traded at a discount of 5.42% below its net asset value, which is worse than its one-year historical average discount of 7.01%.

David P. Cole currently receives a manager quality ranking of 91 (0=worst, 99=best). If you desire an average level of risk, then this fund may be an option.

Data Date	Investment Rating	Net Assets ($Mil)	Price	Performance Rating/Pts	Total Return Y-T-D	Risk Rating/Pts
3-12	C+	564.45	6.98	C / 5.0	5.75%	B / 8.4
2011	B	558.30	6.72	C+ / 6.6	0.89%	B+ / 9.0
2010	B+	563.16	6.90	B / 8.2	15.16%	C+ / 5.8
2009	C+	466.51	6.50	C+ / 6.6	40.23%	C+ / 5.9

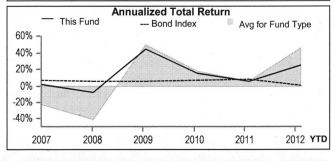

MFS Municipal Income Trust (MFM) A+ Excellent

Fund Family: MFS Investment Management
Fund Type: Municipal - National
Inception Date: November 18, 1986

Major Rating Factors:
Exceptional performance is the major factor driving the A+ (Excellent) TheStreet.com Investment Rating for MFS Municipal Income Trust. The fund currently has a performance rating of A- (Excellent) based on an annualized return of 20.93% over the last three years and a total return of 4.39% year to date 2012. Factored into the performance evaluation is an expense ratio of 1.42% (average).

The fund's risk rating is currently B (Good). It carries a beta of 1.55, meaning it is expected to move 15.5% for every 10% move in the market. Volatility, as measured by both the semi-deviation and a drawdown factor, is considered low. As of March 31, 2012, MFS Municipal Income Trust traded at a premium of 4.14% above its net asset value, which is worse than its one-year historical average premium of 2.78%.

Geoffrey L. Schechter has been running the fund for 19 years and currently receives a manager quality ranking of 81 (0=worst, 99=best). If you desire only a moderate level of risk and strong performance, then this fund is an excellent option.

Data Date	Investment Rating	Net Assets ($Mil)	Price	Performance Rating/Pts	Total Return Y-T-D	Risk Rating/Pts
3-12	A+	271.03	7.29	A- / 9.0	4.39%	B / 8.6
2011	A+	274.80	7.11	A+ / 9.7	0.41%	B / 8.7
2010	C	273.60	6.41	C / 4.6	1.91%	C+ / 6.3
2009	B	221.67	6.78	B / 7.6	70.48%	C+ / 5.9

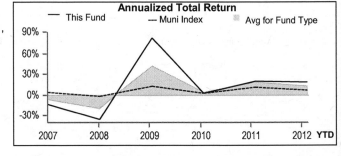

MFS Special Value Trust (MFV)

B+   **Good**

Fund Family: MFS Investment Management
Fund Type: Growth and Income
Inception Date: November 17, 1989

Data Date	Investment Rating	Net Assets ($Mil)	Price	Perfor-mance Rating/Pts	Total Return Y-T-D	Risk Rating/Pts
3-12	B+	46.44	7.09	B / 8.2	12.98%	B / 8.0
2011	B	45.70	6.43	B- / 7.5	3.11%	B- / 7.9
2010	C	49.44	7.38	C+ / 6.6	15.54%	C- / 3.8
2009	C-	36.38	7.03	C+ / 5.7	91.76%	C- / 4.0

Major Rating Factors: Strong performance is the major factor driving the B+ (Good) TheStreet.com Investment Rating for MFS Special Value Trust. The fund currently has a performance rating of B (Good) based on an annualized return of 33.33% over the last three years and a total return of 12.98% year to date 2012. Factored into the performance evaluation is an expense ratio of 1.39% (average).

The fund's risk rating is currently B (Good). It carries a beta of 0.54, meaning the fund's expected move will be 5.4% for every 10% move in the market. Volatility, as measured by both the semi-deviation and a drawdown factor, is considered low. As of March 31, 2012, MFS Special Value Trust traded at a premium of 2.75% above its net asset value, which is better than its one-year historical average premium of 3.45%.

David P. Cole currently receives a manager quality ranking of 93 (0=worst, 99=best). If you desire only a moderate level of risk and strong performance, then this fund is an excellent option.

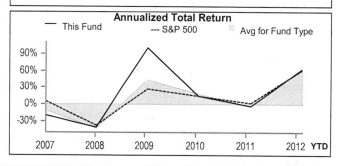

Minnesota Municipal Inc Portfolio (MXA)

C+   **Fair**

Fund Family: US Bancorp Asset Management Inc
Fund Type: Municipal - Single State
Inception Date: June 18, 1993

Data Date	Investment Rating	Net Assets ($Mil)	Price	Perfor-mance Rating/Pts	Total Return Y-T-D	Risk Rating/Pts
3-12	C+	60.00	15.77	C+ / 5.6	-5.17%	B / 8.9
2011	A+	62.70	16.78	A+ / 9.7	0.70%	B+ / 9.0
2010	A-	63.00	14.36	B / 7.7	4.57%	C+ / 6.9
2009	A-	55.51	14.60	B- / 7.5	49.11%	C+ / 6.8

Major Rating Factors: Middle of the road best describes Minnesota Municipal Inc Portfolio whose TheStreet.com Investment Rating is currently a C+ (Fair). The fund currently has a performance rating of C+ (Fair) based on an annualized return of 14.71% over the last three years and a total return of -5.17% year to date 2012. Factored into the performance evaluation is an expense ratio of 1.46% (average).

The fund's risk rating is currently B (Good). It carries a beta of 1.56, meaning it is expected to move 15.6% for every 10% move in the market. Volatility, as measured by both the semi-deviation and a drawdown factor, is considered low. As of March 31, 2012, Minnesota Municipal Inc Portfolio traded at a premium of 1.28% above its net asset value, which is better than its one-year historical average premium of 5.34%.

James D. Palmer currently receives a manager quality ranking of 59 (0=worst, 99=best). If you desire an average level of risk, then this fund may be an option.

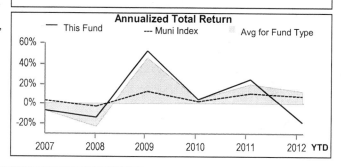

Minnesota Municipal Income Fund II (MXN)

B   **Good**

Fund Family: US Bancorp Asset Management Inc
Fund Type: Municipal - Single State
Inception Date: October 30, 2002

Data Date	Investment Rating	Net Assets ($Mil)	Price	Perfor-mance Rating/Pts	Total Return Y-T-D	Risk Rating/Pts
3-12	B	21.00	15.99	C+ / 6.4	-3.29%	B+ / 9.2
2011	A+	22.10	16.68	A- / 9.0	-2.58%	B+ / 9.2
2010	A+	22.00	15.02	B+ / 8.4	6.58%	B- / 7.8
2009	A+	19.64	14.89	B / 7.9	53.71%	B- / 7.0

Major Rating Factors: Minnesota Municipal Income Fund II receives a TheStreet.com Investment Rating of B (Good). The fund currently has a performance rating of C+ (Fair) based on an annualized return of 15.53% over the last three years and a total return of -3.29% year to date 2012. Factored into the performance evaluation is an expense ratio of 2.25% (high).

The fund's risk rating is currently B+ (Good). It carries a beta of 0.76, meaning the fund's expected move will be 7.6% for every 10% move in the market. Volatility, as measured by both the semi-deviation and a drawdown factor, is considered very low. As of March 31, 2012, Minnesota Municipal Income Fund II traded at a premium of 4.17% above its net asset value, which is better than its one-year historical average premium of 4.18%.

James D. Palmer currently receives a manager quality ranking of 83 (0=worst, 99=best). If you desire an average level of risk, then this fund may be an option.

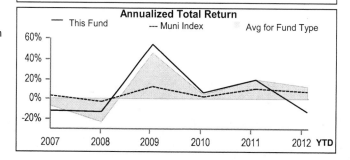

MLP & Strategic Equity Fund Inc. (MTP)   C+   Fair

Fund Family: Nuveen Fund Advisors Inc
Fund Type: Energy/Natural Resources
Inception Date: June 29, 2007

Data Date	Investment Rating	Net Assets ($Mil)	Price	Performance Rating/Pts	Total Return Y-T-D	Risk Rating/Pts
3-12	C+	262.85	17.80	C+ / 6.7	5.63%	B / 8.1
2011	B	274.30	17.08	B / 7.7	-0.06%	B- / 7.9
2010	B-	242.20	17.62	B / 7.8	17.06%	C / 4.8
2009	A	162.86	15.83	A+ / 9.7	74.30%	C / 4.8

Major Rating Factors: Middle of the road best describes MLP & Strategic Equity Fund Inc. whose TheStreet.com Investment Rating is currently a C+ (Fair). The fund currently has a performance rating of C+ (Fair) based on an annualized return of 26.61% over the last three years and a total return of 5.63% year to date 2012. Factored into the performance evaluation is an expense ratio of 1.20% (average).

The fund's risk rating is currently B (Good). It carries a beta of 0.52, meaning the fund's expected move will be 5.2% for every 10% move in the market. Volatility, as measured by both the semi-deviation and a drawdown factor, is considered low. As of March 31, 2012, MLP & Strategic Equity Fund Inc. traded at a discount of 3.73% below its net asset value, which is worse than its one-year historical average discount of 5.89%.

James J. Cunnane, Jr. currently receives a manager quality ranking of 90 (0=worst, 99=best). If you desire an average level of risk, then this fund may be an option.

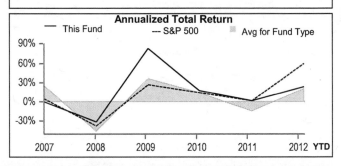

Montgomery Street Inc. Sec. (MTS)   C-   Fair

Fund Family: PIMCO
Fund Type: General - Investment Grade
Inception Date: January 31, 1973

Data Date	Investment Rating	Net Assets ($Mil)	Price	Performance Rating/Pts	Total Return Y-T-D	Risk Rating/Pts
3-12	C-	177.00	15.80	D+ / 2.5	2.40%	B+ / 9.5
2011	C	178.00	15.43	C- / 3.5	-0.13%	B+ / 9.4
2010	C+	170.34	15.78	C / 4.9	12.49%	B- / 7.1
2009	C	164.93	14.68	D+ / 2.9	9.05%	B / 8.0

Major Rating Factors:
Disappointing performance is the major factor driving the C- (Fair) TheStreet.com Investment Rating for Montgomery Street Inc. Sec.. The fund currently has a performance rating of D+ (Weak) based on an annualized return of 10.24% over the last three years and a total return of 2.40% year to date 2012. Factored into the performance evaluation is an expense ratio of 0.71% (very low).

The fund's risk rating is currently B+ (Good). It carries a beta of 0.62, meaning the fund's expected move will be 6.2% for every 10% move in the market. Volatility, as measured by both the semi-deviation and a drawdown factor, is considered very low. As of March 31, 2012, Montgomery Street Inc. Sec. traded at a discount of 10.13% below its net asset value, which is better than its one-year historical average discount of 9.69%.

Mark Kiesel currently receives a manager quality ranking of 78 (0=worst, 99=best). This fund offers only a moderate level of risk but investors looking for strong performance are still waiting.

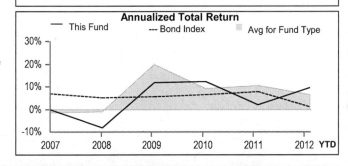

Morgan Stanley Asia Pacific Fund (APF)   C-   Fair

Fund Family: Morgan Stanley Investment Mgmt Inc
Fund Type: Foreign
Inception Date: July 25, 1994

Data Date	Investment Rating	Net Assets ($Mil)	Price	Performance Rating/Pts	Total Return Y-T-D	Risk Rating/Pts
3-12	C-	562.96	14.86	C- / 4.2	13.44%	B- / 7.4
2011	C-	306.30	13.10	C- / 3.6	2.29%	C+ / 6.8
2010	C-	484.77	16.98	C / 5.5	17.90%	C- / 3.9
2009	C-	475.59	14.65	C / 4.8	32.84%	C / 4.3

Major Rating Factors: Middle of the road best describes Morgan Stanley Asia Pacific Fund whose TheStreet.com Investment Rating is currently a C- (Fair). The fund currently has a performance rating of C- (Fair) based on an annualized return of 18.36% over the last three years and a total return of 13.44% year to date 2012. Factored into the performance evaluation is an expense ratio of 1.15% (low).

The fund's risk rating is currently B- (Good). It carries a beta of 0.98, meaning that its performance tracks fairly well with that of the overall stock market. Volatility, as measured by both the semi-deviation and a drawdown factor, is considered low. As of March 31, 2012, Morgan Stanley Asia Pacific Fund traded at a discount of 10.27% below its net asset value, which is worse than its one-year historical average discount of 10.40%.

James K.K. Cheng currently receives a manager quality ranking of 65 (0=worst, 99=best). If you desire an average level of risk, then this fund may be an option.

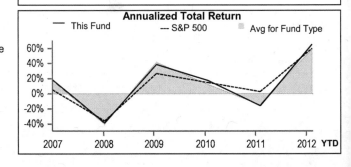

Morgan Stanley China A Share Fund (CAF)   D-   Weak

Fund Family: Morgan Stanley Investment Mgmt Inc
Fund Type: Foreign
Inception Date: September 28, 2006

Data Date	Investment Rating	Net Assets ($Mil)	Price	Perfor-mance Rating/Pts	Total Return Y-T-D	Risk Rating/Pts
3-12	D-	609.84	19.59	D- / 1.1	11.80%	C / 5.5
2011	D	493.20	19.35	D+ / 2.5	2.02%	C / 5.3
2010	D	397.04	27.35	C- / 3.9	-0.73%	C- / 3.3
2009	C	531.73	31.37	B / 8.0	59.50%	C- / 3.3

Major Rating Factors:
Disappointing performance is the major factor driving the D- (Weak) TheStreet.com Investment Rating for Morgan Stanley China A Share Fund. The fund currently has a performance rating of D- (Weak) based on an annualized return of 0.65% over the last three years and a total return of 11.80% year to date 2012. Factored into the performance evaluation is an expense ratio of 1.78% (above average).

The fund's risk rating is currently C (Fair). It carries a beta of 1.02, meaning that its performance tracks fairly well with that of the overall stock market. Volatility, as measured by both the semi-deviation and a drawdown factor, is considered average. As of March 31, 2012, Morgan Stanley China A Share Fund traded at a discount of 9.77% below its net asset value, which is better than its one-year historical average discount of 7.38%.

Homiyar Vasania has been running the fund for 6 years and currently receives a manager quality ranking of 12 (0=worst, 99=best). This fund offers an average level of risk but investors looking for strong performance will be frustrated.

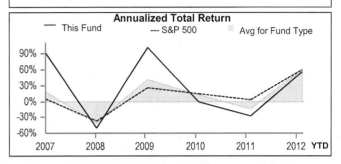

Annualized Total Return — This Fund --- S&P 500 ░ Avg for Fund Type

Morgan Stanley Eastern Europe (RNE)   C+   Fair

Fund Family: Morgan Stanley Investment Mgmt Inc
Fund Type: Foreign
Inception Date: September 24, 1996

Data Date	Investment Rating	Net Assets ($Mil)	Price	Perfor-mance Rating/Pts	Total Return Y-T-D	Risk Rating/Pts
3-12	C+	84.69	16.58	C+ / 6.3	23.18%	B- / 7.3
2011	C-	63.60	13.46	C- / 3.6	1.82%	B- / 7.2
2010	E+	65.42	18.95	E+ / 0.9	21.09%	C- / 3.5
2009	E+	49.14	15.65	D+ / 2.7	77.65%	D+ / 2.6

Major Rating Factors: Middle of the road best describes Morgan Stanley Eastern Europe whose TheStreet.com Investment Rating is currently a C+ (Fair). The fund currently has a performance rating of C+ (Fair) based on an annualized return of 25.29% over the last three years and a total return of 23.18% year to date 2012. Factored into the performance evaluation is an expense ratio of 2.01% (high).

The fund's risk rating is currently B- (Good). It carries a beta of 1.41, meaning it is expected to move 14.1% for every 10% move in the market. Volatility, as measured by both the semi-deviation and a drawdown factor, is considered low. As of March 31, 2012, Morgan Stanley Eastern Europe traded at a discount of 10.14% below its net asset value, which is worse than its one-year historical average discount of 11.86%.

Eric J. Carlson has been running the fund for 16 years and currently receives a manager quality ranking of 59 (0=worst, 99=best). If you desire an average level of risk, then this fund may be an option.

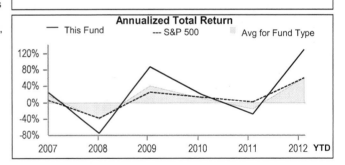

Annualized Total Return — This Fund --- S&P 500 ░ Avg for Fund Type

Morgan Stanley Emerging Markets (MSF)   C   Fair

Fund Family: Morgan Stanley Investment Mgmt Inc
Fund Type: Emerging Market
Inception Date: October 25, 1991

Data Date	Investment Rating	Net Assets ($Mil)	Price	Perfor-mance Rating/Pts	Total Return Y-T-D	Risk Rating/Pts
3-12	C	303.18	14.63	C / 4.5	13.24%	B- / 7.6
2011	C-	248.00	12.92	C / 4.5	1.32%	B- / 7.5
2010	D	240.63	16.36	C / 4.5	17.74%	D+ / 2.7
2009	C	200.61	13.97	C+ / 6.9	62.20%	C- / 3.5

Major Rating Factors: Middle of the road best describes Morgan Stanley Emerging Markets whose TheStreet.com Investment Rating is currently a C (Fair). The fund currently has a performance rating of C (Fair) based on an annualized return of 20.10% over the last three years and a total return of 13.24% year to date 2012. Factored into the performance evaluation is an expense ratio of 1.54% (average).

The fund's risk rating is currently B- (Good). It carries a beta of 1.03, meaning that its performance tracks fairly well with that of the overall stock market. Volatility, as measured by both the semi-deviation and a drawdown factor, is considered low. As of March 31, 2012, Morgan Stanley Emerging Markets traded at a discount of 9.97% below its net asset value, which is better than its one-year historical average discount of 9.55%.

Ruchir Sharma has been running the fund for 21 years and currently receives a manager quality ranking of 30 (0=worst, 99=best). If you desire an average level of risk, then this fund may be an option.

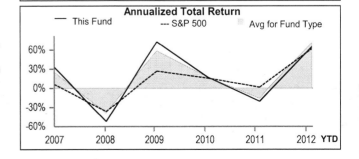

Annualized Total Return — This Fund --- S&P 500 ░ Avg for Fund Type

Morgan Stanley Emerging Mkts Debt (MSD)   C+   Fair

Fund Family: Morgan Stanley Investment Mgmt Inc
Fund Type: Emerging Market
Inception Date: July 16, 1993

Major Rating Factors: Middle of the road best describes Morgan Stanley Emerging Mkts Debt whose TheStreet.com Investment Rating is currently a C+ (Fair). The fund currently has a performance rating of C+ (Fair) based on an annualized return of 22.01% over the last three years and a total return of 5.57% year to date 2012. Factored into the performance evaluation is an expense ratio of 1.19% (average).

The fund's risk rating is currently B (Good). It carries a beta of 0.93, meaning that its performance tracks fairly well with that of the overall stock market. Volatility, as measured by both the semi-deviation and a drawdown factor, is considered low. As of March 31, 2012, Morgan Stanley Emerging Mkts Debt traded at a discount of 10.18% below its net asset value, which is better than its one-year historical average discount of 9.73%.

Eric J. Baurmeister has been running the fund for 10 years and currently receives a manager quality ranking of 91 (0=worst, 99=best). If you desire an average level of risk, then this fund may be an option.

Data Date	Investment Rating	Net Assets ($Mil)	Price	Performance Rating/Pts	Total Return Y-T-D	Risk Rating/Pts
3-12	C+	269.40	10.85	C+ / 5.8	5.57%	B / 8.3
2011	B-	273.30	10.41	C+ / 6.8	0.00%	B / 8.1
2010	B-	267.21	10.48	B- / 7.5	13.75%	C / 5.1
2009	C+	210.80	10.08	C+ / 6.5	47.43%	C+ / 6.2

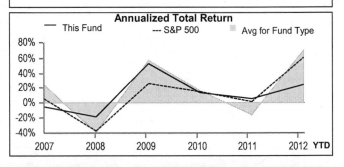

Morgan Stanley Emg Mkts Dom Debt (EDD)   B-   Good

Fund Family: Morgan Stanley Investment Mgmt Inc
Fund Type: Emerging Market
Inception Date: April 24, 2007

Major Rating Factors: Strong performance is the major factor driving the B- (Good) TheStreet.com Investment Rating for Morgan Stanley Emg Mkts Dom Debt. The fund currently has a performance rating of B (Good) based on an annualized return of 27.87% over the last three years and a total return of 16.87% year to date 2012. Factored into the performance evaluation is an expense ratio of 2.07% (high).

The fund's risk rating is currently B- (Good). It carries a beta of 1.57, meaning it is expected to move 15.7% for every 10% move in the market. Volatility, as measured by both the semi-deviation and a drawdown factor, is considered low. As of March 31, 2012, Morgan Stanley Emg Mkts Dom Debt traded at a discount of 7.94% below its net asset value, which is worse than its one-year historical average discount of 8.74%.

Eric J. Baurmeister has been running the fund for 5 years and currently receives a manager quality ranking of 92 (0=worst, 99=best). If you desire only a moderate level of risk and strong performance, then this fund is an excellent option.

Data Date	Investment Rating	Net Assets ($Mil)	Price	Performance Rating/Pts	Total Return Y-T-D	Risk Rating/Pts
3-12	B-	1,255.62	16.24	B / 7.6	16.87%	B- / 7.8
2011	C	1,153.50	14.15	C / 5.4	4.95%	B- / 7.6
2010	B+	1,264.52	16.15	B / 7.6	27.14%	C+ / 5.8
2009	B+	1,029.18	13.68	B / 8.2	36.17%	C+ / 5.6

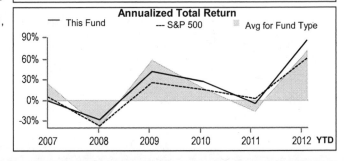

Morgan Stanley Frntier Emrg Mkt Fd (FFD)   D+   Weak

Fund Family: Morgan Stanley Investment Mgmt Inc
Fund Type: Global
Inception Date: August 28, 2008

Major Rating Factors:
Disappointing performance is the major factor driving the D+ (Weak) TheStreet.com Investment Rating for Morgan Stanley Frntier Emrg Mkt Fd. The fund currently has a performance rating of D+ (Weak) based on an annualized return of 13.57% over the last three years and a total return of 9.10% year to date 2012. Factored into the performance evaluation is an expense ratio of 2.03% (high).

The fund's risk rating is currently B- (Good). It carries a beta of 0.69, meaning the fund's expected move will be 6.9% for every 10% move in the market. Volatility, as measured by both the semi-deviation and a drawdown factor, is considered low. As of March 31, 2012, Morgan Stanley Frntier Emrg Mkt Fd traded at a discount of 13.45% below its net asset value, which is better than its one-year historical average discount of 11.27%.

Ruchir Sharma has been running the fund for 4 years and currently receives a manager quality ranking of 65 (0=worst, 99=best). This fund offers only a moderate level of risk but investors looking for strong performance are still waiting.

Data Date	Investment Rating	Net Assets ($Mil)	Price	Performance Rating/Pts	Total Return Y-T-D	Risk Rating/Pts
3-12	D+	84.96	11.39	D+ / 2.6	9.10%	B- / 7.5
2011	D+	79.30	10.44	D / 2.2	1.82%	B- / 7.4
2010	A	94.85	14.61	A+ / 9.6	37.78%	C+ / 6.0
2009	C	70.96	10.75	C / 5.0	20.17%	C+ / 5.7

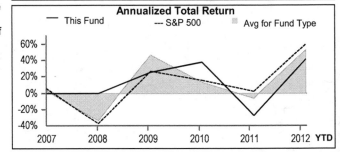

Morgan Stanley Income Sec (ICB)   C   Fair

Fund Family: Morgan Stanley Investment Advisors
Fund Type: General Bond
Inception Date: April 6, 1973

Data Date	Investment Rating	Net Assets ($Mil)	Price	Performance Rating/Pts	Total Return Y-T-D	Risk Rating/Pts
3-12	C	162.03	17.79	C- / 4.0	3.80%	B+ / 9.2
2011	B-	164.40	17.34	C / 5.4	1.04%	B+ / 9.1
2010	C+	165.95	16.83	C+ / 6.4	11.35%	C+ / 6.4
2009	C+	155.32	16.01	C / 4.7	18.94%	B- / 7.6

Major Rating Factors: Middle of the road best describes Morgan Stanley Income Sec whose TheStreet.com Investment Rating is currently a C (Fair). The fund currently has a performance rating of C- (Fair) based on an annualized return of 16.64% over the last three years and a total return of 3.80% year to date 2012. Factored into the performance evaluation is an expense ratio of 0.65% (very low).

The fund's risk rating is currently B+ (Good). It carries a beta of 0.81, meaning the fund's expected move will be 8.1% for every 10% move in the market. Volatility, as measured by both the semi-deviation and a drawdown factor, is considered very low. As of March 31, 2012, Morgan Stanley Income Sec traded at a discount of 4.61% below its net asset value, which is worse than its one-year historical average discount of 5.61%.

Joseph M. Mehlman has been running the fund for 4 years and currently receives a manager quality ranking of 86 (0=worst, 99=best). If you desire an average level of risk, then this fund may be an option.

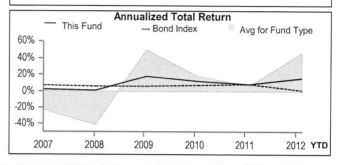

Morgan Stanley India Inv Fund (IIF)   D-   Weak

Fund Family: Morgan Stanley Investment Mgmt Inc
Fund Type: Foreign
Inception Date: February 17, 1994

Data Date	Investment Rating	Net Assets ($Mil)	Price	Performance Rating/Pts	Total Return Y-T-D	Risk Rating/Pts
3-12	D-	613.14	16.56	D / 2.2	18.20%	C / 5.4
2011	D-	350.00	14.01	D / 1.8	2.43%	C / 5.3
2010	D-	553.10	25.65	C- / 3.2	24.45%	D / 2.2
2009	D	372.04	22.61	C / 4.7	68.48%	D+ / 2.3

Major Rating Factors:
Disappointing performance is the major factor driving the D- (Weak) TheStreet.com Investment Rating for Morgan Stanley India Inv Fund. The fund currently has a performance rating of D (Weak) based on an annualized return of 12.39% over the last three years and a total return of 18.20% year to date 2012. Factored into the performance evaluation is an expense ratio of 1.33% (average).

The fund's risk rating is currently C (Fair). It carries a beta of 1.19, meaning it is expected to move 11.9% for every 10% move in the market. Volatility, as measured by both the semi-deviation and a drawdown factor, is considered average. As of March 31, 2012, Morgan Stanley India Inv Fund traded at a discount of 11.21% below its net asset value, which is better than its one-year historical average discount of 8.03%.

Ruchir Sharma has been running the fund for 18 years and currently receives a manager quality ranking of 25 (0=worst, 99=best). This fund offers an average level of risk but investors looking for strong performance will be frustrated.

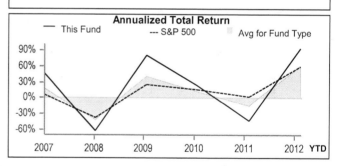

Nasdaq Premium Income & Growth Fun (QQQX)   B-   Good

Fund Family: Nuveen Fund Advisors Inc
Fund Type: Income
Inception Date: January 30, 2007

Data Date	Investment Rating	Net Assets ($Mil)	Price	Performance Rating/Pts	Total Return Y-T-D	Risk Rating/Pts
3-12	B-	260.18	15.74	B / 8.1	23.69%	B- / 7.0
2011	C+	260.20	12.97	B- / 7.3	4.93%	C+ / 6.9
2010	C-	259.73	14.10	C+ / 6.0	7.51%	C- / 4.0
2009	B+	229.87	14.41	A / 9.4	66.91%	C / 4.6

Major Rating Factors: Strong performance is the major factor driving the B- (Good) TheStreet.com Investment Rating for Nasdaq Premium Income & Growth Fun. The fund currently has a performance rating of B (Good) based on an annualized return of 27.68% over the last three years and a total return of 23.69% year to date 2012. Factored into the performance evaluation is an expense ratio of 1.04% (low).

The fund's risk rating is currently B- (Good). It carries a beta of 1.14, meaning it is expected to move 11.4% for every 10% move in the market. Volatility, as measured by both the semi-deviation and a drawdown factor, is considered low. As of March 31, 2012, Nasdaq Premium Income & Growth Fun traded at a discount of 3.38% below its net asset value, which is worse than its one-year historical average discount of 4.39%.

David A. Friar has been running the fund for 1 year and currently receives a manager quality ranking of 60 (0=worst, 99=best). If you desire only a moderate level of risk and strong performance, then this fund is an excellent option.

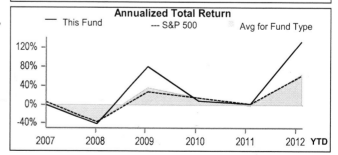

Neuberger Berman CA Inter Muni Fun (NBW)

A-   **Excellent**

Fund Family: Neuberger Berman Management LLC
Fund Type: Municipal - Single State
Inception Date: September 24, 2002

Data Date	Investment Rating	Net Assets ($Mil)	Price	Perfor-mance Rating/Pts	Total Return Y-T-D	Risk Rating/Pts
3-12	A-	83.10	16.04	B / 7.8	6.47%	B+ / 9.2
2011	A-	84.70	15.27	B / 8.2	-0.24%	B+ / 9.2
2010	A-	59.54	14.34	B / 7.7	13.94%	C+ / 6.8
2009	B	92.34	13.27	C / 5.3	31.32%	B- / 7.9

Major Rating Factors:
Strong performance is the major factor driving the A- (Excellent) TheStreet.com Investment Rating for Neuberger Berman CA Inter Muni Fun. The fund currently has a performance rating of B (Good) based on an annualized return of 16.45% over the last three years and a total return of 6.47% year to date 2012. Factored into the performance evaluation is an expense ratio of 1.29% (average).

The fund's risk rating is currently B+ (Good). It carries a beta of 1.62, meaning it is expected to move 16.2% for every 10% move in the market. Volatility, as measured by both the semi-deviation and a drawdown factor, is considered very low. As of March 31, 2012, Neuberger Berman CA Inter Muni Fun traded at a premium of 3.62% above its net asset value, which is worse than its one-year historical average discount of 2.71%.

Thomas J. Brophy has been running the fund for 10 years and currently receives a manager quality ranking of 64 (0=worst, 99=best). If you desire only a moderate level of risk and strong performance, then this fund is an excellent option.

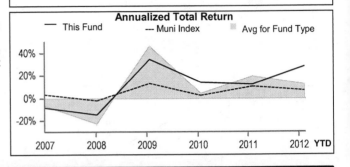

Neuberger Berman High Yield Strat (NHS)

B-   **Good**

Fund Family: Neuberger Berman Management LLC
Fund Type: Corporate - High Yield
Inception Date: July 28, 2003

Data Date	Investment Rating	Net Assets ($Mil)	Price	Perfor-mance Rating/Pts	Total Return Y-T-D	Risk Rating/Pts
3-12	B-	253.17	13.55	B+ / 8.8	1.42%	C+ / 6.5
2011	B	249.40	13.65	A / 9.4	0.37%	C+ / 6.4
2010	B-	138.29	13.50	B+ / 8.6	24.86%	C- / 4.0
2009	C+	111.79	11.95	B / 8.0	103.10%	C- / 4.0

Major Rating Factors: Strong performance is the major factor driving the B- (Good) TheStreet.com Investment Rating for Neuberger Berman High Yield Strat. The fund currently has a performance rating of B+ (Good) based on an annualized return of 37.73% over the last three years and a total return of 1.42% year to date 2012. Factored into the performance evaluation is an expense ratio of 1.68% (above average).

The fund's risk rating is currently C+ (Fair). It carries a beta of 1.77, meaning it is expected to move 17.7% for every 10% move in the market. Volatility, as measured by both the semi-deviation and a drawdown factor, is considered low. As of March 31, 2012, Neuberger Berman High Yield Strat traded at a premium of 1.04% above its net asset value, which is better than its one-year historical average premium of 3.81%.

Ann H. Benjamin has been running the fund for 7 years and currently receives a manager quality ranking of 23 (0=worst, 99=best). If you desire only a moderate level of risk and strong performance, then this fund is an excellent option.

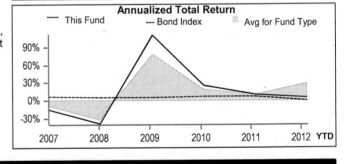

Neuberger Berman Intermediate Muni (NBH)

B+   **Good**

Fund Family: Neuberger Berman Management LLC
Fund Type: Municipal - National
Inception Date: September 24, 2002

Data Date	Investment Rating	Net Assets ($Mil)	Price	Perfor-mance Rating/Pts	Total Return Y-T-D	Risk Rating/Pts
3-12	B+	277.50	16.10	B- / 7.4	2.65%	B+ / 9.3
2011	A	283.20	15.90	B+ / 8.8	-0.69%	B+ / 9.3
2010	B+	62.64	14.01	B- / 7.0	10.26%	B- / 7.1
2009	B	282.36	13.41	C / 5.3	22.50%	B- / 7.8

Major Rating Factors: Strong performance is the major factor driving the B+ (Good) TheStreet.com Investment Rating for Neuberger Berman Intermediate Muni. The fund currently has a performance rating of B- (Good) based on an annualized return of 15.70% over the last three years and a total return of 2.65% year to date 2012. Factored into the performance evaluation is an expense ratio of 1.05% (low).

The fund's risk rating is currently B+ (Good). It carries a beta of 1.34, meaning it is expected to move 13.4% for every 10% move in the market. Volatility, as measured by both the semi-deviation and a drawdown factor, is considered very low. As of March 31, 2012, Neuberger Berman Intermediate Muni traded at a premium of 4.89% above its net asset value, which is worse than its one-year historical average discount of .30%.

Thomas J. Brophy has been running the fund for 10 years and currently receives a manager quality ranking of 75 (0=worst, 99=best). If you desire only a moderate level of risk and strong performance, then this fund is an excellent option.

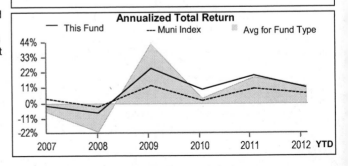

Neuberger Berman NY Int Muni (NBO)   C+   Fair

Fund Family: Neuberger Berman Management LLC
Fund Type: Municipal - Single State
Inception Date: September 24, 2002

Data Date	Investment Rating	Net Assets ($Mil)	Price	Performance Rating/Pts		Total Return Y-T-D	Risk Rating/Pts	
3-12	C+	73.10	14.68	C	/ 4.9	-3.85%	B	/ 8.8
2011	A	74.40	15.47	A-	/ 9.0	-1.36%	B	/ 8.9
2010	C+	62.64	13.50	C+	/ 5.7	8.09%	C+	/ 6.7
2009	B-	74.46	13.13	C+	/ 5.6	30.77%	B-	/ 7.6

Major Rating Factors: Middle of the road best describes Neuberger Berman NY Int Muni whose TheStreet.com Investment Rating is currently a C+ (Fair). The fund currently has a performance rating of C (Fair) based on an annualized return of 12.83% over the last three years and a total return of -3.85% year to date 2012. Factored into the performance evaluation is an expense ratio of 1.29% (average).

The fund's risk rating is currently B (Good). It carries a beta of 1.61, meaning it is expected to move 16.1% for every 10% move in the market. Volatility, as measured by both the semi-deviation and a drawdown factor, is considered low. As of March 31, 2012, Neuberger Berman NY Int Muni traded at a discount of .68% below its net asset value, which is worse than its one-year historical average discount of 1.31%.

Thomas J. Brophy has been running the fund for 10 years and currently receives a manager quality ranking of 49 (0=worst, 99=best). If you desire an average level of risk, then this fund may be an option.

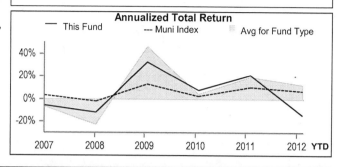

Neuberger Berman Real Est Secs Inc (NRO)   A+   Excellent

Fund Family: Neuberger Berman Management LLC
Fund Type: Growth and Income
Inception Date: October 28, 2003

Data Date	Investment Rating	Net Assets ($Mil)	Price	Performance Rating/Pts		Total Return Y-T-D	Risk Rating/Pts	
3-12	A+	257.20	4.28	A+	/ 9.8	15.79%	B-	/ 7.9
2011	B-	245.60	3.75	B+	/ 8.5	1.07%	C+	/ 6.5
2010	E	260.60	3.99	D-	/ 1.5	40.04%	D	/ 2.1
2009	E	139.73	3.05	E+	/ 0.8	78.23%	C-	/ 3.0

Major Rating Factors:
Exceptional performance is the major factor driving the A+ (Excellent) TheStreet.com Investment Rating for Neuberger Berman Real Est Secs Inc. The fund currently has a performance rating of A+ (Excellent) based on an annualized return of 53.14% over the last three years and a total return of 15.79% year to date 2012. Factored into the performance evaluation is an expense ratio of 2.21% (high).

The fund's risk rating is currently B- (Good). It carries a beta of 1.38, meaning it is expected to move 13.8% for every 10% move in the market. Volatility, as measured by both the semi-deviation and a drawdown factor, is considered low. As of March 31, 2012, Neuberger Berman Real Est Secs Inc traded at a discount of 13.36% below its net asset value, which is better than its one-year historical average discount of 11.89%.

Steve S. Shigekawa currently receives a manager quality ranking of 94 (0=worst, 99=best). If you desire only a moderate level of risk and strong performance, then this fund is an excellent option.

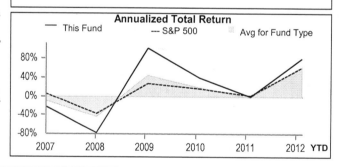

New America High Income Fund (HYB)   B   Good

Fund Family: T Rowe Price Associates Inc
Fund Type: Corporate - High Yield
Inception Date: February 26, 1988

Data Date	Investment Rating	Net Assets ($Mil)	Price	Performance Rating/Pts		Total Return Y-T-D	Risk Rating/Pts	
3-12	B	221.66	10.29	A-	/ 9.1	2.07%	C+	/ 6.6
2011	B	221.50	10.21	A-	/ 9.1	-2.25%	C+	/ 6.5
2010	B-	217.22	9.96	B+	/ 8.6	22.09%	C-	/ 3.7
2009	C+	180.44	9.05	B+	/ 8.4	110.83%	C-	/ 3.7

Major Rating Factors:
Exceptional performance is the major factor driving the B (Good) TheStreet.com Investment Rating for New America High Income Fund. The fund currently has a performance rating of A- (Excellent) based on an annualized return of 37.27% over the last three years and a total return of 2.07% year to date 2012. Factored into the performance evaluation is an expense ratio of 1.46% (average).

The fund's risk rating is currently C+ (Fair). It carries a beta of 1.43, meaning it is expected to move 14.3% for every 10% move in the market. Volatility, as measured by both the semi-deviation and a drawdown factor, is considered low. As of March 31, 2012, New America High Income Fund traded at a premium of 1.08% above its net asset value, which is better than its one-year historical average premium of 1.22%.

Mark J. Vaselkiv has been running the fund for 24 years and currently receives a manager quality ranking of 70 (0=worst, 99=best). If you desire only a moderate level of risk and strong performance, then this fund is an excellent option.

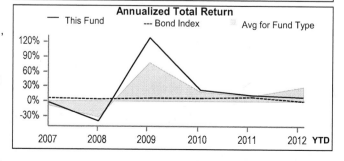

New Germany Fund (GF)

B **Good**

Fund Family: Deutsche Asset Mgmt International G
Fund Type: Foreign
Inception Date: January 24, 1990

Data Date	Investment Rating	Net Assets ($Mil)	Price	Performance Rating/Pts	Total Return Y-T-D	Risk Rating/Pts
3-12	B	241.42	15.08	B+ / 8.7	23.20%	C+ / 6.7
2011	C	241.50	12.24	C+ / 5.9	2.61%	C+ / 6.5
2010	C-	271.35	15.72	C+ / 5.9	32.19%	C- / 3.9
2009	C-	210.18	11.99	C- / 3.9	43.93%	C / 4.8

Major Rating Factors: Strong performance is the major factor driving the B (Good) TheStreet.com Investment Rating for New Germany Fund. The fund currently has a performance rating of B+ (Good) based on an annualized return of 34.59% over the last three years and a total return of 23.20% year to date 2012. Factored into the performance evaluation is an expense ratio of 1.09% (low).

The fund's risk rating is currently C+ (Fair). It carries a beta of 1.40, meaning it is expected to move 14.0% for every 10% move in the market. Volatility, as measured by both the semi-deviation and a drawdown factor, is considered low. As of March 31, 2012, New Germany Fund traded at a discount of 10.50% below its net asset value, which is better than its one-year historical average discount of 9.61%.

Rainer Vermehren currently receives a manager quality ranking of 84 (0=worst, 99=best). If you desire only a moderate level of risk and strong performance, then this fund is an excellent option.

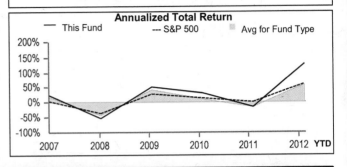

Annualized Total Return

NFJ Dividend Interest & Premium St (NFJ)

B **Good**

Fund Family: Allianz Global Investors Fund Mgmt
Fund Type: Growth and Income
Inception Date: February 23, 2005

Data Date	Investment Rating	Net Assets ($Mil)	Price	Performance Rating/Pts	Total Return Y-T-D	Risk Rating/Pts
3-12	B	1,807.67	17.87	B / 7.6	14.36%	B- / 7.8
2011	C-	1,661.60	16.02	C / 4.4	3.68%	B- / 7.5
2010	C-	1,635.73	17.51	C- / 4.2	22.29%	C+ / 5.8
2009	D	1,481.95	14.75	D- / 1.4	13.27%	C+ / 6.1

Major Rating Factors: Strong performance is the major factor driving the B (Good) TheStreet.com Investment Rating for NFJ Dividend Interest & Premium St. The fund currently has a performance rating of B (Good) based on an annualized return of 27.26% over the last three years and a total return of 14.36% year to date 2012. Factored into the performance evaluation is an expense ratio of 0.97% (low).

The fund's risk rating is currently B- (Good). It carries a beta of 0.96, meaning that its performance tracks fairly well with that of the overall stock market. Volatility, as measured by both the semi-deviation and a drawdown factor, is considered low. As of March 31, 2012, NFJ Dividend Interest & Premium St traded at a discount of 1.54% below its net asset value, which is worse than its one-year historical average discount of 4.73%.

Benjamin J. Fischer currently receives a manager quality ranking of 76 (0=worst, 99=best). If you desire only a moderate level of risk and strong performance, then this fund is an excellent option.

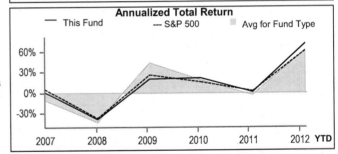

Annualized Total Return

Nuveen AMT/Fr Muni Income (NEA)

C+ **Fair**

Fund Family: Nuveen Fund Advisors Inc
Fund Type: Municipal - National
Inception Date: November 21, 2002

Data Date	Investment Rating	Net Assets ($Mil)	Price	Performance Rating/Pts	Total Return Y-T-D	Risk Rating/Pts
3-12	C+	326.91	14.47	C / 5.1	0.43%	B / 8.7
2011	B+	332.40	14.61	B / 7.8	0.14%	B / 8.7
2010	C-	320.59	13.39	D+ / 2.6	1.90%	B- / 7.7
2009	B-	277.71	13.90	C+ / 6.2	34.27%	B- / 7.8

Major Rating Factors: Middle of the road best describes Nuveen AMT/Fr Muni Income whose TheStreet.com Investment Rating is currently a C+ (Fair). The fund currently has a performance rating of C (Fair) based on an annualized return of 12.71% over the last three years and a total return of 0.43% year to date 2012. Factored into the performance evaluation is an expense ratio of 2.01% (high).

The fund's risk rating is currently B (Good). It carries a beta of 1.96, meaning it is expected to move 19.6% for every 10% move in the market. Volatility, as measured by both the semi-deviation and a drawdown factor, is considered low. As of March 31, 2012, Nuveen AMT/Fr Muni Income traded at a discount of 4.43% below its net asset value, which is worse than its one-year historical average discount of 4.51%.

Paul L. Brennan has been running the fund for 6 years and currently receives a manager quality ranking of 32 (0=worst, 99=best). If you desire an average level of risk, then this fund may be an option.

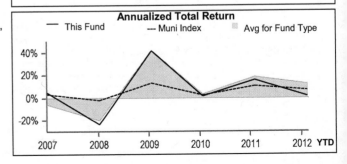

Annualized Total Return

Nuveen AZ Div Adv Muni (NFZ)

B+   **Good**

Fund Family: Nuveen Fund Advisors Inc
Fund Type: Municipal - Single State
Inception Date: January 30, 2001

Major Rating Factors: Strong performance is the major factor driving the B+ (Good) TheStreet.com Investment Rating for Nuveen AZ Div Adv Muni. The fund currently has a performance rating of B (Good) based on an annualized return of 16.72% over the last three years and a total return of 4.90% year to date 2012. Factored into the performance evaluation is an expense ratio of 2.23% (high).

The fund's risk rating is currently B (Good). It carries a beta of 2.11, meaning it is expected to move 21.1% for every 10% move in the market. Volatility, as measured by both the semi-deviation and a drawdown factor, is considered low. As of March 31, 2012, Nuveen AZ Div Adv Muni traded at a discount of 5.39% below its net asset value, which is worse than its one-year historical average discount of 6.93%.

Michael S. Hamilton has been running the fund for 1 year and currently receives a manager quality ranking of 57 (0=worst, 99=best). If you desire only a moderate level of risk and strong performance, then this fund is an excellent option.

Data Date	Investment Rating	Net Assets ($Mil)	Price	Performance Rating/Pts	Total Return Y-T-D	Risk Rating/Pts
3-12	B+	20.63	14.21	B / 7.6	4.90%	B / 8.5
2011	B+	22.60	13.73	B+ / 8.3	-0.15%	B / 8.6
2010	C-	21.98	12.30	D / 2.0	5.01%	B- / 7.4
2009	C	21.52	12.39	C- / 3.8	38.67%	B- / 7.2

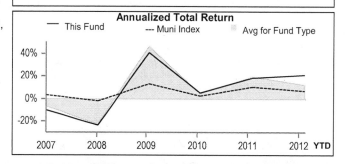

Nuveen AZ Div Adv Muni Fund 2 (NKR)

B+   **Good**

Fund Family: Nuveen Fund Advisors Inc
Fund Type: Municipal - Single State
Inception Date: March 25, 2002

Major Rating Factors: Strong performance is the major factor driving the B+ (Good) TheStreet.com Investment Rating for Nuveen AZ Div Adv Muni Fund 2. The fund currently has a performance rating of B (Good) based on an annualized return of 15.89% over the last three years and a total return of 4.01% year to date 2012. Factored into the performance evaluation is an expense ratio of 2.06% (high).

The fund's risk rating is currently B+ (Good). It carries a beta of 1.96, meaning it is expected to move 19.6% for every 10% move in the market. Volatility, as measured by both the semi-deviation and a drawdown factor, is considered very low. As of March 31, 2012, Nuveen AZ Div Adv Muni Fund 2 traded at a discount of 4.47% below its net asset value, which is worse than its one-year historical average discount of 7.07%.

Michael S. Hamilton has been running the fund for 1 year and currently receives a manager quality ranking of 54 (0=worst, 99=best). If you desire only a moderate level of risk and strong performance, then this fund is an excellent option.

Data Date	Investment Rating	Net Assets ($Mil)	Price	Performance Rating/Pts	Total Return Y-T-D	Risk Rating/Pts
3-12	B+	33.85	14.54	B / 7.6	4.01%	B+ / 9.0
2011	A-	36.30	14.17	B+ / 8.3	0.00%	B+ / 9.0
2010	C	35.73	12.88	D+ / 2.9	3.62%	B / 8.0
2009	B-	35.47	13.17	C / 5.5	39.56%	B- / 7.5

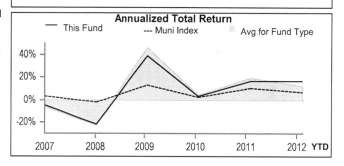

Nuveen AZ Div Adv Muni Fund 3 (NXE)

A   **Excellent**

Fund Family: Nuveen Fund Advisors Inc
Fund Type: Municipal - Single State
Inception Date: September 25, 2002

Major Rating Factors:
Strong performance is the major factor driving the A (Excellent) TheStreet.com Investment Rating for Nuveen AZ Div Adv Muni Fund 3. The fund currently has a performance rating of B+ (Good) based on an annualized return of 18.71% over the last three years and a total return of 5.43% year to date 2012. Factored into the performance evaluation is an expense ratio of 1.43% (average).

The fund's risk rating is currently B+ (Good). It carries a beta of 1.97, meaning it is expected to move 19.7% for every 10% move in the market. Volatility, as measured by both the semi-deviation and a drawdown factor, is considered very low. As of March 31, 2012, Nuveen AZ Div Adv Muni Fund 3 traded at a discount of 6.40% below its net asset value, which is worse than its one-year historical average discount of 8.33%.

Michael S. Hamilton has been running the fund for 1 year and currently receives a manager quality ranking of 65 (0=worst, 99=best). If you desire only a moderate level of risk and strong performance, then this fund is an excellent option.

Data Date	Investment Rating	Net Assets ($Mil)	Price	Performance Rating/Pts	Total Return Y-T-D	Risk Rating/Pts
3-12	A	41.26	13.90	B+ / 8.3	5.43%	B+ / 9.1
2011	A-	44.40	13.36	B+ / 8.3	0.75%	B+ / 9.1
2010	C+	43.28	12.30	C- / 3.5	4.23%	B- / 7.9
2009	B-	42.94	12.50	C+ / 5.9	40.46%	B- / 7.8

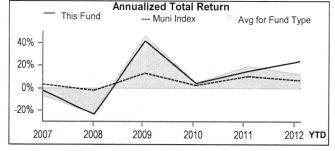

* Denotes ETF Fund

Nuveen AZ Prem Inc Muni (NAZ)

B+   **Good**

Fund Family: Nuveen Fund Advisors Inc
Fund Type: Municipal - Single State
Inception Date: November 19, 1992

Data Date	Investment Rating	Net Assets ($Mil)	Price	Performance Rating/Pts	Total Return Y-T-D	Risk Rating/Pts
3-12	B+	59.26	14.78	B / 8.2	5.89%	B / 8.5
2011	B+	63.90	14.14	B+ / 8.5	0.14%	B / 8.5
2010	C+	62.55	12.72	C / 5.3	4.36%	C+ / 6.9
2009	B-	63.33	12.87	C+ / 6.0	40.82%	B- / 7.4

Major Rating Factors: Strong performance is the major factor driving the B+ (Good) TheStreet.com Investment Rating for Nuveen AZ Prem Inc Muni. The fund currently has a performance rating of B (Good) based on an annualized return of 16.24% over the last three years and a total return of 5.89% year to date 2012. Factored into the performance evaluation is an expense ratio of 1.19% (average).

The fund's risk rating is currently B (Good). It carries a beta of 1.75, meaning it is expected to move 17.5% for every 10% move in the market. Volatility, as measured by both the semi-deviation and a drawdown factor, is considered low. As of March 31, 2012, Nuveen AZ Prem Inc Muni traded at a premium of .14% above its net asset value, which is worse than its one-year historical average discount of 4.18%.

Michael S. Hamilton has been running the fund for 1 year and currently receives a manager quality ranking of 62 (0=worst, 99=best). If you desire only a moderate level of risk and strong performance, then this fund is an excellent option.

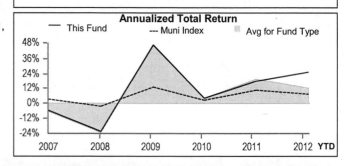

Nuveen Build America Bond Fund (NBB)

B-   **Good**

Fund Family: Nuveen Fund Advisors Inc
Fund Type: Municipal - National
Inception Date: April 27, 2010

Data Date	Investment Rating	Net Assets ($Mil)	Price	Performance Rating/Pts	Total Return Y-T-D	Risk Rating/Pts
3-12	B-	499.02	20.18	C+ / 6.5	-0.08%	B / 8.8
2011	A+	556.80	20.53	A / 9.4	0.58%	B / 8.9

Major Rating Factors: Nuveen Build America Bond Fund receives a TheStreet.com Investment Rating of B- (Good). The fund currently has a performance rating of C+ (Fair) based on an annualized return of 0.00% over the last three years and a total return of -0.08% year to date 2012. Factored into the performance evaluation is an expense ratio of 1.11% (low).

The fund's risk rating is currently B (Good). It carries a beta of 0.00, meaning the fund's expected move will be 0.0% for every 10% move in the market. Volatility, as measured by both the semi-deviation and a drawdown factor, is considered low. As of March 31, 2012, Nuveen Build America Bond Fund traded at a discount of 5.66% below its net asset value, which is better than its one-year historical average discount of 4.72%.

Craig M. Chambers currently receives a manager quality ranking of 21 (0=worst, 99=best). If you desire an average level of risk, then this fund may be an option.

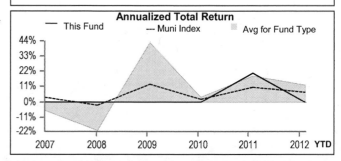

Nuveen Build America Bond Oppty Fd (NBD)

C   **Fair**

Fund Family: Nuveen Fund Advisors Inc
Fund Type: General - Investment Grade
Inception Date: November 24, 2010

Data Date	Investment Rating	Net Assets ($Mil)	Price	Performance Rating/Pts	Total Return Y-T-D	Risk Rating/Pts
3-12	C	163.03	20.97	C- / 3.3	-1.39%	B+ / 9.2
2011	A-	158.80	21.62	B / 8.0	-0.14%	B+ / 9.3

Major Rating Factors: Middle of the road best describes Nuveen Build America Bond Oppty Fd whose TheStreet.com Investment Rating is currently a C (Fair). The fund currently has a performance rating of C- (Fair) based on an annualized return of 0.00% over the last three years and a total return of -1.39% year to date 2012. Factored into the performance evaluation is an expense ratio of 0.84% (very low).

The fund's risk rating is currently B+ (Good). It carries a beta of 0.00, meaning the fund's expected move will be 0.0% for every 10% move in the market. Volatility, as measured by both the semi-deviation and a drawdown factor, is considered very low. As of March 31, 2012, Nuveen Build America Bond Oppty Fd traded at a discount of 7.05% below its net asset value, which is better than its one-year historical average discount of 5.00%.

Daniel J. Close currently receives a manager quality ranking of 88 (0=worst, 99=best). If you desire an average level of risk, then this fund may be an option.

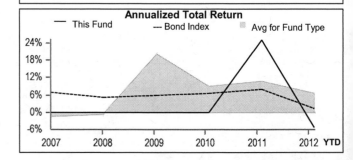

Nuveen CA Div Adv Muni (NAC)   A-   Excellent

Fund Family: Nuveen Fund Advisors Inc
Fund Type: Municipal - Single State
Inception Date: May 25, 1999

Major Rating Factors:
Strong performance is the major factor driving the A- (Excellent) TheStreet.com
Investment Rating for Nuveen CA Div Adv Muni. The fund currently has a
performance rating of B+ (Good) based on an annualized return of 18.58% over the
last three years and a total return of 2.57% year to date 2012. Factored into the
performance evaluation is an expense ratio of 1.18% (low).

The fund's risk rating is currently B (Good). It carries a beta of 2.68, meaning it is
expected to move 26.8% for every 10% move in the market. Volatility, as measured
by both the semi-deviation and a drawdown factor, is considered low. As of March 31,
2012, Nuveen CA Div Adv Muni traded at a discount of 2.77% below its net asset
value, which is worse than its one-year historical average discount of 2.98%.

Scott R. Romans has been running the fund for 10 years and currently receives a
manager quality ranking of 34 (0=worst, 99=best). If you desire only a moderate level
of risk and strong performance, then this fund is an excellent option.

Data Date	Investment Rating	Net Assets ($Mil)	Price	Performance Rating/Pts	Total Return Y-T-D	Risk Rating/Pts
3-12	A-	297.63	14.38	B+ / 8.5	2.57%	B / 8.5
2011	A-	335.30	14.24	B+ / 8.8	-0.07%	B / 8.5
2010	C-	325.79	12.31	D+ / 2.5	6.08%	C+ / 6.5
2009	C	337.10	12.40	C- / 3.9	30.53%	B- / 7.2

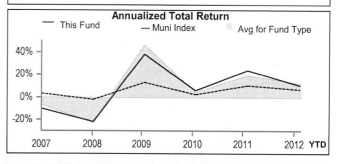

Annualized Total Return

Nuveen CA Div Adv Muni 2 (NVX)   A   Excellent

Fund Family: Nuveen Fund Advisors Inc
Fund Type: Municipal - Single State
Inception Date: March 27, 2001

Major Rating Factors:
Strong performance is the major factor driving the A (Excellent) TheStreet.com
Investment Rating for Nuveen CA Div Adv Muni 2. The fund currently has a
performance rating of B+ (Good) based on an annualized return of 18.57% over the
last three years and a total return of 2.80% year to date 2012. Factored into the
performance evaluation is an expense ratio of 1.28% (average).

The fund's risk rating is currently B (Good). It carries a beta of 2.20, meaning it is
expected to move 22.0% for every 10% move in the market. Volatility, as measured
by both the semi-deviation and a drawdown factor, is considered low. As of March 31,
2012, Nuveen CA Div Adv Muni 2 traded at a discount of 3.18% below its net asset
value, which is better than its one-year historical average discount of 3.05%.

Scott R. Romans has been running the fund for 10 years and currently receives a
manager quality ranking of 59 (0=worst, 99=best). If you desire only a moderate level
of risk and strong performance, then this fund is an excellent option.

Data Date	Investment Rating	Net Assets ($Mil)	Price	Performance Rating/Pts	Total Return Y-T-D	Risk Rating/Pts
3-12	A	198.68	14.93	B+ / 8.3	2.80%	B / 8.8
2011	A	219.70	14.75	B+ / 8.9	0.34%	B / 8.9
2010	C	213.69	13.10	C / 4.9	4.11%	C+ / 6.3
2009	B-	219.78	13.47	C+ / 6.7	45.75%	B- / 7.1

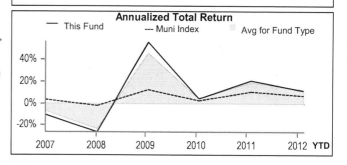

Annualized Total Return

Nuveen CA Div Adv Muni 3 (NZH)   A-   Excellent

Fund Family: Nuveen Fund Advisors Inc
Fund Type: Municipal - Single State
Inception Date: September 25, 2001

Major Rating Factors:
Strong performance is the major factor driving the A- (Excellent) TheStreet.com
Investment Rating for Nuveen CA Div Adv Muni 3. The fund currently has a
performance rating of B+ (Good) based on an annualized return of 18.44% over the
last three years and a total return of 3.59% year to date 2012. Factored into the
performance evaluation is an expense ratio of 1.94% (above average).

The fund's risk rating is currently B (Good). It carries a beta of 2.33, meaning it is
expected to move 23.3% for every 10% move in the market. Volatility, as measured
by both the semi-deviation and a drawdown factor, is considered low. As of March 31,
2012, Nuveen CA Div Adv Muni 3 traded at a discount of .43% below its net asset
value, which is worse than its one-year historical average discount of 1.81%.

Scott R. Romans has been running the fund for 10 years and currently receives a
manager quality ranking of 47 (0=worst, 99=best). If you desire only a moderate level
of risk and strong performance, then this fund is an excellent option.

Data Date	Investment Rating	Net Assets ($Mil)	Price	Performance Rating/Pts	Total Return Y-T-D	Risk Rating/Pts
3-12	A-	292.56	13.77	B+ / 8.5	3.59%	B / 8.6
2011	A-	322.20	13.51	B+ / 8.9	0.67%	B / 8.7
2010	D+	317.86	11.96	D / 2.2	3.36%	C+ / 6.1
2009	C	328.52	12.40	C / 4.6	41.00%	C+ / 6.9

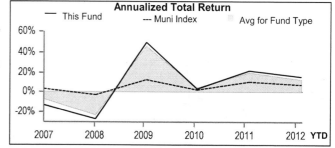

Annualized Total Return

Nuveen CA Inv Quality Muni (NQC)

A+   **Excellent**

Fund Family: Nuveen Fund Advisors Inc
Fund Type: Municipal - Single State
Inception Date: November 20, 1990

Major Rating Factors:
Exceptional performance is the major factor driving the A+ (Excellent) TheStreet.com Investment Rating for Nuveen CA Inv Quality Muni. The fund currently has a performance rating of A (Excellent) based on an annualized return of 21.60% over the last three years and a total return of 5.52% year to date 2012. Factored into the performance evaluation is an expense ratio of 1.36% (average).

The fund's risk rating is currently B (Good). It carries a beta of 2.37, meaning it is expected to move 23.7% for every 10% move in the market. Volatility, as measured by both the semi-deviation and a drawdown factor, is considered low. As of March 31, 2012, Nuveen CA Inv Quality Muni traded at a premium of .07% above its net asset value, which is worse than its one-year historical average discount of 2.15%.

Scott R. Romans has been running the fund for 10 years and currently receives a manager quality ranking of 61 (0=worst, 99=best). If you desire only a moderate level of risk and strong performance, then this fund is an excellent option.

Data Date	Investment Rating	Net Assets ($Mil)	Price	Performance Rating/Pts	Total Return Y-T-D	Risk Rating/Pts
3-12	A+	177.47	15.24	A / 9.3	5.52%	B / 8.7
2011	A	200.00	14.68	A- / 9.2	0.82%	B / 8.7
2010	C-	190.88	12.59	C- / 3.2	4.89%	C+ / 6.0
2009	B-	197.13	12.83	C+ / 5.6	31.27%	B- / 7.1

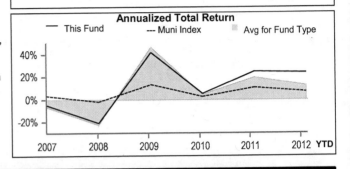

Nuveen CA Muni Market Opportunity (NCO)

A+   **Excellent**

Fund Family: Nuveen Fund Advisors Inc
Fund Type: Municipal - Single State
Inception Date: May 18, 1990

Major Rating Factors:
Exceptional performance is the major factor driving the A+ (Excellent) TheStreet.com Investment Rating for Nuveen CA Muni Market Opportunity. The fund currently has a performance rating of A (Excellent) based on an annualized return of 21.71% over the last three years and a total return of 7.52% year to date 2012. Factored into the performance evaluation is an expense ratio of 1.77% (above average).

The fund's risk rating is currently B (Good). It carries a beta of 2.07, meaning it is expected to move 20.7% for every 10% move in the market. Volatility, as measured by both the semi-deviation and a drawdown factor, is considered low. As of March 31, 2012, Nuveen CA Muni Market Opportunity traded at a premium of .58% above its net asset value, which is worse than its one-year historical average discount of 2.57%.

Scott R. Romans has been running the fund for 10 years and currently receives a manager quality ranking of 74 (0=worst, 99=best). If you desire only a moderate level of risk and strong performance, then this fund is an excellent option.

Data Date	Investment Rating	Net Assets ($Mil)	Price	Performance Rating/Pts	Total Return Y-T-D	Risk Rating/Pts
3-12	A+	103.93	15.50	A / 9.5	7.52%	B / 8.8
2011	A-	120.60	14.64	B+ / 8.9	-0.68%	B / 8.8
2010	C-	115.07	12.73	C- / 3.9	3.08%	C+ / 6.2
2009	C+	119.38	13.16	C / 5.0	44.62%	B- / 7.1

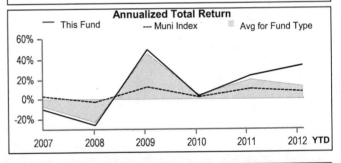

Nuveen CA Muni Value (NCA)

C+   **Fair**

Fund Family: Nuveen Fund Advisors Inc
Fund Type: Municipal - Single State
Inception Date: October 7, 1987

Major Rating Factors: Middle of the road best describes Nuveen CA Muni Value whose TheStreet.com Investment Rating is currently a C+ (Fair). The fund currently has a performance rating of C (Fair) based on an annualized return of 9.46% over the last three years and a total return of 4.27% year to date 2012. Factored into the performance evaluation is an expense ratio of 0.65% (very low).

The fund's risk rating is currently B (Good). It carries a beta of 1.61, meaning it is expected to move 16.1% for every 10% move in the market. Volatility, as measured by both the semi-deviation and a drawdown factor, is considered low. As of March 31, 2012, Nuveen CA Muni Value traded at a discount of 2.49% below its net asset value, which is worse than its one-year historical average discount of 5.43%.

Scott R. Romans has been running the fund for 10 years and currently receives a manager quality ranking of 29 (0=worst, 99=best). If you desire an average level of risk, then this fund may be an option.

Data Date	Investment Rating	Net Assets ($Mil)	Price	Performance Rating/Pts	Total Return Y-T-D	Risk Rating/Pts
3-12	C+	228.95	9.80	C / 5.0	4.27%	B / 8.9
2011	B	248.50	9.51	C+ / 6.5	-0.11%	B / 8.9
2010	C	240.60	8.63	D+ / 2.6	-0.01%	B / 8.7
2009	C+	246.89	9.07	C- / 3.7	9.98%	B / 8.2

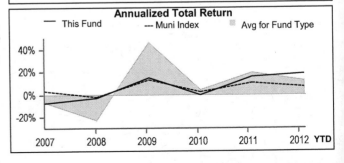

Nuveen CA Performance Plus Muni (NCP)　　　　A+　　Excellent

Fund Family: Nuveen Fund Advisors Inc
Fund Type:　Municipal - Single State
Inception Date:　November 16, 1989

Data Date	Investment Rating	Net Assets ($Mil)	Price	Performance Rating/Pts	Total Return Y-T-D	Risk Rating/Pts
3-12	A+	168.60	15.18	A / 9.3	3.72%	B / 8.7
2011	A	191.30	14.87	A / 9.3	-0.81%	B / 8.7
2010	C-	182.06	12.42	D+ / 2.9	7.12%	C+ / 6.5
2009	B-	188.63	12.39	C / 5.4	40.37%	B- / 7.4

Major Rating Factors:
Exceptional performance is the major factor driving the A+ (Excellent) TheStreet.com Investment Rating for Nuveen CA Performance Plus Muni. The fund currently has a performance rating of A (Excellent) based on an annualized return of 21.30% over the last three years and a total return of 3.72% year to date 2012. Factored into the performance evaluation is an expense ratio of 1.31% (average).

The fund's risk rating is currently B (Good). It carries a beta of 2.19, meaning it is expected to move 21.9% for every 10% move in the market. Volatility, as measured by both the semi-deviation and a drawdown factor, is considered low. As of March 31, 2012, Nuveen CA Performance Plus Muni traded at a discount of .13% below its net asset value, which is worse than its one-year historical average discount of 2.50%.

Scott R. Romans has been running the fund for 10 years and currently receives a manager quality ranking of 68 (0=worst, 99=best). If you desire only a moderate level of risk and strong performance, then this fund is an excellent option.

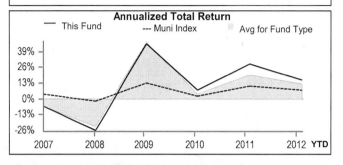

Nuveen CA Prem Inc Muni (NCU)　　　　　　　A+　　Excellent

Fund Family: Nuveen Fund Advisors Inc
Fund Type:　Municipal - Single State
Inception Date:　June 18, 1993

Data Date	Investment Rating	Net Assets ($Mil)	Price	Performance Rating/Pts	Total Return Y-T-D	Risk Rating/Pts
3-12	A+	74.28	15.04	A / 9.5	7.29%	B / 8.7
2011	A	83.80	14.22	A / 9.3	1.05%	B / 8.8
2010	C	78.58	12.44	C / 4.6	9.46%	C+ / 6.1
2009	B-	81.65	12.13	C / 5.5	40.09%	B- / 7.4

Major Rating Factors:
Exceptional performance is the major factor driving the A+ (Excellent) TheStreet.com Investment Rating for Nuveen CA Prem Inc Muni. The fund currently has a performance rating of A (Excellent) based on an annualized return of 22.55% over the last three years and a total return of 7.29% year to date 2012. Factored into the performance evaluation is an expense ratio of 1.69% (above average).

The fund's risk rating is currently B (Good). It carries a beta of 2.17, meaning it is expected to move 21.7% for every 10% move in the market. Volatility, as measured by both the semi-deviation and a drawdown factor, is considered low. As of March 31, 2012, Nuveen CA Prem Inc Muni traded at a discount of .99% below its net asset value, which is worse than its one-year historical average discount of 5.28%.

Scott R. Romans has been running the fund for 10 years and currently receives a manager quality ranking of 71 (0=worst, 99=best). If you desire only a moderate level of risk and strong performance, then this fund is an excellent option.

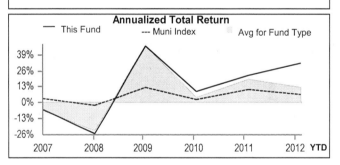

Nuveen CA Quality Inc Muni (NUC)　　　　　　A　　Excellent

Fund Family: Nuveen Fund Advisors Inc
Fund Type:　Municipal - Single State
Inception Date:　November 20, 1991

Data Date	Investment Rating	Net Assets ($Mil)	Price	Performance Rating/Pts	Total Return Y-T-D	Risk Rating/Pts
3-12	A	299.61	15.82	B+ / 8.8	0.89%	B / 8.4
2011	A	337.40	15.94	A / 9.5	-0.56%	B / 8.5
2010	C-	320.56	13.33	C- / 3.8	5.46%	C+ / 6.4
2009	B-	329.60	13.52	C+ / 5.9	38.93%	B- / 7.3

Major Rating Factors:
Strong performance is the major factor driving the A (Excellent) TheStreet.com Investment Rating for Nuveen CA Quality Inc Muni. The fund currently has a performance rating of B+ (Good) based on an annualized return of 19.46% over the last three years and a total return of 0.89% year to date 2012. Factored into the performance evaluation is an expense ratio of 1.55% (average).

The fund's risk rating is currently B (Good). It carries a beta of 2.23, meaning it is expected to move 22.3% for every 10% move in the market. Volatility, as measured by both the semi-deviation and a drawdown factor, is considered low. As of March 31, 2012, Nuveen CA Quality Inc Muni traded at a discount of .25% below its net asset value, which is worse than its one-year historical average discount of .30%.

Scott R. Romans has been running the fund for 10 years and currently receives a manager quality ranking of 60 (0=worst, 99=best). If you desire only a moderate level of risk and strong performance, then this fund is an excellent option.

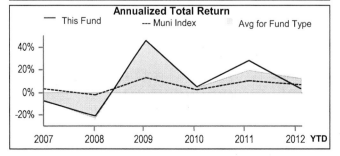

Nuveen CA Select Quality Muni (NVC)　　　　　　　A　　Excellent

Fund Family: Nuveen Fund Advisors Inc
Fund Type: Municipal - Single State
Inception Date: May 22, 1991

Major Rating Factors:
Exceptional performance is the major factor driving the A (Excellent) TheStreet.com Investment Rating for Nuveen CA Select Quality Muni. The fund currently has a performance rating of A- (Excellent) based on an annualized return of 20.63% over the last three years and a total return of 4.83% year to date 2012. Factored into the performance evaluation is an expense ratio of 1.50% (average).

The fund's risk rating is currently B (Good). It carries a beta of 2.24, meaning it is expected to move 22.4% for every 10% move in the market. Volatility, as measured by both the semi-deviation and a drawdown factor, is considered low. As of March 31, 2012, Nuveen CA Select Quality Muni traded at a discount of .32% below its net asset value, which is worse than its one-year historical average discount of .55%.

Scott R. Romans has been running the fund for 10 years and currently receives a manager quality ranking of 65 (0=worst, 99=best). If you desire only a moderate level of risk and strong performance, then this fund is an excellent option.

Data Date	Investment Rating	Net Assets ($Mil)	Price	Perfor-mance Rating/Pts	Total Return Y-T-D	Risk Rating/Pts
3-12	A	302.55	15.56	A- / 9.1	4.83%	B / 8.5
2011	A	345.90	15.09	A / 9.3	0.40%	B / 8.6
2010	C+	329.54	13.04	C / 5.4	5.00%	C+ / 6.2
2009	B-	342.02	13.29	C+ / 5.8	39.57%	B- / 7.1

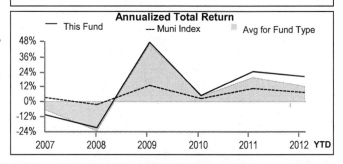

Annualized Total Return

Nuveen CA Select Tax-Free Inc Port (NXC)　　　　　　　B　　Good

Fund Family: Nuveen Fund Advisors Inc
Fund Type: Municipal - Single State
Inception Date: June 26, 1992

Major Rating Factors: Strong performance is the major factor driving the B (Good) TheStreet.com Investment Rating for Nuveen CA Select Tax-Free Inc Port. The fund currently has a performance rating of B- (Good) based on an annualized return of 12.65% over the last three years and a total return of 6.34% year to date 2012. Factored into the performance evaluation is an expense ratio of 0.38% (very low).

The fund's risk rating is currently B+ (Good). It carries a beta of 1.56, meaning it is expected to move 15.6% for every 10% move in the market. Volatility, as measured by both the semi-deviation and a drawdown factor, is considered very low. As of March 31, 2012, Nuveen CA Select Tax-Free Inc Port traded at a discount of 1.79% below its net asset value, which is worse than its one-year historical average discount of 5.51%.

Scott R. Romans has been running the fund for 20 years and currently receives a manager quality ranking of 49 (0=worst, 99=best). If you desire only a moderate level of risk and strong performance, then this fund is an excellent option.

Data Date	Investment Rating	Net Assets ($Mil)	Price	Perfor-mance Rating/Pts	Total Return Y-T-D	Risk Rating/Pts
3-12	B	84.20	14.80	B- / 7.0	6.34%	B+ / 9.0
2011	B	91.40	14.08	C+ / 6.8	0.63%	B+ / 9.0
2010	C	87.55	12.75	D+ / 2.7	4.93%	B / 8.5
2009	C+	89.96	12.77	C- / 3.1	6.56%	B / 8.8

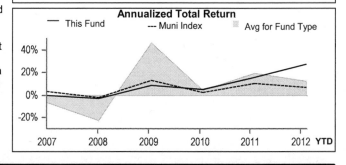

Annualized Total Return

Nuveen California Municipal Value (NCB)　　　　　　　A+　　Excellent

Fund Family: Nuveen Fund Advisors Inc
Fund Type: Municipal - National
Inception Date: April 28, 2009

Major Rating Factors:
Exceptional performance is the major factor driving the A+ (Excellent) TheStreet.com Investment Rating for Nuveen California Municipal Value. The fund currently has a performance rating of A- (Excellent) based on an annualized return of 0.00% over the last three years and a total return of 6.22% year to date 2012. Factored into the performance evaluation is an expense ratio of 0.72% (very low).

The fund's risk rating is currently B (Good). It carries a beta of 0.00, meaning the fund's expected move will be 0.0% for every 10% move in the market. Volatility, as measured by both the semi-deviation and a drawdown factor, is considered low. As of March 31, 2012, Nuveen California Municipal Value traded at a discount of 4.76% below its net asset value, which is worse than its one-year historical average discount of 6.83%.

Scott R. Romans currently receives a manager quality ranking of 86 (0=worst, 99=best). If you desire only a moderate level of risk and strong performance, then this fund is an excellent option.

Data Date	Investment Rating	Net Assets ($Mil)	Price	Perfor-mance Rating/Pts	Total Return Y-T-D	Risk Rating/Pts
3-12	A+	48.94	15.80	A- / 9.2	6.22%	B / 8.6
2011	B+	52.60	15.06	B / 7.6	1.46%	B / 8.6
2010	C-	51.66	14.40	D / 2.0	3.81%	B / 8.1

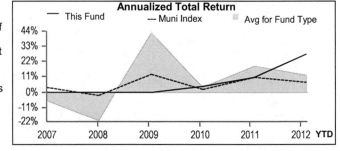

Annualized Total Return

Nuveen Core Equity Alpha Fund (JCE)   B-   Good

Fund Family: Nuveen Fund Advisors Inc
Fund Type: Income
Inception Date: March 28, 2007

Major Rating Factors: Strong performance is the major factor driving the B- (Good) TheStreet.com Investment Rating for Nuveen Core Equity Alpha Fund. The fund currently has a performance rating of B- (Good) based on an annualized return of 27.05% over the last three years and a total return of 13.22% year to date 2012. Factored into the performance evaluation is an expense ratio of 1.05% (low).

The fund's risk rating is currently B- (Good). It carries a beta of 0.94, meaning that its performance tracks fairly well with that of the overall stock market. Volatility, as measured by both the semi-deviation and a drawdown factor, is considered low. As of March 31, 2012, Nuveen Core Equity Alpha Fund traded at a discount of 7.97% below its net asset value, which is better than its one-year historical average discount of 7.11%.

Adrian D. Banner currently receives a manager quality ranking of 77 (0=worst, 99=best). If you desire only a moderate level of risk and strong performance, then this fund is an excellent option.

Data Date	Investment Rating	Net Assets ($Mil)	Price	Performance Rating/Pts	Total Return Y-T-D	Risk Rating/Pts
3-12	B-	222.46	13.85	B- / 7.4	13.22%	B- / 7.9
2011	C+	222.50	12.47	C+ / 6.4	1.84%	B- / 7.6
2010	C	211.37	13.12	C / 5.5	17.29%	C / 5.2
2009	A	203.74	12.21	A- / 9.0	34.51%	C+ / 5.7

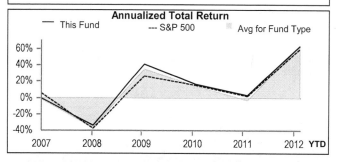

Nuveen Credit Strategies Income (JQC)   A+   Excellent

Fund Family: Nuveen Fund Advisors Inc
Fund Type: Growth and Income
Inception Date: June 25, 2003

Major Rating Factors:
Exceptional performance is the major factor driving the A+ (Excellent) TheStreet.com Investment Rating for Nuveen Credit Strategies Income. The fund currently has a performance rating of A+ (Excellent) based on an annualized return of 43.36% over the last three years and a total return of 14.01% year to date 2012. Factored into the performance evaluation is an expense ratio of 1.65% (above average).

The fund's risk rating is currently B (Good). It carries a beta of 0.87, meaning the fund's expected move will be 8.7% for every 10% move in the market. Volatility, as measured by both the semi-deviation and a drawdown factor, is considered low. As of March 31, 2012, Nuveen Credit Strategies Income traded at a discount of 8.18% below its net asset value, which is worse than its one-year historical average discount of 11.21%.

Gunther M. Stein has been running the fund for 9 years and currently receives a manager quality ranking of 94 (0=worst, 99=best). If you desire only a moderate level of risk and strong performance, then this fund is an excellent option.

Data Date	Investment Rating	Net Assets ($Mil)	Price	Performance Rating/Pts	Total Return Y-T-D	Risk Rating/Pts
3-12	A+	1,250.25	8.98	A+ / 9.6	14.01%	B / 8.6
2011	B	1,250.00	8.05	B / 8.1	3.35%	B- / 7.7
2010	C+	839.85	8.80	C+ / 6.7	24.24%	C / 4.9
2009	D	1,194.98	7.69	C- / 3.4	65.23%	C- / 4.2

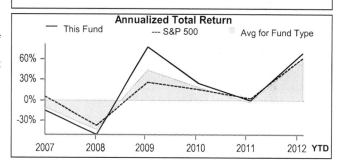

Nuveen CT Div Adv Muni (NFC)   C   Fair

Fund Family: Nuveen Fund Advisors Inc
Fund Type: Municipal - Single State
Inception Date: January 25, 2001

Major Rating Factors: Middle of the road best describes Nuveen CT Div Adv Muni whose TheStreet.com Investment Rating is currently a C (Fair). The fund currently has a performance rating of C- (Fair) based on an annualized return of 10.29% over the last three years and a total return of 0.04% year to date 2012. Factored into the performance evaluation is an expense ratio of 3.08% (high).

The fund's risk rating is currently B (Good). It carries a beta of 1.09, meaning that its performance tracks fairly well with that of the overall stock market. Volatility, as measured by both the semi-deviation and a drawdown factor, is considered low. As of March 31, 2012, Nuveen CT Div Adv Muni traded at a discount of 5.31% below its net asset value, which is better than its one-year historical average discount of 3.89%.

Michael S. Hamilton currently receives a manager quality ranking of 60 (0=worst, 99=best). If you desire an average level of risk, then this fund may be an option.

Data Date	Investment Rating	Net Assets ($Mil)	Price	Performance Rating/Pts	Total Return Y-T-D	Risk Rating/Pts
3-12	C	37.33	14.61	C- / 4.0	0.04%	B / 8.8
2011	B	39.30	14.78	B- / 7.4	0.74%	B / 8.8
2010	C	38.53	13.51	D+ / 2.7	-1.92%	B / 8.0
2009	B-	38.67	14.51	C / 5.2	33.81%	B- / 7.7

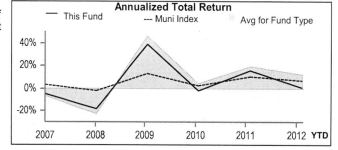

Nuveen CT Div Adv Muni Fund 2 (NGK)   C   Fair

Fund Family: Nuveen Fund Advisors Inc
Fund Type: Municipal - Single State
Inception Date: March 25, 2002

Data Date	Investment Rating	Net Assets ($Mil)	Price	Perfor-mance Rating/Pts	Total Return Y-T-D	Risk Rating/Pts
3-12	C	33.48	14.55	C- / 3.9	-1.54%	B / 8.4
2011	B	35.00	14.96	B / 7.7	0.20%	B / 8.3
2010	C	34.83	13.73	D+ / 2.9	-1.57%	B- / 7.8
2009	B-	35.13	14.70	C / 5.4	38.72%	B- / 7.6

Major Rating Factors: Middle of the road best describes Nuveen CT Div Adv Muni Fund 2 whose TheStreet.com Investment Rating is currently a C (Fair). The fund currently has a performance rating of C- (Fair) based on an annualized return of 10.73% over the last three years and a total return of -1.54% year to date 2012. Factored into the performance evaluation is an expense ratio of 2.83% (high).

The fund's risk rating is currently B (Good). It carries a beta of 1.41, meaning it is expected to move 14.1% for every 10% move in the market. Volatility, as measured by both the semi-deviation and a drawdown factor, is considered low. As of March 31, 2012, Nuveen CT Div Adv Muni Fund 2 traded at a discount of 4.84% below its net asset value, which is better than its one-year historical average discount of 2.33%.

Michael S. Hamilton currently receives a manager quality ranking of 54 (0=worst, 99=best). If you desire an average level of risk, then this fund may be an option.

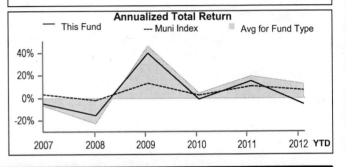

Nuveen CT Div Adv Muni Fund 3 (NGO)   C+   Fair

Fund Family: Nuveen Fund Advisors Inc
Fund Type: Municipal - Single State
Inception Date: September 25, 2002

Data Date	Investment Rating	Net Assets ($Mil)	Price	Perfor-mance Rating/Pts	Total Return Y-T-D	Risk Rating/Pts
3-12	C+	63.06	13.88	C / 5.1	2.63%	B+ / 9.1
2011	B	64.40	13.69	B- / 7.2	0.95%	B+ / 9.1
2010	C	63.06	12.98	C- / 3.3	1.06%	B- / 7.1
2009	B-	63.27	13.52	C+ / 5.7	36.55%	B- / 7.7

Major Rating Factors: Middle of the road best describes Nuveen CT Div Adv Muni Fund 3 whose TheStreet.com Investment Rating is currently a C+ (Fair). The fund currently has a performance rating of C (Fair) based on an annualized return of 12.07% over the last three years and a total return of 2.63% year to date 2012. Factored into the performance evaluation is an expense ratio of 2.87% (high).

The fund's risk rating is currently B+ (Good). It carries a beta of 1.35, meaning it is expected to move 13.5% for every 10% move in the market. Volatility, as measured by both the semi-deviation and a drawdown factor, is considered very low. As of March 31, 2012, Nuveen CT Div Adv Muni Fund 3 traded at a discount of 7.22% below its net asset value, which is worse than its one-year historical average discount of 7.94%.

Michael S. Hamilton currently receives a manager quality ranking of 63 (0=worst, 99=best). If you desire an average level of risk, then this fund may be an option.

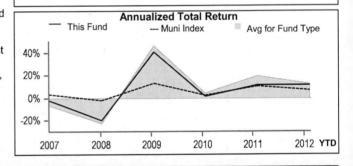

Nuveen CT Prem Inc Muni (NTC)   C+   Fair

Fund Family: Nuveen Fund Advisors Inc
Fund Type: Municipal - Single State
Inception Date: May 20, 1993

Data Date	Investment Rating	Net Assets ($Mil)	Price	Perfor-mance Rating/Pts	Total Return Y-T-D	Risk Rating/Pts
3-12	C+	76.28	14.25	C / 5.4	2.59%	B+ / 9.0
2011	B+	79.80	14.06	B / 7.6	0.85%	B+ / 9.0
2010	C	78.11	13.05	C- / 3.3	0.42%	B- / 7.9
2009	B-	78.03	13.67	C+ / 5.7	33.94%	B- / 7.6

Major Rating Factors: Middle of the road best describes Nuveen CT Prem Inc Muni whose TheStreet.com Investment Rating is currently a C+ (Fair). The fund currently has a performance rating of C (Fair) based on an annualized return of 12.74% over the last three years and a total return of 2.59% year to date 2012. Factored into the performance evaluation is an expense ratio of 2.41% (high).

The fund's risk rating is currently B+ (Good). It carries a beta of 1.84, meaning it is expected to move 18.4% for every 10% move in the market. Volatility, as measured by both the semi-deviation and a drawdown factor, is considered very low. As of March 31, 2012, Nuveen CT Prem Inc Muni traded at a discount of 5.38% below its net asset value, which is worse than its one-year historical average discount of 6.60%.

Michael S. Hamilton currently receives a manager quality ranking of 39 (0=worst, 99=best). If you desire an average level of risk, then this fund may be an option.

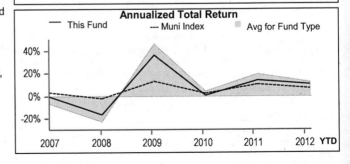

Nuveen Div Adv Muni (NAD)

B+　　**Good**

Fund Family: Nuveen Fund Advisors Inc
Fund Type: Municipal - National
Inception Date: May 25, 1999

Major Rating Factors: Strong performance is the major factor driving the B+ (Good) TheStreet.com Investment Rating for Nuveen Div Adv Muni. The fund currently has a performance rating of B (Good) based on an annualized return of 17.44% over the last three years and a total return of 1.66% year to date 2012. Factored into the performance evaluation is an expense ratio of 2.02% (high).

The fund's risk rating is currently B (Good). It carries a beta of 2.32, meaning it is expected to move 23.2% for every 10% move in the market. Volatility, as measured by both the semi-deviation and a drawdown factor, is considered low. As of March 31, 2012, Nuveen Div Adv Muni traded at a discount of 4.64% below its net asset value, which is better than its one-year historical average discount of 4.17%.

Thomas C. Spalding has been running the fund for 10 years and currently receives a manager quality ranking of 39 (0=worst, 99=best). If you desire only a moderate level of risk and strong performance, then this fund is an excellent option.

Data Date	Investment Rating	Net Assets ($Mil)	Price	Performance Rating/Pts	Total Return Y-T-D	Risk Rating/Pts
3-12	B+	565.36	14.58	B / 7.8	1.66%	B / 8.6
2011	A-	577.40	14.56	B+ / 8.7	-0.27%	B / 8.7
2010	C-	561.83	12.90	C- / 3.7	1.95%	C+ / 6.5
2009	C+	569.67	13.50	C+ / 5.6	38.15%	B- / 7.1

Annualized Total Return

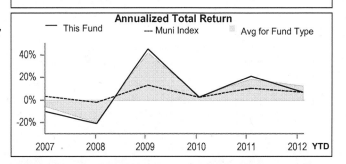

Nuveen Div Adv Muni 3 (NZF)

B+　　**Good**

Fund Family: Nuveen Fund Advisors Inc
Fund Type: Municipal - National
Inception Date: September 25, 2001

Major Rating Factors: Strong performance is the major factor driving the B+ (Good) TheStreet.com Investment Rating for Nuveen Div Adv Muni 3. The fund currently has a performance rating of B- (Good) based on an annualized return of 17.30% over the last three years and a total return of 2.04% year to date 2012. Factored into the performance evaluation is an expense ratio of 1.46% (average).

The fund's risk rating is currently B (Good). It carries a beta of 1.54, meaning it is expected to move 15.4% for every 10% move in the market. Volatility, as measured by both the semi-deviation and a drawdown factor, is considered low. As of March 31, 2012, Nuveen Div Adv Muni 3 traded at a discount of 2.76% below its net asset value, which is worse than its one-year historical average discount of 2.93%.

Paul L. Brennan has been running the fund for 6 years and currently receives a manager quality ranking of 74 (0=worst, 99=best). If you desire only a moderate level of risk and strong performance, then this fund is an excellent option.

Data Date	Investment Rating	Net Assets ($Mil)	Price	Performance Rating/Pts	Total Return Y-T-D	Risk Rating/Pts
3-12	B+	587.05	14.77	B- / 7.4	2.04%	B / 8.8
2011	B+	596.70	14.71	B+ / 8.3	-1.50%	B / 8.8
2010	C	584.56	13.29	C- / 3.9	5.81%	C+ / 6.8
2009	C+	592.68	13.45	C / 5.0	36.58%	B- / 7.4

Annualized Total Return

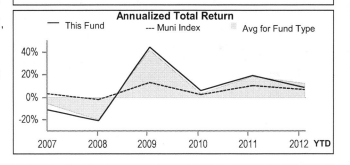

Nuveen Div Adv Muni Income (NVG)

B-　　**Good**

Fund Family: Nuveen Fund Advisors Inc
Fund Type: Municipal - National
Inception Date: March 25, 2002

Major Rating Factors: Nuveen Div Adv Muni Income receives a TheStreet.com Investment Rating of B- (Good). The fund currently has a performance rating of C+ (Fair) based on an annualized return of 13.50% over the last three years and a total return of 0.86% year to date 2012. Factored into the performance evaluation is an expense ratio of 1.84% (above average).

The fund's risk rating is currently B+ (Good). It carries a beta of 1.60, meaning it is expected to move 16.0% for every 10% move in the market. Volatility, as measured by both the semi-deviation and a drawdown factor, is considered very low. As of March 31, 2012, Nuveen Div Adv Muni Income traded at a discount of 4.23% below its net asset value, which is worse than its one-year historical average discount of 4.52%.

Paul L. Brennan has been running the fund for 6 years and currently receives a manager quality ranking of 53 (0=worst, 99=best). If you desire an average level of risk, then this fund may be an option.

Data Date	Investment Rating	Net Assets ($Mil)	Price	Performance Rating/Pts	Total Return Y-T-D	Risk Rating/Pts
3-12	B-	448.07	14.96	C+ / 6.0	0.86%	B+ / 9.1
2011	B+	454.20	15.05	B / 7.8	-0.66%	B+ / 9.1
2010	C+	441.21	13.60	C / 4.9	0.77%	C+ / 6.9
2009	B-	457.06	14.30	C+ / 6.2	31.09%	B- / 7.5

Annualized Total Return

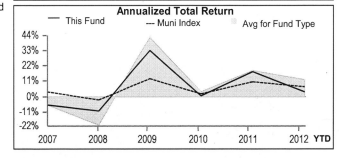

Nuveen Diversified Dividend&Income (JDD)   A   Excellent

Fund Family: Nuveen Fund Advisors Inc
Fund Type: Growth and Income
Inception Date: September 30, 2003

Data Date	Investment Rating	Net Assets ($Mil)	Price	Performance Rating/Pts	Total Return Y-T-D	Risk Rating/Pts
3-12	A	226.70	11.73	A / 9.4	16.73%	B / 8.1
2011	B	226.70	10.26	B+ / 8.4	3.61%	B- / 7.8
2010	C	222.57	10.89	C+ / 6.4	22.16%	C- / 4.0
2009	D	215.83	9.73	D+ / 2.4	63.04%	C / 4.6

Major Rating Factors:
Exceptional performance is the major factor driving the A (Excellent) TheStreet.com Investment Rating for Nuveen Diversified Dividend&Income. The fund currently has a performance rating of A (Excellent) based on an annualized return of 39.04% over the last three years and a total return of 16.73% year to date 2012. Factored into the performance evaluation is an expense ratio of 1.73% (above average).

The fund's risk rating is currently B (Good). It carries a beta of 0.97, meaning that its performance tracks fairly well with that of the overall stock market. Volatility, as measured by both the semi-deviation and a drawdown factor, is considered low. As of March 31, 2012, Nuveen Diversified Dividend&Income traded at a discount of 5.10% below its net asset value, which is worse than its one-year historical average discount of 7.60%.

Gunther M. Stein has been running the fund for 9 years and currently receives a manager quality ranking of 90 (0=worst, 99=best). If you desire only a moderate level of risk and strong performance, then this fund is an excellent option.

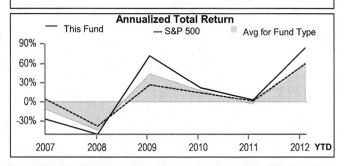

Nuveen Dividend Advantage Muni 2 (NXZ)   B+   Good

Fund Family: Nuveen Fund Advisors Inc
Fund Type: Municipal - National
Inception Date: March 27, 2001

Data Date	Investment Rating	Net Assets ($Mil)	Price	Performance Rating/Pts	Total Return Y-T-D	Risk Rating/Pts
3-12	B+	427.09	15.19	B / 7.8	4.54%	B / 8.8
2011	B+	431.20	14.76	B / 8.1	-0.54%	B / 8.7
2010	C-	436.38	13.30	D / 2.2	-1.17%	B- / 7.6
2009	C+	441.36	14.38	C / 5.3	29.54%	B- / 7.4

Major Rating Factors: Strong performance is the major factor driving the B+ (Good) TheStreet.com Investment Rating for Nuveen Dividend Advantage Muni 2. The fund currently has a performance rating of B (Good) based on an annualized return of 15.47% over the last three years and a total return of 4.54% year to date 2012. Factored into the performance evaluation is an expense ratio of 1.75% (above average).

The fund's risk rating is currently B (Good). It carries a beta of 1.64, meaning it is expected to move 16.4% for every 10% move in the market. Volatility, as measured by both the semi-deviation and a drawdown factor, is considered low. As of March 31, 2012, Nuveen Dividend Advantage Muni 2 traded at a discount of .91% below its net asset value, which is worse than its one-year historical average discount of 2.96%.

Thomas C. Spalding has been running the fund for 11 years and currently receives a manager quality ranking of 64 (0=worst, 99=best). If you desire only a moderate level of risk and strong performance, then this fund is an excellent option.

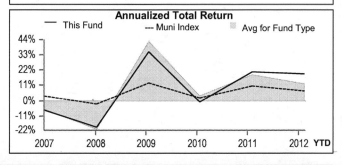

Nuveen Energy MLP Total Return Fun (JMF)   D+   Weak

Fund Family: Nuveen Fund Advisors Inc
Fund Type: Growth and Income
Inception Date: February 24, 2011

Data Date	Investment Rating	Net Assets ($Mil)	Price	Performance Rating/Pts	Total Return Y-T-D	Risk Rating/Pts
3-12	D+	409.91	18.40	C- / 3.5	7.89%	B- / 7.3

Major Rating Factors: Nuveen Energy MLP Total Return Fun receives a TheStreet.com Investment Rating of D+ (Weak). The fund currently has a performance rating of C- (Fair) based on an annualized return of 0.00% over the last three years and a total return of 7.89% year to date 2012. Factored into the performance evaluation is an expense ratio of 1.78% (above average).

The fund's risk rating is currently B- (Good). It carries a beta of 0.00, meaning the fund's expected move will be 0.0% for every 10% move in the market. Volatility, as measured by both the semi-deviation and a drawdown factor, is considered low. As of March 31, 2012, Nuveen Energy MLP Total Return Fun traded at a premium of 1.71% above its net asset value, which is worse than its one-year historical average premium of .45%.

This fund has been team managed for 1 year and currently receives a manager quality ranking of 14 (0=worst, 99=best). If you desire an average level of risk, then this fund may be an option.

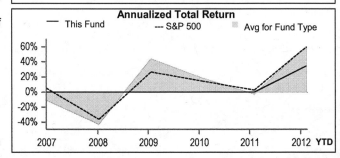

Nuveen EnhancedMunicipal Value (NEV)   B   Good

Fund Family: Nuveen Fund Advisors Inc
Fund Type: General - Investment Grade
Inception Date: September 25, 2009

Major Rating Factors: Strong performance is the major factor driving the B (Good) TheStreet.com Investment Rating for Nuveen EnhancedMunicipal Value. The fund currently has a performance rating of B- (Good) based on an annualized return of 0.00% over the last three years and a total return of 7.47% year to date 2012. Factored into the performance evaluation is an expense ratio of 1.17% (low).

The fund's risk rating is currently B (Good). It carries a beta of 0.00, meaning the fund's expected move will be 0.0% for every 10% move in the market. Volatility, as measured by both the semi-deviation and a drawdown factor, is considered low. As of March 31, 2012, Nuveen EnhancedMunicipal Value traded at a premium of 1.01% above its net asset value, which is worse than its one-year historical average discount of 1.36%.

Steve M. Hlavin currently receives a manager quality ranking of 93 (0=worst, 99=best). If you desire only a moderate level of risk and strong performance, then this fund is an excellent option.

Data Date	Investment Rating	Net Assets ($Mil)	Price	Performance Rating/Pts	Total Return Y-T-D	Risk Rating/Pts
3-12	B	269.05	15.05	B- / 7.3	7.47%	B / 8.2
2011	B+	273.10	14.23	B+ / 8.3	3.23%	B / 8.2
2010	D+	240.98	12.71	E+ / 0.9	2.73%	B- / 7.6

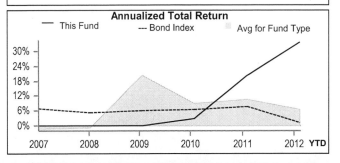

Nuveen Equity Premium & Growth Fun (JPG)   C+   Fair

Fund Family: Nuveen Fund Advisors Inc
Fund Type: Income
Inception Date: November 22, 2005

Major Rating Factors: Middle of the road best describes Nuveen Equity Premium & Growth Fun whose TheStreet.com Investment Rating is currently a C+ (Fair). The fund currently has a performance rating of C (Fair) based on an annualized return of 19.62% over the last three years and a total return of 12.78% year to date 2012. Factored into the performance evaluation is an expense ratio of 0.96% (low).

The fund's risk rating is currently B (Good). It carries a beta of 0.68, meaning the fund's expected move will be 6.8% for every 10% move in the market. Volatility, as measured by both the semi-deviation and a drawdown factor, is considered low. As of March 31, 2012, Nuveen Equity Premium & Growth Fun traded at a discount of 8.57% below its net asset value, which is worse than its one-year historical average discount of 10.73%.

J. Patrick Rogers currently receives a manager quality ranking of 75 (0=worst, 99=best). If you desire an average level of risk, then this fund may be an option.

Data Date	Investment Rating	Net Assets ($Mil)	Price	Performance Rating/Pts	Total Return Y-T-D	Risk Rating/Pts
3-12	C+	225.66	13.33	C / 5.2	12.78%	B / 8.3
2011	C	225.70	12.07	C / 4.5	1.08%	B / 8.0
2010	C	226.19	13.85	C+ / 6.0	14.90%	C / 5.3
2009	C-	217.79	13.09	D+ / 2.8	27.99%	C+ / 6.0

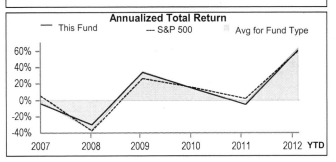

Nuveen Equity Premium Advantage (JLA)   C-   Fair

Fund Family: Nuveen Fund Advisors Inc
Fund Type: Income
Inception Date: May 26, 2005

Major Rating Factors: Middle of the road best describes Nuveen Equity Premium Advantage whose TheStreet.com Investment Rating is currently a C- (Fair). The fund currently has a performance rating of C- (Fair) based on an annualized return of 15.92% over the last three years and a total return of 8.24% year to date 2012. Factored into the performance evaluation is an expense ratio of 0.94% (low).

The fund's risk rating is currently B- (Good). It carries a beta of 0.60, meaning the fund's expected move will be 6.0% for every 10% move in the market. Volatility, as measured by both the semi-deviation and a drawdown factor, is considered low. As of March 31, 2012, Nuveen Equity Premium Advantage traded at a discount of 11.08% below its net asset value, which is better than its one-year historical average discount of 10.36%.

J. Patrick Rogers currently receives a manager quality ranking of 70 (0=worst, 99=best). If you desire an average level of risk, then this fund may be an option.

Data Date	Investment Rating	Net Assets ($Mil)	Price	Performance Rating/Pts	Total Return Y-T-D	Risk Rating/Pts
3-12	C-	340.53	12.12	C- / 3.9	8.24%	B- / 7.7
2011	C	340.60	11.46	C / 5.0	1.66%	B- / 7.5
2010	C-	349.90	12.90	C / 4.4	8.94%	C / 5.3
2009	C-	339.64	13.07	C- / 3.6	34.61%	C+ / 5.8

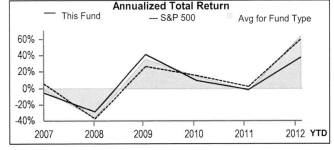

Nuveen Equity Premium Income Fund (JPZ)   C   Fair

Fund Family: Nuveen Fund Advisors Inc
Fund Type: Income
Inception Date: October 26, 2004

Major Rating Factors: Middle of the road best describes Nuveen Equity Premium Income Fund whose TheStreet.com Investment Rating is currently a C (Fair). The fund currently has a performance rating of C- (Fair) based on an annualized return of 17.22% over the last three years and a total return of 9.48% year to date 2012. Factored into the performance evaluation is an expense ratio of 0.84% (very low).

The fund's risk rating is currently B (Good). It carries a beta of 0.69, meaning the fund's expected move will be 6.9% for every 10% move in the market. Volatility, as measured by both the semi-deviation and a drawdown factor, is considered low. As of March 31, 2012, Nuveen Equity Premium Income Fund traded at a discount of 10.20% below its net asset value, which is better than its one-year historical average discount of 10.09%.

J. Patrick Rogers currently receives a manager quality ranking of 63 (0=worst, 99=best). If you desire an average level of risk, then this fund may be an option.

Data Date	Investment Rating	Net Assets ($Mil)	Price	Performance Rating/Pts	Total Return Y-T-D	Risk Rating/Pts
3-12	C	496.09	11.97	C- / 4.2	9.48%	B / 8.1
2011	C	496.10	11.18	C- / 4.2	1.25%	B- / 7.8
2010	C-	502.49	12.76	C- / 4.2	8.13%	C / 5.4
2009	C-	487.49	13.00	C- / 3.5	28.97%	C+ / 5.8

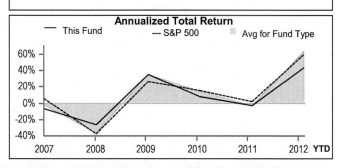

Nuveen Equity Premium Opportunity (JSN)   C-   Fair

Fund Family: Nuveen Fund Advisors Inc
Fund Type: Income
Inception Date: January 26, 2005

Major Rating Factors: Middle of the road best describes Nuveen Equity Premium Opportunity whose TheStreet.com Investment Rating is currently a C- (Fair). The fund currently has a performance rating of C- (Fair) based on an annualized return of 15.67% over the last three years and a total return of 9.11% year to date 2012. Factored into the performance evaluation is an expense ratio of 0.81% (very low).

The fund's risk rating is currently B- (Good). It carries a beta of 0.61, meaning the fund's expected move will be 6.1% for every 10% move in the market. Volatility, as measured by both the semi-deviation and a drawdown factor, is considered low. As of March 31, 2012, Nuveen Equity Premium Opportunity traded at a discount of 8.56% below its net asset value, which is worse than its one-year historical average discount of 9.38%.

J. Patrick Rogers currently receives a manager quality ranking of 67 (0=worst, 99=best). If you desire an average level of risk, then this fund may be an option.

Data Date	Investment Rating	Net Assets ($Mil)	Price	Performance Rating/Pts	Total Return Y-T-D	Risk Rating/Pts
3-12	C-	859.33	12.18	C- / 3.9	9.11%	B- / 7.9
2011	C	859.30	11.42	C / 4.5	0.79%	B- / 7.6
2010	C-	878.32	12.88	C / 4.4	7.85%	C / 5.3
2009	C-	858.14	13.20	C- / 4.0	32.50%	C+ / 5.7

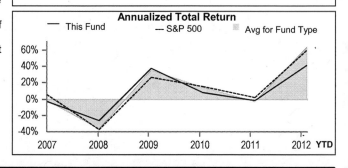

Nuveen Floating Rate Income Fund (JFR)   B+   Good

Fund Family: Nuveen Fund Advisors Inc
Fund Type: Loan Participation
Inception Date: March 26, 2004

Major Rating Factors: Strong performance is the major factor driving the B+ (Good) TheStreet.com Investment Rating for Nuveen Floating Rate Income Fund. The fund currently has a performance rating of B+ (Good) based on an annualized return of 34.20% over the last three years and a total return of 11.73% year to date 2012. Factored into the performance evaluation is an expense ratio of 1.54% (average).

The fund's risk rating is currently B (Good). It carries a beta of -113.91, meaning the fund's expected move will be -1139.1% for every 10% move in the market. Volatility, as measured by both the semi-deviation and a drawdown factor, is considered low. As of March 31, 2012, Nuveen Floating Rate Income Fund traded at a premium of .08% above its net asset value, which is worse than its one-year historical average discount of 2.70%.

Gunther M. Stein currently receives a manager quality ranking of 99 (0=worst, 99=best). If you desire only a moderate level of risk and strong performance, then this fund is an excellent option.

Data Date	Investment Rating	Net Assets ($Mil)	Price	Performance Rating/Pts	Total Return Y-T-D	Risk Rating/Pts
3-12	B+	580.42	11.92	B+ / 8.7	11.73%	B / 8.1
2011	B	543.20	10.86	B / 7.6	2.30%	B- / 7.9
2010	C+	542.46	11.81	B / 7.7	21.16%	C- / 3.7
2009	C-	500.80	10.35	C / 5.3	71.62%	C / 4.7

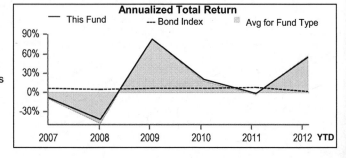

Nuveen Floating Rate Income Opp (JRO)

A   **Excellent**

Fund Family: Nuveen Fund Advisors Inc
Fund Type: Loan Participation
Inception Date: July 30, 2004

Major Rating Factors:
Exceptional performance is the major factor driving the A (Excellent) TheStreet.com Investment Rating for Nuveen Floating Rate Income Opp. The fund currently has a performance rating of A (Excellent) based on an annualized return of 39.73% over the last three years and a total return of 11.19% year to date 2012. Factored into the performance evaluation is an expense ratio of 1.56% (average).

The fund's risk rating is currently B (Good). It carries a beta of -40.13, meaning the fund's expected move will be -401.3% for every 10% move in the market. Volatility, as measured by both the semi-deviation and a drawdown factor, is considered low. As of March 31, 2012, Nuveen Floating Rate Income Opp traded at a premium of 1.43% above its net asset value, which is worse than its one-year historical average discount of .67%.

Gunther M. Stein has been running the fund for 5 years and currently receives a manager quality ranking of 99 (0=worst, 99=best). If you desire only a moderate level of risk and strong performance, then this fund is an excellent option.

Data Date	Investment Rating	Net Assets ($Mil)	Price	Performance Rating/Pts	Total Return Y-T-D	Risk Rating/Pts
3-12	A	364.88	12.05	A / 9.3	11.19%	B / 8.0
2011	B+	340.90	11.04	B+ / 8.6	2.45%	B- / 7.9
2010	C+	322.14	12.08	B / 7.9	19.90%	C- / 3.6
2009	C+	296.41	10.76	B / 7.9	106.49%	C / 4.3

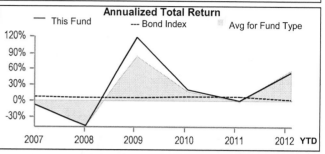

Annualized Total Return

Nuveen GA Div Adv Muni (NZX)

C+   **Fair**

Fund Family: Nuveen Fund Advisors Inc
Fund Type: Municipal - Single State
Inception Date: September 25, 2001

Major Rating Factors: Middle of the road best describes Nuveen GA Div Adv Muni whose TheStreet.com Investment Rating is currently a C+ (Fair). The fund currently has a performance rating of C (Fair) based on an annualized return of 13.92% over the last three years and a total return of 0.21% year to date 2012. Factored into the performance evaluation is an expense ratio of 2.83% (high).

The fund's risk rating is currently B (Good). It carries a beta of 1.16, meaning it is expected to move 11.6% for every 10% move in the market. Volatility, as measured by both the semi-deviation and a drawdown factor, is considered low. As of March 31, 2012, Nuveen GA Div Adv Muni traded at a discount of .20% below its net asset value, which is worse than its one-year historical average discount of .76%.

Daniel J. Close has been running the fund for 5 years and currently receives a manager quality ranking of 73 (0=worst, 99=best). If you desire an average level of risk, then this fund may be an option.

Data Date	Investment Rating	Net Assets ($Mil)	Price	Performance Rating/Pts	Total Return Y-T-D	Risk Rating/Pts
3-12	C+	28.30	15.28	C / 5.4	0.21%	B / 8.6
2011	B+	29.50	15.43	B+ / 8.3	-1.04%	B / 8.6
2010	C-	29.18	13.22	D+ / 2.8	-0.49%	B- / 7.2
2009	C+	29.37	14.00	C / 4.6	45.00%	B- / 7.1

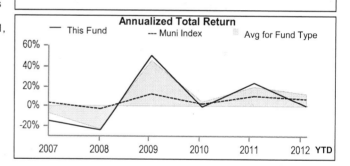

Annualized Total Return

Nuveen GA Div Adv Muni Fund 2 (NKG)

C+   **Fair**

Fund Family: Nuveen Fund Advisors Inc
Fund Type: Municipal - Single State
Inception Date: September 25, 2002

Major Rating Factors: Middle of the road best describes Nuveen GA Div Adv Muni Fund 2 whose TheStreet.com Investment Rating is currently a C+ (Fair). The fund currently has a performance rating of C+ (Fair) based on an annualized return of 13.94% over the last three years and a total return of -1.52% year to date 2012. Factored into the performance evaluation is an expense ratio of 2.75% (high).

The fund's risk rating is currently B (Good). It carries a beta of 1.27, meaning it is expected to move 12.7% for every 10% move in the market. Volatility, as measured by both the semi-deviation and a drawdown factor, is considered low. As of March 31, 2012, Nuveen GA Div Adv Muni Fund 2 traded at a discount of 1.86% below its net asset value, which is better than its one-year historical average discount of .04%.

Daniel J. Close has been running the fund for 5 years and currently receives a manager quality ranking of 71 (0=worst, 99=best). If you desire an average level of risk, then this fund may be an option.

Data Date	Investment Rating	Net Assets ($Mil)	Price	Performance Rating/Pts	Total Return Y-T-D	Risk Rating/Pts
3-12	C+	62.78	14.24	C+ / 5.7	-1.52%	B / 8.8
2011	A-	65.10	14.63	B+ / 8.6	0.00%	B / 8.8
2010	C	64.72	12.58	C- / 3.1	2.09%	B- / 7.4
2009	B-	65.35	12.98	C+ / 6.3	44.26%	B- / 7.5

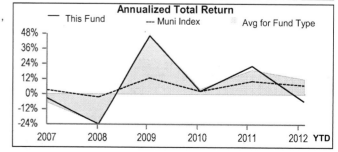

Annualized Total Return

* Denotes ETF Fund

Nuveen GA Prem Inc Muni (NPG)

B-   **Good**

Fund Family: Nuveen Fund Advisors Inc
Fund Type: Municipal - Single State
Inception Date: May 20, 1993

Data Date	Investment Rating	Net Assets ($Mil)	Price	Performance Rating/Pts	Total Return Y-T-D	Risk Rating/Pts
3-12	B-	53.29	14.57	C+ / 6.3	1.83%	B / 8.9
2011	B+	55.60	14.47	B / 8.0	0.55%	B+ / 9.0
2010	C	55.02	12.92	C- / 3.7	-0.83%	C+ / 6.7
2009	B-	55.83	13.70	C+ / 6.3	40.51%	B- / 7.3

Major Rating Factors: Nuveen GA Prem Inc Muni receives a TheStreet.com Investment Rating of B- (Good). The fund currently has a performance rating of C+ (Fair) based on an annualized return of 14.57% over the last three years and a total return of 1.83% year to date 2012. Factored into the performance evaluation is an expense ratio of 2.91% (high).

The fund's risk rating is currently B (Good). It carries a beta of 1.49, meaning it is expected to move 14.9% for every 10% move in the market. Volatility, as measured by both the semi-deviation and a drawdown factor, is considered low. As of March 31, 2012, Nuveen GA Prem Inc Muni traded at a discount of 2.15% below its net asset value, which is worse than its one-year historical average discount of 2.36%.

Daniel J. Close has been running the fund for 5 years and currently receives a manager quality ranking of 66 (0=worst, 99=best). If you desire an average level of risk, then this fund may be an option.

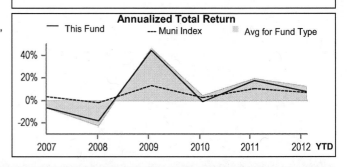

Annualized Total Return — This Fund · · · Muni Index · Avg for Fund Type

Nuveen Glob Govt Enhanced Inc (JGG)

D+   **Weak**

Fund Family: Nuveen Fund Advisors Inc
Fund Type: Global
Inception Date: June 30, 2006

Data Date	Investment Rating	Net Assets ($Mil)	Price	Performance Rating/Pts	Total Return Y-T-D	Risk Rating/Pts
3-12	D+	144.70	14.33	D / 1.9	3.36%	B / 8.1
2011	C-	144.70	14.16	D+ / 2.6	-0.57%	B / 8.1
2010	C+	156.25	15.65	C / 5.2	-0.21%	C+ / 6.9
2009	C	161.34	17.23	C- / 4.1	15.94%	C+ / 6.9

Major Rating Factors:
Disappointing performance is the major factor driving the D+ (Weak) TheStreet.com Investment Rating for Nuveen Glob Govt Enhanced Inc. The fund currently has a performance rating of D (Weak) based on an annualized return of 6.21% over the last three years and a total return of 3.36% year to date 2012. Factored into the performance evaluation is an expense ratio of 1.06% (low).

The fund's risk rating is currently B (Good). It carries a beta of 0.27, meaning the fund's expected move will be 2.7% for every 10% move in the market. Volatility, as measured by both the semi-deviation and a drawdown factor, is considered low. As of March 31, 2012, Nuveen Glob Govt Enhanced Inc traded at a discount of 7.13% below its net asset value, which is worse than its one-year historical average discount of 7.38%.

Steve S. Lee currently receives a manager quality ranking of 71 (0=worst, 99=best). This fund offers only a moderate level of risk but investors looking for strong performance are still waiting.

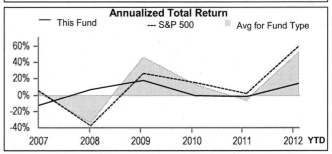

Annualized Total Return — This Fund · · · S&P 500 · Avg for Fund Type

Nuveen Global Value Opportunities (JGV)

C-   **Fair**

Fund Family: Nuveen Fund Advisors Inc
Fund Type: Global
Inception Date: July 25, 2006

Data Date	Investment Rating	Net Assets ($Mil)	Price	Performance Rating/Pts	Total Return Y-T-D	Risk Rating/Pts
3-12	C-	324.96	16.31	C- / 3.9	-0.71%	B- / 7.8
2011	C+	325.00	16.76	C+ / 5.8	-2.15%	B- / 7.7
2010	B+	351.82	20.30	B+ / 8.4	23.36%	C / 5.1
2009	C+	340.16	17.53	C+ / 6.9	52.59%	C+ / 5.6

Major Rating Factors: Middle of the road best describes Nuveen Global Value Opportunities whose TheStreet.com Investment Rating is currently a C- (Fair). The fund currently has a performance rating of C- (Fair) based on an annualized return of 20.66% over the last three years and a total return of -0.71% year to date 2012. Factored into the performance evaluation is an expense ratio of 1.16% (low).

The fund's risk rating is currently B- (Good). It carries a beta of 0.67, meaning the fund's expected move will be 6.7% for every 10% move in the market. Volatility, as measured by both the semi-deviation and a drawdown factor, is considered low. As of March 31, 2012, Nuveen Global Value Opportunities traded at a discount of 4.73% below its net asset value, which is better than its one-year historical average discount of 3.44%.

David B. Iben has been running the fund for 6 years and currently receives a manager quality ranking of 86 (0=worst, 99=best). If you desire an average level of risk, then this fund may be an option.

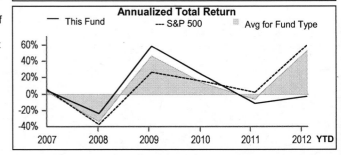

Annualized Total Return — This Fund · · · S&P 500 · Avg for Fund Type

Nuveen Insured CA Div Adv Muni Fun (NKL)

B   **Good**

Fund Family: Nuveen Fund Advisors Inc
Fund Type: Municipal - Single State
Inception Date: March 25, 2002

Data Date	Investment Rating	Net Assets ($Mil)	Price	Performance Rating/Pts	Total Return Y-T-D	Risk Rating/Pts
3-12	B	208.95	15.32	B- / 7.3	-3.30%	B / 8.6
2011	A+	234.00	16.09	A+ / 9.6	0.19%	B / 8.7
2010	C-	224.30	13.22	C- / 3.2	4.38%	C+ / 6.9
2009	C+	231.92	13.51	C / 5.2	32.05%	B- / 7.3

Major Rating Factors: Strong performance is the major factor driving the B (Good) TheStreet.com Investment Rating for Nuveen Insured CA Div Adv Muni Fun. The fund currently has a performance rating of B- (Good) based on an annualized return of 17.33% over the last three years and a total return of -3.30% year to date 2012. Factored into the performance evaluation is an expense ratio of 0.97% (low).

The fund's risk rating is currently B (Good). It carries a beta of 2.35, meaning it is expected to move 23.5% for every 10% move in the market. Volatility, as measured by both the semi-deviation and a drawdown factor, is considered low. As of March 31, 2012, Nuveen Insured CA Div Adv Muni Fun traded at a discount of 3.10% below its net asset value, which is better than its one-year historical average discount of .78%.

Scott R. Romans has been running the fund for 10 years and currently receives a manager quality ranking of 41 (0=worst, 99=best). If you desire only a moderate level of risk and strong performance, then this fund is an excellent option.

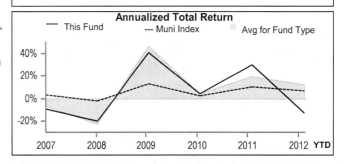

Annualized Total Return

Nuveen Insured CA Prem Inc Muni (NPC)

B-   **Good**

Fund Family: Nuveen Fund Advisors Inc
Fund Type: Municipal - Single State
Inception Date: November 19, 1992

Data Date	Investment Rating	Net Assets ($Mil)	Price	Performance Rating/Pts	Total Return Y-T-D	Risk Rating/Pts
3-12	B-	87.83	15.10	C+ / 6.5	-5.27%	B / 8.8
2011	A+	99.30	16.16	A+ / 9.6	-0.06%	B / 8.9
2010	C	94.94	13.05	D+ / 2.9	6.90%	B- / 7.5
2009	C+	97.63	13.00	C / 4.7	27.19%	B- / 7.7

Major Rating Factors: Nuveen Insured CA Prem Inc Muni receives a TheStreet.com Investment Rating of B- (Good). The fund currently has a performance rating of C+ (Fair) based on an annualized return of 15.53% over the last three years and a total return of -5.27% year to date 2012. Factored into the performance evaluation is an expense ratio of 1.77% (above average).

The fund's risk rating is currently B (Good). It carries a beta of 2.10, meaning it is expected to move 21.0% for every 10% move in the market. Volatility, as measured by both the semi-deviation and a drawdown factor, is considered low. As of March 31, 2012, Nuveen Insured CA Prem Inc Muni traded at a discount of 3.51% below its net asset value, which is better than its one-year historical average discount of 2.49%.

Scott R. Romans currently receives a manager quality ranking of 42 (0=worst, 99=best). If you desire an average level of risk, then this fund may be an option.

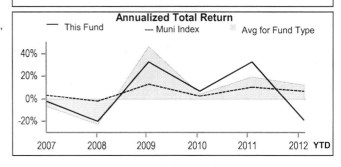

Annualized Total Return

Nuveen Insured CA Prem Inc Muni 2 (NCL)

B   **Good**

Fund Family: Nuveen Fund Advisors Inc
Fund Type: Municipal - Single State
Inception Date: March 18, 1993

Data Date	Investment Rating	Net Assets ($Mil)	Price	Performance Rating/Pts	Total Return Y-T-D	Risk Rating/Pts
3-12	B	165.36	14.58	B- / 7.2	-5.03%	B / 8.6
2011	A+	187.50	15.58	A+ / 9.8	1.54%	B / 8.7
2010	C-	177.17	12.64	C- / 3.6	7.33%	C+ / 6.4
2009	C+	185.25	12.55	C / 5.3	34.03%	B- / 7.4

Major Rating Factors: Strong performance is the major factor driving the B (Good) TheStreet.com Investment Rating for Nuveen Insured CA Prem Inc Muni 2. The fund currently has a performance rating of B- (Good) based on an annualized return of 17.01% over the last three years and a total return of -5.03% year to date 2012. Factored into the performance evaluation is an expense ratio of 1.29% (average).

The fund's risk rating is currently B (Good). It carries a beta of 2.46, meaning it is expected to move 24.6% for every 10% move in the market. Volatility, as measured by both the semi-deviation and a drawdown factor, is considered low. As of March 31, 2012, Nuveen Insured CA Prem Inc Muni 2 traded at a discount of 4.14% below its net asset value, which is better than its one-year historical average discount of 1.95%.

Scott R. Romans currently receives a manager quality ranking of 33 (0=worst, 99=best). If you desire only a moderate level of risk and strong performance, then this fund is an excellent option.

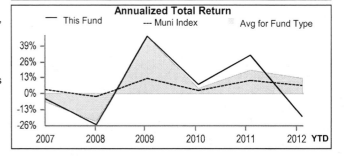

Annualized Total Return

Nuveen Insured CA T/F Adv Muni Fd (NKX)

B   **Good**

Fund Family: Nuveen Fund Advisors Inc
Fund Type: Municipal - Single State
Inception Date: November 21, 2002

Major Rating Factors: Strong performance is the major factor driving the B (Good) TheStreet.com Investment Rating for Nuveen Insured CA T/F Adv Muni Fd. The fund currently has a performance rating of B- (Good) based on an annualized return of 13.77% over the last three years and a total return of -0.51% year to date 2012. Factored into the performance evaluation is an expense ratio of 1.97% (above average).

The fund's risk rating is currently B (Good). It carries a beta of 2.38, meaning it is expected to move 23.8% for every 10% move in the market. Volatility, as measured by both the semi-deviation and a drawdown factor, is considered low. As of March 31, 2012, Nuveen Insured CA T/F Adv Muni Fd traded at a discount of 3.05% below its net asset value, which is worse than its one-year historical average discount of 4.93%.

Scott R. Romans has been running the fund for 10 years and currently receives a manager quality ranking of 26 (0=worst, 99=best). If you desire only a moderate level of risk and strong performance, then this fund is an excellent option.

Data Date	Investment Rating	Net Assets ($Mil)	Price	Performance Rating/Pts	Total Return Y-T-D	Risk Rating/Pts
3-12	B	75.49	14.32	B- / 7.2	-0.51%	B / 8.5
2011	B+	84.50	14.60	B+ / 8.7	-0.36%	B / 8.5
2010	C-	39.30	12.18	D / 1.7	2.01%	B- / 7.8
2009	C+	85.77	12.68	C- / 3.7	26.23%	B / 8.0

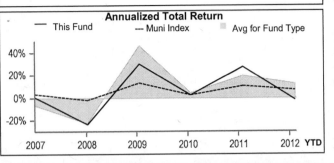

Nuveen Insured MA T/F Adv Muni Fd (NGX)

C   **Fair**

Fund Family: Nuveen Fund Advisors Inc
Fund Type: Municipal - Single State
Inception Date: November 21, 2002

Major Rating Factors: Middle of the road best describes Nuveen Insured MA T/F Adv Muni Fd whose TheStreet.com Investment Rating is currently a C (Fair). The fund currently has a performance rating of C- (Fair) based on an annualized return of 7.24% over the last three years and a total return of 8.18% year to date 2012. Factored into the performance evaluation is an expense ratio of 3.01% (high).

The fund's risk rating is currently B (Good). It carries a beta of 0.71, meaning the fund's expected move will be 7.1% for every 10% move in the market. Volatility, as measured by both the semi-deviation and a drawdown factor, is considered low. As of March 31, 2012, Nuveen Insured MA T/F Adv Muni Fd traded at a discount of .07% below its net asset value, which is worse than its one-year historical average discount of 5.61%.

Michael S. Hamilton currently receives a manager quality ranking of 60 (0=worst, 99=best). If you desire an average level of risk, then this fund may be an option.

Data Date	Investment Rating	Net Assets ($Mil)	Price	Performance Rating/Pts	Total Return Y-T-D	Risk Rating/Pts
3-12	C	39.16	14.80	C- / 4.1	8.18%	B / 8.4
2011	C+	40.20	13.84	C / 5.2	0.14%	B / 8.5
2010	C	40.10	13.68	D+ / 2.6	-1.26%	B- / 7.9
2009	B-	40.40	14.57	C+ / 6.8	34.25%	B- / 7.7

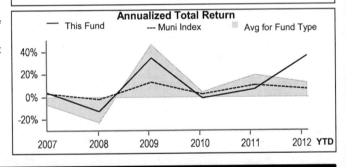

Nuveen Investment Quality Muni Fun (NQM)

B+   **Good**

Fund Family: Nuveen Fund Advisors Inc
Fund Type: Municipal - National
Inception Date: June 21, 1990

Major Rating Factors: Strong performance is the major factor driving the B+ (Good) TheStreet.com Investment Rating for Nuveen Investment Quality Muni Fun. The fund currently has a performance rating of B (Good) based on an annualized return of 16.60% over the last three years and a total return of 1.72% year to date 2012. Factored into the performance evaluation is an expense ratio of 1.50% (average).

The fund's risk rating is currently B (Good). It carries a beta of 1.93, meaning it is expected to move 19.3% for every 10% move in the market. Volatility, as measured by both the semi-deviation and a drawdown factor, is considered low. As of March 31, 2012, Nuveen Investment Quality Muni Fun traded at a discount of 1.14% below its net asset value, which is worse than its one-year historical average discount of 1.69%.

Christopher L. Drahn currently receives a manager quality ranking of 57 (0=worst, 99=best). If you desire only a moderate level of risk and strong performance, then this fund is an excellent option.

Data Date	Investment Rating	Net Assets ($Mil)	Price	Performance Rating/Pts	Total Return Y-T-D	Risk Rating/Pts
3-12	B+	535.52	15.63	B / 7.7	1.72%	B / 8.8
2011	A	552.10	15.61	A- / 9.2	0.64%	B / 8.8
2010	C+	510.91	13.49	C / 4.3	7.98%	B- / 7.1
2009	C+	534.55	13.32	C / 4.8	29.90%	B- / 7.7

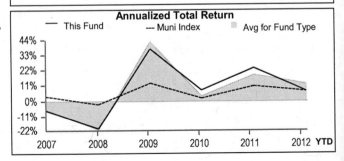

Nuveen MA Div Adv Muni (NMB)   C-   Fair

Fund Family: Nuveen Fund Advisors Inc
Fund Type: Municipal - Single State
Inception Date: January 30, 2001

Major Rating Factors: Middle of the road best describes Nuveen MA Div Adv Muni whose TheStreet.com Investment Rating is currently a C- (Fair). The fund currently has a performance rating of C- (Fair) based on an annualized return of 6.86% over the last three years and a total return of 4.00% year to date 2012. Factored into the performance evaluation is an expense ratio of 3.03% (high).

The fund's risk rating is currently B (Good). It carries a beta of 2.17, meaning it is expected to move 21.7% for every 10% move in the market. Volatility, as measured by both the semi-deviation and a drawdown factor, is considered low. As of March 31, 2012, Nuveen MA Div Adv Muni traded at a discount of 4.67% below its net asset value, which is worse than its one-year historical average discount of 5.18%.

Michael S. Hamilton currently receives a manager quality ranking of 19 (0=worst, 99=best). If you desire an average level of risk, then this fund may be an option.

Data Date	Investment Rating	Net Assets ($Mil)	Price	Performance Rating/Pts	Total Return Y-T-D	Risk Rating/Pts
3-12	C-	27.47	14.28	C- / 3.6	4.00%	B / 8.4
2011	B	28.90	13.90	B- / 7.1	1.44%	B / 8.3
2010	C	28.24	13.60	C / 4.6	4.30%	C+ / 6.7
2009	C+	28.60	13.80	C / 4.9	34.98%	B- / 7.5

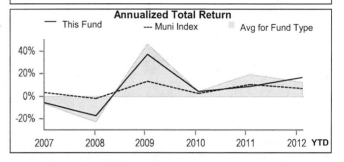

Nuveen MA Prem Inc Muni (NMT)   B-   Good

Fund Family: Nuveen Fund Advisors Inc
Fund Type: Municipal - Single State
Inception Date: March 18, 1993

Major Rating Factors: Nuveen MA Prem Inc Muni receives a TheStreet.com Investment Rating of B- (Good). The fund currently has a performance rating of C+ (Fair) based on an annualized return of 12.71% over the last three years and a total return of 3.77% year to date 2012. Factored into the performance evaluation is an expense ratio of 2.51% (high).

The fund's risk rating is currently B (Good). It carries a beta of 1.64, meaning it is expected to move 16.4% for every 10% move in the market. Volatility, as measured by both the semi-deviation and a drawdown factor, is considered low. As of March 31, 2012, Nuveen MA Prem Inc Muni traded at a discount of 1.19% below its net asset value, which is worse than its one-year historical average discount of 4.45%.

Michael S. Hamilton currently receives a manager quality ranking of 43 (0=worst, 99=best). If you desire an average level of risk, then this fund may be an option.

Data Date	Investment Rating	Net Assets ($Mil)	Price	Performance Rating/Pts	Total Return Y-T-D	Risk Rating/Pts
3-12	B-	67.61	14.97	C+ / 6.4	3.77%	B / 8.7
2011	A-	71.10	14.61	B+ / 8.6	0.92%	B / 8.8
2010	C	69.03	13.35	C / 4.8	4.28%	C+ / 6.5
2009	B-	69.25	13.55	C+ / 6.0	42.87%	B- / 7.4

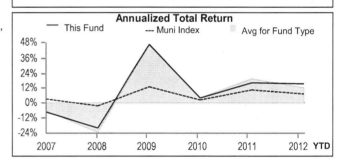

Nuveen MD Div Adv Muni (NFM)   C+   Fair

Fund Family: Nuveen Fund Advisors Inc
Fund Type: Municipal - Single State
Inception Date: January 23, 2001

Major Rating Factors: Middle of the road best describes Nuveen MD Div Adv Muni whose TheStreet.com Investment Rating is currently a C+ (Fair). The fund currently has a performance rating of C (Fair) based on an annualized return of 11.73% over the last three years and a total return of -0.10% year to date 2012. Factored into the performance evaluation is an expense ratio of 2.58% (high).

The fund's risk rating is currently B (Good). It carries a beta of 1.36, meaning it is expected to move 13.6% for every 10% move in the market. Volatility, as measured by both the semi-deviation and a drawdown factor, is considered low. As of March 31, 2012, Nuveen MD Div Adv Muni traded at a discount of 5.94% below its net asset value, which is better than its one-year historical average discount of 5.06%.

Thomas C. Spalding currently receives a manager quality ranking of 53 (0=worst, 99=best). If you desire an average level of risk, then this fund may be an option.

Data Date	Investment Rating	Net Assets ($Mil)	Price	Performance Rating/Pts	Total Return Y-T-D	Risk Rating/Pts
3-12	C+	58.11	14.09	C / 4.6	-0.10%	B / 8.8
2011	B+	61.70	14.29	B / 8.1	-0.49%	B / 8.8
2010	C	60.31	12.92	C- / 3.2	0.90%	B- / 7.3
2009	B-	60.32	13.53	C+ / 5.7	49.03%	B- / 7.0

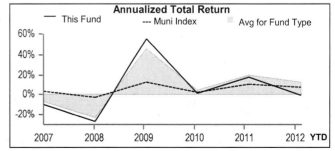

Nuveen MD Div Adv Muni 2 (NZR)

B-   **Good**

Fund Family: Nuveen Fund Advisors Inc
Fund Type: Municipal - Single State
Inception Date: September 25, 2001

Major Rating Factors: Nuveen MD Div Adv Muni 2 receives a TheStreet.com Investment Rating of B- (Good). The fund currently has a performance rating of C+ (Fair) based on an annualized return of 13.21% over the last three years and a total return of 4.77% year to date 2012. Factored into the performance evaluation is an expense ratio of 2.55% (high).

The fund's risk rating is currently B (Good). It carries a beta of 1.72, meaning it is expected to move 17.2% for every 10% move in the market. Volatility, as measured by both the semi-deviation and a drawdown factor, is considered low. As of March 31, 2012, Nuveen MD Div Adv Muni 2 traded at a discount of 3.55% below its net asset value, which is better than its one-year historical average discount of 3.32%.

Thomas C. Spalding currently receives a manager quality ranking of 40 (0=worst, 99=best). If you desire an average level of risk, then this fund may be an option.

Data Date	Investment Rating	Net Assets ($Mil)	Price	Performance Rating/Pts	Total Return Y-T-D	Risk Rating/Pts
3-12	B-	58.42	14.65	C+ / 6.4	4.77%	B / 8.5
2011	B+	61.90	14.17	B / 8.0	1.56%	B / 8.5
2010	C	60.75	12.95	C- / 3.4	1.69%	B- / 7.3
2009	C	60.91	13.46	C / 4.3	39.14%	B- / 7.0

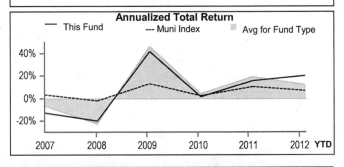

Nuveen MD Div Adv Muni Fund 3 (NWI)

C+   **Fair**

Fund Family: Nuveen Fund Advisors Inc
Fund Type: Municipal - Single State
Inception Date: September 25, 2002

Major Rating Factors: Middle of the road best describes Nuveen MD Div Adv Muni Fund 3 whose TheStreet.com Investment Rating is currently a C+ (Fair). The fund currently has a performance rating of C (Fair) based on an annualized return of 12.91% over the last three years and a total return of 1.07% year to date 2012. Factored into the performance evaluation is an expense ratio of 2.29% (high).

The fund's risk rating is currently B (Good). It carries a beta of 1.92, meaning it is expected to move 19.2% for every 10% move in the market. Volatility, as measured by both the semi-deviation and a drawdown factor, is considered low. As of March 31, 2012, Nuveen MD Div Adv Muni Fund 3 traded at a discount of 6.63% below its net asset value, which is better than its one-year historical average discount of 5.30%.

Thomas C. Spalding currently receives a manager quality ranking of 34 (0=worst, 99=best). If you desire an average level of risk, then this fund may be an option.

Data Date	Investment Rating	Net Assets ($Mil)	Price	Performance Rating/Pts	Total Return Y-T-D	Risk Rating/Pts
3-12	C+	75.70	14.09	C / 5.0	1.07%	B / 8.8
2011	B+	79.30	14.12	B / 8.1	1.27%	B / 8.9
2010	C+	78.27	13.09	C / 5.1	0.07%	B- / 7.2
2009	B-	78.55	13.80	C+ / 6.9	47.52%	B- / 7.3

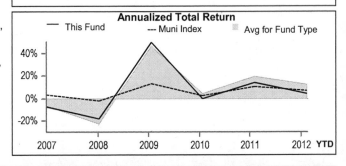

Nuveen MD Prem Inc Muni Fund (NMY)

B   **Good**

Fund Family: Nuveen Fund Advisors Inc
Fund Type: Municipal - Single State
Inception Date: March 18, 1993

Major Rating Factors: Nuveen MD Prem Inc Muni Fund receives a TheStreet.com Investment Rating of B (Good). The fund currently has a performance rating of C+ (Fair) based on an annualized return of 14.79% over the last three years and a total return of 3.73% year to date 2012. Factored into the performance evaluation is an expense ratio of 2.10% (high).

The fund's risk rating is currently B (Good). It carries a beta of 1.60, meaning it is expected to move 16.0% for every 10% move in the market. Volatility, as measured by both the semi-deviation and a drawdown factor, is considered low. As of March 31, 2012, Nuveen MD Prem Inc Muni Fund traded at a discount of .84% below its net asset value, which is worse than its one-year historical average discount of 2.78%.

Thomas C. Spalding has been running the fund for 1 year and currently receives a manager quality ranking of 66 (0=worst, 99=best). If you desire an average level of risk, then this fund may be an option.

Data Date	Investment Rating	Net Assets ($Mil)	Price	Performance Rating/Pts	Total Return Y-T-D	Risk Rating/Pts
3-12	B	153.08	15.30	C+ / 6.7	3.73%	B / 8.8
2011	A	160.60	14.93	A- / 9.0	3.25%	B / 8.9
2010	C+	157.24	13.45	C / 5.5	2.66%	C+ / 6.3
2009	B-	157.09	13.80	C+ / 6.1	45.56%	B- / 7.1

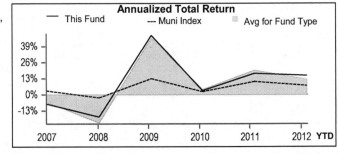

Nuveen MI Div Adv Muni (NZW)   **B+**   **Good**

Fund Family: Nuveen Fund Advisors Inc
Fund Type: Municipal - Single State
Inception Date: September 25, 2001

Data Date	Investment Rating	Net Assets ($Mil)	Price	Performance Rating/Pts	Total Return Y-T-D	Risk Rating/Pts
3-12	B+	27.71	13.87	B / 7.6	3.74%	B+ / 9.1
2011	A-	30.30	13.56	B+ / 8.4	1.62%	B+ / 9.0
2010	C	29.13	12.37	C- / 3.2	7.94%	B- / 7.7
2009	C	30.12	12.17	C- / 3.3	33.95%	B- / 7.4

Major Rating Factors: Strong performance is the major factor driving the B+ (Good) TheStreet.com Investment Rating for Nuveen MI Div Adv Muni. The fund currently has a performance rating of B (Good) based on an annualized return of 17.06% over the last three years and a total return of 3.74% year to date 2012. Factored into the performance evaluation is an expense ratio of 1.69% (above average).

The fund's risk rating is currently B+ (Good). It carries a beta of 1.54, meaning it is expected to move 15.4% for every 10% move in the market. Volatility, as measured by both the semi-deviation and a drawdown factor, is considered very low. As of March 31, 2012, Nuveen MI Div Adv Muni traded at a discount of 7.53% below its net asset value, which is worse than its one-year historical average discount of 8.28%.

Daniel J. Close currently receives a manager quality ranking of 73 (0=worst, 99=best). If you desire only a moderate level of risk and strong performance, then this fund is an excellent option.

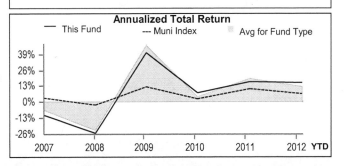

Nuveen MI Prem Inc Muni (NMP)   **A+**   **Excellent**

Fund Family: Nuveen Fund Advisors Inc
Fund Type: Municipal - Single State
Inception Date: December 17, 1992

Data Date	Investment Rating	Net Assets ($Mil)	Price	Performance Rating/Pts	Total Return Y-T-D	Risk Rating/Pts
3-12	A+	106.08	14.83	B+ / 8.8	6.65%	B+ / 9.3
2011	B+	114.20	14.11	B / 8.0	-0.57%	B+ / 9.2
2010	C+	109.62	13.00	C+ / 6.3	12.62%	C+ / 6.4
2009	C	112.18	12.27	C- / 3.8	30.95%	B- / 7.8

Major Rating Factors:
Strong performance is the major factor driving the A+ (Excellent) TheStreet.com Investment Rating for Nuveen MI Prem Inc Muni. The fund currently has a performance rating of B+ (Good) based on an annualized return of 19.48% over the last three years and a total return of 6.65% year to date 2012. Factored into the performance evaluation is an expense ratio of 1.20% (average).

The fund's risk rating is currently B+ (Good). It carries a beta of 1.42, meaning it is expected to move 14.2% for every 10% move in the market. Volatility, as measured by both the semi-deviation and a drawdown factor, is considered very low. As of March 31, 2012, Nuveen MI Prem Inc Muni traded at a discount of 2.95% below its net asset value, which is worse than its one-year historical average discount of 7.02%.

Daniel J. Close has been running the fund for 5 years and currently receives a manager quality ranking of 82 (0=worst, 99=best). If you desire only a moderate level of risk and strong performance, then this fund is an excellent option.

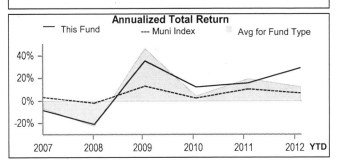

Nuveen MI Quality Inc Muni (NUM)   **A+**   **Excellent**

Fund Family: Nuveen Fund Advisors Inc
Fund Type: Municipal - Single State
Inception Date: October 24, 1991

Data Date	Investment Rating	Net Assets ($Mil)	Price	Performance Rating/Pts	Total Return Y-T-D	Risk Rating/Pts
3-12	A+	163.88	15.11	B+ / 8.7	4.84%	B+ / 9.1
2011	A-	178.30	14.62	B+ / 8.5	-0.41%	B+ / 9.1
2010	C	170.98	13.10	C / 4.8	9.07%	C+ / 6.5
2009	B	175.48	12.75	C / 5.4	34.07%	B- / 7.8

Major Rating Factors:
Strong performance is the major factor driving the A+ (Excellent) TheStreet.com Investment Rating for Nuveen MI Quality Inc Muni. The fund currently has a performance rating of B+ (Good) based on an annualized return of 19.19% over the last three years and a total return of 4.84% year to date 2012. Factored into the performance evaluation is an expense ratio of 1.18% (low).

The fund's risk rating is currently B+ (Good). It carries a beta of 1.50, meaning it is expected to move 15.0% for every 10% move in the market. Volatility, as measured by both the semi-deviation and a drawdown factor, is considered very low. As of March 31, 2012, Nuveen MI Quality Inc Muni traded at a discount of 4.06% below its net asset value, which is worse than its one-year historical average discount of 7.30%.

Daniel J. Close has been running the fund for 5 years and currently receives a manager quality ranking of 81 (0=worst, 99=best). If you desire only a moderate level of risk and strong performance, then this fund is an excellent option.

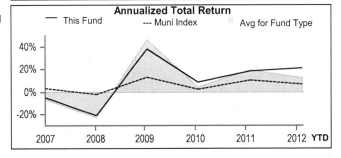

Nuveen Mlt-Cur Sht-Tm Govt Inc (JGT)

D+ | **Weak**

Fund Family: Nuveen Fund Advisors Inc
Fund Type: Global
Inception Date: April 25, 2007

Major Rating Factors:
Disappointing performance is the major factor driving the D+ (Weak) TheStreet.com Investment Rating for Nuveen Mlt-Cur Sht-Tm Govt Inc. The fund currently has a performance rating of D+ (Weak) based on an annualized return of 11.24% over the last three years and a total return of 11.71% year to date 2012. Factored into the performance evaluation is an expense ratio of 1.06% (low).

The fund's risk rating is currently B- (Good). It carries a beta of 1.27, meaning it is expected to move 12.7% for every 10% move in the market. Volatility, as measured by both the semi-deviation and a drawdown factor, is considered low. As of March 31, 2012, Nuveen Mlt-Cur Sht-Tm Govt Inc traded at a discount of 11.51% below its net asset value, which is better than its one-year historical average discount of 11.04%.

Steve S. Lee currently receives a manager quality ranking of 63 (0=worst, 99=best). This fund offers only a moderate level of risk but investors looking for strong performance are still waiting.

Data Date	Investment Rating	Net Assets ($Mil)	Price	Performance Rating/Pts	Total Return Y-T-D	Risk Rating/Pts
3-12	D+	605.96	13.22	D+ / 2.8	11.71%	B- / 7.3
2011	C-	606.00	12.11	D+ / 2.8	1.98%	B- / 7.7
2010	C-	748.96	13.77	C- / 3.0	-1.42%	B- / 7.0
2009	C+	762.97	15.41	C+ / 6.1	21.70%	C+ / 6.4

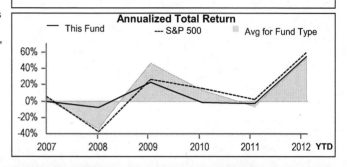

Nuveen MO Prem Inc Muni (NOM)

B+ | **Good**

Fund Family: Nuveen Fund Advisors Inc
Fund Type: Municipal - Single State
Inception Date: May 20, 1993

Major Rating Factors: Strong performance is the major factor driving the B+ (Good) TheStreet.com Investment Rating for Nuveen MO Prem Inc Muni. The fund currently has a performance rating of B (Good) based on an annualized return of 16.85% over the last three years and a total return of 2.70% year to date 2012. Factored into the performance evaluation is an expense ratio of 2.30% (high).

The fund's risk rating is currently B (Good). It carries a beta of 1.16, meaning it is expected to move 11.6% for every 10% move in the market. Volatility, as measured by both the semi-deviation and a drawdown factor, is considered low. As of March 31, 2012, Nuveen MO Prem Inc Muni traded at a premium of 16.10% above its net asset value, which is worse than its one-year historical average premium of 11.32%.

Christopher L. Drahn currently receives a manager quality ranking of 81 (0=worst, 99=best). If you desire only a moderate level of risk and strong performance, then this fund is an excellent option.

Data Date	Investment Rating	Net Assets ($Mil)	Price	Performance Rating/Pts	Total Return Y-T-D	Risk Rating/Pts
3-12	B+	30.60	16.66	B / 7.7	2.70%	B / 8.5
2011	A-	32.80	16.42	A- / 9.0	0.78%	B / 8.5
2010	C+	31.35	14.50	C / 5.0	-1.68%	C+ / 6.5
2009	B+	31.22	15.50	B- / 7.0	34.30%	C+ / 6.7

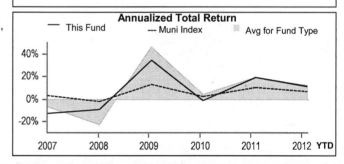

Nuveen Mortgage Opportunity Term (JLS)

C | **Fair**

Fund Family: Nuveen Fund Advisors Inc
Fund Type: Mortgage
Inception Date: November 25, 2009

Major Rating Factors: Middle of the road best describes Nuveen Mortgage Opportunity Term whose TheStreet.com Investment Rating is currently a C (Fair). The fund currently has a performance rating of C (Fair) based on an annualized return of 0.00% over the last three years and a total return of 17.49% year to date 2012. Factored into the performance evaluation is an expense ratio of 1.44% (average).

The fund's risk rating is currently B (Good). It carries a beta of 0.00, meaning the fund's expected move will be 0.0% for every 10% move in the market. Volatility, as measured by both the semi-deviation and a drawdown factor, is considered low. As of March 31, 2012, Nuveen Mortgage Opportunity Term traded at a discount of 1.43% below its net asset value, which is worse than its one-year historical average discount of 3.52%.

John V. Miller currently receives a manager quality ranking of 87 (0=worst, 99=best). If you desire an average level of risk, then this fund may be an option.

Data Date	Investment Rating	Net Assets ($Mil)	Price	Performance Rating/Pts	Total Return Y-T-D	Risk Rating/Pts
3-12	C	346.83	23.38	C / 4.4	17.49%	B / 8.3
2011	D+	346.80	20.35	D- / 1.4	4.67%	B / 8.3
2010	A+	0.00	25.50	B / 8.2	10.44%	B / 8.7

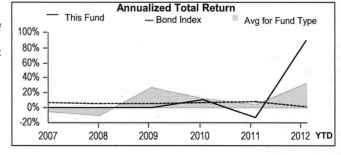

Nuveen Mortgage Opportunity Term 2 (JMT)   C+   Fair

Fund Family: Nuveen Fund Advisors Inc
Fund Type: Mortgage
Inception Date: February 24, 2010

Data Date	Investment Rating	Net Assets ($Mil)	Price	Perfor-mance Rating/Pts	Total Return Y-T-D	Risk Rating/Pts
3-12	C+	104.62	23.46	C / 5.1	17.61%	B / 8.3
2011	D+	104.60	20.40	D / 1.6	3.77%	B / 8.3

Major Rating Factors: Middle of the road best describes Nuveen Mortgage Opportunity Term 2 whose TheStreet.com Investment Rating is currently a C+ (Fair). The fund currently has a performance rating of C (Fair) based on an annualized return of 0.00% over the last three years and a total return of 17.61% year to date 2012. Factored into the performance evaluation is an expense ratio of 1.58% (above average).

The fund's risk rating is currently B (Good). It carries a beta of 0.00, meaning the fund's expected move will be 0.0% for every 10% move in the market. Volatility, as measured by both the semi-deviation and a drawdown factor, is considered low. As of March 31, 2012, Nuveen Mortgage Opportunity Term 2 traded at a discount of 1.39% below its net asset value, which is worse than its one-year historical average discount of 4.38%.

John V. Miller currently receives a manager quality ranking of 95 (0=worst, 99=best). If you desire an average level of risk, then this fund may be an option.

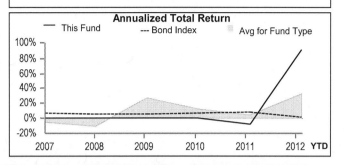

Annualized Total Return — This Fund --- Bond Index Avg for Fund Type

Nuveen Muni Advantage (NMA)   B-   Good

Fund Family: Nuveen Fund Advisors Inc
Fund Type: Municipal - National
Inception Date: December 28, 1989

Data Date	Investment Rating	Net Assets ($Mil)	Price	Perfor-mance Rating/Pts	Total Return Y-T-D	Risk Rating/Pts
3-12	B-	626.62	14.57	C+ / 6.8	0.86%	B / 8.5
2011	B+	634.30	14.68	B / 8.0	-1.57%	B / 8.5
2010	C-	624.08	13.08	C- / 3.0	-1.70%	C+ / 6.5
2009	C+	634.51	14.25	C+ / 6.3	39.72%	C+ / 6.9

Major Rating Factors: Nuveen Muni Advantage receives a TheStreet.com Investment Rating of B- (Good). The fund currently has a performance rating of C+ (Fair) based on an annualized return of 16.08% over the last three years and a total return of 0.86% year to date 2012. Factored into the performance evaluation is an expense ratio of 2.01% (high).

The fund's risk rating is currently B (Good). It carries a beta of 2.00, meaning it is expected to move 20.0% for every 10% move in the market. Volatility, as measured by both the semi-deviation and a drawdown factor, is considered low. As of March 31, 2012, Nuveen Muni Advantage traded at a discount of 2.87% below its net asset value, which is better than its one-year historical average discount of 1.42%.

Thomas C. Spalding has been running the fund for 10 years and currently receives a manager quality ranking of 45 (0=worst, 99=best). If you desire an average level of risk, then this fund may be an option.

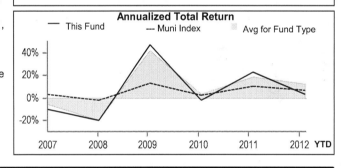

Annualized Total Return — This Fund --- Muni Index Avg for Fund Type

Nuveen Muni High Income Opport (NMZ)   B+   Good

Fund Family: Nuveen Fund Advisors Inc
Fund Type: Municipal - High Yield
Inception Date: November 19, 2003

Data Date	Investment Rating	Net Assets ($Mil)	Price	Perfor-mance Rating/Pts	Total Return Y-T-D	Risk Rating/Pts
3-12	B+	323.09	12.89	B / 8.2	8.33%	B / 8.3
2011	B+	330.90	12.11	B+ / 8.3	1.49%	B / 8.3
2010	D+	288.96	11.45	D- / 1.5	-1.31%	C+ / 6.9
2009	C	300.97	12.60	C / 4.7	51.50%	C+ / 6.0

Major Rating Factors: Strong performance is the major factor driving the B+ (Good) TheStreet.com Investment Rating for Nuveen Muni High Income Opport. The fund currently has a performance rating of B (Good) based on an annualized return of 16.98% over the last three years and a total return of 8.33% year to date 2012. Factored into the performance evaluation is an expense ratio of 1.40% (average).

The fund's risk rating is currently B (Good). It carries a beta of 2.44, meaning it is expected to move 24.4% for every 10% move in the market. Volatility, as measured by both the semi-deviation and a drawdown factor, is considered low. As of March 31, 2012, Nuveen Muni High Income Opport traded at a premium of 3.12% above its net asset value, which is better than its one-year historical average premium of 3.61%.

John V. Miller has been running the fund for 9 years and currently receives a manager quality ranking of 35 (0=worst, 99=best). If you desire only a moderate level of risk and strong performance, then this fund is an excellent option.

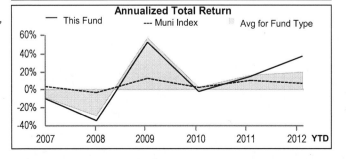

Annualized Total Return — This Fund --- Muni Index Avg for Fund Type

Nuveen Muni High Income Opport 2 (NMD)   B   Good

Fund Family: Nuveen Fund Advisors Inc
Fund Type: Municipal - High Yield
Inception Date: November 16, 2007

Major Rating Factors: Strong performance is the major factor driving the B (Good) TheStreet.com Investment Rating for Nuveen Muni High Income Opport 2. The fund currently has a performance rating of B (Good) based on an annualized return of 15.69% over the last three years and a total return of 7.51% year to date 2012. Factored into the performance evaluation is an expense ratio of 1.61% (above average).

The fund's risk rating is currently B (Good). It carries a beta of 2.33, meaning it is expected to move 23.3% for every 10% move in the market. Volatility, as measured by both the semi-deviation and a drawdown factor, is considered low. As of March 31, 2012, Nuveen Muni High Income Opport 2 traded at a discount of .25% below its net asset value, which is worse than its one-year historical average discount of .76%.

John V. Miller currently receives a manager quality ranking of 39 (0=worst, 99=best). If you desire only a moderate level of risk and strong performance, then this fund is an excellent option.

Data Date	Investment Rating	Net Assets ($Mil)	Price	Performance Rating/Pts	Total Return Y-T-D	Risk Rating/Pts
3-12	B	199.43	12.10	B / 7.8	7.51%	B / 8.3
2011	B	201.80	11.44	B / 7.8	0.52%	B / 8.4
2010	D	174.35	10.82	D- / 1.3	2.47%	C+ / 6.6
2009	A+	183.30	11.46	A+ / 9.6	57.72%	C+ / 6.4

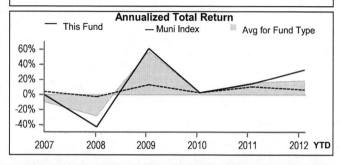

Nuveen Muni Income (NMI)   C   Fair

Fund Family: Nuveen Fund Advisors Inc
Fund Type: Municipal - National
Inception Date: April 20, 1988

Major Rating Factors: Middle of the road best describes Nuveen Muni Income whose TheStreet.com Investment Rating is currently a C (Fair). The fund currently has a performance rating of C (Fair) based on an annualized return of 10.44% over the last three years and a total return of -0.83% year to date 2012. Factored into the performance evaluation is an expense ratio of 0.77% (very low).

The fund's risk rating is currently B (Good). It carries a beta of 1.31, meaning it is expected to move 13.1% for every 10% move in the market. Volatility, as measured by both the semi-deviation and a drawdown factor, is considered low. As of March 31, 2012, Nuveen Muni Income traded at a premium of .53% above its net asset value, which is better than its one-year historical average premium of 1.25%.

Christopher L. Drahn currently receives a manager quality ranking of 50 (0=worst, 99=best). If you desire an average level of risk, then this fund may be an option.

Data Date	Investment Rating	Net Assets ($Mil)	Price	Performance Rating/Pts	Total Return Y-T-D	Risk Rating/Pts
3-12	C	88.49	11.29	C / 4.4	-0.83%	B / 8.8
2011	B+	90.20	11.53	B- / 7.4	0.35%	B / 8.9
2010	C+	84.88	10.30	C- / 3.9	-0.83%	B- / 7.9
2009	B-	87.01	10.95	C / 5.5	18.61%	B- / 7.3

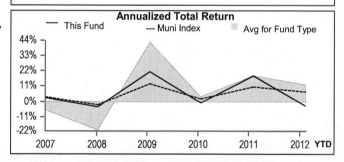

Nuveen Muni Market Opportunity (NMO)   B   Good

Fund Family: Nuveen Fund Advisors Inc
Fund Type: Municipal - National
Inception Date: March 22, 1990

Major Rating Factors: Strong performance is the major factor driving the B (Good) TheStreet.com Investment Rating for Nuveen Muni Market Opportunity. The fund currently has a performance rating of B- (Good) based on an annualized return of 15.78% over the last three years and a total return of 3.42% year to date 2012. Factored into the performance evaluation is an expense ratio of 2.10% (high).

The fund's risk rating is currently B (Good). It carries a beta of 1.90, meaning it is expected to move 19.0% for every 10% move in the market. Volatility, as measured by both the semi-deviation and a drawdown factor, is considered low. As of March 31, 2012, Nuveen Muni Market Opportunity traded at a discount of 2.42% below its net asset value, which is better than its one-year historical average discount of 1.96%.

Thomas C. Spalding has been running the fund for 10 years and currently receives a manager quality ranking of 50 (0=worst, 99=best). If you desire only a moderate level of risk and strong performance, then this fund is an excellent option.

Data Date	Investment Rating	Net Assets ($Mil)	Price	Performance Rating/Pts	Total Return Y-T-D	Risk Rating/Pts
3-12	B	622.82	14.09	B- / 7.3	3.42%	B / 8.6
2011	B+	636.00	13.84	B+ / 8.3	0.87%	B / 8.6
2010	C	636.76	12.87	C / 4.4	3.40%	C+ / 6.4
2009	C+	645.65	13.35	C / 5.5	31.35%	B- / 7.1

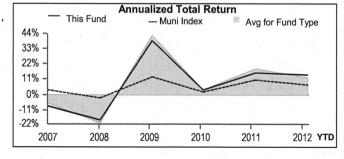

Nuveen Muni Opportunity (NIO)   C+   Fair

Fund Family: Nuveen Fund Advisors Inc
Fund Type: Municipal - National
Inception Date: September 27, 1991

Data Date	Investment Rating	Net Assets ($Mil)	Price	Performance Rating/Pts	Total Return Y-T-D	Risk Rating/Pts
3-12	C+	1,404.81	14.61	C / 5.5	-0.65%	B / 8.9
2011	B+	1,435.40	14.92	B+ / 8.4	-0.80%	B / 8.9
2010	C	1,358.84	13.04	C- / 4.0	3.04%	B- / 7.0
2009	B-	1,205.12	13.44	C / 5.4	29.95%	B- / 7.6

Major Rating Factors: Middle of the road best describes Nuveen Muni Opportunity whose TheStreet.com Investment Rating is currently a C+ (Fair). The fund currently has a performance rating of C (Fair) based on an annualized return of 14.13% over the last three years and a total return of -0.65% year to date 2012. Factored into the performance evaluation is an expense ratio of 1.63% (above average).

The fund's risk rating is currently B (Good). It carries a beta of 1.85, meaning it is expected to move 18.5% for every 10% move in the market. Volatility, as measured by both the semi-deviation and a drawdown factor, is considered low. As of March 31, 2012, Nuveen Muni Opportunity traded at a discount of 4.70% below its net asset value, which is better than its one-year historical average discount of 4.06%.

Paul L. Brennan has been running the fund for 6 years and currently receives a manager quality ranking of 46 (0=worst, 99=best). If you desire an average level of risk, then this fund may be an option.

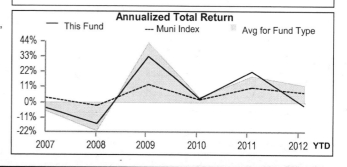

Nuveen Muni Value (NUV)   C+   Fair

Fund Family: Nuveen Fund Advisors Inc
Fund Type: Municipal - National
Inception Date: June 18, 1987

Data Date	Investment Rating	Net Assets ($Mil)	Price	Performance Rating/Pts	Total Return Y-T-D	Risk Rating/Pts
3-12	C+	1,915.23	10.07	C / 4.3	3.96%	B+ / 9.1
2011	B-	1,939.10	9.80	C / 5.4	0.27%	B+ / 9.0
2010	C+	1,872.03	9.19	C- / 3.7	-0.22%	B / 8.1
2009	C+	1,931.30	9.69	C / 4.5	12.15%	B- / 7.8

Major Rating Factors: Middle of the road best describes Nuveen Muni Value whose TheStreet.com Investment Rating is currently a C+ (Fair). The fund currently has a performance rating of C (Fair) based on an annualized return of 9.28% over the last three years and a total return of 3.96% year to date 2012. Factored into the performance evaluation is an expense ratio of 0.65% (very low).

The fund's risk rating is currently B+ (Good). It carries a beta of 1.23, meaning it is expected to move 12.3% for every 10% move in the market. Volatility, as measured by both the semi-deviation and a drawdown factor, is considered very low. As of March 31, 2012, Nuveen Muni Value traded at a premium of .90% above its net asset value, which is worse than its one-year historical average discount of .69%.

Thomas C. Spalding has been running the fund for 25 years and currently receives a manager quality ranking of 48 (0=worst, 99=best). If you desire an average level of risk, then this fund may be an option.

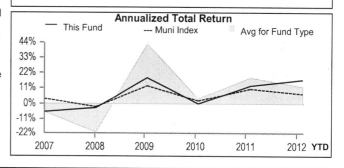

Nuveen Municipal Value Fund 2 (NUW)   C   Fair

Fund Family: Nuveen Fund Advisors Inc
Fund Type: Municipal - National
Inception Date: February 25, 2009

Data Date	Investment Rating	Net Assets ($Mil)	Price	Performance Rating/Pts	Total Return Y-T-D	Risk Rating/Pts
3-12	C	212.87	16.67	C- / 3.6	-2.57%	B / 8.5
2011	A-	215.20	17.32	A- / 9.0	0.40%	B / 8.7
2010	C-	205.71	15.38	D- / 1.0	2.98%	B / 8.1

Major Rating Factors: Middle of the road best describes Nuveen Municipal Value Fund 2 whose TheStreet.com Investment Rating is currently a C (Fair). The fund currently has a performance rating of C- (Fair) based on an annualized return of 9.58% over the last three years and a total return of -2.57% year to date 2012. Factored into the performance evaluation is an expense ratio of 0.71% (very low).

The fund's risk rating is currently B (Good). It carries a beta of 1.37, meaning it is expected to move 13.7% for every 10% move in the market. Volatility, as measured by both the semi-deviation and a drawdown factor, is considered low. As of March 31, 2012, Nuveen Municipal Value Fund 2 traded at a discount of 1.94% below its net asset value, which is better than its one-year historical average premium of .98%.

Thomas C. Spalding has been running the fund for 3 years and currently receives a manager quality ranking of 39 (0=worst, 99=best). If you desire an average level of risk, then this fund may be an option.

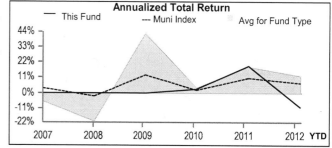

Nuveen NC Div Adv Muni (NRB)
B   **Good**

Fund Family: Nuveen Fund Advisors Inc
Fund Type: Municipal - Single State
Inception Date: January 25, 2001

Major Rating Factors: Strong performance is the major factor driving the B (Good) TheStreet.com Investment Rating for Nuveen NC Div Adv Muni. The fund currently has a performance rating of B- (Good) based on an annualized return of 12.19% over the last three years and a total return of 9.75% year to date 2012. Factored into the performance evaluation is an expense ratio of 2.95% (high).

The fund's risk rating is currently B (Good). It carries a beta of 0.87, meaning the fund's expected move will be 8.7% for every 10% move in the market. Volatility, as measured by both the semi-deviation and a drawdown factor, is considered low. As of March 31, 2012, Nuveen NC Div Adv Muni traded at a premium of 8.70% above its net asset value, which is worse than its one-year historical average premium of 1.56%.

Daniel J. Close has been running the fund for 5 years and currently receives a manager quality ranking of 80 (0=worst, 99=best). If you desire only a moderate level of risk and strong performance, then this fund is an excellent option.

Data Date	Investment Rating	Net Assets ($Mil)	Price	Perfor-mance Rating/Pts	Total Return Y-T-D	Risk Rating/Pts
3-12	B	33.34	17.00	B- / 7.0	9.75%	B / 8.6
2011	B	34.90	15.68	B- / 7.0	0.35%	B / 8.5
2010	C-	34.62	14.19	D+ / 2.8	-5.80%	B- / 7.2
2009	B-	34.82	15.90	C+ / 6.7	35.61%	B- / 7.3

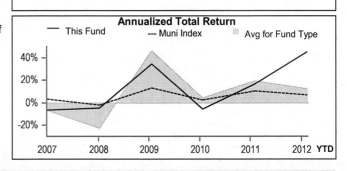

Nuveen NC Div Adv Muni 2 (NNO)
C   **Fair**

Fund Family: Nuveen Fund Advisors Inc
Fund Type: Municipal - Single State
Inception Date: November 15, 2001

Major Rating Factors: Middle of the road best describes Nuveen NC Div Adv Muni 2 whose TheStreet.com Investment Rating is currently a C (Fair). The fund currently has a performance rating of C (Fair) based on an annualized return of 10.64% over the last three years and a total return of 2.40% year to date 2012. Factored into the performance evaluation is an expense ratio of 2.79% (high).

The fund's risk rating is currently B (Good). It carries a beta of 0.99, meaning that its performance tracks fairly well with that of the overall stock market. Volatility, as measured by both the semi-deviation and a drawdown factor, is considered low. As of March 31, 2012, Nuveen NC Div Adv Muni 2 traded at a premium of .58% above its net asset value, which is worse than its one-year historical average discount of .60%.

Daniel J. Close currently receives a manager quality ranking of 69 (0=worst, 99=best). If you desire an average level of risk, then this fund may be an option.

Data Date	Investment Rating	Net Assets ($Mil)	Price	Perfor-mance Rating/Pts	Total Return Y-T-D	Risk Rating/Pts
3-12	C	54.59	15.56	C / 4.5	2.40%	B / 8.7
2011	B+	57.10	15.38	B / 7.6	0.07%	B / 8.7
2010	C+	56.59	14.30	C / 5.2	1.28%	B- / 7.0
2009	B-	56.96	14.89	C+ / 6.9	40.55%	B- / 7.5

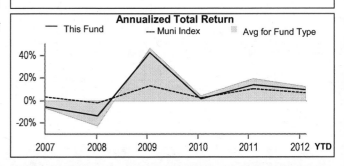

Nuveen NC Div Adv Muni Fund 3 (NII)
C+   **Fair**

Fund Family: Nuveen Fund Advisors Inc
Fund Type: Municipal - Single State
Inception Date: September 25, 2002

Major Rating Factors: Middle of the road best describes Nuveen NC Div Adv Muni Fund 3 whose TheStreet.com Investment Rating is currently a C+ (Fair). The fund currently has a performance rating of C (Fair) based on an annualized return of 10.74% over the last three years and a total return of 2.81% year to date 2012. Factored into the performance evaluation is an expense ratio of 2.75% (high).

The fund's risk rating is currently B (Good). It carries a beta of 1.52, meaning it is expected to move 15.2% for every 10% move in the market. Volatility, as measured by both the semi-deviation and a drawdown factor, is considered low. As of March 31, 2012, Nuveen NC Div Adv Muni Fund 3 traded at a premium of 1.71% above its net asset value, which is worse than its one-year historical average premium of .07%.

Daniel J. Close has been running the fund for 5 years and currently receives a manager quality ranking of 51 (0=worst, 99=best). If you desire an average level of risk, then this fund may be an option.

Data Date	Investment Rating	Net Assets ($Mil)	Price	Perfor-mance Rating/Pts	Total Return Y-T-D	Risk Rating/Pts
3-12	C+	55.96	15.43	C / 4.9	2.81%	B / 8.8
2011	B	58.70	15.19	B- / 7.4	-0.07%	B / 8.6
2010	C-	58.05	13.68	D+ / 2.7	-4.57%	B- / 7.4
2009	A	58.61	15.12	B- / 7.2	40.38%	B- / 7.3

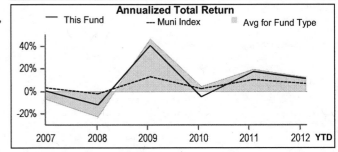

Nuveen NC Prem Inc Muni (NNC)

C+ **Fair**

Fund Family: Nuveen Fund Advisors Inc
Fund Type: Municipal - Single State
Inception Date: May 20, 1993

Major Rating Factors: Middle of the road best describes Nuveen NC Prem Inc Muni whose TheStreet.com Investment Rating is currently a C+ (Fair). The fund currently has a performance rating of C+ (Fair) based on an annualized return of 12.77% over the last three years and a total return of 2.34% year to date 2012. Factored into the performance evaluation is an expense ratio of 2.49% (high).

The fund's risk rating is currently B (Good). It carries a beta of 1.33, meaning it is expected to move 13.3% for every 10% move in the market. Volatility, as measured by both the semi-deviation and a drawdown factor, is considered low. As of March 31, 2012, Nuveen NC Prem Inc Muni traded at a premium of 2.39% above its net asset value, which is worse than its one-year historical average discount of .01%.

Daniel J. Close has been running the fund for 5 years and currently receives a manager quality ranking of 67 (0=worst, 99=best). If you desire an average level of risk, then this fund may be an option.

Data Date	Investment Rating	Net Assets ($Mil)	Price	Performance Rating/Pts	Total Return Y-T-D	Risk Rating/Pts
3-12	C+	91.26	15.43	C+ / 5.7	2.34%	B / 8.9
2011	B+	95.10	15.25	B / 7.7	0.39%	B / 8.8
2010	C+	93.57	13.96	C+ / 6.3	2.69%	C+ / 6.9
2009	B-	93.88	14.30	C+ / 6.3	36.07%	B- / 7.4

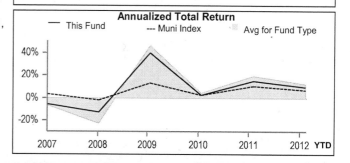

Nuveen New Jersey Municipal Value (NJV)

A+ **Excellent**

Fund Family: Nuveen Fund Advisors Inc
Fund Type: Municipal - National
Inception Date: April 28, 2009

Major Rating Factors:
Exceptional performance is the major factor driving the A+ (Excellent) TheStreet.com Investment Rating for Nuveen New Jersey Municipal Value. The fund currently has a performance rating of A- (Excellent) based on an annualized return of 0.00% over the last three years and a total return of 5.41% year to date 2012. Factored into the performance evaluation is an expense ratio of 0.85% (very low).

The fund's risk rating is currently B (Good). It carries a beta of 0.00, meaning the fund's expected move will be 0.0% for every 10% move in the market. Volatility, as measured by both the semi-deviation and a drawdown factor, is considered low. As of March 31, 2012, Nuveen New Jersey Municipal Value traded at a discount of 2.43% below its net asset value, which is worse than its one-year historical average discount of 4.65%.

Paul L. Brennan currently receives a manager quality ranking of 29 (0=worst, 99=best). If you desire only a moderate level of risk and strong performance, then this fund is an excellent option.

Data Date	Investment Rating	Net Assets ($Mil)	Price	Performance Rating/Pts	Total Return Y-T-D	Risk Rating/Pts
3-12	A+	22.98	16.03	A- / 9.2	5.41%	B / 8.7
2011	B+	24.70	15.38	B+ / 8.3	0.13%	B / 8.7
2010	C+	24.72	14.87	C- / 3.7	5.49%	B / 8.5

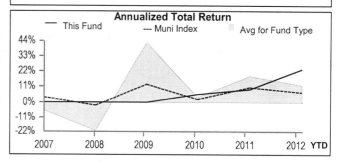

Nuveen New York Municipal Value 2 (NYV)

B **Good**

Fund Family: Nuveen Fund Advisors Inc
Fund Type: Municipal - National
Inception Date: April 28, 2009

Major Rating Factors: Strong performance is the major factor driving the B (Good) TheStreet.com Investment Rating for Nuveen New York Municipal Value 2. The fund currently has a performance rating of B- (Good) based on an annualized return of 0.00% over the last three years and a total return of 6.27% year to date 2012. Factored into the performance evaluation is an expense ratio of 0.77% (very low).

The fund's risk rating is currently B (Good). It carries a beta of 0.00, meaning the fund's expected move will be 0.0% for every 10% move in the market. Volatility, as measured by both the semi-deviation and a drawdown factor, is considered low. As of March 31, 2012, Nuveen New York Municipal Value 2 traded at a discount of 3.10% below its net asset value, which is worse than its one-year historical average discount of 6.25%.

Scott R. Romans currently receives a manager quality ranking of 86 (0=worst, 99=best). If you desire only a moderate level of risk and strong performance, then this fund is an excellent option.

Data Date	Investment Rating	Net Assets ($Mil)	Price	Performance Rating/Pts	Total Return Y-T-D	Risk Rating/Pts
3-12	B	36.04	15.30	B- / 7.1	6.27%	B / 8.7
2011	B	36.10	14.56	B- / 7.3	0.62%	B / 8.7
2010	C-	37.80	13.98	D- / 1.3	2.54%	B / 8.0

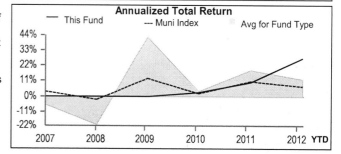

Nuveen NJ Div Adv Muni (NXJ)   A   Excellent

Fund Family: Nuveen Fund Advisors Inc
Fund Type: Municipal - Single State
Inception Date: March 27, 2001

Data Date	Investment Rating	Net Assets ($Mil)	Price	Performance Rating/Pts	Total Return Y-T-D	Risk Rating/Pts
3-12	A	89.40	14.68	B+ / 8.5	6.28%	B / 8.6
2011	B+	97.40	14.00	B+ / 8.6	1.07%	B / 8.7
2010	C	95.30	13.15	C / 5.0	9.08%	C+ / 6.3
2009	C	96.32	12.81	C / 4.4	42.00%	B- / 7.2

Major Rating Factors:
Strong performance is the major factor driving the A (Excellent) TheStreet.com Investment Rating for Nuveen NJ Div Adv Muni. The fund currently has a performance rating of B+ (Good) based on an annualized return of 17.58% over the last three years and a total return of 6.28% year to date 2012. Factored into the performance evaluation is an expense ratio of 1.27% (average).

The fund's risk rating is currently B (Good). It carries a beta of 2.05, meaning it is expected to move 20.5% for every 10% move in the market. Volatility, as measured by both the semi-deviation and a drawdown factor, is considered low. As of March 31, 2012, Nuveen NJ Div Adv Muni traded at a discount of 3.23% below its net asset value, which is worse than its one-year historical average discount of 6.37%.

Paul L. Brennan has been running the fund for 1 year and currently receives a manager quality ranking of 55 (0=worst, 99=best). If you desire only a moderate level of risk and strong performance, then this fund is an excellent option.

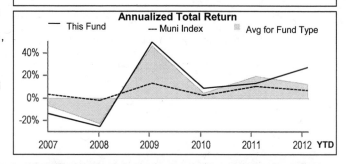

Nuveen NJ Div Adv Muni Fund 2 (NUJ)   B+   Good

Fund Family: Nuveen Fund Advisors Inc
Fund Type: Municipal - Single State
Inception Date: March 25, 2002

Data Date	Investment Rating	Net Assets ($Mil)	Price	Performance Rating/Pts	Total Return Y-T-D	Risk Rating/Pts
3-12	B+	61.50	14.70	B / 7.9	2.53%	B / 8.4
2011	A-	66.40	14.54	B+ / 8.9	0.76%	B / 8.5
2010	C-	65.41	13.08	D+ / 2.9	4.60%	C+ / 6.6
2009	C	65.93	13.30	C / 4.6	43.78%	B- / 7.0

Major Rating Factors: Strong performance is the major factor driving the B+ (Good) TheStreet.com Investment Rating for Nuveen NJ Div Adv Muni Fund 2. The fund currently has a performance rating of B (Good) based on an annualized return of 16.32% over the last three years and a total return of 2.53% year to date 2012. Factored into the performance evaluation is an expense ratio of 1.81% (above average).

The fund's risk rating is currently B (Good). It carries a beta of 2.26, meaning it is expected to move 22.6% for every 10% move in the market. Volatility, as measured by both the semi-deviation and a drawdown factor, is considered low. As of March 31, 2012, Nuveen NJ Div Adv Muni Fund 2 traded at a discount of 2.52% below its net asset value, which is worse than its one-year historical average discount of 4.09%.

Paul L. Brennan currently receives a manager quality ranking of 40 (0=worst, 99=best). If you desire only a moderate level of risk and strong performance, then this fund is an excellent option.

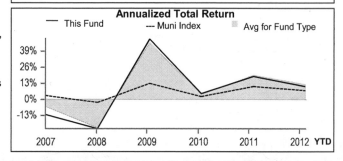

Nuveen NJ Investment Quality Muni (NQJ)   B+   Good

Fund Family: Nuveen Fund Advisors Inc
Fund Type: Municipal - Single State
Inception Date: February 21, 1991

Data Date	Investment Rating	Net Assets ($Mil)	Price	Performance Rating/Pts	Total Return Y-T-D	Risk Rating/Pts
3-12	B+	279.97	14.57	B / 7.7	3.48%	B / 8.7
2011	B+	302.20	14.28	B / 8.2	0.01%	B / 8.8
2010	C+	295.38	13.12	C / 5.2	8.04%	C+ / 6.3
2009	B-	298.16	12.90	C+ / 5.8	37.89%	B- / 7.6

Major Rating Factors: Strong performance is the major factor driving the B+ (Good) TheStreet.com Investment Rating for Nuveen NJ Investment Quality Muni. The fund currently has a performance rating of B (Good) based on an annualized return of 16.35% over the last three years and a total return of 3.48% year to date 2012. Factored into the performance evaluation is an expense ratio of 1.55% (average).

The fund's risk rating is currently B (Good). It carries a beta of 1.71, meaning it is expected to move 17.1% for every 10% move in the market. Volatility, as measured by both the semi-deviation and a drawdown factor, is considered low. As of March 31, 2012, Nuveen NJ Investment Quality Muni traded at a discount of 3.70% below its net asset value, which is worse than its one-year historical average discount of 5.28%.

Paul L. Brennan currently receives a manager quality ranking of 67 (0=worst, 99=best). If you desire only a moderate level of risk and strong performance, then this fund is an excellent option.

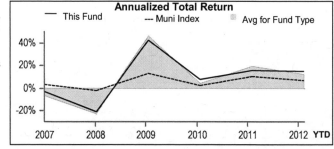

Nuveen NJ Prem Inc Muni (NNJ)

B+   **Good**

Fund Family: Nuveen Fund Advisors Inc
Fund Type: Municipal - Single State
Inception Date: December 17, 1992

Major Rating Factors: Strong performance is the major factor driving the B+ (Good) TheStreet.com Investment Rating for Nuveen NJ Prem Inc Muni. The fund currently has a performance rating of B (Good) based on an annualized return of 16.56% over the last three years and a total return of 2.11% year to date 2012. Factored into the performance evaluation is an expense ratio of 1.59% (above average).

The fund's risk rating is currently B (Good). It carries a beta of 1.33, meaning it is expected to move 13.3% for every 10% move in the market. Volatility, as measured by both the semi-deviation and a drawdown factor, is considered low. As of March 31, 2012, Nuveen NJ Prem Inc Muni traded at a discount of .57% below its net asset value, which is worse than its one-year historical average discount of 3.72%.

Paul L. Brennan currently receives a manager quality ranking of 78 (0=worst, 99=best). If you desire only a moderate level of risk and strong performance, then this fund is an excellent option.

Data Date	Investment Rating	Net Assets ($Mil)	Price	Performance Rating/Pts	Total Return Y-T-D	Risk Rating/Pts
3-12	B+	171.21	15.60	B / 7.9	2.11%	B / 8.8
2011	B+	184.90	15.49	B+ / 8.4	-2.00%	B / 8.8
2010	C	180.02	13.55	C / 4.4	6.43%	C+ / 6.7
2009	B-	182.23	13.47	C+ / 5.8	34.60%	B- / 7.6

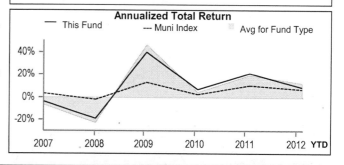

Nuveen NY AMT/Fr Muni Income (NRK)

C+   **Fair**

Fund Family: Nuveen Fund Advisors Inc
Fund Type: Municipal - Single State
Inception Date: November 21, 2002

Major Rating Factors: Middle of the road best describes Nuveen NY AMT/Fr Muni Income whose TheStreet.com Investment Rating is currently a C+ (Fair). The fund currently has a performance rating of C (Fair) based on an annualized return of 13.02% over the last three years and a total return of 3.12% year to date 2012. Factored into the performance evaluation is an expense ratio of 2.89% (high).

The fund's risk rating is currently B+ (Good). It carries a beta of 1.35, meaning it is expected to move 13.5% for every 10% move in the market. Volatility, as measured by both the semi-deviation and a drawdown factor, is considered very low. As of March 31, 2012, Nuveen NY AMT/Fr Muni Income traded at a discount of 5.20% below its net asset value, which is worse than its one-year historical average discount of 6.70%.

Scott R. Romans currently receives a manager quality ranking of 61 (0=worst, 99=best). If you desire an average level of risk, then this fund may be an option.

Data Date	Investment Rating	Net Assets ($Mil)	Price	Performance Rating/Pts	Total Return Y-T-D	Risk Rating/Pts
3-12	C+	52.69	14.40	C / 5.5	3.12%	B+ / 9.0
2011	B+	52.90	14.13	B- / 7.3	1.70%	B+ / 9.0
2010	C+	53.87	13.17	C- / 3.6	2.25%	B / 8.0
2009	B-	53.22	13.57	C+ / 6.3	37.21%	B- / 7.9

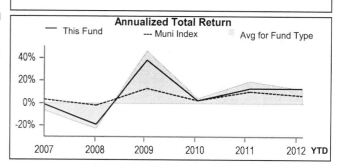

Nuveen NY Div Adv Muni (NAN)

B   **Good**

Fund Family: Nuveen Fund Advisors Inc
Fund Type: Municipal - Single State
Inception Date: May 25, 1999

Major Rating Factors: Nuveen NY Div Adv Muni receives a TheStreet.com Investment Rating of B (Good). The fund currently has a performance rating of C+ (Fair) based on an annualized return of 14.74% over the last three years and a total return of 2.67% year to date 2012. Factored into the performance evaluation is an expense ratio of 2.42% (high).

The fund's risk rating is currently B+ (Good). It carries a beta of 1.71, meaning it is expected to move 17.1% for every 10% move in the market. Volatility, as measured by both the semi-deviation and a drawdown factor, is considered very low. As of March 31, 2012, Nuveen NY Div Adv Muni traded at a discount of 6.60% below its net asset value, which is worse than its one-year historical average discount of 7.66%.

Scott R. Romans currently receives a manager quality ranking of 60 (0=worst, 99=best). If you desire an average level of risk, then this fund may be an option.

Data Date	Investment Rating	Net Assets ($Mil)	Price	Performance Rating/Pts	Total Return Y-T-D	Risk Rating/Pts
3-12	B	139.06	14.43	C+ / 6.7	2.67%	B+ / 9.0
2011	A	140.50	14.24	B+ / 8.7	1.83%	B+ / 9.0
2010	C	140.53	12.90	C- / 3.6	5.84%	B- / 7.8
2009	C+	137.27	12.94	C / 4.5	36.73%	B- / 7.6

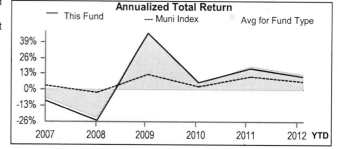

Nuveen NY Div Adv Muni 2 (NXK)

B+   **Good**

Fund Family: Nuveen Fund Advisors Inc
Fund Type: Municipal - Single State
Inception Date: March 27, 2001

Major Rating Factors: Strong performance is the major factor driving the B+ (Good) TheStreet.com Investment Rating for Nuveen NY Div Adv Muni 2. The fund currently has a performance rating of B- (Good) based on an annualized return of 15.88% over the last three years and a total return of 3.03% year to date 2012. Factored into the performance evaluation is an expense ratio of 2.41% (high).

The fund's risk rating is currently B+ (Good). It carries a beta of 1.67, meaning it is expected to move 16.7% for every 10% move in the market. Volatility, as measured by both the semi-deviation and a drawdown factor, is considered very low. As of March 31, 2012, Nuveen NY Div Adv Muni 2 traded at a discount of 5.72% below its net asset value, which is worse than its one-year historical average discount of 7.42%.

Scott R. Romans currently receives a manager quality ranking of 60 (0=worst, 99=best). If you desire only a moderate level of risk and strong performance, then this fund is an excellent option.

Data Date	Investment Rating	Net Assets ($Mil)	Price	Performance Rating/Pts	Total Return Y-T-D	Risk Rating/Pts
3-12	B+	96.94	14.50	B- / 7.3	3.03%	B+ / 9.0
2011	A-	98.00	14.26	B+ / 8.7	1.26%	B+ / 9.1
2010	C+	98.16	13.09	C / 4.8	7.35%	C+ / 6.6
2009	C+	95.75	12.92	C / 4.5	38.97%	B- / 7.3

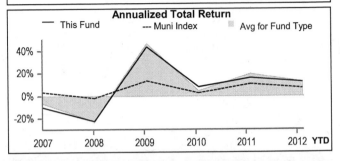
Annualized Total Return

Nuveen NY Div Adv Muni Income (NKO)

B-   **Good**

Fund Family: Nuveen Fund Advisors Inc
Fund Type: Municipal - Single State
Inception Date: March 25, 2002

Major Rating Factors: Nuveen NY Div Adv Muni Income receives a TheStreet.com Investment Rating of B- (Good). The fund currently has a performance rating of C+ (Fair) based on an annualized return of 14.94% over the last three years and a total return of 0.13% year to date 2012. Factored into the performance evaluation is an expense ratio of 1.66% (above average).

The fund's risk rating is currently B+ (Good). It carries a beta of 1.80, meaning it is expected to move 18.0% for every 10% move in the market. Volatility, as measured by both the semi-deviation and a drawdown factor, is considered very low. As of March 31, 2012, Nuveen NY Div Adv Muni Income traded at a discount of 5.32% below its net asset value, which is worse than its one-year historical average discount of 5.93%.

Scott R. Romans currently receives a manager quality ranking of 50 (0=worst, 99=best). If you desire an average level of risk, then this fund may be an option.

Data Date	Investment Rating	Net Assets ($Mil)	Price	Performance Rating/Pts	Total Return Y-T-D	Risk Rating/Pts
3-12	B-	121.78	14.76	C+ / 6.2	0.13%	B+ / 9.0
2011	B+	122.60	14.94	B / 8.2	0.47%	B+ / 9.1
2010	C+	122.24	13.40	C / 4.7	8.08%	C+ / 6.8
2009	C+	120.41	13.10	C / 5.0	34.55%	B- / 7.5

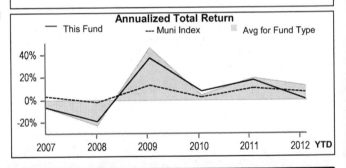
Annualized Total Return

Nuveen NY Investment Quality Muni (NQN)

B-   **Good**

Fund Family: Nuveen Fund Advisors Inc
Fund Type: Municipal - Single State
Inception Date: November 20, 1990

Major Rating Factors: Nuveen NY Investment Quality Muni receives a TheStreet.com Investment Rating of B- (Good). The fund currently has a performance rating of C+ (Fair) based on an annualized return of 14.84% over the last three years and a total return of -1.77% year to date 2012. Factored into the performance evaluation is an expense ratio of 1.73% (above average).

The fund's risk rating is currently B (Good). It carries a beta of 1.85, meaning it is expected to move 18.5% for every 10% move in the market. Volatility, as measured by both the semi-deviation and a drawdown factor, is considered low. As of March 31, 2012, Nuveen NY Investment Quality Muni traded at a discount of 4.05% below its net asset value, which is worse than its one-year historical average discount of 4.54%.

Scott R. Romans currently receives a manager quality ranking of 55 (0=worst, 99=best). If you desire an average level of risk, then this fund may be an option.

Data Date	Investment Rating	Net Assets ($Mil)	Price	Performance Rating/Pts	Total Return Y-T-D	Risk Rating/Pts
3-12	B-	268.79	14.94	C+ / 6.3	-1.77%	B / 8.8
2011	A	270.20	15.41	A- / 9.0	0.39%	B / 8.9
2010	C+	272.03	13.48	C / 5.5	7.17%	C+ / 6.4
2009	B	264.17	13.34	C / 5.5	33.30%	B- / 7.7

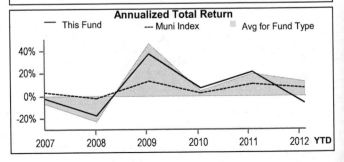
Annualized Total Return

Nuveen NY Muni Value (NNY)   C   Fair

Fund Family: Nuveen Fund Advisors Inc
Fund Type: Municipal - Single State
Inception Date: October 7, 1987

Data Date	Investment Rating	Net Assets ($Mil)	Price	Perfor-mance Rating/Pts	Total Return Y-T-D	Risk Rating/Pts
3-12	C	150.55	9.89	C- / 3.5	0.74%	B+ / 9.1
2011	B	151.80	9.92	C+ / 6.5	1.11%	B+ / 9.2
2010	B	152.03	9.08	C- / 4.2	0.46%	B / 8.8
2009	B-	150.06	9.45	C / 4.6	11.40%	B / 8.3

Major Rating Factors: Middle of the road best describes Nuveen NY Muni Value whose TheStreet.com Investment Rating is currently a C (Fair). The fund currently has a performance rating of C- (Fair) based on an annualized return of 8.00% over the last three years and a total return of 0.74% year to date 2012. Factored into the performance evaluation is an expense ratio of 0.65% (very low).

The fund's risk rating is currently B+ (Good). It carries a beta of 0.97, meaning that its performance tracks fairly well with that of the overall stock market. Volatility, as measured by both the semi-deviation and a drawdown factor, is considered very low. As of March 31, 2012, Nuveen NY Muni Value traded at a discount of 2.37% below its net asset value, which is worse than its one-year historical average discount of 3.18%.

Scott R. Romans currently receives a manager quality ranking of 51 (0=worst, 99=best). If you desire an average level of risk, then this fund may be an option.

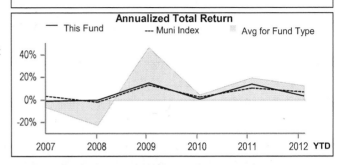

Nuveen NY Performance Plus Muni (NNP)   B   Good

Fund Family: Nuveen Fund Advisors Inc
Fund Type: Municipal - Single State
Inception Date: November 16, 1989

Data Date	Investment Rating	Net Assets ($Mil)	Price	Perfor-mance Rating/Pts	Total Return Y-T-D	Risk Rating/Pts
3-12	B	238.57	15.51	C+ / 6.7	1.81%	B+ / 9.0
2011	A-	240.50	15.44	B+ / 8.4	0.82%	B+ / 9.1
2010	C	241.45	13.98	C / 4.4	6.74%	C+ / 6.6
2009	C+	235.11	13.89	C / 5.1	38.65%	B- / 7.4

Major Rating Factors: Nuveen NY Performance Plus Muni receives a TheStreet.com Investment Rating of B (Good). The fund currently has a performance rating of C+ (Fair) based on an annualized return of 15.71% over the last three years and a total return of 1.81% year to date 2012. Factored into the performance evaluation is an expense ratio of 1.77% (above average).

The fund's risk rating is currently B+ (Good). It carries a beta of 1.74, meaning it is expected to move 17.4% for every 10% move in the market. Volatility, as measured by both the semi-deviation and a drawdown factor, is considered very low. As of March 31, 2012, Nuveen NY Performance Plus Muni traded at a discount of 4.44% below its net asset value, which is worse than its one-year historical average discount of 5.05%.

Scott R. Romans currently receives a manager quality ranking of 63 (0=worst, 99=best). If you desire an average level of risk, then this fund may be an option.

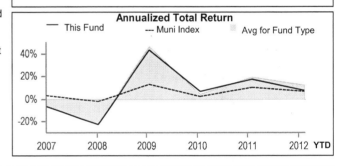

Nuveen NY Prem Inc Muni (NNF)   B   Good

Fund Family: Nuveen Fund Advisors Inc
Fund Type: Municipal - Single State
Inception Date: December 17, 1992

Data Date	Investment Rating	Net Assets ($Mil)	Price	Perfor-mance Rating/Pts	Total Return Y-T-D	Risk Rating/Pts
3-12	B	129.32	15.21	C+ / 6.6	-2.42%	B+ / 9.0
2011	A+	130.30	15.79	A- / 9.1	0.63%	B+ / 9.1
2010	C+	129.68	13.62	C / 5.0	7.23%	C+ / 6.8
2009	B-	126.26	13.39	C+ / 5.9	36.21%	B- / 7.8

Major Rating Factors: Nuveen NY Prem Inc Muni receives a TheStreet.com Investment Rating of B (Good). The fund currently has a performance rating of C+ (Fair) based on an annualized return of 16.02% over the last three years and a total return of -2.42% year to date 2012. Factored into the performance evaluation is an expense ratio of 1.28% (average).

The fund's risk rating is currently B+ (Good). It carries a beta of 1.60, meaning it is expected to move 16.0% for every 10% move in the market. Volatility, as measured by both the semi-deviation and a drawdown factor, is considered very low. As of March 31, 2012, Nuveen NY Prem Inc Muni traded at a discount of 4.52% below its net asset value, which is better than its one-year historical average discount of 4.02%.

Scott R. Romans currently receives a manager quality ranking of 66 (0=worst, 99=best). If you desire an average level of risk, then this fund may be an option.

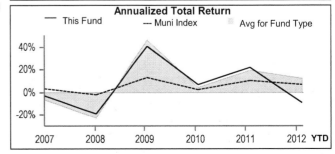

Nuveen NY Quality Inc Muni (NUN)

C+ **Fair**

Fund Family: Nuveen Fund Advisors Inc
Fund Type: Municipal - Single State
Inception Date: November 25, 1991

Major Rating Factors: Middle of the road best describes Nuveen NY Quality Inc Muni whose TheStreet.com Investment Rating is currently a C+ (Fair). The fund currently has a performance rating of C+ (Fair) based on an annualized return of 15.27% over the last three years and a total return of -3.67% year to date 2012. Factored into the performance evaluation is an expense ratio of 1.62% (above average).

The fund's risk rating is currently B+ (Good). It carries a beta of 1.73, meaning it is expected to move 17.3% for every 10% move in the market. Volatility, as measured by both the semi-deviation and a drawdown factor, is considered very low. As of March 31, 2012, Nuveen NY Quality Inc Muni traded at a discount of 4.76% below its net asset value, which is better than its one-year historical average discount of 3.53%.

Scott R. Romans currently receives a manager quality ranking of 62 (0=worst, 99=best). If you desire an average level of risk, then this fund may be an option.

Data Date	Investment Rating	Net Assets ($Mil)	Price	Perfor-mance Rating/Pts	Total Return Y-T-D	Risk Rating/Pts
3-12	C+	362.83	14.81	C+ / 5.6	-3.67%	B+ / 9.0
2011	A-	365.40	15.59	B+ / 8.6	-1.30%	B+ / 9.2
2010	C+	368.51	13.84	C+ / 6.5	10.17%	C+ / 6.4
2009	B-	359.83	13.30	C+ / 5.7	31.80%	B- / 7.6

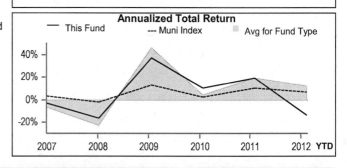

Nuveen NY Select Quality Muni (NVN)

B- **Good**

Fund Family: Nuveen Fund Advisors Inc
Fund Type: Municipal - Single State
Inception Date: May 22, 1991

Major Rating Factors: Nuveen NY Select Quality Muni receives a TheStreet.com Investment Rating of B- (Good). The fund currently has a performance rating of C+ (Fair) based on an annualized return of 15.73% over the last three years and a total return of -2.13% year to date 2012. Factored into the performance evaluation is an expense ratio of 1.73% (above average).

The fund's risk rating is currently B (Good). It carries a beta of 1.78, meaning it is expected to move 17.8% for every 10% move in the market. Volatility, as measured by both the semi-deviation and a drawdown factor, is considered low. As of March 31, 2012, Nuveen NY Select Quality Muni traded at a discount of 4.67% below its net asset value, which is better than its one-year historical average discount of 4.10%.

Scott R. Romans currently receives a manager quality ranking of 61 (0=worst, 99=best). If you desire an average level of risk, then this fund may be an option.

Data Date	Investment Rating	Net Assets ($Mil)	Price	Perfor-mance Rating/Pts	Total Return Y-T-D	Risk Rating/Pts
3-12	B-	366.20	15.11	C+ / 6.3	-2.13%	B / 8.8
2011	A-	363.40	15.65	B+ / 8.6	-1.15%	B+ / 9.0
2010	C+	366.20	13.70	C / 5.2	7.18%	C+ / 6.5
2009	B-	356.49	13.55	C+ / 6.0	35.70%	B- / 7.6

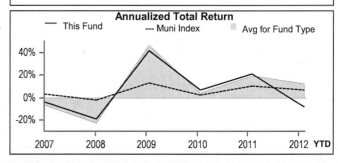

Nuveen NY Select Tax-Free Inc Port (NXN)

C **Fair**

Fund Family: Nuveen Fund Advisors Inc
Fund Type: Municipal - Single State
Inception Date: June 19, 1992

Major Rating Factors: Middle of the road best describes Nuveen NY Select Tax-Free Inc Port whose TheStreet.com Investment Rating is currently a C (Fair). The fund currently has a performance rating of C- (Fair) based on an annualized return of 7.42% over the last three years and a total return of 0.27% year to date 2012. Factored into the performance evaluation is an expense ratio of 0.41% (very low).

The fund's risk rating is currently B+ (Good). It carries a beta of 1.32, meaning it is expected to move 13.2% for every 10% move in the market. Volatility, as measured by both the semi-deviation and a drawdown factor, is considered very low. As of March 31, 2012, Nuveen NY Select Tax-Free Inc Port traded at a discount of 3.36% below its net asset value, which is worse than its one-year historical average discount of 3.82%.

Scott R. Romans currently receives a manager quality ranking of 30 (0=worst, 99=best). If you desire an average level of risk, then this fund may be an option.

Data Date	Investment Rating	Net Assets ($Mil)	Price	Perfor-mance Rating/Pts	Total Return Y-T-D	Risk Rating/Pts
3-12	C	53.71	14.10	C- / 3.2	0.27%	B+ / 9.2
2011	B+	56.70	14.22	B- / 7.1	3.45%	B+ / 9.2
2010	B	55.01	13.09	C- / 4.0	1.30%	B / 8.9
2009	C+	55.65	13.50	C- / 4.2	11.59%	B / 8.4

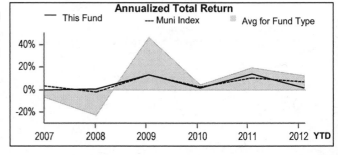

Nuveen OH Div Adv Muni (NXI)   B+   Good

Fund Family: Nuveen Fund Advisors Inc
Fund Type: Municipal - Single State
Inception Date: March 27, 2001

Major Rating Factors: Strong performance is the major factor driving the B+ (Good) TheStreet.com Investment Rating for Nuveen OH Div Adv Muni. The fund currently has a performance rating of B- (Good) based on an annualized return of 15.37% over the last three years and a total return of 1.41% year to date 2012. Factored into the performance evaluation is an expense ratio of 1.33% (average).

The fund's risk rating is currently B (Good). It carries a beta of 1.72, meaning it is expected to move 17.2% for every 10% move in the market. Volatility, as measured by both the semi-deviation and a drawdown factor, is considered low. As of March 31, 2012, Nuveen OH Div Adv Muni traded at a discount of 2.81% below its net asset value, which is worse than its one-year historical average discount of 4.55%.

Daniel J. Close has been running the fund for 5 years and currently receives a manager quality ranking of 57 (0=worst, 99=best). If you desire only a moderate level of risk and strong performance, then this fund is an excellent option.

Data Date	Investment Rating	Net Assets ($Mil)	Price	Performance Rating/Pts	Total Return Y-T-D	Risk Rating/Pts
3-12	B+	60.55	15.21	B- / 7.3	1.41%	B / 8.8
2011	B+	65.00	15.21	B+ / 8.4	1.17%	B / 8.9
2010	C+	64.29	13.56	C / 4.8	2.07%	B- / 7.2
2009	B-	65.57	14.08	C+ / 6.2	33.96%	B- / 7.8

Annualized Total Return

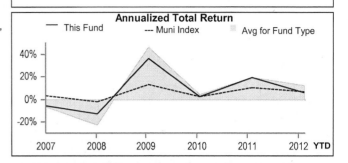

Nuveen OH Div Adv Muni 2 (NBJ)   B+   Good

Fund Family: Nuveen Fund Advisors Inc
Fund Type: Municipal - Single State
Inception Date: September 25, 2001

Major Rating Factors: Strong performance is the major factor driving the B+ (Good) TheStreet.com Investment Rating for Nuveen OH Div Adv Muni 2. The fund currently has a performance rating of B (Good) based on an annualized return of 15.54% over the last three years and a total return of 6.42% year to date 2012. Factored into the performance evaluation is an expense ratio of 1.10% (low).

The fund's risk rating is currently B (Good). It carries a beta of 1.80, meaning it is expected to move 18.0% for every 10% move in the market. Volatility, as measured by both the semi-deviation and a drawdown factor, is considered low. As of March 31, 2012, Nuveen OH Div Adv Muni 2 traded at a discount of 3.13% below its net asset value, which is worse than its one-year historical average discount of 6.75%.

Daniel J. Close has been running the fund for 5 years and currently receives a manager quality ranking of 58 (0=worst, 99=best). If you desire only a moderate level of risk and strong performance, then this fund is an excellent option.

Data Date	Investment Rating	Net Assets ($Mil)	Price	Performance Rating/Pts	Total Return Y-T-D	Risk Rating/Pts
3-12	B+	43.91	14.88	B / 7.6	6.42%	B / 8.8
2011	B+	46.90	14.18	B / 8.1	0.63%	B / 8.8
2010	C+	46.00	13.20	C / 5.0	2.86%	B- / 7.0
2009	B-	46.46	13.60	C+ / 6.9	44.94%	B- / 7.4

Annualized Total Return

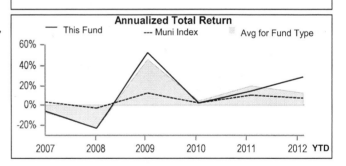

Nuveen OH Div Adv Muni Fund 3 (NVJ)   B-   Good

Fund Family: Nuveen Fund Advisors Inc
Fund Type: Municipal - Single State
Inception Date: March 26, 2002

Major Rating Factors: Nuveen OH Div Adv Muni Fund 3 receives a TheStreet.com Investment Rating of B- (Good). The fund currently has a performance rating of C+ (Fair) based on an annualized return of 14.44% over the last three years and a total return of 2.12% year to date 2012. Factored into the performance evaluation is an expense ratio of 1.10% (low).

The fund's risk rating is currently B (Good). It carries a beta of 1.91, meaning it is expected to move 19.1% for every 10% move in the market. Volatility, as measured by both the semi-deviation and a drawdown factor, is considered low. As of March 31, 2012, Nuveen OH Div Adv Muni Fund 3 traded at a discount of 1.99% below its net asset value, which is worse than its one-year historical average discount of 3.08%.

Daniel J. Close has been running the fund for 5 years and currently receives a manager quality ranking of 38 (0=worst, 99=best). If you desire an average level of risk, then this fund may be an option.

Data Date	Investment Rating	Net Assets ($Mil)	Price	Performance Rating/Pts	Total Return Y-T-D	Risk Rating/Pts
3-12	B-	30.97	15.23	C+ / 6.6	2.12%	B / 8.6
2011	B+	32.90	15.13	B / 8.1	0.86%	B / 8.7
2010	C+	33.06	13.95	C / 4.9	0.45%	C+ / 6.9
2009	A+	33.76	14.73	B- / 7.2	41.71%	B- / 7.6

Annualized Total Return

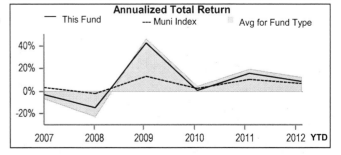

Nuveen OH Quality Inc Muni (NUO)

A-   **Excellent**

Fund Family: Nuveen Fund Advisors Inc
Fund Type: Municipal - Single State
Inception Date: October 11, 1991

Data Date	Investment Rating	Net Assets ($Mil)	Price	Performance Rating/Pts	Total Return Y-T-D	Risk Rating/Pts
3-12	A-	150.56	17.38	B+ / 8.3	5.55%	B / 8.8
2011	B+	162.30	16.70	B+ / 8.5	0.66%	B / 8.8
2010	C+	157.44	14.68	C / 5.1	-2.94%	C+ / 6.9
2009	A	160.55	16.00	B- / 7.3	34.98%	B- / 7.2

Major Rating Factors:
Strong performance is the major factor driving the A- (Excellent) TheStreet.com Investment Rating for Nuveen OH Quality Inc Muni. The fund currently has a performance rating of B+ (Good) based on an annualized return of 17.41% over the last three years and a total return of 5.55% year to date 2012. Factored into the performance evaluation is an expense ratio of 1.14% (low).

The fund's risk rating is currently B (Good). It carries a beta of 1.65, meaning it is expected to move 16.5% for every 10% move in the market. Volatility, as measured by both the semi-deviation and a drawdown factor, is considered low. As of March 31, 2012, Nuveen OH Quality Inc Muni traded at a premium of 2.36% above its net asset value, which is worse than its one-year historical average discount of 3.04%.

Daniel J. Close currently receives a manager quality ranking of 73 (0=worst, 99=best). If you desire only a moderate level of risk and strong performance, then this fund is an excellent option.

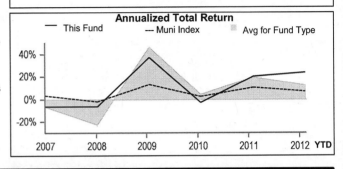

Nuveen PA Div Adv Muni (NXM)

B   **Good**

Fund Family: Nuveen Fund Advisors Inc
Fund Type: Municipal - Single State
Inception Date: March 27, 2001

Data Date	Investment Rating	Net Assets ($Mil)	Price	Performance Rating/Pts	Total Return Y-T-D	Risk Rating/Pts
3-12	B	46.52	14.16	B- / 7.2	2.32%	B / 8.7
2011	B+	49.60	14.04	B / 8.1	1.14%	B / 8.7
2010	C-	48.93	12.97	D+ / 2.8	4.81%	B- / 7.3
2009	C+	49.17	13.20	C / 4.9	43.85%	B- / 7.3

Major Rating Factors: Strong performance is the major factor driving the B (Good) TheStreet.com Investment Rating for Nuveen PA Div Adv Muni. The fund currently has a performance rating of B- (Good) based on an annualized return of 16.33% over the last three years and a total return of 2.32% year to date 2012. Factored into the performance evaluation is an expense ratio of 1.87% (above average).

The fund's risk rating is currently B (Good). It carries a beta of 1.81, meaning it is expected to move 18.1% for every 10% move in the market. Volatility, as measured by both the semi-deviation and a drawdown factor, is considered low. As of March 31, 2012, Nuveen PA Div Adv Muni traded at a discount of 7.09% below its net asset value, which is worse than its one-year historical average discount of 7.25%.

Paul L. Brennan currently receives a manager quality ranking of 64 (0=worst, 99=best). If you desire only a moderate level of risk and strong performance, then this fund is an excellent option.

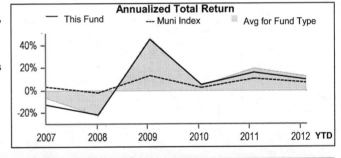

Nuveen PA Div Adv Muni Fund 2 (NVY)

B-   **Good**

Fund Family: Nuveen Fund Advisors Inc
Fund Type: Municipal - Single State
Inception Date: March 25, 2002

Data Date	Investment Rating	Net Assets ($Mil)	Price	Performance Rating/Pts	Total Return Y-T-D	Risk Rating/Pts
3-12	B-	52.47	14.40	C+ / 6.3	4.17%	B / 8.7
2011	B+	54.80	14.03	B / 8.2	0.86%	B / 8.8
2010	C	54.92	13.18	C- / 3.2	6.40%	B- / 7.5
2009	B-	55.38	13.22	C+ / 6.8	57.14%	B- / 7.3

Major Rating Factors: Nuveen PA Div Adv Muni Fund 2 receives a TheStreet.com Investment Rating of B- (Good). The fund currently has a performance rating of C+ (Fair) based on an annualized return of 12.92% over the last three years and a total return of 4.17% year to date 2012. Factored into the performance evaluation is an expense ratio of 1.74% (above average).

The fund's risk rating is currently B (Good). It carries a beta of 1.62, meaning it is expected to move 16.2% for every 10% move in the market. Volatility, as measured by both the semi-deviation and a drawdown factor, is considered low. As of March 31, 2012, Nuveen PA Div Adv Muni Fund 2 traded at a discount of 4.19% below its net asset value, which is worse than its one-year historical average discount of 6.20%.

Paul L. Brennan currently receives a manager quality ranking of 58 (0=worst, 99=best). If you desire an average level of risk, then this fund may be an option.

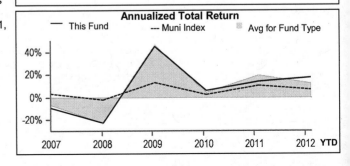

Nuveen PA Investment Quality Muni (NQP)   A   Excellent

Fund Family: Nuveen Fund Advisors Inc
Fund Type: Municipal - Single State
Inception Date: February 21, 1991

Major Rating Factors:
Strong performance is the major factor driving the A (Excellent) TheStreet.com
Investment Rating for Nuveen PA Investment Quality Muni. The fund currently has a
performance rating of B+ (Good) based on an annualized return of 18.06% over the
last three years and a total return of 4.14% year to date 2012. Factored into the
performance evaluation is an expense ratio of 1.60% (above average).

The fund's risk rating is currently B+ (Good). It carries a beta of 1.45, meaning it
is expected to move 14.5% for every 10% move in the market. Volatility, as measured
by both the semi-deviation and a drawdown factor, is considered very low. As of
March 31, 2012, Nuveen PA Investment Quality Muni traded at a price exactly equal
to its net asset value, which is worse than its one-year historical average discount of
3.85%.

Paul L. Brennan currently receives a manager quality ranking of 79 (0=worst,
99=best). If you desire only a moderate level of risk and strong performance, then this
fund is an excellent option.

Data Date	Investment Rating	Net Assets ($Mil)	Price	Performance Rating/Pts	Total Return Y-T-D	Risk Rating/Pts
3-12	A	226.91	15.56	B+ / 8.4	4.14%	B+ / 9.0
2011	A	245.70	15.17	A- / 9.0	-0.07%	B+ / 9.0
2010	C+	238.37	13.33	C / 5.3	7.97%	C+ / 6.3
2009	A	241.54	13.15	B- / 7.0	44.57%	B- / 7.4

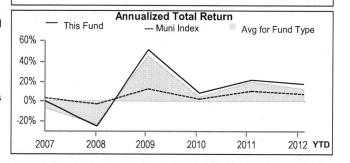

Nuveen PA Prem Inc Muni 2 (NPY)   A   Excellent

Fund Family: Nuveen Fund Advisors Inc
Fund Type: Municipal - Single State
Inception Date: March 18, 1993

Major Rating Factors:
Strong performance is the major factor driving the A (Excellent) TheStreet.com
Investment Rating for Nuveen PA Prem Inc Muni 2. The fund currently has a
performance rating of B+ (Good) based on an annualized return of 18.55% over the
last three years and a total return of 3.85% year to date 2012. Factored into the
performance evaluation is an expense ratio of 1.56% (average).

The fund's risk rating is currently B (Good). It carries a beta of 1.75, meaning it is
expected to move 17.5% for every 10% move in the market. Volatility, as measured
by both the semi-deviation and a drawdown factor, is considered low. As of March 31,
2012, Nuveen PA Prem Inc Muni 2 traded at a discount of 4.35% below its net asset
value, which is worse than its one-year historical average discount of 6.98%.

Paul L. Brennan currently receives a manager quality ranking of 73 (0=worst,
99=best). If you desire only a moderate level of risk and strong performance, then this
fund is an excellent option.

Data Date	Investment Rating	Net Assets ($Mil)	Price	Performance Rating/Pts	Total Return Y-T-D	Risk Rating/Pts
3-12	A	210.84	14.30	B+ / 8.5	3.85%	B / 8.9
2011	A	228.60	13.97	A- / 9.0	0.00%	B / 8.9
2010	C	220.11	12.39	C- / 3.9	5.76%	C+ / 6.5
2009	B-	222.77	12.47	C+ / 6.8	46.95%	B- / 7.3

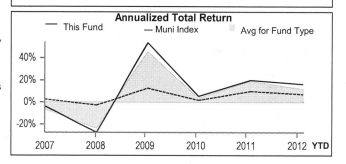

Nuveen Pennsylvania Municipal Valu (NPN)   C   Fair

Fund Family: Nuveen Fund Advisors Inc
Fund Type: Municipal - National
Inception Date: April 28, 2009

Major Rating Factors: Middle of the road best describes Nuveen Pennsylvania
Municipal Valu whose TheStreet.com Investment Rating is currently a C (Fair). The
fund currently has a performance rating of C- (Fair) based on an annualized return of
0.00% over the last three years and a total return of -0.99% year to date 2012.
Factored into the performance evaluation is an expense ratio of 0.87% (low).

The fund's risk rating is currently B (Good). It carries a beta of 0.00, meaning the
fund's expected move will be 0.0% for every 10% move in the market. Volatility, as
measured by both the semi-deviation and a drawdown factor, is considered low. As of
March 31, 2012, Nuveen Pennsylvania Municipal Valu traded at a discount of 7.54%
below its net asset value, which is better than its one-year historical average discount
of 4.65%.

Paul L. Brennan currently receives a manager quality ranking of 11 (0=worst,
99=best). If you desire an average level of risk, then this fund may be an option.

Data Date	Investment Rating	Net Assets ($Mil)	Price	Performance Rating/Pts	Total Return Y-T-D	Risk Rating/Pts
3-12	C	18.03	14.95	C- / 3.6	-0.99%	B / 8.7
2011	B+	19.40	15.26	B / 7.6	-0.07%	B / 8.8
2010	D+	18.81	14.20	E+ / 0.7	-3.16%	B / 8.2

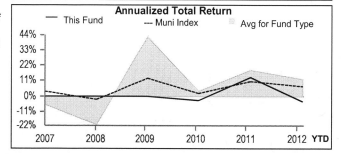

Nuveen Performance Plus Muni (NPP)   B+   Good

Fund Family: Nuveen Fund Advisors Inc
Fund Type: Municipal - National
Inception Date: June 22, 1989

Major Rating Factors: Strong performance is the major factor driving the B+ (Good) TheStreet.com Investment Rating for Nuveen Performance Plus Muni. The fund currently has a performance rating of B (Good) based on an annualized return of 16.45% over the last three years and a total return of 3.12% year to date 2012. Factored into the performance evaluation is an expense ratio of 1.62% (above average).

The fund's risk rating is currently B (Good). It carries a beta of 1.74, meaning it is expected to move 17.4% for every 10% move in the market. Volatility, as measured by both the semi-deviation and a drawdown factor, is considered low. As of March 31, 2012, Nuveen Performance Plus Muni traded at a discount of 2.27% below its net asset value, which is worse than its one-year historical average discount of 3.07%.

Thomas C. Spalding has been running the fund for 10 years and currently receives a manager quality ranking of 65 (0=worst, 99=best). If you desire only a moderate level of risk and strong performance, then this fund is an excellent option.

Data Date	Investment Rating	Net Assets ($Mil)	Price	Performance Rating/Pts	Total Return Y-T-D	Risk Rating/Pts
3-12	B+	892.60	15.52	B / 7.7	3.12%	B / 8.8
2011	A-	918.30	15.28	B+ / 8.7	0.72%	B / 8.8
2010	C+	893.85	13.55	C+ / 5.6	3.45%	C+ / 6.8
2009	B-	906.41	14.06	C+ / 5.8	29.74%	B- / 7.5

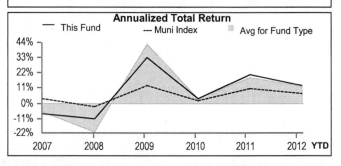

Nuveen Preferref Income Opps (JPC)   A+   Excellent

Fund Family: Nuveen Fund Advisors Inc
Fund Type: Growth and Income
Inception Date: March 26, 2003

Major Rating Factors:
Exceptional performance is the major factor driving the A+ (Excellent) TheStreet.com Investment Rating for Nuveen Preferref Income Opps. The fund currently has a performance rating of A+ (Excellent) based on an annualized return of 44.52% over the last three years and a total return of 13.23% year to date 2012. Factored into the performance evaluation is an expense ratio of 1.70% (above average).

The fund's risk rating is currently B (Good). It carries a beta of 0.92, meaning that its performance tracks fairly well with that of the overall stock market. Volatility, as measured by both the semi-deviation and a drawdown factor, is considered low. As of March 31, 2012, Nuveen Preferref Income Opps traded at a discount of 5.23% below its net asset value, which is worse than its one-year historical average discount of 9.88%.

Gunther M. Stein has been running the fund for 9 years and currently receives a manager quality ranking of 94 (0=worst, 99=best). If you desire only a moderate level of risk and strong performance, then this fund is an excellent option.

Data Date	Investment Rating	Net Assets ($Mil)	Price	Performance Rating/Pts	Total Return Y-T-D	Risk Rating/Pts
3-12	A+	840.64	8.88	A+ / 9.7	13.23%	B / 8.1
2011	B	840.50	8.01	B / 8.2	0.37%	B- / 7.7
2010	C	839.85	8.35	C+ / 6.2	21.28%	C / 4.6
2009	D+	809.16	7.49	C- / 3.5	73.30%	C / 4.6

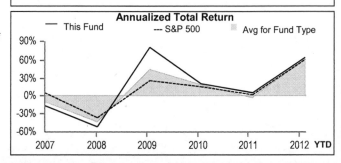

Nuveen Prem Inc Muni (NPI)   B   Good

Fund Family: Nuveen Fund Advisors Inc
Fund Type: Municipal - National
Inception Date: July 21, 1988

Major Rating Factors: Nuveen Prem Inc Muni receives a TheStreet.com Investment Rating of B (Good). The fund currently has a performance rating of C+ (Fair) based on an annualized return of 15.21% over the last three years and a total return of 1.70% year to date 2012. Factored into the performance evaluation is an expense ratio of 1.66% (above average).

The fund's risk rating is currently B (Good). It carries a beta of 1.64, meaning it is expected to move 16.4% for every 10% move in the market. Volatility, as measured by both the semi-deviation and a drawdown factor, is considered low. As of March 31, 2012, Nuveen Prem Inc Muni traded at a discount of 2.23% below its net asset value, which is worse than its one-year historical average discount of 3.20%.

Paul L. Brennan has been running the fund for 6 years and currently receives a manager quality ranking of 61 (0=worst, 99=best). If you desire an average level of risk, then this fund may be an option.

Data Date	Investment Rating	Net Assets ($Mil)	Price	Performance Rating/Pts	Total Return Y-T-D	Risk Rating/Pts
3-12	B	900.46	14.49	C+ / 6.9	1.70%	B / 8.9
2011	B+	922.10	14.47	B / 8.1	-1.31%	B / 8.9
2010	C	875.34	12.82	C- / 4.2	4.00%	C+ / 6.7
2009	C+	915.49	13.15	C / 5.4	27.21%	B- / 7.2

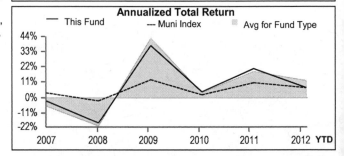

Nuveen Prem Inc Muni 4 (NPT) | B+ | Good

Fund Family: Nuveen Fund Advisors Inc
Fund Type: Municipal - National
Inception Date: February 19, 1993

Major Rating Factors: Strong performance is the major factor driving the B+ (Good) TheStreet.com Investment Rating for Nuveen Prem Inc Muni 4. The fund currently has a performance rating of B (Good) based on an annualized return of 17.31% over the last three years and a total return of 1.24% year to date 2012. Factored into the performance evaluation is an expense ratio of 1.99% (high).

The fund's risk rating is currently B (Good). It carries a beta of 2.05, meaning it is expected to move 20.5% for every 10% move in the market. Volatility, as measured by both the semi-deviation and a drawdown factor, is considered low. As of March 31, 2012, Nuveen Prem Inc Muni 4 traded at a discount of 3.11% below its net asset value, which is worse than its one-year historical average discount of 3.22%.

Christopher L. Drahn currently receives a manager quality ranking of 55 (0=worst, 99=best). If you desire only a moderate level of risk and strong performance, then this fund is an excellent option.

Data Date	Investment Rating	Net Assets ($Mil)	Price	Performance Rating/Pts	Total Return Y-T-D	Risk Rating/Pts
3-12	B+	565.53	13.40	B / 7.8	1.24%	B / 8.7
2011	A	579.30	13.44	A- / 9.2	0.60%	B / 8.7
2010	C+	543.81	11.97	C+ / 6.0	5.19%	C+ / 6.5
2009	B-	568.53	12.15	C+ / 6.2	32.99%	B- / 7.0

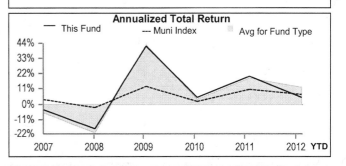

Nuveen Prem Inc Muni Oppty (NPX) | B- | Good

Fund Family: Nuveen Fund Advisors Inc
Fund Type: Municipal - National
Inception Date: July 22, 1993

Major Rating Factors: Nuveen Prem Inc Muni Oppty receives a TheStreet.com Investment Rating of B- (Good). The fund currently has a performance rating of C+ (Fair) based on an annualized return of 14.88% over the last three years and a total return of -0.73% year to date 2012. Factored into the performance evaluation is an expense ratio of 1.80% (above average).

The fund's risk rating is currently B (Good). It carries a beta of 1.88, meaning it is expected to move 18.8% for every 10% move in the market. Volatility, as measured by both the semi-deviation and a drawdown factor, is considered low. As of March 31, 2012, Nuveen Prem Inc Muni Oppty traded at a discount of 5.33% below its net asset value, which is better than its one-year historical average discount of 5.11%.

Douglas J. White currently receives a manager quality ranking of 49 (0=worst, 99=best). If you desire an average level of risk, then this fund may be an option.

Data Date	Investment Rating	Net Assets ($Mil)	Price	Performance Rating/Pts	Total Return Y-T-D	Risk Rating/Pts
3-12	B-	505.77	13.50	C+ / 6.6	-0.73%	B / 8.8
2011	A-	518.10	13.78	B+ / 8.6	-1.89%	B / 8.9
2010	C	484.07	11.90	C- / 4.2	2.35%	C+ / 6.7
2009	B-	501.85	12.32	C+ / 6.2	35.39%	B- / 7.3

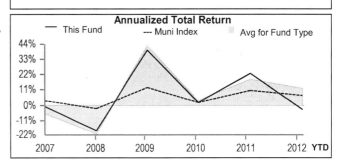

Nuveen Premier Muni Inc (NPF) | B | Good

Fund Family: Nuveen Fund Advisors Inc
Fund Type: Municipal - National
Inception Date: December 18, 1991

Major Rating Factors: Strong performance is the major factor driving the B (Good) TheStreet.com Investment Rating for Nuveen Premier Muni Inc. The fund currently has a performance rating of B- (Good) based on an annualized return of 15.92% over the last three years and a total return of 0.05% year to date 2012. Factored into the performance evaluation is an expense ratio of 1.55% (average).

The fund's risk rating is currently B (Good). It carries a beta of 2.13, meaning it is expected to move 21.3% for every 10% move in the market. Volatility, as measured by both the semi-deviation and a drawdown factor, is considered low. As of March 31, 2012, Nuveen Premier Muni Inc traded at a discount of 3.44% below its net asset value, which is worse than its one-year historical average discount of 3.87%.

Daniel J. Close currently receives a manager quality ranking of 43 (0=worst, 99=best). If you desire only a moderate level of risk and strong performance, then this fund is an excellent option.

Data Date	Investment Rating	Net Assets ($Mil)	Price	Performance Rating/Pts	Total Return Y-T-D	Risk Rating/Pts
3-12	B	287.47	14.59	B- / 7.1	0.05%	B / 8.8
2011	A-	294.90	14.81	B+ / 8.9	-0.47%	B / 8.8
2010	C+	275.67	13.05	C / 5.1	7.17%	C+ / 6.4
2009	B-	290.67	12.96	C+ / 6.0	33.38%	B- / 7.2

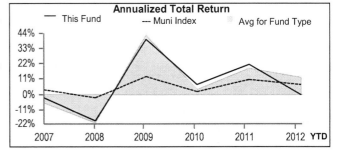

Nuveen Premier Muni Oppty (NIF)

C **Fair**

Fund Family: Nuveen Fund Advisors Inc
Fund Type: Municipal - National
Inception Date: December 18, 1991

Major Rating Factors: Middle of the road best describes Nuveen Premier Muni Oppty whose TheStreet.com Investment Rating is currently a C (Fair). The fund currently has a performance rating of C (Fair) based on an annualized return of 13.02% over the last three years and a total return of -6.29% year to date 2012. Factored into the performance evaluation is an expense ratio of 1.65% (above average).

The fund's risk rating is currently B (Good). It carries a beta of 2.17, meaning it is expected to move 21.7% for every 10% move in the market. Volatility, as measured by both the semi-deviation and a drawdown factor, is considered low. As of March 31, 2012, Nuveen Premier Muni Oppty traded at a discount of 2.66% below its net asset value, which is better than its one-year historical average premium of 1.54%.

Paul L. Brennan has been running the fund for 6 years and currently receives a manager quality ranking of 29 (0=worst, 99=best). If you desire an average level of risk, then this fund may be an option.

Data Date	Investment Rating	Net Assets ($Mil)	Price	Performance Rating/Pts	Total Return Y-T-D	Risk Rating/Pts
3-12	C	287.07	14.99	C / 4.6	-6.29%	B / 8.5
2011	A-	293.60	16.23	A- / 9.2	-2.09%	B / 8.6
2010	C+	279.31	13.50	C / 5.2	3.34%	C+ / 6.6
2009	B-	289.96	13.88	C+ / 6.1	32.10%	B- / 7.2

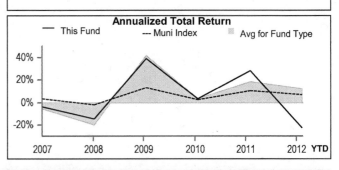

Nuveen Premium Income Muni 2 (NPM)

B **Good**

Fund Family: Nuveen Fund Advisors Inc
Fund Type: Municipal - National
Inception Date: July 23, 1992

Major Rating Factors: Strong performance is the major factor driving the B (Good) TheStreet.com Investment Rating for Nuveen Premium Income Muni 2. The fund currently has a performance rating of B- (Good) based on an annualized return of 15.14% over the last three years and a total return of 2.11% year to date 2012. Factored into the performance evaluation is an expense ratio of 1.48% (average).

The fund's risk rating is currently B (Good). It carries a beta of 1.82, meaning it is expected to move 18.2% for every 10% move in the market. Volatility, as measured by both the semi-deviation and a drawdown factor, is considered low. As of March 31, 2012, Nuveen Premium Income Muni 2 traded at a discount of 2.60% below its net asset value, which is worse than its one-year historical average discount of 4.02%.

Paul L. Brennan has been running the fund for 15 years and currently receives a manager quality ranking of 56 (0=worst, 99=best). If you desire only a moderate level of risk and strong performance, then this fund is an excellent option.

Data Date	Investment Rating	Net Assets ($Mil)	Price	Performance Rating/Pts	Total Return Y-T-D	Risk Rating/Pts
3-12	B	1,039.72	15.00	B- / 7.1	2.11%	B / 8.9
2011	A-	1,064.70	14.92	B+ / 8.5	-0.94%	B+ / 9.0
2010	C	1,003.37	13.24	C- / 3.9	5.79%	C+ / 6.5
2009	B-	603.44	13.33	C+ / 5.7	32.68%	B- / 7.3

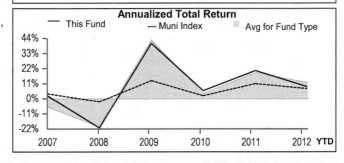

Nuveen Quality Inc Muni (NQU)

B **Good**

Fund Family: Nuveen Fund Advisors Inc
Fund Type: Municipal - National
Inception Date: June 19, 1991

Major Rating Factors: Strong performance is the major factor driving the B (Good) TheStreet.com Investment Rating for Nuveen Quality Inc Muni. The fund currently has a performance rating of B- (Good) based on an annualized return of 14.91% over the last three years and a total return of 3.92% year to date 2012. Factored into the performance evaluation is an expense ratio of 1.92% (above average).

The fund's risk rating is currently B (Good). It carries a beta of 1.65, meaning it is expected to move 16.5% for every 10% move in the market. Volatility, as measured by both the semi-deviation and a drawdown factor, is considered low. As of March 31, 2012, Nuveen Quality Inc Muni traded at a discount of 2.73% below its net asset value, which is worse than its one-year historical average discount of 2.82%.

Thomas C. Spalding has been running the fund for 10 years and currently receives a manager quality ranking of 60 (0=worst, 99=best). If you desire only a moderate level of risk and strong performance, then this fund is an excellent option.

Data Date	Investment Rating	Net Assets ($Mil)	Price	Performance Rating/Pts	Total Return Y-T-D	Risk Rating/Pts
3-12	B	781.06	14.94	B- / 7.2	3.92%	B / 8.8
2011	B+	800.60	14.60	B / 8.0	0.62%	B / 8.8
2010	C+	774.98	13.68	C / 4.8	7.08%	C+ / 6.6
2009	C+	808.36	13.63	C / 4.9	22.37%	B- / 7.5

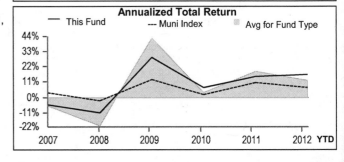

Nuveen Quality Municipal (NQI)   C+   Fair

Fund Family: Nuveen Fund Advisors Inc
Fund Type: Municipal - National
Inception Date: December 19, 1990

Data Date	Investment Rating	Net Assets ($Mil)	Price	Performance Rating/Pts	Total Return Y-T-D	Risk Rating/Pts
3-12	C+	544.50	14.26	C / 4.8	-3.49%	B / 8.7
2011	B+	555.90	15.00	B+ / 8.5	-2.90%	B / 8.7
2010	C-	521.22	12.55	D / 2.1	-1.89%	B- / 7.5
2009	B-	542.09	13.60	C+ / 6.4	39.37%	B- / 7.0

Major Rating Factors: Middle of the road best describes Nuveen Quality Municipal whose TheStreet.com Investment Rating is currently a C+ (Fair). The fund currently has a performance rating of C (Fair) based on an annualized return of 12.66% over the last three years and a total return of -3.49% year to date 2012. Factored into the performance evaluation is an expense ratio of 1.66% (above average).

The fund's risk rating is currently B (Good). It carries a beta of 1.77, meaning it is expected to move 17.7% for every 10% move in the market. Volatility, as measured by both the semi-deviation and a drawdown factor, is considered low. As of March 31, 2012, Nuveen Quality Municipal traded at a discount of 3.58% below its net asset value, which is better than its one-year historical average discount of 1.28%.

Douglas J. White currently receives a manager quality ranking of 38 (0=worst, 99=best). If you desire an average level of risk, then this fund may be an option.

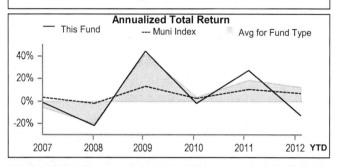

Nuveen Quality Preferred Income (JTP)   A+   Excellent

Fund Family: Nuveen Fund Advisors Inc
Fund Type: Income
Inception Date: June 25, 2002

Data Date	Investment Rating	Net Assets ($Mil)	Price	Performance Rating/Pts	Total Return Y-T-D	Risk Rating/Pts
3-12	A+	533.06	8.16	A- / 9.2	9.78%	B / 8.9
2011	C+	501.80	7.57	B- / 7.5	2.38%	C+ / 6.9
2010	D-	456.19	7.40	D+ / 2.3	21.90%	C- / 3.7
2009	E+	437.92	6.57	D- / 1.1	40.71%	C- / 3.8

Major Rating Factors:
Exceptional performance is the major factor driving the A+ (Excellent) TheStreet.com Investment Rating for Nuveen Quality Preferred Income. The fund currently has a performance rating of A- (Excellent) based on an annualized return of 38.22% over the last three years and a total return of 9.78% year to date 2012. Factored into the performance evaluation is an expense ratio of 1.61% (above average).

The fund's risk rating is currently B (Good). It carries a beta of 0.52, meaning the fund's expected move will be 5.2% for every 10% move in the market. Volatility, as measured by both the semi-deviation and a drawdown factor, is considered low. As of March 31, 2012, Nuveen Quality Preferred Income traded at a discount of 1.81% below its net asset value, which is worse than its one-year historical average discount of 3.36%.

Lewis P. Jacoby, IV currently receives a manager quality ranking of 96 (0=worst, 99=best). If you desire only a moderate level of risk and strong performance, then this fund is an excellent option.

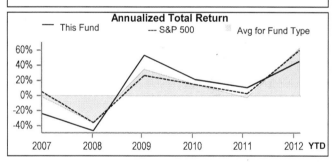

Nuveen Quality Preferred Income 2 (JPS)   A+   Excellent

Fund Family: Nuveen Fund Advisors Inc
Fund Type: Income
Inception Date: September 23, 2002

Data Date	Investment Rating	Net Assets ($Mil)	Price	Performance Rating/Pts	Total Return Y-T-D	Risk Rating/Pts
3-12	A+	1,055.47	8.62	A- / 9.2	12.21%	B / 8.7
2011	C+	979.60	7.83	B- / 7.3	2.81%	C+ / 6.6
2010	D-	922.35	7.90	D+ / 2.5	18.30%	C- / 3.7
2009	E+	881.49	7.25	D- / 1.5	50.53%	C- / 3.6

Major Rating Factors:
Exceptional performance is the major factor driving the A+ (Excellent) TheStreet.com Investment Rating for Nuveen Quality Preferred Income 2. The fund currently has a performance rating of A- (Excellent) based on an annualized return of 37.87% over the last three years and a total return of 12.21% year to date 2012. Factored into the performance evaluation is an expense ratio of 1.58% (above average).

The fund's risk rating is currently B (Good). It carries a beta of 0.65, meaning the fund's expected move will be 6.5% for every 10% move in the market. Volatility, as measured by both the semi-deviation and a drawdown factor, is considered low. As of March 31, 2012, Nuveen Quality Preferred Income 2 traded at a discount of 2.05% below its net asset value, which is worse than its one-year historical average discount of 4.46%.

Lewis P. Jacoby, IV currently receives a manager quality ranking of 95 (0=worst, 99=best). If you desire only a moderate level of risk and strong performance, then this fund is an excellent option.

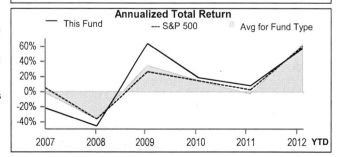

Nuveen Quality Preferred Income 3 (JHP)   A+   Excellent

Fund Family: Nuveen Fund Advisors Inc
Fund Type: Income
Inception Date: December 18, 2002

Data Date	Investment Rating	Net Assets ($Mil)	Price	Perfor-mance Rating/Pts	Total Return Y-T-D	Risk Rating/Pts
3-12	A+	201.14	8.32	A / 9.3	8.11%	B / 8.6
2011	C+	186.50	7.84	B- / 7.4	1.53%	C+ / 6.8
2010	D	176.68	7.74	D+ / 2.8	20.63%	C- / 3.6
2009	E+	168.75	6.95	D- / 1.2	45.67%	C- / 3.8

Major Rating Factors:
Exceptional performance is the major factor driving the A+ (Excellent) TheStreet.com Investment Rating for Nuveen Quality Preferred Income 3. The fund currently has a performance rating of A (Excellent) based on an annualized return of 38.85% over the last three years and a total return of 8.11% year to date 2012. Factored into the performance evaluation is an expense ratio of 1.54% (average).

The fund's risk rating is currently B (Good). It carries a beta of 0.68, meaning the fund's expected move will be 6.8% for every 10% move in the market. Volatility, as measured by both the semi-deviation and a drawdown factor, is considered low. As of March 31, 2012, Nuveen Quality Preferred Income 3 traded at a discount of 2.12% below its net asset value, which is worse than its one-year historical average discount of 3.31%.

Lewis P. Jacoby, IV currently receives a manager quality ranking of 95 (0=worst, 99=best). If you desire only a moderate level of risk and strong performance, then this fund is an excellent option.

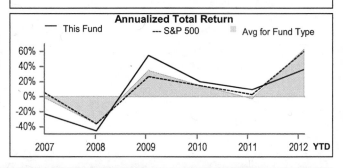

Nuveen Real Estate Inc Fund (JRS)   A   Excellent

Fund Family: Nuveen Fund Advisors Inc
Fund Type: Growth and Income
Inception Date: November 15, 2001

Data Date	Investment Rating	Net Assets ($Mil)	Price	Perfor-mance Rating/Pts	Total Return Y-T-D	Risk Rating/Pts
3-12	A	275.75	11.29	A+ / 9.8	10.47%	B- / 7.5
2011	B	275.80	10.44	A+ / 9.6	-0.19%	C+ / 6.4
2010	C-	230.33	10.11	B- / 7.3	37.66%	D+ / 2.3
2009	E	212.32	8.08	D- / 1.0	77.56%	C- / 3.1

Major Rating Factors:
Exceptional performance is the major factor driving the A (Excellent) TheStreet.com Investment Rating for Nuveen Real Estate Inc Fund. The fund currently has a performance rating of A+ (Excellent) based on an annualized return of 51.67% over the last three years and a total return of 10.47% year to date 2012. Factored into the performance evaluation is an expense ratio of 1.65% (above average).

The fund's risk rating is currently B- (Good). It carries a beta of 1.34, meaning it is expected to move 13.4% for every 10% move in the market. Volatility, as measured by both the semi-deviation and a drawdown factor, is considered low. As of March 31, 2012, Nuveen Real Estate Inc Fund traded at a premium of 8.14% above its net asset value, which is worse than its one-year historical average premium of 6.70%.

Anthony R. Manno, Jr. currently receives a manager quality ranking of 95 (0=worst, 99=best). If you desire only a moderate level of risk and strong performance, then this fund is an excellent option.

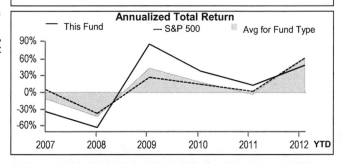

Nuveen Select Maturities Muni (NIM)   D+   Weak

Fund Family: Nuveen Fund Advisors Inc
Fund Type: Municipal - National
Inception Date: September 18, 1992

Data Date	Investment Rating	Net Assets ($Mil)	Price	Perfor-mance Rating/Pts	Total Return Y-T-D	Risk Rating/Pts
3-12	D+	124.55	10.23	D / 1.9	-3.40%	B / 8.8
2011	C+	129.20	10.69	C / 5.4	-0.09%	B / 8.9
2010	B-	126.83	9.97	C / 5.3	0.24%	B- / 7.8
2009	B-	127.58	10.36	C / 5.2	13.82%	B / 8.0

Major Rating Factors:
Disappointing performance is the major factor driving the D+ (Weak) TheStreet.com Investment Rating for Nuveen Select Maturities Muni. The fund currently has a performance rating of D (Weak) based on an annualized return of 4.41% over the last three years and a total return of -3.40% year to date 2012. Factored into the performance evaluation is an expense ratio of 0.59% (very low).

The fund's risk rating is currently B (Good). It carries a beta of 1.01, meaning that its performance tracks fairly well with that of the overall stock market. Volatility, as measured by both the semi-deviation and a drawdown factor, is considered low. As of March 31, 2012, Nuveen Select Maturities Muni traded at a discount of 2.11% below its net asset value, which is better than its one-year historical average premium of 1.02%.

Paul L. Brennan currently receives a manager quality ranking of 30 (0=worst, 99=best). This fund offers only a moderate level of risk but investors looking for strong performance are still waiting.

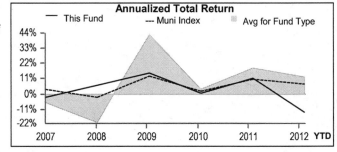

Nuveen Select Quality Muni (NQS)   B+   Good

Fund Family: Nuveen Fund Advisors Inc
Fund Type: Municipal - National
Inception Date: March 21, 1991

Data Date	Investment Rating	Net Assets ($Mil)	Price	Performance Rating/Pts	Total Return Y-T-D	Risk Rating/Pts
3-12	B+	491.45	15.37	B / 8.2	1.04%	B / 8.6
2011	A	501.20	15.47	A / 9.4	0.13%	B / 8.6
2010	C+	481.23	13.64	C / 5.0	4.67%	C+ / 6.3
2009	B-	500.85	14.07	C+ / 5.8	40.53%	B- / 7.2

Major Rating Factors: Strong performance is the major factor driving the B+ (Good) TheStreet.com Investment Rating for Nuveen Select Quality Muni. The fund currently has a performance rating of B (Good) based on an annualized return of 18.57% over the last three years and a total return of 1.04% year to date 2012. Factored into the performance evaluation is an expense ratio of 1.53% (average).

The fund's risk rating is currently B (Good). It carries a beta of 1.94, meaning it is expected to move 19.4% for every 10% move in the market. Volatility, as measured by both the semi-deviation and a drawdown factor, is considered low. As of March 31, 2012, Nuveen Select Quality Muni traded at a premium of 1.45% above its net asset value, which is better than its one-year historical average premium of 1.60%.

Thomas C. Spalding has been running the fund for 10 years and currently receives a manager quality ranking of 66 (0=worst, 99=best). If you desire only a moderate level of risk and strong performance, then this fund is an excellent option.

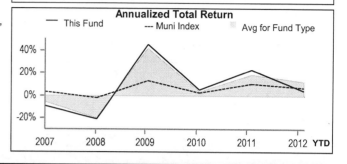

Nuveen Select T-F Inc Portf (NXP)   C   Fair

Fund Family: Nuveen Fund Advisors Inc
Fund Type: Municipal - National
Inception Date: March 19, 1992

Data Date	Investment Rating	Net Assets ($Mil)	Price	Performance Rating/Pts	Total Return Y-T-D	Risk Rating/Pts
3-12	C	224.27	14.57	C- / 3.2	0.67%	B / 8.9
2011	B-	234.20	14.65	C+ / 5.8	0.15%	B / 8.9
2010	C	233.87	13.54	D+ / 2.5	-3.80%	B / 8.5
2009	B-	235.93	14.80	C / 5.2	12.38%	B- / 7.8

Major Rating Factors: Middle of the road best describes Nuveen Select T-F Inc Portf whose TheStreet.com Investment Rating is currently a C (Fair). The fund currently has a performance rating of C- (Fair) based on an annualized return of 7.01% over the last three years and a total return of 0.67% year to date 2012. Factored into the performance evaluation is an expense ratio of 0.32% (very low).

The fund's risk rating is currently B (Good). It carries a beta of 1.15, meaning it is expected to move 11.5% for every 10% move in the market. Volatility, as measured by both the semi-deviation and a drawdown factor, is considered low. As of March 31, 2012, Nuveen Select T-F Inc Portf traded at a premium of .14% above its net asset value, which is better than its one-year historical average premium of .22%.

Thomas C. Spalding has been running the fund for 13 years and currently receives a manager quality ranking of 37 (0=worst, 99=best). If you desire an average level of risk, then this fund may be an option.

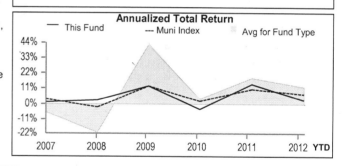

Nuveen Select T-F Inc Portf 2 (NXQ)   C   Fair

Fund Family: Nuveen Fund Advisors Inc
Fund Type: Municipal - National
Inception Date: May 21, 1992

Data Date	Investment Rating	Net Assets ($Mil)	Price	Performance Rating/Pts	Total Return Y-T-D	Risk Rating/Pts
3-12	C	228.02	13.63	C- / 3.2	1.66%	B / 8.9
2011	C	239.50	13.56	C- / 4.2	-1.70%	B / 8.9
2010	C	239.10	12.73	C- / 3.0	-3.73%	B / 8.1
2009	C+	241.15	13.89	C / 4.6	9.06%	B- / 7.8

Major Rating Factors: Middle of the road best describes Nuveen Select T-F Inc Portf 2 whose TheStreet.com Investment Rating is currently a C (Fair). The fund currently has a performance rating of C- (Fair) based on an annualized return of 6.38% over the last three years and a total return of 1.66% year to date 2012. Factored into the performance evaluation is an expense ratio of 0.39% (very low).

The fund's risk rating is currently B (Good). It carries a beta of 1.32, meaning it is expected to move 13.2% for every 10% move in the market. Volatility, as measured by both the semi-deviation and a drawdown factor, is considered low. As of March 31, 2012, Nuveen Select T-F Inc Portf 2 traded at a discount of 1.87% below its net asset value, which is worse than its one-year historical average discount of 2.35%.

Thomas C. Spalding has been running the fund for 13 years and currently receives a manager quality ranking of 26 (0=worst, 99=best). If you desire an average level of risk, then this fund may be an option.

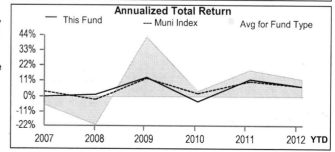

Nuveen Select Tax-Free Inc 3 (NXR)

C- **Fair**

Fund Family: Nuveen Fund Advisors Inc
Fund Type: Municipal - National
Inception Date: July 24, 1992

Major Rating Factors: Middle of the road best describes Nuveen Select Tax-Free Inc 3 whose TheStreet.com Investment Rating is currently a C- (Fair). The fund currently has a performance rating of C- (Fair) based on an annualized return of 5.59% over the last three years and a total return of 1.35% year to date 2012. Factored into the performance evaluation is an expense ratio of 0.37% (very low).

The fund's risk rating is currently B (Good). It carries a beta of 0.78, meaning the fund's expected move will be 7.8% for every 10% move in the market. Volatility, as measured by both the semi-deviation and a drawdown factor, is considered low. As of March 31, 2012, Nuveen Select Tax-Free Inc 3 traded at a discount of .62% below its net asset value, which is worse than its one-year historical average discount of .99%.

Thomas C. Spalding has been running the fund for 13 years and currently receives a manager quality ranking of 52 (0=worst, 99=best). If you desire an average level of risk, then this fund may be an option.

Data Date	Investment Rating	Net Assets ($Mil)	Price	Performance Rating/Pts	Total Return Y-T-D	Risk Rating/Pts
3-12	C-	175.85	14.34	C- / 3.0	1.35%	B / 8.8
2011	C+	183.10	14.31	C / 4.7	-1.40%	B / 8.9
2010	C+	182.78	13.10	C- / 3.0	-6.33%	B / 8.5
2009	B	184.84	14.64	C / 5.3	11.40%	B- / 7.9

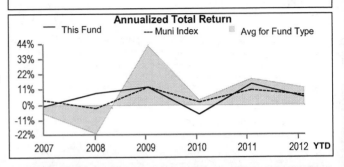

Annualized Total Return

Nuveen Sr Inc (NSL)

A- **Excellent**

Fund Family: Nuveen Fund Advisors Inc
Fund Type: Loan Participation
Inception Date: October 26, 1999

Major Rating Factors:
Strong performance is the major factor driving the A- (Excellent) TheStreet.com Investment Rating for Nuveen Sr Inc. The fund currently has a performance rating of B+ (Good) based on an annualized return of 37.56% over the last three years and a total return of 9.70% year to date 2012. Factored into the performance evaluation is an expense ratio of 1.78% (above average).

The fund's risk rating is currently B (Good). Volatility, as measured by both the semi-deviation and a drawdown factor, is considered low. As of March 31, 2012, Nuveen Sr Inc traded at a premium of .71% above its net asset value, which is better than its one-year historical average premium of .82%.

Gunther M. Stein has been running the fund for 13 years and currently receives a manager quality ranking of 93 (0=worst, 99=best). If you desire only a moderate level of risk and strong performance, then this fund is an excellent option.

Data Date	Investment Rating	Net Assets ($Mil)	Price	Performance Rating/Pts	Total Return Y-T-D	Risk Rating/Pts
3-12	A-	227.99	7.13	B+ / 8.9	9.70%	B / 8.2
2011	B+	216.30	6.62	B+ / 8.5	2.42%	B / 8.1
2010	C	203.26	7.14	C+ / 6.8	7.64%	C- / 4.1
2009	C+	185.99	7.11	B+ / 8.5	127.45%	C- / 4.0

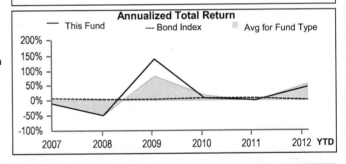

Annualized Total Return

Nuveen Tax-Advant Tot Ret Strat Fd (JTA)

B **Good**

Fund Family: Nuveen Fund Advisors Inc
Fund Type: Income
Inception Date: January 28, 2004

Major Rating Factors: Strong performance is the major factor driving the B (Good) TheStreet.com Investment Rating for Nuveen Tax-Advant Tot Ret Strat Fd. The fund currently has a performance rating of B (Good) based on an annualized return of 28.16% over the last three years and a total return of 18.50% year to date 2012. Factored into the performance evaluation is an expense ratio of 1.73% (above average).

The fund's risk rating is currently B (Good). It carries a beta of 0.96, meaning that its performance tracks fairly well with that of the overall stock market. Volatility, as measured by both the semi-deviation and a drawdown factor, is considered low. As of March 31, 2012, Nuveen Tax-Advant Tot Ret Strat Fd traded at a discount of 9.16% below its net asset value, which is worse than its one-year historical average discount of 9.18%.

Gunther M. Stein has been running the fund for 8 years and currently receives a manager quality ranking of 80 (0=worst, 99=best). If you desire only a moderate level of risk and strong performance, then this fund is an excellent option.

Data Date	Investment Rating	Net Assets ($Mil)	Price	Performance Rating/Pts	Total Return Y-T-D	Risk Rating/Pts
3-12	B	151.89	11.11	B / 7.6	18.50%	B / 8.2
2011	C+	151.90	9.56	C+ / 5.7	4.71%	B- / 7.6
2010	D-	161.40	11.24	D- / 1.1	14.72%	C / 4.3
2009	D-	157.14	10.66	D- / 1.1	46.20%	C / 4.4

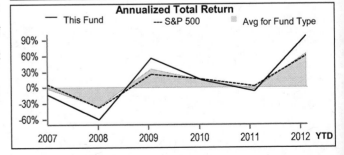

Annualized Total Return

Nuveen Tax-Advantaged Dividend Grt (JTD)   A-   Excellent

Fund Family: Nuveen Fund Advisors Inc
Fund Type: Growth and Income
Inception Date: June 27, 2007

Major Rating Factors:
Strong performance is the major factor driving the A- (Excellent) TheStreet.com Investment Rating for Nuveen Tax-Advantaged Dividend Grt. The fund currently has a performance rating of B+ (Good) based on an annualized return of 33.15% over the last three years and a total return of 14.02% year to date 2012. Factored into the performance evaluation is an expense ratio of 1.87% (above average).

The fund's risk rating is currently B (Good). It carries a beta of 0.92, meaning that its performance tracks fairly well with that of the overall stock market. Volatility, as measured by both the semi-deviation and a drawdown factor, is considered low. As of March 31, 2012, Nuveen Tax-Advantaged Dividend Grt traded at a discount of 7.90% below its net asset value, which is worse than its one-year historical average discount of 9.78%.

James R. Boothe currently receives a manager quality ranking of 89 (0=worst, 99=best). If you desire only a moderate level of risk and strong performance, then this fund is an excellent option.

Data Date	Investment Rating	Net Assets ($Mil)	Price	Performance Rating/Pts	Total Return Y-T-D	Risk Rating/Pts
3-12	A-	196.40	13.75	B+ / 8.8	14.02%	B / 8.3
2011	B-	196.40	12.29	B- / 7.2	2.44%	B- / 7.7
2010	C	189.01	13.01	C+ / 6.0	22.52%	C / 4.6
2009	A-	182.06	11.56	A- / 9.1	40.04%	C / 5.1

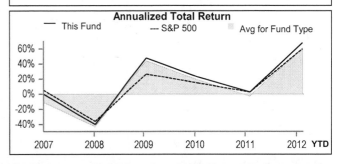

Annualized Total Return
— This Fund   --- S&P 500   Avg for Fund Type

Nuveen Tax-Advantaged Floating Rat (JFP)   D   Weak

Fund Family: Nuveen Fund Advisors Inc
Fund Type: Loan Participation
Inception Date: March 29, 2005

Major Rating Factors:
Disappointing performance is the major factor driving the D (Weak) TheStreet.com Investment Rating for Nuveen Tax-Advantaged Floating Rat. The fund currently has a performance rating of D+ (Weak) based on an annualized return of 7.93% over the last three years and a total return of 20.08% year to date 2012. Factored into the performance evaluation is an expense ratio of 0.59% (very low).

The fund's risk rating is currently C+ (Fair). Volatility, as measured by both the semi-deviation and a drawdown factor, is considered low. As of March 31, 2012, Nuveen Tax-Advantaged Floating Rat traded at a discount of 11.96% below its net asset value, which is better than its one-year historical average discount of 8.88%.

Lewis P. Jacoby, IV currently receives a manager quality ranking of 4 (0=worst, 99=best). This fund offers only a moderate level of risk but investors looking for strong performance are still waiting.

Data Date	Investment Rating	Net Assets ($Mil)	Price	Performance Rating/Pts	Total Return Y-T-D	Risk Rating/Pts
3-12	D	37.66	2.43	D+ / 2.8	20.08%	C+ / 6.3
2011	D-	37.66	2.05	D- / 1.5	1.46%	C+ / 6.0
2010	E	33.89	2.18	E / 0.3	10.66%	D / 2.2
2009	E-	45.64	2.14	E / 0.3	-24.35%	D+ / 2.5

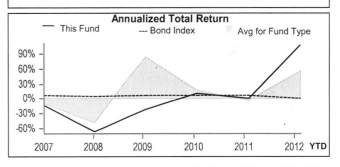

Annualized Total Return
— This Fund   --- Bond Index   Avg for Fund Type

Nuveen TX Quality Inc Muni (NTX)   C+   Fair

Fund Family: Nuveen Fund Advisors Inc
Fund Type: Municipal - Single State
Inception Date: October 17, 1991

Major Rating Factors: Middle of the road best describes Nuveen TX Quality Inc Muni whose TheStreet.com Investment Rating is currently a C+ (Fair). The fund currently has a performance rating of C (Fair) based on an annualized return of 13.38% over the last three years and a total return of 0.75% year to date 2012. Factored into the performance evaluation is an expense ratio of 1.92% (above average).

The fund's risk rating is currently B+ (Good). It carries a beta of 1.29, meaning it is expected to move 12.9% for every 10% move in the market. Volatility, as measured by both the semi-deviation and a drawdown factor, is considered very low. As of March 31, 2012, Nuveen TX Quality Inc Muni traded at a premium of 5.73% above its net asset value, which is better than its one-year historical average premium of 6.32%.

Daniel J. Close currently receives a manager quality ranking of 66 (0=worst, 99=best). If you desire an average level of risk, then this fund may be an option.

Data Date	Investment Rating	Net Assets ($Mil)	Price	Performance Rating/Pts	Total Return Y-T-D	Risk Rating/Pts
3-12	C+	134.85	16.24	C / 5.1	0.75%	B+ / 9.1
2011	B+	143.60	16.34	B / 8.2	0.69%	B+ / 9.1
2010	B+	143.08	14.92	B- / 7.4	4.43%	C+ / 6.6
2009	C+	141.86	15.10	C+ / 6.7	33.58%	C+ / 6.7

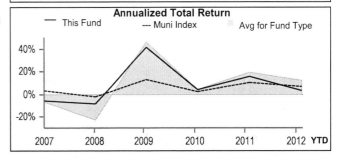

Annualized Total Return
— This Fund   --- Muni Index   Avg for Fund Type

Nuveen VA Div Adv Muni 2 (NNB)

C+ **Fair**

Fund Family: Nuveen Fund Advisors Inc
Fund Type: Municipal - Single State
Inception Date: November 15, 2001

Major Rating Factors: Middle of the road best describes Nuveen VA Div Adv Muni 2 whose TheStreet.com Investment Rating is currently a C+ (Fair). The fund currently has a performance rating of C+ (Fair) based on an annualized return of 10.55% over the last three years and a total return of 5.98% year to date 2012. Factored into the performance evaluation is an expense ratio of 2.74% (high).

The fund's risk rating is currently B (Good). It carries a beta of 1.67, meaning it is expected to move 16.7% for every 10% move in the market. Volatility, as measured by both the semi-deviation and a drawdown factor, is considered low. As of March 31, 2012, Nuveen VA Div Adv Muni 2 traded at a premium of 3.60% above its net asset value, which is worse than its one-year historical average premium of .71%.

Thomas C. Spalding currently receives a manager quality ranking of 28 (0=worst, 99=best). If you desire an average level of risk, then this fund may be an option.

Data Date	Investment Rating	Net Assets ($Mil)	Price	Performance Rating/Pts	Total Return Y-T-D	Risk Rating/Pts
3-12	C+	81.42	15.81	C+ / 5.6	5.98%	B / 8.8
2011	B	85.80	15.11	B- / 7.1	0.60%	B / 8.9
2010	C+	83.77	14.01	C / 5.3	0.02%	C+ / 6.6
2009	B-	84.04	14.79	C+ / 5.7	42.40%	B- / 7.1

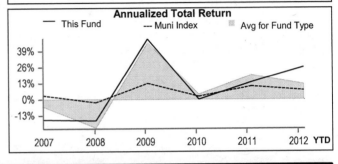

Nuveen VA Div Adv Muni Fund (NGB)

C **Fair**

Fund Family: Nuveen Fund Advisors Inc
Fund Type: Municipal - Single State
Inception Date: January 24, 2001

Major Rating Factors: Middle of the road best describes Nuveen VA Div Adv Muni Fund whose TheStreet.com Investment Rating is currently a C (Fair). The fund currently has a performance rating of C (Fair) based on an annualized return of 9.77% over the last three years and a total return of 4.51% year to date 2012. Factored into the performance evaluation is an expense ratio of 2.96% (high).

The fund's risk rating is currently B (Good). It carries a beta of 1.40, meaning it is expected to move 14.0% for every 10% move in the market. Volatility, as measured by both the semi-deviation and a drawdown factor, is considered low. As of March 31, 2012, Nuveen VA Div Adv Muni Fund traded at a premium of .60% above its net asset value, which is better than its one-year historical average premium of .93%.

Thomas C. Spalding currently receives a manager quality ranking of 48 (0=worst, 99=best). If you desire an average level of risk, then this fund may be an option.

Data Date	Investment Rating	Net Assets ($Mil)	Price	Performance Rating/Pts	Total Return Y-T-D	Risk Rating/Pts
3-12	C	43.47	15.07	C / 4.6	4.51%	B / 8.6
2011	B	46.10	14.60	B- / 7.4	2.47%	B / 8.6
2010	C-	44.61	13.35	C- / 3.3	-0.18%	C+ / 6.5
2009	C	44.94	14.11	C- / 3.4	41.13%	C+ / 6.9

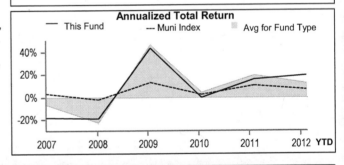

Nuveen VA Premium Income Municipal (NPV)

B- **Good**

Fund Family: Nuveen Fund Advisors Inc
Fund Type: Municipal - Single State
Inception Date: March 18, 1993

Major Rating Factors: Nuveen VA Premium Income Municipal receives a TheStreet.com Investment Rating of B- (Good). The fund currently has a performance rating of C+ (Fair) based on an annualized return of 12.46% over the last three years and a total return of 6.34% year to date 2012. Factored into the performance evaluation is an expense ratio of 2.11% (high).

The fund's risk rating is currently B (Good). It carries a beta of 1.40, meaning it is expected to move 14.0% for every 10% move in the market. Volatility, as measured by both the semi-deviation and a drawdown factor, is considered low. As of March 31, 2012, Nuveen VA Premium Income Municipal traded at a premium of 5.40% above its net asset value, which is worse than its one-year historical average premium of 2.96%.

Thomas C. Spalding currently receives a manager quality ranking of 56 (0=worst, 99=best). If you desire an average level of risk, then this fund may be an option.

Data Date	Investment Rating	Net Assets ($Mil)	Price	Performance Rating/Pts	Total Return Y-T-D	Risk Rating/Pts
3-12	B-	130.03	16.19	C+ / 6.4	6.34%	B / 8.5
2011	B	136.60	15.42	C+ / 6.7	-0.13%	B / 8.6
2010	C+	132.30	14.70	C+ / 6.7	3.78%	C+ / 6.8
2009	B-	133.23	14.94	C+ / 5.9	36.34%	B- / 7.3

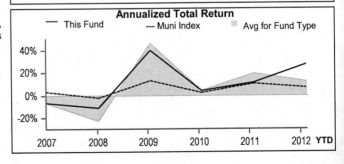

Pacholder High Yield Fund (PHF)   A-   Excellent

Fund Family: JP Morgan Investment Management Inc
Fund Type: Corporate - High Yield
Inception Date: November 16, 1988

Data Date	Investment Rating	Net Assets ($Mil)	Price	Perfor-mance Rating/Pts	Total Return Y-T-D	Risk Rating/Pts
3-12	A-	101.95	9.01	A+ / 9.7	3.82%	B- / 7.4
2011	A	101.90	8.95	A+ / 9.7	1.56%	B / 8.1
2010	C+	100.90	8.45	B / 8.2	21.63%	C- / 3.4
2009	C	77.08	7.38	B+ / 8.3	126.90%	C- / 3.0

Major Rating Factors:

Exceptional performance is the major factor driving the A- (Excellent) TheStreet.com Investment Rating for Pacholder High Yield Fund. The fund currently has a performance rating of A+ (Excellent) based on an annualized return of 46.57% over the last three years and a total return of 3.82% year to date 2012. Factored into the performance evaluation is an expense ratio of 2.17% (high).

The fund's risk rating is currently B- (Good). It carries a beta of 1.32, meaning it is expected to move 13.2% for every 10% move in the market. Volatility, as measured by both the semi-deviation and a drawdown factor, is considered low. As of March 31, 2012, Pacholder High Yield Fund traded at a premium of 8.82% above its net asset value, which is better than its one-year historical average premium of 10.91%.

James E. Gibson currently receives a manager quality ranking of 86 (0=worst, 99=best). If you desire only a moderate level of risk and strong performance, then this fund is an excellent option.

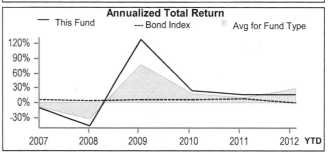

PCM Fund (PCM)   A+   Excellent

Fund Family: Allianz Global Investors Fund Mgmt
Fund Type: Mortgage
Inception Date: August 27, 1993

Data Date	Investment Rating	Net Assets ($Mil)	Price	Perfor-mance Rating/Pts	Total Return Y-T-D	Risk Rating/Pts
3-12	A+	108.81	11.01	A / 9.5	4.56%	B / 8.8
2011	B+	113.02	10.77	B+ / 8.8	1.58%	B- / 7.8
2010	B-	88.29	10.80	B+ / 8.8	48.82%	C- / 4.0
2009	D+	68.87	7.97	C- / 3.1	45.58%	C / 4.8

Major Rating Factors:

Exceptional performance is the major factor driving the A+ (Excellent) TheStreet.com Investment Rating for PCM Fund. The fund currently has a performance rating of A (Excellent) based on an annualized return of 43.06% over the last three years and a total return of 4.56% year to date 2012. Factored into the performance evaluation is an expense ratio of 2.44% (high).

The fund's risk rating is currently B (Good). It carries a beta of -1.13, meaning the fund's expected move will be -11.3% for every 10% move in the market. Volatility, as measured by both the semi-deviation and a drawdown factor, is considered low. As of March 31, 2012, PCM Fund traded at a premium of 7.73% above its net asset value, which is better than its one-year historical average premium of 9.43%.

Daniel J. Ivascyn has been running the fund for 11 years and currently receives a manager quality ranking of 99 (0=worst, 99=best). If you desire only a moderate level of risk and strong performance, then this fund is an excellent option.

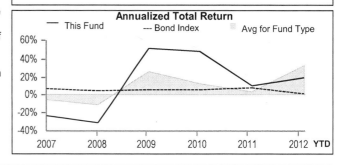

Petroleum and Resources Corp. (PEO)   C-   Fair

Fund Family: Adams Express Company
Fund Type: Energy/Natural Resources
Inception Date: January 21, 1969

Data Date	Investment Rating	Net Assets ($Mil)	Price	Perfor-mance Rating/Pts	Total Return Y-T-D	Risk Rating/Pts
3-12	C-	761.74	25.99	C- / 3.9	6.57%	B- / 7.5
2011	C	732.80	24.48	C / 4.7	1.96%	B- / 7.4
2010	C	650.72	27.02	C / 4.6	19.58%	C+ / 5.8
2009	C-	552.91	23.74	C- / 3.8	22.87%	C+ / 5.9

Major Rating Factors: Middle of the road best describes Petroleum and Resources Corp. whose TheStreet.com Investment Rating is currently a C- (Fair). The fund currently has a performance rating of C- (Fair) based on an annualized return of 17.00% over the last three years and a total return of 6.57% year to date 2012. Factored into the performance evaluation is an expense ratio of 0.64% (very low).

The fund's risk rating is currently B- (Good). It carries a beta of 1.06, meaning that its performance tracks fairly well with that of the overall stock market. Volatility, as measured by both the semi-deviation and a drawdown factor, is considered low. As of March 31, 2012, Petroleum and Resources Corp. traded at a discount of 13.08% below its net asset value, which is worse than its one-year historical average discount of 13.17%.

David D. Weaver has been running the fund for 2 years and currently receives a manager quality ranking of 38 (0=worst, 99=best). If you desire an average level of risk, then this fund may be an option.

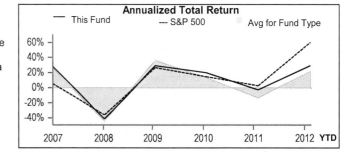

PIMCO CA Municipal Income Fund (PCQ)

B+ **Good**

Fund Family: Allianz Global Investors Fund Mgmt
Fund Type: Municipal - Single State
Inception Date: June 26, 2001

Major Rating Factors: Strong performance is the major factor driving the B+ (Good) TheStreet.com Investment Rating for PIMCO CA Municipal Income Fund. The fund currently has a performance rating of B (Good) based on an annualized return of 15.28% over the last three years and a total return of 7.21% year to date 2012. Factored into the performance evaluation is an expense ratio of 1.48% (average).

The fund's risk rating is currently B (Good). It carries a beta of 2.72, meaning it is expected to move 27.2% for every 10% move in the market. Volatility, as measured by both the semi-deviation and a drawdown factor, is considered low. As of March 31, 2012, PIMCO CA Municipal Income Fund traded at a premium of 4.96% above its net asset value, which is better than its one-year historical average premium of 5.12%.

Joseph P. Deane has been running the fund for 1 year and currently receives a manager quality ranking of 26 (0=worst, 99=best). If you desire only a moderate level of risk and strong performance, then this fund is an excellent option.

Data Date	Investment Rating	Net Assets ($Mil)	Price	Performance Rating/Pts	Total Return Y-T-D	Risk Rating/Pts
3-12	B+	208.15	14.17	B / 8.0	7.21%	B / 8.1
2011	A-	236.00	13.44	A- / 9.1	2.23%	B / 8.3
2010	D+	234.79	12.40	D / 1.7	7.56%	C+ / 6.6
2009	C	192.85	12.39	C- / 4.0	45.39%	C+ / 6.7

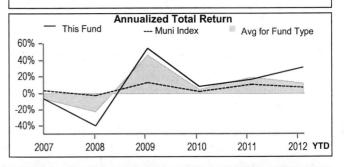

PIMCO CA Municipal Income Fund II (PCK)

B **Good**

Fund Family: Allianz Global Investors Fund Mgmt
Fund Type: Municipal - Single State
Inception Date: June 25, 2002

Major Rating Factors: Strong performance is the major factor driving the B (Good) TheStreet.com Investment Rating for PIMCO CA Municipal Income Fund II. The fund currently has a performance rating of B- (Good) based on an annualized return of 15.59% over the last three years and a total return of 7.04% year to date 2012. Factored into the performance evaluation is an expense ratio of 1.55% (average).

The fund's risk rating is currently B (Good). It carries a beta of 2.74, meaning it is expected to move 27.4% for every 10% move in the market. Volatility, as measured by both the semi-deviation and a drawdown factor, is considered low. As of March 31, 2012, PIMCO CA Municipal Income Fund II traded at a premium of 17.92% above its net asset value, which is better than its one-year historical average premium of 21.74%.

Joseph P. Deane has been running the fund for 1 year and currently receives a manager quality ranking of 27 (0=worst, 99=best). If you desire only a moderate level of risk and strong performance, then this fund is an excellent option.

Data Date	Investment Rating	Net Assets ($Mil)	Price	Performance Rating/Pts	Total Return Y-T-D	Risk Rating/Pts
3-12	B	231.49	9.87	B- / 7.5	7.04%	B / 8.5
2011	B+	247.80	9.40	B+ / 8.3	2.13%	B / 8.6
2010	D-	252.82	8.77	D- / 1.0	10.09%	C- / 4.3
2009	D-	231.42	8.68	D- / 1.2	47.00%	C / 4.8

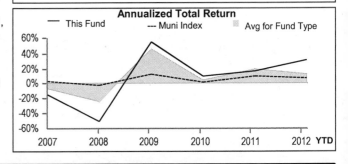

PIMCO CA Municipal Income Fund III (PZC)

A- **Excellent**

Fund Family: Allianz Global Investors Fund Mgmt
Fund Type: Municipal - Single State
Inception Date: October 28, 2002

Major Rating Factors:
Strong performance is the major factor driving the A- (Excellent) TheStreet.com Investment Rating for PIMCO CA Municipal Income Fund III. The fund currently has a performance rating of B+ (Good) based on an annualized return of 17.55% over the last three years and a total return of 8.47% year to date 2012. Factored into the performance evaluation is an expense ratio of 1.48% (average).

The fund's risk rating is currently B (Good). It carries a beta of 2.35, meaning it is expected to move 23.5% for every 10% move in the market. Volatility, as measured by both the semi-deviation and a drawdown factor, is considered low. As of March 31, 2012, PIMCO CA Municipal Income Fund III traded at a premium of 6.23% above its net asset value, which is worse than its one-year historical average premium of 6.03%.

Joseph P. Deane has been running the fund for 1 year and currently receives a manager quality ranking of 50 (0=worst, 99=best). If you desire only a moderate level of risk and strong performance, then this fund is an excellent option.

Data Date	Investment Rating	Net Assets ($Mil)	Price	Performance Rating/Pts	Total Return Y-T-D	Risk Rating/Pts
3-12	A-	198.75	10.40	B+ / 8.6	8.47%	B / 8.6
2011	A-	202.10	9.76	A- / 9.1	2.36%	B / 8.6
2010	D-	210.32	9.01	E+ / 0.9	7.20%	C / 4.9
2009	D	207.17	9.08	D- / 1.3	56.52%	C / 5.5

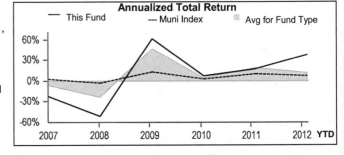

PIMCO Corporate and Income Oppty (PTY)   A+   Excellent

Fund Family: Allianz Global Investors Fund Mgmt
Fund Type: Corporate - High Yield
Inception Date: December 23, 2002

Major Rating Factors:
Exceptional performance is the major factor driving the A+ (Excellent) TheStreet.com Investment Rating for PIMCO Corporate and Income Oppty. The fund currently has a performance rating of A+ (Excellent) based on an annualized return of 46.86% over the last three years and a total return of 9.18% year to date 2012. Factored into the performance evaluation is an expense ratio of 1.09% (low).

The fund's risk rating is currently B (Good). It carries a beta of 1.50, meaning it is expected to move 15.0% for every 10% move in the market. Volatility, as measured by both the semi-deviation and a drawdown factor, is considered low. As of March 31, 2012, PIMCO Corporate and Income Oppty traded at a premium of 20.30% above its net asset value, which is better than its one-year historical average premium of 21.26%.

William H. Gross currently receives a manager quality ranking of 83 (0=worst, 99=best). If you desire only a moderate level of risk and strong performance, then this fund is an excellent option.

Data Date	Investment Rating	Net Assets ($Mil)	Price	Performance Rating/Pts	Total Return Y-T-D	Risk Rating/Pts
3-12	A+	967.20	18.61	A+ / 9.7	9.18%	B / 8.0
2011	C+	1,098.92	17.37	B / 7.9	2.19%	C+ / 6.4
2010	B	962.49	16.97	B+ / 8.7	28.50%	C / 4.3
2009	C+	669.92	14.40	B- / 7.3	54.08%	C / 4.9

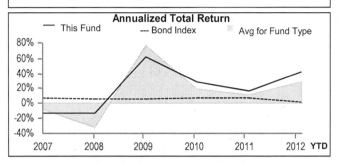

Annualized Total Return

PIMCO Corporate and ncome Strategy (PCN)   A   Excellent

Fund Family: Allianz Global Investors Fund Mgmt
Fund Type: Corporate - High Yield
Inception Date: December 19, 2001

Major Rating Factors:
Exceptional performance is the major factor driving the A (Excellent) TheStreet.com Investment Rating for PIMCO Corporate and ncome Strategy. The fund currently has a performance rating of A (Excellent) based on an annualized return of 40.11% over the last three years and a total return of 2.56% year to date 2012. Factored into the performance evaluation is an expense ratio of 1.30% (average).

The fund's risk rating is currently B (Good). It carries a beta of 1.53, meaning it is expected to move 15.3% for every 10% move in the market. Volatility, as measured by both the semi-deviation and a drawdown factor, is considered low. As of March 31, 2012, PIMCO Corporate and ncome Strategy traded at a premium of 13.36% above its net asset value, which is better than its one-year historical average premium of 15.40%.

William H. Gross currently receives a manager quality ranking of 63 (0=worst, 99=best). If you desire only a moderate level of risk and strong performance, then this fund is an excellent option.

Data Date	Investment Rating	Net Assets ($Mil)	Price	Performance Rating/Pts	Total Return Y-T-D	Risk Rating/Pts
3-12	A	515.04	16.04	A / 9.4	2.56%	B / 8.0
2011	C+	589.03	15.95	B- / 7.4	0.94%	C+ / 6.1
2010	B	529.37	15.49	B+ / 8.5	22.06%	C / 4.8
2009	C	286.56	13.85	C+ / 5.7	36.63%	C / 4.7

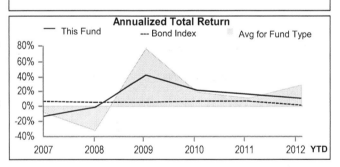

Annualized Total Return

PIMCO Global StocksPLUS&Inc (PGP)   B+   Good

Fund Family: Allianz Global Investors Fund Mgmt
Fund Type: Global
Inception Date: May 26, 2005

Major Rating Factors:
Exceptional performance is the major factor driving the B+ (Good) TheStreet.com Investment Rating for PIMCO Global StocksPLUS&Inc. The fund currently has a performance rating of A+ (Excellent) based on an annualized return of 48.33% over the last three years and a total return of 10.55% year to date 2012. Factored into the performance evaluation is an expense ratio of 2.81% (high).

The fund's risk rating is currently B- (Good). It carries a beta of 1.01, meaning that its performance tracks fairly well with that of the overall stock market. Volatility, as measured by both the semi-deviation and a drawdown factor, is considered low. As of March 31, 2012, PIMCO Global StocksPLUS&Inc traded at a premium of 60.41% above its net asset value, which is better than its one-year historical average premium of 68.05%.

Daniel J. Ivascyn has been running the fund for 7 years and currently receives a manager quality ranking of 96 (0=worst, 99=best). If you desire only a moderate level of risk and strong performance, then this fund is an excellent option.

Data Date	Investment Rating	Net Assets ($Mil)	Price	Performance Rating/Pts	Total Return Y-T-D	Risk Rating/Pts
3-12	B+	150.88	20.18	A+ / 9.7	10.55%	B- / 7.1
2011	B	150.88	18.75	A / 9.3	3.25%	C+ / 6.6
2010	C+	125.37	21.60	A- / 9.2	34.73%	D+ / 2.8
2009	C	103.34	18.02	B+ / 8.4	115.60%	D+ / 2.5

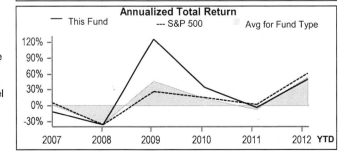

Annualized Total Return

PIMCO High Income Fund (PHK)   A   Excellent

Fund Family: Allianz Global Investors Fund Mgmt
Fund Type: Corporate - High Yield
Inception Date: April 24, 2003

Major Rating Factors:
Exceptional performance is the major factor driving the A (Excellent) TheStreet.com Investment Rating for PIMCO High Income Fund. The fund currently has a performance rating of A+ (Excellent) based on an annualized return of 46.10% over the last three years and a total return of 10.04% year to date 2012. Factored into the performance evaluation is an expense ratio of 1.11% (low).

The fund's risk rating is currently B- (Good). It carries a beta of 1.97, meaning it is expected to move 19.7% for every 10% move in the market. Volatility, as measured by both the semi-deviation and a drawdown factor, is considered low. As of March 31, 2012, PIMCO High Income Fund traded at a premium of 63.15% above its net asset value, which is worse than its one-year historical average premium of 58.16%.

William H. Gross currently receives a manager quality ranking of 42 (0=worst, 99=best). If you desire only a moderate level of risk and strong performance, then this fund is an excellent option.

Data Date	Investment Rating	Net Assets ($Mil)	Price	Performance Rating/Pts	Total Return Y-T-D	Risk Rating/Pts
3-12	A	1,138.19	12.84	A+ / 9.6	10.04%	B- / 7.8
2011	B	1,138.19	12.02	A+ / 9.6	3.58%	C+ / 6.3
2010	C	1,046.24	12.71	B+ / 8.7	32.67%	D / 2.1
2009	C	875.24	10.85	B / 7.9	111.17%	D+ / 2.3

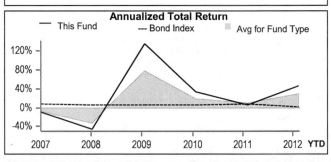

Annualized Total Return

Pimco Income Opportunity Fund (PKO)   B+   Good

Fund Family: Allianz Global Investors Fund Mgmt
Fund Type: Global
Inception Date: November 30, 2007

Major Rating Factors: Strong performance is the major factor driving the B+ (Good) TheStreet.com Investment Rating for Pimco Income Opportunity Fund. The fund currently has a performance rating of B+ (Good) based on an annualized return of 32.67% over the last three years and a total return of 6.99% year to date 2012. Factored into the performance evaluation is an expense ratio of 2.44% (high).

The fund's risk rating is currently B (Good). It carries a beta of 0.56, meaning the fund's expected move will be 5.6% for every 10% move in the market. Volatility, as measured by both the semi-deviation and a drawdown factor, is considered low. As of March 31, 2012, Pimco Income Opportunity Fund traded at a premium of 5.53% above its net asset value, which is better than its one-year historical average premium of 6.74%.

Daniel J. Ivascyn has been running the fund for 5 years and currently receives a manager quality ranking of 97 (0=worst, 99=best). If you desire only a moderate level of risk and strong performance, then this fund is an excellent option.

Data Date	Investment Rating	Net Assets ($Mil)	Price	Performance Rating/Pts	Total Return Y-T-D	Risk Rating/Pts
3-12	B+	359.91	26.35	B+ / 8.4	6.99%	B / 8.5
2011	B	391.73	25.18	B- / 7.4	3.53%	B / 8.2
2010	A-	307.68	25.59	B / 7.9	24.64%	C+ / 6.6
2009	A+	229.21	22.37	B+ / 8.8	39.16%	C+ / 6.1

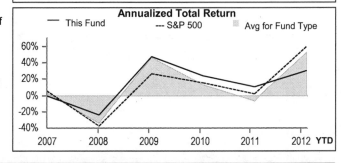

Annualized Total Return

PIMCO Income Strategy Fund (PFL)   A   Excellent

Fund Family: Allianz Global Investors Fund Mgmt
Fund Type: Loan Participation
Inception Date: August 26, 2003

Major Rating Factors:
Exceptional performance is the major factor driving the A (Excellent) TheStreet.com Investment Rating for PIMCO Income Strategy Fund. The fund currently has a performance rating of A (Excellent) based on an annualized return of 41.97% over the last three years and a total return of 11.52% year to date 2012. Factored into the performance evaluation is an expense ratio of 1.51% (average).

The fund's risk rating is currently B- (Good). It carries a beta of -60.41, meaning the fund's expected move will be -604.1% for every 10% move in the market. Volatility, as measured by both the semi-deviation and a drawdown factor, is considered low. As of March 31, 2012, PIMCO Income Strategy Fund traded at a premium of 5.38% above its net asset value, which is better than its one-year historical average premium of 5.93%.

William H. Gross currently receives a manager quality ranking of 99 (0=worst, 99=best). If you desire only a moderate level of risk and strong performance, then this fund is an excellent option.

Data Date	Investment Rating	Net Assets ($Mil)	Price	Performance Rating/Pts	Total Return Y-T-D	Risk Rating/Pts
3-12	A	282.69	11.36	A / 9.4	11.52%	B- / 7.9
2011	C-	282.69	10.40	C+ / 5.6	2.50%	C+ / 5.7
2010	D	262.06	11.50	C- / 4.0	9.80%	D+ / 2.8
2009	D+	165.98	11.29	C / 4.9	71.37%	C- / 3.2

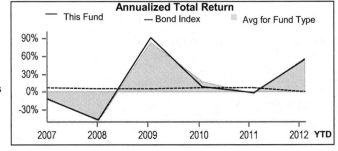

Annualized Total Return

PIMCO Income Strategy Fund II (PFN)   A   Excellent

Fund Family: Allianz Global Investors Fund Mgmt
Fund Type: Loan Participation
Inception Date: October 29, 2004

Major Rating Factors:
Exceptional performance is the major factor driving the A (Excellent) TheStreet.com Investment Rating for PIMCO Income Strategy Fund II. The fund currently has a performance rating of A (Excellent) based on an annualized return of 42.03% over the last three years and a total return of 13.29% year to date 2012. Factored into the performance evaluation is an expense ratio of 1.24% (average).

The fund's risk rating is currently B (Good). It carries a beta of 9.86, meaning it is expected to move 98.6% for every 10% move in the market. Volatility, as measured by both the semi-deviation and a drawdown factor, is considered low. As of March 31, 2012, PIMCO Income Strategy Fund II traded at a premium of 3.67% above its net asset value, which is worse than its one-year historical average premium of 2.91%.

William H. Gross has been running the fund for 3 years and currently receives a manager quality ranking of 99 (0=worst, 99=best). If you desire only a moderate level of risk and strong performance, then this fund is an excellent option.

Data Date	Investment Rating	Net Assets ($Mil)	Price	Performance Rating/Pts	Total Return Y-T-D	Risk Rating/Pts
3-12	A	584.35	10.16	A / 9.5	13.29%	B / 8.1
2011	C	584.35	9.15	C+ / 6.3	2.19%	C+ / 6.6
2010	D-	537.34	9.90	D / 2.1	8.28%	C- / 3.5
2009	D+	341.95	9.88	C / 4.7	78.67%	C- / 3.3

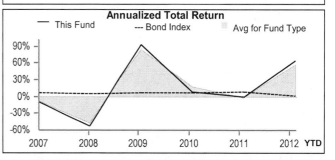

PIMCO Municipal Income Fund (PMF)   B+   Good

Fund Family: Allianz Global Investors Fund Mgmt
Fund Type: Municipal - National
Inception Date: June 27, 2001

Major Rating Factors: Strong performance is the major factor driving the B+ (Good) TheStreet.com Investment Rating for PIMCO Municipal Income Fund. The fund currently has a performance rating of B (Good) based on an annualized return of 18.43% over the last three years and a total return of 3.88% year to date 2012. Factored into the performance evaluation is an expense ratio of 1.44% (average).

The fund's risk rating is currently B (Good). It carries a beta of 2.40, meaning it is expected to move 24.0% for every 10% move in the market. Volatility, as measured by both the semi-deviation and a drawdown factor, is considered low. As of March 31, 2012, PIMCO Municipal Income Fund traded at a premium of 14.06% above its net asset value, which is better than its one-year historical average premium of 16.90%.

Joseph P. Deane has been running the fund for 1 year and currently receives a manager quality ranking of 59 (0=worst, 99=best). If you desire only a moderate level of risk and strong performance, then this fund is an excellent option.

Data Date	Investment Rating	Net Assets ($Mil)	Price	Performance Rating/Pts	Total Return Y-T-D	Risk Rating/Pts
3-12	B+	269.92	14.52	B / 8.0	3.88%	B / 8.3
2011	A-	305.90	14.22	A- / 9.1	1.62%	B / 8.4
2010	D+	294.46	12.61	D+ / 2.8	9.70%	C+ / 5.6
2009	C-	233.51	12.39	C- / 4.0	60.00%	C+ / 5.8

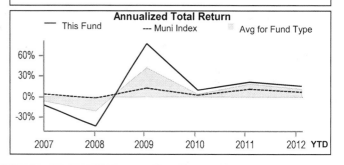

PIMCO Municipal Income Fund II (PML)   A+   Excellent

Fund Family: Allianz Global Investors Fund Mgmt
Fund Type: Municipal - National
Inception Date: June 25, 2002

Major Rating Factors:
Exceptional performance is the major factor driving the A+ (Excellent) TheStreet.com Investment Rating for PIMCO Municipal Income Fund II. The fund currently has a performance rating of A (Excellent) based on an annualized return of 21.03% over the last three years and a total return of 10.14% year to date 2012. Factored into the performance evaluation is an expense ratio of 1.37% (average).

The fund's risk rating is currently B (Good). It carries a beta of 2.85, meaning it is expected to move 28.5% for every 10% move in the market. Volatility, as measured by both the semi-deviation and a drawdown factor, is considered low. As of March 31, 2012, PIMCO Municipal Income Fund II traded at a premium of 5.27% above its net asset value, which is worse than its one-year historical average premium of 3.45%.

Joseph P. Deane has been running the fund for 1 year and currently receives a manager quality ranking of 37 (0=worst, 99=best). If you desire only a moderate level of risk and strong performance, then this fund is an excellent option.

Data Date	Investment Rating	Net Assets ($Mil)	Price	Performance Rating/Pts	Total Return Y-T-D	Risk Rating/Pts
3-12	A+	610.80	12.18	A / 9.4	10.14%	B / 8.5
2011	A+	663.80	11.24	A+ / 9.7	3.02%	B / 8.6
2010	D	645.59	10.05	D- / 1.0	2.71%	C+ / 6.2
2009	C-	534.05	10.52	C- / 3.6	60.32%	C+ / 5.7

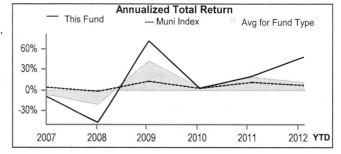

PIMCO Municipal Income Fund III (PMX)

A   **Excellent**

Fund Family: Allianz Global Investors Fund Mgmt
Fund Type: Municipal - National
Inception Date: October 28, 2002

Data Date	Investment Rating	Net Assets ($Mil)	Price	Perfor-mance Rating/Pts	Total Return Y-T-D	Risk Rating/Pts
3-12	A	313.02	11.80	B+ / 8.6	8.74%	B / 8.8
2011	A+	321.10	11.05	A- / 9.2	3.17%	B / 8.9
2010	D-	330.84	10.44	D / 1.6	9.82%	C / 4.4
2009	C-	324.92	10.30	C- / 3.3	68.02%	C / 5.4

Major Rating Factors:
Strong performance is the major factor driving the A (Excellent) TheStreet.com Investment Rating for PIMCO Municipal Income Fund III. The fund currently has a performance rating of B+ (Good) based on an annualized return of 18.55% over the last three years and a total return of 8.74% year to date 2012. Factored into the performance evaluation is an expense ratio of 1.44% (average).

The fund's risk rating is currently B (Good). It carries a beta of 1.90, meaning it is expected to move 19.0% for every 10% move in the market. Volatility, as measured by both the semi-deviation and a drawdown factor, is considered low. As of March 31, 2012, PIMCO Municipal Income Fund III traded at a premium of 13.68% above its net asset value, which is worse than its one-year historical average premium of 13.29%.

Joseph P. Deane has been running the fund for 1 year and currently receives a manager quality ranking of 71 (0=worst, 99=best). If you desire only a moderate level of risk and strong performance, then this fund is an excellent option.

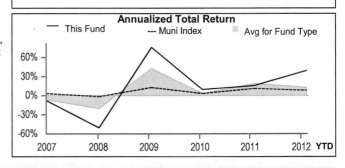

PIMCO NY Muni Income Fund (PNF)

B-   **Good**

Fund Family: Allianz Global Investors Fund Mgmt
Fund Type: Municipal - Single State
Inception Date: June 27, 2001

Data Date	Investment Rating	Net Assets ($Mil)	Price	Perfor-mance Rating/Pts	Total Return Y-T-D	Risk Rating/Pts
3-12	B-	75.73	11.18	C+ / 6.8	0.50%	B / 8.6
2011	A	82.70	11.29	A / 9.4	1.86%	B / 8.7
2010	D+	81.07	10.21	D / 1.8	3.36%	C+ / 6.3
2009	C-	69.48	10.53	C- / 3.7	58.92%	C+ / 5.9

Major Rating Factors: PIMCO NY Muni Income Fund receives a TheStreet.com Investment Rating of B- (Good). The fund currently has a performance rating of C+ (Fair) based on an annualized return of 14.85% over the last three years and a total return of 0.50% year to date 2012. Factored into the performance evaluation is an expense ratio of 1.51% (average).

The fund's risk rating is currently B (Good). It carries a beta of 2.50, meaning it is expected to move 25.0% for every 10% move in the market. Volatility, as measured by both the semi-deviation and a drawdown factor, is considered low. As of March 31, 2012, PIMCO NY Muni Income Fund traded at a discount of .45% below its net asset value, which is better than its one-year historical average premium of .77%.

Joseph P. Deane has been running the fund for 1 year and currently receives a manager quality ranking of 27 (0=worst, 99=best). If you desire an average level of risk, then this fund may be an option.

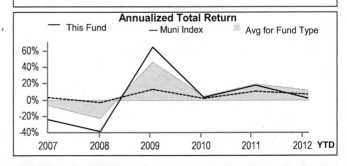

PIMCO NY Municipal Income Fund II (PNI)

B+   **Good**

Fund Family: Allianz Global Investors Fund Mgmt
Fund Type: Municipal - Single State
Inception Date: June 25, 2002

Data Date	Investment Rating	Net Assets ($Mil)	Price	Perfor-mance Rating/Pts	Total Return Y-T-D	Risk Rating/Pts
3-12	B+	109.26	11.92	B / 7.6	5.26%	B / 8.6
2011	B+	115.80	11.52	B+ / 8.7	2.08%	B / 8.6
2010	D	117.16	10.50	D- / 1.2	1.93%	C+ / 6.2
2009	C-	102.13	11.07	C / 4.3	62.39%	C / 5.4

Major Rating Factors: Strong performance is the major factor driving the B+ (Good) TheStreet.com Investment Rating for PIMCO NY Municipal Income Fund II. The fund currently has a performance rating of B (Good) based on an annualized return of 15.40% over the last three years and a total return of 5.26% year to date 2012. Factored into the performance evaluation is an expense ratio of 1.55% (average).

The fund's risk rating is currently B (Good). It carries a beta of 2.22, meaning it is expected to move 22.2% for every 10% move in the market. Volatility, as measured by both the semi-deviation and a drawdown factor, is considered low. As of March 31, 2012, PIMCO NY Municipal Income Fund II traded at a premium of 7.58% above its net asset value, which is worse than its one-year historical average premium of 7.43%.

Joseph P. Deane has been running the fund for 1 year and currently receives a manager quality ranking of 55 (0=worst, 99=best). If you desire only a moderate level of risk and strong performance, then this fund is an excellent option.

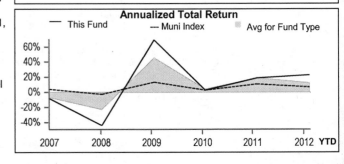

PIMCO NY Municipal Income Fund III (PYN)   **B-**   **Good**

Fund Family: Allianz Global Investors Fund Mgmt
Fund Type: Municipal - Single State
Inception Date: October 28, 2002

Data Date	Investment Rating	Net Assets ($Mil)	Price	Performance Rating/Pts	Total Return Y-T-D	Risk Rating/Pts
3-12	B-	49.49	9.61	C+ / 6.6	3.14%	B / 8.7
2011	A-	50.10	9.47	B+ / 8.7	1.58%	B / 8.8
2010	D-	65.94	8.79	E+ / 0.9	5.63%	C / 4.4
2009	D-	50.53	8.92	D- / 1.2	54.95%	C- / 4.2

Major Rating Factors: PIMCO NY Municipal Income Fund III receives a TheStreet.com Investment Rating of B- (Good). The fund currently has a performance rating of C+ (Fair) based on an annualized return of 13.54% over the last three years and a total return of 3.14% year to date 2012. Factored into the performance evaluation is an expense ratio of 1.73% (above average).

The fund's risk rating is currently B (Good). It carries a beta of 2.44, meaning it is expected to move 24.4% for every 10% move in the market. Volatility, as measured by both the semi-deviation and a drawdown factor, is considered low. As of March 31, 2012, PIMCO NY Municipal Income Fund III traded at a premium of 4.46% above its net asset value, which is better than its one-year historical average premium of 4.58%.

Joseph P. Deane has been running the fund for 1 year and currently receives a manager quality ranking of 25 (0=worst, 99=best). If you desire an average level of risk, then this fund may be an option.

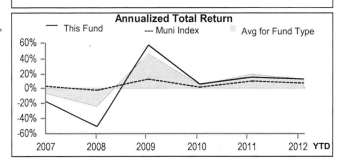

PIMCO Strategic Glob Gov Fund (RCS)   **B-**   **Good**

Fund Family: Allianz Global Investors Fund Mgmt
Fund Type: Mortgage
Inception Date: February 17, 1994

Data Date	Investment Rating	Net Assets ($Mil)	Price	Performance Rating/Pts	Total Return Y-T-D	Risk Rating/Pts
3-12	B-	394.70	11.06	C+ / 6.8	1.32%	B / 8.5
2011	B-	394.70	11.15	C+ / 6.8	2.69%	B- / 7.7
2010	A-	254.12	10.19	B- / 7.5	7.69%	B- / 7.0
2009	C+	313.64	10.27	C+ / 6.8	28.06%	C+ / 6.1

Major Rating Factors: PIMCO Strategic Glob Gov Fund receives a TheStreet.com Investment Rating of B- (Good). The fund currently has a performance rating of C+ (Fair) based on an annualized return of 25.87% over the last three years and a total return of 1.32% year to date 2012. Factored into the performance evaluation is an expense ratio of 1.43% (average).

The fund's risk rating is currently B (Good). It carries a beta of 2.33, meaning it is expected to move 23.3% for every 10% move in the market. Volatility, as measured by both the semi-deviation and a drawdown factor, is considered low. As of March 31, 2012, PIMCO Strategic Glob Gov Fund traded at a premium of 18.80% above its net asset value, which is better than its one-year historical average premium of 21.55%.

Daniel J. Ivascyn has been running the fund for 7 years and currently receives a manager quality ranking of 89 (0=worst, 99=best). If you desire an average level of risk, then this fund may be an option.

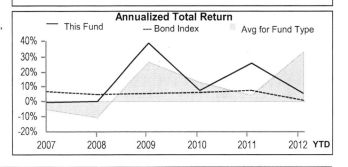

Pioneer Diversified High Income Tr (HNW)   **B+**   **Good**

Fund Family: Pioneer Investment Management Inc
Fund Type: Global
Inception Date: May 24, 2007

Data Date	Investment Rating	Net Assets ($Mil)	Price	Performance Rating/Pts	Total Return Y-T-D	Risk Rating/Pts
3-12	B+	172.88	20.59	B / 8.0	9.47%	B / 8.3
2011	B	154.70	19.27	B / 7.9	0.21%	B / 8.2
2010	B-	165.28	20.20	B+ / 8.3	25.55%	C / 4.4
2009	B-	113.81	17.74	A / 9.3	68.14%	C- / 3.7

Major Rating Factors: Strong performance is the major factor driving the B+ (Good) TheStreet.com Investment Rating for Pioneer Diversified High Income Tr. The fund currently has a performance rating of B (Good) based on an annualized return of 30.78% over the last three years and a total return of 9.47% year to date 2012. Factored into the performance evaluation is an expense ratio of 2.20% (high).

The fund's risk rating is currently B (Good). It carries a beta of 0.46, meaning the fund's expected move will be 4.6% for every 10% move in the market. Volatility, as measured by both the semi-deviation and a drawdown factor, is considered low. As of March 31, 2012, Pioneer Diversified High Income Tr traded at a premium of 5.27% above its net asset value, which is worse than its one-year historical average premium of 2.88%.

Andrew D. Feltus currently receives a manager quality ranking of 97 (0=worst, 99=best). If you desire only a moderate level of risk and strong performance, then this fund is an excellent option.

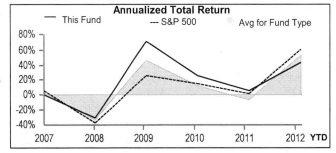

Pioneer Floating Rate Trust (PHD)

B **Good**

Fund Family: Pioneer Investment Management Inc
Fund Type: Loan Participation
Inception Date: December 28, 2004

Major Rating Factors: Strong performance is the major factor driving the B (Good) TheStreet.com Investment Rating for Pioneer Floating Rate Trust. The fund currently has a performance rating of B- (Good) based on an annualized return of 28.01% over the last three years and a total return of 5.22% year to date 2012. Factored into the performance evaluation is an expense ratio of 1.67% (above average).

The fund's risk rating is currently B (Good). It carries a beta of -72.29, meaning the fund's expected move will be -722.9% for every 10% move in the market. Volatility, as measured by both the semi-deviation and a drawdown factor, is considered low. As of March 31, 2012, Pioneer Floating Rate Trust traded at a premium of .15% above its net asset value, which is better than its one-year historical average premium of 1.24%.

Jonathan D. Sharkey currently receives a manager quality ranking of 99 (0=worst, 99=best). If you desire only a moderate level of risk and strong performance, then this fund is an excellent option.

Data Date	Investment Rating	Net Assets ($Mil)	Price	Performance Rating/Pts	Total Return Y-T-D	Risk Rating/Pts
3-12	B	306.82	12.96	B- / 7.2	5.22%	B / 8.3
2011	B+	483.40	12.47	B / 8.1	0.56%	B / 8.3
2010	C-	278.57	12.89	C+ / 6.5	20.27%	C- / 3.6
2009	D+	230.91	11.52	C / 4.4	71.93%	C- / 4.2

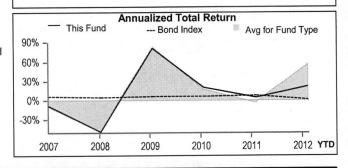

Pioneer High Income Trust (PHT)

A+ **Excellent**

Fund Family: Pioneer Investment Management Inc
Fund Type: Global
Inception Date: April 25, 2002

Major Rating Factors:
Exceptional performance is the major factor driving the A+ (Excellent) TheStreet.com Investment Rating for Pioneer High Income Trust. The fund currently has a performance rating of A (Excellent) based on an annualized return of 41.49% over the last three years and a total return of -2.24% year to date 2012. Factored into the performance evaluation is an expense ratio of 1.11% (low).

The fund's risk rating is currently B+ (Good). It carries a beta of 0.68, meaning the fund's expected move will be 6.8% for every 10% move in the market. Volatility, as measured by both the semi-deviation and a drawdown factor, is considered very low. As of March 31, 2012, Pioneer High Income Trust traded at a premium of 23.77% above its net asset value, which is better than its one-year historical average premium of 26.00%.

Andrew D. Feltus currently receives a manager quality ranking of 98 (0=worst, 99=best). If you desire only a moderate level of risk and strong performance, then this fund is an excellent option.

Data Date	Investment Rating	Net Assets ($Mil)	Price	Performance Rating/Pts	Total Return Y-T-D	Risk Rating/Pts
3-12	A+	401.35	16.66	A / 9.3	-2.24%	B+ / 9.0
2011	A	356.20	17.33	A+ / 9.9	2.71%	B- / 7.9
2010	B-	367.09	15.49	B+ / 8.5	21.64%	C- / 3.9
2009	C	326.42	14.11	B / 7.9	93.64%	C- / 3.0

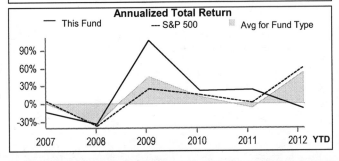

Pioneer Municipal High Income Adv (MAV)

A+ **Excellent**

Fund Family: Pioneer Investment Management Inc
Fund Type: Municipal - High Yield
Inception Date: October 20, 2003

Major Rating Factors:
Exceptional performance is the major factor driving the A+ (Excellent) TheStreet.com Investment Rating for Pioneer Municipal High Income Adv. The fund currently has a performance rating of A+ (Excellent) based on an annualized return of 28.15% over the last three years and a total return of 4.28% year to date 2012. Factored into the performance evaluation is an expense ratio of 1.35% (average).

The fund's risk rating is currently B (Good). It carries a beta of 2.25, meaning it is expected to move 22.5% for every 10% move in the market. Volatility, as measured by both the semi-deviation and a drawdown factor, is considered low. As of March 31, 2012, Pioneer Municipal High Income Adv traded at a premium of 14.37% above its net asset value, which is worse than its one-year historical average premium of 11.39%.

David J. Eurkus currently receives a manager quality ranking of 83 (0=worst, 99=best). If you desire only a moderate level of risk and strong performance, then this fund is an excellent option.

Data Date	Investment Rating	Net Assets ($Mil)	Price	Performance Rating/Pts	Total Return Y-T-D	Risk Rating/Pts
3-12	A+	266.87	14.72	A+ / 9.7	4.28%	B / 8.4
2011	A+	288.40	14.40	A+ / 9.9	2.08%	B / 8.3
2010	D+	281.55	12.42	C- / 3.5	6.42%	C / 4.8
2009	B-	277.65	12.67	B / 7.9	72.76%	C / 5.0

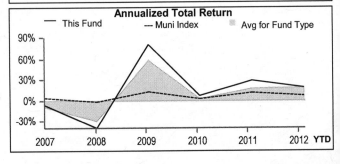

Pioneer Municipal High Income Trus (MHI)

A+   **Excellent**

Fund Family: Pioneer Investment Management Inc
Fund Type: Municipal - High Yield
Inception Date: July 17, 2003

Major Rating Factors:
Exceptional performance is the major factor driving the A+ (Excellent) TheStreet.com Investment Rating for Pioneer Municipal High Income Trus. The fund currently has a performance rating of A (Excellent) based on an annualized return of 24.10% over the last three years and a total return of 1.04% year to date 2012. Factored into the performance evaluation is an expense ratio of 1.12% (low).

The fund's risk rating is currently B (Good). It carries a beta of 2.08, meaning it is expected to move 20.8% for every 10% move in the market. Volatility, as measured by both the semi-deviation and a drawdown factor, is considered low. As of March 31, 2012, Pioneer Municipal High Income Trus traded at a premium of 5.74% above its net asset value, which is worse than its one-year historical average premium of 5.01%.

David J. Eurkus currently receives a manager quality ranking of 80 (0=worst, 99=best). If you desire only a moderate level of risk and strong performance, then this fund is an excellent option.

Data Date	Investment Rating	Net Assets ($Mil)	Price	Perfor-mance Rating/Pts	Total Return Y-T-D	Risk Rating/Pts
3-12	A+	291.05	14.73	A / 9.3	1.04%	B / 8.5
2011	A+	304.60	14.87	A+ / 9.8	0.81%	B / 8.5
2010	C	308.46	13.42	C+ / 5.9	4.92%	C / 5.4
2009	B+	247.56	13.79	B / 8.2	70.35%	C+ / 5.7

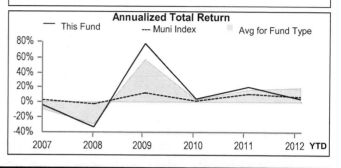

Putnam High Income Securities (PCF)

C+   **Fair**

Fund Family: Putnam Investment Management LLC
Fund Type: General Bond
Inception Date: July 9, 1987

Major Rating Factors: Middle of the road best describes Putnam High Income Securities whose TheStreet.com Investment Rating is currently a C+ (Fair). The fund currently has a performance rating of C+ (Fair) based on an annualized return of 25.49% over the last three years and a total return of 11.80% year to date 2012. Factored into the performance evaluation is an expense ratio of 0.91% (low).

The fund's risk rating is currently C+ (Fair). It carries a beta of -0.01, meaning the fund's expected move will be -0.1% for every 10% move in the market. Volatility, as measured by both the semi-deviation and a drawdown factor, is considered low. As of March 31, 2012, Putnam High Income Securities traded at a premium of 1.81% above its net asset value, which is worse than its one-year historical average discount of 1.11%.

Eric N. Harthun currently receives a manager quality ranking of 96 (0=worst, 99=best). If you desire an average level of risk, then this fund may be an option.

Data Date	Investment Rating	Net Assets ($Mil)	Price	Perfor-mance Rating/Pts	Total Return Y-T-D	Risk Rating/Pts
3-12	C+	139.12	8.45	C+ / 6.8	11.80%	C+ / 6.9
2011	C+	133.80	7.68	C+ / 6.4	3.52%	C+ / 6.9
2010	B	135.78	8.38	B / 8.0	24.09%	C / 5.0
2009	C	123.26	7.21	C / 5.3	43.23%	C+ / 5.7

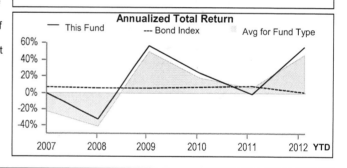

Putnam Managed Muni Inc Tr (PMM)

A-   **Excellent**

Fund Family: Putnam Investment Management LLC
Fund Type: Municipal - National
Inception Date: February 16, 1989

Major Rating Factors:
Strong performance is the major factor driving the A- (Excellent) TheStreet.com Investment Rating for Putnam Managed Muni Inc Tr. The fund currently has a performance rating of B+ (Good) based on an annualized return of 20.54% over the last three years and a total return of 4.66% year to date 2012. Factored into the performance evaluation is an expense ratio of 1.03% (low).

The fund's risk rating is currently B (Good). It carries a beta of 1.77, meaning it is expected to move 17.7% for every 10% move in the market. Volatility, as measured by both the semi-deviation and a drawdown factor, is considered low. As of March 31, 2012, Putnam Managed Muni Inc Tr traded at a discount of .39% below its net asset value, which is better than its one-year historical average premium of .22%.

Paul M. Drury has been running the fund for 23 years and currently receives a manager quality ranking of 76 (0=worst, 99=best). If you desire only a moderate level of risk and strong performance, then this fund is an excellent option.

Data Date	Investment Rating	Net Assets ($Mil)	Price	Perfor-mance Rating/Pts	Total Return Y-T-D	Risk Rating/Pts
3-12	A-	423.92	7.70	B+ / 8.6	4.66%	B / 8.5
2011	A-	429.60	7.47	B+ / 8.9	0.13%	B / 8.6
2010	C+	422.05	6.91	C / 5.5	11.66%	C+ / 6.2
2009	B-	350.83	6.65	C+ / 6.0	38.99%	B- / 7.1

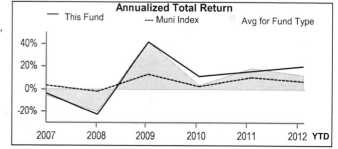

Putnam Master Intermediate Inc Tr (PIM)   D   Weak

Fund Family: Putnam Investment Management LLC
Fund Type: General Bond
Inception Date: April 11, 1988

Major Rating Factors: Putnam Master Intermediate Inc Tr receives a TheStreet.com Investment Rating of D (Weak). The fund currently has a performance rating of C- (Fair) based on an annualized return of 16.13% over the last three years and a total return of 3.11% year to date 2012. Factored into the performance evaluation is an expense ratio of 0.94% (low).

The fund's risk rating is currently C+ (Fair). It carries a beta of 1.72, meaning it is expected to move 17.2% for every 10% move in the market. Volatility, as measured by both the semi-deviation and a drawdown factor, is considered low. As of March 31, 2012, Putnam Master Intermediate Inc Tr traded at a discount of 5.68% below its net asset value, which is better than its one-year historical average discount of 3.76%.

D. William Kohli has been running the fund for 18 years and currently receives a manager quality ranking of 68 (0=worst, 99=best). If you desire an average level of risk, then this fund may be an option.

Data Date	Investment Rating	Net Assets ($Mil)	Price	Performance Rating/Pts	Total Return Y-T-D	Risk Rating/Pts
3-12	D	351.03	5.15	C- / 3.3	3.11%	C+ / 6.1
2011	C-	345.80	5.08	C / 4.7	0.39%	C+ / 6.0
2010	C-	381.36	5.79	C / 5.3	6.52%	C / 4.5
2009	B-	383.39	6.03	B / 7.8	73.93%	C / 5.1

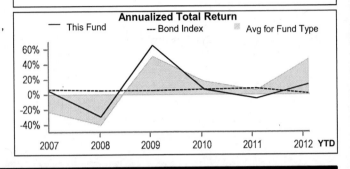

Annualized Total Return

Putnam Muni Opp Tr (PMO)   A-   Excellent

Fund Family: Putnam Investment Management LLC
Fund Type: Municipal - National
Inception Date: May 21, 1993

Major Rating Factors:
Strong performance is the major factor driving the A- (Excellent) TheStreet.com Investment Rating for Putnam Muni Opp Tr. The fund currently has a performance rating of B+ (Good) based on an annualized return of 18.14% over the last three years and a total return of 3.91% year to date 2012. Factored into the performance evaluation is an expense ratio of 1.31% (average).

The fund's risk rating is currently B (Good). It carries a beta of 1.93, meaning it is expected to move 19.3% for every 10% move in the market. Volatility, as measured by both the semi-deviation and a drawdown factor, is considered low. As of March 31, 2012, Putnam Muni Opp Tr traded at a discount of 1.95% below its net asset value, which is worse than its one-year historical average discount of 3.62%.

Susan A. McCormack has been running the fund for 13 years and currently receives a manager quality ranking of 63 (0=worst, 99=best). If you desire only a moderate level of risk and strong performance, then this fund is an excellent option.

Data Date	Investment Rating	Net Assets ($Mil)	Price	Performance Rating/Pts	Total Return Y-T-D	Risk Rating/Pts
3-12	A-	482.53	12.55	B+ / 8.3	3.91%	B / 8.8
2011	A	532.10	12.27	B+ / 8.9	-0.24%	B / 8.8
2010	C+	514.09	10.87	C / 5.2	4.60%	C+ / 6.7
2009	B-	448.68	11.13	C+ / 6.4	34.79%	B- / 7.0

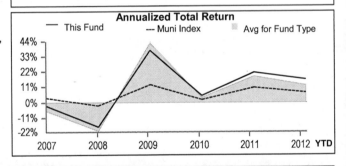

Annualized Total Return

Putnam Premier Income Trust (PPT)   D+   Weak

Fund Family: Putnam Investment Management LLC
Fund Type: General Bond
Inception Date: February 29, 1988

Major Rating Factors: Putnam Premier Income Trust receives a TheStreet.com Investment Rating of D+ (Weak). The fund currently has a performance rating of C (Fair) based on an annualized return of 22.64% over the last three years and a total return of 7.91% year to date 2012. Factored into the performance evaluation is an expense ratio of 0.85% (very low).

The fund's risk rating is currently C+ (Fair). It carries a beta of 0.76, meaning the fund's expected move will be 7.6% for every 10% move in the market. Volatility, as measured by both the semi-deviation and a drawdown factor, is considered low. As of March 31, 2012, Putnam Premier Income Trust traded at a discount of 5.00% below its net asset value, which is better than its one-year historical average discount of 2.16%.

Michael V. Salm has been running the fund for 20 years and currently receives a manager quality ranking of 90 (0=worst, 99=best). If you desire an average level of risk, then this fund may be an option.

Data Date	Investment Rating	Net Assets ($Mil)	Price	Performance Rating/Pts	Total Return Y-T-D	Risk Rating/Pts
3-12	D+	874.40	5.51	C / 4.9	7.91%	C+ / 5.8
2011	C-	794.60	5.19	C / 5.5	1.35%	C+ / 5.9
2010	C+	887.22	6.28	B- / 7.1	14.15%	C / 4.7
2009	C+	803.32	6.13	B- / 7.5	70.88%	C / 5.0

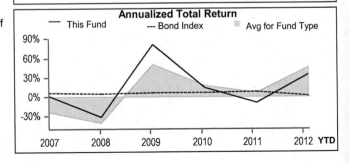

Annualized Total Return

Pyxis Credit Strategies Fund (HCF)   **C-**   **Fair**

Fund Family: Highland Capital Management LP
Fund Type: General Bond
Inception Date: June 26, 2006

Data Date	Investment Rating	Net Assets ($Mil)	Price	Performance Rating/Pts	Total Return Y-T-D	Risk Rating/Pts
3-12	C-	443.05	6.34	C- / 4.0	4.39%	B- / 7.7
2011	C-	445.10	6.18	C- / 3.7	0.32%	B- / 7.5
2010	E+	458.76	7.58	D- / 1.3	30.86%	D+ / 2.8
2009	E+	400.79	6.31	E+ / 0.6	18.33%	C- / 4.0

Major Rating Factors: Middle of the road best describes Pyxis Credit Strategies Fund whose TheStreet.com Investment Rating is currently a C- (Fair). The fund currently has a performance rating of C- (Fair) based on an annualized return of 19.80% over the last three years and a total return of 4.39% year to date 2012. Factored into the performance evaluation is an expense ratio of 3.15% (high).

The fund's risk rating is currently B- (Good). It carries a beta of 0.14, meaning the fund's expected move will be 1.4% for every 10% move in the market. Volatility, as measured by both the semi-deviation and a drawdown factor, is considered low. As of March 31, 2012, Pyxis Credit Strategies Fund traded at a discount of 11.70% below its net asset value, which is better than its one-year historical average discount of 7.83%.

Greg Stuecheli currently receives a manager quality ranking of 93 (0=worst, 99=best). If you desire an average level of risk, then this fund may be an option.

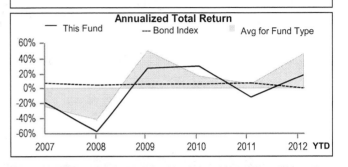

Annualized Total Return

Reaves Utility Income Trust (UTG)   **A+**   **Excellent**

Fund Family: W H Reaves & Company Inc
Fund Type: Utilities
Inception Date: February 24, 2004

Data Date	Investment Rating	Net Assets ($Mil)	Price	Performance Rating/Pts	Total Return Y-T-D	Risk Rating/Pts
3-12	A+	545.02	26.00	A / 9.4	0.97%	B / 8.9
2011	B+	557.60	26.01	A / 9.4	-3.19%	B- / 7.5
2010	B-	438.31	22.35	B / 8.1	29.08%	C / 4.3
2009	C	279.17	18.56	B- / 7.2	61.18%	C / 4.3

Major Rating Factors:
Exceptional performance is the major factor driving the A+ (Excellent) TheStreet.com Investment Rating for Reaves Utility Income Trust. The fund currently has a performance rating of A (Excellent) based on an annualized return of 41.19% over the last three years and a total return of 0.97% year to date 2012. Factored into the performance evaluation is an expense ratio of 1.93% (above average).

The fund's risk rating is currently B (Good). It carries a beta of 1.00, meaning that its performance tracks fairly well with that of the overall stock market. Volatility, as measured by both the semi-deviation and a drawdown factor, is considered low. As of March 31, 2012, Reaves Utility Income Trust traded at a premium of 6.17% above its net asset value, which is worse than its one-year historical average premium of 6.08%.

Ronald J. Sorenson has been running the fund for 8 years and currently receives a manager quality ranking of 95 (0=worst, 99=best). If you desire only a moderate level of risk and strong performance, then this fund is an excellent option.

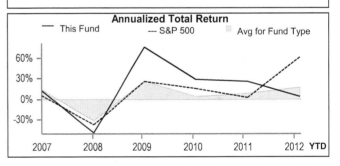

Annualized Total Return

RENN Global Entrepreneurs Fund Inc (RCG)   **E+**   **Very Weak**

Fund Family: RENN Capital Group Inc
Fund Type: Growth and Income
Inception Date: May 25, 1994

Data Date	Investment Rating	Net Assets ($Mil)	Price	Performance Rating/Pts	Total Return Y-T-D	Risk Rating/Pts
3-12	E+	9.50	1.95	E+ / 0.8	7.14%	C / 5.4
2011	D-	9.50	1.82	D- / 1.0	-3.85%	C / 5.1
2010	D-	18.17	1.96	E / 0.3	-24.62%	C / 4.7
2009	E+	17.41	2.60	E / 0.4	-19.75%	C / 4.9

Major Rating Factors:
Very poor performance is the major factor driving the E+ (Very Weak) TheStreet.com Investment Rating for RENN Global Entrepreneurs Fund Inc. The fund currently has a performance rating of E+ (Very Weak) based on an annualized return of -12.49% over the last three years and a total return of 7.14% year to date 2012. Factored into the performance evaluation is an expense ratio of 5.25% (high).

The fund's risk rating is currently C (Fair). It carries a beta of 0.46, meaning the fund's expected move will be 4.6% for every 10% move in the market. Volatility, as measured by both the semi-deviation and a drawdown factor, is considered average. As of March 31, 2012, RENN Global Entrepreneurs Fund Inc traded at a discount of 20.73% below its net asset value, which is worse than its one-year historical average discount of 21.53%.

Russell G. Cleveland has been running the fund for 18 years and currently receives a manager quality ranking of 7 (0=worst, 99=best). This fund offers an average level of risk but investors looking for strong performance will be frustrated.

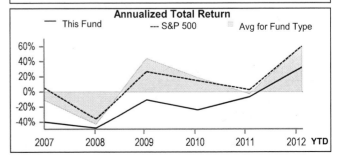

Annualized Total Return

RMR Real Estate Income (RAP)

D+   **Weak**

Fund Family: RMR Advisors Inc
Fund Type: Growth and Income
Inception Date: May 26, 2006

Data Date	Investment Rating	Net Assets ($Mil)	Price	Performance Rating/Pts	Total Return Y-T-D	Risk Rating/Pts
3-12	D+	77.12	16.10	C- / 3.3	16.33%	C+ / 6.8
2011	D	54.80	14.02	D / 2.0	1.78%	C+ / 6.7
2010	D-	72.61	18.37	E+ / 0.9	15.99%	C / 4.4
2009	E+	68.40	16.89	E+ / 0.7	30.41%	C- / 3.7

Major Rating Factors: RMR Real Estate Income receives a TheStreet.com Investment Rating of D+ (Weak). The fund currently has a performance rating of C- (Fair) based on an annualized return of 13.10% over the last three years and a total return of 16.33% year to date 2012. Factored into the performance evaluation is an expense ratio of 1.72% (above average).

The fund's risk rating is currently C+ (Fair). It carries a beta of 1.18, meaning it is expected to move 11.8% for every 10% move in the market. Volatility, as measured by both the semi-deviation and a drawdown factor, is considered low. As of March 31, 2012, RMR Real Estate Income traded at a discount of 17.82% below its net asset value, which is better than its one-year historical average discount of 17.25%.

Craig Dunstan currently receives a manager quality ranking of 16 (0=worst, 99=best). If you desire an average level of risk, then this fund may be an option.

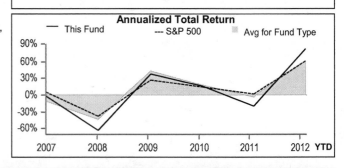

Royce Focus Trust (FUND)

C-   **Fair**

Fund Family: Royce & Associates LLC
Fund Type: Growth
Inception Date: March 2, 1988

Data Date	Investment Rating	Net Assets ($Mil)	Price	Performance Rating/Pts	Total Return Y-T-D	Risk Rating/Pts
3-12	C-	172.29	6.96	C- / 3.9	12.06%	B- / 7.3
2011	C-	175.90	6.30	C / 4.3	3.97%	B- / 7.2
2010	C-	141.50	7.57	C / 4.7	19.59%	C+ / 5.6
2009	D	108.09	6.33	D / 2.2	33.33%	C / 5.4

Major Rating Factors: Middle of the road best describes Royce Focus Trust whose TheStreet.com Investment Rating is currently a C- (Fair). The fund currently has a performance rating of C- (Fair) based on an annualized return of 17.72% over the last three years and a total return of 12.06% year to date 2012. Factored into the performance evaluation is an expense ratio of 1.39% (average).

The fund's risk rating is currently B- (Good). It carries a beta of 1.26, meaning it is expected to move 12.6% for every 10% move in the market. Volatility, as measured by both the semi-deviation and a drawdown factor, is considered low. As of March 31, 2012, Royce Focus Trust traded at a discount of 13.65% below its net asset value, which is better than its one-year historical average discount of 12.73%.

Whitney W. George has been running the fund for 16 years and currently receives a manager quality ranking of 16 (0=worst, 99=best). If you desire an average level of risk, then this fund may be an option.

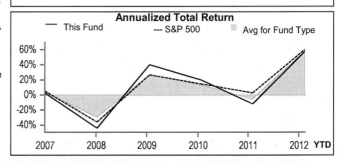

Royce Micro-Cap Trust (RMT)

C+   **Fair**

Fund Family: Royce & Associates LLC
Fund Type: Growth
Inception Date: December 14, 1993

Data Date	Investment Rating	Net Assets ($Mil)	Price	Performance Rating/Pts	Total Return Y-T-D	Risk Rating/Pts
3-12	C+	311.28	9.41	C+ / 6.0	8.78%	B- / 7.5
2011	C	339.30	8.77	C+ / 5.6	1.14%	B- / 7.0
2010	C+	243.16	9.80	C+ / 6.8	34.06%	C / 5.1
2009	D-	196.94	7.37	E+ / 0.9	29.62%	C / 4.8

Major Rating Factors: Middle of the road best describes Royce Micro-Cap Trust whose TheStreet.com Investment Rating is currently a C+ (Fair). The fund currently has a performance rating of C+ (Fair) based on an annualized return of 23.25% over the last three years and a total return of 8.78% year to date 2012. Factored into the performance evaluation is an expense ratio of 1.12% (low).

The fund's risk rating is currently B- (Good). It carries a beta of 1.32, meaning it is expected to move 13.2% for every 10% move in the market. Volatility, as measured by both the semi-deviation and a drawdown factor, is considered low. As of March 31, 2012, Royce Micro-Cap Trust traded at a discount of 13.11% below its net asset value, which is worse than its one-year historical average discount of 13.60%.

Charles M. Royce has been running the fund for 19 years and currently receives a manager quality ranking of 25 (0=worst, 99=best). If you desire an average level of risk, then this fund may be an option.

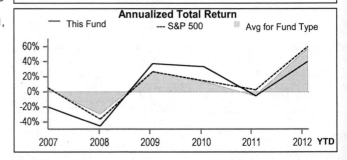

Royce Value Trust (RVT)   C+   Fair

Fund Family: Royce & Associates LLC
Fund Type: Growth
Inception Date: November 19, 1986

Major Rating Factors: Middle of the road best describes Royce Value Trust whose TheStreet.com Investment Rating is currently a C+ (Fair). The fund currently has a performance rating of C+ (Fair) based on an annualized return of 25.40% over the last three years and a total return of 14.77% year to date 2012. Factored into the performance evaluation is an expense ratio of 0.23% (very low).

    The fund's risk rating is currently B- (Good). It carries a beta of 1.47, meaning it is expected to move 14.7% for every 10% move in the market. Volatility, as measured by both the semi-deviation and a drawdown factor, is considered low. As of March 31, 2012, Royce Value Trust traded at a discount of 12.86% below its net asset value, which is worse than its one-year historical average discount of 13.53%.

    Charles M. Royce has been running the fund for 26 years and currently receives a manager quality ranking of 21 (0=worst, 99=best). If you desire an average level of risk, then this fund may be an option.

Data Date	Investment Rating	Net Assets ($Mil)	Price	Perfor-mance Rating/Pts	Total Return Y-T-D	Risk Rating/Pts
3-12	C+	1,105.88	13.89	C+ / 6.8	14.77%	B- / 7.2
2011	C	1,186.90	12.27	C / 5.3	2.44%	C+ / 6.9
2010	C+	849.78	14.54	C+ / 6.6	35.03%	C / 5.2
2009	D-	656.68	10.79	D- / 1.2	28.12%	C / 5.0

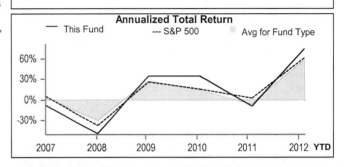

Singapore Fund (SGF)   C+   Fair

Fund Family: Aberdeen Asset Management Asia Ltd
Fund Type: Foreign
Inception Date: July 31, 1990

Major Rating Factors: Strong performance is the major factor driving the C+ (Fair) TheStreet.com Investment Rating for Singapore Fund. The fund currently has a performance rating of B- (Good) based on an annualized return of 28.06% over the last three years and a total return of 18.79% year to date 2012. Factored into the performance evaluation is an expense ratio of 1.83% (above average).

    The fund's risk rating is currently C+ (Fair). It carries a beta of 1.10, meaning it is expected to move 11.0% for every 10% move in the market. Volatility, as measured by both the semi-deviation and a drawdown factor, is considered low. As of March 31, 2012, Singapore Fund traded at a discount of 8.80% below its net asset value, which is better than its one-year historical average discount of 7.25%.

    Hugh Young has been running the fund for 1 year and currently receives a manager quality ranking of 84 (0=worst, 99=best). If you desire only a moderate level of risk and strong performance, then this fund is an excellent option.

Data Date	Investment Rating	Net Assets ($Mil)	Price	Perfor-mance Rating/Pts	Total Return Y-T-D	Risk Rating/Pts
3-12	C+	137.50	12.96	B- / 7.1	18.79%	C+ / 6.7
2011	C-	119.40	10.91	C / 5.0	2.57%	C+ / 6.6
2010	C	146.90	15.19	B- / 7.3	28.33%	C- / 3.5
2009	C	85.06	13.30	B- / 7.0	69.74%	C- / 4.2

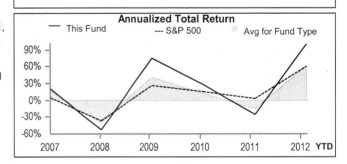

Source Capital (SOR)   C+   Fair

Fund Family: First Pacific Advisors LLC
Fund Type: Income
Inception Date: October 24, 1968

Major Rating Factors: Strong performance is the major factor driving the C+ (Fair) TheStreet.com Investment Rating for Source Capital. The fund currently has a performance rating of B- (Good) based on an annualized return of 26.51% over the last three years and a total return of 12.83% year to date 2012. Factored into the performance evaluation is an expense ratio of 0.98% (low).

    The fund's risk rating is currently B- (Good). It carries a beta of 1.26, meaning it is expected to move 12.6% for every 10% move in the market. Volatility, as measured by both the semi-deviation and a drawdown factor, is considered low. As of March 31, 2012, Source Capital traded at a discount of 12.54% below its net asset value, which is better than its one-year historical average discount of 11.09%.

    Eric S. Ende has been running the fund for 16 years and currently receives a manager quality ranking of 40 (0=worst, 99=best). If you desire only a moderate level of risk and strong performance, then this fund is an excellent option.

Data Date	Investment Rating	Net Assets ($Mil)	Price	Perfor-mance Rating/Pts	Total Return Y-T-D	Risk Rating/Pts
3-12	C+	577.54	52.95	B- / 7.0	12.83%	B- / 7.5
2011	C+	470.00	46.99	B- / 7.0	1.50%	B- / 7.2
2010	B+	490.04	53.13	B / 7.8	30.34%	C+ / 5.8
2009	C-	356.92	42.91	D+ / 2.8	51.58%	C+ / 5.8

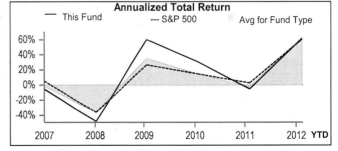

Special Opportunities Fund (SPE)

B   **Good**

Fund Family: Brooklyn Capital Management LLC
Fund Type: Municipal - National
Inception Date: May 28, 1993

Data Date	Investment Rating	Net Assets ($Mil)	Price	Performance Rating/Pts	Total Return Y-T-D	Risk Rating/Pts
3-12	B	109.63	16.06	C+ / 6.5	10.76%	B+ / 9.0
2011	B	106.90	14.50	C+ / 6.9	2.04%	B+ / 9.1
2010	A	294.13	14.75	B / 8.1	4.90%	B- / 7.2
2009	A-	305.27	14.09	B- / 7.5	42.95%	C+ / 6.9

Major Rating Factors: Special Opportunities Fund receives a TheStreet.com Investment Rating of B (Good). The fund currently has a performance rating of C+ (Fair) based on an annualized return of 14.51% over the last three years and a total return of 10.76% year to date 2012. Factored into the performance evaluation is an expense ratio of 1.50% (average).

The fund's risk rating is currently B+ (Good). It carries a beta of 0.39, meaning the fund's expected move will be 3.9% for every 10% move in the market. Volatility, as measured by both the semi-deviation and a drawdown factor, is considered very low. As of March 31, 2012, Special Opportunities Fund traded at a discount of 6.95% below its net asset value, which is worse than its one-year historical average discount of 8.85%.

Andrew Dakos currently receives a manager quality ranking of 87 (0=worst, 99=best). If you desire an average level of risk, then this fund may be an option.

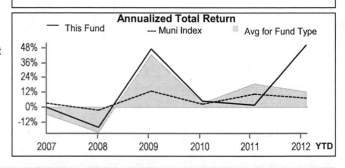

Stone Harbor Emg Markets Income (EDF)

C+   **Fair**

Fund Family: Stone Harbor Investment Partners LP
Fund Type: Emerging Market
Inception Date: December 22, 2010

Data Date	Investment Rating	Net Assets ($Mil)	Price	Performance Rating/Pts	Total Return Y-T-D	Risk Rating/Pts
3-12	C+	0.10	24.58	C+ / 6.5	20.43%	B / 8.0
2011	D+	339.00	20.88	D / 1.6	6.42%	B / 8.0

Major Rating Factors: Middle of the road best describes Stone Harbor Emg Markets Income whose TheStreet.com Investment Rating is currently a C+ (Fair). The fund currently has a performance rating of C+ (Fair) based on an annualized return of 0.00% over the last three years and a total return of 20.43% year to date 2012. Factored into the performance evaluation is an expense ratio of 1.76% (above average).

The fund's risk rating is currently B (Good). It carries a beta of 0.00, meaning the fund's expected move will be 0.0% for every 10% move in the market. Volatility, as measured by both the semi-deviation and a drawdown factor, is considered low. As of March 31, 2012, Stone Harbor Emg Markets Income traded at a premium of 3.93% above its net asset value, which is worse than its one-year historical average premium of 1.21%.

Pablo Cisilino currently receives a manager quality ranking of 93 (0=worst, 99=best). If you desire an average level of risk, then this fund may be an option.

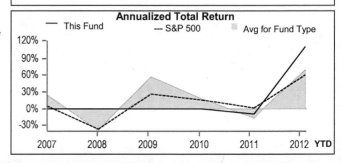

Strategic Global Income Fund (SGL)

B-   **Good**

Fund Family: UBS Global Asset Management
Fund Type: Global
Inception Date: January 24, 1992

Data Date	Investment Rating	Net Assets ($Mil)	Price	Performance Rating/Pts	Total Return Y-T-D	Risk Rating/Pts
3-12	B-	207.56	10.68	B- / 7.3	6.69%	B / 8.0
2011	B	204.10	10.17	B / 8.0	2.36%	B- / 7.9
2010	A-	209.28	11.00	A- / 9.0	28.41%	C+ / 6.0
2009	C+	183.83	10.99	C+ / 6.7	54.09%	C+ / 6.6

Major Rating Factors: Strong performance is the major factor driving the B- (Good) TheStreet.com Investment Rating for Strategic Global Income Fund. The fund currently has a performance rating of B- (Good) based on an annualized return of 28.67% over the last three years and a total return of 6.69% year to date 2012. Factored into the performance evaluation is an expense ratio of 1.17% (low).

The fund's risk rating is currently B (Good). It carries a beta of 1.01, meaning that its performance tracks fairly well with that of the overall stock market. Volatility, as measured by both the semi-deviation and a drawdown factor, is considered low. As of March 31, 2012, Strategic Global Income Fund traded at a discount of 5.15% below its net asset value, which is worse than its one-year historical average discount of 5.94%.

John C. Leonard currently receives a manager quality ranking of 94 (0=worst, 99=best). If you desire only a moderate level of risk and strong performance, then this fund is an excellent option.

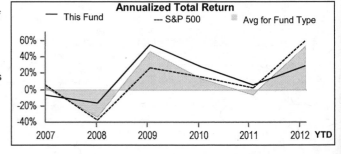

Swiss Helvetia Fund (SWZ)   D+   Weak

Fund Family: Hottinger Capital Corporation
Fund Type: Foreign
Inception Date: August 19, 1987

Data Date	Investment Rating	Net Assets ($Mil)	Price	Performance Rating/Pts	Total Return Y-T-D	Risk Rating/Pts
3-12	D+	467.31	11.21	C- / 4.0	12.66%	C+ / 6.7
2011	D	343.90	9.95	D / 2.1	1.71%	C+ / 6.5
2010	C-	433.93	13.54	C- / 4.1	20.89%	C / 4.9
2009	D-	374.26	11.62	D- / 1.0	-0.53%	C / 5.2

Major Rating Factors: Swiss Helvetia Fund receives a TheStreet.com Investment Rating of D+ (Weak). The fund currently has a performance rating of C- (Fair) based on an annualized return of 17.61% over the last three years and a total return of 12.66% year to date 2012. Factored into the performance evaluation is an expense ratio of 1.34% (average).

The fund's risk rating is currently C+ (Fair). It carries a beta of 0.82, meaning the fund's expected move will be 8.2% for every 10% move in the market. Volatility, as measured by both the semi-deviation and a drawdown factor, is considered low. As of March 31, 2012, Swiss Helvetia Fund traded at a discount of 11.66% below its net asset value, which is better than its one-year historical average discount of 10.67%.

Rudolf S. Millisits has been running the fund for 16 years and currently receives a manager quality ranking of 66 (0=worst, 99=best). If you desire an average level of risk, then this fund may be an option.

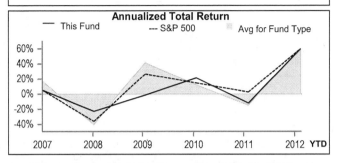

Taiwan Fund (TWN)   C-   Fair

Fund Family: Martin Currie Inc
Fund Type: Foreign
Inception Date: December 16, 1986

Data Date	Investment Rating	Net Assets ($Mil)	Price	Performance Rating/Pts	Total Return Y-T-D	Risk Rating/Pts
3-12	C-	375.17	16.83	C / 4.6	16.15%	B- / 7.0
2011	C-	296.30	14.49	C / 4.8	0.14%	B- / 7.1
2010	B	303.41	19.24	B+ / 8.3	35.64%	C / 4.8
2009	C-	257.06	14.30	C- / 4.2	52.57%	C / 4.8

Major Rating Factors: Middle of the road best describes Taiwan Fund whose TheStreet.com Investment Rating is currently a C- (Fair). The fund currently has a performance rating of C (Fair) based on an annualized return of 19.93% over the last three years and a total return of 16.15% year to date 2012. Factored into the performance evaluation is an expense ratio of 1.43% (average).

The fund's risk rating is currently B- (Good). It carries a beta of 1.08, meaning that its performance tracks fairly well with that of the overall stock market. Volatility, as measured by both the semi-deviation and a drawdown factor, is considered low. As of March 31, 2012, Taiwan Fund traded at a discount of 6.34% below its net asset value, which is worse than its one-year historical average discount of 9.48%.

James Liu currently receives a manager quality ranking of 63 (0=worst, 99=best). If you desire an average level of risk, then this fund may be an option.

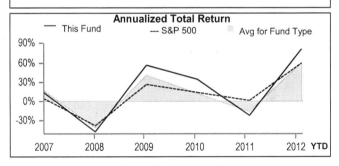

TCW Strategic Income Fund (TSI)   B+   Good

Fund Family: TCW Investment Management Company
Fund Type: Growth and Income
Inception Date: February 26, 1987

Data Date	Investment Rating	Net Assets ($Mil)	Price	Performance Rating/Pts	Total Return Y-T-D	Risk Rating/Pts
3-12	B+	235.23	5.15	B+ / 8.4	7.97%	B / 8.0
2011	B-	262.58	4.85	B- / 7.0	-2.27%	B- / 7.7
2010	B+	227.31	5.22	A- / 9.2	32.52%	C / 4.9
2009	C+	190.35	4.37	B- / 7.1	54.35%	C / 5.5

Major Rating Factors: Strong performance is the major factor driving the B+ (Good) TheStreet.com Investment Rating for TCW Strategic Income Fund. The fund currently has a performance rating of B+ (Good) based on an annualized return of 31.90% over the last three years and a total return of 7.97% year to date 2012. Factored into the performance evaluation is an expense ratio of 1.26% (average).

The fund's risk rating is currently B (Good). It carries a beta of 0.32, meaning the fund's expected move will be 3.2% for every 10% move in the market. Volatility, as measured by both the semi-deviation and a drawdown factor, is considered low. As of March 31, 2012, TCW Strategic Income Fund traded at a discount of 2.46% below its net asset value, which is worse than its one-year historical average discount of 6.33%.

Mitchell A. Flack currently receives a manager quality ranking of 95 (0=worst, 99=best). If you desire only a moderate level of risk and strong performance, then this fund is an excellent option.

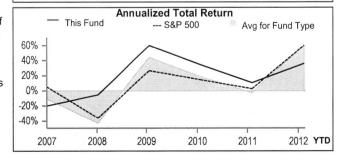

Templeton Dragon Fund (TDF)

C   **Fair**

Fund Family: Templeton Asset Management Ltd
Fund Type: Foreign
Inception Date: September 21, 1994

Major Rating Factors: Middle of the road best describes Templeton Dragon Fund whose TheStreet.com Investment Rating is currently a C (Fair). The fund currently has a performance rating of C (Fair) based on an annualized return of 22.03% over the last three years and a total return of 11.39% year to date 2012. Factored into the performance evaluation is an expense ratio of 1.47% (average).

The fund's risk rating is currently B- (Good). It carries a beta of 0.81, meaning the fund's expected move will be 8.1% for every 10% move in the market. Volatility, as measured by both the semi-deviation and a drawdown factor, is considered low. As of March 31, 2012, Templeton Dragon Fund traded at a discount of 7.59% below its net asset value, which is worse than its one-year historical average discount of 9.43%.

Mark J. Mobius has been running the fund for 18 years and currently receives a manager quality ranking of 83 (0=worst, 99=best). If you desire an average level of risk, then this fund may be an option.

Data Date	Investment Rating	Net Assets ($Mil)	Price	Performance Rating/Pts	Total Return Y-T-D	Risk Rating/Pts
3-12	C	1,258.24	28.35	C / 5.4	11.39%	B- / 7.4
2011	C+	1,054.50	25.45	C+ / 6.3	1.26%	C+ / 6.9
2010	C+	1,092.71	30.74	B / 7.7	19.81%	C- / 4.2
2009	C	968.58	27.25	B- / 7.4	56.75%	C- / 3.8

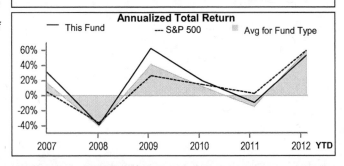

Templeton Emerging Markets Fd (EMF)

C   **Fair**

Fund Family: Templeton Asset Management Ltd
Fund Type: Emerging Market
Inception Date: March 5, 1987

Major Rating Factors: Middle of the road best describes Templeton Emerging Markets Fd whose TheStreet.com Investment Rating is currently a C (Fair). The fund currently has a performance rating of C+ (Fair) based on an annualized return of 25.77% over the last three years and a total return of 9.52% year to date 2012. Factored into the performance evaluation is an expense ratio of 1.46% (average).

The fund's risk rating is currently C+ (Fair). It carries a beta of 1.29, meaning it is expected to move 12.9% for every 10% move in the market. Volatility, as measured by both the semi-deviation and a drawdown factor, is considered low. As of March 31, 2012, Templeton Emerging Markets Fd traded at a discount of 7.82% below its net asset value, which is better than its one-year historical average discount of 5.83%.

Mark J. Mobius has been running the fund for 21 years and currently receives a manager quality ranking of 24 (0=worst, 99=best). If you desire an average level of risk, then this fund may be an option.

Data Date	Investment Rating	Net Assets ($Mil)	Price	Performance Rating/Pts	Total Return Y-T-D	Risk Rating/Pts
3-12	C	397.29	19.56	C+ / 5.9	9.52%	C+ / 6.6
2011	C	343.20	17.86	C+ / 6.4	2.13%	C+ / 6.7
2010	C	355.29	23.57	B / 7.7	20.71%	D+ / 2.7
2009	C	283.40	19.65	B+ / 8.5	110.52%	D+ / 2.9

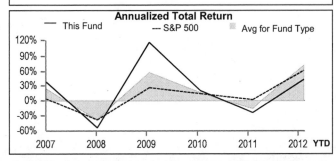

Templeton Emerging Markets Income (TEI)

C+   **Fair**

Fund Family: Franklin Advisers Inc
Fund Type: Emerging Market
Inception Date: September 23, 1993

Major Rating Factors: Strong performance is the major factor driving the C+ (Fair) TheStreet.com Investment Rating for Templeton Emerging Markets Income. The fund currently has a performance rating of B- (Good) based on an annualized return of 29.01% over the last three years and a total return of 2.31% year to date 2012. Factored into the performance evaluation is an expense ratio of 1.20% (average).

The fund's risk rating is currently B- (Good). It carries a beta of 1.24, meaning it is expected to move 12.4% for every 10% move in the market. Volatility, as measured by both the semi-deviation and a drawdown factor, is considered low. As of March 31, 2012, Templeton Emerging Markets Income traded at a discount of .82% below its net asset value, which is better than its one-year historical average premium of 1.92%.

Eddie Chow currently receives a manager quality ranking of 93 (0=worst, 99=best). If you desire only a moderate level of risk and strong performance, then this fund is an excellent option.

Data Date	Investment Rating	Net Assets ($Mil)	Price	Performance Rating/Pts	Total Return Y-T-D	Risk Rating/Pts
3-12	C+	790.00	15.68	B- / 7.2	2.31%	B- / 7.2
2011	B	714.20	15.57	B / 7.8	0.39%	B- / 7.9
2010	B	769.97	16.39	B+ / 8.6	21.06%	C / 4.3
2009	B-	653.99	14.41	B / 7.7	59.87%	C / 5.1

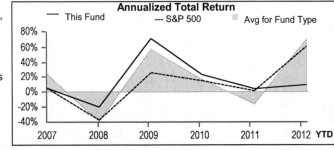

Templeton Global Income Fd (GIM)   C   Fair

Fund Family: Franklin Advisers Inc
Fund Type: Global
Inception Date: March 17, 1988

Major Rating Factors: Middle of the road best describes Templeton Global Income Fd whose TheStreet.com Investment Rating is currently a C (Fair). The fund currently has a performance rating of C (Fair) based on an annualized return of 18.49% over the last three years and a total return of 4.10% year to date 2012. Factored into the performance evaluation is an expense ratio of 0.74% (very low).

The fund's risk rating is currently B (Good). It carries a beta of 1.23, meaning it is expected to move 12.3% for every 10% move in the market. Volatility, as measured by both the semi-deviation and a drawdown factor, is considered low. As of March 31, 2012, Templeton Global Income Fd traded at a premium of 5.23% above its net asset value, which is better than its one-year historical average premium of 6.34%.

Michael Hasenstab has been running the fund for 24 years and currently receives a manager quality ranking of 85 (0=worst, 99=best). If you desire an average level of risk, then this fund may be an option.

Data Date	Investment Rating	Net Assets ($Mil)	Price	Performance Rating/Pts	Total Return Y-T-D	Risk Rating/Pts
3-12	C	1,338.95	9.65	C / 4.3	4.10%	B / 8.0
2011	C	1,338.95	9.45	C / 5.1	-0.21%	B- / 7.9
2010	A-	1,307.68	10.70	B+ / 8.5	19.09%	C+ / 6.3
2009	B-	1,160.28	9.50	C+ / 6.2	28.31%	B- / 7.3

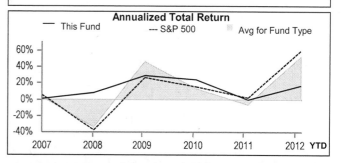

Templeton Russia&East European Fun (TRF)   D   Weak

Fund Family: Templeton Asset Management Ltd
Fund Type: Foreign
Inception Date: June 15, 1995

Major Rating Factors: Templeton Russia&East European Fun receives a TheStreet.com Investment Rating of D (Weak). The fund currently has a performance rating of C- (Fair) based on an annualized return of 19.41% over the last three years and a total return of 20.79% year to date 2012. Factored into the performance evaluation is an expense ratio of 1.79% (above average).

The fund's risk rating is currently C (Fair). It carries a beta of 1.77, meaning it is expected to move 17.7% for every 10% move in the market. Volatility, as measured by both the semi-deviation and a drawdown factor, is considered average. As of March 31, 2012, Templeton Russia&East European Fun traded at a discount of 7.59% below its net asset value, which is better than its one-year historical average discount of 6.70%.

Mark J. Mobius has been running the fund for 17 years and currently receives a manager quality ranking of 17 (0=worst, 99=best). If you desire an average level of risk, then this fund may be an option.

Data Date	Investment Rating	Net Assets ($Mil)	Price	Performance Rating/Pts	Total Return Y-T-D	Risk Rating/Pts
3-12	D	140.06	16.44	C- / 3.7	20.79%	C / 5.3
2011	D-	86.30	13.61	D+ / 2.3	2.57%	C / 5.3
2010	E	119.22	22.90	D / 1.9	26.42%	D / 1.6
2009	E	90.37	18.20	D- / 1.5	79.31%	D- / 1.5

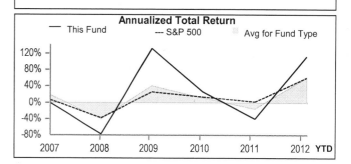

Thai Capital Fund (TF)   B-   Good

Fund Family: SCB Asset Management Co Ltd
Fund Type: Foreign
Inception Date: May 30, 1990

Major Rating Factors:
Exceptional performance is the major factor driving the B- (Good) TheStreet.com Investment Rating for Thai Capital Fund. The fund currently has a performance rating of A+ (Excellent) based on an annualized return of 41.48% over the last three years and a total return of 34.92% year to date 2012. Factored into the performance evaluation is an expense ratio of 2.14% (high).

The fund's risk rating is currently C (Fair). It carries a beta of 0.70, meaning the fund's expected move will be 7.0% for every 10% move in the market. Volatility, as measured by both the semi-deviation and a drawdown factor, is considered average. As of March 31, 2012, Thai Capital Fund traded at a discount of 4.77% below its net asset value, which is worse than its one-year historical average discount of 12.40%.

Sopana Janeborvorn currently receives a manager quality ranking of 96 (0=worst, 99=best). If you desire an average level of risk and strong performance, then this fund is a good option.

Data Date	Investment Rating	Net Assets ($Mil)	Price	Performance Rating/Pts	Total Return Y-T-D	Risk Rating/Pts
3-12	B-	51.20	11.58	A+ / 9.7	34.92%	C / 5.4
2011	C+	35.80	8.59	B / 8.0	1.86%	C / 5.4
2010	B+	36.87	13.63	A / 9.3	71.62%	C / 4.6
2009	C-	31.05	9.83	C- / 4.1	51.36%	C / 5.3

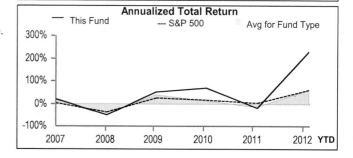

Thai Fund (TTF)　　　　　　　　　　　　　　　　　　A+　　Excellent

Fund Family: Morgan Stanley Investment Mgmt Inc
Fund Type: Foreign
Inception Date: February 17, 1988

Major Rating Factors:
Exceptional performance is the major factor driving the A+ (Excellent) TheStreet.com Investment Rating for Thai Fund. The fund currently has a performance rating of A+ (Excellent) based on an annualized return of 47.49% over the last three years and a total return of 30.02% year to date 2012. Factored into the performance evaluation is an expense ratio of 1.59% (above average).

The fund's risk rating is currently B- (Good). It carries a beta of 0.86, meaning the fund's expected move will be 8.6% for every 10% move in the market. Volatility, as measured by both the semi-deviation and a drawdown factor, is considered low. As of March 31, 2012, Thai Fund traded at a discount of 10.55% below its net asset value, which is worse than its one-year historical average discount of 14.28%.

James K.K. Cheng has been running the fund for 4 years and currently receives a manager quality ranking of 97 (0=worst, 99=best). If you desire only a moderate level of risk and strong performance, then this fund is an excellent option.

Data Date	Investment Rating	Net Assets ($Mil)	Price	Perfor- mance Rating/Pts	Total Return Y-T-D	Risk Rating/Pts
3-12	A+	235.07	15.94	A+ / 9.8	30.02%	B- / 7.9
2011	B+	215.80	12.26	B+ / 8.4	0.00%	B- / 7.9
2010	B+	180.33	12.80	B+ / 8.7	49.50%	C / 5.0
2009	C	139.46	8.93	C / 5.2	48.85%	C / 5.1

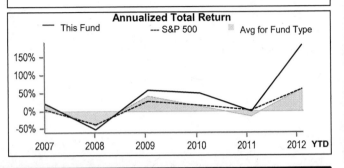

The Cushing MLP Total Return Fund (SRV)　　　　A-　　Excellent

Fund Family: Cushing MLP Asset Management LP
Fund Type: Growth and Income
Inception Date: August 27, 2007

Major Rating Factors:
Exceptional performance is the major factor driving the A- (Excellent) TheStreet.com Investment Rating for The Cushing MLP Total Return Fund. The fund currently has a performance rating of A (Excellent) based on an annualized return of 42.52% over the last three years and a total return of 14.40% year to date 2012. Factored into the performance evaluation is an expense ratio of 3.39% (high).

The fund's risk rating is currently B- (Good). It carries a beta of 0.97, meaning that its performance tracks fairly well with that of the overall stock market. Volatility, as measured by both the semi-deviation and a drawdown factor, is considered low. As of March 31, 2012, The Cushing MLP Total Return Fund traded at a premium of 28.85% above its net asset value, which is worse than its one-year historical average premium of 20.82%.

Daniel L. Spears currently receives a manager quality ranking of 91 (0=worst, 99=best). If you desire only a moderate level of risk and strong performance, then this fund is an excellent option.

Data Date	Investment Rating	Net Assets ($Mil)	Price	Perfor- mance Rating/Pts	Total Return Y-T-D	Risk Rating/Pts
3-12	A-	255.75	9.96	A / 9.4	14.40%	B- / 7.6
2011	B	258.40	8.90	B+ / 8.5	1.57%	B- / 7.4
2010	D	64.51	10.52	C+ / 5.8	33.98%	D- / 1.2
2009	C+	50.46	8.51	A+ / 9.9	118. 95%	D+ / 2.3

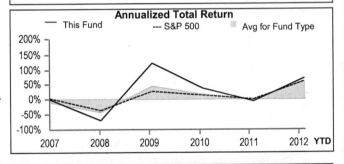

The Denali Fund Inc. (DNY)　　　　　　　　　　　C+　　Fair

Fund Family: Boulder Investment Advisors LLC
Fund Type: Growth and Income
Inception Date: November 25, 2002

Major Rating Factors: Middle of the road best describes The Denali Fund Inc. whose TheStreet.com Investment Rating is currently a C+ (Fair). The fund currently has a performance rating of C+ (Fair) based on an annualized return of 24.15% over the last three years and a total return of 11.87% year to date 2012. Factored into the performance evaluation is an expense ratio of 2.64% (high).

The fund's risk rating is currently B (Good). It carries a beta of 1.05, meaning that its performance tracks fairly well with that of the overall stock market. Volatility, as measured by both the semi-deviation and a drawdown factor, is considered low. As of March 31, 2012, The Denali Fund Inc. traded at a discount of 18.92% below its net asset value, which is better than its one-year historical average discount of 17.19%.

Stewart R. Horejsi currently receives a manager quality ranking of 55 (0=worst, 99=best). If you desire an average level of risk, then this fund may be an option.

Data Date	Investment Rating	Net Assets ($Mil)	Price	Perfor- mance Rating/Pts	Total Return Y-T-D	Risk Rating/Pts
3-12	C+	74.92	14.74	C+ / 6.0	11.87%	B / 8.0
2011	C-	70.50	13.23	C- / 3.8	4.01%	B- / 7.2
2010	C-	73.32	15.22	C- / 4.1	10.10%	C / 5.2
2009	D-	51.89	14.29	D / 1.6	33.76%	C / 4.9

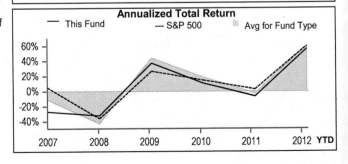

The European Equity Fund (EEA)   D+   Weak

Fund Family: Deutsche Asset Mgmt International G
Fund Type: Foreign
Inception Date: July 18, 1986

Major Rating Factors: The European Equity Fund receives a TheStreet.com Investment Rating of D+ (Weak). The fund currently has a performance rating of C- (Fair) based on an annualized return of 16.31% over the last three years and a total return of 14.14% year to date 2012. Factored into the performance evaluation is an expense ratio of 1.60% (above average).

The fund's risk rating is currently C+ (Fair). It carries a beta of 1.25, meaning it is expected to move 12.5% for every 10% move in the market. Volatility, as measured by both the semi-deviation and a drawdown factor, is considered low. As of March 31, 2012, The European Equity Fund traded at a discount of 9.84% below its net asset value, which is better than its one-year historical average discount of 9.39%.

Theresa M. Gusman currently receives a manager quality ranking of 26 (0=worst, 99=best). If you desire an average level of risk, then this fund may be an option.

Data Date	Investment Rating	Net Assets ($Mil)	Price	Performance Rating/Pts	Total Return Y-T-D	Risk Rating/Pts
3-12	D+	72.02	6.78	C- / 3.4	14.14%	C+ / 6.6
2011	D	72.00	5.94	D / 1.9	-0.17%	C+ / 6.5
2010	E+	97.38	7.58	D- / 1.2	8.61%	D+ / 2.9
2009	D-	77.28	7.03	D- / 1.4	30.74%	C / 4.6

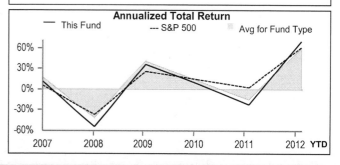

The New Ireland Fund (IRL)   C   Fair

Fund Family: Kleinwort Benson Investors Intl Ltd
Fund Type: Foreign
Inception Date: March 30, 1990

Major Rating Factors: Middle of the road best describes The New Ireland Fund whose TheStreet.com Investment Rating is currently a C (Fair). The fund currently has a performance rating of C+ (Fair) based on an annualized return of 21.68% over the last three years and a total return of 17.00% year to date 2012. Factored into the performance evaluation is an expense ratio of 2.22% (high).

The fund's risk rating is currently C+ (Fair). It carries a beta of 1.18, meaning it is expected to move 11.8% for every 10% move in the market. Volatility, as measured by both the semi-deviation and a drawdown factor, is considered low. As of March 31, 2012, The New Ireland Fund traded at a discount of 13.71% below its net asset value, which is better than its one-year historical average discount of 11.73%.

Noel O'Halloran has been running the fund for 1 year and currently receives a manager quality ranking of 70 (0=worst, 99=best). If you desire an average level of risk, then this fund may be an option.

Data Date	Investment Rating	Net Assets ($Mil)	Price	Performance Rating/Pts	Total Return Y-T-D	Risk Rating/Pts
3-12	C	54.07	8.12	C+ / 5.7	17.00%	C+ / 6.9
2011	D+	51.30	6.94	C- / 3.5	1.59%	C+ / 6.7
2010	E	58.57	6.86	E+ / 0.6	-2.52%	D+ / 2.5
2009	E	47.05	7.10	E+ / 0.6	42.03%	D+ / 2.6

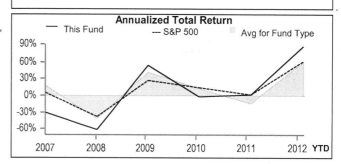

Tortoise Energy Capital (TYY)   B-   Good

Fund Family: Tortoise Capital Advisors LLC
Fund Type: Energy/Natural Resources
Inception Date: May 31, 2005

Major Rating Factors: Strong performance is the major factor driving the B- (Good) TheStreet.com Investment Rating for Tortoise Energy Capital. The fund currently has a performance rating of B- (Good) based on an annualized return of 27.60% over the last three years and a total return of 7.17% year to date 2012. Factored into the performance evaluation is an expense ratio of 3.93% (high).

The fund's risk rating is currently B- (Good). It carries a beta of 0.63, meaning the fund's expected move will be 6.3% for every 10% move in the market. Volatility, as measured by both the semi-deviation and a drawdown factor, is considered low. As of March 31, 2012, Tortoise Energy Capital traded at a premium of 4.85% above its net asset value, which is worse than its one-year historical average premium of 2.51%.

H. Kevin Birzer has been running the fund for 7 years and currently receives a manager quality ranking of 90 (0=worst, 99=best). If you desire only a moderate level of risk and strong performance, then this fund is an excellent option.

Data Date	Investment Rating	Net Assets ($Mil)	Price	Performance Rating/Pts	Total Return Y-T-D	Risk Rating/Pts
3-12	B-	500.13	28.34	B- / 7.4	7.17%	B- / 7.9
2011	B+	532.30	26.83	A- / 9.0	1.90%	B- / 7.9
2010	B-	356.02	27.77	B+ / 8.6	29.80%	C- / 3.9
2009	C+	300.60	22.88	B / 7.8	90.71%	C- / 4.0

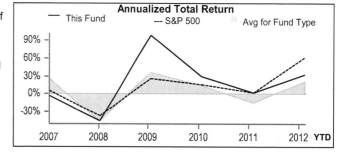

Tortoise Energy Infrastr Corp (TYG)

A **Excellent**

Fund Family: Tortoise Capital Advisors LLC
Fund Type: Energy/Natural Resources
Inception Date: February 27, 2004

Major Rating Factors:
Strong performance is the major factor driving the A (Excellent) TheStreet.com Investment Rating for Tortoise Energy Infrastr Corp. The fund currently has a performance rating of B+ (Good) based on an annualized return of 33.82% over the last three years and a total return of 4.53% year to date 2012. Factored into the performance evaluation is an expense ratio of 3.47% (high).

The fund's risk rating is currently B (Good). It carries a beta of 0.60, meaning the fund's expected move will be 6.0% for every 10% move in the market. Volatility, as measured by both the semi-deviation and a drawdown factor, is considered low. As of March 31, 2012, Tortoise Energy Infrastr Corp traded at a premium of 16.15% above its net asset value, which is worse than its one-year historical average premium of 13.75%.

H. Kevin Birzer has been running the fund for 8 years and currently receives a manager quality ranking of 93 (0=worst, 99=best). If you desire only a moderate level of risk and strong performance, then this fund is an excellent option.

Data Date	Investment Rating	Net Assets ($Mil)	Price	Performance Rating/Pts	Total Return Y-T-D	Risk Rating/Pts
3-12	A	925.42	41.22	B+ / 8.7	4.53%	B / 8.5
2011	A	990.20	39.99	A+ / 9.6	1.23%	B / 8.3
2010	B+	613.60	38.25	B+ / 8.8	32.04%	C / 5.0
2009	B	510.54	31.02	B / 8.0	95.84%	C / 5.4

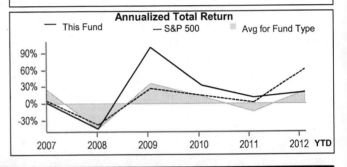

Annualized Total Return

Tortoise MLP Fund Inc (NTG)

C- **Fair**

Fund Family: Tortoise Capital Advisors LLC
Fund Type: Growth
Inception Date: July 30, 2010

Major Rating Factors:
Disappointing performance is the major factor driving the C- (Fair) TheStreet.com Investment Rating for Tortoise MLP Fund Inc. The fund currently has a performance rating of D+ (Weak) based on an annualized return of 0.00% over the last three years and a total return of 0.97% year to date 2012. Factored into the performance evaluation is an expense ratio of 2.33% (high).

The fund's risk rating is currently B (Good). It carries a beta of 0.00, meaning the fund's expected move will be 0.0% for every 10% move in the market. Volatility, as measured by both the semi-deviation and a drawdown factor, is considered low. As of March 31, 2012, Tortoise MLP Fund Inc traded at a premium of .43% above its net asset value, which is better than its one-year historical average premium of .89%.

This is team managed and currently receives a manager quality ranking of 35 (0=worst, 99=best). This fund offers only a moderate level of risk but investors looking for strong performance are still waiting.

Data Date	Investment Rating	Net Assets ($Mil)	Price	Performance Rating/Pts	Total Return Y-T-D	Risk Rating/Pts
3-12	C-	1,140.95	25.62	D+ / 2.6	0.97%	B / 8.5
2011	B-	1,178.50	25.77	C+ / 5.9	-0.31%	B / 8.5

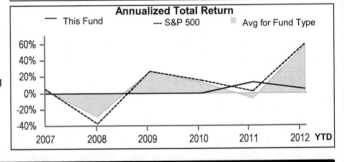

Annualized Total Return

Tortoise North American Energy (TYN)

A **Excellent**

Fund Family: Tortoise Capital Advisors LLC
Fund Type: Energy/Natural Resources
Inception Date: October 31, 2005

Major Rating Factors:
Strong performance is the major factor driving the A (Excellent) TheStreet.com Investment Rating for Tortoise North American Energy. The fund currently has a performance rating of B+ (Good) based on an annualized return of 33.97% over the last three years and a total return of 6.42% year to date 2012. Factored into the performance evaluation is an expense ratio of 2.00% (high).

The fund's risk rating is currently B (Good). It carries a beta of 0.34, meaning the fund's expected move will be 3.4% for every 10% move in the market. Volatility, as measured by both the semi-deviation and a drawdown factor, is considered low. As of March 31, 2012, Tortoise North American Energy traded at a discount of 1.12% below its net asset value, which is worse than its one-year historical average discount of 4.22%.

H. Kevin Birzer has been running the fund for 7 years and currently receives a manager quality ranking of 97 (0=worst, 99=best). If you desire only a moderate level of risk and strong performance, then this fund is an excellent option.

Data Date	Investment Rating	Net Assets ($Mil)	Price	Performance Rating/Pts	Total Return Y-T-D	Risk Rating/Pts
3-12	A	155.94	25.65	B+ / 8.6	6.42%	B / 8.8
2011	A-	162.20	24.46	B+ / 8.9	1.35%	B / 8.5
2010	C+	126.61	25.00	B / 7.8	21.51%	C- / 3.9
2009	C+	77.01	21.93	B+ / 8.4	103.63%	C- / 4.2

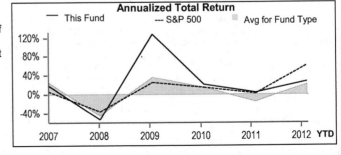

Annualized Total Return

Tortoise Power and Energy Inf Fund (TPZ)   C-   Fair

Fund Family: Tortoise Capital Advisors LLC
Fund Type: Energy/Natural Resources
Inception Date: July 29, 2009

Major Rating Factors: Middle of the road best describes Tortoise Power and Energy Inf Fund whose TheStreet.com Investment Rating is currently a C- (Fair). The fund currently has a performance rating of C- (Fair) based on an annualized return of 0.00% over the last three years and a total return of 3.09% year to date 2012. Factored into the performance evaluation is an expense ratio of 1.65% (above average).

The fund's risk rating is currently B (Good). It carries a beta of 0.00, meaning the fund's expected move will be 0.0% for every 10% move in the market. Volatility, as measured by both the semi-deviation and a drawdown factor, is considered low. As of March 31, 2012, Tortoise Power and Energy Inf Fund traded at a discount of 2.27% below its net asset value, which is worse than its one-year historical average discount of 3.14%.

Zachary A. Hamel currently receives a manager quality ranking of 81 (0=worst, 99=best). If you desire an average level of risk, then this fund may be an option.

Data Date	Investment Rating	Net Assets ($Mil)	Price	Performance Rating/Pts	Total Return Y-T-D	Risk Rating/Pts
3-12	C-	176.33	25.39	C- / 3.1	3.09%	B / 8.6
2011	C+	182.50	24.99	C / 4.6	-0.36%	B / 8.6
2010	A+	0.00	24.49	A / 9.4	29.38%	B / 8.3

Annualized Total Return

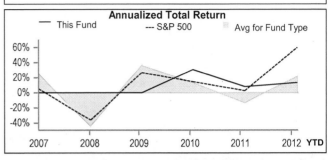

Transamerica Income Shares (TAI)   C+   Fair

Fund Family: Transamerica Asset Management Inc
Fund Type: Global
Inception Date: November 9, 1972

Major Rating Factors: Middle of the road best describes Transamerica Income Shares whose TheStreet.com Investment Rating is currently a C+ (Fair). The fund currently has a performance rating of C (Fair) based on an annualized return of 19.93% over the last three years and a total return of 2.58% year to date 2012. Factored into the performance evaluation is an expense ratio of 0.80% (very low).

The fund's risk rating is currently B+ (Good). It carries a beta of 0.08, meaning the fund's expected move will be 0.8% for every 10% move in the market. Volatility, as measured by both the semi-deviation and a drawdown factor, is considered very low. As of March 31, 2012, Transamerica Income Shares traded at a discount of 1.98% below its net asset value, which is worse than its one-year historical average discount of 2.41%.

Bradley J. Beman currently receives a manager quality ranking of 91 (0=worst, 99=best). If you desire an average level of risk, then this fund may be an option.

Data Date	Investment Rating	Net Assets ($Mil)	Price	Performance Rating/Pts	Total Return Y-T-D	Risk Rating/Pts
3-12	C+	141.91	21.79	C / 4.6	2.58%	B+ / 9.1
2011	B	136.70	21.60	C+ / 6.7	0.49%	B+ / 9.0
2010	C+	139.24	20.70	C+ / 6.7	12.22%	C+ / 6.2
2009	C+	132.60	20.05	C / 5.5	33.33%	C+ / 6.8

Annualized Total Return

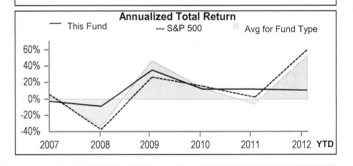

Tri-Continental Corporation (TY)   B-   Good

Fund Family: Columbia Management Inv Advisers LL
Fund Type: Income
Inception Date: N/A

Major Rating Factors: Strong performance is the major factor driving the B- (Good) TheStreet.com Investment Rating for Tri-Continental Corporation. The fund currently has a performance rating of B- (Good) based on an annualized return of 24.71% over the last three years and a total return of 12.62% year to date 2012. Factored into the performance evaluation is an expense ratio of 0.60% (very low).

The fund's risk rating is currently B (Good). It carries a beta of 1.11, meaning it is expected to move 11.1% for every 10% move in the market. Volatility, as measured by both the semi-deviation and a drawdown factor, is considered low. As of March 31, 2012, Tri-Continental Corporation traded at a discount of 14.73% below its net asset value, which is better than its one-year historical average discount of 14.22%.

Brian M. Condon has been running the fund for 2 years and currently receives a manager quality ranking of 47 (0=worst, 99=best). If you desire only a moderate level of risk and strong performance, then this fund is an excellent option.

Data Date	Investment Rating	Net Assets ($Mil)	Price	Performance Rating/Pts	Total Return Y-T-D	Risk Rating/Pts
3-12	B-	1,061.25	15.92	B- / 7.1	12.62%	B / 8.2
2011	C+	1,078.20	14.23	C+ / 6.0	1.97%	B / 8.0
2010	C-	946.34	13.76	D+ / 2.9	21.82%	C+ / 6.1
2009	D	778.22	11.52	D- / 1.0	14.61%	C+ / 5.8

Annualized Total Return

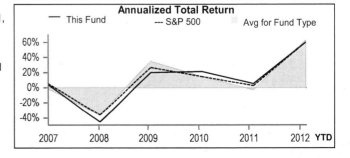

Turkish Investment Fund (TKF)

C+   **Fair**

Fund Family: Morgan Stanley Investment Mgmt Inc
Fund Type: Foreign
Inception Date: December 5, 1989

Data Date	Investment Rating	Net Assets ($Mil)	Price	Perfor-mance Rating/Pts	Total Return Y-T-D	Risk Rating/Pts
3-12	C+	108.28	13.65	B+ / 8.6	23.42%	C+ / 6.2
2011	C-	93.40	11.06	C / 5.1	0.81%	C+ / 6.1
2010	D	97.73	16.50	C- / 3.0	24.92%	C- / 3.8
2009	C	60.26	13.37	C+ / 6.9	112.38%	C- / 3.7

Major Rating Factors: Strong performance is the major factor driving the C+ (Fair) TheStreet.com Investment Rating for Turkish Investment Fund. The fund currently has a performance rating of B+ (Good) based on an annualized return of 36.26% over the last three years and a total return of 23.42% year to date 2012. Factored into the performance evaluation is an expense ratio of 1.05% (low).

The fund's risk rating is currently C+ (Fair). It carries a beta of 1.35, meaning it is expected to move 13.5% for every 10% move in the market. Volatility, as measured by both the semi-deviation and a drawdown factor, is considered low. As of March 31, 2012, Turkish Investment Fund traded at a discount of 11.82% below its net asset value, which is better than its one-year historical average discount of 10.46%.

Paul C. Psaila has been running the fund for 15 years and currently receives a manager quality ranking of 88 (0=worst, 99=best). If you desire only a moderate level of risk and strong performance, then this fund is an excellent option.

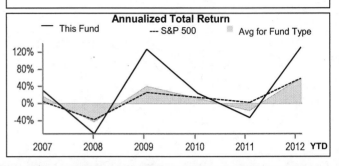

Virtus Total Return (DCA)

A+   **Excellent**

Fund Family: Virtus Investment Advisers Inc
Fund Type: Growth and Income
Inception Date: February 23, 2005

Data Date	Investment Rating	Net Assets ($Mil)	Price	Perfor-mance Rating/Pts	Total Return Y-T-D	Risk Rating/Pts
3-12	A+	111.49	3.80	A+ / 9.7	11.01%	B / 8.2
2011	C+	111.50	3.50	B+ / 8.4	-0.57%	C / 5.5
2010	D-	39.18	3.45	D / 2.1	53.64%	C- / 3.2
2009	E	30.47	2.39	E / 0.4	28.00%	C- / 3.4

Major Rating Factors:
Exceptional performance is the major factor driving the A+ (Excellent) TheStreet.com Investment Rating for Virtus Total Return. The fund currently has a performance rating of A+ (Excellent) based on an annualized return of 49.46% over the last three years and a total return of 11.01% year to date 2012. Factored into the performance evaluation is an expense ratio of 1.38% (average).

The fund's risk rating is currently B (Good). It carries a beta of 1.36, meaning it is expected to move 13.6% for every 10% move in the market. Volatility, as measured by both the semi-deviation and a drawdown factor, is considered low. As of March 31, 2012, Virtus Total Return traded at a discount of 8.65% below its net asset value, which is worse than its one-year historical average discount of 12.99%.

Connie M. Luecke currently receives a manager quality ranking of 91 (0=worst, 99=best). If you desire only a moderate level of risk and strong performance, then this fund is an excellent option.

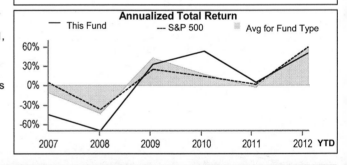

Wells Fargo Avtg Global Div Oppty (EOD)

D+   **Weak**

Fund Family: Wells Fargo Fund Management LLC
Fund Type: Global
Inception Date: March 28, 2007

Data Date	Investment Rating	Net Assets ($Mil)	Price	Perfor-mance Rating/Pts	Total Return Y-T-D	Risk Rating/Pts
3-12	D+	438.08	8.52	C- / 3.5	15.92%	B- / 7.4
2011	D+	413.70	7.59	D+ / 2.4	3.56%	B- / 7.3
2010	D-	561.05	9.55	D- / 1.1	2.46%	C / 5.2
2009	C+	475.34	10.24	B- / 7.3	18.74%	C / 5.4

Major Rating Factors: Wells Fargo Avtg Global Div Oppty receives a TheStreet.com Investment Rating of D+ (Weak). The fund currently has a performance rating of C- (Fair) based on an annualized return of 14.54% over the last three years and a total return of 15.92% year to date 2012. Factored into the performance evaluation is an expense ratio of 1.05% (low).

The fund's risk rating is currently B- (Good). It carries a beta of 0.83, meaning the fund's expected move will be 8.3% for every 10% move in the market. Volatility, as measured by both the semi-deviation and a drawdown factor, is considered low. As of March 31, 2012, Wells Fargo Avtg Global Div Oppty traded at a discount of 2.29% below its net asset value, which is worse than its one-year historical average discount of 3.52%.

Jeffrey P. Mellas currently receives a manager quality ranking of 53 (0=worst, 99=best). If you desire an average level of risk, then this fund may be an option.

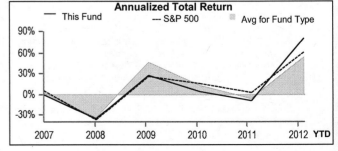

Wells Fargo Avtg Income Oppty (EAD)

B-   **Good**

Fund Family: Wells Fargo Fund Management LLC
Fund Type: Corporate - High Yield
Inception Date: February 26, 2003

Major Rating Factors: Strong performance is the major factor driving the B- (Good) TheStreet.com Investment Rating for Wells Fargo Avtg Income Oppty. The fund currently has a performance rating of B (Good) based on an annualized return of 29.64% over the last three years and a total return of 3.15% year to date 2012. Factored into the performance evaluation is an expense ratio of 1.09% (low).

The fund's risk rating is currently B- (Good). It carries a beta of 1.33, meaning it is expected to move 13.3% for every 10% move in the market. Volatility, as measured by both the semi-deviation and a drawdown factor, is considered low. As of March 31, 2012, Wells Fargo Avtg Income Oppty traded at a premium of 5.79% above its net asset value, which is worse than its one-year historical average premium of 4.24%.

Niklas Nordenfelt currently receives a manager quality ranking of 47 (0=worst, 99=best). If you desire only a moderate level of risk and strong performance, then this fund is an excellent option.

Data Date	Investment Rating	Net Assets ($Mil)	Price	Performance Rating/Pts	Total Return Y-T-D	Risk Rating/Pts
3-12	B-	709.85	10.24	B / 7.7	3.15%	B- / 7.2
2011	B	667.50	10.18	A- / 9.0	0.49%	B- / 7.1
2010	C-	676.14	9.63	C+ / 6.5	12.95%	C- / 3.4
2009	C-	508.60	9.51	C / 5.2	84.05%	C / 4.6

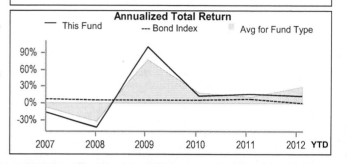

Wells Fargo Avtg Multi-Sector Inc (ERC)

C+   **Fair**

Fund Family: Wells Fargo Fund Management LLC
Fund Type: Global
Inception Date: June 25, 2003

Major Rating Factors: Middle of the road best describes Wells Fargo Avtg Multi-Sector Inc whose TheStreet.com Investment Rating is currently a C+ (Fair). The fund currently has a performance rating of C+ (Fair) based on an annualized return of 22.67% over the last three years and a total return of 4.43% year to date 2012. Factored into the performance evaluation is an expense ratio of 1.14% (low).

The fund's risk rating is currently B (Good). It carries a beta of 0.65, meaning the fund's expected move will be 6.5% for every 10% move in the market. Volatility, as measured by both the semi-deviation and a drawdown factor, is considered low. As of March 31, 2012, Wells Fargo Avtg Multi-Sector Inc traded at a discount of 7.80% below its net asset value, which is worse than its one-year historical average discount of 8.09%.

Anthony J. Norris currently receives a manager quality ranking of 92 (0=worst, 99=best). If you desire an average level of risk, then this fund may be an option.

Data Date	Investment Rating	Net Assets ($Mil)	Price	Performance Rating/Pts	Total Return Y-T-D	Risk Rating/Pts
3-12	C+	679.50	15.14	C+ / 5.6	4.43%	B / 8.7
2011	B	668.70	14.78	B- / 7.0	1.01%	B / 8.6
2010	B-	677.42	15.32	B / 7.7	17.47%	C / 4.9
2009	C+	546.30	14.18	C+ / 6.1	46.45%	C+ / 5.6

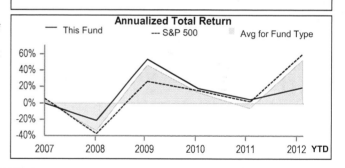

Wells Fargo Avtg Utilities&High In (ERH)

C-   **Fair**

Fund Family: Wells Fargo Fund Management LLC
Fund Type: Utilities
Inception Date: April 28, 2004

Major Rating Factors: Middle of the road best describes Wells Fargo Avtg Utilities&High In whose TheStreet.com Investment Rating is currently a C- (Fair). The fund currently has a performance rating of C (Fair) based on an annualized return of 16.97% over the last three years and a total return of 9.33% year to date 2012. Factored into the performance evaluation is an expense ratio of 1.24% (average).

The fund's risk rating is currently C+ (Fair). It carries a beta of 0.77, meaning the fund's expected move will be 7.7% for every 10% move in the market. Volatility, as measured by both the semi-deviation and a drawdown factor, is considered low. As of March 31, 2012, Wells Fargo Avtg Utilities&High In traded at a premium of 1.44% above its net asset value, which is worse than its one-year historical average discount of 3.82%.

Timothy P. O'Brien has been running the fund for 8 years and currently receives a manager quality ranking of 74 (0=worst, 99=best). If you desire an average level of risk, then this fund may be an option.

Data Date	Investment Rating	Net Assets ($Mil)	Price	Performance Rating/Pts	Total Return Y-T-D	Risk Rating/Pts
3-12	C-	108.15	11.96	C / 4.4	9.33%	C+ / 6.6
2011	D+	107.60	11.15	C- / 3.5	1.08%	C+ / 6.2
2010	D-	103.25	11.59	E+ / 0.6	-14.38%	C / 4.9
2009	D	103.69	14.73	C- / 3.1	40.56%	C / 4.5

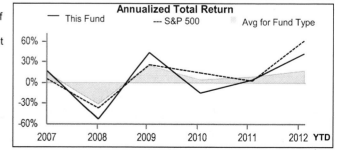

Western Asset Emerging Market Debt (ESD)

B   **Good**

Fund Family: Legg Mason Partners Fund Advisor LL
Fund Type: Emerging Market
Inception Date: December 1, 2003

Major Rating Factors: Strong performance is the major factor driving the B (Good) TheStreet.com Investment Rating for Western Asset Emerging Market Debt. The fund currently has a performance rating of B- (Good) based on an annualized return of 27.60% over the last three years and a total return of 8.35% year to date 2012. Factored into the performance evaluation is an expense ratio of 1.02% (low).

The fund's risk rating is currently B (Good). It carries a beta of 0.81, meaning the fund's expected move will be 8.1% for every 10% move in the market. Volatility, as measured by both the semi-deviation and a drawdown factor, is considered low. As of March 31, 2012, Western Asset Emerging Market Debt traded at a discount of 5.89% below its net asset value, which is worse than its one-year historical average discount of 8.10%.

S. Kenneth Leech currently receives a manager quality ranking of 95 (0=worst, 99=best). If you desire only a moderate level of risk and strong performance, then this fund is an excellent option.

Data Date	Investment Rating	Net Assets ($Mil)	Price	Performance Rating/Pts	Total Return Y-T-D	Risk Rating/Pts
3-12	B	632.27	20.13	B- / 7.5	8.35%	B / 8.4
2011	B	632.10	18.90	B / 7.9	0.74%	B- / 7.9
2010	B-	600.30	18.31	B- / 7.3	13.69%	C / 5.1
2009	C+	452.15	17.36	C+ / 6.8	51.88%	C / 5.3

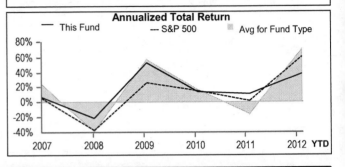

Western Asset Emerging Mkts Inc (EMD)

B   **Good**

Fund Family: Legg Mason Partners Fund Advisor LL
Fund Type: Emerging Market
Inception Date: June 18, 1993

Major Rating Factors: Strong performance is the major factor driving the B (Good) TheStreet.com Investment Rating for Western Asset Emerging Mkts Inc. The fund currently has a performance rating of B (Good) based on an annualized return of 28.27% over the last three years and a total return of 8.28% year to date 2012. Factored into the performance evaluation is an expense ratio of 1.23% (average).

The fund's risk rating is currently B (Good). It carries a beta of 1.04, meaning that its performance tracks fairly well with that of the overall stock market. Volatility, as measured by both the semi-deviation and a drawdown factor, is considered low. As of March 31, 2012, Western Asset Emerging Mkts Inc traded at a discount of 5.68% below its net asset value, which is worse than its one-year historical average discount of 7.35%.

S. Kenneth Leech currently receives a manager quality ranking of 94 (0=worst, 99=best). If you desire only a moderate level of risk and strong performance, then this fund is an excellent option.

Data Date	Investment Rating	Net Assets ($Mil)	Price	Performance Rating/Pts	Total Return Y-T-D	Risk Rating/Pts
3-12	B	430.38	14.28	B / 7.8	8.28%	B / 8.4
2011	B	416.80	13.41	B / 7.9	0.75%	B / 8.0
2010	B	392.18	13.06	B- / 7.4	14.02%	C / 5.5
2009	B-	350.61	12.31	B- / 7.2	61.16%	C+ / 5.6

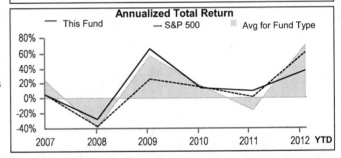

Western Asset Global Corp Def Oppt (GDO)

C+   **Fair**

Fund Family: Legg Mason Partners Fund Advisor LL
Fund Type: Global
Inception Date: November 23, 2009

Major Rating Factors: Middle of the road best describes Western Asset Global Corp Def Oppt whose TheStreet.com Investment Rating is currently a C+ (Fair). The fund currently has a performance rating of C (Fair) based on an annualized return of 0.00% over the last three years and a total return of 9.28% year to date 2012. Factored into the performance evaluation is an expense ratio of 1.40% (average).

The fund's risk rating is currently B (Good). It carries a beta of 0.00, meaning the fund's expected move will be 0.0% for every 10% move in the market. Volatility, as measured by both the semi-deviation and a drawdown factor, is considered low. As of March 31, 2012, Western Asset Global Corp Def Oppt traded at a discount of 2.28% below its net asset value, which is worse than its one-year historical average discount of 5.16%.

Ryan K. Brist currently receives a manager quality ranking of 87 (0=worst, 99=best). If you desire an average level of risk, then this fund may be an option.

Data Date	Investment Rating	Net Assets ($Mil)	Price	Performance Rating/Pts	Total Return Y-T-D	Risk Rating/Pts
3-12	C+	291.50	19.28	C / 5.5	9.28%	B / 8.5
2011	C+	281.90	18.00	C / 4.8	2.06%	B / 8.5
2010	C-	0.00	17.93	D / 2.1	-2.44%	B- / 7.7

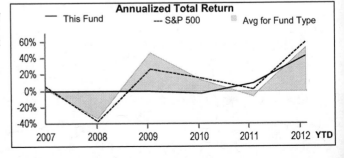

Western Asset Global High Income (EHI)

B+   **Good**

Fund Family: Legg Mason Partners Fund Advisor LL
Fund Type: Global
Inception Date: July 29, 2003

Data Date	Investment Rating	Net Assets ($Mil)	Price	Performance Rating/Pts	Total Return Y-T-D	Risk Rating/Pts
3-12	B+	417.57	13.25	B+ / 8.9	7.50%	B- / 7.3
2011	B-	380.80	12.60	B / 8.2	-0.87%	B- / 7.0
2010	B	369.75	12.88	B+ / 8.6	27.13%	C / 4.3
2009	C	313.21	11.08	C+ / 6.4	63.21%	C / 5.0

Major Rating Factors: Strong performance is the major factor driving the B+ (Good) TheStreet.com Investment Rating for Western Asset Global High Income. The fund currently has a performance rating of B+ (Good) based on an annualized return of 35.46% over the last three years and a total return of 7.50% year to date 2012. Factored into the performance evaluation is an expense ratio of 1.53% (average).

The fund's risk rating is currently B- (Good). It carries a beta of 0.78, meaning the fund's expected move will be 7.8% for every 10% move in the market. Volatility, as measured by both the semi-deviation and a drawdown factor, is considered low. As of March 31, 2012, Western Asset Global High Income traded at a premium of .38% above its net asset value, which is worse than its one-year historical average discount of 1.98%.

S. Kenneth Leech currently receives a manager quality ranking of 97 (0=worst, 99=best). If you desire only a moderate level of risk and strong performance, then this fund is an excellent option.

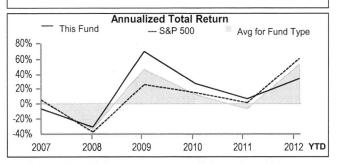

Western Asset Global Partners Inc (GDF)

B   **Good**

Fund Family: Legg Mason Partners Fund Advisor LL
Fund Type: Global
Inception Date: October 21, 1993

Data Date	Investment Rating	Net Assets ($Mil)	Price	Performance Rating/Pts	Total Return Y-T-D	Risk Rating/Pts
3-12	B	179.30	12.90	B+ / 8.7	0.64%	B- / 7.0
2011	B+	172.30	13.12	A+ / 9.6	0.69%	B- / 7.1
2010	C+	178.84	11.87	B / 8.2	13.69%	C- / 4.1
2009	C+	154.06	11.50	B / 8.0	98.86%	C- / 4.0

Major Rating Factors: Strong performance is the major factor driving the B (Good) TheStreet.com Investment Rating for Western Asset Global Partners Inc. The fund currently has a performance rating of B+ (Good) based on an annualized return of 34.72% over the last three years and a total return of 0.64% year to date 2012. Factored into the performance evaluation is an expense ratio of 1.66% (above average).

The fund's risk rating is currently B- (Good). It carries a beta of 1.04, meaning that its performance tracks fairly well with that of the overall stock market. Volatility, as measured by both the semi-deviation and a drawdown factor, is considered low. As of March 31, 2012, Western Asset Global Partners Inc traded at a premium of 8.77% above its net asset value, which is better than its one-year historical average premium of 8.79%.

Stephen A. Walsh currently receives a manager quality ranking of 96 (0=worst, 99=best). If you desire only a moderate level of risk and strong performance, then this fund is an excellent option.

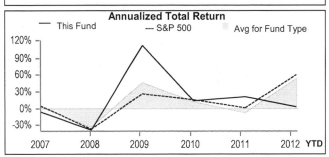

Western Asset High Inc Fd II (HIX)

B+   **Good**

Fund Family: Legg Mason Partners Fund Advisor LL
Fund Type: Global
Inception Date: May 22, 1998

Data Date	Investment Rating	Net Assets ($Mil)	Price	Performance Rating/Pts	Total Return Y-T-D	Risk Rating/Pts
3-12	B+	807.32	9.99	A- / 9.0	6.33%	B- / 7.5
2011	B	709.60	9.64	A / 9.3	1.97%	C+ / 6.6
2010	C+	751.12	9.37	B / 7.8	15.24%	C- / 3.9
2009	C	504.96	9.16	B / 8.0	100.71%	D+ / 2.9

Major Rating Factors:
Exceptional performance is the major factor driving the B+ (Good) TheStreet.com Investment Rating for Western Asset High Inc Fd II. The fund currently has a performance rating of A- (Excellent) based on an annualized return of 37.15% over the last three years and a total return of 6.33% year to date 2012. Factored into the performance evaluation is an expense ratio of 1.61% (above average).

The fund's risk rating is currently B- (Good). It carries a beta of 0.72, meaning the fund's expected move will be 7.2% for every 10% move in the market. Volatility, as measured by both the semi-deviation and a drawdown factor, is considered low. As of March 31, 2012, Western Asset High Inc Fd II traded at a premium of 12.75% above its net asset value, which is worse than its one-year historical average premium of 12.05%.

S. Kenneth Leech currently receives a manager quality ranking of 97 (0=worst, 99=best). If you desire only a moderate level of risk and strong performance, then this fund is an excellent option.

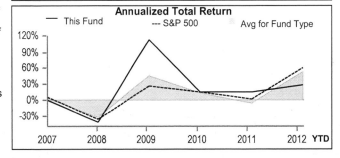

Western Asset High Income Fund (HIF)

C **Fair**

Fund Family: Legg Mason Partners Fund Advisor LL
Fund Type: Corporate - High Yield
Inception Date: January 22, 1993

Major Rating Factors: Middle of the road best describes Western Asset High Income Fund whose TheStreet.com Investment Rating is currently a C (Fair). The fund currently has a performance rating of C (Fair) based on an annualized return of 22.29% over the last three years and a total return of 10.17% year to date 2012. Factored into the performance evaluation is an expense ratio of 1.11% (low).

The fund's risk rating is currently B- (Good). It carries a beta of 0.86, meaning the fund's expected move will be 8.6% for every 10% move in the market. Volatility, as measured by both the semi-deviation and a drawdown factor, is considered low. As of March 31, 2012, Western Asset High Income Fund traded at a premium of 3.77% above its net asset value, which is better than its one-year historical average premium of 4.85%.

S. Kenneth Leech has been running the fund for 6 years and currently receives a manager quality ranking of 69 (0=worst, 99=best). If you desire an average level of risk, then this fund may be an option.

Data Date	Investment Rating	Net Assets ($Mil)	Price	Perfor- mance Rating/Pts	Total Return Y-T-D	Risk Rating/Pts
3-12	C	46.44	9.64	C / 5.3	10.17%	B- / 7.4
2011	C+	46.40	8.93	C+ / 6.5	2.24%	B- / 7.2
2010	B-	46.79	10.05	B+ / 8.4	19.67%	C- / 4.2
2009	C+	40.02	9.24	B- / 7.3	63.57%	C / 5.1

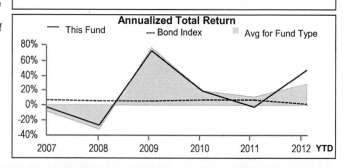

Western Asset High Income Opp Inc. (HIO)

C+ **Fair**

Fund Family: Legg Mason Partners Fund Advisor LL
Fund Type: Corporate - High Yield
Inception Date: October 21, 1993

Major Rating Factors: Middle of the road best describes Western Asset High Income Opp Inc. whose TheStreet.com Investment Rating is currently a C+ (Fair). The fund currently has a performance rating of C+ (Fair) based on an annualized return of 25.73% over the last three years and a total return of 1.92% year to date 2012. Factored into the performance evaluation is an expense ratio of 0.89% (low).

The fund's risk rating is currently B- (Good). It carries a beta of 1.02, meaning that its performance tracks fairly well with that of the overall stock market. Volatility, as measured by both the semi-deviation and a drawdown factor, is considered low. As of March 31, 2012, Western Asset High Income Opp Inc. traded at a premium of .33% above its net asset value, which is better than its one-year historical average premium of 1.13%.

Michael C. Buchanan has been running the fund for 6 years and currently receives a manager quality ranking of 56 (0=worst, 99=best). If you desire an average level of risk, then this fund may be an option.

Data Date	Investment Rating	Net Assets ($Mil)	Price	Perfor- mance Rating/Pts	Total Return Y-T-D	Risk Rating/Pts
3-12	C+	433.00	6.16	C+ / 6.4	1.92%	B- / 7.4
2011	B	443.00	6.17	B / 7.8	0.81%	B- / 7.4
2010	C	457.00	6.08	B / 7.6	12.07%	C- / 3.7
2009	C	423.86	5.98	B- / 7.1	61.55%	C- / 3.7

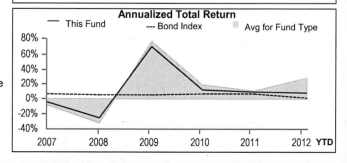

Western Asset High Yld Def Opp (HYI)

B+ **Good**

Fund Family: Legg Mason Partners Fund Advisor LL
Fund Type: Corporate - High Yield
Inception Date: October 27, 2010

Major Rating Factors: Strong performance is the major factor driving the B+ (Good) TheStreet.com Investment Rating for Western Asset High Yld Def Opp. The fund currently has a performance rating of B+ (Good) based on an annualized return of 0.00% over the last three years and a total return of 21.79% year to date 2012. Factored into the performance evaluation is an expense ratio of 0.91% (low).

The fund's risk rating is currently B (Good). It carries a beta of 0.00, meaning the fund's expected move will be 0.0% for every 10% move in the market. Volatility, as measured by both the semi-deviation and a drawdown factor, is considered low. As of March 31, 2012, Western Asset High Yld Def Opp traded at a premium of 8.13% above its net asset value, which is worse than its one-year historical average premium of .63%.

Michael C. Buchanan currently receives a manager quality ranking of 78 (0=worst, 99=best). If you desire only a moderate level of risk and strong performance, then this fund is an excellent option.

Data Date	Investment Rating	Net Assets ($Mil)	Price	Perfor- mance Rating/Pts	Total Return Y-T-D	Risk Rating/Pts
3-12	B+	401.00	19.69	B+ / 8.4	21.79%	B / 8.0
2011	D+	384.80	16.56	D+ / 2.3	5.13%	B- / 7.8

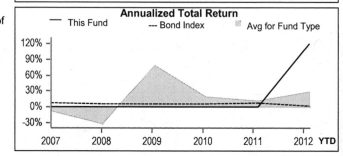

Western Asset Income Fund (PAI)

C+   Fair

Fund Family: Western Asset Management Company
Fund Type: General - Investment Grade
Inception Date: March 15, 1973

Major Rating Factors: Middle of the road best describes Western Asset Income Fund whose TheStreet.com Investment Rating is currently a C+ (Fair). The fund currently has a performance rating of C+ (Fair) based on an annualized return of 21.24% over the last three years and a total return of 6.71% year to date 2012. Factored into the performance evaluation is an expense ratio of 0.74% (very low).

The fund's risk rating is currently B (Good). It carries a beta of 0.71, meaning the fund's expected move will be 7.1% for every 10% move in the market. Volatility, as measured by both the semi-deviation and a drawdown factor, is considered low. As of March 31, 2012, Western Asset Income Fund traded at a premium of 2.46% above its net asset value, which is worse than its one-year historical average discount of 3.13%.

S. Kenneth Leech currently receives a manager quality ranking of 90 (0=worst, 99=best). If you desire an average level of risk, then this fund may be an option.

Data Date	Investment Rating	Net Assets ($Mil)	Price	Perfor-mance Rating/Pts	Total Return Y-T-D	Risk Rating/Pts
3-12	C+	129.90	14.55	C+ / 5.7	6.71%	B / 8.7
2011	B-	129.90	13.81	C+ / 6.1	-0.14%	B / 8.3
2010	C+	127.08	12.89	C+ / 6.3	12.19%	C+ / 6.4
2009	C	111.76	12.75	C- / 4.2	29.94%	C+ / 6.1

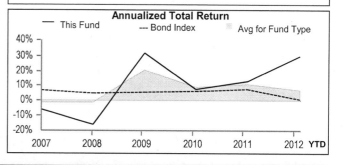

Western Asset Inflation Mgmt (IMF)

C   Fair

Fund Family: Legg Mason Partners Fund Advisor LL
Fund Type: Global
Inception Date: May 25, 2004

Major Rating Factors:
Disappointing performance is the major factor driving the C (Fair) TheStreet.com Investment Rating for Western Asset Inflation Mgmt. The fund currently has a performance rating of D+ (Weak) based on an annualized return of 10.01% over the last three years and a total return of 2.06% year to date 2012. Factored into the performance evaluation is an expense ratio of 0.87% (low).

The fund's risk rating is currently B+ (Good). It carries a beta of 0.14, meaning the fund's expected move will be 1.4% for every 10% move in the market. Volatility, as measured by both the semi-deviation and a drawdown factor, is considered very low. As of March 31, 2012, Western Asset Inflation Mgmt traded at a discount of 8.83% below its net asset value, which is better than its one-year historical average discount of 8.73%.

S. Kenneth Leech has been running the fund for 6 years and currently receives a manager quality ranking of 82 (0=worst, 99=best). This fund offers only a moderate level of risk but investors looking for strong performance are still waiting.

Data Date	Investment Rating	Net Assets ($Mil)	Price	Perfor-mance Rating/Pts	Total Return Y-T-D	Risk Rating/Pts
3-12	C	127.39	17.75	D+ / 2.6	2.06%	B+ / 9.6
2011	C+	137.00	17.49	C- / 4.2	0.69%	B+ / 9.6
2010	B-	127.98	17.65	C+ / 6.8	13.46%	B- / 7.0
2009	C+	115.46	16.13	C- / 4.2	13.03%	B- / 7.6

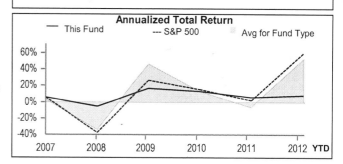

Western Asset Intermediate Muni (SBI)

C+   Fair

Fund Family: Legg Mason Partners Fund Advisor LL
Fund Type: Municipal - National
Inception Date: February 27, 1992

Major Rating Factors: Middle of the road best describes Western Asset Intermediate Muni whose TheStreet.com Investment Rating is currently a C+ (Fair). The fund currently has a performance rating of C+ (Fair) based on an annualized return of 13.16% over the last three years and a total return of 3.58% year to date 2012. Factored into the performance evaluation is an expense ratio of 0.91% (low).

The fund's risk rating is currently B+ (Good). It carries a beta of 0.95, meaning that its performance tracks fairly well with that of the overall stock market. Volatility, as measured by both the semi-deviation and a drawdown factor, is considered very low. As of March 31, 2012, Western Asset Intermediate Muni traded at a discount of 1.86% below its net asset value, which is worse than its one-year historical average discount of 3.13%.

Dennis J. McNamara currently receives a manager quality ranking of 74 (0=worst, 99=best). If you desire an average level of risk, then this fund may be an option.

Data Date	Investment Rating	Net Assets ($Mil)	Price	Perfor-mance Rating/Pts	Total Return Y-T-D	Risk Rating/Pts
3-12	C+	139.00	10.03	C+ / 5.6	3.58%	B+ / 9.2
2011	B	141.60	9.80	C+ / 6.8	-0.15%	B+ / 9.2
2010	B-	137.00	9.43	C+ / 6.9	10.70%	B- / 7.2
2009	B	127.61	8.95	C+ / 5.6	25.03%	B / 8.1

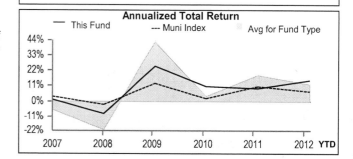

Western Asset Managed High Income (MHY)

B-　　**Good**

Fund Family: Legg Mason Partners Fund Advisor LL
Fund Type: Corporate - High Yield
Inception Date: March 18, 1993

Major Rating Factors: Western Asset Managed High Income receives a
TheStreet.com Investment Rating of B- (Good). The fund currently has a performance
rating of C+ (Fair) based on an annualized return of 24.88% over the last three years
and a total return of 3.85% year to date 2012. Factored into the performance
evaluation is an expense ratio of 0.92% (low).

　　The fund's risk rating is currently B (Good). It carries a beta of 1.00, meaning that
its performance tracks fairly well with that of the overall stock market. Volatility, as
measured by both the semi-deviation and a drawdown factor, is considered low. As of
March 31, 2012, Western Asset Managed High Income traded at a premium of 3.37%
above its net asset value, which is worse than its one-year historical average
premium of 2.94%.

　　Stephen A. Walsh currently receives a manager quality ranking of 55 (0=worst,
99=best). If you desire an average level of risk, then this fund may be an option.

Data Date	Investment Rating	Net Assets ($Mil)	Price	Perfor- mance Rating/Pts	Total Return Y-T-D	Risk Rating/Pts
3-12	B-	291.00	6.14	C+ / 6.3	3.85%	B / 8.6
2011	B-	267.50	6.04	B- / 7.2	0.66%	B / 8.0
2010	B	267.47	6.12	B / 7.9	16.81%	C / 5.1
2009	C-	244.39	5.79	C+ / 5.9	45.34%	C- / 4.1

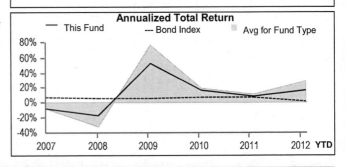

Western Asset Managed Municipals (MMU)

A-　　**Excellent**

Fund Family: Legg Mason Partners Fund Advisor LL
Fund Type: Municipal - National
Inception Date: June 18, 1992

Major Rating Factors:
Strong performance is the major factor driving the A- (Excellent) TheStreet.com
Investment Rating for Western Asset Managed Municipals. The fund currently has a
performance rating of B (Good) based on an annualized return of 17.41% over the
last three years and a total return of 3.40% year to date 2012. Factored into the
performance evaluation is an expense ratio of 0.95% (low).

　　The fund's risk rating is currently B+ (Good). It carries a beta of 1.60, meaning it
is expected to move 16.0% for every 10% move in the market. Volatility, as measured
by both the semi-deviation and a drawdown factor, is considered very low. As of
March 31, 2012, Western Asset Managed Municipals traded at a discount of .07%
below its net asset value, which is worse than its one-year historical average discount
of .35%.

　　Joseph P. Deane has been running the fund for 20 years and currently receives a
manager quality ranking of 70 (0=worst, 99=best). If you desire only a moderate level
of risk and strong performance, then this fund is an excellent option.

Data Date	Investment Rating	Net Assets ($Mil)	Price	Perfor- mance Rating/Pts	Total Return Y-T-D	Risk Rating/Pts
3-12	A-	522.16	13.67	B / 8.0	3.40%	B+ / 9.0
2011	A+	559.40	13.41	A- / 9.2	0.22%	B+ / 9.0
2010	B+	539.18	12.07	B- / 7.3	5.24%	C+ / 6.3
2009	A	494.58	12.19	B- / 7.4	37.29%	B- / 7.2

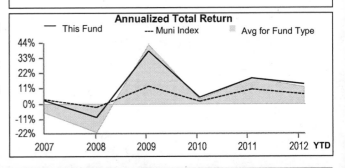

Western Asset Mtge Defined Oppty (DMO)

C　　**Fair**

Fund Family: Legg Mason Partners Fund Advisor LL
Fund Type: Mortgage
Inception Date: February 24, 2010

Major Rating Factors: Middle of the road best describes Western Asset Mtge
Defined Oppty whose TheStreet.com Investment Rating is currently a C (Fair). The
fund currently has a performance rating of C (Fair) based on an annualized return of
0.00% over the last three years and a total return of 13.13% year to date 2012.
Factored into the performance evaluation is an expense ratio of 2.24% (high).

　　The fund's risk rating is currently B (Good). It carries a beta of 0.00, meaning the
fund's expected move will be 0.0% for every 10% move in the market. Volatility, as
measured by both the semi-deviation and a drawdown factor, is considered low. As of
March 31, 2012, Western Asset Mtge Defined Oppty traded at a premium of .46%
above its net asset value, which is worse than its one-year historical average discount
of .79%.

　　S. Kenneth Leech currently receives a manager quality ranking of 77 (0=worst,
99=best). If you desire an average level of risk, then this fund may be an option.

Data Date	Investment Rating	Net Assets ($Mil)	Price	Perfor- mance Rating/Pts	Total Return Y-T-D	Risk Rating/Pts
3-12	C	197.29	21.71	C / 4.5	13.13%	B / 8.7
2011	C-	197.30	19.61	D / 2.1	0.76%	B / 8.7

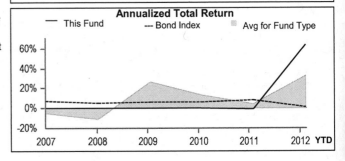

Western Asset Municipal Defined Op (MTT)   C   Fair

Fund Family: Legg Mason Partners Fund Advisor LL
Fund Type: Municipal - National
Inception Date: March 27, 2009

Major Rating Factors: Middle of the road best describes Western Asset Municipal Defined Op whose TheStreet.com Investment Rating is currently a C (Fair). The fund currently has a performance rating of C (Fair) based on an annualized return of 9.14% over the last three years and a total return of 2.74% year to date 2012. Factored into the performance evaluation is an expense ratio of 0.71% (very low).

The fund's risk rating is currently B (Good). It carries a beta of 1.01, meaning that its performance tracks fairly well with that of the overall stock market. Volatility, as measured by both the semi-deviation and a drawdown factor, is considered low. As of March 31, 2012, Western Asset Municipal Defined Op traded at a premium of .31% above its net asset value, which is worse than its one-year historical average discount of .68%.

Robert E. Amodeo currently receives a manager quality ranking of 55 (0=worst, 99=best). If you desire an average level of risk, then this fund may be an option.

Data Date	Investment Rating	Net Assets ($Mil)	Price	Performance Rating/Pts	Total Return Y-T-D	Risk Rating/Pts
3-12	C	256.64	22.41	C / 4.3	2.74%	B / 8.9
2011	A-	260.30	22.06	B+ / 8.5	-0.27%	B+ / 9.0
2010	C-	256.21	19.89	D- / 1.1	0.51%	B / 8.4

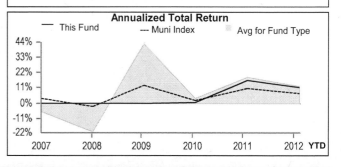

Western Asset Municipal High Inc (MHF)   C+   Fair

Fund Family: Legg Mason Partners Fund Advisor LL
Fund Type: Municipal - High Yield
Inception Date: November 17, 1988

Major Rating Factors: Middle of the road best describes Western Asset Municipal High Inc whose TheStreet.com Investment Rating is currently a C+ (Fair). The fund currently has a performance rating of C (Fair) based on an annualized return of 10.13% over the last three years and a total return of 4.05% year to date 2012. Factored into the performance evaluation is an expense ratio of 0.68% (very low).

The fund's risk rating is currently B (Good). It carries a beta of 1.48, meaning it is expected to move 14.8% for every 10% move in the market. Volatility, as measured by both the semi-deviation and a drawdown factor, is considered low. As of March 31, 2012, Western Asset Municipal High Inc traded at a premium of .88% above its net asset value, which is worse than its one-year historical average discount of 1.11%.

Ellen S. Cammer currently receives a manager quality ranking of 41 (0=worst, 99=best). If you desire an average level of risk, then this fund may be an option.

Data Date	Investment Rating	Net Assets ($Mil)	Price	Performance Rating/Pts	Total Return Y-T-D	Risk Rating/Pts
3-12	C+	164.00	8.04	C / 5.0	4.05%	B / 8.9
2011	B+	166.00	7.83	B- / 7.5	-0.13%	B / 8.9
2010	C+	162.00	7.23	C / 4.9	3.19%	B- / 7.3
2009	C+	145.41	7.43	C / 5.1	18.79%	B- / 7.3

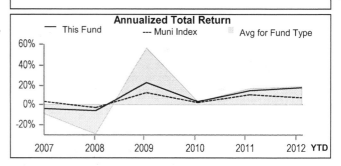

Western Asset Municipal Partners (MNP)   A   Excellent

Fund Family: Legg Mason Partners Fund Advisor LL
Fund Type: Municipal - National
Inception Date: January 22, 1993

Major Rating Factors:
Strong performance is the major factor driving the A (Excellent) TheStreet.com Investment Rating for Western Asset Municipal Partners. The fund currently has a performance rating of B+ (Good) based on an annualized return of 18.33% over the last three years and a total return of 4.16% year to date 2012. Factored into the performance evaluation is an expense ratio of 1.25% (average).

The fund's risk rating is currently B (Good). It carries a beta of 1.79, meaning it is expected to move 17.9% for every 10% move in the market. Volatility, as measured by both the semi-deviation and a drawdown factor, is considered low. As of March 31, 2012, Western Asset Municipal Partners traded at a discount of 1.99% below its net asset value, which is worse than its one-year historical average discount of 3.77%.

Robert E. Amodeo currently receives a manager quality ranking of 70 (0=worst, 99=best). If you desire only a moderate level of risk and strong performance, then this fund is an excellent option.

Data Date	Investment Rating	Net Assets ($Mil)	Price	Performance Rating/Pts	Total Return Y-T-D	Risk Rating/Pts
3-12	A	148.08	15.79	B+ / 8.5	4.16%	B / 8.9
2011	A+	152.10	15.36	A / 9.4	0.20%	B / 8.9
2010	C+	143.85	13.26	C+ / 5.7	5.45%	C+ / 6.6
2009	B-	131.23	13.32	C+ / 6.5	42.02%	B- / 7.5

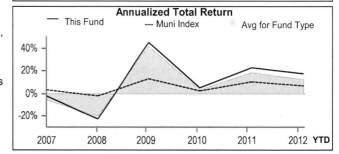

Western Asset Premier Bond Fund (WEA)

B+ Good

Fund Family: Western Asset Management Company
Fund Type: General - Investment Grade
Inception Date: March 25, 2002

Major Rating Factors: Strong performance is the major factor driving the B+ (Good) TheStreet.com Investment Rating for Western Asset Premier Bond Fund. The fund currently has a performance rating of B+ (Good) based on an annualized return of 33.09% over the last three years and a total return of 1.84% year to date 2012. Factored into the performance evaluation is an expense ratio of 1.38% (average).

The fund's risk rating is currently B- (Good). It carries a beta of 0.28, meaning the fund's expected move will be 2.8% for every 10% move in the market. Volatility, as measured by both the semi-deviation and a drawdown factor, is considered low. As of March 31, 2012, Western Asset Premier Bond Fund traded at a premium of 16.65%* above its net asset value, which is worse than its one-year historical average premium of 14.60%.

S. Kenneth Leech currently receives a manager quality ranking of 97 (0=worst, 99=best). If you desire only a moderate level of risk and strong performance, then this fund is an excellent option.

Data Date	Investment Rating	Net Assets ($Mil)	Price	Perfor-mance Rating/Pts	Total Return Y-T-D	Risk Rating/Pts
3-12	B+	163.81	15.90	B+ / 8.4	1.84%	B- / 7.9
2011	B+	154.20	15.95	B+ / 8.8	0.31%	B- / 7.8
2010	B-	154.24	14.13	B / 7.7	17.57%	C / 4.9
2009	C	117.14	13.36	C+ / 6.6	60.72%	C / 4.5

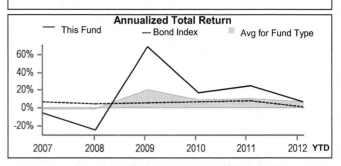

Annualized Total Return

Western Asset Var Rt Strat Fd (GFY)

C Fair

Fund Family: Legg Mason Partners Fund Advisor LL
Fund Type: Global
Inception Date: October 26, 2004

Major Rating Factors: Middle of the road best describes Western Asset Var Rt Strat Fd whose TheStreet.com Investment Rating is currently a C (Fair). The fund currently has a performance rating of C (Fair) based on an annualized return of 20.74% over the last three years and a total return of 13.29% year to date 2012. Factored into the performance evaluation is an expense ratio of 0.99% (low).

The fund's risk rating is currently B (Good). It carries a beta of 0.18, meaning the fund's expected move will be 1.8% for every 10% move in the market. Volatility, as measured by both the semi-deviation and a drawdown factor, is considered low. As of March 31, 2012, Western Asset Var Rt Strat Fd traded at a discount of 5.89% below its net asset value, which is worse than its one-year historical average discount of 8.41%.

Michael B. Zelouf currently receives a manager quality ranking of 92 (0=worst, 99=best). If you desire an average level of risk, then this fund may be an option.

Data Date	Investment Rating	Net Assets ($Mil)	Price	Perfor-mance Rating/Pts	Total Return Y-T-D	Risk Rating/Pts
3-12	C	111.89	16.62	C / 5.0	13.29%	B / 8.3
2011	C	111.90	14.85	C- / 4.0	0.81%	B / 8.3
2010	B+	113.54	16.99	B / 7.9	25.48%	C / 5.5
2009	C-	126.39	14.14	C- / 3.4	26.80%	C+ / 6.2

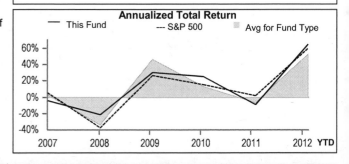

Annualized Total Return

Western Asset Worldwide Inc Fd (SBW)

B Good

Fund Family: Legg Mason Partners Fund Advisor LL
Fund Type: Emerging Market
Inception Date: December 31, 1993

Major Rating Factors: Strong performance is the major factor driving the B (Good) TheStreet.com Investment Rating for Western Asset Worldwide Inc Fd. The fund currently has a performance rating of B- (Good) based on an annualized return of 27.34% over the last three years and a total return of 6.89% year to date 2012. Factored into the performance evaluation is an expense ratio of 1.37% (average).

The fund's risk rating is currently B (Good). It carries a beta of 0.94, meaning that its performance tracks fairly well with that of the overall stock market. Volatility, as measured by both the semi-deviation and a drawdown factor, is considered low. As of March 31, 2012, Western Asset Worldwide Inc Fd traded at a discount of 6.52% below its net asset value, which is worse than its one-year historical average discount of 8.94%.

S. Kenneth Leech currently receives a manager quality ranking of 93 (0=worst, 99=best). If you desire only a moderate level of risk and strong performance, then this fund is an excellent option.

Data Date	Investment Rating	Net Assets ($Mil)	Price	Perfor-mance Rating/Pts	Total Return Y-T-D	Risk Rating/Pts
3-12	B	193.34	14.49	B- / 7.5	6.89%	B / 8.2
2011	B	194.10	13.78	B / 7.7	-0.29%	B / 8.2
2010	B	184.25	13.30	B- / 7.2	11.85%	C+ / 5.7
2009	B-	152.02	12.75	B- / 7.0	54.15%	C+ / 5.9

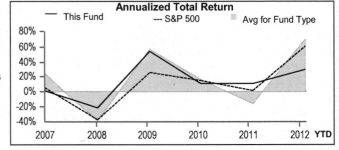

Annualized Total Return

Western Asset/Claymore Inf-Link O& (WIW)   C   Fair

Fund Family: Guggenheim Funds Investment Advisor
Fund Type: US Government/Agency
Inception Date: February 25, 2004

Major Rating Factors:
Disappointing performance is the major factor driving the C (Fair) TheStreet.com Investment Rating for Western Asset/Claymore Inf-Link O&. The fund currently has a performance rating of D+ (Weak) based on an annualized return of 10.47% over the last three years and a total return of 1.96% year to date 2012. Factored into the performance evaluation is an expense ratio of 0.75% (very low).

The fund's risk rating is currently B+ (Good). It carries a beta of 0.05, meaning the fund's expected move will be 0.5% for every 10% move in the market. Volatility, as measured by both the semi-deviation and a drawdown factor, is considered very low. As of March 31, 2012, Western Asset/Claymore Inf-Link O& traded at a discount of 10.75% below its net asset value, which is better than its one-year historical average discount of 10.29%.

S. Kenneth Leech currently receives a manager quality ranking of 84 (0=worst, 99=best). This fund offers only a moderate level of risk but investors looking for strong performance are still waiting.

Data Date	Investment Rating	Net Assets ($Mil)	Price	Perfor-mance Rating/Pts	Total Return Y-T-D	Risk Rating/Pts
3-12	C	811.72	12.79	D+ / 2.6	1.96%	B+ / 9.6
2011	C+	872.60	12.61	C / 4.5	0.87%	B+ / 9.6
2010	B-	813.12	12.51	C+ / 5.7	7.99%	B- / 7.0
2009	C+	749.85	12.04	C / 4.8	16.70%	B- / 7.3

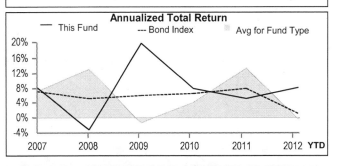

Western Asset/Claymore Inf-Link S& (WIA)   C-   Fair

Fund Family: Western Asset Management Company
Fund Type: US Government/Agency
Inception Date: September 26, 2003

Major Rating Factors:
Disappointing performance is the major factor driving the C- (Fair) TheStreet.com Investment Rating for Western Asset/Claymore Inf-Link S&. The fund currently has a performance rating of D (Weak) based on an annualized return of 7.36% over the last three years and a total return of 1.29% year to date 2012. Factored into the performance evaluation is an expense ratio of 0.76% (very low).

The fund's risk rating is currently B+ (Good). It carries a beta of 0.08, meaning the fund's expected move will be 0.8% for every 10% move in the market. Volatility, as measured by both the semi-deviation and a drawdown factor, is considered very low. As of March 31, 2012, Western Asset/Claymore Inf-Link S& traded at a discount of 10.28% below its net asset value, which is better than its one-year historical average discount of 8.53%.

S. Kenneth Leech has been running the fund for 8 years and currently receives a manager quality ranking of 79 (0=worst, 99=best). This fund offers only a moderate level of risk but investors looking for strong performance are still waiting.

Data Date	Investment Rating	Net Assets ($Mil)	Price	Perfor-mance Rating/Pts	Total Return Y-T-D	Risk Rating/Pts
3-12	C-	383.24	12.74	D / 2.0	1.29%	B+ / 9.6
2011	C+	412.20	12.64	C- / 3.8	0.08%	B+ / 9.6
2010	B-	384.76	12.83	C+ / 6.1	8.11%	B- / 7.1
2009	C	356.52	12.30	C / 4.8	15.64%	C+ / 6.8

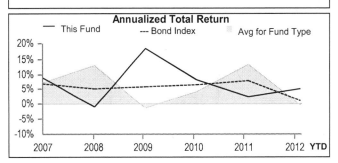

Western Asst Invst Grade Define Op (IGI)   C-   Fair

Fund Family: Legg Mason Partners Fund Advisor LL
Fund Type: Corporate - Investment Grade
Inception Date: June 26, 2009

Major Rating Factors:
Disappointing performance is the major factor driving the C- (Fair) TheStreet.com Investment Rating for Western Asst Invst Grade Define Op. The fund currently has a performance rating of D+ (Weak) based on an annualized return of 0.00% over the last three years and a total return of -0.99% year to date 2012. Factored into the performance evaluation is an expense ratio of 0.80% (very low).

The fund's risk rating is currently B (Good). It carries a beta of 0.00, meaning the fund's expected move will be 0.0% for every 10% move in the market. Volatility, as measured by both the semi-deviation and a drawdown factor, is considered low. As of March 31, 2012, Western Asst Invst Grade Define Op traded at a discount of .51% below its net asset value, which is better than its one-year historical average premium of .21%.

Ryan K. Brist currently receives a manager quality ranking of 85 (0=worst, 99=best). This fund offers only a moderate level of risk but investors looking for strong performance are still waiting.

Data Date	Investment Rating	Net Assets ($Mil)	Price	Perfor-mance Rating/Pts	Total Return Y-T-D	Risk Rating/Pts
3-12	C-	220.35	21.40	D+ / 2.9	-0.99%	B / 8.9
2011	B	224.30	21.93	C+ / 6.5	0.05%	B+ / 9.1
2010	C	217.59	20.04	D+ / 2.6	8.40%	B / 8.4

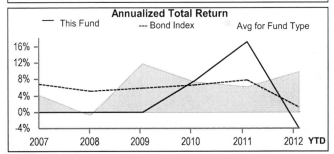

Zweig Fund (ZF)

C   **Fair**

Fund Family: Zweig Advisors LLC
Fund Type: Income
Inception Date: September 25, 1986

Major Rating Factors: Middle of the road best describes Zweig Fund whose TheStreet.com Investment Rating is currently a C (Fair). The fund currently has a performance rating of C (Fair) based on an annualized return of 19.69% over the last three years and a total return of 13.74% year to date 2012. Factored into the performance evaluation is an expense ratio of 1.23% (average).

The fund's risk rating is currently B- (Good). It carries a beta of 0.98, meaning that its performance tracks fairly well with that of the overall stock market. Volatility, as measured by both the semi-deviation and a drawdown factor, is considered low. As of March 31, 2012, Zweig Fund traded at a discount of 12.77% below its net asset value, which is better than its one-year historical average discount of 10.69%.

Carlton B. Neel has been running the fund for 9 years and currently receives a manager quality ranking of 40 (0=worst, 99=best). If you desire an average level of risk, then this fund may be an option.

Data Date	Investment Rating	Net Assets ($Mil)	Price	Performance Rating/Pts	Total Return Y-T-D	Risk Rating/Pts
3-12	C	349.21	3.21	C / 4.8	13.74%	B- / 7.8
2011	C-	310.00	2.90	C- / 4.0	1.38%	B- / 7.6
2010	C-	353.05	3.35	C- / 3.5	13.02%	C+ / 6.5
2009	D	317.86	3.31	D / 1.8	25.34%	C+ / 6.0

Annualized Total Return

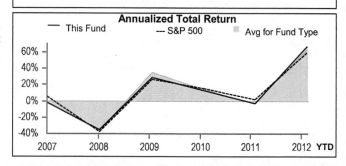

— This Fund   --- S&P 500   ▒ Avg for Fund Type

Zweig Total Return Fund (ZTR)

C-   **Fair**

Fund Family: Zweig Advisors LLC
Fund Type: Growth and Income
Inception Date: September 22, 1988

Major Rating Factors:
Disappointing performance is the major factor driving the C- (Fair) TheStreet.com Investment Rating for Zweig Total Return Fund. The fund currently has a performance rating of D+ (Weak) based on an annualized return of 11.30% over the last three years and a total return of 8.71% year to date 2012. Factored into the performance evaluation is an expense ratio of 1.10% (low).

The fund's risk rating is currently B (Good). It carries a beta of 0.51, meaning the fund's expected move will be 5.1% for every 10% move in the market. Volatility, as measured by both the semi-deviation and a drawdown factor, is considered low. As of March 31, 2012, Zweig Total Return Fund traded at a discount of 12.81% below its net asset value, which is better than its one-year historical average discount of 12.27%.

Carlton B. Neel has been running the fund for 9 years and currently receives a manager quality ranking of 53 (0=worst, 99=best). This fund offers only a moderate level of risk but investors looking for strong performance are still waiting.

Data Date	Investment Rating	Net Assets ($Mil)	Price	Performance Rating/Pts	Total Return Y-T-D	Risk Rating/Pts
3-12	C-	457.04	3.20	D+ / 2.8	8.71%	B / 8.3
2011	C-	513.80	3.03	C- / 3.1	0.66%	B / 8.1
2010	C	473.22	3.56	C- / 3.5	1.07%	B- / 7.6
2009	C	451.62	3.91	C- / 3.7	27.12%	C+ / 6.9

Annualized Total Return

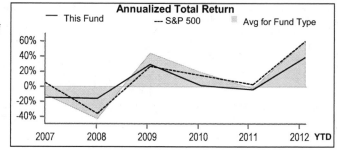

— This Fund   --- S&P 500   ▒ Avg for Fund Type

Section III

Top ETFs and
Other Closed-End Funds

A compilation of those

Exchange-Traded Funds and Other

Closed-End Mutual Funds

receiving the highest TheStreet Investment Ratings.

Funds are listed in order by Overall Investment Rating.

Section III Contents

This section contains a summary analysis of each of the top ETFs and other closed-end mutual funds as determined by their overall TheStreet Investment Rating. You can use this section to identify those mutual funds that have achieved the best possible combination of total return on investment and reduced volatility over the past three years. Consult each fund's individual Performance Rating and Risk Rating to find the fund that best matches your investing style.

1. Fund Type

The mutual fund's peer category based on an analysis of its investment portfolio.

COH	Corporate – High Yield	HL	Health
COI	Corporate – Inv. Grade	IN	Income
EM	Emerging Market	LP	Loan Participation
EN	Energy/Natural Resources	MTG	Mortgage
FS	Financial Services	MUH	Municipal – High Yield
FO	Foreign	MUN	Municipal – National
GEI	General – Inv. Grade	MUS	Municipal – Single State
GEN	General Bond	PM	Precious Metals
GL	Global	USA	U.S. Gov. – Agency
GR	Growth	UT	Utilities
GI	Growth and Income		

A blank fund type means that the mutual fund has not yet been categorized.

2. Fund Name

The name of the mutual fund as stated in its prospectus, which can sometimes differ slightly from the name that the company uses for advertising. If you cannot find the particular mutual fund you are interested in, or if you have any doubts regarding the precise name, verify the information with your broker or on your account statement. Also, use the fund's ticker symbol for confirmation. (See column 3.)

3. Ticker Symbol

The unique alphabetic symbol used for identifying and trading a specific mutual fund. No two funds can have the same ticker symbol.

4. Overall Investment Rating

Our overall rating is measured on a scale from A to E based on each fund's risk-adjusted performance. Please see page 10 for specific descriptions of each letter grade. Also, refer to page 7 for information on how our ratings are derived. Most important, when using this rating, please be sure to consider the warnings beginning on page 11 regarding the ratings' limitations and the underlying assumptions.

5. Price

Closing price of the fund on the date shown.

6.	**Performance Rating/Points**	A letter grade rating based solely on the mutual fund's financial performance over the trailing three years, without any consideration for the amount of risk the fund poses. Like the overall Investment Rating, the Performance Rating is measured on a scale from A to E for ease of interpretation. The points score indicates where the Performance Rating falls on a scale of 0 to 10.
7.	**1-Year Total Return**	The total return the fund has provided investors over the preceeding 52 weeks. This total return figure is computed based on the fund's dividend distributions and share price appreciation/depreciation during the period, net of the expenses and fees it imposes on its shareholders.
8.	**1-Year Total Return Percentile**	The fund's percentile rank based on its one-year performance compared to that of all other closed-end funds in existence for at least one year. A score of 99 is the best possible, indicating that the fund outperformed 99% of the closed-end mutual funds. Zero is the worst possible percentile score.
9.	**3-Year Total Return**	The total annual return the fund has provided investors over the preceeding 156 weeks.
10.	**3-Year Total Return Percentile**	The fund's percentile rank based on its three-year performance compared to that of all other closed-end funds in existence for at least three years. A score of 99 is the best possible, indicating that the fund outperformed 99% of the closed-end mutual funds. Zero is the worst possible percentile score.
11.	**5-Year Total Return**	The total annual return the fund has provided investors over the preceeding 260 weeks.
12.	**5-Year Total Return Percentile**	The fund's percentile rank based on its five-year performance compared to that of all other closed-end funds in existence for at least five years. A score of 99 is the best possible, indicating that the fund outperformed 99% of the closed-end mutual funds. Zero is the worst possible percentile score.
13.	**Dividend Yield**	Most recent quarterly dividend to fund investors annualized, expressed as a percent of the fund's current share price. The dividend yield of a fund can have little correlation to the amount of dividends the fund has received from its underlying investments. Rather, dividend distributions are based on a fund's need to pass earnings from both dividends and gains on the sale of investments along to shareholders. Thus, these dividend distributions are included as a part of the fund's total return.

Keep in mind that dividend income may be taxed at a different rate than capital gains depending on your income tax bracket. |

14.	**Risk Rating/Points**	A letter grade rating based solely on the mutual fund's risk as determined by its monthly performance volatility over the trailing three years. The risk rating does not take into consideration the overall financial performance the fund has achieved or the total return it has provided to its shareholders. Like the overall Investment Rating, the Risk Rating is measured on a scale from A to E for ease of interpretation. The points score indicates where the Risk Rating falls on a scale of 0 to 10.
15.	**Premium/ Discount**	A comparison of the fund's price to its NAV as of the date indicated. The premium (+) or discount (-) indicates the percentage the shares are trading above or below the fund's NAV per share.
		If the price is above the fund's NAV, the fund is said to be trading at a premium. If the price is lower than the fund's NAV, the fund is trading at a discount.
16.	**1-Year Average Premium/ Discount**	The average of the fund's premium/discount over the preceeding year.
		It can be useful to compare the fund's current premium/discount to its one-year average. If the fund is currently trading at a premium/discount that is lower/higher than its one-year average, then there has been less demand for the fund in more recent times than over the past year. Conversely, if the fund is currently trading at a premium/discount that is higher/lower than its one-year average, this indicates that there has been greater demand for the fund in more recent times than over the past year.

Fund Type	Fund Name	Ticker Symbol	Overall Investment Rating	Price As of 3/31/12	Perform-ance Rating/Pts	Annualized Total Return Through 3/31/12			Dividend Yield %	Risk Rating/ Pts	Premium/Discount As of 3/31/12	1 Year Average
	99 Pct = Best / 0 Pct = Worst					1Yr/Pct	3Yr/Pct	5Yr/Pct				
GR	*Direxion Daily Retail Bull 3X	RETL	A+	87.91	A+ / 9.9	59.72 / 99	--	--	0.00	B / 8.5	-0.05	0.06
IN	*ProShares Ultra Consumer Goods	UGE	A+	92.52	A+ / 9.8	24.50 / 85	46.70 / 98	7.50 / 71	0.66	B / 8.0	0.21	-0.10
IN	*iShares FTSE NAREIT Retail Idx	RTL	A+	32.64	A+ / 9.6	18.72 / 81	41.95 / 96	--	3.40	B / 8.0	0.09	-0.02
MUN	*SPDR Nuveen Barclays Bld Amr Bd	BABS	A+	58.72	A- / 9.1	27.82 / 98	--	--	4.54	B+ / 9.0	0.39	-1.05
IN	*SPDR S&P Retail ETF	XRT	A	61.25	A / 9.4	21.16 / 83	36.88 / 93	8.27 / 76	0.65	B / 8.1	0.00	0.01
GR	*Guggenheim S&P 500 Eq WgCon Dsc	RCD	A	54.80	A- / 9.2	14.68 / 77	35.94 / 92	3.94 / 50	1.94	B / 8.0	0.18	-0.04
IN	*Guggenheim S&P 500 Pure Value	RPV	A	32.29	A- / 9.2	5.49 / 57	37.75 / 94	0.69 / 30	2.68	B / 8.1	-0.06	0.04
GR	*Focus Mstar Technology Id ETF	FTQ	A	29.11	A- / 9.1	15.94 / 78	--	--	0.72	B / 8.5	0.31	-0.03
FO	*iShares MSCI Thailand Inv Market	THD	A-	72.79	A+ / 9.8	9.88 / 68	50.49 / 99	--	2.15	B- / 7.1	0.12	0.13
IN	*ProShares Ultra Consumer Service	UCC	A-	68.31	A+ / 9.8	26.85 / 86	51.59 / 99	-0.15 / 27	0.00	B- / 7.2	0.12	0.07
GI	*iShares FTSE EPRA/NAREIT NA Idx	IFNA	A-	45.93	A / 9.5	10.24 / 69	41.41 / 96	--	3.16	B- / 7.7	-0.39	0.09
HL	*ProShares Ultra Health Care	RXL	A-	73.10	A / 9.5	25.06 / 85	36.58 / 92	2.09 / 39	0.83	B- / 7.6	-0.04	-0.02
IN	*iShares Cohen & Steers Realty Ma	ICF	A-	76.64	A- / 9.2	12.50 / 73	37.33 / 93	-1.95 / 19	3.11	B- / 7.8	0.03	N/A
IN	*SPDR DJ REIT ETF	RWR	A-	70.83	A- / 9.2	13.17 / 74	37.02 / 93	-1.01 / 22	2.46	B- / 7.8	-0.04	N/A
IN	*First Trust S&P REIT Index Fund	FRI	A-	17.14	A- / 9.1	12.48 / 73	36.42 / 92	--	1.70	B- / 7.9	0.18	0.04
IN	*Vanguard REIT ETF	VNQ	A-	63.65	A- / 9.1	12.74 / 73	36.60 / 92	0.15 / 28	3.15	B- / 7.8	-0.03	N/A
IN	*iShares FTSE NAREIT Residential	REZ	A-	46.41	A- / 9.0	14.30 / 76	35.75 / 92	--	3.37	B / 8.0	0.00	0.04
GI	*PowerShares Act US Real Estate	PSR	A-	54.33	A- / 9.0	11.69 / 72	35.50 / 91	--	1.67	B / 8.1	-0.24	0.03
IN	*PowerShares Dynamic Leisure&Ente	PEJ	A-	21.89	A- / 9.0	15.69 / 78	33.02 / 88	4.90 / 56	0.99	B- / 7.9	0.23	-0.04
IN	*First Trust Consumer Dis AlphaDE	FXD	A-	22.85	B+ / 8.9	8.09 / 64	34.09 / 89	--	0.81	B / 8.0	0.09	0.01
IN	*iShares FTSE NAREIT Real Estate	FTY	A-	38.18	B+ / 8.9	11.17 / 70	35.41 / 91	--	3.49	B / 8.1	-0.10	N/A
IN	*Vanguard Consumer Discret ETF	VCR	A-	72.20	B+ / 8.7	15.12 / 77	31.53 / 85	4.37 / 53	1.18	B / 8.2	-0.01	N/A
IN	*Guggenheim Spin-Off ETF	CSD	A-	26.57	B+ / 8.6	9.06 / 67	31.80 / 85	0.41 / 29	0.42	B / 8.5	0.08	0.10
GR	*ProShares Ultra QQQ	QLD	B+	118.95	A+ / 9.9	32.11 / 90	57.20 / 99	8.17 / 75	0.00	C+ / 6.9	-0.03	-0.01
IN	*ProShares Ultra Real Estate	URE	B+	61.79	A+ / 9.8	8.79 / 66	58.64 / 99	-26.00 / 2	1.46	C+ / 6.4	-0.10	N/A
GR	*ProShares Ultra Rus Mid Cap Valu	UVU	B+	39.62	A+ / 9.8	-4.98 / 30	47.51 / 98	-9.46 / 7	0.23	C+ / 6.4	0.15	-0.10
GR	*ProShares Ultra Technology	ROM	B+	86.97	A+ / 9.8	30.39 / 89	50.01 / 99	5.83 / 61	0.00	C+ / 6.5	0.02	-0.03
GR	*ProShares Ultra Russell1000 Grow	UKF	B+	64.55	A+ / 9.7	13.00 / 74	43.74 / 97	0.99 / 31	0.20	C+ / 6.9	0.00	-0.05
IN	*Guggenheim 2x S&P 500 ETF	RSU	B+	49.99	A+ / 9.6	10.01 / 68	39.78 / 95	--	1.85	C+ / 6.8	-0.02	-0.04
GR	*ProShares Ultra Dow 30	DDM	B+	70.54	A+ / 9.6	13.63 / 75	40.78 / 96	-1.19 / 22	0.53	B- / 7.0	0.00	0.03
GR	*ProShares Ultra S-P 500	SSO	B+	58.36	A+ / 9.6	9.26 / 67	39.26 / 95	-6.26 / 10	0.94	C+ / 6.8	-0.05	-0.01
GR	*Guggenheim S&P Sm Cap 600 Pure V	RZV	B+	40.99	A / 9.4	1.08 / 44	39.57 / 95	0.32 / 29	1.76	B- / 7.3	-0.12	-0.06
GR	*PowerShares Dynamic Networking	PXQ	B+	28.58	B+ / 8.9	3.17 / 49	33.57 / 88	9.48 / 83	0.00	B- / 7.3	-0.03	-0.02
GR	*PowerShares S&P SC Cnsmr Discr	PSCD	B+	32.06	B+ / 8.9	13.09 / 74	--	--	0.23	B- / 7.4	0.28	0.03
IN	*iShares DJ US Real Estate	IYR	B+	62.30	B+ / 8.8	8.70 / 66	33.76 / 89	-1.93 / 19	3.42	B- / 7.9	0.00	0.01
GR	*Guggenheim S&P Mid Cap 400 Pure	RFV	B+	36.06	B+ / 8.7	0.16 / 41	33.14 / 88	1.61 / 35	2.80	B- / 7.8	-0.08	0.01
GR	*Consumer Discretionary Sel Sec S	XLY	B+	45.09	B+ / 8.6	16.54 / 79	30.21 / 82	4.66 / 55	1.22	B / 8.2	0.04	-0.01
GR	*First Trust US IPO Index Fund	FPX	B+	28.86	B+ / 8.5	14.09 / 76	29.30 / 81	5.39 / 58	1.29	B / 8.1	0.49	0.01
GR	*Guggenheim S&P Mid Cap 400 Pure	RFG	B+	89.64	B+ / 8.5	3.57 / 50	32.78 / 87	10.56 / 90	0.42	B / 8.0	-0.07	N/A
GR	*RevenueShares Small Cap Fund	RWJ	B+	36.34	B+ / 8.5	4.12 / 52	31.36 / 85	--	0.52	B- / 7.7	0.30	-0.04
GR	*WisdomTree SmallCap Earnings Fun	EES	B+	56.79	B+ / 8.5	4.90 / 55	31.35 / 85	4.40 / 53	1.50	B- / 7.8	0.35	0.02
GR	*WisdomTree MidCap Earnings Fund	EZM	B+	61.14	B / 8.2	4.85 / 54	30.39 / 83	5.70 / 60	0.75	B- / 7.9	0.23	0.07
HL	*First Trust Health Care AlphaDEX	FXH	B+	30.81	B / 8.1	7.17 / 62	30.23 / 83	--	0.10	B / 8.4	0.10	0.05
HL	*iShares DJ US Pharmaceuticals	IHE	B+	83.06	B / 8.1	25.66 / 85	27.75 / 75	10.02 / 87	1.44	B / 8.1	-0.04	0.01
FS	*PowerShares Financial Preferred	PGF	B+	17.90	B / 8.0	5.66 / 57	30.74 / 83	1.59 / 34	6.44	B / 8.7	0.28	-0.02
IN	*Guggenheim Multi-Asset Income ET	CVY	B+	21.85	B / 7.9	8.02 / 64	29.90 / 82	1.98 / 38	4.85	B / 8.7	0.14	0.07
IN	*WisdomTree Dividend Ex-Financial	DTN	B+	54.82	B / 7.9	13.66 / 75	28.92 / 80	2.15 / 39	3.33	B+ / 9.0	0.02	0.08
UT	*ProShares Ultra Utilities	UPW	B+	53.34	B / 7.8	19.40 / 82	29.73 / 81	-5.87 / 11	1.59	B / 8.4	-0.19	-0.01
GR	*iShares Russell Top 200 Growth	IWY	B+	35.16	B / 7.6	13.37 / 75	--	--	1.37	B / 8.5	-0.06	0.07
GI	*WisdomTree Equity Income Fund	DHS	B+	44.80	B- / 7.5	15.51 / 78	27.25 / 74	-0.94 / 23	3.67	B+ / 9.1	-0.02	0.14

Fund Type	Fund Name	Ticker Symbol	Overall Investment Rating	Price As of 3/31/12	PERFORMANCE Performance Rating/Pts	Annualized Total Return Through 3/31/12 1Yr/Pct	3Yr/Pct	5Yr/Pct	Dividend Yield %	RISK Risk Rating/ Pts	VALUATION Premium/Discount As of 3/31/12	1 Year Average
IN	F&C/Claymore Preferred Sec Inc Fun	FFC	A+	18.05	A+ / 9.8	16.54 / 79	52.62 / 99	7.06 / 67	9.04	B+ / 9.0	3.97	5.11
FO	Thai Fund	TTF	A+	15.94	A+ / 9.8	22.18 / 83	47.49 / 98	13.33 / 98	1.66	B- / 7.9	-10.55	-14.28
IN	Flaherty&Crumrine Preferred Income	PFD	A+	14.22	A+ / 9.7	24.11 / 84	47.29 / 98	5.24 / 58	7.85	B / 8.8	14.40	14.11
GI	Nuveen Preferref Income Opps	JPC	A+	8.88	A+ / 9.7	14.32 / 76	44.52 / 97	1.03 / 31	8.56	B / 8.1	-5.23	-9.88
COH	PIMCO Corporate and Income Oppty	PTY	A+	18.61	A+ / 9.7	7.23 / 62	46.86 / 98	14.88 / 99	8.03	B / 8.0	20.30	21.26
GI	Virtus Total Return	DCA	A+	3.80	A+ / 9.7	6.76 / 60	49.46 / 99	-16.16 / 3	6.16	B / 8.2	-8.65	-12.99
IN	Flaherty&Crumrine Preferred Inc Op	PFO	A+	10.99	A+ / 9.6	14.90 / 77	45.22 / 98	6.69 / 65	8.24	B / 8.9	7.53	10.43
IN	J Hancock Tax Advantage Div Income	HTD	A+	17.72	A+ / 9.6	18.82 / 81	43.04 / 97	7.57 / 71	6.67	B / 8.9	-7.76	-7.42
GI	Nuveen Credit Strategies Income	JQC	A+	8.98	A+ / 9.6	9.57 / 68	43.36 / 97	1.32 / 32	8.91	B / 8.6	-8.18	-11.21
MUS	BlackRock Invt Qual Muni Inc Tr	RFA	A+	13.43	A / 9.5	31.22 / 99	24.27 / 93	6.63 / 88	6.25	B / 8.5	2.21	1.09
MUN	BlackRock MuniHoldings Fund	MHD	A+	17.76	A / 9.5	30.61 / 99	22.87 / 91	8.78 / 98	6.18	B / 8.9	3.80	0.24
MUN	Eaton Vance Municipal Inc Tr	EVN	A+	13.63	A / 9.5	25.83 / 97	23.32 / 92	4.61 / 68	7.26	B / 8.4	14.35	13.02
MUS	Nuveen CA Muni Market Opportunity	NCO	A+	15.50	A / 9.5	33.72 / 99	21.71 / 88	6.12 / 83	6.19	B / 8.8	0.58	-2.57
MUS	Nuveen CA Prem Inc Muni	NCU	A+	15.04	A / 9.5	32.72 / 99	22.55 / 90	7.37 / 93	5.78	B / 8.7	-0.99	-5.28
MTG	PCM Fund	PCM	A+	11.01	A / 9.5	11.27 / 71	43.06 / 97	10.21 / 88	9.45	B / 8.8	7.73	9.43
MUN	BlackRock Long Term Muni Adv	BTA	A+	12.39	A / 9.4	29.18 / 99	22.45 / 90	4.47 / 67	6.39	B / 8.4	3.08	-1.67
MUN	BlackRock MuniVest Fund II	MVT	A+	16.22	A / 9.4	25.46 / 96	23.85 / 92	7.99 / 97	6.73	B / 8.7	3.64	3.10
MUH	MFS High Inc Muni Tr	CXE	A+	5.35	A / 9.4	22.22 / 92	23.90 / 93	3.37 / 57	7.18	B / 8.7	4.70	4.09
MUH	MFS High Yield Muni Trust	CMU	A+	4.90	A / 9.4	25.00 / 96	22.76 / 91	3.64 / 59	7.10	B / 8.8	6.75	5.37
MUN	PIMCO Municipal Income Fund II	PML	A+	12.18	A / 9.4	28.95 / 98	21.03 / 86	2.07 / 45	6.40	B / 8.5	5.27	3.45
MUS	BlackRock MuniYield Invt Fund	MYF	A+	15.38	A / 9.3	30.41 / 99	21.31 / 87	8.56 / 98	6.16	B / 8.7	0.52	-1.35
MUN	BlackRock Strategic Municipal Tr	BSD	A+	14.19	A / 9.3	27.11 / 97	22.67 / 90	1.20 / 37	6.26	B / 8.8	0.14	-1.44
MUS	Invesco Van Kampen Tr Fr Inv NJ Mu	VTJ	A+	17.78	A / 9.3	31.84 / 99	20.50 / 85	7.90 / 96	6.41	B / 8.8	5.77	1.35
IN	J Hancock Preferred Income II	HPF	A+	21.85	A / 9.3	25.80 / 86	37.80 / 94	7.17 / 68	7.69	B / 8.8	2.53	0.07
COH	MFS Interm High Inc	CIF	A+	3.18	A / 9.3	14.94 / 77	38.28 / 94	10.20 / 87	8.30	B / 8.7	5.65	-0.82
MUS	Nuveen CA Inv Quality Muni	NQC	A+	15.24	A / 9.3	32.50 / 99	21.60 / 88	7.20 / 92	6.54	B / 8.7	0.07	-2.15
MUS	Nuveen CA Performance Plus Muni	NCP	A+	15.18	A / 9.3	32.75 / 99	21.30 / 87	6.98 / 91	6.44	B / 8.7	-0.13	-2.50
IN	Nuveen Quality Preferred Income 3	JHP	A+	8.32	A / 9.3	12.15 / 73	38.85 / 95	-1.37 / 21	7.50	B / 8.6	-2.12	-3.31
GL	Pioneer High Income Trust	PHT	A+	16.66	A / 9.3	11.45 / 71	41.49 / 96	12.28 / 96	9.90	B+ / 9.0	23.77	26.00
MUS	BlackRock MuniYield AZ Fund	MZA	A+	14.59	A- / 9.2	27.36 / 98	20.95 / 86	6.14 / 83	5.72	B / 8.8	0.41	-3.80
COH	Credit Suisse High Yield Bond Fund	DHY	A+	3.12	A- / 9.2	11.50 / 71	39.04 / 95	5.63 / 60	10.19	B / 8.6	6.12	5.54
MUN	DWS Municipal Income Trust	KTF	A+	13.82	A- / 9.2	27.13 / 97	22.45 / 90	11.23 / 99	6.08	B / 8.7	3.68	0.69
MUN	DWS Strategic Municipal Inc Tr	KSM	A+	13.95	A- / 9.2	25.77 / 96	22.18 / 89	9.70 / 99	6.62	B / 8.8	5.52	3.87
IN	J Hancock Preferred Inc	HPI	A+	21.78	A- / 9.2	24.21 / 84	37.86 / 94	7.09 / 68	7.71	B / 8.9	1.82	2.00
IN	John Hancock Premium Dividend	PDT	A+	13.47	A- / 9.2	23.91 / 84	37.61 / 94	10.78 / 91	6.73	B+ / 9.1	-2.60	-3.36
IN	Nuveen Quality Preferred Income	JTP	A+	8.16	A- / 9.2	14.26 / 76	38.22 / 94	-1.14 / 22	7.35	B / 8.9	-1.81	-3.36
IN	Nuveen Quality Preferred Income 2	JPS	A+	8.62	A- / 9.2	13.65 / 75	37.87 / 94	-0.32 / 25	7.66	B / 8.7	-2.05	-4.46
MUN	BlackRock Municipal Income Trust I	BLE	A+	15.50	A- / 9.1	23.53 / 94	22.88 / 91	5.17 / 74	6.58	B / 8.6	1.64	0.95
MUN	BlackRock MuniYield Fund	MYD	A+	15.31	A- / 9.1	25.00 / 96	22.18 / 89	6.38 / 85	6.54	B / 8.6	2.34	1.25
MUS	Invesco Van Kampen Tr Fr Inv NY Mu	VTN	A+	15.85	A- / 9.1	24.99 / 96	21.98 / 89	6.86 / 90	6.36	B / 8.9	3.46	0.65
MUN	BlackRock Municipal Bond Trust	BBK	A+	16.28	A- / 9.0	20.97 / 90	21.83 / 88	4.21 / 64	6.52	B / 8.6	2.07	2.46
MUS	BlackRock MuniYield CA Fund	MYC	A+	15.35	A- / 9.0	27.76 / 98	20.47 / 85	7.93 / 96	6.18	B / 8.7	-4.42	-3.53
IN	J Hancock Preferred Income III	HPS	A+	17.80	A- / 9.0	14.11 / 76	36.79 / 93	4.42 / 53	7.56	B / 8.8	-3.31	-2.71
MUN	MFS Municipal Income Trust	MFM	A+	7.29	A- / 9.0	23.99 / 94	20.93 / 86	4.31 / 65	6.91	B / 8.6	4.14	2.78
IN	BlackRock Credit Alloc Inc Tr II	PSY	A+	10.51	B+ / 8.9	14.29 / 76	35.57 / 92	-3.89 / 14	6.96	B / 8.8	-9.08	-11.40
MUN	BlackRock MuniHoldings Fund II	MUH	A+	15.72	B+ / 8.9	22.69 / 93	21.93 / 89	8.12 / 97	6.34	B / 8.7	-1.81	-1.18
MUS	Invesco New York Quality Muni Sec	IQN	A+	15.79	B+ / 8.8	24.91 / 96	19.73 / 83	7.83 / 96	4.94	B / 8.9	-2.59	-6.37
MUS	Invesco Van Kampen OH Qual Muni	VOQ	A+	16.56	B+ / 8.8	28.08 / 98	18.35 / 77	7.46 / 93	6.16	B / 8.9	5.08	0.54
MUS	Nuveen MI Prem Inc Muni	NMP	A+	14.83	B+ / 8.8	23.13 / 93	19.48 / 82	6.69 / 88	5.91	B+ / 9.3	-2.95	-7.02
MUS	Nuveen MI Quality Inc Muni	NUM	A+	15.11	B+ / 8.7	23.44 / 94	19.19 / 81	6.81 / 89	5.88	B+ / 9.1	-4.06	-7.30

* Denotes ETF Fund, N/A denotes number is not available

Section IV

Bottom ETFs and
Other Closed-End Funds

A compilation of those

Exchange-Traded Funds and Other

Closed-End Mutual Funds

receiving the lowest TheStreet.com Investment Ratings.

Funds are listed in order by Overall Investment Rating.

Section IV Contents

This section contains a summary analysis of each of the bottom closed-end mutual funds as determined by their overall TheStreet.com Investment Rating. Typically, these funds have invested in securities that are currently out of favor, presenting a risky investment proposition. As such, these are the funds that you should generally avoid since they have historically underperformed most other mutual funds given the level of risk in their underlying investments.

1. **Fund Type**   The mutual fund's peer category based on an analysis of its investment portfolio.

COH	Corporate – High Yield	HL	Health
COI	Corporate – Inv. Grade	IN	Income
EM	Emerging Market	LP	Loan Participation
EN	Energy/Natural Resources	MTG	Mortgage
FS	Financial Services	MUH	Municipal – High Yield
FO	Foreign	MUN	Municipal – National
GEI	General – Inv. Grade	MUS	Municipal – Single State
GEN	General Bond	PM	Precious Metals
GL	Global	USA	U.S. Gov. – Agency
GR	Growth	UT	Utilities
GI	Growth and Income		

A blank fund type means that the mutual fund has not yet been categorized.

2. **Fund Name**   The name of the mutual fund as stated in its prospectus, which can sometimes differ slightly from the name that the company uses for advertising. If you cannot find the particular mutual fund you are interested in, or if you have any doubts regarding the precise name, verify the information with your broker or on your account statement. Also, use the fund's ticker symbol for confirmation. (See column 3.)

3. **Ticker Symbol**   The unique alphabetic symbol used for identifying and trading a specific mutual fund. No two funds can have the same ticker symbol.

4. **Overall Investment Rating**   Our overall rating is measured on a scale from A to E based on each fund's risk-adjusted performance. Please see page 10 for specific descriptions of each letter grade. Also, refer to page 7 for information on how our ratings are derived. Most important, when using this rating, please be sure to consider the warnings beginning on page 11 regarding the ratings' limitations and the underlying assumptions.

5.	Price	Closing price of the fund on the date shown.
6.	**Performance Rating/Points**	A letter grade rating based solely on the mutual fund's financial performance over the trailing three years, without any consideration for the amount of risk the fund poses. Like the overall Investment Rating, the Performance Rating is measured on a scale from A to E for ease of interpretation. The points score indicates where the Performance Rating falls on a scale of 0 to 10.
7.	**1-Year Total Return**	The total return the fund has provided investors over the preceeding 52 weeks. This total return figure is computed based on the fund's dividend distributions and share price appreciation/depreciation during the period, net of the expenses and fees it imposes on its shareholders.
8.	**1-Year Total Return Percentile**	The fund's percentile rank based on its one-year performance compared to that of all other closed-end funds in existence for at least one year. A score of 99 is the best possible, indicating that the fund outperformed 99% of the closed-end mutual funds. Zero is the worst possible percentile score.
9.	**3-Year Total Return**	The total annual return the fund has provided investors over the preceeding 156 weeks.
10.	**3-Year Total Return Percentile**	The fund's percentile rank based on its three-year performance compared to that of all other closed-end funds in existence for at least three years. A score of 99 is the best possible, indicating that the fund outperformed 99% of the closed-end mutual funds. Zero is the worst possible percentile score.
11.	**5-Year Total Return**	The total annual return the fund has provided investors over the preceeding 260 weeks.
12.	**5-Year Total Return Percentile**	The fund's percentile rank based on its five-year performance compared to that of all other closed-end funds in existence for at least five years. A score of 99 is the best possible, indicating that the fund outperformed 99% of the closed-end mutual funds. Zero is the worst possible percentile score.
13.	**Dividend Yield**	Most recent quarterly dividend to fund investors annualized, expressed as a percent of the fund's current share price. The dividend yield of a fund can have little correlation to the amount of dividends the fund has received from its underlying investments. Rather, dividend distributions are based on a fund's need to pass earnings from both dividends and gains on the sale of investments along to shareholders. Thus, these dividend distributions are included as a part of the fund's total return.
		Keep in mind that dividend income may be taxed at a different rate than capital gains depending on your income tax bracket.

14. Risk Rating/Points

A letter grade rating based solely on the mutual fund's risk as determined by its monthly performance volatility over the trailing three years. The risk rating does not take into consideration the overall financial performance the fund has achieved or the total return it has provided to its shareholders. Like the overall Investment Rating, the Risk Rating is measured on a scale from A to E for ease of interpretation. The points score indicates where the Risk Rating falls on a scale of 0 to 10.

15. Premium/Discount

A comparison of the fund's price to its NAV as of the date indicated. The premium (+) or discount (-) indicates the percentage the shares are trading above or below the fund's NAV per share.

If the price is above the fund's NAV, the fund is said to be trading at a premium. If the price is lower than the fund's NAV, the fund is trading at a discount.

16. 1-Year Average Premium/Discount

The average of the fund's premium/discount over the preceeding year.

It can be useful to compare the fund's current premium/discount to its one-year average. If the fund is currently trading at a premium/discount that is lower/higher than its one-year average, then there has been less demand for the fund in more recent times than over the past year. Conversely, if the fund is currently trading at a premium/discount that is higher/lower than its one-year average, this indicates that there has been greater demand for the fund in more recent times than over the past year.

Fund Type	Fund Name	Ticker Symbol	Overall Investment Rating	Price As of 3/31/12	Perform-ance Rating/Pts	Annualized Total Return Through 3/31/12 1Yr/Pct	3Yr/Pct	5Yr/Pct	Dividend Yield %	Risk Rating/Pts	Premium/Discount As of 3/31/12	Premium/Discount 1 Year Average
IN	*Brclys ETN+ Sh C Lv I S&P500 TR	BXDC	E-	21.27	E- / 0.0	-39.27 / 3	--	--	0.00	D / 1.9	1.38	0.21
IN	*C-Tracks ETN Citi Volatility Idx	CVOL	E-	11.00	E- / 0.0	-72.12 / 0	--	--	0.00	D / 1.9	3.00	-0.33
GR	*Direxion Daily Real Estate Bear	DRV	E-	27.76	E- / 0.0	-61.04 / 0	--	--	0.00	D / 1.9	-0.07	-0.03
IN	*Direxion Daily Semiconductor Bea	SOXS	E-	29.95	E- / 0.0	-50.17 / 1	--	--	0.00	D / 1.9	-0.20	0.01
GR	*Direxion Daily Small Cap Bear 3x	TZA	E-	17.68	E- / 0.0	-48.95 / 1	-69.01 / 0	--	0.00	D / 1.9	-0.11	-0.01
FS	*Direxion Financial Bear 3x Share	FAZ	E-	20.65	E- / 0.0	-47.42 / 1	-70.20 / 0	--	0.00	D / 1.9	0.00	-0.06
IN	*IPath S&P 500 VIX Sm-Trm Futr ET	VXX	E-	16.78	E- / 0.0	-42.31 / 2	-66.07 / 0	--	0.00	D / 1.9	0.60	0.14
IN	*iPath Shrt Ext Rus 1000 TR Idx E	ROSA	E-	16.01	E- / 0.0	-46.60 / 2	--	--	0.00	D / 1.9	3.49	1.11
IN	*iPath Shrt Ext S&P 500 TR Idx ET	SFSA	E-	16.47	E- / 0.0	-46.07 / 2	--	--	0.00	D / 1.9	2.94	0.02
GR	*ProShares UltraPro Short MidCap4	SMDD	E-	11.65	E- / 0.0	-41.25 / 3	--	--	0.00	D / 1.9	-0.26	0.02
GR	*ProShares UltraPro Short QQQ	SQQQ	E-	10.79	E- / 0.0	-57.44 / 1	--	--	0.00	D / 1.9	0.00	-0.03
GR	*ProShares UltraPro Shrt Russell2	SRTY	E-	8.80	E- / 0.0	-48.45 / 1	--	--	0.00	D / 1.9	-0.11	-0.03
EN	*ProShares UltraShort Silver	ZSL	E-	10.55	E- / 0.0	-54.53 / 1	-72.05 / 0	--	0.00	D / 1.9	0.57	-0.42
GEI	*ProShares VIX Short-Term Futures	VIXY	E-	35.77	E- / 0.0	-43.37 / 2	--	--	0.00	D / 1.9	0.76	0.15
IN	*VelocityShares Daily 2x VIX S-T	TVIX	E-	7.24	E- / 0.0	-79.66 / 0	--	--	0.00	D / 1.9	15.29	2.14
IN	*VelocityShares Dly 2x VIX Med-T	TVIZ	E-	34.55	E- / 0.0	-38.41 / 3	--	--	0.00	D / 2.0	2.80	0.04
GI	*VelocityShares VIX Short-Term ET	VIIX	E-	36.42	E- / 0.0	-42.19 / 2	--	--	0.00	D / 1.9	0.94	0.17
PM	*Direxion Daily Gold Miners Bull	NUGT	E-	16.36	E- / 0.1	-52.83 / 1	--	--	0.00	D+ / 2.4	-0.18	0.01
FO	*Direxion Daily Latin Amer Bear 3	LHB	E-	11.10	E- / 0.1	-23.27 / 9	--	--	0.00	D / 1.9	0.00	0.05
GR	*Direxion Daily Mid Cap Bear 3X	MWN	E-	21.23	E- / 0.1	-40.11 / 3	-64.94 / 0	--	0.00	D / 1.9	0.14	0.03
GR	*Direxion Daily Technology Bear 3	TYP	E-	8.71	E- / 0.1	-58.82 / 0	-62.59 / 1	--	0.00	D / 1.9	0.00	-0.03
EN	*Direxion Energy Bear 3x Shares	ERY	E-	9.75	E- / 0.1	-26.14 / 7	-59.72 / 1	--	0.00	D / 1.9	0.31	-0.06
GR	*Direxion Large Cap Bear 3x Share	BGZ	E-	20.16	E- / 0.1	-42.56 / 2	-57.44 / 1	--	0.00	D+ / 2.3	0.15	-0.04
IN	*iPath Shrt Ext Rus 2000 TR Idx E	RTSA	E-	22.95	E- / 0.1	-7.91 / 25	--	--	0.00	D / 2.0	0.44	-0.02
GR	*ProShares UltraPro Short Dow30	SDOW	E-	19.25	E- / 0.1	-41.95 / 3	--	--	0.00	D+ / 2.7	-0.05	-0.05
GR	*ProShares UltraPro Short S&P 500	SPXU	E-	9.06	E- / 0.1	-42.40 / 2	--	--	0.00	D+ / 2.4	0.11	-0.06
IN	*ProShares UltraShort Real Estate	SRS	E-	29.54	E- / 0.1	-35.81 / 4	-62.75 / 0	-50.77 / 0	0.00	D+ / 2.8	0.24	-0.01
GR	*ProShares UltraShort Russell2000	SKK	E-	26.67	E- / 0.1	-31.49 / 5	-51.15 / 1	-31.53 / 1	0.00	D+ / 2.7	-0.56	0.06
FO	*Direxion Daily China Bear 3x ETF	YANG	E-	12.34	E- / 0.2	-11.60 / 19	--	--	0.00	D / 1.9	0.24	0.09
IN	*ProShares UltraShort Basic Mater	SMN	E-	14.99	E- / 0.2	-9.26 / 23	-52.21 / 1	-38.90 / 0	0.00	D / 2.1	0.00	-0.01
FS	*ProShares UltraShort Financials	SKF	E-	40.40	E- / 0.2	-28.58 / 6	-50.03 / 1	-32.57 / 0	0.00	D+ / 2.7	0.02	-0.03
EM	*ProShares UltraShort MSCI Emg Mk	EEV	E-	25.89	E- / 0.2	-9.06 / 23	-46.30 / 2	--	0.00	D+ / 2.3	0.04	-0.03
IN	*ProShares UltraShort Semiconduct	SSG	E-	32.65	E- / 0.2	-36.96 / 4	-47.80 / 2	-31.53 / 1	0.00	D+ / 2.5	-0.27	-0.02
GR	*Direxion Daily Nat Gas Rel Bull	GASL	E-	34.66	E / 0.3	-57.45 / 1	--	--	0.22	D+ / 2.5	0.03	-0.15
EN	*iPath DJ UBS Ntrl Gas Tot Ret Su	GAZ	E-	3.80	E / 0.3	-57.16 / 1	-41.52 / 2	--	0.00	D / 1.9	80.09	14.86
PM	*PowerShares DB Gold Double Sht E	DZZ	E-	4.61	E / 0.3	-40.73 / 3	-42.23 / 2	--	0.00	D / 1.9	0.00	-0.26
FO	*ProShares UltraShort MSCI PXJ	JPX	E-	40.45	E / 0.3	-17.04 / 13	--	--	0.00	D+ / 2.5	0.75	-0.18
EN	*iPath Cptl Glbl Carbon Tot Ret E	GRN	E-	10.00	E / 0.4	-65.51 / 0	-24.73 / 4	--	0.00	D / 1.9	-11.50	-5.12
PM	*PowerShares DB Base Mtls Dbl Sh	BOM	E-	12.24	E / 0.4	17.58 / 80	-37.33 / 3	--	0.00	D / 1.9	-0.33	-0.10
GR	*PowerShares DB Crude Oil Dbl Sh	DTO	E-	37.92	E / 0.4	-8.85 / 23	-36.70 / 3	--	0.00	D / 1.9	-0.16	-0.19
EN	*ProShares UltraShort DJ-UBS Cr O	SCO	E-	35.16	E / 0.4	-12.49 / 18	-36.37 / 3	--	0.00	D / 2.2	-0.23	-0.21
FO	*ProShares UltraShort FTSE China	FXP	E-	26.09	E / 0.4	0.93 / 43	-38.26 / 3	--	0.00	D+ / 2.6	-0.19	-0.05
FO	*ProShares UltraShort MSCI Brazil	BZQ	E-	14.27	E / 0.4	3.39 / 50	--	--	0.00	D / 2.0	0.28	-0.01
IN	*IPath S&P 500 VIX Mid-Trm Futr E	VXZ	E-	46.23	E / 0.5	-15.42 / 15	-25.39 / 4	--	0.00	D+ / 2.4	1.31	0.09
USA	*PowerShares DB 3x Sh 25+ Yr Tr E	SBND	E-	10.80	E / 0.5	-58.60 / 1	--	--	0.00	D / 1.9	0.84	0.17
GR	*PowerShares DB Agri Double Sht	AGA	E-	16.98	E / 0.5	4.04 / 52	-28.06 / 3	--	0.00	D / 1.9	-1.11	0.21
GR	*PowerShares DB Commodity Double	DEE	E-	30.42	E / 0.5	5.41 / 57	-26.72 / 4	--	0.00	D / 1.9	6.48	0.26
EM	*Direxion Daily India Bull 3X	INDL	E-	23.95	E+ / 0.7	-46.75 / 2	--	--	0.00	D / 2.2	-0.29	-0.11
FO	*Direxion Daily China Bull 3x ETF	YINN	E-	22.25	E+ / 0.8	-58.41 / 1	--	--	0.00	D / 1.9	0.59	-0.04
GR	*Direxion Daily Nat Gas Rel Bear	GASX	E-	18.65	E+ / 0.9	12.79 / 73	--	--	0.00	D / 2.0	-0.11	0.04

* Denotes ETF Fund, N/A denotes number is not available

Fund Type	Fund Name	Ticker Symbol	Overall Investment Rating	Price As of 3/31/12	PERFORMANCE					Dividend Yield %	RISK Risk Rating/ Pts	VALUATION Premium/Discount	
	99 Pct = Best 0 Pct = Worst				Perform-ance Rating/Pts	Annualized Total Return Through 3/31/12						As of 3/31/12	1 Year Average
						1Yr/Pct	3Yr/Pct	5Yr/Pct					
GI	RENN Global Entrepreneurs Fund Inc	RCG	E+	1.95	E+ / 0.8	-5.80 / 29	-12.49 / 5	-25.24 / 2	0.00	C / 5.4	-20.73	-21.53
PM	ASA Gold & Precious Metals Ltd	ASA	E+	25.77	D+ / 2.7	-17.10 / 13	15.95 / 29	5.46 / 59	2.64	D+ / 2.8	-5.78	-9.24
IN	Equus Total Return	EQS	D-	2.27	D- / 1.0	-14.02 / 16	-4.18 / 6	-21.31 / 3	0.00	C / 5.5	-37.12	-42.20
IN	Eaton Vance Risk Mgd Div Eq Inc	ETJ	D-	10.59	D- / 1.1	-5.34 / 30	-0.78 / 7	--	12.07	B- / 7.0	-15.48	-13.96
FO	Morgan Stanley China A Share Fund	CAF	D-	19.59	D- / 1.1	-24.32 / 8	0.65 / 7	7.70 / 72	0.00	C / 5.5	-9.77	-7.38
IN	BlackRock Res & Commdty Strat Trus	BCX	D-	15.13	D- / 1.5	-16.90 / 13	--	--	9.25	C+ / 5.8	-6.02	-5.38
GL	Alpine Total Dynamic Dividend Fund	AOD	D-	4.74	D / 1.7	-12.53 / 18	5.41 / 11	-12.14 / 5	13.92	C / 5.4	-7.42	-5.55
FO	India Fund	IFN	D-	22.30	D / 1.7	-29.73 / 6	8.59 / 14	-0.43 / 25	0.09	C / 5.1	-10.26	-8.00
FO	Morgan Stanley India Inv Fund	IIF	D-	16.56	D / 2.2	-27.77 / 7	12.39 / 20	-0.77 / 24	0.00	C / 5.4	-11.21	-8.03
GL	Alpine Global Dynamic Div Fd	AGD	D-	6.06	D+ / 2.8	-11.69 / 19	11.15 / 18	-11.22 / 6	11.88	C / 5.1	8.02	4.37
EN	ING Risk Managed Nat Resources Fun	IRR	D	12.27	D- / 1.5	-16.01 / 14	5.43 / 11	1.37 / 33	10.76	B- / 7.2	-4.51	-2.62
USA	Federated Enhanced Treasury Income	FTT	D	14.76	D / 1.6	2.46 / 47	--	--	6.10	B- / 7.5	-9.95	-10.89
LP	Avenue Income Credit Strategies	ACP	D	16.58	D / 1.8	-5.12 / 30	--	--	8.69	B- / 7.2	-4.93	-1.45
FO	Japan Smaller Cap Fund Inc.	JOF	D	7.83	D / 2.1	-11.98 / 19	9.33 / 15	-8.52 / 8	0.45	B- / 7.6	-14.43	-11.23
EN	Gabelli Nat Res Gold & Income Trus	GNT	D	15.81	D / 2.2	-10.42 / 21	--	--	10.63	C+ / 6.1	3.20	-2.03
MTG	American Strat Inc Portfolio III	CSP	D	7.00	D+ / 2.4	1.25 / 44	9.41 / 15	-0.08 / 27	6.43	B- / 7.5	-14.32	-14.67
FO	Greater China Fund	GCH	D	11.50	D+ / 2.4	-9.62 / 22	9.14 / 15	0.73 / 30	0.00	C+ / 6.8	-7.63	-10.23
GL	First Trust Active Dividend Inc Fd	FAV	D	8.70	D+ / 2.5	-15.63 / 14	12.84 / 21	--	8.28	C+ / 6.5	-9.28	-3.54
FO	JF China Region Fund	JFC	D	12.73	D+ / 2.5	-17.59 / 12	10.84 / 17	3.36 / 47	0.80	C+ / 6.7	-11.29	-11.79
LP	Nuveen Tax-Advantaged Floating Rat	JFP	D	2.43	D+ / 2.8	11.15 / 70	7.93 / 13	-22.32 / 3	4.94	C+ / 6.3	-11.96	-8.88
FO	BlackRock Intl Grth and Inc Tr	BGY	D	7.85	C- / 3.0	-11.13 / 20	14.19 / 24	--	11.21	C+ / 6.5	-8.61	-5.34
FO	Asia Tigers Fund	GRR	D	13.56	C- / 3.1	-12.08 / 19	14.58 / 25	0.20 / 28	0.00	C+ / 5.8	-8.01	-7.11
GR	ING Infrastructure Indus & Mtrls	IDE	D	18.48	C- / 3.1	-8.56 / 24	--	--	9.74	C+ / 6.7	-6.57	-6.45
IN	Cornerstone Progressive Return Fun	CFP	D	6.67	C- / 3.3	9.13 / 67	12.24 / 20	--	16.44	C+ / 6.3	27.29	25.20
IN	Cornerstone Total Return Fund	CRF	D	6.80	C- / 3.3	-13.91 / 16	17.41 / 34	-14.07 / 4	17.22	C / 5.4	17.44	37.69
GEN	Putnam Master Intermediate Inc Tr	PIM	D	5.15	C- / 3.3	-5.78 / 29	16.13 / 30	4.04 / 51	6.76	C+ / 6.1	-5.68	-3.76
GL	Canadian World Fund Limited	T.CWF	D	3.75	C- / 3.4	-9.86 / 22	17.19 / 33	-10.58 / 6	0.00	C / 4.9	-32.80	-31.83
FO	AGIC Intl & Premium Strategy Fund	NAI	D	10.97	C- / 3.5	-9.35 / 22	15.31 / 28	-5.08 / 12	14.59	C+ / 6.0	-2.58	-3.65
FO	Templeton Russia&East European Fun	TRF	D	16.44	C- / 3.7	-32.07 / 5	19.41 / 40	-10.19 / 7	0.00	C / 5.3	-7.59	-6.70
FO	Canadian General Investments Ltd	T.CGI	D	16.92	C / 4.7	-10.66 / 21	22.07 / 53	-5.35 / 12	1.42	C / 4.6	-24.77	-22.40
LP	Blackstone / GSO Lng-Sht Credit In	BGX	D+	18.27	D / 1.8	-3.28 / 33	--	--	7.09	B / 8.2	-2.19	0.72
GL	Nuveen Glob Govt Enhanced Inc	JGG	D+	14.33	D / 1.9	6.80 / 61	6.21 / 11	2.54 / 42	8.65	B / 8.1	-7.13	-7.38
MUN	Nuveen Select Maturities Muni	NIM	D+	10.23	D / 1.9	8.49 / 74	4.41 / 12	4.99 / 72	3.70	B / 8.8	-2.11	1.02
GL	Global Income & Currency Fund	GCF	D+	13.73	D / 2.0	1.59 / 45	6.40 / 12	1.55 / 34	6.55	B / 8.8	-8.04	-9.27
GL	MFS Government Markets Income Trus	MGF	D+	6.78	D / 2.1	13.85 / 76	6.49 / 12	7.80 / 73	7.49	B / 8.4	-2.45	-3.32
GL	GDL Fund	GDL	D+	12.27	D+ / 2.6	0.29 / 42	10.50 / 17	0.74 / 30	10.43	B / 8.2	-12.79	-12.99
FO	Japan Equity Fund	JEQ	D+	5.67	D+ / 2.7	-6.83 / 27	11.51 / 19	-7.71 / 9	0.92	B- / 7.6	-11.13	-9.75
LP	Apollo Senior Floating Rate Fd Inc	AFT	D+	17.91	D+ / 2.9	-4.16 / 32	--	--	6.45	B- / 7.3	-2.50	-4.65
IN	Eaton Vance Tax Mgd Div Eqty Inc	ETY	D+	9.53	C- / 3.1	-0.27 / 40	11.91 / 19	-1.53 / 21	12.15	C+ / 6.8	-15.21	-12.59
GL	ING Global Advantage and Premium O	IGA	D+	12.06	C- / 3.3	-3.11 / 33	13.88 / 24	0.38 / 29	11.11	B- / 7.4	-5.78	-4.34
GI	RMR Real Estate Income	RAP	D+	16.10	C- / 3.3	-4.45 / 31	13.10 / 22	-12.95 / 5	3.91	C+ / 6.8	-17.82	-17.25
FO	The European Equity Fund	EEA	D+	6.78	C- / 3.4	-16.34 / 13	16.31 / 30	-7.72 / 8	0.24	C+ / 6.6	-9.84	-9.39
FO	Asia Pacific Fund	APB	D+	10.58	C- / 3.5	-11.91 / 19	16.39 / 31	3.10 / 45	0.00	B- / 7.2	-9.34	-9.11
GI	Nuveen Energy MLP Total Return Fun	JMF	D+	18.40	C- / 3.5	-1.29 / 38	--	--	6.87	B- / 7.3	1.71	0.45
GL	Wells Fargo Avtg Global Div Oppty	EOD	D+	8.52	C- / 3.5	-1.67 / 36	14.54 / 25	-3.51 / 15	13.15	B- / 7.4	-2.29	-3.52
GL	Eaton Vance Tax-Mgd Gbl Div Eq Inc	EXG	D+	8.91	C- / 3.7	-2.20 / 35	14.70 / 26	-1.85 / 20	12.76	C+ / 6.7	-14.74	-12.37
FO	Swiss Helvetia Fund	SWZ	D+	11.21	C- / 4.0	-3.96 / 32	17.61 / 34	-2.09 / 19	3.00	C+ / 6.7	-11.66	-10.67
FO	China Fund	CHN	D+	23.30	C- / 4.2	-15.73 / 14	19.66 / 41	9.92 / 86	0.75	C+ / 6.1	-7.47	-10.12
IN	Cornerstone Strategic Value Fund	CLM	D+	7.61	C / 4.3	-12.03 / 19	21.15 / 48	-9.47 / 7	18.94	C+ / 5.6	18.17	35.00
GEN	Putnam Premier Income Trust	PPT	D+	5.51	C / 4.9	-7.59 / 26	22.64 / 55	6.38 / 64	6.53	C+ / 5.8	-5.00	-2.16

* Denotes ETF Fund, N/A denotes number is not available

Section V

Performance:
Best and Worst
ETFs and Other
Closed-End Funds

A compilation of those

Exchange-Traded Funds and Other

Closed-End Mutual Funds

receiving the highest and lowest Performance Ratings.

Funds are listed in order by Performance Rating.

Section V Contents

This section contains a summary analysis of each of the top and bottom ETFs and other closed-end mutual funds as determined by their respective TheStreet Performance Ratings. Since the Performance Rating does not take into consideration the amount of risk a fund poses, the selection of funds presented here is based solely on each fund's financial performance over the past three years.

You can use this section to identify those funds that have historically given shareholders the highest returns on their investments. A word of caution though: past performance is not necessarily indicative of future results. While these funds have provided the highest returns, some of them may be currently overvalued and due for a correction.

1. **Fund Type**

The mutual fund's peer category based on an analysis of its investment portfolio.

COH	Corporate – High Yield	HL	Health
COI	Corporate – Inv. Grade	IN	Income
EM	Emerging Market	LP	Loan Participation
EN	Energy/Natural Resources	MTG	Mortgage
FS	Financial Services	MUH	Municipal – High Yield
FO	Foreign	MUN	Municipal – National
GEI	General – Inv. Grade	MUS	Municipal – Single State
GEN	General Bond	PM	Precious Metals
GL	Global	USA	U.S. Gov. – Agency
GR	Growth	UT	Utilities
GI	Growth and Income		

A blank fund type means that the mutual fund has not yet been categorized.

2. **Fund Name**

The name of the mutual fund as stated in its prospectus, which can sometimes differ slightly from the name that the company uses for advertising. If you cannot find the particular mutual fund you are interested in, or if you have any doubts regarding the precise name, verify the information with your broker or on your account statement. Also, use the fund's ticker symbol for confirmation. (See column 3.)

3. **Ticker Symbol**

The unique alphabetic symbol used for identifying and trading a specific mutual fund. No two funds can have the same ticker symbol.

4. **Overall Investment Rating**

Our overall rating is measured on a scale from A to E based on each fund's risk-adjusted performance. Please see page 10 for specific descriptions of each letter grade. Also, refer to page 7 for information on how our ratings are derived. Most important, when using this rating, please be sure to consider the warnings beginning on page 11 regarding the ratings' limitations and the underlying assumptions.

5. **Price**

Closing price of the fund on the date shown.

<table>
<tr><td>6.</td><td>Performance Rating/Points</td><td>A letter grade rating based solely on the mutual fund's financial performance over the trailing three years, without any consideration for the amount of risk the fund poses. Like the overall Investment Rating, the Performance Rating is measured on a scale from A to E for ease of interpretation. The points score indicates where the Performance Rating falls on a scale of 0 to 10.</td></tr>
<tr><td>7.</td><td>1-Year Total Return</td><td>The total return the fund has provided investors over the preceeding 52 weeks. This total return figure is computed based on the fund's dividend distributions and share price appreciation/depreciation during the period, net of the expenses and fees it imposes on its shareholders.</td></tr>
<tr><td>8.</td><td>1-Year Total Return Percentile</td><td>The fund's percentile rank based on its one-year performance compared to that of all other closed-end funds in existence for at least one year. A score of 99 is the best possible, indicating that the fund outperformed 99% of the closed-end mutual funds. Zero is the worst possible percentile score.</td></tr>
<tr><td>9.</td><td>3-Year Total Return</td><td>The total annual return the fund has provided investors over the preceeding 156 weeks.</td></tr>
<tr><td>10.</td><td>3-Year Total Return Percentile</td><td>The fund's percentile rank based on its three-year performance compared to that of all other closed-end funds in existence for at least three years. A score of 99 is the best possible, indicating that the fund outperformed 99% of the closed-end mutual funds. Zero is the worst possible percentile score.</td></tr>
<tr><td>11.</td><td>5-Year Total Return</td><td>The total annual return the fund has provided investors over the preceeding 260 weeks.</td></tr>
<tr><td>12.</td><td>5-Year Total Return Percentile</td><td>The fund's percentile rank based on its five-year performance compared to that of all other closed-end funds in existence for at least five years. A score of 99 is the best possible, indicating that the fund outperformed 99% of the closed-end mutual funds. Zero is the worst possible percentile score.</td></tr>
<tr><td>13.</td><td>Dividend Yield</td><td>Most recent quarterly dividend to fund investors annualized, expressed as a percent of the fund's current share price. The dividend yield of a fund can have little correlation to the amount of dividends the fund has received from its underlying investments. Rather, dividend distributions are based on a fund's need to pass earnings from both dividends and gains on the sale of investments along to shareholders. Thus, these dividend distributions are included as a part of the fund's total return.

Keep in mind that dividend income may be taxed at a different rate than capital gains depending on your income tax bracket.</td></tr>
</table>

14. Risk Rating/Points

A letter grade rating based solely on the mutual fund's risk as determined by its monthly performance volatility over the trailing three years. The risk rating does not take into consideration the overall financial performance the fund has achieved or the total return it has provided to its shareholders. Like the overall Investment Rating, the Risk Rating is measured on a scale from A to E for ease of interpretation. The points score indicates where the Risk Rating falls on a scale of 0 to 10.

15. Premium/ Discount

A comparison of the fund's price to its NAV as of the date indicated. The premium (+) or discount (-) indicates the percentage the shares are trading above or below the fund's NAV per share.

If the price is above the fund's NAV, the fund is said to be trading at a premium. If the price is lower than the fund's NAV, the fund is trading at a discount.

16. 1-Year Average Premium/ Discount

The average of the fund's premium/discount over the preceeding year.

It can be useful to compare the fund's current premium/discount to its one-year average. If the fund is currently trading at a premium/discount that is lower/higher than its one-year average, then there has been less demand for the fund in more recent times than over the past year. Conversely, if the fund is currently trading at a premium/discount that is higher/lower than its one-year average, this indicates that there has been greater demand for the fund in more recent times than over the past year.

Fund Type	Fund Name	Ticker Symbol	Overall Investment Rating	Price As of 3/31/12	Performance Rating/Pts	1Yr/Pct	3Yr/Pct	5Yr/Pct	Dividend Yield %	Risk Rating/ Pts	Premium/Discount As of 3/31/12	1 Year Average
GR	*Direxion Daily Retail Bull 3X	RETL	A+	87.91	A+ / 9.9	59.72 / 99	--	--	0.00	B / 8.5	-0.05	0.06
GR	*ProShares Ultra QQQ	QLD	B+	118.95	A+ / 9.9	32.11 / 90	57.20 / 99	8.17 / 75	0.00	C+/ 6.9	-0.03	-0.01
HL	*ProShares Ultra Nasdaq Biotech	BIB	B	96.07	A+ / 9.9	39.64 / 96	--	--	0.00	C+/ 6.2	0.20	-0.13
GR	*Direxion Large Cap Bull 3x Share	BGU	C+	86.18	A+ / 9.9	1.51 / 45	55.23 / 99	--	0.00	C / 4.5	-0.22	-0.03
IN	*Brclys ETN+ Lg B Lv S&P500 TR ET	BXUB	C+	97.75	A+ / 9.9	16.86 / 80	--	--	0.00	C- / 3.8	0.00	-0.05
FS	*ProShares Ultra KBW Regional Ban	KRU	C+	49.10	A+ / 9.9	-2.91 / 34	--	--	0.84	C- / 3.7	0.25	0.06
IN	*iPath Long Ext S&P 500 TR Idx ET	SFLA	C+	81.24	A+ / 9.9	18.03 / 81	--	--	0.00	C- / 3.6	-0.01	-0.03
GR	*ProShares UltraPro QQQ	TQQQ	C	119.62	A+ / 9.9	40.51 / 97	--	--	0.00	D / 2.2	-0.04	-0.03
IN	*iPath Long Ext Rus 2000 TR Idx E	RTLA	C	71.24	A+ / 9.9	-3.26 / 33	--	--	0.00	D+/ 2.4	-1.00	-0.01
GR	*Direxion Daily Technology Bull 3	TYH	C-	65.50	A+ / 9.9	39.24 / 96	70.71 / 99	--	0.00	D / 1.9	-0.03	-0.04
GR	*Direxion Daily Mid Cap Bull 3X	MWJ	C-	41.17	A+ / 9.9	-14.80 / 15	67.22 / 99	--	0.00	D / 1.9	-0.34	-0.06
IN	*ProShares UltraPro S&P 500	UPRO	C-	84.88	A+ / 9.9	5.37 / 57	--	--	0.04	D / 1.9	-0.21	-0.02
GR	*Direxion Daily Real Estate Bull	DRN	C-	68.61	A+ / 9.9	16.70 / 79	--	--	0.00	D / 1.9	-0.03	N/A
IN	*Direxion Daily Semiconductor Bul	SOXL	C-	44.07	A+ / 9.9	-20.52 / 11	--	--	0.00	D / 1.9	-0.05	-0.04
GI	*VelocityShares Dly Invs VIX ST E	XIV	C-	12.27	A+ / 9.9	-13.08 / 18	--	--	0.00	D / 1.9	-0.97	-0.18
IN	*ProShares Ultra Consumer Goods	UGE	A+	92.52	A+ / 9.8	24.50 / 85	46.70 / 98	7.50 / 71	0.66	B / 8.0	0.21	-0.10
IN	*ProShares Ultra Consumer Service	UCC	A-	68.31	A+ / 9.8	26.85 / 86	51.59 / 99	-0.15 / 27	0.00	B- / 7.2	0.12	0.07
FO	*iShares MSCI Thailand Inv Market	THD	A-	72.79	A+ / 9.8	9.88 / 68	50.49 / 99	--	2.15	B- / 7.1	0.12	0.13
IN	*ProShares Ultra Real Estate	URE	B+	61.79	A+ / 9.8	8.79 / 66	58.64 / 99	-26.00 / 2	1.46	C+/ 6.4	-0.10	N/A
GR	*ProShares Ultra Technology	ROM	B+	86.97	A+ / 9.8	30.39 / 89	50.01 / 99	5.83 / 61	0.00	C+/ 6.5	0.02	-0.03
GR	*ProShares Ultra Rus Mid Cap Valu	UVU	B+	39.62	A+ / 9.8	-4.98 / 30	47.51 / 98	-9.46 / 7	0.23	C+/ 6.4	0.15	-0.10
IN	*ProShares Ultra Industrials	UXI	B	51.98	A+ / 9.8	-5.72 / 29	48.22 / 98	-4.95 / 13	0.35	C+/ 5.8	-0.13	-0.03
GR	*ProShares Ultra Rus Mid Cap Grow	UKW	B	54.89	A+ / 9.8	-0.99 / 38	48.77 / 99	-2.53 / 18	0.00	C+/ 6.3	0.11	-0.08
GR	*ProShares UltraPro Dow30	UDOW	B	166.24	A+ / 9.8	13.86 / 76	--	--	0.69	C+/ 5.8	-0.05	N/A
GR	*Direxion Daily Small Cap Bull 3x	TNA	C	62.40	A+ / 9.8	-30.06 / 5	48.01 / 98	--	0.00	D+/ 2.5	-0.11	-0.02
GR	*ProShares UltraPro MidCap400	UMDD	C-	81.52	A+ / 9.8	-20.39 / 11	--	--	0.00	D / 1.9	-0.06	-0.05
GR	*ProShares Ultra Russell1000 Grow	UKF	B+	64.55	A+ / 9.7	13.00 / 74	43.74 / 97	0.99 / 31	0.20	C+/ 6.9	0.00	-0.05
GR	*ProShares Ultra MidCap 400	MVV	B	70.84	A+ / 9.7	-7.02 / 27	46.43 / 98	-3.02 / 17	0.00	C+/ 6.1	-0.10	-0.02
GR	*ProShares Ultra SmallCap 600	SAA	B	52.31	A+ / 9.7	-1.60 / 37	45.25 / 98	-6.00 / 11	0.04	C+/ 5.9	0.06	-0.07
IN	*ProShares Ultra Russell 3000	UWC	B	91.97	A+ / 9.7	8.42 / 65	--	--	0.00	C+/ 6.2	0.01	-0.14
GR	*ProShares Ultra Russell2000 Grow	UKK	B-	50.97	A+ / 9.7	-10.01 / 22	44.82 / 97	-5.18 / 12	0.00	C+/ 5.6	0.71	-0.04
FO	*Market Vectors Indonesia Idx ETF	IDX	C+	29.86	A+ / 9.7	-0.18 / 40	48.88 / 99	--	1.52	C / 4.7	-0.40	-0.27
IN	*iShares FTSE NAREIT Retail Idx	RTL	A+	32.64	A+ / 9.6	18.72 / 81	41.95 / 96	--	3.40	B / 8.0	0.09	-0.02
GR	*ProShares Ultra Dow 30	DDM	B+	70.54	A+ / 9.6	13.63 / 75	40.78 / 96	-1.19 / 22	0.53	B- / 7.0	0.00	0.03
GR	*ProShares Ultra S-P 500	SSO	B+	58.36	A+ / 9.6	9.26 / 67	39.26 / 95	-6.26 / 10	0.94	C+/ 6.8	-0.05	-0.01
IN	*Guggenheim 2x S&P 500 ETF	RSU	B+	49.99	A+ / 9.6	10.01 / 68	39.78 / 95	--	1.85	C+/ 6.8	-0.02	-0.04
GL	*PowerShares DB 3x German Bd Fut	BUNT	B-	30.36	A+ / 9.6	54.98 / 99	--	--	0.00	C+/ 5.6	-0.10	-0.05
IN	*ProShares Ultra Semiconductors	USD	C+	45.45	A+ / 9.6	11.46 / 71	38.44 / 94	-6.55 / 10	0.21	C / 5.2	0.02	-0.04
IN	*Brclys ETN+ Lg C Lv S&P500 TR ET	BXUC	C+	164.34	A+ / 9.6	12.97 / 73	--	--	0.00	C / 4.3	0.00	N/A
PM	*UBS E-TRACS S&P 500 Gold Hedged	SPGH	C+	51.27	A+ / 9.6	26.72 / 86	--	--	0.00	C / 4.9	-0.37	0.30
GL	*PowerShares DB 3x Itn Trs B Fut	ITLT	C+	22.00	A+ / 9.6	10.72 / 70	--	--	0.00	C- / 4.0	3.58	-7.03
HL	*ProShares Ultra Health Care	RXL	A-	73.10	A / 9.5	25.06 / 85	36.58 / 92	2.09 / 39	0.83	B- / 7.6	-0.04	-0.02
GI	*iShares FTSE EPRA/NAREIT NA Idx	IFNA	A-	45.93	A / 9.5	10.24 / 69	41.41 / 96	--	3.16	B- / 7.7	-0.39	0.09
PM	*ProShares Ultra Gold	UGL	B	88.40	A / 9.5	25.46 / 85	41.40 / 96	--	0.00	C+/ 6.2	0.69	0.44
GR	*ProShares Ultra Russell2000	UWM	B-	43.76	A / 9.5	-11.81 / 19	40.34 / 95	-9.31 / 7	0.03	C / 5.5	-0.14	-0.02
PM	*PowerShares DB Gold Double Lg ET	DGP	C+	53.17	A / 9.5	24.67 / 85	41.85 / 96	--	0.00	C- / 4.2	-0.21	0.18
USA	*PowerShares DB 3x Lg 25+ Yr Tr E	LBND	C+	37.10	A / 9.5	78.97 / 99	--	--	0.00	C / 4.8	-0.40	-0.08
FO	*Global X/InterBolsa FTSE Col 20	GXG	C	21.20	A / 9.5	5.01 / 55	41.61 / 96	--	0.98	C- / 3.6	-0.14	0.08
GR	*ProShares UltraPro Russell2000	URTY	C-	69.21	A / 9.5	-29.02 / 6	--	--	0.00	D / 1.9	-0.04	-0.05
IN	*SPDR S&P Retail ETF	XRT	A	61.25	A / 9.4	21.16 / 83	36.88 / 93	8.27 / 76	0.65	B / 8.1	0.00	0.01

* Denotes ETF Fund, N/A denotes number is not available

www.thestreetratings.com

Fund Type	Fund Name	Ticker Symbol	Overall Investment Rating	Price As of 3/31/12	Perform-ance Rating/Pts	1Yr/Pct	3Yr/Pct	5Yr/Pct	Dividend Yield %	Risk Rating/ Pts	As of 3/31/12	1 Year Average
GR	*Direxion Daily Small Cap Bear 3x	TZA	E-	17.68	E- / 0.0	-48.95 / 1	-69.01 / 0	--	0.00	D / 1.9	-0.11	-0.01
FS	*Direxion Financial Bear 3x Share	FAZ	E-	20.65	E- / 0.0	-47.42 / 1	-70.20 / 0	--	0.00	D / 1.9	0.00	-0.06
EN	*ProShares UltraShort Silver	ZSL	E-	10.55	E- / 0.0	-54.53 / 1	-72.05 / 0	--	0.00	D / 1.9	0.57	-0.42
IN	*IPath S&P 500 VIX Sm-Trm Futr ET	VXX	E-	16.78	E- / 0.0	-42.31 / 2	-66.07 / 0	--	0.00	D / 1.9	0.60	0.14
GR	*Direxion Daily Real Estate Bear	DRV	E-	27.76	E- / 0.0	-61.04 / 0	--	--	0.00	D / 1.9	-0.07	-0.03
GR	*ProShares UltraPro Short MidCap4	SMDD	E-	11.65	E- / 0.0	-41.25 / 3	--	--	0.00	D / 1.9	-0.26	0.02
GR	*ProShares UltraPro Shrt Russell2	SRTY	E-	8.80	E- / 0.0	-48.45 / 1	--	--	0.00	D / 1.9	-0.11	-0.03
IN	*Brclys ETN+ Sh C Lv I S&P500 TR	BXDC	E-	21.27	E- / 0.0	-39.27 / 3	--	--	0.00	D / 1.9	1.38	0.21
GR	*ProShares UltraPro Short QQQ	SQQQ	E-	10.79	E- / 0.0	-57.44 / 1	--	--	0.00	D / 1.9	0.00	-0.03
IN	*Direxion Daily Semiconductor Bea	SOXS	E-	29.95	E- / 0.0	-50.17 / 1	--	--	0.00	D / 1.9	-0.20	0.01
IN	*C-Tracks ETN Citi Volatility Idx	CVOL	E-	11.00	E- / 0.0	-72.12 / 0	--	--	0.00	D / 1.9	3.00	-0.33
GI	*VelocityShares VIX Short-Term ET	VIIX	E-	36.42	E- / 0.0	-42.19 / 2	--	--	0.00	D / 1.9	0.94	0.17
IN	*VelocityShares Daily 2x VIX S-T	TVIX	E-	7.24	E- / 0.0	-79.66 / 0	--	--	0.00	D / 1.9	15.29	2.14
IN	*VelocityShares Dly 2x VIX Med-T	TVIZ	E-	34.55	E- / 0.0	-38.41 / 3	--	--	0.00	D / 2.0	2.80	0.04
IN	*iPath Shrt Ext Rus 1000 TR Idx E	ROSA	E-	16.01	E- / 0.0	-46.60 / 2	--	--	0.00	D / 1.9	3.49	1.11
IN	*iPath Shrt Ext S&P 500 TR Idx ET	SFSA	E-	16.47	E- / 0.0	-46.07 / 2	--	--	0.00	D / 1.9	2.94	0.02
GEI	*ProShares VIX Short-Term Futures	VIXY	E-	35.77	E- / 0.0	-43.37 / 2	--	--	0.00	D / 1.9	0.76	0.15
GR	*Direxion Daily Retail Bear 3X	RETS	E	12.66	E- / 0.0	-49.26 / 1	--	--	0.00	C- / 3.2	-0.16	-0.08
IN	*ProShares UltraShort Real Estate	SRS	E-	29.54	E- / 0.1	-35.81 / 4	-62.75 / 0	-50.77 / 0	0.00	D+ / 2.8	0.24	-0.01
GR	*ProShares UltraShort Russell2000	SKK	E-	26.67	E- / 0.1	-31.49 / 5	-51.15 / 1	-31.53 / 1	0.00	D+ / 2.7	-0.56	0.06
GR	*Direxion Large Cap Bear 3x Share	BGZ	E-	20.16	E- / 0.1	-42.56 / 2	-57.44 / 1	--	0.00	D+ / 2.3	0.15	-0.04
EN	*Direxion Energy Bear 3x Shares	ERY	E-	9.75	E- / 0.1	-26.14 / 7	-59.72 / 1	--	0.00	D / 1.9	0.31	-0.06
GL	*Direxion Developed Markets Bear	DPK	E-	24.33	E- / 0.1	-29.11 / 6	-56.22 / 1	--	0.00	D / 1.9	0.12	-0.02
GL	*Direxion Emerging Markets Bear 3	EDZ	E-	12.68	E- / 0.1	-25.63 / 8	-64.84 / 0	--	0.00	D / 1.9	0.00	-0.06
GR	*Direxion Daily Technology Bear 3	TYP	E-	8.71	E- / 0.1	-58.82 / 0	-62.59 / 1	--	0.00	D / 1.9	0.00	-0.03
GR	*Direxion Daily Mid Cap Bear 3X	MWN	E-	21.23	E- / 0.1	-40.11 / 3	-64.94 / 0	--	0.00	D / 1.9	0.14	0.03
GR	*ProShares UltraPro Short S&P 500	SPXU	E-	9.06	E- / 0.1	-42.40 / 2	--	--	0.00	D+ / 2.4	0.11	-0.06
FO	*Direxion Daily Latin Amer Bear 3	LHB	E-	11.10	E- / 0.1	-23.27 / 9	--	--	0.00	D / 1.9	0.00	0.05
GR	*ProShares UltraPro Short Dow30	SDOW	E-	19.25	E- / 0.1	-41.95 / 3	--	--	0.00	D+ / 2.7	-0.05	-0.05
PM	*Direxion Daily Gold Miners Bull	NUGT	E-	16.36	E- / 0.1	-52.83 / 1	--	--	0.00	D+ / 2.4	-0.18	0.01
IN	*iPath Shrt Ext Rus 2000 TR Idx E	RTSA	E-	22.95	E- / 0.1	-7.91 / 25	--	--	0.00	D / 2.0	0.44	-0.02
EN	*United States Natural Gas Fund	UNG	E	15.92	E- / 0.1	-64.87 / 0	-49.36 / 1	--	0.00	C- / 3.0	-0.56	-0.02
EN	*US 12 Month Natural Gas Fund	UNL	E	16.28	E- / 0.1	-52.15 / 1	--	--	0.00	C- / 3.9	-0.55	-0.02
HL	*ProShares UltraShort Nasdaq Biot	BIS	E	22.90	E- / 0.1	-47.24 / 2	--	--	0.00	C- / 3.3	0.09	0.12
GR	*Teucrium Natural Gas	NAGS	E+	11.04	E- / 0.1	-53.90 / 1	--	--	0.00	C / 4.5	0.18	-0.20
IN	*ProShares UltraShort Basic Mater	SMN	E-	14.99	E- / 0.2	-9.26 / 23	-52.21 / 1	-38.90 / 0	0.00	D / 2.1	0.00	-0.01
FS	*ProShares UltraShort Financials	SKF	E-	40.40	E- / 0.2	-28.58 / 6	-50.03 / 1	-32.57 / 0	0.00	D+ / 2.7	0.02	-0.03
IN	*ProShares UltraShort Semiconduct	SSG	E-	32.65	E- / 0.2	-36.96 / 4	-47.80 / 2	-31.53 / 1	0.00	D+ / 2.5	-0.27	-0.02
EM	*ProShares UltraShort MSCI Emg Mk	EEV	E-	25.89	E- / 0.2	-9.06 / 23	-46.30 / 2	--	0.00	D+ / 2.3	0.04	-0.03
FO	*Direxion Daily China Bear 3x ETF	YANG	E-	12.34	E- / 0.2	-11.60 / 19	--	--	0.00	D / 1.9	0.24	0.09
GR	*ProShares UltraShort Russell2000	TWM	E	29.62	E- / 0.2	-28.49 / 6	-50.07 / 1	-30.75 / 1	0.00	D+ / 2.8	0.00	-0.01
GR	*ProShares UltraShort MidCap 400	MZZ	E	29.22	E- / 0.2	-24.10 / 9	-47.51 / 2	-28.04 / 1	0.00	C- / 3.1	0.03	-0.03
GR	*ProShares UltraShort QQQ	QID	E	30.28	E- / 0.2	-40.56 / 3	-47.71 / 2	-32.20 / 1	0.00	C- / 3.2	-0.07	-0.03
GR	*ProShares UltraShort SmallCap 60	SDD	E	29.98	E- / 0.2	-33.86 / 4	-50.72 / 1	-29.61 / 1	0.00	D+ / 2.9	-0.56	-0.03
IN	*ProShares UltraShort Consumer Se	SCC	E	12.12	E- / 0.2	-37.14 / 4	-45.44 / 2	-23.66 / 2	0.00	C- / 3.4	-0.41	-0.05
IN	*ProShares UltraShort Industrials	SIJ	E	32.21	E- / 0.2	-23.80 / 9	-48.48 / 1	-25.37 / 2	0.00	D+ / 2.9	-0.03	0.05
GR	*ProShares UltraShort Technology	REW	E	33.69	E- / 0.2	-40.84 / 3	-45.87 / 2	-30.03 / 1	0.00	C- / 3.1	-0.30	-0.05
GR	*ProShares UltraShort Russell MC	SJL	E	38.20	E- / 0.2	-23.06 / 9	-48.57 / 1	-23.76 / 2	0.00	C- / 3.0	0.92	-0.12
IN	*ProShares UltraShort Russell2000	SJH	E	34.07	E- / 0.2	-26.84 / 7	-49.26 / 1	-29.10 / 1	0.00	D+ / 2.8	-0.84	-0.18
FO	*ProShares UltraShort MSCI Europe	EPV	E	35.92	E- / 0.2	-24.06 / 9	--	--	0.00	C- / 3.2	0.11	0.09

* Denotes ETF Fund, N/A denotes number is not available

99 Pct = Best
0 Pct = Worst

Fund Type	Fund Name	Ticker Symbol	Overall Investment Rating	Price As of 3/31/12	Performance Rating/Pts	Annualized Total Return Through 3/31/12			Dividend Yield %	Risk Rating/Pts	Premium/Discount As of 3/31/12	1 Year Average
						1Yr/Pct	3Yr/Pct	5Yr/Pct				
IN	Cohen&Steers REIT& Preferred Incom	RNP	A	16.31	A+ / 9.9	14.47 / 76	66.66 / 99	0.38 / 29	7.36	B- / 7.6	-4.90	-6.73
GI	Cohen&Steers Quality Income Realty	RQI	A-	9.82	A+ / 9.9	6.55 / 60	68.30 / 99	-5.19 / 12	7.33	B- / 7.1	-7.53	-7.91
FO	Thai Fund	TTF	A+	15.94	A+ / 9.8	22.18 / 83	47.49 / 98	13.33 / 98	1.66	B- / 7.9	-10.55	-14.28
IN	F&C/Claymore Preferred Sec Inc Fun	FFC	A+	18.05	A+ / 9.8	16.54 / 79	52.62 / 99	7.06 / 67	9.04	B+ / 9.0	3.97	5.11
IN	F&C/Claymore Total Return Fund	FLC	A+	19.01	A+ / 9.8	14.88 / 77	53.78 / 99	7.76 / 73	8.81	B+ / 9.1	2.92	3.67
GI	Neuberger Berman Real Est Secs Inc	NRO	A+	4.28	A+ / 9.8	9.51 / 67	53.14 / 99	-10.96 / 6	5.61	B- / 7.9	-13.36	-11.89
GI	Nuveen Real Estate Inc Fund	JRS	A	11.29	A+ / 9.8	13.82 / 76	51.67 / 99	-3.40 / 16	8.15	B- / 7.5	8.14	6.70
GI	LMP Real Estate Income Fund Inc	RIT	A	10.32	A+ / 9.8	6.42 / 59	50.88 / 99	-4.72 / 13	6.98	B- / 7.8	-10.65	-10.77
IN	Flaherty&Crumrine Preferred Income	PFD	A+	14.22	A+ / 9.7	24.11 / 84	47.29 / 98	5.24 / 58	7.85	B / 8.8	14.40	14.11
COH	PIMCO Corporate and Income Oppty	PTY	A+	18.61	A+ / 9.7	7.23 / 62	46.86 / 98	14.88 / 99	8.03	B / 8.0	20.30	21.26
GI	Nuveen Preferref Income Opps	JPC	A+	8.88	A+ / 9.7	14.32 / 76	44.52 / 97	1.03 / 31	8.56	B / 8.1	-5.23	-9.88
MUH	Pioneer Municipal High Income Adv	MAV	A+	14.72	A+ / 9.7	27.83 / 98	28.15 / 97	7.20 / 92	8.39	B / 8.4	14.37	11.39
GI	Virtus Total Return	DCA	A+	3.80	A+ / 9.7	6.76 / 60	49.46 / 99	-16.16 / 3	6.16	B / 8.2	-8.65	-12.99
GL	DWS High Income Opportunities Fund	DHG	A+	16.03	A+ / 9.7	20.22 / 82	42.68 / 97	-6.08 / 11	8.92	B / 8.8	2.62	-5.91
MUN	BlackRock Build America Bond	BBN	A+	21.45	A+ / 9.7	31.67 / 99	--	--	7.37	B / 8.5	-4.58	-6.07
EM	Aberdeen Indonesia Fund	IF	A	12.74	A+ / 9.7	4.40 / 53	48.02 / 98	10.30 / 88	2.40	B- / 7.6	-9.19	-8.76
COH	Pacholder High Yield Fund	PHF	A-	9.01	A+ / 9.7	16.38 / 79	46.57 / 98	10.12 / 87	9.32	B- / 7.4	8.82	10.91
GL	PIMCO Global StocksPLUS&Inc	PGP	B+	20.18	A+ / 9.7	-9.11 / 23	48.33 / 99	12.60 / 97	10.91	B- / 7.1	60.41	68.05
FO	Thai Capital Fund	TF	B-	11.58	A+ / 9.7	19.28 / 81	41.48 / 96	11.78 / 95	0.78	C / 5.4	-4.77	-12.40
IN	Flaherty&Crumrine Preferred Inc Op	PFO	A+	10.99	A+ / 9.6	14.90 / 77	45.22 / 98	6.69 / 65	8.24	B / 8.9	7.53	10.43
IN	J Hancock Tax Advantage Div Income	HTD	A+	17.72	A+ / 9.6	18.82 / 81	43.04 / 97	7.57 / 71	6.67	B / 8.9	-7.76	-7.42
GI	Nuveen Credit Strategies Income	JQC	A+	8.98	A+ / 9.6	9.57 / 68	43.36 / 97	1.32 / 32	8.91	B / 8.6	-8.18	-11.21
GI	Cohen&Steers Total Return Realty	RFI	A	13.84	A+ / 9.6	6.31 / 59	42.82 / 97	4.40 / 53	6.36	B- / 7.6	3.98	1.93
COH	PIMCO High Income Fund	PHK	A	12.84	A+ / 9.6	3.36 / 50	46.10 / 98	11.98 / 95	11.39	B- / 7.8	63.15	58.16
MUS	BlackRock NJ Inv Qual Muni Tr	RNJ	A-	14.32	A+ / 9.6	37.08 / 99	22.00 / 89	2.09 / 45	5.49	B- / 7.4	5.60	-1.08
GI	CBRE Clarion Global Real Estate In	IGR	A-	8.04	A+ / 9.6	5.27 / 56	41.95 / 96	-8.42 / 8	6.72	B- / 7.6	-9.46	-11.07
FO	Aberdeen Chile Fund	CH	B	19.23	A+ / 9.6	7.72 / 63	40.27 / 95	15.64 / 99	8.94	C+ / 5.9	14.40	5.98
MUS	Nuveen CA Muni Market Opportunity	NCO	A+	15.50	A / 9.5	33.72 / 99	21.71 / 88	6.12 / 83	6.19	B / 8.8	0.58	-2.57
MUS	BlackRock Invt Qual Muni Inc Tr	RFA	A+	13.43	A / 9.5	31.22 / 99	24.27 / 93	6.63 / 88	6.25	B / 8.5	2.21	1.09
MTG	PCM Fund	PCM	A+	11.01	A / 9.5	11.27 / 71	43.06 / 97	10.21 / 88	9.45	B / 8.8	7.73	9.43
MUS	Nuveen CA Prem Inc Muni	NCU	A+	15.04	A / 9.5	32.72 / 99	22.55 / 90	7.37 / 93	5.78	B / 8.7	-0.99	-5.28
MUN	BlackRock MuniHoldings Fund	MHD	A+	17.76	A / 9.5	30.61 / 99	22.87 / 91	8.78 / 98	6.18	B / 8.9	3.80	0.24
MUN	Eaton Vance Municipal Inc Tr	EVN	A+	13.63	A / 9.5	25.83 / 97	23.32 / 92	4.61 / 68	7.26	B / 8.4	14.35	13.02
LP	PIMCO Income Strategy Fund II	PFN	A	10.16	A / 9.5	4.97 / 55	42.03 / 97	-1.31 / 21	7.68	B / 8.1	3.67	2.91
IN	Foxby Corp	FXBY	B+	1.58	A / 9.5	37.39 / 95	32.45 / 87	-7.74 / 8	0.00	B- / 7.3	-24.40	-29.17
GEN	Helios Advantage Income Fund Inc	HAV	B+	9.30	A / 9.5	31.59 / 90	36.61 / 92	-23.30 / 2	8.06	B- / 7.2	4.38	-6.42
MUH	MFS High Inc Muni Tr	CXE	A+	5.35	A / 9.4	22.22 / 92	23.90 / 93	3.37 / 57	7.18	B / 8.7	4.70	4.09
MUH	MFS High Yield Muni Trust	CMU	A+	4.90	A / 9.4	25.00 / 96	22.76 / 91	3.64 / 59	7.10	B / 8.8	6.75	5.37
MUN	BlackRock MuniVest Fund II	MVT	A+	16.22	A / 9.4	25.46 / 96	23.85 / 92	7.99 / 97	6.73	B / 8.7	3.64	3.10
MUN	PIMCO Municipal Income Fund II	PML	A+	12.18	A / 9.4	28.95 / 98	21.03 / 86	2.07 / 45	6.40	B / 8.5	5.27	3.45
UT	Reaves Utility Income Trust	UTG	A+	26.00	A / 9.4	21.91 / 83	41.19 / 96	9.24 / 82	5.77	B / 8.9	6.17	6.08
MUN	BlackRock Long Term Muni Adv	BTA	A+	12.39	A / 9.4	29.18 / 99	22.45 / 90	4.47 / 67	6.39	B / 8.4	3.08	-1.67
GI	Guggenheim Strategic Opportunities	GOF	A+	20.55	A / 9.4	7.56 / 63	42.12 / 97	--	8.99	B / 8.7	5.60	6.72
MUN	Eaton Vance National Municipal Opp	EOT	A+	21.80	A / 9.4	23.36 / 94	--	--	5.14	B / 8.3	0.74	-3.22
COH	PIMCO Corporate and ncome Strategy	PCN	A	16.04	A / 9.4	10.34 / 69	40.11 / 95	11.61 / 94	8.62	B / 8.0	13.36	15.40
LP	PIMCO Income Strategy Fund	PFL	A	11.36	A / 9.4	4.22 / 53	41.97 / 96	0.19 / 28	8.58	B- / 7.9	5.38	5.93
GI	Nuveen Diversified Dividend&Income	JDD	A	11.73	A / 9.4	12.87 / 73	39.04 / 95	-0.20 / 27	8.53	B / 8.1	-5.10	-7.60
GI	AGIC Convertible & Income Fund II	NCZ	A-	8.76	A / 9.4	-1.74 / 36	41.62 / 96	1.76 / 36	11.64	B- / 7.6	11.88	12.10
GI	The Cushing MLP Total Return Fund	SRV	A-	9.96	A / 9.4	1.30 / 44	42.52 / 97	--	9.04	B- / 7.6	28.85	20.82
GL	Delaware Enhanced Glb Div & Inc Fd	DEX	B+	12.83	A / 9.4	6.58 / 60	38.48 / 95	--	9.59	B- / 7.2	5.86	-1.01

* Denotes ETF Fund, N/A denotes number is not available

99 Pct = Best
0 Pct = Worst

Fund Type	Fund Name	Ticker Symbol	Overall Investment Rating	Price As of 3/31/12	Performance Rating/Pts		Annualized Total Return Through 3/31/12			Dividend Yield %	Risk Rating/Pts		Premium/Discount As of 3/31/12	1 Year Average
							1Yr/Pct	3Yr/Pct	5Yr/Pct					
GI	RENN Global Entrepreneurs Fund Inc	RCG	E+	1.95	E+ /	0.8	-5.80 / 29	-12.49 / 5	-25.24 / 2	0.00	C /	5.4	-20.73	-21.53
IN	Equus Total Return	EQS	D-	2.27	D- /	1.0	-14.02 / 16	-4.18 / 6	-21.31 / 3	0.00	C /	5.5	-37.12	-42.20
FO	Morgan Stanley China A Share Fund	CAF	D-	19.59	D- /	1.1	-24.32 / 8	0.65 / 7	7.70 / 72	0.00	C /	5.5	-9.77	-7.38
IN	Eaton Vance Risk Mgd Div Eq Inc	ETJ	D-	10.59	D- /	1.1	-5.34 / 30	-0.78 / 7	--	12.07	B- /	7.0	-15.48	-13.96
IN	BlackRock Res & Commdty Strat Trus	BCX	D-	15.13	D- /	1.5	-16.90 / 13	--	--	9.25	C+ /	5.8	-6.02	-5.38
EN	ING Risk Managed Nat Resources Fun	IRR	D	12.27	D- /	1.5	-16.01 / 14	5.43 / 11	1.37 / 33	10.76	B- /	7.2	-4.51	-2.62
USA	Federated Enhanced Treasury Income	FTT	D	14.76	D /	1.6	2.46 / 47	--	--	6.10	B- /	7.5	-9.95	-10.89
FO	India Fund	IFN	D-	22.30	D /	1.7	-29.73 / 6	8.59 / 14	-0.43 / 25	0.09	C /	5.1	-10.26	-8.00
GL	Alpine Total Dynamic Dividend Fund	AOD	D-	4.74	D /	1.7	-12.53 / 18	5.41 / 11	-12.14 / 5	13.92	C /	5.4	-7.42	-5.55
USA	BlackRock Enhanced Government	EGF	D+	15.30	D /	1.7	4.86 / 54	4.58 / 10	1.77 / 36	5.49	B /	8.9	-5.20	-5.48
LP	Avenue Income Credit Strategies	ACP	D	16.58	D /	1.8	-5.12 / 30	--	--	8.69	B- /	7.2	-4.93	-1.45
LP	Blackstone / GSO Lng-Sht Credit In	BGX	D+	18.27	D /	1.8	-3.28 / 33	--	--	7.09	B /	8.2	-2.19	0.72
MUN	Nuveen Select Maturities Muni	NIM	D+	10.23	D /	1.9	8.49 / 74	4.41 / 12	4.99 / 72	3.70	B /	8.8	-2.11	1.02
GL	Nuveen Glob Govt Enhanced Inc	JGG	D+	14.33	D /	1.9	6.80 / 61	6.21 / 11	2.54 / 42	8.65	B /	8.1	-7.13	-7.38
GL	Global Income & Currency Fund	GCF	D+	13.73	D /	2.0	1.59 / 45	6.40 / 12	1.55 / 34	6.55	B /	8.8	-8.04	-9.27
USA	Western Asset/Claymore Inf-Link S&	WIA	C-	12.74	D /	2.0	4.62 / 54	7.36 / 13	6.89 / 67	3.27	B+ /	9.6	-10.28	-8.53
FO	Japan Smaller Cap Fund Inc.	JOF	D	7.83	D /	2.1	-11.98 / 19	9.33 / 15	-8.52 / 8	0.45	B- /	7.6	-14.43	-11.23
GL	MFS Government Markets Income Trus	MGF	D+	6.78	D /	2.1	13.85 / 76	6.49 / 12	7.80 / 73	7.49	B /	8.4	-2.45	-3.32
FO	Morgan Stanley India Inv Fund	IIF	D-	16.56	D /	2.2	-27.77 / 7	12.39 / 20	-0.77 / 24	0.00	C /	5.4	-11.21	-8.03
EN	Gabelli Nat Res Gold & Income Trus	GNT	D	15.81	D /	2.2	-10.42 / 21	--	--	10.63	C+ /	6.1	3.20	-2.03
FO	Greater China Fund	GCH	D	11.50	D+ /	2.4	-9.62 / 22	9.14 / 15	0.73 / 30	0.00	C+ /	6.8	-7.63	-10.23
MTG	American Strat Inc Portfolio III	CSP	D	7.00	D+ /	2.4	1.25 / 44	9.41 / 15	-0.08 / 27	6.43	B- /	7.5	-14.32	-14.67
FO	JF China Region Fund	JFC	D	12.73	D+ /	2.5	-17.59 / 12	10.84 / 17	3.36 / 47	0.80	C+ /	6.7	-11.29	-11.79
GL	First Trust Active Dividend Inc Fd	FAV	D	8.70	D+ /	2.5	-15.63 / 14	12.84 / 21	--	8.28	C+ /	6.5	-9.28	-3.54
GEI	Montgomery Street Inc. Sec.	MTS	C-	15.80	D+ /	2.5	5.50 / 57	10.24 / 16	3.46 / 48	3.80	B+ /	9.5	-10.13	-9.69
GL	GDL Fund	GDL	D+	12.27	D+ /	2.6	0.29 / 42	10.50 / 17	0.74 / 30	10.43	B /	8.2	-12.79	-12.99
GL	Morgan Stanley Frntier Emrg Mkt Fd	FFD	D+	11.39	D+ /	2.6	-16.86 / 13	13.57 / 23	--	1.90	B- /	7.5	-13.45	-11.27
GR	Tortoise MLP Fund Inc	NTG	C-	25.62	D+ /	2.6	2.91 / 49	--	--	6.44	B /	8.5	0.43	0.89
USA	Western Asset/Claymore Inf-Link O&	WIW	C	12.79	D+ /	2.6	7.47 / 62	10.47 / 17	6.91 / 67	3.41	B+ /	9.6	-10.75	-10.29
GL	Western Asset Inflation Mgmt	IMF	C	17.75	D+ /	2.6	11.14 / 70	10.01 / 16	6.88 / 67	3.66	B+ /	9.6	-8.83	-8.73
PM	ASA Gold & Precious Metals Ltd	ASA	E+	25.77	D+ /	2.7	-17.10 / 13	15.95 / 29	5.46 / 59	2.64	D+ /	2.8	-5.78	-9.24
FO	Japan Equity Fund	JEQ	D+	5.67	D+ /	2.7	-6.83 / 27	11.51 / 19	-7.71 / 9	0.92	B- /	7.6	-11.13	-9.75
GEI	Duff & Phelps Utilities & Crp Bd T	DUC	C-	11.81	D+ /	2.7	16.33 / 79	9.62 / 16	8.29 / 76	7.11	B /	8.7	0.60	-1.40
MUN	Invesco Value Municipal Securities	IMS	C-	14.33	D+ /	2.7	12.91 / 82	5.53 / 14	4.34 / 65	4.19	B /	8.8	-4.08	-3.48
GL	Alpine Global Dynamic Div Fd	AGD	D-	6.06	D+ /	2.8	-11.69 / 19	11.15 / 18	-11.22 / 6	11.88	C /	5.1	8.02	4.37
LP	Nuveen Tax-Advantaged Floating Rat	JFP	D	2.43	D+ /	2.8	11.15 / 70	7.93 / 13	-22.32 / 3	4.94	C+ /	6.3	-11.96	-8.88
GL	Nuveen Mlt-Cur Sht-Tm Govt Inc	JGT	D+	13.22	D+ /	2.8	3.67 / 51	11.24 / 18	--	9.47	B- /	7.3	-11.51	-11.04
GI	Zweig Total Return Fund	ZTR	C-	3.20	D+ /	2.8	2.95 / 49	11.30 / 18	-0.95 / 23	11.63	B /	8.3	-12.81	-12.27
LP	Apollo Senior Floating Rate Fd Inc	AFT	D+	17.91	D+ /	2.9	-4.16 / 32	--	--	6.45	B- /	7.3	-2.50	-4.65
GL	MFS Intermediate Income Trust	MIN	C-	6.38	D+ /	2.9	14.82 / 77	9.49 / 15	9.20 / 81	8.43	B /	8.6	1.43	-1.02
COI	Western Asst Invst Grade Define Op	IGI	C-	21.40	D+ /	2.9	15.24 / 77	--	--	5.86	B /	8.9	-0.51	0.21
FO	BlackRock Intl Grth and Inc Tr	BGY	D	7.85	C- /	3.0	-11.13 / 20	14.19 / 24	--	11.21	C+ /	6.5	-8.61	-5.34
MUN	Nuveen Select Tax-Free Inc 3	NXR	C-	14.34	C- /	3.0	15.29 / 84	5.59 / 14	5.29 / 75	4.60	B /	8.8	-0.62	-0.99
GL	AllianceBernstein Income Fund	ACG	C	8.19	C- /	3.0	13.81 / 75	11.61 / 18	7.25 / 69	5.86	B+ /	9.3	-9.30	-10.78
FO	Asia Tigers Fund	GRR	D	13.56	C- /	3.1	-12.08 / 19	14.58 / 25	0.20 / 28	0.00	C+ /	5.8	-8.01	-7.11
GR	ING Infrastructure Indus & Mtrls	IDE	D	18.48	C- /	3.1	-8.56 / 24	--	--	9.74	C+ /	6.7	-6.57	-6.45
IN	Eaton Vance Tax Mgd Div Eqty Inc	ETY	D+	9.53	C- /	3.1	-0.27 / 40	11.91 / 19	-1.53 / 21	12.15	C+ /	6.8	-15.21	-12.59
MTG	American Strat Inc Portfolio II	BSP	C-	8.30	C- /	3.1	1.22 / 44	14.25 / 25	2.97 / 44	7.23	B- /	7.9	-15.48	-15.52
EN	Tortoise Power and Energy Inf Fund	TPZ	C-	25.39	C- /	3.1	5.23 / 56	--	--	5.91	B /	8.6	-2.27	-3.14
MTG	BlackRock Income Trust	BKT	C	7.42	C- /	3.1	16.88 / 80	11.90 / 19	8.91 / 79	6.55	B+ /	9.6	-6.08	-9.17

* Denotes ETF Fund, N/A denotes number is not available

Section VI

Top-Rated
ETFs and Other
Closed-End Funds
by Fund Type

A compilation of those

Exchange-Traded Funds and Other

Closed-End Funds

receiving the highest TheStreet Investment Rating

within each type of fund.

Funds are listed in order by Overall Investment Rating.

Section VI Contents

This section contains a summary analysis of the top rated ETFs and other closed-end mutual funds within each fund type. If you are looking for a particular type of mutual fund, these pages show those funds that have achieved the best combination of risk and financial performance over the past three years.

1. Fund Type
The mutual fund's peer category based on an analysis of its investment portfolio.

COH	Corporate – High Yield	HL	Health
COI	Corporate – Inv. Grade	IN	Income
EM	Emerging Market	LP	Loan Participation
EN	Energy/Natural Resources	MTG	Mortgage
FS	Financial Services	MUH	Municipal – High Yield
FO	Foreign	MUN	Municipal – National
GEI	General – Inv. Grade	MUS	Municipal – Single State
GEN	General Bond	PM	Precious Metals
GL	Global	USA	U.S. Gov. – Agency
GR	Growth	UT	Utilities
GI	Growth and Income		

A blank fund type means that the mutual fund has not yet been categorized.

2. Fund Name
The name of the mutual fund as stated in its prospectus, which can sometimes differ slightly from the name that the company uses for advertising. If you cannot find the particular mutual fund you are interested in, or if you have any doubts regarding the precise name, verify the information with your broker or on your account statement. Also, use the fund's ticker symbol for confirmation. (See column 3.)

3. Ticker Symbol
The unique alphabetic symbol used for identifying and trading a specific mutual fund. No two funds can have the same ticker symbol.

4. Overall Investment Rating
Our overall rating is measured on a scale from A to E based on each fund's risk-adjusted performance. Please see page 10 for specific descriptions of each letter grade. Also, refer to page 7 for information on how our ratings are derived. Most important, when using this rating, please be sure to consider the warnings beginning on page 11 regarding the ratings' limitations and the underlying assumptions.

5. Price
Closing price of the fund on the date shown.

6. **Performance Rating/Points**

A letter grade rating based solely on the mutual fund's financial performance over the trailing three years, without any consideration for the amount of risk the fund poses. Like the overall Investment Rating, the Performance Rating is measured on a scale from A to E for ease of interpretation. The points score indicates where the Performance Rating falls on a scale of 0 to 10.

7. **1-Year Total Return**

The total return the fund has provided investors over the preceeding 52 weeks. This total return figure is computed based on the fund's dividend distributions and share price appreciation/depreciation during the period, net of the expenses and fees it imposes on its shareholders.

8. **1-Year Total Return Percentile**

The fund's percentile rank based on its one-year performance compared to that of all other closed-end funds in existence for at least one year. A score of 99 is the best possible, indicating that the fund outperformed 99% of the closed-end mutual funds. Zero is the worst possible percentile score.

9. **3-Year Total Return**

The total annual return the fund has provided investors over the preceeding 156 weeks.

10. **3-Year Total Return Percentile**

The fund's percentile rank based on its three-year performance compared to that of all other closed-end funds in existence for at least three years. A score of 99 is the best possible, indicating that the fund outperformed 99% of the closed-end mutual funds. Zero is the worst possible percentile score.

11. **5-Year Total Return**

The total annual return the fund has provided investors over the preceeding 260 weeks.

12. **5-Year Total Return Percentile**

The fund's percentile rank based on its five-year performance compared to that of all other closed-end funds in existence for at least five years. A score of 99 is the best possible, indicating that the fund outperformed 99% of the closed-end mutual funds. Zero is the worst possible percentile score.

13. **Dividend Yield**

Most recent quarterly dividend to fund investors annualized, expressed as a percent of the fund's current share price. The dividend yield of a fund can have little correlation to the amount of dividends the fund has received from its underlying investments. Rather, dividend distributions are based on a fund's need to pass earnings from both dividends and gains on the sale of investments along to shareholders. Thus, these dividend distributions are included as a part of the fund's total return.

Keep in mind that dividend income may be taxed at a different rate than capital gains depending on your income tax bracket.

14. Risk Rating/Points

A letter grade rating based solely on the mutual fund's risk as determined by its monthly performance volatility over the trailing three years. The risk rating does not take into consideration the overall financial performance the fund has achieved or the total return it has provided to its shareholders. Like the overall Investment Rating, the Risk Rating is measured on a scale from A to E for ease of interpretation. The points score indicates where the Risk Rating falls on a scale of 0 to 10.

15. Premium/Discount

A comparison of the fund's price to its NAV as of the date indicated. The premium (+) or discount (-) indicates the percentage the shares are trading above or below the fund's NAV per share.

If the price is above the fund's NAV, the fund is said to be trading at a premium. If the price is lower than the fund's NAV, the fund is trading at a discount.

16. 1-Year Average Premium/Discount

The average of the fund's premium/discount over the preceeding year.

It can be useful to compare the fund's current premium/discount to its one-year average. If the fund is currently trading at a premium/discount that is lower/higher than its one-year average, then there has been less demand for the fund in more recent times than over the past year. Conversely, if the fund is currently trading at a premium/discount that is higher/lower than its one-year average, this indicates that there has been greater demand for the fund in more recent times than over the past year.

Fund Type	Fund Name	Ticker Symbol	Overall Investment Rating	Price As of 3/31/12	Perform-ance Rating/Pts	Annualized Total Return Through 3/31/12			Dividend Yield %	Risk Rating/Pts	Premium/Discount	
						1Yr/Pct	3Yr/Pct	5Yr/Pct			As of 3/31/12	1 Year Average
COH	PIMCO Corporate and Income Oppty	PTY	A+	18.61	A+ / 9.7	7.23 / 62	46.86 / 98	14.88 / 99	8.03	B / 8.0	20.30	21.26
COH	MFS Interm High Inc	CIF	A+	3.18	A / 9.3	14.94 / 77	38.28 / 94	10.20 / 87	8.30	B / 8.7	5.65	-0.82
COH	Credit Suisse High Yield Bond Fund	DHY	A+	3.12	A- / 9.2	11.50 / 71	39.04 / 95	5.63 / 60	10.19	B / 8.6	6.12	5.54
COH	PIMCO High Income Fund	PHK	A	12.84	A+ / 9.6	3.36 / 50	46.10 / 98	11.98 / 95	11.39	B- / 7.8	63.15	58.16
COH	PIMCO Corporate and ncome Strategy	PCN	A	16.04	A / 9.4	10.34 / 69	40.11 / 95	11.61 / 94	8.62	B / 8.0	13.36	15.40
COH	BlackRock Debt Strategies Fund Inc	DSU	A	4.14	B+ / 8.9	11.60 / 72	36.55 / 92	-0.29 / 26	7.83	B / 8.6	0.49	-1.33
COH	BlackRock High Income Shares	HIS	A	2.28	B+ / 8.6	15.98 / 79	32.42 / 86	8.02 / 74	7.47	B / 8.7	2.70	-3.63
COH	Helios High Yield Fund	HHY	A	10.45	B+ / 8.4	23.79 / 84	29.94 / 82	10.67 / 90	9.33	B+ / 9.0	5.24	0.38
COH	Pacholder High Yield Fund	PHF	A-	9.01	A+ / 9.7	16.38 / 79	46.57 / 98	10.12 / 87	9.32	B- / 7.4	8.82	10.91
COH	Invesco Van Kampen High Inc Tr II	VLT	A-	16.94	B+ / 8.8	10.77 / 70	34.53 / 90	6.68 / 65	8.22	B / 8.2	3.61	3.60
COH	Western Asset High Yld Def Opp	HYI	B+	19.69	B+ / 8.4	14.33 / 76	--	--	8.96	B / 8.0	8.13	0.63
COH	BlackRock Senior High Income Fund	ARK	B+	4.11	B / 7.8	8.46 / 65	29.44 / 81	0.93 / 31	7.30	B / 8.7	-0.72	-3.87
COH	BlackRock High Yield Trust	BHY	B+	7.24	B / 7.7	16.70 / 79	27.54 / 75	6.82 / 66	7.21	B / 8.9	1.26	-2.75
COH	BlackRock Corporate High Yield III	CYE	B	7.59	A- / 9.1	15.39 / 78	36.91 / 93	9.56 / 84	8.06	B- / 7.0	3.27	-0.90
COH	New America High Income Fund	HYB	B	10.29	A- / 9.1	11.08 / 70	37.27 / 93	12.43 / 97	7.58	C+ / 6.6	1.08	1.22
COH	BlackRock Corporate High Yield V	HYV	B	12.55	A- / 9.0	14.89 / 77	35.42 / 91	9.30 / 82	8.22	B- / 7.0	1.87	-1.40
COH	Dreyfus High Yield Strategies Fund	DHF	B	4.65	A- / 9.0	9.70 / 68	37.00 / 93	13.28 / 98	9.46	C+ / 6.4	19.23	18.16
COH	BlackRock Corporate High Yield VI	HYT	B	12.42	B+ / 8.9	14.95 / 77	34.19 / 89	9.19 / 81	8.07	B- / 7.1	3.16	-1.38
COH	BlackRock Corporate High Yield Fun	COY	B	7.35	B+ / 8.5	11.48 / 71	32.92 / 87	8.63 / 78	8.33	B- / 7.1	1.66	1.12
COH	Invesco High Yield Investments Fun	MSY	B	6.36	B / 8.1	16.09 / 79	29.78 / 82	11.73 / 95	8.49	B- / 7.3	2.58	2.16
COH	Credit Suisse Asset Mgmt Income	CIK	B	3.73	B- / 7.4	10.87 / 70	28.40 / 78	8.02 / 74	8.53	B / 8.6	0.27	0.69
COH	BlackRock Strategic Bond Trust	BHD	B	14.07	C+ / 6.4	17.82 / 80	22.57 / 54	9.64 / 84	7.20	B+ / 9.1	-0.35	-4.38
COH	Neuberger Berman High Yield Strat	NHS	B-	13.55	B+ / 8.8	1.44 / 45	37.73 / 94	9.12 / 80	7.97	C+ / 6.5	1.04	3.81
COH	Wells Fargo Avtg Income Oppty	EAD	B-	10.24	B / 7.7	10.96 / 70	29.64 / 81	5.82 / 61	9.96	B- / 7.2	5.79	4.24
COH	Western Asset Managed High Income	MHY	B-	6.14	C+ / 6.3	5.83 / 58	24.88 / 64	7.79 / 73	8.31	B / 8.6	3.37	2.94
COH	DWS High Income Trust	KHI	C+	10.09	B / 8.0	8.44 / 65	31.14 / 84	6.35 / 63	9.66	C+ / 6.7	4.24	6.61
COH	Western Asset High Income Opp Inc.	HIO	C+	6.16	C+ / 6.4	4.25 / 53	25.73 / 67	8.23 / 75	8.28	B- / 7.4	0.33	1.13
COH	Western Asset High Income Fund	HIF	C	9.64	C / 5.3	4.77 / 54	22.29 / 53	9.09 / 80	7.78	B- / 7.4	3.77	4.85
COH	*Guggenhm BltShs 2015 HY Corp Bd	BSJF	C	25.89	D+ / 2.7	6.76 / 61	--	--	3.80	B+ / 9.4	0.47	0.54
COH	*Guggenhm BltShs 2014 HY Corp Bd	BSJE	C	25.92	D+ / 2.5	6.78 / 61	--	--	4.81	B+ / 9.6	0.27	0.41
COH	*SPDR Barclays Cap Hi Yld Bd ETF	JNK	C-	39.37	C / 4.9	6.23 / 59	20.40 / 45	--	7.19	C+ / 6.9	-0.13	0.27
COH	*iShares iBoxx $ High Yld Corp Bo	HYG	C-	90.72	C / 4.3	6.39 / 59	18.10 / 36	--	7.10	B- / 7.1	0.49	0.59
COH	*PowerShares Fundamental High Yie	PHB	C-	18.62	C- / 3.7	6.33 / 59	15.90 / 29	--	5.37	B / 8.0	-0.27	0.14
COH	*Peritus High Yield ETF	HYLD	C-	49.75	D+ / 2.4	2.47 / 48	--	--	6.35	B+ / 9.0	0.42	0.24
COH	*Guggenhm BltShs 2013 HY Corp Bd	BSJD	C-	25.77	D / 2.2	5.29 / 56	--	--	4.38	B+ / 9.6	0.39	0.44
COH	*Guggenhm BltShs 2012 HY Corp Bd	BSJC	C-	25.49	D / 1.7	3.47 / 50	--	--	3.67	B+ / 9.7	0.24	0.63

99 Pct = Best
0 Pct = Worst

* Denotes ETF Fund, N/A denotes number is not available

www.thestreetratings.com

Fund Type	Fund Name	Ticker Symbol	Overall Investment Rating	Price As of 3/31/12	Performance Rating/Pts	Annualized Total Return Through 3/31/12			Dividend Yield %	Risk Rating/ Pts	Premium/Discount	
						1Yr/Pct	3Yr/Pct	5Yr/Pct			As of 3/31/12	1 Year Average
COI	Cutwater Select Income	BDF	C+	19.74	C / 5.2	15.40 / 78	20.08 / 44	8.13 / 75	5.83	B+/ 9.6	-3.14	-7.09
COI	*iShares iBoxx $ Inves Grade Corp	LQD	C	115.63	C- / 3.1	11.14 / 70	12.81 / 21	6.95 / 67	4.18	B+/ 9.4	0.32	0.49
COI	*iShares Barclays Credit Bond Fd	CFT	C	109.72	D+ / 2.8	9.19 / 67	11.86 / 19	6.72 / 66	3.82	B+/ 9.4	0.58	0.50
COI	*Guggenheim BltShs 2017 Corp Bd E	BSCH	C	22.02	D+ / 2.6	8.41 / 65	--	--	2.83	B+/ 9.7	0.32	0.43
COI	*Vanguard Intm-Term Corp Bd Idx E	VCIT	C	83.75	D+ / 2.5	9.69 / 68	--	--	3.44	B+/ 9.7	0.53	0.60
COI	*PIMCO Investment Grade Corp Bond	CORP	C	103.88	D+ / 2.5	9.23 / 67	--	--	3.00	B+/ 9.7	0.27	0.09
COI	*iShares Barclays Intrm Credit Bd	CIU	C	108.85	D+ / 2.4	6.87 / 61	9.50 / 15	6.21 / 62	3.51	B+/ 9.7	0.49	0.35
COI	Western Asst Invst Grade Define Op	IGI	C-	21.40	D+ / 2.9	15.24 / 77	--	--	5.86	B / 8.9	-0.51	0.21
COI	*Vanguard Long-Term Corp Bd Idx E	VCLT	C-	84.98	D+ / 2.8	15.29 / 78	--	--	4.86	B+/ 9.2	0.45	0.94
COI	*Guggenheim BltShs 2016 Corp Bd E	BSCG	C-	21.69	D / 2.1	6.49 / 60	--	--	2.43	B+/ 9.7	0.23	0.60
COI	*Guggenheim BltShs 2015 Corp Bd E	BSCF	C-	21.50	D / 2.0	5.71 / 58	--	--	2.12	B+/ 9.8	0.19	0.61
COI	*Vanguard Short-Term Crp Bd Idx E	VCSH	C-	79.04	D / 1.7	4.51 / 54	--	--	2.32	B+/ 9.9	0.39	0.35
COI	*Guggenheim BltShs 2014 Corp Bd E	BSCE	C-	21.14	D / 1.6	3.20 / 49	--	--	1.76	B+/ 9.9	0.09	0.59
COI	*iShares Barclays 1-3 Year Credit	CSJ	C-	105.09	D / 1.6	2.62 / 48	4.90 / 10	4.20 / 51	1.79	B+/ 9.8	0.25	0.15
COI	*SPDR Barclays Cap S/T Corp Bd ET	SCPB	C-	30.53	D- / 1.5	2.74 / 48	--	--	1.65	B+/ 9.9	0.33	0.25
COI	*Guggenheim BltShs 2013 Corp Bd E	BSCD	C-	20.93	D- / 1.4	2.50 / 48	--	--	1.43	B+/ 9.9	0.34	0.51
COI	*PIMCO Enhanced Short Maturity St	MINT	C-	101.03	D- / 1.3	1.06 / 44	--	--	1.19	B+/ 9.9	0.01	0.01
COI	*Guggenheim BltShs 2012 Corp Bd E	BSCC	C-	20.48	D- / 1.2	0.42 / 42	--	--	0.94	B+/ 9.9	-0.10	0.43
COI	*SPDR Barclays Cap Intl Corp Bd E	IBND	D+	33.96	D / 2.1	2.83 / 49	--	--	3.14	B / 8.7	0.89	0.28
COI	*ProShares Short Inv Grade Corp	IGS	D	35.20	E+ / 0.7	-12.11 / 19	--	--	0.00	B / 8.9	0.37	0.13

99 Pct = Best
0 Pct = Worst

* Denotes ETF Fund, N/A denotes number is not available

99 Pct = Best
0 Pct = Worst

Fund Type	Fund Name	Ticker Symbol	Overall Investment Rating	Price As of 3/31/12	Performance Rating/Pts	Annualized Total Return Through 3/31/12 1Yr/Pct	3Yr/Pct	5Yr/Pct	Dividend Yield %	Risk Rating/Pts	Premium/Discount As of 3/31/12	Premium/Discount 1 Year Average
EM	Aberdeen Indonesia Fund	IF	A	12.74	A+ / 9.7	4.40 / 53	48.02 / 98	10.30 / 88	2.40	B- / 7.6	-9.19	-8.76
EM	Global High Income Fund	GHI	B	13.45	B+ / 8.6	18.89 / 81	31.34 / 84	8.35 / 76	7.93	B- / 7.3	2.91	-1.93
EM	Western Asset Emerging Mkts Inc	EMD	B	14.28	B / 7.8	16.91 / 80	28.27 / 77	10.97 / 92	6.72	B / 8.4	-5.68	-7.35
EM	Western Asset Worldwide Inc Fd	SBW	B	14.49	B- / 7.5	18.79 / 81	27.34 / 74	10.01 / 86	6.54	B / 8.2	-6.52	-8.94
EM	Western Asset Emerging Market Debt	ESD	B	20.13	B- / 7.5	15.18 / 77	27.60 / 75	11.74 / 95	6.86	B / 8.4	-5.89	-8.10
EM	Morgan Stanley Emg Mkts Dom Debt	EDD	B-	16.24	B / 7.6	7.68 / 63	27.87 / 76	--	7.39	B- / 7.8	-7.94	-8.74
EM	Templeton Emerging Markets Income	TEI	C+	15.68	B- / 7.2	2.39 / 47	29.01 / 80	12.14 / 96	6.38	B- / 7.2	-0.82	1.92
EM	*PowerShares DWA Emg Mkts Tech Le	PIE	C+	17.94	C+ / 6.7	-3.78 / 33	25.56 / 66	--	1.14	C+ / 6.9	0.17	-0.12
EM	*WisdomTree Emg Mkts SmCap Div Fd	DGS	C+	48.12	C+ / 6.7	-7.57 / 26	26.01 / 69	--	0.57	C+ / 6.8	0.67	0.40
EM	Stone Harbor Emg Markets Income	EDF	C+	24.58	C+ / 6.5	11.75 / 72	--	--	8.79	B / 8.0	3.93	1.21
EM	*WisdomTree Emg Mkts Eqty Inc Fd	DEM	C+	57.61	C+ / 6.4	-2.38 / 35	24.46 / 62	--	1.40	B- / 7.3	0.49	0.75
EM	*EGShares Emerging Markets Cons E	ECON	C+	24.85	C+ / 6.2	7.70 / 63	--	--	0.49	B- / 7.7	0.32	0.20
EM	Morgan Stanley Emerging Mkts Debt	MSD	C+	10.85	C+ / 5.8	12.07 / 72	22.01 / 52	8.92 / 79	5.16	B / 8.3	-10.18	-9.73
EM	Templeton Emerging Markets Fd	EMF	C	19.56	C+ / 5.9	-16.21 / 14	25.77 / 67	8.08 / 75	1.41	C+ / 6.6	-7.82	-5.83
EM	*SPDR S&P Emerging Latin America	GML	C	78.87	C+ / 5.7	-10.29 / 21	23.05 / 57	7.39 / 70	3.11	B- / 7.0	-0.22	-0.12
EM	*SPDR S&P Emerg Middle East&Afric	GAF	C	71.12	C / 5.1	-4.03 / 32	20.85 / 47	5.10 / 57	5.15	B- / 7.4	0.24	-0.12
EM	Morgan Stanley Emerging Markets	MSF	C	14.63	C / 4.5	-9.69 / 22	20.10 / 44	2.85 / 43	0.00	B- / 7.6	-9.97	-9.55
EM	*Vanguard Total World Stock ETF	VT	C	48.27	C / 4.4	-1.68 / 36	18.24 / 36	--	2.11	B- / 7.8	0.15	0.22
EM	Aberdeen Emerging Mkt Tele & Infr	ETF	C	19.37	C- / 4.2	4.72 / 54	17.08 / 33	1.50 / 34	0.34	B / 8.4	-11.47	-10.49
EM	*PowerShares Emrg Mkt Sovereign D	PCY	C	28.02	C- / 4.0	11.49 / 71	16.71 / 32	--	5.32	B / 8.8	0.00	-0.03
EM	*iShares JPMorgan USD Emg Mkts Bo	EMB	C	112.71	C- / 3.6	10.74 / 70	15.00 / 27	--	4.83	B / 8.9	0.60	0.57
EM	*Vanguard MSCI Emerging Markets E	VWO	C-	43.47	C / 4.8	-10.53 / 21	20.69 / 46	3.87 / 50	2.08	B- / 7.1	0.16	0.09
EM	*PowerShares Emg Mkts Infrastruct	PXR	C-	42.88	C / 4.8	-20.23 / 11	21.85 / 52	--	0.26	C+ / 6.4	-0.23	-0.17
EM	*SPDR S&P Emerging Markets ETF	GMM	C-	66.12	C / 4.7	-10.14 / 21	20.39 / 45	4.90 / 57	2.55	B- / 7.2	-0.08	0.05
EM	*iShares MSCI ACWI ex US IT Index	AXIT	C-	57.32	C / 4.3	-2.24 / 35	--	--	2.60	B- / 7.5	-0.24	-1.22
EM	*SPDR S&P Emerging Asia Pacific E	GMF	C-	74.15	C- / 4.2	-10.83 / 20	18.77 / 38	5.80 / 61	3.26	C+ / 6.9	-0.36	-0.14
EM	*SPDR S&P International Div ETF	DWX	C-	49.97	C- / 4.2	-11.14 / 20	19.89 / 43	--	2.63	B- / 7.3	0.52	0.24
EM	*iShares MSCI Emerging Markets	EEM	C-	42.95	C- / 4.1	-11.48 / 19	18.15 / 36	3.17 / 45	1.62	B- / 7.1	-0.16	0.04
EM	*PowerShares FTSE RAFI Emg Mkts	PXH	C-	22.92	C- / 4.1	-12.24 / 18	18.13 / 36	--	0.39	B- / 7.0	0.09	0.26
EM	*WisdomTree Emg Mkts Local Debt F	ELD	C-	51.89	D+ / 2.6	3.91 / 52	--	--	2.76	B / 8.6	0.33	0.20
EM	*SPDR S&P Emerging Europe ETF	GUR	D+	42.93	C / 4.4	-21.36 / 10	20.41 / 45	-4.51 / 13	3.75	C+ / 6.0	0.37	-0.24
EM	*BLDRS Emerging Market 50 ADR Ind	ADRE	D+	42.22	C- / 3.3	-11.30 / 20	14.93 / 27	3.04 / 44	2.76	B- / 7.3	-0.12	-0.05
EM	*iPath MSCI India Index ETN	INP	D	56.47	C- / 3.6	-22.90 / 9	18.44 / 37	2.32 / 40	0.00	C+ / 5.9	-0.02	0.04
EM	*Guggenheim MSCI Em Mkt Eq Weight	EWEM	D	35.74	D+ / 2.6	-12.15 / 19	--	--	0.90	C+ / 5.9	1.62	1.15
EM	*iShares MSCI Emg Mkts Finls Sctr	EMFN	D	24.24	D+ / 2.3	-12.91 / 18	--	--	9.53	C+ / 6.6	1.59	0.34
EM	*Guggenheim MSCI EAFE Eq Weight E	EWEF	D	38.40	D / 1.8	-7.40 / 26	--	--	2.06	B- / 7.1	-0.78	-0.02
EM	*iShares MSCI ACWI ex US TS Index	AXTE	D	52.89	D- / 1.1	-6.14 / 28	--	--	4.72	B / 8.3	-1.40	-0.11
EM	*Direxion Daily BRIC Bull 3X	BRIL	D-	32.95	C- / 3.5	-31.51 / 5	--	--	0.67	C- / 3.8	-0.48	-0.23
EM	*ProShares Ultra MSCI Emerging Mk	EET	D-	80.36	D+ / 2.5	-30.69 / 5	--	--	0.00	C- / 4.1	0.09	0.02
EM	*Market Vectors Egypt Index ETF	EGPT	D-	12.67	D+ / 2.3	-19.88 / 11	--	--	2.30	C / 4.4	-1.71	-0.60
EM	*IShares MSCI EM Eastern Europe	ESR	D-	27.79	D / 1.6	-21.76 / 10	--	--	3.11	C+ / 5.7	0.47	-0.09
EM	*SPDR S&P Russia	RBL	D-	30.93	D / 1.6	-22.13 / 10	--	--	2.80	C+ / 5.7	0.72	-0.11
EM	*iShares S&P India Nifty 50	INDY	D-	23.71	D- / 1.0	-20.97 / 10	--	--	0.22	C+ / 6.1	0.25	0.19
EM	*iShares MSCI Emg Mkts Matl Sctr	EMMT	D-	21.46	D- / 1.0	-22.42 / 10	--	--	3.95	C+ / 6.1	-0.46	-0.46
EM	*EGShares GEMS Composite ETF	AGEM	E+	23.22	D- / 1.5	-15.68 / 14	--	--	1.68	C- / 3.5	-0.39	-0.49
EM	*EGShares Energy GEMS ETF	OGEM	E+	24.44	D- / 1.3	-18.20 / 12	--	--	2.11	C- / 3.8	-0.57	-0.51
EM	*Market Vectors Poland ETF	PLND	E+	20.60	D- / 1.0	-26.31 / 7	--	--	3.66	C / 5.1	0.44	-0.10
EM	*ProShares Short MSCI Emg Mkts	EUM	E+	29.16	E / 0.5	0.03 / 41	-23.60 / 4	--	0.00	C / 4.4	0.07	N/A
EM	*EGShares Em Mkts Metals&Mining E	EMT	E	15.98	E+ / 0.8	-28.68 / 6	--	--	3.70	D / 2.2	0.06	-0.42
EM	*Direxion Daily India Bull 3X	INDL	E-	23.95	E+ / 0.7	-46.75 / 2	--	--	0.00	D / 2.2	-0.29	-0.11
EM	*ProShares UltraShort MSCI Emg Mk	EEV	E-	25.89	E- / 0.2	-9.06 / 23	-46.30 / 2	--	0.00	D+ / 2.3	0.04	-0.03

* Denotes ETF Fund, N/A denotes number is not available

www.thestreetratings.com

Fund Type	Fund Name	Ticker Symbol	Overall Investment Rating	Price As of 3/31/12	Performance Rating/Pts	Annualized Total Return Through 3/31/12			Dividend Yield %	Risk Rating/ Pts	Premium/Discount As of 3/31/12	1 Year Average
	99 Pct = Best 0 Pct = Worst					1Yr/Pct	3Yr/Pct	5Yr/Pct				
EN	Tortoise Energy Infrastr Corp	TYG	A	41.22	B+ / 8.7	9.85 / 68	33.82 / 89	8.32 / 76	5.41	B / 8.5	16.15	13.75
EN	Tortoise North American Energy	TYN	A	25.65	B+ / 8.6	8.63 / 66	33.97 / 89	8.49 / 77	6.00	B / 8.8	-1.12	-4.22
EN	*United States Gasoline Fund LP	UGA	B	57.16	B+ / 8.5	11.64 / 72	31.17 / 84	--	0.00	B- / 7.5	0.47	0.20
EN	Kayne Anderson Energy Tot Ret	KYE	B	27.48	B+ / 8.4	-7.35 / 26	35.25 / 91	9.98 / 86	6.99	B- / 7.4	-0.18	2.45
EN	First Trust Energy Income&Growth	FEN	B	30.05	B- / 7.5	9.97 / 68	27.39 / 74	8.71 / 78	6.39	B / 8.5	4.56	3.54
EN	*PowerShares Dynamic Energy	PXI	B-	40.76	B / 7.9	-7.17 / 27	31.23 / 84	6.57 / 64	0.25	B- / 7.3	-0.05	N/A
EN	Tortoise Energy Capital	TYY	B-	28.34	B- / 7.4	7.07 / 61	27.60 / 75	6.25 / 63	5.79	B- / 7.9	4.85	2.51
EN	*United States Brent Oil Fund	BNO	B-	86.30	B- / 7.3	9.43 / 67	--	--	0.00	B- / 7.9	-0.01	0.02
EN	Fiduciary/Claymore MLP Opp	FMO	B-	22.66	B- / 7.1	7.35 / 62	26.60 / 71	5.76 / 60	6.41	B / 8.2	7.96	4.26
EN	MLP & Strategic Equity Fund Inc.	MTP	C+	17.80	C+ / 6.7	0.27 / 42	26.61 / 71	--	5.33	B / 8.1	-3.73	-5.89
EN	*PowerShares Dynamic Enrg Exp & P	PXE	C+	25.06	C+ / 6.6	-8.60 / 24	25.41 / 66	4.63 / 55	0.79	B- / 7.3	-0.12	-0.07
EN	Kayne Anderson MLP Inv Co	KYN	C+	31.15	C+ / 6.4	-0.84 / 39	26.35 / 70	5.21 / 58	6.55	B / 8.2	8.95	6.80
EN	BlackRock Energy & Resources	BGR	C+	26.20	C+ / 6.3	-11.56 / 19	26.20 / 70	5.95 / 62	6.18	B- / 7.3	-4.17	-5.64
EN	ClearBridge Energy MLP Fund Inc	CEM	C+	23.60	C+ / 5.9	10.83 / 70	--	--	6.19	B / 8.2	4.66	2.55
EN	*SPDR S&P Oil & Gas Equip & Serv	XES	C	36.41	C+ / 5.9	-16.88 / 13	25.32 / 65	3.13 / 45	0.48	C+ / 6.4	0.05	N/A
EN	*Guggenheim S&P 500 Eq Wght Engy	RYE	C	64.03	C / 5.2	-14.44 / 15	23.24 / 58	4.79 / 56	1.62	B- / 7.1	0.00	-0.03
EN	*Guggenheim S&P Global Water Idx	CGW	C	21.11	C / 4.9	0.98 / 43	20.10 / 44	--	1.95	B / 8.2	0.00	-0.27
EN	*United States Heating Oil Fund	UHN	C	35.99	C / 4.3	-0.80 / 39	18.79 / 39	--	0.00	B- / 7.8	0.70	0.13
EN	*Alps Alerian MLP ETF	AMLP	C	16.67	C- / 3.0	8.10 / 64	--	--	5.83	B+ / 9.2	0.18	0.07
EN	*UBS E-TRACS 2x Levd Lng Alerian	MLPL	C-	41.66	C+ / 6.7	11.42 / 71	--	--	2.30	C / 4.8	0.07	-0.09
EN	*iPath DJ UBS Precious Mtls Tot R	JJP	C-	91.44	C+ / 6.4	6.46 / 59	25.58 / 67	--	0.00	C / 4.8	-0.41	0.06
EN	*ProShares Ultra Oil and Gas	DIG	C-	47.59	C+ / 5.9	-23.54 / 9	24.52 / 63	-7.18 / 9	0.10	C / 5.4	-0.25	-0.01
EN	*iShares DJ US Oil Equip & Svcs	IEZ	C-	53.50	C / 5.2	-20.97 / 10	24.33 / 62	2.05 / 38	0.44	C+ / 6.4	-0.09	N/A
EN	*First Trust Energy AlphaDEX	FXN	C-	20.20	C / 5.1	-18.74 / 11	23.76 / 59	--	0.66	C+ / 6.8	0.00	-0.02
EN	*PowerShares WilderHill Progr Ene	PUW	C-	26.26	C / 4.7	-13.53 / 17	20.01 / 43	-0.38 / 25	1.42	C+ / 6.9	0.04	-0.10
EN	*iShares DJ US Oil & Gas Exp & Pr	IEO	C-	65.79	C / 4.6	-11.42 / 20	20.36 / 44	4.77 / 56	0.60	B- / 7.1	-0.02	N/A
EN	BlackRock EcoSolutions Investment	BQR	C-	9.95	C / 4.4	-6.88 / 27	16.34 / 31	--	9.45	C+ / 6.6	5.51	-1.95
EN	*Vanguard Energy ETF	VDE	C-	105.18	C- / 4.1	-8.82 / 23	18.60 / 38	4.58 / 54	1.54	B- / 7.5	-0.02	0.01
EN	*Energy Select Sector SPDR	XLE	C-	71.75	C- / 4.0	-8.85 / 23	17.97 / 36	4.68 / 55	1.59	B- / 7.5	-0.01	0.01
EN	Petroleum and Resources Corp.	PEO	C-	25.99	C- / 3.9	-8.77 / 23	17.00 / 32	2.45 / 41	0.62	B- / 7.5	-13.08	-13.17
EN	*iShares DJ US Energy	IYE	C-	41.52	C- / 3.8	-7.65 / 25	16.58 / 31	4.45 / 53	1.42	B- / 7.6	-0.05	N/A
EN	*PowerShares Global Water Portfol	PIO	C-	18.10	C- / 3.7	-10.67 / 21	16.40 / 31	--	1.17	B- / 7.4	-0.11	-0.30
EN	Tortoise Power and Energy Inf Fund	TPZ	C-	25.39	C- / 3.1	5.23 / 56	--	--	5.91	B / 8.6	-2.27	-3.14
EN	*ProShares Ultra Silver	AGQ	D+	54.46	B+ / 8.7	-51.76 / 1	42.17 / 97	--	0.00	D / 1.9	-0.80	0.24
EN	*Market Vectors Coal ETF	KOL	D+	31.88	C / 4.9	-36.85 / 4	27.85 / 76	--	1.52	C+ / 6.0	-0.50	-0.33
EN	*PowerShares Dynamic Oil & Gas Sv	PXJ	D+	20.85	C / 4.7	-21.16 / 10	22.40 / 54	-0.29 / 26	0.01	C+ / 6.1	-0.14	-0.04
EN	*Guggenheim Canadian Energy Inc E	ENY	D+	17.20	C / 4.3	-23.34 / 9	21.75 / 51	--	2.74	C+ / 6.5	0.29	-0.17
EN	*PowerShares Global Coal Portfoli	PKOL	D+	24.82	C- / 3.9	-33.62 / 4	22.90 / 56	--	1.90	C+ / 6.5	-0.12	-0.45
EN	*iShares S&P NA Natural Resource	IGE	D+	39.42	C- / 3.6	-14.96 / 15	17.35 / 34	3.08 / 44	0.84	B- / 7.2	-0.05	0.01
EN	*iShares S&P Global Energy	IXC	D+	39.78	C- / 3.2	-9.24 / 23	14.29 / 25	3.24 / 46	2.20	B- / 7.6	0.25	-0.02
EN	*PowerShares DB Energy Fund	DBE	D+	30.05	C- / 3.1	-5.53 / 29	13.25 / 22	2.54 / 42	0.00	B- / 7.4	0.10	0.09
EN	*SPDR SP Intl Energy Sector ETF	IPW	D+	26.12	D+ / 2.7	-12.45 / 18	12.88 / 21	--	2.75	B- / 7.4	-0.38	-0.18
EN	*iPath DJ UBS Sugar Tot Ret Sub	SGG	D	89.67	B- / 7.0	5.77 / 58	28.09 / 77	--	0.00	D+ / 2.8	-0.02	-0.07
EN	*Direxion Energy Bull 3x Shares	ERX	D	51.32	C+ / 6.6	-43.33 / 2	27.50 / 75	--	0.00	D / 2.2	-0.31	N/A
EN	*iPath DJ UBS Tin Tot Ret Sub	JJT	D	52.43	C+ / 6.2	-29.65 / 6	28.17 / 77	--	0.00	C- / 3.4	0.02	-0.49
EN	*United States 12 Month Oil Fund	USL	D	45.81	C- / 3.1	-6.64 / 27	12.49 / 21	--	0.00	C+ / 6.8	0.00	0.04
EN	*PowerShares DB Oil Fund	DBO	D	29.91	C- / 3.0	-8.59 / 24	12.48 / 21	3.28 / 47	0.00	C+ / 6.6	0.13	0.07
EN	*WisdomTree Global Natural Resour	GNAT	D	25.20	D+ / 2.9	-13.84 / 17	13.13 / 22	1.30 / 32	2.53	B- / 7.0	0.16	-0.15
EN	*Focus Mstar Energy Id ETF	FEG	D	23.37	D / 2.2	-7.09 / 27	--	--	1.24	B- / 7.1	0.04	0.02
EN	*PowerShares Gb Nuclear Energy Po	PKN	D	17.03	D / 2.1	-13.41 / 17	9.08 / 15	--	0.20	B- / 7.2	-0.64	-0.53
EN	*iShares S&P Global Nuclear	NUCL	D	35.17	D / 1.7	-12.57 / 18	5.86 / 11	--	2.35	B- / 7.3	-0.34	-0.56
EN	*IQ Global Resources ETF	GRES	D	29.10	D- / 1.1	-10.20 / 21	--	--	0.70	B / 8.2	0.10	0.09

* Denotes ETF Fund, N/A denotes number is not available

99 Pct = Best
0 Pct = Worst

Fund Type	Fund Name	Ticker Symbol	Overall Investment Rating	Price As of 3/31/12	Perform-ance Rating/Pts	1Yr/Pct	3Yr/Pct	5Yr/Pct	Dividend Yield %	Risk Rating/Pts	Premium/Discount As of 3/31/12	1 Year Average
FS	Financial Trends Fund	DHFT	A-	10.81	A- / 9.1	8.57 / 65	33.46 / 88	-5.12 / 12	0.32	B- / 7.9	-9.54	-14.58
FS	First Tr Specialty Finance &Fin Op	FGB	B+	7.12	A- / 9.1	-4.72 / 31	38.97 / 95	--	8.99	B- / 7.5	-4.81	-5.38
FS	*PowerShares Financial Preferred	PGF	B+	17.90	B / 8.0	5.66 / 57	30.74 / 83	1.59 / 34	6.44	B / 8.7	0.28	-0.02
FS	*Guggenheim S&P 500 Eq Wght Finl	RYF	B	28.35	B / 7.8	-0.28 / 40	28.06 / 77	-9.01 / 7	5.91	B- / 7.7	-0.14	-0.08
FS	*First Trust Financial AlphaDEX	FXO	B	15.47	B- / 7.5	1.56 / 45	26.98 / 73	--	1.54	B- / 7.9	0.06	N/A
FS	*ProShares Ultra KBW Regional Ban	KRU	C+	49.10	A+ / 9.9	-2.91 / 34	--	--	0.84	C- / 3.7	0.25	0.06
FS	*ProShares Ultra Financials	UYG	C+	62.82	B+ / 8.5	-10.93 / 20	27.16 / 73	-36.77 / 0	0.71	C / 5.5	-0.16	-0.01
FS	J Hancock Bank & Thrift Oppty Fd	BTO	C+	17.25	C+ / 6.3	4.79 / 54	19.82 / 42	-5.31 / 12	4.94	B- / 7.5	-8.63	-9.84
FS	*RevenueShares Financials Sector	RWW	C	30.48	C+ / 6.1	-4.66 / 31	21.19 / 48	--	1.41	C+ / 6.8	0.03	0.07
FS	*Financial Select Sector SPDR	XLF	C	15.80	C / 5.4	-2.80 / 34	19.34 / 40	-13.11 / 5	1.26	B- / 7.5	0.00	-0.01
FS	*iShares DJ US Financial Sector	IYF	C	58.52	C / 5.3	-0.18 / 40	19.21 / 40	-10.79 / 6	1.20	B- / 7.6	-0.03	-0.01
FS	*Vanguard Financials ETF	VFH	C	32.97	C / 5.3	-1.63 / 37	19.16 / 39	-10.39 / 7	0.51	B- / 7.6	-0.06	0.02
FS	*iShares DJ US Financial Services	IYG	C-	57.22	C / 4.6	-2.00 / 35	15.77 / 29	-13.45 / 5	0.96	B- / 7.2	0.00	0.01
FS	*SP Bank ETF	KBE	C-	23.85	C / 4.6	-6.63 / 28	17.45 / 34	-13.61 / 4	1.19	B- / 7.0	-0.33	N/A
FS	*iShares DJ US Regional Banks	IAT	C-	24.80	C / 4.4	2.59 / 48	15.32 / 28	-10.89 / 6	1.08	B- / 7.4	0.08	0.02
FS	*SP Regional Banking ETF	KRE	C-	28.47	C- / 4.2	7.82 / 63	12.73 / 21	-7.09 / 9	1.36	B- / 7.3	0.11	N/A
FS	*PowerShares Dynamic Financial	PFI	C-	20.30	C- / 3.7	1.01 / 44	13.59 / 23	-3.37 / 16	0.22	B / 8.1	0.10	0.02
FS	First Opportunity Fund	FOFI	C-	7.05	C- / 3.2	-2.76 / 34	13.31 / 22	-9.49 / 7	0.00	B / 8.3	-24.19	-24.81
FS	*Direxion Financial Bull 3x Share	FAS	D+	109.15	B+ / 8.3	-29.49 / 6	22.85 / 56	--	0.00	D / 1.9	-0.08	0.02
FS	*iShares S&P Global Financials	IXG	D+	42.66	C- / 3.5	-9.72 / 22	14.38 / 25	-11.40 / 6	2.19	B- / 7.3	0.49	-0.15
FS	*SPDR SP Intl Finl Sector ETF	IPF	D+	17.46	D+ / 2.7	-14.34 / 16	11.96 / 19	--	1.26	B- / 7.3	-0.40	-0.28
FS	*SP Capital Markets ETF	KCE	D	34.01	D+ / 2.6	-12.85 / 18	8.48 / 14	-11.52 / 6	1.25	C+ / 6.9	0.12	-0.02
FS	*PowerShares Dynamic Banking Port	PJB	D	13.50	D+ / 2.4	5.32 / 56	4.99 / 10	-8.65 / 7	1.40	B- / 7.4	0.15	-0.06
FS	*iShares DJ US Broker-Dealers Idx	IAI	D	25.36	D / 2.1	-15.66 / 14	6.50 / 12	-12.96 / 5	1.49	B- / 7.0	0.12	0.01
FS	*iShares MSCI Far East Finls Sctr	FEFN	D	24.61	D- / 1.2	1.00 / 44	--	--	2.10	B- / 7.5	0.20	-0.04
FS	*Global X China Financials ETF	CHIX	D-	11.00	D- / 1.3	-22.45 / 9	--	--	0.10	C / 5.2	-1.26	-0.40
FS	*iShares MSCI Europ Finls Sctr Id	EUFN	D-	17.78	D- / 1.1	-22.49 / 9	--	--	0.67	C+ / 5.6	-0.34	0.11
FS	*SPDR SP Mortgage Finance ETF	KME	D-	37.74	E+ / 0.9	-7.60 / 26	--	--	1.97	C+ / 5.9	-0.08	-0.10
FS	*iShares MSCI ACWI ex US Fn Sctr	AXFN	D-	20.87	E+ / 0.9	-16.88 / 13	--	--	2.82	C+ / 6.7	-2.61	-0.32
FS	*EGShares Financials GEMS ETF	FGEM	E+	20.30	D / 1.7	-17.56 / 12	--	--	1.71	C- / 3.1	0.35	-0.51
FS	*ProShares Short Financials	SEF	E+	30.96	E / 0.5	-11.24 / 20	-25.62 / 4	--	0.00	C / 4.6	0.06	-0.02
FS	*ProShares Short KBW Regional Ban	KRS	E+	44.28	E / 0.3	-21.17 / 10	--	--	0.00	C+ / 5.6	0.20	-0.08
FS	*ProShares UltraShort Financials	SKF	E-	40.40	E- / 0.2	-28.58 / 6	-50.03 / 1	-32.57 / 0	0.00	D+ / 2.7	0.02	-0.03
FS	*Direxion Financial Bear 3x Share	FAZ	E-	20.65	E- / 0.0	-47.42 / 1	-70.20 / 0	--	0.00	D / 1.9	0.00	-0.06

* Denotes ETF Fund, N/A denotes number is not available

www.thestreetratings.com

Fund Type	Fund Name	Ticker Symbol	Overall Investment Rating	Price As of 3/31/12	PERFORMANCE Performance Rating/Pts	Annualized Total Return Through 3/31/12			Dividend Yield %	RISK Risk Rating/Pts	VALUATION Premium/Discount As of 3/31/12	1 Year Average
						1Yr/Pct	3Yr/Pct	5Yr/Pct				
FO	Thai Fund	TTF	A+	15.94	A+ / 9.8	22.18 / 83	47.49 / 98	13.33 / 98	1.66	B- / 7.9	-10.55	-14.28
FO	*iShares MSCI Thailand Inv Market	THD	A-	72.79	A+ / 9.8	9.88 / 68	50.49 / 99	--	2.15	B- / 7.1	0.12	0.13
FO	*iShares MSCI Philipps Invst Mkt	EPHE	B+	28.74	A / 9.4	18.49 / 81	--	--	0.68	B- / 7.3	0.56	-0.17
FO	Malaysia Fund	MAY	B+	10.26	A- / 9.2	5.15 / 55	37.36 / 94	11.40 / 93	1.90	B- / 7.6	-3.21	-8.40
FO	Mexico Fund	MXF	B+	25.25	B+ / 8.8	-1.83 / 36	34.95 / 91	4.29 / 52	1.53	B- / 7.7	-8.91	-8.72
FO	Mexico Equity & Income Fund	MXE	B+	11.40	B+ / 8.6	-2.65 / 34	34.45 / 89	0.31 / 28	0.00	B / 8.0	-12.58	-10.55
FO	Aberdeen Chile Fund	CH	B	19.23	A+ / 9.6	7.72 / 63	40.27 / 95	15.64 / 99	8.94	C+ / 5.9	14.40	5.98
FO	New Germany Fund	GF	B	15.08	B+ / 8.7	-7.52 / 26	34.59 / 90	0.85 / 30	1.87	C+ / 6.7	-10.50	-9.61
FO	*iShares MSCI Malaysia	EWM	B	14.60	B / 7.6	2.03 / 46	28.83 / 79	8.84 / 79	6.08	B- / 7.9	-0.41	-0.03
FO	Thai Capital Fund	TF	B-	11.58	A+ / 9.7	19.28 / 81	41.48 / 96	11.78 / 95	0.78	C / 5.4	-4.77	-12.40
FO	Aberdeen Latin America Equity Fund	LAQ	B-	35.51	B+ / 8.4	-4.52 / 31	32.45 / 87	10.69 / 91	0.22	C+ / 6.8	-7.91	-9.05
FO	*iShares MSCI Irlnd Capd Inv Mkt	EIRL	B-	23.11	B / 7.9	8.11 / 64	--	--	0.99	B- / 7.3	2.03	0.34
FO	*iShares MSCI All Peru Capped Idx	EPU	B-	46.70	B / 7.9	5.18 / 56	--	--	2.62	B- / 7.0	1.54	-0.21
FO	*iShares MSCI Mexico Inv Market	EWW	B-	62.52	B / 7.7	-0.57 / 39	28.71 / 79	3.74 / 49	1.11	B- / 7.5	0.05	-0.04
FO	*Market Vectors Indonesia Idx ETF	IDX	C+	29.86	A+ / 9.7	-0.18 / 40	48.88 / 99	--	1.52	C / 4.7	-0.40	-0.27
FO	Central Europe & Russia Fund	CEE	C+	35.02	B+ / 8.8	-12.64 / 18	35.37 / 91	-0.96 / 23	2.12	C+ / 5.9	-7.23	-9.49
FO	Turkish Investment Fund	TKF	C+	13.65	B+ / 8.6	-15.78 / 14	36.26 / 92	-1.75 / 21	2.23	C+ / 6.2	-11.82	-10.46
FO	*iShares MSCI Singapore	EWS	C+	12.89	B- / 7.3	-2.44 / 35	27.81 / 76	3.75 / 49	4.30	B- / 7.3	-0.08	-0.11
FO	Singapore Fund	SGF	C+	12.96	B- / 7.1	-8.05 / 25	28.06 / 76	-0.26 / 26	1.03	C+ / 6.7	-8.80	-7.25
FO	*iShares MSCI Chile Inv Market	ECH	C+	68.30	C+ / 6.9	-5.88 / 29	26.15 / 70	--	0.18	C+ / 6.7	-0.55	-0.24
FO	*WisdomTree Australia Divide	AUSE	C+	56.08	C+ / 6.6	-4.26 / 32	25.43 / 66	2.80 / 43	6.83	C+ / 6.9	0.38	0.04
FO	*PowerShares FTSE RAFI Asia Pac E	PAF	C+	51.92	C+ / 6.4	-8.79 / 23	25.64 / 67	--	1.55	B- / 7.0	-0.21	-0.17
FO	*WisdomTree Commodity Country Equ	CCXE	C+	31.43	C+ / 6.3	-2.64 / 34	24.20 / 61	2.16 / 39	3.08	B- / 7.4	-0.03	-0.30
FO	Morgan Stanley Eastern Europe	RNE	C+	16.58	C+ / 6.3	-16.22 / 13	25.29 / 65	-6.74 / 10	0.00	B- / 7.3	-10.14	-11.86
FO	*iShares DJ Intl Select Dividend	IDV	C+	32.60	C+ / 5.8	-5.05 / 30	24.00 / 61	--	3.10	B- / 7.7	0.59	0.32
FO	*iShares MSCI New Zealand Inv Mk	ENZL	C+	31.66	C+ / 5.6	12.00 / 72	--	--	8.94	B- / 7.9	0.38	0.05
FO	*iShares MSCI ACWI xUS Cnsmr Stp	AXSL	C+	67.32	C / 5.0	12.32 / 73	--	--	1.57	B / 8.7	0.73	0.25
FO	*Global X/InterBolsa FTSE Col 20	GXG	C	21.20	A / 9.5	5.01 / 55	41.61 / 96	--	0.98	C- / 3.6	-0.14	0.08
FO	*ProShares Ultra MSCI Mex Invest	UMX	C	37.57	B / 8.1	-14.09 / 16	--	--	0.00	C / 4.6	-1.39	-0.43
FO	*Global X Brazil Consumer ETF	BRAQ	C	18.78	B- / 7.1	-3.25 / 33	--	--	1.16	C+ / 6.1	-0.32	0.23
FO	*iShares MSCI Turkey Inv Market	TUR	C	53.05	B- / 7.0	-17.69 / 12	28.50 / 78	--	0.55	C+ / 5.7	0.51	-0.20
FO	Korea Equity Fund	KEF	C	9.74	C+ / 6.9	-6.68 / 27	28.41 / 78	3.68 / 49	4.72	C+ / 5.8	-8.72	-8.84
FO	Aberdeen Australia Equity Fund	IAF	C	10.75	C+ / 6.7	-2.99 / 34	25.38 / 65	4.23 / 52	10.42	C+ / 6.6	8.81	4.71
FO	*iShares MSCI South Korea	EWY	C	59.54	C+ / 6.2	-8.31 / 24	24.26 / 62	3.69 / 49	1.25	C+ / 6.5	-0.28	-0.35
FO	*iShares MSCI Sweden	EWD	C	29.01	C+ / 6.2	-9.25 / 23	24.58 / 63	-0.29 / 26	3.58	C+ / 6.5	0.31	-0.19
FO	*iShares MSCI South Africa	EZA	C	68.91	C+ / 6.1	-4.31 / 32	23.70 / 59	5.11 / 57	3.10	B- / 7.1	0.91	0.03
FO	Latin American Discovery Fund	LDF	C	16.34	C+ / 5.9	-11.00 / 20	23.99 / 60	4.31 / 52	0.91	C+ / 6.8	-7.53	-8.07
FO	The New Ireland Fund	IRL	C	8.12	C+ / 5.7	5.21 / 56	21.68 / 51	-13.96 / 4	0.25	C+ / 6.9	-13.71	-11.73
FO	*Global X FTSE Andean 40 ETF	AND	C	14.92	C+ / 5.7	1.33 / 44	--	--	1.61	B- / 7.1	-0.20	-0.02
FO	*Global X Brazil Mid Cap ETF	BRAZ	C	17.26	C+ / 5.7	-5.97 / 29	--	--	1.98	C+ / 6.5	-0.29	-0.18
FO	Templeton Dragon Fund	TDF	C	28.35	C / 5.4	-1.79 / 36	22.03 / 52	10.12 / 87	0.36	B- / 7.4	-7.59	-9.43
FO	*WisdomTree Asia Pacific ex-Japan	AXJL	C	64.10	C / 5.4	-2.85 / 34	21.92 / 52	3.41 / 47	1.38	B- / 7.4	0.08	0.09
FO	*iShares MSCI Pacific ex-Japan	EPP	C	43.52	C / 5.3	-7.17 / 27	21.95 / 52	2.44 / 41	4.47	B- / 7.1	0.07	-0.07
FO	*iShares MSCI EAFE Small Cap Idx	SCZ	C	40.13	C / 5.2	-4.77 / 31	21.46 / 50	--	2.89	B- / 7.9	0.48	-0.02
FO	*SPDR S&P International Small Cap	GWX	C	28.77	C / 5.1	-6.21 / 28	21.50 / 51	--	3.33	B- / 7.8	0.52	-0.02
FO	*WisdomTree Intl Small Cap Divide	DLS	C	49.55	C / 5.0	-2.12 / 35	20.71 / 46	-2.95 / 17	2.03	B- / 7.8	0.45	-0.25
FO	*Guggenheim Intl Multi-Asset Inc	HGI	C	17.67	C / 4.8	-5.65 / 29	20.73 / 46	--	4.19	B- / 7.8	0.74	0.25
FO	*PowerShares Intl Dividend Ach	PID	C	15.36	C / 4.7	-3.02 / 33	21.21 / 48	-1.31 / 21	1.85	B / 8.2	0.13	0.11
FO	*iShares FTSE Dev Sm Cap ex-North	IFSM	C	35.54	C / 4.6	-8.49 / 24	19.84 / 42	--	2.72	B- / 7.7	0.42	-0.26
FO	Herzfeld Caribbean Basin Fund	CUBA	C	7.34	C / 4.4	-0.52 / 39	17.83 / 35	-4.09 / 14	0.00	B / 8.2	-6.38	-9.67
FO	*Guggenheim Australian Dollar Sha	FXA	C	103.87	C- / 3.8	3.27 / 49	16.89 / 32	7.91 / 74	3.51	B / 8.6	-0.05	-0.02
FO	*WisdomTree Japan SmallCap Div Fd	DFJ	C	45.58	C- / 3.6	10.52 / 69	14.76 / 26	-0.76 / 24	3.19	B / 8.8	0.29	-0.15

* Denotes ETF Fund, N/A denotes number is not available

Fund Type	Fund Name	Ticker Symbol	Overall Investment Rating	Price As of 3/31/12	Performance Rating/Pts	1Yr/Pct	3Yr/Pct	5Yr/Pct	Dividend Yield %	Risk Rating/Pts	Premium/Discount As of 3/31/12	1 Year Average
GEI	Western Asset Premier Bond Fund	WEA	B+	15.90	B+ / 8.4	13.29 / 74	33.09 / 88	11.64 / 94	8.30	B- / 7.9	16.65	14.60
GEI	Guggenheim Build America Bd Mgd Du	GBAB	B+	21.81	B- / 7.3	26.72 / 86	--	--	7.10	B+ / 9.3	-3.84	-5.94
GEI	J Hancock Investors Trust	JHI	B	23.01	B / 8.1	13.36 / 75	31.05 / 84	14.72 / 98	8.68	B- / 7.6	18.43	11.99
GEI	Nuveen EnhancedMunicipal Value	NEV	B	15.05	B- / 7.3	25.94 / 86	--	--	6.38	B / 8.2	1.01	-1.36
GEI	J Hancock Income Securities Tr	JHS	B	15.25	C+ / 6.7	16.81 / 80	25.41 / 66	9.94 / 86	6.92	B / 8.8	2.28	1.34
GEI	Fort Dearborn Inc. Secs.	FDI	B-	16.17	C+ / 6.1	31.33 / 90	19.82 / 42	11.62 / 94	8.66	B+ / 9.0	-3.58	-6.89
GEI	*VelocityShares Dly Invs VIX M-T	ZIV	C+	15.84	A- / 9.0	2.84 / 49	--	--	0.00	C / 5.4	-1.25	0.01
GEI	Western Asset Income Fund	PAI	C+	14.55	C+ / 5.7	17.32 / 80	21.24 / 49	6.78 / 66	4.95	B / 8.7	2.46	-3.13
GEI	*PowerShares Preferred Port	PGX	C+	14.37	C / 5.0	6.81 / 61	20.78 / 46	--	6.65	B+ / 9.4	0.35	0.09
GEI	BlackRock Core Bond Trust	BHK	C	13.77	C / 4.8	20.01 / 82	18.81 / 39	8.50 / 77	5.84	B / 8.5	-3.30	-6.54
GEI	MFS Charter Income Trust	MCR	C	9.57	C / 4.5	12.27 / 73	17.61 / 34	9.83 / 85	6.83	B / 8.8	-4.97	-7.10
GEI	BlackRock Income Opportunity Trust	BNA	C	10.48	C- / 4.0	18.14 / 81	14.93 / 26	6.77 / 66	6.07	B / 8.6	-5.50	-8.41
GEI	Nuveen Build America Bond Oppty Fd	NBD	C	20.97	C- / 3.3	19.00 / 81	--	--	6.09	B+ / 9.2	-7.05	-5.00
GEI	*SPDR Barclays Cap Lng-T Corp Bd	LWC	C	38.65	C- / 3.3	15.64 / 78	14.73 / 26	--	4.95	B+ / 9.0	0.39	0.77
GEI	*Vanguard Long Term Bd Idx ETF	BLV	C	88.91	C- / 3.0	19.17 / 81	13.06 / 22	--	4.14	B+ / 9.0	0.24	0.33
GEI	*SPDR Barclays Cap Int Corp Bd ET	ITR	C	33.89	D+ / 2.4	7.40 / 62	9.64 / 16	--	3.32	B+ / 9.7	0.68	0.50
GEI	*Schwab US TIPS ETF	SCHP	C	55.95	D+ / 2.3	10.46 / 69	--	--	0.78	B+ / 9.8	0.11	0.12
GEI	Invesco Van Kampen Bond	VBF	C-	20.21	C- / 3.3	19.31 / 82	13.35 / 22	9.01 / 80	4.75	B / 8.6	-1.13	-3.55
GEI	Duff & Phelps Utilities & Crp Bd T	DUC	C-	11.81	D+ / 2.7	16.33 / 79	9.62 / 16	8.29 / 76	7.11	B / 8.7	0.60	-1.40
GEI	Montgomery Street Inc. Sec.	MTS	C-	15.80	D+ / 2.5	5.50 / 57	10.24 / 16	3.46 / 48	3.80	B+ / 9.5	-10.13	-9.69
GEI	*Vanguard Intermediate Term Bond	BIV	C-	86.96	D+ / 2.4	11.07 / 70	9.66 / 16	--	3.20	B+ / 9.6	0.24	0.30
GEI	*iShares 2017 S&P AMT-Free Muni S	MUAF	C-	54.67	D / 2.1	8.92 / 66	--	--	1.91	B+ / 9.4	0.05	0.39
GEI	*iShares 2016 S&P AMT-Free Muni S	MUAE	C-	53.58	D / 2.1	7.72 / 63	--	--	1.75	B+ / 9.7	0.73	0.20
GEI	*Guggenheim Enhanced Core Bond ET	GIY	C-	51.55	D / 2.1	5.87 / 58	8.15 / 14	--	1.17	B+ / 9.4	-0.83	0.21
GEI	*iShares Barclays Aggregate Bd	AGG	C-	109.85	D / 1.9	7.71 / 63	6.66 / 12	6.04 / 62	3.02	B+ / 9.8	0.19	0.15
GEI	*Vanguard Total Bond Market ETF	BND	C-	83.28	D / 1.9	7.71 / 63	6.72 / 12	--	2.82	B+ / 9.7	0.24	0.21
GEI	*Columbia Core Bond Strategy	GMTB	C-	52.44	D / 1.8	8.22 / 65	--	--	2.68	B+ / 9.7	0.40	0.53
GEI	*SPDR Barclays Cap Aggregate Bd E	LAG	C-	57.75	D / 1.8	7.76 / 63	6.20 / 11	--	2.34	B+ / 9.7	0.05	0.12
GEI	*iShares Barclays Intrm Govt/Crdt	GVI	C-	111.12	D / 1.7	5.93 / 58	5.52 / 11	5.60 / 59	2.30	B+ / 9.8	0.17	0.21
GEI	*iShares 2015 S&P AMT-Free Muni S	MUAD	C-	53.46	D / 1.7	5.25 / 56	--	--	1.48	B+ / 9.8	0.64	0.22
GEI	*iShares 2014 S&P AMT-Free Muni S	MUAC	C-	51.90	D- / 1.5	3.51 / 50	--	--	1.09	B+ / 9.7	0.54	0.17
GEI	*Vanguard Short-Term Bd Idx ETF	BSV	C-	80.94	D- / 1.5	3.31 / 50	3.62 / 9	--	1.58	B+ / 9.8	0.01	0.09
GEI	*iShares 2013 S&P AMT-Free Muni S	MUAB	C-	51.23	D- / 1.4	1.68 / 45	--	--	1.00	B+ / 9.9	0.53	0.15
GEI	*SPDR Nuveen S&P VRDO Muni Bond E	VRD	C-	30.01	D- / 1.3	0.89 / 43	--	--	0.26	B+ / 9.9	-0.03	-0.13
GEI	*iShares 2012 S&P AMT-Free Muni S	MUAA	C-	50.84	D- / 1.3	0.44 / 42	--	--	0.67	B+ / 9.8	0.24	-0.27
GEI	*ProShares Short High Yield	SJB	D	35.84	E+ / 0.7	-10.17 / 21	--	--	0.00	B / 8.4	0.03	-0.02
GEI	*ProShares VIX Mid-Term Futures E	VIXM	E+	56.82	E / 0.4	-15.27 / 15	--	--	0.00	C / 5.6	1.55	0.02
GEI	*ProShares VIX Short-Term Futures	VIXY	E-	35.77	E- / 0.0	-43.37 / 2	--	--	0.00	D / 1.9	0.76	0.15

* Denotes ETF Fund, N/A denotes number is not available

www.thestreetratings.com

Fund Type	Fund Name	Ticker Symbol	Overall Investment Rating	Price As of 3/31/12	Perform-ance Rating/Pts	Annualized Total Return Through 3/31/12			Dividend Yield %	Risk Rating/ Pts	Premium/Discount As of 3/31/12	1 Year Average
	99 Pct = Best *0 Pct = Worst*					1Yr/Pct	3Yr/Pct	5Yr/Pct				
GEN	Helios Advantage Income Fund Inc	HAV	B+	9.30	A / 9.5	31.59 / 90	36.61 / 92	-23.30 / 2	8.06	B- / 7.2	4.38	-6.42
GEN	Helios Multi Sector High Income	HMH	B+	6.07	A- / 9.1	28.74 / 88	33.63 / 88	-28.14 / 1	8.40	B- / 7.4	-0.98	-7.31
GEN	Helios High Income Fund Inc	HIH	B+	8.90	A- / 9.1	27.89 / 87	33.70 / 88	-23.95 / 2	8.09	B- / 7.1	4.95	-3.14
GEN	Franklin Templeton Ltd Duration In	FTF	B-	14.01	C+ / 6.4	13.68 / 75	23.59 / 59	8.01 / 74	7.11	B / 8.6	1.45	-2.18
GEN	Helios Strategic Income Fund Inc	HSA	C+	5.94	C+ / 6.8	21.29 / 83	23.69 / 59	-28.99 / 1	7.07	B- / 7.8	-10.27	-11.99
GEN	Putnam High Income Securities	PCF	C+	8.45	C+ / 6.8	5.66 / 57	25.49 / 66	6.61 / 65	6.23	C+ / 6.9	1.81	-1.11
GEN	Eaton Vance Limited Duration Incom	EVV	C+	16.05	C+ / 6.4	8.28 / 65	24.47 / 62	6.58 / 64	7.79	B- / 7.5	-3.02	-5.15
GEN	BlackRock Limited Duration Income	BLW	C+	17.74	C / 5.5	11.50 / 71	20.51 / 45	5.94 / 61	7.10	B / 8.7	3.68	-1.21
GEN	MFS Multimarket Income Trust	MMT	C+	6.98	C / 5.0	11.45 / 71	19.70 / 42	10.97 / 92	7.22	B / 8.4	-5.42	-7.01
GEN	First Trust Strategic High Inc II	FHY	C	17.31	C+ / 6.5	31.95 / 90	15.05 / 27	-9.99 / 7	9.76	C+ / 6.7	4.15	-6.96
GEN	Morgan Stanley Income Sec	ICB	C	17.79	C- / 4.0	14.95 / 77	16.64 / 32	7.85 / 73	4.72	B+ / 9.2	-4.61	-5.61
GEN	Pyxis Credit Strategies Fund	HCF	C-	6.34	C- / 4.0	-9.79 / 22	19.80 / 42	-12.02 / 5	6.62	B- / 7.7	-11.70	-7.83
GEN	Putnam Premier Income Trust	PPT	D+	5.51	C / 4.9	-7.59 / 26	22.64 / 55	6.38 / 64	6.53	C+ / 5.8	-5.00	-2.16
GEN	Putnam Master Intermediate Inc Tr	PIM	D	5.15	C- / 3.3	-5.78 / 29	16.13 / 30	4.04 / 51	6.76	C+ / 6.1	-5.68	-3.76

* Denotes ETF Fund, N/A denotes number is not available

www.thestreetratings.com
713
Data as of March 31, 2012

Fund Type	Fund Name	Ticker Symbol	Overall Investment Rating	Price As of 3/31/12	PERFORMANCE Performance Rating/Pts	Annualized Total Return Through 3/31/12 1Yr/Pct	3Yr/Pct	5Yr/Pct	Dividend Yield %	RISK Risk Rating/Pts	VALUATION Premium/Discount As of 3/31/12	1 Year Average
	99 Pct = Best											
	0 Pct = Worst											
GL	DWS High Income Opportunities Fund	DHG	A+	16.03	A+ / 9.7	20.22 / 82	42.68 / 97	-6.08 / 11	8.92	B / 8.8	2.62	-5.91
GL	Pioneer High Income Trust	PHT	A+	16.66	A / 9.3	11.45 / 71	41.49 / 96	12.28 / 96	9.90	B+ / 9.0	23.77	26.00
GL	BlackRock Credit Alloc Inc Tr III	BPP	A	11.23	B+ / 8.6	13.91 / 76	33.00 / 87	-7.48 / 9	6.79	B / 8.8	-9.51	-12.06
GL	Managed High Yield Plus Fund	HYF	A-	2.19	A / 9.3	5.72 / 58	40.56 / 96	-4.17 / 14	8.55	B- / 7.6	2.34	5.68
GL	Macquarie/FTG Infr/ Util Div&Inc	MFD	A-	16.00	B+ / 8.9	10.25 / 69	34.83 / 90	-0.21 / 27	8.75	B / 8.2	-0.62	-5.14
GL	PIMCO Global StocksPLUS&Inc	PGP	B+	20.18	A+ / 9.7	-9.11 / 23	48.33 / 99	12.60 / 97	10.91	B- / 7.1	60.41	68.05
GL	Delaware Enhanced Glb Div & Inc Fd	DEX	B+	12.83	A / 9.4	6.58 / 60	38.48 / 95	--	9.59	B- / 7.2	5.86	-1.01
GL	Gabelli Global Multimedia Trust	GGT	B+	7.24	A- / 9.1	4.88 / 55	36.91 / 93	-4.57 / 13	11.05	B- / 7.1	-9.95	-12.52
GL	Western Asset High Inc Fd II	HIX	B+	9.99	A- / 9.0	12.24 / 73	37.15 / 93	10.35 / 88	9.91	B- / 7.5	12.75	12.05
GL	Western Asset Global High Income	EHI	B+	13.25	B+ / 8.9	12.20 / 73	35.46 / 91	8.77 / 79	8.72	B- / 7.3	0.38	-1.98
GL	First Trust/Aberdeen Emerg Opp Fd	FEO	B+	20.78	B+ / 8.8	8.25 / 65	33.32 / 88	11.56 / 94	5.05	B- / 7.9	-6.90	-9.69
GL	DWS Strategic Income Fund	KST	B+	14.55	B+ / 8.6	19.83 / 82	31.91 / 86	9.05 / 80	8.49	B- / 7.5	5.05	-1.03
GL	AllianceBernstein Global High Inc	AWF	B+	15.02	B+ / 8.5	11.43 / 71	31.85 / 85	13.94 / 98	7.99	B / 8.4	1.42	-1.13
GL	Pimco Income Opportunity Fund	PKO	B+	26.35	B+ / 8.4	9.15 / 67	32.67 / 87	--	9.37	B / 8.5	5.53	6.74
GL	First Trust/Aberdeen Glob Opp Inc	FAM	B+	17.46	B / 8.1	13.75 / 75	29.77 / 81	9.31 / 82	8.93	B / 8.6	-0.85	-4.17
GL	Pioneer Diversified High Income Tr	HNW	B+	20.59	B / 8.0	6.26 / 59	30.78 / 83	--	10.10	B / 8.3	5.27	2.88
GL	Western Asset Global Partners Inc	GDF	B	12.90	B+ / 8.7	9.78 / 68	34.72 / 90	10.48 / 89	8.84	B- / 7.0	8.77	8.79
GL	Cohen & Steers Global Inc Builder	INB	B	10.70	B+ / 8.4	5.82 / 58	30.84 / 84	--	10.47	B- / 7.4	-7.76	-10.06
GL	Eaton Vance Tax Adv Glob Div Inc	ETG	B	14.47	B / 8.2	5.68 / 57	30.14 / 82	-2.87 / 17	8.50	B- / 7.8	-6.28	-6.82
GL	Macquarie Global Infr Total Return	MGU	B	18.45	B / 7.6	4.42 / 53	28.35 / 78	-2.96 / 17	5.20	B / 8.0	-11.76	-12.72
GL	Aberdeen Global Income Fund	FCO	B	13.98	B- / 7.3	16.80 / 80	26.86 / 72	12.20 / 96	6.01	B / 8.4	3.86	1.87
GL	*PowerShares DB 3x German Bd Fut	BUNT	B-	30.36	A+ / 9.6	54.98 / 99	--	--	0.00	C+ / 5.6	-0.10	-0.05
GL	DWS Multi-Market Income Trust	KMM	B-	10.33	B / 8.1	7.13 / 62	31.79 / 85	9.71 / 85	8.94	B- / 7.1	3.30	5.29
GL	Calamos Global Dynamic Income Fd	CHW	B-	8.80	B- / 7.5	8.89 / 66	25.55 / 66	--	8.45	B- / 7.5	-8.71	-13.13
GL	Strategic Global Income Fund	SGL	B-	10.68	B- / 7.3	6.79 / 61	28.67 / 79	11.12 / 92	0.86	B / 8.0	-5.15	-5.94
GL	*iShares S&P Global Cons Disc	RXI	B-	59.04	C+ / 6.9	9.24 / 67	23.91 / 60	1.32 / 32	1.32	B / 8.1	0.37	-0.03
GL	*PowerShares DB 3x Itn Trs B Fut	ITLT	C+	22.00	A+ / 9.6	10.72 / 70	--	--	0.00	C- / 4.0	3.58	-7.03
GL	*Market Vectors Gaming ETF	BJK	C+	35.83	B+ / 8.6	12.05 / 72	30.92 / 84	--	1.76	C / 5.5	-0.47	-0.31
GL	*Guggenheim Frontier Markets ETF	FRN	C+	21.52	B- / 7.1	0.17 / 41	26.38 / 70	--	3.83	B- / 7.4	0.70	-0.42
GL	Eaton Vance Tax Adv Global Div Opp	ETO	C+	19.58	B- / 7.0	-4.34 / 32	26.70 / 72	-1.44 / 21	7.15	B- / 7.5	-12.00	-11.50
GL	Lazard World Div&Inc Fd	LOR	C+	12.20	C+ / 6.9	-1.99 / 35	27.27 / 74	-0.64 / 24	6.53	B- / 7.8	-10.62	-8.24
GL	*iShares S&P Global Technology	IXN	C+	70.79	C+ / 6.7	14.33 / 76	21.86 / 52	4.63 / 55	0.94	B- / 7.2	0.10	-0.06
GL	*First Trust DJ Glb Sel Div Idx F	FGD	C+	23.59	C+ / 6.5	-1.12 / 38	25.84 / 68	--	1.70	B / 8.2	0.51	0.21
GL	J Hancock Tax Adv Glb Shlr Yield	HTY	C+	13.07	C+ / 6.3	12.18 / 73	23.45 / 58	--	9.79	B / 8.3	9.10	6.21
GL	BlackRock S&P Qual Rkg Glob Eq Mgd	BQY	C+	12.97	C+ / 6.3	5.00 / 55	23.63 / 59	1.20 / 32	9.64	B / 8.2	-5.95	-6.72
GL	*SPDR SP Intl Con Stap Sect ETF	IPS	C+	33.57	C+ / 5.8	10.47 / 69	22.34 / 53	--	2.15	B / 8.8	0.36	0.03
GL	Cohen & Steers Closed-End Opp Fd	FOF	C+	12.76	C+ / 5.8	2.31 / 47	23.47 / 58	0.13 / 27	8.15	B / 8.4	-7.87	-8.03
GL	Global Income Fund	GIFD	C+	4.05	C+ / 5.8	0.02 / 41	24.36 / 62	6.83 / 66	6.42	B / 8.3	-18.18	-17.89
GL	Lazard Global Total Return&Income	LGI	C+	14.96	C+ / 5.7	4.29 / 53	21.54 / 51	-0.04 / 27	6.47	B- / 7.8	-12.26	-11.62
GL	Wells Fargo Avtg Multi-Sector Inc	ERC	C+	15.14	C+ / 5.6	8.33 / 65	22.67 / 55	8.48 / 77	7.93	B / 8.7	-7.80	-8.09
GL	Western Asset Global Corp Def Oppt	GDO	C+	19.28	C / 5.5	13.81 / 75	--	--	7.94	B / 8.5	-2.28	-5.16
GL	*iShares S&P Gl Cons Staples Sect	KXI	C+	70.77	C / 5.5	13.46 / 75	20.83 / 47	6.61 / 65	1.93	B+ / 9.0	-0.16	0.09
GL	*iShares High Dividend Equity	HDV	C+	57.15	C / 5.2	15.68 / 78	--	--	4.60	B+ / 9.4	0.02	0.06
GL	Transamerica Income Shares	TAI	C+	21.79	C / 4.6	10.20 / 69	19.93 / 43	8.54 / 77	6.61	B+ / 9.1	-1.98	-2.41
GL	*Guggenheim Timber ETF	CUT	C	18.84	C+ / 5.9	-17.57 / 12	25.23 / 65	--	2.05	B- / 7.3	0.16	-0.14
GL	First Trust High Income Long/Short	FSD	C	18.13	C / 5.4	5.21 / 56	--	--	8.84	B- / 7.7	-1.79	-5.86
GL	*SPDR SP Intl Con Disc Sect ETF	IPD	C	29.30	C / 5.3	4.23 / 53	19.57 / 41	--	0.39	B / 8.0	0.41	-0.33
GL	*iShares S&P Global Industrials	EXI	C	54.23	C / 5.3	-4.66 / 31	21.48 / 50	0.12 / 27	1.78	B- / 7.6	0.20	-0.05
GL	Aberdeen Asia-Pacific Income Fund	FAX	C	7.29	C / 5.2	11.19 / 70	21.25 / 49	10.25 / 88	5.76	B / 8.0	-2.28	-2.82
GL	Western Asset Var Rt Strat Fd	GFY	C	16.62	C / 5.0	1.63 / 45	20.74 / 46	4.46 / 54	4.84	B / 8.3	-5.89	-8.41
GL	Eaton Vance Sh Dur Diversified Inc	EVG	C	17.08	C- / 4.1	7.84 / 63	17.33 / 33	5.57 / 59	6.32	B+ / 9.0	-4.04	-6.79
GL	MFS InterMkt Inc Tr I	CMK	C	8.37	C- / 3.2	8.07 / 64	13.57 / 23	7.59 / 71	5.45	B+ / 9.5	-9.71	-10.02

* Denotes ETF Fund, N/A denotes number is not available

www.thestreetratings.com

					PERFORMANCE					RISK	VALUATION	
99 Pct = Best *0 Pct = Worst*			Overall Investment Rating	Price As of 3/31/12	Perform-ance Rating/Pts	Annualized Total Return Through 3/31/12			Dividend Yield %	Risk Rating/ Pts	Premium/Discount	
Fund Type	Fund Name	Ticker Symbol				1Yr/Pct	3Yr/Pct	5Yr/Pct			As of 3/31/12	1 Year Average
GR	*Direxion Daily Retail Bull 3X	RETL	A+	87.91	A+ / 9.9	59.72 / 99	--	--	0.00	B / 8.5	-0.05	0.06
GR	*Guggenheim S&P 500 Eq WgCon Dsc	RCD	A	54.80	A- / 9.2	14.68 / 77	35.94 / 92	3.94 / 50	1.94	B / 8.0	0.18	-0.04
GR	*Focus Mstar Technology Id ETF	FTQ	A	29.11	A- / 9.1	15.94 / 78	--	--	0.72	B / 8.5	0.31	-0.03
GR	*ProShares Ultra QQQ	QLD	B+	118.95	A+ / 9.9	32.11 / 90	57.20 / 99	8.17 / 75	0.00	C+/ 6.9	-0.03	-0.01
GR	*ProShares Ultra Technology	ROM	B+	86.97	A+ / 9.8	30.39 / 89	50.01 / 99	5.83 / 61	0.00	C+/ 6.5	0.02	-0.03
GR	*ProShares Ultra Rus Mid Cap Valu	UVU	B+	39.62	A+ / 9.8	-4.98 / 30	47.51 / 98	-9.46 / 7	0.23	C+/ 6.4	0.15	-0.10
GR	*ProShares Ultra Russell1000 Grow	UKF	B+	64.55	A+ / 9.7	13.00 / 74	43.74 / 97	0.99 / 31	0.20	C+/ 6.9	0.00	-0.05
GR	*ProShares Ultra Dow 30	DDM	B+	70.54	A+ / 9.6	13.63 / 75	40.78 / 96	-1.19 / 22	0.53	B- / 7.0	0.00	0.03
GR	*ProShares Ultra S-P 500	SSO	B+	58.36	A+ / 9.6	9.26 / 67	39.26 / 95	-6.26 / 10	0.94	C+/ 6.8	-0.05	-0.01
GR	*Guggenheim S&P Sm Cap 600 Pure V	RZV	B+	40.99	A / 9.4	1.08 / 44	39.57 / 95	0.32 / 29	1.76	B- / 7.3	-0.12	-0.06
GR	*PowerShares S&P SC Cnsmr Discr	PSCD	B+	32.06	B+ / 8.9	13.09 / 74	--	--	0.23	B- / 7.4	0.28	0.03
GR	*PowerShares Dynamic Networking	PXQ	B+	28.58	B+ / 8.9	3.17 / 49	33.57 / 88	9.48 / 83	0.00	B- / 7.3	-0.03	-0.02
GR	*Guggenheim S&P Mid Cap 400 Pure	RFV	B+	36.06	B+ / 8.7	0.16 / 41	33.14 / 88	1.61 / 35	2.80	B- / 7.8	-0.08	0.01
GR	*Consumer Discretionary Sel Sec S	XLY	B+	45.09	B+ / 8.6	16.54 / 79	30.21 / 82	4.66 / 55	1.22	B / 8.2	0.04	-0.01
GR	*First Trust US IPO Index Fund	FPX	B+	28.86	B+ / 8.5	14.09 / 76	29.30 / 81	5.39 / 58	1.29	B / 8.1	0.49	0.01
GR	*WisdomTree SmallCap Earnings Fun	EES	B+	56.79	B+ / 8.5	4.90 / 55	31.35 / 85	4.40 / 53	1.50	B- / 7.8	0.35	0.02
GR	*RevenueShares Small Cap Fund	RWJ	B+	36.34	B+ / 8.5	4.12 / 52	31.36 / 85	--	0.52	B- / 7.7	0.30	-0.04
GR	*Guggenheim S&P Mid Cap 400 Pure	RFG	B+	89.64	B+ / 8.5	3.57 / 50	32.78 / 87	10.56 / 90	0.42	B / 8.0	-0.07	N/A
GR	*WisdomTree MidCap Earnings Fund	EZM	B+	61.14	B / 8.2	4.85 / 54	30.39 / 83	5.70 / 60	0.75	B- / 7.9	0.23	0.07
GR	*iShares Russell Top 200 Growth	IWY	B+	35.16	B / 7.6	13.37 / 75	--	--	1.37	B / 8.5	-0.06	0.07
GR	*ProShares UltraPro Dow30	UDOW	B	166.24	A+ / 9.8	13.86 / 76	--	--	0.69	C+/ 5.8	-0.05	N/A
GR	*ProShares Ultra Rus Mid Cap Grow	UKW	B	54.89	A+ / 9.8	-0.99 / 38	48.77 / 99	-2.53 / 18	0.00	C+/ 6.3	0.11	-0.08
GR	*ProShares Ultra SmallCap 600	SAA	B	52.31	A+ / 9.7	-1.60 / 37	45.25 / 98	-6.00 / 11	0.04	C+/ 5.9	0.06	-0.07
GR	*ProShares Ultra MidCap 400	MVV	B	70.84	A+ / 9.7	-7.02 / 27	46.43 / 98	-3.02 / 17	0.00	C+/ 6.1	-0.10	-0.02
GR	*PowerShares QQQ	QQQ	B	67.55	B+ / 8.4	18.00 / 80	28.55 / 78	9.21 / 81	0.33	B- / 7.5	0.00	0.01
GR	*SPDR S&P 600 Small Cap Growth ET	SLYG	B	124.36	B+ / 8.3	5.41 / 57	30.90 / 84	5.61 / 59	1.10	B- / 7.6	0.10	-0.03
GR	*Guggenheim S&P Sm Cap 600 Pure G	RZG	B	55.42	B / 8.2	7.22 / 62	30.26 / 83	5.93 / 61	0.47	B- / 7.7	0.42	0.02
GR	Columbia Seligman Prem Tech Gro	STK	B	18.90	B / 8.0	7.53 / 62	--	--	9.79	B- / 7.7	-2.53	-3.44
GR	*Guggenheim S&P 500 Pure Growth	RPG	B	49.24	B / 8.0	6.12 / 59	29.36 / 81	6.37 / 63	1.37	B- / 7.6	0.12	0.03
GR	*SPDR S&P 600 Small Cap ETF	SLY	B	73.84	B / 8.0	5.05 / 55	29.06 / 80	4.30 / 52	1.15	B- / 7.7	0.48	0.06
GR	*First Trust NASDAQ-100-Technolog	QTEC	B	28.69	B / 7.8	6.42 / 59	27.32 / 74	7.18 / 68	0.00	B- / 7.8	-0.07	N/A
GR	*First Trust Small Cap Core Alpha	FYX	B	33.48	B / 7.8	4.02 / 52	28.68 / 79	--	0.27	B- / 7.8	0.15	0.03
GR	*iShares Morningstar Small Value	JKL	B	87.64	B / 7.8	1.96 / 46	29.02 / 80	3.23 / 46	2.11	B- / 7.9	0.09	0.02
GR	*First Trust Mid Cap Core AlphaDE	FNX	B	36.69	B / 7.8	1.86 / 46	29.11 / 80	--	0.60	B / 8.0	0.03	0.03
GR	*iShares Morningstar Mid Core	JKG	B	96.43	B / 7.7	5.67 / 57	27.78 / 75	3.54 / 48	1.14	B / 8.1	-0.06	0.02
GR	*SPDR S&P 400 Mid Cap Growth ETF	MDYG	B	83.90	B / 7.7	2.64 / 48	28.57 / 79	6.16 / 62	0.62	B- / 7.9	0.33	-0.02
GR	*WisdomTree MidCap Dividend Fund	DON	B	56.29	B / 7.6	6.86 / 61	28.06 / 77	2.55 / 42	3.04	B / 8.4	0.07	0.10
GR	*WisdomTree SmallCap Dividend Fd	DES	B	49.09	B- / 7.4	5.19 / 56	27.34 / 74	0.98 / 31	3.35	B / 8.1	0.12	0.10
GR	*Guggenheim Mid-Cap Core ETF	CZA	B	32.81	B- / 7.4	4.31 / 53	27.50 / 75	--	0.21	B / 8.2	0.24	0.13
GR	*Vanguard Russell 1000 Gro Idx ET	VONG	B	67.84	B- / 7.2	10.35 / 69	--	--	1.12	B / 8.5	0.10	-0.04
GR	*Guggenheim S&P 500 Eq Wght HC ET	RYH	B	75.41	B- / 7.1	10.44 / 69	25.17 / 65	7.61 / 72	1.11	B / 8.4	0.07	0.01
GR	*ProShares Ultra Russell2000 Grow	UKK	B-	50.97	A+ / 9.7	-10.01 / 22	44.82 / 97	-5.18 / 12	0.00	C+/ 5.6	0.71	-0.04
GR	*iShares DJ US Technology	IYW	B-	77.81	B / 7.9	18.02 / 81	25.79 / 68	7.66 / 72	0.52	B- / 7.4	0.04	N/A
GR	*Vanguard Info Tech Ind ETF	VGT	B-	74.18	B / 7.9	16.75 / 80	26.03 / 69	7.34 / 70	0.65	B- / 7.4	0.08	0.03
GR	*SPDR S&P 600 Small Cap Value ETF	SLYV	B-	75.60	B / 7.6	3.91 / 51	27.18 / 73	3.00 / 44	1.08	B- / 7.8	0.27	0.01
GR	*SPDR DJ Wilshire Mid Cap ETF	EMM	B-	65.49	B- / 7.5	2.26 / 47	27.33 / 74	4.18 / 51	1.01	B- / 7.8	0.15	0.01
GR	*RevenueShares Mid Cap Fund	RWK	B-	32.12	B- / 7.5	1.47 / 45	27.15 / 73	--	4.04	B- / 7.8	0.12	-0.05
GR	*First Trust NASDAQ-100 Equal Wei	QQEW	B-	26.97	B- / 7.4	6.70 / 60	26.38 / 70	5.40 / 58	0.20	B- / 7.8	0.11	0.01
GR	*iShares S&P Small Cap 600 Growth	IJT	B-	82.59	B- / 7.4	5.04 / 55	27.17 / 73	4.70 / 55	1.16	B- / 7.7	0.01	-0.03
GR	*iShares S&P Mid Cap 400 Growth	IJK	B-	112.44	B- / 7.3	2.11 / 47	26.94 / 72	6.31 / 63	0.62	B- / 7.9	-0.04	N/A
GR	*Schwab US Large-Cap Growth ETF	SCHG	B-	34.21	B- / 7.1	8.24 / 65	--	--	0.88	B / 8.0	0.06	0.02
GR	*Vanguard S&P 500 G Indx ETF	VOOG	B-	67.38	C+/ 6.5	11.23 / 71	--	--	1.40	B / 8.8	-0.01	0.03

* Denotes ETF Fund, N/A denotes number is not available

99 Pct = Best
0 Pct = Worst

Fund Type	Fund Name	Ticker Symbol	Overall Investment Rating	Price As of 3/31/12	Perform- ance Rating/Pts	Annualized Total Return Through 3/31/12 1Yr/Pct	3Yr/Pct	5Yr/Pct	Dividend Yield %	Risk Rating/ Pts	Premium/Discount As of 3/31/12	1 Year Average
GI	Neuberger Berman Real Est Secs Inc	NRO	A+	4.28	A+ / 9.8	9.51 / 67	53.14 / 99	-10.96 / 6	5.61	B- / 7.9	-13.36	-11.89
GI	Nuveen Preferref Income Opps	JPC	A+	8.88	A+ / 9.7	14.32 / 76	44.52 / 97	1.03 / 31	8.56	B / 8.1	-5.23	-9.88
GI	Virtus Total Return	DCA	A+	3.80	A+ / 9.7	6.76 / 60	49.46 / 99	-16.16 / 3	6.16	B / 8.2	-8.65	-12.99
GI	Nuveen Credit Strategies Income	JQC	A+	8.98	A+ / 9.6	9.57 / 68	43.36 / 97	1.32 / 32	8.91	B / 8.6	-8.18	-11.21
GI	Guggenheim Strategic Opportunities	GOF	A+	20.55	A / 9.4	7.56 / 63	42.12 / 97	--	8.99	B / 8.7	5.60	6.72
GI	Nuveen Real Estate Inc Fund	JRS	A	11.29	A+ / 9.8	13.82 / 76	51.67 / 99	-3.40 / 16	8.15	B- / 7.5	8.14	6.70
GI	LMP Real Estate Income Fund Inc	RIT	A	10.32	A+ / 9.8	6.42 / 59	50.88 / 99	-4.72 / 13	6.98	B- / 7.8	-10.65	-10.77
GI	Cohen&Steers Total Return Realty	RFI	A	13.84	A+ / 9.6	6.31 / 59	42.82 / 97	4.40 / 53	6.36	B- / 7.6	3.98	1.93
GI	Nuveen Diversified Dividend&Income	JDD	A	11.73	A / 9.4	12.87 / 73	39.04 / 95	-0.20 / 27	8.53	B / 8.1	-5.10	-7.60
GI	Cohen&Steers Quality Income Realty	RQI	A-	9.82	A+ / 9.9	6.55 / 60	68.30 / 99	-5.19 / 12	7.33	B- / 7.1	-7.53	-7.91
GI	CBRE Clarion Global Real Estate In	IGR	A-	8.04	A+ / 9.6	5.27 / 56	41.95 / 96	-8.42 / 8	6.72	B- / 7.6	-9.46	-11.07
GI	*iShares FTSE EPRA/NAREIT NA Idx	IFNA	A-	45.93	A / 9.5	10.24 / 69	41.41 / 96	--	3.16	B- / 7.7	-0.39	0.09
GI	The Cushing MLP Total Return Fund	SRV	A-	9.96	A / 9.4	1.30 / 44	42.52 / 97	--	9.04	B- / 7.6	28.85	20.82
GI	AGIC Convertible & Income Fund II	NCZ	A-	8.76	A / 9.4	-1.74 / 36	41.62 / 96	1.76 / 36	11.64	B- / 7.6	11.88	12.10
GI	*PowerShares Act US Real Estate	PSR	A-	54.33	A- / 9.0	11.69 / 72	35.50 / 91	--	1.67	B / 8.1	-0.24	0.03
GI	Nuveen Tax-Advantaged Dividend Grt	JTD	A-	13.75	B+ / 8.8	11.81 / 72	33.15 / 88	--	7.56	B / 8.3	-7.90	-9.78
GI	AGIC Convertible & Income Fund	NCV	B+	9.50	A / 9.3	-2.56 / 34	40.32 / 95	2.27 / 40	12.32	B- / 7.3	10.34	9.64
GI	Alpine Global Premier Properties F	AWP	B+	6.50	A- / 9.0	0.57 / 42	35.36 / 91	--	9.23	B- / 7.1	-12.28	-13.75
GI	Delaware Inv Div & Inc	DDF	B+	8.15	B+ / 8.7	9.46 / 67	32.19 / 86	1.35 / 33	8.47	B- / 7.7	-4.12	-6.61
GI	*Focus Mstar Cons Cyc Id ETF	FCL	B+	29.07	B+ / 8.5	14.62 / 76	--	--	1.20	B / 8.3	0.03	-0.12
GI	TCW Strategic Income Fund	TSI	B+	5.15	B+ / 8.4	11.77 / 72	31.90 / 86	13.29 / 98	6.72	B / 8.0	-2.46	-6.33
GI	MFS Special Value Trust	MFV	B+	7.09	B / 8.2	-3.82 / 32	33.33 / 88	2.50 / 41	9.66	B / 8.0	2.75	3.45
GI	LMP Capital and Income Fund Inc	SCD	B+	13.39	B / 8.1	8.53 / 65	30.01 / 82	2.07 / 39	8.36	B / 8.3	-4.56	-7.20
GI	*WisdomTree Equity Income Fund	DHS	B+	44.80	B- / 7.5	15.51 / 78	27.25 / 74	-0.94 / 23	3.67	B+ / 9.1	-0.02	0.14
GI	Calamos Strategic Total Return Fun	CSQ	B	10.00	B / 8.2	10.16 / 69	28.65 / 79	0.67 / 29	8.40	B- / 7.7	-7.58	-12.75
GI	Franklin Universal Trust	FT	B	6.88	B / 8.0	13.40 / 75	30.61 / 83	7.23 / 69	6.63	B- / 7.5	-5.62	-7.11
GI	*SPDR DJ Wilshire Glb Real Est ET	RWO	B	39.14	B / 7.8	5.32 / 56	29.25 / 80	--	2.31	B- / 7.9	0.33	0.26
GI	NFJ Dividend Interest & Premium St	NFJ	B	17.87	B / 7.6	7.93 / 64	27.26 / 74	0.21 / 28	10.07	B- / 7.8	-1.54	-4.73
GI	Calamos Global Total Return Fund	CGO	B	15.19	B- / 7.5	7.56 / 63	28.06 / 76	6.79 / 66	7.90	B / 8.0	2.22	0.73
GI	*Schwab US REIT ETF	SCHH	B-	29.57	B- / 7.3	13.27 / 74	--	--	2.54	B- / 7.8	-0.07	0.02
GI	Calamos Convertible Opport&Income	CHI	B-	12.78	C+ / 6.6	5.32 / 56	24.60 / 63	1.43 / 34	8.92	B / 8.3	1.83	-0.58
GI	*WisdomTree LargeCap Dividend Fun	DLN	B-	52.96	C+ / 6.4	13.13 / 74	22.74 / 55	1.08 / 31	2.44	B / 8.8	-0.04	0.10
GI	*Cohen & Steers Global Realty Maj	GRI	C+	36.55	B- / 7.4	2.66 / 48	27.87 / 76	--	1.64	B- / 7.3	0.14	0.17
GI	*First Trust FTSE EPRA/NAREIT Glb	FFR	C+	35.70	C+ / 6.8	1.05 / 44	25.79 / 68	--	1.13	B- / 7.4	-0.28	0.04
GI	Calamos Convertible&High Income	CHY	C+	12.76	C+ / 6.6	1.93 / 46	25.11 / 64	4.11 / 51	7.99	B / 8.1	-1.92	-3.32
GI	*Guggenheim Wilshire US REIT ETF	WREI	C+	34.69	C+ / 6.5	11.90 / 72	--	--	2.14	B / 8.0	-0.29	-0.01
GI	*First Trust Lrg Cap Core AlphaDE	FEX	C+	30.27	C+ / 6.5	2.59 / 48	24.30 / 62	--	1.19	B / 8.2	0.03	0.08
GI	Advent Claymore Cnv Sec & Inc	AVK	C+	16.31	C+ / 6.2	-11.72 / 19	25.75 / 67	-1.87 / 20	7.48	B- / 7.4	-7.38	-8.06
GI	*PowerShares KBW High Div Yield F	KBWD	C+	23.93	C+ / 6.1	9.92 / 68	--	--	11.04	B / 8.4	0.21	0.11
GI	*Vanguard Total Stock Market ETF	VTI	C+	72.26	C+ / 6.1	6.69 / 60	22.09 / 53	2.17 / 39	1.70	B / 8.1	-0.06	0.01
GI	The Denali Fund Inc.	DNY	C+	14.74	C+ / 6.0	-1.36 / 37	24.15 / 61	-5.06 / 12	0.14	B / 8.0	-18.92	-17.19
GI	*Focus Mstar Real Est Id ETF	FRL	C+	27.26	C+ / 5.9	9.65 / 68	--	--	5.86	B / 8.0	0.04	-0.05
GI	*First Trust Value Line Dividend	FVD	C+	16.90	C / 5.4	8.64 / 66	21.12 / 48	2.60 / 42	2.39	B / 8.9	0.18	0.10
GI	*Focus Mstar Cons Def Id ETF	FCD	C+	28.77	C / 5.2	15.54 / 78	--	--	2.27	B+ / 9.3	0.10	0.03
GI	BlackRock Enhanced Capital and Inc	CII	C	13.49	C+ / 5.6	0.03 / 41	21.97 / 52	4.65 / 55	10.67	B- / 7.8	-7.35	-5.80
GI	*db-X 2040 Target Date Fund	TDV	C	21.99	C / 4.9	5.34 / 56	19.00 / 39	--	1.73	B / 8.2	0.78	-1.79
GI	*iShares S&P Target Date 2035 Ind	TZO	C	35.50	C / 4.8	3.39 / 50	19.41 / 40	--	1.15	B / 8.3	0.31	0.07
GI	*iShares S&P Aggressive Allocatio	AOA	C	36.45	C / 4.8	3.15 / 49	19.16 / 39	--	1.13	B / 8.2	0.11	0.08
GI	Ellsworth Fund Ltd	ECF	C	7.35	C / 4.8	0.15 / 41	20.12 / 44	3.11 / 45	3.40	B / 8.4	-13.02	-13.23
GI	*iShares S&P Target Date 2040 Ind	TZV	C	35.76	C / 4.6	2.80 / 49	18.71 / 38	--	1.16	B / 8.2	0.14	-0.03
GI	*iShares S&P Target Date 2025 Ind	TZI	C	35.15	C / 4.3	3.85 / 51	17.82 / 35	--	1.10	B / 8.7	0.49	0.02
GI	*iShares S&P Target Date 2030 Ind	TZL	C	35.31	C- / 4.1	3.33 / 50	17.31 / 33	--	1.12	B / 8.7	0.00	-0.02

* Denotes ETF Fund, N/A denotes number is not available

www.thestreetratings.com

Fund Type	Fund Name	Ticker Symbol	Overall Investment Rating	Price As of 3/31/12	PERFORMANCE Performance Rating/Pts	Annualized Total Return Through 3/31/12 1Yr/Pct	3Yr/Pct	5Yr/Pct	Dividend Yield %	RISK Risk Rating/Pts	VALUATION Premium/Discount As of 3/31/12	1 Year Average
HL	*ProShares Ultra Health Care	RXL	A-	73.10	A / 9.5	25.06 / 85	36.58 / 92	2.09 / 39	0.83	B- / 7.6	-0.04	-0.02
HL	H&Q Life Sciences Investors	HQL	B+	13.83	A- / 9.1	29.16 / 88	31.15 / 84	8.26 / 76	7.52	B- / 7.5	-5.98	-9.23
HL	*iShares DJ US Pharmaceuticals	IHE	B+	83.06	B / 8.1	25.66 / 85	27.75 / 75	10.02 / 87	1.44	B / 8.1	-0.04	0.01
HL	*First Trust Health Care AlphaDEX	FXH	B+	30.81	B / 8.1	7.17 / 62	30.23 / 83	--	0.10	B / 8.4	0.10	0.05
HL	*ProShares Ultra Nasdaq Biotech	BIB	B	96.07	A+ / 9.9	39.64 / 96	--	--	0.00	C+ / 6.2	0.20	-0.13
HL	*PowerShares Dynamic Pharmaceutic	PJP	B	31.43	A- / 9.0	29.39 / 88	32.53 / 87	12.03 / 96	0.23	C+ / 6.9	0.10	0.07
HL	*SPDR S&P Pharmaceuticals ETF	XPH	B	57.10	B+ / 8.6	22.37 / 83	30.59 / 83	11.29 / 93	0.71	B- / 7.3	0.04	0.02
HL	*First Trust AMEX Biotechnology	FBT	B	42.27	B+ / 8.5	2.08 / 47	30.77 / 83	11.60 / 94	0.00	C+ / 6.9	0.07	0.03
HL	H&Q Healthcare Investors	HQH	B	16.47	B / 8.1	24.53 / 85	26.15 / 70	6.75 / 66	7.53	B / 8.0	-7.83	-9.45
HL	*iShares DJ US Health Care Provid	IHF	B	66.88	B / 8.0	7.25 / 62	28.62 / 79	2.98 / 44	0.81	B / 8.1	0.07	-0.01
HL	Gabelli Healthcare & WellnessRx Tr	GRX	B-	8.32	C+ / 6.6	8.76 / 66	23.06 / 57	--	0.00	B / 8.5	-14.58	-15.87
HL	*Focus Mstar Hlth Care Id ETF	FHC	B-	28.86	C+ / 6.1	14.64 / 77	--	--	1.34	B+ / 9.0	0.17	-0.02
HL	*iShares Nasdaq Biotechnology	IBB	C+	123.30	B- / 7.5	22.26 / 83	24.02 / 61	9.58 / 84	0.04	C+ / 6.9	-0.03	-0.02
HL	*SPDR S&P Biotech ETF	XBI	C+	80.46	C+ / 6.6	19.70 / 82	19.87 / 43	10.39 / 89	0.00	B- / 7.0	0.04	0.05
HL	BlackRock Health Sciences Trust	BME	C+	27.47	C+ / 6.5	11.24 / 71	23.02 / 57	8.26 / 76	5.60	B- / 7.9	-1.12	-2.56
HL	*PowerShares Dynamic Hlthcare	PTH	C+	32.43	C+ / 6.5	8.56 / 65	23.12 / 57	2.76 / 43	0.00	B- / 7.6	0.28	0.01
HL	*Vanguard HealthCare Index ETF	VHT	C+	67.57	C / 5.5	13.80 / 75	19.95 / 43	4.50 / 54	1.55	B / 8.6	0.06	0.01
HL	*iShares DJ US Healthcare	IYH	C+	78.20	C / 5.2	14.40 / 76	18.87 / 39	4.26 / 52	1.72	B / 8.6	-0.01	-0.01
HL	*Health Care Select Sector SPDR	XLV	C+	37.61	C / 5.1	15.38 / 78	18.62 / 38	3.66 / 49	1.98	B / 8.7	-0.03	N/A
HL	*iShares DJ US Medical Devices Id	IHI	C	67.84	C+ / 6.1	4.81 / 54	22.68 / 55	4.90 / 57	0.21	B- / 7.2	-0.01	-0.02
HL	*SPDR S&P Health Care Equipment E	XHE	C	55.84	C / 4.7	6.10 / 59	--	--	0.15	B / 8.3	-0.52	0.11
HL	*iShares S&P Global Healthcare	IXJ	C	60.15	C / 4.6	12.95 / 73	17.82 / 35	2.53 / 42	1.40	B / 8.6	0.05	-0.02
HL	*SPDR SP Intl Health Care ETF	IRY	C	32.26	C- / 3.8	5.74 / 58	15.82 / 29	--	3.88	B / 8.5	-0.43	0.16
HL	*iShares MSCI ACWI ex US HlthCre	AXHE	C	60.33	C- / 3.7	9.45 / 67	--	--	0.58	B / 8.5	0.89	0.18
HL	*PowerShares Dynamic Biotech&Geno	PBE	C-	22.68	C+ / 5.6	3.42 / 50	21.38 / 49	4.37 / 53	0.00	C+ / 5.9	-0.09	-0.12
HL	*ProShares UltraShort Health Care	RXD	E	16.89	E / 0.3	-33.58 / 4	-36.00 / 3	-17.46 / 3	0.00	C- / 3.9	-0.30	-0.08
HL	*ProShares UltraShort Nasdaq Biot	BIS	E	22.90	E- / 0.1	-47.24 / 2	--	--	0.00	C- / 3.3	0.09	0.12

99 Pct = Best
0 Pct = Worst

* Denotes ETF Fund, N/A denotes number is not available

99 Pct = Best
0 Pct = Worst

Fund Type	Fund Name	Ticker Symbol	Overall Investment Rating	Price As of 3/31/12	Performance Rating/Pts	Annualized Total Return Through 3/31/12			Dividend Yield %	Risk Rating/ Pts	Premium/Discount As of 3/31/12	1 Year Average
						1Yr/Pct	3Yr/Pct	5Yr/Pct				
IN	*ProShares Ultra Consumer Goods	UGE	A+	92.52	A+ / 9.8	24.50 / 85	46.70 / 98	7.50 / 71	0.66	B / 8.0	0.21	-0.10
IN	F&C/Claymore Preferred Sec Inc Fun	FFC	A+	18.05	A+ / 9.8	16.54 / 79	52.62 / 99	7.06 / 67	9.04	B+ / 9.0	3.97	5.11
IN	F&C/Claymore Total Return Fund	FLC	A+	19.01	A+ / 9.8	14.88 / 77	53.78 / 99	7.76 / 73	8.81	B+ / 9.1	2.92	3.67
IN	Flaherty&Crumrine Preferred Income	PFD	A+	14.22	A+ / 9.7	24.11 / 84	47.29 / 98	5.24 / 58	7.85	B / 8.8	14.40	14.11
IN	J Hancock Tax Advantage Div Income	HTD	A+	17.72	A+ / 9.6	18.82 / 81	43.04 / 97	7.57 / 71	6.67	B / 8.9	-7.76	-7.42
IN	*iShares FTSE NAREIT Retail Idx	RTL	A+	32.64	A+ / 9.6	18.72 / 81	41.95 / 96	--	3.40	B / 8.0	0.09	-0.02
IN	Flaherty&Crumrine Preferred Inc Op	PFO	A+	10.99	A+ / 9.6	14.90 / 77	45.22 / 98	6.69 / 65	8.24	B / 8.9	7.53	10.43
IN	J Hancock Preferred Income II	HPF	A+	21.85	A / 9.3	25.80 / 86	37.80 / 94	7.17 / 68	7.69	B / 8.8	2.53	0.07
IN	Nuveen Quality Preferred Income 3	JHP	A+	8.32	A / 9.3	12.15 / 73	38.85 / 95	-1.37 / 21	7.50	B / 8.6	-2.12	-3.31
IN	J Hancock Preferred Inc	HPI	A+	21.78	A- / 9.2	24.21 / 84	37.86 / 94	7.09 / 68	7.71	B / 8.9	1.82	2.00
IN	John Hancock Premium Dividend	PDT	A+	13.47	A- / 9.2	23.91 / 84	37.61 / 94	10.78 / 91	6.73	B+ / 9.1	-2.60	-3.36
IN	BlackRock Credit Alloc Inc Tr I	PSW	A+	9.88	A- / 9.2	16.62 / 79	37.91 / 94	-6.39 / 10	7.23	B / 8.7	-8.09	-11.32
IN	Nuveen Quality Preferred Income	JTP	A+	8.16	A- / 9.2	14.26 / 76	38.22 / 94	-1.14 / 22	7.35	B / 8.9	-1.81	-3.36
IN	Nuveen Quality Preferred Income 2	JPS	A+	8.62	A- / 9.2	13.65 / 75	37.87 / 94	-0.32 / 25	7.66	B / 8.7	-2.05	-4.46
IN	J Hancock Preferred Income III	HPS	A+	17.80	A- / 9.0	14.11 / 76	36.79 / 93	4.42 / 53	7.56	B / 8.8	-3.31	-2.71
IN	BlackRock Credit Alloc Inc Tr II	PSY	A+	10.51	B+ / 8.9	14.29 / 76	35.57 / 92	-3.89 / 14	6.96	B / 8.8	-9.08	-11.40
IN	Cohen&Steers REIT& Preferred Incom	RNP	A	16.31	A+ / 9.9	14.47 / 76	66.66 / 99	0.38 / 29	7.36	B- / 7.6	-4.90	-6.73
IN	*SPDR S&P Retail ETF	XRT	A	61.25	A / 9.4	21.16 / 83	36.88 / 93	8.27 / 76	0.65	B / 8.1	0.00	0.01
IN	*Guggenheim S&P 500 Pure Value	RPV	A	32.29	A- / 9.2	5.49 / 57	37.75 / 94	0.69 / 30	2.68	B / 8.1	-0.06	0.04
IN	BlackRock Credit Alloc Inc Tr IV	BTZ	A	13.07	B+ / 8.9	15.43 / 78	34.49 / 90	-1.19 / 22	7.21	B / 8.7	-8.86	-11.78
IN	*ProShares Ultra Consumer Service	UCC	A-	68.31	A+ / 9.8	26.85 / 86	51.59 / 99	-0.15 / 27	0.00	B- / 7.2	0.12	0.07
IN	*SPDR DJ REIT ETF	RWR	A-	70.83	A- / 9.2	13.17 / 74	37.02 / 93	-1.01 / 22	2.46	B- / 7.8	-0.04	N/A
IN	*iShares Cohen & Steers Realty Ma	ICF	A-	76.64	A- / 9.2	12.50 / 73	37.33 / 93	-1.95 / 19	3.11	B- / 7.8	0.03	N/A
IN	*Vanguard REIT ETF	VNQ	A-	63.65	A- / 9.1	12.74 / 73	36.60 / 92	0.15 / 28	3.15	B- / 7.8	-0.03	N/A
IN	*First Trust S&P REIT Index Fund	FRI	A-	17.14	A- / 9.1	12.48 / 73	36.42 / 92	--	1.70	B- / 7.9	0.18	0.04
IN	*PowerShares Dynamic Leisure&Ente	PEJ	A-	21.89	A- / 9.0	15.69 / 78	33.02 / 88	4.90 / 56	0.99	B- / 7.9	0.23	-0.04
IN	*iShares FTSE NAREIT Residential	REZ	A-	46.41	A- / 9.0	14.30 / 76	35.75 / 92	--	3.37	B / 8.0	0.00	0.04
IN	*iShares FTSE NAREIT Real Estate	FTY	A-	38.18	B+ / 8.9	11.17 / 70	35.41 / 91	--	3.49	B / 8.1	-0.10	N/A
IN	*First Trust Consumer Dis AlphaDE	FXD	A-	22.85	B+ / 8.9	8.09 / 64	34.09 / 89	--	0.81	B / 8.0	0.09	0.01
IN	*Vanguard Consumer Discret ETF	VCR	A-	72.20	B+ / 8.7	15.12 / 77	31.53 / 85	4.37 / 53	1.18	B / 8.2	-0.01	N/A
IN	*Guggenheim Spin-Off ETF	CSD	A-	26.57	B+ / 8.6	9.06 / 67	31.80 / 85	0.41 / 29	0.42	B / 8.5	0.08	0.10
IN	*ProShares Ultra Real Estate	URE	B+	61.79	A+ / 9.8	8.79 / 66	58.64 / 99	-26.00 / 2	1.46	C+ / 6.4	-0.10	N/A
IN	*Guggenheim 2x S&P 500 ETF	RSU	B+	49.99	A+ / 9.6	10.01 / 68	39.78 / 95	--	1.85	C+ / 6.8	-0.02	-0.04
IN	Foxby Corp	FXBY	B+	1.58	A / 9.5	37.39 / 95	32.45 / 87	-7.74 / 8	0.00	B- / 7.3	-24.40	-29.17
IN	Gabelli Equity Trust	GAB	B+	5.75	A- / 9.1	3.30 / 50	36.16 / 92	1.65 / 35	9.74	B- / 7.8	1.05	-1.16
IN	Guggenheim Enhanced Equity Strateg	GGE	B+	17.20	B+ / 8.8	10.13 / 69	34.49 / 90	-26.20 / 2	7.27	B- / 7.4	-13.00	-11.28
IN	*iShares DJ US Real Estate	IYR	B+	62.30	B+ / 8.8	8.70 / 66	33.76 / 89	-1.93 / 19	3.42	B- / 7.9	0.00	0.01
IN	Gabelli Dividend & Income Trust	GDV	B+	16.38	B / 8.1	4.04 / 52	30.77 / 83	1.85 / 37	5.86	B / 8.1	-11.22	-11.85
IN	*WisdomTree Dividend Ex-Financial	DTN	B+	54.82	B / 7.9	13.66 / 75	28.92 / 80	2.15 / 39	3.33	B+ / 9.0	0.02	0.08
IN	*Guggenheim Multi-Asset Income ET	CVY	B+	21.85	B / 7.9	8.02 / 64	29.90 / 82	1.98 / 38	4.85	B / 8.7	0.14	0.07
IN	Kayne Anderson Midstream/Energy	KMF	B+	27.42	B / 7.7	13.18 / 74	--	--	4.57	B / 8.5	-5.68	-6.52
IN	*ProShares Ultra Russell 3000	UWC	B	91.97	A+ / 9.7	8.42 / 65	--	--	0.00	C+ / 6.2	0.01	-0.14
IN	*PowerShares NASDAQ Internet Port	PNQI	B	41.63	A / 9.3	5.39 / 57	37.23 / 93	--	0.00	C+ / 6.6	0.29	0.07
IN	*ProShares Ultra Russell1000 Valu	UVG	B	33.09	A / 9.3	0.82 / 43	36.56 / 92	-12.30 / 5	0.53	C+ / 6.8	-0.09	0.04
IN	*iShares FTSE NAREIT Indl/Off Idx	FNIO	B	28.26	B+ / 8.4	2.17 / 47	32.40 / 86	--	3.02	B- / 7.5	-0.28	-0.02
IN	*PowerShares FTSE RAFI US 1500 Sm	PRFZ	B	68.07	B+ / 8.4	-0.92 / 38	32.11 / 86	4.73 / 56	0.38	B- / 7.5	0.03	0.02
IN	Cohen&Steers Dividend Majors	DVM	B	13.90	B+ / 8.3	11.77 / 72	29.75 / 81	-0.23 / 26	6.62	B- / 7.8	-7.09	-7.85
IN	Eaton Vance Tax Advantage Div Inc	EVT	B	16.73	B / 8.2	1.78 / 46	30.85 / 84	-1.88 / 20	7.71	B- / 7.9	-9.47	-9.85
IN	*PowerShares Dynamic Retail	PMR	B	25.61	B / 7.8	26.22 / 86	24.32 / 62	5.50 / 59	0.10	B / 8.2	-0.04	-0.02
IN	*First Trust Multi Cap Val AlphaD	FAB	B	32.00	B / 7.7	3.65 / 51	28.29 / 77	--	0.59	B / 8.2	-0.16	0.07
IN	*PowerShares Buyback Achievers	PKW	B	29.35	B- / 7.3	13.26 / 74	25.49 / 66	3.91 / 50	0.53	B / 8.6	0.17	0.05
IN	*iShares S&P USPreferred Stock	PFF	B	39.04	C+ / 6.9	4.43 / 53	26.87 / 72	2.56 / 42	4.57	B / 8.9	0.28	0.04

* Denotes ETF Fund, N/A denotes number is not available

Fund Type	Fund Name	Ticker Symbol	Overall Investment Rating	Price As of 3/31/12	PERFORMANCE Perform- ance Rating/Pts	Annualized Total Return Through 3/31/12			Dividend Yield %	RISK Risk Rating/ Pts	VALUATION Premium/Discount As of 3/31/12	1 Year Average
	99 Pct = Best 0 Pct = Worst					1Yr/Pct	3Yr/Pct	5Yr/Pct				
LP	PIMCO Income Strategy Fund II	PFN	A	10.16	A / 9.5	4.97 / 55	42.03 / 97	-1.31 / 21	7.68	B / 8.1	3.67	2.91
LP	PIMCO Income Strategy Fund	PFL	A	11.36	A / 9.4	4.22 / 53	41.97 / 96	0.19 / 28	8.58	B- / 7.9	5.38	5.93
LP	Nuveen Floating Rate Income Opp	JRO	A	12.05	A / 9.3	6.58 / 60	39.73 / 95	5.64 / 60	7.22	B / 8.0	1.43	-0.67
LP	Nuveen Sr Inc	NSL	A-	7.13	B+ / 8.9	0.98 / 43	37.56 / 94	4.30 / 52	7.24	B / 8.2	0.71	0.82
LP	Invesco Van Kampen Senior Inc Tr	VVR	A-	4.91	B+ / 8.7	3.60 / 50	34.18 / 89	-3.43 / 16	6.48	B / 8.2	0.00	-3.85
LP	Nuveen Floating Rate Income Fund	JFR	B+	11.92	B+ / 8.7	5.36 / 57	34.20 / 89	4.31 / 53	6.90	B / 8.1	0.08	-2.70
LP	Eaton Vance Floating Rate Income T	EFT	B+	16.24	B+ / 8.3	4.52 / 54	31.64 / 85	4.65 / 55	6.28	B / 8.2	3.70	-1.29
LP	Eaton Vance Senior Income Trust	EVF	B+	7.21	B+ / 8.3	3.67 / 51	32.27 / 86	3.44 / 47	6.16	B / 8.5	0.00	-3.48
LP	First Tr Senior Floating Rte Inc I	FCT	B	14.97	B / 7.6	6.49 / 60	28.46 / 78	2.22 / 40	6.01	B / 8.4	1.98	-2.29
LP	Invesco Van Kampen Dynamic Cred Op	VTA	B	11.68	B- / 7.4	-2.44 / 35	29.36 / 81	--	7.71	B / 8.0	-6.26	-6.87
LP	Pioneer Floating Rate Trust	PHD	B	12.96	B- / 7.2	4.99 / 55	28.01 / 76	1.95 / 37	7.52	B / 8.3	0.15	1.24
LP	Eaton Vance Senior Floating Rate	EFR	B-	15.24	B- / 7.5	-0.64 / 39	30.16 / 82	3.30 / 47	6.85	B- / 7.6	-0.59	0.57
LP	BlackRock Floating Rate Inc Strt I	FRB	B-	13.95	B- / 7.3	5.60 / 57	26.71 / 72	3.09 / 44	6.28	B- / 7.6	2.27	-2.97
LP	LMP Corporate Loan Fund Inc	TLI	B-	11.90	C+ / 6.7	1.69 / 45	26.11 / 69	3.27 / 46	6.45	B / 8.6	-5.56	-4.65
LP	BlackRock Diversified Inc Strat	DVF	C+	10.28	C+ / 6.9	0.75 / 43	26.99 / 73	-2.67 / 17	6.83	B- / 7.7	-3.93	-4.23
LP	BlackRock Floating Rate Inc Strat	FRA	C+	14.82	C+ / 6.5	1.70 / 45	24.52 / 63	3.60 / 48	6.23	B- / 7.7	0.07	-2.45
LP	*Focus Mstar Finl Svc Id ETF	FFL	C+	24.66	C+ / 6.5	-1.91 / 36	--	--	1.36	B- / 7.1	-0.04	0.12
LP	BlackRock Floating Rt Income	BGT	C+	14.27	C+ / 6.1	3.88 / 51	23.73 / 59	3.56 / 48	6.52	B- / 7.8	0.63	-0.32
LP	ING Prime Rate Trust	PPR	C+	5.70	C+ / 5.7	0.09 / 41	22.98 / 57	1.60 / 35	6.32	B / 8.1	-2.23	-3.32
LP	BlackRock Defined Opp Credit Trust	BHL	C	13.40	C / 4.5	-5.46 / 30	20.41 / 45	--	5.91	B / 8.2	-3.87	-3.12
LP	Blackstone/GSO Sr Floating Rate Tr	BSL	C	19.95	C- / 4.1	6.71 / 60	--	--	6.62	B / 8.2	3.05	0.99
LP	*PowerShares Senior Loan	BKLN	C-	24.58	D / 2.2	2.91 / 49	--	--	4.93	B+ / 9.5	0.74	0.44
LP	Apollo Senior Floating Rate Fd Inc	AFT	D+	17.91	D+ / 2.9	-4.16 / 32	--	--	6.45	B- / 7.3	-2.50	-4.65
LP	Blackstone / GSO Lng-Sht Credit In	BGX	D+	18.27	D / 1.8	-3.28 / 33	--	--	7.09	B / 8.2	-2.19	0.72
LP	Nuveen Tax-Advantaged Floating Rat	JFP	D	2.43	D+ / 2.8	11.15 / 70	7.93 / 13	-22.32 / 3	4.94	C+ / 6.3	-11.96	-8.88
LP	Avenue Income Credit Strategies	ACP	D	16.58	D / 1.8	-5.12 / 30	--	--	8.69	B- / 7.2	-4.93	-1.45

* Denotes ETF Fund, N/A denotes number is not available

Fund Type	Fund Name	Ticker Symbol	Overall Investment Rating	Price As of 3/31/12	PERFORMANCE					Dividend Yield %	RISK	VALUATION	
			99 Pct = Best *0 Pct = Worst*		Perform-ance Rating/Pts	Annualized Total Return Through 3/31/12					Risk Rating/ Pts	Premium/Discount	
							1Yr/Pct	3Yr/Pct	5Yr/Pct			As of 3/31/12	1 Year Average
MTG	PCM Fund	PCM	A+	11.01	A / 9.5		11.27 / 71	43.06 / 97	10.21 / 88	9.45	B / 8.8	7.73	9.43
MTG	PIMCO Strategic Glob Gov Fund	RCS	B-	11.06	C+ / 6.8		14.44 / 76	25.87 / 68	11.65 / 94	9.40	B / 8.5	18.80	21.55
MTG	American Strat Inc Portfolio	ASP	B-	11.67	C+ / 6.8		13.03 / 74	24.65 / 63	9.26 / 82	7.71	B / 8.2	-7.89	-11.95
MTG	Nuveen Mortgage Opportunity Term 2	JMT	C+	23.46	C / 5.1		4.18 / 52	--	--	8.82	B / 8.3	-1.39	-4.38
MTG	Helios Total Return Fund Inc	HTR	C	6.02	C / 5.3		8.98 / 66	22.04 / 52	2.48 / 41	9.47	B / 8.1	1.01	-0.44
MTG	American Select Portfolio	SLA	C	10.41	C / 4.8		10.82 / 70	19.66 / 41	5.32 / 58	7.78	B / 8.0	-10.57	-12.39
MTG	Western Asset Mtge Defined Oppty	DMO	C	21.71	C / 4.5		6.43 / 59	--	--	8.98	B / 8.7	0.46	-0.79
MTG	Nuveen Mortgage Opportunity Term	JLS	C	23.38	C / 4.4		2.70 / 48	--	--	8.85	B / 8.3	-1.43	-3.52
MTG	BlackRock Income Trust	BKT	C	7.42	C- / 3.1		16.88 / 80	11.90 / 19	8.91 / 79	6.55	B+ / 9.6	-6.08	-9.17
MTG	American Income Fund	MRF	C-	7.99	C / 5.1		8.99 / 66	20.53 / 45	7.88 / 73	7.51	B- / 7.0	-5.89	-8.29
MTG	First Trust Mortgage Income Fund	FMY	C-	19.62	C / 4.4		7.86 / 64	18.61 / 38	12.79 / 97	9.79	C+ / 6.9	9.30	5.24
MTG	Helios Strategic Mortgage Income	HSM	C-	6.32	C- / 4.2		6.40 / 59	18.15 / 36	-3.21 / 16	9.97	B- / 7.5	-0.63	-3.82
MTG	American Strat Inc Portfolio II	BSP	C-	8.30	C- / 3.1		1.22 / 44	14.25 / 25	2.97 / 44	7.23	B- / 7.9	-15.48	-15.52
MTG	*SPDR Barclays Cap Mortg Backed E	MBG	C-	27.52	D / 1.7		6.50 / 60	4.76 / 10	--	1.54	B+ / 9.6	0.00	0.03
MTG	*iShares Barclays MBS Bond	MBB	C-	107.95	D / 1.7		5.86 / 58	5.02 / 10	5.83 / 61	3.37	B+ / 9.7	0.10	0.08
MTG	*Vanguard Mort-Backed Secs Idx ET	VMBS	C-	51.87	D / 1.6		5.52 / 57	--	--	1.60	B+ / 9.8	-0.02	0.22
MTG	American Strat Inc Portfolio III	CSP	D	7.00	D+ / 2.4		1.25 / 44	9.41 / 15	-0.08 / 27	6.43	B- / 7.5	-14.32	-14.67

* Denotes ETF Fund, N/A denotes number is not available

www.thestreetratings.com

Fund Type	Fund Name	Ticker Symbol	Overall Investment Rating	Price As of 3/31/12	PERFORMANCE Perform-ance Rating/Pts	Annualized Total Return Through 3/31/12			Dividend Yield %	RISK Risk Rating/ Pts	VALUATION Premium/Discount As of 3/31/12	1 Year Average
						1Yr/Pct	3Yr/Pct	5Yr/Pct				
MUH	Pioneer Municipal High Income Adv	MAV	A+	14.72	A+ / 9.7	27.83 / 98	28.15 / 97	7.20 / 92	8.39	B / 8.4	14.37	11.39
MUH	MFS High Yield Muni Trust	CMU	A+	4.90	A / 9.4	25.00 / 96	22.76 / 91	3.64 / 59	7.10	B / 8.8	6.75	5.37
MUH	MFS High Inc Muni Tr	CXE	A+	5.35	A / 9.4	22.22 / 92	23.90 / 93	3.37 / 57	7.18	B / 8.7	4.70	4.09
MUH	Pioneer Municipal High Income Trus	MHI	A+	14.73	A / 9.3	23.33 / 94	24.10 / 93	7.37 / 93	8.38	B / 8.5	5.74	5.01
MUH	Nuveen Muni High Income Opport	NMZ	B+	12.89	B / 8.2	17.97 / 87	16.98 / 69	2.03 / 45	6.80	B / 8.3	3.12	3.61
MUH	Nuveen Muni High Income Opport 2	NMD	B	12.10	B / 7.8	18.72 / 88	15.69 / 61	--	6.50	B / 8.3	-0.25	-0.76
MUH	*Market Vectors Hi-Yld Mun Idx ET	HYD	B-	31.34	C+ / 5.9	16.71 / 86	12.81 / 42	--	5.00	B+ / 9.1	0.67	0.32
MUH	Western Asset Municipal High Inc	MHF	C+	8.04	C / 5.0	18.54 / 87	10.13 / 28	5.82 / 80	5.22	B / 8.9	0.88	-1.11
MUH	*PowerShares VRDO Tax-Free Weekly	PVI	C-	24.99	D- / 1.2	0.48 / 43	0.56 / 8	--	0.15	B+ / 9.9	-0.04	-0.01

99 Pct = Best
0 Pct = Worst

* Denotes ETF Fund, N/A denotes number is not available

Fund Type	Fund Name	Ticker Symbol	Overall Investment Rating	Price As of 3/31/12	Performance Rating/Pts	Annualized Total Return Through 3/31/12			Dividend Yield %	Risk Rating/ Pts	Premium/Discount As of 3/31/12	1 Year Average
						1Yr/Pct	3Yr/Pct	5Yr/Pct				
MUN	BlackRock Build America Bond	BBN	A+	21.45	A+ / 9.7	31.67 / 99	--	--	7.37	B / 8.5	-4.58	-6.07
MUN	BlackRock MuniHoldings Fund	MHD	A+	17.76	A / 9.5	30.61 / 99	22.87 / 91	8.78 / 98	6.18	B / 8.9	3.80	0.24
MUN	Eaton Vance Municipal Inc Tr	EVN	A+	13.63	A / 9.5	25.83 / 97	23.32 / 92	4.61 / 68	7.26	B / 8.4	14.35	13.02
MUN	BlackRock Long Term Muni Adv	BTA	A+	12.39	A / 9.4	29.18 / 99	22.45 / 90	4.47 / 67	6.39	B / 8.4	3.08	-1.67
MUN	PIMCO Municipal Income Fund II	PML	A+	12.18	A / 9.4	28.95 / 98	21.03 / 86	2.07 / 45	6.40	B / 8.5	5.27	3.45
MUN	BlackRock MuniVest Fund II	MVT	A+	16.22	A / 9.4	25.46 / 96	23.85 / 92	7.99 / 97	6.73	B / 8.7	3.64	3.10
MUN	Eaton Vance National Municipal Opp	EOT	A+	21.80	A / 9.4	23.36 / 94	--	--	5.14	B / 8.3	0.74	-3.22
MUN	BlackRock Strategic Municipal Tr	BSD	A+	14.19	A / 9.3	27.11 / 97	22.67 / 90	1.20 / 37	6.26	B / 8.8	0.14	-1.44
MUN	Managed Duration Investment Grd Mu	MZF	A+	15.32	A / 9.3	24.62 / 95	23.19 / 92	9.96 / 99	6.46	B / 8.6	2.13	-0.38
MUN	DWS Municipal Income Trust	KTF	A+	13.82	A- / 9.2	27.13 / 97	22.45 / 90	11.23 / 99	6.08	B / 8.7	3.68	0.69
MUN	DWS Strategic Municipal Inc Tr	KSM	A+	13.95	A- / 9.2	25.77 / 96	22.18 / 89	9.70 / 99	6.62	B / 8.8	5.52	3.87
MUN	Nuveen New Jersey Municipal Value	NJV	A+	16.03	A- / 9.2	23.74 / 94	--	--	4.34	B / 8.7	-2.43	-4.65
MUN	Nuveen California Municipal Value	NCB	A+	15.80	A- / 9.2	22.86 / 93	--	--	5.05	B / 8.6	-4.76	-6.83
MUN	*SPDR Nuveen Barclays Bld Amr Bd	BABS	A+	58.72	A- / 9.1	27.82 / 98	--	--	4.54	B+ / 9.0	0.39	-1.05
MUN	BlackRock MuniYield Fund	MYD	A+	15.31	A- / 9.1	25.00 / 96	22.18 / 89	6.38 / 85	6.54	B / 8.6	2.34	1.25
MUN	BlackRock Municipal Income Trust I	BLE	A+	15.50	A- / 9.1	23.53 / 94	22.88 / 91	5.17 / 74	6.58	B / 8.6	1.64	0.95
MUN	MFS Municipal Income Trust	MFM	A+	7.29	A- / 9.0	23.99 / 94	20.93 / 86	4.31 / 65	6.91	B / 8.6	4.14	2.78
MUN	BlackRock Municipal Bond Trust	BBK	A+	16.28	A- / 9.0	20.97 / 90	21.83 / 88	4.21 / 64	6.52	B / 8.6	2.07	2.46
MUN	BlackRock MuniHoldings Fund II	MUH	A+	15.72	B+ / 8.9	22.69 / 93	21.93 / 89	8.12 / 97	6.34	B / 8.7	-1.81	-1.18
MUN	BlackRock Investment Qual Muni Tr	BKN	A	15.50	A- / 9.0	26.20 / 97	21.08 / 87	3.04 / 55	6.50	B / 8.5	2.45	3.85
MUN	BlackRock Municipal Income Trust	BFK	A	14.49	B+ / 8.9	25.95 / 97	20.20 / 84	2.95 / 54	6.63	B / 8.4	1.05	1.85
MUN	Invesco Van Kampen Sel Sector Muni	VKL	A	12.84	B+ / 8.9	22.18 / 92	21.23 / 87	5.92 / 80	6.82	B / 8.6	3.63	0.94
MUN	MFS Invst Gr Muni Tr	CXH	A	10.16	B+ / 8.8	23.55 / 94	19.61 / 82	5.14 / 73	6.44	B / 8.7	0.89	-0.51
MUN	Invesco Municipal Premium Income T	PIA	A	8.89	B+ / 8.7	28.51 / 98	18.39 / 77	5.09 / 73	6.07	B / 8.6	-0.22	-3.66
MUN	Federated Prem Intermediate Muni	FPT	A	14.90	B+ / 8.7	25.50 / 96	17.26 / 71	7.53 / 94	5.23	B / 8.9	3.11	-2.75
MUN	American Municipal Income Portfoli	XAA	A	14.87	B+ / 8.7	24.02 / 94	19.91 / 83	5.59 / 77	6.26	B / 8.8	-2.04	-3.08
MUN	Invesco Van Kampen Adv Muni Inc II	VKI	A	12.95	B+ / 8.7	22.53 / 92	19.54 / 82	5.97 / 81	6.76	B / 8.8	3.11	0.62
MUN	Invesco Quality Municipal Income T	IQI	A	13.90	B+ / 8.6	24.84 / 95	18.62 / 79	5.99 / 81	6.37	B / 8.8	1.83	-2.06
MUN	Invesco Van Kampen Tr Fr Inv Gr Mu	VGM	A	15.15	B+ / 8.6	21.09 / 91	20.45 / 85	6.51 / 86	6.97	B / 8.8	3.41	1.43
MUN	PIMCO Municipal Income Fund III	PMX	A	11.80	B+ / 8.6	19.32 / 89	18.55 / 78	1.43 / 40	7.12	B / 8.8	13.68	13.29
MUN	Western Asset Municipal Partners	MNP	A	15.79	B+ / 8.5	26.13 / 97	18.33 / 77	8.65 / 98	5.32	B / 8.9	-1.99	-3.77
MUN	BlackRock Muni Interm Duration	MUI	A	15.85	B+ / 8.3	21.97 / 92	18.04 / 75	7.32 / 92	5.41	B / 8.9	-0.81	-3.67
MUN	Federated Premier Muni Income	FMN	A-	15.97	B+ / 8.8	28.65 / 98	17.38 / 72	7.33 / 93	6.24	B / 8.4	8.05	2.65
MUN	Putnam Managed Muni Inc Tr	PMM	A-	7.70	B+ / 8.6	19.20 / 88	20.54 / 85	6.63 / 87	6.06	B / 8.5	-0.39	0.22
MUN	Dreyfus Strategic Municipals	LEO	A-	9.12	B+ / 8.5	22.16 / 92	18.85 / 80	5.98 / 81	6.45	B / 8.5	3.52	1.31
MUN	BlackRock MuniYield Quality Fund I	MQT	A-	13.56	B+ / 8.4	25.98 / 97	19.03 / 80	7.76 / 95	6.15	B / 8.5	-2.59	-2.44
MUN	Eaton Vance Muni Bond II	EIV	A-	14.49	B+ / 8.3	24.02 / 94	17.08 / 70	5.54 / 77	6.61	B / 8.8	14.18	11.99
MUN	Putnam Muni Opp Tr	PMO	A-	12.55	B+ / 8.3	22.96 / 93	18.14 / 76	7.12 / 91	6.34	B / 8.8	-1.95	-3.62
MUN	Invesco Van Kampen Muni Opp	VMO	A-	14.58	B / 8.2	19.60 / 89	19.02 / 80	5.89 / 80	7.08	B / 8.7	4.29	3.57
MUN	Western Asset Managed Municipals	MMU	A-	13.67	B / 8.0	23.76 / 94	17.41 / 72	9.89 / 99	5.71	B+ / 9.0	-0.07	-0.35
MUN	Nuveen Select Quality Muni	NQS	B+	15.37	B / 8.2	24.05 / 94	18.57 / 78	6.10 / 82	6.71	B / 8.6	1.45	1.60
MUN	Dreyfus Strategic Muni Bond Fund	DSM	B+	8.69	B / 8.0	20.25 / 89	18.99 / 80	4.77 / 69	6.49	B / 8.7	1.28	1.57
MUN	Invesco Quality Municipal Inv Tr	IQT	B+	13.99	B / 7.9	23.34 / 94	17.76 / 74	6.34 / 85	6.33	B / 8.7	-2.71	-3.23
MUN	Invesco Quality Municipal Sec	IQM	B+	14.83	B / 7.9	22.10 / 92	17.88 / 75	6.42 / 86	6.07	B / 8.8	-3.14	-3.32
MUN	Dreyfus Municipal Income	DMF	B+	9.92	B / 7.9	21.25 / 91	18.07 / 76	7.08 / 91	6.35	B / 8.8	0.40	0.28
MUN	BlackRock MuniVest Fund	MVF	B+	10.42	B / 7.9	20.28 / 90	18.62 / 79	7.51 / 94	6.79	B / 8.9	2.16	2.46
MUN	Nuveen Dividend Advantage Muni 2	NXZ	B+	15.19	B / 7.8	25.35 / 96	15.47 / 60	4.65 / 68	6.32	B / 8.8	-0.91	-2.96
MUN	Nuveen Prem Inc Muni 4	NPT	B+	13.40	B / 7.8	22.62 / 93	17.31 / 71	6.81 / 89	6.36	B / 8.7	-3.11	-3.22
MUN	Nuveen Investment Quality Muni Fun	NQM	B+	15.63	B / 7.7	24.42 / 95	16.60 / 66	6.51 / 86	6.45	B / 8.8	-1.14	-1.69
MUN	Nuveen Performance Plus Muni	NPP	B+	15.52	B / 7.7	22.86 / 93	16.45 / 65	6.97 / 91	6.19	B / 8.8	-2.27	-3.07
MUN	DTF Tax Free Income	DTF	B+	16.60	B / 7.7	21.39 / 91	16.42 / 65	7.72 / 95	5.48	B / 8.9	-0.72	-3.97
MUN	Neuberger Berman Intermediate Muni	NBH	B+	16.10	B- / 7.4	21.39 / 91	15.70 / 61	8.84 / 98	5.22	B+ / 9.3	4.89	-0.30

99 Pct = Best
0 Pct = Worst

* Denotes ETF Fund, N/A denotes number is not available

www.thestreetratings.com

Fund Type	Fund Name	Ticker Symbol	Overall Investment Rating	Price As of 3/31/12	Performance Rating/Pts	Annualized Total Return Through 3/31/12			Dividend Yield %	Risk Rating/Pts	Premium/Discount	
	99 Pct = Best 0 Pct = Worst					1Yr/Pct	3Yr/Pct	5Yr/Pct			As of 3/31/12	1 Year Average
MUS	Nuveen CA Muni Market Opportunity	NCO	A+	15.50	A / 9.5	33.72 / 99	21.71 / 88	6.12 / 83	6.19	B / 8.8	0.58	-2.57
MUS	Nuveen CA Prem Inc Muni	NCU	A+	15.04	A / 9.5	32.72 / 99	22.55 / 90	7.37 / 93	5.78	B / 8.7	-0.99	-5.28
MUS	BlackRock Invt Qual Muni Inc Tr	RFA	A+	13.43	A / 9.5	31.22 / 99	24.27 / 93	6.63 / 88	6.25	B / 8.5	2.21	1.09
MUS	Nuveen CA Performance Plus Muni	NCP	A+	15.18	A / 9.3	32.75 / 99	21.30 / 87	6.98 / 91	6.44	B / 8.7	-0.13	-2.50
MUS	Nuveen CA Inv Quality Muni	NQC	A+	15.24	A / 9.3	32.50 / 99	21.60 / 88	7.20 / 92	6.54	B / 8.7	0.07	-2.15
MUS	Invesco Van Kampen Tr Fr Inv NJ Mu	VTJ	A+	17.78	A / 9.3	31.84 / 99	20.50 / 85	7.90 / 96	6.41	B / 8.8	5.77	1.35
MUS	BlackRock MuniYield Invt Fund	MYF	A+	15.38	A / 9.3	30.41 / 99	21.31 / 87	8.56 / 98	6.16	B / 8.7	0.52	-1.35
MUS	BlackRock MuniYield AZ Fund	MZA	A+	14.59	A- / 9.2	27.36 / 98	20.95 / 86	6.14 / 83	5.72	B / 8.8	0.41	-3.80
MUS	Invesco Van Kampen Tr Fr Inv NY Mu	VTN	A+	15.85	A- / 9.1	24.99 / 96	21.98 / 89	6.86 / 90	6.36	B / 8.9	3.46	0.65
MUS	BlackRock MuniYield CA Fund	MYC	A+	15.35	A- / 9.0	27.76 / 98	20.47 / 85	7.93 / 96	6.18	B / 8.7	-4.42	-3.53
MUS	BlackRock Muni NY Interm Duration	MNE	A+	15.00	B+ / 8.9	23.32 / 94	20.89 / 86	6.89 / 90	5.00	B+ / 9.1	-2.02	-6.52
MUS	Invesco Van Kampen OH Qual Muni	VOQ	A+	16.56	B+ / 8.8	28.08 / 98	18.35 / 77	7.46 / 93	6.16	B / 8.9	5.08	0.54
MUS	Invesco New York Quality Muni Sec	IQN	A+	15.79	B+ / 8.8	24.91 / 96	19.73 / 83	7.83 / 96	4.94	B / 8.9	-2.59	-6.37
MUS	Nuveen MI Prem Inc Muni	NMP	A+	14.83	B+ / 8.8	23.13 / 93	19.48 / 82	6.69 / 88	5.91	B+ / 9.3	-2.95	-7.02
MUS	Nuveen MI Quality Inc Muni	NUM	A+	15.11	B+ / 8.7	23.44 / 94	19.19 / 81	6.81 / 89	5.88	B+ / 9.1	-4.06	-7.30
MUS	Eaton Vance OH Muni Inc Tr	EVO	A	15.05	A / 9.3	22.13 / 92	21.18 / 87	6.45 / 86	5.53	B / 8.2	3.79	-1.04
MUS	BlackRock PA Strategic Muni Tr	BPS	A	15.00	A- / 9.2	24.02 / 94	22.68 / 90	2.59 / 51	6.08	B / 8.4	0.67	-1.48
MUS	Nuveen CA Select Quality Muni	NVC	A	15.56	A- / 9.1	28.52 / 98	20.63 / 85	7.71 / 95	6.63	B / 8.5	-0.32	-0.55
MUS	Eaton Vance OH Muni Bond	EIO	A	14.07	A- / 9.0	32.03 / 99	17.90 / 75	4.12 / 63	5.48	B / 8.3	7.65	4.75
MUS	BlackRock MuniHoldings CA Qly	MUC	A	14.99	B+ / 8.9	27.55 / 98	20.50 / 85	7.14 / 92	6.32	B / 8.7	-4.70	-4.61
MUS	BlackRock MuniYield California Qly	MCA	A	14.86	B+ / 8.9	26.74 / 97	20.09 / 84	6.85 / 90	6.14	B / 8.6	-6.36	-6.57
MUS	Nuveen CA Quality Inc Muni	NUC	A	15.82	B+ / 8.8	31.09 / 99	19.46 / 82	7.36 / 93	6.64	B / 8.4	-0.25	-0.30
MUS	Invesco California Quality Muni Se	IQC	A	13.94	B+ / 8.8	30.62 / 99	18.68 / 79	4.78 / 70	6.03	B / 8.6	-3.86	-5.93
MUS	BlackRock MuniHoldings New York Ql	MHN	A	15.15	B+ / 8.8	25.02 / 96	21.02 / 86	7.73 / 95	6.30	B / 8.6	-0.26	-0.71
MUS	Eaton Vance PA Muni Inc Tr	EVP	A	14.15	B+ / 8.8	22.25 / 92	19.53 / 82	5.58 / 77	6.13	B / 8.7	1.36	-2.21
MUS	Eaton Vance NY Muni Inc Tr	EVY	A	14.64	B+ / 8.7	27.25 / 97	18.10 / 76	5.22 / 75	6.21	B / 8.5	3.32	0.42
MUS	Nuveen NJ Div Adv Muni	NXJ	A	14.68	B+ / 8.5	24.90 / 96	17.58 / 73	4.45 / 66	5.68	B / 8.6	-3.23	-6.37
MUS	Nuveen PA Prem Inc Muni 2	NPY	A	14.30	B+ / 8.5	23.82 / 94	18.55 / 78	6.68 / 88	5.87	B / 8.9	-4.35	-6.98
MUS	Nuveen PA Investment Quality Muni	NQP	A	15.56	B+ / 8.4	26.21 / 97	18.06 / 75	8.39 / 97	6.02	B+ / 9.0	0.00	-3.85
MUS	Nuveen CA Div Adv Muni 2	NVX	A	14.93	B+ / 8.3	24.18 / 95	18.57 / 78	5.77 / 79	6.43	B / 8.8	-3.18	-3.05
MUS	Nuveen AZ Div Adv Muni Fund 3	NXE	A	13.90	B+ / 8.3	19.78 / 89	18.71 / 79	4.94 / 71	5.44	B+ / 9.1	-6.40	-8.33
MUS	BlackRock NJ Inv Qual Muni Tr	RNJ	A-	14.32	A+ / 9.6	37.08 / 99	22.00 / 89	2.09 / 45	5.49	B- / 7.4	5.60	-1.08
MUS	Eaton Vance CA Muni Inc Tr	CEV	A-	13.46	B+ / 8.7	31.44 / 99	17.65 / 73	4.13 / 63	6.58	B / 8.5	0.37	0.25
MUS	PIMCO CA Municipal Income Fund III	PZC	A-	10.40	B+ / 8.6	24.83 / 95	17.55 / 73	-2.63 / 18	6.92	B / 8.6	6.23	6.03
MUS	Nuveen CA Div Adv Muni	NAC	A-	14.38	B+ / 8.5	26.53 / 97	18.58 / 79	5.36 / 76	6.43	B / 8.5	-2.77	-2.98
MUS	Nuveen CA Div Adv Muni 3	NZH	A-	13.77	B+ / 8.5	25.22 / 96	18.44 / 78	4.57 / 67	6.54	B / 8.6	-0.43	-1.81
MUS	Invesco Van Kampen PA Val Muni Inc	VPV	A-	14.57	B+ / 8.4	20.70 / 90	18.98 / 80	6.31 / 85	6.18	B / 8.7	-1.49	-3.93
MUS	Invesco California Muni Income Tr	IIC	A-	15.18	B+ / 8.3	28.72 / 98	17.72 / 74	6.83 / 90	5.34	B / 8.7	-3.74	-5.36
MUS	BlackRock New York Muni Inc Qly	BSE	A-	15.20	B+ / 8.3	28.16 / 98	17.25 / 71	6.28 / 84	5.64	B / 8.6	1.27	-1.65
MUS	BlackRock MuniYield NJ Fund	MYJ	A-	15.77	B+ / 8.3	26.62 / 97	16.95 / 69	6.73 / 88	5.63	B / 8.7	-2.47	-5.57
MUS	BlackRock MuniYield New Jersey Qly	MJI	A-	15.40	B+ / 8.3	25.47 / 96	17.76 / 74	6.89 / 90	5.61	B / 8.7	-1.72	-3.87
MUS	Nuveen OH Quality Inc Muni	NUO	A-	17.38	B+ / 8.3	24.92 / 96	17.41 / 72	7.73 / 95	5.52	B / 8.8	2.36	-3.04
MUS	BlackRock NY Municipal Income Tr I	BFY	A-	15.63	B+ / 8.3	21.52 / 91	19.25 / 81	6.78 / 89	6.41	B / 8.9	0.90	1.75
MUS	MA Health & Education Tax-Exempt T	MHE	A-	14.35	B / 8.2	18.94 / 88	19.48 / 82	8.30 / 97	5.85	B / 8.9	3.16	5.17
MUS	BlackRock MuniYield Michigan Qly I	MYM	A-	13.81	B / 8.1	23.00 / 93	19.96 / 83	6.91 / 90	6.21	B / 8.8	-5.09	-3.41
MUS	Neuberger Berman CA Inter Muni Fun	NBW	A-	16.04	B / 7.8	20.48 / 90	16.45 / 65	7.42 / 93	5.09	B+ / 9.2	3.62	-2.71
MUS	BlackRock FL Muni 2020 Term Tr	BFO	A-	15.43	B- / 7.5	19.30 / 89	17.45 / 72	6.76 / 89	4.35	B+ / 9.4	-1.66	-3.52
MUS	Invesco Van Kampen CA Val Muni Inc	VCV	B+	13.15	B+ / 8.5	27.25 / 97	17.79 / 74	2.94 / 54	6.94	B / 8.4	1.08	2.39
MUS	BlackRock NY Inv Qual Muni Tr	RNY	B+	14.81	B+ / 8.3	24.32 / 95	18.15 / 76	3.41 / 58	5.91	B / 8.5	-1.33	-0.73
MUS	BlackRock Muni Bond Invt Trust	BIE	B+	15.36	B / 8.2	22.44 / 92	18.36 / 77	4.64 / 68	6.33	B / 8.6	-3.70	-2.04
MUS	BlackRock MuniHoldings Inv Quality	MFL	B+	14.59	B / 8.2	18.92 / 88	19.09 / 81	7.43 / 93	6.29	B / 8.6	-3.25	-1.85
MUS	Alliance CA Municipal Income Fund	AKP	B+	14.71	B / 7.9	21.32 / 91	17.09 / 70	6.05 / 82	6.22	B / 8.9	1.31	-1.95

* Denotes ETF Fund, N/A denotes number is not available

www.thestreetratings.com
723
Data as of March 31, 2012

Fund Type	Fund Name	Ticker Symbol	Overall Investment Rating	Price As of 3/31/12	Perform-ance Rating/Pts	Annualized Total Return Through 3/31/12			Dividend Yield %	Risk Rating/ Pts	Premium/Discount As of 3/31/12	1 Year Average
	99 Pct = Best / *0 Pct = Worst*					1Yr/Pct	3Yr/Pct	5Yr/Pct				
PM	*ProShares Ultra Gold	UGL	B	88.40	A / 9.5	25.46 / 85	41.40 / 96	--	0.00	C+ / 6.2	0.69	0.44
PM	*UBS E-TRACS S&P 500 Gold Hedged	SPGH	C+	51.27	A+ / 9.6	26.72 / 86	--	--	0.00	C / 4.9	-0.37	0.30
PM	*PowerShares DB Gold Double Lg ET	DGP	C+	53.17	A / 9.5	24.67 / 85	41.85 / 96	--	0.00	C- / 4.2	-0.21	0.18
PM	*iShares Silver Trust	SLV	C+	31.38	B+ / 8.3	-14.87 / 15	35.55 / 91	18.10 / 99	0.00	C / 5.1	-0.35	0.18
PM	*SPDR Gold Shares	GLD	C+	162.12	C+ / 5.9	16.47 / 79	22.78 / 56	19.38 / 99	0.00	B / 8.2	0.40	0.15
PM	*PowerShares DB Precious Metals F	DBP	C+	58.33	C+ / 5.9	7.54 / 62	23.90 / 60	17.58 / 99	0.00	B- / 7.6	-0.14	0.08
PM	*PowerShares DB Gold Fund	DGL	C+	57.78	C / 5.3	15.15 / 77	21.24 / 49	17.51 / 99	0.00	B / 8.2	-0.19	0.10
PM	*PowerShares DB Silver Fund	DBS	C	56.24	B / 8.2	-15.25 / 15	34.82 / 90	16.79 / 99	0.00	C / 5.0	-0.46	0.05
PM	Central Fund of Canada	CEF	C	21.95	C / 5.5	-1.22 / 38	23.58 / 59	18.25 / 99	0.05	B- / 7.4	3.93	1.81
PM	*ETFS Physical Swiss Gold Shares	SGOL	C-	165.23	C- / 3.7	16.45 / 79	--	--	0.00	B / 8.2	0.38	0.17
PM	Central Gold-Trust	GTU	C-	63.75	C- / 3.6	17.71 / 80	14.12 / 24	19.72 / 99	0.00	B- / 7.9	3.26	3.31
PM	*ETFS Physical Asian Gold Shares	AGOL	C-	164.75	C- / 3.3	15.46 / 78	--	--	0.00	B / 8.0	-0.13	-0.10
PM	GAMCO Global Gold Nat ResandIncome	GGN	D+	16.16	C- / 3.4	-4.78 / 31	13.96 / 24	-0.49 / 25	10.40	C+ / 6.8	9.93	2.63
PM	*PowerShares Glb Gold & Precious	PSAU	D	39.70	D+ / 2.9	-18.01 / 12	17.19 / 33	--	0.29	C+ / 6.0	1.04	-0.06
PM	*ETFS Physical PM Basket Shares	GLTR	D	95.27	D / 1.9	-0.54 / 39	--	--	0.00	C+ / 6.7	0.08	0.14
PM	*ETFS Physical Platinum Shares	PPLT	D	161.72	D / 1.7	-7.79 / 25	--	--	0.00	B- / 7.0	-0.06	0.13
PM	*iShares Gold Trust	IAU	D-	16.27	C+ / 5.9	16.63 / 79	22.86 / 56	19.43 / 99	0.00	D / 1.9	0.43	0.24
PM	*PowerShares DB Base Mtls Dbl Lg	BDD	D-	12.12	C- / 3.7	-37.16 / 4	20.82 / 47	--	0.00	C- / 3.0	-0.33	0.07
PM	*Market Vectors Gold Miners ETF	GDX	D-	49.54	D / 2.1	-16.87 / 13	12.86 / 21	4.35 / 53	0.30	C+ / 5.9	-0.02	N/A
PM	*ETFS Physical WM Basket Shares	WITE	D-	53.55	D- / 1.3	-12.96 / 18	--	--	0.00	C / 5.2	-0.11	0.06
PM	*ETFS Physical Palladium Shares	PALL	D-	64.47	E+ / 0.9	-16.01 / 14	--	--	0.00	C+ / 6.6	0.37	N/A
PM	*iShares MSCI ACWI ex US Mtls Ind	AXMT	D-	55.22	E+ / 0.9	-19.87 / 11	--	--	1.93	C+ / 6.5	-0.65	-0.26
PM	*Global X Silver Miners ETF	SIL	D-	22.23	E+ / 0.8	-20.93 / 10	--	--	0.16	C+ / 6.0	-0.49	-0.14
PM	*Global X Pure Gold Miners ETF	GGGG	D-	11.98	E+ / 0.6	-22.37 / 10	--	--	2.07	C+ / 6.0	-0.58	0.10
PM	ASA Gold & Precious Metals Ltd	ASA	E+	25.77	D+ / 2.7	-17.10 / 13	15.95 / 29	5.46 / 59	2.64	D+ / 2.8	-5.78	-9.24
PM	*Direxion Daily Gold Miners Bear	DUST	E+	42.04	D- / 1.2	-1.33 / 37	--	--	0.00	C- / 3.7	6.46	-0.12
PM	*Global X Copper Miners ETF	COPX	E+	13.64	D- / 1.0	-25.53 / 8	--	--	4.15	C / 4.7	-0.44	-0.27
PM	*First Trust ISE Global Copper Id	CU	E+	31.17	E+ / 0.8	-29.35 / 6	--	--	0.00	C / 4.9	-0.38	-0.21
PM	*FactorShares Gold Bull S&P 500 B	FSG	E+	23.38	E / 0.5	-2.30 / 35	--	--	0.00	C / 4.5	0.00	0.21
PM	*Market Vectors Junior Gold Mnrs	GDXJ	E+	24.55	E / 0.5	-32.97 / 5	--	--	4.94	C / 5.1	0.74	0.27
PM	*First Trust ISE Global Platinum	PLTM	E+	19.33	E / 0.5	-42.14 / 2	--	--	2.48	C / 4.7	-0.21	-0.12
PM	*PowerShares DB Base Metals Sht E	BOS	E	20.12	E+ / 0.7	13.04 / 74	-18.86 / 5	--	0.00	D+ / 2.6	-0.69	0.06
PM	*PowerShares DB Gold Short ETN	DGZ	E	11.95	E+ / 0.6	-20.23 / 11	-22.25 / 4	--	0.00	D+ / 2.6	0.08	-0.12
PM	*PowerShares DB Base Mtls Dbl Sh	BOM	E-	12.24	E / 0.4	17.58 / 80	-37.33 / 3	--	0.00	D / 1.9	-0.33	-0.10
PM	*PowerShares DB Gold Double Sht E	DZZ	E-	4.61	E / 0.3	-40.73 / 3	-42.23 / 2	--	0.00	D / 1.9	0.00	-0.26
PM	*Direxion Daily Gold Miners Bull	NUGT	E-	16.36	E- / 0.1	-52.83 / 1	--	--	0.00	D+ / 2.4	-0.18	0.01

* Denotes ETF Fund, N/A denotes number is not available

99 Pct = Best
0 Pct = Worst

Fund Type	Fund Name	Ticker Symbol	Overall Investment Rating	Price As of 3/31/12	Perform-ance Rating/Pts	1Yr/Pct	3Yr/Pct	5Yr/Pct	Dividend Yield %	Risk Rating/Pts	Premium/Discount As of 3/31/12	1 Year Average
USA	*Direxion Daily 7-10 Yr Trs Bull	TYD	B	73.33	B / 8.1	46.45 / 99	--	--	0.00	B- / 7.5	-0.12	-0.04
USA	*PowerShares DB 3x Lg 25+ Yr Tr E	LBND	C+	37.10	A / 9.5	78.97 / 99	--	--	0.00	C / 4.8	-0.40	-0.08
USA	*Direxion Daily 20+ Yr Treas Bull	TMF	C+	56.36	B+ / 8.7	73.73 / 99	--	--	0.00	C / 5.1	0.02	-0.04
USA	*ProShares Ultra 20+ Year Treasur	UBT	C+	116.15	C+ / 6.5	51.62 / 99	--	--	0.24	B- / 7.1	-0.70	-0.02
USA	*PIMCO Build America Bond Strateg	BABZ	C+	54.45	C / 4.8	24.43 / 85	--	--	3.97	B+ / 9.4	-0.02	-0.08
USA	*PowerShares Build America Bond	BAB	C+	29.06	C / 4.3	21.74 / 83	--	--	5.16	B+ / 9.3	0.03	0.05
USA	*iPath US Treas 10Yr Bull ETN	DTYL	C	65.40	B / 7.9	41.47 / 97	--	--	0.00	C / 5.2	-0.06	-0.12
USA	*PIMCO 25+ Year Zero Coupon US Tr	ZROZ	C	97.14	C+ / 6.0	46.83 / 99	--	--	3.05	B- / 7.1	0.05	-0.19
USA	*ProShares Ultra 7-10 Year Treasu	UST	C	102.77	C / 4.3	28.48 / 87	--	--	0.01	B+ / 9.0	0.02	0.07
USA	*PIMCO 15 Plus Year US TIPS Index	LTPZ	C	64.65	C- / 4.0	21.86 / 83	--	--	1.11	B+ / 9.1	0.09	0.08
USA	Western Asset/Claymore Inf-Link O&	WIW	C	12.79	D+ / 2.6	7.47 / 62	10.47 / 17	6.91 / 67	3.41	B+ / 9.6	-10.75	-10.29
USA	*SPDR Barclays Capl TIPS ETF	IPE	C	58.35	D+ / 2.5	13.02 / 74	9.35 / 15	--	1.51	B+ / 9.7	0.07	0.03
USA	*PIMCO Broad US TIPS Index	TIPZ	C	58.65	D+ / 2.5	11.88 / 72	--	--	1.36	B+ / 9.7	0.03	0.03
USA	*iShares Barclays TIPS Bond	TIP	C	117.65	D+ / 2.4	11.75 / 72	8.78 / 15	7.49 / 71	1.84	B+ / 9.7	0.23	0.12
USA	*iPath US Treas Lng Bd Bull ETN	DLBL	C-	63.59	C+ / 6.1	37.52 / 95	--	--	0.00	C / 5.1	-0.33	-0.09
USA	*Vanguard Long-Term Govt Bd Idx E	VGLT	C-	70.04	D+ / 2.5	21.44 / 83	--	--	3.12	B / 8.7	-0.40	0.06
USA	*PIMCO 7-15 Year US Treasury Inde	TENZ	C-	84.44	D+ / 2.5	14.70 / 77	--	--	1.56	B+ / 9.3	0.66	-0.02
USA	*iShares Barclays 10-20 Yr Treasu	TLH	C-	127.76	D / 2.1	17.58 / 80	7.17 / 13	8.94 / 79	2.46	B+ / 9.1	-0.12	0.03
USA	Western Asset/Claymore Inf-Link S&	WIA	C-	12.74	D / 2.0	4.62 / 54	7.36 / 13	6.89 / 67	3.27	B+ / 9.6	-10.28	-8.53
USA	*PowerShares 1-30 Laddered Treasu	PLW	C-	31.11	D / 1.9	16.22 / 79	6.22 / 12	--	2.55	B+ / 9.1	-0.16	N/A
USA	*iShares Barclays 7-10Yr Treasury	IEF	C-	103.28	D / 1.9	13.71 / 75	6.13 / 11	8.28 / 76	1.97	B+ / 9.3	-0.01	0.04
USA	*iShares Barclays Govt/Credit Bd	GBF	C-	112.96	D / 1.9	8.66 / 66	6.84 / 12	6.22 / 63	2.74	B+ / 9.7	0.31	0.13
USA	*Schwab Intmdt-Term US Treasury E	SCHR	C-	52.83	D / 1.8	9.03 / 66	--	--	0.88	B+ / 9.7	-0.02	0.04
USA	*Vanguard Intm-Term Govt Bd Idx E	VGIT	C-	64.66	D / 1.8	8.72 / 66	--	--	1.54	B+ / 9.6	-0.06	0.10
USA	*PIMCO 3-7 Year US Treasury Index	FIVZ	C-	80.83	D / 1.8	8.03 / 64	--	--	1.63	B+ / 9.6	0.19	-0.04
USA	*iShares Barclays 3-7 Yr Treasury	IEI	C-	121.10	D / 1.6	7.68 / 63	4.46 / 10	6.58 / 65	1.09	B+ / 9.7	0.03	0.04
USA	*PIMCO 1-5 Year US TIPS Index	STPZ	C-	54.06	D / 1.6	3.66 / 51	--	--	0.57	B+ / 9.9	0.02	0.02
USA	*SPDR Barclays Cap Int Tr Treas E	ITE	C-	60.60	D- / 1.5	6.05 / 58	3.47 / 9	--	1.64	B+ / 9.8	-0.05	-0.03
USA	*iShares Barclays Agency Bond	AGZ	C-	112.64	D- / 1.5	4.64 / 54	3.43 / 9	--	1.48	B+ / 9.9	0.28	0.07
USA	*iShares Barclays 0-5 Year TIPS B	STIP	C-	103.32	D- / 1.5	3.34 / 50	--	--	0.23	B+ / 9.9	0.16	0.13
USA	*PIMCO 1-3 Year US Treasury Index	TUZ	C-	50.93	D- / 1.3	1.43 / 45	--	--	0.47	B+ / 9.9	-0.04	-0.01
USA	*iShares Barclays 1-3Yr Treasury	SHY	C-	84.32	D- / 1.3	1.35 / 45	1.48 / 8	3.26 / 46	0.50	B+ / 9.9	0.01	0.02
USA	*Schwab Short-Term US Treas ETF	SCHO	C-	50.42	D- / 1.2	1.31 / 44	--	--	0.26	B+ / 9.9	0.00	0.04
USA	*Vanguard Short-Term Gvt Bd Idx E	VGSH	C-	60.86	D- / 1.2	1.26 / 44	--	--	0.41	B+ / 9.9	0.05	0.06
USA	*iShares Barclays Short Treasury	SHV	C-	110.19	D- / 1.2	-0.01 / 41	0.11 / 7	1.38 / 33	0.00	B+ / 9.9	0.01	0.02
USA	*SPDR Barclays Cap 1-3 Month T-B	BIL	C-	45.82	D- / 1.2	-0.06 / 40	-0.01 / 7	--	0.00	B+ / 9.9	0.00	N/A
USA	*SPDR Barclays Cap Lng-T Treas ET	TLO	D+	65.50	D / 2.2	23.20 / 84	7.74 / 13	--	2.76	B / 8.7	-0.23	-0.06
USA	*iShares Barclays 20+Yr Treasury	TLT	D+	112.20	D / 2.1	26.12 / 86	7.02 / 12	9.42 / 83	2.85	B / 8.4	-0.28	0.03
USA	BlackRock Enhanced Government	EGF	D+	15.30	D / 1.7	4.86 / 54	4.58 / 10	1.77 / 36	5.49	B / 8.9	-5.20	-5.48
USA	*iPath US Treas Flattener ETN	FLAT	D	57.08	C- / 3.9	23.90 / 84	--	--	0.00	C / 5.2	-0.19	-0.03
USA	*iPath US Treas 2Yr Bull ETN	DTUL	D	57.03	D+ / 2.6	15.84 / 78	--	--	0.00	C+ / 5.8	0.07	-0.01
USA	*Vanguard Extnd Durtn Trea Idx ET	EDV	D	107.65	D+ / 2.4	43.33 / 98	7.41 / 13	--	2.99	B- / 7.0	0.49	0.43
USA	Federated Enhanced Treasury Income	FTT	D	14.76	D / 1.6	2.46 / 47	--	--	6.10	B- / 7.5	-9.95	-10.89
USA	*ProShares Short 20+ Year Treas	TBF	D-	33.23	E+ / 0.7	-24.70 / 8	--	--	0.00	C+ / 6.5	0.30	-0.01
USA	*iPath US Treas 2Yr Bear ETN	DTUS	E+	41.65	E+ / 0.8	-16.11 / 14	--	--	0.00	C / 4.9	-0.19	N/A
USA	*iPath US Treas Steepen ETN	STPP	E+	40.77	E+ / 0.6	-23.59 / 9	--	--	0.00	C / 4.4	-1.21	0.08
USA	*Direxion Daily 7-10 Yr Trs Bear	TYO	E+	28.33	E / 0.5	-37.69 / 3	--	--	0.00	C / 4.5	-0.14	0.03
USA	*iPath US Treas Lng Bd Bear ETN	DLBS	E	35.77	E+ / 0.7	-32.56 / 5	--	--	0.00	C- / 3.4	0.39	0.07
USA	*iPath US Treas 10Yr Bear ETN	DTYS	E	33.78	E / 0.5	-36.44 / 4	--	--	0.00	C- / 3.4	0.06	0.04
USA	*Direxion Daily 20+ Yr Treas Bear	TMV	E	81.19	E / 0.4	-62.32 / 0	--	--	0.00	D+ / 2.6	-0.06	0.06
USA	*PowerShares DB 3x Sh 25+ Yr Tr E	SBND	E-	10.80	E / 0.5	-58.60 / 1	--	--	0.00	D / 1.9	0.84	0.17

* Denotes ETF Fund, N/A denotes number is not available

Fund Type	Fund Name	Ticker Symbol	Overall Investment Rating	Price As of 3/31/12	Performance Rating/Pts	1Yr/Pct	3Yr/Pct	5Yr/Pct	Dividend Yield %	Risk Rating/Pts	Premium/Discount As of 3/31/12	1 Year Average
			99 Pct = Best / 0 Pct = Worst			Annualized Total Return Through 3/31/12						
UT	Reaves Utility Income Trust	UTG	A+	26.00	A / 9.4	21.91 / 83	41.19 / 96	9.24 / 82	5.77	B / 8.9	6.17	6.08
UT	Cohen&Steers Infrastructure Fund	UTF	B+	17.60	B+ / 8.6	7.30 / 62	32.89 / 87	1.51 / 34	8.18	B / 8.1	-7.61	-9.10
UT	*ProShares Ultra Utilities	UPW	B+	53.34	B / 7.8	19.40 / 82	29.73 / 81	-5.87 / 11	1.59	B / 8.4	-0.19	-0.01
UT	Gabelli Global Utility&Income Trus	GLU	B-	21.30	C+ / 5.7	11.27 / 71	22.39 / 54	5.83 / 61	5.63	B+ / 9.1	3.50	-0.77
UT	Gabelli Utility Trust	GUT	C+	8.09	B / 7.9	32.62 / 91	24.99 / 64	5.69 / 60	7.42	C+ / 6.4	46.03	32.38
UT	DNP Select Income Fund Inc	DNP	C+	10.10	C / 5.5	15.11 / 77	22.96 / 56	6.67 / 65	7.72	B / 8.7	24.38	30.28
UT	*Guggenheim S&P 500 Eq Wght Util	RYU	C	54.57	C- / 4.0	8.45 / 65	17.32 / 33	1.31 / 32	7.06	B+ / 9.3	-0.04	-0.01
UT	*iShares DJ US Utilities	IDU	C	86.16	C- / 3.7	11.57 / 71	15.72 / 29	0.69 / 30	3.64	B+ / 9.2	-0.03	0.01
UT	*Utilities Select Sector SPDR	XLU	C	35.05	C- / 3.6	13.57 / 75	15.39 / 28	1.11 / 32	3.67	B+ / 9.1	0.00	N/A
UT	*Vanguard Utilities Index ETF	VPU	C	74.84	C- / 3.6	11.61 / 72	15.59 / 28	1.08 / 31	3.78	B+ / 9.2	0.01	0.03
UT	*First Trust Utilities AlphaDEX	FXU	C	17.66	C- / 3.5	2.00 / 46	16.50 / 31	--	1.75	B+ / 9.0	-0.06	0.11
UT	Wells Fargo Avtg Utilities&High In	ERH	C-	11.96	C / 4.4	8.89 / 66	16.97 / 32	-5.82 / 11	7.53	C+ / 6.6	1.44	-3.82
UT	*PowerShares Dynamic Utilities	PUI	C-	16.74	D+ / 2.9	4.21 / 52	12.43 / 21	-0.36 / 25	1.56	B / 8.8	0.00	-0.04
UT	*Focus Mstar Utilities Id ETF	FUI	C-	27.62	D+ / 2.3	10.68 / 69	--	--	2.66	B+ / 9.5	0.07	-0.03
UT	*iShares S&P Global Utilities	JXI	D+	42.67	D / 2.0	-2.84 / 34	7.97 / 14	-3.86 / 14	3.85	B / 8.5	0.28	0.16
UT	*SPDR S&P Transportation ETF	XTN	D	49.25	D+ / 2.7	-7.67 / 25	--	--	0.27	C+ / 6.9	-1.62	-0.01
UT	*WisdomTree Global ex-US Utilitie	DBU	D	18.92	D / 1.9	-6.65 / 27	7.19 / 13	-5.03 / 12	1.83	B- / 7.7	0.11	-0.26
UT	*SPDR SP Intl Utils Sector ETF	IPU	D	17.33	D- / 1.3	-13.95 / 16	3.20 / 8	--	1.08	B- / 7.6	0.41	0.27
UT	*iShares MSCI ACWI ex US Utl Sct	AXUT	D	45.09	D- / 1.1	-10.34 / 21	--	--	3.35	B- / 7.5	1.76	0.16
UT	*ProShares UltraShort Utilities	SDP	E	32.10	E / 0.4	-28.04 / 6	-32.03 / 3	-14.61 / 4	0.00	C- / 3.8	0.19	N/A

* Denotes ETF Fund, N/A denotes number is not available

www.thestreetratings.com

Appendix

What is a Mutual Fund?

Picking individual stocks is difficult and buying individual bonds can be expensive. Mutual funds were introduced to allow the small investor to participate in the stock and bond market for just a small initial investment. Mutual funds are pools of stocks or bonds that are managed by investment professionals.First, an investment company organizes the fund and collects the money from investors. The company then takes that money and pays a portfolio manager to invest it in stocks, bonds, money market instruments and other types of securities.

Most funds fit within one of two main categories, open-end funds or closed-end funds. Open-end funds issue new shares when investors put in money and redeem shares when investors withdraw money. The price of a share is determined by dividing the total net assets of the fund by the number of shares outstanding.

On the other hand, closed-end funds issue a fixed number of shares in an initial public offering, trading thereafter in the open market like a stock. Thus by their very nature, closed-end funds are unique in that they do not always trade at their net asset value (NAV). Unlike their open-end counterparts, closed-end funds trade on an exchange at market prices that are independent of their NAV. If the price is above the fund's NAV, the fund is said to be trading at a premium. If the price is lower than the fund's NAV, the fund trades at a discount. Investing in either class of funds means you own a share of the portfolio, so you participate in the fund's gains and losses.

Exchange traded funds are an increasingly popular subset of closed-end funds. Their portfolios are predefined "baskets" of investments (usually stocks or bonds, but sometimes commodity-related vehicles). Because they are passively managed, their expense ratios are generally much lower than actively managed open-end and closed-end funds. ETFs also incorporate an arbitrage process that keeps their market prices during the trading day extremely close to their respective net asset per share values. So unlike traditional closed-end funds, which frequently trade at premiums or discounts of several percentage points from their respective NAVs, ETFs normally remain within a fraction of a percent of NAV.

There are more than 20,000 different mutual funds, each with a stated investment objective. Here are descriptions for five of the most popular types of funds:

Stock funds: A mutual fund which invests mainly in stocks. These funds are more actively traded than other more conservative funds. The stocks chosen may vary widely according to the fund's investment strategy.

Bond funds: A mutual fund which invests in bonds, in an effort to provide stable income while preserving principal as much as possible. These funds invest in medium- to long-term bonds issued by corporations and governments.

Index funds: A mutual fund that aims to match the performance of a specific index, such as the S&P 500. Index funds tend to have fewer expenses than other funds because portfolio decisions are automatic and transactions are infrequent.

Balanced funds: A mutual fund that buys a combination of stocks and bonds, in order to supply both income and capital growth while ensuring a minimal amount of risk for investors.

Money market funds: An open-end mutual fund which invests only in stable, short-term securities. The fund seeks to preserve its value at a constant $1 per share. Money market funds are not insured by the FDIC, however may be covered by SIPC insurance. Investors should contact the firm administering their investment account to determine the insurance coverage of the funds or contact the FDIC and/or the SIPC directly.

Investing in a mutual fund has several advantages over owning a single stock or bond. For example, funds offer instant portfolio diversification by giving you ownership of many stocks or bonds simultaneously. This diversification protects you in case a part of your investment takes a sudden downturn. You also get the benefit of having a professional handling your investment, though a management fee is charged for these services, typically 1% or 2% a year. You should be aware that the fund may also levy other fees and that you will likely have to pay a commission to purchase the fund through a brokerage firm.

The fund manager's strategy is laid out in the fund's prospectus, which is the official name for the legal document that contains financial information about the fund, including its history, its officers and its performance. Mutual fund investments are fully liquid so you can easily get in or out by just placing an order through a broker.

How Do Open-End and Exchange-Traded Funds Differ?

Similarities:

Both open-end and ETFs…

- may be invested in stocks, bonds, derivatives, commodity-related instruments or a combination thereof.
- provide benefits of diversification by holding a basket of stocks, bonds, derivatives and/or commodity-related instruments.

Differences:

Open-End	Exchange-Traded Funds*
• Open-end funds are more popular. There are more than 16,000 open-end funds available. The general term "mutual funds" typically refers to the much more common, open-end mutual funds.	• Exchange-traded funds are lesser known, and there are significantly fewer in existence.*
• Fund companies may require an initial minimum amount that must be invested.	• There is no minimum initial investment required. *
• Investors cannot utilize limit and stop orders.	• Investors may utilize limit and stop orders. *
• 12b-1 fees are used to pay for marketing the fund.	• 12b-1 fees are not charged. *
• All transactions occur at the end of each business day based upon the movement in the value of the fund's portfolio of securities.	• Shares are traded on an exchange throughout the day. *

* These attributes also apply to traditional closed-end funds. See next page for more information on traditional closed-end funds.

How do "Exchange-Traded Funds" (ETFs) and Traditional Closed-End Funds Differ?

ETFs are an increasingly popular subset of closed-end funds. The funds' portfolios represent "baskets" of securities or commodities, frequently representing components of popular indices such as the S&P 500 or the NASDAQ 100. They differ from traditional closed-end funds in several ways

A traditional closed-end fund issues a set number of shares. The shares outstanding rarely changes and only when approved by a vote of shareholders. ETFs, however, allow an arbitrage process whereby shares are frequently added and redeemed. The arbitrage tends to impact the price of the ETF fund as well as the prices of the individual investments in its portfolio.

While it is not uncommon for investor demand to drive traditional closed-end fund prices to premiums or discounts of several percentage points above or below their respective net asset values per share, the ETF arbitrage process normally keeps the market price of an ETF extremely close to its net asset per share value. ETFs normally trade within a small fraction of 1% above or below net asset value per share.

Only investment organizations pre-approved by an ETF's management company may engage in the normal arbitrage process involving shares of that fund. For a fee, a pre-approved arbitrageur may exchange a fund's shares for a "redemption unit" of actual shares in the component stocks, bonds and/or commodities of the fund's "basket" of securities or commodities. Conversely, the arbitrageur has the option of delivering to the ETF a predefined "basket" of securities or commodities known as a "creation unit." The arbitrage firm then receives in exchange a predetermined number shares in the fund.

How Do Open-End and Traditional Closed-End Funds Differ?

Similarities:

Both open-end and traditional (non-ETF) closed-end mutual funds…

- employ a fund manager or management team to invest assets in various types of securities according to the fund's stated objectives and policies.
- may be invested in stocks, bonds, commodities or a combination thereof.
- provide benefits of diversification by holding a basket of stocks, bonds and/or commodities.

Differences:

Open-End	Traditional Closed-End
• The mutual fund company issues and redeems shares on demand, whenever investors put money into the fund or take it out.	• The mutual fund company issues a set number of shares in an initial public offering and the shares then trade on an exchange.
• There is no limit to the number of shares the fund can issue.	• The fund offers a fixed number of shares.
• The share price is determined by the total value of the assets it holds.	• The share price is determined by investor demand for the fund.
• Fund shares trade at net asset value (NAV).	• Fund shares generally trade at a premium (above NAV) or discount (below NAV).

Performance Benchmark

The following benchmarks represent the average performance for all mutual funds within each ETF and closed-end fund category as of March 31, 2012. Investment returns are averages for all closed-end funds, which include ETFs. Comparing an individual mutual fund's returns to these benchmarks is yet another way to assess its performance. For the top performing funds within each of the following categories, turn to Section VI, Top-Rated ETFs and Other Closed-End Funds by Fund Type, beginning on page 706.

		3 Month Total Return %	1 Year Total Return %	Refer to page:
COH	Corporate - High Yield	6.31%	10.20%	706
COI	Corporate - Investment Grade	2.05%	6.02%	707
EM	Emerging Market Income	13.10%	-7.96%	708
EN	Energy/Natural Res	3.54%	-17.22%	709
FO	Non-US Equity	10.79%	-9.18%	711
FS	Financial Services	15.65%	-8.20%	710
GEI	General Bond - Investment Grade	0.31%	8.81%	712
GEN	Multi-Sector Bond	9.55%	13.13%	713
GI	Growth & Income	8.18%	0.91%	716
GL	Global	9.06%	-1.66%	714
GR	Growth - Domestic	8.91%	-2.47%	715
HL	Health	11.40%	11.21%	717
IN	Equity Income	9.10%	0.02%	718
LP	Loan Participation	11.60%	2.19%	719
MTG	General Mortgage	6.91%	7.78%	720
MUH	Municipal - High Yield	4.34%	18.98%	721
MUN	Municipal - National	2.70%	19.95%	722
MUS	Municipal Single State	2.78%	21.80%	723
PM	Precious Metals	4.26%	-7.23%	724
USA	Government Bond	-0.73%	10.16%	725
UT	Utilities	3.68%	5.45%	726

Exchange-Traded Funds Summary Data

ETF SUMMARY BY INVESTMENT OBJECTIVE *

INVESTMENT OBJECTIVE	NO. OF ETFs	TOTAL NET ASSETS ($MIL.)
Corporate - High Yield	10	27,675.9
Corporate - Investment Grade	31	42,943.2
Emerging Market Equity	47	107,309.6
Emerging Market Income	4	6,802.2
Equity Income	236	125,579.8
General Bd - Investment Grade	30	44,868.8
General Mortgage	4	4,815.2
Global Equity	112	19,220.0
Global Income	31	6,990.7
Government Bond	54	54,612.7
Growth & Income	78	28,581.1
Growth - Domestic	282	392,985.7
Loan Participation	2	265.1
Multi-Sector Bond	1	217.7
Municipal - High Yield	2	878.3
Municipal - National	18	7,703.3
Municipal Single State	2	308.5
Non-US Equity	214	152,457.2
Sector - Energy/Natural Res	95	34,108.6
Sector - Financial Services	30	17,689.1
Sector - Health/Biotechnology	27	11,000.4
Sector - Precious Metals	36	113,514.4
Sector - Utilities	15	8,770.4
TOTALS	**1361**	**1,209,298.0**

* ETFs only (traditional closed-end funds not included).

Exchange-Traded Funds Summary Data cont.

ETF SUMMARY BY FUND GROUP *

FUND GROUP	ETFs #	NET ASSETS ($MIL.)	FUND GROUP	ETFs #	NET ASSETS ($MIL.)
AdvisorShares Investments	12	407.7	IndexIQ Advisors LLC	12	489.7
ALPS Advisors Inc	24	3,678.0	Invesco Powershares Cap Mgmt	115	21,396.4
Bank of New York Mellon	6	44,293.2	JP Morgan	4	4,080.7
Barclays Bank PLC	70	6,086.0	Morgan Stanley Inv Mgmt	4	66.9
BlackRock Fund Advisors	261	503,159.9	Northern Trust Investments	4	664.3
Charles Schwab Inv Mgmt	15	6,322.9	Nuveen Commodities Asset	1	212.7
Citi Fund Management Inc	1	8.9	Pax World Management	2	14.3
Columbia Management Inv Adv	4	19.8	PIMCO	17	3,744.3
Credit Suisse AG	21	1,164.0	Precidian Funds LLC	1	193.0
Credit Suisse Asset Mgmt	5	434.5	ProShare Advisors LLC	127	23,499.8
DB Commodity Services LLC	23	12,844.2	Rafferty Asset Management	52	7,077.5
DBX Advisors LLC	4	48.8	Royal Bank of Scotland NV	6	140.3
DBX Strategic Advisors LLC	5	124.3	Russell Investment Mgmt	19	239.7
Deutsche Bank AG (London)	19	1,050.2	Security Investors LLC	34	8,368.3
ETF Securities USA LLC	7	4,417.4	SSgA Funds Management Inc	104	176,309.1
Factor Capital Management	4	16.4	State Street Bank and Trust Co	2	118,223.8
FFCM LLC	7	43.9	Swedish Export Credit Corp	6	942.6
Fidelity Mgmt & Res Comp	1	187.2	Teucrium Trading LLC	6	82.4
First Trust Advisors LP	64	7,522.9	UBS Global Asset Management	36	801.1
FocusShares LLC	15	89.6	United States Commodity Funds	10	3,394.9
Global X Management Comp	31	1,295.3	Van Eck Associates Corp	44	26,445.0
Goldman Sachs & Co/GSAM	1	71.3	Vanguard Group Inc	64	199,528.2
Greenhaven Commodity Svcs	1	676.8	VTL Associates LLC	6	489.5
Guggenheim Funds Inv Adv	37	3,787.6	WisdomTree Asset Mgmt	47	15,142.7
			TOTALS	**1361**	**1,209,298.0**

* ETFs only (traditional closed-end funds excluded).

Fund Type Descriptions

<u>COH - Corporate - High Yield</u> - Seeks high current income by investing a minimum of 65% of its assets in generally low-quality corporate debt issues.

<u>COI - Corporate - Investment Grade</u> - Seeks current income by investing a minimum of 65% in investment grade corporate debt issues. Investment grade securities must be BBB or higher, as rated by Standard & Poor's.

<u>EM - Emerging Market</u> - Seeks long term capital appreciation and/or income by investing primarily in emerging market equity and/or income producing securities.

<u>EN - Energy/Natural Resources</u> - Invests primarily in equity securities of companies involved in the exploration, distribution, or processing of natural resources.

<u>FS - Financial</u> - Seeks capital appreciation by investing in equity securities of companies engaged in providing financial services. Typically, securities are from commercial banks, S&Ls, finance companies, securities brokerages, investment managers, insurance companies, and leasing companies.

<u>FO - Foreign</u> - Invests primarily in non-U.S. equity securities of any market capitalization. Income is usually incidental.

<u>GEI - General - Investment Grade</u> - Seeks income by investing in investment grade domestic or foreign corporate debt, government debt and preferred securities.

<u>GEN - General Bond</u> - Seeks income by investing without geographic boundary in corporate debt, government debt or preferred securities. Investments are not tied to any specific maturity or duration.

<u>GL - Global</u> - Invests primarily in domestic and foreign equity securities of any market capitalization and/or fixed income securities issued by domestic and/or foreign governments.

<u>GR - Growth</u> - Seeks long term capital appreciation by investing primarily in equity securities of any market capitalization. Income is usually incidental.

<u>GI - Growth and Income</u> - Seeks both capital appreciation and income primarily by investing in equities with a level or rising dividend stream.

<u>HL - Health</u> - Seeks capital appreciation by investing primarily in equities of companies engaged in the design, manufacture, or sale of products or services connected with health care or medicine.

<u>IN - Income</u> - Seeks current income by investing a minimum of 65% of its assets in income-producing equity securities.

<u>LP - Loan Participation</u> - Invests a minimum of 65% of its assets in loan interests.

<u>MTG - Mortgage</u> - Invests a minimum of 65% of its assets in a broad range of mortgage or mortgage-related securities, including those issued by the U.S. government and by government related and private organizations.

<u>MUH - Municipal - High Yield</u> - Seeks tax-free income by investing a minimum of 65% of its assets in generally low-quality issues from any state municipality.

<u>MUN - Municipal - National</u> - Seeks federally tax-free income by investing at least 65% in issues from any state municipality.

<u>MUS - Municipal - Single State</u> - Seeks tax-free income by investing in issues which are exempt from federal and the taxation of a specified state.

<u>PM - Precious Metals</u> - Seeks capital appreciation by investing primarily in equity securities of companies involved in mining, distribution, processing, or dealing in gold, silver, platinum, diamonds, or other precious metals and minerals.

<u>USA - U.S. Government - Agency</u> - Invests a minimum of 65% in securities issued or guaranteed by the Government, its agencies or instrumentalities. Investments are not tied to any specific maturity or duration.

<u>UT - Utilities</u> - Seeks a high level of current income by investing primarily in the equity securities of utility companies.